# THE OXFORD DICTIONARY
## OF THE RENAISSANCE

# THE OXFORD

## DICTIONARY

## OF THE

## RENAISSANCE

GORDON CAMPBELL

OXFORD

UNIVERSITY PRESS

# OXFORD
### UNIVERSITY PRESS

Great Clarendon Street, Oxford OX2 6DP
Oxford University Press is a department of the University of Oxford.
It furthers the University's objective of excellence in research, scholarship,
and education by publishing worldwide in

Oxford  New York

Auckland  Bangkok  Buenos Aires  Cape Town  Chennai
Dar es Salaam  Delhi  Hong Kong  Istanbul  Karachi  Kolkata
Kuala Lumpur  Madrid  Melbourne  Mexico City  Mumbai  Nairobi
São Paulo  Shanghai  Taipei  Tokyo  Toronto

Oxford is a registered trade mark of Oxford University Press
in the UK and in certain other countries

Published in the United States
by Oxford University Press Inc., New York

British Library Cataloguing in Publication Data
Data available

Library of Congress Cataloguing in Publication Data
Data available

ISBN 0–19–860175–1

1 3 5 7 9 10 8 6 4 2

Typeset by Graphicraft Limited, Hong Kong
Printed in the United States of America on acid-free paper

# CONTENTS

# INTRODUCTION

This book describes the cultural history of a long Renaissance, and one with permeable boundaries. The core period covered by the volume is marked by the two Defenestrations of Prague, 1415 and 1618. These dates are not altogether arbitrary: 1415 was not only the year of Agincourt and the capture of Ceuta, but also the year in which Jan Hus was burnt at the stake; the Reformation of which his reforming zeal was a harbinger was to shape the course of European affairs for centuries; similarly, 1618 marked the opening salvoes in the Thirty Years War, which was to change the face of Europe permanently. Most of the material in this volume can be comfortably accommodated within these dates, but in some countries the model of a cultural Renaissance has necessitated the stretching of my chronological limits. In Italy I extend the chronological range back to the early trecento in order to include seminal figures such as Dante and Giotto; in Spain and England I go forward to the mid-seventeenth century, because the death of Lope de Vega in 1635 is often said by Hispanists to mark the end of the *Siglo de Oro*, and the closing of the English theatres in 1642 is usually treated by Anglicists as the conclusion of the English Renaissance. I include no one born after 1595, so there is no Corneille, no Calderón, no Milton; they await a *Dictionary of the Seventeenth Century*.

The geographical centre of the volume consists of the countries whose cultures were touched in significant measure by the revival of classical learning, and so extends to nearly all early modern Europe, including eastern and central Europe. States and territories on the periphery are given slighter treatment, so Arabic, Celtic, and Ottoman territories and cultures are discussed only in terms of political and cultural contacts with the countries at the centre of the volume. The space given to the British Isles is relatively small, because an abundance of material is available in other English-language reference books, such as the *Oxford Companion to British History* and the *Oxford Companion to English Literature*; Spain, on the other hand, is given extensive coverage, because it is not represented in proportion to its importance in most English-language reference books. I have also tried to find extra space for regions whose languages are unfamiliar to British readers, such as the Low Countries, Scandinavia and east-central Europe. Independent Slav states in eastern Europe are included, as is Hungary, but Slav areas occupied by the Ottomans were untouched by the Renaissance, and so are not represented in the volume; the Timurid Renaissance centred in Transoxiana and Herat in the fifteenth century in many ways resembles the European Renaissance, but the cultural differences between Christianity and Islam render it pointless to treat both cultures in a single volume.

This volume is a dictionary of the Renaissance rather than an encyclopedia of early modern Europe, which means that my bias is cultural. Accounts of rulers, for example, often describe their role as patrons. That said, culture is broadly conceived, and includes subjects such as law, theology, medicine, science, and elements of popular culture as well as the high culture of art, architecture, gardens, literature, and music. I have written with three audiences in mind. The first is the academic specialist in one field who requires information in a contiguous field, but lacks the requisite languages, or simply does not know where to look. The second is the student, at whatever level, who needs to know the conventional wisdom or to ascertain a point of entry for any topic within the large area of the European Renaissance. The third is the intelligent general reader in need of a reference book that will act as a guide to the culture of the Renaissance. Entries in areas likely to be of interest to the general reader do not assume prior knowledge, but in learned subjects such as law or Greek I make fewer concessions, because such entries are likely to be consulted only by professionals.

One consequence of this audience profile is that the volume is intended to mediate knowledge about subjects that may be unfamiliar, and so makes concessions that may displease subject specialists: spelling in all European languages is modernized (except for Law French), in Latin the unaspirated aitch (e.g. *Hetruria*) and the digraph *th* (e.g. *Anthonius*) are suppressed (e.g. *Etruria* and *Antonius*) and accents are used in accordance with modern rather than Renaissance usage. Similarly, my aim in transliterating from Arabic, Cyrillic, Greek, and Hebrew scripts has been to give those who do not read those scripts some sense of the form in which they might encounter the terms elsewhere in English-language books; this procedure has of necessity meant that I have not been able to assist those who might want to use my transcriptions either to help with pronunciation or to work out what the form of the words would be in the original alphabets. Alphabetization poses a particular problem, because practice is not consistent across the languages of Europe: in Spanish the compound *ll* follows *lz* and the compound *ch* follows *cz*; in Danish *æ*, *ø*, and *å* all follow *z* and in Polish the crossed 'dark' *ł* follows the uncrossed *l*. In several languages, the modified vowels *ä*, *ö* and *ü* are alphabetized as *ae*, *oe*, and *ue*. My solution has been to run roughshod over all such conventions, and to treat all such letters as if they were their unaccented English counterparts; similarly, I have treated the ligatures *æ* and *œ* as if they were separate letters.

My treatment of proper names sacrifices consistency to clarity. The use of exonyms in place names is declining, but has not disappeared: I therefore print Frankfurt, Livorno, Lyon, Marseille, and Reims instead of Frankfort, Leghorn, Lyons, Marseilles, and Rheims, but I print Cologne, Florence, Geneva, Munich, and Vienna rather than Köln, Firenze, Genève, München, and Wien; when historical events are associated with exonyms no longer in use (e.g. Ratisbon), I record the exonym but explain what it means. I try to acknowledge the cultural balance within the early modern period, and use the German forms Basel, Luxemburg, and Strassburg rather than the French Bâle (or the exonym Basle), Luxembourg, and Strasbourg. The German *eszett* (ß) now in use in Germany (but not in Austria or Switzerland) was not used consistently in the early modern period; I have retained it in book titles and personal names, but not in place names, so I print Strassburg and Meissen, not Straßburg and Meißen. The use of Latin place names on title pages is a particularly problematical area; I have eliminated such names from my text, but have supplied an appendix which lists all such Latin names. In areas that once had substantial German populations, notably Alsace, Bohemia, Hungary, Silesia, and Transylvania, I often give both the German name and the name to be found on modern maps.

Personal names present a more complex problem, in that the modern convention of the surname emerged during the period covered by this volume. If the second name carried a strong sense of place or profession, as was often the case in the fifteenth century, I treat the first name as the main name: Leonardo da Vinci is therefore listed under Leonardo rather than under 'da' or 'Vinci'; if, on the other hand, the surname was no longer felt to be a place of origin, I use it as the main name, so Hans von Aachen is listed under 'Aachen' rather than under 'von' or 'Hans'. In the case of Spanish names, however, I have adhered to the convention of listing names by the patronymic that precedes the final matronymic. In the case of Dutch names ending 'sz.' I have expanded the abbreviated patronymic to 'szoon'. Exonymic personal names are slowly receding, but English speakers still refer to Francis I and Charles V, and in countries in which pronunciation is not obvious to English speakers, recourse to exonyms is normal, so we say King John of Portugal because most English speakers do not know how to pronounce João. My instinct is to suppress exonymic personal names as much as possible, but the exigencies of a volume that covers all of Europe have created a particular problem with respect to rulers: Spanish kings, for example, also ruled Naples and Sicily, and on occasion the same king ruled Poland, Bohemia, and Hungary. In such cases I have often used an exonym to ensure that each person is called by one name. The unhappy effect of this policy is that French entries include kings called Francis but dukes called François and Spanish entries kings called John and artists called Juan; in eastern Europe, King Vladislas II of Bohemia, King Ulászló II of Hungary, and Prince Władysław Jagiełło of Poland are the same person, and I refer to him by the exonym Ladislas II.

The alphabetical sequence of entries is followed by four appendices. The tabulation of ruling houses is simply a ready reference tool, but the other appendices serve more serious purposes. Scholars are often baffled by the place names on title pages, so I have tried to provide a complete list of early modern Latin imprints as well as a selection of other place names that might seem mysterious. Similarly, the lack of a table showing the dates at which European cities and countries changed from the Julian to the Gregorian calendar has often confused historians who assume, for example, that Utrecht changed calendars at the same time as other parts of the Netherlands. Finally, I address the problem of Greek ligatures and contractions, which was memorably formulated by John Buchan's character Sir Edward Leithen in *The Dancing Floor* (1926): 'I was taught Greek at school, though I have forgotten most of it, but I never professed to be able to read even the printed Greek of the fifteenth and sixteenth centuries. This document seemed to be of that date, and its insane ligatures and contractions completely defeated me.' Sir Edward was able to solve his problem by recourse to a chancery barrister whose hobby was medieval Greek, but, since such barristers are now in short supply, I have appended a table that sets out all the ligatures and contractions that are not readily apparent to a scholar with a modest competence in Greek.

G.C.

# ACKNOWLEDGEMENTS

Entries in this volume extend over the cultural and political history of Europe for a period of two centuries. The complexities of such a large geographical range have been compounded by the need to contend with source material written in more than twenty languages. Over the years I have constructed bridgeheads in the Germanic, Romance, and Slavonic languages of Europe, and in the ancient Mediterranean and oriental languages studied during the Renaissance, but my linguistic knowledge is uneven and often alarmingly slight; indeed, in the cases of Hungarian and Turkish, I have, despite considerable exposure, been utterly defeated by the mysteries of grammatical agglutination, and in dealing with episodes in which Hungarians have fought Turks have had to rely on material written in languages other than those of the combatants. Such linguistic shortcomings have also made me particularly reliant on advice given by learned members of the academic community. Much of that expertise has been given by fellow members of the Society for Renaissance Studies, which has been an important source of intellectual companionship for many years. Writing this book has been an exercise in learning how little I know, how much I should know, and how dependent I am on the knowledge of other scholars.

Most Oxford Dictionaries and Companions are edited volumes, written by scores or even hundreds of contributors; the third edition of the *Oxford Dictionary of the Christian Church* (1997), for example, was written by almost 500 authors. I decided to write most or all of this volume myself, and in the event wrote considerably more than 90 per cent of the entries; the range of subjects on which I have written has made me particularly reliant on the advice of specialists. The burden of advice has fallen chiefly on the learned members of my advisory board, and I should like to thank them for their patient assistance even as I acknowledge their formidable command of the matters on which they have offered counsel: every entry has been seen by one of the advisory editors and most entries have been altered in the light of their recommendations. One of their number, J. V. Field, volunteered to draft some of the key entries in the mathematical sciences, and I eagerly accepted that generous offer. My research assistant, Catherine Packham, wrote many of the entries on England, and the composer and musician Eleanor Graff-Baker wrote most of the entries on music. I am grateful to all three for the quality of their work and for their willingness to submit to a tight schedule and to allow me to blend their work into the larger whole.

This will be the last book in which I shall have enjoyed the assistance of Stella Lanham, ostensibly my secretary but in practice a learned and cultured research assistant with a formidable command of European languages, and I am happy to acknowledge her generous contribution to this book and its predecessors. I was assisted for a time by Paula Warrington and in the final months of writing by Catherine Packham, both of whom brought sharp eyes for detail to the project. I should also like to thank those who have responded to my pleas for help on specific matters: Alain Dubois, Kalina Filipova, Neil Forsyth, Susan Frost, John Gough, Mihaela Irimia, Michael Jones, Martin Kayman, Piotr Kuhiwczak, George Lukowski, and Henry Woudhuysen. In the run-up to submission, Elaine Treharne and Anthony Pearson, the heads of my two departments, both affected not to notice that I had abandoned my other duties in order to finish on schedule, and I am grateful for their tolerant understanding. Kent J. Rigsby, the Editor of *Greek, Roman and Byzantine Studies*, graciously gave permission for me to adapt material from his journal for use in Appendix 3.

Finally, I should like to thank friends at Oxford University Press. The editorial process at OUP resembles a race in which the runner is accompanied by a series of sprinters who offer encouragement and support. The first sector, which concluded with the contract, was managed by the scholar-editor Michael Cox, who commissioned the volume and presented the proposal to the Delegates, the body of Oxford academics responsible for the probity of OUP publications. Several Delegates took an interest in the project, and anonymously offered constructive criticism that has substantially affected the nature of this volume; I wish that I could thank them by name. The sector from contract to submission was overseen by Pam Coote, who has a knowledgeable enthusiasm for Renaissance gardens as well as a formidable ability to coax authors to completion; it was she who tactfully shaped the volume. The final lap, from submission to publication, was the responsibility of Rebecca Collins, who worked for countless hours on the project and in her enthusiasm took on some of the work that in a just world would have fallen to me. All three have contributed substantially to this volume; I am grateful for their assistance and for their friendship. I was also fortunate in my copy editors, Edwin Pritchard and Jackie Pritchard, who turned a mildly tumultuous submission into an orderly volume, in my picture editors, Sophie Hartley and Helen Nash, who eased my job very considerably, in my proofreaders, Peter Gibbs, Kathie Gill, Judith Colleran, and Mick Belson, who brought their usual high standards to bear on an exceedingly demanding text, in my production controller, Lisa Begley, whose formidable scheduling skills made it possible to publish the volume on time, and in my designer, Nick Clarke, who was responsible for the clean page layout and the elegant designs of the jacket and binding case.

The idea for this volume was first suggested to me in the mid-1980s by the OUP editor Kim Scott Walwyn, who in the course of a peripatetic conversation outlined what she wanted me to write and edit over the course of the next twenty years. In the years that followed she warmly acknowledged the various projects as they came to fruition, and in the late 1990s cheered on this one as it proceeded. I have enjoyed support from many quarters, but it was she who more than anyone else shaped my career as a scholar; her faith in me always seemed slightly misplaced, but was nonetheless touching, and I have never ceased to be grateful. I should like to inscribe this volume to her memory.

G.C.

*Leicester*
*July 2002*

# EDITORIAL TEAM

THE AUTHOR

**Gordon Campbell** is Professor of Renaissance Literature at the University of Leicester. Professor Campbell's research interests are centred in the history and culture of Renaissance and seventeenth-century Europe; his particular interest is in John Milton. In the past ten years Professor Campbell has edited Milton's *Complete Poems*, inspected and compiled more than 2,000 life records in *A Milton Chronology*, and published a revised edition of the authoritative two-volume biography of Milton by W. R. Parker (Oxford University Press); he has also edited four plays by Ben Jonson (OUP) and the life records and Latin poems of *Edward King, Milton's "Lycidas": Poems and Documents*. Professor Campbell was the founding editor of *Renaissance Studies* (then OUP), and has been the editor of *The Year's Work in English Studies* (now OUP) and the series editor of *Essays and Studies*; he is now the general editor of *Review of English Studies* (OUP). He has served as Chairman of the Society for Renaissance Studies and President of the English Association, of which he is a director. He has been awarded a D.Litt by the University of York and an honorary doctorate by the University of Bucharest; he is a fellow of the Royal Historical Society, a corresponding fellow of the South African Society for Medieval and Renaissance Studies, and a member of the advisory board of the Sociedad Española de Estudios Renacentistas Ingleses.

CONSULTANT EDITORS

**George Holmes** is Chichele Professor Emeritus of Medieval History at the University of Oxford and Emeritus Fellow of St Catherine's College, Oxford. His books include *The Estates of Higher Nobility in Fourteenth-Century England* (1957), *The Later Middle Ages* (1962), *The Florentine Enlightenment, 1400–1450* (1969), *Europe: Hierarchy and Revolt, 1320–1450* (1975, 2nd edn. 2000), *The Good Parliament* (1975), *Dante* (1980), *Florence, Rome and the Origins of the Renaissance* (1986), *The Oxford Illustrated History of Medieval Europe* (1988), *The Oxford Illustrated History of Italy* (1997), and *Renaissance* (1996).

**Brian Vickers** is Professor of English Literature in the Centre for Renaissance Studies at the Eidgenössische Technische Hochschule, Zürich. His many books include *The Artistry of Shakespeare's Prose* (1968; rev. edn. 1979), *Classical Rhetoric in English Poetry* (1970, rev. edn. 1989), *Shakespeare: The Critical Heritage* (6 vols., 1974–81), *In Defence of Rhetoric* (1988), *Returning to Shakespeare* (1989), *Appropriating Shakespeare: Contemporary Critical Quarrels* (1993), *Counterfeiting Shakespeare: Evidence, Authorship, and John Ford's Funerall Elegye* (2002), and *Shakespeare, Co-author: A Historical Study of Five Collaborative Plays* (2002). He has also edited works by Hooker (1995) and Bacon (1996, 1999, and 2002).

**John Woodhouse** is Fiat-Serena Professor Emeritus of Italian Studies at the University of Oxford and Emeritus Fellow of Magdalen College, Oxford. His interests range through the whole of Italian literature, from Dante to Calvino, D'Annunzio and Rossetti. In Renaissance literature his principal publications are *Baldesar Castiglione: A Reassessment of the Courtier* (1978), *From Castiglione to Chesterfield: The Decline in the Courtier's Manual* (1991), and an edited collection on *The Language of Literature in Renaissance Italy* (1988). He has also published the important *inedita* of Vincenzio Borghini, *Scritti sulla lingua* (1971), and *Storia della nobiltà fiorentina* (1974).

ADVISORY EDITORS

**Michael J. B. Allen** (humanism) is Professor of English at UCLA and formerly Co-Editor of *Renaissance Quarterly* and Director of UCLA's Center for Medieval and Renaissance Studies. His books include *The Platonism of Marsilio Ficino* (1984), *Icastes: Marsilio Ficino's Interpretation of Plato's 'Sophist'* (1989), *Nuptial Arithmetic* (1994), *Plato's Third Eye: Studies in Marsilio Ficino's Metaphysics and its Sources* (1995), and *Synoptic Art: Marsilio Ficino on the History of Platonic Interpretation* (1998). He has also edited *Sources and Analogues of Old English Poetry: The Major Latin Texts* (1976, with D. G. Calder), *Shakespeare's Plays in Quarto* (1982, with K. Muir), and *Sir Philip Sidney's Achievements* (1990, with D. Baker-Smith and A. Kinney). Currently he is editing and translating Ficino's *Platonic Theology* (with J. Hankins).

**Francis Ames-Lewis** (Italian art) is Professor of the History of Renaissance Art at Birkbeck College, University of London. His books include *Drawing in Early Renaissance Italy* (1981, 2nd edn. 2000), *Drawing in the Italian Renaissance Workshop* (1983, with J. Wright), *The Library and Manuscripts of Piero di Cosimo de' Medici* (1984), *The Draftsman Raphael* (1986), *Tuscan Marble Carving, 1250–1350* (1997), and *The Intellectual Life of the Renaissance Artist* (2000). His edited collections of essays include *Decorum in Renaissance Narrative Art* (1991, with Anka Bednarek), *Cosimo 'il Vecchio' de' Medici* (1992), *Concepts of Beauty in Renaissance Art* (1998, with M. Rogers), *Sir Thomas Gresham and Gresham College* (1999), and *Art and Politics* (1999, with P. Paszkiewicz).

**Stephen Bamforth** (French literature) is Professor of Renaissance Studies at the University of Nottingham. His interests include early Renaissance court festival, French Renaissance scientific poetry, and seventeenth-century theatre, particularly the writings of Boaistuau, Béroalde de Verville, Jacques Dubois (Jacobus Sylvius), and Molière. His publications include editions of Sylvius' *Francisci Francorum rex et Henrici Anglorum colloquium* (1991, with J. Dupèbe) and Boaistuau's *Histoires prodigieuses* (2001); he has also edited collections of essays on *Forms of Eloquence in French Renaissance Poetry* (1989) and *Molière* (1994).

**Peter Burke** (European periphery) is Professor of Cultural History at the University of Cambridge and a fellow of Emmanuel College Cambridge. Professor Burke's books include *Culture and Society in Renaissance Italy* (1972; 4th edn. 1999), *Venice and Amsterdam: A Study of Seventeenth-Century Elites* (1974; 2nd edn. 1994), *Popular Culture in Early Modern Europe* (1978, 2nd edn. 1994), *The Historical Anthropology of Early Modern Italy* (1987), *The French Historical Revolution: The Annales School, 1929–89* (1990), *The Fabrication of Louis XIV* (1992, 2nd edn. 1994), *History and Social Theory* (1992), *The Art of Conversation* (1990), *The Fortunes of the Courtier* (1995), *Varieties of Cultural History* (1997), *The European Renaissance: Centres and Peripheries* (1998), and *A Social History of Knowledge from Gutenberg to Diderot* (2000).

**Mario Di Cesare** (classical tradition) is Distinguished Professor Emeritus of English and Comparative Literature at the State University of New York. His books include *Vida's Christiad and Vergilian Epic* (1964), *The Altar and the City: A Reading of Vergil's Aeneid* (1974), *Bibliographia Vidiana: A Bibliography of Marco Girolamo Vida* (1974), a translation of Juan Ruíz's *Libro de buen amor* (1977, with Rigo Magnani), a diplomatic edition of the Bodleian manuscript of George Herbert's *The Temple* (1995), and jointly authored concordances of Juan Ruíz's *Libro de buen amor* (1977) and the works of George Herbert (1977), Ben Jonson (1978), and Christopher Marlowe (1982). His edited collections include *Reconsidering the Renaissance* (1992) and *Milton and Italy* (1996). Professor Di Cesare was the founder and Director of *Medieval & Renaissance Texts & Studies* and is the Director of Pegasus Press.

**Iain Fenlon** (music) is Reader in Historical Musicology at the University of Cambridge, fellow of King's College, Cambridge, and Honorary Keeper of Music at the Fitzwilliam Museum, Cambridge. His books include *Music and Patronage in Sixteenth-Century Mantua* (2 vols., 1980 and 1982), *The Italian Madrigal in the Early Sixteenth Century* (1988, with J. Haar), *Music, Print and Culture in Early Sixteenth-Century Italy* (1995), an edition of *Giaches de Wert: Letters and Documents* (1999), and *Music and Culture in Late Renaissance Italy* (2002); he has also published catalogues of music manuscripts in the Barber Institute in Birmingham and (with V. Rumbold) of printed music in the Fitzwilliam Museum. Dr Fenlon is the founding editor of *Early Music History* and was the editor of Cambridge Studies in Medieval and Renaissance Music.

**J. V. Field** (mathematical sciences) is Honorary Visiting Research Fellow in the History of Art at Birkbeck College, London, Visiting Research Fellow at the Royal Institution in London, President of the Leonardo da Vinci Society, and a member of the International Academy of the History of Science. Dr Field's books include *Byzantine and Arabic Mathematical Gearing* (1985, with D. R. Hill and M. T. Wright), *The Geometrical Work of Girard Desargues* (1987, with J. J. Gray), *Kepler's Geometrical Cosmology* (1988), *The Invention of Infinity: Mathematics and Art in the Renaissance* (1997), and a translation of Kepler's *The Harmony of the World* (1997, with E. J. Aiton and A. M. Duncan).

**Susan Foister** (North European art) is Curator of Netherlandish, German, and British Paintings at the National Gallery in London. Dr Foister's principal interest is northern Renaissance painting, particularly Holbein. Her publications include *Dürer to Veronese: Sixteenth-Century Painting in the National Gallery* (1999, with J. Dunkerton and N. Penny), an edition of Anton van den Wyngaerde's *Panorama of London* (1996, with H. Colvin), edited collections on *Robert Campin* (1996, with S. Nash) and *Investigating Jan van Eyck* (2000, with

S. Jones and D. Cool), and a catalogue of *Drawings by Holbein from the Royal Library, Windsor Castle* (1983). Her exhibition catalogues for the National Portrait Gallery and the National Gallery include *Making and Meaning: Holbein's Ambassadors* (1997, with Ashok Roy and Martin Wyld).

**John Dixon Hunt** (gardens) is Professor of the History and Theory of Landscape Architecture at the University of Pennsylvania. Professor Hunt's books include *The Figure in the Landscape* (1976), *William Kent* (1987), *The Anglo-Dutch Garden in the Age of William and Mary* (1988, with Erik de Jong), *Garden and Grove: The Italian Landscape Garden in the English Imagination* (1986), *Gardens and the Picturesque* (1992), and *Greater Perfections: The Practice of Garden Theory* (2000). His many edited collections include *The Genius of the Place: The English Landscape Garden 1620–1820* (1975, with P. Willis), *The Dutch Garden in the Seventeenth Century* (1990), and *The Italian Garden* (1996). Professor Hunt is the founding editor of the *Journal of Garden History* (now *Studies in the History of Gardens and Designed Landscapes*) and of *Word & Image*.

**Robert Knecht** (French history and art) is Emeritus Professor of History at the University of Birmingham. Professor Knecht's principal work is his biography of *Francis I* (1982), which was later revised and expanded as *Renaissance Warrior and Patron: The Reign of Francis I* (1994) and subsequently translated (and again revised) into French as *Un prince de la Renaissance: François I^er et son royaume* (1998). His other books include *French Renaissance Monarchy: Francis I and Henry II* (1984, 2nd edn. 1996), *The French Wars of Religion* (1998, 2nd edn. 1996), *Richelieu* (1991), *Catherine de' Medici* (1998), *The French Civil Wars* (2000), and *The Rise and Fall of Renaissance France, 1483–1610* (2nd edn. 2001).

**John Law** (Italian history) is Reader in History at the University of Wales, Swansea, a fellow of the Royal Historical Society, and editor of *Renaissance Studies*. Dr Law's interests in late medieval and Renaissance Italy cover such subjects as Venice and its empires, the growth of the territorial state, the 'despots', Italian courts, and the 'discovery' of the Italian Renaissance in the nineteenth century. His publications include *Italy in the Age of the Renaissance* (1989, with Denys Hay) and *Venice and the Veneto in the Early Renaissance* (2000). Dr Law is a member of the editorial board established by the Fondazione Cassamarca of Treviso to publish a series of volumes on *Il Rinascimento italiano e l'Europa*. He is currently editing collections of essays on the Victorian and Edwardian response to the Italian Renaissance and on the background to the Italian Renaissance.

**Jeremy Lawrance** (Spain and Portugal) is Professor of Spanish at the University of Manchester. His interests range widely through the literature (both vernacular and neo-Latin) and history of medieval and Renaissance Spain and Portugal; he is at present conducting research on the presentation of Islam in European literature. His principal publications are scholarly editions of works by Alfonso de Cartagena (1979), Nuño de Guzmán and Giannozza Manetti (1989), Francisco de Vitoria (1991, with A. Pagden), and Alfonso de Palencia (2 vols., 1998; with R. B. Tate).

**Ian Maclean** (law) is Professor of Renaissance Studies at the University of Oxford and Senior Research Fellow at All Souls College, Oxford. Professor Maclean's interests centre on Renaissance intellectual history from Valla to Descartes, and on history and theory. His books include *The Renaissance Notion of Woman: A Study in the Fortunes of Scholasticism and Medical Science in European Intellectual Life* (sixth reprinting, 1995), *Interpretation and Meaning in the Renaissance: The Case of Law* (1992), *Montaigne philosophe* (1996), and *Logic, Signs and Nature in the Renaissance: The Case of Learned Medicine* (2001).

**John Monfasani** (Greek) is Professor of History at the State University of New York at Albany and Executive Director of the Renaissance Society of America; he is also a fellow of the Venetian Academy of Science. Professor Monfasani's interests in European intellectual history centre on Greek and Latin humanists in fifteenth-century Italy and also include Byzantine history and Reformation theology. His books include *George of Trebizond: A Biography* (1976) and *Collectanea Trapezuntiania: Texts, Documents, and Bibliographies of George of Trebizond* (1984), *Fernando of Cordova: A Biographical and Intellectual Profile* (1992), *Language and Learning in Renaissance Italy* (1994), and *Byzantine Scholars in Renaissance Italy: Cardinal Bessarion and Other Emigrés* (1995).

**Letizia Panizza** (Italian literature) is Honorary Research Fellow at Royal Holloway, University of London. Dr Panizza has written widely on Italian humanist thought (especially Stoicism and Platonism), on the reconciliation of philosophy and rhetoric, and on Lorenzo Valla, Ariosto, and Tasso; she has also edited Arcangela Tarabotti's *Che le donne siano della spezie degli uomini* (1994). Her recent publications include a collection of essays on *Women in Italian Renaissance Culture and Society* (2000) and *A History of Women's Writing in Italy* (2000, with Sharon Wood). Her current research is on the reception of Lucian in the Renaissance; she is also co-editing a volume on sixteenth- and seventeenth-century European libertinism.

**Tom Scott** (German and Reformation history) is Reader in History at the University of Liverpool and Director of the Liverpool Centre for Medieval Studies. Dr Scott's research interests include town–country relations in late medieval and early modern Europe, the German Peasants' War, and the social history of the Reformation in Germany. His books include *Die Freiburger Enquete von 1476* (1986), *Freiburg and the Breisgau: Town–Country relations in the Age of Reformation and Peasants' War* (1987), *Thomas Müntzer* (1989), *The German Peasants' War* (1991, with Bob Scribner), *Regional Identity and Economic Change: The Upper Rhine, 1450–1600* (1997), and *Society and Economy in Germany, 1300–1600* (2002).

**Paul R. Sellin** (Netherlands) is Emeritus Professor of English at UCLA. His interests are centred in English and Dutch Renaissance literature (including neo-Latin literature), particularly the writings of John Donne, Daniel Heinsius, Ben Jonson, John Milton, and Gerardus Vossius. His books include *Daniel Heinsius and Stuart England* (1968), a translation of Heinsius' *On Plot in Tragedy* (1971, with J. McManmon), *John Donne and 'Calvinist' Views of Grace* (1983), and *So doth, so is religion: John Donne and diplomatic contexts in the Reformed Netherlands, 1619–20* (1988). His current research is on Sir Walter Ralegh and the Orinoco.

**Greg Walker** (England) is Professor of Early Modern Literature and Culture at the University of Leicester. Professor Walker's principal interests are in the liter-ary, dramatic, and political history of the sixteenth century, especially the cultural consequences of the Henrician Reformation and the history of the stage in the period before the building of the professional playhouses. His books include *John Skelton and the Politics of the 1520s* (1988), *Plays of Persuasion: Drama and Politics at the Court of Henry VIII* (1991), *Persuasive Fictions: Faction, Faith and Political Culture in the Reign of Henry VIII* (1996), and *The Politics of Performance in Early Renaissance Drama* (1998).

**Andrew Wear** (medicine) is Reader in the History of Medicine in the Wellcome Trust Centre for History of Medicine (University College London). His books include *Health and Healing in Early Modern England* (1998), *Knowledge and Practice in English Medicine, 1550–1680* (2000), and the jointly written *Western Medical Tradition, 800–1800* (1995). His edited collections include *The Medical Renaissance of the Sixteenth Century* (1985, with R. French and I. Lonie), *Problems and Methods in the History of Medicine* (1987, with R. Porter), *Interpretation and Cultural History* (1990, with J. Pittock), *British Medicine in an Age of Reform* (1991, with R. French), *Medicine in Society* (1992), and *Doctors and Ethics* (1994, with J. Geyer-Kordesch and R. French).

# THEMATIC INDEX

Cisneros, Cardinal Francisco
 Jiménez de
Dolet, Étienne
Ducaeus, Fronto
Estius
Foxe, John
Harvey, Gabriel
Heinsius, Daniel
Karo, Joseph ben Ephraim
Lascaris, Constantinos
Lascaris, Janos Ryndakenos
Meigret, Louis
Sá, Manuel de
Saville, Sir Henry
Sirmond, Jacques
Torres, Francisco

### classical scholarship
Greek scholarship
Homer in the Renaissance
Latin scholarship
mythology and mythographers

### classical scholars
Bessarion, Cardinal Basil
Chalcondyles, Demetrius
Fabricius, Georg
Gaza, Theodore
Gennadios II Scholarios
Gruter, Jan
Laetus, Julius Pomponius
Lambin, Denys
Lipsius, Justus
Musurus, Marcus
Núñez de Toledo, Fernando
Robortelli, Francesco
Salmasius, Claudius
Scaliger, Joseph Justus
Sylburg, Friedrich
Turnèbe, Adrien
Vatable, François
Voss, Gerhard Jan
Xylander, Wilhelm

### biblical scholarship and biblical scholars
Andrewes, Lancelot
Arias Montano, Benito
Baudart, Willem
Bible
Complutensian Polyglot
Pagnini, Santi
Strigel, Viktorin

### Hebrew scholarship and Hebraists
Hebrew scholarship
Buxdorf, Johannes
Fagius, Paul

Lebrija, Antonio Martínez de
 Cala de
Münster, Sebastian
Pellikan, Konrad
Reuchlin, Johann
Tremellius, Immanuel
Zamora, Alfonso de

### humanists
#### ENGLAND
Caius, John
Cheke, Sir John
Colet, John
Elyot, Sir Thomas
Fisher, John
Foxe, Richard
Grocyn, William
Lily, William
Linacre, Thomas
More, Sir Thomas
Rainolds, John
Sellyng, William
Starkey, Thomas

#### FRANCE
Amyot, Jacques
Briçonnet, Guillaume
Casaubon, Isaac
Des Périers, Bonaventure
Dolet, Étienne
Dorat, Jean
Gaguin, Robert
Hervetus, Gentien
Lefèvre d'Étaples, Jacques
Muret, Marc-Antoine de
Ramus, Petrus
Roussel, Gérard
Tissard, François
Turnèbe, Odet de

#### GERMANY AND GERMAN LANDS
Albrecht von Eyb
Brant, Sebastian
Camerarius, Joachim
Celtis, Konrad
Crotus Rubeanus
Cuspinian, Johannes
Denck, Hans
Emser, Hieronymus
Franck, Sebastian
Hegius, Alexander
Peutinger, Conrad
Pirkheimer, Willibald
Reuchlin, Johann
Sabinus, Georgius
Schedel, Hartmann
Steinhöwel, Heinrich
Trithemius, Johannes
Wimpfeling, Jakob

Wimpina, Konrad
Wolf, Hieronymus
Zasius, Ulrich

#### HUNGARY
Pannonius, Janus
Vitéz, János

#### ITALY
Alamanni, Luigi
Alberti Leon Battista
Alciato, Andrea
Amaseo, Romulo
Aurispa, Giovanni
Balbi, Girolamo
Barbaro, Ermolao, the Younger
Barzizza, Gasparino da
Benvenuto da Imola
Beroaldo, Filippo the Elder and
 Filippo the Younger
Bracciolini, Poggio
Bruni, Leonardo
Buonaccorsi, Filippo
Bussi, Giovanni Andrea
Colocci, Angelo
Cortese, Paolo
Decembrio family
Della Fonte, Bartolomeo
Facio, Bartolomeo
Filelfo, Francesco
Forteguerri family
Geraldini family
George of Trebizond
Giustiniani family
Laetus, Julius Pomponius
Landino, Cristoforo
Manetti, Gianozzo
Marsuppini, Carlo
Maturanzio, Francesco
Merula, Giorgio
Niccoli, Niccolò de'
Nogarola, Isotta
Palmieri, Matteo
Panvinio, Onofrio
Parrasio, Aulo Giano
Patrizzi, Francesco
Perotti, Niccolò
Platina, Il
Poliziano, Angelo Ambrogini
Pontano, Giovanni
Rinuccini family
Salutati, Coluccio
Scala, Bartolomeo
Speroni, Sperone
Strozzi, Palla
Traversari, Ambrogio
Valeriano, Pietro
Valla, Lorenzo
Vegio, Maffeo

# ABBREVIATIONS

ADB     *Allgemeine Deutsche Biographie* (56 vols., Leipzig, 1875–1912)

BLBL     *Biographisches Lexikon zur Geschichte der Böhmischen Länder* (2 vols. and 8 fascicles to date, A–Schier, Munich, 1979– )

BLGS     *Biographisches Lexikon zur Geschichte Südosteuropas* (4 vols., Munich, 1974–81)

BNB     *Biographie nationale de Belgique* (28 vols., Brussels, 1866–1919)

CoE     *Contemporaries of Erasmus: A Biographical Register of the Renaissance and Reformation* (3 vols., Toronto 1985–7)

DBC     *Diccionari biogràfic* (4 vols., Barcelona, 1966–70)

DBEH     *Diccionario biográfico español e hispanoamericano* (1 vol., A–F only, Palma de Mallorca, 1950)

DBF     *Dictionnaire de biographie française* (19 vols. to date, A–La Vallée, Paris, 1933– )

DBI     *Dizionario biografico degli italiani* (56 vols. to date, A–Giuletti, Rome, 1960– )

DBL     *Dansk Biografisk Leksikon* (16 vols., Copenhagen, 1979–84)

DSB     *Dictionary of Scientific Biography* (15 vols., New York, 1970–8)

DCLI     *Dizionario critico della letteratura italiana*, ed. Vittore Branca (4 vols., Turin, 1986)

DHBS     *Dictionnaire historique et biographique de la Suisse* (8 vols., Neuchâtel, 1921–34); published simultaneously with minor variations as *Historisch-biographisches Lexikon der Schweiz*

DHE     *Diccionario de historia de España* (2nd edn., 3 vols., Madrid, 1968–9)

DHP     *Dicionário de história de Portugal* (6 vols., Lisbon, 1981)

DLL     *Deutsches Literatur Lexikon* (16 vols. to date, A–Schwaiger, Munich, 1968– )

DNB     *Dictionary of National Biography* (22 vols., 1885–1900); *Oxford Dictionary of National Biography* (forthcoming 2004)

FBH     *Finsk Biografisk Handbok* (2 vols., Helsinki, 1895–1903)

Grove     *The New Grove Dictionary of Music and Musicians* (29 vols., London, 2001)

HWWI     *A History of Women's Writing in Italy*, ed. L. Panizza and S. Wood (Cambridge, 2000)

JNB     *Große Jüdische National-Biographie* (7 vols., 1925–36)

MDA     *The Dictionary of Art* (34 vols., London, 1996)

MEL     *Magyar Életrajzi Lexikon* (2 vols., Budapest, 1967, 1969)

NBL     *Norsk Biografsk Leksikon* (19 vols., Oslo, 1923–83)

NBW     *Nationaal Biografisch Woordenboek* (15 vols., Brussels, 1964–96)

NDB     *Neue Deutsche Biographie* (20 vols. to date, A–Püterich, Berlin, 1953– )

NDBA     *Nouveau Dictionnaire de biographie alsacienne* (36 fascicles to date, A–Tavernier, Strasbourg, 1982– )

NNBW     *Nieuw Nederlandsch Biografisch Woordenboek* (10 vols., Leiden, 1911–37)

OCIL     *The Oxford Companion to Italian Literature*, ed. D. Robey and P. Hainsworth (Oxford, 2002)

PLP     *Prospographisches Lexikon der Palaiologenzeit*, ed. E. Trapp, R. Walther, and H. V. Meyer (12 vols. plus 7 vols. of index and addenda, Vienna, 1976–96)

PSB     *Polski Słownik Biograficzny* (39 vols. and 1 fascicle to date, A–Sokołowski, Kraków, 1935– )

RBS     Русский биографический Словарь (25 vols., St Petersburg, 1896–1918 (omits letters V, E, M, and U and sequences within G, N, P, and T; missing sequences and letters published New York, 1991–3, and Moscow, 1997– ))

SBL     *Svenskt Biografiskt Lexikon* (31 vols. and 1 fascicle to date, A–Silfverstolpe, Stockholm, 1918– )

SBL2     *Slovenski Biografski Leksikon* (4 vols., Ljubljana, 1925–81)

SBS     *Slovenský Biografický Slovník* (6 vols., Martin, 1986–94)

SEK     *Suomen Elämäkerraston Käyttäjille* (Helsinki, 1955)

SMK     *Svenska Män och Kvinnor: Biografisk Uppslagsbok* (8 vols., Stockholm, 1942–55)

# NOTE TO THE READER

This book is designed for ease of use but the following notes may be of help to the reader.

**Alphabetical arrangement** Entries are arranged in letter-by-letter alphabetical order following punctuation of the headword, with the exception that St is ordered as though it were spelt Saint.

**Cross-references** are denoted by small capitals and indicate the entry headword to which attention is being directed. Cross-references appear only where reference is likely to amplify or increase understanding of the entry being read and they are not given in all instances where a headword appears. Cross-references to major figures will not necessarily appear in specialist entries. Also 'see' or 'see also' followed by a headword in small capitals is used to indicate a cross-reference when the precise form of a headword does not appear naturally in the text.

**Spelling** for European languages is mainly in modern form. For other languages encountered in the text it is in a form which non-specialist readers will easily be able to interpret. The use of accents follows modern rather than Renaissance conventions. Exonyms have been used sparingly. For a full explanation of spelling conventions and treatment of names in the book see the Introduction (pp. vii–ix).

**Thematic Index** The list of entries under major topics which appears at the front of the book (see pp. xvii–xlvi) offers another means of accessing the material in the *Dictionary*. It allows the reader to see at a glance all the entries relating to a particular subject.

**Bibliographies** at the end of many entries provide guidance to further reading. Frequently cited works are referred to in abbreviated form (a key to these abbreviated forms can be found on p. xlvii). In the case of entries on music and Italian literature readers are referred to the recently published edition of *Grove* and the new *Oxford Companion to Italian Literature*.

**Appendices** There are four appendices at the back of the book: tables of ruling houses, a list of place names in early modern imprints, a table showing the dates at which European cities and countries changed from the Julian to the Gregorian calendar, and a table of Greek ligatures and contractions. For more information see the Introduction.

**Readers' comments** Every effort has been made to ensure that the information in the text is accurate. Readers are invited to call attention to any minor errors or inconsistencies that they discover, or to comment on individual entries, by writing to:

Rebecca Collins, Trade and Reference Department, Academic Division, Oxford University Press, Great Clarendon Street, Oxford, OX2 6DP, UK.

Readers' comments will be passed to the author.

# A

**AACHEN, HANS VON** (1552–1615), German painter, born in Cologne, the son of a native of Aachen. He studied and worked in Italy from 1574 to 1588, living in Venice and visiting Florence and Rome. On returning to Germany he worked as a portrait and landscape painter; several members of the FUGGER FAMILY commissioned portraits. In 1592 Hans von Aachen was appointed court painter to RUDOLF II, but did not move to Prague until 1597. Once established in Prague, he turned to mythological and allegorical subjects, notably his series of *Allegories on the Wars against the Turks*, of which some survive as oil sketches in the Vienna Kunsthistorisches Museum and the Budapest Museum of Fine Arts. He died in Prague on 5 March 1615.

    *MDA; NDB.*

**AAL, JOHANNES** (*c.*1500–1551), Swiss playwright. Aal's Catholic convictions forced him into exile in Freiburg im Breisgau. When the Catholic Church was reinstated in Solothurn in 1533, he returned and was appointed a canon. He was the author of a play on John the Baptist (*Tragoedia Johannis des Täufers*, 1549).

    *DHBS; DLL; NDB.*

**ABACUS**. The abacus uses counters to carry out operations in arithmetic. In the Renaissance the instrument usually took the form of a board with lines to mark the positions for counters. More recent instruments use beads on strings or rods, but the principle is the same. In western Europe, the use of the abacus was eventually replaced by written methods of calculation. Probably because the mathematics involved was elementary, the abacus lent its name to elementary instruction in mathematics. See ABACUS SCHOOLS.

In architecture, the term abacus was (and is still) used to denote the flat slab on the top of a capital: in the Ionic, Tuscan, and Roman Doric ORDERS it was square with a moulded lower edge, in the Greek Doric order it was a thick square slab, and in the Corinthian and Composite orders it had concave sides and cut corners.

**ABACUS SCHOOLS.** From the late thirteenth century onwards, many towns and guilds paid an 'abacus master' to teach mathematics to a given number of boys who intended to engage in commerce or the crafts. There were also private abacus schools, in all of which teaching was in the vernacular. Such schools are best documented in Tuscany, but similar developments seem to have occurred elsewhere. With the rise of international BANKING and the growth of commerce, the usefulness of mathematics was becoming increasingly obvious.

The schools have no direct connection with the ABACUS but take their name from the *Abacus Book* (*Liber abaci*) written by Leonardo of Pisa (*c.*1170–*c.*1240, sometimes called Fibonacci). This book set the pattern for what was taught in the schools. There was usually a great deal of ARITHMETIC, some ALGEBRA, and a little GEOMETRY. 'Arabic' (more properly Hindu-Arabic) numerals were used throughout, and instruction proceeded by series of worked examples, though surviving abacus texts do sometimes state a general rule before providing a batch of examples. Most problems are proposed as practical, for instance asking the price of a length of cloth, the weight of a fish, or the time for a fountain to be drained. The geometry problems tend to be concerned with such matters as finding the areas of triangles, which have connections with SURVEYING. Texts connected with this tradition often have titles such as 'practical mathematics' or 'commercial arithmetic'.

Abacus schools were important for the development of algebra, which had been absorbed from Islamic sources and was not taught in universities. Although the teaching in the schools was in principle elementary, masters competed for pupils by engaging in public problem-solving contests (see TARTAGLIA, NICCOLÒ). This activity, together with the authors' interest in their subject for its own sake, no doubt explains why surviving abacus texts (which are invariably the copy from which the teacher read) sometimes contain advanced problems that are posed in abstract terms that lift them out of the 'practical' tradition to which they ostensibly belong.

Abacus schools, and the kind of mathematics they taught, were significant for widening not only the intellectual base of mathematics but also its social base. They helped the processes by which mathematical skills became an increasingly important component of the lives of people of all classes. Abacus mathematics first appeared in print in Luca PACIOLI's *Summa de arithmetica . . .* (1494).

**ABAQUESNE, MASSÉOT** (*fl.* 1528–64), French potter who established the manufacturing of FAIENCE in Rouen. His workshop specialized in tile pavements decorated with heraldic designs and mythological, allegorical, and GROTESQUE figures. Some of the finest examples are those designed by Geoffrey DUMONSTIER and made by Abaquesne for MONTMORENCY's Château d'Écouen (now the Musée de la Renaissance) between 1542 and 1549. Italianate elements in his work, particularly his drug jars, may imply that he was trained by an Italian.

DBF.

**ABRAVANEL or Abrabanel, ISAAC** (1437–1508), Portuguese Jewish statesman, banker, and scholar, born in Lisbon and educated in both rabbinical and Latin learning. In 1471 he succeeded his father Judah as treasurer to AFONSO V, but when JOHN II succeeded Afonso in 1481, Abravanel was expelled from the royal court and migrated to Spain, where he entered the service of FERDINAND and ISABELLA, for whom he worked as a financial official (1484–92) and to whom he lent money to finance the war against GRANADA.

The JEWS were expelled from Spain in 1492, and Abravanel migrated to Naples, where he entered the service of FERRANTE I and ALFONSO II. When CHARLES VIII invaded Naples in 1494, Abravanel initially sought refuge in Corfu and Monopoli and in 1503 settled in Venice, where he worked in the spice trade until his death in 1508.

Abravanel wrote numerous works in Hebrew on philosophy, biblical exegesis, and anti-Christian apologetics. His commentaries on Samuel and Kings, in which he often cited Christian authorities (except in the sensitive area of messianic passages), were widely studied in Latin translation by Christian scholars in the sixteenth and seventeenth centuries. Abravanel was the father of LEONE EBREO.

DHE; JNB s.v. Abarbanel, Isaak; Roland Goetschel, *Isaac Abravanel: Conseiller des princes et philosophe* (1996); B.-Z. Netanyahu, *Don Isaac Abravanel: Statesman and Philosopher* (5th edn., 1998).

**ABRIL, PEDRO SIMÓN** (*c.*1530–*c.*1595), Spanish humanist, born in Alcaraz (La Mancha). Abril taught for 25 years at Zaragoza University. His translations into Castilian included Plato's *Cratylus* and *Gorgias*, Aristotle's *Politics* (1584) and *Logic* (1587), speeches by Aechines and Demosthenes, letters by Cicero, the comedies of Terence (1577), Euripides' *Medea*, and Aristophanes' *Pluto*; these translations were instrumental in popularizing classical literature and thought in sixteenth-century Spain. Abril also wrote a pedagogical treatise (*Latini idiomatis docendi ac discendi methodus*, 1561), a treatise on Latin grammar (*De lingua Latina vel de arte grammatica*, 1567), and Greek and Latin grammars in Castilian. His most substantial work in Castilian was *Apuntamientos de como se deben reformar las doctrinas y la manera de enseñarlas* (1589).

DBEH; Margherita Morreale, *Pedro Simón Abril* (1949); Manuel Breva-Claramonte, *La didáctica de las lenguas en el Renacimiento: Juan Luis Vives y Pedro Simón Abril* (1994).

**ACADEMIES.** The learned societies of Renaissance Europe adopted the term 'academy' in imitation of the Academy established by Plato, whose school was named after Academus, the mythical hero who was sacred to the grove on the outskirts of Athens where Plato taught. The first Renaissance academies were established in Florence and Naples.

In the mid-fifteenth century a group of scholars began to meet in the garden of the MEDICI VILLA in Careggi; these meetings, which were a conscious imitation of the meetings in Plato's *Symposium*, were organized by FICINO under the patronage of Cosimo de' MEDICI. Though not formally constituted as an academy, the scholars who met came to be known as the Accademia Platonica. At various times in the Academy's history, meetings were attended by POLIZIANO, LANDINO, PICO DELLA MIRANDOLA, BRUNELLESCHI, DONATELLO, ALBERTI, PULCI, and MICHELANGELO. The study of PLATO and the reconciliation of Platonism with Christianity were the main interests of the Academy, but DANTE and the ITALIAN LANGUAGE also fell within its scholarly purview. The Accademia Platonica declined after the death of Lorenzo de' Medici in 1492, but was revived for a short period early in the sixteenth century under the patronage of Bernardo RUCELLAI; humanists who met in the Orti Oricellari included MACHIAVELLI.

In Naples, the Academy originated in the 1440s under the leadership of Antonio BECCADELLI and the patronage of King ALFONSO V. In the late fifteenth century its most eminent member was Giovanni PONTANO, and so it came to be known as the Accademia Pontaniana.

The Roman Academy, which was founded by Julius Pomponius LAETUS, was a learned antiquarian society which sought to revive ancient Rome by performing classical plays, celebrating ancient festivals, and studying the literature of antiquity; members of the Academy, which met on the Quirinal (the northernmost hill of Rome) to discuss the ancient world, adopted Greek and Latin names; Laetus was styled *pontifex maximus*. In 1468 the Academy was suppressed by Pope PAUL II, who suspected its members of paganism and heresy; Laetus was arrested and tortured, but was eventually acquitted of the charges of heresy and immorality. Thereafter it became an offence even to mention the name of the Academy. Sixtus IV allowed the Academy to reopen, and it became prominent during the pontificates of JULIUS II and LEO X; it finally closed with the SACK OF ROME in 1527.

In the course of the sixteenth century some 700 academies were established in Italy. Some were no more than gentlemen's clubs, but others had serious scholarly, literary, and artistic purposes. In Venice, the NEAKADEMIA promoted the study of Greek language and literature. The Accademia della Crusca (Latin *Furfuratorum*), founded in 1582 in Florence, took a scholarly interest in the Italian language; its dictionary of Italian (*Vocabulario della Crusca*, 1612), which adhered to the view of BEMBO that trecento Tuscan should be regarded as the basis of the literary vernacular, was influential both in terms of the growth of lexicography (many other academies subsequently produced dictionaries) and in the establishment of Tuscan as the standard form of literary Italian.

Academies of the fine arts have their origins in the school of BERTOLDO DI GIOVANNI in Florence and the circle of LEONARDO DA VINCI in Milan, but the first formally constituted fine art academy was the Accademia del Disegno founded on the initiative of Giorgio VASARI in Florence in 1562 and jointly led by Duke COSIMO I DE' MEDICI and Michelangelo; the first fine art academy in Rome was the Accademia di San Luca, which was established in 1593.

The first scientific academy was the Academia Secretorum Naturae (Italian Accademia dei Segreti), which was founded by Giambattista DELLA PORTA in Naples in 1560; the interests of the Academy, which lay at the meeting point of magic and experimental science, attracted the attention of the INQUISITION, which ordered the Academy to close in 1580. The Accademia dei Lincei, founded in Rome in 1603 by Federico Cesi, was another early example of a scientific academy, in this case with an emphasis on biological and medical sciences; its members included Galileo GALILEI.

In France, an unconstituted academy assembled by a guild of troubadours in Toulouse in May 1324 brought together poets to give public recitations of their works at a festival of Floral Games. The games became an annual event and in about 1500 were endowed by a wealthy Toulouse matron; in 1694, the Académie des Jeux Floraux was formally constituted by King Louis XIV. The Floral Games was a poetry festival rather than a forum for philological debate, but nonetheless became the arena in which the literary claims of OCCITAN were advanced; the royal letters patent of 1694 formally imposed the FRENCH LANGUAGE. The first French academy to be officially instituted by royal decree was the Académie de la Poésie et de Musique, which was founded in 1570 by Jean-Antoine de BAÏF, who assembled poets and musicians in his house until the death of King CHARLES IX in 1574; this academy was revived two years later as the Académie du Palais, which met in the Louvre for more cerebral discussions of philosophy and rhetoric than had occurred in Baïf's house; it was permanently suspended in 1584 because of financial problems and the disruptions of the WARS OF RELIGION. The Académie Française, which is now the principal learned society of France, began as a group of writers brought together by Valentin Conrart in about 1629; in 1634 the group was taken over by Cardinal Richelieu and its letters patent were approved by the Parlement of Paris in 1637.

In the Netherlands, the Renaissance institutions comparable to the academies of southern Europe were the CHAMBERS OF RHETORIC. In 1617, Samuel COSTER, a member of a chamber of rhetoric called De Egelantier, declared himself exasperated with the frivolity of the chambers of rhetoric, and so instituted an academy modelled on those of fifteenth-century Italy. His Duijtsche Academie, which held its meetings in Dutch rather than Latin, held meetings on mathematics, philosophy, and philology, and also mounted performances of plays of an anti-Calvinist stripe. Persecuted by the authorities (largely because of the plays), the Academy merged with De Egelantier in 1635.

In the Holy Roman Empire, the forerunners of the academies were the various learned sodalities founded by Konrad CELTIS on the model of the Roman Academy of Julius Pomponius Laetus: these included the Sodalitas Vistulana in Kraków, the Sodalitas Literaria Hungarorum, the Sodalitas

Rhenana in Mainz, and, most influential of all, the Sodalitas Danubiana in Vienna. The first literary academy in Germany was Die Fruchtbringende Gesellschaft ('The Fruitful Society', also known as the Palmenorden), which was established by Prince Ludwig von Anhalt-Köthen in Weimar in 1617, in imitation of the Accademia della Crusca (of which Ludwig was a member); members aspired to encourage the literary use of the GERMAN LANGUAGE (instead of French), but the Academy had little perceptible effect on the development of literary German, and closed in 1680. German academies often produced publications, many of which failed to record the city of origin on the title pages; a list of these academic addresses is printed in Appendix 2.

In England, academies were either fictional (as in Edmund SPENSER's Areopagus) or unrealized. In 1617 the antiquary Edmund Bolton formulated a scheme for a royal academy of letters and science; Bolton drafted a constitution, drew up a list of founding members (including George CHAPMAN, Sir Kenelm Digby, Michael DRAYTON, Ben JONSON, John SELDEN, and Sir Henry WOTTON), and secured the support of King JAMES (who was himself a scholar), but the plan was never implemented; the project was renewed in 1635, this time for an aristocratic academy to be called 'Minerva's Museum', but again the plan was not realized.

The Geneva Academy founded by CALVIN in 1559 was an educational institution designed to produce godly preachers and governors; its first rector was BEZA, and the academic staff (and some of the students) were recruited *en bloc* from Lausanne. The Academy was run on strict disciplinarian lines, and on occasion students were sentenced to death for apostacy or libelling their teachers. The Academy grew rapidly, and by the time Calvin died in 1564, the Academy had 300 students and the preparatory college (the *schola privata*) had 1,000 pupils; this Academy was the antecedent institution of the University of Geneva, which was founded in 1873.

M. Maylender, *Storia delle accademie d'Italia* (5 vols., 1926–30); Frances Yates, *The French Academies of the Sixteenth Century* (1947); Nicholas Pevsner, *Academies of Art* (1940).

**ACANTHUS**, a Mediterranean plant for which the English vernacular name is bear's breech. The scalloped leaves of *Acanthus spinosus* were, according to Callimachus, the model for the distinctive foliage that decorates the capitals in the Corinthian and Composite ORDERS of architecture in antiquity; it was this stylized foliage that was revived in the Renaissance. In French such ornament is (inaccurately) termed *chicorée*.

**ACARIE, BARBE JEANNE, or Sœur Marie de l'Incarnation** (1566–1618), French Carmelite, born in Paris, the daughter of a royal councillor, and educated by the Poor Clares (French Clarisses, the second ORDER of the Franciscans) at Longchamps, near Paris. At the behest of her parents she married Pierre Acarie (a distant relative), by whom she had six children. Her salon at the family home, the Hôtel Acarie (Paris), became an important centre for French spiritualism.

Reading the autobiography of TERESA DE ÁVILA inspired Mme Acarie to establish the Reformed (or Discalced)

Carmelite Order in France, and the first house was opened in 1604; she also helped to bring the URSULINES to Paris. On the death of her husband in 1613 Mme Acarie entered the Carmelite house in Amiens as a lay sister, assuming the name Marie de l'Incarnation; in 1616 she transferred to the Carmelite house in Pontoise, where she died in 1618. She was beatified in 1791. She published nothing during her lifetime, but her devotional writing was published posthumously as *Les Vrais Exercices de la bienheureuse Sœur Marie de l'Incarnation* (1622).

DBF; Lancelot C. Sheppard, *Barbe Acarie, Wife and Mystic: A Biography* (1953).

**ACCIAIUOLI, DONATO** (1429–78), Florentine scholar and statesman, a scion of the ACCIAIUOLI FAMILY. He studied Greek with John ARGYROPOULOS and with his assistance wrote commentaries on Aristotle's *Ethics* and *Politics*. He translated some of PLUTARCH's *Lives* into Latin, and wrote biographies of Hannibal, Scipio, and Charlemagne. In addition to his expertise in Greek, he was regarded as an authority on ARITHMETIC.

Acciaiuoli represented Florence in several diplomatic missions, and in 1473 became GONFALONIERE (i.e. chairman of the governing council) of Florence. In 1478 he embarked on a diplomatic mission to Paris to solicit the support of King LOUIS XI for the struggle of Florence against Pope SIXTUS IV; he died in Milan before reaching France.

DBI.

**ACCIAIUOLI FAMILY.** Members of the Acciaiuoli family migrated to Florence from Bergamo in the twelfth century, and established themselves in business and BANKING. The family opened branches in Naples and Rome and Athens; Niccolò Acciaiuoli (1310–65), who in 1331 founded the Neapolitan branch, was in 1348 appointed grand seneschal to Queen Giovanna I; he was also the founder (in 1342) of the Certosa di Montesanto, the Carthusian monastery in Galluzzo (6 kilometres (4 miles) south of Florence) where he was later buried in a fine Gothic tomb.

In 1345 the Acciaiuoli bank collapsed; it had been weakened by a military tax in Florence and a loss of business in Rome because of difficult political relations, and was finally bankrupted by the failure (from 1341) of King Edward III of England to repay his loans. The banking business disappeared (except in Athens, where Ranieri Acciaiuoli, nephew of Niccolò, established an autonomous branch in 1388), and the family directed its energies towards Florentine politics, siding with the MEDICI against the ALBIZZI oligarchy. This alliance with the Medici enabled members of the family (including Donato ACCIAIUOLI) to fill senior civic and ecclesiastical positions throughout the fifteenth century, and, after the two interregnums (1494–1512 and 1527–30), to enjoy similar positions under the Medici dukes and grand dukes.

DBI s.v. Acciaiuoli, Niccolò; C. Urgugieri della Berardenga, *Gli Acciaiuoli di Firenze* (1961).

**ACCOLTI FAMILY.** The Arezzo family of the Accolti produced jurists, churchmen, and writers for centuries. The family had already produced several distinguished jurists when Benedetto Accolti 'il Vecchio' (1415–66) was appointed professor of jurisprudence at Florence; in 1458 he became chancellor of the Florentine republic. Benedetto wrote a history of the First Crusade, *De bello a christianis contra barbaros gesto pro Christi sepulchro et Judaea recuperandis* (Venice, 1432), which was translated into Italian (1543) and French (1620), and used by TASSO for his *Gerusalemme liberata*. Francesco Aretino (1416/17–88), the brother of Benedetto and Leonardo (his surname derives from the Latin form of 'Arezzo'), was also a distinguished jurist; he wrote several legal commentaries and became professor at Ferrara and Siena; he also translated Leonardo BRUNI's *De bello italico adversus Gothos* into verse (1528).

Bernardo Accolti (1465–1536), the son of Benedetto, was a poet (known as 'L'Unico Aretino') who became famous for his public recitations of impromptu poetry, often to large crowds; his popular following included learned humanists and churchmen (Cardinal BEMBO was among those who praised his performances). His comedy *Virginia*, a dramatized version of a story in BOCCACCIO's *Decameron*, was performed in 1493 and subsequently published in a collection entitled *Virginia, comedia, capitoli e strambotti* (Florence, 1513). Bernardo's brother Pietro (1455–1532) was appointed bishop of Ancona in 1505 and created cardinal by Pope JULIUS II on 17 March 1511. He served as an abbreviator (i.e. a papal draughtsman of letters and writs) to Pope LEO X, and in that capacity drew up the bull EXSURGE DOMINE (promulgated 15 June 1520) against Martin LUTHER. He was bishop of Albano and Sabina (both close to Rome), Cádiz, Maillezais (the fortress of the dukes of Aquitaine), Arras, and Cremona, and in 1524 was appointed archbishop of Ravenna by Pope CLEMENT VII. Pietro's son Benedetto organized an attempt on the life of Pope PIUS II and was executed in 1564. Pietro's nephew Benedetto il Giovane (1497–1549) shared several preferments with his uncle (with whom he is sometimes confused), and on 3 May 1527 was created cardinal by Pope Clement VII; he was also a neo-Latin poet, and his *Epigrammata* were published in *Carmina quinque etruscorum poetarum* (Florence, 1562).

DBI has entries s.v. Accolti on Benedetto il Vecchio, Francesco, Bernardo, Pietro, Benedetto the son of Pietro (wrongly said to be the son of Cardinal Benedetto but corrected in vol. xxxv p. 403), and Benedetto il Giovani; Robert Black, *Benedetto Accolti and the Florentine Renaissance* (1985).

**ACCORAMBONI, VITTORIA** (1557–85), born in Gubbio on 15 February 1557; she moved to Rome as a child, and at the age of 16 married Francesco Peretti, a nephew of Cardinal Montalto (Felice Peretti, later Pope SIXTUS V). Vittoria soon embarked on an affair with Paolo Giordano ORSINI, duke of Bracciano, who had in 1576 murdered his first wife, Isabella de' Medici (sister of Francesco de' Medici, duke of Florence), because of her infidelity with Troilo Orsini. In 1581 Vittoria's brother Marcello, possibly in collusion with Paolo, arranged for Francesco Peretti to be assassinated, whereupon Paolo married Vittoria. Pope GREGORY XIII declared the marriage void and ordered Vittoria to be immured in her family home;

she initially refused, and so was imprisoned in Castel Sant'Angelo in December 1581, and after a year was released at the behest of Cardinal Carlo BORROMEO, who had interceded on her behalf. In 1583 she travelled to the Orsini castle in Bracciano and secretly remarried Paolo.

On 10 April 1585 Pope Gregory died, and while the electoral conclave was in session, Vittoria and Paolo were married for a third time, in a public wedding. When Cardinal Montalto was elected as Pope Sixtus V and the Peretti family renewed its intention to avenge the death of Francesco, Vittoria and Paolo fled to the Veneto (first to Venice, and then to Salò), but on 13 November 1585 Paolo died of an ulcerous infection in his leg, bequeathing his personal fortune to Vittoria. Vittoria retired in grief to Padua, where she was pursued by Paolo's cousin Ludovico Orsini, whose anger because of the murder had been exacerbated by the loss of the Orsini fortune. Ludovico arranged for Vittoria to be assassinated on 22 December 1585; he and his accomplices were subsequently executed.

The violence, political intrigue, and sexual interest of the story rendered it attractive to Protestants, in part because it confirmed rectitudinous and xenophobic Protestant stereotypes about the decadence of Italy. Within 25 years there were more than 100 accounts of the story circulating in Europe. Material from one of these accounts, deriving from a manuscript newsletter (written in German) for the FUGGER banking family (now Codex 8959 in the Österreichische Nationalbibliothek) became the principal source for John WEBSTER's *The White Devil: The Tragedy of Paulo Giordano Ursini Duke of Brachiano and Vittoria Corombona* (1612); Webster retained the original names, but his Francesco Peretti is called Camillo and Cardinal Montalto becomes the fifteenth-century Pope PAUL II instead of Sixtus V. In the nineteenth century Vittoria became the heroine of historical fictions by Ludwig Tieck (*Vittoria Accorombona*, 1840), Stendhal (*Vittoria Accoramboni*, 1839), and a host of Italian novelists, including F. D. Guerrazzi (*Isabella Orsini*, 1844).

DBI; Gunnar Boklund, *The Sources of 'The White Devil'* (1957).

**ACKERMANN, HANS** (*fl.* 1530s), German author of two biblical plays performed in Zwickau; both *Der verlorene Sohn* (1536) and *Tobias* (1539) reflect the values of the Reformation.

DLL; NDB.

**ACONTIUS, JACOBUS, or Giacomo Acontio** (1492–1566), tolerationist theologian and engineer. He was born in Trento (Trentino) and migrated to escape persecution, first to Basel and then to Zürich. His *De methodo, hoc est de recto investigandarum tradendarumque scientiarum ratione* (Basel, 1558) was an exposition of the principles of biblical criticism. He moved to England, possibly in 1559, and there worked as an engineer, draining marshes by the Thames (1562–6). His mechanical inventions were rewarded with an annual pension of £60 by Queen Elizabeth, and he enjoyed the patronage of the earl of Leicester.

Acontius was an active member of the Dutch church in Austin Friars (London) and engaged in theological controversies. In 1564 he published *Stratagemata Satanae* (the title page of which says 1565), in which he sought to establish common theological tenets for all Christian churches and proclaimed his opposition to the death penalty for heresy; the book was soon translated into Dutch, English, French, and German and was added to the 1569 edition of the INDEX.

DBI s.v. Aconcio; DNB; P. Rossi, *Giacomo Aconcio* (1952).

**ACORN CUP**, in late sixteenth- and early seventeenth-century England, a stemmed cup made of silver or gold in which the bowl and lid are shaped like an acorn cup, i.e. the shell (*cupulate involucre*) of the acorn.

**ACOSTA, JOSÉ DE** (1539–1600), Spanish missionary and naturalist, born in Medina del Campo; he joined the JESUITS in 1551. In 1571 he was sent as a missionary to Peru, where he served as provincial of his Order (1576–81) and acted as theological adviser to the Council of Lima (1582). In 1583 Acosta published a catechism in Aymara and Quechua which was the first book to be printed in Peru.

Acosta returned to Spain in 1587. He wrote a natural history of Spanish America, *De natura novi orbis* (Salamanca, 1588–9), which proved to be a preliminary version of his great work, the *Historia natural y moral de las Indias* (Seville, 1590), which was translated into Italian (1596), French (1597), Dutch (1598), German (1601), Latin (1602), and English (1604); this treatise, which is now valued for its ethnography and excoriated for its defence of Spanish colonialism, examines the physical geography and flora and fauna of Mexico and Peru (arguing that the plants and animals had spread from Europe to America along a lost land bridge) and describes the religious and political institutions of the Aztec and Inca empires. His other publications included *De procuranda salute Indorum* (Salamanca, 1588), *De Christo revelato* (Rome, 1590), *De temporibus novissimis* (Rome, 1590), and three volumes of sermons (1596–9).

In 1592, Acosta's opposition to AQUAVIVA led to his imprisonment. He was released in 1593 and, on submitting to Aquaviva the following year, was appointed superior of the Jesuits at Valladolid. In 1598 he was appointed rector of the Jesuit college in Salamanca, where he died on 15 February 1600.

DBEH; DHE; Claudio Burgaleta, *José de Acosta: His Life and Thought* (1999).

**ACQUAVIVA, CLAUDIO.** See AQUAVIVA, CLAUDIO.

**ACUÑA, FERNANDO DE** (*c.*1520–*c.*1580), Spanish soldier, poet, and translator, born in Valladolid; he served as a soldier in Germany, Italy, and Tunisia. His Italianate *Varias poesías* was published by his widow in 1591. He translated the first four books of BOIARDO's *Orlando innamorato*, and versified a prose version of Olivier de LA MARCHE's *Le Chevalier délibéré* from a prose translation said to have been written by CHARLES V; Acuña's version was itself translated into English, and appeared in 1594 as *The Resolved Gentleman*.

DBEH; Gabriele Morelli, *Hernando de Acuña: Un petrarchista dell'epoca imperiale* (1977).

**ADAMSON, PATRICK** (1537–92). Created archbishop of St Andrews in 1576 and ambassador to London between 1583 and 1584, Adamson was an opponent of the presbyterian party in Scotland. Although he had the support of JAMES VI, his continued disfavour with the General Assembly culminated in his excommunication at the Synod of Fife in 1586. His writings include translations into Latin of the Lamentations of Jeremiah and the Book of Revelation (published 1590), a catechism (*c.*1570), and the *Declaration of the King's Intention and Meaning towards the Late Acts of Parliament* (1585).

DNB.

**ADIAPHORA**, a transliteration of the Greek word ἀδιάφορα, which means 'things indifferent'. In theological use, an adiaphoron is a rite or a practice that is not essential to the Christian faith. The Adiaphorists were a Lutheran faction whose members maintained that certain rites and practices were matters of indifference. The controversy came to a head at the LEIPZIG INTERIM of 1548, at which the Wittenberg theologians led by MELANCHTHON insisted in the face of opposition from the ecclesiastical and civic authorities of Saxony that concessions might be made to the Catholic Church on matters such as confirmation, extreme unction, and the veneration of saints, all of which were deemed by the Wittenberg theologians to be adiaphora. The principal opponent of these concessions was the Istrian theologian Matthias FLACIUS ILLYRIUS, who argued in his *De veris et falsis adiaphoris* (1549) that to yield on such matters would fragment the Lutheran cause.

The controversy was not settled by the Peace of AUGSBURG in 1555, but was finally concluded in the Formula of CONCORD (1577), Article 10 of which declared that concessions could not be made in times of persecution, but that in other circumstances, ceremonies not explicitly prescribed or proscribed by Scripture should be regarded as adiaphora and so could be used or discarded at the discretion of individual churches. Thereafter the controversy remained dormant in Germany until the late seventeenth century, when Pietists insisted that worldly pleasures such as dancing and playgoing were sinful but orthodox Lutherans held them to be adiaphora and therefore permissible. This debate was anticipated in England and Scotland by seventeenth-century Puritans, who thought that worldly pleasures should be suppressed.

**ADLERGLAS** or *Adlerhumpen* or *Reichsadlerhumpen*, a German drinking-glass, sometimes with a cover, developed in the mid-sixteenth century. Each glass was decorated in enamel with an image of the eagle of the Holy Roman Empire; the wings of the eagle bore the armorial bearings of the families of the Empire.

**ADMIRAL'S MEN**. Named after their patron, Lord Charles HOWARD, the lord high admiral, this Elizabethan acting company, which included Edward ALLEYN, first appeared at court in 1585. Based in 1590 at the THEATRE, later at the ROSE, and from 1600 at the FORTUNE, their numbers were depleted by the formation of the CHAMBERLAIN'S MEN in 1594. They performed Christopher MARLOWE's plays as part of a large repertoire, but other plays were lost in a fire at the Fortune in 1621. On the death of ELIZABETH, they became Prince Henry's Men and later (1612) Palsgrave's Men; they eventually disbanded in 1631.

**ADMONITION TO THE PARLIAMENT**, a Puritan manifesto issued anonymously by an unknown publisher in June 1572. The manifesto inveighs against senior ecclesiastical and university figures, argues for the replacement of episcopacy by presbyterianism, and attacks practices such as the use of wafer-bread in communion and the obligation to kneel while receiving communion. The London clergymen John Field and Thomas Wilcox attempted to present the manifesto to Parliament, but were rebuffed; they were assumed to be the authors and were committed to Newgate on 7 July 1572.

WHITGIFT's formal response to the manifesto merely prompted the appearance of the *Second Admonition to the Parliament*, which seems to have been written by Thomas CARTWRIGHT. The *Admonition* and the *Second Admonition* were suppressed by royal proclamation on 11 June 1573, and Cartwright fled the country to avoid arrest. The greatest literary product of this debate was Richard HOOKER's *Ecclesiastical Polity* (1594–7).

**ADRIAN VI or Hadrian VI** (1459–1523), pope from 9 January 1522 until his death on 14 September 1523, was born Adriaan Florenszoon Dedal in Utrecht on 2 March 1459. He was educated by the BRETHREN OF THE COMMON LIFE, and entered Louvain University at the age of 17; he was awarded a doctorate in 1492, and successively appointed to a professorship, the rectorship, and in 1497 to the chancellorship of the university. In 1507 the Emperor MAXIMILIAN I charged him with the education of his grandson, the future CHARLES V, and in 1515 he travelled to Spain to oversee his pupil's succession to the Spanish throne. On the death of Ferdinand II of Aragon (FERDINAND V) in 1516, he became co-regent with Cardinal Jiménez de CISNEROS until Charles ascended the throne in 1517.

Adrian was appointed bishop of Tortosa and inquisitor for Aragon and Navarre in 1516; the following year he was created cardinal of Utrecht, and in 1518 his inquisitorial duties were extended to Castile and León. Charles became emperor in 1519, and during his protracted absence (1520–2) for the imperial coronation, Adrian served as regent, in which capacity he presided over the suppression of the Revolt of the COMUNEROS.

Adrian was still in Spain when he was elected pope in January 1522. He sailed to Rome and was frostily received by the ecclesiastical and civic communities, who resented the appointment of a foreign pope with no interest in the artistic or musical culture of Rome. On 1 September 1522 Adrian announced at his first consistory that he proposed to deal with the twin threats of the Lutheran revolt and Ottoman incursions (Belgrade had fallen the previous year) by reforming the Catholic Church, beginning with the papal curia; his contention that the corruption of the curia lay at the heart of the Church's problems was one of the seeds of the COUNTER-

REFORMATION. Adrian made an ascetic virtue of the debt that he had inherited from the profligate LEO X; he campaigned against simony and nepotism, and declined to assert the temporal powers of the papacy.

It was Adrian's hamfisted attempt to unite Europe against the Ottoman threat that finally destroyed his authority and may have precipitated his death. He forfeited the support of Charles V by declaring papal neutrality in the imperial war with France, and his proclamation of a three-year truce for all Christian countries in the wake of the loss of Rhodes to the Ottomans on 21 December 1522 incurred the hostility of FRANCIS I. This rift, which was exacerbated by the arrest of Cardinal Soderini (a furtive ally of Francis I), led Francis to sever the transfer of funds to Rome and to mount an invasion of Lombardy. Adrian's last significant act was the formation of a defensive alliance with the Empire, England, Austria, and several Italian cities on 3 August 1523; he died six weeks later, and jubilant Romans proclaimed his physician as their liberator.

DBI s.v. Adriano; J. Posner, *Der deutsche Papst Adrian VI* (1962).

**ADRIANO FIORENTINO or Adriano di Giovanni de' Maestri** (*c*.1450/60–*c*.1499), Italian sculptor and medallist, born in Florence, where he cast the bronze statuette of *Bellerophon and Pegasus* (Kunsthistorisches Museum, Vienna) by BERTOLDO DI GIOVANNI. At an unknown date in the 1480s Adriano moved to Naples, where he entered the service of King FERRANTE I, for whom he worked as a military engineer, artillery-founder, and portrait medallist; his portrait medal subjects included Giovanni PONTANO and Jacopo SANNAZARO. In the late 1490s he moved to Mantua and then to Saxony, where his work included a bell-metal bust of the Elector FRIEDRICH III (1498, Albertinum, Dresden).

DBI s.v. Maestri, Adriano de; MDA.

**ADVERTISEMENTS, BOOK OF** (1566), the short title of Matthew PARKER's *Advertisements, partly for due order in the public administration of common prayers and using the holy sacraments, and partly for the apparel of all persons ecclesiastical by virtue of the Queen's Majesty's Letters commanding the same*, a statutory document issued in March 1566. The 39 commands included the requirement to kneel when receiving holy communion and the disallowing of the sign of the cross at baptism. The requirements concerning the wearing of the surplice ignited the VESTIARIAN CONTROVERSY.

The Act of UNIFORMITY of 1559 contained an 'Ornaments Rubric' which dealt with many of the same matters as the *Book of Advertisements*, and explained that the rubric would remain in force 'until other order shall therein be taken by order of the Queen's Majesty'. Scholars are uncertain about whether this 'other order' is the *Book of Advertisements*.

**AERSCHOT or Aarschot, PHILIPPE DE CROY, DUKE OF** (1526–95), leader of the Catholic nobility in the southernmost provinces of the Netherlands. In July 1563 Aerschot emerged as the leader of a group of Walloon aristocrats who supported the beleaguered Cardinal GRANVELLE. In 1565 King PHILLIP II appointed Aerschot as head of the Council of State of the Netherlands; he thus became the principal opponent of WILLIAM OF ORANGE. He was a political moderate, and distanced himself from the brutality with which the duke of ALBA suppressed civil unrest and Protestantism. In 1576 the plunder of Antwerp by the forces of Luís REQUESCENS (the episode known as the Spanish fury) enabled Aerschot to assume control and to negotiate the Pacification of GHENT. He supported the appointment of Archduke (later Emperor) MATTHIAS as governor-general of the Netherlands (January 1578), but when he discovered that Matthias was prepared to co-operate with William of Orange, Aerschot realigned himself with the forces of Spain.

**AERTSEN or Aertszoon, PIETER** (*c*.1507/8–1575), Dutch painter who worked both in his native Amsterdam and (from 1535 to *c*.1555) in Antwerp. His paintings, which are often huge, are usually GENRE PAINTINGS or STILL LIFE pictures, characteristically representing butchers and meat. Aertsen also painted ALTARPIECES, most of which have perished or survive only in fragments.

Aertsen's sons Pieter Pieterszoon (1540–1603) and Aert Pieterszoon (1550–1612) were also painters, as were his nephew Joachim BEUCKELAER and his grandson Cabel Arentszoon (*c*.1585–1635).

MDA; NNBW i.

**AFONSINE ORDINANCES.** See ALFONSINE ORDINANCES.

**AFONSO V** (1432–81), king of Portugal, known as 'Africano', succeeded his father DUARTE in 1438; for the next ten years the kingdom was governed by regents, initially Afonso's mother and then his uncle Dom Pedro. At the conclusion of his minority in 1448, Afonso assumed control of the government and married Dom Pedro's daughter Isabella. A quarrel between Afonso and Dom Pedro escalated into a rebellion which culminated in May 1449 with the battle of Alfarrobeira, in which Dom Pedro was killed.

In 1458 Afonso responded to the papal call for a CRUSADE by invading North AFRICA; he returned in 1471 with a larger force, and captured Tangier. In 1475 his aspirations turned to Castile, where he decided to support the claim of his niece JUANA LA BELTRANEJA to the disputed throne, and, as he was now a widower, to marry Juana and assume the throne of Castile himself; he proclaimed himself king of Castile and León on the basis of his betrothal. Juana's aunt ISABELLA of Castile also claimed the throne, and in 1476 the army of her husband FERDINAND defeated Afonso's army at the battle of Toro. Afonso travelled to France in an attempt to secure assistance from King LOUIS XI and, on being betrayed by the French king, abdicated in favour of his son Juan (later JOHN II); on returning to Portugal he was forced by his son to resume the throne. In 1479 he repudiated his claim to the throne of Castile by signing the Treaty of ALCAÇOVAS, and spent the rest of his life in a monastery at Cintra.

DHP; MDA s.v. Aviz (3).

**AFRICA.** The modern geographical idea of Africa evolved gradually from ancient and medieval European and Islamic cosmographical notions about the division of the world into three continents. Before the fifteenth century only the vaguest notions of sub-Saharan Africa were available to the Latin West, and the continent was thought to correspond roughly with Roman North Africa, excluding Egypt east of the Nile, which was, together with Ethiopia, considered to be part of ASIA. In the late fifteenth century the circumnavigation of the continent by the Portuguese transformed this picture, producing more accurate maps of the extent, shape, and ethnographic diversity of black Africa and associating the terms 'African' and 'Ethiopian' more particularly with the sub-Saharan regions. The modern notion of an African continent is a product of European colonialism and the post-colonial legacy, and did not take root in the African continent until the Organization of African Unity was established in 1963; even now, the sub-Saharan notion of Azania excludes Arab and Berber North Africa, and in the north the ancient distinction between Mediterranean Ifriqiyya and al-Sūdān ('the land of the blacks') still obtains.

In learned circles, Africa was associated with early Christianity, because PATRISTIC writers such as Arnobius, Augustine, Cyprian, Lactantius, and Tertullian lived in North Africa. The Arab conquest of the seventh century left North Africa inaccessible to Europeans, but classical ideas lingered for centuries. Biblical ethnology also left its mark on the European consciousness: Noah's son Ham, whose name was known to derive from a Semitic root meaning 'black', was condemned by his father to be a slave of slaves, and this curse was passed to his descendants; in this story lay the aetiological myth that long sustained European notions of cultural and racial superiority over black Africans.

The Ottoman conquerors of Constantinople and the Balkan peninsula turned their sights on North Africa in the early sixteenth century, conquering Mameluke Egypt in 1517 and thereafter vassalizing Algiers (1529), Tripoli (1551), and Tunis (1574); Morocco retained its independence as a Berber sultanate overlaid with Arab institutions. Arabs and Berbers had traversed the desert south of the Maghrib in the fourteenth century: Timbuktu (now Tombouctou, in Mali), for example, had been reached by an Arab traveller in 1352, even though its inhabitants did not convert to Islam until the Moroccan invasion of 1590.

The retreat of the Saracens from Sicily and southern Italy in the eleventh century opened the way for Italian attacks on Tunisia and Libya, and by the end of the fifteenth century the maritime states of northern Italy had established trading links with North Africa. The struggle against the Moors in the Iberian peninsula provided another important point of contact between Europe and North Africa. Long before the final expulsion of the Moors from the kingdom of GRANADA in 1492, Spain and Portugal had attacked and occupied North African ports. In 1415 the Portuguese forces of King JOHN I captured Ceuta, which was destined to become a permanent European enclave in North Africa; it passed to Spain with the ending of Portuguese independence in 1580 and, despite a siege that lasted for 26 years (1694–1720), has remained a Spanish possession. Similarly, Melilla was captured by Spain

in 1490, and is still a Spanish possession. The Spanish enclaves that were subsequently lost were (from west to east) Peñón de Vélez de la Gomera, Tlemcen (1510), Oran (1509–1708, 1732–91) and its port of Mers el Kébir (captured in 1505), Mostaganem, Ténès, Peñón de Alger (1510–29), Bejaïa, Annaba, Bizerte (1535–74), and Tunis; Tripoli was captured by the Spanish in 1510, passed to the Knights of ST JOHN in 1528, and was captured by the Ottomans in 1553. Portugal held Tangier (1471–1580, 1656–62), Alcácer Ceguer (1458–1578; now Ksar-es-Seghir), and enclaves along the Moroccan coast to the south-west from Asilah (1513–41) to Mazagan (1514–1769; now El-Jadida) and Safi. This period of Hispanic domination came to an end in 1578, when the Portuguese were resoundingly defeated at the battle of KSAR-EL-KEBIR. Thereafter Europeans associated the northern coast of Africa with BARBARY PIRATES and slavery: as late as 1631, North African pirates captured an English ship off the north coast of Wales and sold its 150 passengers and crew into slavery.

The combatants at the battle for Ceuta had included Prince HENRY THE NAVIGATOR, who developed an ambition to acquire for Portugal the Atlantic coast of Africa. The voyages of discovery initiated by Prince Henry began with the discovery of Madeira in 1419 and the Azores in 1432; in the same period a series of Portuguese expeditions began to explore the West Africa coast: in 1434 an expedition rounded Cape Bojador, 200 kilometres (125 miles) south of the Canaries and the limit of the world known to Europeans, and in 1444 an expedition led by Nuno TRISTÃO reached the Senegal river. By 1457 Alvise da CADAMOSTO had reached the Gambia river and discovered the Cape Verde Islands. In 1482 Diogo CÃO reached the mouth of the Congo, and in 1488 Bartolomeu DIAS rounded the Cape of Good Hope. In 1498 an expedition commanded by Vasco da GAMA rounded Africa, landed briefly at Sofala (now in Mozambique), Mombasa, and Malindi (both now in Kenya), and reached India; the voyage was celebrated by Luís CAMÕES in his epic poem *The Lusiads*.

Tales of the gold found in West Africa by the Portuguese, together with the nascent market for slaves, attracted other Europeans to the African coast: by the mid-sixteenth century, the European presence on the Ivory Coast (now Côte d'Ivoire), the Gold Coast (now Ghana), and the Slave Coast (now Togo, Dahomey, and Nigeria) included Danish, Dutch, English, French, German (Brandenburger), Ottoman, Portuguese, and Spanish settlements; from 1526 to 1870 some 10,000,000 slaves were to be shipped to the Americas.

The Portuguese established forts and *FEITORIAS* ever further south, and so remained in the vanguard of exploration and exploitation. Luanda (now in Angola) was founded by the Portuguese in 1576, and was held by Portugal until 1974. Rounding the cape, the Portuguese encountered the Arab sultanates of the East African coast; by 1520, all these sultanates had been captured, and were administered from Mozambique. In 1569 the Portuguese began to penetrate the interior of the Zambezi valley in search of gold, and so encountered the indigenous people of the region, establishing settlements on the shores of the Zambezi at Sena and Tele.

The horn of Africa became the seat of a struggle between Islam and Christianity. The north and east coasts of Africa had been Islamic for centuries, but Ethiopia had remained Christian. In the early 1520s the sultan of Adal (now Djibouti and the contiguous part of the Somali Republic) began to move his Islamic forces into Christian Ethiopia; the Portuguese believed that the Christian kingdom of the legendary PRESTER JOHN was at risk, and from 1541 to 1543 a regiment of 400 soldiers under the command of Christovão da Gama fought on the side of Ethiopian Christians. They failed to convert the Ethiopians to Catholicism, as did the Portuguese Jesuits who followed them, but until they were finally expelled in 1665, the Jesuits travelled widely in Ethiopia: in 1615 Pedro Paez visited the sources of the Blue Nile, as did Jerónimo Lobo in 1625. After the expulsion of the Jesuits from Ethiopia in 1663, European contacts were restricted to the coasts of Africa, and no curiosity was evinced about the interior or its inhabitants. As Jonathan Swift wrote in 1773,

> So geographers in Afric maps
> With savage pictures fill their gaps;
> And o'er unhabitable downs
> Place elephants for want of towns.

European exploration only resumed with James Bruce's expedition of 1770–2.

Throughout the sixteenth century, English and Dutch ships bound for India stopped at Table Bay (now the port of Cape Town) to take on fresh water before rounding the Cape. In 1620 two English officers took it upon themselves to protect British interests by claiming Table Bay for King JAMES; on 6 April 1652, the Netherlands founded a settlement at Table Bay. These rival claims sowed the seeds of discord that were to dominate European life in southern Africa for centuries.

Africa was the subject of a substantial European literature, including Francisco Álvarez's *Veradadera informaçam das terras do Preste Joam* (Lisbon, 1540), Leo Africanus, *Della descrittione dell'Africa* (Venice, 1550), Luis del Mármol Carajal, *Descripción general de Africa* (Granada and Málaga, 1573–99), and Diego de Haedo, *Topographia e historia general de Árgel* (Valladolid, 1612).

J. W. Blake, *West Africa: Gold and Slaves, 1454–1578* (1977); C. Boxer, *Four Centuries of Portuguese Expansion* (1961).

**AGARD or Agarde, ARTHUR** (1540–1615), English antiquary. In 1603 Agard was created deputy chamberlain of the exchequer, where he may have been a clerk from an early age. Here he spent three years drawing up a catalogue of the records of the four treasuries of the exchequer, together with a list of the leagues, treatises, and marriages which had been arranged between England and other countries. Both of these were published in 1631. He was a member of the Society of Antiquaries from its foundation in 1572 to the ceasing of its activities in 1604; through this he knew CAMDEN, STOW, and others with antiquarian concerns. His other writings include a Latin treatise on the Domesday Book, and histories of English names, heraldry, land measurements, and other institutions.

**AGATE GLASS or (Italian)** *calcedonio* **or (German)** *Schmelzglas*, an imitation of agate made by blending molten GLASS of two or more colours. The technique was known in antiquity and revived in late fifteenth-century Venice and Germany.

**AGAZZARI, AGOSTINO** (1578–c.1640), Italian composer and music theorist, born in Siena. He worked in Rome as a choirmaster, and in 1607 returned permanently to Siena to become the cathedral organist and choirmaster. His works include *Eumelio*, a pastoral drama performed in Rome in 1606; *Del sonare sopra 'l basso . . . nel conserto* (1607), a treatise on the art of accompanying an ensemble from an unfigured bass; *La musica ecclesiastica* (1638), on the implementation of the decrees of the COUNCIL OF TRENT concerning church music, and several volumes of original compositions.

**AGINCOURT or (French) Azincourt, BATTLE OF** (25 October 1415), a battle in the HUNDRED YEARS WAR. On 13 August 1415 King Henry V of England invaded France with an army of 10,000 men (7,500 archers and 2,500 men-at-arms). His army besieged Harfleur, but the siege was raised on 23 September, partly because the town had excellent defences, but also because the English army was suffering from dysentery. King Henry decided to retreat to England via CALAIS, which was then an English possession.

A French army of c.20,000 soldiers (including a strong contingent of feudal cavalry) contrived to block the line of retreat at Agincourt. By this point the English army had been reduced to 5,000 archers and 1,000 men-at-arms. On 24 October Henry drew up his troops, all on foot, in a narrow defile bordered by trees, placing his archers on the flanks. The next morning the French cavalry charged, but quickly became mired in the muddy terrain, and were forced to dismount amidst volleys of arrows. The French were defeated and suffered huge losses; French prisoners included CHARLES D'ORLÉANS.

The consequences of the battle were the English reconquest of Normandy (1415–17) and the signing of the Treaty of Troyes (21 May 1420), according to which King Henry was betrothed to Princess Catherine, daughter of King Charles VI of France, and acknowledged as heir to the throne of France in place of the dauphin. The battle was later dramatized in *Henry V* by SHAKESPEARE, who glossed over Henry's decision to slaughter his prisoners, which was a breach of CHIVALRIC practice.

Christopher Hibbard, *Agincourt* (London, 1964); Philippe Contamime, *Azincourt* (1964); C. T. Allmand, *Henry V* (rev. edn., 1997).

**AGNADELLO, BATTLE OF, or battle of Ghiaradadda**, fought on 14 May 1509 at Agnadello, on the Milanese–Venetian border. The French forces of the League of CAMBRAI, commanded by Gian Giacomo TRIVULZIO, inflicted on the Venetian army the greatest defeat in its history; the Venetian humiliation included the capture of BARTOLOMEO D'ALVIANO, who was second in command to the count of Pitigliano. This defeat led in October 1511 to the formation of the HOLY LEAGUE, which aspired to drive the forces of LOUIS XII out of Italy.

**AGOSTINO DI DUCCIO** (1418–*c*.1481), Italian sculptor, a native of Florence who worked as a mercenary soldier in his youth. Nothing is known of his training in sculpture, and his style differs so markedly from that of his Florentine contemporaries that it is not possible to associate him confidently with any particular workshop. His principal works are reliefs on the pulpit of Modena Cathedral (1442), on the interior of Sigismondo MALATESTA's Tempio Malatestiano at Rimini (*c*.1450–7), and on the façade of the Oratory of San Bernardino in Siena (*c*.1457–61). A relief of *The Virgin and Child*, which was sculpted while Agostino was in Rimini, is now in the Victoria and Albert Museum in London.

DBI; MDA; Adrian Stokes, *Stones of Rimini* (1934); Marco Campigli, *Luce e marmo: Agostino di Duccio* (1999).

**AGOSTINO VENEZIANO or Agostino de Musi** (*c*.1490–1536/40), Italian engraver who worked in his native Venice from 1509 to 1516, after which he moved first to Florence and then to Rome. His engravings are notable for their GROTESQUE ornament.

DBI s.v. De Musi, Agostino; MDA s.v. Musi, Agostino del.

**AGRICOLA, ALEXANDER** (*c*.1446–1506), Flemish composer who wrote masses, motets, and motet chansons as well as secular vocal and instrumental music. His style betrays the influence of OCKEGHEM and incorporates borrowed material. Recognized with some distinction in his lifetime, he worked in France, Italy, and the Low Countries and died at Valladolid in 1506.

**AGRICOLA or (German) Bauer, GEORG** (1494–1555), German mineralogist who studied philosophy and medicine in Leipzig, Bologna, Padua, and Venice. In the early 1530s he travelled widely in Europe, meeting and becoming friends with ERASMUS, MELANCHTHON, and Joachim CAMERARIUS. On returning to Saxony he first practised as a physician in the new mining town of Joachimstal (now Jáchymov in the Czech Republic), the town which gave its name to the thaler and thence to the dollar. Agricola eventually settled in Chemnitz, of which he became burgomaster, and there turned his attention to mining operations. Chemnitz was at the centre of one of the most advanced and important mining regions in Europe, so there was a happy consonance of Agricola's intellectual interests and his civic concerns.

Agricola's published works include a study of the minerals of Saxony (*Bermannus*, 1530), a taxonomy of minerals (*Natura fossilum*, 1546), and a detailed account of the mining and smelting of metallic ores (*De re metallica*, 1556). These writings, which were widely read in their own time, contain many illustrations and are now important as records of mining techniques and as providing indications of current understanding of the structure of the earth.

DSB; NDB; NBW vii; H. Hartmann, *George Agricola 1494–1555* (1953).

**AGRICOLA, JOHANN** (1494–1566), German reformer, born on 20 April 1494 in Eisleben and baptized as Johann Schneider; he subsequently changed his family name to Schnitter. He studied at Wittenberg under LUTHER, whom he accompanied to the LEIPZIG DISPUTATION; he also became a friend of MELANCHTHON. In 1526 he became headmaster of St Andrew's School in Eisleben, and thereafter worked for the reformed cause in Eisleben and Wittenberg. Agricola's fiery temperament led to a rift with Melanchthon, and in 1536 his advocacy of ANTINOMINANISM led to a heated controversy with Luther. Dissent was not tolerated in Luther's Wittenberg, and Agricola was forced to leave to avoid being tried for heresy. In 1540 he accepted a post in Berlin as court preacher to JOACHIM II, elector of Brandenburg, and later worked with Bishops Julius von PFLUG and Michael Helding on the preparations for the Interim of AUGSBURG (1548). The controversy concerning ADIAPHORA ignited in Augsburg became the final cause of Agricola's life. He died on 22 September 1566 during an outbreak of PLAGUE.

Agricola published two pioneering collections of proverbs: the Low German *Dre hundret Sprikwörde* appeared in 1528 (a High German version followed the next year) and *Sibenhundret und fünfftzig Sprichwörter* was published in 1548. He also wrote a play about Jan HUS that presented his life as a tragedy (*Tragedia Johannis Huß*, 1528).

NDB; Gustav Kawerau, *Johann Agricola von Eisleben: Ein Beitrag zur Reformationsgeschichte* (1881; repr. 1977); Johann Agricola, *Die Sprichwörtersammlung*, ed. Sander L. Gilman (2 vols., 1971).

**AGRICOLA, MARTIN, or (German) Martin Sohr or Sore** (1486–1556), German musician, music theorist, and cantor. Born at Schwiebus in Poland, he became choirmaster of the Protestant Lateinschule at Magdeburg, where he died in June 1550. Mostly self-taught, he was an enthusiastic educator. His *Musica instrumentalis deutsch* (1529), which describes instruments and playing methods, is written in German rather than Latin. Compositions such as his *54 Instrumentische Gesenge* (1561) and *Ein Sangbüchlein aller Sonntags Evangelien* (1541) were intended to be instructive.

**AGRICOLA, MIKAEL** (*c*.1510–1577), Protestant reformer in Finland, born and educated in Viborg. He moved to Turku (Swedish Åbo) and embraced the Reformation. His bishop, the humanist Martin Skytte, sent Agricola to study in Wittenberg (1536–9). On returning to Finland he became headmaster of the school in Turku; from this base he strove to implement the Reformation in Finland.

Agricola was a pioneer of Finnish literature, which perforce began with the establishment of orthographical conventions. Agricola's alphabet book (*ABC-kiria*, Stockholm, 1542 or 1543) was in this sense one of the founding texts of Finnish literature. Agricola also wrote a manual for priests (1545) and translated the New Testament into Finnish (1548).

FBH; Jakko Gummerus, *Mikael Agricola: Der Reformator Finnlands* (1941).

**AGRICOLA, RUDOLFUS, or Rudophus Frisius or Roelof Huysman** (1444–85), Dutch humanist, born in Baflo (near Groningen) and educated at the universities of Erfurt and Louvain, where he graduated in 1465. He spent most of the period between 1469 and 1479 in Italy, studying at the universities of Pavia and Ferrara. In 1479 he returned to northern Europe as a prominent exponent of HUMANISM, and in the last years of his life lectured at Worms and Heidelberg, where he died on 28 October 1485. His most important work was his *De inventione dialectica* (1479), an attack on the philosophy of SCHOLASTICISM, but he also published commentaries on Boethius and Seneca the Elder, orations, poems, and translations from Greek into Latin.

NDB; NNBW; Peter Mack, *Renaissance Argument: Valla and Agricola* (1993).

**AGRIPPA VON NETTESHEIM or Heinrich Cornelius Agrippa** (1486–1535), German philosopher, scholar, and Cabbalist, born near Cologne on 14 September 1486 and educated at the University of Cologne. He travelled relentlessly, working in Spain and Italy as a soldier, as an imperial theologian at the COUNCIL OF PISA, and as a physician in Geneva and Fribourg. In 1524 he became royal physician and astrologer to LOUISE OF SAVOY at her court in Lyon, and from 1528 to 1530 worked as historian and librarian to MARGARET OF AUSTRIA in Brussels. He subsequently returned to Cologne, where he worked in the service of the archbishop; he evinced some sympathies for the ideas of LUTHER, but never left the Catholic Church. He died in Grenoble on 18 February 1535.

Agrippa's philosophy was a syncretic blend of PLATO, CABBALISM, HERMETICISM, and the thought of the medieval Catalan theologian Ramon Llull. His most popular book was a treatise on magic, *De occulta philosophia* (1510, expanded edition 1533); the central statement of his beliefs, *De incertitudine et vanitate scientiarum atque artium declamatio* (1526), rejected science, scholarship, and the possibility of human knowledge in favour of faith in divine revelation.

NDB; Charles G. Nauert, *Agrippa and the Crisis of Renaissance Thought* (1965).

**AICHINGER, GREGOR** (1564/5–1628), German composer, theorist, and organist, born in Regensburg. He was influenced by Giovanni GABRIELI in his writing for large ensembles and vocal concertos, and by VIADANA in his *Cantiones ecclesiasticae* (1607). This collection contains music with thoroughbass and a treatise on thoroughbass notation and performance and was the first of its kind to be published in Germany.

**ALABASTER.** In Renaissance usage the term 'alabaster' was used to denote two distinct kinds of stone, a carbonate of lime and a sulphate of lime. In Latin and Greek the term sometimes denoted the translucent or variegated stalagmitic carbonate of lime used by the ancients (especially the Egyptians) to fashion containers for unguents and now known variously as 'oriental alabaster', 'calcareous alabaster', 'onyx marble', and 'Mexican onyx'. In vernacular languages the term tended to denote the sulphate of lime now known as 'gypsum' (to mineralogists) or 'gypseous alabaster'.

Gypseous alabaster can be white, yellow, or red, but the variety used by medieval and Renaissance artists was usually pure white, and in Renaissance poetry the term denotes whiteness and smoothness. From the fourteenth century alabaster was quarried and carved in the Meuse valley (Lorraine) and in the English Midlands (Derbyshire, Nottinghamshire, and Staffordshire); Lincoln and York also became important centres for the sculpting of alabaster. In medieval and Renaissance art, alabaster was used principally for tombs and religious statues; since the revival of the medium in late eighteenth-century Italy, alabaster has been used chiefly for ornamental objects such as vases and busts.

F. Cheetham, *English Medieval Alabasters* (1984).

**ALAMANNI, LUIGI** (1495–1556), Italian poet and humanist, a native of Florence who was associated with the literary and philosophical circle that met in the RUCELLAI gardens; MACHIAVELLI, who was a member of the same circle, made Alamanni one of the speakers in his *Arte della guerra*. Alamanni was forced to leave Florence after being implicated in an attempt to depose Giulio de' Medici (later Pope CLEMENT VII) in 1522 and again after the restoration of the MEDICI in 1531. On both occasions he sought refuge in France at the court of FRANCIS I, where he subsequently enjoyed the patronage of HENRI II and CATHERINE DE MÉDICIS. His regular visits to Italy made Alamanni an important conduit of cultural influence between Italy and France.

Alamanni's dramatic and literary works include a comedy in the Roman tradition (*Flora*, 1549), a tragedy based on Sophocles (*Antigone*, 1566), and an epic based on Homer (*Avarchide*, 1570). His most influential work was *La coltivazione* (1546), a blank-verse imitation of Virgil's *Georgics*. His satires were imitated by Sir Thomas WYATT.

DBI; H. Hauvette, *Un exilé florentin à la cour de la France au XVIe siècle* (1903).

**ALARCÓN, FERNANDO DE** (c.1500–c.1542), Spanish navigator and cartographer who embarked from Spain on 9 May 1540 as the commander of a royal expedition with instructions to sail to California and await the arrival of an overland expedition led by Francisco VÁZQUEZ DE CORONADO. The two expeditions failed to meet, and Alarcón undertook a detailed survey of the coast of Baja California, establishing that it is a peninsula rather than an island, as had been previously assumed. He also ascended the Colorado river for 85 Spanish miles (c.150 kilometres/90 miles).

DBEH.

**ÁLAVA, JUAN DE** (c.1480–1537), Spanish master mason and architect who first appears as one of the nine master masons assembled in 1512 to plan the cathedral at Salamanca, and in 1513 appears as one of the three master masons (along with Francisco de COLONIA) advising on the recently renewed work on Plasencia Cathedral. From 1513 to 1537 he served as master of the works at Plasencia, where he was responsible for the late Gothic chancel and the magnificent crossing. He began contributing to the construction of Salamanca Cathedral in 1520, and in 1526 succeeded Juan GIL DE HONTAÑÓN the elder as master mason. He designed the cloister of Santiago Cathedral, where he began to work in 1521. His greatest works are the crossing at Plasencia and the Church of San Esteban in Salamanca, which he designed and began to build in 1524.

DBEH; MDA.

**ALBA or Alva, FERNANDO ÁLVAREZ DE TOLEDO, THIRD DUKE OF or (Spanish) duque de** (1507–82), Spanish soldier and minister of PHILIP II, inducted into the arts of war and politics by his grandfather Fernando Álvarez de Toledo. He subsequently fought in the battle of PAVIA (1525) and the battle of TUNIS (1535). He rose steadily in the imperial army, and was appointed commander-in-chief of imperial forces in Italy by CHARLES V. After the abdication of Charles V from the rule of the Netherlands and Naples (1555) and from the thrones of Spain and the Empire (1556), Alba entered the service of PHILIP II, first as viceroy of Naples (1556–9) and eventually as the king's first minister.

In 1567 King Philip sent Alba and an army of 9,000 troops to extirpate civil unrest and the Protestant heresy in the Netherlands. On his arrival, the regent, MARGARET OF PARMA, resigned, and both WILLIAM OF ORANGE and LOUIS OF NASSAU went into exile, so leaving Alba, as governor-general, as the unchallenged head of government. Alba used the tribunal known as the COUNCIL OF BLOOD to remove all opponents of Spanish rule, and in 1568 arrested and executed the leaders of the revolt, the count of EGMONT and the count of HOORNE. Their executions sparked the REVOLT OF THE NETHERLANDS. Alba attempted to suppress the revolt, and also enforced a series of unpopular taxes known as the 'hundredth penny', the 'twentieth penny', and the 'tenth penny'. In 1572 he concentrated his forces in the southern Netherlands in order to repel the threatened invasion of a French army commanded by the Huguenot leader Gaspard de COLIGNY; the rebels took advantage of the reduction of troops in the north to capture the provinces of Holland and Zeeland and to defeat the Spanish fleet dispatched to regain the lost provinces. By the time the ST BARTHOLOMEW'S DAY MASSACRE alleviated the French threat, the SEA BEGGARS had established a defensive cordon, and Alba did not have sufficient naval power to attempt another attack.

In 1573 Alba was recalled from the Netherlands at his own request, but was soon dismissed by King Philip. He returned to royal service in 1580, when he was asked to command the Spanish forces intent on the conquest of Portugal. In a spectacularly successful military operation Alba crossed the border near Badajoz on 27 June 1580 and occupied Lisbon (after a short siege) on 25 August 1580. For the next two years he served as captain-general of Portugal. He died at the age of 74 in January 1583.

DBEH s.v. Alvarez de Toledo, Fernando; DHE; MDA; H. Schubart, *Arias Montano y el duque de Alba en los Países Bajos* (1962); William Maltby, *Alba: A Biography* (1983).

**ALBANIA or (Albanian Tosk) Shkiperia or (Albanian Gheg) Shkipenia.** The Albanian people, who are apparently the most ancient surviving race in south-eastern Europe, are either Ghegs (who inhabit the north of the country) or Tosks (who inhabit the south). The lands of the Albanians stretched inland beyond the boundaries of the modern state to include Kosovo (Albanian Kosova) and the contiguous parts of the modern states of Macedonia and Greece. Strabo asserts that the Via Egnatia (which follows the course of the Shkumb) divided the Illyrians of the north from the Epirots of the south, and this ancient boundary was retained in medieval Albania, when the Shkumb (the course of which runs close to the Via Egnatia) divided the northern Ghegs from the southern Tosks. From 640 till 1360, northern Albania (Ghegería) was ruled by Serbia, but in 1081 Durazzo (Albanian Durrës) was occupied by the Normans, and eventually passed into the realm of the Angevin Sicilians, who from 1271 till 1368 ruled what they called the kingdom of Albania, which consisted of Durazzo in the north and the territory stretching across the Shkumb to Berat in the south; during this period southern Albania passed back and forth between Byzantine and Bulgarian rule, but in 1204 an independent despotate of Epirus was established in the south, centred on what is now Yannina (in northern Greece), and from 1318 to 1358 this despotate was ruled by princes of the ORSINI FAMILY.

The Ottoman occupation of Albania began with the capture of Yannina in 1431. Thereafter the country united in its resistance under the leadership of SKANDERBEG, who mounted thirteen military campaigns against the Ottomans between 1444 and 1466. During this period Tosk Albanian refugees established settlements (which still survive) in southern Italy and Sicily. In 1478, Skanderbeg's fortress at Krujë (Venetian Kroia), which had been garrisoned by Venetians after his death, fell to the Ottomans; in 1479 the Venetian and Montenegrin defenders of Shkodër (Venetian Scutari) were overcome, and in 1502 Durazzo, the last unoccupied city, was captured. The last two Venetian enclaves, Antivari (now Montenegrin Bar) and Dulcingo (Turkish Olgun, now Montenegrin Ulcinj), were conquered in 1571, whereupon the Ottoman conquest was complete.

At this point Albania was a Christian country, and since the end of Serbian rule in 1360 had become substantially Catholic under Venetian and Norman influence. As Albanian was an unwritten language, the literary language was therefore Latin. The earliest surviving composition by an Albanian living in Albania is a baptismal formula of 1462 written by Archbishop Paul Angelus. In Italy, the Albanian refugee community produced two important writers, both born in Shkodër: Marino Becichemo was a humanist rhetorician who taught in both Italy and Dalmatia and published widely on classical literature; Marinus Bartelius, the most famous Albanian writer of the period, wrote an account of the Ottoman siege of Shkodër (*De obsidione Scodrensi*, Venice, 1504) and the celebrated biography of Skanderbeg (*Vita et res praeclare gestae Georgii Castriotae*, Rome, c.1508) which remained in print for three centuries and was widely translated.

Albanian is an Indo-European language with no surviving relatives, and for centuries or even millennia it remained unwritten. The earliest surviving example of written Albanian seems to occur in the Latin comedy *Epirota* (1483) by the Venetian Thomas Medius, in which the Epirote says a few words in Albanian; the first serious attempt to write the language is the *Dictionarium Latino-Epiroticum* (Rome, 1635) of Francisco Bianchi. The two dialects were united in 1969, with Tosk as the dominant form, so the name of the country is now Shkiperia.

M. Prenushi, *Kontribut shqiptar në Rilindjen Evropian* ('The Albanian Contribution to the European Renaissance') (1980).

**ALBARELLO or alberello**, a cylindrical apothecary jar used for the storage of dried herbs and medicines. The neck and foot have a slightly smaller circumference than the body of the jar, and the neck is grooved with a flange to enable a parchment lid to be affixed. Albarelli were manufactured in Spain from the fourteenth century, and from the late fifteenth century they were also made in Italy. From the sixteenth to the eighteenth centuries they were manufactured all over western Europe.

The spouted apothecary jars designed to hold medicinal liquids are often called by their French name, *chevrettes*.

L. Campanile, *I vasi di farmacia* (1973); R. E. A. Drey, *Apothecary Jars* (1978); Henry Wallis: *Italian Ceramic Art: The Albarello, a study in early Renaissance Maiolica* (1904).

**ALBERGHETTI FAMILY**, a family of Venetian gun-founders and bronze casters who worked in the Venetian ARSENALE from the fifteenth to the eighteenth centuries. Until 1582 their ARTILLERY was commissioned by the COUNCIL OF TEN, and thereafter by the Venetian Senate. Their occasional civic commissions include the well-head in the courtyard of the Palazzo Ducale (1556), which is signed by Alfonso Alberghetti.

**ALBERTI, LEON BATTISTA** (1404–72), Italian humanist writer on the theory of art and architecture, designer of buildings, and, in varying degrees, athlete, lawyer, mathematician, moral philosopher, musician, painter, playwright, and satirist, born in Genoa, the illegitimate son of a Florentine exile. He was educated in Padua, where he was inducted into the HUMANIST movement, and later studied law at Bologna. In 1424 he wrote a Latin comedy, *Philodoxeus*, and subsequently wrote satires (*Intercenales* and *Momus*) and works of moral philosophy (*Teogenio* and *Della tranquillità dell'animo*). In 1431 he moved to Rome, where he worked in the papal secretariat and was eventually appointed as papal adviser for the restoration of Rome (1437–55), and so worked alongside Bernardo ROSSELLINO; in 1432 he made his first documented visit to Florence, travelling in the train of Pope EUGENIUS IV.

In 1435, apparently in reaction to the new classicizing style in art that he had seen for the first time in Florence, he wrote *De pictura*, an essay on painting dedicated to Gianfrancesco GONZAGA, marquis of Mantua. In this treatise, which is concerned with the theory of painting rather than the painter's practice of the craft, Alberti draws heavily on the descriptions of ancient Greek paintings given by PLINY in his *Historia naturalis*. Like Pliny, Alberti believed that good art requires an understanding of OPTICS and careful attention to the imitation of nature; the first book of Alberti's treatise is given over almost entirely to a discussion of the geometrical optics of vision and the mathematical rules for correct PERSPECTIVE.

The exterior façade of Palazzo Rucellai, in Florence, designed by Leon Battista **Alberti** and constructed (1446–51) under the supervision of Bernardo ROSSELLINO

Alberti's principal concern, however, is with the *historia*, which is what the picture is about, the story it tells and the way it tells it; these are matters on which a patron would express an opinion when commissioning a work of art. *De pictura* establishes what was to prove to be a long-lived and influential connection between HUMANISM and the new style in art. In 1436 Alberti translated the treatise into Italian (*Della pittura*), introducing some small changes and dedicating the work to BRUNELLESCHI, DONATELLO, MASACCIO, GHIBERTI, and Luca DELLA ROBBIA; the Italian text was not printed until the late nineteenth century. The Latin *De pictura* was printed in 1540, then in a new Italian translation in 1547, and in another new translation in 1568 as part of a collection of Alberti's *Opuscoli morali*.

In 1450 Alberti received his first important architectural commission when he was asked by Sigismondo MALATESTA to refashion the Gothic Church of San Francesco in Rimini into the building now known as the Tempio Malatestiano. Alberti designed a marble shell to encase the church; the front, which was based on a Roman triumphal arch, was never finished. The original design, which included a large dome, is preserved on a commemorative medal.

Alberti's next patron was Giovanni RUCELLAI, for whom he designed the façades of the Church of Santa Maria Novella in

The nave of the Church of Sant'Andrea in Mantua, designed by **Alberti**

Florence (1456–70) and of the Palazzo Rucellai, for which he also designed the Loggia dei Rucellai at right angles with the palace; he designed the Shrine of the Holy Sepulchre (1467) in the Rucellai Chapel in San Pancrazio, and may have been the architect of the chapel. The façade of Santa Maria Novella, which is covered with marble inlay, is based on a geometrical design and on an ideal of harmonic proportion based on ratios derived from music: the pitch of a resonating cord will rise by an octave if its length is halved, by a fifth if its length is reduced by a third, and by a fourth if its length is reduced by a quarter; the ratios 1 : 2, 2 : 3, and 3 : 4 were therefore deemed by Alberti to be as harmonious in architecture as in music. The façade of Santa Maria Novella was the first Renaissance building to embody these ratios in its structure.

Alberti designed buildings, but never worked on site while building was in progress: he designed Palazzo Rucellai, for example, but construction was overseen by Rossellino. The only buildings that he designed in their entirety (unless he was the architect of Cappella Rucellai) were two churches in Mantua, San Sebastiano (from 1460) and San Andrea, neither of which was completed during his lifetime. In 1452 he published *De re aedificatoria*, the first architectural treatise of the Renaissance, and dedicated it to Pope NICHOLAS V; a complete edition appeared in 1485. In this treatise Alberti articulated his understanding of VITRUVIUS, described the architectural ORDERS, and set out the principles of TOWN PLANNING and the ideals of mathematical proportion. His final theoretical work was *De statua* (c.1464).

DBI; MDA; F. Borsi, *Leon Battista Alberti: The Complete Works* (1977); Anthony Grafton, *Leon Battista Alberti: Master Builder of the Italian Renaissance* (2000); Luca Boschetto, *Leon Battista Alberti e Firenze* (2000).

**ALBERTINELLI, MARIOTTO** (1474–1515), Italian painter, a native of Florence, where he trained alongside Fra BARTOLOMEO in the studio of Cosimo ROSSELLI. Albertinelli collaborated with Fra Bartolomeo until the latter entered the Dominican Order in 1499; the products of their collaboration include the ALTARPIECE of Santa Maria della Quercia (3 kilometres (2 miles) from Viterbo). Albertinelli eventually abjured painting and became an innkeeper.

Albertinelli's paintings, which owe much to the style of LEONARDO DA VINCI and PERUGINO, include a *Visitation* (1503, Uffizi) and an *Annunciation* (1510, Accademia, Florence).

DBI; MDA; Ludovico Borgo, *The Works of Mariotto Albertinelli* (1976).

**ALBERTINUS ÄGIDIUS** (*c.*1560–1620), Dutch Counter-Reformation polemicist in Germany, born in Deventer. He left the Netherlands as a religious refugee and seems to have travelled in Spain and Austria before entering the service of Duke Wilhelm der Fromme of Bavaria in 1593; on the duke's death in 1597 Albertinus remained at the court of his son and successor, Maximilian I.

Albertinus's large corpus of COUNTER-REFORMATION polemic was in substantial part based on sources in French, Italian, Latin, and (especially) Spanish. His most important religious translations were works by Fray Antonio de GUEVARA; he also translated Mateo ALEMÁN's *Gusmán de Alfarache* as the distinctly moralistic *Der Landtstörstzer: Gusman von Alfarche oder Picaro genannt* (1615), and so introduced the PICARESQUE novel (German *Schelmenroman*) into German.

**ALBERUS, ERASMUS** (*c.*1500–1553), German satirist and fabulist, born in the village of Sprendlingen (10 kilometres (6 miles) south of Frankfurt), the son of a schoolmaster. He studied in Wittenberg, where he met LUTHER and MELANCHTHON and became a supporter of the Reformation. His polemical verse satire *Der barfüßer Mönche Eulenspiegel und Alkoran* (1542), to which Luther contributed a preface, is an adaptation of the *Liber conformitatum* of the fourteenth-century Franciscan monk Bartolomeo Albizzi of Pisa. Alberus' principal literary work is an adaptation of 49 of Aesop's *Fables*; the setting of the fables is Germany, and the narratives are vehicles for Alberus' views on the relations between Church and state. The satire of the fables is humane and gentle, and so stands in marked contrast to the savage satire of contemporaries such as Thomas MURNER. Alberus also wrote hymns, several of which still survive in Lutheran hymnals.

After the death of Luther, Alberus served as deacon (*Diakonus*) in Wittenberg. He was in Magdeburg during 1550–1, when the city was besieged by MAURICE OF SAXONY. In 1552 he became *Generalsuperintendent* at Neubrandenburg (Mecklenburg), where he died on 5 May 1553.

NDB s.v. Alber, Erasmus.

**ALBIZZI FAMILY.** Members of the Albizzi family migrated to Florence from Arezzo in the twelfth century, and established themselves in communal government. The family was exiled after the CIOMPI REVOLUTION of 1378, but assumed control of the city after its return in 1382, initially under the leadership of Maso Albizzi (1343–1417). On Maso's death in 1417, control of the governing oligarchy passed to his cousin Rinaldo (1370–1442). Rinaldo's unsuccessful war against Lucca (1430–3) was opposed by Cosimo de' MEDICI; Rinaldo exiled Cosimo in 1433, and on Cosimo's return in 1434 the Albizzi family was exiled from Florence.

DBI.

**ALBRECHT V** (1528–79), duke of Bavaria, the son of WILHELM IV of WITTELSBACH, succeeded his father in March 1550. He had married a daughter of Ferdinand of Habsburg (later the Emperor FERDINAND I), and was encouraged by his powerful father-in-law to support the Catholic cause in Bavaria. For the first few years of his rule, Albrecht tolerated the reformers (who were numerous in Bavaria) but in 1553 he began to promote the COUNTER-REFORMATION. In 1564 he suppressed a Lutheran conspiracy and so subjugated the Bavarian ESTATES. He admitted the JESUITS to Bavaria in 1556, and their presence, especially in educational institutions, soon arrested the spread of LUTHERANISM.

Albrecht was an important patron of the arts. His court in Munich attracted artists and musicians (including Orlande de LASSUS) and he commissioned many public buildings and founded the state library. He died in October 1579.

NDB.

**ALBRECHT III ACHILLES** (1414–86), Hohenzollern elector of BRANDENBURG, was born in Tangermünde on 9 November 1414, the third son of Friedrich I of HOHENZOLLERN. As a young man he joined the court of the Emperor SIGISMUND and fought with imperial forces in the HUSSITE WARS; he subsequently fought with the Emperor Albrecht II against the Poles. On the death of Albrecht's father in 1440, the electorate was partitioned, and Albrecht received only the Franconian principality of Ansbach. In 1464, on the death of his brother Johann, Albrecht was able to add Bayreuth to his domain. His surviving brother, the Elector Friedrich II, abdicated in 1470, whereupon Albrecht became elector of Brandenburg. Two years later, under the terms of the Treaty of Prenzlau, he added Pomerania to his realm.

In February 1473 Albrecht issued the *Dispositio Achillea*, which established the principle of primogeniture in Brandenburg by stipulating that the united Mark of Brandenburg should descend to the eldest son in its entirety and that the younger sons should inherit the Franconian possessions of the Hohenzollern family; this was a prudent provision for a man who had six children by his first wife and thirteen by his second. The following year he retired to Franconia, leaving the governance of Brandenburg in the hands of his son Johann. In Albrecht's absence, Brandenburg was invaded by Johann II of Sagan and MATTHIAS CORVINUS, and Pomerania took advantage of the instability of war to rebel. In 1478 Albrecht was forced to return to Brandenburg to expel the invaders and quell the revolt in Pomerania. He participated in the election of MAXIMILIAN as king of the Romans and shortly thereafter died in Frankfurt on 11 March 1486.

NDB.

**ALBRECHT ALCIBIADES or Albert of Bayreuth** (1522–57), Hohenzollern margrave of Brandenburg-Kulmbach, was born in Ansbach on 28 March 1522, the son of Casimir, prince of Bayreuth, a member of the Franconian branch of the HOHENZOLLERN dynasty. Albrecht's father died in 1527, and he was placed under the guardianship of his Protestant uncle, Georg of Ansbach. In 1541 the family lands were divided, and

Albrecht received Bayreuth; the principal town of Bayreuth was Kulmbach, so Albrecht is sometimes described as the margrave of Brandenburg-Kulmbach.

In 1543 Albrecht embarked on a military career, serving with his small private army (commanded by Wilhelm von GRUMBACH) in the Emperor CHARLES V's campaign against France. Charles subsequently recruited Albrecht to assist in his attack on the SCHMALKALDIC LEAGUE. In March 1547 he was captured at Rochlitz by JOHANN FRIEDRICH I, elector of Saxony, but was released the following year in the wake of the imperial victory at the battle of MÜHLBERG.

After his release, Albrecht deserted the imperial cause and instead aligned himself with MAURICE OF SAXONY in his campaign to assist HENRI II of France to overthrow the emperor. When the insurrection was concluded with the Treaty of Passau in August 1552, Albrecht left his new allies and instead used his army to plunder Franconia and to extort money from the burghers of Nuremberg. Charles was eager to have such an effective warrior on his side, and so acquiesced in Albrecht's appropriation of the lands owned by the bishops of Würzburg and Bamberg. In January 1553 Albrecht courageously assisted with the imperial retreat from Metz, but when Charles left Germany the following month, Albrecht renewed his attacks on Franconia. A League was formed to resist his depredations, and Maurice of Saxony led an attack on his former friend and comrade. Albrecht was defeated at Sievershausen on 9 July 1553; he was later defeated by a League army commanded by Heinrich II, the Younger, duke of Brunswick-Wolfenbüttel. Albrecht fled to France and entered the service of Henri II, and was fighting to regain Henri's territories when he died at Pforzheim on 8 January 1557.

NDB.

## ALBRECHT III ANIMOSUS or Albert the Courageous

(1443–1500), duke of SAXONY, was born on 31 July 1443, the son of Friedrich II ('Frederick the Mild'), elector and duke of Saxony, and his wife Margaret, daughter of the duke of Styria. In July 1455, in an incident known as the *Prinzenraub*, Albrecht and his brother Ernst were kidnapped by a knight called Kunz von Kaufungen; the boys were on their way to Bohemia when they were rescued.

After the death of Friedrich II on 7 September 1464, the brothers ruled conjointly, but in 1485 the duchy was divided and Albrecht received Meissen and Osterland; his descendants there are known as the Albertine line of the Wettin family (see Appendix 1).

Albrecht's military abilities were highly valued by Emperor FRIEDRICH III, and he served as an imperial soldier in campaigns against CHARLES THE BOLD (1475) and MATTHIAS CORVINUS (1487). In 1488 he marched the SWABIAN LEAGUE to Bruges to rescue MAXIMILIAN, king of the Romans, from captivity, and when Maximilian was returned to Germany, Albrecht remained behind to restore imperial authority in Holland, Flanders, and Brabant. In 1498 Maximilian rewarded Albrecht's services by appointing him as hereditary governor (*potestat*) of Friesland, but Albrecht had to conquer and subdue his

territory before he could rule it. Shortly after the capture of Groningen, Albrecht died at Emden on 12 September 1500 and was buried at Meissen.

NDB s.v. Albrecht der Beherzte, Herzog von Sachsen.

## ALBRECHT II OF MAINZ or Albert of Brandenburg

(1490–1545), cardinal-archbishop and elector of Mainz, was born on 28 June 1490, the younger son of Johann Cicero, the elector of Brandenburg. He studied at the University of Frankfurt an der Oder and entered the Church, in which he quickly rose to become prebendary of Mainz (1509), archbishop of Magdeburg (1518), archbishop and elector of Mainz (1514), and cardinal (1518).

Albrecht needed to raise money to pay for the expenses of his elevation to the see of Mainz (including his pallium, the expensive archiepiscopal cloak) and therefore took out a loan from the FUGGER FAMILY. In order to repay this loan, Albrecht sought and secured permission from Pope LEO X to sell on a profit-sharing basis the INDULGENCE for the rebuilding of ST PETER'S BASILICA in his diocese. Albrecht chose the Dominican Johann TETZEL to preach the indulgence, and so inadvertently fuelled the nascent reform movement in Germany. The imperial election of 1519 presented the possibility of another income stream, because both Charles (later CHARLES V) and FRANCIS I were eager to secure electoral votes; a large sum of money encouraged Albrecht, who was already his strongest champion, to vote for Charles.

Albrecht's political ambitions and his friendship with humanists such as Ulrich von HUTTEN and ERASMUS raised the hope amongst Protestants that he would embrace Lutheranism; in the event, he temporized during the PEASANTS' WAR of 1524–5 and thereafter aligned himself with the Catholic princes at their assembly in Dessau in 1525. Unlike his brother, the Elector Joachim I of Brandenburg, he was not a persecutor of Protestants: he was a resolute defender of the Catholic cause, but opposed extreme measures against the Protestants and advocated a modicum of toleration, especially when offered financial incentives; the citizens of Magdeburg were allowed to purchase their religious liberty for 500,000 florins.

In 1538 Albrecht joined the Catholic League of NUREMBERG, which opposed the League of SCHMALKALDEN. Under the influence of the JESUIT Pierre FABER, who lived in his diocese for a year, Albrecht became a friend and patron of the new ORDER, encouraging Jesuits to teach in his dominions and curbing his earlier tolerance of the Protestant heresy. He died at Aschaffenburg on 24 September 1545 and was buried in Mainz Cathedral.

Albrecht was an important patron of education and art. Together with his brother Joachim I he founded the University of Frankfurt an der Oder (1506). He also extended his patronage to Lucas CRANACH, Albrecht DÜRER, Matthias GRÜNEWALD, and Peter VISCHER the Elder.

NDB s.v. Albrecht, Markgraf von Brandenburg; Jakob May, *Der Kurfürst, Cardinal und Erzbischof Albrecht II von Mainz und Magdeburg* (2 vols., 1865–75).

## ALBRECHT VON EYB (1420–75), German humanist, born near Ansbach and educated in Padua, Bologna, and Pavia.

On returning to Germany he became a canon of Bamberg Cathedral and then Eichstätt Cathedral. His writings, all of which are imbued with humanist values, included a popular manual on marriage (*Ehebüchlein*, 1472) which contained some translations of BOCCACCIO's *Decameron*, an anthology of Roman poetry (*Margarita poetica*, 1472), and a posthumously published collection of plays (*Spiegel der Sitten*, 1511) which included his German translations of the *Menaechmi* and *Bacchides* of Plautus, much admired for their skilful and idiomatic German.

*NDB.*

**ALBRECHT VON HABSBURG** (1559–1621), archduke, cardinal, and governor of Portugal and the Spanish Netherlands, the son of the Emperor MAXIMILIAN II and the nephew of King PHILIP II of Spain. He was created cardinal (at the age of 18) and archbishop of Toledo, and later served as governor of Portugal. In 1596 Albrecht was appointed governor-general of the Netherlands. By the provisions of the Peace of VERVINS (2 May 1598) King Philip was obliged to surrender control of the Spanish Netherlands to his daughter Isabella, who was to marry Albrecht (who renounced his clerical orders), after which they were to rule the Netherlands as sovereign princes. King Philip died in September 1598, and two months later Albrecht married Isabella. At the end of 1599 they formally entered Brussels, but by then reconciliation with the rebellious northern provinces was no longer possible. Albrecht continued to prosecute the war, but in 1609 acceded to the twelve-year truce which gave independence to the United Provinces. Thereafter Albrecht continued to persecute Protestants in his dominion.

*NDB* s.v. Albrecht VII, Erzherzog von Österreich; *NNBW* iii s.v. Albrecht, Aartshertog van Oostenrijk.

**ALBRECHT VON PREUSSEN or Albert of Prussia** (1490–1568), grand master of the TEUTONIC ORDER and first HOHENZOLLERN duke of Prussia, was born Albert von Brandenburg-Ansbach in Ansbach on 17 May 1490. In 1511 he was elected as grand master of the Teutonic Order in the hope that his family connections (his mother was the daughter of King Casimir IV of Poland) would enable the Order to settle its disputes with Poland. In December 1519 war broke out with Poland, and Prussia was ravished. In 1522 Albrecht attended the Diet of Nuremberg with a view to soliciting support for his struggle with Poland, and there met the reformer Andreas OSIANDER, who converted Albrecht to Lutheranism. Albrecht subsequently decided, with the support of Martin LUTHER, to remove Prussia from the theocratic administration of the Teutonic Order and to reconstitute it as a hereditary duchy.

On 10 February 1525 Albrecht was invested as the first duke of Prussia by SIGISMUND I, king of Poland, to whose suzerainty Albrecht was obliged to submit; he was promptly deposed as grand master by the Order. In the same year he married Dorothea of Denmark, daughter of King FREDERICK I; after her death in 1547, he married Anna Maria, daughter of Erik I, duke of Brunswick.

In 1544 Albrecht founded the avowedly Protestant University of Königsberg, and five years later appointed Osiander to a professorship; when Osiander fell out with MELANCHTHON over the issue of JUSTIFICATION by faith, Albrecht supported Osiander. In the 1560s Albrecht faced opposition to his rule, but dissent was quelled with the assistance of SIGISMUND II. He died at Tapiau (now Russian Gvardeysk, in the Kaliningradskaya Oblast) on 20 March 1568.

*NDB* s.v. Albrecht d. Ä, Markgraf von Brandenburg-Ansbach; P. G. Thielen, *Die Kultur am Hofe Herzog Albrechts von Preussen* (1953).

**ALBUQUERQUE, AFONSO DE** (*c.*1445/62–1515), Portuguese admiral and second viceroy of Portuguese India, born in Alhandra (near Lisbon), the son of a courtier through whom he was illegitimately related to the royal family. He was educated at the court of AFONSO V, and after the king's death in 1481 served as a soldier in AFRICA; on his return to the court he was appointed as equerry (*estribeiro-mor*) to King JOHN II.

In 1503 Albuquerque embarked on the first of his naval expeditions to East Africa, the Red Sea, and the west coast of India. In return for military assistance to the ruler of Cochin, he was given permission to built a Portuguese fort on his territory. Returning home in July 1504, Albuquerque was favourably received by King MANUEL I, who placed him in command of a squadron of five ships in the fleet of sixteen ships bound for India under the command of Tristão da CUNHA; once in India he was to succeed the viceroy, Francisco de ALMEIDA. The expedition attacked and pillaged Muslim towns and settlements on the east coast of Africa, whereupon Albuquerque's squadron split off from the main force and sailed to Hormuz, an island (and commercial centre) in the Persian Gulf. He arrived at Hormuz on 25 September 1507 and quickly overran the island, but was unable to establish a permanent Portuguese presence.

Albuquerque supplemented his squadron with three impounded ships and sailed for the Malabar coast (now Kerala) of India, which he reached at the end of 1508. Almeida refused to recognize Albuquerque's credentials and imprisoned him. Three months later a large Portuguese fleet arrived; Almeida promptly released Albuquerque, resigned in his favour, and sailed for home.

Albuquerque quickly set about laying the foundations for the Portuguese empire in the East. His ambition was centred on the spice trade, which he wanted to service through the route around the Cape as a Portuguese enterprise rather than through the Red Sea route, which was under the control of the Mameluke sultans of Egypt. To that end he used his naval strength to create a network of sea routes whose defence from the depredations of pirates and local rulers was ensured by naval squadrons based in fortified naval bases along the Cape route to India. After a faltering start in which an attack on Calicut was rebuffed in January 1510, Albuquerque captured Goa (which became his viceregal capital) later in the year. Turning his attention to the Malay peninsula, he captured Malacca (1511), where he remained for a year, during which time he made his first contacts with Chinese merchants. In 1512 he sailed for Malabar on board the treasure-laden *Flor de la mar*, but a storm destroyed the ship and

Albuquerque escaped with his life but without his treasure. In 1513 he besieged Aden (in the Yemen) with a view to securing control of the entry to the Red Sea, but he was repulsed, and his exploration of the Red Sea (the first by a European) yielded no military or commercial gains. In 1515 he again attacked Hormuz, which thereafter remained a Portuguese possession until 1622, when it was captured by the English EAST INDIA COMPANY.

On returning from Hormuz to Goa, Albuquerque was informed that he had been dismissed through the efforts of a hostile faction at court, and he sailed for Portugal. He died at sea on 16 December 1515; the ship returned to Goa, where he was buried in the Church of our Lady.

DHP; E. Prestage, *Afonso de Albuquerque* (1929); J. Villiers and T. F. Earle (eds.), *Afonso de Albuquerque, Caesar of the East* (1990).

## ALCAÇOVAS, TREATY OF (1479).

The war of succession to the throne of Castile, in which the rival claimants were JUANA LA BELTRANEJA (supported by her fiancé AFONSO V of Portugal) and ISABELLA of Castile (supported by her husband FERDINAND of Aragon), was won by the forces of Ferdinand and Isabella; the conflict was concluded by the Treaty of Alcaçovas. The treaty also assigned disputed Atlantic territories to either Spain or Portugal: Portugal recognized Spain's possession of the CANARY ISLANDS, and Spain recognized Portugal's claim to the Azores, Cape Verde Islands, and Madeira and also recognized the Portuguese crown's monopoly of West African trade. These provisions made the treaty the first to deal with European possessions overseas, and so inaugurated the process that was to culminate in the Treaty of TORDESILLAS.

## ALCALÁ DE HENARES or (Latin) Complutum,

a Spanish town on the river Henares, 30 kilometres (18 miles) northeast of Madrid. In the sixteenth century Alcalá was an important seat of learning: the richly endowed university founded by Cardinal CISNEROS in 1500 and opened in 1510 quickly became second in reputation only to Salamanca; the university's principal building, the Colegio de San Ildefonso, was completed in 1583; its PLATERESQUE façade (1541–53), the work of Rodrigo GIL DE HONTAÑÓN, is arguably the greatest secular building of the Spanish Renaissance. The BIBLE known as the Complutensian Polyglot was prepared in Alcalá 1514–17. The Emperor FERDINAND I was born in Alcalá, as were CERVANTES and CATHERINE OF ARAGON. The university was moved to Madrid in 1836, and its buildings were used as archives and military barracks, but a new University of Alcalá was founded in the original university buildings in 1977.

## ALCARAZ CARPETS.

The two principal regions for the manufacture of carpets in Spain from the fifteenth to the mid-seventeenth centuries were Alcaraz and CUENCA. Alcaraz carpets typically have a woollen pile dyed red and blue, tied with Spanish knots (i.e. single warp knots) on an undyed woollen foundation. The designs are usually geometrical, though the fifteenth-century sub-group known as 'admiral carpets' incorporates the arms of the Enriquez family and some sixteenth-century Alcaraz carpets depict pine cones and pomegranates.

J. A. Tárrago, *Los alfombras de Alcaraz* (1974).

## ALCHEMY AND CHEMISTRY.

The Arabic origins of the term 'chemistry' are apparent in the cognate term 'alchemy', because *al* is simply the definite article in Arabic. In modern usage the term alchemy refers to the practices devoted to the transmutation of base metals into gold and the search for the ALKAHEST (the universal solvent) and the panacea (the universal remedy), whereas the term chemistry, when used in an early modern context, refers to more obviously practical procedures such as the smelting of metals. In the Renaissance, chemical and alchemical manipulations usually involve elements of ASTROLOGY, and the line between them is drawn largely with hindsight. Even the lexical distinction is largely anachronistic, because the Arabic article did not become separated from the rest of the word until the early seventeenth century, and the new word 'chemistry' was not distinguished in meaning from the older term 'alchemy': early chemistry was alchemy.

Some Renaissance alchemists, such as Jean Baptiste van HELMONT, were engaged in serious research, usually in connection with medicine, but the more common image is that of the charlatan who appears in Ben Jonson's *Alchemist* (1610). The medical chemistry of PARACELSUS assumed considerable importance in the century after his death, and alchemy was prominent in the Prague of RUDOLF II, who invited to his court alchemists such as John DEE, Cornelis DREBBEL, and SENDIVOGIUS.

## ALCIATO or Alciati, ANDREA

(1492–1550), Italian jurist and humanist, born in Milan and from 1518 professor of law at Avignon. In 1529 he moved to Bourges, and his four years there shifted the centre of European jurisprudence from Italy to France (see FRENCH LAW). The tradition that he inaugurated at Bourges was carried on by his successor Jacques CUJAS, and Alciato returned to Italy to teach at Bologna, Ferrara, and Pavia, where he died. He never wrote a systematic treatise on law, but his commentary on the *Tres libri*, the last three books of JUSTINIAN's *Codex* (*Annotationes in tres libros codicis*, Milan, 1517), brought humanist values and a scholarly command of philology and ancient history to bear on the text of Justinian, and so was able to present the Justinian *Tres libri* as a historical document embodying legal formulations arising out of particular historical circumstances. In this as in other legal works, notably the *De verborum significatione* (Lyon, 1530), Alciato was able to champion the values of historical jurisprudence without alienating those who worked in the earlier glossatory tradition (see LAW) of exposition in the interests of practical application. His essays on points of law and interpretation (*Paradoxa, Parerga juris, Dispunctiones*) were cast in humanist form and used humanist classical texts to throw light on the *Corpus iuris civilis*; he also overturned the practices of late medieval commentary, showing in such works as the *Commentariae* and the *De praesumptionibus* a subtlety of approach even more acute than that of his predecessors.

Alciato was also a student of EMBLEMS. His history of Milan (*Rerum patriae, seu historiae Mediolanensis*) was published posthumously in 1625. His *Emblemata* (Augsburg, 1531) was instrumental in the dissemination of knowledge about emblems; it was translated into many languages and appeared in almost 200 editions.

DBI; MDA s.v. Alciati; Paul-Émile Viard, *André Alciat* (1926); Donald R. Kelley, *Foundations of Modern Historical Scholarship: Language, Law and History in the French Renaissance* (1970), 87–115; P. Daly (ed.), *Andrea Alciati and the Emblem Tradition* (1989); Karl-Ludwig Selig, *Studies on Alciato in Spain* (1990); Alciatus, *Opera* (4 vols., 1582).

**ALDANA, FRANCISCO DE** (1537–78), Spanish poet and soldier resident in Naples, called by Cervantes 'el divino capitán'. He wrote voluptuous love sonnets (of which the best known is '¿Cuál es la causa, mi Damón?'), religious poems including 'Canción a Cristo crucificado' (not to be confused with the greatest of Spanish religious sonnets, the anonymous 'A Christo crucificado'), and mythological poems, including a *Fábula de Faetonte*. The most pronounced Italian strain in Aldana's writing is the presence of Neoplatonic motifs, which appear most strikingly in his *Carta para Arias Montano sobre la contemplación de Dios*.

Aldana was killed at the battle of KSAR-EL-KEBIR.

DBEH; *Obras completas*, ed. M. Moragón Maestre (2 vols., 1953).

**ALDEGREVER, HEINRICH** (*c*.1502–1555/61), German engraver and painter who lived and worked in Soest (Westphalia). His engravings show the clear influence of DÜRER, and the small scale of both his engravings and his paintings has led to Aldegrever being associated with the LITTLE MASTERS of Nuremberg. His portraits include engravings of JOHN OF LEIDEN and Bernd KNIPPERDOLLINCK, who were at the time both imprisoned.

NDB; MDA.

**ALDOBRANDINI VILLA.** The baroque villa at Frascati (26 kilometres (16 miles) south-east of Rome) was constructed between 1598 and 1603. The architect was Giacomo DELLA PORTA, who designed the house and garden for Cardinal Pietro Aldobrandini, nephew of Pope Clement VIII; della Porta died in 1602, before construction was completed, and the project was completed by Carlo Maderno.

The steeply sloping site was flattened and, in the area to be covered by the villa, levelled; the garden was built on the flattened incline and an abundant supply of water was provided by an aqueduct; this remarkable feat of engineering is celebrated in an inscription. In front of the villa there are three terraces, and from the house, which is unusually high (but only two rooms deep), there were views over the terraces to the Campagna, Rome, and the sea. The garden terraces contain a *GIARDINO SEGRETO* and a garden room called the Stanza dei Venti (the room of the winds) with *GIOCHI D'ACQUA* that were repeatedly described by seventeenth-century travellers; John Evelyn, for example, enthusiastically describes water-theatres in which storms rage and monsters roar. The sides of the house were planted with plane trees that are now old and twisted. Scattered around the gardens there were statues (of which only a few remain) and FOUNTAINS, two of which are in the form of boats (*barchette*).

The central feature of the garden is a hemispherical water-theatre (a type of NYMPHAEUM) at the rear of the house, the practical purposes of which were to provide relief from summer heat and to retain the hillside. A large retaining wall surmounted by carved ilex trees is cut into the hillside in a huge arc. The area within the semicircle is in effect the stage of a water-theatre, the water for which flows down a staircase (topped with two columns) that divides the ilex trees. The wall has five niches with statues, and there is a water-jet in front of each niche. In the central niche water falls from the roof through a star (the Aldobrandini emblem) onto a statue of Atlas carrying a globe. The small terrace above the water-staircase contains a fountain; originally there were two fountains, and this area was surrounded by clipped hedges, beyond which was woodland. The staged retreat from the formality of the house to the distant woodland is a characteristic feature of baroque gardens.

The villa and gardens were damaged by bombing during the Second World War, but have been restored.

David R. Coffin, *The Villa in the Life of Renaissance Rome* (1979); C. d'Onofrio, *La Villa Aldobrandini di Frascati* (1963); C. L. Franck, *The Villas of Frascati, 1550–1750* (1966); Claudia Lazzaro, *The Italian Renaissance Garden* (1990).

**ALDROVANDI, ULISSE** (1522–1605), Italian naturalist. He was born into a noble family in Bologna, and studied law and medicine in Bologna and Padua. In 1550 he was called before the Roman INQUISITION to answer charges of heresy, but was acquitted. He embarked on a career at the University of Bologna, and in 1560 was appointed to the chair of natural history. In 1568, on his recommendation, the city founded a BOTANICAL GARDEN, of which Aldrovandi became the first director; he used the garden to conduct his research on the medicinal properties of plants. He subsequently published a treatise on drugs and medicines (*Antidotarii Bononiensis epitome*, 1574) and a huge natural history: four volumes were published in his lifetime (three in 1599 and one in 1602), of which three are devoted to ornithology and one to entomology; the remaining volumes were assembled from his notes by former pupils and published posthumously.

DBI; DSB.

**ALDUS MANUTIUS or Aldo Manuzio** (*c*.1450–1515), Venetian printer of texts from the literature of classical antiquity, especially ancient Greek texts. Aldus was born at Bassiano (Velletri), south-west of Rome; he was educated in Ferrara, where he was taught by GUARINO DA VERONA. In 1495 he opened a press and publishing house in Venice, at a house marked by a sign of a dolphin entwined around an anchor, a device originating on coins of the Emperor Titus Vespasianus; the anchor and dolphin became Aldus' *impresa*, and the press and publishing house came to be known as the Aldine Press.

Between 1495 and 1515 Aldus published some 130 editions of classical and classical texts, some 30 of which had never before been printed. Many of the texts that he published were in Greek, including important editions of ARISTOTLE (5 vols., 1495–8), Aristophanes (1498), Thucydides, Sophocles, and Herodotus (1502), Euripides and Xenophon (1503), PLUTARCH (1509), and PLATO (1513); some of the texts in his Greek *editiones principes* (e.g. many of those in his two-volume *Rhetores Graeci* of 1508–9) were not reprinted until the nineteenth century. Aldus edited some of the volumes himself, but Marcus MUSURUS and other members of the NEAKADEMIA also assumed editorial responsibilities. The books were printed in a Greek cursive type that Aldus commissioned; unlike earlier Greek types, which imitated the uncial script (see CALLIGRAPHY) of classical manuscripts, Aldus insisted that his script incorporate the ligatures (and contractions) of contemporary commercial Greek; a list of these ligatures (and those developed by Aldus' successors) is printed in Appendix 4.

Aldus also published Latin texts, including works by PETRARCH and DANTE (both edited by BEMBO) and by contemporaries such as POLIZIANO, SANNAZARO, and Francesco COLONNA; he also published the *Adages* of ERASMUS, who joined the Neakademia in 1508. These Latin texts were printed in an elegant cursive type designed by Francesco GRIFFO, later known as italic; they were often published in small (octavo) formats with large print runs (*c*.1000) and low prices.

Problems with cash flows occasioned by a recession led to the suspension of the massive publication programme in 1505, and the torrent of publications was reduced to a trickle until 1512. On Aldus' death the business passed to his son Paulus (1512–74) and thereafter to his grandson Aldus the Younger (1547–79), who developed a large list of publications in Italian.

G. Orlandi (ed.), *Aldo Manuzio editore* (2 vols., 1975); Martin Lowry, *The World of Aldus Manutius: Business and Scholarship in Renaissance Venice* (1979); N. Barker, *Aldus Manutius and the Development of Greek Script and Type in the Fifteenth Century* (2nd edn., 1992); Susy Marcon and Marino Zorzi (eds.), *Aldo Manuzio e l'ambiente veneziano* (2 vols., 1994); David Zeidberg (ed.), *Aldus Manutius and Renaissance Culture* (1998).

**ALEANDRO, GIROLAMO** (1480–1542), Italian Hellenist and papal diplomat, born in Treviso and educated in Padua and Venice. His interest in Greek developed in Venice, where he moved in the circle of ALDUS MANUTIUS. In 1508 he accepted the advice and assistance of ERASMUS to move to Paris, where Guillaume BUDÉ became one of his private pupils. In 1509 he secured a teaching post in Paris, and taught Greek, Latin, and Hebrew until 1513. During this period Aleandro inaugurated the study of Greek in France, and in 1517 he published a textbook, the *Lexicon Graeco-Latinum*.

Aleandro returned to Italy, and in 1519 was appointed Vatican librarian under Pope LEO X. He subsequently became a papal diplomat, and in that capacity famously clashed with LUTHER when the latter was arraigned before him at Worms. He also became a critic of Erasmus, and the *mot* 'Erasmus laid the egg that Luther hatched' is attributed to him. Aleandro was appointed cardinal in 1536.

*DBI* s.v. Aleandro, Girolamo; *DBF*, s.v. Aléandre, Jérôme; Franco Gaeta, *Un nunzio pontificio a Venezia nel Cinquecento (Girolamo Aleandro)* (1960).

**ALEMÁN, MATEO** (1547–1620), Spanish novelist, born in Seville, the son of a MARRANO prison doctor. He graduated from Seville University in 1564 and later studied medicine at Salamanca and Alcalá, after which he married unhappily (1571) and held a post in the Treasury (1571–88). Alemán was imprisoned for debt in 1580, for malversation in 1594, and again for debt in 1602. He published a life of St Anthony of Padua in 1603. In 1608 he emigrated to Mexico in the train of his patron Archbishop García Guerra, whose biography he later wrote. In Mexico he also wrote his *Ortografía castellana* (1609), which was an attempt to reform the spelling of the SPANISH LANGUAGE.

Alemán's most famous work is his *Guzmán de Alfarache*, one of the earliest and greatest PICARESQUE novels. The first part was published in 1599; in the course of the next five years some sixteen editions were published, as was a translation into French (1600) and a sequel purporting to be by Alemán. The authentic second part was published in 1604. In 1622 James Mabbe translated *Guzmán* into English as *The Rogue*, and the following year a Latin translation was published. The *pícaro* Guzmán presents (in retrospect as a GALLEY slave) scandalous episodes from his peripatetic life; he writes from the perspective of the *atalaya*, or 'watchtower' of repentance, hence the subtitle of part II, *Atalaya de la vida umana*). Guzmán was the progenitor of similar figures in many of the literatures of Europe.

Donald McGrady, *Mateo Alemán* (1968); Edmond Cros, *Mateo Alemán: Introducción a su vida y su obra* (1971).

**ALENÇON, DUKE OF.** See ANJOU, FRANÇOIS, DUC D'.

**ALESIUS or Ales or Alane, ALEXANDER** (1500–65), Scottish reformer in Germany, born in Edinburgh on 23 April 1500 and educated at the University of St Andrews, where he graduated in 1515. He was chosen to refute the Lutheran heresies of Patrick HAMILTON, but was so impressed by the power of Hamilton's arguments and his courage while being burnt at the stake that he was converted to Lutheranism. He was imprisoned for attacking clerical immorality in a sermon, and in 1532 he escaped. He made his way to Wittenberg, where he met LUTHER and MELANCHTHON and signed the AUGSBURG CONFESSION.

Alesius continued to inveigh against the Church in Scotland, writing to King JAMES V to protest against a Scottish clerical decree forbidding access to the New Testament by the laity; Johann COCHLÄUS wrote a reply (also addressed to the king), and Alesius responded with a full exposition of his reformist sympathies. In August 1534 he was excommunicated at Holyrood Palace by the deputy of the archbishop of St Andrews.

Shortly after King HENRY VIII of England broke with the Church of Rome, Alesius travelled to England carrying a letter from Melanchthon to Henry VIII; on arrival in August 1535 he was received by the king, Thomas CROMWELL, and Thomas CRANMER. Cromwell was chancellor of Cambridge University, and arranged for Alesius to be appointed to a lectureship at the university. Alesius' expository lectures on the Psalms aroused such resentment amongst the powerful Catholic party in Cambridge that he was forced to leave. He moved to London, where he worked as a physician and in 1537, at Cromwell's request, attended a convocation of the clergy and participated in a disputation with the bishop of London on the number of the SACRAMENTS; his argument for two sacraments was subsequently published as *Of the Authority of the Word of God Concerning the Number of Sacraments*.

In 1539 Alesius fled to Germany for fear of persecution under the Act of Six ARTICLES, and the following year he was appointed professor of theology at Frankfurt an der Oder. In 1543 he again became embroiled in debate, this time by contending that punishment for fornication lay within the jurisdiction of the civil magistrate; his position offended the university authorities, and he was forced to migrate to a chair at Leipzig. Throughout this period he maintained contact with Thomas Cromwell, who asked Alesius to translate parts of the 1549 Book of COMMON PRAYER into Latin for the benefit of Martin BUCER and Pietro Martire VERMIGLI; it is not clear whether Alesius visited England in order to discharge this task, but his translation was published in Leipzig in 1551. He died in Leipzig on 17 March 1565.

*DNB*; *NDB*; John T. McNeil, 'Alexander Alesius: Scottish Lutheran, 1500–1565', *Archiv für Reformationsgeschichte*, 55 (1964).

**ALESSI, GALEAZZO** (1512–72), Italian architect, born in Perugia and trained in Rome (*c.*1536–42), where he was influenced by MICHELANGELO. By 1548 he had settled in Genoa, where his early work included the Church of Santa Maria Assunta di Carignano, the basilica plan of which was adapted from BRAMANTE's design for ST PETER'S BASILICA. He was the principal architect of the Strada Nuova, a street of palaces in which Alessi overcame the challenge of sloping sites with huge staircases and colonnades and sets of courtyards imaginatively built on different levels. His Genoese palaces include Palazzo Pallavicini (*c.*1550), Palazzo Cataldi (1558, now the Chamber of Commerce), Palazzo Cambiaso (1565, now the Banco d'Italia), and Palazzo Parodi (1567); his Genoese villas include the Villa Cambiaso (1548).

Alessi worked in Milan from the late 1550s until 1569. His surviving Milanese buildings include the Palazzo Marino (1557, now the Municipio; the façade on Piazza della Scala is a nineteenth-century addition), the Church of SS Paolo e Barnaba (1561–7), and the façade of Santa Maria presso San Celso, which was completed in 1573 by Martino Bassi (1542–91).

*DBI*; *MDA*; *Galeazzo Alessi e l'architettura del cinquecento* (1975); N. A. H. Brown, *The Milanese Architecture of Galeazzo Alessi* (2 vols., 1982).

**ALEVIZ or Alevizo Friasin or Alevizo Novi or Aloiso da Carcano** (*fl.* 1505–9), Italian architect, possibly of Venetian origin, invited to Moscow by IVAN III, grand duke of Muscovy. He was the architect of the Cathedral of the Archangel (Arkhangelsky Sobor) in the Moscow Kremlin, a church that combines Russian domes with a north Italian quattrocento façade with scalloped gables.

*DBI* s.v. Aloiso da Carcano.

**ALEXANDER VI** (1431–1503), pope from 11 August 1492 until his death on 18 August 1503, was born in Játiva (Valencia) on 1 January 1431. His baptismal name was Rodrigo de Borja y Borja (Italian Borgia), and his maternal uncle Alfonso de Borja was bishop of Valencia, and showered benefices on Rodrigo. After studying CANON LAW in Bologna, Rodrigo was in February 1456 created cardinal-deacon by his uncle Alfonso, who had been elected Pope CALLISTUS III. The continued patronage of his uncle provided the young cardinal with a large collection of profitable bishoprics and abbeys, culminating in 1457 with his appointment as vice-chancellor of the Holy See, an immensely lucrative post that Rodrigo was to hold under five successive popes.

Cardinal Borgia's appetite for wealth was exceeded only by his voracious sexual appetite. He fathered children by several mistresses, and was particularly fond of the four children that he had by Vannozza Catenei (Juan, Cesare BORGIA, Lucrezia BORGIA, and Goffredo). He campaigned to become pope after the death of Pope SIXTUS V, but was unsuccessful, in part because of resistance to the candidature of a Spaniard. On the death of Pope INNOCENT VIII in 1492, however, Borgia overcame resistance by recourse to bribery and promises of preferments and was elected as Pope Alexander VI.

The securing of the papacy enabled Alexander to indulge his passion for wealth and women, and also allowed him to promote the interests of his relatives, especially the children of Vannozza Catenei. In 1492, when Cesare was 18, Alexander conferred on him several bishoprics (including the particularly lucrative archbishopric of Valencia); the following year he created Cesare cardinal, also conferring a cardinal's hat on Alessandro FARNESE, the brother of Giulia Farnese, his current mistress. Alessandro arranged for his son Juan, duke of Gandía, to marry a Spanish princess, and in 1497 conferred on him the duchy of Benevento, which he sliced out of the PAPAL STATE. For his daughter Lucrezia he arranged advantageous marriages, and assisted in the termination of her marriages (the first by papal annulment, the second by acquiescing in her husband's murder, which was probably arranged by Cesare); he also allowed Lucrezia to act as his unofficial regent when he was absent from Rome.

Alexander's son Juan was murdered in June 1497, and his grief was exacerbated by the suspicion that the assassination had been arranged by Cesare. Alexander vowed to devote himself to his ecclesiastical duties, but his resolve was short-lived, and he soon returned to a life of unbridled sensuality and extravagant nepotism. Cesare, who had renounced his ecclesiastical dignities after the death of his brother, became his father's closest adviser and assumed a new career as a papal soldier.

Alexander's domestic and foreign policies were largely dictated by the interests of his family. He arranged for the marriage of his son Goffredo to a granddaughter of King FERRANTE I of Naples, whose dowry was the wealthy principality of Squillace (Calabria); Alexander had hitherto supported the claims of CHARLES VIII of France to the Angevin inheritance of Naples, but after the marriage of Goffredo in 1493, he changed sides and supported King Ferrante. When Ferrante died on 25 January 1494, Alexander crowned Ferrante's son

ALFONSO II as king of Naples, thus precipitating Charles VIII's invasion of Italy. Alexander realized that he could not defend Rome or his tenure of the papacy, and so appeased King Charles, who went on to occupy Naples. On 31 March 1493 Alexander formed an alliance which forced Charles to withdraw, and in June 1497 he sent his son Cesare to Naples to crown FEDERICO (son of Ferrante I) as king of Naples.

In 1498 Alexander was persuaded by Cesare to change sides in order to secure French support for the subjugation of the Papal State, and he suddenly became an ally of the French crown, obliging LOUIS XII (the new king) with a papal annulment which enabled him to cast off Jeanne de France and marry ANNE OF BRITTANY, the widow of Charles VIII. Alexander then dispatched Cesare to France, and the grateful king created him duke of Valentinois and Dios and donated a princess, Charlotte d'Albret, as Cesare's bride. Alexander ratified the Treaty of Granada (11 November 1500), which partitioned Naples between France and Spain, and Cesare proceeded (with French assistance) to subdue Romagna, the largest province of the Papal State. The Borgia seizure of the Papal State was a costly campaign, and Alexander raised funds by assassinating Roman noblemen and then appropriating their estates, and also by turning the creation of cardinals into a business transaction in which cardinals paid for their elevation. In 1495 Alexander entered into a long struggle with SAVONAROLA which ended with the judicial TORTURE and execution of the friar.

On 4 May 1493 Alexander made his greatest contribution to geopolitics by fixing the line of demarcation between the Spanish and Portuguese zones in the Americas at a point 100 leagues west of the Azores and Cape Verde Islands and giving Spain the territorial rights to the west of the line; Portugal deemed this line to be too generous to Spain, and on 7 June 1494 the Treaty of TORDESILLAS moved the line to 270 leagues further west. In August 1503 Alexander and Cesare were both taken seriously ill; Alexander died on 18 August, and was hastily and ignominiously buried. The cause of Cesare's illness and Alexander's death is not known, but the likelihood is that they either contracted malaria or were mistakenly poisoned at a dinner party at which the poison was intended for Cardinal Adriano CASTELLESI, who was their host.

Alexander was not a lavish patron of learning or the arts, but he supported the University of Rome, which was accommodated in the Palazzo degli Sapienza (which he began in 1497) until 1935; he also lavishly restored Castel Sant'Angelo, persuaded MICHELANGELO to prepare plans for the rebuilding of ST PETER'S BASILICA, and commissioned PINTURICCHIO to decorate the Borgia apartments in the Vatican tower now known as the Torre Borgia, which he built in 1494; these decorations include a fresco of the Resurrection which incorporates a pious portrait of Pope Alexander.

The English playwright Barnabe Barnes wrote *The Devil's Charter: A Tragedy Containing the Life and Death of Pope Alexander the Sixth* (1607), which was performed before King JAMES.

DBI s.v. Alessandro VI; MDA s.v. Borgia (2); P. de Roo, *Materials for a History of Pope Alexander VI, his Relations and his Times* (5 vols., 1924); Michael Mallett, *The Borgias* (1969).

**ALFONSINE ORDINANCES or (Portuguese) Ordenações Afonsinas**, a codification of Portuguese law undertaken by the regents of King AFONSO V and completed in 1446. The ordinances dealt with issues of royal jurisdiction, aristocratic privilege, and succession, and also incorporated a revised code of criminal law. The code restricted the rights of JEWS and so encouraged conversions to Christianity. The ordinances were superseded by the Manueline Ordinances (Ordenações Manuelinas) of 1521.

**ALFONSO II OF ARAGON** (1448–95), king of Naples, was born on 4 November 1448, the son of FERRANTE I, who created him duke of Calabria. Alfonso was educated in his father's humanist court and later became a soldier and a patron of architecture; in the 1480s Alfonso remodelled the city of Naples, straightening roads, constructing FOUNTAINS fed by an aqueduct, and building new churches.

In 1478–9 Alfonso commanded the Neapolitan army in Tuscany, in 1480–1 he expelled the Ottomans from Otranto, and in 1484 he fought Venice. In 1486 his repressive policies towards the Neapolitan barons precipitated a revolt which he suppressed with an excess of cruelty that exacerbated the opposition to Alfonso and his father. He succeeded his father in 1494, but was forced to abdicate on 23 January 1495 in favour of his son FERRANTE II as the army of CHARLES VIII advanced on Naples. Alfonso sought refuge in the Olivetan monastery at Mazara del Vallo, where he died on 18 December 1495.

DBI s.v. Alfonso II d'Aragona; DHE; MDA s.v. Aragon, House of (4).

**ALFONSO V, EL MAGNÁNIMO** (1394–1458), king of Aragon and (as Alfonso I) king of Naples, succeeded to the throne of Aragon in 1416 and quickly began to secure and expand Aragonese possessions in the western Mediterranean. In 1419 he invaded CORSICA and occupied the southern part of the island, and in 1420 he subdued SICILY; SARDINIA was already an Aragonese possession, but Alfonso visited in 1421 with a view to strengthening the administration of the island.

In 1421 Queen GIOVANNA II of Naples, besieged by the forces of King Louis III of Anjou, offered to designate Alfonso as her heir in return for his assistance. In 1424 she disinherited Alfonso and on her death in 1435 left her kingdom to her adopted son RENÉ D'ANJOU. In the ensuing war of succession, Alfonso was defeated and taken captive by the Genoese in the battle of Ponza (1435), but was released after signing a secret treaty with his captor, Filippo Maria VISCONTI.

At the conclusion of the war, Alfonso entered Naples as its king in February 1443 and thereafter made Naples the capital of his empire. He established a magnificent court and became a generous patron of humanists (including Antonio BECCADELLI, who wrote a panegyric biography of Alfonso, Francesco FILELFO, and Lorenzo VALLA); he also commissioned an *Historia Alfonsi* from Bartolomeo Fazio, to whom he paid an annual pension of 500 ducats. His most important building was the triumphal arch (c.1452–71) constructed as an entrance to his castle; a frieze portrays Alfonso entering

Naples in triumph on 26 February 1443. Alfonso supported the University of Naples and in Sicily founded a university in Catania and a school of GREEK in Messina. His piety passed into folklore, both in its religious manifestations (he gave unstintingly to the Church and was a connoisseur of sermons) and in its reverence for the classics: he halted his army in pious respect before the birthplace of a Latin writer, carried copies of Livy and Caesar on his military campaigns, and, according to Beccadelli, was once cured of an illness by having the history of Alexander the Great by Quintus Curtius Rufius read to him.

Alfonso's conquest of Naples gave him a new base for his military exploits. He fought in the war for the succession of Milan (1447–50) and in the war against Francesco SFORZA (1450–3), and declined to submit to the Peace of LODI until 1455; in 1454 he signed an accord with Al-Ashraf Inal, the Mameluke sultan of Egypt, with a view to mounting a crusade (never to be realized) against the Ottomans. Alfonso's empire was divided at his death on 27 June 1458: he was succeeded in Aragon, Sardinia, and Sicily by his brother JOHN II and in Naples by his illegitimate son FERRANTE I.

DBI s.v. Alfonso V d'Aragona; DHE; MDA s.v. Aragon, House of (2); A. Ryder, *The Kingdom of Naples under Alfonso the Magnanimous* (1976).

**ALGEBRA.** Much of the 'practical mathematics' taught in ABACUS SCHOOLS is of medieval Islamic origin, being derived from the work of Leonardo of Pisa, who spent most of his life in Palermo (Sicily). In particular, this is true of algebra. The term is of Arabic origin, though not derived from the name of Geber (an alchemist) as was commonly supposed in the Renaissance. Algebraic work is, moreover, characterized by the use of 'Arabic' (more properly Hindu-Arabic) numerals, which again can be traced to Leonardo of Pisa, whose *Liber quadratorum* (1202) played an important part in the introduction of such numerals in the Latin West. Throughout the Renaissance, algebra was generally regarded as part of ARITHMETIC. This usage was partly vindicated as ancient when the Greek origin of algebra became apparent with the rediscovery of the *Arithmetica* of Diophantus of Alexandria (*fl.* AD 250) in 1572.

In the fifteenth century, there was room for disagreement about what distinguished algebra from ordinary arithmetic. PACIOLI says that 'algibra' is characterized by the taking of square roots. It was more common to consider that algebra involved the use of an explicit 'unknown', in Italian called *cosa* ('thing'), which led to the subject being called *cossa* in Latin (where the unknown becomes *res*) and *coss* in various vernaculars; an English attempt to make the word sound Greek leads to the name 'The Cossic Art'.

In abacus schools instruction proceeded by series of worked examples. Those for algebra were generally presented as practical, for instance asking what each partner takes as his share from a company that carries out various commercial transactions. The choice of problems sheds light on craft and commercial practices. More advanced texts contain some abstract problems, including geometrical ones. Some algebraic techniques seem to have been known in the learned mathematical community; REGIOMONTANUS, for instance, used algebra as part of his work on triangles (written in 1461).

Quadratic equations were solved by EUCLID, in geometrical terms that, by the Middle Ages, had been adapted for numerical examples. One of the great achievements of Renaissance algebraists was to provide a general method of solving cubic equations. It seems that a method of solving at least some cubics was devised by Scipione dal Ferro (1465–1526), who taught mathematics at the University of Bologna. It is not clear whether the general method, that is, the method of solving *any* cubic equation, later published by CARDANO (1545) and its discoverer TARTAGLIA (1546), is the same as Scipione's. However, the general method of solving cubics marks a very important point in the history of mathematics: it makes algebraic methods capable of solving problems that defeat geometrical ones (methods using straight-edge and compasses). Although some examples occur earlier, it seems that mathematicians did not truly recognize what had happened to algebra until after the publication of Descartes's algebraic geometry (1637). The solution of some quartic equations—associated particularly with Cardano's pupil Lodovico Ferrari (see TARTAGLÍA, NICCOLÒ)—and attacks on quintics, are of much less moment than the success with cubics.

The development of algebra also showed up problems with the notion of number. The Latin *numerus*, and its vernacular equivalents, resembled the Greek *arithmos* in denoting the natural numbers 1, 2, 3, and so on. Euclid's GEOMETRY deals with 'magnitudes' that are not limited in this way; it does not deal in negative quantities. The solution of cubic equations involved using the square roots of negative quantities. In any given case, the answer could be shown to be correct by substituting it into the original equation. However, mathematicians were accustomed to proceeding by rigorous methods. The remedy was provided by BOMBELLI (1572), who gave proper definitions and a set of rules for handling the roots of negative quantities. This gave such quantities the same status as the objects handled by Euclid. Little fuss was made over Bombelli's work, but thereafter the notion of a negative quantity, and its square root, gradually became accepted. At the same time, the rise in intellectual respectability of algebra, still seen as based in arithmetic, blurred the once sharp distinction made between number and quantity. Problems of dimensionality in equations were sometimes explicitly obviated by putting in unit magnitudes, but such precautions were more often taken as read. Another important conceptual advance was made by VIÈTE, who was the first to treat equations as entities in their own right, having the same status as the geometrical figures studied by Euclid and, like them, capable of having properties.

The history of Renaissance algebra shows us a part of mathematics wriggling free of the constraints imposed by rigour. At the same time we see the development of a specialized notation, which eventually colonized geometry, and has now become universal. In the fifteenth century there is no specialized notation, except for the numerals. Everything is written out in words. This 'rhetorical algebra', as it is sometimes called, reflects the fact that the abacus master read out the problems for the pupils to write down. Manuscript texts employ the usual scribal abbreviations, which in printed texts eventually become symbols for plus (+) and minus (−). Both these symbols would already have been available to the compositor. These two, together with the square root sign ($\sqrt{}$), derived from a scribal contraction for 'radix', first appear in the work of Michael STIEFEL (1544). The equals sign (=), apparently derived from the symbol for the zodiac sign Libra (the Balance), first appears in the work of Robert RECORDE. However, algebra books, being written in the vernacular, had only local circulation, so such symbols were not adopted either universally or rapidly. Viète was the first to use notation to distinguish between the unknown and given quantities: he used vowels for the former and consonants for the latter; Descartes (1637) introduced the use of letters from the end and the beginning of the alphabet, an innovation that proved popular, as did his style of denoting powers by means of superscripts. The first author whose equations stand entirely free of the verbal text is Thomas HARRIOT (1621).

**ALGIERS or (French) Alger or (Spanish) Argel or (Arabic) Al Jaza'ir** (i.e. 'the islands'), a port on the north coast of AFRICA on the site of ancient Icosium. From the thirteenth century, Algiers was nominally subject to the sultanate of Themcen, but in practice was ruled by its own emirs. In the harbour, the small island known as Peñón de Alger was occupied by the Spanish from as early as 1302, and fortified in 1510. In 1516 Selim bin Teumi, the emir of Algiers, invited Barbarossa and his brother Aruj (Turkish Oruç) to expel the Spaniards from the fort. Aruj arrived in Algiers, assassinated Selim, occupied the town, and became its ruler. Aruj was succeeded two years later by Barbarossa, who in 1529 drove the Spanish garrison from the Peñón. Thereafter Algiers became an Ottoman vassal state, nominally ruled by a bey (from 1587 a pasha) appointed by the PORTE. The city rapidly became the principal base of the BARBARY PIRATES, who in 1669 expelled the pasha and installed a bey from amongst their own numbers.

In October 1541 an imperial army led in person by CHARLES V mounted an assault on the city; Charles landed his troops, but a storm destroyed most of his fleet on the night of 26 October, and his army of 30,000 Spaniards, bereft by the storm of ammunition and provisions, was defeated by the Ottoman army. Thereafter the city became a safe haven for piracy until 1830.

**ALHACEN or Alhazen.** See ḤAṢAN IBN ḤAṢAN IBN AL-HAYTHAM.

**ALISON or Allison, RICHARD** (*fl.* 1592–1606), English composer. His particular interest was in writing consort music. Some of these pieces, written for Lady Frances Sidney, are for mixed consort of treble viol (or violin), flute, lute, cittern, bandora, and bass viol. He also wrote for plucked strings in consort; in his *Psalms of David in Metre* (1599) the four-part

vocal writing is enriched by an accompaniment to be played on the lute or orpharion and cittern.

**ALKAHEST**, the name alchemists gave to the universal solvent. See ALCHEMY AND CHEMISTRY.

**AL-KAZAR AL-KEBIR.** See KSAR-EL-KEBIR, BATTLE OF.

**ALKMAAR, MASTER OF** (*fl.* *c.*1475–*c.*1515), Dutch artist whose name derives from the altarpiece of *The Seven Works of Mercy* painted for the Church of St Lawrence in Alkmaar and now in the Rijksmuseum in Amsterdam. The anonymous artist may be Cornelius Buys (d. 1520), the brother of CORNELISZOON VAN OOSTSANEN. The depiction of peasants in the ALTARPIECE is an early instance of the Dutch form that was later to be known as GENRE PAINTING.
    MDA.

**ALLEN, WILLIAM** (1532–94), English cardinal and Counter-Reformation polemicist. He was educated at Oxford, where he was a fellow of Oriel College, and for four years principal of St Mary's Hall. In 1561 he left England and joined Catholic exiles at Louvain; he devoted the rest of his life to the attempt to reconvert England from Protestantism. In 1568 he founded a college at DOUAI to provide university education for Catholics, and to train priests for the recovery of English Catholicism. He encouraged the Jesuit mission to England, instigated the Douai translation of the Bible (in 1582), and founded the ENGLISH COLLEGE in Rome (1575–9). In 1587 he was created cardinal. His encouragement of Philip II's attempted invasion of England the following year provoked hostility from many English Catholics. He died in Rome.
    DNB.

**ALLEYN, EDWARD** (1566–1626), actor-manager, founder of Dulwich College. Star actor of the ADMIRAL'S MEN and rival of Richard BURBAGE, he had already acquired a following by the age of 18, and played the leading roles in many of MARLOWE's plays. He built the FORTUNE playhouse with Philip HENSLOWE, whose stepdaughter he married, and whose wealth he inherited. He founded Dulwich College, and married John DONNE's daughter as a second wife.
    DNB.

**ALLORI, ALESSANDRO** (1535–1607), Italian painter, trained in the workshop of BRONZINO, who became his adoptive father. The imprint of Bronzino's style is most apparent in Allori's nudes, such as *The Pearl Fishers* (1570–1, Palazzo Vecchio, Florence). As a young man he visited Rome (1554–6), where he saw the work of MICHELANGELO, whose influence can be seen in Allori's *Last Judgement* (1560, Church of SS Annunziata, Florence). His frescoes include GROTESQUES for the Uffizi and historical paintings for the *salone* of the MEDICI VILLA at Poggio a Caiano. Allori's later works include a *Birth of the Virgin* (1602, SS Annunziata).
    DBI; MDA.

**ALMAGEST.** See PTOLEMY IN THE RENAISSANCE.

**ALMAGRO, DIEGO DE** (1478/9–1538), Spanish conquistador, the son of a Castilian peasant. In 1514 he emigrated to Spanish America, where in 1525 he joined Francisco PIZARRO and Fernando de Luque in Panama in an expedition to conquer Peru. Almagro was Pizarro's second in command in the conquest of Cuzco (1533), and in 1535 commanded his own expedition to Chile. On returning from Chile he raised the Inca siege of Cuzco on 18 April 1537 and took possession of the city. A jurisdictional dispute between the Pizarro brothers and Almagro culminated in Almagro's defeat in the battle of Las Salinas on 26 April 1538. Almagro was captured and executed on the orders of Fernando Pizarro. In 1541 Almagro's son Diego avenged his father's death by organizing the assassination of Francisco Pizarro on 26 June 1541, but he was captured after the battle of Chuapas on 16 September 1542 and beheaded at Cuzco.

*DBEH; DHE;* Gerardo Larraín Valdés, *Diego de Almagro: Biografía* (1996).

**ALMANAC**, a book containing a calendar, a list of ecclesiastical festivals and saints' days, and a list of astronomical phenomena, sometimes with astrological predictions of the weather and political events. Almanacs have been compiled since the twelfth century, and were first printed in Germany; the first series appeared annually from 1450 to 1461. The earliest almanac to be printed in England (a translation from a French original) was *The Calendar of Shepherds* (c.1497).

**ALMEIDA, FRANCISCO DE** (c.1457–1510), first Portuguese governor in India. He was a soldier of aristocratic parentage who as a young man fought under King FERDINAND V of Spain in the campaigns to expel the Moors from GRANADA (1485–92). In March 1505 he was appointed as the first viceroy of India by King MANUEL I of Portugal. He sailed from Lisbon around the coast of Africa, pausing on the east coast to capture and plunder the Muslim settlements in Kilwa (now in Tanzania) and Mombasa (now in Kenya).

Almeida established his viceregal residence in Cochin, where Afonso de ALBUQUERQUE had built a fort. On 2 February 1509 he defeated the navy of the sultan of Egypt at the battle of Diu (Gujarat) and so secured Portuguese supremacy in the Indian Ocean.

Albuquerque was sent by Portugal to replace Almeida, but in the first instance Almeida refused to recognize Albuquerque's credentials and imprisoned him. In November 1509 he reluctantly yielded viceregal authority to Albuquerque, and on 1 December set sail for Europe with an escort of three vessels. The fleet stopped for water on the site of what is now Cape Town, and there attacked the Hottentots on 1 March 1510; Almeida was among the 65 Portuguese who died in the skirmish.

*DHP;* J. C. Silva, *O fundador do 'Estado Português da India': D. Francisco de Almeida* (1996).

**ALPHONSO**, the English form of the name of various Spanish and Portuguese kings named after St Ildefonso, a seventh-century archbishop of Toledo; the Castilian form is ALFONSO, the Catalan Alfons, the Galician Affonso, the Leonese Alonso, and the Portuguese AFONSO.

**ALSLOOT, DENIS VAN** (c.1570–c.1627), Flemish LANDSCAPE artist who in 1599 became a painter at the court in Brussels, and for the next decade painted landscapes in a style redolent of Gilles CONINXLOO and Jan BRUEGHEL; during this period the human figures in Alsloot's paintings were often drawn by Hendrik de CLERCK. After 1510 Alsloot increasingly adopted a more naturalistic idiom in his landscapes. He is best known for his depictions of processions and festivals in landscapes that sometimes include biblical or mythological figures. In 1615, at the command of Archduchess Isabella, Alsloot executed a series of paintings of the Ommegang (an annual procession in honour of the Virgin) held in Brussels on 31 May 1615; paintings in the series are now in Brussels (Musée d'Art Ancien), London (Victoria and Albert), Madrid (Prado), and Turin (Galleria Sabauda). He painted another series depicting the festivals at the Abbaye de la Cambre at Brussels.

*BNB; MDA.*

**ALTARPIECE**, the term used in ecclesiastical architecture for a picture or a carved screen behind and above an altar; in theological terms, an altarpiece is a decorative adjunct to an altar and not a liturgical object, so the blessing or consecration of an altar by a bishop does not extend to the altarpiece. The usual subject of an altarpiece is the saint to whom the church is dedicated.

The terms 'reredos' and 'retable' are sometimes used interchangeably with the term 'altarpiece', but the semantic fields of the three terms do not overlap altogether. The term 'reredos' is often used to denote a large construction in wood or stone decorated with carved figures, but is sometimes used in a broader sense for any decoration mounted above and behind or in front of an altar (e.g. the golden Pala d'Oro refashioned in 1345 for the altar of Basilica San Marco in Venice); these reredoses could be very large (e.g. Veit Stoss's painted reredos of 1477–9 in the Church of Our Lady in Kraków, in some cases covering the entire wall (e.g. the restored fifteenth-century reredos in the chapel of All Souls College, Oxford). The 'retable' (Latin *retabulum,* i.e. rear table) evolved from the shelf at the back of the altar on which candlesticks were placed into part of the framework of panels forming a reredos, and eventually came to mean a carved or painted altarpiece made up of panels fixed together rather than hinged like a triptych. The 'predella', which evolved (like the retable) from the shelf at the back of the altar, came also to be used to denote the strip of paintings at the base of an altarpiece; when placed below a triptych so that the doors could be opened and closed, the predella would be painted with scenes related to those on the altarpiece. In Italian an altarpiece consisting of a single picture is called a *pala d'altare,* and an altarpiece with several panels in a single frame is called an *ancona.* Altarpieces sometimes take the form of triptychs, in which two hinged side panels fold over the central panel; the diptych (which consists of two panels) is rare in altarpieces, but there was a tradition of polyptychs, which had at least four panels side by side and sometimes had a crowning panel; two of the most complex polyptychs are the Ghent altarpiece of Jan and Hubert van EYCK and the Isenheim altarpiece of GRÜNEWALD.

In Italy the altarpiece typically consisted of a panel painting in an elaborate gilt frame. The panel was often divided into compartments, but in the course of the fifteenth century the number of compartments was reduced and all the paintings in the frame were organized into a single composition, typically with a SACRA CONVERSAZIONE in the central panel and saints looking towards the Holy Family from the side panels, which shared a landscape background with the central panel. The ascendancy of pictorial values meant that the altarpiece differed from other easel paintings only in the architectural use of the surrounding frame.

In Germany and Flanders, the altarpiece typically consisted of a central panel flanked by hinged leaves. The leaves of this 'winged altar' (German Wandelaltar) would normally be painted on both sides; some altars had a second pair of wings, painted on the outside in GRISAILLE, for use on days of penitence. In France, where altars were usually made of stone, altarpieces were typically mounted in arched architectural frames; the influence of Flanders meant that painted triptychs became increasingly popular. In Spain large retables (Spanish retablos) accommodated extensive narrative cycles of paintings; the enormous carved reredos filled with figures and scenes was also popular (e.g. Damià FORMENT's reredos in the Cistercian abbey of Poblet, which introduced Renaissance sculpture in the Roman style to Catalonia).

In England the wooden reredos developed into a distinctive national form in the fourteenth century, typically a large construction with niches for figures of Christ and the saints; no complete sets of figures survived the Reformation. The painted reredos was always rare; the few that survived the Reformation include an early fourteenth-century Crucifixion with Eight Saints found in its original frame in a stable in 1927 and now restored to the thatched parish church of Thornham Parva in Suffolk.

There were no altarpieces in Orthodox churches (where images were mounted on the iconostasis), and the iconoclastic ideology of the Reformation meant that many altarpieces in Protestant countries were destroyed, though wooden reredoses survived, albeit stripped of their statuary. Strong Counter-Reformation support for altarpieces, including a stipulation that every altar should bear the image of the titular saint of the church in which it was placed, ensured that the genre remained alive in Catholic countries. In the late sixteenth century, large altarpieces tended to be attached to the wall behind the altar and surrounded with architectural frames that reflected structures within the church.

J. Berg Sobré, *Behind the Altar Table: The Development of the Painted Retable in Spain, 1350–1500* (1989); Peter Humfrey, *The Altarpiece in Renaissance Venice* (1993); Peter Humfrey and Martin Kemp (eds.), *The Altarpiece in the Renaissance* (1990); Patricia Meilman, *Titian and the Altarpiece in Renaissance Venice* (2000).

**ALTDORFER, ALBRECHT** (*c.*1480–1538), German painter, born in Regensburg, of which he became a burgher in 1505. His syncretic style reflects the influence of MANTEGNA, CRANACH, and DÜRER. Altdorfer's preferred subject was LAND-SCAPE. His early works experiment with the presentation of figures in landscapes; the best-known painting of this period is *Christ Taking Leave of his Mother* (National Gallery, London). Many of his later works (some of which are miniatures) eschew figures in favour of pure landscapes. From 1526 until his death Altdorfer served as civic architect of Regensburg, in which capacity he built fortifications and a slaughterhouse; his interests in architecture and his skill in perspective are evident in his *Birth of the Virgin* (Alte Pinakothek, Munich). He also painted an important battlepiece, *The Battle of Alexander at Issus* (Alte Pinakothek, Munich). He died in Regensburg on 12 February 1538.

NDB; MDA; O. Benesch, *Der Maler Albrecht Altdorfer* (1939); F. Winzinger, *Albrecht Altdorfer: Zeichnungen* (1952); id., *Albrecht Altdorfer: Grafik* (1963).

**ALTHAUS, JOHANNES, or Althusius** (1557–1638), German jurist and political theorist, from 1590 professor of law at the Calvinist University of Herborn. In law he applied the methods of RAMUS to jurisprudence (*Jurisprudentiae Romanae methodice digestae*, Herborn, 1586) and in his *Dicaeologicae* (1617) he set out a complete legal system centred on private law (i.e. the law that governs the relations of ordinary individuals to one another and to the state). His central work on political theory was *Politica methodice digesta* (1603), in which he advocated popular sovereignty, federalism, and a limited monarchy as means to achieve the national unity of Germany.

NDB s.v. Althusius; K.-W. Dahm, W. Krawietz, and Dieter Wyduckel (eds.), *Politische Theorie des Johannes Althusius* (1988); Thomas Huglin, *Sozietaler Foderalismus: Die Politische Theorie des Johannes Althusius* (1991).

**ALTICHIERO** (1320/30–*c.*1393), Italian painter, born in Zevio, near Verona. His principal surviving works, all of which echo the style of GIOTTO, are a fresco in the Church of Sant'Anastasia in Verona and, in collaboration with another painter called Avanzo, the fresco cycles in the Basilica del Santo and the Oratorio di San Giorgio in Padua.

DBI; MDA; John Richards, *Altichiero: An Artist and his Patrons in the Italian Trecento* (2000).

**ALUM.** The alum which is extracted from alunite during the early modern period is not the alum of the ancients (the *alumen* of PLINY and the στυπτηρία of Dioscorides), which was iron sulphate or aluminium sulphate, nor is it the alum of modern chemistry. The alum derived from alunite is rather a white transparent mineral salt that was used for fixing dyes, tawing skins, glassmaking, and medicine. When the supply of Levantine alum (which had been imported by Genoese merchants) was blocked by the Ottoman invasions, a substitute was discovered in the alum (variously called Roman alum or rock alum) which could be extracted from alunite. A mine was opened at Tolfa (60 kilometres (35 miles) northwest of Rome) in 1462, and by 1550 employed 700 workers. Tolfa was in the PAPAL STATE, and so the substantial profits were passed to the pope and his bankers, first the MEDICI, then from 1500 Agostino CHIGI, and after 1531 the venture capitalists of Genoa.

A second alunite mine was opened at Volterra in 1470, when a group of Volterran citizens financed by Lorenzo de' MEDICI formed a company to exploit the alunite deposits which had been discovered there. As Lorenzo's family held the concession on the papal mine at Tolfa, he decided that he should set the price at which the Volterra alum was to be sold; this decision precipitated the War of VOLTERRA. The Volterra mine closed in 1483.

J. Delumeau, *L'Alun de Rome* (1962).

**ALUMBRISMO**, a sixteenth-century Spanish religious movement centred in Toledo and other cities in New Castile. Adherents, who were called *alumbrados* or *illuminati* ('the enlightened'), withdrew from the secular world and gave their lives to prayer and contemplation; some *alumbrados* experienced visions and revelations. Their advocates within the Church included JUAN DE ÁVILA, the reformed Franciscans, and a significant number of JESUITS. The extent to which *alumbrados* were heterodox in their theology is unclear, but from 1524 the Spanish INQUISITION persecuted them ruthlessly in a futile attempt to link the movement with Protestantism. In 1527, IGNATIUS LOYOLA (who had not yet founded the Jesuit Order) was accused of showing sympathy for *alumbrismo*.

Alastair Hamilton, *Heresy and Mysticism in Sixteenth-Century Spain: The Alumbrados* (1992).

**ALVA, DUQUE DE**. See ALBA, FERNANDO ÁLVAREZ DE TOLEDO, THIRD DUKE OF.

**ALVARADO, PEDRO DE** (1485–1541), Spanish conquistador, born in Badajoz. He travelled to Cuba and in 1518 held a command in an expedition (led by Juan de GRIJALBA) from Cuba to Yucatán, which had been discovered the previous year by the navigator Francisco FERNÁNDEZ DE CÓRDOBA. In February 1519 Alvarado commanded one of the eleven ships in the fleet of Hernán CORTÉS, whose purpose was to conquer Mexico. When Mexico City (Aztec Tenochtitlán) was first occupied, Alvarado was left behind in charge of the garrison when Cortés had to return to the coast to confront Pánfilo de NARVÁEZ. On 1 July 1520 the garrison was forced to withdraw in the face of an Aztec rebellion precipitated by Alvarado's execution of large numbers of the Aztec nobility; Alvarado led the rearguard, and while under attack saved his life with a long leap (Spanish *salto*) in which he used his spear to propel himself forward: this *salto de Alvarado* passed into colonial folklore.

Alvarado led the expedition to conquer Guatemala (1523–4), of which he was appointed governor by the Emperor CHARLES V. In 1534 he led an expedition to subdue the Inca province of Quito, but was intercepted by Diego de ALMAGRO, to whom he sold his soldiers for 100,000 gold pesos and so recovered the cost of the expedition. In 1537, while on a visit to Spain, his governorship was extended to include Honduras.

In February 1540 Francisco VÁZQUEZ DE CORONADO had undertaken an expedition to the legendary kingdom of Cíbola in search of the fabled wealth of its seven cities. He failed to find Cíbola, and Alvarado was persuaded to lead another expedition the following year. He was killed by Indians in Jalisco (Mexico) as he marched north.

*DBEH*; *DHE*; J. E. Kelly, *Pedro de Alvarado, Conquistador* (1932); Jesús García, *Pedro de Alvarado* (1987); Antonio Gutiérrez Escudero, *Pedro de Alvarado: El conquistador del país de los quetzales* (1988).

**AMADEO, GIOVANNI ANTONIO** (1447–1522), Italian sculptor and architect, born in Pavia, and from 1466 employed carving sculptures for the Certosa di PAVIA; from 1481 to 1499 he served as principal architect, in which capacity he designed the façade. His other work includes the sculptures on the COLLEONI Chapel in Bergamo (1470–3) and the dome over the crossing of Milan Cathedral (1490).

*DBI*; *MDA*; Janice Shell and Liana Castelfranchi (eds.), *Giovanni Antonio Amadeo: Sculture e architettura del suo tempo* (1993).

**AMADÍS DE GAULA**, the title and protagonist of a prose romance of which the earliest surviving printed version is an edition in Spanish by García Rodríguez de Montalvo published in Zaragoza in 1515 and surviving in a unique copy in the British Library; Rodríguez claimed to have reworked the first three books from earlier versions but to have written the fourth book himself. In 1955 a fragment of an earlier version was discovered. It is not clear when Amadís was first printed (the 1515 edition is probably not the first), nor is its original language (which may have been Portuguese or Galician) known. Its date is similarly unclear: there are allusions to *Amadís* in the mid-fourteenth century, and its Arthurian elements (Amadís is a version of Lancelot) derive from thirteenth-century French romances of chivalry, which were adapted in Spain as *libros de caballería*, of which *Amadís* is the most distinguished example. The immense popularity of *Amadís* in Spain is attested by a large number of imitations (including one by TERESA DE ÁVILA), sequels (four more books were published by various authors), and adaptations (including Gil VICENTE's play *Amadís de Gaula*) and by the rescue of *Amadís* from the flames in CERVANTES' chapter on literary criticism in *Don Quijote* (1. 6), where it is extolled as 'the finest of all books of its kind that have ever been written' ('el mejor de todos los libros que deste género se han compuesto').

In France, *Amadís* became the most popular chivalric romance of the sixteenth and early seventeenth centuries. In 1540 Heberay des Essarts published a French translation, *Amadis de Gaule*, but by 1591 the four books of Herberay's translation had been expanded into a 21-book version, and in 1615 a 24-book version was published. An abridgement published in 1629 marked the end of the fashion for *Amadís* in France.

In England Anthony Munday translated the book as *Amadis of Gaul* (c.1590); interest in *Amadís* was revived in the nineteenth century by the publication of an abridged version by Robert Southey in 1803.

John O'Connor, '*Amadis de Gaule' and its Influence on Elizabethan Literature* (1970).

**AMALFI, LAWS OF**, a code of MARITIME LAW formulated at Amalfi (near Naples) in the twelfth century. It is usually called the *Tabula Amalfitana*, or, more formally, the *Capitula* *et ordinationes curiae maritimae nobilis civitatis Amalphae.* In the course of the fifteenth century many of its elements were absorbed into the Catalan *Consolato del mare,* and in that form became the maritime law by which the Mediterranean was regulated.

**AMASEO, ROMULO** (1489–1552), Italian humanist. He was born in Udine and educated in Padua, after which he taught at the University of Bologna from 1513 to 1544. His memorable contribution to the QUESTIONE DELLA LINGUA was a two-day oration delivered in 1529 in the presence of the Emperor CHARLES V and Pope CLEMENT VII, when Amaseo argued that Ciceronian Latin was much superior to the vernacular as a literary language.

DBI.

**AMATI FAMILY,** Italian violin-makers in Cremona. Andrea (*c.*1511–1577) is thought to be responsible for the form which the violin, viola, and cello have today. The instruments' design, which used contemporary standards of measurement and proportion, established a model for subsequent generations of instrument-makers; the rules for scroll design remain virtually unchanged. The characteristic tone of these instruments is sweet, if somewhat delicate compared to later models. Antonio (*c.*1540–1607) and his half-brother Girolamo (*c.*1561–1630) were sons of Andrea. Known as 'the brothers Amati', they developed the work started by their father, making alterations to the shape of the soundhole and strengthening the instrument. The superior quality of instruments from the Amati workshop was sustained even allowing for the experimental work they carried out on the outline and arching of instruments; it is possible they were the inventors of the contralto viola (the size commonly used today) at a time when the larger tenor viola was in common use.

The Amati family were the first of many to work as violin-makers in Cremona. Their reputation spread far beyond north Italy, and the influence of their designs was felt as far afield as the Tirol and the Netherlands. The effect of these sophisticated instruments on composers of the period is incalulable.

**AMBERGER, CHRISTOPH** (*c.*1505–1561/2), German portrait painter who worked in AUGSBURG, which by virtue of its position on the principal trade route from the Mediterranean to northern Europe was the first important humanist centre in the north and the first northern city in which painters fell under the influence of Italian artists. The portraits of Amberger, such as his *Charles V* (Gemäldegalerie, Berlin) are in their emphasis on the splendour of dress and their delight in fabric and jewellery products of the Venetian school.

Amberger was the son-in-law and pupil of Leonhard Beck, with whom his portraits are sometimes confused.

NDB; MDA.

**AMBOISE, CHÂTEAU D'**, the birthplace and principal residence of CHARLES VIII. It overlooks the Loire from a triangular rocky outcrop above the town of Amboise. Construction of the castle began in 1434. The principal wing, facing the Loire, is the Logis du Roi (the royal apartments), which was built in the French Gothic style by Charles VIII; the other wing, at a sharp angle to the Logis du Roi, was commissioned by LOUIS XII, and was demolished at the Revolution.

The Italian campaign of Charles VIII instilled in him a taste for Italian gardens, and on his return in 1496 he commanded PACELLO DA MERCOGLIANO to provide a garden for Amboise on a terrace within the castle precincts. A later drawing of the chateau by Jacques DUCERCEAU shows that the garden, which was entirely enclosed by buildings which have since disappeared, was divided into ten square (or rectangular) planted areas, each of which was divided into four smaller squares; on the end of the garden overlooking the Loire there was a gallery pierced by windows. There is also a PAVILION in the Italian Renaissance style, like those which Pacello designed for BLOIS and GAILLON.

LEONARDO DA VINCI was invited to Amboise by FRANCIS I, and died there in 1519; he is said to be buried in the Chapelle Saint-Hubert, an exquisite French Gothic building on the ramparts.

**AMBOISE, CONJURATION D', or (English) Conspiracy of Amboise** (1560), a Huguenot plot possibly led by Louis I de Bourbon, prince of CONDÉ, to capture the youthful King FRANCIS II at the Château d'AMBOISE and destroy the power of Cardinal Charles de GUISE and Duke François de GUISE. The discovery of the plot led to the massacre of more than 1,000 Huguenots. Condé was arrested and sentenced to death (31 October 1560), but spared by the death of King Francis on 5 December; power passed to the queen mother, CATHERINE DE MÉDICIS, who convened the Colloquy of POISSY. The failure of the Colloquy led to the outbreak of the WARS OF RELIGION.

Jacques Debû-Bridel, *La Conjuration d'Amboise* (1963); L. Romier, *La Conjuration d'Amboise* (1923).

**AMBOISE, GEORGES D'** (1460–1510), French cardinal and statesman, successively consecrated as bishop of Montauban (1484), archbishop of Narbonne (1493), and archbishop of Rouen (1492). In 1488 he supported the rebellion of Louis, duke of Orléans, against the regent, ANNE OF FRANCE, and was imprisoned for two years. In 1498 Duke Louis acceded to the throne as King LOUIS XII, and Cardinal Georges was made a cardinal and appointed as the king's chief minister, in which capacity he controlled foreign policy and helped to organize the French invasion of Italy in 1499 (see WARS OF ITALY). He travelled to Italy with the French army and administered the conquered territories; on the death of Pope ALEXANDER VI he aspired to the papacy, but acquiesced in the election of PIUS III and (a month later) JULIUS II. In 1508 he helped to form the League of CAMBRAI. He died in Lyon and was buried in Rouen Cathedral.

DBF; MDA.

**AMBOISE, TREATY OF or Peace of or Pacification of, or (French) L'Édit d'Amboise,** an edict issued by CHARLES IX on 19 March 1563 at the Château d'Amboise in the Loire valley. Under the terms of the agreement, Huguenot nobles were allowed to hold Protestant services in their homes, and one town in each judicial district (*baillage* or *sénéchaussée*), with the exception of Paris, was allowed to hold Protestant services for commoners. The treaty ended the first of the nine WARS OF RELIGION.

**AMBROSIANA LIBRARY or (Italian) Biblioteca Ambrosiana**, the principal library of Milan, named in honour of St Ambrose, the patron saint of Milan; it was the first large LIBRARY to be accessible to the public. The library was founded by Cardinal Federico Borromeo (1564–1631), cousin of Carlo BORROMEO and his successor as archbishop of Milan. It opened on 8 December 1609, at which point its collections consisted of *c*.30,000 books and *c*.12,000 manuscripts.

**AMBROSIAN REPUBLIC or (Latin) Aurea Respublica Ambrosiana**. On 14 August 1447, the day after the death of Filippo Maria VISCONTI (who left no heir to his dukedom), a group of 24 local noblemen constituted the Ambrosian Republic (named in honour of St Ambrose, patron saint of Milan) with a view to replacing signoral rule with free civic government. From the outset the administration was enervated by inter-family strife and popular hostility, and it was unwilling to deal with the aspirations to independence of other cities within the Visconti *signoria*. The republic decided to assign military authority over the disaffected cities to Francesco SFORZA, a *condottiere* who had been employed by Filippo Maria Visconti (whose illegitimate daughter he married) in various campaigns against Venice. Francesco Sforza aspired to the Visconti dukedom, and in 1450 led a Venetian army in an attack on Milan. The Ambrosian Republic capitulated, and on 11 March 1450 the Popular Assembly dissolved the republic and conferred the dukedom of Milan on Francesco Sforza.

**AMERBACH, JOHANNES** (*c*.1440–1513), Swiss humanist printer and art collector, born in Basel and educated in Basel and Paris. In 1484 he established a printing workshop in Basel, specializing in the production of patristic works. The humanist Jean Heynlen, who had taught Amerbach in Paris, later migrated to Basel, where he joined a small circle of humanist scholars (who included REUCHLIN) responsible for the textual accuracy of Amerbach's editions. His most important publication was an eleven-volume edition of Augustine. The presence of a group of humanists associated with the press attracted other humanists to what quickly became an important humanist centre.

In 1511 Amerbach contributed to the advancement of humanist study by engaging the Dominican scholar Johannes Cono of Nuremberg (1463–1513) as a tutor in Greek and Hebrew to his sons Bonifacius (1495–1562) and Basilius (1533–91), and opened the classes (which were held in his house) to anyone who wanted to acquire a proficiency in these languages. Bonifacius was the subject of an important portrait by Hans HOLBEIN (1519, Kunstmuseum, Basel).

*DHBS*; *NDB*.

**AMES, WILLIAM** (1576–1633), Calvinist theologian. Ames was educated at Cambridge, where he was taught by the Puritan William PERKINS. From *c*.1610, he lived for a time in Colchester and then moved to Holland, where he gained a reputation as a prominent Calvinist theologian. In 1622 he was appointed professor of theology at Franeker, a position he held until almost the end of his life, when he moved to Rotterdam to lead the English congregation there. In 1627 he published a comprehensive treatise on Calvinism, *Medulla theologiae*; *De conscientia, eius iure et casibus* (1632) was an influential discussion of casuistry.

*DNB*.

**AMMAN or Ammann, JOST** (1539–91), Swiss engraver. He was born in Zürich but spent most of his working life in Nuremberg. He was a prolific producer of WOODCUTS and ENGRAVINGS for use as illustrations in popular books. The artistry of his illustrations may not achieve the highest standards, but they are nonetheless valuable as documents in the social history of sixteenth-century Nuremberg. Some of his biblical illustrations were later imitated by Rubens.

*NDB*; *MDA*; *DHBS* s.v. Amman II.8.

**AMMANATI, BARTOLOMEO** (1511–92), Italian architect and sculptor, born in Settignano (near Florence) and trained in the workshop of Pisa Cathedral. He worked in Venice with SANSOVINO on the Libreria del Sansovino (which was to house the Biblioteca MARCIANA until 1812) and subsequently moved to Rome, where from 1550 he worked with VASARI and VIGNOLA on the Villa GIULIA. In Florence he built the Ponte Santa Trinita (1567–70, destroyed 1944 and rebuilt) and the rusticated court of the PITTI PALACE (1558–70), completed the Palazzo Grifoni (1557), and supervised the construction of MICHELANGELO's vestibule stairway in the Biblioteca LAURENZIANA; elsewhere in Tuscany, he built the Tempietto della Vittoria near Arezzo (1572) and contributed to the Palazzo Provinciale in Lucca (1578). His last important building was the Collegio Romano in Rome (*c*.1582–5), which Ammanati designed for the JESUIT Order.

Ammanati's principal surviving sculpture is the FOUNTAIN in the Piazza della Signoria in Florence (1571–5), in which a marble *Neptune* is surrounded by bronze nymphs (1571–5).

*DBI*; *MDA*; Michael Kiene, *Bartolomeo Ammannati* (1995).

**AMMERBACH, ELIAS NIKOLAUS** (*c*.1530–1597), German composer and organist, born in Naumburg. In 1561 he was appointed organist of the Thomaskirche in Leipzig. His *Orgel oder Instrument Tabulatur* (1571) is organized into five increasingly difficult sections, each more decorative than its predecessor. The first printed German organ music, it is written in the new German organ tablature where pitch is indicated by letters and note values are defined by rhythm-signs placed above the stave.

**AMMIRATO, SCIPIONE** (1531–1600), historian of Florence, born at Lecce, in the kingdom of Naples. He studied law at his father's behest and classical literature to satisfy his interest in the ancient world. After periods of residence in Venice and Rome (where he entered the service of Pope PIUS IV) he settled in Florence in 1569. He secured the patronage of Duke

COSIMO I DE' MEDICI, who provided him with apartments at the Palazzo Medici and commissioned a history of Florence from its remote beginnings to the present day. The *Istorie fiorentine* (1600) concluded in 1434, the year in which Rinaldo degli ALBIZZI was exiled and Cosimo de' Medici invited to return; a continuation to 1574, the year in which Ammirato's patron Cosimo I died, was published posthumously. The *Istorie* may not be a great imaginative work, but it is securely based on original archive sources, many of which had been previously inaccessible. Ammirato's other works (which were collected in 1594) included discourses on TACITUS and genealogical histories of prominent Neapolitan and Florentine families.

*DBI.*

**AMNER, JOHN** (1579–1641), English composer and organist. He studied music at Oxford, returning in 1610 to Ely, where his family were closely involved with the music at the cathedral. He was appointed *informatur choristarum* and in 1615 his *Sacred Hymns of 3, 4, 5 and 6 Parts for Voices and Viols* was published. His musical vocabulary was sufficiently flexible to conform to the changing religious prescriptions within his lifetime.

**AMPHITHEATRE.** The amphitheatres of ancient Rome, such as the Colosseum, were oval auditoriums used for gladiatorial combats and, when flooded, naval displays; the term 'amphitheatre', which was borrowed from Greek, means 'double theatre', i.e. two elliptical buildings facing each other in an oval. Roman amphitheatres were free-standing buildings, and so differed from Greek theatres, which were elliptical auditoriums scooped out of the side of hills; Roman theatres imitated this construction, but supplemented the natural support of the hillside with concrete vaulting.

In the Renaissance the term 'amphitheatre' was used to denote what the Greeks and Romans would have called a 'theatre', i.e. an open semicircular or elliptical structure. In the garden to the west of the Villa MADAMA, Raphael hollowed out the hillside to build an *exedra*, i.e. a modern imitation of the classical debating theatre. Behind the villa at PRATOLINO there is a vast amphitheatre carved out of the Tuscan hillside. The most celebrated amphitheatre of the sixteenth century is in the BOBOLI GARDENS, where TRIBOLO regulated the shape of a natural hollow so that it resembled a U, and then planted the banks; the seating that later replaced the plantations was not built until 1637.

**AMSDORF, NIKOLAUS VON** (1483–1565), German Protestant reformer, born on 3 December 1483 in Torgau. He studied in Leipzig and in 1502 became one of the first students at the new University of WITTENBERG; in 1508 he joined the academic staff as a lecturer in philosophy and theology. In 1517 Amsdorf declared himself a supporter of LUTHER, whom he accompanied to the LEIPZIG DISPUTATION in 1519 and the Diet of WORMS in 1521. He subsequently worked for the Reformation cause in Magdeburg (1524), Goslar (1528 and 1531), and Einbeck (1534).

Amsdorf was a relentless controversialist who revelled in argument: in 1534 he precipitated a new stage in Luther's debate with ERASMUS; he subsequently quarrelled with both MELANCHTHON and Martin BUCER, entered vigorously into the debates at Schmalkalden that led to the formulation of the SCHMALKALDIC ARTICLES (1537), denounced the bigamy of the Landgrave PHILIP OF HESSE (1540), and in 1541 incurred the wrath of the Emperor CHARLES V at the Conference of REGENSBURG.

On 20 January 1542 Amsdorf was consecrated as bishop of Naumburg by JOHANN FRIEDRICH, elector of Saxony, in the face of opposition from the emperor and the cathedral chapter. After the SCHMALKALDIC WAR Amsdorf had to yield his see to Julius von PFLUG, and retreated to Eisenach. He contributed to the founding of the University of Jena in 1548 and violently opposed the LEIPZIG INTERIM. He joined forces with FLACIUS ILLYRICUS and led the party (now known as the GNESIO-LUTHERANS) who opposed the ADIAPHORISTS. He subsequently became involved, in the wake of the Leipzig Interim, with a debate with Georg MAIER, who defended Melanchthon's position on GRACE. His contention that good works were not merely useless (the classic Lutheran position) but actually harmful was criticized in the Formula of CONCORD, but his adherents created a short-lived sect, the Amsdorfians, which championed his view that good works were an impediment to salvation. He died at Eisenach on 14 May 1565, where his effigy is in the Church of St George.

*NDB; Hans Stiller, Nikolaus von Amsdorf: Sein Leben bis zu seiner Einweihung als Bischof in Naumburg, 1483–1542 (1937); Robert Kolb, Nikolaus von Amsdorf (1483–1542): Popular Polemics in the Preservation of Luther's Legacy (1978).*

**AMSTERDAM**, the principal city of the Dutch province of HOLLAND, so called from its location at the dam constructed across the river Amstel in 1240. In the course of the next 60 years Amsterdam developed from a fishing hamlet into a chartered town; it was originally governed by a bailiff (*schout*) and a panel of judicial assessors (*scheperen*), thereafter by burgomasters and a municipal council (*Vroedschap*). Originally protected by an earthen wall surmounted by a wooden stockade, stone walls were constructed in 1482, and ten years later a Jewish community consisting of refugees from Spain was established in Amsterdam. In the sixteenth century Amsterdam declined to join the REVOLT OF THE NETHERLANDS until 1578; in 1587 Robert Dudley, earl of Leicester, failed in an attempt to capture the city. The population movements arising out of the Revolt of the Netherlands, the French WARS OF RELIGION, the expulsion of the MARRANOS from Spain and Portugal, and the THIRTY YEARS WAR led to successive waves of refugees arriving in Amsterdam. These refugees made Amsterdam one of the wealthiest cities in Europe, and with the fall of Antwerp to Spain in 1585 Amsterdam became Europe's financial capital. The DUTCH EAST INDIA COMPANY was founded in 1602 and thereafter the city became the capital of the Dutch empire and one of the principal European centres of the arts.

**AMYOT, JACQUES** (1513–93), French humanist and translator, born in Melun (on the Seine near Paris); he was the son of a tanner. He attracted the patronage of MARGUERITE

D'ANGOULÉME, and from 1536 until c.1546 taught Greek at the University of Bourges; he subsequently travelled to Italy. In 1554 Amyot entered the service of King HENRI II as tutor to his two sons, the future kings CHARLES IX and HENRI III. His appointments in the Church included abbot of Bellozane (1548), *grand aumônier de France* (1560), and bishop of Auxerre (1570).

Amyot translated Heliodorus (*Histoire éthiopique*, 1547), Diodorus Siculus (*Les Sept Livres*, 1554), Longus (*Les Amours pastorales de Daphnis et Chloé*, 1559), and Plutarch's *Lives* (*Les Vies des hommes illustres grecs ou romains*, 1559) and *Moralia* (*Les Œuvres morales et mêlées* (1572). The translation of Plutarch's *Lives*, which was commissioned by King FRANCIS I, was widely admired (notably by MONTAIGNE) and very influential: in France it was an important influence on the development of French literary prose, and in its English translation of 1579 became the principal source of SHAKESPEARE's Roman plays.

DBF; A. Cioranescu, *Vie de Jacques Amyot* (1941); Robert Aulotte, *Amyot et Plutarque: La Tradition des Moralia aux 16ᵉ siècle* (1975).

**ANABAPTISTS**, the term coined from Greek (meaning 'rebaptizers') used to denote various sixteenth-century reformed communities which had in common a conviction that infant BAPTISM was not efficacious, and so rejected infant baptism in favour of the reinstitution of adult baptism for believers, a practice which had hitherto been used for the admission of converted infidels to the Church. The designation 'Anabaptist' is used of at least five distinct groups; as a description of a theological conviction held by individuals not organized into communities (e.g. Michael SERVETUS and Faustus SOCINUS), it has an even wider application.

The five continental communities, whose doctrine often differs sharply on matters other than baptism, are (1) the ZWICKAU PROPHETS under their leader Nicholas STORCH; (2) the SWISS BRETHREN, including Balthasar HUBMAIER, and the related south German Anabaptist groups; (3) the Moravian community founded by Jakob HUTTER; (4) the disciples of Melchior HOFFMAN, known as Melchiorites or Hoffmanites, in the Netherlands and north-west Germany; (5) the followers of JOHN OF LEIDEN, who established the short-lived Anabaptist kingdom of MÜNSTER, and of MENNO SIMONS, who in the wake of the Münster debacle led a pacifist movement in the Netherlands and north-west Germany.

The Anabaptist heresy was denounced both by the Catholic Church and by reformers such as LUTHER, ZWINGLI, and CALVIN, and Anabaptists were persecuted by both sides, often not simply for their views on baptism (e.g. the Hoffmanites for their aberrant Christology); tens of thousands of Anabaptists were executed in the sixteenth century.

**ANAMORPHOSIS**, a seventeenth-century term transliterated from a Greek word meaning 'transformation' and used to denote images that are distorted when viewed from the front but become properly proportioned when viewed from a particular angle or by reflection in a special mirror. The optical principles were understood and implemented in antiquity by Greek sculptors whose statues were designed to be viewed from below, and this practice was described by Plato (*Sophist* 236). The earliest examples of the technique occur in the notebooks of LEONARDO DA VINCI. The two best-known examples in painting are Guillim SCROTS's portrait of King EDWARD VI (National Portrait Gallery, London) and the skull in HOLBEIN's *Ambassadors* (1533, National Gallery, London); in woodcuts, the most familiar image is Erhard Schön's *Anamorphosis of Emperor Ferdinand* (c.1531–4).

Jurgis Baltrušaitis, *Anamorphoses: Les Perspectives dépravés* (3rd edn., 1986).

**ANATOMY**. In the early modern period, most areas of medical theory remained essentially GALENIC and medical practice evolved very little, but anatomy was transformed, in significant part because of the work of Renaissance humanists and artists who regarded the human body as an important subject of intellectual and empirical enquiry. ALBERTI and GHIBERTI both valued the study of anatomy for the knowledge it could yield about proportion. Artists such as MANTEGNA and SIGNORELLI studied musculature, and VERROCCHIO required his pupils to study flayed bodies. DÜRER and MICHELANGELO both studied anatomy, and LEONARDO DA VINCI filled his notebooks with some 750 anatomical drawings. Leonardo interpreted his investigations through the intellectual framework of Galenic medicine, and so his drawings reinforce traditional understandings of the areas in which he was interested, notably embryology, musculature, and physiology, especially the nervous, respiratory, vascular, and urino-genital systems.

In the universities, dissections for purposes of anatomical study began in Bologna in the fourteenth century. In the sixteenth century the most prominent Bologna anatomist was Jacopo BERENGARIO DA CARPI, who dissected executed criminals (including a pregnant woman). The most important Italian centre of anatomical study was Padua, where the anatomy theatre of 1594 still survives; the anatomists of Padua included VESALIUS, Gabriele FALLOPPIO, and Girolamo FABRICI. In Rome, the most important anatomist was Bartolomeo EUSTACHIO.

Anatomical dissection became a metaphor for analysis. In England, for example, Philip Stubbes wrote *The Anatomy of Abuses* (1583), John Donne wrote 'An Anatomy of the World', and Robert Burton wrote *An Anatomy of Melancholy* (1621). Humanist anatomists such as John CAIUS in Cambridge and Pieter Pauw (1564–1617) in Leiden also saw dissection as a means for demonstrating the observational approach to anatomy, and dissections became public events: at Bologna there were public dissections during Carnival, and in Amsterdam Rembrandt painted *The Anatomy Lesson of Dr Niclaes Tulp* (1632; Mauritshuis, The Hague).

Jonathan Sawday, *The Body Emblazoned: Dissection and the Human Body in Renaissance Culture* (1995); B. Schultz, *Art and Anatomy in Renaissance Italy* (1985).

**ANCHIETA, JOSÉ DE** (1534–97), Spanish Jesuit missionary who travelled in 1553 to Brazil, where he founded a school near what is now São Paulo. His particular interest was the education of Indians, and he became a vociferous campaigner against the enslavement of Indians. He wrote a 'grammar of the most used language on the coast of Brazil' (*Arte da gramática da língua mais usada na costa do Brasil*), which was Tupi, and constructed a theatre in which religious plays were performed in Tupi and Latin.

DHP; Miguel Rodriquez-Pantoja Márquez et al., *José de Anchieta: Vida y obra* (1988); José Fornell (ed.), *José de Anchieta, primer mariólogo jesuita: Texto latino de sus poemas mariólogos* (1997); Décio de Almeida Prado (ed.), *Theatro de Anchieta a Alencar* (1993).

**ANCONA**. The seaport and episcopal see of Ancona, capital of the Marches, was in late antiquity one of the cities of the Pentapolis under the exarchate of Ravenna. The city retained its connections with the Levant as it evolved into an independent maritime republic with consular representation in Constantinople and Acre (modern Akko, in Israel). In 1348 Ancona was captured by Guastafamiglia ('destroyer of families'), ruthless scion of the MALATESTA family. Pope Innocent VI dispatched the equally ruthless Cardinal Albornoz to recapture the city, and thereafter Ancona's independence was in theory compromised by subordination to the papal see.

In practice, however, Ancona constantly reasserted its independence. The city successfully withstood sieges mounted by Francesco SFORZA and ALFONSO V of Aragon and repelled an invasion by Pope INNOCENT VIII in 1477. In 1488 Ancona openly rebelled against the papacy, but the Ottoman expansion had sapped the economic strength of the city, and it was increasingly unable to defend its independence. In 1532 Pope CLEMENT VII sold Ancona to Cardinal Pietro ACCOLTI and ordered the seizure of the city by Frederico II GONZAGA, captain-general of the papal forces. The city was captured, communal rule was terminated (and the communal archive destroyed), anti-papal members of the citizen council and executive were exiled, and the city was thereafter absorbed into the PAPAL STATE.

The Marches (Le Marche) were originally frontier provinces of the Frankish empire and the Papal State, and in the Carolingian period the term 'March of Ancona' (Marca Anconitana) referred to the territory of the Pentapolis. In the late eleventh century the March of Fermo (Marca Fermana), the March of Camerino (Marca Camerinese), and the March of Ancona all came under the control of Robert Guiscard, and from the early twelfth century the term 'March of Ancona' was used as a collective term for all three Marches.

**ANCY-LE-FRANC, CHÂTEAU D'**, an Italian Renaissance house and garden near Auxerre, in Burgundy. The architect was SERLIO, who was employed at the court of Francis I. The house and garden were commissioned by Antoine de Clermont, brother-in-law of DIANE DE POITIERS; construction on a large, level site began *c*.1546.

The house is built around a large rectangular courtyard of majestic proportions. The twelve principal rooms on the ground floor, notably the Chambre des Nudités and the Chambre de Diane, are adorned with tapestries and frescoes. On the first floor, the apartments and galleries were sumptuously decorated by PRIMATICCIO.

A drawing by Jacques DUCERCEAU shows that the original gardens echoed the rectangular shape of the house. A huge rectangular raised terrace was constructed around the house and garden, and this terrace was used as a promenade from which house and gardens could be viewed. In the late seventeenth century *bosquets* (see BOSCO) and PARTERRES *de broderie* were added, and in the mid-eighteenth century a FOUNTAIN was built on an island in the lake.

**ANDELOT, FRANÇOIS D'** (1521–69), French Huguenot leader, the younger brother of Admiral COLIGNY. He fought in the WARS OF ITALY, but in 1551 was captured near Milan by imperial forces. He was imprisoned for five years, during which time he became a Protestant. He became a Huguenot leader, and in 1562, on the outbreak of the WARS OF RELIGION, assumed command of the foreign mercenaries financed by the German Protestant princes. He was a prominent commander in the Wars until he died of a fever in 1569.

DBF.

**ANDREA DEL CASTAGNO or Andrea di Bartolo di Bargilla or Andreino degli Impiccati** (*fl*. 1442, d. 1457), Italian painter and designer of stained glass. He was born in the Castagno (Tuscany) and spent most of his career in Florence. The origin of the nickname that associates him with hanged men (*impiccati*) is not known, unless the aetiological myth that he painted frescoes of condemned men in the Bargello in the aftermath of the battle of ANGHIARI contains a grain of historical truth. His short career ended when he died of plague.

In 1442 Andrea collaborated with an otherwise unknown painter called Francesco da Faenza on frescoes for the Cappella di San Tarasio in the Church of San Zaccaria in Venice; the decoration, which is the earliest example of Tuscan Renaissance painting in Venice, includes naturalistic representations of St John (who is sharpening his quill) and St Luke (who is scratching his ear). From 1444 until his early death in 1457 Andrea lived in Florence, where he designed a window for the cathedral and painted the series of frescoes (including the *Last Supper* or *Cenacolo*) in the Cenacolo di Sant'Apollonia, the refectory of the Monastery of Sant'Apollonia. His other works include an *Assumption* (1449, Gemäldegalerie, Berlin), an equestrian portrait (in fresco) of *Niccolò da Tolentino* (1455–6, Florence Cathedral), and a series of frescoes of *Famous Men and Women* (three soldiers, three women from antiquity, and DANTE, PETRARCH, and BOCCACCIO) for the Villa Carducci in Legnaia, near Florence (now in the Uffizi).

DBI s.v. Andrea di Bartolo; MDA s.v. Castagno.

**ANDREA DEL SARTO** (1486–1530), Italian painter, born in Florence. The son of a tailor (*sarto*), he trained in the studio of PIERO DI COSIMO. His most important paintings, all in Florence, are the GRISAILLE murals *The Life of John the Baptist* in Chiostro dello Scalzo (1511–26), the frescoes of *The Nativity of the Virgin* (1514) and *The Madonna del Sacco* (1524), both in the cloister of the Church of the SS Annunziata, and *The Last Supper* (1526–7) in the refectory of the Convent of San Salvi. He also painted gentle Madonnas, such as *The Madonna delle Arpie* (1517, Uffizi, Florence).

**Andrea del Castagno,** *The Last Supper* (or *Cenacolo*), a fresco on the refectory wall of the Monastery of Sant'Apollonia in Florence

VASARI, who trained in Andrea's studio, declared his paintings to be faultless but condemned him for allowing his life to be ruled by a domineering wife. Robert Browning's dramatic monologue 'Andrea del Sarto' derives from Vasari's account, as does Ernest Jones's influential essay (1913), which links the languor of Andrea's art with his timidity in the domestic arena; this psychoanalytical silliness still colours popular accounts of Andrea's art.

> *DBI* s.v. Andrea d'Agnolo; *MDA* s.v. Sarto, Andrea del; S. J. Freedberg, *Andrea del Sarto* (2 vols., 1963); John Shearman, *Andrea del Sarto* (2 vols., 1965); Antonio Natali, *Andrea del Sarto*, trans. Jeffrey Jennings (1999).

**ANDREA VANNI.** See VANNI, ANDREA.

**ANDREAE, JAKOB** (1528–90), German Lutheran theologian and church leader, raised from humble circumstances by the dukes of Württemberg, who financed his education and appointed him as superintendent (i.e. assistant to the principal Lutheran minister) of Göppingen in 1553 and professor of theology and chancellor of the University of Tübingen in 1561. He sought reconciliation with other churches, negotiating with Catholics in Germany, attending the Colloquy of POISSY in France, and meeting his Calvinist detractors at Montbéliard in 1586. Andreae also strove to unify Lutheranism: he was one of the architects of the Formula of CONCORD and travelled widely to encourage its acceptance. He published his autobiography (in Latin) in 1562.

> *NDB*; Robert Kolb, *Andreae and the Formula of Concord: Six Sermons on the Way to Lutheran Unity* (1977).

**ANDREAE, LAURENTIUS, or (Swedish) Lars Anderson** (1470–1552), Swedish reformer and chancellor of King GUSTAVUS VASA. He was instrumental in securing the appointment of the Lutheran Olaus PETRI as city clerk of Stockholm. After the Diet of Västerås (1527), at which much of the

**Andrea del Sarto,** *The Madonna of the Harpies* (1517), in the Uffizi, Florence

revenue of the cathedrals and monastic houses was vested in the king, Andreae became the king's principal adviser on religious matters, and, together with Petri and Petri's brother Laurentius, translated the New Testament into Swedish. In 1540 Andreae and the Petri brothers fell from royal favour and were condemned to death, but they were reprieved and returned to their posts.

> *SBL* s.v. Laurentius Andreae.

**ANDREOLI, GIORGIO or Maestro, or Giorgio da Gubbio** (*c.*1465/70–*c.*1553), Italian potter, born in Intra (on Lake Maggiore). In the early 1490s he settled in Gubbio (Umbria), where he established a pottery specializing in MAIOLICA, working alongside his brothers Salimbene (d. *c.*1522) and Giovanni (d. *c.*1535). In 1536 Andreoli handed over the workshop to his sons Vicenzo and Ubaldo.

Andreoli specialized in the iridescent metallic surfaces known as 'lustres', and his plates are characteristically finished in a golden or deep red lustre. Pottery bearing his mark is often decorated with GROTESQUES, but his Gubbio factory also produced ISTORIATO pottery.

*DBI; MDA.*

**ANDREWES, LANCELOT** (1555–1626), English bishop and biblical scholar. Educated at Cambridge, Andrewes was successively bishop of Chichester (1605), Ely (1609), and Winchester (1619). Following the HAMPTON COURT CONFERENCE in 1604, which he attended, he worked on the new translation of the Bible. He defended the Oath of Allegiance, repudiating papal authority, which was imposed by JAMES VI following the GUNPOWDER PLOT, and sought Scottish acceptance of episcopacy. He was a key influence on the formation of Anglican theology, and gained a great reputation as a preacher. He was hostile to Calvinism and Puritanism and opposed the LAMBETH ARTICLES. His *Preces privatae* is a collection of devotional texts for private use.

*DNB.*

**ANDRIES FAMILY**, sixteenth-century Antwerp potters. Guido Andries (*Pl.* 1512, d. 1541), a potter of Italian origin (probably from CASTEL DURANTE), began making TIN-GLAZED EARTHENWARE in Antwerp in or before 1512. His sons Lucas (b. before 1535, d. *c.*1573), Frans (b. before 1535, d. after 1565), and Joris (*c.*1535–*c.*1579) inherited the workshop. In 1567 Joris and his brother Jasper (1535/41–*c.*1580) moved from Antwerp to Norwich with a potter called Jacob Jansen (d. 1593), where they founded a pottery workshop specializing in tiles and pharmacy jars.

**ANERIO, FELICE** (*c.*1560–1614) and **GIOVANNI FRANCESCO** (*c.*1567–1630), Italian composers. Felice's musical career started at the age of 8 as a choirboy at Santa Maria Maggiore. In 1594 he followed in PALESTRINA's footsteps and was appointed composer to the papal choir in Rome. He also became musical director at the chapel of Duke Giovanni Angelo Altemps. Most of his compositions are sacred works in the tradition of Palestrina, although he was a keen admirer of Filippo NERI, directing three- and four-choir works in his honour on his feast day. Felice's younger brother Giovanni Francesco was a more forward-looking composer who wrote in the *stile concertato* in his second book of motets (1611) and subsequently published intensely expressive compositions in the *Teatro armonico spirituale* (1619).

**ANET, CHÂTEAU D'**, a Renaissance chateau some 80 kilometres (50 miles) west of Paris. It was built between 1546 and 1552 by HENRI II for his mistress DIANE DE POITIERS. The house

and gardens were designed by Philibert DELORME. The house was built around a large courtyard which was entered through the Portail d'Entrée, which is surmounted with a tympanum by CELLINI depicting Diane as the huntress of classical mythology, a motif repeated in the fountain (now in the Louvre) which stood in the courtyard. On either side of the gateway there was a small garden (one part of which survives) leading through a grove to a terrace that ended in a building designed to resemble a sarcophagus, a gesture towards Diane's widowhood.

The main garden, behind the house, was designed to be viewed from a terrace; the garden was divided into compartments with heraldic designs associated with Diane's family. In the 1570s these compartments were swept away in favour of a *PARTERRE de broderie*, which was surrounded by galleries with pavilions at the corners furthest from the house. Between the pavilions (and beyond the rear gallery) there was a room for bathing which was surrounded on three sides by a moat. These galleries, pavilions, and parterres, which can all be seen in a drawing by Jacques DUCERCEAU, were replaced in the 1680s by a vast parterre, and a canal and lawns were added. In the nineteenth century the grounds were transformed into a park in the English style and the canal was naturalized.

The buildings that survive include the Portail d'Entrée, the left wing of the house, Delorme's domed chapel with its two pyramid-topped towers, and the funerary chapel built in 1566 to accommodate the remains of Diane de Poitiers (which were discarded during the Revolution, when her tomb was used as a horse trough); the statue of Diane kneeling, which is still in the chapel, is attributed to BONTEMPS.

A. Roux, *Le Château d'Anet* (1911); M. Mayer, *Le Château d'Anet* (1952); Kenneth Woodbridge, *Princely Gardens: The Origins and Development of the French Formal Style* (1986).

**ANGELA MERICI** (1474–1540), founder of the URSULINES, was born at Desenzano del Garda (Lombardy). She became a Franciscan tertiary in Brescia and devoted her early life to the education of young girls and the care of sick women. She travelled to Palestine in 1524–5 and there temporarily lost her sight. She returned to Brescia, where in 1535 her visions inspired her to found a religious community for women, which she named after her patron St Ursula (a British princess thought to have been martyred in Cologne together with 11,000 virgins); she was elected superior in 1537. Members of the Order were not enclosed, took no vows, and did not wear a habit, and these characteristics delayed formation into an approved congregation until 1565. Angela was canonized in 1807.

*DBI;* Sister Mary Monica, *Angela Merici and her Teaching Idea, 1474–1540* (1927); Philip Caraman, *St Angela* (1963).

**ANGELICO, FRA GIOVANNI DA FIESOLE, or Guido di Pietro** (1395/1400–1455), Italian painter who entered the Dominican ORDER in Fiesole in 1418, renouncing his secular name, Guido di Pietro, and assuming the name Fra Giovanni da Fiesole; the name Fra Angelico originated in the fifteenth century (when he was called Fra Giovanni Angelico) and is a reflection of the religious quality of his art rather than a formal name.

Fra Angelico's earliest datable work is the *Madonna dei Linaiuoli* (1433, Uffizi), a triptych with a marble frame made by Lorenzo GHIBERTI. The buildings of the Convent of San Marco were restored to the Order in 1436 at the initiative of Cosimo de' MEDICI, and from 1441 Fra Angelico and his assistants painted more than 45 frescoes in the convent, notably the two *Annunciations* (one at the head of the stairs and the other in one of the cells).

In 1447 Fra Angelico executed two frescoes in Orvieto Cathedral (assisted by Benozzo GOZZOLI), part of an *Apocalypse* cycle that was later to be finished by Luca SIGNORELLI. He then moved to Rome at the invitation of Pope EUGENIUS IV, and there decorated the private chapel of Pope NICHOLAS V (the successor of Eugenius) with frescoed *Scenes from the Lives of SS Stephen and Lawrence* (1447–9), again assisted by Gozzoli. He returned to Fiesole to serve as prior of his convent (1449–52) and then went once more to Rome to paint frescoes in the Chapel of the Sacrament (later demolished) in the Vatican.

In the nineteenth century Fra Angelico was championed by the Pre-Raphaelites, and Ruskin declared that he was 'not an artist properly so-called but an inspired saint'. The attitudes that informed this hagiographical proclamation led to his beatification (1984) and still linger on, so obscuring the extent to which Fra Angelico was a professional artist who drew on the work of his predecessors and contemporaries.

DBI s.v. Guido de Pietro; *MDA*; W. Hood, *Fra Angelico at San Marco* (1993); Paolo Morachiello, *Fra Angelico: The San Marco Frescoes* (1996); John Pope-Hennessy, *Fra Angelico* (1989).

**ANGHIARI, BATTLE OF**. On 29 June 1440 a Milanese army (which included many Florentine exiles) commanded by Niccolò PICCININO was overwhelmed by a Florentine army under Francesco SFORZA and Micheletto ATTENDOLO at Anghiari (near Arezzo). Some 300 men were killed, but MACHIAVELLI, advancing the thesis that mercenaries are reluctant to risk their lives in battle, disingenuously claimed in his *Istorie fiorentine* that the only fatality was caused when a soldier was thrown by his horse and trampled.

The battle of Anghiari was the subject of a FRESCO painted in 1504–5 by LEONARDO DA VINCI in the Sala del Maggior Consiglio in the Palazzo Vecchio in Florence. The fresco was described by contemporaries as miraculous, but it deteriorated quickly and disappeared altogether in VASARI's

Peter Paul Rubens, *The Fight for the Standard* (Louvre), a drawing in chalk and ink of the central portion of LEONARDO DA VINCI's lost fresco, *The Battle of Anghiari*

redecoration of the room in 1557; it is now known from preparatory drawings that survive in the Royal Library at Windsor and the Accademia in Venice and from various painted and engraved copies, notably the copies by Rubens (based on a published engraving by Lorenzo Zacchia and lost copies in oils) of *The Fight for the Standard*, the central group which he painted in oil (now in the Vienna Akademie) and drew in chalk and ink on at least two occasions, famously the drawing in the Louvre and, recently discovered, the drawing in the Dutch royal collection at Het Hoo.

**ANGUISSOLA, SOFONISBA** (1531–1626), Italian painter, born in Cremona, the daughter of a Piedmontese nobleman. She trained in the studio of Bernardino CAMPI and thereafter specialized in portrait paintings. She moved to Madrid in 1559 and subsequently worked in Sicily before returning to Cremona at the end of her life. Her surviving paintings include several self-portraits (e.g. Uffizi, Florence, and Althorp House, Northants) and a group portrait of her sisters playing chess (National Museum, Poznań).

DBI; MDA; Ilya Perlingieri, *Sofonisba Anguissola: The First Great Woman Artist of the Renaissance* (1992)

**ANIMUCCIA, GIOVANNI** (*c.*1500–1571), Italian composer. A Florentine by birth, he moved to Rome where, in 1555, he succeeded PALESTRINA as *magister cantorum* at the Cappella Giulia. He sustained links with Florence through his association with the Altoviti family exiled in Rome, and through them came into contact with Orlande de LASSUS and Filippo NERI. In 1565 he published a book of *Madrigali a tre voce . . . con alcuni motetti, et madrigali spirituali* and three years later *Il secondo libro delle laudi, dove si contengono motteti, salmi et altre diverse cose spirituali vulgari et latine*. This use of the vernacular combined with his handling of varied textures and vocal colours were all part of his desire to entice congregations into churches with music. Although overshadowed by his contemporary Palestrina, Animuccia's music helped to establish one prominent trend in Italian sacred music for the next hundred years.

**ANJOU, FRANÇOIS, DUC D', or duc d'Alençon or (English) Francis, duke of Anjou, or duke of Alençon** (1554–84), the fourth son of King HENRI II of France and CATHERINE DE MÉDICIS. He was known as the duke of Alençon until 6 May 1576, when his brother King HENRI III created him duke of Anjou; he was popularly known as 'Monsieur'.

François fought in the WARS OF RELIGION as one of the leaders of the POLITIQUES, and supported the HUGUENOTS against the CATHOLIC LEAGUE. In 1578 he was invited to the Netherlands by one of the Protestant groups in the REVOLT OF THE NETHERLANDS and was created duke of Brabant. In 1579 and 1581 he travelled to London, where he was the last suitor of Queen ELIZABETH. A plan supported by Queen Elizabeth and WILLIAM OF ORANGE to install François as king of the Netherlands in succession to PHILIP II proceeded as far as his arrival at the gates of Antwerp in February 1582, but in January 1583 his French army failed to take the city by force and François withdrew from the Netherlands to France, where he died on

10 June 1584. When he died François was heir to the throne, and thereafter the heir presumptive was the Protestant Henry of Navarre (later King HENRI IV).

DBF s.v. Anjou, Hercule plus tard François; Frédéric Duquenne, *L'Entreprise du duc d'Anjou aux Pays-Bas de 1580 à 1584: Les Responsabilités d'un échec à partager* (1998); Mack Holt, *The Duke of Anjou and the Politique Struggle during the Wars of Religion* (1986).

**ANJOU, HOUSE OF.** The counts and dukes of Anjou, who are known as the Angevins (from Angers, the capital of the duchy), became rulers in southern Italy from 1266, when Charles I, count of Anjou and son of King Louis VIII of France, became king of Sicily and Naples. He lost Sicily in 1282, and on his death in 1285, his son Charles II became king of Naples; thereafter his descendants ruled Naples until 1435 and also reigned as kings of Hungary from 1308 to 1382 (see Appendix 1). Throughout the centuries when Sicily was ruled by the Aragonese, the Angevin kings of Naples continued to style themselves 'kings of Sicily'. Even within the kingdom of Naples there was a protracted succession dispute. GIOVANNA I OF ANJOU had no sons, and her daughters both predeceased her, so she designated as her heir Louis, duc d'Anjou, brother of Charles V of France. In 1382 Giovanna was murdered and was succeeded by the Angevin Charles III of Durazzo (great-grandson of King Charles II of Naples), who later became King Charles II of Hungary.

Charles III's son, LADISLAS OF DURAZZO, acceded to the throne of Naples in 1386, at the age of 6, and was crowned by Pope BONIFACE IX in 1390; his claim was contested by King LOUIS II of Anjou (son of Louis, duc d'Anjou), who had been crowned king of Naples by the antipope Clement VII. On Ladislas's death in 1414 he was succeeded by his sister GIOVANNA II. Giovanna designated her adopted son RENÉ D'ANJOU (Louis's brother) as her successor; he was to be the last Angevin king of Naples. The last male descendant of Louis II (Charles II de Maine) died in 1481, and on the extinction of the male line the rights claimed by the Angevins passed to the French crown and provided the motive for CHARLES VIII's invasion of Naples in 1494, the action that inaugurated the WARS OF ITALY.

E. G. Léonard, *Les Angevins de Naples* (1954).

**ANNE BOLEYN** (1507–36), second wife of Henry VIII, and queen of England. Following several years at the court of France, Anne returned to England in 1522, where she gained a place in the household of CATHERINE OF ARAGON. Anne's sister Mary was already the king's mistress, and by 1527 Henry was seeking an annulment of his marriage. Anne probably became Henry's mistress in 1532; following her pregnancy, she and Henry were married privately in early 1533, and she gave birth to Princess Elizabeth (later Queen ELIZABETH) in September that year. Anne's position appeared strong, but despite two miscarriages she could not produce the looked-for male heir. Henry's interest subsequently transferred to JANE SEYMOUR. In May 1536, Anne was taken to the Tower on charges of adultery and incest, and executed a fortnight later. Although the degree of Anne's commitment to radical religion is hotly debated, ambition, intelligence, and some reformist sympathies were certainly hers.

*DNB.*

**ANNE OF BRITTANY or (French) Anne de Bretagne** (1477–1514), duchess of Brittany and queen of France, was the daughter of Duke François II of Brittany and Marguerite de Foix. She succeeded her father on 9 September 1488, aged 12, and so became prey to European rulers with territorial designs on Brittany. In 1489 the army of CHARLES VIII of France invaded Brittany, and Anne agreed to protect the duchy by marrying Maximilian of Austria (later the Emperor MAXIMILIAN I) by proxy, but under French pressure the marriage was annulled and Anne was instead married to King Charles (December 1491). The marriage contract ensured the independence of Brittany from France.

King Charles died in 1498, and Queen Anne married his successor, King LOUIS XII, who had been granted a divorce from Jeanne de France by Pope ALEXANDER VI. Claude de France, the daughter of Louis XII and Queen Anne, was pledged by the Treaty of BLOIS (1504) to marry the future Emperor CHARLES V, but the treaty was broken, and Queen Anne agreed that Claude could marry François d'Angoulême, who in 1515 became King FRANCIS I of France. The consequence of this marriage was the incorporation of Brittany into France in 1532, though Brittany retained its own ESTATES until the French Revolution.

*DBF s.v. Anne de Bretagne; H. A. Butler, Twice Queen of France: Anne of Brittany (1967); George Minois, Anne de Bretagne (1999).*

**ANNE OF CLEVES** (1515–57), fourth wife of Henry VIII and queen of England. Henry's fourth marriage was an attempt to cement a diplomatic allegiance with Anne's brother the duke of Cleves. A portrait of Anne by Holbein charmed Henry, but the marriage, which took place in January 1540, was not a success. An annulment was declared in July of the same year, and Henry swiftly remarried, making CATHERINE HOWARD his fifth wife. Anne was accorded the status of royal sister and a generous settlement, and until her final years lived comfortably in Chelsea. On her death she was buried with ceremony in Westminster Abbey.

*DNB.*

**ANNE OF FRANCE or Anne of Beaujeu or La Dame de Beaujeu** (1460–1522), regent of France, was the eldest daughter of King LOUIS XI and Charlotte of Savoy. After a long series of betrothals she married Pierre de Beaujeu, a younger brother of the duke of Bourbon. On the death of her father in 1483, Anne became regent of France on behalf of her 13-year-old brother CHARLES VIII. During her regency (1483–91) Anne and her husband successfully asserted royal authority in the face of opposition from the Estates-General (1484) and the conflicts of the 'Mad War' (1485) and the war with Brittany (1488).

Pierre de Beaujeu succeeded his brother as duke of Bourbon in 1488 and died in 1503. For the last twenty years of her life Anne lived in Moulins, the capital of the duchy, and defended the Bourbon interest against her brother and his successor FRANCIS I. In 1505 her daughter Suzanne married her cousin Charles, the future duke of BOURBON and constable of France.

*DBF s.v. Anne de Beaujeu; Paul Pélicier, Essai sur le gouvernement de la dame de Beaujeu 1483–1491 (1882).*

**ANTHONISZOON, CORNELIS** (*c.*1505–*c.*1553), Dutch painter and cartographer who worked as a cartographer in the service of CHARLES V and in that capacity painted a map of Amsterdam (now in the Weigh House, Amsterdam). He also painted several group portraits (Rijksmuseum).

*MDA; NNBW i.*

**ANTICHRIST.** The term 'Antichrist' ($\dot{\alpha}\nu\tau\acute{\iota}\chi\rho\iota\sigma\tau\sigma$) first appears in the Epistles of John (1 John 2: 18, 22; 4: 3; 2 John 7), and is used to describe the prince of Christ's enemies. Early exegetes identified the Antichrist with the Beast of the Book of Revelation. The number of the beast, according to Revelation 13: 18, was 666 or, in some manuscripts, 616. In both Greek and Hebrew each character in the alphabet represented a number as well as a letter, and so every name could be represented by the arithmetical sum of its letters. This calculation led to an identification of the Antichrist with the Emperor Nero, because in Hebrew letters 'Nero Caesar' adds up to 616 and 'Neron Caesar' (which includes 50 in the extra letter *nûn*) to 666. Both AUGUSTINE and JEROME believed that John of the Apocalypse had not died, but was rather sleeping until he was wakened to testify against the reborn Nero (*Nero redivivus*) when he returned as Antichrist.

Throughout late antiquity and the early Middle Ages the Antichrist was variously identified with heresies (e.g. the Arian heresy) and enemies of Christianity (e.g. Caligula, who erected his statue in the temple in Jerusalem). In the twelfth century, the revival of interest in eschatology heralded by Joachim of Fiore led in the Western Church to the habit of identifying enemies with the Antichrist: popes and emperors, GUELFS AND GHIBELLINES, hurled the term at each other. In Germany, the twelfth-century Bavarian play *Ludus de Antichristo* portrays an allegorical Antichrist (supported by Hypocrisy and Heresy) being defeated by the Church with the aid of a divine bolt of lightning, and the fifteenth-century FASTNACHTSPIEL *Des Entchrist Vasnacht* dramatizes Antichrist offering new territories to the emperor in return for his soul.

The identification of the pope with the Antichrist originated with the Franciscans, from whom the idea passed to the pre-Hussite Moravian reformer Jan Milič (*c.*1325–74), the author of a *Libellus de Antichristo*, and thence to Matthias of Janov and Tomáš Štítný, whose eschatology was inherited by the Hussites. In England, the identification of the Antichrist with the pope in the Wycliffite *Commentarius in Apocalypsin ante centus annos editus* (which may be the work of John WYCLIFFE or his disciple John Purvey) was disseminated on the Continent by Martin LUTHER, who edited the text in 1528. Luther's most explicit statement of this identification is contained in the SCHMALKALDIC ARTICLES.

The identification of the pope with Antichrist became a Protestant commonplace, and still has exponents in America and Northern Ireland. The triple-crowned papal tiara (the *triregnum* first recorded in the inventory of the papal treasury in 1316) was popularly thought to confirm the identification, which was mocked by Ben Jonson when he had his Puritan Ananias observe to another character that 'Thou look'st like Antichrist in that lewd hat' (*Alchemist*, IV. vii. 55).

Hans Preuss, *Die Vorstellungen vom Antichrist im späten Mittelalter, bei Luther und in der konfessionellen Polemik* (1906); R. K. Emmerson, *Antichrist in the Middle Ages* (1981); Christopher Hill, *Antichrist in Seventeenth-Century England* (rev. edn., 1990).

**ANTICO or Pier Jacopo di Antonio Alari Bonacolsi** (*c*.1460–1528), Italian sculptor and bronze-founder, born in Mantua, where he trained as a goldsmith. His nickname derives from his practice of making bronze statuettes of ANTIQUE SCULPTURE such as the *Apollo Belvedere* (versions in Vatican Museum and Liebieghaus, Frankfurt) and *Hercules and Antaeus* (versions in the Kunsthistorisches Museum in Vienna and the Victoria and Albert Museum). His principal patron was the GONZAGA FAMILY, especially Isabella d'ESTE.

*DBI* s.v. Alari Bonacolsi; *MDA* s.v. Antico Calari-Bonacolsi.

**ANTINOMIANISM**, a medieval Latin coinage from the Greek (literally 'against law') used to denote the doctrine that Christians are exempted from the moral law, and are instead subject only to the law of grace. At the Reformation, antinomian teaching emerged as a corollary of LUTHER's doctrine of JUSTIFICATION by faith alone. The German reformer Johann AGRICOLA advocated antinomianism, which caused him to become involved in heated controversy with Luther. There was also an antinomian strain in Thomas MÜNTZER's doctrine of inner revelation, which derived from the mystical theology of the fourteenth-century Dominican Johann Tauler; the idea of inner revelation later emerged in England as the Quaker doctrine of 'inner light'. The term 'antinomianism' was introduced into English in 1643 by John Milton in order to describe the sects which were emerging in the 1640s.

**ANTIQUE SCULPTURE IN THE RENAISSANCE.** The rediscovery of classical sculpture and architectural remains exercised a profound influence on Renaissance artists. Artists such as GENTILE DA FABRIANO, PISANELLO, and Giuliano da SANGALLO drew ancient sculpture and buildings, and there were important collections of antique sculpture in the Vatican and Florence, where Lorenzo de' MEDICI placed some of his collection in the Giardino di San Marco. Statues such as the *Apollo Belvedere*, *Laocoön* (rediscovered in 1506), and the *Sleeping Ariadne*, all of which were placed in the Vatican's BELVEDERE COURT (and are now in the Vatican Museum), had a profound effect on artists such as MICHELANGELO. These three statues were copied in bronze by Giacomo da VIGNOLA and placed in the garden of FONTAINEBLEAU; they are now in the Louvre.

Phyllis Bober and Ruth Rubinstein, *Renaissance Sculptors and Antique Sculpture* (1985).

**ANTOINE DE BOURBON or (Spanish) Antonio de Borbón** (1518–62), king of Navarre, was a scion of a cadet branch of the French BOURBON FAMILY. In 1548, when he was duke of Vendôme, Antoine married JEANNE D'ALBRET, the heiress of Navarre, and in 1555 he became king of Navarre.

He converted to the Protestantism of his wife, but was capable of professing Catholicism when it was to his political advantage to do so. When FRANCIS II of France died in 1561 and was succeeded by his 10-year-old brother CHARLES IX, Antonio attempted to secure the regency, but lost to CATHERINE DE MÉDICIS; by way of consolation and appeasement he was given the title lieutenant-general of France. He died of wounds sustained in battle at the outset of the French WARS OF RELIGION and was succeeded by his young son Henri III (later HENRI IV of France).

*DBF*; *DHE* s.v. Borbón, Antonio de.

**ANTONELLO DA MESSINA** (*c*.1430–1479), Sicilian painter, born in Messina. The Flemish qualities in his paintings and his innovative use of oils led VASARI to assume that Antonello had trained in the studio of Jan van EYCK, but Antonello is unlikely ever to have visited the Netherlands; it is more likely that he encountered Flemish painters and paintings in Naples and that he was influenced by the Flemish style of COLANTONIO, in whose studio he may have trained. His early paintings, executed in Messina, include a *Crucifixion* (Brukenthal Museum, Sibiu, Romania) and a *St Jerome in his Study* (National Gallery, London). In the early 1470s his figures became more sculptural but his backgrounds remained Flemish, as is apparent in paintings such as a second *Crucifixion* (National Gallery, London).

In about 1475 Antonello visited Venice, where he painted his San Cassiano altarpiece, of which three fragments survive (Kunsthistorisches Museum, Vienna); this altarpiece was admired by Giovanni BELLINI, who exercised considerable influence on Antonello's style, as is apparent in his *St Sebastian* (Gemäldegalerie, Dresden).

*DBI* s.v. De Antonio, Antonello (Antonello da Messina); *MDA*; Chiara Savettieri, *Antonello da Messina* (Palermo, 1998).

**ANTONINO, FRA, or Antonio Pierozzi or Antonio de Forciglioni** (1389–1459), Dominican archbishop of Florence. Born in Florence on 1 March 1389, he entered the Dominican Order at the age of 15; his allegiance was to the Strict Observants within the Order. After his novitiate in Cortona, Fra Antonino successively served as superior of the Dominican houses in Rome, Naples, Gaetà, Cortona, Siena, and Fiesole. In 1436, assisted by the patronage of Cosimo de' MEDICI the Elder, he restored and enlarged the former Sylvestrine Convent of San Marco in Florence, and in 1439 became its Dominican prior. He served as a papal theologian at the COUNCIL OF FLORENCE from 1439 to 1445. In 1446 Fra Antonino was consecrated archbishop of Florence by Pope EUGENIUS IV, but he continued to live the simple life of a friar, spending the revenues of his see on the relief of the poor. Unlike many of his ecclesiastical contemporaries, he took no interest in art or culture and regarded secular learning as idle curiosity; he was also unusual in taking his pastoral duties seriously, and his work among the victims of plague, earthquake, and war gave rise to a reputation as a worker of miracles. He died on 2 May 1459 and was canonized by Pope ADRIAN VI in 1523. In 1960 Pope John XXIII acceded to a request first made in 1838 that Fra Antonino be made a doctor of the Church.

Antonino's writings include a chronicle of world history, a *Summa theologica* (Venice, 1477), and a textbook for confessors (*Summa confessionalis*, Mondavi, 1472). In his moral and theological works he dissented from the received view that the charging of interest was sinful, arguing that it was legitimate if the money was invested in business, because commerce was essential if the wealth of the Church was to be maintained.

There is a posthumous portrait drawing of Fra Antonino by Fra BARTOLOMMEO in the Museo San Marco in Florence.

*DBI* s.v. Antonino Pierozzi; G. Calzolai, *Fra Antonio, Arcivescovo di Firenze* (1961).

**ANTONIO DE BORBÓN**. See ANTOINE DE BOURBON.

**ANTÓNIO DO CRATO** (1531–95), pretender to the Portuguese throne, the illegitimate son of Luís, duke of Beja (a younger son of King MANUEL I of Portugal), and a Jewish woman called Violante Gomes who may later have become a nun; he was a nephew of King JOHN III of Portugal. António was educated at Coimbra and joined the Order of St John of God (founded by the followers of JUAN DE DIOS); he was endowed with the wealthy priory of the Order's house at Crato (and so is sometimes known as the 'prior of Crato').

When King Manuel died in 1557, António abandoned the Church for the court. He fought with Portuguese troops in North AFRICA, and was with King SEBASTIAN I when he was killed at the battle of KSAR-EL-KEBIR in 1558; António was captured but managed to conceal his identity, and so was released on payment of a small ransom. The next king of Portugal was the elderly and unstable Cardinal HENRIQUE, who was a legitimate son of Manuel I; Henrique refused to name António as his successor because he had forsaken the Church, but when Henrique died in 1580, António was proclaimed king by loyal courtiers. The succession was contested by PHILIP II of Spain, who sent the duke of ALBA to occupy Portugal. António fled to France, from which he mounted an attempt to occupy the AZORES which ended with his defeat in a naval battle of 27 July 1582. In 1585 António moved to England and in 1589 he accompanied Sir Francis DRAKE on his abortive expedition to Portugal in the forlorn hope of stimulating a popular revolt against Spanish rule. António returned to England and in 1592 moved to France, where he spent the final years of his life at the court of HENRI IV; he died in Paris on 26 August 1595.

*DHP*; J. Veríssimo Serrão, *O reinado de D. António, prior do Crato* (1956).

**ANTWERP or (French) Anvers**, a Netherlandish (now Belgian) city and port on the river Scheldt, 80 kilometres (50 miles) from the North Sea. Its greatest period of prosperity and importance was between the late fifteenth century, when the silting of the Zwyn (complete by 1490) closed the port of BRUGES, and the late sixteenth century, when Antwerp was recaptured by Spain (1585).

The advent of HABSBURG rule in 1477 brought prosperity to Antwerp, which soon became an important financial centre; the stock exchange was established in 1531. In the first half of the century Antwerp became the principal Netherlandish centre for TIN-GLAZED EARTHENWARE and for pavement tiles. The first important potters were Guido ANDRIES, who had established his pottery by 1512, and Jan FLORIS DE VRIENDT, who was active in Antwerp from 1533. The city was an important centre for the manufacture of TAPESTRIES, and also produced floral borders for tapestries made in Brussels and Oudenarde. The arrival of PLANTIN in 1548 inaugurated a period in which Antwerp was an important printing centre. The zenith of the city's fortunes was *c*.1560, when more than 1,000 foreign merchants were resident in Antwerp; in that year GUICCIARDINI, the Venetian ambassador, described the arrival of up to 500 ships a day and some 2,000 carts a week, and reported (with some exaggeration) that as much business was transacted in Antwerp in a fortnight as in Venice in a year. Cornelius FLORIS DE VRIENDT's Antwerp Town Hall (1561–6) was the grandest and most influential of Flemish Renaissance buildings.

In 1576 Antwerp was plundered in the 'Spanish fury', in which thousands of citizens were massacred and hundreds of buildings were burnt; in 1583, the 'French fury' unleashed by the troops of François, duke of ANJOU, caused more death and destruction. In 1585, Alessandro FARNESE captured the city after a long siege and sent its Protestant citizens into exile. The death-blow to Antwerp's trade came when the Scheldt was closed by the twelve-year truce of 1609 and the Treaty of Münster of 1648.

**ANTWERP-LOUVRE SCHOOL**, the modern name for a group of unidentified workshops that produced embossed parade armours (see ARMS AND ARMOUR) and shields for the court of HENRI II in the third quarter of the sixteenth century. Some of these armours were produced by Étienne Delaune (1518/19–1583) in a hypothetical French royal workshop assumed to be in Paris and long known as the Louvre School of Armourers. It was subsequently discovered that some of these armours had been decorated in the early 1560s in Antwerp by a goldsmith called Eliseus Libaerts, whose armours were made for the court of ERIC XIV of Sweden. It is possible that Eliseus Libaerts worked for a time in Paris and that some of his armours were designed for the French court. The uncertainties about provenance have led to the designation 'Antwerp-Louvre School'.

**APIANUS, PETRUS**, or (German) Peter Bienewitz (1495–1552), German geographer, mathematician, and astronomer, a native of Leisnig who studied in Leipzig and Vienna and in 1527 was appointed professor of mathematics at Ingolstadt. His best-known publications were a map of the world (1520) and *Cosmographia* (1520 and many later editions), which both used the knowledge gained by recent EXPLORATION to supplement PTOLEMY's *Geographia*. He subsequently published a manual of arithmetic (*Rechnung*, 1527). Apianus' principal astronomical work was *Astronomicum caesareum* (1540), a sumptuous volume which included descriptions of five comets (among them the appearance of Halley's Comet in 1531) and noted that the tails of comets always point away from the sun.

*DSB*; *NDB*.

**APOSTLE SPOONS**, small silver spoons manufactured in England and Germany from the late fifteenth to the late seventeenth centuries. The tops of the handles were each shaped into the figure of an apostle. When manufactured in sets of thirteen, the handle of the 'master spoon' was a figure of Jesus.

C. G. Rupert, *Apostle Spoons* (1929).

**APOSTOLIS, ARSENIOS** (1468/9–1535), Cretan philologist in Italy. Arsenios Apostolis was born in Candia (CRETE), where his father Michael APOSTOLIS had found a safe haven after being imprisoned in Constantinople by the Ottomans. Like his father, he worked as a copyist of Greek manuscripts, and he also taught Greek. In 1492 he visited Venice, and by the end of the year he was working in Florence, transcribing Greek manuscripts which had been collected for Lorenzo de' MEDICI by Janos LASCARIS; by the time he arrived in Florence, Lorenzo had died, but his offer of employment was honoured by Piero de' MEDICI.

In 1494 Apostolis moved to Venice, where he worked as an editor with ALDUS MANUTIUS. A dispute over money led to a rift with Aldus, and in 1497 Apostolis returned to Crete, where he remained until 1504, again working as a copyist and tutor. He then sought ecclesiastical preferment, developing an elaborate plan to become the archbishop of Monemvasia (a Venetian enclave in the south-western Peloponnese); he was rebuffed in his attempt to become the Orthodox archbishop, and so decided to become the Latin archbishop instead. This attempt also failed, and Marcus MUSURUS was appointed in his stead; Apostolis never forgave him. In 1518 or 1519 Apostolis was appointed as the founding director of the Greek Institute in Florence, but the Institute closed shortly after the death of its patron, Leo X, in December 1521, whereupon Apostolis again returned to Crete. In 1523 the see of Monemvasia again fell vacant; Janos LASCARIS wrote to Apostolis in Crete urging him to lobby for the post, which was now a united Latin and Orthodox archbishopric; this time he was successful, and Apostolis held the post until his death, though in his last years he lived in Venice.

Apostolis published extensively with the Monte Cavallo press (the publication arm of the Greek College in Rome) and the Venetian presses of Aldus and Stefano da Sabbio; his publications include the *scholia* on Euripides and various Byzantine works, including Michael Psellus' eleventh-century treatise on MATHEMATICS, which was deemed to consist of arithmetic, MUSIC, geometry, and ASTRONOMY.

*DBI* s.v. Apostolio, Arsenio; D. Geanakoplos, *Greek Scholars in Venice* (1962), 167–200.

**APOSTOLIS, MICHAEL** (*c.*1420–*c.*1486), Byzantine copyist and manuscript collector in Crete. Apostolis was probably a native of Constantinople, where he studied with John ARGYROPOULOS at the Katholikon Mouseion, a school attached to the hospital of the Xenon of the Kral; he remained as a teacher at the Mouseion, and was imprisoned when Constantinople fell to the Turks in 1453.

On his release from prison Apostolis emigrated to Crete; for the rest of his life he divided his time between his home in Crete and the humanist centres of Italy. He was employed by BESSARION to find and secure Greek manuscripts for his library. In cases in which a recovered manuscript could not be purchased, Apostolis would copy it; some 115 manuscripts survive in his hand, mostly in Bessarion's collection, which is now in the Marciana in Venice.

The writings of Apostolis include a collection of proverbs, a large number of literary letters, a polemical defence of the Platonist George Gemistos PLETHO in the Plato–Aristotle controversy, and an essay setting out how Greek should be taught to Italians. Sometime after 1453 he wrote an oration *On Greece and Europe*, in which he acknowledged the demise of Byzantium and the start of a new era in Italy, but nonetheless insisted that the Greek civilization of Byzantium was superior to that of Europe.

*PLP* i. 112; Henri Noiret, *Lettres inédites de Michel Apostolis* (1889); D. Geanakoplos, *Greek Scholars in Venice* (1962), 73–110.

**APPENZELLER, BENEDICTUS** (*c.*1480–after 1558), Flemish composer and singer. In 1536 he became a singer in MARY OF HUNGARY's chapel choir in Brussels, and the following year became master of the choirboys, a post equivalent to *maître de la chapelle*. His works include masses, motets, Magnificats, and secular pieces published in *Des chansons à quatre parties* (1542). His works, bearing only the name 'Benedictus', are often confused with those by two of his contemporaries, the German composer Benedictus Ducis and the Netherlandish organist Benedictus de Opitiis.

**APPIANO** or **Appiani FAMILY**. The Pisan family of the Appiani was prominent in Pisan commerce and public affairs in the thirteenth century, and in 1392 Jacopo d'Appiano (1322–98) assassinated the ruler Piero Gambacorti and succeeded him as tyrant of Pisa. Jacopo bequeathed the state to his son Gherardo Leonardo (d. 1405), who in 1399 sold the city to Gian Galeazzo VISCONTI for 200,000 florins and possession of Piombino (which was a strategic port) and the Tuscan archipelago (including Elba, Pianosa, and Monte Cristo). The family continued to rule this micro-empire until the end of the fifteenth century, and again from the mid-sixteenth century until 1634.

*DBI* s.v. Appiani, Jacopo and Appiani, Gherardo Leonardo.

**AQUAVIVA** or **Acquaviva, CLAUDIO** (1543–1615), fifth general of the JESUITS, born in Naples; he was the youngest son of the duke of Atri, in the Abruzzi. He studied CIVIL LAW and CANON LAW at Perugia, and entered the Jesuit novitiate in Rome in 1567. He became provincial of Naples and then of Rome, and in 1581, at the age of 37, was elected superior general of the Order, a post that he was to hold for 34 years until his death on 31 December 1615. Under his administration the activities of the Order were greatly expanded in Europe, Asia, and the Americas and the number of members rose from a base of 5,000 to 13,000 members in 550 houses and 15 provinces.

Aquaviva's statesmanship and formidable administrative skills enabled him to deal with the considerable problems that arose while he was in office, including the persecutions of English recusants and Jesuits (notably Robert PARSONS and Edmund CAMPION), the HUGUENOT rebellions in France, the expulsion of the Jesuits from Venice, the threat of the INQUISITION to review the constitution of the Order, and, most seriously of all, the Spanish schism of the Order, which was organized by Gabriel VÁZQUEZ and supported by King PHILIP II and Pope SIXTUS V. Aquaviva managed to set the king and the pope against each other, and overcame the obloquy of the pope (who had denounced him), convincing him that the Spanish revolt threatened to damage papal interests.

Aquaviva's statement of the principles of Jesuit education in *Ratio atque institutio studiorum* (Rome, 1586) was denounced by the Dominicans to the Spanish and Roman Inquisitions, both of which condemned it; the offending chapters, which were deemed to contain an incorrect account of the teaching of THOMAS AQUINAS on predestination and on God's foreknowledge of secondary causes, were withdrawn in the edition of 1591. Aquaviva was also active in saving his Order from papal condemnation arising out of the rancorous dispute between Dominican and Jesuit theologians on the subject of divine GRACE. He is commonly adjudged to have been the most able general in the history of the Jesuit Order.

*DBI* s.v. Acquaviva.

**ARABESQUES** (early modern English 'moresques', Italian *rabeschi*), the French and English term for the scrolling plant motifs used in medieval Islamic ornament. The term is used more loosely to denote Renaissance decorative motifs in which geometrical and botanical lines are used to create elaborate patterns. The Italian term *rabeschi* was also used to denote ACANTHUS foliage. In LACE and EMBROIDERY such patterns are usually known as 'moresque' or 'mauresque'. An anonymous *Passements de moresques* published in 1563 was the first pattern book to offer such designs. After *c.*1530 arabesques were often used in GROTESQUE decorative schemes.

**ARAGON or (Spanish) Aragón**, a kingdom in north-eastern Spain which at its greatest extent, in the thirteenth century, included Catalonia, Montpellier, VALENCIA, the Balearics, and SICILY amongst its possessions; in the fourteenth century SARDINIA and the duchy of Athens were acquired, and in the fifteenth NAPLES was conquered (1442).

The empire of Aragon was divided after the death of ALFONSO V in 1458: his brother JOHN II inherited Aragon, and Naples was bequeathed to his illegitimate son FERRANTE I. King John, faced with the loss of much of the Mediterranean empire, sought unification with Castile as a means of protecting Aragon from the ambitions of France. He therefore arranged for the marriage of his son FERDINAND of Aragon to ISABELLA of Castile, sister of King HENRY IV (Enrique IV), who opposed the marriage. After King Henry's death in 1474, the battle for the succession between Isabella and her niece JUANA LA BELTRANEJA was decided at the battle of Toro (1476) in favour of Isabella. In 1479 Ferdinand acceded to the throne of Aragon, and thereafter the two kingdoms were ruled as a joint monarchy, though both kingdoms retained their local institutions. In practice the alliance was dominated by Castile,

and in 1591 there was an uprising in Zaragoza to which PHILIP II responded with further restrictions on Aragon.

**ARAGON, HOUSE OF**, the term used outside Aragon to denote the Aragonese rulers (often from cadet lines) who governed Majorca (1276–1343), NAPLES (1443–1501), SICILY (1282–1410), and Castile (1474–1504). Within Aragon, the rulers came from three distinct dynasties: the House of Navarre (1035–1164), the House of Barcelona (1164–1410), and the House of Trastámara (1412–1516). Some Aragonese rulers in territories outside Aragon also belonged to one of these dynasties: FERDINAND V was regarded as Aragonese in Castile but in Aragon (where he was Ferdinand II) he was regarded as a member of the House of Trastámara. For lists of rulers see Appendix 1.

**ARANJUEZ**, a town 50 kilometres (30 miles) south of Madrid on the left bank of the river Tagus and the summer residence of the court of PHILIP II. The fourteenth-century palace at Aranjuez passed to the Spanish crown in 1522. CHARLES V built a hunting lodge on the site, and this was enlarged by Philip II, who planted the English elms which render the landscape so distinctive. Remnants of the chateau survive only in the east face of the eighteenth-century palace that now dominates the site.

The gardens that Philip II laid out in the early 1560s showed the influence of both FLEMISH GARDENS and ITALIAN GARDENS. The chief Flemish element was the use of small compartments with clipped hedges; the Italian influence is apparent in the large statues of mythological figures. This garden contained many FOUNTAINS, some with stacked basins; some of the fountains now in the garden may date from this early garden. In the 1580s Philip decided to incorporate a nearby island in the Tagus into the garden that is now known as the Jardín de la Isla (where Schiller later set his play *Don Carlos*); this garden, which is bounded by the canal (La Ría) on one side and the river on the other sides, was laid out with avenues of plane trees. Details of the original layout are not known, but by the mid-seventeenth century the Hercules Fountain (which derives from the sixteenth-century Ocean Fountain in the BOBOLI GARDENS) had been constructed, and *GIOCHI D'ACQUA* had been installed, one of which drenched unwitting pedestrians on a path called Los Burladores ('The Jesters'). In the eighteenth century PARTERRES and avenues of lime trees were planted, but elements of the Renaissance gardens can still be seen.

**ARBEAU, THOINOT, or Jehan Tabourot** (1520–95), French cleric and writer on dance. Using a pen name (which is an anagram of his real name) Thoinot Arbeau wrote the dance manual *Orchesographie* (1588, reprinted 1596). Given the strong influence of Italian dancing masters in European courts, it is possible that this work does not accurately reflect the actual practices of the French court at this time. His manual still remains a useful source of information on dance music, being the only known source of Renaissance tabor rhythms as well as giving information about the construction of instruments and different dance tempi.

**ARBEDO, BATTLE OF.** In 1403 Swiss troops occupied the Val Levantina, which was the southern approach along the Ticino valley to the St Gotthard Pass, and in 1419 the cantons of Uri and Obwalden bought Bellinzona. Filippo Maria VISCONTI, the duke of Milan, was alarmed by this expansion further south, and in 1422 dispatched CARMAGNOLA's army to occupy the valley. The armies met in June 1422 in Arbedo, just north of Bellinzona (Switzerland), and the Milanese army of mercenaries decisively defeated the Swiss army.

**ARCADELT or Archadelt, JACQUES** (c.1505–1568), composer. Little is known of Arcadelt's early years, although he is thought to be of Flemish origin. He may have spent his formative years in France. By 1543 he was in Florence in the private service of Duke Alessandro de' MEDICI. Following the duke's murder by his kinsman Lorenzino de Medici in 1537, Arcadelt (who had set Lorenzino's madrigal 'Ver inferno è'l mio petto') moved to Rome and in 1540 was admitted to the Cappella Sistina. He returned to France in 1551 where many of his compositions were published by the Parisian printers Le Roy and Ballard.

Arcadelt's sacred music includes motets, a Magnificat and a set of lamentations which were used at the Cappella Sistina, but he is generally better known for his secular writing, such as the 125 chansons written throughout his career, and the five books of madrigals. These include settings of Petrarch, Bembo, Benedetto Varchi, and Filippo Strozzi. The *Primo libro* (1538) also contains 'Deh dimm' Amor se l'alma' and 'Io dico che fra noi', both by Michelangelo. The enormous popularity of Arcadelt's music is clear from its use in parody compositions, the numerous transcriptions of the madrigals for lute or guitar, and the fact that his music was depicted several times in sixteenth-century paintings.

**ARCADIA IN THE RENAISSANCE.** Arcadia is the bleak and harsh central plateau of the Peloponnese, ringed on all sides by mountains that separate it from the sea. The Arcadia of literature and art, however, is a fertile land populated by shepherds and largely benign gods that seems first to have been discovered by VIRGIL (who never visited Greece) when he embarked on the composition of his *Eclogues* in about 45 BC.

Virgil's idealized landscape was revived by SANNAZARO in his *Arcadia*, a PASTORAL consisting of a prose narrative interspersed with verse eclogues; Sannazaro had written his pastoral in the 1480s, but did not publish it until 1504. In Spain, Lope de VEGA modelled his pastoral romance *Arcadia, prosas y versos* (1598) on MONTEMAYOR's *Diana*, but took his title from Sannazaro, whose *Arcadia* had been published in a Spanish translation in 1547. The title was in turn used by Sir Philip SIDNEY for his posthumously published *Arcadia* (1590), and the young Milton called his fragmentary entertainment *Arcades*, which refers to the inhabitants of Arcadia.

The phrase *Et in Arcadia ego* first appears as the legend (now used as the title) in a painting by Guercino (c.1623, Corsini Gallery, Rome) which depicts shepherds finding a human skull; those who associate the phrase with pastoralism assume that it means 'I too have lived in Arcadia', but the 'I' in Guercino's *ego* is Death, who is asserting that he too is present in Arcadia; in Poussin's *Et in Arcadia ego* (c.1645, Louvre), the tomb represents Death, who is asserting his presence.

Bruno Snell, 'Arcadia: The Discovery of a Spiritual Landscape', in *The Discovery of the Mind* (English trans. 1954); Erwin Panofsky, 'Et in Arcadia ego', in *Philosophy and History*, ed. R. Klibansky (2nd edn., 1963); Petra Maisak, *Arcadien: Genese und Typologie einer idyllischen Wunschwelt* (1981).

**ARCHIMEDES IN THE RENAISSANCE.** Archimedes (c.287–212 BC), was regarded in the Renaissance as the supreme example of the mathematician and of the engineer. Though the text itself was not generally known until the sixteenth century, the approximate value of pi (22/7) that he had derived in *On the Measurement of a Circle* was in common use. The re-emergence of Archimedes' writings, and their publication in learned editions (see COMMANDINO, FEDERICO), constituted an important driving force for Renaissance work on conic sections, on the science of machines, and on the development of methods that eventually led to the invention of the calculus. See CARDANO, GIROLAMO; GALILEI, GALILEO; KEPLER, JOHANNES; TARTAGLIA, NICCOLÒ.

Archimedes' sand-reckoner (*Psammites, Arenarius*), which proposes the use of exponents for writing very large numbers, was the only authoritative source on the heliocentric astronomy of Aristarchus of Samos (c.310–c.230 BC). See COPERNICUS, NIKOLAUS.

**ARCHITECT.** In the fifteenth century, anyone who was concerned with erecting a building, even by supervising financial arrangements, could be called an architect. The specialized profession of architect, in today's sense of the designer of the building and overseer of the building work, developed during the sixteenth century. The first person who can be called an architect in this sense is probably PALLADIO.

**ARCHITECTURE.** The GOTHIC architecture which first emerged in France and then spread (often through Cistercian buildings) to the rest of Europe was succeeded by the new style known as Renaissance architecture; that style was in turn succeeded by MANNERISM. The Renaissance style was inaugurated in Florence by BRUNELLESCHI, in Rome and Mantua by ALBERTI, in Milan by MICHELOZZO and FILARETE, and in Venice by the anonymous architect of the portal of the ARSENALE (1460). In 1499 BRAMANTE moved from Milan to Rome and established what is known as the High Renaissance, a period deemed to last until the SACK OF ROME in 1527. For an account of the dissemination of Renaissance architecture within Italy see ITALIAN ARCHITECTURE. For accounts of Gothic, Renaissance, and mannerist architecture beyond Italy, see BOHEMIAN AND MORAVIAN ARCHITECTURE; DUTCH ARCHITECTURE; ENGLISH ARCHITECTURE; FLEMISH ARCHITECTURE; FRENCH ARCHITECTURE; GERMAN ARCHITECTURE; POLISH ARCHITECTURE; PORTUGUESE ARCHITECTURE; SCOTTISH

ARCHITECTURE; SPANISH ARCHITECTURE; THEATRES AND THE-
ATRE ARCHITECTURE.

    J. Quentin Hughes and Norbert Lynton, *Renaissance Architecture*
(rev. edn. of F. M. Simpson, *History of Architectural Development*,
vol. iv, 1962).

**ARCIMBOLDO or Arcimboldi, GIUSEPPE** (*c*.1527–1593),
Italian painter in Prague, a native of Milan, where he worked
as a designer of stained-glass windows for the cathedral. He
entered the imperial service as a court painter, and from 1562
to 1587 worked in Prague and Vienna in the courts of FERDI-
NAND I, MAXIMILIAN II, and RUDOLF II (who in 1592 ennobled
Arcimboldo as count palatine). His paintings, of which some
twenty survive, are typically bizarre heads composed of
fruits, vegetables, flowers, and leaves (e.g. *Rudolf II as
Vertumnus*, *c*.1591, Skokloster Slott, Skokloster).

    Arcimboldo's paintings were long regarded as curiosities
in questionable taste, but in the twentieth century he was
championed by Salvador Dalí and the Surrealists, who valued
Arcimboldo for his visual punning and use of *objets trouvés*.

    *DBI*; *MDA*.

**ARCINIEGA, CLAUDIO DE** (*c*.1527–1593), Spanish architect
who lived and worked in Mexico from the mid-1540s. In 1559
he designed the Túmulo Imperial, a temporary funeral monument for CHARLES V (now lost). He was appointed as master
of the works (*maestro mayor*) at Mexico Cathedral in 1584, and
promptly changed the plan of the cathedral. He was probably also the architect of Puebla Cathedral. These buildings
displaced the PLATERESQUE style which had previously prevailed in favour of the more austere style of Juan de HERRERA.

    *MDA*.

**ARCTIC EXPLORATION**. Exploration of the Arctic regions
was stimulated by the search for a NORTH-EAST or NORTH-
WEST PASSAGE to China and the Orient, with the lucrative

Arcimboldo, *RUDOLF II as
Vertumnus* (*c*.1591), in Skokloster
Slott, Sweden

trade that would follow. The possibility of a north-east passage was the first to be explored, and in 1553 WILLOUGHBY and CHANCELLOR sailed north-east of Scandinavia. Willoughby was lost, but Chancellor entered the White Sea, and made contact with the tsar, leading to the establishment of the MUSCOVY COMPANY in 1555. In 1594, the Dutchman Willem BARENTSZOON, also in search of a north-east passage, explored the west coast of Novaya Zemlya and discovered the straits leading to the Kara Sea; in 1596, he discovered Bear Island and Spitsbergen. Exploration of the northern reaches of the North American continent gathered pace from the final quarter of the sixteenth century. FROBISHER, on three voyages from 1576, visited Greenland and discovered what is now Frobisher Bay; DAVIS, between 1585 and 1587, explored the Greenland coast and sailed through what is now the Davis Strait into Baffin Bay. Between 1607 and 1611, HUDSON discovered the Hudson river and Hudson Bay; he also discovered Jan Mayen, an island off the east coast of Greenland. Further exploration was made between 1612 and 1616 by BAFFIN, who sailed to the north end of what is now Baffin Bay and discovered sounds leading to the north. Exploration of the west coast of Hudson Bay was furthered by BUTTON, Luke FOX, and Thomas JAMES.

**ARETINO, PIETRO** (1492–1556), Italian author, born in Arezzo (Tuscany), the son of a cobbler; his surname derives from Arretium, the Latin name for Arezzo. He was obliged to leave Arezzo because of his impiety, and settled first in Perugia before moving in 1517 to Rome, where he secured the patronage of Agostino CHIGI, Pope LEO X, and, after the latter's death in 1521, the *condottiere* Giovanni de' MEDICI (Giovanni delle Bande Nere). When Giovanni was killed in 1526, Aretino moved permanently to Venice, where his friends included TITIAN.

Aretino's best-known work is *I ragionamenti*, a series of two sets (1534, 1536) of dialogues conducted by prostitutes on the relative merits of the three states of life for women (the religious life, marriage, prostitution), and on the tricks of the trade necessary to become a good whore and procuress. He also wrote a tragedy (*Orazia*, 1546), five comedies (notably *La cortigiana*, 1525; *Il marescalco*, 1526–7; *La talanta*, 1542), and a set of lewd sonnets (*Sonnetti lussuriosi*) illustrated with sexually explicit engravings by GIULIO ROMANO. In 1538 Aretino published the first of his five collections of letters. These literary, dramatic, and epistolary works are suffused with cheerful cynicism, a delight in sexuality, and a spirited irreverence that was explicitly anticlerical and implicitly blasphemous; his satires led to ARIOSTO's description of Aretino as the scourge of princes (*il flagello dei principe*). Such was his versatility, however, that Aretino was also able to write a devotional work on the Passion and a paraphrase of the penitential psalms.

DBI; MDA; OCIL; P. Larivaille, *Pietro Aretino fra Rinascimento e Manierismo* (1980).

**ARFE or Arphe FAMILY**, a dynasty of Spanish goldsmiths who specialized in monstrances. Enrique de Arfe (*c.*1470–*c.*1545) was born in Germany (probably in Cologne) and by 1500 had settled in León, where he embarked on a huge silver-gilt monstrance (completed 1522, destroyed 1809) for the cathedral. He made similar monstrances for Córdoba Cathedral (1518) and Cádiz Cathedral (1528); his processional cross for Toledo Cathedral (1515–24) is 3 metres (10 feet) high and is decorated with 260 silver-gilt statuettes.

Enrique's style was uncompromisingly Gothic, but the work of his son Antonio de Arfe (1510–*c.*1566) is PLATERESQUE. Antonio's tabernacles include those in Santiago Cathedral (1539–45) and the Church of Santa María in Medina de Rioseco (Valladolid).

Antonio's son Juan de Arfe y Villafañe (1535–1603) made the monstrances for Ávila Cathedral (1564–71) and Seville Cathedral (1580–7, now altered) and the processional cross for Burgos Cathedral (1592). He published a treatise on the goldsmith's art (*Quilatador de la plata, oro y piedras*, Valladolid, 1572), an account of his Seville monstrance (*Descripción del traço y ornato de la custodia de plata de la Sancta Iglesia de Sevilla*, Seville, 1587), and a treatise (partly in verse) on proportions in sculpture and architecture (*De varia comensuración para esculptura y architectura*, 1585).

MDA.

**ARGENSOLA, BARTOLOMÉ LEONARDO DE** (1562–1631), Spanish poet and historian, born in Barbastro; he entered the priesthood and became rector of Villahermosa in 1588. He travelled with his younger brother Lupercio ARGENSOLA to Naples in the train of the count of Lemos, and succeeded his brother as historiographer of Aragon in 1613. He died in Zaragoza on 4 February 1631.

Bartolomé's principal historical works are his *Conquista de las Islas Molucas* (1609) and his supplement to the *Anales de Aragón* of Jerónimo ZURITA, which carried the narrative from 1516 to 1520 (Zaragoza, 1630). His *Rimas* were published (together with those of his brother) by his nephew Gabriel in 1634. His poetry ranges from witty satires to devotional odes; his sonnets and odes are modelled on those of Fray LUIS DE LEÓN.

M. Mir, *Bartolomé Leonardo de Argensola* (1891); J. Aznar Molina, *Los Argensola* (1939).

**ARGENSOLA, LUPERCIO LEONARDO DE** (1559–1613), Spanish poet, playwright, and historian, baptized at Barbastro on 14 December 1559 and educated at the universities of Huesca and Zaragoza. In 1585 he entered the service of the duke of Villahermosa and in 1599 he was appointed historiographer of Aragon, in which capacity he wrote *Información de los sucesos de Aragón en los años de 1590 y 1591* (first published in 1808). In 1610 he accompanied the count of Lemos to Naples (where the count was viceroy), and there served as secretary to the viceroy and founded the Academia de los Ociosos; he died in Naples in March 1613.

Lupercio burnt his poems in Naples, but his son Gabriel had prudently taken copies, and published the surviving poems with those of Lupercio's brother Bartolomé Argensola in 1634. The simplicity of Lupercio's poetic diction stands in marked contrast to the prevailing GONGORISM of contemporary poetry. His classicizing impulse led him to translate and imitate ancient Latin poets, especially Horace and Virgil; his original poems include sonnets, satires, and descriptive poetry (notably a description of ARANJUEZ). He wrote three Senecan tragedies that were widely acclaimed: *Isabela* and *Alejandra* were first published in 1772, and *Filis* is now lost.

Otis Green, *The Life and Works of Lupercio Leonardo de Argensola* (1927; Spanish trans. 1945).

**ARGENTRÉ, BERTRAND D'** (1519–90), Breton jurist and historian. He wrote two important treatises on the CUSTOMARY LAW of Brittany (*Commentaires sur les quatre premiers livres de l'ancienne coutume*, 1568; *Commentarii ad praecipuos juris Britanniae titulos*, 1605). His chief historical work, published in 1619, was the *Traité de l'ancien état de la petite Bretagne* (Brittany is small—*petite*—by contrast with Great Britain).

*DBF*; Ieuan Jones, *D'Argentré's History of Brittany and its Maps* (1987).

**ARGYROPOULOS, JOHN** (*c*.1405–1487), Byzantine scholar in Italy. Argyropoulos studied at the University of Padua from 1441 to 1444, learning Latin and medicine and privately teaching Greek; he was supported throughout this period by the Florentine exile Palla STROZZI. He returned to Constantinople as a champion of the proposed union between the Byzantine and Roman churches, and eventually converted to Catholicism. During this period in Constantinople he taught at the Katholikon Mouseion, a school attached to the hospital of the Xenon of the Kral; his pupils included Michael APOSTOLIS, who later became a teacher in the Mouseion. In 1456 Argyropoulos returned to Florence in the wake of the fall of Constantinople and was appointed to a professorship at the University of Florence, where he lectured on ARISTOTLE for fifteen years. His direct appeal to the Greek texts of ancient philosophers antagonized exponents of the Latin tradition of scholarship, but appealed to the younger generation of humanists, including Lorenzo de' MEDICI, FICINO, and POLIZIANO.

In 1471 Argyropoulos moved to Rome, where he joined the curia of Pope SIXTUS IV, who had been one of his teachers in Padua. He returned to Florence for four years (1477–81), but otherwise spent the rest of his life in Rome, teaching and writing. His translations included Latin versions of Aristotle's *Nicomachean Ethics* and *Physics*, both of which were reprinted regularly, and his original works included a monody for the Emperor JOHN VIII PALAIOLOGOS and a theological treatise on the Holy Spirit. The account of the COUNCIL OF FLORENCE often attributed to Argyropoulos is a ghost, and the mistaken tradition that he attended the Council arises from a confusion between Argyropoulos and Amirutzes (who did attend) in a printed chronicle.

*DBI* s.v. Argiropulo, Giovanni; *PLP* i. 118–19; *DCLI*; G. Cammelli, *Giovanni Argiropulo* (1941); D. Geanakoplos, 'The Italian Renaissance and Byzantium: The Career of the Greek Humanist-Professor John Argyropoulos in Florence and Rome (1415–1487)', *Conspectus of History*, 1/1 (1974); John Monfasani, 'The Averroism of John Argyropoulos and his *Questio utrum intellectus humanus sit perpetuus*', *I Tatti Studies*, 5 (1993).

**ARIAS DE ÁVILA, PEDRO**. See DÁVILA, PEDRARIAS.

**ARIAS MONTANO, BENITO** (1527–98), editor of the Antwerp Polyglot BIBLE, born in Fregenal de la Sierra (Extramadura) and educated in Seville and Alcalá. He took holy orders in 1559 and three years later attended the COUNCIL OF TRENT as a theologian. In 1564 he retired as a hermit to Peña de Aracena, and was subsequently appointed professor of oriental languages and librarian at the ESCORIAL.

Arias was sent to Antwerp at the behest of PHILIP II to edit the eight sumptuous folio volumes of the Antwerp Polyglot, entitled *Biblia sacra Hebraice, Chaldaice, Graece et Latine*, published by Christophe PLANTIN between 1568 and 1573. While working in Flanders, Arias purchased books and manuscripts on a huge scale for the Escorial; he also pursued his interests in Jewish antiquities and in philosophy and theology (on all of which he wrote) and wrote poetry in Latin and Spanish. His Spanish poetry is so indebted to the poetry of his friend LUIS DE LEÓN that problems of attribution have arisen, particularly with respect to 'A la hermosura exterior de Nuestra Señora'. Like Fray Luis, Arias also wrote a vernacular paraphrase of the Song of Solomon, the 'Paráfrasis sobre el cantar de los cantares'.

The emphasis that Arias placed on the Hebrew and Aramaic texts of the Old Testament in his edition of the Antwerp Polyglot was deemed to be heretical by León de Castro (a professor at Salamanca), who denounced Arias to the Inquisition. He travelled to Rome to appear before the tribunal (1575–6), and was eventually acquitted. On returning to Spain Arias was appointed as royal chaplain, but nonetheless withdrew to Peña de Aracena (1579–83). In 1584 he resigned his chaplaincy, and thereafter spent the rest of his life as a hermit at Santiago de la Espada, where he died in 1598.

*DBEH*; *MDA*; B. Rekers, *Benito Arias Montano* (1972).

**ARIOSTO, LUDOVICO** (1474–1533), Italian poet and dramatist, born into a noble family in Reggio (Emilia). He spent his career in the service of the ESTE family, working first for Cardinal Ippolito d'ESTE and then for the cardinal's brother, Duke Alfonso d'ESTE. In Ferrara, to which Ariosto retired in 1527, he supervised the construction of the threatre in which his five comedies (notably *I suppositi*) were performed. These comedies established *commedia erudita* in the Renaissance. His other works include a set of seven Horatian satires composed between 1517 and 1525.

Ariosto's principal literary work was the epic *Orlando furioso* (1516, 1521, 1532), a masterpiece of parody and irony; it was a sequel to BOIARDO's *Orlando innamorato* and established Ariosto's standing as the Renaissance successor to DANTE. He continued to revise and expand *Orlando furioso* for the rest of his life.

*DBI*; *Grove*; *MDA*; *OCIL*; P. Brand, *Ludovico Ariosto* (1974).

**ARISTOTLE IN THE RENAISSANCE**. Many of the works of Aristotle (384–322 BC) were known in medieval Europe, often through Latin translations of Arabic versions, in particular the recovery of his logical treatises (all of which were known in the West by the early twelfth century). Of the Arabic commentators, the most important for the Renaissance was AVERROËS. THOMAS AQUINAS's doctrine of the EUCHARIST, for example, is based on the Aristotelian distinction between substance and accidents (the underlying 'substances' of the bread and wine were deemed to be changed, even though the 'accidents', or external qualities, remained unchanged). Even the notion that fish could be eaten on fast days (including Fridays) is Aristotelian in origin, given Aristotle's contention that fish were produced without sexual activity and were therefore a pure food. The standing of Aristotle as the supreme philosopher was symbolized by Dante's declaration that he was 'the master of those who know'.

At the Reformation the link between Aristotelian logic and scholastic theology led to a reaction against Aristotle amongst Protestants, and to a realization by logicians such as Petrus RAMUS that a reformed theology required a reformed logic. In Catholic circles Thomistic Aristotelianism remained at the heart of orthodox theology. In the humanist circles of the Renaissance, the central Aristotelian works were the *Nicomachean Ethics*, the *Rhetoric*, the *Politics*, and the *Poetics*, all of which were the subject of scholarly editions, detailed commentaries, and translations into various vernaculars. Among scientists, Aristotle's works on natural science were regarded as authoritative, but were slowly subverted, particularly in the field of ASTRONOMY.

Charles Schmitt, *Aristotle and the Renaissance* (1983); id., and *La tradizione aristotelica: Fra Italia e Inghilterra* (1985).

**ARITHMETIC.** In universities arithmetic, one of the sciences of the quadrivium (see LIBERAL ARTS), was taught from the treatise of Nicomachus of Gerasa (*fl.* AD 100), which is a simplified and expanded version of the arithmetical books of EUCLID's *Elements*, books 7 to 9. There is much emphasis on the correct naming of ratios, which is perhaps partly understandable since the principal application of arithmetic was in the theory of MUSIC. There was also an interest in numbers with special properties, such as 'perfect numbers', which are equal to the sum of their factors (6, for instance, which is the sum of 1, 2, and 3), or pairs of 'amicable numbers', in which each is the sum of the factors of the other, such as 284 (factors 142, 71, 4, 2, 1) and 220 (factors 110, 55, 44, 22, 20, 11, 5, 4, 2, 1), and 'figurate numbers' which can be displayed as an array of units that forms a geometrical figure, such as a square, a triangle, a cube, or a pyramid. Most of these properties do not retain their interest today, but one can never be sure that Number Theory, a descendant of arithmetic with a somewhat discontinuous history, will not take a turn that brings them back into favour.

In ABACUS SCHOOLS 'practical' or 'commercial' arithmetic formed a very significant proportion of the syllabus. Elementary books start with writing the 'Arabic' numerals. Such texts provide problems and their solutions, but no details of how the working was done; the most elementary books, however, do show working. One such is the first printed arithmetic text, the 'Treviso *Arithmetic*' of 1478. After

instruction in the basic operations of addition, subtraction, multiplication, and division, and exercises in handling fractions and factorizing numbers, the problems begin with 'the rule of three', that is, exercises of the form 'If 7 *braccia* of cloth cost 12 *lira*, 3 *soldi*, and 2 *denari*, what is the price of 5 *braccia*?' Apart from the units of length and currency, these are exactly like the problems used in teaching children in Europe today. More complicated problems follow, all apparently designed to prepare the pupil for earning a living in the market place or the workshop. Decimal fractions became common only after strong advocacy for their use by STEVIN (1585).

After arithmetic, the abacus texts turn to ALGEBRA. As this was regarded as an advanced form of arithmetic, many books whose titles suggest they are concerned with arithmetic in fact turn out to deal largely with algebra. See also LOGARITHMS.

**ARMADA, SPANISH, or (Spanish) La Armada Invencible**, the naval expedition sent to invade England by King PHILIP II of Spain in 1588. As the husband of MARY I of England, Philip had been king consort of England, and after Mary's death he became increasingly hostile to the Protestantism of Queen ELIZABETH, Mary's half-sister and successor: Elizabeth supported the Dutch Protestant rebels against Spain in the REVOLT OF THE NETHERLANDS and Philip supported the Irish Catholic rebels against England. Military skirmishes began when Sir Francis DRAKE began to attack Spanish ports in the Caribbean. In 1587, while the Armada was being prepared, Drake mounted the CÁDIZ Raid.

As Portugal had been subsumed into Spain, the Armada sailed from Lisbon in July 1588. It consisted of 138 ships crewed by some 7,000 seamen under the command of the count of MEDINA SIDONIA; the ships carried siege equipment and an invasion force of some 17,000 soldiers. The opposing English force under the command of Lord HOWARD OF EFFINGHAM consisted of 34 royal warships and some 170 privately owned ships. The English were outnumbered and could not sustain hand-to-hand combat at sea or on land; their only advantage lay in their firepower, because the English guns had longer ranges and the ships on which they were mounted were more manoeuvrable.

The Spanish plan was to sail to Flanders to join forces with the fleet of Alessandro FARNESE, duke of Parma, and then cross the channel to England. The rendezvous was never to occur. English ships began to harass Medina Sidonia's fleet as soon as it entered the channel, twice breaking its disciplined crescent formation before the Spanish fleet reached Calais on 6 August. Dutch naval forces had sealed off the sea exits of Farnese's fleet, which was unable to reach Calais.

On the night of 7/8 August English forces attacked the tight Spanish formation with six fireships, and in the course of the next day inflicted heavy losses on the Spanish fleet in a protracted battle off the coast of Gravelines. Their route home blocked, the Spanish fleet yielded to deteriorating weather and strong southerly winds and sailed into the North Sea to round Scotland and Ireland: the exhaustion of supplies of food and water, together with the outbreak of disease, cost more lives than had been lost in battle, and more than 30 ships were lost in the Hebrides and along the west coast of Ireland. Only 66 ships and some 10,000 men reached Spain.

England may have been saved by the weather, but in England the weather was regarded as a providential complement to the power of its navy, and the defeat of the Armada became one of the pivotal points of English history as constructed by English historians. The victory certainly enhanced England's reputation as a maritime power, though neither country changed its policies towards the other as a result of the conflict.

Garrett Mattingly, *Armada* (1959); Colin Martin and Geoffrey Parker, *The Spanish Armada* (2nd edn., 1999).

**ARMAGNACS AND BURGUNDIANS**. From 1407 to 1435 the French and Burgundian courts were divided by a quarrel between the dukes of Burgundy (JOHN THE FEARLESS and, from 1419, PHILIP THE GOOD) and the kings of France. In 1407 John, duke of Burgundy, ordered the assassination of Prince Louis of Orléans, the brother of King Charles VI. Prince Louis was succeeded as leader of the anti-Burgundian faction by the count of Armagnac, whose supporters were known by his title. The Armagnacs were weakened by the defeat of France at AGINCOURT and by the death of the count of Armagnac in a massacre in Paris in 1418. In 1419, however, Armagnacs assassinated John, duke of Burgundy, at a meeting with the dauphin (later CHARLES VII) on the bridge of Montereau (now Montereau-faut-Yonne). John's son Philip the Good retaliated by supporting the claim of King Henry V of England to the throne of France, and in 1420 persuaded King Charles VI to accede to the Treaty of Troyes, by which Charles repudiated the dauphin and named Henry V as his successor. The dauphin, supported by the Armagnacs, held the territory south of the Loire, and was supported by JOAN OF ARC. Philip betrayed Joan of Arc to the English, but in the Treaty of Arras (1435), which ended the rift between Armagnacs and Burgundians, he recognized Charles VII as King of France.

J. d'Avont, *Le Querelle des Armagnacs et des Bourguignons* (1943).

**ARMILLARY SPHERE**, literally a sphere made of rings, an openwork model of the heavens consisting of the circles used by astronomers: meridians (passing through the celestial poles), the celestial equator, and smaller circles parallel to it representing latitudes, which always include those of the tropics (of Cancer and of Capricorn), plus the circle of the ecliptic (which intersects the equator at the equinoxes). In the Renaissance, armillary spheres were generally very small and used only for pedagogical purposes. Larger spheres, could be employed as an aid to astronomical calculation. Pictures of armillary spheres are used for symbolic purposes, for instance one appears on the frontispiece of REGIOMONTANUS' *Epytoma* (1496).

**ARMIN, ROBERT** (*c*.1586–*c*.1611), English actor, clown, and writer. A pupil of TARLETON, Armin performed at the CURTAIN and the GLOBE. He performed in SHAKESPEARE's plays, probably succeeding KEMPE as Dogberry in *Much Ado About Nothing*

and other comic roles. He also published works connected to his trade: *Fool upon a Fool* (1600), on the art of clowning, and *Quips upon Questions* (1600), on improvisation. A play, *The Two Maids of Moreclacke* (1609) is also attributed to him.

*DNB.*

**ARMINIANISM**. The theology of GRACE developed by ARMINIUS was formally set out the year after his death in the Remonstrance of 1610, which was drawn up by his friend Johannes Uitenbogaert and signed by 44 Arminians, who were thereafter known as REMONSTRANTS. Arminians argued that the affirmation of human free will did not compromise the sovereignty of God, and rejected the Calvinist doctrines of predestination (in both its supralapsarian and sublapsarian forms), the limited atonement (i.e. Jesus died only for the elect), and the irresistibility and indefectibility of grace.

In England, the theology of the Laudian party was broadly Arminian, and in the eighteenth century the Arminianism of John Wesley, which was at odds with the Calvinism of George Whitefield, led to the separation (which still persists) of Wesleyan and Calvinistic Methodists.

A. W. Harrison, *The Beginnings of Arminianism to the Synod of Dort* (1926); id., *Arminianism* (1937); Nicholas Tyacke, *Anti-Calvinists: The Rise of English Arminianism c.1590–1640* (1987).

**ARMINIUS, JACOBUS, or (Dutch) Jakob Hermanszoon** (1560–1609), Dutch theologian, born in Oudewater, the son of a cutler. He was educated at Utrecht and Marburg, but on learning of the massacre of his family in the REVOLT OF THE NETHERLANDS returned to the Netherlands, initially to Rotterdam and then to Leiden, where he studied from 1576 to 1581; he later studied in Geneva (under BEZA), Basel, Padua, and Rome. In 1587 he again returned to the Netherlands, where he was ordained as a minister in Amsterdam (1588). Arminius began to doubt the Calvinist doctrine of GRACE, and his rejection of predestination led to accusations of Pelagianism. His correspondence with Franciscus JUNIUS and his attempt to refute William PERKINS's Calvinistic *De praedestinationis modo et ordine* (1598) led Arminius to refine his views.

In 1603 Arminius was appointed to a chair of theology at Leiden, but in order to claim his chair was obliged to defend himself against charges of Pelagianism and SOCINIANISM in a disputation held at The Hague on 6 May 1603 in the presence of OLDENBARNEVELT (who was a supporter of Arminius). He assumed his chair at Leiden (where Joseph SCALIGER was his colleague), and remained there for the last six years of his life, constantly immersed in theological controversy because of his campaign to revise the BELGIC CONFESSION and the HEIDELBERG CATECHISM, the two principal statements of the Calvinist theology of the Dutch Reformed Church.

*NNBW* i; Carl Bangs, *Arminius: A Study in the Dutch Reformation* (1971).

**ARMS AND ARMOUR**. Arms are weapons of offence and armour is defensive equipment. Arms wielded by hand in close combat included SWORDS, DAGGERS, axes (including the halberd and the bill), clubs, maces, hammers, lances (cavalry spears fitted with a circular handguard known as a vamplate), pikes (very long spears used by infantry to form a palisade against cavalry), and partisans (spears, still in use in parade grounds, with a triangular blade with pointed lugs at its base). Projectile weapons included bows, crossbows, catapults, guns, and ARTILLERY.

Armour consisted of body armour (including protection for limbs and head) and shields. Metal armour was constructed by one or more of five distinct methods: lamellar (laced overlapping oblong plates), scale (small leaf-shaped plates secured to a textile garment like roof tiles), mail or (popularly) chain mail (interlinked rings), coat-of-plates (small overlapping plates or hoops riveted to a textile garment), and plate (large plates, each of which covers part of the body).

In the second half of the fourteenth century, armour typically consisted of chain mail or coat-of-plates with a solid plate breastplate, covered with a sleeveless surcoat (known as a jupon or as coat-armour) embroidered with the coat of arms of the wearer. The helmet was made of metal, and by the thirteenth century completely enveloped the head; this 'great helm', as it is now known, was used in warfare until the mid-fourteenth century and in tournaments until the sixteenth century. In the late fourteenth century it was replaced on the battlefield by the basinet (or basnet), a new type of helmet with a detachable pointed visor and a chain-mail tippet (called an aventail or gorget) to protect the neck.

In the fifteenth century, the gowns previously worn over armour were discarded, and armour increasingly came to be made from polished steel plates. By the 1410s armour had assumed the form that it was to retain until it ceased to be used at the end of the seventeenth century. A typical fifteenth- and sixteenth-century armour consisted of a cuirass (a linked polished steel breastplate and backplate) with a skirt of iron hoops worn over a quilted undergarment, a coat-of-plates covering for the arms and the front of the legs, and a helmet. The left side of the armour was thicker than the right, because the lance of an opponent was held in the right hand couched diagonally across the horse's neck to the left. In tournament armours this imbalance was exaggerated, and the right arm and shoulder were lightly armoured or left unprotected. In helmets, the chain-mail aventail of the basnet was replaced by plate, and a series of new designs emerged: the Italian *barbuta* was a one-piece helmet that extended to the cheeks; the sallet (or salade) had a visor worn with a separate chin piece (called a beaver); the armet had hinged cheek pieces that fastened at the chin, leaving only the eyes visible; the close-helmet, which was popular in the sixteenth century, looked like an armet, except that the cheek pieces were made from a continuous piece of metal and pivoted like the visor. The close-helmet was worn with full armour, but sixteenth-century light cavalry wore the burgonet (a peaked open helmet with cheek pieces, fitted to the gorget so that the head could be turned without exposing the neck) and infantry wore either the burgonet or the morion (a descendant of the medieval kettle-hat resembling a broad-brimmed hat).

The most important centres for armour production were south Germany (especially Augsburg and Nuremberg) and north Italy (especially Milan and Brescia); in the early sixteenth century MAXIMILIAN I founded an imperial armoury in Innsbruck (1504) and HENRY VIII founded a royal armoury in Greenwich (1515). The most prominent armourers were the HELMSCHMIED FAMILY of Augsburg and the MISSAGLIA FAMILY of Milan. Fifteenth-century German armours were angular, and were decorated with fluting (which survived into the sixteenth century with the 'Maximilian armours' popular from c.1515 to c.1530), whereas Italian armours of the same period had rounded lines. These national styles began to merge at the end of the fifteenth century, and in the sixteenth century there were pan-European fashions in armour; until the 1510s breastplates were rounded, but thereafter they became flatter and featured a vertical ridge down the middle; in the last 30 years of the century the prevailing fashion was a peapod or waistcoat form curving down to a blunt point at the bottom. By the 1520s tournament armour had evolved away from field armour, but thereafter armours that could be used for either purpose were developed, often with alternative or additional pieces (called garnitures) to facilitate the change of use; during the same period a new kind of armour emerged, the decorative parade armour.

Sixteenth-century armours were often decorated with etched and gilt designs which could survive the use of armour in the field or at the tournament. Parade armours, however, were intended only as symbols of the wealth and power of their wearers, so decoration and design were not constrained by practical considerations. Parade armours were sometimes elaborately embossed, etched, or damascened, and designs included adaptations of ancient Roman armour. Artists such as DÜRER and HOLBEIN executed designs for armours, and others, such as Daniel Hoffner and Jörg SORG the Younger, specialized in the decoration of armour. Embossed armour was made by the NEGROLI FAMILY of Milan, Bartolommeo CAMPI of Pesaro, and the ANTWERP-LOUVRE SCHOOL.

The Roman practice of equipping horses with armour was revived intermittently in the twelfth and thirteenth centuries (when horses were sometimes covered with mail), and from the fourteenth to the seventeenth centuries horses were sometimes armoured with plate (though the legs were usually left uncovered). Riders wore a spiked spur until the early fourteenth century, after which the spike was replaced with the rowel that has remained in use to the present day.

*MDA*; Sydney Anglo, *The Martial Arts of Renaissance Europe* (2001).

**ARNDT, JOHANN** (1555–1621), German Lutheran theologian and mystic. He was born in Ballenstedt (Anhalt) and studied from 1576 to 1571 at the universities of Helmstedt, Wittenberg (where he became a follower of MELANCHTHON), Strassburg (where he studied Hebrew under Johannes Pappus (1508–85), an anti-Calvinist Lutheran), and Basel (where he studied under Simon Sulzer (1508–85), who sought to reconcile the Swiss and German churches). In 1583 Arndt was appointed pastor at Badeborn, but his uncompromising Lutheranism alienated the Calvinist city authorities, and when in 1590 he refused to remove pictures from his church and to discontinue the use of exorcism in baptism, he was dismissed. He initially found asylum in Quedlinburg, and in 1599 moved to Brunswick, where he became pastor of St Martin's Church.

Arndt's most influential publication is *Vier Bücher vom wahren Christentum* (1606), which was subsequently translated into many European languages; the most contentious aspect of the volume's 'true Christianity' concerns the doctrine of the ATONEMENT, which bypasses the conventional forensic view in which Christ died for humankind in favour of an emphasis on the presence of Christ in humankind. Arndt's affirmation of the mystical union between Christ and the individual believer led to his posthumous veneration by German Pietists. Arndt's other important publication was his *Paradiesgärtlein aller christlichen Tugenden* (1612), which was eventually translated into English as *The Garden of Paradise* (1716).

NDB; E. Weber, *Johann Arndts Vier Bücher vom wahren Christentum als Beitrag zur protestantischen Irenik des 17. Jahrhunderts* (1969); C. Braw, *Bücher im Staube: Die Theologie Johann Arndts in ihrem Verhältnis zur Mystik* (1986).

**ARNOLFO DI CAMBIO or Arnolfo di Lapo** (*c*.1245–1310), Italian architect, mason, and sculptor, recorded as an assistant to Nicola PISANO in 1266. He was appointed master mason of the new cathedral in Florence in 1296; his design was implemented in the nave and aisles, but the east end is the work of his successor, Francesco TALENTI. Surviving buildings that have been attributed to Arnolfo on stylistic grounds include the Florentine churches of Badia and Santa Croce and the tower of the Palazzo Vecchio.

Arnolfo's work as a sculptor includes a bust of *Pope Boniface VIII* (Grotte Vaticane, Rome), the ciboria in San Paolo fuori le Mura in Rome (1285) and in Santa Cecilia in Rome (1293), and the tomb of Cardinal De Braye (after 1282, San Domenico, Orvieto), which was imitated in wall tombs for more than a century.

DBI; MDA; A. M. Romanini, *Arnolfo di Cambio e lo 'stil novo' del gotico italiano* (1969).

**ARQUEBUS or harquebus or (German) *Hackenbüchse* or (early modern English) hackbut**, a sixteenth-century firearm, the immediate predecessor of the MUSKET. The weight of the gun meant that it could not be raised to the firing position without support, so in battle it was supported by a trestle, which the imperial armies of MAXIMILIAN I later replaced with a portable tripod. The German and Flemish form of the name means 'hook-gun', which refers to the hook with which the gun was joined to whatever was supporting the barrel; the hook steadied the gun and diminished the effect of the recoil. The French form *arquebuse à croc* (hooked arquebus), which appears in early modern English as 'harquebus of crock', is a reduplication formed after the etymology of *arquebuse* had been forgotten.

The firing mechanism of the arquebus was either a matchlock, in which a trigger brought a match down to the priming, or, in more expensive weapons, a wheel-lock, in which the trigger released a sprung wheel which rapidly revolved and emitted sparks that ignited the GUNPOWDER in the pan. Some German arquebuses were rifled: spiral grooves (German *riffeln*, 'to groove') in the bore forced the bullet to rotate, which diminished the effect of irregularities in weight or shape and so increased accuracy.

The arquebus was first deployed in the WARS OF ITALY, in the first instance by Spanish arquebusiers at the battles of BICOCCA (1522) and PAVIA (1525). In about 1530 Filippo STROZZI extended the range of the arquebus to 400 metres (440 yards) and standardized the calibres of the arquebuses of the French forces in Italy. This feature led to the English term 'caliver' to denote a light gun that could be fired without a support for the barrel.

The arquebus continued in use throughout the sixteenth century, but by the 1570s it had been substantially displaced by the musket.

**ARRAS or Atrecht, UNION OF** (7 January 1579), a league consisting of Hainaut (Heregouwen), Artois, and Douai, the southern provinces of the Netherlands, formed with the purpose of defending the Catholic religion. The treaty extended the provisions of the Pacification of GHENT and so moved the southern Netherlands closer to separation from the northern provinces; the northern provinces responded with the Union of UTRECHT (23 January 1579). In May 1579 the Union was ratified by Alessandro FARNESE. The signatories of the treaty recognized King PHILIP II as the sole ruler of the Netherlands and Catholicism as the sole state religion.

**ARRAS TAPESTRIES** (*c*.1313–1477), a group of TAPESTRY workshops in the town of Arras (Artois). The tapestries of Arras are first mentioned in 1313, and by the middle of the fourteenth century Arras had become the most important tapestry centre in Europe. In 1384 Artois was annexed to the duchy of Burgundy, and thereafter Arras enjoyed the patronage of the Burgundian court and gained access to the English export market. In 1477 King LOUIS XI of France captured Arras and dispersed its inhabitants; the workshops were re-established on a small scale, but the centre of production shifted to Tournai, and the Arras workshops closed early in the sixteenth century.

The similarity of Arras and Tournai tapestries creates problems of attribution. The only tapestries for which documentary evidence demonstrates an Arras provenance are the set depicting the lives of St Piat and St Éleuthère (1402, Tournai Cathedral), which formerly bore the signature of Pierrot Feré of Arras. Attributed works (all of which could have been made in Tournai) include a *Passion* series (now divided between the Musée Cinquantenaire in Brussels, Zaragoza Cathedral, and the Vatican Museum) and the *Chatsworth Hunts* (Victoria and Albert Museum; also known as the *Devonshire Hunts*).

G. Wingfield-Digby, *The Devonshire Hunts Tapestries* (1971).

**ARRIGHI, LUDOVICO** (d. 1527), Italian calligrapher, type designer, and printer, a native of Vicenza who worked as a scrivener in the papal chancery. In 1522 he published *Operina da imparare di scrivere littera cancellaresca*, which was the first printed handbook on CALLIGRAPHY. His typeface, which was an elaboration of the chancery hand (*cancelleresca corsiva*) used in the Vatican secretariat, influenced the development of italic type (which had been invented by Francesco GRIFFO), and his script, which combines revived Carolingian minuscules with angular inscriptional majuscules, became the standard correspondence script of sixteenth-century Italy.

DBI.

**ARRUDA, DIOGO DE** (*c.*1470–1531) and **FRANCISCO DE** (*c.*1480–1547), Portuguese architects who introduced the MANUELINE style to Portugal. Diogo's main work is the exuberantly decorated nave and chapter house of the Convento de Cristo in Tomar (1510–14); the sculpted west front of this building, which includes maritime motifs such as sails and ropes (around the windows) and buttresses carved with coral and seaweed, represents the Manueline style at its most extravagant.

Francisco de Arruda, who was probably the brother of Diogo, was the military architect who built the Tower of Belém (1516–21) in subdued Manueline style on an island in the Tagus; the river has since changed course, and the tower is now on the north shore.

MDA.

**ARSENALE**, the walled area in Venice, covering some 32 hectares (79 acres), which contained the naval docks, the armouries, and the ship-construction and dry-dock facilities of the republic. The Arsenale was founded *c.*1104 and expanded in 1304 by Andrea PISANO; subsequent additions were undertaken in 1325 (the Arsenale Nuovo), 1473 (the Arsenale Nuovissimo), 1539 (the Riparto delle Galeazze), and 1564 (the Canal delle Galeazze e Vasca). The monumental gateway to the Arsenale (1457) is the earliest Venetian example of the Renaissance style of ITALIAN ARCHITECTURE. By the fifteenth century the Arsenale had become the largest industrial zone in Europe, employing some 4,000 men. The workers of the Arsenale, who were known as *Arsenalotti*, provided the personal guard of the DOGE and the civic firefighters of the republic. The presence of gunpowder and wooden ships made the Arsenale vulnerable to fires started by explosions, the largest of which occurred in 1509 and 1569.

MDA; Giorgio Bellavitis, *L'Arsenale di Venezia* (1983); Ennio Concina, *L'Arsenale della Repubblicà di Venezia* (1984); Paola Gennaro, *Le fabbriche dell'Arsenale* (1997).

**ARS NOVA**, a term used to distinguish music of the fourteenth century from the *ars antiqua* of the thirteenth century. The term appeared in the title of a treatise by Philippe de Vitry (1325) and the style is evident in the works of Guillaume de Machaut (1300–77). In Italy the enhanced sense of tonality in the writing of Johannes Ciconia (1335–1411) and the madrigals and *ballate* of Francesco Landini (1325–97) paved the way for the developing musical language of the Renaissance.

**ARTESONADO**, an architectural term, derived from Spanish *artesón* (a wooden trough or panel), used to denote a marquetry ceiling in which geometrical ornaments constructed

of small wooden ribs (*lacería*) outline rows of concave projections that resemble the bottoms of troughs. These ceilings, which were painted in bright colours and gilded, were a particular feature of MUDÉJAR design in the fifteenth and sixteenth centuries, and in Spanish America continued to be constructed throughout the seventeenth century.

**ARTICLES, ACT OF SIX, or the Whip with Six Strings**, an Act imposed in June 1539 by King HENRY VIII and interpreted by many as a curb on the spread of Protestantism. The Six Articles confirmed transubstantiation and communion in one kind (see EUCHARIST), enforced clerical celibacy, upheld monastic vows and private masses, and confirmed auricular confession. The Act was repealed in 1547.

G. Redworth, 'A Study in the Formulation of Policy: The Genesis and Evolution of the Act of Six Articles', *Journal of Ecclesiastical History*, 37 (1986).

**ARTICLES, THE THIRTY-NINE**, the confession of faith of the Church of England, based on the Ten Articles of 1536, the Bishops' Book of 1537, the Six Articles of 1539, the King's Book of 1543, and the Forty-Two Articles of 1553. The Thirty-Nine Articles were adopted by a united convocation of the English clergy and promulgated by Queen ELIZABETH in 1563.

In 1571 the original version of the Articles was ratified by the Convocation of Canterbury, with an acknowledgement that those loyal to Rome had seceded from the English Church; a later statute stipulated that ecclesiastical officials and members of the two universities who did not subscribe to the Articles should be deprived of their offices. The Articles remained in force from 1571 until 1865, when the subscription was replaced by an affirmation that the Articles were consistent with Scripture.

The Articles differ from their continental counterparts in not taking the form of a creed or the exposition of the Creed; Article 8 simply accepts the ancient creeds on the grounds that their tenets are biblical. Instead, the Thirty-Nine Articles consist of short statements of dogma, most of which attempt to articulate a distinctively Anglican position on contemporary theological controversies; doctrine is therefore formulated in relation to Catholic, Calvinist, and Anabaptist dogma rather than by means of precise theological definitions. Article 21, for example, repudiates the authority of general councils of the Church, and Article 28, which sets out the doctrine of the EUCHARIST, explicitly repudiates the Catholic and Zwinglian positions. The effect of this tendency to define positions by repudiating the views of other churches is exacerbated by the absence of precise definitions, and the result is deliberate theological ambiguity: Article 28, for example, accommodates both Lutheran and Calvinist interpretations of the eucharist, and the statement on predestination in Article 17 is markedly vague.

**ARTICLES OF WAR.** The military law that governs the discipline and conduct of serving soldiers and regulates institutions such as courts of inquiry and courts martial was not formulated until the late seventeenth century; in Denmark and Norway, for example, the first code was formulated in

1683, and in England the Mutiny Act of 1689 was the first legal instrument to set out a code of discipline for armies during peacetime. The only exception to the lack of any legislative control concerned desertion, which in England had been a felony since the late fifteenth century.

In the absence of codes of military law, the conduct of soldiers was regulated by Articles of War, which were usually promulgated for particular campaigns, because armies were often raised for a specific service, at the end of which they were disbanded; Articles of War were deemed to have lapsed on the cessation of hostilities. The first Articles of War were formulated in 1527 and issued in the name of FERDINAND I (then king of Bohemia, later emperor). These Articles, like their successors, forbade unauthorized plundering and asserted imperial ownership of ARTILLERY, ammunition, and military stores. Sixteenth-century Articles were very severe: the punishment for almost every offence was either amputation or death.

**ARTILLERY.** Mechanical devices for hurling objects at enemies have long been a feature of organized warfare. In the Old Testament, Uzziah is said to have constructed a device 'to shoot arrows and great stones', and the author of Maccabees describes a device that could 'cast fiery darts'. ARCHIMEDES is credited with having constructed many such devices for the defence of Syracuse (212 BC). Such weapons developed into the Roman catapult (*ballista*), and evolved slowly into the siege weapons of medieval Europe. The invention of GUNPOWDER, however, transformed artillery, and in the early fourteenth century the cannon was introduced into warfare. The first use of cannons may have been at the German siege of Cividale (Italy) in 1331, and it is certain that three cannons were fired by the English at Crécy in 1346, but it is not clear in either case that the cannons were intended to do anything more than make a frightening noise.

Cannons began to be used as weapons in the fifteenth century, and for decades their sole use was the battering of fortifications. It was not until the early sixteenth century that cannon became a reliable weapon rather than an impressive threat. Early cannons were huge. In the siege of Constantinople (1453), Sultan Mehmet II deployed a battery of cannons which included two huge mortars capable of hurling stones weighing 400 kilograms (880 pounds) against the walls of the city; one of these cannons was still in use in 1807, when a 300-kilogram (660-pound) stone struck a British warship. 'Mons Meg', which was installed in Edinburgh in 1460, weighed 4,000 kilograms (8,800 pounds) and could hurl a 150-kilogram (330-pound) stone more than a kilometre (half a mile); its contemporary the 'Dulle Griete', which was built in Ghent (where it remains), weighed 10,000 kilograms (22,000 pounds). Such cannons were utterly immobile, and could only be used from fixed positions. These early muzzle-loaded cannons used the technology of bell-founding, and so were cast in bronze. The next generation of cannons were forged from strips of wrought iron bound with hooped rings, a technology adapted from the cooper's art. The cast-iron cannon first appeared in the early sixteenth century.

Light artillery seems to have originated in Germany, where the *Wagenburg*, a cart fitted with several small cannons, was first deployed in the HUSSITE WARS (1420–36); such carts were used in the English Wars of the Roses (1455–85), and a few even survived into the seventeenth century, when their presence was attested in the THIRTY YEARS WAR (Wimpfen, 1622) and the English Civil War (Cropredy Bridge, 1644).

In the WARS OF ITALY of the sixteenth century, artillery played an important role in both siege and field warfare, because it had become much more mobile. In 1495 CHARLES VIII of France brought with his invading army siege guns that could be carried forward at the marching pace of his soldiers. These weapons were primarily used to batter the walls of cities that offered resistance, but were also on occasion used on the battlefield, notably at the battles of FORNOVO (1495), Ravenna (1512), MARIGNANO (1515), and PAVIA (1522). Cannon also played a prominent role in the Ottoman siege of MALTA (1565). The quality of artillery improved throughout the sixteenth century, particularly in France and Spain, and manufacturing specifications became standardized: in 1544 CHARLES V restricted the production of Spanish guns to seven standard models, the balls of which ranged from one kilogram (2 pounds) to 18 kilograms (40 pounds); in 1551, HENRI II of France followed suit, specifying six standard models. Cannons were sometimes named after birds of prey: the light cannon was called a falconet (Spanish *falconete*, French *fauconneau*), the musket is named after a sparrowhawk, and the small cannons known as sakers are named after the lanner falcon.

Cannons were mounted on the upper decks of ships as early as 1338, but they did not become significant naval weapons until the sixteenth century, when ports cut into the hulls enabled cannons to be positioned on the lower decks. The first naval engagement in which cannons were a decisive factor was the battle of LEPANTO in 1571. The Venetians had been very slow to adopt the use of cannon on ships because of their obvious potential for damaging the vessel. It is probable that the cause of the loss of HENRY VIII's favourite ship, *Mary Rose*, in 1545 was caused by gun ports being left open so that the vessel was swamped when it turned into rough seas.

**ARUNDEL, THOMAS HOWARD, EARL OF** (1586–1646), English art collector, the only son of Philip Howard, the first earl of Arundel, who was imprisoned because of his adherance to Catholicism shortly before his son's birth and remained in prison until his death in 1595. In 1604 the title was restored to Thomas Howard, who thus became the second earl of Arundel. After undertaking his first tour of the Continent (1609–10), Howard entered public life, serving as a privy counsellor (1616), as the president of the committee of peers considering the case of Francis BACON (1621), and as joint commissioner of the great seal (1621). He was imprisoned because of his opposition to the duke of Buckingham (1626–8). Howard commanded the army of Charles I against the Scots (1639) and later chaired the court that tried the earl of Strafford (1641). In 1642 he escorted Henrietta Maria into exile, and thereafter spent the rest of his life in Padua.

The earl of Arundel assembled one of England's greatest art collections at Arundel House (demolished 1678), on the Strand. The statuary, which included ancient and modern statues, busts, and marbles (described in SELDEN's *Marmora Arundeliana*, 1628), was in 1677 bequeathed by the duke of Norfolk (Thomas Howard's grandson) to Oxford University; the collection is now in the Ashmolean. In painting, Howard collected works by DÜRER and HOLBEIN, extended his patronage to Rubens and Van Dyck, and brought Wenzel Hollar to England.

DNB s.v. Howard, Thomas; M. F. S. Hervey, *The Life, Correspondence and Collections of Thomas Howard, Earl of Arundel* (1921); David Howarth, *Thomas Howard, Earl of Arundel* (1985).

**ASCHAM, ROGER** (1515–68), English humanist writer. Born in Yorkshire, Ascham was educated at Cambridge, where in 1538 he became college reader in Greek. In 1545 he published a treatise on archery, *Toxophilius*, a model for later treatises in dialogue form. He acted as tutor to both Princess ELIZABETH and the future EDWARD VI, and travelled on the Continent between 1550 and 1553. He served as Latin secretary for MARY I, and remained in favour during the reign of Elizabeth. His best-known work, *The Schoolmaster, or Plain and Perfect Way of Teaching Children the Latin Tongue*, was published posthumously, and was an important influence on SIDNEY's *Defence of Poetry*.

DNB; Lawrence V. Ryan, *Roger Ascham* (1963).

**ASIA.** For early Greek geographers, the term 'Asia' denoted the hinterland of Ionia; for the Romans, 'Asia' was the name of a province; from the fifth century AD, the term 'Asia Minor' emerged as a way of distinguishing the Hellenic western coast of what is now Turkey from the Roman province of Asia. These senses continued in learned use throughout the period of the Renaissance, and what would now be called Asia was then described as the Indies.

The European penetration of Asia famously began with the journeys of MARCO POLO and the Franciscan missionaries of the thirteenth century. The fifteenth-century Venetian traveller Niccolò de' CONTI explored South Asia as far east as Java, but he travelled as an individual rather than as a representative of his country. In Asia, as in AFRICA, European penetration with the objective of enhancing trade was largely the work of Portuguese mariners. Vasco da GAMA reached India in 1498 and ALBUQUERQUE captured Malacca, on the Malay peninsula, in 1511. In 1513 the first Portuguese ship reached Guangzhou (English exonym Canton) and in 1557 Portuguese traders were given the right to live in Macao. In 1543 the Portuguese reached Japan, and six years later Francis XAVIER arrived.

For most of the sixteenth century, the Portuguese were the only European nation active in Asia. The sole exception was the Philippines, which MAGELLAN reached on his voyage across the Pacific in 1521. In 1542 Spain sent an expedition to the Philippines, which was named in honour of Prince Philip (later PHILIP II), the son of the Emperor CHARLES V. The first Spanish settlement in the Philippines was established in 1564, and in 1571 a permanent settlement was established in the Bay of Manila. After a dispute over the Moluccas had been settled in Portugal's favour in 1529, Spanish and Portuguese interests in the region were quite separate, even in the South China Sea: the Portuguese imported spices from the Moluccas through the Indian Ocean route, and Spain imported silk and cinnamon from the Philippines on a ship that made an annual voyage from Acapulco (Mexico).

Peaceful coexistence between the European powers in Asia ended in the 1590s, when the EAST INDIA COMPANIES of England and the Netherlands began to trade in the region. In the early seventeenth century the Dutch supplanted the Portuguese as the most powerful European nation in Asia.

Donald Lach, *Asia in the Making of Europe* (3 vols. in 9 books, 1965–93).

**ASOLA, GIOVANNI MATTEO or Giammateo** (*c*.1532–1609), Italian composer. In 1577 he was appointed *maestro di cappella* at Treviso Cathedral, and a year later moved to Vicenzo Cathedral. A great admirer of PALESTRINA, he was a prolific composer of masses and other sacred pieces as well as some secular madrigals.

**ASPERTINI, AMICO** (*c*.1474/5–1552), Italian painter and sculptor, a native of Bologna. He was trained in the Ferrara studio of ERCOLE DE' ROBERTI and on returning to Bologna worked in 1506 as an assistant to Lorenzo COSTA (who had also been trained by Ercole) and FRANCIA when they were painting the frescoes in the Oratory of Santa Cecilia in the Church of San Giacomo Maggiore. Aspertini's surviving independent paintings include frescoes in the Church of San Frediano in Lucca. As a sculptor he contributed to the doorways (begun by JACOPO DELLA QUERCIA) of the Church of San Petronio in Bologna.

DBI; MDA.

**ASPETTI, TIZIANO** (1559–1606), Italian sculptor, born in Venice, where in 1577 he secured the patronage of Giovanni Grimani, patriarch of Aquilea. His work in Venice includes reliefs of *St Mark* and *St Theodore* for the new Rialto Bridge (1589–90) and a bronze statuette of *Mars* (1590s, Metropolitan Museum, New York). In 1604 he accompanied Bishop Antonio Grimani (great-nephew of Giovanni) to Florence, where he remained for the rest of his life. His only surviving Tuscan work is a bronze relief of *The Martyrdom of St Lawrence* (1604–6, Santa Trinita, Florence).

DBI; MDA.

**ASTON or Ashton, HUGH** (*c*.1485–1558), English composer, and master of the choristers at St Mary Newarke in Leicester from 1525 to 1548. He composed a 'Hornpipe' for the virginals as well as ecclesistical music such as the *Missa Te Deum* and the antiphon 'Te Deum laudamus'. These may have been the works he submitted for his B.Mus. at Oxford in 1510.

**ASTROLABE.** In the second century AD, Claudius PTOLEMY described an *astrolabion* (literally 'star-taker'), that is, an armillary sphere for making observations. In later times, the term 'astrolabe' normally denotes an instrument which includes a flat star map, that is a 'planispheric astrolabe'. In the Renaissance, the so-called 'mariner's astrolabe', a much simpler instrument, was used in NAVIGATION. The mathematics of the planispheric astrolabe was known to the astronomer Hipparchus (c.190–after 126 BC) and it seems likely that the instrument itself was invented in the fourth or fifth century AD, though our earliest unambiguous evidence for its use comes from Islamic sources. Western astrolabes are derived from Islamic models.

The main body of the instrument (the 'mater', literally 'mother') is a recessed disc into which are fitted fixed-coordinate plates and an openwork star map (the *rete*, literally 'net') that is free to turn about a central pin. The back of the instrument carries an alidade, usually with pinhole sights, and the limb is graduated so that one can 'take the height' of a star. The *rete* is then rotated until the star in question is shown at the correct altitude against the coordinate lines on the underlying plate, which sets the instrument to show the state of the sky. If one knows the position of the sun in the ecliptic (that is if one has the date in an adequate calendar), one can then find, say, the time, or how many hours remain before sunrise. There are many other uses of the instrument, ranging from astronomical and astrological calculations to sighting for SURVEYING. There are numerous Renaissance manuals on the structure and use of the astrolabe.

In the standard form of astrolabe, the plate of coordinate lines has to be chosen according to the geographical latitude at which the astronomical observations are made. In the Renaissance several designs were proposed for 'universal' astrolabes that did not require additional plates. The most successful designs were those of Juan de Rojas (1551) and GEMMA FRISIUS (1556), but both were rather awkward to construct, and neither superseded the standard astrolabe. By the later sixteenth century, the main astronomical use of astrolabes seems to have been in teaching.

**ASTROLOGY** was firmly based in standard Aristotelian physics and geocentric COSMOLOGY whereby the movements of the heavens could be transmitted to the earth. The strongest arguments for heavenly bodies affecting terrestrial ones were, first, that the position of the sun in the ecliptic manifestly caused the variations in weather associated with the seasons, and second, which was considered a little more doubtful, that the moon caused the tides. The effects of other heavenly bodies was taken to be weaker, except in special circumstances. It is extremely difficult to describe astrology in general terms because almost every astrologer who explained himself in print has a system that is simultaneously claimed to be age-old and importantly new and different from those of everyone else. Ancient astrology was available in the works of PTOLEMY.

The greatest use of astrology was in medical practice, where it was used for both diagnosis and prognosis, and to choose suitable moments for treatment. A rather similar use of it was made in ALCHEMICAL operations. The next most significant use was in weather forecasting: ALMANACS regularly foretell the weather, sometimes day by day, and declare whether there will be good harvests of corn and wine. These were very significant matters in countries whose economies were all basically agrarian. KEPLER published such astrological calendars, but was exceedingly sceptical about much of traditional astrology, as can be seen from his Latin tract on the subject (1601). The casting of horoscopes and the determination of auspicious or inauspicious hours ('judicial astrology') was generally considered the most doubtful or unreliable kind of astrology, but was frequently used with political intent. Martin LUTHER's horoscope convinced any number of Catholic astrologers that he was the ANTICHRIST and Protestants sometimes found the same significance in horoscopes of popes. After his death (1594) the horoscope of LASSUS (whose date of birth is unknown) was sometimes presented as that of the perfect musician. CARDANO's published horoscopes include one of Christ.

Contrary to popular belief in our own time, it was the Renaissance rather than the Middle Ages that saw the most widespread enthusiasm for what we should now call occult sciences, such as astrology. However, one of its most occult features turned out to be astrology's lasting contribution to modern science: the notion of force, that is, of action at a distance. Action at a distance was not admitted by Aristotle, for whom objects moved either because they were regaining their natural place (earth falling downwards to the centre, fire striving upwards to its sphere) or because they were pushed. Astrologers believed the moon moved the sea by influence, sympathy, or attraction, and that idea turned out to have some scientific mileage in it.

The Copernican system weakens the basis of standard astrology because it means there is no sphere of stars; instead, the stars of the constellations may not actually be associated, but simply seem close to one another because they are seen from the earth. One might thus expect the rise of Copernicanism to undermine belief in traditional astrology (as it did for Kepler), so the decline of belief in standard astrology among the educated classes in the later seventeenth century is perhaps explicable.

**ASTRONOMY.** Until 1582, the need for CALENDAR REFORM was a significant spur to astronomy. Astronomers' reactions to the publication of the Copernican theory (1543) were at first rather friendly (see RHETICUS, GEORG; REINHOLD, ERASMUS), but Reinhold's *Prutenic Tables* (1551) proved to be useful for no more than about fifteen years, after which time they seemed to be no better than their Ptolemaic predecessors. Tycho BRAHE reacted to this by setting about making a huge number of precise observations which he hoped would lead to better models of planetary motions and hence to better tables. COPERNICUS' work required modifications to conventional ideas about terrestrial physics, which in the longer term were supplied by GALILEO, but in the short one tended to have natural philosophers arguing about what would happen if the earth really were moving and (with hindsight) coming up with inadequate answers. Some astronomers, for instance MÄSTLIN, were sympathetic to Copernicanism, and during the sixteenth century there were a number of challenges to parts of standard Aristotelian physics (for example, see BENEDETTI, GIOVANNI BATTISTA), but the first astronomer to see the full sweep of the implications of Copernicanism was KEPLER. His first two Laws of Planetary Motion (1609), which unambiguously relate the planets to the sun, spoke strongly for Copernicanism (though HARRIOT seems to have been one of the few readers to make sense of Kepler's book at the time), and the long-term reliability of the *Rudolphine Tables* (1627), which were based on Tycho Brahe's observations and Kepler's first two laws, eventually persuaded the majority of astronomers that the planetary system was indeed heliocentric.

Several bright comets were proved (by Tycho Brahe and others) to pass through the regions where the planetary spheres should be (see COSMOLOGY). The two New Stars, of 1572 and 1604 (now known as Tycho's supernova and Kepler's supernova, though neither was the first to see the star in question), tended to weaken belief in the ancient notion that the heavens were unchanging, and Galileo's telescopic observations of the moon proved that it was far from the perfection asserted to be the property of every celestial body; observations of sunspots proved that even the sun showed imperfection and change. As can be seen in the work of both Kepler and Galileo, astronomy was clearing the path for a coming together of the traditionally distinct cultures of celestial and terrestrial physics.

**ATONEMENT**, the Christian doctrine of the process, ending in redemption, whereby Christians are reconciled to God through the propitiatory death of Christ; in early modern English, the term retained a strong sense of its origins in the compound 'at-one-ment'.

By the sixteenth century there were four rival theories of the atonement. According to the recapitulation theory, which was formulated by Justin Martyr, Jesus was the *recapitulator generis humani*, recapitulating in his person the entire human race and so achieving redemption for humankind. In the ransom theory, which was formulated by Origen and gained wide support amongst both Latin and Greek fathers, Jesus was the ransom paid to Satan, into whose hands humankind had been delivered by the Fall. In the satisfaction theory, which was formulated by Anselm in *Cur Deus homo?*, God the Father required 'satisfaction' (i.e. reparation) for the sin of humankind, and the death of Jesus satisfied the honour of God by repaying the debt incurred by sin.

Elements of these three theories survive in sixteenth-century theological debate, in that Jesus is variously described as the representative of humankind (the recapitulation theory), the substitute for humankind (the ransom theory), and the debt paid for mankind (the satisfaction theory). The reformers introduced a fourth theory, known as the penal theory: in LUTHER's formulation, Jesus bore the punishment due to humankind, diverting the wrath of God to himself; CALVIN was even more explicit, arguing that Jesus suffered the torture of a condemned man and so paid the penalty for human sin.

The only reformed groups that rejected the doctrine of the atonement were the UNITARIANS; the SOCINIANS, for example, denied the efficacy of the death of Jesus, arguing that its purpose was exemplary rather than expiatory. The doctrine of universal atonement, also known as Huberism, was championed by Samuel HUBER.

**ATTAIGNANT, PIERRE** (*c*.1494–1551/2), French music printer, probably born in Douai. He established a workshop in Paris, where he developed typefaces for music; in 1537 he was appointed printer of the king's music. In his *Chansons nouvelles en musique* (1527) and *Chansons de Maître Clément Janequin* (*c*.1528) he uses characters consisting of a short segment of staff lines to which diamond-shaped notes with stems are attached. This system of single-impression printing obviated the need to print music and staff lines separately. The consequent reduction in costs enabled Attaignant to create a European network for his publications, which in turn disseminated the French chanson all over Europe.

**ATTENDOLO, MICHELETTO, or Michelettus Cotineolanus or Micheletto Sforzesco** (*c*.1390–1451), *condottiere*, born into a Romagnol military family. He established his reputation in the armies of the kingdom of NAPLES and in the PAPAL STATE before entering the service of Florence, on whose behalf he won the battle of ANGHIARI and so conquered the Casentino region (the upper valley of the Arno). He subsequently worked for the Venetians, whose army he commanded in the victory at Cassalmaggiore in 1446 over the Milanese army led by PICCININO.

*DBI*.

**AUBIGNÉ, THEODORE AGRIPPA D'.** See D'AUBIGNÉ, THEODORE AGRIPPA.

**AUGSBURG or (Latin) Augusta Vindelicorum**, a south German city which became an episcopal see in 759, an imperial free city in 1276, and a member of the SWABIAN LEAGUE in 1331. By the fifteenth century, Augsburg's location on the principal trade route between the Mediterranean and northern Europe, together with its proximity to important SILVER mines, had enabled it to develop into an important centre of trade, BANKING, and commerce. Two of Europe's most important banking families, the FUGGERS and the WELSERS, operated from Augsburg, and lent substantial sums to princely families such as the HABSBURGS. At the Reformation the banking families remained loyal to Rome, but many citizens welcomed the reformers, who included Lutherans, Zwinglians, and ANABAPTISTS. In 1537, by which time reformers controlled the city, images were forbidden in the churches. In 1547, the victory of CHARLES V over the SCHMALKALDIC LEAGUE reversed the balance of ecclesiastical power, and Catholic clergy were welcomed back to the city. The Religious Peace of AUGSBURG (1555) gave Catholics and Lutherans equal rights to freedom of worship; Calvinists did not receive the same right until 1648.

Augsburg was one of the earliest centres of HUMANIST culture north of the Alps. Augsburg artists included the HOLBEIN FAMILY and Hans BURGKMAIR, and the city was an important centre for printing. Early modern architecture includes the Gothic Church of SS Ulrich and Afra (1474–1604) and the Town Hall (1615–20) in the Renaissance style. In 1519 construction began on the Fuggerei, Europe's first purpose-built settlement for the poor; it consists of six short streets on which are placed 106 small houses built by the Fugger brothers and let to indigent Catholic families for nominal rents.

W. Zorn, *Augsburg: Geschichte einer Stadt* (1955).

**AUGSBURG, RELIGIOUS PEACE OF, or (German) Augsburger Religionsfrieden**, the treaty that concluded the religious wars of Germany, signed on 25 September 1555. The treaty was the agreement which concluded the Diet of Augsburg (February–September 1555). Because the Emperor CHARLES V was abdicating, the Empire was represented by his brother FERDINAND I; the Protestant side was represented by the electors assembled at Augsburg.

The settlement recognized the legitimacy of both Catholicism and Lutheranism in Germany, but did not recognize Calvinism; the Lutheran faith was prescribed in terms of the AUGSBURG CONFESSION of 1530 and any subsequent recensions. There were four main provisions in the treaty, of which three were agreed: first, that the religion of each state should be decided by its ruler (a principle later known as *cujus regio eius religio*) and that those who would not subscribe to the ruler's religion would be free, after selling their property, to emigrate; second, that in free cities and imperial cities, both religions, if already established, would be allowed to continue; third, that Lutheran towns in Catholic ecclesiastical states could continue in their Lutheranism. The contested fourth provision was that all ecclesiastical land secularized by the Lutherans before the Treaty of Passau in 1552 should be confirmed to them, but that in future the principle of ecclesiastical reservation was to apply, which meant that any cleric converting to Lutheranism could not take his lands and revenues with him; Ferdinand insisted that this provision had been agreed, but the Lutherans refused to accept it.

The Religious Peace of Augsburg is sometimes seen as a victory for religious toleration, but it might more properly be construed as a victory for territorialism; it marked the defeat of imperial attempts to unite Germany as a state with one religion, and accelerated the disintegration of the Empire into hundreds of petty states. The Peace of Augsburg nonetheless remained the foundation of the religious settlement within the Empire until the Treaty of Westphalia concluded the THIRTY YEARS WAR in 1648.

**AUGSBURG CONFESSION or (German) Augsburgische Konfession**, the principal Lutheran confession of faith, drafted by MELANCHTHON, approved by LUTHER, and presented to the Emperor CHARLES V at Augsburg on 25 June 1530. On receiving the Confession, the emperor passed it to a group of Catholic theologians (including Johann COCHLÄUS, Johann ECK, Johann FABER, and Konrad WIMPINA), whose formal reply, the 'Confutatio pontifica', was read on 3 August. Melanchthon responded to the 'Confutatio' with 'An Apology for the Confession' which the emperor declined to receive.

The Confession consists of a preface and two parts. Part I is a statement, in 21 articles, of the theology of Lutheranism. The tone of this part is conciliatory, eschewing any anti-Catholic language and, on the fundamental issue of SOTERIOLOGY (Article 20), setting out the Lutheran position on faith and works with elaborate precision. Part II is a review of ecclesiastical abuses for which remedy is demanded, and the contentious list of such abuses includes communion in one kind (see EUCHARIST), clerical celibacy, private masses, and compulsory confession.

The Confession was published (in a slightly altered text) in the spring of 1531; successive editions contained more alterations on points of doctrine. In 1540 Melanchthon published a revised text known as the 'Variata', and this text is still in use in many Reformed (i.e. Calvinist rather than Lutheran) churches in Germany. In 1580, the compilers of the Book of CONCORD decided to revert to the text presented to the imperial Diet in 1530; in the event, the Concord text, which is known as the 'Invariata', contains some 450 minor differences from the 1530 text. The Invariata is still the standard confession of faith in the Lutheran churches of Germany. Differences between the two texts on the subject of the eucharist led to the failure of the NAUMBURG CONVENTION in 1561.

**AUGSBURG INTERIM.** In February 1548 the Emperor CHARLES V appointed a commission to negotiate a settlement between Protestants and Catholics. When the group failed to agree on the text of a settlement, the emperor commissioned Johann AGRICOLA, Bishop Julius von PFLUG, and Michael Helding (suffragan bishop of Mainz) to draft a doctrinal formula which might win the assent of both parties. The 26 articles of this statement of faith were shown in confidence to both sides and then accepted as the basis of an interim settlement by the Diet of Augsburg on 30 June 1548; it was regarded as a temporary settlement in the expectation that the COUNCIL OF TRENT would negotiate a permanent settlement. The principal concessions yielded to the Protestants were tolerance of a married clergy and of communion in both kinds, i.e. a celebration of the EUCHARIST in which the laity were given consecrated wine as well as bread.

In Catholic south Germany the Interim was firmly imposed, but in the Protestant areas of the north in which the Augsburg Interim failed to win assent, the Elector MAURICE OF SAXONY proposed a more Protestant formulation called the LEIPZIG INTERIM, which was accepted in December 1548.

**AUGUSTA, CRISTÓBAL DE** (*fl.* 1569–84), Spanish potter, born in Estella (Navarre). He moved to Seville, where in 1569 he married the daughter of a potter who manufactured MAIOLICA tiles. From 1577 to 1584 he supplied tiles for the public rooms in the Alcázar. His best-known work is *The Virgin of the Rosary* (1577), a large panel (156 tiles) now in the Museo de Bellas Artes in Seville.

**AUGUSTINE IN THE RENAISSANCE.** Augustine of Hippo (354–430), Latin church father, was born in Numidia, a Roman province in what is now eastern Algeria, and in 390 or

391 became bishop of Hippo (now Arabic Annaba, French Bône, on the coast of Algeria).

The chief conduit through which Augustinian theology was reworked into Reformation theology was Martin LUTHER, who was conversant with at least 25 of Augustine's works; Luther's theology of GRACE owes a direct and substantial debt to Augustine. The influence of Augustine can be discerned to a lesser extent in the reformers of Geneva: Augustine's soteriology was explicitly predestinarian, and his belief that only the inscrutable wisdom of God could account for the apparently arbitrary division between the elect and the damned strongly influenced CALVIN and his successors. Alongside this reformed tradition, Catholic theologians continued to utilize the thought of Augustine: his contention that babies who die unbaptized are condemned eternally to the flames of hell had been developed by THOMAS AQUINAS and his successors, and was stoutly maintained by Counter-Reformation theologians. Augustine's familiarity with classical rhetoric and Platonism created another link with the Renaissance, because his contention that the virtuous elements in classical culture should enrich Christian thought was taken up by Renaissance humanists such as FICINO.

There were three important early collected editions of Augustine's works: the first was published by Johannes AMERBACH (9 vols., Basel, 1506), the second by ERASMUS (10 vols., Basel, 1528–9), and the third was a collaborative edition known as the *Theologi Lovaniensis* (11 vols., Antwerp, 1577).

P. O. Kristeller, 'St Augustine and the Early Renaissance', in *Studies in Renaissance Thought and Letters* (1956, 1969); Charle, Béné, *Érasme et saint Augustin* (1969); F. Tateo, 'S. Agostino e l'umanesimo italiano', in M. Fabbris (ed.), *L'umanesimo di S. Agostino* (1988); H. A. Oberman and F. A. James (eds.), *Via Augustini: Augustine in the Later Middle Ages, Renaissance and Reformation* (1991).

**AUGUSTUS I** (1526–86), elector of Saxony, was born in Freiberg on 31 July 1526, the younger son of Heinrich, duke of Saxony, a member of the Albertine branch of the WETTIN family. Augustus was raised as a Lutheran and educated at the University of Leipzig. In 1541 the dukedom passed to his elder brother MAURICE OF SAXONY, and Augustus became Maurice's representative at the imperial court of FERDINAND I in Vienna. In 1544 he served briefly as administrator of the bishopric of Merseburg, but his extravagance soon led to his return to the Saxon court at Dresden, where he supported his brother in the SCHMALKALDIC WAR and in his wresting of the Saxon electorate from JOHANN FRIEDRICH I (head of the Ernestine branch of the Wettin family; see Appendix 1).

On 7 October 1548 Augustus married Anna, daughter of CHRISTIAN III of Denmark, and took up residence in Weissenfels. In July 1553 Augustus was visiting Denmark when he learnt that his brother had died and that he had succeeded him as elector of Saxony. He secured recognition of his legitimacy as elector from Johann Friedrich in the Naumburg Treaty of February 1554, but his fear of an Ernestine coup long remained an important influence on his domestic and foreign policies. In 1567 Matthias FLACIUS ILLYRICUS supported the Ernestine cause by preaching against

Augustus, and Johann Friedrich's champion Wilhelm von GRUMBACH led a rebellion, for which he was tortured and executed.

Augustus maintained close relations with the Habsburg family, but also sought religious reconciliation, contributing to the Religious Peace of AUGSBURG in 1555 and to the Diet of Augsburg in 1566. His relations with the Habsburgs were strained by the marriage of his daughter Elizabeth to JOHANN CASIMIR (son of the elector palatine FRIEDRICH III), because it was feared that he would support his son-in-law in the REVOLT OF THE NETHERLANDS, but they quickly became estranged. His attempts to unite Protestants in a peaceful relationship with their Catholic opponents also led him into negotiations with the HUGUENOTS.

The religious culture of ducal Saxony differed from that of electoral Saxony, in that the former advocated uncompromising Lutheranism and the latter subscribed to the teaching of MELANCHTHON, which came to be called GNESIO-LUTHERANISM. Augustus was suspicious of what he saw as the crypto-Calvinism of the Gnesio-Lutherans, and when in 1574 his agents discovered letters that criticized Augustus and his electress and expressed the hope that Augustus could be won over to Calvinism, he ordered the arrest, torture, and imprisonment of the Gnesio-Lutheran leaders and declared strict Lutheranism to be binding on all of Saxony.

Augustus was a brutal ruler, but he was nonetheless a conscientious ruler of Saxony, improving the roads, instituting a postal system, regulating the coinage, erecting new buildings in Dresden (where he founded an important library), and improving agriculture; his interest in agriculture led him to write a book on the subject, *Künstlich Obst und Gartenbüchlein*. He was also the author of the Saxon constitution of 1572, which regulated the Church, the universities, the administration of justice, and the raising of taxes. He died in Dresden on 21 January 1586.

*NDB* s.v. August I; *MDA* s.v. Wettin (5).

**AULIC COUNCIL or (German) Reichshofrat**, the executive and juridical council of the HOLY ROMAN EMPIRE, founded by the Emperor MAXIMILIAN I in 1498 and dissolved (together with the Empire) in 1806. For the first century of its existence, the Aulic Council exercised the judicial powers of the emperor with reference to imperial fiefdoms, criminal charges against the immediate vassals of the Empire, and a few special cases reserved to the emperor. In other judicial matters it was in competition with the REICHSKAMMERGERICHT, which had been established under Maximilian I at the great reform Diet of Worms in 1495 as the permanent high court of the Empire. In 1648 the Treaty of Westphalia regulated the competition between the two courts by stipulating that only the court which had first dealt with a case should have the competence to pursue it.

**AURICULAR STYLE or Lobate Style or (Dutch) *Kwab-ornament* or *Ohrmuschel* or (German) *Knorpelwerk***, an early seventeenth-century Dutch silverwork style characterized by curving forms that resemble a human ear (hence its name)

or a sea-shell. Its originator was Paulus van VIANEN, who was using it by 1607, and by 1614 it was in use by his elder brother Adam and Adam's son Christiaen.

**AURISPA, GIOVANNI** (1376–1459), Sicilian humanist, Hellenist, and collector of manuscripts. Aurispa studied in Naples before undertaking two protracted visits to the Byzantine East (1405–13, 1421–3). On his first visit he worked in Constantinople and the Byzantine provinces as a commercial agent, but also studied Greek with John Chrysoloras (nephew of Manuel CHRYSOLORAS). From 1414 to 1419 he taught at Savona (Liguria), after which he entered the service of Pope MARTIN V. When he returned to Constantinople in 1421, he travelled as the ambassador of the GONZAGA family. On his return to Italy Aurispa taught Greek at Bologna and then Florence, where he held the chair of Greek from 1425 to 1427. In 1427 he settled permanently in Ferrara, where he taught Greek privately and on occasion acted in a diplomatic capacity for the ESTE family. In 1438 he was appointed a papal secretary.

Aurispa assembled a collection of some 300 Greek manuscripts during his sojourns in the East, and the hoard that he brought to Italy included important manuscripts of HOMER, Aeschylus, Sophocles, PLATO, Apollonius of Rhodes, the *Homeric Hymns*, and the *Greek Anthology*.

DBI; A. Franceschini, *Giovanni Ausispa e la sua biblioteca* (1976).

**AUSTRIA or (German) Österreich.** The modern state of Austria is one of the successor states of the Austrian Empire and Austria-Hungary. In the early modern period, the term 'Austria' is used to designate the ever-expanding lands of the HABSBURG dynasty, whose acquisitions raised Austria from a small duchy to a major European power. The duchy of Austria was created by the Emperor Friedrich I in 1156, and consisted initially of VIENNA and some countryside along the Danube. In 1276 the duchy of Austria passed into the hands of the Habsburgs, but because the family had not established the rule of primogeniture, the following centuries saw a succession of partitions as well as new acquisitions, including Carinthia (1335), Tirol (1363), Carniola (1364), Istria (1374), and Trieste (1382).

In 1438 Albrecht V of Austria became king of the Romans (i.e. emperor-elect) as Albrecht II, and thereafter the Habsburg rulers of Austria were also the ruling dynasty of the HOLY ROMAN EMPIRE. On the death of Albrecht's father-in-law SIGISMUND, king of Bohemia and Hungary, he assumed both crowns. After his death in 1439, the duchy of Austria and the kingdoms of Bohemia and Hungary passed to his posthumous infant son LADISLAS V POSTHUMUS, and thenceforth the history of Austria was intertwined with that of Hungary and Bohemia. FRIEDRICH III, who ruled the Empire for more than half a century (1440–93), ruled Austria (which he raised to an archduchy in 1453) as Friedrich V, and in the course of his long reign consolidated the Habsburg possessions of Austria, Carniola, Carinthia, Styria, and Tirol under a central government; this process of centralization was continued by his successor MAXIMILIAN I (1493–1519). Maximilian's grandson

CHARLES V became king of the Romans in 1519, and promptly resigned his Austrian possessions, including his claims to the thrones of Bohemia and Hungary, to his brother Ferdinand (later the Emperor FERDINAND I), who consolidated these realms (which included MORAVIA, SLOVAKIA, and SILESIA) under his personal rule and so created the huge central European empire that was to survive until 1918.

In the early sixteenth century Austria faced the external threat of the Ottomans, who twice reached the gates of Vienna (1529 and 1532), and the internal threat of the Reformation, which began with the PEASANTS' REVOLT of 1525, after which ANABAPTISTS became active and Lutheranism spread through the ranks of the nobility. For many years Ferdinand refrained from suppressing the Reformation, but he eventually attempted to stem the spread of Protestantism by admitting the JESUITS to Austria with a view to reconverting Protestants to Catholicism.

Ferdinand's successes in consolidating his empire were reversed by his decision to divide his patrimony amongst his three sons: Maximilian (later MAXIMILIAN II) inherited the duchy of Austria, Archduke Ferdinand inherited Tirol, and Archduke Charles inherited Carniola. In 1576 Maximilian was succeeded by RUDOLF II, a committed Spanish Catholic who intensified attempts to extirpate the Protestant heresy. The Austrian dominions began to drift apart, and in 1606 the archdukes agreed to acknowledge MATTHIAS as head of the Habsburg family in Austria. Matthias became emperor in 1612, but religious and ethnic conflicts continued to destabilize the Empire, and by the time he died in 1619 unrest in Bohemia had erupted into the THIRTY YEARS WAR.

Paula Sutter Fichtner, *Ferdinand I of Austria: The Politics of Dynasticism in the Age of the Reformation* (Boulder, Colo., 1982).

**AUTO-DA-FÉ** (plural *autos-da-fé*), the Portuguese term, literally 'act of faith', for the public ceremonies attending the proclamation of sentences at the conclusion of INQUISITION trials. The Portuguese spelling is also used in French and English; the cognate term in Spanish is *auto de fe*. The first *auto-da-fé* was held in 1481; the last was in Mexico in 1850.

*Autos-da-fé* took place on royal or national anniversaries, but not on ecclesiastical feast days. The ceremony began with a procession in which members of the HOLY OFFICE, together with those who had been tried, were presented to the king and his court. A solemn mass was followed by an oath of allegiance to the Inquisition, a sermon by the grand inquisitor and the reading of the verdicts and sentences delivered by the Holy Office. Condemned heretics were dressed in a ceremonial *sanbenito* (a black penitential garment, embroidered, in the case of impenitent heretics, with flames and demons) with a yellow mitre and handed over to the secular authorities for the imposition and execution of sentences, which usually took the form of burning at the stake.

**AUTOMATA.** An automaton is a machine with a source of movement contained within its own mechanism; in this broad sense it came to be used to describe clocks and watches, but in earlier usage it referred to devices such as mechanical animals (including singing birds), water-organs, water-trumpets and fire-engines that sprayed water at those who accidentally triggered them. In Renaissance Europe automata were used primarily in gardens; water-powered automata in gardens could include GIOCHI D'ACQUA but also included more serious displays. The designs derived both from medieval Arabic technology and from the ancient school of Alexandria. The pneumatic inventions of Ctesibius, an Alexandrian of the third century BC, including a pump with plunger and valve and a water-organ, were described in treatises by Philon of Byzantium, HERON, and VITRUVIUS. Philon's treatise on technology, written in the late third century BC, included a treatise on pneumatic devices operated by air and fluids (book 5) which was transmitted to the Renaissance through Arabic, and another on automata-making (book 6) which is mentioned by Heron but now lost. Automata are also described in the *Hypnerotomachia Polifili* of Francesco COLONNA (1499).

Automata first appear in the gardens of Italy, such as Villa d'ESTE (Tivoli) and Villa LANTE. The hydraulic effects at Villa d'Este were imitated in gardens at PRATOLINO, HELLBRUNN (Austria), and, in England, Wilton and Enstone (a lost garden in Oxfordshire). The English diarist John Evelyn describes his visit in 1645 to the Villa ALDOBRANDINI, where he saw singing birds (constructed c.1600) 'moving and chirping by the force of water'; he also describes devices that spray unwary spectators and 'a copper ball that dances about three foot above the pavement, by virtue of a wind conveyed secretly to a hole beneath it'. Similarly, Descartes, proposing in his early mechanistic *Traité de l'homme* (1629) an analogy between humans and automata, describes the automata at SAINT-GERMAIN-EN-LAYE, noting that water pressure is used to play musical instruments

Alfred Chapuis and Edmond Droz, *Les Automates* (1949), trans. Alec Reid as *Automata: A Historical and Technological Study* (1958); Claudia Lazzaro, *The Italian Renaissance Garden* (1990).

## AUTO SACRAMENTAL

*AUTO SACRAMENTAL* (plural *autos sacramentales*), a Spanish one-act play performed on carts (*carros*) in towns and villages at the Feast of Corpus Christi. The *auto* originated as a dramatic presentation of the eucharist, and although it soon developed elements of farce, even the most robustly comic *autos* end with the discovery of a large host and chalice. The finest writers of *autos* were Lucas FERNÁNDEZ (especially his *Auto de la Pasión*, c.1500), Fernando LÓPEZ DE YANGUAS (whose *Farsa sacramental*, 1520, was the first *auto* to use the eucharist as its central theme), Gil VICENTE (in whose *Auto de la Fe* a personified Faith explains the incarnation to shepherds), Lope de VEGA (*Las aventuras del hombre*), and TIRSO DE MOLINA (*El colmenero divino*). The greatest exponent of the form was Calderón, who in 1649 secured the monopoly for writing *autos* for Madrid; his twelve *autos* were published in 1677. *Autos* continued to be performed in the eighteenth century, but were banned in June 1765; performances nonetheless continued in remote villages, and in 1840 the last known performance of an *auto* before the twentieth century was staged in Valencia.

## AVALOS, FERDINANDO FRANCESCO D'

**AVALOS, FERDINANDO FRANCESCO D'** (1489–1525), marquis of Pescara, born in Naples into a family of Spanish descent. He entered the service of Spain, and in 1512 was captured in the battle of Ravenna (where he had commanded light cavalry), but was allowed to ransom himself for 6,000 ducats. He commanded Spanish troops in the battle of Vicenza or La Morta (7 October 1513), the battle of BICOCCA (1522), and the assault on Genoa (1522). Until 1522 Ferdinando fought alongside Prospero COLONNA, but after the battle of Bicocca, CHARLES V appointed Prosper as commander-in-chief; Ferdinando travelled to Valladolid to protest, but Charles persuaded him to submit to the authority of Prosper. In these meetings Charles had been impressed with Ferdinando, so when Charles invaded Italy in 1524 (see WARS OF ITALY), he appointed Ferdinando as his lieutenant. Ferdinando successfully besieged Pavia and on 24 February 1525 led the imperial army of Charles V to an overwhelming victory at the battle of PAVIA, where he took FRANCIS I prisoner. Giovanni MORONE offered him the throne of Naples if he would support the anti-imperial conspiracy, but Ferdinando revealed the plot to Charles V, arrested Morone, and occupied Milan.

Ferdinando had been married since 1509 to the poet Vittoria COLONNA, to whom he had been betrothed since the age of 6. His early death from consumption on 3 December 1525 prompted the first hundred sonnets of her *Rime*, which by her account she wrote to assuage the pain of bereavement. Paolo GIOVIO wrote a biography of Ferdinando which was published in *Vitae illustrium virorum* (Basel, 1578) and subsequently translated into Italian (Florence, 1551) and Spanish (Antwerp, 1553).

*DBI.*

## AVALOS DEL VASTO, ALFONSO D'

**AVALOS DEL VASTO, ALFONSO D'** (1502–46), marquis of Pescara, soldier, and occasional poet, born on 25 March 1502. He became a distinguished imperial soldier, serving in Provence in 1524 and fighting at the battle of PAVIA in 1525. He was captured by Andrea DORIA during the siege of Naples (1528). On his release he fought against Florence, and in July 1535 commanded the troops of Charles V at the battle of TUNIS. He returned to Provence in 1536 and was appointed imperial governor of Milan in 1538. He died in Vigevano on 31 March 1546.

*DBI.*

## AVELLI, FRANCESCO XANTO

**AVELLI, FRANCESCO XANTO** (1486/7–1542), Italian MAIOLICA painter who worked in Urbino, where he made plates in the ISTORIATO style, usually signing his work 'FLR' or 'FR'. His designs were usually adapted from prints by well-known artists (particularly RAPHAEL) and his favoured subjects were mythological scenes and contemporary events.

*DBI; MDA.*

## AVENTINUS, JOHANNES

**AVENTINUS, JOHANNES** (1477–1534), the Latin name of the German historian Johann Turmair, who was born in Abensberg (Latin Aventium) on 4 July 1477. He studied at Ingolstadt, Vienna, Kraków, and Paris, and in 1507 returned to Ingolstadt, where two years later he became tutor to the sons of the late Albrecht IV, duke of Bavaria. He retained this post until 1517, during which time he wrote a Latin grammar and travelled to Italy. From 1517 to 1521 he wrote *Annales Boiorum*, the Latin version of his history of BAVARIA, which he thereafter translated into German as the *Bayersche Chronik*. The seven books of the *Annales* record the history of Bavaria from its remote beginnings to 1460; it was first published in an expurgated version (stripped of its criticism of the Catholic Church) in 1554, and a complete text was published in Basel in 1560.

Aventinus was a reforming Catholic, but his sympathies for the Protestant movement that he never joined led to his temporary imprisonment in 1528. He died in Regensburg on 9 January 1534.

NDB; G. Strauss, *Historian in an Age of Crisis: The Life and Work of Johannes Aventinus, 1477–1534* (1963).

**AVENTURINE**, a brown GLASS with golden specks, manufactured in antiquity and rediscovered in the sixteenth century by the glassmakers of the Venetian island of Murano; the name (Italian *avventurino*) implies that its rediscovery was accidental. Aventurine was made by the admixture of copper crystals to molten glass, and was used both for glassware and as a porcelain glaze. Since the nineteenth century the term 'aventurine' has also been used in a transferred sense to denote a variety of quartz in which the golden specks are pieces of mica.

**AVERROËS IN THE RENAISSANCE**. The Cordoban Islamic philosopher Abul-Wahid ibn Rushd (1126–98), who was known in Europe as Averroës, was the author of commentaries on ARISTOTLE; his works were read in Europe in Latin and Hebrew translations. The contention of Averroës that theologians cannot achieve the highest level of demonstrative knowledge and are thus unable to interpret the divine will correctly excited the animosity of THOMAS AQUINAS, who attacked Averroës in *Summa contra gentiles* and *De unitate intellectus contra Averroistas*. In 1277 Averroism was formally anathematized and French philosophers who were thought to be tainted with Averroism were excommunicated by the bishop of Paris.

Averroism was extirpated from northern Europe in the early fourteenth century, but it was revived later in the century by John of Jandun and enjoyed a protracted afterlife in Italian universities, especially Padua, as late as the seventeenth century. The Paduan philosophers Agostino NIFO and Giacomo ZABARELLA were distinguished latter-day Averroists.

**AVIGNON**. In 1309 Pope Clement V established his residence in Avignon, which remained the seat of popes until 1377 and antipopes until 1408; the period from 1309 to 1377 was known by residents such as PETRARCH as the Babylonian Captivity. In 1348 the city and its Provençal territories were bought by Pope Clement VI from Queen GIOVANNA I of Naples (who was countess of Provence), and after the papacy was restored to Rome, Avignon was governed by papal legates until 1791, when it was absorbed into France. The town is still surrounded by the walls built by the fourteenth-century popes, and they constitute one of Europe's finest surviving examples of late medieval fortification.

SIMONE MARTINI was the first of a series of Sienese artists to work in Avignon, and the Papal Palace is decorated with frescoes in the Sienese style. After the departure of the papacy French painters such as Nicolas FROMENT and Enguerrand QUARTON worked in the city. The finest product of Avignon art is the *Pietà* of Villeneuve-lès-Avignon (*c*.1460, Louvre).

H. Labande, *Les Palais des Papes et les monuments d'Avignon au XIVᵉ siècle* (2 vols., 1925); G. Mollat, *The Popes at Avignon* (English trans., 1963); B. Guillemain, *La Cour pontificale d'Avignon, 1309–1376* (1964).

**ÁVILA, PEDRO ARIAS DE** See DÁVILA, PEDRARIAS.

**AYALA, BALTHAZAR** (1548–84), jurist of the Spanish Netherlands. His treatise on the law of war (*De jure et officiis bellicis et disciplina militari*, 1582) was an important contribution to the development of INTERNATIONAL LAW. He served as auditor (i.e. judge) of the Spanish forces in the Netherlands, and later became a member of the Great Council and was appointed master of requests.

BNB.

**AYLLÓN, LUCAS VÁZQUEZ DE** (*c*.1473–1526), Spanish colonizer, probably a native of Toledo. In 1502 he accompanied Nicolás de OVANDO to Hispaniola, where he became a colonial administrator, a judge, and a businessman. In 1521 he sent Francisco Gordillo to explore the coast of Florida, and on the basis of his report applied in 1523 for a charter from the Emperor CHARLES V that would enable Ayllón to plant colonies along the Atlantic coast of North America. The charter was granted, and after commissioning a second reconnoitring expedition, Ayllón set sail early in 1526 with 500 colonists and about 100 African slaves. He established a colony called San Miguel de Gualdape at latitude 33 degrees 40 minutes; the remains of the colony have not been found, so its exact location is unknown, but it may have been in or near what is now Jamestown (Virginia) or at the mouth of the Pee Dee river. This colony was the first place in what is now the United States to use African slave labour.

Many of the colonists died of fever, including Ayllón, who died on 18 October 1526. After his death there was civil unrest and many of the slaves escaped into the forest. In December 1526 the colony was abandoned and the remnant of colonists and slaves left for Hispaniola.

**AYRER, JAKOB** (1544–1605), German dramatist, who lived from 1570 to 1593 in Bamberg (where he wrote a rhymed *Chronik der Stadt Bamberg*) and then returned to his native Nuremberg (German Nürnberg), where he became an imperial notary and a public prosecutor (*Stadtprokurator*). Between 1592 and 1602 he wrote 106 plays, of which 69 survive; 66 of these plays were printed in Ayrer's posthumous *Opus theatricum* (Nuremberg, 1618), which consists of 36 FASTHACHTSPIELE and 30 tragedies and comedies; this was the first collection of German plays to include a significant number of stage directions. Ayrer's plays are all written in KNITTELVERSE.

Ayrer was the inheritor of Hans SACHS, but also drew freely on foreign traditions such as the Italian NOVELLA and the ENGLISCHE KOMÖDIANTEN (from whom he borrowed the character of the clown). Two of his comedies have Shakespearian analogues: his *Comedia von der schönen Phaenica* seems to share a common source with *Much Ado About Nothing*, and the action of his *Comedia von der schönen Sidea* resembles the courtship of Ferdinand and Miranda in *The Tempest*, with which it seems to share a source.

DLL; NDB.

**AZORES or (Portuguese) Açores**, a Portuguese island group in the Atlantic Ocean. There are no written records alluding to the Azores in the ancient world, but the discovery of Carthaginian coins implies that at some point the uninhabited islands had been visited. Arab geographers of the twelfth and fourteenth centuries allude to a group of islands beyond the Canaries which seem to be the Azores. The European discoverers of the islands are unknown, but the Azores appear clearly on maps of 1351 and 1375.

This evidence of European discovery undercuts the traditional claim that the islands were discovered in 1427 by the Portuguese mariner Diogo de Silves. His rediscovery of the islands did, however, excite the interest of the Portuguese court, and the navigator Gonzalo Velho Cabral was dispatched to establish a Portuguese presence. Beginning with Santa Maria in 1432, Cabral and his successors colonized the known islands and discovered new ones, and by 1457 all of the islands in the group had been discovered.

In 1466 the island of Faial was presented by King AFONSO V to his aunt Isabella, duchess of Burgundy. Thereafter Faial was colonized by Flemings, who soon settled on other islands in the group, and in some early modern maps the islands are described as the Flemish Isles.

From 1580 to 1640 the islands, together with mainland Portugal, were annexed to Spain, and during this period two important naval battles took place in the Azores. In 1583 the fleet of the Portuguese pretender, which was supported by English and French privateers, was defeated off Terceira by Álvaro de Bazán, marquis of SANTA CRUZ. On 31 August 1591 the English ship *Revenge*, which was commanded by Sir Richard Grenville, famously engaged a Spanish fleet of 53 ships off Flores after the main English fleet had escaped.

C. M. Bento, *History of the Azores* (1994); J. M. dos Santos, *Os Açores nos séculos XV e XVI* (2 vols., 1989).

**AZULEJO**, the Spanish and Portuguese name (from Arabic *al-zulayj*, 'the tile') for a glazed polychrome TILE used in Moorish architecture for exterior and interior walls and for floors. The tiles were typically about 15 centimetres (6 inches) square and brightly coloured, sometimes with geometrical patterns. The reflective surface of *azulejos* caught the sun, and in SPANISH GARDENS and PORTUGUESE GARDENS they were used to reflect water. After the RECONQUISTA the manufacturing of *azulejos* continued, often in MUDÉJAR designs.

The iconoclasm of Sunni Islam meant that designs were geometrical rather than representational, and until the end of the fifteenth century each tile had a self-contained geometrical design which was repeated in adjoining tiles. In about 1498 Francisco NICULOSO of Pisa began to manufacture tiles in Seville, and he introduced the idea of a single pictorial design made up of panels of *azulejos*. Geometrical designs continued to dominate in *azulejos*, but in TALAVERA DE LA REINA pictorial design was favoured, and Talavera tiles were exported to the Spanish and Portuguese empires around the world. The styles of Spanish and Portuguese tiles could not be readily distinguished in the fifteenth and sixteenth centuries, in that all tiles used a similar range of colours, and designs were specific to cities and regions rather than to countries. In the mid-seventeenth century, however, a distinctively Portuguese style developed, characteristically consisting of large pictorial panels with blue designs on a white background, often depicting episodes from history or religion.

From the early sixteenth century *azulejos* were decorated by a technique known as *cuerda seca*, in which the coloured glazes were kept separate by outlining the decorative pattern in a compound consisting of manganese and grease. In the middle of the sixteenth century another technique, known as *cuenca* ('shell'), addressed the problem of colours intermingling by impressing the pattern of the design into the unbaked clay so that thin clay borders separate the different coloured areas.

**AZURARA, GOMES EANES DE.** See ZURARA, GOMES EANES DE.

# B

**BACCHIACCA or Francesco di Ubertino** (1494–1557), Italian painter, trained in the Florentine studio of PERUGINO. His paintings include *Moses Striking the Rock* (*c*.1535, National Gallery, Edinburgh) and *The Gathering of Manna* (*c*.1540, National Gallery, Washington). He also worked as a decorative artist, in which capacity he decorated a *studiolo* in the Palazzo della Signoria in Florence with illusionistic pictures of fish and birds.

DBI s.v. Francesco di Ubertino; *MDA*.

**BACCIO D'AGNOLO or Bartolomeo Baglioni** (1462–1543), Italian woodworker, INTARSIATORO, and architect, a native of Florence. His surviving woodwork from the 1490s includes the choir of the Cappella Maggiore in the Church of Santa Maria Novella in Florence (subsequently altered by VASARI) and the church's organ case (now in the Church of SS Pierre et Paul in Rueil-Malmaison, near Paris) and its gallery (now in the Victoria and Albert Museum). His architectural commissions included the Palazzo Bartolini-Salimbeni in Florence (1520–3).

DBI s.v. Baglioni, Bartolomeo; *MDA*.

**BACCIO DA MONTELUPO or Bartolomeo Sinibaldi** (1469–1535), Florentine sculptor and architect who worked initially as a sculptor of terracotta busts. He became a disciple of SAVONAROLA, and on the death of Savonarola in 1498 fled to Venice. He returned to Florence in 1504 and worked as a decorative sculptor on Orsanmichele and the Church of San Lorenzo; his son RAFFAELO DA MONTELUPO trained in his studio in Florence. Baccio eventually left Florence for Lucca, where he was the architect of the Church of San Paolino.

DBI s.v. Sinibaldi, Bartolomeo; *MDA* s.v. Montelupo; Ricardo Gatteschi, *Baccio di Montelupo: Scultore e architetto* (1993).

**BACCUSI, IPPOLITO** (*c*.1550–1609), Italian composer of sacred and secular music who worked in Venice, Ravenna, Mantua, and Verona. Among his works are two books of madrigals published in 1572, each of which opens with a different sequence of pieces celebrating the defeat of the Turks at LEPANTO.

**BACHELIER, NICOLAS** (*c*.1500–1557), French sculptor, mason, and architect, a native of Toulouse, where he carved stone altarpieces and reredoses in local churches and in the Cathedral of Saint-Étienne. His architectural work, such as the doors of the Hôtel de Ville (1546), is designed in an idiom inspired by SERLIO. His finest work is the Hôtel d'Assézat (1555), but the exact extent of his contribution to the building is unclear: he certainly provided the sculptural decoration (1555–8) and may have designed the building, but construction was supervised by another mason.

DBF; *MDA*; Henri Graillot, *Nicolas Bachelier: Imagier et maçon de Toulouse au XVIe siècle* (1914).

**BACKSTAFF**, a navigational instrument used to take the altitude of a celestial body and so calculate the geographical latitude of the observer. The predecessor of the backstaff was the quadrant, an instrument that was satisfactory for stars but difficult to use for the sun because one had to look at it directly. The English seaman John DAVIS invented the backstaff, a variation on the quadrant in which the observer stood facing away from the sun and measured its altitude from its shadow.

**BAÇO, JAUME.** See JACOMART.

**BACON, FRANCIS** (1561–1626), lawyer, philosopher, and essayist. Educated at Cambridge, Bacon trained as a lawyer, and achieved rapid promotion under James I (see JAMES VI), becoming lord chancellor in 1618. Accused of bribery in 1621 he retired from public life. In his writings, he criticizes scholastic and humanist learning, advocating the study of the book of Nature through careful induction from the particular to the general; his thought was to be a great influence on the scientific revolution. *The Advancement of Learning* (1605) offers a division of knowledge into different branches. *Novum organum* (1620) is a fragment of a proposed project, the *Great Instauration*, to reform the whole of natural philosophy; it outlines, through aphorism, Bacon's theory of method. *New Atlantis* (1627) gives utopian expression to the possibilities of scientific research. The *Essays* (published from 1597) are witty discussions of moral and political conduct, human behaviour, and other topics.

DNB; Brian Vickers (ed.), *Francis Bacon* (1996).

**BACON, SIR NATHANIEL** (1585–1627), English painter, educated at Corpus Christi College, Cambridge; in 1613 he travelled to the Netherlands to study painting. Several of his paintings survive in the collection of the earl of Verulam at Gorhambury (Hertfordshire), including a self-portrait and a portrait of his wife. His best-known picture is *The Cook Maid*, which exists in three versions (one in Tate Britain and two in the possession of his descendants); it is sometimes said to be the earliest naturalistic portrait of a woman in British art. Bacon also painted a miniature (Ashmolean, Oxford) that is the earliest known British LANDSCAPE.

*DNB; MDA.*

**BADIUS, JODOCUS ASCENSIUS, or Josse Bode** (1462–1535), Flemish humanist printer, born in Ghent. He studied in Italy and taught in Lyon before opening a printing workshop in Lyon, where he published an edition of TERENCE (1493). In 1499 Badius moved to Paris, where he opened a workshop in 1503; the emblem of his Paris workshop shows the interior of a printer's shop. His publications included works by Guillaume BUDÉ and ERASMUS. His daughter married Robert ESTIENNE.

*BNB; DBF s.v. Bode.*

**BAENA, JUAN ALFONSO DE** (1406–54), Spanish *converso* poet and anthologist, the eponym of the *Cancionero de Baena*, an anthology of poems presented to King JOHN II in 1445; the collection survives in a single copy in the Bibliothèque Nationale in Paris. The collection is a conspectus of Spanish poetry in the late fourteenth and early fifteenth centuries. It contains 612 poems (mostly in Castilian, but some in GALICIAN) by 54 named poets.

*DBEH; Cancionero de Baena, ed. Brian Dutton and Joaquín González Cuenca (1993).*

**BAFFIN, WILLIAM** (1584–1622), English explorer. He sought a NORTH-WEST PASSAGE to Asia on a number of voyages in the 1610s, using notably accurate measurements and observations. The large island he discovered north of Hudson Bay was later named after him. He was killed in India during a skirmish with the Portuguese.

*DNB.*

**BAGLIONI FAMILY**, the Umbrian family that dominated PERUGIA from the thirteenth century until 1540, when the city was subjected to the direct rule of the PAPAL STATE by Pope PAUL III. The wealth of the family derived from their employment as *condottieri* from the thirteenth century. In 1424, after the death of Andrea FORTEBRACCIO, Malatesta Baglioni (1387–1427) gained control of the city and was awarded additional territories by Pope MARTIN V; thereafter the family dominated Perugia for more than a century.

The rule of the Baglioni was remarkable for its violence, criminality, and internecine hatred. In 1460 Braccio di Malatesta Baglioni (1419–79) murdered his cousin Pandolfo Balglioni and his nephew Niccolò. The rival Oddi family was dispatched in two massacres (1482 and 1484). In 1500 Giampaolo Baglioni (1470–1520) seized power in a violent coup that involved the murder of Carlo Baglioni, Filippo di Braccio Baglioni, Guido Baglioni, Rodolfo Baglioni, and Astorre Baglioni. In 1506 Giampaolo attempted to murder

Pope JULIUS II as he entered Perugia (MACHIAVELLI was later to lament this failure); in 1520 he was lured to Rome and beheaded at the instigation of Pope LEO X. From 1527 to 1530 the family supported Florence against the MEDICI; Malatesta IV Baglioni (1491–1531) commanded the army of Florence and surrendered it to the Medici in 1530. At the end of the SALT WAR of 1540, Rodolfo Baglioni (1518–54), who had murdered the papal legate sent to govern the city, was defeated by the papal army of Pierluigi FARNESE; the city lost many of its privileges and the Baglioni family was sent into exile.

*DBI; B. Astur, I Baglioni (1964); C. F. Black, 'The Baglioni as Tyrants of Perugia, 1488–1504', English Historical Review (1970).*

**BAÏF, JEAN-ANTOINE DE** (1532–89), French poet, translator, and scholar, born in Venice; he was the illegitimate son of Lazare de BAÏF, the French ambassador, and his Venetian lover. He was educated in Paris at the Collège de Coqueret, where his contemporaries included DU BELLAY and RONSARD.

Baïf's literary works include collections of chansons and Petrarchan sonnets addressed to fictitious lovers, including *Méline* (1552) and *Francine* (1555). In 1567 he adapted Plautus' *Miles gloriosus* as *Le Brave*. Baïf was a member of the PLÉIADE, whose interests in scientific poetry are reflected in his *Premier des météores* (1567).

From 1567 to 1573 Baïf was principally occupied with his collaboration with the composer Joachim Thibault de COURVILLE in the establishment of the Académie de Poésie et de Musique, which was founded in 1570. During this period he collected his works as *Œuvres en rime* (1572–3), which consisted of four parts devoted to *Poèmes*, *Amours*, *Jeux* (eclogues and theatrical entertainments), and *Passetemps* (comic epigrams). His second collection, *Mimes, enseignements et proverbes* (1576, 1581, 1597), made Baïf a national figure.

*DBF; Jean Vignes, Jean Antoine de Baïf (1999).*

**BAÏF, LAZARE DE** (c.1496–1547), French ambassador in Venice. He translated Sophocles' *Electra* into alexandrines (1537); this dodecasyllabic line (named after the late twelfth-century *Roman d'Alexandre*) quickly became the standard metre for French tragedy and for much serious poetry, and in the seventeenth century was also used in comedy. Baïf's translation was wooden, but his choice of metre for this translation created a precedent which shaped French drama for centuries.

*DBF s.v. 4. Baïf (Lazare Ier); Yvonne Roberts, Lazare de Baïf and the Valois Court (2000).*

**BAIUS, MICHEL.** See BAY, MICHEL DE.

**BALBI, GIROLAMO** (c.1450–1535), Italian humanist, born in Venice. He moved to Rome, where he became a member of the Roman ACADEMY, which had been suppressed by Pope PAUL II (who suspected its members of paganism and heresy) but been allowed to reopen by Pope SIXTUS IV. In 1489 Balbi moved to Paris, where in 1496 he was accused of heresy and immorality and so fled to England. He later lived in Vienna and Prague and finally settled in Slovakia (then part of Hungary) as bishop of Pressburg (now Bratislava). His itinerant life made Balbi an important conduit for Italian humanism in the various cities in which he lived.

*DBI.*

**BALBI, LUDOVICO** (*c*.1545–*c*.1604), Italian composer of masses, motets, madrigals, and the *Musicale essercitio* (1589), a collection of madrigals. After eight years as a singer at San Marco, Venice, he worked as *maestro di cappella* at Verona, Padua, Feltre, and Treviso.

**BALBOA, VASCO NÚÑEZ DE** (*c*.1475–1517), Spanish conquistador, born into an impoverished family in Jérez de los Caballeros (Estremadura). In 1500 he travelled with the conquistador Rodrigo de Bastidas to Hispaniola, where Balboa became a farmer and sank into debt. In 1510 he escaped his creditors by travelling as a stowaway on a ship bound for San Sebastián, an island off the mainland of what is now Colombia, where OJEDA had founded a colony (later refounded as Cartagena). The expedition arrived at San Sebastián to find the settlement in ruins and Ojeda nowhere in evidence.

Balboa assumed command of the ship and mounted an expedition to the isthmus of Panama, where he founded a new colony, Santa María de la Antigua del Darién, which was known as Antigua. He began to explore the hinterland of Darién and heard rumours of a great ocean beyond the mountains. On 1 September 1513 he set out to find the ocean, leading an expedition of 190 Spaniards (including Francisco PIZARRO) and about 1,000 Indians. On 25 September he reached the summit of the range, where he and his fellow Spaniards became the first Europeans to see the Pacific Ocean. On 29 September he reached the shore and in the name of the Spanish crown took possession of the 'South Sea' (Mar del Sur); the name 'Pacific Ocean' was bestowed seven years later by MAGELLAN. After exploring what is now the Archipiélago de las Perlas, Balboa returned to Antigua, which he entered in triumph on 18 January 1514.

On hearing the news of Balboa's discovery King FERDINAND named him *adelantado del Mar del Sur* (admiral of the South Sea) and governor of Panama and Isla Colba; the king also dispatched an expedition led by Pedrarias DÁVILA, who was to replace Balboa as governor of Darién. Dávila accused Balboa of treachery, and captured him at Acla, on the north coast of the isthmus. After a summary trial Balboa was beheaded in the public square of Acla.

*DHE;* C. L. G. Anderson, *Life and Letters of Vasco Nuñez de Balboa* (1941); Kathleen Romoli, *Balboa of Darién* (1953).

**BALDACCHINO or umbraculum or ciborium**, an architectural canopy, made from wood, stone, metal, silk, or velvet, suspended over an altar or bishop's throne or tomb; it may be portable (and so a form of ceremonial UMBRELLA) or suspended from a ceiling or mounted on a wall. A free-standing canopy mounted on pillars over an altar is called a ciborium.

The baldacchino became an issue of confessional dispute in the sixteenth century. Some reformers argued that the baldacchino turned a portable communion table into a fixed altar; the Catholic Church made the baldacchino obligatory in 1600. From 1564 to 1568 the baldacchino became the subject of a bitter dispute in England, in which the principal protagonists were Bishop John JEWEL and the Catholic apologist Thomas Harding (1516–72).

**BALDI, BERNARDINO** (1553–1617), Italian mathematician and historian, born in Urbino, a pupil of COMMANDINO, whose biography figures prominently in Baldi's collection of lives of mathematicians, from antiquity to his own time, apparently conceived in emulation of VASARI's *Lives*. The work was not published in the Renaissance, but a very much shortened version appeared in 1707.

*DSB;* Bernardino Baldi, *Le vite de' matematici* (the medieval and Renaissance part), ed. with notes and commentary by Elio Nenci (1998).

**BALDOVINETTI, ALESSIO** (1425–99), Italian painter and mosaicist who worked in Florence and its *contado* (dependent territory). His work is documented by the diary of his commissions, one of the few to survive from the fifteenth century. His paintings, which usually include plants and brocades, include a *Sacra Conversazione* painted for the MEDICI VILLA at Caffaggiolo (now in the Uffizi), an *Annunciation* in the Uffizi, a *Madonna* in the Louvre, and a badly damaged fresco of *The Nativity* in the atrium of the Church of the SS Annunziata in Florence. His principal work was a cycle of frescoes in the Cappella Maggiore of Santa Trinita (now largely destroyed). His attributions include *Portrait of a Lady in Yellow* (*c*.1465) in the National Gallery in London.

In 1450 Baldovinetti began to work as a decorator and mosaicist for the cathedral in Florence; he made MOSAICS for the baptistery in Florence (in the soffit of the north door) and for the tympanum over the south door of the cathedral in Pisa.

*DBI; MDA.*

**BALDUNG GRIEN, HANS** (1484/5–1545), German painter who may have been trained in the workshop of DÜRER. He settled in Strassburg, but also worked across the Rhine in Freiburg, where he painted his best-known work, the ALTARPIECE (1512–16) in the cathedral. Baldung was also an accomplished designer of WOODCUTS, in which medium he deployed CHIAROSCURO to create dramatic effects.

*NDB; MDA.*

**BALE, JOHN** (1495–1563), English Protestant reformer and dramatist. Educated at Cambridge and Louvain, he was converted to Protestantism *c*.1533 and spent his life in its vigorous promotion. He wrote several religious plays which gained him the support of CROMWELL, on whose fall in 1540 he fled the country for eight years. In 1552 he became bishop of Ossory, Ireland, but again left the country the following year on MARY's succession; he returned on ELIZABETH's succession in 1559 and retired to Canterbury. He wrote a history of English writers, and plays and polemics in support of the Reformation; often savage, these earned him the sobriquet 'bilious Bale'. His history play *King John* (*c*.1538) was an influential model for later historical dramas.

*DNB.*

**BAMBAIA or Agostino Busti** (c.1483–1548), Italian sculptor, born near Milan and trained in Padua. His tombs include those of the poet Lancino Curzio (1513, Castello Sforzesco, Milan), Gaston de FOIX (1515, Castello Sforzesco), Cardinal Marino Caracciolo (Milan Cathedral), Canon Giovanni Vimercati (Milan Cathedral), and the Venetian *condottiere* Mercurio Bua (Santa Maria Maggiora, Treviso).

> DBI s.v. Busti, Agostino; *MDA*; Giovanni Agosti, *Bambaia e classicismo Lombardo* (1990); Maria Teresa Fiorio, *Bambaia: Catalogo completo* (1990).

**BAMBERGISCHE HALSGERICHTSORDNUNG or (Latin) *Constitutio criminalis Bambergensis*.** In 1507 Johann von Schwarzenburg (1463–1528), the German lay judge and penal reformer, created, in his capacity as president of the bishop of Bamberg's judicial tribunal, the criminal code known as the *Bambergische Halsgerichtsordnung*. The code was in essence a statute dealing with criminal procedure, but it contained interpolations of substantive law (i.e. law dealing with rights and duties). Its origins in German CUSTOMARY LAW were in part obscured by a strong admixture of Roman law. It became the model for the CAROLINA, and so influenced German criminal law until 1870.

**BANCHIERI, ADRIANO** (1568–1634), Italian composer, theorist, and organist whose sacred music includes organ masses and other liturgical organ pieces. These are to be found in *L'organo suonarino* (1605). Other instrumental writing includes original canzonas and fantasias. His madrigal comedy *La pazzia senile* (1598) is based on the *commedia dell'arte* character Pantalone. The *Cartella musicale* (1614) is a theoretical work covering metrical beat, vocal ornamentation, and the modal system.

**BANCROFT, RICHARD** (1544–1610), archbishop of Canterbury. Educated at Cambridge, he held a number of positions in the Church, including the see of London (from 1597), before becoming archbishop of Canterbury on WHITGIFT's death in 1604. He attended ELIZABETH I on her deathbed in 1603. Throughout his career he was a vigorous opponent of Puritanism and presbyterianism, and an advocate of episcopacy, which he helped restore to Scotland. He played a leading role at the HAMPTON COURT CONFERENCE, influencing the strong line taken there against the Puritans. He supported the 1611 translation of the Bible, and attempted to raise both the income and the intellectual standards of the clergy.

> *DNB*.

**BANDELLO, MATTEO** (1485–1561), Italian writer, Dominican friar, diplomat, and soldier, born in Castelnuovo Scrivia (near Tortona) and educated in Milan and Pavia. He worked as a tutor in noble households in Lombardy until 1525, when the Spanish attack on Milan in the wake of the battle of PAVIA led to the destruction of his house and the loss of his possessions. Bandello moved permanently to France, where in 1550 he was consecrated bishop of Agen.

Bandello's principal work was a collection of 214 *Novelle* (1554 and 1573) which earned him a European reputation, and was soon translated into French (1565) and English (1567); his version of the tale of *Giulietta e Romeo* was one of Shakespeare's sources. Bandello also published a collection of Petrarchan sonnets (*Canzoniere*, 1544) and an Italian translation of Euripides' *Hecuba*.

> *DBI*; *OCIL*; T. G. Griffith, *Bandello's Fiction* (1955).

**BANDINELLI, BACCIO or Bartolommeo** (1488–1560), Italian architect and sculptor in marble and bronze. He was born in Florence, the son of a goldsmith; he trained with his father and then with Giovanni RUSTICI. Bandinelli secured the patronage of COSIMO I DE' MEDICI and his duchess ELEANOR OF TOLEDO, whom he served as an architect on the Palazzo della Signoria and on the choir of Florence Cathedral, to which he contributed several fine sculptures, including low-relief sculptures of the *Prophets* (1555).

Bandinelli was disliked by his contemporaries, and the sneers of fellow artists such as Benvenuto CELLINI (who on returning to Florence in 1525 became Bandinelli's rival) have echoed down through the centuries. The obloquy heaped on his work makes it particularly difficult to judge his long succession of unfinished commissions, including the tombs of Pope LEO X and Pope CLEMENT VII in the Church of Santa Maria sopra Minerva in Rome (both commissioned in 1536) and the statue of Duke Cosimo's father, Giovanni de' MEDICI, in Piazza San Lorenzo in Florence (commissioned 1540). His finest competed work is the *Hercules and Cacus* (1534) in the Piazza della Signoria in Florence. He also executed versions of classical statues, notably *Orpheus and Cerberus* (1519, Palazzo Medici-Riccardi, Florence) and *Laocoön* (1525, Uffizi).

> *DBI*; *MDA*.

**BANDORA**, a stringed instrument said to have been invented by John Rose of London in 1562. It had seven metal strings and up to fifteen frets and sounded in the bass register. A member of the lute family, it had a distinctive scallop-shaped body.

**BÁÑEZ, DOMINGO** (1528–1604), Spanish Thomist theologian who studied philosophy at Salamanca and in 1547 entered the Dominican Order, where he became a pupil of Domingo de SOTO. He taught at the universities of Ávila and Valladolid, and in 1577 returned to Salamanca, where he spent the rest of his career. He became a prominent exponent of the teaching of THOMAS AQUINAS, and also a principal combatant in the dispute between the Dominicans and the JESUITS on the subject of divine GRACE, castigating the doctrine of Luis de MOLINA. Báñez was the spiritual adviser and confessor to TERESA DE ÁVILA, and assisted her in her reform of the Carmelites.

> M. Lépée, *Báñez et sainte Thérèse* (1947); Vicente Beltrán de Heredia, *Domingo Báñez y las controversias sobre la gracia* (1968).

**BANG, HIERONYMUS** (1553–1630), German goldsmith and designer of gold ornament. He was born in Osnabrück and worked from 1588 in Nuremberg. His prints include GROTESQUES designed to be engraved on the lips of cups.

**BANKING.** By the fourteenth century the great Italian banking families, such as the ACCIAIUOLI, Bardi, and Peruzzi families of Florence and the Frescobaldi of Lucca, had expanded their operations all over Europe; the Bardi, for example, had branches both within Italy (Ancona, Aquila, Bari, Barletta, Genoa, Naples, Orvieto, Palermo, Pisa, Venice) and beyond (Avignon, Barcelona, Bruges, Constantinople, Cyprus, Jerusalem, London, Majorca, Marseille, Nice, Rhodes, Seville). The recession of the second half of the fourteenth century was inaugurated by the failure of King Edward III of England to repay his debts, initially defaulting in 1341 and finally repudiating his debts in 1350; the king's failure to repay loans bankrupted the Peruzzi (1343), the Acciaiuoli (1345), and the Bardi (1346).

The long recession hampered the development of banking until the fifteenth century, when the the Bank of Barcelona was established (1401), the Banca di San Giorgio was founded in Genoa (1407), and the MEDICI family of Florence began to expand its presence in international banking; the Medici bank collapsed in 1494 when CHARLES VIII captured Florence in the first campaign of the WARS OF ITALY. In the late fifteenth century AUGSBURG emerged as an important financial centre; its banking families included the FUGGERS (who became bankers to the HABSBURGS), the WELSERS, and the HÖCHSTETTERS. In France Jacques CŒUR became banker to King CHARLES VII and in Italy Agostino CHIGI became banker to the PAPACY; within the Church, the MONTES PIETATIS (Italian *monti di pietà*) were in effect banks for ordinary citizens. The political power of the banks was most evident in CORSICA, which was ruled from 1453 to 1460 by the Genoese Banca di San Giorgio.

The papal interdiction against usury was evaded by recourse to the polite fiction that the loans were temporary gifts which were repayable with a monetary gift. Bankers' account books, which had begun to use double-entry bookkeeping from the early fourteenth century, substituted the heading 'profit and loss on exchange' for the unacceptable 'interest'. In practice fifteenth-century banks were lending money and collecting interest, but such activities are recorded in their accounts as the conversion of bills of exchange (which later evolved into promissory notes and then into cheques).

The first public banks were established in the late sixteenth and early seventeenth centuries. The Banco della Piazza di Rialto was established by the Venetian Senate in decrees of 1584 and 1587, the Bank of Amsterdam (Amsterdamsche Wisselbank) on 31 January 1609, the Bank of Middelburg on 28 March 1616, and the Bank of Hamburg (which survived until 1873) in 1619. On 3 May 1619 the Venetian Senate founded a second bank, the Banco del Giro, which eclipsed its predecessor and became known throughout Europe as the Bank of Venice; *giro* has the sense of 'turn' (i.e. turning bills of exchange into money), and the term survives in the Giro Bank established by the British Post Office.

A. Sapori, *La crisi delle compagnie mercantili dei Bardi e dei Peruzzi* (1926); R. de Roover, *The Rise and Decline of the Medici Bank, 1397–1494* (1963); R. Ehrenberg, *Capital and Finance in the Age of the Renaissance* (1963).

**BANQUETING HOUSE or Hall.** Built at Whitehall in classical Palladian style by Inigo JONES between 1619 and 1622, the Banqueting House was one of few buildings to survive the fire at Whitehall palace in 1698. The ceiling, completed by Rubens in 1634, celebrates the wisdom of James I (see JAMES VI); his son Charles I stepped from a window of the Hall onto the scaffold and his death in 1649. The Hall is open to the public and still in use for formal occasions.

**BAPTISM,** the SACRAMENT which confers admission to the Christian Church. From the third century to the Reformation, baptism was the rite of admission for infants from Christian families (infant baptism or paedobaptism), for converts from other religions, and, in some branches of the early Church, for defectors from heretical sects. For centuries baptism took the form of either immersion (which is sometimes called 'infusion'), in which the lower part of the candidate's body was submerged and water was poured over the upper part, or of submersion, in which the candidate was entirely submerged in water. In the Western Church, beginning in the eighth century, immersion and submersion were gradually (but not entirely) replaced by affusion, in which water was poured over the head of the candidate or, in exceptional circumstances, by aspersion, in which the candidate was sprinkled with baptismal water.

The standard view of the efficacy of baptism was articulated by AUGUSTINE, who argued that because baptism removed the stain of original sin, infants who died before they could be baptized were barred from heaven. In the elaboration of this doctrine by THOMAS AQUINAS, baptism remitted the divine punishment due to original and actual sin; it did not mitigate the natural consequences of sin, such as ignorance, pain, sexual appetite, and death.

The reformers were not content to receive the traditional theology of baptism uncritically. The AUGSBURG CONFESSION affirmed in deliberately conciliatory language that baptism was essential to salvation, that it was the rite by which GRACE was offered, and that children were to be baptized and through baptism were received into God's favour. LUTHER struggled to combine belief in the necessity of baptism with his insistence on JUSTIFICATION by faith alone, and so described baptism as a promise of divine grace which when received would ensure that sin is no longer imputed to the sinner. CALVIN argued that baptism was efficacious only for the elect, since only the elect have the faith essential to salvation. ZWINGLI took a more radical position, denying that baptism was essential for salvation and describing it as a public sign of admission to the Christian community. The most fundamental challenge to the traditional theology and practice of baptism came from the ANABAPTISTS, who refused to have their children baptized and instead reinstituted the baptism of adult believers, a practice which had hitherto only been used for converts from other religions.

The Thomist understanding of baptism was reaffirmed by the COUNCIL OF TRENT, which combatively stressed that baptism is an instrument of grace as well as a sign of grace. The position of the Church of England is less clear, because the Book of COMMON PRAYER affirmed traditional Catholic teaching, but the THIRTY-NINE ARTICLES opaquely describe baptism as a 'sign of regeneration' by which 'the promises of forgiveness of sins and of our adoption to be the sons of God by the Holy Ghost are visibly signed and sealed'.

**BARBARI, JACOPO DE'** (1460/70–c.1516), Italian painter and engraver; nothing is known of his early life, save that he was a Venetian. In the first decade of the sixteenth century he worked in Germany in the service of the Emperor MAXIMILIAN, the Elector FRIEDRICH III of Saxony, and the Elector JOACHIM I of Brandenburg. In about 1509 he moved to the Netherlands, where he worked as court painter to the Habsburgs, first for Maximilian's son Duke Philip of Burgundy (later King PHILIP I of Castile) and later for MARGARET OF AUSTRIA.

Jacopo's paintings include a *Dead Bird* (1504, Residenzmuseum, Munich), one of the earliest STILL LIFES. His engravings, many depicting mythological figures, were very influential, and were largely responsible for the dissemination of the Italian depiction of the nude in northern Europe. His best-known woodcut is a large aerial view of Venice (1500), which was the first comprehensive picture of a city as viewed from its highest buildings. Jacopo signed his paintings and his engravings with a caduceus.

DBI s.v. Barbari, Iacopo de'; *MDA*; Giandomenico Romanelli et al. (eds.), *A volo d'uccello: Jacopo de' Barbari e le rappresentazioni di città nell'Europa del Rinascimento* (1999).

**BARBARIGO FAMILY**, a Venetian patrician family. The account books of the merchant Andrea Barbarigo (1399–1449) provided detailed information on Venetian business practices in the first half of the fifteenth century. Marco Barbarigo (1413–86) served as doge in 1485–6 and was succeeded by Agostino Barbarigo (1419–1501), who was doge from 1486–1501. The *PROVVEDITORE* Agostino Barbarigo (1516–71) commanded the Venetian galleys at the battle of LEPANTO (1571), and died of wounds two days after the battle.

DBI; F. C. Lane, *Andrea Barbarigo, Merchant of Venice* (1944).

**BARBARO, DANIELE MATTEO ALVISE** (1513–70), Italian polymath and patron, born into a noble Venetian family. He spent his early life in Padua, where he pursued his interests in philosophy, literature, mathematics, and science. In 1545 he became the founding superintendent of the BOTANICAL GARDEN in Padua, in the planning of which he had represented the Venetian Senate. He and his brother Marcantonio commissioned the Villa BARBARO, which was designed by PALLADIO.

Barbaro served as Venetian ambassador to England from 1548 to 1550. It was apparently under family pressure that he took holy orders, which equipped him to hold (from 1550) the essentially political office of patriarch elect of Aquileia. In this capacity he represented Venetian interests at the COUNCIL OF TRENT.

Barbaro's intellectual interests exemplify the patrician class's growing concern with mathematical learning. He made an Italian translation of VITRUVIUS' *De architectura*, with

illustrations and notes (1556); this was later reprinted together with his edition of the Latin text (1566). These became the standard texts used by scholars for about 150 years. Following on from his annotations to *De architectura*, Barbaro wrote a separate treatise on Vitruvian topics, dealing largely with PERSPECTIVE (in which he draws very heavily upon the treatise by PIERO DELLA FRANCESCA), but also considering SUNDIALS and polyhedra. These discussions contain some interesting mathematical insights. The book, *La pratica della perspettiva* (1568, 1569), was very widely read.

There are fine portraits of Daniele Barbaro by TITIAN, TINTORETTO, and VERONESE.

DBI; *MDA* s.v. Barbaro I.

**BARBARO, ERMOLAO THE YOUNGER, or Almoro di Zaccaria** (1454–93), Italian humanist, distinguished philologist, and diplomat. He was born into a noble family in Venice and studied in Rome under Julius Pomponius LAETUS. In 1477 he became a doctor of civil and canon law and was appointed professor of philosophy at Padua, where he corresponded with FICINO, PICO DELLA MIRANDOLA, and POLIZIANO. He undertook various diplomatic missions and in 1491, while serving as Venetian ambassador in Rome, he was nominated as patriarch of Aquileia by Pope INNOCENT VIII. The Venetian Senate refused to allow Barbaro to accept the post which the pope insisted on his accepting. He obeyed the pope and was banished to Rome, where he died of the plague.

Barbaro's principal scholarly work was *Castigationes Pliniae* (1493; 'Emendations of Pliny'), in which he proposed more than 5,000 emendations of Pliny's *Historia naturalis*, a process to which his formidable knowledge of botany and classical philology was well suited. His other literary works include a translation of the Greek *Paraphrases* of Themistius on Aristotle (1481), an edition of Pomponius Mela (1493), and a posthumously published translation of Aristotle's *Rhetorica* into Latin (1544).

DBI.

**BARBARO, GIOSOFAT** (1413–94), Venetian merchant who travelled in 1436 to the Black Sea ports, and subsequently to Russia and the Caucasus. After returning to Venice in 1451, Barbaro entered the service of the republic, and in 1473 was sent as Venetian ambassador to Persia with a view to negotiating an alliance against the Ottomans; the following year he was joined by Ambrogio CONTARINI. Barbaro remained in Persia for four years, learning the Farsi language and studying Persian culture. He wrote an account of his travels called *Viaggi fatti da Venetia*, which was first published in 1543.

DBI; *I viaggi in Persia degli ambasciatori veneti Barbaro e Contarini*, ed. L. Lockhart et al. (1973).

**BARBARO, VILLA**, a villa and garden in Maser (Veneto), 27 kilometres (17 miles) north-west of Treviso. The villa and gardens were designed by PALLADIO for Daniele BARBARO and his brother Marcantonio, and the villa is fully described in Palladio's *Di architettura* (1570); the villa and garden were built between 1554 and 1558. The interior of the villa is sumptuously decorated with frescoes by VERONESE. The garden made extensive use of water, and was rich in statues, including stone warriors on the boundary walls, within which there were PARTERRES and simple arbours; the main drive was lined with statues of Olympian gods. The villa, which is now called the Villa di Maser, is well preserved, but Palladio's garden has largely disappeared, except for a small GIARDINO SEGRETO.

The *giardino segreto*, which is entirely enclosed by the house and the hill, is dominated by a magnificent semicircular NYMPHAEUM built by Alessandro VITTORIA. The fountain, which is decorated with fourteen statues of classical figures, is cut into the hill. The fountain feeds a round ornamental fish pond, from which the water runs into the kitchen of the villa and thence to the gardens on either side of the access road and to the distant orchards. Palladio's description of the garden does not specify the size of the pool; nineteenth-century photographs show that the pool was then smaller than it is now, but its original size is not known.

MDA s.v. Maser; U. Basso, *Cronaca di Maser: Delle sue chiese e della villa palladiana dei Barbaro* (1968); id. *La villa e il tempietto dei Barbaro a Maser di Andrea Palladio* (1976).

**BARBAROSSA BROTHERS.** See BARBARY PIRATES.

**BARBARY PIRATES.** 'Barbary' is a European name for the coastal areas of North Africa (excluding Egypt); it derives from the Arabic *barbar* (i.e. Berber), but the similarity to Greek and Latin *barbaria* made it easy for Christian Europeans to associate Barbary with the supposed barbarity of infidels.

Pirates had preyed on European vessels and coastal settlements from safe havens in North Africa since late antiquity. In the fourteenth and fifteenth centuries, the principal base for piracy was Bejaia (later French Bougie), 200 kilometres (125 miles) east of Algiers. The scale of such piracy grew enormously with the expulsion of the Moors from Spain in 1492, because many dispossessed Moorish refugees turned to piracy, in the first instance raiding coastal settlements in Spain. Spain responded by conquering and garrisoning the towns that harboured pirates (see AFRICA).

Spain's attempt to suppress piracy was rendered more difficult by the increased presence of Levantine pirates in North Africa, notably the two pirate brothers known to Christians as Barbarossa, whose base was on the island of Djerba, off the coast of what is now Tunisia. The elder brother, Aruj, was killed in battle with the Spaniards in 1518, whereupon the younger brother, Khair-ed-Din, secured military aid from Selim I, the Ottoman sultan. In 1529 Khair captured the Spanish fort of Peñón de Alger (an island in the harbour of Algiers), and thereafter ALGIERS became the principal base for North African pirates as well as the seat of Ottoman rule in North Africa. From 1529 until 1587, when direct government was imposed by Constantinople, piracy was sponsored by the Ottoman beys, and its main activity was slave hunting; after 1587, Algerian pirates also sought to plunder European merchant ships, and 10 per cent of the value of their prizes was paid into the treasury of the pashas. Pirate bases developed in Tunis and Tripoli and in the coastal towns of Morocco, of which the most notorious was Sale (near Rabat).

In the late sixteenth and early seventeenth centuries, SLAVERY reached unprecedented proportions. Until the end of the sixteenth century, pirates used GALLEYS, which restricted their slaving and plundering expeditions to the Mediterranean. The advent of sailing ships in the service of piracy (an innovation introduced by the Flemish pirate Simon Danser) opened the way for piracy in the Atlantic. In this period Europeans began to join the ranks of the pirates, who included the Oxford-educated Englishman Sir Francis Verney (1584–1615), who was based in Algiers, and the Flemish pirate known as Murad Reis, who in 1631 sacked the Irish town of Baltimore and sold many of its inhabitants into slavery in Algiers. There were also Christian pirates in the eastern Mediterranean: the USCOKS operated from bases in Dalmatia, and two military ORDERS, the Knights of ST JOHN and the Order of San Stefano, preyed on both Ottoman and European shipping.

Some captives were able to regain their freedom by converting to Islam, and others were ransomed by their families or countries, but most spent the rest of their lives as slaves. European countries began to pay protection money (thinly disguised as presents or ransom payments) to secure immunity from predation. The ORDERS OF RANSOM (especially, after 1625, the Lazarists) worked to redeem captives both by paying ransoms and by offering themselves as substitutes for enslaved Europeans. North African piracy was not finally suppressed until 1830, when Algiers was conquered by France.

**BARCLAY, ALEXANDER** (*c.*1476–1552), English poet and translator. A divine, probably of Scottish origins, he was successively priest in Devon, Benedictine monk, and London rector. His moral and satirical *Eclogues* (*c.*1513–14) are the earliest English examples of the form. He translated BRANT's *Narrenschiff* into English as *The Ship of Fools* (1509), adding satirical sketches from English culture. Other translations are a life of St George (from Mantuan, a model for his *Eclogues*), and the Roman historian Sallust's *Bellum Jugurthinum* (*c.*1520). DNB.

**BARCLAY, WILLIAM** (1546/7–1608), Scottish jurist and political philosopher in France and England. Barclay was educated at the University of Aberdeen, and left Scotland for France in 1573. He studied CIVIL LAW in Paris and Bourges under CUJAS, DONEAU, and LE CONTE, and was appointed professor of civil law at Pont-à-Mousson (Lorraine) in about 1580. He championed the divine right of kings in his *De regno et regali potestate* (1600), which was a refutation of the arguments of BUCHANAN's *De iure regni apud Scotos* (1578), which sought to restrict royal power. *De regno* also contained a polemical defence of the rights of monarchs in attacks on Junius Brutus (pseudonym of Hubert LANGUET, author of *Vindiciae contra tyrannos*, 1600) and Jean BOUCHET (*De iusta Henrici III abdicatione et Francorum regno*, 1600). In 1603 Barclay travelled to the court of James I of England, where he wrote *In titulo pandectarum de rebus creditis et de jure jurando*, which he dedicated to James I. He returned to France in 1604, and became professor of civil law at Angers, where he lived for the last few years of his life. His posthumously published *De potestae papae* (1609), which acknowledged the spiritual authority of the pope but denied his temporal power over monarchs, was another polemical work, this time directed against BELLARMINE, and it achieved a wide readership all over Europe.

DBF s.v. 3. Barclay; *DNB*.

**BARDI FAMILY**, a family of Florentine merchant bankers who in the late thirteenth century established branches in Italian city-states, England, Flanders, and France. In the early fourteenth century they were the wealthiest family in Florence, lending to rulers in exchange for export monopolies in commodities such as English wool. The family could not sustain the bad debts created by the bankruptcy of King Edward III of England, and the bank collapsed in 1345/6.

The family remained in Florence, and in the late sixteenth century Giovanni Bardi (1534–1612) assembled a group of musical friends known as the CAMERATA in his *palazzo* (and in that of Jacopo CORSI). Their experiments in the use of instruments and solo voices to express emotion soon developed into *dramma per musica*, an early form of opera. The members of the Camerata included Vincenzo GALILEI and Jacopo PERI, for both of whom Bardi wrote libretti.

**BARENDSZOON, DIRK** (1534–92), Dutch portrait painter, born in Amsterdam. He worked in TITIAN's studio in Venice (*c*.1560), and thereafter his pictures combine elements of Dutch realism with an evocative Venetian use of colour. His best-known painting is the triptych *The Adoration of the Shepherds* (Gouda Museum).

NNBW ii; *MDA*.

**BARENTSZOON, WILLEM or (English) William Barents** (1550–97), Dutch explorer in the Arctic. He sailed from Amsterdam with two ships in 1594 in search of a north-east passage to Asia. He reached the west coast of Novaya Zemlya before being forced to turn back. In 1595 he mounted a second expedition with seven ships and sailed as far as Proliv Yugorskiy Shar, the narrow strait between Ostrov Vaygach and the Russian mainland, before being turned back by ice.

In 1596 Barentszoon mounted his third and final expedition, this time with two ships. The expedition sighted Bear Island (Norwegian Bjørnøya) and Spitsbergen (Norwegian Svalbard, in which one of the islands is now called Barentsøya), whereupon the ships separated. Barentszoon's ship rounded the northern tip of Novaya Zemlya and was trapped in the ice. The crew, which included Jacob van HEEMSKERK, spent the winter on Novaya Zemlya; the ship was not released in the spring, so the crew abandoned ship on 13 June 1597 and made their way home in two open boats; Barentszoon died a week later. Knowledge of his three voyages was disseminated by the expedition surgeon, Gerrit de Vere, whose *Waerachtighe beschryvinghe van de drie seylaegien by Noorden* (1598) was translated into English (*The True and Perfect Description of Three Voyages*, 1609) and other European languages.

In 1871 the house in which Barentszoon and his crew had wintered was discovered, and in 1875 part of his journal was found. The Barents Sea, between Spitsbergen, Scandinavia, and Novaya Zemlya, is named after him.

NNBW iv; Rayner Unwin, *A Winter away from Home: William Barents and the North-East Passage* (1995).

**BARILI, ANTONIO, or Antonio di Neri** (1453–1516), Italian civil engineer, architect, engraver, and INTARSIA designer, a native of Siena. As a young man he was employed in the repairing of bridges and the construction of fortifications. From 1483 to 1502 he worked in Siena Cathedral, providing carving and intarsia for the choir stalls in the Chapel of San Giovanni (1483–1502; seven panels survive in La Collegiata in San Quirido d'Orcia and one in the Kunstgewerbemuseum in Vienna) and building the benches for the Piccolomini library (1496) and the cathedral's organ case, organ loft, and cantoria (1510). He also built the choir stalls in Santa Maria Nuova in Fano (1484–9; nineteen survive in the church).

Antonio's nephew Giovanni Barili (d. *c*.1529) worked as his assistant until 1514 and then settled in Rome, where his work included the implementation of RAPHAEL's designs for doors and door-cases in the Vatican *Stanze*.

DBI.

**BARNABITES**, a religious ORDER, formally known as the Clerks Regular of St Paul, founded by Antonio Maria ZACCARIA in Milan in 1530. Priests were bound by vows to regenerate the love of Christian worship and the Christian way of life by preaching and the administration of the sacraments. This emphasis on the eucharist and the prescribed study of the epistles of St Paul are the two distinctive features of the order. The popular name derives from their Church of St Barnabas in Milan; the dedication to St Barnabas reflects the ancient belief that he was the first bishop of Milan.

O. Premoli, Barnabite, *Storia dei Barnabiti nel cinquecento* (1913), *nel seicento* (1922).

**BARO, PETER** (1534–99), French theologian in England. Baro came into contact with Protestantism whilst studying law at Bourges; he transferred his attentions from law to theology, and travelled to Geneva where he became a minister under CALVIN. He found himself unwelcome in France and fled to England, where in 1574 he became professor of divinity at Cambridge. There, he became an opponent of PERKINS and a vigorous critic of predestinarianism, anticipating the Arminianist movement. The LAMBETH ARTICLES were in part designed to refute his teaching, but Baro was able to reconcile them with his beliefs; the following year, however, he left Cambridge for London, where he lived for the rest of his life.

DNB.

**BAROCCI, FEDERICO, or Il Fiori** (*c*.1535–1612), Italian painter and draughtsman. He was a native of Urbino who in 1550 moved to Rome, where he trained and then worked as an assistant to Taddeo ZUCCARO on the CASINO of Pope PIUS IV, painting one of the ceilings (1561–2). In the mid-1560s he returned permanently to Urbino, escaping from an allegation of poisoning. Between protracted bouts of ill health he painted hundreds of religious pictures in a style indebted to CORREGGIO, including *The Madonna of St Simon* (1567, Galleria Nazionale delle Marche, Urbino), *The Martyrdom of St Vitalis* (1580–3, Brera, Milan), *The Virgin with Kitten* (c.1576, National Gallery, London), *The Madonna del Rosario* (1588–91, Palazzo Vescovile, Senigallia, Marches), *The Madonna della popolo* (1579, Uffizi), *The Calling of St Andrew* (1580–3, Musée des Beaux-Arts, Brussels), and *The Circumcision* (1590, Louvre). Barocci also produced a large number of drawings, and was one of the first artists to make extensive use of pastel chalks in his drawings.

*DBI*; *MDA*; Nicholas Turner, *Federico Barocci* (2000).

**BARON, ÉGUINAIRE-FRANÇOIS** (1495–1550), Breton humanist jurist and champion of the MOS GALLICUS. He taught Roman law at Angers, Poitiers, and Bourges, where he was the rival of LE DOUAREN. He wrote prolifically on the JUSTINIAN compilations of Roman law; his two main works are *Pandectarum iuris civilis oeconomica* (1555) and *Commentaria in quatuor institutionum libros* (1574).

*DBF* s.v. 12. Baron.

**BARONCELLI, NICCOLÒ, or Niccolò del Cavallo** (*fl.* 1434, d. 1453), Italian sculptor, born in Florence. In 1436 he moved to Padua, where his surviving works include a terracotta relief of *St Aegidius* made for the Church of San Clemente and now in the Museo Civico. In 1443 he was invited to Padua by Leonello d'ESTE, who commissioned Baroncelli and Antonio di Cristoforo to make an EQUESTRIAN STATUE of Niccolò III d'ESTE; Antonio made the effigy of the duke and Baroncelli made the horse.

*DBI*; *MDA*.

**BARONIUS, CAESAR** (1538–1607), Italian cardinal and historian, born in Sora and educated in Veroli and Naples. In 1557 he moved to Rome, where he became a member of the ORATORY OF DIVINE LOVE under Filippo NERI, whom he succeeded as superior in 1593. He served as confessor to Pope CLEMENT VIII, who created him cardinal in 1596 and Vatican librarian in 1597.

Baronius' greatest work was his *Annales ecclesiastici*, which was published in twelve large folio volumes (1588–1607). The *Annales*, which was undertaken as a Catholic reply to the Protestant MAGDEBURG CENTURIES, was a scrupulous account of the history of the Church in which each year occupies a chapter. The scholarship on the Western Church is excellent, but in Baronius' account of the Orthodox Church he perpetuated the errors of his sources. In volume xi of the *Annales* (1605) Baronius included a section in which he championed the claims of the pope against Spain, and so incurred the enmity of the Spanish Church; after the two conclaves of 1605, in which Leo XI and Paul V were elected as pope, it was rumoured that Spanish opposition had cost Baronius the papacy.

*DBI* s.v. Baronio, Cesare.

**BAROQUE**, an art-historical term of uncertain origin (possibly from Portuguese *barocco* or Spanish *barrueco*, an irregular pearl) for the dominant style of art and architecture from the late sixteenth to the early eighteenth centuries, characterized by curved forms and exuberant decoration; in the conventional sequence of styles, it follows MANNERISM and precedes Rococo. In literary criticism, the Baroque is deemed to follow the Renaissance and precede the Enlightenment. In music the Baroque refers to a style characterized by harmonic complexity, and as a period extends from the early seventeenth to the mid-eighteenth centuries.

**BAROVIER FAMILY**, Italian glassmakers, active on the Venetian island of Murano from at least 1330, when Jacobello Barovier was recorded as a glassmaker. Jacobello's great-grandson Angelo Barovier (d. 1460) was one of three brothers who owned glasshouses on Murano. There is evidence that Angelo was one of the pioneers in the technology for making crystal GLASS (*cristallo*) and LATTIMO. A marriage-cup in the Museo Vetrario Murano was formally attributed to Angelo, but is now thought to have been made after his death and so is likely to have been the work of another member of his family; no other work can be securely attributed to Angelo. After Angelo's death the workshop passed to his son Marino (d. c.1490) and thence to other members of the family. The Barovier glasshouse is now the most prominent of the ancient glasshouses of Murano.

*DBI*; *MDA*.

**BARROS, JOÃO DE** (1496–1570), Portuguese colonizer, humanist, and historian, educated at the royal court in Lisbon. At the age of 20 he wrote a chivalric romance called *Clarimundo* (Lisbon, 1522); in 1530 Barros withdrew from Lisbon to his estate near Pombal to escape an epidemic of plague, and there wrote the first of his moral dialogues, *Rópica Pnefma*. On returning to Lisbon in 1532 he became the overseer of Portugal's trade with its colonies, and in 1539 led a colonizing expedition to Maranhão, in northern Brazil; the colony later failed. Barros then returned to writing, publishing a Portuguese grammar (1540) and composing more moral dialogues. In 1552 he published the first part of his *Décadas da Ásia*, a celebratory account of Portuguese discovery and conquest (4 vols., 1552–1615; Italian translation, 2 vols., 1561–2) which was completed by Diogo do COUTO; Barros's narrative is based on a documentary record some parts of which have subsequently been lost. Barros came to be known as the Portuguese Livy, a sobriquet that links Portuguese historical writing to that of the ancient world and acknowledges the elegance of Barros's style and the range of his scholarship.

*DHP*; C. Boxer, *Three Historians of Portuguese Asia* (1948); António Borges Coelho, *João de Barros, vida e obra* (1997); A. A. Banha de Andrade, *João de Barros, historiador do pensamento, humanista português de quinhentos* (1980).

**BARROWISTS**, an English Puritan sect whose name derives from Henry Barrow (c.1550–93), an English courtier who in the early 1580s began to attack episcopacy and to advocate congregational independence. He was imprisoned in 1586 by order of Archbishop WHITGIFT, and hanged for sedition in 1593. His writings, including *A Brief Discovery of the False Church* (*c*.1590), were published by exiled English Barrowists in Amsterdam. Members of the Amsterdam congregation emigrated to New England, where they founded congregationalist churches.

**BARTOLO DA SASSOFERRATO or Bartolus** (1313–57), Italian jurist and political theorist. He studied law at Perugia and Bologna and practised as a judicial assessor at Todi and Pisa, and from 1343 taught law at Perugia. His early practical experience as a lawyer coloured his perception of Roman law, and in his commentaries on the Justinian *Digest*, on which his reputation as the greatest student of CIVIL LAW in fourteenth-century Italy is based, he developed a theory of statutes which declared statutes based on CUSTOMARY LAW to be exceptions to the general applicability of Roman law; his exposition of the relationship of statutes to Roman law forms the jurisprudential basis of modern principles of international private law (also known as 'conflict of laws'), which centres on issues of jurisdiction.

In his role as political philosopher, Bartolus discussed the nature of political authority and constitutional models in a treatise on the government of cities (*De regimine civitatum*), and his treatise *De tyrannis* described circumstances in which tyrants might be deposed.

DBI; C. N. S. Woolf, *Bartolus of Sassoferrato* (1913); J. L. J. van de Kamp, *Bartolo de Saxoferrato* (1936).

**BARTOLOMEO or Bartolommeo, FRA, or Baccio della Porta** (1472–1517), Italian painter and draughtsman, born in Florence, where he trained in the studio of Cosimo ROSSELLI. He fell under the influence of SAVONAROLA and in 1498 was in the Convent of San Marco when it was raided and Savonarola was captured; in 1500, after witnessing Savonarola's execution, he entered the Dominican ORDER. He became head of the San Marco workshop (a post once held by Fra ANGELICO) in 1504. Visits to Venice (1508) and Rome (1514–15) broadened his artistic experience, and in his own paintings he developed a distinctive style characterized by facial expressions of rapt devotion, deeply folded drapery, and an air of gravity and decorum.

Fra Bartolomeo's surviving paintings include a *Vision of St Bernard* (1504–7, Uffizi), *God the Father with Mary Magdalene and Catherine of Siena* (1507, Villa Guinigi, Lucca), *The Madonna in Glory with Saints* (1512, Besançon Cathedral), at least two versions of *The Mystic Marriage of St Catherine* (Louvre, 1511, and Accademia, Florence, 1512), and many Madonnas, often pictured (like those of RAPHAEL) together with the infant Jesus and his cousin John in a landscape (e.g. *Holy Family*, National Gallery, London).

DBI s.v. Bartolomeo di Paolo; MDA s.v. Bartolommeo; Serena Padovani (ed.), *Fra Bartolomeo e la scuola di San Marco* (1996).

**BARTOLOMEO D'ALVIANO** (1435–1515), Umbrian soldier who commanded Spanish troops in their defeat of the French in the battle of GARIGLIANO (1503) and in 1507 entered the service of Venice, for which he fought for the rest of his career.

In 1508 he led a successful campaign against the army of the Emperor MAXIMILIAN I, but the following year he was captured when Venice was defeated in the battle of AGNADELLO. On his release in 1513 Bartolomeo returned to Venice, where he was again installed as commander-in-chief. His attempts to secure the *terraferma* for Venice were not always successful, but he did reconquer Friuli. At the battle of MARIGNANO his forces fought alongside the army of King FRANCIS I and contributed to the French victory; he died a few weeks later, on 7 October 1515.

DBI s.v. Alviano, Bartolomeo d'; L. Leonij, *La vita di Bartolomeo d'Alviano* (1858).

**BARTOLOMEO VENETO** (*fl.* 1502–d. 1531), Italian painter who worked in Ferrara (1506–8) and in Milan (from 1520). His surviving paintings include *A Courtesan* (Städelsches Kunstinstitut, Frankfurt am Main), *St Catherine* (Glasgow Art Gallery), *The Madonna and Child* (Ambrosiana, Milan), *The Circumcision* (1506, Louvre), and *Ludovico Martinengo* (1530, National Gallery, London).

DBI; MDA; Laura Pagnotta, *Bartolomeo Veneto: l'opera completo* (1997).

**BARTON, ELIZABETH, or the Maid of Kent** (*c*.1506–1534), a servant from Canterbury who in 1525 began to prophesy and, after a public examination, was admitted as a nun to the Convent of St Sepulchre in Canterbury. Her prophetic utterances continued, and she began to denounce the intention of King HENRY VIII to divorce CATHERINE OF ARAGON. In 1533 she was examined by Archbishop CRANMER, who secured a confession that the trances and prophecies were feigned, and she was executed in 1534.

DNB.

**BARZIZZA, GASPARINO DA** (*c*.1360–1431), Italian humanist, educated in Pavia, where he later taught grammar and rhetoric. In 1407 Gasparino moved to Padua, where he established an institute for the study of classical Latin. In 1417 he attended the COUNCIL OF CONSTANCE as a representative of the antipope JOHN XXIII; on returning he spent the 1520s teaching in Milan.

Gasparino was a committed supporter of the humanist view that the grammar of Latin should be restored to what was seen as classical purity. To this end he wrote commentaries on Seneca and Cicero, and attempted to purge Ciceronian texts of medieval accretions. He also composed Latin letters which he designed as models for those aspiring to develop a Latin epistolary style.

DBI s.v. Barzizza; OCIL; R. Mercer, *The Teaching of Gasparino Barzizza* (1979).

**BASEL or (French) Bâle or (Italian and Latin) Basilea or (English exonym) Basle**, a city, bishopric, and canton on the Rhine which in 1501 became the eleventh canton in the SWISS CONFEDERATION. The COUNCIL OF BASEL met in the choir of the cathedral (Münster) from 1431 to 1439, and its committees met in the chapter house. In 1460 Pope PIUS VI authorized the founding of a university; the staff later included REUCHLIN and ERASMUS (who is buried in the city). Basel had one of the first printing presses (1468), and by the end of the fifteenth century had become an important centre for printing. From the mid-fifteenth century the guilds and corporations had secured complete control of the machinery of civic and cantonal government, and during this period the city enjoyed economic as well as cultural prosperity. The craft guilds gained control of the city in 1526, which may have initiated the ensuing period of economic decline. In 1529 Basel adopted the Reformation, which was introduced by OECOLAMPADIUS; in 1534 the Confession of BASEL became the doctrinal basis of the city's churches. During the French WARS OF RELIGION the city welcomed French HUGUENOT refugees whose descendants later constituted the city's French minority.

The city's Renaissance architecture includes the City Hall (Rathaus, 1504–21) and the Renaissance additions to the Münster, which was consecrated in 1019, rebuilt after the huge earthquake of 1356 and completed in 1528. In 1833 the canton of Basel was divided into two cantons, Basel-Stadt and Basel-Land.

P. Burckhardt, *Geschichte der Stadt Basel von der Reformation bis zur Gegenwart* (1942); Hans R. Guggisberg, *Basel in the Sixteenth Century* (1982).

**BASEL, CONFESSION OF**, a confession of faith compiled by Oswald MYCONIUS which became the doctrinal basis of reform introduced at Basel in 1534; this Confession, which is sometimes called the 'First Confession of Basel', was an expanded version of a short confession formulated by OECOLAMPADIUS in 1531. In theology, the Confession treads a middle course between the views of Martin LUTHER and ZWINGLI.

The HELVETIC CONFESSION of 1536 is sometimes known as the Second Confession of Basel.

**BASINIO DA PARMA** (1425–57), Italian neo-Latin poet. He was educated under VITTORINO DA FELTRE and Theodore GAZA, and after a period in the court of Ferrara moved in 1451 to Rimini, where he secured the patronage of Sigismondo MALATESTA. His Latin poems, which skilfully emulate the style of a variety of ancient poets, often describe the accomplishments of his patron. His *Hesperis* is one of the finest Latin poems of the Renaissance.

*DBI; OCIL.*

**BASSANO or Bassani, GIOVANNI** (c.1558–c.1617), Italian composer and wind player in Venice, remembered particularly for his *Ricercate, passaggi et cadentie per potersi ésercitar nel diminuir terminatemente con ogni sorte d'istrumento* (1585). His technique of drawing attention to one of several contrapuntal lines through continuous decoration meant that he was highly regarded as a player; it is thought that GABRIELI's *Canzona in echo (Sacrae symphoniae)* (1597) was written with Bassano in mind.

**BASSANO, JACOPO DAL PONTE** (c.1517/18–1592), Italian painter, born in Bassano, the son of the painter Francesco da Ponte the Elder (c.1475–1539). He trained with his father and then with BONIFAZIO VERONESE DE PITATI in Venice, and

returned permanently to Bassano in the late 1530s. He usually painted religious subjects, the distinctive feature of which is the presence of peasants and animals; he was therefore drawn to the subject of the Adoration of the Magi, of which there are examples in the National Gallery in Edinburgh and the Kunsthistorisches Museum in Vienna. From the late 1560s he sometimes abandoned the religious element altogether, instead painting LANDSCAPES.

Jacopo's four sons included the painters Francesco da Ponte Bassano the Younger (1549–92) and Leandro da Ponte Bassano (1557–1622).

*DBI s.v. Dal Ponte; MDA s.v. Bassano (2); Paolo Berdini, The Religious Art of Jacopo Bassano (1997).*

**BASSE DANSE** was a popular dance in the courts of western Europe during the fifteenth and early part of the sixteenth centuries. By the 1500s it had become a stereotyped dance, generally in slow triple metre with frequent repetitions of melodic material.

**BATAILLE, GABRIEL** (c.1575–1630), French lutenist and composer whose *Airs de différents auteurs, mis en tablature de luth* was published by Pierre Ballard in 1608. In addition to these arrangements, he composed his own songs, most of which were secular airs, including some *chansons pour boire* and others for *ballets de cour*.

**BATESON, THOMAS** (c.1570/5–1630), English composer and cathedral organist at Chester and Christ Church, Dublin. Little sacred music survives but there are two sets of madrigals (1604 and 1618). The first includes the madrigal which missed the deadline for inclusion in The TRIUMPHS OF ORIANA (1601).

**BATTEN, ADRIAN** (1591–1637), English composer. He was a chorister at Winchester Cathedral and a lay vicar at Westminster Abbey. His compositions include several services and anthems; 'Hear my prayer, O Lord' and 'Out of the deep' are fine examples of his verse anthems. He is less well known than his more inventive contemporaries TOMKINS and GIBBONS.

**BATTISTA DA CREMA or Battista Cariono** (1460–1537), Dominican leader and writer. He became a Dominican friar in his native Crema. He contributed to the development of the THEATINES and in 1529 became confessor and spiritual adviser to Ludovica TORELLI. He was also the mentor of Antonio Maria ZACCARIA, founder of the BARNABITES.

*DBI s.v. Cariono, Battista.*

**BAUDART, WILLEM** (1565–1640), Dutch biblical scholar, born in Deinze (near Ghent). His parents became religious refugees in England, and Baudart's education began in Sandwich and Canterbury. In 1577 Baudart returned with his family to the Netherlands, and his education continued in Leiden, Franeker, Heidelberg, and Bremen. By the time he returned to the Netherlands in 1593, Baudart had become a formidable scholar of Greek and Hebrew. He compiled an index to the Hebrew, Greek, and Latin Bibles (1596) and wrote a history of the REVOLT OF THE NETHERLANDS (*Les Guerres de Nassau*, 2 vols., Amsterdam, 1616). He articulated his opposition to the truce with Spain signed in 1609 in his *Morgenwecker* (1610).

NNBW 3 s.v. Baudartius.

**BAUDOUIN, FRANÇOIS** (1520–73), French humanist jurist and theologian. His *Scaevola seu Iurisprudentia Muciana* (1558) is an analysis of works attributed to the second-century Roman jurist Quintus Scaevola. His *Justinianus* of 1560 sets out an *interpretatio duplex* which considers the alternatives of a revival of pure Roman law and an adaptation of Roman law to suit the needs of contemporary France. Baudouin's approach to Roman law was avowedly historical; his synthesis of history and law is *De institutione historiae universalis et eius cum iurisprudentia coniunctione* (1561).

Donald R. Kelley, *Foundations of Modern Historical Scholarship: Language, Law and History in the French Renaissance* (1970), 116–48.

**BAUHIN, GASPARD** (1560–1624), Swiss botanist and anatomist, born in Basel, the son of a French physician who had moved to Basel as a religious refugee. Gaspard was educated in Padua and Montpellier, and in 1580 returned to Basel, where he was appointed to the chairs of Greek (1582) and botany (1588). His botanical books (on which he collaborated with his brother Jean) were *Pinax theatri botanici* (1596 and 1619) and *Historia plantarum generalis* (1619); these volumes, which drew on both the natural histories of antiquity and the Bauhins' observations of the plants growing near Basel, contain descriptions and illustrations of more than 5,000 plants. Gaspard's anatomical books, such as *Theatrum anatomicum infinitis locis auctum* (1592), supplemented the illustrations of VESALIUS and introduced a nomenclature of muscles that is still in use.

DHBS s.v. Bauhin, Caspar; DSB; NDB.

**BAVARIA or (German) Bayern**, a south German duchy ruled by the WITTELSBACH FAMILY (see Appendix 1) from 1180 to 1918. From 1253 to 1504 the duchy was repeatedly partitioned, initially into Upper Bavaria and Lower Bavaria, and then to Upper Bavaria-Ingolstadt, Upper Bavaria-Munich, Lower Bavaria-Landshut, and Lower Bavaria-Straubing. Reunification was achieved by Albrecht IV, duke of Bavaria from 1467 to 1508, who united the duchy in 1504 and established MUNICH as its capital; in 1506 Albrecht solved the problem of partition by instituting the principle of primogeniture. On his death, however, his younger son, Ludwig X, ruled part of the duchy separately from his elder brother Wilhelm IV (duke from 1508 to 1550), but on Ludwig's death in 1545 the duchy was permanently reunited. In 1623 the duke of Bavaria became an elector in succession to the elector of the PALATINATE.

Bavaria declined to adopt the Reformation, and is still predominantly Catholic. Wilhelm IV supported the Empire against the SCHMALKALDIC LEAGUE, and his son ALBRECHT V enforced Catholicism throughout the duchy. Wilhelm V, who inherited the dukedom in 1579, was obliged to abdicate in favour of his son Maximilian I, who ruled from 1597 to 1651.

During the THIRTY YEARS WAR Bavaria was a Catholic stronghold, and so was ravaged by Swedish and French armies.

The first and most important university in Bavaria was established in Ingolstadt by a bull issued by Pope PIUS II on 7 April 1452. Albrecht IV supported the university, which finally opened in 1472 with a complement of twelve professors (two theology, three jurisprudence, one medicine, and six arts). Every student was obliged on graduation to swear an oath of fidelity to the pope, and this oath remained in place throughout the period of the Reformation, when Ingolstadt remained an important centre for Catholic education. In 1556 the JESUITS were invited to work in Bavaria, and they chose to establish their headquarters in the university.

M. Spindler, *Handbuch der bayerischen Geschichte* (4 vols., 1967).

**BAY or (Latin) Baius, MICHEL DE** (1513–89), Flemish theologian, educated in Louvain, where he later taught theology. In the early 1550s he began, together with Jan Hessels (1522–66), to promulgate a doctrine of GRACE that was deemed unorthodox by the university and by the archbishop of Mechelen (Malines). This doctrine, which is known as Baianism, extends the anti-Pelagian teaching of AUGUSTINE in ways that anticipate the Jansenism of seventeenth-century France. Bay's doctrine consisted of three related points: that prelapsarian innocence was a natural human state rather than a supernatural gift of God; that original sin is not the consequence of a withdrawal of divine grace but rather a habitual concupiscence that is transmitted to infants in the womb and is present even in unconscious infants; and that redemptive grace permits the Christian to recover the natural state of prelapsarian innocence, and so to live a morally pure life motivated by charity rather than concupiscence. At the heart of this doctrine is the contention that grace is natural rather than supernatural.

In 1560 eighteen of Bay's propositions were censured by the University of Paris, but he and Hessels were nonetheless chosen to represent the University of Louvain at the COUNCIL OF TRENT. On 1 October 1567 the papal bull *Ex omnibus afflictionibus* condemned many of Bay's theological propositions, but did not name him. Thereafter Bay tried to reword his doctrine to avoid the obloquy of the Church, but in 1579 the papal bull *Provisionis nostri* reaffirmed the censure of the earlier bull, and Bay was forced formally to recant. His later writings on the subject are carefully worded, but seem to imply that he remained faithful to his heterodox convictions.

BNB; NBW I s.v. Bay, Michael de.

**BAYARD, PIERRE TERRAIL, SEIGNEUR DE** (c.1473–1524), Savoyard soldier in the service of France, born in Château Bayard (Dauphiné, near Chambéry). He was educated at the ducal court in Savoy, serving as a page to Duke Charles I, and became a soldier, fighting in the WARS OF ITALY under CHARLES VIII, LOUIS XII, and FRANCIS I. In 1494 he accompanied Charles VIII on his invasion of Italy; he may have been knighted after the battle of FORNOVO, but was captured soon afterwards by the forces of Ludovico SFORZA, who freed him without a ransom. In 1503 he fought a famous duel with Alonso de Sotomayor and later in the year conducted a heroic defence of the bridge over the Garigliano; such exploits helped to create the image of Bayard as a military leader who was also capable of heroism in single combat.

Bayard fought for King Louis XII in Italy from 1508 (the siege of Genoa) to 1512 (the battle of Ravenna). On returning to France he fought in the battle of the SPURS, where he was captured by the forces of HENRY VIII, who released him without a ransom on condition that he not take up arms for six weeks.

On the accession of Francis I in 1515, Bayard was appointed lieutenant-general of Dauphiné, and then returned to Italy. He distinguished himself at the battle of MARIGNANO (1515), at the end of which he supposedly knighted the young King Francis on the battlefield. In 1521 Bayard held Mézières (Ardennes) with a force of 1,000 men against an imperial siege mounted by an army of 35,000 men, and the success of his resistance, which was deemed to have saved France from invasion, made him a national hero. He returned to Italy in 1523, and was killed by an arquebus ball in an engagement with Spanish troops on 30 April 1524.

Within his lifetime Bayard had become an icon of CHIVALRY, a soldier who had been twice released without ransom because of his gallantry and who enjoyed a reputation for heroism, piety, and magnanimity in victory; these qualities were reflected in popular references to Bayard as *le chevalier sans peur et sans reproche* and *le bon cavalier*. Behind this romantic representation of Bayard's character lay a soldier who was a fine strategist and tactician and a firm believer in reconnaissance and espionage but as a champion of knightly cavalry remained stubbornly opposed to the emerging importance of infantry and the use of firearms.

*DBF*; Jean Jacquart, *Bayard* (1987).

**BAYER or Beyer, JOHANN** (1563–1625), German astronomer, born in Augsburg, where he practised law. In his *Uranometria* (Nuremberg, 1603) Bayer depicted twelve new constellations visible from the southern seas and introduced the system (still in use) of naming stars within constellations according to brightness, using letters of the Greek alphabet, so that the brightest star in the Swan becomes $\alpha$ Cygni, the next brightest $\beta$ Cygni, and so on. In a posthumously published treatise, *Coelum stellatum christianum* (1627), he proposed (in vain) a second reform in which classical names for constellations would be replaced by biblical ones, so that Argo, for example, would become Noah's Ark.

**BAZÁN, ÁLVARO DE.** See SANTA CRUZ, ÁLVARO DE BAZÁN, MARQUIS OF.

**BEATON or Bethune, DAVID** (c.1494–1546), Scottish cardinal and diplomat. He was appointed abbot of Arbroath in June 1524, and subsequently undertook a series of diplomatic missions to France on behalf of King JAMES V. Thereafter he was appointed keeper of the privy seal (1529), cardinal (1538), and archbishop of St Andrews (1539). Cardinal Beaton was a resolute opponent of English plans to subjugate Scotland, and of Protestant attempts to introduce the REFORMATION into Scotland. The Scottish reformer George Wishart, who

may have been involved in an English plot to kill Beaton, was captured and on Beaton's orders burnt at St Andrews on 1 March 1546; three months later (29 May) Beaton was assassinated.

*DNB.*

**BEATUS RHENANUS or Beat Bild von Rheinau** (1485–1547), German humanist scholar and printer, born on 22 August 1485 in Schlettstadt (now French Sélestat), in Alsace, the son of a prosperous butcher who had been born in Rheinau (now French Rhinau), close to Schlettstadt. He was educated at the Latin school in Schlettstadt and (from 1503) at the University of Paris. In 1511 he moved to Basel, where he became a friend of ERASMUS and entered the publishing trade, initially with Johann FROBEN.

In 1526 Beatus returned to Schlettstadt, where he worked as a printer and publisher. He edited and published works by TACITUS (1519, excluding the histories), LIVY (1535), Velleius Paterculus (1522, from a manuscript that he discovered), and Erasmus (nine folio volumes, including a biography, 1540–1). His most important original work was *Rerum Germanicorum libri tres* (1531), which is a distinguished example of humanist historiography. He died in Strasbourg on 20 July 1547.

*NDB.*

**BEAUGRANT, GUYOT DE** (c.1500–1549), French sculptor who worked for several years (c.1525–30) in Flanders, where he assisted Lanceloot BLONDEEL in the sculpting of the chimney piece in the council chamber of the Palais de Justice. In 1533 he migrated to Spain, where he made the carvings for the Church of Santiago in Bilbao (Basque Bilbo).

*BNB; MDA.*

**BEAUMONT, FRANCIS** (1584–1616), English playwright. Following Oxford and the Inner Temple, Beaumont collaborated with FLETCHER on over 50 plays between 1606 and 1613. Although the pair wrote some plays alone, they are remembered as a partnership, and attribution of plays or parts of plays to each is a difficult process. Among their best-known collaborations are *The Knight of the Burning Pestle* (1609), *Philaster* (1611), and *The Maid's Tragedy* (1611).

*DNB.*

**BEBEL, HEINRICH** (1472–1518), German humanist poet, born into a peasant family in Württemberg and educated in Kraków and Basel. In 1497 he became professor of rhetoric at Tübingen, and in 1501 he was crowned as POET LAUREATE by Maximilian I. Bebel was the most important German exponent of the *Fazetie* (see FACETIAE); his two collections were *Libri facetiarum incundissimi* (1512) and *Novus liber facetiarum* (1514). He also wrote an anticlerical satirical poem (*Triumphans Veneris*, 1509) and treatises on Latin grammar.

*DLL; NDB.*

**BECCADELLI, ANTONIO, or Il Panormita** (1394–1471), Italian humanist poet, born in Palermo; his nickname derives from Panormus, the Latin name of Palermo. He lived in a series of north Italian courts (1420–34) and in 1425, while in Bologna, published *Hermaphroditus*, a Latin poem (dedicated to Cosimo de' MEDICI) that elegantly described heterosexual and homosexual liaisons as pleasures rather than vices; copies of the poem were publicly burnt.

After a period as court poet at Pavia, Beccadelli returned in 1434 to Naples, where he joined the service of ALFONSO V (and later of FERRANTE I) as a secretary and adviser. He supported humanist scholarship, notably by his foundation in 1442 of the Accademia Pontaniana (see ACADEMIES). His adulatory biography of King Alfonso, *De dictus et de factis Alfonsi regis* (1455), is the principal source of the legends of the king's magnanimity.

DBI; OCIL; *A Panhormitae, Hermaphroditus*, ed. D. Coppini (1990).

**BECCAFUMI, DOMENICO DI PACE** (*c*.1484–1551), Italian painter, born in a village near Siena, the son of a peasant, and trained in Siena and Rome. He later assumed the name of his Sienese patron, Lorenzo Beccafumi. Returning to Siena in 1512, Beccafumi painted frescoes for the Palazzo Pubblico (1529–35), designed 35 biblical scenes for the marble floor in the cathedral, contributed to the decoration of the façade of Palazzo Borghese, decorated the ceiling of the Palazzo Bindi Sergardi, and made a mosaic for the Church of San Bernardino. Many of his panel paintings are in the Pinacoteca in Siena, including *The Trinity and Saints* (1513), *St Catherine Receiving the Stigmata* (*c*.1514), *The Mystic Marriage of St Catherine* (1528), and *Christ in Limbo* (*c*.1536). His *Story of Papirius* (1540–50, National Gallery, London) depicts small figures in an architectural setting.

DBI; MDA; Piero Torriti, *Beccafumi* (1997); Pascale Dubus, *Domenico Beccafumi* (2000).

**BECERRA, FRANCISCO** (1545–1605), Spanish architect in Mexico and Peru, born in Trujillo (Extremadura), where he worked as a master mason before leaving for Mexico in 1573. He was master of the works at Puebla Cathedral from 1575 until about 1580, when he moved to Quito (then in Peru), where he designed the churches of San Agustín and Santo Domingo. In 1582 he moved to Lima, where he was responsible for the severe designs of the cathedrals at Lima (1582–1601) and Cuzco (1582–1654); the heavily baroque façade of Cuzco Cathedral is the work of a later architect.

DBEH; MDA.

**BECERRA, GASPAR** (*c*.1520–1568), Spanish sculptor and painter who studied in Rome, where he assisted VASARI with the decoration of the papal chancellery. He returned to Spain in about 1557 and the following year began work on the ALTARPIECE of Astorga Cathedral. In 1563 he was appointed court painter to PHILIP II.

MDA.

**BECK, LEONHARD** (*c*.1480–1542), German painter and woodcut engraver, born in Augsburg, the son of a manuscript illuminator. He was apprenticed to Hans Holbein the Elder in 1495; he became an independent member of the guild in 1503. Beck collaborated with Hans BURGKMAIR the Elder and Hans SCHÄUFELIN on the cycles of woodcuts commissioned by the Emperor MAXIMILIAN I and known as the *Teuerdank* and the *Weisskunig*. The emperor also commis-

sioned a series called the *Sipp- Mag- und Schwägerschaften* for which Beck designed 123 WOODCUTS of saints. Beck may have been the anonymous artist who between 1502 and 1515 drew a series of chalk portraits of Augsburg artists.

NDB; MDA s.v. Beck (2).

**BECON, THOMAS** (*c*.1513–1567), English Protestant reformer. Becon was influenced by LATIMER whilst at Cambridge, and was ordained priest in 1538. His Protestant preaching caused him to be arrested in 1541 and 1543; he was forced to recant and to destroy his writings. Until the accession of EDWARD VI in 1547, he travelled the country as a layman, and published his popular and polemical writings under the pseudonym Theodore Basil. In 1547 he became chaplain to Protector SOMERSET, and to CRANMER, and he contributed the sermon on adultery to Cranmer's Book of Homilies. He was briefly imprisoned under MARY, and subsequently left the country, but became a canon at Canterbury Cathedral under ELIZABETH.

DNB; D. S. Bailey, *Thomas Becon and the Reformation of the Church in England* (1952).

**BEDLAM.** See BETHLEM HOSPITAL.

**BEDS.** Until the seventeenth century most Europeans spread bedding on the bare floor or on rushes, but in wealthy households bedding was laid on a dais or a raised bed, which from the twelfth century was sometimes surmounted by a canopy which was originally called a celure and from the seventeenth century was known as a tester (a term previously used to denote the headboard). By the early fourteenth century French celures were supported by four posts, a fashion which later spread to England. The state bed of the fifteenth century, which was hung with tapestries, was only used on ceremonial occasions, but by the sixteenth century beds with celures and embroidered curtains had become common in prosperous households; the most famous example is the Great Bed of Ware (*c*.1590) mentioned in Shakespeare's *Twelfth Night*, when it was kept in the Saracen's Head in Ware; it was later removed to Rye House and is now in the Victoria and Albert Museum. Less affluent and spacious houses had press beds that fitted into cupboards when not in use: when hinged at the top the opened door served as a canopy with supporting poles at the foot, and when hinged near the bottom the opened door supported the bedding and rested on supports at the foot.

**BEERT, OSIAS** (*c*.1580–1624), Flemish painter and cork merchant. He became a master in Antwerp in 1602, but continued his business as a cork merchant. He was an early exponent of STILL LIFE and flower pictures and is best known for his pictures of crustaceans (especially oysters).

MDA.

**BEESTON, CHRISTOPHER** (*c*.1570–1638), English actor-manager. Beeston's early career was as an actor, with STRANGE'S MEN and then QUEEN ANNE'S MEN, which he also managed. In 1616–17, he retired from acting and ran the COCKPIT Theatre, which was converted from its original use for cockfighting. Between 1625 and 1636 he managed Queen Henrietta's Men.

*DNB.*

**BEHAIM, MARTIN** (1459–1507), German geographer and navigator in Portugal. He was a native of Nuremberg who moved to Portugal, where he entered the service of King JOHN II and joined the royal commission responsible for maritime exploration. In 1485 he sailed with Diogo CÃO on his second expedition along the coast of Africa and on his return to Portugal was ennobled. He constructed the first terrestrial GLOBE (now in the Germanisches Nationalmuseum in Nuremberg) in 1492 while on a visit to Nuremberg; the globe illustrates Behaim's contention that all parts of the world were accessible by sea.

*DSB; NDB;* E. G. Ravenstein, *Martin Behaim: His Life and Globe* (1908).

**BEHAM, HANS SEBALD** (1500–50) and **BARTEL** (1502–40), Nuremberg engravers, brothers who engraved illustrations for the Bible and for mythological and historical books. Their style is characteristic of the art of the LITTLE MASTERS. In 1525 the brothers were found guilty of blasphemy and sedition and expelled from the city.

*NDB; MDA* s.v. Beham (1) and (2).

**BELALCÁZAR or Benalcázar, SEBASTIÁN DE** (c.1480–1551), Spanish conquistador who participated in the conquest of Nicaragua (1524–7) and then travelled to Peru in the expedition led by PIZARRO, who appointed him to command the garrison in the coastal town of Piura. Belalcázar subsequently led the conquest of Quito (1534) and then travelled north to Popayán (1538) and Cali, reaching Bogotá in 1539. In Bogotá he was welcomed by Gonzalo JIMÉNEZ DE QUESADA and met Nikolaus FEDERMANN. He died in Cartagena de Indias while returning to Spain under indictment for the murder of Jorge Robledo, a powerful local figure.

*DBEH; DHE* s.v. Benalcázar; Diego Garcés Giraldo, *Sebastián de Belalcázar: Estudio biográfico* (1986); J. I. Avellaneda Navas, *La expedición de Sebastián de Belalcázar* (1992).

**BELGIC CONFESSION**. See BRAY, GUIDO DE.

**BELLANO, BARTOLOMEO** (1437/8–1496/7), Italian sculptor and architect, born in Padua, the son of a goldsmith. He was trained in the studio of DONATELLO in Florence. In 1467 he visited Perugia, where he sculpted a life-sized statue of Pope PAUL II (destroyed 1798), and may have worked in the papal service in Rome. By 1469 Bellano had returned to Padua, where he fashioned his most famous work, a marble reliquary chest for the relics of St Anthony of Padua (now in the treasury chapel of the Basilica del Santo in Padua). In 1479 he accompanied Gentile BELLINI on a visit to Constantinople on behalf of the Venetian republic, of which Padua was a dependency. Bellano later made the ten bronze bas-reliefs in the chancel of the Basilica del Santo in Padua (1484–8).

*DBI* s.v. Bellano (Vellano), Bartolomeo; *MDA;* Volker Krahn, *Bartolomeo Bellano: Studien zur Paduaner Plastik des Quattrocento* (1988).

**BELLARMINE or (German)** *Bartmannskrug* ('bearded-man jug'), a type of German glazed stoneware jug produced from the fifteenth to the nineteenth centuries and from the seventeenth century known in English as the bellarmine, the eponym of which was Cardinal Roberto BELLARMINO, who was detested in England because of his anti-Protestant polemics. The jugs, which are decorated with the moulded face of a bearded man (sometimes with a coat of arms below it), are also known as 'Greybeards' and as 'd'Alva bottles'; the latter name alludes to the duke of ALBA, who persecuted Protestants in the Netherlands.

**BELLARMINO, ROBERTO** (1542–1621), cardinal and controversialist, born in Montepulciano (Tuscany) on 4 October 1542. As a young man he became proficient as a composer of Latin verse, a violinist, and a debater. In 1560 he entered the JESUIT ORDER, and after teaching classics in Florence and Piedmont moved to the Netherlands, where he was ordained as a priest in Ghent (1570), lectured on THOMAS AQUINAS in Louvain (where he attacked the teaching of Michel de BAY), and wrote a Hebrew grammar.

In 1576 Bellarmine moved to Rome, where he became professor of 'controversial theology' at the Jesuits' Collegium Romanum; his lectures on theological controversies were collected as *Disputationes de controversiis christiane fidei adversus huius temporis haereticos* (3 vols., Ingolstadt, 1586–93), a learned statement of the Catholic position on a huge range of issues. He played a prominent role in the revision of the Vulgate BIBLE and the publication in 1592 of the version known as the Sixto-Clementine.

Bellarmino was appointed rector of the Collegium Romanum in 1592, provincial of Naples in 1594, cardinal in 1598, and archbishop of Capua in 1602. In 1605 he resigned his see and returned to Rome to become prefect of the VATICAN LIBRARY and a participant in several Roman congregations. He engaged in controversy with King JAMES I and with William BARCLAY. In religious politics, he sought the recognition of HENRI IV as king of France and supported Pope Paul V in his struggle with Venice (in which Bellarmine's pamphleteering ally was Caesar BARONIUS and his opponent Paolo SARPI). He died, aged 79, on 17 September 1621.

Bellarmine was awarded the title 'venerable' in 1627, but his views on the temporal power of the papacy displeased Pope SIXTUS V and delayed his canonization. He was finally canonized in 1930 and named a doctor of the Church in 1931.

J. Brodrick, *Robert Bellarmine, Saint and Scholar* (1961).

**BELLAVERE or Bell'haver, VINCENZO** (1530–87), Venetian composer and organist who worked in Padua and Venice, where he succeeded Andrea GABRIELI as organist at San Marco. In addition to church music, he wrote madrigals and edited an anthology, *Primo libro delle justiniane* (1570), to which he contributed ten items.

**BELLEAU, RÉMY** (1528–77), French poet and member of the PLÉIADE, born in Nogent-le-Rotrou and educated at the Collège de Boncourt in Paris, where his teachers included MURET. In 1556 he published a translation of the odes of

Anacreon and a collection of original poems called *Petites Inventions*. After a brief period of service as cavalry officer in the WARS OF ITALY (1556–7), where his commander was the marquis d'Elbeuf, Belleau returned to France, where he published a commentary on RONSARD's *Second Livre des amours* (1560). He became a tutor in the household of the marquis d'Elbeuf, working at the family seat in Joinville, which became the setting of Belleau's most important poem, *La Bergerie* (1565; revised 1572). Belleau's skill as a descriptive poet, which had been adumbrated in the *blasons* (see BLAZON) of the *Petites Inventions*, found its fullest expression in his lapidary *Les Amours et nouveaux échanges des pierres précieuses* (1576), which also included versions of Ecclesiastes and the Song of Solomon in French verse.

DBF; *Œuvres poétiques*, ed. Guy Demerson (3 vols. to date, 1995–2001).

**BELLECHOSE, HENRI** (d. c.1445), Flemish painter from Brabant who in 1415 succeeded Jean MALOUEL as Burgundian court painter at Dijon. His only documented work is *The Martyrdom of St Denis* (Louvre), which was formerly thought to have been started by Malouel but is now thought to be solely the work of Bellechose.

BNB; MDA.

**BELLEGAMBE, JEAN** (c.1470–c.1535), Flemish painter, architect, furniture designer, and embroiderer, born in Douai (now in France but then in the Spanish Netherlands), the son of a cabinetmaker and musician; he remained in Douai throughout his life. His paintings are a syncretic blend of French and Flemish influences and were remarkable for their skilled use of colour; in the seventeenth century Bellegambe attracted the epithet 'Master of Colours'. He was primarily a painter of ALTARPIECES; his best-known work is the nine-panel polyptych known as the *Credo* altarpiece (Musée Municipal, Douai).

BNB; MDA.

**BELL'HAVER, VINCENZO**. See BELLAVERE, VINCENZO.

**BELLI, GIULIO** (c.1560–1621), Italian composer whose writings are principally masses and motets. There is also some secular vocal music included (with English texts) in MORLEY's *Madrigals to Five Voices* (1598). His sacred music reflects the influence of PALESTRINA; later works include continuo parts.

**BELLI or Bello, PIERINO, or Bellinus** (1502–75), Savoyard jurist, counsellor of state, and legal adviser to the duke of Savoy. His *De re militari et de bello tractatus* (1563) is an important contribution to early modern INTERNATIONAL LAW.

DBI s.v. Belli.

**BELLI, VALERIO, or Il Vicentino** (1468–1546), Italian engraver of gems, especially ROCK CRYSTAL, born in Vicenza. He may have trained in Venice before moving in 1520 to Rome, where Pope CLEMENT VII commissioned an engraved cross and three medallions, all in rock crystal (1524); they are now in the Vatican Library. In 1530 Belli returned to Vicenza, where in 1532 he completed a casket consisting of twenty panels of engraved rock crystal depicting the life of Jesus; the casket was commissioned by Clement VII, who presented it to King FRANCIS I, and it is now in the Museo degli Argenti in the Pitti Palace in Florence.

DBI; MDA; Howard Burns et al. (eds.), *Valerio Belli Vicentino* (2000).

**BELLINI, GENTILE** (c.1429–1507), Italian painter, born in Venice; he was the son of Jacopo BELLINI and elder brother of Giovanni BELLINI. In 1474 he was commissioned by the Venetian Senate to decorate the Sala del Maggior Consiglio in the Ducal Palace, reworking some of the canvases painted by his father; these paintings were lost in the fire of 1577. Gentile lived at the Ottoman court in Constantinople from 1479 to 1481, and there painted the portrait of *Sultan Mehmet II* (National Gallery, London). In 1493 he contributed three paintings to a cycle on *The Legend of the True Cross* (now in the Accademia, Venice) for the Scuola di San Giovanni Evangelista in Venice. His *Martyrdom of St Mark* (begun 1504) and his *St Mark Preaching in Alexandria* (begun 1506) were both left unfinished at his death; the former is still in the Scuola di San Marco in Venice, whilst the latter is now in the Brera, Milan. The finest aspect of his pictures is the treatment of townscapes peopled with crowds attending religious processions, as in the *True Cross* paintings.

DBI; MDA s.v. Bellini: (2); Jürg Meyer zur Capellen, *Gentile Bellini* (1985).

**BELLINI, GIOVANNI, called Giambellino** (c.1431/6–1516), Italian painter, born in Venice; he was the son of Jacopo BELLINI and younger brother of Gentile BELLINI. He was trained in his father's workshop, and, after his sister Nicolosia's marriage to MANTEGNA in 1454, fell under the latter's beneficent influence. Art historians often compare their treatments of *The Agony in the Garden*, both painted in the early 1460s and now hanging together in the National Gallery in London. The composition and the treatment of the foreground figures in Bellini's version is clearly indebted to Mantegna; the landscape background of the two pictures, however, demonstrates the originality which makes Bellini a seminal figure: Mantegna's background is precisely drafted, minutely observed, and rigorously representational, but Bellini's brushwork evokes light and space and colour by moving away from representation in order to capture the effect of the dim sunlight on the contours of the countryside. This break from the sculptural definition of form in favour of a lyrical use of light and colour was passed by Bellini to his pupil PALMA VECCHIO and to GIORGIONE (who may have been his pupil) and later to TITIAN. His innovations changed the course of western art.

Bellini was a prolific painter who continued throughout

---

Giovanni Bellini, *Madonna and Child* (c.1489), formerly in the Palazzo Barberini in Rome and now in the Burrell Collection, Glasgow

**Giovanni Bellini,** *Young Woman with a Mirror* (1515), Kunsthistorisches Museum, Vienna

his long life to innovate in all forms of painting from small devotional pictures to large altarpieces. The landscapes of paintings such as *The Crucifixion* (*c.*1465, Correr, Venice), *St Francis* (*c.*1480, Frick, New York), and *The Madonna of the Meadow* (*c.*1510, National Gallery, London) use light to create a contemplative mood, and increasingly light becomes the unifying force of his paintings; similarly, colour ceases to be representational and decorative, and in a painting such as *The Dead Christ with St John and the Virgin* (Brera, Milan) the cold colour of the clothing and the steely chill of the sky and landscape combine to produce the mood of desolation that Bellini sought.

Bellini's ALTARPIECES also use light and colour to create both coherence and mood. From his early *St Vincent Ferrer* (if it can confidently be said to be his) in SS Giovanni e Paolo in Venice (*c.*1465), in which both figures and landscapes are transfigured by light, to the versions of *The Madonna with Saints* in the Church of the Frari in Venice (which Ruskin thought one of the three finest paintings in the world) and in San Zaccaria in Venice, his altarpieces increasingly show independence from both the early influence of Mantegna and the later influence of ANTONELLO DA MESSINA; in these altarpieces Bellini achieves an unprecedented coherence not only through his use of light and colour but also through his attentiveness to the relationships between the paintings and their settings.

Bellini's small paintings are usually devotional, and he returned on many occasions to the *Madonna and Child*; a particularly fine example is the *Madonna and Child* (*c.*1489) now in the Burrell Collection in Glasgow. He painted a small number of portraits, notably *The Doge Loredan* (*c.*1501), now in the National Gallery in London, in which the light gives the skin a translucent quality. His late works, several of which deploy abstract patterning, include the innovative *Fra Teodoro* (1515) in the National Gallery in London, the comic *Feast of the Gods* in the National Gallery in Washington (1514), and his only known female nude, the reticently sensuous *Young Woman with a Mirror* (1515) in the Kunsthistorisches Museum in Vienna.

Bellini was appointed chief painter to the Venetian republic in 1483 and remained pre-eminent among Venetian painters until his death in 1516.

DBI; MDA; Rona Goffen, *Giovanni Bellini* (1989); Anchise Tempestini, *Giovanni Bellini* (1999).

**BELLINI, JACOPO** (*c.*1400–1470/1), Italian painter, born in Venice, the son of a pewterer, and trained in the studio of GENTILE DA FABRIANO. In 1436 he painted a *Crucifixion* in Verona (destroyed 1759) and in 1441 won a competition in Ferrara to paint the young Lionello d'ESTE (now lost); another portrait was painted by PISANELLO. On returning to Venice he established a studio with his two sons, Gentile BELLINI and Giovanni BELLINI .

Jacopo Bellini's signed paintings include a *Jesus on the Cross* (Museo Civico, Verona), a *Virgin and Child* (Accademia, Venice), and two Madonnas (Louvre and Brera); he also painted a *St Jerome* (Museo Civico, Verona) and an *Annunciation* (Church of Sant'Alessandro, Brescia). Jacopo's two surviving sketchbooks (Louvre and British Museum) contain more than 230 drawings, many of which are experiments in PERSPECTIVE and composition. The drawings were occasionally later adapted by Jacopo's two sons and by his son-in-law MANTEGNA for their own works, although this does not seem to have been one of the acknowledged functions of the books.

DBI s.v. Bellini, Iacopo; MDA; Colin Eisler, *The Genius of Jacopo Bellini* (1989).

**BELVEDERE COURT or (Italian) Cortile di Belvedere**, a Vatican court (built 1503–15) designed by BRAMANTE to link St Peter's with the Villa Belvedere (which no longer exists). The original dimensions of the vast court were *c.*300 × 100 metres (330 × 110 yards). The buildings which enclosed the court now house the Vatican Museums. Originally the court was used for pageants, and at one end there was a garden museum for the display of ancient statues. In 1580 the court was divided by a building designed to accommodate the library of Sixtus V, so what is now the Giardino della Pigna was originally the northern end of the Belvedere Court.

J. S. Ackerman, *The Cortile del Belvedere* (1954); Hans Henrik Brummer, *The Statue Court in the Vatican Belvedere* (1970); David R. Coffin, *Gardens and Gardening in Papal Rome* (1991).

**BEMBO, PIETRO** (1470–1547), Italian poet, courtier, and literary theorist, born in Venice, the son of a diplomat; his education included a period in Messina studying Greek with Constantinos LASCARIS. Bembo entered the service of Pope LEO X, and subsequently lived in the courts of Padua and Urbino; in 1539 he returned to Rome, where Pope PAUL III made him a cardinal. As a young man Bembo had established his literary reputation with *Gli asolani* (1505), a dialogue on the nature of love, and later published a volume of poems (*Rime*, 1530) and a history of Venice. In *Il cortigiano* CASTIGLIONE presented Bembo as the ideal of the humanist courtier.

Bembo was the central figure in the debate known as the QUESTIONE DELLA LINGUA, to which his principal contributions were *De imitatione* (1512) and *Prose della volgar lingua* (1525), in which he advocated the use of Cicero as a model for Latin and trecento Tuscan (Petrarch for poetry and Boccaccio for prose) as the model for literary Italian.

DBI; OCIL; G. Santangelo, *Il Bembo critico* (1950); id., *Il petrarchismo del Bembo* (1967).

**BENEDETTI, GIOVANNI BATTISTA** (1530–90), Italian mathematician and natural philosopher, born in Venice, possibly of a Spanish family. He was one of the ablest geometers of his day. His work is notable for handling problems directly in three dimensions rather than, as was usual, reducing them to two.

For most of his life Benedetti was attached to the court of Savoy (in Turin), but he does not seem to have depended upon patronage for his livelihood. He wrote a substantial and widely read treatise on SUNDIALS (*De gnomonum umbrarumque solarium usu liber*, 1574), which contains some significant mathematical discoveries; his shorter works, together with his replies to correspondents' queries, were published as a collection (*Diversarum speculationum physicarum et mathematicarum liber*, 1585). This latter work includes a brief but important contribution to the theory of PERSPECTIVE (*De rationibus operationum perspectivae*). Benedetti discusses some results in statics and some thought experiments regarding the fall of heavy bodies that were later made famous by Galileo GALILEI (1638). It is not known whether Galileo knew Benedetti's work.

MDA; A. Manno (ed.), *Cultura, scienze e techniche nella Venezia del cinquecento: Atti del convegno internazionale 'Giovan Battista Benedetti e il suo tempo'* (1987).

**BENEDETTO, MAESTRO** (*fl.* 1503–22), Italian potter who established a MAIOLICA workshop in Siena in 1503. His only surviving signed work is a plate depicting St JEROME in blue monochrome (Victoria and Albert Museum, London).

**BENEDETTO DA MAIANO or Benedetto di Leonardo** (1442–97), Italian sculptor, the younger brother of GIULIANO DA MAIANO. He trained in the studio of Antonio ROSSELLINO in Florence. He sculpted the pulpit in the Church of Santa Croce in Florence (1472–5), an altar in the Chapel of Santa Fina in the Cathedral of San Gimignano (*c.*1475) and another in the Chapel of San Bartolo in the Church of Sant'Agostino in San Gimignano (1494), and a reredos in the Church of Monte Oliveto in Naples (*c.*1485), where his brother had worked. His portrait busts include one of Pietro Mellini, the donor of the Santa Croce pulpit (1474, Bargello), and another of Filippo STROZZI (Louvre). It is possible that Benedetto was, like his brother, an architect, if he was indeed responsible for the portico of Santa Maria delle Grazie in Arezzo (1490–1), which is sometimes attributed to him.

DBI s.v. Benedetto di Leonardo; MDA s.v. Maiano; Edgar Lein, *Benedetto da Maiano* (1988).

**BENEDICT XIII** (*c.*1328–1423), antipope from 28 September 1394 until his deposition on 26 July 1417, was born to a noble family in Illueca (Aragon) and was until his election known as Pedro da Luna. He was educated at Montpellier, where he lectured on CANON LAW until he was created cardinal by Pope Gregory XI in 1375. He participated in the strife-torn election of Urban VI, but eventually transferred his allegiance to the antipope Clement VII, and served as his legate in Spain and Portugal for eleven years.

On the death of Clement VII in 1394, the 21 Avignon cardinals each swore an oath to abdicate if the majority thought that abdication of both the Avignon and the Roman popes could heal the rift of the GREAT SCHISM. Pedro da Luna had opposed the oath, but nonetheless took it, albeit reluctantly. Having secured election as Benedict XIII by agreeing to abdicate, and insisting that abdication would be as easy as removing his hat, he then spent the next 30 years refusing to do so, so prolonging the schism. When the COUNCIL OF PISA met in 1409, both Benedict and the Roman pope GREGORY XII were deposed (on 5 June 1409). Benedict refused to be deposed, and retained the obedience of Sicily, Spain, Portugal, and Scotland. In 1415 he retreated to the castle of Peñiscola, a rocky headland on the coast of Valencia which he declared to be the seat of the true Church. On 26 July 1417 the COUNCIL OF CONSTANCE confirmed his deposition and extruded him from the Church, but Benedict again declined to be deposed. On 27 November 1422, in his mid-nineties, he defiantly created four new cardinals. He died on 23 May 1423, still claiming to be the rightful pope.

A. Glasfurd, *The Antipope (Peter de Luna, 1342–1423)* (1965).

**BENEFIT OF CLERGY.** One of the legal consequences of the murder of Thomas à Becket in 1170 was the development of immunity, for clergy accused of felonies, from prosecution by the royal courts, on the grounds that clergy were only accountable to the ecclesiastical courts. Benefit of clergy was claimed either before arraignment or after conviction but before sentence was passed; in theory defendants were then retried by an ecclesiastical court, but in practice these courts simply discharged defendants. Originally benefit of clergy could only be claimed by ordained clerks, monks, and nuns, but by 1350 it had been extended to lay clergy. In the fifteenth century Henry IV declared that only those in holy orders could claim benefit of clergy more than once; by the end of the century, those not in orders were branded (see CORPORAL PUNISHMENT) after their first conviction and prohibited from claiming the benefit a second time.

The restriction of the benefit to clergy gradually disappeared, and it became available to all literate men charged with felonies (except high treason), provided they had only married once; lay women could not claim the privilege until 1692. The convention by which judges satisfied themselves of the legitimacy of the claim to clerical immunity was the reading or recitation of Psalm 51 : 1 ('Have mercy upon me, O God, according to thy loving kindness: according unto the multitude of thy tender mercies blot out my transgressions'), which was known as the 'neck verse'. Convicted murderers, including Ben JONSON, simply recited the verse, whereupon branding on the thumb was substituted for hanging. In 1705 the 'neck-verse' test was abolished, which rendered the privilege available to all; the concomitant branding was abolished in 1779, and the plea was completely abolished in 1827; it survived until the middle of the nineteenth century only in North and South Carolina, a vestige of English COMMON LAW.

**BENING or Benig FAMILY**, a family of fifteenth-century Flemish book illuminators. The family was founded by Sanders (also known as Alexander) Bening (d. 1518), who painted MINIATURES in Bruges and Ghent. The illuminations in the Prayer Book of Ingelbert of Nassau (Bodleian Library, Oxford) are attributed to Sanders Bening, who has also been identified with the Master of Mary of Burgundy, so named from his most celebrated work, the Hours of Mary of Burgundy (Nationalbibliothek, Vienna). Sanders's son Simon Bening (c.1483–1561) adopted a naturalist Flemish style similar to his father's; the magnificent *Grimani Breviary* (Marciana Library, Venice) is the work of Simon Bening.

BNB; MDA.

**BENIVIENI, GIROLAMO** (1453–1542), Italian poet, a native of Florence and a member of the literary circle of Lorenzo de' MEDICI. His poetry, which contains lyrical and narrative verse, includes 'De la amore celeste', a canzona which became famous when it was chosen by PICO DELLA MIRANDOLA as the subject of a commentary. Benivieni later became a disciple of SAVONAROLA and repudiated his secular poetry.

DBI; OCIL; S. Jayne, *A Commentary on a Canzone of G. Benivieni by P. della Mirandola* (1984).

**BENNET, JOHN** (c.1575/80–1614), English composer, thought to have come from the north-west of England. He is remembered as a madrigalist. His style encompasses the joyous 'All creatures now' (1601), which appeared in *The* TRIUMPHS OF ORIANA (1601), and the serious intensity of 'Weepe O mine eyes'.

**BENSON, AMBROSIUS or (Italian) Ambrogio Benzone** (b. late fifteenth century, d. before 12 January 1550), Flemish painter of Italian birth who in 1518 became a citizen of Bruges, where he worked in the studio of Gérard DAVID. Many of his paintings were exported to Spain, including his triptych of *St Anthony of Padua*, which is now in the Musée d'Art Ancien in Brussels. Spanish elements in Benson's work led scholars to believe that he was a Spaniard who had been influenced by Flemish art, and so his works were long attributed to an unidentified Master of Segovia.

MDA.

**BENTIVOGLIO, GIOVANNI II** (1443–1508), ruler of Bologna, born on 15 February 1443, the posthumous son of Annibale Bentivoglio, who was ruler of Bologna until his murder, and Donnina Visconti. Giovanni became 'first citizen' in 1463; he could not be called *signore*, because Bologna was a papal fiefdom and so was nominally ruled by a papal legate. Giovanni ruled Bologna for 43 years, during which time his court was an important centre for literature and the arts and Bologna gained many fine churches and palaces; the artists from whom he commissioned work include Il FRANCIA, Francesco del COSSA, and Lorenzo COSTA. He married Ginevra Sforza, by whom he had twelve children.

In 1500 Cesare BORGIA, as part of his campaign to subjugate Romagna, fixed his attention on Bologna, but Giovanni was saved by French intervention. In 1502 he joined the conspiracy to overthrow Cesare Borgia, but when Borgia secured French assistance, Giovanni changed sides. Pope JULIUS II resolved to conquer the entire PAPAL STATE, and in November 1506 marched on Bologna together with the French army of

King LOUIS XII. Giovanni was deposed and exiled, and chose to seek refuge with the French in order to escape the recriminations of the pope. He died in exile in Milan in February 1508. Giovanni's son Annibale II became ruler of Bologna during the brief rebellion against Julius II (1511–12), but thereafter the city was ruled by papal legates.

*DBI; MDA.*

**BENTIVOGLIO FAMILY**, a Bolognese dynasty established by Giovanni I Bentivoglio (*c.*1358–1402), who seized power in March 1401 and was murdered by a mob in June 1402. In 1420 Giovanni's elder son Antonio Galeazzo (*c.*1390–1435), who taught law at the University of Bologna, seized power in a *coup d'état*, but was quickly deposed; he became a *condottiere* and was assassinated by papal officials. Annibale Bentivoglio (1413–45), the putative son of Anton Galeazzo (whose wife Francesca Gozzadini was uncertain about Annibale's paternity, so the matter was resolved by recourse to dice), led a revolt against the papacy in 1438, but was assassinated in 1445.

Annibale was succeeded by Sante Bentivoglio (1424–63), an apprentice in the wool guild of Florence who may have been the illegitimate son of Ercole (Giovanni's second son), but his paternity is uncertain. Sante ruled Bologna until his death in 1463, and was succeeded by Annibale's son Giovanni II BENTIVOGLIO.

*DBI;* Cecilia Ady, *The Bentivoglio of Bologna* (1937).

**BENVENUTO DA IMOLA** (1320/30–1387/8), Italian humanist. He was born in Imola and subsequently taught at Bologna and Ferrara. His writings include a history of ancient Rome, commentaries on classical literature, and, in 1373, the first commentary on DANTE's *Divina commedia*.

*DBI.*

**BENZI, UGO** (1376–1439), Spanish physician in Italy and France who taught in Bologna, Pavia, and Ferrara, where he was the physician of Niccolò III d'Este; he subsequently became the physician of Charles VII. His treatise on the preservation of health, *Trattato utilissimo circa la conservazione della sanitate*, which circulated in manuscript and was finally printed in 1481, was one of the first medical textbooks to be written in a European vernacular.

*DBI.*

**BENZONI, GIROLAMO** (1519–after 1572), traveller and historian, the son of a Milanese merchant. He travelled in Germany and Spain before sailing in 1542 to the West Indies and Peru; he returned to Spain in 1556. His autobiographical account of the New World, *Historia del mundo nuovo*, was published in 1572 and soon translated into French (1579) and Latin (1581).

*DBI.*

**BEOLCO, ANGELO, or Ruzante** (*c.*1500–1542), Italian actor and dramatist, born in Padua, the illegitimate son of a local landowner and a peasant. He secured the patronage of Alvise Cornaro, for whose literary circle he devised dramatic entertainments, and subsequently toured the Veneto with his troupe. He devised and acted the role of Ruzante, a peasant who is both the object and the voice of social satire. The plays performed by Beolco's company ranged from simple dialogues to five-act comedies in the tradition of *commedia erudita*.

*DBI; OCIL;* N. Dersoti, *Arcadia and the Stage: An Introduction to the Dramatic Art of Angelo Beolco Called Ruzante* (1978).

**BERENGARIO DA CARPI, JACOPO** (*c.*1460–*c.*1530), Italian anatomist who studied medicine at Bologna, where he received his doctorate in 1489. He remained in Bologna, where he worked as a physician and surgeon and (from 1502) lecturer in surgery. He conducted regular dissections for purposes of research and teaching, and developed considerable expertise in internal female anatomy and physiology; his cadavers included at least one pregnant woman who had been executed. He tempered received Galenic wisdom with his own observations, insisting, for example, that the network of blood vessels (*rete mirabile*) said to be seated at the base of the brain simply did not exist in humans (though it does exist in some animals). Berengario's *Isagogae brevis* (Bologna, 1522) contains many anatomical illustrations.

*DSB.*

**BERG, CLAUS** (*c.*1478/80–1532/5), German sculptor, a native of Lübeck. He worked in Denmark (from a workshop in Odense) from 1504/5 till 1532, whereupon he moved to Mecklenburg, possibly as a religious refugee. His religious works, notably the *Güstrower Domapostel* (the carved apostles in Güstrow Cathedral, *c.*1530), are often characterized by dramatic expression of sorrow.

*MDA.*

**BERGAMASCO, IL**. See CASTELLO, GIAMBATTISTA.

**BERGANTINA**, a small GALLEY used widely on the Mediterranean from the fourteenth to the sixteenth centuries, propelled by either sail or oars; in many respects it resembles the English PINNACE of the same period. The bergantina was typically 10 metres (30 feet) long and was fitted with eight to sixteen rowing benches and a small cabin aft for the officers. A single lateen sail was carried by one or two masts. The draught was less than 50 centimetres (20 inches), which suited the bergantina for coastal and river waters. Like the pinnace, the bergantina was routinely carried in pieces in the holds of larger ships bound for any coast on which wood was available for planking; COLUMBUS and his successors carried bergantinas in the holds of their ships.

**BERGOGNONE, AMBROGIO, or Ambrogio da Fossano** (*c.*1453–1523), Italian painter, trained in Milan. He worked from 1488 to 1494/5 on the Certosa di Pavia, for which he painted frescoes, altarpieces, and processional banners. He subsequently painted frescoes at Lodi (now lost) and at the Church of San Satiro in Milan (largely lost, but some fragments survive in the Brera). His figures are calm and still, and are set against delicate landscapes; these features are redolent of an older style, and do not imply any interest in the innovations of his contemporary LEONARDO DA VINCI.

*DBI* s.v. Ambrogio da Fossano; *MDA;* Gianni Carlo Sciolla (ed.), *Ambrogio da Fossano detto il Bergognone* (1998).

**BERLICHINGEN, GÖTZ VON or Gottfried von** (1480–1562), Franconian knight, soldier, and robber baron, born in the castle at Jagsthausen. He became a professional soldier, and in 1497 entered the service of Friedrich IV, margrave of Brandenburg-Ansbach; in 1498 he fought for the Emperor MAXIMILIAN in Burgundy, Lorraine, and Brabant, and in 1499 in the Swiss Confederation. In about 1500 he formed an army of mercenaries which he led in a series of private wars. In 1505, while besieging Landshut on behalf of Albrecht IV of Bavaria, his right hand was shot off; he substituted an iron hand (which is still on display in Jagsthausen Castle) and so became known as Götz 'mit der eisernen Hand' (Götz with the hand of iron).

In 1512 Götz robbed a party of merchants returning from the Leipzig Fair, and in consequence was placed under an imperial ban; the ban was lifted in 1514 in response to Götz's promise to pay a fine of 14,000 gulden, but was imposed again in 1516 after a raid into Hesse in which Götz kidnapped the count of Waldeck and forced him to pay a ransom of 8,400 gold gulden.

In 1519 Götz helped to defend ULRICH, duke of Württemberg, against the attack mounted by the SWABIAN LEAGUE. He was forced to surrender the town of Möckmühl and was taken prisoner; he was released in 1522, thanks to the mediation of Franz von SICKINGEN and Georg von FRUNDSBERG, on the payment of a ransom of 2,000 gulden and the taking of an oath undertaking not to seek revenge on the League. In 1525, during the PEASANTS' WAR, Götz became the leader of the rebels in Odenwald and helped to besiege Würzburg Castle, but later withdrew to his own castle. He was called to account in Speyer for his part in the rebellion, but was acquitted on 17 October 1526. He was lured to Augsburg by a promise of safe conduct proffered by the Swabian League but was arrested there on 28 November 1528 and imprisoned for two years; on the renewal of his oath of 1522 he was released into house arrest at his castle at Hornberg on the Neckar, where he remained until released from his oath by CHARLES V in 1540.

Götz returned to imperial service, fighting against the Ottomans in Hungary in 1542 and two years later fighting alongside Charles V in his invasion of France. He died in Hornberg on 23 July 1562. Berlichingen wrote an autobiography which was first published in 1731 as *Lebensbeschreibung Herrn Götzens von Berlichingen*, which was Goethe's source for the play that bears his name.

NDB; Helgard Ulmschneider, *Götz von Berlichingen* (1974).

**BERMEJO, BARTOLOMÉ** (*c.*1440–1495), Spanish painter and designer of stained glass who worked in Barcelona from 1486. His *Pietà* in the Museum of Barcelona Cathedral, which is executed in the Hispano-Flemish style of SPANISH ART, is signed and dated 1490, and so is one of the earliest surviving oil paintings in Spain.

DBEH; MDA; Eric Young, *Bartolomé Bermejo: The Great Hispano-Flemish Master* (1975).

**BERNARDES, DIOGO** (1530–1605), Portuguese poet, born in the northern province of Minho, the son of a public notary; as a young man he lived for a time at the royal court in Lisbon before returning to Minho to succeed his father. In 1578 Bernardes joined the expedition to KSAR-EL-KEBIR led by King SEBASTIAN I. The king was killed and Bernardes was captured; he was released in 1581, and thereafter held a minor post at the court of PHILIP II.

Bernardes collected his poetry in three volumes: *Rimas ao bom Jesus e à Virgem Gloriosa sua mãe* (1594), *Flores do Lima* (1596), and *O Lima* (1596). His poems are sometimes devotional, but he also wrote fine pastoral poetry in the Italianate style of SÁ DA MIRANDA.

**BERNARDI, GIOVANNI DESIDERIO** (1494–1553), Italian engraver of ROCK CRYSTAL, born in Castel Bolognese, the son of a goldsmith. He moved to Ferrara, where he entered the service of Alfonso I d'ESTE as an engraver and medallist. By 1530 he had moved to Rome, where he secured the patronage of the Medici Pope CLEMENT VII and Cardinal Ippolito de' Medici, for both of whom he executed rock crystal carvings (now lost and known from casts) that had been designed by MICHELANGELO. His best-known work is a set of six rock-crystal panels of the Cassetta Farnese designed by PERINO DEL VAGA and made by Bastiano SBARRI (1561, Museo Nazionale, Naples).

DBI; MDA.

**BERNARDI, STEFANO** (*c.*1585–1636), Italian composer and theorist. He worked in Verona, Rome, and Salzburg, where he contributed to the music at the consecration of the cathedral. He wrote both sacred and secular music, including several instrumental works.

**BERNARDINO OF SIENA or Bernardino degli Albizzeschi** (1380–1444), Franciscan friar. He was born at Massa Marittima, and in 1402 entered the Franciscan Order. He initially lived at Colombaio (near Siena) and then moved to Fiesole, where his cell can still be seen. In 1417 Bernardino moved to Milan and embarked on a career as a popular preacher. He subsequently travelled all over northern and central Italy, always on foot, preaching his message of penitence, reconciliation, the sanctity of poverty, and the wickedness of gambling, WITCHCRAFT, usury, and JEWS to large crowds, often in the open air. His sermons, which were later printed in his *Opera omnia* (Venice, 1591), are remarkable for their colloquial good humour and rhetorical force. He was committed to the 'Holy Name of Jesus', and at the conclusion of his sermons he would hold up for veneration a sign displaying the letters 'IHS'.

In 1437 Bernardino was elected vicar-general of the Strict Observant branch of the Franciscan Order, and under his leadership the number of Observant Franciscans rose more than tenfold; it is likely but not certain that he wrote the statutes for the Observants in 1440. Bernardino established schools of theology in Perugia and Monteripido in the belief that ignorance was as much a spiritual impediment as was wealth. In 1443 Bernardino resigned his post and returned to itinerant preaching, travelling on a donkey rather than on foot because of ill health. The following year he preached for

50 consecutive days in his native Massa Marittima and then set out for Naples, preaching as he travelled; he died in L'Aquila on 20 May 1444. He is buried in a mausoleum (constructed in 1505 and adorned with statues and bas-reliefs by Silvestro dell'Aquila) in the Basilica di San Bernardino, which was designed by Cola dell'Amatrice and erected in L'Aquila between 1454 and 1472; the façade was added in 1527. Many of the fifteenth-century houses in L'Aquila display the IHS monogram.

Bernardino was canonized by Pope NICHOLAS V in 1450. The cult of San Bernardino rapidly expanded throughout Europe; in England the Observant Friars who venerated him established a foundation in Greenwich in 1482 and expanded to a province of five houses in 1499. In Renaissance art San Bernardino is depicted as a small, emaciated figure holding the IHS sign, sometimes with three mitres at his feet (representing his declining of the bishoprics of Siena, Ferrara, and Urbino).

*DBI* s.v. Bernardino da Siena; I. Origo, *The World of San Bernardino* (1963).

**BERNI, FRANCESCO** (1497/8–1535), Italian poet, born in Florence. He became a canon, and served the Church contentedly until he was poisoned by a priest for declining to murder another priest. His poetry has a strong satirical edge, and his use of the lyric for burlesque created a minor literary genre now known as the *bernesco*. Berni's best-known work is his version (*rifacimento*) of BOIARDO's *Orlando innamorato* (1541), in which he substituted Tuscan locutions for Boiardo's Ferrarese idioms.

*DBI*; *OCIL*; Anne Reynolds, *Renaissance Humanism at the Court of Clement VII: Francesco Berni's Dialogue against Poets* (1997).

**BERNINI, PIETRO** (1562–1629), Italian sculptor. He was born in Sesto Fiorentino (Tuscany) but in 1584 moved to Naples, where he worked for twenty years; his finest Neapolitan work is the *Madonna* group in the Certosa di San Martino (1596–8). In 1604 he was called to Rome by Camillo Borghese (then the inquisitor and later Pope Paul V), for whom he collaborated with other sculptors on the Cappella Paolina (Pauline Chapel or Borghese Chapel) in the Basilica of Santa Maria Maggiore, where he carved the large *Assumption* now in the baptistery. He later carved the *St John the Baptist* (1616) in the Barberini Chapel in the Church of San Andrea della Valle.

Pietro Bernini was the father of Gianlorenzo Bernini (1598–1680), the most important BAROQUE architect and sculptor of the seventeenth century.

*DBI*; *MDA*.

**BÉROALDE DE VERVILLE, FRANÇOIS** (1556–1626), French author, born in Paris, the son of the HUGUENOT Hebrew scholar Matthieu Brouard; he studied in Geneva, where his father joined him in 1574. After the latter's death two years later, he travelled to Basel and Lyon, and by 1580 he had left Geneva permanently. He subsequently repudiated the Protestantism of his youth, and in 1593 he was appointed as a canon of the Cathedral of Saint-Gatien in Tours.

Béroalde de Verville's reputation is that of a polymath, and his works include a 1,000-line hexameral poem (*Les Connaissances nécessaires*, 1583) and a treatise on ALCHEMY (*Les Recherches de la pierre philosophale*, 1583). His other writings include a sequence of love sonnets (*Les Soupirs amoureux*, 1583), an epic poem on the ideal state (*L'Idée de la république*, 1584), devotional poety (*La Muse céleste*, 1583), a versification of the Lamentations of Jeremiah (*Les Ténèbres*, 1599), and *La Sérodokimasie* (1600), a poem in 300 quatrains on the breeding of silkworms. There is also a rambling romance, *Les Aventures de Floride* (1594–1601), and *Le Moyen de parvenir*, an imaginary and licentious dialogue between figures of antiquity. He also published a translation of COLONNA's *Poliphile* (1600).

*DBF*; V. L. Saulnier, 'Études sur Béroalde de Verville', *Bibliothèque d'humanisme et Renaissance* (1944); N. Cazauran (ed.), *Béroalde de Verville, 1556–1626* (1996).

**BEROALDO, FILIPPO THE ELDER** (1453–1505) and **FILIPPO THE YOUNGER** (1472–1518), Italian humanists. Filippo the Elder studied in his native Bologna and then taught in Parma and Paris before returning permanently to Bologna in 1478; his scholarly works consist of commentaries on ancient authors, the most famous being that on *The Golden Ass of Apuleius*. His son Filippo the Younger joined the papal court in Rome at the invitation of Pope LEO X; his principal scholarly work was the preparation of the *editio princeps* of the *Annales* of Tacitus (1515).

*DBI*; *OCIL*.

**BERRUGUETE, ALONSO** (c.1488–1561), Spanish painter, the son of Pedro BERRUGUETE. For an unknown period between 1504 and 1517 he lived in Italy, where he completed Filippino LIPPI's *Coronation of the Virgin* (now in the Louvre). The other paintings of his Italian period, notably the *Salome* now in the Uffizi, show a marked debt to MICHELANGELO (who mentions Berruguete in his *Letters*, as did VASARI in his *Lives*); the Uffizi also holds a collection of his ink drawings.

By 1517 Berruguete had returned to Spain to take up an appointment as court painter to CHARLES V. His principal work during this period was the 16-metre (50-foot) high composite ALTARPIECE (painted panels, grisailles, and statues in an architecture frame) made between 1526 and 1532 for the Church of San Benito in Valladolid, now dismantled and shown in three rooms in the Valladolid Museo Nacional de Escultura. His last important work was the tomb of Cardinal Juan de Tavera in the Hospital de Tavera in Toledo (1552–61).

*MDA*; R. de Orueta y Duarte, *Berruguete y su obra* (1917); José María de Azcárete, *Alonso Berruguete: Cuatro ensayos* (1963).

**BERRUGUETE, PEDRO** (c.1450–c.1500), Spanish painter who served as court painter to FERDINAND and ISABELLA. He is the most likely candidate for the unidentified 'Pietro spagnuolo' employed in 1477 alongside JOOS VAN WASSENHOVE and MELOZZO DA FORLÌ to work on the library of the Ducal Palace in Urbino. He worked in Toledo from 1483. His ten panels painted for the Dominican convent at Ávila (now in the Prado) show signs of Renaissance Italian influence, but are nonetheless predominantly in the style of SPANISH ART known as Hispano-Flemish.

*DBEH; MDA;* María Pilar Silva Maroto, *Pedro Berruguete* (1998).

**BERTAUT, JEAN** (1552–1611), French poet. He was the successor of Philippe DESPORTES as court poet to King HENRI III and retained this post under HENRI IV, to whose conversion he contributed; he served as councillor to the Parlement of Grenoble, almoner to MARIE DE MÉDICIS, and in 1606 was consecrated bishop of Sées (Normandy), where he died on 8 June 1611. In his capacity as court poet he wrote heroic verse in the tradition of RONSARD and undemanding celebrations of court life; he also wrote elegant love poetry characterized by philosophical abstractions (*Recueil de quelques vers amoureux,* 1602 and 1606). His best-known work is a narrative poem entitled *Timandre.*

*DBF.*

**BERTOLDO DI GIOVANNI** (*c.*1430/40–1491), Italian bronze sculptor and medallist, born in Florence, where he trained in the studio of DONATELLO; he later completed two pulpits in the Church of San Lorenzo left unfinished by Donatello at his death. Bertoldo specialized in small bronzes which were made for the *studioli* (see CABINET) of private collectors. His most important works are a bronze relief of *The Crucifixion with St Jerome and St Francis* (*c.*1478) and a *Battle* relief, both in the Bargello; attributions include an *Orpheus* statuette in the Bargello and a *Hercules* in the Galleria Estense in Modena. His medals include one depicting the PAZZI CONSPIRACY.

Bertoldo became the first head of the Academy of Art instituted by Lorenzo de' MEDICI in the Giardino di San Marco. His pupils included MICHELANGELO.

*DBI; MDA;* James Draper, *Bertoldo di Giovanni, Sculptor of the Medici Household* (1992).

**BERTRAND, ANTHOINE DE** (*c.*1530/40–*c.*1580/2), French composer. He was assassinated by Protestants who strongly objected to the nature of his hymn writing. Before the influence of the Jesuits was felt in his writing, he had been a composer of 'chansons d'amour follastres', setting texts by the humanists and Ronsardist poets in Toulouse.

**BÉSARD, JEAN BAPTISTE** (1567–after 1617), French composer and lutenist, and writer on philosophy, history, and medicine. He studied in Rome and later became a lute teacher in Cologne. In 1617 he published a dictionary of diseases and cures (*Antrum philosophicum*), a second collection of lute music (*Novus partus*), and a German translation of his manual on lute playing (*Thesaurus harmonicus*). He was by this time living in Augsburg.

**BESSARION, CARDINAL BASIL** (1408–72), Greek scholar in Italy; his Christian name is usually said to be Johannes, but this cannot be right, because in the Greek monastic tradition, the monk assumes upon profession a new name that begins with the first letter or syllable of his Christian name. The error can be traced to an eighteenth-century misreading of a Marciana MS. Bessarion was born on 2 January 1408 (the traditional date of 1403 is almost certainly wrong) in Trebizond, which was then a Greek city. He was educated in Constantinople, where one of his fellow students was Francesco FILELFO, with whom he remained on good terms until Bessarion died. Bessarion became a monk in 1423 and from 1431 to 1436 lived and studied at Mistra, where he acquired a learned enthusiasm for Plato, who was championed at Mistra by PLETHO. In 1436 he returned to Constantinople to become abbot (ἡγούμενος) of the monastery of St Basil; he was appointed metropolitan of Nicaea (now Iznik) in 1437. He favoured reunification of the Byzantine and Roman churches, and wrote several treatises on the subject; he also wrote a panegyric on the glories of Trebizond which contains a detailed account of the geography and daily life of his native city.

Bessarion championed the union at the COUNCIL OF FLORENCE in 1439. His advocacy of the union on terms favourable to the Roman Church so pleased the pope that he granted Bessarion a pension, to which a premium would be attached if Bessarion were to join the Roman curia. Bessarion agreed, converted to Catholicism, and was promptly made a cardinal. He returned to Constantinople for a short period before settling permanently in Italy, initially in Florence (1440–3) and then in Rome, where he remained permanently except for a period as governor of Bologna (1450–5). In his new role as a Catholic churchman Bessarion once again rose to high ecclesiastical office; he became a papal legate, and in 1455 and 1471 he was a candidate for the papacy. Throughout this period he wrote prolifically in both Greek and Latin; his Greek polemic *Against the Detractor of Plato* was an attack on the Aristotelianism of GEORGE OF TREBIZOND. Bessarion accumulated a large collection of Greek and Latin manuscripts, which he bequeathed in 1468 to Venice, where they became the founding collection of the Biblioteca Marciana.

*DBI* s.v. Bessarione; L. Mohler, *Kardinal Bessarion als Theologe, Humanist und Staatsmann* (3 vols., 1923–42); John Monfasani, *Byzantine Scholars in Renaissance Italy: Cardinal Bessarion and Other Emigrés* (1995); G. Fiaccadori et al. (eds.), *Bessarione e l'Umanesimo: Catalogo della mostra* (1994).

**BETHLEM HOSPITAL or Bedlam.** The Hospital of St Mary of Bethlehem was established as a religious house of the Sisters of the Star of Bethlehem in Bishopsgate (London) on 23 October 1247. By 1400 it had become a refuge for the mentally ill. In the early modern period the hospital housed and attempted to cure the harmlessly insane; those deemed to be incurable were not admitted. From 1553, those judged to be criminally insane were diverted to Bridewell, with which Bethlem shared a common governing body until 1948. The treatments consisted of bloodletting, emetics, and purges, all of which were designed to expel whatever was causing the malady (e.g. the black bile that caused MELANCHOLIA).

On the dissolution of the monasteries in 1547 Bethlem Hospital was incorporated as a royal foundation and presented by HENRY VIII to the City of London. In 1675 Bethlem moved to Moorfields, in 1815 to Lambeth (to the buildings that are now the Imperial War Museum), and in 1930 to its present location in Beckenham (Kent).

Bethlem was Europe's second hospital for the insane. The first was established by the Moors in Granada in 1365; Islamic influence lay behind the establishment of a succession of such hospitals in Spain, at Valencia (1407), Zaragoza (1427), Seville (1436), Barcelona (1481), and Toledo (1483).

Jonathan Andrews et al., *The History of Bethlem* (1997).

**BETTISI, LEONARDO, or Don Pino** (*fl.* 1566–89), Italian potter in FAENZA and an important manufacturer of BIANCHI. He worked with Virgiliotto CALAMELLI, on whose death in 1570 Bettisi leased his workshop from his widow. Some of his MAIOLICA services include hundreds of pieces (a set manufactured in 1568 had 307 pieces). Products of his factory are marked 'Don Pino'.

*DBI.*

**BEUCKELAER or Bueckelaer, JOACHIM** (*c.*1535–1573), Flemish painter, the nephew and pupil of Pieter AERTSEN. He painted large STILL LIFES, and his preferred settings were markets and kitchens. He is the earliest painter known to have depicted fish stalls.

*BNB; MDA.*

**BEVIN, ELWAY** (*c.*1554–1638), Welsh composer and theorist. Until his suspension, he was a vicar-choral at Wells Cathedral; he then became an organist in Bristol. His sacred music includes a 'short' Dorian service and he was renowned for his skill as a composer of canons, several examples of which can be found in his *Brief and Short Instruction in the Art of Music* (1631).

**BEZA, THEODORUS, or (French) Théodore de Bèze** (1519–1605), French theologian, historian, and dramatist, born in Vézelay (Burgundy). Beza received a humanist education in Orléans and then in Bourges, where he became a Protestant; he subsequently returned to Orléans, where he studied law (1535–9). In 1548 Beza published a collection of Latin poetry (*Poemata juvenalia*) and in the same year fled as a religious refugee to Lausanne, where he taught Greek; he then moved to Geneva, where he taught theology and in 1564 succeeded CALVIN as pastor. In his role as an ambassador for Calvinism and the church discipline of Geneva, Beza negotiated with Catholics at the Colloquy of POISSY (1561) and with the Lutherans at Montbéliard (1586).

Beza wrote prolifically in both French and Latin. His principal works were a Calvinist confession of faith (*Confession de la foi chrétienne*, 1559; Latin version, 1560), a biography of Calvin (*Vie de Calvin*, 1564), a treatise on Genevan church discipline (*Du droit de magistrats*, 1574), a continuation of MAROT's version of the Psalms (*Psaumes de David*, 1553), and a Calvinist play (*Abraham sacrifiant*, performed by Lausanne schoolboys in 1550) which dramatizes Genesis 22 and portrays Satan as a monk. In Latin his most important work was *De haereticis a civili magistratu puniendis* (1554), a defence of the execution of SERVETUS for heresy.

Beza's principal scholarly work was his Latin translation of the New Testament (1556), to which he added a Greek text in 1565. This edition, together with its textual and theological annotations, was designed as a Protestant corrective to the edition of ERASMUS. One of the texts on which Beza relied was the bilingual (Latin and Greek) text of the Gospels now known as the Codex Bezae (now in the Cambridge University Library).

*DBF; Correspondance*, ed. Hippolyte Aubert (23 vols. to date, 1960–2001).

**BIANCHI or bianco di Faenza** a type of MAIOLICA covered with a thick white glaze. *Bianchi* ware was often extravagantly shaped and pierced but tended to be lightly decorated, usually in blue and orange. The decorative technique was known as *compendiario* (Italian; 'perfunctory') and characteristically consisted of boldly drawn figures which left most of the glazed surface untouched. It was introduced in the FAENZA potteries in the 1540s but was eventually produced all over Europe. The most prominent Faenza manufacturers of *bianchi* were Leonardo BETTISI, Virgiliotto CALAMELLI, and Francesco MEZZARISA.

**BIANDRATA, GIORGIO or (Latin) Giorgius Blandrata** (*c.*1515–1588), physician and Unitarian reformer, born in Saluzzo (then a marquisate in Piedmont). He studied arts and medicine at Montpellier, graduating in 1533, after which he practised medicine as a specialist in women's disorders. He spent 1557 in Geneva, where he had regular discussions with CALVIN and began to champion UNITARIANISM in the Italian Church. The fate of SERVETUS demonstrated how dangerous it was to expound anti-Trinitarian views in Geneva, and in 1558 Biandrata found it prudent to withdraw to Poland, the birthplace of organized Unitarianism.

In Kraków Biandrata was appointed as court physician to Bona Sforza, the dowager queen, who had once been so opposed to Unitarianism that she had ordered the burning (in 1539) of 80-year-old Catharine Weygel because of her anti-Trinitarian views, but under the influence of the writings of Bernardino OCHINO had since become a Protestant with Unitarian sympathies. During this period Biandrata was also active in ecclesiastical politics, serving as a leader of the Unitarian party at the synods of Pinczów (1558) and Ksiaz (1560 and 1562).

In 1563 Biandrata moved to the court of TRANSYLVANIA (which he had first visited in 1544), where the family of the *voivode* had intermarried with the children of Bona Sforza. In 1576 he revisited Poland in the train of STEFAN BÁTORY, who had become prince of Transylvania in 1571 and king of Poland in May 1575, and whose tolerationist policies extending to heresies that elsewhere in Europe were punishable by death. In Transylvania Biandrata worked closely with the anti-Trinitarian bishop Francis DÁVID, but relations broke down when Biandrata was accused of sodomy; in order to win Dávid back to a more moderate anti-Trinitarian position, Biandrata invited Faustus SOCINUS to Transylvania to negotiate on his behalf. The circumstances of Biandrata's death in May 1588 are unclear, but he may have been strangled by his nephew and namesake Giorgio Biandrata.

*DBI.*

**BIBELORGEL or Bibelregal**, a particularly small portable organ which used only reed pipes. Its name derives from the fact that it could be folded together like a book. The Bibelorgel dates from c.1450 and was popular during the sixteenth and seventeenth centuries.

**BIBLE.** Until the last quarter of the fifteenth century the Bible of western Europe was the Latin translation by Jerome known as the Vulgate (*editio vulgata*), which had established itself as the standard Latin text in the Catholic West. The first edition of the Vulgate to be printed was the GUTENBERG Bible of 1456, which was also the first book to be printed; the first scholarly text was printed by Robert ESTIENNE (Paris, 1528). On the debate about the Latin text, see JEROME IN THE RENAISSANCE.

The English translation by John WYCLIFFE (1382) had been instrumental in providing theological ammunition for the LOLLARDS, and thereafter the Church actively but ineffectively discouraged translations into the vernacular. The first printed vernacular version of the Vulgate was a German translation which was printed in Strassburg in 1466; this edition was the first printed version of a translation which had been made more than a century earlier. In the next 50 years, at least fourteen High German and four Low German editions had been printed. During these years translations of the Vulgate into various vernaculars appeared all over Europe. The first Catalan translation was printed in Valencia in 1478; it was burnt, and only survives in fragments, but another translation was published in Barcelona in 1492. A Dutch Old Testament (without the Psalms) was published in Delft in 1477; the Psalter appeared in 1480 and a partial translation of the New Testament in 1513. The Italian translation by Niccolò Malermi was printed in Venice in 1471. A Czech translation was published in Prague in 1488 and reprinted in Kutná Hora the following year.

Alongside these translations into various vernaculars, scholars also produced learned editions in the original languages. The first complete Hebrew text of the Old Testament was published in SONCINO in 1488. In Alcalá, a group of scholars led by Cardinal Ximénez de CISNEROS produced the trilingual text of the Old Testament and bilingual text of the New Testament known as the COMPLUTENSIAN POLYGLOT; their labours began in 1502, and the six volumes were printed between 1514 and 1517, but the edition was not published until 1522. This delay meant that although the Complutensian edition of the Greek text of the New Testament had been printed in 1514, it was not published until long after ERASMUS had published his Greek New Testament, which had appeared in Basel in 1516. The culmination of Catholic scholarship on the Bible in its original languages was the eight-volume *Biblia regia* prepared by Benito ARIAS MONTANO and published by Christophe PLANTIN in Antwerp between 1568 and 1572. Within the Protestant tradition the most important editions were Robert Estienne's editions in Latin (1546), Hebrew (1549), and Greek (1550); censure of these editions by the Sorbonne precipitated Estienne's move from Paris to Geneva in 1551, and his later editions were therefore published in Geneva. Theodorus BEZA, Calvin's successor in Geneva, published ten editions of the Greek text of the New Testament between 1565 and 1611.

The availability of printed texts of the Bible in its original languages led to a second wave of translations; in Protestant circles these translations from the original languages replaced older translations of the Vulgate. The first translation from the Hebrew and Greek into German was LUTHER's; his complete text was published in Wittenberg in 1534. Luther's translation into High German had been published in six parts, beginning with the New Testament in 1522, and as each part appeared various anonymous writers translated Luther's version into Low German, so that a complete Low German version was published in Lübeck in 1534. The first Danish New Testament was published in Wittenberg in 1524, and in 1526 a Swedish New Testament was published in Stockholm; both translations derive in part from Luther's translation. The first complete Bible in Swedish was published in Uppsala in 1541, and the first Danish Bible in Copenhagen in 1550. The first Icelandic translation of the New Testament was published in Roskilde (Denmark) in 1540; in 1584 the first complete Icelandic version (known as the Gudbrand Bible) was printed in Hólar (Iceland). Dutch Protestants had to wait for the monumental Estates-General Bible (*Statenvertaling*) of 1637.

The first Italian translation from the original languages was undertaken by Antonio Brucioli (Venice, 1532); the preface to this edition testifies to the translator's Protestant sympathies. The first officially Protestant Italian translation was printed in Geneva in 1562; the greatest Italian translation in terms of both accuracy and literary merit was published by the Protestant Hebrew scholar Giovanni Diodati in 1607. Bans imposed by the Spanish INQUISITION in the *Indexes* of 1551 and 1559 forbade translations of the Bible into vernaculars, which ensured that there were no translations into Spanish prose before the eighteenth century; similarly, there was no Portuguese translation until a New Testament was published in Amsterdam in 1681. In francophone Europe, a French translation of the New Testament (probably by Jacques LEFÈVRE D'ÉTAPLES) was printed in Paris in 1523, and an Old Testament in Antwerp in 1528; the two Testaments were printed together in 1530. This Bible, which is known as the Antwerp Bible, was placed on the *Index* in 1546. The first Protestant Bible in France was the Neuchâtel Bible of 1535 (also known as the Bible de Serrières), which was largely the work of OLIVÉTAN. This translation was subjected to continuous tinkering by the pastors of Geneva, and in 1588 was comprehensively revised by a committee headed by Beza and the Hebraist Corneille Bertram. In 1555 a rival translation was published in Basel by the Savoyard Sebastiano CASTELLIO; his translation incurred the vociferous obloquy of the pastors of Geneva, but is nonetheless an important early attempt to render the Bible into a French that could be understood, as he explained in his preface, by uneducated people (*les idiots*). The Edict of CHÂTEAUBRIANT (1551) prohibited the printing of prose translations, but towards the end of the sixteenth century the Catholic Louvain Bible of 1550 seems to have been widely tolerated in France. One of the most important translations (from a literary rather than a scholarly perspective) was the verse translation of the Psalms initiated by Clément MAROT with his *Trente Psaumes de David* in 1541 and completed by Beza; this composite Psalter became the badge of French Protestantism, and was sung in battle during the WARS OF RELIGION and by martyrs at the stake.

In eastern Europe, the Czech translation that was to prevail for three centuries (except among the Bohemian Brethren) was the edition printed in Venice in 1509; the Brethren (see UNITY OF THE BROTHERS) produced their own translation, which eventually appeared in six volumes (1579–93), and is now known as the Kralice Bible. The first Hungarian version of the Bible was a New Testament translated from the Greek by Johannes Sylvester (Erdösi), who had been a pupil of MELANCHTHON; a complete Hungarian Bible was published in the translation of the Calvinist Gáspár Károlyi in 1590. In Poland, the first complete translation was the Sárospatak Bible of 1455; after the advent of print, a Catholic translation from the Vulgate by Jan Leopolita Nicz (Kraków, 1561) soon found a formidable Protestant rival in a composite translation published in 1563 in Brest-Litovsk (then in Lithuania, now in Belarus); this translation, when purged of allegedly Arian marginal notes, was published in a revised version in Danzig (Gdańsk) in 1632, and thereafter became the standard Protestant edition. Nicz's Catholic version was replaced by a fine new translation by Jakób Wujek z Wagrowca (1593 and 1599) which after a revision by the Jesuits was accepted as the approved Catholic version in 1607. Polish Socinians needed their own translations, the best known of which was undertaken by the Hebraist Szymon Budny and published in Nieśwież (now Nesvizh, in Belarus) 1570–82. The Styrian Protestant Count Hans Ungard established a Slavonic press for the benefit of Slovene-speaking Austrians, and from 1560 until his death in 1564 published translations of the New Testament into Slovene; he also printed a New Testament in Croatian, which was issued in both the Glagolitic and Cyrillic alphabets. The first Slovene Bible to include both Testaments was printed in Wittenberg in 1584.

The first published translation into English was TYNDALE'S New Testament, which was printed in Cologne and Worms in 1525; in 1535 COVERDALE published an English translation of both Testaments in Cologne. Four years later Coverdale's Great Bible was printed in England. The Geneva Bible published in 1557 (New Testament and Psalter) and 1560 (both Testaments) by refugees from the Marian persecution of Protestants became the Bible of Puritans in England; the Bishops' Bible published in 1568 was the authorized alternative to the Geneva Bible. When James VI of Scotland assumed the throne of England in 1603, he commissioned a new translation, which was published in 1611; it is now known in Britain as the Authorized Version (though it was never authorized) and in America as the King James Version. The Catholic antidote to this series of Protestant translations into English was a translation of the Vulgate by English Catholic refugees in France; their translations were pub-

lished in DOUAI and Reims between 1582 and 1609. Elsewhere in the British Isles, Richard Davies published a Welsh translation of the New Testament in 1567; both Testaments appeared in a Welsh translation (by William Morgan) in 1588. A New Testament in Erse (Irish Gaelic) was printed in 1602.

Many learned Protestants with insufficient Hebrew and Greek preferred to read the Bible in a learned Latin translation rather than in a popular vernacular version. The Bible that was eventually to enjoy the universal approbation of Protestants is known as the Junius–Tremellius Bible. The Latin translation of the Old Testament and Apocrypha (first published 1575–9) was undertaken by Immanuel TREMELLIUS and his son-in-law Franciscus JUNIUS, a native of Bourges who became professor of theology at Leiden; uncertainties about the precise meanings of the Hebrew were dealt with by recourse to alternative translations in the margins. Subsequent editions often included a Latin translation of the Syriac New Testament by Tremellius or a Latin translation of the Greek New Testament by Beza, or both translations.

The chapters into which bibles are divided can be traced to the thirteenth century and were well established by the time the first bibles were printed, though at first chapters were not numbered. The first Bible to divide the chapters into verses was Santi PAGNINI's translation of 1528 into Latin; other bibles followed suit in the 1550s, but there is no consistency of numbering between languages, except that Catholic vernacular versions follow the Vulgate numbering.

S. L. Greenslade (ed.), *The Cambridge History of the Bible: The West from the Reformation to the Present Day* (1963).

**BIBLIANDER** or (German) **Buchmann, THEODOR** (*c.*1504–1564), Swiss orientalist and Protestant reformer, born in Bischofszell (in the canton of Thurgau) and educated in the Latin school in Zürich and at the University of Basel. He taught at the school in Liegnitz (now Polish Legnica) in Silesia (1529–31) and on ZWINGLI's death in 1531 succeeded to his professorship at the University of Zürich. He was a polemical theologian, and attacked CALVIN's theology of GRACE, especially his doctrine of predestination; he also maintained that heathens possessed a natural knowledge of God. Bibliander wrote a HEBREW grammar (Zürich, 1535), published two works of biblical chronology (1551 and 1558), and edited a Latin version of the Koran (Basel, 1543) and Guillaume POSTEL's translation of the *Protevangelium Jacobi* (1552), the apocryphal infancy narrative known in English as the Book of James. He died of the plague on 24 September 1564.

NDB.

**BICCHERNA COVERS**, the painted wooden covers used in Siena for tax account books; the dates of surviving covers range from 1258 to 1682. The covers were adorned with paintings by artists such as Ambrogio LORENZETTI, GIOVANNI DI PAOLO, and Domenico BECCAFUMI.

**BICOCCA, BATTLE OF.** On 27 April 1522 a French army supported by Swiss pikemen was defeated near Milan by the German-Spanish force of Francesco SFORZA (commanded by Ferdinando Francesco d'AVALOS, marquis of Pescara) on behalf of the emperor designate CHARLES V and his allies.

**BIDERMANN, JAKOB** (1578–1639), German Jesuit playwright, born in Ehingen (near Ulm) and educated at Augsburg. He entered the Jesuit Order in 1594, and after serving the Order in Augsburg and Ingolstadt was appointed professor at the Jesuit school in Munich, where he directed the school's plays from 1606 to 1614. Thereafter he taught at the University of Dillingen (1615–22) and Rome, where he died on 20 August 1639.

Bidermann was, together with Jakob GRETSER, one of the finest exponents of the *Jesuitendrama* (see JESUITS). His Latin plays include *Belisar* (1607), *Cenodoxus* (1609), *Macarius* (1613), *Philemon Martyr* (1618), *Josaphatus* (1619), and *Stertinius* (1620). Of these, only the tragedy of *Cenodoxus*, which dramatizes an episode in the life of St Bruno in which Dr Cenodoxus disobeys God and is sentenced by Jesus to eternal damnation, survives in the canon of German drama, in a German translation of 1635.

*DLL; NDB.*

**BIEL, GABRIEL** (*c.*1418–1495), German scholastic philosopher and economist, born in Speyer and educated in Heidelberg, Erfurt, and Cologne. He joined the BRETHREN OF THE COMMON LIFE at Marienthal, and became provost of their houses at Butzbach and (in 1479) Urach. In 1477 he founded, together with Count Eberhard of Württemberg, the University of Tübingen, where he held the founding chair of theology.

Biel's principal theological work, *Epitome et collectorium ex Occamo super libros quatuor sententiarum* (1508 and often reprinted), is an elucidation of the nominalism of William of Ockham. He also wrote a commentary on the *Sentences* of Peter Lombard and an exposition of the canon of the mass. These treatises are firmly in the scholastic tradition, but the epithet *ultimus scholasticorum*, last of the scholastics, is improperly applied to Biel, as SCHOLASTICISM had a long afterlife in Spain, and even continued for a time in Germany.

Biel's treatise on 'the power and utility of money', *De potestate et utilitate monetarum* (Oppenheim, 1516), attempts to dissociate the economics of commerce from the morality of theology: he argued that the 'just price' was determined by supply and demand rather than by the maxims of moral theology and insisted that the merchant was a necessary member of society who contributed to its material well-being.

*NDB;* H. A. Oberman, *The Harvest of Medieval Theology: Gabriel Biel and Late Medieval Nominalism* (1963); Wilhelm Ernst, *Gott und Mensch am Vorabend der Reformation: Eine Untersuchung zur Moralphilosophie und -theologie bei Gabriel Biel* (1972); R. B. Burke (trans.), *Treatise on the Power and Utility of Moneys* (1930).

**BIJNS, ANNA** (1493–1575), Flemish poet, born in Antwerp, where she worked as a teacher; she remained a Catholic, and may have been a lay nun. She published three collections of poems (1528, 1538, 1567) in the verse form known as *refereinen* ('refrains'). The second and third collections are invectives against the religion and character of Martin LUTHER. Her ele-

gant and graceful poems established Dutch as the medium of a vernacular literature of the highest quality.

*NBW* i; F. J. P. van den Branden, *Anna Bijns: Haar leven, haar werken, haar tijd, 1493–1575* (1911); Lode Roose, *Anna Bijns: Een rederijkster uit de Hervormingstijd* (1963).

**BILIVERTI, JACOPO, or (Dutch) Jan Bijlivelt** (1550–1603), Dutch goldsmith. He moved to Augsburg as a young man, and in 1574 was invited to Florence to manage the gallery of Grand Duke Francesco I de' Medici; he remained in Florence for the rest of his life. He made a ducal crown for the Medici (1577–83) which is now lost, and is known only from paintings and a drawing. His only documented work known to have survived is the enamelled gold setting of a lapis lazuli urn designed by Bernardo BUONTALENTI (Museo degli Argenti, Palazzo Pitti, Florence).

*MDA* s.v. Bijlivert.

**BILNEY, THOMAS** (*c.*1495–1531), English reformer. Bilney reputedly converted LATIMER and PARKER to reformist doctrines whilst at Cambridge. In 1527 he was arrested for heresy, but was released on recanting. Arrested again in 1531, he was accused of a number of heretical views. Although he initially recanted once more, he subsequently withdrew the recantation and was burnt at the stake in Norwich. He appears to have accepted church doctrine on transubstantiation, but his vociferous criticism of pilgrimages and the cults of saints attracted the attention of the authorities. With Thomas Arthur, he is the unnamed target of SKELTON's *Replication against Certain Young Scholars* (1528).

*DNB.*

**BINCHOIS, GILLES DE BINS** (*c.*1400–1460), Franco-Flemish composer. Having trained as a chorister, Binchois joined the Burgundian court chapel in the late 1420s. Here he remained until he retired to Soignies in 1452 when, up to his death, he received a generous pension in recognition of his continuous and lengthy service. He is cited by many composers. OCKEGHEM composed a biographical lament ('Mort tu as navré de ton dart') on the death of Binchois. DUFAY, with whom Binchois visited Mons in 1449, expressed his grief at the loss of a friend in 'En triumphant de cruel deuil' in which there are references to two of Binchois's songs. His influence, along with that of DUNSTAPLE, was recognized by TINCTORIS in his *Liber de arte contrapuncti* (1477). Living in France during the English occupation, and being at the Burgundian court in Bruges, Binchois was ideally placed to absorb and reflect styles from across the channel.

**BIONDO, FLAVIO** (1392–1463), Italian historian, philologist, and pioneer of Roman archaeology, born in Forlì and educated in Cremona. Biondo worked for a succession of Italian rulers and in 1433 joined the papal court, where he worked as a secretary (notably as diplomatic secretary to Pope EUGENIUS IV) and scholar for the rest of his life.

Biondo's most important historical work was his *Historiarum ab inclinatione Romanorum imperii decades* (1437–42), a survey of European history from 410 to 1441. This work introduced the notion of the MIDDLE AGES to European HIS-TORIOGRAPHY. His study of the lexis of Roman speech, *De verbis Romanae locutionis* (1435), contributed to the debate about the QUESTIONE DELLA LINGUA by contesting the view that Latin and Italian had always been parallel but distinctive languages. Biondo also published a three-volume account of the topography and human geography of Rome, *Roma instaurata* (1446), *Italia instaurata* (1453), and *Roma triumphans* (1456); the use of surviving remains and artefacts to supplement written records refined the nascent science of chorography, and also influenced artists such as MANTEGNA.

*DBI*; A. Campana, *Flavio Biondo* (1928); Denys Hay, 'The Decades of Flavio Biondo', *Proceedings of the British Academy* (1959); R. Cappelletto, *Recuperi ammianei da Biondo Flavio* (1983).

**BIRINGUCCIO, VANNOCCIO** (1480–1537), Italian metallurgist and military engineer, born in Siena, where he entered the service of Pandolfo PETRUCCI, working in the civic arsenal. In 1526 he was exiled (together with his patron); he worked in Florence, Parma, Ferrara, and Venice, returning to Siena in 1530. In 1538, shortly before his death, he was appointed by Pope PAUL III as superintendent of the papal arsenal in Rome.

Biringuccio's posthumously published *Pirotechnia* (1540) is a liberally illustrated treatise that ranges widely over the field of metalworking and includes sections on mining, the extraction of ores, the design of furnaces for smelting, the casting and boring of cannon, and the manufacture of GUNPOWDER and GLASS; it also contains the earliest printed account of typecasting. The *Pirotechnia* remained in print (in English and French translation as well as Italian) for more than 200 years.

*DBI*; *DSB*.

**BIRÓ, MATHIÁSZ** (c.1500–1545), Hungarian Protestant reformer, a member of the Franciscan Order who became a disciple of LUTHER while studying at the University of Wittenberg (1529–30). On returning to Hungary he preached the Reformation, but in the 1540s began to advocate the Calvinist doctrine of the EUCHARIST, which prompted the censure of Luther.

**BLACKFRIARS PLAYHOUSES**. The first theatre built in the old Dominican monastery in Ludgate, London, was used by the Children of Windsor Chapel from 1576. Another part of the building was adapted as a theatre by James Burbage in 1597. Initially used by the children's company, it reverted to Burbage's son Richard BURBAGE in 1608, and a new company was formed to play there.

**BLACK LEGEND or (Spanish)** *La Leyenda Negra*, the belief that the cruelty of Spaniards towards the inhabitants of subject nations (especially American Indians) exceeded that of other Europeans. In the second half of the sixteenth century Dutch and English pamphleteers mounted polemical attacks on PHILIP II and the duke of ALBA. These polemicists drew on the writings of Bartolomé de LAS CASAS to document their contention that the Spanish treatment of the Indians during the conquest had been brutal and inhumane because the

conquest had been prompted by a lust for gold rather than noble Christian motives. The Protestant polemicists' image of Spaniards as rapacious, cruel, and intolerant was subsequently extended to include such institutions as the Spanish INQUISITION and the AUTO-DA-FÉ.

*DHE*; Charles Gibson (ed.), *The Black Legend: Anti-Spanish Attitudes in the Old World and the New* (1971); W. S. Maltby, *The Black Legend in England* (1971); Ricardo García Cárcel, *La leyenda negra: Historia y opinión* (1992).

**BLACKWELL, GEORGE** (c.1545–1613), English Catholic leader. Educated at Oxford, Blackwell resigned a fellowship at Trinity College due to Catholic sympathies. In 1574 he joined William ALLEN's college at DOUAI and was ordained the following year; in 1576 he returned to England as part of a Catholic mission. Following Allen's death in 1594, Blackwell was created archpriest and leader of the Catholic clergy in England. His pro-Jesuit line provoked hostility from other priests, and although initially supported by Rome, Blackwell was formally rebuked in 1602. Following a period of imprisonment, in 1607 he took the Oath of Allegiance to JAMES VI, recanting his earlier loyalty to Rome, and hence was no longer regarded by Rome as its Catholic leader in England.

*DNB*.

**BLADDER PIPE**, a primitive form of bagpipe where the animal bladder which encloses the reed acts like a wind reservoir. Akin to wind-cap instruments, where the reed is enclosed in a rigid wooden cap, by the end of late fifteenth century the bladder pipe was mainly a folk instrument played by shepherds and itinerant musicians.

**BLADO, ANTONIO** (1490–1567), Italian printer, born in Asola. He moved to Rome c.1516, and from 1546 worked as a printer in the service of the papacy. The publications of his press include MACHIAVELLI's *Il principe* (1532), PALLADIO's *Antichità di Roma* and many scholarly titles in Latin, Greek, and Hebrew; his *Modus baptizandi*, printed in 1549 for the Ethiopic Church, used Ethiopic type. In many fields, including the publishing of music, he was the principal rival to Valerio Dorico.

*DBI*; *Grove*.

**BLAEU, WILLEM JANSZOON** (1571–1638), Dutch cartographer and astronomer, a native of Alkmaar who studied with Tycho BRAHE at Uraniborg and on returning to Amsterdam established a workshop for the manufacture of GLOBES and scientific instruments (1596) and a publishing shop specializing in cartography (1599). He issued a world map (1605) and a three-volume sea atlas entitled *Het licht der Zeevaerdt* (1608–21; 'The Light of Navigation'), and inaugurated the series of atlases that culminated in the *Atlas Maior* (11 vols., 1662) published by his son Jan Blaeu.

*DSB*; *NNBW* x.

**BLARER or Blaurer, AMBROSIUS** (1492–1567), Protestant reformer, born in Constance. From 1514 to 1519 he studied law at Freiburg im Breisgau and then migrated to Wittenberg to study theology. He returned to Constance in 1522 as an advocate of the Reformation, and after 1528 preached the Reformed cause in southern Germany. He moved to Tübingen at the behest of ULRICH duke of Württemberg and worked with Johannes BRENZ to institute Protestantism in the town. After his expulsion he returned to Constance, where he served as mayor from 1537 to 1547. In 1548 he had to flee when the imperial forces of CHARLES V captured the city, which subsequently proscribed Protestantism. Blarer spent the rest of his life as an itinerant preacher. He died in Gyrsburg (Thurgau) on 19 March 1567.

*NDB* s.v. Blarer (1).

**BLAUROCK or Cajacob, GEORG or Jörg** (*c.*1492–1529), Swiss ANABAPTIST leader. He was born in Bonaduz (a village near Chur in the canton of Graubünden) and studied in Leipzig (1513). He worked with the church in Trins (near Chers) from 1516 to 1518. His marriage in 1523 signalled his break with the Catholic Church. Two years later he arrived in Zürich, where he became a follower of ZWINGLI; he became known as 'Blaurock' because of his blue coat. A group of reformers which included Blaurock, Conrad GREBEL, and Felix MANTZ formed a separate church in Zürich, whereupon they were banished from the city. They then baptized each other in Zollikon, and so became the first Anabaptists; they were later known as the SWISS BRETHREN. After the death of Grebel in 1526, Blaurock became the leader of the Anabaptist movement in the Tirol. He was burnt at the stake in Klausen (Italian Chiusa) on 6 September 1529.

*DHBS* s.v. Blaurock, Jörg; *NDB* s.v. Blaurock, Georg; John Allen Moore, *Der Starke Jörg* (1955).

**BLAZON or (French) *blason*.** In heraldry, a blazon is a shield bearing the arms of a family. The term is used in poetry to denote a descriptive genre that became popular in sixteenth-century France and was soon in use all over Europe. The blazon typically lavished extravagant praise on the parts of a woman's body, and so was known in France as the *blason anatomique* or the *blason du corps féminin*. The genre enjoyed its greatest notoriety in the so-called *concours des blasons* of 1535, instigated by the 'Blason du beau tétin' written by Clément MAROT in Ferrara.

Alison Saunders, *The Sixteenth-Century Blazon Poétique* (1981).

**BLES, HERRI MET DE, or Herri Patenier or (Italian) Civetta** (1510–*c.*1550), Flemish LANDSCAPE painter, in 1535 admitted as Herri Patenier to the Antwerp Guild; 'Met de Bles' is a nickname meaning 'with the white forelock', and 'Civetta' (Italian; 'owl') is a nickname bestowed by Italian collectors of his landscapes, which often include depictions of owls. He is likely to have been a relative of Joachim PATINIR (or Patenier), whose painting strongly influenced that of Herri Met de Bles; both artists painted panoramic landscapes which seem to overwhelm the small groups of figures. None of the paintings attributed to him is signed, but the *Mountain Landscape with the Holy Family and St John* (Kunstmuseum, Basel) was attributed to 'Heinrich Blesius' in 1568.

*BNB*; *MDA*.

**BLITHEMAN, JOHN** (*c.*1525–1591), English composer and organist who was a gentleman of the CHAPEL ROYAL and also sang at Christ Church, Oxford. He composed sacred vocal and keyboard music and counted John BULL amongst his pupils.

**BLOCK BOOKS or xylographs** are books printed from WOODCUTS, and so are the product of the technology that preceded GUTENBERG's movable type. Woodcuts appeared in Europe in the early fifteenth century, and by the 1440s binders had begun to assemble woodcut sheets into books. The process was much more labour-intensive than the setting of movable type, because each letter had to be cut into wooden blocks; the technique was best suited to books which were predominantly pictorial. Block books were superseded by books printed from movable type by the end of the fifteenth century, partly because movable type was more efficient, but also because the advent of humanism created a market for books with a high proportion of text.

Block books were printed in Germany and in the Netherlands. At least 37 block books or fragments from block books survive from the fifteenth century, and of these 23 seem to be German and fourteen Dutch.

**BLOEMAERT, ABRAHAM** (1566–1651), Dutch painter based in Utrecht who specialized in historical paintings and LANDSCAPE paintings and drawings, of which there is a large collection in the Utrecht museum. Many of his drawings were etched by his son Frederick and published in a *Konstryk tekenboek* ('drawing book') for the use of students which remained in print for two centuries. Bloemaert trained more than 30 artists in his studio, some of whom, including Jan Both, Jacob Gerritzoon Cuyp, Gerrit van Honthorst, Hendrick TERBRUGGHEN, Cornelius Poelenburgh, and Jan Baptist Weenix, were to become important figures in seventeenth-century Dutch art.

*MDA* s.v. Bloemaert: (1); *NNBW* i; G. Delbanco, *Der Maler Abraham Bloemaert, 1564–1651* (1928).

**BLOIS**, a town 56 kilometres (35 miles) south-west of Orléans, on the right bank of the Loire. It is dominated by a chateau which in the early fifteenth century was the favourite residence of the poet CHARLES D'ORLÉANS. The fort that he inherited contained a Salle des États (in which the Estates-General of 1576 and 1588 were held) and the Tour de Foix, both of which were built in the thirteenth century and still survive. Charles built a gallery (which now bears his name) that combined the use of brick and stone, an innovation that was subsequently to become an important feature of French Renaissance architecture. The gallery originally connected the two ends of the courtyard, but is now only half its original length; the rest was dismantled by François Mansart, who rebuilt Blois for Gaston d'Orléans between 1635 and 1638.

In 1498, when Charles's son Louis succeeded to the throne as King LOUIS XII, Blois became a royal residence, and throughout the sixteenth century assumed the national role that was later to be associated with Versailles under the

Bourbons. Louis XII and his queen, Anne of Brittany, added a wing to the medieval castle, and also built the Chapelle Saint-Calais, of which only the chancel remains; the nave was removed by Mansart. The king also commissioned PACELLO DA MERCOGLIANO to build gardens on the site of what is now Place Victor Hugo. These gardens, which were built on three terraces between 1499 and 1515, were reached by a bridge across the moat. Little is known of the upper garden, which may have been a kitchen garden, but a drawing by Jacques DUCERCEAU shows that the principal garden, on the middle terrace, was divided into ten rectangular compartments, like that at AMBOISE which Pacello had built four years earlier. Each compartment contained geometrically arranged plantings, which included orange and lemon trees in tubs which were moved indoors in winter. The lowest garden, the small Jardin de Bretonnerie, was reached by a staircase descending from the main garden; the Pavillon d'Anne de Bretagne, which is now the Syndicat d'Initiative, is the only surviving remnant of this garden.

FRANCIS I added a new wing, the style of which is distinctly Italianate. It was in this building that Henri duc de GUISE was assassinated in 1588; it later became the home of MARIE DE MÉDICIS when she was banished from the court from 1617 to 1619. The inner façade of this wing is dominated by a magnificent spiral staircase turret which was, until Mansart demolished part of the wing, in the centre of the façade; the staircase (which was rebuilt in 1932 to a design by Mansart) is contained within an octagon, three faces of which are embedded in the main structure; the other five faces, with their sculpted balustrades, project into the courtyard.

William Howard Adams, *The French Garden, 1500–1800* (1979); A. Cospérec, *Blois, la forme d'une ville: Étude topographique et monumentale* (1994); Kenneth Woodbridge, *Princely Gardens: The Origins and Development of the French Formal Style* (1986).

**BLOIS, TREATIES OF.** In the sixteenth century three important treaties were signed in Blois, the city on the Loire which had passed to the French crown in 1498 on the accession of King LOUIS XII. The first two treaties arose out of the WARS OF ITALY. Milan was an imperial fief, and its occupation by France was sanctioned by the Emperor MAXIMILIAN in the first Treaty of Blois (1504), as part of a projected arrangement in which King Louis's daughter Claude would marry Maximilian's grandson, the future CHARLES V. King Louis and King FERDINAND V of Spain then partitioned Naples in the Treaty of Granada (1500), but a boundary dispute renewed hostilities; the Spanish army was victorious in the battles of CERIGNOLA (28 April 1503) and GARIGLIANO (29 December 1503), and in the second Treaty of Blois (1505) King Louis renounced his claim to Naples, leaving the kingdom in control of King Ferdinand.

The third Treaty of Blois (21 April 1572) was an Anglo-French treaty between Queen ELIZABETH (who was represented at Blois by Sir Francis Walsingham) and King CHARLES IX. This treaty was essentially a defence pact, and its most important consequence was the withdrawal of French support for the Scottish adherents of MARY, QUEEN OF SCOTS, which in turn facilitated a Protestant settlement in Scotland.

**BLONDEEL, LANCELOOT** (1488–1581), Flemish painter, architect, and designer of sculptures, tapestries, and pageant decorations. He was a native of Poperinghe who was admitted to the Guild of Painters in Bruges in 1519. His paintings include the triptych *The Martyrdom of SS Cosmas and Damian* (in the Hôpital de Saint-Jean in Bruges) and his sculpture designs the chimney piece (1530) in the Greffe du Franc in Bruges. In 1550 he worked with Jan SCOREL on the restoration of the finest of fifteenth-century Netherlandish ALTARPIECES, *The Adoration of the Lamb* (the Ghent altarpiece) by Hubert and Jan van Eyck.

*BNB; MDA.*

**BOBADILLA, FRANCISCO DE** (d. 1502), Spanish colonial governor who spent his early career as an official in the military ORDER of Calatrava, and in 1499 was appointed as successor to COLUMBUS as governor of the newly discovered Spanish territories in America. He reached Santo Domingo in 1499, arrested Columbus and his brothers and sent them in chains to Spain. Although FERDINAND and ISABELLA freed the Columbus brothers on arrival, they left Bobadilla in post until 1502, when he was replaced by Nicolás de OVANDO. Bobadilla died while sailing back to Spain.

*DBEH; DHE.*

**BOBADILLA, NICOLÁS ALFONSO DE** (1510–90), Spanish Jesuit, born in Valencia. He studied at the University of Paris, where in August 1534 he become one of the seven priests led by IGNATIUS LOYOLA who consecrated themselves to missionary work in Palestine; this group eventually evolved into the JESUIT Order. During the 1540s Nicolás fought the Protestant heresy in Germany, but his opposition to the AUGSBURG INTERIM (on the grounds that it conceded too much to the Protestant schismatics) led to his expulsion from Germany by the imperial court. Nicolás's longevity meant that he eventually became the last survivor of the seven priests who founded the Jesuits, but he never achieved high office in the Order.

*DBEH; Bobadillae monumenta: Nicolai Alphonsi de Bobadilla* (1913).

**BÖBLINGER FAMILY**, a family of south German architects and masons. Hans Böblinger the Elder (1412–82) trained in Constance, where he was a journeyman in 1435, and then became the assistant of Matthäus ENSINGEN at the Frauenkirche in Esslingen; Ensinger moved to Strassburg in 1399, and the following year Böblinger was appointed master mason at Esslingen. Matthäus Böblinger (d. 1505), who was probably one of Hans's sons, seems to have trained in Cologne; he worked for a time with Hans Böblinger at Esslingen and then moved in 1477 to Ulm, where he was appointed master mason of the minster in 1480. He modified the plans for the west tower that he had inherited from his predecessors (Ulrich and Matthäus Ensingen). In 1492 cracks appeared in the tower and Matthäus Böblinger was dismissed and expelled before he could erect his spire; his drawing for the spire survived, and when the spire was finally built 400 years later (1881–90), it became, at 161 metres (528 feet), the world's tallest church spire.

*MDA; NDB.*

**BOBOLI GARDENS**. In 1549 the unfinished PITTI PALACE was bought by ELEANOR OF TOLEDO, the duchess of COSIMO I DE' MEDICI. Niccolò TRIBOLO was quickly commissioned to design a garden; he died the following summer, and the work was completed by Bartolomeo AMMANATI. The garden was laid out symmetrically around a central axis, in the middle of which is a U-shaped AMPHITHEATRE carved out of a natural hollow in the hill; below the amphitheatre there is a large courtyard adjoining the palace, and above it is a pond. A lunette by Giusto UTENS now in the Museo Topografico in Florence shows that the amphitheatre was thickly planted when he painted it in 1599. There were also PARTERRES laid out at the side of the palace. Immediately behind the palace there was a huge FOUNTAIN of Neptune (the Ocean Fountain) by GIAMBOLOGNA; his statue of *Ocean* is now in the Bargello. Bernardo BUONTALENTI added a three-chambered GROTTO (1583–93) filled with statues, the pedestals of which were decorated with sea-shells. The first grotto contained four unfinished statues of *Slaves* by MICHELANGELO, intended for the tomb of Julius II and since 1908 in the Accademia. The third grotto, which is the work of Bernardino Pocetti, contains a statue of *Venus Leaving her Bath* by Giambologna. Originally the grotto was fitted with GIOCHI D'ACQUA designed by Buontalenti.

In the seventeenth century the design of the garden was altered considerably. The plantations around the amphitheatre were uprooted when seats were built on the banks in 1637, at which point festivities were moved from the courtyard to the amphitheatre. Later in the century a GIARDINO SEGRETO (the Giardino de Cavaliere) was built on the ramparts. The narrow track that followed the line of Tribolo's axis up the hill was widened into an avenue with a double series of shallow sloping steps (*cordonate*). The Ocean Fountain, which originally stood by the palace, was moved up the hill to the baroque Piazzale dell' Isolotto, which was designed by Alfonso Parigi in 1618 in exuberant imitation of the Maritime Theatre of Hadrian's villa (Tivoli), which had been excavated in the sixteenth century; Parigi's design was in turn imitated at ARANJUEZ. Finally the area beyond the Isolotto, which was originally planted with *ragnaie* (thickets for netting small birds), was cleared for a monumental avenue lined with cypresses and pines.

The seventeenth-century garden, which is the form in which the garden survives today (the only subsequent addition was a *kaffeehaus* built in 1776), is more monumental than its Renaissance predecessor, but both gardens served the same purpose, which was to provide settings for great pageants. The gardens continue to fulfil that role when events are mounted there by the Maggio Musicale Fiorentino.

Francesco Gurrieri and Judith Chatfield, *Boboli Gardens* (1972); Christina Acidini Luchinet and Elvira Garbera Zorzi, *Boboli 90* (2 vols., 1991).

**BOCCACCINO, BOCCACCINI** (b. before 1466, d. 1525), Italian painter, born in Ferrara, where he trained in the studio of ERCOLE DE' ROBERTI. His early works include *The Death of the Virgin* (Louvre). In 1510, after a long peripatetic period in which he fell out with a series of patrons, Boccaccino settled in Cremona, where he decorated the cathedral with frescoes (1519) depicting scenes from the New Testament and the life of the Virgin Mary.

DBI s.v. Boccacci, Boccaccino, detto il Boccaccino; *MDA*.

**BOCCACCIO, GIOVANNI** (1313–75), Italian author, probably born in Certaldo (Tuscany) or Florence; he was educated in Naples and in 1340 returned to his family in Florence. His literary works, many of which were to exercise an important influence on the literary culture of fifteenth- and sixteenth-century Europe, include the youthful poems *Filostrato* and *Teseida* (the sources of Chaucer's *Troilus and Criseyde* and 'Knight's Tale'), the prose romance *Filocolo*, and mythologized accounts of the ladies of the Angevin court in Naples (*Caccia di Diana*) and of the Florentine nobility (*Ameto*, also known as *Commedia delle ninfe fiorentine*). His scholarly works include *Genealogia deorum gentilium* (the founding text of Renaissance MYTHOGRAPHY) and a series of commentaries (first delivered as lectures) on DANTE, of whom Boccaccio wrote a biography.

Boccaccio's finest and most influential work is the *Decameron*, a collection of NOVELLAS which was to determine the conventions of that genre. The narratorial framework (*cornice*) is the flight of ten aristocratic Florentines (seven ladies and three gentlemen) from the plague of 1348. For ten days they meet in one of the party's villas to recount tales to each other; each participant tells a story every day, so there are 100 tales in all, ranging from the moralistic to the scurrilous. BEMBO was later to propose the *Decameron* as the ideal model for vernacular literary prose. Chaucer was one of the first to adapt the tale of Griselda (10. 10), perhaps from a Latin translation of Petrarch.

DBI; MDA; OCIL; V. Branca, *Boccaccio: The Man and his Work* (1976); D. Wallace, *Giovanni Boccaccio: Decameron* (1991).

**BOCCALINI, TRAIANO** (1556–1613), Italian political satirist, born in Loreto and educated in Perugia. He joined the Vatican secretariat, in which he worked as a judge and administrator, and in 1612 moved to Venice, where he published his dystopian *Ragguagli di Parnaso*, a trenchant satire on the values of contemporary Italy. He then wrote a sequel, published posthumously as *Pietra del paragone politico* (1615), in which the principal object of his satire was the Spanish presence in Italy.

DBI; OCIL; *Ragguagli di Parnaso e scritti minori*, ed. L. Firpo (3 vols., 1948).

**BOCCANEGRA, SIMONE** (c.1301–1363), first doge of Genoa, elected perpetual doge in 1339, when the city was divided by rival GUELF AND GHIBELLINE loyalties. His use of the post to enrich himself through taxation led to his exile to Pisa in 1344, but he returned in 1356 to participate in Genoa's revolt against the VISCONTI FAMILY, and was reinstated as perpetual doge. He died suddenly in 1363, but perhaps not of the poison by which he is killed in the Verdi opera of which he is the protagonist.

DBI.

**BODENSTEIN, ANDREAS RUDOLF.** See KARLSTADT, ANDREAS RUDOLF BODENSTEIN VON.

**BODIN, JEAN** (1530–96), French political philosopher. Bodin was born in Angers, and as a young man entered the Carmelites. He later repudiated his vows and studied law at Toulouse, where he became a professor of Roman law. His first publication, in 1555, was a translation into Latin verse of the *Cynegetica*, a second-century Greek poem on hunting by Oppian of Cicilicia. In 1561 Bodin moved to Paris to practise as an advocate, but he developed interests in a large number of fields and eventually became known as a jurist, an economist, a Latin poet, a cosmologist, and, pre-eminently, as a political philosopher. He also lived a public life as a courtier. He was appointed *procureur du roi*, and in 1576 became a deputy representing the Third ESTATE of Vermandois in the Estates-General of Blois; in this capacity he opposed the noble and clerical supporters of the LEAGUE, which advocated a wholly Catholic France. At court the duc d'Alençon became his patron, and in 1581 Bodin accompanied the duke to England on his embassy to negotiate a marriage with Queen Elizabeth. When his patron died in 1583, Bodin left the court and moved to Laon, where he died of plague.

Bodin's first publication in Paris was *Methodus ad facilem historiarum cognitionem* (1566), an analysis of the laws that govern history. His writings on economics began with an analysis of inflation in France, the *Discours sur les causes de l'extrême cherté qui est aujourd'hui en France* (1574). His contention that inflation had been high excited the wrath of the master of the mint, the seigneur de Malestroit, who contended that France had been free of inflation for centuries. Bodin replied in 1588 with his *Responsio ad paradoxa Malestretti* (published in French as *Réponse aux paradoxes de M. Malestroit*) with an investigation of the price revolution of the sixteenth century. His analyses of prices, wages, trade barriers, and the money supply mark an important stage in the development of economic analysis, as does his essay on public revenues in book 6 of his *République*.

Bodin's most famous work is his *Six Livres de la république* (1576), which describes an ideal state but also advocates reforms in France. He argued that sovereignty is based on human needs, and that the essential unit of the state is the family; the state was therefore conceived as an association of families who recognize the legitimacy of a legislative group or individual. The prime duty of the individual was deemed to be submission to the authority of the acknowledged head of state; in the case of France, he argued that a powerful monarchy was essential for the stability of the state. He did not advocate uniformity of government for all societies; indeed, he argued that types of humanity, and the laws required to regulate societies, corresponded to different climactic zones. Unlike Thomas MORE, he argued in favour of private property. In economics, he advocated both free trade and high taxes on imported manufactured goods; in the essay on public finance in book 6, he constructs detailed arguments about just and appropriate levels of taxation. This treatise became enormously influential, both in France, where it became a cornerstone of political science, and abroad through translations, which include both an English translation (1606) and Bodin's own translation into Latin (1586).

Bodin's other works include a judicial manual on WITCHCRAFT and sorcery (*Démonomanie des sorciers*, 1580) and a cosmological treatise (*Universae naturae theatrum*, 1596, translated into French as *Théâtre de la nature entière*, 1597). His fictional debate between the advocates of seven creeds (Judaism, Islam, Lutheranism, Zwinglianism, Catholicism, Epicureanism, and natural religion), the *Heptaplomeres*, was written in 1588 and widely read throughout Europe in manuscript copies, but was not published until the nineteenth century. The treatise evinces particular sympathies for Judaism and natural religion, and concludes with a tolerationist agreement between the seven speakers to live together in peace and not discuss religious differences.

DBF s.v. 5. Bodin; J. H. Franklin, *Jean Bodin and the Sixteenth-Century Revolution in the Methodology of Law and History* (1963); Ann Blair, *The Theater of Nature: Jean Bodin and Renaissance Science* (1997).

**BODLEY, SIR THOMAS** (1545–1613), English diplomat and patron. Educated at Oxford, he became a fellow of Merton College, and then pursued a career at court. He became an MP in 1584, and subsequently pursued diplomatic missions in Denmark, France, and Holland. On his return to England in 1596, he retired from public service, and undertook the restoration of the Duke Humphrey Library at Oxford; reopened, it was renamed the 'Bodley' in 1604.

DNB.

**BOECE, HECTOR** (c.1465–c.1536), Scottish humanist historian, and author of the earliest history of Scotland. He was educated at university in Paris, before becoming a professor at Montaigu College. In 1498 he helped in the establishment of a university at Aberdeen (later known as King's College), and became its principal. His lives of the bishops of Mortlach and Aberdeen were published in Paris in 1522; the *History of Scotland* from early times to the reign of James III, which was the first such account, appeared five years later.

**BOHEMIA or (Czech) Čechy or (German) Böhmen.** The early modern kingdom of Bohemia, which contained the incorporated provinces of Lusatia, MORAVIA, and SILESIA as well as the traditional Bohemian lands, was ruled from 1310 to 1437 by members of the House of Luxemburg, a dynasty whose last three members, Charles, WENCESLAS IV, and SIGISMUND, were also Holy Roman Emperors; Sigismund was also king of Hungary. Sigismund was succeeded by two HABSBURG rulers, Albrecht of Austria and LADISLAS V POSTHUMUS of Bohemia; after an interregnum (1439–53) and rule by GEORGE OF PODĚBRADY (1458–71) and two members of the Polish royal family, LADISLAS II and LOUIS, Habsburg rule was re-established in 1526 with the accession of FERDINAND I (who later became Holy Roman Emperor). Bohemia remained a Habsburg possession until 1918.

The prosperity of fourteenth-century Bohemia kept ethnic tensions between Germans and Czechs at bay, but the advent of a religious reform movement in the early fifteenth century destroyed the fragile stability of the kingdom. In 1415 Jan HUS was burnt at the COUNCIL OF CONSTANCE, and Bohemia was then divided by the HUSSITE WARS. Peace was temporarily restored in 1436 by the religious concessions of the COUNCIL OF BASEL, but the death of Sigismund the following year led to a renewal of hostilities during the minority and reign of Ladislas Posthumus.

The accession of George of Poděbrady, Bohemia's only Protestant king and only Czech king, led to Catholic revolts in Silesia and Moravia. Catholicism was restored with the two Polish JAGIEŁŁONIAN kings, Ladislas II and Louis II, but religious pluralism was tolerated. The death of King Louis at the battle of MOHÁCS (1526) led to the election of Ferdinand as king of Bohemia, which inaugurated four centuries of Habsburg rule.

F. Siebt (ed.), *Renaissance in Böhmen* (1985); H. B. Harder and H. Rothe (eds.), *Studien zum Humanismus in den böhmischen Ländern* (1988).

## BOHEMIAN AND MORAVIAN ARCHITECTURE.

The dominant architectural style of Bohemia from the fourteenth to the sixteenth centuries was GOTHIC. In the fourteenth century, the German mason Peter Parler (1333–99) completed Prague Cathedral, installing structural features (especially the window tracery and the rib vaults) that were to remain influential in Germany and Austria for more than a century. Parker was also the architect of the chancel in the church at Kolin and began the huge church at Kutná Hora in 1388.

The architect who effected the transition from Gothic to Renaissance in Bohemia was Benedikt RIED, who sometimes worked in Gothic and sometimes combined both styles. His finest work is the Vladislav Hall (1493–1502) in the Old Royal Palace (Starý Královský Palác) on the Hradčany in Prague; this room, which was large enough to accommodate jousting competitions, combines extravagantly decorated Gothic vaulting with windows executed in Italian Renaissance style.

There are only two examples of sixteenth-century Bohemian buildings conceived in a purely Italian Renaissance style. The elegant Belvedere Palace (Czech Belvedér Palác) in Prague (1534–63), set in a fine BOHEMIAN GARDEN, is wholly Italianate in design; the first architect was Paolo della Stella, who died in 1552 and was succeeded as architect by Bonifaz Wohlmut. The other Italian Renaissance building is Hvězda Castle (near Prague), a star-shaped hunting lodge built in 1555 and imaginatively decorated with stucco.

Many Bohemian buildings of the late sixteenth and early seventeenth centuries contain features (especially portals) that show Italian influence mediated through the interpretation of Renaissance conventions in POLISH ARCHITECTURE and GERMAN ARCHITECTURE. In Prague, the Schwarzenberg Palace (on which work began in 1545) has sculpted gables and cut ashlar blocks, and the Ball Court (on the Hradčany) designed by Bonifaz Wohlmut has *sgraffito* (see GRAFFITO) decoration.

In Moravia, the ruler of Telč, Zachariáš of Hradec, visited Genoa in 1546, and returned with Genoese artists and craftsmen who rebuilt and decorated his castle and the houses of the city's wealthy citizens in the style of Renaissance Genoa. The city centre, a Genoese oasis in Moravia, is now a UNESCO world heritage monument.

## BOHEMIAN AND MORAVIAN GARDENS.

The first Renaissance garden in Bohemia was the royal garden (Královská Zahrada) on the west side of Prague Castle, which was built in 1534 as the garden of the summer palace, the Belvedér. Under RUDOLF II, Jan VREDEMAN DE VRIES introduced elements of the Dutch style (see DUTCH GARDENS) into the garden, including tulips from Turkey. He also built GROTTOES lined with mirrors in which music was played; it is not clear whether the music was produced mechanically or by a hidden orchestra. The garden also included an orangery, a fig-house, a famous singing well, and accommodation for Rudolf's menagerie, including an aviary and a lion-court.

There are four other surviving Renaissance gardens in Bohemia. The garden of the royal palace at Brandýs-nad-Labem, 16 kilometres (10 miles) north-east of Prague, is laid out in terraces. In the castle at Kratochvíle by Netolice, south of Prague, the castle and the PARTERRES of the garden are surrounded by a moat. The castle garden of Jindřichčův Hradec, south-east of Prague, is enclosed with an arched gallery in the Renaissance style. In Telč, the Moravian castle was restyled by Italian craftsmen, who also constructed an Italianate walled garden.

Prague's finest garden is the Wallenstein (Valdštejn) Garden, which was designed in 1623 by Andrea Spezza for Count Wallenstein's new palace; it is a baroque garden, but it incorporates some Renaissance features. The garden was laid out with geometrical parterres and an avenue flanked by bronze statues. The garden was restored in the late 1940s, and the original statues (which were taken to Sweden during the Thirty Years War) have been replaced by copies.

Zdeněk Dokoupil, *Historické zahrady v Čechách a na Moravě* (1947).

## BOHEMIAN ART.

The term 'Bohemian School', a translation from the German *Böhmische Malerschule*, refers to the artistic revival of the late fourteenth century, between the accession of Charles to the throne of Bohemia in 1346 (and, as Charles IV, to the HOLY ROMAN EMPIRE in 1348) and the death of his son WENCESLAS IV in 1419. Charles established his principal residence at Prague, where he established in 1348 the university that still bears his name and attracted to his imperial court scholars and artists from all over Europe. Prague thus became an important artistic centre, but its art was international rather than Bohemian, because the artists came from Strassburg, Nuremberg, and the cities of northern Italy. The art that survived the iconoclasm of the HUSSITE WARS is for the most part anonymous, but tends to be Italianate (and specifically Sienese) in the 1350s; by the end of the century, French influences are clearly discernible. By the mid-fifteenth century, Bohemia had declined in importance as an artistic centre, and although BOHEMIAN ARCHITECTURE includes some important Renaissance buildings, no movement in Renaissance painting emerged as the successor to the Gothic art of the Bohemian School.

In the early 1580s RUDOLF II moved the imperial court from Vienna to Prague, and with the court came artists such as Hans von AACHEN, Bartholomäus SPRANGER, Adriaen de VRIES, and Joris HOEFNAGEL. For the next 30 years Bohemia was one of Europe's most important artistic centres. On the death of Rudolf in 1612 the artists were dispersed and the collections gradually moved to Vienna.

A. Matějček and J. Pešina, *Czech Gothic Painting, 1350–1450* (1950).

**BOHEMIAN BRETHREN.** See UNITY OF THE BROTHERS.

**BOHEMIAN MUSIC.** The long tradition of music at the Cathedral of St Vitus in Prague came to an end with the HUSSITE revolution of the early fifteenth century; the Hussites put an end to the use of instruments and the singing of Latin in churches. Thereafter church music consisted of congregational singing, and printed music was restricted to hymn books. The Hussite Jan Blahoslav wrote the first theoretical treatise on music in Czech (*Musica*, 1558). At the end of the sixteenth century, secular music flourished at the court of RUDOLF II, who invited foreign musicians to Prague, including Jacob HÄNDL, Hans HASSLER, and Philippe de MONTE.

**BÖHM or Böheim, HANS** (d. 1476), German visionary, known as the piper or drummer of Niklashausen ('Pauker von Niklashausen'), in the Tauber valley. He was a shepherd and village entertainer who in March 1476, claiming to have received inspiration from the Virgin Mary, became a radical preacher, denouncing the clergy and the nobility and proclaiming the imminence of an egalitarian kingdom of heaven to crowds of peasants and artisans. Böhm was arrested in July 1476 by order of the bishop of Würzburg. On 12 July his followers marched on Würzburg with a view to freeing him, but were dispersed by force. He was tried for sorcery and heresy and burnt at the stake on 19 July 1476.

*NDB*; Klaus Arnold, *Niklashausen 1476* (1980); Richard Wunderli, *Peasant Fires: The Drummer of Niklashausen* (1992).

**BÖHME or Boehme, JACOB** (1575–1624), German Protestant mystic known as 'Philosophus Teutonicus', born in Alt-Seidenberg (now Polish Zawidów, in Upper Lusatia, but then part of Bohemia, hence the surname 'Böhme'), the son of a farmer. He worked as a shepherd, and was then apprenticed to a shoemaker. From 1599 (when he married) until 1613 he worked as a shoemaker in Görlitz (now on the German–Polish border), in Silesia. His mystical *Morgenröte im Aufgang; oder, Aurora* (1612) offended the Lutheran pastor of Görlitz, Gregor Richter, who made Böhme promise to stop writing. In 1613 he forsook shoemaking in favour of dealing in wool, and in 1618 began to write again; a collection of his devotional treatises was published in 1623 as *Der Weg zu Christo*. In 1624 Richter attacked Böhme's views, and Böhme died a few months later, on 17 November 1624.

Böhme's posthumously published writings, which deploy the abstruse vocabulary of PARACELSUS, describe a primal God the Father (the *Ungrund*) who is neither good nor evil but potentially both. The opposing good and evil wills of God, manifested in his love and wrath, make him create the seven spirits of nature (*Quellgeister*), of which the last is man. The two wills of God are described in *Die drei Prinzipien göttlichen Wesens*, and Böhme sets out his cosmology in *Signatura rerum* and *Mysterium magnum* (an allegorical commentary on Genesis); *Von Christi Testamenten* is a treatise on BAPTISM and the EUCHARIST.

In the seventeenth century Böhme's English disciples, the 'Behmenists' were a significant force in the radical religious movements of the Interregnum (including the Quakers) and in the Philadelphian sect; his writings also influenced Peter Sterry, the Cambridge Platonist. Böhme's writings were also an important influence on German Romanticism.

*NDB*; J. J. Stoudt, *Sunrise to Sunset: A Study in Jakob Böhme's Life and Thought* (1957); W. Elert, *Die voluntistische Mystik Jakob Böhmes* (1973).

**BOIARDO, MATTEO MARIA** (1441–94), Italian poet, born into a noble Ferrarese family in Scandiano, of which he later became count. He entered the ducal court in Ferrara, serving Borso, Ercole, and Sigismondo d'ESTE in various capacities, notably as governor of Modena and later of Reggio. His dramatic and literary works include a comedy, a collection of sonnets, and translations of Apuleius and Herodotus. His principal literary work, which was printed the year after his death, was his unfinished epic romance *Orlando innamorato*. The poem was continued by Niccolò degli Agostini and then by Francesco BERNI, whose *rifacimento* of 1541 became the authoritative version; Berni's version, in which a literary Tuscan is imposed on Boiardo's courtly Ferrarese idiom, was the standard version of the poem until the nineteenth century. The most important successor of *Orlando innamorato* was ARIOSTO's *Orlando furioso*, which continued Boiardo's narrative.

*DBI*; *OCIL*; J. Everson, *The Italian Romance Epic in the Age of Humanism* (2001).

**BOITAC or Boytac, DIOGO** (fl. 1498–1525), Portuguese architect (whose name may imply French origins), the architect of some of the earliest MANUELINE buildings in Portugal. He designed and built the Church of Jesus (Igreja de Jesus) at Setúbal (1491–8); this was the first building in Portugal to be decorated in the Manueline style. Boytac planned the Hieronymite monastery at Belém (c.1502), near Lisbon, and was probably the architect of the Manueline stage of Guarda Cathedral (1504–17), which included the window on the north façade and the main doorway on the west façade.

*DHP* s.v. Boitac; *MDA*.

**BOLOGNA or (Latin) Bononia**, a city and archiepiscopal see at the foot of the highway (and trade route) across the Apennines to Florence. The University of Bologna was founded as a school of LAW in the eleventh century, and was Europe's most important centre of legal studies (both CANON LAW and Roman law) until the rise of the humanist school of CUJAS in Bourges in the sixteenth century; ANATOMY was taught at the university from the fourteenth century. The university had no permanent buildings until 1562, when Cardinal Carlo BORROMEO, in the name of Pope PIUS

IV, commissioned a university building (now the Palazzo dell'Archiginnasio, which serves as the library of the *commune*).

In the late twelfth and thirteenth centuries Bologna was a free city, governed by a constitution dating from 1123. In the fourteenth century the city was ruled by papal legates (1325–34, 1360–76), the VISCONTI FAMILY (1350–60), and the *signore* Taddeo Peppoli (1337–47). After 1376 the *commune* was ruled by an oligarchy who governed through a council known as the 'Sixteen Reformers of the State of Liberty'. In the fifteenth century the city was dominated by the BENTIVOGLIO FAMILY, who ruled through the Committee of Sixteen rather than as princes. In 1506 Pope JULIUS II absorbed Bologna into the PAPAL STATE, by which it was ruled until 1796. In the sixteenth century, the Emperor CHARLES V was crowned in Bologna, the historian Francesco GUICCIARDINI served as a particularly brutal papal governor (1531–4), and the city hosted the eighth session of the COUNCIL OF TRENT (March–September 1547), which met in the Palazzo Bevilacqua, the finest surviving Renaissance building in Bologna.

In painting, Bologna produced no great artists before FRANCIA and NICCOLÒ DELL'ARCA in the late fifteenth century, and became a centre of European importance only with the emergence of the CARRACCI family (Agostino, Annibale, and Ludovico) and Bartolomeo PASSAROTTI in the late sixteenth century; in the early seventeenth century, Bolognese artists included Francesco Albani, Domenichino, Guercino, and Guido Reni. The long line of visiting artists included Nicola PISANO, who painted the *arca* (the tomb of St Dominic) in the Church of San Domenico, Lorenzo COSTA, who decorated the Palazzo Bentivoglio, Pellegrino TIBALDI and NICCOLÒ DELL'ABBATE, both of whom contributed to the decoration of the Palazzo Pozzi, and GIAMBOLOGNA (whose name refers to French Boulogne, not Italian Bologna), whose Fountain of Neptune (Fontana del Nettuno, 1566) was commissioned by Pope PIUS IV. In architecture, the main buildings are medieval, but have many Renaissance accretions, notably the doorway in the Basilica of San Petronio by Jacopo della QUERCIA and the Bentivoglio Chapel in the Church of San Giacomo Maggiore.

A. Ferri and G. Roversi (eds.), *Storia di Bologna* (1978); 'Civic Self-Fashioning in Renaissance Bologna', special issue of *Renaissance Studies*, 13 (1999).

## BOLOGNA, CONCORDAT OF

The concordat, which was signed by FRANCIS I and Pope LEO X in August 1516, repealed the PRAGMATIC SANCTION OF BOURGES (7 July 1438), which had asserted that the authority of general councils of the Church was higher than that of the pope. The concordat legitimized the control by the French crown of about 600 of the principal benefices (and so gave the king the right to appoint his own bishops) and allowed the king to sanction or veto the implementation of papal bulls in France; this right later formed the legal basis of the French refusal to implement the decrees of the COUNCIL OF TRENT. The Parlement of Paris objected to the restoration of judicial appeals to Rome, which were thought to be inimical to GALLICANISM, and delayed ratifying the Concordat until forced to do so in March 1518. Once ratified, the Concordat remained in place until the French Revolution.

**BOLSEC, JÉRÔME, or (Latin) Hieronymus Hermes** (d. 1584), French theologian and physician who became a Carmelite friar in Paris and c.1545 became a Protestant. He sought refuge with RENÉE DE FRANCE, duchess of Ferrara, and in 1547 moved to the Chablais (then in the Swiss canton of Bern, now in France), where he worked as a doctor. Bolsec was a regular visitor to Geneva, where he contested CALVIN's doctrine of GRACE, contending that predestination to salvation or damnation was simply a reflection of the individual's faith or infidelity. In October 1551 Bolsec was arrested, tried, and banished. He eventually settled in France, where he returned to the Catholic Church and wrote vituperative biographies of Calvin (1577) and BEZA (1582).

*DBF*; Philip Holtrup, *The Bolsec Controversy on Predestination* (1993).

**BOLTRAFFIO, GIOVANNI ANTONIO** (c.1467–1516), Italian painter and draughtsman, born into an aristocratic family in Milan, where he became a disciple of LEONARDO DA VINCI, who mentioned Boltraffio's silverpoint drawings in his Notebooks. He painted portraits (e.g. *Portrait of a Musician* (Biblioteca Ambrosiana, Milan) and *Portrait of a Gentleman* (National Gallery, London)) and Madonnas, such as the *Madonna of the Bowl* (Museum of Fine Arts, Budapest) and *Madonna of the Flower* (Museo Poldi Pezzoli, Milan).

*DBI*; *MDA*; Maria Fiorio, *Giovanni Antonio Boltraffio* (2000).

**BOMARZO.** See ORSINI, VILLA.

**BOMBELLI, RAFAELLE** (1526–72), Italian engineer and mathematician. He was born in Bologna, but for most of his career lived in Borgo San Sepolcro, working as a hydraulic engineer on the drainage system of the Val di Chiana (then part of Tuscany). The fact that Bombelli did not publish his mathematical work until the very end of his life almost certainly indicates that he did not teach mathematics, but the style of his work is essentially that of the ABACUS SCHOOL tradition.

Bombelli had already finished writing *L'algebra* (1572) when he learned of the rediscovery of the *Arithmetica* of Diophantus of Alexandria (*fl.* AD 250), which proved that there was a Greek origin for ALGEBRA. It was probably in the spirit of emulating ancient models that, in rewriting his book, Bombelli took the important step of establishing a formal system of definitions and axioms that for the first time made it possible to give a rigorous treatment of the new entities that algebraic manipulations had thrown up (see ALGEBRA). In particular, he gives the first rigorous treatment of square roots of negative quantities (now called 'imaginary numbers'). This does not seem to have had any great effect upon his contemporaries or his immediate successors, who apparently preferred to ignore philosophical complexities, but it is nevertheless a very impressive achievement.

*DBI*; *DSB*.

**BOMBERG, DANIEL** (1483–1553), Flemish Christian printer of HEBREW, a native of Antwerp who in 1516 migrated to Venice, where he established a printshop specializing in the printing of Hebrew bibles, notably the rabbinical bible (with commentaries) of 1516–17. Bomberg learned Hebrew himself, but also employed Jewish scholars to assist with the editing of Hebrew texts. He was the publisher of the first complete edition of the Talmud (1520–3). In 1538 he returned permanently to Antwerp.

*BNB; DBI; NBW s.v. Bomberghen, Daniël van.*

**BON, BARTOLOMEO.** See BUON, BARTOLOMEO.

**BONFINI, ANTONIO** (*c.*1427–1503), Italian humanist historian who travelled to Hungary to join the Buda court of MATTHIAS CORVINUS. His principal work was *Rerum Hungaricum decades*, a history of the Magyar people for which he was rewarded with a title of nobility by King LADISLAS II.

*DBI; MEL.*

**BONIFACE IX** (*c.*1350–1404), pope from 2 November 1389 until his death on 1 October 1404, was born into an impoverished aristocratic family in Naples; his baptismal name was Pietro Tomacelli. He seems to have received little formal education, but was nonetheless created cardinal-deacon in 1381 and cardinal-priest in 1385. His pontificate fell during the GREAT SCHISM, and on his election in 1389 he and his Avignon rival, the antipope Clement VII, excommunicated each other.

Boniface took little active interest in the schism, declining to agree to resign if the antipope agreed to step down simultaneously. He concentrated instead on the imposition of Roman papal authority on Italy. In 1390 he intervened in the dynastic quarrels in NAPLES by supporting LADISLAS OF DURAZZO (and crowning him at Gaeta on 29 May 1390) and was rewarded in 1400 with a resumption of obedience to Rome. He appointed his two brothers to govern Ancona and Spoleto, and through this means brought the PAPAL STATE back into Roman control. At one point his relations with the authorities of Rome were so unsatisfactory that he threatened to remove the papacy from the city, but in 1398 he responded to a plot on his life by assuming temporal control of Rome, abolishing its republican independence, and appointing senators himself. His political skills were widely admired, but his pontificate was corrupted by nepotism and simony.

*DBI s.v. Bonifacio IX; L. Zanuto, Il pontificato di Bonifacio IX (1904).*

**BONIFAZIO VERONESE DE PITATI** (1487–1553), Italian painter. He was born in Verona, and by 1528 had settled in Venice, where he established a large workshop; Jacopo BASSANO was one of his pupils. Bonifazio's paintings, which include *The Adoration of the Magi* and *The Virgin of the Tailors* (both in the Accademia in Venice), are chiefly remarkable for the skill with which he deployed colour.

*DBI s.v. Pitati; MDA s.v. Pitati.*

**BONNER, EDMUND** (1496–1569), bishop of London. Educated at Oxford, Bonner was chaplain to WOLSEY and later served HENRY VIII on diplomatic missions to FRANCIS I and CHARLES V. He pleaded with the pope first for Henry's divorce from CATHERINE OF ARAGON and later against his excommunication. Made bishop of Hereford in 1538, and

bishop of London in 1539, he enforced the Six ARTICLES, but his objections to the Book of COMMON PRAYER caused him to lose his position under EDWARD VI. Restored by MARY, he became known as 'bloody Bonner' for his implementation of her Counter-Reformation policy. He refused to swear an oath to ELIZABETH's Act of Supremacy and in 1559 was again deprived and died in Marshalsea prison.

*DNB.*

**BONSIGNORI, FRANCESCO** (*c.*1460–1519), Italian painter, born in Verona. He was employed for a time by the GONZAGA FAMILY in Mantua, for whom his work included a chalk drawing of *Francesco Gonzago* (*c.*1500, National Gallery, Dublin) and an altarpiece, *The Adoration of the Blessed Osanna Andreasi* (1519, Palazzo Ducale, Mantua).

*DBI; MDA.*

**BONTEMPS, PIERRE** (*c.*1512–*c.*1570), French sculptor, who worked as an assistant to PRIMATICCIO at FONTAINEBLEAU. His best-known work, executed in collaboration with François Marchand (d. 1551), is the monument to King FRANCIS I and his family (1547–88) in the Abbey (now Basilica) of Saint-Denis, near Paris (now a northern suburb of Paris); Bontemps's contribution to the monument, which was designed by Philibert DELORME, was the execution of the recumbent figures (*gisants*) and the bas-reliefs. He also contributed to a monument for the heart of King Francis, originally in the priory of Haube-Bruyère. On the outbreak of the WARS OF RELIGION in 1562 Bontemps became a religious refugee.

*DBF; MDA.*

**BOOKBINDING.** In late fifteenth-century Europe, printers employed craftsmen to bind the sheets of their books in simple bindings. By the early sixteenth century, however, it had become standard practice for books to be sold in unbound sheets, so allowing the buyer to exercise personal taste within an individual budget. A few books, such as liturgical books intended for display on altars, were fitted with covers made from metal or ivory and decorated with enamel or gems, but the principal material for bookbinding was leather, which was often decorated with engraved panel stamps. In the mid-fifteenth century gold tooling was introduced in Venice, from which the technique spread throughout Europe.

In the fifteenth century the principal centre of bookbinding was Venice, and the finest bindings were those of ALDUS MANUTIUS. In the early sixteenth century the centre of bookbinding shifted to France, initially to Paris (where GROLIER BINDINGS were made). In the mid-sixteenth century, the principal innovations were MAIOLI BINDINGS made in Paris and LYONESE BINDINGS, both of which took advantage of the new technique of GAUFFERING. The most important stylistic development in late sixteenth-century France was the FANFARE BINDING.

Anthony Hobson, *Humanists and Bookbinders: The Origins and Diffusion of the Humanistic Bookbinding 1459–1559* (1989); Philippa Marks, *The British Library Guide to Bookbinding* (1998); Marie-Pierre Laffitte and Fabienne le Bars, *Reliures royales de la Renaissance: La Librarie de Fontainebleau, 1544–1570* (1999).

**BOOK ILLUSTRATION.** The earliest printed books were illustrated with illuminations added by hand with a view to making the books resemble ILLUMINATED MANUSCRIPTS. Subsequently books were illustrated with WOODCUTS and occasionally with copperplate ENGRAVINGS. The woodcut illustrations include some CHIAROSCURO WOODCUTS (French *gravures en camaïeu*). The practice of making printed books look like illuminated manuscripts disappeared by the end of the fifteenth century except in France, where this tradition survived until the mid-sixteenth century in printed BOOKS OF HOURS in which every page was framed by a decorative woodcut border; in England this convention was imported for a single book known as Queen Elizabeth's Prayer Book but actually entitled *A Book of Christian Prayers* (1578).

The first printer to use woodcuts as illustrations was Albrecht PFISTER of Bamberg, who introduced hand-coloured woodcut illustrations in 1460. Ten years later the AUGSBURG printer Erhard RATDOLT began to use woodcuts to replicate the elaborate borders of illuminated manuscripts on the first page of his books, and so became the inventor of the title page. By the end of the fifteenth century woodcut illustration was established as an important adjunct of printing throughout Europe. In Germany woodcut illustrations became a prominent feature of works such as Bernhard von Breydenbach's *Reise ins Heilige Land* (1486; Latin *Sanctae peregrinationes*), Hartmann SCHEDEL's 'Nuremberg Chronicle' (*Weltchronik*, 1491), and the *Teuerdank* commissioned by the Emperor MAXIMILIAN and illustrated by Hans SCHÄUFELIN (1517). In the sixteenth century German artists such as BURGKMAIR, CRANACH, DÜRER, and HOLBEIN designed woodcut illustrations and decorations, and their designs were used all over Europe.

In Italy the first woodcut illustrations were the line drawings used in Juan de TORQUEMADA's *Meditationes* (Rome, 1463). The most important centres of woodcut illustration were Venice, Verona, and Florence. In Venice, ALDUS MANUTIUS used woodcut illustrations in his editions of classical texts, and in 1499 produced his magnificent illustrated edition of Francesco COLONNA's *Hypnerotomachia Polifili*. In Verona, the most important illustrated book of the fifteenth century was Roberto VALTURIO's *De re militari* (1479), for which the woodcuts were designed by Matteo de' PASTI. In Florence, the most prominent printer was Piero PACINI, who used woodcut illustrations for works such as his edition of Aesop's *Fables* (1496).

In France the earliest centre of woodcut illustrations was Lyon, where the first book with woodcut illustrations was *Miroir de la rédemption* (1478), which was followed by an edition of the comedies of TERENCE (*Commoediae*, 1493) and a book on the DANCE OF DEATH (*La Grande Danse macabre*, 1500). In Paris Jean DUPRÉ published the first illustrated book, a missal published in 1484. In the early sixteenth century the MANIÈRE CRIBLÉE was introduced, but did not supplant woodcut illustration.

In England woodcut illustrations were introduced by CAXTON in *Mirror of the World* (*c.*1481) and more sophisticated woodcuts were used by his successor Wynkyn de WORDE.

Illustrated books were not common in early sixteenth-century England, but books often had decorative woodcut title pages. The first popular book to be illustrated was FOXE's *Book of Martyrs* (1563).

The technique of making copperplate engravings was well known to printers, but the practical difficulties of combining a relief method (printing from type) with an INTAGLIO method (engraving) defeated most printers; the small number of fifteenth-century books illustrated with engravings include Caxton's *Recuyell of the Histories of Troy* (1474–6) and an edition of PTOLEMY's *Cosmographia* (Bologna, 1477). By the late sixteenth century, however, the engraving had replaced the woodcut illustration in learned books, and the woodcut was reduced as a medium to modest tasks such as printers' decorations. At the end of the century Christophe PLANTIN, the most influential printer in Europe, established the convention of confining book illustration to title pages, and for the next two centuries book illustration was a rare exception to a continuous expanse of print.

**BOOK OF HOURS** or (Latin) *Horae* or (French) *Livre d'heures*, a type of breviary intended for lay use and often lavishly illustrated. The finest surviving examples are from the fifteenth-century ducal courts of Burgundy and Berry, notably *Les Très Riches Heures du duc de Berry* (Musée Condé, Chantilly). A Book of Hours always included a calendar in which each month was illustrated by its 'occupation'; a typical calendar might depict feasting (January), warming (February), pruning (March), flower gathering or tending sheep (April), hunting (May), mowing (June), reaping (July), threshing (August), treading grapes (September), gathering acorns and feeding hogs (October), slaughtering hogs (November), feasting (December). The prayers associated with each of the eight canonical Hours of the Virgin were also illustrated with miniatures: *Annunciation* (Matins), *Visitation* (Lauds), *Nativity* (Prime), *Annunciation to the Shepherds* (Sext), *Presentation in the Temple* (None), *Massacre of the Innocents* (Vespers), and *Coronation of the Virgin* (Compline); sometimes a *Flight into Egypt* is substituted in Vespers or Compline.

V. Leroquais, *Les Livres d'heures* (3 vols., 1927–43); Léopold Delisle, *Les Grandes Heures de la Reine Anne de Bretagne et l'atelier de Jean Bourdichon* (1913); Thierry Crétin-Leblond and Myra Orth, *Livres d'heures royaux: La Peinture de manuscrits à la cour de France au temps de Henri II* (1993).

**BORDONE** or Bordon, **PARIS** (1500–71), Italian painter. He was born in Treviso, and by 1518 had settled in Venice. He specialized in SACRA CONVERSAZIONE and mythological pictures which were bought by patrons throughout Europe. His *Presentation of the Ring of St Mark to the Doge* (1538, Accademia, Venice) was painted for the Scuola di San Marco.

DBI; MDA.

**BORGIA, CESARE** (1475–1507), duke of Valentinois and Dios and duke of Romagna, one of the four children of Cardinal Rodrigo Borgia (later Pope ALEXANDER VI) by his mistress Vannozza Cattanei. When his father was elected pope in 1492, Cesare was created archbishop of Valencia, and the following year was raised to the cardinalate. When King CHARLES VIII left Rome on his expedition to conquer Naples in 1495, Cesare accompanied him as a hostage to ensure that the pope would not interfere; Cesare escaped at Velletri and returned to Rome.

In 1497 Cesare's brother Juan, duke of Gandía, was murdered, probably by Cesare. It is possible that Cesare and his brother were rivals in two sexual liaisons, one with Donna Sancha, the wife of their half-brother Goffredo, and the other with their sister Lucrezia BORGIA, but it is difficult to separate fact from anti-Spanish propaganda in this or any other disreputable episode in Cesare's career. Cesare renounced his ecclesiastical dignities after the death of his brother; he became his father's closest adviser and took up a new career as a papal legate and soldier.

In July 1497 Cesare travelled to Naples as a papal legate and crowned FEDERICO of Aragon as king of Naples. Cesare decided to marry Carlotta, the daughter of King Federico, but she and her father declined an alliance with 'a priest and the bastard of a priest'. On 1 October 1498 Cesare set sail for France as papal legate to King LOUIS XII, bearing the pope's bull annulling Louis's marriage to Jeanne de France, which had become an impediment to his desire to marry ANNE OF BRITTANY. In exchange for this favour, King Louis created Cesare duke of Valentinois and Dios and pledged military assistance to Pope Alexander and Cesare in their campaign to subdue the PAPAL STATE. In France Cesare again met Carlotta of Naples, but despite the fact that since their last meeting he had secured permission from his father to renounce the priesthood (August 1498), his suit was again rejected. In May 1499 he married Charlotte d'Albret, sister of King John III of Navarre.

Cesare began the campaign to reclaim the Papal State by capturing Cesena, Imola, and Forlì (where Caterina SFORZA surrendered on 22 January 1500); Cesare returned to Rome (February–October 1500), where his delighted father made Cesare GONFALONIERE of the Church and where Lucrezia Borgia's third husband, the duke of Bisceglie, was murdered in July, probably at the command of Pope Alexander and Cesare. In October 1500 Cesare returned to Romagna, where he captured Rimini and Pesaro without a fight and Faenza after a siege which was ended when Cesare promised to spare the life of their ruler, 18-year-old Astorre Manfredi; the city surrendered and Astorre was sent to Rome, where he was tortured and executed. On this occasion Pope Alexander signalled his pleasure by creating Cesare duke of Romagna. In his next campaign Cesare captured Camerino, Urbino, Piombino, and Elba.

In 1502 several of Cesare's condottieri rose against him in the Conspiracy of La Magione, so named from the castle near Perugia where the plotters met. The skill with which Cesare tricked the conspirators and had them strangled (31 December 1502) was widely admired.

In August 1503 Cesare and his father were both taken seriously ill, either from malaria or from poison intended for Cardinal Adriano CASTELLESI, their host at a dinner party;

Alexander died, and Cesare was too ill to arrange the succession in his family's interests. Pope PIUS III was elected, and immediately confirmed Cesare as gonfaloniere of the Church and papal vicar of Romagna, but died within a month and was succeeded by Pope JULIUS II, an implacable enemy of the Borgias. Cesare was obliged to surrender his conquests and flee for Naples, where in May 1504 the governor, Gonzalo de CÓRDOBA, arrested him at the command of King FERDINAND. Cesare was sent to Spain and imprisoned; two years later he escaped and sought refuge with his brother-in-law, King John III of Navarre, whose service he entered. On 12 March 1507 he was killed while besieging the Castle of Viana.

In *The Prince*, Machiavelli argued (in chapter 7) that Cesare's failure to frustrate the election of Pope Julius II by backing a rival candidate was the only political error in Cesare's life.

*DBI*; *MDA* s.v. Borgia: (3).

**BORGIA, LUCREZIA** (1480–1519), duchess of Ferrara, born in Rome, the illegitimate daughter of Cardinal Rodrigo Borgia (later Pope ALEXANDER VI) and Vannozza Catenei; the four children of this liaison included Lucrezia's brother Cesare BORGIA. The securing of the papacy enabled Alexander to promote the interests of his children, and in the case of Lucrezia he allowed her to act as his unofficial regent when he was absent from Rome and arranged a series of advantageous marriages (though the advantage was his rather than hers). He began by arranging her marriage to Giovanni Sforza, *signore* of Pesaro, a process that began with his dissolving of her earlier marriage to Don Gasparo de Procida; when political circumstances changed Alexander was able to terminate the marriage to Giovanni Sforza by papal annulment (1497) and arrange for a third marriage, this time to Alfonso of Aragon, duke of Bisceglie (the illegitimate son of ALFONSO II of Naples). This husband was murdered, probably on the orders of Cesare Borgia, and Pope Alexander arranged for a fourth marriage, this time to Alfonso d'ESTE, heir to the duchy of Ferrara; this marriage, into which Lucrezia entered at the age of 22, produced seven children (of which four survived infancy), and Lucrezia became a patron of the arts in Ferrara. Anti-Spanish propaganda presented Lucrezia as an evil figure and implied that she was involved in political assassinations and guilty of incestuous relations with her father and brother; there is no evidence to support such allegations. Similarly, the inference from her correspondence with Pietro BEMBO that they were lovers is based on a misapprehension of the epistolary conventions of Neoplatonism.

*DBI* s.v. Lucrezia; *MDA* s.v. Borgia: (4); M. Bellonci, *Lucrezia Borgia* (1960).

**BORGIA FAMILY**, a Hispano-Italian family (called BORJA in Spanish) that came originally from Aragón. In Italy they were always regarded as foreigners, and so were always subject to anti-Spanish propaganda. The first Borgia pope, CALLISTUS III, lavished favours on his relatives, and raised two of his young nephews to the cardinalate; one of them, Rodrigo Borgia, was later elected as Pope ALEXANDER VI. Pope Alexander's children included Juan, duke of Gandía

(1476–97), Cesare BORGIA, and Lucrezia BORGIA. Francisco de BORJA, duke of Gandía (1510–72), became general of the JESUITS and after his death on 30 September 1572 was beatified (1624) and canonized (1671). The Borgias were demonized in Italy because of the voluptuousness of Pope Alexander and the cruelty of Cesare Borgia, but the Spanish Borjas retained an aura of sanctity because of the austere ideals of San Francisco Borja.

> Michael Mallett, *The Borgias: The Rise and Fall of a Renaissance Dynasty* (1969).

**BORGOÑA, JUAN DE** (*fl.* from 1495; d. 1535), Spanish painter who spent most of his working life in Toledo. He worked with Pedro BERRUGUETE on the main ALTARPIECE at Ávila Cathedral (*c.*1508), and later worked extensively in Toledo Cathedral, to which he contributed a fresco of the *Last Judgement* and a polychromed wooden effigy of *King John II*. His style combines Gothic and Renaissance elements, particularly the Florentine style as represented by GHIRLANDAIO.

> *MDA*; D. Angulo Íñiguez, *Juan de Borgoña* (1954).

**BORJA, FRANCISCO DE, or** (Italian) **Francesco Borgia** (1510–72), Valencian educator and third general of the JESUITS, the great-grandson of Pope ALEXANDER VI and of King FERDINAND V of Castile. In 1534 he succeeded his father as duke of Gandía, and in 1539 he was appointed viceroy of Catalonia by CHARLES V. In 1546 his wife died, leaving him with eight children, and two years later he secretly joined the Jesuits, securing a three-year dispensation from his vow of poverty to enable him to set his family affairs in order (which included the resignation of his dukedom to his eldest son). He travelled to Rome in the autumn of 1550, and there made public his profession. He was ordained priest in the Basque country in 1551, and was from 1554 to 1560 commissary of the Jesuit provinces of Spain and Portugal, founding many colleges in both provinces.

The presence of an eminent member of the BORGIA FAMILY in the fledgling Jesuit Order enhanced the public profile of the Society. In 1548 he secured the approval of Pope PAUL III for the publication of IGNATIUS LOYOLA's *Exercitia spiritualia*. He was also influential within the Spanish and Portuguese courts; during the absence of King PHILIP II of Spain Borja acted as spiritual adviser to his regent Princess Juana, whom he admitted to secret membership of the Jesuit Order in 1555. These courtly links did not spare Borja difficulties with the Spanish INQUISITION (1559–61), which were resolved only when he returned to Rome.

Borja was recalled to Rome in 1561 to become the deputy of Diego LAÍNEZ, the second general of the Jesuits; in 1565 he succeeded Laínez as general, and held this post until his death on 30 September 1572. As general his most conspicuous achievements were the inauguration of the Jesuit missions in the Spanish colonies in America, the establishment of the Jesuit's Roman College (later the Gregorian University), the construction of the Church of San Andrea del Quirinale, and the commissioning of VIGNOLA to build the Gesù Church.

Francisco was beatified in 1624 and canonized in 1671 and is now known as San Francisco de Borja.

> *DHE* s.v. Francisco; C. de Dalmases, *Francis Borgia* (1983; English trans. 1991); Cruz Martínez Esteruelas, *Francisco de Borja, el nieto del escándalo* (1988); Mario Scaduto, *L'opera di Francesco Borgia, 1565–1572* (1992); Enrique García Hernán, *Francisco de Borja, grande de España* (1999).

**BORMAN or Borreman, JAN** (*fl. c.*1479–1520), Flemish wood-sculptor who specialized in carved altars; his most famous work is the altar of *St George* (1493), which is now in the Musée du Cinquantenaire in Brussels. Borman's son, who was also called Jan, worked in his father's workshop; his most important independent work is the Saluces altar, which is now in the Municipal Museum in Brussels.

> *BNB* s.v. Borreman; *MDA*.

**BOROUGHS or Burrows, STEPHEN** (1585–84), navigator who accompanied Sir Richard CHANCELLOR and Sir Hugh WILLOUGHBY in search of a NORTH-EAST PASSAGE in 1553; he became the first Englishman to reach the White Sea. Following a voyage to Spain (*c.*1558) and a return visit to Russia (1561), he later worked as a pilot in the Medway.

**BORROMEO, CARLO** (1538–84), Italian cardinal, born on 2 October 1538 in the castle of Arona (on Lake Maggiore), the second son of the count of Arona. At the age of 12 he received the tonsure and his first benefice, the commendatory abbacy of Arona; he assigned the proceeds of the benefice (which he held *in commendam*, i.e. as a secular ecclesiastic who is allowed to possess more than one benefice) to the poor. He studied CIVIL LAW and CANON LAW at Pavia, and took his doctorate in 1559. At the end of the year, his maternal uncle, Cardinal Giovanni Angelo de' Medici, was elected Pope PIUS IV, and Borromeo was soon appointed as prothonotary and then cardinal, with responsibility (at the age of 22) for the administration of Romagna and the March of Ancona (both in the PAPAL STATE) and the supervision of the Franciscan ORDER, the Carmelites and the Military ORDER of the Knights of ST JOHN. He was also appointed archbishop of Milan, but his myriad responsibilities necessitated residence in Rome, so his see was administered by a deputy. He was a patron of PALESTRINA, and took a particular interest in the reforming of church music.

Borromeo persuaded Pius IV to reconvene the COUNCIL OF TRENT and carried the final sessions to a successful conclusion; he presided over the formulation of the doctrinal and disciplinary decrees and took an important part in the drafting of the Roman Catechism. In 1564 Borromeo was ordained as a priest and consecrated as a bishop, and as papal legate with responsibility for the city-states of Italy convened a provincial council in Milan to promulgate the Tridentine decrees.

In 1566 the new pope, PIUS V, granted Borromeo permission to reside in his diocese, and he promptly moved to Milan to implement a programme of reform; he was the first resident bishop for 80 years. In conformity with the austere decrees of Trent, he stripped Milan Cathedral of its sumptuous tombs (including those of his relatives), ornaments, banners, and coats of arms and divided the nave into separate sections for men and women. In his programme of educational reform, in which he was assisted by the JESUITS and BARNABITES, Borromeo established seminaries for the education of the clergy, founded an order of Oblates, and reinvigorated a Confraternity of Christian Doctrine charged with the instruction of children. His reforms of the religious orders were greeted with embittered opposition, and in 1569 members of the Order of the Humiliati conspired to assassinate him in the archiepiscopal chapel in Milan; a shot was fired at close range, but Borromeo escaped, and the belief that his escape was miraculous laid the foundation of his cult. The idea that he was a saint-in-waiting was encouraged by Borromeo's response to the famine of 1570 and the PLAGUE of 1576, in which he organized programmes of relief and played a prominent personal role.

Borromeo took a particular interest in Britain. He was a generous patron of the English College in DOUAI and his confessor was the Welsh physician Griffith Roberts (who published a Welsh treatise on grammar in Milan in 1567). He also venerated John FISHER, whose portrait he always carried with him. In 1580 he received a group of young English Jesuits on their way to England: the group included Ralph Sherwin (1550–81), Edmund CAMPION (both of whom were to be martyred and canonized), and Robert PARSONS.

In 1583 Borromeo was appointed apostolic visitor to the SWISS CONFEDERATION, and in this capacity persecuted Zwinglians and WITCHES; two years after his death, the Catholic Swiss cantons formed a 'Borromean League' with the avowed purpose of expelling heretics from the cantons, if necessary by recourse to arms.

Carlo Borromeo died on 4 November 1584 and was buried in Milan Cathedral. A cult quickly arose, and he was canonized in 1610. A vast bronze and copper effigy, the Colosso di San Carlone, was erected on a hillside near Arona; the statue, which is 23 metres (75 feet) high and stands on a granite plinth 12 metres (39 feet) high, is one of the largest in the world. Federico Borromeo (1564–1631), Carlo's cousin and successor (from 1595) as archbishop of Milan, was the founder of the Biblioteca AMBROSIANA, whose holdings include two posthumous portraits of Carlo Borromeo by Ambrogio Figino.

*DBI* s.v. Carlo; A. Deroo, *Saint Charles Borromée, cardinal reformateur, docteur de la pastorale* (1963); on Federico, see *DBI* s.v. Borromeo.

**BOS, CORNELIUS** (c.1510–c.1566), Netherlandish engraver. He was born in 's-Hertogenbosch (Brabant) and seems to have studied in Rome in the studio of Marcantonio RAIMONDI. He was settled in Antwerp by 1540, but persecution of the proscribed religious sect to which he belonged forced him to leave the city in 1544; he died in Groningen. Many of his engravings are versions of Italian paintings, but he also produced his own designs. His younger brother Balthasar Bos (1518–80) was trained as an engraver in the studio of Cornelius.

*MDA* s.v. Bos, Cornelis; *NNBW* viii.

**BOSCÀ I D'ALMUGÀVER, JOAN**, or (Castilian) **Juan Boscán** (c.1490–1542), Catalan poet (writing in Castilian) and translator, born into an aristocratic Catalan family in Barcelona. He lived most of his life as a courtier in Castile, acting as tutor to the youthful Don Fernando (later the duke of ALBA) and, at the court of CHARLES V, forming a friendship with GARCILASO DE LA VEGA.

In 1526 the poet Andrea NAVAGIERO, who was Venetian ambassador to the Spanish court, invited Boscà to experiment with Italian metres. Boscà had the advantage of familiarity with the hendecasyllabic line of Catalan lyric poetry, and quickly became adept in the composition of Castilian poetry in Italian metres, including those of sonnets and tercets (*terza rima*) but, most importantly, the *octavas reales* that were to become the dominant metre in Spanish Renaissance epic. The *octava real*, which is also known as *octava rima* (a direct translation of Italian *ottava rima*) and the *octava heróica* (especially when used in epic), consists of an eight-line stanza (rhymed *ababababcc*) in which each line has eleven syllables.

Boscà began to collect his poetry in the last year of his life, but in the event the task was completed by his widow Ana Girón de Rebolledo; his poems were published together with those of Garcilaso as *Las obras de Boscan y algunas de Garcilaso de la Vega repartidas en quatro libros* (Barcelona, 1543), which was set in a roman fount that was an innovation in Spanish vernacular printing. Book 1 contains Boscà's early poetry, which celebrates domestic virtues and a principled simplicity of life; book 2 contains his poems in Italian metres; book 3 collects an *Epístola a Mendoza* in tercets, a long allegory in *octava rima* expanding a poem by BEMBO with 85 new octaves, and *Leandro*, a 2,793-line epyllion in blank verse (*versos sueltos*, an adaptation of TRISSINO's *versi sciolti*) based on the *Hero and Leander* of Musaeus, a narrative later to be the subject of an unfinished poem by MARLOWE; book 4 consists of poems by Garcilaso.

Garcilaso presented Boscà with a copy of CASTIGLIONE's *Il cortegiano*, which Boscà translated as *El cortesano* (1534). Boscà's choice of Castilian rather than Catalan for his poems and translations marks the triumph of Castilian and the end of CATALAN LITERATURE until the *Renaixença* of the nineteenth century. In the conventional historiography of SPANISH LITERATURE, the publication of the poems of Boscà and Garcilaso is deemed to inaugurate the Golden Age (SIGLO DE ORO) of literature.

*DBC*; *DBEH*; David Darst, *Juan Boscán* (1978); Margherita Morreale, *Castiglione y Boscán* (1959); Ann Cruz, *Imitación y transformación: El petrarquismo en la poesía de Boscán y Garcilaso de la Vega* (1988); Antonio Prieto, *Libro de Boscán y Garcilaso* (1999).

**BOSCH, HIERONYMUS** (c.1450–1516), Netherlandish painter, born in 's-Hertogenbosch (Brabant); his baptismal name was Jerom van Aken, and the name by which he is known derives from the Latin form of his given name and the final syllable of his birthplace. He spent his entire life in 's-Hertogenbosch, where he became a wealthy lay member of a local religious ORDER. His paintings were admired and collected in orthodox Catholic circles; the finest collection was assembled by King PHILIP II and is now in the Prado in Madrid.

Hieronymus Bosch, *The Garden of Earthly Delights*, in the Prado, Madrid

The canon of Bosch's work consists of some 40 paintings, none of which is dated. It is usually assumed that his relatively conventional paintings are either early (e.g. the *Crucifixion* in the Musée d'Art Ancien, Brussels) or commissioned works (e.g. donor painters such as *The Adoration of the Kings* in the Prado). His paintings are usually religious in subject and are typically peopled by fantastic part-human creatures, many of whom are suffering or inflicting pain on others; his depictions of HELL portray the suffering of sinners with morbid glee. His best-known paintings are *The Haywain* and *The Garden of Earthly Delights*, both of which are in the Prado.

The grotesque and fantastic elements in Bosch's paintings appealed powerfully to the Surrealists, who claimed Bosch as a progenitor. The nightmarish quality of his paintings, especially their representation of horror, has ensured that they continue to appeal to popular taste.

BNB s.v. Aken, Jérôme van; *MDA*; *NBW* ix, s.v. Bosch, Jheronimus.

**BOSCO** (plural *boschi*) **or** (**French**) *bosquet*. The *bosco* of Italian gardens is a woodland descended from the sacred groves of classical antiquity. In Renaissance gardens, the *bosco* was a contrast to the axial geometry of the garden design. It was usually planted with evergreen ilex (holm-oak), which provided deep shade and exotically twisted tree trunks; its dark leaves resemble those of holly, its near relative. The finest surviving examples are the two ilex *boschi* in the garden of the Villa Gamberaia in Settignano (near Florence) and the parkland of the Villa LANTE.

The link between the Italian *bosco* and the French *bosquet* may have been the *boschi* planted *c*.1590 at the Villa Bernadini in Lucca, where the studied anarchy of the woodland is broken with a sequence of geometrical clearings. In France the *bosquet* evolved into an ornamental grove, usually with a lawn and fountain at the centre, and sometimes the *bosquet* was planted as a MAZE. The enclosed space within a *bosquet* was called a *salle de verdure* (a green room) if it was large and a *cabinet de verdure* if it was small. In the early seventeenth century the paths that pierced *bosquets* were laid out in geometrical patterns, but these lines were gradually softened, and this process led to the evolution of the *bosquet* into the wildernesses planted in seventeenth-century ENGLISH GARDENS, of which the first were André MOLLET's wilderness at WIMBLEDON HOUSE (1642) and Wren's wilderness at Hampton Court (1689).

**BOSIO, ANTONIO** (1575–1629), Maltese archaeologist who moved as a child to Rome, where he eventually became the agent of the Knights of Malta. In 1593 he began an extensive study of the catacombs; his discoveries were published posthumously in *Roma sotterranea* (1632).

*DBI*.

**BOSSCHAERT, AMBROSIUS** (1573–1621), Flemish painter. He was born in Antwerp, which he fled in the turmoil of the REVOLT OF THE NETHERLANDS, seeking refuge in Middelburg (1593–1616) and later settling in Utrecht, where he became a member of the Guild in 1616; he died in The Hague while delivering a painting commissioned by the stadtholder MAURICE OF NASSAU. In common with many Flemish artists, Bosschaert chose to concentrate on flowers in his STILL LIFE paintings. Together with his three sons (Ambrosius the Younger, Abraham, and Johannes) and his brother-in-law Balthasar van der Ast, Bosschaert popularized the painting of flowers in the United Provinces. He often chose to paint on copper, and his paintings are remarkable for their colour-tones and for a high degree of finish in which individual brush-strokes are invisible. Examples of his paintings are pre-served in the Mauritshuis (The Hague) and in the Ashmolean Museum in Oxford.

*MDA s.v. Bosschaert (I).*

**BOTANICAL GARDENS**. The purpose of the botanical gardens of the Renaissance was to facilitate the study of plants for medicinal purposes. The origins of these gardens are disputed, but they may combine elements of the physic gardens of earlier centuries and the Aztec gardens that the conquistadors had discovered in Mexico.

Both Pisa and Padua claim to possess the earliest botanical garden in Europe. The founding of the Paduan garden can be dated to 1545 by a bill passed by the Venetian Senate author-izing its foundation. The evidence for Pisa is inconclusive, but the garden is normally dated *c.*1543.

The Orto Botanico in Pisa was planted by Luca Ghini (*c.*1490–1556), who taught botany and medicine at the Uni-versity of Pisa. The garden, which is on a 3-hectare (7-acre) site between the cathedral and the river, was planted with medicinal plants gathered by Ghini and his students on field trips in north Italy. Andrea CESALPINO succeeded Ghini as curator of the garden in 1555, and used the collection as the basis of his taxonomical research, in which he classified plants according to fruits and seeds. An account of the garden written by the French botanist Pierre Belon after his visit in 1555 (*Observations de plusieurs singularités et choses mémorables*) confirms that the garden had already developed an inter-national reputation both for the range of its collections and for its beauty. Pisa was the first garden in Europe to cultivate the horse-chestnut (*Aesculus hippocastanum*), the black walnut (*Juglans nigra*), the ailanthus (*Ailantus glandulosa*), the cam-phor tree (*Cinnamomum camphora*), the Japanese quince (*Chaenomeles japonica*), the magnolia (*Magnolia grandiflora*), and the tulip tree (*Liriodendron tulipifera*). The garden is still owned by the university, but now specializes in lilies, water-lilies, and amaryllis.

The botanic garden in Padua (Giardino Botanico dell'Uni-versità di Padova) occupies a 1.8-hectare (4-acre) site close to the Basilica del Santo; its first curator, Luigi Squalerno, had been a pupil of Ghini at Pisa. The garden, which was jointly owned by the University of Padua and the Venetian republic, was designed by the Bergamese painter Giovanni Battista MORONI and constructed under the supervision of Pietro da Noale (representing the university) and Daniele BARBARO (representing the Venetian Senate). The garden was laid out as an enormous circle, some 82 metres (90 yards) in diame-ter; the broad outline of the original design has survived, but details of the beds have been changed. The circle was enclosed in 1551, but this wall was replaced in the eighteenth century by the one which now surrounds the garden. The

area within the circle was divided into sixteen equal parts, each of which was divided into four beds. The beds were planted with medicinal herbs, which were used for the instruction of medical students. A palm planted in one of the greenhouses in 1585 was later to inspire Goethe's theory of the morphology of plants (*Die Metamorphose der Pflanzen*, 1790), and still survives, as does the chaste tree (*Vitex agnus-castus*) planted in 1550. Padua was the first garden in Europe to cultivate the potato (*c.*1575), the bignonia (*Bignonia radi-cans*), the Indian cedar (*Cedrus deodara*), the common acacia (*Robinia pseudoacacia*), the pelargonium (*Pelargonium cuculla-tum*), the cyclamen (*Cyclamen persicum*), and the winter jas-mine (*Jasminum nudiflorum*), which was rediscovered three centuries later by Scottish plant-collector Robert Fortune.

Botanical gardens were subsequently planted at Florence (1550), Bologna (1568), Leipzig (1580), Heidelberg (1593), and Montpellier (1593; see FRENCH GARDENS), but the most import-ant botanical garden of the late sixteenth century was in Leiden. The Hortus Academicus at Leiden was founded by the University of Leiden in 1587, but planting did not begin until 1594. The delay was caused in part by the difficulty in securing the appointment of CLUSIUS, the greatest living botanist, as the founding curator of the garden. The garden was used for teaching, but also became the main European centre for the collection and dissemination of plants from around the world; most of the world's cultivated geraniums (*Pelargonium*) and evening primroses (*Oenothera*) originate in this garden, which also bequeathed the tulip to the world. The garden is now 2.6 hectares (6 acres), which is slightly larger than the original garden, and is still used for research by the university's botanists. The original design was sub-merged in a new planting plan devised in 1730 (in part by Linnaeus), but the original layout and planting of Clusius and his head gardener Clutius (Dirck Outgaerzoon Cluyts) were replicated in a new garden built in 1931 across the canal from the original garden.

In the seventeenth century botanical gardens were planted in Giessen (1605), Strassburg (1620), Oxford (1621), Altdorf (1625), Jena (1629), Paris (Jardin du Roi, later called the Jardin Royal des Plantes Médicinales, 1635), Uppsala (1657), Edinburgh (1670), Chelsea (1673), and Amsterdam (1682).

John Prest, *The Garden of Eden: The Botanic Garden and the Re-creation of Paradise* (1981); M. Azzi Visentini, *L'Orto botanico di Padova e il giardino del rinascimento* (1984); H. Veendorp and L. G. M. Baas Becking, *Hortus Academicus Lugduno-Batavus, 1587–1937* (2nd edn., 1990; in English).

**BOTANY**. In the fifteenth century the pseudo-Aristotelian treatise on plants was supplemented by the recovery of the botanical works of Pliny the Elder and Dioscorides; Pliny's *Naturalis historia* provided more anecdote than precise description, but Dioscorides' *Materia medica*, the most widely read of all botanical treatises, contained precise descriptions, and many of its plant names are still in use. The *Materia medica* quickly became an authoritative source against which collected specimens could be judged; this process began with the commentary by Pierandrea MATTIOLI. The study of plants was in part motivated by curiosity, but the medicinal application of plants was the principal point of interest, and most botanical treatises were herbals.

In the sixteenth century the principal observational botanists were the Germans Otto BRUNFELS and Leonhard FUCHS, the Flemings Julius DODOENS and Carolus CLUSIUS, the Italian Andrea CESALPINO and, most comprehensively of all, the Swiss Huguenot Gaspard BAUHIN, who described and illustrated some 5,000 plants. The voyages of EXPLORATION produced previously unknown plants, and collections were established in BOTANICAL GARDENS all over Europe.

**BOTELER, NATHANIEL** (*c.*1577–*c.*1643). A member of the Virginia Company, and a participant in an unsuccessful raid on CÁDIZ in 1625, Boteler is chiefly remembered as author of *A Dialogical Discourse* (written from 1621, printed 1634). It addresses a variety of subjects to do with shipping and the sea through six dialogues between an admiral and a captain.

**BOTERO, GIOVANNI** (1544–1617), Savoyard political philosopher and demographer, born in Cuneo (Piedmont) and educated at a JESUIT seminary in Palermo. He taught in the colleges of the Jesuit Order, but did not take final vows. In 1579 he was dismissed because of a sermon in which he was critical of the temporal power of the papacy, but was assisted by Cardinal Carlo BORROMEO, who in 1582 appointed Botero as his secretary; when Carlo Borromeo died two years later, Botero became secretary to his cousin and (in 1595) successor in the see of Milan, Cardinal Francesco Borromeo. In 1599 Botero joined the court of CARLO EMANUELE I, duke of Savoy, in Turin, where his duties included acting as tutor to the duke's son, with whom he visited Spain.

Botero's *Cause della grandezza e magnificenza della città* (1588; Spanish translation 1593; Latin 1602; English 1606) analysed the factors that underlay the demographic and economic growth of cities; he returned to this subject in his *Relazioni universali* (1596; Latin translation 1596; German 1596; English 1601; Spanish 1603; Polish 1609). Botero's *Della ragione di stato* (1589; Spanish translation 1593; French 1599; Latin 1602; German 1657) allows, with MACHIAVELLI, that 'reasons of state' can justify extraordinary means, but nonetheless declares Machiavelli's political morality to be unacceptable, and proposes instead that civic life be governed by an explicitly Christian morality.

DBI; *The Reason of State*, trans. P. J. and D. P. Waley (1956), includes a translation of *The Greatness of Cities*.

**BOTHWELL, JAMES HEPBURN, EARL OF** (1536–78), Scottish royal consort. Succeeding as fourth earl in 1556, Bothwell, a Protestant, was initially a supporter of MARY OF LORRAINE, and later became close to MARY, QUEEN OF SCOTS. In 1567 he was implicated in the plot to murder DARNLEY, and his own divorce and marriage to Mary swiftly followed. Confronted by opposing forces, however, he and Mary fled Edinburgh after less than a month, Bothwell heading for Norway, where he was imprisoned and later died insane.

DNB s.v. Hepburn, James.

**BOTTICELLI, SANDRO, or Alessandro di Moriano Filipepi** (1444/5–1510), Italian painter and draughtsman, born in Florence, the son of a tanner; his youth is not well documented, but he may have trained alongside Filippino LIPPI in the studio of Filippo LIPPI. In the 1470s and early 1480s his most important paintings were pictures of the *Adoration of the Magi* (Uffizi; National Gallery, London; National Gallery, Washington); the Uffizi panel incorporates portraits of many members of the MEDICI family. In 1481 Botticelli was one of the painters invited to contribute to the fresco cycle on the walls of the SISTINE CHAPEL in Rome. He painted a series of mythological paintings, notably *Primavera* (*c.*1478, Uffizi), *Mars and Venus* (*c.*1485, National Gallery, London), *The Birth of Venus* (*c.*1484, Uffizi), and *The Calumny of Apelles* (1490s, Uffizi); the figures in these paintings derive from Ovid's frolicking Olympians, but have been related by scholars to the Florentine Neoplatonism of philosophers such as Marsilio FICINO and to the Virgilian culture of POLIZIANO and Lorenzo de' MEDICI.

Vasari states that Botticelli fell under the spell of SAVONAROLA, repudiated his secular pictures, and forsook painting. This statement cannot be entirely correct, because Botticelli continued to paint, but it is hard to judge the precise nature of the conversion that Vasari is misrepresenting. Botticelli did not repudiate his patron, Lorenzo di Pierfrancesco de' Medici, who was an avowed opponent of Savonarola, nor did Botticelli follow his brother in committing himself to Savonarola's programme of reform. That said, there is some evidence that Botticelli developed millenarian sympathies; the inscription on his *Mystic Nativity* (1500, National Gallery, London), a quotation from the Book of Revelation, seems to imply the expectation that the world would end shortly, and the late *Pietà* in the Alte Pinakothek in Munich has an extraordinary spiritual intensity.

Botticelli's finest drawings are his illustrations for DANTE's *Divine Comedy*, now divided between the Gemäldegalerie in Berlin and the Vatican.

*DBI* s.v. Filipepi; *MDA*.

**BOTTICINI, FRANCESCO DI GIOVANNI DI DOMENICO** (*c.*1446/7–1498), Italian painter, born in Florence, the son of a painter of PLAYING CARDS. His paintings include an *Assumption of the Virgin* (*c.*1474, National Gallery, London) with a view of Florence in the background. The picture is remarkable as the only painting of the Italian Renaissance executed to illustrate a heresy, which was the view of the donor, Matteo Palmieri, that human souls are the angels who remained neutral during Satan's rebellion against God.

*DBI*; *MDA*; Lisa Venturini, *Francesco Botticini* (1994).

**BOUCHET, JEAN** (1476–1557), French poet, chronicler, and polemicist. He was a lawyer in Poitiers associated with the RHÉTORIQUEURS. He wrote a long didactic poem (*Les Renards traversants*, 1503), a chronicle of Aquitaine (*Les Annales d'Aquitaine*, 1524), and a polemical attack on Luther (*Les Triomphes de la noble et amoureuse dame*, 1531).

*DBF*; Jennifer Britnell, *Jean Bouchet* (1986).

**Sandro Botticelli**, *Primavera* (*c.*1478), Uffizi Gallery, Florence

**Sandro Botticelli**, *The Birth of Venus* (*c.*1484), Uffizi Gallery, Florence

**BOURBON, CHARLES, DUKE OF** (1490–1527), constable of France, the second son of the count of Montpensier. In 1505 he married Suzanne, the daughter of ANNE OF FRANCE and the late Pierre de Beaujeu, duke of Bourbon. On his marriage Charles assumed the title of duke of Bourbon and embarked on a military career, fighting for King LOUIS XII in the WARS OF ITALY from 1507 to 1512, notably contributing to the defeat of Venice at the battle of AGNADELLO (1509).

On the accession of FRANCIS I Duke Charles was created constable of France, making him effectively the commander-in-chief of the army under the king. He returned to Italy under King Francis, and after the battle of MARIGNANO (1515) was appointed governor of Milan, in which capacity he staved off an attack mounted by the imperial forces of MAXIMILIAN I. Following Suzanne's death in 1521, Duke Charles's relations with the king gradually deteriorated as Charles asked for a new wife outside France, and in 1523 his properties were confiscated. He eventually defected, and became a commander in the imperial army. In 1525 he led an imperial army to victory in the battle of PAVIA, at which King Francis was captured. In 1527 he led an imperial army against Rome and was killed by an arquebus shot for which credit was claimed by Benvenuto CELLINI. On the duke's death his soldiers savaged the city in the SACK OF ROME.

> DBF; A. Lebey, *Le Connétable de Bourbon 1490–1523* (1904); Vincent Pitts, *The Man who Sacked Rome: Charles de Bourbon, Constable of France (1490–1527)* (1993).

**BOURBON or (Spanish) Borbón FAMILY**, a noble French family which became the ruling dynasty of Navarre (from the accession of ANTOINE DE BOURBON in 1555 until union with France in 1610), France (from the accession of HENRI IV in 1589 until the Revolution), Spain (from 1700 to the present, with several interregnums), Naples (1734–1860), Parma (1731–1802, 1854–9), and Lucca (1815–47).

In France, the Bourbons became related to the VALOIS when Pierre de Beaujeu, the husband of ANNE OF FRANCE (eldest daughter of King LOUIS XI), became duke of Bourbon in 1488. Their daughter Suzanne married her cousin Charles, the future duke of BOURBON and constable of France. After the constable's death the title passed to Antoine de Bourbon, who married JEANNE D'ALBRET, heiress of Navarre. Antoine became king of Navarre and their son Henri became King Henri IV of France.

> A. Leguai, *Histoire de Bourbonnais* (2nd edn., 1974).

**BOURDICHON, JEAN** (1457–1521), French painter and illuminator, active in Tours, where he executed works for the courts of LOUIS XI, CHARLES VIII, and LOUIS XII. His most important surviving work is the illuminated *Book of Hours of Anne of Brittany* (c.1503–8, Bibliothèque Nationale, Paris). None of his paintings is known to survive.

> DBF; MDA; David MacGibbon, *Jean Bourdichon: A Court Painter of the Fifteenth Century* (1933); Raymond Limousin, *Jean Bourdichon, peintre et enlumineur: Son atelier et son école* (1954).

**BOURGEOIS, LOYS** (c.1510/15–1559), French composer and theorist based in Geneva. Calvin personally intervened

when, in 1551, Bourgeois was imprisoned for changing the tunes of some printed psalms. In his theoretical work, *Le Droit Chemin de musique*, and in psalm settings, he sought to weld together Catholic polyphony and Calvinist monody, which resulted in the homophonic settings of *Le Premier Livre des psaumes*, published in Lyon in 1547.

**BOUTS, DIERIC** (c.1415–1475), Dutch painter. He was born in Haarlem but spent most of his working life in Louvain, where his commissions included an ALTARPIECE of *The Holy Sacrament* (1464–8) for the collegiate Church of St Peter. In 1468 the town council commissioned three sets of panels: two sets were to be double panels representing the administration of justice in secular history and the third was to be a triptych depicting the divine justice of the Last Judgement. Bouts completed the triptych of *The Last Judgement* in 1470; the central panel is lost, but the wings may be a set now in the Musée des Beaux Arts in Lille. At the time of his death Bouts was still working on the first set of secular panels; the one completed panel, *Ordeal by Fire*, was installed in the Court of Justice in the Town Hall in 1473, and the other panel in the pair was completed in 1481 by other hands. Bouts also painted a series on the *Life of the Virgin*, of which four panels survive in the Prado in Madrid. His style is individualistic, particularly in its dramatic use of colour, and his background LANDSCAPES are unusually evocative. Bouts died on 6 May 1475; his sons Dieric the Younger (d. 1490/91) and Aelbrecht (d. 1548) were also artists.

> MDA s.v. Bouts: (1) Dieric Bouts I; NNBW x s.v. Bouts, Dirk; NBW i, s.v. Bouts, Dirk (I).

**BOVICELLI, GIOVANNI BATTISTA** (*fl.* 1592–4), Italian singer and writer on music whose *Regole, passaggi di musica, madrigali et motetti passeggiate* (published in Venice, 1594) sheds light on the virtuoso singing style which, with its highly ornamented improvisations, was to become one of the fingerprints of baroque opera.

**BOYTAC, DIOGO**. see BOITAC, DIOGO.

**BRACCIOLINI, POGGIO** (1380–1459), Italian humanist, born in Terranova (Valdarno) and educated in Florence, where he became a formidable Latinist and a member of the circle of SALUTATI. In 1403 he moved to Rome and entered the papal secretariat as a lay scriptor; in the course of the next 50 years he served under eight popes. In 1453 he became chancellor of Florence, where he lived for the rest of his life.

In Rome Poggio developed a lifelong passion for the recovery of manuscripts of Latin authors. He travelled with the papal court to the COUNCIL OF CONSTANCE, which became the base for his four journeys to monastic libraries such as Cluny and St Gallen in search of manuscripts; his discoveries included works or parts of works by Cicero, Livy, Lucretius, Quintilian (complete), Silius Italicus, Statius, Valerius Flaccus, and Vitruvius.

After a brief period in England with Cardinal Henry Beaufort, Poggio returned in 1423 to the papal court, where he wrote a large number of dialogues, some of which are sexually explicit and some poised on the boundary of anti-clericalism and blasphemy; the subjects of his dialogues include avarice (*De avaritia*, 1428), the unhappiness of princes (*De infelicitate principum*, 1440), the vicissitudes of fortune (*De varietate fortunae*, 1448), and hypocrites (*Contra hypocritas*, 1449). He also wrote a popular collection of *FACETIAE* and a history of Florence. His literary feuds included a quarrel with Lorenzo VALLA about the correct form of written Latin (Valla favoured Ciceronian Latin and Poggio was a champion of the living language). He is also credited with inventing the new humanist hand (from which modern Roman type descends) by reconstituting elements of the old Carolingian script. His letters, of which more than 600 survive, provide us with a unique insight into the life of an early humanist.

*DBI*; *MDA*; P. Castelli (ed.), *Un toscano del '400: Poggio Bracciolini 1380–1459* (1980).

**BRADE, WILLIAM** (1560–1630), English string player and composer employed at the Brandenburg court and in the court chapel at Copenhagen. He wrote prolifically, publishing instrumental dance movements; the first collection was published in Hamburg in 1609.

**BRAHE, TYCHO or (Danish) Tygge** (1546–1601), Danish astronomer, born into a noble family at the family seat of Knudstrup, which was then in the Danish province of Scania. In 1562 he went to Leipzig to study law, and while in Germany began to study astronomy. He left Leipzig in May 1565, and subsequently travelled to Wittenberg, Rostock, and Augsburg (where he studied chemistry for two years). In 1571 Tycho returned to Scania, and on 11 November 1572, emerging into the early evening after a long session of alchemical experimentation, he saw a new star in the constellation of Cassiopeia; this was the first New Star (in Latin '[stella] nova', now called a supernova) to have been recorded in the West. Tycho was not the first to see the star, but like many other astronomers he published an account of his observations of it, in *De nova stella* (1573); his observations, like those of WILHELM IV, landgrave of Hesse, helped to establish that the New Star was indeed one of the fixed stars rather than a more local phenomenon.

In 1574 King FREDERICK II of Denmark presented Tycho with the island of Hveen (now a Swedish possession) in the Sound between Denmark and Sweden. There Tycho built the observatory of Uraniborg, laying the foundation stone on 8 August 1576 and getting everyone up at a very early hour in order to ensure that the ceremony took place at an astrologically auspicious moment. Tycho had a lifelong interest in ASTROLOGY; his continuing interest in ALCHEMY can be deduced from the fact that the basements of the observatory were organized as laboratories, but he is not known to have written on the subject. In 1578 Tycho published *De mundi aetherei recentioribus phaenomenis*, of which the main subject was the comet of 1577; Tycho demonstrated that the comet must lie beyond the planet Venus, and thus could not be a local meteorological phenomenon as comets were commonly supposed to be. He also proposed a cosmology in which the five planets revolved around the sun, which itself,

carrying the planets with it, moved around the earth, which was stationary at the centre; the sphere of the fixed stars rotated once every twenty-four hours. If one thinks in terms of transformation of coordinates, the Tychonic system seems like a variant of the Copernican one (though GALILEO chose to ignore it for the opposite reason: that it kept the earth at rest); however, in sixteenth-century terms the Tychonic system seemed original, and it was widely accepted by astronomers.

Tycho worked at his observatory for more than twenty years, during which time his visitors included JAMES VI of Scotland (20 March 1590) and many astronomers. The accession in 1588 of CHRISTIAN IV meant that Brahe fell from royal favour, and in June 1597 he sailed for Rostock. In 1598 he printed on his own presses at Wandsbeck a detailed and richly illustrated account of his observatory buildings and his instruments, *Astronomiae instauratae mechanica*. All the instruments had open sights and many of them were very large. Tycho had taken great care over their precision, that is, he had ensured that the scales were finely divided so that angles could be read precisely, but had also taken care over accuracy, making observations repeatedly with different instruments or the same one in different adjustments so as to check, for instance, that the axis of rotation of some part was correctly oriented. It seems that either on his own or later in conversation with KEPLER Tycho noticed there was a limit to the exactness of his observations, which must have shown up as the irreducible difference between observations taken with different instruments each known to be properly adjusted, or between observations taken with the same instrument on different occasions. This concept, now known as observational error, played a crucial part in Kepler's use of Tycho's observations to find the orbits of Mars and the other planets. By June 1599 Tycho had reached Prague, where he was welcomed to the court of RUDOLF II, where he spent the remaining years of his life as imperial mathematician.

Tycho's principal publication was *Astronomicae instauratiae progymnasmata* (2 vols., Prague, 1602–3), which was edited by Kepler. The first volume was an analysis of the movement of the sun and moon and an account of the location of 777 fixed stars; the second volume was a reprint of Tycho's *De mundi aetherei* of 1577. Kepler's *Rudolphine Tables* (1627) were based on Tycho's observations and his name appears in very large type on the title page.

*DSB*; *DBL* s.v. Brahe, Tyge; Victor E. Thoren, *The Lord of Uraniborg: A Biography of Tycho Brahe* (1990).

**BRAMANTE, DONATO, or Donato di Pascuccio d'Antonio** (*c*.1443/4–1514), Italian architect and painter, born near Urbino. He may have had contact with artists in the ducal court such as FRANCESCO DI GIORGIO, who may have stimulated or created Bramante's interest in PERSPECTIVE. He began his career as a painter: in 1477 he was employed painting the perspectival *Philosophers* on the façade of the Palazzo del Podestà in Bergamo, and subsequently painted the *Men at Arms* frescoes (1480–5) now in the Brera in Milan.

**Donato Bramante, the Tempietto di San Pietro in Montorio (commissioned 1502, constructed c.1510), in Rome**

In about 1479 Bramante entered the service of Duke Ludovico sforza, for whom he worked at Vigevano (Lombardy) on the ducal palace. His first important architectural commission was the rebuilding of the ninth-century Cappella della Pietà (Milan), which he transformed into the Church of Santa Maria presso San Satiro (now known as San Satiro) by encasing the chapel in a drum topped by a dome (the first since antiquity to have a coffered interior) and an octagonal lantern. He remodelled the interior as a Latin cross with a barrel-vaulted nave and incorporated the ancient baptistery, which he rebuilt as an octagonal sacristy (now once again the baptistery); the building could not accommodate a chancel, so Bramante constructed the illusion of a chancel with a TROMPE L'ŒIL painting and relief.

Bramante's next project was the remodelling of the east end of the abbey Church of Santa Maria delle Grazie (Milan), for which he encased the dome in a sixteen-sided drum with an elegant arcaded gallery (c.1488–99); as this church was originally constructed on the plan of a basilica, he is sometimes said to have remodelled the tribune, which in ecclesiastical architecture denotes the apse of a basilican church. In the 1490s Bramante also worked on the ancient Basilica of Sant' Ambrogio, to which he added the Canons' Cloister (1492; only one wing was built) and a further group of four cloisters (1497; two were completed to his plans in the late 1570s).

In 1499 King LOUIS XII of France occupied Milan (see WARS OF ITALY) and dislodged the Sforza rulers who were Bramante's patrons. Bramante fled to Rome, where his architectural style was soon adapted to the Roman taste for gravity and majesty, as is exemplified in his cloister at Santa Maria della Pace (1500) and his circular Tempietto di San Pietro in Montorio (commissioned 1502 by Pope ALEXANDER VI, constructed c.1510). In 1503 Giuliano della Rovere was elected as Pope JULIUS II, who commissioned Bramante to rebuild the Vatican, including ST PETER'S BASILICA; Pope Julius decided to defray the cost of rebuilding by the sale of INDULGENCES, a decision that proved to be one of the sparks which ignited the REFORMATION. Bramante began with a range of buildings later incorporated into the Cortile di San Damaso, and then built the BELVEDERE COURT, in which he incorporated a spiral staircase ramp (c.1505); a humorous account of Bramante by Andrea Guarna (Simia, 1516) suggested that when Bramante arrived in heaven, his remodelling of the celestial city would include a spiral ramp to facilitate disabled access.

For St Peter's Basilica Bramante proposed a huge church shaped like a Greek cross and covered with a dome, with a smaller Greek cross in each of the four arms, each of which would have a corner tower and a dome. Elsewhere in Rome he built the choir of Santa Maria del Popolo (1505–9) and designed Palazzo Caprini (c.1510, subsequently much altered), which had a heavily rusticated ground floor accommodating shops and pedimented windows between half-columns on the upper floor, a design that was to prove immensely influential for centuries. Outside Rome, Bramante's most important project was the Santa Casa at Loreto (begun 1509).

*DBI*; *MDA*; A. Bruschi, *Bramante* (1977).

**BRAMANTINO or Bartolomeo Suardi** (c.1465–1530), Italian architect and painter, born in Milan. He was trained by BRAMANTE, from whom his name derives. His most important architectural work is the octagonal chapel (begun 1512) commissioned by the TRIVULZIO FAMILY for the Church of San Nazaro Maggiore in Milan. His surviving paintings include an *Adoration of the Magi* (National Gallery, London) and a *Crucifixion* (Brera, Milan).

*DBI* s.v. Suardi, Bartolomeo; *MDA*.

**BRANDENBURG**, a margravate and electorate in eastern Germany. The borders of Brandenburg shifted constantly, but at the Reformation it was bordered on the north by Mecklenburg and Pomerania, on the east by POLAND, on the south-east by SILESIA, on the south by SAXONY, on the southwest by the archbishopric of Magdeburg, and on the west by Brunswick-Lüneburg. Since the thirteenth century, Brandenburg had consisted of three provinces: the territory west of the Elbe was the Old Mark (Altmark), the territory between the Elbe and the Oder was the Middle Mark (Mittelmark), which included both Berlin and the city of Brandenburg, and the recently acquired land east of the Oder was the New Mark (later in Prussian Posen, now in Polish Wielkopolska, 'Greater Poland'); for much of the early modern period, Prignitz, an area bordering on Mecklenburg in the northern part of the Middle Mark, was administered as a separate province.

On 30 April 1415 the Emperor SIGISMUND appointed Friedrich I of HOHENZOLLERN as margrave of Brandenburg and attached to the margravate an electorate of the HOLY ROMAN EMPIRE (see Appendix 1 for a list of the electors). Friedrich had invaded Brandenburg in June 1412, and his authority had been recognized in the Middle Mark, but the nobility of Prignitz and of the Old Mark refused to acknowledge his suzerainty; the New Mark, in Pomerania, had been held by the TEUTONIC ORDER since 1402, and was not reunited with the Brandenburg lands until 1455.

At his death on 21 September 1440, Friedrich's territory was divided between his second and his fourth sons, both of whom were named Friedrich. The second son, Friedrich II, who is known as the 'Iron Margrave', became elector, and his authority was recognized in the Middle Mark and, subsequently, in the New Mark; the fourth son, who is known as 'Friedrich the Fat', became margrave of Prignitz and the Old Mark. When Friedrich the Fat died childless in 1453, Friedrich II was able to unite all of Brandenburg.

In 1470 Friedrich abdicated in favour of his brother ALBRECHT ACHILLES and retired to the fortress of Plassenburg (near Kulmbach), where he died on 10 February 1471. Albrecht first subdued Pomerania, with which he had inherited a dispute from his brother, and then settled the problems which might have arisen from the succession by issuing on 24 February 1473 the instrument known as the *Dispositio Achillea*, which decreed that the mark would pass in its entirety to the eldest son of the margrave and so established the principle of primogeniture. On Albrecht's death in March 1486 he was succeeded by his son Johann, who was surnamed 'Cicero' because of his accomplishments as a Latinist and an orator; Johann Cicero moved the capital to Berlin, and actively promoted HUMANISM by bringing Italian scholars to the margravate.

Johann Cicero died in Arneburg on 9 January 1499 and was succeeded by his son JOACHIM I, surnamed Nestor, during whose stern rule (1499–1535) the JEWS were expelled from Brandenburg (1510) and the Reformation was stoutly resisted. Johann set aside the *Dispositio Achillea* and bequeathed the duchy to his two sons: JOACHIM II, surnamed Hector, received the electorate, the Middle Mark, the Old Mark, and Prignitz; his younger brother Johann received the New Mark. Johann took his domain into the Lutheran Reformation in 1538; Joachim granted the Reformers freedom to work within his territories in 1539, but, like HENRY VIII in England, retained the forms of the Church of Rome in a church that was independent of Rome.

The elector and his brother died within ten days of each other early in 1571; Johann left no male heir, so the duchy was reunited under Joachim's son Johann Georg, surnamed Oekonom (the steward), whose rule (1571–98) was unambiguously Lutheran: he accepted the Formula of CONCORD (June 1580), and ensured that his duchy was free of Calvinism. He took little interest, however, in the Protestant cause beyond his borders: he joined the League of Gotha and assented to the League's support for HENRI IV of France in 1591, but declined to assist the Protestant cause in the REVOLT OF THE NETHERLANDS. Like his grandfather, he ignored the *Dispositio Achillea*, and on his death on 8 January 1598 bequeathed the New Mark to a younger son.

The new elector was Joachim Friedrich, who ruled from 1598 to 1608; he contested his father's will, negotiating with his younger brothers to yield any parts of Brandenburg that they or their descendants might inherit in return for compensation in the form of other lands belonging to the Hohenzollern family; this agreement, which is known as the Gera Bond, ratified the *Dispositio Achillea*. Joachim Friedrich attempted in vain to facilitate a union between the Lutherans and the Calvinists, but public opposition forced him to fall back on the Formula of Concord. He died on 18 July 1608 and was succeeded by his eldest son, Johann Sigismund, who in 1613 abandoned the Lutheranism of his family, converted to Calvinism, and conceded freedom of religion to his subjects. He became duke of Prussia in 1618 and died on 23 December 1619.

J. Schultze, *Die Mark Brandenburg* (5 vols., 1961–9); S. B. Fay, *The Rise of Brandenburg-Prussia to 1786* (1964).

**BRANT, SEBASTIAN** (1458–1521), German humanist, born in Strassburg and educated at Basel, where he took his doctorate in law and in 1488 became professor of jurisprudence. He returned to Strassburg in 1500, when he was appointed as a syndic of the city, and died there on 10 May 1521.

Brant wrote Latin poems (*Varia carmina*, 1498), translated classical and neo-Latin works into German (*Liber faceti*, 1496; *Dicta Catonis*, 1498), and edited Freidank's Middle High German *Bescheidenheit* (1508), but he is primarily associated with his long satirical poem *Das Narrenschiff* (1494), which was published in twelve editions (six of them unauthorized) during Brant's lifetime. Elsewhere in Europe the poem was known through the Latin translation by Brant's pupil Jakob Locher, *Stultifera navis* (1497), which sold more copies than the German original and formed the basis of the translations into French (1497), Dutch (1500), and English (Alexander BARCLAY's adaptation, *Ship of Fools*, 1509). Brant's *Das Narrenschiff* inspired Erasmus' *In Praise of Folly*.

*Das Narrenschiff* is a long poem (more than 7,000 lines) with a standard line of four iambic feet, sometimes with a ninth syllable; each of the 115 sections drives home its satirical point by repetitive variations on a central idea (as in a sermon) rather than through narrative development. The central conceit is an allegory in which a ship crewed by fools and laden with fools sails to the fools' paradise of Narragonia. The targets of the satire include gluttony, sexual misdemeanours, and blasphemy; the attacks in the final sections of the poem on ecclesiastical abuse and the corruption of the princes of the Empire (moderated by tactful support for the Emperor MAXIMILIAN I) later made the poem attractive to Protestants. Many editions reproduced the original woodcuts which illustrated the allegory.

*NDB*; *Ship of Fools*, trans. E. H. Zeydel. (1962); E. H. Zeydel, *Sebastian Brant* (1967).

**BRANTÔME, PIERRE DE BOURDEILLE, SEIGNEUR ET ABBÉ DE** (*c.*1540–1614), French writer of historical biographies, born into an aristocratic Périgord family and educated in Paris (from 1549) and Poitiers (from 1555). He was appointed as commendatory abbot (*abbé commandataire*) of Brantôme Abbey by King HENRI II, but nonetheless remained a member of the military aristocracy; his travels as a soldier took him to Italy, Scotland (where he accompanied MARY, QUEEN OF SCOTS), England (1561, 1579), Morocco (1564), Spain, and Portugal; he subsequently fought in the WARS OF RELIGION. His military career was truncated in 1584 after he was injured in a fall from a horse, and thereafter Brantôme began to write exemplary biographies which were collected as *Vies des hommes illustres et des grands capitaines* (lives of his fellow soldiers) and *Vies des dames galantes et des dames illustres* (lives of the ladies of the Valois court), both of which were published in 1665, long after his death on 15 July 1614.

DBF; R. D. Cottrell, *Brantôme: The Writer as Portraitist of his Age* (1970); A. Grimaldi, *Brantôme et le sens de l'histoire* (1971); Madeleine Lazard, *Pierre de Bourdeille, seigneur de Brantôm* (1995).

**BRASS.** The terms 'brass' and 'brazen', which are unique to English, were in early modern English used as generic terms for all alloys of copper with tin or zinc, and so denoted what would now be called bronze as well as brass. In the nineteenth century the term 'bronze' came to denote alloys of copper with tin and the term 'brass' was reserved for alloys of copper with zinc.

The principal centre for the production of brass in medieval Europe was Dinant, near Liège (Flanders, now Belgium), from which the name of the kitchen utensils (especially kettles) known as 'dinanderie' derives. Brass imported to England in flat sheets was long used for engraved monumental brasses, of which some 7,000 survive in English churches. The destruction of Dinant by PHILIP THE GOOD in 1466 made brass a rare commodity and therefore a valuable one; in England no brass was produced until 1568, and then only in small quantities, but sufficient to facilitate a modest revival of the tradition of monumental brasses.

Brass was often used for liturgical objects such as censers, candlesticks, and fonts, such as the paschal candlestick by Renier van Thienen (1483, Church of St Leonard, Zoutleeuw). In Venice it was used for the brass vessels (basins and ewers, candlesticks, caskets, etc.) encrusted with gold and silver and now variously known as 'Venetian-Saracenic metalwork' or 'Azzimina work' or 'All'Aggiamina work'. In Augsburg and Nuremberg, brass was used from the fifteenth to eighteenth centuries to make alms-dishes, the centres of which were decorated with biblical and mythological scenes in relief made with metal stamps.

**BRATISLAVA or (Hungarian) Pozsony or (German) Pressburg or (Latin) Posonium**, on the left bank of the Danube, is now the capital of SLOVAKIA. After the loss of Buda in the wake of the battle of MOHÁCS in 1526, Catholic HUNGARY shifted its centre to Bratislava, which was the Hungarian capital from 1541 to 1784. MATTHIAS CORVINUS founded the university (the Academia Istropolitana) in 1467. For nearly 300 years the kings and queens of Hungary were crowned in the thirteenth-century Gothic Cathedral of St Martin.

**BRAY, GUIDO DE, or Guy de Brès** (1522–67), Flemish Protestant reformer, born in Mons (Bergen). He lived for a time in England as a religious refugee (1548–52), and on returning to the Continent became a preacher in Liège (Luik), Ghent, Tournai (Doornik), and Valenciennes. His Calvinist confession of faith (*Confession de foi des églises des Pays Bas*, 1562), which is known as the Belgic Confession, incurred the disapprobation of the Catholic authorities; it was later to be adopted by the Synod of Antwerp (1566) and endorsed by the Synod of DORT (1619). In August 1566 Bray led a Protestant revolt in Valenciennes, where he was captured and hanged.

NNBW vii; BNB s.v. Brès.

**BREDA, COMPROMISE OF**, a petition submitted on 5 April 1566 to MARGARET OF PARMA, the HABSBURG regent of the Netherlands, by a group of Dutch noblemen and civic officials. The petition objected to the imposition of Catholicism on the Netherlands by PHILIP II of Spain. The petition was rejected, the petitioners denounced as beggars (*gueux*, which later became a party name), and Catholicism was imposed with even greater force. The Protestant rebellion that arose from the rejection of the Compromise of Breda soon evolved into the full-scale REVOLT OF THE NETHERLANDS.

**BREDERO, GERBRAND ADRIAENSZOON** (1585–1618), Dutch poet and playwright, born in Amsterdam, the son of a shoemaker. He trained as a painter, but soon turned to the composition of drama under the patronage of the Amsterdam CHAMBER OF RHETORIC known as the Oude Kammer. From 1611 until his death seven years later he wrote satirical comedies, farces, and romantic dramas. His finest play, *Jerolimo den Spaansche Brabander* ('Jerolimo the Spanish Brabanter', 1617), was an adaptation of *LAZARILLO DE TORMES* in which Bredero satirized the affected declamatory style of the Burgundian refugees who had joined the Amsterdam chambers of rhetoric.

NNBW vi; Jan Cartens, *'T kan verkeren: Leven en werk van Gerbrand Bredero* (1971).

**BREGNO, ANDREA** (1418–1503), Italian sculptor, born in Osteno, near Lugano. In about 1465 he established a workshop in Rome, where he became the principal monumental sculptor in the second half of the fifteenth century, specializing in altars and tombs characterized by innovative uses of the niche. His most important work is in the Roman Church of Santa Maria del Popolo, which Bregno remodelled together with Baccio PONTELLI. Bregno also made the Piccolomini altar (1485) in Siena Cathedral (for which some of the statues of popes and saints were made by MICHELANGELO) and the tabernacle (1490) in the Church of Santa Maria della Quercia near Viterbo.

DBI; MDA.

**BREHON LAWS.** The Anglo-Irish term 'Brehon' derives from Irish *breiteamh*, meaning 'judge' and refers to the ancient laws of Ireland; the correct Irish term for this body of law is *feinechus*. After Henry II seized Dublin and its hinterland, two codes of law sat in uneasy juxtaposition. Within the Pale, ENGLISH LAW obtained; beyond the Pale, the Brehon laws formed the basis of justice. This element of ambiguity was turned to advantage by the English in Ireland: an Englishman who killed an Irishman, for example, would not be executed for his crime under English law, but would instead pay compensation under Brehon law, which did not provide for capital punishment in ordinary circumstances. In 1495 Poyning's Law imposed all English statutes on Ireland and gave England control of all Irish legislation. The Tudors attempted to impose English law and legal institutions (such as sheriffs) on Ireland. The Brehon laws were finally swept away in the legal reforms imposed by James I of England, who substituted the English land system of inheritance through the eldest son for the Brehon conventions of tanistry (succession through the eldest brother) and gavelkind (succession through all sons equally) and dispatched Sir John Davies to Ireland as solicitor-general to establish judicial circuits.

**BRENZ, JOHANNES, or Johannes Witlingius** (1499–1570), German Protestant reformer, born at Weil der Stadt (Württemberg) on 24 June 1499. In 1514 he entered the University of Heidelberg, where OECOLAMPADIUS was one of his teachers and, in 1518, he heard Luther participating in a debate and became one of his supporters. He was ordained as a priest in 1520, and in 1522 was appointed preacher at Schwäbisch Hall, where he openly supported the Reformation; in 1523 he stopped celebrating mass.

The PEASANTS' WAR broke out in 1525, and, like Luther, Brenz refused to support the insurgents. On 25 October 1525 he published *Syngramma Suevicum*, which insisted on the real presence in the EUCHARIST (in the face of opposition from Oecolampadius, a Zwinglian memorialist) and so ensured the acceptance of Lutheranism in most of the territory of Württemberg; similarly, the church order that he formulated for Schwäbisch Hall in 1527 was from 1535 onwards adopted in most parts of Württemberg.

Brenz participated in the Colloquies of MARBURG (1529), WORMS (1540–1), and REGENSBURG (1541) and was actively involved in the reconstitution of the University of Tübingen (1537–8). In the wake of the AUGSBURG INTERIM and the arrival of imperial forces in Schwäbisch Hall in 1548 (on his birthday), he was obliged to flee. He declined an invitation from CRANMER to seek sanctuary in England, and instead travelled from city to city in south Germany. In 1552 he published the WÜRTTEMBERG CONFESSION, and in January 1553 he was appointed by Duke Christoph of Württemberg as provost of the collegiate Church (Stiftskirche) of Stuttgart, where he remained for the rest of his life and where he died on 11 September 1570.

Brenz was an active polemicist, especially in the UBIQUI-TARIAN controversy of the 1560s, but declined to persecute his opponents; his tolerance was noted approvingly by Sebastiano CASTELLIO, who, writing under the pseudonym

Martinus Bellinus in *De haereticis* (1554), cites and praises Brenz (whom he calls Joannes Witlingius) for his view that WITCHES, ANABAPTISTS, and other heretics should not be executed.

Brenz's eldest son, who was also called Johann Brenz (b. 1540), was also a theologian, and was appointed in 1562 to a chair in theology at Stuttgart.

*NDB*; M. Brecht, *Die frühe Theologie des Johannes Brenz* (1966); J. M. Estes, *Christian Magistrate and State Church: The Reforming Career of Johannes Brenz* (1982).

**BRENZONE, VILLA.** The Villa Guarienti di Brenzone was designed by Michele SANMICHELI for the lawyer and humanist philosopher Agostino Brenzone. The house and gardens were built in the early 1540s on the promontory of San Vigilio, overlooking Lake Garda. The garden became famous in the sixteenth century, in part because its owners invited the public to visit it. The gardens of cedars, lemons, and oranges that were described by visitors have now been replaced by lawns, and a Garden of Apollo surrounding a tomb of Catullus has disappeared, but many original features remain, including a pergola on a terrace by the lake, a Tempietto of San Vigilio, and an artificial mound encircled by clipped cypresses and a wall with niches containing busts of Roman emperors which may well be the original of William Kent's temple of British worthies at Stowe. The original avenue still exists, and the cypresses with which it is lined now stand in magnificent maturity.

**BRESCIA or (Latin) Brixia**, a fortified city and episcopal see in Lombardy. In 1426 Brescia passed from the VISCONTI FAMILY to Venice, to which it belonged until 1797. In February 1512, during the WARS OF ITALY, Brescia was sacked by a French army commanded by Gaston de FOIX. The economic importance of the city lay in the exploitation of the nearby iron deposits for the manufacturing of hand-held guns for the military; this tradition still survives in Brescia's Biretta factory.

The most important Renaissance buildings in Brescia are clustered around the Piazza della Loggia: the Municipio was begun in 1492 and its upper floor was completed in the sixteenth century by SANSOVINO and PALLADIO; the Palazzo Monte Vecchio (1484) and the Palazzo Monte Nuovo (1497) both show Venetian influence. The painters of Brescia include Girolamo ROMANINO, MORETTO DA BRESCIA, and his pupil Giovanni Battista MORONI.

Conde Giovanni Treccani degli Alfieri, *Storia di Brescia* (5 vols., 1961).

**BREST-LITOVSK, SYNOD OF**, a meeting of the Catholic and RUTHENIAN CHURCHES in what is now the Belorussian–Polish border town of Brest. The Synod met on 6–10 October 1596, and representatives of Pope CLEMENT VIII and King SIGISMUND III of Poland negotiated the Union of Brest-Litovsk, according to which the Ruthenian Church became a UNIATE church, retaining the Orthodox rite but acknowledging papal supremacy. The Union was opposed by Polish Catholics, who disliked the Byzantine rite, and by the Russian Orthodox Church, which sought, with some measure of success, to encourage Ruthenians to return to the Orthodox fold.

**BRETHREN OF THE COMMON LIFE or (Latin) Fratres Communis Vitae**, a religious association founded in Deventer (in the Netherlands) in the late fourteenth century by Geert de GROOTE, on whose death in 1384 the leadership was assumed by Florens RADEWIJNS; the association was approved by Pope EUGENIUS IV in 1431. Some of the brethren became Augustinian canons, a group of whom founded the WINDESHEIM CANONS; others remained as laymen. Members of the brethren were not required to take vows. Distinguished members of the brethren included Gabriel BIEL, Jan BUSCH, Adrian Florensz (later Pope ADRIAN VI), and THOMAS À KEMPIS.

The brethren were the principal exponents of the pietist movement known as the DEVOTIO MODERNA, and so stressed the inward spirituality of Christianity. They also laid great emphasis on the importance of EDUCATION, founding schools all over the Netherlands and in Germany; some of those who studied at these schools, including ERASMUS, NICHOLAS OF CUSA, and Rudolfus AGRICOLA, later became prominent humanists. The need to supply books for these schools led the brethren into the copying of manuscripts; for the same reason, they were early practitioners of PRINTING. The brethren declined in the late sixteenth century and had disappeared altogether by the end of the seventeenth century.

Albert Hyma, *The Brethren of the Common Life* (1950).

**BREU, JÖRG THE ELDER** (1475/80–1537), German painter who worked in Augsburg. His principal surviving work, the Herzogenburg altarpiece (1501), so called from the survival of eight of its twelve panels at Herzogenburg, was a *Passion* cycle painted for the Carthusian monastery at Aggsbach. He worked alongside Albrecht ALTDORFER and Albrecht DÜRER on the illumination of the margins of the Emperor MAXIMILIAN's prayer book (1513), which is now in the Bayerische Staatsbibliothek in Munich.

Jörg's son and namesake, Jörg the Younger (*c*.1510–1547), was a painter and book illustrator.

*NDB; MDA* s.v. Breu: (1) Jörg Breu (i) and Breu: (2) Jörg Breu (ii); Andrew Morrall, *Jörg Breu the Elder* (2002).

**BRIÇONNET, GUILLAUME** (1470–1534), French humanist, appointed bishop of Lodève by CHARLES VIII (1489) and bishop of Meaux by FRANCIS I (1516). From 1521 to 1524 he corresponded with MARGUERITE D'ANGOULÊME; these letters are the epistolary form of a mystical piety that was also reflected in his theological works. He encouraged the reformation of the Church, and some of his followers converted to Protestantism and were burnt at the stake. Briçonnet, who was suspected of Lutheran sympathies, instituted a programme of reform in his own diocese of Vaux but submitted to the Parlement of Paris (1526) and so avoided prosecution.

*DBF; Guillaume Briçonnet, Marguerite d'Angoulême: Correspondance*, ed. Christine Martineau and Michel Veissière (2 vols., 1975–9).

**BRIGGS, HENRY** (1561–1630), English mathematician, born near Halifax and educated at Cambridge University. In 1596 he became the first professor of geometry at GRESHAM COLLEGE and in 1619 Savillean professor of astronomy at Oxford. In 1615 he visited John NAPIER, with whom he agreed to develop a system of logarithms to base 10. Napier was too frail to contribute to the construction of the tables, so Briggs undertook the task himself and in 1617 published his *Logarithmorum chilias prima*, a table of logarithms to base 10 for the numbers 1 to 1,000, to 14 decimal places. In his *Arithmetica logarithmica* (1624) Briggs extended the tables to numbers up to 20,000 and added numbers from 90,000 to 100,000; logarithms for the intermediate numbers were published by the Dutch mathematician Adriaan Vlacq in 1628.

Briggs's experience of Gresham College encouraged him to explore other matters of practical use, including magnetism (on which he collaborated with William GILBERT) and the mathematics of NAVIGATION.

*DNB; DSB.*

**BRIL, MATTHIJS or Mattheus THE YOUNGER** (1550–83) and **PAUL** (*c*.1554–1626), Flemish painters, born in Antwerp, the sons of Matthijs Bril the Elder. The brothers travelled to Rome (separately) *c*.1575 and received commissions to paint fresco landscapes in the Vatican; both died in Rome. The brothers were both LANDSCAPE painters, and their styles were very similar. After the death of Matthijs, Paul's style evolved away from Flemish mannerism and his landscapes became less fantastic and more plausible. He also painted marine pictures and views of Rome for the tourist trade.

*MDA; BNB*, s.v. Bril, Matheu and Bril, Paul.

**BRIOT, FRANÇOIS** (*c*.1550–*c*.1612), French metalworker, born in Damblain (Lorraine); he was a HUGUENOT, and in 1579 fled to the Protestant sanctuary of Montbéliard (a fiefdom of the duchy of Württemberg), where he established himself as a pewterer and was in 1585 appointed engraver to the Montbéliard mint, where he designed COINS and medals. Briot is widely regarded as the greatest artist to have worked in PEWTER. The work often described as his masterpiece is the *Temperantia* dish (1585–90) now in the Museum für Kunsthandwerk in Dresden; this dish was often copied, notably by ENDERLEIN in pewter and by Bernard PALISSY in FAIENCE.

*MDA;* H. Deminani, *François Briot, Caspar Enderlein und das Edelzinn* (1897).

**BRISSON, BARNABÉ, or Brissonius** (1531–91), French humanist jurist. He served as advocate-general of the Parlement of Paris, and compiled a collection of the *ordonnances* in force during the reign of Henri III (*Code du roi Henri III*, 1584). He also published a legal dictionary, *Lexicon iuris* (1587), which is sometimes cited by its subtitle, *De verborum quae ad ius pertinent significatione*.

*DBF* s.v. 3. Brisson; Paul Gambier, *Le Président Barnabé Brisson, ligueur (1531–1591)* (1957).

**BROCADE or (Spanish and Portuguese)** *brocado* **or (French)** *brocart* **or (Italian)** *broccato*, a fabric woven with a pattern of raised figures. In Renaissance usage the term referred to a cloth in which the figures were woven in silver or gold, but in later use it came to denote any cloth with a raised pattern. Brocades originate in the Islamic world, from which the practice of brocading passed to Sicily (represented in the magnificent twelfth-century imperial robe now in the Bishop's Palace in Regensburg) and Spain; by the fourteenth century brocades were primarily associated with Lucca, Genoa, Florence, and Venice; in the sixteenth and seventeenth centuries the most important centre for the manufacturing of brocades was Lyon.

**BRONZE AND BRONZE SCULPTURE.** In early modern English, the terms 'BRASS' and 'brazen' denoted what would now be called bronze as well as brass. In the nineteenth century 'bronze', like Italian *bronzo* and Spanish *bronce*, came to denote alloys of copper with tin and the term 'brass' came to be reserved for alloys of copper with zinc.

Renaissance bronze statues were cast from clay or plaster models. All but the smallest statues were hollow, which gave a greater degree of flexibility to represent limbs in movement than was possible with marble statues. Hollow statues were made by the method of casting now known as *cire-perdue* ('lost wax'), which is described by CELLINI in his *Trattato della scultura* with reference to the casting of his *Perseus* (1545–54, Loggia dei Lanzi, Florence).

In the *cire-perdue* process a plaster cast taken from a clay model is enveloped in wax, which is then surrounded by a heat-proof mould, usually a mixture of clay, ashes, and pulverized crockery or brick. The composite structure of core, wax layer, and mould is then placed in a kiln; the wax runs out through a vent, whereupon molten bronze is poured into the space previously filled by the wax. Once cooled, the clay envelope can be removed and the core broken up and extracted through a hole in the base.

The grandest bronze monument of the fourteenth century is the tabernacle (almost 10 metres (30 feet) high) in the Marienkirche in Lübeck. In the fifteenth century DONATELLO made the first free-standing bronze nude (*David*, *c*.1434, now in the Bargello) and the first bronze EQUESTRIAN STATUE (*Gattamelata*, 1443–53). Later in the century, the VISCHER workshop manufactured the bronze shrine (1490) mounted over the silver sarcophagus of St Sebaldus in the Sebaldus-kirche in Nuremberg. In England, most bronze monuments of the period are in Westminster Abbey, including TORRIGIANO's effigies of King HENRY VII and Elizabeth of York.

**BRONZINO, IL, or Agnolo Tori di Cosimo di Moriano** (1503–72), Italian painter and poet, born in Florence, where he trained in the studio of Jacopo da PONTORMO, whose *Martyrdom of San Lorenzo* (in the Florentine Church of San Lorenzo) he was to complete in 1569. Bronzino's subjects were often religious (e.g. *Christ in Limbo*, 1552, Uffizi) or mythological (e.g. *An Allegory of Venus and Cupid*, 1540/50, National Gallery, London). His finest and most influential pictures were courtly portraits, such as his *Portrait of a Young Man*, *Portrait of a Lady*, and *Piero de' Medici* (all in the National Gallery in London), *Eleanor of Toledo and her Son* (Uffizi), and *Portrait of a Young Man* (Metropolitan Museum, New York).

*DBI* s.v. Tori, Agnolo; *MDA* s.v. Bronzino, Agnolo; Charles McCorquodale, *Bronzino* (1981); Deborah Parker, *Bronzino: Renaissance Painter as Poet* (2000).

**BROSAMER, HANS** (*c*.1500–1554), German painter and engraver who worked in Fulda and Erfurt. The small scale of his engravings implies the influence of the LITTLE MASTERS of Nuremberg. His woodcut portraits include one of PHILIP OF HESSE (*c*.1546). Brosamer published *Ein neue Kunstbüchlein* (*c*.1548), which contained designs for silver in German Renaissance style; the volume was widely used throughout northern Europe.

*MDA; NDB.*

**BROSSE, SALOMON DE** (*c*.1571–1626), French architect, born in Verneuil, where his maternal grandfather Jacques DUCERCEAU was building the chateau. After the Edict of NANTES (1598) brought a measure of stability to France, he moved to Paris, and in 1608 he was appointed royal architect. He was commissioned to build three important chateaux: Coulommiers (from 1613) for the duchess of Longueville, Blérancourt (1612–19; only one pavilion survives) for Bernard Potier, and the Palais du Luxembourg (from 1615, rebuilt in the nineteenth century) for MARIE DE MÉDICIS. In 1618 he began the Palais du Parlement in Rennes (Brittany). His classical façade for the Church of Saint-Gervais-Saint-Protais (1616–21) was the first in Paris. In 1623 he rebuilt the Protestant Temple at Charenton. Brosse's importance for French architecture is that his classical ideals led him to concentrate on sharply defined mass rather than surface decoration.

*DBF; MDA*; Rosalys Coope, *Salomon de Brosse and the Development of the Classical Style in French Architecture from 1565 to 1630* (1972).

**BROWNE, JOHN** (*fl. c*.1480–1505), English composer. He was a chaplain in the aristocratic household of John de Vere, earl of Oxford. His setting of 'Stabat iuxta Christi crucem' was probably written for Queen Elizabeth following the early death of Prince Arthur in 1502. He wrote in a florid contrapuntal style which, through skilful handling of false relations, was highly expressive. 'O Maria salvatoris mater' and three Marian antiphons are contained in the ETON CHOIRBOOK.

**BROWNE, ROBERT** (*fl*. 1583–1620), English actor-manager in Germany. One of the first actors to become well known as part of the ENGLISCHE KOMÖDIANTEN touring troupes on the Continent. Details of his life are obscure, but he is known to have acted in London before in 1592 heading a troupe in Holland and Germany, and was still touring in 1620.

*DNB.*

**BROWNISTS**, early congregationalists, one of the main Protestant dissenting sects, which held that each congregation was autonomous and self-governing. The first congregations were established in the late sixteenth century, and the groups were initially called 'Brownists' after the influential Robert Browne (*c*.1550–*c*.1633), regarded by many as the sect's founder. Born into a wealthy family in Rutland, Browne was influenced by CARTWRIGHT whilst at Cambridge;

he then became a preacher in London, Cambridgeshire, and East Anglia, denouncing the church government and episcopal ordination. In 1580, he and Robert Harrison established a separatist congregation in Norwich. Browne was arrested and accused of heresy, but his relative CECIL offered some protection, and Browne and his followers emigrated to Middelburg in the Low Countries. There he published literature in support of his beliefs, and in 1583 returned to England. He became a schoolmaster, and then, in 1591, having accepted episcopal ordination, rector in Northamptonshire, where he remained until his death. The number of Brownist congregations increased from the late 1580s, especially in southern England; they were known in the seventeenth-century as INDEPENDENTS.

**BRU, ANYE, or Lurius de Brun or Euricus de Brun** (*fl.* early sixteenth century), German painter in Catalonia who from 1502 to 1507 painted the ALTARPIECE for the Benedictine monastery of Sant Cugat del Valles (near Barcelona); a panel from this altarpiece, now in the Museu d'Art de Catalunya in Barcelona, exhibits both German and Venetian stylistic features.

**BRUEGEL or Brueghel, PIETER THE ELDER** (*c.*1525–1569), Flemish painter; his surname, which he spelt with an 'h' until 1559 and without thereafter, may derive from a village in north Brabant which could have been his birthplace. He is sometimes called 'Peasant' Bruegel to distinguish him from his sons Pieter BRUEGHEL the Younger ('Hell' Brueghel) and Jan BRUEGHEL ('Velvet' Brueghel). Bruegel trained in the Antwerp studio of Pieter COECKE VAN AELST; in 1551, the year after Coecke's death, Bruegel was admitted to the Antwerp Guild of Painters. He soon left for a protracted visit to Italy, and while in Rome collaborated with the Croatian painter Giulio CLOVIO; in Italy he made LANDSCAPE drawings, including *Mountain Landscape in an Italianate Cloister* (1552, Louvre) and *River Valley with Mountain* (Küpferstichkabinett, Berlin), and on returning to Antwerp in 1555 he designed a set of twelve landscapes (now known as the *Large Landscapes*) which were engraved and published by Hieronymus Cock. For the next eight years he concentrated on drawings, many of which have a moral edge, including parables such as *Big Fish Eat Little Fish* (Albertina, Vienna; published 1557); many of these drawings show the influence of BOSCH in their use of fantasy and grotesque. In 1563 Bruegel moved to Brussels,

**Pieter Bruegel the Elder**, *Big Fish Eat Little Fish* (1556, published 1557), drawing with pen and brush and grey and black ink, in the Albertina, Vienna

where he married the youngest daughter of Pieter Coecke van Aelst.

In the last ten years of his life Bruegel worked principally as a painter; some 50 oil paintings survive, fourteen of which are in the Kunsthistorisches Museum in Vienna. His landscapes included an important series on the theme of the calendar, of which five survive: three in the Kunsthistorisches Museum in Vienna (including *Hunters in the Snow*), one in the Metropolitan Museum in New York, and one formerly in the National Gallery in Prague and now in a private collection. His subjects included his famous peasant village scenes (such as *The Peasant Dance* and *Peasant Wedding*, both in Vienna), religious themes (such as *The Adoration of the Kings*, National Gallery, London, and *The Procession to Calvary*, Vienna) and mythological figures (such as *The Fall of Icarus*, Musée d'Art Ancien, Brussels). Some of his allegorical paintings, such as *The Dulle Griet* (1562, Koninklijk Museum voor Schone Kunsten, Antwerp) and *Triumph of Death* (Prado, Madrid), seem to combine overt moral satire with covert criticism of the harshness of Spanish rule in the Netherlands.

*MDA* s.v. Bruegel: (1) Pieter Bruegel I.

**BRUEGHEL, JAN** (1568–1625), Flemish painter, born in Brussels, the second son of Pieter BRUEGEL the Elder and the younger brother of Jan BRUEGHEL; he is sometimes called 'Velvet' Brueghel to distinguish him from his father ('Peasant' Bruegel) and his brother ('Hell' Brueghel). His father died when he was an infant, and so he trained in the studio of another painter, possibly Gillis CONINXLOO. In 1590 he travelled to Rome, where he secured the patronage of Federico Borromeo (1564–1631), Carlo BORROMEO's cousin and successor (from 1595) as archbishop of Milan. Brueghel moved with Cardinal Borromeo to Milan, and in 1596 returned to the Netherlands and settled in Antwerp, where he enjoyed the patronage of ALBRECHT VON HABSBURG and his consort the Infanta Isabella (daughter of PHILIP II).

The subjects and style of Jan Brueghel's paintings are very different from those of his father. In STILL LIFES, he worked in the Flemish tradition of flower painting, and was the most distinguished exponent of this genre. In LANDSCAPE painting he specialized in small forest scenes, typically with mythological figures or horses and carriages in the foreground. He collaborated with many other painters, including Joos MOMPER (for whom he painted foreground figures) and Rubens. A large number of his paintings survive, as do large numbers of similar paintings by his sons Jan Brueghel the Younger (1601–78) and Ambrosius (1617–75).

*MDA* s.v. Bruegel: (3) Jan Breughel I.

**BRUEGHEL, PIETER THE YOUNGER** (1564/5–1637/8), Flemish painter, born in Brussels, the elder son of Pieter BRUEGEL the Elder and the elder brother of Jan BRUEGHEL; he is sometimes called 'Hell' Brueghel to distinguish him from his father ('Peasant' Bruegel) and his brother ('Velvet' Brueghel). His father died when he was 5, and so he had to train in the studio of another painter, probably Gillis CONINXLOO. Like his father and brother, he pursued his career in Antwerp, where he was admitted to the Guild of Painters in

1585. He was, like his son Pieter Breughel III (1589–*c*.1640), primarily a copyist of the paintings of Pieter Bruegel the Elder; as the original paintings had often been sold before his father's death, Pieter the Younger seems to have worked from drawings and engravings.

*MDA* s.v. Bruegel: (2) Pieter Breughel II (the younger).

**BRUGES or (Flemish) Brugge or (Spanish) Brujas**, a city in Flanders on the river Zwyn, close to the North Sea coast. Bruges was the capital of Flanders until 1180, when the seat of the counts of Flanders moved to Ghent, and thereafter was an important mercantile centre, a 'counter' of the HANSEATIC LEAGUE. Bruges was at the height of its prosperity in the fourteenth and early fifteenth centuries, when its Bourse regulated rates of exchange throughout northern Europe. Prosperity led to artistic patronage, and the artists who worked in Bruges included Jan van EYCK and Hans MEMLING. In 1430 Duke PHILIP THE GOOD of Burgundy married Isabella of Portugal in Bruges, and on the occasion of his wedding founded the chivalric Order of the GOLDEN FLEECE, an acknowledgement of the staple industry of Bruges. The silting of the Zwyn, which was complete by 1490, denied the traders of Bruges access to the sea. The enervating effect of the loss of maritime trade was exacerbated in the sixteenth century by the REVOLT OF THE NETHERLANDS, which damaged the economy of Bruges and severely reduced its population.

J. A. van Houtte, *Bruges: Essai d'histoire urbaine* (1967).

**BRÜGGEMANN, HANS** (*c*.1480/90–1540), north German sculptor and woodcarver, known principally for his monumental carved Bordesholm altarpiece (1514–21), which was originally made for a house of Augustinian canons at Bordesholm (south of Kiel) and was moved to its present location in Schleswig Cathedral in 1666. The altarpiece, which is carved from oak, is 16 metres (53 feet) high and contains 392 figures; it draws heavily on DÜRER's *Small Passion* series (1510–11) and the paintings of Hieronymus BOSCH.

*MDA.*

**BRUMEL, ANTOINE** (*c*.1460–*c*.1515), French composer, mainly of sacred music, who worked in Chartres, Geneva, Laon, Paris, and Ferrara. His writing reflected the changes in musical language which were taking place as Franco-Flemish composers travelled south and blended their techniques with elements of the Italian style. He wrote masses, motets, and Magnificat settings, as well as some vocal and instrumental secular music.

**BRUNELLESCHI, FILIPPO, or Filippo di Ser Brunellesco** (1377–1446), Italian architect and engineer, born in Florence, the son of a notary. He trained as a goldsmith and sculptor, and in 1401 he entered the competition for the bronze baptistery doors, which GHIBERTI won. Brunelleschi came to architecture as a builder and construction engineer with an acute sense of practical issues and of the mathematics of natural OPTICS; he was less interested than his successors (e.g. ALBERTI) in the revival of ancient Roman architecture. In or shortly before 1413, Brunelleschi invented a method of giving

The loggia of the Ospedale degli Innocenti, in the Piazza della SS Annunziata in Florence. The building was designed by **Brunelleschi**, and the roundels depicting babies were added by **Andrea** DELLA ROBBIA

a naturalistic impression of depth in flat pictures and made two paintings of city views (the first showed the baptistery and the second the Palazzo Vecchio) to demonstrate how well the method worked; it is not known what the method was. See PERSPECTIVE.

Brunelleschi's architectural commissions, all in Florence, began in 1418. His early projects, some of which cannot be dated precisely, include a domed chapel in San Jacopo Oltrarno (destroyed 1709), the Barbaradori Chapel in the Church of San Felicità (now known as the Capponi Chapel), the Palazzo di Parte Guelfa (now largely rebuilt), and the Church of San Lorenzo (1421–8). In San Lorenzo Brunelleschi first built what is now known as the Old Sacristy (the New Sacristy, 1523–9, was added by MICHELANGELO), a cube surmounted by a dome in which ribs radiate from the lantern at the centre; Brunelleschi described this construction, which mimics the effect of canvas pressed over the ribs, as having 'crests and sails' (*a creste e vele*). The church is designed as a basilica, but differs from the basilicas of late antiquity in its use of the proportions 1 : 2 and 1 : 4 throughout the building. In the interior Brunelleschi used ribbons of the grey Macigno stone mined in Fiesole and known as *pietre serena* to emphasize the architectural lines.

In 1419 Brunelleschi received the commission to design and build the Ospedale (or Spedale) degli Innocenti (constructed 1421–44), which is sometimes said to be the first Renaissance building. The façade of the Ospedale (then a foundling hospital, now a museum) is a loggia consisting on the ground floor of an arcade of thin Corinthian columns (the glazed terracotta roundels depicting babies were later added by Andrea DELLA ROBBIA); above each semicircular arch is a pedimented window, and every detail honours the canons of mathematical proportion. The design proved to be seminal, and created the definitive form of the Renaissance loggia, which was to be imitated for centuries.

In 1420 Brunelleschi began his greatest work, the dome of Florence Cathedral, which was intended to be built in partnership with Ghiberti (with whom he had won the competition jointly) but in the event became Brunelleschi's project; the design is in some respects Gothic, but the engineering that enabled Brunelleschi to raise the dome without supports is an imaginative revival of the ancient Roman technique of herringbone brickwork. Construction was completed in 1436, and a second competition was initiated for the construction of the lantern; this time Brunelleschi was the unequivocal winner, but construction of the lantern was delayed until 1446; in the interval Brunelleschi built the niched semicircular tribunes (1438) beneath the drum of the dome.

In 1429 Brunelleschi began to build the Pazzi Chapel in the cloister of the Church of Santa Croce. In the interior Brunelleschi again used *pietre serena* to emphasize the architectural lines. The façade, which has a blank upper storey with rectangular panels, is so different from Brunelleschi's other work that it seems possible that his designs were replaced with those of another architect when it was constructed after his death.

**Filippo Brunelleschi**, the nave and choir of the Church of Santo Spirito in Florence, begun in 1436

In 1433 Brunelleschi started to build the Scolari Oratory in the Convent of Santa Maria degli Angeli, but construction stopped before the building was roofed; a roof was added in 1503, and the building was 'completed' in 1934, but only the lower parts of Brunelleschi's walls survived this restoration. These remnants clearly delineate the ground plan of the church, which was to have been the first centrally planned church of the Renaissance: the centre of the church was an octagon, and from each of the eight sides a chapel projected; externally the church was to have had sixteen sides.

Brunelleschi's last church, started in 1436, was San Spirito. The church is in some respects a reversion to the geometrical basilican plan of San Lorenzo, but Brunelleschi aspired to create the sense of a central space by constructing an aisle around the whole church; his successors demurred, and the west aisle was never built.

Of attributions to Brunelleschi, the most important is the Palazzo PITTI. The rustication and geometry of the façade make it likely that Brunelleschi was the architect who drew up the initial plans for the central section; construction began in 1435, and the palace was eventually finished in 1570 by AMMANATI.

*DBI; MDA.*

**BRUNFELS, OTTO** (c.1489–1534), German BOTANIST and physician, the author of the first large-scale printed herbal, the *Herbarum vivae eicones ad nature imitationem* (1530–6), which was illustrated by Hans WEIDITZ; the carefully observed detail of the illustrations shows that Weiditz drew collected samples of living plants rather than modified traditional representations. Brunfels included some north European plants in his treatise, but the emphasis is on the Mediterranean medicinal plants described in antiquity by Dioscorides.

*DSB; NDB.*

**BRUNI, LEONARDO** (1370–1444), Florentine humanist, born in Arezzo, and so (like Pietro ARETINO) often called Aretino. He was educated in Florence, where he mastered Greek as well as Latin. Between 1405 and 1415 he worked in the secretariat of the papal court in Rome, initially for INNOCENT VII and then for JOHN XXIII, whom he accompanied to the COUNCIL OF CONSTANCE. In 1415 he returned to Florence, where he became the most important figure in the humanism of the 1430s and 1440s. He became chancellor of Florence in 1427, and, like SALUTATI a generation earlier, used this post to promote the cultural life of the city. His translations from Greek include PLATO's *Phaedo, Gorgias, Crito, Phaedrus,* and *Apology* and ARISTOTLE's *Nicomachean Ethics* and *Politics.* His most important original works were a panegyric on the city of Florence (*Laudatio Florentinae urbis, c.*1401), which is a seminal work in the development of political humanism in Florence, his *Dialogues to Pier of Istria* (i.e. to Pietro Paolo VERGERIO), and a history of the Florentine people (*Historiarum Florentini populi*) which imitates the lofty prose of the historians of antiquity and scrupulously sets evidence in its historical context; these characteristics have led students of HISTORIOGRAPHY to describe this treatise as the founding text of Renaissance historical writing.

*DBI;* Hans Baron, *Leonardo Bruni Aretino, Humanistisch-philosophische Schriften* (1928); *The Humanism of Leonardo Bruni: Selected Texts,* trans. and ed. Gordon Griffiths et al. (1987).

**BRUNO, GIORDANO** (1548–1600), speculative Italian philosopher, born in Nola (near Naples), the son of a soldier. In 1562 he entered the Dominican Order, but fled in 1576 after being accused of heterodoxy. For the next seventeen years he was an itinerant teacher of mnemonics and an exponent of HERMETICISM and Neoplatonism. In 1581 he visited the court of HENRI III in Paris, and from 1583 to 1585 he lived in England, apparently working as a spy for the English government; lecturing at Oxford, he was accused of plagiarizing from FICINO's works. In 1592 he was captured in Venice and taken to Rome to face the INQUISITION. He was imprisoned until 17 February 1600, when he was burnt at the stake on the Campo dei Fiori.

Bruno's eclectic beliefs included an imaginative version of Copernican cosmology in which he envisaged many earths revolving around many suns and, in theology, a pantheistic immanentism in which God was the efficient and final cause of everything. His expounded his monistic ideas in a number of dialogues and treatises including *De la causa, principio ed uno, De l'infinito, universo e mondi,* and *Spaccio della bestia trionfante* (all in 1584).

*DBI;* Frances Yates, *Giordano Bruno and the Hermetic Tradition* (1964); *The Art of Memory* (1966); G. Aquilecchia, *Giordano Bruno* (1971); J. Bossy, *Giordano Bruno and the Embassy Affair* (1991).

**BRUSSELS or (French) Bruxelles or (Flemish) Brussel**, the principal city of Brabant, now the capital of Belgium, was in the fourteenth century a small town on the river Senne (now called Zenne), a tributary of the Scheldt. Brussels received its charter in 1312, and in 1357 the construction of new city walls was commenced; these walls remained in place until the early nineteenth century. In 1383 the duke of Brabant moved his capital from Louvain to Brussels, which remained the capital of an independent duchy until 1430, when Brabant was incorporated into the duchy of Burgundy.

Brussels flourished under Burgundian rule, and became an important centre of learning and the arts; its artists included Rogier van der WEYDEN. The city was ruled by the HABSBURGS from 1477, and under the Habsburgs became the residence of the court and the archducal capital of the Netherlands. In the REVOLT OF THE NETHERLANDS, Brussels was captured by the Calvinists in 1577 but recaptured by Alessandro FARNESE in 1585.

**BRUSSELS TAPESTRIES.** The origins of tapestry manufacturing in Brussels are not known, but by the mid-fifteenth century the city was exporting TAPESTRIES to the Burgundian court, and by 1516, when Pope LEO X sent RAPHAEL's cartoons of *The Acts of the Apostles* (now in the Victoria and Albert Museum in London) to the Brussels weaver Pieter van Aelst (d. *c.*1530), Brussels had become Europe's most important centre for the manufacturing of tapestries; it was to retain this pre-eminence until the middle of the eighteenth century. In the early sixteenth century the Habsburgs commissioned their court painters Bernaert van ORLEY and Jan VERMEYEN to design tapestries which were then woven in Brussels. The most prominent family of weavers was the PANNEMAKER FAMILY.

In 1528 the tapestry factories of Brussels introduced the mark of a shield between two Bs to designate their products. Brussels tapestries made before 1528 are difficult to distinguish from those made elsewhere in Flanders or in France; attributions from the period before 1528 include the *Allegory of the Virgin as a Source of Living Water* (1485, Louvre) and the *Virgin and Child with a Donor* (*c*.1500, Musée des Tissus, Lyon). Differences between the cartoons of the *Acts of the Apostles* series (1516–19) and the finished tapestries sent to Rome to hang on the walls of the SISTINE CHAPEL on important occasions show that the weavers felt free to elaborate the decorative details of the designs from which they were working: the flowers on the robe of Jesus, for example, are not present on Raphael's cartoon.

**BRUYN, BARTEL** (*c*.1493–1555), German painter, born in Cologne. He painted portraits and historical scenes as well as religious pictures; his best-known work is the pair of paintings (1536) illustrating the lives of St Victor and St Helen in the wings of the shrine of St Victor in the Cathedral of St Victor at Xanten, on the Lower Rhine.

NDB; MDA s.v. Bruyn: (1) Bartholomäus Bruyn (i).

**BRY, THÉODORE DE** (1528–1598), Flemish printer and engraver. He was born in Liège and in 1570 settled in Frankfurt, where he established a workshop together with his two sons. The press specialized in illustrated travel books, the most famous of which was the impassioned *Brevíssima relación de la destrucción de las Indias* (1552), by Fray Bartolomé de LAS CASAS; Théodore de Bry's illustrations contributed to the development of the BLACK LEGEND.

BNB; NDB; MDA s.v. Bry, de (1) Theodor de Bry.

**BUCER or Butzer, MARTIN** (1491–1551), Alsatian Protestant reformer, born in Schlettstadt (now French Sélestat), where he entered the Dominican ORDER (*c*.1506–07). He was sent to Heidelberg (*c*.1516–17) to continue his studies and in April 1518 attended a disputation at which Martin LUTHER defended his call for ecclesiastical reform. In 1521 he abandoned his vows by papal dispensation, and shortly thereafter married a nun. He became pastor at Landstuhl (in the Palatinate) in 1522. The following year he was excommunicated and settled in Strassburg, where he was appointed as preacher at St Aurelia, the church of the Gardeners' Guild. He worked as a pastor and also wrote prolifically as a polemicist (against both Catholicism and ANABAPTISM). On the fraught subject of the EUCHARIST, the ambiguity of Bucer's position is exacerbated by the opacity of his Latin: at the Colloquy of MARBURG (1529) Bucer and Wolfgang CAPITO seemed to support the Zwinglian position, but their TETRAPOLITAN CONFESSION of 1530 is equivocal, and Bucer's willingness to sign the WITTENBERG CONFESSION in 1536 implies a measure of acquiescence in MELANCHTHON's slightly modified Lutheran position.

Bucer participated in the Conferences of HAGENAU (1540), WORMS (1540), and REGENSBURG (1541) and subsequently assisted HERMANN VON WIED in his forlorn attempt to impose the Reformation on Cologne. He opposed the AUGSBURG INTERIM of 1548, and the following year accepted the invitation of Thomas CRANMER to settle in England, where he was appointed Regius professor of divinity at Cambridge. He died in Cambridge on 27 February 1551 and was interred in the university church; in 1557, at the command of Queen MARY's commissioners, his body was disinterred and burnt and his tomb destroyed, but the empty tomb was later rebuilt at the command of Queen Elizabeth. Bucer's voluminous writings included *De regno Christi*, part of which has entered the canon of English literature because it was translated by John Milton as *The Judgement of Martin Bucer Concerning Divorce* (1644).

NDB; NDBA; DNB; C. Hopf, *Martin Bucer and the English Reformation* (1946); D. F. Wright (ed.), *Martin Bucer: Reforming Church and Community* (1994).

**BUCHANAN, GEORGE** (1506–82), Scottish humanist poet and political philosopher. Educated at St Andrews and Paris, where he was taught by John MAJOR, he held positions at the universities of Bordeaux, Paris, and Coimbra in Portugal. Influenced by ERASMUS, he repeatedly attacked the clergy, and was imprisoned by the Portuguese INQUISITION. Returning to Scotland in 1561, he declared himself Protestant, and, following the murder of DARNLEY, became a persistent opponent of MARY, QUEEN OF SCOTS. Principal of St Leonard's College, St Andrews, and influential tutor to Mary's son JAMES VI, the writings of this eminent humanist include *De iure regni apud Scotos* (1579), which regards the people as the source of political power and defends resistance to tyranny. His Latin poem *Sphaera* (1582) rejects Copernican astronomy in favour of that of Ptolemy; *Rerum Scoticarum historia* (1582) was an influential history of Scotland.

DNB; Ian McFarlane, *Buchanan* (1981).

**BUCHNER, HANS, or Hans von Constansz** (1483–1538), German composer, organist, and organ builder. He was a student of Paul HOFHAIMER and became organist of Konstanz Cathedral following a recommendation by Emperor Maximilian. His *Fundamentum* (*c*.1520) is a theoretical work and addresses details of organ playing, making organ arrangements of vocal pieces, and the contrapuntal handling of a *cantus firmus*.

***BUCINTORO or (English exonym) bucentaur*** (from Italian *buzino d'oro*, 'golden barque'), the state galley of the doges of Venice. The *bucintoro* led the fleet which sailed to the Porto del Lido on Ascension Day in the ceremony of the marriage of the sea (*sponsalizio del mar*), in which the doge threw a consecrated ring into the Adriatic. The ceremony originated in the commemoration of the Venetian conquest of DALMATIA in AD 1000. The last *bucintoro* was built in 1724 and destroyed by the French in 1798 while its gold ornamentation was being removed; what remains of the galley (a group of carvings by Antonio Corradini) is now in the Museo Correr in Venice; there is a model of the *bucintoro* in the Museo Storico Navale.

**BUDÉ, GUILLAUME, or Budaeus** (1468–1540), French polymath and humanist jurist. Budé was born in Paris, and studied law in Orléans. He enjoyed the patronage of Louis XII, who sent him to Rome as ambassador to Leo X, and of Francis I, who appointed him as secretary and later as the first royal librarian; the library over which he presided at FONTAINBLEAU later became the foundation collection of the Bibliothèque Nationale. Francis I also enabled Budé to found the *lecteurs royaux*, which later evolved into the Collège de France. As a jurist he advocated the philological and historical study of Roman law, an approach that he implemented in his *Annotationes in Pandectas* (1508), which greatly influenced the study of Roman law.

Budé wrote authoritatively on ancient coins and measures (*De asse et partibus*, 1514) and published translations of PLUTARCH. He was a formidable classical philologist, and his *Commentarii linguae Graecae* (1529) is an important analysis of Greek. His religious convictions are unclear, but the fact that after his death on 23 August 1540 his widow moved to Geneva and professed Calvinism aroused suspicions that Budé was a furtive Protestant sympathizer.

DBF s.v. 2. Budé; J. Plattard, *Guillaume Budé et les origines de l'humanisme français* (1923); Donald R. Kelley, *Foundations of Modern Historical Scholarship: Language, Law and History in the French Renaissance* (1970), 53–85; Budaeus, *Opera* (4 vols., 1557).

**BUGENHAGEN, JOHANNES, or Pomeranus** (1485–1558), German Protestant reformer, born on 24 June 1485 in Wollin (now Polish Wolin), an island near Stettin (now Polish Szczecin), in Pomerania. He studied at the university of Greifswald and in 1504 was appointed rector of the city school in Treptow (now Polish Trzebiatow). In 1509 he was ordained as a priest and was appointed to a post in the collegiate Marienkirche in Treptow, and in 1517 he became a lecturer in biblical and patristic studies at the Premonstratensian monastery at Belbuck.

In 1522 Bugenhagen converted to Lutheranism under the influence of Luther's *De captivitate Babylonica*, and his zeal led to the conversion of his abbot. He moved to Wittenberg, where he married (1522) and became a pastor and university lecturer. He organized the Lutheran Church in Brunswick and Hamburg (1528) and in Lübeck and Pomerania (1530). In 1537 he moved to Denmark at the invitation of King CHRISTIAN III and in the course of the next five years reorganized the Danish Church and the University of Copenhagen along the rigorously Protestant lines favoured by the king. Though only a presbyter, he consecrated seven churchmen as bishops (or 'superintendents'), and so the Danish Church forfeited the episcopal Apostolic Succession. He spent the rest of his life in Wittenberg, where he assisted Luther with his translation of the Bible and where he died on 20 April 1558.

NDB.

**BULL, JOHN** (1562/3–1628), English composer, organist, virginalist, and organ builder who worked at Hereford and the Chapel Royal. He studied with John BLITHEMAN and William BYRD. He is principally known for his keyboard writing, which characteristically consisted of highly decorated patterns against a plain *cantus firmus*, their brilliance allowing him to demonstrate his skills as a keyboard player. Thomas TOMKINS described his writing as 'excellent for the hand'. Shortly before he left England for the Netherlands, where he spent the last fifteen years of his life, he wrote the *Prince's Galliard* for his pupil Prince Henry.

**BULLANT, JEAN** (*c*.1515–1578), French architect and geometer, born in Amiens. From *c*.1540 to 1545 he studied classical antiquities in Italy. On returning to France he entered the service of Anne de MONTMORENCY, for whom he designed additions to the Château d'Écouen which include the earliest façade in France in the colossal ORDER. He also built the mannerist bridge and gallery at Fère-en-Tardenois (1552–62) and the Petit Château at Chantilly (*c*.1561).

In 1570 Bullant succeeded Philibert DELORME as architect to CATHERINE DE MÉDICIS, but most of his commissions (including his work on the TUILERIES) have been destroyed; his only surviving building for Queen Catherine is at CHENONCEAUX, for which he designed the gallery on the bridge and the western part of the forecourt. Bullant's publications include an architectural treatise which expounds the five orders (*La Règle générale d'architecture, étude sur les cinq ordres de colonnes*, 1563) and a manual of geometry (*Petit Traité de géométrie*, 1564).

DBF; MDA.

**BULLINGER, JOHANN HEINRICH** (1504–75), Swiss Protestant reformer usually known as Heinrich Bullinger, born in Bremgarten, in the canton of Aargau, on 18 July 1504 and educated at Emmerich (near Nijmegen) and Cologne. He began to take an interest in Luther's call for reform in about 1520, and his reading of the Bible, the church fathers, and MELANCHTHON's *Loci communes* led him first to Lutheranism and then to Zwinglianism. He taught at the Cistercian school in Kappel from 1523 to 1529, and finally broke with the Catholic Church in 1529, when he became pastor of Bremgarten and married a nun, Anna Adlischweiler, by whom he was to have eleven children. On 9 December 1531 he was chosen to succeed ZWINGLI as chief pastor of Zürich, and remained in that post until his death on 11 September 1575.

Bullinger played an important part in the formulation of the HELVETIC CONFESSIONS of 1536 and 1566 and was also one of the architects of the ZÜRICH AGREEMENT. He was also an untiring controversialist, attacking Luther's doctrine of the EUCHARIST in a polemical combat with Johannes BRENZ throughout the 1560s, attacking ANABAPTIST theology in tracts of 1531 and 1560, corresponding with Laelius SOCINUS, and commenting on the VESTIARIAN controversy in England. In 1570 he was asked by Richard COX to prepare a reply to the bull that had excommunicated Queen Elizabeth: his reply was published in Latin (1571), English (1572), and German (1572). His sermons, which were published in Latin as the *Decades* and in German as the *Hausbuch*, were published in English in 1577 and used as a textbook in Canterbury and Lincoln.

DHBS; NDB.

*BUNDSCHUH*, a German peasant's boot fashioned from a single piece of leather and fastened to the ankle with long straps. In the 1490s and in the first two decades of the sixteenth century, the *Bundschuh* became an emblem of popular revolt, and the shoe hanging on a pole became the flag of rebellion. The term quickly came to denote the rebels and the rebellions as well as the boot, and is commonly applied to revolts in Alsace (1493), the bishopric of Speyer (1502), the Breisgau (1513), and the Upper Rhine as a whole (1517).

**BUON or Bon or Bono, BARTOLOMEO** (*c*.1400/10–*c*.1464/7), architect and sculptor, born in Venice, the son of the sculptor Giovanni Buon, in whose workshop he was trained. Bartolomeo built the well-head in the courtyard of the Cà d'Oro (1424–31) and a fine lunette on the Porta della Carta of the Ducal Palace (1438–42); he later built the portals of the churches of Santi Giovanni e Paolo (1458–63) and Madonna dell'Orto (1460–6) and the upper storey of the Arco Foscari in the Ducal Palace (1460–4). His sculpture includes a relief of *The Madonna della Misericordia* (1441–5) carved as a lunette for the façade of the Scuola Grande della Misericordia and now in the Victoria and Albert Museum. Buon's style was almost wholly Gothic, though at his death he was working on the Ca' del Duca on the Grand Canal; had he completed more than the basement he would be regarded as an early exponent of the Renaissance style rather than the last important Gothic architect in Venice.

Buon is sometimes confused with his unrelated namesake Bartolomeo Buon or Bon (d. 1529), a Lombard architect in Venice who built the ground floor of the Scuola di San Rocco.

*DBI* s.v. Bono, Bartolomeo; *MDA* s.v. Buon.

**BUONACCORSI, FILIPPO, or Callimachus Experiens** (1437–96), Italian humanist in Poland, born into a noble family in Rome, where he joined the Roman Academy of Julius Pomponius LAETUS. In 1468 the Academy was suppressed by Pope PAUL II, who suspected its members of paganism and heresy; Laetus was arrested, but Buonaccorsi fled. Two years later he moved to Poland, where he entered the service of CASIMIR IV and (subsequently) JOHN ALBERT. He served as a diplomat in the service of Poland on embassies to Constantinople, Venice, and Rome, and also wrote historical works and Latin poetry.

*DBI; PSB* s.v. Kallimach.

**BUONTALENTI, BERNARDO, or Bernardo delle Giràndole** (1531–1608), Italian architect, military and hydraulic engineer, painter, sculptor, and designer of waterworks and AUTOMATA. He was a native of Florence, where he worked in the service of the MEDICI grand dukes of Tuscany, for whom he built the Casino di San Marco (*c*.1580–8, now the Tribuna), the Galleria and Tribuna of the Uffizi (1584), the façade of the Church of San Trinita (1592–4), and the GROTTOES (1583–93) in the BOBOLI GARDENS; in 1593 he began work on what was to be called the Palazzo Nonfinito, the 'unfinished palace'. He painted a self-portrait (Uffizi)

and fashioned a vase (Museo degli Argenti, Palazzo Pitti, Florence) for which a gold setting was made by Jacopo BILIVERTI.

Buontalenti was the architect of PRATOLINO (for which he designed the automata). His fortifications include the Belvedere of the Medici and the port of Livorno. He built the canal between Livorno and Pisa (where in 1605 he designed the Loggia dei Banchi). The *spettacoli* that he organized for the Medici often included firework displays, which gave rise to his nickname (*giràndole* means 'Catherine wheels').

*DBI; MDA;* Amelio Fara, *Bernardo Buontalenti* (1988; German trans. 1990); Amelio Fara (ed.), *Bernardo Buontalenti* (1998).

**BURBAGE, RICHARD** (*c*.1567–1619), English actor. Son of the actor James Burbage, after working with the ADMIRAL'S MEN, Richard joined the CHAMBERLAIN'S MEN on their formation in 1594. Despite shortness and plumpness, he was an outstanding and versatile actor, noted especially for his performances as Lear, Othello, and Hamlet. He also acted in plays by JONSON, KYD, WEBSTER, and BEAUMONT and FLETCHER, and shared in the management of the THEATRE, as well as the building and management of the GLOBE.

*DNB.*

**BURCHIELLO or Domenico di Giovanni** (1404–49), Italian barber and satirist, born in Florence. His poems, many of which are sonnets, are lightly satirical, but Burchiello's imprudent mocking of members of the MEDICI family led in 1434 to his exile; he initially moved to Siena, and then to Rome. His verse, in which Burchiello delights in playfully recondite allusions and improbable phrasing, inspired imitations (including some by Anton Francesco DONI) of the *maniera burchiellesca*.

*DBI* s.v. Domenico; *OCIL.*

**BÜRGI, JOST** (1552–1632), Swiss clockmaker, instrument-maker, and mathematician. He served from 1579 to 1592 as maker of clocks, mechanical globes, and astronomical instruments to the Landgrave WILHELM IV of Hesse in Kassel; on the landgrave's death in 1592, Bürgi moved to Prague to take up a similar post in the service of RUDOLF II. He was regarded as the leading clockmaker of his day. Bürgi's technical innovations included a device which directed a constant driving force to the escapement; he was one of the first horologists to fit his clocks with sweep hands to measure seconds.

In mathematics, Bürgi devised a system of logarithms in the 1580s, before NAPIER, but it was not printed until 1620 when, apparently after pressure from KEPLER, who had a lively respect for his talents (and says he learned about ALGEBRA from him), he published his *Arithmetische und geometrische Progress-Tabulen*.

*DSB; NDB.*

**BURGKMAIR, HANS THE ELDER** (1473–1531), German engraver and painter, born in Augsburg. He trained with Martin SCHONGAUER in Colmar and returned to Augsburg in 1498. The Venetian elements in his paintings, which include ALTARPIECES in the Alte Pinakothek in Munich and the Städtische Kunstsammlungen in Augsburg, have been adduced as evidence that Burgkmair also studied in Venice, but there is no documentary evidence of any visit to Italy. He contributed the woodcut illustrations to the Emperor MAXI-MILIAN's *Der Weißkunig* (an unfinished autobiography not published until 1775) and some of the illustrations in his *Teuerdank* (1517). He also contributed (as did his friend DÜRER) to the *Triumph of Maximilian*, a series of imperial woodcuts.

*MDA* s.v. Burgkmair (2) Hans Burgkmair I; *NDB*.

**BURGOS, LAWS OF,** a Spanish legal code promulgated in December 1512 with a view to regulating the treatment of American Indians by requiring royal officials in Spanish America to protect the Indians and by requiring all Spaniards in the Americas to treat the Indians humanely. The code, which was a response to the complaints of missionaries, was not enforced, and in 1542 it was replaced by the code known as the Laws of the INDIES.

**BURGUNDY or (French) Bourgogne or (Latin) Burgundia,** a kingdom (411–1032) and duchy (1032–1361) which reverted in 1361 to the crown of France. In 1363 King Jean II of France conferred the duchy on his son Philip the Bold, who expanded his inheritance through marriage to include the counties of Burgundy (which was distinct from the duchy), Artois, and Flanders and through purchase to include the country of Charolais. In May 1404 Duke Philip was succeeded by his son JOHN THE FEARLESS, who in November 1407 precipitated a feud between ARMAGNACS AND BURGUNDIANS that was to last for 28 years.

Duke John was succeeded by PHILIP THE GOOD, who extended the Netherlandish territories of Burgundy by inheritance (Brabant and Holland on his marriage in 1433), conquest (Luxemburg in 1443) and, in 1435, by recognizing Charles VII as king of France, for which he was rewarded with the counties of Auxerre, Bar-sur-Seine, Mâcon, and Ponthieu and the Somme towns of Montdidier, Péronne, and Roye.

Duke Philip was succeeded by CHARLES THE BOLD, who inherited the duchy and county of Burgundy and its territories, which by this time included Artois, Brabant, Flanders, Friesland, Hainaut, Luxemburg, and Zeeland. Charles aspired to add Alsace and Lorraine to these possessions with a view to creating a middle kingdom between France and the Holy Roman Empire. Initially he made progress, defeating the army of LOUIS XI of France at the battle of Montlhéry (16 July 1465), but in 1471 Louis was able to retaliate by capturing the towns on the Somme which had been ceded to Burgundy by the Treaty of Arras. Two years later the duchy of Gelderland was ceded to Charles. Charles was killed in battle in January 1477, and his death marked the conclusion of the Burgundian threat to the French monarchy.

The inheritance of Burgundy passed to Duke Charles's daughter MARY OF BURGUNDY. Louis XI contested the inheritance, claiming Burgundy and its possessions as a fief of the French crown; he seized Burgundy, and Mary turned to her Netherlandish territories for assistance, which she secured in exchange for a transfer of authority to the ESTATES-GENERAL. She married Maximilian of Austria (later the Emperor MAXI-MILIAN I) in Ghent on 18 August 1477. After Mary's death in 1482 the duchy passed to the French crown, but the Netherlandish territories deriving from the inheritance of Charles the Bold passed to the HOLY ROMAN EMPIRE, and in 1512 were constituted as the imperial Circle of Burgundy (i.e. Franche-Comté).

From 1482 to 1792 Burgundy was a *pays d'états* consisting of Autunois, Auxois, Dijonnais, the Pays de la Montagne (Châtillon-sur-Seine), and the counties of Auxerrois, Bar-sur-Seine, Chalonnais, and Mâconnais. The Estates assembled at Dijon, with the bishop of Autun representing the clergy and the mayor of Dijon the third estate. In the administration of justice most of Burgundy fell within the jurisdiction of the Parlement of Dijon, but Auxerrois and Mâconnais were subject to the Parlement of Paris.

**BURLAMACCHI, FRANCESCO** (1498–1548), GONFALONIERE of Lucca. He was born into a wealthy Luccan family and as a young man pursued a career in commerce. He was elected as *gonfaloniere* (head of state for a fixed term) in 1533 and again in 1546. As part of his duties Burlamacchi inspected the militia of the *contado* (dependent territory) of Lucca, and he regularly advocated the strengthening of the militia in the face of the ever-present threat posed by Cosimo de' MEDICI in Florence.

Burlamacchi's interests in the militia were revealed by a treacherous ally to be central to a conspiracy to invade Pisa and encourage its citizens to throw off Medicean rule and establish a free republic. He hoped that Pistoia and Florence would follow the example of Pisa and that eventually Tuscany would become a federation of self-governing republics; this republican vision had a religious dimension that entailed a renewal of the Church. Burlamacchi was arrested, repeatedly tortured, and executed. In the historiography of the Risorgimento Burlamacchi's plan for rebellion was seen as an early attempt to begin the process of unifying Italy; his statue was erected in Lucca in 1863.

*DBI.*

**BUSCH, JAN** (1399–1480), one of the principal BRETHREN OF THE COMMON LIFE. He was born in Zwolle (Overijssel) and from 1420 to 1424 taught at WINDESHEIM. He was ordained as a priest in Bödingen (near Cologne) in 1424 and thereafter worked to reform the monasteries of Germany and the Netherlands as required by the COUNCIL OF BASEL. In this task he worked alongside NICHOLAS OF CUSA, who secured for him the post of visitor apostolic of the Augustinian houses in Saxony and Thuringia. His history (*Chronicon*) of the Windesheim house was published posthumously (Antwerp, 1621).

*NDB* s.v. Busch, Johannes.

**BUSLEIDEN, JEROOM or (French) Jérôme** (c.1470–1517), Flemish humanist poet, patron, and diplomat, educated in Louvain and Bologna. In 1503 he became the leader of the governing council of Brabant. He was employed as an imperial ambassador by the Emperor MAXIMILIAN I, and served as an adviser to CHARLES V. He wrote poetry and Latin letters and was a patron of art and learning. In his will he bequeathed money for the establishment of the Collegium Trilingue, a college of the University of Louvain specializing in the teaching of Latin, Greek, and Hebrew.

*BNB; NBW* i s.v. Busleyden, Jeroom van; H. de Vocht, *Jerome de Busleiden, Founder of the Louvain Collegium Trilingue* (1950).

**BUSNOIS, ANTOINE** (*c.*1430–1492), French composer, singer, and poet. As a professional singer he worked with and wrote for skilful vocal virtuosi. His music caught the attention of his contemporaries with its imaginative use of syncopation and cross-rhythms and its appealing melodies. Thirty years after his death he was credited with the invention of the 'L'Homme armé' tune, which became the basis of over 40 mass settings by composers as diverse as OBRECHT, DUFAY, and PALESTRINA.

**BUSSI, GIOVANNI ANDREA** (1417–75), Italian papal secretary and humanist, born in Vigevano on 14 July 1417. He entered the service of Pope NICHOLAS V in 1451 and thereafter served Cardinal NICHOLAS OF CUSA. He was consecrated as a bishop and eventually became a papal secretary. He edited classical authors, notably LIVY (1469), and collected classical manuscripts for the VATICAN LIBRARY. He died in Rome on 4 February 1475.

*DBI.*

**BUTTON or Batton, THOMAS** (*c.*1577–1634). Button entered the navy in 1589. In 1612 he led an expedition to search for the NORTH-WEST PASSAGE, exploring Hudson Bay, and proving that there was no access from it to the north-west. He also named Nelson River, Button's Bay, and New Wales.

**BUXDORF, JOHANNES** (1564–1629), German Hebraicist, born in Kamen (Westphalia); he studied at Marburg and at the new University of Herborn and then moved first to Heidelberg and then to Basel; he subsequently studied under BULLINGER at Zürich and BEZA at Geneva before returning to Basel, where he remained for the rest of his life. He was appointed professor of Hebrew at Basel in 1591. He was a rare dissenter from the anti-Semitism of the period, entertaining learned JEWS in his house, employing Jews to assist him with the preparation of his edition of the Hebrew BIBLE, and even advising Jews on the minutiae of Jewish ceremonial law; he also corresponded with Jewish scholars in Germany, the Netherlands, and Constantinople.

Buxdorf's monumental edition of the Hebrew Bible (*Biblia Hebraica*, 2 vols., 1618; 4 vols., 1618–19) contained a punctuated and vocalized Hebrew text and the Aramaic *Targumim*. He also published a Hebrew and Aramaic grammar (*Manuale Hebraicum et Chaldaicum*, 1602) and a treatise on Jewish ceremonial law (*Synagoga Judaica*), which appeared first in German (1603) and subsequently in an enlarged Latin translation. The two great projects of his last years, his *Lexicon Chaldaicum, Talmudicum et Rabbinicum* and his *Concordantiae bibliorum Hebraicorum*, were both left unfinished at his death, but were completed by his son (and namesake) Johannes (1599–1664), who also chose to defend polemically his father's

discreetly held position on the central debate in HEBREW SCHOLARSHIP, the date at which the vowel points were added to the text. The younger Buxdorf maintained that the vowel points were at least as old as the reformation of Ezra, and therefore divinely inspired, whereas his French opponent Louis Cappel argued (correctly) that the vowel points were of comparatively recent origin.

*NDB.*

**BUYTEWECH, WILLEM PIETERSZOON** (*c.*1591–*c.*1624), Dutch genre painter and book illustrator. He worked in Haarlem, where he painted a large number of paintings of stylish dandies and fashionable ladies who hover between respectability and the *demi-monde*. His subjects also included domestic scenes and, in his etchings, LANDSCAPES of the Dutch countryside.

*MDA; NNBW* vi.

**BYRD, WILLIAM** (1543–1623), English composer, who enjoyed the patronage and protection of several powerful aristocrats and Queen Elizabeth I. His circle of friends and employers included Catholic activists such as the earls of Oxford, Northumberland, and Worcester. He benefited (with Thomas TALLIS) from the patent granted by the queen for the printing and marketing of music. Even after the death of Edmund CAMPION in 1581 and the consequent tightening up of laws for RECUSANTS, and at a time when Byrd was closely involved with the Jesuits, he was held in sufficiently high royal regard to be asked to set the queen's own words, 'Look and bow down', as an anthem thanking God for the defeat of the Armada.

Sworn in as a gentleman of the Chapel Royal in 1572, he was, after his death, described in its Cheque Book as 'a Father of Music'. Influenced by Alfonso FERRABOSCO, he became an exponent of imitative polyphony which is the hallmark of much of his early sacred music. Byrd's support of the Catholic cause is evident in his Latin motets. After 1593 Byrd moved to Essex where he found a safe haven in the Catholic home of St John Petre, and it was here, in his three masses and the two books of *Gradualia* (1605 and 1607), that he wrote music specifically for the Catholic liturgy.

The influence of this 'Brittanicae Musicae Parens' was apparent in the short term in the music and writing of his pupils Thomas MORLEY and Thomas TOMKINS, and in the keyboard works of John BULL and Orlando GIBBONS. In the long term, his music has scarcely been out of the English cathedral repertoire since his death.

**BYZANTIUM.** In 330 the capital of the Roman Empire shifted to Constantinople, and in the ensuing centuries the eastern half of the Empire evolved into the Greek Byzantine Empire of the Middle Ages. The cultural differences between the Greek East and the Roman West were reflected in the gradual separation of the Orthodox Church in the East and the Catholic Church in the West; in 1054 the churches finally separated, and despite attempts such as the COUNCIL OF FLORENCE to achieve reconciliation, the two churches have remained apart.

The Byzantine Empire began to break up with the battle of Manzikert in 1071, as a result of which the Byzantines lost almost all of Asia Minor to the Seljuk Turks. The forces of the fourth CRUSADE conquered Constantinople in 1204, which led to the establishment of the Latin Empire; the Venetians added to their empire part of Constantinople, bases along the Greek coast, and CRETE, and the French took most of the Balkan lands. Constantinople was recovered by the Byzantines in 1261, but by this time the remaining territories of Byzantium had evolved into three successor states centred in Nicaea, Epiros, and Trebizond. Nicaea, which had been the Byzantine capital during the period when Constantinople was lost, fell to the Ottomans in 1331. The despotate of Epiros, which was from 1224 to 1242 a self-declared empire, was successively annexed by Nicaea (1246–64), administered by the ORSINI family (1318–37), occupied by the Serbs (1348), and eventually conquered by the Ottomans, partially in 1430 and completely in 1449. Trebizond remained an independent empire until 1461, when it fell to the Ottomans; the emperors of Trebizond (see Appendix 1) were members of the Komnenoi family, and used the title Grand Comneno (Μέγας Κομνηνός). Eventually the Byzantine Empire consisted only of Constantinople and its immediate hinterland; Constantinople was finally overrun by the army of Mehmet II on 29 May 1453.

The model of a RENAISSANCE in which scholars look back to a golden age in antiquity inevitably necessitates the deprecation of the immediately preceding civilization. The full force of this slur has been directed towards Byzantium, which has been depicted, like the Rome of late antiquity, as inert and decadent; indeed, the very term 'Byzantine' has become a byword for pointless and stultified complexity. This slander was most elegantly articulated by Gibbon, who ringingly declared that the Greeks of Constantinople 'held in their lifeless hands the riches of their fathers, without inheriting the spirit which had created and improved that sacred patrimony; they read, they praised, they compiled, but their languid souls seemed alike incapable of thought and action.' This is an unnecessarily harsh judgement. It is true that the standards of Byzantine scholarship declined as its territories fell to the Ottoman armies, but the scholarship of Byzantium was nonetheless the conduit through which much of the literature of the ancient world passed to Italy in the fifteenth century and thence to the rest of Europe; in that sense, Byzantium was the begetter of the GREEK SCHOLARSHIP that is an important strand in the European Renaissance and the custodian of the corpus of ancient Greek literature that had been lost in the West.

K. M. Setton, 'The Byzantine Background to the Italian Renaissance', *Proceedings of the American Philosophical Society*, 1 (1956); John Monfasani, *Byzantine Scholars in Renaissance Italy: Cardinal Bessarion and Other Emigrés* (1995); D. J. Geanakoplos, *Greek Scholars in Venice* (1962), repr. as *Constantinople and the West* (1973); N. G. Wilson, *From Byzantium to Italy: Greek Studies in the Italian Renaissance* (1992).

# C

**CABBALA or Kabbala**, a system of Jewish theosophy in which an esoteric interpretation of the Old Testament yielded to its adherents hidden doctrines. In the fifteenth and sixteenth centuries Cabbalism lived on in the Jewish tradition, and exiled Spanish JEWS established Cabbalistic centres all over the Ottoman Empire, notably at Safed (now Zefat, in Upper Galilee), where it was taught by Joseph KARO. There was also a parallel system of Christian Cabbalism, of which the founders were PICO DELLA MIRANDOLA (whose *Conclusiones cabalisticae* of 1486 set out 72 doctrines), Johannes REUCHLIN (who wrote about Cabbalism in his *De verbo mirifico* of 1472 and in his *De arte cabalistica* of 1517), and Cornelius AGRIPPA (who described Cabbalism in his *De occulta philosophia* of 1510, published in 1533). Thereafter Cabbalism became part of the intellectual stock of the Renaissance magus, notably PARACELSUS and Jakob BÖHME. See also GOLEM.

J. L. Blau, *The Christian Interpretation of the Cabala in the Renaissance* (1944); F. Secret, *Les Kabbalistes chrétiens de la Renaissance* (1964).

**CABEZA DE VACA, ÁLVAR NÚÑEZ** (*c.*1500–*c.*1564), Spanish explorer, born in Jerez de la Frontera; he was the grandson of Pedro de Vera, the conquistador of Gran Canaria in the CANARY ISLANDS. In 1527 Cabeza sailed for Florida in the expedition led by Pánfilo de NARVÁEZ. A succession of shipwrecks and other fatal incidents led to the death of all but four members of the expedition. Cabeza survived, and according to his own account, *Naufragios y relación de la jornada que hizo a la Florida con el adelantado Pánfilo de Naváez* (1537), wandered with his three companions for nine years (including a long period of captivity by Indians in Texas) before reaching Mexico City in 1536. His route, which took him as far west as the Gulf of California, made him the first European to cross America.

Cabeza de Vaca later succeeded Pedro de MENDOZA as governor (*adelantado*) of Río de la Plata and Paraguay (1540–5), where he collaborated with his secretary Pedro Hernández in the composition of his *Comentarios*, an account of his overland journey from Buenos Aires to Asunción. A feud with Domingo Martínez de Irala led in 1545 to his arrest; he was sent home to Spain in chains, convicted of exceeding his gubernatorial authority, and imprisoned by the Council of the INDIES. In 1551 he was banished for eight years to Africa, but after a year he was invited to return to Spain and appointed as a judge in Seville.

DHE; C. Hallenbeck, *Álvar Núñez Cabeza de Vaca: The Journey and Route of the First European to Cross the Continent of North America, 1534–36* (1940); José Fernández, *Álvar Núñez Cabeza de Vaca, the Forgotten Chronicler* (1975); José Rodríguez Carrión, *Apuntes para una biografía del jerezano Álvar Núñez Cabeza de Vaca* (1985); Rolena Adorno and P. C. Pautz, *Álvar Núñez Cabeza de Vaca: His Account, his Life, and the Expedition of Pánfilo de Narváez* (3 vols., 1999).

**CABEZÓN, ANTONIO DE** (1510–66), Spanish composer and organist, blind from childhood. In 1538 he became *músico de la cámara* to Charles V, and on the death of Queen Isabella a year later he was entrusted with the musical education of Prince Philip. He accompanied his pupil to London for his marriage to MARY TUDOR. His music is part of the Spanish instrumental tradition, and is written for plucked string instruments and ensembles of string and wind players. His variations on Spanish songs and dance forms were a source of inspiration throughout Europe.

**CABINET**, the fifteenth- and early sixteenth-century term for a room in a palace or scholar's house devoted to the display of a collection of art or natural history; the term could also refer to the objects in a collection. In France such rooms were called *cabinets de curiosités*, in Italy *studioli*, and in Germany *Wunderkammern* or *Kunstkammern*.

In the course of the sixteenth century the term 'cabinet' gradually came to refer to a piece of FURNITURE used to store objects. Cabinets were distinguished from cupboards in having drawers or pigeonholes rather than shelves. The cabinet originated in early sixteenth-century Italy and was soon being manufactured in Spain, Germany, the southern Netherlands, and Bohemia. The Spanish cabinet, which has been known since the nineteenth century as the *vargueño*, consisted of a rectangular case (containing drawers) set on an arcaded stand; the exterior was relatively plain, but the drop-leaf front opened to reveal a highly ornate interior typically decorated with carving and INTARSIA. The German cabinet, which derived from the Spanish *vargueño*, was known as a *Kunstschrank* or *Kabinettschrank*, and was variously decorated with marquetry, metals, and semi-precious stones; Augsburg was the principal centre of production, and early seventeenth-century baroque cabinets are sometimes called *Augsburger Kabinette*. In the southern Netherlands, where the principal centre of production was Antwerp, cabinets were typically made of ebony and decorated with marquetry flowers and mother-of-pearl; the interiors of the doors and the drawer fronts were often painted with biblical or mythological or genre scenes. Cabinets made in the Bohemian town of Cheb (formerly German Eger) were distinguished by panels carved in low relief with religious scenes based on engraved designs. In Florence, where PIETRE DURE was revived in the sixteenth century, a workshop established under the patronage of Grand Duke COSIMO I DE' MEDICI (and refounded in 1588 as the Opificio delle Pietre Dure) manufactured panels of *pietre dure* for assembly into cabinets.

**CABOT, JOHN, or (Italian) Giovanni Caboto** (*c*.1450–*c*.1498), Genoese explorer. After participating in Venetian and Spanish expeditions, Cabot came to Bristol in 1493 in the hope of emulating Columbus' Atlantic crossing. He reached Newfoundland on his second attempt in 1497, but died on a return voyage; his explorations were continued by his son Sebastian CABOT.

*DBI.*

**CABOT, SEBASTIAN** (1476–1557), English navigator. Son of John CABOT, Sebastian shared his father's interest in exploration, and may have been with him on his successful crossing of the Atlantic in 1497. After his father's death, he continued to attempt to find a NORTH-WEST PASSAGE to the East, exploring much of the north-east American coastline in the process. He later participated in Spanish expeditions, before helping to found the company of MERCHANT ADVENTURERS to search for a NORTH-EAST PASSAGE to the Orient.

*DNB.*

**CABRAL, PEDRO ÁLVARES** (*c*.1467–*c*.1520), Portuguese mariner, born into a noble family in Belmonte. In 1499, after the return of Vasco da Gama from India, Cabral was given command of a royal expedition of thirteen ships and 1,200 men and instructed to sail to India. He strayed west and on 22 April 1500 landed on the coast of Brazil near what is now Salvador (formerly Bahia). He claimed the new land on behalf of Portugal and sent one of his ships back to Lisbon to announce the discovery. After ten days in Brazil he then proceeded to India, but lost four ships in storms before landing in Calicut; those lost at sea included Bartolomeu DIAS. Cabral established a FEITORIA in Calicut and then returned home. Cabral's expedition marked the inauguration of the trading route from Portugal to India, but the beginnings were not auspicious: those whom he left in Calicut were later murdered.

Cabral was acclaimed as the first European to reach Brazil, but he was preceded by three months by the Spaniard Vicente Yañez PINZÓN. It is also not clear whether Cabral's course to the west was accidental or whether his route was determined by prior knowledge of the existence of Brazil.

*DHP*; J. R. McClymont, *Pedralvarez Cabral* (1914); E. Metzner Leone, *Pedro Alvares Cabral* (1968).

**CACCINI, GIULIO, or Giulio Romano** (1551–1618), composer, singer, instrumentalist, and gardener. He was born in Rome but was recruited to sing for the wedding of Prince Francesco de' Medici and Johanna of Austria in Florence in 1565. There he met Giovanni de' BARDI and other members of the CAMERATA. He heard the *concerto delle donne* at FERRARA and was renowned as a skilful player of the harp, lira da braccio, theorbo, and chittarone. His involvement in several Medici wedding festivities must have reinforced his sense of theatre, and in 1600 he supplied most of the music for the entertainment at the wedding of MARIE DE MÉDICIS and HENRI IV of France; he also (to 'save' his singers from singing Peri's music) added his own music to Jacopo PERI's setting of Ottavio Rinuncini's *Euridice*. Out of the ensuing rivalry came *Le nuove musiche*, in the preface of which Caccini claims the originality of the new style of song, claiming one *favellare in armonia* as his own. Inspired by the discoveries of the Camerata, Caccini was one of the first to write monody.

**CADAMOSTO, ALVISE DA, or Alvise Ca' da Mosta** (*c*.1426–1483), Venetian traveller in Africa in the service of Portugal. He sailed in 1454 for Flanders, but stopping *en route* in Portugal was persuaded to enter the service of HENRY THE NAVIGATOR. On 22 March 1455 he sailed as the commander of an expedition down the coast of AFRICA via Madeira and the CANARY ISLANDS as far as the river Gambia. The following year he sailed with the Genoese Antoniotto Usodimare (the author of a letter of 12 December 1455 purporting to describe a meeting near the Gambia with the descendants of the Genoese expedition of 1291) on an expedition that discovered the Cape Verde Islands and returned to the Gambia before pushing south to the Rio Grande (now the Corubal) and the Rio Géba (both in Guinea-Bissau). On his return to Portugal Cadamosto pursued a career in commerce until 1463, when he went home to Venice.

In Venice Cadamosto wrote the *Navigazioni*, an account of his Portuguese voyages which was posthumously published in 1507. He describes the indigenous Guanches of the Canary Islands (who are now extinct) and distinguishes the brown-skinned people of the Sahara from the black-skinned people of Senegal, and, unusually amongst explorers, tries to understand how Africans felt about their encounters with Europeans and European technology.

*DBI* s.v. Da Mosta, Alvise; *The Voyages of Cadamosto*, trans. G. R. Crone (1937).

**CADÉAC, PIERRE** (*fl.* 1538–56), French composer and choirmaster in Gascony who wrote sacred and secular music. Despite his provincial background, his reputation was far reaching, and his music was known in Nuremberg, Strassburg, Venice, and Madrid.

**CÁDIZ.** With the discovery of America in 1492, the port of Cádiz in southern Spain became the wealthiest port in Europe, as it was here that Spanish treasure ships returned from the New World. It was repeatedly attacked both by BARBARY PIRATES and, in the late sixteenth century, by English forces. In 1587, DRAKE burnt all the ships in the harbour; in 1596 an English squadron led by ESSEX and Lord HOWARD OF EFFINGHAM sacked the port, sinking most of the shipping in the harbour. A further raid was attempted in 1626 by the duke of Buckingham; despite such attacks, the port grew rapidly in wealth.

**CAESAR, SIR JULIUS** (1557–1636), English judge, born in Tottenham (Middl.), the son of Cesare Aldemare (originally Aldemare Cesare), an Italian physician at the courts of Mary and Elizabeth. He was educated at Magdalen Hall, Oxford, and studied COMMON LAW at the Inner Temple and CIVIL and CANON LAW at the University of Paris. In the course of his career he served as an Admiralty judge (1584), a master of chancery (1588–91), a master of the Court of Requests (1595), chancellor of the exchequer (1606), and master of the rolls (1614–36); he was also a member of Parliament for various constituencies from 1589 to 1622. He wrote, but did not publish, treatises on the Court of Requests and on the Privy Council.
  DNB; L. M. Hill, *Bench and Bureaucracy: The Public Career of Sir Julius Caesar, 1580–1636* (1988).

**CAFAGGIOLO POTTERY.** In 1498 Stefano and Piero di Filippo, who had been trained as potters in MONTELUPO, acquired a pottery housed in the outbuildings of the MEDICI VILLA at Cafaggiolo. The finest work of the pottery was produced between 1500 and 1530, though the manufacture of dated pieces continued until at least 1570 and thereafter the pottery continued to operate until the eighteenth century. The pottery's products included capacious MAIOLICA jugs decorated with designs based on peacock feathers and ISTO-RIATO wares depicting mythological scenes or classical triumphs, often based on Florentine designs. The Cafaggiolo pottery was the only pottery in Tuscany to produce products finished with the iridescent metallic surfaces known as 'lustres'.
  MDA; Galeazzo Cora and Angiolo Fanfani, *La maiolica di Cafaggiolo* (1982).

**CAIMO, GIUSEPPE** (c.1545–c.1584), Italian composer and organist. He became organist at Milan Cathedral where, despite recommendations made on his behalf to Duke Ferdinand of Bavaria, he remained until his death. Much of his music is lost and he is now best remembered as a composer of madrigals.

**CAIUS, JOHN** (1510–73), English medical humanist, born in Norwich and educated at Gonville Hall (Cambridge) and the University of Padua, where he studied under VESALIUS. On returning to England he practised medicine in London and later moved back to Cambridge, where he became a benefactor of Gonville Hall (1557) and then its master (24 January 1559); thereafter the college was known in print as Gonville and Caius and in speech (and occasionally in writing) as 'Gonville and Keys'.

Caius proved to be an aggressive head of his college, and his tenure of office was characterized by litigation and expulsions. His scholarly writings included editions of Hippocratic and Galenic texts, a treatise on the SWEATING SICKNESS (1556), a history of the University of Cambridge (1568), a treatise on rare plants and animals (1570), and a treatise on the pronunciation of Greek and Latin (*De pronunciatione Graecae et Latinae linguae*, 1574). In 1565 Caius received permission for his college to dissect two executed criminals each year; these dissections were important contributions to empirical ANATOMY.

Caius is sometimes described as John Caius the Younger, to distinguish him from his earlier namesake, the fifteenth-century poet.
  DNB; DSB.

**CAJETAN, SAN,** or **Gaetano Thiene** (1480–1547), founder of the THEATINE Order, born to a noble family in Vicenza and educated at the University of Padua, where he embarked on an academic career in theology and law. In 1516 he was ordained priest in Rome, and he subsequently established CONFRATERNITIES (of clergy and laity) dedicated to the service of the sick and poor in Rome, Vicenza, and Venice. In 1524 he founded, together with Pietro Carafa (later Pope PAUL IV) and two other priests, a congregation known as the Theatines, in which clergy bound by vows and living communally were to be engaged in preaching and pastoral work. The spiritual purpose of the Order was to restore apostolic purity to the clergy at a time of clerical corruption. Cajetan served as provost-general of the Order for three years, during which time he worked in Verona, Venice, and Naples. Within ten years the Order had spread throughout Italy and had established houses in Spain and central Europe.

Cajetan was beatified in 1629 and canonized in 1671.
  DBI s.v. Gaetano Thiene; G. B. Mattoni, *San Gaetano Thiene* (1981).

**CAJETAN, TOMMASO** (1469–1534), Thomist theologian, born in Gaetá; his baptismal name was Giacomo de Vio, but he was called Cajetan after his birthplace Gaetà (Latin Caieta) and assumed the name Tommaso in honour of THOMAS AQUINAS. He entered the Dominican Order in 1484, and from 1493 to 1507 taught philosophy and theology at the universities of Padua, Pavia, and Rome; in 1494 he engaged in a public disputation in Ferrara with PICO DELLA MIRANDOLA. He served as general of his Order from 1508 to 1518; he was created cardinal by Pope LEO X in 1517 and bishop of Gaetà in 1519. In 1518 he travelled to Augsburg as a papal legate to present the Church's views to LUTHER, and he subsequently worked for the election of CHARLES V as emperor (1519) and of ADRIAN VI as pope (1522); he also opposed the plans of HENRY VIII of England to secure a divorce. Cajetan's influence waned during the pontificate of CLEMENT VII, and in recommending concessions to the Lutherans (including a married clergy, as in the Greek Church, and communion in both kinds, as agreed at the COUNCIL OF BASEL) he found himself in an ecclesiastical minority. He died in Rome on 9 August 1534.

Cajetan's greatest scholarly work was a commentary on the *Summa theologica* of Thomas Aquinas; the publication of this commentary between 1507 and 1522 precipitated the revival of Thomism in the sixteenth century. Cajetan also published biblical commentaries which are characterized by their recourse to current philological scholarship.

*DBI* s.v. De Vio.

**CALAIS.** The French port of Calais was an English possession from its capture by King Edward III in 1347 to its loss in 1558; Rodin's statue commemorates the six burghers who surrendered to King Edward in order to save the town. During the period of English occupation Calais was garrisoned and fortified, and English settlers replaced expelled French residents; from 1536 Calais was represented in the English Parliament. Its economic strength lay in its role as the staple through which all exported English wool had to be directed.

English possession extended into the hinterland of Calais, which was known in English as its PALE and in French as the Calaisis; after the French reconquest it was known as the Pays Reconquis. When HENRY VIII met FRANCIS I at the FIELD OF THE CLOTH OF GOLD, the meeting took place on the border of the Pale and of France. On 7 January 1558 Calais was captured by the army of Duke François de GUISE. In April 1559 the Treaty of CATEAU-CAMBRÉSIS acknowledged the right of France to occupy Calais for eight years, but in the event it was never returned. Calais was held by Spain from 1595 to 1598, but was restored to France by the Peace of VERVINS.

**CALAMELLI, VIRGILIOTTO** (*fl.* 1531–70), Italian potter in FAENZA; he worked with Francesco MEZZARISA and later with Leonardo BETTISI and became with these colleagues one of the most important manufacturers of BIANCHI. His *bianchi*, which were sold all over Europe, were often decorated with putti. His factory also produced ISTORIATO wares.

*DBI; MDA.*

**CALCAR, JAN STEVEN VAN,** or (Latin) Johannes **Stephanus** (*c.*1499–*c.*1546), Dutch painter and engraver, a native of Calcar (now Kalkar) who is thought to have eloped with a young woman to Venice, where he trained in the studio of TITIAN, whose style he emulated. He subsequently lived in Naples, where he died. He was the engraver of the anatomical figures in VESALIUS' *De humanis corporis fabrica* (1543).

*MDA.*

**CALENDARS AND CALENDAR REFORM.** The Julian calendar in force until the late sixteenth century is named after Julius Caesar, who took advice from the astronomers of the day and revised the calendar of republican Rome to create a civil year that corresponded more exactly with the solar year. He believed the mean length of the solar year as measured from equinox to equinox or solstice to solstice (called the 'tropical year') was 365 days and six hours, so he decreed that each civil year should have 365 days, and the quarter-day should be accommodated by the addition of an extra day

every four years. However, as we now know, his value for the tropical year was slightly too large; the error was a matter of minutes, but over the centuries the gap between calendar and astronomical reality became noticeable: the spring equinox occurred earlier in the civil year. This obtruded itself upon the attention of the Church because it affected the calculation of the date of Easter. Like Julius Caesar, medieval and Renaissance rulers asked astronomers to help; in fact in the period from about 1400 to 1600 it seems that anyone considered a mathematician and astronomer was asked for advice on the matter.

The underlying astronomical problem was more complicated than can be explained here, touching upon different ways of measuring the year, different mathematical models ('theories') for the motion of the sun and of the fixed stars, and ideas about observational results that take no account of what we should now call observational error (a notion first formulated by Tycho BRAHE and KEPLER). In the fifteenth and sixteenth centuries the difficulties with the calendar were an important stimulus to astronomical research. In particular, all were agreed on the usefulness of more precise observations, that is, ones made using larger instruments. Thus in 1472 Paolo dal Pozzo TOSCANELLI used Florence Cathedral as a CAMERA OBSCURA for observing the sun at the summer solstice, and Egnazio DANTI used Santa Maria Novella (Florence) to observe the equinoxes and the winter solstice in the early 1570s.

Slowly, it became clear that only a small change needed to be made in the value of the tropical year, and the reform could be extremely simple. In 1582, by which time the equinox was 11 March, Pope GREGORY XIII commanded that ten days be suppressed and that henceforth there should be an extra day every fourth year except that for years at the end of a century (1600, 1700, and so on), there would be an extra day only if the year was divisible by 400. So 1600 was to be a Leap Year, as it would have been in the Julian calendar, but 1700 would not be. This reform is very simple, and apart from losing the days (which affected the dates of saints' days because those could not be lost), it made little change in the near future, so one must sympathize with those who, knowing little of technical astronomy, and seeing this unspectacular conclusion to centuries of astronomical activity, thought the reform was something of a propaganda exercise. Good Catholics and serious astronomers adopted the change immediately. In Poland, Spain, and Portugal, and in all of the states in Italy, the day after Thursday, 4 October 1582, was Friday, 15 October 1582, and the equinox was restored to 21 March.

These reforms created a discrepancy of ten days between the Julian and Gregorian calendars. The Protestant areas of Europe saw no reason to concur in a reform initiated by a pope, and many remained faithful to the Julian calendar. Details of the gradual adoption of the Gregorian calendar are set out in Appendix 3.

**CALEPINO or Calepio, AMBROGIO** (*c.*1435–1509/10), Italian lexicographer, born in Calepio (near Bergamo). He was the author of the *Cornucopiae*, a Latin–Italian dictionary first published in 1502. In subsequent editions prepared by Calepino and his successors, the dictionary was repeatedly enlarged and the number of languages in which equivalents were given was greatly expanded. The 1590 edition included eleven languages: Dutch, English, French, German, Greek, Hebrew, Hungarian, Italian, Latin, Polish, and Spanish. The word 'calepino' came to be a synonym for 'dictionary'.

*DBI* s.v. Calepio; *OCIL*.

**CALLIERGIS, ZACHARIAS** (*c.*1473–after 1524), Cretan printer and calligrapher in Italy, born into a noble Byzantine family in Rethymnon (Crete). Details of his education are unknown, but by 1493 he was living in Venice, where he established a Greek press in which the principal posts were filled by Cretans. The first publication of the press was a huge dictionary of Byzantine Greek, the *Etymologicum magnum* (1499). ALDUS MANUTIUS advertised books printed by the Calliergis press in his own catalogues, and even sold a copy of the *Etymologicum* to REUCHLIN, which seems to imply that Aldus and Calliergis saw each other as colleagues rather than competitors.

The recession that caused Aldus to suspend his pro-gramme of publications in 1505 claimed Calliergis's press a few years later. By 1515 Calliergis had re-established himself in Rome as the city's first printer of Greek. Greek printing had begun in Milan in 1476 with the *Erotemata* of Constantinos LASCARIS, and in 1484 the publication of the *Erotemata* of CHRYSOLORAS in Venice had inaugurated Greek printing there, but Rome lagged far behind in this respect, and the first Greek book to be published there was Calliergis's edition of Pindar, which appeared on 13 August 1515. Five months later, on 15 January 1516, he published an important edition of Theocritus which included the *scholia*. The last book known to have been published by Calliergis is dated 27 May 1523, and the last surviving manuscript in his hand is dated 1524; thereafter he disappears from the historical record.

*DBI* s.v. Calliergi, Zaccaria; D. Geanakoplos, *Greek Scholars in Venice* (1962), 201–22.

**CALLIGRAPHY.** The earliest surviving examples of writing were produced by sharp tools cutting characters out of rock; in the fifteenth century mechanical means such as WOODCUTS or movable type were again used to produce writing. The usual term for writing produced with tools is 'lettering', and it is to be distinguished from calligraphy, which is the art of fine handwriting; the study of ancient lettering is called epigraphy and the study of early handwriting is called palaeography.

Since Greek antiquity there has been a distinction in European calligraphy between the uncial hands used for lit-erary works and the cursive hands used for documents and correspondence. Greek uncial hands remained in use in litur-gical works until the twelfth century, and were familiar to Renaissance scholars through manuscripts such as the Codex Vaticanus (a fourth-century Greek Bible that has been in the Vatican Library since at least 1475) and the Codex Bezae (a text of the Gospels once owned by BEZA and now in the Cam-bridge University Library). Despite these survivals, uncial hands had for most purposes been superseded by cursive minuscule hands by the ninth century. The alternative to the small letters of minuscules is majuscules, which are large letters written as uncials or capitals. A capital letter, like the capital of a column, is the form used at the head of a word, though some early manuscripts, notably those of VIRGIL's poems, are written entirely in capitals.

The Roman minuscule cursive hand survived the fall of the Roman Empire and slowly evolved into the simple and elegant style known as Carolingian minuscule. It was this style that was revived at the Renaissance and in the hand-writing of humanists displaced the Gothic calligraphy of late medieval Europe, which lived on in the handwriting of merchants. Revived Carolingian minuscule, when combined with majuscules derived from ancient Roman inscriptions (which were chiselled and therefore angular), formed the basis of the 'roman' typeface, which was first used in 1465 by Arnold PANNARTZ and Konrad Sweynheym.

Of the specialist hands, the most important were those of the scriveners of the papal chancery. During the pontificate of EUGENIUS IV (1431–47) a cursive chancery hand known as 'short hand' (*brevi manu*) came to be reserved for documents known as 'briefs'. This hand, which from the sixteenth cen-tury was known as *cancelleresca corsiva*, became the standard correspondence script of sixteenth-century Italy.

The earliest studies of letter formation concentrated on ancient Roman inscriptions, which were written in capital letters. Felice FELICIANO wrote a treatise on the shape of inscriptional letters, and dedicated his collection of ancient inscriptions (the manuscript of which is dated 1463) to MAN-TEGNA, who introduced copies of inscriptions into the fres-coes (largely destroyed in the Second World War) of the Church of the Eremitani in Padua. In 1509 Luca PACIOLI pub-lished his *De divina proportione*, which includes an appendix on letter formation. The first printed handbook on callig-raphy was the *Operina da imparare di scrivere littera cancellaresca* (1522) of Ludovico ARRIGHI.

Italian calligraphy was imitated and assimilated with national styles throughout Europe. In France, where the most important style was a Gothic hand known as *cursive française* (from which the typeface known as *civilité* derived), Italian hands were introduced when FRANCIS I brought Italian calligraphers to FONTAINEBLEAU. The gradual assimilation of *cancelleresca corsiva* into *cursive française* created the *ronde* which in the seventeenth century was codified into three forms (the upright *financière*, the inclined *bâtarde*, and the running style known as *coulée*) and was for centuries the French national hand.

In sixteenth-century England, Gothic, secretary, and italic hands were all in use and were collected by Jean de Beauchesne and John Baildon in *A Book Containing Divers Sorts of Hands* (1571). The English hand known in English as copperplate, in France as *anglaise*, in Italy as *lettere inglese*, and in Spain as *letra inglesa*, was originally a commercial hand which was in the seventeenth century influenced by Dutch commercial calligraphy. This hand was carried to America by early colonists, and in the course of the twentieth century influenced or displaced national hands throughout Europe.

B. L. Ullman, *The Origin and Development of Humanistic Script* (1960).

**CALLISTUS III or Calixtus III** (1378–1458), pope from 8 April 1455 until his death on 6 August 1458, was born in Játiva (Valencia) on 31 December 1378; his baptismal name was Alfonso de Borja (or Borgia). He studied (and later lectured on) CANON LAW at Lleida (Spanish Lérida) and subsequently became private secretary to King ALFONSO V of Aragon, at whose court he exercised both legal and diplomatic skills. In 1429 he successfully negotiated (on behalf of Alfonso) the abdication of the antipope CLEMENT VIII, and his reward was to be appointed bishop of Valencia. In 1443 he helped Alfonso to extricate himself from the machinations of the COUNCIL OF BASEL and effected a reconciliation with Pope EUGENIUS IV; on this occasion his reward was to be created cardinal-priest.

In 1455 Alfonso was elected to the papacy as a compromise candidate. It was widely assumed that because he was 76 years old and crippled with gout, he would be an inactive caretaker pope. Instead he proposed a CRUSADE to reconquer CONSTANTINOPLE (which had fallen two years earlier), and promptly set about raising money by selling indulgences all over Europe and imposing a crusade tithe. In Rome he commissioned the construction of galleys, for which he paid by selling gold and silver artefacts and rare book bindings. His crusade enjoyed some partial success in Giovanni di CAPISTRANO's defeat of the Turks at Belgrade in July 1456 and the defeat of the Turkish fleet near Lesbos in August 1457, but indifference in Europe and hostility to the tithe precluded any extension of the campaign. King Alfonso, his former patron, diverted a papal crusader fleet to attack Genoa in order to further his own territorial ambitions, and Callistus was so unforgiving that he tried to prevent Alfonso's illegitimate son FERRANTE from succeeding his father as king of Naples by asserting that Naples was a fiefdom of the Holy See.

The pontificate of Callistus was dominated by the futile crusade in which he passionately believed, and his court was characterized by xenophobia and nepotism. He surrounded himself with Spaniards and Catalans, and showered favours on his relatives: he appointed one nephew as governor of Castel Sant'Angelo and prefect of Rome, and created two more nephews cardinals while they were still in their twenties; he appointed one of these nephews, Rodrigo Borgia (later Pope ALEXANDER VI), to the lucrative vice-chancellorship of the papal curia. On 16 June 1456 he exonerated JOAN OF ARC, who had been burnt at the stake in 1431, and in the same year he revived the interdiction forbidding social relations between Christians and JEWS. His death was marked by an outbreak of violence against the detested Catalans in Rome.

DBI s.v. Callisto III; Michael Mallett, *The Borgias: The Rise and Fall of a Renaissance Dynasty* (1969).

**CALMO, ANDREA** (1510–71), Italian actor and playwright, born in Venice, where he worked for a time as a gondolier. Some of his comedies were based on classical models (*Rodiana*, 1540; *Travaglia*, 1546), but others were rooted in robust vernacular traditions (*La Spagnola*, 1549; *Saltuzza*, 1551). His plays influenced the subsequent development of COMMEDIA DELL'ARTE. Calmo also composed a popular series of verse epistles in the Venetian dialect.

DBI; OCIL.

**CALVAERT, DENYS, or (Italian) Dionisio Fiammingo** (c.1540–1619), Flemish painter in Italy, a native of Antwerp who moved c.1560 to Bologna, where he trained in the studio of Prospero FONTANA; apart from a short period in Rome in 1570–1, Calvaert remained in Bologna for the rest of his life. In 1572 he established a painting academy in Bologna; more than 100 painters were trained in the academy, including Francesco Albani ('the Anacreon of Rome'), Domenichino, and Guido Reni.

DBI s.v. Calvart, Denis; BNB s.v. Calvaert, Denis; MDA.

**CALVIN, JEAN** (1509–64), French reformer and theologian, born in Noyon (Picardy) on 10 July 1509, the second son of an ecclesiastical lawyer and his wife Jeanne le Franc, the daughter of an innkeeper. His family and the bishop of Noyon intended him for an ecclesiastical career, and on 19 May 1521, at the age of 11 (or 12, according to the Latinate idiom of the chapter register), his head was tonsured and he received his first benefice. He studied humanities at the University of Paris (c.1521–6) and CIVIL LAW at Orléans (c.1526–9) and Bourges (1529–31), where he was taught by ALCIATO. After the death of his father in 1531 Calvin returned to Paris to study Greek and Hebrew, and in 1532 published a commentary on SENECA's *De clementia*.

In the early 1530s Calvin developed pronounced Lutheran sympathies. In November 1533 he fled Paris to escape the religious unrest sparked off by an oration (in which Calvin may have had a hand) given by Calvin's friend Nicolas Cop, the rector of the University of Paris. On 4 May 1534 he resigned his ecclesiastical benefices and the following year settled in Basel, where the first edition of his *Institutio religionis christianae* was published in March 1536.

In July 1536 Calvin visited Geneva, and was persuaded by Guillaume FAREL to assist with the task of implementing the Reformation in the city. Early in 1537 Calvin and Farel drafted articles for church discipline, but these articles were strenuously opposed by the Zwinglians (who enjoyed powerful support from Bern), partly because of the requirement of subscription to a confession of faith but also because excommunication was to be used as an instrument of social policy. The city council decided to prescribe the Zwinglian church discipline of Bern, and when on Easter Day 1538 Calvin publicly declined to submit to the will of the council, he was expelled from the city. Martin BUCER promptly invited him to Strassburg, where, for the next three years, Calvin served as minister to the French congregation. In his Strassburg years Calvin published his commentary on Romans (1539) and an expanded version of the *Institutio* (1539), which he soon translated into French (*Institution de la religion chrétienne*, 1541). In August 1540 he married a widow, Idelette de Bure; their only child, a son born on 28 July 1542, died a few days after his birth.

In September 1541 Calvin accepted the invitation of the city council of Geneva to return to the city, and for the next 23 years he presided over its theocratic government. Two months after he arrived, the city council adopted Calvin's 'Ecclesiastical Ordinances', which reflect his experience of Strassburg and the influence of Bucer. Under these ordinances ecclesiastical discipline was entrusted to a consistory which enforced public morality by laws that were prescriptive (e.g. compulsory church attendance) and proscriptive (e.g. the banning of dancing and gambling). Public dissent from the strictures of the ordinances culminated in the victory of an opposition party in the council elections of 1548. This challenge to Calvin's public authority was soon followed by a private catastrophe: Calvin's wife Idelette died in March 1549, leaving a desolate Calvin with the two children of her previous marriage.

The restoration of Calvin's authority was accomplished at the cost of the life of Michael SERVETUS, who was burnt at the stake in 1553; thereafter Calvin ruled without opposition. In 1559 he was finally made a citizen of Geneva, and in the same year he founded the Genevan ACADEMY, which became a vehicle for Calvin's theology and his model of church government, and trained generations of HUGUENOT pastors. Calvin died on 27 May 1564.

Calvin's principal theological treatise, the *Institutes*, culminated in an 80-chapter edition published in Latin (1559) and French (1560). The Latin version rapidly became the most important theological treatise of the Reformation, the *Summa theologica* of Protestantism; it was translated into English in 1561. The French text, together with Calvin's other theological writings in French, formed a corpus of literature that shaped the literary language of France, chiefly in its protean variety of linguistic register, which ranged from an elegant and dignified high style to a demotic popular idiom uninhibited in its use of humour and sarcasm. On Calvin's theology, see CALVINISM.

DBF; E. Doumergue, *Jean Calvin: Les Hommes et les choses de son temps* (5 vols., 1899–1917); A. E. McGrath, *A Life of John Calvin* (1990); William J. Bouwsma, *John Calvin: A Sixteenth Century Portrait* (1988).

**CALVINISM**, the theological thought and ecclesiastical discipline of Jean CALVIN as articulated in Calvin's *Institutes* and in Theodore BEZA's *Confession de la foi chrétienne* (1559; Latin version, 1560). Calvinism is avowedly hostile to Catholicism, and disputes doctrines such as that of the EUCHARIST, but nonetheless acquiesces in many Catholic doctrines, most centrally Trinitarianism. Calvinism shares with LUTHERANISM a theology that emphasizes the sole authority of the Bible, the bondage of the human will by sin, and JUSTIFICATION of the believer by faith alone. Calvinism differs from Lutheranism in the centrality of SOTERIOLOGY, the stress on election and predestination, the doctrine of the eucharist, and the emphasis on church discipline. Calvinism is distinguished from Zwinglianism chiefly on the doctrine of the eucharist.

The acceptance of Calvinism outside Geneva and the Swiss Confederation often took the form of adoption of the Second HELVETIC CONFESSION (1566), a Calvinist document drafted by BULLINGER with an eye to Zwinglian sensitivities. The HUGUENOTS of France were Calvinist in theology, and in 1622 Calvinism became the state religion of the Netherlands. In the Protestant areas of the German lands, the 'Reformed Church' (the usual term for Calvinist churches) displaced the 'Evangelical Church' (the usual term for Lutheran churches) in the Palatinate, in Brandenburg, and in Transylvania. In England some elements of Calvinist doctrine may be discerned in the Thirty-Nine ARTICLES, but the true English inheritors of Calvinism were the radical Puritans of the seventeenth century; the Westminster Confession of 1648 is in its essentials a Calvinist document. In Scotland the flame of Calvinism was carried by John KNOX, and Calvinist theology is still an important strand in the Scottish Kirk. Similarly, the Calvinism championed by preachers such as Jonathan Edwards still has many exponents in twenty-first-century America.

In its aspirations to intellectual rigour, Calvinism is the inheritor of SCHOLASTICISM. Beza believed that theology could be deduced from general principles, and this conviction constitutes the organizing principle of many theological ordinances in sixteenth- and seventeenth-century Europe. In the case of the central doctrine of predestination, refinement of this deductive process led to the emergence of two competing (post-Calvinist) theories: the supralapsarians (or antelapsarians), such as Francis GOMAR, believed that God decreed the election and damnation of individual human beings before the fall of Adam; the sublapsarians (or infralapsarians or postlapsarians) believed that God delayed his decision until after the fall of Adam, and after the Synod of DORT, sublapsarianism became Calvinist orthodoxy.

M. Prestwich (ed.), *International Calvinism 1541–1715* (1985); A. Duke et al. (eds.), *Calvinism in Europe 1540–1610* (1992).

**CALVINUS, JOHANNES, or (German) Johann Kahl** (*c.*1550–1614), German jurist, best known for his legal dictionary, *Lexicon iuridicum iuris Caesarei simul et canonici* (Frankfurt, 1600). He also wrote on Jewish law (*Themis Hebraeo-Romana*, 1595), Roman jurisprudence (*Iurisprudentiae Romanae synopsis methodica*, 1595), and FEUDAL LAW (*Iurisprudentiae feudalis*, 1611).

ADB.

**CAMBIASO, LUCA** (1527–85), Italian painter, born in Moneglia (near Genoa), the son of the painter Giovanni Cambiaso. He worked in Genoa as a decorator of palaces until 1583, when he moved to Spain to assist in the decoration of the ESCORIAL. His paintings (e.g. *Adoration of the Child*, Brera, Milan) are remarkable for their innovative use of dry paint, and the geometrical forms of his drawings anticipate the work of early twentieth-century Cubists.

DBI; Lauro Magnani, *Luca Cambiaso: Da Genova all'Escorial* (1995); MDA.

**CAMBIO, PERISSONE** (1520–62), Flemish composer and singer who was a member of the chapel at San Marco, Venice, and also, by the 1550s, of the Compagnia di San Marco, a group of ducal singers. He mixed with Parabosco and Baldassare DONATO, and in his madrigal writing was influenced by Cipriano de RORE and Adriaan WILLAERT.

**CAMBRAI, LEAGUE OF**, an alliance formed at Cambrai on 10 December 1508 between the Valois rulers of France, the HABSBURGS, and their allies; the formation of the League broadened the involvement of European powers in the WARS OF ITALY. The League consisted of King LOUIS XII of France, the Emperor MAXIMILIAN I, Pope JULIUS II, King HENRY VII of England, King LADISLAS II of Bohemia and Hungary, and King FERDINAND of Spain; it was later joined by Marquis Gianfrancesco II GONZAGA of Mantua and Duke Alfonso I d'ESTE of Ferrara. The ostensible purpose of the League was to combat the Ottoman threat, but its secret provisions made clear that its underlying purpose was to divest Venice of the mainland territories it had gained in the course of the previous century. Under the terms of the agreement France was to extend its assertion of sovereignty in Milan to Bergamo, Brescia, Crema, Cremona, and the Ghiaradadda; the Empire was to receive the Friuli, Padua, Treviso, Verona, and Vicenza; the papacy was to regain territories in Romagna (including Faenza, Ravenna, and Rimini); Spain was to receive the ports held by Venice in the kingdom of Naples; Mantua was to regain Asola, Lonigo, and Peschiera; and Ferrara was to regain Rovigo.

The League secured victory at the battle of AGNADELLO on 14 May 1509 and thereafter took from Venice most of its possessions (except Treviso), but the allies soon turned against each other and the League was dissolved in 1510. By January 1517 Venice had regained most of its territories, though it did not recapture Cremona.

**CAMBRAI, PEACE OF or Treaty of, or (French) La Paix des Dames**, a treaty signed at Cambrai on 3 August 1529 between LOUISE OF SAVOY (representing her son King FRANCIS I) and MARGARET OF AUSTRIA (representing her nephew the Emperor CHARLES V). By the terms of the treaty King Francis renounced his claims to Artois, Flanders, and Naples and Charles renounced his claim to Burgundy. Francis recovered his two sons who had been held as hostages in Spain since 1526 and, on their release, married Charles's sister Eleanor, whose engagement to Francis had been agreed in the Treaty of Madrid. The peace accord remained in effect until 1536, when hostilities were resumed in the final stage of the WARS OF ITALY.

**CAMBRIDGE.** The university at Cambridge was founded in 1209 by students who left Oxford University following a dispute with the townspeople. Its first college, Peterhouse, was founded in 1284, by the bishop of Ely. Until the fifteenth century Cambridge was controlled by the diocese of Ely, but a period of expansion followed, with the foundation of King's College in 1441 by HENRY VI, and of Trinity College in 1546 by HENRY VIII. ERASMUS, ASCHAM, John FISHER, and other leading figures of the Renaissance had strong associations with Cambridge; the presence of BILNEY and others also made it a stronghold of reformist thinking during this period.

**CAMDEN, WILLIAM** (1551–1623), English antiquary. Educated at Oxford, Camden was from 1575 until 1597 teacher and then headteacher at Westminster School. He is chiefly remembered as a historian: his *Britannia* (1586) surveys the antiquities of Britain, and his *Annals of Queen Elizabeth* (1615) exemplifed the new civic history of his time.
DNB; MDA.

**CAMEO**, an engraved GEM (usually agate or sardonyx) with layers in two different colours in which the upper layer is carved in RELIEF and the lower is used as a ground, so that the design stands up in relief above the surface; the process, which can also be used with glass or shell or ceramics, is the reverse of INTAGLIO, which is incised carving. In Renaissance Europe the finest cameos were made in Nuremberg, where they were often mounted in silver or gold cups. Seventeenth-century German glass engraved in cameo is known as *Hochschnitt* glass.

**CAMERA OBSCURA** (Latin; 'dark chamber'), an optical arrangement that uses a darkened room or even a church (see CALENDAR REFORM), or a box into which light enters through a small aperture. From the late sixteenth century onwards, the aperture was sometimes fitted with a lens. An image is formed on the far wall of the chamber. The *camera obscura* was widely used for astronomical observation of the sun. According to VASARI, a *camera obscura* was first used for drawing by ALBERTI in 1457. LEONARDO DA VINCI likened the human eye to a *camera obscura*. Girolamo CARDANO noted in his *De subtilitate* (1550) how the use of a lens could enhance the quality of the image, as did Giambattista DELLA PORTA, who discussed the instrument in the second edition of his *Magia naturalis* (1559). The first correct account of its theory was given by KEPLER (1604); see OPTICS.

**CAMERARIUS, JOACHIM** (1500–74), German humanist, born in Bamberg and educated at Leipzig, where he studied Greek. He moved to Wittenberg, where he became the friend and biographer of MELANCHTHON. In 1524 he published a Latin translation of Demosthenes, and the following year a substantial commentary on Cicero's *Tusculan Disputations*. In 1526 he was appointed (through the influence of Melanchthon) as professor of Greek and Latin at the new Protestant college in Nuremberg. In 1530 he attended the Diet of Augsburg as a deputy for Nuremberg and assisted Melanchthon in the drafting of the AUGSBURG CONFESSION. He later taught at Tübingen (from 1535) as professor of Greek and finally at Leipzig (from 1541) as professor of Latin and Greek, where he remained.

Camerarius was a prolific editor, grammarian, textbook writer, biographer, historian of church history, and translator, whose work included Greek editions of Aristotle, Galen, Herodotus, Homer, Ptolemy, and Sophocles and a complete edition of PLAUTUS (1552). As a theologian he remained committed to reconciliation, discussing the possibility of a Catholic–Protestant accord with FRANCIS I in 1535 and with the Emperor MAXIMILIAN II in 1568.
NDB.

**CAMERATA**, a small academy made up of professional and amateur musicians, intellectuals, poets, and philosophers, who met at the home of Count Giovanni de' BARDI in Florence (c.1573–87). Many were members of the nobility. They discussed a wide range of subjects from poetry to astrology and other scientific matters. The musician Vincenzo GALILEI's research into the music of ancient Greece resulted in his *Dialogo della musica antica et della moderna* (1581), the principles of which were cited by RINUCCINI, CACCINI, and PERI in their prefaces to *Euridice*.

**CAMILLO DE LELLIS** (1550–1614), founder of the 'Ministers of the Sick' (or 'Camillians'), born at Bocchianico in the Abruzzi, which was then part of the kingdom of Naples. He was a tall man (2 metres (6 feet 7 inches) high) with a short temper and a taste for gambling, and these characteristics suited him for a military career. He joined the Venetian army to fight the Turks, but contracted an incurable disease in his legs and was reduced to poverty by his addiction to gambling.

In 1574 Camillo was employed as a labourer by the CAPUCHINS at Manfredonia, and the following year experienced a religious conversion. He sought to enter the Capuchins (and subsequently the Franciscan Recollects), but his health prevented him from being professed; he instead became a nurse at the hospital of San Giacomo in Rome; he was later appointed bursar.

Camillo was ordained priest in 1584, and the following year, under the guidance of his spiritual mentor San Filippo NERI, he founded the Camillians, a congregation of male nurses who agreed to take a fourth vow committing themselves to the service of the sick, especially prisoners and the victims of plague. The congregation received papal approval in 1586 and five years later was elevated to an Order with the privileges of the Mendicants (notably exemption from episcopal jurisdiction). In 1595 and 1601 members of the Order served as nurses on battlefields in Hungary and Croatia, and in Rome and Naples they founded hospitals and ministered to galley-slaves. By the time Camillo died, the Camillians had established fifteen houses and eight hospitals. Camillo was canonized in 1746, and is patron of nurses and of the sick.

*DBI*; M. Vanti, *S. Camillo de Lellis 1550–1614, apostolo di carità infermiera* (1929); C. C. Martindale, SJ, *St Camillus* (1946).

**CAMÕES, LUÍS VAZ DE** (1517/24–1579), Portuguese poet, born into a noble family in Lisbon and probably educated at the University of Coimbra. As a young man he composed lyrics, many of which were adoringly addressed to Caterina de Ataíde, a lady-in-waiting whom he called 'Natercia'. He wrote both in the native Portuguese metres (*canções, cantigas, endechas, motes, trovas,* and *voltas*) and, more importantly, in the Italianate genres of the Renaissance (elegies, odes, pastorals, sonnets, and *ottava rima*) as well as a number of prose letters. He also wrote three plays, one a Plautine comedy (*Anfitriões*) and two in the Portuguese tradition of Gil VICENTE (*El rei Seleuco* and *Filodemo*). In 1547 he joined a military expedition to Morocco, where he lost an eye in battle. In 1553 he

sailed for India, where he lived for seventeen years, mostly in Goa, and travelled to other Portuguese possessions in Asia. In India he wrote the first draft of his great poem *Os Lusíadas*, which is now regarded as the national epic of Portugal. After returning to Portugal he published *Os Lusíadas* (1572), and was awarded a small royal pension; he remained in Lisbon for the rest of his life and died in an epidemic of plague.

*Os Lusíadas*, an epic in ten cantos written in hendecasyllabic *ottava rima*, celebrates the exploration of the coasts of AFRICA by the Portuguese (the Lusitanians of the title), and is centred on the discovery of the sea route to India by Vasco da GAMA in 1498–9. The poem uses the classical framework of ancient epic (the seas are populated with ancient gods, Venus supporting the expedition against Bacchus) to depict the conquest of paganism by Christianity and to compare favourably the heroes of the Portuguese discoverers with the heroes of classical antiquity.

*DHP*; J. P. Oliveira Martins, *Camões: Os Lusíadas e a Renascença em Portugal* (1986).

**CAMPAGNOLA, DOMENICO** (1500–64), Italian painter, draughtsman, and engraver, the pupil and adopted son of Giulio CAMPAGNOLA. His paintings, such as the fresco of *Joachim and Anna* in the Scuola del Carmine in Padua (1520), show the influence of TITIAN. His LANDSCAPE drawings (e.g. *Landscape with Two Boys*, British Museum), like those of Titian, helped to shape the landscape painting of the seventeenth century.

*DBI*; *MDA*.

**CAMPAGNOLA, GIULIO** (c.1482–after 1515), Italian engraver who trained in the Mantua studio of MANTEGNA, and in 1499 entered the service of the ESTE FAMILY in Ferrara. Many of his engravings are copies of works by DÜRER and were the principal medium through which Dürer's work became known in Italy. In 1509 he moved to Venice, where his engravings show the influence of GIORGIONE.

*DBI*; *MDA*.

**CAMPAÑA, PEDRO (DE)**, or (Flemish) **Pieter de Kempeneer** (c.1503–c.1580), Flemish painter in Italy and Spain, born in Brussels. He worked in various Italian cities, including Bologna and Venice, and sometime before 1537 moved to Seville, where he painted works for the cathedral, including a *Descent from the Cross* (1547) and a *Group of Donors* (1555). On returning to Brussels he was appointed by the city as a designer of tapestry cartoons (28 May 1563) and opened a tapestry factory.

*MDA* s.v. Kempeneer, Peter de.

**CAMPANELLA, TOMMASO** (1568–1639), Italian philosopher and poet. He was born in Stilo di Calabria and in 1582 entered the Dominican Order. He was censured for his TELESIAN views and left Calabria under suspicion of heterodoxy; in Rome he was tortured by the INQUISITION and forced to recant in 1595. He returned to Calabria in 1599 to participate in the rebellion against Spanish rule, and was arrested, tortured, and imprisoned for 30 years. On his release in 1626 he moved to Rome and then (in 1634) to Paris where he was granted a pension by Louis XIII.

Campanella's prison writings include *La città del sole* (*c*.1602), which was first published in Latin as *Civitas solis* (Frankfurt, 1623). In this utopian city of the sun, the resident Solarians regulate their lives by astrological and Hermetic principles, venerating COPERNICUS and deprecating Aristotle. In 1616 he also wrote a defence of Galileo GALILEI (*Apologia pro Galileo*, 1622), a classic plea for freedom of thought. In *Atheismus trionphatus* (1631) he mounted arguments that would triumph over atheism, but the rationalistic deism that he proposed led to the tract being denounced as proclaiming 'atheism triumphant'.

DBI; John M. Headley, *Tommaso Campanella and the Transformation of the World* (1997); G. Ernst, *Religione, ragione e natura: Studi su Tommaso Campanella* (1991).

**CAMPEGGI or Campeggio, LORENZO** (1474–1539), Italian cardinal and diplomat, born in Milan into a noble Bolognese family. He studied CANON LAW in Pavia and Bologna, and had already established a formidable reputation as a canonist by the time he took his doctorate in 1499. In 1500 Lorenzo married Francesca de' Gualtavillani, by whom he had five children; one of their sons (Alessandro) was to become a cardinal in 1551, and another (Gianbaptista) became bishop of Minorca. Shortly after the death of Francesca in 1510, Lorenzo entered the Church, and the following year he was appointed auditor of the Rota. In 1512 he was consecrated bishop of Feltre, and 1513–17 he served as papal nuncio to the imperial court. He was created cardinal-priest of San Tommaso in Pavione on 27 June 1517.

In 1518 Cardinal Lorenzo was sent to England by Pope LEO X with a view to securing the support of HENRY VIII for a crusade against the Ottomans; he arrived in England on 23 July 1518. Cardinal WOLSEY was eager not to be reduced to a subordinate position, and managed to secure his own appointment as senior legate and to suspend Cardinal Lorenzo's legatine status. Campeggi failed to secure support for Leo's crusade, but he did not return home empty-handed: at a meeting of Consistory on 28 November 1519 he presented to the pope Henry's gifts of money, furniture, and the palace of Cardinal Adriano CASTELLESI (now the Palazzo Giraud-Torlonia). Lorenzo was subsequently appointed protector of England in the papal curia. In 1523 Pope ADRIAN VI appointed him archbishop of Bologna, and the next year King Henry VIII appointed him bishop of Salisbury. After attending the imperial Diet in Regensburg in the hope of advancing papal interests, he returned to Rome and became caught up in the SACK OF ROME, sharing the captivity of Pope CLEMENT VII in Castel Sant'Angelo.

In 1528 Cardinal Lorenzo was again sent to England, this time to mediate in the dispute over King Henry's divorce. He arrived on 1 October 1528, and his status was that of co-legate with Cardinal Wolsey. Cardinal Lorenzo carried with him the Decretal, a confidential document which set out the CANON LAW of DIVORCE but did not bind the legatine court that was to decide the issue. The Decretal was to be shown only to King Henry and Cardinal Wolsey; the reason for the secrecy was that Pope Clement was eager to avoid offending CHARLES V, who was the nephew of CATHERINE OF ARAGON. There was also an element of duplicity in the proceedings, in that Cardinal Lorenzo had received secret instructions from Pope Clement (on 16 September 1528) to prolong the debate as long as possible and to refer back to Rome before passing final judgement. The legatine court opened at Blackfriars on 18 June 1529; Cardinal Lorenzo refused to pass judgement and prorogued the court on 23 July. He had failed to oblige the king with the judgement that he required, and on 26 October 1529 left England; his luggage was searched at Dover with a view to retrieving the Decretal, but it had prudently been burnt.

Cardinal Lorenzo returned to Bologna, where he assisted at the coronation of Charles V, whom he subsequently accompanied to the Diet of AUGSBURG. King Henry deprived him of the English protectorate, and, after the adverse judgement on the divorce, deprived him of the see of Salisbury by Act of Parliament (11 March 1535). In 1537 Lorenzo was appointed cardinal-bishop of Sabina by Pope PAUL III. He died in Rome on 25 July 1539; his tomb is in Santa Maria in Trastevere.

DBI s.v. Campeggi; DNB s.v. Campeggio.

**CAMPI, BARTOLOMEO** (d. 1573), Italian goldsmith, armourer, and military engineer, a native of Pesaro. His only surviving documented work is a suit of parade armour made for Duke Guidobaldo II da Montefeltro of Urbino; this armour, which is signed and dated 1546, was later given to King PHILIP II of Spain and is now in the Armería Real in Madrid.

DBI.

**CAMPI FAMILY**, a family of Italian painters from Cremona. Galeazzo Campi (*c*.1477–1536) worked with his sons Giulio (*c*.1508–1573) and Antonio (1523–87) and their relative Bernardino (1522–91) on the frescoes in the Church of San Sigismondo in Cremona. The church had been built by Francesco SFORZA in 1463, in honour of his marriage in 1441 to Bianca Visconti in a chapel that had previously occupied the site; Giulio Campi's fresco *The Madonna Appearing to Francesco and Bianca* commemorates the marriage. Giulio painted the fresco cycle depicting *The Life of St Agatha* for the Church of Sant'Agata in Cremona (1537); Antonio painted the *Pietà with Saints* in Cremona Cathedral (1566), and also published a history of Cremona (1585) which he illustrated with his own engravings. Vincenzo Campi (1530/5–91), Galeazzo's third son, painted STILL LIFES, such as *Fish Market* (Brera, Milan). Bernardino Campi's paintings include a *Pietà* (1574) now in the Brera.

DBI; MDA; Bram de Klarck, *Giulio, Antonio and Vincenzo Campi: Schilderkunst en devotie in het zestiendeeuwse Lombardije, 1565–1591* (1997).

**CAMPIN, ROBERT** (*c*.1375/9–1444), Flemish artist generally believed to be the Master of FLÉMALLE. The pupils in his Tournai studio included Jacques DARET and one Rogelet de la Pâture, who is probably Rogier van der WEYDEN.

**Robert Campin**, *The Nativity*, in the Musée des Beaux-Arts in Dijon

**Robert Campin,** *Portrait of a Woman* (*c.*1430), in the National Gallery in London

Only one picture associated with Campin, the Werl Wings (1438, Prado, Madrid), can be dated on the basis of documentary evidence; attempts to construct a chronology of his work are therefore based only on stylistic evidence. The *Marriage of the Virgin* (Prado) and the Seilern Triptych (Courtauld Institute Galleries, London) may date from the beginning of the fifteenth century. The *Dijon Nativity* (now in the Musée des Beaux-Arts in Dijon) may be a work of the early 1420s. The clothing of the sitters in the matched pair of portraits (painted on marble) *Portrait of a Man* and *Portrait of*

*a Woman* (National Gallery, London, *c.*1430) is consistent with the hypothesis that they are portraits of a Tournai merchant and his wife. The Städelsches Kunstinstitut in Frankfurt, which has the largest collection of Campin's paintings, has a GRISAILLE of the *Trinity* (part of an unprovenanced and otherwise lost ALTARPIECE) and a fragment of the *Crucified Thief* from a lost *Deposition* triptych (which survives in a copy in the Walker Art Gallery in Liverpool). The harsh realism of these pictures stands in marked contrast to what are assumed to be Campin's later pictures, which include the

Mérode altarpiece (Metropolitan Museum, New York), set in a comfortable middle-class room.

*MDA*; Susan Foister and Susie Nash (eds.), *Robert Campin: New Directions in Scholarship* (1996).

**CAMPION, EDMUND** (1540–81), English Jesuit. Educated at Oxford, Campion was initially ordained in the Anglican Church but in 1571 he left England for William ALLEN's English College at DOUAI in accordance with his Catholic sympathies. He made a pilgrimage to Rome and was ordained as a Jesuit in 1578; he then taught at Prague. With PARSONS, he led the Jesuit mission to England in 1580, where he preached to some effect before being caught and imprisoned in the Tower. Despite torture he refused to recant his beliefs; he was convicted of treason and hanged.

**CAMPION, THOMAS** (1567–1620), English poet, composer, theorist, and musician. He entered Peterhouse, Cambridge, as a gentleman pensioner in 1581, and in 1586 was admitted to Gray's Inn, where he became involved in the presentation of MASQUES and plays, some of which were performed for Queen ELIZABETH. From 1607 he provided both words and music for some of the extravagant royal masques at the BANQUETING HOUSE at Whitehall. He was a prolific composer of lute songs and published five books of ayres. His *Observations in the Art of English Poesy* (1602) defends classical metres and deprecates rhyme, and includes his best-known poem, 'Rosy-cheeked Laura'.

**CANAL or Canale, CRISTOFORO DA** (1510–62), Venetian naval commander, born on 12 September 1510 into a poor branch of a patrician family. He entered the navy of the republic and served as a commander in the Turkish War (1537–40). Canal persuaded the Senate that the problem of diminishing numbers of free oarsmen for the republic's GALLEYS could be remedied by using convict labour. The proposal had detractors (who worried that convict oarsmen could not be armed for combat), but proved to be successful. In his subsequent career Canal became an acknowledged authority on naval organization and strategic deployment.

Canal's dialogue *Della milizia marittima*, which was not printed until 1930, provides a wealth of information about the Venetian navy; it is the earliest study of naval warfare to have survived.

*DBI* s.v. Canal; *Della milizia marittima*, ed. M. Nani Mocenigo (1930); A. Tenenti, *Cristoforo da Canal, la marine vénitienne avant Lepante* (1962).

**CANARY ISLANDS or (Spanish) Islas Canarias**, an archipelago 100 kilometres (60 miles) west of the African coast, known to the Romans as unpopulated islands which had previously been inhabited. By the time the islands were visited by Arab sailors in the twelfth century, they had long been settled by a people known as the Guanches. In 1334 a French ship was driven into the archipelago, and in the course of the fourteenth century there was at least one Portuguese expedition (which failed to find the islands) and at least two Spanish expeditions, on one of which a monastic mission was established.

The conquest of the Canaries was initiated by the French adventurers Jean de Béthencourt and Gadifer de la Salle, who arrived in two ships at Lanzarote in July 1402. Jean had suffered a mutiny, and so dislodged his crew and sailed for Castile, where his uncle, Robert de Braquemont, persuaded King Henry III of Castile to confer the title of king of the Canary Islands on Jean in return for Jean's submission to the crown of Castile. On returning to the archipelago in 1404, Jean discovered that Gadifer had conquered Lanzarote and part of Fuerteventura; Gadifer was not prepared to acknowledge the suzerainty of Jean, and promptly left to lodge what proved to be an unsuccessful appeal with Henry III. In 1405 Jean settled Norman colonists on Hierro, and in December 1406 left the islands for the last time; before his death in 1422, he wrote *Le Canarien: Livre de la conquête et conversion des Canaries*. The ownership of the islands was contested for the next 50 years, the main claimants being the relatives of Gadifer and Jean, Prince HENRY THE NAVIGATOR, and FERDINAND and ISABELLA of Castile. In 1479 the Treaty of ALCAçOVAS between Castile and Portugal settled the dispute in favour of Castile.

Settlement of the dispute about sovereignty enabled a bloody conquest to proceed apace: Pedro de Vera subdued Gran Canaria in 1483; La Palma fell to Alonso de Lugo in 1491, and in 1495 Lugo completed the conquest with the securing of Tenerife. The mountain on Tenerife was variously estimated to be 25 to 100 kilometres high; Peter Heylyn reported it to be 'the highest in the whole world' (*Cosmography*, 1652).

Agustín Millares Torres, *Historia general de las Islas Canarias* (6 vols., 1977–81).

**CANDIDA, GIOVANNI or (French) Jean de** (*c*.1450–*c*.1500), Italian medallist, diplomat, and historian. He may have been born in Naples, but by 1477 he had entered the service of the Burgundian court and in the early 1480s he moved to the court of LOUIS XI of France. He wrote a short history of France (in Latin) for CHARLES VIII, and in the 1590s travelled to Italy on a series of diplomatic missions. His portrait MEDALS portray French and Italian statesmen, including a signed portrait of Charles the Bold and his future son-in-law Maximilian of Austria (later the Emperor MAXIMILIAN).

*DBI*; *MDA*.

**CANDIDO, PIETRO.** See WITTE, PIETER DE.

**CANE, FACINO** (*c*.1350–1412), *condottiere*. He became a soldier as a young man, initially fighting in his native Piedmont and in Savoy, where he acquired a reputation for ruthlessness and enjoyed the unflinching loyalty of his soldiers, whom he allowed to pillage and murder at will. In 1394 he was given an important cavalry and infantry command in Genoa, and in 1397 he entered the service of Gian Galeazzo VISCONTI, duke of Milan. He became an influential figure in Milan, and was the chief arbiter in the succession crisis that ensued in the wake of the death of Duke Gian Galeazzo in 1402; during this period the stability of government was wholly dependent on this presence of Facino and his troops.

When the new duke, Giovanni Maria VISCONTI, finally secured his position in 1404, it was Facino who kept him in office and advised on every aspect of government. The prospect of Facino displacing the Visconti dynasty was averted by his death, but such was the power of his name that Filippo Maria VISCONTI, on succeeding to the dukedom on the death of his brother in 1412, promptly married Facino's widow Beatrice; six years later he had her executed on a false charge of adultery.

*DBI*; N. Valeri, *La vita di Facino Cane* (1940).

**CANISIUS or (Dutch) Kanijs, PETRUS** (1521–97), Jesuit priest, educator, and papal nuncio in Germany, born on 8 May 1521 in Nijmegen, the son of a tutor to the sons of the duke of Lorraine. Canisius was educated at Cologne and at Louvain, where he studied CANON LAW and came under the influence of the Jesuit Pierre Lefèvre. He joined the JESUIT Order in Cologne, where he became a PATRISTIC scholar and published editions of Cyril of Alexandria and Pope Leo the Great. After his ordination he became a preacher, and also attended two sessions of the COUNCIL OF TRENT. He then moved to Sicily, where he taught at the first Jesuit school in Messina, and afterwards returned to Rome to work with IGNATIUS LOYOLA.

Canisius' next move was to the University of Ingolstadt, where he served as rector and vice-chancellor and introduced a programme of reform. His success in Ingolstadt led to Canisius being sent in 1552 with a comprehensive reforming brief to Vienna, in which there had been no ordinations for twenty years, the monasteries and parishes had been deserted, and religious practice had been largely abandoned. Canisius set about remedying these defects, and also attended to the victims of PLAGUE; he was offered the archbishopric of Vienna, and declined. In 1554 Canisius published his CATECHISM *Summa doctrinae christianae*, and two years later published an abbreviated version. These catechisms, which were designed as antidotes to LUTHER's *Grosser Katechismus* and *Kleiner Katechismus*, were translated into fifteen languages before the end of the century.

In 1556 Canisius was appointed provincial of the new Jesuit province of Upper Germany, which included Austria, Bavaria, and Bohemia. Canisius moved to Prague, where he founded a college, and from 1559 to 1565 he lived in Augsburg, where he founded another college (as he was later to do in Munich and Innsbruck) and energetically set about converting Protestants and revitalizing lapsed Catholics. He subsequently taught in Dillingen, and helped to facilitate the foundation of Fribourg University. In 1591 he was paralysed by a stroke, but continued to write anti-Protestant polemic by dictating to a secretary until his death on 21 December 1597.

Canisius was an articulate and combative presence at the heart of the COUNTER-REFORMATION in the south German lands and central Europe. He was an unusually courteous controversialist, and believed that debate between Protestants and Catholics on matters of doctrine emphasized differences and so was an impediment to reconciliation with

Rome. Canisius was canonized in 1925 and at the same time was declared to be a doctor of the Church.

*NDB*; O. Braunsberger (ed.), *Beati Petri Canisii societatis Iesu epistolae et acta* (8 vols, 1896–1923); J. Broderick, *Saint Peter Canisius* (1935).

**CANNONS.** See ARTILLERY.

**CANO, JUAN SEBASTIÁN DEL.** See ELCANO, JUAN SEBASTIÁN DEL.

**CANO, MELCHOR or Melchior** (1509–60), Spanish Dominican theologian, born in Tarancón (New Castile); in 1523 he entered the Dominican ORDER in Salamanca, where he was taught by Francisco de VITORIA. He taught at Valladolid (1534–43) and Alcalá (1543–6) before succeeding Vitoria as professor of theology at Salamanca. He attended the COUNCIL OF TRENT and participated in the debates on the EUCHARIST and on penance (which dealt with the issue of INDULGENCES).

In 1552 Cano was appointed bishop of the Canaries at the behest of JESUITS who wanted him out of Spain because of his opposition to their Order; there was unease in Rome about the appointment, and the following year Cano renounced the see. In his *Consultatio theologica* (1556) Cano defended the anti-papal policies of PHILIP II (which included resisting the temporal encroachments of the papacy and assuming control of the administration of ecclesiastical revenues) and so further alienated the papacy; Pope PAUL IV excoriated him as a son of perdition. In 1557 Cano was elected Dominican provincial of Castile, but the Vatican declined to confirm the appointment; he was again elected in 1559, and after an initial refusal the Vatican acquiesced in the appointment.

Cano's most important theological work was his posthumously published *De locis theologicis* (Salamanca, 1563), a major contribution to the New Scholasticism of the Salamanca school. The treatise gained a measure of notoriety because of Cano's contention that in marriage it is the sacerdotal blessing which is the 'form' of the sacrament (i.e. the words that give significance to it), whereas the consent of those being married is merely the matter of the sacrament (and so comparable to the status of the water used in baptism). This view gave rise to disputes at the Council of Trent that subsequently rumbled on for generations.

*DBEH*; *DHE*; E. Marcotte, *La Nature de la théologie d'après Melchior Cano* (1949); J. Sanz y Sanz, *Melchor Cano: Cuestiones fundamentales de crítica histórica sobre su vida y sus escritos* (1959).

**CANON LAW** is the corpus of legislation that regulates the Christian Church. Its origins lie in the general councils and papal legislation of late antiquity. In the Western Church canons were collected in the fifth century, and in the Eastern Church (where imperial laws were added to canons) in the sixth century. In about 1140, Gratian, who may have been a Camaldolese monk, assembled some 4,000 texts of canon law and adapted the work of jurists who had been studying Roman law in order to arrange the canons systematically. Gratian's collection, variously known as the *Decretum Gratiani* or the *Concordia discordantium canonum*, sought to reconcile discrepancies in earlier collections and to establish an authoritative text of the canons. Gratian's text quickly became the subject of a tradition of learned commentary by jurists known as Decretists, who produced *glossae*, *summae*, and *quaestiones* (glosses, summaries, and dialectically framed questions), chiefly in Bologna, but also in Cologne, Oxford, and Paris. Beyond these centres, canon law was studied throughout the universities of Europe alongside Roman CIVIL LAW. Supplements to Gratian were discovered and assiduously edited, and collections of canons and of decretals proliferated. The *Corpus iuris canonici* was declared to be complete in 1317, but extra material continued to be added. By the time the *Corpus* was first printed, in 1499, it consisted of six parts: Gratian's *Decretum*; Raymond of Peñaforte's *Liber extra* (1234; sometimes known as *Decretales Gregorii IX*); the *Liber sextus* of Pope Boniface VIII (1298); the 'Clementines' (or *Liber septimus*) of Clement V (promulgated posthumously in 1317); the 'Extravagantes' (i.e. *extra decretum vagantes*, 'decretals wandering outside') of John XXII (1325); the decrees of various popes promulgated between 1261 and 1471. The COUNCIL OF TRENT declared the *Corpus* to be in need of revision, and in 1582 an authoritative new edition was issued. This edition, together with a supplement approved in 1580, remained the official text for the Western Church until the Code of Canon Law was promulgated in 1917.

Many of the greatest canonists worked in the formative period extending from 1140 to 1350, but the study of canon law nonetheless had a distinguished afterlife in figures such as Nicolò de' Tedeschi (PANORMITANUS), archbishop of Palermo, the French humanist Pierre PITHOU, and the Spanish jurist Antonio Agustín.

In Scotland canon law was abolished by Parliament in 1567, but in practice the new Commissary Court of Edinburgh (established 1563) continued to draw on elements of pre-Reformation canon law that were not contrary to Reformation doctrine until it was finally abolished in 1830. In England Henry VIII converted canon law into national law and so extended its jurisdiction to the entire population, lay and clerical. Convocation (the assembly of the provinces of Canterbury and York) and Parliament both requested that canon law be revised, but acknowledged that the inherited canon law should remain in force until the process of revision had been completed. In 1571 Queen Elizabeth forbade Parliament to discuss the revision, which was known as the *Reformatio legum ecclesiasticarum*; the revision was never ratified by Parliament or Convocation, but new canons were added in 1604. The original canons have never been revoked, but in 1857 the jurisdiction of ecclesiastical courts was severely curtailed, and canon law is now applicable only to such matters as disciplining clergy.

J. F. von Schulte, *Geschichte der Quellen und Literatur des canonischen Rechts* (3 vols., 1875–83); W. M. Plöchl, *Geschichte des Kirchenrechts* (3 vols., 1953–9); R. Naz, *Dictionnaire du droit canonique* (1935); F. W. Maitland, *Roman Canon Law in the Church of England* (1898); R. H. Helmholz, *The Spirit of Classical Canon Law* (1996).

**CANTO CARNASCIALESCO** (plural *canti carnascialeschi*) **or (English) carnival song**, a Florentine processional madrigal used at festivals during the pre-Lenten Carnival and the Calendimaggio, which celebrated the return of spring. These part songs, or *mascheratas*, were presented by groups of boys and masked men and would accompany *tableaux vivants* performed on decorated floats. Encouraged under MEDICI rule, these were replaced by religious processions and the singing of *laudi* under SAVONAROLA.

**CANTO FERMO or (Latin) *cantus firmus*** (literally 'fixed song'), the term used to denote the pre-existing melody used as a basis for a new polyphonic composition. A *cantus firmus* could be drawn from either sacred or secular music.

**CANZONA or (Italian) *canzone***, originally an arrangement, for instruments, of a polyphonic song. It developed into original composition, often making use of fugal imitation as noted by PRAETORIUS in his *Syntagma musicum* (1614–20).

**CÃO, DIOGO** (*fl.* 1482–6), Portuguese mariner who explored the coast of Africa as far south as what is now Cape Cross, on the coast of Namibia north of Walvis Bay. In 1483–4 he became the first European to sail up the Congo river, from which he returned with a cargo of African slaves; he returned in 1485–6 and established a slave-trading agreement with the local Congolese ruler.

    DHP.

**CAPADIFERRO, GIOVANNI FRANCESCO** (d. *c.*1533), woodcutter and *intarsitoro* whose only surviving work is the series of panels (designed by Lorenzo LOTTO) on the choir screen and stalls of Santa Maria Maggiore in Bergamo. Capadiferro began the execution of the designs in INTARSIA in 1522; they were completed by other hands after his death.

    *DBI*; L. Angelini, *Le tarsie in S. Maria Maggiore in Bergamo* (1957).

**CAPECE, SCIPIONE** (*c.*1480–1551), Italian humanist and jurist, born in Naples, where he lectured on CIVIL LAW and joined the Accademia Pontaniana (see ACADEMIES). He later became associated with the circle of Juan de VALDÉS, which led in 1543 to his banishment from Naples. He settled in Salerno, where he wrote Latin poetry and treatises on law.

    *DBI*.

**CAPELLO or Cappello, BIANCA** (1548–87), grand duchess of Tuscany. She was born into a patrician family in Venice and at the age of 15 eloped with a Florentine lover. In Florence she became the mistress of Francesco de' MEDICI, who ordered the murder of her lover. On the death of Cosimo de' MEDICI in 1574 Francesco succeeded his father as grand duke; in 1579 Francesco's wife died and he married Bianca, who was reconciled both to her parents and to the republic of Venice, which bestowed a title of honour on her. In 1587 Francesco and Bianca died within a day of each other, probably by poison.

    *DBI* s.v. Bianca; P. Gauthiez, *La Vie de Bianca Capello* (1929).

**CAPILUPI, GEMIGNANO** (1573–1616), Italian composer. A pupil of Orazio Vecchi, he brought about his dismissal and then succeeded him as *maestro di cappella* at Modena Cathedral in 1604 and later as musical director to the duke of Modena. He wrote madrigals, canzonets, and motets.

**CAPISTRANO, GIOVANNI DI**, or (English) **John of Capistrano** (1386–1456), Franciscan inquisitor and papal legate, born in the village of Capistrano (Abruzzi) into a family which had migrated to Italy with the Angevins. His early life was secular: he studied law at Perugia, married, embarked on a career as a magistrate, and in 1412 was appointed chief magistrate of Perugia. Giovanni subsequently separated from his wife on conditions that are unclear (possibly by mutual consent), and at the age of 30 entered the Franciscan Order. He quickly became an advocate of strict observance and a practitioner of rigorous asceticism.

Giovanni was ordained as a priest in 1420 and thereafter combined the study of theology under BERNARDINO of Siena with a strenuous programme of itinerant preaching. He also contributed energetically to the reform of the Franciscan Observant Order and the sister order of Observant nuns.

Giovanni became an inquisitor and papal legate under Popes EUGENIUS IV and NICHOLAS V. Within Italy, he persecuted the Fraticelli (Franciscan Spirituals) of Ferrara and the JEWS of Sicily. His appointment in 1451 as inquisitor-general to Vienna enabled Giovanni to persecute the Jews of Poland and Moldavia and, with consuming zeal, the Hussites of Bohemia, Hungary, and Germany.

In the wake of the fall of Constantinople in 1453, Giovanni was commanded by Pope PIUS II to preach a CRUSADE against the Ottomans. Austria and Bavaria responded grudgingly, but Hungary, faced with the approach of the Ottomans towards Belgrade, gave generous support. An army under the command of János HUNYADI (and urged on by Giovanni) raised the blockade of Belgrade imposed by the army of Mehmet II. The failure to bury the corpses around the city caused an outbreak of disease which killed both Giovanni (23 October 1456) and Hunyadi. Giovanni was canonized in 1724.

*DBI* s.v. Giovanni; J. Hofer, *Johannes von Capistrano* (1936), trans. as *St John Capistran, Reformer* (1943).

**CAPITAL PUNISHMENT.** In Roman law, the term 'capital punishment' extended beyond the death penalty to punishments that included the stripping of citizenship, such as penal servitude and banishment; Renaissance jurists sometimes use the term in this broader sense, but in the courts it always referred to the death penalty. In most territories of Europe, death was the penalty for treason, heresy, WITCHCRAFT, and all felonies except petty larceny; the boundary between petty and grand larceny was commonly set at a low level (in England, for example, thefts of property worth more than 12 pence were treated as grand larceny), so in practice offences such as sheep-stealing, burglary, and highway robbery were punishable by death.

The means of execution varied between crimes, classes, and countries. Witches were normally burnt at the stake (except in England, where they were hanged), as were heretics; noblemen were often beheaded by axe or sword, but commoners were hanged. Poisoners, such as the bishop of Rochester's cook in 1531, were boiled to death. Breaking on the wheel (in Roman-Dutch and imperial law), slow strangulation, drowning, stoning, and precipitation from rocks were also used. In England traitors were 'drawn' (i.e. disembowelled) before execution and subsequently quartered.

Executed criminals were sometimes dissected for purposes of research or the teaching of ANATOMY. The drawings of hanged men by PISANELLO are in the British Museum.

Michael Weisser, *Crime and Punishment in Early Modern Europe* (1979).

**CAPITO** or (originally) **Köpfel, WOLFGANG** or **Fabricius** (1478–1541), German Protestant reformer, born in Hagenau (now French Haguenau), in Alsace, and educated at Ingolstadt, Heidelberg, and Freiburg im Breisgau. He served as a pastor in Bruchsal for three years and in 1515 moved to a post in the cathedral church of Basel, where he met ERASMUS and ZWINGLI and began to correspond with LUTHER. In 1519 he moved to Mainz at the invitation of ALBRECHT II of Mainz, who appointed him as his chancellor. In 1523 he settled in Strassburg, where he stayed until his death in November 1541. By 1524 he had become a Protestant and had emerged as Martin BUCER's principal ally in the implementation of the Reformation.

Capito was the co-author (with Bucer) of the TETRAPOLITAN CONFESSION and also wrote a Hebrew grammar and a biography of OECOLAMPADIUS. In theology he showed an unusual aversion to dogmatic formulations: on the fraught subject of the EUCHARIST, he evinced Zwinglian sympathies, but nonetheless signed the WITTENBERG CONCORD of 1536.

*NDB*; J. M. Kittelson, *Wolfgang Capito: From Humanist to Reformer* (1975).

**CAPITULATION** or (Renaissance Latin) *capitulum* or (Renaissance Greek) κεφαλαίωσις. Capitulations are grants by treaty of commercial privileges, awarded by a state to foreign residents. Capitulations confer trading rights, but also exempt foreign residents from the jurisdiction of local courts, instead placing the administration of justice in the hands of the state of which the merchant is a citizen; they also confer right of residence and freedom of religion. The term is usually used with reference to Ottoman capitulations, the first of which was granted to France in 1535 by Süleyman I and signed the following year. Under the terms of this capitulation, France was awarded commercial privileges, and was also allowed to appoint French consuls in Turkey to judge the criminal and civil affairs of French citizens according to FRENCH LAW, and to call on the forces of the sultan for assistance in the execution of sentences. Subsequent concessions in Turkey were obtained by Venice (1540), England (1583), and the United Provinces (1613), but France retained the right (in the face of English claims) to represent all European subjects without diplomatic representation in Turkey.

**CAPORALI, BARTOLOMEO** (c.1420–c.1505), Italian painter and illuminator, a native of Perugia who during his lifetime was regarded as the greatest painter in Umbria. His extant works include an *Adoration of the Shepherds* (Galleria Nazionale, Perugia) painted for the convent at Monteluce (Perugia) and a fresco of the *Virgin and Child* in the church at Rocchicciola (near Assisi).

*DBI; MDA.*

**CAPPELLO, BIANCA**. See CAPELLO, BIANCA.

**CAPPONI FAMILY**, Tuscan family resident in Florence from 1210 and prominent in public office from the late fourteenth century to 1530. Gino Capponi (1350–1421) was a prominent supporter of the ALBIZZI, but his son Neri Capponi (1388–1457) supported the MEDICI, recalling Cosimo de' MEDICI from exile in 1434 and representing him on diplomatic missions. Piero Capponi (1446–96) was employed by Lorenzo de' MEDICI as a diplomat and in 1494 succeeded Lorenzo's son Piero II de' MEDICI as head of the restored Florentine republic. It was Piero who, faced with the threat of King CHARLES VIII to sound his trumpets (i.e. sack Florence), famously replied, 'and we shall sound our bells', and tore up the king's ultimatum to the Signoria in his face; Piero was killed on 25 September 1496 while besieging the castle of Soiana. The family's power came to an end with the restoration of the Medici in 1530.

*DBI.*

**CAPRANICA, DOMENICO** (1400–58), Italian cardinal. He was born in Capranica (near Viterbo) on 31 May 1400 and studied theology in Padua and Bologna. Pope MARTIN V appointed him as apostolic secretary in 1423 and two years later created him cardinal. In 1430 he was deprived of his benefices by Pope EUGENIUS IV, whereupon Domenico defected to the COUNCIL OF BASEL together with his secretary Enea Silvio Piccolomini (later Pope PIUS II). In 1434 he was reconciled with Pope Eugenius, after whose death he served as an adviser to Popes NICHOLAS V and CALLISTUS III. After the death of Callistus III on 6 August 1458, Domenico was regarded as a strong candidate for the papacy, but he died eight days later.

*DBI s.v. Capranica.*

**CAPUCHINS or (Latin) Ordo Fratrum Minorum S. Francisci Capuccinorum**. In 1528 Matteo di Bassi (*c*.1449–1552), an Observant Friar, secured the permission of Pope CLEMENT VII to live as a hermit and preach to the poor. This permission extended to anyone who might decide to join Matteo, and soon others did so. The Observants opposed the movement, but the Conventual Franciscans supported it, so Matteo and his companions were formed into a congregation that was called the Hermit Friars Minor, which was constituted as a branch of the Conventuals. By the end of 1529 they had four houses, but as numbers in each house were restricted to twelve, with an ideal of eight, the Order was not large. Its aim was to re-establish the simplicity associated with St Francis, in imitation of whom members wore a pointed cowl (Italian *cappuccio*) and grew a beard; they also went barefoot. The rule of the Order, which was drafted

in 1559, emphasized the Franciscan ideals of poverty and personal austerity of life. Sustenance was to be secured by begging, and the friars were not allowed to touch money.

The early years of the Order were troubled by the desertion of its founders (Matteo returned to the Observant Friars) and the hostility of other Franciscans; in 1541 the defection to Lutheranism of its third vicar-general, Bernardino OCHINO, brought it to the edge of suppression. The Order survived these misfortunes to become (through its preaching and missionary activities) an important conduit of the COUNTER-REFORMATION. In 1619 the Order was freed from its status as a branch of the Conventual Franciscans and became an independent order with its own general; by that time the Order had 1,500 houses in 50 provinces and had embarked on a missionary programme that was to extend to the Americas, Asia, and Africa.

In 1538 an order of Capuchin nuns known as Capuchines was formed in Naples; the extreme austerity of their lives led to their being called the Sisters of Suffering.

Most Capuchins abbreviated the Latin name of the Order as 'OCap' in postnominal initials, but English and Irish Capuchins used (and continue to use) the postnominal letters OSFC (Ordinis Sancti Francisci Capuccinorum).

Fr. Cuthbert [Hess], OSFC, *The Capuchins* (2 vols., 1928).

**CARA, MARCHETTO** (*c*.1470–*c*.1525), Veronese composer of more than a 100 FROTTOLAS who worked as a singer and lutenist for the Gonzaga family in Mantua.

**CARACCIOLO FAMILY**, an ancient Neapolitan family, reputedly of Byzantine origin. The most prominent of the many branches of the family were the Caracciolo of Avellino, who became counts of Gallerate (1539) and Torella (1560), dukes of Atripalda (1572) and Avellino (1589), and hereditary grand chancellors of Naples (1609). Giovanni Caracciolo (d. 1431), who was known as Sergianni, became grand seneschal of Naples and lover of Queen GIOVANNA II; he was assassinated in 1431. Another Giovanni Caracciolo (1480–1539), a scion of the Melfi branch of the family, was a *condottiere* who fought for the last Florentine republic (1527–30) and was later appointed governor of Marseille and Piedmont by King FRANCIS I. Galeazzo Caracciolo (1517–86), who was connected to the CARAFA FAMILY through his mother (whose brother became Pope PIUS IV) and his wife, was a Protestant in the circle of Juan de VALDÉS. In 1551 he fled for Geneva, leaving his wife and son behind.

The Church of San Giovanni a Carbonara in Naples contains two Caracciolo chapels, the Caracciolo di Vico and the Caracciolo del Sole; the pavement laid in 1440 in the latter chapel is the earliest dated example of the ceramic known as lustred MAIOLICA.

*DBI.*

**CARADOSSO or Cristoforo Foppa** (*c*.1452–1526/7), Italian goldsmith, medallist, and sculptor, born in Mondonico (near Pavia); he worked in Rome in 1477 and in 1480 entered the service of Ludovico SFORZA in Milan; in the 1490s he worked in several north Italian cities. In 1505 Caradosso returned to

Rome, where he worked in the service of Popes JULIUS II, LEO X, ADRIAN VI, and CLEMENT VII. His work in gold (which included MEDALS and COINS) was praised by CELLINI and VASARI, but no examples are known to survive. The papal tiara that he made for Pope Julius II in 1510 was destroyed and is known only from a drawing executed in 1725 (now in the British Museum).

*DBI* s.v. Foppa, Caradosso; *MDA*.

**CARAFA or Caraffa FAMILY**, a Neapolitan family that was active in the political and ecclesiastical life of fifteenth- and sixteenth-century Italy. Cardinal Oliviero Carafa (1430–1511) promoted the career of his nephew Giampietro Carafa, who was elected Pope PAUL IV in 1555, the high point of the family's fortunes. Pope Paul in turn raised his nephew, the soldier Carlo Carafa (1518–61), to the cardinalate. On Pope Paul's death popular hatred for him and for the Carafa family resulted in riots in which his statue on the Capitol was toppled and mutilated.

*DBI* and *MDA* s.v. Carafa.

**CARAVAGGIO, BATTLE OF**. On 29 July 1448 a Milanese army defeated Venetian forces near Caravaggio (in Lombardy) and so prevented the Venetians from destroying the AMBROSIAN REPUBLIC in Milan.

**CARAVAGGIO, MICHELANGELO MERISI DA** (1571–1610), Italian painter. He was born in Caravaggio (near Bergamo), and by 1592 had settled in Rome. He fled from Rome in 1606 after killing a man in a brawl, and spent the final years of his life as a fugitive in Naples, Sicily, and Malta. He died of malaria while travelling to Rome in the hope of securing a pardon.

Caravaggio's early works, such as *Boy with a Fruit Basket* (c.1593, Borghese Gallery, Rome), are typically non-dramatic subjects with a strong element of STILL LIFE. His mature habit of using a shaft of light to unify his compositions is apparent in the late 1590s in paintings such as the *Lute Player* (Hermitage, St Petersburg). Caravaggio's public paintings, which were executed between 1599 and 1605, include *The Crucifixion of St Peter* and *The Conversion of St Paul* (both in the Cerasi Chapel of Santa Maria del Popolo), *St Matthew and the Angel*, *The Calling of St Matthew*, and *The Martyrdom of St Matthew* (all in the Contarelli Chapel in the Church of San Luigi de' Francesci, the French church in Rome), *The Deposition* (Vatican), the *Madonna di Loreto* (Church of Sant'Agostino, Rome), and the *Madonna de' Palafrenieri* (Borghese Gallery, Rome). The finest painting of Caravaggio's exile is *The Beheading of John the Baptist* (St John's Co-Cathedral, Valetta, Malta).

In the historiography of art, Caravaggio is depicted as the founder of stylistic naturalism. It is certainly the case that he eschewed idealized beauty in favour of a realistic presentation of his subjects: his *St Matthew* is the earliest representation to show the disciple with dirty feet.

*DBI* s.v. Merisi, Michelangelo; *MDA*; Helen Langdon, *Caravaggio: A Life* (1998); Catherine Puglisi, *Caravaggio* (1998).

**CARAVEL**, a type of small Mediterranean trading vessel in use from the fourteenth to the seventeenth centuries. In the course of this period the caravel evolved from a large boat lateen-rigged on two (or occasionally three) masts (the *caravela latina*) into a small three-masted ship with a square rig on the two forward masts and a lateen sail on the mizzen (the *caravela rotunda*). These three-masted caravels were typically 25 metres (80 feet) long.

COLUMBUS undertook his first voyage with three caravels, the *Santa María*, the *Niña*, and the *Pinta*. The *Niña* sailed from Spain rigged as a *caravela latina*, but was unable to keep up with the others and so was rerigged as a *caravela rotunda* in the Canary Islands. Caravels were also used on the voyages of Bartolomeu DIAS and Ferdinand MAGELLAN.

**CARDANO, GIROLAMO** (1501–76), Italian physician, humanist, natural philosopher, mathematician, and autobiographer, born in Gallerate (near Milan), the illegitimate son of a jurist, and educated at the universities of Pavia and Padua. He earned his living mainly as a physician, but also taught mathematics. (For the links between mathematics and medicine see ASTRONOMY; ASTROLOGY.) He is now best remembered for his contribution to ALGEBRA.

Cardano's most important publication in algebra arose at least partly out of a meeting with TARTAGLIA, who told Cardano his general method of solving cubic equations. Cardano published this method in *Ars magna* (1545), which resulted in the method being ascribed to Cardano himself and set off a priority dispute. The *Ars magna* is important not only for its technical content but also for the fact that it is in Latin, and thus marks algebra as a suitable subject for study by learned mathematicians, rather than being associated only with the 'practical' tradition of the ABACUS SCHOOLS. Cardano himself clearly took the work very seriously indeed: he ends it with the words 'It was written out five times, may it last the same number of millennia' ('quinquies exscriptus, maneat tot millibus annis'). He wrote a further, short, treatise that seems to be conceived as a continuation of the *Ars magna*, called *De regula aliza* (1570); the last word of the title may be derived from Arabic but its meaning is not known. This treatise was published together with a much more substantial work, *Opus novum de proportionibus numerorum, motuum, ponderum, sonorum aliarumque rerum*, which, as the long title suggests, proposes to explain a number of natural phenomena by mathematical rules of proportions. The models for this include ARCHIMEDES' work on the law of the lever.

In 1547 Cardano became professor of medicine at Pavia and four years later embarked on a protracted visit to France, England, and Scotland. In 1562 he moved to Bologna, where he was arrested by the Roman INQUISITION on suspicion of heresy; he was released but forbidden to teach, and spent the rest of his life in Rome. Cardano's many publications include a bulky discursive work on natural philosophy, *De subtilitate* (1550), that among many other things gives a list of notable thinkers rated by their subtlety, in which Archimedes comes top. The work provoked a long philosophical retort from

Julius Caesar SCALIGER. Cardano also wrote prolifically on medicine, on astrology, and on various humanist topics. His autobiography, *De vita propria*, was first published in 1643.

DBI; DSB; Grove s.v. Cardano, Jerome; Anthony Grafton, *Cardano's Cosmos: The Worlds and Works of a Renaissance Astrologer* (2000); Eckhard Keßler (ed.), *Girolamo Cardano: Philosoph, Naturforscher, Arzt* (1994).

**CARDONA, RAMON or (Italian) Raimondo FOLCH DE** (d. 1522), Catalan soldier who served under Gonzalo FERNÁNDEZ DE CÓRDOBA in Italy and was created duke of Cardona (in Catalonia) in 1491. He was appointed viceroy of Naples and in the War of the HOLY LEAGUE (1511–13) commanded the Spanish troops of FERDINAND V and the papal army of JULIUS II. He unsuccessfully besieged Bologna and was defeated by the French at the battle of Ravenna (April 1512). The defeat marked an important stage in the WARS OF ITALY, and led to the sack of Prato and the restoration of the MEDICI in Florence.

DBI; DBEH s.v. Folch de Cardona, Ramón; DHE; Manuel Ballesteros Gaibrois, *Ramón de Cardona: Colaborador del Rey Católico en Italia* (1953).

**CARDOSO, FRAY MANUEL** (1566–1650), Portuguese composer of sacred music. He was *mestre da capela* at the Convento do Carmo in Lisbon. King John IV, to whom he dedicated his music, thought sufficiently of him to keep his portrait in his music library.

**CARIANI, GIOVANNI BUSI** (c.1485–after 1547), Italian painter. He was born near Bergamo and trained in the studio of Gentile BELLINI in Venice, where he worked for most of his life. His religious paintings include *St Agatha* (National Gallery, Edinburgh) and *The Road to Calvary* (Ambrosiana, Milan); his portraits include *Giovanni Benedetto Caravaggi* (Accademia Carrara, Bergamo) and *Giovan Antonio Caravaggi* (National Gallery, Ottawa).

DBI s.v. Busi, Giovanni, detto il Cariani; MDA; Rodolfo Pallucchini, *Giovanni Cariani* (1983).

**CARLETON, NICHOLAS** (c.1570/5–1630), English composer who as a child was at the almonry house attached to St Paul's Cathedral. He wrote keyboard music and was a friend of Thomas TOMKINS.

**CARLO EMANUELE I, 'IL GRANDE'** (1562–1630), duke of SAVOY, was the son of EMANUELE FILIBERTO, whom he succeeded in 1580. He sought to turn the rivalry between France and Spain to his advantage and aspired to conquer Geneva, Saluzzo, and Monferrato. He wrested Saluzzo from France in 1588 and then entered the French WARS OF RELIGION on the Catholic side. When King HENRI III was assassinated in 1589, Carlo Emanuele claimed the throne of France through his mother Margaret, (sister of King Henri II) and his wife Catherine (granddaughter of Henri II and Catherine de Médicis). In 1590 he dispatched troops to Provence to fight for the CATHOLIC LEAGUE and later assumed command himself. The settlement of 1593, in which Henry of Navarre became King HENRI IV, put an end to Carlo Emanuele's ambitions in France. In the Peace of Lyon (1602), Carlo Emanuele ceded all possessions beyond the Rhône, but his occupation of Saluzzo was recognized as legitimate.

On the night of 11/12 December 1602 Carlo Emanuele attempted to capture Geneva with the assistance of Spain, but his plan failed; the attack is known as the *Escalade* because ladders were used to scale the city walls. The 83-year-old BEZA assembled the victorious citizens of Geneva in the cathedral, where they sang Psalm 124, which is still sung on the anniversary of the attack. In 1612 Carlo Emanuele seized Monferrato from the GONZAGA FAMILY, but the combined forces of Venice, Tuscany, Spain, and the Holy Roman Empire forced him to relinquish his conquest.

DBI; R. Bergadani, *Carlo Emanuele I* (1926).

**CARLOS, DON** (1545–68), prince of Asturias and heir to the Spanish throne, born in Valladolid, the son of King PHILIP II and his first wife Maria of Portugal, who died a few days after giving birth. Don Carlos was an unstable youth, and relations with his father were strained. In 1559 he was betrothed to Elizabeth of Valois, daughter of King HENRI II, but a few months later she became King Philip's third wife. In 1560 Don Carlos was recognized as heir to the throne of Castile and in 1563 to the throne of Aragon. In January 1568 King Philip arrested his son and imprisoned him for reasons that are still unclear; Don Carlos died in prison six months later, which led to the popular belief that King Philip had ordered the murder of his son.

The legend of Don Carlos derives from the speculative belief that Don Carlos resented the loss of Princess Elizabeth to his father; the fact that she died shortly after Don Carlos fuelled the romantic notion that she died of grief. The story has been the subject of plays and fictions in many languages, notably Schiller's *Don Carlos*, which formed the basis of Verdi's libretto.

DBEH s.v. Carlos de Austria; DHE s.v. Carlos, príncipe don; F. W. C. Lieder, *The Don Carlos Theme* (1930).

**CARLTON, RICHARD** (c.1558–c.1638), English composer based in Norfolk and, for fourteen years, master of the choristers at Norwich Cathedral. He wrote madrigals and was one of the composers represented in *The* TRIUMPHS OF ORIANA (1601).

**CARMAGNOLA, COUNT FRANCESCO BUSSONE DA** (c.1385–1432), *condottiere*, born in Carmagnola (near Turin). At the age of 12 he became a soldier under the command of Facino CANE, who was then in the service of Gian Galeazzo VISCONTI. After Facino's death in 1412, Francesco succeeded him as the principal *condottiere* of Filippo VISCONTI, reconquering on his behalf the towns and cities that had seceded from the duchy in the tumultuous years following the death of Gian Galeazzo in 1402. Francesco successfully besieged Alessandria, Bergamo, Brescia, Cremona, Lodi, and Monza and then defeated the Swiss army at the battle of ARBEDO.

Francesco's growing reputation for invincibility unnerved Filippo Visconti, who was apprehensive of Francesco's political support and territorial ambitions. Instead of offering him further military commands, Filippo offered Francesco the governorship of Genoa. Francesco's request for a personal interview was refused, and he reacted by resigning his commission and offering his services to Venice. The doge, Francesco FOSCARI, was fearful of Visconti expansionism, and was eager to join forces with Florence in a war against the Visconti.

Francesco entered the service of Venice in 1425, and the following year war was declared on the Visconti. Francesco was appointed captain-general of the campaign. The war dragged on inconclusively, and Francesco failed to follow up his one great victory at the battle of MACLODIO in 1427. Venice offered huge rewards for victory, including the lordship of Milan, but the Visconti also offered huge rewards if Francesco abandoned Venice for Milan. This contact with Filippo Maria Visconti aroused the wrath of Venice, which recalled Francesco on 29 March 1432, ostensibly to discuss future military operations. Francesco was arrested, tried for treason, and beheaded between the columns on the Piazzetta on 5 May 1432.

DBI s.v. Bussone, Francesco; A. Battistella, *Il conte di Carmagnola* (1889).

**CARNESECCHI, PIETRO** (1508–67), heretic and victim of the INQUISITION, a Florentine nobleman whose early career was spent in the service of Pope CLEMENT VII. He became notary to the curia and first secretary to the pope, whom he accompanied to Marseille in October 1533; on that occasion he made a favourable impression on CATHERINE DE MÉDICIS and her court. In Rome he joined the humanist salon of his maternal uncle Cardinal Bernardo DOVIZI, and also met the Spanish reformer Juan de VALDÉS. On the accession of Pope PAUL III, Carnesecchi withdrew from the curia, and in 1536 he followed Juan de Valdés to Naples, where Juan's circle included future Protestants such as Bernardino OCHINO and Pietro Martire VERMIGLI and the Catholic reformer Giulia GONZAGA.

Carnesecchi's advocacy of the doctrine of justification by faith attracted the attention of the Inquisition. In 1546 he was tried and condemned for heresy, but the trial was annulled and Carnesecchi was pardoned; he retreated for safety to France, and was accommodated by friends from the French court. In 1552 he moved to Venice, where he became a prominent advocate of Catholic reform. In 1557 he was again required to appear before the Inquisition in Rome, but he declined to attend. The death of Pope PAUL IV and the accession of PIUS IV removed the threat of a second trial, and Carnesecchi returned to Rome in 1559 in the belief that he would be safe. The accession of Pope PIUS V in 1565, however, signalled a renewal of the murderous zeal of the Inquisition. Carnesecchi was in Venice when news of the election reached him, and he decided to seek refuge in Florence. He was betrayed by Cosimo de' MEDICI, and handed over to the Inquisition in July 1566. He was interrogated about his associates, especially Cardinal Giovanni MORONE, but declined to implicate anyone else; he nonetheless confessed to heresy under torture. He was sentenced to death (along with sixteen others) on 21 September 1567; Florentine ambassadors knelt before the pope in a vain attempt to secure mercy, and on 1 October Carnesecchi was publicly beheaded and then burnt. The records of his trial are an important source of information about evangelism.

DBI.

**CARO, ANNIBALE** (1507–66), Italian courtier, poet, and letter-writer, born in Civitanova Marche (near Ancona) and educated in Florence. He became secretary to Pierluigi FARNESE, and after his employer's murder in 1547 entered the service of Cardinal Alessandro Farnese. His antipathy to Ludovico CASTELVETRO led to the latter leaving Italy to avoid persecution by the Inquisition.

Caro's dramatic and literary works include the prose comedy *Gli straccioni* (1554; 'The Ragamuffins') and a large corpus of Petrarchan sonnets (*Rime*, 1557) and verse satires (many of which were sonnets). More than 1,000 of his letters were published as *Lettere familiari* in 1573 and 1575, and his blank-verse translation of Virgil's *Aeneid* was published in 1581.

DBI; OCIL; A. Greco, *Annibale Caro* (1950).

*CAROLINA* or (Latin) *Constitutio Carolina Criminalis* or (German) *Peinliche Gerichtsordnung des Karls V*, a criminal code enacted by the Emperor Charles V (hence *Carolina*). The code was modelled on the BAMBERGISCHE HALSGERICHTS-ORDNUNG of 1507 and was initiated at the Diet of WORMS in 1521; the fourth and final draft was finally adopted by the Diet of Regensburg in 1532. Like its Bamberg model, the code centred on criminal procedure, but also contained substantive law. It was the first national code to combine German CUSTOMARY LAW with Roman law. Although it contained a clause that deferred to local law, it became the law of criminal procedure throughout the Empire and remained in force for three centuries. The decline of imperial authority in Italy after the thirteenth century meant that imperial legislation seldom affected Italy, but the *Carolina* was a notable exception, and it became the standard code of criminal procedure in north Italy.

**CARON, ANTOINE** (1521–99), French painter associated with the second FONTAINEBLEAU SCHOOL. Caron worked as an assistant to PRIMATICCIO at Fontainebleau and later became court painter to CATHERINE DE MÉDICIS and a supporter of the CATHOLIC LEAGUE. His historical paintings include *Massacres under the Triumvirate* (1566, Louvre; the title alludes to the anti-Protestant triumvirate of the maréchal de SAINT-ANDRÉ, Anne de MONTMORENCY, and François, duke of GUISE) and *Augustus and the Sybil* (c.1575–80, Louvre).

DBF; MDA; Jean Ehrmann, *Antoine Caron: Peintre des fêtes et des massacres* (1986).

**CARPACCIO, VITTORE** (c.1460/6–1525/6), Italian painter, born in Venice and probably trained in the studio of Lazzaro Bastiani (c.1425–1512); his paintings show the influence of both Bastiani and Gentile BELLINI. Carpaccio's most important paintings were cycles of *The Life of St Ursula* (painted in the 1490s and now in the Accademia in Venice) and of *The Lives of SS George and Jerome* (painted in the early 1500s for the Scuola di San Giorgio degli Schiavone in Venice, where they remain). Carpaccio was one of the first artists to paint townscapes, and his depictions of contemporary Venice have considerable documentary value.

DBI; MDA; Vittorio Sgarbi, *Carpaccio* (English trans. 1994); Stefania Mason Rinaldi, *Carpaccio: The Major Pictorial Cycles* (2000).

**CARPETS AND RUGS**. The term 'carpet' now refers primarily to a floor covering, but until the eighteenth century floors were normally covered with rush matting, and carpets were used either as coverings for furniture such as beds and tables or as wall hangings. Domestic carpets were often made by NEEDLEWORK (working threads through a cloth mesh), but more sumptuous carpets were TAPESTRIES made by WEAVING on a loom; the laborious medieval knotted-pile carpets had largely ceased to be manufactured in the early modern period, except for a small number of German wall-carpets. Most carpets were made from wool, but some contained silk threads and decorative motifs woven in gold and silver threads.

In addition to these indigenous European carpets, merchants imported large numbers of Middle Eastern carpets, principally from the Ottoman Empire. Sunni Islam is iconoclastic, so carpets from Egypt and what is now Turkey were woven in geometrical patterns; Shia Islam, however, has a rich pictorial tradition, so Persian carpets and those from Mughal India often portrayed subjects such as animals, gardens, vases, and hunting scenes. Both types of designs were widely imitated by European designers. The knots used to make these carpets differed markedly: the Persian knot (also known as the Sehna knot) used in Persian, Mughal, central Asian, and Chinese carpets was effected by twisting the yarn around one warp thread and under the adjacent thread, a process which produced carpets with a very close pile; the Ghiordes knot (also known as the Turkish knot) used in Turkey, Egypt, and the Caucasus was tied symmetrically on two adjacent warp threads, and produced a coarse pile.

The types of Anatolian carpets (and their European imitations) named after artists such as BELLINI, CRIVELLI, HOLBEIN, LOTTO, MEMLING are those represented in their paintings. The carpet in Holbein's *Madonna of Burgomaster Meyer* (c.1526, Kunstmuseum, Basel), for example, has a border of illegible Kufic lettering and a red ground with octagonal motifs decorated in blues and yellows; the carpet in Lorenzo Lotto's portrait of *Giovanni Giuliano* (c.1520, National Gallery, London) is similar, but the motifs are of stylized palmettes rather than octagons. Painters were not always consistent in the types of carpets that they depicted, but their repeated use of the same carpets renders the taxonomy sufficiently stable to be of use. In the early seventeenth century Ushak and Transylvanian carpets became popular in western Europe. Ushak carpets were made in the Turkish province of Ushak (now spelt Uşak), and typically depicted a large medallion ('medallion Ushaks') or a repeated eight-pointed star ('star Ushaks'). Transylvanian carpets, which were either Anatolian carpets or Transylvanian imitations, were hung in the Protestant churches of Transylvania; their colours were more subdued than those of Ushak carpets, and their designs typically consisted of two halves that mirrored each other, and so were vertically but not horizontally symmetrical.

**CARPI, GIROLAMO DA, or Girolamo da Ferrara** (c.1501–1566), Italian painter, a native of Ferrara, where he trained in the studio of GAROFALO. He painted pictures on religious themes for churches in Bologna (notably his *Marriage of St Catherine* in San Salvatore and his *Adoration of the Magi* in San Martino Maggiore) and Ferrara (of which three survive in Ferrara Cathedral) and portraits in the style of PARMIGIANINO. He lived for a time in Rome, where he compiled a sketchbook of antiquities which is the most important early modern compilation of Roman antiquities.

DBI; MDA; Norman Canedy, *The Roman Sketchbook of Girolamo da Carpi* (1976); A. Mezzetti, *Girolamo da Ferrara detto da Carpi* (1977).

**CARRACCI, AGOSTINO** (1557–1602), Italian artist, born in Bologna; he was the elder brother of Annibale CARRACCI and the cousin of Ludovico CARRACCI. Agostino painted a well-known altarpiece, *The Communion of St Jerome* (1593–4, Pinacoteca, Bologna). His engravings include a portrait of TINTORETTO, whom Agostino visited in Venice in 1582. His most important drawings were ANATOMICAL studies which were engraved after his death and used in European drawing schools for centuries. In 1597 Agostino left Bologna for Rome, where he assisted his brother Annibale in the decoration of the Farnese Gallery. In 1600 he moved to Parma, where he decorated the vault of a room in Palazzo del Giardino and where he died in 1602.

DBI; MDA.

**CARRACCI, ANNIBALE** (1560–1609), Italian artist, born in Bologna; he was the younger brother of Agostino CARRACCI and the cousin of Ludovico CARRACCI. As a young man in Bologna he specialized in GENRE PAINTINGS such as *The Butcher's Shop* (Christ Church, Oxford) and *The Bean Eater* (Colonna Gallery, Rome). Between 1583 and 1595 he painted a series of altarpieces (notably *The Almsgiving of St Roch*, Gemäldegalerie, Dresden) and LANDSCAPES (e.g. *Fishing* and *Hunting*, both in the Louvre).

In 1595 Annibale moved to Rome at the invitation of Cardinal Odoardo Farnese, and in the course of the next ten years decorated the Farnese Palace with fresco cycles on *The Legend of Hercules* and *The Loves of the Gods*. These cycles, for which Annibale made more than 1,000 preparatory drawings, are one of the masterpieces of early baroque art; they exercised an important influence on seventeenth-century Roman art and on the development of the baroque style, and until the nineteenth century were thought fit to stand alongside MICHELANGELO's Sistine Chapel and RAPHAEL's Stanza della Segnatura, to both of which Annibale was indebted.

DBI; MDA; Charles Dempsey, *Annibale Carracci: The Farnese Gallery, Rome* (1995).

**CARRACCI, LUDOVICO** (1555–1619), Italian artist, born in Bologna; he was the cousin of Agostino CARRACCI and

Annibale CARRACCI. His finest pictures, which were painted in the late 1580s and early 1590s, include a portrait of *The Tacconi Family* (c.1588–90, Pinacoteca Nazionale, Bologna), a *Madonna and Child with St Joseph and St Francis* (1591, Pinacoteca Civica, Cento), and *The Preaching of St John the Baptist* (Pinacoteca, Bologna).

DBI; MDA.

**CARRACK**, a type of large trading vessel in use from the fourteenth to the seventeenth centuries. Carracks were rigged like the three-masted CARAVEL (*caravela rotunda*) with a square rig on the two forward masts and a lateen sail on the mizzen, but were altogether larger ships with high forecastles and aftercastles. Carracks were used by Spanish and Portuguese merchants in Asia and America throughout the sixteenth and early seventeenth centuries, but were then superseded by the GALLEON.

**CARRANZA, BARTOLOMÉ** (1503–76), Spanish Dominican theologian, born into a noble family in Miranda de Arga (Navarre) and educated at Alcalá de Henares (1515–20). He entered the Dominican Order (1520) and then continued his studies at Salamanca (1521–5) and Valladolid, where from 1527 he taught theology. His reputation for learning was rivalled only by that of Melchor CANO, and his lectures attracted national attention. In 1530 he was denounced to the Spanish INQUISITION for advocating limitations in papal power and sympathizing with the thought of ERASMUS, but he was acquitted. In the 1530s he was appointed professor and then regent in theology at Valladolid.

In 1539 Carranza travelled to Rome as a representative to the chapter-general of his Order. While in Rome he received the degree of doctor of theology and enjoyed the confidence of Pope PAUL III; on the other hand, he was in contact with the suspect circle of Juan de VALDÉS. On returning to Valladolid he was appointed censor (*cualificador*) of books, including suspect versions of the Bible, for the Inquisition. In 1540 he was nominated for the bishoprics of the Canary Islands and Peru, but declined both.

In 1546 the Emperor CHARLES V appointed Carranza as an envoy to the COUNCIL OF TRENT, where he delivered a discourse advocating the view (which he presented as divine law, *iuris divini*) that bishops and other clergy should reside in their benefices; he published his discourse as *De necessaria residentia personali* (Venice, 1547). His reformist sympathies were also apparent in his choice of JUSTIFICATION as the theme of his Lenten sermon to the Council. While in Italy he also returned to one of the subjects that had first attracted the attention of the Inquisition in his *Summa conciliorum et pontificum* (Venice, 1546; successive editions to 1821).

On returning to Spain Carranza was appointed provincial of his Order for Castile. In 1554 he was sent by the emperor to England on the occasion of the marriage of his son Philip (later PHILIP II) to Queen MARY. In England he became the queen's confessor and endeavoured to re-establish Catholicism in Oxford. On returning to Spain he was appointed archbishop of Toledo (1557) and in September 1558 attended the emperor on his deathbed, administering extreme unction. By the end of the year he had again been denounced to the Inquisition, this time for his *Comentarios sobre el catechismo* (Antwerp, 1558); he was arrested early in 1559 at Tordelaguna and imprisoned for almost eight years. His book was placed on the INDEX, but in 1563 was approved by a commission appointed by the Council of Trent.

Carranza was able to appeal against the judgment of the Spanish Inquisition, and in December 1566 he was taken to Rome, where he was imprisoned for ten years in Castel Sant'Angelo while his case was considered by the papal tribunal. The final judgment acquitted Carranza of heresy but convicted him of error, and he was obliged to abjure sixteen errors; he was sentenced to suspension from his see for five years and immured in the Dominican cloister at Santa Maria sopra Minerva in Rome. He died on 2 May 1576, exactly a week after his abjuration, and was succeeded in his see by Gaspar Quiroga, the Spanish inquisitor-general. Pope GREGORY XIII, who shared the common view that Carranza had been persecuted for his commitment to reform rather than heresy, commissioned a laudatory plaque for Carranza's tomb in Santa Maria sopra Minerva.

DBEH; DHE; J. I. Tellechea Idígoras, *Bartolomé Carranza, arzobispo* (1958); id., *Fray Bartolomé Carranza: Documentos históricos* (8 vols., 1962–94).

**CARRARA or Carraresi FAMILY**, a family whose members ruled Padua from 1318 to 1388 and, after a two-year interregnum during which the city was held by Gian Galeazzo VISCONTI of Milan, from 1390 to 1405. Giacomo Carrara was elected *dominus generalis* in 1318, and Marsiglio Carrara became *signore* in 1328. The most prominent of the nine Carraresi rulers was Francesco da Carrara il Vecchio (1325–88), who succeeded his murdered brother in 1350. Francesco waged two wars against Venice (1372–3 and 1378–81). In 1362 Francesco curtailed the civil liberties of Paduans and thereafter ruled as a putative prince. He commissioned a series of coins and frescoes commemorating famous men; his choices were guided by PETRARCH, who had bequeathed most of his library to Francesco.

Francesco's son Francesco da Carrara il Novello (1359–1406) recaptured Padua from Gian Galeazzo Visconti. He ruled until November 1405, when he surrendered his besieged city to the Venetians. He was taken to Venice together with his two elder sons Francesco III and Jacopo; all three were tried and judicially strangled. Francesco Novello's third son Marsiglio attempted to recover Padua in 1435, but his plot was discovered and he was killed.

DBI; MDA s.v. Carrara, da.

**CARRILLO Y SOTOMAYOR, LUIS DE** (1581/2–1610), Spanish literary theorist, poet, and translator, born into a noble family in Córdoba and educated at Salamanca; he subsequently lived in the viceregal court in Naples, where he became part of the literary circle of Giambattista MARINO. He published translations of Ovid and Seneca, and a *Fábula de Acis y Galatea*.

Carrillo's most important work is his *Libro de la erudición poética*, which advocates a Latinate style and tone in Spanish poetry, which should, in his view, be addressed to an educated audience capable of understanding an allusive framework that is centred in classical antiquity. This treatise subsequently came to be regarded as the manifesto of GONGORISM.

Angelina Costa Palacios, *La obra poética de Luis Carrillo y Sotomayor* (1984).

**CARTAGENA, ALFONSO DE, or García de Santa María** (1384–1456), Spanish humanist, born in Burgos, the son of the chief rabbi of Burgos. In July 1390 Alfonso's father became a *converso* when he was baptized as Pablo de Santa María, and in 1401 was appointed bishop of Cartagena. Alfonso followed his father into the Church and was nominated bishop of Burgos in 1435; his consecration was delayed for several years because he was absent in Basel, where he was the representative of Castile at the COUNCIL OF BASEL. At the Council he made a speech claiming the supremacy of Spain over England (*Sobre la precedencia del rey de Castilla sobre él de Inglaterra en el Concilio de Basilea*), and published a claim that the CANARY ISLANDS belonged to Castile rather than Portugal (a claim eventually ratified in the Treaty of ALCAÇOVAS of 1479).

Cartagena translated Seneca (*Cinco libros de Séneca*, Seville, 1491) and Cicero (*Tullio de Officiis*, Seville, 1501), and wrote works on moral philosophy, education, and lay devotion in both Latin and the vernacular, including an extensive theological treatise (*Defensorium unitatis christianae*, 1450) in defence of Jewish converts to Christianity (like his own family) in the face of a rising tide of anti-Semitism in Spanish society.

Luciano Serrano, *Los conversos Don Pablo de Santa María y Don Alfonso de Cartagena* (1940).

**CARTIER, JACQUES** (1491–1557), French explorer, born in Saint-Malo (Brittany). He became a sea captain, and from 1534 to 1541 undertook three voyages across the North Atlantic in search of a NORTH-WEST PASSAGE to the Pacific. On his second voyage he entered the estuary of the St Lawrence river and sailed upstream to the site of what is now Montréal; he named both the St Lawrence River and Montréal (the latter denoted the mountain; the settlement was later called Ville Marie), and called the whole region 'Canada', a French rendering of the Huron and Iroquois term meaning 'village'. On this voyage he carried Indians back to France, and there persuaded King FRANCIS I to finance a third journey; the gold ore that he brought back on his third voyage turned out to be iron pyrite. Cartier's *Brief Récit de la navigation faite aux isles de Canada* (1545) remained unpublished for centuries.

*DBF*; *The Voyages of Jacques Cartier*, ed. Ramsay Cook (1993).

**CARTOGRAPHY**, the science and craft of drawing maps and charts; on the latter, see CHARTS AND CHART-MAKING. In Babylonian and Greek antiquity the world was thought to be a disc surrounded by a circular river, the Oceanus; from the sixth century BC Greeks such as Pythagoras had concluded that the earth was spherical, but for many centuries the idea of the disc suited European map-makers, who in the Middle Ages continued to represent the world as three continents (EUROPE, ASIA, and AFRICA) surrounded by a circular ocean; the centre of such maps was usually Jerusalem.

The *Mappa mundi* (1457) of Fra MAURO, which is circular, was one of the last world maps to have been designed without reference to PTOLEMY's *Geography*, which had been translated into Latin *c.*1407. The first representation of the earth to show an awareness of Ptolemy was the GLOBE made by Martin BEHAIM in 1492. Columbus' discovery of lands unknown to Europeans meant that cartographers had to represent these new territories (and expanses of ocean) on maps; in 1500 Juan de la COSA became the first person to publish a map of the world that included America. The first cartographer to separate America and Europe with a wide ocean was Martin WALDSEEMÜLLER, whose *Cosmographiae introductio* (1508) contained a twelve-page map of the world showing the new continent, which Waldseemüller called America on the grounds that Amerigo VESPUCCI had discovered it.

More world maps followed in quick succession, including those of Petrus APIANUS (1520), Reinerus GEMMA FRISIUS (1540), Abraham ORTELIUS (1564, a heart-shaped map), and Willem BLAEU (1605), all of which used traditional projections. In 1569 Gerardus MERCATOR had published a world map in eighteen sheets using his new projection, in which parallels of latitude and meridians of longitude cross each other at right angles. This projection had important implications for cartography and NAVIGATION, but both cartographers and navigators were slow to adopt it; the first cartographer to devise maps using Mercator's projection was Jodocus HONDIUS. In the area of provincial maps, the principal innovators were the English cartographers Christopher SAXTON and John SPEED.

**CARTOON or (French)** *carton* **or (Italian)** *cartone*, the art-historical term for a full-size design on paper, drawn in charcoal or chalk for the purpose of transferring the design to an easel painting, a fresco, or a large work such as a MOSAIC or TAPESTRY. The designs of early frescoes were drawn directly onto the walls, but cartoons seem to have been introduced for fresco painting early in the fifteenth century; the idea may have been borrowed from the use of cartoons in the production of STAINED GLASS. Surviving cartoons include LEONARDO's *Virgin and Child with St Anne and St John* (National Gallery, London) and RAPHAEL's designs (Victoria and Albert Museum) for the tapestries depicting *The Lives of SS Peter and Paul* woven for the SISTINE CHAPEL. Sometimes the cartoons were cut out and then used both forwards and backwards: in MICHELANGELO's paintings in the Sistine Chapel, for example, each pair of putti supporting a cornice is a mirror image of another pair.

Tapestry cartoons such as Raphael's *Peter and Paul* series differed from other cartoons in two important respects: they were painted in full colour, and they were drawn in reverse for the benefit of tapestry weavers using low-warp looms; that is why the figures in Raphael's cartoons appear to be left-handed.

Cartoons were normally used for large-scale works, but some finished drawings for small works were used as cartoons. Raphael's small oil painting of *The Vision of a Knight* (c.1504) hangs beside the pen and ink sketch on which it is based (National Gallery, London). Small oil paintings used as cartoons (such as those painted by Rubens) are known in Italian as *cartoncini*.

> Carmen Bambach, *Drawing and Painting in the Italian Renaissance Workshop: Theory and Practice 1300–1600* (1999).

**CARTWRIGHT, THOMAS** (1535–1603), English Puritan. Educated at Cambridge, his career there was interrupted by his expulsion in MARY's reign. He returned to Cambridge under ELIZABETH, and, after two years in Ireland (1565–7), was made Lady Margaret professor of divinity at Cambridge (1569). His criticism of the established Church and his support for Puritanism and presbyterianism led to him being deprived after a year, however. A period of preaching on the Continent and in England followed. In 1590 he was arrested and imprisoned for two years. He played a key role in the preparation for the HAMPTON COURT CONFERENCE, but died before he could represent the Puritan cause there. He remained opposed to the BROWNISTS and BARROWISTS and is remembered as the leading Puritan of his day.

> DNB; A. F. Scott Pearson, *Thomas Cartwright and Elizabethan Puritanism* (1925).

**CARVAJAL, JUAN DE** (c.1399–1469), Spanish cardinal and legate, born in Trujillo (Extremadura) and educated in CANON LAW and CIVIL LAW. In 1440 he was appointed as governor of Rome, and subsequently served as a papal diplomat in Germany, securing the support of the German princes for Pope EUGENIUS in his opposition to the COUNCIL OF BASEL; in 1446 he was created cardinal by his grateful pope. In 1455 he travelled with Giovanni CAPISTRANO to Hungary to preach a crusade against the Ottomans, and he remained in Hungary until 1461; his final legation was to Venice, where in 1466 he again attempted to raise a crusade. Carvajal died in Rome on 6 December 1469. His accounts of his diplomatic missions and his polemical defences of the papacy remained unpublished during his lifetime.

> DBEH; DHE.

**CARVER, ROBERT** (c.1490–c.1546), Scottish monk and composer who became a canon of the Augustine abbey at Scone (c.1511). He appears to have had royal connections, and it is likely that his *Missa 'Dum sacrum mysterium'* was sung at the coronation of the infant JAMES V, after the death of his father at the battle of Flodden (1513). The Carver Choirbook, akin to the ETON CHOIRBOOK, contains music from Scotland, England, and also a piece by DUFAY.

**CASA DA ÍNDIA**, the commission established by the Portuguese government to regulate trade with the Portuguese empire in Asia. Its antecedent institution was the Casa da Guiné e Mina, which had governed trade with West Africa, but the establishment of Portuguese outposts in India and in the Far East led to an extension of its jurisdiction. Like the Spanish CASA DE CONTRATACIÓN, the Casa da Índia was responsible for the inspection of the merchant fleet and for

crown monopolies such as the slave trade; it also collected taxes from subjugated peoples of the empire.

**CASA DE CONTRATACIÓN DE LAS INDIAS**, a commission established by Juan Rodríguez de Fonseca to regulate Spanish trade with the Americas; the commission met in Seville from 1503 to 1718. The responsibilities of the Casa included the inspection of ships and the collection of taxes, including the 20 per cent tax on precious metals mined in America. The Casa also functioned as a law court which dealt with commercial disputes.

> DHE; H. and P. Chaunu, *Séville et l'Atlantique* (8 vols., 1955).

**CASAUBON, ISAAC** (1559–1614), French humanist, born into a Huguenot family in Geneva and raised at Crest (Dauphiné). In 1578 he returned to Geneva, where he became professor of Greek (1581–96); in 1586 he married the daughter of Henri ESTIENNE. In 1596 Casaubon moved to Montpellier and in 1599, at the invitation of HENRI IV, to Paris, where he worked in the royal library. After the assassination of King Henri in 1610, Casaubon moved to England, where he secured the patronage of King James I and remained for the rest of his life. Casaubon's scholarly works include editions of Suetonius, Theophrastus, and Polybius and of the collected works of Aristotle; he also wrote commentaries on Athenaeus, Persius, and Strabo. Casaubon was the first scholar to date correctly the collection of treatises known as the *Corpus Hermeticum* (see HERMETICISM). He is the original of George Eliot's pedantic Mr Casaubon in *Middlemarch*.

> DBF; DNB.

**CASCINA, BATTLE OF.** On 28 July 1364 a Florentine army defeated the forces of Pisa at Cascina, a small town on the Arno near Pisa. Some of the Pisan soldiers were the victims of a surprise attack while they were bathing in the river. This battle subsequently became the subject of a BATTLEPIECE fresco commissioned from MICHELANGELO and LEONARDO DA VINCI by the Signoria of Florence for the Council Chamber in the Palazzo Vecchio. MICHELANGELO embarked on the full-sized cartoon in the winter of 1504 and worked intermittently on the fresco until 1506. The project was never completed, but is known from a copy by Bastiano da Sangallo of the portion of the cartoon which depicted the attack on the bathers (now in the collection of the earl of Leicester in Holkham Hall, Norfolk), by an engraving, and by drawings by Michelangelo now scattered in various collections. In sixteenth-century Florence the cartoon influenced a generation of artists (including RAPHAEL) and became the model for mannerist depictions of the male nude engaged in violent action.

> C. Gould, *Michelangelo's Battle of Cascina* (1966).

**CASIMIR IV JAGIEŁŁO** (1427–92), king of Poland, was the son of VLADISLAV II. He succeeded his brother VLADISLAV III in 1446 and ruled Poland for the next 46 years, during which time he preserved the fragile Polish–Lithuanian union and fought the TEUTONIC knights in a protracted war (1453–66) which ended with the knights recognizing Casimir as their sovereign and so giving Poland access to the Baltic. In domestic politics, Casimir promoted the privileges of the SZLACHTA at the expense of the landed aristocracy.

In the wake of the death of GEORGE OF PODĚBRADY in 1471, Casimir disputed the succession to the crown of Bohemia with MATTHIAS CORVINUS; in 1478 he succeeded in securing Bohemia for his son LADISLAS II, who in 1490 also gained the crown of Hungary.

*PSB* s.v. Kazimierz, Andrzej Jagiełłończyk.

**CASINO** (plural *casini*). In Italian VILLAS, a *casino* is either a term for the main house, if it is small by comparison with the scale of the gardens, or for a secondary house or PAVILION in the grounds of a grand house. There are *casini* at Villa LANTE (where there is no large house), the MEDICI VILLA at Castello, and in the *GIARDINO SEGRETO* of the FARNESE PALACE. See also MONDRAGONE, VILLA; PIA, VILLA; GAILLON.

**CASOLA, PIETRO** (1427–1507), Milanese pilgrim, who travelled to Palestine in 1494. His account of the pilgrimage, first published in Milan in 1885 under the title *Viaggio a Gerusalemme verso la fine del 1400*, not only describes the holy sites, but also contains a detailed description of Venice, which was the usual point of embarkation for pilgrimages.

*DBI*; Margaret Newett, *Canon Pietro Casola's Pilgrimage to Jerusalem* (1907).

**CASSANDER, GEORG** (1515/18–1556), Flemish Catholic theologian, born at Pitthem (near Bruges) and educated in Louvain. He subsequently taught at Bruges, Ghent, and (from *c*.1549) Cologne. He was by temperament and principle eirenic, and attempted to reconcile Catholic and Protestant opinion; the concessions to Protestantism that he advocated included communion in both kinds (in *De sacra communione christiani populi in utraque panis et vini specie*, 1564) and a married clergy. His principal theological work, *De officio pii ac publicae tranquillitatis vere amantis viri in hoc religionis dissidio* (published anonymously in Basel in 1561), argued from the precedent of the early Church that clerical abuse did not justify separation from the Church; the treatise was submitted to the Colloquy of POISSY, where it was denounced by both Catholics and Protestants. In 1564, at the behest of the Emperor FERDINAND I, Cassander attempted a sympathetic Catholic interpretation of Protestant doctine in his *Consultatio de articulis religionis inter catholicos et protestantes controversis* (published 1577), and was again denounced by both sides. His tolerance of Protestantism did not extend to the ANABAPTISTS, against whose doctrine he wrote *De baptismo infantium* (1563).

*BNB* s.v. Cassander, Georges; *NDB*.

**CASSONE** (plural *cassoni*), a large Italian chest, often a dower chest, manufactured in Italy in the fifteenth and sixteenth centuries and used principally to hold clothing. A *cassone* could be built from planks which were then covered with friezes executed in GESSO and then painted; alternatively, it could be made from wooden panels and then painted. The subjects of *cassone* paintings include mythological and religious scenes, battles, and tournaments. In the sixteenth century painted *cassoni* were displaced by a new fashion for carved decoration, usually on thick walnut and typically depicting a mythological scene.

P. Schubring, *Cassoni: Truhen und Truhenbilder der italienischen Frührenaissance* (1923); Cristelle Baskins, *Cassone Painting, Humanism and Gender in Early Modern Italy* (1998).

**CASTAGNO, ANDREA DEL.** See ANDREA DEL CASTAGNO.

**CASTANHEDA, FERNÃO LOPES DE** (d. 1559), Portuguese historian, the illegitimate son of a royal administrator. In 1528 he accompanied his father to India, and for the next ten years worked in Goa and the Spice Islands (now Moluccas). In 1538 he returned to Portugal and began to assemble materials for a huge account of the Portuguese conquest of India and the Indies. The ten volumes of his *História do descobrimento e conquista da Índia pelos Portugueses*, of which the last three were published posthumously, were based on the documentary record and on oral sources. Selections from the *História* were soon translated into major European languages (including Italian 1577, French 1581, and English 1582), and the treatise became established as the authoritative account of its subject.

*DHP*; Ana Paula Menino, *Fernão Lopes de Castanheda: Historiador dos portugueses na Índia ou cronista do governo de Nuno da Cunha?* (1997).

**CASTEL DURANTE**, a small town near Urbino which was renamed Urbania (in honour of Pope Urban VIII) in 1636. Castel Durante was an important centre for MAIOLICA, and in the sixteenth century developed with the potters of Urbino the display pottery known as ISTORIATO ware.

**CASTELLESI or Corneto, ADRIANO** (*c*.1461–*c*.1521), cardinal, born in Corneto (now Tarquínia). In 1488 he was appointed nuncio to Scotland by Pope INNOCENT VIII with a view to reconciling James III of Scotland to his people. Adriano's mission was unsuccessful (King James was murdered), and he moved to England, where he was appointed collector of Peter's Pence in 1489, prebend of St Paul's Cathedral, and rector of St Dunstan in the East in 1492. He returned to Rome as English ambassador, and there was appointed clerk to the papal treasury; while absent from England he was appointed bishop of Hereford (1502) and bishop of Bath and Wells (1504), but he never lived in either diocese. He bought a vineyard in the Borgo near the Vatican and commissioned a large palace there (now the Palazzo Giraud-Torlonia). He was created cardinal on 31 May 1503 in return for a large bribe to Pope ALEXANDER VI. Shortly after his elevation Cardinal Adriano entertained the pope and his son Cesare BORGIA at his *palazzo*; Adriano and his two guests all fell ill, and Pope Alexander died. Adriano deemed it prudent to withdraw from Rome because of widespread suspicion that he had poisoned the pope and his son; he returned on the election of Pope LEO X in 1511. He was implicated in the plot to murder Pope Leo in 1517, but a payment of 25,000 ducats enabled him to avoid being executed. He was stripped of his ecclesiastical offices and fled to Venice. His subsequent history is unclear, but he may have been murdered by a servant while travelling to Rome after the death of Pope Leo in December 1521.

Cardinal Adriano was one of the earliest writers of revived Ciceronian Latin. His publications include *De vera philosophia ex quatuor doctoribus ecclesiae* (Bologna, 1507), *De sermone Latino* (Basel, 1513), and a poem, *De Venatione* (Venice, 1534).

DBI s.v. Castellesi; DNB s.v. Adrian.

**CASTELLIO, SEBASTIANO, or (French) Sébastien Châteillon or (pseudonym) Martinus Bellius** (1515–63), Savoyard humanist reformer and translator, born in Saint-Martin-du-Fresne, near Geneva (in territory that belonged to the duchy of Savoy), and educated in Lyon; he converted to Protestantism and in 1540 moved to Strasbourg, where he studied under Jean CALVIN. When Calvin returned to Geneva the following year, he arranged for Castellio to be appointed rector of the Collège de Genève. He resigned because of failing health in 1544, but during his short tenure of the rectorship wrote his *Dialogi sacri* (dated 1543 but published 1542), a manual of biblical dialogues that enjoyed a wide readership for two centuries.

Castellio was an independent thinker, and his refusal to accept the canonicity of the Song of Solomon together with his heterodox view of Christ's descent into HELL led to a rift with Calvin, and Castellio was forced to leave Geneva in 1545. He settled in Basel, working as a proofreader for eight years and then accepting the chair of Greek at the university. In 1551 he published a translation of the Bible into Ciceronian Latin, and four years later he produced a French translation. This controversial edition, which was dedicated to King Edward VI of England, defended the freedom of the human will (in a note on Romans 9: 13) and advocated freedom of worship; the former was an affront to Calvin's theology of GRACE and the latter an assault on the rigorous church discipline of Geneva.

In 1554 one 'Martinus Bellius' published *De haereticus an sint persequendi* in Latin and in a French translation; this book roundly condemned the burning of SERVETUS in Geneva and advocated religious toleration. Castellio was the driving force behind this volume; he was certainly the principal author, and may have been the sole author. His most eloquent plea for religious toleration is contained in *Conseil à la France désolée* (1562), which was written in the wake of the massacre of Wassy, one of the most brutal acts of the WARS OF RELIGION. Castellio's humanist interests are most apparent in his Latin translations of ancient Greek authors, including Homer and Xenophon.

S. Zweig, *The Right to Heresy: Castellio against Calvin* (1936); Hans Guggisberg, *Sebastian Castellio 1515–1563: Humanist und Verteidiger der religiösen Toleranz im konfessionellen Zeitalter* (1997).

**CASTELLO, GIAMBATTISTA, or Il Bergamasco** (*c.*1509–1569), Italian painter and architect who worked as a painter in Genoa before turning to architecture. His Gothic palaces and churches in Genoa include the Church of San Matteo (1554). He also built palaces, including the Palazzo Podestà in the Strada Nuova (*c.*1563–1565) and the Palazzo Vincenzo Imper-

iale in Campetto (*c.*1560–1566). In 1567 he moved to Spain to enter the service of PHILIP II, but died before completing any substantial work.

DBI s.v. Castello, Giovanni Battista; MDA.

**CASTELNAU, MICHEL DE, SIEUR DE LA MAUVISSIÈRE** (1520–91), French soldier and diplomat. He was born into a noble family in Touraine and as a young man fought in the WARS OF ITALY. He became a diplomat, in which capacity he negotiated an agreement with Queen ELIZABETH in which England acknowledged the right of France to occupy CALAIS for eight years; the terms of the agreement were incorporated into the Treaty of CATEAU-CAMBRÉSIS (1559). He attempted to reconcile Elizabeth to MARY, QUEEN OF SCOTS, but was unsuccessful. In 1562 he returned to France, where he reverted to his earlier military vocation, and fought on the Catholic side in the early phases of the WARS OF RELIGION; during this period he also travelled on diplomatic embassies to the Netherlands, Savoy, and Rome. In 1574 he returned to England on an embassy that was to last for ten years; for much of this period he was occupied with an attempt to secure a French husband for the queen. In the last years of his life he became a military commander in the service of King HENRI IV. His *Memoires* of 1559–70 were published in 1621.

Gustave Hubault, *Michel de Castelnau ambassadeur en Angleterre* (1856).

**CASTELVETRO, LUDOVICO** (1506–71), Italian scholar, philologist, literary theorist, and polemicist, born in Modena, where he lived for most of his life. In 1560 he was accused of Lutheran sympathies by Annibale CARO and condemned for doctrinal error by the Roman INQUISITION, and he fled to the Swiss Confederation and then to France; he died in self-imposed exile in Chiavenna, north of Lake Como.

Castelvetro's principal works were his commentaries on Aristotle's *Poetics* (1570), Petrarch's *Rime* (1582), and the first 29 cantos of Dante's *Inferno* (unknown until its discovery in the nineteenth century). He also wrote a supplement to BEMBO's *Prose* (*Giunta fatta al Ragionamento di Pietro Bembo*, 1563) in which he discussed the historical development of Italian, and published a set of corrective responses to Benedetto VARCHI's *L'Ercolano* (1572). His commentary on Aristotle's *Poetics* contains the earliest statement of the dramatic unities that Castelvetro thought implicit in Aristotle's text; these unities, which are largely Castelvetro's invention, are now popularly attributed to Aristotle.

DBI; OCIL; B. Weinberg, *A History of Literary Criticism in the Italian Renaissance* (2 vols., 1961); G. Norton (ed.), *The Cambridge History of Literary Criticism*, iii: *The Renaissance* (1999).

**CASTIGLIONE, BALDASSARE** (1478–1529), Italian courtier, diplomat, and writer, born in Casàtico to a land-owning family that served the rulers of nearby Mantua as soldiers and administrators. In 1496 Castiglione entered the service of Ludovico SFORZA in Milan. He left Milan after Ludovico's defeat and capture at the battle of Novara in 1500, and entered the service of Gianfrancesco II GONZAGA in Mantua. In 1504 he moved to Urbino, where he became a diplomat at the courts of Guidobaldo I MONTEFELTRO and (from 1508) Francesco Maria I DELLA ROVERE. In 1513 he moved to Rome, where he represented the interests of the duke of Urbino in the papal court, and in 1516 he returned to Mantua, where he worked in the service of Gianfrancesco II Gonzaga and (from 1519) Federico II GONZAGA, latterly as Mantuan ambassador to Rome. In 1524, by which time his wife had died, Castiglione was ordained and sent to Spain by Pope CLEMENT VII as his papal nuncio. Castiglione died in Toledo five years later. His portrait by RAPHAEL now hangs in the Louvre.

Castiglione wrote poetry in both Latin and Italian, but his principal literary work was the dialogue-treatise *Il cortegiano* ('The Courtier'; Castigliane's Lombard spelling is sometimes Tuscanized as *cortigiano*), which is set in the court of Urbino in 1506; he completed a draft while still in Urbino, but continued to revise his manuscript until its publication in Venice in 1528. In *Il cortegiano* Castiglione sketched a portrait of the ideal courtier, one whose accomplishments in literature, music, sport, conversation, and the art of war should be presented modestly, in accordance with the ideal of SPREZZATURA. The graceful deportment and modesty of an ideal courtier would, in Castiglione's view, render him acceptable as an adviser to princes, a role particularly timely in the tumult of the WARS OF ITALY. Book 3 is a pioneering portrait of the lady at court, presented as the moral and intellectual equal of the courtier.

*Il cortegiano* was widely read throughout Europe, both in Italian and in translations into Latin, English, French, and Spanish. Castiglione's idealized Urbino court became a model for courtly behaviour all over Europe, and its precepts were absorbed into the burgeoning literature of etiquette.

*DBI*; J. R. Woodhouse, *Baldesar Castiglione: A Reassessment of 'The Courtier'* (1978); Peter Burke, *Fortunes of the Courtier: The European Reception of Castiglione's 'Courtier'* (1995).

**CASTILLEJO, CRISTÓBAL DE** (c.1491–1550), Spanish poet and satirist, born in Ciudad Rodrigo; he became a page to the future Emperor FERDINAND I and subsequently joined the Cistercian ORDER. After several years as a monk Castillejo moved to Vienna to rejoin the service of Ferdinand, who in 1521 had been entrusted by his brother CHARLES V with the governance of the Habsburg possessions in the East; in Vienna he wrote an *Historia de Píramo y Tisbe*. In 1539 he moved to Venice to enter the household of the Spanish ambassador (and poet) Diego HURTADO DE MENDOZA, but later returned to Vienna, where he died.

In his poems and his writings on poetry Castillejo resisted the fashion for Italianate poetry in favour of traditional Spanish forms, mocking Italianate poets (especially BOSCÀ and GARCILASO) in his *Contra los que dejan los metros castellanos y siguen los italianos* (c.1540). In his poetry Castillejo used a traditional octosyllabic line, often in *quintillas* (five-line stanzas) or the 'broken foot stanzas' (*coplas de pie quebrado*) popularized by Jorge MANRIQUE, and favoured traditional Spanish forms, such as the ballad and *villancicos* (a popular genre consisting of a song with a refrain, used for Christmas carols and other folk songs).

Castillejo's works include satires on courtly deportment (*Diálogo y discurso de la vida del corte*) and sexual morality (*Aula de courtesanos*), a treatise on flattery and compliment (*Diálogo entre la verdad y la lisonja*), a satire on women (*Diálogo de mujeres*), and a satirical dialogue between the author and his pen (*Diálogo entre el autor y su pluma*).

*DBEH*; C. J. Nicolay, *The Life and Works of Cristobal de Castillejo* (1910).

**CASTILLO, FERNANDO DEL** (*fl.* 1510), Spanish anthologist who compiled the *Cancionero general de muchas y diversas obras de todos los mas principales trovadores de España en lengua castellana* (Valencia, 1511), which was to become the most important collection of courtly fifteenth- and early sixteenth-century Spanish poetry before the irruption of Italianate metres introduced by GARCILASO DE LA VEGA. The first edition contains 1,033 poems by 128 named and many unnamed poets; subsequent editions printed in Toledo (1520), Valencia (1540), Zaragoza (1554), and Antwerp (1557) contained slightly different selections. The anthology summed up the course of Spanish poetry in the century preceding its publication, and had an important influence on court taste in music and literary fashion throughout the HABSBURG Empire in the Renaissance.

**CASTRO, ANTONIO DE** (*fl.* 1565), Portuguese silversmith and goldsmith in Genoa, known principally for a magnificent silver ewer and basin (1565) decorated with fifteen scenes depicting a fourteenth-century private war. The ewer and basin are now in the Palazzo Cini (formerly Grassi) in Venice.

**CASTRO Y BELLVÍS, GUILLÉN DE** (1569–1631), Spanish playwright, a founder member of the Academia de los Nocturnos, a literary academy active in Valencia in the early 1590s. His plays include three adaptations of CERVANTES: *Don Quijote de la Mancha* (a dramatization of the story of Cardenio and Lucinda), *El curioso impertinente*, and *La fuerza de la sangre*. His *comedias de capa y espada* ('cloak-and-sword plays') include *Los mal casados de Valencia* and *El Narciso en su opinión* (of which the protagonist, Don Gutierre, is a self-absorbed fop). He also wrote historical and exemplary plays (*Pagar en propria moneda*, *La humildad soberbia*, and *La justicia en la piedad*), domestic tragedy (*El amor constante*, which contains an apology for tyrannicide), mythological plays (*Progne y Filomena* and *Los amores de Dido y Eneas*) and dramatic adaptations of the ballad tradition known as the *Romancero*, notably the two-part *Las mocedades del Cid* (which later formed the basis of Corneille's *Le Cid*), *El conde de Irlos*, and *El conde Alarcos*.

William Wilson, *Guillén de Castro* (1973); James Crapotta, *Kingship and Tyranny in the Theater of Guillén de Castro* (1984); Luciano García Lorenzo, *El teatro de Guillén de Castro* (1976).

**CATALAN LANGUAGE.** Catalan is a Romance language that now has 11 million speakers, the largest language group in Europe not to occupy its own country. It is the principal language of Catalonia (Catalunya), which has since 1833 been divided into the four provinces of Barcelona, Girona, Lleida

(Castilian Lérida), and Tarragona, and is also spoken in the provinces of Castelló, València, Alacant (Castilian Alicante), and the Balearic Islands. To the north of Spain, Catalan is also the official language of Andorra. It is closely related to the *langue d'oc* (see OCCITAN LANGUAGE AND LITERATURE) of the old Catalan provinces (now French regions) of Roussillon and Cerdagne. This congruence has led some linguists to describe Catalan as a Gallo-Romance language, but others, including those eager to emphasize Catalonia's cultural links with the rest of Spain, insist that it is more accurately described as Ibero-Romance.

In early modern Europe, Catalan was spoken in an even wider area, because, as the official language of the chanceries of the crown of Aragon, it became the cultural medium of the viceregal courts in Sardinia (where it survived into the twentieth century in the district of Alghero), Corsica, Naples, and Sicily. Written Catalan was standardized in the Barcelona chancery in the fourteenth century, but the Valencian variety became equally important in the fifteenth; the two dialects remain distinct, with many regional variations, and this has led to debates on the unity of the language with important political dimensions in modern times.

A. M. Badia y Margarit, *Gramática histórica catalana* (1951).

## CATALAN LITERATURE.

Until the second half of the thirteenth century, the literary language of Catalan troubadours was OCCITAN. The first major writer to use Catalan was Ramon Llull, the only figure in Catalan literature read widely beyond the confines of Spain in the Middle Ages. Llull wrote in a Catalan prose still heavily coloured by Occitan; the fact that Llull also worked in Latin and Arabic is a useful reminder that Catalan was not the only literary language of Catalonia.

The fifteenth century represents the high-water mark of poetry in Catalan, which was typically written in the hendecasyllabic line used in Provençal literature. The most prominent poet was in fact a Valencian, Ausiàs March (c.1397–1459), one of the greatest European poets of the age. His poems, of which 128 survive, are Provençal in genre and form, but resolutely Valencian in language, which strips away the courtly associations of the Provençal tradition. He also drew substantially on the poetry of DANTE and PETRARCH. Many of his love poems are addressed to married women, one of whom he praises for her liveliness of mind (under the poetic pseudonym or *senhal* of Plena de seny) and the other (though she may be the same person) for a beauty that makes her a lily among thorns (*Llir entre cards*) but for whom he harbours a sensual desire that he feels will lead him to hell. His finest religious poem is the *Cant espiritual*, a monologue in which the poet confesses that his love is surpassed by his fear of God. A selection of March's poems was published in a bilingual Catalan–Spanish edition in Valencia in 1539; the first collected edition was published in Barcelona in 1543. The first Renaissance poet in Catalan literature was Joan BOSCÀ; the fact that he chose to write in Spanish rather than Catalan signalled the triumph of Castilian and the end of courtly Catalan poetry until the twentieth century.

Apart from Llull's mystical works, medieval Catalan prose reached its first flowering in an outstanding series of chronicles; this tradition was continued in the fifteenth century, though at a much inferior level, by the *Feyts d'armes de Catalunya* of Bernat Boades, which chronicles military history to 1420, and Pere Tomich's *Històries e conquestes del reialme d'Aragó* (1448). Cultural leadership had by this time passed to Valencia, where, besides the poetry of Ausiàs March, prose was represented by the remarkable romance of chivalry *Tirant lo blanc*, most of which was written by Joanot Martorell, the brother-in-law of Ausiàs March. After Martorell's death in 1470, the work was completed by Martí Joan de Galba, though the extent of his contribution is uncertain; *Tirant lo blanc* was first printed in Catalan (Valencia, 1490) and then in Castilian (Valladolid, 1511), in which form it influenced CERVANTES.

The union of Aragon and Castile in 1469 began the process whereby Catalan was reduced to a culturally peripheral language, a process exacerbated by the adoption of Castilian as an everyday language by the upper classes in Valencia. The sixteenth century produced few poets of note, the best known of which is Pere Serafí, whose poems were printed in Barcelona in 1547. With a few isolated exceptions, Catalan ceased to be a literary language until the *Renaixença* of the nineteenth century was inaugurated by the publication in 1814 of the first systematic modern grammar of Catalan, the *Gramàtica y apologia de la llengua Cathalana* of Joseph Pau Ballot y Torres.

M. de Riquer, A. Comas, and J. Molas, *Història de la literatura catalana* (11 vols., 1984–8); Arthur Terry, *Catalan Literature* (1972).

## CATEAU-CAMBRÉSIS, TREATY OF

(2–3 April 1559), the set of treaties between England, France, and Spain that concluded the WARS OF ITALY, which had begun in 1494. Under the terms of the treaties England recognized the French conquest of Calais for eight years, France returned Piedmont-Savoy to Duke EMANUELE FILIBERTO and recognized the Spanish claim to Franche-Comté, Milan, Naples, Sardinia, and Sicily, Spain renounced its claim to Burgundy, and Florence gained Siena and its territories. France agreed not to intervene in Scotland with respect to the claim of MARY, QUEEN OF SCOTS (who was married to the dauphin) to the English throne. The provisions of the treaty also include the marriage of PHILIP II of Spain to Elizabeth of Valois, the daughter of HENRI II of France.

England later renewed its claim to Calais (1562–4), but in other respects the treaty proved to be binding.

Alphonse, Baron de Ruble, *Le Traité de Cateau-Cambrésis* (1889).

## CATECHISMS.

The term 'catechism' was originally used to describe the oral instruction that preceded baptism, but the term later came to be used to describe popular manuals of Christian doctrine. Pre-Reformation catechisms, such as GERSON's *ABC des simples gens* and the German *Christenspiegel*, tended to be gently expository, but with the Reformation catechisms acquired a confessional edge. LUTHER's *Kleiner Katechismus* of 1529 was the first of the new, combative catechisms, and it remains the standard Lutheran manual. In Calvinist communions, the comparable catechism is the *Heidelberger Katechismus* of 1563. In England, the catechism was incorporated into the Book of Common Prayer, and from 1549 to 1662 it was printed as a preliminary to the rite of confirmation rather than as a separate item.

The Catholic response to the advent of Protestant catechisms was a new generation of Catholic catechisms, of which the most important was the *Summa doctrinae christianae* published by Petrus CANISIUS in 1554 and (in a shorter version) 1556. The 'Roman Catechism' produced by Pope PIUS V (*Catechismus ex decreto Concilii Tridentini*, 1566) was intended for priests rather than for laity.

**CATENA, VINCENZO** (*c.*1470/80–1531), Italian painter born into a patrician family in Venice and apparently trained in the studio of GIORGIONE. His best-known paintings, typical of the Venetian School in their soft colours and suffused light, are the *Martyrdom of S Christina* (1520, Santa Maria Mater Domini, Venice) and the *Holy Family with a Kneeling Warrior* (National Gallery, London).

*DBI; MDA.*

**CATHERINE OF ARAGON** (1485–1536), first wife of HENRY VIII, and queen of England. Daughter of Ferdinand and Isabella of Spain, Catherine came to England in 1501 as a wife for Prince Arthur, eldest son of HENRY VII. He died five months after the marriage, and in 1509 Catherine married his brother, HENRY VIII, on his succession to the throne. An initially happy marriage, marked by the birth of MARY in 1516, later soured as the looked-for male heir was not forthcoming. Henry cited the biblical injunction not to marry one's brother's wife as a reason to separate and seek an annulment; Catherine's assertion that her marriage to Arthur had not been consummated failed to prevent her downfall. From 1531, she lived in seclusion, deprived of her title and separated from her daughter; on her death she was buried in Peterborough Cathedral.

*DNB.*

**CATHERINE OF GENOA or Caterina Fieschi Adorno** (1447–1510), Italian mystic. She was born into a noble Ligurian family in Fieschi and at the age of 16 married Giuliano Ligurio. Ten years later she experienced a religious conversion, and eventually her husband experienced a similar conversion; Giuliano became a Franciscan tertiary, but Catherine did not join a religious order. Her principal activity was her care for the sick in the Genoese hospital of Pammatone. The principal account of her visions and spiritual doctrine is contained in the book published in 1551 as her *Vita e dottrina*, but her role in the composition of the book is unclear.

Catherine was beatified in 1737 and canonized shortly thereafter; in 1944 she was proclaimed by Pius XII as patroness of Italian hospitals.

*DBI s.v. Caterina Fieschi Adorno; HWWI;* L. Scaraffia and G. Zarri, *Women and Faith: Catholic Religious Life in Italy from Late Antiquity to the Present* (1999).

**CATHERINE HOWARD** (1522–42), fifth wife of HENRY VIII, and queen of England. Niece of the duke of Norfolk, Catherine married Henry in 1540, weeks after the annulment of his marriage to ANNE OF CLEVES. By the end of the following year, rumours of her adultery with Thomas Culpepper, and of an earlier relationship with Francis Dereham, were circulating; she was imprisoned and beheaded in February 1542.

*DNB.*

**CATHERINE DE MÉDICIS or (Italian) Caterina de' Medici** (1519–89), queen of France, was born on 13 April 1519 in Florence, the daughter of Lorenzo de' Medici, duke of Urbino, and Madeleine de la Tour d'Auvergne. She was orphaned at an early age and in October 1533 married the future HENRI II of France as part of an arrangement between Pope CLEMENT VII and King FRANCIS I. She had five sons and five daughters by King Henri, and on his death on 10 July 1559 their eldest son assumed the throne as King FRANCIS II. When Francis died on 5 December 1560, he was succeeded by Catherine's second son CHARLES IX, who was then 10 years old, and Catherine became regent of France.

Catherine sought to dispel the rising tensions between Catholic and Protestant factions by sponsoring the Colloquy of POISSY (September–October 1561) and issuing the January Edict (January 1562), which allowed HUGUENOTS to worship freely outside towns and in private houses within towns. The first of the eight WARS OF RELIGION broke out in April 1562, and was concluded on 19 March 1563 when Catherine made further concessions to the Huguenots in the Treaty of Amboise. In June 1565 she met her daughter Queen Elizabeth of Spain together with PHILIP II's minister, the duque de ALBA; Huguenot fears that these talks were a prelude to a suppression of Protestantism by Spanish troops led to the second War of Religion (September 1567–March 1568).

Catherine lost sympathy with the Protestants, and may have ordered the assassination of COLIGNY in 1572. It was his murder that inaugurated the ST BARTHOLOMEW'S DAY MASSACRE (23–4 August 1572). Thereafter Catherine was detested by the Huguenots and the positions of authority within her court passed to the Guises. Catherine's ambitions then became focused on her family. She arranged for her son Henri to be elected king of Poland, and on the death of her son Charles IX on 30 May 1574 ensured that Henri was able to return from Poland to claim his throne (as HENRI III). King Henri remained under his mother's control until 1588, when he asserted his independence by dismissing the ministers that she had appointed. Catherine died of pneumonia at Blois on 5 January 1589.

*DBF; MDA s.v. Valois* (16); Paul Van Dyke, *Catherine de Medici* (2 vols., 1927); Ivan Cloulas, *Catherine de Médicis* (1979); R. J. Knecht, *Catherine de' Medici* (1998).

**CATHERINE PARR** (1512–48), sixth wife of HENRY VIII and queen of England. On her marriage to Henry she was 32 years old and twice widowed. She acted as regent during Henry's absence in France in 1544, and concerned herself with the education of both ELIZABETH and MARY. She was the author of a number of reformist religious texts, including *The Lamentation of a Sinner*. Following Henry's death in 1547, she remarried but died after giving birth to a daughter.

*DNB.*

## CATHERINE DE' RICCI or Alessandra Lucrezia Romola

(1522–90), Italian mystic, a native of Florence who in 1535 entered the Dominican convent in Prato, which was closely associated with the reform programme of SAVONAROLA; from 1552 until her death she alternated as prior and sub-prior of this convent. Her mystical raptures and reputation for sanctity attracted many visitors to the convent, some of whom became her 'spiritual children'. Her correspondents included Cardinal Carlo BORROMEO and Filippo NERI.

Catherine de' Ricci was beatified in 1732 and canonized in 1746.

*DBI s.v. Caterina Ricci; L. Scaraffia and G. Zarri, Women and Faith: Catholic Religious Life in Italy from Late Antiquity to the Present (1999).*

## CATHERINE OF SIENA or Caterina Benincasa (1347–80),

Italian mystic, born in Siena, the twenty-third of 25 children born to a dyer. She entered the Dominican order of penance (later known as the Dominican third or tertiary order), and after several years of seclusion began to travel widely in Italy, always accompanied by a band of disciples. She mediated in local conflicts, and acted as an intermediary between Florence and Pope Gregory XI; in 1375 she received the stigmata. Her teaching is articulated in her *Dialogo* and in her 383 surviving letters, the first collection of letters written in Italian, published by ALDUS MANUTIUS in 1500. It heralded a great century of letters and letter collections.

Catherine of Siena was canonized in 1461 and declared a doctor of the Church in 1970.

*DBI s.v. Caterina da Siena; HWWI; I, Catherine: Selected Writings of Catherine of Siena, ed. K. Foster and M. J. Ronayne (1980).*

## CATHOLIC LEAGUE or the League or (French) La Ligue or La Sainte Union

(1576–95), a political and military force representing the Catholic party in France during the central years of the WARS OF RELIGION; individual members of the League were known as Ligueurs. The League was led by Duke Henri de GUISE, and in the first instance was formed to resist the Peace of Monsieur, which had extended a measure of religious freedom to Protestants.

In December 1584 the League was reformed with an altogether more serious purpose. The death on 10 June 1584 of the duke of ANJOU, the younger brother and heir of King HENRI III, left the Protestant Henry of Navarre (later King HENRI IV) as heir presumptive. The renewed League resolved to prevent the French throne from falling into the hands of a heretic, and the next year secured the formal support King PHILIP II of Spain.

King Henri III supported the League of 1576, but was an opponent of the League of 1584, and ordered the murder of the duke of Guise at Blois on 23 December 1588. Seven months later, on 31 July 1589, King Henri III was assassinated,

and the League refused to recognize Henri IV as his successor, instead declaring cardinal de Bourbon to be King Charles X. Thereafter the military victories of Henri IV, together with his diplomatic successes in winning the support of moderate Catholics, sapped the strength of the League. When King Henri reverted to Catholicism (July 1593) and entered Paris (March 1594), the League began to dissolve, and by the time he received absolution from Pope CLEMENT VIII (September 1595) it had disappeared.

In 1594 a group of writers (including Pierre PITHOU and Nicolas RAPIN) published *La Vertu du Catholicon d'Espagne* (later known as *La Satire Ménippée*), in which two charlatans, a Spaniard and a Ligueur, attempt to sell their intolerant religion as a cure for all evils. The disparagement of the League, partly on the grounds of its alliance with a foreign power (which was deemed to be unpatriotic) but also because of a distaste for religious fanaticism, continued for centuries, notably in Voltaire's epic *La Ligue* (1723, republished as *La Henriade* in 1728).

*Élie Barnavi, Le Parti de Dieu (1980); F. J. Baumgartner, Radical Reactionaries: The Political Thought of the French Catholic League (1976); J. M. Constant, La Ligue (1996); Ann Ramsay, Liturgy, Politics, and Salvation: The Catholic League in Paris and the Nature of Catholic Reform, 1540–1630 (1999).*

## CATTANEO, DANESE

(c.1509–72), Italian architectural sculptor and epic poet, trained in the Roman studio of Jacopo SANSOVINO, whom he accompanied to Venice, where he spent the rest of his life, working for many years as a sculptor on Sansovino's buildings. His literary works include a romance, *L'amor di Marfisa* (Venice, 1562).

*DBI; MDA.*

## CAURROY, FRANÇOIS EUSTACHE DE

(1549–1609), French composer and singer in the Royal Chapel of Charles IX. His *Missa pro defunctis* became an official requiem for the funerals of French kings, having been first performed after the death of HENRI IV. He was influenced by JOSQUIN, WILLAERT, and ZARLINO and most of his music was published posthumously.

## CAUS or Caux, SALOMON DE

(1576–1626), Huguenot engineer and architect. Caus was a native of Normandy who, as a young man, had lived in Italy; during this period (1595–8) he studied the design and waterworks of PRATOLINO. In 1605 he was employed as an engineer in Brussels by Archduke Albrecht. In 1610 he was brought to the English court as mathematics tutor to Henry, prince of Wales, advising him on the construction of waterworks at Richmond; his treatise on *La Perspective, avec les raisons des ombres et miroirs* (1612) is dedicated to Henry. Caus also worked for the queen, Anne of Denmark, at Somerset House and Greenwich, and for Robert Cecil at HATFIELD HOUSE. On the marriage in 1613 of Princess Elizabeth to Friedrich V, the elector palatine, Caus moved with her court to Heidelberg, where he laid out the castle gardens known as the HORTUS PALATINUS. In 1623 Caus left the service of the elector and returned to France. His *Raisons des forces mouvantes* (1615) explains the hydraulic principles on which garden waterworks were built and illustrates AUTOMATA built for GROTTOES; it also adumbrates the technology of the steam-engine.

*DBF s.v. 2. Caus; NDNB s.v. De Caus; MDA; Christina Maks, Salomon de Caus, 1576–1626 (1935); Roy Strong, The Renaissance Garden in England (1979).*

**CAUSTON or Cawston, THOMAS** (*c.*1520/5–1569), English composer, arranger, and church musician who became a gentleman of the Chapel Royal (*c.*1563/4). His syllabic, homophonic settings of the words from the Book of COMMON PRAYER demonstrate his sympathy with Protestant reform.

**CAVALIERI, EMILIO DE'** (*c.*1550–1602), Italian composer, whose career started in Rome. By 1588 he was in Florence where he supervised the *intermedi* for the wedding of Ferdinando de' Medici and Christine of Lorraine (1589). In so doing, he worked with Giovanni de'BARDI, Ottavio Rinuccini, CACCINI, and PERI. In 1600 he produced Rinuccini's *Euridice* for the wedding of Henri IV of France and Marie de Médicis, after which he returned to Rome where his *Rappresentatione di anima, et di corpo* (1600) was performed. This, the first surviving play set to music throughout, is a pastoral piece comprising speech-like recitative, madrigals, and songs.

**CAVENDISH, MICHAEL** (*c.*1565–1628), English composer of songs and madrigals, who came from a musical family in Suffolk and later served in the household of JAMES VI's son Prince Charles. His 'Come gentle swains' is in THE TRIUMPHS OF ORIANA (1601).

**CAVENDISH or Candish, THOMAS** (1555–92), English privateer and circumnavigator. Active in British exploration of North Carolina in 1585, Cavendish became the second English sailor to circumnavigate the globe. A skilled seaman and pirate, the capture of a Spanish treasure ship made him rich, but he later lost his fortune and died at sea in 1592.

*DNB.*

**CAVICEO, JACOPO** (1443–1511), Italian author, a native of Parma who as a young man was ordained as a priest but lived so riotously that he was forced to flee abroad; for several years he lived in Constantinople. He eventually returned to Parma, and in the final years of his life lived in the court at Ferrara, where he wrote *Il pelegrino*, an amorous romance which is a landmark in the development of the Italian novel; its sexual explicitness and cheerful anticlericalism made *Il pelegrino* immensely popular, and it was reprinted and translated throughout the sixteenth century.

*DBI; OCIL.*

**CAXTON, WILLIAM** (*c.*1422–1492), English printer. A merchant from Kent, Caxton learned printing in the Low Countries, where from 1465 to 1469 he was governor of the English merchants in Bruges. He successfully exploited his skill with a press set up at Westminster in 1476, on which he published nearly 100 volumes on a variety of subject matter, including literary works by Chaucer and Malory.

*DNB; MDA.*

**CECIL, SIR WILLIAM** (1520–98), English statesman. Son of a Lincolnshire gentleman, Cecil moved in humanist circles during his education at Cambridge. His political career progressed swiftly during the final years of HENRY VIII's reign, and that of EDWARD VI, culminating in a knighthood in 1551 and membership of the Privy Council from 1550 until 1553. He served ELIZABETH as principal secretary and private secretary before becoming lord treasurer in 1572. Able at the administrative work which these posts entailed, Cecil also addressed more political concerns; he pressed Elizabeth to marry and settle the English succession, and drew up plans for the government of the country in the event of her death. A staunch Protestant, he was exercised by fears of attacks on England by her Catholic enemies. A patron of learning and a historian of the crown, he was created Lord Burghley in 1571.

*DNB; MDA; Pauline Croft (ed.), Patronage, Culture and Power: The Early Cecils, 1558–1612 (2002).*

**CELLINI, BENVENUTO** (1500–71), Italian sculptor, goldsmith, medallist, and autobiographer, born in Florence, where he trained as a goldsmith. He lived from 1519 to 1540 in Rome, working as a goldsmith and medallist. During the SACK OF ROME (1527) Cellini defended Castel Sant'Angelo, and according to his own account shot Charles, duc de BOURBON. In 1540 Cellini moved to FONTAINEBLEAU at the invitation of King FRANCIS I, for whom Cellini fashioned a bronze relief of the *Nymph of Fontainebleau* (Louvre). His golden salt cellar, the finest surviving goldsmith's work of the Renaissance, was begun in Rome in 1540 for Cardinal Ippolito d'ESTE and completed in France for King Francis; King CHARLES IX presented it in 1570 to Archduke FERDINAND of Tirol; it is now in the Kunsthistorisches Museum in Vienna. This oval salt cellar, which is some 25 centimetres (10 inches) high, is surmounted by two voluptuous nude statuettes: a female figure representing Earth reclines beside an Ionic temple which holds the pepper; opposite her sits Neptune, who represents the source of salt, which is held in a small ship. The recumbent figures around the base are modelled on MICHELANGELO's Medici tombs.

In 1545 Cellini returned to Florence, where he spent the rest of his career in the service of Duke Cosimo de' MEDICI, of whom he made a bronze bust (Bargello). During this period Cellini cast his finest sculpture, the bronze *Perseus* (1545–54) now in the Loggia dei Lanzi. His sculptures in marble from this period include *Apollo and Hyacinth* (Bargello), *Narcissus* (Bargello), and a *Crucifix* (Escorial).

Cellini's autobiography, which he began in 1558, was first printed in Naples in 1728. It was translated into German by Goethe, and so became a central document of the Romantic ideal of the artist. He also wrote treatises on the art of the goldsmith (*Trattato della oreficena*) and the art of the sculptor (*Trattato della scultura*).

*DBI; MDA; John Pope-Hennessy, Cellini (1985); Angela Biancofiore, Benvenuto Cellini, artiste-écrivain (1998).*

**CELTIS or Celtes, KONRAD** (1459–1508), German humanist, born in Wipfeld (near Schweinfurt); his original surname was Bickel or Pickel, of which Celtis is a Greek translation,

**Benvenuto Cellini**, golden salt cellar (begun 1540), in the Kunsthistorisches Museum, Vienna

the spelling of which is shaped by Low Latin *celtis*, a chisel. He left home to avoid following his father into the wine trade, and travelled to Heidelberg, where he was taught by Rudolfus AGRICOLA. On Agricola's death in 1485, Celtis became a wandering scholar, studying in Cologne and Erfurt and later teaching at universities in Italy, Poland, and Hungary. As he travelled he established learned societies on the model of the Roman ACADEMY of Julius Pomponius LAETUS: these sodalities included the Sodalitas Vistulana in Kraków, the Sodalitas Literaria Hungarorum, the Sodalitas Rhenana at Mainz, and, most influential of all, the Sodalitas Danubiana in Vienna.

In 1486 Celtis published *Ars versificandi et carminum*, which so enhanced his reputation that the Emperor FRIEDRICH III crowned him as the first imperial POET LAUREATE in a ceremony at the Diet of Nuremberg in 1487. In 1492 Celtis became a professor at Ingolstadt, in 1497 he moved to Vienna as professor of poetry and rhetoric, and in 1502 the Emperor MAXIMILIAN I created the Collegium Poetarum et Mathematicorum in his honour. He died in Vienna on 4 February 1508.

The scholarship of Celtis included the discovery, in the Convent of St Emmeram in Regensburg, of a manuscript containing the six Latin plays of the tenth-century nun Roswitha of Gandersheim, of which he published an edition (Nuremberg, 1501); he also found the map of the Roman Empire known as the *Tabula peutingeriana* (named after Conrad PEUTINGER, to whom he presented it) and the historical poem *Ligurinus sive de rebus gestis Frederici primi imperatoris*,

which he edited for publication (Augsburg, 1507). He planned a historical survey of Germany, the *Germania generalis*, but the only surviving portion of this uncompleted work is an account of Nuremberg (*De origine, situ et institutis Norimbergae libellus*, 1501). His historical writing is tinged with xenophobia and racism, as in the *Oration* delivered at Ingolstadt in 1492, so that Celtis can be seen as the chief exemplar of a specifically German nationalist strand of humanism. His poetry, all of which was written in Latin, included elegies, epigrams, odes, plays, and an unfinished epic, the *Theodoriceis*. His erotic poems (*Amores*, 1502) are often assumed to be autobiographical, but there is no evidence to support such a reading.
  *NDB; DLL* s.v. Celtes; L. W. Spitz, *Conrad Celtis, the German Arch-Humanist* (1957).

**CENCI, BEATRICE** (1577–99), Italian noblewoman, born in Rome, the daughter of Francesco Cenci. Francesco's cruelty towards his daughter prompted her to organize a household conspiracy to assassinate him. Beatrice was tried together with her brother, stepmother, lover, and servants; all were found guilty and executed, whereupon Pope CLEMENT VIII confiscated the family's property. Beatrice was thereafter represented as the innocent victim of a cruel father and a grasping pope by generations of poets, playwrights, and novelists. The most important dramatic and literary narratives of her life are Shelley's *The Cenci* (1819) and Alberto Moravia's *Beatrice Cenci* (1958).
  *DBI; OCIL.*

**CENNINI, CENNINO** (c.1370–c.1440), Italian painter and art theorist, trained in the Florentine studio of Agnolo Gaddi, the son of Taddeo GADDI; none of Cennini's paintings is known to survive. Cennini was the author of the *Libro dell'arte*, the first Renaissance treatise on painting. The treatise is a practical guide, and so discusses matters such as TEMPERA techniques, and also contains art history and theory (such as the contention that Nature is the master of the artist). The earliest extant manuscript is dated 1437, 'in the Debtors' Prison in Florence'.

DBI; MDA.

**CENTILOQUIUM.** See ASTROLOGY; PTOLEMY IN THE RENAISSANCE.

**CERAMICS or (French) céramique**, a nineteenth-century term, derived from Greek, for POTTERY and the art of making pottery. In specialist usage, when PORCELAIN is distinguished from pottery, the term 'ceramics' is deemed to encompass both arts.

Timothy Wilson, *Ceramic Art of the Italian Renaissance* (1987); Howard Coutts, *The Art of Ceramics: European Ceramic Design, 1500–1800* (2001).

**CERIGNOLA, BATTLE OF.** This decisive battle in the struggle between France and Aragon for the control of the kingdom of NAPLES was occasioned by a Spanish attack on the French supply depot in Cerignola, a village south-east of Foggia, in Apulia. A Spanish force under the command of Gonzalo FERNÁNDEZ DE CÓRDOBA captured the lightly defended village and quickly occupied and fortified it. On 28 April 1503 the regrouped French forces attacked the village, and were repulsed and later routed. This defeat eventually led to the administration of the kingdom of Naples by Aragon (and later by Spain) and to the abrogation of the Treaty of Granada (1500), according to which Naples had been divided between Aragon and France.

**CERTON, PIERRE** (c.1515–1572), French composer who, by 1536, was master of the choristers at the Sainte-Chapelle in Paris. He wrote masses, motets, chansons, and *voix de villes*, a kind of strophic song fashionable at the French court.

**CERVANTES DE SALAZAR, FRANCISCO** (c.1514–1575), Spanish historian of Mexico, born in Toledo and educated at Salamanca University. He taught briefly at Osuna before leaving in 1551 for Mexico, where he initially worked as a schoolmaster and in 1553 moved to the newly founded University of Mexico. He was ordained as a priest the following year.

Cervantes de Salazar knew CORTÉS personally, and drew on his *Relaciones* and other sources (notably the *Historia* of Francisco LÓPEZ DE GÓMARA) for his *Crónica de la Nueva España*, which remained unpublished until 1914 (when part I was published in Madrid) and 1936 (when parts II and III were published in Mexico City). His miscellaneous works (*Obras*, 3 vols., Alcalá, 1546) include translations of Latin dialogues, based on those of Luís VIVES, that document the early years of the University of Mexico and contemporary life in the city.

A. Millares Carlo, *Apuntes para un estudio bio-bibliográfico del humanista Francisco Cervantes de Salazar* (1958).

**CERVANTES SAAVEDRA, MIGUEL DE** (1547–1616), Spanish novelist, poet, playwright, and soldier, born in Alcalá, the fourth son of an apothecary-surgeon. In 1569 he travelled to Italy, where he entered the service of Cardinal AQUAVIVA and then became a soldier. In 1571 he fought in the battle of LEPANTO, where his left hand was shattered by an Ottoman bullet. He recuperated in Messina, and subsequently returned to active service in Corfu, Navarino (now Greek Pylos), and Tunis. He was discharged with letters of commendation from Don JUAN DE AUSTRIA, and while sailing back to Spain in 1575 was captured by BARBARY PIRATES and taken to Algiers. The letters from Don Juan gave the Moors an exaggerated impression of Cervantes's standing, and so the price required for his ransom was more than his family could afford. After several failed escape attempts he was finally ransomed in October 1580, after five years in captivity; the ransom had been paid after the intercession of the ORDER of Trinitarians.

On returning to Spain Cervantes worked as a government official in Seville, where his tasks included procurement for the Spanish ARMADA. He was twice imprisoned for alleged financial improprieties. In 1601 he followed the court of Philip III to Valladolid, and was again jailed, this time because of a stabbing incident involving his illegitimate daughter Isabel which ended with the death of a man on Cervantes's doorstep. He subsequently separated from his wife Catalina de Salazar y Palacios, with whom he had entered into an unhappy marriage in 1584, but they were eventually reconciled. In 1606 he moved with the court to Madrid, and there wrote some of his finest work. He died on 23 April 1616 and was buried in the Convent of Trinitarian Nuns which stood in the street now known as Calle de Lope de Vega.

The poetry of Cervantes includes *Epístola a Mateo Vázquez*, a remarkable verse epistle (in tercets), written from Algiers to the secretary of Philip II, in which Cervantes pleads for an early ransom. His prose works (especially *La Galatea*) contain a significant amount of verse, sometimes in traditional Spanish metre (e.g. ballads, *quintillas dobles*) and sometimes in Italian metres (*octavas reales*, *liras*, and *tercets*). At the end of his career he wrote a 3,000-line *Viaje del Parnaso* (1614) based on a poem of the same title (*Viaggio in Parnaso*) by the Italian poet Cesare Caporali (1531–1601).

The early plays of Cervantes include the autobiographical *El trato de Argel* (later imitated by Lope de VEGA in *Los cautivos de Argel*), in which a character called Saavedra describes the lighter side of captivity in Algiers, and a fine patriotic tragedy based on an episode in Hispano-Roman history, *El cerco de Numancia*. In 1615 he collected his comic interludes (*entremeses*) and eight full-length plays as *Ocho comedias y ocho entremeses nuevos* (1615), a title to which he added the rueful phrase *nunca representados* ('never acted'), an accurate indication of the total failure of his classicizing drama to find success in the face of the *comedia nueva* ('new theatre') of Lope de Vega.

Two of the *entremeses* are in verse (*La elección des los alcaldes de Daganzo* and *El rufián viudo*), the others in prose: *El juez de la divorcios* is a satire on marriage, *El retablo de las maravillas* a village comedy on the dangerous subject of anti-Semitic prejudices about purity of blood, while *La cueva de Salamanca* mocks complacent husbands, *El vizcaíno fingido* is an anti-feminist satire, and *La guarda cuidadosa* depicts a love feud between a soldier and a priest.

The prose of Cervantes consists of *La Galatea* (Alcalá, 1585), *Novelas ejemplares* (1613), *Los trabajos de Persiles y Sigismunda* (1617), and the two parts of *Don Quijote de la Mancha* (1605 and 1615). The *Primera parte de La Galatea* (of which the second part never appeared) is an episodic pastoral novel in the tradition of SANNAZARO and Jorge de MONTEMAYOR in which poems and tales are interpolated into a loose narrative of the loves of shepherds and of aristocrats disguised as shepherds. *Novelas ejemplares* is a collection of twelve short stories which include picaresque, comic, naturalistic, and satirical narratives. *Los trabajos de Persiles y Sigismunda*, which occupied the final years of Cervantes's life, is a sprawling Byzantine novel of adventure with strong elements of romance and allegory in its characterization.

The first part of *El ingenioso hidalgo Don Quijote de la Mancha* (in the seventeenth century spelt 'Quixote') is, as Cervantes mischievously claims in his preface, a satire on chivalric romances ('una invectiva contra los libros de caballerías') in which an elderly nobleman living in a village in La Mancha (Castile) becomes inspired by the romances of chivalry (*libros de caballerías*) that he is reading and sets out on his horse Rocinante on a journey inspired, as he imagines, by the fair Dulcinea del Toboso; Quijote's idealistic madness is balanced by the worldly foolishness of his squire, Sancho Panza. The comic narrative, which contains some 700 characters, is interpolated with digressions, dialogues (including one on the art of writing romances in chapter 47), and secondary narratives. Part I of *Don Quijote* proved to be enormously popular: it was reprinted in Madrid (1608), Brussels (1607 and 1611), and Milan (1610) and translated into English (1612) and French (1614).

The success of part I of *Don Quijote* prompted an otherwise unknown author who styled himself Alonso Fernández de Avellaneda (probably a pseudonym) to publish the *Segundo tomo del ingenioso hidalgo Don Quijote de la Mancha* (Tarragona, 1614). The following year Cervantes published his own sequel, *Segundo parte del ingenioso cavallero Don Quixote de la Mancha* (Madrid, 1614). This is a more disciplined narrative and its humour more profound, being shot through with a tragic humanity lacking in the more innocent farce of part I; the secondary narratives are deftly integrated into a more unified plot, which ends with the death of Quijote, who has returned home cured of his folly.

Jean Canavaggio, *Cervantes* (1986; Spanish trans. 1987; English trans. 1990).

**CESALPINO, ANDREA** (1524/5–1603), Italian botanist, physician, anatomist, and metallurgist. He was born in Arezzo and studied medicine in Pisa, where in 1555 he became director of the BOTANICAL GARDEN. In 1592 he moved to Rome, where he taught at the Sapienza and served as physician to Pope CLEMENT VIII. His most important publication was *De plantis* (Florence, 1583), which introduced a taxonomy of plants based on fruits and seeds.

DBI; DSB.

**CESARI, GIUSEPPE, or Il Cavaliere d'Arpino** (1568–1640), Italian painter, born into a family of Spanish descent in Rome. From 1588 to 1591 he lived in Naples, where he decorated the choir of the Certosa di San Martino. He was employed by the Vatican from 1590 to 1615; his work included two *Scenes from the Life of John the Baptist* in the Lateran Baptistery (1598) and the unfinished frescoes of *The History of Ancient Rome* in the Great Hall of the Palazzo dei Conservatori.

DBI; MDA s.v. Arpino, Cavaliere d'.

**CESARINI, GIULIANO or Julian** (1398–1444), cardinal and diplomat. He was born into a noble Roman family and studied at Perugia and Padua, where he became a friend of NICHOLAS OF CUSA. He entered the papal curia and was employed as a diplomat. In 1419 he undertook his first mission to BOHEMIA to confront the Hussites. In 1425 he travelled as a papal legate to France, where he met John of Lancaster, duke of Bedford, who was HENRY VI's regent in France. The following year Giuliano was created cardinal and transferred to England, where he met Cardinal Henry Beaufort and the circle of humanists associated with Humphrey, duke of Gloucester.

On 1 February 1431, three weeks before his death, Pope MARTIN V appointed Cardinal Giuliano president of the COUNCIL OF BASEL. Giuliano had to be recalled from Germany, where he had recently travelled as papal legate to Bohemia, Hungary, Poland, and the Holy Roman Empire with a view to leading a crusade against the Hussites. Once installed at the Council, Giuliano attempted to persuade Martin's successor Pope EUGENIUS IV to temper his insistence on papal supremacy. At the subsequent COUNCIL OF FLORENCE in Ferrara and Florence, Giuliano participated in the negotiations for reconciliation with the Greek Church. In 1442 he was sent to Hungary to preach the crusade against the Turks. He succeeded in persuading King LADISLAS V POSTHUMUS to abrogate the Peace of Szegedin (July 1444), as a result of which the war was resumed. The Christians were routed by the Turks at Varna (Bulgaria) on 10 November 1444, and Cardinal Giuliano was killed in the retreat.

DBI; R. C. Jenkins, *The Last Crusader: The Life and Times of Cardinal Julian* (1861).

**CÉSPEDES, PABLO DE** (c.1545–1608), Spanish painter, sculptor, architect, and poet, born near Toledo. He travelled to Rome to study oriental languages, and there began to paint. He settled in Córdoba in 1575 and spent the rest of his career as a painter. His best-known painting is *The Last Supper* (1595, Córdoba Cathedral). He also composed a poem on the art of painting (*Poema de la pintura*), which survives only in fragments.

MDA.

**CHAIRS, SETTLES, AND STOOLS**. The chair existed in antiquity, but survived in the Middle Ages only in the form of thrones and other ceremonial chairs, such as the doge's chair. In the church, the bishop's seat (*sedes*) or throne (*cathedra*) was the symbol of his authority; the *sedia gestatoria* was the portable throne on which the pope was carried by twelve bearers (*palafrenieri*). The throne of England was (and is) the Gothic oak chair occupied by the monarch in the House of Lords (not the coronation chair in Westminster Abbey). In France and the Netherlands, the seigneurial chair was the remote ancestor of the modern armchair. The notion of the chair as the seat of authority survives in attenuated form in the conventions whereby meetings are 'chaired' by the person in authority and in the idea of the professorial chair in universities.

In the fifteenth century the chair ceased to be used only as an apanage of Church and state and began to be used as a form of seating in wealthy houses. Chairs were normally made from oak or walnut, and were sometimes elaborately carved. Specialized chairs in use as seating included the French *caquetoire* (a small low chair favoured by women who wished to chatter, i.e. *caqueter*), the chair-table (an armchair with a hinged back that could be swung forward to rest on the arms as a table), the farthingale chair (the modern name for a sixteenth-century upholstered chair with a low back and no arms) and the chair known in Spain as the *sillon de caderas* and in England as the Dante chair or Savonarola chair (a chair with no back in which the seat is supported on an X-shaped frame). Some chairs were extravagantly decorated for purposes of display, such as the iron chair (now in Longford Castle in Wiltshire) made in 1574 by Thomas RUCKER, and the twelve sumptuous chairs (of which seven survive) commissioned in 1585 by the Elector AUGUSTUS I and made by Giovanni Maria NOSSENI.

In taverns and farmhouses, the settle, which was a bench with a straight back and arms, provided seating for more than one person; settles remained in use until the nineteenth century. The settee, which was the predecessor of the nineteenth-century sofa, was introduced in early seventeenth-century England as a comfortable alternative to the settle.

From the Middle Ages to the nineteenth century the most common type of seat in European houses was the three-legged stool known in Italy as a Strozzi stool; the Cambridge term 'tripos', which now refers to final examinations, originates in the three-legged stool on which sat the person appointed to conduct mock disputations with candidates for degrees. The cucking stool or pining stool (known from the eighteenth century as the ducking stool) was used to duck scolds and disorderly women into ponds and rivers; in Scotland the repentance stool was one placed in a conspicuous position in a church for the use of sinners repenting publicly for sins of a sexual nature. The type of stool known as the *tabouret* (which was shaped like a drum mounted on four upright legs) was used in the French court (where a protocol of entitlement to sit on the *tabouret* evolved) and later in the English court.

**CHALCONDYLES, DEMETRIUS, or (Italian) Demetrio Calcondila** (1423–1511), Greek scholar in Italy. Chalcondyles was an Athenian who lived in the circle of BESSARION in Rome and in 1464 became the first holder of the professorship of Greek at Padua, where his pupils included foreigners such as LINACRE and GROCYN and many Italians who were to achieve distinction, including PICO, POLIZIANO, and Giovanni de' Medici (the future LEO X). In 1475 he was invited by Lorenzo de' MEDICI to accept the chair of Greek in Florence, where he succeeded Andronicus Callistus; in this capacity he produced the first printed edition of HOMER (1488). In 1491 he moved to Milan, where he lived until his death, working as an editor of Greek texts and as a teacher of Greek; his pupils included CASTIGLIONE and TRISSINO.

*DBI* s.v. Calcondila, Demetrio; Giuseppe Cammelli, *Demetrio Calcondila* (1954).

**CHAMBERLAIN'S MEN**. Formed in 1594, based initially at the THEATRE, and drawing actors from the ADMIRAL'S MEN, this acting company is strongly associated with SHAKESPEARE, and performed most of his plays. In 1599 they moved to the GLOBE Theatre, built for them by BURBAGE, their leading actor. In 1603 they came under the direct patronage of JAMES I and were renamed the King's Men; in 1613 they began using BLACKFRIARS Theatre for winter performances.

**CHAMBERS OF RHETORIC or (Dutch) Rederijkerskamers or Kamers van Rhetorica**. The literary and dramatic societies of the Netherlands in the fifteenth and sixteenth centuries derived from the late medieval theatrical companies known as *Gesellen van den Spele*. The *rederijkers* who were members of these societies were amateur enthusiasts who had formed organizations analogous to guilds in order to promote poetry and drama. Like the MEISTERGESANG in Germany and *collèges de rhétorique* in France, their literary and dramatic tastes were conservative, and they resisted the forces of the Renaissance and Reformation. Writers associated with the chambers included Anna BIJNS, Dirck COORNHERT, Hendrick SPIEGEL, and Matthijs de Castelein (1488–1550), founder of the Flemish chamber Pax Vobiscum at Oudenarde and author of *De conste van rhetorijcken* (Ghent, 1573), the first Dutch treatise on poetry.

In the fifteenth and early sixteenth centuries, the chambers functioned principally as civic dramatic societies, and they therefore played an important role in the development of DUTCH DRAMA, especially secular drama, and so contributed to the development of secular drama throughout northern Europe. Every town and city in the Netherlands eventually acquired a chamber, invariably with a fanciful name and motto: the principal Amsterdam chamber, which was founded in 1496 and was to achieve national prominence, was called *De Egelantier* ('The Eglantine'), and its motto was *In Liefde Bloeyende* ('Blossoming in Love'). The chambers produced mystery and miracle plays for civic occasions, and also commissioned music. The play most familiar to English readers is *Elckerlijk* (c.1495), of which the English morality play *Everyman* is a version.

In the northern provinces, membership of the chambers consisted of middle-class burghers, but in Flanders and Brabant there was a pronounced aristocratic presence: noblemen financed civic events, but also extended patronage to tournaments of rhetoric (*landjuweelen*) at which valuable prizes were given for the best literary and dramatic compositions. Among the 66 festivals known to have taken place in the southern provinces between 1426 and 1620, the most splendid was said to be the *landjuweel* celebrated in Antwerp on 3 August 1561, when Brussels sent a delegation of 340 members who entered on horseback in crimson mantles, and Antwerp donated a ton of gold to be shared as prizes amongst the 1,893 rhetoricians.

**CHAMBORD, CHÂTEAU DE**, a royal chateau on the left bank of the Cosson, a tributary of the Loire. The chateau was commissioned by FRANCIS I and construction began in 1519 on the site of a former hunting lodge; the architect may have been DOMENICO DA CORTONA, to whom the wooden model (now lost, but known through drawings) which formed the basis of the design is attributed. The structure of the chateau was inspired by the MEDICI VILLA at Poggio Caiano and its 440 rooms are laid out and decorated in the style of the Italian Renaissance. Internal features include a double spiral staircase, almost certainly inspired by LEONARDO DA VINCI, in which the spirals are superimposed but do not meet; the central nucleus is pierced so that each spiral can be seen from the other.

Chambord was rarely used by Francis I, but became the favourite residence of HENRI II; it was only used intermittently by HENRI III and HENRI IV, but again became an important royal residence under Louis XIV, during whose reign Molière wrote and produced *Monsieur de Pourceaugnac* and *Le Bourgeois Gentilhomme* at the chateau.

Monique Chatenet, *Chambord* (2001).

**CHAMBRE ARDENTE**, a French court of justice convened for the trial of heretics who had been arraigned after examination by the inquisitorial tribunal. The court first sat in 1535, and was abolished in 1682.

N. Weiss, *La Chambre Ardente, 1540–1550* (1889).

**CHAMPLAIN, SAMUEL DE** (1567–1635), French explorer and colonial governor, born in Brouage (on the Bay of Biscay), the son of a sea captain. As a young man he fought for the CATHOLIC LEAGUE in Brittany, and at the conclusion of the WARS OF RELIGION in 1598 he sent his uncle (who commanded one of the ships on which Spanish troops were returning home) to Cádiz, whereupon Champlain secured the command of one of the ships in an expedition bound for the Caribbean. His account of his two years on the islands and mainland of central America includes the first recorded suggestion that a canal could usefully be dug across Panama.

In 1603 Champlain made his first voyage to Canada, sailing up the St Lawrence river as far as the rapids above Montréal. He returned to America the following year, exploring the coast as far south as Cape Cod and establishing settlements on an island at the mouth of the St Croix river (now the border of Canada and the USA) and at Port Royal (now Annapolis, Nova Scotia). Vested interests in France managed to have Champlain's colonial patent revoked, and he returned with his colonists to France.

Champlain's patron managed to secure a modified patent, and in July 1608 Champlain established a French settlement on the site of what is now Québec, which he named. The following spring Champlain aligned his forces with the coalition of Algonquin and Huron Indians fighting the Iroquois, and while on a war party visited the lake that now bears his name. In the years to come the Iroquois were to seek alliances with Dutch and then English armed bands, and so the divisions of Europe became aligned with those of the Indians.

Champlain returned to Canada in 1611 and established a trading post at Mont Royal (now Montréal). On his return to France he was appointed as governor of New France. For many years he crossed the Atlantic annually, exploring his territories as far as Lake Ontario and Lake Huron, and in France promoting the interests of the colony. In 1629 he was captured by an English expedition intent on securing Canada and taken to England as a prisoner. On his release four years later, when Canada was returned to France, Champlain returned to Québec, where he died on 25 December 1635.

DBF; Samuel Eliot Morison, *Samuel de Champlain: Father of New France* (1972); Conrad Heidenreich, *Explorations and Mapping of Samuel de Champlain, 1603–1632* (1976).

**CHANCELLOR, RICHARD** (d. 1556), English Arctic explorer. Following early sailing experience around the Mediterranean, in 1553 he joined WILLOUGHBY's expedition to find a NORTH-EAST PASSAGE to the Orient. He sailed into the White Sea and continued overland to Moscow, where he established the trade agreements which first secured English–Russian contacts.

DNB.

**CHANDELIER**, a branched ornamental light fixture hanging from a ceiling; the English term derives from the French word for candlestick, but since the eighteenth century the French term for such a hanging fixture has been *lustre*. The progenitor of the chandelier was the late medieval candle beam, a suspended piece of wood with candles on it. The type of chandelier used in churches was called a corona or *corona lucis* (crown of light), which was a suspended iron hoop with spikes for candles or cups for oil. By the sixteenth century chandeliers used in domestic and civic settings contained up to 24 branches; these chandeliers were fashioned from precious metals and suspended by chains from the ceiling. Glass chandeliers were not manufactured until the eighteenth century, when they were produced in Venice and in the Spanish glasshouse at La Granja.

**CHAPEL ROYAL**, a term derived from the meaning of the word chapel as a place where the relics of saints were safeguarded. The guardians were priests or chaplains, and also clerks trained in singing, and thus the term came to be applied to private groups of musicians. Court chapels existed throughout Europe and musical styles were exchanged by musicians as they moved from one chapel to another. While many chapels employed instrumentalists as well as singers, the Chapel Royal in England was made up of singers and an organist. The Children of the Chapel Royal was a company of boy actors.

**CHAPMAN, GEORGE** (c.1559–1634), English poet and translator. Following a university education, Chapman may have been a soldier in the Low Countries before spending ten years as a playwright. Seven comedies and three tragedies survive; especially notable is *The Revenge of Bussy D'Ambois* (1613), which, like SHAKESPEARE's *Hamlet*, reworks the revenge play formula with a hero reluctant to take action. In 1605 he was briefly imprisoned due to an attack on the Scottish in *Eastward Hoe*, on which he collaborated with JONSON and MARSTON. He published his translations of Homer from 1598, issuing a completed translation of the *Iliad* and the *Odyssey* in 1616; amongst his early poetry is a completion of MARLOWE's *Hero and Leander* (1598).

DNB.

**CHARLES V or (German) Karl V** (1500–56), Holy Roman Emperor and (as Carlos I) king of Spain, born on 24 February 1500 in Ghent; he was the son of PHILIP I and JUANA LA LOCA; his maternal grandparents were FERDINAND V and ISABELLA THE CATHOLIC and his paternal grandparents were the Emperor MAXIMILIAN I and MARY OF BURGUNDY. Through these grandparents he was heir to four distinct inheritances, to each of which he added new territories. From King Ferdinand he acquired Aragon, Naples, Sardinia, and Sicily, and to this inheritance he added Milan and Tunis in 1535. From Isabella he acquired Castile, Granada, and the West Indies, and to this inheritance he added Mexico (1519) and Peru (1543). From the Emperor Maximilian he acquired the Holy Roman Empire, Alsace, Austria, Carinthia, and Tirol, and to this inheritance he added Bohemia, Moravia, Silesia, and part of Hungary. From Mary of Burgundy he acquired the southern and central Netherlands, to which he later added the north-eastern provinces (1523–43).

Charles also used marriage as a means of acquiring territory and new spheres of influence. His sister Isabella was married to CHRISTIAN II of Denmark, his sister Mary (MARY OF HUNGARY) to King LOUIS II of Hungary, his brother Ferdinand (later the Emperor FERDINAND) to Anna Jagiełło (King Louis's sister), his sister Eleanor to King MANUEL I of Portugal, his sister Catherine to King JOHN III of Portugal. In 1526 Charles married the Infanta Isabella of Portugal, and he later arranged for their son Philip (later PHILIP II) to marry his cousin Maria Manuela of Portugal and, after her death in childbirth, Queen MARY I of England. The Portuguese matches led in 1580 to the Spanish annexation of Portugal.

King Philip died in 1506, by which time Queen Juana's insanity precluded her raising her son. Charles spent his childhood in the household of his aunt MARGARET OF AUSTRIA, who was regent of the Netherlands. In 1507 Charles's religious education was entrusted by the Emperor Maximilian

Titian, *Charles V* (1548), in the Alte Pinakothek, Munich

to Adriaan Dedal of Utrecht (later Pope ADRIAN VI). Charles was recognized by the Estates as ruler of the Netherlands in 1515 (aged 15). In September 1517 he travelled to Spain with a Burgundian retinue (including Adriaan Dedal); he quickly learnt to speak Spanish, but his appointment of Burgundians to important positions aroused hostility within the Spanish court. In 1518 Charles was formally proclaimed king of Aragon and co-regent of Castile with his mother. The Emperor Maximilian died in 1519, and Charles promptly left for Germany to claim the crown of the HOLY ROMAN EMPIRE. In the imperial election he defeated his rival, King FRANCIS I, by bribing the Electors with money lent by the FUGGER family. Charles was elected in Frankfurt on 28 June 1519 and crowned as king of the Romans in Aachen on 23 October 1520.

The coronation of Charles was to be postponed for a decade because of a series of crises in the 1520s: war with France (part of the WARS OF ITALY), the eruption of Protestantism in Germany, Ottoman incursions in eastern Europe

(Belgrade fell in 1521), and the Revolt of the COMUNEROS in Spain. In 1521 Charles attended the Diet of WORMS with a view to securing a settlement with the German Protestants, but the following year he had to return to Spain to deal with the final stages of the Revolt of the Comuneros; he was to remain in Spain from 1522 to 1529. In 1522 his former tutor Adriaan Dedal was elected as Pope Adrian VI, which for a short time gave Charles a formidable ally in Italy; in the same year Charles handed over the government of his possessions in eastern Europe to his younger brother Ferdinand. In 1525 King Francis was captured at the battle of PAVIA and sent to Spain as a prisoner. He was forced by Charles to sign the Treaty of Madrid (14 January 1526), by which Francis surrendered his claims to Flanders, Artois, and Burgundy and his Italian claims (Milan, Genoa, Asti, and the kingdom of Naples).

In April 1526 Francis was released, and promptly repudiated the Treaty of Madrid on the grounds that he had signed under duress. The coalition known as the League of COGNAC (which included the new pope, CLEMENT VII) was formed to fight the emperor, who retaliated with the SACK OF ROME (1527), which broke the military power of the papacy. In June 1529 Clement was reconciled to Charles in the Treaty of Barcelona, in which they pledged common cause against Lutheran heretics and the Ottoman army that was advancing on Vienna. Two months later the Peace of CAMBRAI suspended hostilities between France and the Empire, and Charles was at last able to go to Italy for his coronation. Rome was still in ruins, so Pope Clement travelled to Bologna, where he crowned Charles as Holy Roman Emperor on 24 February 1530; this was to be the last imperial coronation by a pope. Charles showed his good will to Clement by overthrowing the Florentine republic and installing Alessandro de' MEDICI as duke of Florence.

Charles then had to attend the Diet of Augsburg, where on 25 June 1530 he was presented with the AUGSBURG CONFESSION, which had been drafted by MELANCHTHON and approved by LUTHER. On receiving the Confession, the emperor passed it to a group of Catholic theologians (including Johann COCHLÄUS, Johann ECK, Johann FABER, and Konrad WIMPINA), whose formal reply, the 'Confutatio pontifica', was read on 3 August. Melanchthon responded to the 'Confutatio' with 'An Apology for the Confession' which the emperor declined to receive. His rejection of the Confession led the following year to the formation of the SCHMALKALDIC LEAGUE by the Protestant princes of Germany.

In 1532 Charles travelled to Vienna to assist his brother Ferdinand in the defence of Vienna against the Ottoman army of Sultan Süleyman. Eventually Charles decided to take the war to the Turks. In 1535 Barbarossa (see BARBARY PIRATES) conquered Tunis in the name of the Ottoman sultan; Mohammed al-Hafsi, the Berber claimant to the kingdom, appealed to Charles for assistance. He responded in July 1535 with an invasion of Tunis which he led in person. The imperial forces, commanded by Andrea DORIA at sea and Alfonso d'AVALOS on land, stormed Tunis and installed Mohammed as a Spanish vassal. The victory in the battle of TUNIS was acclaimed all over Europe as a Christian triumph over the infidel Turk, but proved to be short-lived.

From 1536 to 1538 Charles was again at war with France, and in 1540 he returned to the Netherlands to suppress a rebellion in his native Ghent. In 1541 he returned to North Africa for a failed assault on ALGIERS, and the following year he was yet again at war with France; this stage of the war ended with the imperial invasion of northern France in 1544 and the signing of the Treaty of Crépy-en-Laonnois (September 1544).

In 1546 Charles returned to Germany to conduct the SCHMALKALDIC WAR against the Schmalkaldic League of Protestant princes. The turning point in the war was Charles's conclusion of a secret agreement with MAURICE OF SAXONY, which eased the imperial conquest of southern Germany. Charles then advanced north, and defeated the League at the battle of MÜHLBERG on 24 April 1547; his prisoners included JOHANN FRIEDRICH I, elector of Saxony. Two months later PHILIP OF HESSE was persuaded to surrender to Charles by his son-in-law Maurice of Saxony and JOACHIM II, elector of Brandenburg, who promised Philip that he would be pardoned; in the event he was not pardoned, and was instead imprisoned.

In February 1548 Charles appointed a commission to negotiate a settlement between Protestants and Catholics. When the group failed to agree on the text of a settlement, he commissioned Johann AGRICOLA, Bishop Julius VON PFLUG, and Michael Helding (suffragan bishop of Mainz) to draft a doctrinal formula which might win the assent of both parties. This statement of faith was accepted as the basis of an interim settlement by the Diet of Augsburg on 30 June 1548, and is known as the AUGSBURG INTERIM; it was regarded as a temporary settlement in the expectation that the COUNCIL OF TRENT would negotiate a permanent settlement. In Catholic south Germany the Interim was firmly imposed, but in the Protestant areas of the north in which the Augsburg Interim failed to win assent, Maurice of Saxony proposed a more Protestant formulation called the LEIPZIG INTERIM, which was adopted in Saxony in December 1548.

In 1552 the forces of Maurice of Saxony surprised Charles near Innsbruck and almost managed to take him prisoner as he escaped to Villach (Carinthia). Charles was forced to sign the Treaty of Passau, which reaffirmed the religious freedom of the Protestants and contained a clause stipulating that Philip of Hesse be released. Charles then turned his attention to Metz, which he hoped to wrest from HENRI II of France, but his will to conquer was beginning to ebb. His withdrawal from the religious conflict that had riven the Empire was signalled by his appointment of his brother Ferdinand as his representative at the Diet of Augsburg (February–September 1555); Ferdinand made concessions that Charles would not have countenanced, and negotiated the Religious Peace of AUGSBURG (25 September 1555), which concluded the religious wars of Germany. On 25 October 1555 Charles abdicated as duke of Burgundy (i.e. ruler of the Netherlands) and king of Naples; on 15 January 1556 he abdicated as king of Spain (in favour of his son Philip II) and Holy Roman Emperor (in favour of his brother Ferdinand). Charles retired to a small palace adjoining the Hieronymite monastery of Yuste (Estremadura), where he lived until his death on 21 September 1558.

Willem Blockmans, *Emperor Charles V* (2001); Alfred Kohler, *Karl V, eine Biographie* (1999), Spanish trans. *Carlos V, una biografía* (2000).

**CHARLES VII** (1403–61), king of France, was born in Paris on 22 February 1403, the fifth son of King Charles VI and Isabeau of Bavaria; before his accession in 1422 Charles was known as count of Pontieu and (from 1416) duke of Touraine. The last of his elder brothers died in 1417, whereupon Charles became dauphin. In December 1418 Charles became regent of France, because his father's insanity had rendered him incapable of ruling.

In 1419 the murder of JOHN THE FEARLESS in the presence of Charles exacerbated the rift between ARMAGNACS AND BURGUNDIANS, and Duke John's son PHILIP THE GOOD retaliated by supporting the claim of King Henry V of England to the throne of France, and in 1420 persuaded King Charles VI to accede to the Treaty of Troyes, by which the king repudiated the dauphin and named Henry V as his successor.

Paris was occupied by the English, and Charles established his capital at Bourges. His rule was recognized south of the Loire, and was supported by JOAN OF ARC, who raised the siege of Orléans and two months later accompanied Charles to his coronation as Charles VII at Reims in July 1419. Philip the Good betrayed Joan of Arc to the English, but in the Treaty of Arras (1435) he recognized Charles VII as king of France. The following year his troops recaptured Paris.

In ecclesiastical politics King Charles was an important proponent of GALLICANISM. During the COUNCIL OF BASEL he supported the French delegation by promulgating the PRAGMATIC SANCTION OF BOURGES (1438). In this period Charles was served by a group of loyal advisers of bourgeois origin (such as Jacques CŒUR), and his choice of such councillors was one of the reasons for the disaffection of the nobility. In 1440 the aristocratic revolt known as the PRAGUERIE broke out in Poitou in protest against King Charles's proscription of the private militias of feudal nobles. The rebellion was soon suppressed, and after the suspension of hostilities with England (Treaty of Tours, 1444) and Burgundy (Treaty of Arras, 1435) Charles created a regular army which was able to suppress the brigandage of the aristocratic armed bands known as *écorcheurs* and to regain the territories held by the English. During this period Charles's mistress was Agnes Sorel, who inaugurated the French tradition of royal mistresses playing a prominent role in matters of state. Charles completed the conquest of Normandy in the battle of Formigny (15 April 1450) and conquered Guienne in expeditions of 1451 and 1453; at his death only CALAIS remained in English hands.

King Charles was married to Marie d'Anjou (daughter of Duke LOUIS II of Anjou), by whom he had his son and successor, LOUIS XI. In 1446 Charles exiled Louis to the Dauphiné, and they never met again. When Charles invaded the Dauphiné in 1456, Louis sought refuge at the court of PHILIP THE GOOD of Burgundy, where he remained until his father's death on 22 July 1461. Charles believed that he had been poisoned by order of his son, but there is no evidence for this contention apart from Louis's wish that his father would die so that he could assume the throne of France.

DBF; MDA s.v. Valois, (8); M. G. A. Vale, *Charles VII* (1974).

**CHARLES VIII** (1470–98), king of France, was the only son of King LOUIS XI; he was raised far from the court in the royal chateau at AMBOISE, which was his principal residence throughout his short life. He succeeded his father in 1483, aged 13, but until 1492 was content to allow France to be governed by his sister ANNE OF FRANCE and her husband Pierre de Beaujeu. In 1491 he married ANNE OF BRITTANY and assumed control of his kingdom.

King Charles nourished ambitious plans, including the reclaiming of the Neapolitan inheritance of the House of Anjou, which would give Charles a forward base from which to reconquer Constantinople and proclaim himself Byzantine emperor. He invaded Italy in 1494, so inaugurating the WARS OF ITALY, and on 12 May 1495 entered NAPLES. He garrisoned the city and in the course of the next year subdued the kingdom, whereupon he set out for home. The forces of the HOLY LEAGUE attempted to cut off Charles's retreat at the battle of FORNOVO, but his army cut its way through the forces of the League and continued its march to France.

Charles returned to Amboise to plan his return to Italy, but on 8 April 1498 died at his chateau as a result of a head injury sustained when he accidentally hit his head on a door. He was succeeded by his brother-in-law (and cousin) LOUIS XII, duke of Orléans, who had married his sister Jeanne of France.

DBF; MDA s.v. Valois, (11).

**CHARLES VIII** (1408/9–70), king of Sweden, was born into a noble Swedish family. Sweden had been ruled by Denmark since 1389, and in 1436 Charles participated in a revolt against King ERIC of Denmark; two years later he was appointed regent of Sweden, but retained secessionist ambitions. In 1448 he was elected king of Sweden by the Estates, but the legitimacy of his rule was disputed by King CHRISTIAN I of Denmark. Charles was temporarily deposed by the nobility in favour of King Christian (1464–7), and although he was restored, his powers were limited by the nobility.

SBL s.v. Karl Knutsson.

**CHARLES IX** (1550–74), king of France, was the second son of King HENRI II and CATHERINE DE MÉDICIS; before his accession he was known as duke of Orléans. In 1560, aged 10, he succeeded his brother FRANCIS II as king of France; the regent was his mother Queen Catherine. Charles was declared to be of age on 17 August 1563, but throughout the 1560s he was content to allow his mother to take important decisions, even after the outbreak of the WARS OF RELIGION in 1562. In 1570 he married the Archduchess Elizabeth of Austria, daughter of the Emperor MAXIMILIAN II; there were no children of the marriage, but by his mistress Marie Touchet Charles had one son, Charles, duke of Angoulême.

In the early 1570s the Huguenot leader Gaspard de COLIGNY attempted to persuade the king to offer military assistance to the Dutch in the REVOLT OF THE NETHERLANDS. Queen Catherine, however, convinced him that he should accede to the decisions that led to the murder of Coligny and the ST BARTHOLOMEW'S DAY MASSACRE. On 30 May 1574 he died of tuberculosis at Vincennes.

Charles was a cultured man who wrote poetry and extended his patronage to RONSARD and other poets of the PLÉIADE. He also granted privileges to the ACADEMY founded by Jean-Antoine de BAÏF (later the Académie du Palais). His treatise on hunting, *Traité de la chasse royale*, was posthumously published in 1625.

DBF.

**CHARLES IX** (1550–1611), king of Sweden, was the third son of King GUSTAVUS VASA, the younger half-brother of King ERIC XIV, and the younger brother of King JOHN III. In 1568 Charles and John deposed Eric, who was insane, and John acceded to the throne. When King John died in 1592, his son SIGISMUND, who had been king of Poland since 1587, claimed the Swedish throne. Sigismund's Catholicism was unacceptable to many Protestant Swedes, and a civil war ensued. When Sigismund invaded Sweden in 1598 with a view to claiming his throne, he was beaten back by Charles, who had been regent since 1595.

In 1599 Sigismund was deposed by the Swedish Estates, and in 1604 Charles became King Charles IX. His reign was characterized by war, first with Sigismund, then with Russia, and finally with Denmark.

SBL s.v. Karl IX.

**CHARLES THE BOLD or (French) Charles le Téméraire** (1433–77), duke of Burgundy, was born on 10 November 1433 in Dijon, the son of Duke PHILIP THE GOOD and Isabella of Portugal; until his accession he was known as the count of Charolais. On 12 April 1465 the ailing Duke Philip transferred to Charles the responsibility for the territories of Burgundy, which included Artois, Brabant, Flanders, Friesland, Hainaut, Luxemburg, and Zeeland as well as the duchy and county of Burgundy. Charles aspired to add Alsace and Lorraine to these possessions with a view to creating a middle kingdom between France and the Holy Roman Empire. Initially he made progress, defeating the army of LOUIS XI of France at the battle of Montlhéry (16 July 1465), but his victory did not enable him to prevent the king from re-entering Paris. In 1468 he sought to create an alliance with England by marrying Margaret of York, sister of King EDWARD IV of England, and later in the year he arrested King Louis in Péronne, accusing him of supporting rebels in Ghent. In 1471 Louis was able to retaliate with the aid of Swiss troops who helped him to seize the towns on the Somme which had been ceded to Burgundy by the Treaty of Arras. Two years later the duchy of Gelderland was ceded to Charles.

Charles prepared to be crowned king of Burgundy in Trier by the Emperor FRIEDRICH III in September 1473, but the emperor withdrew at the last moment. The following year King Louis was able to bring to his side the former allies of Charles, including Duke René of Lorraine, the free towns of Alsace, and the Swiss Confederation. In 1475 Edward VI, who had invaded France on behalf of Duke Charles, agreed to withdraw his troops and signed the Treaty of Picquigny with King Louis (29 August 1475), and Charles was subsequently defeated in battles with the Swiss at Granson (December 1475) and Morat (22 June 1476). On 6 January 1477 he met the combined forces of Lorraine and the Swiss Confederation outside the walls of Nancy and was killed in battle. His death signalled the conclusion of the Burgundian threat to the French monarchy.

Charles the Bold is a central figure in Walter Scott's *Anne of Geierstein*, which was first translated into French as *Charles le Téméraire*.

DBF s.v. Charles 22; Richard Vaughan, *Charles the Bold: The Last Valois Duke of Burgundy* (1973); Anne Le Cam, *Charles le Téméraire* (1992).

**CHARLES D'ORLÉANS** (1391–1465), French poet. He was raised in the court of his uncle King Charles VI of France; in 1407 his father, the duke of Orléans, was assassinated. In 1415 Charles was captured at the battle of AGINCOURT, and spent the next 25 years as a prisoner in England. During his long incarceration Charles wrote poetry, of which the finest examples are chansons and *ballades*. After his release in 1440 he lived at BLOIS, where he extended his patronage to artists and poets, notably VILLON. During this period his preferred genre was the *rondeau*.

DBF s.v. Orléans; J. Fox, *The Lyric Poetry of Charles d'Orléans* (1969); D. A. Fein, *Charles d'Orléans* (1983).

**CHARONTON, ENGUERRAND.** See QUARTON, ENGUERRAND.

**CHARRON, PIERRE** (1541–1603), French religious and philosophical writer. He was born in Paris where he studied law and became a priest. He became caught up in the French WARS OF RELIGION and in 1589 he defected from the CATHOLIC LEAGUE to the POLITIQUES. In 1593 he published *Les Trois Vérités*, in which the 'three truths' were that the existence of God necessitates institutional religion, that Christianity is a revealed and not necessarily rational truth, and that Catholicism is the only true version of Christianity. His best-known work is *De la sagesse* (1601), a statement of Renaissance SCEPTICISM and STOICISM that draws substantially on the writings of LIPSIUS and Charron's friend MONTAIGNE, from whom he borrows entire chapters of the *Essais*.

DBF; J. B. Sabrie, *De l'humanisme au rationalisme: Pierre Charron* (1913); Renée Kogel, *Pierre Charron* (1972).

**CHARTIER, ALAIN** (c.1395–c.1430), French humanist poet and prose writer. He was from 1417 to 1428 a diplomat in the service of the future CHARLES VII. His official diplomatic writing was in Latin, but his imaginative writing was normally in French; his preferred genre in both poetry and prose was the debate. His best-known poems are *La Belle Dame sans merci* (1424), in which the poet reports a conversation between a mournful lover (Amant) and a sceptical Belle Dame who coolly rejects his impassioned pleas, and the *Débat du héraut, du vassal et du villain* (written at an unknown date after 1415), a conversation between a dispirited knight, a herald nostalgic for a lost world, and a gruff peasant. In prose, Chartier's most important work is the *Quadrilogue invectif* (1422), a debate between a personified France and her three ESTATES, who are represented as a feckless nobility, a hedonistic clergy, and a whingeing populace.

DBF; F. Rouy, *L'Esthétique du traité moral après les œuvres d'Alain Chartier* (1980).

**CHARTS AND CHART-MAKING.** From the thirteenth century, Mediterranean sailors used charts known as portulan (or portolan) charts for NAVIGATION. These charts were characterized by the prominent use of compass roses and extended rhumb lines and by outlines of coasts with markings of ports together with their flags. The earliest portulan charts were made in Venice and Genoa, but in the fourteenth century some of the finest portulan charts were made by Catalan chart-makers in Palma (Majorca); these Catalan charts have scales representing distances in 'Portulan miles' which are *c*.6,000 metres (6,500 yards) long.

In 1420 Prince HENRY THE NAVIGATOR invited Jafuda Cresques, a prominent Majorcan cartographer, to work in Sangres; Cresques was happy to accept, because persecution of the JEWS in Aragon made staying in Majorca problematical. As a result of the work of Cresques and his fellow cartographers, the primacy in chart-making passed to Portugal. By the end of the century Vasco da GAMA had rounded AFRICA and COLUMBUS had sailed to America, and these and other voyages of EXPLORATION stimulated the art of chart-making in Portugal and Spain. Both countries established institutions to regulate commerce with their new possessions (the CASA DA ÍNDIA in Portugal and the CASA DE CONTRATACIÓN DE LAS INDIAS in Spain), and these Casas both kept sets of up-to-date charts, many of which survive.

In 1530 King JOHN III of Portugal appointed Pedro NUNES as his principal hydrographer in the Casa da Índia, and it was he who successfully addressed the problems associated with plotting oceanic courses on portulan charts. At the heart of Nunes's revision of the methodology of chart-making lay his realization that meridians converge towards the poles; the navigational implication of this insight is that a course that crosses the meridians at a constant angle is actually a spiral rhumb line that leads to the pole.

There is little evidence of the use of charts in northern Europe, but in the late sixteenth century the implications for chart-making of the maps of MERCATOR and ORTELIUS became clear to Edward WRIGHT, who described the Mercator projection in his *Certain Errors of Navigation* (1599). The Dutch seaman Lucas WAGHENAER was similarly influenced by the maps of Ortelius, and published an atlas of sea charts (*paskaerten*) entitled *Spieghel der Zeevaerdt*; these charts did not, however, avail themselves of Mercator's projection, nor did those of Waghaener's successor Willem BLAEU. Indeed, as late as 1693, when *Great Britain's Coasting Pilot* (which had been commissioned by Samuel Pepys) was published, British cartographers remained unaware of the navigational implications of Mercator's projection.

**CHASSENEUZ, BARTHÉLEMY DE** (1480–1541), French jurist and counsellor of the Parlement of Paris. His *Catalogus gloriae mundi* (1528) is an important text on precedence, and was widely reprinted. He also wrote *Commentaria in consuetudines ducatus Burgundiae* (1517) and *Repertorium consiliorum* (1531).

DBF.

**CHASTELLAIN or Chastelain, GEORGES** (1405–75), Flemish poet and historian, nicknamed 'le grand Georges', born in Aalst. As a young man he served as a soldier in the Burgundian army of PHILIP THE GOOD. He lived for a time in France, and in 1466 entered the service of the dukes of Burgundy, for whom he worked as an administrator and diplomat. In 1455 he was appointed official chronicler to the duchy of Burgundy, in which capacity he wrote a prose *Chronique des ducs de Bourgogne* which eventually covered the years 1419 to 1474. His verse includes moralizing poems (e.g. *Les Princes* and *Le Miroir de mort*), a celebration of the defeat of the English (*Le Trône azuré*), an embittered attack on France (*Dit de vérité*), and a large number of short topical poems.

BNB; DBF; K. Urwin, *Georges Chastellain: La Vie, les œuvres* (1937).

**CHÂTEAUBRIANT, EDICT OF** (27 June 1551), a decree signed by King HENRI II of France restricting the growth of Protestantism in France. The Edict codified earlier decrees, and strengthened the strictures with respect to the publication of Protestant books.

**CHÂTEAU, PALAIS, AND HÔTEL** (plurals *châteaux, palais,* and *hôtels*), the French terms for a large house. The *château* is a large country house, the *palais* is a royal or episcopal residence or a building representing the authority of the crown (such as a court of justice), and the *hôtel* is a large urban residence or a building representing a civic authority (such as a town hall); the distinctions are not rigid, so the house of Jacques CŒUR (1442–53) in Bourges, which is arguably the finest private house in France, is called Palais Jacques Cœur.

The designs of chateaus and the residential *palais* derive from the architecture of the Italian PALACE, designs for which were disseminated all over Europe through engravings and architectural treatises. The most important Renaissance palaces in France were the LOUVRE, the TUILERIES (destroyed 1871), and SAINT-GERMAIN-EN-LAYE, and the principal chateaus were AMBOISE, ANET, BLOIS, CHAMBORD, CHENONCEAUX, and FONTAINEBLEAU. Public buildings were often built in the older GOTHIC style; the Hôtel de Ville in Compiègne is one of the finest surviving examples.

**CHATILLON, CARDINAL DE.** See COLIGNY, ODET DE.

**CHEKE, SIR JOHN** (1514–57), English humanist. Regius professor of Greek at Cambridge, and tutor to EDWARD VI, Cheke was an eminent scholar who promoted a simple prose style in the vernacular and followed Erasmus in the debate over Greek pronunciation. Imprisoned by MARY in 1553, and again in 1556, his edition of sermons by St John Chrysostom (1543) was the first text published in England in Greek type; he also translated the Gospels and wrote an introduction, published posthumously in 1561, to a translation of Castiglione's *The Courtier*.

*DNB*.

**CHELČICKÝ, PETER** (*c*.1390–*c*.1460), Bohemian peasant religious leader, a prominent figure in the UNITY OF THE BROTHERS. In theology and church discipline he represented a radical antinomian alternative to the Hussite Church, interpreting the life of a self-sufficient peasant as a realization of the Christian ideal of a return to the purity of the early Church. His *Sít víry* ('Net of Faith') is a seminal work in Czech literature.

*BLBL*.

**CHEMNITZ, MARTIN** (1522–86), German Protestant theologian, born in Treuenbrietzen (Brandenburg) on 9 November 1522, the third son of a cloth worker of noble origins. Chemnitz was orphaned at the age of 11 and thereafter worked in his father's trade. A relative financed three years of schooling at Magdeburg (1539–42), after which Chemnitz taught for a year and then entered the University of Frankfurt an der Oder (1543), migrating two years later to the University of Wittenberg.

In Wittenberg Chemnitz enjoyed the patronage of MELANCHTHON, who encouraged his studies of MATHEMATICS and ASTROLOGY and in 1547 introduced him to his son-in-law Georgius SABINUS in Königsberg, where in 1548 he became rector of the Kneiphof. Chemnitz's expertise in astrology brought him to the attention of ALBRECHT VON PREUSSEN, who in 1550 appointed him as his librarian. Chemnitz immersed himself in BIBLICAL and PATRISTIC SCHOLARSHIP and entered into a controversy with Andreas OSIANDER on the subject of IMPUTATION; Chemnitz defended the Lutheran position against Osiander's advocacy of a doctrine of infused righteousness in which the righteousness of Christ was said to be transferred rather than imputed to the believer; Duke Albrecht sided with Osiander, and Chemnitz therefore resigned his librarianship and returned to Wittenberg.

In Wittenberg Chemnitz lectured on MELANCHTHON's *Loci communes*; his lectures, which were published posthumously as *Loci theologici* (1591), became the standard exposition of the theology of Melanchthon. In 1554 he resigned his lectureship to take up the post of coadjutor to the superintendent (i.e. assistant to the principal Lutheran minister), Joachim Mörlin, in Brandenburg, where he arrived on 15 December 1554 and stayed for the rest of his life. There he became a prominent controversialist, defending the Lutheran doctrine of the EUCHARIST in *Repetitio sanae doctrinae de vera praesentia* (Latin edition 1560, German edition 1561), attacking the JESUITS in *Theologiciae Jesuitarum praecipua capita* (1562), writing a hostile account of the COUNCIL OF TRENT in *Examen concilii Tridentini* (4 vols., 1565, 1566, 1572, and 1573; English translation by F. Kramer, 4 vols., St Louis, 1971–86) and combating SOCINIANISM in his *De duabus naturis in Christo* (1570).

In 1567 he published the influential *Corpus doctrinae Prutenicum* ('Corpus of Prussian Doctrine') with Joachim Mörlin, whom he succeeded in the same year as super-

intendent of Brunswick, in effect becoming the head of the Lutheran Church in Lower Saxony. He subsequently worked with Jakob ANDREAE and Nikolaus Selnecker (1530–92) on the composition of the Formula of CONCORD. In 1584 Chemnitz resigned his post on grounds of ill health, and died on 8 April 1586.

*NDB*; E. F. Klug, *From Luther to Chemnitz on Scripture and the Word* (1971), 115–248.

**CHENONCEAUX, CHÂTEAU DE.** The chateau was built by Thomas Bohier between 1513 and 1521. The site is the river Cher, which the chateau spans. After the death of Bohier and his widow the chateau passed to the crown in lieu of debts to the royal treasury. When HENRI II ascended the throne in 1547, he gave Chenonceaux to his mistress DIANE DE POITIERS, who commissioned Philibert DELORME to build a bridge carrying a two-storey gallery (La Grande Galerie) to link the chateau (which extended from the medieval keep on the north bank of the Cher) to the south bank; she also commissioned the garden that bears her name on the north bank. On Henri's death in 1559, Diane was displaced at Chenonceaux by the regent, CATHERINE DE MÉDICIS, who forced her to trade Chenonceaux for Chaumont. When Henri was killed, work was suspended on the bridge; the arches was completed, but the gallery had not been built. Catherine ordered work on the gallery to be resumed. During this period great pageants were staged to mark the arrival of important guests. One was mounted for the arrival of FRANCIS II and Mary Stuart (MARY, QUEEN OF SCOTS), and another for the arrival of Catherine's son HENRI III in 1574. On the latter occasion guests were welcomed by singers dressed as mermaids and wood nymphs, and there were fireworks, masquerades, and a naval battle on the Cher. On Catherine's death she bequeathed Chenonceaux to her daughter-in-law Louise of Lorraine, wife of Henri III. When Henri was assassinated in 1589, Louise retired in mourning to the chateau for the rest of her life. Thereafter Chenonceaux fell into desuetude, though it enjoyed a revival in the eighteenth century, when the salon of Mme Dupin attracted visitors such as Voltaire, Montesquieu, and Lord Chesterfield, and Rousseau acted as tutor to the Dupin boys, for whom he wrote *Émile* (1762), his treatise on education.

The gardens constructed for Diane de Poitiers were laid out between 1551 and 1555 on a 1-hectare (2½-acre) terrace east of the entrance to the chateau. The garden was planted with fruit trees, flowers, and vegetables in rectangular beds which are depicted in a drawing by DUCERCEAU. When Catherine took possession of the chateau, she built a garden (now named after her) on the west side of the entrance; this garden was dominated by a circular FOUNTAIN in the form of a rock. Both gardens are now laid out in a French classical style rather than a Renaissance style, though the site of the fountain is marked by a circular depression in the west garden. Catherine also laid out a garden and park on the south side of the river, arranged around an axis that is an extension of the approach road and the line of the chateau as it crosses the river.

William Howard Adams, *The French Garden, 1500–1800* (1979); Kenneth Woodbridge, *Princely Gardens: The Origins and Development of the French Formal Style* (1986).

**CHETTLE, HENRY** (*c*.1560–1607), English playwright. Although Chettle wrote at least thirteen plays, and contributed to more, only one is extant: *Hoffman* (*c*.1602), a revenge tragedy, which describes the death of a Danish pirate and his son's revenge. Chettle also wrote satirical pamphlets and an elegy for ELIZABETH on her death. Partner in a printing business, he published Robert GREENE's *Groatsworth of Wit* (1592), which famously attacks SHAKESPEARE as an 'upstart Crow'. His hand, together with one which may be Shakespeare's, is present on an incomplete manuscript transcript of the play *Sir Thomas More*, submitted to the MASTER OF THE REVELS *c*.1593.

*DNB.*

**CHEVRON**, the term used in heraldry for an inverted V; the term derives from rafters meeting at an angle at the ridge. In the fifteenth and sixteenth centuries the chevron was used as a decorative motif on wood (in which it was carved or inlaid) and plaster. When used in mouldings the chevron was known as a dancette.

**CHIABRERA, GABRIELLO** (1552–1638), Italian poet, born in Savona and educated in the household of an uncle in Rome. He spent a riotous youth in a succession of north Italian courts and in 1581 returned permanently to Savona. Although he composed ambitious long poems on religious and moral themes, his best-known works are his poised and gracious lyrics, short songs (canzonettas), and brief jocular poems (*scherzi*), many of which evince the influence of the PLÉIADE poets.

*DBI; OCIL; Grove;* F. Neri, *Il Chiabrera e la Pléiade francese* (1920).

**CHIAROSCURO** (Italian; 'bright-dark'), a late seventeenth-century oxymoron used to denote monochrome paintings (such as GRISAILLES), woodcuts (see next entry), and engravings (particularly those of Rembrandt) characterized by the dramatic use of gradations of lightness and shade. The term is also used in a broader sense to denote the use of light and shadow to model form in paintings such as those of LEONARDO DA VINCI.

**CHIAROSCURO WOODCUT or** (French) *gravure en camaïeu*, a WOODCUT in which the illusion of depth is created by printing from a succession of blocks in which the intensity of the tone is varied. The earliest dated CHIAROSCURO woodcut is Hans BURGKMAIR's equestrian portrait of the Emperor MAXIMILIAN (1508). German artists who subsequently made chiaroscuro woodcuts include Albrecht ALTDORFER, Hans BALDUNG GRIEN, and Lucas CRANACH. In Italy, where the medium remained popular until the advent of colour wood engraving in the nineteenth century, UGO DA CARPI was the most important exponent of the form; many of his prints were designed by RAPHAEL and PARMIGIANINO (the most prolific chiaroscuro woodcut designer of the Renaissance).

**CHIGI, AGOSTINO** (1465–1520). The banker, patron, and printer known as 'Il Magnifico' was a member of a prominent Sienese family. He amassed a huge fortune in shipping and property, founded an important Roman bank, and acted as financier to a succession of popes from ALEXANDER VI to LEO X. In 1500 he was awarded the lease of the papal ALUM mines at Tolfa and in 1507 he was appointed as an apostolic secretary. After the death of his wife and of his Roman mistress, the courtesan Imperia, he took into his household a young woman by whom he had five children before marrying her in 1519.

Chigi's villa outside Rome, which later came to be known as the Villa Farnesina, was designed by Baldassare PERUZZI; the ground floor was decorated by RAPHAEL and the first floor by SODOMA. His patronage also extended to scholarship, notably the establishment by Zacharias CALLIERGIS of the first Greek press in Rome, which produced an important edition of Pindar in 1515. Chigi was commemorated by monumental chapels in two Roman churches, Santa Maria della Pace and Santa Maria del Popolo; the latter was designed by Raphael and decorated with a painting by SEBASTIANO DEL PIOMBO.

The Chigi family remained prominent for centuries. In 1655 Fabio Chigi became Pope Alexander VII, and in 1712 the family was appointed as the hereditary marshals of the Church and guardians of the papal conclave.

*DBI; MDA* s.v. Chigi: (1) Agostino Chigi (i); F. Gilbert, *The Pope, the Banker, and Venice* (1980).

**CHILDREN OF PAUL'S.** A popular London company of boy actors in the sixteenth and early seventeenth centuries, drawn from the choristers of St Paul's Cathedral. Like their rivals, the CHILDREN OF THE CHAPEL, they performed regularly at court, and also at St Paul's School. LYLY's plays were in their repertoire.

**CHILDREN OF THE CHAPEL.** One of the most popular groups of boy actors in London in the sixteenth and early seventeenth centuries, the Children of the Chapel were drawn from the choristers of the Chapel Royal. First performing at court in 1517, they eventually rivalled the professional adult acting companies, and gave the first performances of plays by JONSON, CHAPMAN, and others. The acting careers of FIELD and others began with such companies.

**CHIMNEY PIECE** Until the end of the seventeenth century, the term 'chimney piece' denoted an ornament, typically a painting or a tapestry, placed over a fireplace. In the eighteenth century the term acquired its modern sense of an ornamental structure built around the open recess of a fireplace. By the fourteenth century, the hearth, which had traditionally stood in the middle of a room, had begun to be set in the thickness of one of the walls. The decoration of the protruding hood or chimney breast soon evolved into chimney pieces that dominated the rooms in which they were built.

The earliest surviving high-quality chimney pieces are those installed by Luciano LAURANA in the Palazzo Ducale in Urbino (1464–72). In the sixteenth century chimney pieces became popular in northern Europe, and designs were often taken from those printed in Sebastiano SERLIO's *Architettura* (1537), Jacques Androuet DUCERCEAU's *Second Livre d'architecture* (1561), Philibert DELORME's *Architecture* (1567), and Wendel Dietterlin's *Architectura und Ausstheilung der V. Seuln* (1593–4).

**CHIOGGIA, WAR OF** (1378–81). In the course of the fourteenth century, control of the eastern Mediterranean passed from Genoa to Venice in a series of naval conflicts; the last and decisive engagement was the War of Chioggia. In August 1379, the Genoese fleet evaded Venice's coastal patrols, landed its soldiers on the edge of the Venetian lagoon, and, with the assistance of the Paduan forces of Francesco I CARRARA, occupied Chioggia and Malamocco, which control the southern entrances to the lagoon. Genoese and Paduan forces were encamped within sight of Venice, but were not sufficiently strong to mount an assault on the city. Venetian forces were unable to dislodge the invaders, and even when in January 1380 the main Venetian fleet returned to port after a successful campaign against Genoese shipping in the Levant, the beleaguered garrisons were able to hold out until June.

The war continued at sea, but the mounting threat from Venice's enemies (Francesco I Carrara of Padua, Duke Albrecht III of Austria and Hungary) led the republic to sue for peace through the mediation of Amadeus VI, count of Savoy. The settlement did not favour Venice, but the war exhausted Genoa's challenge to Venice's maritime supremacy in the eastern Mediterranean.

**CHITTARONE** literally means a large kithara and was used synonymously with THEORBO. It was a member of the lute family used to accompany voices, and as a continuo instrument initially in the early years of monody writing (1590–1630) by composers such as Jacopo PERI and Giulio CACCINI.

**CHIVALRY.** By the fifteenth century the medieval code of chivalric behaviour, which promoted virtues such as valour and honour, had evolved into a ceremonial system of courtly etiquette and a set of literary conventions derived from the tradition of courtly love (*amour courtois*). Courtly romances such as AMADÍS DE GAULA and ARIOSTO's *Orlando furioso* perpetuated chivalric values, which were parodied at a later stage in works such as CERVANTES' *Don Quijote*. The chivalric code survived in attenuated form in chivalric ORDERS and in courtly traditions such as jousting. Countries developed chivalric courts which decided on disputes about matters such as rights to arms, precedence, and descent.

In England the medieval High Court of Chivalry declined in the sixteenth century and now rarely meets (and never met between 1737 and 1954); most of its functions are discharged by the College of Arms (also known as the Heralds' College), which was established by royal charter in 1556. The three kings of arms (Garter, Clarenceux, and Norroy and Ulster), six heralds (Windsor, Chester, Lancaster, Somerset, York, and Richmond), and four pursuivants (Rouge Croix, Rouge Dragon, Bluemantle, and Portcullis) have since the

foundation of the college dealt with matters such as peerage claims and the granting of arms.

R. M. Ruggieri, *L'umanesimo cavalleresco italiano da Dante al Pulci* (1963).

**CHORALE or (German)** *Choral*, a Lutheran metrical hymn tune sung by the congregation in unison, the *Achtlieder* book of 1524 being one of the earliest sources. That year also saw the publication of Johann Walter's *Geistliches Gesang büchlein*, supervised by Martin Luther; its polyphonic motets used the chorale melody as a *cantus firmus* in the tenor line. Although chorale melodies continued to be treated in a contrapuntal style, one departure from this technique was the 'cantional' style created by Lucas Osiander, where the melody is in the soprano part and the text is musically punctuated with cadences and pauses. This type of chorale setting was widely adopted in Germany. PRAETORIUS' *Musae Sionae* (1609–10) contains 742 harmonizations to 458 hymn texts.

**CHRISTIAN I** (1426–81), king of Denmark, Norway, and Sweden, secured his three thrones in 1448, when his uncle (the crown prince) resigned the succession in Christian's favour. The Swedish Estates declined to recognize his accession, and instead elected CHARLES VIII. Christian fought to secure his Swedish throne, but except for a brief period (1464–7) when Charles was temporarily deposed, he remained king of Sweden only in name.

King Christian developed trading links with the HANSEATIC LEAGUE, and, on returning from a visit to Italy in 1474, founded the University of Copenhagen.

*DBL*; *NBL*; *NDB*; *SMK* s.v. Kristian I.

**CHRISTIAN II** (1481–1559), king of Denmark, Norway, and Sweden, became viceroy of Norway in 1506 and succeeded to the three thrones of his father King JOHN in 1513. In 1515 Christian married Isabella, sister of the Emperor CHARLES V, but the marriage did not significantly diminish the influence of his Dutch mistress Dyveke Villoms and her mother Sigbrit, who was one of Christian's closest advisers; the sudden death in 1517 of Dyveke was widely believed to be murder, and led to strained relations with the Danish nobility.

In 1518 Christian began to prosecute his claim to subdue Sweden, where the regent Sten STURE the Younger strenuously opposed the union with Denmark. Christian was eventually able to defeat Sture (and afterwards his widow Christina), but opposition continued, and in the wake of Christian's coronation in Stockholm in November 1520 more than 80 noblemen were beheaded (allegedly for heresy) in the judicial massacre now known in English as the 'Stockholm Bloodbath'. These executions precipitated the rebellion of GUSTAVUS VASA, which led to the secession of Sweden in 1523.

In 1522 King Christian introduced a new legal code (the *Landelove*) which had the effect of shifting power away from the nobility and increasing the authority of the burghers and the legal rights of the peasantry. In April 1523 the nobility, led by Christian's uncle FREDERICK I, rose in revolt, and Frederick usurped the throne. Christian fled to the Netherlands to seek refuge in the court of Charles V. In 1531 Christian attempted to mount an invasion of Norway, but he was captured; he spent the last 27 years of his life in a Danish prison.

DBL, NBL, SMK s.v. Kristian II.

**CHRISTIAN III** (1503–59), king of Denmark and Norway, was the son of King FREDERICK I and his first wife Anne of Brandenburg. As a young man he attended the Diet of WORMS (1521), where he began to sympathize with LUTHER'S views. In 1533 Frederick I died, and the following year Christian was proclaimed king; the result was a civil war (the Grevens Fejde or 'Count's War') on confessional lines. In 1535 King Christian, supported by Lutheran nobles and burghers, besieged Copenhagen, which fell to his German mercenaries in 1536.

In 1537 Christian invited BUGENHAGEN to Denmark to reorganize the Danish Church on Lutheran lines. Christian seized episcopal property and repudiated the pope in favour of a national church of which the monarch was the head; the most important cultural event of his reign was the publication of a Danish translation of the Bible in 1550. Christian's foreign policy was also shaped by his Lutheranism: he sought alliances with the Protestant princes of Germany and in 1542 he declared war on CHARLES V and closed the Baltic to ships from Catholic countries. The deleterious effect of the blockade on the economy of the Netherlands forced Charles to negotiate a peace with Christian at the Diet of SPEYER (23 May 1544) and to abandon his attempt to place his niece (the daughter of CHRISTIAN II, who was imprisoned in Denmark) on the throne.

DBL; NBL; NDB.

**CHRISTIAN IV** (1577–1648), king of Denmark and Norway, was the son of King FREDERICK II of Denmark and Sophia of Mecklenburg. He succeeded his father in 1588 and began to rule in his own right in 1598. A long period of peace was ended by war with Sweden (the War of Kalmar or First Swedish War, 1611–13) and by intervention in the THIRTY YEARS WAR in the hope of incorporating some of the north German HANSE cities into Denmark.

Christian's court was one of the most splendid in Europe, particularly with respect to music and architecture. In 1599 he sent a group of young musicians to study with Giovanni GABRIELI in Venice, and as a result Venetian music (particularly the MADRIGAL) was introduced to Denmark. Christian also invited Dutch singers and English instrumentalists to his court, notably John DOWLAND, who lived at the royal court from 1598 to 1606. In architecture, Christian rebuilt three royal residences (notably Frederiksborg, which became the architectural image of his regal authority), fortified many cities and towns, and instituted a programme of church building. He also amassed a huge collection of European and Danish art.

DBL; NBL; NDB; Grove; MDA s.v. Oldenburg; J. Skovgaard, A King's Architecture: Christian IV and his Buildings (1973).

**CHRISTINE DE PIZAN or (Italian) Cristina da Pizzano** (c.1364–c.1430), Italian-French poet, born in Venice, the daughter of the Italian royal astrologer at the court of King Charles V of France. As a young woman she married and was soon widowed (1390), and during this period wrote lyric poetry, typically *ballades* and *rondeaux*. In 1399 she entered the long debate now known as the *querelle des femmes* (conducted in Latin and French from the thirteenth to the seventeenth centuries) with her *Épître au dieu d'amours*; her subsequent works on women include *Livre de la cité des dames* (1404–5) and *Livre des trois vertus* (1406; also known as *Trésor des dames*). She also wrote a life of JOAN OF ARC (*Ditié de Jeanne d'Arc*, 1429).

DBI s.v. Cristina da Pizzano; MDA; C. C. Willard, Christine de Pizan (1984).

**CHRISTMAS, GERARD or Garrett** (1576–1634), English sculptor. He was appointed carver to the navy (1614–34) and designed pageantry for lord mayor's shows from 1619 to 1632. His works include an equestrian figure of King James I (JAMES VI) on the city gate at Aldersgate (demolished 1761), through which James had entered London for the first time as king; he also carved (and perhaps designed) a three-tiered frontispiece on Northumberland House on the Strand (demolished 1874). Christmas worked together with his sons John and Matthias; their workshop produced a large number of sculpted tombs, of which the best known is the tomb of George Abbot, archbishop of Canterbury, in Holy Trinity, Guildford.

DNB; MDA.

**CHRISTUS, PETRUS** (c.1410–1475/6), Netherlandish painter who became a master in Bruges in 1444 and worked there throughout his career. The style of his paintings is indebted to Jan van EYCK and Rogier van der WEYDEN. In the case of Jan van Eyck, Petrus Christus copied some of his paintings and may have completed some of the paintings that Jan van Eyck left unfinished at his death; the influence of Rogier van der Weyden is apparent in Petrus Christus' *Lamentation* (c.1450, Musée d'Art Ancien, Brussels), which is based on Rogier's *Deposition* (Prado, Madrid). He differed from his predecessors in eschewing their dark backgrounds in favour of interiors or landscapes seen through a window in paintings such as *St Eligius with Two Saints* (1449, Metropolitan Museum, New York), *Portrait of Edward Grimston* (1446, on loan to the National Gallery in London), and the undated *Portrait of a Young Man* (National Gallery, London). His innovative treatment of PERSPECTIVE is evident in *Virgin and Child with SS Francis and Jerome* (1457, Städelsches Kunstinstitut, Frankfurt am Main), which is the earliest dated painting in northern Europe to use geometrical perspective.

MDA.

**CHRYSOLORAS, MANUEL** (c.1350–1415), the founder of GREEK SCHOLARSHIP in Italy. Chrysoloras was a friend of the Emperor MANUEL II, and led many imperial missions to Europe in search of military aid to combat the Turks. His visits to Venice in the 1390s brought him into contact with Italian scholars, and in 1397 he moved to Florence to take up a professorship in Greek which Coluccio SALUTATI had persuaded the Florentine government to offer to him. He taught in Florence from 1397 to 1400; his pupils, in whom he instilled a lasting passion for Greek language and literature, included Leonardo BRUNI, Niccolò NICCOLI, Palla STROZZI, and VERGE-RIO. These three years in Florence had a decisive impact, in that, together with Salutati, he inaugurated the humanist school of fifteenth-century Florence.

In 1400 Chrysoloras resumed his career in the diplomatic service of the empire, initially travelling to northern Europe to meet the emperor and then in 1403 returning to Constantinople. Between 1406 and 1410 he visited Venice, Padua, and Bologna, and travelled to England, France, and Spain. He converted to Catholicism and subsequently spent two years in Rome (1411–13) lobbying for the convening of a church council. John XXIII was persuaded to convoke the COUNCIL OF CONSTANCE, to which Chrysoloras travelled; he died in Constance on 15 April 1415, when the Council had only been in session for five months.

Chrysoloras wrote relatively little. His most influential book was a textbook of Greek grammar called *Erotemata* (c.1471); this text, which was later abridged and translated into Latin by his student GUARINO DA VERONA (to whom he had taught Greek in Constantinople) was eventually printed in 1484, and was subsequently used by humanists such as ERASMUS and REUCHLIN. Chrysoloras also wrote an important Greek epistle addressed to the co-emperor (later JOHN VIII PALAIOLOGOS) entitled *A Comparison of the Old and New Rome*. In this epistle he describes the classical antiquities and Christian shrines of Rome, but contends that these marvels cannot hold a candle to the glories of Constantinople, such as Hagia Sophia.

G. Cammelli, *Manuele Crisolora* (1941); H. Homeyer, 'Zur *Synkrisis* des Manuel Chrysolaras, einem Vergleich zwischen Rom und Konstantinopel', *Clio*, 62 (1980).

## CHURCHYARD, THOMAS

**CHURCHYARD, THOMAS** (c.1520–1604), English poet and soldier. Churchyard served SURREY as a page before becoming a soldier in France, Ireland, Scotland, and the Low Countries. His writings include *A Mirror for Man* (before 1553), *Shore's Wife* in the *Mirror for Magistrates* (1563; see SACKVILLE, THOMAS), and the *General Rehearsal of Wares* (1579). Amongst his minor writings are some accounts of contemporary events.

*DNB*.

## CICERO IN THE RENAISSANCE

**CICERO IN THE RENAISSANCE**. The Roman orator and politician Marcus Tullius Cicero (106–43 BC), who is often called 'Tully' in English Renaissance texts, was revived by PETRARCH, who, together with Poggio BRACCIOLINI, was responsible for the recovery of many of Cicero's texts: Petrarch discovered the *Letters to Atticus* in Verona in 1345 and Poggio, in the course of his visit to the COUNCIL OF CONSTANCE, found ten of Cicero's *Orations*. Petrarch valued Cicero both as a moralist and as an exemplary prose stylist. Cicero's pursuit of a public career became central to the Renaissance debate about the rival claims of the active life of public service (*vita activa*) and the contemplative life of scholarly enquiry and spiritual meditation (*vita contemplativa*). His most influential Renaissance champion in this respect was Coluccio SALUTATI, whose appropriation of Cicero as a model

for public life shaped the views of humanists in Florence. In his philosophical writings Cicero articulated a form of STOICISM that Renaissance humanists were able to reconcile with Christian belief.

The term 'Ciceronianism' refers to the standing of Cicero as a model for Latin prose. Humanists such as Lorenzo VALLA and GUARINO DA VERONA advocated a Latin style based on Cicero's orations, letters, and philosophical treatises, but others, including POLIZIANO and ERASMUS, deplored the excesses of Ciceronianism, and Erasmus' satire *Ciceronianus* (1528) mercilessly mocked pedantic adherence to Ciceronian models.

Charles Schmitt, *Cicero scepticus: A Study of the Influence of the 'Academica' in the Renaissance* (1972); Emile Telle, *L'Erasmianus sive Ciceronianus d'Étienne Dolet (1535)* (1974); J. W. Binns, 'Ciceronianism in Sixteenth-Century England: The Latin Debate', *Lias*, 7 (1980); J. H. M. Salmon, 'Cicero and Tacitus in Sixteenth-Century France', *American Historical Review*, 85 (1980).

**CICOGNA, VILLA**, a VILLA and garden in Bisuschio (Piedmont), near Lake Lugano. The villa was built in the fifteenth century as a hunting box to which the Mozzoni family invited the dukes of Milan for boar-hunts. In the sixteenth century the villa was rebuilt in the Renaissance style, with two decorated loggias: one leads to the villa, and the other to a porticoed court bordering a sunken garden with clipped hedges, gravel paths, and small FOUNTAINS; below this level there are two ornamental fish ponds. The most remarkable features of the garden are the water-staircase and the large terrace that runs at right angles to it. The elegant water-staircase leads from the sunken garden to the meadows above the house. The terrace was used as a sheltered promenade from which the Lombard countryside and the PARTERRES of the lower gardens could be viewed; the arcaded retaining wall of the terrace contains an underground gallery (imitative of the ancient Roman cryptoporticus) that was intended as a cool retreat from the heat of summer. Both house and garden have survived in their sixteenth-century form.

**CICONIA, JOHANNES** (c.1370–1412), Walloon composer, active in Italy, who by 1403 was *cantor et custos* of Padua Cathedral. He wrote motets and secular songs for Francesco Zabarella, his patron, and for the Carrara family who were rulers of Padua.

**CIECO, FRANCESCO, or Francesco Bello** (d. 1505), Italian poet. He was probably born in Ferrara, and in the course of his career worked in several north Italian courts; the name 'Cieco' refers to his blindness. His principal literary work was *Il Mambriano*, a chivalric romance modelled on BOIARDO's *Orlando innamorato*.

*DBI* s.v. Francesco, detto il Cieco di Ferrara; *OCIL*.

**CIEZA DE LEÓN, PEDRO** (1518–60), Spanish soldier and historian who participated in the conquest of Peru and later supported Pedro de la GASCA in his suppression of the rebellion of Gonzalo PIZARRO. The first part of his *Crónica del Perú*, which contains the first account of its physical geography, was published in Seville in 1553. The remaining parts, which deal with the civilization of the Incas and the Spanish conquest, remained unpublished until the nineteenth and twentieth centuries.

*DBEH; DHE*; Harriet de Onis (ed.), *The Incas of Pedro de Cieza de León* (1979); Francesca Cantù, *Pedro de Cieza de León e il 'Descrubrimiento y conquista del Perú'* (1979).

**CIFRA, ANTONIO** (1584–1629), Italian composer who became *maestro di cappella* at the Santa Casa in Loreto and was also active in Rome. He wrote madrigals, *ricercares*, and canzonas as well as sacred music, notably several *concertato* motets for voices and organ.

**CIGOLI or Ludovico Cardi** (1559–1613), Italian painter, architect, and writer on perspective, a native of Cigoli (Tuscany); he trained in the Florentine studio of Alessandro ALLORI. His surviving paintings include frescoes in the Church of Santa Maria Novella in Florence (1581–4) and a fine *Madonna and Child* (1582, Szépmüvészti Múzeum, Budapest); in Rome he painted *St Peter Healing the Lame Man* (St Peter's Basilica). Cigoli's principal surviving architectural work is the courtyard of BUONTALENTI's Palazzo Nonfinito, the 'unfinished palace' in Florence. The manuscript of Cigoli's unpublished *Trattato della prospettiva pratica* is in the Uffizi.

*DBI* s.v. Cardi, Lodovico, detto il Cigoli; *MDA* s.v. Cigoli, Lodovico; Roberto Confini, *Il Cigoli* (1991).

**CIMA, GIOVANNI PAOLO** (c.1570–c.1622), Italian composer, organist of Santa Maria presso San Celso in Milan, where he also assumed the duties of *maestro di cappella*. He composed for organ and other instruments; his *Concerti* (1610) includes a significantly early experiment with a trio sonata format of violin, CORNETT, and continuo.

**CIMABUE or Cenni di Pepe** (c.1240–1302), Italian painter, probably a native of Florence. He was famously said by DANTE to have 'held the field in painting' and then to have been eclipsed by GIOTTO ('Credette Cimabue nella pintura | tener lo campo, e ora ha Giotto il grido | sì che la fama di colui è scura' *Purgatorio* II. 94–6). This passage was the basis of the subsequent belief that Cimabue was the harbinger of Giotto and therefore the progenitor of Italian Renaissance painting. The only documented work by Cimabue is a mosaic of *St John* (1301), which was his restoration of a considerably older and larger mosaic (possibly by a twelfth-century artist) in the apse of Pisa Cathedral. Attributions, all of which are contested, include the *Madonna of Santa Trinita* (c.1285/6, Uffizi), a crucifix in the Church of Santa Croce in Florence (seriously damaged in the flood of 1966), and a cycle of damaged murals in the Upper Church of San Francesco in Assisi.

*DBI* s.v. Cenni di Pepe, detto Cimabue; *MDA*; Luciano Bellosi, *Cimabue* (English trans. 1998).

**CIMA DA CONEGLIANO, GIOVANNI BATTISTA** (1459/60–1517/18), Italian painter. He was born in Conegliano, on the Venetian terraferma, and spent his career in Venice.

Although Cima painted a considerable number of small devotional works, his reputation rests on his altarpieces, of which he painted a large number. In the early years of the sixteenth century he painted altarpieces for several Venetian churches, including Santa Maria della Carità (c.1510, now in the Accademia), Corpus Domini (c.1505, now in the Brera, Milan), and Santa Maria dei Carmini (c.1510, still in the church). His later works include a pair of secular tondi (*Endymion Asleep* and *The Judgement of Midas*, c.1505–10, Galleria Nazionale, Parma) and a signed and dated *Incredulity of St Thomas* (1504, National Gallery, London) painted for a flagellant community in Portogruaro.

*DBI; MDA*; Peter Humfrey, *Cima da Conegliano* (1983).

**CIMINELLI, SERAFINO DE', or L'Aquilano** (1466–1500), Italian poet and musician, a native of Aquila who became a page in the viceregal court in Naples and then moved to the papal court in Rome. His reputation as a poet, and to a lesser extent as a musician, led to invitations to the courts of Milan, Urbino, and Mantua. His poems were collected as *L'opera d'amore* (Venice, 1530).

*DBI; OCIL.*

**CINQUECENTO**, an apheretic form of *mil cinque cento* ('one thousand five hundred'), the Italian term for the sixteenth century (15—) and for the art and architecture of the period.

**CINTHIO, IL**. See GIRALDI, GIAMBATTISTA CINZIO.

**CIOMPI REVOLUTION or (Italian) Tumulto dei Ciompi**. The *ciompi* were the day-labourers in the wool industry in Florence; they were not allowed to join the Wool Guild or form their own association. They were subject to summary dismissal, and they had no legal redress other than to appeal to their employer, the Arte della Lana. In July 1378 the *ciompi*, with the aid of other disaffected groups, staged an armed rebellion against the civic government, which they forced to grant their status as a guild and to improve their wages. In late August the employers in other industries, alarmed at the prospect of a workers' dictatorship, joined forces with the Arte della Lana and crushed the rebellion. The oligarchy centred on the ALBIZZI FAMILY was reinstated and promptly repealed all the legislation that had been passed under pressure from the *ciompi*.

G. Brucker, 'The Ciompi Revolution', in N. Rubinstein (ed.), *Florentine Studies* (1968); Istituto Nazionale di Studi sul Rinascimento, *Il Tumulto dei Ciompi* (1981).

**CIRIACO D'ANCONA or Ciriaco Pizzicolli or Cyriac of Ancona** (c.1390–1455), epigraphist and collector of antiquities. Ciriaco collected antiquities in Constantinople (where he travelled as a merchant in 1418) and in subsequent visits to Greece and Egypt. His collection centred on epigraphs (which were published posthumously in his *Commentaria*), but he also amassed manuscripts, gems, and medallions. Most of his collection was eventually destroyed in a fire, and so his sketches of artefacts sometimes constitute the only evidence of lost classical antiquities.

*DBI* s.v. Pizzicolli, Ciriaco; C. C. van Essen, *Ciriaque d'Ancone en Égypte* (1958); *Cyracus of Ancona's Journeys in the Propontis and the Northern Aegean, 1444–1445*, ed. E. W. Bodnar and C. Mitchell (1976).

**CISNEROS, CARDINAL FRANCISCO JIMÉNEZ or Ximénez DE** (1436–1517), Spanish statesman and scholar, born in Torrelaguna (Castile) and educated at Alcalá de Henares and Salamanca before being ordained as a priest in 1459 and moving to Rome. He returned to Spain in 1465, bringing with him an expectative letter from Pope SIXTUS IV appointing him as archpriest of Uceda in the diocese of Toledo; the appointment was to take effect in 1473. When Cisneros claimed his benefice, his diocesan, Archbishop Carrillo of Toledo, opposed the appointment and imprisoned Cisneros. Six years later, Carrillo yielded to Cisneros's obstinacy and restored him to his benefice, which Cisneros promptly exchanged for a chaplaincy in Sigüenza, where Cardinal MENDOZA appointed him as his vicar-general.

Cisneros was a markedly successful churchman, and seemed assured of further advancement in the ranks of the SECULAR CLERGY, but he suddenly resolved to become a friar. He resigned his benefices, set aside his baptismal name of Gonzalo in favour of Francisco, and entered the Observant Franciscan monastery of San Juan de los Reyes, which had recently been founded in Toledo by FERDINAND and ISABELLA. He surpassed the usual severities of the novitiate by sleeping on the ground, wearing a hair-shirt, doubling his fasts, and scourging himself mercilessly. His conspicuously extreme austerity attracted large crowds of penitents, and he therefore withdrew to the remote Monastery of Our Lady of Castañar, near which he built a hut in which he lived as a hermit.

Cisneros's life changed again in 1492, when he reluctantly accepted the post of confessor to Queen Isabella, for which he had been nominated by Cardinal Mendoza. The queen, moved by the severe sanctity of her confessor, submitted to his advice on affairs of state as well as on spiritual matters. In 1494 she secured his appointment as provincial of the Franciscans in Castile, and in the face of intense opposition (especially from the Conventual Franciscans, who followed a mitigated rule that allowed them to accumulate property) he set about reducing all Franciscans to the uncompromising austerity of the Observants. On the death of Cardinal Mendoza in 1495, Queen Isabella secured from Pope ALEXANDER VI a bull designating her confessor as Mendoza's successor as archbishop of Toledo, an office that carried with it the chancellorship of Castile. Cisneros resisted, but his 'nolo episcopari' ('I decline to become a bishop') was overruled by a second papal bull commanding him to accept consecration. He was ordered by Rome to live in a style appropriate to his high office, but he contrived to live a severely ascetic life. At Toledo Cisneros reintroduced the Mozarabic rite and endowed a chapel in the cathedral and six parish churches in the city to ensure its survival; it still survives, albeit in Spanish rather than Latin, and is, together with the Ambrosian rite in Milan, the only non-Roman rite in the Catholic Church in the West.

In 1499 Cisneros followed the royal court to Granada, and set about converting the Moors who had elected to remain in Spain after the conquest of the Islamic sultanate in 1492. Deploying a combination of bribes and compulsory sermons, Cisneros succeeded in securing so many converts that they had to be baptized by aspersion (sprinkling *en masse*) rather than affusion (pouring individually). The mass conversions occasioned a rebellion amongst those who remained faithful to Islam. Cisneros quelled the civil unrest, and offered the rebels the choice of baptism or exile; most chose baptism, and Isabella rejoiced at her confessor's service to Christianity.

On 24 November 1504 Isabella died, and was succeeded by her daughter JUANA LA LOCA and Juana's husband Archduke Philip of Burgundy (PHILIP I); King Ferdinand declared himself to be regent of Castile. It was Cisneros who arranged a meeting between Ferdinand and Philip and facilitated the retirement of Ferdinand from Castile. The sudden death of Philip in September 1506, together with the mental incapacity of Juana, the youth of the future CHARLES V, and the absence in Naples of Ferdinand, combined to make Cisneros the virtual ruler of Spain until the return in May 1507 of Ferdinand, who brought with him a cardinal's hat for Cisneros and his appointment as grand inquisitor-general of Castile and León.

The next great cause in the life of Cardinal Cisneros was the securing of the enclave of Oran on the north coast of AFRICA. The port of Mers el Kebir (10 kilometres (6 miles) from Oran) had been captured in 1505, and in 1509 Cisneros accompanied the army that stormed the city. On 28 January 1516 Ferdinand died, and once again Cisneros became regent of Castile, this time on behalf of Charles, a youth of 16 who lived in the Netherlands. Charles landed in Asturias in September 1517; Cisneros hastened to meet him, but fell ill at Roa, possibly because he had been poisoned; he received a letter from Charles coldly thanking him for his services and giving him permission to retire to his diocese. Cisneros died a few hours later, on 8 November 1517.

Cisneros was a generous patron of learning. In 1500 he founded the University of ALCALÁ DE HENARES out of his private income; the university was opened in 1508, and attracted some of Europe's finest scholars to work on the COMPLUTENSIAN POLYGLOT. His Complutensian University was to be removed to Madrid in 1836, and its splendid buildings in Alcalá handed over to the military, but a new Universidad de Alcalá was founded in the original buildings in 1977.

The life of Cisneros had an odd postscript: in the seventeenth century, King Philip IV of Spain attempted to secure the beatification of Cisneros by commissioning research on his miracles; the result was Pedro de Quintanilla's *Oranum Ximenii virtute catholicum* (Rome, 1658), which demonstrated that, in the 140 years since his death, Cisneros had miraculously intervened to extend the faith from Oran (where, in life, he had established the INQUISITION) throughout Africa and the Americas.

*DHE* s.v. Cisneros; J. García Oro, *Cisneros y la reforma del clero español* (1971); id., *El cardenal Cisneros: Vida y empresas* (2 vols., 1992–3).

**CITTERN**, a pear-shaped, fretted instrument on which the wire strings pass over a movable bridge. The bulk of the neck is reduced on the bass side to allow rapid shifting of the left hand. It was seen as a modern equivalent of the ancient Greek kithara, though its immediate medieval forebear was the citole. Late sixteenth-century cittern-making was centred at Brescia in the workshops of G. P. Maggini (c.1581–c.1632) and Gasparo da Salò (1540–1609). It was used for playing continuo.

**CIVIL LAW or (Latin)** *ius civile*. The term 'civil law' was originally used to denote the law applicable to Roman citizens as opposed to the law applicable to foreigners in Rome. The term was gradually extended to refer to the law applicable to Roman citizens throughout the Empire. In the Renaissance the term retained this historical sense, but was also used to distinguish state law from CANON LAW. The term *Corpus iuris civilis* to describe the Justinian compilation of Roman civil law was first used in GODEFROY's edition of 1583, and was intended to echo the title of the *Corpus iuris canonici*. In popular usage the term 'civil law' referred to the law applicable to ordinary individual citizens, as opposed to the law for clergy or the LAW MERCHANT or MARITIME LAW.

The collapse of the Roman Empire in the west meant that for centuries European law was Germanic CUSTOMARY LAW. The Roman origins of canon law ensured that Roman law never disappeared altogether, and in eleventh-century Italy Roman civil law was rediscovered. The study of Roman law spread across Europe, and eventually Roman law was incorporated into the legal systems of northern Europe in the process known as the RECEPTION. The civil law systems of modern continental Europe (as opposed to the COMMON LAW systems of England and Ireland) are all rooted in Roman civil law, either in its Napoleonic codifications (France, Belgium, Italy, Luxemburg, Spain, and Latin America) or on the model of German codification (Germany, Switzerland, and most of eastern and central Europe).

**CIVITALI, MATTEO** (1436–1501), Italian sculptor, born in Lucca. He trained in the Florentine studio of Antonio ROSSELLINO and later introduced the Florentine style to Lucca, where his first important work was the marble tomb of Piero da Noceto (1472) in Lucca Cathedral; his other work for the cathedral includes a pulpit (1494–8) and the Tempietto del Volto Santo (1484), a marble reliquary which contains a wooden image of Jesus believed to have been fashioned by Nicodemus. Civitali also designed the Palazzo Pretorio (1492) in Lucca, and his statue now stands in the portico. Beyond Lucca, Civitali sculpted a lectern and candelabra in Pisa Cathedral and six free-standing statues of patriarchs in Genoa Cathedral (1496).

> *DBI; MDA;* Martina Harms, *Matteo Civitali: Bildhauer der Frührenaissance in Lucca* (1995).

**CLAUDIAN IN THE RENAISSANCE.** Claudian was a Greek-speaking Alexandrian (known in Latin as Claudius Claudianus) who moved to Italy at an unknown date before AD 395. He adopted the Latin tongue of his hosts, and soon became a court poet under the patronage of the Emperor Honorius. His poetry demonstrates that he was an adherent of the old religion rather than of Christianity, but he was nonetheless appropriated in medieval Italy not only as a Christian, but also as a Florentine; the latter misapprehension derives from the dedication of one of Claudian's poems to someone named Florentinus. The *editio princeps* was printed in Vicenza in 1482.

Claudian is the last significant poet of the classical tradition in Latin, and so was deemed by fifteenth-century educators to be the last exponent of pure and correct Latin; this judgement led to his poetry being used in schools as a model for imitation. The most important feature of Claudian's poetry for the Renaissance was *ekphrasis*, the description of works of art; he is the source of these descriptive set pieces for writers from POLIZIANO (in the *Stanze per la giostra*) to SHAKESPEARE (in *The Rape of Lucrece*), and of the passages in epics such as ARIOSTO's *Orlando furioso* and SPENSER's *Fairy Queen* in which the narrative is suspended in favour of sumptuous descriptions of buildings.

> S. Döpp, 'Claudian und lateinische Epik zwischen 1300 und 1600', *Res publica literarum*, 12 (1989).

**CLAVICYTHERIUM**, an upright harpsichord (looking similar to a portative organ) with a vertical soundboard. The instrument is mentioned in a treatise by Paulus Paulirinus of Prague (1459–63). Unlike the more familiar type of harpsichord, the jacks, being set horizontally, do not have the benefit of gravity to assist them in their return; in consequence they do not share the lightness of touch enjoyed by their descendants.

**CLAVIORGANUM**, a keyboard instrument where the sound comes from both strings and pipes. The inventories of HENRY VIII (1547) list five spinets or virginals 'with pipes underneath' and different types existed elsewhere on the Continent. From 1580 several large organs were built incorporating one or two rows of harpsichord strings.

**CLAVIUS or (German) Klau, CHRISTOPH** (1537–1612), German mathematician and astronomer, born in Bamberg. He entered the JESUIT Order in 1555, studied in Coimbra and became professor of mathematics at the Order's Collegio Romano. Clavius was the principal apologist for the CALENDAR REFORMS of Pope GREGORY XIII, and between 1588 and 1603 published five treatises on the subject. In 1611 he was asked to advise Pope Paul V on the cosmological implications of Galileo GALILEI's astronomical observations; Clavius' report approved Galileo's work but argued that it did not prove that the cosmos was heliocentric. Clavius wrote two elementary mathematical textbooks, *Epitome arithmeticae* (1583) and *Algebra* (1608); these books were in Latin because they were for use by the Jesuits whose work was international.

> *DSB; NDB.*

**CLEMENS NON PAPA or Jacobus Clement** (c.1510/15–1555/6), Flemish composer active in Bruges and Ypres. In 1550 he worked as *sanger ende componist* to the Marien Brotherhood in 's-Hertogenbosch. He is best remembered for his settings of the Psalms in Dutch (*souterliedekens*); other compositions suggest connections with Philippe de Croy, duke of Alva, and Charles V.

**CLEMENT VII** (1478–1534), pope from 19 November 1523 until his death on 25 September 1534, was born Giulio de' MEDICI in Florence on 26 May 1479; he was the illegitimate son of Giuliano de' MEDICI and his mistress Fioretta. His father was murdered in the PAZZI CONSPIRACY before he was born, so he was raised and educated by his grandfather, Lorenzo de' MEDICI.

In 1513 Giulio's cousin Pope LEO X swept aside the impediment of bastardy and created him archbishop of Florence and cardinal; in 1517 he was appointed vice-chancellor of the Holy See, a post that was immensely lucrative but brought with it responsibility for the formulation of policies to combat the Lutheran reformation in the north and to free Italy from foreign domination. In May 1519 Giulio assumed responsibility for the government of Florence and took a solicitous interest in its administration even as he extended the influence of his family. He was largely responsible for the formation of an imperial-papal alliance in 1521, and retained his responsibility for the alliance under Pope ADRIAN VI.

On 19 November 1523, at the end of a bitter and contentious 50-day conclave, Giulio was elected pope and assumed the conciliatory name Clement. He was rightly regarded as the imperial candidate, but he declined to become a puppet of CHARLES V. He refused to renew the defensive alliance with Charles V for which he had been responsible under the two previous popes, and further alienated Charles by entering into alliances with FRANCIS I (December 1524) and Venice (January 1525). Francis had reconquered Milan in October 1524, but his defeat and capture at the battle of PAVIA in February 1525 prompted Clement to renew his allegiance to the Empire. In May 1526 he again changed sides, joining the anti-imperial alliance of France, Florence, Milan, and Venice which was ratified by the League of COGNAC. Charles responded with the imperial invasion of Italy which culminated in the SACK OF ROME on 6 May 1527. Clement retreated to Castel Sant'Angelo, where he became a prisoner of the Empire; one of the many consequences of his incarceration was the loss of control of Florence, where in May 1527 the Medici were ejected by the restored republic. Clement eventually secured his release (on 6 December 1527) by acceding to the imperial occupation of much of the PAPAL STATE, by pledging neutrality, and by paying a large ransom (400,000 scudi). On being released he left Rome, first for Orvieto and subsequently for Viterbo, only returning to Rome in October 1528.

In June 1529 Clement was reconciled to Charles in the Treaty of Barcelona, in which they pledged common cause against Lutheran heretics and the Ottoman army that was advancing on Vienna. Clement crowned Charles as Holy Roman Emperor in Bologna on 24 February 1530; this was to be the last imperial coronation by a pope. Charles reciprocated by overthrowing the Florentine republic and installing Alessandro de' MEDICI as duke of Florence. The following year, moved by unease about the imperial domination of Italy, Clement renewed his alliance with France, this time by travelling to Marseille in October 1533 to conduct the wedding of his grand-niece CATHERINE DE MÉDICIS to Henri d'Orléans (later King HENRI II), second son of Francis I.

The long series of catastrophes which beset the pontificate of Clement often arose out of his troubled relationship with the Empire. In 1524 Clement had sent Cardinal CAMPEGGI as his legate to the Diet of Nuremberg to assure the emperor of continued papal support for the imperial ban on Luther pronounced at the Diet of WORMS, but the emperor's nine-year absence from Germany after the Diet, occasioned in significant part by his struggle with the papacy, allowed the Reformation to grow unchecked, and in June 1526 the Diet of SPEYER overthrew the edict banning Luther. Similarly, Clement was unable to deal effectively with the spread of Lutheranism in Scandinavia and of Zwinglianism in Switzerland. In England, his hesitation in granting a divorce to HENRY VIII to enable him to dispose of CATHERINE OF ARAGON in order to marry ANNE BOLEYN was in part a result of pressure from Charles V, who was Catherine's nephew; Clement's vacillation led inexorably to the English schism.

Clement was a generous patron of learning, literature, and the arts, as befitted a Medici pope. He extended his patronage to Benvenuto CELLINI, GUICCIARDINI, MICHELANGELO, and RAPHAEL. His commissions to Michelangelo included the Medici monuments in the Sagrestia Nuova in the Church of San Lorenzo in Florence and, shortly before his death, the ceiling of the SISTINE CHAPEL. The magnificent portrait of Clement by SEBASTIANO DEL PIOMBO now hangs in the Palazzo di Capodimonte in Naples.

*DBI* s.v. Clemente VII; *MDA* s.v. Medici, de' (8).

**CLEMENT VIII** (1563–1605), pope from 30 January 1592 until his death on 5 March 1605, was born Ippolito Aldobrandini in Fano on 24 February 1536, the son of a lawyer who had been exiled from Florence. Through the patronage of Cardinal Alessandro FARNESE, Ippolito was able to study CANON LAW at Padua, Perugia, and Bologna, after which he was appointed consistorial advocate by Pope PIUS V, the protector of the Aldobrandini family. In 1569 Pope Pius appointed Ippolito *auditorus* ('auditor', i.e. a judge who hears cases) of the *Rota Sacra Romana*, the principal tribunal of the Holy See. On 15 May 1585 Pope SIXTUS V appointed him datary of the papal court and seven months later (18 December) created him cardinal-priest. The following year he was appointed grand penitentiary, and in that capacity presided over the tribunal which deals with cases pertaining to the sacraments. In 1588–9 he visited Poland as a papal legate, and successfully mediated a dispute between King SIGISMUND III VASA and the house of HABSBURG. He was a serious candidate for the papacy in the three conclaves of 1590–1 and was elected on 30 January 1605.

Clement was a reforming pope who was determined to implement the decrees of the COUNCIL OF TRENT, but his undoubted personal piety did not inhibit his unblushing nepotism: in 1593 he raised his nephews Cinzio and Pietro Aldobrandini to the cardinalate, and he subsequently created a grand-nephew cardinal at the age of 14. More honourably, he promoted to the cardinalate Caesar BARONIUS (who was his confessor) and Roberto BELLARMINO, and his closest adviser was Filippo NERI.

In 1592 Clement reissued a revised edition of JEROME's translation of the Bible; the Clementine text was to be the definitive text for centuries. He also authorized revised versions of the principal liturgical texts (the pontifical of 1596, the *Caeremoniale episcoporum*—the liturgical book for bishops —of 1600, the breviary of 1602, and the missal of 1604) as well as an expanded INDEX LIBRORUM PROHIBITORUM (1596) which proscribed all books by JEWS. He stiffened the resolve of the INQUISITION to extirpate heresy, and the dozens of heretics that were sent to the stake included Giordano BRUNO. He also hounded Beatrice CENCI to the stake, partly out of moral outrage, but, in the view of her defenders, with an eye to the prospect of confiscating her estate. Such episodes show that Clement could be brutally decisive, but there is also evidence of a tendency to dither: for ten years he studied the dispute between the JESUITS and the DOMINICANS about the doctrine of GRACE, but refused to arbitrate.

In foreign policy, Clement courageously recognized HENRI IV as king of France, and on 17 September 1595 absolved him from the excommunication enacted by Pope Sixtus V. The cost of this recognition was acceptance of the Edict of NANTES, which granted civil and religious rights to HUGUENOTS. The corresponding benefit was the curbing of Spanish power within the curia, and Clement was instrumental in negotiating the Peace of VERVINS in 1598. When the ESTE dynasty in Ferrara was extinguished, Clement was able to deploy the power of Henri IV to fend off Spanish and imperial opposition to his absorption of Ferrara into the PAPAL STATE in 1597.

In 1595 the metropolitan of Kiev and five Ruthenian bishops petitioned for communion with Rome. On 23 December Clement agreed to an arrangement whereby the millions of Orthodox Ruthenian Christians in Poland could enjoy communion with Rome while still retaining their liturgy; these proposals were ratified by the Synod of BREST-LITOVSK (6–10 October 1596). He supported the COUNTER-REFORMATION in Switzerland by appointing FRANÇOIS DE SALES as coadjutor bishop (1599) and bishop (1602) of Geneva.

Clement's foreign policy successes in France and Poland were counterbalanced by failures elsewhere in Europe. Clement was unable to realize his ambition to form a Christian coalition to fend off the Ottomans, who were threatening Hungary and Austria. Similarly, he carried on a futile dialogue with King James I (JAMES VI) of England in the forlorn hope (sustained by the Catholic sympathies of Queen Anne) of reconciling Britain with Rome. Clement's hopes for a Catholic restoration in Sweden (sustained by the accession of the Catholic SIGISMUND III VASA to the throne in 1593) were crushed when he was deposed in 1598 by his Protestant uncle, Karl of Södermanland (later King CHARLES IX).

*DBI* s.v. Clemente VIII; *MDA* s.v. Aldobrandini, (1).

**CLEMENT VIII** (*c*.1360–1446), antipope from 10 June 1423 until his abdication on 26 July 1429, was born Gil Sanchez Muñoz in Teruel and was later known as Aegidius. At the time of his election, Sanchez was provost of Valencia and archpriest of Teruel. His predecessor BENEDICT XIII had created four new cardinals in 1422, and when he died six months later the three who were in Peñiscola chose Sanchez; the absentee, Cardinal Jean Carrier (who declared that the election had been invalidated by simony), was later punished by being stripped of his cardinalship and excommunicated.

Upon his election the tiny promontory of Peñiscola was promptly blockaded by the forces of Queen Maria of Aragon (regent of ALFONSO V, who was absent in Naples), but Clement continued to preside over his miniature papal court, which he increased to five by the creation of two new cardinals. In 1429 Alfonso V (who had lifted the royal blockade late in 1423) sent a delegation to Peñiscola led by his private secretary Alfonso de Borja (later Pope CALLISTUS III). Alfonso negotiated successfully with Clement and his curia, and on 26 July 1429 Clement abdicated at a ceremony in which his cardinals formally elected Cardinal Odda Colonna as pope, a post that he had held (as Pope MARTIN V) since 1417. On 14 August the legate of Martin V formally reconciled Sanchez, and twelve days later Martin V appointed Sanchez bishop of Majorca, a post which he held until his death on 28 December 1446. His tomb is in the chapter house of Palma Cathedral.

M. Garcia Miralles, *La personalidad de Gil Sanchez Muñoz y la solución del cisma de Occidente* (1954).

**CLERCK, HENDRIK DE** (*c*.1570–1630), Flemish painter, born in Brussels; he was long thought to have trained in the Antwerp studio of Maarten de VOS, but it now seems clear that in 1587 he was working in Rome as an apprentice to the Flemish painter Frans van de Kasteele. He settled in Brussels, where he was appointed court painter to Archduke ALBRECHT VON HABSBURG. One of his finest paintings is *Holy Kinship*, the central panel of his first dated triptych (1590, Brussels, Musée d'Art Ancien).

*MDA.*

**CLÉREAU, PIERRE** (*fl.* 1539–67), French composer, based in Lorraine. He wrote sacred music and songs, setting poetry by Ronsard, Tyard, Baïf, Belleau, Masures, Bembo, Tansillo, and Ariosto.

**CLES or Clesio, BERNARDO** (1485–1539), Italian cardinal and patron, born in the castle in Cles (Trentino) on 11 March 1485. He studied at Bologna, and in 1514 Pope LEO X appointed him bishop of Trent, of which he was already the secular ruler. In 1530 he was created cardinal by Pope CLEMENT VII, who bestowed other bishoprics on him. Cardinal Bernardo was a firm ally of the HABSBURGS and a counsellor of FERDINAND I, Habsburg governor of Austria (and later Holy Roman Emperor). He died of complications arising from SYPHILIS on 30 July 1539.

Cardinal Bernardo was the patron of ARETINO, BEMBO, and ERASMUS, and brought the architecture of the Renaissance to

Trentino, notably in the Palazzo Assessoriale in his native Cles.

*DBI* s.v. Cles.

**CLOCKS AND WATCHES**. The first mechanical clocks were the turret clocks of the late thirteenth century. These clocks were structures of iron wheels mounted in open-work frames set in the bell towers of churches and civic buildings, and their purpose was to sound the hours; they had no clock face. The central machinery of the mechanical clock is a set of toothed wheels with an escapement device to regulate the turning of the wheels. Turret clocks were driven by weights suspended by ropes wound around wooden drums that were connected to the first toothed wheel of the clock movement. The earliest surviving turret clock is the Salisbury cathedral clock of 1386, which has been restored and now sounds the hours. The earliest surviving clock that sounds the quarter-hour is the one in Rouen Cathedral (1389); the Wells Cathedral clock (1392), the movement of which is now in the Science Museum in London, also chimes the quarter-hours. Some early clocks were fitted with AUTOMATA, such as the one in Strassburg Cathedral (1574), in which the Magi pass in front of the Virgin and Child while a cock flaps its wings, and Sebastian LINDENAST's Männleinlaufen (1506–9), the clock with animated figures of the electors mounted above the porch of the Liebfrauen-kirche in Nuremberg.

The earliest domestic clocks were scaled-down versions of these ecclesiastical and civic clocks, and were fitted with faces. These clocks were fitted in iron cases, and were known as Gothic clocks because of the style of their decorative mouldings. In the sixteenth century the most prominent makers of Gothic clocks were the LIECHTI family, whose workshop was in Winterthur. Early domestic clocks (like turret clocks) were driven by suspended weights, and this technology eventually led to the long-case clock (or grandfather clock) of the seventeenth century. In the mid-fifteenth century, however, the spring-driven clock was developed, and this technology was used in the TABLE CLOCKS AND TABERNA-CLE CLOCKS of the sixteenth century; it also made possible the development of the watch. The technology of the clock continued to develop through the sixteenth century, at the end of which one of the most important centres of horology was the court of RUDOLF II in Prague, where Jost BÜRGI was the court clockmaker and Christoph Margraf developed a type of clock driven by a ball running down an inclined plane; examples of their work are preserved in the Kunsthistorisches Museum in Vienna.

The watch evolved out of the table clock. The earliest examples, which were suspended from the waist or the neck rather than carried in a pocket, are the portable box clocks made from c.1510 by the Nuremberg locksmith Peter HEN-LEIN, the inventor of the mainspring. Spherical box clocks in this style, which are known as Nuremberg eggs (*Nürnberger Eier*), were made throughout the sixteenth century. Most sixteenth-century watches, however, retained the drum shape of the table clock, and like those clocks had the dial mounted on the top of the drum; the dial was not covered by glass, but was rather placed under a hinged cover or (in a small number of early seventeenth-century watches) provided with a ROCK-CRYSTAL cover. Some sixteenth-century watches were fitted with striking mechanisms as well as dials. The pocket watches of the first quarter of the seventeenth century, which were usually enclosed in silver cases, are normally oval rather than circular.

**CLOUET or Cloet family**, a family of French painters. Jean (or Janet) Clouet (*c.*1485–1540/1), who was the son and namesake of a Flemish painter who worked in France and Burgundy, worked in Burgundy before being appointed court painter to King FRANCIS I of France. He drew and painted members of the royal court, including portraits of *Francis I on Horseback* (Uffizi) and a *Man Holding Petrarch's Works* (Royal Collection, Windsor).

Jean's son François Clouet (*c.*1516–72) was a portraitist and painter of GENRE scenes. His signed portraits include *Charles IX* (1570, Kunsthistorisches Museum, Vienna) and *Lady in her Bath* (*c.*1570, National Gallery, Washington), which may represent Marie Touchet, the mistress of Charles IX.

*DBF; MDA*; Étienne Jollet, *Jean et François Clouet* (1997); Peter Mellen, *Jean Clouet* (1971).

**CLOVIO, GIULIO, or (Croatian) Julije Klovic or Il Macedone** (1498–1578), Croatian painter and illuminator who moved to Venice in 1516 and from 1523 worked at the imperial court in Bohemia and Hungary. He returned to Rome in 1526, and was captured in the SACK OF ROME (1527) but escaped and became a Benedictine monk in Mantua. When Pieter BRUEGEL visited Rome in the course of his long Italian journey (1551–5), he collaborated with Clovio, who owned several works by Bruegel (now lost). Giulio Clovio's illuminations include a series on the victories of CHARLES V (British Library), the Towneley Lectionary (New York Public Library) and St Paul's Epistle to the Romans (Sir John Soane's Museum, London); he also painted the Farnese Hours (Pierpont Morgan Library, New York), which was bound in silver by Antonio GENTILI. Clovio's oil paintings include a *Pietà* of 1553 now in the Uffizi.

*DBI* s.v. Clovio, Giorgio Giulio; *MDA*.

**CLUSIUS, CAROLUS, or Charles de l'Écluse** (1526–1609), Flemish botanist. Clusius was born in Artois; he first studied law, but then turned to medicine at Wittenberg and Montpellier. His interest in plants ranged far beyond their medical applications, and he travelled widely to collect plants, exploring the south of France (1550) and Spain and Portugal (1565–6). In 1573 Clusius accepted the invitation of the Emperor Maximilian I to establish a physic garden in Vienna. He served as prefect of the imperial gardens until 1577, during which time he collected plants in Austria and Hungary, and also received and cultivated seeds and bulbs from a former imperial ambassador to the Turkish court. After leaving Vienna Clusius settled in Frankfurt where, in 1592, he was partially crippled by a fall. He was at this point approached by the academics responsible for the new BOTANICAL GARDEN in

Leiden to see if he would become its first curator. He initially declined on grounds of health, but was finally persuaded to accept the post on the condition that a head gardener (*hortulanus*) be employed to assist him; Dirck Outgaerzoon Cluyts (Clutius) was appointed, and together Clusius and Clutius laid out and planted the garden. Clusius established Leiden as the most important centre in Europe for the study of botany. He was responsible for the cultivation and dissemination of species such as crocuses, crown imperials, gladioli, hyacinths, narcissi, irises (both Spanish and Siberian), lilies, African marigolds, marvels of Peru, sunflowers, and windflowers. His work on the tulip, on which he published widely, led in the mid-1630s to an explosion of interest in variegated tulips in the Netherlands and eventually became the cornerstone of the Dutch bulb industry.

Clusius described hundreds of previously unknown species of Spanish plants in his *Rariorum aliquot stirpium per Hispanias* (1576), and performed the same service for the flora of Austria and north-western Hungary (Pannonia) in *Rariorum aliquot stirpium per Pannoniam, Austriam* (1583). He also published Latin translations of a book by the Portuguese botanist Garcia de ORTA on the medicinal plants of India and of Nicolas Monardes's treatise on American plants, *Joyful News out of the New Found World*.

BNB s.v. De L'Escluse; *NBW* i; F. W. T. Hunger, *Charles de l'Escluse (Carolus Clusius), Nederlandsch kruidkundige 1526–1609* (1927).

## COCHLÄUS or Cochlaeus or Wendelstinus, JOHANN

(1479–1552), German Catholic polemicist, born in Wendelstein (near Nuremberg); his family name was Dobeneck, but his nickname, which derived from a pun on the name of his village (the first element of which means 'spiral'), was Cochlaeus (Latin 'spiral'), which in German became Cochläus. He studied at Cologne (1504–7) and in 1507 published (as Wendelstinus) *In musicam exhortationum*. In May 1510 he became a teacher in Nuremberg, but by 1515 he was living in Italy, where he heard Johann ECK's disputation on usury (Bologna, 1515), was awarded a doctorate (Ferrara, 1517), and was ordained priest (Rome, 1518/19).

In 1520 Cochläus returned to Germany, where he became dean of the Liebfrauenkirche in Frankfurt am Main and began his long career as polemicist whose bitter energy was directed against the Reformation, which he attributed to rivalry between the Dominicans and the Augustinians. He attended the diets of WORMS (1521), SPEYER (1526), AUGSBURG (1530), and REGENSBURG (1541) as a representative of the Catholic side, but his services were little used, because his rhetoric was too vitriolic to be useful in negotiations.

In 1525 Cochläus was driven from Frankfurt by the PEASANTS' REVOLT and became a canon at Mainz. In 1529 he entered the service of GEORG DER BÄRTIGE as ducal secretary in Dresden and Meissen (where he became a canon in 1534), but again had to flee when his patron died in 1539. He moved to Breslau (now Polish Wrocław), in Silesia, where he was appointed to a canonry in September 1539 and where he died on 10 January 1552.

Cochläus was a prolific writer. His best-known polemical works, both published in 1549, were *Historiae Hussitarum* and *Commentaria de actis et scriptis M. Lutheri, 1517–1546*.

NDB; Remigius Bäumer, *Johannes Cochlaeus (1479–1552): Leben und Werk im Dienst der katholischen Reform* (1980).

## COCKPIT, THE.

Originally built for cockfighting in 1609, the building in Drury Lane was converted for play performances in 1616 by the influential actor-manager BEESTON. Although burnt down and rebuilt in 1617, it remained in use until the closure of the theatres in 1642 (and perhaps beyond); reopened in 1651 by Beeston's son, it provided an important link between Elizabethan and Restoration theatre. Another Cockpit theatre at Whitehall was used for the private performances of Charles I's and Charles II's MASQUES.

## CODUSSI or Coducci, MAURO

(*c*.1440–*c*.1504), Italian architect. He was born near Bergamo and by 1469 had settled in Venice, where, together with Pietro LOMBARDO, he supplanted Venetian Gothic with a syncretic Byzantine-Renaissance style of architecture. His first church, on Venice's cemetery island, was San Michele in Isola (1469–77), the earliest Renaissance church in Venice; it has a Renaissance façade indebted to the design of ALBERTI's Tempio Malatestiano at Rimini but topped with a Veneto-Byzantine semicircular pediment. Codussi subsequently completed the Church of San Zaccaria (1480–1500), which had been begun by Antonio Gambello in 1458, designed the campanile of San Pietro di Castello (1482–8), which was the cathedral of Venice until 1807, and built San Giovanni Crisostomo (1497–1504). He also restored the Church of Santa Maria Formosa on a twelfth-century plan (1492–1504); the present interior is largely Codussi's, but the exterior and dome are later accretions.

Codussi excelled in the design of staircases. His staircase at the Scuola di San Marco (1490–5) was destroyed in the nineteenth century, but his elegant double staircase at the Scuola di San Giovanni Evangelista (1498) is one of the finest works of Venetian architecture.

There is no documentary evidence to link Codussi with any Venetian palace, but attributions include Palazzo Corner-Spinelli (*c*.1485–90) and Palazzo Loredan (from 1502, later completed by Pietro LOMBARDO and now called Palazzo Vendramin-Calergi). The clock tower in Piazza San Marco has also been attributed to Codussi.

DBI; MDA; Loredana Olivato Puppi and Lionello Puppi, *Mauro Codussi e l'architettura veneziana del primo rinascimento* (1977); Vittorio Polli, *Mauro Codussi: Architetto bergamasco* (1993).

## COECKE VAN AELST, PIETER

(1502–50), Flemish painter, architect, sculptor, translator, designer of tapestries and stained glass, born in the south Netherlandish village of Aelst (where his father was deputy mayor) on 14 August 1502. He was trained in the Brussels studio of Bernaert van ORLEY and was admitted to the Antwerp guild in 1527. He visited Rome and in 1533–4 went on to Constantinople in the hope of soliciting tapestry commissions from Süleyman the Magnificent; the drawings that he made on his journey were later published by his widow as woodcuts and were collected in 1873 as *The Turks in 1533*. In 1549 he became a member of the group of artists who prepared the pageant decorations for the ceremonial entry of CHARLES V and his son Philip (later King PHILIP II). Artists trained in his studio included Pieter BRUEGEL the Elder, who married his daughter.

Coecke's best-known painting is his *Last Supper* (Musée d'Art Ancien, Brussels). His greatest services to architecture were his translations of VITRUVIUS' *De architectura* into Flemish (Antwerp, 1539) and SERLIO's *L'architettura* into High German, Flemish, and French (Antwerp, 1539–53).

Coecke is sometimes confused with his namesake Pieter van Aelst (d. *c*.1530), the Brussels weaver to whom Pope LEO X sent RAPHAEL's cartoons of *The Acts of the Apostles*.

*BNB* s.v. Coecke, Pierre; *MDA*; *NBW* iii.

**COELHO, MANUEL RODRIGUES.** See RODRIGUES COELHO, MANUEL.

**CŒUR, JACQUES** (1395–1456), French merchant and banker, born in Bourges, the son of a wealthy merchant. In the 1430s he began to trade with Damascus, importing carpets and silks and amassing a vast fortune. In 1436 King CHARLES VII appointed Cœur as master of the mint and began to use him as banker, diplomat, and (from 1438) steward of the royal treasury. Cœur lent money to finance the war against the English in Normandy, negotiated a trade agreement between the Knights of ST JOHN in Rhodes and the sultan of Egypt, and in 1448 represented King Charles at the papal court of NICHOLAS V, where he helped to arrange an agreement with the antipope FELIX V and so contributed to the ending of the GREAT SCHISM. His wealth was reflected in the construction of a Flamboyant Gothic house in Bourges now known as the Palais Jacques Cœur (1442–53) and regarded as the finest private house in France.

Cœur's wealth and influence made him vulnerable to court intrigues, and in 1451 he was falsely accused of having poisoned Agnes Sorel (the king's mistress, by whom the king had four daughters). He was arrested and his property was confiscated, but in 1455 he escaped from prison and fled to Rome, when Nicholas V offered him the command of an expedition to relieve Rhodes. He died in Chios before reaching Rhodes.

*DBF*; A. B. Kerr, *Jacques Cœur, Merchant Prince of the Middle Ages* (1927); Michel Mollet, *Jacques Cœur; ou, L'Esprit d'entreprise au XVᵉ siècle* (1988).

**COG**, a type of north European merchant ship in use from the thirteenth to the fifteenth centuries. It was clinker-built (i.e. the side planks overlapped), broad in the beam, and had a rounded bow and stern.

**COGNAC, LEAGUE OF** (22 May 1526), an anti-imperial alliance in the WARS OF ITALY. The founding members of the League, FRANCIS I of France, Francesco SFORZA of Milan, the republic of Venice, and Pope CLEMENT VII, were later joined by HENRY VIII of England. The purpose of the League was to prevent Italy from becoming a Spanish fiefdom and to contain the power of the Emperor CHARLES V. The Empire

responded in May 1527 with the SACK OF ROME, and on 21 June 1529 the French army in Milan was defeated at Landriano. The League was dissolved in August 1529 by the Peace of CAMBRAI.

**COINS**, metal discs struck or cast with the head or effigy of a person on the obverse and a design related to the state for which they were produced on the reverse. Coins are primarily a medium of exchange, and it is their monetary value that distinguishes coins from MEDALS (which are primarily commemorative). Printed banknotes were not in public use until the end of the eighteenth century, so for most purposes, beyond the specialized world of BANKING (where bills of exchange were used), coins were the only form of money. Coins also differ from medals in that they were issued by states, whereas all Renaissance medals except those of the PAPAL STATE were privately manufactured.

Coins were usually made from copper and silver alloys. Whereas medals were usually cast, coins were normally struck by hand with hammers. Dies could be used repeatedly, but until the mid-sixteenth century all coins were manufactured by hand. Such coins were irregular in shape, partly because the blank discs were not uniform, but also because the force of the hammer often caused the blank to spread unevenly. These irregularities left coins vulnerable to clipping, a criminal process whereby small quantities of precious metal were pared from the edges (which were not milled) and made into new coins.

In the second half of the sixteenth century, new technologies were developed which enabled coins to be mass produced: rolling mills produced sheets of metals with a consistent depth, cutting presses facilitated the production of uniform discs, and screw-driven vices (developed in Augsburg *c*.1550) enabled mints to make coins by placing a heated metal disc between two engraved dies, which were then forced together with a screw-driven vice.

M. H. Crawford, C. R. Ligota, and J. B. Trapp (eds.), *Medals and Coins from Budé to Mommsen* (1990).

**COKE, SIR EDWARD** (1552–1634), English jurist. Coke (whose name is pronounced 'cook') was educated at Trinity College, Cambridge, and studied law at Clifford's Inn and Lincoln's Inn. In 1592, through the patronage of Lord Burghley, he became reader in the Inner Temple, recorder of London, and solicitor-general; the following year he became a member of Parliament and speaker of the House of Commons, and a year later was appointed attorney-general. In this capacity he presided with ferocity and rancour over the trials of the earl of ESSEX (1600), Sir Walter RALEGH (1603), and the conspirators of the GUNPOWDER PLOT (1605), the last of which suited his deep-seated hatred of Catholicism.

In 1606 Coke became chief justice of the common pleas, and in 1613 chief justice of the King's Bench (which, despite its name, was a COMMON LAW court); these roles brought him into conflict with the king in the dispute over the rival jurisdictions of common law and equity courts which dominated ENGLISH LAW for much of the seventeenth century. Coke became the champion of the common law and the chief opponent of the exercise of royal power through the equity courts.

Coke was a learned jurist with a good command of medieval ENGLISH LAW, and these qualities, together with his public position and the clarity and power of his expository prose, meant that his publications had a lasting effect on English jurisprudence and on the development of English law. His early works include the *Book of Entries* (a collection of pleadings published in 1614), *The Complete Copyholder* (1630), and *A Treatise of Bail and Mainprise* (1635). His two most important publications are his *Reports* and the *Institutes*. The *Reports*, which he published in eleven parts between 1600 and 1615 (two final parts were published in 1655 and 1658), collect cases to illustrate various points and principles of law; his presentation is historical in its tendency to preserve early forms of law and political in its advocacy of the constitutional ideal of the rule of law, and the cases that he collects form a corpus of common law (both civil and criminal) that is a conspectus of the law of the period.

The *Institutes* is the central text of English COMMON LAW. The first of its four books, which is commonly known as *Coke on Littleton* (1628), is an edition of LITTLETON's *Tenures* with an erudite commentary of encyclopedic range and proportions. Book 2 deals with Magna Carta and other medieval statutes, book 3 with criminal law, and book 4 with the jurisdictional dispute between common law and equity courts. The last three books, which were published in 1641, were welcomed by advocates of the view that Parliament and the common law are the highest authority in the state as a vindication of their position; as the struggle between king and Parliament was in the end won by Parliament, these three books became the basis of English constitutional law.

DNB; Jean Beauté, *Un grand juriste anglais, Sir Edward Coke, 1552–1634* (1975).

**COLA DI RIENZO** (*c.*1313–1354), a Roman notary who twice seized power in Rome (1347 and 1354), styling himself 'tribune' of Rome; on the second occasion he was murdered by a mob. Cola was an early exponent of the idea that the Roman republic of classical antiquity should be a model for the governance of contemporary Rome.

In the nineteenth century Cola was idealized as an early revolutionary rather than as a political philosopher: Napoleon carried a biography of Cola to Waterloo, Bulwer-Lytton wrote *Rienzi, Last of the Tribunes*, on which Wagner based his opera *Rienzi, der letzte der Tribunen*, Friedrich Engels wrote a play called *Cola di Rienzi: Ein unbekannter dramatischer Entwurf*, and Gabriele d'Annunzio wrote a *Vita di Cola di Rienzo*.

DBI; *Life of Cola di Rienzo*, trans. John Wright (1975).

**COLANTONIO, NICCOLÒ** (*c.*1420–*c.*1460/70), Italian painter, based in Naples, where he painted religious paintings in a style marked by Flemish influence. His surviving paintings include his early *St Jerome in his Study Removing the Thorn from the Lion's Paw* (Museo Nazionale, Naples), which was painted as part of an altarpiece for the Church of San Lorenzo in Naples, and his later *St Vincent* (San Pietro

Martire, Naples). Colantonio's pupils may have included ANTONELLO DA MESSINA.

DBI; MDA.

**COLASCIONE**, a small-bodied lute with a long neck and as many as 24 frets and two or three strings. Thought to have come from the Middle East, it became popular in Naples in the mid-sixteenth century.

**COLET, JOHN** (*c.*1466–1519), English humanist and educational reformer. Following his education at Oxford, Paris, and in Italy, he gained a reputation with his teaching at Oxford on the epistles of St Paul (*c.*1497); his Neoplatonism drew especially on PICO DELLA MIRANDOLA. He also attacked clerical worldliness, and was suspected of heresy. From 1505 until his death, he was dean of St Paul's, London. He refounded St Paul's School with money inherited from his father, twice lord mayor of London; William LILY was appointed as the school's first headmaster. Friend of MORE and patron of ERASMUS, on whose advice he drew in formulating the curriculum at St Paul's School, he was a leading figure in the first substantial wave of English humanism. *On the Basis of Study* (1511) records his views on education; the Latin grammar which he wrote for St Paul's School later became a standard text.

DNB; J. B. Gleason, *John Colet* (1989).

**COLIGNY, GASPARD DE** (1519–72), French Huguenot leader and admiral of France, born into a noble family; his father and namesake was *maréchal de France*, and his mother was Louise of Montmorency, the sister of Anne de MONTMORENCY. He served in the WARS OF ITALY in the campaign of 1544 and in 1552 was appointed *amiral de France*. He was appointed governor of Picardy, and in that capacity commanded the defence of Saint-Quentin; the French were defeated at the battle of SAINT-QUENTIN (August 1557), and Coligny was captured. He was imprisoned until April 1559, when he was released as part of the Treaty of CATEAU-CAMBRÉSIS.

While in prison Coligny had become a Protestant, and in the three years following his release he worked alongside Louis, prince of CONDÉ, and Theodorus BEZA to secure a peaceful compromise. On the outbreak of the WARS OF RELIGION he became one of Condé's commanders, and on Condé's death Coligny was elected commander-in-chief of the Hugenot army at a conference in Cognac (March 1569).

Coligny was defeated at the battle of Poitou in October 1569, but nonetheless secured favourable terms in the Treaty of Saint-Germain (August 1570). He displaced the GUISES at court and became an adviser to the youthful CHARLES IX (who called him *mon père*), but alienated CATHERINE DE MÉDICIS. On 22 August 1572 he was wounded in a failed assassination attempt mounted by the Guise faction; two days later he became the principal victim of the ST BARTHOLOMEW'S DAY MASSACRE.

DBF; Comte Jules Delaborde, *Gaspard de Coligny: Amiral de France* (3 vols., 1879–82); Arthur Whitehead, *Gaspard de Coligny: Admiral of France* (1904); J. Shimizu, *Conflict of Loyalties: Politics and Religion in the Career of Gaspard de Coligny* (1970).

**COLIGNY, ODET DE, CARDINAL DE CHATILLON** (1517–71), French rebel cardinal and Huguenot leader, the elder brother of Gaspard de COLIGNY. In 1561 Odet became the last of the three Coligny brothers (the other brother was the marquis d'Andelot) to convert to Protestantism. He fought on the Protestant side in the early stages of the WARS OF RELIGION and in 1569 fled to England, where he died two years later, probably poisoned by a member of his entourage.

*DBF* s.v. Chatillon.

**COLLEGE OF ARMS.** See CHIVALRY.

**COLLEONI, BARTOLOMEO** (1400–75), *condottiere*, born near Bergamo into an aristocratic family with a long military tradition. As a young man he served several *condottieri*, including Andrea FORTEBRACCIO and CARMAGNOLA. In 1431 he joined the service of Venice and fought the Visconti under the command of GATTAMELATA, whom he again served in the war against Milan in 1438–41. After the death of Gattamelata, Colleoni fought under Francesco SFORZA in 1448. When the Peace of LODI (1454) settled the disputes between Venice and Milan, Colleoni was appointed captain-general of Venice. In the ensuing years of idleness occasioned by Venice remaining at peace, Colleoni retired to his castle at Malpaga, where he became a lavish patron of the arts and where he died on 2 November 1475.

Colleoni's posthumous fame arises from his bequest to the Venetian republic to help finance the Turkish War. The bequest was accompanied by a request that an equestrian statue of Colleoni be erected in the Piazza San Marco. VERROCCHIO made the statue, but Venice was not willing to make an exception to its interdiction against monuments in Piazza San Marco, and so chose to interpret 'super platea S. Marco' as 'on the square of St Mark's School', and therefore erected the statue on the Campo Santi Giovanni e Paolo (Venetian San Zanipolo) beside the Scuola Grande di San Marco.

*DBI; MDA;* R. Belotti, *La vita di Bartolomeo Colleoni* (1923).

**COLOCCI, ANGELO** (1474–1549), Italian humanist, romance philologist, and antiquarian, born in Isei. From 1497 he worked in the Vatican secretariat of Popes LEO X and CLEMENT VII; in 1537 he was consecrated as bishop of Nocera Umbria. Colocci was a learned student of Old Portuguese, Provençal, and medieval Italian, and took an educated interest in the origins of Italian poetry in Provence. In the QUESTIONE DELLA LINGUA he favoured the *lingua cortigiana*; he is represented as one of the speakers in VALERIANO's *Dialogo della volgar lingua*.

Colocci wrote poetry in Italian and Latin, and his house in Rome was an important centre for humanist discussion as well as a repository for his large collection of manuscripts, statues, coins, and medals. His collections were looted during the SACK OF ROME, but some manuscripts survived and are now in the Vatican Library.

*DBI; OCIL.*

**COLOGNE or (German) Köln,** a free imperial city (from 1475), archiepiscopal see, and member of the HANSEATIC LEAGUE. Incumbents of the see, which was established in 313, acquired territorial authority in 1180, when the duchy of SAXONY was partitioned and the duchy of Westphalia was assigned to the archbishops of Cologne. In the Golden Bull of 1356 the archbishops were numbered amongst the seven electors of the Empire, and there was a continuous succession of archbishop-electors until 1801, though the city and the electors feuded constantly, and from 1273 to 1671 the archbishop lived in Bonn rather than in Cologne. In 1396 a long period of civic instability came to an end when a constitution based on the trade and craft guilds was adopted; this constitution was to remain in place for 400 years. The city was an important manufacturing centre, particularly of leather, textiles, and metal goods, and after 1464 became the principal centre of PRINTING in north-west Germany.

The University of Cologne was founded by the burghers of Cologne in 1389, and by the mid-fifteenth century had grown into an important European university whose 1,000 students came from as far afield as Scandinavia and Scotland. Despite the protracted dispute with the archbishop-electors, Cologne remained loyal to the Catholic Church in the face of the Reformation, as a result of which the university, a redoubt of SCHOLASTICISM and opposition to HUMANISM, was unable to recruit students; it was virtually empty by the time the JESUITS instituted a programme of revival, and the university did not return to the top rank of European universities until the nineteenth century.

Cologne was a resolutely Catholic city. The JEWS were expelled in 1414, and after the Reformation Protestants were denied citizenship, excluded from the magistracy, and encouraged to leave the city. The reforming efforts of HERMANN VON WIED (archbishop 1515–46) were stoutly resisted, and when in 1582 the archbishop-elector Gebhardt Truchsess von Waldburg converted to Protestantism, the result was a war between Protestant and Catholic princes, as a result of which Cologne entered the sphere of influence of the WITTELSBACH family.

R. W. Scribner, 'Why was there no Reformation in Cologne?', *Bulletin of the Institute of Historical Research,* 49 (1976).

**COLOGNE SCHOOL or (German) Kölner Schule.** Cologne was an important centre of painting from the late fourteenth to the early sixteenth centuries, but there was no local style with distinctive characteristics that would warrant the use of the term 'school'. The notion that there was such a school was developed in early nineteenth-century Germany, when the founder of the school was said to be one Master Wilhelm. No surviving pictures can be securely attributed to Wilhelm, who is probably a mythical figure.

The spuriousness of this historiography does detract from the importance of Cologne as an artistic centre. Early fifteenth-century pictures are painting in the INTERNATIONAL GOTHIC style, and the proximity of Flanders and Burgundy meant that Gothic was gradually blended with realist elements. The paintings of Stefan LOCHNER (who is sometimes said to be the leader of the Cologne School) are among the finest examples of this blend of German Gothic and Flemish realism.

**COLOMBE, MICHEL** (*c*.1430–*c*.1514), French sculptor. Little is known of his early life, but in the early sixteenth century he was commissioned by ANNE OF BRITTANY to work with Jean PERRÉAL on the tomb (1502–7) of her father Duke François II of Brittany in Nantes Cathedral. Colombe also made the relief carving for an altarpiece of *St George* at Gaillon (now in the Louvre).

*DBF; MDA;* Pierre Pradel, *Michel Colombe: Le Dernier Imagier gothique* (1953); Jean-René Gaborit (ed.), *Michel Colombe et son temps* (2001).

**COLÓN, DIEGO** (1478/9–1526), Spanish colonist, the son of Christopher COLUMBUS. He was educated at the Spanish court and on the death of his father in 1506 inherited his titles (including viceroy and admiral of the Indies) and claims on the territories that he had discovered. In 1509 Diego travelled with his family to Hispaniola, where he assumed control of the government of the growing number of Spanish possessions in America. Six years later he was recalled to Spain to answer charges that he had exceeded his gubernatorial powers. He spent the next five years following the Royal Council on progress around Spain, and in 1520 finally received provisional recognition of his rights as governor, whereupon he returned to Hispaniola. In 1523 he was again recalled to Spain to face new charges, and three years later died in Spain while awaiting the Council's decision.

The dispute over his rights continued until 1536, when it was agreed that Diego's son Luis Colón would retain the title admiral of the Indies and receive a large annuity and substantial estates in Jamaica and Panama in return for his renunciation of all other claims.

*DHE;* Luis Arranz Márquez, *Don Diego Colón: Almirante, virrey y gobernador de las Indias* (1 vol. to date, 1982).

**COLONIA, JUAN DE** (d. 1481), **SIMÓN DE** (d. *c*.1511), and **FRANCISCO DE** (d. 1542), a family of architects naturalized in Burgos. Juan de Colonia came from Cologne to Burgos in about 1540, and built the distinctively German late Gothic spires on the west towers of the cathedral.

Juan's son Simón succeeded his father as master of the works at Burgos Cathedral in 1481, and built the distinctively Spanish late Gothic (i.e. PLATERESQUE) Chapel of the Constable (1486–98). He was also responsible for the Plateresque façade of San Pablo, Valladolid (1486–99), which is an early example of a façade designed in the manner of a sculpted reredos; the fashion for such church fronts in Spain and in Spanish America may be traced at least in part to this church. In 1497 Simón was appointed as master mason of Seville Cathedral.

Simón's son Francisco assisted his father on the façade of San Pablo, and was responsible for the retable above the altar of San Nicolás in Burgos (*c*.1503–5), which mingles Plateresque and Renaissance elements. He succeeded his father as master of the works at Burgos Cathedral in 1511, and was responsible for the Puerta de la Pellejería (1516, in early Renaissance style) and, together with Juan de Vallejo, for the late Gothic crossing tower, on which work began in 1540. In 1513 Francisco was appointed as master mason of Plasencia Cathedral

together with his rival Juan de Álava, but the collaboration was not a success, because they quarrelled constantly.

*DBEH* (Simón and Francisco); M. Dezzi Bardeschi, *La cattedrale di Burgos* (1965).

**COLONNA, FRANCESCO** (1433–1527), Italian author, a Dominican friar who wrote *Hypnerotomachia Polifili*, a philosophical allegorical romance published in Venice in 1499 by ALDUS MANUTIUS. It is written in a hybrid Latin-Italian language entirely its own; some editors provided Italian summaries. Much of the importance of the Aldine edition lies in the beauty of the typography and its exquisite woodcut illustrations (by an unidentified artist), which include many imaginative architectural fantasies. Translations were subsequently published in a fine French edition with additional illustrations (1546) and in an unambitious English edition entitled *The Strife of Love in a Dream* (1592).

*DBI; OCIL.*

**COLONNA, VITTORIA** (1490–1547), Italian poet, born into the COLONNA FAMILY in Rome. She was betrothed at the age of 4 and married at the age of 19 to Ferdinando Francesco d'AVALOS, marquis of Pescara, who died of consumption on 3 December 1525. By her own account Vittoria eased the pain of bereavement by composing the first 100 sonnets of the collection that was later to be published as her *Rime* (1538). After losing her husband Vittoria lived mainly in convents, eventually settling in Rome, where she joined the Catholic reform circle of Juan de VALDÉS, which included Pietro CARNESECCHI, Giulia GONZAGA, Bernardino OCHINO, and Pietro Martire VERMIGLI. Some members of the circle became Protestants, but Vittoria remained within the Church, in significant part because of the influence of her spiritual adviser Cardinal Reginald POLE. The sonnets of her final years are largely on religious and philosophical themes, and are characterized by a disciplined austerity rather than emotional intensity. A collection of her lyrics was dedicated to MICHELANGELO. Colonna was a role model for later women poets in the cinquecento.

*DBI; HWWI.*

**COLONNA FAMILY**, a Ghibelline family that held large estates in the PAPAL STATE south of Rome and in the kingdom of NAPLES; the Colonna were the perpetual rivals of the ORSINI, whose estates lay north of Rome. The election of Cardinal Oddo Colonna as Pope MARTIN V in 1409 enabled him to enrich his family with further grants of property within the Papal State; he also persuaded Queen GIOVANNA II of Naples to present his brothers with large fiefdoms within her realm. Pope Martin commissioned the Palazzo Colonna in Rome.

Pope EUGENIUS IV attempted to restore the Colonna territories to the papacy, but little progress was made until the depredations of Cesare BORGIA began the process of reconquering Colonna territories, and the family remained a threat to the papacy until the pontificate of Pope PAUL IV in the mid-sixteenth century. At the battle of LEPANTO, the papal fleet was commanded by Marcantonio Colonna (1535–84).

*DBI; MDA.*

**COLT or Coult, MAXIMILIAN, formerly surnamed Poultrain or Poutrain** (*fl.* 1595–1641), a sculptor from Arras who migrated to England *c.*1595. From 1605 to 1608 he carved monuments in Westminster Abbey, notably the canopied tomb of Queen ELIZABETH, which was painted by Johan DE CRITZ. He entered the service of Robert Cecil, earl of Salisbury, and worked extensively at HATFIELD HOUSE, where his commissions included fireplaces and the memorable tomb of Robert Cecil, in which his effigy lies on a black marble slab which is supported by four kneeling Virtues. In 1608 Colt was appointed master sculptor to King James, in which capacity he carved the decorations on the royal barges (1611–24). His post was renewed by King Charles I, but Colt received only a few minor commissions. He disappeared from the historical record while a prisoner in the Fleet in 1641.

*DNB; MDA.*

**COLUMBINE CUP.** The term 'columbine', which derives from the Latin *columbinus* ('like a dove'), was used in a transferred sense both to suggest the mildness of the dove (as in Columbina, the character in COMMEDIA DELL'ARTE) and to suggest the shape of a group of doves (as in the Columbine flower *Aquilegia vulgaris*). Silver goblets shaped like the flower of the Columbine were manufactured in Nuremberg in the sixteenth century (they were first mentioned in 1513), often by candidates applying for admission to the guilds of goldsmiths. There are two fine examples in the Victoria and Albert Museum and another in the British Museum. Georg WECHTER is sometimes said (in error) to have been the inventor of the Columbine cup, but his influential design was not published until 1579.

**COLUMBO, REALDO** (*c.*1510–1559), Italian anatomist, an apothecary's son who studied medicine and surgery at the University of Padua, where he succeeded VESALIUS in 1544. His *De re anatomica* (1559) records his analysis of the heartbeat and his discovery of the pulmonary transit. He overturned the received wisdom of the heartbeat by observing that the contraction of the heart (systole) was more powerful than its dilation (diastole); in Galenic medicine it was assumed that the heart's motion was concentrated on dilation, the process by which it sucked blood in. On pulmonary transit, Colombo conducted vivisection experiments which demonstrated that blood passed from the right side of the heart through the lungs to the left side, that the pulmonary vein contained blood (in Galenic medicine it was deemed to contain air), and that the mixing of blood with air took place in the lungs (where it assumed the robust colour of arterial blood) rather than in the left ventricle. These were the observations that led in 1628 to William Harvey's demonstration of the circulation of the blood.

*DBI; DSB.*

**COLUMBUS or (Italian) Cristoforo Colombo or (Spanish) Cristóbal Colón** (1451–1506), explorer and colonist, born in Genoa, the son of a weaver. In 1476 he joined an expedition bound for England, but the ships were attacked by French corsairs as they rounded Cape St Vincent (the south-western tip of Portugal); Columbus swam ashore and made his way to Lisbon, where his younger brother Bartolomeo was a cartographer and bookseller. The following year Columbus completed his voyage to England and sailed on to Iceland, and on returning to Portugal married Filipa Moniz Perestrelo, a noblewoman who became the mother of his only legitimate son, Diego COLÓN; he subsequently had an illegitimate son, Fernando, by Beatriz Enríquez.

From 1477 to 1483 Columbus lived in Lisbon and Madeira, during which time he formulated his plan for a westward voyage to India. The circumference of the earth was variously estimated, and Columbus favoured the 'small earth' hypothesis, which assumed a circumference of some 28,000 kilometres (16,800 miles). The Florentine mathematician and geographer Paolo TOSCANELLI was an advocate of the 'small earth' hypothesis, and on 14 June 1474 sent a letter and map to AFONSO V of Portugal. On the basis of this information, which Columbus saw in the early 1480s, he concluded, with characteristic incompetence, that the distance from the CANARY ISLANDS to the Cathay described by MARCO POLO was no more than 9,600 kilometres (6,000 miles).

Columbus was unable to persuade King JOHN II of Portugal to support an expedition, and decided to seek Spanish sponsorship for his plan to establish contact with the Mongol khan of Cathay by the western route, in order to circumvent the Islamic world. In 1486 he met Queen ISABELLA, who appointed a commission to evaluate the proposal. In 1491 the commission recommended that the proposed voyage not be supported, arguing (correctly) that Columbus' geographical calculations were grossly underestimated. Nevertheless, Columbus found independent financial support and appealed successfully to the queen's religious fervour; she conferred on him the hereditary rights over any territories that he might discover and claim during his mission to the khan.

On 3 August 1492 Columbus sailed from Palos (Huelva) with an expedition of some 120 men in three CARAVELS; he commanded the *Santa María*, his flagship, and the PINZÓN brothers commanded the *Pinta* and the *Niña*. The expedition stopped at Las Palmas (Canary Islands) to rerig the *Niña*, which had left Palos as a three-masted *caravela latina* rigged on all three masts with lateen sails and at Las Palmas was rerigged with square sails to enable her to keep up with the other two caravels.

Thereafter the expedition sailed west, and on 12 October sighted land; the precise location of the island on which he first landed, traditionally said to be Watlings Island (now San Salvador), is not known. Despite clear evidence to the contrary, Columbus insisted that he had arrived in China, Japan, or India, but this conviction did not prevent him from raising the Spanish flag and declaring the land and its inhabitants to be subject to Spain. He sailed along the coasts of Cuba and Hispaniola (now Haiti and the Dominican Republic); on Christmas Eve 1492 the *Santa María* was wrecked on a coral reef in Caracol Bay (Haiti); her timbers were used to build a fort on the shore. The expedition left 39 settlers behind on

Hispaniola and returned to Spain, where Ferdinand and Isabella awarded Columbus the hereditary titles of admiral of the Ocean Sea and viceroy of the Indies.

When Columbus published an account of his discovery, learned opinion in Europe quickly came to the conclusion that Columbus had stumbled onto a previously unknown land mass. Columbus refused to admit the truth, and persisted in his dream of reaching the court of the khan, as Marco Polo had done. Determined to prove the point, he departed on 25 September 1493 on his second voyage, sailing from Cádiz with seventeen ships and some 1,200 men. As he entered the Caribbean he landed at Guadeloupe and Puerto Rico before proceeding to his settlement in Hispaniola; on arrival he discovered that the settlers had been massacred. Undeterred, he established the settlement of Isabela (now Santo Domingo, the oldest surviving European city in the Americas) and from that base further explored the Caribbean, sailing along the coast of Cuba (or Japan, as he preferred to call it) and in May 1494 landing in Jamaica. After a further period of exploration he returned to Spain, arriving in Cádiz on 11 June 1496.

On his third voyage Columbus departed from Sanlúcar (at the mouth of the river Guadalquivir) on 30 May 1498 with six ships and 200 passengers as well as his crew. He landed in Trinidad (July 1498), and then sailed to the mouth of the Orinoco (August 1498), which was his first sighting of the mainland of America; he instantly declared that the river was the Ganges and that he had discovered the Earthly Paradise, though he did not put his theory to the test by risking a landing. On returning to Hispaniola he assumed control of the colony in Santo Domingo. In September 1500, Francisco de BOBADILLA, who had been appointed the previous year as Columbus' successor as governor of the newly discovered Spanish territories in America, reached Santo Domingo, arrested Columbus and his brothers, and sent them in chains to Spain; they were promptly released, though Columbus' standing with Ferdinand and Isabella never fully recovered.

On 9 May 1502 Columbus, whom the failure to prove his Indian thesis had by now driven to an almost messianic conviction about his mission, embarked from Cádiz with four ships on his fourth and final voyage, when he sailed along the coasts of Honduras, Nicaragua, and Panama. At last, it seemed to Columbus, he had reached the definitive terra firma of the coastline of Asia. The triumph was short-lived; the expedition was dogged by mutinies and shipwreck and, stranded on Jamaica, he wrote the despairing *Lettera rarissima*, in which he shows signs of what would now be called megalomania and paranoia about the scepticism of his contemporaries. Columbus was rescued by the bravery of one of his companions and returned to Spain, landing in Sanlúcar in November 1504. He spent the last seventeen months of his life embroiled in legal actions and petitions to the crown in vain attempts to recover the honours and wealth that had been promised to him; he died in relative obscurity, still convinced that he had not discovered America.

Columbus was not the first European to cross the Atlantic (Norse EXPLORATION had led to the establishment of a settlement in Newfoundland c.1000). Nevertheless, the particular significance of his voyage was instantly recognized, especially in his native Italy, where he was extolled as the bearer of Christianity to the New World. In this role he became the central figure in at least nine epics written between 1581 and 1650, and was mentioned in many others (including Milton's *Paradise Lost*). The notion of Columbus as the discoverer of America is in part a myth, since his exploration was largely confined to the islands of the Caribbean and he refused to recognize that they were unknown; besides, the islands which he visited were already populated, and their residents had probably established contact with mainland America (and possibly with Africa) long before. More recently, historians of the Americas have presented Columbus, equally partially and inaccurately, as the first exploiter of America, the man who introduced genocide to the native Americans and inaugurated the destruction of its ancient civilizations. What is certain, however, is his pioneering role in the creation of the Atlantic economy of the modern world. In his voluminous writings he also bequeathed to posterity one of the most vivid accounts of early modern voyages.

Samuel Morison, *Admiral of the Ocean Sea* (2 vols., 1942); Charles Verlinden, *Cristóbal Colón y el descubrimiento de América* (1967); Jacques Heers, *Christophe Colomb* (1981); Felipe Fernández Armesto, *Columbus* (1991); Cristóbal Colón, *Textos y documentos completos*, ed. C. Varela (2nd edn., 1992).

**COMEDY.** Renaissance comedy evolved from two quite distinct sources. Popular comedy drew on the medieval tradition of farce, which evolved into more sophisticated forms such as the SOTIE in France, the COMMEDIA DELL'ARTE in Italy, and the *entremese* in Spain, all of which retained elements of farce.

Learned comedy (*commedia erudita*) drew on the classical tradition, especially on the plays of PLAUTUS and TERENCE. In the sixteenth century these plays were performed in Italian translation to courtly audiences in cities such as Ferrara, Florence, and Rome; the earliest known revival of an ancient comedy was a production of Plautus' *Menaechmi* mounted by Duke Ercole d'ESTE in Ferrara in 1486. The conventions of Latin comedy were reproduced in the earliest original Italian comedies, such as those of ARIOSTO and ARETINO (each of whom wrote five comedies), Cardinal DOVIZI (whose celebrated *Calandria* was first performed in 1513), MACHIAVELLI (whose *Mandragola* was published in 1524), and FIRENZUOLA.

In France, Plautus and Terence were translated and adapted by playwrights such as Jean-Antoine de BAÏF, Rémy BELLEAU, Charles ESTIENNE, Jacques GRÉVIN, Jean de LA TAILLE, and Octavien SAINT-GELAIS. In 1548 Joachim DU BELLAY called for the revival of the ancient genre of comedy in his *Défense et illustration de la langue française*. By this date adaptation had begun to blend imperceptibly into original writing, but the first original French comedy is traditionally said to be Étienne JODELLE's *Eugène* (1552), a classical comedy which retains strong elements of medieval farce. Greek comedy was less well known, but RONSARD translated the *Plutus* of Aristophanes. French comedy before Molière was traditionally written in octosyllabic verse, but a few dramatists, including La Taille, Pierre de LARIVEY, and Adrien TURNÈBE, chose to write in prose.

In Spain, Bartolomé de TORRES NAHARRO proposed (in his *Propalladia* of 1517) a taxonomy of comedy that distinguished realistic *comedias a noticia* from fanciful *comedias a fantasía*, but the distinction proved to be inadequate for the huge scope of Spanish comedy, which ranged from popular farce in the *entremeses* to *comedias de capa y espada* (amorous cloak-and-dagger plays) and translations intended to be read rather than performed (such as Pedro Simón ABRIL's translation of Terence). Late sixteenth- and early seventeenth-century SPANISH DRAMA was among the finest in Europe, and comedies were written by the greatest playwrights of the period, including Juan de la CUEVA, Guillén de CASTRO, Luis VÉLEZ DE GUEVARA, Juan RUIZ DE ALARCÓN, TIRSO DA MOLINA, and Lope de VEGA. Lope repudiated classical strictures against the mixing of genres in his *Arte nuevo de hacer comedias* (*c.*1607), in which he advocated the mingling of tragic and comic elements.

The earliest significant English comedies were Nicholas UDALL's *Ralph Roister Doister* (performed at Westminster School *c.*1553), the anonymous *Gammer Gurton's Needle* (performed at Christ's College, Cambridge, in 1566), and George GASCOIGNE's *Supposes* (performed at Gray's Inn, one of the INNS OF COURT, in 1566), which was based on Ariosto's *I suppositi* (and was the first prose comedy in English). English Renaissance comedy culminated in the plays of JONSON and SHAKESPEARE. Ben Jonson remained faithful to classical models, but in the 1590s Shakespeare developed a new form of love comedy in which the central character is an intelligent woman who in the course of the play overcomes various obstacles and at the end of the play is betrothed. Jonson's comedies were imitated for centuries, but Shakespeare's comedies had no significant dramatic progeny, although their structure was eventually replicated in the English novel, most successfully in the novels of Jane Austen.

**COMMANDINO, FEDERICO** (1509–75), Italian humanist, mathematician, and physician, born into a noble family in Urbino. He was taught Latin and Greek by a humanist at Fano before, in 1534, going to the University of Padua, where for ten years he studied philosophy and medicine, and would therefore have attended classes in mathematics (that is, the four subjects of the quadrivium (see LIBERAL ARTS), arithmetic, geometry, astronomy, and music). However, he actually took his medical degree at the University of Ferrara. He then returned to Urbino where, having two daughters to provide for, he practised for some years as a physician before turning his attention to the editing, translating, and annotation of Greek mathematical texts. He became a mathematical tutor and medical adviser in the household of the DELLA ROVERE FAMILY; he later moved to Rome as physician to a cardinal. In Urbino Commandino had access to the ducal library, which was a good one, but there were many more libraries open to him in Rome; he also obtained access to Greek manuscripts in Venice.

Commandino naturally worked on ARCHIMEDES, and his edition was published in 1558; it included all the works of Archimedes then known and some ancient commentaries on them. These works are not elementary but rather research treatises addressed to serious students of mathematics, and in Commandino's intelligently annotated editions they proved intellectually stimulating to future generations of mathematicians. He also edited the Latin fragment of PTOLEMY's *Planisphaerium* (1558), which concerns the mathematics of making a flat image of a sphere (as on a planispheric ASTROLABE) and which Commandino notices is equivalent to the construction of a flat PERSPECTIVE image. This edition is dedicated to Rannuccio FARNESE. There followed an edition of Ptolemy's *De analemmate* (1562), a fragmentary text on SUNDIALS which is of both antiquarian and mathematical interest as providing a supplement to the unsatisfactory treatment of the subject by VITRUVIUS. Commandino adds a short original discussion of the mathematics of the types of sundial in Vitruvius, drawing on the information supplied by Ptolemy's text. Other important editions included the first four books of Apollonius' *Conics*, the only ones to survive in Greek (1566), Euclid's *Elements* (with full mathematical commentaries, 1572), and the posthumously published edition of Pappus' *Mathematical Collection* (1588).

Commandino's pupils included Bernardino BALDI and Galileo GALILEI's friend and patron Guidobaldo del MONTE.
DBI.

***COMMEDIA DELL'ARTE***, a genre of improvised drama which flourished in Italy in the sixteenth and seventeenth centuries and exercised an important influence on French drama, where it evolved into the *comédie italienne*. The phrase *commedia dell'arte* carries the sense of comedy improvised by the profession (of actors), and so distinguishes the genre from the written plays of the *commedia erudita*. The contemporary names for the genre are indicative of its most prominent features: *commedia a soggetto* is indicative of the practice of improvising within the framework of an agreed synopsis (*scenario*); *commedia all'improviso* emphasizes the element of improvisation; *commedia dei zanni* alludes to the comic servants; *commedia delle maschere* recalls the masks worn by the actors.

Each actor represented a character of a certain social type, and characterization was established through speech, gesture, costume, and the mask. The principal stock characters were the elderly Venetian merchant Pantalone, the clever servants Arlecchino (the antecedent of Harlequin), Pedrolino, and Scapino, the artless servant Pulcinella (who evolved into Punch), and the coarse female servant Franceschina. The companies, which normally consisted of nine women and four men, included I GELOSI, Accesi, Desiosi, Uniti, and the two troupes known as I Confidenti.

C. Cairns (ed.), *The 'Commedia dell'arte' from the Renaissance to Dario Fo* (1989).

***COMMEDIA ERUDITA.*** See COMEDY.

**COMMINES or Commynes, PHILIPPE DE** (*c.*1446–*c.*1511), Flemish historian in France, born in Renescure (Flanders).

In 1465 he entered the household of Charles, count of Charolais (later duke of Burgundy), and in 1468, at peace talks in Péronne, he negotiated a treaty between Duke Charles and King LOUIS XI. He subsequently entered the service of the king, for whom he helped to shape French policy towards Burgundy (1472–7) and travelled as an ambassador in Italy. On the accession of the youthful CHARLES VIII in 1483 Commines was gradually excluded from the court, and eventually defected to the anti-royalist duke of Orléans (later King LOUIS XII). He was arrested, imprisoned (1487–9), and, on his release, confined to his estates. The French invasion of Italy in the opening campaign of the WARS OF ITALY led to Commines being recalled from retirement; in Italy he served as French ambassador to Venice and fought in the battle of FORNOVO (1495).

Commines was the author of historical *Mémoires* in which he looks with disillusioned eyes at the history of his own time. The first six books, which describe the reign of King Louis XI, were published in 1524; books 7 and 8, which describe the invasion of Italy by Charles VIII, were published in 1552. The *Mémoires* were subsequently translated into every major European language, and so helped to shape the historiography of the period that they describe.

BNB; *DBF* s.v. Comines; J. Dufourmet, *Études sur Philippe de Commynes* (1975); J. Demers, *Commynes mémorialiste* (1975).

**COMMON LAW or** (Latin) *ius commune* **or** (French) *droit commun* **or** (German) *Gemeinrecht*. The English term 'common law' is now used to distinguish the legal systems of England, Ireland, and the Commonwealth from the CIVIL LAW systems of western Europe; in Renaissance England, however, the term was used to distinguish common law courts from equity courts (see ENGLISH LAW). In continental usage the equivalent terms were (and continue to be) used to distinguish national law common to entire states from local law. Within the context of CANON LAW, the Latin term *ius commune* referred to the general law of the Church as opposed to local CUSTOMARY LAW.

**COMMON PRAYER, BOOK OF**. The desire of CRANMER and others to reform the Latin services of the medieval Church, as well as evangelical demand for prayers, readings, and services in the vernacular, led to the issue of the first Book of Common Prayer in 1549. An English litany had already been issued in 1544, a King's Primer in 1545, and a vernacular communion service three years later. In 1548, under EDWARD VI, a commission of twelve bishops and clergy was established to oversee the production of a uniform order of service; the Prayer Book issued the following year, however, was largely the work of Cranmer. Its exclusive use was ordered by the 1549 Act of UNIFORMITY, but resisted in the western rebellion of the same year. A second Book of Common Prayer was issued in 1552, again largely prepared by Cranmer; its modifications reflected the latest reformist thinking, but with the succession of MARY in 1553, and the return to Catholic services, it was little used. Slight revisions were made to the Book of Common Prayer under ELIZABETH

in 1559, and again by JAMES VI, whose modifications following the HAMPTON COURT CONFERENCE offered some minor concessions to the Puritans. The book was issued in its final form in 1662.

**COMPASS**. The simplest form of compass was a magnetized needle lodged in a straw or piece of cork and floating in a basin of water. From the twelfth century compass needles were placed on a pivot above a card on which the compass points were marked. In the late fifteenth century mariners discovered that the compass needle did not point to true astronomical north. The problem of compensating for varying magnetic declination was addressed with the azimuth compass, which was first described in 1514 in João de Lisboa's *Livro de Marinharia*; the azimuth compass took a bearing from the sun, the moon, or a star, and the difference between this reading and that of the magnetic compass generated the magnetic declination.

**COMPÈRE, LOYSET** (*c.*1445–1518), Flemish composer in France and Italy who sang in the *cappella* of Galeazzo Maria Sforza, duke of Milan; by 1486 he was a *chantre ordinaire* to Charles VIII. He was also active in Cambrai and Douai and composed masses, motets, and chansons.

**COMPLUTENSIAN POLYGLOT**. In about 1502 a group of biblical scholars led by Cardinal Jiménez de CISNEROS started work in Alcalá (Latin Complutum) on the trilingual text of the Old Testament (in Hebrew, Greek, and Latin) and bilingual text of the New Testament (in Greek and Latin) known as the Complutensian Polyglot (Spanish *Biblia políglota Complutense*). The Hebraists included Antonio LEBRIJA and three Jewish converts to Catholicism, the most eminent of which was Alfonso de ZAMORA. The principal Greek specialist was Hernán NÚÑEZ DE TOLEDO. The six volumes were printed between 1514 and 1517, but the edition was not authorized by Pope LEO X until 1520 and was probably not published until 1522. This edition included the first printed text of the Septuagint (the Greek version of the Old Testament).

The pointing of the Hebrew text of the Old Testament does not conform to the norms of Massoretic vocalization, and the pausal accents are omitted altogether, except for the *Athnach* (the breathing or rest within each verse), the usage of which is eccentric. It has been hypothesized that these oddities can be attributed to the eclectic use of Massoretic manuscripts together with a pre-Massoretic manuscript which embodies the Babylonian system of vocalization and pausal accents; as no manuscript embodying the Babylonian system survives amongst the manuscripts of Cardinal Cisneros now in Madrid, this explanation remains conjectural.

**COMUNEROS, REVOLT OF THE, or** (Spanish) **Comunidades de Castilla or Guerra de las Comunidades**, a rebellion in Castile by a group of towns called the Comuneros. The rebellion was social in nature, but was precipitated by the accession of Charles I (later CHARLES V) to the throne of Castile and his subsequent departure for Flanders. Charles was regarded as a foreigner who spoke no Spanish, and he had aggravated Castilian resentment with a series of foreign appointments, notably the Burgundian Guillaume de Croy as archbishop of Toledo and the Dutchman Adriaan of Utrecht (later Pope ADRIAN VI) as co-regent (together with Cardinal CISNEROS) of Castile. In May 1520 Juan López de PADILLA emerged as the leader of the insurrectionists in the Revolt of the Comuneros. His forces captured the castle at Tordesillas where Queen JUANA LA LOCA was incarcerated, vainly hoping that she could lead a national government. Padilla at first attracted some aristocratic support for the revolt, but he soon forfeited it by proposing egalitarian measures, and was deposed as leader in favour of the grandee Pedro Girón. After Girón's defeat, Padilla was reinstated, but after several military successes his army was defeated at Villalar (near Toro) on 23 April 1521; Padilla and the other leaders were captured and publicly executed the following day. Padilla's widow María Pacheco prolonged the revolt for another six months by defending Toledo against the royal army, but she eventually had to flee to Portugal, and the revolt was concluded; the noble participants were pardoned, the commoners punished.

There was a simultaneous revolt in Valencia known as the Germanía, so called from the name of the committee that organized the insurgency. This revolt was not so much a reaction against Charles as an attack by Christian townsmen and sailors against landowners and their MUDÉJAR and MORISCO serfs, many of whom were murdered or forced to convert on pain of death.

DHE; H. L. Seaver, *The Great Revolt of Castile* (1928); J. A. Maravall, *Las comunidades de Castilla* (1963); Joseph Pérez, *La Révolution des 'Comunidades' de Castille* (1970).

**CONCILIAR MOVEMENT**, the movement within the Catholic Church which represented the view that supreme authority lay with the general councils of the Church rather than with the papacy. Conciliar theory had been debated by thirteenth- and fourteenth-century canonists in relation to the theoretical possibility of a heretical pope. The implications of the debate were realized with the advent of the GREAT SCHISM in 1378. The COUNCIL OF CONSTANCE declared in its fourth and fifth sessions that all Christians, including popes, were bound by the decisions of general councils, which derived their authority directly from God, but in resolving the schism the Council subverted the position of the conciliarists by creating an unchallenged pope. In 1418 Pope MARTIN V prepared but did not promulgate a bull forbidding any pope to appeal to a general council (and thereby acknowledge the superior authority of a council). NICHOLAS OF CUSA proposed a modified conciliarism in his *De concordantia catholica* (1433), but by 1437 had become a supporter of the pope. Support for conciliar ideas faded in the fifteenth century, and in 1460 Pope PIUS II, who had been a conciliarist early in his career, promulgated a bull forbidding his successors to appeal to any future general council.

The death of the conciliar movement was one of the causes of discontent that eventually led to the Reformation, which was in part directed against papal authority. Within the Church, conciliar sentiment survived in the form of GALLICANISM in the French Church.

Antony Black, *The Conciliar Movement and the Fifteenth-Century Heritage* (1979); G. Alberigo, *Chiesa Conciliare: Identità e significatio del conciliarismo* (1981); H. J. Sieben, *Traktate und Theorien zum Konzil von Beginn des Großen Schismas bis zum Vorabend der Reformation, 1378–1521* (1983).

**CONCORD, BOOK OF** or (Latin) **Liber concordiae** or (German) **Konkordienbuch**, the collective name for the six founding documents of the Lutheran confession, consisting of the Formula of Concord (Formula Concordiae), the AUGSBURG CONFESSION of 1530 (Confessio Augustana), MELANCHTHON's *Apologia Confessionis Augustanae*, the SCHMALKALDIC ARTICLES (Articula Smalcaldici) and Luther's *Catechismi Major* (*Grosser Katechismus*) and *Catechismi Minor* (*Kleiner Katechismus*). The German version of the Book of Concord was published in Dresden in 1580; the Latin edition followed in 1584.

The most important of these documents is the Formula of Concord, which was issued on 25 June 1580—the fiftieth anniversary of the Augsburg Confession—by the Lutheran Church; its purpose was to reconcile uncompromising Lutherans with crypto-Calvinist Lutherans. The 24 articles of the Formula of Concord had been drafted in March 1577 by Jakob ANDREAE, Martin CHEMNITZ, and Nikolaus Selnecker (1530–92) in Bergen (near Magdeburg). In the event its reception was uneven. The German states of Saxony, Württemberg, and Baden-Durlach accepted the Formula, but Hesse, Holstein, and Nassau rejected it. The free cities were similarly divided: Hamburg and Lübeck accepted it, but Frankfurt am Main and Bremen rejected it. Beyond Germany, the Formula was accepted by the churches of Hungary and Sweden; Denmark initially rejected it, and declared publication of the Formula to be an offence punishable by death, but eventually recanted and accepted the Formula.

F. Bente, *Historical Introductions to the Book of Concord* (1965); L. Spitz and W. Lohff (eds.), *Discord, Dialogue and Concord: Studies in the Lutheran Reformation's Formula of Concord* (1977; German edn. 1977).

**CONDÉ, PRINCES OF**, the title of a French dynasty (a branch of the BOURBONS) whose ancestral home was in Condé sur l'Escaut (in Hainaut, close to what is now the Belgian border).

The first prince of Condé was the HUGUENOT leader Louis de Bourbon, son of the duke of Vendôme and younger brother of ANTOINE DE BOURBON, king of Navarre. He became a soldier, and as a young man fought in Piedmont. He led the reinforcements in the relief of the imperial siege of Metz (November 1552–January 1553), fought at the battle of SAINT-QUENTIN (10 August 1557) and participated in the capture of CALAIS (7 January 1558). He was implicated as a conspirator in the Conjuration d'AMBOISE (March 1560), which aimed to capture FRANCIS II; when the plot was discovered Condé was arrested in Orléans (31 October 1560) and sentenced to death, but spared by the death of King Francis on 5 December. Under the conciliatory regency of CATHERINE DE MÉDICIS

Condé was appointed governor of Picardy and participated in the Colloquy of POISSY, but on the outbreak of the WARS OF RELIGION he became the military and political leader of the Huguenot side. In September 1562 he signed the Treaty of Richmond, which ceded Le Havre to England in exchange for military support. On 13 March 1569, at the battle of Jarnac (Poitou), Condé imprudently charged the entire Catholic army with a small troop of cavalry; he eventually yielded his sword in surrender, whereupon he was shot by an officer in the Catholic army.

The second prince of Condé was Louis's son Henri (1552–88), who became leader of the Huguenot side in the Wars of Religion, but was captured and imprisoned; he died of poison popularly believed to have been administered by his wife.

The third prince of Condé was Henri's posthumous son, who was also called Henri (1588–1646). He married Charlotte de Montmorency, and in order to prevent her from becoming the mistress of King HENRI IV fled to Spain and then to Italy. They returned to France in July 1610, after the assassination of the king. The prince plotted against the regent, MARIE DE MÉDICIS, and was imprisoned at Vincennes from 1616 to 1619; his wife, who had planned to divorce her husband, voluntarily joined him in captivity. Their son Louis, who is known as the Great Condé (1621–86), assembled the paintings, tapestries, stained glass, jewels (including the Condé Rose Diamond), and illuminated manuscripts (including *Les Très Riches Heures du duc de Berry*) housed in the Musée Condé in Château de Chantilly.

DBF.

**CONDIVI, ASCANIO** (1525–74), Italian painter, and the biographer of MICHELANGELO; his *Vita di Michelagnolo Buonarroti*, which was published in 1553, was in part a reaction to the view of Michelangelo advanced by VASARI in his *Lives*, which had been published in 1550. Condivi was a close associate at Michelangelo, and at times his biography seems to encapsulate Michelangelo's perspective so sympathetically that its subject seems to be a silent collaborator in the biography.

DBI; MDA; *Vita di Michelagnolo Buonarroti*, ed. Giovanni Nencioni (1998); *The Life of Michelangelo*, trans. A. S. Wohl (2nd edn., 1999).

**CONDOTTIERE** (plural *condottieri*), a soldier who held a military contract (*condotta*) to raise and command mercenary troops. The soldiers were equipped as armoured cavalry, which was in the fifteenth century increasingly supplemented with infantry and artillery. The city-states of Italy began to issue *condotte* in the late thirteenth century and the system survived until the mid-sixteenth century. In the early sixteenth century independent infantry regiments began to emerge; their commanders were called *conquestabili*.

Families such as the BAGLIONI, the FARNESE, the ORSINI, the PICCOLOMINI, the SAVORGNAN, and the TRIVULZIO supplied generations of *condottieri*. The most prominent *condottieri* of the period were Micheletto ATTENDOLO, Alfonso d'AVALOS, BARTOLOMEO D'ALVIANO, Facino CANE, Francesco CARMAGNOLA, Bartolomeo COLLEONI, Andrea DORIA, Alfonso d'ESTE, Alessandro FARNESE, FEDERICO II DA MONTEFELTRO, Francesco FERRUCCI, Andrea FORTEBRACCIO (Braccio da Montone), Il GATTAMELATA (Erasmo da Narni), Federico I GONZAGA, Gianfrancesco I GONZAGA, Celio MALESPINA, Giovanni de' MEDICI (Giovanni della Banda Nere), NICCOLÒ DA TOLENTINO, Niccolò PICCININO, SAMPIERO DA BASTELICA, and Francesco SFORZA. The qualities of an ideal *condottiere* were outlined by Roberto VALTURIO.

Michael Mallett, *Mercenaries and their Masters: Warfare in Renaissance Italy* (1974); J. R. Hale, *War and Society in Renaissance Europe, 1450–1620* (1985).

**CONFRATERNITIES** or (Italian) *confraternite* or *compagnie* or (in Venice) *scuole*, religious associations that offered to their members support in life (through social gatherings and benevolent funds) and death (through masses and prayers). From the thirteenth century confraternities increasingly served as expressions of lay piety, occasionally even denouncing the sinfulness of the clergy. In Italy, the *compagnie dei disciplinati*, which arose from the flagellant movement that appeared in 1260, sought to relieve poverty, appease civil strife, expose heresy, and extirpate sodomy. The Venetian *scuole grande* (such as the Scuola Grande di San Marco and the Scuola Grande di San Rocco), which also arose from the flagellant movement, had by the sixteenth century evolved into mutual aid societies that administered charitable funds, but never altogether abandoned their ritualized flagellant practices.

In the fifteenth century, confraternities arose from the mendicant ORDERS, notably the Dominicans, whose Confraternity of the Blessed Virgin Mary evolved into the Confraternity of the Rosary (Italian Confraternita del Rosario) after the battle of LEPANTO (1571), when in thanksgiving for the victory Pope PIUS V instituted (1572) the Feast of the Blessed Virgin Mary of the Rosary.

Another group of fifteenth-century confraternities, commonly called *compagnie di San Girolamo* (i.e. JEROME) or *compagnie del Divino Amore*, offered discreet assistance for the 'shamefaced poor' (*poveri vergognosi*), the group now described by a British charity as 'distressed gentlefolk'. The Roman ORATORY OF DIVINE LOVE is a product of this movement. In the sixteenth century these confraternities also developed specialized institutions that included hospitals for the *incurabili* (SYPHILIS patients, orphans, and beggars), such as the Venetian Incurabili on the Dorsoduro, and convents of *convertite* (reformed and retired prostitutes); some confraternities offered relief to imprisoned debtors, and others, devoted to the ideals of the *buona morte*, prepared condemned prisoners for their executions.

In the course of the sixteenth century confraternities in Italy, France, and Spain became important forces in the process of Catholic reform.

Nicholas Terpstra, *The Politics of Ritual Kinship: Confraternities and Social Order in Early Modern Italy* (2000); J. P. Donnelly and M. W. Maher, *Confraternities and Catholic Reform in Italy, France and Spain* (1999); B. Wisch (ed.), *Confraternities and the Visual Arts in Renaissance Italy* (2000); Maureen Flynn, *Confraternities and Social Welfare in Spain, 1400–1700* (1989).

**CONFRÉRIE DE LA PASSION** (1402–1675). *Confréries*, like the CONFRATERNITIES of Italy, were religious associations of lay people; some *confréries* were attached to guilds (French *corporations*) and most were associated with a saint or a feast day. The Confrérie de la Passion, which held its meetings (*puys*) in Paris, performed mystery plays. In 1548 the Confrérie adapted as a playhouse the l'Hôtel de Bourgogne on the right bank of the Seine.

Sophie Holsboer, *Le Théâtre de l'Hôtel de Bourgogne* (2 vols., 1970).

**CONINXLOO, GILLIS VAN** (1544–1607), Flemish LANDSCAPE painter, born in Antwerp. He lived in Frankenthal from 1587 to 1595, and then settled permanently in Amsterdam. His early landscapes are backdrops to biblical or mythological figures, but in his later works, such as the *Forest* (Kunsthistorisches Museum, Vienna), his voluptuous landscapes become the subject of his paintings. He died in Amsterdam, where he was buried on 4 January 1607.

*MDA* s.v. Coninxloo, van (i): (2); *BNB* s.v. Coninxlo, Gilles van.

**CONNAN or Conan or Connat, FRANÇOIS DE, or Connanus** (c.1508–1551), French jurist, a friend of CALVIN. Connan's dissatisfaction with what he saw as the muddle of the JUSTINIAN *Corpus* led him to systematize Justinian with a view to identifying and extracting coherent principles of CIVIL LAW. In his *Commentarii iuris civilis* (2 vols., Paris, 1538) Connan inaugurated a tradition of systematic law which was to be developed in the seventeenth century by jurists such as Jean Dornat.

*DBF* s.v. 5. Conan.

**CONQUISTADORES** (Spanish; 'conquerors'), the sixteenth-century Spanish conquerors of Mexico and Peru, principally in the period 1519–40; the two most famous *conquistadores* were CORTÉS and PIZARRO. The term 'conquistador' (plural 'conquistadors') has been naturalized in English since the nineteenth century.

F. A. Kirkpatrick, *The Spanish Conquistadores* (1934).

**CONSEJO DE LAS ÍNDIAS.** See INDIES, COUNCIL OF THE.

**CONSTANTINOPLE, FALL OF** (29 May 1453). Constantinople, the Byzantium of antiquity (657 BC–AD 330), was the capital of the Roman Empire in the east from 330 to 1453 and the capital of the Ottoman Empire from 1453 to 1922. The event known to the West as the 'fall of Constantinople' is celebrated by Turks as the 'conquest of Istanbul'. The borders of Christian BYZANTIUM gradually contracted under the Ottoman onslaught, and with the fall of Trebizond in 1461, the Byzantine Empire consisted only of Constantinople and its immediate hinterland.

Constantinople had been besieged by the Ottomans in 1393 and 1422. The third and final siege, by the army of Sultan Mehmet II, began on 7 April 1453; the city fell 53 days later, on 29 May 1453, and among the dead was Constantine XI Palaiologos, the last Byzantine emperor. The Ottomans referred to Constantinople as 'the city' ('Istanbul' derives from Greek *'s ten polin*, 'the city'), and rejoiced in having con-

quered what they regarded as the capital of Christendom. Mehmet was a magnanimous conqueror, and granted extensive privileges to the defeated Greeks and their patriarch.

In the traditional historiography of the RENAISSANCE, the fall of Constantinople precipitated the recovery of knowledge of classical antiquity because Greeks in Constantinople fled to Venice with copies of ancient texts. This model of cultural descent is only useful in the limited sense that some Greek texts were only known through manuscripts that originated in Constantinople.

**CONSTITUTIONES MARCHIAE ANCONTIAE or (Italian) Constitutiones de la Marca de Ancona**, a recension of the law of the Marches published in 1357; it remained in effect for two centuries. It is popularly known as the *Collectio Aegidiana*, with reference to Cardinal Aegidio Albornoz, who appointed the papal commission which drafted the law. The law, which regulated government with a view to limiting the power of local officials, was later extended to all the papal states, and lasted until 1816.

**CONTARINI, AMBROGIO** (1429–after 1496), Venetian traveller, born into a patrician family. In 1474 he was sent on a diplomatic mission to Persia to join Giosofat BARBARO in his negotiations for a military alliance against the Ottomans. He travelled through Poland and the Ukraine to the Caucasus and in 1475 arrived in Isfahan, where he met Barbaro. He was expelled in 1476 and returned to Venice via Tiflis (now T'bilisi, in Georgia) and Astrakhan (then a Tatar city, now Russian). His account of his voyage was published in 1486.

*DBI; I viaggi in Persia degli ambasciatori veneti Barbaro e Contarini*, ed. L. Lockhart et al. (1973).

**CONTARINI, GASPARO** (1483–1542), cardinal and political philosopher, born into a Venetian patrician family that provided the republic with eight doges. He was educated at the University of Padua and became a diplomat, representing Venice at the court of the Emperor CHARLES V and in this capacity attending the Diet of WORMS in 1521, and subsequently serving on missions to England, Spain, and the Vatican. These diplomatic activities on behalf of Venice (1520–34) came to an end in 1535, when Pope PAUL III created him a cardinal, despite the fact that he was a layman.

In 1536 Contarini was appointed bishop of Belluno and joined the commission charged with the planning of the general council which was convoked nine years later as the COUNCIL OF TRENT, and in this capacity issued a set of reform proposals entitled *Consilium de emendanda ecclesia*. In 1541 Contarini attended the Conference of REGENSBURG as a papal legate (but not as a delegate); while residing in Regensburg he wrote his *Epistola de justificatione* (25 May 1541), in which he sought reconciliation with the Lutheran party on the fraught issue of JUSTIFICATION by elaborating the conciliatory doctrine of DOUBLE JUSTICE. The attempt failed to convince the Lutherans and aroused suspicions of heterodoxy amongst Catholic theologians.

In 1516 Contarini published a treatise on the office of bishop (*De officio viri boni ac probi episcopi*) and a treatise asserting the immortality of the soul (*De immortalitate animae*), a response to Pietro POMPONAZZI's *De immortalitate animae* (1516); in 1530 he published a courteous riposte to Martin LUTHER, *Confutatio articulorum seu quaesionum Lutheri*. Contarini's treatise on political philosophy, *De magistratibus et republica Venetorum* (written 1523–4, revised 1531, published 1543), is an impassioned defence of the Venetian form of government, and it became a seminal text in constitutional debates all over Europe. In England, the translation by Lewis Lewkenor (*The Commonwealth and Government of Venice*, 1599) was graced by a prefatory sonnet by Edmund SPENSER, and in *Volpone* (1607) Ben JONSON's character Sir Politic Would-Be reads Contarini's treatise in Venice.

Contarini died in Bologna, apparently of poison administered by the Church; as he lay dying he advised Bernardino OCHINO to flee Italy.

DBI; P. Matheson, *Cardinal Contarini at Regensburg* (rev. edn., 1995).

**CONTI, NICCOLÒ DE'** (*c*.1395–1469), Venetian traveller, born into a noble merchant family in Chioggia. In 1419 he left Venice on a journey that was to last for 25 years. He travelled to Damascus and thence to Baghdad, where he boarded a ship and sailed down the Tigris to Basra and the head of the Persian Gulf. He visited the island of Ormus (now Iranian Hormuz) and then sailed along the Indian Ocean coast of Persia to Cambay (now Khambhat, in Gujarat). He travelled down the west coast to Goa (then a *haj* port) and inland to Vijayanagar (modern Hampi, in Karnataka), the Hindu capital which was to be destroyed in 1555 and is now a wilderness of ruins. He travelled on to Mylapore (now a suburb of Madras), where he visited the shrine of St Thomas, which MARCO POLO had visited while returning from Cathay.

Conti travelled on to Sumatra, where he stayed for a year, and then turned back. He stopped in Tenasserim (on the Malay peninsula in what is now southern Myanmar) and sailed up the Ganges to Burdwan (modern Barddhamän, in West Bengal) before turning south-east again and sailing up the Irrawaddy to Ava (near Mandalay). He then settled for a time in Pegu (near Rangoon), from which he sailed to Java, his furthest point east. He stayed in Java for nine months and then sailed back to India, possibly visiting Ceylon (now Sri Lanka) and certainly calling at Cochin (Kochi), Calicut (Kozhikode), and Cambay (Khambhat) before sailing west to Socotra (now Yemeni Suquṭrä, then a Nestorian bishopric) and Aden. He sailed up the Red Sea to Jeddah, the *haj* port of Mecca, and thence overland to Cairo and home to Venice, where he arrived in 1444.

Conti had been obliged to renounce Christianity during his travels, and as a penance he was ordered by Pope EUGENIUS IV to dictate an account of his travels to Poggio BRACCIOLINI, the papal secretary. His tales of cinnamon in Sri Lanka, bamboo in the Ganges valley, polyandry in Kerala, cockfighting in Java, and Indian *suttee* are the finest account by a European of travel in fifteenth-century south Asia.

DBI; English translation of Conti's *Travels* in R. H. Major (ed.), *India in the Fifteenth Century* (1858).

**CONTRAPPOSTO**, the Renaissance Italian term (literally 'opposite') for the pose of the erect human figure as portrayed in sculpture. The robed human figure is relatively unproblematical for the sculptor, but the naked figure constitutes a practical problem of balance, particularly if the sculptor seeks to avoid the impersonality and solemnity of a symmetrical figure.

Renaissance sculptors such as DONATELLO, VERROCCHIO, and MICHELANGELO studied ANTIQUE SCULPTURE, and also experimented with the classical pose in their live models. The most innovative and radical treatment of the *contrapposto* is the statuary of Michelangelo, who boldly balanced projecting masses of stone against one another. In his *David* (Accademia, Florence), the forward motion of the left knee is balanced by the backward movement of the left shoulder, which means that the chest is twisted on its axis; similarly, the forward movement of the upper arm is balanced by the backward movement of the head. This interpretation of *contrapposto* was to set the style of Italian and German sculpture until the end of the eighteenth century. The term *contrapposto* is also used to denote a posture in which the weight is carried on one leg and the other leg is relaxed.

**COOKERY**. Modern European cookery has its origins in fifteenth-century Italy, when cooks began to prepare and serve food imaginatively and to experiment with new recipes. The *Diarii* of Marino SANUTO record the menus and prices of the banquets enjoyed by Venetian noblemen, and Ortensio Lando describes the regional dishes of Italy in his *Commentario delle più notabili e mostruose cose d'Italia* (Venice, 1550); VERONESE depicts a Venetian banquet in his *Wedding at Cana* (1563). Ices were an Italian invention, and the idea of serving slices of meat with sauce (*fricandeaux*) was invented by the chef of Pope LEO X; such dishes (and the cooks who prepared them) were taken to France by CATHERINE DE MÉDICIS, and the novelty of her Italianate food was noted by MONTAIGNE; in the kingdom of Naples, pizza is recorded in the fifteenth century. The use of the fork as a dining implement originated in Venice; the Englishman Thomas CORYATE records in his *Crudities* (1611) that he was mocked as a *furciferus* (Latin 'pitchfork handler') because of his use of those 'Italian neatnesses called forks'. A fork first appears in a depiction of *The Last Supper* in Jacopo BASSANO's painting of 1599. Ben Jonson offers a classicized description of an ideal meal in his poem 'Inviting a Friend to Dinner'.

Emilio Faccioli, 'La cucina italiana nel Rinascimento', in Giulio Einaudi (ed.), *Storia d'Italia* (6 vols. in 10, Turin, 1972–6) vol. v.

**COORNHERT, DIRCK VOLCKERTSZOON** (1522–90), Dutch humanist, translator, poet, dramatist, politician, notary, and engraver, born in Amsterdam, the son of a cloth merchant. In 1547 he settled in Haarlem, where he worked as an engraver for Maarten van HEEMSKERK. His translations into Dutch include Boethius, BOCCACCIO (several tales from the *Decameron*), Cicero, Homer (*Odyssey*), and Seneca. Coornhert's most important original literary work was a STOIC treatise on 'morality, or the art of virtuous living' (*Zedekunst dat is Wellevenkunste*, 1586). He lived for several years (1568–72) as a religious exile in Cleves, where he taught the art of engraving to GOLTZIUS; he returned to Haarlem (where he worked as a notary) and then moved to Delft and (in 1588) to Gouda. His engravings include illustrations to the German edition of Jan van der NOOT's epic *Das Buch Extasis* (1576).

*MDA; NNBW* x; Henk Bonger, *Leven en werk van Dirck Volckertszoon Coornhert* (1978); Henk Bonger (ed.), *Dirck Volckertszoon Coornhert* (1989); Gerrit Voogy, *Constraint on Trial: Dirck Volckertsz Coornhert and Religious Freedom* (2000).

**COPERNICUS, NICOLAUS, or (Polish) Mikołaj Kopernik** (1473–1543), Polish astronomer, born into a merchant family in Thorn (now Polish Toruń). He studied mathematics at Kraków (1491–4) and then moved to Italy, where he studied CANON LAW and medicine in Bologna, Ferrara, and Padua. While in Padua he learned some Greek, and probably met FRACASTORO; Copernicus also visited Rome. On returning to Poland in 1505 he served as physician to his maternal uncle, who was a scholarly bishop. His uncle died in 1512, whereupon Copernicus moved to Frauenburg (now Polish Frombork), where he worked for the rest of his life as a canon and physician.

There Copernicus worked on writing up his heliocentric theory, whose final manuscript draft survives, in Copernicus' tidy humanistic cursive hand, with the title *De revolutionibus*. It is not at all clear why Copernicus decided to consider a heliocentric model of the universe. One possible contributory factor is that the revival of Greek, in Padua and other universities in Italy, had led to an increased interest in the various ancient theories that Aristotle had described and rejected in the introductory paragraphs of his writings on natural philosophy. Copernicus knew that in proposing a heliocentric model of the cosmos he was reviving a Pythagorean idea (rejected in Aristotle's *On the Heavens*). The Pythagorean system is now believed to make the sun move about the central fire together with the moon and the planets, but in the Renaissance the Pythagorean central fire was identified as the sun. Copernicus began to discuss a heliocentric cosmos while he was still in Italy, and a conversation with friends in Rome led to his writing a short account of his ideas in an essay called the *Commentariolus*, probably completed about 1513, which circulated in manuscript. A copy later came into the possession of Tycho BRAHE.

The system sketched in the *Commentariolus* is simpler than standard geocentric astronomy, but the detailed theory described in *De revolutionibus* is not. In the introduction to the later document, Copernicus says that his reason for rejecting the current geocentric model is that the motions it ascribes to the planets involve circular movements that are not uniform about their own centres but about a point some distance from it (called the 'equant point'). Such movement Copernicus considers contrary to Aristotelian physics. This is only one of several indications that Copernicus took a 'realist' view of astronomical theories, that is, he believed the models represented physical truth, and were not mere calculation devices. This is to operate a fusion between the concerns of astronomers, who were mathematicians, and natural philosophers, who considered the physical facts. In his preliminary chapters, Copernicus points out that his system is indeed systematic in the sense that it allows the orbs to be related one to another since their order and sizes can be known from observation, but in the remainder of the work he makes nothing further of this (it was taken up by KEPLER) and presents a separate model for the motion of each planet. This is in the manner of the *Almagest*, which at the time he began to write Copernicus apparently knew only from REGIOMONTANUS' *Epytoma*, and Copernicus' models are constructed in exactly the same way as PTOLEMY's, even to the extent that the centre of the system, the point to which motions are referred, is the centre of the orb of the earth, a point near the sun but not identifiable with it. Thus Copernicus' planetary system should properly be described as heliostatic rather than heliocentric. Copernicus does, however, place the sun in the centre of the universe, albeit noting that since the heavens are no longer taken to move there is no need to assume that the fixed stars belong to a sphere and their distance may be infinite (see COSMOLOGY).

It is not known when Copernicus finished writing *De revolutionibus* (his own declaration that he delayed publication for Pythagorean reasons is not wholly convincing), but news of his work reached the outside world. The Wittenberg mathematician Georg RHETICUS visited Copernicus in Frauenburg, and secured permission to publish the work. The volume, dedicated to Pope PAUL III and edited by Andreas OSIANDER, appeared shortly before Copernicus' death in 1543; it is said that Copernicus, who it seems had suffered a stroke, was given a copy of the printed book on his deathbed. The book had to fight its battles without help from the author. Matters were complicated by Osiander's preface. As we have seen, Copernicus believed his model represented the physical truth of the cosmos. In his preface, Osiander took an opposite view, stating that the models were calculation devices whose apparent physical absurdity did not matter. The preface was unsigned and was thus likely to be taken as written by Copernicus himself; a small number of people knew at once that it was not; MÄSTLIN told Kepler that the preface was by Osiander.

*DSB; NDB; PSB* s.v. Kopernik; Paolo Casini, *L' antica sapienza in Italia: Cronistoria di un mito* (1998).

**COPLAND, ROBERT** (d. 1547), English printer, poet, and translator who worked in the printhouse of Wynkyn de WORDE. He translated several works from French, including three romances and *The Rutter of the Sea* (see, RUTTIER). His best-known original poem, the 'High Way to the Spital House', is of documentary value because of its account of beggars and vagabonds.

*DNB;* F. C. Francis, *Robert Copland* (1961).

**COPPENHOLE, JAN VAN** (d. 1492), Netherlandish leader of the rebellion of Ghent, who emerged as a national figure in 1484, when he led the resistance to the claim of Maximilian of Austria (later the Emperor MAXIMILIAN I) to the regency of his son PHILIP THE HANDSOME. Coppenhole fled to France in

1485, but returned to Ghent two years later to lead another insurrection against Maximilian. The city held out against Maximilian until Coppenhole was murdered in 1492, whereupon Ghent capitulated.

**COPRARIO, GIOVANNI, or John Cooper** (*c.*1570/80–1626), English composer whose name was Italianized possibly after spending time there. His principal patron was Robert Cecil, earl of Salisbury. He collaborated with Thomas CAMPION on *The Lords' Masque* (1613) for the marriage of Princess Elizabeth to the Elector Friedrick, to whom he had dedicated his *Songs of Mourning: Bewailing the Untimely Death of Prince Henry*. He also wrote fantasias for keyboard and viols.

**CÓRDOBA, GONZALO FERNÁNDEZ DE.** See FERNÁNDEZ DE CÓRDOBA, GONZALO.

**CORFINI, JACOPO** (*c.*1540–1591), Italian composer, active in Ferrara and Lucca, where he was organist at San Martino. He wrote sacred and secular music; his *Concerti* of 1591 displays the influence of the GABRIELI.

**CORIO, BERNADINO** (1459–*c.*1519), Milanese historian, a member of the household of Ludovico SFORZA, who commissioned from him a history of Milan and put at his disposal a large body of archival material. *Patria historia* (1503), which traces the history of Milan from its remote origins to 1499, is the earliest scholarly study of Italian history to be written in Italian rather than Latin.
*DBI*; *Patria historia*, ed. A. Morosi Guerra as *Storia di Milano* (2 vols., 1978).

**CORI SPEZZATI**, a term used to describe the use of groups of singers in different parts of a building, or the technique of music composed for them. It became widely used in the sixteenth century, reflecting the popularity of Italian polychoral music in that period.

**CORNAGO, JOHANNES** (*c.*1400–after 1474), Spanish composer and chaplain to King Alfonso I of Naples. It is possible that he met OCKEGHEM in Paris; a mass, a motet, and eleven Spanish and Italian songs survive.

**CORNARO, CATERINA** (1454–1510), Italian queen of CYPRUS, born in Venice, the daughter of the patrician Marco Cornaro, who owned large properties in Cyprus. In 1468 Caterina was married by proxy to King James II of Cyprus, and in 1472 she went to join her husband. He died the following year when Caterina was pregnant with their son James III. She became the infant's regent, and when he died in 1474, Caterina became queen regnant. She struggled to fend off Ottoman attacks, and in 1489 was persuaded by her brother Giorgio to abdicate in favour of the Venetian republic.

Caterina returned to Italy and settled in Asolo (near Treviso), where her court became the fictitious setting of BEMBO's dialogues on love, *Gli asolani*.
*DBI* s.v. Caterina Cornaro, regina di Cipro; *OCIL*.

**CORNARO, LUIGI** (1475–1566), Italian slimmer. He was born into a patrician family in Venice and for several decades indulged his prodigious appetite for food and drink. On the advice of his physician he reduced his diet to 350 grams (12 ounces) of food a day and 350 grams (12 fluid ounces) of wine; his food intake was eventually reduced to one egg a day. Details of his diet, which may have been responsible for his long life, are recorded in his *Discorsi della vita sobria* (1558), which was translated into many languages (including English, French, and Latin) and proved to be influential throughout Europe.

**CORNAZZANO or Cornazano, ANTONIO** (*c.*1430–1483/4), Italian author, a native of Oiacenza who spent most of his career in the service of the SFORZA rulers of Milan and his final years in the ESTE court in Ferrara. His works include a poem in praise of the Sforza dynasty (the *Sforzeide*), a treatise on DANCE, a treatise on the art of war (*Opera belissima de l'arte militare*, 1493), and a collection of amorous tales (*I proverbi*, 1525).
*DBI*; *Grove* s.v. Cornazano; R. Bruni and D. Zancani, *Antonio Cornazzano* (1992).

**CORNEILLE DE LYON or Corneille de la Haye** (1500/10–1575), Dutch painter. He was born in The Hague and *c.*1540 moved to Lyon, where he worked as a painter of portrait miniatures. The canon of his paintings was long regarded as unstable, but in 1976 the Louvre acquired Corneille's recently recovered portrait of *Pierre Aymerie*, which has become the basis of subsequent attributions. In 1536 the royal court visited Lyon, and Corneille painted three of the children of FRANCIS I: the Dauphin Henri (Galleria Estense, Modena), Madeleine (Musée Municipal, Blois), and Charles d'Angoulême (Uffizi).
*DBF*; *MDA*; Anne Dubois de Groër, *Corneille de la Haye dit Corneille de Lyon* (1996).

**CORNELISZOON, CORNELIS, or Corneliszoon van Haarlem** (1562–1638), Dutch mannerist painter, born in Haarlem, where he founded an academy with Hendrik GOLTZIUS and Karel van MANDER. His paintings are typically large pictures that depict biblical or historical scenes in which life-sized nudes are sharply foreshortened. The largest collection of his paintings is in the Frans Hals Museum in Haarlem.
*MDA*; *NNBW* x.

**CORNELISZOON VAN OOSTSANEN or van Amsterdam, JACOB** (*c.*1472/7–1533), Dutch painter, book illustrator, and designer of woodcuts and stained glass. He was Amsterdam's most prominent and innovative designer of woodcuts, of which the best surviving examples are a series on *The Passion*. His surviving paintings include a *Self-Portrait* (1533, Rijksmuseum, Amsterdam) and a *Nativity* (1512, Palazzo di Capodimonte, Naples); he died before 18 October 1533.
*MDA*; *NNBW* vi.

**CORNET, PIETER** (1570/80–1633), Flemish composer and organist from a musical family in Brussels, where he became organist at St Nicholas in 1603. He later became a chapel musician, where his colleagues included Peter PHILIPS and John BULL. He composed keyboard fantasias.

**CORNETT.** Its name (little horn) points to its origin as an animal horn, although it came to be made of wood. It was played by vibrating the lips against a cup-shaped mouthpiece and the pitch was altered by the use of finger-holes. The treble instrument was considered more important than its companions, the tenor and the small treble. It was used in conjunction with trombones to support choral music, doubling or replacing the vocal lines. From 1600 it was sometimes used in place of the violin in ensemble pieces and achieved greater prominence through the elaborate parts written by Giovanni GABRIELI.

**CORNISH or Cornysche, WILLIAM** (c.1465–1523), English composer, poet, dramatist, and actor. He was a gentleman of the Chapel Royal and had links with Westminster Abbey. From 1509 he was a significant and versatile figure in the court entertainments, writing and appearing in several, including *The Golden Arbour* (1511). He also oversaw the festivities at the FIELD OF THE CLOTH OF GOLD (1513).

**CORPORAL PUNISHMENT** is the judicial infliction of bodily pain for criminal offences for which the death sentence is deemed to be inappropriate; it normally takes the form of flogging, mutilation, or branding. It is in law distinguished from TORTURE, except when torture is a preliminary part of a death sentence. Corporal punishment was widely used in the Spanish INQUISITION, which burnt alive some 2,000 heretics but mutilated a further 17,000. In England the Court of Star Chamber (see ENGLISH LAW) inflicted a range of mutilations (including excision of ears and slitting of nostrils) on those whom it condemned.

Branding was used extensively in England after 1487 for those who had claimed BENEFIT OF CLERGY: murderers (including Ben JONSON) were branded on the thumb with the letter M and thieves with the letter T. Under the terms of the Statute of Vagabonds (1547), men and women who refused to work were branded on the breast with a V (for 'vagabond') and assumed the legal status of a slave for two years; if such a slave escaped, he was branded on the face with an S (for 'slave'). From 1551, those who brawled in church were excommunicated and branded with an F (for 'felon').

**CORREGGIO or Antonio Allegri** (1494–1534), Italian painter who took his name from his birthplace, the small town of Correggio (east of Parma). Nothing is known of his youth or training, but the indebtedness of his style to MANTEGNA may imply an apprenticeship in Mantua. His early paintings, which are characterized by elegant poses and the use of SFUMATO, include a *St Francis* altarpiece (1514, Gemäldegalerie, Dresden) and *Jesus Taking Leave of his Mother* (National Gallery, London).

By 1518 Correggio had settled in Parma, where his first important commission was the decoration of the ceiling of the Camera di San Paolo (1519), the dining room of the abbess of the Convento di San Paolo; the painting is entirely secular, and includes depictions of Diana (goddess of chastity), Adonis, putti, the Graces, and the Fates. In 1520 Correggio painted an illusionist fresco of *The Vision of St John* (who sees Christ ascending and the apostles) on the dome of the Church of San Giovanni Evangelista, and in 1526 he painted a similar fresco of *The Assumption of the Virgin* on the dome of Parma Cathedral. His altarpieces include *The Virgin with St Jerome* (1527–8, Galleria Nazionale, Parma) and *The Nativity* (Gemäldegalerie, Dresden). His mythological paintings include a series (started in 1530) on *The Loves of Jupiter* for Federico GONZAGA, which is now dispersed; surviving paintings include *Io*, in which Jupiter appears as a cloud, *Ganymede* (both in the Kunsthistorisches Museum, Vienna) and *Leda* (Louvre).

DBI s.v. Allegri, Antonio, detto il Correggio; *MDA*; David Ekserdjian, *Correggio* (1997).

**CORREIA, GASPAR** (c.1495–c.1561), Portuguese historian of India who sailed in 1512 for India, where he became the secretary of Afonso de ALBUQUERQUE; he remained in India and the Portuguese East for the rest of his life, which ended with his murder in Malacca. His *Lendas da Índia*, which remained unpublished until 1858, is an account of Indian culture, a chronicle of events from 1495 to 1550, and an indictment of the colonial administration.

DHP; Aubrey Bell, *Gaspar Corrêa* (1924).

**CORRER, GREGORIO** (1409–64), Italian humanist educationalist, dramatist, translator, and autobiographer. He was born into a patrician family in Venice, and after an education entrusted to VITTORINO DA FELTRE he was taken to Rome by his uncle (a cardinal), who inducted him into an ecclesiastical career. In 1433 Correr attended the COUNCIL OF BASEL, where he supported the CONCILIAR position. This alienated the papacy, and when living in 1443 in Florence (where the papal court was in temporary residence), he was excluded from preferment. Correr was elected patriarch of Venice in the last year of his life, but he died before Pope PAUL II had ratified the appointment.

Correr's writings included a Latin play, a translation of Aesop into Latin, several works on education, and an autobiography.

DBI; OCIL; C. A. Riccio, *Gregorio Correr* (1900).

**CORSI, JACOPO** (1561–1602), Florentine patron of music and literature and composer. He shared an interest with PERI and RINUCCINI in the relationship between music and dramatic poetry which led to the beginnings of opera. In 1600 he produced their *Euridice* for MARIE DE MÉDICIS on the occasion of her wedding to HENRI IV of France, during which he played the harpsichord; he also collaborated with Peri in writing *Daphne*.

**CORSICA or (French) Corse.** The Mediterranean island of Corsica, which lies 12 kilometres (7 miles) north of SARDINIA, is now a *département* of France, but has at various points in its medieval and modern history been governed by Pisa, Genoa, Milan, Aragon, and Britain. For much of the period from 1347 to 1768, Corsica was a Genoese possession; fifteen months later Napoleon was born in the capital, Ajaccio. In the eleventh century the north and south of Corsica instituted separate mechanisms of governance: the south was ruled by feudal barons and the north was a loosely knit republic known as the Terra di Commune, in which administration was in the hands of a Council of Twelve and of hereditary local rulers (*caporali*). Under the terms of the settlement of 1347, in which Corsica submitted to Genoese suzerainty, Corsica agreed to pay a regular tribute to Genoa, and in return was allowed to keep its own legal system and to administer its affairs locally, under the Council of Twelve in the north and a Council of Six in the south. In the first three years of Genoese rule the epidemic of PLAGUE known as the Black Death killed two-thirds of the population.

In 1396 Genoa was conquered by France, and the ensuing political instability in Corsica was exacerbated by rival allegiances in the GREAT SCHISM. In 1419 ALFONSO V of Aragon invaded and occupied the southern part of the island: thereafter the Genoese ruled the Terra di Commune in the north and the Aragonese the feudal area in the south. In 1453 the Terra de Commune offered the government of the island to the Genoese Bank of San Giorgio, whose forces soon expelled the Aragonese; the Bank was in turn driven out by local barons in 1460, and two years later Francesco SFORZA claimed Corsica for Milan. In the course of the next 90 years power changed hands repeatedly, and the island, when it was governed at all, was ruled by the FREGOSO FAMILY of Genoa, the Sforza of Milan, and the Bank of San Giorgio.

On 1 February 1553 HENRI II of France set in motion a plan to conquer Corsica by entering into a military alliance with the Ottoman Sultan Süleyman I. The combined forces of France and the Ottomans quickly overran the island; only Calvi remained in Genoese hands. The Emperor CHARLES V decided to intervene on behalf of Genoa, and invaded with an army of Genoese and imperial forces. The next three years were a bloodbath, during which the patriot SAMPIERO DA BASTELICA, now the national hero of Corsica, fought for the French. A truce agreed in 1556 left Corsica in the hands of the French (except for Bastia), but three years later, under the terms of the Treaty of CATEAU-CAMBRÉSIS (1559), the island was passed to the Bank of San Giorgio, who in turn demitted authority to the republic of Genoa.

Genoa promptly levied a tax on Corsica and (in violation of the treaty) confiscated the property of Sampiero, who responded to these two impositions by organizing a national uprising. After a failed attempt to place Corsica under Ottoman suzerainty, Sampiero landed in June 1564 in Valinco with a band of 50 men; his forces, which quickly grew to 8,000 men, waged war against Genoa until 1567, when the rebellion was broken by the assassination of Sampiero. A peace settlement negotiated in 1568 proved to be lasting, and there were no new rebellions until 1729.

Pierre Antonetti, *Histoire de la Corse* (1973).

**CORTECCIA, FRANCESCO** (1502–71), Florentine composer and organist active in Florence. He composed madrigals some of which were used as *intermedi* for Francesco d'Ambra's *Il furto* (1544) and *La cofanaria*, performed at the Medici court in Florence.

**CORTE REAL FAMILY**, a family of Portuguese explorers of the North Atlantic. João Corte Real sailed *c*.1472 to what may have been Newfoundland. His son Gaspar (*c*.1450–1501) sailed in 1500 to Greenland and Newfoundland (three years after CABOT). In Newfoundland he named Conception Bay and Portugal Cove; he disappeared on his second expedition. Miguel (*c*.1450–1502), Gaspar's brother, may have reached what is now Massachusetts, but he also disappeared; his disappearance gave rise to a legend that he had become an Indian chief.

A third brother, Jerónimo Corte Real (1535–88), was a soldier, painter, and poet. He wrote epics on the siege of the Portuguese Indian island fortress of Diu (*O segundo cerco de Diu*, 1574; Spanish version, 1597), on the battle of LEPANTO (*Austríada*, 1578; written in Spanish), and on a shipwreck off the coast of South Africa (*Naufragio de Sepúlveda*, published posthumously in 1592).

*DHP*; M. Lopes del Almeida (ed.), *Obras de Jerónimo Corte Real* (1979).

**CORTÉS, HERNÁN** (1485–1547), Spanish conquistador of Mexico, born into an impoverished noble family in Medellín (Extremadura) and educated in law at Salamanca. He ran away to Hispaniola in 1504 (aged 19) and fought in the conquest of Cuba (1511–13) under the command of Diego VELÁZQUEZ. In February 1519 he landed on the coast of Mexico with a force of 600 soldiers (supported by thirteen muskets, seven cannons, and sixteen horses). He first landed at what is now Tabasco, and then sailed along the coast and founded the settlement of Villa Rica de Vera Cruz (now the city of Vera Cruz). He then destroyed his eleven ships to ensure that there would be no turning back.

Cortés planned to conquer the Aztec capital of Tenochtitlán (now Mexico City), and to that end reached an accommodation with the Mayans of Tlaxcala, who were hostile to the Aztecs, and used them to reach Tenochtitlán (November 1519), which was on an island accessible only by guarded causeways. Montezuma, the Aztec emperor, mistook Cortés for the god Quetzalcoatl, so entry to the city was unimpeded. Cortés promptly imprisoned Montezuma with a view to using him as a means to conquer and convert the 5 million people of the Aztec empire.

Diego Velázquez dispatched a force under the command of Pánfilo de NARVÁEZ to replace Cortés, who had no inclination to relinquish control of the city. He garrisoned Tenochtitlán and then defeated the forces of Narváez at Cempolán, incorporating Narváez's soldiers into his own army. On returning to Tenochtitlán, Cortés discovered that the brutality of his garrison had led to an Aztec uprising in which Montezuma had been killed by his own people. Cortés was obliged to retreat from Tenochtitlán (June 1520); he rebuffed his pursuers at Otumba (July 1520) and then sought refuge in Tlaxcala in order to prepare a counter-attack.

On 20 May 1521 Cortés besieged Tenochtitlán, which fell after three months, in part because Cortés had been able to cut off its water supply. He entered the ruined city with a view to establishing his authority throughout the Aztec empire. In October 1522 the Emperor CHARLES V acknowledged the conquest of the Aztec capital by appointing Cortés governor and captain-general of New Spain. Cortés used Indian slave labour to rebuild the city in a Spanish style; Mexico City thus became the capital of New Spain, and was soon more populous than any city in metropolitan Spain.

Cortés spent the next six years establishing an administration and (in 1524) exploring his newly conquered territory in a journey to Guatemala and Honduras. In Spain, the court of Charles V was increasingly resentful of the independence of the conquistadors, to whom Cortés had allocated large ENCOMIENDAS, and wanted to replace feudal overlords with the representatives of the Spanish government. Cortés returned to Spain (1528–30) in an attempt to have his authority restored and to answer accusations that he had murdered his wife and Juan de GARAY and embezzled gold that rightly belonged to the crown. He was exonerated and created marqués del Valle de Oaxaca (the site of his own capacious encomienda) and confirmed as captain-general, but was denied the post of viceroy of New Spain, for which he had supplicated. After his return to Mexico, Cortés continued his programme of exploration and conquest (notably an expedition to Baja California in 1533–5) and retired to Spain in 1539. He subsequently took part in the emperor's unsuccessful attack on Algiers (October 1541) and thereafter lived in retirement.

The official history of Cortés's conquest of Mexico was written by LÓPEZ DE GÓMARA, and answered on behalf of those who fought with Cortés by Bernal DÍAZ DEL CASTILLO. Cortés's own reports took the form of five letters to Charles V. The first of these letters is lost, and is replaced in editions of the Cartas de relación by a letter from the regent of Vera Cruz. The second letter (dated 30 October 1520 and published in Seville in 1520) describes Cortés's exploration of the hinterland of Vera Cruz and the sorrowful night (noche triste) of 30 June 1520, when 500 of his soldiers were killed in the retreat from Tenochtitlán and 40 captured and later sacrificed to the gods of the Aztecs. The third letter (dated 15 May 1522 and published in Seville in 1523) describes the conquest and siege of Tenochtitlán. The fourth letter (dated 15 October 1524 and published in Toledo in 1525) describes the treachery of Diego Velázquez and enjoins the emperor to send settlers to New Spain. The fifth letter (dated 3 September 1526 and not published at the time) complains of the treachery of Cristóbal de Olid, whom Cortés had appointed as commander of the expedition sent to conquer Guatemala.

DBEH; DHE; S. de Madariaga, Hernán Cortés (1942); Cortés: Letters from Mexico, ed. and trans. A. R. Pagden (1972); Maurice Collis, Cortés and Montezuma (1994).

**CORTÉS DE ALBACAR, MARTÍN** (c.1510–1582), Spanish geographer, the author of El arte de navegar (Cádiz, 1551), a treatise on navigation that was translated into English in 1561. He confirmed the belief of transatlantic sailors in the vari-

ability of magnetic declination, and postulated the existence of a magnetic pole.

DSB.

**CORTESE, PAOLO** (1465–1510), Italian humanist and literary historian of neo-Latin. He spent his career in the papal secretariat, where in 1481 he succeeded PLATINA as head of the department responsible for the drafting of Latin correspondence. His writings include a history of writing in Latin from Dante to his own time (De hominibus doctis, 1489) and the posthumously published De cardinalatu, a portrait of the ideal cardinal which has analogies to CASTIGLIONE's ideal courtier.

DBI.

**CORVINUS, JÁNOS** (1473–1504), duke of SLAVONIA, the illegitimate son of MATTHIAS CORVINUS, king of Hungary, and his father's designated heir. When Matthias died in 1490 János failed to gain the support of the Hungarian nobility, who instead placed King LADISLAS II of Bohemia on the throne of Hungary. Thereafter János served as a military commander, and from 1499 to 1502 successfully resisted the Ottoman advance on Bosnia.

MEL s.v. Corvin, János.

**CORVUS, JOANNES, or (Flemish) Jan Rav or (English) John Raven** (fl. 1512–44), Flemish painter, probably a native of Bruges. He worked in England for most of the 1520s, and subsequently in France; he may have returned to England on leaving France, but there is no firm evidence. His best-known work is a portrait of Bishop John Foxe (not the martyrologist) in Corpus Christi College, Oxford.

MDA s.v. Rav, Jan.

**CORYATE, THOMAS** (c.1577–1617), English traveller. In 1611 Coryate published Coryate's Crudities, an account of his journeys, largely on foot, three years earlier, through France, Italy, Switzerland, Germany, and the Low Countries. This, with its shorter sequel, and an abstract of its accompanying verses, was published separately as The Odcombian Banquet (1611), gained him much repute, in his lifetime and beyond, as an amusing eccentric. Between 1612 and 1616 he travelled overland to India; he died at Surat.

DNB; M. Strachan, The Life and Adventures of Thomas Coryate (1962).

**COSA, JUAN DE LA** (d. 1510), Spanish mariner and cartographer. He was the owner of COLUMBUS' flagship the Santa María, and may have accompanied Columbus on his first voyage. He travelled on Columbus' second expedition as his cartographer. In 1499 he sailed with Alonso de OJEDA and Amerigo VESPUCCI on a voyage along the coast of what is now Guyana and Venezuela. His map of the world, which was the first to include America, was published in 1500. He continued to visit America regularly, and on his seventh voyage was killed by Indians near Cartagena.

DBEH.

**COSIMO I DE' MEDICI** (1519–74), duke of Florence (1537–69) and grand duke of Tuscany (1569–74), was the son of the condottiere Giovanni de' MEDICI (d. 1526) and Maria

Salviati (d. 1543). In the wake of the assassination of Alessandro de' MEDICI in January 1537, and the consequent extinguishing of the Medici line that extended back through five generations to Cosimo, the Council of 48 chose as Alessandro's successor 17-year-old Cosimo de' Medici, a fourth-generation descendant of Cosimo's brother Lorenzo.

Cosimo had been raised in the country by his widowed mother and had no experience of Florentine politics, but he nonetheless did not falter in his new role. His army defeated the patrician exiles who opposed him at the battle of MONTE-MURLO (1 August 1537). Cosimo coldly executed the leaders of the rebellion and went on to execute another 430 opponents in the course of the next three years; during his reign 1,040 men and six women were executed in Tuscany and an unknown number fell to the daggers of his assassins in other Italian states. He not only disinherited all those whom he executed, but also disinherited their heirs as a way of financing his expansionist wars.

Duke Cosimo was twice married: his first wife, by whom he had eight children, was Eleanor of Toledo (d. 1562); his second wife was Camilla Martelli. Cosimo's son Francesco, who succeeded him as grand duke, was the father of MARIE DE MÉDICIS.

*DBI* s.v. Cosimo; H. M. M. Acton, *The Last Medici* (1958).

**COSMOLOGY** was generally considered the province of natural philosophers or theologians. This allowed purely qualitative descriptions. The planetary system, which seemed to be a very large component of the universe, was believed to consist of a series of planetary orbs, each composed of several mainly hollow spheres rolling against one another. The outer surface of the orb has the form of a spherical shell, centred on the earth. Pictures of the internal structure of orbs are provided in textbooks, such as that of PEURBACH, and confusion is sometimes introduced by referring to them as spheres. The orbs were in contact with one another, and the outermost was in contact with the sphere (spherical shell) of the fixed stars, which in turn was (perhaps) in contact with some further spheres, and the whole system was driven from the outside by the movement of the *primum mobile*, the first moving sphere, beyond which lay heaven, which of course had some structure of its own. The order of the planetary orbs is determined by the periods of revolution of the bodies concerned, so that, working inwards, one has the fixed stars, Saturn, Jupiter, Mars, the sun, Venus, Mercury, and the moon. Below the moon is the 'natural' or 'sublunary' world which, still working inwards, comprised the spheres of fire, air, water, and earth. This is the universe of Dante, whose dissolution is proclaimed by DONNE in *The Second Anniversary* (1611). The spheres were crystalline in the sense that one could see through them; whether they were solid was apparently a matter for debate in the fifteenth and sixteenth centuries. COPERNICUS seems to have been on the side of solidity. It was not possible to construct a model using solid orbs for the Tychonic system (see BRAHE, TYCHO).

Making the assumption that the orbs were in contact, and no thicker than they needed to be, it was possible to calculate cosmic dimensions, but the serious turning point came with the Copernican theory, which made it possible to find the dimensions from observations. Copernicus kept tactfully silent about the huge gaps he had revealed to exist between the paths of the planets. KEPLER decided to try to explain their size, and his two models mark the beginnings of mathematical cosmology. Given that, for Kepler, the universe was created by God, a cosmological model is necessarily a cosmogonic one, a Divine Archetype for Creation. Kepler's first model, published in his *Mysterium cosmographicum* (1596), the only one of his works to go into a second edition in his lifetime (in 1621), explains why there are six planets (the moon now being effectively part of the earth), and the sizes of the spaces between their paths, by appealing to the five Platonic solids. These solids, so called because they are mentioned in Plato's *Timaeus*, are discussed in detail at the end of EUCLID's *Elements*; they are the tetrahedron (four triangular faces), the cube (six square faces), the octahedron (eight triangular faces), the dodecahedron (twelve pentagonal faces), and the icosahedron (twenty triangular faces). The faces are all regular polygons. Euclid proves that there are exactly five solids each having faces that are regular polygons of only one kind. In Kepler's model, the fact that there are five such solids explains why there are six planets, and the sizes of the five gaps between the paths is determined by the ratio between the diameters of the sphere that will just fit outside one of the solids and the sphere that just fits inside the solid. To today's readers this model inevitably seems bizarre, but it is in rather close agreement with the dimensions available from Copernicus' *De revolutionibus*. Dimensions calculated from much more accurate observations by Tycho Brahe failed to bring closer agreement, however, and Kepler duly modified his theory to include ratios of extreme speeds of planets, which (as it turned out) corresponded to the notes of musical scales (one of each of the types that correspond to today's major and minor). The agreement with the notes of the scales is very close indeed; the phenomenon is now known as 'resonance' and the subject of elaborate mathematical explanations. Kepler's new model was published in *Harmonices mundi libri V* (1619).

As Copernicus had noted, the fact that in his heliocentric universe the 'fixed stars' (those that form the constellations) no longer moved made it possible for them to be at an infinite distance. At the time it was impossible to determine their distances by observation and no consensus was ever reached. In the seventeenth century, however, astronomers show an increasing tendency to believe the universe is infinite.

**COSS or cossa.** See ALGEBRA.

**COSSA, FRANCESCO DEL** (*c.*1435–1476/7), Italian painter who worked in his native Ferrara, where he painted some of the frescoes of the *Months* commissioned by Borso d'ESTE for the Palazzo Schifanoia. These paintings, with their astrological symbols and complex iconography, exemplify the intellectual dimension of the culture of mid-fifteenth century north Italian courts. Cossa later left Ferrara for Bologna, where he worked as a painter of ALTARPIECES, portions of at least three of which survive, including a *Crucifixion* in the National Gallery in Washington which was part of a polyptych for the altar of San Petronio in Bologna.

DBI s.v. Del Cossa, Francesco; MDA; Andrea Bacchi, *Francesco del Cossa* (1991).

**COSTA, LORENZO** (*c.*1460–1535), Italian painter. He began his career in Ferrara, where he painted *The Concert* (National Gallery, London). In about 1483 Costa moved to Bologna, where he entered into a partnership with FRANCIA, with whom he worked for the BENTIVOGLIO family on the decoration of the Bentivoglio Palace; the palace has since been destroyed, but some of Costa's frescoes survive in the nearby Bentivoglio Chapel. In 1506 Costa left Bologna for Mantua, where he succeeded MANTEGNA as court painter to the GONZAGA family. His Mantua paintings include an allegorical *Isabella d'Este in the Garden of the Muses* (now in the Louvre) painted for Isabella d'ESTE, marchioness of Mantua.

DBI; MDA.

**COSTELEY, GUILLAUME** (*c.*1530–1606), French composer, active in Paris and, after 1560, organist at the court of Charles IX. He wrote chansons and in his four-part 'Seigneur Dieu ta pitié' experimented with the use of microtones. He was also president of a society in honour of St Cecilia, the patron saint of music.

**COSTER, SAMUEL** (1579–1665), Dutch playwright and surgeon, a native of Amsterdam who studied medicine at Leiden and practised in Amsterdam, where he was a member of the CHAMBER OF RHETORIC known as De Egelantier. In 1617 he founded the Duijtsche Academie, which was modelled on the ACADEMIES of fifteenth-century Italy. His Academy mounted Catholic plays, and so was opposed by the Calvinist authorities; it merged with De Egelantier in 1635.

Coster wrote farces in the style favoured by the chambers of rhetoric (notably *Teeuwis de Boer*, 1612), but also wrote tragedies modelled on SENECA, including the gruesome *Ithys* (1615) and *Polyxena* (1619) and the anti-Calvinist *Iphigenia* (1617).

NNBW vi.

**COSYN, BENJAMIN** (*c.*1570–after 1652), English composer and organist. His collection, the *Cosyn Virginal Book* (1620), contains music by Thomas TALLIS, William BYRD, John BULL, and Orlando GIBBONS as well as most of Cosyn's own works.

**COTTON, SIR ROBERT** (1571–1631), English antiquarian. Cotton's collection of manuscripts and antiquities, largely made up of articles previously in monastic libraries, included the Lindisfarne Gospels, and manuscripts of *Beowulf*, *Sir Gawain and the Green Knight*, and other early literature. It was used by such scholars as BACON and CAMDEN. What remains of the collection, following a benefaction to the Bodleian Library on its foundation, and a fire in 1731, is now in the British Library.

DNB; MDA.

**COUNCIL, FIFTH LATERAN** (1512–17). The Palazzo del Laterano (1586) and its antecedent buildings served as the setting of church councils in Rome from the seventh century to the eighteenth. Four medieval councils (1123, 1139, 1179, and 1215) are deemed by the Western Church to be of ecumenical standing, and it is this enumeration that accounts for the early sixteenth-century Council being unofficially reckoned as the Fifth Lateran Council.

The Council was convoked by Pope JULIUS II in response to the French-dominated COUNCIL OF PISA of 1511, which had decreed the suspension of Pope Julius. The Fifth Lateran Council, which convened on 3 May 1512, devoted the five sessions conducted during the pontificate of Pope Julius to the condemnation of the Council of Pisa and the PRAGMATIC SANCTION OF BOURGES.

Pope Leo X pledged in his election oath to continue the Lateran Council, and opened the sixth session on 27 April 1513. At the eighth session (19 December 1513) he received the condemnation of the Council of Pisa by King LOUIS XII of France and ratified a theological definition of the individuality of the soul; in the ninth session (5 March 1514) he accepted the adhesion of the French episcopate. Later sessions ratified the abrogation of the Pragmatic Sanction of Bourges and Pope Leo's concordat with King FRANCIS I (the Concordat of BOLOGNA). The final sessions established a reform commission and levied a three-year tax on benefices to finance the CRUSADE against the Turks decreed by Pope Leo, who closed the Council on 16 March 1517.

**COUNCIL OF BASEL** (1431–49), a general council convoked by Pope MARTIN V and convened in 1431 under the presidency of Cardinal Giuliano CESARINI. Pope EUGENIUS IV, who was the successor of Martin V, became dissatisfied with the conduct of the Council and dissolved it in a bull of 18 December 1431. The Council invoked the decrees of the COUNCIL OF CONSTANCE asserting the superior authority of general councils over popes and carried on with its business. In the course of the next two years it grew from a small assembly of bishops and abbots into an authoritative body which represented interests such as the secular princes and the universities as well as the Church; the scholars present included NICHOLAS OF CUSA.

The authority of the Council, which enjoyed the support of the Emperor SIGISMUND and powerful states such as Venice, forced Pope Eugenius to revoke his former decision and recognize the legitimacy of the Council (15 December 1433). Eugenius watched with growing alarm as the Council confirmed its commitment to the CONCILIAR MOVEMENT by reaffirming the conciliar decrees of the Council of Constance, circumscribing the powers of papal legates, and prescribing an oath to be taken by popes after their elections; in 1436 he finally dissociated himself from the Council in a letter to all Catholic princes denouncing the usurpations of the papal prerogative by the Council.

In 1437 the Council defied the pope by reversing its earlier decision condemning the Compactata of Prague, and so endorsed the concession of the chalice to the UTRAQUISTS of

Bohemia. In the same year the Council divided over the issue of the location of the negotiations for reunion with the Orthodox Church. Pope Eugenius, with the support of the Greek delegates and a minority of supporters in the Council, removed the Council to Ferrara, where he convoked the COUNCIL OF FERRARA-FLORENCE. The rump that remained at Basel deposed Pope Eugenius and renewed the schism by electing Amadeus VIII of Savoy as Pope FELIX V in 1439. In 1448 the Council was expelled from Basel and migrated to Lausanne, where Pope Felix abdicated (7 April 1449) and the Council decreed its own closure.

J. W. Stieber, *Pope Eugenius IV, the Council of Basel and the Secular and Ecclesiastical Authorities in the Empire* (1978); G. Christianson, *Cesarini: The Conciliar Cardinal: The Basel Years, 1431–1438* (1979).

**COUNCIL OF BLOOD** (1567–8), a tribunal, officially known as the 'Council of Troubles', established by the duke of ALBA with a view to quelling the REVOLT OF THE NETHERLANDS. The seven-man tribunal, which was personally chaired by Alba, had no legal authority, but nonetheless tried 12,302 Netherlanders, of whom 1,105 were executed or banished. The most prominent victims were the counts of EGMONT and HOORNE, who were executed on 5 June 1568.

**COUNCIL OF CONSTANCE** (1414–18), a general council convoked in Konstanz (Germany) in 1414 by Pope JOHN XXIII at the behest of the Emperor SIGISMUND. Its threefold purpose was to resolve the GREAT SCHISM, to initiate a programme of ecclesiastical reform, and to extirpate heresy.

The problem of the schism had previously been addressed by the COUNCIL OF PISA, which succeeded only in exacerbating the schism by adding a third candidate to the claimants. By 1414 there were three putative popes: BENEDICT XIII of Avignon, GREGORY XII of Rome, and JOHN XXIII of Pisa. Pope John had convoked the Council of Constance, and so had the inestimable advantage that all the delegates were loyal to the Pisan obedience, but in the event the Council decided to depose all three claimants in favour of a fourth. Pope John realized his refusal to abdicate would incur the wrath of the Council, so he offered to resign if his competitors would do so and then fled Konstanz in disguise on the night of 20/21 March 1415.

In the absence of its papal convener, the Council lost its judicial authority. At its fourth and fifth sessions (30 March and 15 April 1415) the Council enacted decrees which ringingly declared that general councils of the Church held their authority directly from God and that everyone, including popes, must obey the decrees of the councils. These decrees, which became the credo of the CONCILIAR MOVEMENT, were soon subverted when the Council succeeded in resolving the schism. Pope John was captured, returned to Konstanz as a prisoner, and in the twelfth session (29 May 1415) deposed. In the fourteenth session (4 July 1415) Pope Gregory abdicated, but only after his cardinal Giovanni Dominici read aloud his bull convoking the Council. Pope Benedict declined to abdicate, and was eventually deposed in the 37th session (26 July 1417). Having deposed all three claimants, the Council then elected Oddo Colonna as Pope MARTIN V on 11 November 1417.

The Council's programme of ecclesiastical reform began with a decree reforming the Franciscan ORDER (23 September 1415) and culminated in the enactment of five reforming decrees (9 October 1417) which stipulated the convocation of general councils at regular intervals, set out procedures for resolving schisms, formulated the profession to be made by popes, regulated the translation of bishops, and prohibited *spolia* (the plundering of benefices for personal gain).

The Council inaugurated its contribution to the extirpation of heresy by condemning more than 200 propositions associated with John WYCLIFFE and ordering that his body be removed from consecrated ground. Jan HUS travelled to the Council protected by an imperial safe conduct, but was arrested, tried, and burnt at the stake on 6 July 1415; his colleague JEROME OF PRAGUE followed him to the stake on 30 May 1416. The Council was dissolved on 22 April 1418.

W. Brandmüller, *Das Konzil von Konstanz 1414–18* (2 vols., 1991–8).

**COUNCIL OF FLORENCE or Council of Ferrara-Florence** (1438–45), an ecumenical council held successively in Ferrara (1438–9), Florence (1439–42), and Rome (1442–5). The purpose of the Council was to reunify the Byzantine Church in the east with the Roman Church in the west. The Greek delegates invited to the COUNCIL OF BASEL had pleaded for a more convenient venue; most delegates were opposed to a change, but Pope EUGENIUS IV decided to convoke a new council in Ferrara, which opened on 8 January 1438.

The Byzantine delegation was led by the emperor, JOHN VIII PALAIOLOGOS, and its theologians and scholars included BESSARION and PLETHO; the leading theologian in the Roman delegation was Cardinal CESARINI. The pope declared himself unable to bear the costs of the Council; the city of Florence offered to finance the Council, which transferred on 26 February 1439 to Florence.

There were four main theological points at issue. The oldest theological issue, which had been smouldering since the Third Council of Toledo in 589, was the double procession of the Holy Spirit as embodied in the *filioque* (Latin; 'and the son') clause; the Roman theologians argued that the Holy Spirit was generated conjointly by the father 'and the son', and the Greek theologians insisted that the Spirit was generated by the Father alone. Delegates debated this issue for three months, during which time Bessarion wrote his discourse arguing that the doctrine of the double procession was taught explicitly by both the Greek and Latin fathers. This argument, when strengthened with an offer of military assistance for Byzantium, persuaded the Greeks to accept the Roman doctrine. The second and third issues, the use of unleavened bread for the eucharist and the doctrine of purgatory, were quickly settled in favour of Roman doctrine, but the fourth issue, that of papal primacy, caused difficulties until the Greeks accepted a watered-down version of papal supremacy.

Once the theological debates had been settled, the Decree of Union was proclaimed in a papal bull on 6 July 1439. The bull is known from its opening words as *Laetentur coeli* (Latin 'Let the heavens rejoice'), a phrase meant to recall the opening phrase of the Greek Formulary of Union of 23 April 433.

The Greek delegation returned home to a cool reception from the Byzantine synod, which eventually repudiated the Union; the minority who accepted the Union became a separate denomination, known as the Greek Uniate Church. The Council continued in session in order to deal with the schismatic Council of Basel, all members of which were declared heretics and excommunicated. The age-old dispute of the relative authority of the pope and the councils was settled in favour of the pope in the bull *Etsi non dubitemus* of 20 April 1441. Union with the Syrian Monophysites ('Jacobites') was effected in 1442, and the following year the Council was transferred to Rome. Its activities in Rome are not well documented, except that reconciliations with the Copts of Egypt (1443), the Mesopotamian Nestorians (1444), the Cypriots, the Chaldeans, and the Maronites (1445) were successfully negotiated; all of these unions proved to be ephemeral, though the Maronites were eventually reconciled in 1736 and the Chaldean Church in 1830.

J. Gill, *The Council of Florence* (1959).

## COUNCIL OF PISA

**COUNCIL OF PISA**, a church council convoked by cardinals in 1409 with a view to ending the GREAT SCHISM and deciding between the rival claims of BENEDICT XIII and GREGORY XII. The Council, which met from 25 March until 7 August 1409, deposed both popes on 5 June, and on 26 June elected Pietro Philarghi (Peter of Candia) as Pope Alexander V, who died on 3 May 1410. The authority of the Council has been much debated by Catholic historians, and Alexander V is variously described as a pope, an antipope, and a 'council pope'. In the short term the Council exacerbated the Great Schism by adding a third pope to the claimants, but its debates led the way to the final resolution of the schism at the COUNCIL OF CONSTANCE.

A second Council of Pisa was convened in 1511 at the instigation of King LOUIS XII of France, who wished to facilitate the deposition of Pope JULIUS II. The Council made little progress, because the imperial delegates of MAXIMILIAN I quarrelled with the French. In 1512 the Council was declared schismatic by Pope Julius, who convened the Fifth Lateran COUNCIL. The French retreat from Italy later in the year brought the Council of Pisa to an undignified close.

## COUNCIL OF TEN

**COUNCIL OF TEN or (Italian) Consiglio dei Dieci**, the Venetian body with responsibility for state security. The Council was first constituted in 1310 to investigate the conspiracy of Baiamonte Tiepolo. Membership was for one year, and consecutive terms of office were not allowed.

The Council employed spies, received security reports from rectors (*rettori*) in Venetian territories abroad, conducted secret diplomacy on behalf of the state, and on occasion ordered assassinations (seldom successfully) and the poisoning of enemy water supplies (never successfully). In 1539 the Council appointed three inquisitors of state (*sindici inquisitori*) to conduct secret investigations of crimes which they then punished. In 1582 the Council was reformed and its jurisdiction narrowed: its responsibility for the production, storage, and distribution of artillery, ammunition, and gunpowder was transferred to the Senate.

Martin Lowry, 'The Reform of the Council of Ten', *Studi veneziani* (1971).

## COUNCIL OF TRENT

**COUNCIL OF TRENT**, the general council of the Church that met in Trento (Italy; English exonym Trent) from 1545 to 1563. The Council was convoked in response to calls for reform within the Catholic Church and to the emergence of Protestantism in northern Europe; the decrees of the Council embody the dogma and ideals of the COUNTER-REFORMATION. Pope PAUL III convoked a council to meet in Mantua on 23 May 1537, but yielded to French objections; a second attempt the following year, this time for a council in Vicenza, foundered on the objections of the Emperor CHARLES V. In 1542 Pope Paul issued his third summons, on this occasion calling delegates to Trento. After one postponement, the Council finally opened on 13 December 1545 in Trento; the small assembly consisted of three papal legates, one cardinal (Cristoforo MADRUZZO), four archbishops, 21 bishops, and four generals of religious ORDERS. The Council assembled in 25 sessions and was closed on 4 December 1563; its decrees were approved on 26 January 1564 by Pope PIUS IV, who on 13 November 1564 published *Professio fidei Tridentinae* ('Profession of the Tridentine Faith'), a summary of doctrine (also known as the 'Creed of Pius IV') to which all holders of important ecclesiastical offices were obliged to subscribe until 1967.

Voting at the COUNCIL OF CONSTANCE had been by nation, but at Trent it was by individual, which meant in practice that bishops from the city-states of Italy exerted a disproportionate influence. The opening debate considered the question of whether dogma or church discipline should be considered first; it was agreed that the subjects should be treated concurrently. The 25 sessions of the Council fell into three discrete periods (1545–7, sessions 1–8; 1551–4, sessions 9–14; 1562–3, sessions 15–25).

In the first period, the decrees of session 4 (8 April 1546) countered Protestant assertions of the sole sufficiency of the Bible with an affirmation that the Bible and unwritten traditions were of equal authority (*pari pietatis affectus ac reverentia*), session 5 (17 June 1546) set out the doctrine of original sin, session 6 (13 January 1547) addressed the fraught issues of JUSTIFICATION and IMPUTATION, making clear that the Protestant position was mistaken but evading the points still in contention amongst Catholic theologians, and session 7 (3 March 1547) dealt with the SACRAMENTS, insisting on the institution of all seven sacraments and their necessity for salvation. An outbreak of plague in Trento caused session 8 (11 March 1547) to be transferred to Bologna, whereupon the proceedings were abandoned for four years.

In the second period, sessions were resumed in 1551 in Trento (which some delegates had refused to abandon) at the command of Pope JULIUS III. The decrees of session 13 (11 October 1551) dealt with the EUCHARIST, affirming the truth of transubstantiation and repudiating the LUTHERAN, CALVINIST, and Zwinglian positions. The Protestants present at this session demanded that the debates be reopened, that bishops be released from their oaths of allegiance to the papacy, and, in a revival of the issues first aired in the CONCILIAR MOVEMENT, insisted that the Council affirm the supremacy of general councils over popes. The revolt of the Protestant princes against CHARLES V led to the suspension of the Council on 28 April 1552. Pope PAUL IV would not consider any dialogue with Protestants, and so the Council remained suspended during his pontificate.

The Council reassembled for its third period on 18 January 1562 at the command of Pope PIUS IV. By this time the hope of reconciliation with the Protestant reformers had been extinguished, and the Catholic delegates were divided: the papal party, which was skilfully led by Giovanni MORONE, was supported by the JESUITS, who were now a powerful force within the Church, but was opposed by imperial, Spanish, and French bishops. The decrees of session 21 returned to the subject of the eucharist in order to affirm the doctrine of concomitance, affirming that both the body and the blood of Jesus are present in each of the consecrated species and thereby justifying an insistence on the adequacy of communion in one kind in the face of UTRAQUIST demands for communion in both kinds. Session 25 dealt perfunctorily with a series of contentious issues, including INDULGENCES, the invocation of saints in prayer, PURGATORY, and the veneration of relics and images.

In session 4 (8 April 1546) the Council had asserted the authority of the Vulgate text of the BIBLE and ordered that the text be revised. The huge process of revision could scarcely be started while the Council was still in session, and was finally completed under Pope CLEMENT VIII in 1592; similarly, the reform of the INDEX was undertaken by Pope PIUS V, who in 1571 established the Congregation of the Index to implement the process of reform that he had initiated by publishing the 'Roman Catechism' (*Catechismus ex decreto conciliarii Tridentini*, 1566), which the Council had requested as an antidote to the proliferation of Protestant catechisms, and by publishing revised editions of the *Breviary* (1568) and the *Missal* (1570).

The Council of Trent failed to reconcile Protestant reformers to the Catholic Church, but nonetheless provided the Church with an agreed statement of doctrine and a programme for the reform of church discipline.

H. Jedin, *Geschichte des Konzils von Trent* (4 vols., 1949–75); vols. i and ii trans. as *A History of the Council of Trent* (1957–61).

**COUNTER-REFORMATION.** The movement of Catholic renewal represented in the COUNCIL OF TRENT has long been seen as a reaction to the REFORMATION in Germany and the struggle against the Protestant heresy. The term *Gegenreformationen* (in the plural) was first used in 1760 by Johann Stephan Pütter (a Lutheran jurist) to denote reversions to Catholicism in Lutheran areas; when appropriated by Leopold von Ranke a century later, it became a historiographical orthodoxy; reduced to the singular and translated into English by Sarah Austin in the mid-nineteenth century,

the *Gegenreformationen* became the 'Counter-Reformation'. This term satisfied historians who wanted to interpret Catholic reform as a reaction to Protestantism. Historians who wanted to trace the origins of renewal to the pre-Tridentine reform of the religious ORDERS needed another model, and this was supplied in 1880 by Wilhelm Maurenbrecher, who introduced the term 'Catholic Reformation'.

Many of the decrees of the Council of Trent reflected concerns that were shared by Protestants about abuses such as nepotism, simony, pluralism, and absenteeism, but whereas German Protestants saw these abuses as a reason for rejecting the hegemony of Rome, Catholic reformers saw them as the impetus for the reform of ecclesiastical discipline. On matters of doctrine, however, Protestant and Catholic reformers differed: Protestant reformers wanted to reassess doctrines such as JUSTIFICATION and sweep away medieval practices such as the veneration of saints and the sale of INDULGENCES; Catholic reformers wanted to reaffirm traditional beliefs and justify religious practices that had long been sanctioned by tradition.

The Counter-Reformation continued the process of reforming the religious orders by imposing disciplinary measures on the established orders and sanctioning the creation of new orders, such as the BARNABITES, CAPUCHINS, THEATINES, and JESUITS. The discipline of the laity took the form of the institution of the INQUISITION and the *INDEX LIBRORUM PROHIBITORUM*. The rationalism of Protestantism may account for the revival of Catholic mysticism in the sixteenth century. The greatest achievements of the Counter-Reformation were the resubmission of Poland and southern Germany to the Roman obedience and the extirpation of the nascent Protestant movement in Italy.

A. G. Dickens, *The Counter Reformation* (1968); Michael A. Mullett, *The Catholic Reformation* (2000).

**COURLAND or (German) Kurland**, a Baltic duchy, the territory of which occupied the coastal and southern portion of what is now Latvia; to the north of Courland lay LIVONIA and to the south LITHUANIA. From 1237, Courland was part of the territory of the TEUTONIC knights. In 1561, the prospect of a Russian invasion led the grand master of the Order, Gotthard Kettler, to submit the Order and its territories to the protective suzerainty of Poland, whereupon Kettler became the first duke of Courland; in the same year, the duchy adopted Lutheranism.

**COURT, JEAN DE** (*fl.* 1541–64) and **SUZANNE DE** (*fl.* 1600), French enamellers in Limoges. Jean de Court typically painted bright colours on black backgrounds; many of his designs are taken from prints by other artists, including Étienne DELAUNE. Suzanne de Court, who may have been the daughter of Jean de Court, was the last important Limoges enameller; she painted brightly coloured figures on a large range of decorative objects such as plates and caskets.

*DBF* (Jean); *MDA* (Suzanne).

**COURTOIS, JEAN** (*fl.* 1530–45), south Netherlandish composer active in Cambrai. He was *maître de chapelle* there in

1540 when Charles V would have heard his motet 'Venite populi terrae' on his way to Ghent. He composed sacred music and chansons.

**COURTOIS, LAMBERT** (*c.*1520–*c.*1585), French composer, singer, and trombonist in Italy and Dalmatia. After performing in Rome and Verona during the Carnival season he settled in Ragusa (Dubrovnik), where he played in the court wind ensemble, conducted, and taught. Some madrigal collections and motets survive.

**COURVILLE, JOACHIM THIBAULT DE** (d. 1581) composer, singer, lutenist, and lyre player. With Jean-Antoine de BAÏF, he co-founded the Académie de Poésie et Musique in 1570, and, in accordance with the Académie's rules, none of his works was published. His official position at court was as a *joueur de lyre*.

**COUSIN, JEAN THE ELDER** (*c.*1500–1560) and **JEAN THE YOUNGER** (1522–94), French painters and engravers. Jean the Elder was born near Sens, and in 1538 moved to Paris, where he worked as a painter and designer of stained glass. Attributions include the *Eva Prima Pandora* (Louvre), the stained-glass *Life of St Eutropius* (1536) in Sens Cathedral, and a tapestry cycle on *The Life of St Mammès* (eight panels, of which two survive in Langres Cathedral and one in the Louvre).

Jean's son, Jean the Younger, was a book illustrator and glass painter. His only authenticated work is a painting of *The Last Judgement* (1616, Louvre). His most famous work is an emblem book, the *Livre de fortunes* (Bibliothèque de l'Institut de France).

DBF; MDA.

**COUTO, DIOGO DO** (1542/3–1616), Portuguese historian, born in Lisbon, where he was educated at the Jesuit College. In 1559 he sailed as a soldier to India, where he became a friend of CAMÕES. He returned to Portugal for two years (1569–71), but then returned to India and lived in Goa for the rest of his life. He was appointed royal historiographer by King PHILIP II of Spain, in which capacity he wrote *Diálogo do soldado prático* (first published in 1790), which was critical of the Portuguese administration in India. In 1595 he was appointed as archivist in Goa, and thereafter he devoted his time to the completion of the *Décadas da Ásia* of João de BARROS.

DHP; A. F. G. Bell, *Diogo do Couto* (1924); C. R. Boxer, *Three Historians of Portuguese Asia: Barros, Couto and Becarro* (1948).

**COVARRUBIAS, ALONSO DE** (1488–1570), Spanish mason, architect, and decorative sculptor, one of the nine architects who were called in to advise on the plans for the Gothic New Cathedral in Salamanca in 1512. His own work is often described as Renaissance-PLATERESQUE: his structures are Gothic, but his decoration is conceived in a light and elegant early Renaissance style. He worked on Sigüenza Cathedral early in his career (from 1515) and returned in his maturity to build the tunnel-vaulted sacristy (1532–4). He built the

Church of the Piedad at Guadalajara (1526; now in ruins) and the staircase of the Archbishop's Palace in Alcalá de Henares (*c.*1530, destroyed 1939).

Covarrúbias was appointed master mason at Toledo Cathedral, where he built the magnificent Chapel of the New Kings (Capilla de los Reyes Nuevos, 1531–4). He was appointed as architect to the royal palaces in 1537, and proceeded to convert the Alcázar in Toledo into a palace. His other works in Toledo include the Hospital de Tavera (from 1537) and the reconstruction of the Bisagra Gate (from 1559). In his late Toledo buildings Covarrubias moved away from Renaissance-Plateresque lightness towards the austere severity epitomized by Juan de HERRERA.

DBEH; MDA.

**COVERDALE, MILES** (1488–1568), translator of the Bible. Educated at Cambridge, and ordained in 1514, Coverdale became an enthusiast for ecclesiastical reform; his attacks on church doctrines led to an enforced exile from the country. Whilst abroad, Coverdale produced, in 1535, the first complete English translation of the Bible, for which TYNDALE's translation of the New Testament was an important source. Thomas CROMWELL interceded with HENRY VIII to obtain approval for its publication in England, and also assigned to Coverdale the task of preparing the 'Great Bible': a revised, official translation for use in every church, published by GRAFTON in 1539. Bishop of Exeter under EDWARD VI, Coverdale fled the country on MARY's succession, returning in ELIZABETH's reign to become a leading voice of the Puritans.

DNB.

**COVILHÃ, PÊRO DA** (*fl.* 1487, d. 1525), Portuguese explorer, a native of Covilhã (Beira). He left Portugal on 7 May 1487 at the behest of King JOHN II, who wished to ascertain where cinnamon could be found and to establish an overland route to the land of PRESTER JOHN, whose capital was thought to be in Ethiopia; at the same time Bartolomeu DIAS was dispatched to find the sea route. Covilhã sailed to Naples and then on to Rhodes, Alexandria, and Cairo before travelling through the Red Sea to Aden. His companion Afonso de Paiva then went to Ethiopia, but Covilhã travelled to India, where he visited Calicut (Kozhikode), Cannamore (Kannur), and Goa. He then returned to Africa, travelling down the east coast as far as Sofala (now in Mozambique), where he was probably the first European visitor. He then sailed north and travelled back to Cairo, where he met two Portuguese Jews (Rabbi Abraham of Beja and a former shoemaker called Joseph of Lamego) who had been sent by King John to meet Covilhã and Afonso de Paiva (who had died in Ethiopia).

Covilhã sent an account of his journey to India back to Portugal with Joseph of Lamego, describing the cinnamon, pepper, and clove trade in Calicut and advising on the ocean route that Vasco da GAMA was later to take. Covilhã then travelled with Rabbi Abraham to Hormuz (which ALBUQUERQUE was to overrun in 1507), where he left Rabbi Abraham, and then sailed to Jeddah, from which he visited the cities of Mecca and Medina. In 1490 Covilhã travelled to Ethiopia, where he was to remain as an honoured prisoner of state for the last 35 years of his life. In 1520 he was visited by an embassy led by Rodrigo da Lima; he acted as an interpreter for the embassy, but was unable to escape. Francisco Álvares, a priest who accompanied Rodrigo's expedition, published an account of Covilhã's life in his *Verdadera informaçam das terras do Preste João* (1540).

DHP.

**COX, RICHARD** (1500–81), English bishop and ecclesiastical reformer. Cox held various church appointments following his education at Cambridge, and was from 1540 tutor to EDWARD VI. On Edward's accession, Cox became extensively involved in church and liturgical reform. He aided in the publishing of a vernacular communion service in 1548, and assisted CRANMER in the preparation of the Book of COMMON PRAYER in 1549 and 1552. Between 1546 and 1553 he was the first dean of Christ Church, Oxford, and was concurrently chancellor of Oxford University (1547–52). Much university reform was enacted whilst he held these positions, designed to eradicate traces of Catholic religious doctrine. On MARY's accession, Cox was deprived and imprisoned for a time; he later travelled to Frankfurt where he disputed with John KNOX. In 1559, under ELIZABETH, he became bishop of Ely, where he continued to express hostility both to the old religion and to elements of ritual retained in the new English Church.

DNB.

**CRABETH, DIRCK PIETERSZOON** (*fl.* 1539, d. 1574) and **WOUTER PIETERSZOON** (*fl.* 1559, d. 1589), Dutch brothers in Gouda who were makers of stained glass and designers of maps. On 1 January 1552 a fire in St Jans Church in Gouda destroyed 46 of the stained-glass windows. Dirck was commissioned to make nine of the new windows and Wouter was commissioned to make four. The windows completed by 1566 survived the iconoclastic attacks of Protestants and are still in the church, but work on the other windows was soon discontinued; the full-scale cartoons for the most of the windows survive and are still stored in the church.

MDA; NNBW iii.

**CRAIG, SIR THOMAS** (1538–1608), Scottish jurist and constitutionalist. He was educated at St Andrews and studied law in Paris from 1555 to 1561. He returned to Scotland and in 1574 was appointed justice-depute, in which capacity he presided over criminal trials until 1573, when he was appointed sheriff-depute of Edinburgh.

Craig's four constitutional works all remained unpublished during his lifetime. In about 1603 Craig wrote *Ius feudale*, one of the founding texts of SCOTTISH LAW; it was published in 1655 and translated into English in 1934. *Ius feudale* is the first scholarly account of Scottish law, and its central accomplishment is the skill with which it relates Scottish CUSTOMARY LAW to the CANON LAW, Roman law, and FEUDAL LAW traditions of the Continent. In 1603 he wrote, but again left unpublished, a *Treatise on the Succession* in vindication of the claim of James VI of Scotland to the English crown. In 1604 he became

one of the Scottish commissioners charged with the task of negotiating a union of England and Scotland that extended beyond the union of the crowns, and in furtherance of that end wrote *De unione regnorum Britanniae tractatus*. His final work was *Scotland's Sovereignty Asserted, or a Dispute Concerning Homage*, which contested English claims for homage from Scotland.

Craig's only publications during his lifetime were four poems in Latin written to celebrate royal occasions.

DNB.

**CRANACH, LUCAS** (1472–1553), German painter, sometimes styled Lucas Cranach the Elder to distinguish him from his son Lucas Cranach the Younger (1515–86). He was born in Kronach (in Upper Franconia) and trained with an otherwise unknown painter called Hans Maler (i.e. Hans the Painter). Cranach first appears in the historical record as a portrait painter in Vienna in about 1500. Pictures from Cranach's Vienna period include the portraits of *Dr Johannes Cuspinian* and his wife *Anna Cuspinian* (Winterthur, Switzerland), *The Crucifixion* (Alte Pinakothek, Munich), and *The Rest on the Flight into Egypt* (1504, Gemäldegalerie, Berlin).

In 1505 Cranach moved to Wittenberg as court painter to FRIEDRICH III, elector of Saxony. He embraced the Reformation and soon became its principal visual apologist. His woodcut *Luther as Junker Jörg* (1521–2) inaugurated a long series of portraits of Martin LUTHER (mostly in oil). He also painted nudes, sometimes clad in transparent veils, and these paintings, which often have a classical or biblical theme, have a mildly erotic quality. His pictures, which often exist in several versions, are signed with his initials or with a winged snake.

Cranach followed the Elector JOHANN FRIEDRICH I to Augsburg and then to his prison cell in Weimar; he died in Weimar a year after the release of the deposed elector.

MDA s.v. Cranach: (1) Lucas Cranach I; NDB.

**CRANE, RALPH** (*c.*1550/60–*c.*1621), English scrivener associated with the King's Men (see CHAMBERLAIN'S MEN). Eight of Crane's transcriptions of Jacobean plays survive (including plays by JONSON, FLETCHER, and MIDDLETON), and he seems to have prepared the transcriptions that served as printer's copy for the Folio texts of six Shakespeare plays: *Two Gentlemen of Verona, Merry Wives of Windsor, Measure for Measure, The Winter's Tale, Cymbeline,* and *The Tempest.*

**CRANMER, THOMAS** (1489–1556), archbishop of Canterbury. A fellow of Jesus College, Cambridge, from 1523, Cranmer rose to sudden prominence in 1529 allegedly as a result of suggestions to HENRY VIII that he consult the universities on the legitimacy of his attempt to 'divorce' CATHERINE OF ARAGON. On a diplomatic mission to CHARLES V in 1532, he secretly married Margaret, the nice of Katharina Preu, wife to the reformer Andreas OSIANDER of Nuremberg. He became archbishop of Canterbury the following year, and presided over the annulment of Henry's marriages to Catherine and later ANNE BOLEYN. He opposed the Six ARTICLES and supported CROMWELL in the dissemination of the

Bible in the vernacular. Under EDWARD VI, he issued a revised liturgy for the new Church of England, preparing the first and second Books of COMMON PRAYER and a Book of Homilies (or standard sermons); he is also associated with the preparation of the Thirty-Nine ARTICLES. He welcomed reformist thinkers from the Continent and drew on their thinking in the second Book of Common Prayer. Imprisoned under MARY I, he signed documents admitting the supremacy of Rome, but he later recanted and was burnt at the stake in Oxford. The style of the English liturgy stems largely from Cranmer.

DNB; D. MacCulloch, *Thomas Cranmer: A Life* (1996).

**CRÉCQUILLON, THOMAS** (*c.*1480/1500–1557), French-Flemish composer, many of whose works were published by Tylman Susato from 1543. He was a singer and chaplain in the Imperial Chapel of Charles V. This would have involved extensive travel to Spain and Germany, through which his music would have reached a wide audience.

**CREDI, LORENZO DI**. See LORENZO DI CREDI.

**CREMONA**, a city and episcopal see in Lombardy, incorporated into the duchy of Milan in the early fifteenth century. Cremona was occupied by Venice (1499–1509). Thereafter it was subject to the rulers of Milan, who from 1535 were Spanish governors. In the sixteenth century the AMATI family of viol-makers laid the foundation for Cremona's reputation for the manufacturing of fine stringed instruments, which culminated in the instruments of Stradivarius Cremonensis (1644–1737).

**CRETE or Candia**. In the partition of the Byzantine Empire that followed the Latin conquest of Constantinople in 1204, Crete was given to Boniface of Montferrat, who sold it to Venice; it remained under Venetian administration until 1669, when it fell to the Ottomans; a vestigial Venetian presence was permitted in three areas in the north (Vouxa, Souda, and Spinalonga) until 1718, when these enclaves reverted to the Turks. The seat of the Venetian government was Candia (now Herakleion); in Venetian documents Crete was known as 'the island of Candia', and so Candia became a name for the entire island as well as its capital.

Venetian rule was harsh, and there were revolts both by Venetian colonists against the republic (culminating in the revolt of 1361–4) and by colonized Greeks (notably the revolt of Siffius Vlasto in 1453). In ecclesiastical affairs, a Latin archbishop presided uneasily over Orthodox clergy, whose numbers were restricted to 130. The collapse of Byzantium led to an influx of refugees into Crete, some of whom were scholars; educated Venetians resident in Crete extended literary patronage to learned exiles, and so nourished the GREEK SCHOLARSHIP which flowered into the Cretan Renaissance of the late fifteenth century.

The juxtaposition of Greek and Venetian cultures in Crete facilitated a degree of contact that was unusual, and bicultural Cretans such as Arsenios and Michael APOSTOLIS, GEORGE OF TREBIZOND, and Zacharias CALLIERGIS moved easily into the humanist circles of Italy, and Demetrius DUCAS moved in similar circles in Spain. In 1409–10 the Cretan Pietro Philarghi briefly became the antipope Alexander V. The links between Crete and Venice were not untroubled, but they nonetheless constituted an important conduit for the dissemination of Greek culture to the West.

Alexandre Embiricos, *La Renaissance crétoise: XVIe et XVIIe siècles* (1960); D. Geanakoplos, *Greek Scholars in Venice* (1962), 41–52.

**CRÉTIN, GUILLAUME** (*c.*1460–1525), French poet associated with the RHÉTORIQUEURS. He pursued a career in the Church and also composed a substantial corpus of poetry, some of which is associated with the courts of LOUIS XII and FRANCIS I. His poems are normally short, and range over a wide number of genres, including *ballades*, *rondeaux*, and verse epistles. His longer poems include a *Déploration sur le trépas de feu Okergan*, a lament for the death of the musician Johannes OCKEGHEM.

DBF; *Œuvres poétiques*, ed. Kathleen Chesney (1932).

**CRIVELLI, CARLO** (1430/5–*c.*1495), Italian painter, born in Venice, where he probably trained in the VIVARINI workshop. After a period of imprisonment for adultery, Crivelli left Venice in 1468 and spent the rest of his life in Ascoli Piceno (Marches). His paintings usually have religious subjects and are characterized by the presence of ornamental decorative motifs. Eight of his paintings are held by the National Gallery in London, including a perspectival *Annunciation* (1486).

DBI; MDA; Pietro Zampetti, *Carlo Crivelli* (2nd edn. 1988).

**CROATIA**. See DALMATIA.

**CROCE, GIOVANNI** (*c.*1557–1609), Italian composer, singer, and priest. He was appointed *maestro di cappella* at San Marco, Venice, in 1603; his *Sacre cantilene concertate* (1610) are a blend of Viadana's *concertato* techniques with the grand Venetian style. He composed motets, masses, canzonettas, and madrigals. His influence was widespread and reached as far as England, where his pieces were included in Thomas MORLEY'S The TRIUMPHS OF ORIANA (1601).

**CROCUS, CORNELIUS** (*c.*1500–1550), Dutch playwright and educationalist, born in Amsterdam and educated at Louvain. He was ordained as a priest and in 1528 became a headmaster in Amsterdam. He wrote a Latin textbook for his pupils, and also wrote as a controversialist against LUTHER and the ANABAPTISTS. His Latin plays, which were intended for performance in schools, included the *Comedia sacra Ioseph* (1535), which was printed in at least twenty editions and adapted in various vernaculars: in 1543 Mikołaj REJ (who was still a Catholic) published a Polish version, *Żywot Józefa*. In 1549, the year before he died, Crocus resigned his headship and walked to Rome, where he was received by IGNATIUS LOYOLA into the JESUIT Order.

NNBW iii; Albertus Kölker, *Alardus Aemstelredamus en Cornelis Crocus: Twee Amsterdamse priester-humanisten* (1963).

**CROMWELL, THOMAS** (*c.*1485–1540), English statesman and reformer. Cromwell rose from humble origins to become secretary to Cardinal WOLSEY and then, following Wolsey's fall, HENRY VIII. A supporter of Protestantism and the royal supremacy, in 1535 he was created vicar-general and vicegerent in spirituals; in this position Cromwell was Henry's principal agent in church matters. An MP in 1523, he was also an intermediary between Henry and Parliament. Between 1536 and 1540 he arranged for the visitation and the dissolution of the MONASTERIES. In 1536 he arranged for COVERDALE's English Bible to be printed in England, and commissioned the official English translation known as the Great Bible, copies of which were placed in every church. Cromwell advocated alliance with the Protestant princes in Germany, and to this end negotiated Henry's marriage to ANNE OF CLEVES, the failure of which brought about his downfall. Created earl of Essex in April 1540, he was accused (almost certainly falsely) of SACRAMENTARIAN views and executed for treason three months later.

*DNB.*

**CRONACA, IL, or Simone del Pollaiuolo** (1457–1508), Italian architect and stonemason, a native of Florence who as a young man spent several years in Rome (1475–85). On returning to Florence he collaborated with Giuliano da SANGALLO on the sacristy of Santo Spirito and the Casa Horne and with BENEDETTO DA MAIANO on the Palazzo Strozzi, for which Il Cronaca designed the elegant courtyard and the magnificent cornice. His finest independent work is the aisleless Church of San Salvatore al Monte (1487–1504), which reflects Il Cronaca's study of ancient buildings in Rome and Romanesque buildings in Florence (which were thought to be ancient). Il Cronaca also contributed to the Salone dei Cinquecento which was built in the Palazzo Vecchio (July 1495–February 1496) to accommodate SAVONAROLA's Grand Council.

*DBI* s.v. Simone de Tommaso d'Antonio Pollaiolo; *MDA.*

**CROSS-STAFF**, also called Jacob's staff, a sighting instrument for measuring angles invented by Levi ben Gerson (see REGIOMONTANUS). It could, for example, be used to measure the altitude of a heavenly body and so calculate the geographical latitude of the observer. It consisted of a staff, with square cross-section, typically about a metre (3 feet) long, along which a transom or cross-piece was free to slide, held at right angles to the shaft. The observer held one end of the staff to his eye and adjusted the transom so that its upper and lower edges appeared to touch the heavenly body and the horizon directly beneath it; a scale on the staff showed the corresponding angle. The use of the cross-staff for navigation at sea was first mentioned *c.*1514, and its construction and use were described in detail in the *Arte de navegar* of Martín CORTÉS (1551).

**CROTUS RUBEANUS or Rubianus or (German) Johannes Jäger** (1480–1545), German humanist, born in Dornheim and educated in Erfurt, where he met Ulrich von HUTTEN, with whom he later collaborated on the *EPISTOLAE OBSCURORUM VIRORUM* (1515). He studied in Rome and Italy from 1517 to 1520, and on his return to Germany was appointed rector of the University of Erfurt, where he entertained LUTHER as he travelled to the Diet of WORMS. He subsequently worked for the Lutheran ALBRECHT VON PREUSSEN in Königsberg, but in 1530 reverted to Catholicism and at the behest of ALBRECHT II OF MAINZ became a canon at Halle. He defended his apostasy in an *Apologia* (Leipzig, 1531) that prompted several angry Protestant responses.

*NDB.*

**CRUCIGER or (German) Creutziger, CASPAR THE ELDER** (1504–48) and **CASPAR THE YOUNGER** (1525–97), German reformers. Caspar the Elder was born in Leipzig, and in 1521 travelled to Wittenberg to study theology. He became a pastor in Magdeburg and in 1528 returned to Wittenberg to assist Luther in the implementation of the Reformation. He contributed to the translation of the Bible into German and took copious notes on Luther's sermons which later became the basis of their publication; he also initiated the Wittenberg edition of Luther's works. In 1539 he returned to his native Leipzig to supervise the establishment of the Reformation. His son Caspar the Younger became the successor of MELANCHTHON at Wittenberg.

*NDB*; Timothy Wengert, 'Caspar Cruciger, 1504–1548: The Case of the Disappearing Reformer', *Sixteenth Century Journal*, 20 (1989).

**CRUMHORN**, sometimes known as a *Krummpfeife* ('curved pipe'), which gives some indication of its shape and points to Germany as its place of origin. It had a double reed which was covered with a wind-cap which formed a wind chamber. Although the reed was not touched by the player's lips, its vibrations were set in motion by the air in the chamber. It was frequently depicted in paintings, often being played by angels.

**CRUSADES**, a series of expeditions from western Europe to the eastern Mediterranean with the avowed purpose of wresting the sepulchre of Jesus in Jerusalem from its Islamic possessors and placing it under Christian administration. The term is normally used to denote the expeditions mounted between 1095 and the final collapse of the Latin states in Jerusalem in 1291, but the phrase 'later crusades' is often used to describe the armed response of west Europeans to the Ottoman incursions into eastern Europe from the fourteenth to sixteenth centuries.

In the late fourteenth century campaigns against Smyrna (1344, now İzmir), Alexandria (1365), and Tunis (1390) culminated in a huge crusade to the Balkans that ended in an Ottoman victory at Nicopolis (now Bulgarian Nikopol) in 1396. In the early fifteenth century territories were regained in Albania, Bosnia, and Bulgaria, and in 1443 crusaders defeated an Ottoman army in Niš (Serbia), but the crusade was destroyed in the Ottoman victory at Varna (1444), and in 1453 CONSTANTINOPLE fell to the Ottomans.

Later crusades were never fully realized. In 1454 PHILIP THE GOOD organized a huge banquet at which his crusaders ceremoniously launched their campaign of conquest, but then everyone went home. In 1464 Pope EUGENIUS IV died at

Ancona while he awaited the assembling of his crusading fleet. Thereafter the idea of the crusade survived only in attenuated form in the ideology of the RECONQUISTA, in Spanish campaigns in North AFRICA, in CHARLES V's raid on Tunis in 1535, and finally in the imaginative literature of the late sixteenth century, notably Tasso's *Gerusalemme liberata* (1581).

> Norman Housley, *The Later Crusades, 1270–1580* (1992); J. Muldoon, *Popes, Lawyers and Infidels: The Church and the Non-Christian World 1250–1550* (1979).

**CRUTCHED FRIARS GLASS.** In 1565 Jean Carré, a native of Amiens, established a glass factory in Hart Street (London) on the site of the monastery of the Friars of the Holy Cross (of which 'crutched' is a corruption). He employed glass-makers from Lorraine and Venice to produce crystal glass-ware in the Venetian fashion. On Carré's death in 1572 the factory was taken over by the Venetian Giacomo VERZELINI. The factory was destroyed by fire in 1572, but Verzelini rebuilt it and continued to manufacture glass until his retirement in 1592.

**CRUZ, AGOSTINHO DA** (c.1590–c.1632), Portuguese composer and theorist, who became *mestre di capela* at the monastery of St Vicente de Fora in Lisbon. He played and wrote for the organ and the rebec, dedicating his compositions to King John IV and João Mascarenhaus, count of Santa Cruz.

**CRYPTOGRAPHY,** the present-day term for the arts of devising, using, and breaking ciphers, was not introduced until about 1600. From about 1550, at least in Germany, the more usual term was 'steganography' (which today has a more specialized significance). The single term that would have been understood from about 1350 to 1750 is 'cipher'.

Ancient ciphers were, it seems, constructed by letter substitution. Medieval and Renaissance sources describe this type of cipher and show how it can be broken. ALBERTI proposed a more complicated variant using many more symbols. Johannes TRITHEMIUS proposed in his *Polygraphia* (1518) and *Steganographia* (published 1606) the use of a rectangular table of alphabets; this method was refined by Giovanni Belaso in *La cifra* (1553) and Giambattista DELLA PORTA in *De furtivis litterarum notis* (1563). Blaise de VIGENÈRE surveyed the work of his predecessors in his *Traité des chiffres* (1586) and proposed the additional refinement of an autokey.

It is, however, clear that these writings about ciphers have an ambiguous relationship to actual practice. For instance, keys to hundreds of ciphers employed by the SFORZA in the second half of the fifteenth century (preserved in a manuscript now in Vienna) show that in every cipher multiple symbols were used to stand for a given letter and symbols were used for common letter sequences, common words, and proper names. This form of cipher, now called a 'nomenclator', is designed to defeat the known methods of attack. Instead of 23 symbols each standing for one of the 23 letters, one might see 100 or 200 symbols, each standing for a letter, a letter sequence, a word, a name, or even for nothing. As far as we know, this was the only kind of cipher actually used to any great extent up to about 1800.

It seems that courts regularly employed specialists to break ciphers. Sicco Simonetta, who did this work for the Sforza in the 1470s, left a written account of his methods (1474). The most famous of the court cipher-breakers is François VIÈTE, now best remembered for his very important contributions to ALGEBRA.

> David Kahn, *The Codebreakers: The Story of Secret Writing* (1967).

**CUENCA CARPETS.** The two principal regions for the manufacture of carpets in Spain from the fifteenth to the mid-seventeenth centuries were Cuenca and ALCARAZ. There is documentary evidence of carpet manufacturing in Cuenca from the twelfth century, but the earliest surviving examples were woven in the fifteenth century. From the fifteenth to the mid-seventeenth centuries designs were based on Turkish carpets, but the pile was tied with the Spanish knot (i.e. single warp knot).

> J. Ferrandis, *Alfombras antiguas españolas* (1941).

**CUEVA, JUAN DE LA** (1550–1609), Spanish playwright and poet, a native of Seville. He lived in Mexico in the mid-1570s and on returning to Seville became a writer and producer of plays. He wrote four tragedies and ten comedies, of which the finest are historical, including *La muerte del rey don Sancho* and *La libertad de España por Bernardo del Carpio*, which seem to admonish PHILIP II for his aspirations to secure the succession to the Portuguese crown. Cueva's poems include mildly erotic Petrarchan lyrics (collected in Cueva's *Obras*, 1582), an epic (*Conquista de la Bética*, 1603), and a treatise in verse, *Ejemplar poético, o Arte poética española*, which discusses historical drama as well as poetry.

> DBEH; Anthony Watson, *Juan de la Cueva and the Portuguese Succession* (1971); Richard Glenn, *Juan de la Cueva* (1973).

**CUIR BOUILLI** (French; 'boiled leather'), the term used in England from the fourteenth to the sixteenth centuries to denote leather moulded or pressed into forms; if the moulded leather was designed to hold a liquid (e.g. in jugs and goblets) it was lined with pitch or resin, and if it was moulded into a case for a precious object, the surfaces were impregnated with wax and then incised or tooled in gold. The spelling now in use corresponds to modern French, but in fourteenth- and fifteenth-century English it variously appears as *qwyrbolle* and *coerbuille*.

**CUJAS, JACQUES or (Latin) Jacobus Cujacius** (1522–90), the pre-eminent jurist of the French Renaissance and the founder of the humanist school of jurisprudence at Bourges, which became the most important centre of legal studies in sixteenth-century Europe. Cujas was the son of a fuller in Toulouse, and there he taught himself Greek and Latin and studied at the university; he became a lecturer in law at Toulouse and an acknowledged authority on Justinian. After a brief period in 1554 as professor of law at Cahors, he accepted the invitation of Michel de L'HÔPITAL to a chair at Bourges, where the presence of ALCIATO had stimulated the introduction of humanist jurisprudence in a part of France in which FRENCH LAW was primarily customary. Academic jealousies quickly precipitated a rift with LE DOUAREN, and Cujas left to take a chair at Valence, where he remained until Le Douaren died in 1559, whereupon he returned to Bourges. He left once again for Valence in 1567, and in this period his pupils included Joseph Justus SCALIGER and Jacques-Auguste de Thou (THUANUS). After a short sojourn in Turin, he returned to Bourges, but soon moved to Paris at the command of the king to lecture at the University of Paris. A year later he returned to Bourges for the rest of his life, declining invitations to move elsewhere, including one from Gregory XIII to teach at Bologna. Cujas taught and wrote throughout the WARS OF RELIGION, but remained resolutely detached from the conflict, replying when asked about his own convictions that 'nihil hoc ad edictum praetoris' ('this has nothing to do with the edict of the magistrate').

Cujas's reputation as the most distinguished jurist of his generation was founded on the study of Justinian's *Corpus*, to which he brought formidable skills of textual analysis as well as historical and philological expertise. His textual studies of Justinian and various authors of classical antiquity (literary as well as juristic) were collected in his *Observationes et emendationes*, the first three volumes of which were published in 1557. He also wrote on FEUDAL LAW (*Consuetudines feudorum*) and on CANON LAW. He recovered and published part of the *Codex Theodosianus* (a fifth-century compilation of laws) and also recovered the manuscript of the *Basilica* (the tenth-century compilation of canon and civil law that lies at the heart of Byzantine jurisprudence). His posthumous publications include a commentary on Papinian. His teaching and his publications were enormously influential, and secured the ascendancy of humanist jurisprudence over the earlier traditions of the glossators and commentators (see LAW). The tradition of scholarly jurisprudence which he inaugurated at Bourges was maintained by his successors, who included Hugues DONEAU, François BAUDOUIN, and François HOTMAN.

DBF; Donald R. Kelley, *Foundations of Modern Historical Scholarship: Language, Law and History in the French Renaissance* (1970).

*CULTERANISMO*. See GONGORISM.

**CUNHA, TRISTÃO DA** (c.1460–1540), Portuguese navigator who commanded a fleet which left Portugal in 1506 to sail around Africa to India. In the South Atlantic he discovered the three uninhabited volcanic islands which now bear his name. Sailing up the east coast of Africa, he captured several Arab trading posts, and in India he fought on behalf of the governor, Francisco de ALMEIDA. In 1507 Cunha sailed with ALBUQUERQUE on the expedition that captured Socotra (now Yemeni Suqutra), the inhabitants of which professed a form of Christianity which has since disappeared. He returned to Portugal in 1508 and in 1513 led a diplomatic embassy to Pope LEO X; he was later appointed to the Portuguese Privy Council.

DHP.

**CURE, CORNELIUS** (*fl.* 1574, d. c.1609), Netherlandish stonemason and sculptor who emigrated to England and established a workshop in Southwark, on the south bank of the Thames opposite London. Cure was appointed master mason to Queen ELIZABETH and King James I (JAMES VI). He was responsible for the design and construction of the monuments of Queen Elizabeth and MARY, QUEEN OF SCOTS in Westminster Abbey. The effigy of Queen Elizabeth was carved by Maximilian COLT, but Cornelius carved that of Queen Mary himself. The tomb was finished after Cure's death by his son William (d. 1632), who succeeded his father as master mason to King James and worked under Inigo JONES on the BANQUETING HOUSE.

MDA.

**CURTAIN THEATRE** (1577), a round, wooden, circular, unroofed theatre building, opened in 1577, in Curtain Close, Shoreditch, London. It was occupied in turn by the CHAMBERLAIN'S MEN, QUEEN ANNE'S MEN, and PRINCE CHARLES'S MEN. The first performances of some of SHAKESPEARE's plays, including *Romeo and Juliet* (1595) and *Henry V* (1599), may have been seen there.

**CURTAL or curtall**, the name used in England for a double reed instrument which was a forebear of the bassoon. Its predecessor was the bombard (a low-pitched shawm), which was made up of a straight tube, whereas the curtal's tube was folded, thus making the instrument appear shorter, hence the German name *Kortholt*. A more extreme version of a folded tube wind instrument was the aptly named RACKET.

**CUSPINIAN, JOHANNES, or (German) Hans Spiesshaymer** (1473–1529), German humanist, a native of Leipzig who was educated at the University of Vienna, where he remained throughout his life. In 1493 he was crowned POET LAUREATE by the Emperor MAXIMILIAN I, who in 1500 appointed Cuspinian as rector of the university. He subsequently served the emperor as a councillor and diplomat and promoted humanist scholarship at the university (in 1497 he had been responsible for the invitation that led to the appointment of Konrad CELTIS). Cuspinian's writings include Latin poetry and a series of historical works, among them a history of Austria and an account of the Ottoman Turks and their religion.

NDB.

**CUSTOMARY LAW**. Customs that have been fixed over a broad area for a considerable period assume the force of law when they are regarded as obligatory, and assume the form of law when they are codified. The collapse of the Roman Empire in the West meant that much of Europe was for centuries regulated by Germanic customary law, and the RECEPTION of Roman law was impeded, sometimes permanently, in areas affected by comprehensive compilations of customary law. The most influential compilations were the *Sachsenspiegel* ('Mirror of the Saxons') of the thirteenth-century Saxon judge Eike von Repgow, which is an important presence in GERMAN LAW, and the *Coutumes de Beauvaisis* of the thirteenth-century lord of Beauvais, Phillipe de Remy, which was long influential in FRENCH LAW as formulated and practised in the north, where customary law prevailed over Roman law; the influence of customary law in France was further strengthened by the *Ordonnance de Montil-les-Tours* of 1453, in which Charles VII ordered that local and regional customary law be systematically collected. Apart from France, the strongest redoubt of customary law was Scandinavia, in which codes ranging from the Norwegian codes of 1274 and 1276 to the Danish Law of 1683 were essentially compilations of customary rules, which included criminal and CIVIL LAW but excluded ecclesiastical law. The Scandinavian codes are largely independent of Germanic customary law; in criminal law, for example, Germanic customary law simply regulated the custom of blood-feud, so punishment remained the prerogative of the victim or the victim's family, whereas Scandinavian customary law provided for punishments to be administered by judicial authority.

H. Maine, *Dissertation on Early Law and Custom* (1883).

**CUTWORK or (Italian)** *punto tagliato*, an openwork linen fabric made by cutting away portions of the fabric and filling the gaps with ornamental designs made with needle and thread. The technique was evolved prior to that of LACE, of which it is an early form, and cutwork clothing became fashionable in sixteenth-century Italy. The most important designer of cutwork patterns was Mateo PAGANO.

Cutwork patterns were also used in garden design in the cutwork PARTERRES (French *parterres de pièces coupées*) of Jan VREDEMAN DE VRIES.

**CYPRUS.** The position of Cyprus has made it a prey to invaders since antiquity, when it was occupied by Phoenicians, Greeks, and Romans. With the division of the Roman Empire Cyprus was absorbed into the Byzantine Empire, of which it remained a part for six centuries, despite two Arab invasions. In 1192 the island passed from Richard Cœur-de-Lion to the Knights Templar and thence to the kings of Jerusalem; members of this dynasty (listed in Appendix I) ruled Cyprus until King James II married the Venetian Caterina CORNARO; after the death of James and his son James III, Caterina despaired of fending off the Ottomans, and so abdicated in 1489 in favour of the Venetian republic. Cyprus remained a Venetian possession until 1571, when it finally fell to the Turks, who ruled it until 1878. Most of Shakespeare's *Othello* (1604) is set in Cyprus at a time when it was still a Venetian dependency and so garrisoned by Venetian soldiers.

J. Richard (ed.), *Cypre sous les Lusignans: Documents chypriotes des archives du Vatican (XIVᵉ et XVᵉ siècles)* (1962); G. Hill, *A History of Cyprus*, vols. ii and iii (1948).

**CYRIAC OF ANCONA.** See CIRIACO D'ANCONA.

**CZECH BRETHREN.** See UNITY OF THE BROTHERS.

**CZECH LANGUAGE.** Czech is a West Slavic language spoken in BOHEMIA and MORAVIA; it is closely related to Slovak, the language of SLOVAKIA. The most important Czech writer of the fourteenth century, Thomas of Štitný, chose to write in Czech (rather than Latin) in his theological and philosophical treatises. In the next century, the Bohemian reformer Jan HUS, a champion of the Czech language, wrote a treatise called *Orthographia Bohemica*. In this book Hus grappled with the problem of writing a Slavic language in a Latin alphabet, and proposed a system of diacritics (e.g. the čarka, an acute accent which lengthens the vowel, and the háček, an inverted circumflex which softens a consonant) which, in modified form, is still in use. In the sixteenth century, Jan Blahoslav wrote the first *Grammatika Česká* (1571). In 1608 the ESTATES of Bohemia declared Czech to be the only official language of the state and made competence in Czech a condition of citizenship. The subjugation of Bohemia to the Emperor Ferdinand in the wake of the battle of the White Mountain (Bila Hora) on 8 November 1620 led to the attempt to suppress the Czech language in some domains, and the destruction of all books in Czech; the written form of the language was not revived until the nineteenth century.

**CZECH LITERATURE.** Late medieval Czech literature consists of hymns, saints' lives, chronicles, and the fragments of several epics. In the early fifteenth century, the standing of Jan HUS as a religious leader and then as a martyr made his writings (in both Czech and Latin) more influential than they might otherwise have been; his exposition of the Creed, the decalogue, and the Lord's Prayer (*Výklad viry, desatera Boziho prikazani, a patere*) was widely read, and helped to shape the development of literary Czech. The other important literary figure of the fifteenth century was Peter CHELČICKÝ, whose *Sit víry* ('Net of Faith') is one of the foundation stones of Czech literature. He shared with his co-religionists in the UNITY OF THE BRETHREN a principled preference for Czech over Latin, and it was this group who a century later published the first translation of the Bible into Czech; it was published in Králíky (Moravia) in six volumes (1579–93) and is now known in English as the Kralice Bible.

# D

**DADDI, BERNARDO** (*fl. c.*1320–48), Italian painter, a native of Florence. His triptych of the *Madonna* (1328), painted for the Church of the Ognissanti (the predecessor of the present church) and now in the Uffizi, is indebted to GIOTTO's *Madonna Enthroned* (Uffizi), which was painted for the same church; it therefore seems possible that Daddi was a pupil or assistant of Giotto. His surviving paintings include two frescoes depicting the *Martyrdoms of St Lawrence and St Stephen* (Church of Santa Croce), a large altarpiece of the *Madonna* in Orsanmichele, and a triptych now in the National Gallery in Edinburgh. He also painted small panels, often with detailed depictions of domestic interiors (e.g. the predella on the *Life of the Virgin* in the Uffizi).

   *DBI; MDA.*

**DAGGERS.** At least ten types of dagger (or poniard) were in use in early modern Europe; all were worn on the right side for use with the left hand, and so balanced the sword. The quillon dagger had a triangular blade, a cross-guard consisting of two quillons, and a wheel pommel. The rondel dagger had a cross-guard (and sometimes a pommel) shaped like a disc. The ballock knife (now politely known as a kidney dagger) had a cross-guard consisting of two rounded lobes; it evolved in Scotland into the dirk, which still survives in attenuated form in the stocking knife (*sgian dubh*) worn with Highland dress. The baselard, which probably derives its name from Basel, where it was first manufactured, was a dagger used by civilians; it had a hilt shaped like a capital I with serifs. The Swiss dagger resembled a baselard, but had a shorter blade; it is also known as a Holbein dagger, because HOLBEIN was one of the artists who designed gilt-copper and brass scabbards for Swiss daggers. The *cinquedea* was an Italian civilian dagger with sloping quillons and a long blade that was often etched with mythological scenes. The ear dagger was a Spanish dagger with a pommel formed of two discs set at an angle to each other like ears. The left-hand dagger (or *main-gauche*), which was made with a matching rapier, was a quillon dagger used for parrying; the quillons were sometimes arched with a view to trapping an opponent's sword. The stiletto (sometimes *stiletta*) was a short dagger with a triangular blade used principally in late sixteenth- and early seventeenth-century Italy. The bayonet, which was introduced in the early seventeenth century, was initially intended for use in the muzzle of a gun (which could then be used as a spear); in the late seventeenth century it began to be fitted with a socket attachment for fitting to the muzzle, and it remained in use in this form until the twentieth century.

   The dagger worn by the figure of Vice in English morality plays was recalled in Elizabethan plays as a 'dagger of lath', i.e. a counterfeit weapon made of wooden lath.

   Logan Thomas, *Daggers and Bayonets: A History* (1999).

**DALMATIA or (Croatian) Dalmacija or (Italian) Dalmazia or (German) Dalmatien.** The maritime city-states on the Adriatic coast of the Balkan peninsula were Italian-speaking outposts of the Venetian empire; the hinterland around these towns was settled by Slavs. The principal towns of Dalmatia, from north-east to south-west, were Zara (Croatian Zadar), Sebenico (Croatian Šibenik), Traù (Croatian Trogir, Latin Tragurium), Spalato (Croatian Split), Almissa (Croatian Omiš), Macarsca (Croatian Makarska, Latin Mocum), RAGUSA (Croatian Dubrovnik), and Cattaro (Montenegrin Kotor). From 1102 until 1420 Dalmatia was the subject of rivalry between Venice and Hungary. In 1420 all but two cities fell to the Ottomans: Almissa held out until 1444, and Ragusa retained its independence.

   The Ottoman conquest of the Balkan peninsula continued apace: Serbia fell in 1459, Bosnia in 1463, and Herzegovina in 1483. In 1508 the League of CAMBRAI forced Venice to withdraw its garrisons, and the Hungarians withdrew after their defeat at the battle of MOHÁCS in 1526. Dalmatia was thereafter easy prey for the Ottomans, and a settlement of 1540 left the Venetian maritime cities stripped of their hinterlands, which were absorbed into an Ottoman province. Christian refugees from the interior flocked into the towns, for the most part abandoning Orthodox Christianity for Catholicism, but retaining their Croatian language, which eventually supplanted Italian. Some refugees, notably the USCOKS, became pirates; others became mercenaries, notably the Dalmatian squadron that fought against the Turks at the battle of LEPANTO.

**DALMAU, LLUÍS** (*fl.* 1428–61), Valencian painter who worked in Valencia and became court painter to ALFONSO V of Aragon, under whose patronage he lived in Bruges from 1431 to 1437, after which he returned to Valencia (though he also worked in Barcelona). His sojourn in Flanders is significant for the history of SPANISH ART because it is the earliest known connection between a Spanish painter and the traditions of FLEMISH ART. His *Virgin of the Counsellors* (1443–5), now in the Barcelona Museum, was influenced by the Ghent ALTARPIECE of Jan van EYCK.

*DBC; MDA.*

**DAMASCENING**, a process used to decorate steel, usually sword blades, with a watered pattern; the name derives from Damascus, which was one of the early centres in which the process was developed. The term is also used to denote an inlaying process in which steel is decorated with gold or silver that is beaten into grooves.

**DAMASK**, the term used variously to denote a wavy pattern on steel (see DAMASCENING), a pink rose, a figured silk fabric, and a twilled linen fabric. In general English usage 'damask' could simply mean 'silk', but with reference to table linen (sometimes known as 'linen damask') the term referred specifically to a richly figured textile in which a surface sheen is created by opposing reflections of light from two faces of the same weave. In the fifteenth and sixteenth centuries linen damask was woven in the Netherlands, from which tablecloths and napkins were exported all over Europe. In the seventeenth century it began to be manufactured elsewhere in Europe, notably Ireland and Germany.

G. T. Yssesteyn, *White Figured Linen Damask* (1962).

**DAMHOUDER, JOOS DE, or Jodocus** (1507–81), Flemish jurist and magistrate who wrote on criminal law (*Praxis rerum criminalium*, 1555) and CIVIL LAW (*Praxis rerum civilium*, 1567). The treatise on criminal law was translated into Dutch and French and became accepted all over Europe as a definitive exposition of its subject. The indebtedness of the treatise to the *Practycke Crimineele* of Philip Weilant (1439–1519) is by modern standards tantamount to plagiarism, but the less confining conception of authorship in sixteenth-century Europe meant that the issue was never raised.

*NBW V.*

**DAMON or Daman, WILLIAM** (c.1540–1591), Italian composer and recorder player who was in London by 1571. In 1579 he became a musician to Queen Elizabeth, and the same year saw the publication of his *The Psalms of David in English Metre with Notes of Four Parts Set unto them.*

**DANCE** underwent increasingly sophisticated organization during the first half of the fifteenth century, with the advent of instruction manuals and the rise of the dancing master, beginning with Domenico da Piacenza (c.1390–c.1470). The most commonly found dance was the *basse dance* in the north; in Italy the *bassadanza* was joined by the balli and ballettos each with their own tunes appropriate to their choreography. In the sixteenth century new dances such as the galliard, the branle, and the moresca became part of the

repertoire; the last two were practised by courtiers and artisans alike. Dance manuals by Fabritio Caroso, Thoinot Arbeau, and Cesare Negri appeared between 1581 and 1604; they describe stylistic changes, give guidance on social etiquette, and provide information about dances such as the *volta* and the *matachin*. The theatrical context of dance overlapped with its role as a courtly pastime in the elaborate spectacles of the *intermedio*, the *ballet de cour*, the MASQUE, and early opera; the second act of MONTEVERDI's *Orfeo* relies heavily on dance. Dance strongly influenced the musical language with its requirements for a regular metre and repeated strong beats; it also impinged on the organization of musical material into ostinato variations and binary or ternary forms. These ideas were transferred into collections, either for solo instrument (the FITZWILLIAM VIRGINAL BOOK) or for ensembles. The pairing of dances such as the pavan and galliard translated into musical terms which ultimately led to the baroque dance suite.

**DANCE OF DEATH or** (French) *danse macabre* **or** (German) *Totentanz*, a pictorial or literary representation of a procession or a dance in which both the living and the dead participate. The term was first used by Jean Lefèvre in 1376, who introduced the term *macabré* (which was consistently so spelt until the sixteenth century) into French; the word clearly has Semitic origins, but its precise meaning is unknown. The earliest known pictorial Dance of Death is a *Danse macabre* mural that was painted in 1424–5 in the cloisters of the Cimetière des Innocents in Paris; the procession consisted of a series of couples, one living and one dead, arranged in an order of precedence beginning with pope and emperor and ending with a hermit and a baby. Underneath each dancer an eight-line octosyllabic stanza offered a moralistic commentary with a distinct social edge: death treats all ESTATES equally. The wall was destroyed in 1669, but the verses had been copied by the Parisian printer Guyot Marchant, who in 1485 published an illustrated *Danse macabre* in which the woodcuts were accompanied by short verses; these woodcuts were often reprinted, and created a genre which spread throughout Europe.

In England there was a *Dance of Death* mural in the old St Paul's Cathedral, but the mural was destroyed in 1549 (and the cathedral in 1666). John STOW said that the pictures were similar to those in Paris; the verses under the pictures were translated from those in Paris by the poet John Lydgate. Sir Thomas MORE recorded in his *Four Last Things* that

we were never so greatly moved by the beholding of the Dance of Death pictured in Paul's, as we shall feel ourselves stirred and altered by the feeling of that imagination in our hearts. And no marvel. For those pictures express only the loathly figure of our dead, bony bodies, bitten away the flesh, which though it be ugly to behold, yet neither the light thereof, nor the sight of all the dead heads in a charnel house, is half so deep as the deep conceived fantasy of death in his nature, by the lively imagination graven in thine own heart.

This passage represents one of the rare occasions in which sixteenth-century viewers yield some sense of how they looked at pictures.

The only known sculpted representation of a Dance of Death in England was in Coventry Cathedral, and was destroyed along with the cathedral in 1944. There are, however, two surviving painted versions of the Dance of Death in English churches: one is in the priory at Hexham (Northumberland) and the other is in the Church of St Mary Magdalen in Newark (Nottinghamshire). Elsewhere in Europe, there is a painted *Dance of Death* in the Marienkirche in Lübeck and sculpted series in the Church of St Maclou (Rouen) and in the Dreikönigskirche in Dresden Neustadt; the latter is the work of Christoph Walther (d. 1546).

The most famous representation of the Dance of Death is the series of 40 woodcuts designed by Hans HOLBEIN the Younger (*c.*1523–6) and executed by the German woodcutter Hans Lützelburger (*fl. c.*1517–26). Holbein's designs may be indebted to a fourteenth-century *Totentanz* fresco made for the nunnery at Klingenthal and moved in the mid-fifteenth century to the Predigerkloster in Basel, where it was restored in 1568 and destroyed when the wall collapsed in 1805. The first edition of these designs was published in Lyon in 1538; a Basel edition reached proof stage but was not printed. Holbein's designs have shaped all subsequent representations of the Dance of Death. The finest products of the revival of interest in the Dance of Death in the nineteenth century were Liszt's *Totentanz* for piano and orchestra, Saint-Saëns's symphonic poem *Danse macabre*, and Strindberg's two *Dödsdansen* plays; in the twentieth century Ingmar Bergman portrayed the Dance of Death in his film *The Seventh Seal*.

> J. M. Clark, *The Dance of Death in the Middle Ages and the Renaissance* (1950).

**DANIEL or Danyel, JOHN** (1564–*c.*1626), English composer and lutenist. He was the brother of the poet Samuel DANIEL and his contemporary reputation as a player linked him with John DOWLAND. He was awarded a B.Mus. at Christ Church, Oxford, in 1603 and dedicated his first book of songs to his pupil Mrs Anne Green. In 1618 he replaced his brother as 'allower of the plays' at Blackfriars Playhouse.

**DANIEL, SAMUEL** (*c.*1562–1619), English poet, brother of the composer John DANIEL. Following education at Oxford and travels in Italy, Daniel became a private tutor. His sonnet collection *Delia* was published in 1592, and two tragedies, *Cleopatra* (1594) and *Philotas* (1604), followed. A verse dialogue 'in defence of learning', *Musophilius*, appeared in 1599, a *Defence of Rhyme c.*1603, and a verse epic of the Wars of the Roses, *Civil Wars*, in 1595 and 1609. He also wrote MASQUES for the court of James I (JAMES VI).

> DNB.

**DANIELE RICCIARELLA DA VOLTERRA** (1509–66), Italian painter and sculptor, born in Volterra and trained in the studio of Il SODOMA in Siena. He moved to Rome *c.*1541 and executed frescoes such as the *Deposition* in the Orsini Chapel in the Church of Santa Trinita dei Monti.

Daniele became a close associate of MICHELANGELO, of whom he made a bronze portrait bust (*c.*1564, Bargello) after attending him on his deathbed. His best-known commission was the painting of draperies on the nude figures that Michelangelo had painted on the ceiling of the SISTINE CHAPEL, a task that led to the nickname 'Il Braghettone' ('maker of breeches').

> *DBI* s.v. Ricciarelli, Daniele; *MDA* s.v. Daniele da Volterra.

**DANISH ART AND ARCHITECTURE.** The principal citizens of the seaports of fifteenth-century Denmark were German traders, and the art that they installed in their churches was German, notably Bernt NOTKE's carved and painted altarpiece in Århus and Claus BERG's altarpiece in Odense. With the advent of the Reformation, art became secularized and its purpose to satisfy the tastes of the royal court. In the late sixteenth and early seventeenth centuries Kings FREDERICK II and CHRISTIAN IV invited large numbers of Dutch and German architects, painters, sculptors, and musicians to Denmark. The most important monuments of this artistic renaissance are the buildings constructed by Dutch architects in the style of the Netherlandish Renaissance: Antonius van Opbergen (1543–1611) and Hans Steenwinckel the Elder (*c.*1545–1601) built Frederick II's palace of Kronborg at Helsingør (Hamlet's Elsinore) and Hans Steenwinckel the Younger (1587–1639) and his brother Lourens (*c.*1585–1619) built Christian IV's magnificent palace at Frederiksborg (now the Museum of National History). The Steenwinckels were also responsible for the Exchange (Børsen) in Copenhagen (1619–25); its spire is one of the city's landmarks. The summer palace at Rosenborg (1606–17), which was then outside the walls of Copenhagen, was designed by Bertel Lange. In Scania, which was Danish until 1658, the church at Kristianstad (1618), which may be the work of the Steenwinckels, is one of the finest Protestant churches ever built; it is a hall church (i.e. its aisles are as high as the nave) with slender piers, and its gables are Netherlandish in style.

**DANISH LANGUAGE AND LITERATURE.** Danish is a North Germanic language of which the principal forms are West Jutlandish (which, unlike other forms of Danish, still has three genders), East Jutlandish, and the island dialects of Funen, Zealand, and Bornholm; Faroese is a sister language rather than a dialect. In the early modern period, Scania (Swedish Skåne), in southern Sweden, was part of Denmark, and the language spoken there, Scanir, was a form of Danish that has since been supplanted by Swedish.

The literary languages of Denmark were Latin and Danish, and the principal centre of literary activity was Copenhagen, where the university was established in 1479 and the first printing press in 1490. In 1495 the press issued its first vernacular publication, a *Rimkrønike* which recorded in rhymed verse the history of Denmark to 1481 (the death of CHRISTIAN I). In the sixteenth century the principal subjects of Denmark's poetry and prose were religious, and ranged from devotional poetry to polemical prose.

The commanding literary figure of sixteenth-century Denmark was Christiern PEDERSEN, who through his publication of historical, imaginative, and religious literature (notably his Bibles) exercised an influence on Danish literary culture that has led to his being regarded as the father of Danish literature. The tradition of Danish drama that was to culminate in Holberg was inaugurated by the *Ludus de Sancto Kanuto* (c.1530), an anonymous play which, despite its Latin title, is written in Danish. The most important dramatist was Hieronymus Justesen Ranch (1539–1607), a priest from Viborg who wrote plays on the crowning of King Solomon (*Kong Solomons Hylding*), the imprisonment of Samson (*Samsons Fængsel*), and a farce about a miser (*Karrig Niding*). Ranch was also a poet (and the author of *Fuglevise*, a well-known moralizing poem about birds), but the first great poet in Danish was Anders Christensen Arrebos (1587–1637), the bishop of Trondheim (subsequently deprived for immorality) whose works included a hexameral poem modelled on the *Divine Semaine* of DU BARTAS.

**DANISH MUSIC.** Late medieval Denmark had a robust tradition of ecclesiastical music which in the early sixteenth century was enriched by the presence of Flemish composers and performers at the royal court. The Reformation in Denmark was Lutheran rather than Calvinist; church music continued to flourish throughout the sixteenth century. In the late sixteenth century the court of CHRISTIAN IV became an important centre for secular music. King Christian sent Danish musicians abroad to study in London and Venice, and also invited English musicians, including William BRADE, John DOWLAND, John MAYNARD, Thomas ROBINSON, and Thomas SIMPSON, to Denmark.

**DANTE IN THE RENAISSANCE.** The standing of Dante Alighieri (1265–1321) as Italy's national poet is a product of the Risorgimento; in the fifteenth and sixteenth centuries, he was Tuscany's greatest poet, a citizen and patriot who represented Florentine aspirations to cultural hegemony. The poetry of the *Vita nuova*, which contains the story of Dante's love for Beatrice, formed the opening section of Lorenzo de' MEDICI's anthology of Tuscan verse (*Raccolta aragonese*, 1477). In 1481 Cristoforo LANDINO published his commentary on Dante's *Divina commedia*, presenting its author as a Florentine opposed to the power of the papacy. The public lectures on Dante inaugurated by BOCCACCIO in 1373 were an important statement of Dante's cultural standing.

The *Commedia* and Dante's treatise *De vulgari eloquentia* ('On Elegance in the Vernacular') were central points of reference in the debate known as the QUESTIONE DELLA LINGUA. Dante's preference for vernacular Tuscan over Latin caused some difficulties for humanists, and in the fifteenth century linguistic controversialists such as Pietro BEMBO declared Dante's language to be base and indecorous and instead recommended as literary models the poetry of Petrarch and the prose of Boccaccio. Thereafter Dante was admired more for his learning and exemplary morality than for his literary style, and the *Commedia* became the preserve of learned commentators. In the sixteenth century Protestant commentators seized on the anti-papal passages in the *Commedia*, but otherwise Dante is strikingly absent from the religious and cultural debates of the sixteenth century.

Michael Caesar, *Dante: The Critical Heritage, 1314–1870* (1989); Cecil Grayson, 'Dante and the Renaissance', in C. P. Brand (ed.), *Italian Studies Presented to E. R. Vincent* (1962).

**DANTI, EGNAZIO** (1536–86), Italian mathematician and geographer, born in Perugia; he was the younger brother of the sculptor Vincenzo DANTI, and the great-nephew of Giovanni DANTI. In 1555 he entered the Dominican Order, and from 1562 to 1574 worked in the service of Duke Cosimo de' MEDICI. In the early 1570s, in connection with a possible reform of the CALENDAR, he made observations of the sun using instruments attached to the façade of Santa Maria Novella (Florence) and made a small hole in the round window to allow sunlight to enter the church at the equinoxes, and others in the façade and the vault to allow it to enter at the winter solstice, thus making it possible to use the building as a *CAMERA OBSCURA*; perhaps confusingly, this kind of arrangement is called a gnomon. Danti later set up a smaller gnomon in Rome, where he was appointed papal cosmographer by GREGORY XIII, for whom he made a series of large and decorative, but accurate, maps to adorn the walls of a long gallery.

Danti's mathematical works include editions of Euclid's *Optica* (1574, in which Danti describes his first Florentine gnomon), the mathematical works of Proclus, and the treatise *Scienze matematiche ridotte in tavole* (Bologna, 1577); he edited VIGNOLA's treatise on PERSPECTIVE *Le due regole della prospettiva pratica* (1583); Danti's extensive and learned notes and commentaries probably account for the book being widely read well into the following century. Danti participated in the calendar reform of 1582.

Some very elegant astronomical instruments ascribed to Danti are in the collection of the Istituto e Museo di Storia della Scienza in Florence.

*DBI; DSB.*

**DANTI, GIOVANNI** (1478–1517), Italian military engineer and mathematician, the great-uncle of Egnazio and Vincenzo DANTI. He was born in Perugia and settled in Venice as a teacher of mathematics. He invented a flying machine, and in 1503, near Lake Trasimene, made his initial attempt to fly with the assistance of two artifical wings.

*DSB s.v. Danti, Egnazio.*

**DANTI, VINCENZO** (1530–76), Italian sculptor, goldsmith, and writer on perspective, born into a family of goldsmiths in Perugia. His first important work was a monumental bronze statue of Pope JULIUS III (1555) still in its original position outside Perugia Cathedral. In 1557 he moved to Florence to enter the service of COSIMO I DE' MEDICI, and thereafter his works show the marked influence of MICHELANGELO, for whose funeral (1564) he supplied sculpture and paintings. In 1567 he published a treatise on proportion, *Delle perfette proporzioni*, which is dedicated to Grand Duke Cosimo. His Florentine sculptures include a small bronze *Venus Anadyomene* (Palazzo Vecchio), a marble *Honour Overcoming Falsehood* (Bargello), and a bronze group of *The Beheading of John the Baptist* made for the baptistery (completed 1571). In 1573 Danti returned to

Perugia, where he became city architect and a founding professor at the Accademia del Disegno.

*DBI*; *MDA*; Giovan Battista Fidanza, *Vincenzio Danti* (1996).

**DANZIG or (Polish) Gdańsk**, a HANSA city and maritime fortress at the mouth of the Vistula (Polish Wisła). The city was governed by the TEUTONIC KNIGHTS from 1308 to 1466, when it was ceded to King CASIMIR IV of Poland; thereafter it became a German city under Polish rule. When the Reformation was proclaimed in 1525, King Sigismund I intervened to suppress the rebellion. Danzig was the most prosperous of the Baltic ports, shipping vast quantities of grain from its hinterland to the Low Countries, and developed an important shipbuilding industry which still survives; its first warship was launched in 1572. The most important surviving Renaissance buildings are the sixteenth-century 'high gate' (modelled on a Roman triumphal arch) at the western entrance to the 'main town' (Glowne Miasto) and the façade of Dwór Artusa in the 'old town' (Stare Miasto).

**DARET, JACQUES** (*c*.1400/5–*c*.1468), Flemish painter, born in Tournai and trained from 1427 to 1432 in the studio of Robert CAMPIN, where his fellow pupil was one Rogelet de la Pâture, who is assumed to be Rogier van der WEYDEN. His principal surviving works are four panels from the *St Vaast* altarpiece, now divided: the *Nativity* is in the Thyssen Collection in Madrid, the *Visitation* and the *Adoration* are in the Gemäldegalerie in Berlin, and the *Presentation* is in the Petit Palais in Paris.

*BNB*; *MDA*.

**DARNLEY, HENRY STUART** (1545–67), royal consort. Darnley married MARY, QUEEN OF SCOTS, in 1565. Grandson, by her second husband, of Margaret Tudor, sister of HENRY VIII and queen of JAMES IV, Darnley was second only to his wife in the line of succession to the English throne: their marriage, and the birth in 1567 of a son, the future JAMES VI of Scotland, thus threatened the unmarried ELIZABETH. Having betrayed his Protestant allies in the RIZZIO murder, Darnley's position became increasingly insecure; his murder, in which Mary and BOTHWELL may have been implicated, unleashed a series of events which would lead to Mary's own enforced abdication.

*DNB* s.v. Stuart, Henry.

**DASER, LUDWIG** (*c*.1525–1589), German composer who, having spent most of his early life in Munich at the Bavarian Hofkapelle, became *Kapellmeister* in 1552. As a Protestant in a Catholic court he encountered some difficulties, and in 1572 he became *Kapellmeister* at the Württemberg court in Stuttgart, which had been separated from Rome over 30 years earlier. He was highly regarded for his well-crafted sacred works.

**DATINI, FRANCESCO** (*c*.1335–1410), merchant and banker. He was born in Prato, and after being orphaned worked in Florence while still a child. In 1350 he moved to Avignon, where he became wealthy as a supplier of goods to the papal court. In 1383 he returned to Prato, and thereafter divided his time between Prato and Florence. His trading company developed branches in Avignon, Barcelona, Florence, Genoa, Majorca, Pisa, and Valencia and agencies in northwest Europe and the Levant. Datini died on 16 August 1410, and left most of his fortune to charity.

The records of Datini's company were preserved in his palace in Prato, and the scale of the archive has made it a valuable resource for the economic history of the period and has made Datini the most studied international businessman of early modern Italy.

*DBI*; I. Origo, *The Merchant of Prato* (1957); *La 'pratica di mercatura' datiniana*, ed. C. Ciano (1964); *Comptes du sel (Libro di ragione e conto di salle) de Francesco di Marco Datini*, ed. C. Villain-Gandossi (1969).

**D'AUBIGNÉ, THEODORE AGRIPPA** (1552–1630), French poet, historian, satirist, Protestant polemicist, and soldier. He was educated in Paris and Geneva and later fought on the side of Henry of Navarre (later HENRI IV) in the WARS OF RELIGION. In the early 1570s d'Aubigné composed a remarkable sequence of Petrarchan love poems (*Le Printemps*) for Diane Salviati, the niece of RONSARD's Cassandre; the poems remained unpublished until 1874. He was absent from Paris during the ST BARTHOLOMEW'S DAY MASSACRE (1572), which nonetheless marked his subsequent writings, notably *Les Tragiques* (completed 1579, published 1616), a poetic history of the Wars of Religion from a Protestant perspective. He later wrote a prose history of the same period (*L'Histoire universelle*, 1618–20). In 1620 d'Aubigné moved as a religious exile to Geneva, where he spent the last decade of his life.

*DBF* s.v. Aubigné; Madeleine Lazard, *Agrippa d'Aubigné* (1998); *Histoire universelle*, ed. André Thierry (11 vols. to date, 1981–2000).

**DAUCHER, ADOLF** (*c*.1460–1523/4) and **HANS** (*c*.1485–after 1538), German sculptors in Augsburg who worked in the service of the FUGGER family. Adolf's best-known work is the high altar of the Annenkirche in Annaberg-Buchholz; the altar was commissioned by GEORG DER BÄRTIGE in 1519 and is still in the church. Hans entered the service of CHARLES V and also accepted commissions from the dukes of Württemberg. His best-known work is *Christ with the Virgin and St John*, which he made for the altar of the Fugger Chapel in Augsburg.

*MDA*; *NDB*.

**DAVANZATI, BERNARDO** (1529–1606), Italian author and translator, born in Florence. After a period as a businessman in Lyon, he returned to Florence, where he translated the *Annals* of Tacitus into Italian and wrote treatises on subjects such as agriculture and economics. His religious works include *Scisma d'Inghilterra* (1602), a translation from Latin to Italian of a treatise on the English Reformation by the Jesuit Nicholas SANDERS.

*DBI*; *OCIL*.

**DÁVID, FRANCIS, or (Latin) Franciscus Davidis or (Hungarian) Ferenc Dávid or (German) Franz Hertel** (*c*.1520–1579), Transylvanian Protestant, born into a Saxon family in Kolozsvár (Romanian Cluj, German Klausenburg).

His education abroad is not well documented, but he may have studied at Wittenberg and Frankfurt an der Oder. He returned c.1551 to TRANSYLVANIA, and in 1556 was appointed as town pastor of Kolozsvár, a post that he held until 1579, when he was imprisoned in Deva (German Diemrich) for the final months of his life.

Dávid was born into a Lutheran family, and until 1558 worked for the Lutheran cause in Germany. In 1559 he adopted Zwinglian views on the EUCHARIST, and in 1564 he became superintendent of the Calvinist Church. By 1567 he had completed his tour of the Protestant churches and become a UNITARIAN, but thereafter his theology became radical even by the radical standards of the Unitarians; by 1575 he was not only preaching against the divinity of Christ but was also opposing the invocation of the name of Jesus in prayer.

At this point Giorgio BIANDRATA invited Faustus SOCINUS to Kolozsvár to negotiate with Dávid. Socinus arrived in November 1578, and for the next four months the two men debated the finer points of the doctrine of invocation. Socinus argued that the worship of Christ (adoratio Christi) was obligatory for Christians even though prayer to Christ (invocatio Christi) was simply permissive, but Dávid's radical anti-Trinitarianism extended to non-adorationism, and he would not be persuaded otherwise. At the end of their fruitless negotiations, Socinus left for Poland and Dávid was tried for heresy and imprisoned; he died in prison on 15 November 1579. His friends published Defensio Francisci Davidis in negotio de non invocando Jesu Christo in precibus, a defence of Dávid's non-adorationist principles.

Dávid had been raised in a German-speaking Saxon family, but he always chose to write in Latin or Hungarian. He was twice married, and in 1576 divorced his second wife, Katherine Münich-Barát, after four years of marriage; he is the only churchman in sixteenth-century Europe known to have been divorced.

NDB s.v. Davidis, Franz; Dávid Ferenc, 1579–1979 (1979).

**DAVID, GÉRARD** (c.1460–1523), Netherlandish painter. He was a native of Oudewater (near Gouda) and worked in Bruges from 1484 and in Antwerp from 1515. His finest pictures are those that depict domestic scenes from the life of Jesus; the popularity of these paintings ensured that they were often copied, and many exist in several versions: the Virgin Feeding the Christ-Child with Porridge, for example, exists in four versions. David's compositional skills are apparent in works such as his triptych The Baptism of Christ (Groeninge Museum, Bruges) which, despite the fracturing effect of three panels separated by frames, is a single picture in which the viewers on the wings are integrated with the baptism in the central panel, in the background of which a landscape recedes without an artificial break.

BNB; MDA; NBW xii.

**DÁVILA, PEDRARIAS, or Pedro Arias de Ávila** (c.1440–1530), Spanish conquistador who fought as a young man in the final stages of the RECONQUISTA. In 1514 he was appointed successor to BALBOA as governor of Darién, and three years later executed Balboa on a charge of treason. Despite his age, Dávila led the conquest of what is now Costa Rica and Nicaragua. In 1519 he moved Balboa's settlement at Antigua to Panama, and so founded the oldest surviving European town on the mainland of America.

DHE; María del Carmen Mena Garcia, Pedrarias Dávila (1992).

**DA VINCI, LEONARDO.** See LEONARDO DA VINCI.

**DA VINCI, PIERINO.** See PIERINO DA VINCI.

**DAVIS, JOHN** (1550–1605), English sailor and inventor. Following in the footsteps of FROBISHER, Davis undertook a series of expeditions, in 1585–7, in pursuit of the NORTH-WEST PASSAGE, sailing west of Greenland on the strait now named after him. He later fought the Armada, and died in the East Indies. He is also remembered as the inventor of the BACKSTAFF.

DNB.

**DAVY, RICHARD** (c.1465–c.1507), English composer, active in Oxford, Exeter, and possibly at Fotheringay College in Northamptonshire. He was a major contributor to the ETON CHOIRBOOK, along with BROWNE and LAMBE, and was reputed to have written the antiphon 'O Domine caeli terraeque' in a single day.

**DAY, JOHN** (c.1574–c.1640), English playwright. Day produced plays for the ADMIRAL'S MEN, both on his own and in collaboration with DEKKER, CHETTLE, and ROWLEY. The Parliament of Bees (c.1607), a MASQUE in which bees and other insects represent virtues and vices, is his best-known sole production.

DNB.

**DECEMBRIO FAMILY**, a family of Italian humanists. Uberto Decembrio (c.1350–1427) was a secretary in the service of the VISCONTI rulers of Milan; his surviving works include letters and treatises on philosophical and civic matters. Pier Candido Decembrio (1392–1477), Uberto's elder son, inherited his father's civic posts, but lived from 1466 to 1474 in Ferrara, where he worked as a secretary to Borso d'ESTE; he translated Appian, Homer (part of the Iliad), and Plutarch from Greek, and wrote biographies of Italian princes. Angelo Decembrio (c.1415–c.1466), Uberto's younger son, studied under Gasparino da BARZIZZA and GUARINO DA VERONA, and subsequently worked in Ferrara, Naples, and Spain; his works include Politia litteraria, an account of the circle of Guarino da Verona in Ferrara.

DBI; OCIL.

**DECIO, FILIPPO, or Decius** (1454–1535), Italian jurist and political theorist. He studied law at Pavia and Pisa, and subsequently taught at those universities and at Padua and Siena. He became an auditor of the Rota (the papal ecclesiastical court), but his propensity for controversy led at one point to his excommunication and a period of exile in France (1512–15). As a political theorist he argued that rulers were contractually bound to their subjects. As a jurist he wrote prolifically on subjects such as the JUSTINIAN *Digest* (1507–10), the *Decretals* (1543), feudal law (*Usus feudorum*, 1483), and the law of actions (*De actionibus*, 1483).

*DBI; CoE.*

**DE CRITZ, JOHAN or John** (*c.*1551/2–1642), Flemish painter. He left his native Antwerp for England as a refugee *c.*1570. He was appointed serjeant-painter to the crown in 1603, and in this capacity was responsible for the decorative work in the royal palaces, though he did not undertake all of the painting himself. He was associated with a group of painters that included Marcus GHEERAERTS the Elder and the Younger, Isaac and Peter OLIVER, and Sir Robert Peake (1592–1667), to all of whom he was related by marriage. Some court portraits are attributed to more than one member of this group, and it is possible that in some cases they collaborated on portraits. In his capacity as serjeant-painter, de Critz painted Maximilian COLT's tomb of Queen Elizabeth in Westminster Abbey.

The title of serjeant-painter was inherited by reversion by Johan's son Johan (or John) the Younger (*c.*1591–*c.*1642) in 1610; he was active as a decorator but apparently not as a portrait painter, and died fighting for the king in defence of Oxford. One of Johan's other sons, Emmanuel de Critz (*c.*1608–1665), painted scenery for court MASQUES. A third son, Thomas de Critz (1607–53), may have been the painter of a series of portraits of the TRADESCANT family executed in the 1640s (and formerly attributed to Emmanuel) and now in the Ashmolean Museum in Oxford.

*DNB; MDA s.v. Critz, de (family).*

**DEDEKIND, FRIEDRICH** (1524–98), German satirist, a Lutheran pastor in his native Neustadt am Rübenberge (1551) and in Lüneburg (1575), and the author of *Grobianus sive De morum simplicitate* (1549), a satire in two books which was translated into German by Kaspar SCHEIDT (1551). The huge popularity of *Grobianus* led Dedekind to compose a third book, *Grobiana* (1552). These satires ridicule vulgar behaviour, especially at the dinner table, and ironically champion boorishness; in addition to their literary merits they are also important documents in the history of manners. Dedekind's later works were *Der christliche Ritter* (1590) and *Papista conversus* (1596).

*NDB; E. Rühl, Grobianus in England (1904).*

**DEE, JOHN** (1527–1608), English astrologer, alchemist, and mathematician, educated at St John's College, Cambridge, and at Louvain. He subsequently lectured in Paris on EUCLID. On returning to England he was appointed astrologer to Queen MARY, but was tried (and acquitted) by the Star Chamber for using sorcery against the queen. After further travels on the Continent (where he visited the imperial court in Buda) and a voyage to St Helena, he returned to the court of Queen ELIZABETH, where he worked as an astrologer and also lectured on NAVIGATION. From 1583 to 1589 Dee lived in Bohemia and Poland, where he conducted experiments in alchemy and the occult sciences. On returning to England he was appointed warden of Manchester College (1595–1604).

He wrote a long preface to the first English translation of Euclid's *Elements*, by Henry Bilingsley, published in 1570. Dee's preface makes much of the practical usefulness of the mathematical arts but also contains hints of occult interests such as those found in Dee's *Monas hieroglyphica* (1564).

*DNB; DSB.*

**DEFENESTRATION OF PRAGUE** (30 July 1419). The execution of Jan Hus in 1415 had aroused popular opposition in Bohemia. King WENCESLAS IV controlled dissent in Prague through a town council consisting for the most part of German merchants. The council's persecution of Hussite reformers led to a popular rising. On 30 July 1419 the Hussite priest John of Želiv (German Selau) led a procession through the streets of Prague, and stones were thrown at the procession from the Town Hall. The Hussites, led by Jan ŽIŽKA, stormed the Town Hall and hurled the magistrates out of its windows; in some accounts of the incident, they were impaled on spikes held by the rioters below. Within a fortnight Wenceslas had died of a stroke and the course had been set for the eruption of the HUSSITE WARS. The incident has come to be called the First Defenestration of Prague by analogy to the Defenestration of 1618.

*Thomas A. Fudge, The Magnificent Ride: The First Reformation in Hussite Bohemia (1998).*

**DEFENESTRATION OF PRAGUE or (German) Prager Fenstersturz** (23 May 1618). In December 1617, the archbishop of Prague and the Benedictine abbot of Broumov (German Braunau) forbade Protestant religious services in churches within their jurisdictions. The UTRAQUISTS organized an assembly of all Protestant members of the Diet; the assembly, which met in Prague on 21 May 1618, decided to march to the royal palace to petition the councillors of the Emperor MATTHIAS. On 22 May, the Protestant leaders held a secret meeting at which they decided to murder the most influential of Matthias's Catholic councillors.

On 23 May 1618 the Protestants marched to the castle to meet the royal councillors in the chancellery. The Protestants accused two of the king's councillors, Jaroslav Martinic and Vilém Slavata, of having advised the king to approve the suppression of the Protestants. The meeting concluded when the Protestants hurled the two councillors out of the window together with Fabricius, the secretary of the royal council; their fall of about 20 metres (65 feet) was broken by a dunghill, and only Slavata was slightly injured. The incident, which is known as the Defenestration of Prague, set in train the events that soon erupted in the THIRTY YEARS WAR.

Franz Grillparzer's play *Ein Bruderzwist in Habsburg* (planned 1824, performed 1872), which dramatizes the events of 1581–1618, cavalierly brings forward the Defenestration from 1618 to 1612, the year in which RUDOLF II died.

**DEI, BENEDETTO** (1418–92), Italian traveller and historian, born in Florence on 4 March 1418. He fled the city after participating in an abortive coup, and travelled for many years in Africa and Asia, settling in Constantinople for several years. He returned to Florence in 1486 and spent the rest of his life in the service of the MEDICI; he died in Florence on 28 August 1492. His *Le memorie storiche* is a wide-ranging account of Ottoman Turkey.

*DBI*; M. Pisani, *Un avventuriero del quattrocento: La vita e le opere de Benedetto Dei* (1923).

**DEKKER, THOMAS** (*c*.1572–1632), English playwright. Over 40 of the plays which Dekker wrote, or more often collaborated on, are now lost; the fifteen which survive, however, are comedies, often reflecting London life and its vivid cast of characters. *The Shoemaker's Holiday* (1599) describes the part Simon Eyre, shoemaker to the lord mayor of London, plays in the wooing by Rowland Lacy of the mayor's daughter. In *Old Fortunatus* (1600), a beggar is granted his wish of riches, and *The Honest Whore* (1604), to which MIDDLETON contributed, dramatizes the good-hearted harlot Bellafront's love for Count Hippolito.

*DNB*.

**DELAUNE, ÉTIENNE** (1518/19–83), French engraver and medallist who published influential designs for armourers, cabinetmakers, enamellers, jewellers, and silversmiths, typically filled with fanciful human figures and sea monsters and decorated with fruit and flowers. His medals include one of *Henri II* (of which an example survives in the Bibliothèque Nationale in Paris).

*MDA*.

**DEL CHIERICO, FRANCESCO D'ANTONIO** (1433–84), Italian illuminator in Florence. He may have been trained by Fra ANGELICO, whose style he imitated; his illuminations are not merely decorations, but often consist of small paintings. From 1463 to 1471 he illuminated a series of books for the cathedral in Florence. His patrons included the MEDICI, the MONTEFELTRO dukes of Urbino, the Aragonese kings of Naples, and MATTHIAS CORVINUS of Hungary. His books include a breviary now in the Biblioteca LAURENZIANA and Petrarch manuscripts in the Bibliothèque Nationale in Paris (commissioned by Lorenzo de' Medici) and Castello Sforzesco in Milan.

*DBI* s.v. Francesco d'Antonio del Chierico; *MDA* s.v. Francesco di Antonio del Chierico.

**DELFTWARE, ENGLISH**, the modern term for TIN-GLAZED EARTHENWARE manufactured in England; the term is anachronistic, because such earthenware was introduced into England from Antwerp in 1567, when Jasper and Joris ANDRIES established a pottery in Norwich, but Delft did not emerge as an important pottery centre until the 1650s. In the Netherlands the pottery was called 'Delf' and in Britain 'English Delfware'; the addition of the paragogic *t* to the name of the town in modern Dutch was in turn adopted in Britain. Jacob Jansen (d. 1593), who had accompanied the Andries brothers to Norwich, established a pottery in Aldgate (London), and soon 'English Delftware' factories were established in Lambeth, Southwark (both on the south bank of the Thames opposite London) and Bristol.

L. L. Lipski and M. Archer, *Dated English Delftware* (1984); F. Britten, *London Delftware* (1987).

**DELLA CASA, GIOVANNI** (1503–56), Italian archbishop, poet, and writer on etiquette, born into a prominent Florentine family, probably in Mugello. He studied law at Bologna and Greek at Padua before moving in 1532 to Rome, where he pursued a career in the Church. He became archbishop of Benevento and in 1544 was appointed papal nuncio to Venice. He withdrew to Venice during the pontificate of JULIUS III, but was recalled to Rome by Pope PAUL IV, and in the last year of his life served as secretary of state for the Vatican.

In 1558 della Casa published a collection of Petrarchan sonnets (*Rime*) and a prose work, *Il Galateo, ovvero dei costumi*, which is a letter of advice from an old man to a young man, mostly on the subject of correct conduct. This treatise, which is based on the courtly ideals of CASTIGLIONE, was widely translated, and became one of Europe's most important manuals of courtly etiquette.

*DBI*; *OCIL*; *Il Galateo*, ed. C. Cordié (1960), trans. R. R. Pine-Coffin (1958); A. Santosuosso, *Vita di Giovanni della Casa* (1979).

**DELLA FONTE, BARTOLOMEO** (1445–1513), Italian humanist, born in Florence, where he was educated under ARGYROPOULOS and LANDINO. He lived for a time in the ESTE court in Ferrara (1468–72) and subsequently at the papal court. In 1489 he visited Hungary at the invitation of MATTHIAS CORVINUS, and then returned permanently to Florence. His publications include commentaries, translations, a collection of letters, the *editio princeps* of the *Artes* of Aulus Cornelis Celsus, and the first Renaissance treatise devoted exclusively to poetics, *De poetice* (1490–2).

*DBI*.

**DELLA GATTA, BARTOLOMEO, or Pietro Dei** (1448–1502), Italian painter, born in Florence, where he became a Camaldolese monk. He worked in Rome as an assistant to PERUGINO and SIGNORELLI on the frescoes in the SISTINE CHAPEL, and subsequently became abbot of his ORDER's house in Arezzo. His surviving paintings include an *Assumption of the Virgin* (*c*.1475, Museo Diocesano, Cortona).

*DBI* s.v. Dei, Pietro, detto Bartolomeo della Gatta; *MDA* s.v. Bartolomeo della Gatta.

**DELLA PORTA, ANTONIO, or Il Tamagnino** (*fl.* 1491–1501), Italian sculptor. He worked as a decorative sculptor at the Certosa di Pavia (1491–9), but no works by his hand can now be identified. In 1501 he moved to Genoa, where his work included carved doors for the city's palaces, one of which survives in Palazzo Grillo-Cattaneo; he also collaborated with Pace Gagini on a series of tombs.

*DBI* s.v. Della Porta, Antonio, detto Tamagnino; *MDA* s.v. Porta, Antonio della.

**DELLA PORTA, GIACOMO** (1532–1602), Italian architect, born in Porlezza and trained in the Roman studio of MICHELANGELO, whom he succeeded as architect of the Capitol. He completed several works by Michelangelo, including the Palazzo dei Conservatori and (with Domenico FONTANA) the dome of ST PETER'S BASILICA; in both cases he altered Michelangelo's designs. He also completed the façade of Il Gesù, the mother church of the JESUITS, after the death of Giacomo VIGNOLA in 1573, again altering the design; this façade was subsequently copied in Jesuit churches all over the world. His secular designs include the Palazzo della Sapienza (from 1575), the Palazzo Marescotti (c.1590) and the Villa ALDOBRANDINI in Frascati (1598–1603). His Roman churches include Santa Maria dei Monti (1580–1), Sant'Atanasio (1580–3), the nave of San Giovanni dei Fiorentini (1582–92) and the initial stage of Sant'Andrea della Valle (1591, completed by Carlo Maderno, 1608–23).

DBI; MDA s.v. Porta, Giacomo della; Vitaliano Tiberia, *Giacomo della Porta: Un architetto tra manierismo e barocco* (1974).

**DELLA PORTA, GIAMBATTISTA** (c.1535–1615), Italian dramatist, exponent of natural magic, and cryptographer, a native of Naples who in 1558 published *Magica naturalis*, a compendium of unexplained phenomena which was soon translated into Italian, French, and Dutch. Della Porta distinguished between sorcery, which he deplored, and natural magic, which in his view included unexplained aspects of chemistry, hydraulics, magnetism, and optics. Della Porta's other works include a treatise on cryptography (*De furtivis literarum*, 1563).

In 1560 della Porta founded the Neapolitan Academia Secretorum Naturae (Italian Accademia dei Segreti), which was the first scientific academy; the interests of the Academy, which lay at the intersection of magic and experimental science, attracted the attention of the INQUISITION, which ordered the Academy to close in 1580. In 1610 della Porta became a member of the Accademia dei Lincei in Rome (see ACADEMIES).

In 1589 della Porta began to publish his plays, of which he had written at least seventeen. Some of the plays were translated into French and English, and three (*La Cintia, La fantesca*, and *Astrologo*) were performed in Latin translation at Trinity College, Cambridge, between 1598 and 1615.

DBI; OCIL; L. G. Clubb, *Giambattista della Porta, Dramatist* (1965).

**DELLA PORTA, GUGLIELMO** (c.1490–1577), Italian sculptor, trained in his family's workshop in Milan. He subsequently worked in Genoa with his uncle Giovanni Giacomo della Porta (from c.1534) and then Rome (from c.1540), where he entered the papal service, succeeding SEBASTIANO DEL PIOMBO as *piombatore* (keeper of the papal seal) in 1547. His principal commission was the tomb of Pope PAUL III (d. 1549), over the design and location of which he quarrelled with MICHELANGELO; the tomb, which includes a seated effigy in bronze, now stands against the wall to the left of the high altar of St Peter's Basilica.

DBI; MDA.

**DELLA ROBBIA, ANDREA** (1435–1525), Italian decorative sculptor and potter, the nephew of Luca DELLA ROBBIA. The most famous of his reliefs is the set of roundels of babies on the façade of BRUNELLESCHI's Ospedale degli Innocenti (1463–6) in Florence.

DBI; MDA.

**DELLA ROBBIA, GIROLAMO** (1488–1566), Italian sculptor and potter, the son of Andrea DELLA ROBBIA. He was trained in the family workshop in Florence and in 1527 moved to Paris, where he worked from 1529 on pictorial tiles for the Château de Madrid; fragments of the tiles survive in the Musée de Sèvres.

DBI; MDA s.v. Robbia, della (4) Girolamo (Domenico) della Robbia.

**DELLA ROBBIA, LUCA** (1399–1482), Italian sculptor, trained in the workshop of Florence Cathedral, for which he carved a marble cantoria (singing gallery) that now hangs in the Museo dell'Opera del Duomo opposite a similar cantoria by DONATELLO; the ten relief panels of Luca's cantoria depict angelic child musicians.

Luca was the first important artist to use a ceramic medium for sculpture; he invented 'glazed TERRACOTTA' which was impervious to damp and so could be used in outdoor architectural settings. His surviving reliefs include *The Resurrection* (1442–5) and *The Assumption of Jesus* (1446–51) in lunettes above the sacristy doors of the cathedral, and *The Labours of the Months* (c.1460) in the *studiolo* of Piero de' MEDICI, which is now in the Victoria and Albert Museum.

Luca was the originator of a sub-genre of representations of the Virgin, a half-length *Madonna with Child* in glazed white terracotta set against a blue background. These sculptures were innovative not only in their use of terracotta but also in the sweetness of temperament with which Luca endowed his Madonnas.

Luca della Robbia's workshop passed to his nephew Andrea DELLA ROBBIA and then to Andrea's five sons, who included Girolamo DELLA ROBBIA. The della Robbia workshop is the eponym of a type of glazed terracotta relief, typically portraying a Virgin and Child in a circular frame formed like a wreath of leaves, fruit, and flowers.

DBI; MDA s.v. Robbia, della Luca; John Pope-Hennessy, *Luca della Robbia* (1980).

**DELLA ROVERE FAMILY**, the dynasty which ruled Urbino from 1508 to 1631; 'rovere' means 'oak tree' in Italian, and the family coat of arms depicted an oak. The family originally came from Savona (Liguria), and become prominent when Francesco della Rovere was elected pope as SIXTUS IV in 1471. Pope Sixtus quickly abjured his election oath by appointing his two young nephews, Pietro Riario and Giuliano della Rovere (later Pope JULIUS II), as cardinals and lavishing lucrative benefices on them. He invested another nephew, Giovanni della Rovere (1457–1501), as *signore* of Senigállia (on the Adriatic coast near Ancona), and so provided him with the rank requisite for his marriage to Giovanna, daughter of FEDERICO II DA MONTEFELTRO. Federico's successor GUIDOBALDO DA MONTEFELTRO had no heir, and devised the duchy to Francesco Maria della Rovere (1490–1538), the son of Giovanni and Giovanna.

Francesco Maria succeeded to the duchy in 1508, and so became the first of the della Rovere dukes of Urbino. He was succeeded by Guidobaldo II (ruled 1538–74), Francesco Maria II (ruled 1574–1621 and 1623–31), and Federico Ubaldo (1621–3).

Luca della Robbia, marble cantoria (singing gallery) carved for Florence Cathedral and now in the Museo dell'Opera del Duomo, Florence

**DELLA SCALA or Scaligeri FAMILY**, the dynasty that ruled VERONA and its territory from 1259, when Mastino I became *capitano*, until 1387, when the family was dislodged by Gian Galeazzo VISCONTI. After the death of Mastino in 1277, power passed to Alberto della Scala (d. 1301). Alberto had three sons who succeeded him as *signore*: Bartolomeo (d. 1304), who was confirmed as ruler by popular vote, Alboino (d. 1311), and Cangrande (1291–1329).

Cangrande (born Canfrancesco della Scala) had been joint ruler of Verona with his brother Alboino since 1308, but on his brother's death in 1311 he became sole lord of the city; his authority was given imperial sanction in the same year by his designation as imperial vicar. Like his brother Bartolomeo, Cangrande had given refuge to DANTE, and his reputation for courtliness, kindness, and hospitality is rooted in the respect accorded him in the writings of Dante and BOCCACCIO. Cangrande expanded the rule of his family by the conquest of Vicenza (1312), Padua (1328), Belluno and Feltre (1322), and Treviso (1329), and his imperial authority was further strengthened by his appointment as vicar of Mantua (1327).

The final years of the dynasty marked a decline in its fortunes. Mastino II (1308–51) built the family's fine equestrian tombs (*arche Scaglieri*) but lost all of its territories except Verona and Vicenza. Cangrande II (1332–59) built the castle (the Castelvecchio, now an art gallery) and the Ponte Scaligero (destroyed by bombs in 1945 and subsequently rebuilt), and was murdered by his brother Cansignorio (1340–75), who commissioned the Ponte Navi and the fountain in Piazza Erbe. The family was forced into exile by Gian Galeazzo Visconti in 1387, but refused to surrender their claims to Verona. Guglielmo della Scala (*c*.1350–1404), the illegitimate son of Cangrande II, was briefly restored in

1404, but died almost immediately. After the annexation of Verona by Venice in 1405, Brunoro della Scala (d. 1437) retained imperial protection, but was unable to recapture the city.

G. M. Varanini (ed.), *Gli Scaligeri, 1277–1389* (1988); *DBI* has entries s.v. Della Scala on Alberto, Alboino, Bartolomeo, Brunoro, Cangrande, Cangrande II, Cansignorio, Guglielmo, Mastino, and Mastino II.

**DELLA VIOLA, ALFONSO** (*c*.1508–*c*.1570), Italian composer and instrumentalist. He was employed by the ESTE family and became *maestro di cappella* in 1563. He wrote music for the classical pastoral plays performed at Ferrara and his madrigals include settings of ARIOSTO's verse.

**DELORME or de L'Orme, PHILIBERT** (1514–70), French architect, born in Lyon, the son of a master mason. He visited Rome as a young man (*c*.1533–6), and the influence of the Roman High Renaissance is apparent in the work that he executed after his return to France. Most of his buildings have been destroyed, but surviving examples of his work include the tomb of Francis I at Saint-Denis and parts of Château d'ANET, which he built for DIANE DE POITIERS; his frontispiece for the chateau is now in the École des Beaux Arts in Paris. The most complete survival is the Hôtel Bulliod in Lyon. At the end of his life Delorme began to build the Palace of the TUILERIES (never completed, and burnt in the Commune of 1871) for CATHERINE DE MÉDICIS.

Delorme was an important influence on the development of FRENCH ARCHITECTURE, partly through his buildings, but also through his writings, *Nouvelles Inventions* (1561) and *L'Architecture* (1567).

MDA s.v. L'Orme, Philibert de; Anthony Blunt, *Philibert de l'Orme* (1958); Philippe Potié, *Philibert de l'Orme: Figures de la pensée constructive* (1996); Catharine Coats, *Philibert de L'Orme, Protestantism and Architecture: Peculiarities of Style* (1997); Jean-Marie Pérouse de Montclos, *Philibert de l'Orme: Architecte du roi, 1514–1570* (2000).

**DEL TASSO FAMILY**, a large family of Florentine woodworkers of whom the most prominent was Domenico di Francesco del Tasso (1440–1508). Domenico completed the choir stalls in Perugia Cathedral after the death of GIULIANO DA MAIANO in 1490; it was he who made most of the delicate INTARSIA panels of flowers in vases. He also carved the seats in the Sala del Cambio in Perugia.

Giovan Battista di Marco del Tasso (1500–55), who was Domenico's nephew, trained in the studio of Benvenuto CELLINI in Rome (1519). His most important commission was the ceiling of the Biblioteca LAURENZIANA, which he carved together with Antonio Carota (1485–1568) to MICHELANGELO's design.

DBI s.v. Del Tasso, Domenico; MDA s.v. Tasso, Giovan Battista di Marco del.

**DEMANTIUS, JOHANNES CHRISTOPH** (1567–1643), German-Bohemian composer, poet, and writer on music. He studied at Wittenberg and was *Kantor* at Zittau, Saxony, and in Freiberg, for whose annual choral festival he wrote secular songs. He and Valentin HAUSSMANN imported ideas from Polish folk music into the German secular style. He wrote the first German alphabetical music dictionary.

**DE' MARCHI, FRANCESCO** (1504–76), Italian soldier and military engineer, born in Bologna. He became a specialist in ARTILLERY and FORTIFICATIONS, and constructed defences in Rome for Pope PAUL III and in Parma for the FARNESE family; he also built fortifications in Flanders for MARGARET OF PARMA. He was the author of *Della architectura militare*, an authoritative treatise on fortifications.

DBI.

**DENCK or Denk, HANS** (*c.*1500–1527), German humanist and Anabaptist leader. He was born near Munich and studied at Ingolstadt, where he was trained in the classical languages. He moved to Basel, where he fell under the influence of OECOLAMPADIUS. He settled in Nuremberg, but in January 1525 was forced to leave when OSIANDER accused him of heresy. Thereafter he became an itinerant preacher, travelling throughout southern Germany to promote the Anabaptist cause. He sought refuge in Basel in 1527 but was killed in November 1527 by the plague.

NDB s.v. Denk, Hans; A. Coutts, *Hans Denck, Humanist and Heretic* (1927); G. Godbach, *Hans Denck und Thomas Müntzer* (1969); Clarence Bauman, *The Spiritual Legacy of Hans Denck* (1991); *Selected Writings of Hans Denck*, ed. E. J. Furcha and F. L. Battles (1975).

**DENISOT DU MANS, NICOLAS,** or (pseudonym) **le comte d'Alsinois** (1515–59), French poet, the editor of the poetical *Tombeau* for MARGUERITE D'ANGOULÊME and the author of the *Cantique du premier avènement de Jésus-Christ* (1553), which attempts to adapt the quasi-pagan Neoplatonism of the PLÉIADE for a Christian poem. It is possible that Denisot was the author of the Christian and Neoplatonic prose work *L'Amant ressuscité de la mort d'Amour* (1558), which was published by a pseudonymous 'Théodose Valentinian'.

DBF; Margaret Harris, *A Study of Théodose Valentinian's L'Amant ressuscité de la mort d'Amour and its Possible Connections with Denisot du Mans* (1966).

**DENMARK or (Danish) Danmark.** Early modern Denmark included within its borders Scania (Swedish Skåne) and Blekinge, both of which were in what is now southern SWEDEN. In 1397, by the Union of Kalmar, Denmark became the senior partner in the 'triple bond' of Denmark, Sweden, and Norway. Sweden was a restless member of the union, and at the conclusion of a rebellion that lasted from 1448 to 1523 finally secured its independence (see SWEDEN). Norway was reduced to the level of a Danish province in 1536, and was destined to be subject to Danish rule until 1814, when it was ceded to Sweden by Denmark; in 1905 it became independent. From 1448 to 1863, when Denmark was ruled by members of the House of Oldenburg, many Danish kings were also dukes of Holstein.

The reigns of Kings ERIC, CHRISTIAN I, JOHN, and CHRISTIAN II were dominated by wars with the secessionists of Sweden. The Danish Reformation was implemented during the reigns of FREDERICK I and CHRISTIAN III. The long reign of FREDERICK II was marred by war with Sweden over Estonia (1563–70). In the late sixteenth and early seventeenth centuries the patronage of King CHRISTIAN IV made Denmark an important centre for music and architecture, but in 1611 another war with Sweden broke out, and in 1618 Denmark joined in the THIRTY YEARS WAR.

**DERING or Deering, RICHARD** (*c.*1580–1630), English composer and organist who, being Catholic, lived in Brussels (as did John BULL and Peter PHILIPS). He worked as a musician to Charles I shortly after being appointed organist to Queen Henrietta Maria in 1625. He wrote Anglican and Latin church music as well as some canzonettas and continuo madrigals.

**DERUTA POTTERIES**, a pottery centre in Umbria, active since the fourteenth century and in the sixteenth century one of the most important centres (together with Gubbio) of MAIOLICA finished with the iridescent metallic surfaces known as 'lustres'. Its finest and most distinctive pieces were made in the first half of the sixteenth century, typically apothecary jars or large dishes painted in blue with a gold lustre. In the second half of the sixteenth century the Deruta potteries introduced GROTESQUE motifs in imitation of Urbino pottery. Examples are collected in the Museo Regionale della Ceramica di Deruta.

L. De Mauri, *La maioliche di Deruta* (1924).

**DES AUTELS, GUILLAUME** (1529–81), French writer, the PLÉIADE poet to whom RONSARD dedicated his famous *Élégie* of 1560. His writings include a corpus of lyric poetry, commentaries on public affairs (notably the Conjuration d'AMBOISE), a treatise on orthography that attacked Louis MEIGRET's proposals for spelling reform (1548), and an imitation of RABELAIS (1574).

DBF.

**DESCHAMPS, EUSTACHE, or Eustache Morel** (c.1346–c.1406), French poet, born in Vertus (near Éparnay) and privately educated by Guillaume de Machaut, who may have been his uncle; he subsequently studied law at Orléans. He worked in the service of King Charles V and King Charles VI in a variety of posts, including *maître des eaux et forêts* in Champagne and Brie.

Deschamps's vast corpus of poetry includes more than 1,000 *ballades* (one of which is addressed to Geoffrey Chaucer) and almost 200 *rondeaux*; his experiences of foreign travel as a courtier and soldier are distilled in his poems, the best of which are laments about the discomforts of travel and the shortcomings of foreign food. He also wrote the first French treatise on poetry (*L'Art de ditier*, 1392), a vast misogynist satire on women (*Le Miroir de mariage*), and many plays (notably *La Farce de Maître Trubert et d'Antroignant* and *Dit des quatre offices de l'Hôtel du Roi*).

DBF.

**DESIDERIO DA SETTIGNANO** (1429/32–1464), Italian sculptor, born in Settignano (near Florence). His surviving work, which shows the pronounced influence of DONATELLO, includes the *Panciatichi Madonna* (now in the Bargello in Florence) and the tomb of Carlo MARSUPPINI in Santa Croce (Florence).

DBI; MDA; I. Cardellini, *Desiderio da Settignano* (1962).

**DES MASURES, LOUIS** (c.1515–1574), French Protestant playwright, born in Tournai. He left France on the accession of HENRI II in 1547 and converted to Protestantism while on a visit to Geneva c.1550. In 1563 Des Masures published a trilogy of biblical plays (*David combattant*, *David triomphant*, and *David fugitif*) that bridge the gap between the Catholic mystery plays and the revival of classical tragedy; they were also a modern parable, encouraging Huguenot perseverance in the face of persecution. His other works include a morality play (*Bergerie spirituelle*) and translations of Virgil and the Psalms.

DBF.

**DES PÉRIERS, BONAVENTURE** (c.1510–1544), French humanist, born in Arny-le-Duc (Burgundy) and raised by the abbot of Saint-Martin in Autun. As a young man he lived in Lyon, assisting OLIVÉTAN with his translation of the Bible (1533–4) and collaborating with Étienne DOLET on the *Commentarii linguae Latinae* (1536–8). He is said to have been *valet de chambre* and secretary to MARGUERITE D'ANGOULÊME and to have assisted her with the transcription of her *Heptaméron*. He was almost certainly the author of the anonymous *Cymbalum mundi* (1537), a set of four Lucianic dialogues that satirized Christianity and so were publicly burnt. He was hounded by the Church as an atheist, and died, apparently by

suicide, in 1544. A collection of his short prose narratives, *Nouvelles Récréations et joyeux devis*, was published posthumously in 1558.

DBF; Bernard Leblanc, *Bonaventure Des Périers* (1986).

**DESPORTES, PHILIPPE** (1546–1606), French poet, born in Chartres, the son of a wealthy merchant. He was ordained as a priest and as a young man travelled in Italy with his bishop. On returning to France in 1567 he entered the service of Henri, duke of Anjou, following him to Poland (1573–5) and returning to France on Henri's accession as King HENRI III. After the king's assassination, Desportes joined the CATHOLIC LEAGUE; he later shifted his allegiance to King HENRI IV.

Desportes's early collections of love poems, *Imitations d'Arioste* (1572) and *Amours* (1573), relaunched the vogue for Petrarchan love poetry at the court of Henri III. His later work is religious, and includes a verse translation of the Psalms (1591) that was championed by FRANÇOIS DE SALES and came to be regarded as the Catholic antidote to MAROT's version. His poetry was excoriated by MALHERBE in the marginal notes to the edition of the *Œuvres* published in 1600.

DBF; M. T. Marchand-Roques, *La Vie de Philippe Desportes* (1949); Jean Balsamo (ed.), *Philippe Desportes: Études* (2000).

**DEUTSCH, NIKLAS MANUEL.** See MANUEL, NIKLAS.

**DEVOTIO MODERNA** (Latin; 'modern devotion'), a spiritual revival which began in the Netherlands and at the end of the fourteenth century spread to the Upper Rhineland and to parts of France and Italy. The movement originated in the mysticism of Geert de GROOTE; its emphasis on the methodically contemplative life was famously articulated in the *De imitatione Christi* of THOMAS À KEMPIS. The principal vehicle of the Devotio Moderna amongst the laity was the schools of the BRETHREN OF THE COMMON LIFE; in the world of the monasteries, the comparable body was the WINDESHEIM CANONS.

R. R. Post, *The Modern Devotion* (1968); J. Andriessen et al. (eds.), *De doorwerking van de Moderne Devotie Windesheim 1387–1987* (1988).

**DIALOGUE**, a prose genre, originating in classical antiquity for purposes of instruction and entertainment, consisting of a conversation between two or more people. The interlocutors are sometimes fictional, but often have the names of real people (either living or dead) and articulate arguments consistent with the views of their flesh-and-blood originals. The genre was revived at the Renaissance in conscious imitaion of Plato and was soon represented in every literature in Europe.

David Marsh, *The Quattrocento Dialogue* (1980); Virginia Cox, *The Renaissance Dialogue* (1992).

**DIAMONDS.** See GEMS AND DIAMONDS.

**DIANE DE POITIERS** (1499–1566), duchess of Valentinois, born into a noble family in the Dauphiné. In 1515 she married Louis de Brézé, grand seneschal of Normandy, by whom she had two daughters; Louis died in 1533, and two years later Diane became the mistress of Prince Henri (later King HENRI

II of France); she was 36 and he was 16. Henri acceded to the throne in 1547, and throughout his reign Diane was a more prominent figure in the court than Queen CATHERINE DE MÉDICIS, who lived in relative obscurity. Henry gave her the chateau of CHENONCEAUX and the duchy of Valentinois.

After Henri's death in 1559 Diane was ousted from the court by Catherine de Médicis, who forced her to return the crown jewels and to exchange Chenonceaux for the Loire chateau of Chaumont. After a brief stay at Chaumont Diane retired to her chateau at Anet, also given to her by Henry II.

DBF; Françoise Bardon, *Diane de Poitiers et le mythe de Diane* (1963); Ivan Cloulas, *Diane de Poitiers* (1997).

**DIAS DE NOVAES, BARTOLOMEU** (*fl.* 1478, d. 1500), Portuguese navigator and the first European to round the Cape of Good Hope. He sailed along the African coast in 1478 (to Guinea) and 1481 (to the Gold Coast, now Ghana), and in 1487 sailed from Lisbon with a fleet of three ships, intent on sailing beyond the furthest point reached by Diogo CÃO (21 degrees 50 minutes south). He reached what is now known as Diaz Point (26 degrees 38 minutes south), and there erected a pillar, of which fragments still exist. From there the fleet was blown south by a storm, and so approached the southern coast of Africa from the southwest, landing at Bahia dos Vaqueiros (now Mossel Bay) on 3 February 1488. They then sailed east along the coast past Bahia de Roca (now Algoa Bay) to Rio do Ifante (now the Great Fish river), where they turned back. On the return voyage he named what is now the Cape peninsula Cabo Tormentoso, the Cape of Storms; it was subsequently renamed Cabo da Boa Esperança, the Cape of Good Hope. He returned to Lisbon in December 1488.

Dias supervised the construction and outfitting of VASCO DA GAMA's fleet and in 1497 sailed with it as far as the AZORES before being ordered to go to El Mina (in what is now Ghana). In 1500 he sailed with CABRAL, and so was present when Brazil was first sighted by Europeans on 22 April 1500; he was supposed to guide the fleet around the Cabo Tormentoso to India, but drowned when his ship was lost in a storm as it rounded the Cape.

DHP s.v. Dias, Bartholomeu.

**DÍAZ DEL CASTILLO, BERNAL** (1495/6–1584), Spanish soldier and historian, born in Medina del Campo; in 1514 he sailed to Central America with Pedrarias DÁVILA. He subsequently participated in the conquest of Mexico (1519) under the command of CORTÉS and later served in the expedition to Honduras (1524–6); he then settled in Guatemala. Irritated by the *Historia de las Indias* of Francesco LÓPEZ DE GÓMARA, Díaz embarked on his own 'true history' of the conquest (*Historia verdadera de la conquista de Nueva España*), which was published in 1632; the simplicity of its style and the directness of its observations ensured the popularity of Díaz's *Historia* for centuries.

DBEH; DHE; Alfonso Mendiola Mejía, *Bernal Díaz del Castillo: Verdad romanesca y verdad historiográfica* (1991); Carmelo Sáenz de Santa María, *Historia de un historia: La crónica de Bernal Díaz del Castillo* (1984).

**DÍAZ DE SOLÍS, JUAN** (1470–1516), Spanish explorer who sailed with Vicente Yáñez PINZÓN along the Atlantic coast of Central America (1507) and South America (1509). In 1515 FERDINAND V appointed him as chief pilot (*piloto mayor*) in succession to Amerigo VESPUCCI. In 1515 Diaz led an expedition of three ships down the coast of South America in search of a passage to the Pacific; he left Huelva on 8 October 1515, reached the estuary of Río de la Plata early in 1515, and then turned into the mouth of the Paraná, where he was killed by Indians whom he was attempting to capture.

**DIETTERLIN, WENDEL** (1550/1–1599), German architect and engraver. He was born in Pfullendorf, near Konstanz, and died in Strassburg. He was the author and engraver of *Architectura und Ausstheilung der V. Seuln* (1593–4), which contains designs for architectural decoration in the northern mannerist idiom at its most extreme; the designs include improbably interlaced strapwork and human figures that range from the erotic to the macabre. A second edition with additional plates was published in Nuremberg in 1598–9. Both editions were widely used by architects and decorative artists.

Wendel Dietterlin's son and namesake was a goldsmith who worked for a time in Lyon and published engraved designs for GROTESQUE decorations.

NDB; MDA.

**DIGGES, LEONARD** (*c.*1515–*c.*1559), English mathematician, born in Kent and probably educated at Oxford; he entered Lincoln's Inn in 1537. He was implicated in the rebellion of Sir Thomas WYATT in 1554 and sentenced to death, but was pardoned later that year. Digges belonged to the first generation that published mathematical books in English. His interest in practical mathematics led to his publication of manuals on surveying (*Tectonicon*, 1556) and on geometry (*Pantometria*, edited by his son Thomas, 1571).

DNB; DSB.

**DIGGES, THOMAS** (*c.*1546–1595), English mathematician, the eldest son of Leonard DIGGES. After his father's death (1559), Thomas's education was entrusted to John DEE. Thomas Digges's first publication was his father's *Pantometria* (1571), as an appendix to which he published his own treatise *A Mathematical Discourse of Geometrical Solids*. In response to the appearance of the New Star of 1572 Digges wrote about astronomy and astronomical observation in *Alae seu scalae mathematicae* (1573); he concluded that the New Star was indeed a celestial phenomenon rather than a nearby meteorological event. Digges seems to have been inclined to believe in the Copernican system rather than standard geocentric astronomy.

DNB; DSB.

**DIPLOMACY.** Until the fifteenth century, diplomacy was conducted by ambassadors (and sometimes their rulers) who travelled abroad for particular purposes and returned to their own countries when they had discharged the tasks associated with a particular journey. The idea of resident ambassadors had been adumbrated by the trade consuls established in the Levant by Florence, Genoa, and Venice, by semi-permanent representation of the Church by resident legates, and by the use of representatives to create military alliances (e.g. the League of CAMBRAI in 1508) and peace congresses (e.g. the Peace of CAMBRAI in 1529), but the notion of a permanent representation staffed by a succession of ambassadors first arose in the city-states of late fifteenth-century Italy, in the half-century between the signing of the Peace of LODI in 1454 and the outbreak of the WARS OF ITALY in 1494. During this period the states of Italy established diplomatic missions both with each other and with other European states that took an interest (sometimes a threatening interest) in Italian affairs. Diplomats were expected to keep their governments informed through regular correspondence and at the conclusion of their tours of duty to submit reports. In the case of Venice, these *relazioni* were read to the Senate and then filed; these Venetian diplomatic archives are one of the central resources of early modern European history.

King FERDINAND V of Spain was the first ruler of a nation-state to establish permanent legations: in the course of the 1490s he established embassies in Rome, Venice, London, Brussels, and in the imperial court. In 1519 King HENRY VIII of England established an embassy in Paris (his first ambassador was Thomas Boleyn, father of ANNE BOLEYN) and the following year he agreed to exchange resident ambassadors with the Emperor CHARLES V. In 1534 France sent its first resident ambassador to the Sublime PORTE; the Ottoman sultan did not reciprocate, because his policy, and that of his successors, was that the flow of ambassadors should be entirely in his direction.

By the mid-sixteenth century, the conventions of diplomatic etiquette, notably the reluctance to interfere in the domestic affairs of the host country, had become established, and the hierarchical distinction between ambassadors and agents was strengthened by the development of diplomatic privileges for ambassadors, which included *droit de chapelle* (the entitlement to practise the religion of their home country), *droit de quartier* (exemption from local civil and criminal jurisdiction), and *droit de l'hôtel* (exemption from local taxation and, at a later stage, extraterritoriality). One of the earliest examples of diplomatic immunity was the incident in 1584 in which Bernardino de MENDOZA, the Spanish ambassador in London, was implicated in a conspiracy to depose Queen ELIZABETH in favour of MARY, QUEEN OF SCOTS; he was expelled (much to the annoyance of PHILIP II) but not punished.

Garrett Mattingly, *Renaissance Diplomacy* (1955).

## DIPLOVATATIUS, THOMAS, or Diplovatatzes (1468–1541), Greek jurist and legal historian in Italy. Diplovatatius was a native of Corfu who studied law in Padua from 1486 to 1489 and became a magistrate in Pesaro. Book 9 of his treatise *De praestantia doctorum* is a valuable biographical account of jurists from Roman antiquity to his own time, entitled *Liber de claris jurisconsultis*.

*DBI* s.v. Diplovatazio, Tommaso.

**DISCOVERIES.** See EXPLORATION.

**DISSECTION.** See ANATOMY.

**DIVORCE.** In western CANON LAW marriage was deemed to be indissoluble. This injunction meant that in the Western Church divorce *a vinculo matrimonii* (from the bond of marriage) was forbidden unless there was a judicial decree of annulment. However, a form of judicial separation called divorce *a mensa et toro* (from table and bed; the Renaissance Latin form is *thoro*) was granted by ecclesiastical courts. The essential difference between these two forms of divorce was that divorce *a vinculo matrimonii* permitted remarriage, whereas divorce *a mensa et toro* did not. Canon law recognized six grounds for divorce *a mensa et toro*: sexual offences (adultery, sodomy, and bestiality), impotence, physical cruelty, religious disbelief, entering holy orders, and consanguinity; canon law also allowed three grounds on which divorce could be contested: equal guilt (*compensatio criminis*), such as both parties having committed adultery; condonation, when an offence was deemed to have been forgiven by virtue of the resumption of sexual relations; and connivance, when, for example, a husband was deemed to be the agent of his wife's infidelity.

The alternative to divorce was annulment, a procedure which allowed ecclesiastical courts to grant divorce *a vinculo matrimonii* on the grounds that the original marriage contract was void. The twelve grounds for nullification are memorably satirized in the penultimate scene of JONSON's *Epicene*. This process was famously used by Henry VIII to divorce Catherine of Aragon. In that case annulment was based on Henry's contention that the marriage had been illicit because Catherine had previously been married to his brother Arthur.

In Protestant countries divorce was more easily secured, though in England, until 1857, divorce could only be granted by Parliament, and so was not available to ordinary citizens. In Scotland, divorce on grounds of adultery has been permitted since 1560 and on grounds of malicious desertion since 1573 (in England desertion did not constitute grounds for divorce until the Act of 1857), and in both cases remarriage was permitted, though marriage to the other party in the adultery was forbidden. In other Protestant countries the grounds for divorce were extended: in Denmark, for example, absolute divorce was allowed on grounds of incest, transportation, flight from justice, and the contracting of leprosy, and in the Netherlands permanent imprisonment constituted grounds for divorce.

**DOCTORS' COMMONS**, the popular name for the College of Advocates founded in the 1490s by Richard Blodwell, dean of the arches (i.e. the judge of the provincial court of the archbishop of Canterbury). Members of the College practised either in ecclesiastical courts or in Admiralty courts. Admission was restricted to doctors of law, who had to be DCL of Oxford or LL D of Cambridge. The English universities taught CIVIL LAW rather than COMMON LAW, and the only areas of law in which civilians could practise were international MARITIME LAW and ecclesiastical law (which was founded on

CANON LAW), both of which were unusual in ENGLISH LAW in having their principles and practices rooted in Roman law. In 1567 the College acquired the site in Paternoster Row (on Knightrider Street, near St Paul's Cathedral) later known as Doctors' Commons, and there erected buildings for ecclesiastical and Admiralty courts and for the accommodation of judges. The College was incorporated in 1768 as 'The College of Doctors of Law exercent in the Ecclesiastical and Admiralty Courts' and was abolished in 1857.

G. D. Squibb, *Doctors' Commons* (1977); Daniel Coquillette, *The Civilian Writers of Doctors' Commons* (1988).

**DODOENS, JULIUS REMBERT, or Rembert van Joenckema** (1516–85), Flemish botanist and physician, the author of the *Cruydeboeck* (1554), an influential herbal which draws freely on the descriptions and illustrations of Leonhard FUCH's herbal but also adds a large number of new plants. The *Cruydeboeck* was translated into French by CLUSIUS (1557), whose version in turn became the basis of Henry Lyte's *New Herbal* (1578).

*BNB; DSB; NBW* iv.

**DOGE**, the Italian term for the heads of state of the republics of Genoa (1339–1797) and Venice (697–1797); the word *doge*, which is disyllabic in Italian, is monosyllabic in French and English. It derives from the Latin *dux*, which is normally translated as 'duke'; from the fourteenth century, the Latin title of the doge of Venice was *dux Venetiarum*. In other parts of Italy, *dux* evolved into *duca* (duke) and *duce* (leader): the former term is used for nobles such as the dukes of Florence and Milan; the latter can be used of military leaders, but was only used of a political leader by Mussolini.

The dogeship of Venice was hereditary until the eleventh century, and thereafter it became an elective office. In medieval Venice the doges exercised very considerable authority, but, as power passed to the MAGGIOR CONSIGLIO and other communal councils, the executive authority of the doge was diminished.

In Genoa the office remained in the domain of the nobility until 1339, when the introduction of the popular dogeship rendered the institution unstable. For centuries civil unrest, warring families, and private armies left the city without effective government. The dogeship was supposed to be permanent, but only four doges died in office, several were forced to abdicate on the day of their election and only one ruled for more than eight years. Stability awaited the reforms of Andrea DORIA, who instituted a system of biennial elections.

V. Lazzarini, 'I titoli dei doge di Venezia', *Archivio Veneto*, 5 (1903); R. Cessi, *Venezia ducale* (2 vols., 1963–5).

**DOLCE, LUDOVICO** (1508–68), Italian dramatist; little is known of his life. His plays include an original tragedy, *Mariamna* (1565), which presents the story of Herod and his wife Mariamne. He also wrote *Giocasta*, an adaptation of Euripides' *Phoenician Women* which was performed in English translation at Gray's Inn in 1566.

*DBI; OCIL;* P. F. Grenler, *Critics of the Italian World, 1530–1560: Anton Francesco Doni, Niccolò Franco, and Ortensio Lando* (1969).

**DOLET, ÉTIENNE** (1509–46), French printer and humanist scholar. He was born in Orléans and briefly studied law in Toulouse; as a young man he worked in Venice as secretary to the French ambassador. On returning to France he published his *Dialogus de imitatione Ciceroniana* (1535), which defended his fellow Ciceronians against the strictures of ERASMUS, and *Commentarii linguae Latinae* (1536–8), which enabled him to secure the patronage of King FRANCIS I. He established a printing press in Lyon, where he published his translations of the Psalms and of Platonic dialogues into French, editions of classical Latin literature, and the works of his friends RABELAIS and Clément MAROT.

Dolet was imprisoned on at least four occasions, once for killing a painter and three times as a suspected atheist; the charge of atheism arose from his sympathy for the SCEPTICISM of classical antiquity and from publications deemed to be heretical, including his *Cato christianus* (1542) and his edition of the pseudo-Platonic dialogues *Axiochus* (1544), which denied the immortality of the soul and advocated contempt for death. He was twice condemned to death (1536 and 1542) but on both occasions was spared by a royal pardon. On the third occasion he was tried by the theologians of the Sorbonne and burnt at the stake at Place Maubert in Paris in 1546.

*DBF;* Jacques Pineaux, *Étienne Dolet* (1986).

**DOMENICO DA CORTONA or Domenico Bernabei or Le Boccador** (c.1470–c.1549), Italian architect and woodcarver who moved to France in 1495 at the invitation of King CHARLES VIII. He was probably the designer of the wooden model (now known only from engravings) which may have formed the basis of the design of the Château de CHAMBORD. The model contains innovative features such as a double central staircase and a keep laid out as a Greek cross with a suite of apartments in each corner, an idea derived from Giuliano da SANGALLO which was to be very influential in France. Domenico's other work includes the design of the Hôtel de Ville in Paris (1532).

*DBI* s.v. Bernabei, Domenico; *MDA.*

**DOMENICO DA NOLA** (d. 1592), Italian composer and poet. He was a founder member of the Accademia dei Sereni and *maestro di capella* at SS Annunziata in Naples from 1563. Here he taught singing and wrote two books of *Canzoni villanesche* (1541), which were in turn arranged by several composers including Orlande de LASSUS and WILLAERT. His madrigal book of 1545 includes 22 settings of Petrarch.

**DOMENICO DI BARTOLO or Domenico Ghezzi** (c.1400–c.1445), Italian painter. He was born in Asciano (near Siena) and may have trained in the studio of Il SASSETTA in Siena, where he was admitted to the Guild of Painters in 1428. His principal surviving work is a series of five frescoes in the Ospedale della Santa Maria della Scala in Siena (1440–3). His Madonnas include a *Madonna with Five Angels* in the Pinacoteca in Siena. Domenico's depictions of contemporary dress and customs have considerable documentary value.

*DBI* s.v. Ghezzi, Domenico; *MDA.*

**DOMENICO VENEZIANO** (*fl. c.*1438–61), Italian painter, mostly active in Florence; little is known about his life, though his name may imply that he was Venetian by birth or origin. VASARI credited Domenico with the introduction of OIL PAINTING into Tuscany; this claim is mistaken, but Domenico did use an exceptional amount of linseed oil in his fresco cycle on *The Life of the Virgin* (1438–45) in the Church of Sant'Egidio in Florence; his assistants on this cycle (now lost) included PIERO DELLA FRANCESCA.

Domenico's two surviving works, both in egg tempera, are the *Carnesecchi Madonna* (*c.*1440, National Gallery, London) and the *St Lucy* altarpiece (*c.*1445), of which the *Madonna* is in the Uffizi and the panels from the predella are dispersed in the Gemäldegalerie in Berlin, the Fitzwilliam Museum in Cambridge, and the National Gallery in Washington. Attributions include a tondo of the *Adoration of the Magi* (*c.*1440, Gemäldegalerie, Berlin) and a portrait of *Matteo Olivieri* (National Gallery, Washington).

MDA; Helmut Wohl, *The Paintings of Domenico Veneziano* (1980).

**DOMINIS, MARCO ANTONIO DE** (1566–1624), Italian ecclesiastical polemicist in England. Following positions as professor of mathematics at Padua, and of rhetoric and logic at Brescia, in 1602 de Dominis was created archbishop of Spalato and primate of Dalmatia. In 1616 conflict arose between Venice and Rome, and he resigned his office and travelled to England. There he was welcomed by JAMES VI and received into the Church of England; in 1617 he was made dean of Windsor. The same year, he published *De republica ecclesiastica*, which attacked Rome and defended national churches. He felt threatened by negotiations for the marriage of the future Charles I and the Infanta Maria, sister of PHILIP III, and in 1622 left England. He sought a reconciliation with Rome and now turned his polemics against the Church of England. He was imprisoned by the Inquisition, however, and died in Rome.

DBI s.v. De Dominis; DNB.

**DONATÁRIOS**, the Portuguese term for the colonial system (and its administrators) introduced by the Portuguese crown in the fifteenth century for the governance of Madeira and the AZORES and then subsequently used in Brazil and Angola. Under the terms of the system the crown awarded to individuals the right to colonize and govern a designated area within a colonial possession. The *donatários* assumed powers which exceeded those of a chief magistrate, in that they could distribute land to individual settlers and were also responsible for the administration of justice.

**DONATELLO or Donato di Niccolò di Betto Bardi** (1386/7–1466), Italian sculptor, born in Florence; his training included a period in the workshop of GHIBERTI (1404–7), so he may have contributed to the bronze baptistery north doors. His early work includes a series of marble statues for niches in the façade of Florence Cathedral (*St John the Evangelist*, 1408, now in the Museo dell'Opera del Duomo) and in Orsanmichele (*St Mark*, 1411–13, *in situ*, and *St George*, *c.*1415, now in the Bargello). Between 1415 and 1436 he made four

**Donatello**, *Judith and Holofernes*, a bronze statue now in the Palazzo Vecchio in Florence

**Donatello,** *David* (1430–2), a bronze statue now in the Bargello in Florence

statues of prophets for the campanile of the cathedral (now in the Museo dell'Opera del Duomo). His shallow reliefs in marble include *St George and the Dragon* (c.1415, Bargello), *The Feast of Herod* (Musée des Beaux-Arts, Lille), and the *Ascension of Christ* (c.1425, Victoria and Albert Museum).

Donatello's bronzes include *St Louis of Toulouse* (c.1418–22), made for Orsanmichele and now in the refectory of Santa Croce, the effigy of the antipope JOHN XXIII for the baptistery (c.1424), on which he collaborated with MICHELOZZO, and several gilt-bronze statuettes for the font of Siena Cathedral, on which he collaborated with JACOPO DELLA QUERCIA and Ghiberti. His finest bronze, a statue of *David* (1430–2), was commissioned to stand in the courtyard of the Palazzo Medici and is now in the Bargello; this celebrated statue was the first life-size nude statue of the Renaissance.

From 1443 to 1453 Donatello lived in Padua, where he worked primarily in bronze. His greatest Paduan work was the EQUESTRIAN STATUE of the *condottiere* GATTAMELATA, which now stands outside the Basilica del Santo. His other important commission in Padua was the group of 22 bronze reliefs, seven bronze figures (including the bronze crucifix), and a stone *Entombment* for the high altar of the Basilica.

Donatello returned to Tuscany in 1453, and thereafter worked in Florence and Siena. His three most important statues from this period, all intensely dramatic, were a bronze *John the Baptist* for Siena Cathedral, a bronze *Judith and Holofernes* for the garden of the Palazzo Medici (now in Palazzo Vecchio), and a wooden *St Mary Magdalene* (c.1456–60, Museo dell' Opera del Duomo). His final statues, commissioned by Cosimo de' MEDICI, were bronze narrative reliefs for the twin pulpits of the Church of San Lorenzo.

*DBI* s.v. Bardi, Donato; *MDA*; John Pope-Hennessy, *Donatello* (1993).

## DONATO or Donati, BALDASSARE (c.1525/30–1603), 

Venetian composer whose career centred on San Marco where, in 1590, he succeeded ZARLINO as *maestro di cappella*. He composed sacred and secular music, the popularity of which was demonstrated by numerous reprints, and by its inclusion in anthologies at home and abroad.

## DONEAU, HUGUES or (Latin) Hugo Donellus (1527–91), 

French humanist jurist and religious controversialist. He was a colleague and rival of CUJAS at Bourges, and also taught at Orléans and Heidelberg. He was a distinguished analyst of Roman legal texts, and wrote a systematic commentary on the JUSTINIAN *Corpus* (*Commentarii iuris civilis*).

*DBF*; Donellus, *Opera omnia* (12 vols., 1762–70).

## DONI, ANTON FRANCESCO (1513–74), 

Italian popular writer and satirist, born in Florence, the son of a scissors-maker; he entered the Servite Order and then travelled for many years in northern Italy, publishing some seventeen vernacular works in Venice; he boasted that he wrote in the printer's shop and that each page was printed as soon as he had filled it. Doni's best-known work is *I marmi* (1552), a collection of imaginary conversations said to have been overheard on the marble steps of the cathedral in Florence.

Doni also composed a utopian fiction, *I mondi* (1553), and a dystopian companion piece, *Gl'inferni* (1553). Doni was by temperament a dissenter, and his books are critical both of the world in which he lived and of the received wisdom of its intellectuals.

*DBI*; *OCIL*; P. F. Grendler, *Critics of the Italian World, 1530–1560: Anton Francesco Doni, Niccolò Franco, and Ortensio Lando* (1969).

## DONNE, JOHN (c.1572–1631), 

English poet and dean of St Paul's. Born into a Catholic family, Donne attended Oxford University, though his religion, which he was later to reject, barred him from taking a degree. In 1596, he joined the earl of ESSEX's attack on CÁDIZ and, the following year, RALEGH's pursuit of Spanish treasure ships off the Azores, before training in law and becoming an MP. By 1598 he had expressed his allegiance to Protestantism and became secretary to Sir Thomas Egerton, the lord keeper. A secret marriage in 1601 to Ann More, Egerton's niece, was discovered the following year; he was dismissed from service and he spent the next ten years in poverty, dependent on charity and the aid of friends. Many of his religious poems are the product of this period; he also occupied himself with religious pamphleteering. With the help of powerful patrons, Donne gradually re-established himself, and was ordained in 1615 on the advice of JAMES I; in 1621 he became dean of St Paul's, and gained fame for his preaching both there and at court. Donne is remembered both for the witty 'metaphysical' poetry of his youth, which combines wordplay, intellectual jesting, and passionate feeling, and for his religious writings: his *Sermons* are a record of a celebrated preacher, and his *Devotions* attest to a fervent, if not untroubled faith.

*DNB*; R. C. Bald, *John Donne: A Life* (1970); John Carey, *John Donne: Life, Mind and Art* (1981).

## DONOR PORTRAIT, 

a portrait depicting the giver of a work of art or architecture in company with holy figures (Jesus, the Virgin, or saints); the convention goes back at least as far as the sixth century. By the fourteenth century donors were inevitably portrayed kneeling in prayer, usually on a smaller scale than the sacred figures. The last of GIOTTO's 38 frescoes in the Arena Chapel (or Cappella della Scrovegni) in Padua (1303–6) portrays Enrico Scrovegni (who had built the chapel in expiation for his father's usury) kneeling before the *Last Judgement*; similarly, ALTICHIERO's frescoes in Sant'Anastasia in Verona depict the knights of the Cavalli family who had commissioned the murals and in Burgundy Claus SLUTER sculpted portraits of Philip the Bold and his duchess Margaret of Flanders on the porch of the Chartreuse de Champmol in Dijon.

In the fifteenth century donor portraits became more naturalistic, and donors became integrated into the compositions, as exemplified in the donors in MASACCIO's *Trinity* (Santa Maria Novella, Florence) and Jan van EYCK's Ghent altarpiece, and, later in the century, GOZZOLI's portraits of the MEDICI among the retinue accompanying the Magi to Jerusalem (in the chapel of the Medici-Riccardi Palace), Hugo van der GOES's portrayal of the Portinari family in the wings of the Portinari altarpiece (Uffizi), and GHIRLANDAIO's portraits of the Sassetti family in the Church of Santa Trinita in Florence.

By the earlier seventeenth century the donor portrait had all but disappeared: Rubens's *Ildefonso* altarpiece of 1630–2, now in the Kunsthistorisches Museum in Vienna, is the last great exemplar of the tradition. Thereafter the donor portrait has survived only in the self-consciously archaic iconography of stained glass.

**DORAT or Daurat, JEAN** (1508–88), French humanist scholar and poet. He taught from 1547 at the Collège de Coqueret (where his pupils included Jean-Antoine de BAÏF, Joachim DU BELLAY, and RONSARD) and from 1556 at the Collège Royal. His legendary erudition is widely attested, but Dorat's only published scholarly work is an annotated edition of the Greek text of Aeschylus' *Prometheus Unbound* (1548). He also wrote original poems in Latin (collected as *Poemata*, 1596) and French.

DBF; Henri Demay, *Jean Dorat* (1996).

**DORIA, ANDREA** (1466–1560), Genoese *condottiere* and admiral, born in Oneglia on 30 November 1466 into an ancient and noble Genoese family. As a young man Doria served as a member of the papal guard of Pope INNOCENT VIII and as a *condottiere* in the service of a series of Italian princes. In 1503 he fought in CORSICA in the service of Genoa, and thereafter established himself as a naval commander, searching the Mediterranean for BARBARY PIRATES and Ottoman galleys. In the WARS OF ITALY Doria initially worked as captain-general of the French forces of King FRANCIS I, in whose service he relieved (in 1524) the city of Marseille, which had been besieged by an imperial army, and helped to place Genoa under French control.

When King Francis gave commercial privileges to Savona instead of handing it back to Genoa, Doria changed sides and allied himself with the Emperor CHARLES V. In 1528 he drove the French from Genoa and established a new republican constitution under imperial protection. Thereafter he declined the dogeship but nonetheless became the stern ruler of Genoa, suppressing the FIESCHI CONSPIRACY in 1547. Doria continued to serve the emperor as a naval commander, and from 1553 to 1555 fought the French in Genoa; at the end of the campaign, by which time he was 89 years old, he retired to Palazzo DORIA PRINCIPE in Genoa, where he died on 25 November 1560, five days short of his ninety-fourth birthday.

DBI; I. Luzzati, *Andrea Doria* (1943).

**DORIA, GIAN ANDREA** (1539–1606), Genoese statesman and naval commander, the great-nephew and heir of Andrea DORIA. The elder Doria had maintained a policy of neutrality with respect to the factional disputes of Genoa, but on Andrea's death in 1560 Gian Andrea promptly declared himself for the old nobility, inviting Spain to intervene on their behalf. Andrea had handed over the command of his naval squadron to Gian Andrea in 1555, but the young commander failed to distinguish himself in war: he was unable to capture Djerba in 1560, and in 1571, when he commanded a squadron under JUAN DE AUSTRIA at the battle of LEPANTO, his perform-

ance was harshly judged by contemporaries and by later historians.

R. Bracco, *Il principe Gian Andrea Doria* (1960).

**DORIA PRINCIPE, PALAZZO, or Palazzo Doria Pamphili**, the Doria villa at Fassolo, outside the city walls of Genoa, so named to distinguish it from the Palazzo Doria Tursi (now the Palazzo Municipale) built in 1564 in the city centre.

The Palazzo Doria Principe was designed by Domenico Caranca for Andrea DORIA between 1521 and 1529. Pierino del Vaga, who had earlier assisted RAPHAEL with the decoration of the Vatican loggias, worked from 1527 until c.1540 on the frescoes and stuccoed decoration of the palace and its loggias. The gardens and the loggias on the main building were designed by Giovanni MONTORSOLI. The magnificent fireplace was the work of Giambattista CASTELLO. The palace was badly damaged by bombing during the Second World War, but has been restored, as has the garden.

The garden consisted of three terraces descending to the sea, embellished with FOUNTAINS, PARTERRES, and pergolas and planted with orange trees, lemon trees, pomegranates, and beds of flowers; there were also pools, one of which was sufficiently large to be used by Admiral Doria to test models of his galleys. The garden climbing the hill behind the house was structured around linking staircases. In front of the house there was a level enclosed garden which contained what John Evelyn described in 1644 as a 'colossal Jupiter, under which is the sepulchre of a beloved dog'; the statue ('Gigante') and the tomb of the Emperor CHARLES V's dog Roland are all that survive of this garden. The view from the house over the garden was painted in 1561 by Jan Massys as the background to his picture of *Flora* (or *Venus Cythereia*?), which is now in the National Museum in Stockholm.

At the sea front there was a long terrace supported by marble columns, beside which there was an aviary supported by ironwork which Evelyn described as 'stupendous'. It was on this terrace or on a ship moored close to it that Andrea Doria entertained the Emperor Charles V and his son Philip (later PHILIP II of Spain), famously ordering that the three silver services from which they had eaten be hurled into the sea; prudence lay beneath the ostentation, for Admiral Doria had arranged for fishermen to catch the plates with their nets. The focal point of the sea-front garden was a large stucco statue of Neptune. This was replaced in 1599 by a marble Fountain of Neptune on a sea chariot pulled by horses by Taddeo Carlone and his brother Giuseppe; this fountain is all that survives of the lower terrace garden.

G. L. Gorse, 'The Villa of Andrea Doria in Genoa: Architecture, Gardens and Suburban Setting', *Journal of the Society of Architectural Historians*, 44 (1985).

**DORT, SYNOD OF** (1618–19), the second national convocation of the Dutch Reformed (i.e. Calvinist) Church, which met in Dordrecht (Dort) from 13 November 1618 to 9 May 1619 to contend with the issue of ARMINIANISM. The assembly, which enjoyed the support of MAURICE OF NASSAU, welcomed Calvinist delegates from other European countries, including England, the Palatinate, and the Swiss Confederation. Dutch

Arminians, who were known as REMONSTRANTS, were admitted on 6 December 1618 in a delegation led by Episcopius (the assumed name of Simon Bisschop, professor of theology at Leiden). On 23 April 1619 the Synod affirmed five sets of articles which asserted the doctrines of unconditional election to salvation, limited atonement (i.e. Jesus died for the elect, not for everyone), the total depravity of humankind, the irresistibility of GRACE, and the final perseverance of the saints. In its final session (the 154th) on 9 May 1619 the Synod agreed on 93 canonical rules and confirmed the authority of the BELGIC CONFESSION and the HEIDELBERG CATECHISM.

The endorsement of Calvinism as the official orthodoxy led to the persecution of Arminians, and in the aftermath of the Synod Jan van OLDENBARNEVELT was beheaded, Hugo GROTIUS was sentenced to life imprisonment, and some 200 Remonstrant clergy were deprived of their pulpits. The authority of the Synod in defining Calvinist orthodoxy extended beyond the Netherlands to England (the Westminster Assembly), France (the Huguenots), and America (the Puritan settlers).

**DOSIO or Dosi, GIOVANNI ANTONIO** (1533–1609), Italian architect and sculptor. He was born in Florence, but worked for many years in Rome, where in 1569 he published *Urbis Romae*, an illustrated treatise on the antiquities of Rome. From 1576 to 1590 he worked mostly in Florence, initially as an assistant to Bartolomeo AMMANATI and then as an independent architect; his Florentine buildings include Palazzo Giacomini-Larderel. He spent his last years in Naples, where he worked as an engineer at the royal court; his work in Naples included the tabernacles (1598) in the Brancaccio Chapel in the cathedral.

*DBI s.v. Dosi; MDA.*

**DOSSI, DOSSO, or Giovanni Luteri** (c.1490–1541/2), Italian painter sometimes described as the last painter of the Ferrarese School. He may have been born in Mantua or Ferrara; little is known of his early life, but, according to VASARI, Dossi was trained in the studio of Lorenzo COSTA. His early paintings include a sentimental *Nymph and Faun* (Pitti Palace, Florence). In 1512 Dossi was working with his brother Battista (d. 1548) on the decoration of the Ducal Palace in Mantua, but by 1517 both brothers had entered the service of the ESTE family in Ferrara, where they remained for the rest of their lives, working with ARIOSTO on court entertainments and triumphs as well as painting and designing tapestries.

Dosso Dossi's paintings, which often imitate the Venetian style of GIORGIONE, include a misnamed *Circe* in the Borghese Palace in Rome (which probably portrays Melissa, the sorceress in Ariosto's *Orlando furioso*), the *Poet and the Muse* (National Gallery, London), *St John the Baptist* (Pitti Palace, Florence), and *Circe and her Lovers in a Landscape* (National Gallery, Washington). His paintings characteristically use light to create an unworldly atmosphere; their most individualistic feature is a tendency to portray characters with parted lips.

*DBI s.v. Luteri; MDA s.v. Dossi (1) Dosso Dossi; Peter Humfrey, Dosso Dossi: Court Painter in Renaissance Ferrara (1998).*

**DOUAI**, a Flemish town (now in France) which in 1384 became part of the duchy of Burgundy and in 1477 passed with the rest of the Netherlands to the Spanish crown; Douai was ceded to France in 1713. In 1562 King PHILIP II of Spain founded a university in Douai and appointed English Catholics to its founding chairs. In 1568 William ALLEN founded the English College in Douai, which soon became an important centre of English Catholicism; there was also a Scottish College (founded 1580) and an English Benedictine house. The university and its colleges were suppressed in 1793, whereupon the English College migrated first to Crook Hall (now St Cuthbert's College, near Durham) and then to St Edmund's Old Hall (Ware); the Benedictine community also returned to England, and has since 1814 been accommodated at Downside.

The Douai Bible, which is also known as the Douai-Reims Bible, is an English Catholic translation of the Vulgate version of the BIBLE. The translation was undertaken by a group of exiled Oxford scholars, initially in Douai, and then in Reims (where the English College was located from 1578 to 1593); the New Testament was published in Reims in 1582 and the Old Testament in Douai in 1609–10.

**DOUAREN, FRANÇOIS.** See LE DOUAREN, FRANÇOIS.

**DOUBLE JUSTICE or (Latin)** *duplex iustitia*, a doctrine in the theology of GRACE which conceded some ground to LUTHER's doctrine of JUSTIFICATION by distinguishing between inherent justice (acquired through good works and sanctifying grace) and imputed justice (acquired by faith through the imputed justice of Christ). The doctrine was proposed by Johann GROPPER and later elaborated by Gasparo CONTARINI and Girolamo SERIPANDO and discussed at the Conference of REGENSBURG in 1541, but the COUNCIL OF TRENT declined either to support or to condemn it.

**DOUKAS or Ducas** (c.1400–after 1462), Byzantine historian. His baptismal name is not known, though historians sometimes assume that he was called Michael, which was his grandfather's name. Doukas first appears in the historical record in Nea Phokia (Italian Foglia, Turkish Foça), on the Bay of Smyrna. Nea Phokia was an important centre of the ALUM trade, and was administered by the Genoese until 1455; by 1421, Doukas was secretary to the chief magistrate (*podestà*), Giovanni Adorno. He subsequently moved to Lesbos, where he spent the rest of his life in the service of the ruling Gattilusio family, acting as both an envoy to the Ottoman sultan and as an historian of the last days of the Byzantine Empire, of which Lesbos had been an important outpost for centuries, until it was granted to the corsair Francesco Gattilusio in 1354.

The *History* of Doukas, which survives in the Greek text and in an early Italian translation, records the history of Byzantium from 1341 to 1462. The authority of his account increases as it reaches his own time, because he was present at some of the events that he chronicles, and his command of Greek, Italian, and Turkish gave him access to a wide range of sources. He characterized the Ottoman Sultan Mehmet

II as dissolute and cruel, and argued that the Ottoman conquests were the punishment inflicted by God for the immorality of Byzantium. The contention that God intervened in history to punish those who had displeased him was mitigated by an insistence on the importance of Fortune (Greek τύκη, Italian *Fortuna*) in the historical process.

> Doukas, *History*, ed. and trans. into Romanian as *Istoria Turco-Bizantină*, ed. V. Grecu (1958), trans. into English by H. Magoulias as *Decline and Fall of Byzantium to the Ottoman Turks* (1975).

**DOVIZI, BERNARDO, or Il Bibbiena** (1470–1520), Italian cardinal and playwright, born in Bibbiena (near Florence). He secured the patronage of Cardinal Giovanni de' Medici (later Pope LEO X) and followed him into exile in 1494. Dovizi worked tirelessly for his patron, and when Cardinal Giovanni was elected to the papacy, Dovizi was rewarded with a cardinal's hat and an appointment as Pope Leo's treasurer-general.

Bibbiena was a friend of RAPHAEL, who painted his portrait (now in the Pitti, though it may be a copy), and his character is sympathetically sketched in CASTIGLIONE's *Il cortegiano*. He wrote elegant *Lettere* and a *commedia erudita* entitled *La calandria*, which was first performed in Urbino in 1513 and often revived thereafter; it was this play that introduced to the stage the familiar motif of the woman disguised as a man.

> *DBI*; *OCIL*; R. Andrews, *Scripts and Scenarios: The Performance of Comedy in Renaissance Italy* (1993); G. L. Moncallero, *Il cardinale Bernardo Dovizi da Bibbiena umanistia e diplomatico* (1953).

**DOWLAND, JOHN** (1563–1626), English composer and lutenist. Repeatedly passed over in royal circles, Dowland worked in Paris, Wolfenbüttel, and Denmark, where he was in the service of CHRISTIAN IV. In 1604 he dedicated his *Lachrimae or Seven Tears* to Christian's sister Anne, the new queen of England. He received patronage from Theophilus, Lord Howard of Walden, whose father was lord chamberlain; in 1612, thanks to the creation of a new post, Dowland joined four other lutenists at court.

**DÓZSA, GYÖRGY** (1470–1514), Hungarian peasant leader, born into a prominent SZEKLER family. He became a professional soldier, and in 1514 was appointed by Cardinal Tamás Bakócz, the Hungarian chancellor, to lead a crusade against the Ottomans. Thousands of landless peasants, friars, parish priests, and students moved to regional centres to join Dózsa's armies. These *Kuruczok* (a corruption of *Cruciati*) soon began to protest about the lack of provisions for their volunteer armies. As the harvest approached the landlords insisted that the soldiers return to their fields, and when they declined to do so the landlords began to mistreat the soldiers' families. The soldiers quickly abandoned their intention to fight the Turks and instead rose against the landlords.

The rebellion spread through Hungary: hundreds of manor houses were burnt and thousands of landlords were cruelly murdered, sometimes by crucifixion. The papal bull ordering the crusade was revoked and the peasants were ordered to return to their homes, but to no avail: by this time the rebellion had become a revolution.

Dózsa had directed the pillaging and burning from his camp in Cegléd (south-east of Budapest), but when the king began to hire mercenaries from Venice, Bohemia, and the Holy Roman Emperor, Dózsa took the offensive. He captured the city and fortress of Szerb Csánad and publicly impaled the bishop and the castellan; he then captured Arad, where he tortured the lord treasurer to death. He was finally defeated at Temesvár (Romanian Timişoara) by the combined forces of János ZÁPOLYA and STEFAN BÁTORY. He was sentenced to be executed in a mock coronation: he was seated on a red-hot iron throne, forced to hold a burning sceptre, and crowned with a red-hot iron crown before being fed to his fellow rebels, who had been starved for the occasion.

MEL.

**DRAGONI, GIOVANNI ANDREA** (*c.*1540–1598), Italian composer, active in Rome. He was a pupil of PALESTRINA, whose influence is reflected in his style; he composed madrigals and secular and sacred works. He was *maestro di cappella* at San Giovanni in Laterano in Rome from 1576, and in 1594 was commissioned by Cardinal del Monte to assess the revisions that had been made to liturgical chant.

**DRAKE, SIR FRANCIS** (1545–96), English sailor. Chiefly remembered for his part in the defeat of the Spanish Armada (1588), Drake's career contributed to the establishment of English, and the decline of Spanish, naval power. Early expeditions in the 1560s and 1570s saw Drake, at times with his relation HAWKINS, dabbling in the slave trade between Africa and the Caribbean and skirmishing with Spanish treasure ships. He circumnavigated the globe in 1577–80 and was knighted by ELIZABETH on his return. Further raids on Spain, including the Armada, followed; he died at sea during an expedition to the West Indies.

*DNB*.

**DRAPERY.** The artistic depiction of draped clothing in classical antiquity was not recovered at the Renaissance, but rather had a continuous history from antiquity to the Renaissance. For centuries after the disappearance of the Greek chlamys and the Roman toga as articles of clothing, sculptors and painters continued to depict Jesus and the apostles in classical attire. In the INTERNATIONAL GOTHIC art of northern Europe, drapery was depicted with the soft folds characteristic of woollen fabrics.

The soft lines of late medieval drapery are evident in the sculptures of GHIBERTI, but many artists chose instead to stress the heaviness of the material and the angularity of folds characteristic of linen; the most extreme example of this reaction against the soft style was the work of Konrad WITZ, but it also finds clear echoes in Jan van EYCK, MASACCIO, and DONATELLO. In the late fifteenth and early sixteenth centuries the emphasis on angular folds became even more marked, both in northern Europe (Tilman RIEMENSCHNEIDER, Martin SCHONGAUER, and Veit STOSS) and in Italy (e.g. Cosimo TURA). The finest painter of drapery was RAPHAEL, who in his *School of Athens* (Stanza della Segnatura, Vatican) clothed his philosophers in robes of great dignity.

**DRAWING or (Italian) disegno**. Renaissance artists drew with chalk, charcoal, pens, and silverpoint. Drawing was usually undertaken as a preparation for a painting, sculpture, or building, but as early as the thirteenth century it also existed as a semi-autonomous form, as is evident in the pattern book of the French architect Villard d'Honnecourt (c.1235, Bibliothèque Nationale).

The earliest surviving fully autonomous drawings date from the fourteenth century. The first treatise to outline the techniques of drawing (and the first treatise on painting) was Cennino CENNINI's *Libro dell'arte*, which proclaimed drawing as the triumphal arch to painting. The largest surviving collections of Italian drawings are those by PISANELLO (now in the Louvre), Jacopo BELLINI (Louvre and British Museum), and LEONARDO DA VINCI (now mostly in Windsor Castle). Leonardo's drawings, which range over his vast field of artistic and scientific interests, include the earliest drawings to be executed in red chalk. RAPHAEL, the greatest draughtsman of the Renaissance, used red chalk for drawings such as his *Girl Holding a Mirror* (Louvre). MICHELANGELO, whose early pen drawings are often as close-hatched as an engraving, made presentation drawings for his friends and patrons, such as the *Jesus on the Cross* (British Museum) drawn for Vittoria COLONNA.

The principal centre of drawing was Tuscany, but in Venice artists such as Jacopo Bellini, Vittore CARPACCIO, and TINTORETTO were accomplished draughtsmen; the first centre outside Tuscany where drawing was taught was the Bologna academy of the CARRACCI family.

In northern Europe the tradition inaugurated by Jan van EYCK in drawings such as his portrait of *Cardinal Albergati* (1434, Gemäldegalerie, Dresden), which has colour notes in the margins, was continued by DÜRER, HOLBEIN, and Pieter BRUEGEL. Many of Dürer's drawings survive in the Albertina in Vienna; drawings in other collections include those in the margins of the Emperor MAXIMILIAN's prayer book (1513), which is now in the Bayerische Staatsbibliothek in Munich. Holbein followed Jan van Eyck in drawing portraits, but his preferred medium was coloured chalk rather than ink. Bruegel's drawings of LANDSCAPES are, like his paintings, minutely observed.

Francis Ames-Lewis, *Drawing in Early Renaissance Italy* (1981).

**DRAWING FRAME**, a rectangular frame fitted with vertical and horizontal wires or threads placed between the artist and his subject; the transference of the image to paper was sometimes further assisted by the use of paper squared in the same way as the drawing frame. LEONARDO described a drawing frame in one of his notebooks (and advocated the use of squared paper). DÜRER described and illustrated a drawing frame in his treatise on measurement (*Unterweisung der Messung*, 1525).

**DRAYTON, MICHAEL** (1563–1631), English poet, a prolific writer, details of whose personal life are obscure. His poems include SPENSERIAN eclogues, *Idea: The Shepherd's Garland* (1593), the sonnet sequence *Idea's Mirror* (1594, revised 1619), the fairy poem *Nimphidia*, and the topographical sequence *Poly-Olbion* (1612 and 1622), which celebrates the beauties of England in 30 songs.

*DNB.*

**DREBBEL, CORNELIS JACOBSZOON** (1572–1633), Dutch alchemist and hydraulic engineer, a native of Alkmaar who emigrated to England and secured the patronage of James I (JAMES VI), to whom he presented a machine for producing perpetual motion. He later visited the court of Rudolf II in Prague, and in 1620 was imprisoned when the city fell to the elector palatine. He was freed at the behest of King James (the elector's father-in-law) and returned to England. He contributed to plans to drain the Fens, and continued to produce (or claim credit for) inventions, including the thermometer and a submarine which he demonstrated in the Thames.

*DNB; DSB; NNBW vi.*

***DROIT DE SEIGNEUR** or (Latin) ius primae noctis* ('right of the first night'), the alleged right of a feudal lord in medieval or early modern Europe to spend the first night with the bride of any of his vassals. The right is a sixteenth-century myth, and is not enshrined in any legal system, but records of payments in lieu of the exercising of such a right do exist, which may indicate that the practice existed in the remote past. These payments were probably a form of feudal taxation analogous to the 'avail of marriage' (payable to a ward's guardian on her marriage) or a redemption payment to transfer the lord's right to select a bride for his vassal. The *seigneur* in the Latin phrase may originally have referred to God rather than the feudal lord: the Council of Carthage (398) required Christians to remain celibate on their wedding night, and there is some evidence that the first night was regarded as 'God's right'; this prohibition, exacerbated by the subsequent clerical extention of the period of abstention to three nights, may be the remote original of the legal myth.

Louis Veuillot, *Le Droit du seigneur au moyen âge* (1854).

**DRYPOINT**, a method of making or enhancing PRINTS in which a design is scratched on a copper plate with a sharply pointed tool (sometimes called an etching needle) which is held like a pen. The scoring of the plate creates a burr which retains ink when the plate is wiped with a cloth, and so the lines on the prints are slightly fuzzy; the darkness of these blurred lines varies with the pressure applied to the etching needle. Drypoint was sometimes used by ENGRAVERS to sketch their designs before applying the burin, and was also used in combination with other methods (usually engraving) to create special effects. Prints made exclusively by drypoint are relatively rare, but include DÜRER's *St Jerome in the Wilderness* (1512) and his *Agony in the Garden* (1515).

**DUARTE or (English exonym) Edward** (1391–1438), king of Portugal from 1433 to 1438, the eldest son of King JOHN I (João I) of Portugal and Queen Philippa of Lancaster (daughter of John of Gaunt); Duarte's brothers included Prince HENRY THE NAVIGATOR and Prince Fernando. In the course of his short reign he supported Portuguese navigators as they sailed ever further down the coast of AFRICA and sought to extend the Portuguese presence in North Africa by means of military force. In October 1437 Duarte led an attack on Tangiers, supported by Prince Henry and Prince Fernando. The attack was repulsed, and Prince Fernando was surrendered as a hostage to avoid the destruction of the Portuguese army. King Duarte died less than a year later; Fernando, who became known as 'the Constant Prince' for his fortitude in captivity, died unransomed in 1443.

Duarte was the author of *Leal conselheiro*, a guide to the morality of kingship, and *Livro da ensinança de bem cavalgar toda sela*, a treatise on horsemanship. He was also a collector of manuscripts and the patron of the historian Fernão LOPES.

*DHP*; A. Soares Amora, *El-rei D. Duarte e o 'Leal conselheiro'* (1948).

## DU BARTAS, GUILLAUME DE SALLUSTE (1544–90),

French poet, soldier, and diplomat who studied law at Toulouse. After securing his doctorate in 1567, Du Bartas retired to his estate, where he wrote a series of Calvinist poems (notably *Judith*, *Uranie*, and *Le Triomphe de la foi*) which he published together with a treatise on Protestant poetry (*La Muse chrétienne*) in 1574. He subsequently wrote his two biblical epics, *La Première Semaine ou Création du monde* (1578) and the unfinished *Seconde Semaine ou Enfance du monde* (1584). The *Première Semaine*, which is written within the Christian tradition of hexameral poetry and the French Renaissance tradition of scientific poetry, was regularly reprinted and widely translated, and was an important influence on seventeenth-century European poetry.

Du Bartas became caught up in the WARS OF RELIGION, in which he fought for Henry of Navarre (later HENRI IV), for whom he undertook diplomatic missions in Scotland and Denmark. He died in battle with the CATHOLIC LEAGUE.

*DBF*; J. Dauphiné, *Guillaume Salluste du Bartas, poète scientifique* (1983); *La Sepmaine*, ed. Yvonne Bellenger (2 vols., 1981).

## DU BELLAY, GUILLAUME, SIEUR DE LANGEY (1491–

1543), French soldier and diplomat, born in the chateau of Glatigny (near Montmirail), the eldest of the six sons of Louis de Bellay-Langey; his younger brother was Jean DU BELLAY, who was to become a cardinal. Guillaume was taken prisoner at the battle of PAVIA (1525) and shared the captivity of King FRANCIS I. After his release he regularly travelled as a diplomat to England, Germany, Italy, and Spain; in England, which he visited on three missions in 1529–30, he negotiated the implementation of the Peace of CAMBRAI and also assisted with the divorce of HENRY VIII from CATHERINE OF ARAGON, obtaining through the influence of his brother Jean (then bishop of Paris) an opinion supporting Henry from the University of Paris (2 July 1530).

In the early 1530s Du Bellay continued to visit England, but was principally occupied with the need to unite the German princes against CHARLES V. In 1536 SAVOY was occupied by the French army, and Du Bellay served as governor of Turin (1537–9) and the whole of Piedmont (1540–2). He returned in France and died near Lyon on 9 January 1543; RABELAIS witnessed his death, of which he gave an account in *Pantagruel* (3. 21 and 4. 27).

Du Bellay was the author of *Ogdoades*, an unfinished treatise in the style of Livy on the rivalry between Francis I and Charles V.

*DBF*.

## DU BELLAY, JEAN (1498–1560), French cardinal and diplomat, born in the chateau of Glatigny (near Montmirail), one of the six sons of Louis de Bellay-Langey; his elder brother was Guillaume DU BELLAY, who was to become a distinguished soldier and diplomat. Jean entered the Church and successively became the first bishop of Bayonne (1526), bishop of Paris (1532), bishop of Limoges (1541), archbishop of Bordeaux (1544), and bishop of Le Mans (1546); he was created cardinal in 1535. In his parallel secular career he served King FRANCIS I as a diplomat in England (1527–34) and Rome (1534–6) and as the lieutenant-general in charge of preparing the defences of Paris against an imperial attack.

Du Bellay was an important patron of literature, humanist scholarship, and religious reform, supporting figures as various as Guillaume BUDÉ, Étienne DOLET, the neo-Latin poet Salmon Macrin (1490–1557), and RABELAIS (his doctor and secretary). After the death of King Francis in 1547 Du Bellay retired to Rome (taking with him his young cousin Joachim DU BELLAY), where in 1549 he received eight votes in the conclave that elected Pope JULIUS III. His Latin poems were printed by Robert Estienne (together with Macrin's *Odes*) in 1546.

*DBF*.

## DU BELLAY, JOACHIM (1522–60), French poet of the PLÉIADE, born into a noble family in Liré (Anjou) and educated at the Collège de Coqueret under DORAT. In the course of 1549 and 1550 Du Bellay published the first Petrarchan sonnet sequence in French (*L'Olive*), two collections of Horatian odes (*Vers lyrique* and *Recueil de poésie*), and an allegorical account of a battle between poetry and ignorance (*La Musagnœomachie*). Du Bellay set out the principles underlying his poetry in a theoretical treatise, *La Défence et illustration de la langue française* (1549), a response to SEBILLET's *Art poétique* (1548); in this treatise, which subsequently became the manifesto of the Pléiade, Du Bellay advocated the creation of a French literary language based on the imitation of the poetry of classical antiquity, a process he termed *innutritio*.

In 1550 Du Bellay became seriously ill, and in the course of the next two years lost most of his hearing and became prematurely aged. He recovered sufficiently to accompany his cousin Cardinal Jean DU BELLAY to Rome in April 1553. He returned to Paris in 1557, and the following year published four collections of poetry: *Poemata* (Latin verse), *Divers Jeux rustiques* (a satirical miscellany), and two sonnet sequences, *Antiquités de Rome* and *Les Regrets*. The fifteen allegorical sonnets of the *Songe* that follows the *Antiquités* (which consists of 32 sonnets) were translated by Edmund SPENSER as *The Visions of Bellay*. The 191 sonnets of *Les Regrets* contain an account of Du Bellay's illness, a lament for the decadence of the papal court, and a satirical account of Renaissance Rome.

*DBF*; G. H. Tucker, *The Poet's Odyssey: Joachim Du Bellay and the 'Antiquitez de Rome'* (1990).

**DU BELLAY, PIERRE** (*fl.* 1587), French lawyer, the first political theorist to publish a substantial exposition of the theory of the divine right of kings. He maintained in his *De l'autorité du roi* (1587) that temporal authority was created and conferred by God, and that the king, who was God's viceroy, was responsible only to God.

**DUBOIS, JACQUES**. See SYLVIUS, JACOBUS.

**DU BROEUCQ, JACQUES** (*c.*1505–1584), Flemish sculptor and architect. He was born near Mons and travelled as a young man to Italy, where he is believed on the basis of stylistic evidence to have studied the work of GHIBERTI, MICHELANGELO, and SANSOVINO. He returned to the Netherlands and in 1535 received a commission to undertake the carvings for the Cathedral of St Waltrudis in Mons; he worked in the cathedral until 1548, and in the late 1540s had as his pupil GIAMBOLOGNA. Most of his carvings were destroyed during the French Revolution, but much of the rood-screen survived the destruction. In 1545 he was appointed as an imperial painter to CHARLES V, and in this capacity designed and built for MARY OF HUNGARY (regent of the Netherlands and sister of Charles) the chateaus of Binche (15 kilometres (9 miles) east of Mons) and Mariemont (Hainaut) and the Castle of Marienbourg (Namur).

*BNB; MDA.*

**DUCA, GIACOMO DEL** (*c.*1520–1604), Sicilian architect and sculptor who worked as an assistant to MICHELANGELO on the tomb of Pope JULIUS II (1542) and on the Porta Pia (1562). His most important independent works in Rome are the Church of Santa Maria in Trivio (*c.*1575) and the cupola of Antonio da SANGALLO the Younger's Church of Santa Maria di Loreto. He returned to Messina in 1588, but most of his Sicilian buildings have been destroyed by earthquakes.

*MDA s.v. Duca (1) Giacomo del Duca; Sandro Benedetti, Giacomo del Duca e l'architettura del Cinquecento (1973).*

**DUCAEUS, FRONTO, or Fronton du Duc** (1559–1624), French patristic scholar. He entered the JESUIT Order in 1577 and in 1604 was appointed librarian of the College of Clermont in Paris. He specialized in the editing of the Greek fathers, including Chrysostom (12 vols., 1609–36), Gregory of Nyssa (2 vols., 1615), and Basil the Great (3 vols., 1618–38). He also wrote as a controversialist, refuting the doctrine of the EUCHARIST set out by the Huguenot Philippe DUPLESSIS-MORNAY.

*DBF s.v. Du Duc.*

**DUCAS or Doukas, DEMETRIUS** (*c.*1480–*c.*1527), Cretan Hellenist in Venice and Spain. Ducas was probably born in Candia (modern Herakleion), where he witnessed a will in 1500. By 1508 he was established as a printer-scholar in Venice, working with ALDUS MANUTIUS and Marcus MUSURUS; his editions for the Aldine Press include a collection of Greek treatises on rhetoric (*Rhetores Graeci*, 1508) and the first edition of PLUTARCH's *Moralia.* (1509).

The recession in Venice reduced to a trickle the production of books in Greek, and Ducas eventually left Venice. His whereabouts for the next few years are unknown, but by 1512 Ducas was holding a chair of Greek at the University of ALCALÁ, near Madrid. On 10 April 1514 Ducas inaugurated Greek printing in Spain with the publication of a volume of six Byzantine grammatical treatises, including works by CHALCONDYLES, CHRYSOLORAS, and GAZA; his second publication, which was printed later in the same year, was an edition of Musaeus' poem on Hero and Leander.

Ducas had come to Alcalá at the invitation of Cardinal Jiménez de CISNEROS, and quickly became involved in the COMPLUTENSIAN POLYGLOT; he was one of the five scholars responsible for the Greek text of the New Testament, and presumably also had a hand in the Septuagint.

Ducas seems to have resigned his chair in 1517, and he disappears from the historical record until October 1526, when his name appears on an edition of three Byzantine liturgies published in Rome. A few months later, in January 1527, he was described in a papal privilege as professor of Greek at the University of Rome. In common with many other scholars, he disappeared in the SACK OF ROME in May 1527.

D. Geanakoplos, *Greek Scholars in Venice* (1962), 223–55.

**DUCCIO DI BUONINSEGNA** (*fl.* 1278–1319), Italian painter active in Siena; little is known of his life. His early commissions include the *Rucellai Madonna* (1285, Uffizi) and a *Virgin in Majesty* for the Palazzo Pubblico in Siena (1302, now lost).

**Duccio**, *Madonna of the Franciscans*, in the Pinacoteca in Siena

His only surviving fully documented work (and the basis of all attributions) is an altarpiece of the *Virgin in Majesty* commissioned in 1308 for the high altar of Siena Cathedral; most of this *Maestà* is in the Museo dell' Opera del Duomo, but the predella panels depicting the life of Jesus and the Virgin Mary are dispersed in the National Galleries of London and Washington, the Frick Collection in New York, and the Kimbell Art Gallery, Fort Worth, Texas. The two most important paintings attributed to Duccio are the triptych of the *Virgin and Child with Saints* (National Gallery, London) and the tiny *Madonna of the Franciscans* (Pinacoteca, Siena).

Duccio's Madonnas are indebted to the Byzantine tradition of hieratic poses, but he softens the poses with naturalistic gestures: the infant of the *Madonna of the Franciscans* struggles in order to bless the three kneeling friars. Duccio was also an innovator in his handling of space, in that his figures are integrated with their surroundings. The most remarkable feature of his panels is the mastery of narrative, which was well established as a component of fresco cycles but had not previously been a pronounced feature of panel paintings.

DBI; MDA; Luciano Bellosi, *Duccio: The Maestà* (1999).

**DUCERCEAU or Du Cerceau FAMILY**, a family of French architects and engineers. Jacques Androuet the Elder (*c.*1515–1585) was an architect, decorator, engraver, and publisher. During his life he was famous as an engraver with a relish for decorative detail and fantastic ornament, but he is now valued chiefly for the images that his engravings supply of the buildings and gardens of sixteenth-century France, which he collected in the two volumes of his *Les Plus Excellents Bâtiments de France* (1576 and 1579). Ducerceau's *Livre d'architecture* (1539) was the first French textbook of architecture, and his *Second Livre d'architecture* (1561) contains designs of buildings and gardens in a mannerist idiom. His engravings include designs for the chateaus at Verneuil-sur-Avre and Charleval, east of Rouen; in both cases Ducerceau wilfully disregarded classical principles of composition and so incurred the obloquy of architectural historians who regard Mannerism as decadent.

Three of Jacques's sons followed him into the profession, and his daughter Julienne was the mother of Salomon de BROSSE. His son Baptiste (*c.*1545–1590) succeeded Pierre LESCOT as the architect responsible for the reconstruction of the LOUVRE, and built the Pont Neuf, the oldest surviving bridge in Paris, between 1578 and 1604. Jacques the Younger (1550–1614) was responsible for parts of the Louvre and the TUILERIES. Charles (d. 1600) is known to have worked on the chateau at Châtellerault. Baptiste's son Jean (*c.*1585–*c.*1649) designed the Hôtel Brentonvilliers (of which only a small part survives) on the Île Saint-Louis and the horseshoe staircase at FONTAINEBLEAU.

DBF s.v. Andronet du Cerceau (5: Jacques; 3: Baptiste; 4. Charles); MDA s.v. Du Cerceau (Jacques the Elder, Baptiste, Jacques the Younger, and Jean); H. von Geymüller, *Les Du Cerceau: Leur Vie et leur œuvre* (1887).

**DUFAY, GUILLAUME** (*c.*1400–1474), French composer whose early years were spent as a chorister at Cambrai Cathedral. In 1420 he was employed by Carlo Malatesta da Rimini, whom he would have met at the COUNCIL OF CONSTANCE (1414–18). He was also active in Bologna and Rome, where he was a papal chaplain. From the 1430s he worked alternately in the courts of Savoy and Burgundy, affected as they were by the schism resulting from the papal election in 1439. During the 1440s he was *maître des petits vicaires* at Cambrai, where he embarked on the task of revising the cathedral liturgical books and composing a new polyphonic repertoire. His final appointment as *magister capellae* at the Savoy chapel was almost a formality as he was, by then, a friend and adviser to the duke's family.

Dufay was an important and influential figure, composing prolifically and in a variety of genres, including masses (notably a *Missa L'Homme armé*), Magnificats, motets, antiphons, and hymns, as well as *ballades*, *rondeaux*, and *virelais*. He met BINCHOIS, Martin le Franc, OCKEGHEM, and TINCTORIS; following his death, lamentations in his memory were composed by BUSNOIS and Ockeghem.

**DUMONSTIER FAMILY**, a family of French portrait painters active in Rouen in the sixteenth and seventeenth centuries. Étienne Dumonstier the Elder (d. 1501) was an illuminator in the service of Cardinal Georges d'AMBOISE. His relationship to the painter and illuminator Jean Dumonstier (d. *c.*1535) is unknown. Jean's son Geoffrey Dumonstier (*c.*1510–1573) was an illuminator whose best-known work is the frontispiece to the *Registre du chartier de l'hospice général de Rouen* (Bibliothèque Municipale, Rouen); he also designed the tile pavements made by Masséot Abaquesne for the Château d'Écouen (now the Musée de la Renaissance). Geoffrey's sons Étienne Dumonstier the Younger (*c.*1540–1603) and Pierre Dumonstier the Elder (*c.*1545–1625) both made portrait drawings of members of the French court (including King HENRI IV, CATHERINE DE MÉDICIS, and MARGUERITE DE VALOIS), now in the Bibliothèque Nationale.

DBF; MDA.

**DUMOULIN, CHARLES, or (Latin) Carolus Molinaeus** (1500–66), French jurist and political theorist, known as the French Papinian (or the 'prince of jurists'). He practised as an advocate at the Parlement of Paris, but his sympathies for Calvinism made him liable to persecution, and so he left for Strassburg and then Besançon (both of which were then independent of France). During his exile he wrote *Commentaire sur l'édit du roi Henri II sur les petites dates* (1552), which was condemned by the Sorbonne. He returned to France in 1557 and wrote prolifically for the next few years. In 1564 he published *Conseil sur le fait du Concile de Trente*, which earned him the enmity of both Calvinists and Catholics and resulted in his being briefly imprisoned by the Parlement.

Dumoulin was an erudite and prolific jurist. He published a learned attack on FEUDAL LAW (*De feudis*, 1539), a Calvinist commentary on CANON LAW (*Commentarius in regulas iuris pontifici*, 1548), and a treatise on the law of surety (*Extricatio labyrinthi dividui et individui*, 1561). His most important works examine CUSTOMARY LAW: he published a commentary on the customary law of Paris (*Commentarii in consuetudines Parisiensis*, 1539), and his last book, published posthumously, was *Le Grand Coutumier du royaume de France et des Galles* (1567), a systematic presentation of French customary law. The account in *Le Grand Coutumier* of the principles that underlie customary law formed the basis of Robert Pothier's recasting of customary law in terms of Roman jurisprudence and so led ultimately to the French Civil Code of 1804.

> DBF s.v. 3. Dumoulin; Donald R. Kelley, *Foundations of Modern Historical Scholarship: Language, Law and History in the French Renaissance* (1970), 151–82.

**DUMOULIN, PIERRE** (1568–1658), French Protestant leader, born in the chateau at Buhy (near Nantes), where his parents were religious refugees. In 1588 Pierre became tutor to the young earl of Rutland, and lived in England until 1592, when he moved to a chair in philosophy and Greek at Leiden. From 1599 to 1620 he was minister of the Protestant church at Charenton, and from 1620 until his death minister and professor at Sedan. He was a prolific controversialist, and published more than 80 works. His son Peter Dumoulin the Younger (1601–84) was a prominent Anglican divine.

> DBF.

**DUNOIS, JEAN, COUNT OF LONGUEVILLE,** or Le **Bâtard d'Orléans** or (English) the **Bastard of Orléans** (*c.*1403–1468), French soldier, born in Paris, the illegitimate son of Duke Louis of Orléans (brother of King Charles VI) and Mariette d'Enghien, Mme de Canny. In 1421 he entered the service of the dauphin (later CHARLES VII). He commanded the defences of Orléans during the siege of 1429, which was lifted through the intervention of JOAN OF ARC. He later led the French army to a series of victories over the English (including the raising of the sieges of Chartres and Lagny) which culminated in the liberation of Paris on 13 April 1436. In 1439 he was ennobled as the count of Dunois.

In 1440 Dunois joined the revolt against King Charles known as the PRAGUERIE, but soon changed sides and resumed command of the royal army. In the 1440s he expelled the English from Normandy and Guienne (where the English had held Bordeaux for more than 300 years); in recognition of his services Dunois was created count of Longueville. After the accession of King LOUIS XI he joined the League of the PUBLIC WEAL, but was eventually reconciled to the king.

> DBF.

**DUNSTAPLE** or **Dunstable, JOHN** (*c.*1390–1453), English composer, mathematician, and astronomer. He was associated with a number of royal and noble households, notably those of Queen Joan and Humphrey, duke of Gloucester, whose links with Leonello d'ESTE might explain the amount of Dunstaple's music in an important contemporary Ferrarese manuscript. Described by TINCTORIS as 'primus inter pares', he was thought to have influenced several significant musical figures including DU FAY, BINCHOIS, OCKEGHEM, and BUSNOIS. His masses, Magnificats, motets, and carols are in what Martin le Franc described as 'a sweet new English style', where the interval of the third predominates.

**DU PÉRAC or Du Pérat, ÉTIENNE** (1525/35–1604), French architect and garden designer. He moved to Rome in 1550 and stayed for twenty years; the Italian form of his name was Stefano du Perac. His engravings of sixteenth-century Rome are valued not so much for their technical or artistic excellence as for the records that they provide of the ruins of antiquity (*I vestigi dell'antichità di Roma*, 1575), the contemporary architecture of Rome, the gardens at Tivoli (*Vues perspectives des jardins de Tivoli*, 1570), and especially the work of MICHELANGELO, including some of his unrealized plans. He returned to France in 1570, and in 1595 was appointed by HENRI IV as *architecte du roi*. In that capacity he painted the decoration in the bathroom at FONTAINEBLEAU and may have contributed to the design of its gardens; he also continued the work of Philbert DELORME at SAINT-GERMAIN-EN-LAYE, where he laid out the terraces.

> DBF s.v. Duperac; MDA s.v. Dupérac.

**DUPERRON or Du Perron, JACQUES DAVY** (1556–1618), French cardinal and polemicist, born in Saint-Lô (Normandy), the son of a physician who became a Protestant and moved his family to Bern. Duperron received a humanist education in Bern, and in 1576 returned to France, where he abjured Protestantism and entered the service of King HENRI III; he subsequently became a supporter of HENRI IV. Duperron became a Catholic priest and reader to the king, in which capacity he was commissioned to write the eulogies for RONSARD and MARY, QUEEN OF SCOTS. He became bishop of Évreux in 1591, and three years later travelled to Rome to secure absolution for King Henri IV, who had converted to Catholicism. Duperron was created cardinal in 1604 and consecrated as archbishop of Sens in 1606.

Cardinal Duperron became a prominent polemicist, and in 1611–12 conducted a controversial correspondence with King JAMES I of England on the meaning of catholicity; this debate culminated in the posthumous publication of Duperron's *Réplique à la réponse du . . . roi de la Grande Bretagne* (1620). He also defended the Ultramontanist position against advocates of GALLICANISM; his 'Harangue' on his subject to the Estates-General (1615) provoked another response from King James, who argued that the powers of kings were divine but independent of the pope.

> DBF.

**DUPLESSIS-MORNAY or Du Plessis-Mornay, PHILIPPE** (1549–1623), Huguenot leader known as Philippe de Mornay and 'Le Pape des Huguenots', born in Normandy; after the death of his father in 1559, the family converted to Protestantism. He studied in Paris and then embarked on a tour of Europe; on his return he fought with the prince of CONDÉ in the second of the WARS OF RELIGION. He escaped from the ST BARTHOLOMEW'S DAY MASSACRE and fled to England, where he became a friend of Sir Philip SIDNEY. On returning to France he fought on the Protestant side; in 1576 he was wounded and captured, and after he was ransomed served as a diplomatic agent for Henry of Navarre (later HENRI IV of France) and WILLIAM OF ORANGE.

In 1578 Duplessis-Mornay published in London his *Traité de l'Église*, which was printed in English translation the following year. His *De la vérité de la religion chrétienne* was completed in 1579 and published in Antwerp in 1581 and in an English translation by Sir Philip SIDNEY in 1587. He may also have been the author of the VINDICIAE CONTRA TYRANNOS (1579). In 1589 he became governor of Saumur, where he built a Protestant church and in 1593 founded a Protestant academy.

In 1593 King Henri converted to Catholicism; Duplessis-Mornay was horrified, but carried on as a champion of Protestantism and helped to secure the Edict of NANTES (1598). He published a treatise on the EUCHARIST, *De l'institution, usage et doctrine du saint sacrement de l'eucharistie en l'Église ancienne* (1598), and was accused by Bishop DUPERRON of misquoting the church fathers. The dispute culminated in a public debate held in the presence of the king at Fontainebleau on 4 May 1600; Duplessis-Mornay was defeated, though very few misquotations were identified. In 1611 Duplessis-Mornay published his *Mysterium iniquitatis seu historia papatus*, an attack on BARONIUS and BELLARMINO which was quickly translated into French and English. In 1621 Duplessis-Mornay was deprived of his governorship of Saumur by King Louis XIII and retired to his castle at La Fôret sur Sèvres (Poitou).

*DBF*; R. Patry, *Philippe du Plessis-Mornay* (1933).

**DUPRAT or Du Prat, ANTOINE** (1463–1535), French cardinal, jurist, and statesman, born in Issoire. He trained as a lawyer, and in 1507 became the first president of the Parlement of Paris. He was employed by LOUISE OF SAVOY as an adviser. On his succession, King FRANCIS I appointed Duprat as his chancellor. In 1516 Duprat negotiated the Concordat of BOLOGNA with Pope LEO X and after the meeting of the FIELD OF THE CLOTH OF GOLD (1520) engaged in unsuccessful negotiations with Cardinal WOLSEY. He played a prominent part in the regency of Louise of Savoy, working on her behalf against Charles, duke of BOURBON, and in 1532 overseeing the incorporation of Brittany into France.

Duprat's wife died in 1507, whereupon he took holy orders. In the course of the next twenty years he was consecrated as bishop of Valence, Die, Meaux, and Albi and as archbishop of Sens (1525) and cardinal (1527).

*DBF*; François Albert-Buisson, *Le Chancelier Antoine Duprat* (1935).

**DUPRÉ, JEAN** (*fl.* 1481–8), French printer, active in Paris and Lyon from 1481. He was the first French printer to abjure editions of classical texts in favour of popular mass-produced books with copious illustrations. In 1488 he published the Arthurian *Roman des chevaliers de la table ronde* and the next year published *Legenda aurea*, a collection of some 200 saints' lives by the thirteenth-century hagiographer Jacobus de Voragine.

**DÜRER, ALBRECHT** (1471–1528), German painter and engraver, born on 21 May 1471 in Nuremberg, the son of a goldsmith; his earliest surviving self-portrait, a silverpoint drawing now in the Albertina in Vienna, was drawn in 1484, when Dürer was 13, which implies that he was trained in drawing by his father before entering the workshop of Michael WOLGEMUT in 1484. Dürer's godfather was the printer Anton KÖBERGER, and through him the young Dürer had access to the humanists of Nuremberg, particularly Koberger's close friend Willibald PIRKHEIMER.

In 1490 Dürer embarked on a journey to the western part of the German lands. His itinerary is not fully understood, but he certainly visited Colmar (in a vain attempt to visit Martin SCHONGAUER, who died before Dürer arrived), Basel (where he worked as a book illustrator, contributing woodcuts to Sebastian BRANT's *Narrenschiff*), and Strassburg (again working as an illustrator) and he may have visited the Netherlands. He returned to Nuremberg on 7 July 1494 and a few weeks later married Agnes Frey, a merchant's daughter. He travelled to Italy *c*.1495, and on this journey began to paint his innovative WATERCOLOURS, which were Europe's first important LANDSCAPE PAINTINGS. On returning to Germany, Dürer established a workshop in Nuremberg. As well as painting, including a *Self-Portrait* in 1500 and the Paumgärtner altarpiece in 1504 (both in the Alte Pinakothek, Munich), he also worked on WOODCUTS and ENGRAVINGS, notably his series on *The Apocalypse* (1498), *The Great Passion* (1510), and *The Life of the Virgin* (1510).

Dürer's interest in PERSPECTIVE seems to have developed in the early years of the sixteenth century: he discussed perspective with Jacopo de' BARBARI, who lived in Nuremberg from 1500 to 1503, and read VITRUVIUS' *De architectura*; engravings such as *Nemesis* (1501–3) and *The Nativity* (1504) reflect Dürer's experiments in perspective. In 1505–6 he undertook a second journey to Venice, where he painted his *Feast of the Rose-Garlands* (National Gallery, Prague), which reflects the influence of BELLINI.

In the years following his return to Nuremberg, Dürer painted several altarpieces, including *The Assumption of the Virgin* (1509; now lost, but the drawings survive in the Albertina in Vienna) and *The Adoration of the Trinity* (1511, Kunsthistorisches Museum, Vienna). He also produced two series of woodcuts, the *Great Passion* (1510) and the *Little Passion* (1511). In 1514 he produced two of the finest of Renaissance engravings, *Melancholia I* (the 'I' seems to be an allusion to the taxonomy of melancholy in Florentine Neoplatonism rather than the first number in a series) and *St Jerome in his Study*. He also began to experiment with DRYPOINT, and with this technique produced prints of *St Jerome* and *The Agony in the Garden* (1515).

In 1520–1 Dürer travelled with his wife to the Netherlands to seek a renewal of his imperial pension from CHARLES V. His journal, of which copies survive in the Bamberg Staatsarchiv and the Nuremberg Archiv, records his visual and verbal impressions of the artists and humanists that he met (who included ERASMUS, who praised him as 'the Apelles of black lines') and the news that he heard (including the kidnapping of LUTHER after the Diet of Worms, which Dürer thought the work of malefactors), and is the earliest of its kind to survive.

Dürer returned to Nuremberg on 12 July 1521, and in the years that followed, his work, with the exception of a small number of portraits, was mostly related to religious subjects, including a second engraved *Passion* series (1521–3) and two panels depicting the *Four Apostles* (Alte Pinakothek, Munich). He also wrote and designed three important theoretical treatises, one a book of instruction in measurement (*Unterweisung der Messung*, 1525), a second a treatise on FORTIFICATION (*Etliche Unterricht zu Befestigung der Stett, Schloss und Flecken*, 1527), and the third a four-book examination of human proportion (*Vier Bücher von menschlicher Proportion*, 1528). He died in Nuremberg on 6 April 1528.

*MDA; NDB.*

**DUTCH ARCHITECTURE.** The prevailing style of architecture in the northern Netherlands from the thirteenth to the fifteenth centuries is known as 'Dutch Gothic', which in ecclesiastical architecture is distinguished by a large nave, usually without side chapels, by a preference for brick rather than stone, and by a principled plainness with respect to decorative detail; the best example of Dutch Gothic is the Great Church in The Hague, and the most important exception to the eschewing of ornamentation is the Church of St John at 's-Hertogenbosch (Brabant), of which both interior and exterior are richly decorated. In the secular architecture of the thirteenth to fifteenth centuries there was less inhibition about decoration, notably in the façades of town halls (e.g. Middelburg, 1412–1599, destroyed in the Second World War and since rebuilt) and in the stepped gables of merchants' houses.

Renaissance architecture was introduced in the 1530s in buildings constructed by Italians, including the Bolognese architects Alessandro Pasqualini (who built the tower of Ijsselstein church, 1532–5) and Tommaso Vincidor (who built the courtyard of Breda Castle, on which work began in 1536). Dutch architects began to use Renaissance decorative motifs on the façades of town halls such as Nijmegen (*c.*1555) and The Hague (1564–5) and Pieter COECKE translated VITRUVIUS (1537) and SERLIO (1539) into Dutch. The interpenetration of indigenous Dutch structures and Italianate decoration produced a distinctive style of Dutch Renaissance architecture characterized by the adventurous mixture of stone and brick and the elaborate and varied development of the gable. The most important Dutch architect to use this style in secular buildings was Lieven de KEY. In Dutch Renaissance ecclesiastical architecture, interiors were adapted to the Protestant ideal of a focus on the pulpit rather than the altar, most successfully in the Amsterdam churches of Hendrick de KEYSER.

Dutch Renaissance buildings were also constructed in Denmark and along the Baltic as far as Danzig (now Polish Gdańsk).

**DUTCH ART.** In the late fourteenth century the dukes of Burgundy began to integrate the duchies, marquisates, and counties of the Netherlands into a single administrative unit, albeit one in which Frisian was spoken in the north, Dutch in the central provinces, and French in the south. The importance of Burgundian patronage, which extended to all parts of the Netherlands, meant that in the fifteenth century there was a common culture of Netherlandish art, within which there were regional centres. As north and south gradually

separated, distinctive Dutch and Flemish artistic cultures began to emerge. Population movements in the wake of the REVOLT OF THE NETHERLANDS made the north more Protestant and the south more Catholic, and by 1579, when the UNITED PROVINCES declared their independence, Dutch culture had become a distinctive part of Netherlandish culture.

The scale and quality of Dutch sculpture is difficult to judge; expatriates such as Claus SLUTER and Claux de WERVE produced fine work in Burgundy, but much of the work of sculptors from the northern Netherlands was destroyed in the iconoclasm of the late sixteenth century. In the sixteenth century Dutch painting achieved great distinction, and the fact that it seems to have been overshadowed by FLEMISH ART is exaggerated by the loss of so many northern paintings. It is nonetheless true that Flanders benefited from proximity to the Burgundian court, and many Dutch artists either moved to the south (e.g. Pieter AERTSEN and Gérard DAVID) or adopted a style influenced by painting in Antwerp (e.g. Cornelis ENGELBRECHTSZOON and LUCAS VAN LEIDEN). The link with Flanders was also maintained in Catholic Utrecht, where late sixteenth- and early seventeenth-century painters such as Abraham BLOEMART, Paulus MOREELSE, and Hendrick TERBRUGGHEN worked in a distinctively Flemish idiom.

In the late fifteenth century Haarlem was the home of artists such as Albert van OUWATER and GEERTGEN TOT SINT JANS, and early in the sixteenth century of Jan JOEST and Jan MOSTAERT. At the end of the sixteenth century Haarlem emerged as the most important centre of Dutch art; during this period the city's artists included Cornelis CORNELISZOON, Hendrik GOLTZIUS, and Karel van MANDER.

**DUTCH DRAMA.** In the fifteenth century the Netherlands, in common with many other parts of Europe, had a strong tradition of religious drama that took the form of mystery plays (on biblical subjects) and miracle plays. There was also a tradition of secular farces, which were performed by itinerant companies (*gesellen van den spele*), out of which grew the CHAMBERS OF RHETORIC. These chambers produced religious plays, notably *Elckerlijk* (*c.*1495), of which the English morality play *Everyman* is a version; the chambers also fostered secular drama, which reached its apogee in the comic plays of Gebrand BREDERO. His younger contemporary Theodore Rodenburg introduced the work of other European playwrights to Dutch audiences and readers; he adapted several plays by Lope de VEGA and in 1618 adapted the anonymous English play (possibly by TOURNEUR) *The Revenger's Tragedy*.

In 1617 Samuel COSTER founded the 'first Dutch academy', which was the first playhouse to be independent of the chambers of rhetoric; his own plays included both farces and tragedies. Dutch drama culminated in the seventeenth century with the 32 plays of Joost van den Vondel (1587–1679), the greatest of Dutch writers; in the same period Hebrew drama became established in Amsterdam.

**DUTCH EAST INDIA COMPANY.** On 20 March 1602 the Estates-General of the UNITED PROVINCES issued a charter creating the company known in Dutch as the Vereenigde

Oost-Indische Compagnie (or the Oostindische Vereenigde Maatschappij). The company was thereafter responsible for the regulation and protection of Dutch trade in the Indian Ocean and assumed an important role in the overseas theatres of the REVOLT OF THE NETHERLANDS.

Until Spain conquered Portugal in 1580, the principal carriers of African and Asian goods from Lisbon to northern Europe had been Dutch merchant vessels. The fall of Lisbon cost the Dutch their access to the Portuguese trade, and Dutch mariners therefore decided to trade directly with the Spice Islands (now Moluccas, Dutch Molukken, Indonesian Moluku). The possibility of an Arctic route was explored by Jan Huyghen van LINSCHOTEN, but his failure to establish a viable northern route led Dutch merchants to the alternative of the Cape route, which was the traditional preserve of the Portuguese and so brought them into conflict with Spain.

The first Dutch expedition to Asia sailed for the Cape of Good Hope on 2 April 1595 under the command of Cornelius de Houtman, a Dutch merchant who had formerly worked in Lisbon; Houtman secured a trade agreement with the sultan of Banten (now Bantam, in Java) and returned to the United Provinces with a rich cargo on 20 August 1597. The success of this voyage precipitated the creation of 'Van Verre' ('distant seas') companies which in the course of the next five years dispatched scores of ships to South and East Asia. The effect of what was sometimes violent competition between these companies was to raise the prices at which goods were bought in Asian markets and to depress the prices at which they were sold in domestic markets. The Estates-General therefore decided, largely at the instigation of Jan van OLDENBARNEVELT, to unite these companies in a Dutch East India Company which could regulate trade (and so stabilize prices), represent the government of the United Provinces, and, in its military capacity, prosecute the war with Spain. Capital was raised by national subscription in shares of 3,000 florins, which created an initial capital of some 6.5 million florins.

The governance of the company reflected the federal structure of the new republic, in that local boards were created in provincial capitals, the general directorate of 60 members was chosen by the local boards, the 'collegium' of seventeen members that managed the company was chosen from the general directorate on the basis of the proportion of joint stock raised by each branch, and the governors-general appointed from 1608 onwards were nominated by the collegium; dealings with the Estates-General were conducted through a committee of ten members in The Hague.

The charter granted to the company (renewable every 21 years) endowed it with huge powers. It was given a trading monopoly in Asia, from the Cape of Good Hope to Cape Horn, and within that huge region enjoyed full administrative, judicial, and legislative authority. The company was allowed to import goods into the United Provinces without paying any customs duty; in return, the Estates-General received rent from the company, and levied a tax of 3 per cent on its exports. In its governmental role, the company was empowered to negotiate trade agreements, to declare wars

and sue for peace, to establish colonies, and to coin money; in its military capacity, it was authorized to raise and maintain land armies and warships and to build and garrison forts.

The company established its operational headquarters in Batavia (now Jakarta, in Java). It established outposts of government in Amboina (Dutch and Indonesian Ambon), the Banda Islands (i.e. the islands in what is now the Banda Sea), the Cape of Good Hope, Ceylon (now Sri Lanka), Macassar (now Makasar, in the Celebes), Malacca (now in Malaysia), and Ternate (North Moluccas). Of these, only the Cape settlement grew into a permanent colony (established 1652), though most of Java was acquired by the company in succeeding centuries.

In the first half of the seventeenth century, the company expelled the English from the Spice Islands (Moluccas) and the Malay peninsula, leaving them only with a precarious toehold in Banten; similarly, the company ousted the Portuguese from Ceylon and Malacca. In England, the episode that caught the popular imagination was the trial and judicial execution of English merchants in Amboina in 1623: in 1654 Oliver Cromwell secured compensation (£300,000) from the company for the descendants of those who died in what had come to be known as the 'Amboina Massacre', and in 1673 John Dryden wrote his tragedy *Amboyna; or, The Cruelties of the Dutch to the English Merchants*.

In the eighteenth century the company ceased to earn its revenue from trade, instead levying taxes on its subjects. It was finally dissolved in 1798. The monumental history of the first century of the company, published in eight sumptuous folio volumes, is François Valentyn's *Beschryving van oud en nieu oost Indien* (Dordrecht, 1724).

C. R. Boxer, *Jan Compagnie: In War and Peace 1602–1799: A Short History of the Dutch East India Company* (1979).

**DUTCH GARDENS.** The Dutch Renaissance garden derives from three distinct traditions. First, the medieval Dutch garden, of which examples survive in attenuated form in Het Binnenhof in The Hague and at Rosendael in Gelderland, bequeathed the idea of outdoor rooms variously containing ornamental and fragrant flowers, pavilions with statues, lakes, orchards, vineyards, and menageries. Second, the example of Italian Renaissance gardens influenced the design of Dutch gardens. Third, the insistent piety that is a distinctive feature of the Dutch Renaissance is responsible for Christian images in Dutch gardens; this is a marked contrast to the paganism typical of ITALIAN GARDENS that prompted the remark of Queen Christina of Sweden, on seeing the gardens of the Villa FARNESE, that 'I dare not speak the name of Jesus lest I break the spell.'

A strong sense of spirituality pervades the ideal and emblematical garden of Erasmus' *Convivium religiosum* ('The Godly Feast', 1522). Erasmus proclaims the protector of his garden to be Jesus rather than Priapus, and at the entrance visitors encounter the FOUNTAIN of St Peter rather than pagan monsters. His square garden is bounded on three sides by a pillared gallery accommodating a library and an aviary. The walls of the gallery are covered with TROMPE-L'ŒIL frescoes depicting plants and animals. The garden is divided by a brook which drains a fountain and flows into a decorated stucco basin; the purpose of the water is to refresh and cleanse the soul. The ornamental and fragrant plants are laid out in beds, and each species is labelled with its name and virtues. Beyond the galleried garden there are two summer houses and a kitchen garden, bordered on one side by a meadow and on the other by an orchard containing trees not native to Europe and beehives.

All the elements of this garden of the godly mind were present in Dutch gardens of the sixteenth century. The gardens of Jan VREDEMAN DE VRIES, the most influential designer of the century, contained medieval and Erasmian elements laid out with a painterly attention to detail and form; he was the first landscape architect to present the garden as a work of art. The most important architectonic element in his gardens was the Erasmian gallery, which overlooked complementary structures containing fountains and PARTERRES. The galleries and parterres of early seventeenth-century gardens are illustrated in the engravings of Crispijn van de PASSE in *Hortus floridus* (1614).

The intricate parterres of Dutch gardens included a much higher proportion of rare foreign plants than did gardens elsewhere. This predilection for the exotic was encouraged by the establishment in Leiden of what was to become Europe's most important BOTANICAL GARDEN, not least because of the cultivation of tulips by CLUSIUS.

Spanish recognition of the independence of the northern provinces in 1609 exacerbated the cultural (and horticultural) distinctions between north and south, in that FLEMISH GARDENS perpetuated the mannerist tradition of the sixteenth century, whereas the Dutch gardens of the United Provinces championed classical principles of harmony and proportion as articulated by ALBERTI and VITRUVIUS. The finest embodiment of these principles was the Buitenhof, a garden in The Hague laid out c.1620 by the stadtholder, MAURICE OF NASSAU. This garden, which is portrayed in an engraving in Hendrick Hondius' *Institutio artis perspectivae* (The Hague, 1622), was designed as a double square containing two circles. The only vestige of the Italian mannerist tradition was the fantastic GROTTO (the first in the Netherlands) designed by Jacques de GHEYN the younger.

Maurice's younger brother Frederik Hendrik, who succeeded him as stadtholder in 1625, was an amateur architect and landscape designer of distinction. There were pronounced classical elements in the design of his garden at Noordeinde Palace in Het Hof (Princessetuin, 1610), and his classical garden at Honselaarsdijk, laid out on 8 hectares (20 acres) on a polder south of The Hague, inaugurated the Dutch tradition of the canal garden; this garden, which was destroyed in 1815, was the first large garden in northern Europe to be designed on Albertian principles of harmonic ratios.

Anna Bienfait, *Oude Hollandsche Tuinen* (1943); Erik de Jong, *Natuur en kunst: Nederlandse tuin- en landschapsarchitectuur 1650–1740* (1993); John Dixon Hunt (ed.), *The Dutch Garden in the Seventeenth Century* (1990).

**DUTCH LANGUAGE**, the principal language of the Netherlands (where FRISIAN and FRENCH are also spoken) and of Dutch possessions in southern Africa (where it evolved into Afrikaans), the West Indies (the Leeward Islands of Sint Maarten, St Eustatius, and Saba, the Lesser Antilles islands of Aruba, Curaçao, and Bonaire, and the mainland settlements of Dutch Guiana, later Surinam, and Stabroek, now Georgetown or Demerara, in Guyana), North America (New Amsterdam, later New York), India (Cochin, in Kerala, and Chinsura, in Bengal), Ceylon (now Sri Lanka), the Malay peninsula (Malacca), Java (Banten, now Bantam, and Batavia, now Jakarta), Macassar (now Makasar, in Sulawesi), and Zeelandia (now T'ain-nan, in Taiwan); the dialect of Dutch spoken in Flanders (including the French *département* of Nord as well as what is now Belgium) is known in English as 'Flemish' and in Flemish as 'Vlaams'. The importance of the Netherlands both within Europe and in international trade made Dutch a more important language than it is now, and in the early modern period it was acquired for purposes of trade by speakers of other languages.

Dutch is, together with Frisian and English, a Low German branch of the West Germanic languages. The resemblance of Dutch to German has caused some confusion in English speakers, in part because the English term 'Dutch' derives from the early modern Dutch word *duytsch* but resembles German *deutsch*. In early modern English, the word 'Dutch' was used to mean what would now be called 'German', and the language and people of the Netherlands were described as 'Low Dutch' or 'Low German'. After the creation of the UNITED PROVINCES in 1581, the English term 'Dutch' gradually came to be restricted to the language and people of the Netherlands (though the old sense survives in the American term 'Pennsylvania Dutch', which refers to a community from the Rhine Palatinate and Switzerland). English usage thus differs from Dutch and German, because modern Dutch *duits* and modern German *deutsch* refer to the language and people of Germany rather than those of the Netherlands and Friesland.

**DUTCH LAW**. Medieval law in the Netherlands was based on an early unwritten system of CUSTOMARY LAW which had later been formulated in the Salic law and the Frisian code of the eighth century. The various feudal dependencies of the Holy Roman Emperor in the Netherlands gradually developed independent legal systems. A unified system of Dutch law became possible with the establishment in 1446 of a central judicial council, the Groote Raad; a national court of appeal, the Parlement van Mechelen (French Parlement de Malines), first emerged in 1473. The RECEPTION of Roman law, CANON LAW, and FEUDAL LAW in Germany influenced legal theory and practice in the Netherlands, but never entirely displaced early Germanic law. The thirteenth-century *Sachsenspiegel* of Eike von Repgow, which gave Saxon law its distinctive character for 700 years, appeared in the fourteenth century in Dutch translation as the *Hollandscher Saksenspiegel* and, together with local formulations of customary law, formed a bulwark against the wholesale adoption of Roman

CIVIL LAW; the coexistence of these two systems eventually led to the emergence of the hybrid system known as Romano-Dutch law, which was implemented when the Netherlands became independent in 1648. Romano-Dutch law was the subject of important treatises by Nicolaus EVERARDUS, JOOS DAMHOUDER, Pierre Goudelin, and the German jurist Andreas von GAIL. The Flemish jurist Philip Wielant wrote on civil and criminal procedure (*Practijcke civile*, 1517; *Practijcke crimineele*, 1558), Petrus Peck on testaments and arrest (*Tractatus de testamentis conjugum*, 1556; *Tractatus de jure sistendi et manuum injectione*, 1564, both of which were translated into Dutch) and Paul van Merel ('Merula') on procedure (*Manier van procederen*, 1592). Romano-Dutch law received its classic formulation at the hands of Hugo GROTIUS in his *Inleidinge tot de Hollandsche Rechtsgeerheid* (1631). Romano-Dutch law remained at the heart of Dutch law till 1795, and is still the basis of the COMMON LAW system of South Africa, where it was introduced in 1652.

**DUTCH LITERATURE.** The courtly poets of the Netherlands in the Middle Ages first began to adapt Italian models when Dirk Potter van der LOO (*c*.1365–1428), a secretary at the court of the counts of Holland, travelled to Rome on a diplomatic embassy (1411–12) and wrote *Der minnen loep*, a long poem, loosely modelled on BOCCACCIO, in which he charts the amorous adventures of classical and biblical figures. This courtly poetry continued to be composed on a small scale, but the most important institutions for Dutch poetry and DUTCH DRAMA in the fifteenth and sixteenth centuries were the CHAMBERS OF RHETORIC rather than the courts.

The poetry and drama of the chambers excluded Renaissance influences until the mid-sixteenth century, when rhetoricians in Brabant and Flanders began to use classical models for Dutch poetry. Jean Baptista HOUWAERT wrote classical plays for the Brussels chamber, and also composed a long poem on earthly love, the *Pegasides Pleyn* ('Palace of Maidens', Antwerp, 1582–3). In the same period Cornelis van Ghistele of Antwerp translated portions of Horace, Terence, Ovid, and Virgil into Dutch, and the painter Karel van MANDER translated Homer's *Iliad* and Virgil's *Eclogues* from French into Dutch.

The first poet capable of rising above the rather pedestrian poetry of the chambers was Anna BIJNS, whose elegant and graceful Dutch poems in the verse form known as *refereinen* ('refrains') are the fountainhead of Dutch literature. In the next generation, the most important writers were the theologian Philipp van MARNIX and the humanist Dirck COORNHERT.

The upheaval of the REVOLT OF THE NETHERLANDS reduced literary activity in the southern Netherlands, and Flemish poets such as Jonker Jan Baptist van der NOOT moved abroad. In the northern Netherlands, however, Amsterdam became an important literary centre. The most important poets of sixteenth-century Amsterdam were Hendrick SPIEGEL and Roemer VISSCHER, whose two daughters, Anna Roemers Visscher and Maria Tesselschade Roemers Visscher, were to be numbered among the greatest poets of the seventeenth century.

**DU VAIR, GUILLAUME** (1556–1621), French STOIC philosopher and statesman who became immersed in the French WARS OF RELIGION, first on the side of the CATHOLIC LEAGUE and then on that of the POLITIQUES. He supported the Salic law of succession, according to which persons descended from a previous sovereign through a female are excluded from the succession, and so secured the patronage of HENRI IV.

Du Vair's writings on Stoic philosophy include an edition of the *Enchiridion* of Epictetus (1591), *De la constance et consolation dans les calamités publiques* (1597), *De la philosophie morale des stoïques* (1598), and *De la sainte philosophie* (1600). In these works Du Vair sought to formulate a Christian version of Stoicism in which the Christian god was deemed to provide the fortitude requisite for the enduring of suffering. He also wrote an influential rhetorical treatise, *Traité de l'éloquence française* (1594).

*DBF*; R. Radouant, *Guillaume du Vair, l'homme et l'orateur* (1907).

**DUVET, JEAN or Jehan, or The Master of the Unicorn or (French) Le Maître à la Licorne** (*c*.1485–*c*.1561), French goldsmith and copperplate engraver who worked in his native Langres. The name 'Master of the Unicorn' derives from a set of prints (engraved in the 1540s) on the subject of the hunting of the unicorn. Duvet's best-known work is a series of 24 etchings which depict *The Apocalypse* (1546–56), which were published together in 1561 in Lyon. His style seems untouched by the elegance valued by artists of the School of FONTAINEBLEAU, and instead articulates the emotional intensity associated with Italian Mannerism.

*DBF* s.v. Duvet, Jehan; *MDA*; Colin Eisler, *The Master of the Unicorn: The Life and Work of Jean Duvet* (1979).

# E

**EAST, MICHAEL** (*c*.1580–1648), English composer and nephew of Thomas EAST, who sang at Ely Cathedral and later moved to Lichfield. He received a Mus.B. from Cambridge in 1606. He contributed to *The* TRIUMPHS OF ORIANA (1601) and, in addition to madrigals, wrote anthems for voices and viols, as well as some purely instrumental consort music.

**EAST, THOMAS** (*c*.1550–1608), English music printer and publisher in London whose publications include *Musica transalpina* (1588 and 1597), and *The* TRIUMPHS OF ORIANA (1601), which contained music by his nephew Michael EAST. He also printed music by William BYRD, Thomas MORLEY, John DOWLAND, Francis PILKINGTON, and John DANIEL. *The Whole Book of Psalms, with their Wonted Tunes* (1592 and 1594) contained harmonizations of the English Metrical Psalter with settings by Giles FARNABY, Richard ALISON, Michael CAVENDISH, and Dowland; it was followed in 1598 by Orlande de LASSUS's *Novae cantiones*. Despite the uncertainties of the day, with a risky market and a number of printing monopolies in operation, East was optimistic and enterprising, even planning to export English music to Italy.

**EAST INDIA COMPANY**, The English term for the eight incorporated companies established in the seventeenth and eighteenth centuries for the purpose of trade with Asia. The first and most prominent companies were the DUTCH EAST INDIA COMPANY and the (English) Honourable EAST INDIA COMPANY. Companies were subsequently established by Austria, Denmark, France, Scotland, Spain (the Ostend Company), and Sweden.

**EAST INDIA COMPANY, THE HONOURABLE.** First formed in 1599 to challenge Dutch supremacy in the spice trade, the energies of the company focused mainly on the Indian subcontinent. The frequent revocation (and reissue) of the company's charter dogged its progress in the seventeenth century, although trading relations established then provided a foundation for its later prosperity, and such further developments as the acquisition of territory, in the eighteenth century and beyond.

**EBERLIN VON GÜNZBURG, JOHANN** (*c*.1470–1534), German popular reformer and translator of TACITUS, born in Günzburg (near Augsburg) and educated at the universities of Basel and Freiburg im Breisgau. He entered the Observant Franciscan ORDER, but in about 1520 became a supporter of Martin LUTHER. He was the author of *Fünfzehn Bundesgenossen* (Basel, 1521) which, in the demotic voices of its fifteen speakers, demanded social reforms to alleviate the hardship of the lower classes. They included the sketch of a Christian commonwealth, called Wolfaria (from German *Wohlfahrt*, 'welfare'), which echoed many of the concerns of contemporary humanists and reformers, even if orthodoxly Catholic, such as Thomas More's *Utopia*. He later spent time with Luther in Wittenberg, where his preaching lost its radical edge, and towards the end of his life became a preacher in Erfurt. He translated the *Germania* of Tacitus into German.

*NDB*; Geoffrey Dipple, *Antifraternalism and Anticlericalism: Johann Eberlin von Günzburg and the Campaign against the Friars* (1996); Steven Ozment, *The Reformation in the Cities* (1975).

**EBOLI, RUY GOMEZ DE SILVA, PRINCE OF or (Spanish) príncipe de** (1516–73), Spanish statesman, born into a noble Portuguese family; he entered the Spanish court as a royal page. He became a close friend of the future King PHILIP II, on whose accession to the throne in 1556 he became councillor of state. The 'Eboli faction' associated with his name was the group within the Spanish court that deplored the harsh policies of the duke of ALBA in the Netherlands; after the prince's death the leadership of the faction passed to his widow, the princess of EBOLI, and her lover Antonio PÉREZ.

*DHE.*

**EBOLI, ANA DE MENDOZA Y LA CERDA, PRINCESS OF or (Spanish) princesa de** (1540–92), leader of the Eboli faction at the Spanish court, and the daughter of the Spanish viceroy of Peru. In 1559 she married the prince of EBOLI, and after his death in 1573 became the lover of Antonio PÉREZ; King PHILIP II was also rumoured to have been her lover. The princess assumed (together with Pérez) the leadership of the 'Eboli faction' at court, but in 1579 Pérez was arrested and she was banished. The princess spent the final years of her life immured in the Ducal Palace at Pastrana, where she is said to have been allowed to appear at the window for one hour each day; this romantic legend is commemorated in the name of the square, which is known as the Plaza de la Hora.

José García Mercadal, *La princesa de Éboli* (1944).

**ECCARD, JOHANNES** (1553–1611), German composer who sang at the Weimar court and the Bavarian Hofkapelle in Munich, where he studied with Orlande de LASSUS. He moved to Königsberg and finally to Berlin, where he was *Kapellmeister* to Elector Joachim Friedrich of Brandenburg. His *Geistlicher Lieder auf den Choral* (1597) are simple polyphonic settings of Lutheran chorales with the melody in the top line, appropriate for congregational participation. More complex music is found in the chorale motets of his *Preussischen Festlieder* (1642 and 1644), where his debt to the teachings of Lassus becomes more apparent.

**ECK or Eckius, JOHANN** (1486–1543), German Catholic theologian, born Johann Maier (or Mayer) in Egg an der Günz (Swabia) on 13 November 1486, the son of a village bailiff (*Amtmann*), and educated at Rothenburg, Heidelberg, Tübingen (MA 1501), and Cologne. From 1502 to 1510 Eck was at the University of Freiburg (*doctor theologiae* 1510), where he studied theology, mathematics, geography, and law (under Ulrich ZASIUS) and taught philosophy.

In 1510 Eck was appointed professor of theology and vice-chancellor (*Prokanzler*) at the University of Ingolstadt, where he was to remain for 30 years. He participated in public disputations in Augsburg (1514, on the legitimacy of interest in investments), Bologna (against usury, 1515), Vienna (1516), and Leipzig (1519) and in the imperial diets in Augsburg (1530), HAGENAU, Worms, and REGENSBURG (1540–1). In the LEIPZIG DISPUTATION, his opponents were KARLSTADT and LUTHER.

Eck's confrontation with Luther made him a central figure in the struggle against the Lutheran heresy. In January 1520 Eck travelled to Rome to secure the means of suppressing the German heretics; there he was created a protonotary apostolic, and in July he returned to Germany bearing the papal bull EXSURGE DOMINE. In Germany he was attacked in the anonymous Latin satire *Eccius dedolatus* (1520), and was forced to flee from Saxony. On 18 February 1521 he appealed to the Emperor CHARLES V in *Epistola ad Carolum V*, asking him to crush the Lutherans by force.

Eck devoted the rest of his life to combating Protestantism, travelling back and forth between Germany and Rome. He eventually became frustrated by Luther's silence in the face of Eck's torrent of anti-Lutheran tracts, which included eight weighty volumes published between 1522 and 1526, and decided instead to shift his attack to the Zwinglians of Switzerland. In May and June 1526 he took part in a disputation along with Thomas MURNER against OECO-LAMPADIUS on the subject of the EUCHARIST, championing the Catholic doctrine of transubstantiation against the memorialism of the Zwinglians. In 1530 he was a prominent member of the group commanded by CHARLES V to draw up a refutation of the AUGSBURG CONFESSION. In 1540 he attended the Conference of WORMS and in 1541 participated in the Colloquy of REGENSBURG.

Eck was the principal combatant for the Catholic cause in Germany, and he brought to the fight the skills of an orator and the learning of a scholar. His principal anti-Lutheran tract, the *Enchiridion locorum communium adversus Lutherum* (1525), was published in 46 editions in 50 years, and his collected anti-Lutheran writings, *Opera contra Ludderum* (4 vols., 1530–5), testify to his relentless energy. His principal scholarly work is a treatise on the papacy, *De primata Petri* (1519). Anti-Catholic tracts routinely described Eck as drunken, greedy, sexually profligate, and self-promoting, and these charges have clung to his posthumous reputation. He died in Ingolstadt on 10 February 1543.

*NDB*; A. Seifert, *Logik zwischen Scholastik und Humanismus: Das Kommentarwerk Johann Ecks* (1978); E. Iserloh, *Johannes Eck (1486–1543): Scholastiker, Humanist, Kontroverstheologe* (1981).

*ÉCORCHEURS* (literally 'skinners'), armed bands led by local noblemen who between 1435 and 1444, when the English controlled much of Flanders and northern France, took advantage of the political instability to plunder throughout the region; the term implies that they 'skinned' their victims of all their possessions. The truce of 1444 between England and France put an end to their ravages, and thereafter they were absorbed into the forces of the French crown.

*EDITIO PRINCEPS* (plural *editiones principes*), the first printed edition of a classical text.

**EDUCATION.** The schools of fifteenth-century Europe include grammar schools, court schools, choir schools, and schools maintained by the guilds and by religious ORDERS. The medium of instruction was normally Latin, which was the language of scholarship and the Church, and also the international language of Europe. The syllabus centred on the seven LIBERAL ARTS, and there was a particular emphasis on RHETORIC; Latin literature was studied as a model for style. The purpose of education was to equip boys with the skills requisite for their contribution to the governing elite; there were no schools for girls until Ludovica TORELLI founded a Jesuit school in Milan in 1557.

Renaissance education was informed by the values of humanism. In about 1402 the early humanist Pietro Paolo VERGERIO wrote *De ingenuis moribus et liberalibus studiis*, a treatise on 'good manners and liberal studies' which proposed an integrated programme of education designed to develop a sound mind in a healthy body; this treatise was to be widely read for three centuries.

The first humanist schools were established by VITTORINO DA FELTRE and GUARINO DA VERONA. Vittorino established schools in Padua and Venice, but his most important school (which included a small number of young women among its pupils) was established in Mantua under the patronage of the GONZAGA family; the traditional syllabus was taught by new methods, including the use of arithmetical and geometrical games to teach mathematics. In 1429, Guarino, one of the early exponents of Greek, accepted the invitation of Niccolò d'Este, marquis of Ferrara, to act as tutor to his son; a school soon developed, and in the course of the next 30 years Ferrara developed a European reputation as a centre of education; it was this school that inaugurated the classical literary education that was to dominate European education for centuries. The court schools of Mantua and Ferrara were to be replicated all over Europe. Queen ISABELLA of Spain, for example, founded a school for young noblemen and appointed as its first headmaster the Italian humanist Pietro MARTIRE D'ANGHIERA.

In northern Europe the most influential school was the Deventer school run by the BRETHREN OF THE COMMON LIFE, who subsequently established schools throughout the Netherlands and Germany. The first humanist headmaster at Deventer was Alexander HEGIUS, and through his influence the schools introduced a syllabus that was to shape the thinking and values of influential humanists such as ERASMUS, NICHOLAS OF CUSA, and Rudolfus AGRICOLA. In England the schools of Deventer, Mantua, and Ferrara were important models for institutions such as St Paul's School in London (which was refounded in 1508 by John COLET, a friend of Erasmus).

The advent of the Reformation brought with it a new emphasis on vernaculars. In the Protestant areas of Germany education was reorganized by reformers such as BUGENHAGEN and MELANCHTHON; Latin remained central to the syllabus, but the written form of the German language was taught and German was adopted as the medium of religious instruction. The Counter-Reformation led to the creation of a new generation of Catholic schools, notably those established by the JESUITS. The syllabus (*ratio studiorum*) of the Jesuit schools shared with that of the German Protestant *gymnasium* an emphasis on morality, manners, and classical literature and a conviction that religious instruction was a central feature of education.

Educational theorists of the sixteenth century included Sir Thomas ELYOT (*The Book Named the Governor*, 1531), Roger ASCHAM (*The Schoolmaster*, 1570), and Juan Luís VIVES, whose writings on education include *De institutione feminae christianae*, a pioneering book on the education of women which was translated into Spanish (1528) and English (*The Instruction of a Christian Woman*, 1540).

On higher education, see UNIVERSITIES.

E. Garin, *L'educazione in Europe, 1400–1600* (1957); P. Grender, *Schooling in Renaissance Italy* (1989); A. T. Grafton and L. Jardine (eds.), *From Humanism to the Humanities: Education and the Liberal Arts in Fifteenth- and Sixteenth-Century Europe* (1986).

**EDWARD IV** (1442–83), king of England. Edward came to power when the rule of HENRY VI was challenged in 1461 by his father, the duke of York and heir to the throne; York was killed in battle but Edward seized the crown. Feuding between different factions within England, variously aided by Scottish and French allies, meant that his position was far from secure, and the rebellion of Warwick caused Edward to flee to the Netherlands in 1470. During his absence Henry was briefly restored to the throne, but Edward successfully invaded and regained power. The remainder of his reign was spent re-establishing stability in England; a war with France was planned but not pursued.
*DNB.*

**EDWARD V** (1470–83). Son of EDWARD IV, Edward was 12 years old when he succeeded to the throne on his father's death. He was however never to be crowned: he was captured by his uncle Gloucester (RICHARD III) and put in the Tower of London with his younger brother while Richard seized the throne. Despite SHAKESPEARE's dramatization of their death in *Richard III*, details of what must be assumed to be their murder are not known, although it may be that two skeletons found in the Tower grounds in 1674 constitute their remains.

**EDWARD VI** (1537–53), king of England. Son of JANE SEYMOUR, and HENRY VIII's much-sought male heir, Edward came to the throne in 1547, at the age of 9. His youth meant that protectors saw to the running of the kingdom during much of his reign, a period in which the Protestant character of Henry VIII's separated Church was consolidated through the repeal of the Six ARTICLES and the issue of the Book of COMMON PRAYER. NORTHUMBERLAND's plan, to which Edward complied, to divert the succession from MARY to Lady Jane GREY as Edward's health failed, was ultimately unsuccessful.
*DNB.*

**EDWARDS, RICHARD** (1524–66), English composer, dramatist, and poet who studied at Oxford and became a member of the Chapel Royal where, in 1561, he was appointed master to the children. About twenty of his poems appear in *The Paradise of Dainty Devices* (1576); the tragicomedy *Damon and Pythias* (1564) is the only surviving example of his work for theatre. He wrote songs for plays; some appear as keyboard arrangements in the Mulliner Book. One of these, 'When griping griefs', is quoted in SHAKESPEARE's *Romeo and Juliet*.

**EGAS FAMILY**, a family of architects of Flemish origin who worked in Toledo in the fifteenth and sixteenth centuries. The family came from Brussels, where their name may have been Coeman. The first member of the family to appear in the records of Toledo Cathedral was Hanequín de Bruselas (*fl.* 1448–70), who is sometimes erroneously called 'Hanequín de Egas'. Hanequín was responsible for the late Gothic Portal of the Lions (1452) in the south transept of the cathedral.

Hanequín's brother was Egas Cueman de Bruselas (*fl.* 1452, d. 1495); his early work includes the tomb of Alfonso de Velasco in Guadalupe (1467–8). He later assisted Juan GUAS on the carved screen around the sanctuary of Toledo Cathedral (1483–c.1491).

Antón Egas (*fl.* 1495, d. by 1532), son of Egas Cueman, succeeded his father as assistant master of the works at Toledo Cathedral in 1495. In 1510 he collaborated with Alfonso Rodriguez (d. 1513) on the plans for the new cathedral at Salamanca, and two years later he was included in the nine architects convened to discuss the plans for the construction of the cathedral.

Enrique Egas (*fl. c.*1480, d. 1534), son of Egas Cueman, worked with his brother Antón at Toledo Cathedral from about 1480. Enrique designed the royal hospital at Santiago de Compostela (1501–11); his cruciform design, which shows the influence of north Italian Renaissance architecture, was soon repeated in his designs for the royal hospitals in Toledo (Santa Cruz, 1504–14) and Granada (from 1511). In 1505 Enrique was appointed as master of the works at Granada, where he built the Chapel Royal (from 1506) and designed the cathedral in the Gothic style; construction began according to his plan in 1521, but in 1528 Enrique was succeeded by Diego de SILOÉ, who completed the building in the Renaissance style. Enrique's reputation meant that he was often consulted on the construction of cathedrals; there are records of his consultations on the cathedrals in Zaragoza (1505), Seville (1512 and 1525), Málaga (1528), and Segovia (1529).

MDA.

**EGIDIO DA VITERBO** (1469–1532), Italian cardinal and humanist. He joined the Augustinian Order in 1488 and eventually rose to become his Order's prior-general. He was subsequently employed as a papal diplomat by Popes JULIUS II and LEO X, and in 1517 was created cardinal. Egidio wrote learned theological works in Latin and essays and poetry in Italian.

DBI; OCIL.

**EGMONT, COUNT OF, or (Dutch) Lamoraal, Graaf van Egmont or (French) Lamoral, comte d'Egmont** (1522–68), soldier and Dutch nationalist. He was born into a noble family in Hainaut and became a soldier in the expedition to Algiers of the Emperor CHARLES V, who in 1553 appointed him prince of Gaveren. In 1554 he travelled to England as head of a delegation to secure the agreement of Queen MARY to marry Philip of Spain (later King PHILIP II), and subsequently attended the wedding ceremony in Winchester. He commanded imperial troops against France in the battle of SAINT-QUENTIN (1557) and the battle of Gravelines (1558), at which he captured the French commander, the Seigneur de THERMES.

In 1559 Egmont was appointed as stadtholder of Flanders and Artois and a member of the Council of State of MARGARET OF PARMA, regent of the Netherlands. His resistance to Spanish rule in the Netherlands led him, together with the count of HOORNE and WILLIAM OF ORANGE, to oppose the plan of King Philip to make the Netherlands a Spanish dependency. In 1564 he secured the withdrawal of Cardinal GRANVELLE from the Netherlands. He suequently travelled to Spain in what proved to be a vain attempt to persuade the king to yield more autonomy to the Low Countries, where there was widespread resistance to the adoption of the decrees of the COUNCIL OF TRENT and the institution of the Spanish INQUISITION.

In 1566 the opposition of the Netherlandish nobility to Spanish rule began to move towards open rebellion. Egmont equivocated, and although he attempted to contain influential Flemish Protestants, he declined to inaugurate a campaign of persecution and even showed some sympathy for the demands of the protesters. In September 1567 the duke of ALBA arrived from Spain and promptly instituted the COUNCIL

OF BLOOD with a view to restoring order. He arrested Egmont and Hoorne and imprisoned them in Ghent. On 5 June 1568 they were beheaded in Brussels.

Egmont and Hoorne died as Catholics loyal to King Philip, but their deaths nonetheless fuelled the rebellion, and in death Egmont became a martyr to Flemish freedom. His life became the subject of a tragedy by Goethe and of Beethoven's overture and incidental music to Goethe's play.

BNB; NNBW iii; NBW i; B. de Troeyer, Lamoraal van Egmont: Een critische studie over zijn rol in de Jaren 1559–1564 (1961); Herman van Nuffel, Lamoraal van Egmont in de geschiedenis, literatuur, beelende kunst en legende (1971).

**EGYPTOLOGY.** The study of ancient Egypt, for which the principal authorities were Plutarch (especially De Iside et Osiride), Herodotus, Iamblicus, Pliny, and Plotinus, was stimulated by the discovery in 1419 of a Greek manuscript containing the Hieroglyphica attributed to Horapollo, an emblematic treatise of the fifth century AD. Thereafter hieroglyphs became the principal stimulus of interest in ancient Egypt, though the emphasis was always on the mystical significance of the hieroglyphs rather than the investigation of the possibility that they represented a lost language; indeed, the idea that the hieroglyphs represented a language was not entertained until the seventeenth century, when Athanasius Kircher (1601/2–80) attempted to decipher hieroglyphs; there was no significant progress in this endeavour until the discovery of the Rosetta stone in 1799 and the subsequent deciphering of the language by Jean-François Champollion. Renaissance scholars interpreted each pictorial sign as an emblem, and interpreted these emblems through the Neoplatonic analysis of Plotinus.

CIRIACO D'ANCONA visited Egypt in 1435, and there transcribed a hieroglyphic inscription for Niccolò NICCOLI. The Hieroglyphica, which was welcomed by FICINO as a key document in the understanding of how the religion of the Egyptians related to the philosophy of Plato, was first printed by ALDUS in 1505 and first published in Latin translation in 1517. In 1556 VALERIANO published his Hieroglyphica, a compendious examination of ancient Egyptian writing based on ancient sources and on the study of inscriptions on obelisks in Rome. Valeriano also studied the bronze tablet known as the Bembine Table, which had been excavated in Rome in the 1520s and was in 1527 passed to Pietro BEMBO; an engraving of the hieroglyphs on the tablet was published in 1559, and a full analysis was published in 1605 by Lorenzo Pignorio in his 'exposition of the sacred symbols of the Egyptians on a very ancient bronze tablet' (Vetustissimae tabulae aenaea sacris Aegyptiorum simulachris coelatae accurata explicatio). Public interest was stimulated by the erection of Egyptian obelisks in sixteenth-century Rome: Domenico FONTANA placed one in St Peter's Square in 1586, and two years later another was erected in front of the Lateran Palace.

L. Volkmann, Bilderschriften der Renaissance: Hieroglyphik und Emblematik in ihren Beziehungen und Fortwirkungen (1923).

**EIGHT SAINTS, WAR OF THE, or (Italian) Guerra di Otto Santi**, a war between Florence (in alliance with Bernabò

VISCONTI) and the papacy waged between August 1375 and July 1378. The 'saints' were the eight Florentine officials who raised money by levying a war tax on church property, but in the traditional name of the conflict they are confused with the Eight of War (Otto della Guerra) who employed John HAWKWOOD and orchestrated the military operations of Florence.

The war was a struggle for the control of central Italy, and its effect was to break up the GUELF alliance: advocates of the war (notably Coluccio SALUTATI) were pitted against appeasers in the *Parte Guelfa*, and these divisions were exacerbated by Pope Gregory XI's excommunications and his placing of Florence under an interdict. The prospect of the fall of Rome prompted Pope Gregory to end the 70-year exile of the papacy in Avignon, and so led to the GREAT SCHISM. In Florence, war taxes and economic sanctions helped create the deprivation that led to the CIOMPI REVOLUTION. The war was concluded, in part through the mediation of CATHERINE OF SIENA, with the Peace of Tivoli in 1378; the treaty stipulated that the pope would lift the interdiction in return for a payment of 200,000 florins.

R. C. Trexler, *The Spiritual Power: Republican Florence under Interdict* (1974).

**ELBA or (Italian) Ilva**, the principal island in the Tuscan archipelago (which also includes Gorgona, Pianosa, Capraia, Montecristo, Giglio, and Giannutri), since antiquity an important source of iron ore; lack of fuel meant that smelting was carried out on the mainland. From the eleventh to the fourteenth centuries Elba belonged to Pisa, and in 1399 it became part of the lordship of Piondino, which was held by the APPIANO FAMILY. In 1548 Elba was ceded to Florence, and thereafter belonged to Spain (1596–1709), Naples (1709–1802), and France (1802–15). During Napoleon's exile on Elba (1814–15), the island and its neighbour Pianosa were constituted as a private Napoleonic principality.

When Florence acquired Elba in 1548, Cosimo de' MEDICI fortified the harbour and built the town, which he called Cosimopolis (modern Portoferraio). The Spanish fortress in Porte Longone (modern Porto Azzurro) was built in 1603 and is now used as a prison.

**ELCANO or Cano, JUAN SEBASTIÁN DEL** (1475–1526), Basque mariner, born in the province of Guipúzcoa on the Bay of Biscay. He was given the command of the *Vitoria*, one of the five ships in MAGELLAN's fleet. When Magellan was killed in the Philippines, Elcano assumed command of the expedition. He sailed on to the Moluccas and then returned around Africa to Spain; the only ship to survive the voyage was the *Vitoria*, which landed in Seville on 6 September 1522 with eighteen European survivors and four Indians. He was lauded as the first circumnavigator of the world and rewarded with a royal pension and the motto *primus circumdedisti me*. In 1526 Elcano embarked on another expedition to the Moluccas, but died at sea on 4 August.

DBEH; Mairin Mitchell, *Elcano: The First Circumnavigator* (1958); Victor Maria de Sola, *Juan Sebastián de Elcano: Ensayo biográfio* (1962).

**EL DORADO** (Spanish; 'the gilded man'), a legendary South American king or chief priest who was believed to cover himself in gold dust at an annual religious festival held near what is now Bogotá, in Colombia. The term was subsequently applied to a city of gold called Manoa or Omoa and to a fabled country in which gold and precious gems were to be found in abundance. The legend is first reported in the 1530s: in an expedition commanded by Diego de Ordáz (1480–c.1532), his lieutenant Martínez claimed to have survived a shipwreck and been taken to Omoa where he was entertained by El Dorado, and Sebastián de BELALCÁZAR described how the kings, covered in gold dust, would sacrifice themselves in a lake. In 1541 Gonzalo PIZARRO led the first of a series of Spanish expeditions up the Amazon to find the kingdom and in 1595 Sir Walter RALEGH led an English expedition to what is now Guyana; Ralegh, who described Manoa as a city on the fabled lake of Parimá (in what is now Brazil), published an account of his expedition in *Discovery of Guiana* (1596). El Dorado continued to appear on maps for centuries, and belief in its existence only ebbed away after Alexander von Humboldt's expedition to the Upper Orinoco in 1800. El Dorado's presence in literature includes an allusion in *Paradise Lost* 6. 411, two chapters (18 and 19) in Voltaire's *Candide*, and Edgar Allan Poe's poem 'Eldorado'.

DHE s.v. Dorado, El.

**ELEANOR OF TOLEDO** (1522–62), duchess of Florence, was the daughter of Pedro de TOLEDO, Spanish viceroy in Naples. In 1539 she married Duke Cosimo de' MEDICI. The marriage constituted an important military alliance, and also produced eight children. Eleanor was an important patron of artists and architects, notably BRONZINO.

DBI; OCIL.

**ELIZABETH I** (1533–1603), queen of England and Ireland. Daughter of HENRY VIII and ANNE BOLEYN, Elizabeth's long reign (from 1558 to 1603) is credited with the further consolidation of the Protestant Church in England, including the issue of the Thirty-Nine ARTICLES, after the divisive reign of Catholic MARY; the rise of English power at sea, through the talents of DRAKE and RALEGH; and, despite campaigns in Scotland and the threat of Spainish attack, manifested in the Armada, a period of relative stability, peacefulness, and prosperity. Advised by CECIL, caution characterized much of Elizabeth's dealings in the fraught, religiously charged politics of the period: she allowed the death of the Catholic MARY, QUEEN OF SCOTS, only when her presence in England provided a focus for dissent which threatened her own crown; she maintained advantageous relations with PHILIP of Spain well into the 1580s; and she intervened in Scottish politics only with reluctance. Caution did not eclipse strength of character, however: Elizabeth's rousing speeches to her troops are still remembered, and her decision not to marry, against pressure from all sides, reflects her care in protecting her own position. Literature and drama, including a cult of the 'Virgin Queen', flourished in her reign. She was succeeded by JAMES VI of Scotland.

DNB; Grove.

**ELSEVIR or Elzevir or Elsevier**, a family of Dutch printers and publishers. The firm was founded in Leiden in 1580 by Louis Elsevir (1540–1617), a native of Louvain who had trained in the Antwerp workshop of Christophe PLANTIN. The Elsevir workshop specialized in editions of classical authors which were prepared for the staff and students of Leiden University. In the course of the next century members of the family opened branches in several Dutch cities, and their books were sold all over Europe. The firm closed in 1712, but the name has been revived by a modern Dutch publisher.

D. W. Davies, *The Work of the Elzevirs, 1580–1712* (1954).

**ELSHEIMER, ADAM** (1578–1610), German painter and designer of engravings, a native of Frankfurt. His early work, such as his *Sermon of St John* (Alte Pinakothek, Munich), is painted in a Flemish realist idiom that reflects the influence of exiled Netherlandish landscape painters; similarly, the illustrations published in *Messrelationen* (1598) are modelled on recently published Dutch designs. Elsheimer's visit to Strassburg in 1596 introduced the influence of south German and Swiss designs to his work.

In 1598 Elsheimer moved to Italy, living first in Venice and from 1600 in Rome, where he became part of the Flemish community of artists (which included Rubens). His pictures, which are always small, eschew the contemporary mannerist idiom in favour of lyrical depictions of biblical and mythological scenes set against idyllic landscapes. *St Paul in Malta*, the *Baptism of Christ*, and *St Lawrence Prepared for Martyrdom*, all in the National Gallery in London, are painted in oil on copper. Elsheimer died in 1610 shortly after his release from imprisonment for debt.

*MDA*; *NDB*; Gottfried Sello, *Adam Elsheimer* (1988).

**ELSINORE TAPESTRIES or (Danish) Kronborg tapeterne**, a set of tapestry panels woven between 1581 and 1584 for FREDERICK II's palace of Kronborg at Helsingør (Hamlet's Elsinore) to designs provided by a Flemish painter, Hans Knieper (d. 1587). The panels are imaginary portraits of Danish kings (both historical and legendary) depicted in outdoor settings which include hunts and battlefields. The fifteen surviving panels are now divided between Kronborg and the Nationalmuseum in Copenhagen.

M. Mackeprang and S. F. Christensen, *Kronborg Tapeterne* (1950).

**ELYOT, SIR THOMAS** (*c*.1490–1546), English humanist, administrator, and diplomat. Elyot's *Book Named the Governor* (1531) outlined the benefits of a humanist education to those serving king and state. His use of English in this work, his medical and scientific works, and his translations of a number of classical treatises concerned with political counsel did much to promote the status of writing in the vernacular.

*DNB*; J. M. Major, *Sir Thomas Elyot and Renaissance Humanism* (1964).

**EMANUELE FILIBERTO** (1528–80), duke of SAVOY, was born on 8 July 1528, the son of Duke Charles II and Beatrice of Portugal, who presided over a duchy that was occupied by imperial troops engaged in the WARS OF ITALY. In 1545 Emanuele became a soldier in the service of the Empire. He was appointed lieutenant-general of the imperial army in Flanders (1553) and governor of the Netherlands (1556). Emanuele's victory over the French at the battle of SAINT-QUENTIN (1557) replenished his treasury, and he was able to use the income from ransomed French prisoners to create a small Savoyard navy.

In 1559 the Treaty of CATEAU-CAMBRÉSIS marked an end to hostilities, and Emanuele regained his duchy, but on terms that rankled: France was to garrison several Piedmontese fortresses (including Turin and Pinerolo) for up to three years, Spain was to garrison Asti and Vercelli (which was later exchanged for Santhià) for the same period, and Emanuele was to marry Margaret, duchess of Berry, the sister of King Henri II. After his marriage in Paris Emanuele returned to a jubilant welcome in his despoiled duchy, established himself as an absolutist ruler, and began to rebuild the institutions of the duchy. On the question of religious toleration, he initially persecuted the WALDENSIANS, but in 1561 retreated from this policy and condoned a measure of religious liberty; he later renewed his persecution at the behest of the papacy, but again withdrew in response to the pleas of his duchess and the Protestant princes of Germany.

In December 1562 the French army finally departed for a payment of 100,000 scudi, retaining only Pinerolo and Savigliano. The departure of the Turin garrison enabled Emanuele to re-establish his capital in Turin. He also exchanged territories with the Swiss cantons, settling all points of conflict except the suzerainty of Geneva, where the government steadfastly resisted the claims of Savoy. By 1575 France and Spain had withdrawn the last of their garrisons and the duchy was free of foreign troops for the first time in 39 years. Emanuele expanded his seaboard by purchasing Tenda (since 1947 French Tende) and Oneglia, and towards the end of his life entered into protracted but fruitless negotiations to obtain Monteferrato, which the GONZAGA FAMILY held under Spanish protection, and Saluzzo, which was a French fiefdom.

*DBI*.

**EMBLEMS AND EMBLEM BOOKS.** An emblem is a pictorial and literary representation of an abstraction. The emblem has a tripartite structure, and consists of a motto, a woodcut illustration, and an epigrammatic gloss (often in verse but sometimes in prose). The first emblem book was Andrea ALCIATO's *Emblemata* (Augsburg, 1531), which was translated into many languages and appeared in almost 200 editions; thereafter emblem books appeared all over Europe, initially in Latin and later in the vernaculars. The emblem is sometimes distinguished from the device, which is deemed to be personal rather than public and so deliberately enigmatic, but the terms are often used interchangeably, as in Georgette de Montenay's *Emblèmes, ou Devises chrétiennes* (1571).

Alison Adam et al., *A Bibliography of French Emblem Books of the Sixteenth and Seventeenth Centuries* (1999).

**EMBRIACHI or Ubriachi, BALDASSARE DEGLI** (*fl. c.*1390–1410), Italian carver in wood, bone, and ivory who worked with his sons Antonio and Giovanni in Florence and, from about 1400, in Venice. Their workshops produced both luxurious secular goods (notably caskets and CASSONI) and ALTARPIECES. The frames of their mirrors and altarpieces and the surfaces of their *cassoni* are characteristically composed of *certosina*, a geometrical inlay with polygonal tesserae made from wood, bone, ivory, and mother-of-pearl.

Embriachi received commissions for altarpieces from Duke Philip the Bold of Burgundy (Musée de Cluny, Paris), the duke of Berry (Louvre), and Gian Galeazzo VISCONTI (Certosa di Pavia).

*DBI* s.v. Ubriachi; *MDA*.

**EMBROIDERY or (Italian) *ricamo*,** the ornamentation of textiles with decorative NEEDLEWORK. The ground was usually linen, but leather and silk were also used. The thread was usually wool or (for delicate work such as flowers) silk; gold and silver thread were in occasional use, sometimes twisted into wire known as 'bullion'. There are more than 300 named embroidery stitches, many of which were developed in the early modern period. Needles were usually made from twisted wire, which was supplanted in the early sixteenth century by steel; needles used for embroidery include bead needles, bodkins, chenilles, crewels, and tapestry needles. For large embroideries the ground was stretched over a wooden frame, but small embroideries were made with the cloth held loose in the hand. This technique is one of the features of embroidery that distinguish it from TAPESTRY, which from the perspective of the embroiderer is a technique in which bare warps are embroidered with the weft; embroidery and tapestry have in common the use of a CARTOON, a design prepared by the embroiderer or commissioned from an artist.

In medieval and Renaissance Europe, embroidery had a prestige that derived from centuries of use in ecclesiastical vestments (e.g. the Syon Cope of 1300–20 in the Victoria and Albert Museum) and the clothing and domestic furnishings of the aristocracy. This prestige, which was protected by SUMPTUARY LAWS, meant that embroidery was a craft practised both by artisans (who were organized into guilds) and also by aristocratic women who typically embroidered small items such as gloves with silk and gold threads and designed embroideries that were executed by their attendant needlewomen.

The finest embroidery was made in France, where the principal centre of commercial production was Caen. The ARMOUR of French noblemen was worn under richly embroidered surcoats, and their houses were hung with embroidered curtains (called *salles*, because they hung from the ceiling and partitioned large rooms into smaller ones); the soft furnishings of noble houses (e.g. bed-curtains and canopies) were also elaborately embroidered, and were known as *courtepointerie* (a term now associated with QUILTS). In the sixteenth century the designers of French embroidery included RAPHAEL, from whom FRANCIS I commissioned

embroideries now in the Musée Cluny in Paris. CATHERINE DE MÉDICIS made embroideries, and taught the techniques to MARY, QUEEN OF SCOTS. In 1578 the establishment of the Order of the Holy Spirit by King HENRI III led to a revival of heraldic embroidery at his court.

In Italy, where embroidered hangings had been made in Palermo since the twelfth century, embroidery attracted noble patrons in the fifteenth century, and by the end of the sixteenth century Italian embroidery enjoyed a European reputation, partly because of the quality of its designs (designers included Dosso DOSSI, Antonio POLLAIUOLO, Raphael, and Cosimo TURA), but also because Italian pattern books for embroidery were widely disseminated throughout Europe. The finest Italian embroidery was linen, mostly in openwork patterns. Embroidery needles were manufactured in Milan. As in the rest of Europe, most embroidery was made by women in homes and in convents, but some was made in urban workshops by men such as PAOLO DA VERONA.

In Spain the Moorish influence in design was particularly apparent in embroidery, where black scrolled patterns, often in the form of vines, leaves, and flowers, were set against white backgrounds; Spanish designs were also influenced by the Inca designs of pre-conquest tapestries brought from Peru. In Andalusia fine nettings were embroidered with designs that resemble those of LACE; in Castile the embroidery in blue and tan threads was known as *toallas*. In Portugal, where embroidery was principally a craft associated with aristocratic women, early Moorish influences on design began in the late sixteenth century to be displaced by oriental influences which are apparent in the depiction of birds, flowers, butterflies, and dragons.

In the German lands, where the aristocratic tradition of embroidery was already established in the Carolingian court, the principal centre for the production of linen embroideries was Cologne. In the fifteenth century, when linen was displaced by wool in embroideries for wall hangings and soft furnishings, the Cistercian convents at Lüneburg and Wienhausen (near Celle) emerged as important centres; both convents (now women's retreats) show their collections of embroideries once a year. During the fifteenth and sixteenth centuries German embroideries with coloured linen thread were made in designs that resembled those of needlepoint lace.

In England there was a continuous aristocratic tradition of embroidery throughout the Middle Ages: Queen Edith embroidered the coronation robe of her husband Edward the Confessor and Queen Matilda, the wife of William the Conqueror, was sufficiently well known as an embroiderer for her name to be associated with the Bayeux Tapestry (which is technically an embroidery rather than a tapestry). English ecclesiastical embroidery, which was known as *opus Anglicanum*, was favoured by many popes; continental embroidery in the style of *opus Anglicanum* was known as *façon Angleterre*.

Embroidery in English religious houses ended with the dissolution of the MONASTERIES (1536 and 1539), but the aristocratic secular tradition remained buoyant: CATHERINE OF

ARAGON was an embroiderer, and introduced Spanish styles to English embroidery which persisted for more than a century. Queen MARY I was an embroiderer, as was Queen ELIZABETH, who in 1561 granted a charter to the Broderers' Company, which had been incorporated since 1376; their hall in Gutter Lane (1515) was burnt in 1666. Elizabethan embroideries were usually floral, and in the late sixteenth century designs became increasingly botanical: the woodcuts in GERARD's *Herbal* (1597) were used as designs by embroiderers, and botanical designs were published by Richard Shoreleyker in *The School House of the Needle* (1624) and by John Taylor, the 'Water Poet', in *The Needle's Excellency* (1631). During this period many English embroideries took the form of 'paned work' in which varied embroidery materials were juxtaposed in contrasting panels. Another distinctly English style was embroidery on velvet, which was really a form of appliqué: velvet resists needlework, so designs were fashioned from linen or silk, embroidered and then attached to a foundation of velvet, which achieves a result similar to BROCADES; curtains and hangings decorated with such embroidery are preserved in Penshurst Place in Kent and Oxburgh Hall in Norfolk.

Pamela Warner, *A History of Western Embroidery* (1991); Lanto Synge, *Art of Embroidery: A History of Art and Design* (2001).

**EMSER, HIERONYMUS** (1478–1527), German humanist and Catholic polemicist, born in Ulm on 20 March 1477. He was educated at Tübingen (where he studied Greek) and Basel (where he studied law) and in 1504 became a lecturer in classics at Erfurt and secretary to GEORG DER BÄRTIGE, duke of Saxony.

In the early years of the Reformation, Emser evinced some sympathy for the cause of reform, and as late as 1519 LUTHER could refer to him as *Emser noster*. In that same year, however, the LEIPZIG DISPUTATION proved to be a watershed, because Emser did not share Luther's view that reformation could only be achieved in the context of a church that was independent of Rome. The enmity that sprang up between Emser and Luther was symbolized by Luther's decision to burn Emser's books along with the bull *EXSURGE DOMINI* on 10 December 1520. Thereafter the exchange of insults and polemical tracts continued unabated until Emser's death on 8 December 1527.

Emser's long series of polemical exchanges with Luther included a German translation of HENRY VIII's *Assertio septem sacramentorum contra Lutherum* (1523) and a version of Luther's 'December Bible' of 1522; this counter-edition, which Emser published in 1527, imitated the design of Luther's Bible, but contained a polemical introduction and notes. In 1530 a Low German translation of Emser's Bible was published by the BRETHREN OF THE COMMON LIFE. In the course of the next two centuries Emser's Bible was reprinted in more than 100 editions.

NDB; H. Smolinsky, *Augustin von Alveldt und Hieronymus Emser* (1983).

**ENAMEL or (French)** *émail* (plural *émaux*). In modern usage 'enamel' can refer to any hard, smooth surface, but in early modern usage it specifically denotes the inlaying or encrusting of metal with a vitreous composition, usually lead-soda or lead-potash glass, applied to the surface by fusion; if the surface to be covered is pottery, the covering is called a GLAZE. Five types of enamel are usually distinguished: *cloisonné*, *champlevé*, *basse-taille*, encrusted, and painted; the French terms have no agreed equivalents in English.

*Cloisonné* ('cell-work') enamel is made by constructing wire cells (*cloisons*) on the surface of the metal, filling the cells with vitreous paste, and firing the object to melt and then fuse the enamel to the surface. *Cloisonné* was the principal technique of Byzantine enamelling, and from Byzantium the technique was taken to Venice, where the finest example of *cloisonné* is the golden reredos known as the Pala d'Oro, which was refashioned in 1345 for the altar of the Basilica di San Marco in Venice; the Pala d'Oro contains 83 *cloisonné* enamelled panels of Byzantine origin. Enamel FILIGREE is a form of *cloisonné* enamel that was to flourish for centuries. Another form of *cloisonné* enamel is *plique à jour* ('against the light'), in which the backing metal is melted away, so leaving the enamel suspended in the *cloison*. The only surviving example of this technique is the Mérode Cup (*c.*1430, Victoria and Albert Museum), which was made in Burgundy or France.

*Champlevé* ('raised field') enamel, which is also known as *émail en taille d'épargne*, is made by incising the design on a copper ground and placing vitreous paste in the incisions before firing. From the twelfth to the fifteenth centuries the technique is particularly associated with LIMOGES ENAMELS.

*Basse-taille* ('shallow cut') enamel, which is known in English as 'translucent enamel' and in Italian as *lavoro di basso rilievo*, is a refinement of *champlevé* in which the depth to which the reliefs are cut is varied, so that when enamelled the higher parts of the relief are paler than the lower parts. This technique for producing graduated effects of light and shade seems to have originated in late thirteenth-century Italy; the earliest surviving Italian example of *lavoro di basso rilievo* is a chalice made during the pontificate of Pope Nicholas IV (1288–92) by the Sienese goldsmith Guccio di Mannaia and now in the treasury of the Basilica of San Francesco in Assisi, and the finest surviving example is UGOLINO DI VIERI's gilt-brass reliquary of the Sacro Corporale (1337–8) in Orvieto Cathedral, which is decorated with enamel panels. In the early fourteenth century the art of *basse-taille* enamel was perfected by the goldsmith-enamellers of Paris, whose work includes the Royal Gold Cup (mentioned in an inventory of 1391) in the British Museum, a triptych in Namur Cathedral, a crozier in Cologne Cathedral, and one secular piece, a silver ewer (*c.*1330–40) in the National Museum in Copenhagen. From Paris the techniques of *basse-taille* enamel spread throughout western Europe, and it was widely used to decorate ecclesiastical objects, including chalices (notably those made in fourteenth-century Stockholm) and portable triptychs.

Encrusted enamel (French *émail en ronde bosse*) is a technique introduced in the fifteenth century to cover figures or decorative devices moulded in the round. In the late fourteenth and early fifteenth centuries the goldsmith-enamellers of Paris produced pieces such as the Reliquary of the Holy Thorn (formerly in the Geistliche Schatzkammer in Vienna and now in the British Museum), which includes an enamel figure of GOD, the Goldenes Rössel (1403, in the pilgrimage church of Altötting, in Bavaria), the reliquary from the Chapel of the Order of the Saint-Esprit (Louvre), and the Monkey Cup (Metropolitan Museum, New York) made by Netherlandish goldsmiths for the Burgundian court.

Painted enamel is a technique developed in Limoges in the late fifteenth century. The metal surface (usually copper) was covered with white enamel and then fired; the design was then applied in a series of colours, each of which was fired separately. From the mid-sixteenth century the first covering was black or dark blue enamel, which then formed the basis for the type of GRISAILLE painting known as camaïeu, in which a layer of white enamel paste spread on the dark enamel ground was carved to make a design consisting of exposed dark enamel; the technique is analogous to that of CAMEO carving.

The technique of enamelling on glass, which was developed in Venice in the fifteenth century (the earliest surviving piece is a blue glass goblet dated 1465), transformed the technology of STAINED-GLASS windows in the sixteenth century. Enamelled armorial glasses were made by Venetian glass-makers for the German market, and from the mid-sixteenth century were also made in Germany (notably in Nuremberg), where they continued to be produced until the eighteenth century.

**ENCINA, JUAN DEL** (1468–c.1529), Spanish poet, playwright, and musician, born in Encinas (near Salamanca); he studied law at the University of Salamanca and took minor orders. In the 1490s Encina was a courtier in the household of the second duke of Alba at Alba de Tormes (23 kilometres (14 miles) south-east of Salamanca), where he worked as a playwright, actor, musician, and producer of entertainments (including *Triunfo de la fama*, a celebration of the fall of GRANADA). In 1498 he competed unsuccessfully with Lucas FERNÁNDEZ for the post of cantor of Salamanca Cathedral, and shortly thereafter left for Rome, where he joined the court of the Spanish pope, ALEXANDER VI, who appointed him choirmaster. In 1509 Pope JULIUS II appointed Encina archdeacon of Málaga Cathedral, and the following year Pope LEO X appointed him prior of the cathedral in León, where he remained for the rest of his life.

Encina collected his poetry and his early pastoral entertainments (produced at Alba de Tormes) in his *Cancionero* (Salamanca, 1496); the collection is prefaced by *Arte de trobar*, a prose treatise on poetry in Spain. His best plays draw on the Italian tradition of pastoral drama, and one play, *Zambardo y Cardonio*, is an adaptation of a play by Antonio TEBALDEO. His finest play, *Égloga de Plácida y Vitoriano* (Burgos, 1520), was performed in Rome in 1513. In the historiography of Spanish drama, Encina is proclaimed as the father of the Renaissance style. It is certainly the case that the style of his plays was the most important model for Spanish playwrights until Lope de VEGA. Encina's principal innovation lay in dialogue: he developed the art of giving each character a distinctive speech pattern, and also introduced to drama the comic peasant dialect known as *sayagués*. His musical compositions consist of a large corpus of songs for three or four voices.

*DBEH s.v. Enzina; Grove; J. R. Andrews, Juan del Encina (1959); Françoise Maurizi, Théâtre et tradition populaires: Juan de Encina et Lucas Fernández (1994); Manuel Morais (ed. and transcriber), La obra musical de Juan del Encina (1997); Javier Guijarro Ceballos (ed.), Humanismo y literatura en tiempos de Juan del Encina (1999).*

**ENCOMIENDAS**, the grants of estates conferred on conquistadors by the Spanish crown; recipients of the grant were called *encomenderos*. The possession of an *encomienda* did not confer ownership of land, but rather the right to collect taxes and demand services from Indians who lived in villages within the area designated by the *encomienda*; in return, the *encomendero* was required to provide a Christian education for the Indians. *Encomiendas* reverted to the crown on the death of the *encomienda*.

*Encomenderos* demanded that *encomiendas* be made hereditary, and so came into conflict with the crown, which was becoming uneasy about clerical reports of the mistreatment of Indians. The crown administered its overseas territories through the legal instrument of the Laws of the INDIES (Spanish *Leyes de los Reinos de las Indias*). The first attempt to provide civic protection to the Indians within this legal framework was the compilation known as the Laws of Burgos (1512). This legislation was unsuccessful in curtailing atrocities, and it was replaced by the 54 New Laws of 1542, which abolished Indian slavery by restricting the *encomienda*. Spanish colonists in Peru rebelled against the New Laws, which were reissued in amended form in 1552.

*DHE; L. B. Simpson, The Encomienda in New Spain (2nd edn. 1966).*

**ENDERLEIN, CASPAR** (1560–1633), German metalworker, a native of Basel who settled in Nuremberg in 1583. He established his reputation as a master of display PEWTER with a copy of BRIOT's famous *Temperantia* dish. He collaborated with Jacob Koch the Younger (d. 1619) on pewter tableware, notably jugs and tankards. His moulds remained in use until the eighteenth century, but no surviving piece is known to bear Enderlein's stamp.

*MDA; NDB; H. Deminani, François Briot, Caspar Enderlein und das Edelzinn (1897).*

**ENGELBRECHTSZOON or Engelbrechtsen, CORNELIS** (1460/5–1527), Dutch painter, was born in Leiden and trained in Brussels; he worked for a time in Antwerp before returning permanently to Leiden, where one of his pupils was LUCAS VAN LEIDEN. His most important works, two triptychs painted for the Marienpoel convent and now in the Municipal Museum in Leiden, are remarkable for their intensity of emotion.

*MDA; NNBW ix.*

**ENGLAND.** At the beginning of the fifteenth century, England enjoyed a 200-year-old system of parliamentary representation, and had a developed legal system, with regular assizes held throughout the country for administering justice and maintaining order. King Henry IV, who came to power in 1399, was nevertheless occupied in the first years of his reign with crises throughout his kingdom. WALES, which had been conquered by Edward I, was in rebellion, led by Owain Glyndŵr with French assistance, and was out of English control between 1405 and 1408. There were wars with Scotland, at sea, and the HUNDRED YEARS WAR threatened English territories in France. By the mid-century, baronial rebellion within the kingdom had also been ignited: the revolts of the duke of York against the Lancastrian Henry's reign in 1455 and 1459 commenced the series of disturbances known, by reference to the red rose of Lancaster and the white rose of York, as the Wars of the Roses. Although suppressed in 1455, the duke of York claimed the throne in 1459; he was defeated and killed at the battle of Wakefield the following year, but his heir Edward seized the throne. As EDWARD IV, he faced rebellions in turn, however, and Henry VI was temporarily restored to the throne in 1470–1. Edward's victory over the Lancastrians in 1471 appeared to end the Wars of the Roses, but disturbances began again when his brother RICHARD III seized the throne in the infancy of EDWARD V. It was only with Henry Tudor's successful challenge to Richard, and, as HENRY VII, his establishment of the TUDOR dynasty, that the Wars of the Roses finally concluded: an ending cemented with Henry's marriage to Elizabeth of York. Henry's reign, between 1485 and 1509, bequeathed stability and relative prosperity to his son HENRY VIII.

Henry VIII's break with Rome in the 1530s opened the door to the English REFORMATION, and the establishment of the English Church with the monarch at its head. This policy inevitably met with strong opposition from parts of the political and ecclesiastical establishment, with some, such as John FISHER and Thomas MORE, losing their lives through their belief in the supremacy of the pope; others, such as CRANMER, were equally eager for religious reform, and worked to consolidate the new Church in such institutions as the Book of COMMON PRAYER and the authorized translation of the Bible. MARY's attempt to return the country to Catholicism had little long-lasting result, and ELIZABETH and her ministers worked to secure the settlement, and steer a middle way between Rome and Puritan or Calvinist extremes. In foreign politics, the loss of Calais in Mary's reign marked the end of English ambitions on territories in France, which Henry VIII had still seriously pursued. An Act of Union in 1536 had integrated Wales into the English political and administrative system, and no real disturbance now stemmed from that quarter; IRELAND, however, remained a source of unrest in the sixteenth and seventeenth centuries. The English achieved three notable victories over the Scots in the sixteenth century, at Flodden in 1513, Solway Moss in 1542, and Pinkie Cleugh in 1547, and the crowns of Scotland and England were united with JAMES VI's succession to the English throne in 1603. Although James sought political union between the two countries, that was not to come until 1707.

**ENGLISCHE KOMÖDIANTEN.** The first troupe of English touring comic actors on the Continent appear to have accompanied LEICESTER to the Netherlands when he was made governor-general there in 1585. Performing short comic sketches, clowning routines, and even full-length plays, adapted for a foreign audience, such troupes became common at fairs, festivals, and other occasions, especially in Germany, Denmark, and the Netherlands, from the late sixteenth to the mid-seventeenth centuries. Their numbers were especially boosted during the Puritan closing of the theatres in 1642. Robert BROWNE's troupe gained an early reputation; the clown KEMPE also spent some time touring abroad.

**ENGLISH ARCHITECTURE.** English ecclesiastical architecture has long drawn on continental styles but articulated those styles in ways that are distinctly English. Norman architecture in England clearly shares many features with French Romanesque architecture north of the Loire, but English architects eschewed the tunnel vaults of France and the groin vaults of Germany in favour of rib vaults, which were developed at Durham and later imitated on the Continent. Similarly, the distinctive features of English Gothic require a taxonomy of styles separate from those used on the Continent. English Gothic architecture is divided into three phases: Early English, Decorated, and Perpendicular.

The Perpendicular architecture of late medieval England is so called from the upright lines of the window tracery and the panels of churches, and is sometimes divided into Early Perpendicular in the late fourteenth and early fifteenth centuries (e.g. the chancel of Gloucester Cathedral) and Late Perpendicular in the late fifteenth and early sixteenth centuries (e.g. King's College Chapel in Cambridge). The most striking feature of Late Perpendicular architecture is the fan vault, of which there are fine examples in King's College Chapel in Cambridge, the Divinity Schools in Oxford, Sherborne Abbey, Trinity Church in Ely, Gloucester Cathedral, St George's Chapel in Windsor, and the Chapel of Henry VII in Westminster Abbey.

The architecture of sixteenth- and early seventeenth-century England retains strong Perpendicular features, but nonetheless reflects the advent of Flemish, French, and Italian influences. There is no agreed nomenclature for the architecture of this period. Sixteenth-century architecture is sometimes called Tudor (the Tudor monarchs ruled from 1485 to 1603) and sometimes Elizabethan (Queen Elizabeth ruled from 1558 to 1603); the term Elizabethan is sometimes extended to include the architecture of the first half of the seventeenth century, which is more accurately described as Stuart or, more precisely, Jacobean (James I ruled in England from 1603 to 1625) and Caroline (Charles I ruled from 1625 until his execution in 1649).

The decorative features of Italian Renaissance architecture first appeared in the Henry VII Chapel in Westminster Abbey, where the Florentine Pietro TORRIGIANO built the Italianate tombs of King HENRY VII and Elizabeth of York (1512–18), who are represented in bronze effigies. Until the middle of the sixteenth century Italian Renaissance style was restricted to architectural decoration (such as the detail on the screen and stalls in the Chapel of King's College, Cambridge, and GIOVANNI DA MAIANO's terracotta roundels of Roman emperors at Hampton Court) and did not affect structural designs. The first building to articulate in its structure the style of the Italian Renaissance was Somerset House (1547–50, demolished 1775), the predecessor of the present building on the Strand; the first Somerset House had symmetrical façades in the Italian fashion, decorative details drawn from FLEMISH ARCHITECTURE (including STRAPWORK, which originated at FONTAINEBLEAU), and large transomed and mullioned windows in the Perpendicular tradition.

Somerset House was enormously influential, and soon houses with large Perpendicular windows and Flemish decorative motifs in wood and plaster began to appear in the English countryside, notably in Elizabethan houses such as Burghley House in Northamptonshire (1552–87), Charlecote in Warwickshire (from 1558), Loseley House in Surrey (from 1562), Haddon Hall in Derbyshire (1567–84), Longleat House in Wiltshire (from 1568), Kirby Hall in Northamptonshire (1570, unfinished), Longford Castle in Wiltshire (from 1578), WOLLATON HALL in Nottinghamshire (1580–5), Montacute House in Somerset (1580–99), and Hardwick Hall in Derbyshire (1591–7); in the seventeenth century similar features appeared in Jacobean houses such as Audley End in Essex (1603–16), Chastleton House in Oxfordshire (1603–14), Knole House in Kent (from 1605), HATFIELD HOUSE in Hertfordshire (1607–12), and Cope Castle (now Holland House) in Kensington (from 1607). This was also a period of considerable building at the universities, notably of the Old Schools (now the BODLEIAN Library) in Oxford.

In the early seventeenth century Inigo JONES introduced the classical principles of PALLADIO into English architecture, beginning with the Queen's House in Greenwich (1616) and culminating in his BANQUETING HOUSE in Whitehall (1619–22). This Palladian strain was continued in the work of John Webb (who built the state rooms at Wilton House), Sir Roger Pratt (whose buildings have all been destroyed or rebuilt), and Hugh May (who built Eltham Lodge, now the Royal Blackheath Golf Club) and culminated after the Great Fire of 1666 in the buildings of Christopher Wren.

**ENGLISH ART.** In the late fourteenth and fifteenth centuries England was an important centre of ALABASTER sculptures, STAINED GLASS, and EMBROIDERY. The finest painting of the period is the Wilton Diptych (c.1395–9, National Gallery), a depiction in the style of INTERNATIONAL GOTHIC of the presentation of King Richard II to the Virgin by his patron saints; the artist may have been English or French. Towards the end of the fifteenth century, the style of FLEMISH ART began to influence English painting; the best surviving example of this style is William Baker's series of wall paintings (1479–83) in the chapel of Eton College depicting the miracles of the Virgin.

In the sixteenth century the English Reformation stifled religious art and architecture, but the secular art of portrai-

ture flourished early in the century with Hans HOLBEIN's two visits to England and late in the century with portrait MINIATURISTS such as Nicholas HILLIARD and Isaac OLIVER; in the seventeenth century the principal portrait painters in England were Flemish (Sir Anthony Van Dyck), Dutch (Sir Peter Lely), or German (Sir Godfrey Kneller), and King Charles commissioned Rubens to paint the ceiling of the Banqueting House. The ENGLISH ARCHITECTURE of the period achieved great distinction, notably in country houses, but in art England was more remarkable for its art collections and the presence of foreign artists than for indigenous traditions.

**ENGLISH COLLEGE, THE VENERABLE**, the seminary in Rome where English Catholics were trained for the priesthood. The College was founded in 1362 as a resthouse for English pilgrims, and in 1578 was reconstituted by Pope GREGORY XIII as a seminary whose graduates were intended for service in England. The College later passed into the hands of the JESUITS, who governed it until 1773.

English visitors to the College included the playwright Anthony MUNDAY, who seems to have been sent as a Protestant spy to report on the College; later visitors included the uncompromisingly Protestant John Milton. The College mounted productions of English and Latin plays, mostly imitations of ancient Roman comedies.

Michael Williams, *The Venerable English College, Rome: A History, 1579–1979* (1979); Suzanne Gossett, 'Drama in the English College, Rome, 1595–1660', *English Literary Renaissance*, 3 (1973).

**ENGLISH DRAMA.** Prior to 1567, there were no purpose-built playhouses in England, Scotland, or Wales. Drama was performed in a range of public and private spaces from innyards and churchyards to the great halls of aristocratic and royal homes, the Inns of Court, livery company halls, schools, and colleges. In many cities, including York, Chester, and Wakefield, the streets themselves provided the stages for the annual religious 'mystery plays'.

In Elizabethan and Jacobean England there were eleven permanent playhouses, all in London and its suburbs. There were seven public playhouses, of which the first were the Red Lion (1567) and the THEATRE (1576); although the English playhouses are now often called 'theatres', the Theatre was the only playhouse to use this classical term (from Latin *theatrum*). The other public playhouses, in chronological order of opening, were the CURTAIN, the ROSE, the SWAN, the GLOBE, the FORTUNE, and the RED BULL. The three private playhouses were the BLACKFRIARS, the WHITEFRIARS, and the playhouse of the CHILDREN OF PAUL'S.

Plays were also mounted in the yards of inns (see THEATRE IN LONDON INNS); on stages in the palaces of Whitehall (in the Great Hall and in the Jacobean Banqueting House) and Hampton Court (in the Great Hall), and in the halls of the universities (notably St John's, Cambridge) and the INNS OF COURT (notably the Middle Temple).

English TRAGEDY was inaugurated in 1562 with *Gorboduc*, a Senecan play written by two members of the Inner Temple, NORTON and SACKVILLE. In the same period COMEDIES such as UDALL's *Ralph Roister Doister* (c.1550) and the anonymous

*Gammer Gurton's Needle* (c.1560) borrow from the ancient comedy, and GASCOIGNE's *Supposes*, acted at Gray's Inn in 1566, is based on ARIOSTO's *I suppositi*, behind which lies the *Captivi* of Plautus.

The 30 years from 1585 to 1615 encompass the greatest achievements of English drama, including the plays of MARLOWE, KYD, LYLY, PEELE, DEKKER, GREENE, SHAKESPEARE, JONSON, BEAUMONT, and FLETCHER. In the decades leading up to the closing of the public theatres in 1642, the principal playwrights were MARSTON, TOURNEUR, MIDDLETON, MASSINGER, and FORD.

**ENGLISH GARDENS.** The burgeoning of English gardens in the eighteenth and nineteenth centuries often obliterated earlier gardens on the same sites, so English medieval and Renaissance gardens are usually known only from written and pictorial documentation. An illumination of a royal couple playing chess in an English garden made c.1400 shows that the herbaceous border was already a feature of gardens by that date, and the diamond-shaped earthworks of a pleasance (the Pleasance en Marys, i.e. on the marsh) 1.5 kilometres (1 mile) to the west of KENILWORTH CASTLE, which are the remains of a garden and summer house constructed for Henry V between 1414 and 1417, constitute one of the few surviving remnants of the English double-moated garden with rows of trees planted on the lists between the moats. There is evidence that monastic gardens dedicated to the cultivation of edible plants and medicinal herbs also contained roses, lilies, and violets, but such flowering plants may have been valued for their emblematic and medicinal qualities as much as for their beauty.

Many of the plants that were to become important elements in Renaissance gardens had been established in the preceding century. Rosemary had been introduced in 1340, and its advent had ushered in a fashion for evergreens. Juniper, holly, box, and bay (*laurus nobilis*) were all cultivated in early fifteenth-century gardens. By this time evergreens were being clipped, KNOT GARDENS were being laid out in heraldic patterns, and the double-clove gillyflower (i.e. carnation) had become highly valued for its beauty and aroma.

The transition from the *hortus conclusus* (on which see GIARDINO SEGRETO) of the Middle Ages to the pleasure garden of the Renaissance was effected by the Burgundian influences which began to be felt in English gardens at the end of the fifteenth century. The earliest large Renaissance garden was laid out at HENRY VII's palace at Richmond (1498–1501); this garden, which did not survive the destruction of the palace in the eighteenth century, was laid out in enclosures linked by covered walks and galleries.

Three important gardens were built by HENRY VIII at Hampton Court Palace (1531–4), Whitehall (1545), and Nonsuch Palace (1538–47). All three evinced the direct influence of FRENCH GARDENS in their common situation beneath the windows of the state apartments and in their common geometrical design, consisting of a square surrounded by a covered walk and divided into quarters; each quarter was laid out in knot gardens, and at the centre of each garden was a

FOUNTAIN. The only markedly English element was painted heraldic decoration. At Hampton Court Palace the Privy Garden on the south side contained a MOUNT constructed from 250,000 bricks, covered with earth, and planted with hawthorns; it was topped by a three-storey lantern-arbour with a cupola roof crowned by a wind-vane in the form of a heraldic lion. The mount had originated in Italy (there is one in the BOTANICAL GARDEN at Padua), but came to England through France, where Olivier de SERRES had attempted to introduce it into French gardens. The Privy Garden was decorated with painted heraldic models of the King's Beasts; it also contained sixteen sundials and a kitchen garden, and Queen ELIZABETH later added a knot garden. Thomas Platter the Younger (grandson of the humanist Thomas PLATTER) visited the garden in 1599, and described its elaborate TOPIARY. This Privy Garden was lost when Queen Mary laid it out in parterres at the end of the seventeenth century, and Queen Anne comprehensively redesigned the other gardens; the gardens now called the 'Tudor Gardens' were laid out in the eighteenth century.

The garden at Nonsuch (which, together with the palace, has disappeared) was laid out afresh between 1579 and 1591, and in this version reflected Italian influences originating in a visit to Italy by its owner, the antiquarian John Lumley; the most Italianate element was a GROTTO with polychrome statutes of Diana and Actaeon. Elsewhere in the garden, the Italian influence was mediated through France, because the design was a copy of the garden of FRANCIS I at FONTAINEBLEAU (not the later HENRI IV version); the Nonsuch garden contained woodland, a MAZE, imitation animals, and an outdoor banqueting hall which seems to have been the first in England.

In the second half of the sixteenth century innovation in garden design shifted from the royal palaces to the houses of the aristocracy, notably KENILWORTH CASTLE, THEOBALDS PARK, and WIMBLEDON HOUSE, all of which show the direct influence of French or FLEMISH GARDENS and the indirect influence of ITALIAN GARDENS in their designs. One of the most ambitious designs was that of Lyveden New Bield (Northants), which included a moated garden with a raised terrace and two mounts; the garden was never finished, but its structural features still survive. In smaller houses knot gardens became fashionable; designs and advice on the selection and care of plants began to appear in printed form with Thomas Hill's *The Profitable Art of Gardening* (1564). One small garden that is particularly well documented is William TURNER's garden at Kew; Turner records that he grew fruit trees (peaches, apricots, medlars, figs, and almonds) and a large number of ornamental flowers which must have originated in continental gardens. The most surprising flower in Turner's garden is the French marigold (*Tagetes patula*), which, despite its common name, came from Mexico: the Aztec capital did not fall to Cortés until 1521, and yet by 1544 its flowers were being grown in English gardens.

Salomon de CAUS only lived in England for a few years, but he brought with him a knowledge of Italian and French gardens (notably PRATOLINO, SAINT-GERMAIN-EN-LAYE, and

Fontainebleau), and his incorporation of elements of these gardens in his designs for the royal gardens at Somerset House, Greenwich Palace, and Richmond Palace (all laid out between 1610 and 1612) changed the face of English design. In all three commissions he produced designs in which house and garden were conceived as integrated parts of single designs, so that the gardens were extensions of the houses. His enthusiasm for hydraulics greatly increased the importance of water in the English garden, because the fountains, grottoes, and AUTOMATA that he installed in the royal gardens quickly became features of aristocratic gardens that were built between 1610 and 1615, including Ham House (in Richmond, overlaid with a garden built in 1671, and rebuilt as a late seventeenth-century garden in 1975), Twickenham Park, Ware Park (Hertfordshire), Gorhambury (near St Albans), and Chastleton (Oxfordshire; both house and garden survive); hydraulics were also introduced into established gardens, such as those at Wimbledon House and Theobalds Park. The influence of de Caus waned after his departure for Germany, but was revived by the arrival in England of his kinsman (son or brother or nephew) Isaac de Caus, who in the 1620s and early 1630s designed new gardens (all with grottoes) at the Whitehall Banqueting House, Woburn Abbey, Moor Park (Hertfordshire, now overlaid with a Capability Brown garden), and Wilton House (Wiltshire).

In 1613, when Salomon de Caus left for Germany, Inigo JONES travelled to Italy, and he returned the following year as the principal English exponent of PALLADIO. English gardens constructed between 1615 and 1640—Arundel House (London), Oatlands Palace (Surrey), Albury Park (Surrey; the garden was redesigned in 1677 by John Evelyn), and Danvers House (Chelsea)—were all constructed on the Palladian principles championed by Jones.

Just as Erasmus envisaged an imaginary garden that described the features of DUTCH GARDENS, so Francis BACON, in his essay *On Gardens* (1625), imagined an ideal English garden, though in his case he spoke with horticultural authority, as he had overseen the gardens at the family home at Gorhambury and had redesigned the gardens at Gray's Inn, one of the INNS OF COURT. The princely garden that Bacon planned (but never built) was intended to fill 12 hectares (30 acres). In some ways his garden adhered to English conventions, in that it contained features such as ornamented galleries, covered walks, and a mount topped with a banqueting hall. In other respects, however, his garden adumbrates later English tastes, in that he eschews topiary and knot gardens but enthusiastically advocates lawns in which the grass was to be shorn.

Roy Strong, *The Renaissance Garden in England* (1979); John Dixon Hunt, *Garden and Grove: The Italian Renaissance Garden and the English Imagination, 1600–1750* (1986).

**ENGLISH LANGUAGE.** In early modern England, two languages were spoken. Most of the country spoke English, but in the south-west Cornish, a member (together with Breton and Welsh) of the Brittonic group of Celtic languages, was spoken, and was the language of a cycle of mystery plays.

Early modern English was a language in transition. In the third person singular of the present tense in the indicative mode, forms such as *hath*, *doth*, and *saith* jostled alongside modern forms ending in *-s* and *-es*. Similarly, many perfect participles were used both in weak forms that are now archaic (*blowed*, *weaved*, *shaked*) as well as strong forms (*blew*, *wove*, *shaken*). The possessive case of the neuter personal pronoun was *his*: the form *its* is an innovation of the early seventeenth century. *Thee* and *thou* belonged to a linguistic register appropriate only to intimates and inferiors, whereas now they are archaic and reverential. *Which* could be used to refer to persons as well as things, so the Lord's Prayer began 'Our Father which art in heaven'. In the writing of early modern English, the *s* was long (∫) unless written or printed at the end of a word. The letters *u* and *v* could be used both as consonants and vowels, but at the beginning of a word printers always used *v* and thereafter always used *u*, so *universal* was written *vniuersal*; similarly, *i* and *j* were both used as vowels, but until about 1630 *j* could not be used as a consonant, but was only used in an *ij* collocation, typically in roman numerals, where 8 was written *viij*.

Charles Barber, *Early Modern English* (1976); M. Görlach, *An Introduction to Early Modern English* (1990).

**ENGLISH LAW** from the fifteenth to the seventeenth centuries differed fundamentally from the legal systems of continental Europe in three important respects. First, English law was (and remains) uncodified and its rules were unclassified; second, statutes played a very minor role in setting out the law, which until 1830 was instead established almost wholly by judicial precedent; third, there were separate (and rival) principles and jurisdictions for common law and equity.

The Roman administration of England, which ended in AD 409, left no traces of Roman law in England. Until 1066 English law consisted of a series of Anglo-Saxon codes, some elements of which survived as CUSTOMARY LAW after the Norman conquest. The Normans introduced elements of continental law, the most important of which was Frankish FEUDAL LAW. England soon became the most comprehensively feudal society in Europe; the feudal structures of English society were gradually dismantled, but English property law remained feudal until 1925, when fundamental reforms were enshrined in statutes. Under the feudal administration of the Norman monarchs, justice was dispensed by royal judges in the name of the crown. The first great formulation of the decisions of royal judges was Henry of Bracton's *De legibus et consuetudinibus Angliae* ('Law and Customs of England'); the introduction to this treatise, which was compiled in the 1250s, shows the clear influence of Roman law, but its substance, a statement of the practice and procedures of the courts, is based entirely on judicial decisions. The treatise was published by TOTTELL in 1569.

During the reign of Edward I a series of royal courts was established in Westminster and elsewhere, and these courts eventually ousted the old feudal shire courts. In 1362 the spoken language of the courts changed from Norman French to

English, though legal records continued to be kept in Latin and LAW FRENCH. Under the Lancastrian monarchs (1399–1485) the gulf between common law and equity began to develop, and an increasingly powerful King's Council began to rule on petitions submitted by litigants unable to secure remedies in common law. The point in 1474 when the chancellor issued a decree in his own name marks the formal beginning of equity. A few years later, c.1481, Sir Thomas LITTLETON published his *Tenures*, which was the most important English common law book between Bracton and COKE.

The gap between the jurisdiction of the common law and the equitable jurisdiction of chancery courts widened into a chasm under the Tudors and Stuarts (1485–1649). Chancery courts increasingly granted injunctions against proceedings under common law judgments. In 1616 James I ruled in favour of the chancery view that principles of equity could overturn common law, and this ruling turned common lawyers into the enemies of equity. The most infamous of the equity courts was the Court of Star Chamber, which was a court of criminal equity that dealt with offences imperilling the safety of the state. The relationship of this court to the state was replicated in the relationship of the Court of High Commission to the Church, in that its task was to suppress movements that endangered the Church. Both courts persecuted Puritans and acted without regard to the protection afforded to citizens by the common law, and so incurred the enmity of Puritans and common lawyers, who were instrumental in the abolition of both courts in 1641. The leading English jurist of this period was Sir Edward Coke, who expounded the law of England in his *Institutes* and played an important part in the constitutional struggles of the early seventeenth century. His contemporaries included his opponent Sir Francis BACON and the legal historian John SELDEN.

English law remained isolated from continental law except in three important respects. First, the LAW MERCHANT was absorbed into English common law, one important consequence of which was the establishment by the mid-sixteenth century of bills of exchange, the predecessors of cheques. Second, an English form of CANON LAW emerged after the Reformation. Third, Henry VIII founded Regius professorships of CIVIL LAW in the universities, and so exacerbated the rift between academic civil law and the common law of the INNS OF COURT; civil lawyers were appointed to sit in ecclesiastical courts, but civil law was never woven into the fabric of English law.

William Holdsworth, *History of English Law* (16 vols., 1936–66);
J. H. Baker, *An Introduction to English Legal History* (4th edn., 2002).

**ENGLISH MUSIC**. The Old Hall manuscript, the Trent Codices, and the works of John DUNSTAPLE and Lionel POWER all suggest that the early fifteenth century was a period of great activity in English music. The English style, with its emphasis on the interval of the third, was to influence the Burgundian school of composers (DUFAY and BINCHOIS) and in turn European musical language. The English also had their own polychoral style, as demonstrated by composers such as John BROWNE, Walter LAMBE, Richard DAVY, and others in the ETON CHOIRBOOK. Musical styles and genres were subject to foreign and political influences following the Reformation, evident in the works of William BYRD, Thomas TALLIS, and madrigalists such as Thomas MORLEY, Thomas WEELKES, and John WILBYE.

**ENGLISH SWEAT**. See SWEATING SICKNESS.

**ENGRAVING**, a process for making PRINTS in which the design is engraved on a metal plate with a burin (a short steel rod cut obliquely at the end to provide a point) which is pushed through the surface of the plate; the process is sometimes called 'line engraving' to distinguish it from the nineteenth-century process of wood engraving.

Engraving seems to have originated in the workshops of goldsmiths in mid-fifteenth-century Germany and Italy; the early German engravers, such as the MASTER OF THE PLAYING CARDS, MASTER E.S., and Martin SCHONGAUER, were certainly goldsmiths as well as engravers, as was the early Italian engraver Maso FINIGUERRA; the exception was MANTEGNA, who was not a goldsmith, but, like POLLAIUOLO and Schongauer, a painter.

In the early sixteenth century, the most important engravers were DÜRER, RAIMONDI (who often engraved designs by RAPHAEL), and LUCAS VAN LEIDEN (who engraved his first plate, *The Milkmaid*, at the age of 14). In the late sixteenth century the engraving increasingly came to be used as a means of reproducing designs rather than a medium for the creation of original designs.

**ENSINGEN FAMILY**, a family of south German masons and architects. In 1393 Ulrich von Ensingen (c.1360–1419) was appointed master mason of the cathedral at Ulm, where he remodelled what had been a hall church in which the aisles were the same height as the nave into a five-aisled basilica. Ensingen worked on Milan Cathedral (possibly as an adviser) in 1394–5 and then returned to Ulm, where in 1397 he was appointed master mason for life. He designed a west tower and supervised the construction of the lower stage, which is faced with a magnificent porch; the upper stages of the tower were later built by Matthäus BÖBLINGER, who altered Ensingen's plans.

Ensingen's post at Ulm did not inhibit him from accepting simultaneous commissions for other buildings. In 1398 he began to work at the Frauenkirche (1321–1516) in Esslingen, where he designed the west tower; the tower was eventually completed by Hans Böblinger, who may have altered the design. In 1399 Ensingen moved to Strassburg, where he established an office from which he directed work at Ulm and Esslingen and also attended to his latest commission, the completion of the west tower of Strassburg Cathedral. He designed and began the tower and built it as far as the octagon stage, but the openwork spire with its extraordinary spiral staircase was built by his successor, Johann Hültz; at 142 metres (466 feet), this spire was the tallest to be completed in the Middle Ages.

Ulrich had three sons who became masons. Of these the most prominent was Matthäus Ensinger (c.1390/1400–1463), who was trained by his father at Strasburg and then became master mason at Bern, where he designed the minster (1420–1). From his base in Bern he also worked in Esslingen, continuing his father's work on the tower, but in 1440 he was succeeded by Hans Böblinger. In 1446 he was appointed master mason at Ulm, where he was eventually succeeded by Matthäus Böblinger.

MDA; NDB; L. Mojon, *Der Münsterbaumeister Matthäus Ensingen* (1967).

**ENZINAS, FRANCISCO DE, or (English) Francis Dryander or (French) François du Chesne** (1520–53), Protestant Spanish humanist and reformer, born in Burgos and educated in Louvain and Wittenberg. He became a Lutheran and published a short systematic theology (*Breve y compendiosa institución cristiana*, 1540). He then translated the New Testament (*Nuevo Testamento de Nuestro Redemptor*, Antwerp, 1543) from the Greek text of ERASMUS, for which he was imprisoned in Brussels, partly for defying a decree against vernacular bibles, but also because his marginalia expressed unorthodox opinions. Two years later Enzinas escaped from prison. In 1546 he moved to England, where he was appointed professor of Greek at Cambridge, but on the accession of MARY I he left England and became an itinerant reformer. He travelled as far east as Constantinople, where he founded a Protestant colony. He visited Calvin in Geneva, and while travelling to Strasburg died of plague.

Enzinas's humanist works include translations of Livy, Lucian, and Plutarch. His most important works are all written in Latin: they consist of letters and an autobiographical treatise on the 'religion of Spain' in the Netherlands, *Historia de statu Belgico atque religione Hispanica* (1545), which was first published in French (1558).

DBEH; DHE; Francisco de Enzinas, *Epistolario*, ed. I. J. García Pinilla (1995); Jonathan Nelson, 'Francisco de Enzinas (Dryander) and Spanish Evangelical Humanism before the Council of Trent' (Ph.D. thesis, 1999).

**EPIC.** An epic is a long narrative poem, usually distinguished from the ballad by its greater length and by the use of stichic rather than stanzaic verse. The history of epic in the Renaissance is intertwined with the survival and rediscovery of classical epic and ancient critical analysis of the genre, with the development of romance, and with the inheritance of DANTE's *Divina commedia*, which is in some respects an epic without a hero. The recovery of HOMER and Hesiod (first published in Milan in 1493) gave access to the earliest surviving epics, and the survival of VIRGIL's *Aeneid* and OVID's *Metamorphoses* ensured that the two greatest epics of Augustan Rome left their mark on Renaissance epic. The late fifteenth century also saw the publication of the imperial Roman epics: Lucan's *Bellum civile*, Statius' *Thebais* and *Achilleis*, and CLAUDIAN's *Raptus Proserpinae* had been known throughout the Middle Ages, but Silius Italicus' *Punica* was discovered by Poggio BRACCIOLINI in 1416 or 1417 (possibly in Constance), and in 1417 Poggio discovered the first four and a half books of Valerius Flaccus' *Argonautica* in St Gallen.

The recovery of ARISTOTLE's *Poetics*, albeit in mutilated form, stimulated theoretical discussion of the epic genre. In the fifteenth century the *Poetics* was largely known through the commentary of AVERROËS, but sixteenth-century readers could consult new Latin translations (1498 and 1536) and an Italian translation (1549). The use of Aristotle to analyse the epic genre is apparent in the treatises of TRISSINO (*La poetica*, 1529), GIRALDI (*Discorsi intorno al comporre dei romanzi*, 1548), MINTURNO (*L'arte poetica*, 1564), CASTELVETRO (*Poetica d'Aristotele volgarizatta et sposta*, 1570), and TASSO (*Discorsi del poema eroico*, 1594).

Some Renaissance epics were, in the tradition of PETRARCH's *Africa*, resolutely classical: SANNAZARO's *De partu virginis*, Vida's *Christiad*, and Trissino's *La Italia liberata da' Gotthi* all attend carefully to classical precept and precedent. Other Renaissance epics, in the tradition of BOCCACCIO's *Teseida*, combined elements of classical form with the materials of romance (stories of Arthur, Charlemagne, and the *douzepers* (the twelve peers or Paladins)) to produce romance epics, a mixed genre discussed by Tasso in his *Discorsi del poema eroico* (1594). The most prominent Italian examples of romance epics are PULCI's *Morgante Maggiore*, BOIARDO's *Orlando innamorato*, Francesco Bello's *Mambriano* (1497), ARIOSTO's *Orlando furioso*, Bernardo TASSO's *Amadigi*, and Torquato Tasso's *Gerusalemme liberata*; the genre was in due course parodied, famously by Teofilo Falengo in *Baldus* and later by Alessandro Tassoni in *La secchia rapita* ('The Theft of the Bucket', 1622).

In France the secular epic never flourished, with the arguable exception of RONSARD's unfinished *Franciade* (1572), but the hexameral epics of DU BARTAS were widely read throughout Europe. In England Edmund SPENSER began a romance epic, *The Fairy Queen* (1590 and 1596); in the seventeenth century Abraham Cowley began a biblical epic, *Davideis* (1656), and John Milton wrote *Paradise Lost* (1667), the only modern epic of a stature comparable to its ancient originals and to CAMÕES's *Os Lusíadas*. In Spain, where the twelfth-century epic *Canto* (or *Poema*) *de mio Cid* had provided Castile with a national epic, Golden Age writers of epics in the Italian tradition included Cristóbal de VIRUÉS, Juan de la CUEVA, and Alonso de ERCILLA Y ZÚÑIGA.

The countries outside Italy that are richest in Renaissance epic are CROATIA and PORTUGAL. On the Dalmatian coast of Croatia, Marko Marulić (1450–1524) wrote a biblical epic (in Latin) called *Davidas* and Jacov Bunić (1469–1534) published a Latin epic *De vita et gestis Christi* (1515). In Croatian, Mauro Vetranić Čavčić (1482–1576) wrote an allegorical epic on the theme of the pilgrim, Brno Krnarutić (1520–72) wrote an epic on the defence of Szigetvár (Hungary) during the Ottoman siege of 1566, Juraj Baraković (1548–1638) wrote *Vila Slovinka*, a heroic account of the history of Zara (now Zadar), and, finest of all, Ivan Gundulić (1588–1638) wrote *Osman*, an epic account of heroic resistance to the Ottomans. In Portugal, the success of Camões's *Os Lusíadas*, the greatest of Renaissance epics, overshadowed the work of his many successors, who included Jerónimo CORTE REAL.

**EPICURUS IN THE RENAISSANCE.** The moral and natural philosopher Epicurus (341–270 BC) was a native of the Athenian colony in Samos who in *c.*307/6 bought a house with a garden which became his residence and the home of his disciples. The Epicurean School was the subject of suspicion and libel in antiquity, because its self-sufficient privacy and its admission of slaves and women encouraged outsiders to interpret its moral philosophy of principled hedonism as profligacy, whereas in practice it was closer to asceticism. With the advent of Christianity, Epicureanism became anathema, because its advocates, who championed a form of atomism derived from Democritus, denied the existence of a provident creator god and of an afterlife, and argued that the good life could be secured by kindness, friendship, and moderation of appetite.

Accounts of Epicureanism were transmitted to the Renaissance by sympathetic Stoics such as SENECA and CICERO and by LUCRETIUS, whose *De rerum natura* embodied Epicurean natural philosophy. The revival of these authors in the fifteenth century stimulated an interest in Epicureanism in philosophers such as Lorenzo VALLA and Francisco de QUEVEDO. The only fragments of Epicurus that could be read at first hand were three letters included in the account of Epicurus in Diogenes Laertius' *Lives of the Philosophers*, which became available in a Latin translation in the 1420s. Despite the emphasis on asceticism in these accounts, Epicureanism continued to be a byword for shameless voluptuousness; as a character in Giordano BRUNO's *De gli eroici furori* observes, the notion of Epicurus as a sensualist can only be maintained by those who do not read his writings. In England, Ben JONSON caricatured Epicureanism as principled shallowness in the character of Sir Epicure Mammon in *The Alchemist*. In the seventeenth century the atomism of Epicurus was rediscovered and developed into the corpuscular philosophy of the period, which in turn evolved into a branch of the modern discipline of physics.

Howard Jones, *The Epicurean Tradition* (1992).

**EPIPHANIUS OF EVESHAM** (*c.*1570–*c.*1623), English sculptor, born into a prominent Herefordshire family. The scanty documentary record of his early life shows that Epiphanius was working in 1592 in the London studio of an exiled Brabantine sculptor whose English name was Richard Stevens (and who died in the same year). In 1601 Epiphanius established a studio in Paris, where he remained until *c.*1614, but no work from his Paris studio is known to survive. On returning to England he specialized in the carving of tombs; he was responsible for the tomb of Edmund West (1618, Marsworth, in Essex), which is decorated with engraved brasses, and for the signed tomb of Lord Teynam (1632, Lynsted, Kent), which includes a kneeling figure of Lady Teynam and reliefs portraying their grieving children. Epiphanius was probably the sculptor of the tomb (*c.*1619) of Robert Rich, earl of Warwick (the first husband of Penelope Devereux, Sir Philip SIDNEY's Stella) in Felsted (Essex), which contains a series of allegorical reliefs.

*MDA* s.v. Evesham, Epiphanius.

**EPISCHOFER, HANS** (d. 1585), German goldsmith, a native of Augsburg who in 1561 moved to Nuremberg, where he specialized in the engraving of scientific instruments, especially globes, astrolabes, and navigational instruments. Examples of his work are preserved in the Germanisches Nationalmuseum in Nuremberg.

***EPISTOLAE OBSCURORUM VIRORUM*** (Latin; 'Letters of Obscure Men'), a two-part pamphlet (published in 1515 and 1517) that constitutes the most important literary product of the dispute between Johannes REUCHLIN and the Dominicans of Cologne. The title parodies that of a collection of genuine letters to Reuchlin which he had published in 1514 as *Clarorum virorum epistolae*. The authors were both supporters of Reuchlin: part I was written by CROTUS RUBIANUS (1486–1540), part II is substantially the work of Ulrich von HUTTEN.

The imaginary letters were addressed to a real person, a humanist called Ortwin Gratius (1491–1542) who was a supporter of the Dominicans. These letters, which are cast in a hilarious parody of monastic Latin, are a satire on the laborious reasoning of late SCHOLASTICISM and on ecclesiastical abuses. The propaganda war unleashed by the *Letters* helped to create a favourable milieu for the reception of Luther's doctrines. The *Epistolae* were read by humanists all over Europe, and contributed to the discrediting of SCHOLASTICISM in the mid-sixteenth century.

H. Holborn (ed.), *On the Eve of the Reformation: 'Letters of Obscure Men'* (1964); R. P. Becker, *A War of Fools: The Letters of Obscure Men. A Study of the Satire and the Satirized* (1981).

**EQUESTRIAN STATUES.** The most important models for the equestrian statues of the Renaissance were the four bronze horses of San Marco (Venice) and the statue of *Marcus Aurelius* preserved outside San Giovanni in Laterano for centuries (in the belief that it was a statue of Constantine, the first Christian emperor) and transferred in 1538 to its present location in Piazza del Campidoglio. Painted GRISAILLE equestrian monuments, such as Paolo UCCELLO's *Sir John Hawkwood* (1436) and ANDREA DEL CASTAGNO's *Niccolò da Tolentino* (1456), both in Florence Cathedral, were a common memorial form in fifteenth-century Italy, but the first free-standing equestrian statue to be executed since classical antiquity was DONATELLO's *Il Gattamelata* (*c.*1446), which stands outside the Basilica del Santo in Padua. Later in the century, the most important equestrian statue was VERROCCHIO's *Colleoni* (1485–8) on the Campo SS Giovanni e Paolo in Venice. The technical problems of depicting a rearing horse had been anticipated by LEONARDO DA VINCI in his plans for a prancing horse in the Sforza and Trivulzio monuments, but the only legacies of Leonardo's intentions are his drawings and a few small sixteenth-century bronzes.

**EQUICOLA, MARIO** (*c.*1470–1525), Italian courtier and philosopher. He was educated in Florence under FICINO and then entered the service of the ESTE court in Ferrara, where he spent his entire career except for a short period at the court of Isabella d'ESTE in Mantua. His most important

literary work was *Libro de natura de amore* (1525), an exhaustive treatise on Neoplatonic love, and *De mulieribus* (1501).
DBI.

**ERASMUS, DESIDERIUS** (c.1466–1536), Dutch humanist and theologian, born in Rotterdam, the illegitimate son of a priest, and educated in Deventer by the BRETHREN OF THE COMMON LIFE. In 1487 he became an Augustinian canon at Steyn and five years later he was ordained as a priest. He studied and taught in the Collège de Montaigu in Paris (1499), Louvain (1502–4, 1517–21), Italy (1506–9), England (1509–14), and Basel and Freiburg (1529–36). In Venice Erasmus worked with ALDUS MANUTIUS, and in Basel with Johann FROBEN. In England, he taught at Cambridge and became a member of the circle of Sir Thomas MORE and John COLET.

Erasmus' didactic and satirical works, which urged the need for Catholic reform but opposed separation, included *Enchiridion militis christiani* (1503), Μωρίας Ἐγκώμιον (*Moriae encomium*, 1511), *Colloquia familiaria* (1522–33), and *Ciceronianus* (1528). The *Enchiridion* is a 'handbook of the Christian soldier' in which the emphasis is on piety and learning. *Moriae encomium*, which is known in English as *The Praise of Folly*, is a satire on clerical abuse written at the suggestion of Sir Thomas More. The *Colloquies* are vivid and witty dialogues with a caustic satirical edge. *Ciceronianus* is an important document in the debate about the correct form of LATIN, and satirizes those who carry the imitation of CICERO to extremes.

Erasmus' most important controversial works centred on his debate with LUTHER, which Erasmus inaugurated with a tract on the freedom of the human will (*Diatribe de libero arbitrio*, 1524). The most important of his many scholarly works were his edition of the Greek New Testament with a Latin translation (1516), and his *Adagia*, a massive collection of classical proverbs. He also edited classical and patristic texts, including works by Ambrose, Aristotle, Arnobius, Augustine, Basil, Chrysostom, Cicero, Irenaeus, Jerome, Livy, Ptolemy, Seneca, Suetonius and Terence, all of which were published by Froben; many of these editions were collaborative, and it is often difficult to identify the precise extent of Erasmus' contribution.

Erasmus was the most influential scholar of his age, and his wide-ranging correspondence disseminated humanist values all over Europe. Many of his writings were posthumously placed on the INDEX.

NDB; *Collected Works of Erasmus* (76 vols. to date, 1974–99); M. M. Phillips, *Erasmus and the Northern Renaissance* (1950); E. W. Kohls, *Die Theologie des Erasmus* (2 vols., 1966); L. E. Halkin, *Érasme et l'humanisme chrétien* (1969); J. Tracy, *The Politics of Erasmus* (1978); M. O'Rourke Boyle, *Rhetoric and Reform: Erasmus' Civil Dispute with Luther* (1983); R. J. Schoek, *Erasmus of Europe* (1990); A. G. Dickens and W. R. D. Jones, *Erasmus the Reformer* (1994).

**ERASTIANISM** is the theological affirmation of the ascendancy of the state over the Church in ecclesiastical matters. Its eponym is Thomas ERASTUS, who in 1568 took part in a disputation in Heidelberg in which the Englishman George Wither (not to be confused with the poet of the same name)

had proposed a doctoral disputation opposing vestments (part of the VESTIARIAN CONTROVERSY), and when the university disallowed the topic, successfully proposed a disputation affirming the excommunicating power of the presbytery. In 1589 the reply of Erastus, *Explicatio gravissimae questionis ultrum excommunicatio*, was published posthumously by Giacomo Castelvetri, who had married his widow. This book bears the imprint *Pesclavii*, and so claims to have been printed in Poschiavo, in the Swiss canton of Graubünden; it was in fact printed in London by John Wolfe, with whom Castelvetri was staying.

The *Explicatio* was not translated into English until 1659, when it appeared as *The Nullity of Church Censures*, but the Latin text was widely read in England. Richard HOOKER incorporated Erastian views in his *Ecclesiastical Polity* (1594), in which he asserted the supremacy of the secular power, and the Westminster Assembly (1643–9) contained an Erastian party, of which the most prominent members were Thomas Coleman, John Lightfoot, John SELDEN, and Bulstrode Whitelocke; an anti-Erastian chapter 'Of Church Censures' was incorporated into the Westminster Confession, but was not ratified by Parliament.

Erastus defended the authority of the state in ecclesiastical matters, but did not discuss the relationship between the Church and the state. The central Erastian principle of the supremacy of the state over the Church is therefore one on which Erastus never stated a view; in that sense, the principle would more accurately be associated with GROTIUS. The term acquired its modern sense during the Westminster debates of 1643. In this modified sense, Erastianism survived into the secular modern state: in 1928, for example, Parliament rejected the revision of the Book of COMMON PRAYER proposed by the Church of England.

**ERASTUS, THOMAS** (1524–83), Swiss-German theologian, born on 7 September 1524, probably in Baden, in the Swiss canton of Aargau; his surname was Lüber or Lieber. He studied theology in Basel, and philosophy and medicine in Bologna and Padua. In 1558 he became court physician to the elector palatine, Otto Heinrich, and at the same time took up a chair in medicine at Heidelberg; in 1559, FRIEDRICH III (Otto Heinrich's successor) appointed him as a privy counsellor and as a member of the church consistory.

In theology Erastus was a Zwinglian. He defended the Zwinglian memorialist view of the EUCHARIST in the sacramentarian conferences of Heidelberg (1560) and Maulbronn (1564) and engaged in oral and written polemical exchanges with the Lutheran Johann Marbach of Strasbourg. The Zwinglian position on church discipline set Erastus in opposition to the CALVINISM of Caspar Olevianus, who in 1570 sought to impose Genevan ecclesiastical discipline on the Palatinate. Excommunication is one of the central features of the Geneva system, and Erastus was quickly excommunicated on the grounds of his SOCINIAN sympathies, for which the evidence was his correspondence with TRANSYLVANIA; the excommunication was not revoked until 1575. In 1580 Erastus returned to Basel, where he was made professor of ethics in

1583 and where he died on 31 December 1583. See the separate entry on ERASTIANISM.

*NDB* s.v. Erast.

**ERBACH, CHRISTIAN** (1568/73–1635), German composer, organist, and teacher who enjoyed the patronage of Marcus Fugger in Augsburg, and became organist at the Church of St Moritz, and city organist and head of the *Stadtpfeifer* (town pipers). In 1614 he became assistant organist at Augsburg, which required him to teach composition and organ playing to cathedral choir school pupils. His repuation as a teacher grew and he attracted both Catholic and Protestant students from Augsburg and beyond. He composed about 120 keyboard works and sacred, polyphonic vocal music which betrayed a Venetian influence.

**ERCILLA Y ZÚÑIGA, ALONSO DE** (1533–94), Spanish soldier and epic poet, born into a noble family in Madrid. As a young man Ercilla travelled in Europe and then sailed to America, where in 1555 he participated in the invasion of the Arauco valley (Chile); he subsequently fought in Peru. In 1560 he became seriously ill, and on recovering returned to Spain, where he spent the rest of his life at court.

Ercilla's *La Araucana*, the greatest of Spanish Golden Age epics, celebrates the conquest of the Arauco valley. The first 35 cantos were published in three parts (Madrid, 1569; Zaragoza, 1578; Madrid, 1589); a revised edition (Madrid, 1597) contained 37 cantos, but the authorship of the two extra cantos has been contested. The poem is written in *octavas reales*, the Italianate form introduced to Spanish literature by BOSCÀ. In his epic Ercilla praises both the brutality of the conquistadors (who cut off the hands of one of the Indian leaders) and the courage of the Indians, and includes prophetic visions of the battles of SAINT-QUENTIN (1567) and LEPANTO (1571). The first of several imitations of Ercilla's *La Araucana* was Pedro de Oña's *Arauco domado* (Lima, 1596), a rival epic commissioned by Ercilla's commanding officer García Hurtado de Mendoza, who felt that he had been given an insufficiently prominent part in Ercilla's epic.

*DBEH*: Frank Pierce, *Alonso de Ercilla y Zúñiga* (1984).

**ERCOLE DE' ROBERTI or Ercole da Ferrara** (1455/6–1496), Italian painter, born in Ferrara, where he may have been a pupil of Francesco del COSSA, whom he assisted on works such as the *Months* in the Schifanoia. He also worked with Cossa in Bologna, assisting with Cossa's altarpieces. His earliest independent work is the *Madonna Enthroned with Saints* (1480) painted for the Church of Santa Maria in Porto in Ravenna and now in the Brera (Milan). Ercole was appointed court painter to the BENTIVOGLIO family in Bologna, and in this capacity painted portraits of Giovanni II Bentivoglio and his wife Ginevra (1486, National Gallery, Washington).

In 1486 Ercole returned to Ferrara, where he succeeded Cosimo TURA as court painter to the ESTE FAMILY. In this period he painted *Harvest of the Madonna* (National Gallery, London), a *Pietà* (Walker Art Gallery, Liverpool), and *Way of the Cross* (Gemäldegalerie, Dresden), which was part of a predella painted for the Church of San Giovanni in Monte, Bologna.

Ercole was formerly confused with the Bolognese painter Ercole di Giulio Cesare de' Grande (d. 1531), none of whose pictures is known to survive.

*DBI*; *MDA* s.v. Roberti, Ercole de.

**ERIC** (*c*.1382–1459), king of Denmark, Norway, and Sweden, was the son of the duke of Pomerania and the grand-nephew of Queen Margaret I, who designated Eric as heir to her three thrones. In 1396 Margaret abdicated in Eric's favour, but continued to exercise considerable power until her death in 1412. Eric's reign was dominated by constant warfare with Holstein, Sweden, and the cities of the HANSEATIC LEAGUE. He was deposed in 1439 and retired to Pomerania.

*DBL* s.v. Erik VII af Pommern; *NDB* s.v. Erich I; *NBL* and *SBL* s.v. Erik av Pommern.

**ERIC XIV** (1533–77), king of Sweden, was the son of King GUSTAVUS VASA and his first wife Catherine of Saxe-Lauenburg. He acceded to the throne in 1561, and for the eight years of his reign was constantly at war with Denmark and Poland; in 1567 he ordered the murder of the STURE family, which forfeited the support of many Swedish noblemen. His rivalry with his half-brother John (later King JOHN III), which led to John's imprisonment in 1562 (because he had married the daughter of King SIGISMUND I of Poland), culminated in Eric's deposition by John in 1569, whereupon Eric spent the rest of his life in prison. A man with cultural interests, the Renaissance at last won a foothold in Sweden during his reign, for much of which, however, he was subject to periods of insanity.

*SBL* s.v. Erik XIV.

**ERSKINE, JOHN** (1509–91), Scottish reformer. Following the death of his near relatives at Flodden in 1513, Erskine was brought up by his uncle Sir Thomas Erskine, secretary to JAMES V. He was educated possibly at Aberdeen, and then on the Continent; on his return, he brought with him a French teacher of Greek, whom he established at the family home in Montrose, and whose presence hastened the advance of Reformation ideas in Scotland. He was on the Continent again from 1537 to 1540, and between 1542 and 1544. A convinced reformist, he welcomed KNOX to his home on the latter's visit to Scotland in 1555, and negotiated between the rebellious Protestant leaders and the regent, MARY OF LORRAINE, in the disturbances of 1558–9, but also signed the suspension of her regency in October 1559. He retained influence within the reforming party on the return to Scotland of MARY, QUEEN OF SCOTS, and served as moderator of the general assembly in 1564, and subsequent assemblies of 1565 and 1566. Following Mary's flight in 1567, he assisted in the coronation of the infant JAMES VI, and remained a leading reformist voice in Scotland until his death.

**ESCOBAR, PEDRO DE** (*c*.1465–after 1535), Portuguese composer active in Spain, where he sang at the court of Isabella I. He became *magister puerorum* at Seville Cathedral in 1507, but resigned four years later. He composed in a contrapuntal style and wrote sacred music as well as eighteen *villancicos* (secular songs).

## ESCORIAL, SAN LORENZO DE EL

**ESCORIAL, SAN LORENZO DE EL**, a monastery, royal palace, and royal mausoleum near Madrid. On 10 August 1557, the feast day of St Lawrence, the Spanish army of King PHILIP II defeated the French army of Duke Anne de MONT-MORENCY at the battle of SAINT-QUENTIN. King Philip decided to commemorate the victory by building a monastery assigned to the Hieronymite Order and dedicated to St Lawrence; the building, which was originally known as San Lorenzo el Real, is now known as El Escorial.

In 1563 Juan Bautista de TOLEDO, the royal architect, drew up the ground plan for the Escorial and began the construction of the two-storeyed Patio de los Evangelistas (modelled on SANGALLO's Palazzo Farnese in Rome) and the forbiddingly severe south façade. On his death in 1567 Juan Bautista was unofficially succeeded by his assistant Juan de HERRERA, who in completing the building modified the plans of Juan Bautista. Philip II entrusted the various tasks on which Juan Bautista had embarked to several architects, including Giambattista CASTELLO (who built the monumental staircase), Francesco PACIOTTO (who designed the church), and Antonio de Villacastín (who proposed the extra storey to increase the monastic accommodation). Juan de Herrera co-ordinated the entire project and personally designed the infirmary and chapel. The building was completed within 21 years (1563–84).

The vast scale of the Escorial is apparent in its external measurements (206 metres/680 feet by 161 metres/531 feet), its 1,200 doors, and its 2,600 windows. Inside, the principal painter of frescoes was TIBALDI, who in the library (54 metres (177 feet) long) painted the ceiling with allegorical representations of the LIBERAL ARTS; Luca CAMBIASO also contributed to the decoration, and Federico ZUCCARO painted altarpieces. The private apartments of King Philip were decorated with TALAVERA tiles. The royal mausoleum (Panteón de los Reyes), which is reached by a marble and jasper staircase, contains the remains of all but three Spanish monarchs from CHARLES V to the present (the exceptions are Philip V, Ferdinand VI, and Amadeus I).

G. Kubler, *Building the Escorial* (1982).

## ESPINEL Y GÓMEZ ADORNO, VICENTE MARTÍNEZ DE

**ESPINEL Y GÓMEZ ADORNO, VICENTE MARTÍNEZ DE** (1550–1624), Spanish poet, novelist, and musician, born in Ronda and educated at Salamanca University, from which he was expelled in 1572. He subsequently became a soldier in Flanders, serving with the army of Alessandro FARNESE at the siege of Maastricht in 1579. He returned to Spain *c.*1584, entered the Church, and in 1591 was appointed chaplain (i.e. a priest in charge of a chapel) at Ronda, a post of which he was deprived because of his absences. His musical abilities enabled him to secure a post as choirmaster at Plasencia.

In 1591 Espinel collected his poems and his verse translations of Horace as *Diversas rimas, con el Arte poética y algunas odas de Oracio traduzidas en verso castellano*. He revived the form known as *décimas*, a stanza consisting of ten octosyllabic lines; his adept use of this measure led to its becoming known as *espinelas*. Espinel was also an innovative student of the guitar, and is thought to have been responsible for the addition of the fifth string to the *vihuela de mano*, the predecessor of the guitar.

Espinel was the author of *Relaciones de la vida del escudero Marcos de Obregón* (1618), an elegant novel which is in some respects PICARESQUE (though its ageing narrator is not a rogue) and in some measure autobiographical.

DBEH; George Haley, *Vicente Espinel and Marcos Obregón: A Life and its Literary Representation* (1959).

## ESPINOSA, DIEGO DE

**ESPINOSA, DIEGO DE** (1502–72), Spanish cardinal and statesman who studied CIVIL LAW at Salamanca, where he later became a professor. He was appointed as a crown judge in Seville, and was subsequently appointed by PHILIP II as president of the Council of Castile (1565) and inquisitor-general (1566), in which capacity he framed the royal decree of January 1567 that rendered the language and culture of the MORISCOS illegal and required Muslims to renounce their culture and hand over their children to be educated by Christian priests; this decree led to the revolt of the Granadine Moriscos which erupted on 24 December 1568. Espinosa became a confidant of the king, and within the Church became bishop of Sigüenza and cardinal (1568).

DBEH; DHE.

## ESPINOSA, GASPAR DE

**ESPINOSA, GASPAR DE** (d. 1537), Spanish conquistador, born in Medina del Campo. He became known as 'el licenciado Espinosa', which may imply that he had been a student of law. He travelled to Spanish America and assisted Pedrarias DÁVILA in the trial and execution of BALBOA. He subsequently founded the city of Panamá and then led an expedition to what is now Costa Rica.

After a period in Spain Espinosa returned to South America as an administrator in Peru, where he attempted (without success) to reconcile PIZARRO to his rebellious second in command Diego de ALMAGRO.

DBEH.

## ESQUIVEL, JUAN DE

**ESQUIVEL, JUAN DE** (*fl.* 1494–1519), Spanish explorer who accompanied COLUMBUS on his second voyage (1494) and assisted Nicolás de OVANDO in the conquest of Hispaniola. In 1509, at the command of Diego COLÓN, Esquivel led the conquest of Jamaica, which thereafter became a Spanish possession until 1658. Esquivel's brutality towards the Indians was described and condemned by LAS CASAS in his *Brevíssima relación de la destrucción de las Indias* (1552).

DBEH; DHE.

## ESQUIVEL Y BARAHONA, JUAN GIL DE

**ESQUIVEL Y BARAHONA, JUAN GIL DE** (*c.*1563–after 1613), Spanish composer who was *maestro de capilla* at the cathedrals of Oviedo, Calahorra, and Ciudad Rodrigo, whose bishop, Pedro Ponce de León, paid for his Latin church music to be printed. His works were in use throughout Spain and Portugal and by 1610 had reached Mexico.

**ESSEX, ROBERT DEVEREUX, EARL OF** (1567–1601). Stepson of ELIZABETH's favourite LEICESTER, Essex's capture of CÁDIZ (1596) was an early triumph. A mission in Ireland, where he was sent to subdue TYRONE's rebellion, ended unsuccessfully with his premature return home; he later mounted an attempted coup, currying popular favour in part with a staging of Shakespeare's *Richard II*, but this led only to his own execution.

*DNB* s.v. Devereux, Robert.

**ESTATE or** (Latin) *status* **or** (Dutch) *staat* **or** (French) *état* **or** (German) *Stand* **or** (Italian) *stato*. In the political sphere the term 'estate' denoted a class or order that participated in government either directly or through its representatives. The system of representation through estates arose in Europe in the thirteenth century, and remained in place until it was displaced by popular representation; the French Revolution precipitated the end of representation by estates in France (though the last assembly had been convened in 1614), but Navarre maintained representation by estates till 1828, Hungary till 1848, Sweden till 1866, and the duchy of Mecklenburg till 1918.

Societies were traditionally divided into three classes according to whether they prayed, fought, or laboured. In England, for example, Edmund Dudley, president of the King's Council under Henry VII, divided society into 'clergy, chivalry and commonalty' (*Tree of Commonwealth*, 1509). The most important formulation of the tripartite division of society is contained in the *Traité des ordres et simples dignités* (Paris, 1610) of the French jurist Charles Loyseau (1566–1627). The contention that the estates were the central feature of early modern society is reflected in the use of the term *Ständestaat* by German historians.

This ancient theory of social stratification, which may derive from the Roman hierarchy of senators, equestrians, and plebeians, was formalized in the assemblies of late medieval Europe. In the English Parliament the three estates were the lords spiritual (the clergy), the lords temporal (barons and peers), and the Commons. Until the Parliament of 1428 the estates in Scotland were prelates, tenants-in-chief, and townsmen; thereafter they became the lords (lay and clerical), the commissioners of shires, and the burgesses. In France the three estates of the États-Généraux (Estates-General) were the clergy, the nobility, and the townsmen, and assemblies such as the Bohemian *sněm*, the Castilian *cortes* and Catalan *corts*, the Dutch *staaten generaal*, the Polish *sejm*, the Hungarian *országgyüles*, and the independent *Landtage* of Germany were similarly divided. The first two estates are not normally known by their numbers, but the third estate in English refers to the Commons and *le tier état* in French to the *roturiers* (the commonalty). The number and constitution of estates was not consistent across western Europe. The Aragonese *corts* contained four *brazos* (arms): clergy, *ricohombres* (magnates), *infanzones* (lesser nobility), and townsmen; similarly, the Swedish *riksdag* contained four estates: clergy, barons, townsmen, and peasants. Peasants also constituted a separate estate in Denmark (until 1627), Friesland, and the Tirol.

Some writers on constitutional affairs used the term 'three estates' in a quite different sense to refer to rival forms of government, i.e. monarchy, aristocracy, and democracy, and in English usage the three estates were sometimes said to be the crown, the House of Lords, and the House of Commons. In Sir David Lindsay's *A Satire of the Three Estates*, which was performed before the regent Mary of Guise and her court in 1554, the three estates are the Nobility, the Spirituality, and the Merchants.

G. Duby, *Les Trois Ordres ou l'imaginaire du féodalisme* (1978); O. Niccoli, *I sacerdoti, i guerrieri, i contadini: Storia di un'immagine della società* (1979); M. L. Bush, *Social Orders and Social Classes in Europe since 1500* (1992).

**ESTE, ALFONSO I D'** (1476–1534), duke of Ferrara, the son of Ercole I d'ESTE and Eleanor of Aragon, the daughter of King FERRANTE I of Naples. In 1491 he married Anna Sforza, daughter of Galeazzo Maria SFORZA, duke of Milan; in 1497 she died in childbirth and in 1501 Alfonso married Lucrezia BORGIA, daughter of Pope ALEXANDER VI. He succeeded his father as duke in 1505 and soon had to suppress a conspiracy against him mounted by his brothers Ferrante and Giulio.

Alfonso was a leading soldier in the WARS OF ITALY, and he left much of the cultural side of his court in the capable hands of Lucrezia Borgia, but he had an interest in art, and commissioned paintings by Giovanni BELLINI (*The Feast of the Gods*) and TITIAN for his palace. He was a knowledgeable student of GUNS and ARTILLERY, and established a foundry for casting large cannons. On the formation of the League of CAMBRAI in 1508 he was appointed commander of the papal troops by Pope JULIUS II, and destroyed the Venetian fleet on the river Po. In 1512 he fought for the French in the battle of Ravenna, at which he successfully deployed his advanced artillery.

Alfonso carried on a long feud with Pope LEO X, who persuaded CHARLES V to assist him in the conquest of Ferrara; Leo's death in 1521 enabled him to retain his duchy.

*DBI* s.v. Alfonso I; *MDA* s.v. Este (i) (8) Alfonso I d'Este.

**ESTE, ALFONSO II D'** (1533–97), duke of Ferrara, the elder son of Duke Ercole II d'ESTE and RENÉE OF FRANCE. He lived in France at the court of King HENRI II from 1551 to 1559, serving in the French army against the HABSBURGS in the final stages of the WARS OF ITALY. In 1559 Alfonso succeeded to the dukedom and returned to Ferrara. In April 1559 the Treaty of CATEAU-CAMBRÉSIS signalled the end of the Wars of Italy, and Alfonso enjoyed a 38-year reign that was never disrupted by war. The splendour of his court in Ferrara was renowned throughout Europe, and Alfonso presided over an unending succession of hunts, balls, and tournaments in a spirit of cultivated Epicureanism. Alfonso was the patron of TASSO, whom he later imprisoned.

Duke Alfonso was married three times. His first wife was Lucrezia de' Medici, daughter of Duke Cosimo; his second wife, Barbara of Austria, was the daughter of the Emperor FERDINAND I; his third wife, Margherita Gonzaga, was daughter of Guglielmo, duke of Mantua. None of these marriages produced a successor for the dukedom. Alfonso designated his cousin Cesare d'Este (1533–1628) as his successor, but the papacy ruled that Cesare was illegitimate and hence ineligible, and on Alfonso's death the duchy reverted to the PAPAL STATE. The dramatic monologue known as 'My Last Duchess', by Robert Browning, seems to be part of an imaginary conversation between Duke Alfonso, whose wife Lucrezia has died, and a marriage agent representing Barbara of Austria.

*DBI* s.v. Alfonso II; *MDA* s.v. Este (i) (12) Alfonso II d'Este.

**ESTE, BEATRICE D'** (1475–97), duchess of Milan, the second daughter of Duke Ercole I d'ESTE of Ferrara and Eleanor of Aragon, and the younger sister of Isabella d'ESTE, with whom she was educated at the ducal court. At the age of 5 Beatrice was betrothed to Ludovico SFORZA, the 29-year-old regent of Milan; ten years later they were married (January 1491), and six years after her marriage she died in childbirth on 3 January 1497, aged 22.

In her six years at the court of Milan Beatrice was active in both politics and patronage. In 1492 she visited Venice in an effort to secure for her husband recognition as duke of Milan. The following year, in the wake of the battle of FORNOVO, Beatrice worked alongside her husband in the peace settlement that was negotiated at Vercelli between CHARLES VIII and the Italian princes. At the court in Milan, Beatrice extended her patronage to a circle of writers and artists that included BRAMANTE and LEONARDO DA VINCI; the many buildings to which she contributed through her patronage include the Castello Sforzesco in Milan and the Certosa di Pavia.

*DBI* s.v. Beatrice; *MDA* s.v. Este (i) (7) Beatrice d'Este; Julia Cartwright, *Beatrice d'Este, Duchess of Milan* (1902).

**ESTE, BORSO D'** (1413–71), duke of Modena and Ferrara, the second son of Niccolò III d'Este (1383–1441); his elder brother was Leonello d'ESTE, and on Leonello's death in 1450 Borso succeeded him as ruler of Ferrara. Borso was created duke of Modena and Reggio by the Emperor FRIEDRICH III in 1452, and in 1471 was created duke of Ferrara by Pope PAUL II. His patronage centred on humanist scholars and writers (for whom he established a printing press in Ferrara) and on art: he appointed Cosimo TURA as his principal court painter in 1458 and commissioned Francesco del COSSA to paint the frescoes in the Palazzo Schifanoia; he also established contact with MANTEGNA and PIERO DELLA FRANCESCA. He is the eponym of the *Bibbia di Borso*, one of the finest manuscript books of the century. He was succeeded by his half-brother Ercole I d'ESTE.

*DBI* s.v. Borso; *MDA* s.v. Este (i) (4) Borso d'Este.

**ESTE, ERCOLE I D'** (1431–1505), duke of Ferrara, the third son of Niccolò III d'Este (1383–1441) and the younger half-brother of Leonello d'ESTE and Borso d'ESTE. He spent his youth in Naples, and in 1463 returned to Ferrara at the behest of Borso, whom he succeeded in 1471. He married Eleanor of Aragon, daughter of King FERRANTE I of Naples; their children included Alfonso I d'ESTE (Ercole's successor), Beatrice d'ESTE, Isabella d'ESTE, and Cardinal Ippolito d'ESTE. Ercole's nephew Niccolò attempted to stage a coup when Ercole was absent from Ferrara, but Eleanor had him beheaded.

Ercole's patronage was extended to humanist scholars, artists (including Cosimo TURA, Ercole de' ROBERTI, and Lorenzo COSTA), and writers (including BOIARDO and ARIOSTO); he particularly encouraged the performance of vocal music and plays. During his rule Ferrara expanded considerably, and in the project known after its patron as the Herculean Addition (*Addizione Erculea*), designed by Biagio ROSSETTI, trebled the land within the city walls and built four new churches and eight new palaces.

Duke Ercole became caught up in the conflict known as the War of FERRARA (1482–4), at the conclusion of which he was forced to cede the salt-rich Polesine to Venice. He did not oppose the French invasion of Italy of 1494 which inaugurated the WARS OF ITALY, and again remained neutral when France invaded for a second time in 1499. In 1500, after protracted negotiations with Pope ALEXANDER VI, Ercole consented to the proposed marriage of his son and successor Alfonso to Lucrezia BORGIA, the pope's daughter.

*DBI* s.v. Ercole I; *MDA* s.v. Este (i) (5) Ercole I d'Este; W. L. Gundersheimer (ed.), *Art and Life at the Court of Ercole I d'Este: The 'De triumphis religionis' of Giovanni Sabadino degli Arienti* (1972); Thomas Tuohy, *Herculean Ferrara: Ercole d'Este and the Invention of a Ducal Capital* (1996).

**ESTE, ERCOLE II D'** (1508–59), duke of Ferrara, the son of Duke Alfonso I d'ESTE and his second wife Lucrezia Borgia, the daughter of Pope ALEXANDER VI. In 1528 he married RENÉE DE FRANCE, the daughter of King LOUIS XII of France, and in 1534 succeeded his father as duke of Ferrara. In 1536 Renée received CALVIN at the ducal court and later became a Protestant; in 1554 the duke removed her children and briefly imprisoned her.

In the WARS OF ITALY, Duke Ercole was for many years a supporter of Spain and the Empire, but in 1551 changed sides and became an ally of HENRI II of France and Pope PAUL IV in their war against the Emperor CHARLES V. He was defeated in 1558 but was allowed to retain most of his territory.

*DBI* s.v. Ercole II; *MDA* s.v. Este (i) (10) Ercole II d'Este.

**ESTE, IPPOLITO D'** (1479–1520), Italian cardinal, the son of Duke Ercole I d'ESTE and the younger brother of Duke Alfonso I d'ESTE. He became an abbot at the age of 5 and an archbishop at 7, and in 1496, aged 17, became archbishop of Milan. He took little interest in the Church, but was an accomplished military commander and a generous patron of the arts. He fought with Ludovico SFORZA against the French and defended Ferrara against Venice and against Pope JULIUS II. His secretary was ARIOSTO, who dedicated *Orlando furioso* to Cardinal Ippolito. He is sometimes confused with his nephew and fellow archbishop of Milan Cardinal Ippolito d'ESTE, the builder of Villa d'ESTE.

*DBI* s.v. Este, Ippolito d'; *MDA* s.v. Este (i) (9) Ippolito I d'Este.

**ESTE, IPPOLITO D'** (1509–72), Italian cardinal, the son of Duke Alfonso I d'ESTE and his second wife Lucrezia Borgia, the daughter of Pope ALEXANDER VI; he was the younger brother of Duke Ercole II d'ESTE. In 1520, aged 10, he succeeded his uncle and namesake Cardinal Ippolito d'ESTE (with whom he is sometimes confused) as archbishop of Milan. Ippolito worked as a papal legate in France and later came to be associated with the French party in the papal curia. He built the Villa d'ESTE at Tivoli, where he assembled a large collection of paintings and sculptures.

DBI s.v. Este, Ippolito d'; MDA s.v. Este (i) (11) Ippolito II d'Este.

**ESTE, ISABELLA D'** (1474–1539), marchioness of Mantua, the daughter of Duke Ercole I d'ESTE of Ferrara and Eleanor of Aragon, and the sister of Beatrice d'ESTE. Isabella received a formidable education at the ducal court (where her tutors included Battista GUARINI), and on 15 February 1490, aged 16, married Gianfrancesco II GONZAGA, marquis of Mantua, by whom she was to have six children. Gianfrancesco pursued his military career in theatres of war far from Mantua, and took little interest in the governance of his duchy, so the presiding spirit of the ducal court was Isabella d'Este, who was in any case better educated and more intelligent than her husband, who lacked both her diplomatic skills and her broad cultural interests. The most remarkable product of her diplomacy was her agreement of 1502 with Cesare BORGIA, who had toppled Duke Guidobaldo da MONTEFELTRO of Urbino, husband of Isabella's sister-in-law Elisabetta Gonzaga; Isabella offered refuge to the deposed duke and duchess at her court. After her husband's death in 1519, Isabella acted as an adviser to their eldest son Federico II

LEONARDO DA VINCI, portrait of **Isabella D'Este**, drawing in red chalk, in the Louvre, Paris

GONZAGA. Her visit to Bologna in 1529, shortly before the coronation of CHARLES V in February 1530, raised the profile of Mantua in imperial circles and so was probably instrumental in securing a dukedom for Federico; she also secured a cardinalate for Ercole, her second son.

Isabella extended her patronage to artists such as CORREGGIO, Lorenzo COSTA, FRANCIA, GIULIO ROMANO, LEONARDO DA VINCI (whose portrait drawing of Isabella is now in the Louvre), MANTEGNA, PERUGINO, RAPHAEL, and TITIAN, to writers such as ARIOSTO, BANDELLO, Bernardo DOVIZI, CASTIGLIONE, Paolo GIOVIO, MANTOVANO, and TRISSINO, and to musicians such as Bartolomeo TROMBONCINO (whose motifs are inlaid in her *studiolo* in the *castello* in Mantua) and Marchetto CARA.

MDA s.v. Este (i) (6) Isabella d'Este; Clifford Brown, *Isabella d'Este and Lorenzo da Pavia: Documents for the History of Art and Culture in Renaissance Mantua* (1982).

**ESTE, LEONELLO D'** (1407–50), *signore* of Ferrara, the eldest son of Niccolò III d'Este (1383–1441), *signore* of Ferrara. He succeeded his father in 1441, and became an important patron of art and literature. He was a friend of ALBERTI and a patron of Jacopo BELLINI, and he owned a painting by Rogier van der WEYDEN, possibly the *Entombment*.

DBI s.v. Este, Leonello; MDA s.v. Este (i) (3) Leonello d'Este.

**ESTE, VILLA D'.** Two Renaissance villas are now called Villa d'Este. The villa that belonged to the Este family is at Tivoli (ancient Tibur), a hill town 30 kilometres (20 miles) east of Rome. The other Villa d'Este, at Cernobbio, on Lake Como, has never had any connection with the ESTE family; it was built for Cardinal Tolomeo Gallio (1527–1607), and whimsically renamed Villa d'Este by Caroline of Brunswick when she bought it in 1815; this villa, which is now a hotel, was once surrounded by a Renaissance garden, but the only original feature that survives in the present gardens is a double water-staircase framed by an avenue of cypresses and magnolias.

Villa d'Este in Tivoli was transformed from a Benedictine monastery into a villa for Cardinal Ippolito d'ESTE, the son of Lucrezia BORGIA and Alfonso d'Este, who was appointed governor of Tivoli in 1550. The house is a typical Roman villa, but the magnificence of the greatest of ITALIAN GARDENS reduces the house to a supporting role; the house retains a niche in literary and musical history, however, as the place where TASSO wrote his *Aminta* and Franz Liszt lived for many years.

The gardens were laid out between 1560 and 1575 on a steep slope on the west side of Tivoli. The architect, Pirro LIGORIO, drew on two nearby classical sites as models. One was Praeneste (now Palestrina), a Roman villa resort that in the first century BC boasted the largest temple in Italy; in the sixteenth century all that remained was a series of vast descending terraces linked by sweeping ramps. Ligorio's carefully surveyed drawings of the site testify to its impact on him, and it seems likely that the terraces and ramps of Praeneste inspired the terraces of the Villa d'Este. The other important classical model was Hadrian's villa in Tivoli, which Ligorio had excavated for Cardinal Ippolito between

1550 and 1560, plundering many statues which were subsequently placed in the garden of the Villa d'Este.

The central axis of the garden is marked by a grand stairway that climbs from a gateway at the bottom of the garden across a series of majestic terraces to the villa. The two lowest terraces descend in staircases from the house and in ramps (cordonate) from the hill on the north-west side, which is the source of the water used to such spectacular effect in the garden. The main source of water is a conduit built by Ligorio to supply water from the river Aniene. The conduit delivered a constant flow of water (at 1,140 litres (250 gallons) per second) under the pressure required to lift water through the FOUNTAINS and AUTOMATA.

The centre of the lowest terrace is dominated by a round plantation of cypresses (the Rotonda dei Cipressi), outside of which were four MAZES. Beyond the cypresses, the first water feature was the Fountain of the Organ, which fed a series of waterfalls linked by three fish ponds. The Fountain of the Organ contained a water-organ that could imitate the sound of a trumpet and play in harmony; DU PÉRAC even claimed that it could play madrigals in four or five parts, but MONTAIGNE complained that it only played a single note.

On the next terrace, the most important water feature is the Fountain of the Owl, Ligorio's realization of a contrivance described in late antiquity by HERON. Small birds perched on branches, their singing facilitated by the ingenious use of water; when an owl turned towards them to remonstrate with a water-driven hoot, the birds fell silent. Above this level, the central staircase divides in two in order to encircle the Fountain of the Dragons, whose fearsome roaring noises delighted Montaigne and John Evelyn.

Beyond the Fountain of the Dragons, the path reunites to climb still higher, to the Terrace of a Hundred Fountains, which consists of three magnificent rows of fountains. Behind the middle row there were 100 terracotta reliefs depicting scenes from Ovid's Metamorphoses. The north-west end of the pathway is dominated by the Fountain of the Ovata, in which a waterfall flows from beneath the feet of a giant statue of the Tiburtine Sibyl mounted on a rounded loggia cut into the hillside. At the other end of the terrace Ligorio built the Rometta, a TOPIARY garden (of which little now remains) depicting ancient Rome on its seven hills. Beyond the Terrace of a Hundred Fountains, a series of ramps (now open, but originally thickly planted with evergreen ilex) leads to the highest terrace, at the end of which there is a triumphal arch which frames the distant spectacle of Rome; in 1620 Fulvio Teste described this view over the Roman Campagna as unequalled in the world.

The Villa d'Este is one of the finest of Italy's gardens, and the maturity of the plantations has created effects that would not have been possible in the Renaissance garden, but much has nonetheless been lost. The greatest loss is the antique statuary; the statues (not all of which were installed) were the central features of the iconography of the garden, little of which survives—though the visitor must still choose between the path of virtue that leads to the Grotto of Diana or the path of vice that leads to the Grotto of Venus. The special effects of the fountains have largely disappeared, as have the GIOCHI D'ACQUA that sprayed unsuspecting visitors.

In the seventeenth century the gardens were maintained and a few new features added, such as the Fountain of the Bicchierone built in 1660 by Gianlorenzo Bernini. In the eighteenth century the gardens were neglected and the statues disappeared, but the decay was deemed to be picturesque, and in this decayed state the garden was recorded by Jean-Honoré Fragonard and Hubert Robert. Fragonard's chalk drawings of the fountains are in the Museum of Besançon and his luxuriant Gardens of the Villa d'Este hangs in the Wallace Collection in London; Robert's chalk drawings and his evocative wash drawing of the Fountain of the Ovata are now in the Louvre.

David Coffin, The Villa d'Este at Tivoli (1960); C. Lamb, Die Villa d'Este in Tivoli: Ein Beitrag zur Geschichte der Gartenkunst (1966); David Dernie, The Villa d'Este at Tivoli (1996).

**ESTE FAMILY**, the dynasty that ruled FERRARA from 1196 to 1579 and Modena from 1289 to 1803. In the early fifteenth century Niccolò III d'Este (1383–1441) ruled Ferrara, Modena, Parma, and Reggio. He was succeeded in turn by his three sons Leonello d'ESTE, Borso d'ESTE, and Ercole I d'ESTE; Borso became duke of Modena (1452) and duke of Ferrara (1479). Ercole's children included Alfonso I d'ESTE (his successor), Beatrice d'ESTE, Isabella d'ESTE, and Cardinal Ippolito d'ESTE (the builder of the Villa d'ESTE). Alfonso, who became the third husband of Lucrezia BORGIA, was succeeded by his son Ercole II d'ESTE, who married RENÉE DE FRANCE. Ercole's son Alfonso II d'ESTE (the patron of TASSO) was the last Este duke of Ferrara: on his death in 1597 the duchy reverted to the PAPAL STATE and was henceforth ruled by a cardinal legate. The Este had to leave the duchy after a reign of more than three centuries, and thereafter their seat shifted to Modena, where they ruled until 1803.

L. Chiappini, Gli Estensi (1967); W. L. Gundersheimer, Ferrara: The Style of a Renaissance Despotism (1973); Trevor Dean, Land and Power in Late Medieval Ferrara: The Rule of the Este 1350–1450 (1988).

**ESTIENNE or (Latin) Stephanus or (modern French) Étienne or (Victorian English) Stephens**, a dynasty of French scholar-printers active in Paris and Geneva from 1502 to 1674. The founder of the family was Henri Estienne the Elder (c.1460–1520), who opened his Paris workshop c.1502. On his death his three sons were too young to assume control of the business, so he was succeeded by his partner Simon de Colines, who in 1521 married Henri's widow. Robert ESTIENNE the Elder ran the business from 1526 (when he introduced the device of the olive-tree on his books) to 1551, when he moved to Geneva and opened a branch of the press there. He was succeeded in Geneva by his sons Henri ESTIENNE the Younger (1531–98) and Francis (1537–82). Paul Estienne (1567–1627), son of Henri the Younger, inherited the business from his father but eventually returned to Paris. Paul's son Antoine (d. 1674) was the last printer in the dynasty.

After the departure of Robert Estienne for Geneva in 1550, the Paris workshop was run by his younger brother Charles ESTIENNE, who was in turn succeeded by his nephew Robert

Estienne the Younger (1530–71), who was appointed royal printer in 1564.

*DBF*.

**ESTIENNE or (Latin) Stephanus, CHARLES** (1504–64), French printer, lexicographer, and physician, the third son of Henri Estienne the Elder and the younger brother of Robert ESTIENNE. He studied medicine at Paris and in 1545 published an illustrated treatise on ANATOMY, *De dissectione partium corporis humani*. His other publications include an *Épître* (1542) on classical drama, an encyclopedic *Dictionarium historicum et poëticum* (1553, often reprinted), and a treatise on agriculture (*Praedium rusticum*, 1554). On the departure of his brother Robert for Geneva in 1551, Charles assumed control of the family workshop, but in 1561 he became bankrupt; the business passed to his nephew Robert Estienne the Younger, and Charles died in a debtors' prison.

*DBF*.

**ESTIENNE or (Latin) Stephanus, HENRI THE YOUNGER** (1531–98), French printer, lexicographer, and traveller, born in Paris, the son of Robert ESTIENNE the Elder; he claims in the preface to his edition of Aulus Gellius (1585) that the various backgrounds of those working at the press led to the adoption of Latin as the common language, and that he also learnt Greek as a child. He travelled as a young man in Italy (where he collected manuscripts), England (where he was received by King EDWARD VI), and Flanders (where he learnt Spanish). He followed his father to Geneva and in 1559 succeeded him as head of the family workshop in Geneva. His press published early Christian authors (including the *editio princeps* of Athenagoras), classical authors (including the *editiones principes* of pseudo-Anacreon, which proved to be an important influence on the PLÉIADE, and of Plutarch).

Henri Estienne was a prominent champion of Greek. In 1562 he translated the *Hypotyposes* of Sextus Empiricus (later a source for MONTAIGNE's knowledge of SCEPTICISM) and published a five-volume *Thesaurus linguae Graecae* (1572) to complement the Latin thesaurus first published by his father in 1531. In French he published a lively and salacious *Apologie pour Hérodote* (1566; 12th edition 1582) and a satire on Italianate scholars and courtiers at the court of CATHERINE DE MÉDICIS (*Épître de Monsieur Celtophile aux Ausoniens*, 1578). His polemical treatises include *Traité de la conformité du langage français avec le grec* (1566), *Deux Dialogues du nouveau français italianisé* (1578), and *De la précellence du langage français* (1579), all of which advance the dubious hypothesis that French, the finest of modern languages, is more indebted to Greek, the finest of ancient languages, than to Latin.

Estienne's tracts incurred the obloquy of the Geneva Consistory, which was even more given to censorship than were the theologians of the Sorbonne. After the publication of his *Deux Dialogues* Estienne returned to the French court for a year, and on returning to Geneva was deemed to be contumacious with respect to the Consistory Court and was jailed for a week. Thereafter he lived an itinerant existence in cities such as Basel, Heidelberg, Pest, and Vienna, rarely returning to Geneva. Late in 1597 he visited his daughter Florence and her husband Isaac CASAUBON in Montpellier, and on the return journey, in January 1598, he died in Lyon.

*DBF*; *Henri Estienne* ('actes du colloque', 1988).

**ESTIENNE or (Latin) Stephanus, ROBERT THE ELDER** (1503–59), French printer and lexicographer, the second son of the scholar-printer Henri Estienne the Elder (d. 1520). He was trained in his father's workshop, and in 1526 succeeded his stepfather Simon de Colines as head of the workshop; two years later he married Perrette Bade, the daughter of the Flemish printer Jodocus BADIUS. His titles, which were influenced by those of ALDUS MANUTIUS both in their relatively small size and in their founts, included the Bible in Latin (1528, 1532, 1540), the Old Testament in Hebrew (1539–41, 1544–6), and the New Testament in Greek (1544–51); this New Testament, which also included a Latin text, was the first Bible to divide the chapters into numbered verses. Robert also published editions of church fathers (including Eusebius), classical authors (including Plautus and Terence), and contemporary neo-Latin writers (including BUDÉ). His finest scholarly work was the *Thesaurus linguae Latinae* (1531, enlarged edition 1536, 3-volume edition 1543), which he later supplemented with a *Dictionarium Latinogallicum* (1538) and a *Dictionnaire Français–Latin* (1539). In 1539 he was appointed royal printer for Hebrew and Latin, and in 1540 he additionally became royal printer for Greek.

Robert Estienne's annotations of his bibles incurred the obloquy of the theologians of the Sorbonne, but as royal printer he enjoyed the protection of FRANCIS I and so was able to continue publishing his bibles. On the death of King Francis in 1547 Robert lost his protector, and in 1551 he moved to Geneva, where he continued to publish bibles and also published works by CALVIN and BEZA. He died in Geneva on 7 September 1559.

*DBF*; *MDA*; Elizabeth Armstrong, *Robert Estienne, Royal Printer* (rev. edn. 1986).

**ESTIUS or Willem Hessels van Est** (1542–1613), Dutch Catholic exegete and martyrologist, born in Gorcum (Gorinchem) and educated at Utrecht and (from 1561) Louvain, where one of his teachers was Michel de BAY. He became professor of theology at Douai in 1582 and chancellor in 1595. His most influential work was *Historia martyrum Gorcomiensium* (1603), an account of the 'Gorcum martyrs', a group of nineteen priests who were executed in Briel by Calvinists on 9 July 1572; eleven of the martyrs were Franciscan friars at the Gorcum convent. Estius' account was an important document in the beatification (1675) and canonization (1867) of the martyrs. His principal exegetical work was the posthumously published *Commentarii in omnes divi Pauli et catholicas epistolas* (1614–16), which remained in print for three centuries.

*NNBW* vii s.v. Est.

**ETCHING**, a method of making PRINTS in which a design is bitten into a metal plate with acid. The metal plate is first covered with an acid-resistant compound (typically made of wax, bitumen, and resin) which is melted onto the plate; this covering is called the 'etching ground', and is the medium in which the etcher draws the design with an etching needle held like a pen. The plate is then immersed in acid, which bites into the exposed metal of the design. The ground is later removed from the plate, which is then ready for inking and printing.

Etching was less labour-intensive than ENGRAVING, and so was often used to save time: plates were sometimes begun as etchings and finished as engravings. Similarly, portions of etchings were sometimes finished with DRYPOINT.

Etching found its greatest exponent in Rembrandt, and his Renaissance predecessors, some of whom were great artists, were nonetheless not able to produce work of the highest quality in etchings. Artists who experimented with etching included ALTDORFER, DÜRER (whose *Landscape with a Cannon* of 1518 is an etching), Urs GRAF, LUCAS VAN LEIDEN, and PARMIGIANINO.

**ETON CHOIRBOOK.** One of the chief sources of Latin sacred music in England in the period *c.*1490–1530, this large parchment choirbook contains nine Magnificat settings, one Passion, and 54 motets. Work by BROWNE, DAVY, LAMBE, and WILKINSON is included in it. Of the original 93 contents, 29 are missing.

**EUCHARIST.** The term 'eucharist' is a transliteration of the Greek εὐχαριστία. which means 'thanksgiving'. In English, the SACRAMENT of the eucharist is variously called 'Holy Communion', the 'Lord's Supper', and the 'mass'. The Protestant term 'Lord's Supper', which derives from I Corinthians 11: 20 (τὸ κυριακὸν δεῖπον), achieved wide currency as a result of its use by Nicholas RIDLEY in his *Brief Declaration of the Lord's Supper* (1554). The Catholic term 'mass' (German *Messe*) derives from the late Latin *missa*, a term that may originate in the formula by which the congregation was dismissed (*Ite, missa est*) at the end of a service in which the eucharist was celebrated; the only Protestants to retain the term were the Lutherans of Scandinavia, where *messa* (Swedish) and *messe* (Danish) remained (and still remain) in use.

The theology of the eucharist has been a matter of debate since the ninth century. The relationship between the body and blood of Christ in heaven and the bread and wine of the eucharist was clarified at the Fourth Lateran Council in 1215 and subsequently described in detail by THOMAS AQUINAS, who deployed the Aristotelian distinction between 'substance' and 'accidents' to explain that, at consecration, the 'accidents' (and hence the apparent properties) of the bread and wine remained unchanged, but the underlying 'substance' was transformed into the body and blood of Christ. This doctrine, which was termed 'transubstantiation', was to remain unchallenged in the Western Church until the Reformation.

The first Reformation alternative to transubstantiation was consubstantiation, which is associated with Martin LUTHER, its most prominent advocate. Proponents of consubstantiation retained the Aristotelian distinction between substance and accidents, but denied that the substance of the bread and wine was altered by consecration, maintaining instead that the substance of the bread and wine was co-present with the substance of the body and blood of Christ. Luther proposed the analogy of an iron in the fire: the fire and the iron are united in the glowing iron, and yet neither has been transformed into the other. Luther's insistence on the corporeal presence of Christ in the eucharist was based on his belief in UBIQUITARIANISM.

In Switzerland, ZWINGLI maintained that the eucharist was simply a commemorative rite, and that the bread and wine were not changed in any way. Luther described advocates of such a view as SACRAMENTARIANS; they are now also known as memorialists. Attempts were made, notably at the Colloquy of MARBURG in 1529, to heal the rift between the Lutheran and Zwinglian positions, but to no avail; the eucharist remained the ideological issue that divided the German and Swiss churches.

In Geneva, Calvin proposed another alternative, which became known as 'virtualism'. In this view, the bread and wine were not changed, but the act of receiving the bread and wine was deemed to transmit to the communicant the power (or 'virtue') of the body and blood of Christ. Calvin's virtualism was soon adopted in England by Anglican reformers, and was popular amongst seventeenth-century theologians: in this variant, which has since 1867 been known as 'receptionism', the bread and wine are not changed by consecration, but the communicant nonetheless receives the body and blood of Christ alongside the bread and wine. The Church of England rejected transubstantiation in the twenty-eighth of the Thirty-Nine ARTICLES, but the ambiguity of the formulation accommodated both Lutheran and Calvinist interpretations.

Controversy about the eucharist prompted the delegates at the COUNCIL OF TRENT to clarify the Catholic position, and at the thirteenth session, on 11 October 1551, the doctrine of transubstantiation was reaffirmed, but without reference to the Aristotelian distinction between substance and accidents; although most Catholic theologians drew on Aristotle to explain the doctrine, the revival of interest in atomism may have encouraged caution. Counter-Reformation theologians such as Melchor CANO and Francisco SUÁREZ continued to refine Catholic doctrine, and the INQUISITION kept a wary eye on threats to the doctrine of transubstantiation; indeed, it is possible that the trial of Galileo GALILEI was prompted not so much by his cosmology as by his atomism, which posed a threat to the Aristotelian basis of transubstantiation.

Debate about the theology of the eucharist was exacerbated by a parallel argument about who was entitled to receive the two 'species' of bread and wine. Until the twelfth century, the general (but not universal) practice was for the laity to receive communion in both kinds, i.e. to partake of both bread and wine. By the thirteenth century, the practice had been discontinued: the Synod of Lambeth in 1281, for example, restricted the consecrated wine to the celebrant, and the laity were entitled only to the bread, a practice known as communion 'in one kind'. The Hussites, especially the CALIXTINES, demanded the chalice, for which they were condemned by the COUNCIL OF CONSTANCE in 1415; this Hussite doctrine is called UTRAQUISM. The chalice was conceded to the Calixtines at the COUNCIL OF BASEL in 1437, but the decision was never ratified by the Vatican, and was revoked in 1462. The reformers advocated communion in both kinds, but the COUNCIL OF TRENT insisted that the practice of communion in one kind was justified by the doctrine of concomitance, according to which both the body and the blood of Christ are present in each of the consecrated species.

## EUCLID or (Greek) Eukleides IN THE RENAISSANCE.
Euclid (*fl. c.*300 BC), the author of the *Elements of Geometry*, is now believed to have lived and worked in Alexandria (Egypt), but in the Renaissance was usually identified with the philosopher Euclid of Megara who appears in Plato's dialogue *Theaetetus*. In the Renaissance Euclid's *Elements* provided the basis for all teaching in learned mathematics, and thirteenth-century writings clearly derived from his optical works formed the basis for the study of OPTICS and PERSPECTIVE. His formal system of definitions and axioms (which he separates into Common Notions and Postulates) set the universal standard for rigorous deductive proof.

Euclid's concern is with GEOMETRY, but the *Elements* was also significant for ALGEBRA, since some of the work on equality of areas is equivalent to solving quadratic equations. These solutions are geometrical, and thus presented as concerning general magnitudes. Euclid treats ARITHMETIC as subsidiary to geometry since it deals only with the natural numbers (1, 2, 3, . . . ) which are magnitudes of a specific, limited kind. An edition of the *Elements*, in the thirteenth-century Latin version of Giovanni Campano (Campanus), was one of the first books published in Venice (1482). Bartolommeo Zamberti's translation from the Greek (1505) made very little difference to mathematicians, except that the manuscript Zamberti had used indicated that books 14 and 15, long accepted as part of the *Elements*, were not in fact by Euclid. Many learned Latin editions followed, together with some translations into the vernacular. The Greek text was first printed in 1533, together with Proclus' philosophical commentary on the first book of Euclid's work.

## EUGENIUS IV (*c.*1383–1447), pope from 3 March 1431 until his death on 23 February 1447, was born Gabriele Condulmer in Venice, the son of a wealthy merchant. He became a monk at an Augustinian house in the Venetian lagoon. His uncle, Pope GREGORY XII, appointed him bishop of Siena in 1407 and cardinal-priest of San Clemente in May 1408. After the abdication of Pope Gregory, Gabriele participated in the COUNCIL OF CONSTANCE and Pope MARTIN V appointed him governor of the March of Ancona and of Bologna.

On being elected as pope, Eugenius immediately restored to the PAPAL STATE the vast tracts of land that Pope Martin V had alienated to his relatives; the violence with which Eugenius imposed sequestration caused widespread resentment throughout the Papal State and incurred the lifelong enmity of the COLONNA family.

The COUNCIL OF BASEL had been summoned by Martin V and opened on 23 July 1431. Eugenius, who was suspicious of the Council's intentions, took advantage of the low attendance at the opening sessions and dissolved the Council on 18 December 1431, undertaking to convoke a new Council (which he would lead personally) eighteen months hence. Members of the Council declined to disperse, and on 18 December 1432 invoked the GALLICAN decree of the Council of Constance affirming the conciliar supremacy. On 18 December 1432 the Council issued an ultimatum demanding that Eugenius withdraw the bull of dissolution. A schism was avoided through the mediation of SIGISMUND, whom Eugenius crowned as Holy Roman Emperor in May 1433. On 15 December 1433 Eugenius was humiliatingly forced to annul his bull and acknowledge both the legitimacy and the continuity of the Council.

Eugenius soon had to deal with a crisis in domestic politics. Francesco SFORZA had occupied much of the Papal State and the aggrieved Colonna established an insurrectionary republic in Rome in May 1434. Eugenius was pelted by crowds as he left the city in an unsuccessful disguise; civic order was restored in Rome in October 1434, but Eugenius remained in Florence and Bologna until September 1443. The Council of Basel took advantage of the weakened papacy by suppressing annates (the revenue of the first year of an ecclesiastical benefice, which was payable to the curia) and other papal dues in a decree of 9 June 1435, and proceeded to reduce the size of the curia and the authority of the papacy.

The central agendum of the Council of Basel became union with the Greek Orthodox Church, and members of the Council proposed that the negotiations take place in the relatively neutral setting of Basel or Avignon or Savoy. Eugenius managed to elicit the support of the Greek delegation to transfer the council to Ferrara on 18 September 1437. The Council was opened on 8 January 1438, but Eugenius moved it to Florence on 26 February 1439. At the COUNCIL OF FLORENCE a Decree of Union was promulgated on 6 July 1439. At the behest of the emperor in Constantinople, Eugenius financed a CRUSADE in 1444, but on 10 November 1444 his army was defeated by Murat II at Varna (Bulgaria), before it even reached Constantinople.

The rump of the Council in Basel suspended Eugenius on 24 January 1438, deposed him as a heretic on 25 June 1439, and elected in his stead the antipope FELIX V on 5 November 1439. Eugenius responded on 4 September 1439 by annulling the earlier phases of the Council of Constance and condemning the Council of Basel. The attempt by the Council of Basel to circumscribe papal authority was supported by France, which declared itself neutral in the schism, but nonetheless incorporated 23 of the reform decrees of the Council into the PRAGMATIC SANCTION OF BOURGES (7 July 1438), which asserted the right of the French church to administer its temporal property without reference to the Vatican and disallowed papal nominations to French benefices. Germany was also neutral, and on 26 March 1439 the Diet of Mainz had deprived the pope of most of his powers in the Empire.

In the spring of 1443 Eugenius recognized the claim of ALFONSO V OF ARAGON to the throne of Naples; Alfonso withdrew his bishops from the Council of Basel, which reduced its already depleted authority. Eugenius returned to Rome in triumph on 28 September 1443. He had already been reconciled with Felix's influential secretary, Enea Silvio Piccolomini (later Pope PIUS II), and in September 1445 Piccolomini mediated an agreement between Eugenius and FRIEDRICH III, king of the Romans (i.e. emperor elect); in February 1447 the HOLY ROMAN EMPIRE abandoned its neutrality in favour of Eugenius.

Eugenius died without having dislodged the antipope, but had nonetheless successfully asserted the authority of the papacy over the councils of the Church. His private life was austere, but he was nonetheless a patron of scholarship and the arts: he brought artists and architects to Rome, employed Poggio BRACCIOLINI and Flavio BIONDO in the papal chancery, and in 1431 re-established the University of Rome.

DBI s.v. Eugenio IV; J. Gill, *Eugenius IV: Pope of Christian Union* (1961).

**EULENKRUG** (German; 'owl-jug'), a type of TIN-GLAZED EARTHENWARE jug shaped like an owl and manufactured in Nuremberg in the mid-sixteenth century. The design may be the work of Augustin HIRSCHVOGEL.

**EUPHUISM**, style based on LYLY's prose romance *Euphues* (1578, 1580), and anticipated by PETTIE's *Petite Palace of Pettie his Pleasure* (1576). It is characterized by excessive use of antithesis, by alliteration, and by allusion to classical natural history, and to figures from history, myth, and legend.

**EUROPE**. The classical term 'Europe' was in the Middle Ages displaced by 'Christendom', and when 'Europe' was revived by the HUMANISTS in the late fifteenth century, it was a geographical term used to distinguish the land mass of Europe from those of ASIA, AFRICA, and America rather than, as it became in the nineteenth century, a political and cultural term. The idea of a united Christendom was one of the ideals of the HOLY ROMAN EMPIRE.

D. de Rougemont, *The Idea of Europe* (1966); Peter Burke, 'Did Europe Exist before 1700?', in *History of European Ideas*, I (1980); Bronisław Geremek, *The Common Roots of Europe* (1996).

**EUSTACHIO or Eustachi, BARTOLOMEO** (*c*.1500–1574), Italian anatomist, born in San Severino (Marches), the son of a physician. He studied medicine in Rome and in 1539 joined the Urbino court as the physician of Guidobaldo II DELLA ROVERE. In 1549 he moved to Rome in the suite of Cardinal Giulio della Rovere, the duke's brother; in Rome he became professor of anatomy (1555) and papal physician.

Eustachio published *Opuscula anatomica* (1564), a study of the cardiovascular system that contains treatises on the kidneys (including the first account of the adrenal glands), the ear, and the venous system.

Eustachio's anatomical drawings, engraved on copper, were discovered long after his death and published in 1714. He is the eponym of the Eustachian tube and the Eustachian valve.

DBI; DSB; C. J. Imperatori, *Bartholomaeus Eustachius: His Contribution to the Anatomy of the Ear, Larynx and Bronchi* (1943).

**EVERARDUS, NICOLAUS** (1462–1532), Dutch jurist, president of the Court of Holland (1509–28) and of the Great Court of Mechelen (at the southern tip of what is now Limburg). His legal writings, which include *Topica* (1516) and *Responsio sive Consilia* (1554), are important contributions to the development of the Romano-Dutch law that was to become central to DUTCH LAW.

**EWORTH or Ewouts, HANS** (*fl.* 1540–*c*.1573), Flemish portrait painter, born in Antwerp. He emigrated to England in the late 1540s. The evolution of the style of his portraits from Flemish Mannerism (often with allegorical elements in the FONTAINEBLEAU tradition) to an Elizabethan concentration on details of clothing and drapery or tapestry is a barometer of changing tastes in the third quarter of the sixteenth century. His early portraits are typified by an allegorical portrait of Sir John Luttrell (1550, Courtauld Institute Galleries, London) in which Sir John is portrayed standing half-naked in a stormy sea with his clenched fist raised. His other sitters included Lady Dacre (*c*.1555, National Gallery, Ottawa), Queen MARY I (1554, Society of Antiquaries, London), and Lady Burghley (Hatfield House). He may have been the painter of the allegorical portrait of *Queen Elizabeth and the Three Goddesses* (1569, Hampton Court, London), but this traditional attribution is now regarded as insecure. Eworth also worked as a painter for pageants and masques.

Eworth was long confused with Lucas de HEERE; portraits signed with an 'HE' monogram were formerly attributed to Lucas de Heere, but most are now believed to be the work of Eworth.

MDA.

**EXPLORATION**. The greatest travellers of the Middle Ages were the Arabs and the Norsemen. Arab travellers, who benefited from Arabic translations of the works of ancient Greek geographers, explored Asia, Africa, and Europe; the tenth-century traveller Masudi, for example, wrote about his experience of travelling in countries from Spain to China. Norse sailors, who were in contact with Arab traders (early medieval Arabic coins have been found in Gotland), explored Russia, France (where they settled in what is now Normandy), the Mediterranean (where they established a base in Sicily), the Arctic, Iceland (where they established permanent colonies), and Greenland. The archaeological evidence of the eleventh-century Norse settlement at L'Anse aux Meadows (discovered in 1960) in Newfoundland demonstrates that the Norse preceded COLUMBUS as the first Europeans to cross the Atlantic; the discovery on the site of butternuts (which do not grow so far north) implies that the Norse settlers at L'Anse aux Meadows sailed south along the American coast.

In the twelfth century, the Venetian MARCO POLO travelled to China and wrote a description of the world (*Devisement du monde*) which described his experiences in China. Marco Polo's description of Japan (which he never visited), which he had heard described as rich in gold, provided a central motive for the expeditions of Columbus, who owned and annotated a printed copy of the Latin version of the

*Devisement*. Venice was the European centre of trade with ASIA, and Venetians continued to travel in the East; in the fifteenth century, the most resolute of these explorers to have left a record of his travels was Niccolò de' CONTI.

In the fifteenth century the most important centres for the exploration of the world by sea were Portugal and Spain, both of which employed Italian merchant navigators as well as their own subjects. The Portuguese took the lead in the exploration of AFRICA and the eastward route to Asia; Columbus, a Genoese in the service of Spain, directed Spanish exploration to the West with his journeys to the Americas. Spanish conquistadors soon penetrated to Mexico (CORTÉS), the Pacific (BALBOA), and Peru (PIZARRO). Alvaro de Mendaña sailed west from Peru in search of the Antarctic continent believed to extend northwards into the Pacific, and so became the first European to cross the Pacific. Ferdinand MAGELLAN, a Portuguese mariner in the service of the Spanish crown, sailed around the south tip of South America and across the Pacific to the Philippines, where he was killed; his lieutenant Juan de ELCANO sailed on around Africa and back to Spain, and was heralded as the leader of the first expedition to circumnavigate the world.

English exploration was inaugurated by Giovanni Caboto (John CABOT), a Venetian sailor who settled in Bristol and sailed with a patent from the English crown to Newfoundland and the coast of America. In 1553 Sir Hugh WILLOUGHBY and Richard CHANCELLOR made the first of a series of voyages aimed at discovering a north-east passage to Asia, and so became the first English Arctic explorers. The search for a north-west passage to Asia was another English preoccupation; the most important voyages were those of Martin FROBISHER (1576), John DAVIS (1585), Henry HUDSON (1607), and William BAFFIN (1616). In Pacific exploration, the most important English navigators were Sir Francis DRAKE (circumnavigation 1577–80) and Thomas CAVENDISH (1586–8). In the Indian Ocean, the first English navigator was Sir James LANCASTER, whose first voyage (1591–4) led to the formation of the EAST INDIA COMPANY (1599).

Dutch exploration began with the voyage of Willem BARENTSZOON (1594–7) in search of a north-east passage to Asia. In 1595 a Dutch trading fleet followed the Portuguese route to Asia around the tip of Africa, so inaugurating the long struggle for power between the Dutch and the Portuguese in Asia. In 1598 a Dutch expedition embarked for Asia by the Spanish route through the Straits of Magellan. A DUTCH EAST INDIA COMPANY was formed in 1602. Conflict with Spain over the rights to the western route culminated in a naval battle off the coast of Chilca (Peru) on 5 May 1615. Thereafter the Dutch decided to seek a route further south than that used by the Spanish, and in January 1616 a Dutch fleet commanded by Willem SCHOUTEN rounded the tip of South America, passing south of Tierra del Fuego; the southern extremity was named Cape Horn, with reference to the town of Hoorn (West Friesland), of which Captain Schouten was a native. This fleet subsequently sailed along the coast of New Guinea before reaching the Moluccas. Claims for the discovery of the southern continent (Terra Australis) have been advanced

on behalf of French, Portuguese, and Spanish mariners, but the earliest documented landings on the mainland of Australia are those of the Dutch in the first half of the seventeenth century.

French exploration of North America began with the voyages of French and Breton fishermen to the Grand Banks off the coast of Newfoundland. The first official French expedition was commanded by a Florentine, Giovanni da VERRAZZANO, who in 1524 was sent by King FRANCIS I to explore the east coast of North America. The discoveries of this voyage were consolidated by Jacques CARTIER; the first European known to have penetrated the interior of what is now Canada was Samuel CHAMPLAIN. Further south, Gaspard de COLIGNY and Jean RIBAUT attempted to establish colonies in Florida, thus provoking rivalry with Spain; the French coastal colonies were soon eradicated by Pedro MENÉNDEZ DE AVILÉS, and France did not re-establish a significant presence in the American south until Louisiana was claimed (and named) in 1682.

***EXSURGE DOMINE***, the papal bull drafted by Pietro ACCOLTI and issued by LEO X on 15 June 1520. The bull denounced Martin LUTHER as the *novus Porphyrius*, the 'new Porphyry', a reference to the third-century pagan Neoplatonist philosopher who had written a treatise in fifteen books 'against the Christians' (Κατὰ Χριστιανῶν), and ordered that Luther's writings be burnt and Luther himself restrained or sent to Rome. The bull condemned 41 propositions which it attributed to Luther, excoriating his teaching on matters such as INDULGENCES, PURGATORY, GRACE, and papal authority, and denouncing his associates, including KARLSTADT.

The bull was promulgated in Germany by Johann ECK, who encountered fierce opposition in Leipzig (29 September) and Wittenberg (3 October), where the Elector FRIEDRICH III declined to implement the bull. Luther responded on 17 November with an appeal for a general council of the Church, and, when this was refused, he broke with the papacy on 10 December 1520 by publicly burning the bull in Wittenberg. This action led to Luther's excommunication on 3 January 1521 in the bull *Decet Romanum pontificem*.

**EYB, ALBRECHT VON.** See ALBRECHT VON EYB.

**EYCK, HUBERT VAN** (*c*.1385/90–1426), Flemish painter, born in Maastricht (or in nearby Maaseik); he was probably the elder brother of Jan van EYCK. There are no surviving pictures known to be entirely the work of Hubert. Scholars have speculated that he may have collaborated with Jan on *The Three Marys at the Sepulchre* (Boymans Museum, Rotterdam). His contribution to the Ghent altarpiece is better attested, but is nonetheless disputed, because the authenticity of the inscription on the frame that describes it as being left unfinished at Hubert's death and then finished by Jan has been called into doubt.

   *MDA.*

**EYCK, JAN VAN** (*c*.1395–1441), Flemish painter, probably the younger brother of Hubert van Eyck. In 1422 he moved to

Hubert and Jan van Eyck, the Ghent altarpiece (1432), also known (from the subject of its central panel) as *The Adoration of the Lamb*, in the Cathedral of St Bavo in Ghent

The Hague to enter the service of John of Bavaria, uncle (and opponent) of Jacqueline, countess of Holland, and three years later was appointed court painter and *valet de chambre* to Jacqueline's cousin PHILIP THE GOOD, whose court was in Lille; Duke Philip sent Jan on diplomatic missions to Spain (1426) and Portugal (1428). In about 1430 he left Lille for Bruges, where he married (1434) and lived for the rest of his life.

In many of Jan van Eyck's paintings, such as *The Virgin in the Church* (Gemäldegalerie, Berlin), *The Annunciation* (National Gallery of Art, Washington), the *Van der Paele Madonna* (Groeninge Museum, Bruges), and the triptych of *The Virgin* (Gemäldegalerie, Dresden), figures are characteristically set against meticulously precise architectural backgrounds; in *The Madonna of Chancellor Rolin* (Louvre), however, the figures are set against a panoramic landscape. Hubert and Jan's most celebrated work is *The Adoration of the Lamb* (Cathedral of St Bavon, Ghent), usually known as the Ghent altarpiece, which was finished in 1432; its twelve panels (eight of which are painted on both sides) are based on the Book of Revelation.

Jan van Eyck's portraits include *Portrait of a Man* (1432), which is also known as *Léal Souvenir* ('Loyal Remembrance'), *Man in a Red Turban* (1433), which may be a self-portrait, and *Arnolfini and his Wife* (1434), all in the National Gallery in London; the Arnolfini double portrait, which was formerly known as the *Arnolfini Marriage* (because it was mistakenly thought to be a wedding painting), depicts the Luccan merchant Giovanni di Nicolao Arnolfini standing with his wife Giovanna (and their dog) in an interior setting. Jan's portrait of *Cardinal Albergati* survives as both an annotated drawing (1431, Kupferstichkabinett, Dresden) and a finished portrait (*c*.1433, Kunsthistorisches Museum, Vienna).

Jan van Eyck's unprecedented technical mastery of light and space, together with his innovative use of oils, gained him the admiration of painters (notably DÜRER) and collectors (particularly in Italy). VASARI attributed the invention of OIL PAINTING to Jan van Eyck; this claim is inaccurate, but it is an extraordinary testimony to Jan van Eyck's reputation in fifteenth- and sixteenth-century Europe.

*MDA*; Elisabeth Dhanens, *Hubert and Jan van Eyck* (1982).

**Jan van Eyck,** *Arnolfini and his Wife* (1434), in the National Gallery in London; the painting was formerly (and mistakenly) known as *The Arnolfini Marriage*

**FABER, HEINRICH** (*c*.1500–1552), German music theorist and composer who was rector of the cathedral school of Naumburg until his Lutheran views caused a rift with the Catholic authorities. His *Compendiolum musicae* (1548) is a musical textbook for beginners and, as an educator, he declared himself (in his *Musica poetica*, 1548) in favour of composed music as opposed to improvised singing. He lectured in music at Wittenberg in 1551 and died the following year in Oelsnitz.

**FABER or Fabri, JOHANN** (1478–1542), German Catholic theologian and polemicist. He was born in Leutkirch (Swabia) and studied CANON LAW at Tübingen and (from 26 July 1509) Freiburg im Breisgau. After taking his doctorate he became vicar of Lindau and Leutkirch, and was then appointed canon of Basel. In 1518 he became vicar-general of the bishop of Constance and papal protonotary of Pope LEO X. He was sympathetic to the call for reform, and in 1519–20 corresponded with ZWINGLI; he was also willing to defend LUTHER against ECK, though he never adopted Lutheran views.

In the autumn of 1521 Faber travelled to Rome, and by the conclusion of his visit he had become an opponent of Protestantism. In 1522 he attacked Luther in his *Opus adversus nova quaedam dogmata Lutheri*, and the following year he opposed Zwingli in a disputation in Zürich. In 1524 he renewed his assault on Luther with *Malleus in haeresim Lutheranam*; this work earned him the sobriquet 'hammer (= *malleus*) of the heretics'.

In 1526 Faber became court preacher to Emperor FERDINAND I, and in 1527 and 1528 he visited Spain and England as an imperial emissary. He approved the burning in Vienna of the Anabaptist Balthasar HUBMAIER on 10 March 1528 and subsequently became bishop of Vienna, where he died on 21 May 1541.
*NDB.*

**FABER or (French) Favre or Lefèvre, PIERRE** (1506–46), French Jesuit. He studied in Paris, where he lived with IGNATIUS LOYOLA and Francis XAVIER and became one of the founders of the JESUIT Order. He attended the Conference of REGENSBURG (1541), and concluded that there could be no compromise with the Protestant reformers. Thereafter he worked for Catholic reform in Germany, establishing the first Jesuit educational institutions in the Rhineland. He was beatified on 5 September 1872.

**FABRICI, GIROLAMO, or Hieronymus Fabricius ab Aquapendente** (*c*.1533–1619), Italian anatomist and embryologist who studied medicine at Padua under FALLOPPIO, whom he succeeded as professor of ANATOMY in 1565. He became the most influential anatomist of the late sixteenth and early seventeenth centuries, and was largely responsible for the raising of the status of anatomy within European universities. His treatise on the valves of the venous system, *De venarum ostiolis* (1603), was an important influence on William Harvey, who was his pupil. His works on embryology include a comparative study which ranges across a large number of species in its examination of the mechanisms of fetal development, nourishment, and birth (*De formato foetu*, 1600) and a treatise on the formation of the egg and chick (*De formatione ovi et pulli*, 1612).
*DBI; DSB; De venarum ostiolis*, ed. K. J. Franklin (1933); *The Embryological Treatises*, ed. H. B. Adelmann (1942, 1967).

**FABRICIUS, GEORG** (1516–71), German poet and classical scholar, born in Chemnitz (in Saxony) on 23 April 1516 and educated in Leipzig. In the course of a protracted visit to Rome he made a detailed study of Roman antiquities which he published in *Roma* (1550), in which he attempts to link the artefacts recovered from ancient Rome with references to such objects in classical Latin literature. In 1546 he was appointed rector of the college of Meissen, where he died on 17 July 1571. He published editions of TERENCE (1548), VIRGIL (1551), and HORACE (1555) and several collections of Latin poems in which he fastidiously avoided allusions to pagan gods. His posthumous works include a history of Saxony published in 1609.
*DLL; NDB.*

**FABRIZI, ALVISE CINZIO** (*fl.* 1526), Italian poet. In 1526 Fabrizi published in Venice a collection of obscene proverbs, the *Libro della origine delli volgari proverbi*, which he dedicated to Pope CLEMENT VII. The collection was a popular success, but incurred the obloquy of the Venetian clergy, whose displeasure led to the imposition of literary censorship in Venice the following year.

*DBI; OCIL.*

**FACETIAE or (German) Fazetien**, a neo-Latin genre of wittily phrased anecdotes and jokes, usually of an erotic or anticlerical nature, circulated throughout Europe by humanists. The first (and seminal) collection of *facetiae* was the *Liber facetiarum* of Poggio BRACCIOLINI, a collection of indecent anticlerical anecdotes that became enormously popular. The *facetia* is treated as a distinctive genre in PONTANO'S *De sermone*.

In Germany the earliest author of *Fazetien* was Augustin Tünger, a civic official in Konstanz whose bilingual collection is entitled *Facetiae Latinae et Germaniae* (1486). The most important German collections of the sixteenth century are those of Heinrich BEBEL (*Facetiae*, 1508–12) and Nikodemus FRISCHLIN (*c*.1600). Although the collections of Tünger and Frischlin contain some *Fazetien* in German, the genre is mostly Latin, and the vernacular equivalent is the SCHWANK.

Barbara Bowen, 'Renaissance Collections of Facetiae, 1344–1490: A New Listing', *Renaissance Quarterly*, 39 (1986).

**FACIO, BARTOLOMEO** (*c*.1400–1457), Italian humanist. He was educated under GUARINO DA VERONA and then became a tutor in Venice, Florence, and Genoa. In 1444 the Genoese republic sent Facio to Naples, where he entered the service of ALFONSO V of Aragon as secretary and court astrologer. Facio wrote a history of the reign of Alfonso that contains a large amount of information about fifteenth-century Naples. He also compiled a collection of exemplary biographies (*De viris illustribus*) whose subjects include some of his contemporaries. Facio was for many years embroiled in a public dispute with Lorenzo VALLA, whose history of the reign of FERDINAND OF ARAGON Facio had imprudently criticized.

*DBI; OCIL.*

**FAENZA POTTERIES.** The Italian city and episcopal see of Faenza (ancient Faventia), 50 kilometres (30 miles) southeast of Bologna, was a pottery centre as early as 1142, but the scale of production remained small until the mid-fifteenth century, when Faenza potters began to make the fine MAIOLICA that soon came to be known in northern Europe as FAIENCE. The earliest dated maiolica from Faenza is a plaque dated 1466 now in the Musée de Cluny in Paris. The maiolica produced in Faenza in the last quarter of the fifteenth century used bold colour schemes, often dominated by blue, purple, and orange, on its dishes, ALBARELLI, religious plaques, and tiles; designs typically included human figures surrounded by scrolling foliage. Surviving examples of Faenza maiolica from this period include a plaque of the *Virgin and Child* (1489, Victoria and Albert Museum) and a set of over 1,000 tiles (one of which is dated 1487) in the Cappella dei Vaselli in the Basilica of San Petronio, Bologna.

In 1501 Faenza was captured by Cesare BORGIA, who drowned the surviving members of the ruling Manfredi family in the Tiber. After a few years under the control of Venice,

Faenza was incorporated into the PAPAL STATE in 1509. In the course of these turbulent years the style of Faenza pottery changed to accommodate changing tastes and new markets. Colours were toned down, and in 1515 ISTORIATO wares began to be manufactured, typically with a blue glaze called *berettino*; the most prominent of the istoriato painters was Baldassare MANARA. New potteries included Casa Pirota, which produced two of the finest surviving pieces of maiolica, a plaque dated 1525 (Musée National de la Céramique, Sèvres) and a plaque depicting the coronation of Charles V in 1530 (Museo Civico, Bologna). In the 1540s BIANCHI (or *bianco di Faenza*) production began in Faenza; the most prominent Faenza manufacturers were Leonardo BETTISI, Virgiliotto CALAMELLI, and Francesco MEZZARISA.

Many fine examples of Faenza maiolica were lost when the city's Museo della Ceramica was destroyed during the Second World War, but the collection has been rebuilt in a new museum.

F. Liverani and R. Bosi, *Maioliche di Faenza* (1974).

**FAGIUS, PAUL** (1504–49), German Hebraist, born in Rheinzabern, in the Palatinate, and educated in Strassburg under the Hebraist Wolfgang CAPITO. He became a schoolmaster at Isny im Allgäu (1527–35) and after two years of study in Strassburg returned to Isny as its Protestant pastor (1537–42); while in Isny he established a printing press that specialized in HEBREW. He became professor of Hebrew at Strassburg (1544–6) and then at Heidelberg (1546–9), from where he was dismissed for refusing to support the LEIPZIG INTERIM. In 1549 he was appointed reader in Hebrew at Cambridge, but died of a fever before he gave any lectures.

*DNB; NDB.*

**FAIENCE**, the name used in France, Germany, Scandinavia, and Spain to denote TIN-GLAZED EARTHENWARE; the word derives from the Italian potteries in FAENZA; in Italy such pottery is called MAIOLICA and in Britain and the Netherlands it is called DELFTWARE.

**FAIRFAX or Fayrfax, ROBERT** (1464–1521), English composer. He was a gentleman of the Royal Household Chapel and held D.Mus. degrees from Oxford and Cambridge. In 1502 he joined a guild familiar to many professional musicians, known as the City Fraternity of St Nicholas. He wrote masses, Magnificats and part songs, and his 'Magnificat regale' and the votive antiphons 'Ave lumen gratiae' and 'Salve Regina' appear in the ETON CHOIRBOOK.

**FALCONETTO, GIOVANNI MARIA** (1468–1535), Italian architect and painter. He was born in Verona but spent most of his career in Padua. His Odeon Cornaro (finely decorated with stucco on the inside) and Loggia in Padua (1524), built for the amateur architect and theorist Alvise Cornaro, were later incorporated into the Palazzo Giustiniani. His city gates for Padua, Porta San Giovanni (1528) and Porta Savonarola (1530), are modelled on Roman triumphal arches. He also completed the hilltop Villa dei Vescovi (i.e. of the bishops of Padua) at nearby Luvigliano, using loggias and staircase ramps to accommodate the steepness of the site. PALLADIO, who owned architectural drawings by Falconetto, greatly admired these buildings.

Falconetto's surviving paintings include architectural frescoes (1503) in the cathedral in Verona and a fresco of *The Annunciation* (1514) in the Church of San Pietro Martire in Verona.

*DBI*; *MDA*.

**FALIER or Falieri or Faliero, MARIN or Marino** (1274–1355), doge of Venice. He was born into an ancient patrician family and had a long career as a soldier, naval commander, and diplomat. The high point of his military career came in 1346: he was the commander of the Venetian land forces at the siege of Zara (now Zadar, in Croatia), where he defeated the army of Louis I of Hungary and occupied the city.

In September 1354 Falier was elected doge whilst absent in Avignon on a mission to Pope Innocent IV; the honour may have been wholly unsought. Soon after his election Falier entered into a conspiracy with a group of commoners, including a sea captain and a stonemason, with a view to overthrowing the patrician government on 15 April 1355 and proclaiming Falier prince of Venice. The plot was discovered and Falier was executed on 17 April 1355. In the place where his portrait should be in the Sala del Maggior Consiglio in the Doge's Palace, there is an inscription which bleakly explains that 'this is the place of Marino Falier, beheaded for his crimes' ('Hic est locus Marino Falier decapitati pro criminibus').

It is not altogether clear why a distinguished septuagenarian should have entered into such a conspiracy. In the tragedies of Byron (*Marino Faliero*, 1821) and Swinburne (*Marino Faliero*, 1885), Faliero is motivated by an insult to himself and his wife written on the doge's chair by Michele Steno; this tradition appears not to be attested in any contemporary record.

*DBI* s.v. Falier; V. Lazzarini, *Marino Faliero* (1963).

**FALLOPPIO, GABRIELE** (*c*.1523–1562), Italian anatomist. He was born in Modena, and after a brief period in the Church turned to the study of medicine in Ferrara; he subsequently taught in Ferrara and in Pisa. In 1551 he moved at the invitation of Grand Duke Cosimo de' MEDICI to Padua, where he was professor of anatomy (and so responsible for the annual dissections previously undertaken by VESALIUS) and director of the BOTANICAL GARDEN. He was later accused of practising human vivisection, and it is possible that he experimented on condemned criminals.

Falloppio's *Observationes anatomice* (1561) contains his research on musculature and on the female reproductive system. He described the sexual organs, including the uterine tubes that now bear his name, and also described and named the clitoris, placenta, and vagina. This research was supported by his huge clinical practice, in which he claimed to have examined the genitals of more than 10,000 patients with SYPHILIS.

*DBI*; *DSB*.

**FAMILY OF LOVE or** (Latin) **Familia Caritatis or** (Dutch) **Huis der Liefde or** (Flemish) **Hus der Lieften or** (French) **Famille d'Amour or** (German) **Haus der Liebe**, an Anabaptist sect, the members of which were known in English as 'Familists', founded by Hendrik NICLAES, a native of Münster who arrived in Amsterdam *c*.1531 and in 1539 or 1540 obeyed what he believed to be the command of God to found a new church, the Family of Love. His teachings, which combined elements of mystical pantheism and antinomianism, derived in some measure from the thought of the Dutch Anabaptist David JORIS.

The Family of Love attracted adherents in the Netherlands and in Germany, and attracted the attention of the Inquisition, which placed all of Niclaes's books on the INDEX. Niclaes travelled to England, probably in 1552 or 1553, and it was there that the sect enjoyed its greatest success. In 1580 Queen Elizabeth issued a 'Proclamation against the Sectaries of the Family of Love', which commanded its members to be incarcerated and the books of its leaders to be burnt, but the sect continued to prosper. Thomas MIDDLETON mocked the cult in his city comedy *The Family of Love* (written 1602, printed 1608). Persecution of the sect did not let up until the Interregnum, when the works of Niclaes (known in England as Henry Nicholas) were reprinted. The sect disappeared at the end of the seventeenth century, by which time many of its members had been absorbed into other dissenting groups, mainly the Quakers.

Alastair Hamilton, *The Family of Love* (1981); Christopher Marsh, *The Family of Love in English Society, 1550–1630* (1993).

**FANCELLI, DOMENICO DI ALESSANDRO** (1469–1519), Italian sculptor, born in Settignano, near Florence. He established his studio close to the MARBLE quarries in Carrara, and specialized in tombs for the Spanish market; he regularly visited Spain to install his work. His tombs, which were among the earliest Italian Renaissance works in Spain, include those of Cardinal Hurtado de Mendoza (1509, Seville Cathedral), FERDINAND and ISABELLA (1517, Capilla Real, Granada), and their only son, 10-year-old Prince Juan (1512, Monasterio de Santo Tomás, Ávila).

*DBI*; *MDA*.

**FANFARE BINDINGS**, a decorative style of BOOKBINDING used by Parisian binders between 1578 and 1634. The STRAPWORK recalls the decoration of the GROLIER and MAIOLI BINDINGS, but is reduced to a geometrical design of oval and circular patterns based on the figure 8. The spaces between the patterns were often decorated with tooled clusters of olive, bay, or laurel leaves.

The use of the epithet 'fanfare' to denote these bindings dates from 1829, when the French binder Thouvenin revived the style on his binding of a book entitled *Fanfares et corvées abbadesques des Roules-Bontemps* (1613). The introduction of the style is sometimes attributed to Nicolas and Clovis Ève, who were successively the royal binders from 1578 to 1634, but there is no evidence that they invented the style and little evidence that they used it extensively.

G. D. Hobson, *Les Reliures à la fanfare* (1935).

**FAREL, GUILLAUME** (1489–1565), French Protestant reformer, associated with Jacques LEFÈVRE D'ÉTAPLES, with whom he worked in Meaux in the reform movement inaugurated by Bishop Guillaume BRIÇONNET. In 1524 he was obliged to flee, and settled in Basel, where his attacks on ERASMUS led to his expulsion. He subsequently lived in Neuchâtel (1530), where he introduced the Reformation, and then moved to Geneva, where, together with Pierre VIRET, he persuaded John CALVIN to settle. When Farel and Calvin were forced to leave Geneva in 1538, Farel returned to Neuchâtel, where he implemented the Reformation on the Genevan model. In 1549 he contributed to the ZÜRICH AGREEMENT known as the Consensus Tigurinus. His *Sommaire* (1529) is an important statement of early Calvinist doctrine.

DBF; Henri Heyer, *Guillaume Farel: An Introduction to his Theology* (English trans. 1990).

**FARNABY, GILES** (*c.*1563–1640), English composer and joiner, active in London although he spent some years near Lincoln where he taught the children of Sir Nicholas Saunderson of Fillingham. He contributed nine settings to Thomas EAST's *Whole Book of Psalms* (1592) and in 1598 he dedicated his *Canzonets to Four Voices* to Ferdinando Heybourne, a courtier. He composed keyboard fantasias, dances, and other pieces such as his famous *Tower Hill*; much of his keyboard writing can be found in the FITZWILLIAM VIRGINAL BOOK.

**FARNESE, ALESSANDRO** (1545–92), duke of Parma, soldier, and statesman, born in Rome on 27 August 1545, the son of Ottavio FARNESE, duke of Parma, and MARGARET OF AUSTRIA. He accompanied his mother to the Netherlands when she was appointed regent and was educated at the Spanish court alongside his contemporaries Don CARLOS and Don JUAN DE AUSTRIA; in 1565 he married the Infanta Maria of Portugal (who died in 1577). He served with Don Juan in Italy, where he fought in the battle of LEPANTO (1571), and in 1577 followed him to the Netherlands (where he was governor-general), where he contributed to Don Juan's victory at the battle of Gembloux (Brabant) on 31 January 1578. When Don Juan died on 1 October 1578, Farnese was appointed as his successor.

Farnese negotiated successfully with the Walloon noblemen in the far south, whose Union of ARRAS he ratified (May 1579), and then attended to the military conquest of Brabant and Flanders. He captured Oudenaarde (1582), Dunkirk (1583), Bruges (1584), Ghent (1584), and Brussels (1585) and then turned his attention to Antwerp, which his army had besieged in June 1585. Antwerp had access to the sea through the river Scheldt, which Farnese cut off with a bridge of boats constructed under constant attack from the city's defenders, who were led by Philipp van MARNIX. On 17 August 1585 the starving city surrendered; Farnese required all Protestant citizens to leave within two years. He went on to capture Grave and Venloo (June 1586) and then took towns defended by the English, including ZUTPHEN (October 1586), where Sir Philip SIDNEY was killed, and Deventer (January 1587).

By 1588 Farnese's diplomatic and military conquest of the southern Netherlands was complete, and he had established bridgeheads from which he might mount an invasion of the northern provinces. King Philip, however, deflected Farnese to theatres of war that were in his view more important than the conquest of the secessionist provinces. In 1588 he ordered Farnese to lead his armies to Dunkirk and Nieuwpoort with a view to boarding the ships of the Spanish ARMADA and invading England; neither Nieuwpoort nor Dunkirk could accommodate the draught of the Armada ships, so troops had to be ferried to the warships on canal barges, and vulnerability to Dutch naval guns meant that the plan had to be abandoned. Farnese returned to the war in the Netherlands, but King Philip then insisted that he invade France to assist the CATHOLIC LEAGUE, first to relieve Paris from the siege of HENRI IV (August–September 1590) and then to relieve Rouen (April 1591); at the outset of a third expedition he died, aged 47, at the Abbey of St Vaast near Arras (3 December 1592).

DBI s.v. Alessandro.

**FARNESE, VILLA.** In 1556 Cardinal Alessandro FARNESE (1520–89), patron of BEMBO and VASARI, commissioned Giacomo VIGNOLA to build a villa at Caprarola, 55 kilometres (35 miles) north of Rome; the building was erected on the foundations of an earlier villa begun by Antonio SANGALLO the Younger. The villa was finished in 1583, and is widely considered to be the finest in Italy. Villa Farnese is built on the scale of a palace, and so is sometimes called Palazzo Farnese; it is sometimes confused with the Palazzo Farnese in Rome, which was built by Sangallo for an earlier Cardinal Alessandro Farnese (later Pope PAUL III).

Villa Farnese stands theatrically above terraces joined by enormous horseshoe staircases. The house has five floors; above the basement separate floors were built for clerics, noblemen, knights, and servants. The apartments are decorated with frescoes by the brothers Federico and Taddeo ZUCCARO and Antonio TEMPESTA.

The decision to retain the pentagonal shape of the original foundations created a difficulty for the design of the garden. By 1578 a walled summer garden had been laid out squarely in front of one face and a walled winter garden squarely in front of its neighbour; this design left an awkward triangle between the two gardens. Each of the two gardens was about 70 metres (80 yards) square, and divided into four PARTERRE squares, and they were linked to the principal rooms on the first floor (*piano nobile*) of the house by bridges. The winter garden had a GROTTO and a sheltered walk for inclement weather; the summer garden, which is now lined with camellias (and alive with birdsong), was planted with fruit trees, and contained a fish pond with a gilded FOUNTAIN.

The best feature of the garden lies through a woodland some 365 metres (400 yards) beyond and above the summer garden. There is an ornamental PAVILION (the Casino Villino) of a quality matched only by the pair at Villa LANTE, and behind it is a *GIARDINO SEGRETO* (finally completed in 1620) that is commonly judged to be the world's finest; VASARI memorably declared it to have been born rather than built. The garden is approached by a walled ramp, down the centre of which runs a sculpted cascade (*catena d'acqua*) similar to the one at Villa Lante; at the top of the ramp two river gods lounge against a large fountain. A curved stairway climbs around the fountain to the parterre adjoining the *CASINO*. The garden of the *casino* is enclosed by stone *canephori* (female caryatides with baskets on their heads) on a low wall, beyond which stand stately cypresses. The ground level is mostly on the level of the floor of the house, and the sense of interpenetration of house and garden is enhanced by the carpeting of the garden with pebble mosaics. The fountains now in the garden are the survivors of a much larger number of fountains adorned with statues that once stood in this superb garden.

Gerard Labrot, *Le Palais Farnèse de Caprarola* (1970); I. Faldi, *Il Palazzo Farnese de Caprarola* (1981); Claudia Lazzaro, *The Italian Renaissance Garden* (1990).

**FARNESE FAMILY.** The Farnese were the dynasty that ruled Parma from 1545 to 1731. The association of the family with the papacy goes back at least as far as the early twelfth century, when one Pietro Farnese commanded the army of Pope Paschal II. A later Pietro Farnese led a Florentine force to victory against Pisa in 1363. The labours of Ranuccio Farnese in the service of Pope EUGENIUS IV were rewarded with large fiefs. Later in the fifteenth century, Giulia Farnese became the mistress of Pope ALEXANDER VI, who in 1493 created her brother Alessandro Farnese a cardinal.

The accession of Cardinal Alessandro Farnese to the papacy as Pope PAUL III in 1534 marked the apex of the family's ecclesiastical fortunes and the beginning of its political power. Pope Paul showered papal wealth on his family, alienating vast estates in the PAPAL STATE to his illegitimate children. Soon after his election he appointed his son Pierluigi Farnese (1503–47), who had served at different times in the papal army and in the imperial army that perpetrated the SACK OF ROME, as captain-general of the Church, and passed to him the duchy of Castro (in the Maremma) and a clutch of fiefdoms, including Frascati, Nepi, and Montaldo. Pierluigi was a brutal soldier, and suppressed a rebellion in Perugia in 1540 by recourse to a massacre. In 1545 his father created him duke of Parma and Piacenza. Pierluigi embarked on the construction of a castle in Piacenza, and this symbol of his ducal authority was deeply resented by the noblemen whom he had deprived of their privileges; he had also by this point become the embittered enemy of the Emperor CHARLES V. A plot to assassinate Pierluigi was organized by the marquis of Anguissola with the support of Don Ferrante Gonzaga (imperial governor of Milan) and Andrea DORIA (the imperial admiral, who sought revenge for Pierluigi's role in the FIESCHI CONSPIRACY). On 10 December 1547 Duke Pierluigi was murdered while superintending the construction of his castle, and Piacenza was thereafter occupied by imperial forces.

Pope Paul III made generous provision for Pierluigi's sons Alessandro (1520–89), Ottavio (1521–86), and Orazio (1532–53). He created Alessandro a cardinal at the age of 14. Alessandro developed into a skilled papal diplomat and a learned patron

of scholarship and the arts; writers who enjoyed his patronage included BEMBO, VASARI, Annibale CARO, Giovanni DELLA CASA, and Paolo GIOVIO. He was responsible for the completion of the Palazzo Farnese in Rome, which had been commissioned by his grandfather; its architects were Antonio SANGALLO the Younger (1514–46), MICHELANGELO (till 1564), Giacomo da VIGNOLA (until 1573), and Giacomo DELLA PORTA (till 1589); the palace is now the French embassy. Alessandro also commissioned the Villa FARNESE in Caprarola.

In 1542 Ottavio, Pierluigi's second son, married MARGARET OF PARMA, the illegitimate daughter of CHARLES V and the widow of Alessandro de' MEDICI. After the imperial occupation of Piacenza in 1547, Pope Paul determined to regain the duchies of Piacenza and Parma for the papacy. He therefore set aside Ottavio's claim to the dukedom of Parma and installed a legate; he then claimed Piacenza from the emperor. Ottavio attempted, with the support of his brother Alessandro, to recapture Parma by military force; he failed, but on 10 November 1549 Pope Paul died, and in 1551 his successor JULIUS III restored the duchy of Parma to Ottavio. This left the problem of Piacenza unresolved, because the imperial occupation remained in place; Ottavio therefore resolved to seek the support of France. Pope Julius was eager to retain the support of CHARLES V for the COUNCIL OF TRENT, and so ordered Ottavio to hand over Parma to the papacy. Ottavio declined: Julius stripped him of his Roman fiefs and Charles stripped him of his Lombard fiefs. A French army arrived to protect Parma, war broke out and Gonzaga besieged the city. In the event Ottavio negotiated a peace with his father-in-law, and his titles were restored.

Orazio Farnese, the third son of Pierluigi, inherited the dukedom of Castro on the death of his father and married Diane, an illegitimate daughter of King HENRI II of France. Alessandro FARNESE, the son of Duke Ottavio and Margaret of Parma, was a soldier and statesman in the Netherlands. On his death in 1592 the dukedom passed to his son Ranuccio I (1569–1622); the line became extinct in 1731, and the dukedom passed to the House of Bourbon.

*DBI* has entries s.v. Farnese on the fourteenth-century Pietro and on Pierluigi's son Alessandro; on the Alessandro who became Pope Paul III, see s.v. Paolo III; E. N. Rocca, *I Farnese* (1969).

**FARRANT, RICHARD** (*c.*1525/30–1580), English composer who was a gentleman of the Chapel Royal and master of the choristers. From 1564 he was organist at St George's Chapel, Windsor, where, under his direction, the choristers formed a company to perform plays at court. Only two stage songs survive and are in effect consort songs. Amongst a small repertoire of church music, 'When as we sat in Babylon' is one of the earliest examples of the verse anthem.

**FARTHINGALE or (Spanish)** *verdugado*, a hooped petticoat worn by aristocratic women in England, France, and Spain. In the late sixteenth century, when the farthingale became the height of fashion in England, it consisted of a frame of whalebone hoops that extended the skirt from the hips. The farthingale was the ancestor of the eighteenth-century bustle and the nineteenth-century cane and whalebone crinoline.

*FASTNACHTSPIEL*. Shrovetide (German *Fastnacht*) plays were performed by the citizens of German towns throughout the sixteenth century. The father of the genre was Hans ROSENPLÜT, the master gunner of Nuremberg. In the sixteenth century, the most distinguished writers of *Fastnachtspiele* were Hans SACHS, Hans FOLZ, and the Swiss playwrights Pamphilius GENGENBACH, Niklas MANUEL, and Hans Rudolf Manuel.

*Fastnachtspiele* were normally comedies of marriage or of benignly miscreant peasants and soldiers, often dramatized at a court hearing. After the Reformation, they often treat religious issues. They vary in length from 300 to 4,000 lines and range from simple dramatizations of SCHWÄNKE to highly crafted plays of considerable complexity. They are typically written in KNITTELVERSE.

In the late eighteenth century the *Fastnachtspiel* was revived as a literary form by Goethe in his satirical *Ein Fastnachtspiel vom Pater Bray* (1773), which is written in *Knittelverse*.

**FAUCHET, CLAUDE** (1530–1601), French historian, a native of Paris, where he wrote an important work on medieval France, *Recueil des antiquités gauloises et françaises* (1579 and 1599), which used manuscript sources and attended carefully to philological evidence. He also wrote one of the first histories of French literature, *Recueil de l'origine de la langue et poésie française* (1581).

DBF; J. G. S. Espiner, *Claude Fauchet* (Paris, 1938).

**FAUST, JOHANN, or (Latin) Sabellicus** (1480–1539/40), German magus around whom the Faust legend is constructed; little is known of his life beyond his presence at the universities of Heidelberg, Erfurt, Wittenberg, and Ingolstadt. The legends of his ability to produce wine with the aid of magic and to call from the dead figures from Homer were current in his lifetime. In 1587 an anonymous account of Faust, *Historia von Dr Johann Fausten*, was published in Frankfurt. This book and subsequent elaborations of the legend of a theologian who enters a pact with the devil provided the material for MARLOWE's *Doctor Faustus* and Goethe's *Faust*.

NDB.

**FAUSTO, VETTOR or Vittore** (*c*.1480–*c*.1540), Italian shipwright, a self-educated Venetian who in 1519 was appointed public lecturer in Greek. In 1526 he secured permission from the Senate to construct in the Arsenale a replica of the ancient Greek quinquereme (a fighting ship believed to have five banks of oars on different levels). In trials conducted in 1529 it proved to be faster than a light GALLEY over short distances, but its ineffectiveness over long distances meant that no other quinqueremes were built.

DBI.

**FAWKES, GUY** (1570–1606), one of a group of Catholic conspirators in the GUNPOWDER PLOT against JAMES I who planned to blow up the king and the Houses of Parliament in 1605. The plot was however discovered and Fawkes was executed.

This defeat of Catholic rebellion is celebrated on Bonfire Night, 5 November.

DNB.

**FEDERICO or Federigo II DA MONTEFELTRO** (1422–82), duke of Urbino, was the illegitimate son of Count Guidantonio da MONTEFELTRO of Urbino. Federico was educated in Mantua at the school of VITTORINO DA FELTRE. In 1444 he became a *condottiere*, fighting for Francesco SFORZA of Milan and then for Florence; in 1461 he entered the service of King FERRANTE I of Naples. In 1469 Federico commanded the combined forces of Naples, Florence, and Milan in a successful attack on the papal army and in 1474 was created duke of Urbino by Pope SIXTUS IV, who also acknowledged the legitimacy of Federico's extensive conquests in Romagna. In 1479, by now an ally of the papacy, Federico commanded a papal army in a battle with Florence.

Federico's patronage was extended to artists and architects such as Pedro BERRUGUETE, FRANCESCO DI GIORGIO MARTINI, Luciano LAURANA, MELOZZO DA FORLÌ, PIERO DELLA FRANCESCA, Baccio PONTELLI, and Giovanni SANTI. Piero's celebrated portrait of Federico (1466), now in the Uffizi in Florence, is painted in profile in part to obscure the eye lost in a tournament and a disfiguring injury to his nose; a similar profile is adopted in a portrait (probably by JOOS VAN WASSENHOVE or Pedro Berruguete) now in the Palazzo Ducale in Urbino in which the military and humanist aspects of Federico's life are represented by Federico being shown reading a manuscript while dressed in armour. He abhorred the innovation of printing, choosing instead to collect manuscripts; his LIBRARY was among the largest in Europe. In 1444 Federico commissioned the Palazzo Ducale in Urbino; construction began under the supervision of Luciano Laurana and was completed in 1482 by Francesco di Giorgio Martini. The study (*studiolo*) of Federico, which is arguably the finest small room in Renaissance Italy, is decorated with wooden inlays surmounted with portraits of famous men painted by Pedro Berruguete and Joos van Wassenhove.

DBI; W. Tommasoli, *La vita di Federico da Montefeltro* (1978);
C. H. Clough, *The Duchy of Urbino in the Renaissance* (1981).

**FEDERICO or Federigo D'ARAGONA** (1451–1504), king of Naples from 1496 to 1501, was the second son of King FERRANTE I of Naples and the brother of King ALFONSO II of Naples. As a young man he lived at the court of King LOUIS XI of France before returning to Naples in 1482. Despite his French sympathies, he fought in defence of Naples against the invasion of King CHARLES VIII. In 1496 his nephew King FERRANTE II died, and Federico became king of Naples. In 1501 he abdicated in favour of King LOUIS XII of France, who by way of recompense appointed him count of Maine. He died in Tours.

DBI s.v. Federico d'Aragona.

**FEDERMANN, NIKOLAUS** (*c*.1505–1542), German explorer, an agent of the WELSER banking house. The family was granted exploration rights in Venezuela by the Emperor CHARLES V, and in 1530 Federmann was appointed governor of the infant colony. In 1531 he led an expedition from Coro to Lake Maracaibo. After a sojourn in Spain Federmann returned to Venezuela, and between 1536 and 1539 explored the Orinoco basin and crossed the Andes to Bogotá, where he met the conquistador Gonzalo Jiménez de Quesada. His account of his travels was published posthumously as *Indianische Historia* (1557).

    NDB.

**FEITORIA** is the Portuguese term, cognate with English 'factory', for a trading post. Portuguese *feitorias* were established along the coasts of Africa, India, and Brazil, and were normally garrisoned. Similar trading posts were later established along the coast of Africa by Dutch, French, and English merchants. In early modern English the term for such posts was 'factory' and the official in charge was a 'factor'.

**FELICIANO, FELICE, or Feliciano da Verona or L'Antiquario or (Latin) Antiquarius** (1433–*c*.1479), Italian epigraphist, calligrapher, poet, alchemist, and antiquarian, born in Verona. Feliciano's interest in epigraphy led him to deduce from ancient inscriptions in Rome and Ravenna the mathematical principles on which Roman monumental columns were constructed. His treatise on the shapes of inscription letters, *Alphabetum Romanum* (*c*.1460), was written in a hand which was to influence later manuals on penmanship.

    DBI; MDA.

**FELIX V** (1383–1451), antipope from 5 November 1439 until his abdication on 7 April 1449, was born in Chambéry on 4 December 1383, the son of Count Amadeus VII of SAVOY. He succeeded his father as Amadeus VIII in 1391, and gradually expanded his realm, which eventually included Piedmont and extended from Neuchâtel to the Ligurian coast. SIGISMUND, king of the Romans (i.e. emperor elect), raised Savoy to a duchy in 1416.

    Duke Amadeus was widowed in 1422 and lost his eldest son in 1431, and in October 1434 retired in mourning to the chateau of Ripaille (on Lake Geneva, near Thonon), where he founded and governed the Order of knights-hermits of St Maurice (the patron saint of Savoy, Piedmont, and Sardinia and of the papal SWISS GUARD); he retained responsibility for foreign affairs, but delegated domestic affairs to Louis, his second son.

    Duke Amadeus was elected pope by the rump of the COUNCIL OF BASEL, in opposition to Pope EUGENIUS IV; the electoral college consisted of one cardinal and 32 electors nominated by a commission. He reluctantly accepted the papacy on 14 December 1439, renounced his dukedom in favour of his son Louis on 6 January 1440, and after ordination as a priest and consecration as a bishop was crowned in Basel as Pope Felix V on 24 June 1440.

    Felix created several cardinals (though others declined his invitation) and for a time employed as his secretary Enea Silvio Piccolomini (later Pope PIUS II). He was, however, unable to extend his papal sovereignty significantly beyond the territories that he had controlled as duke of Savoy. His relations with the rump of the Council quickly soured, and

on 17 November 1442 Felix withdrew, first to Lausanne and thence to Geneva. In 1449, through the mediation of King CHARLES VII of France, he reached an agreement with NICHOLAS V, the new Roman pope. At a ceremony on 7 April 1449 he withdrew all of his papal censures of his adversaries and abdicated in favour of Pope Nicholas, who in return appointed him on 18 June cardinal-bishop of Santa Sabina (with a large pension) and also papal vicar and legate in Savoy and its adjacent dioceses. He died in Geneva on 7 January 1451 and was buried at Ripaille, the last of the antipopes.

    DBI s.v. Amadeo VIII, duca di Savoia; F. Cognasso, *Amadeo VIII* (1930).

**FENTON, EDWARD** (d. 1603). English mariner accompanied FROBISHER on his second voyage to seek a NORTH-WEST PASSAGE in 1577, and was second in command on the third voyage for the same purpose the following year. In 1588 he commanded the *MARY ROSE* during the ARMADA.

**FENTON, SIR GEOFFREY** (*c*.1539–1608), English translator. His *Certain Tragical Discourses* (1567) rendered into English, from a French translation, thirteen Italian tales by BANDELLO. He also translated (from a French version) GUICCIARDINI'S *Storia d'Italia*, and works by Fray Antonio de GUEVARA.

    DNB.

**FERDINAND I or (Spanish) Fernando I** (1503–64), Holy Roman Emperor, was born on 10 March 1503 in Alcalá, the second son of PHILIP I and JUANA LA LOCA and the younger brother of the future CHARLES V; his maternal grandparents were FERDINAND V and ISABELLA and his paternal grandparents were the Emperor MAXIMILIAN and MARY OF BURGUNDY. Charles became king of Spain in 1516 and Holy Roman Emperor in 1519. In April 1521, by the Partition of Worms, the emperor awarded to Ferdinand the administration of the HABSBURG territories that he had inherited from Maximilian, which consisted of the archduchies and duchies of Austria, Carinthia, Carniola, and Styria. Charles soon added to Ferdinand's lands the county of Tirol, Vorarlberg, the Outer Austrian lands on the Upper Rhine, and the governorship of the duchy of Württemberg. In Austria Ferdinand created a centralized administrative system that was to last for centuries; its most enduring institutions were the Privy Council (Geheimer Rat) and the Treasury (Hofkammer), both established in 1527, and the Council of War (Hofkriegsrat) instituted in 1556.

    In May 1521 Ferdinand married Anna Jagiełło, the sister of King LOUIS II of Bohemia and Hungary. In the same year he was made president of the Council (*Reichsregiment*) appointed by Charles to act as his regent during his absence from the German lands. After the battle of MOHÁCS in 1526, Ferdinand became king of Bohemia and ruler of Moravia, Silesia, and Lusatia, but the crown of Hungary was disputed by János ZÁPOLYA. Ferdinand was crowned as king of Hungary at Székesfehérvár in November 1527, but was not able to take possession of his kingdom until February 1538, when the war of succession was ended and Ferdinand was forced under the terms of the Treaty of Grosswardein to agree to the partition of Hungary; Ferdinand's share was the western portion, which was thereafter threatened by the Ottomans. On János Zápolya's death in 1540 Ferdinand was finally recognized as king, but the Ottomans advanced further into Hungary, and Ferdinand was able to hold only a narrow strip of the country, for which he later agreed to pay an annual tribute of 30,000 Hungarian ducats to the PORTE. Although he held only a small portion of Hungary, Ferdinand had created a union of Austria, Bohemia, and Hungary which was to last until 1918.

In January 1531 Ferdinand had been chosen as king of the Romans in Cologne and crowned in Aachen. The following year he acquiesced in the Peace of NUREMBERG (a treaty between the emperor and the SCHMALKALDIC LEAGUE), in return he gained Protestant support for his war against the Ottomans in Hungary. In Germany his authority was undermined by the success of the invasion of Württemberg by PHILIP OF HESSE on behalf of the exiled Duke ULRICH; on 13 May 1534 the Habsburg armies of Charles V and his brother Ferdinand were defeated by the forces of Ulrich and Philip of Hesse at the battle of Lauffen. In the final settlement Ulrich was formally restored to the duchy under the terms negotiated in June 1534 in the Treaty of Kaaden, under which Ulrich was recognized as the lawful duke but was subject to the suzerainty of Austria, of which Ferdinand was archduke.

On 25 October 1555 Charles abdicated as emperor in favour of Ferdinand, who was crowned in Frankfurt as emperor on 24 March 1556. On 15 January 1556 Charles had abdicated as king of Spain (which included the Spanish Netherlands and the overseas empire) in favour of his son PHILIP II. Thereafter the Habsburg possessions were permanently divided into Spanish and Austrian branches. Ferdinand's brief imperial reign (1556–64) was dominated by his efforts to negotiate with the Protestants of Germany and by his prosecution of his war with the Ottomans. In religion he remained resolutely Catholic, and although he was willing to make the concession of communion in both kinds to the UTRAQUISTS of Bohemia, he was unwilling to compromise with the Lutherans of Germany by abrogating the clause concerning ecclesiastical reservation in the Peace of AUGSBURG, and was also a firm supporter of the Jesuits in Germany.

In November 1562 Ferdinand secured the election of his son Maximilian (later MAXIMILIAN II) as king of the Romans, and then arranged a partition of his lands among his three surviving sons. Ferdinand died in Vienna on 25 July 1564 and was succeeded as emperor and king of Bohemia and Hungary by Maximilian, his eldest son; his second son, Ferdinand, received Tirol, Vorarlberg, and the Outer Austrian lands on the Upper Rhine; his third son, Charles, received Carinthia, Carniola, Styria, and the lands on the Adriatic.

DHE s.v. Fernando I; NDB.

**FERDINAND V or (Spanish) Fernando V or Ferdinand the Catholic** (1452–1516), king of Castile and León (from 1474), of Aragon (as Ferdinand II), Sardinia, and Sicily (from 1479), and Navarre (from 1512), was born in Sos del Rey Católico, Aragon; he was the son of King JOHN II (Juan II) of Aragon

and his second wife Juana Enríquez. On 19 October 1469 Ferdinand married his cousin Isabella of Castile (later ISABELLA THE CATHOLIC) with a view to securing the crown of Castile should King HENRY IV (Enrique IV), Isabella's brother, die without legitimate heirs. When Henry died in 1474 Isabella assumed the throne of Castile and León; Ferdinand was not formally recognized as king regnant (though he was allowed to append his signature after hers on royal decrees), but rather as king consort. In 1479 Ferdinand succeeded to the throne of Aragon, Sardinia, and Sicily, and thereafter Ferdinand and Isabella ruled their possessions as a joint monarchy, though Aragon and Castile retained their local institutions.

In many of the most important initiatives of the reign of Ferdinand and Isabella, including the establishment of the Spanish INQUISITION (1479), the voyages of COLUMBUS (1492–1504), the expulsion of the JEWS from Spain (1492), and the conquest of GRANADA (1492), Ferdinand was the supporter of Isabella rather than the initiator. Ferdinand's passions lay elsewhere, in the conquest of ports on the north coast of AFRICA and in the securing of NAPLES, which had been overrun by France in the opening campaign of the WARS OF ITALY. Ferdinand dispatched an army commanded by FERNÁNDEZ DE CÓRDOBA to Naples, and supplemented his military campaign by arranging strategic marriages for his daughters: he arranged for his daughter CATHERINE OF ARAGON to marry Prince Henry (later HENRY VIII) of England and for his daughter JUANA LA LOCA to marry Philip of Habsburg (later PHILIP I), son of the Emperor MAXIMILIAN. His other two daughters, Isabella and Maria, were married in succession to MANUEL I of Portugal.

In 1494 Pope ALEXANDER VI is said to have granted the title of *reyes católicos* ('Catholic sovereigns') to Ferdinand and Isabella, who were thereafter known as 'their Catholic Majesties', but the precise circumstances in which the title was conferred are not known. Queen Isabella died in 1504, and the succession to the crown of Castile was contested; after the death of Philip I in 1506, Ferdinand regained control of Castile as regent, as his daughter Juana was incapable of ruling the kingdom. In 1512 Ferdinand conquered and annexed the kingdom of Navarre, which remained a viceroyalty until incorporated into Spain in 1833; French Navarre remained a tiny independent kingdom until 1589, when it was united with France.

In 1505 Ferdinand married Germaine de Foix, niece of King LOUIS XII of France; their only son died in infancy. Ferdinand died on 23 February 1516 in Madrigalejo (Extremadura) and was succeeded by his grandson, the future Emperor CHARLES V.

DBEH and DHE s.v. Fernando V El Católico; J. Vicens Vives, *Historia crítica de la vida y reinado de Fernando II de Aragón* (1962); Ernest Belenguer Cebrià, *Fernando el Católico* (1999).

**FERDINAND OF TIROL, ARCHDUKE** (1529–95), governor of Tirol, Catholic zealot, connoisseur, and playwright, born in Linz, the second son of the Emperor FERDINAND I (hence 'Archduke', German *Erzherzog*, the title borne by sons of emperors since 1453). In 1557 he married Philippine Welser, the daughter of Bartolomäus WELSER; the emperor denied rights of succession to her children, who became margraves of Burgau. After the death of the Emperor Ferdinand in 1564, Archduke Ferdinand became governor of Tirol and promptly instituted a campaign to extirpate Protestantism within his territories. He amassed a huge collection of art and sculpture at his castle of Ambras (or Amras) near Innsbruck. His *Speculum vitae humanae* (1584) is a nine-act play in which the first and last acts are a frame (German *Rahmen*) and the seven internal acts each portray a deadly sin and a godly virtue.

Philippine Welser is depicted in German literature as a woman wronged by her father-in-law; she is the subject of Emanuel Schikaneder's play *Philippine Welser, die schöne Herzogin von Tirol* (1792) and Georg Hesekiel's novel *Lux et umbra* (1861).

NDB.

**FERNANDES, ÁLVARO** (*fl.* 1440s), Portuguese explorer, raised as a page in the court of HENRY THE NAVIGATOR. As a young man he sailed to 'Guinea' (the European term for the west coast of equatorial Africa), and in 1445 he was entrusted by his uncle (joint governor of Madeira and commander of Funchal) with the command of a caravel in the expedition of 1445 led by Alvise da CADAMOSTO; his ship passed beyond Cape Verde to the most southerly point attained by a European. He returned the following year and sailed a further 110 leagues south, probably to what is now Conakry (Guinea). No European sailed further south along the coast until 1461, when Sierra Leone was sighted and named (Portuguese Sierra Leoa) by Pedro da Sintra.

DHP.

**FERNÁNDEZ, ALEJO** (*c.*1475–1545), Spanish painter who appears in the documentary record as 'Maestro Alexos—pintor Alemán', which would seem to indicate German birth or ancestry. He married the daughter of the painter Pedro Fernández and assumed her patronymic surname. The works attributed to Alejo are all in Seville, where he was employed to work on the main ALTARPIECE in the cathedral in 1508. His best-known work is the unsigned *Virgen de los navegantes* (now in the Archivo de Indias in Seville), which is attributed to Alejo on stylistic grounds by analogy to signed works such as the *Virgen de la rosa* in the Church of Santa Ana de Triana in Seville (1510–20) and the altarpiece of the *Lamentation of Christ* in Seville Cathedral (1527).

MDA; D. Angulo Iñíguez, *Alejo Fernández* (1946).

**FERNÁNDEZ or Hernández, GREGORIO** (*c.*1576–1636), Spanish sculptor of reredoses, probably born in Ponferrada; he worked in Valladolid from about 1605. Like JUAN DE JUNI, his predecessor in Valladolid, Gregorio executed sculptures (subsequently painted) on religious subjects, but his work is markedly more dramatic (especially in gesture) than that of Juan. His colouring technique also differs, because whereas Juan's painters used gold and brilliant colours, Gregorio directed his polychromists to use more naturalistic colours. His principal works are the reredoses in the Church of San Miguel in Valladolid (1606) and in the cathedral in Plasencia (1624–34). The room in the Museo Nacional de Escultura in Valladolid devoted to Fernández has several of his works, including a *Baptism of Christ*, a gruesome *Cristo yacente* ('Recumbent Christ'), and a *Pietà* in which the legs of the thieves have been viciously slashed; the Convento de la Encarnación in Madrid has a *Flagellation* and another of his many recumbent Christs. He also sculpted the statues of San JUAN DE LA CRUZ and of *Christ at the Column* in the Convento de Carmelitas Descalzas in Ávila.

MDA; J. J. Martín González, *El escultor Gregorio Fernández* (1980).

**FERNÁNDEZ, JUAN** (1528/30–99), Spanish mariner who explored the west coast of South America. He speculated that the prevailing south wind which retarded voyages from Peru to Chile could be avoided by travelling far out to sea; his hypothesis was correct, and he sailed from Callao (Peru) to Valparaiso (Chile) in only 30 days, as a result of which he was called before the Inquisition on suspicion of sorcery.

In 1563, while sailing from Callao to Valdivia, Fernández discovered the islands that now bear his name. In 1572 he was granted the concession of the islands, and established a colony on Isla Más-a-Tierra (now Isla Robinson Crusoe); the colony soon failed, but the feral descendants of the goats that were left behind were later hunted by Alexander Selkirk. In 1574 Fernández discovered the tiny and remote Islas de los Desventurados (San Félix and San Ambrosio); it is possible that the distant island which he sighted on a voyage in 1576 was Easter Island.

DBEH; DHE.

**FERNÁNDEZ, LUCAS** (*c.*1474–1542), Spanish playwright, born in Salamanca, where in 1498 he competed successfully with Juan del ENCINA for the post of cantor of Salamanca Cathedral. Apart from a visit to Portugal (*c.*1502), Fernández remained in Salamanca, where he taught music at the university for the last twenty years of his life.

The plays of Lucas Fernández survive in a unique copy of his *Farsas y églogas al modo y estilo pastoril y castellano* (Salamanca, 1514) in the Biblioteca Nacional in Madrid, and consist of six plays (three secular comedies and three AUTOS SACRAMENTALES) and a sung dialogue between two shepherds. The secular plays are *Farsa o cuasi comedia del soldado* (an adaptation of the figure of the braggart soldier, following Fernando de ROJAS's *Celestina*), *Comedia de Bras-Gil y Berenguella* (a comic betrothal play in which the figure of the viejo, a gruff but benign elderly figure, is first introduced to Golden Age drama from Roman comedy), and *Farsa o cuasi comedia de una doncella, un pastor y un caballero* (in which the traditional folkloric theme of a shepherd's unrequited love for a noble lady is given a contemporary social setting).

Of Fernández's three *autos*, the most important is the *Auto de la Pasión* (*c.*1500), which was written for performance during Easter week. The play depicts an imaginary meeting between Dionysius the Areopagite and St Peter which eventually leads to the conversion of the Areopagite.

John Lihani, *Lucas Fernández* (1973); A. Hermenegildo, *Renacimiento, teatro y sociedad: Vida y obra de Lucas Fernández* (1975); Françoise Maurizi, *Théâtre et tradition populaires: Juan del Encina et Lucas Fernández* (1994).

**FERNÁNDEZ DE CÓRDOBA, GONZALO, or Gonzalo Fernández y Aguilar de Córdoba or El Gran Capitán** (1453–1515), Spanish soldier in Italy. He was born in Montilla (near Córdoba), the second son of the adelantado of Andalusia, but was orphaned as child. He became a soldier in the service of Castile and as a young man fought the Portuguese and the Moors. In 1492 he was among the officers who received the surrender of the Moors of GRANADA.

In 1495 Gonzalo was given the command of the Spanish force dispatched by King FERDINAND V to relieve FERRANTE II of Naples, which had been occupied by a French army in the opening campaign of the WARS OF ITALY. In the course of his three years in Naples, Gonzalo introduced a new infantry formation in which a central body of men with long pikes was flanked by soldiers armed with ARQUEBUSES; this formation (known as the Swiss Square) was to be used by Spanish armies throughout the next century. After the expulsion of the French army in 1498 the *gran capitán* returned to Spain, but in 1501 he was again sent to Italy, this time as general and viceroy of Naples; in 1503, following his victories at the battle of Cerignola (28 April) and Garigliano (27 December), the French were again expelled from Italy, thus ensuring the Spanish domination of southern Italy. In 1507 Gonzalo was recalled by King Ferdinand and given a royal pension, but no further military commands.

DBEH; DHE; Gerald de Gaury, *The Grand Captain: Gonzalo de Cordoba* (1955); Mary Purcell, *The Great Captain: Gonzalo Fernandez de Cordoba* (1962); J. A. Vaca de Osma, *El Gran Capitán* (1998).

**FERNÁNDEZ DE NAVARRETE, JUAN** (c.1538–1579), Spanish painter, known as 'El Mudo' ('the silent one') because he was a deaf mute. After a long period of study in northern Italy, Navarrete returned to Spain in about 1567 and was appointed court painter to PHILIP II, in which capacity he was commissioned to paint 32 ALTARPIECES for the ESCORIAL, of which he completed eight before he died. His dramatic use of light shows the influence of Venetian art, notably in the *Burial of St Lawrence* painted for the Escorial in 1579. This emphatic use of CHIAROSCURO in Spanish painting is called *tenebrismo*, and so Navarrete is sometimes described as the first of the *tenebristas*; the same term is used of seventeenth-century Neapolitan painters, but the similarities in the use of light between the works of Navarrete and the art of early seventeenth-century Naples seem to reflect a common debt to CARAVAGGIO rather than the influence of Navarrete.

DBEH; MDA s.v. Navarrete; Rosemary Mulcahy, *Juan Fernández de Navarrete, el Mudo: Pintor de Felipe II* (1999).

**FERNÁNDEZ DE OVIEDO, GONZALO** (1478–1557), Spanish historian, born in Madrid. He participated in the capture of GRANADA in 1492 and subsequently fought in Italy under the command of Gonzalo FERNÁNDEZ DE CÓRDOBA. He became a page and chronicler at the court of FERDINAND and ISABELLA, and in that capacity undertook six voyages to Spanish America (1514, 1520, 1526, 1532, 1536, 1549), on the last of which he died in Santo Domingo. His *Sumario de la natural y general istoria de las Indias* (Toledo, 1526) led to his appoint-

ment as royal historiographer of the Indies, and was an early sketch for his *Historia natural y general de las Indias, islas y tierra firme del Mar Océano* (vol. i, Seville, 1535; vol. ii, Valladolid, 1537), which is an unapologetic account of the Spanish discovery and conquest of America. The imperial values and factual inaccuracy of Oviedo's accounts were immediately attacked by Fray Bartolomé de LAS CASAS.

Manuel Ballesteros Gaibrois, *Gonzalo Fernández de Oviedo* (1981).

**FERNÁNDEZ DE QUIRÓS, PEDRO** (1565–1615), Portuguese navigator in the service of Spain. On 21 December 1605 he left Callao in search of a southern continent, the fabled Terra Australis ('southern land'); the following year he discovered Espíritu Santo Island (in the New Hebrides), which he named La Australia del Espíritu Santo in the belief that he had found the southern continent. His crew mutinied and forced Quirós to sail for Mexico. He went on to Spain in 1607 and in 1614 successfully petitioned the king to sponsor an expedition to follow up the discovery of 'Australia', but he died *en route* to the South Pacific and was buried in an unknown grave in Panama.

DHE.

**FERNEL, JEAN FRANÇOIS** (1497–1558), French physician and applied mathematician, the son of an innkeeper who studied medicine at the University of Paris, where he was appointed professor of medicine in 1534. He became physician to DIANE DE POITIERS and then to her lover, King HENRI II.

Fernel's first important publication was *Cosmotheoria* (1528), a treatise on geodesy in which he tried to determine the length of a meridian degree; his calculations were largely vindicated by the work of Willebrord SNEL 90 years later. In 1548 he published a dialogue on the 'hidden causes of things' (*De rerum abditis causis*) in which he tried to establish medicine as a science free from the influence of astrology and the occult sciences. His textbook on medicine (*Medicina*, 1554), which was reprinted in more than 100 editions by the end of the seventeenth century, introduced the terms 'physiology' and 'pathology' to medicine.

DBF; DSB.

**FERRABOSCO, ALFONSO THE ELDER** (1543–88), and **ALFONSO THE YOUNGER** (c.1575–1628), Italian composers in England. Alfonso the Elder, after a youthful career as an instrumentalist and singer in France, moved to England where he was a musician to the queen from 1562. By 1581 he was employed by CARLO EMANUELE I, the duke of Savoy, with whom he travelled to Spain for the duke's wedding in 1585. He died in Bologna. Alfonso the Younger was involved with the musical life at court from 1604, teaching Prince Henry, writing vocal music for MASQUES, and as a string player. He collaborated with Inigo JONES and Ben JONSON on *The Black Masque* performed at court and wrote songs for Jonson's *Volpone*, produced in 1606 at the GLOBE.

**FERRANTE I or (Spanish) Fernando I or (English) Ferdinand I** (1423–94), king of Naples, was the illegitimate son of ALFONSO V of Aragon, king of Sicily and Naples (as

Alfonso I). In his will Alfonso designated Ferrante as his successor to the throne of Naples. Alfonso died on 27 June 1458 and Ferrante claimed his throne. Pope CALLISTUS III declared the line of Aragon to be extinct and claimed Naples for the Church, but he died on 6 August, before he could prosecute his claim. Several months later, his successor, Pope PIUS II, decided to crown Ferrante as king and to dismiss the claims of his rival, RENÉ D'ANJOU. In the intervening period of instability, Jean, duke of Calabria (René's eldest son), invaded Naples and, with the assistance of the disaffected noblemen of Naples, defeated Ferrante at Sarno in July 1460. Ferrante secured the assistance of Alessandro SFORZA and the Albanian leader SKANDERBEG, and by 1464 was able to re-establish his authority throughout the kingdom.

In 1478 Ferrante allied Naples with Pope SIXTUS IV in his struggle with Lorenzo de' MEDICI, but Lorenzo travelled to Naples as his own ambassador and managed to negotiate a peace settlement. Ferrante's style of government became increasingly authoritarian, and in 1485 he was faced with a revolt by Neapolitan noblemen, who were supported by Pope INNOCENT VIII. Ferrante appeased the rebels with promises of an amnesty and then ordered the murder of the leaders. In 1493 he realized that the threat posed by the plans of CHARLES VIII to prosecute the Angevin claim by invading Italy would have grave consequences for other Italian princes, but his attempts to construct a defensive alliance with Pope ALEXANDER VI and Ludovico SFORZA of Milan failed, and he died in January 1494 on the eve of the French invasion.

Ferrante had been educated by Lorenzo VALLA, and throughout his life was a generous patron of the arts.

DBI; DHE s.v. Fernando I.

**FERRANTE II or Ferrantino or (Spanish) Fernando II or (English) Ferdinand II** (1469–96), king of Naples, was the son of ALFONSO II of Aragon, king of Naples, and the grandson of FERRANTE I. In 1494 Alfonso abdicated in favour of Ferrante II as the army of CHARLES VIII approached in the opening campaign of the WARS OF ITALY. Ferrante was unable to defend the city and so fled to Ischia. King Charles garrisoned Naples and then marched north to return home, whereupon Ferrante recaptured the city and, with the assistance of the Spanish soldier Gonzalo FERNÁNDEZ DE CÓRDOBA, expelled French soldiers from the entire kingdom. He died shortly thereafter (7 September 1406) and was succeeded by his uncle, FEDERICO D'ARAGONA.

DBI; DHE s.v. Fernando II.

**FERRARA**, a city, duchy, and episcopal see at the eastern end of the Po valley, ruled by the ESTE FAMILY from 1196, when Azzo I d'Este was nominated as *podestà*, until 1597, when Ferrara was absorbed into the PAPAL STATE by Pope CLEMENT VIII. Under the Este marquises and (from 1472) dukes of Ferrara, the city grew into an elegant regional capital whose wealth was based on riverine commerce (which produced tolls as well as trade), agriculture (the alluvial soil of the flood plain is rich in nutrients), and revenues from subject territories.

The architectural symbol of Este dominance is the castle (Castello Estense), a moated brick fortress constructed by Bertolino da Novaro in 1385 and restored in 1554, when the marble balustrades and the pavilions on top of the towers were added; the castle contains three lavishly frescoed state rooms and a Protestant chapel built for RENÉE DE FRANCE, duchess of Ferrara. The castle was joined by an elevated gallery (c.1475) to the thirteenth-century Ducal Palace (now the Palazzo del Comune, i.e. Town Hall), the official residence of the Este family. The façade of the Ducal Palace (restored 1924) faces the Romanesque-Gothic cathedral (with a baroque interior of 1712), which has a Renaissance campanile (1451–93, with the top floor added a century later). The three principal Renaissance palaces, all of which survived the devastation of the Second World War, are the Schifanoia, the Palazzo dei Diamante, and the Palazzo di Ludovico il Moro. The Schifanoia ('carefree'), which contains frescoes by Francesco del COSSA and ERCOLE DE' ROBERTI, is now the municipal museum. The Palazzo dei Diamanti, built by the Ferrarese architect Biagio ROSSETTI, owes its name to the 12,500 diamond-shaped blocks of marble in its façade; it is now the city art gallery. The Palazzo di Ludovico il Moro, which was built for Ludovico SFORZA (husband of Beatrice d'ESTE), is now an archaeological museum. A smaller palace, the Palazzina Marfisa d'Este (1559), was the home and salon of the Marfisa of TASSO's poems. Rossetti extended the city walls, and so trebled the space within the walls; his extension is called the Herculean Addition (*Addizione Erculea*), named in honour of his patron Ercole I d'ESTE.

The city's university was founded in 1391, and in 1586 moved to its present location in the Palazzo del Paradiso. In literature, Ferrara was the city of Battista GUARINI's *Il pastor fido* and of three masterpieces of Italian romance epic, ARIOSTO's *Orlando furioso*, BOIARDO's *Orlando innamorato*, and Tasso's *Gerusalemme liberata*. The house built for Ariosto survives, as does his tomb in the university library (the Biblioteca Civica Ariostea). The Ospedale di Santa Anna, in which Tasso was confined while insane (1579–86), also survives; Shelley later took a brick from his cell as a memento. In art, Ferrara was the city of Francesco del Cossa, Dosso DOSSI, Benvenuto Tisi GAROFALO, Ercole de' Roberti, Cosimo TURA, and (for short periods) of Rogier van der WEYDEN, PISANELLO, and TITIAN.

In music, Heinrich ISAAC and JOSQUIN DESPRÈS worked at the court of Ercole I d'Este, and in the 1580s the 'three ladies of Ferrara' (*tre nobilissime giovani donne*) sang at the court of Alfonso II d'ESTE (and in Mantua and Florence) and inspired works by Giaches de WERT (the lover of Tarquinia Molza, one of the ladies), MONTEVERDI (in *Terzo libro de madrigali*, 1592), and the Ferrarese organist Luzzasco LUZZASCHI. The composer Carlo GESUALDO came to the city and married Eleanor d'Este, niece of Alfonso II d'Este. Eminent temporary residents of Ferrara also included CALVIN and COPERNICUS.

W. L. Gundersheimer, *Ferrara: The Style of a Renaissance Despotism* (1973); A. Frizzi, *Memorie per la storia di Ferrara* (5 vols., 1791); Anthony Newcomb, *The Madrigal at Ferrara, 1579–1597*

(2 vols., 1980); Trevor Dean, *Land and Power in Late Medieval Ferrara: The Rule of the Este 1350–1450* (1988); Thomas Tuohy, *Herculean Ferrara: Ercole d'Este and the Invention of a Ducal Capital* (1996).

**FERRARA, WAR OF**, a conflict between Venice and Ferrara that began on 2 May 1482 and concluded with the Peace of Bagnolo on 4 August 1484. Ferrara was in theory a secessionist papal fief (a claim that was to be realized in 1598). Pope SIXTUS IV secured the assistance of Venice in his campaign against the kingdom of NAPLES by demitting to Venice the Polesine, the area at the mouth of the Po which contained Comacchio (52 kilometres (32 miles) south-east of Ferrara) and its valuable SALT pans and eel fishery. The Polesine, which was at times claimed by Ravenna, Genoa, and Venice, was a dependency of Ferrara, so the Venetian occupation of the area was regarded by Ferrara as a hostile act.

The conflict quickly escalated: Spain aggressively declared its willingness to defend the Aragonese claim to Naples, and Milan and Florence prepared to go to war in defence of Ferrara's claim. Pope Sixtus withdrew from his alliance with Venice, which responded by urging France to invade Naples in defence of the Angevin claim and to invade Milan in defence of the claim of the Orléans family. The Peace of Bagnolo ended the war, which had consisted for the most part of diplomatic disputes rather than military engagements, but ten years later the tensions revealed in this conflict erupted into the WARS OF ITALY that were to dominate Europe for more than half a century.

E. Piva, *La guerra di Ferrara* (1893).

**FERRARA TAPESTRY WORKSHOP**. In 1445 Flemish weavers who had been working in Ferrara for at least ten years were organized into a large workshop which wove tapestries for the ESTE court to designs by Cosimo TURA. Ferrarese tapestries deriving from Tura's designs include a *Deposition* (c.1475, Cleveland Museum of Art) and may include the *Ryerson Annunciation* (c.1500, Art Institute, Chicago), though the presence of the GONZAGA arms on the latter may imply that it was made in Mantua.

In the mid-sixteenth century the Ferrara factory continued to attract Flemish weavers, notably Nicolas KARCHER; he left for Mantua in 1539, but the Ferrara workshop continued under his nephew Luigi Karcher (d. 1580), whose tapestries included a *Life of the Virgin* (1569–90, Como Cathedral).

N. F. Grazzini, *L'arazzo ferrarese* (1982).

**FERRARI, GAUDENZIO** (1475/80–1576), Italian painter. He was born in Valduggia (Piedmont) and worked in Piedmont and Lombardy. His paintings are characterized by emotional intensity and by bold illusionism. In his *Crucifixion* in the mountain shrine of Sacro Monte (above the Piedmontese town of Varollo), the foreground figures are modelled in terracotta in full relief and the rest of the composition is painted. He also painted an illusionistic *Assumption* or *Concert of Angels* (1534–7) in the dome of Santa Maria dei Miracoli in Saronno (Lombardy). His other works include the *Madonna degli Aranci* (1529, San Cristoforo, Vercelli) and two paintings of the *Annunciation* (National Gallery, London).

DBI; MDA; Vittorio Viale, *Gaudenzio Ferrari* (1969).

**FERRARI, LODOVICO** (1522–65), Italian mathematician. He was born in Milan, where he became a servant in the household of Girolamo CARDANO. He became Cardano's pupil, then his assistant, and in 1540 his successor as public lecturer in mathematics. His method of solving quartic equations, published by Cardano in 1540, was accepted as a significant contribution to ALGEBRA. Ferrari wrote on behalf of Cardano in the dispute with TARTAGLIA over the solution of cubic equations. His part in this written version of a public equation-solving contest shows Ferrari to be an exceedingly able algebraist. Ferrari later taught at Mantua and finally became professor of mathematics at Bologna.

DBI; DSB; Lodovico Ferrari and Niccolò Tartaglia, *Cartelli di sfida matematica, riproduzione in facsimile delle edizioni originali 1547–1548*, introd. Arnaldo Masotti (1974).

**FERREIRA, ANTÓNIO** (1528–69), Portuguese poet, playwright, and humanist, born in Lisbon and educated at the University of Coimbra (1548–51), where he became a lecturer. When the academic climate in Coimbra turned sour as a result of inquisitorial trials, he moved to Lisbon (1567), where he worked as a magistrate (*desembargador da Casa do Cível*) and died in an epidemic of plague. The style of his poetry (which was published in 1598 as *Poemas lusitanos*) and plays is consciously classical, assertively Portuguese (he declined to write in Latin or Spanish) and also draws on the Italian elements in the style of SÁ DE MIRANDA; his poems include epigrams, eclogues, odes, and Italianate sonnets. Ferreira wrote two comedies in prose (*Bristo* and *O Cioso*) and a five-act historical tragedy in blank verse, *Tragédia de Dona Inês de Castro*, which dramatizes the adulterous love of Prince Pedro for the Spanish lady Inés de Castro, who was murdered in 1355 by order of King Afonso IV, Prince Pedro's father. Ferreira's play is regarded as the most important tragedy of Renaissance Portugal, but his true greatness is to be found in the poetry, which is the finest example of classicism in the language, and earned him the sobriquet of 'the Portuguese Horace'.

T. E. Earle, *The Muse Reborn: The Poetry of António Ferreira* (1988).

**FERRETTI, GIOVANNI** (c.1540–after 1609), Italian composer whose *napolitane* were much admired in northern Europe; some of his pieces were included in Thomas MORLEY's collections of madrigals. He was *maestro di cappella* at Ancona Cathedral and at the Santa Casa in Loreto.

**FERRUCCI, FRANCESCO** (1497–1585), Italian sculptor, born in Fiesole or Florence. He was the most distinguished Renaissance sculptor in PORPHYRY. His most important surviving work in this medium is the basin of VERROCCHIO's Putto with Dolphin Fountain in the courtyard of the Palazzo Vecchio in Florence (1555). He also carved relief portraits, including one of Cosimo de' MEDICI the Elder (1569, Victoria and Albert Museum).

MDA.

**FERRUCCI or Ferruccio, FRANCESCO** (1489–1530), *condottiere*, born in Florence on 14 August 1489. He initially worked as a merchant's clerk, but in 1527 joined the roving mercenary force known as the *Bande Nere*. Two years later, when Pope CLEMENT VII and the Emperor CHARLES V decided to reinstate the MEDICI in Florence by force of arms, Ferrucci was appointed military governor of Empoli, where he successfully harassed the imperial army. In 1530 Volterra declared itself free of Florence and declared for the emperor, whose troops garrisoned the city. Ferrucci recaptured the city in a surprise attack, but while he was securing Volterra imperial troops captured Empoli, so cutting off an important access route to Florence. Ferrucci's plan to march on Rome and force Pope Clement VII to make peace with Florence on terms favourable to the republic was rejected by Florence, but he was allowed to mount an attack on the imperial rearguard. On reaching Pisa he contracted fever, and during the month that he lay immobilized, the imperial troops were able to prepare for his attack.

In July 1530 Ferrucci left Pisa at the head of a force of 4,000 men; his plan was to rendezvous with a Florentine army commanded by Malatesta BAGLIONI, but the Florentine troops were withheld by the treachery of Baglioni. Ferrucci marched without his Florentine allies to Gavinana, where he was defeated by the much larger imperial army on 3 August 1530. Ferrucci was wounded, captured, and promptly executed. The defeat sounded the death knell of the Florentine republic, which surrendered nine days later.

DBI; G. Romagnoli, *Brevi cenni storici sulla vita di Francesco Ferruccio* (1897).

**FESTA, COSTANZO** (*c.*1490–1545), Piedmontese composer active in Rome, where he sang in the papal chapel from 1517. He wrote music for the liturgy as well as some motets and, while the form was still in its infancy, about 100 madrigals.

**FEUARDENT, FRANÇOIS** (1539–1610), French polemicist and patristic scholar, born in Coutances and educated in Bayeux and Paris. He entered the Franciscan Order and was ordained as a priest in 1561. He supported the CATHOLIC LEAGUE through a programme of polemical preaching in Paris, where he also became a spokesman for the League. The most important of Feuardent's many anti-Calvinist polemics was his *Theomachia Calvinistica* (1604), in which he attempted to refute some 1,400 Calvinist errors. His patristic scholarship included editions of Ildefonsus of Toledo (1576), Irenaeus (1576), Michael Psellus (1577), Ephraem Syrus (1579), and Arnobius (1596).

DBF.

**FEUDAL LAW**. Feudalism (medieval Latin *feudum* or *feodum*) was a system of land tenure based on the relationship of lord and vassal arising out of the holding of land by the vassal 'in feud' or 'in fee' or 'in fief', that is, as a rightful and heritable possession, in return for service, which could in certain circumstances be commuted as payment. In its purest form (as in England and Scotland), all land was held by the king's tenants-in-chief in exchange for agreed obligations to the king; the tenants-in-chief let the land to subtenants, and so the land passed down the chain of tenure, which could be long and complex, to the occupiers of the land. Feudalism declined in late medieval Europe, but the RECEPTION of Lombard feudal law ensured that feudal law continued to be an important feature of DUTCH LAW and GERMAN LAW. Feudalism was introduced into England by William the Conqueror and into Scotland by David I, and feudal law became enshrined in both legal systems: in England land law remained feudal until 1925 and in Scotland feudal land law still survives in attenuated form.

The system of laws that governed feudal relationships was subject to considerable jurisprudential scrutiny and exposition in the fifteenth and sixteenth centuries, because it formed the basis of the rights of the nobility, endowing them with their lands, titles, and administrative and judicial functions. Jurists CALVINUS, Sir Thomas CRAIG, CUJAS, DECIO, DUMOULIN, and LE DOUAREN wrote extensively on feudal law.

**FEUILLANTS**. The congregation of reformed Cistercians of Les Feuillans (near Toulouse) was founded in 1577 by Abbot Jean de la Barrière (1544–1600), who imposed a strict new rule and expelled monks who would not submit to his reform. The reform was approved by Pope GREGORY XIII in 1581, and the Feuillants were instituted as a separate religious ORDER by Pope SIXTUS V in 1589; the Order was actively encouraged by King HENRI III. A parallel order for women, the Feuillantines, was founded in 1588. Feuillant houses were established in Italy, where they were known as Bernardines. The order was disbanded during the Napoleonic Wars.

The name of the Feuillants was assumed by a separatist Jacobin association during the French Revolution, because its members met in the elegant Paris headquarters of the Order in rue Saint-Honoré.

**FÉVIN, ANTOINE DE** (*c.*1470–1511/12), French composer. He was well regarded by his contemporaries and was involved with the royal court from 1507, when Louis XII requested that one of his chansons be sent to Italy. He wrote masses, motets, and chansons in a style similar to that of JOSQUIN DESPRÈS.

**FEYERABEND, SIGMUND** (*c.*1528–1590), printer and publisher. He was born in Heidelberg and became a publisher in Frankfurt am Main. He published in Latin and in German, and many of his books were illustrated with woodcuts by artists such as Jost AMMAN. His publications included an edition of LUTHER's Bible and *Das Buch der Liebe* (1578), a collection of thirteen VOLKSBÜCHER.

Grove; MDA; NDB s.v. Feyerabend, Sigismund.

**FICINO, MARSILIO** (1433–99), influential Italian Neoplatonist philosopher and magus. He was born in Figline (Valdarno) and received a medical education in Florence. He embarked on the study of Greek *c.*1456, and at the behest of Cosimo de' MEDICI translated the *Corpus Hermeticum* (completed 1463; see HERMETICISM), the complete works of Plato (published 1484) and Plotinus (1492), and selected works of other Neoplatonists. Ficino was the moving force of Renaissance Neoplaton-ism and his wide circle has often been called the Florentine Platonic Academy. His original works included comment-aries on Plato, notably on the *Symposium* (1469), which was an explication of Plato's theory of love, the massive *Theologica platonica* (1482), which examined the immortality of the soul, the *De triplici vita* (1489), which dealt with magic, medicine, and astrology and called his orthodoxy into question; and twelve books of letters to many well-known correspondents. He was ordained in 1473, made a canon of Florence's cathe-dral in 1487, and initially supported and then condemned SAVONAROLA.

*DBI*; M. Allen, *The Platonism of Marsilio Ficino* (1984); M. Allen and U. Rees, *Marsilio Ficino: His Theology, his Philosophy and his Legacy* (2002).

**FIELD, NATHAN** (1587–1620), English actor and playwright whose career began with the CHILDREN OF THE CHAPEL; he later played leading roles in plays by JONSON and CHAPMAN. In 1615 he joined the King's Men (see CHAMBERLAIN'S MEN), possibly in succession to SHAKESPEARE. He also wrote two comedies: *A Woman is a Weathercock* (1609) and *Amends for Ladies* (1610). He collaborated with MASSINGER on a tragedy, *The Fatal Dowry* (c.1617–19).

*DNB*.

**FIELD OF THE CLOTH OF GOLD or (French) Camp du Drap d'Or** (5–24 June 1520), a meeting between King HENRY VIII of England and King FRANCIS I of France, held on the Plain of Ardres, near Calais (which was an English possession). The meeting was more important for its lavish courtly spec-tacle than for its political consequences, in that Francis failed to prevent King Henry from joining the anti-French alliance of the Emperor CHARLES V.

Joycelyne Russell, *The Field of the Cloth of Gold* (1969); Stephen Bamforth and Jean Dupèbe (eds.), *Francisci Francorum regis et Henrici Anglorum Colloquium*, Renaissance Studies, 5 (1991).

**FIESCHI or Fiesco CONSPIRACY**, a failed *coup d'état* in which the patrician Fieschi family of Genoa attempted to overthrow the government of Andrea DORIA on the night of 2 January 1547. The conspirators murdered Giannettino Doria, Andrea's nephew and heir, but the coup collapsed when its leader, Giovanni Luigi Fieschi, was accidentally drowned. Andrea Doria escaped the assassins, and on returning to Genoa on 4 January mounted a campaign of reprisals, executing two of Giovanni Luigi's brothers and seizing their estates.

The Fieschi Conspiracy was for centuries a popular subject for republican tracts, poems, and plays, notably Cardinal de Retz's *Conjuration de Fiesque* (1655) and Schiller's *Die Verschwörung des Fiesco zu Genua: Ein republikanisches Trauerspiel* (1783).

**FIESCO, GIULIO** (*fl.* 1550–70), Italian composer who dedi-cated his music to members of the Este family, which implies that he was active in Ferrara. This inerence is strengthened by his *Musica nova* (1569), which sets verse by GUARINI, who was then at the Ferrarese court. His *Primo libro* (1554)

is somewhat experimental, with a self-conscious use of chromaticism.

**FIGUREHEADS**. Late medieval figureheads were carved directly onto the beakhead or stem of a ship, but with the advent of the CARRACK and the GALLEON, both of which had forecastles above and beyond the stem, there was no place for the figurehead, which disappeared from ship design. The figurehead was revived in 1546, when two English ships had figureheads affixed to their beakheads. In the course of the next century, as the beakhead came to be flanked by cheeks and then to be enveloped in a rounded bow, the position and stance of the figurehead gradually changed. In the mid-sixteenth century the figurehead was almost horizontal, but as the beakhead was incorporated into the bow, the angle of the figurehead moved upwards; by 1700 it was vertical and by 1800 it was leaning backwards.

Figureheads usually represented animals: of the thirteen largest ships in Queen Elizabeth's navy, five had a lion, five had a dragon, one (the MARY ROSE) had a unicorn, one a tiger, and one an image of Jupiter on an eagle. Sixteenth-century Dutch and Netherlandish ships favoured the lion and French ships mythological figures such as Neptune and Jupiter. The Swedish warship *Vasa* (launched 1628, salvaged 1961, and now in the Vasa Museum in Stockholm) has a magnificent 3-metre (9-foot) figurehead of a lion. The figure of a bare-breasted woman was not used as a figurehead until the advent of clipper ships in the nineteenth century.

**FILARETE or Antonio Averlino** (*c*.1400–*c*.1469), Italian sculptor, architect, and goldsmith, born in Florence; his nick-name is an Italian form of the Greek 'lover of virtue'. In 1445 Filarete completed the bronze doors on the Old ST PETER'S BASILICA in Rome (now rehung as the west door of the new St Peter's), on which his reliefs depict religious figures and scenes in large panels, with mythological subjects portrayed in the borders; scenes from the pontificate of Pope EUGENIUS IV and especially the Council of Ferrara of 1438–9 are also shown. He subsequently moved to Milan, where he prac-tised as an architect; in 1456 he began work on the Ospedale Maggiore (subsequently enlarged from 1625 to 1649, largely destroyed during the Second World War, and since rebuilt). Filarete's work as a sculptor includes a bronze equestrian statuette of Marcus Aurelius (a reduced version of the ancient statue which stood outside San Giovanni in Laterano and since 1538 in Piazza del Campidoglio) which was then believed to represent the Emperor Constantine. This piece, which was made in the early 1440s, was presented to Piero de' MEDICI in 1465; it is now in the Albertinum in Dresden. It is the earliest datable bronze statuette of the Renaissance and the earliest known copy of an ancient statue.

Filarete was the author of *Il trattato d'architettura* (1461–4), an illustrated dialogue in 24 books (21 of architecture and three of painting and drawing) which includes a utopian vision of a star-shaped city called Sforzinda (named in hon-our of Francesco SFORZA, Filarete's patron) and a coastal town called Plousiapolis; the symmetrical layout of Sforzinda is an early example of TOWN PLANNING in the Renaissance style. The buildings that Filarete planned included a ten-storey Tower of Vice and Virtue with a brothel on the ground floor and an observatory on the roof. VASARI condemned the treatise as ridiculous, but its readers included BRAMANTE, MICHELANGELO, and SCAMOZZI.

DBI s.v. Averlino, detto Filarete; MDA; *Treatise on Architecture*, trans. J. R. Spencer (2 vols., 1965).

**FILELFO, FRANCESCO** (1398–1481), Italian humanist scholar, Hellenist, and polemicist. Filelfo was born in Tolentino (in the Marches), and studied under Gasparino da BARZIZZA in Padua before moving in 1420 to the Byzantine court in Constantinople, where, in the course of seven years, he became fluent in contemporary Greek and acquired a competence in classical Greek; one of his fellow pupils was BESSARION, with whom he remained in contact in Italy until Bessarion's death in 1472.

Filelfo secured a teaching post in Bologna in 1428, and the following year he was appointed to a chair of Greek at Florence, where his pupils included Enea Silvio Piccolomini (late Pope PIUS II) and Carlo MARSUPPINI and his supporters included Niccolò NICCOLI; in 1431 he was displaced in favour of Marsuppini after a quarrel with members of the Florentine humanist establishment. He fled from Florence when Cosimo de' MEDICI returned from exile in 1434, first teaching in Siena (1434–8), then returning to Bologna (1439), and finally settling in Milan, from the security of which he issued a series of vitriolic polemics against his Florentine detractors. After 35 years in Milan he moved in 1474 to Rome, where he lived for the rest of his life.

Filelfo's translations included the *Rhetorica ad Alexandrum* (then attributed to ARISTOTLE), PLATO's *Euthyphro*, two treatises by Hippocrates, four of PLUTARCH's lives, and an influential educational treatise, Xenophon's *Cyropaedia*.

DBI; C. de' Rosmini, *Vita di Francesco Filelfo* (3 vols., 1808); *Francesco Filelfo nel quinto centenario della morte* (1986); *Filelfo in Milan: Writings 1451–1477*, ed. Diana Maury Robin (1991).

**FILIGREE AND FILIGREE ENAMEL.** Filigree (French *filigrane*, Italian and Spanish *filigrana*, German *Drahtegeflecht*) is ornamental openwork of gold or silver wire twisted and plaited into a design. In sixteenth-century Germany, where the most important centre for filigree was Siedenburg (near Bremen), large caskets and dishes made from filigree were laboriously manufactured for the *Kunstkammer* market. Thereafter filigree survived only in attenuated form as a folk art, and the craft still survives in Italy and Norway for the manufacturing of tourist souvenirs.

In fourteenth- and fifteenth-century Venice filigree was used for mounting ROCK-CRYSTAL cups and was on occasion enriched with ENAMEL by soldering twisted silver wires to a silver base, so forming partitions to separate the applications of polychrome enamels. Filigree enamel became a distinctive art form which spread from Venice to northern Italy (e.g. the reliquary of the cross in the treasury of the cathedral in Padua), Spain, and eastern Europe. In the late fourteenth century Hungary became an important centre of filigree enamel, and from there it spread to Prague, Kraków, Vienna, and (as a folk art) Russia. In Hungary the enamel was made on small plates which were then attached to the object to be decorated; the enamel covered the entire surface of each plate, not only the spaces within the wire design. Decorations consisted of flowers and foliated scrolls, and characteristically depicted the carnation and the pomegranate; the tulip was introduced into HUNGARIAN GARDENS in the sixteenth century, and was soon added to the plants depicted in filigree enamels. Several examples of Hungarian filigree enamel survive in the treasury of Esztergom Cathedral, including the Nyitra Evangelistary (c.1370), on which the silver cover is decorated with floral filigree medallions at each corner, the Széchy Chalice (c.1450), in which bubbles of gilded silver are soldered to the filigree wire, and the Suky Chalice (c.1440). The National Museum in Budapest has a viaticum casket (for carrying the eucharist to the dying) dated 1451 and the Támas Bakócz Chalice.

Transylvanian filigree enamels of the mid-sixteenth century resemble Hungarian filigrees, but the designs are characteristically outlined with a silver frame rather than with filigree wire, and the details of the design are often overpainted in a contrasting colour. The finest surviving example of Transylvanian filigree is the helmet made for STEFAN BÁTORY now in the Muzeum Czartoryskich in Kraków.

Thale Riisøen and Alf Bøe, *Om filigran/Filigree* (1959).

**FINCH, SIR HENRY** (1558–1625), English jurist. He was educated at Oriel College, Oxford, and studied law at Gray's Inn. He served as MP for Canterbury (1614) and in 1616 was appointed serjeant-at-law, the highest order of counsel at the English bar (also known as the Order of the Coif). His *World's Great Restoration; or, Calling of the Jews* (1621) was suppressed as demeaning of the royal prerogative.

Finch worked with BACON and other jurists on what proved to be an abortive attempt to codify the statute law of England. His main juristic publication was *Nomotechnia* (1613), a treatise written in LAW FRENCH examining in its four books jurisprudence, COMMON LAW, procedure, and special jurisdictions; an English translation was published in 1627 as *Law; or, A Discourse Thereof in Four Books*. It remained the authoritative work on common law until William Blackstone published his *Commentaries* (1765–70) and the definitive work on English jurisprudence until John Austin published his *Province of Jurisprudence* in 1832.

DNB.

**FINCK, HERMANN** (1527–1558), German composer and theorist, active in Wittenberg at the university and as an organist. His *Pratica musica* is a treatise setting out the rules of music and citing the works of JOSQUIN DESPRÈS as examples. The section on the history of music distinguishes between older composers (GAFFURIO, TINCTORIS, and DUFAY) and more recent ones (Josquin and GOMBERT). It finishes with a discourse on the performance practice of polyphony.

**FINIGUERRA, MASO** (1426–64), Florentine goldsmith and engraver who from 1456 to 1464 worked with Antonio

POLLAIUOLO. His finest silverware was decorated with NIELLO; most examples of his niello silverware are known only from casts, but one important surviving example is a silver pax in the Museo Nazionale in Florence.

*DBI* s.v. Finiguerra, Tommaso (Maso); *MDA*; Lorenza Merli, *Maso Finiguerra* (1995).

**FIORAVANTI, ARISTOTELE** (1415/20–c.1486), Italian engineer and architect, born into a family of architects in Bologna. He worked in Bologna, Milan, Mantua, and Rome and in 1475 travelled via Hungary to Moscow to build the Cathedral of the Assumption (Uspensky Sobor, 1475–9), which dominates the churches of the Kremlin and was Russia's principal church until 1917, when it became a museum; there are few hints in the design of the church that it is the work of an Italian Renaissance architect.

*DBI*; *MDA*; Stanislav Zemtsov, *Aristotel' F'oravanti* (1985).

**FIORENZO DI LORENZO** (c.1445–c.1522), Italian painter and architect, a native of Perugia, where he worked as a painter of frescoes throughout his career. His principal surviving work is a polyptych of *The Madonna and Child with Saints* (1487–93, Church of Santa Maria Nuova, Perugia). None of his frescoes is now in good condition; his *Madonna of Mercy* (1476), painted in the Hospital of Sant'Egidio during a plague epidemic, is now in the Galleria Nazionale in Perugia following the destruction of the hospital.

*MDA*.

**FIRENZUOLA, AGNOLO, or Michelangelo Girolamo** (1493–1543), Italian author, a native of Florence who studied law, became a Vallombrosan monk (1517), and was released from his monastic vows by papal dispensation in 1526. In 1534 he returned to Florence, and then settled in Prato as the abbot of a church. His wide-ranging literary and dramatic works include two comedies, *Lucidi* and *La trinutia* ('The Triple Marriage'), a collection of amorous *novelle* called *Ragionamenti d'amore*, an adaptation of Apuleius' *Golden Ass* (*Asino d'oro*, 1550), and *Prima veste dei discorsi degli animali* (1548), which is a version (derived from a Spanish translation) of the fables of *Pancha Tantra* (Sanskrit; 'Five Sections'); his dialogues include one on women's beauty (*De la bellezza delle donne*) and another attacking TRISSINO's *Epistola* (*Discacciamento de la nuove lettere*).

*DBI*; *OCIL*; *Opere*, ed. A. Seroni (1958); G. Fatini, *Agnolo Firenzuola e la borghesia letterata del Rinascimento* (1907).

**FISCHART, JOHANN** (1546–90), German satirist and translator of Rabelais. He was probably born in Strassburg, where he received his early education in the school founded by Johannes STURM; he then moved to Worms, where he was educated in the house of his uncle Kaspar SCHEIDT. He subsequently travelled in Italy, France, England, and the Netherlands, in every case learning the language and studying the literature; on his return he took a doctorate in law at Basel. From 1571 to 1582 Fischart worked as a proofreader for his brother-in-law Bernhard Jobin, who was a printer in Strassburg. In 1582 he became an advocate at the REICHSKAM-

MERGERICHT in Speyer, and the following year he married and became principal magistrate (*Amtmann*) in Forbach (near Saarbrücken), where he lived for the rest of his life.

The canon of Fischart's satires is uncertain, partly because he wrote under many pseudonyms, but also because he is a reasonable candidate for the authorship of any anonymous moral satire with a strongly Protestant perspective. More than 50 satires in prose and verse can be confidently attributed to Fischart, including a versified version of TILL EULEN-SPIEGEL (*Eulenspiegel Reimensweis*, 1572), a misogynist satire related to the tradition of FLEA POETRY that describes a battle between fleas and women (*Der Flöhhatz*, 1573), a comic account of gout (*Das Podagrammatische Trostbüchlein*, 1577), and an account of a visit at the height of confessional tensions by Zürich councillors to Strassburg, waterborne on the Rhine, carrying a cauldron of hot millet gruel (*Das Glückhafft Schiff von Zürich*, 1577).

Fischart's most famous work is his *Gargantoa und Pantagruel* (1575) a free translation of RABELAIS in which German puns of great verbal ingenuity replace the French originals and Fischart's own moralistic view of the world is substituted for Rabelais's humanism; the second edition of 1575 was entitled *Geschichtklitterung*, which is the title by which the translation is now known.

Fischart was one of Europe's greatest satirists, but his reputation outlived him by no more than 30 years; his satires were revived in the eighteenth century by J. J. Bodmer and G. E. Lessing and are now part of the canon of German literature.

*DLL*; *NDB*; H. Sommerhalder, *Johann Fischarts Werk* (1960).

**FISHER, JOHN** (1469–1535), English humanist bishop. Following his education at Cambridge, Fisher progressed from a readership in divinity to becoming vice-chancellor in 1501; three years later he was made bishop of Rochester and chancellor of Cambridge University. Fisher supported humanist learning, and was a friend of ERASMUS, whom he encouraged to teach at Cambridge. He was also an eminent scholar and celebrated preacher and bishop. He became a leading defendant of Catholicism in the 1520s. His *Assertionis Lutheranae confutatio* (1523) was an influential attack on Luther and a defence of the Catholic doctrine on the eucharist. A vocal opponent of HENRY VIII's annulment of his marriage with CATHERINE OF ARAGON, he published several works in defence of Catherine's position, and resisted Henry's challenge to the papacy. In 1535 he was tricked into openly denying Henry's supremacy over the Church in England, and was executed shortly after being made a cardinal. He was canonized in 1935.

*DNB*.

**FITZHERBERT, SIR ANTHONY** (1470–1538), English judge and jurist. As a judge he signed articles of impeachment against WOLSEY in 1529 and served as a member of the judicial tribunal which tried FISHER and MORE in 1535.

Fitzherbert's juristic writings are characterized by a vast knowledge of ENGLISH LAW and a lucid expository prose style in his chosen medium of LAW FRENCH. His *La Grande Abridgement* (3 vols., 1516) is a summary account of more than

14,000 cases under 260 headings; it was the first attempt to systematize English law. He also compiled *La novelle natura brevium* (1534), a classic text on procedure. His other writings include *Diversité de courts et lour jurisdictions* (1526), *L'Office et auctorité de justices de peace* (1538) and *L'Office de viconts, bailiffes, escheators, constables, coroners* (1538). Attributed works include *A Book of Surveying and Improvement* (1523) and *A Book of Husbandry* (1523); the latter was the earliest published book on agriculture written in English.

*DNB.*

**FITZWILLIAM VIRGINAL BOOK**. An important source of information on music for virginals in the fifteenth and sixteenth centuries, this book, copied c.1609–19 and now in the Fitzwilliam Library in Cambridge, contains 200 pages of music by BULL, BYRD, and others.

**FLACIUS ILLYRICUS or (German) Flach or (Croatian) Matthias Vlakich** (1520–75), Istrian Protestant theologian in Germany, born in the Venetian town of Albona (now Labin, in Croatia) and educated at the School of San Marco in Venice. In 1539 Flacius was sent to Switzerland by his uncle, the Franciscan provincial Baldo Lupetina (who was later judicially drowned because of his Reformation sympathies), and studied Greek at Basel under Simon Grynaeus. He next moved to Tübingen, where he studied Greek under Matthias Gerbitius and Hebrew under the radical Lutheran Johannes Forster.

In 1541 Flacius moved to Wittenberg, where he was welcomed by MELANCHTHON and became a supporter of LUTHER. He was appointed professor of Hebrew at Wittenberg in 1544, and the following year he contracted his first marriage (which was to produce twelve children) at a ceremony attended by Luther. Throughout this period Flacius sought to defend Lutheranism against the teachings of Melanchthon and his followers. He attempted to rally the theological faculty at Wittenberg to oppose the AUGSBURG INTERIM and the LEIPZIG INTERIM, and on failing to do so was obliged on 9 November 1551 to leave for Magdeburg, where he stayed until 1557, battling against the ADIAPHORISTS as one of the leaders (with Nikolaus von AMSDORF) of the GNESIO-LUTHERAN faction and organizing the MAGDEBURG CENTURIES. He also published *Catalogus testium veritatis* (1556), a learned treatise which sought to demonstrate the historical basis of Lutheran theology; his belief that history was the basis of correct doctrine (*historia est fundamentum doctrinae*) later became a commonplace, but was at the time an innovation.

On 17 May 1557 Flacius moved to Jena to take up a chair in New Testament theology, but he refused to sign the FRANKFURT RECESS and eventually fell out with the SYNERGISTS. In August 1560 Flacius and Victorinus STRIGEL were obliged to hold a disputation before a court in Weimar on the issue of the place of the human will in relation to GRACE in the process of conversion. It was this occasion that led Flacius to coin his aphorism that original sin is the substance of the natural man.

In December 1561 the Synergists managed to have Flacius dismissed from his chair in Jena, whereupon he moved in February 1562 to Regensburg under the patronage and protection of the count of Ortenburg, who converted his territory to Protestantism the following year. In 1564 his wife died, and in the same year he remarried; this marriage was to produce additional children. The most important publication of this period was his *Clavis scripturae sacrae* (1567), in which the key to the Holy Scriptures was a method of biblical exegesis that drew both on philological BIBLICAL scholarship and on the manuals of RHETORIC of Melanchthon and Andreas Hyperius. On the death of his protector Flacius was obliged to leave Regensburg, first settling in Antwerp (1566–7) and then fleeing because of the war to Frankfurt am Main (where he was refused asylum); he proceeded to Strassburg, where he settled and published his *Glossa compendiaria in Neuen Testamentum* (1570), which he dedicated to the city council. He was expelled from Strassburg in 1573, and sought refuge with the Magdalenes (the 'Convent of the White Ladies') in Frankfurt, where the prioress, Katharine von Meerfeld, shielded him against an expulsion order issued by the city authorities; he died on 11 March 1575.

Flacius is the founding father of modern ecclesiastical history and stands second only to Lorenzo VALLA in the history of biblical hermeneutics. He was also the eponym of the *Missa Illyrica*, an eleventh-century 'ordinary of the mass' published by Flacius in Strassburg in 1557. The distinctive feature of the mass is the large number of apologies (*apologiae*) for personal unworthiness interpolated into the liturgy by the celebrant. Flacius dated the mass to c.700, and argued that this early date rendered it free from medieval corruptions of the doctrine of the EUCHARIST. The issue was widely debated by sixteenth-century liturgists and theologians.

*NDB*; L. Haikola, *Gesetz und Evangelium bei Matthias Flacius Illyricus* (1952); P. Polman, 'Flacius Illyricus, historien de l'Église', *Revue d'histoire ecclésiastique*, 27 (1931).

**FLAGEOLET**, a wind instrument similar to a recorder in that the upper end is stopped by a plug leaving a narrow slit or flue. The player's breath is directed towards the sharp edge of an opening below the plug. Unlike the recorder the flageolet has only four finger-holes at the front and two thumb-holes behind. The term also referred to a variety of 'pastoral' pipes.

**FLAMINIO, MARCANTONIO** (1498–1550), Italian neo-Latin poet, a child prodigy who was welcomed by Pope LEO X to the papal court in 1514 and published his first volume of Latin poetry in 1515. He eventually became associated with Catholic reformers, visiting Juan de VALDÉS in Naples and working for a short period as the secretary of Cardinal Reginald POLE. Flaminio's early poems are wholly secular, but in the 1440s he wrote religious verse, including hymns and a Latin paraphrase of 30 psalms (1546).

*DBI; OCIL.*

**FLANDERS or (Dutch) Vlaanderen or (French) Flandre**, a region in the southern Netherlands; the inhabitants of the region are called Flemings. Early modern Flanders consisted of what is now the Dutch province of Zeeland, the Belgian

provinces of East and West Flanders, and the area of northern France centring on Ypres; the principal cities were Bruges
(Brugge, in East Flanders), Ghent (in West Flanders), and
Ypres (Ieperen). Medieval Flanders was an independent state
(or pair of states), but in 1384 it was absorbed into the duchy
of Burgundy. In the first half of the fifteenth century Flanders
was a prosperous region that exported its manufactures
and its culture throughout Europe. It began to decline in the
second half of the century, in part because of the shift of trade
and commerce to Antwerp. The REVOLT OF THE NETHER-
LANDS, which eventually led to the establishment of a separate state in the north (the United Provinces) but failed in
Flanders, had a ruinous effect on its economy. By the end of
the sixteenth century the central sectors of the economy—
commerce, industry (especially cloth), and agriculture—had
collapsed and the population of the cities was in sharp
decline. In 1633 Flanders reverted to Spanish rule, and in 1648
north-west Flanders was ceded to the United Provinces. In
the late seventeenth century, a series of treaties ceded territories in southern Flanders to France.

The adjectival form of 'Flanders' is 'Flemish' (Dutch
*Vlaams*, Spanish *Flamenco*), which in terms such as FLEMISH
ART, FLEMISH ARCHITECTURE, FLEMISH GARDENS, and FLEMISH
MUSIC refers to the culture of the adjacent counties of Brabant
and Hainaut as well as that of Flanders.

**FLEA POEMS**, a genre of poems in which a flea is satirically
presented as the rival of the lover, who is jealous of the flea's
access to his beloved's body. In Romance languages, such as
French, the poems take advantage of a pun on *puce* ('flea')
and *pucelle* ('virgin'). The principal collection of poems on the
subject is Étienne PASQUIER's *La Puce de Madame des Roches*
(1583), which includes poems by various authors written in
French, Spanish, Italian, Latin, and Greek. In English the
best-known contribution to the genre is John DONNE's 'The
Flea'.

**FLECHA, MATEO THE YOUNGER** (*c*.1530–1604), Spanish
composer and nephew of Matheo Flecha. He was a chorister
to the daughters of CHARLES V, remaining in the service of
Juana until 1552 when he became a Carmelite friar. From 1568
he was in Austria as chaplain to the empress and musician to
the emperor. In 1601 he became abbot of the Benedictine
Monastery of San Pedro de Portella, near Berga, where he
died. He was unusual amongst Spanish composers in writing madrigals; his *Il primo libro de madrigali* was published
in Venice in 1568.

**FLÉMALLE, MASTER OF** (*fl. c*.1420–*c*.1440), Netherlandish
painter whose name derives from paintings in Frankfurt
that were wrongly assumed to have come from Flémalle
(near Liège). The scholarly consensus is that the Master of
Flémalle can be securely identified as Robert CAMPIN.

*MDA.*

**FLEMISH ARCHITECTURE**. Gothic ecclesiastical architecture in fourteenth- and fifteenth-century Flanders was a
syncretic and distinctive blend of south German *Sondergotik*

traditions in its exteriors (especially its very tall towers) and
its vaultings and French Flamboyant elements in its interior
fittings (especially rood-screens and pulpits). These stylistic
features were characteristic of the work of masons from
Brabant who dominated architecture during this period, and
so the style is known as the Brabantine School. The earliest
example of the style is the Church of the Béguinage in
Louvain; this church, which has a wooden roof instead of
stone vaults, was planned, like its better-known counterpart
in Bruges, as part of a community for women, an enclosed
town within a town. The finest churches from the Brabantine
period are those of Antwerp Cathedral (with its 130-metre
(425-foot) tower) and Mechelen/Malines Cathedral (with
its 100-metre (330-foot) tower, originally planned to be 170
metres (560 feet)). The same architectural elements are
evident in secular architecture of the period, notably in the
town halls of Bruges (*c*.1376–1482), Brussels (1402–55), Louvain
(1448–63), Ghent (1517), and Oudenaarde (1525–30), but also in
the guildhalls and merchants' houses that survive in Bruges,
Ghent, and Tournai.

In 1517 MARGARET OF AUSTRIA rebuilt part of her palace in
Mechelen (which was the capital of the Netherlands from
1517 to 1530) in a resolutely Italianate Renaissance idiom;
although two years earlier Bruges had been decorated in the
Italian style (with GROTESQUES and relief medallions) for the
triumphal entry of the future Emperor CHARLES V, the façade
of Margaret's palace, with its Italianate scrolls and swags, was
the first monumental embodiment of the Renaissance style.
This style was used again in the design of GRANVELLE's palace
in Brussels (*c*.1550), but in most sixteenth-century buildings
the Renaissance style was either restricted to decorative
details or combined with indigenous styles; surviving examples of this mixed mode include the courtyard of the Bishop's
Palace in Liège (1526), the Hôtel du Saumon in Mechelen
(1530–4), the Maison de l'Ancien Greffe ('Old City Clerk's
Office', now the courthouse) in Bruges (1535–7), with its
magnificent CHIMNEY PIECE commemorating the Peace of
CAMBRAI, the home of the PLANTIN family in Antwerp (1550,
now the Musée Plantin-Moretus), the Town Hall in Ypres
(1575–1621, destroyed in the First World War and replaced by
a replica), and Cornelius FLORIS DE VRIENDT's Antwerp Town
Hall (1561–6), the grandest and most influential of Flemish
Renaissance buildings. Awareness of Italian architecture
models was enhanced by the publication of Pieter COECKE's
Dutch translation of SERLIO in Antwerp in 1539.

The most influential decorative element in Flemish
Renaissance architecture was the combination of French
STRAPWORK (which originated at FONTAINEBLEAU) and Italian
grotesques. This Flemish motif was widely disseminated in
the pattern books of Jan VREDEMAN DE VRIES.

**FLEMISH ART**. In the fifteenth century Burgundian patronage extended all over the Netherlands, and there was a common culture of Netherlandish art, within which there were
regional centres. As north and south gradually separated,
distinctive Flemish and Dutch artistic cultures began to
emerge, and this process was accelerated by the population

movements in the wake of the REVOLT OF THE NETHERLANDS, which made the north more Protestant and the south more Catholic. The proximity of Flanders to the Burgundian and Habsburg courts meant that patronage was centred there rather than in the north, and the artistic culture of Flanders soon assumed a European importance on a scale wholly disproportionate to the small size of Flanders.

In fifteenth-century Flanders the most important painters were Dieric BOUTS, Robert CAMPIN, Petrus CHRISTUS, Jan van EYCK, Hugo van der GOES, Hans MEMLING, and Rogier van der WEYDEN. Their art grew out of the indigenous tradition of manuscript illumination, and was not significantly indebted to the art of Italy; indeed, influence ran in the other direction, because fifteenth-century Flemish art had an influence on painting all over Europe. In the late fifteenth and early sixteenth centuries this pattern changed, and Flemish art, such as that of Jan GOSSAERT and Quentin MASSYS, came to be influenced by the style of Italian artists (especially LEONARDO, MICHELANGELO, and RAPHAEL), though Pieter BRUEGEL the Elder remained firmly rooted in Flemish traditions and Hieronymus BOSCH had a highly individualistic style.

In the early sixteenth century the centre of Flemish art shifted from Bruges to Antwerp, where the artists included JOOS VAN CLEVE, Jan Sanders van HEMESSEN, MARINUS VAN REYMERSWAELE, and visitors such as DÜRER and HOLBEIN. Fifteenth-century Flemish artists such as JOOS VAN WASSEN-HOVE had travelled to Italy as artists and teachers, but their sixteenth-century successors increasingly went to Italy to learn the art of painting and then returned home as northern MANNERISTS. In the traditional historiography of the Flemish Renaissance, the moment deemed to symbolize the advent of the Renaissance style in Flanders was the arrival of Raphael's cartoons for the tapestries in the SISTINE CHAPEL in Brussels in 1517; it is true that the cartoons influenced artists such as Bernaert van ORLEY, but Italian motifs had been apparent in the art of Flanders for at least a generation before the arrival of the cartoons. The most important sixteenth-century Flemish artists to paint in an Italian idiom were Lanceloot BLONDEEL, Pieter COECKE VAN AELST, Franz FLORIS, Hendrik GOLTZIUS, Willem KEY, and Lambert LOMBARD. In sixteenth-century sculpture, the influence of Italy can be seen in the work of Konrad MEIT, Jean MONE, and Jacques DU BROEUCQ, whose pupil GIAMBOLOGNA, the greatest of Flemish sculptors, pursued his career in Italy.

The most important indigenous tradition of sixteenth-century Flemish art was LANDSCAPE PAINTING, of which the finest exponents were Herri Met de BLES, Pieter Bruegel the Elder, Gillis CONINXLOO, and Joachim PATINIR. This tradition was continued in the late sixteenth and early seventeenth centuries in the art of painters such as Jan BRUEGHEL the Elder, Joost de MOMPER II and Roelandt SAVERY, whose works reflect the transition from constructed to naturalistic landscapes. There was also a tradition of STILL LIFE painting which was distinguished from the parallel tradition in the northern Netherlands by a predilection for flowers (notably in the work of Jan Brueghel) and the absence of any overt didactic element.

**FLEMISH GARDENS** of the fifteenth and sixteenth centuries inevitably had much in common with DUTCH GARDENS, but Spanish influence was always more pronounced in the southern Netherlands than in the northern provinces. The most important southern gardens of the period were in Brussels and Antwerp. Brussels Court was a palace set in parkland which in the fifteenth century had been developed in two sections. At the bottom of the hollow that lay between the palace and a large area of woodland, there was a flower garden with a loggia, a fish pond, a palm-court, an orangery, an aviary, and a menagerie. On the upper slope of the hollow there was a second garden for the private use of the court. In the fourteenth and fifteenth centuries this garden had consisted of an orchard in which a wooden summer house and a fountain decorated with statues had been built. In about 1520 the Emperor CHARLES V redesigned this private garden in the Renaissance style. He retained the summer house, but placed it on marble piles in the middle of a bathing pool. The single FOUNTAIN was replaced with a large number of fountains set in a garden that was designed to look like a labyrinth. The old mixed plantings were uprooted in favour of groups of trees of the same species, pruned to form walls flanking paths and porticoes and outdoor rooms (*cabinets de verdure*); the overall effect was of a giant labyrinth. The fashion for elaborate pruning spread beyond the confines of Brussels Court to the public squares and private gardens of the region, some of which included bowers sculpted from trees and supported by wooden frameworks; one such bower survives at Mâcon, a small town on the Belgian–French border.

Italian influence on garden design became more pronounced in the late sixteenth century. The blend of Italian influence and native Flemish traditions is clearly articulated in Jan VREDEMAN DE VRIES's collection of garden plans, published as *Hortorum viridariorumque formae* (Antwerp, 1568 and 1583). Gardens in this period tended to be flat, not so much because of French influence, but rather because the terraces of Italian gardens could only be achieved if the land was already hilly and if gardens were being constructed on a grand scale; neither was the case in the southern Netherlands. The other difference between Italian and Flemish gardens in this period is that although there were fountains, water played a relatively small part in Flemish gardens, whereas it was the central feature of many of the great ITALIAN GARDENS, such as Villa d'ESTE. A continued medieval influence manifested itself in a tendency to enclose gardens with walls and hedges. Gardens were laid out in PARTERRES, and the geometrical intricacy of the patterns of planting became the most characteristic feature of Flemish design. The shrubs planted in the parterres were pruned into geometrical shapes, and were laid out in regular patterns. Individual parterres were typically enclosed with palisades, rows of trees clipped into green walls reaching to the ground. Architectural features tended to be restricted to fountains and statues. Instead of the stone loggias of Italian gardens, Flemish designers favoured outdoor rooms walled entirely by clipped hedges, often supported on wooden frames.

Sometimes even the expected statue at the centre of the parterre was replaced by a bare-trunked tree with sculpted foliage. The introduction of exotic plants was encouraged by the publications of the Flemish botanist Julius DODOENS. There was particular enthusiasm for the tulip and the lily, but collectors' gardens, such as the one established in Borgerhout (near Antwerp) in about 1550, built up collections of hundreds of foreign plants.

French influence became more pronounced in about 1600, when Salomon de CAUS revamped and enlarged the private garden at Brussels Court. He imposed a more geometrical form on the labyrinth, which was reorganized as a sloping rectangle bordered and bisected by clipped greenery; within these green borders he laid out parterres and built fountains. In the extended part of the garden he built GROTTOES decorated with shells in the Italian style, and fitted them with ornamental waterworks and AUTOMATA, including water-organs. This new emphasis on constructed elements in the garden gradually softened the tendency of Flemish gardens to use only plants as architectonic structures. Salomon de Caus also inaugurated a fashion for embroidered parterres (*parterres de broderie*), in which box was planted in intricate patterns, often imitating botanical shapes.

J. Balis, *Hortus Belgicus* (1962).

**FLEMISH MUSIC.** With the sole exception of SWEELINCK, the creative musical life of the Netherlands was centred in the southern provinces, where a succession of composers created one of the richest musical traditions in Europe. The development of polyphonic vocal writing can be traced through the works of DUFAY, OCKEGHEM, JOSQUIN, Philippe de MONTE, and LASSUS. Elsewhere in Europe a significant concentration of Flemish composers and musicians was in Venice, where the Basilica San Marco employed WILLAERT and Cipriano de RORE.

**FLETCHER, JOHN** (1579–1625), English playwright. Cambridge educated, Fletcher is remembered chiefly for his collaboration with BEAUMONT, between 1605 and 1613, on over 50 plays. These include the romantic tragicomedy *Philaster* (c.1609) and *The Maid's Tragedy* (c.1610), in which the spurned Aspatia loses her life in her revenge on her fiancé, who at royal command has married the king's mistress. He also collaborated with MASSINGER and others, and with SHAKESPEARE on *The Two Noble Kinsmen* (c.1613) and *Henry VIII* (1613).

DNB.

**FLORENCE or (Italian) Firenze or (Latin) Florentia,** the principal city of Tuscany, is situated on both banks of the river Arno. The territory of Florence included Fiesole, on the hill above the city, but the *contado* (dependent territory) did not extend far into Tuscany; the other Tuscan city-states, which included LUCCA, PISA, and SIENA, were from 1222 engaged in a series of wars with Florence.

In common with many other Italian cities, Florence was riven by GUELF AND GHIBELLINE rivalries, and the banishing in 1249 of the Guelf leaders inaugurated Florence's long tradition of using exile as a political weapon. Some entire families, such as the MEDICI, were exiled, and sometimes individuals: DANTE, who had White Guelf sympathies, was exiled in 1301 when the Black Guelfs assumed power in the city.

In the fourteenth century, Florence was intermittently at war with its neighbours. In 1315 Florence was defeated by Pisa at Montecatini, and in 1325 it was defeated at Altopascio by the Ghibelline Castruccio Castracani. In 1348 the population of Florence was halved by the advent of PLAGUE (the Black Death). Human misery was compounded by a temporary collapse of trade, but economic recovery was rapid, in part because plague spread more quickly in the slums of the poor than in the prosperous districts of the merchant class. Plague was followed by a war with Milan, the War of the EIGHT SAINTS, and the CIOMPI REVOLUTION of 1378.

In 1387 Maso ALBIZZI, a powerful figure in the Wool Guild (Arte della Lana), became the unofficial leader of the city, which he ruled for 30 years. Under Albizzi the city became enmeshed in a series of wars (1390–1402) with Gian Galeazzo VISCONTI of Milan and conquered Pisa (1406). It also acquired Arezzo (1384), Montepulciano (1390), Cortona (1411), and Livorno (1421). In the course of the fifteenth century the city became more prosperous as banking developed and trade increased (notably by the addition of SILK).

The rise of the Medici family in the early fifteenth century was inaugurated by the banker Giovanni di Bicci de' Medici, whose wealth helped to secure the power of his descendants. In 1434, Giovanni's son Cosimo de' MEDICI Il Vecchio, who had inherited his father's fortune, became the unofficial first citizen of Florence. Cosimo was succeeded in 1464 by his son Piero I de' MEDICI, and thereafter leadership of the city passed in succession to Lorenzo de' MEDICI, Il Magnifico (whose brother Giuliano was killed in the PAZZI CONSPIRACY), and Piero II de' MEDICI (whose brother became Pope LEO X). In 1494 Piero II was deposed during the French invasion and the family was banished. During this interregnum the most prominent figures were SAVONAROLA (who was executed in 1498) and Piero SODERINI, who was elected as permanent GONFALONIERE in 1502.

In 1512 the Medici were restored and Giuliano de' MEDICI became the leader of Florence. Giuliano was succeeded by his nephew (Piero II's son) Lorenzo, duke of Urbino, and on his death in 1519 the leadership of Florence passed to Giulio de' Medici (illegitimate grandson of Piero I), who ruled the city until he was elected as Pope CLEMENT VII in 1523. On his election he was succeeded in Florence by Ippolito de' Medici, the illegitimate son of Giuliano, duke of Nemours.

In 1527 the Medici family was again exiled, and Florence established the republic now known as the Last Republic. When the Medici were again restored in 1530, this time by the Emperor CHARLES V, the leadership passed to Alessandro de' MEDICI, the illegitimate son of Lorenzo, duke of Urbino. In 1532 Alessandro was created duke of Florence by CHARLES V; in 1537 he was assassinated, and with his death the direct line of descent from Cosimo il Vecchio was extinguished. The dukedom passed to COSIMO I DE' MEDICI, son of the *condottiere* Giovanni de' MEDICI (Giovanni delle Bande Nere) and the fifth-generation descendant of Lorenzo, the brother of Cosimo de' Medici il Vecchio. In 1569 Duke Cosimo was created grand duke of Tuscany by Pope PIUS V, and so inaugurated a succession of seven Medici grand dukes of Tuscany, the last of whom died in 1737 (see Appendix I). Under Cosimo Florence ceased to be a city-state that dominated some of its neighbours and instead became the capital of the duchy of Tuscany.

The architects and artists of Renaissance Florence included ALBERTI, BRUNELLESCHI (who designed the dome on the cathedral), CELLINI, DONATELLO, GHIBERTI, LEONARDO DA VINCI, MASACCIO, UCCELLO, and VASARI; Florence was also the city of BRUNI, GALILEO, GUICCIARDINI, and MACHIAVELLI. The city's surviving Renaissance buildings include churches (notably San Lorenzo, Santa Croce, and Santa Maria Novella), palaces (notably the Medici, the PITTI PALACE, the Rucellai, the Strozzi, and Vasari's Uffizi, which contained the administrative offices—Italian *uffizi*—of the Medici), and public buildings (notably the Biblioteca LAURENZIANA and the Ponte Vecchio), and its gardens include the BOBOLI GARDENS.

J. R. Hale, *Florence and the Medici* (1977); George Holmes, *The Florentine Enlightenment 1400–1450* (1992).

## FLORENCE POTTERIES or Tuscan potteries,

a group of factories in Florence and its *contado* or dependent territory (notably CAFAGGIOLO, MONTELUPO, Pistoia, and Prato), prominent as the finest makers of MAIOLICA until the late fifteenth century, when the Florence potteries were superseded by the FAENZA POTTERIES. Maiolica was made in Florence from about 1300 until the 1530s, and soft-paste PORCELAIN from 1575 to 1587; some of the potteries in the *contado* have a continuous history until the present day.

The products of the potteries, which included ALBARELLI, dishes, and tiles, were generally intended for use rather than display, though some pottery busts were produced, notably one of a black woman now in the Musée de Cluny (Paris) and one of *John the Baptist* in the Ashmolean (Oxford). The most distinctive products of the potteries were oak-leaf jars, which were rounded pots with short necks and a pair of handles, typically decorated with dark blue birds, animals, or humans set amidst stylized leaves that resemble oak. These jars, which were designed to hold medicines, were made throughout the first half of the fifteenth century; in 1430–1 the Hospital of Santa Maria Novella ordered 1,000 oak-leaf jars from the Florentine potter Giunta di Tugo, who marked his products with a manganese asterisk beneath the handle.

G. Cora, *Storia della maiolica di Firenze e del contado: Secoli XIV–XV* (1973); H. Wallis, *Oak-Leaf Jars* (1903).

## FLORENTINE MOSAIC,

the English term for the type of decorative mosaic panels known in Italian as *commeso di pietre dure*. Irregularly shaped pieces of PIETRE DURE were assembled into mosaics to form geometrical or representational designs which were used to adorn furniture or even interior walls (such as the Cappella dei Principi in the Church of San Lorenzo in Florence). In 1588 a workshop that had originally been established under the patronage of Grand Duke COSIMO I DE' MEDICI was refounded as the Opificio delle Pietre Dure, which has continued to manufacture mosaics up to the present day.

**FLORENTIUS**. See RADEWIJNS, FLORENS.

## FLORIO, JOHN

(c.1553–1626). Son of an Italian Protestant refugee, Florio was educated at Oxford and became reader in Italian to Anne of Denmark, wife of James I (JAMES VI). He is noted for his translations of Montaigne's *Essais*, which influenced SHAKESPEARE in *The Tempest* and elsewhere. He also wrote Italian–English dialogues, *First* and *Second Fruits*, and an Italian–English dictionary, *World of Words* (1598 and 1611).

*DNB.*

## FLORIS DE VRIENDT FAMILY,

a Flemish family of artists and architects of which the most prominent were three brothers, Cornelius the Younger (an architect and decorative artist), Frans the Elder (a painter), and Jan (a potter). Cornelius and Frans lived and worked in Italy (c.1540–5) before settling in their native Antwerp, where their work had a distinctly Roman style; Jan pursued an independent career in Spain.

Cornelius Floris de Vriendt the Younger (c.1513/14–1575) published influential engravings of Italian decorative motifs. His greatest achievement was Antwerp Town Hall (1561): the four storeys of the façade (which is 100 metres (110 yards) long) consist of a rusticated arcaded ground floor surmounted by a floor in the Doric ORDER, then one in the Ionic, and finally an open gallery beneath the roof; at the centre of the façade a large three-bayed pavilion culminates in gables in which there are statue niches. Inside the building the grandest room is the Marriage Room, which has a fine sixteenth-century CHIMNEY PIECE. Cornelius also built the House of the German Hansa in Antwerp (c.1566) and the rood-screen in Tournai Cathedral (1572).

Jan Floris de Vriendt (1514–75), who was known in Spanish as Juan Flores, worked in Antwerp as a potter until 1553, when he moved to Spain. He worked in Plasencia (Extremadura) until 1562, when King PHILIP II appointed him royal tile-maker and made him responsible for the design of tiles produced at TALAVERA DE LA REINA and for the decoration of the royal palaces in Madrid and Segovia.

Frans Floris de Vriendt the Elder (1519/20–70) trained as a painter in the studio of Lambert LOMBARD in Liège before travelling with his brother Cornelius to Rome, where in 1541 he attended the unveiling of MICHELANGELO's *Last Judgement* in the SISTINE CHAPEL. The muscular nudes that populate his large religious and mythological paintings (such as his *Fall of the Rebel Angels* of 1554, now in the Koninklijk Museum voor Schone Kunsten in Antwerp) seem to have their origins in Michelangelo's paintings. His portraits, such as his *Portrait of a Woman with a Hound* (1558, Musée des Beaux-Arts, Caen), are painted in a wholly different idiom, in that they are more concerned with characterization than with the physical features of his sitters.

*MDA* s.v. Floris; *BNB* s.v. Floris de Vriendt; *NBW* vii.

## FLOTA,

the Spanish term for the convoy system adopted by Spain to enhance the safety of vessels returning from America laden with treasure. Convoys had long been in use

The Antwerp Town Hall (1561), designed by Cornelius Floris de Vriendt the Younger

amongst the cities of the HANSEATIC LEAGUE, and Venice required its six trading squadrons to sail in convoy. The Spanish system was an elaboration of such practices that was codified in legislation.

Each year two Spanish fleets crossed the Atlantic from Cádiz to Spanish America: one was bound for Mexico and the other for Panama and the islands of the Caribbean. After discharging their cargoes and taking on board the precious metals produced by the mining industry, the two fleets would meet in Havana and return in an armed convoy to Cádiz. The *flota* system reached its final form in 1564 and markedly reduced the depredations of foreign PRIVATEERS, though in an infamous raid in 1628 the entire cargo was taken by Dutch privateers. The *flota* system remained in place until the mid-eighteenth century.

C. H. Haring, *Trade and Navigation between Spain and the Indies at the Time of the Hapsburgs* (1918).

**FLÖTNER or Flettner, PETER** (*c*.1486/95–1546), Swiss–German architect, ornamental designer, sculptor, and engraver, born in the Swiss protectorate of Thurgau. By 1518 he was working on the FUGGER Chapel in Augsburg, after which he travelled in Italy. He settled in Nuremberg in 1522, and, except for a second visit to Italy in the early 1530s, remained there for the rest of his career. He published engravings of many of his designs for furniture, decorative motifs, and precious metals. He made two fine fountains that survive: one is in the market place in Mainz (1526) and the other, one of the greatest of Renaissance FOUNTAINS, is the Nuremberg Apollo Fountain (1532, Stadtmuseum Fembohaus, Nuremberg). He was the architect of what was arguably the finest example of Renaissance domestic architecture in Germany, the Hirschvogelsaal in Nuremberg (1534, destroyed 1945). He died in Nuremberg on 23 October 1546.

*MDA; NDB;* Martin Angerer, *Peter Flötners Entwürfe* (1984).

**FLOWER, BERNARD** (d. 1517), glass stainer of Dutch or German origin. He settled in England *c*.1496 and in 1505 was appointed king's glazier. He was responsible for the windows in the Henry VII Chapel in Westminster Abbey (now destroyed). In 1515 he began to work on the glass for the Chapel of King's College, Cambridge, for which the windows had been designed by Dirick VELLERT; the series was completed by Galyon HONE.

Hilary Wayment, *The Windows of King's College Chapel Cambridge* (1972).

**FLUDD, ROBERT** (1574–1637), English physician and Rosicrucian, born in Bearstead (Kent); he studied at St John's College, Oxford, and then migrated to Christ Church to study medicine. After several years of travel on the Continent studying chemistry and the occult traditions of the Rosicrucians, Fludd settled in London, where he became a fellow of the College of Physicians (on the fourth attempt) and practised medicine. He entered into a controversy with KEPLER and Gassendi and published an *Apologia* (1616) in defence of the Rosicrucians.

*DNB; DSB.*

**FOGLIANO, GIACOMO** (1468–1548), Italian composer and brother of Lodovico FOGLIANO. He was organist at Modena Cathedral where he was expected to teach singing, composing, and organ playing to the choirboys. He composed sacred music, FROTTOLAS, madrigals, and keyboard *ricercares*.

**FOGLIANO, LODOVICO** (d. *c*.1539), Italian composer and theorist, who sang in the Cappella Giulia and later moved to Venice where his *Musica theorica* was published in 1529. It is a discourse on the nature of sound, looked at from a mathematical viewpoint, and applied to musical intervals. A *quodlibet*, 'Fortuna d'un gran tempo', and a mass setting survive.

**FOGLIETTA, OBERTO or Uberto** (1518–81), historian of Genoa who moved *c.*1538 from his native Genoa to work in the papal court in Rome. In 1559 he published *Delle cose della repubblica di Genova*, which was officially proscribed in Genoa because of its hostility to the ruling oligarchy. He described his villa in Tivoli in *Tyburtium* (1569) and subsequently published an account of the FIESCHI CONSPIRACY (Naples, 1571). The papal-Spanish intervention in Genoa in 1576 changed the political climate and enabled Foglietta to return to the city, where he was appointed official historiographer, in which capacity he wrote a history of Genoa up to 1527 which was published in Latin (*Historiae Genuensium*, 1585) and in Italian translation (*Dell'istoria di Genova*, 1597).

DBI.

**FOIX, GASTON DE, DUKE OF NEMOURS** (1489–1512), French soldier in the WARS OF ITALY, the nephew of King LOUIS XII of France. At the age of 22 Gaston was given the command of the French army in Italy in its struggle with the army of the HOLY LEAGUE, which was commanded by Pope JULIUS II. Gaston led his army to victory over the Spanish forces of the League in Bologna and subsequently defeated the Venetians at Brescia. On 11 April 1512 Gaston was killed as he led his army to victory in the battle of Ravenna.

DBF.

**FOLENGO, TEOFILO** (1491–1544), Italian poet, born in Mantua, where he joined the Benedictine Order in 1508; he left the Order by papal dispensation in 1524, but returned in 1530. He wrote poetry in both Latin and Italian. His best-known poem is *Baldus* (1517), a macaronic parody of courtly epic in which stately Latin hexameters are juxtaposed with Italian dialect terms to which Folengo has added Latin inflections.

DBI; G. Billanovich, *Tra don Teofilo Folengo e Merlino Cocaio* (1948).

**FOLZ, HANS** (*c.*1435/40–1513), Meistersinger and barber-surgeon. He was born in Worms and in 1459 settled in Nuremberg, where he became a Meistersinger and an innovator in the tradition of MEISTERGESANG. The element of innovation lay in his refusal to confine his compositions to the traditional melodies: he devised 27 new *Töne* which soon became part of the tradition. He wrote SPRÜCHE and bawdy SCHWÄNKE and six FASTNACHTSPIELE. His poem *Von der collation Maximilians in Nürnberg* is an eyewitness account of a visit by the Emperor MAXIMILIAN I to Nuremberg in 1491.

DLL; Grove; NDB.

**FONSECA, PEDRO DA** (1528–99), Portuguese logician and commentator on Aristotle. Fonseca was born in Cortiçada (now Proença-a-Nova), and joined the Jesuit order in Coimbra in 1548. From 1551 to 1555 he studied and taught at the newly established University of Évora. In 1555 he returned to Coimbra, where he taught philosophy at the Colégio das Artes until 1561. From 1464 to 1471 he again worked in Évora, initially as professor of theology and later as chancellor of the university. He lived in Rome as a scholar and ecclesiastical administrator from 1572 to 1582.

Fonseca's most important scholarly work was a commentary on Aristotle's *Metaphysics* (4 vols., 1577–89). In logic, where his thinking was more closely aligned with late SCHOLASTICISM than with HUMANISM, his main publications were *Institutionum dialecticarum* (1564), *Isagoge philosophica* (1591), and *In universam dialectam* (1606).

J. Ferreira Gomes, 'Pedro da Fonseca, Sixteenth-Century Portuguese Philosopher', *International Philosophical Quarterly*, 6 (1966).

**FONTAINEBLEAU, CHÂTEAU DE**, a royal palace set in a forest 65 kilometres (40 miles) south-east of Paris. It was FRANCIS I who in 1528 began the transformation of the small twelfth-century chateau-fortress of Louis VII into a great Renaissance palace. Francis first commissioned Gilles de Breton (*c.*1500–*c.*1552) to build the Cour de l'Ovale on the site of the old chateau; the finest features of this building are its southern entrance, the Porte Dorée (an imitation of the entrance to the ducal palace at Urbino), which was decorated by Benvenuto CELLINI, and the Salles des Fêtes. Gilles de Breton subsequently built the Galerie François I and the lower storey of the left wing of the Cour de la Fontaine and the Chapelle Saint-Saturnin. The decoration of the Salle des Fêtes, which was commissioned by HENRI II and executed by Francesco PRIMATICCIO and NICCOLÒ DELL'ABBATE, created what is arguably the finest Renaissance interior in France. The Galerie François I was sumptuously decorated by Il ROSSO FIORENTINE and Primaticcio. Gilles de Breton's last commission at Fontainebleau was the Cour du Cheval Blanc (now called the Cour des Adieux, with reference to Napoleon's farewell to his Old Guard in 1814), including the Chapelle de la Sainte-Trinité and the Galerie d'Ulysse (decorated by Primaticcio but subsequently destroyed and rebuilt by Louis XV). The rusticated GROTTO (Grotte des Pins) built as part of this gallery between 1541 and 1543 survives unaltered; it was one of the earliest grottoes in France.

Building was continued on a small scale by Henri II, whose architect was Philibert DELORME; the ballroom that he created is one of the greatest rooms in France. CATHERINE DE MÉDICIS commissioned Primaticcio to enclose the Cour de la Fontaine; the façade of this building, which is now known as the Aile de la Belle Cheminée, is the finest exterior in the palace, and its blend of Italian and French elements proved to be very influential. HENRI IV added the court that now bears his name, together with the attached Cour des Princes and the adjoining Galerie de Diane and Galerie des Cerfs. Henri IV also placed the splendid baptistery at the entrance to the Cour de l'Ovale (which he enlarged). In the seventeenth century, Louis XIII commissioned Jean DUCERCEAU to build the elegant horseshoe staircase in the Cour du Cheval Blanc.

The gardens were laid out between 1528 and 1547. A causeway was constructed, and to the west of it a lake was dug, as a setting for the Cour de la Fontaine. On the west side of the lake there was a walk bordered by clipped hedges (the Allée Royale) where scrofula sufferers could come to be healed by the king's touch; there was a fountain (the Fontaine Belleau) on the west side of the road, beyond which a Jardin de Pins was planted; this area is still covered with pines. To the east of the causeway the Grand Jardin was laid out for FRANCIS I, and this garden was transformed into the Parterre du Tibre by Henri IV. The new name referred to the statue and fountain which were installed at its centre by the designer, Alexandre Francini (see FRANCINI, THOMAS); he laid the garden out in two pairs of matched PARTERRES, each with a fountain at the centre. In 1595 Henri IV created an island garden (the Jardin de l'Étang) laid out as a *parterre de broderie*; the island was destroyed in 1713. Henri IV also added the vast Grand Canal (1609), which is 35 metres (40 yards) wide and 1,100 metres (1,200 yards) long. In the park to the north of the palace Catherine de Médicis commissioned a pleasure house called Mi-Voye and a garden which was then known as the Jardin de la Reine; it was laid out in intricately planted parterres and furnished with a wooden gallery. Bronze statues cast in imitation of classical marbles (including *Apollo Belvedere*, *Laocoön*, and the *Sleeping Ariadne*) by Giacomo de VIGNOLA for Francis I were placed in the garden; the marble originals are now in the Vatican and the bronze copies in the Louvre. Henri IV added a FOUNTAIN with a statue of Diana, and the garden acquired its present name, the Jardin de Diane; in 1813 the original statue of Diana was replaced with a bronze Diana taken from the TUILERIES. The gardens were redesigned by André Le Nôtre in 1645, and Napoleon commissioned still another design, but the outlines of the Renaissance garden are still visible.

MDA; P. Dan, *Trésor des merveilles de la maison royale de Fontainebleau* (1642); F. Hebert, *Le Château de Fontainebleau* (1937); William Howard Adams, *The French Garden, 1500–1800* (1979); Kenneth Woodbridge, *Princely Gardens: The Origins and Development of the French Formal Style* (1986).

**FONTAINEBLEAU, SCHOOLS OF.** Two schools of decorative painting are usually distinguished, but references in the singular to the School of Fontainebleau refer to the first school. The first School of Fontainebleau was instituted by the group of Italian artists brought to France by King FRANCIS I to decorate the royal palace of FONTAINEBLEAU. The decoration was carried out between 1528 and 1558, and the principal artists were Il ROSSO FIORENTINO, NICCOLÒ DELL'ABBATE, and Francesco PRIMATICCIO. The style of the murals at Fontainebleau is clearly Italian in origin, but has been adapted to the courtly ideals of France. The style was disseminated both by the French and Flemish assistants who contributed to the murals and by guests at Fontainebleau. Original features of the style include STRAPWORK and the unprecedented combination of mural painting and stucco which came to be known as the French style.

The decorative painting of royal palaces was for the most part suspended during the WARS OF RELIGION (1562–98) but revived by King HENRI IV, who employed the Flemish and French decorative artists of the second School of Fontainebleau, who included Amboise Dubois (1543–1614), Toussaint Dubreuil (1561–1601), and Martin FRÉMINET.

**FONTANA, ANNIBALE** (*c*.1540–1587), Italian sculptor and medallist. He seems to have been a native of Milan, but was probably trained in Rome; he married into the SARACCHI FAMILY, and the style of his work is very similar to theirs. His early work includes five engraved ROCK-CRYSTAL panels set into a casket commissioned by ALBRECHT V, duke of Bavaria (*c*.1565–70, Residenzmuseum, Munich). His sculpture includes four fine bronze candlesticks made for the Certosa di Pavia (1580). His portrait medals include one of LOMAZZO.

*DBI; MDA.*

**FONTANA, DOMENICO** (1543–1607), Italian architect and engineer, born near Lugano. He settled in Rome *c*.1563, and in 1574 entered the service of Cardinal Montalto; on the accession of Cardinal Montalto as Pope SIXTUS V in 1585, Fontana worked with the pope to redesign Rome as a baroque city. In 1585–6 Fontana famously transported the Egyptian obelisk to its present location outside ST PETER'S BASILICA and also laid out the four streets radiating from Santa Maria Maggiore. He was the architect of the Lateran Palace (1586) and the VATICAN LIBRARY (1587–90), and worked as an engineer with Giacomo DELLA PORTA on the completion of the dome of St Peter's. In 1592 Fontana moved to Naples, where he was appointed as royal engineer, in which capacity he built the viceregal palace (1600–2, now substantially altered) in the Piazza del Plebiscito.

*DBI; MDA; A. Muñoz, Domenico Fontana, architetto (1944).*

**FONTANA, GIOVANNI** (*c*.1390–*c*.1454), Italian engineer and natural philosopher. He was a native of Venezia da Michele who studied medicine at Padua and from 1420 to 1433 served as a physician with the Venetian army in Brescia. His treatise on war machines (*Bellicorum instrumentum*), which survives in a single illustrated manuscript, describes hydraulic devices such as siphons and AUTOMATA. His other writings were an encyclopedic account of the natural world (*De omnibus rebus naturalibus*) and a treatise on PERSPECTIVE addressed to Jacopo BELLINI.

*DBI; Marshall Clagett, 'The Life and Works of Giovanni Fontana', Annali dell' Istituto e Museo di Storia della Scienza di Firenze (1976).*

**FONTANA, GIOVANNI BATTISTA** (*c*.1589–*c*.1630), Italian composer and violinist originally from Brescia who was active in Venice, Rome, and Padua. He wrote violin sonatas and, with Biagio Marini (*c*.1587–1663), was an important figure in the development of that form.

**FONTANA, LAVINIA** (1552–1614), Italian painter, the daughter of the painter Prospero FONTANA. She specialized in historical scenes and portraits. Her portraits include a *Self-Portrait at the Harpsichord* (Galleria dell'Accademia di San Luca, Rome) and *Senator Orsini* (Musée des Beaux-Arts, Bordeaux). Her finest religious painting is a *Noli me tangere* (1581, Uffizi, Florence).

*DBI; MDA.*

**FONTANA, ORAZIO** (d. 1571), Italian potter, the son of Guido Durantino (d. 1576), the owner of a pottery and MAIOLICA workshop in Urbino; in 1553 the family name was changed to Fontana. Orazio was active in Urbino from 1540 to 1544, during which time he signed and dated several surviving ISTORIATO plates. His whereabouts and activities for the next twenty years are unknown, but in 1564 he is known to have been working in the service of EMANUELE FILIBERTO, duke of Savoy, and the following year he returned to Urbino and established his own workshop. After the death of Orazio (who predeceased his father), the workshop was managed by his nephew Flaminio Fontana.

The products of the Fontana workshops in Urbino include maiolica of the highest quality, some of which was designed by Battista FRANCO and Taddeo ZUCCARO. It is likely that the table service designed by Zuccaro for presentation by Duke Guidobaldo II della Rovere to King PHILIP II of Spain was made in the workshop of Orazio Fontana.

**FONTANA, PROSPERO** (1512–97), Italian painter, a native of Bologna who worked in a number of Italian cities (including Florence and Rome) on decorative projects, acting as an assistant to painters such as PERINO DEL VAGA, VASARI, and Taddeo ZUCCARO. In 1560 he worked for a short time at FONTAINEBLEAU as the assistant of PRIMATICCIO. He then returned to Bologna, where he established a studio; his pupils included Ludovico CARRACCI and Denys CALVAERT. Most of his paintings are portraits, in which genre his most talented pupil was his daughter Lavinia FONTANA.

*DBI; MDA.*

**FOOLS** had significant roles both in folk festivals and at court from early medieval times through to the sixteenth century. In the former, they were associated with ritual disruption of established order, a role deriving from the New Year 'Feast of Fools' revelries, in which church and cathedral hierarchies were reversed, and inferiors temporarily usurped the roles of their superiors. The fool's traditional costume of parti-coloured hood and suit, with bells, a fool's head on a stick, and sometimes ears and a tail, was also adopted by the court fool, or king's jester, the 'licensed buffoon' whose foolery was tolerated both for entertainment and on the principle that there is wisdom in madness. His foolery might be 'natural', reflecting the genuine stupidity of the simpleton, or 'allowed', a more knowing jesting, indulged for its amusement or insightfulness. Famous fools include Edward I's Martinet of Gasconet, John Scogan at EDWARD IV's court, HENRY VIII's fool Will Somers, and WOLSEY's fool Patch. The fools of SHAKESPEARE are a composite of both the folk and the court types, participating in the disruption of order in *Twelfth Night*, *As You Like It*, and *King Lear*, but also playing a commenting role, both to elicit humour, and to moralize melancholically on the brevity of happiness and the inevitable transience of life.

**FOPPA, VINCENZO** (1427/30–1515/16), Italian painter. He was born near Brescia and probably trained in Padua before settling in Milan, where he painted fresco cycles, notably his *Life of St Peter Martyr* in the Portinari Chapel in the Church of Sant'Eustorgio. His surviving paintings include a *Crucifixion* (1486, Accademia Carrara, Bergamo), an early *Boy Reading* *Cicero* (Wallace Collection, London), and a late *Epiphany* (National Gallery, London).

*DBI; MDA; Maria Balzarini, Vincenzo Foppa (1997).*

**FORD, JOHN** (1586–1638), English playwright. Ford wrote or contributed to nearly twenty plays, of which seven are now lost. He worked in collaboration with others, including DEKKER and ROWLEY from 1620, but from 1625 appears to have worked alone. His poetic blank verse is easily identifiable, and he pursues bold and often dark themes of human suffering, passion, courage, and dignity. *'Tis Pity She's a Whore* (c.1630), his best-known play, is a tragedy depicting the incestuous love between Giovanni and his sister Annabella. Other plays explore the Spartan values of bravery and endurance (*The Broken Heart*, 1633), the folly of love (*Love's Sacrifice*, 1633), and MELANCHOLIA (*The Lover's Melancholy*, 1629); *Perkin Warbeck* (1634) is a historical play set in Scotland at the time of JAMES IV.

*DNB.*

**FORD, THOMAS** (c.1580–1648), English composer and viol player active in London, who played for Prince Charles. His *Music of Sundry Kinds* (1607) contains ayres and duets for the lyra viol, some requiring a pizzicato technique. Two of his anthems are in Sir William Leighton's *Tears or Lamentations of a Sorrowful Soul* (1614); he also wrote six-part anthems and madrigals.

**FORLORN HOPE or** (Dutch) *verloren hoop* **or** (German) *verlorene Haufe* **or** (French) *enfants perdus*, the sixteenth- and seventeenth-century military term for a body of men deputed to initiate a tightly focused skirmish; they fought in front of the vanguard of the army. In English, the derivation of 'hope' from Dutch *hoop* (meaning 'a body of troops') was lost, and the phrase gradually came to mean 'a faint hope'.

**FORMENT, DAMIÀ** (c.1480–1540), Valencian sculptor of alabaster reredoses whose work embodies the transition in SPANISH ART from the Gothic style to that of the Renaissance. His reredoses in the Cathedral of Santa María del Pilar in Zaragoza (finished in 1512) and the cathedral in Huesca (started c.1520) place sculptures carved in the Renaissance manner into settings that are resolutely Gothic. The magnificent reredos (damaged but now restored) in the Cistercian abbey of Poblet (Tarragona) introduced Renaissance sculpture in the Roman style to Catalonia, and marks Forment's abandonment of Gothic structures. In 1539 Forment forsook alabaster for wood when he began work on the reredos (now gilded and polychromed) for the Cathedral of Santo Domingo de la Calzada (Rioja).

*DBEH; MDA; Francisco Fernández Pardo, Damián Forment, escultor renacentista: Retablo mayor de la Catedral de Santo Domingo de la Calzada (1995).*

**FORMULA MISSAE ET COMMUNIONIS**, the Reformed communion service drafted by Martin LUTHER in December 1523, initially for use in Zwickau. This rite, upon which Luther's 'German mass' of 1526 and subsequent Lutheran liturgies were based, retained both the Latin language and the traditional form of the Catholic mass, but Luther insisted that the form of service was intended to be suggestive rather than prescriptive.

The most significant changes to the traditional mass are contained in the mass of the faithful (*missa fidelium*), which is the final part of the mass that begins with the offertory (in which the bread and wine are offered for consecration). Luther reworked this section with a view to safeguarding his doctrine of the EUCHARIST and introducing communion in both kinds.

**FORNOVO, BATTLE OF, or battle of Taro**, a battle in the WARS OF ITALY fought on the banks of the river Taro near Fornovo (20 kilometres (12 miles) south-west of Parma) on 6 July 1495 between the forces of the HOLY LEAGUE (an alliance of the pope, the emperor, Spain, Milan, and Venice) commanded by Gianfrancesco II GONZAGA and the army of CHARLES VIII of France, which was returning from Naples. The battle lasted for only fifteen minutes, because the French army cut its way through the forces of the League and continued its retreat to France; both sides claimed victory.

**FORSTER, GEORG** (*c.*1510–1568), German musician and physician who sang at the court of Elector Ludwig V at Heidelberg, where he started to collect songs. While studying medicine at Ingolstadt he met Martin LUTHER, whose encouragement probably led to the choice of Biblical texts in his *Frische deutsche Liedlein*. This is a collection of 382 songs by several composers including ISAAC and HOFHAIMER, and illustrates a wide range of genres and styles of writing. Some of Forster's own secular songs are also included.

**FORTEBRACCIO, ANDREA, or Braccio da Montone** (1368–1424), *condottiere*, born into a noble Perugian family that had been dispossessed and exiled. In 1414 Braccio entered the service of Pope JOHN XXIII and in 1416, as captain-general of the Church, captured Perugia. The following year he occupied Rome for 70 days. Braccio eventually became the ruler of much of Umbria and part of the Marches. He died of wounds sustained in a battle before the walls of Aquila (Abruzzi) against a Neapolitan army commanded by Francesco SFORZA.

Braccio's hallmark was his deployment of small units in constant support of one another. His soldiers, who were known as the *Braccheschi*, played a conspicuous part in Italian warfare throughout the fifteenth century.

*DBI.*

**FORTEGUERRI FAMILY**, a Pistoian family which included several prominent humanists, churchmen, and writers. Niccolò Forteguerri (1419–73) was a papal legate who was created cardinal by Pope PIUS II. The humanist Scipione Forteguerri (1466–1515) was a Greek scholar who assisted ALDUS MANUTIUS in Venice. Giovanni Forteguerri (1508–82) served as governor of Pistoia on behalf of Duke COSIMO I DE' MEDICI and published a collection of comic tales.

*DBI.*

**FORTESCUE, SIR JOHN** (*c.*1394–*c.*1476), English jurist and constitutional theorist, from 1442 chief justice of the King's Bench. In 1461 he was attainted by Edward IV for his adherence to the Lancastrian claim, and subsequently wrote several treatises in support of that claim, chiefly *De natura legis naturae*. He followed the court of Henry VI into exile in Scotland and Flanders, and while abroad wrote *De laudibus legum Angliae*, a dialogue between Fortescue and Edward, prince of Wales, designed to induct the young prince into the principles of English law, which is described encomiastically. Fortescue also wrote (but did not publish) the treatise variously entitled *The Governance of England* and *The Difference between an Absolute and a Limited Monarchy*, in which he contrasts the governments of fifteenth-century France and England with a view to evaluating the rival merits of despotic and constitutional forms of government.

*DNB; Anthony Gross, The Dissolution of the Lancastrian Kingship: Sir John Fortescue and the Crisis of Monarchy in Fifteenth-Century England (1996).*

**FORTIFICATION AND SIEGECRAFT**. Fortification is the defensive military art of strengthening positions against attack; siegecraft is the complementary offensive art of capturing fortified positions by isolating the fortified town or castle and then attacking its defences. In the thirteenth and fourteenth centuries the enhanced fortifications of castles had given a clear superiority to defence, though in the case of fortified towns the chances of a successful attack were improved. The central structure in fortification was the tall, thin wall with a narrow walkway on the top sheltered by crenellations and with fortified towers at intervals along the wall. Walls were defended from the top, and attack was increasingly directed at the top: the battering ram was displaced by the siege tower and its bridge. One of the principal means of attack was mining, so the rat (the protective structure mounted over the ram) continued in use as protection for the miners. The designers of fortifications made provision for countermining by building chambers at the base of towers and walls and by projecting masonry beyond towers. Attackers used wheeled mantlets to protect bowmen and crossbowmen, and used machines to hurl stones against the parapets and barrels of burning pitch over the parapets.

In the fifteenth century the introduction of GUNPOWDER shifted the balance between fortification and siegecraft. In the late fourteenth century gunpowder had been stuffed into cannon as a loose mixture, but in the fifteenth century it was produced by moistening, shaping, drying, and granulating the compound, a process that created a more powerful and more reliable weapon. Early cannon were so light that they could not breach masonry, and so were more useful to defenders than attackers: the English siege of Orléans (1428) was defeated because the cannon of the French could be used with greater effect than those of the English. By the middle of the century, however, cannon-founding had made many advances in France, and stronger cannon were able to fire iron cannon balls that could penetrate masonry: the ARTILLERY carried in the siege train of King CHARLES VII in 1450 enabled him to capture every castle in Normandy held by the English.

In 1494 CHARLES VIII invaded Italy in the opening campaign of the WARS OF ITALY, and the superiority of the artillery in his siege train enabled him to capture castles and fortified towns with relative ease. The Italian reaction to his success was a rethinking of the art of fortification. Fortification became an art in which Italian military engineers led the rest of Europe; of the 33 treatises published in the sixteenth century on the subject of fortification, only six were written by non-Italians, one of whom was DÜRER (whose *Etliche Underricht, zu Befestigung der Stett, Schlosz und Flecken* was published in 1527). Fortification was one of the arts in which Italian artists and architects developed unrivalled expertise: in Italy the tradition of artists taking an educated interest in military engineering include GIOTTO, BRUNELLESCHI, LEONARDO (who made designs for Piombino), BUONTALENTI (who designed the Belevedere fortress in Florence), and the builders of the fortifications (now Forte Michelangelo) at Civitavecchia (the port of Rome) who included BRAMANTE (who designed the fort and the Rossa), SANGALLO (who built the fort), and MICHELANGELO (who added the dungeons to the fort).

The defence of fortified positions against artillery capable of destroying masonry at long range necessitated improvements both in defensive artillery and in the design of defences. In the case of artillery, roof towers were removed and replaced with gun platforms, and the loopholes in the lower storeys of towers, formerly used to admit air and light and to view the enemy approach from a safe position, were converted into casemates with embrasures from which grazing fire could be directed over the ditch, albeit in a narrow field of fire.

Defences were improved by the innovation of the bulwark, strengthening of walls, the redesigning of ditches and the invention of the bastion. The bulwark was designed to shield the gates against cannonfire, and typically consisted of a semicircular outwork made from earth, reinforced with timber, and faced with masonry. Bulwarks protected the gates and also afforded a forward defensive position which was useful for flanking fire; this latter quality led military architects to place bulwarks in front of towers and at intervals along walls.

Walls consisting of rubble faced by thin masonry proved particularly vulnerable to artillery, and so were banked with soil on the inside. This defence increasingly proved ineffectual against ever more powerful artillery, because the effect of a breach was to allow soil to collapse into a ramp that was convenient for attackers. The refinement that prevented the formation of such ramps was the reinforcement of the banks of soil with layers of brushwood and timber. The occasional use of masonry in the reinforcement of banks of earth developed into counterforts, which were buttresses facing inward from the wall. A refinement attributed to Dürer is the invention of the counterarched revetment, a series of arches between the counterforts with their axes at right angles to the wall; these counterarches, which were sometimes tiered,

both strengthened the wall and constituted an additional obstacle should the wall be breached.

The ditch was primarily an obstacle to prevent attackers from bringing siege towers within range of the walls, and also supplied soil for the reinforcement of the walls. Ditches had traditionally been sloped at the sides, but were redesigned with vertical masonry sides. On the inside of the ditch the defensive walls were extended downwards to the bottom of the ditch, and on the outside of the ditch a masonry counterscarp in effect turned the ditch into a dry canal. This innovation increased the value of the ditch as an obstacle, but also prevented the mounting of sorties by defending troops, who before the advent of the counterscarp had been able to assemble unseen in the ditch and then ascend the slope to attack the enemy.

The ground plan of fortifications, which in military architecture is called the trace, had for centuries consisted of an enclosure wall surmounted by a walkway and reinforced at intervals by towers. In the early sixteenth century Italian engineers began to reconceive the trace with a view to overcoming three problems: the gun platforms on the towers were too small to accommodate more than one or two guns, the field of fire afforded by the embrasures was too narrow, and the forward bulwarks were vulnerable because they were detached from the main defences. The solution to these problems was the bastioned trace. The earliest bastions were modified bulwarks that extended back to join the walls; the semicircular earthworks of the bulwark evolved into the angular projecting masonry bastion, which constituted a forward artillery position connected by flanks to the main wall. In the bastioned trace, flanks faced each other, thus obviating the need for inefficient casemate positions in the main walls, because every position in the ditch could be reached by artillery in the bastions.

The first example of a complete bastioned trace was Francesco PACIOTTO's fortification of Antwerp in 1568. In the seventeenth century the initiative in bastion design passed from Italy to France, and French military engineers continued to dominate European bastion design until the end of the nineteenth century, when increasingly powerful artillery rendered the bastion ineffective.

J. R. Hale, *Renaissance Fortification: Art or Engineering* (1977).

**FORTUNE PLAYHOUSE.** Built at Cripplegate in London in 1600, along the lines of the GLOBE, the Fortune was the home of the ADMIRAL'S MEN. It was capable of holding audiences of up to a thousand people, and was especially popular with the fashionable and prosperous. A fire in 1621 destroyed the building and valuable play-books, but it was rebuilt and remained open until the closing of the theatres in 1642.

**FOSCARI, FRANCESCO** (1373–1457), doge of Venice, born on 19 June 1373 into a noble Venetian family. He held many of the highest offices of state, including ambassador, president of the Forty, member of the COUNCIL OF TEN, inquisitor, and procurator of San Marco. In 1423 the doge, Tommaso Mocenigo, reportedly warned the Senate as he lay dying that if Foscari were to be elected as his successor, he would plunge the republic into war. Foscari was nonetheless elected as doge, and held the post for 34 years.

Mocenigo's words were prescient. The war of 1425–8 enabled Venice to incorporate Bergamo and Brescia into its *terraferma* empire, but two wars against the VISCONTI of Milan (1431–3 and 1435–41) depleted precious resources at a time when the Ottomans were drawing nearer.

In 1444 the domestic tragedy that was to darken the remainder of Foscari's life began to unfold. His son Jacopo was accused of having accepted bribes. He escaped to Trieste, which was then under Austrian protection, and was tried in his absence by the Council of Ten, who sentenced him to be dispossessed and banished to the Venetian fortress of Napoli di Romania (now Greek Návplion); in 1446 his sentence was commuted to banishment at Treviso. In 1450 a member of the Council of Ten that had tried Jacopo was assassinated. Jacopo was accused, but refused to confess, and this time he was banished to Candia (Venetian Crete) for life with an annual pension of 200 ducats.

In 1456 the Council was informed by the governor (*rettore*) of Candia that Jacopo had been in treasonous correspondence with Duke Francesco SFORZA and Sultan Mehmet II. Jacopo was returned to Venice for a third trial and sentenced to a year's imprisonment followed by a return to exile in Candia. His aged father was allowed to visit his son in prison but refused to intercede on his behalf. At the end of the year Jacopo was returned to Candia, where he died in January 1457. The doge was broken by grief and utterly unable to attend to his duties. He reluctantly agreed to the Council's request that he abdicate, and was given an annual pension of 1,500 ducats. Within a week his successor had been elected, and two days later, on 1 November 1457, Foscari died.

Imaginative representations of the story, notably Byron's verse tragedy *The Two Foscari* (1820), the tale in Samuel Rogers's *Italy* (1821), and Verdi's opera *I due Foscari* (1844), have presented the judges as harsh and corrupt, but by the usual standards of Venetian justice Jacopo was treated with extraordinary leniency.

*DBI.*

**FOUNTAIN or (Renaissance Latin)** *fontana*, a decorated water outlet or projection. In antiquity fountains were endowed with mystical and medicinal qualities, and were often dedicated to gods who were thought to frequent the original springs represented by the fountains. There is also evidence—in the form of ancient Breton fountains flowing from dolmens—of an early Celtic fountain cult. The notion that the water of certain fountains had supernatural healing powers was absorbed into Christian folk-belief, and in medieval Europe statues of the Virgin Mary were often placed in the arch that was constructed to cover springs; this form of fountain, which is usually reached by descending a few steps, is known in France as a *fontaine grotte*. Public fountains of the fifteenth and sixteenth centuries survive in many parts of Europe, including the Fontaine Joubert at Poitiers and the fountain by the church of St Mary Wickford in Lincoln.

In the private gardens of the Renaissance fountains tended to be purely ornamental, and often featured *jets d'eau*. In Italy the fountain was the centrepiece of the garden, and the design of fountains attracted many of the great artists of the period. The most important architect of fountains was GIAMBOLOGNA, whose many designs included the Fountain of Venus at the Villa Petraia near Florence, the Hercules Fountain at the nearby MEDICI VILLA of Castello, the Ocean Fountain in the BOBOLI GARDENS, and the huge Apennine Fountain for PRATOLINO. The most dramatic and extensive use of fountains was at the Villa d'ESTE in Tivoli and at the Villa ALDOBRANDINI, in which the architectonic use of water eclipsed the statuary. In some ITALIAN GARDENS, notably that of Villa LANTE, fountains feed or are fed by water-staircases.

FRENCH GARDENS of the fifteenth and sixteenth centuries were usually flatter than Italian gardens, and water was scarce. The great fountains at ANET and GAILLON, for example, produced only trickles of water; the effect was to emphasize the architecture of the fountains and the form of their sculptures rather than the shapes of the water. The revival of HERON in the Renaissance stimulated an interest in hydraulics, and there were occasional successes in artificially fed fountains, such as the high-pressure fountain at CHENONCEAUX in the mid-sixteenth century, but aquatic effects on an Italian scale were not achieved until the seventeenth century, when technology developed by Italian engineers (notably the FRANCINI brothers) was deployed to feed the fountains of Versailles with water under pressure.

In Germany the finest fountains are in Nuremberg. The fourteenth-century Gothic fountain known as the Schöner Brunnen ('Beautiful Fountain'), which is 19 metres (62 feet) high, has many figures around the base, including the seven electors. Peter FLÖTNER was the architect of the Apollo Fountain (1532). The Gänsemännchen Brunnen ('Goose-Boy Fountain', *c.*1555), which depicts a Franconian peasant carrying two geese with water flowing from their beaks, may be the work of Pankraz Labenwolff (1492–1563).

N. Miller, *French Renaissance Fountains* (1977); Elisabeth MacDougall (ed.), *'Fons Sapientiae': Renaissance Garden Fountains* (1978).

**FOUQUET or Foucquet, JEAN** (*c.*1415/20–*c.*1481), French painter and manuscript illuminator. He was a native of Tours who visited Italy in the 1440s, and is known to have lived in Rome from 1443 to 1447. On returning to France he entered the royal court as a painter of portraits and portrait miniatures; the style of his pictures is structurally French, in that his designs are distinctly sculptural, but Fouquet's experience of Italian art is nonetheless reflected in his art. In 1475 he was belatedly appointed *peintre du roi*.

Fouquet's only authenticated works are illustrations in the manuscript of Josephus known as *Antiquités Judaïques* (1470–6, Bibliothèque Nationale) and a signed self-portrait medallion (Louvre). His best-known surviving work is the Book of Hours (*c.*1450–60) made for Étienne Chevalier, the royal treasurer; the book is now incomplete and dismembered, but

40 of the surviving 47 leaves are in the Musée Condé in Chantilly.

DBF; MDA; Sandro Lombardi, *Jean Fouquet* (1983); Claude Schaefer, *Jean Fouquet: An der Schwelle zur Renaissance* (1994).

## FOURQUEVAUX, RAIMOND DE BECCARIE DE PAVIE

(1508–74), French soldier and author, born into a noble family in Toulouse. He fought in the WARS OF ITALY under King FRANCIS I and subsequently fought on the Catholic side in the French WARS OF RELIGION; he also served as governor of Narbonne and as a diplomat in Spain and Scotland. Fourquevaux is the presumed author of *Instructions sur le fait de la guerre* (1548), a treatise on WARFARE based on MACHIAVELLI and VEGETIUS.

DBF.

## FOX or Foxe, LUKE

(1586–1636). Born in Hull, Fox went to sea at an early age. He was turned down for a voyage to Greenland in 1606, but in 1629 received money from the king for an expedition to seek the NORTH-WEST PASSAGE. In 1631 he reached Frobisher Bay, Hudson Strait, and Coates Island. Foxe Channel and Foxe Basin are named after him.

## FOXE, JOHN

(1516–87), English martyrologist. Educated at Oxford, Foxe was a fellow of Magdalen College from 1539, but resigned the position in 1545. On the accession of MARY he left England for the Continent living successively in Strasburg, Frankfurt, and Basel. Here he worked on his *Acts and Monuments of Matters Happening in the Church*, published initially in Latin at Strassburg in 1554, and later in English editions in England in 1563, 1570, 1576, and 1583. The book justifies the Reformation, extols the Protestant martyrs of Mary's reign, and presents England as God's chosen nation. The work was given approval by the bishops, and achieved wide popularity. Under ELIZABETH, Foxe returned to England and was made canon of Salisbury.

DNB.

## FOXE, RICHARD

(c.1448–1528), English humanist. Educated at Oxford, and possibly Cambridge and Paris, Foxe met the future HENRY VII whilst in Paris and, on his gaining the throne, was made bishop of Exeter, secretary to the king, and lord privy seal (1487). Employed greatly on diplomatic missions, he became successively bishop of Bath and Wells (1492), Durham (1494), and Winchester (1501). A close adviser to Henry VII, he lost his place to WOLSEY on the succession of HENRY VIII. His support for the new humanist learning was expressed as master of Pembroke College, Cambridge (1507–19), and in founding Corpus Christi College, Oxford (1515–16).

DNB.

## FRACASTORO, GIROLAMO, or (Latin) Hieronymus Fracastorus

(1478–1553), Italian poet and physician who studied medicine in Padua, and then returned to his native Verona to practise as a physician. In 1530 he published a neo-Latin poem (dedicated to Pietro BEMBO) entitled *Syphilis, sive Morbus Gallicus*. The protagonist of the poem, a shepherd called Syphilis, contracts the 'unknown pestilence' which now bears his name; in the course of the poem Fracastoro describes the symptoms of SYPHILIS and the use of guaiac, bleeding, and mercury as remedies.

Fracastoro's other works include a treatise on epidemiology (*De contagione et contagiosis morbus curatione*, 1546) in which he draws on Epicurus and Lucretius to formulate a theory in which contagion is attributed to *seminaria* ('seeds'), which could infect at a distance, and fomites, which were hosts (such as clothing) that could sustain and transmit 'disease seeds'. This notion differs from the germ theory developed in the late nineteenth century by Louis Pasteur in that Pasteur's germs were independent micro-organisms, whereas Fracastoro's *seminaria* were analogous to spores or leaven.

Fracastoro also published works on cosmology and philosophy. His letters to Giovanni Battista RAMUSIO were published in 1564.

DBI; DSB; *Fracastoro's Syphilis*, ed. and trans. G. Eatough (1984); Enrico Peruzzi, *La nave di Ermete: La cosmologia di Girolamo Fracastoro* (1995).

## FRANCAVILLA, PIETRO, or Pierre de Francheville or Francqueville

(1548–1615), Flemish sculptor, born in Cambrai. He trained in Paris and in 1566 travelled to Innsbruck, where he worked on the tomb of the Emperor MAXIMILIAN. In 1571 or 1572 he moved to Italy, where he spent 30 years as an assistant to GIAMBOLOGNA. His principal independent works are statues of *Janus* and *Jupiter* (1585) for the Grimaldi Palace in Genoa, six statues for the Cathedral of San Lorenzo in Genoa, and five statues in the Niccolini Chapel in the Church of Santa Croce in Florence. He was recalled to France in 1604 by MARIE DE MÉDICIS, who commissioned him to erect Giambologna's EQUESTRIAN STATUE of HENRI IV on the Pont Neuf in Paris; Francavilla modelled the figures of four slaves for the pedestal of the statue. The monument was destroyed during the French Revolution, but bronze casts of Francavilla's four slaves, cast after his death by a pupil, are now in the Louvre.

DBF s.v. Francheville; DBI s.v. Francqueville; MDA.

## FRANCE.

The possessions of the French monarchy in the fifteenth century constituted only a portion of the land occupied by the modern state of France. Most of what is now France consisted of independent counties (i.e. areas ruled by counts) and duchies. Until 1430, most land north of the Loire was controlled by BURGUNDY or England, and south of the Loire the French crown controlled less than half the territory of what is now France. The reconquest of Normandy and Gascony in the 1440s doubled the size of the royal domain, and thereafter the crown added the lands of the dukes of Burgundy (1477, including Artois and Picardy as well as Burgundy), Anjou (1481, including Maine and Provence as well as Anjou), Brittany (1491), and Bourbon (1527, including Auvergne, Forez, and La Marche as well as Bourbon). King LOUIS XII added Blois and Orléanais (1498) and King FRANCIS I added Angoulême and Valois (1515). Most of the remaining fiefdoms (Albret, Armagnac, Béarn, Foix, Limoges, Périgord, Rodez, and Vendôme) reverted to the crown in 1589, when Henry of Navarre ascended the throne as King HENRI IV.

By the end of the sixteenth century the only remaining independent fiefdoms were the contiguous territories of Astarac, Bigorre, and Comminges (in the south-west), the papal enclave of AVIGNON (in the south-east), the Habsburg enclave of Charolais, the dukedom of Nevers, and the Rhineland principalities of Bar and Rethel (all in the east).

For much of the fifteenth and sixteenth centuries France was at war, initially with England in the HUNDRED YEARS WAR (which ended in 1453) and then with Italy and the Habsburgs in the WARS OF ITALY (1494–1559); in the second half of the sixteenth century France was ravaged by a series of civil wars, the WARS OF RELIGION (1562–98). The preoccupation with war meant that France did not compete on a scale appropriate to its size and importance with other European countries in EXPLORATION or in the establishment of overseas colonies, though CARTIER and CHAMPLAIN began French settlement in Canada, and RIBAUT and VILLEGAIGNON established short-lived colonies in Florida and Brazil.

See the separate articles on FRENCH ARCHITECTURE; FRENCH ART; FRENCH GARDENS; FRENCH LANGUAGE AND ORTHOGRAPHY; FRENCH LAW; FRENCH MUSIC.

R. J. Knecht, *The Rise and Fall of Renaissance France, 1483–1610* (2001).

**FRANCESCO DI GIORGIO MARTINI** (1439–1501), Italian painter, sculptor, military engineer, and architect, born in Siena, the son of a poultry dealer, and trained in the Sienese studio of VECCHIETTA. As a young man he worked primarily as a painter; his surviving works include a *Coronation of the Virgin* (1472–4) and a *Nativity* (1475; his only signed work), both in the Pinacoteca in Siena. By 1477 he had moved to Urbino, where he worked for FEDERICO DA MONTEFELTRO as a fortress designer and military engineer; he constructed more than 70 fortresses and designed many military machines and weapons, including the first landmine. He may have contributed to the design of Luciano LAURANA's Ducal Palace at Urbino. He wrote an architectural treatise, *Trattato di architettura civile e militari*, which was largely devoted to ecclesiastical architecture but also included a section on TOWN PLANNING; a manuscript copy of the treatise was owned by LEONARDO DA VINCI, on whom it exercised a considerable influence. From 1491 to 1497 Francesco lived at the courts of ALFONSO II and FERRANTE II in Naples, where he made drawings of ancient remains while working as a military engineer; he then returned to Siena for the final years of his life.

Francesco's only documented work as an architect is the Church of Santa Maria del Calcinaio, near Cortona, for which he provided a model (1485); the church, which is designed as a Latin cross, was completed in 1516. He also seems to have provided the design for the austere Palazzo della Signoria in Jesi (1486–90); later additions include a courtyard by Andrea SANSOVINO. Attributions include the churches of Santa Maria degli Angeli in Siena and San Bernardino in Urbino and the Palazzo Ducale in Gubbio.

*DBI; MDA; Luciano Bellosi (ed.), Francesco di Giorgio e il Rinascimento a Siena, 1450–1500 (1993); F. P. Fiore and M. Taturi (eds.), Francesco di Giorgio architetto (1994).*

**FRANCESCO DI PAOLO or (French) François de Paule or (English) Francis of Paula** (1416–1507), founder of the ORDER of MINIMS. He entered the Franciscan Order as a boy in compliance with a vow made to his parents. In 1431 he began to live as a hermit, initially in a cave on the Tyrrhenian Sea near Paolo and subsequently in a nearby forest. In about 1435, the traditional date at which the Minims were founded, he was joined by disciples who lived nearby as hermits. The group began to live in community in about 1452. By 1474 the Order had secured papal recognition and established houses throughout southern Italy and Sicily.

In 1482 Francesco travelled to Paris at the behest of the dying King LOUIS XI, and after the king's death remained in France as the spiritual adviser of King CHARLES VIII, who constructed two monasteries for Francesco's Order. Francesco remained in France for the rest of his life, and died at the house of his Order in Plessis-lès-Tours. He was canonized in 1519 and declared the patron saint of Italian seafarers by Pope Pius XII in 1943.

*DBI.*

**FRANCESCO DURANTINO** (*fl.* 1543–54), Italian potter who specialized in ISTORIATO ware. He worked from 1543 to 1547 in the studio of Guido di Merlino in Urbino, and then moved to Monte Bagnolo (near Perugia), where he worked until 1554 or possibly later. His best-known surviving piece is a MAIOLICA wine cistern (1553) made in Monte Bagnolo and now in the Art Institute in Chicago.

**FRANCIA or Francesco Raibolini** (*c.*1450–1517), Italian goldsmith, medallist, and painter, a native of Bologna. He worked as a goldsmith until the mid-1480s; his two surviving pieces are niello paxes dated 1480 (a *Crucifixion*) and 1481 (a *Resurrection*), both now in the Pinacoteca Communale in Bologna. He turned to painting and formed a partnership with Lorenzo COSTA that lasted until 1506, when Costa departed for Mantua; their principal surviving collaborative work is the cycle of the frescoes in the Oratory of Santa Cecilia in the Church of San Giacomo Maggiore. The influence of RAPHAEL is apparent in many of Francia's paintings, such as his *Madonna Enthroned with Saints* (Pinacoteca, Bologna).

*DBI s.v. Raibolini, Francesco; MDA.*

**FRANCIABIGIO or Francesco di Cristofano or Francesco Giudici** (1484–1525), Italian painter, a native of Florence, where he trained in the studio of PIERO DI COSIMO. He collaborated with ANDREA DEL SARTO on the decoration of the cloisters of the Church of the SS Annunziata and of the Chiostro dello Scalzo (to which he contributed *The Last Supper*). He also painted a *Triumph of Cicero* in the Salone of the MEDICI VILLA at Poggio a Caiano. The influence of both RAPHAEL and Andrea del Sarto is apparent in paintings such as *The Holy Family* (Kunsthistorisches Museum, Vienna) and *The Madonna del Pozzo* (Accademia, Florence).

*DBI s.v. Giudici, Francesco; MDA; Susan McKillop, Franciabigio (1974).*

**FRANCINI, THOMAS** (1571–1651), a Florentine hydraulic engineer who moved to France c.1599 at the invitation of HENRI IV. Together with his brothers Alexandre (*fl.* 1608, d. 1648) and Camille (*fl.* 1608–20) he designed and installed the waterworks at SAINT-GERMAIN-EN-LAYE, and subsequently designed waterworks for FONTAINEBLEAU, Versailles, the Luxembourg Gardens in Paris (where he designed the aqueduct) and Cardinal Richelieu's garden at Rueil.

Thomas's son François de Francine (1617–88) was the architect of the fountains of Versailles; Pierre de Francine (1621–86) assisted his brother François at Versailles and maintained the waterworks at Fontainebleau.

*DBF* s.v. Francini ou Francine (Les); *DBI* s.v. Francini, Tommaso.

**FRANCIS I or François I** (1494–1547), king of France, born at Cognac on 12 September 1494, the son of Charles of Valois (count of Angoulême) and LOUISE OF SAVOY and the younger brother of MARGUERITE D'ANGOULÊME. On the accession of LOUIS XII to the throne of France in 1498, Francis became heir presumptive. He was educated together with his sister at the royal chateau at AMBOISE, where they were taught Italian and Spanish by their mother and other subjects by a series of distinguished tutors. In 1508 Francis moved to the royal court, and in 1512 he assumed his first military commands, fighting in Guienne (1512) and Picardy (1513). On 18 May 1514 he married Claude de France, the daughter of Louis XII. She died ten years later, having given birth to seven children; at the time of her death in 1524, their surviving children were Henri (later King HENRI II), Madeleine (later queen of Scotland), Charles d'Angoulême, and Margaret (later duchess of Savoy).

When Louis died on 1 January 1515, Francis ascended the throne and ruled France under the watchful eye of his mother, who participated fully in his government. In 1519 he became a candidate for the imperial crown, and was defeated by Charles I of Spain, whose victory united Spain and the Holy Roman Empire under a common HABSBURG ruler. The enmity of Francis and the Emperor CHARLES V was to dominate European politics for generations, and the bloody consequences of their rivalry lasted until the battle of SAINT-QUENTIN in 1567. In 1520 Francis attempted to secure the support of King HENRY VIII of England, and the two young kings met at the FIELD OF THE CLOTH OF GOLD.

From the perspective of King Francis, his Italian territories of Genoa and Milan assumed an importance far beyond his ancestral claims, because they constituted the last barrier to complete Habsburg encirclement on his land frontiers from Provence to Artois. Francis declared war on 22 April 1521, and seven months later Charles V captured Milan (19 November 1521); he subsequently defeated the French at the battle of BICOCCA (24 June 1522). By 1523 the French had been expelled from Genoa and Milan. In 1524 Francis led his army to Italy, and retook Milan (26 October 1524). He was, however, defeated at the battle of PAVIA (24 February 1525), where he was captured and dispatched to Spain as a prisoner. Francis eventually secured his release by signing the Treaty of Madrid (January 1526), which made important territorial concessions and surrendered his sons Charles and Henri as hostages; the boys were to remain in Spain until the signing of the Peace of CAMBRAI in 1529, because as soon as their father was released (April 1526) he repudiated the Treaty of Madrid on the grounds that he had signed under duress. He did, however, honour the terms of the Peace of Cambrai by marrying Eleanor, sister of Charles V. This alliance did not preclude a lifelong struggle with the Habsburgs in the WARS OF ITALY.

In domestic policy the principal issue with which Francis had to contend was the Reformation. In his foreign policy he was willing to form alliances across confessional lines (in 1536, for example, he formed an alliance with the Ottoman Sultan Süleyman and the Protestant princes of Germany), and within France he oscillated between the toleration advocated by some of his advisers (including his mistress the duchesse d'Étampes) and the uncompromising Catholicism of others (including MONTMORENCY). The Affaire des PLACARDS (18 October 1534) angered him deeply, and in the course of the following year hundreds of HUGUENOTS were arrested and some were burnt at the stake. In 1545 he condoned a massacre of the WALDENSES.

Francis's domestic governance was innovative, and some of the institutions that he established were to last for centuries. He ruled through a Conseil du Roi which allocated specific days to the different branches of government; matters of policy were decided by a small group known as the Conseil des Affaires. He appointed Antoine DUPRAT as his chancellor, and supported his reforms. In the field of law, he used a court known as the Grand Conseil as an instrument of centralization, and accelerated the process whereby French CUSTOMARY LAW was codified. His rule was increasingly absolutist, in that he never convened the Estates-General and carefully circumscribed the powers of the *parlements*.

In the course of his reign Francis extended his domains to include the lands of the dukes of BOURBON (from 1523), Alençon (1525), Albret (1527), Burgundy (1529), and Brittany (1532). In the Concordat of BOLOGNA (1516) he ratified the power of the French crown to fill some 600 of France's principal benefices; this right later formed the legal basis of the French refusal to implement the decrees of the COUNCIL OF TRENT.

Francis was a munificent patron of learning and the arts. He founded the antecedent institution of the Collège de France, instituted the *lecteurs royaux* and (in the face of opposition from University of Paris) licensed them to lecture on ancient languages, supported humanists (notably Guillaume BUDÉ) and poets (notably the Protestant Clément MAROT), and employed Italian artists such as CELLINI, LEONARDO, PRIMATICCIO, and ROSSO FIORENTINO. The buildings that he commissioned or rebuilt include BLOIS, CHAMBORD, FONTAINEBLEAU, and SAINT-GERMAIN-EN-LAYE.

*DBF*; *Grove* s.v. François I; *MDA* s.v. Valois (14); R. J. Knecht, *Renaissance Warrior and Patron: The Reign of Francis I* (1994).

**FRANCIS II or (French) François II** (1544–60), king of France, the eldest son of King HENRI II and CATHERINE DE MÉDICIS. In 1558, at the age of 14, he married the 16-year-old MARY, QUEEN OF SCOTS. The following year King Henri died in a jousting accident and Francis acceded to the throne. His short rule was dominated by the GUISES, who wished to extirpate Protestantism. The prince of CONDÉ was implicated in the Conjuration d'AMBOISE, a plot to capture the youthful king at Château d'AMBOISE and destroy the power of the Guises. The conspiracy failed, and on 5 December King Francis died of an abscess in the ear.

*DBF.*

**FRANCIS, DUKE OF ALENÇON.** See ANJOU, FRANÇOIS, DUC D'.

**FRANCK or Franck von Wörd or Frank or (Latin) Francus, SEBASTIAN** (1499–1542), German humanist, historian, heretical reformer, and collector of proverbs, born in Donauwörth and educated (from 26 March 1515) at the University of Ingolstadt and subsequently at the Dominican College in Heidelberg. He was ordained as a priest and in 1524 became a curate near Augsburg, but the following year he went to Nuremberg, where he became a Lutheran; he then became a Lutheran priest in Gustenfelden. In 1527 Franck translated (from Latin to German) a treatise directed against SACRAMENTARIANS and Anabaptists; the following year the treatise was published, but in the same year (on 17 March 1528) Franck married Ottilie Beham, whose brothers (pupils of DÜRER) had Anabaptist sympathies.

Franck's spiritualist theology gradually became more radical than that of the Lutherans, and he began to advocate a measure of religious tolerance that was not countenanced by any church. In the autumn of 1529 he moved to Strassburg, which tolerated a comparatively wide range of religious opinion, and became a close friend of Kaspar SCHWENCKFELD; he was expelled in 1533 and, after a period working as a soap-boiler in Esslingen, moved to Ulm, from which he was expelled in January 1539. He spent the last three years of his life working as a printer in Basel.

In 1530 Franck published a translation (from Latin) of a chronicle of Turkey, to which he added an appendix contrasting the religious tolerance of Islam with the strictures of Lutheranism, Zwinglianism, and Anabaptism. In 1531 he published his *Chronica, Zeitbuch und Geschichtsbibel*, a reworking of the 'Nuremberg Chronicle' that evinced an unacceptable measure of sympathy for heretics and heterodox thought, and in 1538 he published a second historical work, the *Germaniae Chronikon*. His *Weltbuch* of 1534 is a geographical treatise intended as an appendix to his *Chronica*. Franck's radical and tolerationist religious views are set out in *Paradoxa* (1534), *Die Guldin Arch* (1539), and *Das verbütschiert Buch* (1539); his pacifist sympathies are articulated in *Kriegbüchlein des Friedens* (1539). The finest product of his philological interests is a collection of German proverbs (*Die deutschen Sprichwörter*, 1541) assembled with a view to documenting the richness of German proverbial speech.

*NDB*; Patrick Hayden-Roy, *The Inner Word and Outer World: A Biography of Sebastian Franck* (1994).

**FRANCK, MELCHIOR** (c.1579–1639), German composer who, in 1600, was in the choir at Augsburg. He met HASSLER at Nuremberg the following year and by 1603 was *Kapellmeister* to Duke Johann Casimir of Saxe-Coburg. He composed secular music (motets, polyphonic songs, *quodlibets*, and instrumental dance music) and sacred music (a Magnificat, a mass, sacred concertos, and chorale settings).

**FRANCKE, MASTER** (*fl.* 1424–36), German painter in Hamburg and the principal exponent of the style known as north German INTERNATIONAL GOTHIC. His best-known work is an ALTARPIECE commissioned by the Englandfahrer (a guild of Hamburg merchants engaged in trade with England) which depicts scenes from the Passion of Jesus and the life of St Thomas of Canterbury (now in the Kunsthalle in Hamburg).

*MDA; NDB* s.v. Meister Francke.

**FRANCKEN, AMBROSIUS I** (1544–1618), **HIERONYMUS I** (1540–1610), and **FRANS I** (1542–1616), Flemish painters, members of a Flemish dynasty of painters that extended over at least five generations. The three brothers, whose work is amply represented in the Musée d'Art Ancien in Brussels, all favoured religious and historical subjects. Attributions are often problematical, not least because their relatives copied their pictures, but those of Ambrosius are marked by the influence of RAPHAEL, those of Hieronymus I by the influence of MICHELANGELO, and those of Frans I (at least in his later period) by a movement away from large canvases in favour of small paintings on copper.

*MDA.*

**FRANCO, BATTISTA** (c.1510–1561), Italian painter, probably a native of Venice. By 1530 he was living in Rome, where he was one of the first painters to copy the frescoes in the SISTINE CHAPEL; his copies of MICHELANGELO and his drawings of antique sculptures were all executed in ink.

In 1536 Franco received his first commission for decorative painting when he was asked to paint the decorations on Ponte Sant'Angelo for the triumphal entry of CHARLES V into Rome on 5 April 1536. His later paintings include a *Baptism* (c.1555) in the Church of San Francesco della Vigna in Venice.

In about 1545 Franco received a commission from Duke Guidobaldo II della Rovere to make ISTORIATO designs for MAIOLICA table services. Many of the designs that Franco produced for Duke Guidobaldo over the course of the next six years have survived, as have some of the plates made from these designs in the FONTANA and Patanazzi workshops in Urbino (not, as VASARI mistakenly thought, in CASTEL DURANTE). The two most important table services, a *History of Troy* and a *Labours of Hercules*, do not survive in complete sets, but many individual plates survive in museums.

*DBI; MDA.*

**FRANCO, NICCOLÒ** (1515–70), Italian poet. He was born into an impoverished Venetian family, but rose to become the Venetian secretary of Pietro ARETINO. They parted acrimoniously, and Franco subsequently attacked Aretino in his poems. His *Priapea*, which enjoyed a wide clandestine circulation, led to his excommunication. In 1558 Franco was imprisoned in Rome by Pope PAUL IV; by the time he was released in 1560 Pope Paul was dead, but Franco nonetheless denounced him. Franco was tried by the Roman Inquisition and hanged. Franco's most famous works are his satirical collection of dialogues, *Dialoghi piacevoli*, and his collection of *Lettere*.

DBI; OCIL; P. F. Grendler, *Critics of the Italian World, 1530–1560: Anton Francesco Doni, Niccolò Franco, and Ortensio Lando* (1969).

**FRANCO, VERONICA** (1546–91), Italian poet and courtesan, a native of Venice, where she left her husband, a Venetian physician, and became the republic's most prominent courtesan. In 1575 she collected her love poems as *Terze rime*, and in 1580 she retired in order to found a home for impoverished courtesans.

DBI; M. Rosenthal, *The Honest Courtesan: Veronica Frano* (1989).

**FRANÇOIS, DUC D'ALENÇON.** See ANJOU, FRANÇOIS, DUC D'.

**FRANÇOIS DE SALES or (English) Francis of Sales** (1567–1622), Savoyard devotional writer, born in the chateau of Sales (Savoy) and educated in Annecy, Paris (1578–88), and Padua (1588–92). In 1593 he was ordained as a priest, after which he worked as a missionary in Chablais (then in the Swiss canton of Bern, now in France), converting Calvinists to Catholicism. He became bishop of Geneva in 1602, but as Catholicism was not permitted in Geneva, Bishop François administered his diocese from Annecy (then in Savoy, now in France). His principal devotional works were the *Introduction à la vie dévote* (1609) and the *Traité de l'amour de Dieu* (1616).

François de Sales was beatified in 1661 and canonized in 1665; in 1877 he was declared a doctor of the Church and in 1923 he was declared to be the patron saint of Catholic writers and journalists. Several religious orders are named after him, notably the Order of Salesians founded in Turin in 1859; the Order now has some 17,000 members.

**FRANKFURT**, the name of two German cities. Frankfurt am Main (English exonym Frankfort-on-Main), on the right bank of the river Main near the confluence with the Rhine, was from 1372 to 1866 one of Germany's most important imperial cities. The biannual Frankfurt Fair, which was first mentioned in 1150 (by which time it had been long established), made the city an important commercial centre for centuries, and European publishers still converge there annually; the Stock Exchange (Börse), now the largest in Germany, was founded in 1585. The Golden Bull of 1356 declared Frankfurt to be the seat of the imperial elections (German *Wahlstadt*) and in 1495 the Diet of Worms chose Frankfurt as the seat of the REICHSKAMMERGERICHT. This imperial chamber met in Frankfurt until 1527, when it was removed to Speyer. At the Reformation Frankfurt declared for the Protestant party (1533), so incurring the obloquy of the Emperor CHARLES V. The city belatedly joined the SCHMALKALDIC LEAGUE in 1536, but when the League began to lose ground in the SCHMALKALDIC WAR opened its gates to an imperial army on 29 December 1546. The city was garrisoned

by almost 10,000 imperial soldiers until the following October; these soldiers brought PLAGUE to the city, which greatly decreased the population. In 1552 the city was besieged for three weeks by MAURICE OF SAXONY, but a peace was concluded before the city fell. From 1612 to 1616 the city was consumed by a popular revolt called (after the rebel leader Vincenz Fettmilch) the Fettmilch Insurrection.

Germany's other Frankfurt is in Brandenburg: Frankfurt an der Oder (English exonym Frankfort-on-Oder), on the left bank of the Oder (on what is now the Polish border). Frankfurt was a member of the HANSE league from 1368 until c.1450. In 1506 JOACHIM I, elector of Brandenburg, founded the University of Frankfurt, which, except for a brief period in Cottbus from 1516 to 1539 and a dispersal during the THIRTY YEARS WAR, remained in Frankfurt an der Oder until 1811, when it was relocated in Breslau (now Polish Wrocław). In the fifteenth century Frankfurt withstood four sieges, two by the HUSSITES (1429 and 1432), one by the Poles (1450), and one by the duke of Sagan (1477), but in the Thirty Years War it was repeatedly occupied.

F. Bothe, *Geschichte der Stadt Frankfurt am Main* (1966).

**FRANKFURT, MASTER OF** (*fl.* 1500), Flemish artist whose name derives (inappropriately, as he was Flemish rather than German) from the *St Anna* altarpiece (now in the Staedel Institute in Frankfurt) painted for the Dominican monastery in Frankfurt. Some 40 pictures are attributed to this painter, whose style implies some form of association with Quentin MASSYS.

MDA; Stephen Goddard, *The Master of Frankfurt and his Shop* (1984).

**FRANKFURT RECESS.** The Protestant princes of Germany were eager to present a common front against the Catholic foe, and attempted to reconcile the two principal factions of the Lutheran Church in a document dated 18 March 1558 and known as the Frankfurt Recess because it was issued at Frankfurt am Main. The party led by MELANCHTHON approved the document, but the GNESIO-LUTHERAN faction led by Nikolaus VON AMSDORF and FLACIUS ILLYRICUS refused to accede to the agreement.

**FREDERICK I** (1471–1533), king of Denmark and Norway, was the second son of King CHRISTIAN I, who had been succeeded by his sons JOHN and CHRISTIAN II. In 1522 Frederick led a revolt against Christian II, who fled to the Netherlands, and assumed the throne himself; when Christian attempted to mount an invasion of Norway in 1531, Frederick captured and imprisoned him. In the course of Frederick's reign the Reformation was introduced into Denmark by Hans TAUSEN.

DBL s.v. Frederik I; NDB s.v. Friedrich I.

**FREDERICK II** (1534–88), king of Denmark and Norway, was the son of King CHRISTIAN III and Dorothea of Saxe-Lauenburg (elder sister of Catherine of Saxe-Lauenburg, the mother of ERIC XIV of Sweden). Frederick acceded to the throne in 1559, and thereafter his reign was dominated by his enmity for his cousin King Eric. From 1562 to 1570 they were at war in the conflict known in English as the 'Seven Years War in the North'. Thereafter Frederick's reign was peaceful, but from 1571 he strove to secure Danish dominance of the North Sea and the Baltic, attacking pirates and insisting that all foreign ships in those seas strike their topsails to Danish men-of-war in acknowledgement of Denmark's claim to the sovereignty of the seas; these claims, which were contested by England in the North Sea and Sweden in the Baltic, later became part of the debate known as MARE CLAUSUM, MARE LIBERUM.

DBL s.v. Frederik II; NDB s.v. Friedrich II.

**FREGOSO FAMILY**, a Genoese merchant family that supplied GENOA with thirteen doges and several admirals, churchmen, and writers. In 1370 Domenico Fregoso deposed Gabriele Adorno and so inaugurated a feud between the Fregoso and Adorno families that was to dominate Genoese politics for two centuries. In the sixteenth century the Fregoso lost their power under the stern rule of Andrea DORIA, and from 1528 to 1576 the family name disappeared when it was subsumed into the Albergo de Fornari and the Albergo de Ferrari.

DBI.

**FRÉMINET, MARTIN** (1567–1619), French painter and etcher. He was born in Paris and in 1592 travelled to Italy, where he lived principally in Rome, and later in Venice and in Turin. He returned to France in 1602 and entered the service of King HENRI IV, for whom he decorated the ceiling of the Chapelle de la Sainte-Trinité at FONTAINEBLEAU. Fréminet is one of the painters associated with the second School of FONTAINEBLEAU.

DBF; MDA; Sylvie Béguin, L'École de Fontainebleau (1960).

**FRENCH ARCHITECTURE.** The Gothic style that was to dominate European architecture in the late Middle Ages originated in France, where it is known as the *style ogivale*. Individual features of Gothic architecture had long been apparent in late Romanesque architecture (and, in the case of pointed arches, Islamic architecture), but Gothic first emerged as an integrated style in the Île de France in the mid-twelfth century: the first building to be conceived in what later became known as the Gothic style was the choir and chevet (i.e. apse and ambulatory) of the Abbey of Saint-Denis (1140–4). In the second half of the twelfth century construction began on the Gothic cathedrals of Sens, Noyon, Laon, Soissons, Paris, Bourges, and Chartres, and in the early thirteenth century the cathedrals built or rebuilt in the Gothic style included Reims, Amiens, and the abbey Church of Saint-Denis. The style of these buildings is characterized by soaring vertical lines and the use of pointed arches, rib vaults, flying buttresses, traceried stained-glass windows, high clerestory windows, and pinnacles.

The Gothic style of French churches and cathedrals changed very little from the early thirteenth to the late fourteenth centuries, when Flamboyant tracery (which derived from English cathedrals) began to appear in France. Flamboyant Gothic survived into the sixteenth century in structures such as the west porch of the Church of Saint-Maclou in Rouen (c.1500–14) and the west front of Troyes Cathedral (from c.1507).

In secular architecture, the country house began to replace the castle in the fifteenth century, initially in the Gothic style (e.g. Plessis-lès-Tours, 1463–72) that was also favoured in towns for both large private houses (e.g. the Palais Jacques Cœur in Bourges, 1442–53) and civic buildings (e.g. the fifteenth-century Hôtel de Ville in Compiègne and the Palais de Justice in Rouen, 1499–1509). The style of the Italian Renaissance began to appear as decorative motifs in the closing years of the fifteenth century, but did not begin to affect structural design until the early sixteenth century, when some of France's finest palaces and CHATEAUS were built. The most important Renaissance palaces were the LOUVRE, the TUILERIES (destroyed 1871), and SAINT-GERMAIN-EN-LAYE, and the principal chateaus were AMBOISE, ANET, BLOIS, CHAMBORD, CHENONCEAUX, and FONTAINEBLEAU.

By the middle of the sixteenth century Italian motifs introduced into the structures and decorative schemes of chateaus such as Blois, Chambord, and Fontainebleau had been adapted to French tastes and conditions to the point at which distinctive French Renaissance buildings were being designed by French architects such as Philibert DELORME, Pierre LESCOT, Jean BULLANT, Jacques DUCERCEAU the Elder, and (later in the century) Salomon de BROSSE.

Anthony Blunt, *Art and Architecture in France, 1500–1700* (5th edn., 1999).

**FRENCH ART.** Late medieval and early modern France was neither politically united nor culturally homogeneous. In fifteenth-century Burgundy, which was not part of France, the artistic culture was more Flemish than French (especially after the ducal court moved from Dijon to Bruges in 1420); in AVIGNON, which was a papal possession from 1348, the artistic culture was more Sienese than French, and in the fifteenth century, when artists such as Enguerrand QUARTON and Nicholas FROMENT worked in Avignon, the dominant influence was Flemish.

In the fourteenth century, Paris was Europe's most important centre of book illumination, and artists such as Jean PUCELLE were among the first to deploy the iconography and techniques of perspective that derive from the early period of the Italian Renaissance. In the fifteenth century the court at Tours offered patronage to artists such as Jean FOUQUET, who lived for several years in Rome and introduced Italian elements into his paintings and illuminations. These isolated examples of Italian influence did not become an important force in French art until the end of the fifteenth century, when the onset of the WARS OF ITALY exposed French patrons to Italian art.

Italian decorative motifs began to appear in FRENCH ARCHITECTURE, and the interior decoration of French chateaus became the most important means by which Italian art entered France. The most influential chateau was FONTAINEBLEAU, to which King FRANCIS I brought Italian artists such as Il ROSSO FIORENTINO, PRIMATICCIO, and NICCOLÒ DELL'ABBATE.

King Francis also bought and commissioned paintings by artists such as RAPHAEL and TITIAN, and persuaded LEONARDO DA VINCI and ANDREA DEL SARTO to come to France.

Italian mannerist art was quickly adapted to French courtly tastes to produce a distinctive French style characterized by emotional restraint, a secular treatment of mythological themes, and a taste for elegant etiolated nudes. Flemish influence was most important in portraiture, as is apparent in the work of the CLOUET FAMILY. In sculpture, the presence of Benvenuto CELLINI in France from 1540 to 1545 was to have a lasting influence on sculptors such as Jean GOUJON; similarly, the work of Germain PILON was shaped by his period as an assistant to Primaticcio at Fontainebleau.

Anthony Blunt, *Art and Architecture in France, 1500–1700* (5th edn., 1999).

**FRENCH GARDENS** of the Renaissance were influenced but not overwhelmed by the design of ITALIAN GARDENS. In the early sixteenth century the Italian elements were usually incidental: at GAILLON, for example, marble fountains were imported from Italy, and at FONTAINEBLEAU bronze casts of ancient marbles were brought from Italy. The fundamental design of gardens of this period, however, was rooted in the tradition of the enclosed garden wholly independent of the house rather than in the Italian ideal of the interpenetration of house and garden in a unified design. The major difference between Italian and French design was that Italian gardens were usually terraced, but French gardens, with the important exception of the Italianate garden at SAINT-GERMAIN-EN-LAYE (and the mid-seventeenth-century garden at Vaux-le-Vicomte), tended to be flat. An important consequence of this distinction is that flowing water was a relatively minor feature in French gardens of the sixteenth century; until the gardens at Versailles were constructed, French FOUNTAINS produced mere trickles of water, whereas Italian fountains produced torrents.

The rediscovery of VITRUVIUS affected garden design in both Italy and France, in that it shifted the conceptual emphasis of the garden from the traditional horticultural stress on fruit, vegetables, and medicinal herbs to an architectural stress on form and harmony. In France the dominant architectural features of gardens were PAVILIONS, such as those at AMBOISE, BLOIS, and Gaillon, and galleries, such as the monumental wooden gallery at Montargis (the castle of RENÉE DE FRANCE), the stone gallery at Gaillon, the gallery beyond the moats at Chantilly, and the free-standing painted gallery at Fontainebleau.

The ideal of a design encompassing both house and garden was first achieved by Philibert DELORME, who established at ANET (1546–52) the prerogative of the architect to design the garden as well as the house. At about the same time SERLIO retrospectively imposed a unified design on ANCY-LE-FRANC by enclosing both house and garden within a huge rectangular terrace. The influence of the gardens of Roman cardinals, especially the Villa FARNESE, ensured the continued life of small gardens set apart from the main house: in the 1550s cardinal de Bourbon built such a private retreat at Gaillon,

constructing a canal, a *CASINO* (the Maison Blanche), and a hermitage carved out of a rock; at about the same time another independent garden was constructed at Vallery (near Sens, in Yonne), where a canal was flanked by twin pavilions linked by a gallery in the Italian style. Such canals were one of the distinctive features of French gardens of the sixteenth century; at Fleury-en-Bière, the first of these canals (c.730 metres (800 yards) long) still survives, and is thought to have inspired the Grand Canal at Fontainebleau; Philibert Delorme subsequently incorporated a canal into the garden at Anet. In the seventeenth century grand canals became an important element in Le Nôtre's gardens at Vaux-le-Vicomte, Chantilly, Maintenon, Sceaux, and Versailles.

Plantings in French gardens were arranged in PARTERRES, which were well established by the time Serlio printed designs for geometrical parterres in *L'architettura* (1537). A comparison of this volume to the 1572 edition of *L'Agriculture et maison rustique*, by Charles ESTIENNE and Jean Liébault, shows how parterres had developed in the intervening half-century: in 1537 parterres were individual creations sealed in separate compartments (*compartiments de broderie*), but by 1572 parterres had been integrated into an overall architectonic plan. Claude MOLLET, who traced this development to Anet, designed parterres for Fontainebleau, Saint-Germain-en-Laye and the TUILERIES; his designs are printed in the *Théâtre d'agriculture* (1600) of Olivier de SERRES. The parterre was further developed by Mollet's sons at the Luxembourg Palace in Paris; these early seventeenth-century parterre designs for royal gardens were collected by Jacques Boyceau in his *Traité du jardinage* (1638).

The first BOTANICAL GARDEN in France was the Jardin des Plantes at Montpellier, which was built by Richer de Belleval between 1593 and 1607. It is one of the few French examples of a garden with a terraced MOUNT (which still survives). Every plant in the garden was labelled, and 1,332 species and varieties are listed in Belleval's *Onomatologia* (1598). The garden was destroyed during Richelieu's siege of Montpellier in 1622, and subsequently rebuilt on a smaller scale; in the late seventeenth century one of the curators was the taxonomist Pierre Magnol, the eponym of the magnolia. PEIRESC was the other important collector of rare plants, which he cultivated in his gardens at Aix-en-Provence and Belgentier (Provence).

The grand gardens of France, like the BOBOLI GARDENS in Florence, were used as settings for large entertainments, and by the middle of the sixteenth century gardens had been extended or reshaped to incorporate capacious open areas in which such events could be staged. Such provision is most pronounced in the gardens commissioned or enlarged by CATHERINE DE MÉDICIS at CHENONCEAUX, Fontainebleau, Montceaux-en-Brie, and, most capaciously, at the Tuileries, where the open area was more than 550 metres (600 yards) wide.

Many French Renaissance gardens have disappeared, but the drawings of Jacques DUCERCEAU record the chateaus and gardens of France in the 1560s and 1570s; his drawings also include plans for chateaus and gardens that were never executed.

A. Marie, *Jardins français crées à la Renaissance* (1955); William Howard Adams, *The French Garden, 1500–1800* (1979); Mirka Benes, *Villas and Gardens in Early Modern Italy and France* (2001); Kenneth Woodbridge, *Princely Gardens: The Origins and Development of the French Formal Style* (1986).

**FRENCH LANGUAGE AND ORTHOGRAPHY.** French is the most important of the three languages of France (the others being OCCITAN and Breton) and the principal language of the southern part of the Spanish Netherlands (now Belgium) and of Geneva; in the early modern period it was the second language (after German) of Alsace and Lorraine and of the eastern cantons of the SWISS CONFEDERATION. Southern France spoke Occitan (which is also known as Provençal), and on the borders of the two languages intermediate dialects were spoken.

In the course of the sixteenth century French gradually displaced Latin as the language of official documents, and 1539 French became the legal language of France with the signing of the *Ordonnance de Villers-Cotterêts*. In the meantime the gradual Gallicization of southern France meant that French became the language of the literate minority of the south. In religion, the HUGUENOTS preferred French to Latin, and although the universities continued to teach through the medium of Latin, learned subjects such as science and logic were expounded in books written in French as well as in Latin. The French language became a subject for scholarly scrutiny, initially by foreign learners of French (e.g. John Palgrave's *L'Éclaircissement de la langue française*, London, 1530). The first grammar of French to be written by a French scholar was the *In linguam Gallicam isagoge* (1531) of Jacobus SYLVIUS (Jacques Dubois), and the first to be written in French by a French scholar was the *Traité de la grammaire française* (1550) of Louis MEIGRET.

Grammarians such as Meigret, Petrus RAMUS, and Jacques PELETIER DU MANS all participated in a debate about orthography. The point at issue was the need to adapt the Latin alphabet to French pronunciation. Scholars such as Meigret advocated a new spelling system, but the common view was that the alphabet could best be refined through the use of accents. Modern French uses four typographical accents: acute, grave, circumflex, and cedilla. Accents were first used by the Italian printers of Latin books and were adopted in France in the early sixteenth century, first in Lyon and then in Paris. Geofroi Tory's *Horae . . . ubi orthographia, puncta et accentus suis locis habentur*, which appeared in French translation as *Heures . . . en bonne orthographie de points, d'accents et diphtongues* (1525), inaugurated the use of accents in French, but thereafter there was no consistency in the use of accents. With respect to the letter *e*, for example, accents could be used to denote vowel length or the range of sounds represented by the letter (as in modern *été* and *père*) or even gender (Sylvius used a grave accent for feminine nouns).

The acute accent was first used systematically by Robert ESTIENNE in a book of 1530 (Mathurin Cordier's *De corrupti sermonis emendatione*), where the letter *e* in a final syllable was given an acute accent if it was to sound like modern *été*;

Étienne Dolet extended the use of the acute accent for *-ee* endings (like modern *soirée*), but it was not used in the beginning or interior of words until the eighteenth century, until which time the sound was represented by 'es': the ESTIENNE family gradually came to spell their name Étienne. The grave accent, which since the eighteenth century has been used to distinguish two sounds of the letter *e*, was used in early modern French (although not consistently) to distinguish homonyms (*a* and *à*, *ou* and *où*, *la* and *là*). The circumflex was introduced into French by Sylvius in his *In linguam Gallicam isagoge* to signal the lengthening of a vowel resulting from either the contraction of two vowels or the levelling of a diphthong; in 1549 Thomas SEBILLET used this accent to represent the suppression of an *s* before a consonant (e.g. Old French *honeste* became *honnête*). The cedilla is a zed written as a subscript: it originated in Spain and later spread to Italy and France as a way of representing the sound *ts*. It was first used in France for the printing of Spanish books, and was introduced into French in 1531 by Geofroi Tory in his *Le Sacre et couronnement de la reine* and popularized by its use in the French translation of AMADÍS DE GAULA (1540).

Edmond Huguet, *Dictionnaire de la langue française du seizième siècle* (7 vols., 1925–67); M. K. Pope, *From Latin to Modern French* (1934).

**FRENCH LAW.** The feudal monarchs of twelfth- and thirteenth-century France presided over a devolved system of seigneurial courts. The legal frameworks within which these courts operated varied greatly between northern and southern France. South of a line from Bordeaux to Lyon, which broadly corresponds to the line between the *langue d'oc* of the south and the *langue d'oïl* of the north, lay *le pays du droit écrit*, where the written law was Roman law in its JUSTINIAN codification, which was adapted as a customary system for the entire region, though at municipal and even village level, local statutes often modified Roman law; in the struggle between Roman law and CUSTOMARY LAW, the former prevailed throughout the south. In northern France, *le pays du droit coutumier*, it was customary law that prevailed; Roman law was studied in the universities (except at Paris, where it had been banned since 1219), but its considerable authority amongst jurists was not reflected in the courts, where it was subsidiary to customary law, which was a blend of Frankish capitularies, CANON LAW, and Germanic customary law.

The royal court, the *curia regis*, was both a consultative body for the king and a judicial body which functioned as a court of appeal. Eventually these two functions evolved into separate institutions: the consultative body became the *conseil du roi* and the judicial body became the *parlement*. The Parlement of Paris was formally constituted in 1296, and for more than a century exercised its jurisdiction throughout the royal domain, but eventually twelve provincial *parlements* were established at Toulouse (1420), Grenoble (1456), Bordeaux (1462), Dijon (1477), Rouen (1499), Aix-en-Provence (1501), Rennes (1553), Pau (1620), Metz (1633), Douai (1668), Besançon (1676), and Nancy (1775); they were all abolished in 1789. These provincial *parlements*, together with cognate regional courts in Arras, Bastia, Colmar, and Perpignan, had the power to revise laws and to decline to promulgate them altogether; it was the provincial *parlements* that refused to receive the decrees of the COUNCIL OF TRENT.

Local *parlements* represented regional rather than national interests, and in this respect the fact that customary law in northern France had never been consolidated abetted the process of fragmentation. It was hoped that the first step towards a harmonized system would be a compilation of the customary law in each area of local jurisdiction, and to that end Charles VII commanded in 1454 (in the *Ordonnance de Montil-lès-Tours*) that *coutumiers* be assembled for each *coutume*. The project proceeded slowly and unevenly, and despite the fact that in 1495 Charles VIII established a royal commission to oversee the project, substantial numbers of *coutumiers* did not start to appear until the sixteenth century. When the assembling of *pays coutumiers* drew near to completion, the community of learned jurists expressed so much dissatisfaction with the quality of the *coutumiers* that in the second half of the seventeenth century a programme for re-editing the entire collection was set in motion. By the time the project was aborted by the Revolution, there were still 60 provincial *grandes coutumes* and some 300 local *coutumes*. French customary law was not wholly disunified, however, because in 1510 the first compilation of the customary law of Paris had been published, and courts, both in metropolitan France and in overseas possessions, eventually came to regard the *Coutume de Paris* as the national customary law of France. In many areas of law, however, France had no national code prior to the *Code Napoléon*.

French customary law lived on in the Channel Islands. The customary law of Normandy had been compiled in 1205 as the *Grand Coutumier du pays et duché de Normandie*, and is still the basis of Channel Islands law. In 1583 Queen Elizabeth declared the official formulation to be Terrien's *Commentaires de droit civil* (1574) as interpreted in the *Approbation des loix, coutume et usages de l'Île de Guernesey différentes du Coutumier de Normandie d'ancienneté observés en la dite île*.

The distinguished tradition of humanist jurisprudence in France was centred in Bourges, where Andrea ALCIATO inaugurated the most important school of jurisprudence of the sixteenth century. The first of the great French jurists in this humanist tradition was Guillaume BUDÉ, who was followed by Jacques CUJAS, Hugues DONEAU, François LE DOUAREN, François BAUDOUIN, and François HOTMAN. The most learned students of customary law were Michel de L'HÔPITAL and Charles DUMOULIN.

F. Olivier-Martin, *Histoire générale du droit français* (1948, 1961); Henri de Bastard d'Estang, *Les Parlements de France* (1857); Donald R. Kelley, *Foundations of Modern Historical Scholarship: Language, Law and History in the French Renaissance* (1970); A. Gouron and O. Terrin, *Bibliographie des coutumes de France* (1975).

**FRENCH MUSIC.** In the thirteenth and fourteenth centuries France had the richest musical culture in Europe, but in the fifteenth century courtly patronage of music declined, and France produced no major composers. In the sixteenth

century choral music was written by a succession of HUGUENOT composers, including BOURGEOIS, GOUDIMEL, and Claude LE JEUNE.

**FRESCO** (Italian plural *freschi*, English plural frescos or frescoes), a method of wall painting in which powdered pigments dissolved in water are applied to a wet, freshly applied plaster ground. The colour is absorbed into the drying plaster, which acts as the binding medium. The process is described in detail in Cennino CENNINI's early fifteenth-century *Libro dell'arte*. Fresco, which was sometimes called *buon fresco* or *fresco buono*, was distinguished by the wetness of the plaster from paintings executed on dry walls, which were called SECCO or *fresco secco*. The plaster dried quickly, and details were sometimes added in *secco* after the plaster was dry, a practice decried by purists such as VASARI but used to great effect in frescoes such as Fra ANGELICO's series in the Convent of San Marco in Florence. In the 1430s the CARTOON was introduced, but until then the design was sketched on a rough underlying layer of plaster.

Frescoes were primarily an Italian form; the deleterious effect of dampness on plaster meant that frescoes never became an important medium in Venice or in northern Europe. Many Italian artists painted frescoes, including GIOTTO (Arena Chapel, Padua), MASACCIO (Brancacci Chapel, Florence), PIERO DELLA FRANCESCA (Church of San Francesco, Arezzo), RAPHAEL (the Vatican *Stanze*), and MICHELANGELO (the ceiling of the SISTINE CHAPEL in Rome).

**FRESCOBALDI, GIROLAMO** (1583–1643), Italian composer regarded as a child prodigy, particularly as a keyboard player. He was a pupil of LUZZASCHI and his formative years were influenced by the musical life around Duke Alfonso II d'Este in Ferrara. When Ferrara reverted to the papacy (following the duke's death in 1597) Frescobaldi, along with some other musicians, went to Rome where, in 1608, he became organist of the Cappella Giulia. In addition to his duties there, he taught the keyboard and was employed in various ecclesiastical and secular musical establishments. He was a composer of instrumental music, predominantly for the keyboard.

**FRIEDRICH II or Friedrich der Weise or Frederick the Wise** (1482–1556), elector palatine of the Rhine, shares the epithet 'the Wise' with FRIEDRICH III, elector of Saxony, with whom he is sometimes confused. He was born on 9 December 1482, the fourth son of the WITTELSBACH Elector Philip. As a young man he served as a soldier in the imperial armies of MAXIMILIAN I and CHARLES V, and in 1535 he married Princess Dorothea, the daughter of CHRISTIAN II, the deposed king of Denmark; Friedrich failed in his attempt to claim the throne of Denmark.

In March 1544 Friedrich's brother the Elector Ludwig V died, and Friedrich became elector palatine. The following year he joined the SCHMALKALDIC LEAGUE and in 1546 he became a Lutheran. He offered little assistance to the Protestant side in the SCHMALKALDIC WAR, and eventually submitted to the emperor and accepted the AUGSBURG INTERIM of May 1548. Friedrich died on 26 February 1556; he left no children, and so the electorate passed to his nephew Otto Heinrich.

*NDB.*

**FRIEDRICH III or (as king of the Romans) Friedrich IV or (as archduke of Austria) Friedrich V** (1415–93), Holy Roman Emperor, was born in Innsbruck on 21 September 1415, the son of Ernst of Habsburg, the duke of Styria and Carinthia. On his father's death in 1424 he ruled Styria and Carinthia jointly with his brother Albrecht until Albrecht died in 1463. In 1439 the two senior members of the HABSBURG FAMILY, Albrecht II (king of the Romans) and Friedrich of Tirol, both died, and Friedrich became head of the Habsburg family. The following year he also became the guardian of LADISLAS POSTHUMUS, the posthumous son of Albrecht II and heir to the Habsburg possessions of Austria, Bohemia, and Hungary. On 2 February 1440 Friedrich was elected as king of the Romans at Frankfurt am Main, and after a delay occasioned by his absence from Germany, he was crowned at Aachen on 17 June 1442.

In 1445 Friedrich negotiated a secret treaty with Pope EUGENIUS IV, which was eventually signed by his successor NICHOLAS V in 1448. By this treaty, which is known as the Concordat of Vienna, Friedrich pledged the obedience of the Empire to Rome in exchange for a large sum of money and the promise of the imperial crown. In 1452 he travelled to Rome, where on 16 March he married Eleanor, sister of AFONSO V of Portugal, and on 19 March was crowned Holy Roman Emperor by Pope Nicholas V.

When Friedrich had embarked on his journey to Rome he was abandoning rebellions in Austria and Hungary, and when he returned he found that the ELECTORS, angry about Friedrich's capitulation to Rome and his failure to respond to the Ottoman menace, had attempted to depose him, but had been unable to agree on a rival candidate for emperor. In 1457 Ladislas Posthumus died, so vacating the crowns of Bohemia and Hungary and the archdukedom of Austria. Friedrich failed to secure either crown, but occupied Lower Austria; he was soon driven out of Austria by his brother Albrecht, who ruled Upper Austria from Vienna. When Albrecht died in 1463, Friedrich was able to unite Upper and Lower Austria under his rule, but his territories were constantly subjected to the depredations of GEORGE OF PODĚBRADY (king of Bohemia) and MATTHIAS CORVINUS (king of Hungary). In 1485 Matthias finally drove Friedrich from Vienna, whereupon Friedrich handed over the governance of his lands to his son MAXIMILIAN, who was elected as king of the Romans in 1486. Friedrich then withdrew to Linz, where he studied ALCHEMY, ASTRONOMY, and BOTANY until his death on 19 August 1493. His tomb is in St Stephen's Cathedral in Vienna.

Older charges that Friedrich was an inept ruler and an ineffective soldier have yielded to the view that Friedrich was caught between the defence of his Habsburg patrimonial lands in the east and the interests of the electors, whose lands lay largely in the west. Yet he surprised them all by summoning a feudal host to raise the siege of Neuss in 1475, under attack from Duke Charles the Bold of Burgundy. His redeeming qualities were a love of science and scholarship and a conviction of the future greatness of the Austrian branch of the Habsburg dynasty. These two passions were symbolized in the letters AEIOU that he inscribed in his books and had engraved on his tableware: in Latin, *Austria est imperare orbi universo* ('It is Austria's destiny to rule the entire world'), and in German, *Alles Erdreich ist Oesterreich unterthan* ('All the earth is subject to Austria'). His biographer was Enea Silvio Piccolomini (later Pope PIUS II), who had mediated the negotiations for the Concordat of Vienna and later written *De rebus et gestis Friderici III*.

*NDB*; B. Haller, *Kaiser Friedrich III im Urteil der Zeitgenossen* (1965).

**FRIEDRICH III or Friedrich der Fromme or Frederick the Pious** (1515–76), WITTELSBACH elector palatine of the Rhine, was born in Simmern on 14 February 1515, the eldest son of Johann II, duke of Simmern. He was raised as a Catholic, but through his marriage in 1537 to Maria of Brandenburg-Kulmbach he gradually developed Protestant sympathies. In 1557 he became duke of Simmern on the death of his father, and two years later succeeded to the PALATINATE on the basis of being fifth in descent from Ruprecht III (elector 1398–1410).

Friedrich's religious sympathies lay with the Reformed (i.e. Calvinist) Church rather than with the Evangelical (i.e. Lutheran) Church, but he was eager to secure unity amongst Protestants. Efforts to achieve reconciliation failed, and in 1563 Friedrich authorized the formulation and imposition of the HEIDELBERG CATECHISM, which persecuted both Lutherans and Catholics. Thereafter Friedrich refused to recognize German Lutherans as his co-religionists and instead forged links with Calvinists abroad, supporting the HUGUENOTS in the WARS OF RELIGION and the Calvinists in the REVOLT OF THE NETHERLANDS.

The Lutheran princes of Germany were aggrieved by the presence of a Calvinist ruler in the Palatinate, but had no wish to exclude the Palatinate from the Religious Peace of AUGSBURG, which had divided Germany into Lutheran and Catholic sectors but excluded Calvinists. The matter was debated at the imperial Diet of 1566, but Friedrich stood firm in the face of warnings from the emperor. He died in Heidelberg on 26 October 1576 and was succeeded by his son Ludwig VI, who promptly carried the Palatinate into the Lutheran fold.

*NDB.*

**FRIEDRICH III or Friedrich der Weise or Frederick the Wise** (1463–1525), elector of Saxony, shares the epithet 'the Wise' with FRIEDRICH II, elector palatine of the Rhine, with whom he is sometimes confused. Friedrich was born in Torgau on 17 January 1463, the eldest son of Ernst, elector of Saxony. Friedrich succeeded his father as elector in 1486, and in 1500 became president of the newly instituted Council of Regency (Reichsregiment).

Friedrich had strong humanist sympathies: he was a friend of Georg SPALATIN and in 1502 founded the University of WITTENBERG. In 1493 he had undertaken a pilgrimage to Jerusalem, where he was invested as a knight of the Holy Sepulchre, and at the advent of the Reformation he remained loyal to the Catholic Church. This loyalty was tempered with strong sympathies for the reformers: Friedrich appointed LUTHER and MELANCHTHON to posts at his new university and later declined to implement the bull EXSURGE DOMINI, which ordered that Luther be restrained and his books burnt. In 1521, when Luther was placed under an imperial ban at the Diet of WORMS, Friedrich arranged for him to be spirited away to the safety of his castle at the Wartburg.

At the imperial election of 1519 Friedrich declined to stand as a candidate and instead supported the candidacy of CHARLES V. He died, unmarried, at Langau (near what is now Annaberg-Buchholz) on 5 May 1525, and the electorate passed to his brother Johann.

*NDB.*

**FRISCHLIN, (PHILIPP) NIKODEMUS** (1547–90), German humanist playwright, born in Balingen (Württemberg) on 22 November 1547, the son of the parish priest, and educated at the University of Tübingen, where he was appointed professor of poetry and history in 1568. On a visit to Regensburg in 1575 Frischlin read his Latin comedy *Rebecca* to the Emperor MAXIMILIAN, who created him POET LAUREATE; two years later he was made count palatine.

Frischlin's volatile temperament led to quarrels with his colleagues at Tübingen, and he was twice forced to leave. From 1582 to 1584 he taught in Laibach, in Carniola (now Ljubljana, in Slovenia), and in 1587 he left for Frankfurt am Main and then travelled widely through Europe. In Mainz he wrote letters deemed to be libellous, and was arrested. He was imprisoned in the castle at Urach (now Hohenurach), near Reutlingen, and on the night of 29 November 1590 was killed while trying to lower himself from the window of his cell.

Frischlin's Latin plays (six comedies and two tragedies) include *Rebecca* (1576), *Susanna* (1578), and *Judith* (1584), a comedy called *Phasma* (1592), and *Julius redivivus* (1584), in which Caesar and Cicero visit sixteenth-century Germany; his only surviving German play is *Frau Wendelgard* (1579). His *Opera poetica*, which by 1636 had reached its twelfth edition, consisted of a Latin epic on the biblical history of the JEWS (*Hebraeis*, 1590), a collection of Latin *Elegiaca* (1604), and 22 books of lyric poetry. He also translated Callimachus and Aristophanes into Latin and wrote commentaries on Persius and VIRGIL.

*DLL; NDB.*

**FRISIAN LANGUAGE.** Frisian, which Frisian-speakers call Frysk, is the second language of the northern Netherlands and the closest living relative of English. In early modern Europe Frisian was spoken in the Dutch province of Friesland (the West Frisian dialect), in the north German states of Saterland and Niedersachsen (the East Frisian dialect), and in what were then the Danish territories of Schleswig (Danish Slesvig) and Holstein (the North Frisian dialect). Frisian survived in southern Denmark until the 1860s, and is still spoken in the Netherlands (where West Frisian has been influenced by Dutch) and in parts of north-

ern Germany (where East Frisian has been influenced by German).

Frisian is, together with Dutch and English, a Low German branch of the West Germanic languages. The kinship with Dutch and English led philologists such as Johannes de Laet (1581–1649) and Franciscus Junius the Younger (1589–1677) to study the form of the language now known as Old Frisian (1200–1500). Middle Frisian (1500–1800) was not the subject of formal academic study, but Middle West Frisian was the language of one great poet, Gysbert Japix (1603–66), whose style links his poetry with the Renaissance.

R. H. Bremmer, Jr., G. Van der Meer, and O. Vries (eds.), *Aspects of Old Frisian Philology* (1990).

**FROBEN, JOHANN** (*c*.1460–1527), German humanist printer, born in Hammelburg (Bavaria). He moved to Basel in 1491, and trained as a printer and scholarly editor in the workshop of AMERBACH, where he worked until Amerbach's death in 1516, whereupon Froben established himself as an independent publisher with a particular interest in the printing of biblical and patristic works (notably a nine-volume edition of JEROME), and engaged HOLBEIN and Urs GRAF to design decorative initials and borders for his books; Holbein also painted his portrait (of which a copy is in Windsor Castle). He became a close friend of ERASMUS, who lived in Froben's house, and was the publisher of Erasmus' Greek New Testament (the first to be published). He also published tracts by Luther, but when Luther and Erasmus clashed over the doctrine of GRACE, Froben supported his houseguest. After Froben's death the publishing house was managed by his descendants until 1603.

*CoE; NDB.*

**FROBISHER, SIR MARTIN** (1535–94), English explorer. Between 1576 and 1578, he made a number of attempts to find the North-West Passage to Asia, sailing into the Hudson Strait and discovering Baffin Island, where Frobisher Bay bears his name. He later fought with DRAKE in the Armada.

*DNB;* James McDermott, *Martin Frobisher, Elizabethan Privateer* (2001).

**FROMENT, NICHOLAS** (*c*.1425/30–*c*.1480/6), French painter, a native of Uzès (Languedoc) who worked in Avignon, where he painted in a style influenced by that of Flanders. His most important surviving paintings are a triptych of the *Resurrection of Lazarus* (1461, Uffizi, Florence), which has portraits of the donors on the outside, and a triptych of *The Burning Bush* (1475–6, Aix-en-Provence Cathedral).

*DBF; MDA.*

**FROSCHAUER, CHRISTOPH** (*c*.1490–1564), Swiss printer who established a workshop in Zürich in the early 1520s. He was an early disciple of ZWINGLI, whose complete works he published. He sold religious books, including large annotated editions of the Bible in Latin and German. After Froschauer's death the workshop was managed by his nephew until 1590. The Froschauer press was the most important publishing house in the Reformed Swiss Cantons (see SWISS CONFEDERA-

TION), and issued more than 900 titles in the course of the sixteenth century.

*NDB.*

**FROTTOLA** is a term which covers various types of Italian secular song. Its origins lie in a fifteenth-century performance practice of reciting poetry to a musical accompaniment. The improvisatory quality of this practice was formalized through the patronage of Isabella d'ESTE in Mantua, who commissioned poets to provide verses which she then had set to music by Italian composers. PETRUCCI printed eleven books of frottolas in Venice between 1504 and 1514.

**FRUEAUF, RUELAND THE ELDER** (*c.*1440/50–1507), Austrian painter, born in Salzburg, where from 1478 he worked principally for the Benedictine monastery. His paintings, notably his *Man of Sorrows* (Alte Pinakothek, Munich), show the stylistic influence of his older contemporary Conrad LAIB. In 1497 Frueauf moved to Passau, where he remained for the rest of his life. His son Rueland the Younger also worked as a painter in Passau, where he died at an unknown date after 1545.

*MDA; NDB.*

**FRUNDSBERG, GEORG VON** (1473–1528), German imperial soldier, born in Mindelheim on 24 September 1473. In 1499 he fought with the imperial army of MAXIMILIAN against the Swiss and with Ludovico SFORZA against the French; in 1504 he fought with imperial forces in the war over the succession of Bavaria-Landshut, and subsequently commanded imperial forces in the Netherlands. During this period he assisted Maximilian with the formation of the LANDSKNECHTE, and established their reputation in the war against Venice in 1509. He returned to the WARS OF ITALY in 1513 and 1514, when he defeated Venetian and French armies.

Frundsberg returned to Germany in 1514 and soon became a commander in the SWABIAN LEAGUE, whose infantry he used to expel ULRICH, duke of Württemberg, from his duchy. In 1521 he was present at the Diet of WORMS, where he spoke encouragingly to Martin LUTHER. In the following year tensions between France and the Holy Roman Empire once again erupted into war and Frundsberg fought for CHARLES V, invading Picardy and then subduing Lombardy in a campaign that culminated in the battle of BICOCCA (1522); he also contributed to the defeat of the French at the battle of PAVIA (1525). On returning to Germany, he used both diplomacy and force of arms to quell the PEASANTS' REVOLT.

War once again broke out in Italy, and Frundsberg raised an army at his own expense and in Piacenza joined forces with the Constable Charles, duc de BOURBON, with whom he marched towards Rome. Frundsberg was unable to pay his troops, who became mutinous; he fell ill and was unable to pacify the rebellion, and so resigned his command and returned to Mindelheim, where he died on 20 August 1528.

Georg von Frundsberg's son Kaspar (1500–36) and grandson Georg were also distinguished imperial soldiers; when the latter died in 1586 the line became extinct.

*NDB.*

**FUCHS, LEONHARD** (1501–66), German botanist who studied at the University of Ingolstadt, where in 1526 he was appointed professor of medicine. In 1535 he moved to a chair of medicine at Tübingen, where he remained for the rest of his life. In 1542 he published *De historia stirpium*, a treatise on medicinal plants which describes some 400 indigenous plants and about 100 foreign plants, including North American maize. Fuchs is the eponym of the fuchsia, a garden plant imported from South America to Europe in the nineteenth century.

*NDB;* E. Stübler, *Leonhart Fuchs* (1928).

**FUENLLANA, MIGUEL DE** (*c.*1500–after 1568), Spanish vihuelist and composer, active in Seville and Lisbon. His *Orphenica lyra* (1554) is a collection of fantasias, *tientos*, duos, and contrapuntal arrangements of sacred and secular melodies for vihuela and guitar.

**FUGGER FAMILY**, a German banking dynasty which traced its origins to Johann Fugger, a weaver from Graben (near Augsburg), whose son Johann (d. 1408) settled in Augsburg in about 1367, and combined weaving with trade in textiles. Johann the Younger's two sons Andreas and Jakob greatly expanded the family's textile interests, as did their sons. Lukas, the son of Andreas, was the first member of the family to enter civic politics; he became enormously wealthy, but was bankrupted when the town of Louvain defaulted on a debt. In 1452 Lukas's brother Jakob successfully applied for a coat of arms, which contained a roe (German *Reh*), and so became the founder of the Fugger vom Reh branch of the family, which became extinct in 1583 on the death of Ulrich Fugger vom Reh, Jakob's great-grandson.

Johann the Younger's son Jakob had seven sons, of whom three inherited the family business: Ulrich (1441–1510), Georg (1453–1506), and Jakob (1459–1525). In 1473 Ulrich secured from the Emperor FRIEDRICH III the right for the three brothers to bear arms, and during the 1470s began to act as banker to the HABSBURGS, a role that was to give the Fuggers an important place in European finance for centuries. Ulrich's brother Jakob, who had learned the banking trade in Venice, extended the family's interests in mining to silver mines in the Tirol and copper mines in Hungary; Jakob also developed the family's interest in spices, wool, and silk in markets throughout Europe.

By the end of the fifteenth entry the Fuggers were enormously wealthy, and so were able to extend huge loans to the Emperor MAXIMILIAN I; in return, they received pledges of land and a range of privileges. Jakob built the Castle of Fuggerau in Carinthia, and also commissioned the Fuggerei, a settlement in AUGSBURG built specifically to house the poor. He also financed the election of the Emperor CHARLES V in 1519.

Jakob died without male heirs, as did the two sons of his brother Ulrich, who were called Ulrich (d. 1525) and Hieronymus (d. 1536). The family line was continued by Georg, the third brother (1453–1506), whose two sons Raimund (1489–1535) and Anton (1493–1560) carried the family to the apogee of its fortunes. The Fuggers made vast loans to Charles V, and also administered the revenues from his Spanish possessions, which included mining (mercury in Almadén and silver in Guadalcanal) and the estates that had passed from the military ORDERS to the Spanish royal family. In the course of the sixteenth century the Fuggers extended their mining and mercantile activities to Asia and America. The loyalty of the family to the Catholic Church brought rewards—Jakob, for example, was made a count palatine (*Pfalzgraf*)—but also forfeited markets in areas of northern Europe that had declared for the Protestant cause.

Four of Raimund's sons became important figures in sixteenth-century Europe. Sigmund (1542–1600) entered the Church and became bishop of Regensburg; Johann Jacob (1516–75) was the author of *Wahrhaftigen Beschreibung des österreichischen und Habsburgischen Nahmens* and of *Geheim Ernbuch des Fuggerischen Geschlechtes*, and was also an important patron of art; Ulrich (1526–84) entered the service of Pope PAUL III, but subsequently became a Protestant and escaped to the Rhineland PALATINATE, where he amassed a collection of Greek manuscripts that he bequeathed to the University of Heidelberg; Georg (d. 1579) inherited the palatinates of Kirchberg and Weissenhorn. Of Anton's three sons, the most prominent was Marcus (1529–97), who wrote a book on horse-breeding (*Wie und wo man ein Gestüt von guten edeln Kriegsrossen aufrichten soll*, 1578) and translated into German the *Historia ecclesiastica* of the Byzantine historian Nicephorus Callistus, which had been translated into Latin in 1555 and quickly been appropriated by the Catholic party in the religious debates of the later sixteenth century, because it offered support for the role of relics and images in Christian worship.

In 1593 a *Pinacotheca Fuggerorum* containing portraits of the Fuggers engraved by the Flemish artist Dominique Custos was published in Augsburg. Expanded editions containing 127 portraits appeared in 1618 (with a genealogy in Latin) and 1620 (with a genealogy in German).

*NDB*; V. Klarwill (ed.), *The Fugger News-Letters* (1924); R. Ehrenberg, *Capital and Finance in the Age of the Renaissance: A Study of the Fuggers* (1963).

**FURNITURE.** Late Roman law and subsequent legal systems have distinguished between moveables (which are subject to ownership) and immoveables (which are subject to possession). The legal status of furniture as moveables is reflected in the terms used to denote furniture, such as French *meuble*, Italian *mobilio*, Spanish *mueblaje*, Portuguese *movéis*, German *Möbel*, and Danish *møbler*. The practice of noble families of travelling on progress through their territories meant that secular furniture was constructed in sections to facilitate it being moved on wagons from castle to castle. As late as the seventeenth century, much furniture was designed to be portable; in the late sixteenth century, furniture that was installed was said to be dormant: a 'dormant table' is one that is nailed to the floor. The visual balance between textiles and wooden furniture favoured the former: TAPESTRIES hung on walls, and CARPETS covered beds, tables, and chairs; floors were covered with rush matting.

In the fifteenth century, the courtly furniture of northern Europe was dominated by the INTERNATIONAL GOTHIC style. The most important centre for the commercial production of furniture was Antwerp. Medieval furniture had been constructed from planks, but this method was superseded in Flanders in the early fifteenth century, when the advent of joined PANELLING enabled much lighter furniture to be made. In northern Europe the preferred wood was oak, and elm was used as a cheaper substitute; in southern Europe the finest furniture was made from walnut, though cypress and several fruitwoods were also used.

North European furniture was often carved but not painted; in Italy the emphasis was on painted decoration until the sixteenth century: the fifteenth-century CASSONE was painted, but its sixteenth-century successor was usually carved. The Italian emphasis on colour is even apparent in unpainted furniture, because the development of INTARSIA allowed colour contrasts to be achieved without the use of paint.

In France and Burgundy, Renaissance decorative motifs are apparent in sixteenth-century furniture, which was often adorned with ACANTHUS or PUTTI. The Italian style, as interpreted at FONTAINEBLEAU, became the model for French furniture design. In about 1550 Jacques Androuet DUCERCEAU the Elder published a set of engraved designs for household furniture; in Burgundy, a set of designs was published by Hugues SAMBIN in Dijon in 1572. In Germany, Peter FLÖTNER published engraved designs for furniture; an oak and ash cupboard built to one of his designs in 1541 is preserved in the Germanisches Nationalmuseum in Nuremberg. In the Netherlands Jan VREDEMAN DE VRIES published a pattern book (*c*.1580) that set the austere decorative style for Protestant furniture later adopted in the Evangelical Swiss Cantons and adapted in Scandinavia (where some courtly refinement survived). In Spain and Portugal a syncretic Iberian style of furniture blended European design with MUDÉJAR decorative traditions.

The most important pieces of furniture were BEDS, CABINETS, TABLES, and various kinds of seats (CHAIRS, SETTLES, AND STOOLS).

**FUST, JOHANN** (*c*.1400–1466), German printer, a Mainz lawyer who in 1450 lent Johann GUTENBERG 800 gulden to finance the publication of the 42-line Bible. He subsequently invested another 800 gulden and became Gutenberg's partner. When Gutenberg became bankrupt in 1455, Fust assumed control of the press together with his son-in-law Peter SCHÖFFER. On 14 August 1457 Schöffer and Fust published the elegant Mainz Psalter, which was the first book to use colours, and in 1462 they published a two-volume Latin Bible. Their edition of CICERO's *De officiis* (1465) was the first book to contain Greek characters. Fust died of plague whilst on a business trip to Paris and was succeeded by Schöffer.

*NDB*.

**FUSTIAN**, a coarse cloth with a cotton weft and a flax warp, first made in Fustat, the Arab capital of Egypt in the seventh and eighth centuries AD (now a set of ruins south of Cairo).

The principal centres of fustian manufacturing in fourteenth- and fifteenth-century Europe were Spain, Tuscany, and southern Germany (especially Ulm) and Flanders. Until the end of the fifteenth century, fustians were bleached but not dyed. In England, fustian was imported (and much admired) in the fifteenth century, an indigenous industry developed in the later sixteenth century with the arrival in Norfolk and Lancashire of Flemish refugees from the REVOLT OF THE NETHERLANDS. The use of 'fustian' to mean gibberish originates (like 'bombast') in its association with Dutch; in MARLOWE's *Doctor Faustus* a clown replies to a phrase in Latin with 'God forgive me, he speaks Dutch fustian'.

**GABRIEL SEVERUS** (1541–1616), Greek theologian in Venice. Gabriel was a native of the Morea (the Peloponnese); he was consecrated metropolitan of Philadelphia (now Alaşehir, in Turkey) in 1577, but as the town was in Ottoman hands, he migrated to Venice, where he acted as bishop for the resident Greek community and became a noted polemicist in defence of the theology and practices of the Byzantine Church. His most important work was a defence of the Greek practice of venerating the eucharistic bread and wine during the procession that carries the elements from the table on which the eucharist is prepared (the prothesis) to the altar; Gabriel argued that because the elements had already been dedicated for consecration, they were no longer merely bread and wine, but had become holy by participation ($\mu\epsilon\tau o\chi\iota\kappa\hat{\omega}\varsigma$) and so warranted a degree of reverence second only to the adoration appropriate to the consecrated host.

**GABRIELI, ANDREA** (c.1532–1586), Venetian composer. He became organist of San Marco in 1566 and remained there for nearly twenty years, during which time his colleagues included ZARLINO (*maestro di cappella*), MERULO (another organist), and a growing number of able singers and instrumentalists, such as the dalla Casa brothers and the cornettist Giovanni BASSANO. Gabrieli's composing style, influenced as it was by Orlande de LASSUS, and in conjunction with the presence of considerable musical resources, was fundamental to San Marco's becoming a centre for the development of sacred and secular polyphony on a grand scale. This is demonstrated in his *Concerti*, posthumously published in 1587 by his nephew Giovanni GABRIELI, a collection of music for ceremonial occasions of the Venetian Church and state.

**GABRIELI, GIOVANNI** (c.1552–1612), Venetian composer and nephew of Andrea GABRIELI. He studied in Munich with Orlande de LASSUS at the court of Duke ALBRECHT V, and then returned to Venice, where he joined his uncle as an organist at San Marco from 1584. After the death of Andrea he edited many of his uncle's works as well as composing his own. He continued Andrea's work as the principal composer of Venetian ceremonial music although his *Sacrae symphoniae* (1597) probably contains music written, not only for San Marco, but also for the Scuola Grande di San Rocco, where

he held the post of organist from 1585. This collection quickly brought him pupils from Germany and as far away as Denmark. His music is characteristic for mixed vocal and instrumental ensembles and on a large scale; prior to 1597 he uses *CORI SPEZZATI*.

**GABUSSI, GIULIO CESARE** (c.1555–1611), Italian composer in Milan, Forlì, and Warsaw, where he was briefly employed by King SIGISMUND III. He wrote sacred and secular music and was one of the first composers to apply the Council of Trent's instructions to the writing of polyphony.

**GADDI, AGNOLO** (fl. 1369, d. 1396), Italian painter, the son of Taddeo GADDI. As a young man he worked with his brother Giovanni in the Vatican. He contributed frescoes to the chancel (1374) and choir (1388–93) of the Church of Santa Croce in Florence, to the Chapel of the Holy Girdle (Cappella del Sacro Cingolo) in Prato Cathedral (1392–5), and to San Miniato al Monte in Florence (1393–6).
  *DBI; MDA;* Bruce Cole, *Agnolo Gaddi* (1977).

**GADDI, TADDEO** (fl. 1325, d. 1366), Italian painter, a native of Florence; he was for 24 years the assistant of GIOTTO. His finest surviving paintings were executed for the Church of Santa Croce in Florence, including a fresco series on *The Life of the Virgin* in the Baroncelli Chapel (1332–8), a fresco of *The Last Supper* in the refectory, and a series of panel paintings on *The Lives of Christ and St Francis* (c.1330) intended for the doors of a cupboard in the sacristy and now divided between the Accademia in Florence, the Residenzmuseum in Munich, and the Gemäldegalerie in Berlin. Gaddi subsequently worked in Pisa and Pistoia (where in 1353 he painted the polyptych altarpiece for San Giovanni Fuorcivitas), but eventually returned to Florence, where he was a member of the commission charged with responsibility for works on the cathedral.
  *DBI; MDA;* Andrew Ladis, *Taddeo Gaddi* (1982).

**GAFFURIO, FRANCHINO** (1451–1522), Italian musical theorist, exponent of Netherlandish music in Mantua, Verona, Genoa, and Naples; in 1484 he became choirmaster at Milan Cathedral, where he revised his *Theorica musicae* (1492) and *Practica musicae* (1496), two of the most influential Renaissance music treatises.

**GAGGINI or Gagini, NIBILIO** (*fl.* 1586, d. 1607), Sicilian goldsmith, the last prominent member of a family of Lombard sculptors who migrated to Sicily in the fifteenth century. His surviving works include an elaborate monstrance of 1586 (Chiesa Madre, Polizzi Generosa) and a reliquary of 1599 (Chiesa di San Giacomo, Caltagirone). His works disseminated the designs described in the treatises of Juan de ARFE.
*DBI.*

**GAGUIN, ROBERT** (1433–1501), French-Flemish humanist, poet, prosodist, and historian. He was a member of the Trinitarian Order who taught CANON LAW at the University of Paris and served as a diplomat in the service of LOUIS XI and CHARLES VIII, on whose behalf he led embassies to Italy, England, and Germany. His writings include theological treatises, translations of Latin authors, and an influential historical work, *De origine et gestis Francorum compendio* (1495).
*DBF*; Franck Collard, *Un historien au travail à la fin du XVᵉ siècle: Robert Gaguin* (1996).

**GAIL or Gaill, ANDREAS VON** (1526–87), German judge and jurist. His treatise on procedure, *Practicarae observationes* (Cologne, 1578), was widely read in northern Europe, and was an important influence on the development of the DUTCH LAW of procedure.
*NDB* s.v. Gail(l).

**GAÏLDE, JEAN** (*fl.* 1490–*c.*1519), French mason and sculptor who worked in Troyes, where he made the rood-screen in the Church of Sainte-Madeleine (1508–17), beneath which he is buried. The screen is one of the last great monuments of the GOTHIC tradition.
*DBF; MDA.*

**GAILLON**, a chateau and garden near Rouen. The medieval fortress on the site was rebuilt in 1502 for Cardinal Georges d'AMBOISE, minister of LOUIS XII; the castle was remodelled in the Renaissance style, and is now regarded as the first Renaissance chateau in France. The garden, which was designed by PACELLO DA MERCOGLIANO without architectural reference to the house, was laid out between 1502 and 1509 on a level terrace overlooking the Seine valley. The garden was bordered on two sides with galleries, and contained a wooden PAVILION sheltering a FOUNTAIN that had been made in Genoa and presented by the Venetian Senate. Planting was organized in ornamental PARTERRES in square beds, each of which was planted individually with flowers, fruit trees, or herbs against backgrounds of coloured earth, gravel, or terracotta; initially the beds were bordered with wooden fretwork, but this was later replaced by clipped box. One square was planted as a MAZE, and others were designed as coats of arms. Within the garden there was a private retreat called Le Lidieu, with its own house, chapel, and small garden. In the 1550s Charles, cardinal de Bourbon, aggrandized this private retreat in imitation of similar gardens built by the Italian princes of the Church, notably the Villa FARNESE; the house was transformed into a sumptuous *CASINO*, the Maison Blanche, a canal was dug, and a rock hermitage was constructed in the middle of a pool. In the same period a second garden was built at a lower level. Both gardens were redesigned by Le Nôtre between 1691 and 1707, and have since disappeared, as has the chateau.
Elisabeth Chirol, *La Château de Gaillon: Un premier foyer de la Renaissance en France* (1952).

**GAISMAIR, MICHAEL** (*c.*1490–1532), German peasant leader, from a family with mining interests in south Tirol. He captained the PEASANTS' WAR in Tirol and subsequently in Saltzburg. The rebellion began on 10 May 1525 in Brixen (Bressanone), which led to concessions by Archduke FERDINAND. In the winter of 1525 Gaismair was on Swiss territory, where he made contact with ZWINGLI in Zürich. In spring 1526 he returned to lead a combined Salzburg-Austrian peasant army, whose siege of Radstadt was ended by the arrival of troops of the SWABIAN LEAGUE. Gaismair fled to Venetian territory, from where he continued his attempts to launch an international campaign against Habsburg rule, but was assassinated in Padua in 1532 by agents of Archduke Ferdinand. Gaismair's blueprint of a new society, contained in the so-called Territorial Constitution for Tirol, was deeply indebted to Zwingli's vision of a Christian theocratic commonwealth, but also advocated economic improvement along mercantalist lines.
*NDB*; Tom Scott, 'The Reformation and Modern Political Economy: Luther and Gaismair Compared', in Thomas A. Brady Jr. (ed.), *Die deutsche Reformation zwischen Spätmittelalter und Früher Neuzeit* (2001).

**GALEN IN THE RENAISSANCE.** The second-century physician Galen of Pergamum was the principal ancient authority for academic medicine (particularly ANATOMY, physiology, and humoral medicine) in the Renaissance. A collected version of his works in Latin translation was published in 1490, and in 1525 the ALDINE Press published the *editio princeps* of the Greek texts. In anatomy Galen's authority was gradually subverted by the observational anatomy of VESALIUS and FALLOPPIO. In physiology, the Galenic model of vital spirits being transmitted through the arterial system, natural spirits through the venous system, and animal spirits through the nervous system, with centres of convergence in the liver, heart, and brain, remained the conventional wisdom of the medical profession, and enjoyed an afterlife even after the discovery of the circulation of the blood by William Harvey in 1628. In humoral medicine, Galen's notion of illness, which was rooted in Hippocratic medicine and based on analogies between the elements (fire, water, air, and earth), the four bodily fluids known as humours (blood, phlegm, choler or yellow bile, and black bile), and the four qualities (hot, cold, dry, and wet), remained the prevailing orthodoxy throughout the early modern period; physicians regarded disease as the result of a humoral imbalance, and understood the process of healing (and therefore of treatment) as the restoration of balance through diet. Balance was also achieved by herbal and chemical remedies that would counter the qualitative nature of disease, so a hot remedy would cure a cold disease. Evacuative procedures such as bloodletting and purging were also extremely popular; such measures were deemed to expel an excess of a humour or a humour which had become corrupt and putrid inside the body, and so had caused illness.

**GALICIAN LANGUAGE AND LITERATURE.** Galician is the language of the old kingdom of Galicia (the modern Spanish provinces of La Coruña, Lugo, Ourense, and Pontevedra) and of the Vierzo district of the province of León. Linguists classify Galician (*galego* in Galician, *gallego* in Castilian) together with the PORTUGUESE LANGUAGE, which is a more evolved variety of the same language written in a distinct orthography.

Between 1196 and 1350 Galician achieved a special cultural prestige as the chosen literary language of courtly lyric poetry in the western Iberian kingdoms, just as OCCITAN did in Catalonia and Italy. The surviving corpus of surviving Galician poetry includes some 1,679 secular lyrics and satires and a set of 427 religious poems, the latter by the Castilian King Alfonso X, the Wise. Prose includes many translations into Galician from French, Castilian, and Latin works of literature, history, and religion. After 1350 Galician was largely displaced by Castilian as the literary language of Spain, while Portuguese was gradually adopted in Portugal.

**GALILEI, GALILEO** (1564–1642), usually known simply by his given name, Italian mathematician and natural philosopher and astronomer. He was born in Pisa into a family that had been established in Florence for several generations; this is the meaning of the phrase *gentiluomo fiorentino* which his father Vincenzo uses to describe himself. In 1581 Galileo entered the University of Pisa, but left in 1585 and continued study of mathematics and natural philosophy in private. It may have been at this time that he began to reflect on the possibility that all objects fall at the same speed regardless of their weight, a view that was at variance with the standard Aristotelian physics of the day, though it had been discussed, indeed proved to be correct, in 'thought experiments' designed by Giovanni Battista BENEDETTI. In 1592, thanks to support from Guidobaldo del MONTE, Galileo obtained a post teaching mathematics at the University of Padua, where he remained for eighteen years.

In Padua Galileo pursued interests in physics (he admired the work of William GILBERT) and astronomy. The astronomy that Galileo taught was standard geocentric astronomy, and many of his students would have been prospective physicians (see LIBERAL ARTS), but by 1597 Galileo apparently had some knowledge of the work of COPERNICUS.

In 1609, after being told about a TELESCOPE that a visitor had shown in Venice, Galileo began to think about how lenses might be combined, and set to work to make a telescope himself. As he combined optical knowledge with manual dexterity he made instruments whose performance was far better than the one shown in Venice; he used his instruments to make a series of observations that were published in *Sidereus nuncius* (1610). The book caused a sensation, and made Galileo instantly famous. It is notable for its vivid and meticulous descriptions of what Galileo actually saw: the changing shadows that proved the moon had mountains, the changing patterns of the moons as they moved round Jupiter as well as with it, and the fact that the Milky Way could be seen to be made up of stars. Pirated editions of the book appeared almost immediately. KEPLER wrote an open letter to Galileo to express his vigorous approval, published as *Dissertatio cum Nuncio sidereo* (1610).

Galileo had named the moons of Jupiter 'the Medicean stars'; later in 1610 Galileo moved to Florence, where he was appointed mathematician and philosopher to Grand Duke Cosimo II de' Medici. In 1613 he published a book on sunspots (*Historia e dimonstrazioni intorno alle macchie solari*) in which he announced his support for the heliocentric theory of the cosmos. The religious authorities in Florence publicly deplored this, and Galileo, in a letter to Grand Duchess Christina, whose careful wording was no doubt agreed in advance, defended his right to conduct scientific enquiries without reference to the authority of churchmen. However, in 1616 Galileo was admonished by a papal commission chaired by Cardinal BELLARMINE.

Galileo continued to be interested in Copernicanism; he composed *Dialogo dei due massimi sistemi de mondo*, a series of dialogues that compared the Ptolemaic and Copernican cosmologies, but ignored the most popular system of the time, that of Tycho BRAHE, in which, as in Ptolemy, the earth is at rest. Galileo argues largely in terms of terrestrial physics, specifically maintaining that the tides prove the earth moves. He held his book back until the accession of a new pope, Urban VIII, with whom he had been on friendly terms while he was still a cardinal. The *Dialogo* was licensed and published in 1632, but Galileo was summoned to Rome to appear before the INQUISITION. At his trial in 1633 he was found to be 'vehemently suspected of heresy' and forced to recant (he probably did say 'Eppur si muove', 'All the same it does move') and was eventually sentenced to house arrest at his villa in Arcetri, just above Florence. By the standards of the time, it was a rather mild sentence. Attention had been paid to Galileo's international reputation and his connections with the Medici, but at a time of conflict with Protestantism the Church could not be seen to be weak on the literal interpretation of Scripture, which indicated that the earth was at rest. Galileo's eyesight was now failing. His last book, a study of motion and the strength of materials, based on experiments and practical know-how learned from workers in the Arsenale in Venice, *Discorsi e dimonstrazioni matematiche intorno a due nuove scienze*, was published in Leiden in 1638. When Galileo died in February 1642 he was buried the same day in the family vault in Santa Croce (Florence), giving the church authorities no time to object.

*DBI* and *DSB* s.v. Galilei; Stillman Drake, *Galileo at Work* (1978).

**GALILEI, VINCENZO** (1525/30–91), Florentine musical theorist and father of Galileo GALILEI. He enjoyed the patronage of Giovanni de' BARDI who enabled him to study in Venice with ZARLINO. He returned to Florence where he was also supported by Jacopo CORSI. He wrote several theoretical works including the *Dialogo della musica antica et della moderna* (1581) in which he explains theories about the music of ancient Greece, upon which he based the idea of monody. He took part in Bardi's CAMERATA and his theories influenced CAVALIERI.

**GALLEASS or galleasse**, a Mediterranean warship with both oars and sails which emerged in the sixteenth century as a hybrid between the GALLEY (which was rowed) and the GALLEON (which was sailed). The presence of masts and rigging necessitated a broader beam and a deeper draught than the galley, and when being propelled by oars it was therefore slower and harder to manoeuvre than the galley; similarly, the need to accommodate banks of oarsmen necessitated a hull design that could only support lateen rigging, and when being propelled by sail it was therefore slower than the square-rigged galleon. Six galleasses were included in the Spanish fleet for the ARMADA invasion, but proved inadequate to the stormy waters of northern seas. Thereafter the galleass only survived in a civilian version (with a single bank of oars) which was used to convey freight around the Mediterranean and (in the summer months) northern Europe.

**GALLEGO, FERNANDO** (*fl.* 1468–1507), Spanish painter of Galician extraction and the principal exponent of the Hispano-Flemish style in SPANISH ART. Between 1479 and 1493 he painted the ceiling of the Old Library at the University of Salamanca, but this now survives only in fragments; the university museum now houses the fresco that Fernando painted in 1494 for the semi-cupola of the old chapel, which was badly damaged in the Lisbon earthquake of 1755 (which was felt from Scotland to the Levant). Fernando also painted the reredos of *San Idelfonso* for Zamora Cathedral, the retable of the Church of San Lorenzo in Toro, the triptych of *The Virgin, St Andrew, and St Christopher* in the New Cathedral in Salamanca, and the macabre triptych of *St Catherine* in the Old Cathedral. His *Piedad* and *Calvario* are now in the Prado.
MDA.

**GALLEON or (Spanish)** *galeon*, a type of ship designed in 1570 by the privateer Sir John HAWKINS, whose design was based on the CARRACK. Hawkins concluded through experimentation on his slaving voyages that the high forecastle of the carrack (and of other large ships) caught the wind and so forced the bow to leeward, which created difficulties on any course to windward; by lowering the forecastle he was able to ease the problem and to create a ship better able to cope with strong winds. In the late 1580s the design was adopted in Spain, where the term *galeon* was first used; thereafter *galeon* and its cognates (French *galion*, Italian *galeone*, Portuguese *galeão*, and English *galleon*) always denoted Spanish ships.

**GALLEY**, the oared warship used in Mediterranean conflicts for 5,000 years. Originally oarsmen all sat at the same level, but in classical antiquity oars were arranged at different levels; such ships were known as biremes (two banks of oars), triremes (three banks), quadreremes (four banks), and quinqueremes (five banks). From antiquity till the thirteenth century galleys were usually triremes, but in the early modern period they were usually biremes, manned with three or four oarsmen on each oar; Vettor FAUSTO attempted in vain to revive the quinquereme.

The principal weapon of the war galley was a pointed metal ram fixed on the bow or just below the waterline and used to pierce the hull of enemy ships with a view to sinking or disabling them. In the sixteenth century GUNS were mounted on the bows in fixed positions; the guns could not be trained on a target, so the galley had to be manoeuvred so that the guns could be fired directly ahead. Galleys were gradually displaced by warships under sail, and were last used in battle in the Mediterranean in 1717 and in the Baltic in 1809.

F. C. Lane, *Navires et constructeurs à Venise pendant la Renaissance* (1965); M. E. Mallett, *Florentine Galleys in the Fifteenth Century* (1967).

**GALLIARD or (Italian)** *gagliarda*, an energetic court dance of the sixteenth and early seventeenth centuries which originated in Italy. The steps were a vigorous variation of the *cinq pas* with a particularly high leap on the fifth step. The music was generally homophonic and in compound duple time; in time it found its way into purely instrumental music, such as the examples in William BYRD's *Parthenia* (1613). Like its close relation the saltarello, the galliard is frequently paired with a pavan.

**GALLICANISM**, the belief that the French Church should be free from the ecclesiastical authority of the papacy. During the GREAT SCHISM French reformers such as Jean GERSON and Pierre D'Ailly articulated the Gallicanism of the University of Paris, which based the claim to the *libertés de l'Église gallicane* on prerogatives associated with the French crown. The Gallican position was enshrined in the PRAGMATIC SANCTION OF BOURGES (1438), which was issued by the French clergy while the COUNCIL OF BASEL was in session; this statement, restricted the power of the pope in France by upholding the right of the French Church to adminster its temporal property without reference to the papacy and to disallow papal nominations to vacant benefices.

In 1516 the Pragmatic Sanction of Bourges was superseded by the Concordat of BOLOGNA, which legitimized the control by the French crown of about 600 of the principal benefices (and so gave the French king the right to appoint his own bishops) and allowed the king to sanction or veto the implementation of papal bulls in France; this right later formed the legal basis of the French refusal to implement the decrees of the COUNCIL OF TRENT. The most distinguished post-Tridentine exponent of Gallicanism was Pierre PITHOU, whose *Recueil des libertés de l'Église gallicane* (1594) ringingly declared that the papacy had no temporal jurisdiction in France and that its spiritual jurisdiction was limited to conciliar decrees recognized by the French king.

Opposition to Gallicanism is known as Ultramontanism, the belief that authority in the Church should rest with the papacy.

V. Martin, *Les Origines du gallicanisme* (2 vols., 1939).

**GALVÃO, ANTÓNIO** (*c*.1490–1557), Portuguese historian who travelled to India in 1527 and later served as governor of the Moluccas (1536–40); he was said to have declined the throne of Ternate (in the Moluccas). He returned to Portugal in 1540, fell out of favour with the court, and died in poverty. His posthumously published *Livro dos descobrimentos das Antilhas de Índia* (Lisbon, 1563), which was translated into English by HAKLUYT in 1603, was a comprehensive account of the European exploration of Asia up to that time.

*DHP.*

**GAMA, VASCO DA** (*c*.1468–1524), Portuguese mariner, born in the small Atlantic seaport of Sines, the son of an admiral. As a young man he fought in the wars against Castile. King MANUEL I subsequently entrusted him with the command of an expedition that was to follow up the discovery of the southern limit of Africa by Bartolomeu DIAS, who supervised the construction and outfitting of Vasco's fleet.

On 8 July 1497 Vasco sailed down the Tagus from Lisbon with a fleet of four ships and 160 men. He rounded the Cape of Good Hope in November 1497 and in March 1498 landed in Sofala (now in Mozambique), where the sultan provided the expedition with a Gujarati pilot. He subsequently landed in Mombasa and Malindi (both now in Kenya) and then sailed across the Indian Ocean to Calicut, on the Malibar (now Kerala) coast of India, where he landed on 20 May 1498. Vasco was regarded as an unwelcome competitor by Arab and Indian merchants in Calicut, and eventually had to retreat under fire. He finally left India in August 1498, and his first ship reached Lisbon in July 1499; Vasco's flagship arrived on 9 September 1500. His fleet was laden with valuable spices, and Vasco was rewarded with an estate and a title of nobility. His voyage was later to be celebrated by Luis CAMÕES in *The Lusiads*.

Vasco's second expedition, which left Lisbon in November 1502, consisted of twenty ships (of which five followed later). Warships were included in the squadron because one of Vasco's purposes was military. The men whom Pedro CABRAL had left behind in Calicut had been murdered, and on arriving in Calicut intent on vengeance, Vasco bombarded the town and massacred many of its inhabitants. He then proceeded to Cochin, where he established a FEITORIA and signed a treaty with the ruler. At sea he preyed on Arab traders, both because they were Islamic (and therefore infidels) and because they controlled the Red Sea route to Europe, which was the principal competitor to Portugal's ambitions for the Cape route. He then retraced his route, reaching Lisbon in September 1503, again with richly laden ships.

Vasco retired to his estate in Évora with his wife and six sons, and in December 1519 was created count of Vidigueira, which conferred on him considerable judicial privileges (in both criminal and civil jurisdictions) and powers of ecclesiastical patronage. In 1524 he was recalled from retirement by King JOHN III to become the sixth viceroy of India. He sailed to India, but died in Cochin after a short illness.

*DHP*; Anthony Disney and Emily Booth (eds.), *Vasco da Gama and the Linking of Europe and Asia* (2000).

**GAMBARA, VERONICA** (1485–1550), Italian poet and patron, born into a noble family near Brescia. She married the *signore* of Correggio, but the death of her husband in 1518 left Veronica with responsibility for their two sons and the governance of Correggio. She was an educated and cultivated ruler who enjoyed the friendship of BEMBO and Vittoria COLONNA and corresponded with ARETINO. The small corpus of her verse (which includes 37 Petrarchan sonnets) ranges elegantly over subjects such as the death of her husband, the devastation wrought by the WARS OF ITALY, and the pleasures of her domestic and social life.

*DBI*; *HWWI*; C. Bozzetti, P. Gibellini, and E. Sandal (eds.), *Veronica Gambara e la poesia del suo tempo* (1989).

**GANSFORT, WESSEL.** See WESSEL GANSFORT.

**GANTE, PEDRO DE** (1486–1572), Flemish missionary in Mexico, educated in Flanders by the BRETHREN OF THE COMMON LIFE and then at the University of Louvain. He entered the Franciscan Order and travelled to Mexico in 1532 with the first group of Franciscan friars. He settled in Mexico City, where he learnt the Nahuatl language and embarked on a programme of conversion and education that entailed the construction of large numbers of churches, schools, and hospitals. His instruction in European art and Christian iconography introduced the teaching of western art in the Americas.

**GARAMOND, CLAUDE** (1480–1561), French type founder, a native of Paris who worked as a type founder for several Parisian printers. He designed the roman typeface now known as *typi regii* and the Greek type (now known as *grecs du roi*) used by Robert ESTIENNE in an edition of Eusebius (1544) commissioned by King FRANCIS I. Garamond's typefaces were to influence French typography for centuries, and a modernized form of his *typi regii* is now known as Garamond.

*DBF.*

**GARAY, JUAN DE** (1528–83), Spanish colonizer of Argentina. He was taken as a boy to Peru, where he became a soldier and colonial administrator. In 1568 he was commissioned to colonize Río de la Plata. He sailed south from Asunción (Paraguay) and in 1573 founded the town of Santa Fé near the confluence of the Salado and Paraná rivers, near the abandoned settlements of San Espíritu and Corpus Christi. In 1580 he refounded Buenos Aires, which was the third attempt to settle the site first colonized by Pedro de MENDOZA (1536) and CABEZA DA VACA (1542); Garay slaughtered the Indians who tried to defend the town and subsequently used Indian slave labour on the ranches that he established around its perimeter. Garay renamed the town Ciudad de la Santísima Trinidad and endowed it with a council (*cabildo*) with municipal privileges; the port retained the old name of Santa María de Buenos Aires. Three years later Garay was murdered by a party of aggrieved Indians while imprudently sleeping on a river bank near the ruins of San Espíritu.

*DHE*; Eduardo Tijeras, *Juan de Garay* (1987).

**GARCILASO DE LA VEGA** (*c*.1501–1536), Spanish poet and soldier. He was born into a noble family in Toledo and in 1502 entered the court of CHARLES V, in whose service Garcilaso spent most of his life. In 1522 he fought in the unsuccessful attempt to relieve Rhodes (which fell to the Ottomans on 21 December) and in 1535 he participated in the battle of TUNIS. He was banished from the court in 1532 as a punishment for attending the forbidden wedding of a nephew of the emperor, and travelled first to Schütt (an island in the Danube, then Hungarian Csallóköz, now Slovakian Ostrov) and then to Naples, where he met Luigi TANSILLO, Torquato TASSO, and Juan de VALDÉS. In 1536 he was killed in the imperial invasion of France whilst leading an attack on the fort of Le Muy (near Fréjus).

In 1525 Garcilaso married Elena de Zúñiga, but legend tells that in the following year he became enamoured of a Portuguese lady, Isabel Freire, to whom he addressed his finest love poems. The biographical inference is quite gratuitous: modern research has revealed that Garcilaso indeed had a long extramarital affair (though not with Isabel Freire), but his exquisitely crafted verses observe the courtly conventions of the Petrarchan tradition with a deeply classical decorum which deliberately eschews any crudely direct personal references. Garcilaso's surviving poetry includes 38 sonnets, two elegies in *terza rima* (one of which is addressed to his friend JOAN BOSCÀ), an epistle to Boscà in blank verse (*versos sueltos*, an adaptation of TRISSINO's *versi sciolti*), five *canciones* (Spanish versions of the Italian *canzone*), three eclogues (one in *octavas reales*, the metre that was to become the dominant metre in Spanish Renaissance epic), poems in Spanish metres, and poems in Latin. The Italian metres used by Garcilaso in many of his poems had been introduced to Spain by Boscà at the suggestion of the poet Andrea NAVAGIERO, who was Venetian ambassador to the Spanish court. Garcilaso was a much more accomplished poet than Boscà, and it was Garcilaso's use of these metres that created the first great Spanish poetry in the Italian style.

Garcilaso's finest poems are his three pastoral eclogues, all written in Naples in the final two years of his life. *Eclogue I* (1534–5) portrays a pair of love-sick shepherds bemoaning the unfaithfulness or loss of their respective shepherdesses; the second couple, Nemoroso and Elisa, have often been interpreted as Garcilaso lamenting the death in childbirth of Isabel Freire, an identification to which the poet seems to allude in *Eclogue III*; the poem ends with a remarkable evocation of the Neoplatonic idea of a love that can transcend death. *Eclogue II* (1533), which was written before *Eclogue I*, is a long poem (1,885 lines), or perhaps a play, about the unrequited love of the shepherd Albanio for the shepherdess Camila; in this poem Nemoroso describes his own all-consuming love, which is cured by Salicio, his shepherd friend. The characters are sometimes leadenly identified with Garcilaso's circle (he is Nemoroso, Salicio is a Neapolitan friend or perhaps Boscà, the duke of ALBA is Albanio, and the duke's tutor Fra Severo Varini appears as himself), but the poem transcends such reductive identifications to articulate at a wider level the grief felt in the aftermath of the premature death of someone who has been intensely loved. Perhaps the most profound transformation of this intensity into elegant classical imagery occurs in *Eclogue III* (1536), which returns to the death of Elisa and the grief of Nemoroso by recounting the weaving of a tapestry of tragic loves by the river-nymphs of the Tagus.

Garcilaso's poems were published together with those of Boscà as *Las obras de Boscan y algunas de Garcilaso de la Vega repartidas en quatro libros* (Barcelona, 1543), typeset in a roman fount that was an innovation in the printing of Spanish vernacular books. The first three books contain poems by Boscà, and book 4 consists of markedly superior poems by Garcilaso. In the historiography of SPANISH LITERATURE, the publication of the poems of Boscà and Garcilaso is deemed to inaugurate the Golden Age (SIGLO DE ORO) of literature.

Daniel Heiple, *Garcilaso de la Vega and the Italian Renaissance* (1994).

**GARCILASO DE LA VEGA, EL INCA** (1539–1616), historian of Peru and Florida, born in Cuzco, the son of the conquistador Sebastián de la Vega and the Inca princess Isabel Chimpu Ocllo; he is known as 'El Inca Garcilaso', which was his usual signature. On the death of his father, he travelled to Spain in 1560 in an unsuccessful attempt to claim his inheritance. He became a soldier and fought against the Moors, but incurred the enmity of PHILIP II and was imprisoned at Valladolid. He subsequently took holy orders, and died in Spain in 1616.

El Inca Garcilaso translated into Spanish the *Dialoghi d'amore* of LEONE EBREO (Madrid, 1590) and wrote a history of Florida, *La Florida del Inca* (Lisbon, 1605). His most important work as ethnographer and historian was his two-part *Comentariois reales*: part I, *Del origen de los Incas, reyes que fueron del Perú*, was published in Lisbon in 1608 (though the title page says 1609), and part II, the *Historia general del Perú*, was published in Córdoba in 1617.

J. Fitzmaurice-Kelly, *El Inca Garcilaso de la Vega* (1921); R. Porras-Barrenechea, *El Inca Garcilaso en Montilla, 1561–1614* (1955); J. G. Varner, *El Inca: The Life and Times of Garcilaso de la Vega* (1968); D. G. Castanien, *El Inca Garcilaso de la Vega* (1969).

**GARDENS.** The renaissance of garden art was inaugurated by ALBERTI's publication of *De re aedificatoria* in 1452, and first implemented in ITALIAN GARDENS near Florence. With the construction of the BELVEDERE COURT and the Villa MADAMA, the centre of garden art and architecture shifted from Florence to Rome, and in the early sixteenth century Roman gardens became the model for the rest of Italy and, at a later stage, the rest of Europe. Italian influence was often mediated through FRENCH GARDENS, which differed from their Italian originals in that they tended to be flat rather than terraced, and used water on a more modest scale. In the north, DUTCH GARDENS and FLEMISH GARDENS exercised an influence all over northern Europe; they differed from their Italian originals in their repudiation of the exuberant paganism of Italian statuary and in the intricate detail in which beds were laid out. Elsewhere in Europe, the impact of Renaissance design can be seen in BOHEMIAN AND MORAVIAN GARDENS, ENGLISH GARDENS, GERMAN GARDENS, HUNGARIAN GARDENS, POLISH

GARDENS, PORTUGUESE GARDENS, SCOTTISH GARDENS, and SPANISH GARDENS.

The plants in Renaissance gardens were usually secured from the BOTANICAL GARDENS of Europe, of which the first were at Padua and Pavia; in the late sixteenth century a botanical garden was established in Leiden, and it soon became the most important source of exotic plants in Europe.

Marie Luise Gothein, *Geschichte der Gartenkunst* (2 vols., 1914), trans. and expanded as *A History of Garden Art* (2 vols., 1928); T. Comito, *The Idea of the Garden in the Renaissance* (1977); V. Vercelloni, *European Gardens: An Historical Atlas* (1990).

**GARDINER, STEPHEN** (c.1485–1555), English bishop and statesman. Master of Trinity Hall, Cambridge (1525–49), and bishop of Winchester from 1531, Gardiner was a prominent churchman and minister under HENRY VIII, for whom he undertook diplomatic missions in Henry's attempt to secure a divorce from CATHERINE OF ARAGON. Although he initially accepted the royal supremacy, he was conservative in religious matters, promoting the Six ARTICLES and opposing the more reformist policy of CROMWELL. By the 1540s he was regarded as the chief opponent of reformist opinion amongst church leaders. He lost his bishopric and was imprisoned under EDWARD VI but was restored under MARY, and made lord chancellor.

*DNB.*

**GARIGLIANO, BATTLE OF** (29 December 1503). At a crossing on the river Garigliano (or Liri) 15 kilometres (9 miles) east-north-east of Gaeta, a French army that had invaded Italy with a view to reconquering Naples was defeated by a Spanish army commanded by Gonzalo FERNÁNDEZ DE CÓRDOBA. The victory left the entire kingdom of NAPLES in Spanish hands. The casualties included Piero II de' MEDICI, who was drowned whilst fighting on the side of the French.

**GARNIER, ROBERT** (1534–90), French playwright and poet. He was born in La Ferté-Bernard and studied law at Toulouse, after which he became a provincial magistrate. He wrote seven tragedies, a tragicomedy based on ARIOSTO's *Orlando furioso* (*Bradamante*, 1582), and a small number of poems (notably *Hymne de la monarchie*, 1567). Of the seven tragedies, all of which are constructed on the SENECAN model, one is biblical (*Les Juives*, 1583), three are based on Greek tragedies and their Roman adaptations (*Hippolyte*, 1573; *La Troade*, 1579; *Antigone*, 1580), and three on Roman history (*Porcie*, 1568; *Cornélie*, 1574; *Marc-Antoine*, 1578).

*DBF*; J. Holyoake, *A Critical Study of the Tragedies of Robert Garnier* (1987).

**GAROFALO or Benvenuto Tisi** (1481–1559), Italian painter. He studied in Cremona, and after periods in Venice and Rome settled in Ferrara, where he worked with Dosso DOSSI and executed paintings for the churches of the duchy (e.g. *Madonna of the Clouds*, c.1514, Pinacoteca Nazionale, Ferrara). The onset of blindness forced him to retire from painting in 1550.

*MDA*; Anna Maria Fioravanti Baraldi, *Il Garofalo: Benvenuto Tisi, pittore* (1992); Louisa Ciammitti (ed.), *Garofalo e Dossi* (1998).

**GASCA, PEDRO DE LA** (1485–1567), Spanish inquisitor and colonial governor, educated at the universities of Alcalá and Salamanca; he pursued a career in the Church which culminated in his appointment to the Council of the INQUISITION. In 1547 la Gasca was sent by the Emperor CHARLES V to Peru as the first president of the Court of Justice (Audiencia), in which capacity he suppressed the rebellion of Gonzalo PIZARRO. After executing Pizarro for treason, la Gasca consolidated the Spanish conquest of Peru and extended Spanish domination to the south. In 1550 he returned to Spain, where he became bishop of Palencia and then bishop of Sigüenza.

*DHE*; Teodoro Hampe Martínez, *Don Pedro de la Gasca: Su obra política en España y América* (1989).

**GASCOIGNE, GEORGE** (c.1534–1577), English author. Educated at Cambridge, Gascoigne worked for over a decade as a lawyer, and served as a soldier in the Low Countries between 1572 and 1574. His *Posies of George Gascoigne* (1574) collects secular and devotional verses, two plays (a tragedy, *Jocasta*, and a comedy, *Supposes*), and a novella, *The Adventures of Master F. J.* Other writings include *The Glass of Government* (1575), *The Drum of Doomsday* (1576) and *The Steel Glass* (1576), a verse satire.

*DNB.*

**GASPARINO DA BARZIZZA.** See BARZIZZA, GASPARINO DA.

**GASTOLDI, GIOVANNI GIACOMO** (c.1555–1622), Italian composer active in Mantua where, in 1588, he became *maestro di cappella*. The popularity of his ballettos was also shared by his sacred music which, in keeping with Counter-Reformation views, he believed should be accessible. He also composed music for GUARINI's *Il pastor fido* and *L'idropica* which was one of the *intermedi* at the Gonzaga wedding of 1608, when MONTEVERDI's *Ananna* was also performed.

**GATTAMELATA, II, or Erasmo da Narni** (1370–1443), Paduan *condottiere* who fought in the service of Florence and the papacy before accepting a Venetian command in 1434. For the rest of his life he fought for Venice in the war against the VISCONTI of Milan. His boldness was epitomized by a famous incident in 1438–9, in which he brought 30 Venetian vessels (including five galleys) up the Adige and then hauled them 10 kilometres (6 miles) over land from Mori to Lake Garda in order to launch a surprise attack on Milan's transport vessels and warships; in the event, the attack failed.

The origin of Erasmo's nickname ('Tabby Cat') is unknown, but could refer to stealth or to some aspect of his appearance. At his death he was Venice's captain-general. Venice mounted a state funeral in his honour and his family commissioned an equestrian statue from DONATELLO, who had recently arrived in Padua. The commission, together with separately commissioned marble reliefs and bronze figures (including the bronze crucifix) for the high altar, kept

Donatello in Padua for ten years; the statue now stands outside the Basilica del Santo.

DBI s.v. Erasmo; G. Eroli, *Erasmo Gattamelata da Narni* (1897).

**GATTINARA, MERCURINO DI** (1465–1530) Italian imperial counsellor. He entered the service of MARGARET OF AUSTRIA in 1501, and when she became regent of the Netherlands in 1507 became her counsellor and one of her ambassadors. In 1519 Mercurino helped to secure the election of CHARLES V as king of the Romans, and subsequently remained in the imperial court as a counsellor. His opposition to France during the electoral process remained the basis of his advice for the rest of his career, and after the battle of PAVIA (1525) he was aggrieved at the leniency shown to King FRANCIS I. He was created cardinal by Pope CLEMENT VII in 1529.

DBI.

**GAUFFERING**, a technique in BOOKBINDING in which the gilded edges of a book are decorated with the use of heated finishing tools. The technique was introduced in the mid-sixteenth century in France, where binders used pointed tools which they had heated to create dotted designs.

**GAZA or Gazes, THEODORE** (c.1415–1475/6), Greek scholar in Italy. Gaza was born in Thessaloniki, and may have lived there in the first half of his life, of which little is known. The city surrendered to Venice in 1423, and the Venetian occupation may have occasioned Gaza's first contacts with Italy. He left Thessaloniki shortly before it fell to Murat II on 29 May 1430 and in about 1440 he settled in Italy. He became lecturer in Greek at Ferrara; his pupils are often said to include Rudolfus AGRICOLA, the father of German humanism, but in fact Agricola arrived in Ferrara long after Gaza had left, and possibly after he had died. At Ferrara Gaza delivered a seminal oration on the importance of Greek studies, arguing that the study of Greek was a valuable preparation for public life.

In 1451 Gaza moved to Rome, where he joined the circle of BESSARION. He had come to Rome as one of the group of Greek translators assembled by Pope NICHOLAS V, and there translated Theophrastus, ARISTOTLE, and pseudo-Alexander of Aphrodisias into Latin and CICERO's *De senectute* into Greek. Gaza's attempt to reconcile Aristotle's notion of substance with Christian theology occasioned an exchange of polemics with PLETHO, who was a committed Platonist. When Gaza wrote a treatise on the history of the Turks (in the form of an epistle to Francesco FILELFO), he again attacked Pletho, this time about the nature of history: Pletho had depicted the Ottoman conquest as the revenge of fate for Alexander the Great's earlier conquest; Gaza demurred, and, in appealing to sources such as the history of the Turks by the eleventh-century chronicler John Skylitzes, contributed significantly to the development of analytical historical criticism.

In 1455 Gaza moved to Naples, where he lived until 1458, enjoying the patronage of ALFONSO V; during this period he translated some of the sermons of Chrysostom and Aelian's *Tactica*. He remained in southern Italy in the late 1450s and early 1460s, and then returned to Rome until 1474, when he left for Policastro (in Calabria), where he died. The most popular work of his later life was a primer on Greek grammar (the *Eisagogé*), which was praised by ERASMUS and consulted by humanists all over Europe; the major scholarly work of his later years was a translation of Aristotle's zoological works, which he dedicated to Pope SIXTUS V.

D. J. Geanakoplos, 'Theodore Gaza, a Byzantine Scholar of the Palaeologan "Renaissance" in the Italian Renaissance', *Medievalia et humanistica*, 12 (1984); J. Irmscher, 'Theodoros Gazes als griechischer Patriot', *Parole del passato*, 78 (1961).

**GEERTGEN TOT SINT JANS** ('Little Gerard of the Brethren of St John') **or Geertgen van Haarlem** (*fl.* 1475–95), Dutch painter, born in Leiden. He probably trained in the studio of Albert van OUWATER in Haarlem, where he subsequently worked for the religious ORDER from which his name is taken. His only surviving documented works are two panels from an altarpiece painted for the Order's church, the *Lamentation of Christ* and the *Burning of the Bones of St John the Baptist* (both now in the Kunsthistorisches Museum in Vienna). These paintings depict brightly painted figures against landscape backgrounds; the doll-like features of the female figures are the most distinctive feature of Geertgen's style. The small canon of some fifteen pictures attributed to Geertgen on stylistic grounds includes a *Nativity at Night* in the National Gallery in London.

MDA; NNBW x.

**GEIGENWERK**, a bowed keyboard instrument invented in Nuremberg in 1575 by Hans Haiden. In principle it was similar to a hurdy-gurdy. It was similar to a large harpsichord in appearance and had wire or gut strings that were drawn against five parchment-covered, treadle-driven wheels. Haiden claimed that the sounds produced by this 'bowing' technique could be enhanced through varying dynamics and even vibrato.

**GEILER VON KAYSERSBERG, JOHANN** (1445–1510), German preacher, born in Schaffhausen (which had not yet joined the SWISS CONFEDERATION), on 16 March 1445, and educated at Ammerschwihr (German Ammerschweier) (between Colmar and Kaysersberg, from which he derived his name) and, from 1460, the University of Freiburg im Breisgau. From 1465 to 1471 he lectured on Peter Lombard and ARISTOTLE at Freiburg, and immersed himself in the study of the mystic and conciliarist Jean le Charlier de Gerson (1363–1429), who was an important influence on his thinking and whose works he was later to edit (4 vols., 1488–1502). Geiler was ordained as a priest in 1470, and in 1471 he moved to Basel, where he lectured on theology and preached in the cathedral until 1476, when he returned to Freiburg as professor and, a few months later, rector.

In 1478 Geiler abandoned his academic life and became a preacher in the cathedral at Strasbourg, where he worked until his death on 10 March 1510; the chapel in which he was to preach proved too small for the crowds that wanted to hear Geiler preach, and in 1481 a Flamboyant GOTHIC pulpit which is still in the church was erected for him in the nave.

His vivid and denunciatory sermons, which survive in transcriptions taken down by his listeners, evince the mysticism of Gerson and the zeal of a SAVONAROLA (hence Geiler's posthumous epithet 'the German Savonarola'). His sermons include a series based on Sebastian BRANT's Ship of Fools (Narrenschiff) which was later translated from Latin to German by Johannes PAULI.

NDB; E. J. Dempsey Douglass, *Justification in Late Medieval Preaching: A Study of John Geiler of Keisersberg* (2nd edn., 1989).

**GELLI, GIAMBATTISTA** (1498–1563), Italian cobbler, playwright, translator, and champion of the vernacular, born in Florence, where as a young man he worked as a cobbler while studying Latin and philosophy. He secured the patronage of Duke Cosimo de' MEDICI, with whose assistance he helped to found the Florentine Academy, where he became the official commentator on Dante (1553). Gelli was an advocate of living, colloquial Italian, and strove to capture that idiom in his writing. His works include ten moral essays written in the voice of a cooper (*I capricci di Giusto bottaio*, 1546) and *La Circe* (1549), a conversation between Homer's Ulysses and his eleven companions whom Circe had transformed into animals (in *Odyssey* 10); with the exception of the elephant, the animals all decline the opportunity to forsake their contented animal state in order to return to the miseries of human life.

DBI s.v. Gelli, Giovan Battista; A. L. de Gaetano, *Giambattista Gelli and the Florentine Academy: The Rebellion against Latin* (1976).

**GELOSI, I**, a prominent COMMEDIA DELL'ARTE company which first visited France in 1571. Six years later the company returned to France, and, after playing before King HENRI III at Blois, went on to perform in Paris, where they inaugurated a long tradition of Italian actors playing in Paris. The company returned to Paris in 1602, but the principal actress, Isabella Canale, writer of poetry and a pastoral play *Mirtilli*, died on the return journey, whereupon her husband Francesco Andreini disbanded the troupe.

C. Cairns (ed.), *The 'Commedia dell'arte' from the Renaissance to Dario Fo* (1989).

**GEMMA FRISIUS, REINERUS** (1508–55), Frisian cartographer, astronomer, mathematician, and physician who studied at the University of Louvain, where he was appointed professor of medicine in 1541.

In 1530 Gemma published *De principiis astronomiae et cosmographiae*, in which he addressed the traditional navigational problem of establishing longitude by proposing the use of portable clocks, which at the time was a completely unreasonable proposition since even the best mechanical clocks were unreliable; two centuries later astronomers were amazed when the use of a clock proved to be realistic. In 1533 Gemma published the *Cosmographia* of Petrus APIANUS, into which he incorporated his own 'short treatise on a method for delineating places' (*Libellus de locorum describendorum ratione*); the method that he had devised was triangulation. Gemma also published a map of the world (*Charta sive mappa mundi*, 1540), a treatise on the ASTROLABE (*De astrolabio*, 1556),

and an immensely popular book on arithmetic (*Arithmeticae practicae methodus facilis*, 1540; another 58 editions before 1600); he also made GLOBES and astronomical instruments.

DSB; NNBW vi; G. Kish, *Medecina, Mensura, Mathematica: The Life and Work of Gemma Frisius* (1967).

**GEMS AND DIAMONDS**. Gems are precious stones from a small number of mineral species, including corundums (e.g. sapphire, ruby, emerald, oriental amethyst), feldspars (e.g. moonstone), beryls (e.g. beryl, chrysoberyl, emerald, aquamarine), and quartzes (e.g. agate, amethyst, chalcedony, jasper, onyx, ROCK CRYSTAL, sardonyx). Gems are distinguished from diamonds, which consist of pure carbon crystallized into regular octahedrons, and from JET, which is fossilized driftwood.

Diamonds and the hardest corundums, such as rubies and sapphires, were considered too hard to be cut until the fifteenth century, when diamonds were first cut into a pyramidical shape known as a 'diamond point' or *point naïve*; the top of the diamond (known to lapidaries as the 'table') was sometimes flattened with a grindstone, and by the sixteenth century the 'table cut' was in use all over Europe for diamonds and gems. The modern 'rose cut', in which the table is replaced by a ring of six triangular facets rising to a single point and the surrounding crown consists of a further eighteen facets, was introduced in France in the mid-seventeenth century.

Engraved gems are either INTAGLIOS, with the design cut into the stone, or CAMEOS, with the design in relief; the art of engraving gems is sometimes called 'glyptics' or 'glyptography'. The principal centre of gem-engraving was Milan. Milanese gems were sold all over Europe, and collectors included Pope PAUL II, Lorenzo de' MEDICI, and the Emperor RUDOLF II. Gems were valued for their natural beauty and for their craftsmanship, which sometimes aspired to virtuosity, as in the crowded intaglio *The Education of Bacchus* (fancifully known as the Signet of Michelangelo because its design derives from the Sistine Chapel) in the Bibliothèque Nationale in Paris; they were also valued for their magical and medicinal properties. Diamond-cutting was the particular province of JEWS, particularly the Jewish communities in Amsterdam and Antwerp.

**GENEVA** or (French) **Genève** or (German) **Genf** or (Italian) **Ginevra** or (classical Latin) **Genava** or (medieval Latin) **Gebenna**, which was known in Renaissance Latin as Geneva, has since 1815 been a city and canton in Switzerland, but from 1290 to 1530 was a semi-autonomous French-speaking part of SAVOY, and not a member of the SWISS CONFEDERATION, which was essentially German and German-speaking.

The rights and privileges of the citizens of Geneva were codified in 1387, and thereafter the city was in effect ruled by its prince-bishop. Amadeus VIII of Savoy attempted to buy Geneva from its bishop, but the offer was refused by both the bishop and the citizens. When Amadeus eventually became the antipope FELIX V, he appointed himself to the vacant see of Geneva (1444), which he retained after resigning the papacy in 1449 until his death in 1451. For the next 80 years (1451–1522) the bishopric was held almost continuously by members of the house of Savoy.

The fairs of Geneva, which were established in the thirteenth century, were from the early fifteenth century the principal outlet for the cloth manufactured in Freiburg (which was then independent of the Swiss Confederation), and by the mid-fifteenth century had grown into one of Europe's most important trading institutions. In 1462 Duke Louis of Savoy persuaded his son-in-law King LOUIS XI of France to forbid French merchants to attend the Geneva fairs and to change the dates of the fairs at LYON to coincide with those at Geneva. These sanctions caused a rapid economic decline that was exacerbated by the need to pay the Swiss army for the defence of the city against the ambitions of Duke Louis.

The struggle for control of Geneva became more acute after 1519, when the syndic of the city was executed for signing a formal accord with Freiburg (which had joined the Swiss Conferation in 1481). Thereafter the citizens of Geneva were divided into the supporters of the dukes of Savoy (the party of *Memelus* or Mamelukes) and the supporters of the link with Freiburg and the Swiss Confederation (the party of *Eidgenots*). In 1526 the Eidgenots managed to renew the link with Freiburg and negotiate an additional alliance with Bern (which had been part of the Swiss Confederation since 1353). The duke of Savoy was displeased and in 1530 decided to take the city by force, but the arrival of a large contingent of Swiss troops early in October forced him to capitulate, and on 19 October he signed the Treaty of Saint-Julien, in which he undertook to respect the autonomy of Geneva.

In 1533 Guillaume FAREL settled in Geneva and began to preach the Reformation. Bern supported the Reformation, but Freiburg dissented, and in 1534 withdrew from the alliance, so precipitating yet another attack by the duke of Savoy. On 10 August 1535 Geneva formally adopted the Protestant faith, and on 21 May 1536 a programme to implement religious reform was ratified. Two months later Jean CALVIN arrived from France, and quickly became an ally of Farel. Both Farel and Calvin were expelled in 1538; Farel never returned, but Calvin was recalled in September 1541, and quickly established a theocratic government which he administered with a strong hand (burning SERVETUS in 1553) until his death in 1564, when he was succeeded by Theodore BEZA. In 1559 Calvin founded the Genevan ACADEMY (of which the first rector was Beza), the antecedent institution of the University of Geneva (1873).

In 1564 Bern restored Geneva to the duke of Savoy, who tried to bring the city back to Catholicism. The struggle continued until December 1602, when FRANÇOIS DE SALES was appointed bishop of Geneva; the appointment was symbolic (since 1523 the bishops of Geneva had lived in exile in Annecy), but was followed within a few days by a surprise attack on Geneva by the forces of Duke CARLO EMANUELE I of Savoy, who on the night of 11/12 December 1602 tried to capture Geneva; the attack is known as the *Escalade* because ladders were used to scale the city walls. The 83-year-old Beza assembled the victorious citizens of Geneva in the cathedral, where they sang Psalm 124, which is still sung on the anniversary of the attack. On 21 July 1603 Duke CARLO EMANUELE signed the Peace of Saint-Julien, which marked the end of the period of Savoyard domination which had begun in 1290.

**GENEVAN CATECHISM**, the term given to two separate catechisms drafted by Jean CALVIN. The *Catechismus Genevensis prior* issued early in 1537 was a distillation of the doctrine of Calvin's *Institutes*, published in French as *Instruction et confession de foi dont on use en l'Église de Genève*; the formal Confession of Faith which was published in the spring (on 27 April) was either the work of Calvin or of Guillaume FAREL. All inhabitants of Geneva were required to submit to the teaching of both documents. As this catechism did not insist on Trinitarianism as an essential part of the doctrine of GOD, it left some room for cautious dissent on this contentious issue.

The *Catechismus Genevensis*, which was also drafted by Calvin, was a question-and-answer catechism published in a French version in 1542 and in an official Latin version in 1545. This catechism was treated as a fundamental document of the Genevan theocracy. Its five sections outline the official positions on faith, the law, prayer, the Bible, and the SACRAMENTS.

**GENGA, GEROLAMO** (1476–1551), Italian painter and architect, born in Urbino, where he may have trained with Luca SIGNORELLI. In 1502 he accompanied PERUGINO to Florence; several years later he moved to Siena, where his attributed works include frescoes (now detached) of *The Ransoming of Prisoners* and *The Flight of Aeneas from Troy* (Pinacoteca, Siena). On returning to Urbino in 1522 he worked as a court painter and architect. His commissions for the DELLA ROVERE dukes of Urbino included the restoration and decoration of the Sforza Villa Imperiale (at Colle San Bartolo near Pesaro), to which he contributed stuccoed ceilings, MAIOLICA floors, and a fresco cycle (c.1529–32) extending over eight rooms. He subsequently built a second villa on the same site; this villa, which is known as the Della Rovere Villa Imperiale, was not completed until the early twentieth century.

DBI; MDA s.v. Genga, Girolamo.

**GENGENBACH, PAMPHILUS** (c.1480–c.1525), Swiss poet, playwright, and printer, a native of Basel and the author of several moralizing FASTNACHTSPIELE. As a printer he published Johann EBERLIN VON GÜNZBURG's *Fünfzehn Bundesgenossen* and other pro-Lutheran tracts. The anonymous author of *Die Totenfresser* (1521), who seems to have been Gengenbach, was a declared Lutheran who dramatized the Reformation commonplace that the ANTICHRIST could be identified with the pope.

NDB; R. Raillard, *Pamphilus Gengenbach und die Reformation* (1936).

**GENNADIOS II SCHOLARIOS** (c.1400/5–c.1472), Greek scholar, theologian, and patriarch, born in Constantinople. By 1438 he had been appointed teacher of theology (διδάσκαλος) at Hagia Sophia, senator (σύγκλητος), and one of the four 'universal judges' (κριταὶ καθολικοι) of the empire. He attended the COUNCIL OF FLORENCE as a delegate representing the view of those who advocated the reunion of the Byzantine and Roman churches, but by 1444 had defected to the side of those opposed to the union and become leader of the anti-unionist party. This change of allegiance led to his dismissal from his various ecclesiastical offices, whereupon he took monastic vows and entered the Charsianeites monastery, which was at an unknown location in or near Constantinople. He was captured by the Turks in 1453, and on his release served three times as patriarch of Constantinople (1454–6, 1463, 1464–5); between his patriarchies he lived in the Prodromos monastery near Serres (modern Serrai, north-east of Thessaloniki), where he died.

Gennadios sought an accommodation with the Turks, and his voluminous theological writings include expositions of Christian theology prepared for Mehmet II, the conqueror of Constantinople. He had an excellent command of Latin and a learned interest in the scholasticism of the Roman Church. He wrote a polemic against PLETHO in defence of ARISTOTLE, and sought to incorporate the Aristotelianism of THOMAS AQUINAS into Byzantine theology.

*Œuvres complètes*, ed. L. Petit, X. A. Sidéridès, and M. Jugie (8 vols., 1928–36); C. J. Turner, 'The Career of George-Gennadius Scholarius', *Byzantion*, 39 (1969).

**GENOA or (Italian) Genova or (Latin) Genua or (French) Gênes**, a city, archiepiscopal see, and port in Liguria. The need to protect a burgeoning population meant that the line of circumvallation had to be extended three times between the twelfth and seventeenth centuries. The second extension (1320–30) was a 5-kilometre (3-mile) rampart which can still be traced through the modern city; the most recent fortifications (1626–32), which form a 20-kilometre (12-mile) line that rises to 500 metres (1,600 feet) on the hills surrounding the city, are centred on the fort at Sperone.

Medieval Genoa was politically weak but economically and militarily strong. It was, in common with its neighbours, divided by GUELF AND GHIBELLINE rivalries, and on occasion submitted to foreign authority to achieve civic stability. The long rivalry with Pisa was finally resolved when Genoa defeated Pisa in the naval battle of Meloria on 6 August 1284. In 1339 Genoa appointed its first doge, Simone BOCCANEGRA, who was sent into exile to Pisa in 1344, but returned to Genoa in 1356 to participate in the revolt against the VISCONTI FAMILY, and was reinstated as perpetual doge. A series of wars with Venice followed in the late fourteenth century, and although Genoa won the War of CHIOGGIA, it was Venetian rather than Genoese naval power that ruled the Mediterranean.

Genoa periodically secured a measure of internal accord by surrendering its civic authority to foreign governments, including Savoy (1382–3 and 1390–2), France (1396, 1499, and 1527), Monferrato (1409), and Milan (1463). Throughout this period, the most stable institution in Genoa was not the government, but the Banca di San Giorgio; in 1453 it was the bank rather than the government of Genoa that assumed control of CORSICA. Genoa became a reluctant participant in the WARS

OF ITALY, and in May 1522 was sacked by Spanish troops; in 1527 the city was retaken for France by Cesare FREGOSO, but in 1528 Andrea DORIA expelled the French and established a republic under imperial (Spanish) protection; the FIESCHI CONSPIRACY of 1547 threatened to topple the government, but in the event the republican constitution, which was a form of mercantile oligarchy, remained in place until the establishment of the Ligurian republic in the wake of the French Revolution.

The artistic culture of Renaissance Italy arrived late in Genoa, though there was a long tradition of humanist historians, culminating in Oberto FOGLIETTA and the Dominican scholar Agostino GIUSTINIANI. In the first quarter of the sixteenth century, the most important artist in Genoa was not an Italian, but the Fleming JOOS VAN CLEVE. Italian art became prominent through the patronage of Andrea Doria, who commissioned Pierino del VAGA to decorate the Palazzo DORIA PRINCIPE. In the 1550s the Perugian architect Galeazzo ALESSI designed magnificent palaces for the Genoese patriciate. The Cathedral of San Lorenzo is French Gothic, with French influence apparent in the triple portal and the rose window; the fifteenth-century Chapel of John the Baptist (which, under an edict of Pope INNOCENT VIII, women are forbidden to enter) is said to contain the bones of the saint, and the treasury in the archiepiscopal palace contains the Holy Grail (Sacro Catino), brought from Caesarea in 1101 and believed to have been given to Solomon by the queen of Sheba and later used by Jesus at the Last Supper.

J. Heers, *Gênes au XVᵉ siècle* (1961); M. Buongiorno, *Il bilancio di uno stato medievale: Genoa 1340–1529* (1973).

**GENRE PAINTING**, the art-historical term for pictures that depict scenes and subjects from everyday life. The French term *genre* was first used of paintings in eighteenth-century France, where it distinguished paintings that depicted scenes and subjects from everyday life from paintings that depicted subjects such as LANDSCAPE and STILL LIFE. The term was imported into English in the mid-nineteenth century. The publication of Jakob Burckhardt's lecture on *Netherlandish Genre Painting* in 1874 narrowed the meaning of the term, which is now used primarily with reference to the subject matter of Dutch painters.

The origins of genre painting lie in northern Europe, where the iconoclasm of the Reformation severely reduced the market for paintings with religious subjects. Painters such as Pieter AERTSEN and Pieter BRUEGEL the Elder portrayed peasants in their everyday surroundings, and so inaugurated a tradition that in the seventeenth century developed into the Dutch School of genre painters, who included Gerrit Dou, Pieter de Hooch, Gabriel Metsu, Adriaen van Ostade, Jan Steen, David Teniers, and Gerard Terborch, and reached its apogee in the paintings of Vermeer.

Genre painting came late to Italy, but at the end of the sixteenth century the characteristic subjects of genre painting began to appear in the paintings of CARAVAGGIO and the CARRACCI family.

Gentile da Fabriano, *The Adoration of the Magi* (1423), in the Uffizi, in Florence; the painting was the main panel of an altarpiece commissioned for the sacristy of the Church of Santa Trinita in Florence

**GENTILE DA FABRIANO** (*c*.1385–1427), Italian painter, born in Fabriano (Marches); by 1408 he was employed in Venice painting frescoes (now lost) for the Doge's Palace; his pupils in Venice included Jacopo BELLINI. His most important painting from his Venetian period is the polyptych of *The Coronation of the Virgin* (Brera, Milan). In 1413 Gentile entered the service of Pandolfo MALATESTA, and for the next five years lived in Brescia, where he painted frescoes in the chapel of the courthouse (fragments have recently been recovered). In 1420 Gentile moved to Florence, where in 1423 he painted *The Adoration of the Magi*, an altarpiece commissioned for the sacristy of the Church of Santa Trinita in Florence and now in the Uffizi; this painting is now regarded as one of the finest surviving examples of the INTERNATIONAL GOTHIC style in panel painting. In 1425 Gentile painted the Quaratesi Polyptych, of which the elegant *Madonna* is in the Royal Collection in London (on loan to the National Gallery), the saints in the Uffizi, and the predella panels in the Vatican (which has four) and the National Gallery in Washington (which has the fifth, *Pilgrims at the Tomb of St Nicholas*). Both pictures influenced the subsequent development of Florentine art.

In 1425 Gentile left Florence for Siena and Orvieto, and in 1427 moved to Rome, where he painted frescoes (now lost) in the Basilica of San Giovanni in Laterano.

*DBI* s.v. Gentile di Niccolò; *MDA* s.v. Gentile da Fabriano; Keith Christiansen, *Gentile di Fabriano* (1982).

**GENTILI, ALBERICO** (1552–1608), Italian jurist in Oxford. Gentili was born near Ancona and studied law at Perugia, but as a Protestant was exiled by the Inquisition. He arrived in Oxford in 1580. His Italian doctorate was incorporated as an Oxford DCL and he was appointed to a readership in law; in 1586 he was appointed, through the patronage of Walsingham, Regius professor of civil law. He retained his chair even after he began to practise as an advocate in London in 1590, leaving most of his teaching in the hands of deputies. He was admitted to Gray's Inn in 1600, and in 1605 became the permanent advocate of the Spanish crown.

Gentili was the founder of the discipline of international law, and the most important precursor of GROTIUS. In his reliance on principles of NATURAL LAW rather than theological principles and CANON LAW, Gentili became the first jurist to advocate wholly secular legal principles for the governance of relations between communities of nations.

Gentili wrote prolifically in a prose style that is prolix, imprecise, and obscure, but the breadth of his learning is irreproachable. His publications include dialogues on Roman law in which he attacks the humanist school of jurisprudence (*De iuris interpretibus*, 1582), an expanded version of an Oxford disputation at which Sir Philip SIDNEY was present (*De legationibus*, 1585), an important treatise on the law of war (*De iuri belli*, 1598), a collection of his notes on cases in which he represented Spain (*Hispanicae advocationis*, 1613), and a constitutional essay on the union of England and Scotland (*De unione Angliae et Scotiae*, 1605). The Bodleian Library in Oxford holds fifteen volumes of his manuscripts.

DNB; G. Molen, *Alberico Gentili and the Development of International Law* (rev. edn., 1968); Diego Panizza, *Alberico Gentili, giurista ideologo nell'Inghilterra elisabettiana* (1981).

**GENTILI, ANTONIO** (1519–1609), Italian silversmith, born in Faenza, the son of a goldsmith. He moved to Rome, where he was admitted to the guild in 1552, and served as assayer to the papal mint from 1586 to 1602, when he resigned in favour of his son Pietro. Gentili specialized in ecclesiastical silver, but very little of his work can now be identified.

In 1578, two years after the death of Manno SBARRI, Cardinal Alessandro FARNESE asked Gentili to complete the altar set (a cross and two monumental candlesticks) which Sbarri had been making for St Peter's. Gentili completed the task and signed the altar set before it was placed in the sacristy of St Peter's in 1582, but his precise role in this collaborative work has been the subject of scholarly debate.

The only silverwork known to be entirely Gentili's own work is the silver binding of the Farnese Hours, a Book of Hours painted by Giulio CLOVIO for Cardinal Alessandro Farnese and now in the Pierpont Morgan Library in New York.

MDA.

**GEOMETRY** was one of the four mathematical sciences of the QUADRIVIUM taught in universities, where geometry was perceived as finding its application in ASTRONOMY. Geometry was taught from EUCLID's *Elements*, which had been used continuously since ancient times; study did not usually extend beyond the first three or four books of the work, which deal with theorems relating to triangles (Pythagoras' theorem is proved in *Elements* book 1, proposition 47) and circles. The new techniques of PERSPECTIVE construction, which were based on the old geometrical optics taught in universities, used no new mathematics at all, but only results from Euclid.

It was mainly outside universities that, in the sixteenth century, humanists began to concern themselves with the recovery of Greek mathematical texts that, unlike those of Euclid, had largely dropped out of use in the Latin West. The work of some scholars, such as Francesco Maurolico, tended to produce interpretations of texts, or commentaries on them, but later the editions of COMMANDINO set a standard for separating editing from rewriting. These editions were in use for centuries afterwards. The recovery of more advanced Greek work at first stimulated attempts to reconstruct the parts that still seemed to be missing; for instance the final four books of the *Conica* of Apollonius (Commandino edition 1566), whose content had been described briefly by Pappus in his *Mathematical Collection* (Commandino edition 1588), attracted attention from VIÈTE and SNEL, who reconstructed the missing theorems, as well as from KEPLER, who made use of the *Conica* in his work on OPTICS (1604) in connection with the geometry of burning mirrors. However, the radically new results of Kepler's work on the orbit of Mars (1609) were obtained by the use of Euclid, and G. B. BENEDETTI's new theorems about conic sections (1574) use ARCHIMEDES and Euclid.

It was certainly the recovery of works by Archimedes (Commandino edition 1558) that had most effect upon Renaissance mathematics and indeed upon the development of what is now called Science. In particular, Archimedes' method of finding the area of a circle by using successive approximations, drawing a series of polygons inside the figure and outside it, lay behind the invention by Kepler, Cavalieri (c.1598–1647), and others of the 'method of indivisibles' that led to the invention of the differential calculus in the seventeenth century. The algebraic geometry of Descartes's *Géometrie* (1637) is also partly indebted to ancient work.

In ABACUS SCHOOLS, the study of geometry took third place after ARITHMETIC and ALGEBRA, and was mainly confined to results about triangles that would be useful for SURVEYING. There is, however, no use of angles; all problems are set and solved in terms of lengths, which no doubt reflects low-level surveying practice. The abacus tradition is important for seeing the beginnings of treating geometrical problems in three dimensions, instead of reducing them to two as was the ancient practice. The pattern is well seen in the rediscovery of the Archimedean polyhedra. These are solids which have faces that are regular polygons, meeting in the same way at each corner of the solid, and a list of them, identified only by the types and numbers of faces, is given by Pappus, who ascribed their discovery to Archimedes. The rediscovery of the solids in the Renaissance proceeds largely through the work of painters, important parts being played by PIERO DELLA FRANCESCA and by DÜRER, the mathematicians involved being PACIOLI (who in this case may have had some help from LEONARDO DA VINCI) and Daniele BARBARO. So the solids reappear from the practical tradition, but the final mathematical work, providing illustrations of all thirteen solids and proving there are exactly thirteen with such properties, comes from Kepler (1619). One of the important ways in which the Renaissance tradition of practical mathematics was to influence the learned one was by making geometers think in three dimensions.

**GEORG DER BÄRTIGE or George the Bearded or Georg von Sachsen** (1471–1539), duke of Saxony, succeeded his father ALBRECHT III ANIMOSUS as duke in 1500. In the early years of his rule Georg supported both ecclesiastical reform and humanist culture. His experience of the LEIPZIG

DISPUTATION, at which he participated in the debate with Martin LUTHER, turned Georg against the Reformation. In 1525 he was instrumental in suppressing the PEASANTS' REVOLT at the battle of Frankenhausen.

In the course of Georg's long rule he enriched his treasury with the income from the Saxon mining industry and shifted power away from the ESTATES and towards the ducal administration. He remained faithful to the Catholic Church, but on his death his brother Heinrich opened Saxony to Lutheranism.

*NDB* s.v. Georg von Sachsen.

## GEORGE OF PODĚBRADY (1420–71), king of Bohemia,

was born into a noble family in Poděbrady (east of Prague). He became leader of the UTRAQUIST party and in 1448 captured Prague. He ruled Bohemia as regent for the young LADISLAS POSTHUMUS until 1453, when Ladislas was crowned. Four years later Ladislas died and George was elected as his successor.

The papacy and the Holy Roman Empire were alarmed at the election of an Utraquist king: Pope PIUS II planned a crusade against George and on 23 December 1466 Pope PAUL II excommunicated him. In 1465 the Emperor FRIEDRICH III and the emperor's son-in-law MATTHIAS CORVINUS of Hungary began to mount a series of military attacks and to sponsor armed risings. In 1469 Matthias managed to secure the support of the Catholic nobility of Bohemia for his claim to the throne, and captured much of Moravia, where he was crowned as a rival king of Bohemia on 3 May 1469. George nonetheless managed to retain his throne and to name as his successor LADISLAS II, son of King Casimir IV of Poland. In popular Czech historiography George of Poděbrady is honoured as the country's only Czech monarch.

*BLBL*; *NDB* s.v. Georg von Podiebrad.

## GEORGE OF TREBIZOND or Giorgios Trapezountios

(1396–1472/3), Greek humanist scholar in Italy. George was born in Crete, which was then a Venetian dependency, into a family which had originally come from Trebizond (now Trabzon, in Turkey). The juxtaposition of Greek and Latin cultural traditions in fifteenth-century Crete facilitated a high degree of biculturalism, which made George an unusually able mediator between the two cultures. He migrated to Italy *c.*1416 and converted to Catholicism in 1426. He taught Greek in Vicenza, Venice, and Rome, and later attended the COUNCIL OF FLORENCE in the service of the papacy; he was subsequently employed as a secretary in the papal curia. In 1465 he travelled to Constantinople on a mission to convert Mehmet II, the conqueror of Constantinople, but his embassy was unsuccessful, and he failed even to meet Mehmet; when he returned to Rome in 1466 he imprudently sang the praises of Sultan Mehmet, and consequently was briefly imprisoned.

George translated ARISTOTLE, Demosthenes, PLATO, and the Cappadocian fathers (Basil the Great, Gregory of Nyssa, and Gregory of Nazianzus) into Latin; these translations were all attacked in various quarters; his translation of PTOLEMY'S *Almagest* was cautiously praised, but the accompanying commentary was vilified.

George's original writings included polemical and eschatological works. He championed Aristotle in a tract comparing Plato and Aristotle, and so drew the wrath of BESSARION, who replied with his polemical *Against the Detractor of Plato*. George, in his turn, attacked the Platonism of Bessarion, GAZA, and PLETHO, arguing that it was Aristotle who had anticipated Christian teachings such as creation *ex nihilo*, the immortality of the soul, and the Trinity. George's eschatological views are set out in his Greek treatise *On the Truth of the Christian Faith*, in which he envisages the Ottoman sultan converting to Christianity and conquering the world, an expectation arising out of his apocalyptic vision of a revived Roman Empire led by the pope fighting the Antichrist.

John Monfasani, *George of Trebizond: A Biography and a Study of his Rhetoric and Logic* (Leiden, 1976); *Collectanea Trapezuntiana: Texts, Documents and Bibliographies of George of Trebizond*, ed. John Monfasani (1984).

## GERALDINI FAMILY, a prominent family from Amelia, an

episcopal see in southern Umbria in the Papal State. In the fifteenth and sixteenth centuries the family produced a number of distinguished ecclesiastics, humanists, and servants of the papacy. Alessandro Geraldini (1455–1525) became a tutor to members of the Spanish royal family, including CATHERINE OF ARAGON, whom he accompanied to England for her marriage to Prince Arthur (elder son of King HENRY VII) and for her brief residence in Ludlow as princess of Wales. Geraldini's overenthusiastic account of the success of the marriage may have been a central reason for his subsequent fall from favour at the English and other courts, and his dispatch to Santo Domingo (1520) as the first (and probably reluctant) resident bishop in the New World. His *Itinerarium ad regiones sub aequinoctuali plaga constitutas* (eventually published in Rome in 1631) is an account of his journey and of his life in Santo Domingo; his tomb there is a fine example of the Spanish Renaissance style. Six other members of his clan are buried rather closer to home in the family chapel of Sant'Antonio in the Church of SS Filippo e Giacomo in Amelia; early memorials are the work of AGOSTINO DI DUCCIO.

E. Menesto (ed.), *Alessandro Geraldini e il suo tempo* (1993).

## GERARD, JOHN (1545–1612), English herbalist. He was born

in Nantwich (Cheshire) and after a period on the Continent settled in London to pursue a medical career. He joined the Company of Barber-Surgeons in 1595 and served as master in 1607. In 1596 Gerard published a list of the plants in his garden in Holborn (then a suburb of London); the following year he published the first edition of his *Herbal*, which in its analysis of wild and cultivated plants drew freely on the earlier work of DODOENS, L'OBEL, and TURNER (and borrowed woodcuts from a German herbal), but also contained many of his own observations and analyses. Gerard's *Herbal* was to remain the authoritative English work on the subject for two centuries.

*DNB*; *DSB*.

## GERHAERT VAN LEIDEN, NICOLAAS or (German)

**Nicolaus** (*fl.* 1462–73), Dutch sculptor in Strassburg (of which he became a citizen in 1464), Trier, Constance, Baden, and

Vienna; virtually nothing is known of his life, but the style of his warmly sympathetic portraits of contemporary and biblical figures is so distinctive that the canon of his work is relatively stable. His best-known work is the tomb of the Emperor FRIEDRICH III in St Stephen's Cathedral in Vienna.

*MDA; NDB; NDBA; NNBW x.*

**GERHARD, HUBERT** (*c.*1545–*c.*1620), Dutch sculptor in Germany who worked in the service of the FUGGER family in Augsburg (from 1581) and the WITTELSBACH ducal court in Munich (from 1584) and Innsbruck (from 1597). His surviving work includes the FOUNTAINS made for the city of Augsburg (Augustus Fountain, 1594) and for the Fugger castle (1583–95) at Kirchheim unter Teck (for which he also made many decorative fittings) and sculptures for the ducal Residenz in Munich.

*MDA; NDB; NNBW x.*

**GERHARD, JOHANN** (1582–1637), Lutheran theologian, polemicist, and devotional writer, born on 17 October 1582 in Quedlingburg. He studied philosophy and medicine at Wittenberg (1599–1603) and theology at Jena (1603–5). From 1606 to 1616 he worked in the duchy of Coburg as a teacher and ecclesiastical reformer. In 1616 he became a professor of theology at Jena, where he remained for the rest of his life and where he died on 17 August 1637.

Gerhard's two most important polemical works were *Confessionis catholicae* (4 vols. in 2, 1634–7), which seeks to support the AUGSBURG CONFESSION by drawing on the writings of Catholic theologians, and *Bellarminus ὀρθοδοξίας testis* (3 parts, 1631–3), a collection of 30 disputations in which Gerhard was involved; the volume pummels Catholicism and its principal champion, Roberto BELLARMINO, and also elucidates the differences between Catholic and Lutheran theology. His devotional manual, *Meditationes sacra* (1606), was for centuries regularly reprinted and translated into a variety of European languages, including German, English, Greek, and Swedish. Gerhard was also a learned student of BIBLICAL and PATRISTIC SCHOLARSHIP: his principal work in the former field was the completion of the harmony of the Gospels that had been left unfinished by Martin CHEMNITZ and Polycarp Leyser (*Harmonia Evangelistarum Chemnitio-Lyserianae*, 1627); his patristic writings were published posthumously by his son (*Patrologia*, 1653).

The process of refining LUTHER's theology which had begun with MELANCHTHON and continued with Martin Chemnitz culminated in Gerhard's vast *Loci communes theologici* (9 vols. in 10, 1610–22), which quickly achieved canonical status as the authoritative exposition of Lutheran theology. The scholasticism of Luther's methodology and terminology had in some measure been eroded by his successors, who had been influenced by Calvinist and Zwinglian formulations (while not acceding to their doctrinal content); Gerhard restored scholasticism to Lutheranism, and so created a theology that was Protestant in sentiment and in church discipline but in many respects close to Catholic thinking in dogma.

*NDB; J. A. Steiger, Johann Gerhard (1582–1637): Studien zu Theologie und Frömmigkeit des Kirchenvaters der Lutherischen Orthodoxie (1997).*

**GERMAN ARCHITECTURE.** The late Gothic (*Spätgotik*) architecture of late fourteenth- and fifteenth-century Germany took different forms in northern and southern Germany. In north Germany the preferred building material was brick, and the simplified Gothic of its churches and public buildings, notably the brick town halls in Thorn (now Polish Toruń), Lübeck, and Stralsund, is called *Backsteingotik*. The corresponding style in south Germany, Austria, and Bohemia is called *Sondergotik*, which finds its fullest expression in the hall churches of the PARLER FAMILY; in these churches the aisles are approximately the same height as the naves, and so the naves are lit from the windows of the aisles rather than from above; the preferred building material was stone, though Hans STETHAIMER chose to work in brick.

The transition from Gothic to Renaissance styles first becomes apparent in the work of Benedikt RIED VON PIESTING in the Vladislav Hall (1493–1502) of the Hradčany in Prague; this huge room (which was large enough for jousting tournaments) is roofed with Gothic rib vaults but decorated with Italian Renaissance motifs. Elsewhere in the German territories, the earliest example of the Italian Renaissance style is the FUGGER funeral chapel (Fuggerkapelle) in St Anne's Church in Augsburg (1509–18). The small number of monumental buildings in the Renaissance style included Schloss Hartenfelds in Torgau (1483–1622) and the Stadtresidenz at Landshut (1537–43), of which the Italian wing may be the work of GIULIO ROMANO.

In the second half of the sixteenth century, the imitation of Italian forms yielded to a distinctive German Renaissance style, which was characterized by the use of gables, of relatively short columns, and of a decorative style that derives as much from Flanders as from Italy. The most important surviving German Renaissance buildings are the town halls of Leipzig (1556), Altenburg (1562–4), Lemgo (1565–1612), Rothenburg ob der Tauber (1573–8), and Augsburg (1615–20, by Elias HOLL), the Plassenburg in Kulmbach (rebuilt in 1559), the eastern façade of the Gewandhaus (Linen Hall) in Brunswick (1592), the Pellerhaus in Nuremberg (1602–7, reduced to a shell during the Second World War and since rebuilt); the greatest of the lost buildings was the Neues Lusthaus in Stuttgart (1584–93) by George Beer (d. 1600) and Heinrich SCHICKHARDT. Contemporaneous with these buildings are syncretic German Renaissance buildings that incorporate elements from other architectural traditions: Schloss Johannisburg in Aschaffenburg (1605–14, reduced to a shell in 1944 and since rebuilt) is in some respects French, the Ottheinrichsbau in Heidelberg (1556–9) and the portico of the Town Hall in Cologne (1567–70) are both Flemish, as is the work of Pieter de WITTE, and many of the buildings of Hans KRUMPPER and Frederick SUSTRIS are distinctly Italianate, as is the Jesuit Michaelskirche in München (1583–97), which is modelled on the Order's Gesù Church in Rome.

H.-R. Hitchcock, *German Renaissance Architecture* (1981).

**GERMAN ART**. The state of Germany is a creation of the nineteenth century, and its antecedent state, the HOLY ROMAN EMPIRE, extended far beyond the borders of modern Germany. The establishment of the imperial court in Prague (where the first German university was built) led in the late sixteenth century to the emergence of Prague as the most important artistic centre in the Empire. Within what is now Germany the principal artistic centre was Nuremberg, which had strong commercial and artistic links with Italy; Augsburg, Basel (which joined the SWISS CONFEDERATION in 1501), and Cologne were the other important centres for the arts. Germany produced some of Europe's greatest painters, notably DÜRER and HOLBEIN; Germany was also the home of PRINTING and the principal European centre for ENGRAVING (including book illustrations).

The first signs of the influence of the Italian Renaissance on German art become apparent in the 1490s (Dürer first visited Italy in 1494), but the transition from Gothic to Renaissance styles is a phenomenon of the 1520s. During this period Mathias GRÜNEWALD painted the finest of Gothic paintings, the Isenheim altarpiece, but at the same time artists such as Holbein and CRANACH began to incorporate Italian elements into their work.

**GERMAN DRAMA**. In Germany as elsewhere in Europe, drama evolved out of the liturgy of the Church, the public entertainments of the festivals, and the recovery by HUMANISTS of the plays of classical antiquity.

In the course of the fourteenth and fifteenth centuries plays that had originally been performed in Latin and inside churches slowly developed into secularized vernacular plays that were performed outdoors in the churchyard or the market place. The plays that celebrated Christmas (the *Weihnachtsspiel*), Easter (the *Osterspiel*), and the Passion (*Passionsspiel*) became largely secular, and new semi-secular plays were written, most famously the *Spiel von Frau Jutten* (1480), a play about the legendary Pope Joan by the Alsatian Dietrich Schernberg. The *Passionsspiel* (1566) of the Augsburg Meistersinger Sebastian Wild was in 1634 incorporated into the *Oberammergauer Passionsspiel*, which since 1680 has been performed at ten-year intervals.

Alongside this drama of ecclesiastical origin, the sketches performed at festivals evolved, initially at Nuremberg, into the *FASTNACHTSPIEL*. It was in Nuremberg that indigenous German drama untouched by the classicism of the humanists survived well into the sixteenth century, most notably in the plays of Hans SACHS.

The first imitations of classical comedy were, like their originals, written in Latin, beginning with Jakob Wimpfeling's *Stylpho* (1470) and Johann REUCHLIN's *Scena progymnasmata sive Henna* (1497). In the sixteenth century the principal Latin dramatists, Thomas KIRCHMAIER and Nikodemus FRISCHLIN, also wrote vernacular plays and so inaugurated the use of classical genres in German plays.

In the early sixteenth century the biblical subject matter of religious drama was reshaped according to the conventions of classical drama, most notably in Protestant plays such as the *Parabell vam vorlorn Szohn* by Burkard WALDIS (1527) and the plays of the schoolmasters Sixtus Birck (1501–54) and Paul Rebhun (c.1505–1546).

In the late sixteenth century, troops of ENGLISCHE KOMÖDIANTEN began to visit Germany, beginning with the visit of Lord Leicester's players to Dresden in 1586. The presence of these players may account, at least in part, for the development of a more theatrical and less narrative drama in late sixteenth- and early seventeenth-century Germany. The direct influence of the English players can be discerned in the plays of Jakob AYRER and Duke HEINRICH JULIUS of Brunswick.

D. van Abbe, *Drama in Renaissance Germany and Switzerland* (1964).

**GERMAN GARDENS**. The Renaissance garden in Germany is confined to the few years between 1590 and the outbreak of the Thirty Years War in 1618; it was stimulated during this period both by travellers who had seen the gardens of Italy and by the translation into German of French and Italian books on gardening. In 1597 Johann Peschel published the first German book on gardening, which contains a series of garden plans with rectangular layouts and covered walks. The engraver Josef Furttenbach of Ulm (1591–1667) published designs for PARTERRES which combined French and Italian elements (*Architectura recreationis*, Augsburg, 1640); he was the first garden designer in Europe to advocate the use of a garden for the education of children, and so became the remote progenitor of Friedrich Froebel's *Kindergarten*.

Many German Renaissance gardens, including four important Italianate gardens in Munich, are known only from the descriptions provided by Philipp Hainhofer in his *Reise-Tagebuch* (travel diary) of 1612. Only one Renaissance garden within what is now Germany is fully documented, and that is the HORTUS PALATINUS at Heidelberg. In Austria, the chief Renaissance gardens are HELLBRUNN (near Salzburg), Ambras (near Innsbruck), and Neugebäude ('New Building', near Vienna). Ambras was the chateau of Archduke Ferdinand, second son of the Emperor FERDINAND I; it was described by a visitor in 1574 as a garden with large FOUNTAINS, TOPIARY, pergolas, GROTTOES, and a PAVILION for banqueting. The principal parterre was divided into nine squares, in the centre of which was another pavilion, mounted on pillars; this parterre is the only French element in what was otherwise an Italian garden in Innsbruck. Neugebäude, which was at first called 'The Pheasantry', was the garden of Maximilian, the elder son of the emperor (later MAXIMILIAN II); it was built in 1569 by an unknown designer who was probably Italian but could have been French; the upper garden was a square surrounded by an arcaded gallery with pavilions at the corners, laid out in sixteen parterres and decorated with fountains, and the lower garden fell away towards the Danube in four terraces.

BOTANICAL GARDENS were established at many universities, of which the most important were at Leipzig (1580) and Heidelberg (1593). One outstanding book to emerge from this tradition was Basil Besler's *Hortus Eystettensis* (2 vols., 1613), an enormous *florilegium* which depicted and labelled more than 1,000 plants in the botanical garden established on the Willibaldsburg by Johann Conrad von Gemmingen, bishop of Eichstätt.

Dieter Hennebo and A. Hoffman, *Geschichte der deutschen Gartenkunst* (3 vols., 1962–3).

**GERMAN LANGUAGE.** German is one of the West Germanic group of LANGUAGES. In the early modern period it was spoken beyond the borders of modern Germany and Austria in regions and states such as Alsace, Lorraine, Bohemia, Moravia, Livonia, Silesia, and the Tirol, and still survives in some of these regions; within what is now Germany the SORBS spoke (and continue to speak) Sorbian, a Slavonic language. The term *Deutsch* now denotes the German language, but for many centuries *Deutsche Sprache* encompassed cognate languages, including DUTCH and FRISIAN. In the early modern period, German consisted of two related languages, Early New High German and Low German.

Early New High German (*Frühneuhochdeutsch*) was the language of central and southern Germany from c.1350 to c.1650; it was the successor of Old High German (*Althochdeutsch*, c.770–c.1050) and Middle High German (*Mittelhochdeutsch*, c.1050–c.1350) and the predecessor of New High German (*Neuhochdeutsch*, c.1650 ff.). The spoken form of Middle High German was dialectally varied, but the written form was the standardized literary language of medieval German courtly literature. The early modern period saw the development of an official administrative language characterized by 'chancery style' (*Kanzleistil*); this 'chancery speech' (*Kanzleisprache*) developed dialects in the main administrative centres, and philologists speak of the *Kanzleisprachen* of cities such as Mainz, Meissen, Prague, and Vienna. Luther consciously used the chancery style of Saxony in his Bible, and so was instrumental in creating a new literary language; the wide dissemination of his Bible, even in Catholic areas, created a standardized literary language (*Schriftsprache*) throughout Germany. This literary language was not, however, free from dialectal variations: in 1593, Sebastian Helber, a Swiss schoolmaster and notary, distinguished three High German dialects used by printers (*Druckersprachen*): the printers of Leipzig, Erfurt, Nuremberg, Würzburg, Frankfurt, Mainz, Speyer, Strassburg, and (problematically) Cologne used what Helber termed *Mitteldeutsch*; the printers of south Germany, particularly Bavaria and Swabia, used the Augsburg dialect which Helber termed *Donauisch*; the third dialect, which Helber called *Höchst Rheinisch*, was used in the SWISS CONFEDERATION (and continued to be used there until the mid-seventeenth century).

The evolution of the German language was marked by two 'sound shifts' (*Lautverschiebungen*), which were changes in consonantal pronunciation. The first, in late antiquity, created Primitive Germanic out of Indo-European; the second (the *Zweite* or *Hochdeutsche Lautverschiebung*), which occurred between the fifth and tenth centuries, affected central and southern Germany, and created Old High German. Northern and western Germany were not affected by the second sound shift, and the language that evolved in those

areas is known as Low German; this is the language that evolved into more recent languages such as Dutch/Flemish, Frisian, Letzebürgisch, and, in some measure, English and Scots. Within Germany, Low German is known as *Plattdeutsch*, and now survives only as a collection of dialects; in the early modern period, however, the hegemony of Early New High German did not extend to northern Germany, where *Plattdeutsch* had both a written literary language (*Schriftsprache*) and an *Umgangssprache*, i.e. spoken language standardized amongst educated speakers. As a written language, however, Low German was a victim of Luther's success; the last Low German Bible was printed in 1621, and Low German was not revived as a literary language until the nineteenth century.

The first grammar of the German language was Johannes Clajus' *Grammatica Germaniae linguae* (1578).

**GERMAN LAW.** Germany did not enjoy a national system of law until the German Empire, the Second Reich, emerged at the conclusion of the Franco-Prussian War in 1871. Even the Holy Roman Empire, which the term 'second Reich' was meant to evoke, remained legally diverse from its inception in 800 until its demise in 1806. The German lands at the heart of the Empire were governed in the thirteenth and fourteenth centuries by formulations of CUSTOMARY LAW, which began with the *Sachsenspiegel* of Eike von Repgow (c.1230), elements of which are still echoed in German CIVIL LAW. An annotated German translation of this text from its Latin original initiated a series of derivative texts which appeared in regional versions, notably the *Deutschenspiegel* (*Spiegel der Deutschen Leute*, c.1250) and the *Kaiserliches Land und Lehnrecht* (popularly and misleadingly called the *Schwabenspiegel*, c.1260). In about 1330 an anonymous jurist produced a *Kleines Kaiserrecht*, which aspired to present a corpus of Carolingian COMMON LAW that would prevail throughout the Empire. Such legal unity was unachievable, because imperial edicts had little importance beyond the imperial court, and in practice laws were formulated on a local basis.

The belief that the Holy Roman Empire was the successor of the Roman Empire of antiquity led to the movement known as the RECEPTION, a revival of Roman law, CANON LAW, and Lombard FEUDAL LAW which was introduced at the beginning of the fifteenth century and dominated German legal thinking and practice until the seventeenth century. One of the earliest legal texts to incorporate Roman law in its exposition was Raymund von Wiener Neustadt's *Summa legum* (c.1345), which brought to the study of private and criminal law both an academic command of Roman law and a practical awareness of German legal practices and institutions. Early in the fifteenth century an anonymous 'mirror of legal plaints' (*Der richterliche Klagspiegel*), compiled from Italian sources, brought Roman law and the tradition of Italian legal commentary to bear on civil law and on criminal law and procedure. The establishment in 1495 of the Imperial Court of Chancery (the REICHSKAMMERGERICHT), a court required to dispense justice in accordance with the principles of Roman law, led to an implementation of Roman law in lower courts, and by this date the universities were teaching Roman law on an equal footing with canon law, which itself had Roman origins.

By the sixteenth century German law had become more Roman than German, except in the areas of criminal law and procedure. Imperial legislation of this period was almost exclusively constitutional, save for regulations touching the Reichskammergericht. The most important legal statute of the period was the CAROLINA of 1532, which was to dominate the German code of criminal procedure for two centuries. In the semi-independent territories of the Empire local legislation unevenly reflected the Reception, in that legislation ranged from the wholly Roman to the wholly German. Academic jurists, such as Gregor HALOANDER, Andreas von GAIL, and Joachim Münsinger (author of *Observationes iudicii imperialis camerae*, 1563), however, were overwhelmingly supporters of the Reception.

The seeds of dissent from the hegemony of Roman law were sown by two groups of distinguished jurists. German jurists such as Johann OLDENDORP and Johannes ALTHAUS had become exponents of NATURAL LAW, and the definitive exposition of natural law by the Dutch jurist GROTIUS in his *De iuri belli ac pacis* (1625), which was taken up (and enriched by debate with Hobbes) by Samuel von Pufendorf in his *De iure naturae et gentium* (1672), ultimately led to Rousseau and his *contrat social*. The other group were German national jurists of the seventeenth century, notably the legal historian Hermann Conring and Benedikt Carpzov, the first great systematizer of German law. These jurists and their successors (notably Christian Thomasius, who was both a German nationalist jurist and an exponent of natural law) sought to replace the Roman law of the Reception with an indigenous German law.

Adalbert Erler, Ekkehard Kaufmann, et al., *Handwörterbuch zur deutschen Rechtsgeschichte* (5 vols., 1971–98); Ernst Andersen, *The Renaissance of Legal Science after the Middle Ages: The German Historical School no Bird Phoenix* (1974).

**GERMAN LITERATURE.** The model of a Renaissance revival of the forms and ideals of classical literature is of limited usefulness in understanding German literature of the early modern period. The humanist tradition in Germany produced a distinguished corpus of Latin literature in the late fifteenth and sixteenth centuries, but German vernacular literature was not influenced by classical literature until the seventeenth century, when the *Oden und Gesänge* (1618) of Georg Weckherlin (1584–1653) inaugurated German Renaissance poetry; shortly thereafter, Martin Opitz (1597–1639) and the dramatist Andreas Gryphius (1616–64) created a distinguished latter-day German Renaissance literature.

The vernacular literature of the sixteenth century is better understood as a development of Middle High German literature than as a reflection of the humanist ideals of the Renaissance. Poems such as *Teuerdank* and *Der Weißkunig*, the autobiographical poems planned and partly executed by MAXIMILIAN I, are firmly set in an earlier vernacular tradition, and owe little to ancient literature. Similarly, the sixteenth-

century poetry and music of the MEISTERSANG is rooted in the earlier tradition of *Minnesang*. In popular literature, the VOLKSBÜCHER reproduced material that was entirely medieval in origin, and the SCHWANK was a richly vernacular form: collections such as TILL EULENSPIEGEL exalt the clever peasant, not the humanist scholar.

The literary form that dominated sixteenth-century German literature (in both German and Latin) was satire, a genre particularly well suited to the vituperative exchanges that characterize Reformation writing. The prototype of German satire is Sebastian BRANT's *Narrenschiff* (1494), which transforms the anecdote of the *Schwank* into a medium of caustic satire. Throughout the sixteenth century, embittered vernacular satire ran a course parallel to that of wittily ironic humanist satire in Latin, of which EPISTOLAE OBSCURORUM VIRORUM (1515 and 1517) is a distinguished example. Of the vernacular satirists, the most powerful was Thomas MURNER, whose scurrilousness knew no limits; he had no Protestant counterpart of comparable abilities until the emergence later in the century of the Rabelaisian Johann FISCHART.

**GERMAN MUSIC** enjoyed a strong tradition of secular song since the twelfth century troubadour movement had spread from Provence, and was continued through the efforts of the Minnesingers and Renaissance Meistersingers. The popularity of song was to have an impact through Lutheran CHORALES and the secular compositions of Heinrich ISAAC and Ludwig SENFL. Other sacred music reached Germany with the arrival of Franco-Flemish and Italian composers visiting the Bavarian Munich court, and polychoral techniques were taken up by Jacob Gallus, Hans Leo HASSLER, and Michael PRAETORIUS. Arnoldt SCHLICK and Paul HOFHAIMER were important as organists and composers of organ music, paving the way for the German organ masters of the Baroque.

**GERMANY or (German) Deutschland.** The modern state of Germany is the descendant of the German Empire (*Deutsches Reich*) of the nineteenth century and of the HOLY ROMAN EMPIRE (800–1806), which included areas such as AUSTRIA and BOHEMIA. The Golden Bull of 1356 had formalized the division of what is now Germany into some 350 autonomous principalities and imperial cities ruled by secular and ecclesiastical princes and unified only in the sense that they all acknowledged the supremacy of the emperor. The sense of disunity was exacerbated by the Reformation, which divided Germany into Lutheran, Calvinist, and Catholic areas.

For much of the fifteenth century, Germany was ruled by the Emperors SIGISMUND and FRIEDRICH III. During this period the power of the TEUTONIC ORDER was receding in the German settlements in the Baltic, the HANSEATIC LEAGUE was losing its former dominance, and the HUSSITE WARS erupted in Bohemia. The families that were to dominate German politics for centuries to come were consolidating their power in BRANDENBURG (see HOHENZOLLERN FAMILY), SAXONY (see WETTIN FAMILY), and BAVARIA and the PALATINATE (see WITTELSBACH FAMILY) and within the institution of the Holy

Roman Emperors, which reverted to the HABSBURGS on the accession of Albrecht II in 1437. In banking, families such as the FUGGERS and WELSERS were establishing AUGSBURG as a European financial centre. The establishment of a series of new German UNIVERSITIES in the fifteenth century was complemented by the advent of PRINTING.

At the turn of the century, under the Emperor MAXIMILIAN (1493–1519), new legal institutions were introduced, notably the REICHSKAMMERGERICHT and the AULIC COUNCIL. During his reign HUMANISM became an important force in German intellectual life, and artists such as Albrecht ALTDORFER, Lucas CRANACH, and Albrecht DÜRER introduced Italian elements into German art.

The first half of the sixteenth century was dominated by the REFORMATION precipitated by Martin LUTHER in 1517, a series of rebellions such as the KNIGHTS' REVOLT and the PEASANTS' WAR, and the pan-European concerns of the Emperor CHARLES V, which included military campaigns arising out of the WARS OF ITALY and the expansion of the Ottomans into Austria and Hungary. Within Germany, Charles had to struggle with a series of opponents such as PHILIP OF HESSE, the Saxon Elector JOHANN FRIEDRICH I, and MAURICE OF SAXONY. This religious strife was concluded by the Religious Peace of AUGSBURG (1555), in which FRIEDRICH I and the electors agreed on a means whereby Catholics and Lutherans might coexist; the settlement excluded the CALVINISTS, who were subsequently established in the Palatinate.

Religious strife emerged again in the early seventeenth century, when the Protestant Union of 1608 and the Catholic League of 1609 set Germany on a course that was to lead to the THIRTY YEARS WAR, a conflict that was to cause greater destruction in Germany than any war in its history until the advent of the Second World War.

**GERSON, JEAN LE CHARLIER DE** (1363–1429), French ecclesiastical reformer, born near Rethel (in the Ardennes) and educated at the College of Navarre in Paris; he was a pupil of Pierre D'Ailly, whom he succeeded as chancellor of Notre-Dame and the University of Paris in 1395. After three years in Bruges (1397–1400) spent writing a treatise on schism he returned to Paris with a view to ending the GREAT SCHISM. He travelled to the COUNCIL OF CONSTANCE with d'Ailly, and there articulated the position of the CONCILIAR MOVEMENT and of GALLICANISM.

At the conclusion of the Council Gerson moved to the Benedictine abbey of Melk (near Vienna), and in 1419 he moved to France, where he lived in seclusion in Lyon for the rest of his life. His prolific writings include treatises on conciliar theory, moral theology (in which he defended the Nominalist view that nothing was intrinsically sinful and that the sinfulness or goodness of an act depended on the will of God), the spiritual life (notably *The Mountain of God*, his principal work), and commentaries on the Magnificat and the Song of Solomon.

DBF; D. C. Brown, *Pastor and Laity in the Theology of John Gerson* (1987); G. H. M. Posthumus Meyjes, *Jean Gerson, Apostle of Unity: His Church Politics and Ecclesiology* (1999).

**GERVAISE, CLAUDE** (*fl.* 1540–60), French composer, arranger, and editor in Paris, where he was employed by Pierre ATTAIGNANT. He wrote and edited instrumental dance music and polyphonic chansons. His editions of ensemble dance music include dances modelled on chansons by CERTON and JANEQUIN.

**GESNER, KONRAD** (1516–65), Swiss biologist, philologist, and bibliographer. He was born in Zürich and educated in Basel, where he studied medicine, and then in Paris and Montpellier. On returning to the Swiss Confederation he initially taught Greek at Lausanne and then retired to Zürich, where he practised as a physician and conducted zoological and botanical research. He published some 80 books on a large range of subjects. His principal work was a huge zoological survey of mammals, birds, and fishes, the *Historia animalium*, which was published in four volumes (1551–8); a fifth volume, on snakes, was published posthumously in 1587. His botanical *Historiae plantarum*, which contains some 1,500 illustrations, was published in the eighteenth century (1751–9). Gesner's other books include a treatise on palaeontology (*De omni rerum fossilium genere*, 1565) in which he proposes an organic origin for fossils, and a *Biblioteca universalis* (1545–9) in which he attempts to list all known works in Greek, Latin, and Hebrew.

DSB; NDB.

**GESSO**, a paste based on gypsum (plaster of Paris), used primarily by sculptors as a medium for casts, but also used for the decoration of furniture, especially CASSONI, and as the ground laid onto panels for panel paintings. It was usually mixed with linseed oil and then applied in thin layers to the surface; it could be moulded when still malleable and carved and gilded when hardened.

**GESUALDO, CARLO** (*c*.1561–1613), prince of Venosa, and a composer in Naples until, after murdering his wife Maria and her lover, the duke of Andria, he retreated to Gesualdo. His reputation as a composer has been enhanced by the notoriety which resulted from the assassination. His subsequent marriage to Eleonora d'Este at Ferrara in 1594 increased his visibility as a composer. He wrote for the Ferrarese *concerto delle donne*, met Jacopo CORSI, and published books of madrigals. The melancholy he suffered is reflected in moments of intense expression in his madrigals.

**GHEERAERTS, MARCUS THE ELDER** (*c*.1520–*c*.1590) and **MARCUS THE YOUNGER** (1561–1636), Flemish artists in England. Marcus the Elder was active as an engraver in England from 1568, but no painting from this period can be confidently attributed to him. His son Marcus the Younger, who had been trained by his father and Lucas de HEERE, worked alongside the DE CRITZ and OLIVER families. Attributions are problematical, but one painting that can be securely attributed to Marcus the Younger is his portrait of *Queen Elizabeth I* (National Portrait Gallery, London); this portrait, which portrays the queen standing on a map of

Marcus Gheeraerts the Younger, *Queen Elizabeth*, in the National Portrait Gallery, London; the queen is standing on a map of England

England, has been cut back on both sides, but is nonetheless the largest extant portrait of the queen.

DNB; MDA; NBW s.v. Gerards; Edward Hodnett, *Marcus Gheeraerts the Elder of Bruges* (1971).

**GHENT or (Flemish) Gent or (French) Gand**, a Flemish city (now in Belgium) at the junction of the Scheldt and the Lys. Ghent was from 1180 the seat of the counts of Flanders, but in 1384 was incorporated with the rest of Flanders into the duchy of Burgundy and in 1477 became part of the HABSBURG Empire. The city rebelled against Duke PHILIP THE GOOD in 1450 and against the Emperor CHARLES V (who was born in the city) in 1540; on both occasions the revolts were firmly quelled. In November 1576 the anti-Spanish Pacification of GHENT was signed in the city, but in 1584 Ghent was regained for Spain by Alessandro FARNESE. The economy of the city was broken by the REVOLT OF THE NETHERLANDS, and its population was severely reduced by the exodus of Protestant refugees. The closing of the Scheldt to trade at the conclusion of the THIRTY YEARS WAR (1648) was the final blow to the commerce of a city that had once been prosperous.

Jan and Hubert van EYCK's *Adoration of the Lamb*, usually known as the Ghent altarpiece, is in the Cathedral of St Bavon. Surviving Renaissance buildings include the Town Hall, which has one Gothic façade (1518–33) and one Renaissance façade (1595–1628). Ghent is also the home of the largest surviving piece of Renaissance ARTILLERY, the 10,000-kilogram (10-ton) bronze cannon known as Dulle Griete.

H. van Werveke, *Gand, esquisse d'histoire sociale* (1946).

**GHENT, PACIFICATION OF or (Flemish) Pacificatie van Gent**, a treaty concluded on 8 November 1576 by all seventeen provinces of the Netherlands, who united in agreement that Spanish troops should be expelled and that questions of religious toleration should be resolved by a representative assembly. The treaty was primarily the work of Philippe de Croy, duke of AERSCHOT, who as the forces of Luís de REQUESENS sacked Antwerp in the episode known as the 'Spanish fury' (4–14 November 1576) assumed control and negotiated the treaty. The new governor, Don JUAN DE AUSTRIA, ratified the treaty in the 'Eternal Edict' of February 1577, but the REVOLT OF THE NETHERLANDS soon erupted again.

**GHETTO**, the quarter of a city in which JEWS lived by custom and civic injunction; the etymology of the term is uncertain, but it may be an abbreviated form of *borghetto*, the diminutive of *borgo*, i.e. a small borough. Walled ghettos were established in the city-states of Italy by the eleventh century, and they later spread all over Europe. The degree of regulation varied: some communities were self-governing, but nearly all were forbidden to leave the ghetto at night or on Sundays or Christian holy days. In 1556 Pope PAUL IV established a ghetto in Rome which was not abolished until 1870. There were important ghettos in Venice (initially in the Ghetto Vecchio and then in the Campo del Ghetto Nuovo), Frankfurt, Prague (perhaps as early as the tenth century), and Trieste.

S. Waagenaar, *The Pope's Jews* (1974).

**GHEYN, JACQUES DE, THE YOUNGER** (1565–1629), Dutch painter and engraver, the son of Jacques de Gheyn the Elder (1537/8–1581), a glass painter and miniaturist from Antwerp. Jacques the Younger studied in the late 1580s with Hendrik GOLTZIUS, whose influence is discernible both in the lushness of his LANDSCAPE paintings and in the satirical edge of his depictions of contemporary fashions in clothing and behaviour. He entered the service of the Orange family at The Hague, and in 1620 contributed the GROTTO (the first in a DUTCH GARDEN) to the garden commissioned by MAURICE OF NASSAU.

MDA; NNBW vii.

**GHIBERTI, LORENZO** (1378–1455), Italian bronze sculptor, born in Florence, where he trained as a goldsmith and painter. In 1401 he won the competition sponsored by the Arte di Calimala (Guild of Cloth-Dealers and Refiners) to execute a pair of bronze doors intended for the east portal of

**Lorenzo Ghiberti,** *Jacob and Esau,*
a panel on the east doors of the
baptistery in Florence

the baptistery in Florence; the six sculptors that he defeated included BRUNELLESCHI and JACOPO DELLA QUERCIA; the trial pieces depicting *Abraham and Isaac* prepared by Ghiberti and Brunelleschi are both now in the Bargello. Work on the east doors occupied the first half of Ghiberti's career, from 1403 to 1424, and their completion (and removal to the north portal, where they remain) led to the commission of new doors for the east portal (1425–52), which MICHELANGELO famously described as the 'gates of paradise'. The 28 panels of the north doors, which are modelled on Andrea PISANO's earlier doors and executed in an INTERNATIONAL GOTHIC style, depict the life of Jesus (twenty panels) and portray the four evangelists and four doctors of the Church; Ghiberti's assistants during the years when he worked on the doors included DONATELLO and Paolo UCCELLO. The ten panels of the east doors, which depict scenes from the Old Testament (compressed from a cycle of 24 scenes suggested by Leonardo BRUNI), show many features of Renaissance art, including attentiveness to the possibilities of perspective.

Ghiberti's other commissions include three large bronze statues for Orsanmichele: *St John the Baptist* (1412), *St Matthew* (1419), and *St Stephen* (1426–8). He also made two reliefs for the baptistery at Siena and smaller pieces such as bronze reliquaries. His writings, which were unpublished during his lifetime, comprised three volumes of *Commentaries* in which he discusses fourteenth-century Tuscan artists and drafts his autobiography, the first autobiography by a Renaissance artist.

DBI; MDA; Richard Krautheimer, *Lorenzo Ghiberti* (1956).

**GHIRLANDAIO, DOMENICO BIGORDI** (1448/9–94), Italian painter, born in Florence, the son of a goldsmith. He established a workshop together with his two younger brothers, and this *bottega* specialized in altarpieces, of which many survive. Ghirlandaio's unassisted work consisted largely of frescoes, of which the earliest example is the *Last Supper* (1480) in the refectory of the Ognissanti in Florence. He populated his fresco of *Jesus Calling the First Apostles* in the SISTINE CHAPEL in Rome (1481–2) with portraits of prominent Florentines living in Rome, and it seems likely that this pictorial flattery led to further commissions in which Ghirlandaio immortalized wealthy patrons in his paintings, such as the cycle on *The Life of Saint Francis* in the family chapel of Francesco Sassetti in the Church of Santa Trinita in Florence.

Ghirlandaio's most important commission, given to him by Giovanni Tornabuoni (a partner in the Medici Bank), was

**Ghirlandaio**, *St Francis Raising a Child from the Dead*, in the Church of Santa Trinita in Florence

**Ghirlandaio**, *Pope Honorius III Approves the Franciscan Rule*, in the Church of Santa Trinita in Florence

a fresco cycle on *The Lives of the Virgin and St John the Baptist* (1486–90) in the choir of Santa Maria Novella in Florence; this cycle contains portraits of the Tornabuoni family, and in the domestic settings of the two birth scenes provides a visual record of middle-class life in late fifteenth-century Florence. This documentary impulse is also apparent in Ghirlandaio's panel paintings, notably in his *Old Man and his Grandson* (Louvre), which is at once tender in its representation of human emotions and harsh in its uncompromising representation of elephantiasis.

Ghirlandaio's most famous pupil was MICHELANGELO, who through CONDIVI, his ghost-writer, attempted to play down the influence of Ghirlandaio; VASARI contested this attempt to deny Ghirlandaio's influence, which is most readily apparent in the cross-hatching of Michelangelo's early drawings. Ghirlandaio's son Ridolfo Bigordi (1483–1561) was a portrait painter and a friend of RAPHAEL.

*DBI* s.v. Bigordi, Domenico; *MDA*; Jean Cadogan, *Domenico Ghirlandaio: Artist and Artisan* (2000).

**GHISELIN, JOHANNES** (d. 1508), Flemish composer in Ferrara, where he worked with JOSQUIN DESPRÈS and OBRECHT. He wrote masses, some of which were published by PETRUCCI.

**GIAMBOLOGNA or Giovanni Bologna or Jean Boulogne** (1529–1608), Flemish sculptor. He was born in Douai and trained as a sculptor with Jacques DU BROEUCQ in Mons; the 'Bologna' in his name refers to the French port of Boulogne, not the Italian city of Bologna. In 1554 or 1555 he set out on a journey to Italy; he spent two years in Rome and then moved to Florence, where he settled permanently.

Many of Giambologna's finest works are FOUNTAINS, the first of which was the bronze Fontana del Nettuno (1563–6) commissioned by Pope PIUS IV for Bologna and still *in situ*. He subsequently built the Fountain of Venus at the Villa Petraia near Florence, the Ocean Fountain in the BOBOLI GARDENS, and the huge Apennine Fountain for PRATOLINO; his *Hercules and the Centaur* (now in the Loggia dei Lanzi in Florence) and *Samson and a Philistine* (Victoria and Albert Museum) were designed as centrepieces for fountains. Giambologna's other works, some of which were executed to his designs by collaborators such as Pietro FRANCAVILLA and Antonio Susini, included the bronze statues and reliefs for the Grimaldi Chapel in Genoa, and EQUESTRIAN STATUES of HENRI IV for Paris (erected on the Pont Neuf and damaged at the French Revolution and now in the Musée des Beaux-Arts in Dijon) and of Grand Duke Cosimo de' MEDICI (1587–93, Piazza della Signoria, Florence). His most important marble group is the spiralling *Rape of a Sabine* (1579–83) in the Loggia dei Lanzi in Florence, which was carved from a single block of marble.

Until the eighteenth century the canons of artistic taste placed Giambologna's accomplishment as a sculptor second

**Giambologna**, *Rape of a Sabine* (1579–83), in the Loggia dei Lanzi in Florence (facing page; front view)

**Giambologna**, *Rape of a Sabine* (right; rear view)

only to that of MICHELANGELO, and throughout the nine-teenth century popular acclaim ensured that reproductions of his bronze statuettes (especially the *Medici Mercury* of 1564 in the Museo Civico in Bologna) were sold in large numbers.

*DBI* s.v. Boulogne, Jean; *MDA*; *NBW* i s.v. Boulogne, Jean; Charles Avery, *Giambologna: The Complete Sculpture* (1978).

**GIAN CRISTOFORO ROMANO**. See ROMANO, GIAN CRISTOFORO.

**GIANNOTTI, DONATO** (1492–1573), Florentine political philosopher and playwright. He studied law at Pisa and served the Florentine republic of 1527–30 as a chancery secretary; he was banished for life when the MEDICI were restored. He served several churchmen and was eventually appointed as secretary to Pope PIUS V.

Giannotti's principal work as a political philosopher is the *Libro della repubblica de' Viniziani* (written 1526–7, published 1540) which extols the republican constitution of Venice; this dialogue remained permanently in print and was also translated into German, and so became one of the works that nourished the MYTH OF VENICE. Giannotti also wrote a comedy (in imitation of PLAUTUS), *Il vecchio amoroso*. His last work was the *Discorso delle cose d'Italia*, which advocated an alliance with France against the HABSBURGS.

*DBI*; R. Ridolfi, 'Sommario della vita di Donato Giannotti', *Opuscoli* (1942).

**GIARDINO SEGRETO**. The tradition of the *hortus conclusus* (Latin; 'enclosed garden') was long associated with the virginity of MARY, and the roses that it contained were deemed to represent her virtue. The analogies originate in the Song of Solomon 4: 12 ('a garden enclosed is my sister, my spouse, a spring shut up, a fountain sealed'); the fountain metaphor was also related to the biblical metaphor of the fountain of life (Latin *fons vitae*). In literature the *hortus conclusus* (or 'Mary garden') was an allegorical garden compared to the prelapsarian garden of Eden. When implemented in stone and soil, the enclosed garden became a walled or hedged rose garden with a FOUNTAIN, covered walks, and arbours; there was often a turfed seat built against the outer wall or a central fountain or tree, or set into a hedge.

The Renaissance *giardino segreto* (Italian; 'secret garden') is the secular progeny of the medieval *hortus conclusus*. It first appeared in ITALIAN GARDENS of the fifteenth century as an enclosed outdoor room, and quickly became adapted to the secular purposes of those gardens. In the MEDICI VILLA at Fiesole and the Villa Piccolomini in Pienza, for example, it became a place from which to admire distant vistas. In the VILLAS of Frascati, notably ALDOBRANDINI, the *giardini segreti* are tucked away on one side of the villas, and at the FARNESE Palace, the finest *giardino segreto* of the Renaissance is hidden at the end of a path some 365 metres (400 yards) long.

**GIBBONS, ORLANDO** (1583–1625), English composer whose career started as a chorister at King's College, Cambridge. He became a gentleman of the Chapel Royal in 1605 and was later one of the organists. He was one of several musicians, including Alfonso FERRABOSCO (the younger), Thomas FORD, and Giovanni COPRARIO, who worked in the household of Prince Charles. His sacred music includes service settings, anthems, and verse anthems to be accompanied variously by keyboard or instrumental ensembles. His *Madrigals and Motets* (1612) includes 'The silver swan'. He also wrote fantasias for viols and for keyboard; some of his keyboard writing are in *Parthenia* (1613) together with works by William BYRD and John BULL.

**GIBERTI, GIAN MATTEO** (1495–1543), bishop of Verona, born in Genoa; the fact that his birth was illegitimate may explain the otherwise puzzling fact that he was never created cardinal. Giberti entered the service of Cardinal Giulio de' Medici, who was elected as Pope CLEMENT VII; Giberti became datary to the new pope and from that position was able to control the papal curia; he also had the ear of Clement, and urged him to stand firm in his opposition to the Empire. After the SACK OF ROME by imperial troops (1527) Giberti, who had been appointed bishop of Verona, withdrew to his diocese and there introduced a comprehensive programme of ecclesiastical reform. In 1534 the success of this reform induced Pope PAUL III to appoint Giberti to the reforming commission (Consilium de Emandanda Ecclesia) that prepared the general council that was eventually convoked as the COUNCIL OF TRENT. Giberti was also a student of PATRISTIC SCHOLARSHIP, and produced editions of writers such as Chrysostom and John of Damascus.

*DBI*; A. Grazioli, *Gian Matteo Giberti, vescovo di Verona, precursore della riforma del Concilio di Trento* (1955); A. Prosperi, *Tra evangelismo e Controriforma: G. M. Giberti (1495–1543)* (1969).

**GILBERT, SIR HUMPHREY** (c.1539–1583). Half-brother of RALEGH, Gilbert's early life was spent as a soldier in France, Ireland, and the Netherlands. In 1576 he published a *Discourse* on the NORTH-WEST PASSAGE, and two years later, having been granted a charter by ELIZABETH, he led an expedition in its pursuit. The expedition was attacked by the Spanish, however, and returned home unsuccessfully. A second expedition in 1583 reached Newfoundland and established an English colony there; Gilbert was lost at sea on his return home.

**GILBERT, WILLIAM** (1544–1603), English natural philosopher, physician, and astronomer, born in Colchester and educated at Cambridge, where he became a fellow of St John's College and qualified as a physician; in 1600 he became president of the College of Physicians, and the following year physician to the queen. Gilbert's *De magnete, magneticisque corporibus* (1600) describes the numerous experiments that led him to conceive of the earth as an enormous magnet, a contention that explained phenomena such as the movement of a magnetized needle in a COMPASS.

*DNB*; *DSB*; D. H. D. Roller, *The De magnete of William Gilbert* (1959).

**GIL DE HONTAÑÓN, JUAN THE ELDER** (c.1480–1526), **JUAN THE YOUNGER** (*fl.* 1521–31), and **RODRIGO** (1500–77), the family of Spanish architects responsible for the sixteenth-century Gothic cathedrals of Salamanca and Segovia. Juan Gil the Elder was one of the nine architects assembled in 1512 to discuss the construction of the new cathedral at Salamanca, and he was commissioned to build the cathedral. He was also the architect of Segovia Cathedral, and embarked on its construction c.1525. He served as master of the works at Seville Cathedral from 1513 to 1517. In the early 1520s he was assisted by his son Juan Gil the Younger, who succeeded him as architect at Salamanca, where he worked from 1526 to 1531.

Rodrigo Gil was another son of Juan Gil the Elder, and he worked as cathedral architect at Segovia (1521–9) and at Salamanca (from 1538); he also served as master of the works on the cathedrals of Astorga and Palencia. All four of these cathedrals are uncompromisingly Gothic in style. Rodrigo was, however, capable of working at the highest level in the markedly different idiom of the Renaissance-Plateresque style: the façade that he constructed for the University of Alcalá (1541–53) is one of the greatest secular buildings of the Spanish Renaissance.

*MDA* s.v. Gil de Hontañón; Antonio Casaseca Casaseca, *Rodrigo Gil de Hontañón* (1988).

**GILES, NATHANIEL** (c.1558–1634), English composer, organist, and choirmaster who held appointments at Worcester Cathedral and St George's Chapel, Windsor. He received the B.Mus. from Oxford in 1585 and in 1597 became master of the children of the Chapel Royal. A short-lived collaboration with Henry Evans at the BLACKFRIARS Theatre to produce choirboy plays ended in 1602. Two of his anthems are in Sir William Leighton's *Tears and Lamentations* (1614).

**GILI, PAOLO** (*fl.* 1518–66), Sicilian goldsmith whose studio was in Palermo. His early work, such as his reliquary of 1531 for the arm of Sant'Agata (Palermo Cathedral), is wholly Gothic in design and decorative detail, but he later adopted a Renaissance style with distinctive Spanish elements which is represented in a crozier in the Galleria Nazionale in Palermo and a reliquary of 1540/66 for Santa Cristina (Palermo Cathedral).

*DBI.*

**GILIO DA FABRIANO, GIOVANNI ANDREA** (d. 1584), Italian art theorist who articulated the position taken by the COUNCIL OF TRENT on the subject of art. His *Dialogo degli errori della pittura* (1564), which was dedicated to Cardinal Alessandro FARNESE, inveighed against nudity in pictures and enjoined artists to conform to biblical sources and official dogma.

*DBI; MDA.*

**GILLES DE RETZ or Rais** (c.1404–1440), soldier and paedophile sadist who fought at the side of JOAN OF ARC at Orléans in 1429, and was appointed *maréchal de France*. He retired to his castle in Brittany and there indulged his interests in necromancy and his sexual appetites. He was tried in an ecclesiastical court for heresy and sorcery; he confessed to the murder of more than 100 boys, and was hanged

at Nantes. Gilles may have been the model for Charles Perrault's Barbe Bleue (Bluebeard), who murdered his wives and hid their bodies in a locked room.

J. Benedetti, *Gilles de Rais* (1971); Dirk Berents, *Gilles de Rais: De moordenaar en de mythe* (1982).

**GIOCHI D'ACQUA** (Italian; 'water-games'). The term is sometimes used with general reference to water-powered AUTOMATA in gardens such as Villa ALDOBRANDINI and Villa PRATOLINO, but usually refers specifically to devices in sixteenth- and seventeenth-century gardens designed to drench the unsuspecting visitor. The technology that underlay *giochi d'acqua* was transmitted through the Arabic tradition from its origins in HERON. In 1588 MONTAIGNE described such a device at the MEDICI VILLA at Castello, explaining that it could be operated by remote control from a distance of 200 paces. Visitors who strayed onto a certain path in the garden at ARANJUEZ were sprayed when they triggered the mechanism. The Fontana della Girandola built in 1614 at the Borghese villa of MONDRAGONE in Frascati contained polypriapic *giochi d'acqua* which soaked visitors who risked playing a water-game. To modern tastes these devices may seem puerile and, at Mondragone, vulgar, but they were repeatedly described by contemporaries as the most remarkable features of gardens, partly because of their technical ingenuity, but also because they appealed to contemporary tastes.

**GIOCONDO, FRA, or Fra Giovanni Giocondo da Verona** (1433–1515), Italian architect, engineer, and humanist. He was born in Verona, and as a young man seems to have become a Dominican friar. He worked in Naples as an architectural consultant (1489–93), and there designed fortifications and gardens. He subsequently moved to France, where he replanned the irrigation system at BLOIS and then built the Pont Notre-Dame in Paris (1500–8), which had collapsed in 1413; he lined the bridge with identical houses with sumptuous façades. This bridge was in turn destroyed, and the present bridge was erected in 1913.

Fra Giocondo returned to Italy, where he was initially employed by the Venetian republic as an hydraulic engineer on the river Brenta and then as a military architect responsible for the construction of fortifications at Cremona, Legnano, Padua, and Treviso. In 1514 he was called to Rome, where he assumed responsibility for the construction of ST PETER'S BASILICA during BRAMANTE's final illness; after Bramante's death Fra Giocondo shared responsibility for the basilica with RAPHAEL.

Fra Giocondo was a humanist scholar with a particular interest in manuscripts, which he collected and published. In Paris he discovered the correspondence of the Emperor Trajan and Pliny the Younger, and he later published the first illustrated edition of VITRUVIUS (Venice, 1511). His posthumous publications include a collection of ancient Roman inscriptions.

*MDA*; Vincenzo Fontana, *Fra Giovanni Giocondo, architetto* (1988).

**GIOLITO PRESS**, a publishing house founded in Venice in 1536 by Giovanni Giolito de' Ferrari and subsequently managed by his son Gabriele (d. 1578). In the 1540s and 1550s Gabriele established the press as the most important vernacular publisher in Italy, producing a large number of dialogues, novellas, and collections of poems and letters by authors such as ARETINO, ARIOSTO, CASTIGLIONE, Ludovico DOLCE, Anton Francesco DONI, and TULLIA D'ARAGONA. In the 1560s the emergence of the COUNTER-REFORMATION led to many secular authors being added to the INDEX, and Giolito therefore began to publish popular religious works. By the end of the century, when the business closed, the Giolito Press had published more than 1,000 titles, each of which bore the emblem of a phoenix rising from the flames.

DBI s.v. Giolito de' Ferrari, Giovanni and Gabriele; S. Bongi, *Annali di Gabriel Giolito de' Ferrari da Trino di Monferrato, stampatore in Venezia* (2 vols., 1890–5).

**GIORGIONE or Giorgio da Castelfranco or Giorgio Barbarelli** (*c.*1478–1510), Italian painter, born in Venice, where he may have trained in the studio of Giovanni BELLINI alongside Lorenzo LOTTO and PALMA VECCHIO. In 1507 he received a commission to paint pictures for the Audience Chamber in the Doge's Palace (all of which have been destroyed) and frescoes for the façade of the Fondaco dei Tedeschi (now discernible only in faint traces; a few fragments are preserved in the Ca' d'Oro). Little documentation exists for Giorgione's other paintings, none of which is signed or dated and many of which were completed by his pupils (including TITIAN) after his premature death by plague.

Giorgione's early paintings include the *Castelfranco Madonna* (Church of San Liberale, Castelfranco, Veneto) and *Judith* (Hermitage, St Petersburg), both of which have a symmetrical rigidity of composition softened by the subtle use of colours that recalls Bellini's late paintings. The painting that marks a change in Giorgione's style is the *Tempesta* (Accademia, Venice), the subject of which (possibly the infant Paris) is not clear; this is the first painting in which both the figures and the landscape have been subordinated to the intensity of mood, which is expressed in the storm that breaks over the city. In the *Three Philosophers* (Kunsthistorisches Museum, Vienna), which may represent the Magi waiting for the guidance of the star, Giorgione abandons

**Giorgione,** *Tempest,* in the Accademia, Venice

**Giorgione**, *Sleeping Venus*, Gemäldegalerie, Dresden; the painting was left unfinished at Giorgione's death, and was completed by TITIAN

symmetry and articulates mood in his presentation of the landscape; the picture may have been finished by SEBASTIANO DEL PIOMBO. The portrait of *Laura* (Kunsthistorisches Museum, Vienna) in front of a laurel that puns on her name was attributed to Giorgione in the sixteenth century, when someone wrote on the back that it was the work of 'Zorzo di Castelfranco'; the use of SFUMATO may imply a familiarity with the portraits of LEONARDO, who had visited Venice in 1500.

The paintings left unfinished on Giorgione's death include the *Sleeping Venus* (Gemäldegalerie, Dresden) and *Fête champêtre* (Louvre). Titian finished both paintings, and the latter may be entirely his work, though the two nude women are sometimes claimed for Giorgione.

The surviving corpus of Giorgione's paintings is not large, and several are imperfectly understood both with respect to their subjects and to the precise extent of Giorgione's involvement. In the historiography of Venetian painting, however, Giorgione is recognized as an innovator who built on the achievements of Bellini in the use of colour and proportion by uniting his figures and landscapes through the evocation of atmosphere and the secularization of feeling, and so changing the course of Venetian art.

DBI s.v. Giorgio da Castelfranco; *MDA*; Jaynie Anderson, *Giorgione: The Painter of Poetic Brevity* (1997).

**GIOTTO DI BONDONE** (1267/75–1337), Italian painter and architect, a native of Florence. The documentary record of his life is sparse: he owned a house in Florence in 1305, joined the Guild of Painters in 1311, lived from 1329 to 1333 in Naples as court painter to Robert of Anjou, became *capomaestro* (master mason) of Florence Cathedral in 1334, lived in Milan in the service of the Visconti in 1335–6 and died in January 1337. No contemporary record associates Giotto with an extant painting.

The attribution to Giotto of the fresco cycle of *The Lives of the Virgin and Christ* (completed in 1305) in the Arena Chapel in Padua is widely regarded as secure, and the altarpiece of *The Madonna Enthroned* painted for the Church of the Ognissanti in Florence (and now in the Uffizi) is in the same style. The fresco cycle of *The Life of St Francis* in the Upper Church of San Francesco in Assisi (1297–*c*.1305) was for centuries attributed to Giotto, but is now attributed to an unidentified 'Master of the St Francis Legend'; the last three scenes in the cycle, which are executed in a different style, are attributed to an anonymous 'Master of St Cecilia'. The attribution of this cycle to Giotto is the central plank of VASARI's argument that 'Giotto alone succeeded in resuscitating art and restoring it to a true path'; Vasari's comment later became embedded in the historiography of RENAISSANCE painting, of which Giotto became the founding father.

Giotto's only architectural work was the campanile of Florence Cathedral, which he began in 1334, when he was appointed *capomaestro* of the cathedral and the city. By the time of his death he had completed only the first story of the socle (Italian *zoccolo*); the tower was later

**Giotto**, *Madonna Enthroned*, in the Uffizi, Florence; this altarpiece was painted for the Church of the Ognissanti in Florence, and so is also known as the *Ognissanti Madonna*

completed (to altered plans) by Andrea PISANO and Francesco TALENTI.

DBI; MDA; Andrew Ladis (ed.), *The Arena Chapel and the Genius of Giotto* (1998); id., *Giotto: Master Painter and Architect* (1998).

## GIOVANELLI, RUGGIERO (1560–1625), Italian composer.

He was a member of the Virtuosa Compagnia dei Musici di Roma and by 1594 had succeeded PALESTRINA as *maestro di cappella* of the Cappella Giulia in Rome. He was appointed *maestro di cappella* of the Cappella Sistina in 1614, having sung there since 1599. His sacred music includes masses and motets and he also wrote madrigals, setting texts by TASSO, GUARINI, and SANNAZARO.

## GIOVANNA I OF ANJOU or (French) Jeanne I or (English) Joan I or Joanna I (1327–82), queen of Naples, was the daughter of Carlo, duke of Calabria; she succeeded her grandfather Roberto to the throne of Naples in 1343, at the age of 16. Her husband Andrew (son of Charles I of Hungary, and also an Angevin) was assassinated in 1345, possibly at the instigation of the queen; Giovanna immediately married Luigi, son of Filippo, prince of Taranto.

King Louis of Hungary at once travelled to Naples to avenge his brother's death, but Giovanna escaped to Provence, of which she was the ruling countess. She also secured a pardon from Pope Clement VI in exchange for selling Avignon to the papacy. King Louis returned to Hungary, so Giovanna returned to Naples in 1352. Her consort died in 1362, and she subsequently married Iago of Majorca; when he died in 1375, Giovanna took a fourth husband, Otto of Brunswick, prince of Taranto.

Giovanna had no sons, and her daughters both predeceased her, so she designated as her heir Louis, duke of Anjou, brother of Charles V of France. Charles of Durazzo, great-grandson of King Carlo II of Naples, considered himself the rightful heir, and sought to assert his claim by invading Naples, ostensibly because of Giovanna's support for the antipope CLEMENT VII. Giovanna was imprisoned and, on 22 May 1382, murdered. She was succeeded by Charles as Carlo III (later Charles II of Hungary).

Queen Giovanna was a cultured woman with marked scholarly and literary interests; the poets that she knew included Petrarch and Boccaccio.

E. G. Léonard, *Histoire de Jeanne I^re* (1932–7).

## GIOVANNA II DI DURAZZO or (French) Jeanne II de Duras or (English) Joan II or Joanna II (1371–1435), queen of Naples, the daughter of King Carlo III of Naples and sister of King LADISLAS OF DURAZZO; she was married to Duke Wilhelm of Austria, who died in 1406. Giovanna succeeded her brother Ladislas to the throne in 1414, aged 45. She took as her lover the 26-year-old Pandolfo Alopo, whom she appointed as chief seneschal. In 1415 she married James of Bourbon, who promptly declared himself king, ordered the murder of Pandolfo, incarcerated Muzio Attendolo Sforza (Giovanna's chief constable), and restricted his wife's movements. The barons of Naples rebelled, forcing James to release Muzio Attendolo, resign the crown, and leave the kingdom.

The Neapolitans had been expelled from Rome after the death of Ladislas, and in 1416 Giovanna sent Muzio Attendolo with an army to the city, which was guarded by the *condottiere* Andrea FORTEBRACCIO; he was forced to flee, and Muzio Attendolo entered Rome. The accession of Pope MARTIN V in 1417 changed the political climate, because he chose to enter into an alliance with Queen Giovanna, who in turn agreed to give up Rome. Muzio Attendolo returned to discover that he was no longer in favour, because the queen was completely dominated by her latest lover, Giovanni CARACCIOLO. Muzio Attendolo chose to reassert his position by joining Pope Martin in supporting the claim of Louis III of Anjou to succeed Giovanna. Giovanni Caracciolo detested Muzio Attendolo, and persuaded the queen not to designate Louis III as her successor, but instead to nominate King ALFONSO V of Aragon.

War soon broke out, with Giovanna and Spain pitted against Louis III, Muzio Attendolo Sforza, and Pope Martin

Giotto, *The Lamentation*, in the cycle on *Lives of the Virgin and Christ* (1305–8), in the Arena Chapel, Padua

V. At the conclusion of a protracted war prosecuted on land and sea, Alfonso entered Naples, and a fragile peace was secured in 1422. Alfonso had Giovanni Caracciolo arrested, and Giovanna fled to Aversa with the assistance of Muzio Attendolo, who shortly thereafter accidentally drowned. Disillusioned with Alfonso, she designated Louis as her successor. Alfonso garrisoned Naples and returned to Spain, whereupon an Angevin army (assisted by a Genoese navy) retook the city. Once again there was a short period of peace, but in 1432 Giovanni Caracciolo quarrelled with the queen and was murdered, and soon a revolt against Giovanna was organized in Apulia by Gian Antonio ORSINI, prince of Taranto. Louis died in 1434 while trying to suppress the rebellion, and Giovanna designated her adopted son RENÉ D'ANJOU as her successor; he was to be the last Angevin king of Naples. Giovanna died on 11 February 1435.

**GIOVANNI DALMATA or Ivan Duknović** (*c.*1440–after 1509), Dalmatian sculptor and architect. He was born in Traù (Croatian Trogir), moved to Italy as a young man, and

trained in the studio of Andrea BREGNO in Rome. He subsequently collaborated with another sculptor (possibly MINO DA FIESOLE) on the tomb of Pope PAUL II in Old St Peter's Basilica (1474–7; destroyed, but fragments are preserved in the Grotte Vaticane and the Louvre) and also carved the tomb of Cardinal Barto Lommeo Roveralla in the Church of San Clemente in Rome (1476–7); his work as an architect included part of the Palazzo Venezia in Rome. From 1480 to 1491 he worked in Hungary in the service of MATTHIAS CORVINUS; his surviving works from this period include a statue of *Hercules with the Hydra of Lerna* (Višegrad Palace) and a bas-relief of the *Virgin with Two Saints* (Museum of Fine Arts, Budapest).

*MDA*; Johannes Röll, *Giovanni Dalmata* (1994).

**GIOVANNI DA MAIANO** (*fl.* 1520–5), Tuscan sculptor. He worked on the construction of Hampton Court, where he carved the terracotta roundels of Roman emperors (for which he submitted a bill in 1525) and may have sculpted the relief of putti holding the Wolsey arms on the same building.

This decorative sculpture is one of the earliest examples of the Italian Renaissance style in England.

**GIOVANNI DA UDINE or Giovanni Recamador** (1487–1561/4), Italian painter and architect, born in Udine. He moved to Rome and entered the workshop of RAPHAEL, for whom he assumed responsibility for the decoration of the Vatican Loggias (1517–19) and the Villa MADAMA (1519). Giovanni made extensive use of GROTESQUES in his decorative work, which was executed in a combination of fresco and stucco; his style remained influential for centuries, especially in the work of eighteenth-century neoclassical designers. He later returned to Udine, where he became city architect in 1522.

MDA s.v. Udine, Giovanni da; Nicole Dacos and Catherine Furlan, *Giovanni da Udine* (1987).

**GIOVANNI DA VERONA, FRA** (*c.*1457–1525/6), Italian woodworker and INTARSIA craftsman, best known for his work in the Church of Santa Maria in Organo in Verona, where he built the choir, candelabra, and lectern (1494–9); he subsequently returned to build the sacristy cupboards (1519–23). Fra Giovanni was also responsible for the panels in the choir (commissioned 1502) of the abbey of Monte Oliveto Maggiore (35 kilometres (2 miles) south-east of Siena), which he built with the assistance of Fra Raffaele da Brescia (1479–1538); the *intarsia* includes depictions of birds, architectural perspectives, musical instruments, and the Town Hall of Siena.

MDA; DBI; Pier Luigi Bagatin, *Preghiere di legno: Tarsie ed intagli di Fra Giovanni da Verona* (2000).

**GIOVANNI DI PAOLO** (*c.*1399–1482), Italian painter, the most individual painter and the most aggressive exponent of an archaic style in fifteenth-century Siena. His surviving paintings include *Paradise* and the *Creation and Expulsion from Paradise* (both in the Metropolitan Museum in New York). He also painted a series of illustrations for DANTE's *Divine Comedy* (1438–44, British Museum). His reputation was revived by Bernard Berenson, who proclaimed Giovanni di Paolo 'the El Greco of the *Quattrocento*'.

MDA; John Pope-Hennessy, *Paradiso: The Illuminations to Dante's Divine Comedy by Giovanni di Paolo* (1993); John Pope-Hennessy, *Giovanni di Paolo* (London, 1937).

**GIOVANNI MARIA DI MARIANO** (*fl.* 1508–30), Italian MAIOLICA painter who worked in CASTEL DURANTE (1508), Urbino (1508 and 1530), and Venice (1523). The canon of his works has been reduced by scholarly scrutiny, but those that remain secure are typically plates decorated with allegorical subjects surrounded by GROTESQUE borders.

**GIOVIO, PAOLO, or (Latin) Paulus Jovius** (1483–1552), Italian historian and collector, born on 19 April 1483 in Como, the scion of an ancient and noble family. He studied medicine at Padua and practised in Rome. He then left medicine in order to work for Cardinal Giulio de' Medici, and later served Pope ADRIAN VI (who appointed him to a canonry in Como). When Giulio de' Medici was elected as Pope CLEMENT

VII, he brought Giovio into lavish quarters in the Vatican and awarded him a series of benefices culminating in the bishopric of Nocera. During the siege that preceded the SACK OF ROME, Giovio attended the pope in his flight from the Vatican to Castel Sant'Angelo. He served the Medici in other ways, accompanying Ippolito de' MEDICI to Bologna for the coronation of the Emperor CHARLES V and accompanying CATHERINE DE MÉDICIS (daughter of Lorenzo de' MEDICI) to Marseille for her marriage to the duc d'Orléans (later King HENRI II).

Clement was succeeded in 1534 by Pope PAUL III, who chose not to extend his patronage to Giovio, partly because he was tainted by his service to the Medici but also because he was insufficiently discreet about his voluptuous private life. Giovio withdrew to his villa on Lake Como and became a collector of antiquities and paintings (especially portraits); the collection is now dispersed. Giovio died on a visit to Florence in 1552.

Paolo Giovio wrote in both Italian and Latin. His Italian works include a study of the Ottomans (*Commentari delle cose de' Turchi*, Rome, 1531), a treatise on IMPRESE (*Dialogo delle imprese militari et amorose*, Venice, 1541), and a collection of letters (*Lettere volgare*, Rome, 1555). His Latin works, which are written in an elevated style and use humanist diction, include his history of his own time (*Historiae sui temporis ab anno 1494 ad annum 1547*, Florence, 1550–2) and a long series of biographies, including Pope Leo X, Pope Adrian VI, Ferdinando d'AVALOS, FERNÁNDEZ DE CÓRDOBA, Alfonso d'ESTE of Ferrara, and the SFORZA dukes of Milan; these works were all published in Italian translations soon after the Latin editions appeared. He also wrote geographical works (*Descriptio Larii Lacus*, Venice, 1559; *Descriptio Britanniae*, Venice, 1548) and a treatise on ichthyology (*De piscibus romanis*, Rome, 1524).

MDA; T. C. Price-Zimmermann, *Paolo Giovio: The Historian and the Crisis of Sixteenth-Century Italy* (1995).

**GIPSIES or Roma** (singular *Rom*, feminine *Romni*). The earliest known Gipsy migrations into Europe occurred in the fifteenth century. Their place of origin was thought to be either Egypt (hence the the Greek name *Gyftos*, the Spanish *Gitano*, the sixteenth-century German *Aegypter*, the English *Gipsy* or *Gypsy*, and the various terms meaning 'Pharaoh's people', such as Romanian *Faraon* and Hungarian *Pharao Nephka*) or Byzantium, where they were assumed to be associated with a Judaizing sect known as the Athinganoi, meaning 'untouchables' (hence Byzantine Greek *Adsincanoi*, German *Zigeuner*, French *Tsigane*, Hungarian *Cigány*, Italian *Zingari* and *Acingani*, Slav (Bulgarian, Polish, Serbian) *Cigan*, Romanian *Tigan*, and the English *tinker*); terms such as *Walachi*, *Saraceni*, *Agareni*, *Nubiani*, French *Bohémiens*, and German *Tartars* also refer to assumed origins. German *Heydens* refers to the non-Christian religion of the Gipsies and Greek *Katsibeloi* and Russian *Kochevniki* to their nomadic traditions.

The Gipsy language is Romani (normally spelt 'Romany' in English), a group of some 60 dialects (or, as some linguists believe, related languages) deriving ultimately from the Dravidian languages of India, which seems to have been the original homeland of the Gipsies. Romany seems first to have been recorded in England, where in 1542 Andrew Boorde collected thirteen sentences. In the Netherlands, some 53 words and sentences were collected by Johan van Ewsum and published in *Clene Gijpta Sprake* (Leiden, *c*.1565), and the 71 words collected by Antoine Morillon (who thought they were Nubian) were published by Bonaventura Vulcanius in 1597.

The first recorded appearance of Gipsies in Europe is in Corfu in 1326; they had settled in Nauplia (Greek Návplion) by 1378, when the Venetian governor conferred privileges on the 'Acingani' in the colony. By the end of the fifteenth century there were substantial Gipsy settlements in the Balkan peninsula and in the Carpathians, especially Transylvania and Wallachia. In western Europe, the first recorded arrival of Gipsies is in Hesse in 1414; thereafter they appeared in Hamburg (1418), Augsburg (1419), Provence (1427), Switzerland (1428), and Bologna (1422). By the end of the century Gipsies had reached England, and on 5 July 1505, JAMES IV of Scotland gave letters of recommendation to the 'earl of Little Egypt' to present to King JOHN of Denmark; on 15 February 1540 JAMES V of Scotland recognized the rights of Gipsies to be judged by their own laws by granting to the 'earl of Little Egypt' the authority to hang and otherwise punish all 'Egyptians' within the kingdom of Scotland.

In central Europe there was also a moment of tolerance before the centuries of oppression set in. On 18 April 1423, the Emperor SIGISMUND granted to the *voivode* of the Tsigani (*Wayvoda Ciganorum*) the same powers that James V was to confer on the earl of Little Egypt, and granted to the Gipsy people his imperial safe conduct; this 'Gipsy Charter' may have been the precedent that encouraged the prince of Moldavia to grant protection and freedom to Gipsies within his realm in 1478.

Imperial immunity from persecution was soon forgotten as east European Gipsies were reduced to serfdom; the last official auction of Gipsy families took place in Bucharest in 1845, when 200 families were sold in batches of five. The knowledge among Gipsy women of the occult and their work as soothsayers rendered them liable to persecution by the INQUISITION and to their fatal identification as WITCHES. From the end of the fifteenth century onwards, Gipsies were often exiled on pain of death; in 1611, for example, four Gipsies were hanged in Edinburgh 'for abiding within the kingdom, they being Egyptians', and in 1636, in nearby Haddington, 'Egyptian' men were sentenced to be hanged, the women to be drowned, and the children to be branded. The practice of transporting Gipsies to the Americas was taken up by England, France, Germany, the Netherlands, Spain, and Sweden, and in the nineteenth century, after the abolition of serfdom, was revived by Russia.

The earliest reference to PLAYING CARDS is the *Chronicle* of Nicolas of Cavellazzo, who says that cards were brought to Viterbo in 1379 from the land of the Saracens; similarly, the early fifteenth-century Bolognese game of *tarocco* migrated to France, where it was known as *le Tarot des Bohémiens*. It therefore seems likely that it was the Gipsies who introduced playing cards to Europe.

**GIRALDI, GIAMBATTISTA CINZIO, or Il Cinthio** (1504–73), Italian dramatist and literary theorist. He was born in Ferrara, where he attended the university, and eventually became professor of philosophy (1525) and professor of literature (1537). From 1542 to 1559 he acted as secretary to Ercole II d'ESTE; on the accession of Alfonso II d'ESTE Giraldi fell from favour, and the following year left Ferrara, finally settling in Pavia as a teacher of rhetoric.

Giraldi wrote nine plays, including the famously gruesome tragedy *Orbecche* (1541), and two treatises on genre: he examined dramatic genres in his *Intorno al comporre delle comedie e delle tragedie* (1543) and imaginative prose in his *Intorno al corporre dei romanzi* (1548). His collection of 113 novellas, entitled *Ecatomitti* (1565), was read all over Europe; Shakespeare seems to have drawn on two of the tales for *Measure for Measure* and *Othello*.

*OCIL*; P. R. Horne, *The Tragedies of G. B. Giraldi* (1962).

**GIRDLE-BOOKS**, small devotional books with lavish bindings decorated with gold, enamel, and jewels. The books were worn hanging from the belt, for which the sixteenth-century English word is 'girdle'. The British Museum has a girdle-book attributed to Hans van Antwerpen (1540–5). The girdle-book of Princess Augusta of Denmark (1617) is in the Rosenburg Palace in Copenhagen.

**GIROLAMO DA CARPI** (1501–56), Italian painter and architect. He trained in the Ferrara studio of GAROFALO and subsequently worked in the service of the ESTE FAMILY as an architect and decorator; he also worked in Parma, Modena, and Rome; his Roman notebook (now dispersed) reflects his interest in the decorative motifs of antiquity. Girolamo's paintings include copies of works by CORREGGIO and PARMIGIANINO and original paintings for churches in Bologna (notably an *Adoration of the Magi* for San Martino) and Ferrara (including three paintings in the cathedral).

*MDA* s.v. Carpi; Norman Canedy, *The Roman Sketchbook of Girolamo da Carpi* (1976).

*GISANT*. See TOMBS AND MAUSOLEUMS.

**GIULIA, VILLA, or Villa de Papa Giulio**, a Roman VILLA built by Giacomo VIGNOLA, Bartolomeo AMMANATI, and Giorgio VASARI for Pope JULIUS III (1551–5), who consulted MICHELANGELO on details of its construction. The villa was connected to a dock on the Tiber by a majestic walk lined by 36,000 trees; visitors of state requiring a ceremonial entry to Rome proceeded up the path to the villa where they were accommodated.

The principal courtyard, which is modelled on the imperial villas of antiquity, is built as a porticoed semicircle; the curved façade of the villa embraces the courtyard and is extended by a colonnade that meets the screen dividing the courtyard from a sunken NYMPHAEUM with a mosaic on the floor. At the end of the garden there is a small GIARDINO SEGRETO.

The villa was richly decorated with *topia* (landscape paintings) and statues, but the internal decoration has disappeared, and on the death of Julius III the collection of statues was removed to the Vatican; the boats carrying the statues had to undertake 160 journeys to complete the job. By 1569 the villa had been completely emptied; it now accommodates an Etruscan museum.

**GIULIANO DA MAIANO** (1432–90), Italian architect, the elder brother of BENEDETTO DA MAIANO. As a young man he worked as a woodcarver and INTARSIATORO, notably on the choir stalls in Pisa Cathedral and on the cupboards (still in place) in the New Sacristy of Florence Cathedral (1463–5). He subsequently worked as an architect in Tuscany and in Naples, and from 1477 served as architect to Florence Cathedral. His greatest surviving building is Faenza Cathedral (1474–86), on which the façade was left unfinished; he also built the Chapel of Santa Fina in the cathedral in San Gimignano (1468), Palazzo Spannocchi in Siena (1473) and Palazzo Venier (1477, later rebuilt), and the doorway of the Church of San Domenico in Recanati. In Naples he built the Porta Capuana (1484) and was probably the architect of three chapels in the Church of Monte Oliveto.

MDA s.v. Maiano; Francesco Quinterio, *Giuliano da Maiano: 'Grandissimo domestico'* (1996).

**GIULIO ROMANO or Giulio Pippi or Giuliano Giannuzzi** (*c*.1499–1546), Italian painter and architect, born in Rome, where he trained in the studio of RAPHAEL. He worked as Raphael's assistant on the Sala del Incendio (1515), and after Raphael's death in 1520 finished several of his works, including the *Transfiguration* and the Sala di Costantino frescoes in the Vatican; he also worked with GIOVANNI DA UDINE on the painted and stucco decorations of Raphael's Villa MADAMA.

Giulio's earliest independent paintings were a *Madonna* for the Church of Santa Maria dell'Anima in Rome and *The Stoning of St Stephen* for the Church of Santo Stefano in Genoa. He began his career as an architect in Rome, where his first buildings were the Palazzo Adimari Salviati (from 1520, later altered), the Villa Lante on the Gianicolo (from 1520/1, now the Finnish Academy), and the Palazzo Stati Maccarani in Piazza Sant'Eustachio (from 1522/3, now the Palazzo di Brazza).

In 1524 Giulio designed a set of erotic prints that displeased the Vatican and was obliged to leave Rome. He sought refuge in Mantua, where he entered the service of Federico II GONZAGA, who commissioned Giulio's finest building, the Palazzo del Tè (1525–35). Giulio painted frescoes in the Palazzo del Tè (notably those in the Sala de' Giganti) and in the Sala di Troia (1536–9) of the Palazzo Ducale in Mantua. His other architectural projects in Mantua were the Cortile della Cavallerizza in the Palazzo Ducale (from 1539), the remodelling of the cathedral (from 1545), and the construction and decoration of his own house (1544–6), which is now a museum. Beyond Italy, Giulio may have been the architect of the Italian wing of the Stadtresidenz at Landshut (1537–43), in Germany.

Giulio Romano is mentioned in Shakespeare's *Winter's Tale* as a sculptor, but is not known to have worked as one.

MDA; Manfredo Tafuri et al., *Giulio Romano* (Italian edn. 1989; English trans. 1998).

**GIUNTI PRESS**, a group of three publishing houses, the first of which was established in Venice by Luca Antonio Giunti the Elder (1457–1538), a Florentine who had moved to Venice in 1477. The first book to be published by the press was an Italian translation of the *De imitatione Christi* of THOMAS À KEMPIS, which appeared on 26 November 1489; by the end of the century another 52 titles had been published. The press specialized in liturgical works, and throughout the sixteenth century the Venetian branch of the Giunti Press was the largest publisher of liturgical works in Europe. In the last quarter of the sixteenth century the press was managed by Luca Antonio Giunti the Younger (1542–1602), who ruthlessly protected his virtual monopoly of liturgical works; by the time of his death the press had published more than 1,000 books. By the time it closed in 1657, the Venetian Giunti Press had published almost 1,500 books.

The Florentine branch of the Giunti Press was founded by Filippo Giunti (1450–1517) in 1497. It published vernacular texts, but also competed with the Aldine Press of ALDUS MANUTIUS by publishing classical texts in Latin and Greek; by 1600 it had published some 500 volumes. The Lyon branch of the Giunti Press was founded by Giacomo Giunti (nephew of Luca Antonio) in 1520 and survived until 1592. Its books include many counterfeit versions of Aldine editions, prepared with the connivance of Luca Antonio the Elder.

All three branches of the press affixed the family emblem (an adaptation of the Florentine lily) to their books, except for forgeries.

D. Decia et al., *I Giunti tipografia di Firenze: Annali 1497–1625* (2 vols., 1978); William Pettas, *The Giunti of Florence* (1980).

**GIUSTI, GIARDINO DEI**. The Giardino dei Giusti in Verona has been owned by the same family for centuries. Its origins are unknown, but the fact that the family incorporated the garden into their surname (the full family name is Giusti del Giardino—the Giusti of the Garden) implies that it must have been the earliest important garden in Verona. The designer is not known, nor does any documentation survive, so details of the original garden can only be inferred from the enthusiastic descriptions of generations of travellers for whom this was one of Italy's greatest gardens. Thomas CORYATE extolled the garden as a second paradise, and described its terraces planted with figs, oranges, and apricots, its 33 rows of cypress trees, and a small refectory containing an artificial rock decorated with scallop shells; this last detail reflects the Tuscan origins of the family, as decorative shells are a feature of GROTTOES in Tuscan gardens such as the BOBOLI GARDENS. John Evelyn was chiefly impressed by the cypresses, describing one by the gate as 'the goodliest in Europe'.

In the nineteenth century the garden was redesigned as an English landscape garden, and the only original features to survive this restoration were a small CASINO and some of the cypresses; most of the remaining cypresses were destroyed by bombs during the Second World War.

**GIUSTINIANA** was a type of fifteenth-century song related to the sung poetry of Leonardo Giustiniani. It reappeared in the 1560s and 1570s with Girolamo Scotto's *Primo libro delle justiniae a tre voci* and Andrea GABRIELI's *Greghesche et iustiniae a tre voci*.

**GIUSTINIANI FAMILY**, a prominent Venetian family of statesmen, *condottieri*, churchmen, and humanists; the family had branches in Genoa, Corsica, and Crete. Lorenzo Giustiniani (1380–1465) became general of the ORDER of canons of St George in Alga (1433), bishop of Venice (c.1433), and the first patriarch of Venice (1451); he was canonized and appears in the Roman calendar as Laurentius Justinianus.

Leonardo Giustiniani (1388–1446), the brother of Lorenzo, was a Venetian senator and became procurator of San Marco (1443); he wrote love poetry and religious poetry, translated PLUTARCH's lives of Cinna and Lucullus into Italian, and set songs to music. He is the eponym of the song known as the GIUSTINIANA.

Bernardo Giustiniani (1408–89), the son of Leonardo, was educated by Battisto GUARINI and GEORGE OF TREBIZOND and became a prominent Venetian diplomat and historian. He represented Venice in France and Rome and in 1485 was elected to the COUNCIL OF TEN. He wrote a history of the origins of Venice, *De origine urbis Venetiarum rebusque ab ipsa gentis historia* (1492), in which Venetians are said to have revived the liberties of ancient republican Rome. This treatise, both in its original Latin and in the Italian translation of 1545, helped to support the MYTH OF VENICE.

Pietro Giustiniani, a sixteenth-century senator, wrote an *Historia rerum Venetarum*, a sequel to Bernardo's history, and also wrote an account of Pietro MOCENIGO (*De gestis Petri Mocenigi*) and an account of the conflict between Venice and CHARLES VIII that culminated in the battle of FORNOVO (*De bello Venetorum cum Carolo VIII*). Orsatto Giustiniani (1538–1603), another Venetian senator, translated the *Oedipus tyrannus* of Sophocles and also published a collection of Petrarchan *Rime*.

Paolo Giustiniani (1476–1528), who was born Tommaso Giustiniani, entered the ORDER of Camaldolese hermits in 1511 and, together with his fellow Venetian Pietro Querini, established a particularly austere body within the Order; their group eventually became the Monte Corona Congregation. In 1513 Giustiniani and Querini attended the Fifth Lateran COUNCIL in order to present to Pope LEO X a proposal (*libellus*) for ecclesiastical reform (*Libellus ad Leonem X*) that centred on the education of clergy.

Another Paolo Giustiniani (1444–1502), who is also known as Paolo di Moniglia, was a member of the Genoese branch of the family. He became prior of the Dominican convent at Genoa, inquisitor-general for Genoa and its possessions, bishop of Scio, and papal legate to Hungary.

Agostino Giustiniani (1470–1536) was another member of the Genoese branch of the family. He joined the Dominican Order in 1487 and studied Greek, Hebrew, Aramaic, and Arabic with a view to preparing a polyglot Bible. He published the Psalter (*Psalterium Hebracum, Graecum, Arabicum et Chaldaicum*, Genoa, 1516) in an edition of 2,000 copies (including 50 vellum copies for presentation to heads of state) at his own expense, but sales were too low to justify printing the New Testament polyglot that he had prepared. He also translated Maimonides' *Moreh Nevochim* ('Guide to the Perplexed') as *Director dubitantium aut perplexorum* (1520), produced Latin editions of Aeneas Platonicus' *Aureus libellus* and Calcidius' translation of Plato's *Timaeus*, and wrote a history of Genoa which was posthumously published as *Castigatissimi annuali di Genova* (1537).

Geronimo Giustiniani, a late sixteenth-century member of the Genoese branch of the family, translated Euripides' *Alcestis* and three plays by Sophocles. He also wrote two tragedies, *Jephte* and *Christo in Passione*.

Pompeio Giustiniani (1569–1616), who was born in Corsica, was a *condottiere* who fought for Alessandro FARNESE and Ambrogio Spinola in the Netherlands, where he lost an arm in battle; his artificial arm was made of iron, hence his *nom de guerre* 'Bras de Fer'. He fought the Ottomans in Crete and was killed in an engagement in Friuli. His account of the war in Flanders was written in Italian but published in a Latin translation (*Bellum Belgicum*, Antwerp, 1609).

Giovanni Giustiniani (1513–56), who was born in Candia (Venetian Crete), published translations of ancient Latin texts into Italian, including CICERO's *In Verrum*, TERENCE's *Andria* and *Eunuchus*, and book 8 of VIRGIL's *Aeneid*.

Marchese Vicenzo Giustiniani (1564–1638) was a patron of artists (including CARAVAGGIO) who, together with his younger brother Cardinal Benedetto Giustiniani (d. 1621), assembled Rome's finest collection of ancient sculpture in the Palazzo Giustiniani (which Vicenzo built). An account of their collection of paintings and sculptures was published as *Galleria Giustiniana* (Rome, 1631). The collection was moved to Paris in 1807 and was partly broken up; antiquities and 157 pictures purchased by King Friedrich Wilhelm III of Prussia were exhibited in Berlin in 1826, but many paintings in the collection were lost in the fire in the Friedrichshain bunker in 1945.

MDA; P. H. Labalme, *Bernardo Giustiniani: A Venetian of the Quattrocento* (1969); J. Leclercq, *Un humaniste ermite, le bienheureux P. Giustiniani* (1951).

**GLAREAN, HEINRICH** (1488–1563), Swiss music theorist, geographer, humanist, and poet who studied philosophy, theology, mathematics, and music at Cologne University. He went to Basel (where he met and was admired by ERASMUS), Pavia, Milan, and Paris. Here he came into contact with Heinrich FABER, Guillaume BUDÉ, and MOUTON. Disagreeing with the Reformation movement which was gaining strength in Basel, he became professor of poetry and theology at Freiburg im Breisgau. His theoretical *Dodecachordon* (1547) outlines a new system of modal theory; it made a considerable impression on ZARLINO, HOFFMAN, MORLEY, and others, and several composers including the GABRIELIS, who put his theories to practical use in their writing.

**GLASS**, an artificial compound made by fusing a silica (usually sand or quartz) with an alkaline flux (usually soda-ash or potash) in a furnace. The silica was usually sand, but quartz was also in use for fine glass: the quality of Venetian glass was enhanced by the use of white quartz pebbles quarried from local river beds. In Mediterranean glasshouses the usual alkali was soda-ash, which since antiquity had been derived from soda-bearing seaweeds; in northern centres such as Bohemia, Germany, and England, potash (brushwood ash) was used as the alkali. Until the fifteenth century, the presence of iron in the silicates resulted in glass that was tinted with green or brown. Venetian glassmakers discovered that the addition of manganese dioxide to the compound would remove the tints and clarify the glass (an effect later achieved with arsenic and nickel); the clarity of their glass was comparable to that of ROCK CRYSTAL and so came to be known as *vetro di cristallo* (crystal glass), from which English 'crystal' and Spanish *cristal* derive. Lead oxide was added in small quantities to the compound to give weight and clarity to glass, but did not become a major ingredient until the late seventeenth century, when English glassmakers replaced imported Venetian quartz with indigenous flint, which caused interior cracks in the glass; the solution to the problem was a substantial admixture of lead, which produced the glass now known as lead crystal. In Venice, Bohemia, and Germany a similar effect was achieved by the use of lime rather than lead.

The two techniques for making glass were moulding and blowing. Moulding was a technique in which ductile glass was pressed onto a shaped mould. This technique was particularly useful for the production of CAMEO glass, which consisted of two layers of glass of contrasting colours; the technique was known in antiquity (the finest surviving example is the first-century Portland Vase in the British Museum) and was revived at the Renaissance. The blowing of glass through a hollow rod, which seems to be of Syrian origin, had been practised since antiquity for the production of containers. In the fourteenth century Arab glassmakers began to fashion swan-necked decanters, an art that was perfected in fifteenth-century Venice; such glass is still blown on the Venetian island of Murano.

Glass could be decorated by adding coloured strands to make LATTIMO (or *Latticino*) or by engraving by hand with a diamond point or with a grindstone, the lapidary's wheel. The technique of enamelling on glass was developed in Venice, probably by the BAROVIER FAMILY, in the fifteenth century; the earliest surviving piece is a blue glass goblet dated 1465. Enamelled armorial glasses were made by Venetian glassmakers for the German market, and from the mid-sixteenth century were also made in Germany (notably in Nuremberg), where they continued to be produced until the eighteenth century. In the sixteenth century the technique of enamelling glass transformed the technology of STAINED GLASS windows.

The most important centre for the production of glass in Renaissance Europe was Venice, where in 1292 the production of glass was transferred to the island of Murano as a precaution against fire. Venetian glass was made from soda-ash (usually imported), quartz (from river beds), and lime (from powdered marble). The guild system distinguished makers of different types of glass: coloured beads, which accounted for the largest proportion of foreign income, were made for

the religious market (principally for rosaries) by the craftsmen variously known as *paternosteri* or *margaritai* or *perlai*, glass for windows was made by *fioleri*, optical glass for eye-glasses by *cristallai*, and glass for MIRRORS by *specchiai*. The technology of glass was protected by the Venetian state, which forbade glassmakers to emigrate on pain of death. In the late sixteenth century Venetian exiles nonetheless established centres of glassmaking elsewhere in Italy, initially at Altare (near Genoa), where from 1495 craftsmen were required to work for a time abroad; Altarese craftsmen and Venetian exiles took Italian styles to northern Europe, principally Bohemia, Germany, and Flanders. In 1569 a Venetian glassmaker established a workshop in Florence at the request of Grand Duke Cosimo de' MEDICI, and from 1619 a small factory in the BOBOLI GARDENS made glass for the grand ducal household, including optical lenses for Galileo GALILEI.

In the German lands, the most important centres of glass production in the fifteenth and sixteenth centuries were Bohemia (which made the finest glass), Moravia, Franconia, Hesse, Saxony, Thuringia, and Carinthia. The most common German glass was *Waldglas* (forest glass, sometimes known in English as 'green glass'), so named because the alkaline was potash derived from the ashes of forest woods, principally beech. Most German glass was utilitarian, and *Waldglas* was most commonly used for the production of the *Römer*, a wineglass which in the fifteenth century was a simple beaker decorated with raspberry prunts; the descendants of the *Römer*, which gradually acquired a hemispherical bowl and hollow foot, are still used in the Rhineland (and the Netherlands) for white wine. Other common glasses included the *Krautstrunk* (a fifteenth-century glass tumbler, also known as a *Warzenbecher*, decorated with reliefs modelled on cabbage stems), the *Nuppenbecher* (a fifteenth-century drinking-glass decorated with drops of glass drawn out to points), the *Passglas* (a sixteenth-century communal glass in which individual shares were marked by rings), the *Humpen* (a sixteenth-century beer glass, often with a handle like a tankard), and the *Reichsadlerhumpen* (a mid-sixteenth-century glass, also known as *Adlerglas* or *Adlerhumpen*, decorated in enamel with the eagle of the HOLY ROMAN EMPIRE, displaying on its wings the armorial bearings of the 56 noble families of the Empire). The finest German glass was made in Hall-in-Tirol, where a glasshouse was established in 1534, and in Innsbruck, where Archduke FERDINAND OF TIROL founded a glasshouse soon after becoming regent of the Tirol in 1567; a beaker said to have been blown personally by the duke is now in the Kunsthistorisches Museum in Vienna.

In Bohemia the *Krautstrunk* and the *Passglas* were made on a small scale, but production was centred on the manufacturing of fine glass for the imperial court. The most important glassmaker was Kaspar LEHMANN, who developed the art of wheel engraving on glass.

In the early sixteenth century an influx of Venetian craftsmen to Flanders (especially Antwerp and Liège) created a fashion for Venetian glass, which when made in the Venetian style under the influence of expatriate Venetian craftsmen came to be known as *façon de Venise*.

Elsewhere in Europe glass was predominantly utilitarian, even in countries which were later to become important centres of glass manufacturing, such as England (Newcastle), France (Saint-Louis and Baccarat, both in the Vosges), and Spain (La Granja). The equivalent of *Waldglas* in France was *verre de fougère*, which was made with bracken. In England the comparable product was Weald glass, in which, as in Germany, the alkaline was potash derived from the ashes of forest woods. In the 1580s deforestation forced glassmakers to move first to Hampshire and Gloucestershire and then north to Staffordshire and the Scottish borders; in 1615 the use of wood for glassmaking was prohibited. Glass in the Venetian style was first made in England by Giacomo VERZELINI.

D. Klein and W. Lloyd, *The History of Glass* (1984); G. Malandro, *I vetrai di Altare* (1983); D. Heikamp, *Studien zur Mediceischen Glaskunst* (1986); E. Egg, *Die Glashütten zu Hall und Innsbruck im 16 Jahrhundert* (1962); C. Sellner, *Der Gläserne Wald* (1988); G. H. Kenyon, *The Glass Industry of the Weald* (1967).

**GLAZE**, a vitreous surface applied to pottery to make it watertight. Clay pottery that is unglazed can only be vitrified (and so made impermeable) by firing it at a temperature so high that there is a considerable risk of fracturing or melting. The glazing of pottery is the solution to the problem of rendering vessels watertight at comparatively low temperatures. Glazes are made of clay to which is added a fluxing agent (such as lead) that will melt at a low temperature. The glaze is applied as a liquid after the pottery has been fired and (usually) after it has been painted. The pottery is then fired at a low temperature, which causes the glaze to melt and to adhere to the pottery.

The principal glazes in use in Renaissance Europe were the lead glaze, the tin glaze, and the salt glaze. Lead glazes were used for domestic pottery from remote antiquity until the nineteenth century, when its use was restricted by law because of the risk of lead poisoning when lead oxide (litharge) and lead carbonate were in their raw state. TIN-GLAZED EARTHENWARE was used for the display potteries known as MAIOLICA in Italy, FAIENCE in France, Germany, Scandinavia, and Spain, Delft in the Netherlands, and English DELFTWARE in Britain. Salt glazes were used for STONEWARE pottery such as BELLARMINES.

**GLOBE PLAYHOUSES** (1599–1613, 1614–44). Built in 1599 on Bankside in Southwark by Richard BURBAGE and his brother, using materials from the demolished THEATRE, this circular building contained an apron stage, a pit for standing spectators, galleries for seated spectators, and an open roof, which meant it was used only for summer play performances. SHAKESPEARE was a shareholder and actor at the Globe, where some of his plays were first performed. In 1613 the building burned down; it was later rebuilt, but closed in 1642. A replica of the original building, which is open to the public, now stands on Bankside.

**GLOBES**, revolving spheres, mounted at the poles, depicting either the earth (terrestrial globes) or the heavens (celestial globes). A celestial globe constructed from rings representing the circles used by astronomers is known as an ARMILLARY SPHERE. In western Europe, the first terrestrial globe was made by Martin BEHAIM in 1492, and is now in the Germanisches Nationalmuseum in Nuremberg. Pairs of globes were made as library furniture, but were sometimes also used for astronomical and navigational purposes. A globe enabled a navigator either to determine latitude from two altitude observations of the sun (or two stars) or to fix position by determining the azimuth of a celestial body or to determine the rhumb line course (and distance) between any two points on the globe. Manuals such as the *Tractatus de globis et eorum usu* (1592; translated 'for the benefit of the unlearned' 1632) of Robert Hues (1553–1632) offered instruction on the navigational use of globes (in this case those of the English globe-maker Emery Molyneux). CHART-MAKERS were slow to realize that MERCATOR's projection (in which rhumb lines were straight) provided a cheap and efficient alternative to globes, which remained in use throughout the seventeenth century (as did successive editions of Hues's manual), but thereafter globes fell into disuse for purposes of navigation.

In the Renaissance a few wealthy patrons, such as the Landgrave WILHELM IV, commissioned mechanical globes that reproduced the motions of the sun, moon, and planets and the movement of the sphere of fixed stars.

**GNESIO-LUTHERANS**, the modern term (coined from German *Gneiss*, 'rock') for the party of uncompromising Lutherans who opposed the LEIPZIG INTERIM of December 1548. The leaders of the Gnesio-Lutherans were Nikolaus von AMSDORF and Matthias FLACIUS ILLYRICUS, and their principal opponents were Philipp MELANCHTHON and his followers (the 'Philippists'), who had accepted the terms of the Leipzig Interim on the grounds that the concessions to Catholicism were merely ADIAPHORA. As the controversy developed, the Gnesio-Lutherans accused the Philippists of covert Calvinism in their doctrine of the EUCHARIST and of covert Catholicism in their SOTERIOLOGY; the latter issue was pursued through the 1550s and 1560s in the controversies about SYNERGISM, Majorism (see MAIER, GEORG), and Osiandrism (see OSIANDER, ANDREAS). Attempts to restore unity amongst the Lutherans failed at the Diet of WORMS in 1557 and at the Diet of Naumburg in 1561, but after the principal controversialists had died, unity was finally achieved in the Formula of CONCORD in 1577.

R. Kolb, 'Dynamics of Party Conflict in the Saxon Late Reformation: Gnesiolutherans vs Philippists', *Journal of Modern History*, 49 (1977).

**GOD**. The Christian god of early modern Europe differed from his modern counterpart in the extent to which he could be described anthropomorphically. If man had been created in the image of God, then it followed that God resembled man in his physical composition and was capable of experiencing human emotions. God was invariably described as male, and the anthropomorphic attributes mentioned in the early books of the Old Testament (where the god has arms and legs and is able to turn his back and lose his temper) were regarded by most Christians as unproblematical. God appeared on the stages of Europe as a character in the mystery plays of England (speaking Cornish and Latin as well as English) and France. As late as the mid-seventeenth century, Ludowick Muggleton could speculate about the height of God, which he estimated to be six feet.

Professional theologians took a more complex view of God. The Catholic view, affirmed at the COUNCIL OF TRENT, was essentially a recapitulation of the doctrine of God developed by THOMAS AQUINAS, who sought to balance an anthropomorphic conception of God with an assertion of divine transcendence that derives from AUGUSTINE. The Reformers reacted against this coolly speculative conception of God by constructing an intensely personal god with whom the individual believer had a one-to-one relationship. One important difference, however, was that the God of Catholicism continued to perform miracles, whereas the God of Protestantism had ceased to intervene in the natural world after Pentecost, and restricted his miracles to the operation of GRACE in the souls of believers. Alongside these orthodox views of God, there was an abundance of heterodox views: NICHOLAS OF CUSA's emphasis on the immanence of God in the world introduced a strain of pantheism into Christian thought that was later developed by Giordano BRUNO, who was burnt because of his belief in a god who was the world-soul. The first stirrings of atheism are heard in the sixteenth century, and the robust tradition of detesting the God in whom one perforce believed emerged in literary figures such as RABELAIS and Christopher MARLOWE.

The god of the Renaissance was a father, and in most theological circles God the Father was the senior member of a holy trinity. The divine trinity originated in the tricephalous gods of prehistoric Europe and entered the Christian tradition through the neo-Plotinian triads of late antiquity. In the Orthodox churches of the East, the insistence on the primacy of God the Father ensured that the Holy Spirit was deemed to have been generated by the Father alone. In the Catholic tradition of the West, the procession of the Holy Spirit was attributed equally to Father and Son, which in some measure safeguarded the co-equality of the three persons; in practice, however, the veneration of Mary as mother of God, together with the fact that the Holy Spirit, except in a few portrayals of the Trinity as identical triplets (e.g. Bernaert van ORLEY's *Dormition of the Virgin*, 1520, in the Brussels Municipal Hospital), was not represented as a person but rather as a dove or as tongues of fire, meant that the Spirit was occluded in the popular imagination by Mary. In the Protestant traditions of northern Europe, the emphasis on SOTERIOLOGY created a different balance, in that the Son became the most important member of the Trinity because of his centrality in the process of salvation. The only serious dissent from the Trinitarian consensus came from Socinianism (see SOCINUS) and UNITARIANISM.

In the art of late antiquity, God the Father was portrayed as a young man: in the fifth-century mosaics of Santa Maria Maggiore in Rome, for example, a distinctly youthful God

the Father presides over scenes from the Old Testament. This young god survived as late as the thirteenth century, as may be seen in mosaics in St Mark's Cathedral in Venice and sculptures in Chartres Cathedral. Throughout this early period God the Father is usually represented by his right hand, which is protruding downwards from the clouds; this tradition, variously known as *Dextera Domini* (the right hand of the Lord) or *Dextera Dei* (the right hand of God), survived as late as the fifteenth century in Annunciation scenes.

God was transformed in the art of the Renaissance into an elderly bearded man, the biblical Ancient of Days whose 'garment was white as snow and the hair of his head like the pure wool' (Daniel 7: 9). From about 1300 this elderly god looks benignly down on the baptism of Jesus (e.g. GIOTTO's Arena Chapel in Padua, BELLINI's painting in Santa Corona in Vicenza, and GHIBERTI's carved font in San Giovanni, Siena), and he soon begins to appear in representations of the Annunciation (MELOZZO DI FORLI's painting in the Pantheon and Fra BARTOLOMEO's in SS Annunziata in Florence) and the Creation (most famously in MICHELANGELO's paintings on the ceiling of the SISTINE CHAPEL). Sometimes God the Father forsakes his simple robes in favour of papal regalia, as in the VAN EYCK altarpiece in Ghent and BOTTICELLI's *Coronation of the Virgin* in the Accademia in Florence. The grandest depictions of God the Father include those in RAPHAEL's *Disputa* (Stanza della Segnatura, Vatican, 1509–11) and TITIAN's *Gloria* (Prado, 1551–4). On depictions of Jesus, see JESUS IN THE RENAISSANCE.

Protestantism, like Judaism, is iconoclastic, and God the Father is not represented pictorially in Protestant art. Protestants did, however, inherit from their Catholic forebears the tradition of representing God the Father visually through the tetragrammaton, i.e. the four-lettered Hebrew word יהרה. In the Jewish tradition, the name of God was too sacred for utterance, so when the name was read aloud, the Hebrew 'Adonai' (a word of Phoenician origin meaning 'Lord', hence the Greek 'Adonis') was substituted; JEROME made the same substitution in his rendering of Exodus 6: 3, and John WYCLIFFE followed Jerome's example in his English translation, in which he used 'Adonay'. Similarly, in the Greek text of the Septuagint, ὁ κύριος ('the Lord') was substituted, and this convention entered the Latin tradition through Vulgate *dominus* and thence migrated into vernacular traditions, such as the English Authorized Version, where JHVH is translated as 'the Lord'. In 1516, Petrus Galatinus (in *De arcanis catholice veritatis*) superimposed the Massoretic vowels of 'Adonai' on the consonants of 'JHVH' and produced the conflated form 'JeHoVaH', which became in its various vernacular variants the name of God; 'Jehovah' was introduced into English by TYNDALE in his translation of 1530.

Gods other than the Christian god were given short shrift, but their existence was not normally denied. Such gods, together with the moribund gods of the Old Testament (e.g. Baal), were usually thought to be fallen angels.

**GODEFROY, DENIS, or Dionysius Gothofredus** (1549–1622), French humanist jurist. He was educated at the Collège de Navarre and studied law at Louvain, Cologne, and

Heidelberg. He returned to Paris in 1573, but his conversion to Calvinism led to his appointment as professor of law at Geneva, where in 1587 he became a member of the Council of the Two Hundred. At the invitation of Henri IV he returned to France and became grand bailiff of Gex, but shortly after he arrived to take up his post, the town was destroyed (and his library burnt) by the forces of the duke of Savoy. In 1591 he became professor of Roman law at Strassburg, but in 1600 accepted the invitation of the elector palatine, Friedrich IV, to become professor of law at Heidelberg. In 1621, when imperial troops were poised to sack Heidelberg, he returned to Strassburg, where he died the following year.

Godefroy wrote widely on Roman law, but his reputation as a jurist rests on his *Corpus iuris civilis cum notis* (Geneva, 1583), which brought together a humanist edition of the *Digest* and the Accursian and other glosses; it appeared in more than twenty editions and was long regarded as the definitive work on the Justinian *Corpus*. Godefroy's two sons also became eminent jurists: Théodore (1580–1649), who reverted to Catholicism and settled in France, wrote a classic work on royal ceremonial (*Le Cérémonial de France*, 1619), and Jacques (1587–1652), who remained loyal to Calvinism and Geneva, prepared a masterly edition of the *Codex Theodosianus* (1665).

DBF, s.v. 15. Godefroy (Denis and Jacques) and 40. Godefroy (Théodore).

**GODUNOV, BORIS** (1551–1605), tsar of Russia from 1598, a nobleman of Tartar origin who entered the service of IVAN IV. In 1580 his sister married the Tsarevich Fyodor, on whose accession four years later Godunov became the regent of Russia. He remained the most powerful figure in Russia throughout the reign of Fyodor, and in 1598 was elected as his successor. Godunov maintained links with the West, allowing members of the English MUSCOVY COMPANY to trade and admitting some Protestant missionaries. His reign was dramatized in Pushkin's play and Mussorgsky's opera.

RBS s.v. Boris Fyodorovich Godunov.

**GOES, HUGO VAN DER** (*c*.1440–1482), Flemish painter, born in Ghent, where he entered the Guild of Painters in 1467; the following year he worked in Bruges on the design of a pageant for the wedding of CHARLES THE BOLD and Margaret of York, and in 1473 he designed the pageantry for the funeral of PHILIP THE GOOD. He then entered the monastery of the Rode Kloster in Brussels as a lay brother, but continued to paint. In the final year of his life he became insane.

Hugo's major work was the Portinari altarpiece, which was commissioned by Tommaso Portinari (the Bruges agent of the MEDICI bank) for the church of the Hospital of Santa Maria Nuova (on the site of what is now the University of Florence). The central panel of this huge altarpiece, which is now in the Uffizi, is a *Nativity*; Hugo's mastery of the Flemish tradition of STILL LIFE is apparent in the symbolic flowers in the foreground. The wings of the altarpiece depict the donor and his family when open, and an *Annunciation* when closed.

None of Hugo's paintings is signed or dated, but the securely documented attribution of the Portinari altarpiece facilitates other attributions on stylistic grounds, though dating remains problematical. His other important paintings are the Monforte altarpiece (Gemäldegalerie, Berlin), the diptych of *The Fall of Adam and Eve* (Kunsthistorisches Museum, Vienna), the *Death of the Virgin* (Groeningemuseum, Bruges), and the wings of an altarpiece (or possibly the shutters of an organ) commissioned by Edward Bonkil for Trinity College, Edinburgh (National Gallery of Scotland, Edinburgh); on the reverse of one of the panels Hugo depicts one of the music-making angels playing an organ.

BNB; MDA; NBW xi; Elisabeth Dhanens, *Hugo van der Goes* (French trans. 1998).

**GÓIS, DAMIÃO DE** (1502–74), Portuguese humanist and historian, educated at the court of King MANUEL I. In 1523 King JOHN III sent Góis to Antwerp as the representative in the Portuguese FEITORIA; this post proved to be the first of a series of diplomatic appointments in European courts. He lived for four years in Padua (where he met Pietro BEMBO) and six years in Louvain (where he married the aristocratic Johanna van Hargen). Góis moved in radical humanist circles, and his acquaintances included Cardinal Jacopo SADOLETO, Martin LUTHER, and ERASMUS; these contacts eventually attracted the attention of the Portuguese INQUISITION, which repeatedly interviewed Góis and finally arrested him in 1571; he died shortly after his release from prison.

Góis's first scholarly work was *Fides, religio, moresque Aethiopum* (1540), a study of Ethiopian Christianity based on the reports of Portuguese travellers who had visited Ethiopia in search of the legendary kingdom of PRESTER JOHN. He subsequently wrote on the Lapps and on Portuguese imperialism in India. His most important Portuguese works were accounts of the reigns of the two monarchs whom he had served, a four-volume *Crónica do felicíssimo rei Dom Manoel* (1566–7) and a shorter *Crónica do príncipe Dom João* (1568).

DHP; Elisabeth Hirsch, *Damião de Góis: The Life and Thought of a Portuguese Humanist* (1967); Jeremy Lawrance, 'Damião de Góis on Prester John and the Ethiopians', *Renaissance Studies*, 6 (1992); José Fernando Tavares, *Damião de Góis: Um paradigma erasmiano no humanismo português* (1999).

**GOLDEN FLEECE, ORDER OF THE, or** (French) **Ordre de la Toison d'Or**, a chivalric ORDER instituted on 29 January 1430 by PHILIP THE GOOD, duke of Burgundy, in honour of his marriage to Isabella of Portugal. The origin of the name has been disputed from the outset, and is variously understood to refer to the quest of Jason for the golden fleece, the biblical story of Gideon, the Flemish wool trade (the wedding took place in Bruges), and the golden hair of Philip's mistress Marie de Rambrugge. Membership was in the first instance restricted to the grand master (the sovereign) and 24 noblemen and then expanded to 30 noblemen. The sovereign undertook to consult the knights of the Order before declaring war, and the knights were given the right to be tried by their fellow knights on charges of heresy, rebellion, or treason. This right was to be violated when the duke of ALBA refused the request of the counts of EGMONT and HOORNE to be tried by their fellow knights of the Golden Fleece.

The Order was dissolved on the death of CHARLES THE BOLD in 1477, but revived the following year by his son-in-law Archduke Maximilian (later the Emperor MAXIMILIAN I), who used the knights as mediators with his Netherlandish subjects. In 1516 CHARLES V opened membership to Spanish noblemen. During the sixteenth century the knights were used as a consultative body by Charles V and MARGARET OF PARMA.

The Habsburg dynasty in Spain was extinguished in 1700, and in 1713 the Emperor Charles VI instituted the Order in Austria, since which time there have been separate Orders of the Fleece in Austria and Spain. Although the Order was preceded by the English Order of the Garter (1348), it was the Burgundian Order of the Golden Fleece that became the model for chivalric orders such as the Order of the Elephant founded by King CHRISTIAN I of Denmark in 1462, the Order of St Michael founded by King LOUIS XI of France in 1469, and the Order of the Holy Ghost (Saint Esprit) founded by King HENRI III of France in 1578.

**GOLDEN ROSE or Papal Rose**, a flowering ornamental rose made of gold, decorated with gems, and mounted in a vase. Golden Roses have for centuries been blessed by popes on Rose Sunday (the fourth Sunday in Lent) and then presented to rulers and communities who have served the Church. The origin of the practice is unknown, but in 1049 Pope Leo IX described it as an ancient institution. The Golden Rose given by Pope Clement V (pope 1305–14) to the prince-bishop of Basel is now in the Musée de Cluny in Paris and the one given by Pope PIUS II to Siena in 1459 is now in the Palazzo Pubblico in Siena. The Golden Rose is now often sent to the queens of Catholic countries.

**GOLDEN SECTION**, the nineteenth-century name for what EUCLID and his successors knew as 'extreme and mean proportion' (*Elements*, book 6, proposition 3), which in the Renaissance was sometimes called 'divine proportion'. In his treatise of this title (1509) PACIOLI suggests that the proportion would be useful to architects, but there is no evidence that it proved to be so. In particular, it is not found in the list of useful proportions provided by SERLIO (1545). There is no evidence that 'divine proportion' played any part in the work of painters or sculptors. What is now known about the Renaissance suggests very strongly indeed that the supposed importance of the 'golden section' is an artefact of nineteenth-century historiography.

**GOLEM** is the name given to a living human being modelled from clay and brought into full existence by the power of CABBALA. The concept of the golem exists in ancient Jewish sources; in Christian accounts the process of creating a golem usually involves little more than writing letters, including the name of GOD (the tetragrammaton), on the forehead of the model, with suitable incantations. From the later seventeenth century onwards, Christian sources ascribe golem-making to the Jews of various GHETTOS, mainly in Poland, in

the sixteenth century. The story that Rabbi Loew of Prague (Yehudah ben Bezalel, the Maharal, 1513–1609) made a golem to protect the Jews in the reign of RUDOLF II seems to be a nineteenth-century invention, possibly a tribute to the rabbi's fame or possibly an attempt to explain the fact that the Jews did indeed suffer little persecution during the reign of Rudolf II. Rabbi Loew's writings show that he had no interest in cabbala.

Moshe Idel, *Golem: Jewish Magical and Mystical Traditions on the Artificial Anthropoid* (1990).

**GOLTZIUS, HENDRIK** (1558–1617), Dutch engraver of German ancestry, trained in the studio of Dirck COORNHERT. He worked as an engraver in Haarlem, and in 1590 travelled to Rome to study Italian art. The work that Goltzius produced after his return to the Netherlands shows the stylistic influence of his Italian experience. His finest works are landscape and portrait drawings.

Hendrik Goltzius is sometimes confused with Hubert Goltzius (1526–83), a Flemish printmaker.

*MDA* s.v. Goltzius, Hendrick; *NNBW*.

**GOMAR, FRANCIS, or (Latin) Franciscus Gomarus** (1563–1641), Dutch Calvinist leader, born in Bruges and educated in Strassburg, Oxford, Cambridge, and Heidelberg. In 1586 he was appointed pastor of the Dutch church in Frankfurt, and in 1594 he returned to the Netherlands to assume the chair of theology at Leiden. He opposed the theology of GRACE set out by ARMINIUS, who became his colleague at Leiden in 1603; the fact that they worked in the same faculty served only to intensify the bitterness of their dispute. A year after the death of Arminius in 1609, the vacated chair was filled by the Arminian Conradus VORSTIUS, whom Gomar denounced as a heretic. Gomar resigned in 1611, and subsequently taught at Middelburg (1611–15), Saumur (1615–18), and Groningen (1618–41).

*BNB* and *NNBW* vii, s.v. Gomarus.

**GÓMARA, FRANCISCO**. See LÓPEZ DE GÓMARA, FRANCISCO.

**GOMBERT, NICOLAS** (c.1495–c.1560), French composer who from 1526 was in the service of CHARLES V at the imperial court. He wrote motets, masses, and secular songs.

**GOMES, DIOGO** (*fl.* 1440, d. 1482), Portuguese mariner and historian, a courtier who was employed from 1440 as a receiver of the royal customs at Cintra and from 1466 as 'judge' of the royal customs (*juiz das causas e feitorias contadas de Cintra*). He twice commanded expeditions down the coast of AFRICA, travelling as far as the Cape Verde Islands; like CADAMOSTO before him, he claimed to have named São Tiago, the largest of the islands. He also sailed up the estuary of the Gambia river.

Gomes wrote one of the first European accounts of the ethnography and physical geography of West Africa. He composed for the benefit of the geographer Martin BEHAIM a three-part account of the exploration of the coast of Africa initiated by HENRY THE NAVIGATOR, whose navigational aspirations (and final illness) he describes in detail. Gomes's story of the discovery of Guinea (*De prima inventione Guineae*), the progressive discovery of islands in the Atlantic (*De insulis primo inventis in mare* [*sic*] *Occidentali*), and the discovery of the AZORES (*De inventione insularum de Açores*) was translated by Behaim into Latin, and is preserved in a manuscript that belonged to Conrad PEUTINGER.

*DHP.*

**GONÇALVES, NUNO** (*fl.* 1450–71), Portuguese painter who appears fleetingly in the documentary record in 1463, when he was a court painter to King AFONSO V. Gonçalves is assumed to be the artist who in the 1460s painted the *St Vincent* reredos (now in the Museu Nacional de Arte Antiga, Lisbon), which portrays in a realistic idiom members of the court and the ESTATES, including what may be lifelike portraits of the royal family.

DHP; MDA; R. Dos Santos, *Nuno Gonçalves: The Great Portuguese Painter of the Fifteenth Century* (1955); Lita Scarlatti, *Os painéis de Nuno Gonçalves* (1990).

**GONDOLA or** (Renaissance Latin) *cymba*. The flat-bottomed boats of Venice, with their characteristic metal-work at bow and stern (*ferri* or *delfini*) and platform (*poppa*) for the gondolier, who propels the boat with one oar, are first mentioned in 1084. Until SUMPTUARY legislation promulgated in 1562 required all gondolas to be painted black, all cabins (*felzi*) to be plain, and all *ferri* to be ungilded, gondolas were shaded by brightly coloured awnings, sometimes richly embroidered, mounted on an arched framework that was open at both ends. Such gondolas are depicted in the late fifteenth-century paintings of CARPACCIO and Gentile BELLINI.

Giovanni Marangoni, *Gondola e gondolieri* (1970); Dennis Romano, 'The Gondola as a Marker of Station in Venetian Society', *Renaissance Studies*, 8 (1994).

*GONFALONIERE.* A *gonfalone* was a military banner which by metonymy came to represent an administrative district within a city responsible for raising a portion of the civic militia; the *gonfaloniere* was the head of the district. In Florence the term *gonfaloniere* was also used to designate the chairman of the Signoria, or principal political council.

**GÓNGORA Y ARGOTE, LUIS DE** (1561–1627), Spanish poet, born in Córdoba, the son of Francisco de Argote, *corregidor* of the city, and Leonora de Góngora, who was descended from an ancient family whose name Luis used as his surname. He attended the University of Salamanca, ostensibly to study civil law and canon law, but an enthusiasm for gambling and prostitutes is said to have cost him his degree and incurred considerable debts. He took minor orders, and on returning to Córdoba accepted a canonry arranged by his father. In 1589 he was summoned before his bishop and accused of neglecting his duties in the choir in favour of gambling dens, theatres, and bullfighting arenas; Góngora replied that he could not possibly sing in the choir, because he had been placed between one prebend who sang too loudly and another who was deaf. Góngora was ordained

priest in 1605 or 1606, and thereafter lived principally in Valladolid and Madrid; he was eventually appointed chaplain to King PHILIP III, a post arranged by his patron the duke of LERMA, whom he rewarded with his long *Panegírico al duque de Lerma* (1617). In 1609 he began to suffer from arteriosclerosis; in 1627, as he was collecting his poems for publication, he died of apoplexy. His poems were published later in the year as *Obras en verso del Homero español*, edited by Juan López de Vicuña.

Góngora's early reputation as a poet was established by his publication of twelve ballads in the *Flor de romances nuevos* (Huesca, 1589) compiled by Pedro de Moncayo, and various sonnets and *canciones* in the *Flores de poetas ilustres* (Valladolid, 1605) compiled by Pedro Espinosa. He continued to write in these genres, and also wrote *silvas* (an Italian verse form combining hendecasyllabic and heptasyllabic lines, used by Góngora in his *Soledades*), *letrillas* (lyrics in which the same line, an *estribillo*, concludes each verse), two plays (*Las firmezas de Isabela* and *El doctor Carlino*), and three long poems (the panegyric on the duke of Lerma, *Polifemo*, and *Soledades*). It is on the last two and on his sonnets that Góngora's reputation as one of Europe's finest baroque poets rests. His *Fábula de Polifemo y Galatea* (1613) is an evocation in *octavas reales* of the Ovidian story of Acis, Galatea, and the jealousy of Polyphemus in book 13 of the *Metamorphoses*. *Soledades*), issued in an edition with a commentary by García de Salcedo Coronel (1636), was planned as a four-book poem written in *silvas*, but Góngora completed only the *Soledad primera* (a narrative set in the solitude of the countryside) and a substantial section of the *Soledad segunda* (the solitude of the seashore); the other 'solitudes' were probably going to be enacted in the forests and the deserts.

These poems mark the apogee of the style known in Spanish as *culteranismo*, a mannerist exaggeration of classical *imitatio* involving a heavily Latinized diction and syntax, an erudite battery of allusions, a profusion of witty conceits, and an abundance of hyperbolic sensual imagery. Although Góngora's learned style is not easily accessible, its extraordinary linguistic density and vividly sensual colour is instantly exciting. The verbal pyrotechnics also mask a delicate sensibility that enables Góngora to link his human figures to their pastoral environments with a natural immediacy that few poets can command. Perhaps the most remarkable feature of the poems, however, is their utter lack of moral theme or narrative; their descriptions of nature have an austere purity and a concentration on the senses which is almost abstract in its intensity, and without parallel in contemporary art. Perhaps for this reason, perplexed seventeenth-century detractors of Góngora's style deplored its surface obscurity, which came to be known as GONGORISM.

A. A. Parker, *Polyphemus and Galatea: The Interpretation of a Baroque Poem* (1977); Ángel Pariente, *Góngora* (1982).

**GONGORISM**, a baroque literary movement and style in Spanish poetry known by its detractors as *gongorismo* or *culteranismo*. The eponym of gongorism is Luis de GÓNGORA Y ARGOTE; the term *culteranismo*, which was coined in the seventeenth century, carried both the pejorative connotation of a religious cult (by analogy to *luteranismo*, i.e. Lutheranism) and the similarly hostile denotation, much inflamed by the anti-Andalusian prejudices of Castilian critics, of a coterie literary style characterized by artificiality and ostentatious erudition. An apologia for the gongorist movement, which came to be regarded as its manifesto, was the *Libro de la erudición poética* by Góngora's younger contemporary and fellow Andalusian Luis de CARRILLO Y SOTOMAYOR, which was published in his posthumous *Obras* of 1611.

The foremost embodiment of the principles of gongorism was the work of Góngora himself, particularly his three long poems *Polifemo* and *Soledades*. The style, which was imitated by gongorist writers such as the count of VILLAMEDIANA, Pedro Soto de Rojas (1584–1658), Gabriel Bocángel y Unzueta (1603–58), and Salvador Jacinto Polo de Medina (1603–76), was Latinate in its syntax, sentence length, and sentence structure (phrases and clauses are often balanced), learned in its range of reference to classical and contemporary foreign literatures, and elevated in its poetical diction, in which neologisms, recondite archaisms, and elaborate paraphrasis were favoured over more comprehensible forms.

Beyond Spain, gongorism was most prominent in Portugal (where it became the dominant style of seventeenth-century poetry). The style has parallels in England (where it was known as EUPHUISM) and in southern Italy, where its champion was Giambattista MARINO.

Andrée Collard, *Nueva poesia: Conceptismo, culteranismo en la crítica española* (1967); María Cristina Quintero, *Poetry as Play: Gongorismo and the Comedia* (1991).

**GONZAGA, ERCOLE** (1505–63), cardinal and regent of Mantua, the second son of Francesco GONZAGA and Isabella d'ESTE. He was consecrated bishop at the age of 16, and was then educated at the University of Bologna (1521–5) before being created cardinal in 1527. From 1540 he governed Mantua as regent for his nephews, first for Francesco III (1540–50) and then for Guglielmo (1550–63). In 1562 he presided over the final session of the COUNCIL OF TRENT.

*MDA* s.v. Gonzaga (10) Ercole Gonzaga.

**GONZAGA, FEDERICO I** (1441–84), marquis of Mantua, the son of Ludovico II GONZAGA and Barbara of Brandenburg, the niece of the Emperor SIGISMUND. He succeeded his father in 1478. Federico was a distinguished *condottiere* who fought for Bona of Savoy (widow of Gian Galeazzo SFORZA and regent of Milan) and Lorenzo de' MEDICI; he also fought for the ESTE against Pope SIXTUS IV and for his dominions of Ferrara and Mantua against the Venetians.

*DBI* s.v. Federico I; *MDA* s.v. Gonzaga (4) Federico I Gonzaga.

**GONZAGA, FEDERICO II** (1500–40), marquis of Mantua (from 1519), duke of Mantua (from 1530), and marquis of Monferrato (from 1536), the eldest son of Francesco GONZAGA and Isabella d'ESTE. He served as captain-general of the papal army in its struggle with the Empire, but then changed sides and supported CHARLES V. His reward after the Peace of CAMBRAI was an expansion of the Gonzaga territories and a dukedom conferred by the emperor. Federico's lavish patronage of the arts culminated in the construction of the Palazzo del Tè, which was designed by GIULIO ROMANO.

*DBI* s.v. Federico II; *MDA* s.v. Gonzaga (9) Federico II Gonzaga.

**GONZAGA, FRANCESCO I** (1366–1407), *signore* and captain-general of Mantua and captain-general of Venice, the son of Ludovico I Gonzaga, whom he succeeded in 1382. His rule was dominated by the need to defend Mantua against the attempts of Gian Galeazzo VISCONTI to acquire Mantua. As captain-general of Venice, he conquered Verona and Padua in 1406.

In 1395 Francesco commissioned Bartolino da Novara to build the fortress of Castello San Giorgio, which is the most important surviving monument of his fortifications. He also commissioned the Church of Santa Maria delle Grazie (consecrated 1399) a few miles outside the town in thanksgiving for relief from PLAGUE. His library included an important collection of French manuscripts.

*DBI*; *MDA* s.v. Gonzaga (1) Francesco I Gonzaga.

**GONZAGA, GIANFRANCESCO I** (1395–1444), *signore* (captain-general) of Mantua (from 1407) and marquis of Mantua (from 1433), the son of Francesco I GONZAGA, whom he formally succeeded in 1407 under the regency of his uncle Carlo I MALATESTA; Gianfrancesco assumed the government of Mantua in 1413. He was primarily a *condottiere*, and fought first for Venice and then for Filippo Maria VISCONTI of Milan; he later fought again for Venice and finally fought against Venice. In 1433 the Emperor SIGISMUND conferred on him the title of marquis. He invited VITTORINO DA FELTRE to his court and supported Vittorino's school in Mantua.

*DBI*; *MDA* s.v. Gonzaga (2) Gianfrancesco Gonzaga.

**GONZAGA, GIANFRANCESCO II or Francesco II** (1466–1519), marquis of Mantua, the son of Federico I GONZAGA, whom he succeeded in 1484; on 15 February 1490 he married Isabella d'ESTE. Gianfrancesco was primarily a soldier. He served as captain-general of Venice (1489–98) and in that capacity commanded the forces of the HOLY LEAGUE at the short-lived battle of FORNOVO (1495), and subsequently entered the service of LOUIS XII of France, resigning his command shortly before the French defeat at the battle of GARIGLIANO (1503). He then fought for Florence, and when he was dismissed in 1505 entered the service of Pope JULIUS II, for whom he occupied Bologna in 1506. In 1509 Gianfrancesco fought in the papal army for the League of CAMBRAI and was captured by the Venetians, who imprisoned him for a year.

During Gianfrancesco's lengthy absences Mantua was governed by Isabella d'Este, who also exercised most of the patronage during his rule. He did, however, commission the Palazzo San Sebastiano, to which he retired after his release by Venice, and also promoted music in the cathedral.

*DBI*; *MDA* s.v. Gonzaga (8) Francesco II Gonzaga.

**GONZAGA, GIULIA** (1513–66), Italian patron of artists and heretics. She was widowed in 1528 after one year of marriage to the count of Fondi and retained the small principality of Fondi (between Rome and Naples), where her court attracted artists and writers, including TASSO and ARIOSTO. Her reputation reached the ears of Barbarossa (see BARBARY PIRATES), who in 1534 attempted to kidnap her in order to send her as a present to Süleyman I the Magnificent. In 1533 Countess Giulia abandoned her court and retired to a convent near Naples, where she became a member of the Catholic reform circle of Juan de VALDÉS, which included Pietro CARNESECCHI, Vittoria COLONNA, Bernardino OCHINO, and Pietro Martire VERMIGLI. She was suspected of heresy by the Spanish INQUISITION, but died in her convent before she could be arrested.

*DBI.*

## GONZAGA, LUDOVICO II (1412–78), marquis of Mantua,
the son of Gianfrancesco I GONZAGA. He received a humanist education from VITTORINO DA FELTRE. He became a military commander, and in the war between Venice and Milan fought first for Venice and then (from 1437) for Milan. In 1443 Ludovico married Barbara of Brandenburg, the niece of the Emperor SIGISMUND. He succeeded his father in 1444, and for the next ten years was preoccupied with the ongoing war with Venice, during which time he became an ally of Francesco SFORZA. The Peace of LODI (1454) brought an end to hostilities, and Ludovico ruled in peace for the rest of his life.

Ludovico's extensive patronage included humanists such as Francesco FILELFO and Bartolomeo PLATINA and the artist MANTEGNA, whose fresco (completed 1474) in the Castello San Giorgio depicts Ludovico and his wife Barbara listening to the reading of an apostolic letter announcing the appointment of their son Francesco as a cardinal. Ludovico's alliance with Florence led to his employment of ALBERTI, who designed the Church of Sant'Andrea (subsequently built by Luca Fancelli), where Mantegna is buried and blood from the side of Jesus is preserved, and the Chapel of the Crowning of the Virgin in the cathedral.

*DBI*; *MDA* s.v. Gonzaga (3) Ludovico II Gonzaga.

## GONZAGA FAMILY, an Italian princely family which
ruled MANTUA from 1328 to 1708, first as captains-general (1328–1407) and imperial vicars (from 1329), then as marquises (1407–1519), and finally as dukes (1519–1627); from 1328 to 1354 they were also counts of Mirandola and Concordia. The five Gonzaga captains-general of Mantua were Luigi (1328–60), Guido (1360–9), Ludovico (1369–82), Francesco (1382–1407), and Gianfrancesco I GONZAGA (1407–44).

In 1433 the Emperor SIGISMUND created Gianfrancesco marquis of Mantua; his four successors as marquis were Ludovico II GONZAGA, Federico I GONZAGA, Francesco II GONZAGA, and Federico II GONZAGA.

In 1530 the Emperor CHARLES V created Federico II duke of Mantua. His successors as duke were his sons Francesco III (1540–50) and Guglielmo (1550–87); during the lifetime of Francesco (who drowned in 1550) and the minority of Guglielmo, Mantua was ruled by their uncle, Ercole GONZAGA. The third duke was Guglielmo's son Vicenzo I (1587–1612), who brought the young Rubens to Mantua as his court

painter; Vicenzo was succeeded by his three sons Francesco IV (1612), Ferdinando (1612–27), and Vicenzo II (1626–7); the Gonzaga art collection was sold by Vicenzo II in 1628, mostly to King Charles I of England, and was dispersed after the execution of King Charles in 1649. The War of the Mantuan Succession (1628–31) interrupted Gonzaga rule, but after their restoration they continued to rule until 1708.

In 1565 Luigi Gonzaga married Henrietta of Cleves, duchess of Nevers, and so this branch of the family became dukes of Nevers, where they introduced the manufacturing of FAIENCE and built the Ducal Palace (now the Palais de Justice), and overlords of Charleville (now Charleville-Mézières), where they built the magnificent Ducal Palace (dismantled in the nineteenth century) and laid out the Place Ducale; in 1659 Charles Gonzaga sold the dukedom of Nivernais to Cardinal Richelieu. The Gonzaga also ruled Monferrato, where they were marquises (1536–75) and dukes (1575–1708). The rule of the family ended in 1708, when Mantua was absorbed into the Empire and Monferrato was incorporated into Savoy.

G. Coniglio, *I Gonzaga* (1967); *Mantova e i Gonzaga* (1977), esp. A. Sestan, 'La storia dei Gonzaga nel Rinascimento'.

## GONZALO DE CÓRDOBA. See FERNÁNDEZ DE CÓRDOBA,
GONZALO.

## GÓRNICKI, ŁUKASZ (1527–1603), Polish educator and
chronicler of social life and customs. He was educated in Padua and on his return joined the court of SIGISMUND II AUGUSTUS. His most influential work was *Dworzanin polski* (1566), an imitation of CASTIGLIONE's *Il cortigiano*. He later concentrated on legal matters, and wrote *Rosmowa z Włochem*, a 'dialogue between a Pole and an Italian' on the subject of Polish freedoms and Polish laws.

## GOSNOLD, BARTHOLOMEW (d. 1607), English navigator and colonizer. In the early years of the seventeenth century, he explored the North American coast, giving Martha's Vineyard and Cape Cod their present names. His trade with native Americans raised interest in the New World, and led to the establishment of the London and Plymouth companies. In 1607 he was among the first colonists at Jamestown, Virginia, where he died of swamp fever.

*DNB.*

## GOSSAERT or Gossart, JAN, or Jan Mabuse (c.1478–1532),
Flemish painter, draughtsman, and printmaker, probably a native of Maubeuge (then in Flemish Hainaut, now in France). He was admitted to the Antwerp guild in 1503, and in 1508/9 visited Rome in the train of the Burgundian ambassador; thereafter his paintings show a marked Italian influence, which may mean that the *Adoration of the Kings* in the National Gallery in London was painted before his journey to Italy. Later works such as the Malvagna Triptych (Galleria Nazionale della Sicilia, Palermo) and *Neptune and Amphitrite* (Gemäldegalerie, Berlin) include many Italianate features such as putti. DÜRER admired the technical achievement of Gossaert's art, which he described as being 'nit

so gut im Haupstreichen als im Gemäl' ('not as good in inventiveness as in execution'), and VASARI praised Gossaert as 'quasi il primo che portasse d'Italia in Fiandra il vero modo di fare storie piene di figure ignude' ('virtually the first artist to carry the true method of representing nude figures from Italy to Flanders'); Gossaert's sensuous *Hercules* (Barber Institute, Birmingham) is a fine example of his Italianate nudes.

*MDA s.v. Gossart; NBW xii.*

**GOTHA, LEAGUE OF, or League of Torgau**, an alliance of German Protestant princes against the Catholic states of Germany, signed in February 1526 in Torgau, which was then the seat of the electors of SAXONY; the coalition is also known as the League of Torgau. The alliance, which was the initiative of the Landgrave PHILIP OF HESSE, included Magdeburg, Prussia, and Saxony.

**GOTHIC**, an architectural and art-historical term for a style of architecture and art that emerged in the twelfth century and in architecture lived on until the Gothic revival of the nineteenth century. In ecclesiastical architecture, with which the term 'Gothic' was primarily associated, the style (which emanates from the skeletal structure) is characterized by soaring vertical lines and the use of pointed arches, rib vaults, flying buttresses, traceried stained-glass windows, high clerestory windows, and pinnacles. In the conventional sequence of styles, Gothic follows Romanesque and precedes Renaissance. The term was first used in the Renaissance to disparage the architecture of earlier generations by recourse to a spurious association with the Gothic tribes that sacked Rome in late antiquity.

Individual features of Gothic architecture had long been apparent in late Romanesque architecture (and, in the case of pointed arches, Islamic architecture), but Gothic first coalesced into an integrated style in the Île de France in the mid-twelfth century: the first building to have been conceived in what later became known as the Gothic style was the choir and chevet (i.e. apse and ambulatory) of the Abbey of Saint-Denis (1140–4), and this was soon followed by Notre-Dame of Paris (begun 1163) and the cathedrals of Bourges and Laon. The Gothic style soon dominated FRENCH ARCHITECTURE, and spread from France to the rest of Europe, often through the buildings of the Cistercians. For the development of Gothic architecture beyond France, see the country entries (e.g. ENGLISH ARCHITECTURE; GERMAN ARCHITECTURE; ITALIAN ARCHITECTURE).

In sculpture and painting, the term 'Gothic' refers to the style of such works in Gothic buildings. In sculpture it refers to the naturalistic style of the sculpture of cathedral portals, which was then replicated in tombs. In painting the term refers to the style of late medieval illuminated manuscripts, and of altarpieces such as DUCCIO's *Maestà* for Siena Cathedral and the Wilton Diptych (National Gallery, London). The term 'Gothic' is also used with reference to objects into which Gothic architectural motifs have been incorporated (e.g. reliquaries and tabernacles) and to a style in which lightness and intricacy are central features. The term INTERNA-

TIONAL GOTHIC was coined in 1892 by Louis Courajod to denote a style in painting and related arts which emerged in the courts of Burgundy and France.

Cecil Stewart, *Gothic Architecture* (rev. edn. of F. M. Simpson, *History of Architectural Development*, vol. iii, 1961).

**GOUDIMEL, CLAUDE** (1514/20–72), French Huguenot composer, music publisher, and editor who worked with Nicholas de Chemin. By 1557 he was in Metz but a decade later was in Lyon where he was killed in the ST BARTHOLOMEW'S DAY MASSACRE. Amongst his sacred music his psalm settings are particularly accomplished.

**GOUJON, JEAN** (*c.*1510–*c.*1565), French sculptor and engraver. He lived in Rouen in the early 1540s, and there carved the columns supporting the organ loft in the Church of Saint-Maclou; he may also have been the designer of the tomb of Louis de Brézé (husband of DIANE DE POITIERS) in Rouen Cathedral, though the execution seems to be the work of another hand. In about 1543 Goujon moved to Paris, where he worked as a decorative sculptor with the architect Pierre LESCOT. Their collaborations include the Hôtel Carnavalet, for which Goujon carved allegorical figures representing the *Seasons* (1547), the Fontaine des Innocents (1547–9, now reconstructed), and the LOUVRE, for which Goujon made the classical caryatides in the Salle des Caryatides (1550–1). Goujon left Paris at the outbreak of the WARS OF RELIGION, and spent his final years in Bologna. He is now regarded as France's finest Renaissance sculptor. His work as an engraver includes the plates for the first French translation of VITRUVIUS (1547).

*DBF; MDA.*

**GOVÉA or Gouvean, ANTOINE, or Gouveanus** (1505–66), Portuguese humanist jurist in France, and one of the most distinguished students of Roman law in the sixteenth century. In his legal works, such as *De iure accrescendi* (1549) and *De iurisdictione* (1550), his approach was historical, and he sought to relate the development of Roman law to the history of the Roman Empire. He was also an accomplished Latin poet; his early epigrams were collected in *Epigrammatum libri duo* (1539). After his second marriage, in 1565, he moved to Turin, where he lived for the rest of his life.

*DBF s.v. Govéa.*

**GOWER, GEORGE** (*c.*1540–1596), English portrait painter. He became established as a portrait painter in London in the 1570s and in 1581 was appointed serjeant-painter to Queen Elizabeth. His portraits include *Sir Thomas Kitson* and *Lady Kitson* (1573, Tate Gallery, London), a *Self-Portrait* (1579, Milton Park, Cambridgeshire), and (probably) the 'Armada' portrait of *Queen Elizabeth* (Woburn Abbey, Bedfordshire).

*DNB; MDA.*

**GOZZOLI, BENOZZO DI LESE** (*c.*1421–1497), Italian painter, a native of Florence, where he was apprenticed as a goldsmith; he subsequently worked as an assistant to GHIBERTI on the baptistery doors in Florence (*c.*1444–7) and to Fra ANGELICO in the Vatican and in Orvieto Cathedral (*c.*1447–9).

In 1459 Piero de' MEDICI commissioned Gozzoli to decorate the chapel in the Medici Palace (now Palazzo Medici-Riccardi) in Florence. His fresco cycle *The Journey of the Magi*, which covers three walls of the chapel, represents members of the Medici family amongst the attendants. In 1467 Gozzoli painted another fresco cycle (which survives only in fragments) in the Camposanto in Pisa.

*MDA*; Diane Cole Ahl, *Benozzo Gozzoli* (1997); Cristina Luchinat (ed.), *Benozzo Gozzoli: La Cappella dei Magi* (1993).

**GRACE.** In Christian theology, grace is the supernatural assistance bestowed by God upon humankind to facilitate sanctification. The doctrine has been the subject of bitter dispute since late antiquity, when AUGUSTINE maintained that the comprehensiveness of human sinfulness meant that everyone deserved damnation and that grace was a prerequisite for the performance of good works, whether it was fully bestowed in the baptism of Christians or, in the case of Jews, heretics, and pagans, existed in attenuated form as a vestige of prelapsarian grace. Pelagius demurred, arguing that sin was only the following of an evil example, and that grace was not necessary for the performance of good works, but had been given to make it easier for Christians to obey the will of God. The third position, that of Cassian, mediated between the two and so is called semi-Pelagianism: in this compromise, grace was deemed to be universally necessary (as Augustine argued), but was not irresistible, because the human will remained free (as Pelagius argued).

The arguments were refined and complicated by the scholastics of the thirteenth century, but the Reformation and Counter-Reformation debates were essentially continuations of the debates of late antiquity. The logical (but unarticulated) inference from Augustine's position was predestination to damnation; this position was adopted by Luther in his early period and by Calvin, who fortified it with his doctrine of the indefectibility of grace. The Arminians in the Netherlands and the Laudian Church in Caroline England, however, favoured a doctrine that is recognizably Cassian; a similar argument, sometimes called SYNERGISM, was mounted by MELANCHTHON, who contended that the Holy Spirit was the prime cause of the act of conversion, but that the human will could co-operate with the Spirit.

In the Catholic Church, the debate about grace set the Dominicans in bitter opposition to the Jesuits. In 1597 Pope CLEMENT VIII decided to deal with the problem by establishing the Congregatio de Auxiliis to settle the question of how divine grace operated. The Jesuit position, as articulated by Luis de MOLINA in his *De concordia liberi arbitrii cum gratiae donis* (1598), was that the efficacy of grace did not reside within the substance of grace itself (*ab intrinseco*) but rather in God's foreknowledge of free human acceptance of this gift. This position, which is sometimes called Molinism, is a strict form of the doctrine known as congruism (*gratia de congruo*), according to which God confers grace in accordance with circumstances that in his foreknowledge he realizes will be conducive to its use; Jesuits such as AQUAVIVA, BELLARMINO, and SUÁREZ were congruists, whereas Gabriel VÁZQUEZ

defended Molinism against the congruism of Suárez. The Dominican position, which was championed by Domingo BÁÑEZ, was essentially an elaboration of the views of THOMAS AQUINAS, which was Augustinianism sharpened by the distinction between predestination to grace and predestination to glory and modified by an emphasis on free will.

The Congregation reported on 19 March 1598, condemning 90 propositions in Molina's treatise; Pope Clement refused to ratify the condemnation, so the Congregation reconvened and reduced the number of condemned propositions to twenty. Again the pope declined to acquiesce, so the debate was stalled until the accession of Pope Paul V in 1605, whereupon a third attempt to secure papal approval was rebuffed. The debate was officially closed on 5 September 1607, when Pope Paul decreed that the Dominicans could not justly be accused of Calvinism, nor the Jesuits of Pelagianism, and forbade either side to declare the teachings of the other camp to be heretical.

**GRAF, URS** (*c.*1485–1527/9), Swiss goldsmith, designer, and engraver, born in Solothurn, the son of a goldsmith. He worked as an apprentice in Strasburg and then settled in Bern. He produced large numbers of designs for goldsmiths, woodcut engravers, and glass stainers, and also executed many low-life drawings (some with a satirical edge) of peasants, prostitutes, and mercenaries; he was employed by Johann FROBEN to produce ornamental borders for his books. His principal work as a goldsmith was a reliquary (now lost) executed in 1514 for the Monastery of St Urban.

*MDA*; *NDB*.

**GRAFFITO** (plural *graffiti*) or *sgraffito*, a drawing scratched on a wall. In decorative art, the term refers to a method of decoration (used on the façades of Renaissance palaces and occasionally on interiors) in which successive layers of differently coloured plasters were applied, and a scratched design then exposed a ground of a different colour from that of the surface. The same technique was used in north Italian pottery (especially in Venice) from the thirteenth century onwards; such pottery, which is known in English as incised slipware, was a cheap alternative to MAIOLICA. Some maiolica factories, notably those in Bologna and Ferrara, used the technique to produce *maiolica graffita*.

The form *sgraffito* appears to be an English pseudo-Italian coinage formed on the analogy of terms such as *sgrammaticato* in which the prefixional 's' represents the Latin 'ex'.

**GRAFTON, RICHARD** (d. 1572), English printer. A London merchant with reformist beliefs, Grafton, in conjunction with WHITCHURCH, arranged for the printing of 'Matthews's Bible' in Antwerp *c.*1536. A further edition followed, printed at Paris, and as did the printing of the 'Great Bible' in 1539. Grafton also printed the first Book of Homilies in 1547 and the first and second Books of COMMON PRAYER.

*DNB*; *Grove*; J. A. Kingdon, *Richard Grafton* (1901).

**GRANACCI or Grannacci, FRANCESCO** (1469–1543), Italian painter, a native of Florence, where he trained in the studio of GHIRLANDAIO. His fellow pupil was MICHELANGELO, with whom he formed an enduring friendship. His paintings include *The Arrest of Joseph* (c.1515, Palazzo Davanzati, Florence).

MDA; Christian von Holst, *Francesco Granacci* (1974).

**GRANADA or (Arabic) Gharnāṭa, KINGDOM OF.** By 1275 the RECONQUISTA had been completed except for the kingdom of Granada, which remained an Islamic sultanate until 1492. The importance of Granada began to increase in the eleventh century as the caliphate of Córdoba declined. In 1238 the Almohads were displaced by the Naṣrid dynasty, which nominally acknowledged the suzerainty of King Ferdinand III of Castile. Under the 25 Naṣrid rulers who governed Granada from 1238 to 1492 the city of Granada became wealthy; the architectural symbol of its prosperity was the Alhambra. The kingdom was fatally weakened by dynastic rivalries and harem intrigue: in 1462 the sultan took a second wife, a converted Spanish slave, and so incurred the wrath of his first wife, who responded by organizing a coup and placing her son Abu 'Abdullah (Spanish Boabdil) on the throne. Prominent Moorish families were divided in their allegiance, which left Granada increasingly unable to defend itself. The final campaign was initiated by FERDINAND and ISABELLA, who captured Abu 'Abdullah and in 1482 instituted a series of sieges. The Moors finally surrendered on 2 January 1492, and Abu 'Abdullah was allowed to go into exile; the legend that he looked back at Granada from the Motril road and sighed as his mother berated him is commemorated by the place name Suspiro del Moro (and by Salman Rushdie's *The Moor's Last Sigh*). Under the terms of the surrender the Moors were allowed to retain their property and their religion, but in 1499 Islam was proscribed and a policy of forcible conversion was implemented; in 1502 all unconverted Muslims were expelled from Spain. Those who were not converted were called MORISCOS, and were subsequently persecuted by the INQUISITION and by PHILIP II, who in 1566 forbade the use of Arabic and the wearing of Moorish clothing. In the Las Alpujarras Revolt which followed, the *moriscos* proclaimed Fernando Válor as King Aben Humeya; the revolt was crushed in 1571 by the forces of Don JUAN DE AUSTRIA.

The fall of Granada in 1492 was celebrated all over Europe. In England a service of thanksgiving was held in St Paul's Cathedral at the command of King HENRY VII, and two centuries later the conquest was recalled by John Dryden in his two-part *Conquest of Granada* (1670).

In the sixteenth century Spain sought to turn Granada into a Spanish city. The cathedral is the work of Diego de SILOÉ, who supervised its construction from 1528 until his death in 1563; it was completed according to his plans, except for the façade of 1667. The adjoining Chapel Royal (Capilla Real) was commissioned by Ferdinand and Isabella and built by Enrique EGAS as the tomb of the Catholic monarchs. The Emperor CHARLES V commissioned Pedro MACHUCA to build an imperial palace (now called the Palacio de Carlos V) to rival the Alhambra. Surviving Renaissance buildings also include the Casa Castril (now the Museo Arqueológico),

which has a fine PLATERESQUE doorway, and Diego de Siloé's Monasterio de San Jerónimo.

**GRANJON, ROBERT** (1513–after 1589), French type founder, born in Paris, the son of a printer. He worked as a type founder in Paris before moving in 1566 to Lyon (where he designed characters for the printing of music) and thence Rome (where he designed oriental fonts, including Arabic); on returning to Paris he continued to develop new fonts, including one in Greek. In 1557 he designed a cursive typeface known as *Civilité*, which was widely used in France but was eventually displaced by italic. Granjon's Greek, Syriac, and *Civilité* fonts were used by Christophe PLANTIN in his Polyglot Bible (1568–73).

DBF; Grove.

**GRANVELLE, ANTOINE PERRENOT DE** (1517–86), cardinal and minister of Spain in the Netherlands, the son of Nicholas Perrenot de Granvelle, a notary who later became the imperial chancellor of CHARLES V. Antoine studied law at Padua and theology at Louvain, and in 1540, at the age of 23, was appointed bishop of Arras, in which capacity he attended the opening sessions of the COUNCIL OF TRENT. His parallel career in the service of the Empire included the negotiation of the peace at the conclusion of the SCHMALKALDIC WAR (1547), the drafting of the Treaty of Passau which concluded the war between the emperor and MAURICE OF SAXONY (1551), the negotiation of the wedding of the future PHILIP II of Spain and Queen MARY of England (1554), and attendance as a Spanish delegate at the conference that drafted the Treaty of CATEAU-CAMBRÉSIS, where his multilingualism made him a central figure.

On leaving the Netherlands for Spain in August 1559, King Philip appointed Granvelle to the Council of State, made him the principal adviser to the regent, MARGARET OF AUSTRIA, and arranged for his consecration as archbishop of Mechelen (Malines). In 1561 Granvelle became a cardinal. His loyalty to King Philip's anti-tolerationist religious policies incurred the displeasure of noblemen such as WILLIAM OF ORANGE and the count of EGMONT, and in January 1564 King Philip was obliged to dismiss Granvelle.

King Philip then sent Cardinal Granvelle to Italy, where he helped to form the HOLY LEAGUE of 1571 and to plan the battle of LEPANTO. He served as viceroy of Naples (1571–5) and Spanish ambassador to Rome (1575–9), and was then recalled to Spain to replace Antonio PÉREZ. He organized the conquest of Portugal, and advised King Philip to recall the duke of ALBA from retirement in order to command the invading army. His final diplomatic task was the arranging of the marriage of Catherine, daughter of King Philip II, to Duke CARLO EMANUELE I of Savoy, which consolidated the alliance between the Habsburgs and the House of Savoy.

M. van Durme, *Antoon Perrenot van Granvelle* (1953).

**GRASSER, ERASMUS** (c.1445/50–1518), German sculptor and woodcarver who trained in his native Tirol and subsequently worked in Bavaria. His best-known work is the late

Gothic *Moreska Tänzer* (1480), now in the Bayerisches Nationalmuseum in Munich.

*MDA; NDB.*

**GRAZZINI, ANTON FRANCESCO, or Il Lasca** (1503–84), Italian poet, playwright, and academician, born in Florence, where he worked as an apothecary while pursuing his literary and academic interests; in 1540 he became one of the founding members of the Accademia degli Umidi (later the Accademia Fiorentina) and, in 1582, of the Accademia della Crusca (see ACADEMIES). Grazzini wrote satirical poems and seven comedies, but his best-known work is a collection of *novelle* (*Le cene*, 1558).

*OCIL;* R. J. Rodini, *A. F. Grazzini, Poet, Dramatist, and Novelliere* (1970).

**GREAT SCHISM.** The term denotes both the rift between the Eastern and Western churches (1054–1965), which is sometimes called the 'Eastern Schism' or (in French) 'le schisme byzantin', and the period (1378–1417) when the Western Church was divided by the creation of antipopes.

The breach of 1054, which encompassed theological, ecclesiastical, and political differences, resulted in each side directing anathemas at the other. Attempts to reconcile the two churches were made at the Council of Lyon (1274) and the COUNCIL OF FLORENCE (1439), but the Union of Florence was formally repudiated by the Synod of Constantinople of 1484. The churches remain divided, but in 1965 Pope Paul VI and Patriarch Athenagoras simultaneously nullified the anathemas of 1054.

Gregory XI, the last pope of the Avignon exile, died in 1378, and his successor, Urban VI, so antagonized the French cardinals (who were in the majority) that they withdrew to Anagni, deposed Urban VI, and elected Cardinal Robert of Geneva as Pope Clement VII, who established his court in Avignon; his coronation on 31 October 1378 inaugurated the Great Schism of the Western Church. All but three Italian cardinals remained faithful to Urban VI, whose court was in Rome, and declared Clement to be an antipope, whereupon both popes excommunicated each other. Clement's successor in the Avignon obedience was BENEDICT XIII; in the Roman obedience, Urban VI's successors were BONIFACE IX, Innocent VII, and GREGORY XII. The COUNCIL OF PISA was convened in 1409 to resolve the split, and decided to do so by electing a Pisan pope, Alexander V, who was recognized by neither Avignon nor Rome; Alexander's successor in the Pisan obedience was JOHN XXIII. The schism was ended by the COUNCIL OF CONSTANCE, which elected MARTIN V in 1417. Thereafter two antipopes, CLEMENT VIII and the obscure Benedict XIV, formally prolonged the schism, but their followings were minute, and in reality the Western Church had been reunited.

S. Runciman, *The Eastern Schism* (1955); Walter Ullmann, *The Origins of the Great Schism* (1948); J. H. Smith, *The Great Schism, 1378* (1970).

**GREBEL, CONRAD** (c.1498–1526), Swiss Anabaptist leader, born into a patrician family in Zürich and educated in Basel,

Vienna, and Paris. On returning to Zürich he became a Zwinglian, probably early in 1522. By December 1523 Grebel had become a radical critic of the authorities in Zürich, disapproving of the Council's decision to continue the celebration of mass in the interests of civic order. Earlier in the year Grebel had become an ally of Andreas Bodenstein von KARLSTADT and Thomas MÜNTZER, and two letters to the latter written in September 1524 show that Grebel had become an opponent of infant BAPTISM. The final break with the Zwinglian Church came on 21 January 1525, when Grebel baptized Georg BLAUROCK, who then baptized other members of their dissenting group. Grebel was imprisoned in Zürich, but managed to escape; he died of plague in May 1526.

*DHBS; NDB;* J. L. Ruth, *Conrad Grebel, Son of Zurich* (1975); Leland Harder (ed.), *The Sources of Swiss Anabaptism: The Grebel Letters and Related Documents* (1985).

**GRECO, EL, or (Greek) Domenikos Theotokopoulos** (c.1541–1614), Cretan painter in Spain, born in Phodele (near Candia, now Herakleion). He lived in Venice in the late 1560s and from 1570 to 1577 worked in Rome. His surviving paintings from this period include *The Purification of the Temple* (Institute of Arts, Minneapolis), *The Healing of the Blind Man* (Galleria Nazionale, Parma), and portraits of *Giulio Clovio* (Museo Nazionale, Naples) and *Vincenzo Anastagi* (Frick, New York).

In 1577 Domenikos moved to Toledo, where he lived for the rest of his life. In Spain he was known as El Greco ('the Greek'); he signed his paintings 'El Greco' in Greek characters, sometimes adding *Kres* (Cretan). El Greco's earliest surviving painting to have been executed in Toledo is *Christ Stripped of his Garments* (1579, sacristy, Toledo Cathedral). His finest surviving painting from the 1580s is *The Burial of Count Orgaz* (1586, Church of San Tomé, Toledo), which contains all the elements of El Greco's mature style: harsh colour, unremitting light, and figures infused with intense religious emotion. The same features are apparent in late paintings such as *The Assumption* (1613, Church of San Vicente, Toledo), but as his style matured his figures became longer. The development of El Greco's tendency to elongate his figures can be seen in his portrayals of St Francis, of which more than 100 are recorded. These distortions are sometimes attributed to madness or astigmatism, but may simply reflect the influence of Greek icon painting and the MANNERIST idiom in which El Greco worked.

El Greco was primarily a painter of religious pictures, but he also painted some 40 portraits (e.g. *Cardinal Guevara*, c.1601, Metropolitan Museum, New York; *Gentleman with his Hand on his Breast*, 1577–9, Prado, Madrid) and a small number of paintings on classical subjects (*Laocoön*, c.1610, National Gallery, Washington); the influence of Flemish art is apparent in his LANDSCAPE without figures, *Toledo Landscape* (Metropolitan Museum, New York).

*MDA;* Fernando Marías, *El Greco: Biografía de un pintor extravagante* (1997).

**GREEK LANGUAGE.** The late Byzantine Greek of the Renaissance is the classic example of what linguists call a diglossic language, which is one in which a formal, consciously archaic language is used alongside a demotic language. In the case of Byzantine Greek, the formal language was a preserved and reconstituted form of ancient Attic Greek, and was the official language of education, government, and the Church; in its written form, this language stretched back to antiquity and had a long afterlife in 'pure' Greek (*katharevousa*), which was not officially abandoned until 1976. Alongside this language there was a robust demotic Greek which had evolved from the common language (*koiné*) of the ancient eastern Mediterranean, and which had been written since the twelfth century. When Greece became monoglossic in 1976, demotic Greek was the victor, though it incorporated many forms from 'pure' Greek.

Demotic Greek changed very little during the life of the Byzantine Empire, apart from a partial restructuring of its inflectional morphology and some significant phonological changes that lay at the heart of the Renaissance debate about the correct pronunciation of ancient Greek. After 1453 the fragmentation of the Byzantine Empire accelerated the process of change in the language, which was reflected partly in the formation of tenses, but more importantly in significant lexical depletion and a corresponding influx of loan words from Turkish and Venetian Italian; there was also a great deal of dialect differentiation during the Ottoman period.

The pronunciation of Greek was a matter of contention and confusion. In the East, the process of evolution from the Greek of antiquity had reduced several vowels and diphthongs to the sound of a single vowel, iota; this change was condemned by linguistic antiquarians as the error of iotacism, or, when the changed vowel was an eta, itacism, so spelt to indicate the pronunciation. Beta became fricative, as did upsilon in diphthongs. The distinction between omicron and omega was lost, and the diphthong alpha-iota came to be identical with epsilon. All of these changes are reflected in spellings in the manuscript tradition. This late Byzantine pronunciation was the medium used by Greeks in western Europe to teach classical Greek, and its main advocate in the West was REUCHLIN, whose itacistic pronunciation was championed by MELANCHTHON in his *Institutiones linguae Graecae* (1518).

The evidence that this modern pronunciation differed from the pronunciation of Greek in antiquity was accumulated by Antonio LEBRIJA and various members of the NEAKADEMIA. The discovery of this discrepancy is conventionally attributed to ERASMUS, who presumably learned of it in Venice. Erasmus did not claim to have developed the revived classical pronunciation, but it came to be known as the Erasmian pronunciation because he wrote a response to Melanchthon (*De recta Latini Graecique sermonis pronuntiatione*, Basel, 1528). Thereafter Reuchlin's pronunciation prevailed in northern Europe and Erasmus' pronunciation was favoured in southern Europe.

Byzantine Greek had inherited an alphabet of 24 letters that derived from the ancient East Ionic alphabet, and at an early stage added the accents (acute, grave, and circumflex) and breathings (rough and smooth) that remained in use in

modern Greek until 1976. In the cursive form of the language written by Byzantine merchants, there were many ligatures and contractions that are so far removed from the original letters that they function as ideograms. As it was these forms that were adopted in the printed and written Greek of western Europe, reading Renaissance Greek poses considerable problems for modern readers trained only in classical Greek. For a table of the ligatures and contractions, see Appendix 4.

**GREEK SCHOLARSHIP.** From the ninth to the thirteenth centuries, knowledge of Greek in the West was patchy, except in the isolated Greek communities of southern Italy and Sicily, and for centuries western intellectuals had been content to read Greek works in either Latin translations dating from late antiquity or more recent translations from Arabic versions. One of the first westerners to try to learn Greek was PETRARCH, who took lessons from a Greek diplomat (Barlaam) and a Calabrian monk (Leonzio Pilato) but never succeeded in being able to read his beloved copy of the *Iliad*, the gift of a Byzantine ambassador (now Ambrosian MS I 98 inf.). Between 1360 and 1362 Pilato lectured in Florence on HOMER and Euripides; these lectures were probably funded by BOCCACCIO, who organized the lectures and later claimed to have introduced the study of Greek to Tuscany at his own expense.

The traditional date at which Greek scholarship was introduced in Italy is 1397, when SALUTATI persuaded the Florentine government to invite CHRYSOLORAS to teach Greek in Florence; Pilato's lectures were clearly earlier, but scholars have been slow to relinquish the traditional date. The lectures of Chrysoloras did not inaugurate the study of Greek, but they had important cultural consequences, in that Greeks such as PLETHO, ARGYROPOULOS, BESSARION, GEORGE OF TREBIZOND, and GAZA were welcomed into Italian humanist circles as the inheritors of the Hellenic culture of classical antiquity. The first Italian to achieve what he described as total fluency in Greek was the polymath POLIZIANO, who ringingly declared that he had a better command of Greek than most Greeks and any Italian in the previous 800 years; FILELFO and GUARINO also spoke and wrote Greek fluently. The first chair of Greek in western Europe was established at Padua in 1463; Demetrius CHALCONDYLES was appointed as the founding professor in 1464.

Elsewhere in Europe, Greek was revived by expatriate Greeks (often from CRETE) and visiting Italian humanists. In France, Janos LASCARIS and Girolamo ALEANDRO introduced the study of Greek, and rapidly produced a generation of learned French Hellenists, including BUDÉ, Robert ESTIENNE, Étienne DOLET, and RABELAIS. English scholars such as William SELLYNG, William GROCYN, and Thomas LINACRE had been taught Greek in Italy by teachers such as Chalcondyles and Poliziano, and in turn had taught Greek in England; Grocyn began teaching Greek at Exeter College, Oxford, in 1491, and his pupils included ERASMUS and Sir Thomas MORE. Erasmus published his Greek New Testament in 1516, and so inaugurated a tradition of textual debate that was destined to become vituperative in much of northern Europe. In Germany REUCHLIN introduced the scholarly study of Greek, but there as in other countries embroiled in religious controversy, Greek became more of a weapon for religious polemic than a means of access to the literature of the ancient world.

The grammar and lexis of ancient Greek had long been studied in Byzantium, but there were for centuries no textbooks accessible to foreigners. Publishers of Greek such as ALDUS MANUTIUS and Zacharias CALLIERGIS included such texts in their lists alongside scholarly editions of texts. The first Greek grammar for foreigners was the *Erotemata* ('Questions') of Constantinos LASCARIS (Milan, 1476). The grammar of Chrysoloras, also called *Erotemata*, was first published in 1484; it was abridged and translated into Latin by Chysoloras's former pupil GUARINO DA VERONA, and was widely used all over Europe. By the end of the century Lascaris's grammar had appeared in a bilingual Greek and Latin version, and Aldus Manutius had published (in 1495) a volume containing the grammatical primer of Theodore Gaza and the manual of syntax by the second-century Alexandrian Apollonius Dyscolus, a copy of which had been brought from the East to Venice by Giovanni AURISPA in 1423.

The first Greek dictionary for foreigners was published by Giovanni Crastoni in Milan in 1478; it had Greek headwords and Latin definitions. The tradition inaugurated by this modest volume culminated in Henri ESTIENNE's *Thesaurus Graecae linguae* (5 vols., Geneva, 1572), which provided Latin definitions, etymological explanations, and illustrative quotations. In the case of demotic Greek, dictionaries were provided for three distinct purposes: commerce, missionary endeavour, and scholarship. The needs of commerce were first met by the *Corona preciosa* (Venice, 1527), which had Italian headwords and Latin, modern Greek, and ancient Greek equivalents. The first dictionary designed for missionary use was Giroloma Germano's *Vocabulario italiano e greco* (Rome, 1622), which was intended to assist Jesuits working in the East by providing Italian headwords and modern Greek translations. Scholars were served by the glossaries of Ioannes Meursis (Leiden, 1610) and, eventually, Du Cange (Lyon, 1688), both of which provided headwords in Byzantine and modern Greek and Latin definitions.

N. G. Wilson, *From Byzantium to Italy: Greek Studies in the Italian Renaissance* (1992); Roberto Weiss, *Medieval and Humanist Greek* (1977); R. Pfeiffer, *History of Classical Scholarship 1300–1850* (1976).

**GREENE, ROBERT** (1558–92), English playwright and poet. He was educated at Cambridge and then moved to London, where he worked as a writer of plays, pamphlets, romances, and moral dialogues, and cultivated the literary image of a profligate. Among his plays are *James the Fourth* (1598), a romantic comedy set in a fictionalized Scottish court, and *Friar Bacon and Friar Bongay* (1594), a comic treatment of the legends associated with the thirteenth-century churchmen Roger Bacon and Thomas Bungay. His romance *Pandosto* provided the plot for Shakespeare's *Cymbeline*; his *Groatsworth of Wit* (1592) famously describes Shakespeare as an 'upstart Crow beautified with our feathers'.

*DNB*.

**GREENWICH ARMOURY**. See ARMS AND ARMOUR.

**GREGORY XII** (*c*.1325–1415), pope from 30 November 1406 until his abdication on 4 July 1415, was born Angelo Correr in Venice, the son of a nobleman. He was successively appointed bishop of Castello (1380), Latin patriarch of Constantinople (1390), cardinal-priest of San Marco (1405), and papal secretary. At the papal conclave following the death of Pope Innocent VII, all fourteen Roman cardinals swore, if elected, to abdicate in the event of the antipope BENEDICT XIII abdicating or dying, to refrain from creating new cardinals except to maintain parity with Avignon, and to arrange a meeting with his rival with a view to healing the GREAT SCHISM.

On his election Gregory honoured his commitment by sending a delegation to Marseille to negotiate a meeting with Benedict XIII. On 21 April 1407 the two sides agreed that the two popes and all of their cardinals would meet in Savona (which was obedient to Avignon) on 29 September or by 1 November at the latest. Allies in Naples, Bohemia, and Hungary, fearful of the consequences of any concession to Avignon, counselled Gregory to postpone the proposed meeting. Negotiations dragged on between Gregory in Lucca and Benedict in Portovenere, and Gregory became convinced that Benedict had no intention of abdicating. Gregory became suspicious of the loyalties of his own cardinals, and on 4 May 1408 created four new cardinals, two of whom were his nephews. All but three of his original cardinals deserted him and fled for Pisa, where they appealed to the Christian kings of Europe for assistance in ending the schism; they then met four of Benedict's cardinals in Livorno, and in July the two groups issued a united summons to a council to be convened in Pisa in March 1409.

Both popes were invited to the Council and both refused, and both summoned councils of their own. Nonetheless, the COUNCIL OF PISA met in the cathedral in Pisa on 25 March 1409. At the fifteenth session of the Council, on 5 June 1409, both Gregory and Benedict were deposed as schismatics, heretics, and perjurers and the Holy See was declared to be vacant. On 26 June the united college of cardinals elected Alexander V as the next pope. Neither Benedict nor Gregory was willing to yield. Benedict had fled to Perpignan without his cardinals and there summoned a council. Gregory opened his council at Cividale (near Aquileia) on 6 June 1409; attendance was sparse, but Gregory nonetheless excommunicated Popes Benedict XIII and Alexander V before abandoning the Council on 6 September. Fearful of the hostility of the patriarch of Aquileia, Gregory fled to Gaetà, but on being banished from the kingdom of Naples on 31 October 1411 sought refuge with Carlo I MALATESTA in Rimini. Representatives of the COUNCIL OF CONSTANCE entered into negotiations with Gregory, who agreed to abdicate on the condition that he could formally convoke the assembled prelates as a general council. This condition was accepted, and on 4 July 1415 Gregory's cardinal Giovanni Dominici proclaimed Gregory's bull convoking the council, whereupon Carlo Malatesta announced Gregory's abdication. The two colleges of cardinals were united and together ratified the acts of Gregory's pontificate. Gregory was created cardinal-bishop of Porto and appointed legate of the March of Ancona, but was declared ineligible for election as pope. He died at Recanati (near Ancona) on 18 October 1417, three weeks before the election of Pope MARTIN V.

**GREGORY XIII** (1502–85), pope from 14 May 1572 until his death on 10 April 1585, was born Ugo Buoncompagni in Bologna in January 1502, the fourth son of a local merchant. He studied CANON LAW at the University of Bologna, where he took his doctorate and remained as professor of law for eight years (1531–9); during this period he fathered an illegitimate son, Giacomo, whom he later appointed governor of Castel Sant'Angelo.

In 1539 Ugo went to Rome, where he was ordained and entered the service of Pope PAUL III, who valued his legal and administrative abilities and appointed him to a succession of judicial positions. He fell under the influence of Carlo BORROMEO and gradually forsook his early secularism in favour of reformist piety. Under Pope PAUL IV he became a papal diplomat to France (1556) and Brussels (1557) and was appointed bishop of Vieste (July 1558). From 1561 to 1563 he attended the COUNCIL OF TRENT as a canon lawyer and participated in the drafting of its decrees. On 12 March 1565 Pope PIUS IV created him cardinal-priest of San Sisto and appointed him to lead a legation to Spain. The confidence that Ugo inspired in PHILIP II was a key factor in his subsequent election as Pope Gregory XIII.

Gregory committed his pontificate to the cause of reform and the implementation of the decrees of the Council of Trent. He concurred with the Tridentine view that a reformed church required an educated clergy, and so established colleges in Rome and elsewhere, usually entrusting them to the JESUITS. In 1572 he reconstructed and richly endowed the Roman College (the Collegium Romanum founded in 1551 by IGNATIUS LOYOLA), which was later renamed the Pontifica Università Gregoriana in Gregory's honour. He founded a series of colleges designed to train missionary priests for work in their Protestant homelands, including a Greek College, a Maronite College, a Hungarian College (later integrated into the German College, which Gregory had revived), and an ENGLISH COLLEGE.

When news of the ST BARTHOLOMEW'S DAY MASSACRE (23–4 August 1572) reached Rome, Pope Gregory, in common with many churchmen, believed that France had been miraculously delivered from the prospect of HUGUENOT treachery, and joyously celebrated the massacre with Te Deums in thanksgiving for the victory of the Church in France over infidelity. This militant attitude to the COUNTER-REFORMATION cause characterized many of Gregory's foreign policies. He gave financial support for the CATHOLIC LEAGUE, but was frustrated in his efforts to have the decrees of the Council of Trent accepted in France. He dreamt of an attack on the England of Queen Elizabeth, and encouraged Philip II of Spain to concentrate his efforts on the Netherlands and Ireland, which would be ideal countries from which to

mount an invasion of England. He was pleased by the Union of ARRAS (6 January 1579) which united the southern provinces of the Netherlands in defence of the Catholic faith. He negotiated with King JOHN III of Sweden, but the king's insistence on clerical marriage, suppression of the invocation of saints, and communion in both kinds proved to be an insuperable barrier, and Sweden remained Lutheran. He negotiated with the churches of the East, fruitlessly in the case of the Russian Orthodox Church but successfully in the case of the Church in Poland, where on 1595, after Gregory's death, the RUTHENIAN CHURCH renounced communion with Constantinople and submitted to Rome in the Union of BREST-LITOVSK. In Germany, Gregory's support contributed to the arrest of the spread of Protestantism and to the recovery of Catholic territory; in the pursuit of Catholic property rights in Bavaria, ever the practical politician, he allowed Ernst of Bavaria (youngest son of Duke ALBRECHT V) to accumulate five bishoprics, in direct contravention of the Tridentine prohibition on the holding of more than one benefice.

Gregory was a strong supporter of the religious orders. He encouraged Jesuit missions in India, China, Japan, and Brazil, approved the Congregation of the Oratory of Filippo NERI (1575), and sanctioned the reform of the Discalced Carmelites by TERESA DE ÁVILA (1580).

The Council of Trent had decreed that a new edition of the Corpus of CANON LAW (*Corpus iuris canonici*) be prepared; Gregory oversaw the preparation of the edition and arranged for it to be published in 1582. His sense of the importance of the early Church was demonstrated by his quick appreciation of the importance of the rediscovery of the Roman catacombs in 1578. He also brought to fruition the CALENDAR reform that had been contemplated by his predecessors, establishing a commission that met at the Villa MONDRAGONE, where on 24 February 1585 Gregory signed the bull that ordered the suppression of 5–14 October 1585 throughout the Catholic world.

Gregory was an important patron of architecture in Rome. He completed the Gesù (the mother church of the Jesuits), commissioned the Quirinal Palace, and built the Gregorian chapel at ST PETER'S BASILICA and the FOUNTAINS of Piazza Navona. The cost of his lavish expenditure on these and other buildings, on his various colleges and foundations, and on subsidies for various Catholic causes abroad, depleted the considerable resources of the papacy, and Gregory chose to raise money through papal monopolies and customs duties, and by the more dubious method of confiscating estates if title deeds were found to be in any way defective. Recourse to confiscation and extortion created widespread disaffection amongst dispossessed noblemen, and the ensuing civil unrest was exacerbated by the unchecked rise of banditry in the PAPAL STATE and even in the city of Rome. Gregory bequeathed to his successor Pope SIXTUS V a lawless and ungoverned state.

L. Karttunen, *Grégoire XIII comme politicien et souverain* (1911); MDA.

**GREGORY XIV** (1535–91), pope from 5 December 1590 until his death ten months later on 16 October 1591, was born Niccolò Sfondrati in Somma (now Somma Lombarda), north-west of Milan, on 11 February 1535. He studied at Perugia and Padua, graduated with a doctorate in CANON LAW at Pavia, and was then ordained. During this period of his life he formed a close friendship with Carlo BORROMEO, many of whose views he came to share. Pope PIUS IV appointed Sfondrati as bishop of Cremona in 1560, at the age of 25. In 1562–3 he participated in the reconvened COUNCIL OF TRENT, where he argued that bishops were required under divine law to reside in their dioceses and denounced the common practice of holding more than one benefice at a time. He spent the next twenty years in his diocese, and on 12 December 1583 was created cardinal of Santa Cecilia in Trastevere by Pope GREGORY XIII. In Rome, he was associated with the cause of reform and with the ideals of Filippo NERI and the Oratorians.

Cardinal Sfondrati was elected as Pope Gregory XIV, and came to the pontificate without significant curial or political experience. On 19 December 1590 he created his 29-year-old nephew Paolo Emilio Sfondrati a cardinal, and appointed him as secretary of state; Paolo promptly appointed members of his family to posts throughout the PAPAL STATE. Gregory strove to alleviate PLAGUE, famine, and renewed banditry in the Papal State, but to little avail.

Pope Gregory was a Milanese, and therefore had Spanish sympathies, and at the time of his election had been one of the seven candidates on the Spanish list. Whereas his predecessor Pope SIXTUS V had artfully balanced French and Spanish interests, Gregory was unapologetically pro-Spanish, and supported Spain's aspirations in France: he sent a monthly subvention to Paris to ward off the forces of King HENRI IV (who was still a Protestant), supported the Spanish-backed CATHOLIC LEAGUE, renewed Sixtus' excommunication of Henri IV (1 March 1591), barring him from the French throne, and sent a papal army to France. The vigour of Gregory's campaign alienated moderate Catholic thinking in France and so increased support for Henri, and may even have hastened his conversion.

Gregory grew increasingly ill during his pontificate, but continued to advance the cause of reform from his sickbed. On 21 March 1591 he banned all betting on the outcome of papal elections, the length of pontificates, and the creation of cardinals. On 15 May he set out qualifications for bishoprics, forbade mass being said in private houses, and commissioned a revision of Pope Sixtus V's defective edition of St JEROME's Vulgate translation of the Bible.

M. Facini, *Il pontificato di Gregorio XIV* (1911); D. L. Càstano, *Gregorio XIV* (1957).

**GRENIER, PASQUIER** (d. 1496), Flemish tapestry contractor and weaver, the head of a workshop in Tournai; he was also a tapestry merchant, so it is possible that some of his tapestries were made in other centres, despite their execution in the style of Tournai. Grenier's principal patron from 1459 was PHILIP THE GOOD, duke of Burgundy, for whom Grenier made his finest work, a series of sumptuous tapestries illustrating *The Life of Alexander* (two panels survive in the Palazzo Doria Pamphili in Rome). Grenier's workshop also produced tapestries illustrating *Esther and Ahasuerus* (of

which panels survive in the Louvre and in the Musée Lorrain in Nancy), *The Knight of the Swan* (of which panels survive in the Museum für Angewandte Kunst in Vienna and the Church of St Catherine in Kraków), and *The Passion* (of which panels survive in the Vatican and in the Musées Royaux d'Art et d'Histoire in Brussels).

MDA.

**GRENVILLE, SIR RICHARD** (1542–91), English privateer. A relative of RALEGH, Grenville served as a soldier in Ireland before becoming sheriff of Cornwall and MP. He is best remembered for a heroic last stand off Flores (AZORES) in which his ship, the *Revenge*, alone fought over 50 Spanish warships, inflicting considerable damage before surrendering. Grenville died of wounds he sustained.

DNB.

**GRESHAM, SIR THOMAS** (1518–79), English merchant. Son of the lord mayor of London and friend of CECIL, Gresham spent over twenty years as ELIZABETH I's financial agent in Antwerp, where he secured loans for the purchase of military equipment; he also advised Elizabeth on monetary policy, warning against heavy and extended borrowing. In 1565, he financed the building of the Royal Exchange in London as a place for merchants and bankers to do business; he also founded GRESHAM COLLEGE. He is the eponym of 'Gresham's Law', that 'bad money drives out good'.

DNB.

**GRESHAM COLLEGE.** In 1565 Sir Thomas GRESHAM proposed to the Court of Aldermen of London that he build at his own expense an 'exchange' modelled on the Bourse in Antwerp, where he had worked for many years. This institution, which became the Royal Exchange (which is still on the same site), gave Gresham an annual income of c.£750 from the rental of the shops at the top of the building. Gresham died of apoplexy in November 1579, and stipulated in his will that on the death of his wife his various estates (which yielded an annual income of c.£2,300), his home in Bishopsgate Street (on the site of what is now the NatWest Tower), and the rental income arising from the Royal Exchange should be vested in the Corporation of London and the Mercers' Company with a view to establishing a college to which seven professors would be appointed.

The seven professors were to be accommodated in Gresham's Bishopsgate home, and each was to lecture on the subject associated with his professorship to an audience envisaged as consisting of mariners, merchants, and the general public. Gresham professors were appointed in astronomy, geometry, physic (i.e. medicine), law, divinity, rhetoric, and music, and lectures began in 1597. The lectures were intended to have a practical bias, so that astronomy, for example, was expected to concentrate on navigation, but this ideal was not realized; indeed, the professors were recruited from the two universities, where all teaching was in Latin, so the Gresham lectures were also in Latin, except for the lectures on music. Latin was the universal language of European education, and the choice of Latin enabled foreign visitors to attend the lectures, but it also excluded many of the mariners and merchants who were supposed to constitute the audiences for the lectures.

Gresham College remained in Bishopsgate until 1768, and thereafter lectures were given in the Royal Exchange. The college is now in Barnard's Inn, a former Inn of Chancery (see INNS OF COURT AND CHANCERY).

Richard Chartres and David Vermont, *A Brief History of Gresham College* (1998); Francis Ames-Lewis (ed.), *Sir Thomas Gresham and Gresham College* (1999).

**GRETSER or Gretscher, JAKOB** (1562–1625), German Jesuit playwright, born in Markdorf (Swabia). He entered the Jesuit Order in 1578, and served as a professor at Ingolstadt from 1588 to 1616. He was, like Jakob BIDERMANN, an exponent of the *Jesuitendrama* (on which see JESUITS). His plays, all of which were written in Latin, include *Comoedia de Timone* (1584), *Comoedia de Lazaro resuscitato* (1584), *Dialogus de Nicolao episcopo* (1586), *Comoedia de Nicolai Unterwaldio* (1586; see NICHOLAS OF FLÜE), and *Comoedia de Itha Doggia* (1587). Gretser's best-known play is his *Dialogus de Udone Archiepiscopo* (1587), which dramatizes the life of a wicked archbishop.

**GREVILLE, FULKE, FIRST BARON BROOKE** (1554–1628), English statesman and writer. Educated at Cambridge, Greville's career at court culminated in his being made first Baron Brooke in 1621. His *Life of Sir Philip Sidney* (published 1652), a close friend, includes observations on ELIZABETH's reign. Other writing includes a sequence of poems, *Caelica*, *Letter to an Honourable Lady* (1589), two tragedies, and a verse *Treatise of Monarchy* (c.1600).

*DNB.*

**GRÉVIN, JACQUES** (1538–70), French playwright and poet. He studied in Paris at the Collège de Boncourt, where his teachers included BUCHANAN and MURET. In 1560 Grévin published his poems, which were collected as *Olimpe*; this miscellany included odes, a PASTORAL, love sonnets, and satirical sonnets. In 1561 Grévin published his three plays, a tragedy (*César*) which he claimed to be the first in the French language and two fine comedies (*La Trésorière* and *Les Ébahis*). At about this time Grévin became a Protestant, after which he moved to Turin, where he lived for the rest of his short life.

*DBF.*

**GREY, LADY JANE** (1537–54). Daughter of the duke of Suffolk, Lady Jane was nominated as his successor by her cousin EDWARD VI on his deathbed, taking precedence over the claims of his half-sisters MARY and ELIZABETH. Edward's lord protector, NORTHUMBERLAND, married Jane to his fourth son, Guildford Dudley. On Edward's death, Jane was declared queen, and her husband declared himself king, but within nine days Mary's claim to the throne had been asserted, and Jane was executed.

*DNB.*

**GRIFFO, FRANCESCO** (c.1450–1518), Italian type founder. He was a native of Bologna who moved to Venice, where he was appointed as the principal type founder of ALDUS MANU-TIUS. Griffo was the inventor of italics, the fount modelled on the cursive chancery hand (*cancelleresca corsiva*) used in the Vatican secretariat; italic was used from 1501 for classical texts printed on small pages. He also designed Roman founts, including the one used for Francesco COLONNA's *Hypnerotomachia Polifili* (1499).

**GRIJALBA, JUAN DE** (c.1480–1527), Spanish explorer, born in Cuéllar (between Segovia and Valladolid). In 1511 he was a member of Diego VELÁZQUEZ's expedition that conquered Cuba. In 1518 he commanded an expedition to Yucatán, which had been discovered the previous year by the navigator Francisco HERNÁNDEZ DE CÓRDOBA, and in exploring the coasts of Mexico became the first European to establish contact with the Aztec Empire. Velázquez censured Grijalba for failing to establish a colony, and in the second expedition to Mexico (1519) replaced him as commander by CORTÉS. Grijalba was killed in an Indian rebellion in Nicaragua.

*DHE.*

**GRIMALDI FAMILY**, a Genoese family which was prominent in government and in military service from the twelfth century, and later became one of the most important BANKING families in Genoa. In 1458 a branch of the family became rulers of Monaco, where they had lived among the Monégasques since the tenth century. The Grimaldi were lords of Monaco until 1612, when they assumed the title of princes of Monaco, which their descendants still hold; the demise of the House of SAVOY in 1946 means that the Grimaldi dynasty is now the oldest continuous ruling house in Europe.

**GRIMANI, DOMENICO** (1461–1523), Venetian cardinal and collector of art and antiquities, the son of Doge Antonio Grimani. Grimani used the income from his numerous benefices to assemble his vast collection, most of which he bequeathed to the republic on his death. His antiquities are one of the foundation collections of the Museo d'Antichità; many of his Flemish and Italian paintings are now in the Doge's Palace; his illuminated breviary, the work of Simon BENING, passed to the republic in 1593 and is now in the Biblioteca MARCIANA. The Palazzo Grimani on the Grand Canal was designed by Michele SANMICHELI, and is now the Court of Appeal.

*MDA* s.v. Grimani (2) Domenico Grimani; M. Perry, 'Cardinal Domenico Grimani's Legacy of Ancient Art to Venice', *Journal of the Warburg and Courtauld Institutes* (1978).

**GRIMMER, JACOB** (c.1526–c.1590) and his son **ABEL** (c.1570–c.1619), Flemish landscape painters who worked in Antwerp. Their landscapes and townscapes, many of which are preserved in the Koninklijk Museum voor Schone Kunsten in Antwerp, are executed in the style of Pieter BRUEGEL the Elder.

*MDA.*

**GRINGORE, PIERRE** (c.1475–1538), French actor, playwright, and poet, a native of Normandy who became a

*RHÉTORIQUEUR* and a writer in the service of King LOUIS XII. He also worked as a writer and actor (using the stage name Mère Sote) for the *confrérie* known as Les Enfants Sans Souci. Gringore wrote SOTIES for the company, notably the *Jeu du prince des sots* (1512), and also wrote a full-length mystery play, *La Vie de monseigneur saint Louis*.

DBF; *Pierre Gringore's 'Les Fantasies de Mère Sote'*, ed. R. L. Frautschi (1962).

**GRISAILLE**, the English and French term used since the nineteenth century to denote a method of decorative painting in grey (French *gris*) monochrome with a view to representing solid objects in relief. In Renaissance painting and stained glass grisaille was characteristically used to depict sculpture (e.g. in the figures of the two St Johns in Hubert and Jan van EYCK's *Adoration of the Lamb* in Ghent) or architectural decoration such as friezes and mouldings (e.g. on the ceiling of the SISTINE CHAPEL).

**GRITTI, ANDREA** (1455–1538), doge of Venice, the last military figure to be elected as doge. As a young man he travelled overseas as a merchant, and on returning to Venice was appointed as a military *PROVVEDITORE*. He fought in the campaign against the League of CAMBRAI and in 1512 he was captured and taken as a prisoner to France. He returned to Venice the following year and was again employed as *provveditore*. He prepared a report on the defence of Venetian possessions on the *terraferma*; the report formed the basis of the programme to enhance FORTIFICATIONS for the rest of the century. Gritti was elected doge in 1523 after a career that had

TITIAN, *Doge Andrea Gritti*, in the Samuel H. Cress Collection, National Gallery, Washington

culminated in a series of army and naval commands. His tenure of office was marked by the relentless approach of the Ottomans. He died during the first Turkish War (1537–40).

**GROCYN, WILLIAM** (c.1449–1519), English humanist, educated at Winchester and New College, Oxford, of which he became a fellow; in 1481 he became reader in divinity at Magdalen College, Oxford. From 1488 to 1490 he was in Italy with LINACRE, studying Greek under POLIZIANO and CHALCONDYLES. On his return to Oxford, where he helped to introduce the study of Greek, he gained a reputation as England's finest classical scholar. His students and friends included COLET, ERASMUS, and MORE.

DNB.

**GROLIER BINDINGS.** The French bibliophile and statesman Jean Grolier de Servières (1479–1565) amassed a library of some 3,000 volumes, of which approximately 600 books are known to survive. Grolier lived in Milan (which was occupied by the French) from 1510 to 1520, serving as treasurer of the duchy; during this period he commissioned a small number of bindings from local craftsmen; these bindings are typically decorated with medallions illustrating classical scenes.

Most of the bindings now known as Grolier bindings were executed in Paris in the twenty years following Grolier's return in 1520. Grolier commissioned bindings from a number of Parisian binders, the identities of which are mostly unknown. These bindings are in calf, and the designs executed in the 1520s tend to consist of geometrical STRAPWORK. In the 1530s the designs became more complex, and often included intricate interlacing patterns. The surviving examples from the 1540s and 1550s are more elaborate, often including ARABESQUES hatched with parallel lines and strapwork coloured black or red; these bindings may have influenced the development of FANFARE BINDINGS in the late sixteenth century.

Anthony Hobson, Renaissance Book Collecting: Jean Grolier and Diego Hurtado de Mendoza, their Books and Bindings (1999).

**GROOTE, GEERT DE,** or (Latin) **Gerardus Magnus** (1340–84), Dutch religious leader and mystic, born in Deventer and educated in Paris; he subsequently taught at Cologne University. In 1374 Geert repudiated his considerable wealth and entered the Carthusian monastery of Munnikhuizen; five years later he became a missionary preacher in the diocese of Utrecht, where he founded the community known as the BRETHREN OF THE COMMON LIFE. Geert's attacks on clerical corruption led to the suspension of his preaching licence in 1383; he appealed against the suspension, but died of the plague before receiving a reply.

NNBW i; T. P. Van Zijl, Gerard Groote: Ascetic and Reformer (1963).

**GROPPER, JOHANN** (1503–59), German Catholic theologian who studied jurisprudence and theology at Cologne and in 1532 was appointed a canon of Xanten. He attended a synod in Cologne, after which Archbishop HERMANN VON WIED asked Gropper to write a theological handbook

(Enchiridion) to combat the teachings of the reformers. Gropper's Enchiridion (1538) included expositions of the Catholic position on the Creed, the SACRAMENTS, the Lord's Prayer and the Ten Commandments, and proposed a conciliatory doctrine of GRACE known as DOUBLE JUSTICE.

The Enchiridion was welcomed by the theologians of Cologne and by theologians such as Gasparo CONTARINI, Giovanni MORONE, and Reginald POLE, all of whom could see its potential for the reconciliation of Protestants to the Catholic Church. It was eventually (1596) placed on the INDEX LIBRORUM PROHIBITORUM, but during the 1540s was widely regarded as a useful basis for negotiation. Gropper negotiated with Martin BUCER in 1540 and succeeded in securing agreement on the doctrines of grace and JUSTIFICATION, but not on papal authority and the EUCHARIST.

In 1541 Gropper participated in the Conference of REGENSBURG, where the doctrine of double justice was discussed. Archbishop Hermann von Wied became a Lutheran in 1546, and Gropper secured his deposition, restoring Catholicism to the archbishopric. He was appointed provost of Bonn in 1547 and created cardinal in 1556.

NDB; R. Braunisch, Die Theologie der Rechtfertigung im 'Enchiridion' (1538) des Johannes Gropper (1974); J. Meier, Der priesterliche Dienst nach Johannes Gropper (1977).

**GROSSO, NICCOLÒ,** or **Caparra** (fl. c.1500), Italian ironsmith, praised by VASARI as the best of ironsmiths; his nickname 'Caparra' ('payment in advance') presumably refers to his financial arrangements. His finest work is mounted on the exterior of the Palazzo Strozzi in Florence and includes a lantern shaped like a temple and flag-pole holders decorated with fabulous creatures.

**GROTESQUE.** The rooms of ancient Roman buildings revealed by excavation seem to have been known as grotte; the murals on the walls of rooms in ancient houses such as Nero's Domus Aurea (excavated c.1480) on the Esquiline were decorated with distorted representations (sometimes in low relief) of human and animal forms (typically monkeys and sphinxes) interwoven with foliage and flowers. 'Grotesque' is the French and English term, cognate with Spanish and Portuguese grutesco, for this decorative style, which was principally used in decorative painting and sculpture; the modern Italian term for works of art in this style is grotteschi. In early modern usage 'grotesque' is never a pejorative term; such senses evolved in the eighteenth century.

Grotesque motifs first appear in ornament in the 1480s in paintings such as Carlo CRIVELLI's Annunciation (1486, National Gallery, London), and were soon incorporated into decorative schemes such as PINTORICCHIO's ceiling for the Piccolomini Library in Siena Cathedral (1503) and SIGNORELLI's frescoes for Orvieto Cathedral (1499–1504). The earliest decorative scheme in the grotesque style was executed by RAPHAEL in Cardinal Bibbiena's bathroom (stufetta) in the Vatican; Raphael subsequently used grotesques in the Vatican Loggias (c.1519), and GIOVANNI DA UDINE, who had been largely responsible for the execution of Raphael's designs in the Vatican Loggias, later used grotesques in the Villa

MADAMA (1520–1). From the 1530s onwards, the foliage associated with grotesques was usually executed in ARABESQUES.

Engravings of Raphael's grotesques were soon circulating all over Europe, and established a fashion for grotesques that was to persevere for centuries, not only in decorative painting, but also in arts such as tapestries, maiolica, and sculpture.

F. Piel, *Die Ornament-Groteske in der Italienischer Renaissance* (1962); N. Dacos, *La Découverte de la Domus Aurea et la formation des grotesques à la Renaissance* (1971); C. P. Warncke, *Die Ornamentale Grotescke in Deutschland 1500–1650* (1979); A. Chastel, *La Grottesque* (1988).

**GROTIUS, HUGO, or Huig van Groot** (1583–1645), Dutch jurist. Grotius was born in Delft and rapidly grew into a child prodigy. At 9 he was a competent Latin poet and at 12 he entered the University of Leiden, where he was taught by J. J. SCALIGER. When he was 15, Grotius prepared an edition of the *Satyricon*, an encyclopedia by the fifth-century Latin writer Martianus Capella, and travelled to France with OLDENBARNEVELT on a diplomatic mission. After a year in France, during which he met many important scholars, he returned home and took the degree of doctor of law in Leiden, and embarked on his legal career. In 1600 (aged 17) he published an edition of the *Phaenomena*, an astronomical poem by the Greek poet Aratus, together with the Latin versions of the poem by Cicero, Germanicus, and Avienius. In 1603 (aged 20) he was appointed historiographer of the United Provinces and in 1607 advocate fiscal of the provinces of Holland, Zeeland, and West Friesland. In his capacity as official historiographer he composed a constitutional treatise justifying the REVOLT OF THE NETHERLANDS against Spain (*De antiquitate reipublicae Batavicae*, 1610). In 1613 he was sent as an ambassador to England, where he briefed King James on the religious disputes arising out of the rival creeds of ARMINIUS and GOMAR; Grotius was an Arminian, but although he was received with the respect of a fellow scholar by King James, he was unable to change the opinions of the king. On returning to the United Provinces he was appointed *pensionaris* (i.e. chief magistrate) of Rotterdam. The moderate and eirenic sympathies evidenced in his *Ordinum pietas* (1613) incurred the enmity of the Calvinist leader Maurice of Nassau, and these sympathies, together with his friendship with Oldenbarnevelt, led to a sentence of life imprisonment in 1618. While in prison he wrote an introduction to Dutch legal science (*Inleidinge tot de Hollandsche Rechtsgeerheid*, 1631), an account of DUTCH LAW which described the relationship between elements of CUSTOMARY LAW and Roman law.

After twenty months of incarceration, Grotius was smuggled out of prison by his wife, who arranged for him to be carried out in a laundry basket. He fled to Paris, arriving in April 1621, and there composed *De iure belli ac pacis* (Paris, 1625), which was a greatly expanded version of a treatise called *De iure praedae*, which he had written in the winter of 1604 but left unpublished. The twelfth chapter of this early treatise had been published (apparently without Grotius' permission) as *Mare liberum* (1609); it was this tract that prompted a riposte by SELDEN (see MARE CLAUSUM, MARE LIBERUM).

Grotius returned to the United Provinces in 1631 in a vain attempt to settle there permanently, but religious intolerance eventually forced him to return to France, where he accepted an appointment as Swedish ambassador to France. He retained this post for ten years, during which time he wrote a history of the Netherlands (*Annales et historiae de rebus Belgicis*, published posthumously in 1657) and a treatise on the origin of the American Indians (*De origine gentium Americanarum*, 1642), and translated the history of the wars of Justinian by the fifth-century Greek historian Procopius (*Historia Gothorum Vandalorum et Longobardorum*, 1655). His attempts to negotiate on behalf of Protestant interests in Germany were unsuccessful, in part because he never established good relations with Richelieu. In 1645 he arranged to be recalled to Stockholm, but left after a few months on a ship bound for Lübeck; his ship was wrecked on the coast near Danzig (now Gdańsk), and Grotius struggled on to Rostock, where he was taken ill and died.

*De iuri belli ac pacis* is the founding text of modern INTERNATIONAL LAW; in this respect its title is misleading, in that the law of war occupies a relatively small part of the treatise. In *De iuri belli* Grotius severed law from theology by proposing that human actions are shaped by NATURAL LAW rooted in the nature of individuals as social beings rather than in divine command. This law of nature (*ius naturale*), he argued, could be deduced through the exercise of reason; it was as immutable as the axioms of mathematics and so could be deployed to construct a coherent code of law of universal applicability. Natural law was distinct from the laws of specific communities (later termed 'positive law'), and could therefore be used to judge the rightness of those laws.

Grotius' most influential theological work was his *De veritate religionis christianae* (1627), a statement of moderate Protestantism designed to bridge sectarian differences; this treatise became the standard apologetic work for missionary purposes, and was translated into Arabic (by Pococke, 1660), Farsi, Chinese, Welsh, and many other languages. In terms of the development of biblical criticism, his most important work was *Annotationes in Vetus et Novum Testamentum* (1642), which set aside the usual assumption of divine inspiration in favour of the historical and philological approach championed by Scaliger; just as this method mirrors Grotius' approach to Roman law, so his insistence on the centrality of the ecclesiastical tradition reflects his jurisprudential view of the importance of customary law. In 1642 he returned to the advocacy of religious reconciliation with *Via ad pacem ecclesiasticam* and *Votum pro pace ecclesiastica*.

Grotius wrote three plays in Latin: *Christus patiens* (c.1608), which was later translated into English by George Sandys (1640); *Sophomphaneas*, a play about Joseph and his brothers which was translated into Dutch by Vondel (1635) and into English by Francis Goldsmith (1652); and *Adamus exul*, an important precursor of John Milton's *Paradise Lost*. Grotius was also a fine Latin poet, and published his collected poems (*Poemata collecta*) in 1617.

W. S. M. Knight, *The Life and Works of Hugo Grotius* (Grotius Society Publications No. 4, 1962).

**GROTO, LUIGI, or Cieco d'Adria** (1541–85), Italian poet and playwright, born in Adria; his nickname ('Il Cieco') refers to his blindness. Groto's works, which are variously written in Italian, Venetian, Latin, and Spanish, include metrically ambitious poems (*Rime*, 1577), tragedies (including the Senecan *Dalida*, 1572, and the love tragedy *Hadriana*, 1578), and three comedies (*Emilia*, 1579; *Tesoro*, 1580; *Alteria*, 1584).

OCIL.

**GROTTO.** In garden art a grotto is an artificial recess designed to resemble a natural cave. The term is sometimes used to refer to a NYMPHAEUM, but more commonly refers to a rusticated cave containing FOUNTAINS and other waterworks and decorated with statues and shells. The statuary sometimes reflects the contemporary fashion for the GROTESQUE, which can be seen in related features such as the garden monsters of the Villa ORSINI. The Renaissance grotto was thought to be a revival of the grottoes of classical antiquity; ALBERTI, for example, assured his readers that the ancients applied rough dressings to the walls of their caverns, and daubed them with green wax in imitation of slime (*De re aedificatoria* 9. 4). Rustic grottoes were constructed in the BOBOLI GARDENS and in the gardens of the Villa D'ESTE, the Villa MADAMA, the MEDICI VILLA at Castello, and the Palazzo del TÈ. In France grottoes were constructed at Meudon (by PRIMATICCIO), Bastie d'Urfé (Loire), Écouen, CHENONCEAUX, and the TUILERIES. Grottoes sometimes incorporated AUTOMATA into their waterworks, most memorably at PRATOLINO and SAINT-GERMAIN-EN-LAYE.

In the late sixteenth century grottoes were used as the setting of plays and entertainments, and in the early seventeenth century grottoes were transplanted from gardens onto stages by designers such as Inigo JONES. The garden grotto became less popular in the early seventeenth century, but was revived in the eighteenth-century English landscape garden.

Barbara Jones, *Follies and Grottoes* (1955); N. Miller, *Heavenly Caves: Reflections on the Garden Grotto* (1982); Malgorzata Szafranska, 'The Philosophy of Nature and the Grotto in the Renaissance Garden', *Journal of Garden History*, 9 (1989).

**GRUMBACH, WILHELM VON** (1503–67), German soldier and the eponym of the Grumbach Feuds (Grumbachsche Händel) in which the German knights sought to wrest power from the territorial princes. He was born into an ancient Franconian family on 1 June 1503. His military career began when he fought the peasants in the PEASANTS' WAR of 1524–5. In about 1540 Grumbach entered the service of ALBRECHT ALCIBIADES, whom he served as a military commander for thirteen years.

In his role as a landowner, Grumbach was a vassal of the bishops of Würzburg. In 1544 the bishopric was filled by Melchior von Zobel, who resented Grumbach's earlier pillaging of his lands in Franconia. The defeat of Albrecht at Sievershausen on 9 July 1553 and his subsequent flight to France left Grumbach bereft of powerful patronage, and Zobel took advantage of this moment of weakness to seize Grumbach's lands. Grumbach secured an order of restitution from the REICHSKAMMERGERICHT, but Zobel refused to hand

back the land. In April 1558 a group of Grumbach's partisans murdered the bishop; Grumbach insisted that he had played no part in the crime, but was nonetheless forced to flee to France. He returned to protest his innocence at the Diet of Augsburg in 1559, but again was not believed.

After Albrecht fled to France, Grumbach found a new patron in JOHANN FRIEDRICH II, duke of Saxony, whose father JOHANN FRIEDRICH I had been forced to surrender the electorate to the Albertine branch of the family. In 1563 he captured and plundered Würzburg and forced the new bishop to restore his lands. In 1566 Grumbach sought to restore the electorate to the Ernestine branch of the WETTIN FAMILY (see Appendix 1) by assassinating AUGUSTUS I, the Albertine elector of Saxony. Grumbach was captured by Augustus in Gotha, and tortured and executed on 18 April 1567.

J. Voigt, *Wilhelm von Grumbach und seine Händel* (2 vols., 1846–7); Volker Press, 'Wilhelm von Grumbach und die deutsche Adelskrise der 1560er Jahre', *Blätter für deutsche Landesgeschichte*, 113 (1977); repr. in id., *Adel im Alten Reich: Gesammelte Vorträge und Aufsätze* (1998).

**GRÜNEWALD, MATHIAS** (1475/80–1528), German painter. No records of Grünewald's early life are known to survive; he may have been born in Würzburg, but he first emerges in the historical record in the small town of Seligenstadt (near Frankfurt), where he had his workshop from 1501 to 1525. His name, however, was not Grünewald, that being a name first used (in error) by Joachim von Sandrart in his *Teutsche Akademie* of 1675. The artist's real name, Mathis Neithardt, together with the name by which he was called, Gothardt, was established in 1938; this discovery explains the monogram MGN that appears on four of Grünewald's paintings. He was employed by two successive archbishops of Mainz (1516–25), the second of whom (ALBRECHT II OF MAINZ) commissioned a series of ALTARPIECES for Cathedral in Halle an der Saale; the few surviving works commissioned by Cardinal Albrecht include a *Lamentation* (Schloss Johannisburg, Aschaffenburg) and a panel depicting *SS Erasmus and Maurice* (Alte Pinakothek, Munich). No paintings have survived from the final years of his life; he died in Halle in 1528, when he was described as a painter and *Wasserkunstmacher* (i.e. hydraulic engineer).

Grünewald's early paintings include a *Derision of Christ* (Alte Pinakothek, Munich), datable to 1503 by an inscription which is now lost, and the wings (depicting saints) for DÜRER's *Helleraltar* (c.1510, now divided between the Städelsches Kunstinstitut in Frankfurt and the Fürstlich-Fürstenbergische Sammlungen in Donaueschingen). His late works include a *Carrying of the Cross* and a dramatic *Crucifixion*, both now in the Staatliche Kunsthalle in Karlsruhe.

Grünewald's masterpiece is the Isenheim altarpiece, now in the Musée d'Unterlinden in Colmar, where it was moved in 1852, 60 years after the suppression of the Isenheim monastery. Its date is unknown, but it is probably a work of the 1510s. The central image on the front wings of the altarpiece depicts the tortured body of Jesus on the cross, his hands twisted by the pain of the nails and his feet contorted by the single nail driven through them. This distortion,

Mathias Grünewald, *The Crucifixion*, which is the central panel of the Isenheim Altarpiece, in the Musée d'Unterlinden, in Colmar

together with the wounds on the body and the look of suffering on Jesus' face, make this painting the most powerful expression of the horror of crucifixion in western art. Within the monastic hospital for which it was commissioned, the degraded and tortured body of Jesus must have been a reflection of the afflictions of the patients and so an affirmation that spiritual grace can survive the destruction of the body.

MDA s.v. Grünewald, Matthias; *NDB*.

**GRUTER, JAN or Janus** (1560–1627), Anglo-Flemish epigraphist and classical scholar in England and Germany, born in Antwerp, the son of a Flemish father and an English mother. Gruter was educated in Cambridge and Leiden, and subsequently taught at Heidelberg. He published an important collection of ancient inscriptions (*Inscriptiones antiquae totius orbis Romani, in corpus absolutissimum redactae*, Heidelburg, 1602 and 1616) and many commentaries and editions of ancient authors, including CICERO, LIVY, Martial, PLAUTUS, PLINY THE YOUNGER, Sallust, Suetonius, and TACITUS.

*NDB*; Leonard Forster, *Janus Gruter's English Years* (1967).

**GUADAMECÍ**, the Spanish term, derived from the Libyan oasis of Ghadāmis (Spanish Ghadamés), for wall hangings made from sheepskin leather decorated with hand-tooled designs in bright colours. For centuries the principal centre for the production of *guadamecí* was Córdoba, but in the seventeenth century Flemish leatherworkers captured much of the market by using stamps to impress designs on the leather and so reducing labour costs and retail prices.

**GUARDATI, TOMMASO**. See MASUCCIO SALERNITANO.

**GUARINI, BATTISTA** (1538–1612), Italian poet and playwright, born into a distinguished humanist family in Ferrara, where in 1567 he entered the service of Alfonso II d'ESTE, duke of Ferrara. After TASSO's disgrace in 1577, Guarini became the court poet. He acted as an ambassador for Duke Alfonso, and subsequently worked in other north Italian courts.

Guarini was the author of *Il pastor fido* (1590), the most influential PASTORAL drama of the sixteenth century; as Lady Politic explains in Ben JONSON's *Volpone*, 'all our English writers, | I mean such as are happy in the Italian, | will deign to steal out of this author mainly'. *Il pastor fido* was performed abroad, notably in Cambridge in 1605, and was widely translated; the English translations include Sir Richard Fanshawe's *The Faithful Shepherd* (1647). Guarini also wrote a defence of tragicomedy, the *Compendio della poesia tragicomedia* (1601); his other works include a treatise on government, a dialogue on letter-writing, and a comedy called *La idropsica* (1583).

OCIL; N. J. Perella, *The Critical Fortune of Battista Guarini's 'Il pastor fido'* (1973).

**GUARINO DA VERONA** (1374–1460), educator and Hellenist. Guarino was the orphaned child of an artisan family in Verona, but he secured a good education in Padua and Venice; from 1403 to 1408 he lived in Constantinople, where he acquired an excellent command of Greek and built up a collection of Greek manuscripts. He taught in Venice in

1408–9, and subsequently moved to Florence, where he taught from 1410 to 1414; he resigned his post after a quarrel with Niccolò NICCOLI and returned to Venice, where he taught until 1419. He spent the next ten years teaching in Padua and Verona, and in 1429 accepted the invitation of Niccolò III d'Este, signore of Ferrara, to act as tutor to his son Leonello. He spent the last 30 years of his life in Ferrara, which at his hands developed a European reputation as a centre of EDUCATION, the birthplace of the classical literary education that was to dominate European education for centuries. His students in Ferrara included several from England, notably William Grey (bishop of Ely) and Robert Flemmyng (later dean of Lincoln).

The education that Guarino provided for his pupils centred on the languages and literatures of classical antiquity. He inculcated a sound command of grammar in his pupils, taught them ancient history and mythology, and required pupils to imitate the style of ancient authors in both verse and prose. His bias was philological rather than speculative, so his lectures on ancient texts dealt exclusively with the minutiae of textual analysis. He was the first educator to place Greek on an equal footing with Latin as an essential element in the education of a gentleman.

Guarino wrote no original literary or educational works, though he did revise the textbook of Greek grammar written by his former teacher CHRYSOLORAS and he translated the influential treatise *On the Education of Children* (then attributed to PLUTARCH) and Strabo's *Geography*. His educational innovations were disseminated throughout Europe by his pupils, by his contemporary VITTORINO DA FELTRO, and by his son Battista, who wrote an educational treatise describing his father's methods.

Remigio Sabbadini, *Vita di Guarino Veronese* (1891); id., *La scuola e gli studi di Guarino Guarini Veronese* (1896).

**GUAS, JUAN** (*c*.1430–1496), Spanish architect and sculptor of French descent. He arrived in Toledo, possibly from Brussels, in about 1450. In 1459 Juan and his father are recorded as working with Hanequín of Brussels (see EGAS FAMILY) on the Puerto de los Leones at Toledo Cathedral. He served as master of works in the cathedrals of Segovia (1473–91) and Toledo (*c*.1483–95). He received the royal commission to design Queen ISABELLA's monastery of San Juan de los Reyes (1479–80), and was also the principal architect of the Infantado Palace at Guadalajara (1480–*c*.1483). It is likely that he designed the exuberant late Gothic façade of San Gregorio in Valladolid (1487–96), but that has also been attributed to Gil de SILOÉ.

MDA.

**GUCCI FIORENTINO, SANTI** (*c*.1530–1599/60), Italian sculptor and architect in Poland, born in Florence, where he trained in the workshop of his father Giovanni Gucci, who had worked on the restoration of Florence Cathedral. In about 1550 Santi Gucci moved to Poland, where he settled in Kraków. He served as court architect to SIGISMUND II, Anna Jagiełło, and STEFAN BÁTORY, and eventually carved their tombs in Kraków Cathedral. Gucci's surviving buildings in Kraków include the Boners' house (1560; now 6 Market Square) and a chapter house (after 1582; now 21 Kanonicza Street).

MDA; PSB.

**GUÉDRON, PIERRE** (*c*.1570–1619/20), French composer, singer, and singing teacher. He became *maître des chanteurs de la chambre* at the court of HENRI IV which he had joined two years earlier as a singer, and by 1614 had risen to *surintendant des musiques de la chambre du roi*. His principal interest as a composer was with the *airs du cour*, which were lute songs set to his own texts or those of François de MALHERBE. He also wrote vocal music for the *ballet de cour*, including expressive recitatives in which he confronted the rhythmic difficulties of setting the French language in a declamatory style.

**GUELFS or Guelphs** and **GHIBELLINES**, the terms used in thirteenth- and fourteenth-century Italy to denote rival supporters of the papacy (the Guelfs) and the Holy Roman Emperors (the Ghibellines). As the glossator of SPENSER's *Shepherd's Calendar* explained in 1579, 'all Italy was distraict [i.e. divided] into the factions of the Guelfs and Ghibellines'.

The term 'Guelf' (Italian *Guelfo*, medieval Latin *Guelphus*) derives from Middle High German *Welf*, the name of the founder and successive chiefs of the Bavarian princely family that produced five dukes of Bavaria (and from which the British royal family descends).

The etymology of the term 'Ghibelline' (Italian *Ghibellino*, medieval Latin *Ghibellinus*) is uncertain, but may derive from Middle High German *Waiblingen*, the name of an estate owned by the Hohenstaufen family; the term Waiblingen is said to have been used as a battle cry by the soldiers of the Hohenstaufen Emperor Conrad III.

From 1198 to 1218 there was a struggle for central Italy between the supporters of the Emperor Otto IV Welf and the supporters of the rival Hohenstaufen emperors, Philip of Swabia and his nephew Friedrich II. Between 1235 and 1250, the Emperor Friedrich II was in dispute with the papacy, and during those years chroniclers began to use the term 'Guelfs' to denote supporters of the papacy and the term 'Ghibellines' to denote supporters of the Empire. From 1266 to 1442, when Naples was ruled by the house of Anjou, the term 'Guelf' acquired the additional connotation of 'pro-French', because the papacy supported the Angevin claim. The Guelf alliance that emerged in the late thirteenth century linked the kingdom of Naples, the Papal State, Provence (ruled by the counts of Anjou from 1246 to 1481), and France; the trade that arose out of this alliance was financed by the merchant bankers of Florence.

In the early fourteenth century, the Emperors Heinrich VII of Luxemburg (ruled 1308–13) and Ludwig IV of Bavaria (ruled 1314–47) invaded northern Italy and formed alliances with the VISCONTI FAMILY of Milan and the DELLA SCALA FAMILY of Verona; these noble families became the most prominent supporters of the Ghibelline party.

Florence was divided between Guelf and Ghibelline: the merchant banks supported the Guelfs, and the noble families the Ghibellines. This class difference enabled the Guelfs to depict themselves as the champions of republican liberty and their Ghibelline opponents as apologists for tyranny. The *Parte Guelfa* was formally incorporated, and despite occasional splits (notably the moderate White Guelf and aggressive Black Guelf factions) remained a powerful force in Florence until the War of the EIGHT SAINTS between Florence and the papacy (1375–8) fractured the Guelf alliance within the city. In the early fifteenth century the palace of the Guelfs (Palazzo dei Capitani della Parte Guelfa) was rebuilt to the design of BRUNELLESCHI.

Daniel Waley, *The Italian City Republics* (2nd edn., 1978).

**GUERRERO, FRANCISCO** (1528–99), Spanish composer who held a series of posts in Spanish, Portuguese, and Italian churches. In 1551 he was appointed as assistant choirmaster at Seville Cathedral, and in 1574 became the choirmaster. His large corpus of church music includes 'O sacrum convivium' (1570), a motet for six voices; he also wrote secular madrigals. Francisco's elder brother Pedro (b. c.1520) emigrated to Rome, where he sang in the choir of Santa Maria Maggiore; he was a composer of madrigals, motets, and lute music.

**GUEVARA, FRAY ANTONIO DE** (c.1480–1545), Spanish writer, born into a noble family at Treceño (near Santander) and educated in the court of FERDINAND and ISABELLA, where he was a page to their son Prince Juan until the latter's death in 1497. In 1504 Guevara entered the Franciscan Order, and seventeen years later returned to the court as preacher of the Royal Chapel; in 1526 he was appointed royal historiographer to the Emperor CHARLES V, whom he accompanied to the battle of TUNIS (1535). He was appointed bishop of Gaudix (1528) and then bishop of Mondoñedo (1537).

Guevara's most important book was his *Reloj de príncipes y libro áureo de Marco Aurelio* (Seville, 1529), a treatise on the ideal Christian ruler (a 'mirror for princes' or *De regimine principum*) combined with a biography of the Roman Emperor Marcus Aurelius; the treatise was reprinted in an expanded version the following year (*Libro llamado reloj de príncipes*, Valladolid, 1529), and thereafter both versions were frequently reprinted. A French translation was published in 1544.

In 1539 Guevara published several works in Valladolid, including a collection of biographies of Roman emperors (*Década de Césares*), a handbook for courtiers (*Libro llamado aviso de privados y doctrina de cortesanos*), the first volume of his 112 *Epístolas familiares* (the second volume followed in 1541), a treatise contrasting rural purity with urban vice (*Libro llamado menosprecio de corte y alabanza de aldea*), and a book of advice for those about to embark on a sea voyage (*De los inventores del marear*). His final works were guides to the religious life, *Oratorio de religiosos y ejercicio de virtuosos* (Valladolid, 1542) and the two-part *Libro llamado Monte Calvario* (Salamanca, 1542 and 1549).

Guevara's extravagant prose style and miscellaneous erudition won him a large readership, especially in Spain and France, but he also had detractors, notably Pedro de Rúa, who published *Cartas de Rhúa lector en Soria sobre las obras del reverendo señor Obispo de Mondoñedo* (Burgos, 1549), which

solemnly exhorted Fray Antonio to write plain prose and check his facts.

J. Gibbs, *La vida de Fray Antonio de Guevara* (1961); Joseph Jones, *Antonio de Guevara* (1975); Asunción Rallo, *Antonio de Guevara en su contexto renacentista* (1979); Pilar Concejo, *Antonio de Guevara: Un ensayista del siglo XVI* (1985); Pedro Díaz Fernández (ed.), *Frai Antonio de Guevara e a cultura do Renacemento en Galicia* (1994).

**GUGLIELMO DELLA PORTA.** See DELLA PORTA, GUGLIELMO.

**GUICCIARDINI, FRANCESCO** (1483–1540), Florentine historian, born into a patrician family that had served Florence for generations; his godfather was Marsilio FICINO. He studied classics and law at the universities of Ferrara and Padua, and in 1508 married Maria Salviati, whom he chose because of the political support that an alliance with her family would secure. In 1511 Guicciardini was sent as an ambassador to Spain; he was still absent from Florence when the MEDICI FAMILY was restored, but, unlike MACHIAVELLI, Guicciardini was not deemed to have been tainted by his association with the republic, and was able to continue in public service. He became a member of the Signoria in 1515 and was subsequently appointed to a series of papal posts by the Medici popes: Pope LEO X appointed him governor of Modena (1516), Reggio (1517), and Parma (1519) and Pope CLEMENT VII appointed him as regent of Romagna (1524), papal councillor and lieutenant-general of the papal army (1526), papal representative in Florence (1530), and governor of Bologna (1531). On the election of Pope PAUL III in 1534 Guicciardini left the papal service and became a councillor to Duke Alessandro de' MEDICI from 1534 until his assassination in 1537, whereupon he entered the service of Alessandro's successor, Duke COSIMO I DE' MEDICI.

Duke Cosimo soon dismissed Guicciardini, who withdrew to his villa and used his enforced leisure to turn his avocation as a historian into a full-time occupation. His greatest work is the *Storia d'Italia*, a history of Italy that begins with the outbreak of the WARS OF ITALY in 1494 and concludes with the death of Pope Clement VII in 1534. *Storia d'Italia* was published posthumously in 1561 and was soon translated into Dutch, English, French, German, Latin, and Spanish. Its stature was later affirmed by Gibbon, who declared Guicciardini to be the equal of Thucydides and proclaimed the *Storia d'Italia* to be, 'from the point of view of intellectual power, the most important work to have issued from an Italian mind'. Macaulay took a cooler view, and tells the story of an Italian criminal 'who was suffered to make his choice between Guicciardini and the galleys. He chose the History. But the war of Pisa was too much for him. He changed his mind and went to the oar.'

Guicciardini's minor works remained in manuscript until 1857, when his *Opera inedite* was published in Florence in ten volumes. These hitherto unknown works include a youthful history of Florence (*Storie fiorentine dal 1378 al 1509*), series of essays written during his residence in Spain (*Discorsi politici*), a collection of political aphorisms (*Ricordi politici*), and a dialogue on the government of Florence (*Dialogo del reggimento di Firenze, c.1524–5*). This collection does not include

Guicciardini's scholarly account of Florentine affairs first published as *Cose fiorentine* in 1945.

R. Ridolfi, *The Life of Francesco Guicciardini*, trans. Cecil Grayson (1967); M. Phillips, *Francesco Guicciardini: The Historian's Craft* (1977).

**GUIDI, GUIDO, or (Latin) Vidus Vidius** (1508–69), Italian anatomist, a native of Florence who in 1542 went to France as court physician to King FRANCIS I, who invited Guidi to lecture at the Collège de France. In 1547 he returned to Florence at the behest of Grand Duke Cosimo de' MEDICI, who arranged his appointment to a chair at the University of Pisa. His most important anatomical work was *De anatomia corporis humani* (1611). Guidi is the eponym of several features of the anatomy of the head, notably the Vidian artery, the Vidian canal, and the Vidian nerve.

*DSB.*

**GUIDOBALDO or Guidubaldo DA MONTEFELTRO** (1472–1508), duke of Urbino, was the last MONTEFELTRO ruler of Urbino. He succeeded his father FEDERICO II DA MONTEFELTRO in 1482. He fought as a *condottiere* against France in the opening campaign of the WARS OF ITALY. In 1497 he was captured in a feud with the ORSINI FAMILY and released after payment of a large ransom. Urbino was attacked by Cesare BORGIA in 1502, but Guidobaldo managed to escape. He recovered his duchy the following year, in the wake of the death of Pope ALEXANDER VI, Cesare Borgia's father. He had no natural heirs, and so in 1504 adopted as his successor Francesco Maria DELLA ROVERE, a nephew of Pope JULIUS II, who had appointed Guidobaldo as captain-general of the papal army.

Guidobaldo da Montefeltro was the patron of CASTIGLIONE, whose *Cortegiano* depicts Guidobaldo's court in 1506. When King HENRY VII of England invested Guidobaldo with the chivalric ORDER of the Garter, Castiglione was dispatched to England with a letter of thanks and the gift of RAPHAEL's *St George and the Dragon* (1504); the painting remained in the royal collection until it was dispersed in 1649, and is now in the Louvre.

C. H. Clough, *The Duchy of Urbino in the Renaissance* (1981).

**GUILDS or gilds.** The guild system of medieval Europe can be traced to late antiquity, when associations of masters in particular crafts and trades were first formed. Medieval guilds protected monopolies and supported the religious, social, and professional needs of their members. From the thirteenth century, guilds began to regulate standards of workmanship and to convene courts that worked within a body of CUSTOMARY LAW to settle disputes between members. Guilds also developed corporate characteristics, including a patron (typically the chief magistrate of a city or the bishop) and a governing body of masters, and so were able to play an increasingly prominent role in civic government. Guilds were also important patrons of art (commissioning paintings for guildhalls) and music and in the field of drama were responsible for sponsoring the mystery plays (a collocation in which the word 'mystery' means 'pertaining to a craft') of late medieval Europe.

In the sixteenth century new industries (notably mining) could not easily be accommodated to the guild system, and the needs of overseas trade were more effectively met by joint-stock companies. In England, their successors are the livery companies of London.

On religious guilds, see CONFRATERNITIES.

**GUISE, CHARLES DE, or Cardinal de Lorraine** (1525–74), French cardinal, the younger brother of François de Lorraine, second duke of GUISE. He was destined for a career in the Church, to which end he was appointed archbishop of Reims at the age of 13 and a cardinal at the age of 22. He was a stalwart opponent of Protestantism and rejected the idea of offering toleration to HUGUENOTS in the WARS OF RELIGION. He participated in the COUNCIL OF TRENT with a view to containing the Protestant heresy. An advocate of rapprochement with the Lutherans, he was resolutely opposed to CALVINISM, which, in contrast with Luther, rejected the 'real presence' of Christ at the EUCHARIST. He was a patron of humanist learning and the founder of the University of Reims.

*DBF*; H. Outram Evennett, *The Cardinal of Lorraine and the Council of Trent: A Study in the Counter-Reformation* (1930).

**GUISE, FRANÇOIS DE LORRAINE, SECOND DUKE OF** (1519–63), French soldier and leader of the Catholic side in the WARS OF RELIGION, the son of Claude de Lorraine (the first duke) and the elder brother of Charles de GUISE, the future cardinal of Lorraine. As a young man François fought in the WARS OF ITALY, in which he defended Metz against a siege mounted by CHARLES V (November 1552–January 1553) and led the French armies that captured Naples from the Spanish (1557) and CALAIS from the English (1558). His niece Mary Stuart (MARY, QUEEN OF SCOTS) married the future King FRANCIS II, during whose brief reign (1559–60) Guise became the most powerful figure in France.

On the accession of the youthful CHARLES IX, political power passed to the regent CATHERINE DE MÉDICIS, whereupon Guise allied himself with Anne de MONTMORENCY and the maréchal de SAINT-ANDRÉ in the group known as the Triumvirate. He withdrew from the royal court in protest against the concessions to the Protestants that Queen Catherine had allowed in the January Edict (January 1562). In May 1562 his troops massacred a congregation of HUGUENOTS at Vassy (Champagne), and so started the Wars of Religion that were to last for 36 years. Guise was shot by a Huguenot partisan at the siege of Orléans and died of his wounds on 24 February 1563.

*DBF.*

**GUISE, HENRI DE LORRAINE, THIRD DUKE OF** (1550–88), French soldier and leader of the CATHOLIC LEAGUE in the WARS OF RELIGION, the son of François, the second duke of GUISE. He became a soldier as a young man, fighting in the second War of Religion (September 1567–March 1568). He helped to plan the ST BARTHOLOMEW'S DAY MASSACRE and was responsible for the murder of Gaspar de COLIGNY and other prominent Protestants. He subsequently took part in the siege of La Rochelle (November 1572–June 1573) and in the battle of Dormans (on the Marne) against an Anglo-German army (May 1576); the facial wound that he received in this battle left a scar, so he became known as Henri le Balafré ('Henry the Scarred'). When the Catholic League was instituted later in the year, Henri became its first leader, and on 9 May 1588 entered Paris at the head of an armed force of 30,000 men. On 23 December 1588 he was assassinated at Blois by order of King HENRI III, whom Henri had aspired to succeed.

Henri is the eponym of *The Duke of Guise* (1682), a tragedy by John Dryden and Nathaniel Lee.

DBF.

**GUNPOWDER** is an inflammable mixture consisting of charcoal, sulphur, and saltpetre (potassium nitrate). The predecessor of gunpowder, which was known as 'Greek fire', was probably made from naphtha, and had been used in Byzantine warfare since late antiquity. The earliest references to the mixture of substances associated with gunpowder come from ninth-century China; the thirteenth-century Arabic name for gunpowder was 'Chinese snow'. The first western author to describe gunpowder was Roger Bacon, who outlined its nature and history in *De mirabili potestate artis et naturae* (1242), but seemed unaware of its potential as a propellant.

The earliest illustration of a gun is in an Oxford manuscript (*De officiis regnum*) of 1325. Guns and gunpowder were made in Florence by 1326, in France by 1338, and in England by 1344; in Germany, powder-works were established in Augsburg (1340), Spandau (1344), and Liegnitz (1348; now Legnica, in Poland).

The deployment of gunpowder altered the nature and conduct of warfare. It was used in artillery in the early fourteenth century and was later used in hand-held weapons, first in the ARQUEBUS and then in the MUSKET. Gunpowder was initially stuffed into cannon as loose powder, but in the fifteenth century it was produced by moistening, shaping, drying, and granulating the mixture.

Gunpowder remained expensive throughout the early modern period, chiefly because of the difficulty of extracting saltpetre from its only known source, animal urine. Theoreticians extolled its potential, but soldiers remained conscious that it was unreliable because of the tendency of the mixture to disaggregate and the susceptibility of gunpowder to dampness. The literature of gunpowder includes Machiavelli, *Della arte della guerra* (1521), Vanucchio Biringuccio, *De la pirotechnia* (Venice, 1540), Tartaglia, *Quesiti e invenzioni diversi* (Venice, 1546), and Peter Whitehorn, *How to Make Saltpetre, Gunpowder etc.* (London, 1573).

A. Marshall, *Explosives* (3 vols., 1917–32); J. R. Partington, *A History of Greek Fire and Gunpowder* (1960).

**GUNPOWDER PLOT**, the name given to the attempt by Guy FAWKES and others to blow up JAMES I and the Houses of Parliament during the opening of a new parliamentary session in November 1605. Fawkes's plot was in part an extreme response to the fierce opposition which had thwarted James's attempts to relax penal laws against Catholics on his succes-

sion to the English throne in 1603. The conspirators were betrayed, captured, and executed; their failure is celebrated with the burning of the 'Guy' on Bonfire Night, every 5 November.

**GUSTAVUS VASA** (1496–1560), king of Sweden and founder of the VASA dynasty, was born into an aristocratic family in Lindholm. In 1514 he moved to the court of his cousin Sten STURE, and so became part of the movement to secure Swedish independence from CHRISTIAN IV of Denmark. In 1518 he was delivered as a hostage to Denmark, but in September 1519 he escaped. By May 1520 he had made his way back to Sweden. On 8 November 1520 the massacre known in English as the Stockholm Bloodbath precipitated a nationalist uprising, and on 6 June 1523 Gustavus was elected king at Strängnäs.

The reign of Gustavus was dominated by the advent of the Reformation, which was gradually introduced from 1527 (when Gustavus gained control of the property of the Church) to 1550 (when a national church on the Lutheran model was established). The most significant constitutional change effected by Gustavus was abandonment of an elected monarchy in favour of a hereditary monarchy; this change was endorsed by the Swedish Riksdag in 1544.

SBL s.v. Gustav I.

**GUTENBERG, JOHANN** (*c.*1394/9–1468), inventor of printing, born in Mainz, the son of Friele Gensfleisch; the name Gutenberg derives from the name of the family home, Haus zum Gutenberg. He trained as a goldsmith and in 1430 moved to Strassburg, where he worked with a goldsmith and began to experiment with printing techniques. He returned to Mainz *c.*1448 and in 1450 borrowed 800 gulden from Johann FUST (who was later to invest another 800 gulden and become his business partner) in order to establish a printing workshop. He worked with Fust and with Peter SCHÖFFER (Fust's son-in-law) until 1455, when Fust foreclosed on his loans and Gutenberg became bankrupt. Thereafter the workshop was run by Fust and Schöffner, and Gutenberg was gradually excluded from the business; he seems to have printed nothing after 1460. In 1465 he entered the service of the archbishop of Mainz, whose patronage he enjoyed until his death.

It was Gutenberg who developed the technology of printing, which included cutting punches and casting type; the method for stamping matrices may have been the invention of Schöffner. It is difficult to assign specific books to any one of the three partners, especially as they often collaborated, but Gutenberg is traditionally accredited with the 42-line Latin Bible published between 1452 and 1456; of its 180 copies (of which 48 survive in whole or in part), 30 were printed on vellum and the rest on paper. This Bible is also known as the Mazarin Bible, because the first copy to be identified was in Cardinal Mazarin's library.

The Gutenberg Museum in Mainz has Gutenberg's hand-press and a collection of his books, including a 42-line Bible.

MDA; NDB; Janet Ing, *Johann Gutenberg and his Bible* (1988).

# H

HABSBURG or (erroneously) Hapsburg, HOUSE OF, the most important dynasty in European history, which produced dukes and archdukes of AUSTRIA from 1276, HOLY ROMAN EMPERORS intermittently from 1273 and continuously from 1438 to 1806, kings of Bohemia intermittently from 1306 and continuously from 1526, kings of Hungary intermittently from 1437 and continuously from 1526, and kings of Spain (which included the Netherlands, southern Italy, and the overseas empire) from 1516 to 1700. The original family seat was the castle of Habsburg (from 'Habichtsburg', castle of the hawk), on the river Aare near its confluence with the Rhine, in what is now Switzerland.

The first Habsburg to assume a European role was Rudolf I (1218–91), who became emperor in September 1273. Five years later he killed Přemysl Ottokar II, king of Bohemia, and annexed the Bohemian duchies of Austria and Styria, investing them in his sons Albrecht and Rudolf. These investitures were the first stage in the process by which the power base of the Habsburgs shifted from the Rhine to the Danube. In 1306 King Wenceslas III of Bohemia died, and the crown of Bohemia was seized by Rudolf of Austria.

In the fourteenth century the Empire passed out of the hands of the Habsburgs, but the family continued to rule Austria, Styria, Carinthia, and Tirol as well as its ancestral lands in Alsace. In December 1437 the Emperor SIGISMUND, who was also king of Hungary and Bohemia, died without male heirs, bequeathing his kingdoms to his son-in-law Albrecht von Habsburg, duke of Austria, who was crowned king of Hungary on 1 January 1438, elected king of the Romans (as Albrecht II) on 18 March 1438, and crowned king of Bohemia in June 1438.

On 27 October 1439 Albrecht was killed while fighting the Ottomans. He left no sons, but his widow was pregnant, and on 22 February 1440 gave birth to their son, who was called LADISLAS POSTHUMUS. The Empire passed to Albrecht's second cousin FRIEDRICH III, who administered the eastern possessions of the infant king. Shortly after his coronation as emperor in 1453, Friedrich legitimized the Habsburgs' use of the term 'archduke' (German *Erzherzog*), which had been in occasional use since 1453. When Ladislaus died unmarried in 1457, the thrones of Hungary and Bohemia passed from the Habsburgs, who managed to retain only Austria, Tirol,

Carinthia, and their lands on the Upper Rhine, including Alsace; in 1460 the Habsburgs lost the last vestiges of their authority in the SWISS CONFEDERATION.

In August 1493 Friedrich was succeeded by his son MAXIMILIAN, who in 1477 had married MARY OF BURGUNDY, daughter of CHARLES THE BOLD, duke of Burgundy, and so absorbed many Burgundian territories, including the NETHERLANDS (but excluding Artois and the duchy of Burgundy), into the Habsburg Empire. Maximilian's son Archduke Philip married JUANA LA LOCA in 1496; their two sons were Charles (later the Emperor CHARLES V) and Ferdinand (later the Emperor FERDINAND I).

Charles inherited territories from each of his four grandparents. From Ferdinand II of Aragon (FERDINAND V), his maternal grandfather, he inherited Aragon, Naples, Sicily, and Sardinia, to which he added Milan and Tunis in 1535; from ISABELLA THE CATHOLIC, his maternal grandmother, he inherited Castile, Granada, and the Spanish colonies in America, to which he added Mexico (1519) and Peru (1543); from Mary of Burgundy, his paternal grandmother, he inherited the Netherlands, to which he added Friesland, Groningen, Gelderland, Lingen (now in Germany), Overijssel, and Utrecht; from Maximilian, his paternal grandfather, he inherited Austria, Tirol, Carinthia, the Outer Austrian lands on the Upper Rhine, and the HOLY ROMAN EMPIRE.

Charles succeeded his father in 1519, and two years later passed the Austrian archduchies to his brother Ferdinand, who married Anna, the daughter of King LADISLAS II of Bohemia and Hungary. After the battle of MOHÁCS in 1526, Ferdinand became king of Bohemia and ruler of Moravia, Silesia, and Lusatia, but the crown of Hungary was disputed, and in 1538 he was forced to agree to the partition of Hungary; Ferdinand's share was the western portion, which was thereafter threatened by the Ottomans. Charles and his brother Ferdinand ruled a European empire that stretched from Spain in the west to a strip of Hungary in the east, and from the Netherlands in the north to Sicily in the south. A military corridor known as the Spanish road connected the Habsburg possessions from the Netherlands to Genoa and thence east through Lombardy to Tirol.

On 25 October 1555 Charles abdicated as emperor in favour of his brother Ferdinand; on 15 January 1556 he abdicated as king of Spain (which included the Spanish Netherlands and the overseas empire) in favour of his son PHILIP II. Thereafter the family was permanently divided into Spanish and Austrian branches. The last Habsburg king of Spain died without an heir in 1700, and his possessions became the prize in the War of the Spanish Succession. In Austria, Ferdinand's son MAXIMILIAN II inherited Austria, Bohemia, Hungary, and the Empire. Maximilian's sons RUDOLF II and MATTHIAS succeeded in turn to the Empire and the thrones of Bohemia and Hungary.

R. J. W. Evans, *The Making of the Habsburg Monarchy, 1550–1700* (1979).

**HAGENAU, CONFERENCE OF, or (German) Hagenauer Religionsgespräch.** From 25 June to 28 July 1540 the Emperor CHARLES V presided over a conference in the twelfth-century imperial palace in Hagenau (now the French town of Haguenau, 15 kilometres (9 miles) north-east of Strasbourg). The purpose of the meeting was to reconcile the Protestant and Catholic parties in Germany. Delegates were unable to agree on an agenda and on procedural rules, and the conference was dissolved without any result save the decision to reassemble in Worms; see WORMS, CONFERENCE OF.

**HAGENAUER or Hagnower, NIKOLAUS or Niclas** (*fl.* 1493–before 1538), German woodcarver responsible for the figures on the Isenheim altar (now in the Musée d'Unterlinden in Colmar), of which the wings were painted by GRÜNEWALD ten years later.

MDA; NDB; W. Vöge, *Niclas Hagnower, der Meister des Isenheimer Hochaltars und seine Frühwerke* (1931).

**HAKLUYT, RICHARD** (*c.*1552–1616), English writer on exploration. Hakluyt realized the extent of other countries' New World exploration whilst serving between 1583 and 1588 as chaplain to the English ambassador in Paris. He devoted the rest of his life to collecting and producing accounts of English explorations, hoping to stimulate further such exploits. His *Principal Navigations, Voyages, Traffics and Discoveries of the English Nations*, which discussed the voyages of the CABOTS, DRAKE, FROBISHER, WILLOUGHBY, and others, first appeared in 1589; an extended three-volume version was published in 1598–1600. Further writings were published by PURCHAS after his death.

DNB; J. A. Williams, *Richard Hakluyt and his Successors* (1946).

**HALLER, BERCHTOLD or Bertold** (1492–1536), reformer of Bern, born at Aldingen (Württemberg) and educated at Pforzheim (where he met MELANCHTHON) and Cologne. He moved to Bern, where he taught in the gymnasium, and became chaplain of the Bakers' Guild (1513) and canon of the cathedral (1520). In 1521 he met ZWINGLI and became an advocate of reform; he was charged with heresy in 1523, but acquitted. Thereafter he became, together with Thomas WYTTENBACH and the painter Niklas MANUEL, one of the three leaders of the Reformation party in Bern. He participated in the Disputations of Baden (1526) and Bern (1528).

The Disputation of Bern (6–26 January 1528) debated ten theological propositions (known as the Theses of Bern) com-

piled by Haller in collaboration with Franz Kolb. The city council had convened the disputation in order to establish the Reformation in Bern and to confute the Disputation of Baden (1526), which had attempted to consolidate Swiss opposition to the Reformation. The ten Theses, which articulate the Zwinglian position on the PAPACY, the authority of tradition, the ATONEMENT, the EUCHARIST, the sacrifice of the mass, mediation through saints, PURGATORY, images, and clerical celibacy, were debated by Catholics and Protestants at the Disputation and then embodied in an edict of 7 February 1528 (drafted by Haller and Kolb) which instituted the Reformation in Bern. In 1532 Haller and Wolfgang CAPITO took part in the synod which ratified the Reformation in Bern and established Haller as the canton's religious leader. In the final years of his short life Haller became embroiled in controversy with the Swiss ANABAPTISTS and in a futile attempt to establish Protestantism in Solothurn. He published nothing, but some of his letters are printed in Zwingli's works. He died on 25 February 1536.

NDB; M. Kirchhofer, *Bertold Haller oder die Reformation von Bern* (1828); C. Pestalozzi, *Bertold Haller* (1861); I. Backus, *The Disputations of Baden, 1526, and Berne, 1528* (1993).

**HALLMARK,** an eighteenth-century term for the marks or stamps used by guilds to certify the standard of gold and silver articles assayed by them; in London the stamp was applied at the Goldsmiths' Hall, hence the term 'hallmark'. The standard of English silver was first regulated by statute in 1238, and a revised statute of 1300 set the standard of silver (for coin and plate) at 925 parts of silver and 75 of base metals (usually copper) and required the Assay Office in London to certify the standard by stamping a leopard's head on objects deemed to meet the standard; in the language of weights and measures used by goldsmiths, this 'sterling standard' was said to be 11.1 ounces troy of silver alloyed with 0.9 ounce of copper in each troy pound. From 1363 to 1697 makers were required to affix a symbol that would enable the source of any substandard silver to be traced; after 1697 makers were instead required to affix their initials. English silver can be dated from 1478, when makers were required to indicate the year of manufacture with a letter of the alphabet which was changed every May, at first on 19 May and later on 29 May (and from 1975 on 1 January); when one alphabet was exhausted, another with a different fount was introduced.

In 1544 the significance of the leopard's head hallmark changed when a national mark, a lion passant gardant, was introduced; thereafter the leopard's head (which was crowned from 1300 to 1820) became the mark of the Goldsmiths' Hall in London, even though some provincial assay offices continued to use it alongside their own marks. The new national mark was in part a recognition of the existence of provincial assay offices, but it was occasioned by the need to reassure purchasers of silver plate throughout the country that the standard of silver in plate was being maintained even though the standard of silver coin was being debased. After 1544 the leopard's head came to be regarded as the mark of London and the lion passant as the sterling mark.

In France, gold had to be stamped with a mark (French *poinçon*) from 1313; early modern gold marks consist of a marker's mark surmounted by a fleur-de-lis and the guild mark. In the Netherlands hallmarks first appeared in the fourteenth century, but the system was not regulated until 1814. Similarly, Augsburg and Nuremberg goldsmiths marked their products from the fourteenth century, but the system was unregulated until Augsburg introduced a city mark in 1529 and Nuremberg regulated its marks in 1550.

> M. Rosenberg, *Der Goldschmiede Merkzeichen* (4 vols., 1922–8); E. Beuque, *Dictionnaire de poinçons officiels français et étrangers* (2 vols., 1925–8); C. J. Jackson, *English Goldsmiths and their Marks* (1921).

**HALOANDER, GREGOR** (1501–31), German jurist who wrote on both Roman law and CANON LAW. He was the son of a Zwickau tailor, and studied law at Leipzig. From 1525 to 1527 he lived in Italy, studying law in Bologna and Venice. He then moved to Nuremberg, where PIRKHEIMER persuaded the town council to pay for Haloander's monumental edition of the JUSTINIAN *Corpus* (4 vols., 1529–31). When he had completed the edition, Haloander returned to Italy, and died suddenly in Venice.

> *NDB; CoE.*

**HAMILTON, JOHN** (1511–71), Scottish opponent of the Reformation. An illegitimate son of the first earl of Arran, Hamilton spent his youth in a Benedictine monastery. Between 1540 and 1543 he studied in Paris, and on his return he became keeper of the privy seal, through the influence of his half-brother the second earl of Arran, then acting as regent during the minority of MARY, QUEEN OF SCOTS. In 1544 he became bishop of Dunkeld, and three years later archbishop of St Andrews and primate of Scotland. He became a persecutor of Protestant heresy and an opponent of reformist opinion. Between 1548 and 1559 he called four synods, seeking to raise levels of religious understanding amongst the laity; in 1552 *Hamilton's Catechism* in the vernacular was published. He was imprisoned in 1563 for saying mass, but Mary intervened and he was released. He remained her staunch supporter, and in 1567 his questionable annulment of BOTHWELL's first marriage opened the way for Bothwell and Mary's marriage. As support for Mary collapsed, and she fled to England, Hamilton was captured and accused of complicity in the murder of DARNLEY; although his involvement is unlikely, he was found guilty and hanged.

> *DNB.*

**HAMILTON, PATRICK** (1503–28), Scottish reformer. Hamilton studied at St Andrews and Paris, where he became interested in the ideas of LUTHER. In 1527 he travelled on the Continent, visiting Luther at Wittenberg, and the Protestant university at Marburg. He also published *Loci communes* ('Patrick's Places'), before returning to Scotland. In 1528 he was charged with heresy and burnt at the stake.

> *DNB.*

**HAMPTON COURT CONFERENCE**, a conference convened in January 1604 by King JAMES I, which brought together English bishops and Puritan leaders at Hampton Court Palace, the royal palace on the Thames south-west of London; the bishops were led by Richard BANCROFT and the Puritans by John RAINOLDS.

Puritan demands for ecclesiastical reform had been articulated in the Millenary Petition of April 1603, and stated their objection to such practices as the sign of the cross in baptism, the rite of confirmation, the wearing of the surplice, the regulation of the length of church services, the profanation of Sundays, the requirement to bow at the name of Jesus, the churching of women, and the requirement to read from the Apocrypha in church services. At the Conference, Rainolds also set out the Puritan objections to episcopacy. However, James supported the bishops' opposition to Rainolds, asserting that he had learned in Scotland 'no bishop, no king'. He also rejected most of the requests in the Millenary Petition, conceding only a few changes in the Book of COMMON PRAYER.

The most significant result of the Hampton Court Conference was the commissioning of a new translation of the BIBLE, eventually issued as the Authorized Version in 1611; Rainolds was given a prominent role in its translation.

**HÄNDL, JACOB, or Jacob Gallus** (1550–91), Slovenian composer active in Austria, Bohemia, Silesia, and Moravia. Having served as choirmaster to the bishop of Olomouc, by 1586 he was cantor of St Jan na Brzehu in Prague. His *Opus musicum* (1587) is a collection of motets for festivals of the liturgical calendar, music for Marian festivals, and three settings of the Passion.

**HANDSTEIN** (German; 'hand stone'), a sixteenth-century German collectors' object, the size of a human hand, carved from a lump of ore mounted on a silver stand and decorated with enamel figurines to illustrate mining or biblical scenes.

**HANDWRITING.** See CALLIGRAPHY.

**HANS VON REUTLINGEN** (*fl.* 1492–1524), German goldsmith and seal-engraver who worked in Aachen, where he engraved seals for the emperors MAXIMILIAN I and CHARLES V. His most famous piece is the silver-gilt case (now in the Weltliche Schatzkammer in the Kunsthistorisches Museum, Vienna) made for the *Reichsevangeliar* ('Imperial Gospels'), probably on the occasion of Maximilian's coronation in 1500. The Aachen cathedral treasury (Domschatzkammer) holds several pieces by Hans, including a reliquary statue of St Peter (*c.*1510).

**HANSEATIC LEAGUE**, a confederation of mercantile cities in north Germany and the Baltic. In the thirteenth century the League was an association of merchants, but in the half-century following its first plenary diet (1356), the League became a powerful commercial, political, and military force. It sought to secure trading monopolies throughout the Baltic and North Sea region and waged a campaign against pirates. By the mid-fourteenth century there were more than 70 Hansa cities and towns, including Bremen, COLOGNE, DANZIG, Hamburg, LÜBECK, and Riga; the League's depots, known as 'factories', extended from London to Novgorod, and it acquired trading privileges in the Netherlands (Antwerp, Bruges, Ghent), in England (e.g. Bristol, Hull, Ipswich, Norwich, Yarmouth, York), and throughout Scandinavia. Each of these branches was called a 'counter' (German *Kontor*); the London 'counter' is first identified as the Steelyard in 1422. In the late fifteenth century the collective power of the League began to decline as its traditional markets were penetrated by Dutch and English merchants, but individual Hanseatic cities continued to flourish.

The governing body of the League was an assembly of representatives (*Hansetage*) that met at Lübeck. The legal status of the League was clarified at the assembly of 1469, when the terms *societas*, *collegium*, and *universitas* (all of which were in use in England to describe the League) were rejected in favour of *firma confederatio*. The assembly promulgated MARITIME LAWS, but these were not formally codified until 1667, when they were published as *Ius maritimum Hanseaticum*. At the last plenary assembly of the League (1669) only nine members attended.

P. Dollinger, *The German Hansa* (1970; repr. 1999).

**HARDENBERG, ALBRECHT** (*c.*1510–1574), Netherlandish reformer. He was educated by the BRETHREN OF THE COMMON LIFE in Groningen and *c.*1527 entered the Order's house in Aduard (north-east of Groningen). He studied first at Louvain University and then at Mainz, where he met the Polish Protestant reformer Jan ŁASKI. On returning to teach at Louvain he quickly aroused the opposition of the university for advocating the doctrine of JUSTIFICATION by faith. He withdrew to the monastery at Aduard, but maintained his contact with prominent reformers, including HERMANN VON WIED, the archbishop-elector of Cologne, Philipp MELANCHTHON, and Łaski.

In 1542 Hardenberg joined the Reformers, leaving his monastery and moved initially to Wittenberg and then to Cologne, where he worked with Hermann in the reformed cause; he also participated in the diets of SPEYER (1544) and WORMS (1547). In 1546 Hermann was excommunicated by Pope PAUL III and deposed by the Emperor CHARLES V, and Hardenberg left Cologne for Bremen, where he was appointed cathedral-preacher in 1547. He remained in this post until 1561, when he was expelled because of his dissent from the Lutheran doctrine of consubstantiation (see EUCHARIST). Hardenberg sought refuge in Oldenburg, where he lived privately under the protection of the count until 1565, when he was appointed pastor at Sengwarden, on the coast of Oldenburg. In 1567 he was appointed preacher at Emden, in East Frisia, where he worked until his death on 18 May 1574.

NDB.

**HARINGTON, SIR JOHN** (1561–1612), English courtier, wit, and poet. Godson of ELIZABETH I, Harington's translation of Ariosto's *Orlando furioso* (1591) may have been produced at her request; its prefatory *Apology of Poetry* echoes SIDNEY's closely. A subsequent treatise calling for the introduction of water-closets, *The Metamorphosis of Ajax* (1596), the first of

which he may have had installed at his estate near Bath, was more contentious. He accompanied ESSEX to Ireland and shared in the royal displeasure at the early conclusion of that visit. Harington's satires, epigrams, and other writings demonstrate an observational talent and extravagant personality which even royal reproach could not fully repress.

DNB.

**HARPSICHORD**, a stringed keyboard instrument where the sound is produced by a plectrum mounted on a jack plucking the string. The jack then returns to its original position and a felt damper touches the vibrating string to deaden the sound. It was a generic term applied also to the spinet and the virginals, an instrument favoured by ELIZABETH I. These differed in shape since, unlike the harpsichord, the strings were in a transverse position on the virginals and in an oblique position on a spinet. The word harpsichord was first mentioned in 1397; it was used both as a solo instrument and in ensemble playing, particularly in the realizing of figured bass, until the end of the eighteenth century.

**HARRIOT, THOMAS** (*c.*1560–1621), English mathematician, astronomer, and natural philosopher. He was born in Oxford and educated at Oxford University. He became the mathematical tutor to Sir Walter RALEGH, who in 1585 included Harriot as surveyor in his expedition to Virginia; Harriot's report was subsequently published as *A Brief and True Report of the New-Found Land of Virginia* (1588). In the 1590s Harriot entered the service of Henry Percy, ninth earl of Northumberland, later known as 'the Wizard Earl', who was imprisoned in the Tower after the Gunpowder Plot (1605). After 1588, Harriot wrote prodigiously but published nothing. He was even reluctant to discuss his work in private letters: despite KEPLER's explicit request, Harriot did not tell him the results of his work on the law of refraction of light (now named after Willebrord SNEL). Harriot's observations of the moon apparently antedate those of Galileo GALILEI (1610); he was also interested in ALCHEMY.

Harriot's most important work on ALGEBRA was published posthumously as *Artis analyticae praxis ad aequationes algebraicas resolvendas* (1631). The editor of Harriot's text was probably Walter Warner (*c.*1557–1643), another member of the Northumberland circle. Warner seems also to have introduced certain modifications of his own, particularly in the notation. As printed, Harriot's work is systematic and clearly draws on the writings of VIÈTE; it is important as marking the progress of Viète's largely posthumous reputation and for using purely symbolic notation. Harriot's equations have very much the look of today's mathematics, which is to say that they can be read independently of the language of the surrounding text.

DNB; DSB; Robert Fox (ed.), *Thomas Harriot, an Elizabethan Man of Science* (2000).

**HARRISON, WILLIAM** (1535–93), English historian. Educated at Oxford, Harrison was ordained and became canon of Windsor. His *Description of England*, an account of English life and customs, was incorporated into HOLINSHED's *Chronicles*. He translated into English Bellenden's Scots version of BOECE's *Description of Scotland*, which was also included in Holinshed.

*DNB.*

**HARVEY, GABRIEL** (*c*.1545–1630), English scholar and literary critic. Educated at Cambridge, Harvey became a fellow of Pembroke Hall, where his interests included rhetoric and Latin poetry. His *Letters* (1580) to SPENSER discuss the difficulties of writing English verse in classical metres. His *Four Letters* (1592) and *Pierce's Supererogation* (1593) include an attack on NASHE. His surviving library is of interest for its marginalia.

*DNB.*

**HAṢAN IBN HAṢAN IBN AL-HAYTHAM** (965–*c*.1040), known in the Latin West as Alhacen or (later) Alhazen, Egyptian astronomer, mathematician, and natural philosopher who wrote an advanced mathematical treatise on OPTICS parts of whose contents became known in the West because they were used in treatises by Witelo (died after 1281) and Roger Bacon (*c*.1220–*c*.1292). Latin and Italian translations of Ibn al-Haytham's work survive in manuscripts. The first printed edition was *Alhazeni Opticae thesaurus* (ed. Risner, 1572). Ibn al-Haytham proposed that sight was by the reception of light rays, a theory that found rather few adherents until it was proved correct by KEPLER in 1604.

**HASSLER, HANS LEO** (1562–1612), German composer, son of Isaak Hassler and brother of Kaspar and Jakob. He left Nuremberg in 1584 to study with Andrea GABRIELI in Venice and in 1586 became *Cammerorganist* to Octavian Fugger II in Augsburg. He was a consultant in organ design and even involved himself in building mechanical instruments, such as a clockwork organ bought by Emperor RUDOLF II, whom he later served as 'Kaiserlieder Hofdiener'. His vocal music appeared in the anthologies *Rosetum Marianum* (1604) and *Florilegium selectissimarum cantionum* (1603). His final appointment was at the court of Elector Christian II of Saxony in Dresden.

**HATFIELD HOUSE**, a house and garden in Hertfordshire built for Robert Cecil, earl of Salisbury, between 1607 and 1612. The U-shaped house is a distinguished example of a Jacobean nobleman's house, with a central hall and two symmetrical wings. The large two-storeyed hall with its minstrels' gallery and plastered ceiling is a development of the English medieval hall. The state apartments are on the first floor, in the Italian style. The oak staircase that leads to these apartments is one of the finest in England.

The east garden was initially laid out on two terraces by Thomas Chandler, but in 1611 Salomon de CAUS redesigned the garden, though he retained the services of Simon Sturtevant, Chandler's water engineer. Water ran from the grand Fountain of Neptune in a garden laid out in PARTERRES down to a water-garden for which Sturtevant built the hydraulics, which included a stream and FOUNTAINS on an

island with a PAVILION. The collection of plants from the BOTANICAL GARDENS of the Netherlands, France, and Italy was entrusted to John TRADESCANT. The garden has evolved continuously since the early seventeenth century, but the outlines of the Jacobean garden are still visible.

**HAUSMANN, VALENTIN** (*c*.1565–*c*.1614), German composer, music editor, and poet. Based in Gerbstedt, he travelled widely. He visited Poland and Prussia in 1598–9, and collected Polish dances which appeared in his *Venusgarten* (1602) and *Rest von polnischen und andern Tantzen* (1603). He wrote secular and sacred music and popularized Italian vocal music in his publications of music by MARENZIO, VECCHI, and GASTOLDI.

**HAWES, STEPHEN** (*c*.1474–1511 / 23), English poet. Courtier to HENRY VII, his *Pastime of Pleasure* (1509) is a chivalric verse allegory. *Example of Virtue* (1512) is a similar allegory of the pursuit of perfection.

*DNB.*

**HAWKINS, SIR JOHN** (1532–95), English privateer and slaver. A prominent Elizabethan seaman, Hawkins's career encompassed transporting slaves from West Africa to Spanish colonies in America, fighting the Armada, and sailing with DRAKE on further anti-Spanish expeditions. His exploits, together with those of Drake and RALEGH, are associated with England's expansion of its naval power, and the beginnings of its concerns in the New World.

*DNB.*

**HAWKWOOD, SIR JOHN or (Italian) Giovanni Acuto** (*c*.1320–1394), English *condottiere*, a native of Essex who fought in France in the Hundred Years War, and in 1350 moved with his armed band to Italy, where he spent 35 years in the service of various rulers, including Pisa, Milan, Padua, and the papacy. In 1377 he entered the service of Florence, where he became a citizen with tax exemption for life. On his death he was granted a state funeral and a frescoed monument (replaced in 1436 by Paolo UCCELLO's fresco) in Florence Cathedral.

*DNB.*

**HAYTHAM, HAṢAN IBN HAṢAN IBN AL-**. See HAṢAN IBN HAṢAN IBN AL-HAYTHAM.

**HEBREW SCHOLARSHIP.** Hebrew was the literary and liturgical language of the Jews of Europe, and from the end of the tenth century, when the centre of Hebrew studies shifted from Babylon to Europe, there was a tradition of Hebrew scholarship amongst the learned JEWS of France (Rashi in the north and the Kimchi family in Provence), Spain (from Abraham ibn Ezra to Isaac ABRAVANEL), Italy, and Germany. The anti-Semitic attitudes of European Christians meant that many Christian scholars purposefully eschewed Hebrew lest they be tainted by a language associated with Jews. The movement that overcame the aversion to Semitic studies in some scholarly circles was the humanist ideal that the biblical scholar had to be *trium linguarum gnarus* ('familiar with the three languages'): Latin, Greek, and Hebrew. This ideal was embodied in the trilingual university established by Cardinal Jiménez de CISNEROS in Alcalá, in Richard Foxe's foundation of Corpus Christi College in Oxford, in FRANCIS I's *noble et trilingue Académie* (later the COLLEGE DE FRANCE), in the trilingual college in Louvain, and in the provision by FRIEDRICH III, elector of Saxony, of professorships in the three languages at the University of Wittenberg.

One of the earliest Christian students of Hebrew was PICO DELLA MIRANDOLA, who in 1490 met Johann REUCHLIN and encouraged his nascent study of Hebrew. Reuchlin was eventually to become the greatest Christian Hebraist of his generation, perhaps surpassed only by his younger contemporary Sebastian MÜNSTER.

The chief difficulty of Hebrew for Christian students of the language was that the sacred texts were consonantal; this posed no problem for learned Jews who could speak the language, but Christians were tongue-tied without vowels. As Johannes Campensis wrote to Daniel BOMBERG in 1528, 'legere sine punctis non legere puto sed divinare' ('reading Hebrew without the punctuation is not reading but guessing'). The punctuation also proved to be theologically contentious, in that Christians could not agree whether the divine inspiration of the Old Testament included the vowels as well as the consonants.

Christians inadvertently compounded the difficulties of studying Hebrew by choosing to describe the language in terms of Latin grammatical categories. Confusion quickly arose about matters such as the description of articles, of which Latin has none. Hebrew has a definite article (*ha* plus a doubling of the following consonant) which can also be used to express what in Latin would be called a vocative; even Reuchlin became confused, declaring a prefix consisting of the letter *sin* to be an article rather than an abbreviated particle corresponding to the Latin relative pronoun. The first attempt to write a Christian grammar of Hebrew was the *De modo legendi et intelligendi Hebraeum* of the Alsatian Minorite Konrad PELLIKAN, which was published in Strassburg in 1503 or 1504. Reuchlin subsequently published *De rudimentis Hebraicis* (1506) and *De accentibus et orthographia linguae Hebraicae* (1518), and so laid the scholarly foundation for the study of Hebrew in Germany. Wolfgang CAPITO published a Hebrew grammar in Basel in 1518. Santi PAGNINI wrote a Hebrew grammar (1546) and also translated the Old Testament from Hebrew into Latin. Renaissance Hebrew scholarship culminated in Sebastian MÜNSTER, whose prodigious output included the first grammar of Aramaic to be written by a Christian. Münster also produced Latin translations of works by the eminent Jewish grammarian Elijah Bachur (known to Christians as Elias Levita), including his Hebrew grammar (Rome, 1508); Bachur (1469–1549) had taught Hebrew to Cardinal EGIDIO DA VITERBO, who became an important patron of Hebrew studies in early sixteenth-century Italy. The Christian Paul FAGIUS, who as a young schoolteacher had established a Hebrew printing press in Isny, translated the Onkelos Targum into Latin and later held chairs of Hebrew at Strassburg and Cambridge.

Hebrew printing began in northern Italy in about 1475; early printed works include a consonantal Psalter (Bologna, 1477) and a Pentateuch with vowel points and accents (Bologna, 1482). The landmarks of German printing were achieved through the labours of south German Jews in SONCINO, near Mantua. In 1488 a complete Old Testament (with vowel points and accents) was published in Soncino; a second edition dating from 1491–3 may have been published by the Soncino printers working in Naples. The Soncino firm then moved to Brescia, where they produced a two-part edition of the Old Testament (1492 and 1494); it was this edition that LUTHER used for his translation into German. Christian printers of Hebrew texts lacked the linguistic skills of the Soncino family, and so engaged Jewish scholars as editors and proofreaders: Daniel Bomberg, for example, worked with the Christian Jew Felix Pratensis on the production of the first printed rabbinical Bible (1516–17), which contained the *mishnah* and the *targumim* as well as a Hebrew text of the Old Testament; for the second edition of 1524–5 Bomberg used the formidable Massoretic scholarship of the Tunisian refugee Jacob ben Chayim to produce what eventually came to be regarded as the standard Massoretic text. In Spain, the converted Jew Alfonso de ZAMORA worked on the COMPLUTENSIAN POLYGLOT with the Christian Hebraist Antonio LEBRIJA. The two final important editions of the sixteenth century were Robert ESTIENNE's edition of Jacob ben Chayim's text (1539–44) and Christophe Plantin's *Biblia regia*, the first four volumes of which contained the Old Testament (using a modified form of the Complutensian Hebrew text) and the *targumim* (Antwerp, 1569–72).

G. Lloyd Jones, *The Discovery of Hebrew in Tudor England* (1983).

**HEDIO, KASPAR** (1494–1552), German humanist and Protestant reformer, born in Ettlingen and educated in Pforzheim, Freiburg, Basel (where he was ordained as a priest), and Mainz (where he took his doctorate in theology in 1523). In 1520 he became a preacher at the court of ALBRECHT II OF MAINZ, but in 1523 he converted to Protestantism and moved to Strassburg, where he married (May 1524). He took part in the Colloquy of MARBURG (1529) and promoted the Protestant cause both in Strassburg (where he worked with Martin BUCER in the establishment of educational provision) and elsewhere in Germany.

Helio was a champion of both classical scholarship (especially Greek) and PATRISTIC SCHOLARSHIP; he translated the church fathers (notably the *Ecclesiastical History* of Eusebius) and Josephus into German and translated the *Ursberger Chronicle*; in bringing this account up to the present Helio became the first Protestant chronicler. He died of the plague on 17 October 1552.

*NDB*; Hartwig Keute, *Reformation unt Geschichte: Kaspar Hedio als Historiograph* (1980).

**HEEMSKERK, JACOB VAN** (1567–1607), Dutch seaman who sailed with Willem BARENTSZOON on his second and third voyages (1595–6); he was one of the twelve survivors of the third voyage, and their survival was attributed to his leadership. He subsequently commanded a Sea Beggar (see

PRIVATEER), and in 1607 sailed with a fleet of 26 ships in pursuit of a Spanish fleet which was bound for Asia to attack Dutch trading settlements. On 25 April 1607 Heemskerk intercepted the Spanish fleet at Gibraltar Bay; his forces destroyed the Spanish fleet, but Heemskerk died of wounds sustained in the battle. He is now regarded as one of the great naval heroes of the Netherlands.

*NNBW.*

**HEEMSKERK, MAARTEN VAN** (1498–1574), Dutch painter, born in Heemskerck (near Alkmaar). He trained with local artists in Haarlem and Delft and then entered the Haarlem studio of Jan van SCOREL, who was only one year older than Heemskerk; the influence of Jan van Scorel on Heemskerk's style of portraiture was so strong that it is sometimes difficult to attribute their unsigned portraits. Heemskerk was similarly overwhelmed by the work of MICHELANGELO when he lived in Italy (mostly in Rome) from 1532 to 1536. While in Rome he drew ancient and modern buildings and sculptures; leaves from his sketchbooks are now preserved in two albums in the Kupferstichkabinett in Berlin.

On his return to the Netherlands Heemskerk, still mesmerized by Michelangelo, painted large muscular figures in energetic movement, a stark contrast to the sombre realism of his portraits. Heemskerk's portraits include a self-portrait now in the Fitzwilliam Museum in Cambridge. His huge ALTARPIECE for the Church of St Laurentius in Alkmaar (1538–41) was sold to a Russian buyer in 1581, but the ship on which it was sent was wrecked off the coast of Sweden; the altarpiece was salvaged and is now in Linköping Cathedral. He died in Haarlem on 1 October 1574.

*MDA; NNBW* vi; I. M. Veldman, *Maarten van Heemskerk and Dutch Humanism in the Sixteenth Century* (1977).

**HEERE, LUCAS DE** (*c*.1534–1584), Flemish painter and poet, born in Ghent and trained in the Antwerp studio of Frans FLORIS. On returning to Ghent he established a school of painting; his pupils included Karel van MANDER. His painting of *Solomon and the Queen of Sheba* (1559) is in St Bavon's Cathedral in Ghent. Lucas lived in France from 1559 to 1561, working in Paris and Fontainebleau as a TAPESTRY designer in the service of CATHERINE DE MÉDICIS. After his return to Ghent, Lucas became a member of the CHAMBER OF RHETORIC and in 1565 published *De Hof en Bloomgaerd der Poësien* ('The Garden and Orchard of Poetry').

In April 1567 Lucas was banished because of his Calvinism, and sought refuge in London, where his pupils included Johan DE CRITZ and Marcus GHEERAERTS the Younger. In 1577 he returned to Ghent, where he designed the pageants for the entry of WILLIAM OF ORANGE into the city. He is also thought to have been the designer of the Valois Tapestries (now in the Uffizi in Florence) woven in Flanders in 1582 to celebrate the arrival of François, duke of ANJOU.

Many of the portraits formerly attributed to Lucas on the basis of the 'HE' monogram used as a signature are now attributed to Hans EWORTH.

*DNB* s.v. De Heere or D'Heere; *MDA* s.v. Heere, de (1) Lucas de; *NBW* vii.

**HEGIUS, ALEXANDER** (1433–98), German humanist educator. He was a student of Rudolfus AGRICOLA and in 1465 became rector of the school of the BRETHREN OF THE COMMON LIFE in Deventer. His introduction of humanist ideals and methods into the school made it one of the first humanist schools in northern Europe. His pupils included ERASMUS and Adriaan Florenszoon Dedal (later Pope ADRIAN VI).

*NDB*; Jan Bedaux, *Hegius poeta: Het leven en de latijnse gedichten van Alexander Hegius* (1998).

**HEIDELBERG**, a town on the Neckar in south-west Germany which was the capital of the Rhineland PALATINATE from *c*.1225 to 1720. The University of Heidelberg, the oldest in Germany (though younger than the German university in Prague established in 1347), was founded by the Elector Ruprecht I and received its charter from Pope Urban VI on 23 October 1385. By the terms of its charter the university was licensed to teach theology, medicine, arts, and CANON LAW; it was not empowered to teach CIVIL LAW, but nonetheless did so from the outset. In the late fifteenth century the university became an important humanist centre under the leadership of Rodolfus AGRICOLA.

At the Reformation both the town and the university declared firmly for the Reformation: the Elector FRIEDRICH III welcomed Calvinist refugees to the city and the university, and in 1562 promulgated the HEIDELBERG CATECHISM. The city's importance as a centre of Calvinism led to its being repeatedly plundered during the THIRTY YEARS WAR. In 1622 the Catholic prince Maximilian I of Bavaria sent the Biblioteca PALATINA to Rome.

Some Renaissance buildings have survived the depredations of war, notably the magnificent sixteenth-century and early seventeenth-century additions to the medieval castle: the Otto-Heinrichsbau (1556–9), the Friedrichsbau (1601–7), and the Elisabethenbau or Englischebau (1618) named in honour of the daughter of JAMES I. The late sixteenth-century electoral residence is now the finest ruin in Germany.

**HEIDELBERG CATECHISM or (German) Heidelberger Katechismus** (1562), the Protestant confession of faith prepared at the behest of the Elector FRIEDRICH III by Zacharias URSINUS and Kaspar Olevian (1536–87) and published on 19 January 1563. Later in the year an official Latin version and a Dutch translation were published; an English version appeared in 1572. The conventional structure of the catechism (decalogue, Creed, Lord's Prayer, Church, and sacraments) is eschewed in favour of a tripartite structure (sin, redemption, and the redeemed life) modelled on the Epistle to the Romans (except for chapters 9–11).

The theology of the Catechism is broadly Calvinist, but many specific points of doctrine were modified by BULLINGER and other theologians with Lutheran sympathies. The Catechism was nonetheless bitterly attacked by GNESIO-LUTHERANS (led by FLACCIUS ILLYRICUS) for its failure to affirm Luther's doctrine of the EUCHARIST and, more predictably, by the Emperor MAXIMILIAN II, who denounced the Catechism as a violation of the Peace of AUGSBURG.

Within the Palatinate, the Catechism became the official statement of faith, though its authority faded under the electorate of Ludwig VI (1576–83). Its influence also extended well beyond the Palatinate: it was adopted in Germany (Anhalt, Brandenburg, Bremen, and Hesse), the Netherlands (where it was adopted in 1588 and ratified by the Synod of DORT in 1619) and the Protestant churches of Hungary, Transylvania, and Poland. It was also influential in the churches of England, Scotland, France, and America, and was eventually translated into a huge number of languages.

W. Hollweg, *Neue Untersuchungen zur Geschichte und Lehre des Heidelberger Katechismus* (1961 and 1968).

**HEINRICH JULIUS, DUKE OF BRUNSWICK or (German) Herzog von Braunschweig-Wolfenbüttel** (1564–1613), German playwright who succeeded to the dukedom in 1589. Although he was a Lutheran, he had been installed bishop of Halberstadt in 1578 and became a friend of the Emperor RUDOLF II.

In 1592 a troupe of English players (the ENGLISCHE KOMÖDIANTEN), probably led by Thomas SACKVILLE, earl of Dorset, visited Wolfenbüttel (capital of Brunswick), and Duke Heinrich was so impressed by what he saw that in the course of the next two years he wrote ten plays in German prose; the English influence is readily apparent in the realism of the dialogue and in the character of the fool, who speaks Low German. The ten plays consist of four tragedies, two tragicomedies, and four comedies, all of which are insistently moral. The tragedies, which all contain gruesome scenes, are *Der Fleischawer* (in which the dishonest butcher is executed), *Buler and Bulerin* (in which the adulterous lovers die), *Die Ehebrecherin* (in which the wicked husband and wife both die), and *Von einem ungeratenen Sohn* (a grisly version of the life of Nero); the tragicomedies are *Susanna* (based on Nikodemus FRISCHLIN's Latin play) and *Von einem Wirte oder Gastgeber*; the four comedies are *Von einem Wirte* (a different play from the tragicomedy), *Vicentius Ladislaus* (in which the fool exposes a braggart soldier taken from the COMMEDIA DELL' ARTE), *Von einem Edelmann* (which asserts the moral superiority of the godly poor over the wealthy classes), and *Von einem Weibe* (which mocks the foolishness of a cuckold).

Duke Heinrich is the benign Julius Herzog von Braunschweig of Franz Grillparzer's play *Ein Bruderzwist in Habsburg* (planned 1824, performed 1872), in which an eirenic RUDOLF II invests the loyal Protestant duke with the *Friedensritterorden*, a symbol of the emperor's desire for peace.

**HEINSIUS, DANIEL** (1580–1655), Dutch scholar and poet. He was born in Ghent, and spent his childhood as a religious refugee in Veere (Zeeland), London, Rijswijk, and Vlissingen (English exonym Flushing). In 1594 he went to the University of Franeker to study Greek, and six months later moved to Leiden, where his teachers included Joseph SCALIGER. In Leiden, where he was to remain for the rest of his long life, Heinsius was appointed professor of Latin (1602), professor of Greek (1605), and librarian (1607).

Heinsius published scholarly editions of Hesiod (1603), Theocritus, Bion and Moschus (1604), Horace (1610),

Aristotle and Seneca (1611), Terence (1618), Livy (1620), and the *Epistles* of Joseph Scaliger (1627). His original works included three volumes of Latin poems (*Iambi*, 1602; *Elegiae*, 1603; *Poemata*, 1605), a bilingual collection in Dutch and Latin (*Emblemata amatoria*, 1604), a tragedy on the *Massacre of the Innocents* (1613), a collection of poems in Dutch (1616), a collection of Latin orations (1609), and treatises on political philosophy (*De politica sapientia*, 1614) and tragedy (*De tragediae constitutione*, 1611).

Heinsius was the father of Nikolaes Heinsius (1620–81), one of the finest scholars of the seventeenth century.

*NNBW* ii.

**HELL.** Early modern eschatology distinguished 'Four Last Things': death, judgement, heaven, and hell. The idea of hell was elaborated from the Hebrew *Sheol*, the place of the dead, and Greek *Gehenna*, where the wicked spend eternity. The torments of hell, which were a favourite subject of preachers, especially during Advent, consisted of *poena sensus*, the physical pain of hellfire, and *poena damni*, the pain of loss occasioned by separation from God. Augustine had insisted that unbaptized babies would roast eternally in hell, though he allowed that the pain that they experienced would be of the mildest degree. This notion of gradations of suffering is represented in the circles of DANTE's *Inferno*, and in succeeding centuries an iconography of hell, which had been adumbrated in mosaics in Torcello and in the baptistery of Florence, was developed through manuscript illustrations of Dante's poem. Artists such as SIGNORELLI and MICHELANGELO (in the *Last Judgement*) perpetuated the tradition of Dante. The most extravagant depictions of the torments of hell were produced in the Netherlands by BOSCH and Pieter BRUEGEL the Elder. The mouth of hell is often represented as the gaping jaw of a toothed whale, as in El GRECO's *Adoration of the Name of Jesus*, of which there are versions in the Escorial and the National Gallery in London.

Augustine's uncompromising view was mitigated by the folk-doctrine of limbo, which was never sanctioned by the Church but was nonetheless widely held. Its advocates distinguished the *limbus patrum*, in which the godly who lived before Christ awaited his redemption, and the *limbus infantum*, the eternal state of unbaptized infants.

The idea that Jesus descended into hell (or, in some accounts, into limbo, on the outskirts of hell) between his death and resurrection first arises in the Arian formularies of the fourth century, and was eventually codified in the Apostles' Creed and the Athanasian Creed (but not the Nicene Creed); it is the subject of Article 3 of the Thirty-Nine ARTICLES. This doctrine, which was known in English as the Harrowing of Hell, was a popular subject of both art and drama.

Piero Camporesi, *The Fear of Hell* (1991); D. P. Walker, *The Decline of Hell* (1964).

**HELLBRUNN**, a castle and garden on the south side of Salzburg, was built between 1613 and 1615 for Markus Sittikus von Hohenems (1574–1619), prince-archbishop of Salzburg; the designer was the Italian architect Santino Salari. Stone for the castle was quarried from the grounds of the estate, and Sittikus turned the quarry into an AMPHITHEATRE called the Felsentheater. On 31 August 1617 MONTEVERDI's *Orfeo* was performed in the Felsentheater, which is still used for plays and concerts. The grounds were laid out in aquatic PARTERRES, and there were temples, summer PAVILIONS, and balustraded galleries. The fashion for GROTTOES was at its zenith when Hellbrunn was built, and it is amply provided with grottoes in the castle and ranged along a walk in the garden. The grottoes contained AUTOMATA and *GIOCHI D'ACQUA* inspired both by examples in ITALIAN GARDENS and by the rediscovery of HERON. The grotto of Orpheus and the sleeping Eurydice contained water-driven mechanical songbirds, the grotto of Midas featured a crown floating on a jet of water, and the dragon grotto housed a dragon who drank from a fountain before vanishing. The *giochi d'acqua* included FOUNTAINS with stone tables on which drinking-glasses were filled from a spout; unsuspecting visitors who sat on the seats were promptly drenched, and as they tried to escape they were soaked in rain from small pipes in the ceiling.

The gardens were altered in the 1730s, and a water-powered marionette theatre was added between 1748 and 1752, but many features of the original gardens survive, and many of the automata are still in good working order; the garden also has a zoo which is the descendant of the menagerie which was established before 1424.

## HELMONT, JEAN BAPTISTE VAN (1579–1644), Flemish medical chemist and physician, born into a noble family in Brussels. He studied medicine at Louvain. In 1609, after travelling extensively in the Swiss Confederation, Italy, France, and England, he settled in Vilvorde (near Brussels), where he worked as a physician and experimental chemist. In the course of his experimental work he discovered that air is not the only gas; he identified *gas sylvestre* (now known as carbon dioxide), and coined the word 'gas' from a Greek term. His work on medicinal drugs emphasized their chemical properties, and he became an influential advocate of the superiority of chemical drugs to herbal remedies. His chemically based system of medicine, like that of PARACELSUS, developed into an attempt to supplant the qualitative humoral system of GALEN. In the late seventeenth century Helmontian medicine became one of the constituent parts of the 'new science' of the period, but it was dislodged as Robert Boyle's chemistry grew in influence.
*DSB.*

## HELMSCHMIED FAMILY, a dynasty of German armourers whose original surname, Kolman, was replaced by one reflecting their profession as 'makers of helmets'; their armours (see ARMS AND ARMOUR) are signed with the mark of a helmet. Throughout the late fifteenth and sixteenth centuries, members of the family produced armours in their Augsburg workshop for emperors and princes. In 1477 Lorenz Helmschmied (1445–1516) made a complete set of armour for the Emperor FRIEDRICH III and his horse (Kunsthistorisches Museum, Vienna), and in 1491 was appointed as principal

armourer to Friedrich's son Maximilian (later MAXIMILIAN I). Lorenz's son Kolman (1471–1532) produced armours for the Emperor CHARLES V, including the 'KD' garniture (*c*.1526) of which portions survive in the Armería Real in Madrid. Kolman's son Desiderius (1513–78) produced parade armours for King PHILIP II of Spain. Kolman's daughter became the second wife of Jörg Sorg the Elder, an armour etcher in the Helmschmied workshops, and their son, Jörg SORG the Younger, also became an armour etcher.
*NDB.*

## HELVETIC CONFESSIONS. The First Helvetic Confession, which is also known as the Second Confession of Basel, was intended to be a national confession of faith for the SWISS CONFEDERATION, which was known in Latin as Helvetia. It was compiled in 1536 by a group of Protestant theologians including Heinrich BULLINGER and Oswald MYCONIUS. The Confession was Zwinglian, especially on the fraught subject of the EUCHARIST, but the wording was intended to be conciliatory to Lutherans. It was accepted by the Reformed Swiss Cantons but rejected by Strassburg and Konstanz.

The Second Helvetic Confession, also known as the Confessio Helvetica Posterior, was the work of Bullinger, who drafted it in 1561. This Confession was issued in 1566 at the behest of the Elector Palatine FRIEDRICH II. Its theology is broadly Calvinist, but its wording attends to Zwinglian sensitivities. It was accepted by the Zwinglian churches of the Reformed Swiss Cantons, but was also welcomed by Reformed (i.e. Calvinist) churches outside the Swiss Confederation.
E. Koch, *Die Theologie der Confessio Helvetica Posterior* (1968).

## HEMESSEN, JAN SANDERS VAN (*fl.* 1519–56), Flemish painter, admitted to the Antwerp guild in 1524; he may have moved to Haarlem in 1550, but the evidence is inconclusive. Similarities to the style of the MASTER OF THE BRUNSWICK MONOGRAM have encouraged some scholars to think that Hemessen is the Master, but the evidence is again inconclusive. Hemessen's documented work consists of portraits (some of which are satirical), GENRE scenes (of which he was one of the earliest Flemish exponents), and popular religious pictures, including *The Parable of the Prodigal Son* (1536, Musée d'Art Ancien, Brussels) and *Judith with the Head of Holofernes* (*c*.1549, Chicago, Art Institute).
*MDA.*

## HEMMINGSEN, NIELS (1513–1600), Danish reformer, theologian, and jurist, born on the island of Lolland and educated in Roskilde and Lund and at the University of Wittenberg (1537–42), where he became a follower of MELANCHTHON. On returning to Denmark in 1542 Hemmingsen was appointed Professor of Greek at the University of Copenhagen, migrating in 1545 to the chair of dialectics and exegesis and again in 1553 to the chair of theology; he also served as pastor of the Church of the Holy Spirit in Copenhagen. He published a handbook of theology (*Enchiridion theologicum*) in 1555, a textbook on homiletics (*Evangeliepostil*) in 1561 (which was translated from Latin

into Danish, German, and English), and a textbook on pastoral theology (*Pastor*) in 1562; all three remained in print for generations.

In the 1540s and 1550s Hemmingsen was a loyal Philippist, but sometime after 1557 he began to shift his theological thinking away from Melanchthon and towards CALVINISM. In 1571 he attacked the GNESIO-LUTHERANS and UBIQUITARIANS in *Demonstratio indubitatae veritatis de Domino Jesu*, and three years later he published a systematic theology (*Syntagma institutionum christianorum*, 1574) in which he took a Calvinist position on the EUCHARIST. Calvinism was not an acceptable faith in Lutheran Denmark, and in 1579 Hemmingsen was dismissed from his posts by King FREDERICK II. Loyalty to Hemmingsen was one of the reasons why the churches in Denmark, Norway, and Iceland resisted the Formula of CONCORD.

DBL.

**HENLEIN, PETER** (*c.*1485–1542), German locksmith and horologist who worked in his native Nuremberg. The accuracy of his clocks was considerably enhanced by his invention of the mainspring in about 1510. His portable clocks, which were shaped like small boxes and were intended to be hung from the belt, were the predecessors of the pocket watch. One of his box clocks, now in the Fridericianum in Kassel, is known as the Egg of Nuremberg; versions of this clock manufactured in Nuremberg after Henlein's death were popularly known as Nuremberg eggs (*Nürnberger Eier*).

NDB.

**HENRI II** (1519–59), king of France, the second son of FRANCIS I and Queen Claude; he was the younger brother of François, the dauphin. In 1526, at the age of 7, he was sent with François to Spain as a hostage for his father; the brothers remained in Spain until the Peace of CAMBRAI was signed (1529). In 1533 he married CATHERINE DE MÉDICIS; both bride and groom were 14 years old. Two years later Henri became the lover of DIANE DE POITIERS, who was twenty years older than the prince. On the death of his elder brother in 1536 Henri became dauphin, but did not enjoy good relations with his father: in 1541 he supported MONTMORENCY after his exclusion from the court and in 1544 he dissented publicly from the Treaty of Crépy-en-Laonnais, in which FRANCIS I and CHARLES V reached a temporary accommodation.

In 1547 Henri succeeded his father as king, and promptly dismissed his father's principal allies (including Cardinal Tournon and the duchesse d'Étampes), whose influence passed to Diane, Montmorency, and the GUISES. The twelve years of his reign were dominated by the suppression of Protestantism, against which he deployed the CHAMBRE ARDENTE, and the struggle against the HABSBURG rulers Charles V and PHILIP II, which was concluded in the Treaty of CATEAU-CAMBRÉSIS of 1559. In the celebrations following the signing of the treaty King Henri was wounded in the temple with a lance while tilting with the count of Montgomery. He was attended by Ambroise PARÉ, but died ten days later, on 10 July 1559.

At the time of his death seven of Henri's children by Catherine de Médicis were alive: Elizabeth (queen of Spain), Claude (duchess of Lorraine), François (who succeeded his father as FRANCIS II), Charles (later King CHARLES IX), Henri (later HENRI III), Marguerite (later Queen MARGUERITE of Navarre), and François, duke of Alençon (later duc d'ANJOU).

DBF; MDA s.v. Valois (15); Frederic Baumgartner, *Henry II, King of France 1547–1559* (1988).

**HENRI III** (1551–89), king of France and Poland, was born at Fontainebleau, the third son of King HENRI II and CATHERINE DE MÉDICIS, the younger brother of François (later FRANCIS II) and Charles (later CHARLES IX), and the elder brother of MARGUERITE DE VALOIS; before his accession he was known as the duke of Anjou. As a young man Henri fought in the WARS OF RELIGION, and in 1569 commanded the royal army that defeated the armies of Louis, prince of CONDÉ, at Jarnac (Poitou) and of COLIGNY at Moncontour (Poitou). He co-operated in fomenting the ST BARTHOLOMEW'S DAY MASSACRE (1572) and the following year Queen Catherine succeeded in having Henri elected as king of Poland.

Henri travelled to Poland to assume his crown, but on the death of his brother Charles in 1574 he became king of France, and returned to claim his throne; the following year he was deposed as king of Poland by STEFAN BÁTORY. In France he agreed terms of peace with the Huguenots (1576), but the violence of the Catholic reaction made him resume the war. In 1584 the death of his younger brother François, duc d'ANJOU, made the Huguenot leader Henry of Navarre (later HENRI IV) the heir to the throne.

The succession crisis led to the War of the Three Henrys (1585–7). The third Henry was Duke Henri de GUISE, leader of the CATHOLIC LEAGUE, who on 9 May 1588 ended the war by entering Paris at the head of an army. Three days later, on the JOURNÉE DES BARRICADES, Henri fled from Paris to Chartres, where he decided to assassinate Duke Henri and his brother Cardinal Louis de Lorraine at Blois on 23 December 1588. He then joined forces with Henry of Navarre. While besieging Paris alongside Henry of Navarre, King Henri was assassinated by Jacques Clément, a Dominican friar.

DBF; MDA s.v. Valois (17); Nicola Le Roux, *La Faveur du roi* (2000); P. Chevallier, *Henri III* (1995).

**HENRI IV** (1553–1610), king of France and Navarre, born in Pau on 14 December 1533, the son of ANTOINE DE BOURBON (duke of Vendôme) and JEANNE D'ALBRET (queen of Navarre); he was baptized as a Catholic but raised as a Protestant, and until his succession to the throne of France was known as Henry of Navarre. In the WARS OF RELIGION he fought on the Protestant side under Gaspard de COLIGNY (August 1568–August 1570). He became king of Navarre on 9 June 1572, and two months later (18 August) married MARGUERITE DE VALOIS in Paris; the next week he was captured during the ST BARTHOLOMEW'S DAY MASSACRE but was spared after abjuring of his Protestantism. He remained under house arrest in the Louvre until 2 February 1576, when he escaped, recanted his abjuration, and joined the Huguenot army.

On the death of François, duc d'ANJOU (fifth and only surviving son of CATHERINE DE MÉDICIS), on 10 June 1584, Henri became the heir to the French throne. Henri was recognized as heir by King HENRI III, but the CATHOLIC LEAGUE instead recognized Henry's uncle Cardinal Charles de Bourbon, and this choice was ratified in a secret treaty with Spain (Treaty of Joinville, December 1584) and in the excommunication of Henri de Navarre by Pope SIXTUS V (September 1585). In the ensuing War of the Three Henrys (March 1585–August 1589), the other two Henrys (Henri, duc de GUISE, and King HENRI III) were both assassinated, and Henry of Navarre became king of France on 1 August 1589.

On his accession King Henri was still at war with the Catholic League and with Spain, and for the next nine years he struggled to secure the peace. On 25 July 1593 Henri converted to Catholicism, shocking his Protestant supporters but precipitating a collapse in Catholic opposition. The citizens of Paris, which had remained loyal to the League, joyfully admitted him to the city (22 March 1594) and Pope CLEMENT VIII granted him absolution (September 1595). In 1598 Henri negotiated truces with the Protestants (Edict of NANTES) and with Spain (Peace of VERVINS). King Henri and Queen Marguerite had separated in 1583, and their marriage was annulled in 1599. The following year Henri married MARIE DE MÉDICIS.

For the next decade Henri ruled France with an iron hand, instituting financial reforms through his chief minister, the duc de SULLY. His foreign policy was driven by hostility towards the Habsburgs in Spain and Austria, and so his allies were the enemies of the Habsburgs, who included the Ottomans, the papacy, Tuscany, Venice, the Dutch Protestant rebels, and the Protestant princes of Germany. Henri was assassinated on 14 May 1610 by a Catholic zealot, François Ravaillac, who disapproved of the king's alliances with Protestant heretics.

Henri's children by Marie de Médicis were Louis (later King Louis XIII), Gaston (duke of Orléans), Elizabeth (later the queen of Philip IV of Spain), Christine (later duchess of Savoy), and Henrietta Maria (later the queen of Charles I of England). Henri also had a large number of illegitimate children.

DBF; MDA s.v. Bourbon I (5); D. Buisseret, *Henry IV* (1984); Michael Wolfe, *The Conversion of Henri IV: Politics, Power, and Religious Belief in Early Modern France* (1993).

**HENRIQUE, CARDEAL or (English exonym) Henry the Cardinal** (1512–80), king of Portugal from 1578, born in Lisbon on 31 January 1512, the third son of King MANUEL I. He was intended for the Church, and in 1532 was appointed archbishop of Braga; in 1542 he was created cardinal, and he later added the archbishoprics of Lisbon and Coimbra and the wealthy abbacy of Alcobaça to his portfolio.

In August 1579 Cardinal Henrique's grand-nephew King SEBASTIAN was killed at the battle of KSAR-EL-KEBIR, and Henrique succeeded to the throne. Henrique had flourished as a learned churchman, but floundered as a king, and the seventeen months of his reign rendered Portugal unstable.

He refused to nominate his illegitimate nephew ANTÓNIO DO CRATO as his successor, and this failure opened the way for the conquest of Portugal by PHILIP II.

DHP.

**HENRY IV, THE IMPOTENT, or (Spanish) Enrique IV** (1425–74), king of Castile, was born in Valladolid on 6 January 1425, the son of King JOHN II (Juan II) of Castile and León and his wife Maria, daughter of King Ferdinand I of Aragon and Sicily. His first marriage, to Blanche of Navarre, was annulled in 1453 on grounds of impotence, but this did not constitute an impediment to his marriage in 1468 to Juana of Portugal. Juana gave birth to a daughter, JUANA LA BELTRANEJA, whose father was widely believed to be the king's favourite Don Beltrán de la Cueva. In 1465 Enrique was deposed by his half-brother AFONSO V of Portugal, but on his death within the year Enrique was once again recognized as king. He reluctantly designated his half-sister ISABELLA as successor to the throne, but when in 1469 she married FERDINAND of Aragon against the wishes of Enrique, he excluded her from the succession. Enrique died in Madrid on 12 December 1474; on his death the succession was contested between Isabella and Juana.

DHE s.v. Enrique IV; Rogelio Pérez-Bustamente, *Enrique IV de Castilla* (1998); Ana Bélen Sánchez Prieto, *Enrique IV, el Impotente* (1999).

**HENRY VI** (1421–71), king of England. Henry inherited the crowns of England and France from his father Henry V when less than a year old. The period until his coming of age was one of stability in both kingdoms, but on his maturity, Henry's weaknesses of character soon produced instability. Uninterested in French wars, he lost the kingdom of Normandy, and corrupt and ineffectual government in England was challenged by widespread revolt, briefly first in 1450, and then in the civil war of 1461, in which Henry lost the crown to EDWARD IV. Henry's impaired mental capacity, following a coma in 1453, contributed to the confusion. Briefly restored to the throne in 1470 by challengers to Edward's crown, Henry never experienced a real return of power, and was killed shortly after Edward regained his hold on the throne. A cult, which regarded him as a saint, flourished after his death.

DNB; MDA s.v. Lancaster (3).

**HENRY VII** (1457–1509), king of England. Nephew of HENRY VI, Henry Tudor came to the throne in 1485, following his defeat of RICHARD III at the battle of Bosworth. His claim, and the stability of the kingdom, was cemented by his marriage to Elizabeth of York, daughter of EDWARD IV, which united the warring factions of York and Lancaster. Bar some easily quelled disturbances, Henry's reign ended over half a century of national division. It also founded the TUDOR dynasty; the marriage of his daughter Margaret to JAMES IV of Scotland, meanwhile, paved the way for the eventual unification of Scotland and England by their great-grandson JAMES VI. Although England's hold on Brittany was lost during his reign, Henry's close attention to government administration, and his frugal finances, meant that on his death HENRY VIII inherited a stable and prosperous nation.

*DNB; MDA s.v. Tudor (1).*

**HENRY VIII** (1491–1547), king of England. The most far-reaching event of Henry VIII's long reign was the establishment of a separate Church of England with Henry at its head. Henry's desire for a male heir, and the apparent inability of CATHERINE OF ARAGON to provide one, prompted the break with Rome, which refused to grant a divorce. Henry's second wife ANNE BOLEYN, mother of ELIZABETH, was executed following allegations of adultery and incest; a male heir was secured when Henry's third wife JANE SEYMOUR gave birth to the future EDWARD VI. Following Jane's death soon after giving birth to Edward, a short-lived marriage to ANNE OF CLEVES was negotiated by CROMWELL as part of an allegiance with the reformist duke of Cleves. Henry's final marriages were to CATHERINE HOWARD and CATHERINE PARR. Wars with Scotland and France, which drained the coffers, occupied the final years of Henry's reign.

*DNB; MDA s.v. Tudor (2); Grove; J. J. Scarisbrick, Henry VIII (1968).*

**HENRY GRÂCE À DIEU**, the name of the largest warship of Renaissance Europe, known in England as *Great Harry*. It was built at the command of HENRY VIII and launched in June 1514; a painting in Hampton Court by Vincento Volpe depicts King Henry departing from Dover in May 1520 on *Henry Grâce à Dieu* for Calais and the FIELD OF THE CLOTH OF GOLD. The square and lateen sails mounted on the ship's four masts for state occasions were made with cloth damasked with gold. When fitted for war, the ship had a complement of 700 men and artillery consisting of 21 bronze cannon. The *Henry Grâce à Dieu* was accidentally destroyed by fire at Woolwich in August 1553.

**HENRY THE NAVIGATOR or (Portuguese) Infante Dom Henrique** (1394–1460), Portuguese infante, born on 4 March 1394 in Oporto, the fifth son (and third living son) of King JOHN I (João I) and Philippa, daughter of John of Gaunt. Henry was the younger brother of the future King DUARTE, with whom he led their father's army in 1415 at the siege of Ceuta, which was destined to become a permanent European enclave in North Africa. In 1419 Prince Henry was appointed governor of Algarve, the southernmost province of Portugal. He established his residence on the Sagres peninsula near Cape St Vincent (Cabo de São Vicente). The town of Sagres (now a village), which subsequently became known as Vila do Ifante (the infante's town), became the base of a large naval arsenal (Tercena Naval) and the port of departure for royal expeditions.

Prince Henry was Europe's greatest patron of naval EXPLORATION, and he inaugurated a systematic search for a sea route to India along the coast of AFRICA. The voyages of discovery initiated by Prince Henry began with the discovery of Madeira in 1419 and the Azores in 1432; in the same period a series of expeditions sponsored by Henry began to explore the West African coast: in 1434 an expedition rounded Cape Bojador, 200 kilometres (125 miles) south of the Canaries and the limit of the world known to Europeans, and in 1444 an expedition led by Nuno TRISTÃO reached the Senegal river. From 1455 to 1457, Alvise da CADAMOSTO reached the Gambia river and discovered the Cape Verde Islands. After Prince Henry's death there was a hiatus in exploration for more than twenty years, but when exploration was renewed in the 1480s by Diogo CÃO and Bartolomeu DIAS, the Portuguese were on the verge of their reconnaissance of the entire world.

*DHP s.v. Henrique, Infante; Peter Russell, Prince Henry 'The Navigator': a Life (2000).*

**HENSLOWE, PHILIP** (d. 1616), English theatre manager, and owner of the ROSE, FORTUNE, and HOPE playhouses. His diary is an important record of Elizabethan theatrical life, including his relations with actors contracted by him to perform in his theatres. This unusual arrangement caused tensions between actors and manager, and differed from that at the GLOBE, where actors shared in ownership of the theatre building and acting company. Part of Henslowe's hold over his actors may have been a practice of keeping them in his debt. ALLEYN, who married Henslowe's daughter, shared in many of his business dealings, and inherited his wealth after his death.

*DNB.*

**HERALDRY**. Originating in the identifying symbols used on banners in battle from the mid-twelfth century, heraldic devices quickly became used to denote family and status in other contexts, such as seals and on buildings. Their use was regulated by heralds until the foundation of the COLLEGE OF ARMS in 1484, which took over such functions.

**HERBALS**. See BOTANY.

**HERING, LOY** (*c*.1485–*c*.1554), German sculptor, born in Eichstätt; he worked as a sculptor in Eichstätt, Augsburg, and in other Bavarian towns. His subjects were usually religious but sometimes courtly (such as the relief *The Garden of Love* in the Gemäldegalerie, Berlin), and for his designs he often adapted figures from DÜRER's prints. His sculptures contain Gothic elements but are predominantly executed in the style of the Italian Renaissance, which he is deemed to have introduced into German sculpture. His most important surviving monumental sculpture is the seated figure of St Willibald as an old man (*c*.1514) in Eichstätt Cathedral.

*MDA; NDB.*

**HERLIN, FRIEDRICH** (*c*.1425–1500), German painter. He may have been born in Ulm; he was active in Rothenburg ob der Tauber and in Nördlingen. His paintings, mostly of religious subjects, are executed in the manner of Rogier van der WEYDEN. His *Presentation in the Temple*, a panel from the altarpiece painted in 1466 for the Jakobskirche in Rothenburg (and still in the church), characteristically borrows its architectural setting from Rogier.

*MDA; NDB.*

**HERMANN VON WIED** (1477–1552), archbishop-elector of COLOGNE, was born on 14 January 1477, the fourth son of

Friedrich, count of Wied. In 1515, while still a subdeacon, he became archbishop-elector of Cologne. He was a firm ruler of his principality and took strenuous steps to suppress the Protestant heresy in both its Lutheran and ANABAPTIST manifestations. In the late 1530s Hermann gradually became sympathetic to the idea that reform of the Church was necessary, and from 1536 he worked with his friend Johann GROPPER to reform his archdiocese.

In the early 1540s Hermann became openly supportive of the Reformation, inviting Martin BUCER to Cologne in 1542 and MELANCHTHON in 1543. He set out his proposals for the reform of the Church in his *Einfaltigs Bedencken einer Christlichen Reformation*, which was published in German in 1543 and in a revised version translated into Latin by Albrecht HARDENBERG in 1545; two years later this Latin text was translated into English as *A Simple and Religious Consultation*, and became an important source for the Book of COMMON PRAYER. This treatise ruptured Hermann's friendship with Gropper, who replied in 1544 with his *Antididagma*.

Hermann's conversion to Lutheranism was welcomed by Protestants, and the League of SCHMALKALDEN quickly pledged military support in the event of an imperial attack on Hermann's principality. In common with other archbishop-electors of Cologne, Hermann lived in Bonn rather than Cologne, whose citizens remained loyal to the Catholic Church. Hermann was summoned before both emperor and pope, and in 1546 was excommunicated and deposed by Pope PAUL III. Hermann resigned his offices (which included the bishopric of Paderborn) in February 1547 and retired to Wied, where he died on 15 August 1552.

C. Varrentrapp, *Hermann von Wied und sein Reformationsversuch* (1878); A. Franzen, *Bischof und Reformation: Erzbischof Hermann von Wied in Köln vor der Entscheidung zwischen Reform und Reformation* (1971).

## HERMETICISM

**HERMETICISM**, a set of esoteric doctrines based on the *Corpus Hermeticum*, a collection of ancient texts attributed to Hermes Trismegistus, sometimes identified with the Egyptian god Thoth. These texts, together with a treatise on ceremonial magic known as the *Asclepius*, were believed to contain the ancient Egyptian wisdom imparted to Moses and Plato. The first and most important treatise in the *Corpus* is the *Poimandres*, which describes a vision and contains cosmological and astronomical teaching and an account of the ascent of the soul to God through the seven spheres of the planets.

In 1460 a Greek manuscript of the *Hermetic Corpus* was brought to Florence, and Lorenzo de' MEDICI commissioned FICINO to translate the works in this manuscript (which include the *Poimandres* and the *Asclepius*) into Latin; the translation was published in 1471. The belief that the *Corpus* represented the source of Platonic wisdom was sustained until CASAUBON addressed the problem in 1614. Hermetic doctrine was a particularly important strain in the thought of PICO DELLA MIRANDOLA (who began his *Oratio* (later subtitled *De dignitate hominis*) with a quotation from the *Asclepius*), Giordano BRUNO, and John DEE.

Frances Yates, *Giordano Bruno and the Hermetic Tradition* (1964).

**HERNÁNDEZ DE CÓRDOBA, FRANCISCO** (d. 1517), Spanish navigator sometimes confused with his namesake the conquistador. He participated in the conquest of Cuba under the command of Diego VELÁZQUEZ, who placed Hernández in command of an expedition charged with the discovery of new slave-hunting grounds. Hernández sailed with three ships and in February 1517 discovered the east coast of Yucatán, where he made the first European contact with the Mayan civilization; this first encounter caused many deaths on both sides. Hernández's discovery of Yucatán was consolidated in subsequent expeditions led by Juan de GRIJALBA (1518) and Hernán CORTÉS.

DHE.

**HERNÁNDEZ DE CÓRDOBA, FRANCISCO** (d. 1526), Spanish conquistador sometimes confused with his namesake the navigator. He was sent in 1523 by Pedrarias DÁVILA to Nicaragua and what is now Costa Rica. He discovered the Río Desaguadero (now Río San Juan) and sailed up it to Lago de Nicaragua, which he circumnavigated. In 1526 he was executed by Dávila.

DHE; Carlos Meléndez Chaverri, *Hernández de Córdoba, capitán de conquista en Nicaragua* (2nd edn., 1993).

**HÉROËT, ANTOINE** (1492–1568), French humanist poet, a courtier in the service of MARGUERITE D'ANGOULÊME and (from 1552) bishop of Digne. His writings include *L'Androgyne* (composed 1535, published 1542), a poetic imitation of part of Plato's *Symposium* which draws substantially on FICINO's commentary, and *La Parfaite Amie* (1542), a Neoplatonic meditation on love.

DBF.

**HERON or Hero OF ALEXANDRIA IN THE RENAISSANCE.** Heron (*fl.* AD 60) was a mathematician and engineer. In the Renaissance the best known of his works were the *Pneumatica*, a treatise on the construction of devices powered by compressed air, steam, and water, and the *Automatopoietica*, on the construction of AUTOMATA for temples. In the sixteenth century the Greek texts of both treatises were published, as were translations into Latin and Italian.

Pirro LIGORIO read a manuscript of the *Pneumatica*, and constructed some of the waterworks described by Heron at Villa d'ESTE in Tivoli. The clearest debt to Heron at Villa d'Este is the Owl Fountain (1566–8): Heron had described a device in which flowing water was used to make birds sing and fall silent by turns, and in Ligorio's Owl Fountain a group of birds whose song was generated by the pressure of water stopped singing whenever the owl (which was also water-driven) turned towards them.

The influence of Heron's *Automatopoietica* is most apparent in Salomon de CAUS's *Raisons des forces mouvantes* (1615), which draws heavily on the treatise for the descriptions of automata such as water-organs, trumpets, and fire-engines.

**HERRERA, FERNANDO DE** (1534–97), Spanish poet known as 'El Divino', born in Seville, where he spent most of his life. He was a prominent member of a literary circle (*tertulia*) associated with the count of Gelves, to whose countess, Leonor Millán, Herrera addressed adoring Petrarchan lyrics; he always addresses the countess in ways that obscure her identity, though the name of his *amanda* was known to his friends. Besides his Petrarchan sonnets, Herrera's most important poems are three *canciones* (odes): *Canción al señor don Juan de Austria vencedor de los moriscos en las Alpujarras* celebrates Don JUAN DE AUSTRIA's suppression of the MORISCO rebellion in Granada (1568–71), *Canción en alabanza de la Divina Majestad por la victoria del señor don Juan* is a hymn of praise for the divine intervention that ensured Don Juan's triumph at the battle of LEPANTO (1571) and *Canción por la pérdida del rei don Sebastián* mourns the death of King SEBASTIAN I of Portugal at the battle of KSAR-EL-KEBIR (1578). In 1580 Herrera published a collection of his own poems (a fuller edition was to appear in 1619) and an annotated edition of the works of GARCILASO DE LA VEGA; these lengthy *anotaciones* contain influential formulations of Herrara's own views of poetry, which, he insists, should aspire to technical proficiency and clarity (*claridad*) of expression. Herrera also published a prose account of the battle of Lepanto (1571) and a biography of Sir Thomas MORE (1592). His interests included orthography, and he devised his own system of orthography and punctuation.

Mary Randel, *The Historical Prose of Fernando de Herrera* (1971); Oreste Macrí, *Fernando de Herrera* (Spanish trans. from Italian 1959).

**HERRERA, JUAN DE** (1530–97), Spanish architect. He was educated in Valladolid and in 1548 entered the service of Prince Philip (later PHILIP II), in whose retinue he travelled to Italy and thence to Flanders. He remained in Brussels to study MATHEMATICS before returning to Spain in 1551. By 1553 he was serving as a soldier in Italy and Flanders, and he later joined the personal bodyguard of CHARLES V. Throughout his architectural career he maintained his interest in mathematics: he assembled a large scientific library, invented instruments to assist NAVIGATION, and in 1582 founded the Academy of Mathematics in Madrid.

In 1563 Herrera was appointed as an assistant to Juan Bautista de TOLEDO at the ESCORIAL. On Juan Bautista's death in 1567, Philip II entrusted the various tasks on which he had embarked to several architects, including Giambattista CASTELLO (who built the monumental staircase), Francesco PACIOTTO (who designed the church), and Antonio de Villacastín (who proposed the extra storey to increase the monastic accommodation). Herrera was not formally appointed as architect, but it was he who co-ordinated the efforts of others, designed the infirmary and chapel, imposed his personal stamp on the style of the Escorial, and ensured that it was finished in 1584. Herrera also worked as an architect at ARANJUEZ (1569) and in the Exchange at Seville. His last important project was the cathedral in Valladolid, which he began in 1585 on the foundations laid by Rodrigo GIL DE HONTAÑÓN. On the influence of the *estilo desornamentado*, as Herrera's style came to be known, see SPANISH ARCHITECTURE.

MDA; Catherine Wilkinson-Zerner, *Juan de Herrera: Architect to Philip II of Spain* (1993).

**HERRERA Y TORDESILLAS, ANTONIO DE** (1549–1625), Spanish historian. He was born into a noble family in Cuéllar, near Segovia, and after a period in Italy was appointed royal historiographer of the Spanish empire in America by King PHILIP II. His account of the Spanish conquest of America up to 1554, based on official documents as well as printed sources, was published as *Décadas; o, Historia general de los hechos de los castellanos en las islas y tierra firme del Mar Océano* (4 vols., Madrid, 1601–15).

In the seventeenth century Herrera's *Historia* was widely regarded as the authoritative work on its subject. Herrera also published a translation of TACITUS (*Los cinco primeros libros de los Annales de Cornelio Tácito*, 1615) and a history of his own times from 1559 to 1598 (*Historia general*, 3 vols., 1601–12).

DHE.

**HERVETUS or (French) Hervet, GENTIEN** (1499–1584), French humanist, patristic scholar, and religious polemicist, born in Olivet, near Orléans, where he was educated. He became a formidable Greek scholar, and in 1519 moved to England, where he worked as a tutor to the younger brother of Cardinal POLE and dedicated an English translation of Erasmus' *De immensa misericordia Dei* to Pole's mother (Margaret, countess of Salisbury).

After a short period as professor of Greek at Orléans, he moved to Rome, where he translated many works by Greek classical and patristic writers into Latin and participated in the COUNCIL OF TRENT (1545). He became professor of Greek at Bordeaux, but then returned to Rome, where he was ordained and worked in the service of Cardinal Cervini (later Pope MARCELLUS II). On returning to France he became vicar-general of Noyon and in 1561 joined the group of theologians formed by Charles de GUISE to combat Protestantism. In 1562 he became a canon at Reims, where he spent the rest of his life.

Hervetus contributed to the edition of the Bible planned by the COUNCIL OF TRENT, and collated the Codex Bezae (now in Cambridge University Library). He also produced French translations of the decrees of the Council of Trent (1564) and AUGUSTINE's *Civitas Dei* (1572), a substantial number of polemical works directed against the Huguenots, and a treatise advocating rigorous church government (especially episcopal residence) in the cause of Catholic reform (*De reparanda ecclesiasticorum disciplina*, 1561).

DBF.

**HEYWOOD, JOHN** (*c.*1497–*c.*1580), English dramatist and musician, worked as a court singer and virginal player, and then turned to the composition of INTERLUDES, most notably *The Four Ps* (performed *c.*1520), in which a palmer, pardoner, 'potycary', and pedlar compete to speak the best lie. Other writings include *The Play of the Wether*, *A Play of Love*, and *The Dialogue of Wit and Folly* (all 1533), and a satirical poem, *The Spider and the Fly* (1556). Heywood was married to the niece of Thomas MORE.

DNB.

**HEYWOOD, THOMAS** (*c*.1570–1641), English actor and playwright. As well as acting for the ADMIRAL'S MEN and QUEEN ANNE'S MEN, Heywood wrote over 200 plays, mostly for HENSLOWE, the majority of which are now lost. His best-remembered play is the domestic tragedy *A Woman Killed with Kindness* (1603), in which an unfaithful wife is punished by 'kindness', and dies of remorse. His 1612 *Apology for Actors* is a defence of the stage.

DNB.

**HILLEBRANDT, FRIEDRICH** (d. 1508), German goldsmith and engraver, born into a Nuremberg family of goldsmiths and engravers. He became a master in 1579 and thereafter specialized in vessels shaped like large birds, some of which incorporate NAUTILUS SHELLS. Several of his pieces are displayed in the Grünes Gewölbe in the Albertinum in Dresden.

**HILLIARD, NICHOLAS** (*c*.1547–1619), English MINIATURE painter, goldsmith, and carver, born in Exeter, the son of a goldsmith, and trained as a jeweller. He was appointed as court limner (i.e. miniaturist), goldsmith, and carver to Queen ELIZABETH in about 1570, and in 1586 designed and engraved her second great seal of England in collaboration with Derick Anthony (*fl.* 1550, d. 1599), engraver to the mint. There is some evidence that he visited France: in 1577 François, duke of ANJOU, employed one 'Nicholas Belliart, peintre anglais', and the subject of a miniature portrait by Hilliard (dated 1577) in the Pierpont Morgan Library in New York is a maid of honour at the French court.

Hilliard painted a miniature self-portrait at the age of 13 (versions of which survive in the collection of the duke of Buccleuch and in Welbeck Abbey, Notts.). He painted two portraits of Queen Elizabeth (1572, National Portrait Galley, and a later portrait in the Victoria and Albert Museum) and in 1578 painted a portrait of MARY, QUEEN OF SCOTS (versions of which survive in Windsor Castle and the Victoria and Albert Museum). On 5 May 1617 Hilliard was granted the exclusive right (for twelve years) to execute portraits of King JAMES I. He painted miniature portraits of many of his contemporaries; his royal sitters included Anne of Denmark, Prince Charles, and Princess Elizabeth (all in the Victoria and Albert Museum). He is praised in John DONNE's 'The Storm'. His most famous pupil was Isaac OLIVER. Hilliard died early in January 1619 and was buried in St Martin-in-the-Fields. A draft of his treatise on the *Art of Limning* survives in Edinburgh University Library.

DNB; MDA; *A Treatise Concerning the Arte of Limning*, ed. R. K. R. Thornton and T. G. S. Cain (1992); Raphaëlle Costa de Beauregard, *Nicholas Hilliard et l'imaginaire élisabéthain* (1983); id., *Silent Elizabethans: The Language of Colour in the Miniatures of Nicholas Hilliard and Isaac Oliver* (2000).

**HILTON, JOHN** (*c*.1560–1608), English composer and church musician. He sang at Lincoln Cathedral and in 1594 became organist of Trinity College, Cambridge, where he was responsible for the provision of instruments, including the rebuilding of the organ and the acquisition of viols. His madrigals 'Fair Oriana' and 'Beauty's Queen' appeared in *The TRIUMPHS OF ORIANA* (1601); he also wrote liturgical music.

**HIRSCHVOGEL, AUGUSTIN** (1503–53), German etcher, potter, glass painter, medallist, cartographer, and mathematician, born in Nuremberg, the son of a stained-glass artist. He specialized in the etchings of landscapes and maps; his best-known work is a large map of Austria commissioned by the Emperor FERDINAND I in 1542. Hirschvogel's pottery consists of Italianate TIN-GLAZED EARTHENWARE; he may have been the inventor of the EULENKRUG, of which he made the earliest known examples. He died in Vienna in February 1553.

MDA s.v. Hirschvogel (2); NDB; K. Schwartz, *Augustin Hirschvogel, ein deutscher Meister der Renaissance* (1917).

**HISTORIOGRAPHY.** Medieval history was primarily descriptive, and characteristically took the form of a detailed chronicle. The advent of HUMANISM in the fifteenth century created a new kind of historical writing, one characterized by a greater attention to motives and causes, by a conviction that the study of history had direct applications to governance and military science, and (under the influence of classical historians such as Livy and Tacitus) by a belief that historical change should be understood in the context of overarching values: Leonardo BRUNI, one of the earliest humanist historians, therefore presents the history of Florence as a battle between tyranny and civil liberty. The ancient Greek ideal of the independent city-state was appropriated by historians in areas of Europe ruled by local princes, notably the Holy Roman Empire, the Swiss Confederation, and Italy, so a historian such as SABELLICUS presents Venice as the successor of the ancient city-state. The sense that political history was a discipline useful to rulers was made clear by writers such as MACHIAVELLI and Polydore VERGIL.

Religious history shed much of its piety with the Reformation, which enhanced the sense of the confessional perspective of the historian: FLACCIUS and his colleagues produced the *MAGDEBURG CENTURIES*, a Protestant version of the history of the Church; BARONIUS replied with *Annales ecclesiastici*, a Catholic antidote to the Protestant perspective. Similarly, in legal and constitutional history, the importance of a document came to be related to the political position of the historian: in England, the Magna Carta remained an obscure document until the end of the sixteenth century, so Shakespeare's *King John*, a product of the 1590s, does not mention it; in the constitutional debates that followed the accession of King JAMES, however, Sir Edward COKE could ringingly proclaim the Magna Carta to be the foundation of the rights and liberties of Englishmen.

Contemporary events first began to be treated as history in the making by historians such as Piccolomini (later Pope PIUS II), Paolo GIOVIO, and THUANUS. Similarly, Spanish historians began to write about the conquest of America as it happened, and were soon divided into apologists (notably OVIEDO) and detractors (notably LAS CASAS).

N. Struever, *The Language of History in the Renaissance* (1970); E. B. Fryde, *Humanism and Renaissance Historiography* (1983).

**HOBY, SIR THOMAS** (1530–66), English diplomat and translator. After education at Cambridge, Hoby travelled frequently on the Continent, recording observations, notably on Italy, in his notebooks (published 1902). His influential translation of Castiglione's *Il cortegiano* (1561) was in turn translated into Latin (1577).

*DNB.*

**HÖCHSTETTER FAMILY**, German dynasty of bankers and merchants in Augsburg, where they became members of the patrician class in the early fifteenth century. By the beginning of the sixteenth century the Höchstetter were the third largest banking house in Augsburg (after the FUGGERS and the WELSERS) and among the most important bankers in Europe. The family fortunes reached their zenith under Ambrosius Höchstetter (1463–1534). In 1529 Ambrosius' attempt to capture the European market in mercury ended in bankruptcy; he spent the rest of his life in prison.

*NDB s.v. Hoechstetter.*

**HOEFNAGEL, JORIS** (1542–1601), Flemish painter, born in Antwerp, the son of a diamond merchant. He travelled in France and Spain (1561–7), England (1569), and Italy (1577), often in the company of Abraham ORTELIUS. Many of his paintings and drawings of towns were reworked as illustrations for the *Civitates orbis terrarum* (1572–1618) of Georg Braun and Franz Hogenberg. Hoefnagel worked for the FUGGERS in Augsburg and in 1591 entered the imperial service of RUDOLF II in Prague, where the subjects of his drawings included many plants and animals. He was the illuminator of *Mira calligraphiae monumenta*, a work on CALLIGRAPHY by the Hungarian Georg Bocskay.

*BNB s.v. Hoefnaeghel, Georges; MDA; Mira calligraphiae monumenta, ed. Lee Hendrix and Thea Vignau-Wilberg (1992).*

**HOEN, CORNELIUS HERICXZOON** (d. 1534), Dutch Protestant reformer, a native of Gouda who established a legal practice in The Hague. Hoen wrote a treatise on the EUCHARIST (c.1521) in which he rejected the doctrine of transubstantiation in favour of a symbolic understanding of the sacrament; this was a position later to be associated with the SACRAMENTARIANS. The book was read in manuscript by ZWINGLI, and may have shaped his view of the eucharist as a purely commemorative rite. Hoen was summoned to appear before the Spanish INQUISITION in The Hague, where he was fined and imprisoned. His book was published posthumously as *Von dem brot und weyn des Herren, christlicher beriecht* (Strassburg, 1525).

*NNBW vi.*

**HOFFMAN or Hofman, MELCHIOR** (c.1500–1543), German Anabaptist leader, born at Hall (Swabia). He was by trade a furrier, and was working in LIVONIA in 1523 when he emerged as a Lutheran lay preacher. He came into conflict with the Livonian authorities and left for Sweden on a business trip with another evangelical furrier, Melchior Rinck; the two furriers were accompanied by a wealthy cloth merchant, Bernd KNIPPERDOLLINCK. In Stockholm the three

godly merchants inveighed against the worship of images and were promptly expelled.

Hoffman arrived in Tartu (Dorpat) in November 1524, and on being expelled the following January travelled to Riga and thence to Wittenberg, where he was warmly received by Martin LUTHER. He soon set out again on his travels, first to Tartu and Magdeburg and then to Holstein, where he secured the patronage of FREDERICK I of Denmark and was appointed by royal ordinance as a preacher at Kiel.

At Kiel Hoffman adopted a Zwinglian memorialist position on the EUCHARIST, which upset Luther. At a colloquy held in Flensburg on 8 April 1529 Hoffman maintained his Zwinglian position and was in consequence banished. He travelled to Strassburg, where he was welcomed until his ANABAPTIST tendencies became apparent. He worked with Kaspar SCHWENCKFELD and KARLSTADT, but increasingly assumed the mantle of a prophet. From 1530 to 1533 he worked amongst artisans in East Friesland, founding a spiritual community in Emden in 1532.

In 1533 Hoffman returned to his family in Strassburg, which he proclaimed as the New Jerusalem. He was arrested in May 1533, and seems to have spent the last ten years of his life in prison; the last notice of his incarceration is dated 19 November 1543, and he probably died shortly thereafter. His followers, who were known as Melchiorites or Hoffmanites, long remained a distinctive party in the Anabaptist movement.

*NDB; P. Kalerau, Melchior Hoffman als religiöser Denker (1954); K. Deppermann, Melchior Hoffman: Soziale Unruhen und apokalyptische Visionen im Zeitalter der Reformation (1979; English trans. 1987).*

**HOFFMEISTER, JOHANNES** (c.1509–1547), German Catholic leader and Augustinian hermit who entered the Augustinian monastery at Colmar as a young man and became its prior in 1533. He was an indefatigable reformer, but believed in reform from within the Church and so became an entrenched opponent of Lutheranism.

Hoffmeister's formidable oratorical skills led to invitations to preach at important meetings such as the Diet of WORMS (1545) and the Colloquy of REGENSBURG (1546), and also accelerated his rise within his religious ORDER. He was an accomplished polemicist, notably in his *Dialogues* of 1538; he contributed to PATRISTIC SCHOLARSHIP with a collection of extracts published as *Loci communes* (Mainz, 1547), which appeared in many editions. He died prematurely in 1547.

*NDB; N. Paulus, Der Augustinermönch J. Hoffmeister: Ein Lebensbild aus der Reformationzeit (1891).*

**HOFHAIMER, PAUL** (1459–1537), Austrian composer and organist. From the late 1470s he served both Duke Sigismund of Tirol and MAXIMILIAN I. In 1515, knighted and ennobled, he became the imperial 'obrister Organist'. His last appointment was as organist at Salzburg Cathedral and to the archbishop of Salzburg. He was recognized as a skilled organist, an expert adviser on organ construction, and a teacher of several future cathedral organists. There are only two liturgical organ compositions ('Recordare' and 'Salve regina') amongst his surviving works.

**HOHENZOLLERN FAMILY**, a German family established in the eleventh century as counts of Zollern; the name derives from their castle on the hill of Zollern, near Hechingen; the castle now on the hill was built between 1850 and 1867 on the site of the medieval castle, which was destroyed in 1423. The Franconian and Swabian branches of the family rose to prominence in the fifteenth century. In 1415, Friedrich, burgrave of Nuremberg and head of the Franconian line, received the margravate and electorate of BRANDENBURG from the Emperor SIGISMUND, and his descendants ruled Brandenburg until 1701 (see Appendix 1); thereafter they became kings of Prussia and, from 1871 to 1918, German emperors. The authority of the Swabian branch of the family was weakened by a long series of partitions, but members of the family were associated with the courts of MAXIMILIAN I and CHARLES V, and from 1866 to 1947 served as kings of Romania.

NDB s.v. Hohenzollern, Dynastengeschicht; O. Hintze, *Die Hohenzollern und ihr Werk* (1915); H. Eulenberg, *The Hohenzollerns* (1929).

**HOLANDA, FRANCISCO DE** (1517–84), Portuguese miniaturist and art historian of Dutch extraction, known to have been in Rome in 1538; his drawings of Italian artists (including MICHELANGELO) and antiquities are now in the ESCORIAL. By 1545 Francisco had returned to Portugal, where he worked as a court painter, executing portraits of the royal family. He also drew up plans for a comprehensive redesign of Lisbon on the Roman model, with new walls, roads, bridges, fortifications, and churches.

In 1548 Francisco completed a treatise on ancient painting (*Da pintura antigua*). The first book deals with the theory and practicalities of art, and the second contains four dialogues in which Francisco conducts conversations about art with contemporary figures such as Vittoria COLONNA, Giulio CLOVIO, and Michelangelo; in 1549 he added ten more dialogues on the subject of drawing from nature (*Do tirar polo natural*). The treatise was not published until the nineteenth century (1890–6), but nonetheless circulated in manuscript and so exercised a significant influence in its advocacy of Italian models for PORTUGUESE ART.

MDA; José Stichini Vilela, *Francisco de Holanda: Vida, pensamento e abra* (1982).

**HOLBEIN, HANS THE YOUNGER** (1497/8–1543), German painter, born in Augsburg, the son of the painter Hans Holbein the Elder (*c*.1465–1524), in whose studio he trained. In about 1514 he moved to Basel, where he worked as a designer for the printer Johann FROBEN and where he also met ERASMUS. In Basel he painted the portraits of Burgomaster Meyer and his wife (1516, Kunstmuseum, Basel); the drawings for the portraits survive, and show that from the outset of his career it was Holbein's practice to draw his sitters and then to paint from his drawings.

From 1517 to 1519 Holbein worked in Lucerne, where he decorated the Haus zum Tanz (demolished 1907) for the von Hertenstein family. In the years following his return to Basel he painted the portrait of *Bonifacius Amerbach* (1519, Kunst-

museum, Basel). Paintings executed by Holbein in the next few years include *Christ in the Tomb* (1522, Kunstmuseum, Basel), *The Last Supper* (Kunstmuseum, Basel; the painting has been cut down), and *The Madonna and Child with Saints* (1522, Museum der Stadt, Solothurn). In this period he also accepted a commission from the city of Basel to decorate the Town Hall with scenes illustrating Justice (now mostly lost) and continued to work as a designer, in which field his most important commissions were the title page of LUTHER's Bible of 1522 and the series of 51 plates illustrating the DANCE OF DEATH (1523–6, published Lyon, 1538). His portraits in the early 1520s include three of *Erasmus* (Louvre; Kunstmuseum, Basel; earl of Radnor, on loan to the National Gallery, London). In 1524 Holbein visited France, and two years later painted *The Madonna of Burgomaster Meyer* (1526, Altschloss, Darmstadt).

From 1526 to 1528 Holbein lived in London, where a letter of introduction from Erasmus to Sir Thomas More led to a commission to paint a group portrait of the More family; the portrait is lost, and is known only from drawings in Windsor and Basel and copies in Nostell Priory (Yorkshire) and the National Portrait Gallery in London. Surviving portraits from Holbein's first visit to London include those of *Sir Thomas More* (Frick Collection, New York), *Sir Henry Guildford* (Windsor) and *Lady Guildford* (St Louis Art Museum), *Nicolaus Kratzer* (Louvre), *Archbishop Warham* (Louvre and Lambeth Palace), and an unidentified *Lady with a Squirrel and a Starling* (National Gallery, London).

In 1528 Holbein returned to Basel, which was becoming a Protestant centre under the leadership of OECOLAMPADIUS. In 1529 the city adopted the Reformation and Holbein accepted the new Zwinglian orthodoxy. The iconoclasm of the Reformation put an end to religious art, but Holbein was able to resume his commission to decorate the Town Hall and to design stained glass. During this period he painted a portrait of his wife and two children (Kunstmuseum, Basel).

In 1532 Holbein left his family in Basel and returned to London, and about this time he painted what seems to have been his last religious picture, *Noli me tangere* (Hampton Court). Sir Thomas More was no longer in a position to exercise patronage, but Holbein found new patrons in the merchants of the Steelyard, the London 'counter' of the HANSEATIC LEAGUE. His portraits of German merchants include those of *Georg Gisze* (Gemäldegalerie, Berlin) and *Derick Born* (Windsor Castle); he also decorated the Banqueting House of the Steelyard merchants with pictures of *The Triumph of Riches* and *The Triumph of Poverty* (destroyed).

Holbein's other important patron in London was Thomas CROMWELL, whose portrait he painted (Frick Collection, New York) and through whom he may have received the commission for *The Ambassadors* (1533, National Gallery, London), a double portrait filled with books and scientific and musical instruments and with a distorted skull (see ANAMORPHOSIS), an image of mortality, in the foreground. Cromwell may also have been the link that enabled Holbein to secure royal patronage. His paintings of King HENRY VIII include a panel now in the Thyssen Collection in Madrid, a large group portrait for the Company of Barbers and Surgeons (Barber-Surgeons' Hall), and a wall painting in the Palace of White-hall of the king with his parents (Henry VII and Elizabeth of York) and his third consort (Jane Seymour); the painting was destroyed in the fire of 1698, but part of the cartoon survives (National Portrait Gallery, London), as do copies of the mural (Hampton Court) and of the figure of Henry VIII (Walker Art Gallery, Liverpool); he also included a small portrait of King Henry in his design for the title page of the Coverdale Bible (1535), the first Bible in English. His other portraits in this period include those of *Jane Seymour* (Kunsthistorisches Museum, Vienna), *Anne of Cleves* (1539/40, Louvre), *Christina of Denmark, Duchess of Milan* (1538, National Gallery, London), and the miniature *Mrs Pemberton* (c.1540, Victoria and Albert Museum, London). He died in London, probably of the plague.

*MDA*; *NDB*; John Rowlands, *Holbein: The Paintings of Hans Holbein the Younger* (1985); Oskar Bätschmann and Pascal Griener, *Hans Holbein* (1997).

**HOLBORNE, ANTHONY** (d. c.1602), English composer. He wrote consort music which was published in two volumes: *The Cittham School* (1597), which includes six airs by his brother William, and *Pavans, Galliards and Allemandes* (1599). There are also works for lute, bandora, and cittern and some sacred music.

**HOLINSHED, RAPHAEL** (d. 1580), English historian. Author and compiler of the first continuous authoritative history of Britain in English, his *Chronicles of England, Scotland and Ireland* was published in 1577. Politically sensitive passages were removed from the second edition of 1587 (issued by STOW), which became a useful source for playwrights, and was used by SHAKESPEARE for many of his history plays.

*DNB*.

**HOLL, ELIAS** (1573–1646), German architect, born in Augsburg into a family of masons that long enjoyed the patronage of the FUGGERS. He travelled in Italy, pausing in Venice for a protracted period (1600–1), and then returned to Augsburg, where he was appointed city architect in 1602. In this capacity he presided over a huge building programme which included provision for the guilds (guildhalls, market halls, warehouses, merchants' houses), schools, hospitals, fortifications (gates and towers for the city walls, the Arsenal) and the Town Hall. His Protestantism became increasingly problematical during the THIRTY YEARS WAR, and led to his suspension from 1630 to 1632 and his dismissal in 1635.

Holl was the leading exponent of Renaissance architecture in Germany. Most of his work was undertaken in Augsburg, but Holl also built the residence of the prince-bishops (the Willibaldsburg) in Eichstätt and is likely to have been the architect responsible for the design of Bratislavský Hrad (1632–49), the four-towered castle of Pressburg (Hungarian Pozsony, now Bratislava) that was burnt in 1811 and restored from 1953 to 1968, whereupon it became the emblem of the city. Holl's building programme within Augsburg began with the Arsenal (1602–7) and finished with the Hospital of the Holy Ghost (1626–30). His buildings typically had court-yards surrounded by arcades (e.g. St Anne's School, 1612–16) and exteriors characterized by symmetry (especially in fenestration) and classical proportion. Such features are even apparent in Holl's fortifications: his remodelled Red Gate (Rotes Tor) of 1622 is part of an ensemble with a central courtyard. Holl's masterpiece is the Augsburg Town Hall (1615–20), which was badly damaged in the Second World War and has since been rebuilt.

*MDA*; *NDB*; B. Roeck, *Elias Holl Stadtbaumeister und Architekt vom Europäischen Rang* (1984); Wolfram Herausgeber et al., *Elias Holl und das Augsburger Rathaus* (1985).

**HOLLAND**, the principal province of the Netherlands, now used by synecdoche to refer to the entire country. Holland was an independent county from 916 to 1433, when it was incorporated into the duchy of Burgundy; for lists of the counts of Holland and dukes of Burgundy see Appendix 1. In 1579 Holland became one of the founding members of the Union of UTRECHT, and two years later it became part of the UNITED PROVINCES. After 1608 the ESTATES of Holland (formally known as De Edele Groot Mogende Heeren Staaten von Holland en Westfriesland), which met at The Hague, consisted of a representative of the nobility (*ridderschap*) and representatives of the eighteen largest cities and towns, which included AMSTERDAM, Delft, Dordrecht, Edam, Gouda, Haarlem, LEIDEN, and Rotterdam. Holland's financial preponderance made it predominant over all other provinces and, virtually, over the republic.

**HOLLAND, PHILEMON** (1552–1637), schoolmaster at Coventry from 1628, and English translator of Pliny's *Natural History* (1601), Plutarch's *Moral Essays* (1603), CAMDEN's *Britannia* (1610), and Xenophon's *Cyropaedia* (1632), among other works.

*DNB*.

**HOLY LEAGUE**, a term used to denote five wholly distinct alliances. When used without a date, the term normally refers to the Holy League of October 1511, a political alliance between Pope JULIUS II, King FERDINAND V of Spain, King HENRY VIII of England (who fought for the League in the battle of the SPURS), and the republic of Venice. The League was formed to fight France and its Italian allies in the WARS OF ITALY. After the French army defeated the army of the League in the battle of Ravenna (April 1512), the Emperor MAXIMILIAN I joined the League.

The other four leagues were formed in 1495, 1538, 1571, and 1576. The Holy League of Venice, which consisted of the pope, the emperor, Spain, Milan, and Venice, was formed on 31 March 1495 to drive the French out of Italy; on 6 July 1495 the League met the French army of CHARLES VIII in the battle of FORNOVO, after which Charles retreated with his army to France. The League of February 1538, which consisted of the pope, the emperor, and the republic of Venice, was formed to fight BARBAROSSA and the Ottomans. Similarly, the League of May 1571 was an alliance of Spain, the pope, and Venice formed to fight the Ottomans; the League defeated the

Ottomans in the battle of LEPANTO on 7 October 1571. The French Holy League (1576–95), which is also known as the CATHOLIC LEAGUE or La Sainte Union, was a Catholic alliance in the French WARS OF RELIGION.

**HOLY OFFICE or (Latin) Congregatio Sancti Officii or Congregatio Romanae et Universalis Inquisitionis or (officially) Sacra Congregatio Romanae et Universalis Inquisitionis seu Sancti Officii**, the Roman Congregation founded in 1542 by Pope PAUL III to govern the Roman INQUISITION. The Holy Office initially consisted of six cardinals, but when it was reorganized by Pope SIXTUS V in 1588, it was expanded to thirteen cardinals. Thereafter the pope was deemed to be the Congregation's prefect, but in practice he was represented by a cardinal-secretary.

**HOLY ROMAN EMPIRE or (Latin) Sacrum Romanum Imperium**. The ideal of a Holy Roman Empire was proclaimed at the coronation of Charlemagne as emperor on Christmas Day 800 and dissolved when Franz II abdicated on 6 August 1806. This Second Empire, or Second Reich, was conceived as a revival of the Roman Empire that had begun with Augustus in 27 BC, adopted Christianity in 325, and had ended in the West with the deposition of Romulus Augustus in 476. The Roman Empire lived on in Constantinople until 1453, but the gradual estrangement of the Eastern and Western churches allowed the imperial ideal to fade in the West; it was revived with the coronation of Charlemagne, king of the Franks, and thereafter the Western Church dated its documents by the regnal years of Charlemagne and his successors rather than by those of eastern emperors.

This revived Roman Empire did not acquire the epithet 'Holy' (*Sacrum Imperium*) until 1157, by which time the empire and the papacy were struggling for supremacy; the term Sacrum Romanum Imperium is first used in 1254. From the late tenth century the lands of the Empire had included northern Italy as well as the German-speaking lands (modern Germany, Austria, Switzerland, the Netherlands, eastern France, and parts of the Czech Republic and Poland), but the accession of Rudolf of HABSBURG in 1273 marked the end of any serious claim to Italy. The Empire became pan-European under CHARLES V, but on his abdication in 1556, the Empire became a loose federation of German princedoms and the emperor became the president of a German confederation; in nineteenth-century historiography, the emperor is often described as the king of Germany. In the sixteenth century the official term for the Empire became Sacrum Romanum Imperium Nationis Germanicae (abbreviated 'SRING'), which appears in German documents as Das Heilige Römische Reich Deutscher Nation, first officially recorded in 1492.

From the mid-thirteenth century, the post of emperor was elective, though election often followed hereditary lines. From 1273 to 1623, there were seven electors (German *Kurfürsten*), and the Golden Bull of 1356 settled disputes about the composition of the electoral body, which thereafter consisted of the three Rhenish archbishops (Cologne, Mainz, and Trier) and four lay magnates (the count Palatine of the Rhine, the duke of Saxony, the margrave of Brandenburg, and the king of Bohemia). The electoral body was not dissolved after each election, but rather constituted itself as a political entity (*Kurfürstenverein*) that continued to function between elections. In 1519, at the election of CHARLES V, the electors arrogated new powers to themselves by insisting that the *Kurfürstenverein* should be able to make the election of the emperor contingent on his agreement to exercise his office in accordance with terms that the electors had stipulated. This *Wahlkapitulation*, which resembled the *Pacta conventa* that limited the powers of elected kings of Poland, remained the prerogative of the electors until 1648.

In 1500 the Diet of Augsburg divided the Empire into six circles (German *Kreise*), which were increased to ten in 1512. The institutions of the Empire included the AULIC COUNCIL (established in 1498 as the executive and judicial council of the Empire) and the REICHSKAMMERGERICHT (established in 1495 as the high court of the Empire).

From the eleventh century until 1508, the emperor was styled *Romanorum rex* ('king of the Romans') until his coronation, and was thereafter known as *Romanorum imperator* ('emperor of the Romans'); in German the king of the Romans was usually styled *Deutscher König* (though the term *Römischer König* was in occasional use) and the emperor was known as *Deutscher Kaiser*, a title that remained in use until the abdication of Kaiser Wilhelm II in 1918. Kings of the Romans were elected in Frankfurt and crowned in Aachen; emperors were crowned by the Pope in Rome. On 4 February 1508 MAXIMILIAN, unable to reach Rome for his imperial coronation, assumed the title 'Roman emperor elect', which Pope JULIUS II subsequently approved; thereafter the successor-designate of the emperor was styled 'king of the Romans'.

**HOMBERG, SYNOD OF**, a synod convoked by PHILIP OF HESSE which met at Homberg (30 kilometres (18 miles) south of Kassel) on 21 October 1526 to establish a Protestant constitution for the churches of Hesse. The discussions were based on 158 articles (*paradoxa*) prepared by François LAMBERT (published Erfurt, 1517). The Synod appointed a committee to formulate a church order for Hesse; this order, the Reformatio Ecclesiarum Hassiae (German Hessische Kirchenordnung) advocated autonomy in church discipline for each congregation. The congregationalism of the order displeased LUTHER, who persuaded Philip of Hesse not to promulgate it. The order was therefore never enforced, and remained unpublished until 1748.

W. Schmitt, *Die Synode zu Homberg und ihre Vorgeschichte* (1926).

**HOMER IN THE RENAISSANCE**. The works of Homer were unknown in western Europe until Leonzio Pilato, a fourteenth-century Calabrian monk, was appointed in 1360 as a lecturer in Greek in Florence. Pilato was persuaded to translate the *Iliad* and the *Odyssey* into Latin verse; his translations were literal and leaden, so Coluccio SALUTATI assumed the task of improving the Latinity of Pilato's translation. In the fifteenth century there were translations into

Latin prose by Leonardo BRUNI and Lorenzo VALLA, and a translation into Latin hexameters by POLIZIANO, who gave his inaugural lecture on Homer. The first printed edition of the Greek text (the *editio princeps*) was published in Florence in 1488.

A. Pertusi, *Leonzio Pilato fra Petrarca e Boccaccio: Le sue versioni omeriche* (1964).

**HONDIUS, JODOCUS, or (Flemish) Josse de Hondt** (1563–1611), Flemish cartographer, a native of Ghent who *c.*1583 moved to London, where he established himself as an engraver and type founder specializing in cartography; in 1593 he returned to the Netherlands, where he re-established his business in Amsterdam. His best-known works were his two maps constructed on the MERCATOR projection, one containing an image of a Christian knight and the other marking the voyages of CAVENDISH and DRAKE. His other work included the maps that he engraved for John SPEED's *Theatre of the Empire of Great Britain* (1611–12). In 1604 Hondius bought Mercator's plates, and in 1606 he produced a Mercator atlas which contained 37 new plates; this atlas was to sell in large numbers for decades.

BNB s.v. De Hondt, Josse; *DNB* and *MDA* s.v. Hondius.

**HONE, GALYON** (*fl.* 1492–1526), Flemish glass stainer who was admitted to the Antwerp guild in 1492 and subsequently moved to England, where he was appointed royal glazier, in which capacity he succeeded Bernard FLOWER as the glass stainer responsible for the windows of the Chapel of King's College, Cambridge, including the magnificent east window; the windows had been designed by DIRICK VELLERT.

H. G. Wayment, *The Windows of King's College Chapel Cambridge* (1972).

**HOOKER, RICHARD** (*c.*1554–1600), English divine and jurist. Educated at Oxford, Hooker became a fellow of Corpus Christi College in 1575 and in 1579 deputy professor of Hebrew. In 1584 he married and assumed the first of a series of country livings; he was also, in 1585, master of the Temple. His *Of the Laws of Ecclesiastical Polity* (books 1–4 published in 1593, book 5 in 1597, and books 6–8 posthumously) offered a substantial defence of the Anglican Church under Elizabeth, and elaborated a theory of law which was to influence later theorists such as John Locke. According to Hooker, church and civil policy were subservient to the natural law of the universe, which was expressive of God's reason. He offered an essentially contractual account of political government. He also attacked the Puritan literal reading of the Bible, and argued that the contemporary Church had a continuity with the medieval Church; more controversially, he was prepared to cede that episcopal ordination was not always necessary. The work is the most effective statement of the foundations of Anglicanism ever written, and a key work of Elizabethan political theory.

*DNB.*

**HOOPER, JOHN** (1475–1555), English Protestant reformer. Following education at Oxford, Hooper entered a Cistercian priory in Gloucestershire. On the dissolution of the MONASTERIES, he became interested in the extreme reformist opinions of ZWINGLI, and was exiled for heresy following a disputation with Stephen GARDINER. In Zürich, he became friends with Zwingli; he was to become the chief exponent of Zwinglianism in England. He returned to England on EDWARD VI's accession, and became chaplain to Protector SOMERSET. In 1550 he was offered the see of Gloucester, and after prolonged disagreement over VESTMENTS was consecrated fully robed. In 1552 his diocese was merged with Worcester. Under MARY, he was imprisoned and tried for heresy, and was burnt at the stake. His writings, which include *A Godly Confession and Protestation of the Christian Faith* (1551) and *A Brief and Clear Confession of the Christian Faith* (1581), were formative influences on later Puritan opinion.

*DNB.*

**HOORNE, PHILIPPE DE MONTMORENCY-NIVELLE, COUNT OF** (1518–68), Flemish statesman who served CHARLES V as stadtholder of Gelderland and admiral of Flanders and was appointed knight of the GOLDEN FLEECE. In 1559 he commanded the fleet that carried King PHILIP II to Spain, and remained at the Spanish court until 1563. On returning to the Netherlands he allied himself with WILLIAM OF ORANGE and the count of EGMONT in opposition to the policies of Cardinal GRANVELLE, who was attempting to introduce the Spanish INQUISITION into the Netherlands. When King Philip dispatched the duke of ALBA to the Netherlands, Hoorne and Egmont decided to remain in the Netherlands. They were arrested, tried by the COUNCIL OF BLOOD, and on 5 June 1568 beheaded in Brussels. Their deaths became a rallying cry in the REVOLT OF THE NETHERLANDS.

BNB s.v. Hornes.

**HOPE THEATRE** (1613). Built on the old Bear Garden on Bankside in 1613 by HENSLOWE for LADY ELIZABETH'S MEN, the Hope was a circular, wooden building, capable of holding 3,000 people. Its removable stage meant that bearbaiting and cockfights could also still be held there. It initially attracted audiences unable to attend the GLOBE when it burned down, but was not greatly successful, and in 1617 the site reverted to its original use as a venue for bearbaiting.

**HOPFFER or Hopfer, DANIEL** (*c.*1470–1536), German armourer and etcher. He was born in Kaufbeuren (60 kilometres (37 miles) south of Augsburg) and became a burgher of Augsburg in 1493. He worked as an engraver of parade armour (see ARMS AND ARMOUR) and designed architectural decoration, including Gothic foliage and Renaissance gargoyles. He seems to have been the first person to have made prints on paper by ETCHING iron plates rather than by line ENGRAVING. He developed this technique in order to facilitate the decoration of armour, but soon became a printmaker, the first maker of mass-produced etchings. His huge range of etchings included religious scenes, GENRE scenes such as village festivals, many reproductions of Italian art, and some of the earliest etched portraits.

*MDA* s.v. Hopfer (1) Daniel Hopfer; *NDB*.

**HORACE IN THE RENAISSANCE**. Quintus Horatius Flaccus (65–8 BC), Latin satirist and lyric poet, was important in the Renaissance both as a poet and as a literary theorist. His *Odes*, *Epodes*, *Satires*, and *Epistles* were widely reprinted, and influenced both the forms and the values of Renaissance lyric poetry, particularly the ode and the verse epistle.

Horace's *Epistula ad Pisones*, which was known as the *Ars poetica*, was one of the two founding texts from which Renaissance poetics was constructed; the other seminal treatise was Aristotle's *Poetics*, which was known only in part and was often discussed as if it were wholly consistent with Horace's *Ars poetica*. Horace's treatise was the subject of an endless stream of commentary; in the last two decades of the fifteenth century, more than twenty commentaries were published in Italy alone. Horace's notion that literature should both profit and delight the reader ('aut prodesse volunt aut delectare poetae') became an article of faith for many poets and literary theorists.

R. Lebègue, 'Horace en France pendant la Renaissance', *Bibliothèque d'humanisme et Renaissance*, 3 (1936); E. Schäfer, *Deutscher Horaz: Conrad Celtis, Georg Fabricius, Paul Melissus, Jacob Balde. Das Nachwirkung des Horaz in der neulateinischen Dichtung Deutschlands* (1976).

**HORNICK, ERASMUS** (d. 1583), Flemish goldsmith and designer. He may have worked in Antwerp in the 1540s, but first enters the historical record in 1555, by which time he was living in Augsburg. In 1559 Hornick moved to Nuremberg, where he was admitted to the guild in 1563 and where he lived until 1566, when he returned to Augsburg. In 1582 he was appointed imperial *Kammergoldschmeid* to the Emperor RUDOLF II in Prague, where he died the following year.

No examples of Hornick's goldsmith work are known to survive, though 83 etchings and some 600 drawings are attributed to him or to his workshop on the basis of his printed designs. These designs, typically for vases, medallions, and jewellery, were published in a series of books with engraved illustrations, and were intended for execution in a wide range of materials, including rock crystal, mollusc shells, and precious metals.

*MDA.*

**HORTUS PALATINUS**, a garden built in the grounds of Heidelberg Castle. The designer was Salomon de CAUS, who had followed Princess Elizabeth to Heidelberg after her marriage to the elector in 1613. The gardens, on which work began in 1615, are constructed on five narrow terraces with high retaining walls. The terraces were divided into compartments by hedges and pergolas, and are embellished in the Renaissance style with a MAZE, statues, gazebos, and ornamental ponds. These characteristic features are supplemented by waterworks and GROTTOES with AUTOMATA, including water-organs for which Caus composed the music. Caus described and illustrated the garden in his *Hortus palatinus* (1620), but the abandonment of the garden in 1619 when Friedrich was forced to leave Heidelberg creates uncertainties about the extent to which Caus's designs were

implemented. The terraces and a grotto remain today, but the planting is modern and Caus's buildings are in ruins.

Richard Patterson, 'The "Hortus Palatinus" at Heidelberg and the Reformation of the World', *Journal of Garden History*, 1 (1981).

**HOSIUS, STANISLAUS**, or (Polish) **Stanisław Hozjusz** (1504–79), Polish Catholic leader. He was born in Kraków into a family of German origin and studied law in Kraków, Bologna (where he met Reginald POLE), and Padua. In 1549 he was appointed bishop of Kulm (now Polish Chełmno) and two years later he was translated to the diocese of Ermland (now Polish Warmia), where he preached in Latin, Polish, and German. In 1558 he was called to Rome to act as an adviser to Pope PAUL IV, and in 1560 Pope PIUS IV appointed him as papal nuncio to the Emperor FERDINAND I, in which capacity he prepared the reconvening of the COUNCIL OF TRENT, to which he later became the papal legate with particular responsibility for doctrinal issues.

In 1561 Hosius was created cardinal, and in 1564 returned to Ermland, where he published the decrees of the Council of Trent at the Synod of Parczew. He also invited the JESUITS to open a college in Braunsberg (now Polish Braniewo) which was later to be renamed as the Lyceum Hosianum. In 1566 Pope PIUS V nominated him as a legate *a latere* (a rank indicating that authority derives 'from the side' of the pope), and from 1569 he lived permanently in Rome as the representative of the Church in Poland.

Hosius' principal work was *Confessio catholicae fidei* (1552–3), in which he attempted to show that both the Bible and the traditions of the Church supported the contention that Catholicism was true Christianity and Protestantism was an error. His polemical works include an attack on Johannes BRENZ (*Confutatio prolegomenorum Brentii*, 1558), who dissented from Hosius' view that it was proper to torture and execute heretics.

*NDB*; *PSB* s.v. Hozjusz, Stanisław; L. Bernacki, *La Doctrine de l'eglise chez le cardinal Hosius* (1936).

**HOTHBY, JOHN** (c.1410–1487), English Carmelite composer and theorist in Italy. In 1479 he became *lector* in sacred theology in Lucca, where he also taught music, grammar, and mathematics. His original thinking on rhythm, notation, and the hexachord is set out in his treatises *Calliopea legale* and *Tractatus quarundam regularum artis musicae*. Only nine of his compositions survive.

**HOTMAN, FRANÇOIS**, or **Hotomanus** (1524–90), French jurist and political theorist, successor to CUJAS at Bourges. He was born in Paris to a family of Silesian origin, and studied law at Orléans. In 1546 he was appointed lecturer in law at the University of Paris. He converted to Protestantism and left Paris, initially for Lyon and Geneva and then for Lausanne, where, on the recommendation of CALVIN, he was appointed professor of literature and history. In 1556 he was appointed professor of law at Strassburg, in succession to François BAUDOUIN, his former colleague in Paris.

In Strassburg Hotman assumed a parallel career as a diplomat, accompanying Calvin to the Diet at Frankfurt in 1558, representing the Huguenots to German princes, and acting on behalf of CATHERINE DE MÉDICIS. In 1560 he was one of the conspirators in the Conjuration d'AMBOISE and when Francis II died a few months later, joined ANTOINE DE BOURBON; in 1562 he allied himself with CONDÉ.

In 1564 Hotman was appointed to the chair of CIVIL LAW at Valence, and in 1567 succeeded CUJAS in the chair of jurisprudence at Bourges. A few months later his house was sacked and his library burnt by a Catholic mob, and he fled to Paris, where he was appointed royal historiographer through the influence of L'HOPITAL. He returned to Bourges, and when hostilities broke out again fled to Sancerre, where, trapped by a siege, he wrote his *Consolatio a sacris litteris*, which was published by his son in 1593. He returned to Bourges, and then fled for a third time in the wake of the ST BARTHOLOMEW'S DAY MASSACRE. He lived abroad for the rest of his life in Geneva (where he was professor of Roman law) and Basel, and served as councillor of state to Henry of Navarre (later HENRI IV).

Despite the itinerant life forced on Hotman by the WARS OF RELIGION, he was a prolific writer, and brought his erudition and his elegant Latin prose style to a wide range of subjects. In jurisprudence, his most influential work was *Antitribonian* (1567), in which he argued that FRENCH LAW could not be based on the Justinian code prepared by the Byzantine jurist Tribonian, and that law had to be studied in the context of its applications. Hotman's religious writings range from the contemplative *Consolatio* to the polemical *Brutem fulmen* (1585), directed against a bull of SIXTUS V. He also wrote volumes of history, biography (including a life of COLIGNY, 1585), politics, and classical scholarship. His most important constitutional works were *De iure successionis regiae in regno Francorum* (1588) and *Franco-Gallia* (1573), in which he disputed the historical legitimacy of royal absolutism in France, and advocated representative government and an elective monarchy.

DBF s.v. 4. Hotman; NDB s.v. Hotomanus, Fritz; Donald R. Kelley, *François Hotman: A Revolutionary's Ordeal* (1973).

**HOUWAERT, JEAN BAPTISTA** (1533–99), Flemish playwright and poet, a courtier at the ducal court in Brabant and a member of the Brussels CHAMBER OF RHETORIC. His cycle of mythological plays (1583) contained plays on subjects such as *Aeneas and Dido, Leander and Hero, Mars and Venus*, and *Narcissus and Echo*. His poems included the sixteen-book *Palace of Maidens* (1582–3), an examination of love. Houwaert was known to his admiring contemporaries as the 'Homer of Brabant'.

NBW i.

**HOWARD OF EFFINGHAM, CHARLES, LORD** (1536–1624). Remembered as the supreme naval commander during the defeat of the Spanish ARMADA in 1588, Howard's was a career of long and varied naval and political service. Lord chamberlain to ELIZABETH, he participated in the quelling of the NORTHERN REBELLION of 1569, oversaw the defeat of the Armada, and with ESSEX captured CÁDIZ in 1596. He remained in diplomatic and political service in JAMES I's reign, and was patron of the ADMIRAL'S MEN.

DNB s.v. Howard, Charles.

**HUBER, SAMUEL** (c.1547–1624), Protestant controversialist, born in Burgdorf (near Bern). He championed Lutheran theology against the Calvinism of the Reformed Church in the SWISS CONFEDERATION. The doctrine known as 'Huberism' refers to Huber's advocacy of universal ATONEMENT: he argued that Jesus died for the sins of all mankind (*Christum Jesum esse mortuum pro peccatis totius generis humani*), whereas Calvinists argued that Jesus died only for the elect.

Huber was banished from the Confederation on 28 June 1588 and subsequently signed the Formula of CONCORD. He held a series of posts in the Lutheran Church in Germany, but eventually his theology of the atonement proved too strong even for the Lutheran Church, and he was stripped of his offices. He died in Osterwieck on 23 March 1624.

NDB.

**HUBER, WOLF** (c.1485–1553), German painter who worked in Passau. His religious paintings include a crowded *Raising of the Cross* (c.1522–4, Kunsthistorisches Museum, Vienna). His three-quarter-length portraits include portrayals of *Anton Hundertpfundt* (1526, National Gallery, Dublin), master of the Bavarian mint, and of his wife *Marggret Hundertpfundt* (1526, Johnson Collection, Philadelphia).

MDA s.v. Huber, Wolfgang; NDB; Franz Winzinger, *Wolf Huber* (2 vols., 1979).

**HUBMAIER, BALTHASAR** (c.1485–1528), German Anabaptist who studied under Johann ECK at Freiburg im Breisgau and Ingolstadt, where he became professor at the university and parish priest. He was appointed preacher of Regensburg Cathedral in 1516, and in 1521 became parish priest at Waldshut, where he met the Swiss Reformers.

In 1523 Hubmaier declared himself a Zwinglian, but he soon forsook Zwingli's doctrines for those of the ANABAPTISTS. His *Von dem Tauf der Gläubigen* (May 1525) advocated believers' baptism and condemned infant baptism as idolatry. He became involved in the PEASANTS' REVOLT, having rejected tithing and other feudal dues. Unlike many Anabaptists, Hubmaier was not a pacifist, but defended the power and office of the civil magistrate and the use of the sword. When Waldshut was occupied by Austrian troops in December 1525, Hubmaier fled to Zürich, where Zwingli forced him to recant his Anabaptist doctrines. Hubmaier left Zürich early in 1526, retracted his abjuration and in July 1526 settled in Nikolsburg (now Mikulow), in Moravia, where he wrote Anabaptist pamphlets. In 1527 he was extradited to Vienna, where he was burnt at the stake on 10 March 1528; a few days later his wife was executed by drowning.

NDB; C. Windhorst, *Tauferisches Taufverständnis: Balthasar Hubmaiers Lehre zwischen traditioneller und reformatorischer Theologie* (1976); Torsten Bergsten, *Balthasar Hubmaier, Anabaptist Theologian and Martyr* (1978); James M. Stayer, *Anabaptists and the Sword* (2nd edn., 1976).

**HUDSON, HENRY** (d. 1611), English explorer. Uncertainty surrounds much of Hudson's life. It is known, however, that he was employed as navigator and explorer by the MUSCOVY COMPANY, for whom he travelled as far as Spitsbergen. His explorations on behalf of the Dutch of the Hudson river inland from New York, and of the Delaware and Chesapeake bays, laid the foundations of Dutch holdings in North America. He perished when abandoned by a mutinous English crew during a search for a northern passage to Asia.

*DNB.*

**HUGUENOTS**, French Calvinist Protestants. The origin of the term is disputed, but it may derive from *Eigenotz*, a Gallicized German term (*Eidgenossen*) meaning 'confederates'. In Geneva, where the term *Eigenotz* originated, it referred to members of the SWISS CONFEDERATION, but in France it came to refer to French Protestant adherents of Calvin. The Huguenots were first constituted at a synod in Paris in 1539, and by the time of their second synod (Poitiers, 1561) had become a significant minority in many areas of France; their churches were called *temples*, and so were distinguished from Catholic *églises*. The conflict between Huguenots and Catholics, combined with the dynastic rivalries of the time, eventually erupted into the French WARS OF RELIGION.

**HUGUET, JAUME** (*c.*1415–1492), Catalan painter, the most prominent Catalan artist of the late fifteenth century. He was born in Tarragona and settled in Barcelona in about 1448. Attributed work thought to pre-date his arrival in Barcelona includes the *St George and the Princess* (Museu d'Art de Catalunya, Barcelona). Jaume's earliest documented work was the ALTARPIECE of *Sant Antoni Abat* for the Confraría dels Tractants en Animals in Barcelona (1455), which was destroyed in 1909. His principal surviving works are *The Consecration of St Augustine* (commissioned 1463, completed 1486; Museu d'Art de Catalunya, Barcelona) and an *Epiphany* (1463) now in the Chapel Royal in Barcelona.

*DBC; MDA;* J. Ainaud de Lasarte, *Jaime Huguet* (1955).

**HUMANISM**. In popular modern usage, humanism is thought of as an alternative to religious belief. In the Renaissance, however, humanism was entirely consistent with religious belief, and related not to secularism but rather to the *studia humanitatis*, the LIBERAL ARTS now known as the humanities. A Renaissance humanist was a scholar engaged in the study of humanistic subjects (e.g. grammar, rhetoric, and history) with particular reference to the languages and literatures of classical antiquity. Humanists reformed the writing of Latin according to classical precedents and revived the study of Greek and Hebrew. The values of humanism were applied to statecraft in the civic humanism of public figures such as Coluccio SALUTATI and Leonardo BRUNI and in the works of MACHIAVELLI and GUICCIARDINI.

The recovery of the works of classical antiquity was initiated by scholars such as Giovanni AURISPA, Poggio BRACCIOLINI, CIRIACO D'ANCONA, and Niccolò NICCOLI. In education, early humanists included GUARINO DA VERONA, VITTORINO DA FELTRE, and VERGERIO. Scholarly editing, which was initiated by Lorenzo VALLA and taken up by scholars such as POLIZIANO, led after the advent of print to the establishment of the scholarly presses of Venice (notably that of ALDUS MANUTIUS). In philosophy, fifteenth-century humanists included FICINO (who translated all of Plato and Plotinus into Latin) and Giovanni PICO DELLA MIRANDOLA.

By the end of the fifteenth century humanism had become a movement and a set of values that had been diffused throughout Europe by travelling humanists such as Desiderius ERASMUS. Early northern humanists include Konrad CELTIS and Johann REUCHLIN in Germany, LEFÈVRE D'ÉTAPLES in France, and John COLET in England; in Spain the principal humanist was VIVES.

Jill Kraye (ed.), *The Cambridge Companion to Renaissance Humanism* (1996); D. R. Kelley, *Renaissance Humanism* (1991); V. R. Giustiniani, 'Homo, Humanus and the Meanings of "Humanism"', *Journal of the History of Ideas,* 46 (1985).

**HUME, TOBIAS** (*c.*1569–1645), English composer, viol player, and soldier who served in the Russian and Swedish armies. His *First Part of Ayres* (1605) is a collection of instrumental dances for the lyra viol. They are descriptive, sometimes suggestive, pieces, with instructions (unusual for the time) to play 'pizzicato' and 'col legno'. His second collection, *Captain Hume's Poetical Music* (1607), is more serious and was dedicated to Queen Anne.

**HUNDRED YEARS WAR.** This potentially misleading term denotes the series of conflicts between England and France between 1337 and 1453. Edward III's claim to the French throne, via his mother Isabella of France, initiated hostilities which were fuelled also by territorial disputes in France. Edward's military successes in France led to his claiming the title king of France in 1340. Fighting resumed thirty years later, with a series of French victories, but Henry V's armies established a period of English control of much of northern France, and his son HENRY VI was crowned king of France in 1431. In his reign, however, English grip on their territories weakened, and Normandy (in 1450) and Gascony (in 1453) were lost, though, with their control of Calais, the English retained a foothold in France until 1558.

**HUNGARIAN GARDENS.** There is fragmentary evidence of an early fifteenth-century royal garden in Buda commissioned by SIGISMUND, but the earliest documented gardens are those laid out by MATTHIAS CORVINUS in Buda and at his summer residence at Višegrad. Matthias imported plants and trees from Italy, and laid out his Buda garden in symmetrical PARTERRES which were adorned with FOUNTAINS. The garden has since been destroyed, but it was described by Stephanus Taurinus (*Stauromachia*, Vienna, 1519) and Antonio BONFINI (*Rerum Hungaricum decades*, Basel, 1572) and depicted in engravings by Erhard Schön (1541) and Georg Hufnagel (1672). Little is known of the garden at Višegrad beyond the fact that, like the Buda garden, it was terraced and had a MAZE.

There is documentary evidence of a number of aristocratic gardens in the period, but no descriptions are known to have survived; similarly, nothing is known of the garden of the humanist János VITÉZ. The Ottoman occupation of most of Hungary from 1541 to 1686 arrested the development of European gardens (except in Transylvania), but throughout this period plants from other parts of the Ottoman Empire—pomegranates, shrubs, herbs, and, most importantly, tulips—were imported into Hungary, and were introduced from there into western Europe.

Raymund Rapaics, *Magyar kertek: A kertmüvészet magyarországon* (1940).

**HUNGARIAN LANGUAGE AND LITERATURE.** Early modern HUNGARY was a multi-ethnic kingdom which included speakers of German, Croatian, Romanian, Romany, Serbian, Slovakian, Slovenian, and Turkish. The principal language, Hungarian (or Magyar), is a Uralic language whose only living relatives in the Ugric sub-group of the Finno-Ugrian node are Mansi and Khanty, which are spoken in north-west Siberia; the SZEKLER language of Transylvania is a dialect of Hungarian. Scholarly study of the Hungarian language began in 1539 with the publication of PANNONIUS' *Grammatica Hungaro-Latina*.

Until the end of the eighteenth century, the principal language of Hungarian literature was Latin, which was the language of the markedly literary court of MATTHIAS CORVINUS. The most important writers of Latin in Hungary were János VITÉZ, Pannonius (whose poetry included epigrams, panegyrics, and epics), the Italian Antonio BONFINI (who wrote an important history of Hungary, the *Rerum Hungaricarum decades IV*, Basel, 1568), and the Hungarian SAMBUCUS, who wrote a continuation of Bonfini's history. In the Hungarian language, the most influential works were a series of translations of the Bible into Hungarian. The first great lyric poet of Hungary was Valentine Bálint Balassi (1554–95).

**HUNGARIAN MUSIC.** Musical education during the Middle Ages was centred on the cathedral and monastic schools where the syllabus covered theory and notation and was based on Gregorian chant. Several town churches had organs and there is evidence of regional pipers, bagpipe players, and violinists. Singing in the vernacular existed as congregational singing in church and in the tradition of epic singing which had been augmented by the introduction of themes from the Christian tradition, mythology, and Hungarian history.

A court chapel existed from the establishment of the royal court at Buda, and during the fifteenth century its musicians were French and German as well as native Hungarians; they performed Netherlandish, Burgundian, German, and Italian polyphony. The high standard of musical literacy deteriorated during the late sixteenth century, when much of the country became subject to the Ottomans. Even in the fragment of Hungary retained by the Habsburgs, Protestantism spread at the expense of Catholic polyphony.

**HUNGARY or (Hungarian) Magyarország.** From 1001 until 1301 Hungary was ruled by the 23 kings of the Árpád dynasty. When Andrew III, the last Árpád king, died without an heir in 1301, Hungary became an elective monarchy; this system gave considerable power to the Hungarian nobility, but for the next 300 years Hungary was ruled by a series of foreign monarchs. From 1307 to 1395 Hungary was ruled by an Angevin dynasty; in 1385 the last member of the dynasty, Queen Maria, married SIGISMUND of Luxemburg, who was crowned as king of Hungary in 1387 and for the next nine years sought to secure his kingdom against the rival claim of King Ladislas of Naples, son of Charles II of Hungary; Sigismund subsequently became king of the Romans (1410), king of Bohemia (1419) and Holy Roman Emperor (1433), so creating links with Bohemia (which included MORAVIA and SILESIA) and the Empire that were to last for centuries.

In 1438 Sigismund was succeeded by Albrecht V of Austria, who had married his daughter Elizabeth. After Albrecht's death in 1439, the throne passed to 15-year-old King VLADISLAV III of Poland, who was crowned as King Vladislas I of Hungary. After his premature death at the battle of Varna, the duchy of Austria and the kingdoms of Bohemia and Hungary passed to Sigismund's posthumous infant son LADISLAS V POSTHUMUS, and thenceforth the history of Hungary became intertwined with Austria as well as Bohemia and the Empire. During this period Hungary and its territories became the centre of European resistance to the Ottoman advance; the principal figure in the defence of Europe was János HUNYADI, whose son MATTHIAS CORVINUS became the next king of Hungary. Matthias left no legitimate heir, and on his death in 1490 was succeeded as king of Hungary by LADISLAS II, king of Bohemia (and the son of King CASIMIR IV of Poland). On the death of Ladislas in 1516 the thrones of Hungary and Bohemia passed to his 10-year-old son King LOUIS II, who was to be killed ten years later at the battle of MOHÁCS.

In 1519 the Emperor MAXIMILIAN had resigned his claim to his Austrian possessions (including Carniola, Carinthia, Styria, and Tirol) and the thrones of Hungary (including Slovakia, which had been Hungarian territory since 1308) and Bohemia (including Moravia and Silesia) to his brother Ferdinand (later the Emperor FERDINAND I), who was elected as king of Hungary in 1526. In 1558 Ferdinand consolidated his realms under his personal rule and so created the huge central European empire that was to survive until 1918.

In 1541 Buda fell to the Ottomans, and thereafter Hungary was divided: a narrow strip in the north-west was ruled by the Habsburgs (who paid tribute to the sultans), central Hungary was an Ottoman province, and TRANSYLVANIA was an Ottoman protectorate.

Hungary's most important patron of the arts was Matthias Corvinus, who extended his patronage to many Italian artists (including BENEDETTO DA MAIANO, ERCOLE DE' ROBERTI, MANTEGNA, and VERROCHIO), assembled a magnificent library, and commissioned many works of architecture and architectural decoration, including the friezes in Buda Castle (now in the Castle Museum) and the well in the royal palace in Višegrad. The most important product of private architecture patronage to have been executed in the Italian Renaissance style is the red marble Bakócz Chapel (*c*.1506, now in the nineteenth-century Esztergom Cathedral). See also HUNGARIAN GARDENS; HUNGARIAN LANGUAGE AND LITERATURE; HUNGARIAN MUSIC.

**HUNT, THOMAS** (*fl. c*.1600), English composer and organist who sang at Canterbury Cathedral as a boy and received a Mus. B. from Cambridge in 1601. A madrigal 'Hark! Did you ever hear so sweet a singing' and a four-part service survive.

**HUNYADI, JÁNOS** (*c*.1387–1456), Transylvanian soldier and regent, born into a noble Transylvanian family. He fought in the army of King SIGISMUND in the HUSSITE WARS and in 1441 was appointed *voivode* of Transylvania by King VLADISLAV III, a post that included the governorship of the fortress of Belgrade and the responsibility for the defence of the Balkans against the Ottomans. In 1443 he defeated Sultan Murat II in a series of engagements, and forced Murat to sign a ten-year truce. The following year Hunyadi chose to violate the treaty himself and committed his army to the battle of Varna, in which King Vladislav was killed. In 1446 Hunyadi was appointed regent of Hungary on behalf of the youthful LADISLAS POSTHUMUS, who was in Prague. When Ladislas returned to Hungary in 1453, Hunyadi became his captain-general. In 1455 Hunyadi again defended Belgrade from an Ottoman attack, but died of plague a few months later. Hunyadi's son MATTHIAS CORVINUS later became king of Hungary.

MEL.

**HURTADO DE MENDOZA, DIEGO DE** (1503–75), Spanish humanist, soldier, historian, poet, and diplomat. He was born into a noble family in Granada, and studied in Granada and Salamanca, where he studied Hebrew and Arabic as well as Latin and Greek; he subsequently fought in the battle of PAVIA (1525) and the battle of TUNIS (1535). The Emperor CHARLES V sent Mendoza on a marital embassy to HENRY VIII of England, but he failed to negotiate either of the marriages that Charles envisaged (Henry VIII with Charles's niece, the duchess of Milan, and the future MARY I with Don Luis of Portugal). From 1539 to 1547 Mendoza lived in Venice as the ambassador of Charles V, and there patronized the press of ALDUS MANUTIUS and commissioned searches for Greek manuscripts in Ottoman Greece; three of his manuscripts formed the basis of the *editio princeps* of Josephus in 1544.

In 1547 Mendoza was sent to Rome to deliver an imperial rebuke to Pope JULIUS III, an act that marked the high point of his authority. Shortly thereafter he was accused of financial improprieties in Siena; the case dragged on for years, and he was finally declared to be innocent in 1578, three years after his death. He was recalled to Spain in 1554, and in 1568 was banished from the court by King PHILIP II after a court feud. Mendoza withdrew to Medina del Campo and then to his native Granada, where he participated in the suppression of the MORISCO rebellion of 1568–71.

Mendoza's most important historical work is *La guerra de Granada*, an account of the *morisco* rising (published in part in 1610 and in whole in 1730) which is distinguished in its style as well as important in its content. Mendoza was also a talented poet; he composed Petrarchan sonnets, a *Fábula de Adonis, Hipómenes y Atalanta* (written in *octavas reales*), and a large corpus of satirical or humorously indecent poems, such as the *Fábula de cangrejo*. He translated Aristotle's *Mechanica* into Spanish, and may have been the author of the Lucianic satire on the assassination in 1547 of Pietro Luigi FARNESE,

duke of Piacenza and Parma, the *Diálogo entre Caronte y el ánima de Pedro Luis Farnesio, hijo del Papa Paulo III*, which contains a fine dialogue between Charon and the assassinated duke on the subject of clerical abuses and the COUNCIL OF TRENT. Because of his elegant style and pungent wit Mendoza was long thought to have been the author of *LAZARILLO DE TORMES*, the finest Spanish novel of the age. Though this honour is now denied to him, he was nonetheless the finest and most typical example of a 'Renaissance man' ever produced by Spain, and as a poet he is not significantly inferior to his relative GARCILASO DE LA VEGA.

*DHE*; A. González Palencia and E. Mele, *Vida y obra de don Diego Hurtado de Mendoza* (3 vols., 1941–3); Anthony Hobson, *Renaissance Book Collecting: Jean Grolier and Diego Hurtado de Mendoza, their Books and Bindings* (1999).

**HUS or Huss, JAN** (*c*.1372–1415), Bohemian reformer, born into a peasant family in the market village of Husinec (near the Bavarian border), of which his surname is an abbreviation, and educated at University of Prague, where he took degrees in theology (1394) and arts (1393 and 1396). After graduating he remained at the university; he was appointed dean of the faculty of philosophy in October 1401 and served as rector from October 1402 to April 1403. He had been ordained as a priest in 1400, and two years later became rector (*capellarius*) of the Bethlehem Chapel in Prague, where he preached in Czech.

The marriage (1382) of Anne, sister of King Wenceslas IV of Bohemia, to King Richard II of England forged a cultural conduit through which flowed the writings of John WYCLIFFE, and Hus became a Wycliffite sympathizer, particularly in his advocacy of Wycliffe's radical political doctrines (the rejection of private property and of the hierarchical organization of society), which resembled the Czech radical tradition represented by JEROME OF PRAGUE, but also in his adoption of Wycliffe's theological doctrines of GRACE (predestination and the idea of a church consisting of the elect).

In 1383 a fire in the church of Wilsnack (near Wittenberg) left three consecrated hosts unharmed but flecked with blood, and the village became an important pilgrimage centre; Hus's first publication, *De omni sanguine Christi glorificatio* (1404), denounced the miracle as a fraud. Hus was himself subjected to a series of denunciations: a university disputation held on 28 May 1403 condemned the doctrines of Wycliffe, and on 20 May 1408 the university formally condemned 45 Wycliffite propositions. Hus defiantly translated Wycliffe's *Trialogus* into Czech and began to attack the immorality of the clergy in his sermons; when Archbishop Sbinko of Prague forbade him to preach, Hus responded with an attack on the suppression of clergy (*De arguendo clero pro concione*).

In 1409 the COUNCIL OF PISA elected Alexander V as pope, and so exacerbated the GREAT SCHISM by establishing another rival to GREGORY XII and BENEDICT XIII. King Wenceslas IV supported Alexander, as did Hus and the Czech 'nation' at the university; Sbinko and the other three 'nations' (Saxons, Bavarians, and Poles) supported Gregory. By a royal decree of 18 January 1409 control of the university had been awarded to the Czech 'nation' (which led to the withdrawal of thousands of foreigners and the subsequent establishment of the University of Leipzig), and in October Hus became rector. Sbinko was isolated, and so transferred his allegiance to Pope Alexander in return for the promulgation of a bull (20 December 1409) commanding that Wycliffe's doctrines be abjured and his books be burnt. The bull was published in Prague on 9 March 1410; Hus appealed to the new pope (JOHN XXIII) in vain, and in July Sbinko burnt more than 200 Wycliffite books in the courtyard of his palace. In February 1411 Pope John excommunicated Hus, and the next year placed his followers under an interdiction and pronounced the greater excommunication on Hus (the lesser deprived the censured of access to the sacraments and to ecclesiastical office, and the greater added an interdiction against all contact with members of the Church).

King Wenceslas expelled Hus from Prague, and in his exile in the homes of various noblemen Hus wrote his most important work, *De ecclesia* (1413), the first ten chapters of which are adapted from Wycliffe. In 1414 he travelled to the COUNCIL OF CONSTANCE to pursue his appeal against the judgement of the papal curia, travelling with a safe-conduct pass issued by the Emperor SIGISMUND. He arrived on 3 November 1414 and was soon imprisoned. The emperor endeavoured in vain to secure Hus's release, and on 6 July 1415 he was burnt at the stake. The news of his death ignited the HUSSITE WARS.

BLBL s.v. Hus, Johannes; M. Spinka, *John Hus and the Czech Reform* (1941); id., *John Hus' Concept of the Church* (1966); id., *John Hus: A Biography* (1968).

**HUSSITE WARS** (1420–36). Jan HUS was burnt at the stake in Constance on 6 July 1415, and when news of the execution reached Prague, his followers (who were called 'Hussites' or 'Wycliffites') denounced the city authorities, the emperor, and the papacy in a protest (the *protestatio Bohemorum*) sent to the COUNCIL OF CONSTANCE on 2 September 1415. The Hussites began to expel priests loyal to Rome from their Bohemian parishes, and SIGISMUND, king of the Romans, threatened to 'drown all Wycliffites and Hussites'.

King WENCESLAS IV, Sigismund's brother, attempted to suppress the rebellion, but to no avail. The First DEFENESTRATION OF PRAGUE (30 July 1419) and the death of Wenceslas (16 August 1419) exacerbated the tensions, and in November 1419 there was fighting between the Hussites and the mercenaries of Queen Sophia (widow of Wenceslas and regent of Bohemia). War was formally declared on 17 March 1420, when Pope MARTIN V issued a bull proclaiming a CRUSADE to 'destroy all Wycliffites, Hussites, and other heretics in Bohemia'. The crusaders, led by Sigismund, invaded Bohemia and marched on Prague, which they besieged (30 June–14 July 1420). The Hussites set out their demands in a document known as the Articles of Prague, and Sigismund, under pressure from the papal legates, rejected the demands. Sigismund garrisoned the castles of Vyšehrad and Hradčany and then withdrew from the city. The citizens of Prague

promptly besieged the Vyšehrad, and at the end of October, by which time the garrison was facing starvation, Sigismund returned to lift the siege. On 1 November his forces were defeated by the Hussites at the nearby village of Pankrác, whereupon the garrisons in both castles capitulated and Bohemia fell into the hands of the Hussites.

The following year a new invasion was mounted, and in August 1421 imperial troops besieged Žatec (German Saaz); Sigismund arrived from Hungary at the end of the year and captured Kutná Hora (German Kuttenberg), but on 6 January 1422 was defeated by Jan ŽIŽKA's forces at Německy Brod (German Deutschbrod).

The next stage of the conflict was civil war between the TABORITES and the UTRAQUISTS. This conflict culminated in the battle of Horic (27 April 1423) in which a Taborite army led by Žižka defeated the Utraquist forces of Čeněk of Vartenberk (Czech Stráž); shortly thereafter a peace treaty was signed at Konopišt. The Hussites then invaded Moravia, where most of the population sympathized with the Hussite rebellion, but soon withdrew because of internal dissension. The Utraquist city of Králové Hradec (German Königgrätz) defected to the Taborite cause and called Žižka to their aid. The military conflicts that followed in 1423 and 1424 were finally resolved in a peace treaty between the warring Hussite factions signed on 13 September 1424 at the village of Lilen (now a district of Prague).

In 1426 imperial forces again invaded, and were defeated at Ustí nad Labem (German Aussig); the following year an imperial army led by the English cardinal Henry Beaufort was defeated at Tachov (German Tachow). Thereafter the Hussites repeatedly invaded Germany, but made no attempt to secure territorial gains.

Peace negotiations were scheduled to take place at the COUNCIL OF BASEL, which convened on 3 March 1431, but the Catholic Church decided to pre-empt the negotiations by subduing the Hussites by force. On 1 August 1431 an army led by Friedrich, margrave of Brandenburg, and accompanied by Cardinal Giuliano CESARINI, the papal legate, invaded Bohemia. On 14 August the army reached Domažlice (German Taus), but retreated in the face of an advancing Hussite army.

On 15 October the delegates of the Council of Basel formally invited the Hussites to participate in its deliberations. The Hussite delegation arrived in Basel on 4 January 1433, but negotiations failed. The following year civil war again erupted in Bohemia, and on 30 May 1434 the Taborites were decisively defeated at the battle of Lipany (7 kilometres (4 miles) south-east of Český Brod (German Böhmisch Brod)). The victorious Utraquists formulated a peace proposal with the Church of Rome known as the Compactata of Prague. The four compacts, which included communion in both kinds for Bohemia and Moravia, were signed on 5 July 1436 at Jihlava (German Iglau), in Moravia, by the Hussites and by Sigismund, whom the Hussites thereby acknowledged as their king.

The Compactata were eventually repealed in 1567, but the Czech national church established by the Hussite Wars remained independent until Catholicism was imposed after the battle of the White Mountain in 1620.

H. Kaminsky, *A History of the Hussite Revolution* (1967); F. M. Bartoš, *The Hussite Revolution, 1424–1437* (1986); Thomas A. Fudge, *The Magnificent Ride: The First Reformation in Hussite Bohemia* (1998).

**HUT, HANS** (c.1490–1527), German ANABAPTIST preacher, a bookbinder and distiller from the borders of Franconia and Thuringia who deployed his eloquence in the service of a series of radical Anabaptist communities. After four years as a sexton in Bibra, which he left because he refused to have his child baptized, he fought alongside Thomas MÜNTZER in the PEASANTS' WAR and later joined Hans DENCK in Augsburg. He subsequently moved to HUBMAIER's Anabaptist community in Nikolsburg (now Mikulow), in Moravia. On a visit to Augsburg he was arrested; he died while in prison on 6 December 1527, either by setting himself alight or by suffocation from smoke.

*NDB.*

**HUTTEN, ULRICH VON** (1488–1523), German humanist and satirist, born on 21 April 1488 in the castle at Stechelberg (near Fulda, in Hesse), the eldest son of an impoverished noble family. He was sent by his father to the Benedictine monastery in Fulda, but his thirst for learning and his distaste for monastic routine drove him in 1505 to flee his monastery in search of an education. For the next ten years Ulrich wandered from university to university, first to Cologne and Erfurt, and in 1506 to the new university at Frankfurt an der Oder; thereafter he moved to Leipzig, but by 1508 he had become a shipwrecked beggar on the coast of Pomerania. In 1509 he joined the University of Greifswald, but he offended his patrons and was forced to leave, and as he did so was robbed of his clothes and books. In the midst of a cold German winter he arrived destitute in Rostock and was taken in by the HUMANIST community, but he imprudently directed satires against his protectors and moved on to Wittenberg, then back to Leipzig and on to Vienna, where he sought the patronage of the Emperor MAXIMILIAN with a nationalistic poem on the war with Venice. His overtures were rebuffed and Ulrich travelled on to Pavia, where he lived (1511–12) until forced to flee the siege of Pavia; he was robbed as he left, and arrived destitute in Bologna, where he became a private soldier in the imperial army.

In 1514 Ulrich returned to Germany, secured the patronage of the Archbishop-Elector ALBRECHT II OF MAINZ, and devoted himself to scholarship and poetry. The following year his life was permanently changed by the murder of his kinsman Hans von Hutten by ULRICH, duke of Württemberg. He carried on with his humanist endeavours, which culminated in his substantial contribution to part II of EPISTOLAE OBSCURORUM VIRORUM (1517), in which he sided with REUCHLIN against the Dominicans of Cologne, and in 1517 was crowned POET LAUREATE by Maximilian, but became obsessed with the perfidy of Duke Ulrich, against whom he directed a stream of vituperative satires, scathing public letters, Ciceronian orations, and a Latin dialogue (*Phalarismus*, 1516) which began with a

denunciation of Duke Ulrich and developed into a generalized attack on princely tyrants.

In 1519 Ulrich collected his attacks on Duke Ulrich in a single volume, and in the same year fought with the SWABIAN LEAGUE in the war that dislodged Duke Ulrich. This conflict brought Ulrich into contact with Franz von SICKINGEN, and the two men exerted a strong influence on each other: Ulrich had recently become a Lutheran, and eventually persuaded Franz to fight for the Protestant cause; the fact that Franz persuaded Ulrich to join his campaign to assert the right of the knights of the Empire (*Ritterstand*) against the German princes may imply that his hatred of princes was stronger than his devotion to the Lutheran cause. In 1520, however, he turned against the papacy in his Latin dialogue *Vadiscus*, partly with an eye to attracting the sympathetic attention of CHARLES V; Pope LEO X ordered that Ulrich be arrested, Albrecht expelled him from his court, and Charles V declined to give him refuge, so Ulrich turned once again to Franz von Sickingen. When Franz was killed, Ulrich fled to Basel, where he was rebuffed by ERASMUS, who feared both contagion and beggary. Ulrich turned his pen against Erasmus, who replied in kind and drove Ulrich out of his temporary refuge in Mühlhausen (French Mulhouse). Ulrich travelled to Zürich, where he was welcomed by ZWINGLI, who arranged for him to live with the pastor of Ufnau, a small island on Lake Zürich. There he died late in August or early in September 1523, aged 35, of the SYPHILIS that he had contracted several years earlier and on which he had written a treatise, the *De morbo Gallico*, in 1519.

Hutten's life may have been reckless and ill managed, but his prodigious talent made him Germany's greatest neo-Latin writer and, when he translated his Lucianic dialogues into vigorous German (*Gesprächsbüchlein*, 1521), he set a standard for German satire that has seldom been matched. In both languages he was a central figure in the development of the Renaissance DIALOGUE.

*NDB*; H. Holborn, *Ulrich von Hutten and the German Reformation* (1937).

**HUTTER, JAKOB** (d. 1536), German ANABAPTIST leader, born in Moos (Tirol); he joined the Swiss Anabaptists and became a prominent figure amongst the Anabaptists of the Tirol. Persecution led him to take his followers to Moravia, where from 1533 to 1535 he organized agricultural collectives in which property was owned communally; in common with several other Anabaptist groups, the Hutterites were pacifists. In 1536 Hutter was arrested and burnt at the stake in Innsbruck and his followers were dispersed. Some eventually settled in Russia, and in the nineteenth century many of their descendants emigrated to the United States and Canada, where they are known as Hutterites or Hutterite Brethren.

H. Fischer, *Jakob Hutter* (1956); J. W. Bennett, *Hutterian Brethren* (1967).

**HYMNS** were, in ancient Greece, poems in honour of a god. By the fifteenth century polyphonic settings of Latin hymns were in regular use; most being set to a chant melody with alternating verses being sung polyphonically. After 1500, different polyphonic settings for alternate verses were based on the same *cantus firmus*. Composers who wrote hymns include DUNSTABLE, DUFAY, WILLAERT, VICTORIA, PALESTRINA, and LASSUS. Germany, having had a tradition of vernacular hymn singing since the fourteenth century, was fertile ground for the growth of the Protestant hymn, assisted by the advent of printing. The first Protestant hymn book was Michael Weisse's *Ein new Gesengbuchlen* (1531), which translated Czech hymns published by the UNITY OF THE BROTHERS in 1501. LUTHER recognized the potential of metrical religious lyrics to popularize his reforming beliefs. The hymns and chorales that he wrote himself include 'Ein' feste Burg ist unser Gott' (a mighty fortress is our God), the tune of which he adapted from a plainsong melody. Calvinist churches would only allow Biblical words to be set to music, so Lutheran hymns were eschewed in favour of metrical psalters.

***HYPNEROTOMACHIA POLIFILI***. See COLONNA, FRANCESCO.

# I

**IBN ḤASAN IBN AL-HAYTHAM**. See ḤASAN IBN ḤASAN IBN AL-HAYTHAM.

**IGNATIUS LOYOLA or (Spanish) Ignacio de Loyola** (1491–1556), Spanish founder of the Jesuits, born into a noble Basque family in the castle at Loyola, near Azcoitia (Guipúzcoa). As a young man he worked as a soldier. In the French invasion of 1521 Loyola fought in defence of Pamplona, and suffered a leg wound that resulted in a permanent limp. During his protracted convalescence he read devotional works, and the following year, while living in a cave near the abbey of Montserrat (Catalonia), wrote the *Exercitia spiritualia* (Rome, 1548), which was to become a seminal work in sixteenth- and seventeenth-century religious thought.

The purpose of the spiritual exercises is to suppress worldly desires and purify the mind in readiness for devotion. After focusing on the subject of the meditation, which may be represented visually in a painting or statue, the supplicant intensifies the spiritual state by recourse to the three powers of the soul (memory, understanding, and will); the exercise then culminates in a prayer. The Ignatian exercises are enacted in much of the devotional literature of the next century, notably the sonnet *A Cristo crucificado*, which is probably the work of Fray Miguel de Guevara (*c*.1585–1640).

In 1523 Ignatius made a pilgrimage to Palestine, and on returning to Spain studied Latin at Barcelona (1526) and then theology at Alcalá de Henares, where he assembled a group of like-minded students committed to principled poverty. The INQUISITION mistrusted asceticism, especially if tinged with mysticism, so Ignacio was arrested and imprisoned; he was released on condition that he forbear to discuss religion in public or in private. Ignacio moved to Salamanca in order to preach, but was again jailed.

In 1528 Ignatius moved to Paris, where he graduated from the university in 1534. In the same year (15 August) he took vows of poverty and chastity with a group of six friends who included Nicolás BOBADILLA, Diego LAÍNEZ, Alfonso Salmerón, and Francis XAVIER. The seven students met again in 1537 in Venice, where they were ordained as priests. Unable to proceed to Palestine because of the outbreak of hostilities between Venice and the Ottomans, they went to Rome, determined to start a new religious ORDER. In 1540 the statutes of the JESUIT Order were approved by Pope PAUL III, and the next year Ignatius was elected head of the nascent Order. He remained in Rome for the rest of his life, directing the Society that he had founded, compiling its constitution and rules, and founding its Roman and German colleges.

Ignatius died suddenly on 31 July 1556, by which time more than 1,000 Jesuits were working in nine European provinces and in foreign missions. He was beatified in 1556 and canonized in 1622. His birthplace was converted into a sanctuary at the end of the seventeenth century, and is now the Santuario de San Ignacio de Loyola, where large crowds converge annually on 31 July, his feast day.

*DHE*; H. Rahner, *Ignatius von Loyola als Mensch und Theologe* (1964); Philip Caraman, *Ignatius Loyola* (1990).

**IHS**, a monogram derived from the uncial form of the Greek name of Jesus—ΙΗΣΟΥΣ—in which the Greek *eta* was mistaken for a Latin *aitch* and the abbreviation was incorrectly expanded to 'Ihesus'. In the fifteenth century Franciscan devotees of the 'Holy Name of Jesus', notably San BERNARDINO OF SIENA and Giovanni CAPISTRANO, encouraged the use of the monogram (often surrounded by rays) as an object of veneration. The letters were sometimes interpreted as *Iesus Hominum Salvator* (Jesus the Saviour of Mankind) or *In Hoc Signo [Vinces]* (in this sign [you will conquer]), and JESUITS sometimes interpreted it as *Iesum Habemus Socium* (we have Jesus as our companion).

**ILLUMINATED MANUSCRIPTS**. The term 'illuminate' in the context of medieval manuscripts does not have its modern sense of lighting up an object, but rather has a specialized meaning, denoting the embellishment of a manuscript with gold, silver, and luminous colours or with elaborate tracery and miniature pictures which are sometimes illustrative; this embellishment may be restricted to initial letters and words or may extend to borders or entire pages. The word 'miniature' is also used in a specialized sense distinct from the usual sense of a portrait MINIATURE: in manuscript illumination, the minium was the red lead colouring used by the miniator to decorate initial letters; medieval Latin *miniatura* did not refer to size, but rather derived from the verb *miniare*, to rubricate or illuminate. The decoration sometimes took the form of a small picture in an initial letter; such letters are called 'historiated initials'.

The manuscripts chosen for embellishment during the thousand-year period (c.500–c.1500) in which illuminated manuscripts were produced varied over the centuries, and by the fourteenth and fifteenth centuries the older taste for illuminated Gospels (from late antiquity to the eleventh century) and psalters (from the eleventh to the thirteenth centuries) had been supplanted by illuminated BOOKS OF HOURS, famously the early fifteenth-century *Très Riches Heures* in part illuminated by the LIMBOURG brothers for Jean, duc de Berry, and now in the Musée Condé in Chantilly. Later in the fifteenth century, the most important illuminators were Sanders BENING and Jean FOUQUET.

The advent of print rendered illuminated manuscripts an anachronism. There are instances of illuminations being added to printed books, and in the early sixteenth century a few very fine illuminated manuscripts were made, notably Simon BENING's Grimani Breviary (now in the Marciana in Venice) and the Hours of Anne of Brittany (now in the Bibliothèque Nationale in Paris).

**IMPRESA** (Italian plural *imprese*), an emblem or device consisting of a picture accompanied by a motto. The impresa was distinguished from other emblems by virtue of the fact that it was regulated by ACADEMIES. The idea of the impresa was originally French, and was transmitted to Italy through the French occupation of Milan early in the sixteenth century. Thereafter Italian humanist courtiers commissioned MEDALS bearing a portrait on one side and an impresa on the obverse. Paolo GIOVIO set out five rules for the impresa in his *Dialogo dell'imprese militari et amorose* (1555): it must be properly proportioned, strike a middle course between obscurity and transparency, be attractive to the eye, eschew the human figure, and be accompanied by a motto in a language different from that of the formulator of the device.

**IMPUTATION**. In the Lutheran doctrine of JUSTIFICATION, the righteousness of Christ is said to be imputed or accounted to the believer, despite being extrinsic to the person of the believer; the imputation of the extrinsic righteousness of Christ is said to be followed immediately by the advent of personal righteousness. The Catholic view, as articulated at the COUNCIL OF TRENT, is that justification is effected by an imparted or infused righteousness which is intrinsic to the person of the believer. A third position was maintained by Andreas OSIANDER, who insisted that the righteousness of Christ was substantially transferred rather than merely imputed to the believer.

**INCUNABULA**, the Latin term (literally 'swaddling clothes') for books printed before 1500, in the 'infancy' of printing; the singular form is incunabulum. In English the terms 'incunable' and 'incunables' are sometimes used as alternatives to the Latin forms.

**INDEPENDENTS**, an alternative term for congregationalists or BROWNISTS, who upheld the separate or independent nature of each congregation.

**INDEX LIBRORUM PROHIBITORUM** ('List of Forbidden Books'). Universities began to proscribe books in the 1540s, but the first official *Index* was issued in the name of Pope PAUL IV by the Congregation of the Roman INQUISITION in 1557; the first revised edition appeared in January 1559. In 1571 Pope PIUS V established the Congregation of the Index to be in charge of maintenance and revision of the list; the secretary of the Congregation (which was reorganized in 1588) was always a Dominican. The list proscribed all the works of some authors, but in other cases banned specific books by authors who could otherwise be read by Catholics. The penalty for reading books on the list was excommunication. The Congregation of the Index administered the list until 1917, when its duties were transferred to the Holy Office. The *Index* was abolished in 1966.

In Spain and its territories the censorship of books was placed in the hands of the state by FERDINAND and ISABELLA in 1502. In 1521 the Spanish INQUISITION, which was an instrument of the state, assumed responsibility for detecting and prohibiting books containing the LUTHERAN heresy. In 1546 an Index of Prohibited Books was drawn up by scholars at the University of Louvain, and the next year it received official sanction in Spain; updated lists were produced from 1551 onwards. The Inquisition's book police, the *revisores de libros*, could confiscate books from any shop or library; in 1558 the penalty for possession of banned books became death and the confiscation of property. The censorship of books was eventually abolished in 1812.

**INDIA**. European contact with India began with the overland journeys of Venetian travellers such as MARCO POLO and Niccolò de' CONTI, but permanent links were first established by the Portuguese, who established a sea route to the western coast of the Indian subcontinent. Naval communication with India was inaugurated with the landing of Vasco da GAMA near Calicut on 17 May 1498. In the course of the next ten years Portuguese merchants established *FEITORIAS* on the Malabar coast (now Kerala). In 1503 Afonso de ALBUQUERQUE embarked on the first of his naval expeditions to India, and in March 1505 Francisco de ALMEIDA was appointed as the first viceroy of India by King MANUEL I of Portugal. He established his viceregal residence in Cochin, where Albuquerque had built a fort. On 2 February 1509 Almeida defeated the navy of the sultan of Egypt at the battle of Diu (Gujarat) and so secured Portuguese supremacy in the Indian Ocean and control of the Indian spice trade.

In 1510 Albuquerque acquired Goa for Portugal. Goa became the headquarters of the Portuguese Estado da Índia, and remained a Portuguese possession until 1961, when India annexed Goa and Diu. Goa was also the regional centre of Portuguese Christianity: Francis XAVIER arrived in 1542, and fifteen years later Goa became a diocese. Surviving ecclesiastical buildings in Goa include examples of MANUELINE architecture (notably Church of the Rosário, 1543) and of Portuguese Renaissance architecture (cathedral 1562–1631; Bom Jesus 1594). In the early seventeenth century, the most important European Christian missionary in India was the

Jesuit Roberto de Nobili (1577–1656), who worked there from 1606 to 1643 and, with the reluctant approval of the Vatican (given in 1623), adapted his presentation of Christianity to the caste system of southern India.

The first Dutch fleet arrived in India in 1595 and the first English fleet in 1601. Both countries established a commercial presence in India, and within twenty years had dismantled the Portuguese monopoly. Eventually eight European EAST INDIA COMPANIES were formed (by Austria, Denmark, England, France, the Netherlands, Scotland, Spain, Sweden), all of which traded with India. The English company eventually emerged as the dominant European power in India, which it administered until the government was handed over to Britain in 1858.

R. S. Whiteway, *The Rise of Portuguese Power in India, 1497–1550* (1952).

**INDIES, COUNCIL OF THE, or (Spanish) Consejo de las Indias**, the body created by CHARLES V in 1524 to govern the Spanish dominions in America. The Council initially consisted of six members and later expanded to ten. It was responsible for the preparation of successive versions of the LAWS OF THE INDIES and also acted as the highest court of the dominions. In 1571 the Council created the post of historian and cosmographer of the Indies.

DHE; E. Schäfer, *El consejo real y supremo de las Indias* (2 vols., 1935–47).

**INDIES, LAWS OF THE, or (Spanish) Leyes de los reinos de las Indias**. The Laws of the Indies is the compilation of SPANISH LAW used by Spain for the administration of its colonies. The first attempt to regulate the treatment of American Indians by Spaniards was the Laws of Burgos of 1512, a compilation of 32 laws, produced in response to clerical complaints about the ill treatment of Indians, that gave civic protection to Indians. This legislation was unsuccessful in curtailing atrocities, and it was replaced by the 54 New Laws of 1542, which abolished Indian slavery by restricting the ENCOMIENDA. Spanish colonists in Peru rebelled against the New Laws, which were reissued in amended form in 1552.

Codification of the Laws of the Indies began in 1524, and volumes were published in 1563, 1596, and 1628, but the great *Recopilación de las leyes de los reinos de las Indias* was not published until 1680. The code, which contains more than 6,000 laws, was primarily civil rather than mercantile in nature, and was unequivocal about the requirement that Indians be treated humanely. In most parts of South America the Laws were repudiated as countries became independent between 1808 and 1826, but the code survived until 1898 as the law of the island colonies of Cuba, Puerto Rico, and the Philippines.

**INDULGENCES** are remissions, awarded by the pope, of the temporal penalties for sins that have been forgiven. In 1095 Pope Urban II announced the first plenary indulgences, which would comprehensively remit all temporal punishment for the sins of any crusader who had confessed his sins. The question of whether plenary indulgences covered penances that should have been imposed as well as those that were actually imposed was debated by theologians for the next two centuries. With the inauguration of JUBILEE YEARS in 1300, confessors in Rome were authorized to issue plenary indulgences during these particular years; the promise of such indulgences ensured good attendances until 1500, but when they became available elsewhere, attendance fell in 1525.

The sale of indulgences was an excellent source of income for the servants of the medieval Church, and professional pardoners (such as Chaucer's Pardoner) sold indulgences all over Europe until forbidden to do so by Pope PIUS V in 1567. By that time, the sale of indulgences had ignited the Reformation in Germany: in 1516 Pope LEO X had issued an indulgence to finance the rebuilding of ST PETER'S BASILICA in Rome, and in Germany Archbishop ALBRECHT OF MAINZ charged Johann TETZEL with the responsibility for preaching the indulgence, the income from which was to be divided between the archbishop and the Vatican. The indulgence was forbidden in Saxony, but LUTHER travelled to nearby Jüterbog to hear Tetzel preach, and was so scandalized by Tetzel's assurances that cash payments would deliver donors from PURGATORY that he returned to Wittenberg and issued his 95 Theses. In the Swiss Confederation, the sale of indulgences (German *Ablasskram*) was denounced by Niklas MANUEL.

**INFESSURA, STEFANO** (*c*.1436–*c*.1500), Italian historian, born in Rome, where he worked in the service of the COLONNA family. His *Diario della città di Roma*, written in Italian with an admixture of Latin, narrates the history of Rome from 1303 to 1494.

**INGEGNERI, MARCANTONIO** (1535/6–92), Italian composer and instrumentalist who was a chorister at Verona Cathedral and in his teens a *suonadoro di violino* for Venetian processions. By 1566 he was in Cremona and later became *maestro di cappella* at the cathedral. He wrote both sacred and secular music including madrigals which reflect the tuition he had received from RORE. Amongst his own pupils was Claudio MONTEVERDI.

**INGLÉS, JORGE** (*fl.* 1455), Spanish painter, possibly of English origin, who was one of the earliest exponents of the Hispano-Flemish style of SPANISH ART. Contemporary documents associate him with only one work, the ALTARPIECE mentioned in the will of the marqués de SANTILLANA (1455), who had commissioned a series of panels to illustrate a poem that he had written in honour of the Virgin; the surviving panels are now in the private collection of the present marquis. Other works are attributed to Inglés on stylistic grounds, notably the altarpiece *St Jerome in his Study* (Museo Nacional de Escultura, Valladolid).

**INGLOTT, WILLIAM** (1554–1621), English composer and organist who sang at Norwich Cathedral and was organist there and at Hereford Cathedral. He wrote church music; some of his keyboard compositions are contained in the FITZWILLIAM VIRGINAL BOOK.

**INNOCENT VIII** (1432–92), pope from 29 August 1484 until his death on 25 July 1492, was born Giovanni Battista Cibò in Genoa in 1432, the son of a former Roman senator. He spent his profligate youth in the court of Naples and then studied in Padua and Rome. After taking holy orders he was appointed bishop of Savona in 1467, a post which he secured from Pope PAUL II through the influence of Cardinal Calandrini (half-brother of the late Pope NICHOLAS V). He became bishop of Molfetta (near Bari) in 1472 and was created a cardinal in 1473 by Pope SIXTUS V. He spent the evening before he was elected to the papacy endorsing the petitions for favours of cardinals whose votes were not yet committed to him.

Pope Innocent took no interest in church reform, but he had of necessity to attend to the dire state of the papal finances, which was worsened in 1485 by the refusal of King FERRANTE I of Naples to pass on clerical revenues. This financial disaster was the direct result of Innocent having accepted the advice of Giuliano della Rovere (later Pope JULIUS II) to side with rebellious Neapolitan noblemen against King Ferrante; in the event, Innocent was forced to accept a costly and disadvantageous peace in August 1486. The treaty broke down in 1489, and on 11 September Innocent deposed and excommunicated Ferrante and awarded his kingdom to CHARLES VIII of France; in the reconciliation agreed in January 1492 the PAPAL STATE lost L'Aquila.

Innocent was a brazenly corrupt pope. His preferred method of raising income was the creation and sale to the highest bidder of prestigious but unnecessary posts in the curia. His principal concern was the provision of princely marriages for the illegitimate children that he had fathered as a young man. He arranged for his son Franceschetto (to whom he gave several towns near Rome) to marry the daughter of Lorenzo de' MEDICI, whose 13-year-old son Giovanni (later Pope LEO X) he created a cardinal.

Innocent took little interest in theology, but nonetheless hated heresy. On 5 December 1484 he promulgated a bull authorizing the INQUISITION in Germany to punish WITCHES with the utmost severity; in 1486 he prohibited on pain of excommunication the reading of the propositions of PICO DELLA MIRANDOLA; in 1487 he appointed Tomás de TORQUEMADA as grand inquisitor in Spain, and in the same year issued a bull ordering that the WALDENSES be exterminated.

In 1486 Innocent formally declared King HENRY VII to be the lawful king of England by virtue of conquest, inheritance, and popular choice and sanctioned his marriage to Elizabeth of York. His other important decision in foreign policy was his conclusion of an agreement with Sultan Beyazit II, which was the first treaty between the papacy and the Ottoman Empire. Beyazit's brother (and rival) Jem had escaped to Rhodes, where the grand master of the Knights of St John had accepted a cardinalate from Innocent in exchange for his valuable prisoner. In 1489 Innocent agreed with Beyazit to detain Jem under guard in Rome in exchange for 40,000 ducats a year and the gift of the Holy Lance which pierced the side of Jesus at his crucifixion; the lance is now in ST PETER'S BASILICA. In 1492 news reached Rome of the expulsion of the Moors from GRANADA on 2 January; Rome was jubilant, and Innocent presided over the celebrations.

Rome and the Papal State were virtually ungoverned during Innocent's pontificate, and on his death the citizens of Rome rioted. Innocent is buried in St Peter's Basilica in a magnificent bronze tomb by Antonio POLLAIUOLO which contains the earliest sepulchral effigy to replicate the features of the living man.

**INNOCENT IX** (1519–91), pope from 29 October 1591 until his death two months later on 30 December, was born Giovanni Antonio Fachinetti on 20 July 1519 in Bologna, where his family had moved from Verona. He studied CANON LAW, and after securing his doctorate in 1544 moved to Rome, where he joined the staff of Cardinal Alessandro FARNESE, who sent him to Avignon as his representative and four years later transferred him to Parma. In 1560 Pope PIUS IV appointed him bishop of Nicastro (Calabria) and two years later he participated in the closing sessions of the COUNCIL OF TRENT. From 1566 to 1572 he served as papal nuncio in Venice (under Popes PIUS V and GREGORY XIII) and negotiated the formation of the coalition that defeated the Turks in the battle of LEPANTO in October 1571. In 1575 Fachinetti resigned his bishopric because of ill health and returned to Rome. Surprisingly, Pope Gregory appointed him to senior positions in the curia and the Inquisition and named him patriarch of Jerusalem (12 November 1576) and cardinal (12 December 1583).

Fachinetti was elected as a Spanish candidate, but his age and ill health made him an acceptable candidate for the anti-Spanish faction. He sustained the support accorded by his predecessor Pope GREGORY XIV to the campaign of PHILIP II and the CATHOLIC LEAGUE against HENRI IV (still a Protestant) and subsequently allocated 36,000 ducats to maintain the papal army which was attempting to raise the siege of Rouen. At home, he strengthened the ban instituted by Pope Pius V on the alienation of land within the PAPAL STATE and reorganized the Vatican secretariat into sections (one for France and Poland, a second for Italy and Spain, and a third for Germany). Beyond the Vatican, he took steps to suppress banditry in the vicinity of Rome, to regulate the course of the Tiber, and to improve sanitary conditions. On 18 December he fell ill, and his insistence on proceeding to the seven pilgrimage churches of Rome may have hastened his death a fortnight later. His scholarly writings, all of which remained unpublished, include a commentary on ARISTOTLE's *Politics*.

**IN NOMINE** (Latin; 'in the name') is the title of sixteenth- and seventeenth-century English instrumental music based on a *cantus firmus* from John Taverner's mass *Gloria tibi Trinitas*. Employed by many composers including William BYRD, Christopher TYE, Orlando GIBBONS, Thomas TALLIS, John BULL, and both FERRABOSCOS, it was deployed in both consort and keyboard music.

**INN SIGNS.** The English practice of erecting a sign in front of an inn is of great antiquity, and probably originated during the Roman occupation, when shops and businesses displayed pictorial signs for the benefit of customers who could not read. In early modern Europe inn signs could be found on the Continent, but legislation requiring signs was uncommon, and very few examples of non-English signs survive.

In the course of the fourteenth century English towns gradually imposed a requirement on alehouses and inns to display signs. Many signs displayed heraldic emblems of the reigning monarch, such as the Rising Sun (the emblem of Edward III), the White Hart (Richard II), the Swan (Henry VI), and the Red Lion (JAMES VI), and occasionally royal events are commemorated: the Rose and Crown, for example, marks the marriage of HENRY VII to Elizabeth of York. Inn signs often portrayed the arms of the landowner on whose property the inn stood (the Eagle and Child, for example, is part of the arms of the earls of Derby) or a local GUILD (e.g. the Weavers' Arms). A substantial number of inns displayed religious signs that reflect origins in pilgrim hostels, such as the Cross Keys (emblem of St Peter), the Star (the star of Bethlehem), the Anchor (in Hebrews 6: 19, hope is the anchor of the soul), the Ship (Noah's ark), the Seven Stars (the seven-starred crown of the Virgin Mary), and the Lamb and Flag (the Lamb of God and its banner). Signs were mounted on buildings or on posts, and large signs (called gallows signs or beam signs) hung across streets: surviving gallows signs include the Fox and Hounds in Barley (Herts.), the Green Man and Black's Head in Ashbourne (Derbys.), the Swan in Stroud (Glos.), and the Old Starre in York.

There is a substantial collection of inn signs at the Guildhall Museum in London. The Inn Sign Society, founded in 1990, amasses information on inn signs and publishes a quarterly journal, *At the Sign of*.

E. R. Delderfield, *Introduction to Inn Signs* (1969).

**INNS OF COURT AND CHANCERY**. Inns of Court are London legal societies originating in the thirteenth century. Scholars at Oxford and Cambridge studied CIVIL LAW, whereas the Inns of Court were the centre of COMMON LAW in England. The Inns offered legal training and accommodation for common lawyers, and so were populated by both apprentices-at-law and distinguished lawyers. In Tudor and Stuart times the Inns resembled the universities, in that they offered collegiate facilities which were taken up by young men, not all of whom had a vocation for the Church (in the case of the universities) or the law (in the case of the Inns). It was common for gentlemen to study for a few terms at one of the universities and then to move to one of the Inns of Court; others proceeded directly from grammar school to an Inn of Chancery and thence to an Inn of Court. Those intending to practise law remained in residence for about seven years. The Inns offered social facilities, including masques and 'revels'. Shakespeare's *Twelfth Night* was performed at a revel in the Middle Temple in February 1601; the hall in which the play was performed is one of the finest surviving Elizabethan buildings, and contains the only stage used by Shakespeare to have survived unaltered.

There were four Inns of Court, the Honourable Societies of Lincoln's Inn, the Inner Temple, the Middle Temple, and Gray's Inn, each of which had three grades of membership: benchers, barristers, and students. Meetings of benchers, who were senior members of the profession, were variously called parliaments (in the Inner and Middle Temples), pensions (in Gray's Inn), and councils (in Lincoln's Inn). There were ten Inns of Chancery, which were subordinate to the Inns of Court: Thavie's Inn and Furnival's Inn were attached to Lincoln's Inn; Clifford's Inn, Clement's Inn, and Lyon's Inn were attached to the Inner Temple; New Inn was attached to the Middle Temple; Staple Inn and Barnard's Inn were attached to Gray's Inn; the formal affiliations of Scrope's Inn and Chester (or Strand) Inn are not known. There were also two Serjeants' Inns, and when a barrister became a serjeant-at-law, joining the Order of the Coif, he forsook his own inn for either the Inn on Chancery Lane (founded 1416) or the one on Fleet Street (founded 1443). The only Inn of Court outside of London was King's Inns, which was established in Dublin in 1542, and is now the Inn of Court of the Republic of Ireland. The Inns of Chancery and the Serjeants' Inns were dissolved in the nineteenth century, but the four Inns of Court continue to provide legal training and chambers for practising barristers and judges.

J. H. Baker, *The Third University of England: The Inns of Court and the Common Law Tradition* (1990); Wilfred Prest, *The Inns of Court under Elizabeth I and the Early Stuarts, 1590–1640* (1972); D. S. Bland, *Three Revels from the Inns of Court* (1984); B. T. Duhigg, *History of the King's Inn* (1806).

**INQUISITION, PORTUGUESE, or (Portuguese) Inquisição Portuguesa**. In 1515 King MANUEL I of Portugal sought permission from Pope LEO X to institute a Portuguese Inquisition modelled on the Spanish INQUISITION, which had been active since 1480. Permission was refused, but in 1531 the request was renewed by JOHN III; Pope CLEMENT VII refused, but his successor, PAUL III, allowed the Inquisition to be established in 1536; it was extended to Goa in 1561. Unlike the Spanish Inquisition, which was under the direct control of the crown, the Portuguese Inquisition was an instrument of the papacy (which appointed the inquisitors-general nominated by the kings of Portugal) and of the nobility. After 1580, when Portugal was annexed by Spain, the Portuguese Inquisition was replaced by the Spanish Inquisition.

The Portuguese Inquisition was chiefly used for the persecution and prosecution of MARRANOS. The number of *marranos* grew after the forced conversion of all Portuguese Jews in 1497, but the introduction of the Inquisition into Portugal in 1536 caused the number of Portuguese *marranos* to fall, because thousands of families were assured that the Spanish Inquisition would not try them for crimes (i.e. practising Judaism) committed in Portugal, and so emigrated to Spain.

A. J. Saraiva, *A Inquisição Portuguesa* (1956); id., *Inquisição e Cristãos-Novos* (1969).

**INQUISITION, ROMAN or (Italian) Inquisizione Romana**. In 1542 Pope PAUL III established the HOLY OFFICE and the Inquisition to detect and prosecute heresy. The Holy Office is a Roman congregation, and so the Inquisition became known as the Roman Inquisition, a term which also distinguished it from the Spanish INQUISITION and the Portuguese INQUISITION, both of which were associated with the secular power. The designated leader of the Roman Inquisition was Cardinal Caraffa (later Pope PAUL IV). In theory the writ of the Roman Inquisition extended throughout France, Germany, and the Austrian lands of the Habsburgs. In practice, however, it was not a strong institution in northern Europe, and even within Italy, where its authority extended everywhere except Sicily (which was subject to the Spanish Inquisition), it depended on the goodwill of the secular rulers; in the case of Venice, the Inquisition was a restricted presence. The authority of the Roman Inquisition was unchallenged only in the Papal State, where Giordano BRUNO, the most famous victim of the Roman Inquisition, was burnt on 17 February 1600.

The Roman Inquisition was a success in that it eliminated Protestantism in Italy. It was also used to stifle the threats posed by the teachings of Copernicus (posthumously declared a heretic in 1616) and Galileo (declared a heretic and placed under house arrest in 1632).

P. F. Grendler, *The Roman Inquisition and the Venetian Press* (1977); R. Canosa, *Storia dell'Inquisizione in Italia dalla metà del Cinquecento alla fine del Settecento* (5 vols., 1986–90).

**INQUISITION, SPANISH, or (Spanish) Inquisición or Santo Oficio or (formally) Tribunal de la Santa Inquisición**. The papal Inquisition was an ecclesiastical tribunal charged with the detection and prosecution of heresy; in the Middle Ages it had never operated in Castile. In 1478, FERDINAND and ISABELLA, bowing to growing public anti-Semitism and the urging of Tomás de TORQUEMADA, secured permission from Pope SIXTUS IV to establish the Inquisition in Castile and its territories for the special purpose of combating heresy among recent converts to Christianity. Proceedings began in 1480, and in 1483 Torquemada was appointed inquisitor-general. In 1484, despite an appeal by *conversos* (see MARRANOS) to the papacy, the Inquisition was extended to Aragon and all of its territories except for Naples, which remained subject to the Roman INQUISITION; eventually the Spanish Inquisition was implemented in the Netherlands and in the Spanish colonies. From 1507 to 1517 the inquisitor-general was Cardinal CISNEROS.

In the early years of its operation, the Spanish Inquisition was exclusively concerned with the *marranos*, whose numbers had grown after a series of pogroms against the Jews during the fifteenth century. In some tribunals, the Inquisition began to prosecute crimes other than Judaizing heresy: in Aragon (but not in Castile) the tribunal tried sodomites, and in Navarre (though not elsewhere) the Inquisition tried WITCHES.

In the sixteenth and seventeenth centuries, Protestants and ALUMBRADOS joined *marranos* and *moriscos* as the principal victims of the Inquisition, which also assumed responsibility for the censorship of religious books. The Inquisitor-General Fernando de VALDÉS requested papal approval to burn all LUTHERANS, even if they wished to be reconciled, and in 1560 three foreign Protestants (two Englishmen and a Frenchman) were burnt. Both Valdés and Melchor CANO were sus-

picious of the Spanish mystical tradition: *cosas de alumbrados* were detected in the writings of Fray LUIS DEL GRANADA, the *Conceptos del amor divino* of TERESA DE ÁVILA was proscribed by the inquisitorial censors, and IGNATIUS LOYOLA was twice imprisoned by the Inquisition. Reputation may have saved these mystics from the flames of the Inquisition, but hundreds, perhaps thousands, of visionaries and *alumbrados* were burnt alive.

The procedures of the Spanish Inquisition allowed anonymity of witnesses and provided for TORTURE if there was a reasonable belief of guilt that required a confession to make the case incontrovertible. Despite an unusually conscientious concern for due process of law and precise records, trials were inexorable, inappellable, and unaccountable, and the consequences for the accused usually devastating, even if acquitted. Until the mid-sixteenth century substantial numbers of those accused were handed over to the secular authorities to be burnt, and public AUTOS-DA-FÉ further encouraged the view that the Inquisition was the instrument of a reign of terror.

H. C. Lea, *History of the Inquisition in Spain* (4 vols., 1922); H. A. F. Kamen, *The Spanish Inquisition: An Historical Revision* (2000).

**INTAGLIO** (Italian plural *intagli*), an engraved or incised GEM in which the design is sunk beneath the surface; the process, which can also be used with glass or shell or ceramics, is the reverse of CAMEO, which is carved in relief. Intaglio gems were sometimes used as seals, which were pressed onto wax to produce a likeness in relief.

**INTARSIA or tarsia**. In fifteenth-century Italy the generic term for inlay and marquetry was *tarsia*; the infinitive form was *intarsiare* and those who practised the craft were called *intarsiatori*. In the nineteenth century the term *tarsia* fell out of use and was replaced by the back formations *intarsio* and *intarsia*; modern Italian has settled on the masculine form, *intarsio*, while English has chosen the feminine form, *intarsia*.

The art of intarsia decoration was developed in the fourteenth century by Sienese craftsmen, initially for the backs of choir stalls; early examples include the work of Giovanni Ammannati (d. 1340) in Orvieto Cathedral and of Domenico de' Cori (c.1362–1450) in the chapel of the Palazzo Pubblico in Siena. In the fifteenth century the principal centre of pictorial intarsia was Florence, where *intarsiatori*, often trained in the studio of Francesco di Giovanni (1428–95; also called Francione), decorated furniture (including CASSONI) and wall panels with intarsia STILL LIFES, pictorial scenes, and architectural perspectives. A favourite motif was the TROMPE L'ŒIL partly opened cupboard door revealing a collection of books and instruments; one of the finest examples is in the *studiolo* of the Palazzo Ducale in Urbino (1479), which may be the work of the architect Baccio PONTELLI. The dual vocation of architect and *intarsiatoro* is also apparent in the work of BACCIO D'AGNOLO and GIULIANO DA MAIANO.

Intarsia was memorably used to decorate *studioli* in Gubbio (now in the Metropolitan Museum in New York) and Urbino, but its principal application in fifteenth- and

An intarsia panel in the *studiolo* (1479) of the Palazzo Ducale in Urbino

early sixteenth-century Italy was the decoration of choir-stall panels, notably those of Fra GIOVANNI DA VERONA in Monte Oliveto Maggiore near Siena, Domenico DEL TASSO in Perugia Cathedral, Agostino de Marchi (1458–90) in San Petronio in Bologna, and Francesco Zambello (d. 1549) in San Lorenzo in Genoa.

In the Veneto and Lombardy a kind of intarsia called *certosina* or *intarsia della certosina* (from an association with Carthusian monasteries) became a common feature of *cassoni* in the fifteenth century; it consisted of abstract geometrical patterns (derived from Arabic designs) and was made with polygonal tesserae of inlaid bone, ivory, wood, metal, or mother-of-pearl. In the early sixteenth century geometrical intarsia was introduced to Slovakia by Johannes MENSATOR.

Pictorial intarsia was introduced in south Germany by the carver Peter FLÖTNER and the painter Lorenz Stoer, who collaborated on *Geometria und Perspectiva* (1567), a collection of woodcut designs for intarsia panels. South German cabinet-makers (especially in Augsburg and Nuremberg) used intarsia panels for wall panels, doors, and furniture. The most common motif, that of the exterior of a real or fanciful building, spread from south Germany to the Netherlands and then to England, where intarsia panels (often illustrating buildings) were used in Elizabethan and Jacobean furniture, especially the fronts of chests and the headboards of beds.

In France, the group of 22 Italian craftsmen taken to France by CHARLES VIII after the capture of Naples in 1495 included two *intarsiatori*, Domenico da Corona and Bernardo da Brescia. Their work was immensely influential, and through their intarsia they introduced colour to French furniture.

E. Bruggemann, *Kunst und Technik des Intarsia* (1988).

**INTERLUDES.** A short dramatic sketch performed at court, in nobles' houses, or elsewhere in the fifteenth and sixteenth centuries, the interlude is a key transitional form between medieval morality plays and Elizabethan drama. The allegorical nature of the drama is weakened, though characters may still be broadly representative of a quality or trait, and there is a greater emphasis on comedy, dialogue, and plot. John HEYWOOD and RASTELL are noted authors. The name may refer to the performance of these short pieces in intervals between courses at banquets. The interlude was related to the Italian INTERMEZZO, the French *intermède* (or *entremet*) and the Spanish *entremez* (or *entremés*).

**INTERMEZZO or intermedio or (French) intermède**, a musical interlude between acts of a play. This tradition, which originated at the Ferrarese court in the late fifteenth century, evolved from being purely musical into a visual spectacle, which was one of the antecedents of opera. As it developed it grew into lavish court spectacles with specially designed costumes and elaborate stage sets. These were based on pastoral, mythological, and allegorical scenes and devised for particular occasions such as the wedding of Ferdinando de' Medici and Christine of Lorraine in 1589, when the music was written by Cristofano Malvezzi, MARENZIO, and CACCINI, among others. In France the *intermède* evolved into ballet, of which the first was the *Ballet comique de la reine* (1581).

**INTERNATIONAL GOTHIC**, an art-historical term coined in 1892 by Louis Courajod to denote a style prevalent between *c*.1375 and *c*.1425 in painting and related arts such as illuminations, mosaics, tapestries, enamels, and stained glass. The style, which is characterized by an elegant and sometimes sensuous curvilinear stylization in its representation of natural objects, emerged in the courts of Burgundy and France. In the late fourteenth century the most important centres of International Gothic were Mehun-sur-Yèvre (seat of the dukes of Berry), Bourges (the capital of Berry), Dijon (seat of the dukes of Burgundy), and Paris; beyond Burgundy and France, International Gothic found important exponents in northern Italy (GENTILE DA FABRIANO, PISANELLO, and STEFANO DA ZEVIO), Bohemia (in paintings such as the Trebon altarpiece in the National Gallery in Prague), the Rhineland (Master FRANCKE), and England (in paintings such as the Wilton Diptych, now in the National Gallery in London). In the early fifteenth century the style became unfashionable in Burgundy and France, but continued to flourish in Italy and Spain, notably in Catalonia (Lluís DALMAU, Jaime HUGUET, and Bernat MARTORELL).

**INTERNATIONAL LAW or (Latin) *ius gentium* or (French) *droit des gens* or (German) *Völkerrecht***, Roman law distinguished between *ius civile*, the law applicable to Roman citizens, *ius gentium*, the law applicable to foreigners, and *ius naturae*, the law of nature which enabled Roman jurists to appropriate reasonable and just elements in foreign laws for their own purposes. Medieval Europe did not have a developed system of international law, but the RECEPTION of Roman law provided jurists with the conceptual framework on which international law was to be built. The growth of international trade, the establishment of courts to administer MARITIME LAW and the LAW MERCHANT, and the development of international DIPLOMACY all required increasingly detailed international laws.

The sphere of WAR was the first arena in which international conventions of honourable practice began to be formulated as if they were laws. In the fourteenth and fifteenth centuries there was a nascent *ius fetiale* for the declaration of war and peace and an uncodified *ius belli* which imposed limits on the savagery of war, but in practice the application of these notions was confined to the conventions of CHIVALRY, which included pledges of safe conduct for heralds and rules for the ransom of important prisoners. There was, however, no distinction drawn between combatants and civilians, so civilian populations were often massacred. Similarly, the notion of neutrality was not developed until the end of the sixteenth century, and its first practical application was the proclamation of Britain's neutrality by James I in 1604 with respect to the hostilities between Spain and the United Provinces; the first important jurisprudential treatment of neutrality was the *Hispanicae advocationis* (1613) of Alberico GENTILI, the Regius professor of civil law in Oxford.

The literature of international law first emerged in Italy in the writings of jurists such as BARTOLO DA SASSOFERRATO and Petrus Baldus (1327–1406), who wrote about relations between the conflicting legal systems of the city-states. In the same period, Joannes de Lignano (c.1320–1383) wrote treatises on war (De bello et represaliis et de duello, published 1477) and peace (De pace) that form the basis of later international law on the subject. Despite such treatises, international law remained relatively neglected by jurists until the great burgeoning of writing on the subject in the sixteenth century was inaugurated by the ecclesiastical jurists of Spain. Relations between nation-states, the Empire, and the papacy, for example, were the subject of treatises by Fray Francisco de VITORIA (Relectiones theologicae, 1557) and Fernando Vázquez de Menchaca (who, like Vitoria, also wrote on war). Balthazar AYALA examined the legal aspects of war in De iure et officiis bellicis et disciplina militari (1581). Francisco SUÁREZ advocated in his Tractatus de legibus et Deo legislatore (1612) a ius gentium that regulated relations between states that were at once independent, interdependent, and dependent on God. In Savoy the jurist Pierino BELLI published his influential De re militari et de bello (1563) and in England Gentili wrote De iuri belli (1588–9). The debate over the law of war culminated in the De iure belli ac pacis (1625) of GROTIUS, the principles of which were implemented in the Peace of Westphalia which concluded the Thirty Years War in 1648; Grotius' treatise is now regarded as the founding text of modern international law.

In Germany the most distinguished writer on international law was Conrad Braun, author of De legationibus (1548). In France Jean BODIN's Six Livres de la république (1576) discussed international law extensively, and in translation (his own Latin text of 1586 and the English translation of 1606) was widely disseminated across Europe. In 1607 Bodin's countryman the duc de SULLY recommended to Henri IV that Europe secure perpetual peace by forming a federation of fifteen states ruled by a general council; his scheme was finally realized when the European Union was expanded to fifteen members in 1995. International law was first presented as an ordered system by the English jurist Richard Zouche (1590–1661) in his Iuris et iudicii fecialis, sive iuris inter gentes explicatio (1650), the title of which reflects his preference for the term ius inter gentes rather than ius gentium; he also separated the law of warfare from the main body of international law, and relegated it to a secondary position.

The law governing sovereignty of the sea was not seriously debated until the early seventeenth century, when it emerged as the dispute known as MARE CLAUSUM, MARE LIBERUM.
J. B. Scott, The Spanish Origin of International Law (1933); E. Nys, Les Origines de droit international (1894); T. A. Walker, History of the Law of Nations (1899).

## IRALA, DOMINGO MARTÍNEZ DE. See MARTÍNEZ DE IRALA, DOMINGO.

## IRELAND. The English lordship over Ireland was established by Henry II in 1171, and colonization of Ireland gave England control of around two-thirds of the island by the end of the thirteenth century. English energies were largely focused on France in the fifteenth century, however, and, although the PALE around Dublin was established, the rest of the island remained largely under the control of Anglo-Irish lords. The separatist impulses of that community were expressed in the declaration of parliamentary independence in 1460, a move countered in 1494 by Poyning's Law, which forbade parliaments to be held without a licence from the king. The earls of Kildare nevertheless remained effective controllers of the country, although nominally representatives of the king. Thomas Fitzgerald's rebellion against HENRY VIII in the mid-1530s gave the king a chance to reestablish English power in Ireland; the rebellion was crushed, and in 1536 Henry was declared supreme head of the Church in Ireland. In 1541 the lordship of Ireland was replaced with the title of king. Unrest continued in ELIZABETH's reign, however, notably with TYRONE's Spanish-supported rebellion, which ESSEX failed to put down, and which lasted from 1595 to Tyrone's eventual defeat in 1602.

## ISAAC, HEINRICH, or Henricus (c.1450–1517), Flemish composer in Italy. By 1485 he was a singer at Florence Cathedral; he also worked at the Baptistery of San Giovanni, and moved within the circle of Lorenzo de' MEDICI's musicians. After the death of Lorenzo he became court composer to MAXIMILIAN I's chapel in Vienna and travelled to Augsburg, Wels, Innsbruck, Nuremberg, and Konstanz, where he wrote the Choralis Constantinus. He spent his final years in Florence where, with the Medici family restored to power, he again benefited from their patronage, and was appointed provost of the chapter at the cathedral.

## ISABELLA THE CATHOLIC or (Spanish) Isabel la Católica (1451–1504), queen of Castile, was born at Madrigal on 22 April 1451, the daughter of King JOHN II of Castile and his second wife Isabella (granddaughter of King JOHN I of Portugal); John of Gaunt was therefore her paternal and her maternal great-grandfather. Isabella's father died in 1454 and was succeeded by HENRY IV (Enrique IV), his son by his first wife Maria (daughter of Ferdinand I of Aragon and Sicily). On her half-brother's accession 3-year-old Isabella was withdrawn by her mother to the castle at Arévalo (26 kilometres (16 miles) from Segovia), where she received her early education. In 1462 Isabella was moved with her uterine brother Alfonso to the court. In the course of the next six years King Henry was forced to repudiate his own daughter JUANA LA BELTRANEJA and to recognize Isabella as his heir; he negotiated a series of proposed marriages, which collapsed either because Isabella refused her consent or (in one case) because her proposed husband died. Meanwhile she had secretly agreed with the king's opponents, who had unsuccessfully attempted to depose him and crown Prince Alfonso, to marry the son of Castile's traditional enemy, the king of Aragon, her cousin Prince Ferdinand of Aragon (FERDINAND V).

On 19 October 1469 Ferdinand and Isabella, having forged a papal dispensation for consanguinity, were married in Valladolid; when the enraged King Henry found out, he took immediate steps to exclude her from the succession, reinstating Juana la Beltraneja. Henry died on 13 December 1474; the succession was contested, but Isabella was proclaimed queen of Castile and León; Ferdinand was recognized as consort, but was required to obtain his wife's signature on all royal decrees. In 1479 Ferdinand succeeded to the throne of Aragon, and thereafter the kingdoms were united under a dual monarchy until 1519, though each continued to function separately in all internal matters. Isabella sought to strengthen royal authority in Castile, and so curbed the powers of the military ORDERS and nobility while strengthening the royal army and the institution of the *corregidores*, officials who governed each town on behalf of the crown.

Isabella was responsible for cultural initiatives such as the patronage of architecture, printing, learning, and the establishment of a court school for young noblemen, of which the first head was the Italian humanist Pietro MARTIRE D'ANGHIERA. She was also the principal supporter of the voyages of COLUMBUS. Her piety also led Isabella to agree to the introduction of the Spanish INQUISITION, to drive the Moors from Spain (both Isabella and Ferdinand were present at the conquest of GRANADA), and, very reluctantly, to persecute and then banish the JEWS of Spain. In 1494 Pope ALEXANDER VI granted the title of *reges catholici* ('Catholic sovereigns') to Ferdinand and Isabella, who were thereafter known as 'their Catholic Majesties', but the precise circumstances in which the title was conferred are not known.

Isabella had one son (Juan, who died in 1497) and four daughters: JUANA LA LOCA, CATHERINE OF ARAGON, and Isabella and Maria, who successively married King MANUEL I of Portugal. Queen Isabella died at Medina del Campo on 24 November 1504 and was succeeded as queen of Castile by her daughter Juana la Loca, who reigned with her husband Philip of Habsburg (later PHILIP I) until 1506; Ferdinand still occupied the throne of Aragon (and, from 1512, Navarre), and after the death of Philip I became regent of Castile in his daughter's name.

DHE s.v. Isabel I la Católica; Tarsicio de Azcona, *Isabel la Católica* (3rd edn. 1993).

**ISTORIATO**, a form of Italian display MAIOLICA in which the polychrome decorations consist of narratives (*istoriato* means 'storied') drawn from history, classical mythology, or the Bible. The principal centres of production were CASTEL DURANTE, FAENZA, and Urbino. In the nineteenth century this maiolica came to be known in English as Raffaelle ware or Raphael's ware, because it was (mistakenly) believed that Raphael had painted some of the pottery. His designs were certainly used, as were designs by painters such as Battista FRANCO and Taddeo ZUCCARO, but the principal istoriato painters were Orazio FONTANA, NICOLA DA URBINO, and Francesco Xanto AVELLI.

**ITALIAN ARCHITECTURE**. In the late twelfth century the Romanesque and Byzantine traditions of Italian architecture began to be penetrated by GOTHIC architecture, which in Italy as elsewhere was introduced from France by the Cistercian ORDER, initially with Fossanova Abbey, in Lazio (begun 1187, consecrated 1208), which has a fine Gothic chapter house (c.1250); this was the first Cistercian building in Italy, and its fame was enhanced by the presence of the grave of THOMAS AQUINAS, who had died in the guesthouse on 7 March 1274. Cistercian architecture in Italy culminated in the construction of the Certosa di Pavia (1396–1481).

Italian Gothic soon became a distinctive architectural style. The powerful vertical lines of Gothic architecture north of the Alps is subdued in Italian Gothic churches by horizontal cornices and string courses. Italian Gothic churches typically have a flat roof, a circular window in the west front, stripes of coloured marble instead of mouldings, and small windows without tracery; unlike northern churches, they have neither pinnacles nor flying buttresses. By the fourteenth century, Italy's Gothic churches had become much more spacious than their French prototypes, principally because the openings in the arcades are typically twice the width of those in French Gothic churches. The most important exception to this range of characteristics is the abbey Church of Sant'Andrea in Vercelli (1219–27), a Gothic building with Romanesque columns, two western bell towers, and a plan redolent of English Gothic churches.

Many of the finest Gothic ecclesiastical buildings of the thirteenth and fourteenth centuries are Franciscan churches, such as the Church of San Francesco in Assisi (begun 1228, apparently modelled on Angers Cathedral), the Church of San Francesco in Bologna (which began in 1236 with a French ambulatory with radiating chapels), the Church of Santa Maria Gloriosa dei Frari in Venice (1250–1417; Gothic with a Veneto-Byzantine campanile), the Church of Santa Croce in Florence (begun 1294, attributed to ARNOLFO DI CAMBIO on stylistic grounds), and the Church of San Francesco in Siena (begun 1326). The Dominicans also built Gothic churches, notably SS Giovanni e Paolo in Venice (1246–1430) and Santa Maria Novella in Florence (1278–1470). In the ecclesiastical architecture of Rome, the Gothic style made little impact; the only Gothic church in Rome is the Dominican Santa Maria sopra Minerva (c.1290). Elsewhere in Italy, there are important Gothic churches in Bologna (San Petronio, 1390–1437), Padua (Basilica del Santo, 1232–1307), and Verona (Sant'Anastasia, 1261). The principal Gothic cathedrals in Italy are those in Florence (1296–1462), Milan (1385–1485), Orvieto (1290–1310), and Siena (1245–1380); the Gothic Cathedral of Santa Maria Assunta in Naples dates from 1294, but was destroyed in the earthquake of 1456 and rebuilt by ALFONSO V.

In secular architecture, Italy's greatest Gothic building is the Doge's Palace in Venice (1309–42). Gothic buildings continued to be built in Venice throughout the fifteenth century, including the Ca' d'Oro (1421–36), the upper part of the Campanile of San Marco (collapsed 1902 and subsequently rebuilt), and several palaces on the Grand Canal, notably the Foscari (where HENRI III of France was sumptuously entertained in 1574), the Contarini-Fasan (now advertised as Casa di Desdemona), the Cavalli (now Francetti), the Corner Contarini dai Cavalli, and the Pisani. Elsewhere in Italy, there are important secular buildings in the Gothic style in Bologna (Mercanzia, 1382–4), Cremona (Torrazzo, 1261),

Milan (Ospedale Maggiore, 1457), Piacenza (Palazzo Pubblico, 1281), and Verona (Palazzo del Comune, 1206–45). The Ponte Vecchio in Florence (1345) is Gothic, as are the towers of San Gimignano; the finest example of an Italian Gothic city is Siena.

The Renaissance style was inaugurated in Florence by BRUNELLESCHI, who in 1421 began work on the Ospedale degli Innocenti (Foundling Hospital), which has a loggia with a classical colonnade, semicircular arches, and hemispherical domes; the design, like those of his subsequent buildings, observes the mathematical proportions of classical antiquity. Brunelleschi also designed the sacristy (now known as the Old Sacristy) of San Lorenzo (from 1419), the dome of the cathedral (1420–34), the churches of San Lorenzo (1425) and San Spirito (1436–82), the Pazzi Chapel (from 1429/30), and the PITTI PALACE. Brunelleschi's successors included MICHEL-OZZO, who built the Palazzo Medici-Riccardi (begun 1444), which has the first three-storeyed façade and the first palace courtyard (cortile) in the new style, and Giuliano da SAN-GALLO, who erected many buildings on the principles established by Brunelleschi.

The Renaissance style was introduced to Rome by ALBERTI, who also built the first Renaissance church in Mantua (San Sebastiano, begun 1460). Michelozzo and FILARETE took the style to Milan in the 1450s. The earliest Renaissance structure in Venice is the portal of the ARSENALE (1457). In Urbino, construction on the Palazzo Ducale began in the 1460s; Luciano LAURANA was appointed architect in 1468 and the palace was later completed by FRANCESCO DI GIORGIO.

In 1499 BRAMANTE moved from Milan to Rome and inaugurated what is known as the High Renaissance, a period deemed to last until the SACK OF ROME in 1527. Bramante began ST PETER'S BASILICA (1506) and built the BELVEDERE COURT in the Vatican; RAPHAEL built the Villa MADAMA and PERUZZI built the Villa Farnesina for Agostino CHIGI.

The High Renaissance was followed by the style known as MANNERISM, in which motifs are used in deliberate opposition to their original purposes and contexts. The most important Italian mannerist architects are MICHELANGELO (especially his Biblioteca LAURENZIANA in Florence, which has columns that carry no cornices, but also his contributions to St Peter's in Rome), GIULIO ROMANO (especially his Palazzo del TÈ in Mantua, which has keystones out of line and twisted pilasters), VIGNOLA (especially his Villa FARNESE and Villa GIU-LIA), LIGORIO (especially the CASINO of Pope PIUS IV), VASARI (especially the UFFIZI), SANSOVINO (especially the Libreria Vecchia), and SANMICHELE (the palaces of Verona).

Vignola's Il Gesù Church in Rome, which was begun in 1568, had chapels instead of aisles, transepts, and an oval dome. This was the design that led to the development of BAROQUE architecture in the seventeenth century.

**ITALIAN ART.** A national style of art began to emerge in Italy in the mid-thirteenth century, some 600 years before Italy was united as a single state. In the historiography of the Renaissance, this artistic commonality led nineteenth-century historians to place the beginning of the RENAISSANCE

in about 1250. In sculpture, the classical elements in the work of artists such as Nicola and Giovanni PISANO and ARNOLFO DI CAMBIO formed a style that was imitated all over Italy. Even in Angevin Naples, the Sienese sculptor-architect TINO DI CAMAINO, a member of the circle of Giovanni Pisano, sculpted and designed influential works for the court. In the historiography of painting it is said to be CIMABUE who was the harbinger of GIOTTO and therefore the progenitor of Italian Renaissance painting. It is difficult to be confident of Cimabue's importance in this respect, but the dramatic realism of Giotto was undoubtedly an important influence on the development of Italian art, and forms an important element in the style of successors such as Ambrogio and Pietro LORENZETTI. In Siena, the most important painters were DUCCIO and his follower SIMONE MARTINI. In the late fourteenth century INTERNATIONAL GOTHIC emerged as the dominant style in northern Italy; Italian exponents of the style included GENTILE DA FABRIANO, PISANELLO, SASSETTA, and STEFANO DA ZEVIO.

In the sculpture of the early fifteenth century, DONATELLO and GHIBERTI revived features of the art of classical antiquity. Classical elements soon permeated the wall tombs of Florentine artists such as Antonio and Bernardo ROSSELLINO, DESIDERIO DA SETTIGNANO, and MINO DA FIESOLE and the terra-cotta reliefs of Luca DELLA ROBBIA. In painting MASACCIO drew on BRUNELLESCHI for his understanding of PERSPECTIVE and Donatello for the classical modelling of the human figure; the Brancacci Chapel shows that he was also an innovator in the use of light to unify a composition extending over several walls by creating the illusion of a single source of light. In the middle decades of the fifteenth century the Florentine inheritors of Masaccio included DOMENICO VENEZIANO, Fra ANGELICO, Filippo LIPPI, and ANDREA DEL CASTAGNO. In late fifteenth- and early sixteenth-century Florence, the most important artists were BOTTICELLI, PIERO DI COSIMO, Filippino LIPPI, GHIRLANDAIO, POLLAIUOLO, and VERROCCHIO.

The accomplishments of Florentine art were reflected in the art of neighbouring states, which nonetheless retained distinctive identities. In Umbria Verrocchio and PIERO DELLA FRANCESCA shaped the style of Perugian painters such as PERUGINO and PINTORICCHIO. Artists such as Piero and Paolo UCCELLO worked in Urbino, where the court of FEDERICO DA MONTEFELTRO became an important cultural centre, and LEONARDO DA VINCI worked primarily in Milan. In Padua, the sculptures of Donatello shaped the sculptural paintings of MANTEGNA. Mantegna was in turn an important influence on the work of his brother-in-law Giovanni BELLINI (and through him the paintings of GIORGIONE and TITIAN), and may also have influenced the fresco painters of the ESTE court in Ferrara, including Cosimo TURA, Francesco del COSSA, and ERCOLE DE' ROBERTI.

In the sixteenth century Florence produced painters such as ANDREA DEL SARTO, PONTORMO, and Fra BARTOLOMEO and sculptors such as Andrea SANSOVINO and CELLINI. The death of Lorenzo de' MEDICI in 1492, the French invasion of Italy in 1494, and the iconoclastic rule of SAVONAROLA (1494–8) all took their toll, however, and in the early years of the sixteenth century the most important artistic centre in Italy was the Rome of Pope JULIUS II. Artists such as MICHELANGELO, who continued the decoration of the SISTINE CHAPEL (inaugurated by SIXTUS IV), and RAPHAEL, who painted the Vatican *Stanze*, enjoyed his patronage. This period is sometimes known as the High Renaissance.

The calamity of the SACK OF ROME by imperial troops in 1527 created a hiatus in the cultural life of Rome, and when order was eventually re-established much of Italy was under Spanish control. Artistic patronage was affected by these changes, and the COUNTER-REFORMATION led to the regulation of art. In the remainder of the sixteenth century, the period of the style known as MANNERISM, the principal artists were GIULIO ROMANO, PARMIGIANINO, and the sculptors AMMANATI, BANDINELLI, CELLINI, and GIAMBOLOGNA. In Venice the most important painters were TINTORETTO and VERONESE.

Frederick Hartt, *History of Italian Renaissance Art* (rev. edn. 1987).

**ITALIAN GARDENS.** Accounts of fourteenth-century Italian gardens give little sense of the remarkable course that garden design in Italy was to take over the next 200 years, or of the pervasive influence that Italian gardens were to have all over Europe for centuries to come. BOCCACCIO described the royal Neapolitan gardens of the 1340s in his *Visione amorosa*; the most surprising feature of these gardens is the abundance of statues, which were unknown in northern gardens of this period. In the *Decameron* (1348) Boccaccio memorably described the walled garden of the Villa Palmieri in Florence; this garden contained arbours, vine pergolas, walks shaded by citrus trees and jasmine, a marble fountain, and a square flower garden with 1,000 varieties of flowers—the standard features of a medieval garden. This garden was uprooted before 1697 and replaced with the baroque terrace overlooking a lemon garden that still survives amidst the nineteenth-century gardens.

In the fifteenth century the one important garden to be laid out in southern Italy was Poggio Reale, the summer residence of Alfonso of Aragon, crown prince of Naples (later ALFONSO II). The fruit trees and fish ponds are briefly described by Sebastiano SERLIO, but a full account is provided in an anonymous poem, *Le Vergiez d'honneur*; the poem describes many features of the garden (PAVILIONS, loggias, antique statues, FOUNTAINS, GROTTOES, and herb and fruit gardens), but gives no hint of how the garden was laid out. The gardens so impressed CHARLES VIII when he visited Poggio Reale in 1495 that he took the Neapolitan garden designer PACELLO DA MERCOGLIANO back to France with him; the gardens that Pacello designed at AMBOISE, BLOIS, and GAILLON all perpetuated traditions of Neapolitan gardening that declined in southern Italy during the period of Spanish rule from 1503 to 1707.

The renaissance of gardening in Florence was inaugurated by ALBERTI's publication of *De re aedificatoria* in 1452. The garden of the Villa Quaracchi, which was built by Giovanni RUCELLAI in about 1459, contains various medieval elements (arbours, pergolas, a rose garden, and a MOUNT), but it conforms in so many respects to the principles enunciated by Alberti that its design has been confidently attributed to him. The house was built on a small hill, as Alberti had recommended, and the axis of the garden was extended beyond the *GIARDINO SEGRETO* along a tree-lined avenue to the river Arno; box and scented evergreens amenable to clipping were planted and shaped into hedges and figures, apparently in imitation of the first-century gardens of Pliny the Younger. The absence of statues in the Quaracchi gardens may be another gesture towards Pliny, who eschewed statues in favour of features constructed out of plants and soil.

Quaracchi had a central axis, and in that respect anticipated one of the central features of later gardens, but the garden was designed independently of the house. The transition from separate designs for house and garden to fully integrated designs can be seen in two gardens designed by MICHELOZZO DI BARTOLOMEO. In about 1451 Michelozzo laid out a garden at Il Trebbio, the Medici hunting box at Cafaggiolo; the garden is a walled rectangle detached from the house. A lunette by UTENS shows that the garden was laid out in eight square beds of flowers and vegetables; it was originally bounded by vine pergolas (one of which survives with its original brick columns), and the enclosure blocks out the views. This inwardness is a medieval feature; Il Trebbio is the last of the great medieval gardens of Tuscany. In 1458 Michelozzo began work on the MEDICI VILLA at Fiesole, and there he constructed open gardens on two terraces. The house opens out directly onto the upper terrace, which overlooks Florence in the valley below; the enclosure has shrunk to a *giardino segreto*, which still survives. In this design the essential features of the sixteenth-century Italian Renaissance garden are adumbrated. Michelozzo was not, however, the first architect to integrate house and garden: that ideal had already been realized in Rome in the BELVEDERE COURT and the VILLA MADAMA. It was these Roman buildings, and others now lost, that became the model for garden design in Tuscany.

Sixteenth-century Italian gardens were fully integrated with the houses to which they were attached, and retained the use of terraces with attractive views; to this late fifteenth-century outline, designers added four distinctive features that were to influence gardens all over the world: symmetry, statues, water, and a balance between constructed and natural materials. The first garden to have a symmetrical layout around a central axis was Niccolò TRIBOLO's garden at the MEDICI VILLA at Castello; Tribolo subsequently laid out the BOBOLI GARDENS in accordance with the same principle. In the second half of the sixteenth century some designers adopted the principle of the axial design, notably the architect of the Villa Bernadini in Saltocchio (now overgrown), but others chose to place features in opportunistic ways: PRATOLINO, for example, has an avenue that formed a central axis, but BUONTALENTI chose to scatter features around the garden rather than arrange them symmetrically on either side of the axis.

The gardens of classical antiquity were furnished with statues. The first garden to revive this tradition was the Belvedere Court, which contained a collection of ancient statues. Statues modelled on those of antiquity soon began to adorn the fountains at the focal point of gardens such as the Medici villa at Castello and the Palazzo DORIA PRINCIPE in Genoa. At the Villa D'ESTE in Tivoli, ancient statues excavated from the nearby villa of Hadrian were placed in the garden, and at the Villa ORSINI in Bomarzo monstrous statues were carved out of rock outcrops.

The terraces of Italian gardens often contained springs that provided natural sources of water, and in some gardens aqueducts and conduits were used to ensure a constant supply of water under pressure. The Renaissance garden that uses water to greatest advantage is the Villa d'Este at Tivoli, which has scores of magnificent fountains and an abundance of AUTOMATA which include singing birds and a roaring dragon. Some gardens, such as the Villa LANTE, the Villa d'Este at Cernobbio, the Villa CICOGNA, and the Villa FARNESE at Caprarola, have water-staircases or water contained within sculpted channels (catene d'acqua) flanked by dry staircases, and Frascati villas such as Villa ALDOBRANDINI had water-theatres. Water was also used to power GIOCHI D'ACQUA which may seem jejune to modern tastes but delighted visitors for several centuries.

The sculptor Baccio BANDINELLI decreed that 'le cose che si murano debbono essere guidi e superiori a quelle che si piantano' ('that which is constructed should be the model and master of that which is planted'). This principle was implemented in every major Italian garden of the sixteenth century. Sometimes, as in the Boboli Gardens, an architectonic structure was achieved by adapting a natural AMPHITHE-ATRE, but in most cases the effect was achieved with stone. The form of gardens was outlined with galleries (modelled on the ancient Roman cryptoporticum), covered walks, and staircases, and fountains were placed at focal points. The interpenetration of house and garden was often achieved by having elements of the house extended into the garden, as at Villa GIULIA. Gardens were furnished with pavilions, and many contained elaborate GROTTOES. In some gardens, CASINI were built in giardini segreti, of which the finest is at the Villa FARNESE.

Italian gardens influenced the development of garden design throughout Europe, both in layout and in content. This influence also extended to the proliferation of new species of plants, because the first BOTANICAL GARDENS were in Italy.

Georgina Masson, Italian Gardens (1961); J. G. Shepherd and G. A. Jellicoe, Italian Gardens of the Renaissance (1925; 4th edn., 1986); John Dixon Hunt, Garden and Grove: The Italian Renaissance Garden and the English Imagination, 1600–1750 (1986); Claudia Lazzaro-Bruno, The Italian Renaissance Garden (1990); David Coffin, Gardens and Gardening in Papal Rome (1991); Mirka Benes, Villas and Gardens in Early Modern Italy and France (2001).

**ITALIAN LANGUAGE.** The languages spoken in what is now Italy included Occitan and Provençal (in Piedmont), German (in Tirol), Slovene (in Veneto), and Albanian, Catalan, Croatian, and Greek (in southern Italy), as well as dialects and the language now known as 'standard' Italian. Renaissance Italy had neither a national written language nor a standardized spoken language; the former was not achieved until the seventeenth century and the latter until the late twentieth century.

The term 'Italian language' is used in two distinct senses. When used to denote the spoken language, it refers to a group of some fifteen romance languages, many of which are as mutually incomprehensible as French and Spanish; the areas in which these languages were (and are) spoken are approximately conterminous with political units, so one can speak of the Ligurian, Lombard, Tuscan, Venetian, Neapolitan, and Sicilian languages. Nearly all have their own literature. The Italian term dialetto is cognate with English dialect, but is used to refer to these different languages, which in English would be referred to as sibling or cognate languages rather than dialects. A few of these languages (Sardinian, Ladin, and especially Friulian) are so remote from the principal family of Italian languages that some linguists group them separately. These languages are all still alive, but many Italians are now diglossic, and can speak both a local language and the national form of spoken Italian; in the Renaissance, no such national form existed.

The term 'Italian language' is also used to denote the literary language of Italy, which is based on the language of fourteenth-century Tuscany. This language was only established in the seventeenth century; the Vocabulario (1612) of the Accademia della Crusca is the founding document. In earlier centuries, the question of whether the literary language should be the language of the northern courts (the lingua cortigiana) or the language of contemporary Tuscany or the archaic language of fourteenth-century Tuscany was central to the debate known as the QUESTIONE DELLA LINGUA.

T. C. Griffith, The Italian Language (1966).

**ITALIAN LAW.** The official status of Roman law in Italy disappeared with the fall of the Roman Empire in the West in AD 476, but under the Ostrogoths and their successors the Lombards, Roman law continued to be treated as native CUSTOMARY LAW. The Lombard conquest of AD 567 led to the introduction of Lombard law, a body of pure Germanic law which was regularly codified for a millennium, and eventually became the law of Italy, prevailing over the strong force of Roman law. The force of Lombard law waned after the twelfth century, but it was in the north-west an important element of law until the early seventeenth century, and was not altogether displaced until the introduction of the Napoleonic code in 1804. The edicts of Lombard kings, beginning with the Edictus Langobardorum of AD 643, were sufficiently substantial to vie with Roman law for the attention of scholars; an important school of jurists arose in Pavia in the early ninth century, and Lombard law was still being studied there in the sixteenth century. The most important centre of legal studies from the twelfth century onwards was Bologna, where Roman law was revived and studied alongside CANON LAW. Bologna retained its pre-eminence as the most important European centre for the study of law until ALCIATO's foundation of the humanist school at Bourges created a rival centre in the sixteenth century.

As the Lombard empire dissolved into the independent principalities of Italy, strands of Lombard law merged with elements of canon law and Roman CIVIL LAW in the statutes of individual states. There was very considerable variation between states in the laws that emerged in statutes, and for that reason there was no unified legal system in Italy until reunification in 1861. In Lombardy the *Constitutiones dominii Mediolanesis*, a collection of the constitutions of the rulers of Lombardy, was promulgated in 1541 and remained at the heart of Lombard law until the end of the eighteenth century. The principalities of Savoy were administered from 1430 to 1723 by a code issued by Amadeus VIII. In Venice, between 1232 and 1244, Doge Iacopo Tiepolo undertook a comprehensive review and codification of criminal and procedural law, and compiled civil statutes; these codes and statutes were frequently revised over the ensuing centuries, but nonetheless remained in force for five centuries. The Papal State was regulated by Roman law and canon law, but individual provinces also legislated separately. The most important provincial legislation arose in the Marches, where the CONSTITUTIONES MARCHIAE ANCONTIAE was promulgated in 1357 and remained the law of the Marches for two centuries; it was later extended to the rest of the Papal State, where it remained in force until 1816.

In the south of Italy, Lombard rulers were succeeded by the Normans and then by German emperors. In Sicily the *Liber Augustalis*, a code based on the principles of Roman jurisprudence, was promulgated by Frederick II in 1231 and remained in force until the eighteenth century. In Naples the Angevins regulated French citizens with FRENCH LAW, and the Aragonese introduced SPANISH LAW.

In the area of MARITIME LAW, the ports of Amalfi, Ancona, Genoa, Pisa, Trani, and Venice all codified their customary maritime law in the twelfth and thirteenth centuries; the most influential of these formulations was the 'Laws of AMALFI'. These codes were later embodied in the Catalan *Libro del consolato del mare*, which became the maritime law of the Mediterranean.

C. Calisse, *Storia del diritto italiano* (3 vols., 1903–30); E. Merkel, *Geschichte des Langobardenrechts* (1850).

**ITALIAN MUSIC.** After the flowering of Italian polyphony in the *ars nova*, the focus of attention switched to northern Europe until DUFAY, OBRECHT, JOSQUIN DESPRÈS, and Heinrich ISAAC moved south. Italian secular music had continued to flourish in the FROTTOLA and the CANTI CARNASCIALESCHI and these forms, handled by the Franco-Flemish polyphonists, influenced the MADRIGAL. The cultural environment of the courts of Mantua, Florence, and Ferrara and the intellectual liveliness of the CAMERATA in the second half of the sixteenth century played a part in turning Italy into a centre of musical innovation, with the development of the *intermedi* (see INTERMEZZO) and the invention of OPERA. At about the same time Rome, with PALESTRINA, and Venice, with VIADANA and the GABRIELIS, were taking the lead in the area of sacred music, providing opportunities for new MASS settings, MOTETS, and MAGNIFICATS; the thirteenth-century monophonic *laude* had

become a polychoral, instrumentally supported manifestation of northern Italian splendour.

**ITALIC,** a fount invented by Francesco GRIFFO for ALDUS MANUTIUS, who used it from 1501 on editions of classical texts in small formats. The fount was modelled on the cursive chancery hand (*cancelleresca corsiva*) used in the Vatican secretariat. The same humanistic script became the basis of a more elaborate cursive hand which was first published in 1522 by Ludovico ARRIGHI in his *Operina da imparare di scrivere littera cancellaresca*, which was the first printed handbook on CALLIGRAPHY. Both script and fount were known as Italic to distinguish them from Gothic hands and Roman and Gothic types.

In France italic type was introduced by Simon de Colines in 1528. His designs were modelled on Roman types, but introduced an italic slope into lower-case letters. The style of French italics was permanently fixed later in the sixteenth century by Robert GRANJON. Inclined italic upper-case letters were first made in Vienna in 1532, and by mid-century were in general use.

In the early sixteenth century italics were used to set entire texts, but thereafter they were increasingly used to distinguish parts of a book other than the main text, such as commendatory verses. In the 1550s the Antwerp type founder François Guyot introduced the first italic fount designed to match a roman fount.

**ITALY or (Italian) Italia.** The Italian peninsula was not organized into a single political unit until the Risorgimento of 1815–70; even now the process of unification is arguably incomplete, because CORSICA, San Marino, and the Vatican City (the last remnant of the PAPAL STATE) are not part of Italy. In the fourteenth century the papacy was in exile in Avignon (1305–78) and Italy consisted of city-states and principalities that were often at war with each other. During this period in northern Italy republics such as FLORENCE, GENOA, PISA, SIENA, and VENICE coexisted with states ruled by dynasties such as the BENTIVOGLIO in Bologna, the ESTE in Ferrara, the GONZAGA in Mantua, the MALATESTA in Rimini, the MONTEFELTRO in Urbino, the counts of SAVOY in Savoy-Piedmont, and the VISCONTI in Milan. In the fifteenth century the Visconti yielded to the SFORZA in Milan and the MEDICI rose to power in Florence.

In central Italy, the Papal State included Lazio, the Marches, Romagna, and Umbria. In the sixteenth century the territories of the State were extended to include Modena. The State extended from sea to sea, bounded on the northwest by Venice and Lombardy, on the west by Tuscany, and on the south by the kingdom of NAPLES. In the south, Naples was an Angevin kingdom (1266–1442) and an Aragonese kingdom (1443–1501) before being ruled directly from Spain (1501–1707) and SICILY was an Aragonese kingdom (1282–1410) before being ruled directly from Spain (1412–1713); to the east, Istria and the coast of DALMATIA were part of the Venetian empire; and to the west Corsica was a contested Genoese possession (1347–1768) and SARDINIA an Aragonese protectorate (1326–1478) before being ruled directly by Spain (1478–1708).

In the late fifteenth century, between the Peace of LODI (1454) and the outbreak of the WARS OF ITALY (1494–1559), the five great powers of the peninsula—Milan, Venice, Florence, the Papal State, and Naples—coexisted in relative peace and increasing prosperity. Except for this 40-year period, the Italian peninsula was almost constantly at war, and the suffering accorded by this internal strife was exacerbated by running battles with the Ottomans (culminating in the battle of LEPANTO), the depredations of BARBARY PIRATES, and foreign invasions.

**IVAN III** (1440–1505), grand duke of Muscovy from 1463, enlarged the territories of his duchy by incorporating contiguous principalities, notably the republic of Novgorod. Ivan renewed the ancient link with Byzantium in 1472 by marrying the niece of Constantine IX, the last Byzantine emperor, and declaring himself to be the successor of Constantine, whose insignia he adopted. Ivan was the first Russian prince to establish links with western Europe, and the Italians at his court included Aristotele FIORAVANTI, who built the Cathedral of the Assumption (Uspensky Sobor, 1475–9), Pietro SOLARIO, who designed several of the fortification towers in the Moscow Kremlin and collaborated with another Italian architect on the 'Faceted Palace' (Granovitaya Palata, 1487–91), and ALEVIZ, who built the Cathedral of the Archangel (Arkhangelsky Sobor, 1505–9) in the Moscow Kremlin.

*RBS* s.v. Ioann III Vasil'evich.

**IVAN IV or (English) Ivan the Terrible** (1530–84), tsar of Russia, became grand duke of Muscovy at the age of 3 and in 1546 became the first Russian ruler to be crowned as tsar. He extended his realm to the east with the conquest of Kazan (1552), Astrakhan (1556), and Siberia (from 1581), and in his attempt to establish a Russian presence on the Baltic fought several wars with Poland, but to no significant effect. Richard CHANCELLOR visited Moscow in 1553, and Ivan concluded a trading agreement with England; two years later the MUSCOVY COMPANY was founded.

The English translation of *Groznyi* as 'Terrible' reflects a western historiography in which Ivan is portrayed as a monster; the term simply means 'awe-inspiring', and is used in the same sense that the God of the 1611 Bible is described as 'mighty and terrible'.

*RBS* s.v. Ioann IV Vasil'evich, Groznyi.

**IVORY or (Latin)** *ebur*. The term 'ivory' is used in a narrow sense to refer to the tusk of the elephant, but carved ivory artefacts may derive from the tusk of various animals (narwhal, walrus, hippopotamus, fossil mammoth) or the horn of the rhinoceros or the teeth of various mammals (including whales and humans) or of the crocodile. Ivory carving was an important art form in medieval Europe and in Byzantium, but in the mid-fifteenth century it declined in importance. In the sixteenth century ivory was little used for sculpture, but was an important material in the decorative arts, and was widely used for articles such as handles (of DAGGERS and table-knives), sword pommels, hunting horns, powder flasks, and domestic objects (combs and mirror cases). In the same period, Portuguese traders were importing West African ivories fashioned for the European market (and so termed 'Afro-Portuguese ivories') such as salt cellars and hunting horns by Benin and Sherbo carvers (examples are preserved in the British Museum). Ivory carving was revived in the seventeenth century by German, Flemish, and French carvers, but the art form died in the early nineteenth century, surviving until the ivory bans of the late twentieth century only in attenuated form, chiefly Chinese 'magic balls' of concentric spheres of openwork which are more remarkable as feats of patience and skill than as works of art.

William Fagg and Ezio Bassani, *Africa and the Renaissance: Art in Ivory* (1988–9).

# J

**JACOBELLO DEL FIORE** (*c*.1370–1439), Italian painter, born in Venice, the son of a painter; he trained with his father and with GENTILE DA FABRIANO. His surviving works include a *Lion of Saint Mark* (1415, Ducal Palace, Venice), the *Triptych of Justice* (1421, Accademia, Venice), and *The Life of St Lucy* (*c*.1410, Pinacoteca Comunale, Fermo).

    MDA.

**JACOMART or Jaume Baço** (*c*.1413–1461), Spanish painter. He worked in Valencia before being summoned to Naples in 1440 by ALFONSO V of Aragon, for whom he worked as a court painter. The incomplete paintings that he had to abandon in Valencia were completed by Juan Rexach (*fl.* 1431–84). In Naples he painted an ALTARPIECE (now lost) depicting the appearance of the Virgin to King Alfonso.

    By 1451 Jacomart was back in Valencia, where he continued to enjoy royal patronage, executing an altarpiece for the Royal Chapel. The work of his second Valencian period, in which his Hispano-Flemish idiom may have been accentuated by his years in Naples (where the style was popular), is attributed to Jacomart on the basis of stylistic comparisons to the only surviving documented work, an altarpiece (executed with assistants) representing the martyrdom of St Peter and St Lawrence painted for the parish church of Catí.

    MDA s.v. Jacomart; E. Torno y Monzó, *Jacomart y el arte hispano-flamenco cuatrocentista* (1913).

**JACOPINO DEL CONTE** (1510–98), Italian painter, born in Florence, where he trained in the studio of ANDREA DEL SARTO. The finest of his Florentine paintings is a *Virgin and Child with John the Baptist and St Elizabeth* (*c*.1535, National Gallery, Washington). Jacopino moved *c*.1538 to Rome, where he painted two fresco cycles in the Oratory of San Giovanni Decollato (the Roman church of the Florentine Confraternity of the Misericordia). Thereafter he became a portrait artist; his sitters included *Michelangelo* (Metropolitan Museum, New York) and *Pope Paul III* (Church of San Francesco Romano, Rome).

    MDA s.v. Conte.

**JACOPO DA TREZZO** (*c*.1514–1589), Italian goldsmith and medallist in Spain, a native of Milan who in 1555 travelled to the Netherlands to enter the service of King PHILIP II; his finest surviving work from this period is a portrait MEDAL of Queen MARY I of England (British Museum). In 1559 he followed the court to Spain. He established workshops in Madrid and at the Escorial, and brought to Spain several members of the MISERONI FAMILY. His jasper monstrance (1579–86) mounted in gilt bronze is in the Escorial.

    MDA; Jean Babelon, *Jacopo da Trezzo et la construction de l'Escurial* (1922).

**JACOPO DELLA QUERCIA** (*c*.1374–1438), Italian sculptor, born in Siena. VASARI records that in 1401 Jacopo was an unsuccessful entrant in the competition to design new baptistery doors in Florence; his sample panel is lost. His earliest surviving work, the tomb of Ilaria del Carretto in Lucca Cathedral (*c*.1406), combines Gothic drapery with Renaissance putti and scrolls; it was an obscure work of art until lavishly praised by Ruskin. A similarly syncretic style is apparent in Jacopo's Fonte Gaia (1409–19), a FOUNTAIN designed for the Campo of Siena; substantial fragments survive in the Palazzo Pubblico in Siena. From 1417 to 1431 Jacopo collaborated with DONATELLO and GHIBERTI on the font in the baptistery in Siena, for which he supplied a relief. He interrupted this task in 1425 to sculpt panels depicting biblical scenes for the central portal of the Church of San Petronio in Bologna. His surviving work in wood includes a pair of statues depicting *The Annunciation* (1421) in the Cathedral (Collegiata) of San Gimignano.

    MDA; A. C. Hanson, *Jacopo della Quercia's Fonte Gaia* (1965); C. Seymour Jr., *Jacopo della Quercia* (1973); James Beck, *Jacopo della Quercia* (1991).

**JACOPO DEL SELLAIO** (1441–93), Italian painter, born in Florence, the son of a saddler (Italian *sellaio*); he may have trained in the studio of Fra Filippo LIPPI. His earliest documented paintings are an *Angel Annunciate* and a *Virgin Annunciate* (1477, Santa Lucia dei Magnoli). His later paintings include a huge *Crucifixion with the Virgin and Seven Saints* (Church of San Frediano, Florence).

    MDA.

**JAGIEŁŁO FAMILY**, a Lithuanian dynasty that ruled Poland from 1386 to 1572. Its members were VLADISLAV II, VLADISLAV III, CASIMIR IV, JOHN ALBERT, Alexander, SIGISMUND I, and

SIGISMUND II. Beyond Poland, Vladislav III was also king of Hungary and Casimir IV's son LADISLAS II and grandson LOUIS II became kings of Hungary and Bohemia. See Appendix I.

**JAMES IV** (1473–1513), king of Scotland. James came to the throne at the age of 15 at the head of a rising against the unpopular rule of his father James III. On his maturity he proved himself an active and successful king, travelling throughout his kingdom, spending on court patronage, royal buildings, and the navy, and pursuing an aggressive foreign policy which was to lead to his early death. In 1497 his invasion of Northumberland was quickly put down by HENRY VII, and the peace treaty between England and Scotland sealed with James's marriage to Margaret, Henry's sister. Their great-grandson JAMES VI would eventually inherit both the Scottish and English thrones. The traditional Scots-French alliance proved stronger than the new peace with the English, however, and whilst HENRY VIII was fighting France, James again led a strong Scottish force into northern England. His army was defeated, and James himself killed, at the battle of Flodden.
*DNB.*

**JAMES V** (1512–42), king of Scotland. Not two years old on the death of his father JAMES IV, the early years of James's reign were characterized by power struggles between different factions. On his coming of age, James followed his father's policy of artistic patronage and extensive travel throughout the kingdom, the better to display royal power. Royal coffers were replenished through heavy taxation of both the clergy and laity. Marriages, first with Madeleine, daughter of the French king FRANCIS I, and then with MARY OF LORRAINE, renewed traditional Scots-French allegiances, and gave James an heir in MARY, QUEEN OF SCOTS. Meanwhile, hostilities with England had resumed; in 1542, a Scottish force was defeated at Solway Moss, near Carlisle, by Henry VIII's army. James died of an unrelated illness shortly afterwards.
*DNB.*

**JAMES VI** (1566–1625), king of Scotland and (as James I) England. Son of MARY, QUEEN OF SCOTS, and DARNLEY, Mary's forced abdication brought James to the Scottish throne before he was 2 years old. Factions divided the country before his coming of age, but a stable government and moderate church were encouraged by James on his formal accession to power. On the death of his cousin ELIZABETH in 1603, James succeeded to the English throne. His plans to unite the governments, as well as the crowns, of the two kingdoms were derailed by the English Parliament, with whom James's relations remained fractious throughout his reign. His extravagance and firm sense of royal authority were perennial points of conflict. James followed a tolerant religious policy, to which the HAMPTON COURT CONFERENCE contributed, and which even the GUNPOWDER PLOT did not jeopardize. Among his writings are *Basilikon Doron* (1599) on the art of government, *A Counterblast to Tobacco* (1604), theological works, and poetry in Scots, Latin, and English; he also wrote a treatise on rules for writing Scots. He was succeeded by his son Charles I.
*DNB.*

**JAMES, THOMAS** (c.1593–1635) In 1631, James led an expedition to discover a NORTH-WEST PASSAGE to the South Seas. He met Luke FOX in Hudson Bay before exploring the area further, naming Cape Henrietta Maria and wintering off Charlton Island. He returned the following year without having found a north-west passage, and published an account of the voyage in 1633.

**JAMNITZER, WENZEL** (1508–85), German goldsmith. He was born into a Viennese family of goldsmiths, but moved with his father Hans Jamnitzer the Elder (d. c.1549) and his brother Albrecht (d. 1555) to Nuremberg at an unknown date before 1534, when he became a burgher of the city and a master of the Guild of Goldsmiths. He was appointed in 1543 as the die-cutter of the city's coins and seals and in 1552 he became master of the city mint, a post that brought with it *de facto* recognition as Nuremberg's leading goldsmith. He was also appointed to a series of increasingly prestigious civic appointments, beginning with membership of the city council in 1556, and served as *Kaiserlicher Hofgoldschmeid* (imperial goldsmith) to the Emperors CHARLES V, FERDINAND I, MAXIMILIAN II, and RUDOLF II.

Jamnitzer seems to have been the originator of the fashion for casting minutely realistic ornamental figures of small animals (*alle Tier auf Erden*, 'all animals on earth') such as beetles, frogs, and lizards; extravagant examples of these silver menageries include a silver writing case made for Archduke Ferdinand II (c.1570, Kunsthistorisches Museum, Vienna) and a table clock (1560, Residenzmuseum, Munich) for which the design survives (Kupferstichkabinett, Berlin). Some of Jamnitzer's finest pieces are table-centres, of which the best known are the *Merckelsche* (Mother Earth) centrepiece (Rijksmuseum, Amsterdam) of 1549, which is named after the Nuremberg merchant who in 1809 saved it from the melting-pot, and the *Lustbrunnen* of 1556, a table-centre with a FOUNTAIN commissioned by Maximilian II and completed for Rudolf II; it is now lost except for the four gilt-bronze supporting figures of Flora, Ceres, Bacchus, and Vulcan (Kunsthistorisches Museum, Vienna).

Jamnitzer's workshop trained goldsmiths such as Mathias ZÜNDT and many members of his own family. His son Hans Jamnitzer the Younger (1539–1603), who became a master in 1563, may have been the maker of a handbell covered with silver wildlife (British Museum), but the bell has also been attributed to his father. Albrecht's son Bartel (c.1548–1618), who became a master in 1575, was the maker of a pair of NAUTILUS SHELL cups now in the Hessisches Landsmuseum in Kassel. Hans the Younger's son Christoph (1563–1618), who became a master in 1592, was the maker of several well-known pieces, including a cup in the shape of an angel (Armoury Museum, Moscow), the extravagant Trifoni ewer and basin (1603, Kunsthistorisches Museum, Vienna), and, most appealing to modern tastes, a table-fountain shaped like an elephant (c.1610, Kunstgewerbemuseum, Berlin). He also

Wenzel Jamnitzer, the *Merckelsche* (1549), a table-centre (decorated with casts of insects and reptiles) now in the Rijksmuseum in Amsterdam

published a pattern book of GROTESQUE ornaments (*Neue Grotesken buch*, Nuremberg, 1610).

MDA; NDB; G. Bott, *Wenzel Jamnitzer (1508–1585) und die Nürnberger Goldschmiedekunst 1500–1700* (1985).

**JAMYN, AMADIS** (1540–93), French poet associated with the PLÉIADE. He was a student of DORAT and Adrien TURNÈBE and subsequently became the secretary and companion of RONSARD. He wrote love poetry and religious poetry, and also translated portions of the *Iliad* and the *Odyssey*.

DBF.

**JANEQUIN, CLÉMENT** (*c*.1485–1558), French composer whose early years were spent in Bordeaux. In 1531 he was master of the choirboys at Auch Cathedral; from there he moved to Angers where he was *maître de chapelle* from 1534 until 1537. In the 1550s he became *chantre ordinaire du roi* and finally *compositeur ordinaire du roi*. He wrote over 250 chansons, which were popular with singers and instrumentalists throughout the sixteenth century. These were famous for their musical imitations of natural and sounds, for instance in 'Le Chant des oiseaux', and 'Les Cris de Paris'. His sacred music includes his *Missa super 'La Bataille'* and settings of *chansons spirituelles* and psalms in French translation.

**JANE SEYMOUR** (d. 1537), queen of England, and third wife of HENRY VIII. Jane attracted Henry's attention whilst lady-in-waiting to his second wife ANNE BOLEYN. Following Anne's fall from favour and execution in 1536, Jane and Henry married. She died shortly after giving birth to a son and heir, the future EDWARD VI, for whom her elder brother SOMERSET later acted as protector.

DNB.

**JANSSENS, ABRAHAM** (*c*.1575–1632), Flemish painter who worked in Antwerp, where he became dean of the guild in 1606. He visited Rome in 1598, and may have returned to Italy *c*.1604; the influence of Italian models is readily apparent in his paintings. His most important civic commission was the *Scaldis and Antwerpia* (1610) painted for the States Chamber of the Town Hall and now in the Koninklijk Museum voor Schone Kunsten in Antwerp. His religious paintings include a *Lamentation* (St Janskerk, Mechelen) and a *Scourging of Christ* (1626, St Michielskerk, Ghent).

BNB; MDA s.v. Janssen.

**JEANNE D'ALBRET or (English) Joan III** (1528–72), queen of Navarre, was the daughter of Henri II d'Albret, king of Navarre, and MARGUERITE D'ANGOULÊME, sister of King FRANCIS I. She married ANTOINE DE BOURBON, who succeeded his father-in-law as king of Navarre in 1555. As queen she publicly professed Protestantism. On King Antoine's death in 1562, Queen Jeanne acted as protector to her young son King Henri III of Navarre (later King HENRI IV of France), whom she raised as a Protestant. Shortly before her death in June 1572 she arranged the marriage of her son to MARGUERITE DE VALOIS, daughter of CATHERINE DE MÉDICIS and sister of King CHARLES IX.

DBF; Yves Cazaux, *Jeanne d'Albret* (1973).

**JENA**. The Thuringian city of Jena, on the left bank of the Saxon Saale, passed from the margraves of Meissen to the WETTIN electors of Saxony in 1423, and after the division of SAXONY in 1485 was ruled by the Ernestine line of the house of Wettin until reunification in 1547. The university is said to have been conceived by the Elector JOHANN FRIEDRICH I while a captive of CHARLES I. The university was established on 2 February 1558 by the elector's three sons, who secured a charter from the Emperor FERDINAND I. From the outset the university stood for Protestantism and humanist scholarship; its zenith was the twenty-year period from 1787 to 1806, when its staff included Fichte, Hegel, Schelling, Schlegel, and Schiller.

The Stadtkirche of St Michael (1438–1528), which was in the early modern period the principal landmark of the city, is now overshadowed by the 26-storey Universitäts-Hochhaus; the church contains the bronze relief of Martin LUTHER originally intended for his tomb in Wittenberg. The university was for its first three centuries housed in what is now the Collegium Jenense, which still has its original students' prison (*Karzer*) with its drawings and inscriptions by student inmates.

**JENSON, NICOLAS** (*c*.1420–1480), French type founder and publisher in Venice. He was born near Troyes and trained in Germany before settling in Venice. He published more than 70 books, mostly in Greek and Latin; some of his books were illuminated by hand, as if they were manuscripts. Some of his books are printed in Gothic founts (notably his Latin Bible of 1476), but Jenson is best known for his invention of a clear roman typeface which by 1467 was in use in Strassburg and Rome as well as Venice.

DBF; Martin Lowry, *Nicholas Jenson and the Rise of Venetian Printing in Renaissance Europe* (1991).

**JÉREZ, FRANCISCO LÓPEZ DE** (*c*.1500–*c*.1547), historian of Peru. He was born in Jerez (Andalusia) and travelled to Peru as a child. He was appointed by PIZARRO to chronicle the conquest of Peru, and accompanied him on his campaigns in 1524, 1526, and 1530. In 1534 Jérez returned to Spain, and published his account of the conquest of Peru, *Verdadera relación de la conquista del Perú* (Seville, 1534). The detached and objective tone of the writing lends credence to Jérez's endorsement of the myth of vast Inca wealth, which was spread through translations of his book throughout Europe.

DHE.

**JEROME IN THE RENAISSANCE**. Jerome (Latin Hieronymus) (*c*.341–420) was a monk and scholar from Strido, in northern Dalmatia. He left his native Dalmatia for Rome, where he was educated by the grammarian Donatus. By 366 he had been baptized as a Christian, and he subsequently travelled in Italy and Gaul before becoming a monk in Aquileia (now an Italian village, but then an important Roman city). He left his monastery after a quarrel, and travelled to Antioch, where he had a dream in which a heavenly voice accused him of being a Ciceronian rather than a Christian (*Ciceronianus es, non Christianus*). Jerome became a hermit in the desert of Chalcis (near Aleppo) and abjured pagan classical literature, instead studying Hebrew with a view to reading the Old Testament in the original language. He was already competent in Greek and had achieved a formidable mastery of Latin style, and the addition of Hebrew was the final skill necessary for his revision of older translations of the BIBLE into a standard Latin text that later became known as the Vulgate. Jerome had a foul temper and a caustic tongue, and was constantly accused of behaviour that was distinctly unsaintly, but after his death he nonetheless came to be regarded as one of the four Latin doctors of the Church (*doctores ecclesiae*).

In the Renaissance Jerome was valued by scholars such as Leonardo BRUNI as an exemplar of the humanist contention that the study of the pagan literature of classical antiquity could be of benefit to Christian readers. Beyond humanist circles, Jerome was chiefly valued as the originator of the Vulgate (*editio vulgata*), which had established itself as the standard Latin text in the Catholic West. There was, however, no consensus on the precise wording of Jerome's text, which had been corrupted in late antiquity by recollections of readings in Old Latin versions and by scribal errors. The first edition of the Vulgate to be printed was the GUTENBERG Bible of 1456; the first scholarly text was printed by Robert ESTIENNE (Paris, 1528). On 8 April 1564 the COUNCIL OF TRENT declared the Vulgate to be the only authentic Latin text of the Bible. What was intended to be the definitive text was issued by SIXTUS V, who declared in his bull that the text was unalterable. Scholars spotted some 3,000 textual errors, and the edition was quickly recalled. A revised edition was issued in 1592 by CLEMENT VIII, and so is known as the Clementine edition; because the bull two years earlier had forbidden any change to the 1590 text, the title page of Clement's revised text declares it to be the edition of Sixtus V ('Biblia Sacra editionis Sixti Quinti Pont Max jussu recognita atque edita'). The Clementine text was soon seen to depart from Jerome's text in many particulars, but papal interdictions against further emendations meant that the Clementine text remained authoritative until the Vatican embarked on a new text with the publication of a new edition of Jerome's Genesis in 1926.

The first collected edition of Jerome's writings was edited by ERASMUS in nine volumes (Basel, 1516). In Renaissance art Jerome is depicted either as a cardinal (with a red cardinal's hat) or as a hermit in his cave (with a lion at his feet).

E. F. Rice, Jr., *Saint Jerome in the Renaissance* (1985).

**JEROME OF PRAGUE or** (Czech) **Jeroným Pražský** (*c*.1370–1416), Bohemian reformer, educated in Prague, where he became a disciple of Jan HUS and an advocate of WYCLIFFE's theology. After graduating at Charles University he travelled in 1398 to Oxford, where he continued his study of Wycliffe, especially the *Dialogus* and the *Trialogus*, copies of which he took to Paris and Prague. He became a wandering scholar, visiting Jerusalem (1403) and universities in Paris (1402 and 1404), Heidelberg (1405), and Cologne (1406) before returning to Prague in 1407. He proselytized for the Wycliffite cause amongst the students of Prague and in 1410 met King

SIGISMUND of Hungary to discuss corruption amongst the clergy.

Jerome's advocacy of Wycliffe prompted suspicions of heresy, and he fled to Moravia in fear of his life. By 1412, however, he had returned to Prague, where he denounced the bull promulgated by the antipope JOHN XXIII proclaiming an INDULGENCE to raise money for the crusade against LADISLAS OF DURAZZO. In 1413 he travelled to Russia and Lithuania in the train of the grand duke of Kraków, and again aroused suspicion, this time for taking a sympathetic view of the rites of the Orthodox Church. In 1415 he followed Jan Hus to the COUNCIL OF CONSTANCE; he fled when he realized that Konstanz was dangerous, but was captured and brought before the Council in chains.

The Council executed Hus on 6 July, but the violent reaction in Bohemia convinced the Council that a second execution would be imprudent, so an attempt was made to persuade Jerome to recant. On 11 September 1415 he read aloud a document in which the teachings of Wycliffe and Hus were anathematized and the authority of the papacy and the Council was affirmed. When doubt was cast on the genuineness of this public abjuration, Jerome's trial was resumed. He defended himself with formidable oratorical skills, but at the conclusion of his speech withdrew his abjuration, declared the innocence of Hus and affirmed his concurrence with Wycliffe's teaching in all points of theology except the EUCHARIST. He was burnt at the stake on 30 May 1416. Poggio BRACCIOLINI's praise of his Stoic courage as he died gave Jerome a place in the pantheon of reforming martyrs that he might otherwise have been denied.

BLBL s.v. Hieronymus von Prag; F. Šmahel, *Jeroným Pražský* (1966); R. R. Betts, 'Jerome of Prague', *University of Birmingham Historical Journal*, I (1947).

**JESUITS or Society of Jesus or (Spanish) Compañía de Jesús or (French) Compagnie de Jésus or (Italian) Compagnia de Giesu or (German) Gesellschaft Jesu**, a religious ORDER that originated in a vow of poverty and service taken in Paris on 15 August 1534 by seven students, including IGNATIUS LOYOLA, Francis XAVIER, Nicolás BOBADILLA, and Diego LAÍNEZ. The seven students met again in 1537 in Venice, where they were ordained as priests. Unable to proceed to Palestine because of the outbreak of hostilities between Venice and the Ottomans, they went to Rome, determined to start a new religious order. In 1540 this group, which had expanded to ten, became the foundation members of the Society of Jesus, which was approved in the papal bull *Regimini militantis ecclesiae*, promulgated by Pope PAUL III on 27 September 1540. Ignatius Loyola was elected as the first general of the Jesuits, and promptly instituted a programme to establish foreign missions, beginning with Francis Xavier in Asia and Manuel da NÓBREGA in Brazil; he was succeeded as general by Diego Laínez. The Society had not been formed to combat the Reformation, but within ten years of its foundation had been drawn into that role, initially in southern Germany (led by Petrus CANISIUS) and then elsewhere in northern Europe. In the sixteenth century the Society's members included José de ACOSTA, José de ANCHIETA, Claudio AQUAVIVA (the fifth general), Francisco de BORJA (the third general), Roberto BELLARMINO, Edmund CAMPION, Pierre FABER, Robert PARSONS, Antonio POSSEVINO, Matteo RICCI, and Francisco SUÁREZ. By 1600 the Society had more than 8,500 members in 23 provinces; it now has some 25,000 members, many of whom teach in schools and universities.

The most important institutions of the Jesuits were its schools and colleges, the first of which was opened in Messina in 1548. In Rome, Ignatius founded the Roman College (Collegium Romanum, refounded in 1572 by GREGORY XIII and later renamed the Pontificia Università Gregoriana) and the German College; the Jesuits later assumed control of the ENGLISH COLLEGE. In the late sixteenth and early seventeenth centuries, Jesuits teaching in schools wrote Latin plays for performance by their pupils. The genre became popular in the German lands, especially in Vienna and Munich. German exponents of *Jesuitendrama* included Jakob BIDERMANN and Jakob GRETSER.

J. Cretineau-Joly, *Histoire religieuse, politique et littéraire de la Compagnie de Jésus* (6 vols., 1844–6); W. V. Bangert, *A History of the Society of Jesus* (2nd edn. 1986); J. W. O'Malley, *The First Jesuits* (1993).

**JESUS IN THE RENAISSANCE**. The Christological debates of late antiquity centred on two related questions: the precise meaning of the divinity of Jesus and the relationship between the human and divine elements in his person. Arius, the fourth-century heresiarch, sought to affirm the unity of the godhead by denying the full divinity of Jesus; his subordinationist doctrine re-emerged at the Reformation in SOCINIANISM and UNITARIANISM. Martin LUTHER, in developing his doctrine of the EUCHARIST, supported his UBIQUITARIANISM by an appeal to the patristic notion of *communicatio idiomatum* ('interchange of the properties'), according to which the attributes of either the human or divine elements in Jesus could be predicated on the other, because both are united in the person of Jesus. CALVIN, whose God was a more transcendent and less immanent deity than Luther's, favoured a clear distinction between the two natures of Jesus; this doctrine is known as the *extra Calvinisticum*.

The debate about the precise sense in which Jesus can be considered divine revolved around three terms: substance (*substantia*), essence (*essentia*), and person (*persona*). Augustine had maintained that *essentia* and *substantia* were the same thing, and that Jesus shared the essence or substance of GOD the Father but was a separate person. The Catholic view (derived from Tertullian), endorsed by the COUNCIL OF TRENT and shared by some Protestants, was that Jesus shared the substance of God but was a separate person; most Protestant theologians, however, agreed with Calvin that it was the essence of God that Jesus shared and that he was a separate person. Those inclined to subordinationism contended that Jesus shared the substance of God but had a separate essence.

The physical appearance of Jesus is not described in the New Testament, but authentic representations were thought to have been preserved in VERNICLES such as the Turin

Shroud and in the *volto santo* ('sacred face'), a large wooden cross in Lucca Cathedral depicting a robed Jesus which was said to have been a portrait executed by Nicodemus; this portrait is the original of the many *volti santi* dating from the twelfth to the fifteenth centuries found all over Europe. One vestige of the iconoclasm of the early Church is that Jesus is often represented by his monogram (see IHS), which in Counter-Reformation art largely superseded the ancient chi-rho symbol; the ancient representation of Jesus as a lamb survived into the Renaissance in depictions of John the Baptist with a lamb, such as TITIAN's painting in the Accademia in Venice. Representational images of Jesus sometimes depict a bearded figure, as in the Byzantine tradition, and sometimes a beardless man, as in Carolingian art.

In Renaissance art, the depiction of Jesus varied according to the incident in his life being portrayed. In Nativity paintings, the medieval tradition of Mary seated beside the manger yields in the late fourteenth century to depictions of Mary kneeling in adoration before the child, as in an anonymous fourteenth-century fresco in Santa Maria Novella in Florence and the Portinari altarpiece (1473–5) of Hugo van der GOES now in the Uffizi; in the second half of the sixteenth century, more naturalistic depictions become common, and in 1609 CARAVAGGIO depicted a reclining Mary holding the infant Jesus (Museo Nazionale, Messina). In Renaissance depictions of the Adoration of the Magi, the earlier tradition of small groups was displaced by pictures crowded by the attendants of the Magi, which in the case of Benozzo GOZZOLI's *Adoration* of 1459 (now in the Palazzo Riccardi in Florence) included many members of the MEDICI family.

The Virgin and Child was one of the most popular subjects of Renaissance painting. In Italy GIOTTO and his successors had turned away from the solemnity of the Byzantine tradition in favour of an increasingly naturalistic depiction of Mary and the infant Jesus. In the fifteenth century mother and child were depicted either against a landscape or against a formal interior; the culmination of this tradition is RAPHAEL's treatment of the theme. Sometimes the family group is expanded to include Joseph and other relatives, such as the infant John the Baptist; this type of group portrait is known in English as the Holy Family and in Italian as the *Sacra Famiglia*, and is a domestic variation on the SACRA CONVERSAZIONE. The COUNCIL OF TRENT condemned the domestic intimacy of the *Sacra Famiglia*, and prescribed that paintings should depict Jesus, Mary, and Joseph as the earthly equivalents of the three persons of the Trinity; Murillo's *Holy Family* (National Gallery, London) reflects these Tridentine strictures.

Depictions of the BAPTISM (which from the twelfth century onwards often include a portrait of God the Father in the clouds above the dove representing the Holy Spirit) reflect the debate over modes of baptism: medieval pictures, such as GIOTTO's in the Arena Chapel in Padua (1305–6), show a modified version of baptism by immersion, in which Jesus either stands immersed to his waist and has water poured over him or stands under a natural or artificial waterfall; from the twelfth to the fourteenth centuries, both immer-

sion and infusion were depicted, but in the fifteenth and sixteenth centuries, immersion is the invariable rule, as in PIERO DELLA FRANCESCA's *Baptism* in the National Gallery in London. The Transfiguration occurs occasionally in early fifteenth-century art (e.g. in GHIBERTI's baptistery doors in Florence), yet it only became popular with the proclamation of the Feast of the Transfiguration in 1457. Jesus is typically portrayed flanked by Moses and Elijah and either standing on the top of a small hill (e.g. Bellini's version in the Correr in Venice) or, in a revival of a Byzantine tradition, floating above the summit (e.g. RAPHAEL's version in the Vatican).

In depictions of the Last Supper, Jesus and the disciples were in late antiquity and the Middle Ages shown reclining around a semicircular table, dining like ancient Romans; eventually the diners were shown seated on chairs along one side and both ends of a rectangular table. Renaissance treatments of the theme, notably LEONARDO's painting in Santa Maria delle Grazie in Milan, sometimes dramatized the announcement by Jesus that one of his disciples would betray him. The emphasis on the institution of the EUCHARIST in the Last Supper led to the regular depiction of the chalice and wafer, and in some theologically partisan pictures, of only one kind: one of DÜRER's woodcuts (1583) pointedly shows the chalice standing on an otherwise empty table.

In Crucifixions, Jesus had been portrayed in late antiquity as still alive, nailed to the cross by four nails and looking up to heaven, but not apparently suffering inordinately. The depiction of the crucified Jesus after death began in the Byzantine Church, and did not become common in the West until the late thirteenth century. The influence of St Francis of Assisi, who emphasized the suffering of Jesus, led to a tradition in which Jesus was degraded by his suffering; the replacement of the separate nails in the feet of Jesus by a single nail through both feet (as in CIMABUE's painting in the Upper Church in Assisi) both accentuates the suffering of Jesus (because his body must be twisted) and emphasizes the doctrine of the Trinity (because there are three nails). GRÜNEWALD brought to its pinnacle this tradition of grisly realism in his representation of the 'Man of Sorrows' in the Isenheim altarpiece (Colmar). In Crucifixions the principal companions of Jesus are his mother Mary and his disciple John; as the cult of the Virgin developed, Mary was increasingly depicted sharing the sufferings of her son, and in Renaissance art is often depicted fainting. In the fifteenth century painters often depicted a large crowd of spectators around the central characters, but Tridentine condemnations of the indecorum of such scenes produced a generation of painters who banished the spectators and concentrated on a sombre depiction of the central characters, as in El GRECO's *Crucifixion* in the Louvre.

The resurrection of Jesus was not portrayed in Italian art until the fourteenth century. He is usually seen floating in the sky above the empty tomb guarded by the sleeping soldiers, but Piero della Francesca shows him standing with one foot on the tomb (San Sepolcro) and GHIBERTI, in his relief on the Baptistery doors in Florence, shows him standing on the tomb.

In depictions of the Last Judgement, which in Renaissance art often appear on ALTARPIECES, Jesus is portrayed seated as a judge in the central panel, and heaven and HELL are shown on the wings. He is normally dressed in a tunic, but his right side is often uncovered to show his wounds. The greatest challenge to this tradition is MICHELANGELO's depiction in the SISTINE CHAPEL, in which Jesus stands naked like a classical figure and at his sides huge numbers of people move upwards to heaven and downwards to hell; in the gulf between the saved and the damned Michelangelo depicts Charon and his barque, so presenting pagan classical myth as an adumbration of Christian theology.

**JET or (French) *jais* or (German) *Gagat*,** a highly polished black stone that derives from the fossilized driftwood of the *araucaria* (monkey-puzzle tree) genus. Jet was mined in Whitby (Yorkshire), the Lias of Württemberg, and the Aude, but the principal source of jet in the early modern period was Villaviciosa de Asturias, on the north coast of Spain. Jet has been valued for its amuletic properties since antiquity, and for millennia personal ornaments carved from jet have been used to ward off the evil eye and attacks by demons and serpents; they also afford protection from diseases of the eye.

The proximity of Villaviciosa to the pilgrim route to Santiago de Compostela enabled Santiago craftsmen to carve jet for the pilgrim trade. In the fifteenth century the jet carvers of Santiago organized themselves into guilds, each of which had its own retail outlet and its own regulations (including the presentation of 'master works' by apprentices seeking admission). In the sixteenth century production reached its highest levels, and large numbers of crucifixes, paxes, and rosaries were produced, as were carvings of the soldiers of the *reconquista* (*matamoros*) and of pilgrims.

**JEWEL, JOHN** (1522–71), apologist for the Church of England. Educated at Oxford, where in 1542 he was elected a fellow of Corpus Christi College, Jewel was from the late 1540s a leading exponent of reformist opinion in England. On MARY's accession, he signed papers of anti-Protestant principles, but was forced to flee the country in 1555; at Frankfurt he debated with John KNOX. He returned to England under ELIZABETH and in 1560 became bishop of Salisbury. His 1562 *Apologia ecclesiae Anglicanae* was a defence of the Anglican settlement and an argument for the necessity of the church reform which had been undertaken. Jewel's treatise anticipated the later work of HOOKER, whose education Jewel supported; his own teaching was given official approval by Archbishop BANCROFT.

*DNB.*

**JEWS.** Christian hatred of Jews, which culminated in the crime of the Holocaust, has a continuous history that extends back to the Christian Gospels, which attempt to exonerate the Romans who killed Jesus by shifting the blame to the Jews, who throughout Christian history have been charged with deicide. Compulsory baptism of Jews was introduced in the seventh century in France, Spain, and the Byzantine Empire, and during the CRUSADES, from 1095 onwards,

Christian preachers incited their congregations to attack Jews.

In 1215 the Fourth Lateran Council imposed SUMPTUARY LAWS that obliged Jews to wear clothing that distinguished them from Christians. Jews were regularly accused of desecrating the host, murdering children for ritual purposes, and poisoning the water supply; these myths were expressed in ballads and popular drama. Jews were expelled from England in 1290 and from France in 1306 and 1394. In Germany, the PLAGUE of 1348–9 (the Black Death) was attributed to Jews having poisoned the wells, and Jews were driven from many cities; in the next century Jews were expelled from many cities and principalities, including Saxony (1423), Augsburg (1439), Bavaria (1450), Mainz (1483), Magdeberg (1493), Nuremburg (1499), and Ulm (1499); by the end of the fifteenth century, Germany, together with huge tracts of Europe, was *Judenrein* ('free of Jews').

In the Iberian peninsula, Jews were forcibly baptized in both Spain (1391 and 1492) and Portugal (1497) on pain of expulsion. In practice many were expelled from Spain in 1492 and from Portugal in 1494. Jews who converted were known as *conversos* or *nuevos Cristianos* or MARRANOS (Spanish; 'pigs'); in the Balearic Islands, the *marranos* were known as *chuetas*. In 1480 the INQUISITION was established in Aragon, and its first targets were the *marranos* and MORISCOS. The number of *marranos* grew after the expulsion of the Jews from Spain in 1492 and the forced conversion of all Portuguese Jews in 1497.

Exiled *marranos* formed congregations in the Ottoman Empire (which, unlike Catholic Europe, was tolerant of Judaism), notably in Constantinople, Adrianople (now Turkish Edirne), Selanik (now Greek Thessaloniki), and North Africa; some Jews even achieved prominent positions in the Ottoman administration. In Protestant northern Europe, Jews were initially welcomed, but tolerance gave way to expulsions when it became clear that there was no prospect of widespread conversions. The pre-eminent community of *marranos* was the congregation formed in Amsterdam in 1597. There were also substantial Jewish communities in Antwerp, Mantua, Venice, and Rome. The first Jewish GHETTO was established in Rome by Pope PAUL IV in 1556 (abolished 1870); other ghettos followed in Venice (which had isolated Jews since 1516), Frankfurt, Prague, and Trieste.

Jews subsisted on the margins of European society, but were tolerated in certain occupations: the courts of Italy often had Jewish musicians, and in many European courts Jews worked as physicians. Such posts did not allay Christian suspicions: Rodrigo LOPEZ, the principal physician of Queen ELIZABETH, was of Jewish descent, and his execution set off a wave of anti-Jewish sentiment that is reflected in Shakespeare's *Merchant of Venice* and the revival of MARLOWE's *Jew of Malta*. Jewish poets and dramatists produced a body of literature in Hebrew, and the philosopher LEONE EBREO wrote the influential *Dialoghi di amore*.

Humanist interest in HEBREW SCHOLARSHIP produced in a few Christians—notably REUCHLIN, but also PICO DELLA MIRANDOLA—a measure of tolerance that was virtually unique in the late fifteenth and early sixteenth centuries. By the end of the sixteenth century such attitudes had become more widespread amongst humanists, of whom the most tolerant was Johannes BUXDORF. In the seventeenth century, a prosperous Jewish community became established in the United Provinces and the Jews were readmitted to England in 1655.

C. Roth, *The Jews in the Renaissance* (1959); M. A. Shulvass, *The Jews in the World of the Renaissance* (1973).

## JIMÉNEZ DE QUESADA, GONZALO (*c*.1509–1579), Spanish conquistador. He was probably a native of Córdoba, where he practised law until 1535, when he was appointed as a magistrate in Santa Marta, a Spanish colony on the north coast of what is now Colombia. In April 1536 he embarked with 900 soldiers on an expedition up the Magdalena river to subdue the Andean Indian people known as the Chibchas and to capture their capital (now Bogotá); he named the country Nuevo Reino de Granada. In 1538 he founded Santa Fé de Bogotá and the following year welcomed the expeditions of BELALCÁZAR and FEDERMANN. On returning to Spain Quesada was appointed *regidor* (alderman) for life and awarded an ENCOMIENDA. He settled permanently in Bogotá, where in 1569 he mounted an expedition to search for EL DORADO.

DHE; Juan Friede, *El adelantado don Gonzalo Jiménez de Quesada* (2 vols., 1979).

## JOACHIM I, surnamed Nestor (1484–1535), elector of Brandenburg, born on 21 February 1484, the son of Johann Cicero, elector of BRANDENBURG. He succeeded his father as elector in January 1499 and subsequently married Elizabeth, the daughter of King JOHN of Denmark. As the imperial election of 1519 approached he listened sympathetically to the entreaties and promises of both FRANCIS I and the future CHARLES V and even considered standing himself, but in the event he calculated that Charles was likely to win and so voted for him; as an act of ingratiation this proved ineffective, and relations remained strained for many years.

Joachim was a committed Catholic: he urged Charles V to enforce the Edict of WORMS and subsequently opposed the reformers at imperial diets. His wife, however, became a Lutheran, and in 1528 was forced to flee to Saxony for sanctuary. Joachim founded the University of Frankfurt an der Oder in 1506. He died in Stendal on 11 July 1535.

NDB.

## JOACHIM II, surnamed Hector (1505–71), Elector of Brandenburg, born on 12 January 1505, the elder son of JOACHIM I, elector of BRANDENBURG. He received his education at the imperial court. In 1524 he married Magdalene, daughter of GEORG DER BÄRTIGE, duke of Saxony; on her death he married Hedwig (Polish Jadwiga), daughter of King SIGISMUND I of Poland. He succeeded to the electorate in July 1535 and thereafter governed the Old and Middle Marks; the New Mark passed as an apanage to his brother Johann.

In 1532 and 1542 Joachim served as a commander in the imperial army in its campaigns against the Ottomans. He did not join the SCHMALKALDIC LEAGUE, and when the SCHMAL-KALDIC WAR broke out in 1546 he tried to remain neutral, but was eventually obliged to send troops to fight for the emperor. He worked with MAURICE OF SAXONY to persuade PHILIP OF HESSE to surrender to CHARLES V after the battle of MÜHLBERG in 1547, and was angered that the emperor declined to honour his pledge that Philip would not be prosecuted, but he refused to assist Maurice in his retributive attack on Charles.

Joachim shared the Catholicism of his father, but after 1539 allowed Lutheran preaching within his territories, which gradually went over to the Reformation. Like HENRY VIII in England, Joachim instituted a new ecclesiastical organization within Brandenburg, but retained much of the ritual of the Roman Church. He supported the AUGSBURG INTERIM of 1548 and in August 1552 participated in the negotiations that led to the Treaty of Passau, which concluded the insurrection mounted by HENRI II of France and Maurice of Saxony to overthrow the emperor; he was also involved in the negotiations that led to the Religious Peace of AUGSBURG (1555). Joachim died in Köpenick (14 kilometres (9 miles) south-east of Berlin) on 3 January 1571 and was succeeded as elector by his son Johann Georg.

NDB.

## JOAN OF ARC or the Maid of Orléans or (French) Jeanne d'Arc or Jeanne la Pucelle (1412–31), French visionary, born into a peasant family in the village of Domrémy (Champagne). At the age of 13 she began to hear voices which she identified as those of SS Michael, Catherine of Antioch, and Margaret of Antioch. The voices urged her to liberate France from the English, and to that end she was instructed to raise the siege of Orléans and conduct King CHARLES VII to his coronation at Reims. Having accomplished these tasks she wanted to return home, but yielded to calls from French patriots to continue the struggle. PHILIP THE GOOD, duke of Burgundy, betrayed Joan and sold her to the English; Charles VII made no attempt to rescue her. She was tried for heresy and witchcraft by a French ecclesiastical court presided over by Pierre Cauchon, bishop of Beauvais. The court condemned her as a heretic, and Joan was therefore handed over to the civil power for execution; Rouen was an English possession from 1419 to 1449, so she was passed to the English authorities to be burnt at the stake on 30 May 1431. Her sentence was revoked by Pope CALLISTUS III in 1456; in 1920 she was canonized as a holy virgin, though not as a martyr.

In the late nineteenth century Joan of Arc became a French national heroine. She appears in Shakespeare's *1 Henry VI* and is the subject of Voltaire's *La Pucelle*, Schiller's *Die Jungfrau von Orleans*, Southey's *Joan of Arc*, Mark Twain's *Personal Recollections of Joan of Arc*, George Bernard Shaw's *Saint Joan*, and Anouilh's *L'Alouette*.

DBF; P. Doncœur and Y. Lanhers, *Documents et recherches relatives à Jeanne la Pucelle* (5 vols., 1952–61); P. Tisset and Y. Lanhers, *Procès de Jeanne d'Arc* (3 vols., 1960–71); Deborah Fraioli, *Joan of Arc: The Early Debate* (2000).

## JOAN, PERE (1398–after 1458), Catalan sculptor in the Gothic tradition who carved the gilded alabaster reredos in the

central apse of Tarragona Cathedral (1426–33); the reredos depicts scenes from the life of St Tecla, the patron saint of the city. He started work on the reredos of Zaragoza Cathedral, but was called to Naples by ALFONSO V in 1447. In Naples he contributed to the triumphal arch built to commemorate the king's entry into Naples on 26 February 1443.

*DBC.*

**JODELLE, ÉTIENNE, SIEUR DE LYMODIN** (1532–73), French dramatist and Pléiade poet, born in Paris, where he was educated at the Collège de Boncourt. His best-known play, *Cléopâtre captive* (1552–3), was the earliest French TRAGEDY. He wrote a second tragedy, *Didon se sacrifiant* (composed 1555, published 1574), and a classical comedy, *Eugène* (composed 1552, published 1574). In 1558 he was excluded from the court because of a botched entertainment for HENRI II, and although he wrote anti-Protestant poems (including one rejoicing in the ST BARTHOLOMEW'S DAY MASSACRE) and deferential court poetry in an attempt to regain favour, he died in poverty.

*DBF; Enea Balmas, Un poeta del Rinascimento francese: Étienne Jodelle (1962).*

**JOEST, JAN** (c.1450–1519), Dutch painter, born in Wesel, near Rocklinghausen. He moved to Haarlem in about 1510. His most important surviving work is a *Life of Christ* (1505–8) in the Church of St Nicholas in Calcar on which he was assisted by JOOS VAN CLEVE. He was also commissioned (1505) to paint an altarpiece for Palencia Cathedral; it consists of seven panels of *Sorrows of the Virgin* and one of the donor with Mary and St John.

*MDA; NDB; Ulrike Wolff-Thomson, Jan Joest van Kalkar: Ein niederlaendischer Maler um 1500 (1997).*

**JOHANN CASIMIR** (1543–92), count palatine of the Rhine, the fourth child of FRIEDRICH III, elector of the Palatinate. He was by upbringing and conviction a Calvinist, and from 1567 to 1575 fought on the HUGUENOT side in the French WARS OF RELIGION; he subsequently contributed to the Protestant cause in the REVOLT OF THE NETHERLANDS by commanding an army (in part financed by Queen ELIZABETH of England) sent by Dutch Calvinists to relieve GHENT. On the death in 1583 of his elder brother the Elector Ludwig VI, Johann Casimir became regent of the Palatinate during the minority of his nephew, the future Elector Friedrich IV; in this capacity he restored Calvinism to the Palatinate.

*NDB s.v. Johann Casimir, Pfalzgraf bei Rhein.*

**JOHANN FRIEDRICH I, THE MAGNANIMOUS or (German) der Großmütige** (1503–54), elector of Saxony, born at Torgau on 30 June 1503, the son of the Elector Johann, who was the head of the Ernestine branch of the WETTIN family. Johann Friedrich was educated as a Lutheran and in 1531 became involved in the activities of the SCHMALKALDIC LEAGUE. In 1532 he succeeded his father as elector of SAXONY, the territories of which consisted of western Saxony and Thuringia; in 1542 he relinquished Coburg as an apanage for his brother Johann Ernst. On succeeding as elector Johann Friedrich

continued the religious policies of his Lutheran father and became, with PHILIP OF HESSE, joint leader of the Schmalkaldic League, although he disapproved of Philip's bigamy.

In 1541 MAURICE OF SAXONY succeeded to the duchy of Saxony and became head of the Albertine branch of the Wettin family. Casting a covetous eye on the electoral title, Maurice sought to provoke a confrontation. The see of Naumburg had chosen Julius von PFLUG as its bishop, but Maurice imposed a Protestant intruder, Nikolaus von AMSDORF; he also sequestered the property of the bishop of Meissen, whose see was a joint protectorate of ducal and electoral Saxony. Johann Friedrich prepared for war, which was only averted through the intervention of Philip of Hesse. In July 1546, when CHARLES V mounted an attack on the Schmalkaldic League, he revived the earlier quarrel by promising Maurice the electoral title in exchange for assistance disguised as neutrality. In September Johann Friedrich was placed under an imperial ban and in November Charles invaded the electorate. Johann Friedrich repelled the invasion, captured ALBRECHT ALCIBIADES, and overran ducal Saxony.

At the climactic battle of MÜHLBERG on 24 April 1547, Johann Friedrich was taken prisoner and condemned to death. On 19 May he escaped the death penalty by signing the Wittenberg Capitulation, in which he ceded to Maurice the electoral title and the province that contained Wittenberg. He refused, however, to accede to the AUGSBURG INTERIM of May 1548, and so remained in prison until May 1552. He died in Weimar on 3 March 1554.

Johann Friedrich was a man of voracious appetites whose strengths became most apparent in adversity. His fortitude earned the praise of Roger ASCHAM and MELANCHTHON and the appellation *der Großmütige*. His patronage centred on education: while still in prison he founded the Lutheran gymnasium which was finally granted a charter as the University of Jena on 2 February 1558; he was also a generous patron of the University of Leipzig.

*NDB s.v. Johann Friedrich (I) der Großmütige.*

**JOHANN FRIEDRICH II** (1529–95), duke of Saxony, born in Torgau on 8 January 1529, the eldest son of JOHANN FRIEDRICH I, elector of Saxony. During his father's imprisonment (1547–52) he administered the remaining territories of Ernestine Saxony; on the death of his father in 1554, Johann Friedrich ruled together with his two brothers until 1557, when he became sole ruler.

Johann Friedrich was determined to regain the electoral title of which his father had been stripped, and to that end employed Wilhelm von GRUMBACH, who had formerly been in the service of ALBRECHT ALCIBIADES. He protected Grumbach from 1557 to 1566, when his refusal to hand over Grumbach led the Emperor MAXIMILIAN II to impose an imperial ban on Johann Friedrich. The execution of the ban was entrusted to AUGUSTUS I, the elector of Saxony, and Johann Friedrich's surviving brother Johann Wilhelm (1530–73). Augustus and Johann Wilhelm marched on Gotha, whose citizens mutinied and handed over Johann Friedrich in April

1567. He was imprisoned in Vienna until his death in Steyr on 6 May 1595.

In 1565 Johann Friedrich had ceded much of his territory as an apanage for Johann Wilhelm, retaining only Gotha and Weimar, and on his incarceration his remaining territories were given to Johann Wilhelm. His first wife Agnes, the daughter of PHILIP OF HESSE and the widow of MAURICE OF SAXONY, died in 1555. His second wife Elizabeth was the daughter of FRIEDRICH III, elector palatine of the Rhine; she shared her husband's imprisonment for 22 years.

*NDB* s.v. Johann Friedrich II der Mittlere.

## JOHANN VON SPEYER (d. 1470) and WENDELIN VON SPEYER (d. *c*.1477),

German printers, brothers from Speyer (English exonym Spires) who arrived in Venice in 1467. Johann was awarded a printing monopoly, and in 1469 the two brothers opened a printing workshop. Their first book was an edition of Cicero's *Epistolae ad familiares* (1469) printed in roman type in an edition of 300 copies. After Johann's death, Wendelin continued the business until 1477; his books included an Italian translation of the Bible (1471), an edition of Petrarch, and many classical works in Latin.

## JOHN or Hans (1455–1513),

king of Denmark, Norway, and Sweden, was the son of CHRISTIAN I. Although his father died in 1481, a dispute in the Danish Diet about the limits of royal power delayed his accession to the throne of Denmark and Norway until 1483. In Sweden, Sten STURE declined to recognize John as the rightful king of Sweden, so John did not accede to the Swedish throne until 1497, after Stur had resigned the regency. Four years later the Swedish nobility rebelled, and for the rest of his reign John was only nominally king of Sweden.

*DBL, NBL,* and *SBL* s.v. Hans.

## JOHN I or (Portuguese) João I (1357–1433),

king of Portugal, was born in Lisbon on 22 April 1357, the illegitimate son of King Pedro I, and in 1364 was created grand master of Aviz. When John's legitimate half-brother King Fernão I died without a male heir in October 1383, efforts were made to secure the succession for Princess Beatriz, King Fernão's daughter, but her marriage to King John I of Castile would have meant that Portugal, like León in 1230, would in effect become a province of Castile. King John of Castile invaded Portugal, but his army, weakened by plague, was defeated at the battle of Aljubarrota on 14 August 1385; thereafter the throne of John I of Portugal was secure for the 48 years of his reign, though tensions persisted until the death of John of Castile (who died without heirs by Beatriz) in 1390.

King John was married to Philippa, daughter of John of Gaunt. Their five sons included DUARTE (who was to succeed his father) and HENRY THE NAVIGATOR, who in 1415 led their father's army in the siege of Ceuta, which was destined to become a permanent European enclave in North Africa. The capture of Ceuta inaugurated the long period of Portuguese expansion in AFRICA that was the most important feature of the reign of John I.

*DHP.*

## JOHN II or (Spanish) Juan II (1397–1479),

king of Aragon, Sardinia, and Sicily (from 1458) and king of Navarre (from 1425), was born on 29 June 1397, the son of King Ferdinand I of Aragon and the younger brother of Alfonso (later ALFONSO V). Alfonso acceded to the throne in 1416 and thereafter spent much of his life in Naples (where he reigned as Alfonso I), and Prince John acted as his brother's lieutenant-general in Aragon.

King John's first wife was Queen Blanche of Navarre, and on her death in 1441 he was left in sole possession of Navarre for the rest of his life, whereupon the kingdom was to revert to Prince Carlos of Viana, his son by Blanche. King John regarded his son as a threat to his possession of Navarre, and his second wife Juana Enríquez fuelled his dislike for Prince Carlos. In 1461 Prince Carlos died, possibly by poison administered at the instruction of his stepmother. In the intervening years, however, the cause of Prince Carlos had been taken up by the Aragonese and the Catalans, and much of John's reign was taken up with the suppression of rebellions in Aragon and Catalonia; in 1472 he quelled the Catalan revolt, but throughout the 1470s he was at war with King LOUIS XI of France, to whom he was forced to cede Roussillon. In this period he was also blinded by cataracts, but he recovered his sight through the operation known as couching, in which each eye is pricked with a needle to displace the opaque crystalline lens below the axis of vision.

King John was succeeded by Ferdinand II (FERDINAND V, his son by Juana Enríquez), who was already joint sovereign of Castile with his wife ISABELLA.

*DHE;* Jaime Vicens Vives, *Juan II de Aragón* (1953).

## JOHN II or (Spanish) Juan II (1405–54),

king of Castile and León, was born on 6 March 1405, the son of King Henry III (Enrique III, known as 'Henry the Sickly') and his wife Catherine, daughter of John of Gaunt. King John succeeded his father on Christmas Day 1406 (at the age of 21 months), and throughout his long reign his kingdom was ruled by regents and favourites. The authority of the most powerful figure in Castile, Álvaro de LUNA, was finally displaced by Isabella of Portugal, King John's second wife, who had Álvaro executed on a charge of bewitching the king.

King John was succeeded by HENRY IV (Enrique IV), his son by his first wife Maria (daughter of Ferdinand I of Aragon and Sicily); ISABELLA I was his daughter by Isabella of Portugal.

*DHE;* Didier Tisdel Jaén, *John II of Castile and the Grand Master Álvaro de Luna: A Biography* (1978).

## JOHN II, THE PERFECT, or (Portuguese) João II, O Perfeito (1455–95),

king of Portugal, was the son of King AFONSO V, whom he succeeded in August 1481. John proved to be a firm ruler, ordering the execution of the duke of Bragança for conspiring with Castile (1483) and personally killing the young duke of Viseu as a punishment for conspiracy. King John sent Pêro da COVILHÃ on his journey to India and Africa and initiated the voyage in which Bartolomeu DIAS rounded the Cape of Good Hope (1488). His plan to commission a voyage to India had to be delayed until the rivalry between Portugal and Castile over rights to overseas territories was settled by the Treaty of TORDESILLAS (7 June 1494). King John died without a male heir, and the throne passed to his cousin MANUEL I.

DHP; Elaine Sanceau, *The Perfect Prince: A Biography of the King Dom João II* (1959).

**JOHN III or (Portuguese) João III** (1502–57), king of Portugal, was born in Lisbon on 6 June 1502, the son of King MANUEL I, whom he succeeded in December 1521. In 1524 King John married Catherine, sister of the Emperor CHARLES V, and the emperor married the Infanta Isabella, King John's sister. These marriages were ultimately to lead to the annexation of Portugal by Spain. King John was pious, and during his reign the Church gained very considerable authority in Portugal. The Portuguese INQUISITION was established in 1536 and the JESUITS were welcomed to Portugal and to its overseas possessions. The Portuguese colonization of Brazil was effected during King John's reign, and in 1549 he consolidated the captaincies of Brazil into a single colony and appointed the first governor-general. King John died of apoplexy on his 55th birthday and was succeeded by his 3-year-old grandson SEBASTIAN.

DHP.

**JOHN III** (1537–92), king of Sweden, was the son of GUSTAVUS VASA. In 1560 John's half-brother ERIC XIV succeeded their father, and two years later he removed John from his post as governor of Finland (to which he had been appointed in 1556) and imprisoned him. John was freed in 1567 after five years of incarceration, and the following year joined his younger brother Charles (late King CHARLES IX) in a rebellion which culminated in the deposition of their brother Eric, who was later murdered in prison. John was crowned as king of Sweden in 1569, and immediately began to negotiate with Denmark, with whom Sweden had been at war since 1563; in 1570 he concluded a treaty which ended the seven-year war.

In religion King John was a nominal Lutheran with strong Catholic sympathies, and his attempts to effect a reconciliation with Rome ranged from the restoration of Catholic rituals to the placing of his son SIGISMUND III VASA (who had been raised as a Catholic) on the throne of Poland.

SBL s.v. Johan III.

**JOHN VIII PALAIOLOGOS** (1392–1448), emperor of Byzantium. He was made co-emperor before 1408, regent and emperor-designate ($\alpha\dot{\upsilon}\tau o\kappa\rho\dot{\alpha}\tau\omega\rho$) on 19 January 1421, and emperor in mid-1425, in succession to his father MANUEL II. In 1438 he travelled to Italy with a view to reconciling the Byzantine and Roman churches and seeking military aid to fight the Turks. He participated in the COUNCIL OF FLORENCE and signed the decree unifying the churches on 6 July 1439; the decree took the Roman position on the primacy of the papacy and the theological issue of the double procession of the Holy Spirit (the *filioque* controversy), so the settlement was unacceptable in Constantinople, and was repudiated by the Byzantine Church shortly after the empire collapsed in 1453. The attempt to secure military aid also proved to be ineffectual, in that the CRUSADE of 1444 raised to defend the East was defeated by Murat II at Varna, before it even reached Constantinople. By the time John died in 1448, the Turks had reduced the authority of the government to Constantinople and its immediate vicinity. He was succeeded by his brother Constantine XI, who was the last emperor; he died on the ramparts as the Turks overran the city.

**JOHN XXIII** (1370–1419), antipope to Popes BENEDICT XIII and GREGORY XII from 17 May 1410 until his deposition on 29 May 1415, was born Baldassare Cossa, the son of an impoverished Neapolitan nobleman. As a young man he was a sailor (and apparently a pirate) in the naval war between LOUIS II OF ANJOU and LADISLAS OF DURAZZO. He studied CANON LAW at Bologna and, after taking his doctorate, was appointed archdeacon of the city by his fellow Neapolitan Pope Boniface IX. The pope did not regard Baldassare's greed and profligacy as impediments to advancement, and appointed him to the post of papal treasurer, in which capacity his administrative abilities, together with his lack of any ethical scruples, enabled him to implement the pope's money-raising policies, which included the marketing of benefices and the commercial exploitation of INDULGENCES.

In 1402 Pope Boniface created Baldassare cardinal-deacon of Sant'Eustachio and dispatched him to the Romagna and Bologna as his legate; his military skills and ruthless brutality enabled him to regain Bologna for the PAPAL STATE, and he was also able to indulge his voracious sexual appetite, allegedly seducing 200 women in the course of his papal legation.

In May 1408, when the GREAT SCHISM reached a point of crisis, Baldassare broke with Pope Gregory XII and joined the dissident cardinals of Benedict XIII in a third college of cardinals, which assembled in March 1409 at the COUNCIL OF PISA. The Council deposed Popes Gregory and Benedict and elected Pietro Philarghi (Peter of Candia) as Pope Alexander V. When Alexander died suddenly on 3 May 1410 (possibly poisoned by Baldassare), the Pisan cardinals elected Baldassare as Pope John XXIII. Simony was of course a determining factor in the election, but the electors were also mindful that Baldassare's private army would be the likeliest means to recover Rome from Ladislas of Durazzo, king of Naples, and the protector of Gregory XII.

Of the three popes claiming to be the only true pope, John commanded the broadest power base in Europe, enjoying the recognition of England, France, and several Italian and German states. The defeat of Ladislas by the army of Louis II at Roccaseca on 19 May 1411 cleared the way for Pope John to establish his papacy in Rome. John summoned a council to meet in Rome on 1 April 1412, but poor attendance hampered its proceedings, and it accomplished little more than the 'greater excommunication' (which severed all contact with Christians, in addition to the lack of access to the sacraments of the 'lesser excommunication') of Jan HUS in August 1412 (for denouncing John's crusade against Ladislas) and a condemnation of the writings of John WYCLIFFE on 10 February 1413; the Council of Rome was adjourned on 3 March 1413.

At this point Pope John decided to abandon Louis II in favour of Ladislas, with whom he came to an agreement by which Ladislas would repudiate Pope Gregory (which he did on 15 June 1412) in return for being enfeoffed with the kingdom of Naples. This arrangement collapsed in 1413 when Ladislas turned against Pope John and invaded Rome (8 June 1413); Pope John escaped and fled to Florence, where the civic authorities refused to open the gates of the city for fear of the wrath of Ladislas. John appealed to SIGISMUND, king of the Romans, who made his support contingent on a large payment and on John's convoking of a council to be held in Konstanz (Constance); John reluctantly agreed (he would have preferred a council in friendly territory) and on 9 December 1413 proclaimed the COUNCIL OF CONSTANCE, which was to meet in November 1414.

The sudden death of Ladislas on 6 August 1414 altered the political and ecclesiastical balance, but John was persuaded by his cardinals to proceed with the Council of Constance rather than endeavour to secure the PAPAL STATE, and on 5 November he opened the Council. John's delegation pressed for ratification of the decrees of the Council of Pisa, which had excommunicated Popes Gregory and Benedict, but the Council decided instead that all three popes should abdicate. John negotiated for a week about the conditions under which he would abdicate, but then sought to disrupt the proceedings of the Council by fleeing on the night of 20/1 May, disguised as a groom. The tactic did not work: John was captured and returned as a prisoner, and the Council carried on its work. At the fourth and fifth sessions (30 March and 6 April 1415) it promulgated decrees asserting the superiority of the Council over the pope. The Council then suspended John from the papacy (14 May), tried him for simony, perjury, and gross misconduct, and at the twelfth session (29 May) deposed him. Baldassare Cossa, as he had now become, acquiesced in the judgement of the Council, which he declared to be infallible. He was imprisoned in Germany for the next three years, and in 1419 purchased his liberty from the Elector Ludwig III of Bavaria. He used his liberty to travel to Florence in order to submit himself to the legitimate pope, MARTIN V, who created him cardinal-bishop of Tusculum (Frascati), a post which he held for the last few months of his life.

Cardinal Baldassare died on 22 November 1419 and was buried in the baptistery beside the cathedral in Florence in a tomb by DONATELLO and the youthful MICHELOZZO.

**JOHN ALBERT or (Polish) Jan I Olbracht** (1459–1501), king of Poland, was the second son of King CASIMIR IV. In 1492 he acceded to the throne, and in 1497 led an army to Moldavia to fight the Ottomans. He was attacked by the Christian *voivode* of Moldavia, who had formed a defensive alliance with the Turks, and was forced to withdraw. In the course of his reign John Albert subdued the TEUTONIC ORDER and confiscated hundreds of estates owned by the SZLACHTA.

*PSB s.v. Jan I Olbracht.*

**JOHN OF LEIDEN or (Dutch) Jan van Leiden or Jan Beukelszoon or (German) Johann Bockelson** (1509–36),

leader of the Anabaptist kingdom of MÜNSTER, the illegitimate son of the burgomaster of Soevenhagen (near Leiden) who later married John's mother. John was apprenticed to a tailor, and travelled widely in pursuit of his trade, including a four-year sojourn in London. He had been influenced by the radicalism of Thomas MÜNTZER, and in September 1533 joined the Anabaptist movement led by the Haarlem baker Jan Matthyszoon.

On 13 January 1534 John arrived in Münster as an apostle of Matthyszoon. He was already married, but was by conviction a polygamist, and so was able to marry Bernd KNIPPERDOLLINCK's daughter Clara. After Matthyszoon's death, John added his widow to his clutch of wives. On 9 February 1534 the Münster Anabaptists launched their rebellion; a theocratic constitution was introduced, and in August John emerged as the king of this self-proclaimed Zion. Münster was retaken by its prince-bishop on 24 June 1535. John was tried together with his colleagues on 19 January 1536, and on 22 January they were tortured and executed.

*NDB s.v. Bockelson.*

**JOHN THE FEARLESS or (French) Jean sans Peur** (1371–1419), duke of Burgundy, born in Dijon, the son of Duke Philip the Bold (Philippe le Hardi); from 1384, when his maternal grandfather died, he was known as the count of Nevers. On 28 September 1396 he was taken captive by the Ottomans at the battle of Nicopolis (now Nikopol, Bulgaria), and released after payment of a ransom. He succeeded his father as duke of Burgundy in 1404 and became embroiled in a feud with Duke Louis of Orléans, brother of King Charles VI of France. In November 1407 he ordered the assassination of Duke Louis, and so began a rift between ARMAGNACS AND BURGUNDIANS that was to last for 28 years. Duke Jean's troops did not participate in the battle of AGINCOURT, which was a confrontation urged by the Armagnacs. On 30 May 1418 Duke Jean attacked Paris, massacring the Armagnacs (including their leader, the count of Armagnac) and imposing his will on Charles VI.

In 1419 Duke Jean met the dauphin (later CHARLES VII) with a view to settling the dispute. At their second meeting, in September 1419 on the bridge of Montereau (now Montereaufault-Yonne), Duke Jean was killed with an axe by one of the king's attendants. His tomb by JUAN DE LA HUERTA was installed in the Chartreuse de Champmol near Dijon and is now in the Musée des Beaux Arts in Dijon. He was succeeded by his son PHILIP THE GOOD.

*DBF; Richard Vaughan, John the Fearless (1966).*

**JOHNSON, EDWARD** (*fl.* 1570–1602), English composer, employed by the Kytson family in Suffolk. One of his madrigals is published in *The TRIUMPHS OF ORIANA* (1601). He performed in the 1575 entertainment staged at KENILWORTH CASTLE by the earl of Leicester for Queen ELIZABETH and wrote songs for a similar event at Hampshire in 1591.

**JOHNSON, GERARD THE ELDER, or (Dutch) Geraert Janssen** (d. 1611), Dutch sculptor and mason who emigrated to England from Amsterdam, a refugee from the violence of the REVOLT OF THE NETHERLANDS which erupted in 1567. He settled in Southwark (on the south bank of the Thames opposite London) and established a workshop that specialized in tombs but also made CHIMNEY PIECES and basins for FOUNTAINS. His most important tombs are the ALABASTER monuments of the third and fourth earls of Rutland (1587 and 1588) in Bottesford Church in Leicestershire.

Johnson's four sons by his English wife, Bernard, John, Nicholas, and Gerard (or Garat) the Younger, all followed him into the profession: Bernard (*fl.* 1610) was principal mason at Northumberland House in the Strand (demolished 1874) and Audley End in Essex, Nicholas (d. 1624) made the tomb for the fifth earl of Rutland (1612), and Gerard the Younger (*fl.* 1611–16) achieved posthumous fame as the sculptor of SHAKESPEARE's monument in Holy Trinity Church in Stratford, though the attribution is not wholly secure.

*MDA.*

**JOHNSON, JOHN** (*c.*1540–*c.*1595), English composer and lutenist, father of Robert JOHNSON. In 1579 he was appointed as lutenist to Queen ELIZABETH; he wrote dances for solo lute and some lute duets.

**JOHNSON, ROBERT** (*c.*1583–1633), English composer and lutenist, son of John JOHNSON. He was lutenist to James I (JAMES VI) and Princes Henry and Charles; from 1607 he was also involved in theatrical productions and MASQUES, collaborating with Ben JONSON, Alfonso FERRABOSCO, and Thomas CAMPION. His original compositions from this period reflect Italian influence in their declamatory style and the provision of an unfigured bass line for theorbo.

**JONAS, JUSTUS** (1493–1555), German reformer, born in Nordhausen (Thuringia) on 5 June 1493. His baptismal name was Jodokus (or Jobst) Koch, but on entering the University of Erfurt in 1506 he followed the common custom of changing his name, and was thereafter known as Justus Jonas. He studied law and humanities at Erfurt, and after graduating in 1510 migrated to Wittenberg, where he studied law.

On returning to Erfurt Jonas was ordained as a priest, awarded doctorates in both law and humanities, and appointed to a wealthy canonry to which a chair of law was attached; in 1519 he was appointed rector of the university. Jonas was a progressive scholar whose respect for ERASMUS had encouraged his study of GREEK and BIBLICAL scholarship. He had remained loyal to the Catholic Church, but converted to Lutheranism as a result of the LEIPZIG DISPUTATION of June 1519. He accompanied LUTHER to the Diet of WORMS in 1521, and there FRIEDRICH III, elector of Saxony, appointed him to a professorship of CANON LAW at Wittenberg.

In Wittenberg Jonas worked as a translator for both Luther and MELANCHTHON, translating their works from German to Latin and Latin to German; he also worked as a diplomat with the Protestant princes. In 1541 he began to preach in Halle, and the following year became superintendent of its churches. In 1546 he preached Luther's funeral sermon, but in the same year was banished from the duchy by MAURICE OF SAXONY. He became an itinerant preacher, and in 1553 settled in Eisfeld, where he died.

*NDB*; M. E. Lehmann, *Justus Jonas: Loyal Reformer* (1963).

**JONES, INIGO** (1573–1652), English architect and stage designer, born in London, the son of a recusant cloth worker. As a young man he secured the patronage of the earl of Pembroke, at whose expense he visited Italy. In 1605 Jones began to design scenery and costumes for MASQUES, initially those of Ben JONSON but subsequently for many other writers of masques. From 1613 to 1615 he was again in Italy, this time accompanying the earl of Arundel. It seems to have been on this journey that he began to study the architecture of PALLADIO, whose principal English exponent he was soon to become.

In 1615 Jones was appointed surveyor of the king's works, and in this capacity designed the Queen's House in Greenwich (1616–18 and 1629–35), an Italianate VILLA which is the first classical house in England, and the Queen's Chapel in St James's Palace (1623–5), which was the first classical church in England. He was also the architect of the BANQUETING HALL in the Palace of Whitehall (1619–22) and the likely architect of Lincoln's Inn Chapel (1617–23), of which the foundation stone was laid by John DONNE. His lost works include the Corinthian portico of St Paul's Cathedral (destroyed 1666) and Covent Garden, the first London square (of which only the church survives). Many of his drawings survive in Worcester College, Oxford (which also has his annotated copy of Palladio's *Quattro libri dell'architettura*), and at Chatsworth House in Derbyshire.

*DNB*; *Grove*; *MDA*; Stephen Orgel and Roy Strong, *Inigo Jones: The Theatre of the Stuart Court* (1973).

**JONES, ROBERT** (*c.*1570–*c.*1615), English (or Welsh) composer and lutenist, who published five books of ayres for lute and *The First Set of Madrigals* in 1607, as well as contributing a madrigal to *The* TRIUMPHS OF ORIANA (1601).

**JONGHELINCK, JAKOB** or **Jacques** (1530–1606), Flemish sculptor and medallist, born in Antwerp. He studied in Milan, where he may have worked with Leone LEONI, and returned to Flanders in 1555. From 1558 to 1560 he fashioned the bronze table-tomb of CHARLES THE BOLD (who had died in 1477) for the Church of Our Lady in Bruges. The tomb was (and is) situated beside the fifteenth-century tomb of Charles's only daughter MARY OF BURGUNDY (who had died in 1482). Most medieval and Renaissance artists were happy to juxtapose radically different styles, but Jonghelinck took the unusual step of imitating the style of his predecessor who had sculpted Mary's tomb.

Jonghelinck executed many portrait bronzes, notably the bronze bust of the *Duque de ALBA* (1571, Frick Collection, New York). His lifesize bronze of the *Duque de Alba* (1571), formerly in Antwerp Castle (the Steen), was destroyed in the 'Spanish fury' that engulfed Antwerp in November 1576.

*MDA*; Luc Smolderen, *Jacques Jonghelinck: Sculpteur, médailleur et graveur de sceaux* (1996).

**JONSON, BEN** (1572–1637), English playwright and poet. Jonson joined HENSLOWE's employ as actor and playwright at the age of 25, his first play, *Every Man in his Humour*, was performed in 1598. Over the next thirty years he built up a reputation to rival that of his great friend SHAKESPEARE. His plays include the Roman tragedy *Sejanus* (1603); the comedy *Volpone* (1605), in which Volpone tests his family's loyalty by feigning death; *Epicene* (1609), in which Morose's objection to noise is severely tested by his new wife, who is revealed at the end to be a boy; *The Alchemist* (1610), a comic play of misrule; and *Bartholomew Fair* (1614), which presents a satirical, anti-Puritan account of London festival culture. His satirical playwriting twice brought him controversy: *Sejanus* and an early play, *The Isle of Dogs*, now lost, were considered seditious; Jonson was imprisoned for his part in the latter. Jonson also used his art to uphold and celebrate contemporary authority: between 1605 and 1612 he wrote eight MASQUES which were produced at court, with scenery by Inigo JONES. Although his late plays are less well regarded, he was the preeminent literary and dramatic figure of JAMES I's reign. Two collections of his poems and epigrams were also published during his lifetime.

*DNB; Grove;* Anne Barton, *Ben Jonson, Dramatist* (1984).

**JOOS VAN CLEVE** or Joos van der Beke (*c*.1490–*c*.1540), Flemish painter, admitted to the guild in Antwerp in 1511; his name implies that he was a native of the city or province of Cleves. Joos travelled widely as a portrait painter. The subjects of paintings attributed to him include King HENRY VIII (*c*.1536, Hampton Court) and King FRANCIS I (Philadelphia Museum of Art). He also painted religious pictures, such as the *Holy Family* in the National Gallery in London.

The Master of the Death of the Virgin, whose name derives from the triptych of *The Death of the Virgin* in the Wallraf-Richartz Museum in Cologne, is now agreed to be Joos van Cleve. The canon of Joos's works includes ten prints, including the unique surviving impression of a *Battle Scene* now in the Louvre.

*MDA* s.v. Cleve, van.

**JOOS VAN WASSENHOVE** or (English) Justus of Ghent or (French) Juste de Gand or (Italian) Giusto da Guanto (*fl.* 1460–80), Flemish painter, admitted to the Antwerp guild in 1460. He lived from 1464 to 1465 in Ghent, where he was admitted to the guild and met Hugo van der GOES. His early paintings include an *Adoration of the Magi* (Metropolitan Museum, New York). In 1475 he entered the service of Duke FEDERICO II DA MONTEFELTRO, and remained in Urbino until 1475. During this period he painted *The Communion of the Apostles* (Palazzo Ducale, Urbino) and a series on the seven LIBERAL ARTS, of which *Music* and *Rhetoric* survive in the National Gallery in London and *Astronomy* and *Grammar* were destroyed in Berlin in 1945. The *Crucifixion* in Ghent Cathedral is usually considered to be the work of Joos. The series of 28 *Famous Men* now divided between the Palazzo Ducale in Urbino and the Louvre in Paris is sometimes attributed to Joos, but it is more likely that it is

the work of a group of painters, including Joos and Alonso BERRUGUETE.

*BNB* s.v. Juste de Gand; *MDA* s.v. Justus of Ghent.

**JORIS, DAVID,** or (Dutch) **Jan Joriszoon** or **Jan van Brugge** or (German) **Johannes von Bruck** (1501–56), Dutch Anabaptist leader, the son of a shopkeeper and amateur actor at Delft; his father had acted the part of King David, and passed the name to his son, but the name seems not to have been confirmed in baptism. Joris became a glass painter, and in 1522 painted the windows for the church in Enkhuisen (Holland).

In 1524 Joris married, and in the same year he became a Lutheran. He began to inveigh in Dutch verse and prose against the mass and against the pope, whom he castigated as the ANTICHRIST. On Ascension Day 1528 he defiled the host, for which he was placed in the pillory, had his tongue bored, and was exiled from Delft for three years. He became an Anabaptist, and in 1533 was rebaptized. He worked as an itinerant preacher and maintained friendly relations with Jan ŁASKI and MENNO SIMONS; he became a follower of Melchior HOFFMAN, but was hostile to JOHN OF LEIDEN and the Münster rebels.

In 1537 Joris's mother Marytje was executed as an Anabaptist, and shortly thereafter Joris began to experience visions and to prophesy. On 1 April 1544 he appeared with a group of disciples in Basel, which he declared to be the New Jerusalem. In Basel he styled himself Jan van Brugge and wrote more than 200 tracts; he wrote exclusively in Dutch, because his intended readers were his followers in Holland and Friesland. Joris died on 25 August 1556, three days after his wife, and was buried in the Church of St Leonard in Basel. Three years later he was posthumously accused of heresy by his son-in-law; he was convicted of heresy and his exhumed body was burnt on 13 May 1559.

The portrait of Joris in the Kunsthistorisches Museum in Basel was formerly attributed to Jan van SCOREL, but is now thought to be a self-portrait.

*NDB; NNBW* vii.

**JOSQUIN DESPRÈS** or Desprez or Des Près (*c*.1450/5–1521), Netherlandish composer. He sang in the chapel of RENÉ D'ANJOU in Aix-en-Provence in the late 1470s and may subsequently have sung in the service of LOUIS XI in Paris. By 1484 he was chaplain to Cardinal Ascanio Sforza in Milan, where he wrote *motetti missales* which were substituted for mass sections. He served in the papal chapel from 1489 under INNOCENT VIII and ALEXANDER VI; his contributions to the chapel repertoire include a setting of the Ash Wednesday tract 'Domine, non secundum', and hymn stanzas which were added to DUFAY's hymn cycle. Towards the end of the decade he re-established his links with Ascanio Sforza and is likely to have been present once more in northern Italy. With the political upheavals and French invasion of the 1490s, Josquin made his way north and into the service of CHARLES VIII; amongst the works of this period is a setting of Psalm 143, 'Memor esti verbi tui servo', which is said to have shamed the king into fulfilling a hitherto unkept promise. Meetings between LOUIS XII and Ercole d'ESTE in 1499 and 1502 are the likely catalyst which brought about his one-year service as *maestro di cappella* in Ferrara starting in 1504, after which he spent his final years as provost at the collegiate Church of Notre-Dame in Condé-sur-l'Escaut. He was a major figure in the evolution of both the sacred and secular music of the period.

**JOURNÉE DES BARRICADES or (English) Day of Barricades** (12 May 1588), a Catholic rebellion in Paris which proved to be a decisive moment in the final years of the French WARS OF RELIGION. Parisian supporters of the CATHOLIC LEAGUE invited Duke Henri de GUISE to come to Paris in defiance of an order by King HENRI III forbidding Duke Henri to enter the city. On his arrival Parisian Catholics erected barricades to block the king, who fled from the Louvre to Chartres, where he decided to assassinate Duke Henri and his brother Cardinal Louis de Lorraine in December 1588.

**JUANA I, LA LOCA, or Joanna the Mad** (1479–1555), queen of Castile, was born in Toledo on 6 November 1479, the second daughter of FERDINAND V and ISABELLA; her youngest sister was CATHERINE OF ARAGON, who was to become the first wife of King HENRY VIII of England. In 1496 she married Archduke Philip (later PHILIP I) at Lille. The deaths of her brother John (heir of Ferdinand and Isabella), of her eldest sister Isabella (Queen of Portugal), and of Isabella's infant son Miguel made Juana the heir to the throne of Spain. On the death of her mother in November 1504 Juana inherited the crown of Castile, but by this time her violent mental instability had rendered her incapable of ruling the kingdom. Her mental condition was exacerbated by her jealous rage at her husband's infidelities, by the tumultuous events of the contested succession, and by a shipwreck off the English coast, after which Juana and Philip became the guests of Henry VII at Windsor. On the death of her husband in 1506, Juana refused to relinquish his body. She lived for the last 49 years of her tormented life at Tordesillas (near Valladolid), nominally as queen (her name always appeared beside that of her son Charles in public documents) but in fact incapable of understanding affairs of state; she died on 11 April 1555. Juana had six children: her two sons were the future Emperors CHARLES V and FERDINAND I, and her four daughters included Maria (1505–58), wife of King LOUIS II of Hungary and Bohemia.

DHE; José Luis Olaizola, *Juana la Loca* (1996); Manuel Fernández Álvarez, *Juana la Loca* (2000).

**JUANA LA BELTRANEJA or Juana de Castilla** (1462–1530), Spanish princess and pretender to the throne of Castile. She was ostensibly the daughter of King HENRY IV (Enrique IV) of Castile (known as 'Henry the Impotent') and his second wife Juana of Portugal, but was widely believed to be the daughter of the queen's lover Beltrán de la Cueva. In 1468, after a civil war with his discontented nobles and his half-brother Alfonso, Henry reluctantly named his half-sister ISABELLA

as successor to the throne, but when in 1469 she married FERDINAND of Aragon against the wishes of Henry, he excluded her from the succession. On his death in 1474 Isabella and Ferdinand assumed the throne, but the succession was still not resolved. Supporters of Juana devised a plan whereby Juana would marry her powerful uncle, the widowed AFONSO V of Portugal, but before this scheme could be realized her supporters were defeated at the battle of Toro (1476). In 1479 Juana retired to a convent for the last 50 years of her life.

DHE; Tarsicio de Azcona, *Juana de Castilla, mal llamada la Beltraneja* (1998).

**JUAN DE AUSTRIA or Don John of Austria** (1545–78), Spanish soldier, born in Regensburg, the illegitimate son of the Emperor CHARLES V and the daughter of a wealthy citizen of Regensburg. Don Juan was raised in Spain by foster parents who called him Jerónimo and did not reveal his parentage to him. The emperor died in 1558, and in a codicil to his will acknowledged Don Juan as his son and enjoined PHILIP II, his legitimate son and heir, to care for his half-brother. In accordance with his father's wishes, King Philip publicly recognized Don Juan as a member of the royal family in September 1559. For the next three years he was educated at Alcalá de Henares, where his companions were the Infante Don CARLOS (who was his exact contemporary) and Alessandro FARNESE.

Don Juan chose to embark on a military career. In 1568 he was given the command of a squadron of 33 galleys which he deployed against BARBARY PIRATES. On 24 December 1568 the Granadine MORISCOS staged an armed rising, and Don Juan spent the next two years containing the revolt; once the rebellion was suppressed, the *moriscos* were deported in chains from Granada. Don Juan's finest hour was the battle of LEPANTO (1571), at which he was the commander-in-chief of the victorious forces of the HOLY LEAGUE. In 1573 Don Juan captured TUNIS, but it was soon to be lost again.

In 1576 Don Juan was appointed governor-general of the Netherlands, where his task was to suppress the REVOLT OF THE NETHERLANDS. At the point when Don Juan arrived to assume his duties, all seventeen provinces had united around the Pacification of Ghent, a treaty that proposed a common defence against Spanish oppression. After failing to secure a settlement through negotiation, Don Juan defeated the rebels at the battle of Gembloux in Brabant (31 January 1578), in which Alessandro Farnese fought with great distinction at the head of reinforcements sent by Philip II. Eight months later, at the age of 33, Don Juan died of a fever.

Don Juan is occasionally confused with a later Don Juan de Austria (1629–79), the illegitimate son of Philip IV who became viceroy of Aragon.

DHE; J. M. González Cremona, *Juan de Austria, héroe de leyenda* (1994); Fernando Ponce, *Juan de Austria, el vencedor de Lepanto* (1999).

**JUAN DE ÁVILA** (1500–69), Spanish mystic and writer, born into a wealthy family at Almodóvar del Campo (Ciudad Real); on his father's side Juan was of Jewish descent, and so suffered from the anti-Semitism of the Church throughout his life. Juan studied law at Salamanca (1513–17) and arts at Alcalá de Henares (where he was taught by Domingo SOTO). He was ordained in 1525 and three years later moved to Andalusia, where he preached for the rest of his life. In 1531 he was brought before the Seville INQUISITION accused of spreading sedition and being unduly partisan in his championing of the poor, but was released after a year in prison (1532–3). He founded at least fifteen colleges and schools, and was an active supporter of clerical reform, which became the subject of two *Memoriales* (1551 and 1561). He supported the nascent JESUIT Order, encouraging his young followers to join the Society, but did not attempt to do so himself because of the prejudice against applicants with Jewish backgrounds.

Juan de Ávila's most popular book was *Audi, filia, et vide*, which began as a sermon on Psalm 44 (and an eloquent denunciation of worldly vanities), written in 1530 for an aristocratic nun. An expanded version was published in Alcalá de Henares in 1556 without his consent; this edition was placed on the INDEX of 1559. Juan also wrote an influential set of *c*.150 letters of spiritual guidance, originally published as *Epistolario espiritual para todos estados* (1578) and now known as *Cartas espirituales*.

Juan's disciples and admirers included PEDRO DE ALCÁNTARA, Francisco de BORJA, LUIS DE GRANADA, and TERESA DE ÁVILA (who sought his advice in the final months of his life). Juan was beatified in 1894 and canonized in 1970.

Baldomero Jiménez-Duque, *El maestro Juan de Ávila* (1988).

**JUAN DE DIOS or (Portuguese) João de Deus or (English) John of God** (1495–1550), Portuguese founder of the religious ORDER of St John, which is also known as the 'Brothers Hospitallers' and as the 'Order of Charity for the Service of the Sick'. He was a Portuguese soldier, born in Montemor O Novo, who fought for Spain against the French and also fought the Ottomans in Hungary. At the age of 40 Juan experienced a religious conversion and travelled to Morocco in the hope of achieving martyrdom in defence of Christian slaves, but on failing to be killed he returned to Spain, where he opened a religious bookshop in Granada. In 1538 he experienced a second conversion, this time at the hands of JUAN DE ÁVILA, and embarked upon a life of extreme deprivation in which sanctity shaded into insanity. In a subsequent encounter with Juan de Ávila he was persuaded to divert his piety to the care of the sick and poor in Granada.

The Order of St John, which consists mostly of laymen, began in Granada when, after his death, Juan's followers constituted themselves as an Order and claimed Juan as their founder; in 1572 the Order was formally approved by Pope PIUS V. The rule of the Order is Augustinian, and members take a fourth vow committing themselves to service in hospitals. The Order now has some 200 hospitals all over Europe.

Juan de Dios was canonized in 1690 and declared by Pope Leo XIII in 1886 to be the celestial patron of hospitals and the sick. He is also the unofficial heavenly patron of printers and booksellers.

**JUAN DE FLANDES** (*c*.1465–*c*.1519), Flemish painter in Castile, employed by Queen ISABELLA. In the late 1490s, while living in Burgos, he painted a polyptych known as the *Oratorio de la reina católica*; 27 of its 47 small panels are known to survive. He lived from 1505 to 1508 in Salamanca, and then spent the final years of his life in Palencia, where he painted an altarpiece for the Church of San Lázaro (of which three panels are in the Prado and three in the National Gallery in Washington) and a series of panels on *The Life of Christ* for the Cathedral, where the twelve panels are still in place.

*MDA*; E. Bermejo, *Juan de Flandes* (1962).

**JUAN DE JUANES.** See MAÇIP, VICENT AND JOAN VICENT.

**JUAN DE JUNI or (French) Jean de Joigny** (*c*.1507–1577), Burgundian sculptor in Spain who worked in León and Salamanca in the 1530s and settled in Valladolid in 1540. The subject of his sculptures is always religious, and they are characterized by the dramatic expression of strong emotion, a feature that anticipates the advent of the BAROQUE in SPANISH ART. Juan's best-known works are depictions of *The Entombment*: the early version executed for the Monastery of San Francisco in Valladolid (1545) is now in the Valladolid Museum, and the later version (1571) is in the Capilla del Entierro in Segovia Cathedral. Between 1545 and 1561 he was chiefly occupied with the vast MANNERIST reredos for the Church of Santa María la Antigua in Valladolid (now in Valladolid Cathedral).

*MDA* s.v. Juni, Juan de.

**JUAN DE LA CRUZ or (English) John of the Cross** (1542–91), Spanish poet and co-founder of the Discalced Carmelite Order. He was born into an impoverished family in Fontiveros (Ávila) and entered the Carmelite monastery of Medina del Campo in 1563, taking the name Juan de Santa María; he studied theology at Salamanca (1564–8) and was ordained priest in 1567. By this time TERESA DE ÁVILA had established her Reformed Carmelite Order (1562) of nuns, and with her encouragement and assistance Juan extended her reform to include friars. Like the nuns, Discalced Carmelite Friars lived in uncompromising poverty, hardship, and solitude, subsisting on a meagre vegetarian diet and wearing a coarse brown woollen habit. Teresa's nuns wore leather sandals, but Juan's discalced friars were even more rigorous in their abjuring of comfortable footwear, always going barefooted and so truly 'discalced' (from Latin *discalceare*, to make unshod). Juan became sub-prior of the Discalced Carmelite monastery at Duruelo (1568–71), master of the Discalced Carmelite college at Alcalá de Henares (1571–2), and confessor of the Convent of the Incarnation at Ávila (1572–7), where Teresa had returned as prioress in 1571.

In 1575 the General Chapter of the unreformed (and anti-reformist) Calced Carmelites, the Carmelites of the Mitigated Observance, met in Piacenza (Italy), and as a result of their hostility to Juan's reforms he was imprisoned for nine months (1577–8) in the Order's house in Toledo; he escaped to the Hospital of Santa Cruz in Toledo, where he was nursed back to health, and thence to the Monastery of El

Calvario in Andalusia. Thereafter the formal process of separating the Calced and Discalced Carmelites was begun, and the orders became independent in 1580. Juan served as rector of the Discalced Order's college at Baeza (1579–82), prior of the Granada house (1582–8), and prior of the Segovia house (1588–91). After a falling out with Nicolás Doria, the vicar-general of the Discalced Carmelites, he was banished in mid-1591 to Úbeda (Andalusia), where he died a few months later.

In 1577–8, whilst imprisoned in Toledo, Juan de la Cruz wrote three mystical poems that are among the greatest works of Spanish literature; he subsequently constructed extensive commentaries on these poems. *Canciones del alma en la íntima comunicación de unión de Dios*, which is normally known from part of its opening line as *Llama de amor viva*, later became the subject of Juan's prose commentary *Llama de amor* (1584). *Canciones entre el alma y el Esposo*, which is normally known as the *Cántico espiritual* (or sometimes, from its opening line, as *¿Adónde te escondiste, Amado?*), is a dialogue (based on the Song of Solomon) between a lover and her absent beloved which allegorizes the longing of the Soul for the Creator and the Created; it later became the subject of his prose commentary *Cántico espiritual*. The third poem, *Canciones del alma que se goza de haber llegado al alto estado de la perfección, que es la unión con Dios, por el camino de la negación espiritual*, which is normally known either as *Noche oscura* (from its opening phrase) or as *Canción de la subida del Monte Carmelo*, is on a literal level an account of Juan's own escape from prison, but also enacts a young woman's flight to join her beloved and the flight of the soul from the prison of the body to join its divine bridegroom; the first two stanzas later became the subject of Juan's prose commentaries *Noche oscura* and *Subida del Monte Carmelo*.

Juan de la Cruz was beatified in 1675, canonized in 1726, and declared a doctor of the Church in 1926; his feast day was 24 November, but was changed in 1969 to 14 December.

Juan de la Cruz is sometimes confused with two Dominican namesakes, both from Talavera and both called John of the Cross in English. The elder Dominican Juan de la Cruz studied at Salamanca and in 1538 was sent with a group of Spanish friars to reform the Dominican Order in Portugal, where he spent the rest of his life; he was the author of a work on vocal prayer (*Diálogo sobre la necesidad de la oración*, 1555) and of a chronicle of his Order (published posthumously in 1567). The younger Dominican Juan de la Cruz studied at Valladolid (1583) and later published *Epitome de statu religionis* (1613) and *Directorium conscientiae* (1620).

G. Brenan, *Saint John of the Cross, his Life and Poetry* (1973).

**JUAN DE LA HUERTA** (*fl.* 1431–62), Spanish sculptor who in 1443 succeeded Claux der WERVE as the artist responsible for the tomb of John the Fearless, duke of Burgundy (d. 1419), and his wife in the Chartreuse de Champmol near Dijon. Juan imitated the nearby tomb of Philip the Bold in his carving of the minor figures, but left in 1457 without finishing the tomb, which was eventually completed by Antoine MOITURIER. The Charterhouse is now a psychiatric hospital,

and the tombs of the dukes of Burgundy have been moved to the Musée des Beaux-Arts in Dijon.

*MDA.*

**JUAN DE LOS ÁNGELES, FRAY** (*c.*1536–1609), Spanish Franciscan writer. He was born in Oropesa (Toledo) and studied at the University of Alcalá de Henares. He entered the Franciscan Order, where he eventually held several senior positions. His Neoplatonic *Triunfos de amor de Dios* (Medina del Campo, 1590) was revised as *Lucha espiritual y amorosa entre Dios y el alma* (1600). His *Diálogos de la conquista del espiritual y secreto reino de Dios* (2 vols., 1595) drew on medieval north European traditions of mysticism, especially the writings of the Flemish mystic Jan van Ruysbroek and the sermons of the German Dominican Johannes Tauler.

**JUBILEE YEAR or holy year or** (Italian) *anno santo* **or** (German) *Jubeljahr*. In 1300 Pope Boniface VIII declared the first holy year of jubilee, during which Christians who undertook a PILGRIMAGE to Rome would be rewarded with a plenary INDULGENCE if they visited the churches of the apostles Peter and Paul for a specified number of days (30 days for residents of the PAPAL STATE, 15 days for foreigners) during the year. Pope Boniface intended the interval between holy years to be 100 years, but in 1343 Pope Clement VI reduced the interval to 50 years; in 1389 Pope Urban VI further reduced the interval to 33 years (the length of the earthly life of Jesus) and in 1470 Pope PAUL II settled on 25 years, which has been the interval down to the present time. Jubilee years were declared in 1300, 1350, 1390, 1423, 1450, 1475, 1500, and every 25 years thereafter, and in each of these years large numbers of pilgrims travelled to Rome to secure the cherished dispensation. Until 1500 the jubilee dispensation could only be obtained in Rome, but thereafter it could be secured in any church in Christendom during the six months following the Roman year; as a result of this decision, attendance at the jubilee festivities of 1525 was severely reduced.

H. Thurston, SJ, *The Holy Year of Jubilee: An Account of the History and Ceremony of the Roman Jubilee* (1900); P. Bargellini, *L'Anno Santo: Nella storia, nella letteratura e nell'arte* (1974).

**JUD, LEO** (1482–1542), Swiss reformer known to his contemporaries as Meister Leu, born in Alsace and educated in Basel, where he studied medicine and, after becoming a Zwinglian, theology. Jud served for four years (1518–22) as pastor of Einsiedeln and then joined ZWINGLI in Zürich. In Zürich Jud devoted himself to translation: he was the principal translator of the Zürich Bible and also translated the Old Testament into Latin. He died on 19 June 1542.

*DHBS; NDB.*

**JUDENKÜNIG, HANS** (*c.*1450–1526), German composer and lutenist whose family came from Württemberg. He was a lutenist in the Corpus Christi confraternity at St Stephen's Cathedral in Vienna and moved in humanist circles. His *Utilis et compendiaria introductio* (*c.*1515–19) is an early instruction manual for the lute.

**JÜLICH-CLEVES SUCCESSION, WAR OF** (1609–14). By 1521 the duchy of Cleves, on the Lower Rhine, had become a principality which included the duchies of Cleves, Jülich, and Berg, and the counties of Ravensberg and Mark; the principality was sometimes called Jülich-Cleves. When Johann Wilhelm, ruler of the united duchy, died childless and insane on 25 March 1609, there were three claimants to the succession: the Protestants were Johann Sigismund of Brandenburg and Wolfgang Wilhelm of Pfalz-Neuburg, and the Catholic claimant was Christian II, elector of Saxony, whose claim was prosecuted by the Emperor RUDOLF II. Imperial troops led by Archduke Leopold of Passau were sent to dislodge the Protestant claimants and in 1610 Dutch and English troops commanded by MAURICE OF NASSAU joined the war. Wolfgang Wilhelm, who became count palatine in September 1610, converted to Catholicism, and Spanish troops entered the war to support his claim. The conflict was resolved in November 1614 in the Treaty of Xanten, which awarded Jülich, Cleves, and Berg to Brandenburg and the other territories to the count palatine.

**JULIUS II** (1443–1513), pope from 1 November 1503 until his death on 21 February 1513, was born Giuliano della Rovere in Albissola (near Savona) on 5 December 1453. His uncle Francesco (later Pope SIXTUS IV) arranged for Giuliano to be educated by the Franciscans at Perugia, but he does not seem to have entered the Order. Francesco became pope on 9 August 1471, and heaped benefices on his nephew Giuliano, who in the course of his uncle's pontificate became bishop of Carpentras, bishop of Bologna, bishop of Vercelli, archbishop of Avignon, cardinal-priest of San Pietro in Vincoli and of SS Dodici Apostoli, cardinal-bishop of Sabina, cardinal-bishop of Frascati, cardinal-bishop of Ostia, and cardinal-bishop of Velletri. In 1480 he was appointed papal legate *a latere* to France with a view to settling the dispute between King LOUIS XI of France and MAXIMILIAN I over the Burgundian inheritance; the successful conclusion of those negotiations in 1482 enhanced Giuliano's influence in the college of cardinals.

Giuliano was prominent in the pontificate of Pope INNOCENT VIII (whose election he had secured by recourse to bribery), notably in his defence of Rome against the predations of FERRANTE I, king of Naples, in the Barons' War of 1484–6. His position changed abruptly with the election of his rival Rodrigo Borgia as Pope ALEXANDER VI; Giuliano retired promptly to Ostia and then (in 1494) fled to France, where he encouraged King CHARLES VIII to undertake the conquest of Naples. He accompanied the king on his military campaign, but failed to secure his support for the convocation of a council to depose Pope Alexander on grounds of simony. For the remainder of Alexander's pontificate, Giuliano remained in France and northern Italy lest he be assassinated, but after a formal reconciliation in 1498 he subjugated his personal animosity for the pope to the need to represent papal interests. He therefore negotiated the treaty of 1498 with King Louis XII, and the following year negotiated the marriage of Cesare BORGIA to a French princess, Charlotte d'Albret. On the death of Pope Alexander, Giuliano returned to Rome, and supported the election of Pope PIUS

III, who died three weeks after his election. In the ensuing conclave Giuliano bribed his way to the papacy; the fact that he had fathered three daughters as a cardinal was not deemed to be an impediment.

Julius was a ruthless and violent pope (his nickname was 'Il Terribile'), but he displayed diplomatic skills and a measure of integrity. He repudiated the nepotism of his predecessors and sought to restore and extend the PAPAL STATE, large tracts of which had been alienated under the Borgias, and to free Italy from foreign domination. He was at first willing to retain the services of Cesare Borgia, whom he used to subdue a revolt in Romagna, but soon forced him into exile and imprisonment in Spain. He negotiated with Venice for the restoration of the parts of Romagna that Venice had occupied earlier in 1503 and, when diplomacy failed, allied himself with France and the Empire and wrested most of the occupied territory back for the papacy; after 1504, only Rimini and Faenza remained in Venetian hands. In 1506 he attacked Perugia and Bologna, personally leading his papal army into combat, dressed in full armour, and restored both cities to the papacy, so ending the rule of the BAGLIONI in Perugia and of the BENTIVOGLIO family in Bologna. In March 1509 he joined the League of CAMBRAI, which had been formed on 10 December 1508 by King Louis XII of France and the Emperor Maximilian I; on 27 April he excommunicated Venice and in May the League defeated Venice comprehensively and secured the return of Rimini and Faenza.

Having humiliated Venice, Julius decided that French forces in the north of Italy posed a greater danger, and early in 1510 he therefore absolved and negotiated peace with Venice, whose allegiance would be vital for any war with the Turks. In order to win Spanish support, Julius set aside the claims of Francis, duke of Valois (later FRANCIS I), to the kingdom of Naples and on 3 July 1510 enfeoffed Ferdinand II of Aragon (FERDINAND V) with Naples. He then captured Modena and early in the new year seized Mirandola, but these successes were counterbalanced by his failure to secure Ferrara and the temporary loss of Mirandola and Bologna, where Julius narrowly escaped being captured by the French. In order to secure the Vatican, Julius instituted the SWISS GUARD, whose uniforms were designed by MICHELANGELO. He also supported the restoration of the MEDICI in Florence in 1512.

King Louis XII sought to subvert the authority of Pope Julius by holding a synod at Tours in September 1510; the Synod renewed the PRAGMATIC SANCTION OF BOURGES and convoked (in the name of a group of dissident cardinals) a council to meet at Pisa on 1 September 1511 with a view to deposing Pope Julius. The Council, which enjoyed the support of the Emperor Maximilian I, met on 1 October and, after retiring to Milan, decreed the suspension of Julius, who responded militarily by forming the HOLY LEAGUE in October 1511 and responded ecclesiastically by convening the Fifth Lateran COUNCIL in Rome in 1512. The armies of the League were defeated at Ravenna on 11 April 1512, but reinforcement by Swiss troops enabled Julius to reverse the course of the war; by the end of 1512 French troops had been driven out of

Italy and Parma, Piacenza, and Reggio Emilia had been incorporated into the Papal State.

The pontificate of Julius was dominated by war; his military enthusiasms were caricatured by ERASMUS in his *Praise of Folly* (1509), GUICCIARDINI remarked that there was nothing of the priest in him except for his dress and title, and MACHIAVELLI admired him unreservedly. He was not, however, inactive as a churchman. In 1503 he issued the dispensation which allowed HENRY VIII to marry his brother's widow CATHERINE OF ARAGON, and on 14 January 1505 he published a bull declaring that, henceforth, papal elections would be nullified by simony. He also instituted the first episcopal sees in South America.

Julius was a frugal administrator of Vatican finances, but nonetheless a munificent patron of artists and architects, notably Michelangelo (from whom he commissioned the ceiling of the SISTINE CHAPEL and his tomb, for which Michelangelo sculpted the *Moses* in San Pietro in Vincoli and the two *Slaves* now in the Louvre), RAPHAEL (from whom he commissioned the Stanza della Segnatura), and BRAMANTE (from whom he commissioned plans for the new ST PETER'S BASILICA); his decision to raise the requisite capital for the new basilica (for which the foundation stone was laid on 18 April 1506) by the sale of INDULGENCES later incurred the wrath of Protestant reformers, and occasioned LUTHER'S 95 Theses. Julius also greatly expanded the VATICAN LIBRARY and founded the Vatican's collection of sculptures from classical antiquity.

Julius died of fever on 21 February 1513 and was mourned as the liberator of Italy from foreign domination. Julius moulded the Papal State into the form that it was to retain for four centuries; in later Italian historiography he came to be regarded as an early champion of the unification of Italy. Raphael's portrait of Julius hangs in the National Gallery in London.

Christine Shaw, *Julius II: The Warrior Pope* (1993); F. Seneca, *Venezia e Papa Giulio II* (1962); L. Partridge and R. Starn, *A Renaissance Likeness: Art and Culture in Raphael's Julius II* (1980).

**JULIUS III** (1487–1555), pope from 8 February 1550 until his death on 23 March 1555, was born Giovanni Maria Ciocchi de Monte in Rome on 10 September 1487, the son of a jurist. He studied CANON LAW at Perugia and Siena and became chamberlain to Pope JULIUS II. In 1511 he succeeded his uncle as archbishop of Sipontum (the ancient colony close to modern Manfredonia, in Apulia). Pope LEO X appointed him as bishop of Pavia (1520) and Pope CLEMENT VII twice appointed him to the governorship of Rome. He was taken hostage by the emperor during the SACK OF ROME in May 1527. In 1535 he was appointed vice-legate of Bologna by Pope PAUL III, who subsequently created him cardinal-priest (December 1536) and cardinal-bishop of Palestrina (October 1543). He was appointed as one of the three co-presidents of the COUNCIL OF TRENT, and opened its first session on 13 December 1545; it was in his co-presidential capacity that he shared the responsibility for the transference of the Council from Trento to Bologna, and so angered CHARLES V.

In 1550 Giovanni Maria was elected as Pope JULIUS III by a single vote; the loser was Cardinal Reginald POLE. The pontificate of Julius was characterized by a combination of personal indulgence and enlightened patronage. His personal life was never remarkable for its restraint, but public scandal reached its apex when Pope Julius became besotted with a 15-year-old boy called Innocenzo whom he had picked up on a street in Parma; he arranged for Innocenzo to be adopted by his brother and then created him cardinal.

Julius had sworn in a pre-election oath that if elected he would reconvene the suspended Council of Trent, and after protracted negotiations he announced on 14 November 1550 that the Council would reassemble at Trento on 1 May 1551. The Council met as directed, and conducted six sessions (11–16), sometimes with representation from the German Protestant ESTATES. King HENRI II of France, however, refused to countenance French participation in what he saw as a HABSBURG council. This Habsburg–Valois dispute proved to be the undoing of the restored Council. Julius had reluctantly acceded to the wish of his predecessor Pope PAUL III that his grandson Ottavio FARNESE be given Parma. When the emperor claimed Parma, Julius tried to dislodge Ottavio, but to no avail; the combined papal and imperial armies failed to defeat the French, and the revolt of the German princes against Charles V in 1552 forced him to leave Innsbruck. On 28 April 1552, at the sixteenth session, Julius was forced to suspend the Council indefinitely, and the following day he signed a truce with France which restored Parma to Ottavio.

Until 1552 Julius had combined affairs of state with an endless round of banquets, the theatre, and hunting, but the collapse of the Council of Trent and the humiliating truce with France which restored Parma to Ottavio Farnese occasioned Julius' withdrawal from public life to a private life of voluptuous indulgence. He spent most of his time at the Villa GIULIA, but occasionally ventured into political and ecclesiastical affairs. His attempts to act as a peacemaker between Henri II and Charles V succeeded only in alienating both parties from the papacy. He was more successful with ecclesiastical reform, curtailing the practice of holding more than one benefice, restoring monastic discipline, and reorganizing the machinery of curial government. On 21 July 1550 he confirmed the constitution of the JESUIT Order, which had been founded in 1534, and on 31 August 1552, at the urging of IGNATIUS LOYOLA, founded the German College (Collegium Germanicum) for the training of German priests to be sent as missionaries to their homeland. Julius' finest hour in foreign policy was the restoration of England to the obedience of Rome in the wake of the accession of Queen MARY I on 6 July 1553; the announcement was greeted with jubilation in Rome. Pope Julius appointed Cardinal Pole as his legate in England, and on 30 November Cardinal Pole absolved England from schism. Julius was not to live to see how ephemeral the recantation of England was to be. Shortly before his death from gout Julius acceded to the request of Charles V to send Cardinal MORONE to the Diet of AUGSBURG in what proved to be the vain hope that German Protestants could be persuaded to submit to the authority of Rome.

Pope Julius was a generous patron of scholarship and the arts. He appointed Marcello Cervini (later Pope MARCELLUS II) as the founding cardinal-librarian of the VATICAN LIBRARY, MICHELANGELO as chief architect of ST PETER'S BASILICA, and PALESTRINA as choirmaster of the Capella Giulia. He also commissioned the Church of Sant'Andrea della Via Flaminia in thanksgiving for his survival when held hostage after the Sack of Rome.

**JUNIUS, FRANCISCUS, or** (French) **François du Jon** (1545–1602), Protestant theologian and translator. He studied law in his native Bourges and subsequently moved to Geneva to study Hebrew and theology. In 1565 he became a pastor in Antwerp, but was forced to emigrate two years later; he settled in Schonau (near Heidelberg), where he became pastor of the refugee church; during this period he composed a grammar of the FRENCH LANGUAGE. From 1573 to 1579 he collaborated with Immanuel TREMELLIUS on a translation of the Old Testament into Latin. In 1578 he was appointed to a chair of theology and Hebrew at Neustadt; he moved to a chair at Leiden in 1592, and remained there for the rest of his life.

The scholarly Junius–Tremellius translation of the Old Testament was destined to become the standard edition for learned Protestants. Junius' other influential work was his *Eirenicum de pace ecclesiae catholicae*, a plea for mutual tolerance for Christians who acknowledged the authority of the Bible and the redemptive death of Jesus; these strictures set the limits of toleration at Protestants who subscribed to the doctrine of the Trinity.

*DBF* s.v. Du Jon; Christiaan de Jonge, *De Irenische Ecclesiologie van Franciscus Junius, 1545–1602* (1980).

**JUNIUS BRUTUS.** See LANGUET, HUBERT.

**JUSTE, JEAN** (1485–1549), Italian sculptor in France. He was born in San Martino (near Florence) and in the early years of the sixteenth century settled in Tours with his two brothers; in 1513 he was appointed royal sculptor. The finest work of the three brothers was the tomb of LOUIS XII and ANNE OF BRITTANY, which was made in their workshop in Tours (1517–18) and installed in the Abbey of Saint-Denis, near Paris (1531). The tomb depicts the kneeling king and queen attended by the twelve apostles (who are seated) and four allegorical figures representing Virtues; reliefs depict the king's victories in Italy. The tomb is executed in an Italian Renaissance idiom except for the presence of corpses (*gisants*) on the sarcophagus, which represents the continuation of a medieval tradition.

*DBF.*

**JUSTIFICATION or** (German) *Rechtfertigung*. In Christian theology, the term 'justification' derives ultimately from the Latin phrase *iustum facere*, 'to make just'. *Justificatio* was used by THOMAS AQUINAS and subsequent Catholic theologians to refer either to the act whereby God conveys sanctifying GRACE to the human soul and so renders the soul just or to the change effected by grace whereby a person passes from sin to righteousness. In Protestant thought, justification was deemed to be an act of divine clemency in which a person is made righteous by the grace of God, not because of any merit on the part of the sinful believer, but by virtue of the sacrifice of Christ, who is deemed to have borne the punishment due to humankind because of its sinful state.

Martin LUTHER famously contended that justification could only be secured *per solam fidem* ('by faith alone'). In his view, justification was analogous to a legal fiction in which God regards sinful believers as righteous because of the imputed merits of Christ. He insisted that good works were utterly inefficacious: in his hymn 'Ein' feste Burg ist unser Gott' (translated into English as 'A mighty fortress is our God'), Luther epitomized his sense of the vanity of human endeavour in the line 'Est ist doch unser Tun umsonst, auch in dem besten Leben' ('everything we do is vain, even in the best life'). Faced with the inconvenience of the contention in the Epistle of James that 'faith, if it hath not works, is dead, being alone' (James 2: 17), Luther simply omitted it from his translation of the Bible.

Catholic theologians such as Johann GROPPER, Gasparo CONTARINI, and Girolamo SERIPANDO proposed a conciliatory doctrine of DOUBLE JUSTICE, but this doctrine failed both to appease the Lutherans and to gain general acceptance within the Catholic Church.

**JUSTINIAN IN THE RENAISSANCE.** Justinian (AD 483–565) was emperor of the Eastern or Byzantine Empire. The modern term for the body of Roman law that he commissioned is *Corpus iuris civilis*; this title was first used by GODEFROY in his 1583 edition, with a view to distinguishing the CIVIL LAW of Justinian from the CANON LAW of the *Corpus iuris canonici*.

On his accession in 527 Justinian commanded ten commissioners to collect and revise the imperial constitutions of Rome; this collection, which is known as the *Codex Justinianus*, was promulgated in 529, but remained in force only until 534, because it was thought to be unreliable. In 530 Justinian enacted a series of constitutions known as the Fifty Decisions (*quinquaginta decisiones*), the purpose of which was the resolution of points of law on which earlier jurists had been divided. A commission of five was appointed to prepare a revised version of the *Codex*, which was promulgated in 534 as the *Codex repetitae praelectionis*. The text of the original version has not survived, except in a few fragments, but it probably embodies the substance of the Fifty Decisions. It is the text of this second version that was known to Renaissance jurists as the *Codex Justinianus*. It consists of twelve books: book 1 deals with the history of law, with ecclesiastical law, and with the duties of senior imperial administrators; books 2–8 contain private law, book 9 criminal law, and books 10–12 administrative law. In Renaissance editions of Justinian, the last three books (known as the *Tres libri*) are often published separately from the first nine.

In 530 Justinian appointed Tribonian and fifteen other commissioners to prepare a selective compilation of the commentaries of the classical jurists. This collection was promulgated in 533, and was known in the Renaissance both as the *Digest* (from its Latin name, *Digesta*) and as the *Pandects* (from *Pandectae*, the Latin form of its Greek name). According to the Constitution Tanta, which authorized publication, the sixteen commissioners read some 3,000,000 lines in 2,000 books, and selected about a twentieth of this material for inclusion. The excerpts are arranged in 50 books, each of which is divided into sections known as titles. Medieval Bolognese jurists divided the *Digest* into three parts, and this division survives in Renaissance editions: the *Digestum vetus* (book 1 to book 24, title 2), the *Digestum infortiatum* (book 24, title 3 to book 38), and the *Digestum novum* (books 39–50). The most important Renaissance edition of the *Digest* was prepared from the Florentine text by Lelius Torelli (1489–1576) and published in three volumes in 1553 as *Digestorum seu Pandectarum libri L ex Florentinis Pandectis repraesentati*. In Renaissance commentaries passages are often cited by incipit (a tradition long perpetuated in German scholarship), but in modern texts citations are numerical, by book, title, *lex* (or fragment), and paragraph.

After the *Digest* was promulgated, Justinian commissioned the *Institutes*, an elementary textbook on Roman law which was based on (and designed to replace) the *Institutionum iuris civilis commentarii quatuor* of the second-century Roman jurist Gaius.

Finally, Justinian issued supplementary laws known as *Novels* (*leges novellae*) or the *Novellae constitutiones post codicem*. These laws, which deal with public, private, and ecclesiastical law, were usually in Greek, though some are in both Greek and Latin. There was no authorized collection of the *novellae*, but there were three unofficial collections: the *Epitome Juliani* (*c*.555) of the Byzantine professor Julianus, which contained abridged Latin versions of 124 constitutions; the *Authenticum* (*c*.557), a collection of 134 constitutions in Latin or in Greek translated into Latin, possibly intended for promulgation in Italy; and the Greek collection (*c*.580), which contains 168 constitutions.

It was these four works—*Codex, Digest, Institutes*, and *Novels*—that were termed by Godefroy the *Corpus iuris civilis*. The *Corpus* was normally printed in five volumes: volume i was the *Digestum vetus*, volume ii the *Infortiatum*, volume iii the *Digestum novum*, volume iv the *Codex* books 1–9, and volume v (which was known as the *volumen parvum* because of its relative slimness) the *Codex* books 10–12 (the *Tres libri*), the *Institutes*, and the *Novels* (in the form of the *Authenticum*); volume v also contained the *Libri feudorum* (a post-Justinian compilation of FEUDAL LAW added to the *Novels* as the *Decima collatio*) and a collection of imperial statutes.

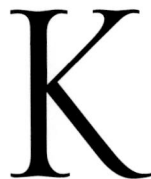

# K

**KABBALA**. See CABBALA.

**KALTEMAIL** (German; 'cold enamel'), a form of lacquer used as a substitute for enamel on ceramics, metals, and wood when they could not be fired, because of either fragility or size.

**KARCHER, NICOLAS or Nicola** (*fl.* 1517, d. 1562), Flemish TAPESTRY weaver who worked with his brother Jan (Italian Giovanni) in the ESTE tapestry workshop in Ferrara; hangings produced in the workshop depicted classical themes drawn from Ovid. From 1539 to 1541 Nicolas worked in the service of the GONZAGA family in Mantua; his Mantua workshop wove a series of *Playing Boys* designed by GIULIO ROMANO (Gulbenkian Museum, Lisbon; Museo Poldi Pezzoli, Milan). He subsequently moved to Florence, where he established a tapestry workshop for Duke COSIMO I DE' MEDICI; the products of this workshop include a *History of Joseph* designed by BRONZINO (Palazzo Vecchio, Florence).

    *MDA.*

**KARLSTADT, ANDREAS RUDOLF BODENSTEIN VON** (*c.*1477–1541), German Protestant reformer often known from his birthplace as Carlstadt (German Karlstadt), educated in Erfurt (1499–1503) and Cologne (1503–4). In the winter of 1504–5 he moved to the newly established University of Wittenberg, where he taught initially in arts and later in theology. In 1508 he became a canon of the university's collegiate church, the Allerheiligenstift, and in 1510 took his doctorate in theology. He was appointed to the chair of theology in 1513 and in 1515 he went to Rome to take his doctorate in CANON LAW.

    Karlstadt returned from Rome as a confirmed champion of SCHOLASTICISM and engaged in a controversy with LUTHER, who maintained that scholasticism misrepresented both the biblical and the Augustinian doctrine of GRACE. Karlstadt abandoned his position and became an advocate of Luther's emphasis (drawn from AUGUSTINE) on the powerlessness of the human will; on 16 September 1516 he proclaimed 151 Theses (published in 1517) setting out his position on grace. Had these theses been known before the nineteenth century, the historiography of the German Reformation would have given a larger role to Karlstadt.

Karlstadt supported Luther's 95 Theses (31 October 1517) in his *Invectiones* (1518) and the following year debated publicly with Johann ECK in the LEIPZIG DISPUTATION. In 1520 he was named in the bull *EXSURGE DOMINE* which threatened Luther with excommunication. Karlstadt formally repudiated his link with the papacy and on Christmas Day 1521 became the first Reformer to celebrate mass in the vernacular; he eschewed vestments, passed over the canon of the mass in silence, made no reference to sacrifice, and offered communion in both kinds to the laity. Three weeks later, on 19 January, he married a noblewoman, Anna von Mochau; he had been the first priest to write against clerical celibacy and through his marriage became the first priest to marry. His reforms were too radical. The pace of reform, and the methods used by Karlstadt to implement reform, alarmed Luther (who denounced Karlstadt in his *Invocavit* sermons), the elector (who believed in a celibate clergy), and the university, and when Luther returned from the Wartburg (the castle near Eisenach where Luther had taken refuge after the Diet of WORMS) on 6 March 1522, Karlstadt was deposed as the spiritual leader of Wittenberg.

    In 1523 Karlstadt resigned his academic post and moved to Orlamünde (south of Jena), where he preached the Reformation but took a memorialist position on the EUCHARIST and refused to baptize infants. Despite his sympathetic theological position, he declined to join Thomas MÜNTZER's uprising, because he had become a pacifist. In 1524 he was expelled from Saxony; he returned to Wittenberg, and on the basis of an ambiguous recantation was allowed to live close to the town. In 1529, fearing arrest, he left the town, first seeking refuge with Melchior HOFFMAN in Holstein and eventually settling in the SWISS CONFEDERATION, first in Zürich, and then in Basel. He abandoned his opposition to infant baptism, and in 1534, on the recommendation of BULLINGER, was appointed professor of Hebrew and preacher in the university church at Basel, where he died on 24 December 1541.

    *NDB s.v. Bodenstein (2); Hermann Barge, Andreas Bodenstein von Karlstadt (2 vols., 1905; repr. 1968); R. J. Sider, Karlstadt's Battle with Luther (1978); id., Andreas Bodenstein von Karlstadt: The Development of his Thought, 1517–1525 (1974).*

**KARO or Caro or Qaro, JOSEPH BEN EPHRAIM** (1488–1575), formulator of Jewish law, expelled from Spain together with most other JEWS in 1492. He led a peripatetic existence until 1535, when he moved to Palestine and settled permanently in Safed (now Zefat, in Upper Galilee), which had become an important CABBALISTIC centre after Rabbi Isaac Lourie had moved there in 1531. There Karo wrote a commentary called *Beit Yosef* before composing an influential legal treatise, *Shulkhan Arukh* ('Table Prepared'), which was completed in 1555 and published in 1565. Karo's code set out details of ritual, law (including sumptuary law), and ethics that were to be honoured for centuries by European Jews.

R. J. Zwi Werblowsky, *Joseph Karo: Lawyer and Mystic* (1962).

**KELLERTHALER, HANS or Johann** (*c.*1562–1611), German goldsmith who worked in Dresden. He made the silver plaques (1585) for the Schmuckschrank (jewellery cabinet) of the Electoral Princess Sophia of Saxony (now in the Grünes Gewölbe in the Albertinum in Dresden).

*MDA*; *NDB*.

**KELS, HANS THE YOUNGER** (*fl.* 1546–*c.*1570), German woodcutter who worked in Augsburg for the FUGGER family. The doors and door-cases executed for Schloss Donauwörth (now the Bayerisches Nationalmuseum, Munich) in 1546 are attributed to Kels. He collaborated with a local carver, Thomas Heidelberger von Memmingen (*c.*1541–*c.*1597), on the carved and inlaid sacristy furniture in the church of the Benedictine abbey at Ottobeuren (near Memmingen), for which Heidelberger made the organ-case and choir stalls (later incorporated into a sacristy cupboard).

**KEMPE, WILLIAM** (d. 1603), English actor. One of the best-known Elizabethan clowns, Kempe was the original Dogberry in SHAKESPEARE's *Much Ado About Nothing*, and also performed in JONSON's plays. Originally with QUEEN ELIZABETH'S MEN, he joined the CHAMBERLAIN'S MEN on their formation in 1594. Famous for his extemporizing, he left the company in 1600. That year he fulfilled a bet by morris dancing in nine days from London to Norwich, and later toured with the ENGLISCHE KOMÖDIANTEN on the Continent.

*DNB*.

**KEMPENEER, PIETER DE.** See CAMPAÑA, PEDRO (DE).

**KENILWORTH CASTLE.** In 1265 the medieval castle at Kenilworth (Warwickshire) was granted by Henry III to his second son Edmund Crouchback, earl of Lancaster, and for the next three centuries it was passed back and forth between the crown and various noble families. In 1563 the castle was granted by Queen ELIZABETH to her favourite Robert Dudley, earl of Leicester, who decided to convert the castle into a great house fit to receive occasional visits from the queen. He retained the banqueting hall that had been built in 1392, and redesigned the Norman keep (built 1120), inserting mullioned and transomed windows on the first floor and renovating the accommodation within the building. He also demolished part of the curtain wall to construct the magnificent guest house that has been known since the seventeenth century as Leicester's Building.

Dudley also built a gatehouse, beside which a large garden was laid out. The design shows indirect French influence, mediated through the English royal palace gardens. Like the gardens at Hampton Court Palace, Whitehall, and Nonsuch Palace, Dudley's gardens consisted of a square divided into quarters, laid out in KNOT GARDENS; at the centre of the square there was a fountain. One important factor separated Dudley's garden from those at the royal palaces: whereas the royal gardens could all be viewed from the state apartments on the first floor, the Kenilworth gardens could not be seen from the castle, and so a large terrace was constructed from which the gardens could be viewed. The terrace was decorated with obelisks and heraldic animals on posts; this distinctly English element, which also appeared in the fountain at the centre of the garden (which was topped by Dudley's personal device, the bear and 'ragged staff', i.e. a staff with projecting knobs), seems to derive from the royal garden at Hampton Court.

Queen Elizabeth visited the castle on three occasions. The entertainments on the last of these visits, from 9 to 27 July 1575, were vividly described by one of her courtiers, Robert Laneham (or Langham), who is also the source of many details of the castle and gardens (*A letter wherein part of the entertainment unto the Queen's Majesty at Killingworth Castle is signified, in this summer's progress 1575*). Laneham's description of a water pageant on the large lake which then adjoined the castle seems to be echoed by Shakespeare's Oberon in *A Midsummer's Night's Dream* (II. i); it is possible that the 11-year-old Shakespeare was present, as his father had been a senior civic official in nearby Stratford, or that he had read Laneham's account.

**KEPLER, JOHANNES** (1571–1630), German astronomer and mathematician, born in Weil de Stadt (Württemberg), the eldest child of a mercenary soldier and an innkeeper's daughter. Throughout his life, Kepler was a deeply religious Lutheran. When young he intended to be ordained, and he was educated at the University of Tübingen, then as now a guardian of Lutheran orthodoxy. However, his astronomy teacher, Michael MÄSTLIN, encouraged him to become an astronomer rather than a priest. In his normal classes, Mästlin taught standard geocentric astronomy, but particularly able pupils, Kepler among them, were introduced to the work of COPERNICUS. Kepler's reasons for believing in Copernicus' system were philosophical; as he says in his first astronomical publication, *Mysterium cosmographicum* (1596), the Copernican system allows one to give rational answers to questions that geocentric astronomy cannot answer, such as why the planets Mercury and Venus are never seen far from the sun (answer: because they lie between the earth and the sun). Moreover, the Copernican system allowed the actual distances of the planets to be calculated from observations. Their paths proved to be widely spaced and in the *Mysterium cosmographicum* Kepler is concerned to explain the sizes of the gaps by means of the five regular polyhedra described by EUCLID (see COSMOLOGY). At the time he wrote this work, Kepler was district mathematician at Graz, but faced dismissal for his Protestantism. Tycho BRAHE had been in correspondence with Mästlin about a possible mathematical assistant to help him use his observations to confirm his own model of the planetary system, and between the two it was decided that Kepler would be suitable. So in 1600 Kepler moved to Prague, where Tycho was then imperial mathematician to RUDOLF II. Rudolf hoped that Tycho's observations would lead to astronomical tables of unexampled accuracy which would bear Rudolf's name and make it famous. As it turned out, the emperor's wish was fulfilled.

Tycho set Kepler to work on the path of the planet that was proving most awkward, Mars. In October 1601 Tycho died and Kepler eventually succeeded him as imperial mathematician. It was May 1605 before Kepler won what he called 'my battle with Mars' and there are 986 surviving pages of arithmetic that record the struggle. Kepler proved that, given the known level of accuracy of Tycho's observations, the orbit of Mars must be an ellipse with the sun in one of its foci, and that as the planet moved round its orbit a line joining the planet to the sun would sweep out equal areas in equal times. At intermediate stages of his calculations, Kepler uses approximate methods, based on ARCHIMEDES, relying on checking the answers against more observations to ensure that the method is giving reliable results, but the final stages, when he obtains the ellipse, rely entirely on the precise geometry of Euclid, using only the properties of straight lines and circles. He recognizes the ellipse from properties treated by Archimedes. Kepler's work on Mars was published as *Astronomia nova . . . tradita commentariis de motibus planetae Martis . . .* (1609). More work with Tycho's observations showed that the other planets moved in the same way as Mars. The ellipse and area rules are now known as the first two of Kepler's Laws of Planetary Motion.

Kepler had hoped that more accurate dimensions, derived from Tycho's observations, would confirm the cosmological model he had proposed in 1596. They did not. Kepler devised a modified version of the model, using musical theory (in a refined version of the technique of PTOLEMY's *Harmonica*), and the result was published as *Harmonices mundi libri V* (1619). This work also contains Kepler's Third Law, which states that the square of the period of the planet is proportional to the cube of the major axis of its elliptical orbit.

After more arithmetic (Kepler was an early enthusiast for LOGARITHMS) the *Rudolphine Tables*, based on Kepler's first two laws, were published in 1627. All astronomical tables that used new observations were reliable for a few years. The *Rudolphine Tables* proved to be reliable for many decades, and over the years their continuing accuracy did much to persuade astronomers to accept Kepler's first two laws, and thus the Copernican system. By the end of the seventeenth century it was for these tables that Kepler was chiefly known. He had, however, done very important work on OPTICS: in *Ad Vitellionem paralipomena quibus astronomiae pars optica traditur* (1604) he gives the first correct explanation of the working of the CAMERA OBSCURA and of the human eye, and his *Diopritice* (1611) contains a design for a TELESCOPE using two convex lenses.

Kepler is the earliest major scientific figure whose papers survive in quantity. The extensive information about personal matters has tempted some historians to write heavily psychologized studies that underestimate the operation of Kepler's powerful rational intellect.

DSB; NDB; J. V. Field, *Kepler's Geometrical Cosmology* (1987); A. E. L. Davis, 'Kepler's Unintentional Ellipse: A Celestial Detective Story', *Mathematical Gazette*, 82/493 (1998).

**KERLE, JACOB VAN** (*c*.1531/2–1591), Flemish composer and organist, educated in Ypres. He was a singer at Cambrai Cathedral from 1548 and then *magister cappellae* in Orvieto. From 1561–2 he composed the *Preces speciales*, commissioned by Cardinal Otto Truchsess von Waldeburg, bishop of Augsburg, for the COUNCIL OF TRENT. At the end of 1565 he was appointed director of music at Ypres Cathedral from which, following a dispute with the chapter, he was dismissed and excommunicated. Further appointments took him to Augsburg, Cambrai, and Prague, where he was chaplain at the imperial court chapel. Most of his compositions are sacred music, in a Flemish polyphonic style and with emphasis on the clarity of the text in accordance with the ideals of the Council of Trent.

**KESSLER, JOHANNES** (1502–74), Swiss Reformer and educator, educated at the Latin school in St Gallen and at the University of Basel (for a short time in 1521) and University of Wittenberg (1522–3), where he attended MELANCHTHON's lectures but did not graduate. In 1523 Kessler returned to St Gallen, where for the next ten years he earned his living as a harness-maker and organized meetings in guildhalls for worship and study; his activities earned him the friendship of VADIANUS, the reformer of St Gallen, and the enmity of the abbot of the Benedictine monastery of St Gallen.

In 1537 Kessler was appointed schoolmaster of St Gallen, and after the death of Vadianus in 1555 was appointed curator of his large personal library; in 1571 Kessler was appointed chief preacher of the city. His *Sabbata* is a chronicle and conversion narrative that describes how Christians in St Gallen were led by their study of the Bible to true Christianity; it contains accounts, sharply focused on St Gallen, of the Reformation, of the PEASANTS' WAR, and of the development of ANABAPTIST congregations.

Ingeborg Wissman, *Die St Galler Reformationschronik des Johannes Kessler, 1503–74* (1972).

**KETEL, CORNELIS** (1548–1616), Dutch portrait and history painter and draughtsman, born in Gouda, where he received his early training from his uncle Cornelis Jacobszoon. He trained for one year (*c*.1565) in the Delft studio of Anthonis Bloklandt van Montfoort (1532/4–83) and then worked at FONTAINEBLEAU (1566) and in Paris (1567–8) and London (1573–*c*.1581) before settling permanently in Amsterdam. His surviving individual portraits include one of Martin FROBISHER (1577, Bodleian Library, Oxford) and another of *Queen Elizabeth Holding a Sieve* (Pinacoteca, Siena); his surviving group portraits include the *Company of Captain Rosencrantz and Lieutenant Paul* (1588, Rijksmuseum, Amsterdam).

MDA; NNBW viii.

**KETT'S REBELLION** (1549). Opposition to the dissolution of the MONASTERIES, as well as local factors, sparked this revolt in the summer of 1549, which was led by Robert Kett, a Norfolk landowner. The rebellious forces occupied Norwich, then England's second city, and defeated the first of two forces sent to quell them; a second attack was more successful, however. Kett was hanged, but many peasants accepted a pardon. The threat posed to the government of SOMERSET by the insurrection was magnified by simultaneous disturbances in the west of England.

**KEY, ADRIAN THOMASZOON** (c.1544–after 1589), Flemish portrait painter, the pupil (and possibly a relative) of Willem KEY. He was admitted to the Antwerp Guild in 1568. His portrait of WILLIAM OF ORANGE exists in several versions, of which the best known is in the Rijksmuseum in Amsterdam.

*BNB s.v. Key, Adrien-Thomas; MDA.*

**KEY, LIEVEN DE** (1560–1627), Dutch mason and architect, born in Ghent. He worked in London for many years (1580–91) and then returned to the Netherlands; in 1593 he was appointed as a civic architect in Haarlem, where he settled permanently. He was responsible for churches and public buildings in Haarlem and Leiden. He built the Meat Hall in Haarlem (1602–3) and the Town Hall in Leiden (1593–7), in which the centre of the façade is topped with a scrollwork gable and the octagonal flèche that rises in storeys above the building incorporates Moorish elements. Key was also the architect of the tower on the Nieuwe Kerk in Haarlem (1613).

*MDA; NNBW ii; Ad van der Blom, Lieven de Key: Haarlems stadsbouwmeester (1995).*

**KEY, WILLEM ADRIAENSZOON** (c.1515–1568), Flemish portrait painter, trained in the studio of Lambert LOMBARD in Liège; in 1542 he was admitted to the Guild in Antwerp, where he settled permanently. His surviving works include *Susanna and the Elders* (1546, Schloss Weissenstein, Pommersfelden), *The Holy Family* (1551; sold London, Christie's 1988), and a *Lamentation* (1553, private collection).

*BNB s.v. Key, Guillaume; MDA; NNBW x.*

**KEYSER, HENDRICK CORNELISZOON DE** (1565–1621), Dutch architect and sculptor, appointed city architect of Amsterdam in 1595. His most important large secular buildings are the Amsterdam Exchange (1608) and the Delft Town Hall (1618). His austere churches, notably the South Church (1603–14) and West Church (begun 1620) in Amsterdam, were long influential in Protestant church design in the Netherlands and in Germany, in significant part because they successfully shifted the focus of the interior from the altar to the pulpit. A similar urge to subdue decoration and emphasize structural lines is apparent in Keyser's domestic architecture, in which he reduced the number of steps in gables and introduced the classical ORDERS of architecture. Many of Keyser's buildings were engraved by Salomon de Bray and published as *Architectura moderna* (1631). His most important sculptural works are the tomb of WILLIAM OF ORANGE at Delft (1614–c.1621) and a statue of

ERASMUS (1618) in Grote Kerkplein, in front of St Laurenskerk in Rotterdam.

Hendrick's son Thomas (1596/7–1667) became an architect and portrait painter; his subjects included the poet and statesman *Constantin Huygens and his Clerk* (1627, National Gallery, London). Thomas's brothers Pieter and Willem both became sculptors.

*MDA; NNBW ii; Jochen Becker, Hendrick de Keyser: Standbeeld van Desiderius Erasmus in Rotterdam (1993).*

**KIRBYE, GEORGE** (c.1565–1634), English composer who was in the service of Sir Robert Jermyn of Rushbrooke Hall near Bury St Edmunds; WILBYE was employed at the nearby Hengrave Hall. One of Kirbye's madrigals is published in *The TRIUMPHS OF ORIANA* (1601); he also made a significant contribution to EAST's Psalter (1592).

**KIRCHMAIER, THOMAS** or (Latin) **Naogeorgus** (1511–63), German humanist and playwright. He was born near Straubing and served as a Lutheran clergyman in Saxony (Salza and Kahla) and Bavaria (Kaufbeuren and Kempten). Kirchmaier wrote a series of aggressively Protestant Latin plays which attacked the Roman Catholic clergy and the papacy. His *Pammachius* (1538), which represents the pope as ANTICHRIST, was performed in Cambridge in 1545; his comedy *Mercator* (1540) is a Protestant version of the story of Everyman which had been dramatized in Dutch, English, and German (*Jedermann*). His later polemical plays include *Incendia* (1541), *Hamanus* (1543), *Hieremias* (1551), and *Judas* (1552). Kirchmaier also translated the plays of Sophocles into Latin.

*NDB s.v. Naogeorg, Thomas.*

**KLESL** or **Khesl, MELCHIOR** (1552–1630), Austrian bishop and statesman, born in Vienna, the son of a Protestant baker. He converted to Catholicism, and, after completing his education in Vienna and Ingolstadt, was appointed chancellor of the University of Vienna and vicar-general of the bishop of Passau. He became bishop of Vienna in 1598, and at about that time began to ally himself with Archduke MATTHIAS, who was attempting to wrest control of the Empire from his brother RUDOLF II. Klesl helped Matthias to secure the imperial throne in 1612 and thereafter counselled reconciliation with the Protestants of Bohemia and Hungary. In 1615 Klesl was created cardinal.

The Archdukes Maximilian and Ferdinand (later the Emperor Ferdinand II) opposed Klesl's policy of reconciliation and in June 1618, in the wake of the DEFENESTRATION OF PRAGUE, had him arrested and imprisoned in Schloss Ambras, in Tirol. In 1622 he was transferred to Rome by order of Pope Gregory XV, who released him from imprisonment. In 1627 Ferdinand II allowed Klesl to return to his see in Vienna, where he died on 18 September 1630.

*NDB s.v. Klesl.*

**KNIGHTS' REVOLT** or **Knights' War** or (German) **Sickingische Fehde** (1522–3) supposedly a rebellion by the imperial knights of SWABIA and Franconia (the *Ritterstand*), eager to assert their political independence from the ruling princes of Germany and to secularize the ecclesiastical territories of the Empire, in reality a feud by Franz von SICKINGEN, abetted by Ulrich von HUTTEN, against the archbishop of Trier, in the hope of advancing at one fell swoop into the ranks of the imperial princes who possessed *Reichsstandschaft*. In August 1522 Sickingen besieged the archbishop of Trier in his city, but he was attacked by the forces of the SWABIAN LEAGUE and forced to lift the siege. The revolt was ended in the summer of 1523 when Sickingen was killed and Hutten fled to Basel. The castles of many Franconian knights were subsequently destroyed to prevent any further rebellion.

W. R. Hitchcock, *The Background of the Knights' Revolt, 1522–1523* (1958).

**KNIPPERDOLLINCK or Knipperdolling, BERND or Bernt or Bernhardt** (*c.*1490–1536), German Anabaptist leader. He was a wealthy cloth merchant in Münster when in 1524 he joined the ANABAPTIST furriers Melchior HOFFMAN and Melchior Rinck on a business trip to Stockholm. There the three godly merchants inveighed against the worship of images and were promptly expelled.

In Münster Knipperdollinck allied himself with the religious movement led by Berndt ROTHMANN, who became pastor of the Lambertikirche in Münster in January 1532. When a new bishop directed a mandate against Rothmann (17 April 1532), Knipperdollinck led the group of radicals who imprisoned the nobles considering the case in nearby Telgte. The crisis was resolved when PHILIP OF HESSE declared Münster to be an evangelical city in a charter of 14 February 1533. Knipperdollinck was made a burgomaster of the city in February 1534.

On 1 January 1534 Heinrich Roll, an Anabaptist refugee, preached Anabaptist doctrines in a city church, and shortly thereafter JOHN OF LEIDEN and Jan Matthyszoon, the radical Dutch Anabaptist, arrived in the city. Knipperdollinck fell under the charismatic spell of John of Leiden, and his daughter Clara joined John's collection of wives. Matthyszoon moved into Knipperdollinck's house, which became the centre of a movement that sought to establish Münster as the New Jerusalem instead of Strassburg, which had been Hoffman's preferred location. On 5 April 1534 Matthyszoon was killed and John of Leiden became the undisputed leader of the movement. Knipperdollinck became John's second-in-command, though he took no part in the defence of the besieged city.

When Münster fell on 25 June 1535, Knipperdollinck hid in a house in the city wall, but was betrayed by his landlady and captured. He was tried together with his colleagues on 19 January 1536; on 22 January he was tortured and executed.

*NDB.*

**KNITTELVERSE**, a popular sixteenth-century German verse form in which lines (usually in rhyming pairs) contain a varying number (from four to eleven) of unstressed syllables, but always have four stresses.

**KNOPKEN, ANDREAS** (*c.*1468–1539), German reformer, born near Küstrin (now Polish Kostrzyn) and educated at Frankfurt an der Oder and from 1514 to 1517 at Treptow (now Polish Trzebiatow), where his teachers included Johannes BUGENHAGEN. He was ordained and became a chaplain in Riga (1517–19). He returned to Riga in 1521 and began to champion the Reformation, which was also supported by the LIVONIAN ORDER. Knopken was declared the winner in a disputation held in June 1522, as a result of which the city adopted the Reformation and Knopken was elected archdeacon.

*NDB.*

**KNOT GARDENS or (French) *entrelacs***. The term 'knot garden' is sometimes used in fifteenth-century English to refer to a MAZE and in sixteenth- and seventeenth-century English to a French PARTERRE. The term is now used by garden historians to refer to a small garden laid out in a series of continuous interlacing bands. Knot gardens seem to have originated in the knot designs of CARPETS AND RUGS imported into Europe from the Middle East in the fifteenth century. The earliest published designs of garden knots are the woodcuts in Francesco COLONNA's *Hypnerotomachia Polifili* (Venice, 1499), where the flowers and herbs planted in the knots are explicitly said to resemble a carpet. The knot garden reached its apogee in England and France. Anyone thinking of building one could consult designs printed in Thomas Hill's *The Profitable Art of Gardening* (1568, 1608) and in *L'Agriculture et la maison rustique* (1564, 1570, 1572, 1582) by Charles ESTIENNE and Jean Liébault; the 1572 edition was translated into English as *Maison rustique; or, The Country Farm* by Richard Surflet in 1600, and the 1608 edition of Hill's text replaces the knot design of the earlier edition with one borrowed from the 1582 edition of *L'Agriculture*.

Thomas Hill suggested that the knots be set in thyme or hyssop. In the seventeenth century John PARKINSON recommended box because of its strong lines, but allowed that the same effect could be achieved with 'lead, boards, bones, tiles or pebbles' (*Paradisus*, 1629).

Kenneth Woodbridge, 'Rise and Decline of the Garden Knot', *Architectural Review* (June 1979).

**KNOX, JOHN** (*c.*1513–1572), Scottish reformer. Educated in Glasgow and St Andrews, Knox was initially ordained as a Catholic priest before being influenced by reformist views. Captured during the French raid on St Andrews in 1547, he was kept prisoner for two years, and travelled to England on his release. There he became known for his uncompromising reformist stance; in 1551 he became chaplain to EDWARD VI and assisted CRANMER in the preparation of the second Book of COMMON PRAYER. On Mary's accession he left England, meeting Calvin at Geneva and ministering to English Protestants at Frankfurt. His *First Blast of the Trumpet against the Monstrous Regiment of Women* (1558), attacking women rulers, caused him to be banned from England. In 1559 he returned to Scotland and became an influential reformist voice, framing the Scottish Confession of Faith and the Scottish Book of Common Order, or service book; he was unremittingly hostile to the Catholic MARY, QUEEN OF SCOTS. His *History* *of the Reformation of Religion in Scotland* was published in 1587 incomplete, and in 1644 in the first complete edition.

*DNB.*

**KÖBERGER or Koburger, ANTON** (*c*.1440–1513), German publisher who introduced printing to Nuremberg in 1470 and sold his books through his sixteen shops and his network of agents throughout Europe. He published more than 200 folio INCUNABULA, many of which were lavishly illustrated with woodcuts, including Hartmann SCHEDEL's 'Nuremberg Chronicle'. On his death the business passed to his heirs, but went bankrupt in 1526.

*NDB.*

**KOCHANOWSKI, JAN** (1530–84), Polish poet, playwright, and humanist. He was born into a noble Polish family and educated in Kraków and Königsberg (now Russian Kaliningrad) and subsequently travelled extensively in Italy and France. On returning to Poland in 1559 he joined the court of King SIGISMUND II. Kochanowski was the first significant Polish poet to use Polish rather than Latin as the language of his verse. His poems range over religious, secular, and patriotic subjects, and incorporate many motifs and stylistic devices taken from Italian and French Renaissance poetry. His best-known works are a set of elegiac lamentations (*Treny*) on the death of his daughter Ursula.

*PSB.*

**KOSTER or Coster, LAURENS JANSZOON** (*c*.1370–*c*.1440), Dutch xylographer, born in Haarlem, where he worked as a printer of BLOCK BOOKS (or xylographs) and from 1417 to 1434 held a series of important civic posts, including member of the Great Council, assessor (*scabinus*), and city treasurer; his surname, which means 'sacristan', reflects the position that he held in the church in Haarlem.

The claim that GUTENBERG was the originator of printing with movable type was challenged for centuries by champions of Koster. The rival claims of Mainz and Haarlem to be the birthplace of printing were long prosecuted with a view to claiming an honour for a nation or denying an honour to an unpopular nation, and these nationalist considerations overwhelmed the scholarly debate. The balance of argument now favours Mainz.

**KOTTER, HANS** (*c*.1485–1541), Alsatian composer and organist who studied with Paul HOFHAIMER. Expelled from Fribourg, where he was organist, for his Protestant inclinations, he became a schoolmaster in Bern. Some of his compostions and arrangements appear in the keyboard tablature belonging to Bonifacius Amerbach along with works by Hofhaimer, ISAAC, and others.

**KRAFT or Krafft, ADAM** (*c*.1455/60–1509), German sculptor, born in Nuremberg. His principal surviving work is the huge ciborium (a canopy supported by columns) in the choir of the Lorenzkirche in Nuremberg. This richly decorated Gothic structure, which is almost 20 metres (65 feet) high, includes many sculpted figures of humans and animals; the tradition that one of the figures is a self-portrait is not supported by documentary evidence.

*MDA; NDB; Wilhelm Schwemmer, Adam Kraft (1958).*

**KRAKÓW or (German) Krakau or (English exonym) Cracow**. The city of Kraków, on the left bank of the Vistula in Polish Galicia, was the seat of Poland's kings from 1305 until 1569, when it was agreed in the Union of LUBLIN that Warsaw would be the capital of a united Poland and Lithuania. It was 40 years before the royal residence was actually moved (in 1610) by SIGISMUND III, and until 1764 Kraków's cathedral of St Stanislas remained the coronation and burial place of Polish kings.

The University of Kraków (Uniwersytet Jagielloński) was founded in 1364; its students included COPERNICUS. The Church of St Mary (Kościół Mariacki) contains the enormous ALTARPIECE of the Virgin carved between 1477 and 1489 by Veit STOSS (Polish Stwosz); it was dismantled by German forces during the Second World War and rediscovered by Allied forces at the end of the war; it has now been reassembled, and is ceremonially unveiled every day at noon. The medieval royal castle (Zamek Wawelski) on the rocky outcrop known as the Wawel was rebuilt in the Italian Renaissance style by King SIGISMUND I, who in 1518 had married Bona Sforza of Milan; under her influence the royal court became an important centre for Renaissance culture. The Sigismund Chapel (1519–30) in the cathedral is constructed in Italian Renaissance style.

**KRANTZ, ALBERT** (1448–1517), German historian. He was born in Hamburg and studied law, theology, and history at the universities of Rostock and Cologne. He travelled widely in western and southern Europe, and on returning to Rostock he was appointed to a chair of philosophy and then to a chair of theology before becoming rector in 1482. In 1493 he returned to Hamburg as a lecturer, canon, and prebend in the cathedral, and in 1508 he became dean of the cathedral chapter. Throughout this period he worked publicly as a diplomat for the Senate of Hamburg and as an ecclesiastical reformer, and privately as a historian. His career as a diplomat culminated in 1500, when he was asked by the king of Denmark and the duke of Holstein to arbitrate in their dispute about the province of Dithmarschen. As a reformer he became a scourge of ecclesiastical abuses, but was unsympathetic to Luther's protests about the abuse of INDULGENCES. He heard of the 95 Theses on his deathbed and cried out for Luther to repent; he died on 7 December 1517.

Krantz was a historian who made reasoned historical judgements rather than a chronicler; in modelling his own writing on that of Pope PIUS II, Krantz became one of the first exponents of humanist historiography in Germany. His most important historical works were *Vandalia, sive Historia de Vandalorum vera origine* (Cologne, 1518), *Saxonia* (Cologne, 1520), *Chronica regnorum aquilonarium Daniae, Sueciae et Norwagiae* (Strassburg, 1546), and *Metropolis, sive Historia de ecclesiis sub Carolo Magno in Saxonia* (Basel, 1548).

*NDB; V. A. Nordman, Die Wandalia des Albert Krantz: Eine Untersuchung (1934).*

**KRAUSE, JAKOB** (c.1531–1586), German bookbinder, based in Dresden, where he was the first bookbinder to use gold tooling and the first to use French and Italian designs. In 1566 he was appointed court binder to the Elector AUGUSTUS I of Saxony, a post which he held for the rest of his life. The library of the electors (now in the Sächsische Landesbibliothek in Dresden) contains many volumes bound by Krause in gilded bindings with portrait stamps and initials of members of the electoral family.

*NDB*; Konrad von Rabenau, *Deutsche Bucheinbände der Renaissance um Jakob Krause* (2 vols., 1994).

**KRUG, LUDWIG** (c.1488/90–1532), German goldsmith, born in Nuremberg, the son of a goldsmith; he became a master in 1484 and served as master of the Nuremberg mint from 1494 to 1509. The only documented artefact known to survive from his workshop is not metalwork, but rather the Solnhofen stone relief of *Adam and Eve* (1514) now in the Skulpturengalerie in Berlin. His attributed works in stone include a large red marble relief (c.1524) now in the Bayerisches Nationalmuseum in Munich. Attributions of work in precious metals are based on a design for a covered cup which is known from a drawing in an inventory of the treasury at Halle; this drawing (c.1526), which is now in the Hofbibliothek in Aschaffenburg, is the basis of attributions of cups in Budapest, Berlin, and Vienna and NEFS in Nuremberg and Padua.

*MDA.*

**KRUMPPER or Krumper, HANS** (c.1570–1634), German sculptor, architect, designer and painter, born in Weilheim (35 kilometres (21 miles) south-west of Munich). In 1584 he entered the service of Duke Wilhelm V in Munich, where he was trained as a sculptor in the studio of Hubert GERHARD and then sent to Italy (1590–2) to study Italian art and architecture. He married the daughter of Frederich SUSTRIS, the court architect, and from 1594 was employed by the court; after Duke Wilhelm's abdication in 1598, Krumpper continued to work for him in a private capacity. Duke Wilhelm's successor Maximilian I additionally appointed him to the post of court painter (1609). Krumpper presided over the reconstruction of the Ducal Palace (Residenz) in Munich and also worked as a sculptor and a producer of designs for goldsmiths.

*MDA* s.v. Krumper; *NDB*.

**KSAR-EL-KEBIR or (Portuguese) Alcácer Quibir or (Spanish) Alcazarquivir, BATTLE OF**. El-Ksar el-Kebir (Arabic; 'the great castle'), a town south-west of Tangier, was the site of the last great battle between Portugal and the Moors of North Africa. In 1578, Mohammed XI, the deposed emir of Morocco, requested King SEBASTIAN I of Portugal to defend him against his uncle Abd el Malik, who had usurped the emirate. On 4 August 1578 King Sebastian led his army into battle against the army of Abd el Malik in what is sometimes known as the 'battle of the Three Kings'. The Portuguese army was defeated, and all three rulers were killed in the battle. The emirate passed to Ahmet IV, who extended his rule as far south as Timbuktu and established diplomatic relations with various European leaders, including Queen Elizabeth.

The battle was the subject of George PEELE's play *The Battle of Alcazar* (1594).

**KULMBACH, HANS SÜSS or Suess VON** (c.1485–1522), German painter. He was born in Kulmbach and studied in the Nuremberg studio of Albrecht DÜRER. He subsequently worked for several years as Dürer's assistant, often collaborating in the design of woodcuts, and in 1511 became a burgher of Nuremberg and an independent artist. He designed stained-glass windows and painted portraits, and after Dürer stopped painting ALTARPIECES (c.1510) Kulmbach became the city's principal supplier of triptychs. Of his numerous surviving altarpieces the best known is his *Adoration of the Magi* (1511, Gemäldegalerie, Berlin), which formed the central panel of an altarpiece on *The Life of the Virgin* originally in the Pauline monastery in Kraków, which he visited in 1514; in the years immediately following his visit Kulmbach painted wings for two more altarpieces in Kraków, one of *St Catherine* (in the Church of St Mary) and another of *St John* (in the Church of St Florian).

*MDA*; *NDB*; F. Winkler, *Hans von Kulmbach: Leben und Werk eines fränkischen Künstlers der Dürerzeit* (1959); Alexander Löhr, *Studien zu Hans von Kulmbach als Maler* (1995).

**KYD, THOMAS** (1558–94), English playwright. A friend of MARLOWE, with whom he shared lodgings; the association led to Kyd's torture and imprisonment. Attributions of Kyd's plays are problematic as they were published anonymously. He is most famous for one of the most popular of Elizabethan dramas, *The Spanish Tragedy* (c.1589). In its account of Hieronimo's revenge for the murder of his son, it anticipated many later revenge tragedies, and its use of a play-within-a-play was echoed in SHAKESPEARE's *Hamlet*.

*DNB.*

# L

**LABÉ, LOUISE** (1524–66), French poet, known as 'La Belle Cordière' because her elderly husband was a wealthy rope-maker (*cordier*). She was a member of the group of Lyon poets in the circle of Maurice SCÈVE. Her works in poetry and prose, which she collected in 1555, consist of three classicizing elegies and 24 emotionally intense sonnets, a prose *Débat de Folie et de l'Amour* in the tradition of ERASMUS, and 24 poems by admirers. For centuries the sonnets were reprinted and translated, but critical attention has now shifted to Labé's prefatory epistle, a rallying cry to women urging the repudiation of traditional women's interests in clothing and jewellery in favour of the cultural pursuits (including literature) traditionally dominated by men.

DBF; Guy Demerson, *Louise Labé: Les Voix du lyrisme* (1990); Keith Cameron, *Louise Labé: Renaissance Poet and Feminist* (1990).

**LA BOËTIE, ÉTIENNE DE** (1530–63), French poet and political philosopher who studied law at Orléans and subsequently became a magistrate in the Bordeaux Parlement, where MONTAIGNE became his colleague in 1557. Their friendship was the subject of Montaigne's 'De l'amitié' (*Essais* I. 28). After La Boëtie's early death his writings were collected by Montaigne, who chose to suppress the *Contr'un* (or *Discours de la servitude volontaire*), which had been published by the HUGUENOTS who, in the wake of the ST BARTHOLOMEW'S DAY MASSACRE, had presented the tract as an attack on the Catholic monarchy. La Boëtie's uncompromising Catholic views are set out in his *Mémoire touchant l'édit de janvier*, the title of which was later broadened from specific reference to the January Edict to a *Mémoire sur la pacification des troubles*; in this treatise La Boëtie argues that Catholicism should be the only religion permitted in France.

DBF; Jacques Desplat, *La Boëtie, le magistrat aux nombreux mystères* (1992).

**LACE**, an openwork fabric, normally made of linen but also made with silk or wool and sometimes supplemented with gold and silver threads. It is often called after its place of manufacture (Brussels lace, Venetian lace) or its particular purpose (e.g. bride lace, which is sometimes made of silk or gold and used to bind the sprigs of rosemary carried at weddings). Lace is made by one of two techniques. Bobbin lace, which is also known as pillow lace, bone lace, and bonework lace, is made on a pillow with bobbins made of bone or wood. Needlepoint lace, which is also known as point lace (French *point à l'aiguille*, Italian *punto in aco*), is made with a needle rather than with bobbins; it is a form of NEEDLEWORK derived from medieval spiderwork (Latin *opus araneum*) and fifteenth-century LACIS, RETICELLA, and PUNTO IN ARIA. These two kinds of lace differ in appearance, in that bobbin lace is more delicate (and so was used to decorate personal clothing) and needlepoint lace is more sculptural (and so was used for ceremonial vestments), but each technique was on occasion used to imitate the effects of the other; the two types can be distinguished by the groundwork threads, which in bobbin lace are twisted or plaited and in needlepoint lace untwisted.

The earliest laces were made in Italy and Flanders at the end of the fifteenth century. In Italy, Venetian lace was made by the needlepoint technique and Genoese lace by the bobbin technique. In the late sixteenth century Venetian pattern books (initially those of Mateo PAGANO) were available all over Europe, and the term 'Venetian lace' (French *point de Venise*) came increasingly to denote style rather than provenance; in Flanders, where the most important centre for the manufacturing of lace was Brussels, needlepoint lace was known as *point de gaze* and bobbin lace included varieties known as *point plat* and *point d'Angleterre*. In the early 1620s bobbin lace began to be manufactured in Honiton (Devon); Honiton lace used Antwerp thread to execute floral designs, and Honiton became the principal centre of English lace until the eighteenth century.

M. Simeon, *The History of Lace* (1979); S. M. Levy, *Lace: A Visual History* (1983); S. Thompson, *Introduction to Honiton Lace* (1985).

**LACIS or filet lace or darned netting**, a form of NEEDLEWORK in which a net of threads, knotted at the crossing points, was used as the background for an ornamental pattern. Both the network and the darned pattern were normally made of linen, but occasionally coloured silks and gold thread were used for the pattern. Lacis evolved into the forms of LACE known as RETICELLA and PUNTO IN ARIA.

**LADISLAS II or (Czech) Vladislas II or (Hungarian) Ulászló II or (Polish) Władysław Jagiełło** (1456–1516), king of Bohemia and Hungary, was the son of CASIMIR IV of

Poland, through whose influence he was elected king of Bohemia in 1471 following the death of GEORGE OF PODĚBRADY. The rival candidate was King MATTHIAS CORVINUS, to whom Ladislas was eventually reconciled, and whom he succeeded as king of Hungary in 1490.

**LADISLAS OF DURAZZO** (1380–1414), king of Naples. He acceded to the throne of NAPLES in 1386, at the age of 6, and was crowned by Pope BONIFACE IX in 1390. For the next nine years he was preoccupied with the defence of his crown in the face of the rival claim of King LOUIS II of Anjou, who had been crowned king of Naples by the antipope Clement VII. In 1404 Ladislas began to expand his realm, conquering Rome, Latium, and Umbria, and in 1409 he secured Cortona. Ladislas's aspiration to create a kingdom of Italy was felt as a threat by Florence, which formed an alliance with his Angevin enemies. He died on 6 August 1414 and was succeeded by his sister GIOVANNA II.

A. Cutolo, *Re Ladislao d'Angiò Durazzo* (1936).

**LADISLAS V POSTHUMUS** (1440–57), king of Hungary and Bohemia, was the posthumous son of Albrecht II (king of Hungary and king of the Romans) and Elizabeth, daughter of the Emperor SIGISMUND. In the four-month interval between the death of Albrecht and the birth of Ladislas, the Hungarian Estates had elected VLADISLAV III of Poland as their king, but Elizabeth arranged for the infant king to be crowned at Székesfehérvár and placed him under the protection of his uncle the Emperor FRIEDRICH III. On the death of Vladislav III in 1444, Ladislas was elected by the Estates as king of Hungary, but his imperial guardian retained Ladislas until 1452, when he was released into the care of his uncle, Count Ulrich of Cilli. In 1453 Ladislas was crowned as king of Bohemia, and thereafter lived in Prague and Vienna. A rift with János HUNYADI, regent of Hungary, led in 1457 to the murder of Count Ulrich and the execution of Hunyadi's son Laszló. Ladislas retreated to Prague, where he died suddenly, probably of plague but possibly of poison.

BLBL; NDB.

**LADY ELIZABETH'S MEN**, a company of actors founded in 1611 under the patronage of JAMES VI's daughter. In 1614 they moved into the HOPE theatre on Bankside, built for them by HENSLOWE, but despite including FIELD in their number, they did not prosper there. The company dispersed in 1616, on Henslowe's death. In 1622, another company, based at the COCKPIT under BEESTON, took the same name, and met with some success. Among the plays they performed was MIDDLETON's great tragedy *The Changeling* (1622).

**LAETUS, JULIUS POMPONIUS, or (Italian) Giulio Pomponio Leto** (1425–98), Italian humanist, classical scholar and philologist. Laetus was born in Salerno and educated in Rome, where he was eventually appointed to a chair of Latin in the Gymnasium Romanum in succession to Lorenzo VALLA. He was the founder of the Roman Academy, a learned antiquarian society which sought to revive ancient Rome by performing classical plays, celebrating ancient festivals, and studying the literature of antiquity; members of the Academy, which met on the Quirinal (the northernmost hill of Rome) to discuss the ancient world, adopted Greek and Latin names; Laetus was styled *pontifex maximus*. In 1468 the Academy was suppressed by Pope PAUL II, who suspected its members of paganism and heresy; Laetus was arrested and tortured, but was eventually acquitted of the charges of heresy and immorality.

Laetus continued to teach until his death in Rome on 9 June 1498. His publications, which were collected as *Opera Pomponii Laeti varia* in 1521, centred on Roman history. He also wrote a commentary on Virgil and edited Sallust and Vegetius. A biography by SABELLICUS was published in Strassburg in 1510.

Vladimiro Zabughin, *Giulio Pomponio Leto* (2 vols., 1909–12).

**LAFRÉRY, ANTOINE or Antonio** (1512–77), Burgundian engraver and publisher who settled in Rome, where he secured many of the copperplates of Marcantonio RAIMONDI. Throughout the 1540s he produced engraved views of ancient and contemporary Rome, some 130 of which he collected as *Speculum romanae magnificentiae* ('The Mirror of Rome's Magnificence').

DBF; MDA.

**LAIB, CONRAD** (*fl.* 1440–60), German painter. He was born in the Riesgau and settled in Salzburg *c.*1440. His style has a strong realist element, as evinced in details such as his depiction of fabric, and his facial expressions are highly individualized, even in his depictions of crowds in pictures such as the *Crucifixion* (1449, Belvedere, Vienna), which is the central panel of an altarpiece now dispersed (Palazzo Vescovile, Padua, and Seminario Patriarcale, Venice).

MDA s.v. Laib, Conrad; NDB.

**LAÍNEZ, DIEGO** (1512–65), Spanish Jesuit and the second general of the JESUITS. He was born in Castile and studied at the University of Alcalá, and subsequently joined IGNATIUS LOYOLA in Paris, where he was one of the seven priests who in August 1534 assembled in the Montmartre church and committed themselves to missionary work in Palestine, so laying the foundations for the establishment of the Jesuit Order. He was later appointed as professor of theology at the University of Rome, where he established a reputation for combating the Protestant heresy in Rome and in the cities of northern Italy. He was a prominent papal theologian at the COUNCIL OF TRENT, where he unyieldingly defended papal authority and a conservative position on the issues of JUSTIFICATION and GRACE. In 1552 Laínez was appointed provincial of the Italian Jesuits, and on the death of Ignatius Loyola in 1556 Laínez succeeded him, initially as general-vicar and from 1558 as general. His tenure of office was characterized by the centralization of authority in the Order and by a huge increase in its missionary endeavours. Laínez died in Rome on 19 January 1565. His two-volume *Disputationes Tridentinae* was not published until 1886.

DHE; Feliciano Cereceda, *Diego Laínez en la Europa religiosa de su tiempo* (2 vols., 1945–6).

**LA MARCHE, OLIVIER DE** (*c.*1425–1502), French historian of Burgundy, born into a noble family and educated at the ducal court in Dijon, where he was a page at the court of PHILIP THE GOOD and a secretary and diplomat in the service of CHARLES THE BOLD. In January 1477 Duke Charles was killed at Nancy and La Marche was taken prisoner. After his release he entered the service of MARY OF BURGUNDY (daughter of Charles the Bold) and her husband Maximilian (later the Emperor MAXIMILIAN I) and in 1480 was charged with the education of their son Philip (later King PHILIP THE HANDSOME of Castile).

La Marche's works include encomiastic poetry, a letter of advice to Maximilian I written at the outbreak of the ITALIAN WARS (1494), and his *Mémoires*, a chronicle of Burgundy from 1435 to 1488 which contains detailed descriptions of court life and its festivities. He also wrote a treatise on courtly etiquette, *Le Chevalier délibéré*, which was later reworked in Spanish verse by Fernando de ACUÑA from a prose translation said to have been written by CHARLES V; Acuña's version was itself translated into English, and appeared in 1594 as *The Resolved Gentleman*.

DBF.

**LAMBE, WALTER** (*c.*1450–1499), English composer and a member of the choir at St George's Chapel, Windsor, and at Holy Trinity, Arundel. He is one of the main contributors to the ETON CHOIRBOOK. His motets are in a florid contrapuntal style, covering a wide compass of notes and sometimes composed on a *cantus firmus* not connected to the text, as for instance in 'O Maria plena gratia' and, in the case of 'O regina caelestis gloriae', using two plainchants simultaneously.

**LAMBERT, FRANÇOIS or** (German) **Franz** (1486–1530), French Protestant reformer in Hesse who entered the Franciscan Order in Avignon at the age of 15. In 1522 he met ZWINGLI in Zürich, whereupon he left his Order and travelled incognito to Wittenberg (1523), where LUTHER secured a pension for him from the Elector FRIEDRICH III of Saxony and where he married.

In 1524 Lambert moved to Metz, but after eight days fled to Strassburg, where he stayed for two years and wrote exegetical works on the Old Testament. In 1526 PHILIP OF HESSE invited Lambert to Hesse, where he participated in the Synod of HOMBERG, assumed responsibility for the preparation and implementation of a new 'church order' for Hesse, and in 1527 was appointed as the founding professor of theology at the new University of Marburg. After the Colloquy of MARBURG in 1529, Lambert adopted the Zwinglian position on the EUCHARIST. His writings in Hesse include a commentary on the Book of Revelation (1528).

DBF; NDB; G. Müller, *Franz von Avignon und die Reformation in Hessen* (1958).

**LAMBERTI, NICCOLÒ** (*c.*1370–1451) and **PIERO** (*c.*1393–1435), Italian sculptors from Florence. Niccolò worked on carved doors depicting the four Evangelists for the façade of Florence Cathedral, and in 1416 moved to Venice, where he worked with his son Piero (who predeceased him) and with

Paolo UCCELLO on sculptural decorations for the Basilica San Marco.

Piero's work in Florence includes sculptures in Orsanmichele (including *St James*) and the tomb of Onofrio Strozzi in the Church of Santa Trinita. In 1424 he became *capomaestro* of the new wing of the Ducal Palace in Venice, for which he executed many sculptures; he also carved the tomb of Doge Tommaso MOCENIGO in the Church of SS Giovanni e Paolo.

MDA.

**LAMBETH ARTICLES**, nine theological propositions formulated in 1595 by a committee that met at the archiepiscopal Lambeth Palace. The committee, which was chaired by John WHITGIFT, archbishop of Canterbury, represented current Puritan thinking, and the Articles have a pronounced Calvinist flavour. The soteriological position at the heart of the Articles was supralapsarianism, a doctrine originating in Calvinism (but not advocated by CALVIN) which affirmed that, before the Fall, God had by immutable decree elected certain individuals to salvation, and that God had selected these individuals not because he had foreseen their merits but rather because it was his unaccountable pleasure to select these individuals rather than others.

The Lambeth Articles were not authorized by the Church, and incurred the displeasure of ELIZABETH, but their theological substance nonetheless represented the mainstream Calvinist view, at least until the Synod of DORT, when the advocacy of a sublapsarian position (according to which God drew up his list after the Fall) gradually secured consensus.

**LAMBIN, DENYS**, or (Latin) **Dionysius Lambinus** (1520–72), French classical scholar, born in Montreuil-sur-Mer in Picardy and educated in Paris, where he arrived sometime before 1634. In 1561 he accepted the chair of Latin at the COLLÈGE DE FRANCE, but soon migrated to the chair of Greek. He edited HORACE (1561), LUCRETIUS (1563), CICERO (1566), Cornelius Nepos (1569), Demosthenes (1570), and PLAUTUS (1576). He was conservative in textual matters, but was nonetheless capable of proposing emendations that were condemned as ill considered. His vast commentaries were sometimes (unjustly) said to be rambling accounts weighed down with trivial detail (hence the French eponym *lambiner*, 'to dawdle'). Lambin's learning was daunting, but his scholarship was not helpful to his successors, because his references to his manuscript sources are disconcertingly vague, and so his readings are often difficult to evaluate.

DBF.

**LANCASTER, SIR JAMES** (*c.*1555–1618). In 1601–2, Lancaster commanded the first EAST INDIA COMPANY expedition to the Indies, accompanied by John DAVIS as his chief pilot. His five ships reached Achin, Sumatra, in June 1602 and established a trading post there. Lancaster had previously sailed to Achin in 1592.

**LANDINO, CRISTOFORO** (1424–1504), Italian humanist, poet, and philologist, who during his years as a professor in Florence attempted in his teaching to reconcile Platonism with Aristotelianism and Christian revelation with the wisdom of classical antiquity. During these years Landino wrote influential commentaries on Virgil, Horace, and Dante and translated PLINY THE ELDER into Italian. His most important original work was his *Disputationes Camaldulenses* (1508), a series of dialogues on Virgil's *Aeneid*. In book 1 Lorenzo de' MEDICI and ALBERTI debate the relative merits of the *vita activa* and the *vita contemplativa*; in book 2 Alberti and FICINO discuss the *summum bonum*; in books 3 and 4 Alberti exemplifies the first two discourses through a detailed allegorical reading of the first six books of the *Aeneid*; books 5 and 6 shift the emphasis from moral philosophy to art, arguing that Virgil embodied Platonic doctrine in his imaginative passages. At the end of these discussions Lorenzo is summoned back to the active life.

Pompeo Giannantonio, *Cristoforo Landino e l'umanesimo volgare* (1971); C. Landino, *Disputationes Camaldulenses*, ed. Peter Lohe (1980); id., *Scritti critici e teorici*, ed. R. Cardini (2 vols., 1984); C. Kallendorf, 'Cristoforo Landino's *Aeneid* and the Humanist Critical Tradition', *Renaissance Quarterly*, 36 (1983); Mario di Cesare, 'Cristoforo Landino on the Name and Nature of Poetry', *Chaucer Review*, 21 (1986).

**LANDSCAPE PAINTING.** Elements of landscape appeared as background in some strands of the visual art of classical and medieval Europe, but the notion that the landscape itself could constitute a suitable subject for a painting did not emerge until the sixteenth century. Indeed, there is no evidence that the natural world was perceived as a unified scene (as opposed to an unending assemblage of natural objects) until artists taught viewers of paintings to view nature as 'picturesque'. The idea of the picturesque was not introduced into English until the eighteenth century, but it can be traced back through French *pittoresque* and Italian *pittoresco* to Dutch and Flemish *schilderachtig*, which has the sense of a landscape worthy of artistic representation. It was in FLEMISH ART that landscape painting was to find its finest expression.

Landscape painting began with the watercolour drawings made by Albrecht DÜRER in the course of his visit to Italy in 1495. The first artist to make a career out of landscape art was Albrecht ALTDORFER, who painted (in oils and watercolours) and etched landscapes, sometimes without figures in the foreground. The abandoning of figures signalled a break with the tradition that pictures containing landscape had to have a narrative element. For Altdorfer, the landscape became an autonomous subject, and even in paintings such as the *Rest on the Flight into Egypt* (Gemäldegalerie, Berlin), the true subject is the scenery rather than the resting figures; indeed, this motif was to become an important pretext for landscape painting for centuries to come, as evidenced in paintings such as the *Rest on the Flight into Egypt* by CORREGGIO (Uffizi), Joachim PATINIR (Koninklijk Museum voor Schone Kunsten, Antwerp), Rembrandt (National Gallery, Dublin), and Claude Lorraine (Galleria Doria, Rome).

In fifteenth-century Flanders, landscape played an increasingly prominent part in paintings ostensibly devoted to other subjects, and in the sixteenth century Flemish artists such as Joachim Patinir, Henri met de BLES, and Pieter BRUEGEL the Elder transformed landscape painting into a major genre. Flemish artists soon introduced the landscape painting to other parts of Europe. Gillis CONINXLOO was one of the most important disseminators of the genre: in 1587 he migrated as a Protestant refugee to Frankenthal (in the Palatinate) and there formed an artists' colony specializing in woodland scenes that influenced German landscape painters such as Adam ELSHEIMER; in 1595 Coninxloo moved to Holland, where he became an important influence on the Dutch school of landscape painters in the seventeenth century.

The growth of landscape painting in both Protestant and Catholic regions may in part be a product of its confessional neutrality. Edward Norgate, who bought pictures on behalf of King Charles I, commented with respect to the collecting of paintings that landscapes were 'of all kinds of pictures the most innocent, and which the Devil himself could not accuse of idolatry'. This quality was a particular advantage in northern Europe, where the iconoclastic strain in Protestantism had discouraged religious art.

In sixteenth-century landscape painting, landscapes were formally constructed, particularly in respect of colour: the foreground tended to be brown, the middle distance green, and the background blue, though Pieter Bruegel the Elder and Joos MOMPER II both resisted this convention. In early seventeenth-century Rome, where artists such as Annibale CARRACCI, Adam Elsheimer, and Paul BRIL were active as landscape painters, the notion of the idealized landscape began to supplant the constructed landscapes of the sixteenth century. These Edenic landscapes were to become typical of painters such as Claude Lorraine and Nicolas Poussin, and were to have a profound influence on garden design.

*LANDSKNECHTE* (German; 'men of the plain'), the sixteenth-century imperial German infantry, so called to distinguish them from the Swiss mercenaries, whose Confederation had seceded from the Empire. In the fifteenth century the Swiss were thought to be the finest foot soldiers in Europe, but their defeat at the battle of MARIGNANO in 1515 by a force that contained large numbers of *Landsknechte* tarnished the reputation of the hitherto invincible Swiss and marked the emergence of the Swabian *Landsknechte* as Europe's most respected infantry.

The *Landsknechte* were formed by the Emperor MAXIMILIAN I, and always constituted the core of imperial armies. They also fought in organized bodies in other countries, notably France, where they fought both for the HUGUENOTS and for the CATHOLIC LEAGUE. Their typical weapon was a long pike or lance known as a *langer Spiess*; this lance is the origin of the common names for the *Landsknecht* in German (*Lanzknecht*), French (*Lansquenet*), and English ('lance-knight'); this etymological slippage meant that *land* gave way to *lanz* and the *Landsknechte* came to be associated with their weapons rather than their geographical origins. Their light weaponry and their mobility meant that they could be used tactically in conjunction with ARTILLERY and cavalry regiments. The most famous commander of the *Landsknechte* was Georg von FRUNDSBERG.

The *Landsknechte* were raised and commanded by colonels (*Obersten*) whose regiments were divided into companies or 'colours' (*Fähnlein*) commanded by captains (*Hauptmänner*) who were assisted by ensigns (*Fähnrichen*). The organization of the *Landsknechte* into regiments and companies and the detailed sets of responsibilities associated with each rank proved to be the model that was to prevail in later armies, and is still recognizably the organizing principle of modern armies.

**LANG, MATTHÄUS** (1468–1540), German cardinal and statesman, born in Augsburg and educated at the universities of Ingolstadt, Tübingen, and Vienna. In 1494 he became secretary to the Emperor MAXIMILIAN I. He enjoyed many ecclesiastical benefices, including the archbishopric of Salzburg, and in 1508 was appointed imperial chancellor. In 1512 he was created cardinal by Pope JULIUS II, and in 1519 he was belatedly ordained as a priest. After Maximilian's death Cardinal Matthäus helped to secure the election of CHARLES V, and afterwards encouraged the young emperor to suppress Martin LUTHER's rebellion.

*NDB* s.v. Matthäus.

**LANGUAGES.** The principal languages of early modern Europe consist of six language families (Germanic, Romance, Slavic, Balto-Slavic, Finno-Ugric, and Celtic), a number of isolates (GREEK, ALBANIAN, Basque, and Romany, the language of the GIPSIES), and the languages associated with the two most important conquests, Arabic (in Spain) and Turkish (in the Balkans); Maltese is in its origins a dialect of Arabic. Within each of the language families there is room for debate about the distinction between languages and dialects; when languages are defined by nationalist aspirations or political boundaries, it is sometimes appropriate to think of a language as a dialect with an army. Of the ancient languages, LATIN, classical and biblical Greek, and HEBREW were widely studied, and BIBLICAL scholarship also encompassed the study of Aramaic, SYRIAC, Samaritan, and Ethiopic; the science of EGYPTOLOGY had not yet deciphered the hieroglyphs on ancient Egyptian monuments.

The East Germanic languages (Gothic, Burgundian, and Vandalic) had all died out before the early modern period, but Gothic was nonetheless studied, especially by Dutch scholars. The North Germanic languages were DANISH, SWEDISH, Norwegian, Icelandic, Faeroese, and Norn (the language of Orkney and Shetland, which survived until the eighteenth century). The West Germanic languages were ENGLISH, Scots (see SCOTTISH LANGUAGES), GERMAN, Low German, Letzebürgisch (see LUXEMBURG), DUTCH/Flemish, FRISIAN, and Yiddish.

The Romance languages, all of which derived from Latin, were SPANISH (including Ladino), PORTUGUESE, CATALAN, FRENCH, ITALIAN, Provençal (also known as OCCITAN and the Langue d'Oc), Romanian, SARDINIAN, Galician (see SPANISH LANGUAGE), and Rhaeto-romanic (Swiss Romansch, South Tirolese, and Friulian).

The Slavic languages (which in British English are called 'Slavonic') are divided by linguists into three groups. The East Slavic languages are Russian, Belorussian (formerly called White Ruthenian), and Ukrainian (formerly called Ruthenian). The South Slavic languages are Bulgarian-Macedonian, Serbo-Croatian, and Slovenian (or Slovene); nationalist linguists distinguish Bulgarian from Macedonian and Serbian from Croatian. The West Slavic languages are CZECH, Slovak, POLISH, SORBIAN (also known as Wendish and Lusatian), Polabian (spoken on the Lower Elbe until the mid-eighteenth century), and Cassubian (or Kashubian, which survives in the area west of Gdańsk).

The Balto-Slavic languages, the relationship of which to Slavic languages is debated by linguists, are LITHUANIAN, Latvian (also known as Lettish), and Old Prussian (which survived until the early eighteenth century).

The principal Finno-Ugric languages were HUNGARIAN and Finnish. Hungarian is the only European language in the Ugrian sub-group, but Finnish had relatives in the north (Saamic, formerly called Lapp), the east (Karelian, Veps, and Votian), and the south, where Estonian, LIVONIAN (which now has only 150 speakers), and Ingrian (in Ingermanland, which was Swedish until 1721 and is now Russian) were spoken. Only Hungarian and Finnish were written languages.

The Celtic languages are divided by linguists into the Brittonic and the Goidelic groups. The Brittonic languages were Cornish (which survived until the eighteenth century), Welsh, and Breton; the Goidelic languages were Manx Gaelic (which survived until the twentieth century), Irish Gaelic, and Scots Gaelic.

**LANGUET, HUBERT**, or (pseudonym) Junius Brutus (1518–81), French Huguenot diplomat and political philosopher, born in Vitteaux in Burgundy (of which his father was governor) and educated at the universities of Poitiers (1536–9), Bologna, and Padua (where he received his doctorate in 1548). In Bologna he read the *Loci communes theologiae* of MELANCHTHON, and in 1549 he travelled to Wittenberg to meet its author; he lived in Wittenberg until Melanchthon died in 1560, though throughout this period he travelled widely in Germany, France, Italy, Spain, and Scandinavia (including Finland and Lapland). In 1559 Languet entered the service of AUGUSTUS I, the elector of Saxony, representing the elector at the French court (1561–72) and the imperial court (1573–7). In 1567 Languet witnessed the siege of Gotha (see JOHANN FRIEDRICH II), of which he wrote an account. The WARS OF RELIGION sometimes forced him to retreat to Saxony, and he only escaped death in the ST BARTHOLOMEW'S DAY MASSACRE through the intervention of Jean de Morvilliers, bishop of Orléans.

Languet spent his final years in the Netherlands. He remained nominally in the service of the elector of Saxony, but in practice worked for other patrons, undertaking a mission to England on behalf of JOHANN CASIMIR and acting as a councillor to WILLIAM OF ORANGE. Languet died in Antwerp on 30 September 1581.

Much of Languet's official and personal correspondence was published in the course of the seventeenth century. His 329 letters to Augustus I (17 November 1565–8 September

1581), 111 letters to the Saxon chancellor Ulrich von Mordeisen (1559–65), 108 letters to Joachim CAMERARIUS, and 96 letters to Sir Philip SIDNEY (22 April 1573–28 October 1580) are one of the most important epistolary sources of sixteenth-century history. Languet's fame as a political philosopher rests on the traditional but uncertain attribution to him of VINDICIAE CONTRA TYRANNOS, which was published under the pseudonym Junius Brutus.

*DBF; ADB.*

**LANIER, NICOLAS** (1588–1666), English composer, singer, and lutenist. In 1613 he composed and sang 'Bring away this sacred tree' at court in CAMPION's MASQUE at the marriage of Lady Frances Howard and Robert Carr, earl of Somerset. He wrote music for Ben JONSON's masques and served as a court musician. He later acted as an agent for Charles I, and in 1628 purchased the picture collection of the dukes of Mantua.

**LA NOUE, FRANÇOIS, SEIGNEUR DE,** or Bras de Fer (1531–91), French Huguenot soldier and historian. He was born into a noble Breton family in Nantes and fought with distinction in the first two WARS OF RELIGION. In 1570 he lost his left arm at the siege of Fontenay, and replaced it with an iron arm (hence his nickname 'Bras de Fer') ending in a hook designed to hold his reins. He commanded the Huguenot fortress of La Rochelle (1572–3), and afterwards went to fight on the Protestant side in the REVOLT OF THE NETHERLANDS. In 1580 he captured Count Egmont but was himself captured by Spanish forces a few weeks later. He was imprisoned in Limburg for five years, during which time he wrote his *Discours politiques et militaires*, an account of the Wars of Religion which was first published in Basel in 1587; this treatise was reprinted and translated into German (1592) and English (1597) and so shaped the Protestant historiography of the Wars. In 1585 La Noue was released in exchange for Egmont and other prisoners. He subsequently fought alongside King HENRI IV at the battle of Ivry (14 March 1590) and later in the year died at Moncontour of wounds sustained at the siege of Lambelle (Brittany).

*DBF.*

**LANTE, VILLA,** a villa in Bagnaia, 5 kilometres (3 miles) east of Viterbo; the architect was almost certainly Giacomo VIGNOLA. Construction began *c.*1566, when the villa was commissioned by Cardinal Gambara, bishop of Viterbo; it was completed by his successor, Cardinal Montalto, and in 1655 passed to the Lante family, from whom it takes its name. There is no imposing house, but rather two elegant CASINI that are treated as ornamental features in the finest of all ITALIAN GARDENS.

The axis of the garden is marked by a stylized stream that falls from a wooded hillside over a series of low terraces to a pool. The water falls from the top of the hill through the Fountain of the Deluge between two PAVILIONS to the Fountain of the Dolphins; this fountain has replaced the Fountain of Coral built in 1596. The water is then channelled into a sculpted cascade (*catena d'acqua*) shaped at its head like

an elongated crayfish (a visual pun on the literal meaning of *gambero*) and falls into the Fountain of the Giants, from which it emerges as a channel that runs the length of a stone table, which is the centrepiece of a graceful outdoor dining room; the channel was used to cool wine, and dinner dishes may have been floated on the water, in imitation of the practice at the Tuscan villa of Pliny the Younger. Finally, the water passes through the Fountain of Lights, which is flanked by GROTTOES dedicated to Neptune and Venus, and flows between the two *casini* to a square pool in the centre of which is a fountain with four youths holding aloft the arms of Cardinal Montalto, surmounted by water jets that spray the water into the lake. The lake is divided into four sections, each with a stone boat crewed, as MONTAIGNE noted, by a musketeer and a trumpeter who shoot water into the lake; the features contribute to the imaginative recreation of a naval battle known as a *naumachia*. The lake is set in a square terrace that is now laid out in four PARTERRES de broderie (in Italian, *ricami*), which replaced the eight original flower parterres in the seventeenth century.

The *casini* are both cubes some 23 metres (25 yards) square. The Palazzina Gambara (the one on the left as the viewer looks up the hill) was completed in 1578; its loggia contains wall paintings depicting the Villa FARNESE, the Villa d'ESTE at Tivoli, and the Villa Lante itself. Gambara did not build the other *casino*, instead diverting the money to build a hospital; the second *casino*, the Palazzina Montalvo, was eventually built by Carlo MADERNO.

The garden of the Villa Lante is the best-preserved garden of the Italian Renaissance. In the seventeenth century Montaigne described it as the supreme water-garden, and in the twentieth century Sacheverell Sitwell, who declared that 'Villa Lante is as much a work of art as any poem, painting, piece of music', memorably reflected that 'were I to choose the most lovely place of the physical beauty of nature in all Italy or all the world that I have seen with my own eyes, I would name the gardens of the Villa Lante at Bagnaia'.

A. Cantoni, F. Fariello, M. Brugnoli, and G. Briganti, *La Villa Lante di Bagnaia* (1961); Francesco Negri Arnoldi, *Villa Lante in Bagnaia* (1963); Claudia Lazzaro, *The Italian Renaissance Garden* (1990).

**LA PÉRUSE, JEAN BASTIEN DE** (1529–54), French dramatist and humanist associated both with the PLÉIADE and with the humanists of the Collège de Boncourt. His *Médée* (1556), an imitation of SENECA, was one of the earliest neoclassical plays to embody the ideals of the Pléiade.

*DBF s.v. Bastien de.*

**LARIVEY, PIERRE DE** (*c.*1540–1612), French playwright and translator of Italian plays. He published collections of prose comedies in 1579 (six plays) and 1611 (three plays). All nine plays are imitations of Italian *commedia erudita* (see COMEDY), and so can be traced to remote Latin originals. His best-known play is *Les Esprits* (1579), in which the central character is a miser who is kept out of his house by spirits (*esprits*) invented as part of a ruse.

*DBF.*

**LA RUE, PIERRE DE** (c.1460–1518), Franco-Flemish composer, educated in Tournai. After working in Cologne, in 1489 he went to the Confraternity of Our Lady at 's-Hertogenbosch until 1492, when he became a member of the Habsburg-Burgundian chapel serving MAXIMILIAN, PHILIP THE HANDSOME, and his widow JUANA LA LOCA. He then returned north where Philip's sister MARGARET OF AUSTRIA was regent. Extensive travel went hand in hand with court service and he visited Spain and England. He was a prolific composer whose works cover nearly every occasion in the liturgical calendar. Influenced by JOSQUIN, his style was distinctive in using accidentals and a low compass.

**LA SALE, ANTOINE DE** (1386–c.1460), French writer who spent his career in the service of the dukes of Anjou and the family of Louis de Luxembourg. His work as a tutor is reflected in his two early compilations of exemplary tales, *La Salade* (1441) and *La Sale* (1451). His experience of bereavement in a noble household is articulated in *Le Réconfort de Madame du fresne* (c.1448), a formal letter of consolation to a mother whose first child had died. La Sale's most famous work is a courtly romance in prose, *Le Petit Jehan de Saintré* (1456). His final work, *Des anciens tournois et faits d'armes* (1459), is a treatise on CHIVALRY in which La Sale recalls the tournaments of his youth.

DBF.

**LASCARIS or Laskaris, CONSTANTINOS** (1434–1501), Byzantine scholar in Italy. Lascaris, who was a member of an aristocratic Constantinople family, emigrated to Italy in the wake of the Ottoman capture of Constantinople in 1453. In 1458 he settled in Milan, where Francesco SFORZA employed him as a tutor to his daughter Ippolita until 1465. He moved to Naples on Ippolita's marriage to Alfonso, duke of Calabria (later ALFONSO II), and subsequently taught briefly at Rome (where he became a friend of BESSARION). In 1466 he moved to Messina, where he lived until 1501, when he died of plague. His pupils in Messina included the humanist scholar Pietro BEMBO. His Greek grammar, the *Erotemata*, was the first book to be printed in Greek (Milan, 1476). Much of his library is now in the Biblioteca Nacional in Madrid.

A. de Rosalia, 'La vita di Costantino Lascaris', *Archivio storico siciliano*, 3 (1957–8); Teresa Martinez Manzano, *Konstantinos Lascaris: Humanist, Philologe, Lehrer, Kopist* (1994).

**LASCARIS or Laskaris, JANOS RYNDAKENOS** (1445–1535), Byzantine scholar in Italy and France, possibly the younger brother of Constantinos LASCARIS. He emigrated to Italy as a child, and later taught Greek in Florence, where in 1492 he succeeded CHALCONDYLES in the chair of Greek. He was also employed by Lorenzo de' MEDICI to scour the Byzantine provinces in search of manuscripts; he added about 200 manuscripts to the Medici Library, of which some 80 were of hitherto lost texts. In 1494 he published his most important work, the first printed edition of the *Greek Anthology*, an ancient collection of epigrams. His other publications included editions of Callimachus (the *Hymns*), Apollonius of

Rhodes (the *Argonautia*), and Euripides (*Alcestis, Andromache, Hippolytus*, and *Medea*).

In 1495 Lascaris moved to France, where he taught Greek in Paris. He was appointed as ambassador to Venice (1503–5) by LOUIS XII. He died in Rome.

Börje Knös, *Un ambassadeur de l'hellénisme: Janus Lascaris et la tradition gréco-byzantine dans l'humanisme français* (1945); *Giano Lascaris, Epigrammi greci*, ed. A. Meschini (1976).

**LAS CASAS, FRAY BARTOLOMÉ DE** (1474–1566), 'Apostle of the Indies', born in Seville and educated in Salamanca. In 1498 he accompanied his father (who had sailed with COLUMBUS in 1492) on Columbus' third voyage, and in 1502 he travelled with Nicolás de OVANDO to Hispaniola, where in 1510 he became the first priest to be ordained in the Americas. The following year he moved to Cuba, where colonization was at an early stage and the Indians still hostile. He was assigned a village to which a group of Indians was attached, and so became a beneficiary of the system known as the *repartimiento* ('sharing'), the allotment of land to CONQUISTA-DORES together with dominion over the inhabitants of the land. The status of Indians under the *repartimiento* system was legally that of vassals (whereas in the mines Indians were legally enslaved), but in practice they were treated as serfs or slaves. Las Casas became wealthy, but his unease about *repartimiento* was exacerbated by his experience of witnessing (and trying to prevent) a massacre of Indians, and he eventually released his own Indian serfs and began to preach against *repartimiento*.

Las Casas became so distraught by the abuse of the Indians by Spanish soldiers and settlers that he assigned his estate to his partner and returned to Spain with a view to establishing a mechanism for protecting the Indians. In 1516 Cardinal CISNEROS appointed Las Casas as head of a commission to reform abuse of the Indians, giving him the title 'protector of the Indians'. Las Casas set about his task in Santo Domingo, but was quickly frustrated by the timidity of his coadjutors in the face of resistance by the resident Spaniards. He returned to Spain in July 1517 with a new scheme in which Indians would be liberated at the expense of enslaved Africans: each colonist would be given twelve African slaves in return for freeing Indians indentured to them under the *repartimiento* system. Las Casas later abjured this plan, and took up the defence of Africans against the slave trade.

Las Casas's schemes failed, because sufficient numbers of colonists could not be attracted. In 1522 he entered the Dominican Order and took up residence in their friary in Hispaniola, where he devoted the rest of his life to campaigning for the abolition of slavery and the peaceful evangelization of the Indians. On one of his protracted visits to Europe (1539–44) he wrote his *Veinte razones* (1542), a defence of the rights of the American Indians, and his impassioned *Brevíssima relación de la destrucción de las Indias* (written 1542, published 1552) on the cruelty and greed of his fellow countrymen; this was the book that was largely responsible for the creation of the BLACK LEGEND. In 1544 Las Casas was appointed bishop of Chiapas in Mexico, but three years later resigned and returned to Spain; he died in Madrid in 1566. The most enduring of his voluminous works, a history of the Spanish conquest of America, which he wrote at intervals from 1527 to 1561, remained in manuscript until its publication as *Historia general de las Indias* in 1875.

In his apologetic treatises Las Casas depicts the Indians as virtuous and peaceful by nature but corrupted by the presence of Spain, thus adumbrating the Enlightenment notion of the noble savage. He attacked the imperialist account of the conquest of Gonzalo FERNÁNDEZ DE OVIEDO and was in turn attacked by the humanist Juan Ginés de SEPÚLVEDA, who wrote his reply to Las Casas in the form of a Latin dialogue entitled *Democrates alter; sive, De iusti belli causis* (1542). The two men met in a public disputation at the imperial tribunal convoked at Valladolid to debate the Dominican campaign against crown policy in the Indies. In defence of the conquistadors Sepúlveda cited the just war principles formulated by Aristotle to legitimize the conquest and enslavement of inferior races. Las Casas was able to show that Sepúlveda's views were heretical, using the legal arguments developed by leading Dominican theologians such as Francisco de VITORIA. The tribunal, which dragged on inconclusively until 1550, refused to sanction the publication of Sepúlveda's book (in effect a victory for Las Casas), and meanwhile the revision of the Laws of the INDIES as the New Laws of 1543 implemented (though to little avail) the policy advocated by Las Casas.

DHE s.v. Casas; Marcel Bataillon, *Études sur Bartolomé de las Casas* (1965; Spanish trans. 1976); J. Friede and B. Keen (eds.), *Bartolomé de las Casas in History* (1971); J. Friede, *Bartolomé de Las Casas, precursor del anticolonialismo, su lucha y su derrota* (1974).

**ŁASKI, JAN THE YOUNGER, or Johannes à Lasco** (1499–1560), Polish Protestant reformer, born into a noble Polish family; the sobriquet 'the younger' distinguishes him from his eminent uncle, the chancellor and archbishop Jan Łaski the elder (1456–1531). Łaski the younger was educated in Bologna (1514–18) and in 1524 he visited Basel, where he lived in the house of ERASMUS for nearly a year. He returned to Poland in 1526 with a humanist commitment to ecclesiastical reform but a Catholic aversion to LUTHER's Protestantism, and was appointed, through the influence of his uncle, to a series of posts including a canonry of Kraków and a position in the secretariat of King SIGISMUND I; in 1529 King János ZAPOLYA appointed him to the Hungarian bishopric of Veszprem, and in 1538 he became archdeacon of Warsaw.

In 1540 Łaski converted to CALVINISM, fled from Poland, married, and accepted a post as Reformed (i.e. Calvinist) minister in Emden. In 1548 he accepted the invitation of Thomas CRANMER and John HOOPER to visit England as an adviser on ecclesiastical reform. In 1550 he returned to England as superintendent of the *ecclesia peregrinorum*, a congregation of exiled Germans who had emigrated in the wake of the AUGSBURG INTERIM, and is thought to have contributed to the 1552 Book of COMMON PRAYER. On the accession of Queen MARY in 1553 Łaski was exiled, and sought refuge first in Denmark and then in Frankfurt am Main, where he wrote a series of three letters (printed at Basel) to Poland urging the conversion of the country to Protestantism. When the Protestant party wrested control of Poland in 1556, Łaski returned to direct the Calvinist Church in southern Poland. He died in Pińczów in January 1560.

Łaski's writings include an account (in Latin) of London's *ecclesia peregrinorum* (1560) and a history (in Polish) of the persecution of Protestants in Poland (1567). He also contributed to the Polish translation of the Bible which was published in 1563.

NDB; DNB; PSB; G. Pascal, *Jean de Lasco, baron de Pologne* (1894); B. Hall, *John à Lasco, 1499–1560: A Pole in Reformation England* (1971).

**LASSUS, ORLANDE DE, or Orlando di Lasso** (1532–94), Franco-Flemish composer. As a boy he went to Mantua in the service of Ferrante Gonzaga. After some time in Milan and Naples, in 1551 he went to Rome where, two years later and still very young, he became *maestro di cappella* at San Giovanni in Laterano in Rome. In 1555 he visited Antwerp where Tylman Susato published a collection of his 'madrigali, vilanesche, canzoni francesi e motetti'. The following year he became a member of the court of Duke Albrecht V of Bavaria in Munich, where he sang tenor under Ludwig DASER, whom he succeeded in 1563. His court duties required him to compose masses, Magnificats, motets, and secular music, such as the 'Tafelmusik' he wrote for banquets, for state occasions. He was also required to travel on state business and visited Flanders, Prague, Frankfurt, Ferrara, Venice, Vienna, Trento, Mantua, Bologna, Rome, and Naples. He was highly regarded, with music being published in Munich, Paris, and Nuremberg as well as by the Flemish and Venetian printers, who had published his early compositions. In 1574 Pope Gregory XIII made him a knight of the Golden Spur. He was a prolific and influential composer whose pupils included Andrea and Giovanni GABRIELI.

**LASTMAN, PIETER PIETERSZOON** (1583–1633), Dutch painter, born in Amsterdam. He visited Italy from 1604 to 1607, and there met Adam ELSHEIMER, whose style was to influence his own. Lastman is best known as the teacher of Rembrandt, who studied in his studio for six months (c.1625) and subsequently copied Lastman's paintings for the next ten years. Lastman was a painter of historical and religious subjects, and was particularly adept at the portrayal of crowds at emotionally charged moments.

MDA; NNBW vi.

**LA TAILLE, JEAN DE** (1537–1608), French humanist playwright, the author of two Senecan tragedies (*Saul le furieux*, 1572; *La Famine*, 1573) and two prose comedies (also 1573) based on Italian models: *Le Nécromant*, modelled on ARIOSTO and *Les Corrivaux*, an adaptation of BOCCACCIO. He was also the author of a theoretical treatise, *De l'art de la tragédie* (prefixed to *Saul le furieux*), in which he articulates the conventions of tragedy as understood in the late sixteenth century, including the five-act structure, the unities of time, place, and action, a morally exemplary protagonist, and the reporting rather than the representation of violence.

DBF.

**LATIMER, HUGH** (*c.*1492–1555), English reformer. Educated at Cambridge, and then ordained, Latimer reputedly became influenced by the reformist opinions of Thomas BILNEY and his preaching soon came to the attention of church authorities. In 1525 he refused to preach a sermon against LUTHER, but defended himself successfully when called before WOLSEY. On HENRY VIII's formal break with Rome in 1534, Latimer became first royal chaplain and, in 1535, bishop of Worcester. He supported the dissolution of the MONASTERIES but opposed the Six ARTICLES, resigned, and was briefly imprisoned. Under EDWARD VI, he resumed his career as a popular preacher with a direct and accessible style, but on MARY's succession he was imprisoned and excommunicated. On refusing to accept the doctrines of the old religion, he was burnt at the stake in Oxford, together with RIDLEY.

DNB.

**LATIN LANGUAGE.** Spoken Latin had been kept alive since antiquity in professional disciplines such as the Church, the courts, and the universities. It was the language in which European intellectuals and diplomats spoke and wrote to each other, and as late as the eighteenth century it was the language of educated travellers: Dr Johnson, for example, spoke Latin rather than French when visiting France. Until the tenth century, Latin was the only significant literary language in Europe, and until the middle of the eighteenth century it was the language of learned discourse in subjects such as history, law, theology, geography, science, and medicine; in Hungary and Croatia, Latin was valued as an antidote to the imposition of German, and so remained in official use until 1848.

This living language was deemed by Renaissance humanists to be decadent because of its post-classical coinages and its failure to adhere to the word-order and syntax of classical Latin. Some modern scholars have argued that the artificial language of humanist Latin asphyxiated the natural language of medieval Latin, but Latin had not been anyone's cradle language for centuries, and it seems more sensible to see the change as a shift from one artificial language to another. Humanists sought to recover what they saw as the purity of ancient Latin, for which CICERO was the preferred model. In the view of BEMBO, only those words and constructions sanctioned by their appearance in Cicero could be used in Latin prose. Such extreme Ciceronianism created problems, not least in the Church, because there were no Ciceronian terms for Christian ideas adopted from the Jewish tradition (e.g. angels) or for Christian institutions (e.g. monasteries). There was also a debate about the language that ancient Romans had actually spoken. Leonardo BRUNI contended in 1435 that uneducated Romans had spoken a *sermo vulgaris*, whereas cultured Romans used a *sermo litteratus*. Bruni's hypothesis was intended to account for the variations in ancient Latin, but other humanists offered other explanations: Flavio BIONDO, for example, argued that the differences were caused by class rather than education, and Poggio BRACCIOLINI pointed to the presence of speakers of other languages in Rome.

The architect of the revival of classical Latinity was Lorenzo VALLA, whose philological treatise on the elegance of the Latin tongue (*De elegantia linguae latinae*, Rome, 1471) inaugurated the LATIN SCHOLARSHIP of the period.

**LATIN LITERATURE.** Latin was the principal literary language of early medieval Europe, and it remained an important literary medium throughout the centuries in which the vernaculars gained the ascendancy. In the Renaissance, Latin was the language of learned discourse, and it was used extensively in poetry, prose fiction, and drama throughout Europe. Latin was an international language in the sense that it was understood all over Europe, but literature in Latin often has a national context as well as an international audience, and writers moved back and forth between Latin and their vernaculars in conformity with the demands of decorum and anticipated readership. Northerners such as LUTHER moved freely between Latin and German, but in southern Europe the choice of literary language became the subject of considerable debate; this controversy, which is known as the QUESTIONE DELLA LINGUA, was particularly acute in Italy, because Italian was not yet a unified language, and so Latin had a nationalist dimension.

The linguistic disunity of Italy rendered that nation uniquely receptive to the flourishing of Latin as a literary language. The first major writer whose Latin can be said deliberately to recall the Latin of classical antiquity is PETRARCH, though minor writers such as Lovato Lovati (1241–1309) preceded him. The Latin of Petrarch and his successors was an imperfect realization of ancient Latin, both in substance (e.g. in the predilection for opaque allegory) and in style. By the mid-fifteenth century, however, the transition to Renaissance Latin was complete. Initially this revived classical Latin was preponderantly used by historians: Leonardo BRUNI and Poggio BRACCIOLINI set out the history of classical antiquity, Flavio BIONDO created an enduring historiography of the Middle Ages, and Enea Silvio Piccolomini (later PIUS II) wrote histories of medieval Europe, of BOHEMIA, of ASIA, and of the COUNCIL OF BASEL. Piccolomini also chose Latin as the medium for love poetry, a comedy, and an erotic novella, and so became a forerunner of the torrent of Latin poets and sprinkling of Latin playwrights in fifteenth- and sixteenth-century Italy. Beyond Italy, there are significant bodies of Renaissance Latin literature in many European countries, including Spain, Portugal, France, Germany, Switzerland, the Netherlands, England, Scotland, Ireland, Poland, Hungary, Bohemia, Scandinavia, and the Baltic states; in some cases the quality of this Latin literature rivals that of the vernacular literature, but the death of Latin as a scholarly language means that few accounts of national literatures now survey the work of writers whose medium was Latin.

P. van Tieghem, *La Littérature latine de la Renaissance* (2nd edn. 1966); J. IJsewijn, *Companion to Neo-Latin Studies*, i: *History and Diffusion of Neo-Latin* (2nd edn. 1990), ii: *Literary, Linguistic, Philological and Editorial Questions* (1998); J. W. Binns, *Intellectual Culture in Elizabethan and Jacobean England: The Latin Writings of the Age* (1990).

**LATIN SCHOLARSHIP.** In fifteenth-century Italy there was a consensus that the Latin language derived from Greek. This (erroneous) view was championed in the early sixteenth century by Pietro BEMBO in his *Prose della volgar lingua* (1525), but contested by Ludovico CASTELVETRO in his *Giunta* (addition) to Bembo's *Prose* (1563).

Systematic study of ancient Latin was prompted by the desire of humanists to write like the greatest writers of antiquity; this aspiration extended beyond vocabulary and grammar to an ancient style which the humanists termed *elegantia*. The treatise that first embodied this aspiration was Lorenzo VALLA's *Elegantiae linguae Latinae*, which was written in the mid-1440s. This treatise presents the words, phrases, and syntactical constructions sanctioned by their usage in the works of approved ancient writers, but does not contain a grammar of ancient Latin. That lacuna had been filled by GUARINO DA VERONA in his *Regulae grammaticales*; this book first appeared *c*.1418, and was the first humanist grammar of Latin.

The first comprehensive grammar of Latin was Niccolò PEROTTI's influential *Rudimenta grammatices* (Rome, 1473), which expanded Guarino's account of Latin grammar and added material on morphology and style. Perotti also published *Cornucopia*, a commentary on Martial's *Epigrams* which provided word-lists that were the first lexical account of ancient Latin. Similarly, Antonio de LEBRIJA published an important Latin grammar (*Introductiones Latinae*, Salamanca, 1481) which included an orthographical dictionary, and also compiled Latin–Spanish and Spanish–Latin dictionaries. The lexicology of ancient Latin later became the subject of treatises by Ambrogio CALEPINO (*Dictionarium*, Reggio, 1502) and Robert ESTIENNE (*Latinae linguae thesaurus*, Paris, 1531).

In the field of grammatical theory, which often contained anti-medieval polemic, there were at least five important treatises: Thomas LINACRE's *De emendata structura Latini sermonis* (London, 1524), Julius Caesar SCALIGER's *De causis linguae Latinae* (Lyon, 1540), Petrus RAMUS' *Scholae grammaticae* (Paris, 1559), the Portuguese Jesuit Manuel Alvares's *De institutione grammatica* (Lisbon, 1572), and Francisco Sánchez de los Brozas's *Grammatica Latina* (Salamanca, 1587).

G. A. Padley, *Grammatical Theory in Western Europe 1500–1700: The Latin Tradition* (1976); R. Sabbadini, *La scoperte dei codici latini e greci ne' secoli XIV e XV* (2 vols., 1905–14); R. Pfeiffer, *History of Classical Scholarship* (1976); P. O. Kristeller and F. Edward Cranz (eds.), *Catalogus translationum et commentarium: Mediaeval and Renaissance Latin Translations and Commentaries*, (6 vols. to date, 1960–86); R. R. Bolgar, *The Classical Heritage and its Beneficiaries* (1954); id. (ed.), *Classical Influences on European Culture A.D. 1500–1700* (1976).

**LATTIMO** or *opalia* or *vetro latteo* or (English) **milk glass** or **opaque white glass** or (German) *Milchglas* or *Porzellanglas* or (French) *blanc-de-lait*, an opaque white glass manufactured on the Venetian island of Murano from the early sixteenth century. It was the preferred glass for the background of ENAMEL painting.

When threads of *lattimo* were alternated with clear glass, the glass was called *Latticino* or *Lattincino* and the pattern was termed *vetro a filograna* (now known as *vitro de trina*); more complex patterns were known as *vetro a reticelli* or *vetro a retortoli*.

**LAUBER, DIEBOLD** (*fl.* 1425–67), German manuscript illuminator who had a workshop in Hagenau (now French Haguenau) in Alsace, 15 kilometres (9 miles) north-east of Strassburg. His workshop is known to have produced more than 50 manuscripts (in both German and Latin) between 1425 and 1467.
*NDB; NDBA.*

**LAURANA, FRANCESCO or François** (*c*.1430–*c*.1502), Dalmatian sculptor and medallist, born near Zara (then a Venetian possession, now Croatian Zadar). He worked from 1453 on the sculptural decoration of the triumphal arch erected in the Castelnuovo in Naples in honour of ALFONSO V of Aragon. His other work in Naples includes portrait busts of female members of the viceregal court, including those of Battista Sforza (Bargello, Florence) and Beatrice of Aragon (Kunsthistorisches Museum, Vienna). In Sicily, Laurana worked on the Mastrantonio Chapel (1468) in the Church of San Francesco in Palermo.

Laurana also worked in France, where he made several medals for RENÉ D'ANJOU, titular king of Naples, a relief altarpiece of *Jesus Carrying the Cross* (Church of Saint-Didier, Avignon), and the Chapel (and altarpiece) of St Lazarus (1481) in the Ancienne Cathédrale de la Major in Marseille.
*MDA;* R. W. Kennedy, *Four Portrait Busts by Francesco Laurana* (1962); H.-W. Kruft, *Francesco Laurana: Ein Bildhauer der Frührenaissance* (1995).

**LAURANA, LUCIANO** (*c*.1420–1479), Dalmatian architect, born at Lo Vrana, near Zara (then a Venetian possession, now Croatian Zadar). His principal work is the Palazzo Ducale at Urbino, of which he was appointed architect in 1468, by which time construction had already begun. In the course of his four years in Urbino he designed many interior features such as CHIMNEY PIECES and door-cases; he was probably the architect of the graceful arcaded courtyard in the Florentine style and of the west façade. The palace was later completed by FRANCESCO DI GIORGIO.
*MDA;* Werner Lutz, *Luciano Laurano und der Herzogpalast von Urbino* (1995).

**LAURENZIANA, BIBLIOTECA, or (English) Laurentian Library**, the Florentine library built to accommodate the collection of books and some 10,000 manuscripts founded by Cosimo de' MEDICI and expanded by Piero de' MEDICI, Giovanni de' MEDICI, and Lorenzo de' MEDICI. The building was designed in 1523 by MICHELANGELO for Pope CLEMENT VII; it is named after the Church of San Lorenzo (not after Lorenzo de' Medici), in the cloisters of which it stands. The carved ceiling, carved benches, and mosaic floor were all made to Michelangelo's designs; the staircase was completed by Bartolomeo AMMANATI and Giorgio VASARI in 1571. The library was opened to the public in 1571. In 1808 the Biblioteca MARCIANA was combined with the Laurenziana to form the Biblioteca Medicea Laurenziana.

The entrance hall, **Biblioteca Laurenziana**, Florence. The building was designed by MICHELANGELO and the staircase was completed by Bartolomeo AMMANATI and Giorgio VASARI

**LA VALETTE, JEAN PARISOT DE** (1494–1568), grand master of the Order of the Knights of ST JOHN, was born into a noble family in Toulouse. He was elected grand master of his Order in 1557, and in 1565 commanded the defences during the siege of MALTA in 1565. He subsequently constructed the new capital of the island, which was called Valetta in his honour.

**LAW**. Legal historians distinguish two groups of late medieval jurists: the glossators were exegetes who elucidated the meaning of legal texts, and the commentators (or post-glossators) were scholars who applied dialectical methods to legal texts with a view to adapting them to municipal statutes, canon law, and customary law. The Renaissance successors of these groups were the humanist jurists of the fifteenth and sixteenth centuries, who sought to restore the principles of the Roman law of antiquity and to produce the legal compilations of JUSTINIAN.

In France the most important early humanist jurist was Guillaume BUDÉ, who published his annotations on the Justinian *Digest* (*Annotationes in Pandectas*) in 1508; in German-speaking Europe the comparable figure was Ulrich Zäsy (ZASIUS), who published his 'nocturnal studies' (*Lucubraciones*) in 1518. In Switzerland the most prominent humanist jurist was Hippolyt von Colli (1561–1612).

The most important figures in humanist jurisprudence were Andrea ALCIATO and, in the next generation, Jacques CUJAS. Alciato published an influential commentary on the Justinian *Tres libri*, and in his academic posts in Avignon, Bologna, Milan, and Pavia influenced many of his contemporaries. Italian humanist jurists of his generation include Lelius Torelli (1489–1576), who in 1553 published his three-volume edition of the Florentine text of the Justinian *Pandects*; in the succeeding generation, one of the most important jurists was Scipio Gentili (1563–1616; the younger brother of Alberico GENTILI) who edited Donellus (Hugues DONEAU) and wrote widely on Roman law.

In the school of humanist jurisprudence founded by Alciato in France, the central figure was Jacques Cujas, who is often said to have inaugurated the golden age of jurisprudence.

Prominent jurists associated with the French humanist school included Charles DUMOULIN ('the French Papinian'), Barnabé BRISSON, François LE DOUAREN, and Denis GODEFROY and his son Jacques. Legal historians refer to this group as the 'Elegant School of Law'. Reaction against Cujas took the form of a revival of the thought of BARTOLO DA SASSOFER-RATO. The major figures in the Bartolist group, who contended that law had to be studied in its applied context, were François HOTMAN (Cujas's successor at Bourges) and Hugues Doneau.

The process whereby Roman law was absorbed into the legal systems of northern Europe is known as the RECEPTION. On national legal systems, see the entries on DUTCH LAW; ENGLISH LAW; FRENCH LAW; GERMAN LAW; ITALIAN LAW; SCOT-TISH LAW; SPANISH LAW. On particular aspects of early modern law, see the entries on CANON LAW; CIVIL LAW; COMMON LAW; CUSTOMARY LAW; INTERNATIONAL LAW; LAW MERCHANT; MAR-ITIME LAW; SUMPTUARY LAWS; and the law of TORTURE.

> Guido Kisch, *Studien zur humanistischen Jurisprudenz* (1972); John Gilissen, *Introduction historique du droit* (1979); O. F. Robinson, T. D. Fergus, and W. M. Gordon, *An Introduction to European Legal History* (1985); Vincenzo Piano Mortari, *Gli inizi del diritto moderno in Europa* (1986); Ian Maclean, *Interpretation and Meaning in the Renaissance: The Case of Law* (1992).

**LAW FRENCH.** From the Norman conquest till the deposition of Richard II in 1399, the language of the English royal court and its judicial system was Anglo-Norman French, which survived in English courts for another two centuries; it became a technical judicial language known as 'Law French'. The Year Books that record debate on points of pleading in an unbroken account till 1535 are written in Law French. Its use diminished in the late sixteenth century, but it nonetheless had eminent exponents in the seventeenth century, notably Sir Henry FINCH. Law French was abolished by Parliament in 1650, restored in 1660, and finally abolished in 1733. The language conflated Anglo-Norman structures and vocabulary with English inflections and word-order. The phrase traditionally cited in law texts is 'fuit assault per prisoner la condemne pur felony que puis son condemnation ject un brickbat a le dit justice que narrowly mist'.

> J. H. Baker, *Manual of Law French* (2nd edn., 1990).

**LAW MERCHANT or (Latin) *lex mercatoria*.** Roman CIVIL LAW distinguished between the law applicable to merchants and the law applicable to ordinary citizens. This distinction survived in the commercial law of Italy, where a system for settling disputes between merchants gradually evolved. Merchants appointed consuls (*consules mercatorum*) from amongst their own numbers, and endowed consuls with judicial powers in commercial matters; the courts convened by consuls were eventually absorbed into the judicial systems of the Italian city-states, and their enactments were incorporated as laws. In the thirteenth century this system began to spread through Europe; consuls were appointed in France (*juges consuls* or *consuls marchands*) and Spain, and when west European merchants settled in eastern Europe they continued to appoint consuls to administer the

burgeoning bodies of customs and law known collectively as the Law Merchant.

There was never a unified Law Merchant all over Europe, but the southern states achieved a considerable measure of uniformity in mercantile and maritime regulations. The most highly developed system was the Italian Law Merchant: here as elsewhere the regulations were rooted in customary law, but Roman civil law contributed a technical vocabulary and the law of obligations (which in civil law systems constitutes a distinctive strand), and CANON LAW supplied the ethical principles of fair dealing and good faith.

In northern Europe the Law Merchant was readily absorbed, because the RECEPTION had facilitated the process whereby CUSTOMARY LAW was formulated in terms of Roman civil law. Whereas in southern Europe the Law Merchant had evolved from the judgements of mercantile courts, in northern Europe the system of franchises and privileges meant that the Law Merchant developed differently, because the ruler who granted franchises for trade at fairs and markets retained the right to administer the law. In practice, however, merchants acted as assessors in the courts, and by 1500 it had become normal practice for merchants to preside over the courts. As markets developed in north European towns, the institutions of the Law Merchant were absorbed into municipal constitutions. Variations between constitutions meant that the Law Merchant was always subject to local conditions, but the practice of adapting constitutions from neighbouring towns led to a measure of uniformity. Eventually the towns and territories of northern and central Europe began to reform their institutions of trade and commerce along Italian lines, because northern merchants never achieved the power of Mediterranean merchants, who in Italy and in parts of France and Spain assumed control of government.

The large international fairs that sprang up at the intersection of trade routes all over Europe from the twelfth to the sixteenth centuries accelerated the development of the international element in the Law Merchant, and there was soon a well-established international commercial law which was formulated (usually on the Italian model) and administered by European merchants for their own collective benefit. The Law Merchant thus began to supplant the protectionist legislation of individual states, which were forced to abandon protectionist claims and rights in order to attract foreign merchants to their fairs. The privileges granted to companies of foreign merchants to regulate their affairs by reference to the Law Merchant rather than by local law facilitated the development of a European system of commercial law in which the conflicts between the competing claims of Roman and customary law were subsumed in the Law Merchant of the international fairs.

The origins in Roman law of the legal systems of continental Europe meant that a separate strand of commercial law was congenial to the legal culture. In England, however, the COMMON LAW system and the willingness of Parliament to legislate on commercial matters meant that commercial law was administered in common law courts rather than in specialist courts. These factors, together with the relative commercial isolation of England before the Reformation, meant that a body of commercial law was slow to develop, and that by the time the volume of trade necessitated the formulation of detailed commercial law, the international Law Merchant could only be articulated through the machinery of equity and common law courts. The only jurisdiction in which the Law Merchant completely displaced the common law was the group of English, Irish, and Welsh towns constituted by the Statute of the Staple in 1353. These towns established Courts of the Staple in which the local mayor and his two constables were assisted by two foreign merchants in the application of the Law Merchant. At fairs in England the Law Merchant was administered by Courts of Piepowder (Latin *pedes pulverosi*, French *pieds poudrés*, so called after the dusty feet of the itinerant pedlars who traded at the fairs); JONSON's *Bartholomew Fair* (II. i) portrays in Justice Overdo a magistrate who had presided over such a court.

The reception in the sixteenth and early seventeenth centuries of the continental Law Merchant by English common law and equity courts and by the Privy Council and Parliament is debated, but the consensus is that it led to the gradual absorption of the Law Merchant into English mercantile law; courts continued to insist that merchants plead specially until, in the eighteenth century, Lord Mansfield extracted and organized the principles of the Law Merchant and then incorporated them into common law.

Gerard Malynes, *Consuetudo vel Lex Mercatoria* (1622); W. Mitchell, *Early History of the Law Merchant* (1904); J. H. Baker, 'The Law Merchant and the Common Law before 1700', *Cambridge Law Journal*, 38 (1979).

**LAYOLLE, FRANCESCO DE** (1492–c.1540), Italian composer and organist. In his youth he sang at SS Annunziata in Florence. His friends in Florence included Luigi ALAMANNI, Zonobi Buondelmonte, and Antonio Brucioli, all conspirators in the 1522 attempt to overthrow the Medici. Subsequently he moved to Lyon where, with Jacques Moderne, he edited collections of sacred music, some of which he had composed. His style is a fusion of Franco-Flemish and Italian styles and he employs both *cantus firmus* and parody techniques. His secular works are mostly set texts by Petrarch, Alamanni, and Machiavelli and the Strozzi, though some have French words.

**LAZARILLO DE TORMES**, an anonymous Spanish novella which became the most influential model for the PICARESQUE novel in Spain; its full title is *La vida de Lazarillo de Tormes y de sus fortunas y adversidades*. Editions were published in 1554 in Alcalá de Henares, Antwerp, and Burgos, and it is possible that there was an Antwerp edition of 1553 of which no copy is known to survive. The protagonist is Lázaro, a poor boy from a criminal family, who narrates his story in the first person, perhaps the first occasion in European literature in which a member of the lower classes was given an authentic voice. Lázaro meets a succession of characters whose occupations represent the objects of the novel's satire: a fraudulent priest, a vain but impoverished nobleman, a profligate Mercedarian friar, a vendor of papal bulls, a painter, a chaplain, and a constable.

An anonymous *Segunda parte de Lazarillo de Tormes* was published in Antwerp in 1555, and is clearly the work of another author; a second *Segunda parte*, written by Juan de Luna, was published in Paris in 1620. *Lazarillo de Tormes* was translated into every major European language, including English in 1578 and Dutch in 1579; the Dutch translation formed the basis of one of Gerbrand BREDERO's finest comedies, *Jerolimo den Spaansche Brabander* (1616).

**LEAD**, a base metal which in medieval Europe was valued for its impermeability (and so was used for roofs, water pipes, and font linings) and for its malleability. The principal sources of lead were mines in England (Derbyshire and the Mendip Hills), Germany (Saxony), Austria (Carinthia), and southern Spain. In the sixteenth century the Roman practice of using lead for outdoor sculptures was revived. Lead was sometimes hammered or beaten into shape, but could also be melted and cast. It was also alloyed with tin to make PEWTER. Lead was also used for taking casts of objects made in more costly metals; there is a large collection of lead casts in the Historisches Museum in Basel.

The use of lead in water pipes and cisterns caused the stomach disorders known in England as Devon colic and in France as Poitou colic; in the eighteenth century medical scientists realized that the disorders could be attributed to lead poisoning.

**LEAGUE, FRENCH.** See CATHOLIC LEAGUE.

**LE BÉ, GUILLAUME** (1525–98), French type founder, born in Troyes and trained in the workshop of Robert ESTIENNE. In 1545 he moved to Venice, where he worked as a type founder for several printers. He designed Latin and Greek founts, but his best-known founts are Hebrew.

**LEBRIJA or Nebrija, ANTONIO MARTÍNEZ DE CALA DE, or (Latin) Aelius Antonius Nebrissensis** (1442–1522), Spanish humanist, born in Lebrija (Andalusia) and educated at Salamanca and Bologna. He returned to Spain in 1473 and taught first at Salamanca and then at Alcalá de Henares, where he lectured until his death at the age of 78. Lebrija was Spain's greatest humanist scholar. His numerous works include commentaries on classical authors (Persius and Sedulius), a compendium of ancient rhetoric (based on Aristotle, Cicero, and Quintilian), a Latin history of the reign of FERDINAND and ISABELLA (*Rerum in Hispania gestarum decades*, based on the official Spanish chronicle by Fernando de Pulgar), and a Spanish–Latin dictionary. His grammar of Spanish (*Gramática sobre la lengua Castellana*, Salamanca, 1492) was the first published analysis of a modern European language. Lebrija wrote Latin poetry and important works of biblical analysis and also contributed to the COMPLUTENSIAN POLYGLOT published under the patronage of Cardinal CISNEROS.

*CoE* s.v. Nebrija; Francisco Rico, *Nebrija frente a los bárbaros* (1978); Marcel Bataillon, *Érasme et l'Espagne* (rev. edn., 3 vols., 1991; rev. Spanish trans. 1979); J. H. Bentley, *Humanists and Holy Writ* (1983).

**LECHNER, LEONARD** (*c*.1553–1606), Austrian composer who studied with Ivo de Vento and Orlande de LASSUS when he was at the Munich Hofkapelle. From 1575 he taught at Nuremberg, where he became 'archimusicus' and was commissioned to write for festive occasions. In 1583 he became *Kapellmeister* to Count Eitelfriedrich IV von Hohenzollern-Hechingen, who was a Catholic. Lechner was a keen Lutheran and, feeling threatened by the count, fled to Tübingen and thence to the Stuttgart Hofkapelle, where he sang for Duke Ludwig of Württemberg. He finally suceeded Ludwig DASER as *Kapellmeister* in 1595. He wrote sacred and secular music including 'Laudate Dominum, quoniam bonus est', a psalm setting, for the marriage of Princess Sibylle Elizabeth to Duke Johann Georg, the future elector of Saxony.

**LE CLERC, FRANÇOIS, or Jambe de Bois** (d. 1563), French HUGUENOT privateer whose nickname ('wooden leg') derived from the artificial limb that he wore after losing a leg in a sea battle. He was employed by King HENRI II of France to attack Spanish merchant vessels and Spanish settlements in America. In 1553 he attacked settlements in Hispaniola, and the following year attacked Cuba. In 1555 he preyed on Spanish ships sailing to and from the Canary Islands. He fought in the opening campaign of the WARS OF RELIGION but died at sea in 1563.

**LE CONTE, ANTOINE, or Contius** (*c*.1525–1586), French humanist jurist. He was the editor of the JUSTINIAN *Corpus iuris civilis*, the author of a commentary on the Justinian *Institutes* (*Notae in libros institutionum*) and of *Disputationes iuris civilis*; in the jurisprudential quarrels of the time, he was the opponent of LE DOUAREN and HOTMAN.
    *DBF.*

**LE DOUAREN or Douaren, FRANÇOIS, or Duarenus** (1509–59), French humanist jurist and religious controversialist. He was a rival of CUJAS at Bourges. He published a polemical treatise on the French Church (*Pro libertate ecclesiae Gallicae*, 1551) and commentaries on the JUSTINIAN *Digest* and on FEUDAL LAW (*Tractatus de feudis*, 1558).
    *DBF* s.v. 'Douaren'.

**LEFÈVRE D'ÉTAPLES, JACQUES, or (Latin) Faber Stapulensis** (*c*.1460–1536), French humanist. He travelled as a young man in Italy where his induction into Florentine Neoplatonism stimulated his subsequent editions of pseudo-Dionysius the Areopagite, Origen, and the medieval Catalan mystic Ramon Llull. His principal biblical works were a Latin translation with commentary on the Pauline Epistles (1512), a commentary on the Gospels (1522), and French translations of the New Testament (1523) and the Old Testament (1528–30). His interest in biblical texts incurred the hostility of the Sorbonne, but Lefèvre enjoyed the protection of FRANCIS I and MARGUERITE DE NAVARRE, at whose court in Nérac he died.
    J.-F. Pernot (ed.), *Jacques Lefèvre d'Étaples* (1995).

**LEHMANN or (later) Lehmann von Löwenwald, KASPAR** (1563/5–1623), German lapidary, born in Uelzen. He entered the service of Duke Wilhelm V of Bavaria and in 1588 moved to Prague, where he worked at the court of the Emperor RUDOLF II, who in 1595 ennobled him as Kaspar Lehmann von Löwenwald; he worked from 1606 to 1608 at the court of the elector of Saxony in Dresden, but thereafter returned permanently to Prague. In 1610 the emperor appointed him *Kaiserliche Kammer-Edelgestein und Glasschneider* ('imperial jeweller and glass engraver') and awarded him a monopoly of glass engraving in the HABSBURG territories.

Lehmann was widely regarded as a distinguished carver and engraver of rock crystal, but no example of his work in this medium can now be identified. He was also an innovative worker in glass, developing the art of wheel engraving on glass (which led to the production of a strong potash-lime glass with the strength requisite for such engraving) and the technique of engraving hard stones with a lapidary's wheel for use in the decoration of crystal. The only signed example of his work in glass is an armorial beaker of 1605 in the Museum of Decorative Arts in Prague; attributions include an engraved glass plaque depicting Perseus and Andromeda in the Victoria and Albert Museum in London.
    *NDB; MDA* s.v. Lehmann (von Lewenwaldt), Caspar.

**LEICESTER, ROBERT DUDLEY, EARL OF** (1532–88), English soldier and statesman. Son of NORTHUMBERLAND, in whose plot to crown Lady Jane GREY he participated, Leicester is remembered as a favourite of ELIZABETH I. He may also have had marital designs on her, and certainly contemporaries interpreted the suspicious death of his first wife in this light; at one stage, however, Elizabeth regarded him as a possible husband for MARY, QUEEN OF SCOTS. As well as his political career at the heart of Elizabeth's court, where he was privy counsellor, Leicester served as general of the English forces in the Netherlands from 1585.
    *DNB* s.v. Dudley, Robert.

**LEICESTER'S MEN.** Formed in 1559, Leicester's Men were the earliest Elizabethan acting company, formed, as their name suggests, under the patronage of LEICESTER. They performed at court from 1560. In 1572 they moved into the first playhouse in London, the THEATRE, built by one of their number, James Burbage, father of Richard BURBAGE. The issue of a patent in 1574 authorizing them to play in all towns, without hindrance from authorities, caused conflict with the corporation of London, and contributed to the establishment of the office of the MASTER OF THE REVELS. Many of them joined QUEEN ELIZABETH'S MEN on its formation in 1583, and the company dispersed on Leicester's death in 1588.

**LEIDEN or Leyden or (Latin) Lugdunum Batavorum**, a city on the Old Rhine (Oude Rijn) in the Dutch province of Holland, had a larger population at the end of the sixteenth century (*c*.100,000) than at the end of the twentieth century. By the end of the fifteenth century the city had become an important centre for weaving, and for centuries Leiden broadcloth, baize, and camlet were exported on a large scale. The city was unsuccessfully besieged by Spanish forces from May till October 1574, and the following year the university was founded by WILLIAM OF ORANGE in celebration of the lifting of the siege, which had been achieved by opening the dykes to enable ships carrying relief supplies to reach the city. In the course of the next 50 years the presence of scholars such as Jacobus ARMINIUS, Francis GOMAR, Hugo GROTIUS, Daniel HEINSIUS, Justus LIPSIUS, Joseph Justus SCALIGER, and Gerhard Jan VOSS established the university as one of the most celebrated in Europe. The university's BOTANICAL GARDEN was founded in 1587.

**LEIDEN, PHILIP OF**. See PHILIP OF LEIDEN.

**LEINBERGER, HANS** (1475/80–1530), German woodcarver and sculptor; his principal surviving work is the Gothic altarpiece (1514) carved for the former collegiate Church of St Castulus in Moosburg (50 kilometres (30 miles) north-east of Munich), in Bavaria; it remains in the church, but is not in its original state.

*MDA*; *NDB*; Claudia Behle, *Hans Leinberger* (1984).

**LEIPZIG**, the second city of SAXONY (after Dresden), was in the early Middle Ages primarily a SORBIAN city; its name derives from the Slav root *lipa*, meaning 'lime tree'. A tenth-century German settlement was gradually expanded with new settlers, and by the late Middle Ages the population was primarily German. Leipzig became a trading city; at first its most important commodity was the SALT mined in Halle, and then it became a depot for Nuremberg merchants who were trading with Poland. The city's university was founded in 1409, and by the end of the century had become an important centre for humanist studies, particularly in Greek.

When Saxony was divided in 1485, Leipzig fell to the Albertine branch of the WETTIN family. Leipzig's two annual markets became imperial fairs in 1497, and imperial privileges granted in the early sixteenth century helped the commercial sector to expand, especially in the fur trade. The Albertine Duke GEORG DER BÄRTIGE ordered the LEIPZIG DISPUTATION and afterwards persecuted the reformers; this policy was reversed by his successor Heinrich (1539–41). In 1547 the city was besieged by JOHANN FRIEDRICH I, elector of Saxony, in the course of the SCHMALKALDIC WAR; the suburbs were destroyed, but the city was not captured. In the course of the sixteenth century the city became an important publishing centre and attracted visitors from all across Europe to its annual book fair.

**LEIPZIG DISPUTATION**, a public disputation held at Leipzig from 27 June to 16 July 1519 at the command of GEORG DER BÄRTIGE, duke of Saxony, who participated in the debate. The origins of the disputation lay in a dispute between Martin LUTHER and Johann ECK. In 1517 Luther had sent Eck copies of his 95 Theses. Eck did not reply publicly, but in 1518 began to circulate his hostile response, the Obelisci, in which he denounced Luther as a Hussite. Luther entrusted his defence to KARLSTADT, who proposed 400 counter-theses in opposition to Eck and challenged him to a public disputation.

On 27 and 28 June and 1 and 3 July Eck and Karlstadt debated the doctrine of GRACE. On 4 July Luther arrived, and the debate shifted to the question of the doctrinal authority of the Church. From 4 to 14 July Eck and Luther debated papal supremacy and contentious doctrines such as PURGATORY, with Eck setting his formidable command of PATRISTIC SCHOLARSHIP and the conciliar tradition against Luther's constant appeals to the authority of the Bible. The arbitrators declined to declare a winner, but Eck was widely regarded as the victor, forcing Luther to admit at one point that councils were not only capable of error but in the case of the COUNCIL OF CONSTANCE had actually erred in condemning Hussite doctrines and in affirming the primacy of the pope over general councils.

The disputation clarified the theological differences between the two sides, but also provided Eck and the Roman authorities with new evidence of Luther's heterodoxy which enabled them to intensify their campaign to suppress Lutheran teaching.

J. C. Seidemann, *Die Leipziger Disputation im Jahre 1519* (1843); K.-V. Selge, 'Der Weg zur Leipziger Disputation zwischen Luther und Eck im Jahre 1519', in B. Moeller and G. Ruhbach (eds.), *Bleibendes im Wandel der Kirchengeschichte* (1973).

**LEIPZIG INTERIM**, a religious settlement drafted by MELANCHTHON at the behest of MAURICE OF SAXONY and adopted by Saxony in December 1548. The formulation of the Interim was prompted by the failure of the AUGSBURG INTERIM to win assent in the Protestant areas of northern Germany. The Leipzig Interim affirmed the Lutheran doctrine of JUSTIFICATION by faith, but tried to adopt a conciliatory position by describing Catholic sacraments, including the mass, as ADIAPHORA rather than condemning them outright.

The effect of the Leipzig Interim was to divide the Lutherans. Its supporters, who were called 'Philippists', had to defend the theology of the Interim against its detractors, who were later called GNESIO-LUTHERANS.

**LE JEUNE, CLAUDE** (*c.*1528/30–1600), French composer. He was *maître des enfants de musique* at the court of François, duke of ANJOU. In 1590, despite having powerful Huguenot contacts, he was forced to flee a besieged Paris. In 1596 he was appointed *maître compositeur ordinaire de la musique de notre chambre* by HENRI IV. He composed sacred and secular music. In his approach to word setting, he adhered to the principles of BAÏF's Académie de Poésie et de Musique, of which he was a member, where the emphasis was on clarity. In 1583 he printed his airs to Baïf's 'measured' poems and the Académie's secret *musique mesurée à l'antique*. He also set Baïf's translations of psalms in his *Psaumes en vers mesurés* (1606).

**LELAND, JOHN** (*c.*1506–1552), English antiquarian. Librarian to HENRY VIII, in 1533 he received a royal commission to research 'the histories and antiquities' of England and Wales in monastic, ecclesiastical, and collegiate libraries. The work was not completed, but extensive notes both of his tour, made between 1535 and 1543, were eventually published as Leland's *Itinerary*, in 1710. Willam CAMDEN and John STOW drew on his scholarship in their works.

*DNB*.

**LE MAIRE, ISAAC AND JACOB**. See SCHOUTEN, WILLEM CORNELISZOON.

**LEMAIRE DE BELGES, JEAN** (*c*.1473–1525), French RHÉTORIQUEUR, born in Bavay (Hainaut) and educated in Valenciennes, Paris, and Lyon before entering the service of MARGARET OF AUSTRIA (regent of the Netherlands) in 1503. His poems include *La Couronne margaritique* (1504–5, on the death of Margaret's second husband Duke Philibert of Savoy), *Les Chansons de Namur* (1507, in support of a popular revolt), *Le Concorde des deux langages* (1511, on French and Italian), and *Épîtres de l'amant vert* (1505, poems placed in the mouth of Princess Margaret's green parrot, whose distress at the absence of the princess leads to its suicide). The debt of these poems to Italian literature makes Jean Lemaire de Belges an important precursor of the PLÉIADE. His principal work in prose, written at the court of ANNE OF BRITTANY, is *Illustrations de Gaule et singularités de Troie* (1510–13), a version of the nationalist legend according to which France was founded by the son of Hector.

Pierre Jodogne, *Jean Lemaire de Belges* (1972).

**LENCKER FAMILY**, German goldsmiths in Augsburg. Hans Lencker (1523–85) was admitted to the guild in 1549 and became a burgher the following year; his works, which are remarkable for their enamel decoration, include the silver binding of the prayer book of the Emperor MAXIMILIAN I (Staatsbibliothek, Munich). Hans's brother Elias Lencker (d. 1591), who was also a skilled decorator in enamel, became master in 1562; his works include a ceremonial cup (*c*.1565–70, Germanisches Nationalmuseum, Nuremberg) and a book-rest (*c*.1590, Kunsthistorisches Museum, Vienna).

Another branch of the Lencker family is represented by Christoph Lencker (*c*.1556–1613) and his sons Zacharias (d. 1612) and Johannes (1573–1637). Christoph was appointed assay master of Augsburg in 1610; his best-known work is a silver-gilt ewer and basin embossed with scenes from the legend of Europa; the ewer is lost, but the basin is in the Kunsthistorisches Museum in Vienna. The work of Zacharias is represented by a relief of *The Infant Jesus with Angels* (Kunsthistorisches Museum, Vienna). Johannes was appointed assay master in 1616 and served for many years as burgomaster of Nuremberg; the last ewer made by his father is known by a copy made by Johannes in 1620 and now in a private collection.

*MDA*; *ADB* (Hans Lencker); *NDB* (Christoph Lencker).

**LEO X** (1475–1521), pope from 11 March 1513 until his death on 1 December 1521, was born Giovanni de' Medici in Florence on 11 December 1475, the second son of Lorenzo de' MEDICI. His family determined that Giovanni should enter the Church: he received the tonsure at the age of 7 and in March 1489 was created cardinal-deacon of Santa Maria in Domenica by Pope INNOCENT VIII at the age of 13, though he did not receive his insignia for another three years. Giovanni was educated in Florence by a succession of distinguished humanists (including POLIZIANO, Marsilio FICINO, PICO DELLA MIRANDOLA, and the poet Bernardo DOVIZI) and from 1489 to 1491 he studied theology and CANON LAW at Pisa, where his teachers included Filippo DECIO. On 23 March 1492 he joined the Sacred College in Rome, and on that occasion received a famous letter of advice from his father. Lorenzo died a few weeks later (8 April) and Cardinal Giovanni returned to Florence. He followed his family into exile in November 1494, and for the next six years travelled in northern Europe, visiting France, the Netherlands (where he met ERASMUS), and Germany. He returned to Rome in May 1500 and established himself at the heart of the cultural life of the city, moving in literary and artistic circles and attending plays and concerts. With the accession of Pope JULIUS II in 1503, Cardinal Giovanni began to move closer to the papacy, and on 1 October 1511 he was appointed papal legate to Bologna and the Romagna, a post that involved responsibility for the papal army as well as diplomacy. On 11 April 1512 the armies of the HOLY LEAGUE were defeated by French forces at Ravenna; Cardinal Giovanni was taken prisoner, but escaped. On 14 September 1512, with the support of Julius II, he was able to re-establish the Medici as rulers of Florence; his younger brother Giuliano de' MEDICI was appointed as head of the Florentine republic, but Cardinal Giovanni remained the *de facto* ruler for the rest of his life.

Cardinal Giovanni was elected as pope on 11 March 1513, at the age of 37; on 15 March he was ordained to the priesthood, on 17 March he was consecrated bishop, and on 19 March he was enthroned with the name Leo X. The proscription of simony in papal elections by Julius II meant that Giovanni's election reflected the judgement of the college (who envisaged a kindly and peace-loving successor to the brutal warrior-pope Julius II) more than the pecuniary interests of the electors. In the event, Pope Leo proved to be a cultured, pleasure-loving, and duplicitous prince with a consuming interest in extending the interests of his family beyond Florence and a blind spot for the significance of the Lutheran revolt in northern Europe.

Pope Leo quickly became embroiled in the WARS OF ITALY. On 5 April 1513 he joined Spain, England, and the Holy Roman Empire in the League of Mechelen, which was a military pact designed to prevent France (with the assistance of Venice) from recovering Milan and the kingdom of Naples. After the victory over France at Novara on 6 June 1513, Leo negotiated a settlement with King LOUIS XII which obliged France to withdraw support from the COUNCIL OF PISA. When King Louis's successor FRANCIS I renewed France's claims and defeated the Swiss defenders of Milan at the battle of MARIGNANO on 13/14 September 1515, Leo disregarded the advice of his cardinals and sued for peace. Leo met King Francis in Bologna, and in August 1516 they signed the Concordat of BOLOGNA, which abrogated the PRAGMATIC SANCTION OF BOURGES; Leo also ceded Parma and Piacenza, but in return secured Florence for the Medici family. The following year he sought to extend the interests of his family by deposing Francesco Maria I DELLA ROVERE as duke of Urbino and installing his nephew Lorenzo (son of Piero II de' MEDICI) in his stead; this campaign proved to be a political and financial disaster, and in 1521 Francesco Maria was reinstated.

In 1517 a group of disaffected cardinals attempted to poison Pope Leo, who promptly executed the principal conspirator, Cardinal Alfonso Petrucci, and adjusted the balance of the Sacred College in his favour by creating 31 new cardinals (31 July 1517). He was not as decisive in the matter of the imperial election, in which he oscillated between support for Francis I and the Elector FRIEDRICH III of Saxony; when Charles I of Spain was eventually elected as CHARLES V, Leo entered into negotiations with him, and in May 1521 concluded an alliance against France with the new emperor.

Leo had undertaken in his electoral oath to reconvene the Fifth Lateran COUNCIL, and he honoured his pledge by opening the sixth session on 27 April 1513. In later sessions the Council ratified the Concordat of Bologna and abrogation of the Pragmatic Sanction of Bourges. Leo tolerated rather than directed the Council, and formally closed it on 16 March 1517, having levied a tax on benefices to finance a new CRUSADE against the Turks.

Such taxes reflected Leo's perpetual need for funding: his personal tastes were costly, his patronage was lavish, and the cost of rebuilding ST PETER'S BASILICA was enormous. To raise money he sold ecclesiastical preferments, including cardinalships. His principal source of income for the construction of St Peter's was a renewal of the INDULGENCE authorized by Julius II, the income from which he enhanced by simoniacal arrangement with ALBRECHT OF MAINZ (archbishop of Magdeburg and Mainz), who arranged for indulgences to be marketed by preachers in his dioceses. When one of these preachers, the Dominican Johann TETZEL, began to promote the sale of the indulgence in January 1517, the Augustinian monk Martin LUTHER reacted by posting his 95 Theses on the door of the Schlosskirche in Wittenberg. When news of this disturbance reached Rome, Leo regarded the episode as a breach of monastic discipline, and ordered the general of the Augustinian Order to silence Luther. When this course of action failed, Leo tried to persuade Luther's protector, Friedrich III of Saxony, to silence him, but to no avail. On 15 June 1520 Leo condemned Luther on 21 counts in the bull EXSURGE DOMINE; Luther burnt the bull, and Leo responded on 3 January 1521 with another bull (Decet Romanum pontificem), this time excommunicating Luther. Among those who came to Leo's defence was King HENRY VIII of England, who wrote a book defending the seven sacraments against Luther's onslaught; Pope Leo gratefully bestowed on King Henry the title 'defender of the faith'. On 1 December 1521 Leo died suddenly of malaria, leaving the papal treasury depleted and the Lutheran revolt spreading unchecked across northern Europe.

Leo's patronage included the refounding of the University of Rome on 5 November 1513, and by the end of the next year it had a staff of 88 professors. While still a cardinal he commissioned the restoration of Santa Maria in Domenica by RAPHAEL, and after his election commissioned the construction of San Giovanni on the Via Giulia by Jacopo SANSOVINO and the construction of St Peter's. He invited LASCARIS to Rome to teach Greek, and founded a Greek printing press. He appointed Raphael as custodian of the classical antiquities of Rome, and appointed Pietro BEMBO, Jacopo SADOLETO, and Bernardo ACCOLTI as papal secretaries; he also employed in various capacities writers such as Matteo BANDELLO, Marco Girolamo VIDA, Gian Giorgio TRISSINO, and Bernardo Dovizi.

W. Roscoe, The Life and Pontificate of Leo the Tenth (1853); G. B. Picotti, La giovanezza di Leone X (1927); E. Rodocanachi, Le Pontificat de Léon X (1931).

**LEO AFRICANUS** or **Johannes Eliberitanus** (i.e. of Granada) or **Johannes Leo** or (Italian) **Giovanni Leo** or (Arabic) **Al-Hassan Ibn Mohammad al-Wezaz al-Fasi** (c.1495–c.1550), traveller in AFRICA, lexicographer, and geographer, born into a prominent Moorish family in GRANADA and educated in Fez. In 1512–13 he travelled extensively in the Maghrib, visiting Morocco, Bugia (now Arabic Bejaïa or French Bougie), Constantine (now Arabic Qacentina), and Tunis. From 1513 to 1515 he undertook a series of journeys to sub-Saharan Africa, visiting Timbuktu (now Tombouctou, in Mali), Guinea, the Niger basin, and (apparently) Borno (now a province of Nigeria) and Lake Chad. In 1516–17 he travelled to Constantinople, and between 1517 and 1520 he visited Egypt three times, on one occasion travelling up the Nile from Cairo to Aswan. At some point he visited the 'three Arabias' (Deserta, Felix, and Petraea), Armenia, and what he calls Tartary (by which he may mean Tabriz).

In about 1520 Al-Hassan was captured by BARBARY PIRATES off the island of Djerba and presented to Pope LEO X as a slave. He was persuaded to convert to Christianity, and Pope Leo stood sponsor at his baptism, honouring him with his own names, Johannes and Leo.

At the pope's suggestion Leo wrote an account of his travels. The original Arabic manuscript was preserved in the library of Vincenzo Pinelli (1535–1601) but is now lost; the Italian version, Descrizione dell'Africa, was issued in Rome on 10 March 1526, but not printed until 1550, when Giovanni Battista RAMUSIO included it in the first volume of his Delle navigationi e viaggi. A French translation by Jean Temporal was published in Lyon in 1556 and twice appeared in pirated editions in Antwerp later in the same year. A Latin translation by Joannes Florianus was printed in Antwerp (1556) and Zürich (1559), and this version was in turn translated into English (1600) by John Pory at the suggestion of Richard HAKLUYT.

Leo also wrote a collection of biographies of Arab physicians and philosophers entitled De viris quibusdam illustribus apud Arabes (1527). He returned to Tunis at an unknown date before his death. His later life is obscure, but he may have renounced Christianity and returned to Islam.

**LEONARDO DA VINCI** (1452–1519), Italian artist and polymath, born in the village of Anchiano, near the Tuscan town of Vinci; he was the illegitimate son of a Florentine notary and a young peasant called Caterina. He was probably trained in the Florentine studio of VERROCCHIO, to whose Baptism (c.1472, Uffizi) Leonardo contributed the head of an angel. His early works, all painted in Florence, include an

*Annunciation* (Uffizi) painted in Verrocchio's workshop, the *Benois Madonna* and the attributed *Madonna Litta* (both in the Hermitage in St Petersburg), the portrait of a young woman known traditionally as *Ginevra de' Benci* (National Gallery, Washington), and the unfinished *Adoration of the Kings* (Uffizi), which was commissioned in 1481; the rearing horses in the background of the *Adoration* were to become an important motif in Leonardo's drawings.

In 1482 Leonardo left Florence for Milan, where he entered the court of Ludovico SFORZA, possibly as a musician. Leonardo shared Ludovico's interest in the arts of WAR and was soon designing FORTIFICATIONS, waterways, weapons (including a tank), and flying machines. The drawings from Leonardo's seventeen years in Milan include these designs and innumerable drawings of the natural world, including flowers, birds, and unborn children. In Milan Leonardo painted at least four portraits, one of *Cecilia Gallerani*, the mistress of Ludovico Sforza, holding an ermine (c.1483, Muzeum Czartoryskich, Kraków), portraits of a *Musician* and of a *Woman in Profile* (both in the Biblioteca Ambrosiana, Milan), and the *Portrait of a Woman* (Louvre; also known as *La Belle Ferronière*). He also began work on the Sforza Monument, a bronze EQUESTRIAN STATUE of Francesco SFORZA which might have been one of his greatest works; Leonardo's preliminary drawings survive, but his full-sized clay model of the horse was damaged in the French invasion of Milan in 1499 and then moved to Ferrara, where it eventually disintegrated.

It was in Milan that Leonardo painted two of his greatest works, *The Virgin of the Rocks* and *The Last Supper*. *The Virgin of the Rocks*, which was commissioned in 1483, exists in two versions, and the relationship between the two is not entirely clear, though it is usually assumed that the version in the Louvre is earlier than the one in the National Gallery in London. *The Last Supper* (1495–7) was painted in the refectory of the Church of Santa Maria delle Grazie (for which BRAMANTE built the dome and cloisters), and began to flake away in the sixteenth century; VASARI reported that in 1556 it consisted largely of blots, and it was subsequently restored on several occasions. On 16 August 1943 the church was hit by an Allied bomb, and one of the side walls of the refectory collapsed; the *Last Supper* had been protected, and survived the attack.

In 1499 the French occupation of Milan led to the dispersal of Ludovico's court. Leonardo left Milan, and after visits to Mantua and Venice, returned to Florence, where he lived from 1500 to 1516, during which time he also worked in Rome and Milan. In 1504–5 he worked on the cartoon and mural of *The Battle of Anghiari* (now lost; see ANGHIARI, BATTLE OF) in the Sala del Maggior Consiglio in the Palazzo della Signoria in Florence. His other work in Florence includes *Leda and the Swan* (now lost; known from copies, including one by Cesare da Sesto in Wilton House) and the enigmatic *St John* (c.1515, Louvre); another painting of St John was later taken to Fontainebleau and converted into a *Bacchus* (Louvre). Similarly, he began work on *The Virgin and Child with St Anne* (Louvre) while still in Florence, but some of the later drawings are on French paper, which must reflect an intention to complete the painting in France. The most famous of Leonardo's Florentine paintings (and of all paintings) is the *Mona Lisa* (c.1503–7, Louvre), which is also known as *La Gioconda* and (in French) *La Gioconde*; the sitter was Lisa Gherardini, the wife of the Florentine merchant Francesco del Giocondo; 'Mona' is an abbreviation of 'Madonna'.

In 1517 Leonardo travelled to France at the invitation of King FRANCIS I; the projects that he proposed to the king included the regulation of the waters of the Loire. He died on 2 May 1519 at the Manoir du Clos Lucé (now a Leonardo museum) near Château d'Amboise. He was buried in the chapel of the chateau, which was destroyed in the French Revolution; his remains were recovered in 1863 and reinterred in the nearby Chapelle Saint-Hubert.

The interests reflected in the 3,500 pages of Leonardo's notebooks include anatomy, architecture, astronomy, athletics, botany, colour, drawing, geography, geology (including stratigraphy), mathematics, music, optics, painting, perspective, philosophy, sculpture, town planning, zoology, and several branches of engineering (notably hydraulic, nautical, mechanical, military, and structural), but his innovative thinking on these and other subjects made no impact on sixteenth-century culture or science, because there was no public awareness of their existence until 1570, when his pupil Francesco Melzi, to whom Leonardo had left them, died; even then, the notebooks were a mass of notes rather than a series of treatises, a tribute to intelligent curiosity on a heroic scale but not a readily publishable work. The largest collection of Leonardo's notes and drawings is in Windsor Castle, but there are also important collections in the Biblioteca Ambrosiana in Milan, the Bibliothèque Nationale in Paris, the British Museum, the Louvre, the Biblioteca Reale in Turin, the Uffizi, and the Vatican Library.

*MDA*; Martin Kemp, *Leonardo da Vinci* (1981); Pietro Marani, *Leonardo: The Complete Paintings* (2000).

**LEONARDO DI SER GIOVANNI** (*fl.* 1358–71), Italian goldsmith, a native of Florence. In 1361 he assumed responsibility for the chasing and gilding of the nine silver relief panels on the south side of the silver altar of St James (1217–1456) in Pistoia Cathedral; he later designed and made the nine relief panels of *The Life of St James the Greater* on the north side of the altar (1367–71). In Florence Leonardo collaborated with Betto di Geri (*fl.* 1366–1402) on a silver altar depicting scenes from *The Life of St John the Baptist* (now in the Museo dell'Opera del Duomo).

*MDA*.

**LEONE DA MODENA** or (Hebrew) **Jehuda Arje ben Isaac** (1571–1648), Jewish writer and preacher, born in Venice to a French family that had migrated to Venice after the expulsion of the JEWS from France, and educated by the learned Jews of Venice. He had no settled occupation and was a habitual gambler, but his erudition gave him a European reputation amongst Christian humanists. His *Riti Ebraici*, which was translated into English in 1650, was regarded as

**Leonardo da Vinci**, *The Virgin of the Rocks*, in the National Gallery, London

Leonardo da Vinci, *The Last Supper* (1495–7), in the refectory of the Church of Santa Maria delle Grazie, in Milan

the authoritative account of Jewish customs; he also wrote an attack on the CABBALA (*'Ari Nohemin*, first published 1840) in which he demonstrated that the *Zohar*, purportedly a second-century commentary on the Pentateuch, was a work of the thirteenth century.

> *JNB* s.v. Modena; C. Roth, *Leone da Modena and the Christian Hebraists of his Age* (1927); E. Rivkin, *Leon da Modena* (1952).

**LEONE EBREO or (Hebrew) Judah ben Isaac Abarbanel or (Latin) Leo Hebraeus** (*c*.1460–*c*.1521), Portuguese philosopher, born in Lisbon, the son of the Jewish statesman and scholar Isaac ABRAVANEL. He studied and then practised medicine in Lisbon, where the forced baptism of his infant son occasioned his poetic lament *Telunah 'al ha Zeman*. Leone then followed his father first to Toledo (1483–92) and then, after the expulsion of the Jews, to Naples, where he became physician to Gonzalo FERNÁNDEZ DE CÓRDOBA. In Italy he

Leonardo da Vinci, *Mona Lisa* (*c*.1503–7), in the Louvre, Paris

began to read PICO DELLA MIRANDOLA and FICINO, and under their influence (and that of Maimonides and Shelomoh ibn Gabirol) wrote his *Dialoghi d'amore*, three Neoplatonic dialogues on love first published in 1535 and thereafter often republished and translated into Hebrew, Latin, French, and Spanish.

> *DBI* s.v. Abarbanel, Giuda; *JNB* s.v. Abarbanel, Juda Leon; S. Damiens, *Amour et intellect chez Léon l'Hébreu* (1971).

**LEONI, LEONE, or Aretine** (*c*.1509–1590), Italian goldsmith, medallist, and bronze sculptor, born in Menaggio on Lake Como. He was trained as a goldsmith. In the 1530s he worked as a medallist in Padua and then moved to Rome, where he engraved COINS for the papal mint (1537–40). He subsequently engraved coins for the mint in Milan (1542–6) and then entered the imperial service of CHARLES V, working in Germany and the Netherlands (and possibly in Spain) before settling in Milan.

None of Leoni's work in precious metals is known to survive, but his goldsmith's skills are apparent in a sardonyx CAMEO (1550) now in the Metropolitan Museum in New York.

His portrait MEDALS include depictions of ARETINO, BEMBO, Andrea DORIA, Cardinal GRANVELLE, MICHELANGELO, and TITIAN. His portrait sculptures include depictions of *Philip II* (1553–5, Prado), *Mary of Hungary* (1553–4, Prado), and *Charles V Victorious over a Fury* (1549–64, Prado), in which the effigy of the emperor is fitted with removable armour. In Italy Leoni's sculpted bronze tombs include those of Vespasiano GONZAGA (Church of the Incoronata, Sabbioneta) and Gian Giacomo Medici (1560–2, Milan Cathedral).

Leoni's son Pompeo Leoni (c.1533–1608) was also a sculptor, medallist, and goldsmith. He worked in Spain, where he finished bronze statues sent by his father (notably the retable of the Capilla Mayor of the ESCORIAL) and also executed tombs. Leoni possessed and preserved many of the papers and drawings of LEONARDO DA VINCI.

*MDA.*

**LEONI, LEONE** (c.1560–1627), Italian composer, active in Verona and Vicenza where he became *maestro di cappella* in 1588. He was a member of the Accademia Olimpico and the Confraternity of Divine Love, and was elected *maestro della musica* of the Pia Opera dell'Incoronata in 1610. He wrote madrigals and sacred music, employing the *stile concertato* in the motets of his *Aurea corona* (1615).

**LEOPARDI, ALESSANDRO** (*fl.* 1482–1522), Italian architect, bronze sculptor, and goldsmith, born in Venice, where he worked at the mint before turning to bronze casting. In 1492 he completed the casting of VERROCCHIO's equestrian statue of the *condottiere* Bartolomeo COLLEONI. He later collaborated with Antonio LOMBARDO on the tomb of Cardinal Zen in the Basilica San Marco (1503–4). His principal architectural work was the Church of Santa Giustina in Padua.

*MDA.*

**LEPANTO, BATTLE OF**, a naval battle fought in the Ionian Sea near the Gulf of Corinth on 7 October 1571, when 200 GALLEYS and eight GALLEASSES of the HOLY LEAGUE commanded by Don JUAN DE AUSTRIA defeated 273 light Ottoman galleys; the forces of the Holy League captured 117 galleys (and sank many more) and freed some 12,000 Christian galley slaves. Casualties were extremely high on both sides (20,000 Ottomans and 8,000 Europeans). The victory was heralded all over Europe as the defeat of the Islamic Ottomans by the united forces of Christendom, but a year after the battle the Ottoman shipyards in Constantinople had replaced the galleys lost in the battle and regained their naval superiority. In 1573 Venice relinquished its claim to CYPRUS (which had been captured by the Ottomans) as part of a peace treaty, and the following year the Turks recaptured TUNIS from the Spaniards. This resurgence of Ottoman power did little to mitigate the popular European view that Lepanto was a turning point, the first victory after a long series of Ottoman victories.

The victory at Lepanto was celebrated in paintings (e.g. VASARI's) and in poems, particularly in Spain and Portugal: Fernando de HERRARA and Bartolomé Leonardo de ARGEN-

SOLA wrote odes. The Portuguese poet Jerónimo de Cortereal wrote a Spanish poem in fifteen cantos entitled *Felicísima victoria concedida del ciel al señor don Juan d'Austria* (1578), and in 1625 Sebastián de Nieva Calvo clarified this heavenly intervention in *La mejor mujer madre y vírgen, poema sacro*, in which he described the miraculous intercession of the Virgin Mary in the battle. CERVANTES was a combatant, and his left hand was shattered by an Ottoman bullet; Cristóbal de VIRUÉS was also a combatant, and later described the battle in his epic *Monserrate* (1587). Three centuries later the battle was sufficiently familiar to an English audience for G. K. Chesterton to celebrate the victory in his poem 'Lepanto' (in *Poems*, 1915).

Lepanto is also remembered by the Church. In 1572 Pope PIUS V instituted the Feast of the Blessed Virgin Mary of the Rosary on 7 October to commemorate the victory; in 1573 the feast was moved to the first Sunday in October, but it reverted in 1969 to 7 October.

M. Lesure, *Lepante: La Crise de l'Empire Ottoman* (1972); J. F. Guilmartin, *Gunpowder and Galleys* (1974).

**LERMA, FRANCISCO GÓMEZ DE SANDOVAL Y ROJAS, MARQUIS OF DENIA AND DUKE OF** (1553–1625), Spanish statesman, born in Seville, the son of the fourth marquis of Denia and his wife Isabella de Borja. Francisco became a courtier during the reign of PHILIP II and rose to prominence as a favourite (*privado*) in the court of PHILIP III, who conferred a dukedom on him (1599) and made him his chief minister. For the next twenty years the duke of Lerma was the most powerful political figure in Spain, and greatly enriched himself at public expense. He pursued the suppression of the REVOLT OF THE NETHERLANDS without regard to cost, and in 1609 he agreed to a twelve-year truce largely because the Spanish treasury had become too depleted to carry on. In the same year he began the expulsion of some 300,000 MORISCOS from Spain (1609–14). He fell from power in October 1618, the victim of a palace intrigue in which his son Cristóbal was a prominent figure.

The duke of Lerma is the subject of Sir Robert Howard's play *The Great Favourite; or, The Duke of Lerma* (1668).

DHE s.v. Lerma, duque de; B. J. García García, *La Pax Hispanica: Política exterior del duque de Lerma* (1996).

**LESCOT, PIERRE** (1510/15–1578), French architect who collaborated with the sculptor Jean GOUJON on the reconstruction of the LOUVRE (in which Lescot's square court of 1546–51 survives), the Hôtel Carnavalet (c.1545–50, now substantially altered), and the Fontaine des Innocents (1547–9, now reconstructed). Little of Lescot's work survives unaltered, but his Italianate square courtyard (Cour Carrée) for the Louvre was a seminal influence on the development of the French classical style in architecture.

**LESLIE, JOHN** (1527–96), Scottish bishop and historian. Educated in St Andrews and France, Leslie was a committed opponent of church reform in Scotland. In 1566 he was made bishop of Ross. He was a strong supporter of MARY, QUEEN OF scots, serving as her ambassador to ELIZABETH in 1569. He was imprisoned in 1571 for his part in the attempted marriage of Mary and the duke of Norfolk, but released in 1573 on condition that he left the country. He spent his remaining years pursuing Catholic interests on the Continent, and planned to kidnap the young JAMES VI in order to educate him in the old religion. In 1579 he was appointed vicar-general of Rouen, and in 1593 bishop of Coutances. His *De origine, moribus, et rebus gestis Scotorum* was published in 1578.

*DNB.*

**LESSIUS, LENAERT** (1554–1623), Flemish Jesuit theologian, was born in Brecht (near Antwerp) and educated in Louvain. He joined the JESUITS in 1572 and subsequently taught at the Jesuit college in Douai (1574–81). He then moved to Rome, where he studied under Francisco SUÁREZ, an exponent of the theology of GRACE expounded by his fellow Jesuit Luis de MOLINA; Lessius also became a Molinist, a position that was to become problematical after he returned to Louvain, where he was appointed to a professorship in 1585. His theology was unacceptable to his colleagues, who in 1587, led by Michel de BAY, censured 34 theses derived from the writings of Lessius.

Lessius' principal work on the theology of grace was *De gratia efficaci* (Antwerp, 1610). His most important work on moral theology was *De iustitia et iure* (1605), which explored the ethics of commerce and the charging of interest.

*BNB* s.v. Leys, Léonard; *NBW* xiv, s.v. Lessius, Leonardus.

**L'ESTOILE, PIERRE TAISAN DE** (1546–1611), French chronicler. He was born in Paris and studied law in Bourges. After a career in the service of the French crown he retired and wrote his *Mémoires-journaux* (published posthumously in 1621), a personal account of the years 1574 to 1611 (and so of the WARS OF RELIGION) written from the perspective of a Catholic observer who favoured reconciliation rather than the extirpation of Protestantism.

*The Paris of Henry of Navarre as Seen by Pierre de l'Estoile* (1958).

**LE TAVERNIER, JEAN** (*fl.* 1434–60), Flemish painter of book illuminations, a native of Oudenaarde (50 kilometres (30 miles) west of Brussels) who entered the service of the dukes of Burgundy; his best-known work is the illumination of *The Miracles of Our Lady* (Bibliothèque Nationale, Paris). He also seems to have worked in Bruges, though the Bruges illuminations are sometimes attributed to a 'Jean Le Tavernier the Younger' (*fl.* 1450–70), who was almost certainly the same person.

*BNB* s.v. Tavernier, Gheraert de; *MDA* s.v. Le Tavernier, Jean.

**LEU, HANS** (*c.*1490–1531), Swiss painter and draughtsman, born in Zürich. He was trained by DÜRER in Nuremberg and in about 1514 settled in Zürich, where his work included the painting of small altarpieces and of LANDSCAPE pictures and the design of stained-glass windows. His surviving paintings include *St Jerome* (1515) and *Orpheus* (1519), both in the Kunstmuseum in Basel, and a series of chiaroscuro drawings, including *Landscape with Mountains and Lake* (Kunstmuseum, Basel).

*MDA*; *NDB*; H. Debrunner, *Der Zürcher Maler Hans Leu im Spiegel von Bild und Schrift* (1941).

**L'HÔPITAL, MICHEL DE** (1505–73), chancellor of France, humanist, and jurist. L'Hôpital was born in the Auvergne, the son of a physician to Charles, duc de Bourbon. His education in Toulouse was cut short by the involuntary removal of his family to Padua, where he studied law for six years. When he had completed his studies L'Hôpital moved to Rome, initially in the suite of CHARLES V and then working in the papal court. In about 1534 he returned to France to practise as an advocate, and three years later was appointed counsellor to the Parlement of Paris. In 1547 he was sent by the king to Bologna, where the COUNCIL OF TRENT was sitting, and sixteenth months later successfully petitioned to be recalled to France. In 1553 he was appointed master of requests, and subsequently president of the Chambre des Comptes. Finally, in 1559, he was appointed chancellor of France.

As chancellor L'Hôpital was chiefly remarkable for his efforts to encourage religious toleration. One of his first acts as chancellor was to register an edict suppressing the INQUISITION. In September 1561 he established (in the name of MARIE DE MÉDICIS) the Colloquy of POISSY to enable Protestant and Catholic leaders to meet, and he subsequently encouraged the queen regent to issue her edict of 17 January 1562 conferring limited recognition on Huguenots. In 1564 he was instrumental in persuading the Conseil du Roi to forbid the publication of the Council of Trent's, proceedings on the grounds that they were inconsistent with the liberties enshrined in French CUSTOMARY LAW. L'Hôpital also strove to encourage judicial reform, and to this end issued the Ordonnance de Moulins, which restructured judicial administration, and wrote a *Traité de la réformation de la justice*.

L'Hôpital's policy of placing the interests of the state before those of either of the warring religious parties incurred the enmity of the Catholic Church, whose allies finally managed, after the renewal of hostilities in 1567, to force him from office the following year. He retired to Vignay, where he composed *Le But de la guerre et de la paix; ou, Discours du chancelier L'Hôpital pour exhorter Charles IX à donner la paix à ses sujets* (1570). His *Poemata* were collected posthumously.

*DBF.*

**LIBERAL ARTS**, the seven branches of learning, recognized in late antiquity by scholars such as AUGUSTINE, and organized in medieval and Renaissance schools and universities as a preliminary trivium (consisting of grammar, RHETORIC, and logic, which is sometimes called dialectic) and an advanced quadrivium (consisting of ARITHMETIC, GEOMETRY, ASTRONOMY, and MUSIC). 'Liberal' has the sense of 'pertaining to a free man', and so the liberal arts studied by those of a superior social station were distinguished from the mechanical arts (which included painting) and the servile arts; the term 'arts' was meant to include speculative science.

By the thirteenth century each of the liberal arts had acquired exemplars and pictorial identities that were to persevere for centuries. One of the best-preserved pictorial representations of the seven liberal arts is TIBALDI's cycle of frescoes on the vault of the library of the ESCORIAL. Grammar is represented by the *School of Babylon* and the *Tower of Babel*, rhetoric by *Hercules the Gaul* and *Cicero Defending Gaius Rabirius*, logic by *Zeno of Elea Showing the Gates of Truth and Error* and *SS Ambrose and Augustine*, arithmetic by the *Gymnosophists* and *Solomon and Sheba*, geometry by the *Death of Archimedes* and the *Priests of Egypt Dividing the Lands*, astronomy by the *Solar Eclipse at Heliopolis after the Death of Jesus* and *King Hezekiah Contemplating the Orbit of the Sun*, and music by *Orpheus and Eurydice*.

**LIBERALE DA VERONA** (c.1445–c.1529), Italian painter and illuminator, trained in Verona. From 1467 to 1474 he worked as a book illuminator in the library of Siena Cathedral and in Monte Oliveto Maggiore, near Siena. He subsequently worked in Florence and Venice, and c.1488 returned to Verona, where he established an independent workshop. His paintings include a *Madonna with Saints* (Gemäldegalerie, Berlin), a *Pietà* (Residenzmuseum, Munich), an *Adoration of the Magi* (Verona Cathedral), and a *St Sebastian* set against a Venetian canal (Brera, Milan).

 MDA; Carlo Del Bravo, *Liberale da Verona* (1967).

**LIBRARIES**. In the fourteenth century, libraries were small collections (numbered in hundreds rather than thousands) of manuscripts stored in monasteries, universities, and royal palaces. In the fifteenth century, humanist evocations of the libraries of antiquity (notably Alexandria) encouraged the amassing of classical texts by scholars and their patrons. Manuscripts of ancient Latin authors were discovered in the monasteries by scholars such as Poggio BRACCIOLINI, Niccolò NICCOLI (whose 800-volume library was opened to the public after his death in 1436), and Lorenzo VALLA, and manuscripts of ancient Greek authors were recovered by Cardinal BESSARION, Constantinos LASCARIS, and Janos LASCARIS.

By the mid-fifteenth century, the foundation collections of several great libraries had been established. Pope NICHOLAS V spent huge sums on the acquisition of manuscripts; the 1,200 Greek and Latin manuscripts that he collected became the foundation collection of the VATICAN LIBRARY. In 1433 Cosimo de' MEDICI was living as an exile in Venice when he began to assemble the manuscripts that formed the nucleus of the Florentine Biblioteca LAURENZIANA, which was designed by MICHELANGELO, completed by AMMANATI and VASARI, and opened by Grand Duke COSIMO I DE' MEDICI in 1571. In Venice, the MARCIANA was opened by Cardinal Bessarion in 1468. The fourth great library of fifteenth-century Italy, the collection of FEDERICO DA MONTEFELTRO in the Palazzo Ducale in Urbino, was memorably described by its first benefactor, Vespasiano da Bisticci.

In Hungary, MATTHIAS CORVINUS assembled what was probably the largest library in Europe at his palace in Buda. In Germany, the greatest collectors were Hartmann SCHEDEL and Willibald PIRKHEIMER. In late sixteenth-century England, Sir Robert COTTON assembled the earliest foundation collections of what is now the British Library and Sir Thomas

BODLEY endowed the first large institutional library, the Bodleian Library in Oxford. The first large library to be accessible to the public was the AMBROSIANA, which opened in Milan on 8 December 1609.

**LICHFIELD, HENRY** (*fl.* 1613), English composer, employed by Lady Cheyney of Toddington near Luton though not specifically as a musician. The madrigals he wrote to be performed by her family were published in *The First Set of Madrigals of 5 Parts, Apt Both for Viols and Voices* (1613/14).

**LIECHTI FAMILY**, a Swiss family of horologists active in Winterthur from c.1500 for more than 300 years. Their turret clocks (i.e. clocks set in the bell towers of churches and civic buildings to sound the hours) and domestic clocks (known as Gothic clocks because of their mouldings) were made almost entirely of iron and were (with one exception) driven by suspended weights. The collection of the family's clocks in the Heimatsmuseum in Winterthur includes a turret clock made in 1529 by Laurenz Liechti (d. 1545) which contains the earliest known example of epicyclic gearing, a device that enabled the astronomical dial on the face to display the position of the sun and the position and phase of the moon.

**LIÉDET, LOYSET** (c.1420–1479), Flemish manuscript illuminator, active in Bruges from 1468 to 1479. His surviving work includes seven illuminations in a copy of Froissart's *Chronique de France* now in the Deutsche Staatsbibliothek in Berlin and three illuminations in a copy of Philippe de Megière's *Songe du vieil pelerin* (Bibliothèque Nationale, Paris).
 MDA.

**LIESBORN, MASTER OF** (*fl.* c.1460–90), German painter whose name derives from an ALTARPIECE painted for the Benedictine abbey in Liesborn (near Münster); six of the fourteen surviving fragments are in the National Gallery in London.
 MDA.

**LIGHTING, STAGE**. Stage lighting, not necessary in open-air theatre, began to be a practical concern with the growth of enclosed theatres and playhouses during the Renaissance. From the mid-sixteenth century, commentators noted the intensifying effect of heightened lighting on the stage, especially if contrasted with darkness in the auditorium, although the latter was not always practical. SERLIO's *Architettura* (1545) describes three kinds of lighting: general stage light, provided by torches and chandeliers above and in front of the stage, 'decorative light', and 'mobile light'. Leone de' Sommi's *Quattro dialoghi in materia di rappresentazioni sceniche* (c.1565) describes the use of coloured light to heighten mood: a bright orange light for comic scenes, and a dark or dim light for tragedy. English theatres in the Elizabethan and Jacobean periods were slower to develop complex lighting arrangements, but nevertheless use some simple devices. Candles and lamps, sometimes combined with mirrors or reflective surfaces to brighten, or coloured glass to give particular hues, were frequently placed in the wings or behind the backcloth to throw light onto the stage; these could be extinguished at significant moments for dramatic effect. Candle footlights were also used for added illumination.

**LIGORIO, PIRRO** (*c*.1510–1583), Italian architect, garden designer, painter, archaeologist, and antiquarian. Ligorio was born in Naples, but spent most of his professional life in Rome. As a young man he excavated Hadrian's villa at Tivoli. He turned to landscape design and architecture and produced two masterpieces: the garden of the Villa D'ESTE in Tivoli and the CASINO that he built for Pius IV (the Villa PIA) in the Vatican gardens. He was appointed as MICHELANGELO'S successor at St Peter's, but was quickly dismissed for changing Michelangelo's designs, and subsequently moved to Ferrara. He wrote prolifically but published little: some 50 manuscripts survive, but his only book was a small treatise on the antiquities of Rome (*Delle antichità di Roma*, Venice, 1553). He was an authority on classical inscriptions, but his reputation as an epigrapher was posthumously compromised by the contention that he had interpolated skilful forgeries into the corpus of Roman inscriptions.

MDA; R. W. Gaston (ed.), *Pirro Ligorio: Artist and Antiquarian* (1988).

**LIGOZZI, JACOPO** (1547–1627), Italian painter, born in Verona; he migrated to Florence, where he was appointed court painter to the MEDICI family in 1575, in which capacity he painted a cycle of frescoes depicting the history of Florence in the Salone del Cinquecento in the Palazzo Vecchio. He was also an accomplished draughtsman; many of his drawings are preserved in the Ashmolean Museum in Oxford.

MDA.

**LILY, WILLIAM** (*c*.1468–1522), English humanist, grammarian, and the first headmaster of St Paul's School, London. He contributed the rules of syntax to COLET and ERASMUS' Latin grammar written for use at the school: the so-called 'Lily's grammar'. A friend of MORE, he was at the head of the revival of Greek learning in England. His grandson was John LYLY.

DNB.

**LIMBOURG or Limburg FAMILY**, French manuscript illuminators. The brothers Pol, Hennequin, and Herman were responsible for the paintings in the most famous illuminated manuscript of the fifteenth century, the *Très Riches Heures du duc de Berry* (Musée Condé, Chantilly). The *Très Riches Heures* was left unfinished at the death of the duke of Berry in 1416, and was completed *c*.1486 by Jean Colombe (brother of Michel COLOMBE).

MDA.

**LIMOGES ENAMELS**. The French city of Limoges was an important centre for the production of ENAMEL from the mid-twelfth to the sixteenth centuries. Initially production was in monastic workshops, but secular workshops were soon active in the manufacturing and export of ecclesiastical enamels such as candlesticks and reliquaries. Limoges enamel was of the type known as *champlevé enamel* (or *émail en taille d'épargne*), which is made by incising the design on the metal ground and placing vitreous paste in the incisions.

In the fifteenth century Limoges enamellers developed a technique for producing painted enamel, of which the city remained the principal European centre for two centuries. In the fifteenth and early sixteenth centuries the metal surface (usually copper) was covered with white enamel and then fired; the design was then applied in a series of colours, each of which was fired separately. From the mid-sixteenth century the first covering was black enamel, which then formed the basis for GRISAILLE painting.

The fifteenth-century revival of enamelling in Limoges is traditionally associated with the Monvaërni workshop, the work of which is represented by some 40 painted enamels which have in common the use of German designs, often adapted from prints by DÜRER and SCHONGAUER. The existence of such a workshop is not supported by the documentary record, and it is possible that the enamels are the work of independent enamellers. In sixteenth-century Limoges, the most important enamellers were Léonard LIMOSIN, Pierre REYMOND, Jean and Suzanne de COURT, and the members of the PÉNICAUD family.

E. Rupin, *L'Œuvre de Limoges* (1890).

**LIMOSIN or Limousin, LÉONARD** (*c*.1505–*c*.1576), French enamel painter who, alone amongst his distinguished contemporaries, left LIMOGES to serve in the royal court. He enjoyed the patronage of FRANCIS I and then of HENRI II, who appointed him royal enamel painter (*émailleur peintre du roi*). His early work includes a series of eighteen scenes from the Passion (1532, Musée de Cluny, Paris) modelled on DÜRER'S *Small Passion*. He later adopted the mannerist style associated with the School of FONTAINEBLEAU for his portraits (notably that of *Anne de Montmorency* in the Louvre) and religious works, notably twelve enamelled plaques of the Apostles (commissioned by Francis I in 1545 and now in the Musée des Beaux-Arts in Chartres) and a *Crucifixion* altarpiece of 1553 made for the Saint-Chapelle in Paris (now in the Louvre).

MDA.

**LINACRE, THOMAS** (*c*.1460–1524), English medical humanist, educated in Canterbury by his uncle William SELLYNG, and at Oxford, where he became a fellow of All Souls. He studied medicine at Padua, and after some seven years in Italy returned to England in 1492. In 1509 he became one of HENRY VIII's physicians, and thereafter he received many lucrative ecclesiastical preferments. He was one of the founders of the College of Physicians (1518). His friends included COLET, ERASMUS, and Thomas MORE.

Linacre's works include a Latin grammar written for the future Queen MARY (*Rudimenta grammatica*), treatises on medicine and grammar, and translations of ancient Greek works, notably editions of three works by GALEN.

DNB; DSB; C. D. O'Malley, *English Medical Humanists: Thomas Linacre and John Caius* (1965).

**LINCK, WENCESLAS** (1483–1547), German Protestant reformer, born in Colditz (Saxony) and educated at the

Pol de Limbourg, *April*, in *Les Très Riches Heures du duc de Berry*, a BOOK OF HOURS now in the Musée Condé in Chantilly

University of Leipzig before joining the Augustinian ORDER, in which he rose to become prior of the Order's convent in Wittenberg, of which Martin LUTHER was sub-prior. In 1520 he succeeded Johann von STAUPITZ as vicar-general of the Augustinian Order in Germany. He converted to Lutheranism and in 1523 he became a preacher in Altenburg, where he successfully pleaded with FRIEDRICH III of Saxony to spare the peasants captured during the PEASANTS' WAR, except for their two leaders. In Altenburg Linck was married by Martin Luther to Margarethe Schweizer, by whom he was to have ten children. In 1525 Linck moved to Nuremberg, where he served as pastor of the New Hospital Church until his death on 12 March 1547.

*NDB.*

**LINDENAST, SEBASTIAN** (*c*.1460–1526), German copper-smith, born into the Nuremberg family that held the mono-poly on gilded and silvered copperware manufactured in the city and was to hold the monopoly till the mid-sixteenth century. His best-known work is the *Männleinlaufen*, a clock with animated figures mounted above the porch of the Liebfrauenkirche in Nuremberg; at noon every day the action commemorates the Golden Bull of 1356 when the jacks appear as the seven electors coming to swear allegiance to the Emperor Charles IV. Attributions to Lindenast include a silvered copper bowl with the statuette of a hart in the cen-tre, a silvered and gilded copper relic statuette of St James the Greater (both in the Germanisches Nationalmuseum in Nuremberg), and a gilded and enamelled copper castle cup with a lid decorated with miniature buildings (now in the Victoria and Albert Museum in London).

*MDA* s.v. Lindenast, Sebastian, the elder.

**LINE ENGRAVING.** See ENGRAVING.

**LINEN,** a textile woven from the bast fibres of flax (*linum usitatissimum*) and then bleached. In early modern Europe it was the most important woven textile; it was cheaper than cotton and silk and in most of Europe was preferred to wool. From the fifteenth to the eighteenth centuries the principal European centre for the production of linen was the Netherlands, where most of the factories were in Haarlem. Elsewhere in Europe a linen warp was woven with a cotton weft to make FUSTIAN.

A linen-armourer was a maker of gambesons (military tunics), but as a proper noun the term denoted a member of the Merchant Taylors' Company, which was officially called the Guild of Taylors and Linen-Armourers (Latin Cissoribus et Armurariis Linearum).

'Linenfold' is a nineteenth-century term for a decorative pattern carved on wall-panels and furniture (especially wardrobe doors); it was so named because it represents or resembles linen arranged in vertical folds. Linenfold decoration originated in fifteenth-century Flanders and by the end of the century was in use in France, Germany, and England. It is one of a small number of late Gothic woodworking motifs that does not have an architectural precedent.

**LINSCHOTEN, JAN HUYGHEN VAN** (1563–1611), Dutch explorer, born in Haarlem. In 1583 he travelled on a Portuguese ship to India, where he remained for six years in the service of the archbishop of Goa; his account of his travels was published in his *Itinerario* (1595–6), which was soon translated into German (1598), English (1598), Latin (two translations in 1599), and French (1610). On returning to Europe Linschoten was shipwrecked on the AZORES, where he remained for two years (1589–91); his presence on the island of Flores on 31 August 1591, when the English ship *Revenge* engaged a Spanish fleet of 53 ships, enabled him to write an authoritative account of the battle. On returning to the Netherlands Linschoten sailed with Willem BARENTSZOON on his second expedition (1595). His account of this Arctic voyage is contained in his *Journalen* (1601). In 1598 he settled permanently in Enkhuizen.

*NNBW* iv; C. M. Parr, *Jan van Linschoten: The Dutch Marco Polo* (1964).

**LIPPI, FILIPPINO** (1457–1504), Italian painter, born in Florence, the illegitimate son of Fra Filippo LIPPI and a novice nun called Lucrezia Buti. He was trained in his father's workshop and, after his father's death in 1469, in the workshop of BOTTICELLI, where he painted CASSONI and devotional pictures such as *Adoration of the Magi* and *Virgin and Child with St John the Baptist* (both in the National Gallery, London).

Botticelli's departure for Rome in 1481 marked the beginning of Filippino's independent career, of which one of the finest paintings is his *Vision of St Bernard* (1486, Badia,

Florence). This celebrated picture led to an important series of commissions, including the completion of the Brancacci Chapel in Santa Maria del Carmine (which MASOLINO and MASACCIO had left unfinished) in 1484 and the decoration of the Strozzi Chapel in Santa Maria Novella in 1487 (postponed for many years and finally completed in 1502).

From 1488 to 1493 Filippino lived in Rome, where his principal commission was the decoration of the Carafa Chapel in Santa Maria Sopra Minerva. On returning to Florence he was commissioned to paint an *Adoration of the Magi* (now in the Uffizi) for the Monastery of San Donato a Scopeto to replace the *Adoration* (also in the Uffizi) left unfinished by LEONARDO.

*MDA*; Luciano Berti and Umberto Baldini, *Filippino Lippi* (1991).

**LIPPI, FRA FILIPPO** (*c*.1406–1469), Italian painter, born in Florence, the son of a butcher; on being orphaned in 1421 he was placed in the Monastery of Santa Maria de Carmine. He became a Carmelite friar, a life for which he was not suited. His early paintings include a fresco (now damaged) in Santa Maria del Carmine entitled *Institution of the Carmelite Rule* (*c*.1432), a theme that understates his relaxation of the rule: in the years to come he faced a criminal charge of fraud, and abducted Lucrezia Buti, a novice nun; their son was Filippino LIPPI.

Fra Filippo's *Tarquinia Madonna* (1437, Palazzo Barberini) and *Annunciation* (*c*.1438, Church of San Lorenzo, Florence) reflect the compositional style of MASACCIO as well as a burgeoning interest in PERSPECTIVE and a precociously strong response to contemporary Netherlandish painting. In the 1440s and 1450s Fra Filippo's style changed: his figures became more linear, and he became interested in delicate decorative motifs; in some respects this new style recalled the style of Gothic painting. In 1452 he painted *The Madonna and Child with Scenes from the Life of the Virgin* (Pitti Palace, Florence) and in the same year moved to Prato, where he painted the fresco cycle on *The Lives of SS Stephen and John the Baptist* in the cathedral. His greatest paintings from this period often portray graceful Madonnas, notably *The Adoration of the Child* (Gemäldegalerie, Berlin) and *The Madonna Adoring her Child with St Bernard* (*c*.1453, Uffizi). Fra Filippo's last commission took him to Spoleto, where, together with his son Filippino, he painted scenes from *The Life of the Virgin* in the apse of the cathedral and where he died in October 1469.

Fra Filippo is the speaker of Browning's dramatic monologue 'Fra Lippo Lippi', which is based on Vasari's account; he also became an important model for the Pre-Raphaelites.

*MDA* s.v. Lippi (1) Fra Filippo (di Tommaso) Lippi; Megan Holmes, *Fra Filippo Lippi: The Carmelite Painter* (1999); Jeffrey Ruda, *Fra Filippo Lippi* (1993).

**LIPPO MEMMI** (*fl.* 1317–50), Italian painter, a native of Siena. He was the brother-in-law of SIMONE MARTINI, with whom he sometimes collaborated, notably on the *Annunciation* in the Uffizi (1333), which they both signed. Some of Lippo's finest works, such as the *Virgin in Majesty* in the San Gimignano Palazzo del Popolo (1317, restored by Benozzo GOZZOLI *c*.1467), are imitations of paintings by Simone;

Filippino Lippi, *The Triumph of St Thomas*, in the Carafa Chapel in the Church of Santa Maria sopra Minerva, Rome

others, such as the *Servi Madonna* (Pinacoteca, Siena), evince a delicacy of palette and sentiment that exceeds that of Simone. The *New Testament* cycle in the Collegiata at San Gimignano has recently been attributed to Lippo Memmi.

*MDA.*

**LIPSIUS, JUSTUS, or Joest Lips** (1547–1606), Flemish classical scholar and Neostoic philosopher, born into a Catholic family in Overyssche, near Brussels. As a young man he studied with the Jesuits in Louvain, visited Rome with Cardinal GRANVELLE, and published his *Variae lectiones* (1567), which was dedicated to the cardinal. He subsequently studied at the University of Jena (1572–5), where he converted to Lutheranism. A few years later he moved to the University of Leiden (1579–90), where he professed Calvinism. On a visit to Mainz in 1590, he publicly reaffirmed the Catholicism of his youth. In 1592 he moved to University of Louvain, where he remained for the rest of his life, faithful to the Catholic Church. This shifting religious allegiance reflects not so much expedience as a principled indifference to Christian dogma and debate. Lipsius' interest in classical history and philosophy is reflected in his editions of TACITUS and SENECA;

he also wrote an influential political treatise urging reconciliation (*Politicorum sive civilis doctrinae*, 1589).

Lipsius is the principal Renaissance exponent of STOICISM. His *De constantia* (1584), a dialogue on the Stoic virtue of steadfastness, inaugurated the revival of ancient Stoicism. In 1604 he published two major works on Stoicism, the *Physiologia stoicorum* and *Manuductio ad stoicam philosophiam*, which sought to reconcile the Stoicism of Seneca and Epictetus with Christian moral theology.

*NBW; NDB;* J. L. Saunders, *Justus Lipsius: The Philosophy of Renaissance Stoicism* (1955).

**LISMANINO, FRANCESCO or (Polish) Franciszek Lismanin** (1504–66), Italian Protestant reformer in Poland, born into an Italian family in Corfu (which had been a Venetian possession since 1401) and brought to Kraków as a boy. He joined the Franciscan ORDER and was educated in Padua, and returned to Poland *c*.1546 as court preacher to Queen Bona Sforza, whose son SIGISMUND II AUGUSTUS encouraged him to visit the SWISS CONFEDERATION in 1553. Lismanino was converted to Calvinism by BULLINGER and CALVIN; he lived in Geneva from November 1554 to February 1555, and

Filippino Lippi, *The Exorcism of the Demon in the Temple of Mars*, in the Strozzi Chapel in the Church of Santa Maria Novella, Florence

there married a Huguenot. He returned to Poland determined to advance the Protestant cause, and worked with Jan Łaski to unite the Protestant groups in Poland. He died in Königsberg (Polish Kroliewiec, now Russian Kaliningrad) in mysterious circumstances: his body was discovered naked in a well. It is possible that the cumulative strains of religious controversy, the infidelity of his wife, and the payment of his pension in counterfeit money drove Lismanino to suicide.

*PSB.*

**LITHUANIA or (Lithuanian) Lietuva**. In the late fourteenth century the Lithuanian people controlled a large tract of land between Poland and Russia, and retained their traditional pagan religion. In 1386 Grand Duke Jagiełło converted the duchy to Christianity and married Jadwiga, queen of Poland, whereupon he assumed the throne of Poland as King VLADISLAV II. The marriage created a dynastic link between Lithuania and Poland. In 1501 Grand Duke Alexander of Lithuania succeeded his brother JOHN ALBERT as king of Poland, and he and his successors were both grand dukes of Lithuania and kings of Poland. The duchy and the kingdom were formally united by SIGISMUND II in the Treaty of LUBLIN (1569).

J. Jurginis, *Renesansas ir humanizmas Lietuvoje* (1965).

**LITTLE MASTERS**, the traditional English translation of German Kleinmeister, a group of sixteenth-century German engravers; the term would more accurately (but less idiomatically) be translated 'masters of the small', because it refers to artists who chose to engrave large subjects (typically biblical or mythological or GENRE scenes) on very small plates. The school of 'Little Masters' centred on a group of DÜRER's pupils in Nuremberg, including Hans Sebald BEHAM, his brother Bartel BEHAM, and Georg PENCZ. The term is sometimes extended to engravers elsewhere in Germany who worked on a similar scale, including Heinrich ALDEGREVER, Albrecht ALTDORFER, and Hans BROSAMER.

**LITTLETON, SIR THOMAS** (1402–81), English jurist who became king's sergeant in 1455, served as a judge on the

Fra Filippo Lippi, *Madonna Adoring her Child* (*c*.1453), in the Uffizi, in Florence

northern circuit, and in 1466 became a justice of the common pleas. His *Tenures* (*c*.1481), which was the earliest printed treatise on ENGLISH LAW, is an account (written in LAW FRENCH) of land tenure, which was then the most important branch of COMMON LAW. The *Tenures* is wholly based on English case law, never referring to codifications of Roman law; in the sixteenth century it was repeatedly printed in English translation. It was appropriated by COKE as the basis of his First Institute: *Coke upon Littleton* (1628).

**LIVERY COMPANIES**, organizations of master tradesmen which developed in LONDON from medieval guilds. Livery companies, which were often wealthy, regulated their chosen trade, provided benefits for members and their dependants, and yielded influence on city government. 'Livery' originally referred to the uniform of their servants, but came to be applied to the distinctive dress worn by important company members on special occasions.

**LIVONIA or (German) Lifland or (Russian) Liflandia**, a Baltic state occupying what is now northern Latvia and southern Estonia; it bordered Estonia on the north and COURLAND on the south. The eponymous Livs were a tribe who spoke Livonian, a Finno-Ugrian language akin to Finnish and Estonian; Livonian is now spoken by about 150 people, and will soon be extinct. Roman Christianity was officially instituted in 1201, when the first bishop of Livonia was installed in the German colony of Riga. The LIVONIAN ORDER evangelized Livonia, converting by the sword, and embarking on a series of wars with Lithuania (till 1435), Russia (till 1466), and Poland (till 1483). The city of Riga joined the HANSEATIC LEAGUE, and declined to recognize the authority of either the bishop or the Order. In 1420 the bishop was able to reassert his authority over the city, but the city became Lutheran in 1524 and in 1566 abolished the bishopric.

In 1527, the master of the Order, Walter von Plettenberg, was recognized by CHARLES V as a prince of the HOLY ROMAN EMPIRE. A war between the Order and IVAN IV of Russia in 1558 led to the division of Livonia: the northern part, including Tartu (Dorpat), was occupied by Russia, and the southern part by Poland. From 1561 to 1582 both Poland and Russia claimed Livonia, but in 1582 Poland withdrew its claim. From 1629 to 1721, Livonia was part of the Swedish empire.

**LIVONIAN ORDER or Brothers of the Sword**, a German military ORDER established in the Baltic in the thirteenth century. In 1237 the Order became a branch of the TEUTONIC knights, but retained an identity separate from that of its Prussian counterpart. In the fourteenth century the Order controlled LIVONIA, COURLAND, and Estonia and the cities of Tartu, Riga, and Lyndantse (German Reval, now Estonian Tallinn). In the fifteenth century the Order successfully defended its territories against LITHUANIA and Russia. At the Reformation the Order followed the example of ALBRECHT ACHILLES, grand master of the Teutonic Knights, in welcoming Protestantism within its domains.

The Livonian Order's rule was terminated by the Livonian War of 1558–82.

**LIVORNO or (French) Livourne or (English exonym) Leghorn**, a Tuscan city, Tyrrhenian port, and bishopric. Livorno was for centuries a possession of Pisa, but in 1407 it passed to Genoa and in 1421 to Florence. It remained a tiny place until the mid-sixteenth century: in 1551 it had only 749 inhabitants. The sudden expansion of Livorno in the late sixteenth century was the initiative of COSIMO I DE' MEDICI, who decided that the port of Pisa was becoming unviable because of silting and that Tuscany should have a new port in Livorno. A programme of land reclamation, quay construction, and house-building transformed the village into a substantial town; the first jetty was built in 1571, the canal linking Livorno with Pisa was dug in 1573, and in 1620 the main port (the Porto Mediceo) was completed by Cosimo II de' Medici; the façade of the cathedral (destroyed in the Second World War) was designed by Inigo JONES.

The freedom from political tribute, together with low harbouring and warehousing costs, the promise of a fifteen-year tax holiday, and of permanent freedom of trade, attracted a large number of settlers, who responded to the invitation to settle in Livorno that was extended to Italians, Armenians, Germans, Greeks, Jews (the synagogue opened in 1581), Moors, Persians, Portuguese, Spaniards, Turks, and 'other men of the East and West'; by 1606, when Livorno became a city, the population exceeded 5,000.

English traders with the Levant used Livorno as a staging post, and the English 'factory' remained open until 1825; English residents included Tobias Smollett, who is buried in the Protestant cemetery. The English exonym Leghorn derives from the early Italian spelling Legorno.

F. Braudel and R. Romano, *Navires et marchandises à l'entrée du port de Livourne, 1547–1611* (1951).

**LIVY IN THE RENAISSANCE.** Titus Livius (59 BC–AD 17 or 64 BC–AD 12) was born in Padua (ancient Padavium) and divided his life between Padua and Rome. His monumental history of Rome was composed in 142 books, of which 35 (1–10, 21–45) survive in something like their original form,

and others are known in fragments or in epitomized versions; in the manuscript tradition the books are divided into 'decades'. At the beginning of *Inferno* 28 DANTE alludes to Livy's account of the war of Hannibal in Italy and then cites his source: 'con Livio scrive, che non era' ('as Livy, who does not make mistakes, writes'). This judgement was based on repute rather than first-hand knowledge, as Dante had not seen a complete text. Livy scholarship began with PETRARCH, who established a text of decades 1, 3 and 4; his lavish manuscript is now in the British Library. These decades constituted all that was known of Livy until part of decade 5 was discovered and published in 1533.

The most eminent students of Livy in Renaissance Italy were Lorenzo VALLA and POLIZIANO, whose distinguished philological works pale into insignificance by comparison to the impact of Livy on vernacular prose. As a young man BOCCACCIO had translated decades 3 and 4, and the prose style that he developed as he translated was markedly indebted to the Latin original. The *Decameron* was later cast in this same Livian prose, and so the dominant Italian prose style of Italian literature from Boccaccio to Manzoni can be traced to the influence of Livy.

The central attraction of Livy for fifteenth-century Italy lay in the fact that the Rome he described was a republic. When Livy was published in Venice in 1470, it was as an exemplary republican text, but it was also read by learned monarchs: ALFONSO V was sent a manuscript copy by Cosimo de' MEDICI, and insisted that it be read to him, despite being warned that it contained poison. The zenith of Livy's standing was marked by MACHIAVELLI in his *Discorsi* (*c*.1516–19), which were essays on the first decade of Livy; in Machiavelli's pages Livy achieves his apotheosis as the recording angel of the virtues of republican Rome before the decadence of the empire.

Livy's fortunes were bound up with republican ideals, and when those ideals were frustrated by the SACK OF ROME in 1528 and the fall of the Florentine republic in 1530, Livy ceased to embody the governing ideology, and he was quickly supplanted by TACITUS; the only significant afterlife of Livy in sixteenth-century Italy was fostered by Jacopo NARDI, who in the 1540s completed a translation of Livy.

Giuseppe Billanovich, *Tradizione e fortuna di Livio tra medioevo e umanesimo* (1981); E. Lefèvre and E. Olshausen (eds.), *Livius: Werk und Rezeption* (1983).

**L'OBEL or Lobel, MATTHIAS** (1538–1616), French botanist and herbalist. He studied medicine at Montpellier and then settled with a fellow student, Pierre Pena, in London. They explored the botany of England, and the results of their labours were published in the form of a herbal (*Stirpium adversaria nova*, 1571) in which plants were classified according to the characteristics of their leaves. L'Obel moved to Flanders in the late 1570s, and in 1576 the Antwerp printer Christophe PLANTIN published an enlarged edition of the herbal, which was followed five years later by a translation into Flemish (*Kruydtboeck*). In 1581 L'Obel became a physician to WILLIAM OF ORANGE, and in 1584 he returned to England, where he assumed responsibility for Baron Zouche's garden at Hackney. In 1607 L'Obel was appointed royal gardener (*botanicus regius*) to King JAMES. L'Obel is the eponym of the lobelia.

*DSB.*

**LOBO, FRANCISCO RODRIGUES** (1580–1622), Portuguese pastoral writer, born into a noble family in Leira and educated at Coimbra before returning to Leira for the rest of his life. His pastorals in verse and prose include the prose *Primavera* (1601), which is regarded as the finest evocation of landscape in Portuguese literature; its sequels were *Pastor peregrino* (1608) and *Desenganado* (1614). Lobo also wrote an historical epic, *O condestabre de Portugal* (Lisbon, 1627), in praise of Nuno Alvares Pereira, who led the Portuguese war of independence against Spain at the end of the fourteenth century; in the context of the annexation of Portugal by Spain (1580–1640), this subject evoked nationalist aspirations.

Richard Preto-Rodas, *Francisco Rodrigues Lobo: Dialogue and Courtly Lore in Renaissance Portugal* (1971).

**LOCHNER, STEFAN** (*fl. c.*1440–1454), German painter, born in Meersburg (on Lake Constance). In 1442 he settled in Cologne, where he became a prominent painter; in the nineteenth century he came to be described as the founder of the COLOGNE SCHOOL, but the existence of such a school is now doubted. The principal work associated with Lochner is an ALTARPIECE painted for the Town Hall in Cologne; it is now in Cologne Cathedral and so is known as the *Dombild*. Albrecht DÜRER greatly admired this altarpiece, noting in the diary of his journey to the Netherlands that he had to pay in order to see the painting.

*MDA; NDB.*

**LODGE, THOMAS** (1558–1625), English writer. Son of the lord mayor of London, and educated at Oxford, Lodge is now chiefly remembered for his prose romance *Rosalynde* (1590), which tells the same story as SHAKESPEARE's *As You Like It*. Other romances include *Scillaes Metamorphosis* (1589) and *A Margarite of America* (1596); he also wrote a play and published a collection of satirical verse, before training as a physician.

*DNB.*

**LODI, PEACE OF.** On 9 April 1454 Venice and Milan signed a peace treaty at Lodi, south-east of Milan. On 30 August 1454, Venice, Milan, and Florence signed a second treaty forming a defensive pact. Despite the fact that the second treaty was signed in Venice, both treaties are known as the Peace of Lodi. On 26 June 1455 ALFONSO of Naples and Pope NICHOLAS V joined the defensive pact. The result was a non-aggression treaty that was signed by the five great powers (Venice, Milan, Florence, the kingdom of Naples, and the Papal State) and their various satellites (the duchies of Savoy and Urbino, the marquisates of Ferrara and Mantua, and the republics of Bologna, Perugia, and Siena). The non-aggression pact was at times strained by the alliance of Florence and Milan against the axis of Venice, the Papal State, and Naples, and by local disturbances such as the War of FERRARA and the papal-Neapolitan campaign against Lorenzo de' MEDICI in the wake of the PAZZI CONSPIRACY, but was nonetheless destined, despite the absence of Genoa from the signatories, to secure a measure of peace for Italy until the outbreak of the WARS OF ITALY in 1494, four years beyond the 25-year period specified in the treaty.

**LOGARITHMS** were invented as an aid to calculation. By converting numbers to their logarithms, the operations of multiplication and division are reduced to addition and subtraction. Logarithms replaced an earlier method, apparently mainly used by astronomers, called prosthaphaeresis, which worked in somewhat the same way by converting numbers to sines and cosines of angles.

The first tables of logarithms were published by John NAPIER in *Mirifici logarithmorum canonis descriptio* (1614; translated in 1618 as *A Description of the Admirable Table of Logarithms*), but this book gave no hint of why the system worked. The first explanation of the mathematical basis of logarithms was provided by KEPLER (1624), using the propositions of book 6 of EUCLID's *Elements*. Napier's logarithms were 'natural logarithms' (that is, they were to base *e*). Henry BRIGGS drew up tables of logarithms to base 10, which are much easier to use. Some years before Napier, work had been done on logarithms by the clockmaker Jost BÜRGI, but he had not published his work. When they were both working for RUDOLF II in Prague (1600–11) Bürgi became friends with Kepler, who seems to have put pressure on him to publish his work, which appeared in 1620.

**LOLLARDS.** Originally those influenced by the views of WYCLIFFE, the term lollard (probably from the middle Dutch *lollaerd*, 'mumbler') came to be applied in a looser sense to those critical of the Church and sympathetic to various reformist principles. Lollards especially emphasized the right of each man to read the Bible, sole source of authority in religious matters, for himself, and unofficial translations were circulated. Personal faith, the need for priests to be in a state of grace, and opposition to the doctrine of transubstantiation, to indulgences, devotion to images, pilgrimages, and endowments, also characterized the movement. Following Wycliffe's expulsion from Oxford in 1382, lollardy lost its brief period of academic support, and the persecution and execution of lollard heresy in the early fifteenth century extinguished support for the movement in aristocratic circles. Pockets of lollard sympathizers, predominantly amongst yeomen farmers and artisans, remained however. Whether or not the existence of such opinion prepared the ground for the later REFORMATION, or delayed necessary reform by extremism and simple-mindedness, remains a subject of debate.

J. A. F. Thompson, *The Later Lollards, 1414–1520* (1965).

**LOMAZZO, GIOVANNI PAOLO** (1538–1600), Italian painter, art theorist, and poet, born in Milan, where he trained in the studio of Gaudenzio FERRARI. At the age of

33 he went blind, and thereafter dictated two important treatises on the theory of art, *Trattato dell'arte della pittura, scultura e architettura* (1584) and *Idea del tempio della pittura* (1590). The seven books of the *Trattato* examine proportion, colour, light, PERSPECTIVE, technique, and the history of art, the last of which describes classical and Christian ICONOGRAPHY. The *Tempio* is a NEOPLATONIC work which delineates the complex symbolism of ASTROLOGY and of numbers and relates these symbols to seven artists who are deemed to govern art: Gaudenzio Ferrari, MICHELANGELO, POLIDORO DA CARAVAGGIO, LEONARDO DA VINCI, RAPHAEL, MANTEGNA, and TITIAN. In 1587 Lomazzo also published a collection of *Rime* with an autobiography.

*MDA.*

**LOMBARD, LAMBERT** (1505–66), Flemish painter, engraver, architect, and antiquarian, born in Liège. He trained in Antwerp and Middelburg before travelling in the Netherlands, France, and Germany and studying Italian painting in Rome (1537–9). On returning to Liège he founded an academy of painting; his pupils included Frans FLORIS, Hendrik GOLTZIUS, and Willem KEY. Karel van Mander described Lombard as 'no less a teacher than learned in the arts of painting, architecture, and perspective; one can confidently rank him amongst the best Netherlandish painters, both past and present'. This judgement echoes that of VASARI (with whom Lambert had corresponded), who praised Lombard as the finest of Flemish artists, 'a man well versed in literature, and painter of judgement, a learned architect, and, not least, the master of Frans Floris and Willem Key'.

These generous judgements cannot now be evaluated, because most of Lombard's paintings are known only through copies, drawings, and engravings: the large collection in the episcopal palace in Bonn was lost in a fire in 1703, and those in the churches of Liège were destroyed in the French Revolution. Surviving works include scenes from the life of St Denis (c.1533, now divided between the Musée de l'Art Wallon in Liège, the Church of Saint-Denis in Liège, and the Musée de l'Art Ancien in Brussels), the *Rejection of Joachim's Offer* (Musée de l'Art Wallon, Liège), and *Judith, Esther, Claudia Quinta*, and the *Tiburtine Sibyl* (all in the Church of St Amand in Stokrooie, near Hasselt).

*MDA; Godelieve Denhaene, Lambert Lombard: Renaissance et humanisme à Liège (1990).*

**LOMBARDO FAMILY**, a dynasty of Venetian sculptors and architects, including Pietro (c.1433–1515), Tullio (c.1455–1532), and Antonio (c.1458–1516). Pietro Lombardo was born in Carona (Lombardy), the son of an architect. He probably worked in Florence and certainly worked in Padua, where, as well as his principal work, the Roselli monument, he sculpted the tomb of Giannantonio, the son of GATTAMELATA, in the Basilica del Santo. Moving c.1467 to Venice, he designed and carved decorations for the distinctly Florentine chancel of San Giobbe (1471–85) and built the syncretic Church of Santa Maria dei Miracoli (1481–9), which has

marble panels on both interior and exterior, a Veneto-Byzantine dome, and Florentine decorative motifs; he also began the façade of the Scuola di San Marco (1488–90), of which the upper levels were completed by Mauro CODUSSI.

In sculpture Pietro introduced to Venice the large architectural tomb adorned with classical sculpture; his most important Venetian tombs are those of Doge Pasquale Malipiero (d. 1462), Doge Pietro MOCENIGO (d. 1476), and Doge Niccolò Marcello (d. 1474), all in the Church of SS Giovanni e Paolo; he was probably the sculptor of the effigy and tomb of DANTE in Ravenna (1482, rebuilt 1780) and the Zanetto tomb in Treviso Cathedral (1485). Various Venetian palaces have been attributed to Pietro, notably Palazzo Dario (c.1487) and Palazzo Loredan (1500–9; now Palazzo Vendramin-Calergi), which had been begun by Codussi and is one of the most elegant buildings in Venice, despite the jungle of television masts on its roof.

Pietro Lombardo employed his sons Tullio and Antonio in his workshop, notably in the work for Santa Maria del Miracoli. Tullio's independent work includes the tombs of Doge Giovanni Mocenigo (d. 1485) and Doge Antonio Vendramin (d. 1478), both in the Church of SS Giovanni e Paolo, the effigy of Guidarello Guidarelli now in the Accademia in Ravenna (1525), and various reliefs, including the *Bacchus and Ariadne* in the Kunsthistorisches Museum in Vienna and the *Coronation of the Virgin* in the Church of San Giovanni Crisostomo in Venice. Antonio sculpted one of the reliefs of *The Miracles of St Anthony* for the Basilica del Santo in Padua and a *Madonna della Scarpa* for the Zeno Chapel in Basilica San Marco in Venice; he also sculpted reliefs on mythological subjects (now mostly in the Hermitage in St Petersburg) commissioned by Alfonso I d'ESTE for the Camerini d'Alabastro in the Castello Estense at Ferrara.

Antonio's sons Aurelio (c.1501–1563), Girolamo (c.1505–1589), and Ludovico (c.1507–1575), were also sculptors, as was Sante Lombardo (1504–60), the son of Tullio Lombardo.

*MDA; R. Luciani, Pietro Lombardo architetto (1987); Alison Luchs, Tullio Lombardo and the Ideal Portrait Sculpture in Renaissance Venice (1995).*

**LONDON.** As the seat of government and a centre for finance and overseas trade, London grew rapidly during the fifteenth and sixteenth centuries. In 1500, its population stood at an estimated 50,000; in a century that number had quadrupled to an estimated 200,000, and it was to double again by the mid-seventeenth century. Such growth put inevitable strains on city government, which was divided between the Court of Aldermen, the Common Council, and the Common Hall. Aldermen, usually wealthy merchants, were chosen for life, and were often close to the national government; the 200 members of the Common Council were elected annually; members of the Common Hall, which elected two sheriffs, ran into thousands. The lord mayor was chosen by the aldermen from Common Hall nominations. City government was also administered at ward and parish level. Although outside such structures, the LIVERY COMPANIES also wielded considerable influence.

**LONGHI, MARTINO.** See LUNGHI, MARTINO THE ELDER.

**LOPES, FERNÃO** (c.1380–1460), Portuguese historian. He had served as Portugal's royal archivist for at least fifteen years when on 19 March 1434 King DUARTE commissioned him to write a series of chronicles on the reigns of his predecessors. Lopes's surviving chronicles describe the reigns of Pedro I (1357–67), Fernão I (1367–83), and JOHN I; the two earlier chronicles were first published in 1760, and were preceded by the *Crónica del rei dom João I de boa memoria*, which was published in 1644. The quality of Lopes's prose and his ability to evoke figures in a few well-crafted phrases led to his being praised as the Portuguese Froissart and honoured as the patriarch of Portuguese historians.

DHP; A. de Magalhães Basto, *Fernão Lopes e a Crónica de 1419* (1959).

**LOPES, GREGÓRIO** (c.1490–c.1550), Portuguese court painter to MANUEL I and JOHN III, primarily a painter of ALTARPIECES. His subjects are invariably religious, but his depiction of faces and clothing distinguishes carefully between individuals, and in his backgrounds he depicts in extraordinary detail the life of sixteenth-century Portugal in towns, villages, and, pre-eminently, in the court. His principal works are the altarpieces that he executed for the Convento de Cristo in Tomar, of which the most celebrated is the *Last Supper* in the nearby Church of John the Baptist (in what is now the Praça da República).

MDA; J. A. Seabra Carvalho, *Gregório Lopes* (1999).

**LOPEZ, RODRIGO** (d. 1594), Hispano-Jewish physician in England. Lopez settled in England in 1559 and quickly established a successful medical practice, ministering to the highest reaches of society. He was the first house physician at St Bartholomew's Hospital, and was by 1569 a member of the College of Physicians. In 1586 he became chief physician to Elizabeth, who three years later granted him a monopoly on the importation of aniseed. In 1590 Antonio PÉREZ moved to England as a refugee from the court of PHILIP II. Lopez agreed to act as his interpreter, and became implicated in a plot to poison both Perez and Elizabeth. No evidence against him was found amongst his papers, but in January 1594 he was taken to the Tower, tried, and found guilty of treason. He was hanged at Tyburn in June of that year. His trial and execution inaugurated a wave of anti-Semitism that was reflected in SHAKESPEARE's *Merchant of Venice* and in the revival of MARLOWE's *Jew of Malta*.

DNB; JNB.

**LÓPEZ DE GÓMARA, FRANCISCO** (1511–66), Spanish historian, born in Gómara (Soria), and educated at Alcalá de Henares, where he was ordained as a priest. On the final return of Hernán CORTÉS to Spain in 1540, López became his secretary-chaplain and wrote the encomiastic *Historia de las Indias y conquista de México* (Zaragoza, 1552), which was banned on 17 November 1553 because of its questioning of some of the policies of CHARLES V, to whom it was dedicated.

López's adulatory account of the role of Cortés prompted Bernal DÍAZ DEL CASTILLO to write an alternative history, but that was not published until 1632, whereas López's *Historia* achieved a European reputation through translations into Italian (1560), English (*The Pleasant History of the Conquest of West India*, 1578), and French (1606).

DHE; *Cortés: The Life of the Conqueror of Mexico by his Secretary*, trans. L. B. Simpson (1964).

**LÓPEZ DE YANGUAS, FERNANDO** (c.1470–c.1540), Spanish playwright and collector of proverbs, born in Soria. He became a schoolmaster and later took holy orders. His early work includes a Christmas eclogue, *Égloga en loor de la natividad de Nuestro Señor*, and an allegorical play on the Assumption, *Farsa del mundo*. He wrote at least two dialogues, *Diálogo de mosquito* (Valencia, 1521) and El 'Nunc dimittis' trovado; in the latter a lover speaks the liturgical lines as he leaves his beloved. López's *Farsa sacramental* was the first AUTO SACRAMENTAL to use the eucharist as its central theme. His collection of proverbs was published as *Cincuenta preguntas bivas con otras tantas respuestas* (Valencia, 1550).

**LOREDAN or Loredano, LEONARDO** (1438–1521), doge of Venice from 1501 to 1521 who presided over Venice at the nadir of its fortunes in the years following defeat at the battle of AGNADELLO (1509), after which it gradually regained its mainland possessions in a series of campaigns that lasted till 1517. Loredan is the subject of Giovanni BELLINI's portrait (National Gallery, London).

**LOREDAN or Loredano, PIETRO** (1481–1571), doge of Venice from 1567 to 1571 who presided over Venice in the early years of the war with Turkey (1570–3) that ended after his death with the battle of LEPANTO and the loss of CYPRUS to the Ottomans.

**LORENZETTI, PIETRO** (*fl.* c.1316–1345) and **AMBROGIO** (*fl.* c.1317–1348), Italian painters, brothers who lived in Siena. Pietro's earliest datable work is a polyptych of *The Madonna and Child with Saints* (1320) in the Church of Santa Maria della Pieve in Arezzo. Other works are attributed to Pietro and dated by reference to the Pieve altarpiece: panels of the *Maestà* in Cortona Cathedral and the *Deposition* in the Lower Church of San Francesco in Assisi seem to have been painted before the Pieve altarpiece; later works include a *Madonna* in the Uffizi and frescoes of the *Crucifixion* in the Church of San Francesco in Siena and a *Birth of the Virgin* (1342) in the Museo dell' Opera del Duomo in Siena.

Ambrogio's earliest datable work is a *Madonna and Child* (1319, Museo Diocesano, Florence). The documentary record shows that he was in Florence in the early 1320s, but no paintings survive from this period. His most important painting is a fresco cycle (traditionally entitled *Good and Bad Government*) in the Palazzo Pubblico in Siena; this picture contains the earliest significant portrayal of LANDSCAPE in Italian art. Ambrogio's other surviving paintings include frescoes in the Church of San Francesco in Siena and pictures of the

**Ambrogio Lorenzetti,** *Good Government*, part of a fresco in the Palazzo Pubblico in Siena

*Madonna and Child* in the Pinacoteca in Siena and in the Palazzo Pubblico in Massa Marittima and of the *Presentation in the Temple* (1342) in the Uffizi.

The only known collaboration between the brothers is the fresco cycle of *The Life of Mary* (1335) painted on the façade of the Spedale di Santa Maria della Scala in Siena and now lost.

MDA.

**LORENZO DI CREDI** (*c.*1457–1536), Italian painter, born in Florence, the son of a goldsmith; he trained in the studio of VERROCCHIO, where his fellow pupils may have included LEONARDO. Lorenzo worked as an assistant to Verrocchio and eventually became the manager of his workshop. In 1497 Lorenzo became a disciple of SAVONAROLA, and is said to have destroyed his secular paintings. His surviving works include the altarpiece of the *Madonna di Piazza* in Pistoia Cathedral and a self-portrait drawing (1490) in the National Gallery in Washington.

MDA; Robert Brewer, *A Study of Lorenzo di Credi* (1970).

**LORENZO MONACO** (1370/5–1425/30), Italian painter, born in Siena. He entered the Camaldolese Monastery of Santa Maria degli Angeli in Florence and became a miniature painter; several of his illuminated manuscripts are now in the Biblioteca Laurenziana. He painted many altarpieces for his ORDER, notably two versions of *The Coronation of the Virgin* (1414, Uffizi; *c.*1415, National Gallery, London). His frescoes include a cycle on *The Life of the Virgin Mary* in the Bartolini

Chapel of Santa Trinita in Florence. His late polyptych of *The Deposition* (Museo San Marco, Florence) was finished by Fra ANGELICO.

MDA; Marvin Eisenberg, *Lorenzo Monaco* (1989).

**L'ORME, PHILIBERT DE**. See DELORME, PHILIBERT.

**LOTTO, LORENZO** (*c.*1480–1556), Italian painter, born in Venice and trained in the studio of Giovanni BELLINI, where, according to VASARI, his fellow pupils included GIORGIONE and TITIAN. His early paintings include *Madonna with St Peter Martyr* (1503, Museo Nazionale, Naples) and *St Jerome* (1506, Louvre). Lotto lived in Rome in the service of the Vatican from *c.*1508 to 1512, but no work from this period is known to survive. The latter part of his career was largely spent in Bergamo, and the paintings of this period combine Roman and Venetian elements. His late works include *Man on a Terrace* (Museum of Art, Cleveland) and a *Madonna and Child with St Catherine* (Accademia Carrara, Bergamo). In 1552 he entered the Monastery of Santa Casa in Loreto, where he stayed for the rest of his life. The account book (*Libro di spese diverse*) that he kept from 1538 to 1554 (now in the Archivo della Santa Casa in Loreto) is a chronicle of financial hardship.

MDA; Peter Humfrey, *Lorenzo Lotto* (1997).

**LOTZER, SEBASTIAN** (b. *c.*1490), journeyman furrier and lay preacher, born in Horb (Württemberg). He was an early adherent of the Reformation, and in 1523–4 published five

Ambrogio Lorenzetti, *The Presentation of Christ in the Temple* (1342), in the Uffizi, in Florence

pamphlets advocating religious reform. In 1525 he took part in the PEASANTS' WAR in Upper Swabia as clerk to the Baltringen band, whose list of grievances he systematized into the TWELVE ARTICLES, with biblical commentary provided by Christoph SCHAPPELER, the reforming preacher of Memmingen, where the Articles were drawn up. After the suppression of the rebellion by the SWABIAN LEAGUE both Lotzer and Schappeler fled to St Gallen, where their eyewitness accounts provided the material for Johannes KESSLER's narrative of the war in his *Sabbata*.

ADB.

**LOUIS II** (1506–26), king of Hungary and Bohemia, was the son of King LADISLAS II, whom he succeeded at the age of 10. In 1526 King Louis commanded the army that was defeated by the Ottomans at the battle of MOHÁCS, and was killed while attempting to escape.

*NDB* s.v. Ludwig II, König von Ungarn und Böhmen; *BLBL* s.v. Ludwig II Jagiello.

**LOUIS II, DUKE OF ANJOU** (1377–1417), titular king of NAPLES, was born in Toulon, the son of Duke Louis I. On his father's death in 1384 Louis II inherited the Angevin claim to the throne of Naples, and in 1389 he was crowned as king of Naples by the antipope CLEMENT VII. He was unable to take possession of his kingdom and so continued to live in France, but in 1411 he invaded Naples and defeated LADISLAS OF DURAZZO at the battle of Roccoserra. Louis was unable to consolidate his victory and was soon driven back to France, where he remained for the rest of his life.

**LOUIS XI** (1423–83), king of France, was born in Bourges, where his parents, King CHARLES VII and Queen Marie d'Anjou, had taken refuge from the English, who occupied large areas of France. Louis grew up in the castle of Loches and in June 1436, shortly before his thirteenth birthday, married 11-year-old Margaret of Scotland, the daughter of King James I of Scotland. In 1440 Louis joined the PRAGUERIE, and six years later was exiled by his father to the Dauphiné, where he established what was in effect an independent kingdom; his father lived for another fifteen years, but they never met again. Margaret died in 1445, and in 1452 Louis married Charlotte of Savoy, by whom he had five daughters (including ANNE OF FRANCE) and a son (later CHARLES VIII). In 1456 Louis's father invaded the Dauphiné, and Louis sought refuge at the court of PHILIP THE GOOD of Burgundy, where he remained until his accession in 1461.

King Louis soon alienated his former protector Philip the Good, and within France lost the support of the clergy (by abrogating the PRAGMATIC SANCTION OF BOURGES) and the nobility. From 1465 to 1472 he faced a series of rebellions mounted by the Leagues of the PUBLIC WEAL. He was defeated by CHARLES THE BOLD at the battle of Montlhéry (16 July 1465), but in 1472 defeated Duke Charles, who had been assisted by EDWARD IV of England (whom Louis had attempted to subvert by supporting the Lancastrian claimants to the English throne). During this period Louis also conquered French lands in the south, and pushed the southern boundary of France to the Pyrenees.

In 1474 Louis formed the Union of Constance, which brought to his side the former allies of Charles the Bold, including Duke René of Lorraine, the free towns of Alsace, and the Swiss Confederation. King Edward IV invaded France, but King Louis met King Edward at Picquigny, where they signed a treaty (29 August 1475) agreeing that Edward would withdraw his troops in return for a substantial payment. Louis's Swiss allies defeated Charles the Bold at Granson (December 1475), Morat (22 June 1476), and finally Nancy (6 January 1477), where Duke Charles was killed. Charles's heir was MARY OF BURGUNDY, but Louis contested the inheritance, claiming Burgundy and its possessions as a fief of the French crown. Louis seized Burgundy (but not the Burgundian Netherlands) and soon added to his possessions the duchies of Anjou and Bar (1480) and the counties of Maine and Provence (1481). In 1482 Louis concluded the Treaty of Arras with Mary's widower Maximilian of Austria (later the Emperor MAXIMILIAN I), by which he retained the disputed Somme towns in Artois and Picardy. He spent the final years of his life in virtual seclusion at his chateau at

Plessis-lès-Tours; he died on 30 August 1483, eschewing a state funeral at Saint-Denis in favour of a private interment at Cléry.

King Louis created a unified eastern border for France (with the exception of Lorraine) and united France under a centralized monarchy. He levied centralized taxes such as the *taille* (a property tax from which the nobility and clergy were exempted) and the *gabelle* (a salt tax) and stimulated the economy by encouraging textile production in northern France, introducing the SILK industry to Lyon and developing trade through the newly acquired port of Marseille. On the only occasion on which he convened the ESTATES-GENERAL (1468), his purpose was to secure a declaration of Normandy as an inalienable part of the territories of the French crown. He was constantly in dispute with the Parlement of Paris, but aspired to unify the CUSTOMARY LAW of northern France (see FRENCH LAW) on the model of the Coutume de Paris. In his personal demeanour he was the least regal of France's Renaissance kings, but he was in many respects the creator of France's strong centralized monarchy.

J. Farier, *Louis XI* (2001).

**LOUIS XII** (1482–1515), king of France, the son of CHARLES D'ORLÉANS. In 1476 he married his cousin Jeanne of France, the daughter of King LOUIS XI. In 1488 he led a rebellion against the regent, ANNE OF FRANCE, and on being defeated was imprisoned for three years. In 1494 he accompanied CHARLES VIII on the French invasion of Italy; he occupied Genoa and remained in northern Italy while King Charles marched south to Naples.

King Charles had no living children, and on his death in 1498 the throne passed to Louis, who promptly secured an annulment of his marriage from Pope ALEXANDER VI and married ANNE OF BRITTANY, the widow of Charles VIII. In 1499 he renewed the WARS OF ITALY by invading Italy in pursuit of his family's claim to the duchy of Milan, which originated in the marriage of his grandfather (Louis I, duke of Orléans) to Valentina Visconti, daughter of Gian Galeazzo VISCONTI, duke of Milan. The French army and its Venetian allies captured Milan on 6 October 1499 and went on to occupy Genoa.

King Louis marched south to Naples, where he reached an accommodation with King FERDINAND for the partitioning of the kingdom. A boundary dispute renewed hostilities; the Spanish army defeated the French in the battles of CERIGNOLA (28 April 1503) and GARIGLIANO (29 December 1503), and in a second Treaty of BLOIS (1505) King Louis was obliged to renounce his claim to Naples, leaving the kingdom in control of King Ferdinand.

On 10 December 1508 King Louis and the Emperor MAXIMILIAN joined forces in the League of CAMBRAI, and, together with the forces of Pope JULIUS II, invaded the Veneto. The victory of the League at the battle of AGNADELLO on 14 May 1509 was followed by the occupation of the entire Venetian *terraferma* (except for Treviso). In October 1511 the opposition to France was brought together in a HOLY LEAGUE which consisted of Venice, the Empire, Spain, Pope Julius II

(who had changed sides), and HENRY VIII of England. At the battle of Ravenna on 11 April 1512, the French lost their initial advantage when their commander Gaston de FOIX was killed, and the French army had to retreat. King Louis instigated the convening of the second COUNCIL OF PISA in the hope that Julius II could be deposed, but the Council could not agree, and the French retreat from Italy brought the Council to an undignified close.

In 1513 King Louis dispatched an army to dislodge Massimiliano Sforza from Milan, but his army was defeated by the Swiss troops protecting Massimiliano at the battle of Novara on 6 June 1513. By this time members of the Holy League had begun to attack France itself: in 1512 an Anglo-Spanish force attempted to invade Aquitaine and Ferdinand's army occupied Navarre, and the following year Henry VIII invaded northern France, defeating a French army at the battle of the SPURS near Thérouanne (Artois) on 16 August 1513, and the Swiss Confederation, which had entered the fray when it was forced out of Lombardy, invaded Burgundy as far as Dijon.

Queen Anne died in January 1514, and on 9 October 1514 King Louis married Mary Tudor, sister of Henry VIII of England; he died less than three months later (1 January 1515) and was succeeded by FRANCIS I. Louis's campaigns in Italy had accomplished little at great cost to the French treasury, but one important cultural consequence of his interventions in Italy was to further the introduction of Italian Renaissance styles into French decorative art.

**LOUIS, COUNT OF NASSAU, or** (Dutch) **Lodewijk, Graaf van Nassau** (1538–74), Dutch leader in the REVOLT OF THE NETHERLANDS, the son of William of Nassau and the younger brother of WILLIAM OF ORANGE. He was raised in the Lutheran faith of his parents, and in the 1560s became a prominent figure in the resistance of Dutch aristocrats to the harshness of Spanish rule. In 1566 he organized the Compromise, an alliance of moderate Catholic and Protestant noblemen who demanded religious toleration. The next year King PHILIP II responded by sending the duke of ALBA to the Netherlands to quell civil unrest and religious dissent. Count Louis went into exile in Germany to organize armed resistance, and in 1568 returned with an army and invaded Friesland, defeating a Spanish force at Heiligerlee on 23 May 1568. Two months later, on 21 July 1568, he was defeated by the duke of Alba at Jemgum, and escaped by swimming across the Ems. In October 1568 he joined forces with his brother William in an invasion of Flanders, but was obliged to retreat because of a lack of popular support.

After the failure of the invasion of Flanders, Louis turned to diplomacy, and worked to secure the support of influential foreign figures such as Gaspard COLIGNY (the HUGUENOT leader), Francis Walsingham (the English ambassador in France), the German Protestant princes, and Poland. He organized the SEA BEGGARS (whose port was La Rochelle, which was controlled by Coligny), who captured Brill, in Zeeland (1 April 1572), and subsequently led the army that captured Mons (Hainaut) on 23 May 1572 and held it till 17 September. His diplomatic efforts bore some fruit in 1573, when he assembled the German princes, Poland, and CATHERINE DE MÉDICIS in Blamont (Lorraine) to forge an alliance against Spain. In 1574 he led an army into the Netherlands, and died (together with his brother Henry) fighting the army of Luis de REQUESENS at Mook (near Nijmegen) on 14 April 1574.

*NNBW* i.

**LOUISE OF SAVOY or (French) Louise de Savoie** (1476–1531), duchess of Angoulême, was born into a cadet branch of the house of SAVOY. Her mother was Marguerite de Bourbon, who was the sister of Pierre de Beaujeu (husband of ANNE OF FRANCE and younger brother of the duke of Bourbon). At the age of 12 Louise married Charles of Valois, count of Angoulême, by whom she had two children, MARGUERITE D'ANGOULÊME (later queen of Navarre) and François. On the accession of LOUIS XII to the throne, François became heir presumptive, and when Louis died on 1 January 1515 François ascended the throne as King FRANCIS I.

King Francis awarded his mother the counties of Angoulême (which he raised to a duchy), Maine, and Beaufort and the duchy of Anjou. Thereafter she participated in the government of King Francis, and had to assume control of the kingdom when Francis was captured at the battle of PAVIA. In 1529 she signed the Peace of CAMBRAI (La Paix des Dames) with MARGARET OF AUSTRIA (representing her nephew the Emperor CHARLES V). Louise died in 1531, whereupon her domains, which consisted of Anjou, Angoumois, Auvergne, Bourbonnais, Beaujolais, Maine, and Marche, were incorporated into France.

Dorothy Mayer, *The Great Regent: Louise of Savoy, 1476–1531* (1966).

**LOUVRE.** The Louvre first became a royal residence in the fourteenth century when Charles V converted the fortress built *c.*1200 into a palace, in one wing of which he installed his library, which was later to evolve into the founding collection of the Bibliothèque Nationale. The palace was plundered by British troops in the wake of their victory at Agincourt in 1415, and was subsequently neglected by French kings until Francis I announced in 1528 that he was going to take up residence in the Louvre. He demolished the great keep, thereby opening up a courtyard, but waited till 1546 before commissioning Pierre LESCOT to build a new royal palace consisting of four wings around a square court. When Francis died the following year, the foundations were barely above the ground, but construction continued until it was disrupted by the outbreak of the WARS OF RELIGION in 1562. Francis never saw the building that he had commissioned, so in a sense his memorial at the Louvre is the royal collection of art that it still houses, including two of Francis's early acquisitions, LEONARDO's *Mona Lisa* and RAPHAEL's *Belle Jardinière*. Lescot completed the west wing with the assistance of the decorative sculptor Jean GOUJON; of Lescot's plans only the Italianate square courtyard (Cour Carrée) was executed according to his design.

While the Louvre was under construction it became the principal residence of FRANCIS II and CHARLES IX, but their brother HENRI III lived mostly in Paris. The last French king to use the Louvre as his principal residence was HENRI IV, who instructed Jacques DUCERCEAU the Younger to build the gallery facing the Seine. Construction continued throughout the seventeenth century, but was suspended in 1675; the building was completed in the nineteenth century (1806–78) and the glass pyramid at the entrance was added in the twentieth century (1986–9).

D. Thomson, *Renaissance Paris* (1984).

**LOYET, GÉRARD** (*fl.* 1466, d. 1502–3), Flemish goldsmith and seal engraver, born in Lille. He entered the service of CHARLES THE BOLD, who commissioned a gold enamelled reliquary (1466–71) which includes a statuette of Duke Charles in a kneeling position; it is now in the cathedral treasury in Liège. In 1477 Loyet was appointed master of the mint in Antwerp.

*MDA*; Hugo van der Velden, *The Donor's Image: Gerard Loyet and the Votive Portraits of Charles the Bold* (2000).

**LUBBERTUS, SIBRANDUS** (1556/7–1625), Germano-Dutch Calvinist theologian, born in Langwarden (Oldenburg) and educated at the Latin school in Bremen and then at Wittenberg, Geneva (under BEZA), Marburg, and Neustadt (under URSINUS). In 1585 he became the founding professor of theology at the University of Franeker, where he remained for the rest of his life.

Lubbertus was a polemical theologian whose principal opponent was Roberto BELLARMINO, against whom he wrote four books: *De principiis christianorum* (1591), *De papa Romano* (1594), *De conciliis* (1601), and *De ecclesia* (1607). Lubbertus also wrote against Faustus SOCINUS (*De Jesu Christo servatore contra Faustum Socinum*) and several exponents of ARMINIANISM, including GROTIUS (*Responsio ad pietatum Grotii*, 1614). He was a prominent member of the Synod of DORT, where he deprecated GOMAR's supralapsarian Calvinism.

*NDB*; *NNBW* ii; C. van der Woude, *Sibrandus Lubbertus: Leven en Werken* (1963).

**LÜBECK**, a German port on the Baltic and the most important city in the HANSEATIC LEAGUE. From the twelfth century the city was ruled exclusively by its merchants in accordance with statutes adopted from Soest (Westphalia), and the guilds and nobility were obliged to submit to the authority of the merchants. In 1226 Lübeck became an imperial free city, and did not finally surrender its independence until it joined the German Customs Union (*Zollverein*) on 11 August 1868. By the mid-thirteenth century, the city dominated the herring trade in the Baltic and was exercising its regional authority as an ally of the TEUTONIC knights in the eastern Baltic. By the end of the century Lübeck's statutes had been adopted by scores of Baltic towns with large German populations, and its courts functioned as courts of appeal for all of these cities and even for the small German communities in towns as far afield as Novgorod.

In the fourteenth century Lübeck presided over a league of Baltic cities. It was the principal member of the coalition that fought Denmark, captured Copenhagen, and forced the Danes to sign the peace of Stralsund on 24 May 1370. At the beginning of the fifteenth century, by which time the population had risen to 20,000, both the military power of the Hanseatic League and the commercial standing of the city had begun to decline. Tensions between guilds and merchants led to the exclusion of the merchants from government between 1408 and 1416. In the early sixteenth century Lübeck engaged in a war with Denmark (1501–12) and supported GUSTAVUS VASA in Sweden (1520–3). The most important figure of the sixteenth century was Jürgen Wullenwever, a popular tribune who introduced the Reformation to the city (1530), suspended the constitution (1534–6), and led the city into a protracted naval war with Sweden (1536–70).

Lübeck was devastated by the THIRTY YEARS WAR, and the last Hanseatic diet met in the city in 1630.

**LUBLIN, UNION OF**, the act of 1 July 1569 whereby the grand duchy of LITHUANIA and the kingdom of POLAND were united under one king and one assembly of the ESTATES, so creating the largest state in Europe.

**LUCAS VAN LEIDEN** (c.1494–1533), Dutch painter and engraver, printer, and draughtsman, born in Leiden, the son of a painter, Hugo Jacobszoon. He trained as a painter in the studios of his father and of Cornelis ENGELBRECHTSZOON. Lucas was admitted to the Leiden Guild of Painters in 1514. He is known to have travelled occasionally, visiting Antwerp in 1521 (where he could have met DÜRER) and Middelburg in 1527 (where he met Jan GOSSAERT), but he spent most of his short life in Leiden.

In painting Lucas favoured GENRE subjects in works such as his *Chess Players* (Gemäldegalerie, Berlin) and *Card Players* (Wilton House, Wiltshire), and also painted religious subjects, notably the triptych of *The Last Judgement* (1526, Municipal Museum, Leiden).

It is not known where Lucas trained as an engraver, but he must have learnt the technique at an early age: his skilful *Mohammed and the Monk* is dated 1508, when Lucas was 15 years old, and it displays an assured grasp of foreshortening and the setting of groups of figures against landscapes. Two years later he produced *Ecce homo*, a large engraving in which the figures are placed in a complex architectural setting. Thereafter his engravings (all of which are dated) continued to depict religious subjects, but the seriousness of his themes was habitually subverted by elements of genre painting that border on the satirical. His work was greatly admired by VASARI (who thought Lucas a greater artist than Dürer) and by Rembrandt.

*MDA*; *NNBW* vii s.v. Leyden, Lucas van; Elise Smith, *The Paintings of Lucas van Leyden* (1992).

**LUCCA**, a town and ancient episcopal see in Tuscany. In 1300 feuding between 'black' and 'white' GUELF factions led to the exile of the white Guelfs and their return in 1314 under the command of the Ghibelline Uguccione della Faggiuola, who was DANTE's host during his visit to the city. The city was ruled by the *condottiere* Castruccio Castracani (1320–8) and was then ruled by various other city-states and lordships; thereafter it alternated between republican and oligarchic governments. The first republic lasted from 1369 to 1400, when Paolo Guinigi became *signore*; he was deposed in 1430, when Francesco SFORZA occupied the city on behalf of Filippo Maria VISCONTI and restored the republic. The forces of Milan fended off the attempts of Florence to secure Lucca, which ended when Cosimo de' MEDICI was exiled from Florence in 1433; during this period Lucca lost Carrara and its marble quarries to the Malaspina family and the area north of the Serchio river known as the Garfagnana to the ESTE FAMILY. Lucca remained independent and neutral during the WARS OF ITALY and successfully resisted the attempts of COSIMO I DE' MEDICI to place it under Tuscan control. Francesco BURLAMACCHI was elected GONFALONIERE in 1546 and after his execution in 1548 Lucca drifted into oligarchy.

In 1561 Lucca's rulers decided that it needed protection from the territorial ambitions of Cosimo I de' Medici and commissioned the fortifications (pierced by four gates) that were eventually finished in 1645; they are the best-preserved city walls in Italy.

Lucca enjoyed some eminence as a PILGRIMAGE resort because of the fame of the VERNICLE known as the *volto santo* ('sacred face') in the cathedral; this large wooden cross contains a depiction of a robed JESUS said to have been executed by Nicodemus.

C. Meek, *Lucca 1369–1400: Politics in an Early Renaissance City-State* (1978); Michael Brachel, *Lucca, 1430–1494: The Reconstruction of an Italian City-State* (1996).

**LUCIAN IN THE RENAISSANCE**. Lucian of Samosata (AD c.120–c.200) was author of some 80 prose works in Greek, many of which are satirical dialogues. He was revived by humanists such as Thomas MORE, who translated some of his dialogues into Latin. The mock encomium by ERASMUS in *Encomium moriae* ('The Praise of Folly') gave Lucianic irony a European reputation. The book known in English as *The True History*, which described a voyage to the moon, created a genre of imaginary voyages that extends from Joseph Hall's satirical novel *Mundus alter et idem* (1605) to Swift's *Gulliver's Travels*.

C. Robinson, *Lucian and his Influence in Europe* (1979); E. Mattioli, *Luciano e l'umanesimo* (1980); C. Lauvergnat-Gagnière, *Lucien de Samosate et le lucianisme en France au XVI⁰ s.: Athéisme et politique* (1988).

**LUCRETIUS IN THE RENAISSANCE**. Titus Lucretius Carus (94–55 BC), Roman poet and philosopher whose only known work, *De rerum natura*, is at once a masterpiece of Latin literature and also the chief conduit through which the philosophy of EPICURUS was transmitted to Renaissance Europe and beyond. By the tenth century *De rerum natura* was a forgotten poem, surviving only in quotations in other works, but it was rediscovered by Poggio BRACCIOLINI in 1417, and thereafter was cautiously admitted to the canon of classical texts. The reason for this caution was not the style of Lucretius' elegant poem, which was often the subject of extravagant praise, but rather its Epicurean content. When ALDUS MANUTIUS published the poem in 1500, he was careful to explain in his preface that he was publishing the poem because of its style rather than its content. Similarly, FICINO eventually decided that his youthful commentary on Lucretius should be burnt rather than published. In the case of both Aldus and Ficino, the heart of the problem was that the didactic import of the poem could not be reconciled with Christian teaching or with Platonic and Aristotelian thinking. For these reasons, scholarly commentary on Lucretius had a distinctively defensive tone. Giovan Battista Pio stressed in his commentary of 1511 that the Epicureanism of Lucretius consisted for the most part in advocating the securing of spiritual tranquillity through the investigation of nature. Denys LAMBIN argued in his edition and commentary (1563) that much of the poem was consistent with traditional philosophical teaching, and that the elements that were inconsistent with Christian teaching could simply be repudiated. Hubert van Giffen took a similar line in his commentary of 1566, arguing that the ethical judgements of Lucretius encouraged virtuous living.

Despite the widespead unease about Lucretius being one of the few ancient writers whose doctrines seemed to be in direct conflict with Christianity, the poem continued to be read throughout the period, and was an important influence on the thought of cosmologists such as Giordano BRUNO.

M. D. Reeve, 'The Italian Tradition of Lucretius', *Italia medioevale e umanistica*, 23 (1980).

**LUINI, BERNARDINO** (*c.*1480/5–1532), Italian painter. He was born in a village on Lake Maggiore and by 1512 was working in Milan. Throughout his career his style was indebted to that of LEONARDO DA VINCI. Luini's youthful fresco cycle *Cephalus and Procris* (*c.*1520) in the Casa Rabia (near Monza) survives in fragments now in the National Gallery in Washington. There are many examples of his later paintings in the Brera (Milan) and the churches and monasteries of Lombardy.

*MDA.*

**LUIS DE GRANADA, FRAY** (1504–88), Spanish religious writer, born in Granada to a poor family of Galician origin; his original name was Luis de Sarriá. Luis lost his father when he was 5, and the family survived through the meagre income of his mother, who worked as a laundress in the Dominican monastery in Granada. In the monastery he was introduced to the count of Tendilla, Íñigo López de Mendoza, in whose household he became a page. He entered the Dominican monastery in 1525, and three years later was sent to further his education in Valladolid, where he met the Dominican theologian Melchor CANO; in Córdoba he met JUAN DE ÁVILA, whose biography he was later to write.

Fray Luis found his vocation as an itinerant preacher, travelling throughout Spain. In 1547 he founded the Dominican monastery of Badajoz, where he wrote the *Guía de pecadores* (2 vols., Lisbon, 1556–7), a devotional work which sets out the twelve obligations and the twelve privileges of Christian believers and concludes with an exposition of the three principles that lay at the heart of Luis's asceticism: mortification of the senses, charitable works, and duty to God, to humankind, and to self. He also wrote a *Libro de la oración y meditación* (Salamanca, 1554), which was subsequently condensed by PEDRO DE ALCÁNTARA; this treatise was placed on the INDEX from 1559 to 1576.

Fray Luis was appointed as provincial of the Dominican ORDER in Portugal, and declined the archbishopric of Braga in order to preach and write in Portuguese, Spanish, and Latin. In Portugal he wrote *Libri sex ecclesiasticae rhetoricae*, an important treatise on ecclesiastical RHETORIC in which Luis used the precepts of CICERO and Quintilian to construct a model of the exemplary sermon, which, in marked contrast to his own sermons (which are characterized by long sentences and a vocabulary of baroque exuberance), is marked by the Ciceronian virtues of clarity and brevity. Fray Luis's most famous work is his *Introducción del símbolo de la fe* (Salamanca, 1583), a five-part devotional treatise that begins with a rapturous account of the created world that forms the classic account of the Franciscan doctrine of the brotherhood of animals.

John Moore, *Fray Luis de Granada* (1977); Pedro Laín Entralgo, *La antropología en la obra de fray Luis de Granada* (2nd edn. 1988); Álvaro Huerga, *Fray Luis de Granada: Una vida al servicio de la Iglesia* (1988).

**LUIS DE LEÓN, FRAY** (*c.*1527–1591), Spanish poet and translator, born into a family of jurists in Belmonte (Castile). In about 1541, when his father was appointed as a judge (*oidor*) in Granada, Luis was sent to study in Salamanca, where his uncle was professor of law. A few months later Luis entered the Augustinian ORDER, and in 1544 he returned to Salamanca University, where he made his profession as an Augustinian hermit and entered the university to study theology, first under Melchor CANO, and from 1551 under Domingo de SOTO. On graduating Luis taught at Salamanca and Alcalá de Henares, and in 1561 he was appointed to a professorship at Salamanca; his pupils included JUAN DE LA CRUZ and Francisco SUÁREZ.

In 1566 Fray Luis defied an edict of the COUNCIL OF TRENT by comparing the Vulgate Old Testament unfavourably with the Hebrew original; his position aroused the opposition of the Dominicans, particularly Bartolomé MEDINA, whose appointment to a chair at Salamanca Luis subsequently opposed. In 1572 his Dominican enemies denounced Fray Luis to the INQUISITION, and for the next four years Luis was imprisoned. He was acquitted of all charges in 1576 and returned to his teaching at Salamanca. On returning to his classroom (which is still preserved with its sixteenth-century furnishings) he reputedly began his first lecture with the customary formula 'as we were saying yesterday' ('hesterna die dicebamus'), but this famous story cannot be documented from a contemporary source. In 1578 Luis was appointed to the chair of moral philosophy and in 1579 to the chair of biblical studies. In 1591 he was elected provincial of his Order for Castile, but died nine days later.

During his lifetime Fray Luis was known as a scholar and as a victim of the internal feuds within the Spanish Church, but he is now celebrated as one of the great lyric poets and prose stylists of Spain. Fray Luis's poetry was published in 1631 by QUEVEDO, who wished to deprecate the mannered style of GONGORIST poetry by using Fray Luis's verse as an example of the classical virtues of clarity, precision, and poise. His poetry uses classical models and articulates classical values, principally those of Horace: his 'La vida retirada' is based on Horace's 'Beatus ille', and poems such as his 'Oda a Salinas', which is dedicated to the organist and music theorist Francisco de SALINAS, celebrate the power of music in the language of Neoplatonism and in the form of an Horatian ode. The transmutation of the Horatian ode into the Spanish *lira* (a five-verse line in which lines two and five are hendecasyllabic and the others heptasyllabic) had been accomplished by GARCILASO DE LA VEGA, but its greatest exponent, together with JUAN DE LA CRUZ, was Fray Luis de León.

Fray Luis's Latin prose consists of commentaries on the Bible, notably the *Triplex explanatio* (1589), a commentary on the Song of Solomon. In Spanish he wrote a treatise on the duties of a wife (*La perfecta casada*, 1583) and a devotional work on the biblical names of Jesus (*De los nombres de Cristo*, 1583–95). He also edited the works of TERESA OF ÁVILA (1588).

David Hildner, *Poetry and Truth in the Spanish Works of Fray Luis de León* (1992); Victor García de la Concha and Javier San José Lera (eds.), *Fray Luis de León: Historia, humanismo y letras* (1996).

**LUNA, ÁLVARO DE** (1388–1453), Spanish soldier, statesman, and poet, the illegitimate son of an Aragonese nobleman. In 1420 he entered the service of King JOHN II (Juan II) of Castile, who three years later appointed him constable of Castile. In 1427 King ALFONSO V of Aragon accused him of conspiring against the Aragonese in Castile, and Luna was banished for two years; he returned to the Castilian court in 1429, but ten years later was again banished. In 1453 he was accused of bewitching the king and decapitated at Valladolid. Luna subsequently became famed throughout Europe as a symbol of the overweeningly proud royal favourite who eventually suffers a disastrous nemesis.

Luna was the author of the *Libro de las claras y virtuosas mujeres* (1446), which defends the standing of women by reference to honourable women in classical and biblical antiquity. Sixteen of his poems are printed in the *Cancionero* of his client Juan Alfonso de BAENA (1445), and he is the protagonist of *El laberinto de Fortuna* of Juan de MENA.

DHE; Nicholas Round, *The Greatest Man Uncrowned: A Study of the Fall of Don Alvaro de Luna* (1986); J. M. Calderón Ortega, *Álvaro de Luna* (1998).

**LUNGHI or Longhi, MARTINO THE ELDER** (c.1534–c.1591), Italian architect, born near Milan. In 1573 he moved to Rome, and two years later he was appointed papal architect. He added the tower of the Senate to MICHELANGELO's Capitol and built the Church of San Girolamo degli Schiavoni (1588–90) and the Chiesa Nuova (1575–1605). He also completed the Palazzo Altemps, built part of the Borghese Palace, and contributed a CASINO to the Villa MONDRAGONE in Frascati.

In 1612 Martino's son Onofrio (c.1569–1619) was appointed as architect of the Church of San Carlo al Corso in Rome; he was succeeded by his son Martino Lunghi the Younger (1602–57), who later built the baroque façade of SS Vicenzo ed Anastasio (1646–50).

*MDA* s.v. Longhi.

**LUTE**, a plucked fretted stringed instrument with a body shaped like half a pear, introduced to Europe by the Moors. A fifth course was added during the fifteenth century and by 1500 the range of the open strings was two octaves, produced by the addition of a sixth course. A hundred years later, it was not uncommon to find ten-course lutes, though some of these had been added to facilitate easier fingerings. The sound was originally produced with a plectrum, but this was abandoned in the mid-fifteenth century in favour of the fingertips, which allowed several lines to be played together. The lute could be used as an accompanying instrument, a solo instrument, and (as lutes came to be made in different sizes) as a consort instrument. Lute notation was written in tablatures of different kinds, according to country of origin.

**LUTHER, MARTIN** (1483–1546), founder of the German Reformation, born on 10 November 1483 in Eisleben (Saxony), the second son of Hans Luther, a prosperous peasant miner from Thuringia, and his wife Margarethe Ziegler. He was educated in the village school at Mansfeld, in a Magdeburg school managed by the BRETHREN OF THE COMMON LIFE, in St George's School in Eisenach and at the University of Erfurt. Six months after graduating in January 1505 he entered the Erfurt house of the Observantine Augustinians. He was ordained as a priest in 1507 and the following year became a lecturer in moral philosophy at the newly founded University of Wittenberg. In 1510 he was sent by his ORDER to Rome, where he seems not to have shown any of the disapproval of the secularism of the papal court that he was later to express. On returning to Wittenberg he was awarded a doctorate in theology and appointed professor of biblical studies at the university, a post that he held for the rest of his life. In 1515 he was made vicar of his Order, and so became responsible for eleven monasteries. In the years 1512–19 Luther developed his distinctive doctrine of JUSTIFICATION by faith alone; the notion that the doctrine was a sudden revelation (known as the *Turmerlebnis* or 'tower experience') is part of the Luther legend.

In 1516 Pope LEO X issued an INDULGENCE to finance the rebuilding of ST PETER'S BASILICA in Rome, and Johann TETZEL was charged by his archbishop ALBRECHT OF MAINZ with the responsibility for preaching the indulgence. On 31 October 1517 Luther responded to Tetzel's assurances that cash payments would automatically deliver donors from PURGATORY by posting his 95 Theses on indulgences on the door of the castle church in Wittenberg. The Latin text of the Theses was quickly translated into German, and within a month was being debated all over Europe. Luther was obliged to defend his position in the Heidelberg Disputation of April 1518; one of those persuaded by Luther's arguments was the Dominican Martin BUCER. In the same year Luther was tried for heresy (in his absence) in Rome and summoned to appear before Cardinal CAJETAN in Augsburg. He refused to recant, and sought refuge in Wittenberg under the protection of FRIEDRICH III, elector of Saxony. In 1519 Luther confronted Johann ECK in the LEIPZIG DISPUTATION. He was denounced and threatened with excommunication in the bull EXSURGE DOMINE (12 June 1520), and when Luther replied by publicly burning the bull in Wittenberg (10 December 1520), he was excommunicated by the bull *Decet Romanum pontificem* on 3 January 1521.

Luther's advocacy of ecclesiastical reform attracted the interest of learned HUMANISTS such as ERASMUS, and his tracts in German appealed to a broad audience within Germany. Three tracts published in the months before his excommunication were particularly influential. The first tract was *An den christlichen Adel deutscher Nation*, 'an address to the Christian nobility of the German nation' which urged the princes to summon a reformation Council of the Church and to abolish tributes to Rome and a variety of practices such as clerical celibacy and prayers for the dead. The second tract, which appeared in Latin as *De captivitate Babylonica ecclesiae* and in German as *Von der babylonischen Gefangenschaft der Kirche*, attacked the Catholic doctrine of the EUCHARIST both in theory (the doctrine of transubstantiation) and in practice (the denial to the laity of communion in both kinds); the metaphor of the Babylonian Captivity of the Church, which had been used by PETRARCH and other writers to describe the exile of the papacy in Avignon (1309–77), is used by Luther to denote the 'bondage' in which the Church had been held by Catholic teaching on the eucharist. The third tract, *Von der Freiheit eines Christenmenschen*, proclaimed 'the liberation of the Christian' from the bondage of works on the grounds that justification was achieved through faith alone.

In the wake of his excommunication Luther was summoned before the Diet of WORMS, where he again refused to recant and, according to a contemporary but unsubstantiated tradition, concluded his testimony with the words 'Hier stehe ich. Ich kann nicht anders. Gott helfe mir. Amen' ('Here I stand. I cannot do otherwise. God help me. Amen'). On 26 May 1521 the Edict of Worms formally condemned Luther, and to ensure his safety the elector arranged for Luther to be kidnapped and taken to the Wartburg (a castle near Eisenach which Luther described as his Patmos), where he lived for the next ten months under the pseudonym 'Junker Georg'. Luther took advantage of this enforced inactivity by embarking on his German translation of the New Testament, which was published in September 1522. The complete Bible, including Luther's translation of the Old Testament from the Hebrew, was published in 1534.

In Luther's absence from Wittenberg the town was seized by anticlerical agitation and iconoclasm, spearheaded by the preacher Gabriel ZWILLING and KARLSTADT. On his return to Wittenberg on 6 March 1522 Luther worked with the civic authorities to restore order and to reassert his leadership. He issued the FORMULA MISSAE ET COMMUNIONIS in December 1523 and the following year finally discarded his Augustinian habit. Johann Friedrich continued to uphold clerical celibacy, but his death in 1554 opened the way for priests, monks, and nuns to marry, and on 13 June 1525 Luther married the former Cistercian nun Katharina von Bora. During this period Luther alienated some of his natural supporters: in the PEASANTS' WAR he sided with the authorities against the peasants, and he fell out with Erasmus on the issue of free will, answering Erasmus' *De libero arbitrio* with the polemical *De servo arbitrio* (1525); similarly, his *Contra Henricum regum Anglicanum* (1522) attacked HENRY VIII's *Assertio septem sacramentorum adversus Martinum Lutherum* with such vehemence that Luther alienated his sympathizers in England.

The *Protestatio* at the Diet of SPEYER (1526) gave its name to Protestantism and also strengthened the Lutheran Reformation. Luther was forbidden by the imperial ban imposed by the Edict of Worms to attend the Diet of Augsburg in 1530, but nonetheless approved the AUGSBURG CONFESSION. His own SCHMALKALDIC ARTICLES articulated the doctrinal dispute with the Church of Rome. The doctrine of the eucharist, however, was beginning to dissolve the Reformed consensus, and it became apparent at the Colloquy of MARBURG (1529) that Luther and ZWINGLI could not be reconciled. The eucharistic controversy was to absorb much of Luther's polemical energy for the rest of his life. He also attracted criticism because of his covert endorsement of the bigamous marriage of PHILIP OF HESSE and of the appointment of Nikolaus von AMSDORF as bishop of Naumburg in 1541. He died on 18 February 1546 and was buried in the castle church in Wittenberg. His image is familiar because his portrait was repeatedly painted and engraved by CRANACH the Elder.

Luther wrote a large number of polemical works, two important catechisms (*Grosser Katechismus* and *Kleiner Katechismus*, both 1529), a series of biblical commentaries, and many HYMNS, of which the most famous is 'Ein' feste Burg ist unser Gott' ('A mighty fortress is our God', c.1528). His attack on the JEWS, *Von den Juden und ihren Lügen* (1543), is an important document in the history of German anti-Semitism. Luther's theology differs from the theology of LUTHERANISM as articulated in the Formula of CONCORD in several respects: in *De servo arbitrio*, for example, Luther defends the doctrines of double predestination and of God as the 'author of sin' (*auctor peccati*), both of which were subsequently adopted by Calvinists but rejected by Lutherans. His works have been collected in the 'Weimarer Ausgabe' an edition of more than 100 volumes (1883–1983) which has since 1986 been supplemented by a series of indexes and new editions, and in English translation as the 'Philadelphia edition' (55 vols., 1955–86).

Martin Brecht, *Martin Luther* (3 vols., 1981–7; English trans. 1985–92); Heiko A. Oberman, *Luther: Man between God and the Devil* (1989); A. G. Dickens, *The German Nation and Martin Luther* (1974).

**LUTHERANISM**, a confessional movement inaugurated by Martin LUTHER and his fellow reformers, distinguished from Catholicism, the churches loyal to CALVIN and ZWINGLI, and radical ANABAPTISM; in the sixteenth and seventeenth centuries, the Lutheran churches were often described as 'Evangelical', whereas the Calvinist churches were called 'Reformed'. The theology of Lutheranism, which is contained in the Book of CONCORD and affirmed by the AUGSBURG CONFESSION and the SCHMALKALDIC ARTICLES, centres on Luther's doctrine of JUSTIFICATION by faith and includes doctrines of the EUCHARIST, GRACE, and ADIAPHORA which distinguish Lutheranism from other churches.

After Luther's death in 1546, the movement divided. The GNESIO-LUTHERANS were led by Nikolaus von AMSDORF and Matthias FLACIUS ILLYRICUS; the Philippists (named after their leader, Philipp MELANCHTHON, 'Dr Philippus'), who were also known as crypto-Calvinists and Synergists, were accused by the Gnesio-Lutherans of covert Calvinism in their doctrine of the eucharist and of covert Catholicism in their SOTERIOLOGY; the latter issue was pursued through the 1550s and 1560s in the controversies about SYNERGISM, Majorism (see MAIER, GEORG) and Osiandrism (see OSIANDER, ANDREAS). Some measure of harmony was reached in the Formula of CONCORD of 1577.

In the course of the sixteenth century Lutheranism spread through Germany, Scandinavia, and the parts of eastern and central Europe not occupied by the Ottomans, though it later suffered reversals as countries such as POLAND and HUNGARY reverted (together with much of southern Germany) to Catholicism.

**LUXEMBURG or (French) Luxembourg**, a region in the Netherlands which was a duchy from 1354 till 1815, when it became a a grand duchy. On the death of the Emperor SIGISMUND in 1437, Luxemburg became a HABSBURG possession, because his daughter Elizabeth had married the Habsburg Emperor Albrecht II. In 1443 the duchy was seized by PHILIP THE GOOD, duke of Burgundy, who based his claim on an agreement with Elizabeth, niece of Sigismund. In 1477 Luxemburg reverted to the Habsburgs when Mary, daughter of CHARLES THE BOLD, married the Emperor MAXIMILIAN, and so eventually became part of the Burgundian inheritance of CHARLES V. The duchy remained part of the HOLY ROMAN EMPIRE (and so subject to GERMAN LAW) when it passed to PHILIP II of Spain in 1555.

The territories of the duchy included what is now the Belgian province of Luxemburg as well as the modern state of Luxemburg. The capital was (and is still) Luxemburg or Lützelburg (i.e. the little fortress). The language of Luxemburg, which is known as Luxemb(o)urgish or Lëtzebuergesch, is in its origins an outlier of the Moselle Franconian dialects of German, but centuries of contact with France and the southern Netherlands has arguably carried Luxemburgish across the ill-defined border between a dialect and a separate language.

The Palais du Luxembourg in Paris is so called because it stands on the site of the mansion of Duke Francis of Luxembourg-Piney, which MARIE DE MÉDICIS bought in 1612 in order to build her palace and gardens.

**LUZZASCHI, LUZZASCO** (c.1545–1607), organist and composer in Ferrara, where he was organist at the Este court, Ferrara Cathedral, and the Accademia della Morte. By 1570 he was responsible for the private *musica da camera* which included the famous singing ladies of FERRARA (*concerto delle donne*) for whom he composed the *Madrigali per cantare et sonare a 1–3 soprani* (1601). He was highly regarded as a composer and keyboard player whose influence was felt as far away as Rome and Naples; amongst his pupils was FRESCOBALDI.

**LYLY, JOHN** (c.1554–1606), English writer. Grandson of LILY, Lyly was educated at Oxford and Cambridge and served as an MP for three years from 1598. The distinctive style of his popular and digressive prose romance *Euphues: The Anatomy of Wit* (1578, 1580) gave rise to the term EUPHUISM. His satirical pamphlet *Pap with a Hatchet* (1589) defended the bishops in the MARPRELATE controversy. Among a number of plays written for children's acting companies are *Endymion* (1588), *Campaspe* (1583/4), and *Sappho and Phao* (1584).
*DNB.*

**LYON or (English exonym) Lyons or (Latin) Lugdunum**. The city of Lyon was in the early modern period confined to the peninsula at the confluence of the Rhône and the Saône; the two rivers met at what is now the Place Bellecour, which was built on land reclaimed in the eighteenth century. Lyon was a Roman town, and after periods of Burgundian and Frankish rule became a fiefdom of the HOLY ROMAN EMPEROR (1032); French rule was established in 1312, whereupon the town began to grow substantially; when the HUNDRED YEARS WAR disrupted commercial routes in northern France, Lyon became an important centre for business and commerce diverted from the north, including Italian banks. In the late fifteenth century Lyon became an important centre for the SILK industry and for printing: LOUIS XI granted a monopoly in silk in 1460 and settled Italian silk workers in the city in 1466, and the first printing press was established in 1466; by the end of the sixteenth century there were more than 40 presses, many run by German printers. It was also the foremost banking centre in France with many Italian bankers being represented there. The city's annual fairs expanded throughout the fifteenth and sixteenth centuries, and with increased wealth the arts flourished. During the WARS OF RELIGION Lyon was held by Protestants from 1562 and by Catholics after the ST BARTHOLOMEW'S DAY MASSACRE in 1572; under HENRI III the city was broadly supportive of the CATHOLIC LEAGUE, but was quick to support HENRI IV once he had been welcomed by Paris.
M. Bresard, *Les Foires de Lyon aux XVᵉ et XVIᵉ siècles* (1914).

**LYONESE BINDINGS**, a style of mid-sixteenth-century French BOOKBINDING, often (but not always) used to cover books printed in Lyon. Covers are typically decorated with polychrome STRAPWORK panels which are then painted, lacquered, or enamelled; some covers are decorated with ARABESQUES. The style was used in late sixteenth-century England, where bindings typically had a large central device and corner ornaments on a dotted ground. Unlike GROLIER BINDINGS, which were hand-tooled, Lyonese bindings were usually impressed with a panel stamp, a process that yielded considerable savings in labour with very little diminution of quality.

# M

**MACHIAVELLI, NICCOLÒ** (1469–1527), Italian political philosopher and dramatist, born in Florence, where in 1498 he entered the service of the republic as secretary to the TEN OF WAR; his duties included diplomatic missions to France (1500 and 1510), a visit to the camp of Cesare Borgia (October 1502–January 1503), where he witnessed the execution of Vitellozzo Vitelli, and missions to the court of Pope JULIUS II and the Emperor MAXIMILIAN I. On the restoration of the MEDICI in 1512 Machiavelli was abruptly dismissed because of his loyalty to the previous regime and his friendship with Piero SODERINI, and thereafter he lived in forced retirement on his small estate near San Casciano, 12 kilometres (7 miles) south of Florence.

In retirement Machiavelli had the leisure to write. His principal political and historical works were *Il principe* (1513; 'The Prince'), *Discorsi sopra la prima deca di Livio* (c.1516–19; a commentary on the first ten books of Livy), *Dell'arte della guerra* (1519–20; on the art of war), and *Istorie fiorentine* (c.1520–5; a history of Florence). He also wrote *Mandragola* (c.1518; 'The Mandrake Root'), the finest of Italian Renaissance comedies, satirical poems, a novella, and an impressive collection of letters.

The image of Machiavelli as the advocate of cruelty and deceit originates in part in the *Discours d'état contra Machiavel* (also known as the *Anti-Machiavel*) published in 1576 by Innocent Gentillet, a French Protestant magistrate living in exile in Geneva. Gentillet used Machiavelli's *Il principe* as a weapon against CATHERINE DE MÉDICIS, who had been implicated in the assassination of Gaspard COLIGNY. This tendentious reading of Machiavelli contributed to the image of 'Machevil', to whom Christopher MARLOWE attributed blasphemous sentiments in the prologue to *The Jew of Malta*, where Machevil says, 'I count religion but a childish toy'.

Such readings are an important part of the reception history of Machiavelli, but they occlude the principles on which *Il principe* rests. Machiavelli believed that experience (such as his own) in a harsh political world provided more workable solutions to political problems than did the application of an abstract moral code that worked from first principles rather than political reality. He also thought that the study of history enabled the advisers to the prince to base their counsel on patterns of political behaviour that extend back to classical antiquity. As a former servant of the republic, Machiavelli believed that republicanism was the best form of government for politically mature citizens living in a state with unchallenged boundaries, but thought that until such conditions could be met, princely government was a preferable alternative. As the citizen of a state surrounded by rival states that had a history of becoming enemy states, Machiavelli felt that military security should be the responsibility of local troops rather than foreign mercenaries whose loyalty was open to doubt. He also believed passionately in the need to observe sensitively and act decisively. These principles, which are the product of personal experience rather than the formulations of moral philosophy, underlie the statecraft of Machiavelli.

J. R. Hale, *Machiavelli and Renaissance Italy* (rev. edn. 1972); Sydney Anglo, *Machiavelli: A Dissection* (1969); Q. Skinner, *Machiavelli* (1981).

**MACHUCA, PEDRO** (d. 1550), Spanish architect and painter who worked as a painter in Italy before returning to Spain between 1517 and 1520. His *Madonna del sufragio* (now in the Prado), which is signed and dated 1517, seems to have been painted in Italy. In 1520, Machuca undertook the colouring of a carved reredos in Jaén Cathedral. He settled in Granada, where he worked as a painter of ALTARPIECES between 1521 and 1549; the surviving examples all contain Italian stylistic features.

Machuca's reputation as an architect rests on the palace of CHARLES V in the grounds of the Alhambra in Granada. The idea for the palace was mooted during the emperor's visit to Granada in 1526; construction began in 1531 and continued until 1568, but the original design was never fully realized. The structural features of the design are resolutely Italian, and are reminiscent of RAPHAEL and GIULIO ROMANO, but some of the decorative features, such as the garlanded window frames, are PLATERESQUE.

E. E. Rosenthal, *The Palace of Charles V in Granada* (1985); M. Gómez-Moreno, *Las águilas del Renacimiento español: Bartolomé Ordóñez, Diego Siloé, Pedro Machuca, Alonso Berruguete* (1941).

**MAÇIP, VICENT** (d. c.1550) and **JOAN VICENT** (c.1523–1579), Valencian painters. Vicent's principal work was the main ALTARPIECE at Segorbe Cathedral, which he finished in 1535.

Vicent's son and collaborator Joan Vicent, who is often known as Juan de Juanes, strengthened the Italianate influence on Valencian art. His *Assumption of the Virgin* in the Provincial Museum in Valencia, for example, is clearly influenced by the style of RAPHAEL. His best-known work is the altarpiece series depicting *The Life of St Stephen*, painted for the parish Church of St Esteve (Valencia) and now in the Prado.

*DBC*; *MDA*; J. Albi Fita, *Joan de Joanes y su círculo artístico* (1979).

**MACLODIO, BATTLE OF.** On 17 October 1427 a Venetian force under Francesco CARMAGNOLA defeated a Milanese army near Maclodio, a village 15 km (9 miles) south-west of Brescia. Venice had already captured Brescia, and this victory secured Bergamo and its territories.

**MADAMA, VILLA.** The Villa Madama is now absorbed into the north-eastern edge of Rome (close to the Olympic Stadium), but when it was built it lay well outside the city; it was the first Renaissance VILLA to be built outside the walls of Rome. The villa was commissioned by Cardinal Giulio de' Medici (later Pope CLEMENT VII) as a place for entertainment rather than habitation. The architect was RAPHAEL, who began work in 1516; after his death in 1520 the commission passed to Antonio da SANGALLO the Younger, whose drawings are preserved in the Uffizi. The decoration is the work of Raphael's two assistants, GIULIO ROMANO and GIOVANNI DA UDINE, who squabbled so much that the pope had to send an emissary to reconcile them; Cardinal Maffei discharged this task with difficulty, declaring both artists to be madmen. The villa was only partly completed when it was burnt during the SACK OF ROME in 1527. In about 1537 the house was bought by Princess Margaret of Austria, the illegitimate daughter of the Emperor CHARLES V and the young widow of Alessandro de' MEDICI; she is the *madama* from whom the villa takes its name. Margaret later married Ottavio FARNESE, through whom the villa eventually passed to the Bourbon kings of Naples. Most of the statuary disappeared in the occupation that followed the Sack of Rome, but one of the finest pieces, an ancient statue of Jove admired by Isabella d'ESTE when she was entertained at the Villa, survived and is now in the Caryatid Gallery of the Louvre.

The villa was intended to recreate the ideal Roman villa of classical antiquity. In Raphael's original design, it was conceived as a circular central court surrounded by a series of reception rooms and loggias. These external buildings merged into four distinct formal landscapes. The garden façade was on the east, which overlooked terraces and the Tiber valley, beyond which lay the city of Rome. To the south the large entrance court opened onto the main approach, which was a monumental staircase. To the west a loggia was supposed to have opened onto an open-air AMPHITHEATRE, hollowed out of Monte Mario in the Greek style, but this side of the building was never completed. To the north, a loggia led to terraced gardens which contain a *GIARDINO SEGRETO* that is the sole remnant of the original gardens; of the garden architecture all that survives is GIOVANNI DA UDINE's richly decorated Elephant Fountain; VASARI says that this fountain was carefully modelled on one in a recently excavated Temple of Neptune, but no such elephant's head is known to have survived. All that now remains of the main building is part of the central circle and the magnificent north loggia, which is richly decorated with frescoes and *stucchi*.

The villa was never completed, but it was, together with the BELVEDERE COURT, one of the most influential buildings of the Renaissance. It achieved an unprecedented integration of house and garden, and this design was copied in villas all over Italy.

Renato Lefevre, *Villa Madama* (1973); Guy Dewez, *Villa Madama* (1993).

**MADONNA.** See MARY.

**MADRID.** The city and archbishopric of Madrid, since 1607 the capital of Spain, was captured from the Moors in 1083, and remained a relatively obscure town until the fifteenth century, when King JOHN II of Castile convened a parliament in Madrid (1421) and his favourite Álvaro de LUNA established a residence in the town. In the sixteenth century CHARLES V made Madrid his occasional residence and gave it the sonorous title of Imperial y Coronada Villa, though the principal seats of his court remained in Valladolid and Toledo. In 1561 PHILIP II moved the court from Toledo to Madrid, which he declared to be his 'only court' (*única corte*). Madrid was greatly expanded in the seventeenth century during the reigns of PHILIP III (who built the Plaza Mayor) and Philip IV, but the finest buildings of Madrid were constructed by the Bourbon kings of eighteenth-century Spain. Although Madrid is the seat of an archbishop and the capital of Spain, it has through the centuries formally remained a town (*villa*) rather than a city (*ciudad*).

**MADRIGAL**, a popular and influential form of secular vocal polyphony of the sixteenth century; its main early composers were Philippe VERDELOT and Jacques ARCADELT, who set the words of humanist poets in a new refined and expressive style. In the hands of later composers such as Cipriano de RORE, Andrea GABRIELI, and Orlande de LASSUS the music became more imitative and attentive to the text until, with later composers (Claudio MONTEVERDI, Luca MARENZIO, Carlo GESUALDO), the style was altogether more mannered, using chromaticism, word painting, and dramatic writing for expressive effect. The madrigal also became popular in England through the works of Thomas MORLEY, Nicolas YONGE, Thomas WEELKES, and John WILBYE.

**MADRIGAL, ALFONSO DE, or El Tostado** (c.1400–1455), Spanish philosopher, theologian, and polymath, born in Madrigal (Ávila); his nickname does not derive from a sunburnt complexion but rather alludes to his father's name, Alfonso Tostado. Madrigal's extraordinary erudition won him a post as professor of theology in Salamanca, where his unorthodox views on the SACRAMENTS led to a dispute with the papalist theologian Juan de TORQUEMADA. Madrigal defended his views in Rome, where he impressed Pope EUGENIUS IV with his erudition. He returned to Salamanca and was rewarded by King JOHN II, who secured for him the bishopric of Ávila.

The corpus of Madrigal's writings is so large that it has become proverbial: a prolific writer is said *escribir más que El Tostado* ('to write more than El Tostado'). In Latin he wrote important commentaries on Genesis and Eusebius, and numerous treatises on subjects ranging from friendship and political theory to confession. His best-known vernacular works are *Las catorce cuestiones del Tostado* (on various scientific and moral issues including classical mythology) and a treatise on love.

**MADRUZZO, CRISTOFORO** (1512–78), Italian cardinal, a native of Trento, of which he became prince-bishop in 1539. He was consecrated cardinal in 1543 and two years later opened the first session of the COUNCIL OF TRENT. Madruzzo was more interested in politics than in religious controversy, and in 1556 his long-standing support for the HABSBURG family was rewarded with his appointment as governor of Milan by King PHILIP II. In 1567 he resigned his governorship and his see (the latter in favour of his nephew Ludovico Madruzzo) and retired to Rome.

**MAESTRI, ADRIANO DI GIOVANNI DE'.** See ADRIANO FIORENTINO.

**MAGDEBURG CENTURIES or (German) *Magdeburger Zenturien*,** the popular name for the *Ecclesiastica historia secundum singulas centurias*, the first Protestant history of the Church, which was published in Basel in thirteen parts between 1559 and 1574; the early volumes were published in German translation in Jena (1560–5). The project was financed by the Protestant princes of Germany. The title reflects the fact that it was composed in the Saxon city of Magdeburg and organized into periods of 100 years each.

The *Centuries* is the work of a group of Lutheran historians led by FLACIUS ILLYRICUS; members of the committee are called the Centuriators. It delineates the history of Christianity as a story of decline from the purity of the apostolic Church to the decadence of the Church in 1400; this degenerative process is deemed to have been reversed by the Lutheran revolt, which restored the Church to its early purity.

The Catholic response to the *Magdeburg Centuries* was the *Annales ecclesiastici* of Caesar BARONIUS, who exposed the flawed scholarship of the Centuriators, especially their practice of adapting the texts of early documents to support their arguments.

J. Massner, *Kirchliche Überlieferung und Autorität im Flaciuskreis: Studien zur den Magdeburger Zenturien* (1964); H. Scheible, *Die Entstehung der Magdeburger Zenturien* (1966)

**MAGELLAN, FERDINAND, or (Portuguese) Fernão de Magalhães or (Spanish) Fernando Magallanes** (1480–1521), Portuguese mariner, born into a noble family in Sabrosa (Vila Real) and educated at the Portuguese court. In 1505 he sailed to India with Francisco de ALMEIDA, the first viceroy, and remained in the East for seven years; in 1511 he fought under the command of ALBUQUERQUE in the attack on Malacca (on the Malay peninsula) and then sailed on to the Moluccas. In 1512 he returned to Portugal, and the following year was wounded in the leg in the conquest of Azemmour, in what is now Morocco; he limped for the rest of his life.

In Morocco Magellan had been accused of trading with the Moors, and although the allegation was eventually withdrawn, Magellan fell into disfavour with King MANUEL. He therefore decided to offer his services to Spain, where he married Beatriz Barbosa (the daughter of a Portuguese expatriate). He met CHARLES V in Valladolid and was given command of an expedition that was to seek a westerly route to the Moluccas, in compliance with the Treaty of TORDESILLAS, which had reserved the eastern route for the Portuguese. His first task was to find a way through or around the Americas.

On 20 September 1519 Magellan departed from Sanlúcar de Barrameda with a fleet of five ships. He sailed south along the coast of Brazil, explored the Río de la Plata estuary in the hope that it contained a route through America, and spent the southern winter (March–August 1520) at Puerto San Julián, on the coast of what is now Argentina; there he quelled a mutiny, executing one of his Spanish captains and marooning another, and met the indigenous people that he called Patagonians ('big feet'). In the spring he sailed south, where he discovered the straits that now bear his name (Estrecho de Magallanes, English Straits of Magellan) and spent five weeks (October–November 1520) negotiating a passage through to the South Sea (Mar del Sur), of which the eastern shore had previously been seen by a European when BALBOA crossed Panama seven years earlier. Magellan later called this sea the Océano Pacífico, with reference to the gentle winds that drove his fleet across the ocean. He called the principal island on the southern shore of the straits Tierra del Fuego ('Land of Fire'), with reference to the fires that he had seen from his ship.

The expedition, by now reduced to three ships, sailed west across the Pacific for fourteen weeks, suffering from hunger and scurvy, and finally made landfall on 6 March 1521 at Guam, an island (now an American possession) in the group now known as the Northern Mariana Islands and then known to the Spaniards as the Ladrones (i.e. the Islands of Thieves). They sailed on to the islands now known as the Philippines (named after PHILIP II of Spain), where, as in Guam, they were the first European visitors. The expedition then proceeded to Mactán, a tiny island off the coast of Cebu (Philippines), where on 27 April 1521 Magellan and 40 of his men were killed in a local war.

The survivors burnt one of their ships and sailed on the two surviving ships, the *Vitoria* and the *Trinidad*, to the Moluccas, where they established a trading station and took on cargoes of spices. The *Trinidad* set off to return to Portugal across the Pacific, but was captured by the Portuguese. The *Vitoria*, under the command of Sebastián del CANO, sailed across the Indian Ocean and round the Cape of Good Hope to the Atlantic, reaching Spain on 6 September 1522.

*DHP*; Charles Parr, *Ferdinand Magellan, Circumnavigator* (1964); Yvon Mauffret, *Fernão de Magalhães* (Portuguese trans. of French ed., 1994).

**MAGGI, GIROLAMO** (c.1523–1572), Italian scholar, poet, and engineer, born in Anghiari and educated at the universities of Perugia, Pisa, and Bologna. In 1560 Maggi settled in Venice, where he worked as a proofreader. In 1564 he wrote *Della fortificatione della citto*, a treatise on military engineering that proposed a series of defences for CYPRUS. He was dispatched to Cyprus to construct defences, and captured by the Ottomans at the fall of Famagusta in 1571; he died in captivity in Constantinople.

**MAGGINI, GIOVANNI PAOLO** (1580–c.1630), Italian maker of violins, who studied with Gasparo da Salò in Brescia. His instruments produced a darker and perhaps more responsive tone than those of the AMATI, which was to influence Stradivarius and other Cremonese makers as well as providing a model copied by French and German makers in the nineteenth century. His work in reducing the size of both the viola and the cello resulted in different members of the violin family producing a more homogeneous sound.

**MAGGIOR CONSIGLIO or (English) Greater Council**, the governing council of Venice, on which all adult male members of patrician families were entitled to sit in perpetuity. The restriction (*serrata*) to about 200 patrician families was formally agreed in 1297, and from 1325 the names of eligible members were recorded in the 'golden book' (*Libro d'oro*) maintained by the Council. Those listed in the *Libro d'oro* were also eligible for membership of the Venetian Senate, the college, and the COUNCIL OF TEN.

The republican government established in Florence during the exile of the MEDICI (1494–1512) established a council modelled on the Maggior Consiglio of Venice.

**MAGNIFICAT**, the liturgical text from Vespers, set polyphonically for use on Sundays and feast days. Fifteenth-century Magnificats such as those by DUFAY and BINCHOIS tended to be simple chordal settings in three parts with the canticle tone in the top part. A more elaborate style was evident in the sixteenth century when the tone was used as a *cantus firmus* with imitative techniques, generally in four parts. This technique was developed as the tone was paraphrased in the other voices (JOSQUIN DESPRÈS) and used for points of imitation (PALESTRINA). LASSUS developed a parody Magnificat, using *canti firmi* from unrelated, sometimes secular, sources. Ten of the 24 Magnificats from the ETON CHOIRBOOK (1490–1504) such as those by Robert Fayrfax (1464–1521) and Nicholas Ludford (1485–1557), are earlier examples of parody settings. The English style was characterized by three-voice settings, not on the canticle tone but using a plainchant *cantus firmus* in the middle voice and an improvised fa-burden in the tenor.

**MAGNY, OLIVIER DE** (1529–61), French poet associated with the PLÉIADE who wrote courtly love poetry in the style of RONSARD, collected as *Amours* (1553), *Gaietés* (1554), and *Soupirs* (1557).

**MAIER or Major, GEORG** (1502–74), Lutheran theologian, born in Nuremberg on 25 April 1502 and educated at the University of Wittenberg, where his teachers included LUTHER and MELANCHTHON. On graduating he taught at a school in Magdeburg (1529–37) before returning to Wittenberg, initially as a preacher at the court of the Elector JOHANN FRIEDRICH I and, from 1545, as a lecturer in theology at the university. In 1558 Maier succeeded Johannes BUGENHAGEN as dean of the faculty of theology, and retained this post for the rest of his life. He died in Wittenberg on 28 November 1574.

Maier is the eponym of the 'Majoristic Controversy' which erupted in the wake of the LEIPZIG INTERIM. Maier was attacked by Nikolaus von AMSDORF for his role in the Interim, and replied with *Auf des Ehrenwirdigen Herren Nicholaus von Amsdorf* (1552), in which he contended that good works were essential to holiness and so contributed to salvation. This view was roundly denounced by the GNESIO-LUTHERANS, including Amsdorf and FLACIUS ILLYRICUS, as a betrayal of the Lutheran doctrine of JUSTIFICATION by faith alone. In the ensuing controversy Maier reformulated his position, insisting that good works were only a manifestation of justification and that his opponents were wrong to construe his views as inconsistent with Luther's SOTERIOLOGY.

*NDB* s.v. Major; R. Kolb, 'Georg Major as Controversialist: Polemics in the Late Reformation', *Church History*, 45 (1976).

**MAINARDI, BASTIANO** (1466–1513), Italian painter, born in San Gimignano, the son of an apothecary, and trained in Florence by GHIRLANDAIO, whose sister he married. His principal work is a fresco cycle in the Cappella di San Bartolo in the Church of Sant'Agostino in San Gimignano. His surviving paintings include Madonnas in the Museo Civico in San Gimignano, the Museo Civico in Pisa, the National Gallery in London, and the Metropolitan Museum in New York.

*MDA.*

**MAIOLI BINDINGS**, a group of almost 100 BOOK BINDINGS made in Paris in the 1550s, possibly by the same craftsmen who supplied GROLIER BINDINGS. Each volume is stamped with the name 'Thos Maioli', who is probably Thomas Mahieu (Latin Maiolus), secretary to CATHERINE DE MÉDICIS and one of Jean Grolier's successors as treasurer of France. The sumptuous bindings are decorated with ARABESQUES and STRAPWORK, sometimes set against backgrounds in which gold has been rubbed into the leather.

G. D. Hobson, *Maioli, Canevari and Others* (1926).

**MAIOLICA**, the Italian name for TIN-GLAZED EARTHENWARE, which is known as FAIENCE in France, Germany, Scandinavia, and Spain and as DELFTWARE in Britain and the Netherlands; cognate terms exist in French (*majolique* and *maïolique*) and English (*majolica*). According to Julius Caesar SCALIGER, the term derives from the name of the island of Majorca (for which the medieval name was Majolica), which was the source of the finest earthenware; in fact Majorca was not the ultimate source of the pottery, which came from the Spanish mainland but was carried to Italy by Catalan merchants from Majorca.

The Italian maiolica of the fourteenth and fifteenth centuries was decorated with Gothic designs and painted green

and purple. In the last quarter of the fifteenth century, FLO-
RENCE POTTERIES and FAENZA POTTERIES began to develop new
designs (often with oak-leaf motifs) and to extend the colour
range to include orange and yellow.

In the sixteenth century the decorative patterns often consisted of allegorical figures, sometimes based on paintings.
Maiolica factories were established in many Italian centres,
including CAFAGGIOLO, CASTEL DURANTE, DERUTA, and MON-
TELUPO. The potters of Castel Durante developed a form of
display maiolica known as ISTORIATO ware, and in the 1550s
they began to introduce designs based on GROTESQUES by
RAPHAEL set against white backgrounds; in the nineteenth
century this maiolica came to be known in English as Raffaelle
ware or Raphael's ware, because it was (mistakenly) believed
that Raphael had painted some of the wares. In Faenza,
where white backgrounds soon came to dominate pottery
(and some tableware was entirely white), such wares were
called *bianchi di Faenza*.

The most important treatise on maiolica was Cipriano
PICCOLPASSO's *Tre libri dell'arte del vasaio* (1556–9).

G. Ballardini, *Corpus della maiolica italiana* (2 vol., 1933–8; repr.
1988); Timothy Wilson, *Ceramic Art of the Italian Renaissance*
(1987).

**MAITLAND, SIR RICHARD** (1496–1586), Scottish statesman, poet, and collector of poetry. After education at
St Andrews and Paris, Maitland became courtier to JAMES V,
and keeper of the seal under MARY, QUEEN OF SCOTS (1562–7).
His collection of poetry included his own largely satirical
works, as well as poems by William Dunbar, Gavin Douglas,
and Robert Henryson; the collection was continued by his
daughter, and is now at Magdalene College, Cambridge.

*DNB.*

**MAJESTÄTSBRIEF**, the royal charter granted to the ESTATES
of Bohemia on 9 July 1609 by the Emperor (and king of
Bohemia) RUDOLF II; the charter was extended to SILESIA on
20 July 1609. The charter granted freedom of religion, and so
offered protection to the LUTHERANS and UTRAQUISTS and the
Moravian Brethren (see UNITY OF THE BROTHERS) against
enforced Catholicism. Under the terms of the charter,
Protestants were allowed to build churches and schools and
to attend universities, and the Estates could elect 30 *defensors*
to guard these rights and to administer the Church and the
University of Prague.

The charter momentarily made Bohemia and Silesia the
most tolerant states in Europe, but the toleration was to be
short-lived. In January 1611 Rudolf suppressed the Estates
with an ill-disciplined army hired from his nephew, the
bishop of Passau. The Estates responded by transferring their
loyalty to Rudolf's brother MATTHIAS, who was elected as
king of Bohemia on 23 May 1611 and succeeded him as
emperor in 1612. The tensions that ensued eventually
erupted in the THIRTY YEARS WAR.

**MAJOR or Mair, JOHN** (1467–1550), Scottish theologian and
historian. Educated at Cambridge and Paris, Major became
doctor of theology at the latter before teaching logic and

theology at Glasgow and St Andrews from 1518. In 1525 he
returned to Paris. He published a *Commentary on the Sentences
of Peter Lombard* (published 1509–17) and *History of Greater
Britain, Both England and Scotland* (1521), both in Latin. He
was Scotland's last great exponent of medieval scholastic
learning.

*DNB.*

**MALATESTA, SIGISMONDO** (1417–68), ruler of Rimini,
born in Brescia, the illegitimate son of Pandolfo MALATESTA
(1370–1427). He became a *condottiere* and from 1433 to 1464
fought in virtually every war in the Italian peninsula, loyally
serving Pope EUGENIUS IV and Francesco SFORZA and disloy-
ally deserting King ALFONSO V of Naples (1447). His rejection
of unfavourable peace terms proposed by Pope PIUS II caused
the pope to excommunicate him (1460), and his murderous
hostility towards his neighbours, the MONTEFELTRO of Urbino
and the SFORZA of Pesaro, created an image of Malatesta as
perfidious and violent. This demonization was encouraged
by Pope Pius II, who in April 1462, in a ceremony that appears
to be unique in the history of the Church, formally consigned
Malatesta to HELL. After the siege of Fano in 1463, Malatesta
was deprived of all his territories except Rimini. Paradox-
ically, he then entered the service of Venice to fight the
Ottomans in southern Greece; he died in Rimini on 7 October 1468, aged 51. He had been married three times: first, to
Ginevra d'Este, daughter of Niccolò d'ESTE, lord of Ferrara;
second, to Polissena, daughter of Francesco Sforza; third, to
Isotta degli Atti.

Malatesta was a minor poet and a major patron of the
arts and military sciences. He commissioned ALBERTI to build
the Tempio Malatestiano in Rimini, which was decorated
by PIERO DELLA FRANCESCA (who painted the portrait of
Sigismondo kneeling before St Sigismund) and AGOSTINO DI
DUCCIO. His educated interest in FORTIFICATION was reflected
in his patronage of VALTURIO and in the large number of
fortified buildings which he commissioned, including his
Rimini seat, Castel Sismonde (1446).

Malatesta was accused by his contemporaries of treachery,
bestial cruelty, unconstrained immorality, and blasphemy,
and in the popular imagination he was for centuries seen as
the epitome of the evil Renaissance prince in whom refined
artistic tastes were belied by an essential lack of humanity.
These charges are somewhat overstated. His habit of changing sides was common practice amongst *condottieri*, and his
cruelty was no more extreme than that exercised by officials
such as inquisitors who operated under laws that sanctioned
TORTURE. His sexual immorality consisted of a passion for
Isotta degli Atti that began in his youth and remained constant through two marriages; for her sake he became a poet,
exalting her as Dante did Beatrice, and in 1456, seven years
after the death of his second wife, he married her. As for
blasphemy, Malatesta was certainly not pious, but he was not
enough of a speculative intellectual to contemplate atheism;
the theological significance of the enigmatic design of the
Tempio Malatestiano is not clear, and although some of its
decorative features are classical rather than Christian, their

The Tempio Malatestiano in Rimini. The building was commissioned by **Sigismondo Malatesta** (1450) and designed by Leon Battista ALBERTI. The interior was decorated by PIERO DELLA FRANCESCA and AGOSTINO DI DUCCIO. The façade was never finished

meaning is insufficiently understood to sustain a charge of impiety.

M. Tabanelli, *Sigismondo Pandolfo Malatesta* (1977).

**MALATESTA FAMILY**, a Romagnol family of *condottieri* and landowners that ruled Rimini from 1334 to 1500 and for two periods in the 1520s. In 1216 Rimini granted citizenship to the *condottiere* Giovanni Malatesta (d. 1247), who was elected *podestà* in 1237; he was succeeded as head of the family by his son Malatesta da Verrucchio (1212–1312), who was repeatedly elected *podestà* for long terms of office and lived to be 100. Malatesta had four sons: Malatestino (d. 1317), Giovanni Sciancato (d. 1304), Paolo (d. 1285), and Pandolfo (d. 1326).

Giovanni Sciancato ('the Lame') was a soldier in the service of Giovanni da Polenta of Ravenna, whose daughter Francesca was given to him in marriage. His bride, now Francesca da Rimini, had no affection for her husband and entered into an adulterous affair with her brother-in-law Paolo. The story of how Giovanni Malatesta surprised Francesca and Paolo and murdered them both is told by DANTE in the *Inferno* (canto 5) and repeated by PETRARCH in his *Trionfi*.

Malatesta da Verruchio was succeeded as lord of Rimini by Malatestino, after whose death in 1317 the lordship passed to Pandolfo, his only surviving brother. Pandolfo's two sons, Malatesta 'Guastafamiglia', whose epithet means 'destroyer of families', and Galeotto, inherited territories that included the inland towns of Cesena and Fossombrone as well as the coastal towns of Pesaro, Fano, and Rimini. In 1355 Pope Innocent VI dispatched the ruthless Cardinal Albornoz to subdue the Romagna, which he effected with his characteris-

tic brutality. In the settlement that followed, the Malatesta brothers were awarded a papal vicariate and divided their territories. Malatesta Guastafamiglia became lord of Pesaro, which his descendants held down to the brothers Carlo and Galeazzo. Carlo was the father of Parisina, who was beheaded in Ferrara; she is the eponym of Byron's poem. Galeazzo is known as 'l'Inetto' (the unfit), because he sold the lordship of Pesaro to the SFORZA in 1447.

Galeotto became lord of Rimini, and with the approval of the papacy added Cérvia, Cesena, and Bertinoro to his tiny empire. On his death in 1385, his elder son Carlo (1368–1429) became lord of Rimini and his younger son Pandolfo (1370–1427) became lord of Fano. Carlo enjoyed good relations with the papacy, and was appointed military captain of the Church and rector of Romagna; in the former capacity he helped to secure Lombardy after the death of Gian Galeazzo VISCONTI in 1402, and in the latter he contributed to the resolution of the GREAT SCHISM by receiving GREGORY XII at Rimini and acting as proctor for his abdication at the COUNCIL OF CONSTANCE in 1415. Carlo was an important patron of arts and letters, but his learned piety sometimes turned him against the classical tradition; in Mantua, where he enjoyed some authority through his marriage to Elisabetta GONZAGA, he ordered (1397) the destruction of a statue of VIRGIL on the grounds that it had become the object of a cult. He died without an heir, so his territories passed to his brother Pandolfo.

Pandolfo was a *condottiere*; he participated in the Lombard wars that followed the death of Gian Galeazzo VISCONTI in 1402 and for a time became ruler of Bergamo and Brescia. He left three illegitimate sons, Galeotto (1411–32), Sigismondo

(1417–68), and Novello (1418–65). On the death of Pandolfo in 1427, Pope MARTIN V averted a succession crisis by declaring the three boys to be legitimate and appointing Pandolfo's brother Carlo as regent. Galeotto died in 1432, bequeathing Rimini to his brother Sigismondo; Novello became lord of Cesena. On the rule of Sigismondo MALATESTA, see the separate entry.

In 1468 Sigismondo was succeeded by his widow Isotta and their son Sallustio (d. 1470), but the succession was disputed by an elder illegitimate son, the *condottiere* Roberto Malatesta (d. 1482), who was sent by Pope PAUL II to conquer Rimini on behalf of the papacy, and on arriving on 20 October 1469 told Isotta and Sallustio that he wished to rule conjointly with them. Pope Paul dispatched an army to depose Roberto, who, with the assistance of Duke FEDERICO II DA MONTEFELTRO of Urbino, managed to repel the papal army. The death of Paul II in 1471 removed the papal threat to Roberto's sovereignty, but he prudently strengthened his alliance with Urbino by arranging his betrothal to the daughter of Federico da Montefeltro. He then attended to his fellow rulers: on 8 August 1470 Sallustio was found murdered in a well, and a few months later Isotta died, apparently from poison; Isotta's surviving son Valerio was accused by Roberto of treason and then executed. In 1475 Roberto entered the service of the new pope, SIXTUS IV, on whose behalf he defended Rome against the duke of Calabria; he died of his wounds in 1482. His widow became regent of Rimini on behalf of their son Pandolfo (d. 1534).

On coming of age, Pandolfo consolidated his power by killing relatives who had contested his authority. He was a *condottiere* who distinguished himself in the fight against the French in the battle of FORNOVO. He fled Rimini when Cesare BORGIA was unleashed on Romagna by his father Pope ALEXANDER VI, but returned after the fall of the Borgias in 1503. He sold the lordship of Rimini to Venice in exchange for a cash payment, the promise of a pension, and the lordship of Cittadella. Pope JULIUS II retaliated by setting the League of CAMBRAI against Venice, which was defeated in 1509 at the battle of AGNADELLO. Having crushed Venice in battle, Julius then forged an alliance with the broken republic, together with Spain and the Swiss Confederation, and marched on the French army at Ravenna. France was the victor in the battle of Ravenna (1512), but the death of Gaston de FOIX soured the victory and forced the French army to withdraw. Pope Julius thereby became the new master of Rimini.

Pandolfo attempted to win back Rimini, but was repeatedly rebuffed, and in 1528 Pope CLEMENT VII stifled the final attempt by the Malatesta to return to the city, and two and a half centuries of Malatesta rule came to an end. On his death in 1534 Pandolfo left three indigent children, a daughter and two sons: the elder son, Sigismondo, was a *condottiere* who died at Reggio d'Emilia in 1543; the younger son, Malatesta, went to fight in the English and Scottish wars of the 1540s, and seems never to have returned to Italy. Sigismondo's sons attempted to regain Rimini in 1555, whereupon Pope PAUL IV formally deposed them in perpetuity. The Malatesta became citizens of Venice and were admitted to the MAGGIOR CON-

SIGLIO. The last member of the Rimini branch of the family was Christina Malatesta, who died in 1716.

Gino Franceschini, *I Malatesta* (1973); P. Jones, *The Malatesta of Rimini* (1974).

**MALDONADO, JUAN** (c.1485–1554), Spanish humanist and vicar-general of Burgos. Maldonado's first published work (*Paraenesis ad politiores literas adversus grammaticicorum vulgus*, 1529) was a defence of humanist studies which included an indirect attack on the philological pedantry of his rival Antonio de LEBRIJA, together with a fanfare, again indirect, for the ethical ideal of his admired mentor ERASMUS. Maldonado's own works constitute the most original Spanish contribution to Renaissance neo-Latin literature; they range from Ciceronian moral and spiritual treatises of an Erasmian cast (*De felicitate christiana* and *Praxis sive de lectione Erasmi*, both 1541; *De senectute christiana* and *Paradoxa*, both 1550) to poetry and drama on historical and moral themes (*Hispaniola*, 1535; *Chartarum triumphans* and *Desponsa cauta*, both 1541; *Pastor bonus*, *Tridunus*, and *Geniale iudicium sive Bacchanalia*, all 1550), a remarkable Lucianic dream-vision of Spain's utopia (or dystopia) in the New World (*Somnium*, 1541), a history of the Revolt of the COMUNEROS (*De motu Hispaniae*), and an elegant humanist reworking of *Vitae sanctorum* (1550).

Juan Maldonado is sometimes confused with his Jesuit namesake Juan MALDONADO.

Eugenio Asensio and Juan Alcina Rovira, *Paraenesis ad litteras: Juan Maldonado y el humanismo español en tiempos de Carlos V* (1980); Heliodoro García García, *El pensamiento comunero y erasmista de Juan Maldonado* (1983).

**MALDONADO, JUAN** or **(Latin) Maldonatus** (1533–83), Spanish biblical commentator. He was educated at the University of Salamanca and entered the JESUIT Order in 1562. In 1564 he became a professor at the Collège de Clermont, the Jesuit College in Paris. His lectures on theology attracted huge audiences, and he became a notable opponent of Calvinism. In 1574 he was accused of malpractice in recruiting novices, but was exonerated by the Parlement of Paris. In 1576 Maldonado was sent to Toulouse, but accusations of rash opinions and pride forced him to resign his teaching post, whereupon he withdrew to Bourges to devote himself to biblical studies; he was later appointed by Pope GREGORY XIII to the Roman commission charged with the revision of the Septuagint (the Greek version of the Old Testament).

In his exegetical writings Maldonado repudiated the arcane language and methodology of traditional commentaries in favour of a marked clarity of expression and simplicity of approach. His *Commentarii in quatuor Evangelistas* (2 vols., 1596) was, like all his writings, published posthumously, and was rightly valued by succeeding generations. The textual accuracy of some of Maldonado's writings is problematical, because they derive from notes taken by his students at lectures.

Juan Maldonado is sometimes confused with his humanist namesake Juan MALDONADO.

**MALESPINI, CELIO** (1531–*c*.1609), Venetian *condottiere* and translator who served as a soldier in the Spanish army in the Netherlands during the REVOLT OF THE NETHERLANDS and later fought in Italy. He translated the *Trésor* of Brunetto Latini (Dante's friend) from French to Spanish and Antonio de TORQUEMADA's *Jardín de flores curiosas* from Spanish to Italian. His collection of 202 tales (*Duecento novelle*, Venice, 1609) combined reworkings of BOCCACCIO with original stories.

**MALHERBE, FRANÇOIS DE** (1555–1628), French poet, born in Caen (Normandy), the son of a Protestant lawyer. He was educated in Basel and Heidelberg, and in 1577, having converted to Catholicism, entered the service of Henri, duke of Angoulême, in Aix-en-Provence; he was to live in Provence 1577–86 and 1595–1605, with the intervening years in Caen. In 1605 Malherbe was appointed court poet by HENRI IV (on the recommendation of Guillaume DU VAIR) and after the king's death in 1610 was confirmed in this post by MARIE DE MÉDICIS.

Malherbe's early poetry, such as his baroque *Les Larmes de saint Pierre* (1587), was in its learned diction heavily influenced by the PLÉIADE. His later poems repudiate such diction in favour of a clarity of style and thought that was to be an important model for French poetry in the seventeenth century; he was later to be hailed by Nicolas Boileau-Despréaux with the phrase 'Enfin, Malherbe vint!' as the founder of the classical style. His writings in prose include translations, letters, and a hostile commentary on the poetry of Philippe DESPORTES in which he articulates the principles of his reform of French poetry.

Gilles Henry, *François de Malherbe* (1984).

**MALOUEL, JEAN** (*c*.1365–1415), Flemish painter, probably a native of Nijmegen; he worked in Paris before being appointed in 1397 as court painter to the court of the dukes of Burgundy in Dijon, working first for Philip the Bold and then for Philip's successor John the Fearless. His principal surviving works, both of which are attributions, are a *Martyrdom of St Denis* and a *Pietà* tondo, both now in the Louvre.

BNB; MDA.

**MALTA.** From the thirteenth century Malta was ruled by the Aragonese kings of Sicily through a Consiglio Popolare that administered the will of the kings (including the expulsion of the JEWS in 1492) but had no legislative powers. In 1530 the Emperor CHARLES V presented Malta, Gozo, and Tripoli (now the capital of Libya) to the Order of the Knights of ST JOHN; the Order remained in Malta until 1798, but from 18 May to 8 September 1565 had to defend themselves against an Ottoman siege.

The principal literary language of Malta was Latin. The oldest known poem in Maltese, which was discovered in 1968, is a Maltese version of the Latin *Cantilena* composed by the Maltese notary Pietro Caxaro (1438–85).

**MANARA, BALDASSARE** (*fl.* 1526, d. 1546/7), Italian MAIOLICA painter in Faenza whose signed ISTORIATO work includes a bowl decorated with a *Triumph of Time* in the Ashmolean Museum in Oxford.

MDA.

**MANDER, KAREL** or **Carel VAN** (1548–1606), Flemish painter, poet, and biographer, trained in the Ghent School established by Lucas de HEERE and then by Pieter Vlerick (1539–81) in Kortrijk (Courtrai) and Tournai (Doornik). In 1583 he settled in Haarlem, where he worked as a religious and allegorical painter and together with Cornelis CORNELISZOON and Hendrik GOLTZIUS founded an academy.

In 1604 Mander published *Het schilderboeck* ('The Painter's Book'), a three-part handbook for artists which forms the basis of his reputation as the 'Dutch VASARI'. The first part consists of biographical accounts of some 175 Netherlandish and German artists from Jan van EYCK to Mander's contemporaries; this was the first collection of biographies of north European artists and is in some cases a unique source of information. The second part is an abbreviated translation into Dutch of the second edition of Vasari's *Lives* (1568) and also contains accounts of more recent Italian artists; material for this continuation of Vasari was for the most part assembled when Mander lived in Italy (1573–7) but also draws on information derived from his network of friends and correspondents. The third and final part of the book, entitled *Lehrgedicht*, is a long poem in fourteen parts; much of the poem mediates between the views of Italian theorists and the practical needs of young Dutch artists, and some parts, such as the material on LANDSCAPE painting, are Mander's original work.

BNB s.v. Mander, Charles van; *MDA*; *NBW* xi.

**MANETTI, GIANOZZO** (1396–1459), Italian humanist. He was born into a prominent banking family in Florence, where he entered the political life of the republic. In 1453 Manetti resigned his civic posts and left for Rome, where he entered the service of Pope NICHOLAS V, for whom he prepared a Latin translation of the Greek text of the New Testament. In the final years of his life he lived in Naples at the court of ALFONSO V.

Manetti's works, which are suffused with his formidable knowledge of Latin, Greek, and Hebrew, include historical accounts of Pistoia and ancient Greece and biographies of ancient and contemporary figures. The fullest statement of his humanist principles is his Neoplatonic and Hermetic treatise *De dignitate et excellentia hominis* (first published in Basel in 1532).

OCIL.

**MANFREDI, BARTOLOMEO** (1582–1622), Italian painter, born near Mantua and trained in Rome. His depictions of gamblers, fortune-tellers, and soldiers, which derive from CARAVAGGIO's early paintings, became one of the conduits through which Caravaggio's subjects and his dramatic CHIAROSCURO were transmitted to painters from the Netherlands and France.

MDA.

**MANFREDI FAMILY**, Romagnol family that emerged as a military and political force in the thirteenth century and became lords of Faenza (1313–1501), papal vicars (from 1412), and counts of Val di Lamone. In 1377 Astorre I Manfredi was elected *signore* of Faenza. Astore II Manfredi (ruled 1448–68) and Carlo II Manfredi (ruled 1468–77) were both important patrons of education, the arts, and urban renewal. Galeotto Manfredi (ruled 1477–88) encouraged the production of MAIOLICA, of which Faenza became an important centre; the term FAIENCE derives from 'Faenza'. Galeotto extended his patronage to the visual arts and also assembled a LIBRARY that was remarkable by the standards of the late fifteenth century. Galeotto was assassinated, apparently with the connivance of his wife, who resented her husband's mistress. Their young son Astorre III (ruled 1488–1501) sought the protection of Venice, but in April 1501 Cesare BORGIA captured Faenza after a protracted blockade and ended the rule of the Manfredi family; in June 1502 Astorre and the last legitimate members of the family were drowned in the Tiber. Faenza was held briefly by Venice and in 1509 was absorbed into the PAPAL STATE.

*MANIÈRE CRIBLÉE* (French; 'dotted manner'), a term deriving from the word *crible* (sieve), denoting a type of relief ENGRAVING on metal (usually copper) that first appeared in the mid-fifteenth century. The prints, which resemble nineteenth- and twentieth-century wood engravings, consist of a white design made from lines and dots set against a dark background. The lines were engraved with a burin and the dots were added with punches of various sizes.

Plates engraved in the *manière criblée* were sometimes used to make paste prints, a type of embossed print in which the raised portions have a contrasting colour.

**MANNERISM**, the art-historical term used to designate the style of Italian art from the 1520s to the 1590s; it is therefore the style that follows the RENAISSANCE style and precedes the BAROQUE. The term derives from Italian *maniera*, which was used by VASARI to denote the style of artists who produced works of idealized grace (*grazia*) in the elegant 'manner' of MICHELANGELO. In the nineteenth century Mannerism became an issue in the debates between German cultural historians about stylistic periods in art and literature. In the view of historians such as Heinrich Wölfflin, Mannerism was tainted with the notion of degeneracy, and represented a decline from the standards achieved by RAPHAEL. A subsequent generation of German historians, led by Max Dvořák, portrayed Mannerism as a European movement that began with late Michelangelo and culminated in the religious vision of El GRECO. In the second quarter of the twentieth century, nationalist historians attempted to reclaim Mannerism for Germany by representing it as a revival of the Gothic spirit.

The notion of a repudiation of the ideals of Raphael and early Michelangelo by the artists of the period 1530 to 1590 is a fiction invented to support a historiographical theory. Such artists were not, however, content merely to replicate the achievements of their predecessors. The importance of NEOPLATONISM in sixteenth-century thought encouraged a movement away from realism towards idealism and fantasy, and also encouraged a taste for novelty (which reached its apogee in ARCIMBOLDO and the court of RUDOLF II) and for esoteric allusion. In the representation of figures, mannerist artists developed the ascending corkscrew (or *figura serpentina*) of Michelangelo into an ideal of etiolated elegance typified in the paintings of PARMIGIANINO and PONTORMO and the statuary of GIAMBOLOGNA as represented in *The Rape of the Sabine Women* in the Loggia dei Lanzi in Florence. In France, *maniérisme* was introduced through the decoration of FONTAINEBLEAU by Il ROSSO FIORENTINO and PRIMATICCIO.

Mannerism is also used as a term in architectural history, and is used of sixteenth-century buildings in which motifs are used in deliberate opposition to their original purposes and contexts. The most important Italian mannerist architects are Michelangelo (especially his Biblioteca LAURENZIANA in Florence, which has columns that carry no cornices), GIULIO ROMANO (especially his Palazzo del TÈ in Mantua, which has keystones out of line and twisted pilasters), VIGNOLA (especially his Villa FARNESE and Villa GIULIA), LIGORIO (especially the *CASINO* of Pope PIUS IV), VASARI (especially the UFFIZI), Jacopo SANSOVINO, and SANMICHELE. In France, the principal mannerist architects were Jean BULLANT and Jacques Androuet DUCERCEAU the Elder.

W. F. Friedlander, *Mannerism and Anti-Mannerism in Italian Painting* (1957); John Shearman, *Mannerism* (1967).

**MANRIQUE, GÓMEZ** (*c*.1412–*c*.1490), Spanish playwright and poet, the nephew of the marquis of SANTILLANA and the uncle of the soldier and poet Jorge MANRIQUE. He fought against the army of Álvaro de LUNA at the battle of Olmedo (1445), where his side was defeated, and took part in the rebellions against Kings JOHN II (Juan II) and HENRY IV (Enrique IV) of Castile, fighting on the side of the infantes of Aragon, Prince Alfonso and his sister Princess Isabella. In 1465 he defended Ávila against the pretender Prince Alfonso, and in 1470 was among the Castilian noblemen who forced Henry IV to sign the Treaty of Toros de Guisando, by which Princess (later Queen) ISABELLA of Castile was designated as heir to the throne of Castile. When FERDINAND and Isabella succeeded to the throne in 1474, Manrique was appointed as their representative (*corregidor*) in Toledo.

Manrique's poetry is by turns satirical, amorous, and memorial. His finest satires, which are directed against the government of Henry IV and the archbishop of Toledo, are *Exclamación y querella de gobernación* and *Coplas para Diego Arias de Ávila*. He wrote an elegy in *arte mayor* (an irregular anapaestic metre) entitled *Defunción del muy noble Garci Lasso de la Vega*, which set a pattern for future funerary poems, and, perhaps his finest work, a consolation to his wife on the death of their children from the plague.

Manrique's plays are among the earliest examples of drama in Spanish. They include *La representación del Nacimiento de Nuestro Señor*, a Christmas play written for the convent of Calabozanos (where his sister was abbess), and a Holy Week play called *Lamentaciones hechas para Semana Santa*, a dramatic

493

elaboration of the liturgical *Planctus Mariae* in which the crucified Jesus is mourned with the refrain *¡Ay dolor!* Manrique also wrote allegorical masquerades (*momos*) to celebrate the birth of his nephew Jorge and the fourteenth birthday of Prince Alfonso; in the latter play, which was performed at Arévelo in 1467, Princess (later Queen) Isabella was one of the participants in what was to be her only recorded performance as an actor.

Kenneth Scholberg, *Introducción a la poesía de Gómez Manrique* (1984).

**MANRIQUE, JORGE** (1440–79), Spanish poet and soldier, born in Paredes de Nava. He was the son of Rodrigo Manrique, count of Paredes and grand master of the military ORDER of Santiago, and the nephew of the playwright and poet Gómez MANRIQUE. Like his father and uncle, he fought on the side of the infantes of Aragon, Don Alfonso and (after his death) Princess (later Queen) ISABELLA, against HENRY IV (Enrique IV). He died in battle, fighting against the forces of the king's favourite, the marquis of Villena, before the walls of the castle of Garci-Muñoz.

Manrique's poetry consists of some 50 lyric poems and a long elegy on his father, *Coplas por la muerte de su padre* (composed 1476, published in Seville in 1494). The elegy, which is written in the *coplas de pie quebrado* (broken-foot stanzas) popularized by the marqués de SANTILLANA (Manrique's great-uncle), is a meditation on death that transcends the conventional expression of the brevity and vanity of human life to celebrate Count Rodrigo's worldly and spiritual achievements; it has become the best-known poem in the Spanish language.

Pedro Salinas, *Jorge Manrique, o tradición y originalidad* (1947).

**MANSFELD FAMILY**, a German dynasty seated in Mansfeld (Saxony) from the eleventh century till 1780, when it became extinct. The counts (*Grafen*) of Mansfeld included Albrecht III (1480–1560), the territorial lord of LUTHER's family. Albrecht became a friend of Luther and was one of the first German princes to declare for the Reformation; in 1525 he helped to crush the PEASANTS' REVOLT and in 1531 he joined the SCHMALKALDIC LEAGUE. His kinsman Johann Gebhard (who is sometimes confused with Albrecht's brother Gebhard) was elector of Cologne from 1558 to 1562.

A collateral branch of the Mansfeld family produced distinguished soldiers, including Prince (*Fürst*) Peter Ernst (1517–1604), the governor of Luxemburg, who fought for CHARLES V (in Tunis and France) and PHILIP II (in France and the Netherlands) and succeeded Alessandro FARNESE as governor-general of the Spanish Netherlands. His illegitimate son Prince Ernst von Mansfeld (c.1580–1626) was one of the greatest commanders of the THIRTY YEARS WAR.

NDB.

**MANSUETI, GIOVANNI DI NICCOLÒ** (*fl.* 1485–1526/7), Italian painter who spent his working life in Venice, of which he may have been a native; he was trained in the studio of Gentile BELLINI. He was, like CARPACCIO, one of the first artists to paint townscapes, and his large paintings depict contemporary Venetian architecture and costume with an attentiveness to detail that gives them considerable documentary value. His finest surviving painting is *The Miracle of the True Cross* (1494, Accademia di Belli Arti, Venice).

MDA.

**MANTEGNA, ANDREA** (1430/1–1506), Italian painter, engraver, and antiquarian, born near Vicenza, and trained in the Paduan studio of Francesco SQUARCIONE. He lived in Padua until 1460, during which time he developed the mastery of foreshortening that is one of the most remarkable features of his art. His paintings from this period include a triptych of *The Madonna and Saints* for the Church of San Zeno Maggiore in Verona (1459), one of the finest fifteenth-century altarpieces to have survived in its entirety, and his fresco cycle on *The Lives of SS Christopher and James* in the Ovetari Chapel of the Church of the Eremetani in Padua (1459); the church was badly damaged in 1944, and the frescoes now survive only in fragments.

In 1460 Mantegna was appointed court painter to the Gonzaga family in Mantua, where his finest work was the decoration (completed 1474) of the Camera Depicta (known since 1648 as the Camera degli Sposi) in the Castello San Giorgio. Group portraits of the GONZAGA FAMILY are arranged on two walls, culminating in the depiction of Marquis Ludovico II GONZAGA and his wife Barbara of Brandenburg listening to the reading of an apostolic letter announcing the appointment of their son Francesco as a cardinal. The wholly unprecedented achievement of the room is the illusion that the actions depicted on the paintings on the walls appear to be happening within and outside the space of the room; this illusion is even extended to the ceiling, which has an oculus that depicts the sky framed by a balcony from which figures leaning over the rails look down into the room.

In 1486 Mantegna began to work on a cycle of nine large paintings on *The Triumph of Caesar*; these paintings were bought by King Charles I of England in 1628 and are now at Hampton Court. Mantegna's allegorical paintings of *Parnassus* (1497) and *The Triumph of Virtue* (c.1500), both now in the Louvre, were painted for Francesco's marchioness, Isabella d'ESTE.

In 1453 Mantegna married the daughter of Jacopo BELLINI, and thereafter became a formative influence on Giovanni BELLINI, his brother-in-law. Their respective versions of *The Agony in the Garden* hang on the same wall in the National Gallery in London.

MDA.

**MANTOVANO, BATTISTA, or Giovanni Battista Spagnoli or (English) Mantuan** (1448–1516), Italian Carmelite and neo-Latin poet, born in Mantua and educated in Padua. He joined the Discalced Carmelite Order, and in 1483 became its vicar-general in Mantua; in 1513 he became general of his Order. He was canonized in 1883.

Mantovano was the author of ten Latin pastoral eclogues (published 1498), of which eight were composed while he was a student in Padua and two after he had become a Carmelite friar. These eclogues achieved a European

The Camera Picta in Castello di San Giorgio, Mantua, painted by **Andrea Mantegna**

**Andrea Mantegna**, *The Agony in the Garden* (c.1460), in the National Gallery, London

reputation, and were widely imitated; in England they were an important influence on SPENSER's *Shepherd's Calendar.* Mantovano also wrote a collection of seven hymns in praise of the Virgin (*Pathenices*, 1481) and a treatise deploring secular humanist culture (*De calamitatibus nostrorum temporum*).

*OCIL.*

**MANTUA or (Italian) Mantova**, a Lombard city and episcopal see on the river Mincio, ruled from 1328 to 1627 by members of the GONZAGA FAMILY. The city is built in the loop of the river at a point where it consists of swampy lakes that surround the city on three sides, and has a marsh on the fourth side; in the early modern period Mantua was effectively a pair of islands separated by a narrow channel (the Argine del Mulino) that was bridged at several points. The natural fortification of Mantua's location has been reinforced by walls since at least the sixth century.

Mantua was one of the most important cultural centres of Renaissance Italy. Its court, which reached its apogee under Isabella d'ESTE, received ALBERTI, ARIOSTO, BEMBO, BOIARDO, CASTIGLIONE, the Emperor CHARLES V, GIULIO ROMANO, LEONARDO, MANTEGNA, PETRARCH (who famously described Mantua as foggy and full of frogs), Pope PIUS II, PLATINA, POLIZIANO, POMPONAZZI, PRIMATICCIO, RAPHAEL, Rubens, TASSO, TITIAN, and VITTORINO DA FELTRE, and the quality of its musical life exceeded that of any other city of comparable size. The appropriation of VIRGIL (who was born near Mantua) as a cultural ancestor was asserted in 1225, when the statue of Virgil (seated) was erected on the façade of Palazzo Broletto.

Mantua was sacked in 1630, shelled by Napoleon in 1796/7, and badly damaged in the Second World War, but many of its finest Renaissance buildings survive. The cathedral was redesigned by GIULIO ROMANO and constructed after his death. Similarly, the Church of Sant'Andrea was designed by Alberti and constructed after his death by Luca Fancelli; it contains the tombs of Pietro STROZZI (designed by Giulio Romano) and Mantegna. Three important Gonzaga buildings are grouped together close to the cathedral: the Palazzo Ducale, the Castello San Giorgio (which contains the celebrated Camera degli Sposi with frescoes by Mantegna) and the ducal Capella di Santa Barbara. The Palazzo del TÈ and the Palazzo San Sebastiano are suburban palaces outside the walls.

*Mantova: La storia, le lettere, le arti* (9 vols., 1958–63); Iain Fenlon, *Music and Patronage in Sixteenth-Century Mantua* (2 vols., 1980–2).

**MANTUAN.** See MANTOVANO, BATTISTA.

**MANTZ, FELIX** (*c.*1500–1527), Swiss ANABAPTIST, a priest who in 1519 became a supporter of ZWINGLI and in 1523 joined a group of radicals led by Conrad GREBEL. In January 1525 the first ceremony of believers' BAPTISM took place at his house near Zürich. Mantz was imprisoned and subsequently banished, but returned and again began to attack infant baptism and advocate believers' baptism. He was recaptured and judicially executed by drowning on 5 January 1527.

*DHBS; ADB.*

**MANUEL, NIKLAS, or Niklas Manuel Deutsch** (*c.*1484–1530), Swiss painter, poet, playwright, and anti-Catholic polemicist, a native of Bern, where in 1512 he became a member of the city council. As a young man he worked as a painter, executing ALTARPIECES, murals, drawings, and woodcuts (now mostly in the Basel Kunstmuseum) in the style of the Italian Renaissance. In 1522 he joined a military expedition to Italy; on his return, he became a propagandist for the Reformation. He attacked the sale of INDULGENCES and masses for the dead in two plays performed in 1523, *Vom Papst und seiner Priesterschaft* (also known as *Die Totenfresser*) and *Von Papsts und Christi Gegensatz*, and renewed his attack on the sale of indulgences in *Der Ablaßkrämer* (1526) and *Testament der Messe* (1528).

Manuel's most famous painting, a *Dance of Death* painted for the Dominican monastery in Bern, did not survive and is known only from copies. His preoccupation with death and with the DANCE OF DEATH is evident also in his surviving drawings.

Hans Rudolf Manuel (1525–71), the sixth son of Niklas, was the author of a FASTNACHTSPIEL known as *Die Weinspiel* (1548), a 4,000-line celebration of wine.

*DHBS; MDA* s.v. Deutsch; *NDB*; on Hans Rudolf, see *ADB.*

**MANUEL I or (English) Emanuel** (1469–1521), king of Portugal, was born near Setúbal; his parents were Duke Fernando of Viseu and Beatriz de Beja, who were both grandchildren of King JOHN I (João I) of Portugal. In 1495 Manuel succeeded his cousin JOHN II (João II) as king, and two years later he married Isabella, daughter of FERDINAND V and ISABELLA and the widow of Prince Afonso, the heir of King John II. Queen Isabella died in childbirth in 1496, and her son Miguel died two years later. In 1500 Manuel married Maria, another daughter of Ferdinand and Isabella; two of their sons, João and Henrique, later became kings of Portugal (JOHN III and Cardinal-Prince HENRIQUE). Maria died in 1516 and two years later King Manuel married her niece Eleanor, sister of the Emperor CHARLES V.

King Manuel was the patron of Portuguese expansion during the period when Portuguese navigators, building on the programme of exploration initiated by HENRY THE NAVIGATOR, achieved their most remarkable successes, including Vasco da GAMA's establishment of the sea route to India, Pedro CABRAL's adventitious landing in Brazil, and Gaspar CORTE REAL's establishment of a Portuguese presence in Newfoundland. Manuel expelled the JEWS from Portugal, urged a crusade against the Muslim Ottomans, and in his burgeoning overseas possessions initiated missionary enterprises. His lavish patronage of ecclesiastical architecture included the erection of 26 monasteries and two cathedrals, notably the Hieronymite monastery (Mosteiro dos Jerónimos) at Belém, the harbour of Lisbon.

Manuel is the eponym of the MANUELINE style of architecture and architectural decoration and of the Manueline Ordinances (Ordenações Manuelinas), the reformed legal code of Portugal.

*DHP.*

**MANUEL II PALAIOLOGOS** (1350–1425), Byzantine emperor. Manuel was the second son of the Emperor John V Palaiologos; after the rebellion of his elder brother Andronicus IV in 1373, Manuel was named co-emperor and emperor-designate (αὐτοκράτωρ). In 1376 Andronicus again rebelled, and this time occupied Constantinople, where Manuel and his father were imprisoned until 1379. John V was forced to designate Andronicus as his heir in 1381; Manuel was excluded from the succession, and retreated to Thessaloniki, where he ruled as an independent emperor from 1382 until the Turkish conquest of April 1387. On the death of Andronicus in 1385, Manuel supported John V against the rival claim of John VII (the son of Andronicus), and eventually succeeded John as emperor in 1391. Manuel attempted to sue for peace with the Turks, but also sought military assistance to fight them. A CRUSADE was raised on his behalf, but the army of SIGISMUND was defeated by the forces of Beyazit at Nicopolis (now Nikopol, Bulgaria) in 1396. From 1399 to 1403 Manuel travelled in western Europe in search of further military aid to fight the Turks, who besieged Constantinople from 1394 to 1402.

Manuel was scholarly and contemplative (he became a monk shortly before he died), and his literary skills are attested in a wide range of writings, which include theological treatises, rhetorical exercises (including a description of a TAPESTRY now in the Louvre), and, most famously, his 68 literary letters, which describe his travels in Europe, the Ottoman conquest of Turkey, and contemporary literature.

*The Letters of Manuel II Palaeologus*, ed. G. T. Dennis (1977);
J. W. Barker, *Manuel II Palaeologus (1391–1425): A Study in Late Byzantine Statesmanship* (1969).

**MANUELINE**, a style of PORTUGUESE ARCHITECTURE and architectural decoration named after King MANUEL I, with whose reign (1495–1521) it is primarily associated. It is essentially a blend of late GOTHIC and MUDÉJAR elements, and so is the Portuguese variant of the PLATERESQUE, by which it was influenced. The feature that distinguishes Manueline architecture from the Plateresque is that structures as well as decorations are influenced by Mudéjar styles: the Plateresque is essentially lavish surface decoration, but the Manueline integrates decoration and structure by transforming structures; the clearest example of such transformation is the twisted pier, a spiral column that appears in many Portuguese churches. In sculpted decoration, the Manueline is also said to be characterized by eastern influences from the overseas explorations of Manuel's reign, notably in its extensive use of vegetation (laurel leaves, roses, poppy heads, artichokes, etc.), maritime images (anchors, ropes, terrestrial globes, and ARMILLARY SPHERES), and the ever-present Cross of the Order of Christ.

The Royal Palace (Palácio Real) at Sintra, in which Manuel I added Mudéjar features, such as Moorish windows (*ajimeces*), to the Gothic building erected in the fourteenth century by King John I, is sometimes described as Manueline (not least because Manuel I commissioned the work), but would perhaps be more accurately described as Portuguese Plateresque, because the Mudéjar elements are decorative rather than structural. The greatest of Manueline monuments is the nave of the Convento de Cristo at Tomar, in which Diogo de ARRUDA has produced Portugal's most exuberantly Manueline building, the windows of which are a mass of twisting coral, ropes, corks, masts, seaweed, anchor chains topped by an armillary sphere, and the Cross of the Order of Christ.

The most prominent exponents of the Manueline were Diogo and Francisco Arruda and Diogo BOYTAC (who inaugurated the Manueline style in his Church of Jesus at Setúbal). The influence of these architects and their contemporaries such as Mateus Fernandes and João de Castilho extended beyond metropolitan Portugal to Funchal (Madeira) and Goa and even to mission churches in Mexico sustained by ORDERS that recruited from both Spain and Portugal. The most famous example of portable Manueline decorative art is the enamelled and gilded Belém monstrance (1506) made by Gil VICENTE and now in the Museu Nacional de Arte Antiga in Lisbon.

R. Dos Santos, *O estilo manuelino* (1952).

**MAPS.** See CARTOGRAPHY.

**MARBLE.** In Renaissance Italy the marble preferred by sculptors was the pure white Carrara marble which had been quarried since antiquity (when it was known as *marmor carystium*) in the mountains near Carrara and in the nearby quarries at Massa and Pietrasanta; MICHELANGELO is known to have visited Carrara to select marble, and Domenico FANCELLI was based there. In northern Europe the black marble used by Netherlandish, French, and German sculptors was quarried near Tournai and known as Tournai marble; it is now called Belgian black marble.

**MARBURG, COLLOQUY OF, or (German) Marburger Religionsgespräch**, a meeting convened by PHILIP OF HESSE in the castle of Marburg an der Lahn, Philip's residence, which had embraced Lutheranism when it became the territorial religion of Hesse in 1527. The meeting, which took place from 1 to 3 October 1529, was an attempt to reconcile the Lutherans (represented by LUTHER and MELANCHTHON) and the Zwinglians (represented by ZWINGLI, OECOLAMPADIUS, and Martin BUCER). The agenda of the meeting was set by the fifteen 'Marburg Articles' that Luther had prepared. The conference failed, chiefly because the article setting out the Lutheran doctrine of the EUCHARIST was unacceptable to the Zwinglians.

After the conference Luther and his colleagues revised his articles, which in this revised form (in seventeen articles) became known as the Articles of Schwabach, which in turn became an important influence on the formulation of the AUGSBURG CONFESSION.

**MARCELLUS II** (1501–55), pope from 9 April 1555 until his death three weeks later on 1 May, was born Marcello Cervini in Montepulciano (near Siena) on 6 May 1501, the son of an official in the Sacred Penitentiary (the Vatican tribunal that deals with matters affecting the sacrament). He studied at Siena and Rome, and subsequently received a commission from Pope CLEMENT VII to complete a revision of the CALENDAR started by his father.

Marcello left Rome in 1526 because of the plague, and in the course of the next five years translated Greek works into Latin and Latin works into Italian. He returned to Rome in 1531, where he enjoyed the patronage of Cardinal Alessandro Farnese; when Farnese was elected as Pope PAUL III (October 1534), he appointed Marcello protonotary apostolic and tutor to his nephew Cardinal Alessandro Farnese. The increasing reliance of Pope Paul on Cardinal Alessandro worked in Marcello's favour, and his influence grew apace. Between 1539 and 1544 he was appointed to the bishoprics of Nicastro, Reggio Emilia, and Gubbio, and on 10 December 1539 he was created cardinal-priest of Santa Croce in Gerusalemme. He served as a papal diplomat in France, and in 1543 was appointed papal legate to the HOLY ROMAN EMPIRE. On 6 February 1545 he was chosen as one of the three co-presidents of the COUNCIL OF TRENT, where his unconditional support for the papal view provoked the wrath of the emperor. In 1548 he was charged with the reorganizing of the VATICAN LIBRARY, and so became the first *Cardinale Bibliotecario*. In the same year he was appointed to the reform commission established by Pope Paul; on the accession of Pope JULIUS III he became president of the commission, but his denunciation of the pope's nepotism, indolence, and taste for the comforts of wealth necessitated his withdrawal to Gubbio.

On his election Marcellus instantly established himself as a reforming pope, reducing the budget for his coronation and reducing the size of his court; he avoided any hint of nepotism by banning his relatives from Rome. He was in the process of distilling the reform documents prepared under Julius III into a wide-ranging reform bull when he died of a stroke. Pope Marcellus is commemorated by the *Missa Papae Marcelli*, a mass in six voices which PALESTRINA (then a singer in the SISTINE CHAPEL) wrote *c.*1561 in response to Marcellus' complaint about the poor quality of the liturgical chants for Good Friday.

**MARCIANA, BIBLIOTECA** (Florence). See SAN MARCO, BIBLIOTECA DI.

**MARCIANA, BIBLIOTECA, or St Mark's Library** (Venice). The origin of the Marciana is said to be the presentation by Petrarch (in 1362) of a collection of manuscripts, all of which were subsequently lost. Whatever its prehistory, the library was formally constituted by Cardinal BESSARION in 1468; its vast collection of manuscripts includes more than 1,000 Greek manuscripts donated by Bessarion.

The library was eventually housed in the Libreria del Sansovino, on the Piazzetta facing the Doge's Palace. The building was designed by SANSOVINO; construction began in 1536 and the exterior was completed by SCAMOZZI in 1582; the interior is decorated with stuccoes by VITTORIA. In 1812 the library was moved to the Palazzo Ducale and in 1904 it migrated to its present accommodation in the Palazzo della Zecca (the mint); the Libreria del Sansovino (now called the Libreria Vecchia) now houses the Museum of Archaeology.

L. Labowsky, *Bessarion's Library and the Biblioteca Marciana* (1979).

**MARCOLINI, FRANCESCO** (*c.*1500–1559), Italian printer and type founder, born in Forlì. He moved to Venice, where he established himself as a printer in 1534. His books include the revised version of ARETINO's comedy *La cortigiana* (1534), parts of SERLIO's *L'architettura* (1537–51), and works by contemporary authors such as Anton DONI. He also experimented with the printing of MUSICAL NOTATION.

**MARCO POLO** (1254–1324), Venetian traveller who wrote a description of the world (*Devisement du monde*) which described his experiences in China. This account was translated from the original French into Latin and several vernaculars, and became a seminal influence on the European conception of ASIA in the fifteenth and sixteenth centuries. The accounts of Asia were thought to be exaggerated (hence the nickname *il milione*, implying a collection of fabricated tales), but Marco Polo's description of Japan (which he never visited), which he had heard described as rich in gold, provided a central motive for the expeditions of COLUMBUS, who owned and annotated a printed copy of the Latin version of the *Devisement*.

In the sixteenth century Portuguese navigators returned to Europe with reports of the country that they called China, and attempts to reconcile this country with the one that Marco Polo called Cathay (which appeared on maps such as the Carta Catalana in 1375) led to the mistaken conclusion that they were separate countries with separate capitals (Cambalu and Peking), and that Cathay lay to the north of China. This error persisted into the late seventeenth century, when Milton's *Paradise Lost* could distinguish 'Cambalu, seat of Cathayan khan' from 'Paquin of Sinaean kings' (11. 388–90).

John Larner, *Marco Polo and the Discovery of the World* (1999).

**MARE CLAUSUM, MARE LIBERUM** (Latin; 'closed sea, free sea'). In the early seventeenth century sovereignty of the seas was a central issue in INTERNATIONAL LAW. The treatise which laid the foundations of the debate was the *Illustrium controversiarum aliorumque usu frequentium* (1564) of Fernando Vázquez de Menchaca, who argued that maritime nations had no right to claim dominion over the seas on which they bordered. In 1609 GROTIUS published *Mare liberum*, in which he argued that the high seas could not be private property, because property can only be owned if it is occupied. On these grounds he disputed the Spanish claim to the Caribbean and the Pacific and the Portuguese claim to the South Atlantic and the Indian Ocean, and, in particular, denied the right of the Portuguese to exclude the Dutch from trading in the East Indies. The same arguments challenged Venetian claims to the Adriatic, Genoese claims to the Ligurian Sea, and English claims to the Channel and the North Sea.

Venetian jurists continued to defend the sovereignty of Venice over the seas under its control, but none of their treatises mentions Grotius, whose *Mare liberum* seems not to have attracted attention in Venice. Replies to Grotius were, however, published in Scotland, Spain, and England. In Scotland William Welwood, professor of law at St Andrews, published his *Abridgement of All Sea Laws* in 1613, one chapter of which, on 'the community and propriety of the sea', challenges Grotius' arguments; the following year Welwood published an expanded Latin version of this chapter as a separate book entitled *De dominio maris*. Welwood was particularly concerned with fishing rights in seas adjacent to coasts; in part this was a theoretical argument about usufruct (the right to use property without changing its character), but it was clearly conceived with an eye to King James's concerns about the assize-herring, which was the royalty due three times a year to the kings of Scotland of 1,000 herrings from each boat in the herring fleet. It was long assumed that Grotius ignored Welwood, but his reply, *Defensio capitis quinti Maris liberi oppugnati a Welwodo*, was discovered in manuscript in 1864 and subsequently published.

The Iberian response to Grotius was a large volume entitled *De iusto imperio* (1625), by Seraphin de Freitas, a Portuguese monk and professor at Valladolid who learnedly disputes Grotius point by point. Grotius did not reply to this treatise, but his colleague Dirk Graswinkel did so in *Maris liberi vindiciae* (1652).

In England GENTILI had touched on the argument, contending in *Hispanicae advocationis libri duo* (1613) that English rights over its adjacent seas extended as far as America, and several common lawyers, including COKE, upheld the propriety of the *Mare Anglicanum*, but the classic response to Grotius was John SELDEN's *Mare clausum, seu De domino maris* (1635), which supported English claims to the Channel and the North Sea by arguing that the sea was no different from land in being a subject of private property. Selden attacked what he took to be the tendentiousness of Grotius in using learned debate to justify the predations of Dutch fishermen in British waters. His argument also extended far beyond fishing rights to the issue of dominion, in part because King Charles required Danish, Dutch, and French ships to strike to the English flag in the Channel and the North Sea.

Grotius was by this time in the service of Sweden, whose claims to the Baltic were well served by Selden's argument, so he was not inclined to reply. The debate carried on in works such as Julius Pacius' *De dominio Maris Hadriatici* (1669) and Cornelis van Bynkershoek's *De dominio maris* (1702), but claims to sovereignty declined in the eighteenth century, except in Denmark, which continued to claim dominion over the Baltic (and levy dues for entering the Sound) until the mid-nineteenth century.

**MARENZIO, LUCA** (1553/4–99), Italian composer of madrigals. He was in the service of Cardinals Cristoforo Madruzzo, Luigi d'ESTE, Ferdinando de Medici and, by 1593, Cinzio Aldobrandini. In 1596, he became *maestro di cappella* at the Polish court of SIGISMUND III; he returned to Italy in 1598 where he died the following year. Known principally as a madrigal composer, he also wrote the music for two of the six *intermedi* for *La pellegrina*, written for the Medici wedding of 1589, and was commissioned by Pope CLEMENT VIII to continue the work of PALESTRINA in revising the chant of the Roman liturgy in accordance with the ideals of the Council of Trent.

**MARGARET OF AUSTRIA** (1480–1530), duchess of Savoy and regent of the Netherlands, was the daughter of Maximilian of Austria (later the Emperor MAXIMILIAN I) and MARY OF BURGUNDY, and the sister of Philip (later King PHILIP I of Castile). At the age of 2 she was betrothed to Charles, the French dauphin (later CHARLES VIII), and was thereafter raised at the French court. In 1489 Charles, who had become king, repudiated his betrothal to Margaret in order to marry ANNE OF BRITTANY. Maximilian chose as Margaret's husband Don Juan, the son and heir of FERDINAND and ISABELLA, but he died a few months after their marriage in 1497. Four years later she married Philibert II, duke of Savoy, but he died in 1504. Her brother Philip died in September 1506, and the following year Margaret was appointed as regent of the Netherlands, ruling on behalf of Philip's son Charles (later the Emperor CHARLES V), who allowed her to remain regent for the rest of her life.

*NDB* s.v. Margarethe, Erzherzogin von Österreich; Jane de Iongh, *Margaret of Austria* (English trans., 1954).

**MARGARET OF PARMA or Margaret of Austria** (1522–86), duchess of Parma and regent of the Netherlands, was the illegitimate daughter of CHARLES V and a Flemish woman, Margaret van Ghent. She was raised in the Netherlands by her great-aunt MARGARET OF AUSTRIA (regent 1507–30) and her aunt MARY OF HUNGARY (regent 1530–55). In 1533 she married Alessandro de' MEDICI, who was assassinated in 1537, and in 1542 she married Ottavio FARNESE, duke of Parma.

In 1559 King PHILIP II left the Netherlands for Spain and appointed Margaret as his regent; Cardinal GRANVELLE, her principal minister, advised her on the persecution of Protestantism. Margaret's troubled regency was dominated by resistance to the implementation of the Spanish INQUISITION and the civil unrest that led to the REVOLT OF THE NETHERLANDS. In 1567 she resigned in favour of the duke of ALBA and retired to Italy. Her son Alessandro FARNESE became regent of the Netherlands in 1578.

*NDB* s.v. Margarethe, Herzogin von Parma.

**MARGUERITE D'ANGOULÊME or d'Alençon or de Navarre** (1492–1549), queen of Navarre, author, and patron, was the daughter of Charles of Valois, count of Angoulême, and LOUISE OF SAVOY. In 1509 she married Charles, duke of Alençon, and in 1527, two years after his death, married Henri II d'Albret (Spanish Enrique II), king of Navarre. Their daughter JEANNE D'ALBRET was to become the mother of King HENRI IV of France.

In 1515 Marguerite's younger brother François became King FRANCIS I of France, and thereafter she became a patron of learning; unlike her daughter, Marguerite did not convert to Protestantism, but she sympathized with the cause of ecclesiastical reform. She extended her patronage to RABELAIS, Bonaventure DES PÉRIERS, and Clement MAROT, and defended the reformers of Meaux, Bishop BRIÇONNET and LEFÈVRE D'ÉTAPLES; in 1546 she failed in her attempt to save Étienne DOLET from the stake. She also played an important political role: she travelled to Spain when Francis I was a prisoner there, and attempted to negotiate his release in 1525.

Marguerite was a writer of poetry, plays, and imaginative prose. Her poems, which are usually religious in theme, include *Le Miroir de l'âme pécheresse* (1531), which was banned by the theologians of the University of Paris in 1533. The two principal collections of her poetry were *Marguerites de la Marguerite des Princesses* and *Suite de Marguerites* (both 1547). Her plays were sometimes religious (notably the *Comédie de la nativité de Jésus Christ*) and sometimes secular (e.g. the *Comédie jouée à Mont de Marsan*).

Marguerite's principal work was the prose *Heptaméron*, a cycle of 72 stories modelled on BOCCACCIO, whose *Decameron* had been published in French translation in 1545; it was first published in 1558 as *Histoire des amants fortunés* and assumed its familiar title in an edition of 1559. The tales range from the sexually explicit (often involving Franciscans) and excremental to philosophical accounts of human and divine love. In her representation of the tension between the male urge for sexual conquest and the female ideal of chastity, Marguerite acquiesces in the traditional male view of women, but she is alert and sympathetic to the difficulties of women in a male society.

P. Jourda, *Marguerite d'Angoulême, duchesse d'Alençon, reine de Navarre* (2 vols., 1930); Marcel Tétel, *Marguerite d'Angoulême's Heptaméron* (1973); Nicole Cazauran, *L'Heptaméron de Marguerite d'Angoulême* (2nd edn., 1991).

**MARGUERITE DE VALOIS** (1553–1615), French poet, patron, and autobiographer, the daughter of King HENRI II of France and CATHERINE DE MÉDICIS. In 1572 she married Henry of Navarre, who later became King HENRI IV; they were separated in 1583 and the marriage was annulled in 1599. Thereafter she held court in Paris, where she was popularly and affectionately known as 'la reine Margot'; she wrote poetry and an autobiography and became an important patron of literature.

The name Marguerite de Valois was also borne by MARGUERITE D'ANGOULÊME and by Marguerite the daughter of FRANCIS I, who were respectively the great-aunt and the aunt of 'la reine Margot'.

Janine Garrisson, *Marguerite de Valois* (1994); Éliane Viennot, *Marguerite de Valois* (1995).

**MARIANA, JUAN DE** (1536–1623/4), Spanish historian, political philosopher, and jurist, born in Talavera, the illegitimate son of the dean of the collegiate church, and educated at Alcalá de Henares. He entered the JESUIT Order in 1553 and in 1561 moved to Rome to lecture on theology; his students included BELLARMINE. He lived in Sicily (1564–9) and Paris (1569–74) and then settled in Toledo. In 1592 he published a scholarly history of Spain (*Historia de rebus Hispaniae*) in twenty books, which he soon extended to 30 books (1605) to cover the reigns of CHARLES V, PHILIP II, and PHILIP III and which he himself translated into Spanish (1601, *Historia*

*general de España*). This treatise is distinguished by purity of style and by the cool rationality of its approach to national legends, though its tone remains celebratory.

Juan de Mariana's most important work as a political philosopher is *De rege et regis institutione* (1598), a manual for princes in which Mariana examines the nature and origins of the state and defends tyrannicide. Mariana was reviled by Protestants and Catholics alike: Protestants read *De rege* as evidence that the Jesuits were responsible for the GUNPOWDER PLOT in England and the murder of HENRI IV in France, and regarded Mariana as the Jesuit apologist for such atrocities; on the Catholic side Mariana's teaching was condemned by Claudio AQUAVIVA (the general of the Jesuits) in 1610 and regarded as suspect by the INQUISITION, which repeatedly examined Mariana's works in the final years of his life.

G. Lewy, *Constitutionalism and Statecraft during the Golden Age of Spain: A Study of the Political Philosophy of Juan de Mariana* (1960); Alan Soons, *Juan de Mariana* (1982); D. Ferraro, *Tradizione e ragione in Juan de Mariana* (1989).

**MARIE DE MÉDICIS or (Italian) Maria de' Medici** (1573–1642), queen and regent of France, was born in Florence, the daughter of Grand Duke Francesco de' Medici and the granddaughter of Grand Duke COSIMO I DE' MEDICI. In 1600 she married King HENRI IV of France, by whom she had three daughters and two sons. On the accession of her 9-year-old son Louis XIII, Queen Marie became regent until he was declared of age on 2 October 1614, and in effect ruled for several years thereafter. She established a Spanish alliance by arranging for the marriage of her son King Louis to Anna of Austria (the Spanish infanta) and of Louis's sister Elizabeth to the future Philip IV of Spain. Henri, the prince of Condé, plotted against Marie, and forced the calling of what was to be the last Estates-General before 1789. This assembly (October 1614–Febuary 1615) was the first stage in a revolt that lasted until May 1616, when the Treaty of Loudun was signed.

Queen Marie ruled with the support of her childhood friend Leonora Galigai and Leonora's husband Concino Concini, whom she had ennobled as the marquis and marchioness of Ancre. Concini imprisoned Condé and dispatched troops to quell provincial rebellions, but with the approval of the young king was assassinated outside the Louvre; Leonora was burnt as a witch, and Queen Marie was banished to Blois. She twice revolted against her son and his ally Cardinal Richelieu, but never recovered her former power. In 1631 she escaped to Brussels, and never returned to France.

Michel Carmona, *Marie de Médicis* (1981).

**MARIGNANO or Marignan, BATTLE OF**. In the early sixteenth century, the western passes of the Alps were guarded by Swiss and papal troops. In August 1515 an invading French army raised in Lyon and led by King FRANCIS I crossed the Col de l'Argentière (near Chamonix) on footpaths that had never been used by a military force and surprised and overwhelmed a papal unit at Villafranca (near Pinerolo, southwest of Turin). The papal army retreated to Milan, which enabled Francis to rendezvous with a Venetian force. In order to avoid a costly and protracted siege of Milan, Francis offered to pay the defending Swiss army to return home; the Swiss had not received the payments promised by Pope LEO X and FERDINAND II, and were preparing to accept the offer when the arrival of a new tranche of Swiss mercenaries persuaded the Swiss army to stay and fight.

On the afternoon of 13 September 1515 the French army with its Venetian reinforcements grouped in front of the village of Marignano (now Melegnano), 15 kilometres (9 miles) south-east of Milan. The French and Gascon infantry (who were armed with ARQUEBUSES) were supplemented by a large body of LANDSKNECHTE; the army was commanded by Gian Giacomo TRIVULZIO. The opposing Swiss force (largely armed with pikes) advanced in three columns, and fought hand to hand until midnight; at dawn battle was renewed, with the infantries in the centre of the battlefield and the artillery firing into the mêlée at short range; one of the French units was commanded by the engineer Pedro NAVARRO. Twenty-eight hours after the battle had begun, Swiss resistance was broken, and the 3,000 survivors of the Swiss force of 25,000 fled; on the French side there were 8,000 deaths. At the end of the battle young King Francis may have been knighted on the field by BAYARD.

The consequence of Francis's victory was a renewal of the French occupation of Milan, and later of Genoa. The involvement of Swiss infantry on the losing side tarnished their image as Europe's finest foot soldiers, and the SWISS CONFEDERATION played no further part in the WARS OF ITALY, though its soldiers continued to serve as mercenaries. A settlement between France and the Swiss Confederation in 1516 included an agreed boundary with Milan which is for the most part the Italian–Swiss border of the twenty-first century.

The battle of Marignano was memorably and fancifully described by Thomas NASHE in *The Unfortunate Traveller* (1594). The battlefield was the site of a second battle in 1859.

E. Usteri, *Marignano* (1974).

**MARINO, GIAMBATTISTA** (1569–1625), Italian poet, born in Naples, the son of a lawyer. In 1598 he was arrested on suspicion of having murdered his mistress, and in 1600 he was again imprisoned, this time for forgery. He subsequently lived in Rome under the protection of Cardinal Pietro Aldobrandini, and then moved to Turin (1608–15), where he was imprisoned for his part in a duel with another poet. On being released he travelled to Paris to seek the protection of MARIE DE MÉDICIS, returning to Naples in 1623.

Marino's poems include *Canzone de' baci* (1592), the mythological *Adone* (1623), and *La strage degli innocenti* (1632), which was translated into English as *The Slaughter of the Innocents by Herod* (1675). Marino and his followers (the Marinisti) were an important influence on the development of baroque poetry in seventeenth-century Italy.

*OCIL*; G. G. Ferrero (ed.), *Marino e i Marinisti* (1956).

**MARINUS VAN REYMERSWAELE** (c.1490/5–c.1567), Flemish painter of whom little is known, save that his works show stylistic affinities with the Antwerp painting of the period. His paintings, which exist in many versions, return repeatedly to two subjects: St JEROME in his study and GENRE scenes depicting bankers, usurers, and excisemen; his *Two Tax Collectors* (or *Two Excisemen*) survives in at least 25 versions, one of which is in the National Gallery in London.

*BNB* s.v. Marinus Claeszoon; *MDA* s.v. Reymerswaele, Marinus van.

**MARITIME LAW.** Two bodies of maritime law—one Catalan, one French—dominated the seas of Renaissance Europe, but if the European periphery is taken into account, there were five important codes. In the eastern Mediterranean the Assizes of Jerusalem (sometimes called the Letters of the Holy Sepulchre), the codification of CUSTOMARY LAW used by the crusaders to govern the kingdom of Jerusalem, were lost when Saladin conquered Jerusalem in 1187. The text of the Assizes was reassembled in the course of the thirteenth century. In Euboea (Italian Negroponte, modern Greek Evvoia) the Venetian authorities recognized the legitimacy of the Assizes, which remained in force till Euboea fell to the Ottoman Turks in 1470. The Assizes retained their authority in Cyprus from the time when Guy de Lusignan assumed the throne in 1192 until the Venetian acquisition of Cyprus in 1489. The Venetian government decided to honour the efficacy of the Assizes, which were translated into Italian in 1531 and remained in force until the Turkish conquest of 1571. Throughout this period trading disputes in the eastern Mediterranean were regulated in maritime courts which applied the Assizes of Jerusalem.

In the western Mediterranean the seminal formulation of maritime law was the *Consolato del mare* ('Book of the Consulate of the Sea'), which first appeared *c.*1370 and was published (in Catalan) in Barcelona in 1494. The *Consolato* consisted of an Aragonese code of practice for the sea consuls who presided over maritime courts in Valencia, a collection of maritime customary law (much of which was based on the laws of Italy's ports, notably the Laws of AMALFI), and a body of ordinances for the regulation of military vessels. The code of practice reflected judicial procedures throughout the western Mediterranean, and so quickly spread from Barcelona and Valencia to Majorca, Roussillon, and Sicily. It was subsequently translated into many languages and eventually became the maritime law of Christians throughout the Mediterranean.

On the Atlantic coast, the compilation that corresponded to the Mediterranean *Consolato del mare* is known as the Rules (or Rolls or Laws) of Oléron. The Île d'Oléron, just north of the mouth of the Gironde, was for centuries the commercial centre of the trade in wine and oil with Brittany, Normandy, England, and Flanders. The Rules of Oléron, a collection of the judgments of its maritime court, were translated into Flemish (the 'Purple Book of Bruges') and French ('La Charte d'Oléron des jugements de la mer') during the fourteenth century, and in the same period were adopted in England as the law by which the Admiralty courts settled maritime disputes. The first printed English version was published as *The Rutter of the Sea* (see RUTTIER) in 1536.

In the North Sea and the Baltic Sea maritime courts (including those in Scotland) drew on a compilation known as the Visby Sea Laws, which contained the Rules of Oléron, but also incorporated elements of the customary law of Amsterdam and Lübeck. In the Hanseatic ports maritime law was Roman in character; this body of law was not formally codified until 1667, when it was published as *Ius maritimum Hanseaticum*.

The development of a relatively unified European system of mercantile law (the LAW MERCHANT) helped to bring together the codes and institutions of maritime law, and eventually the specialist maritime courts of the Mediterranean were replicated in England and France. In England the Rules of Oléron were implemented by local courts in English ports, but in the fifteenth and sixteenth centuries their jurisdictions were gradually absorbed by the High Court of Admiralty, and the only local court that now retains its Admiralty jurisdiction is the Court of the Lord Warden of the Cinque Ports, which was both the first and last English court to administer the Rules of Oléron.

Jean Marie Pardessus, *Collection des lois maritimes antérieures au XVIIe siècle* (1828–45).

**MARKWART or (Spanish) Macuarte FAMILY**, a family of German gunsmiths in Spain. In about 1530 Simon Markwart and his brother Peter, sons of the Augsburg gunsmith Bartholomäus, travelled to Madrid at the invitation of CHARLES V and remained in Spain as gun-makers to PHILIP II and PHILIP III; in the next generation the most prominent gunsmith was Simón Macuarte the Younger. The family's guns, which were regarded as the finest in Europe, were marked with a sickle.

**MARLOWE, CHRISTOPHER** (1564–93), English playwright and poet. Educated at Cambridge, Marlowe had a significant influence on the early plays of SHAKESPEARE, and more generally on the development of Elizabethan drama beyond the form of the medieval morality play. His plays address ambition, the acquisition and effect of power, and its consequences and loss. This is evident from an early play, written with NASHE, the *Tragedy of Dido*, through to the highly popular *Tamberlaine the Great* (c.1587, which traces the shepherd-warrior's rise to power), *The Jew of Malta* (c.1590, which provided a model for Shakespeare's Shylock), *Edward II* (c.1592, an influence on Shakespeare's *Richard II*), and *Doctor Faustus* (c.1594). The power and beauty of his blank verse is evident also in his poem *Hero and Leander* (published in 1598). A controversial figure because of his homosexuality and alleged atheism, Marlow died in an inn brawl.

DNB.

**MARMION, SIMON** (c.1425–1489), Franco-Flemish painter and illuminator, born in Amiens and admitted to the guild at Tournai (1468) before settling in Valenciennes. He is best known for an attributed work, the retable of St Bertin (1459), which is now divided: it is mostly in the Gemäldegalerie in Berlin but there are fragments in the National Gallery in London. His paintings are typically populated with many small figures, and he used an unusually large range of colours.

BNB; MDA.

**MARNIX VAN SINT ALDEGONDE, PHILIPS VAN** (1540–98), Flemish poet and theologian, born into a noble family in Brussels. He became a Calvinist and studied in Geneva under CALVIN and BEZA (1560–1). Marnix subsequently became a prominent figure in the REVOLT OF THE NETHERLANDS, in which he played an important part in the Pacification of GHENT (1576) and the Union of UTRECHT (1579) and later commanded the unsuccessful defence of Antwerp (of which he was burgomaster) during the siege mounted by Alessandro FARNESE (1584–5).

Marnix's works include a defence of Dutch iconoclasm in Flanders (*Vraie Narration et apologie*, 1567), a Rabelaisian prose satire on the 'beehive' of the Catholic Church (*De Biëncorf der heilige roomsche kercke*, 1569, translated into English, German, and French), and a translation of the Psalms from Hebrew into Dutch (1580); he is popularly believed to have been the author of the Dutch national anthem, 'Het Wilhelmus' (1568).

NNBW i; *Œuvres* (8 vols., 1857–60); Wilhelmus Ornée, *Calvinisme en humanisme bij P. van Marnix* (1966); C. E. H. J. Verhoef, *Philips van Marnix* (1985).

**MAROT, CLÉMENT** (1496–1544), French Protestant poet. He was born in Cahors, and moved to Paris when his father was appointed as secretary to ANNE OF BRITTANY. He became a page in the household of Nicolas de Neufville (1510–19) and then entered the service of MARGUERITE D'ANGOULÊME, whose patronage and protection Marot enjoyed for the rest of his life. In 1526 Marot succeeded his father as *valet de chambre* to King FRANCIS I.

Marot's Protestant sympathies first became apparent in 1526, when he was imprisoned for eating meat during the Lenten fast. In 1534, in the wake of the Affaires des PLACARDS, he fled to Navarre (where Marguerite had become queen) and then to Ferrara (where RENÉE DE FRANCE sheltered Protestants). Marot returned to France when King Francis declared an amnesty in 1536, but the publication of his *Trente Psaumes de David* (1541) led to a renewal of his exile, initially in Geneva and then in Turin, where he died of plague.

Marot was an immensely versatile poet who wrote in many genres (most successfully in the verse epistle) and registers (from frivolous to pious to savagely satirical). His early poems, which were collected in *L'Adolescence clémentine* (1532) and *Suite de l'Adolescence clémentine* (1533), include allegories, verse epistles, and what may be the earliest SONNETS to have been written in French. Marot also wrote translations of Virgil, Ovid, and Petrarch.

C. A. Mayer, *Clément Marot* (1972); Pauline Smith, *Clément Marot: Poet of the French Renaissance* (1970).

**MAROT, JEAN** (c.1465–1526), French poet associated with the *RHÉTORIQUEURS*. He served as secretary to ANNE OF BRITTANY from 1506 and *valet de chambre* to King FRANCIS I from c.1514. He wrote versified accounts of King LOUIS XII's two military expeditions to Genoa and Venice during the WARS OF ITALY, *Le Voyage de Gênes* (1507) and *Le Voyage de Venise* (1509).

**MARPRELATE TRACTS** (1588–9), a collection of satirical pamphlets issued by the fictitious 'Martin Marprelate' from a secret press, attacking the church hierarchy and WHITGIFT's attempts to impose uniform liturgical practices. They were effective because highly entertaining, and swift measures were taken to counter their arguments and round up those thought responsible for them. These included the playwright UDALL, but the Puritan Job Throckmorton, who may also have played a part, escaped punishment. NASHE, LYLY, and Gabriel HARVEY wrote 'anti-Marprelate' replies.

**MARQUETRY**, a term now used to denote a technique developed in the seventeenth century whereby a decorative veneer consisting of pieces of material shaped into a mosaic is glued to a rough surface, typically the carcass of a piece of furniture. Renaissance marquetry, however, is a form of inlay, on which see INTARSIA.

*MARRANOS*, the Spanish and Portuguese term for Jews who were ostensibly converted to Christianity in the fourteenth and fifteenth centuries, but secretly practised Judaism, and for their descendants. Converts were known as *conversos* or New Christians (Spanish *Nuevos Cristianos*, Portuguese *Cristãos-Novos*), while *marranos* (probably 'pigs') was used to denote heretical Judaizers. However, with the advent of the Spanish INQUISITION all three terms came to be used as pejoratives by Hispanic 'Old Christians' to distinguish themselves from the despised and persecuted descendants of Spain's numerous former Jewish and Muslim minorities (MORISCOS), who by imputation, and in many cases doubtless unfairly, were accused of clinging treacherously to their own ethnic and cultural identities and customs. In the Balearic Islands, the *marranos* were known as *chuetas*.

In Spain, anti-*converso* riots broke out from 1449 onwards, and the crown was forced to accept local racial laws in which 'purity of blood' (*limpieza de sangre*) was used to exclude all New Christians from municipal and ecclesiastical posts. In 1480 the Inquisition was established in Spain with the express purpose of rooting out the *marranos*. The number of Judaizers was assumed by the Inquisition to have increased after the expulsion or conversion of the Jews of Spain in 1492 and those of Portugal in 1497. The introduction of the Inquisition into Portugal in 1536 caused many *marranos* to re-emigrate to Spain or to leave for distant sanctuaries such as the Netherlands and the Ottoman Empire. *Marranos* continued to be persecuted by the Inquisition in both countries (along with subsequent victims such as Protestants and *moriscos*) until the eighteenth century.

It is impossible to ascertain the extent to which the thousands of *marranos* condemned by the Inquisition were in fact Judaizers; certainly many were innocent, but prima facie evidence for the clandestine survival of the Jewish faith after the expulsions of the 1490s is given by the numbers of exiled *marranos* who subsequently reconverted, forming new Sephardi congregations in the Ottoman Empire (which, unlike Catholic Europe, was tolerant of Judaism), in Protestant northern Europe, and in America; the pre-eminent community of *marranos* was the congregation formed in Amsterdam in 1597.

Cecil Roth, *A History of the Marranos* (4th edn. 1974); Benzion Netanyahu, *The Marranos of Spain* (3rd edn. 1999); Haim Beinart, *Conversos on Trial: The Inquisition in Ciudad Real* (1981).

**MARSTON, JOHN** (1576–1634), English playwright, educated at Brasenose College, Oxford, and best remembered for the tragicomedy of court corruption *The Malcontent* (1604), which has resemblances to SHAKESPEARE's *Measure for Measure* of the same year. With JONSON and CHAPMAN, he wrote *Eastward Hoe* (1605), a comedy of London life; a derogatory passage on the Scots caused royal offence and Marston temporarily fled abroad. Other plays include the Italian tragedy *Antonio and Mellida* (1602) and the comedies *The Dutch Courtesan* (1605) and *Parasitaster* (1606). In 1609, Marston took holy orders and retired from playwrighting.

*DNB.*

**MARSUPPINI, CARLO** (1399–1453), Italian humanist and Hellenist, born in Arezzo and educated in Florence, where he enjoyed the patronage of the MEDICI family. He had an excellent command of Greek, and in 1431 was appointed to the chair of Greek at Florence through the influence of the humanist coterie that had edged FILELFO out of the post. In 1444 he succeeded Leonardo BRUNI as chancellor of the republic.

Marsuppini's writings, which testify more to the breadth of his learning than to the originality of his mind, include poems, literary letters, and a translation of book I of the *Iliad* from Greek into Latin. He worked for several years as a papal secretary, and his translation of Homer was praised by Pope NICHOLAS V, but he never shook off the widespread suspicion of paganism.

**MARTIN V** (1368–1431), pope from 11 November 1417 until his death on 20 February 1431, was born Oddo Colonna in Gennazano; his father Agapito, a prominent member of the COLONNA family, later became a bishop and a cardinal. Oddo studied CANON LAW at Perugia and was subsequently appointed protonotary by Pope Urban VI; Pope Innocent VII created him cardinal-deacon of San Giorgio in Velabro. In November 1406 Pope GREGORY XII was elected, and Cardinal Oddo became a member of his Sacred College; less than two years later, in the summer of 1408, Oddo seceded from Gregory and joined the rebel cardinals who were organizing the COUNCIL OF PISA. In 1409 this Council deposed Popes Gregory and BENEDICT XIII and elected Pietro Philarghi as Pope Alexander V. When Alexander died suddenly on 3 May 1410, the Pisan cardinals elected Baldassare Cossa as Pope John XXIII. Oddo remained loyal to Pope John until his flight from the COUNCIL OF CONSTANCE. The Council deposed John XXIII and Benedict XIII, received the abdication of Gregory XII, declared the Holy See vacant, and created an electoral conclave consisting of 22 cardinals and 30 representatives of the five nations present at the conference. Cardinal Oddo was elected on St Martin's Day, and so chose to style himself Pope Martin V. Although the two deposed popes declined to accept their deposition, their followings were so small that the election of Pope Martin can be said to have brought the GREAT SCHISM to a close.

Pope Martin had in effect been elected by a council, but he quickly began to tilt the balance of authority away from councils and towards the papacy. He reorganized the curia as stipulated by the Council, employing officials of both the Avignon and Roman obediences, but the regulations for his chancery that he promulgated on 26 February 1418 left the collation of benefices in the hands of the papacy. Similarly, his reforms of 20 March 1418 diminished the papal prerogative in matters such as the right to revenue from vacant sees, but a subsequent series of papal concordats embodied clauses which meant that power eventually reverted to the papacy. He closed the Council of Constance on 22 April 1418, and in a constitution read in consistory on 10 May 1418 (but never published) he forbade any party to appeal to a council against the judgement of a pope in matters of faith.

Martin resisted pressure to establish his papacy in Avignon or in the HOLY ROMAN EMPIRE, and left Konstanz six days after he closed the Council. He paused for protracted visits to Mantua and Florence, and after negotiating successfully with Queen GIOVANNA II of Naples for the withdrawal of Neapolitan troops from Rome, entered Rome on 28 September 1420. He then needed to secure the PAPAL STATE, which necessitated the dislodging of Andrea FORTEBRACCIO, the Perugian condottiere who dominated much of central Italy; Martin began with appeasement by recognizing Fortebraccio's lordship of various cities that he controlled, but then defeated him in battle at L'Aquila on 2 June 1424. In 1429 Martin again had recourse to arms to suppress a rebellion which started in Bologna and threatened to engulf northern Italy. Martin's increased control of the Papal State enabled him to alienate vast tracts of land to his Colonna relatives.

Pope Martin's foreign policies were well intentioned but ineffectual. He tried in vain to mediate in the Hundred Years War between England and France, and attempted without success to arrange a reunion council in Constantinople; similarly, he was unable to elicit support for the CRUSADES that he declared against the adherents of Jan HUS in Bohemia. He showed a rare tolerance for JEWS, denouncing violent anti-Jewish preaching and banning the compulsory baptism of Jewish children under the age of 12.

Martin disliked councils and conciliar authority, but nonetheless acquiesced in the decree passed by the Council of Constance on 5 October 1417 requiring that councils be convoked at regular intervals. He accordingly summoned a council to assemble in Pavia on 22 September 1423, but failed to attend in person. The Council was transferred by his legates to Siena because of an outbreak of PLAGUE in Pavia, and in the Siena sessions delegates began to deprecate papal authority. Pope Martin therefore dissolved the Council in March 1424 (on the pretext of low attendance) and proclaimed the COUNCIL OF BASEL, which was commanded to

assemble in 1431. On 1 February 1431 he nominated Cardinal Giuliano CESARINI as president of the Council (with full authority to suspend or dissolve it if he deemed it appropriate to do so); three weeks later he died suddenly of apoplexy. He was buried in the Basilica of San Giovanni in Laterano; his tomb includes a recumbent brass effigy.

Martin was an active patron of art and architecture, and carried out an extensive programme of rebuilding ruined churches and public buildings in Rome.

P. Partner, *The Papal State under Martin V* (1958).

**MARTÍNEZ DE IRALA, DOMINGO** (*c*.1512–1557), Spanish conquistador, born in the Basque province of Guipúzcoa. He travelled to Buenos Aires, where in 1537 he commanded an expedition to Paraguay commissioned by Pedro de MENDOZA, governor (*adelantado*) of Río de la Plata and Paraguay. In 1537 Irala settled in Asunción (which had been founded in 1535 by Juan de Ayolas), where he married a succession of Indian wives. In 1545 Álvar Núñez CABEZA DE VACA, who had succeeded Pedro de Mendoza, sought to displace Irala, who responded by organizing a rebellion in which Cabeza de Vaca was deposed and dispatched to Spain in chains. This success consolidated Irala's position as the most powerful figure in Paraguay.

*DHE.*

**MARTÍNEZ DE TOLEDO, ALFONSO** (1398–1470), Spanish satirist, born in Toledo; he entered the Church, and eventually became prebendary of Toledo Cathedral as archpriest of Talavera (1448). His writings include hagiography (*Vidas de San Ildefonso y San Isidoro*) and history (*Atalaya de las crónicas*), but his best-known work is a satire on lust and the wiles of wicked women, *Arcipreste de Talavera* (composed 1438, published 1495), which is sometimes known as El *Corbacho*, after BOCCACCIO's *Corbaccio*.

E. M. Gerli, *Alfonso Martínez de Toledo* (1976).

**MARTINI, SIMONE.** See SIMONE MARTINI.

**MARTINUZZI, GIORGIO** (1482–1551), Croatian cardinal, the son of a Venetian mother, from whom he took his Italian name. He became an adviser to János ZÁPOLYA, on whose death in 1540 Martinuzzi became regent of Transylvania on behalf of Zápolya's young son János Sigismund. In order to combat the rival claim of Archduke FERDINAND of Hungary to the principality of Transylvania, Martinuzzi permitted the country to become an Ottoman protectorate, which allowed a considerable measure of independence. In 1545 he repudiated this policy and formed an alliance with Ferdinand against the Ottomans. Six years later, at the Diet of Kolozsvár (now Romanian Cluj-Napoca), Martinuzzi accepted the incorporation of Transylvania into Hungary. He attempted to appease the wrath of the Ottomans in order to prevent an invasion, but these negotiations were interpreted as treacherous, and Martinuzzi was murdered by Ferdinand's agents.

*MEL* s.v. Fráter György.

**MARTIRE D'ANGHIERA, PIETRO,** or (Spanish) **Pedro Mártir de Angleria** or (Latin) **Petrus Martyr de Angleria**

(1459–1526), Italian humanist, soldier, and historian in Spain, born into a family from Angera (near Arona) on Lake Maggiore. He received a humanist education before moving to Rome to assume a series of administrative posts, and in 1487 travelled to Spain in the train of the returning Castilian ambassador. He became a soldier and fought in the campaigns to conquer GRANADA, and after the defeat and expulsion of the Moors in 1492 entered the service of Queen ISABELLA of Castile; he initially worked as head of a school for young noblemen at the royal court and then became involved in the administration of the Spanish empire in America. His personal knowledge of COLUMBUS, Vasco da GAMA, Amerigo VESPUCCI, Hernán CORTÉS, and MAGELLAN gave Pietro Martire an authoritative command of the process of discovery, conquest, and colonization, and his three-volume *De orbe novo* (1511, 1516, 1530) is the first published account; an English version by Richard Eden, entitled *Decades of the New World*, was published in 1555.

DBI; Llorenç Riber, *El humanista Pedro Mártir de Angleria* (1964); A. L. Stoppa and R. Cicala (eds.), *L'umanisto aronese Pietro Martire Anghiera: Primo storico del Nuovo Mondo* (1992).

**MARTORELL, BERNAT** (*fl.* 1433–52), Catalan painter and miniaturist. His most important documented work is the ALTARPIECE of Púbol Castle (1437–42), now in the Gerona Museum. Paintings attributed to him include panels from an altarpiece of *St George* now divided between the Louvre and the Art Institute in Chicago.

DBC; MDA; J. M. Gudiol Ricart, *Bernardo Martorell* (1959).

**MARTYROLOGIES** are collective compilations of those who have died for the Christian faith, and so are distinguished from accounts of the suffering of individual martyrs. In their simplest form, martyrologies are lists of names and places of martyrdom, usually ordered by the dates of their feasts. These lists, of which the earliest surviving example dates from the fourth century, were in the eighth century (Bede) and the ninth (Usuard) expanded to include historical (or fictional) accounts of the circumstances of martyrdom. Usuard was widely read in the Middle Ages, and formed the basis of the Roman martyrology issued in 1584 by Pope GREGORY XIII and subsequently revised up to the present day.

The early modern martyrology is primarily a Protestant genre. The Catholic Church suffered comparatively few deaths, and the literature of Catholic martyrology is correspondingly thin. The most important Catholic martyrology was Maurice Chauncy's *Historia aliquot nostri saeculi martyrum* (Mainz, 1550), which concentrated on English martyrs; a subsequent edition by Erasmus Vendius added Scottish and French martyrs (Munich, 1573). This martyrology reached its final form in Richard Verstegan's *Theatrum crudelitatum haereticarum nostri temporis* (Antwerp, 1587); it remained in print in the seventeenth century in both Latin and French editions. Apart from specialist martyrologies, such as those produced by the Franciscans commemorating Franciscan martyrs, the only other significant Catholic contribution to Renaissance literature is the anti-martyrology: Nicholas

Harpsfield's *Dialogi sex* (Antwerp, 1566) inaugurated a tradition of disparaging Protestant martyrologies that culminated in Jacques Severt's *L'Anti-martyrologe* (Lyon, 1622).

The *annus mirabilis* of the Protestant martyrology is 1554, when the first Lutheran, Calvinist, and Anglican martyrologies were published. In February Ludwig Rabus (1524–92), a Lutheran minister in Strassburg (1544–56) and Ulm (1556–90), founded the Protestant tradition of martyrologies (German *Märtyrerbücher*) with a *Märtyrerlexikon* published in Latin and (subsequently) in German; this volume was supplemented with a long series of German martyrologies (1554–8) which, like the original volume, described martyrs of the early Church and of the fifteenth and sixteenth centuries but ignored the intervening millennium. In August Jean Crespin, a Calvinist lawyer from Arras who in 1548 settled as a religious refugee in Geneva, published the first edition of his *Livres de martyrs*, a compilation of Calvinist martyrs published in French, Latin, German, and (in the seventeenth century) Dutch. In September John FOXE published the first edition of his *Acts and Monuments*, initially in Latin and in 1563 as *Acts and Monuments of Matters Happening in the Church*, the book popularly known as 'Foxe's Book of Martyrs'; Fox was the first scholarly martyrologist, and weighed evidence in the spirit of humanist historiography. His martyrs were mostly English, but his publishers signalled with the phrase *pars prima* that more martyrs could be added in a supplementary volume; a *pars secunda* containing French, Italian, and German martyrs was prepared by Heinrich Pantaleon (1522–59) and published posthumously in 1563.

Elsewhere in Europe, the most important martyrologies were published in the Netherlands and in Poland. The first Dutch martyrology, which drew on all three of the 1554 compilations, was Adriaan Corneliszoon van Haemstede's *De Gheschiedenisse ende den doodt der vromer Martelaren* (1559), a Calvinist martyrology which was published in ten ever-expanding editions up to 1616, culminating in the 1,000-page folio *Historien der vromer Martelaren* in 1633; grisly illustrative engravings first appeared in the edition of 1604. The Netherlands was also the source of the seminal Anabaptist martyrology, the *Het Offer des Heeren* of 1562; this account of Anabaptists who constituted 'the sacrifice of the Lord' was supplemented the following year by the *Liedtboecxken*, a hymn in praise of martyrs which was for generations published together with the prose account.

Fredrik Pijper, *Martelaarsboeken* (1924).

**MARY or (Latin) Maria**, the mother of Jesus, who was deemed to have conceived without losing her virginity. This feat was often said to have been accomplished by her having conceived through the ear, a doctrine known as the *conceptio per aurem*. In medieval and Renaissance art this doctrine was depicted by the dove representing the Holy Spirit flying towards the ear of the Virgin (e.g. Jan van EYCK's *Annunciation* in the National Gallery in Washington). Conception and birth were through the right ear, except when the doctrine was being parodied: RABELAIS's Gargantua 'sortit par l'oreille senestre'. The doctrines that accumulated around Mary in the Western Church included the immaculate conception, perpetual virginity, and corporeal assumption.

The doctrine of the immaculate conception was essentially an affirmation that from the moment of her conception, Mary was free from the stain of original sin. In the fourteenth century the Franciscans became the principal proponents of the doctrine and the Dominicans (following the lead of St THOMAS AQUINAS) its principal opponents. The debate was quelled when the COUNCIL OF BASEL affirmed in 1439 that the doctrine was consistent with Catholic dogma, reason, and the Bible. In 1449 the Sorbonne required all candidates for degrees to subscribe to the doctrine, and other universities soon exacted the same requirement. In 1476 Pope SIXTUS IV approved the Feast of the Immaculate Conception (8 December) with its own mass and office. The COUNCIL OF TRENT supported the doctrine by exempting Mary from its decree on original sin, and thereafter the doctrine was generally accepted, though it did not become dogma until 1854.

The doctrine of perpetual virginity affirms that Mary conceived as a virgin, remained *virgo intacta* while giving birth to Jesus, and had no subsequent sexual relations with Joseph. In Mark 6: 3 Jesus is described as the brother (ἀδελφός; Vulgate *frater*) of four boys and several girls; the Western Church accepted JEROME's view that these children were the cousins of Jesus, and the Eastern Church followed Epiphanius in asserting that they were the children of Joseph by a former marriage. Many reformers, suspicious of the Catholic ideal of celibacy, denied the doctrine and asserted that these children were born to Mary and Joseph and so were the younger siblings of Jesus. In art the doctrine of Mary's perpetual virginity is usually illustrated by a representation of the Virgin and Child in a walled garden (Latin *hortus conclusus*) or by the *Virgo inter Virgines*, in which Mary is surrounded by female virgin saints (e.g. DAVID's *Virgo inter Virgines* of 1509 in the Musée des Beaux-Arts in Rouen) or by a depiction of *Mary in the Burning Bush* (e.g. Nicholas FROMENT's altarpiece of 1476 in Aix-en-Provence Cathedral) in which the burning bush unconsumed by fire (Exodus 3: 2–6) is deemed to represent her perpetual virginity.

The doctrine of corporeal assumption affirms that at the end of her earthly life Mary was 'assumed' (i.e. taken to heaven) in body and soul. This doctrine, which originated in the sixth century, enjoyed wide support in the Western Church, but was not formally defined until 1950. The Feast of the Assumption was celebrated on 15 August, but because the reformers flatly rejected the doctrine, it disappeared in Protestant countries; in England the feast was excluded from the Book of Common Prayer in 1549, but it remained in the Calendar of Oxford University and is still in the Oxford University *Almanack*. In the Eastern Church, where the doctrine of corporeal assumption has never been formally adopted, 15 August is celebrated as the Feast of the Dormition.

The principal events in the life of Mary are marked by feasts, of which the most significant was the Feast of the Annunciation (25 March), which was the new year until CALENDAR REFORM displaced it in favour of 1 January. Feasts also mark the Birth (8 September), the Purification (2 February; known in English as Candlemas and in the Catholic Church known since 1960 as the Presentation of the Lord), the Visitation (2 July; in 1969 changed to 31 May), the Seven Sorrows of the Virgin (15 September), the Presentation of the Virgin Mary in the Temple (21 November; first permitted in 1372, incorporated into the breviary by SIXTUS IV, removed by PIUS V, and reinstituted by SIXTUS V in 1585), Our Lady of the Snows or Santa Maria ad Nives (5 August; now known as the Dedication of the Basilica of St Mary, i.e. Santa Maria Maggiore, the plan of which was designed by Mary when she left her footprints in snow that fell on 5 August), Our Lady of Mount Carmel (16 July; now optional), and Holy Name of Mary (12 September; now suppressed). In 1572 Pope Pius V instituted the Feast of the Blessed Virgin Mary of the Rosary on 7 October to commemorate the victory of the battle of LEPANTO, in which Mary was thought to have intervened; in 1573 the feast was moved to the first Sunday in October, but it reverted in 1969 to 7 October.

With the possible exception of Jesus, Mary is the most commonly represented figure in Western art. In narrative art she is portrayed in the various scenes in which she was a participant, and so appears in representations of the *Annunciation*, the *Nativity*, the *Adoration of the Magi*, the *Visitation* (to her cousin Elisabeth), the *Crucifixion*, the *Dormition*, and in many other scenes from the canonical and apocryphal Gospels, such as the *Rest on the Flight into Egypt*, which is a common composition in LANDSCAPE PAINTING. The seminal narrative cycle of Mary's life is GIOTTO's sequence in the Arena Chapel in Padua. When portrayed in iconic paintings and statues (usually with the infant Jesus) she is normally described as the Madonna.

Until the mid-fifteenth century, Italian representations of the Madonna, usually holding the infant Jesus in her arms or enthroning him on her knees, show an unsmiling Mary, her head covered by the capacious Byzantine veil known as a *maphorion*; such pictures are not intended to represent the fatigue of motherhood, but rather to affirm the doctrine of the incarnation. In the mid-fifteenth century Italian Madonnas begin to shed this hieratic image in favour of a secularized representation of a loving mother holding her baby. In the art of the Netherlands and Germany the Virgin's head is usually unveiled, and instead a diadem or crown sits on her blond hair. When saints were added to the group in Italian paintings of *The Madonna and Child with Saints*, the saints were placed on wings or in frames on either side of the main panel. When these divisions were abandoned by artists such as Fra ANGELICO, the saints were placed around the central group in a composition known as the SACRA CONVERSAZIONE. In the composition known as the *Holy Family* (Italian *Sacra Famiglia*), the Virgin and child are accompanied by Joseph and sometimes by other relatives. When the Madonna is shown cradling the body of her dead son, the composition is known as a PIETÀ. The cult of the Madonna of the Rosary can be traced to the festivity of a Piacenza CONFRATERNITY in 1250; this popular tradition is represented in art by works such as DÜRER's *Madonna of the Rose Garden* (c.1506–7, National

Gallery, Prague) and CARAVAGGIO's *Madonna of the Rosary* (c.1605, Kunsthistorisches Museum, Vienna).

The *Mater dolorosa* (Mother of Sorrows), which is known in Spanish as the *Virgen de los dolores* (Virgin of Sorrows), is a representation of Mary grieving for her son, either on his way to Calvary (in which case it tends to be one of the Stations of the Cross) or standing beneath the cross (the *Stabat mater*) or holding her dead son (the *Pietà*). Belief in the efficacy of Mary's intercession is reflected in art in the *Misericordia*, an image popular with charities and guilds in which votaries (often guild members) shelter beneath the Madonna's cloak, as in PIERO DELLA FRANCESCA's polyptych in Borgo Sansepolcro. The most familiar image of the *Madonna expectans*, in which Mary is heavily pregnant, is Piero's fresco (now detached) of the *Madonna del Parto* (c.1460) in the cemetery chapel in Monterchi (near Arezzo). The *Madonna del latte*, in which Mary is shown feeding the infant Jesus, is a common image in the Italian art of the fourteenth century (e.g. Nino PISANO's marble *Madonna and Child* of 1367/8 in the Museo Nazionale in Pisa) and fifteenth century (e.g. LEONARDO DA VINCI's *Madonna litta* of 1485/90 in the Hermitage). The *Maestà* (Italian 'majesty') is a large painting in which an enthroned Madonna (the queen of heaven) surrounded by angels and saints holds the infant Jesus.

**MARY I or Mary Tudor** (1516–58), queen of England. Daughter of CATHERINE OF ARAGON and HENRY VIII, her succession to the throne appeared unlikely following the birth of EDWARD VI. Attempts were made to divert the succession from her with the naming of Lady Jane GREY as Edward's heir in the last days of his reign, but nevertheless Mary was proclaimed queen in 1553. Her mother's Catholic faith had sustained Mary through the trials of her early life, and her primary aim as queen was to return the English Church to Rome. A marriage to Philip of Spain (later PHILIP II) forged an alliance with Catholic forces on the Continent. Overly zealous and ignoring advice to be cautious, however, Mary sought to force the pace by having key opponents of her policy burnt at the stake, but the deaths of CRANMER, RIDLEY, LATIMER, and others merely created Protestant martyrs. On Mary's death, ELIZABETH was quick to reassert royal control over the English Church.

*DNB.*

**MARY OF BURGUNDY or (French) Marie de Borgogne or (German) Maria von Burgund** (1457–82), duchess of Burgundy, was the daughter and only child of CHARLES THE BOLD and Isabella of Bourbon. On the death of her father on 5 January 1477, Mary inherited all his possessions, which included Alsace, Artois, Brabant, Flanders, Friesland, Hainaut, Lorraine, Luxemburg, and Zeeland as well as the duchy and county of Burgundy. King LOUIS XI of France contested the inheritance, claiming Burgundy and its possessions as a fief of the French crown; he seized Burgundy (but not the Netherlands) with a view to Mary marrying his son Charles and so securing the inheritance for his successors.

Mary declined the alliance and turned to her Netherlandish subjects for assistance, which was secured at a price:

on 11 February 1477 Mary was obliged to sign the agreement known in English as the 'Great Privilege', which ceded to the ESTATES-GENERAL very considerable rights. She was bound by the treaty not to declare war, sue for peace, or raise taxes without the consent of the Estates, and to restrict employment in the administration of the Netherlands to local people. Having secured a measure of stability in the face of the French threat, Mary married Maximilian of Austria (later the Emperor MAXIMILIAN I) in Ghent on 18 August 1477.

Mary died in a fall from her horse on 27 March 1482 and was buried beside her father in a bronze tomb in the Church of Our Lady in Bruges. Mary's three children included PHILIP THE HANDSOME, father of the Emperor CHARLES V.

*NDB s.v. Maria, Herzogin von Burgund.*

**MARY OF HUNGARY** (1505–58), queen consort of Hungary and regent of the Netherlands, was the daughter of King PHILIP I of Spain and JUANA LA LOCA and the sister of the Emperor CHARLES V; as a child she was known as Mary of Austria. In 1522 she married King LOUIS II of Hungary and Bohemia, who was killed four years later at the battle of MOHÁCS. She was appointed regent of the Netherlands in 1531, and there became a moderate opponent of Protestantism and an important patron of the arts: she employed Jacques DU BROEUCQ to build the chateaus of Binche (15 kilometres (9 miles) east of Mons) and Mariemont (Hainaut) and the Castle of Marienbourg (Namur), and collected works of art by Flemish and Italian artists (notably TITIAN). When Charles abdicated in 1555 she retired to Spain, settling in the Castle of Cigales, near Valladolid.

*NDB s.v. Maria, Erzherzogin von Österreich; MEL s.v. Mária;*
*Jane de Iongh, Mary of Hungary (English trans. 1958).*

**MARY OF LORRAINE or Mary of Guise** (1515–60), queen and regent of Scotland. Mary's marriage to JAMES V of Scotland cemented Scots-French allegiances and brought a fervent Catholic to the consort's throne in Scotland. Their daughter MARY, QUEEN OF SCOTS, inherited the crown when only a week old, and, as regent, Mary trod carefully to uphold Catholic interests in Scotland without alienating the Protestant nobility. There was less need for such circumspection following the marriage of her daughter in 1558 to FRANCIS II of France, and Protestant rebellion, supported by ELIZABETH I, followed. Mary died during the ensuing tumult.

*DNB.*

**MARY, QUEEN OF SCOTS, or Mary Stuart** (1542–87), queen of Scotland and France. Daughter of JAMES V and MARY OF LORRAINE, she came to the throne at one week old. An early betrothal to the future EDWARD VI came to nothing, and an alliance with France was instead sought, through a marriage with the future FRANCIS II in 1558. As a descendant of HENRY VII, through his daughter's marriage to JAMES IV of Scotland, Mary had a claim on the English throne which in Catholic eyes was stronger than that of ELIZABETH, whose legitimacy they did not recognize. Potentially then, Mary and Francis could have controlled England and Ireland as well as Scotland and France, but his death in 1560 put an end to such a possibility. Mary now hoped to be recognized by Elizabeth as her heir; a marriage to DARNLEY further strengthened her claim. Despite the birth of a son, the future JAMES VI of Scotland, relations with Darnley soured, and his murder, and Mary's own speedy remarriage to BOTHWELL, rendered her position precarious. She fled Scotland in 1567 in the midst of a Protestant rebellion, seeking refuge in England, where she was kept under house arrest; eventually persistent evidence of Mary's involvement in Catholic plots against her persuaded Elizabeth to have her executed.

*DNB.*

**MARY ROSE, HMS.** The second largest ship in HENRY VIII's navy, the *Mary Rose* was built between 1512 and 1514. She sank in 1545, within eyeshot of the shore, when setting forth from Portsmouth to join Henry's campaign against France; the king, who was there to see her off, witnessed the loss of a valuable ship, hundreds of men, and his vice-admiral. The ship was rescued from the seabed in 1982 and is now on display to the public in Portsmouth.

**MASACCIO or Tommaso di Ser Giovanni di Monte Cassai** (1401–*c*.1428), Italian painter, born in San Giovanni Valdarno (Tuscany). He lived in Florence from about 1422, and in 1428 moved to Rome, where he died at the age of 27.

The canon of Masaccio's surviving paintings consists of only four works, of which two are collaborative. He worked with MASOLINO on the panel painting of *The Virgin and Child with St Anne* (Uffizi) and the frescoes in the Brancacci Chapel of Santa Maria del Carmine in Florence. His independent paintings are the fresco of *The Trinity* in the Church of Santa Maria Novella in Florence and the polyptych painted in 1426 for Santa Maria del Carmine in Pisa; the surviving panels are now dispersed: the central panel of *The Madonna and Child Enthroned* is in the National Gallery in London, the predella panels in the Gemäldegalerie in Berlin, and the *Crucifixion* in the Museo Nazionale in Naples. There are also smaller panels in Pisa and the Getty Museum.

Masaccio's importance was fully recognized by VASARI, who noted Masaccio's debt to BRUNELLESCHI for his understanding of PERSPECTIVE and his debt to DONATELLO for the classical modelling of the human figure. The most original aspect of Masaccio's art was his innovative use of light to delineate his human figures and their clothing and, in the case of the Brancacci Chapel, to unify a composition extending over several walls by creating the illusion of a single source of light.

*MDA*; P. Joannides, *Masaccio and Masolino* (1993); J. Spike, *Masaccio* (1996).

**MASCHERA, FLORENTIO** (*c*.1540–*c*.1584), Italian composer, string player, and organist. He studied with Claudio MERULO, whom he succeeded as organist at Brescia Cathedral. He played the lira da braccio and violin and his compositions were mostly four-part instrumental canzonas, some of which appeared also as organ arrangements.

**MASNELLI, PAOLO** (*fl.* 1578–1609), Italian composer in Verona. Well known for his madrigals, some of which appeared in *De' floridi virtuosi d'Italia* (1583, 1585, and 1586), he

Masaccio, *The Trinity* (1427–8), a fresco in the Church of Santa Maria Novella in Florence

was also organist of the *ridotto* in Verona, which met under the patronage of Count Mario Bevilacqua and, from 1593, of the Accademia Filarmonica.

**MASO DI BANCO** (*fl.* 1335–50), Italian painter to whom Lorenzo GHIBERTI attributes the fresco cycle *The Life of St Sylvester* in the Bardi di Vernio Chapel of the Church of Santa Croce in Florence. The style of the cycle, which resembles that of GIOTTO, is sufficiently distinctive for other murals to be attributed to Maso, but the canon of his works remains unstable and even his identity is uncertain.

*MDA.*

Masaccio, *Peter Curing the Sick with his Shadow*, a fresco in the Brancacci Chapel of the Church of Santa Maria del Carmine in Florence

**MASOLINO or Tommaso da Panicale or Maso di Cristofano Fini** (c.1383–after 1435), Italian painter, born near Florence, where he was admitted to the Guild of Painters in 1423. He collaborated with MASACCIO on *The Virgin and Child with St Anne* (Uffizi) and the frescoes in the Brancacci Chapel of Santa Maria del Carmine; his style became so similar to Masaccio's that attributions were long regarded as problematical. He subsequently lived in Rome (c.1428–31), where he painted a fresco cycle on *The Life of St Catherine* in San Clemente and may have been responsible for part of the triptych of *The Miracle of the Snow* for Santa Maria Maggiore; the panel depicting *St Jerome and St John* (now in the National Gallery in London), however, is now generally attributed to Masaccio. Masolino eventually moved to northern Italy, where his surviving works include frescoes of *The Life of the Virgin* in the collegiate church at Castiglione Olona (near Como).

MDA; Perri Lee Roberts, *Masolino da Panicale* (1993).

**MASQUE**, a courtly spectacle, deriving ultimately from Italy, but which received distinctive development in England, especially at the court of JAMES I, under the encourage-

ment of his wife Anne. The masque, usually performed by amateurs, offered an entertainment combining dance, disguise, poetry, and music; it characteristically contained little narrative or plot, but offered allegorical representation and celebration of virtues or, in its more political form, authority and order. Spectators often participated in the masques in some way, for instance in a concluding dance. JONSON, the most skilled writer of masques, added an 'antimasque' whose disorder and confusion emphasized the harmony of the main spectacle. Scenery also played an important part in the entertainment, although Jonson quarrelled with his collaborator Inigo JONES over its relative importance. Masques were also produced by Samuel DANIEL, CHAPMAN, and MIDDLETON.

**MASS**, the ritualistic celebration of the EUCHARIST. The meaning of the term as a polyphonic setting of the mass ordinary was established during the Renaissance. The different sections were linked through musical devices, the most obvious being in the *cantus firmus* mass where all the movements are based on the same melody, generally in the tenor line. A *cantus firmus* could have a liturgical source (e.g. JOSQUIN's *Missa Pange lingua*) or secular origins (DUFAY's *Missa Se la face ay pale* and numerous *L'Homme armé* settings). Borrowing material in a more elaborate way occurred in parody mass settings where entire segments from another polyphonic source (often a motet) were incorporated into each mass movement. Examples can be found in the works of PALESTRINA, LASSUS, GOMBERT, and CLEMENS NON PAPA.

**MASSINGER, PHILIP** (1583–1640), English playwright. Author, alone and in collaboration, of over 50 plays, of which some 30 survive, Massinger is a significant figure in Jacobean drama. Following FLETCHER's retirement in 1613, he became BEAUMONT's chief writing partner; sixteen of his plays survive. His best-known work is *A New Way to Pay Old Debts* (1633), a comedy of revenge against the exploitative Overreach; *The City Madam* (acted 1632, published 1658) is another comedy, and *The Roman Actor* (acted 1626, published 1629) is a revenge tragedy set in the reign of the Emperor Domitian. With Fletcher he wrote the bawdy tragicomedy *The Custom of the Country* (c.1620) and the tragedy *Barnavelt* (1619), on OLDENBARNEVELT. From 1625 he was chief playwright of SHAKESPEARE's old company, the King's Men.

DNB.

**MASSYS or Matsys or Metsys, QUENTIN** (1466–1530), Flemish painter, born in Louvain, the son of a clockmaker. His early life is not well documented, but in 1491 he settled permanently in Antwerp. The mastery and majesty of his earliest known paintings, the *St Anne* Altarpiece (1507–9, Musée d'Art Ancien, Brussels) and the *Lamentation*, the central panel of a *St John* altarpiece (1508–11, Koninklijk Museum voor Schone Kunsten, Antwerp), may imply an early œuvre that has been lost. He is not known to have visited Italy, but Italian influence is evident in his paintings: in the altarpiece St Anne is depicted in an Italianate building, and the

Quentin Massys, *The Banker and his Wife* (1514), in the Louvre, Paris

influence of LEONARDO DA VINCI is apparent in his portraits (e.g. *Profile of an Elderly Man*, Musée Jacquemart André, Paris) and devotional paintings (e.g. *Magdalene*, in the Koninklijk Museum voor Schone Kunsten, Antwerp). His pictures of merchants and bankers (notably *The Banker and his Wife*, Louvre, 1514) have a satirical edge (in this case deprecating avarice) that may imply the influence of ERASMUS; Massys painted a portrait of *Erasmus* (1517, Hampton Court) which Erasmus intended as a gift for Sir Thomas MORE.

*BNB* and *MDA* s.v. Metsys; Emmanuelle Revel, *Le Prêteur et sa femme de Quentin Metsys* (1995).

**MASTER E.S. or Master of 1466** (*fl.* mid-fifteenth century), German engraver and goldsmith whose engravings are signed with what are assumed to be his initials; one of his engravings is dated 1466. He was one of the most innovative of early German engravers. His predecessors had largely been content to engrave outlines, whereas Master E.S. created sophisticated tonal effects by the adept use of parallel and cross-hatchings. His subjects were usually devotional, and include representations of the Annunciation, the Nativity, and the Man of Sorrows.

*MDA* s.v. Master E.S. (*fl. c.*1450–1467).

**MASTER OF.** For place names see under the name of the place.

**MASTER OF MARY OF BURGUNDY.** See BENING FAMILY.

**MASTER OF ST GILES** (*fl.* 1480–1500), French artist whose name derives from two panels representing *The Life of St Giles* (National Gallery, London); the style of these panels is the basis of attributions of other works to the same artist. The topographical views of Paris and (in the case of one of the National Gallery panels) of the interior of Saint-Denis have been taken as evidence that the Master lived in or near Paris and may have been French.

*MDA.*

**MASTER OF ST MARTHA or Master of Chaource** (*fl.* 1510–30), French sculptor whose name derives from the statue of St Martha (*c.*1515) in the Church of La Madeleine in Troyes. The emotionally restrained figure of Martha, with her fastidiously carved draperies, forms the basis of attributions of other statues from the same area, including a *Pietà* in the Church of Saint-Jean in Troyes and an *Entombment* in the Church of Saint-Jean-Baptiste in Chaource (the source of the Master's alternative name).

*MDA* s.v. Master of Chaource.

**MASTER OF THE BRUNSWICK MONOGRAM** (*fl.* 1520–40), Flemish artist whose name derives from the monogram on a painting of *The Parable of the Last Supper* (Herzog-Anton-

Ulrich Museum, Brunswick); there is no scholarly consensus about the meaning of the monogram. Pictures attributed to the same hand share a common style characterized by fine drawings and by an unusual ability to depict figures in landscapes; the subject matter of these pictures, however, is sharply divided into those that depict religious subjects in landscapes and those that portray scenes in brothels. The Master has been identified with various artists, including Jan Sanders van HEMESSEN, but is now thought by many scholars to be Jan van Amstel (c.1500–42), the brother of Pieter AERTSEN.

The Master of the Brunswick Diptych (*fl.* 1480–1510) is a different painter, named after a diptych also in the Herzog-Anton-Ulrich Museum in Brunswick.

*MDA* s.v. Masters (III) Monogrammists.

## MASTER OF THE DEATH OF THE VIRGIN. See JOOS VAN CLEVE.

**MASTER OF THE HOUSEBOOK or (formerly) Master of the Amsterdam Cabinet** (*fl.* c.1470–1500), German painter and engraver in the Middle Rhineland whose present name derives from a collection of his drawings in a commonplace book (*Hausbuch*) in Castle Wolfegg (Upper Swabia); his former name derives from the fact that the largest collection of his drawings is held in the Print Room of the Rijksmuseum in Amsterdam. His engravings are characterized in technique by their use of drypoint and in subject by their wholly secular character. The influence of these engravings can be discerned in several of the early drawings of DÜRER, who either took copies or committed details to memory.

*MDA* s.v. Housebook; Alfred Stange, *Die Hausbuchmeister* (1958); Jane Hutchison, *The Master of the Housebook* (1972); J. P. Filedt Kok, *Livelier than Life: The Master of the Amsterdam Cabinet* (1985).

**MASTER OF THE LEGEND OF ST BARBARA** (*fl.* 1470–1500), Netherlandish painter whose name derives from the subject of a triptych of which the right panel is lost, the centre panel is in the Musée d'Art Ancien in Brussels, and the left panel is in the Confrérie du Saint-Sang in Bruges. The Master's hand is apparent in fragments of an altarpiece on *The Legend of St Géry* in the National Gallery of Ireland and the Mauritshuis in The Hague.

*MDA.*

**MASTER OF THE LIFE OF THE VIRGIN** (*fl.* 1460–80), German painter based in Cologne whose name derives from a series of eight panels illustrating the life of the Virgin Mary; seven of the panels are in the Alte Pinakothek in Munich and the eighth, *The Presentation in the Temple*, is in the National Gallery in London. Four other panels in the National Gallery (painted for Werden Abbey, near Essen) are likely to be products of the same workshop, as may a *Crucifixion* at Kues (on the Mosel).

This artist was formerly known as the 'Master of the Lyversberg Passion', whose name derives from a *Passion*

sequence in the Wallraf-Richartz Museum in Cologne. This cycle is now thought to be the work of another artist.

*MDA.*

**MASTER OF THE PLAYING CARDS** (*fl.* 1425–50), German engraver of a set of PLAYING CARDS which contain finely drawn pictures of people, animals, and plants. Examples of the cards are preserved in the Bibliothèque Nationale in Paris and the Kupferstichkabinett in Dresden.

*MDA.*

**MASTER OF THE REVELS.** From the end of the fifteenth century, this was a temporary position for an English official overseeing court entertainment, but the position was made permanent from 1545. From 1574, as a result of conflicts between the London City corporation, which sought to limit plays, and ELIZABETH's court, which sought to promote them, the master of the revels took on the role of licensing plays. From 1581 he had power to send offenders to prison; however, regulation was fitful and addressed political and religious controversies, rather than exercising censorship on moral questions. From 1606, he also issued licences for the printing of plays. Playwrights who fell foul of the master of the revels include JONSON, whose *Sejanus* (1603) was considered seditious, and MASSINGER, who was forced to rewrite his play *Believe as You List* (1631), transferring its action from recent Spanish and Portuguese history to the time of the Roman Empire. From 1622, Sir Henry Herbert was master of the revels; his records provide a wealth of detailed information about drama in this period.

**MASTER OF THE VIEW OF SAINTE-GUDULE** (*fl.* 1470–90), Netherlandish painter whose name derives from a panel (now in the Louvre) which has in its background a view of the façade of the Church of Sainte-Gudule in Brussels. The same artist's *Portrait of a Young Man Holding a Heart-Shaped Book* (National Gallery, London) contains in its background a view of another Brussels church, Notre-Dame-du-Sablon.

*MDA.*

**MASTER OF THE VIRGO INTER VIRGINES** (*fl.* 1483–98), Netherlandish painter based in Delft whose name derives from a picture of the Virgin Mary in the midst of a group of virgins (Rijksmuseum, Amsterdam). His surviving pictures, notably the *Crucifixion* (Uffizi) and the *Lamentation* (Walker Art Gallery, Liverpool), convey the intensity of devotional passion through the depiction of gaunt figures and bleak landscapes painted in vivid colours.

*MDA*; Marc Rudolf de Vrij, *De Meester van de Virgo into Virgines* (1999).

**MÄSTLIN, MICHAEL** (1550–1631), German astronomer, educated at the University of Tübingen. He became a Lutheran minister (1576) and subsequently held chairs of mathematics at Heidelberg and Tübingen. He observed the New Star of 1572 and studied the comets of 1577 and 1580. His writings are concerned with the standard geocentric

(Ptolemaic) system, but at some stage he had developed an interest in the COPERNICAN cosmology and at Tübingen he held extra classes at which his more able students were introduced to the Copernican system. In the 1580s, these students included Johannes KEPLER. Mästlin wrote an account of Copernican planetary theory as an appendix for Kepler's first astronomical publication, *Mysterium cosmographicum* (1596). For the remainder of his life Kepler continued to think of Mästlin as his teacher and wrote him long letters about the progress of his researches, sometimes asking him very difficult questions.

Mästlin's reputation now tends to be eclipsed by that of his famous pupil, but he was in fact one of the most respected astronomers of his generation.

*DSB; NDB.*

**MASUCCIO SALERNITANO or Tommaso Guardati** (*c*.1410–*c*.1475), Italian satirist. He was a native of Salerno, where he entered the service of Roberto Sanseverino, prince of Salerno, and became a friend of Aragonese humanists at the viceregal court in Naples. Masuccio's *Novellino* (posthumously published in Venice in 1492) is a collection of 50 NOVELLAS in which a narrator called Masuccio addresses each tale to a member of the Aragonese court. The tales are characterized by a skilled rendering of dialect and by anticlerical and anti-feminist satire.

*OCIL*; G. Petrocchi, *Masuccio Guardati e la narrativa napoletana del Quattrocento* (1953).

**MATARAZZO, FRANCESCO.** See MATURANZIO, FRANCESCO.

**MATHEMATICS.** See ARITHMETIC.

**MATHEMATICS, PRACTICAL.** See ABACUS SCHOOLS; ALGEBRA.

**MATRIMONIAL LAW.** Marriage is a social institution, but in Renaissance law it was a contract in which the phrase 'two shall become one' meant that the woman's legal personality was submerged in that of her husband. In CANON LAW the Church was deemed to have exclusive jurisdiction over marriage, and the COUNCIL OF TRENT anathematized reformers such as LUTHER for contending that marriage should fall within the jurisdiction of civil courts. See DIVORCE.

**MATTEO DI GIOVANNI** (*c*.1435–1495), Italian painter, born in Sansepolcro (Borgo Sansepolcro, Umbria), the son of a tinker, and trained in VECCHIETTA's studio in Siena. He eventually became Siena's most prominent painter, specializing in elegant Madonnas (e.g. *Virgin and Child with Angels*, Pinacoteca, Siena). He also added the wings to PIERO DELLA FRANCESCA's *Baptism of Jesus*. Matteo's other paintings include an *Assumption*, a *Christ Crowned with Thorns*, and a *St Sebastian* (all in the National Gallery in London). His dramatic *Massacre of the Innocents* survives in four versions, three paintings (1482–91) and an inlaid marble mosaic in the floor of the cathedral in Siena.

*MDA.*

**MATTHIAS** (1557–1619), Holy Roman Emperor, was born on 24 February 1557 in Vienna, the third son of the Emperor MAXIMILIAN II and his wife Maria (daughter of CHARLES V) and the younger brother of the future Emperor RUDOLF II. In January 1578 he became governor-general of the Netherlands in the hope that a successful resolution of the REVOLT OF THE NETHERLANDS would secure a throne for him; in the event the abjuration of PHILIP II in July 1581 ended his governorship, and he returned to Austria, where, in 1595, he was appointed governor on the death of his brother Ernst. In Austria he helped to suppress the Protestants, and also took part in Rudolf's TURKISH WAR. He assumed control of Hungary in May 1605, and concluded a peace with the Transylvanian rebels in June 1606 (the Treaty of Vienna) and with the Ottoman Sultan Ahmet I in November 1606 (the Treaty of Zsitvar-Torok).

Rudolf's instability led the HABSBURG family to appoint Matthias as their head in April 1606. He secured the allegiance of Hungary, Austria, and Moravia by offering religious concessions (the Treaty of Liběň or Lieben), and twice invaded Bohemia (1608 and 1611) before being proclaimed king on 23 May 1611. On the death of his brother Rudolf on 20 January 1612, Matthias became Holy Roman Emperor. He died in Vienna on 20 March 1619, just as the THIRTY YEARS WAR was beginning to devastate his empire.

*NDB.*

**MATTHIAS CORVINUS or Mátyás Hunyadi** (1443–90), king of Hungary, was born in Kolozsvár (now Romanian Cluj-Napoca), the second son of János HUNYADI. He received a humanist education that included military training, and in 1454 (aged 14) was knighted during the siege of Belgrade. On the death of his father he was seized by the agents of King LADISLAS POSTHUMUS, and after the king's death in 1457 he was entrusted to the care of GEORGE OF PODĚBRADY, whose daughter Catherine he married. In 1458 he was elected king of Hungary.

The reign of Matthias was dominated by war with the Ottomans in Bosnia (which was part of his realm), a protracted struggle with the Emperor FRIEDRICH III, and a dispute with his father-in-law George of Poděbrady, who had become king of Bohemia in 1458. The last of these conflicts concerned the throne of Bohemia, to which Matthias was elected in 1458 by the Catholic party that opposed King George; the issue was not resolved until 1471, when, on the death of George of Poděbrady, Matthias secured Moravia and Silesia but relinquished his claim to the throne of Bohemia in favour of LADISLAS II (Czech Vladislas II).

In 1481 Matthias renewed his war with the emperor, and four years later captured Vienna. His courts in Buda and (from 1485) Vienna were important centres of humanist scholarship and the arts. He amassed a vast library known as the Biblioteca Corvina which was dispersed after his death. Matthias left no legitimate heir, and was succeeded by his illegitimate son János CORVINUS.

*NDB; MEL* s.v. Mátyás I; J. Balogh, *Die Anfänge der Renaissance in Ungarn: Matthias Corvinus und die Kunst* (1975); C. Csapoki, *The Corvinian Library* (1973).

**MATTIOLI, PIERANDREA** (1501–77), Italian botanist and physician, a native of Siena who studied medicine in Padua and worked as a physician in Siena, Rome, Trento, Gorizia, and at the imperial court in Prague. His principal botanical work was an annotated edition of the *De materia medica* of Dioscorides (*Comentarii a Dioscoride*, Venice, 1544) which was often reprinted, sometimes in Italian, German, French, and Czech translation; many editions were lavishly illustrated (notably the Prague edition of 1562), and later editions included accounts of newly discovered plants in America and Asia.

*DSB* s.v. Mattioli, Pietro Andrea.

**MATURANZIO or Matarazzo, FRANCESCO** (*c*.1443–1518), Italian humanist, historian, and Hellenist. He was born near Perugia, and his education included a year in Rhodes, where he studied Greek. He settled in Perugia under the patronage of the BAGLIONI family. His most important work is a history of Perugia from 1492 to 1503.

Guglielmo Zappacosta, *Francesco Maturanzio: Umanista perugino* (1970).

**MAURICE, COUNT OF NASSAU, or** (Dutch) **Maurits, Graaf van Nassau** (1567–1625), stadtholder of the UNITED PROVINCES and (from 1618) prince of Orange, was the second son of WILLIAM OF ORANGE, the grandson (through his mother) of MAURICE OF SAXONY, and the nephew of Count LOUIS OF NASSAU. After the assassination of his father on 10 July 1584, Maurice became the military leader of the REVOLT OF THE NETHERLANDS and, with the assistance of Jan van OLDENBARNEVELT, secured appointments in each of the provinces (as captain-general and stadtholder) except Friesland. He reformed the army, in part modelling his reforms on the armies of classical antiquity described in contemporary manuals of WARFARE: he organized his army into small battalions of infantry (*c*.550 officers and men) and specialized artillery and supply units, and in battle arranged his troops in lines rather than squares. With this professional, well-fed, and well-equipped army he was able to expel the Spanish from the northern provinces in the course of ten years (1588–98).

Oldenbarnevelt wanted to extend the war to the south and expel the Spanish from the southern provinces. Maurice did not share this aspiration, but nonetheless invaded Flanders, defeating a Spanish army at Nieuwpoort (2 July 1600); he then withdrew rather than following up his victory. Maurice subsequently disapproved of the twelve-year truce that Oldenbarnevelt negotiated (April 1609). The split between the two men, which reflected deep divisions in the Dutch Church (see DORT, SYNOD OF) and state, came to a head in 1619, when Maurice had Oldenbarnevelt executed. When the twelve-year truce expired in 1621, Maurice resumed the war with Spain in the broader context of the THIRTY YEARS WAR, but his military prowess was in decline, and he suffered a series of reverses; when he died Spinola was advancing into the Netherlands.

*NNBW* i.

**MAURICE OF SAXONY or** (German) **Moritz von Sachsen** (1521–53), elector of Saxony, was born in Freiberg on 21 March 1521, the son of Heinrich, who in 1539 became duke (*Herzog*) of Saxony. In 1485 SAXONY had been divided between two branches of the WETTIN family: the Albertine branch of the family inherited ducal Saxony and the Ernestine branch electoral Saxony. In January 1541 Maurice married Agnes, the 14-year-old daughter of PHILIP OF HESSE, and the same year he succeeded his father as duke of Saxony; he had been raised as a Lutheran, and so continued his father's policy of implementing the Reformation within his territories and using confiscated church property for educational purposes. Maurice's ambition was to secure the electorate, and as he was untroubled by religious considerations, he was happy to fight for CHARLES V against the Turks in 1542.

When Charles decided to attack the SCHMALKALDIC LEAGUE, of which Maurice was a nominal member, the emperor and the duke came to a private arrangement at a meeting held in Regensburg in July 1546: Maurice offered public neutrality and covert assistance in exchange for immunity for his subjects from the decrees of the COUNCIL OF TRENT, and also discussed the possibility of transferring the electorate. When the SCHMALKALDIC WAR broke out, Maurice declared war on JOHANN FRIEDRICH I, the elector of Saxony. The League was defeated at the battle of MÜHLBERG on 24 April 1547, and Johann Friedrich was taken prisoner; on 19 May 1547 he signed the Capitulation, by which he ceded to Maurice the electoral title and the province that contained Wittenberg.

Maurice's relations with Charles were strained by the continued imprisonment of Philip of Hesse (Maurice's father-in-law) and by the emperor's decision to limit the indignities suffered by the family of Johann Friedrich. Maurice changed sides, and in January 1552 signed the Treaty of Chambord, so aligning himself with the Protestant princes and King HENRI II of France. The ensuing campaign against Charles V concluded with the Treaty of Passau, in which Maurice and FERDINAND I (Charles's deputy) agreed on terms that gave religious freedom to Protestants. Maurice was soon at war again, this time in Hungary, fighting the Ottomans on behalf of Ferdinand. His last campaign was directed against his former friend and comrade ALBRECHT ALCIBIADES, whom he defeated at Sievershausen (Selling) on 9 July 1553. Albrecht escaped, but Maurice died of his wounds two days later. His only daughter Anna later became the second wife of WILLIAM OF ORANGE.

*NDB* s.v. Moritz, Herzog von Sachsen.

**MAURO, FRA** (d. 1459), Italian cartographer, a Camaldolese monk who lived in his Order's house on the Venetian island of Murano. In 1457 he received a commission from King AFONSO V of Portugal to produce a map of the world. His circular *Mappa mundi* (190 centimetres (75 inches) in diameter), which draws on sources ranging from MARCO POLO to the Portuguese voyages sponsored by HENRY THE NAVIGATOR, was completed in 1459 and is now in the Biblioteca Marciana in Venice.

*DSB*; T. Gasparrini Leporace, *Il mappamundo di Fra Mauro* (1970).

**MAXIMILIAN I** (1459–1519), Holy Roman Emperor, was born on 22 March 1459 at Wiener Neustadt, the son of the Emperor FRIEDRICH III and Eleanor, daughter of King DUARTE of Portugal. On 18 August 1477 he married MARY OF BURGUNDY, who had recently inherited BURGUNDY (an archduchy which included the Netherlands—modern Holland, Belgium, and Luxemburg—and Franche-Comté as well as Burgundy) from her father CHARLES THE BOLD, so extending the lands of the Habsburgs to an important new area of Europe. Maximilian had to defend his wife's inheritance against an attack mounted by King LOUIS XI of France, whose army Maximilian defeated at Guinegate (modern Enguinegatte, in Artois) on 7 August 1479, so adding Artois to his territories.

Mary of Burgundy died on 27 March 1482, and, because Maximilian's claim to the Netherlands was through her, several provinces were reluctant to recognize the regency claimed by Maximilian on behalf of his 3-year-old son Philip (later PHILIP I, king of Castile), and there was widespread civil unrest. Maximilian was obliged to sign the Treaty of Arras (December 1482) between the ESTATES of the Netherlands and Louis XI. Under the terms of the treaty, Maximilian's daughter MARGARET OF AUSTRIA was betrothed to the Dauphin Charles (later CHARLES VIII) and her dowry was to include Charolais, Auxerre, and the disputed provinces of Artois and Franche-Comté; Maximilian also tacitly acknowledged the suzerainty of Louis XI over the duchy of Burgundy.

Maximilian travelled to Germany, where he was elected king of the Romans at Frankfurt (16 February 1486) and crowned at Aachen (9 April 1486). Returning to the Netherlands, where ANNE OF FRANCE was prosecuting an increasingly unpopular war with Francis II, duke of Brittany, Maximilian entered Bruges, where he was imprisoned from February to May 1488, when he was rescued by his father's imperial army. Maximilian departed for Austria in December 1489, and the following year married by proxy Anne, duchess of Burgundy, daughter of and successor to Francis II; King Charles VIII retaliated by breaking off his betrothal to Maximilian's daughter Margaret and instead marrying Anne, duchess of Burgundy (December 1491), whose marriage to Maximilian had not been consummated because she was inaccessible in French-occupied Brittany. This marital war led to a martial struggle in which Maximilian successfully defended Salins (Franche-Comté) against a French invasion in January 1493 and four months later, in the Treaty of Senlis, secured the return of Artois and Franche-Comté. In August 1494 Maximilian passed responsibility for the Netherlands to his son Philip; after Philip's death on 26 September 1506, his sister Margaret of Austria ruled as regent (1509–30) on behalf of Philip's son Charles (later CHARLES V).

In December 1489 Maximilian had left the Netherlands to attend to problems in the Habsburg possessions centred on Austria. He took over the governance of Tirol in 1490 from the hapless Archduke Sigismund, who was deposed. MATTHIAS CORVINUS had conquered Carinthia and Styria and occupied Vienna in 1485 and Wiener Neustadt in 1487; his death on 6 April 1490 opened the way for Maximilian to reconquer all of his Austrian lands. He recaptured Vienna and expelled the Hungarians from Austria, but could not afford to garrison his newly recovered possessions, and on 7 November 1491 signed the Treaty of Pressburg (now Bratislava, in Slovakia) with LADISLAS II of Bohemia, who had secured the throne of Hungary; by the terms of the treaty it was agreed that Maximilian would succeed to the throne of Hungary if Ladislas were to die without legitimate male heirs. The following year Maximilian repelled an Ottoman attack at Villach.

On the death of the Emperor FRIEDRICH III in August 1493 Maximilian inherited the Empire and became the senior member of the HABSBURG FAMILY. On 16 March 1494 he married (in Innsbruck) Bianca Maria Sforza, daughter of the late Galeazzo Maria SFORZA, duke of Milan; the marriage had been arranged by Galeazzo's brother and successor Ludovico SFORZA, who paid the enormous dowry of 440,000 ducats. He also arranged a strategic double marriage for his children by Margaret of Austria: in 1496 his daughter Margaret was married (in Antwerp) to Don Juan, son and heir of FERDINAND and ISABELLA, and in 1497 his son Philip was married (in Burgos) to Don Juan's sister, who was later known as JUANA LA LOCA. In 1515 he arranged another double marriage, this time between two of his grandchildren and LOUIS II of Hungary and his sister Anna; the eventual result of this union was the addition of Bohemia and Hungary to the Habsburg Empire.

From 1494 till 1516 Maximilian's energies were largely concentrated on the WARS OF ITALY; he sought to expel the French from Italy (and so force CHARLES VIII to abandon his claim to Milan) and to expel the Venetians from Verona and the *terraferma*. As the German princes refused to fund Maximilian's participation in the Wars of Italy, he fought in 1496 as a *CONDOTTIERE* in the service of Milan; he returned humiliated to Germany and was eventually forced to recognize the French annexation of Milan in the Treaty of BLOIS (September 1504). In 1508 he attempted to reach Rome in order to be crowned as emperor, but Venice would not allow him to cross its territory, so Maximilian declared himself to be Roman emperor elect, a title quickly ratified by Pope JULIUS II. When Venice became the enemy that he most desired to defeat, he formed the League of CAMBRAI with France (December 1508); three years later he turned against France and joined the HOLY LEAGUE to fight the French (this time working in the pay of HENRY VIII of England) and on 16 August 1513 participated in the battle of the SPURS at Guinegate (modern Enguinegatte). After FRANCIS I emerged victorious from the battle of MARIGNANO (13/14 September 1515), Maximilian launched his final invasion of Italy, capturing Milan for a day (25 March 1516) before retreating.

In Italy Maximilian had attempted to restore the authority of the Empire; he failed to do so, and in the process weakened the authority of the Empire in Germany. He aspired to reign over a centralized state, but he was opposed by the ESTATES, who had no wish to dismantle the range of governmental structures established in some 350 autonomous principalities and imperial cities. In 1495 an 'eternal public peace' was negotiated at the Diet of Worms: Maximilian established the important legal institutions of the REICHSKAMMERGERICHT and (in 1498) the AULIC COUNCIL, but declined to accept the Diet's proposal that he be subject to an executive council (*Reichsregiment*); his military reforms included the establishment of the LANDSKNECHTE. Maximilian's attempt to subdue Rhaetia drew him into a war with the entire Swiss Confederation known as the Swabian (or, more properly, the Swiss) War, which led to the secession of the Confederation *de facto*, if not *de jure*, from the Empire under the terms of the Treaty of Basel (September 1499). A revised programme of reform negotiated at the Diet of Augsburg in 1500 led to the creation of a twenty-member *Reichsregiment* of which the Emperor was to be president and also divided the HOLY ROMAN EMPIRE into six circles; in the event, the Reichsregiment was dissolved in 1502, but the circles (expanded to ten in 1512) lasted for centuries. At his final diet (Frankfurt, 1518) he set about trying to bribe the imperial electors to choose his grandson Charles (later CHARLES V) as king of the Romans; he left the Diet without having accomplished his purpose and travelled to Wels (Upper Austria), where he died on 12 January 1519. He was buried in the Church of St George in Wiener Neustadt and a magnificent monument was erected in Innsbruck.

Maximilian was a polyglot who had informed interests in art, education, literature, music, and theology; he extended his patronage to artists such as BURGKMAIR and DÜRER (whose superb charcoal drawing of Maximilian, now in the Albertina in Vienna, was the basis of two painted portraits) and to the universities of Vienna (which he reorganized), Ingolstadt, and Freiberg. He was also a writer, though it is difficult to be certain how much of his writing was ghosted by others. The short treatise on hunting written for his grandchildren (*Geheimes Jagdbuch*) is probably his own work, but autobiographical poems such as *Teuerdank* (which describes his journey to marry Mary of Burgundy) and *Der Weißkunig* (an unfinished autobiography not published until 1775) were planned and partly executed by Maximilian but substantially written by others.

*NDB*; *MDA* s.v. Habsburg; H. Wiesflecker, *Kaiser Maximilian I* (5 vols., 1971–86); one-vol. summary (1991).

**MAXIMILIAN II** (1527–76), Holy Roman Emperor, was born in Vienna on 31 July 1527, the eldest son of the HABSBURG Emperor FERDINAND I and his wife Anna, daughter of Ladislas, king of Hungary and Bohemia. Maximilian was educated in Spain and embarked on a military career, fighting with CHARLES V against France in 1544 and in the SCHMALKALDIC WAR of 1546–7. In September 1548 he married his cousin Maria, daughter of Charles V, and for the next two years served as Charles's deputy in Spain. Thereafter he established his court in Vienna, where he was occupied with the defence of the Austrian dominions against the Ottomans.

Maximilian was a humanist in the tradition of ERASMUS, and so was not an energetic opponent of the Reformation. His Lutheran sympathies and his friendly relations with the reformers gave rise to fears that he would leave the Catholic Church; in the event he remained faithful to Rome. In 1562 Maximilian was elected king of the Romans and in July 1564 he succeeded his father as Holy Roman Emperor and king of Bohemia and Hungary. As emperor Maximilian sought to facilitate reconciliation by attempting to persuade Pope PIUS IV to accede to marriage of the clergy; Pius refused, and four years later his successor, Pope PIUS V, withdrew the concession of communion in both kinds to the laity. For his part, Maximilian allowed religious freedom to Lutheran nobles in Austria and refused to license the publication of the decrees of the COUNCIL OF TRENT.

In March 1566 Maximilian travelled to AUGSBURG to preside over his first diet. He declined to agree to the demands of the Lutheran princes, but refrained from instituting any measures to suppress the Reformation. The only important result of the Diet was a large grant which enabled Maximilian to finance the latest campaign against the Ottomans. There were no significant military engagements in the following year, and in 1568 Maximilian agreed to a truce which obliged him to pay tribute for Hungary to the Ottoman Sultan Selim II.

In 1568 Don CARLOS, the heir to the Spanish throne, died while under house arrest, so opening the way for Maximilian (or one of his sons) to succeed his cousin PHILIP II as king of Spain. This possibility, which was never to be realized, led Maximilian in 1570 to forge a marital alliance by which his daughter Anna became the fourth wife of King Philip. In the final years of his reign Maximilian's principal concern was the defence of his territories: the REVOLT OF THE NETHERLANDS created instability on his north-western borders, the Ottomans threatened the eastern borders, and foreign armies passing through Germany posed an internal threat. Maximilian died on 12 October 1576, refusing on his deathbed to receive the last rites of the Church. Maximilian had nine sons and six daughters by his wife Maria: he was succeeded as emperor by his son RUDOLF II, who was in turn succeeded by another son, MATTHIAS.

*NDB*.

**MAYENNE, CHARLES DE LORRAINE, DUKE OF** (1554–1611), leader of the CATHOLIC LEAGUE in the French WARS OF RELIGION, the son of François, second duke of GUISE, and the younger brother of Henri, third duke of GUISE, and Cardinal Charles de GUISE. When his brothers were assassinated in 1588 by order of King HENRI III, Charles marched to Paris (a stronghold of the Catholic League) and was declared by the Parlement to be lieutenant-general of France. When the king was assassinated the following year, Charles proclaimed the elderly cardinal of Bourbon as King Charles X of France and fought with Spanish troops against King HENRI IV. Charles eventually came to favour a policy of reconciliation, and so distanced himself from the Parisian extremists in the League (known as 'the Sixteen', from the sixteen administrative units into which they had divided Paris) and in October 1595 reached an accord with the king, in return for which he was appointed governor of Île de France and received a large indemnity.

**MAYNARD, JOHN** (1577–c.1615), English composer, lutenist, and lyra viol player. In 1600 he was appointed a commissary of muster in Ireland. In 1611 his *XII Wonders of the World*, which were settings of twelve satirical texts on well-known figures (the Courtier, the Lawyer) by Sir John Davies, were published; they are set for 'viola da Gamba, the Lute and the Voice'.

**MAZEROLLES, PHILIPPE DE** (c.1420–1479), Flemish miniaturist who worked in Paris as a young man and in 1467 became court painter to CHARLES THE BOLD in Bruges. His best-known work is the illumination of *The Conquest of the Golden Fleece* (Bibliothèque Nationale, Paris).

MDA s.v. Philippe de Mazerolles.

**MAZES AND LABYRINTHS**. Mazes are sometimes called labyrinths, with reference to the four famous labyrinths of antiquity in Knossos (the original labyrinth), Egypt (the funeral temple of Amenemhet), Lemnos (which survived in Pliny's time), and Italy (the tomb of Porsena at Clusium, now Chiusi). All four labyrinths were lost, but their memory was preserved in literature, and they were depicted on Cretan coins, Greek vases, and Roman mosaics; the recovery of such artefacts revived interest in the form. The four great labyrinths of antiquity were all buildings, but when the form was revived it was implemented in three forms: floor mazes in churches (of which the best Renaissance example was built in 1495 in the collegiate Church of Saint-Quentin), the medieval turf maze, and the garden maze.

In the sixteenth century garden mazes were usually constructed from low shrubs and herbs; the hedge maze was an invention of the seventeenth century. There were mazes in gardens all over Europe: the first to be built in an ENGLISH GARDEN was at Nonsuch; in Germany, there was a maze in the HORTUS PALATINUS; in France, *bosquets* (see BOSCO) were sometimes planted as mazes; in Italy, the garden of the Villa d'ESTE had four mazes.

W. H. Matthews, *Mazes and Labyrinths: Their History and Development* (1922); J. Bord, *Mazes and Labyrinths of the World* (1976); R. Coate, A. Fisher, and G. Burgess, *A Celebration of Mazes* (1976); N. Pennick, *Mazes and Labyrinths* (1990); H. Kern, *Through the Labyrinth: Designs and Meanings over 5,000 Years*, trans. A. Clay (2000).

**MAZZOLINI, SILVESTRE, or Silvestre Prierias** (1456–1523), Italian Dominican polemicist, a native of Priero (Piedmont). In 1471 he entered the Dominican ORDER at Savona. He served as regent master in Bologna (1492–1502) and Venice (1502–8); while working in Venice he also served as professor of Thomistic theology at Padua. He served as prior in Milan, Verona, and Genoa, vicar-general of the Lombardy congregation of his Order (1508–10), inquisitor of Brescia (1508) and Milan (1512), regent master and prior of Bologna (1510–12), and prior of Cremona and Venice (1512–15).

In 1512 Pope LEO X appointed Mazzolini as 'master of the sacred palace', inquisitor for Rome, and professor of Thomistic theology at the University of Rome (Sapienza). He took part in the proceedings against Johann REUCHLIN and Martin LUTHER and in the investigations into the writings of ERASMUS and Pietro POMPONAZZI. He was killed during the SACK OF ROME.

Mazzolini wrote prolifically on theology, logic, homiletics, and spirituality. His best-known book is his dialogue on papal power (*Dialogus de potestae papae*), a response to Luther's *Theses*, copies of which arrived in Germany in January 1518 and fuelled the debate about Luther's rebellion; his subsequent polemics directed against Luther were *Replica ad fratrum Martinum Luther* (1518), *Epitoma responsionis ad Lutherum* (1519), and *Errata et argumenta Martini Lutheris* (1520). Mazzolini also published sermons (*Rosa aurea*, 1503), moral theology (*Summa Silvestriana*, 1514), a treatise on WITCHCRAFT (*De strigimagarum daemonumque mirandis*, 1521), and an unfinished commentary on THOMAS AQUINAS (*Conflatum ex S. Thoma*, part I, 1519).

C. Lindberg, 'Prierias and his Significance for Luther's Development', *Sixteenth-Century Journal*, 3 (1972).

**MAZZONI, GUIDO, or Paganino** (c.1450–1518), Italian sculptor. He was born in Modena, and worked there and in Ferrara, Venice, and Naples. The sculptures that he carved in Italy include many dramatic *Lamentation* scenes (e.g. Santa Anna dei Lombardi, Naples). In 1495 he travelled with CHARLES VIII from Naples to France; his EQUESTRIAN STATUE of *King Charles* (1498) in the Abbey of Saint-Denis was destroyed in 1789; his equestrian statue of *King LOUIS XII* at the Château de BLOIS was also destroyed. The realism to which he aspired in his effigies was achieved through his use of life and death masks. In 1516 he returned to Modena.

MDA.

**MECHANICS**. See TECHNOLOGY.

**MECKENEM, ISRAHEL VON, THE YOUNGER** (1440/5–1503), German engraver, born in Bamberg and trained by his father (and namesake) and by MASTER E.S. Most of his work, which runs to at least 600 copperplate engravings, consists of copies of designs by other engravers. His most important original work is a series of illustrations of *The Passion*. He was the first German artist to engrave a self-portrait, which appears in a double portrait with his wife.

MDA; NDB.

**MEDAL**, a metal disc struck or cast with the head or effigy of a person on the obverse and a related design (normally an IMPRESA in Italy or a coat of arms in northern Europe) on the reverse; its purpose is to commemorate a person or an event. It is this commemorative purpose that distinguishes Renaissance medals from COINS (which are primarily a medium of exchange), PLAQUETTES (which have mythological or religious subjects), and modern military medals (which reward acts of heroism and distinguished service); this element also points to the origin of the medal as a revival of the Roman imperial commemorative medallion. All Renaissance medals except those of the PAPAL STATE were privately manufactured.

Medal (1601) by Guillaume Dupré depicting King HENRI IV of France and MARIE DE MÉDICIS (British Museum)

Medal (1438) by PISANELLO depicting the Byzantine Emperor JOHN VIII PALAIOLOGOS (British Museum)

Italian medals were usually made from bronze, which had not been systematically used for coinage since the sixth century; silver, lead, and gold were also used. In the fifteenth and early sixteenth centuries, medals were normally cast by a variation on the *cire-perdue* ('lost-wax') method of casting statues: a wax model of the medal (each side of which had been separately moulded) was surrounded by a heat-proof mould, typically a paste made from ashes or chalk; the molten wax was then melted out through a vent, and molten bronze was poured into the space formerly filled by the wax. The casting of medals disappeared with the introduction of struck medals in Augsburg in 1550; in this method a heated metal disc was placed between two engraved dies, which were then hammered together or forced together with a screw-driven vice. In cast medals the mould could only be used once, and so medals were made in relatively small numbers; the advent of struck medals allowed for mass production, because dies could be used repeatedly.

The first Renaissance medallist was PISANELLO, who in 1438 cast a portrait medal of the Emperor JOHN VIII PALAEOLOGUS, who was visiting the COUNCIL OF FLORENCE: on the obverse there was a relief profile of the emperor, and on the reverse a scene in which the emperor, mounted on his horse, rides past a cross; the emperor's title surrounding the portrait on the obverse is in Greek, but the signature of Pisanello on the reverse is in both Latin (OPUS PISANI PICTORIS) and Greek. Pisanello subsequently struck medals for many north Italian princes and for ALFONSO V, king of Naples (1448–9). Other Italian medallists followed in Pisanello's wake, notably BERTOLDO DI GIOVANNI (who struck a medal commemorating the PAZZI CONSPIRACY), Giovanni BERNARDI, CARADOSSO, Costanzo da Ferrara (notably his portrait of Sultan Mehmet II), Annibale FONTANA, FRANCIA, Francesco LAURANA, Leone LEONI, Matteo de' PASTI, Savelli SPERANDIO, ADRIANO FIORENTINO (notably his Giovanni PONTANO), Niccolò Fiorentino (notably his Giovanni Albizzi, SAVONAROLA, Lorenzo de' MEDICI, and CHARLES VIII of France), and Domenico and Gianpaolo POGGINI.

In Germany medals were struck by Italian craftsmen as early as 1477, when the Archduke Maximilian (later Emperor MAXIMILIAN) commissioned a medal from Giovanni Candida to commemorate his wedding. German medallists used the same methods as their Italian predecessors, but often cast in silver rather than bronze. The first German medallist was Hans SCHWARZ of Augsburg. His numerous successors included DÜRER, whose most memorable portrait medals are those of his aged father and the youthful CHARLES V. In the Netherlands, the finest medallist was the painter Quentin MASSYS, whose magnificent portrait medal of ERASMUS is his only known medal.

In France the court employed a succession of Italian medallists, but in the sixteenth century native artists received commissions, notably the sculptor Germain PILON, who made portrait medals of HENRI II, HENRY III, and CATHERINE DE MÉDICIS. The French tradition culminated in the early seventeenth century with Guillaume Dupré, the greatest of north European medallists, whose early work includes a double portrait medal of HENRI IV and MARIE DE MÉDICIS (1601).

M. H. Crawford, C. R. Ligota, and J. B. Trapp (eds.), *Medals and Coins from Budé to Mommsen* (1990); S. Scher, *The Currency of Fame: Portrait Medals of the Renaissance* (1994).

**MEDICI, ALESSANDRO DE'** (*c*.1510–1537), duke of Florence, the illegitimate son of Lorenzo de' Medici (1492–1519), duke of Urbino. In 1523 Alessandro and his cousin Cardinal Ippolito (illegitimate son of Giuliano de' MEDICI) were appointed joint rulers of Florence by their uncle Pope CLEMENT VII. The cousins were expelled in 1527, but in 1530 Alessandro was restored with the assistance of the Emperor CHARLES V; on 10 August 1535 Cardinal Ippolito died by poison administered at the command of Alessandro. In 1532 Alessandro, who was already duke of Città di Penna, was created duke of Florence by Charles V; in 1533 he married MARGARET OF PARMA, the emperor's illegitimate daughter.

Alessandro enjoyed the counsel of Francesco GUICCIARDINI and Francesco VETTORI, but nonetheless neglected his civic responsibilities in order to lead a life of pleasure. On 5 January 1537 he was assassinated by a distant relative, Lorenzino de' Medici; with his death the elder line of the Medici, descended from Cosimo de' MEDICI il Vecchio, became extinct. He was succeeded by COSIMO I DE' MEDICI, scion of the cadet branch of the family descended from Lorenzo, brother of Cosimo il Vecchio. Alessandro's legitimate half-sister Caterina married the future King HENRI II of France, where she was known as CATHERINE DE MÉDICIS.

## MEDICI, COSIMO I DE'. See COSIMO I DE' MEDICI.

## MEDICI, COSIMO DE', IL VECCHIO (1389–1464),
Florentine statesman, called 'il Vecchio' (i.e. the elder) to distinguish him from Grand Duke COSIMO I DE' MEDICI. Cosimo was the son of the banker Giovanni di Bicci de' Medici and Piccarda Bueri. As a young man he pursued interests in commerce and politics; he accompanied Pope JOHN XXIII to the COUNCIL OF CONSTANCE, where he transacted a large volume of business, and on returning to Florence worked as an ambassador for the republic. In 1429, at the age of 40, Cosimo inherited his father's vast fortune, which he used to support literature and art and to advance his political career. He initially supported the ALBIZZI FAMILY in the war with Lucca, but when the campaign turned in Lucca's favour, Cosimo became an opponent of the war and those who conducted it. Cosimo was imprisoned, and on 3 October 1433 he was sent into exile in Padua; he was later permitted to move to Venice.

In 1434 Florence was defeated by Niccolò PICCININO, and public opinion turned against the Albizzi. On 1 September 1434 the Florentine Signoria invited Cosimo to return. The Albizzi withdrew from the city after a failed attempt to seize power, and Cosimo returned on 6 September. He quickly consolidated his position within the city by exiling his rivals, and also used his fortune to secure useful alliances elsewhere in the peninsula: he supported Cardinal Tommaso Parentucelli, who in 1447 became Pope NICHOLAS V and thereafter used the Medici bank in Rome to finance the curia; he also befriended and financed Francesco SFORZA, who in 1450 became duke of Milan.

The republican traditions of Florence made it imprudent for Cosimo to assume a formal title, but he nonetheless extended his patronage like a prince. He commissioned the MEDICI VILLAS at Fiesoli and Careggi and continued the

rebuilding of the Church of San Lorenzo in Florence; the artists and architects whom he supported included BRUNELLESCHI, DONATELLO, GHIBERTI, LUCA DELLA ROBBIA, and MICHELOZZO. Cosimo's enthusiasm for humanist scholarship was stimulated by his conversations with PLETHO during the COUNCIL OF FLORENCE and expressed in his large collection of Greek and Latin manuscripts of ancient authors (which became the foundation collection of the Biblioteca LAURENZIANA) and in his patronage of LIBRARIES in the monasteries of San Marco (Florence) and San Francesco (Fiesole); he also paid for the education of Marsilio FICINO to enable him to undertake a complete translation of PLATO from Greek to Latin and extended his patronage to ARGYROPOULOS. Cosimo's reverence for Plato lasted until the end of his life: he died on 1 August 1464, aged 75, while listening to one of Plato's dialogues. He was succeeded by his son Piero I de' MEDICI.

Francis Ames-Lewis (ed.), *Cosimo 'il Vecchio' de' Medici, 1389–1464* (1992); Dale Kent, *Cosimo de' Medici and the Florentine Renaissance* (2000).

## MEDICI, GIOVANNI DE', or Giovanni delle Bande Nere
(1498–1526), Florentine *condottiere*, born into a cadet branch of the MEDICI FAMILY, descended from Lorenzo, the brother of Cosimo de MEDICI il Vecchio. Giovanni's father, also called Giovanni (1467–98), died in the year that he was born, and his mother, Caterina SFORZA Riario, died in 1509. Giovanni became a *condottiere*; he fought in the papal army of LEO X, and when Pope Leo died in 1521, the soldiers in Giovanni's regiments changed their banners from white to black; these banners (*bande nere*), which were again used when Giovanni was killed, gave rise to his *nom de guerre*.

Giovanni was wounded in the battle of PAVIA (1525) while fighting on the side of the French. He subsequently fought for the League of COGNAC, in whose service he was killed. Giovanni married Maria Salviati, the daughter of his guardian; their son Cosimo later became Grand Duke COSIMO I DE' MEDICI.

## MEDICI, GIULIANO DE' (1478–1516), duke of Nemours,
the third son of Lorenzo de' MEDICI. When Giuliano's brother Piero II de' MEDICI was deposed in 1494, Giuliano fled Florence and sought refuge at the court of GUIDO DA MONTEFELTRO. In 1512 he returned to Florence with the assistance of his other brother, Cardinal Giovanni de' Medici, who when he was elected as Pope LEO X in 1513 appointed Giuliano as captain-general of the papal army and subsequently arranged for his marriage to Filiberta of Savoy, the niece of King FRANCIS I of France, who in 1515 created him duke of Nemours. Giuliano died the following year and achieved posthumous fame because of his monument by MICHELANGELO in the Church of San Lorenzo in Florence. His illegitimate son Ippolito de' Medici (1511–35) later became a cardinal.

Giuliano's namesakes include his uncle Giuliano (1453–78), the brother of Lorenzo de' MEDICI, and his distant relative Giuliano, bishop of Beziers.

**MEDICI, LORENZO DE', IL MAGNIFICO** (1449–92), Florentine statesman, the son of Piero I de' MEDICI (Piero the Gouty) and Lucrezia Tornabuoni (d. 1482) and the grandson of Cosimo de' MEDICI, Il Vecchio. Lorenzo was educated by humanists, including FICINO, and at the age of 18 embarked on a tour of Italian courts. He succeeded his father in 1469, nominally sharing power with his younger brother Giuliano (1453–78). The epithet *il magnifico* is a title of respect which Lorenzo was accorded because he was a *de facto* head of state but lacked a princely title.

Lorenzo was only 20 when he assumed control of Florence, but from the outset his rule was vigorous and uncompromising. He committed the republic to an unpopular war against Volterra (1472) over the issue of the ALUM mines; six years later opposition to Lorenzo and the Medici culminated in the PAZZI CONSPIRACY, in which his brother Giuliano was killed. Pope SIXTUS IV, who shared the wish of the conspirators to overthrow the Medici, excommunicated Lorenzo, imposed a papal interdict on Florence, and joined King FERRANTE I of Naples in a military alliance against Florence. In 1480 Lorenzo's army was defeated, and Lorenzo travelled to Naples to sue for peace. Thereafter his increasingly tyrannical rule of Florence was unopposed.

Lorenzo's patronage extended to artists and architects (BOTTICELLI, GHIRLANDAIO, Filippino LIPPI, LEONARDO DA VINCI, MICHELANGELO, Giuliano da SANGALLO, VERROCCHIO), philosophers (Ficino and PICO DELLA MIRANDOLA), and poets (POLIZIANO and PULCI). His own writings include popular poetry, a play, and a treatise on falconry (*Caccia del falcone*).

Lorenzo's six children by Clarice ORSINI (d. 1488) included three sons: Piero II de' MEDICI (who succeeded his father), Giovanni de' MEDICI (who became Pope LEO X), and Giuliano de' MEDICI (later duke of Nemours).

Lorenzo's namesakes include his grandson Lorenzo (1492–1519), duke of Urbino, his great-uncle Lorenzo (1395–1440), the brother of Cosimo il Vecchio, and his great-uncle's grandson Lorenzo (d. 1503).

*Lettere*, ed. Riccardo Fubini et al. (8 vols. to date, 1977–2001);

C. M. Ady, *Lorenzo dei Medici and Renaissance Italy* (1955);

A. Chastel, *Art et humanisme à Florence au temps de Laurent le Magnifique* (1959).

**MEDICI, PIERO I DE', or Piero the Gouty** (1416–69), Florentine statesman and banker, the son of Cosimo il Vecchio de' MEDICI and Contessina de' Bardi. In 1464 Piero succeeded his father as head of the banking family and *de facto* ruler of Florence. He suffered so gravely from gout that he had to be carried. He extended his patronage to humanists and artists such as Luca DELLA ROBBIA and Benozzo GOZZOLI. Piero died on 3 December 1469, leaving two sons, Lorenzo de' MEDICI and Giuliano (1453–78), and three daughters (one of whom was illegitimate); Giuliano's illegitimate son Giulio later became Pope CLEMENT VII.

Francis Ames-Lewis, *The Library and Manuscripts of Piero di Cosimo de' Medici* (1984).

**MEDICI, PIERO II DE', or Pietro de'** (1472–1503), ruler of Florence, the eldest son of Lorenzo de' MEDICI, whom he suc-

ceeded in 1492 as head of the family and *de facto* ruler of Florence. When the French army passed through Tuscany on its way to Naples at the outset of the WARS OF ITALY, Piero visited the camp of CHARLES VIII of France to offer his assistance. This policy shift occasioned a revolt in Florence on 9 November 1494, as a result of which the Medici were deposed and exiled. Piero secured the support of Pope ALEXANDER VI in his attempts to return to Florence, but failed on every occasion. He was drowned fighting on the side of the French at the battle of GARIGLIANO on 29 December 1503 and buried in the cloister of Monte Cassino.

Piero was married to Alfonsina Orsini (d. 1520); their son Lorenzo, duke of Urbino, became the father of the future CATHERINE DE MÉDICIS, and their daughter Clarice (d. 1528) married Filippo STROZZI.

**MEDICI FAMILY**, a Florentine family of bankers, statesmen, churchmen (including two popes), *condottieri*, and patrons of the arts. The family migrated to Florence in the thirteenth century from the Mugello valley (Tuscany). Its first prominent member was the banker Giovanni di Bicci de' Medici (1360–1429), who accumulated a vast fortune and was said to be the wealthiest man in Italy. In 1434, Giovanni's son Cosimo de' MEDICI, Il Vecchio, who had inherited his father's fortune, became the unofficial first citizen of Florence. Cosimo was succeeded in 1464 by his son Piero I de' MEDICI (Piero the Gouty), who had two sons: his elder son Lorenzo de' MEDICI, Il Magnifico, succeeded him in 1469; his younger son Giuliano (who was killed in the PAZZI CONSPIRACY) had an illegitimate son, Giulio de' Medici, who later became Pope CLEMENT VII.

Lorenzo the Magnificent had three sons: Piero II de' MEDICI, the eldest, succeeded him in 1492; Giovanni, the second son, became Pope LEO X; Giuliano de' MEDICI, the third son, became duke of Nemours and found posthumous fame because his tomb was the work of MICHELANGELO. In 1494 Piero II was deposed during the French invasion and the family was banished. Piero died before the family was restored, and in 1512 it was his brother Giuliano who, supported by his brother Giovanni (soon to be elected pope), became the leader of Florence. Giuliano was succeeded by his nephew (Piero's son) Lorenzo, duke of Urbino, and on his death in 1519 the leadership of Florence passed to Giulio de' Medici (illegitimate grandson of Piero I), who ruled the city until he was elected as Pope CLEMENT VII in 1523. On his election he was succeeded in Florence by Ippolito de' Medici, the illegitimate son of Giuliano, duke of Nemours.

In 1527 the Medici family was again exiled, and when they were restored in 1530 the leadership passed to Alessandro de' MEDICI, the illegitimate son of Lorenzo, duke of Urbino. In 1532 Alessandro was created duke of Florence by CHARLES V; in 1537 he was assassinated, and with his death the direct line of descent from Cosimo il Vecchio was extinguished. The dukedom passed to COSIMO I DE' MEDICI, son of the *condottiere* Giovanni de' MEDICI (Giovanni delle Bande Nere) and the fifth-generation descendant of Lorenzo, the brother of Cosimo de' Medici, Il Vecchio. In 1569 Duke Cosimo was created grand duke of Tuscany, and so inaugurated a succession of seven Medici grand dukes of Tuscany (see Appendix I); this line of the family expired in 1737.

Caterina, the daughter of Lorenzo, duke of Urbino, married the future King HENRI II of France, where she was known as CATHERINE DE MÉDICIS; she became regent of France and the mother of three French kings. Maria, the daughter of Francesco de' Medici and the granddaughter of Grand Duke Cosimo I de' Medici, married King HENRI IV of France, where she was known as MARIE DE MÉDICIS; she also became regent of France.

Nicolai Rubenstein, *The Government of Florence under the Medici* (1966).

**MEDICINE.** In the mid-fourteenth century leprosy began to disappear from Europe, but new diseases arose to take its place: PLAGUE broke out in 1347, SWEATING SICKNESS in 1485, TYPHUS in 1489, and SYPHILIS in 1495. In medical science, the revival of GALEN shaped academic medicine, and the field in which most change occurred was ANATOMY. In medical education, the principal centres were PADUA and, in the late sixteenth century, LEIDEN. The study of herbs for their medicinal properties was an important element in BOTANY and in the establishment of BOTANICAL GARDENS.

A. Wear, R. K. French, and I. M. Lonie (eds.), *The Medical Renaissance of the Sixteenth Century* (1985).

**MÉDICIS, CATHERINE DE.** See CATHERINE DE MÉDICIS.

**MEDICI VILLAS.** The MEDICI family had a suite of fourteen VILLAS near Florence, of which the most important were situated in Careggi, Castello, Fiesole, and Poggio a Caiano; in the sixteenth century the family also acquired a villa in Rome.

The Villa Careggi, in what is now a northern suburb of Florence, is the creation of Cosimo de' MEDICI the Elder, who in 1457 commissioned MICHELOZZO DI BARTOLOMEO to convert an old manor house that Cosimo's brother Giovanni de' Bicci had bought in 1417. In rebuilding the fortified manor house as a contemporary villa, Michelozzo chose to leave much of the original exterior intact, but added a graceful double loggia which overlooked a garden. The garden was intended to revive the ancient Roman villa garden, and so was planted with bay, box, cypress, myrtle, pomegranates, quince, lavender, and scented herbs and flowers; the only post-classical plants were carnations from the Levant and orange and lemon trees from North Africa. One of the FOUNTAINS added to the garden by Lorenzo de' Medici contained VERROCCHIO's bronze *Boy with a Dolphin* (c.1480), which is now in the court of the Palazzo Vecchio in Florence.

The Villa Careggi was the home of the loosely constituted Platonic Academy (see ACADEMIES) over which Marsilio FICINO presided. The foundation of the Academy in the early 1460s was prompted by the admiration for Plato which Cosimo shared with Ficino. Meetings of the Academy, which were a conscious imitation of the meeting in Plato's *Symposium*, were patronized by Cosimo and his successors Piero de' MEDICI

and Lorenzo de' MEDICI, and were attended by philosophers, scholars, and artists such as POLIZIANO, LANDINO, PICO DELLA MIRANDOLA, BRUNELLESCHI, DONATELLO, and later MICHELANGELO. Careggi thus became the cradle of HUMANISM.

After Lorenzo's death and the expulsion of the Medici the villa was vandalized and looted. It was later restored by BRONZINO and PONTORMO for Alessandro de' MEDICI and COSIMO I DE' MEDICI. The garden in which the Academy met has since disappeared, and the villa is now part of a hospital complex.

The Medici villa in Fiesole, on a hill overlooking Florence from the north, was constructed by Michelozzo between 1458 and 1461; it was commissioned by Cosimo the Elder for Giovanni, his second son. Massive foundations were dug to secure the house on the steep slope of the hill, and the cellars were used to accommodate stables as well as wine and oil presses and storage rooms. The rooms above included reception rooms, a music room, and a library which were used for entertainment, initially by Giovanni, but more expansively by his nephew Lorenzo de' MEDICI, who entertained his circle of humanist friends, including Poliziano, who wrote *Il rusticus* while staying at the villa. The interior decoration of the villa did not survive the ministrations of Lady Walpole, the dowager countess of Oxford, who redecorated it in 1772.

The villa opens out directly onto the upper terrace, which overlooks Florence in the valley below; the original planting on this terrace has been replaced with grass, but the *GIARDINO SEGRETO* still survives, with its box PARTERRES, subdued fountain, and stone balusters through which can be seen a vista of Florence and the Arno valley. There was originally no access from the upper terrace to the lower terraces, which were reached from the cellars of the house; connecting stairs and ramps were to become a feature of this and other ITALIAN GARDENS in the sixteenth century. The second terrace is dominated by a pergola flanked on its retaining wall by a raised border; the border and the pergola were part of the original garden, though the original supporting columns of the pergola do not survive. On the lowest terrace an elegant Renaissance garden with a fountain and rectangular parterres surrounded and intersected by box has been reconstructed, but the extent to which this garden replicates the layout of the original is not clear.

The Medici villa in Poggio a Caiano, to the west of Florence, was commissioned in 1480 by Lorenzo de' Medici, who instructed Giuliano da SANGALLO to convert the old Villa Ambra (which had previously belonged to the STROZZI and RUCELLAI families) into a contemporary villa. By 1485 the house had been surrounded by a balustraded loggia which acts as a balcony for the rooms on the first floor (*piano nobile*). Lorenzo's son Giovanni (later Pope LEO X) continued to commission additions to the house, notably a six-columned (hexastyle) portico on the first floor, with a frieze and pediment; the structure is modelled on the pedimented temple fronts of classical antiquity, and its use in this building inaugurated the Renaissance revival of the form, which later became the distinguishing feature of PALLADIO's buildings. Villas were traditionally built around a court, but at the centre of the Poggio a Caiano villa there is a large two-storey salon with a gilded stucco ceiling (containing the arms of Leo X) and frescoes by ANDREA DEL SARTO and Pontormo which use classical subjects to record and glorify the history of the Medici family.

CHARLES V was entertained at Poggio a Caiano in 1536, which subsequently became the home of Bianca CAPELLO and her lover (later husband) Francesco, son of Cosimo I de' Medici; they were visited in 1581 by MONTAIGNE. The gardens were uprooted in the nineteenth century to make way for an English garden with a mock-Gothic ruin, and much of the interior was ruthlessly modernized at the same time; Bianca Capello's beautiful bedroom, however, survives in its original form. The house is now a museum.

The Medici villa at Castello, to the north of Florence, had been in the family for a century when Cosimo I de' Medici commissioned the gardens. The garden was begun c.1540 by Niccolò TRIBOLO, and completed after his death by Bartolomeo AMMANATI and Bernardo BUONTALENTI. Its design is in some respects anachronistic, in that the garden is shaped as a square enclosed by a wall and planted as a series of rectangular beds with a statue at the centre; this was the layout characteristic of Italian gardens a century earlier. There are, however, distinctive sixteenth-century features: there is a central axis rising to a magnificent GROTTO (1546–69), and there are many statues (and there were many more, both free-standing and in relief) and fountains. The grotto, which is built into the enclosing wall, is decorated with shell mosaics and fountains in the form of animal statues from whose beaks, ears, noses, and wings water pours. In the Fountain of Hercules and Antaeus, water spews from the mouth of Antaeus as Hercules strangles him; this was the first time that water had been incorporated into the narrative of a sculpture rather than merely issuing from a convenient orifice. A second fountain, GIAMBOLOGNA's Fountain of Venus squeezing the water from her hair, was removed in the eighteenth century to the nearby Villa Medici in Petraia, and the Fountain of Hercules, which originally stood near the house, was put in its place. The Fountain of Venus had been surrounded by a BOSCO in the form of a MAZE of bay, cypress, and myrtle, which meant that the statue emerged from a crown of evergreen; the Fountain of Hercules now in its place stands nakedly above flat geometrical parterres.

The garden still contains some elements of its original layout, but a lunette by UTENS and the account given by Montaigne of his visit in 1580 record additional features that have since disappeared. The Utens lunette shows the house standing on a terrace used for riding and jousting, and Montaigne describes a *cabinet de verdure* (see BOSCO) with a spring rising from a marble table and also describes GIOCHI D'ACQUA that could be triggered by remote control at a distance of 200 paces. In Utens's picture, and in Vasari's description of the garden, there was a wall decorated with fountains at the back of the main garden, beyond which was a lemon garden. There were *giardini segreti* on either side of the main garden: the one on the left, according to Montaigne, contained a tree house approached by a stair decorated with ivy that concealed *giochi d'acqua* that played tunes and squirted

visitors; the one on the right, according to Vasari, contained a herb garden. Vasari said that the gardens, had they been completed, would have been the finest in Europe, and singled out the central fountain for particular praise: 'la più bella fonte e la più ricca, proporzionata e vaga, che sia stata fatta mai' ('the most beautiful fountain, the richest, the best proportioned, the most charming that has ever been made').

The Villa Medici in Rome was built c.1544 on the site of an ancient villa of Lucullus; it was designed by Annibale Ricci for Cardinal Ricci. The villa was subsequently acquired by the Medici family, and has since the early nineteenth century been the home of the Académie de France, which had been founded in Rome in 1666. The most remarkable feature of the villa is its garden, which has preserved its sixteenth-century layout and includes statues (both classical fragments and contemporary *stucchi*), a MOUNT crowned with cypresses and two ilex *boschi* (see BOSCO). In the seventeenth century, Galileo GALILEI lived in the villa and John Evelyn visited the gardens, which were painted by Velázquez and Poussin.

J. Kliemann, *Politische und humanistische Ideen der Medici in der Villa Poggio a Caiano: Untersuchungen zu den Fresken der Sala grande* (1976); P. Foster, *A Study of Lorenzo de' Medici's Villa at Poggio a Caiano* (1978); S. Bordazzi and E. Castellani, *La Villa medicea di Poggio a Caiano* (2 vols., 1978); L. Châtelet-Lange, 'The Grotto of the Unicorn and the Garden of the Villa di Castello', *Art Bulletin*, 50 (1968).

**MEDINA, BARTOLOMÉ** (1527–80), Spanish Dominican theologian who taught theology at Alcalá de Henares and in 1576 migrated to a chair in Salamanca, where he taught for the last few years of his life. His principal works are commentaries on THOMAS AQUINAS. He was the first prominent exponent (and possibly the first exponent) of the doctrine of probabilism, which he sets out in his commentary on the 'Prima secundae' of Thomas Aquinas (1572).

Medina's probabilist doctrine consisted of the contention that if two opinions are probable in unequal degree, the less probable may be followed (*Si est opinio probabilis, licitum est eam sequi, licet opposita probabilior sit*); in moral theology, the consequence of probabilism is that if the licitness of an action is in doubt, it is lawful to choose a probable opinion favouring liberty rather than a more probable opinion favouring the law. This doctrine was soon adopted by other Dominicans, notably Domingo BÁÑEZ, and the notion of the probable was elaborated by Jesuits as well as Dominicans; eventually Jesuits became the principal proponents of the doctrine and Dominicans its principal detractors.

**MEDINA SIDONIA or Medinasidonia, ALONSO PÉREZ DE GUZMÁN, DUKE OF** (1550–1619), commander of the Spanish ARMADA, born into an ancient, noble, and wealthy Spanish family. In 1565 he was betrothed to Ana de Silva de Mendoza, the 4-year-old daughter of the prince and princess of EBOLI, whom he subsequently married; the marriage was consummated by papal dispensation in 1572, when Ana was 10 years old. In 1581 Medina Sidonia was named as captain-general of Lombardy, but he was excused on grounds of poverty and ill health.

King Philip had originally given the command of the invasion of England to the marquis of Vera Cruz, but on the latter's fatal illness the king turned to Medina Sidonia, who on 9 February 1588 was put in charge of the invasion, despite his limited naval experience and lack of military distinction. On being offered the command he tried to decline on the grounds that he suffered from seasickness. After the defeat of the Armada he maintained his good relations with King Philip and continued in post as admiral of the ocean and captain-general of Andalusia. He was subsequently responsible for the loss of Cádiz (1596) to English and Dutch forces.

DHE; Peter Pierson, *Commander of the Armada: The Seventh Duke of Medina* (1989).

**MEIGRET, LOUIS** (*c.*1500–after 1558), French grammarian and humanist translator, a prominent figure in the national debate about spelling reform, advocating in his *Traité touchant le commun usage de l'écriture française* (1542) an orthography based on pronunciation rather than etymology. He wrote the first grammar of the FRENCH LANGUAGE to appear in French, which is now known as the *Traité de la grammaire française* (1550) but which Meigret spelt *Tretté de la grammere françoeze*.

Franz Josef Hausmann, *Louis Meigret: Humaniste et linguiste* (1980).

**MEISTERGESANG or *Meistersang*,** a fifteenth- and sixteenth-century literary and musical tradition in Germany, cultivated by the guilds of craftsmen and which gave the urban middle classes a religious and secular education. The *Meistergesang* were subject to rules regarding the invention of new poems (*Lied, Gesang*) and music (*Ton, Weise*) as illustrated in Wagner's *Die Meistersinger von Nürnberg* (1868).

**MEIT, KONRAD** (*fl. c.*1506–1550), German sculptor and woodcarver, born at Worms. He worked from 1511 in Wittenberg in the service of the Elector FRIEDRICH III, and subsequently moved to the Netherlands, where from 1526 to 1532 he executed his finest works, the tombs of MARGARET OF AUSTRIA and her family in the Church of St Nicholas of Tolentino in Brou (on the outskirts of Bourg-en-Bresse). In 1536 Meit settled in Antwerp, where he worked for the rest of his career. His best-known small-scale work is the ALABASTER statuette of *Judith* now in the Bayerisches Nationalmuseum in Munich.

MDA; NDB.

**MELANCHOLIA,** the temperament associated in Renaissance psychology with intellectual seriousness and distinction. In the GALENIC theory of the humours, melancholia was the cold and dry humour which characterized the scholar, the poet, and the philosopher. In physiology melancholy was associated with black bile and in ASTROLOGY with Saturn, the patron of the mathematical sciences, and so DÜRER's *Melancholia I* depicts a woman in melancholic contemplation who is surrounded by mathematical instruments.

In the late sixteenth century the fashion for melancholic contemplation was transmitted from Italy to England, where in 1621 Robert Burton published his erudite *Anatomy of Melancholy*.

**MELANCHTHON, PHILIPP** (1497–1560), reformer and humanist, born at Bretten (Baden) on 16 February 1407, the son of George Schwartzerd, a royal armourer, and his wife Barbara Reuter, a niece of Johann REUCHLIN. Reuchlin took an interest in Philipp Schwartzerd, and renamed him Melanchthon, which is the Greek form of Schwartzerd, meaning 'black earth'. Melanchthon studied at the universities of Heidelberg (from 1509) and Tübingen (from 1512), and 1518 he was appointed professor of Greek at Wittenberg by FRIEDRICH III, elector of Saxony, who acted on the advice of Johann Reuchlin. Melanchthon participated in the LEIPZIG DISPUTATION and defended Bodenstein von KARLSTADT in his dispute with Johann ECK and again when he celebrated mass in the vernacular. In 1520 Melanchthon married Catharine Krapp of Wittenberg, and the following year, when Luther was confined in the Wartburg, Melanchthon became the acting leader of the Reformation. In 1521 he published his most important book, a systematic theology called *Loci communes rerum theologicarum*, and in the course of the next six years corrected Luther's translation of the New Testament from Greek to German, and wrote several biblical commentaries.

Melanchthon's theology was until the mid-1520s a cerebral version of Luther's theology: Melanchthon supported with formidable erudition and a speculative intelligence the same doctrines that Luther set out with passion in his demotic German and pellucid Latin. By 1527, however, Melanchthon had begun to formulate a theology that was more Catholic than Luther's, especially on issues such as ADIAPHORA, biblical law (which he believed binding on Christians), and GRACE; on the fraught issue of the EUCHARIST, Melanchthon's position was essentially Lutheran, but his wish for reconciliation and his intellectual capaciousness enabled him to tolerate more readily than Luther the rival Calvinist and Zwinglian doctrines of the eucharist. These differences were considerable, but they did not compromise the personal and professional relationships between Melanchthon and Luther, and they presented a common front at the Diet of SPEYER (1529), the Colloquy of MARBURG (1529), and the Diet of AUGSBURG (1530), where Melanchthon drafted the AUGSBURG CONFESSION. His residual sympathies for the Roman Church were made public in 1537 when he became the sole opponent of the condemnation of the papacy in the SCHMALKALDIC ARTICLES, appending to his signature a reservation that a papacy not claiming divine right could be tolerated. Thereafter he attended the Conferences of WORMS (1540–41) and REGENSBURG (1541).

When the Protestant cause suffered setbacks through the death of Luther (February 1546) and the battle of MÜHLBERG (April 1547), a new willingness to negotiate led to the formulation of the AUGSBURG INTERIM (1548). Melanchthon's liberal sense of the doctrines that might be regarded as adiaphora meant that he did not reject the interim settlement out of hand, but his willingness to negotiate within the terms of the settlement incurred the obloquy of many Lutherans, who objected to his SYNERGISM (which was said to be covert Pelagianism) and his alleged crypto-Calvinism.

Melanchthon died on 19 April 1560 and was buried beside Luther in the Schlosskirche at Wittenberg.

*NDB*; W. Maurer, *Der junge Melanchthon zwischen Humanismus und Reformation* (2 vols., 1967–9); S. Wiedenhofer, *Formalstrukturen humanistischer und reformatorischer Theologie bei Philipp Melanchthon* (2 vols., 1976); Heinz Scheible, *Melanchthon* (1997).

**MELOZZO DA FORLÌ** (1438–94), Italian painter, a native of Forlì (Emilia). Little is known of his early life, but he worked in the ducal court in Urbino (1465–76) and came into contact with PIERO DELLA FRANCESCA, to whose style he is indebted. The debt to Piero is readily apparent in Melozzo's best-known painting, *Platina Appointed Librarian of the Vatican by Pope Sixtus V* (1477, Pinacoteca Vaticana). He also painted the frescoes in the Sacristy of San Marco in the Santuario della Santa Casa in Loreto and frescoes (which survive only in fragments) in the cupola of the Church of SS Apostoli in Rome. Much of Melozzo's work is lost, but his contemporary standing is attested by Giovanni SANTI, who praised Melozzo in verse as a master of perspective.

*MDA*; Nicholas Clark, *Melozzo da Forlì: Pictor papalis* (1990).

**MELVILLE, ANDREW** (1545–1622), Scottish presbyterian reformer and theologian. Educated at St Andrews, Paris, and Poitiers, Melville became professor of humanities at Geneva in 1569. In 1574 he returned to Scotland and became principal of Glasgow University, where his educational reforms, including the development of a new plan of studies and the establishment of chairs in theology, science, philosophy, and other subjects, met with success. He later became principal of St Mary's College, St Andrews (1580), and rector of St Andrews (1590). His presbyterianism, pursued as moderator of the General Assembly in 1582 and 1587, brought him into conflict with JAMES VI, and he was imprisoned, briefly, in 1584 and again, for attacks on Anglican worship, in 1607. In 1611 he became professor of biblical theology at Sedan University, a position he retained until his death.

*DNB.*

**MEMLING, HANS** (1430/5–94), German/Flemish painter. He was born in Seligenstadt (near Mainz), but in 1465 became a free mason of Bruges, where he spent the rest of his life. His style, which is characterized by its attention to detail and colours, remained stable throughout his career, and reflects the influence of Rogier van der WEYDEN, which may imply that he was trained in Rogier's studio. His patrons included the Hôpital de Saint-Jean in Bruges, which now has the best collection of his paintings; the Martin van Nieuwenhove Diptych (1482), which portrays the donor together with the Madonna and Child, demonstrates Memling's virtuosity as a portrait painter, and its background shows his mastery of LANDSCAPE. His surviving paintings are widely scattered, because his clients also included the Burgundian court and several Italians who were resident in Bruges; one of the finest products of such commissions is the double portrait of *Tommaso Portinari and his Wife* (Metropolitan Museum, New York). His other works include the Donne Triptych (1468, National Gallery, London) and *Portrait of a Young Man* (Thyssen Collection, Madrid).

*MDA*; *NBW* xii; *NDB*; Dirk de Vos (ed.), *Hans Memling: The Complete Works* (1994); id., *Hans Memling: Essays* (1994).

**MEMMI, LIPPO.** See LIPPO MEMMI.

**MENA, JUAN DE** (1411–56), Spanish poet, born in Córdoba and educated in Salamanca and Italy. He became a loyal courtier at the court of King JOHN II (Juan II) of Castile, where he was appointed as royal chronicler and secretary of Latin letters, and managed to maintain amicable relations with both Álvaro de LUNA (to whose *Libro de las virtuosas y claras mujeres* he contributed a prologue) and Luna's enemy, the marquis of SANTILLANA; both became subjects of important poems by Mena.

In the 1440s Mena translated a Latin version of Homer's *Iliad*, which was published many years later as *Iliada de Homero en romance* (Valladolid, 1519), and is normally known as the *Omero romanzado*. In 1444 he completed *El laberinto de Fortuna*, also formerly known as *Las trescientas* because it has 300 stanzas (although the last three are probably spurious); in this Dantesque allegory the guide is Providence rather than Virgil, and at the conclusion of the tour of the seven circles and the three wheels of fortune (past and future at rest, present perpetually in motion), Mena embarks on a long catalogue of historical figures (including a eulogy of Álvaro de Luna which associates his cause with Providence). The poem is remarkable for its Latinate diction and classical allusions, which represent the first attempt to introduce into Spanish poetry the tenets of humanist imitation of ancient literature.

In 1448 Mena wrote *Coronación del marqués de Santillana* (published in Salamanca in 1498), to which he added a prose commentary; this long allegory in 51 double *quintillas* (i.e. stanzas of ten octosyllabic lines) begins in hell and rises to Parnassus, the setting of the crowning with poetic laurels of Santillana. In Mena's *Claro-escuro* ('bright-dark', like Italian CHIAROSCURO), the vocabulary of the *claro* sections is simple, and that of the *escuro* sections is recondite. His unfinished last poem, published as *Coplas de los siete pecados mortales* (Salamanca, 1500), was completed by three other poets, one of whom was Gómez MANRIQUE.

*DHE*; M. R. Lida de Malkiel, *Juan de Mena, poeta del prerrenacimiento español* (2nd edn., 1984).

**MENDIETA, JERÓNIMO or Gerónimo DE** (1525–1604), Spanish missionary and historian, born in Vitoria, in the Basque country. He became a Franciscan friar and in 1554 travelled to Mexico, where he worked among the Indians; apart from one further period in Spain (1569–73), Mendieta spent the rest of his life in Mexico. His *Historia eclesiástica indiana* (completed 1596, first published 1870) describes the evangelization of Spanish America from the arrival of Columbus, and is deeply critical of Spanish colonialism.

John Phelan, *The Millennial Kingdom of the Franciscans in the New World: A Study of the Life and Writings of Gerónimo de Mendieta* (1956); Patricia Nettel Díaz, *La Utopía franciscana en la Nueva España: El apostolado de Fray Gerónimo de Mendieta* (1989).

**MENDOZA, ANTONIO DE** (1490–1552), the first of the 64 viceroys of New Spain. He was born into a noble family in Granada and served CHARLES V as a diplomat before being sent to Mexico as viceroy in 1535. In Mexico he established the administrative systems that were to sustain Spanish colonial rule in Mexico for three centuries. He supported the new ENCOMIENDA system in the face of considerable resistance, exacted tribute from the Indians, and established a mint, a foundry, and schools for the sons of the Indian nobility; he was powerless to stem the epidemic of European diseases that swept through the Indian population. In 1551 Mendoza was transferred to Peru to introduce similar systems, but died the following year.

DHE; A. S. Aiton, *Antonio de Mendoza, First Viceroy of New Spain* (1927); Germán Vázquez, *Antonio de Mendoza* (1987).

**MENDOZA, BERNARDINO DE** (c.1540–1604), Spanish diplomat, soldier, and writer on warfare who travelled in the entourage of the duke of ALBA to Italy and Flanders in 1567. In 1578 he was appointed ambassador to England, where his conversations with the Catholic conspirator Francis Throckmorton eventually led to Throckmorton's execution (1585); Mendoza was expelled and soon England was at war with Spain.

Mendoza's account of the first ten years of the REVOLT OF THE NETHERLANDS was published in French translation in 1591; the Spanish original, *Comentarios de lo sucedido en las guerras de los Payses Bajos desde el año de 1567 al de 1577*, was published in 1592. He also published a treatise on the art of war, *Teórica y prática de la guerra* (1595).

De Lamar Jensen, *Diplomacy and Dogmatism: Bernardino de Mendoza and the French Catholic League* (1964).

**MENDOZA, FRAY ÍÑIGO DE** (c.1422–c.1492), Spanish poet, born in Guadalajara. He entered the Franciscan Order and subsequently enjoyed the patronage of Queen ISABELLA. His poems include a *Vita Christi por coplas* (Zamora, 1482), an adaptation of Ludolf of Saxony's devotional account of the infancy of Christ that uses traditional Spanish forms such as the ballad and the *villancicos* (a courtly genre consisting of a song with a refrain, traditionally used for Christmas music) to celebrate the Christian faith in a popular idiom. He may also have been the author of *Coplas de Mingo Revulgo*, a savage satire of HENRY IV (Enrique IV) of Castile written in the form of a pastoral dialogue.

J. Rodríguez Puértolas, *Fray Íñigo de Mendoza y sus 'Coplas de vita Christi'* (1968).

**MENDOZA, PEDRO DE** (c.1499–1537), Spanish conquistador, born into a noble family in Almería. As a young man he served as a soldier in Italy and joined the household of CHARLES V, who awarded him a grant (*asiento*) of land that extended southwards from the southern boundary of Brazil, in what is now Uruguay, Argentina, and Paraguay.

In August 1534 Mendoza sailed from Sanlúcar de Barrameda at the head of a lavishly equipped expedition of eleven ships, bound for South America, where he was to be governor (*adelantado*) of Río de la Plata and Paraguay. He sailed to the harbour of Rio de Janeiro and then travelled down the coast to the Río de la Plata, where he founded the colony of Buenos Aires; the foundation stone was laid on 2 February 1535. One of the colonists, Juan de Ayolas, led a colonizing expedition up the Paraná and Paraguay rivers, where his surviving colleagues founded a settlement at Asunción on 15 August 1536; this was to be the earliest permanent Spanish settlement in the interior of South America. Mendoza subsequently sent Domingo MARTÍNEZ DE IRALA on an expedition to Paraguay.

Mendoza's colony in Buenos Aires was under constant attack from Indians, and he decided to abandon the settlement and return to Spain; he died on the return voyage and was succeeded as governor by Álvar Núñez CABEZA DE VACA.

DHE.

**MENDOZA, PEDRO GONZÁLEZ DE, or El Gran Cardeal** (1428–95), Spanish cardinal, statesman, and patron, born in Guadalajara, the fourth son of the marquis of SANTILLANA. He studied at Salamanca, and a year after graduating was appointed bishop of Calahorra (1452). During the reign of King HENRY IV (Enrique IV) he fought for the king, and on 20 August 1467 was wounded at the second battle of Olmedo. In 1468 he became bishop of Sigüenza and in 1473 he was created cardinal and archbishop of Seville and appointed chancellor of Castile. In the succession dispute he supported Queen ISABELLA's right to succeed her brother and on 1 March 1476 was present at the battle of Toro, when the forces of FERDINAND and Isabella defeated the supporters of JUANA LA BELTRANEJA. Mendoza's chancellorship was confirmed by Ferdinand and Isabella, and in 1482 he became cardinal-archbishop of Toledo and primate of Spain. On 2 January 1492 he occupied GRANADA in the name of Ferdinand and Isabella. He died in his native Guadalajara on 11 January 1495.

As a young man Mendoza translated Homer, Ovid, and Virgil into Spanish, and in the course of his ecclesiastical career he undertook the reform of the Spanish Church, founded the College of Santa Cruz in Valladolid, and contributed substantially to the establishment of the Spanish INQUISITION. He was an important collector and patron of art and of the new humanist learning. The beneficiaries of his patronage included Pietro MARTIRE D'ANGHIERA. His mistresses included Doña Mencia de Lemus, a Portuguese lady-in-waiting by whom he had two sons, Rodrigo (who was once betrothed to Lucrezia BORGIA) and Diego (who was to be the grandfather of the princesa de EBOLI).

DBE s.v. González de Mendoza; V. J. Villalba de Toledo, *El Cardeal Mendoza* (1988).

**MENÉNDEZ DE AVILÉS, PEDRO** (1519–74), Spanish naval commander, born in Avilés (Asturias) on 15 February 1519; he was one of nineteen children of a noble family. He ran away to sea at the age of 14 and for the next sixteen years sailed on PRIVATEERS. In 1549 he was commissioned by the Emperor CHARLES V to rid the north coast of Spain and the waters around the Canaries of French pirates. In 1554 Charles V ignored the vigorous protests of the CASA DE CONTRATACIÓN and appointed Avilés as captain-general of the FLOTA. In 1559, when Spain and England were at war with France, Avilés commanded troop carriers travelling from Spain to Flanders, and when peace was restored he commanded the fleet that brought PHILIP II back from Flanders to Spain. Despite the continuing opposition of the Casa, Avilés was reappointed to the captaincy of the *flota* in 1560, and he continued to command the annual crossings until he was arrested on the orders of the Casa in 1563. The nature of the charges is not known, but Avilés was imprisoned for twenty months awaiting trial and then freed.

On being released Avilés was offered a contract (*asiento*) by King Philip II to found a colony in Florida (which included part of the coast of what is now South Carolina); Avilés signed the contract on 20 March 1565. Spain regarded the recent arrival of French Huguenot settlers in Florida as a challenge to its sovereignty and, because of the proximity of its southern peninsula to the *flota* route, a threat to its trade. On 28 June 1565 Avilés sailed for Florida with a fleet consisting of a 600-ton flagship and ten sloops (small cutter-rigged armed ships) and a force of 2,600 sailors and soldiers. On 28 August (the feast of St AUGUSTINE) the fleet entered and named the Bay of St Augustine and constructed a fort in which to base their military operations to remove the French garrison and the Huguenot settlers.

Fort Caroline was a French fort and colony at the mouth of what is now the St Johns river (near Jacksonville). On the same day that Avilés arrived in St Augustine (28 August), a French force of some 300 men under the command of the Huguenot Jean RIBAUT arrived to reinforce the garrison. On 20 September Avilés attacked the fort, killed his prisoners, and gibbeted the bodies of the dead with the inscription 'no por franceses sino por herejes' ('not as Frenchmen but as heretics', i.e. Protestants). The following month the two ships (commanded by Ribaut's son) that had escaped the massacre were shipwrecked; the crews surrendered to Avilés, who promptly executed them. Three years later a French force under Dominique de Gourgue avenged the attack by hanging the Spanish garrison at Fort San Mateo (as the fort had been renamed) and inscribing on a pine tablet the words 'non comme Espagnoles mais comme assassins' ('not as Spaniards but as murderers').

Avilés remained in St Augustine until 1567 and then returned to Spain. He made one more voyage to Florida and died in Santander on 17 September 1574.

DHE; Eugene Lyon, *The Enterprise of Florida: Pedro Menéndez de Avilés and the Spanish Conquest of 1565–1568* (1976); Eugenio Ruidíaz y Caravia, *La Florida: Su conquista y colonización por Pedro Menéndez de Avilés* (2 vols. 1893; repr. 1989).

**MENNICKEN FAMILY**, a family of German potters who worked at Raeren (10 kilometres (6 miles) south of Aachen

in what is now Belgium); in the second half of the sixteenth century their workshop produced large STONEWARE jugs decorated with reliefs. Until the late 1570s the jugs were brown, and usually depicted mythological scenes; thereafter the jugs were often grey, and usually depicted religious scenes. The most prominent member of the family was Jan Emens Mennicken (*fl.* 1568–94). He was the first (*c.*1580) to apply cobalt-blue glaze to wares, a technique that was later to become characteristic of wares produced at Westerwald potteries. The surname was so common in Raeren that the Mennicken potters, including Jan Emens, used only their given names or initials to sign their wares. Jan Emens's relatives included Baldem Mennicken (*fl.* 1577–90) and his son Jan Baldems (*fl.* 1589–1613). Johann Mennicken moved to Westerwald in about 1595, and the Leonard and Wilhelm Mennicken who were working there in 1615 may have been his sons.

MDA s.v. Jan Emens Mennicken; H. Lippe (ed.), *Steinzeug aus dem Raeren und Aachener Raum* (1977).

**MENNO SIMONS** (1496–1561), Dutch Anabaptist leader. He was born in Witmarsum (in Dutch Friesland) and became a parish priest at the nearby village of Pingjum. He developed doubts about the Catholic doctrines of the EUCHARIST and of GRACE; he began to read LUTHER and the New Testament, and the latter led him to doubt Catholic teaching on BAPTISM. In March 1531 a rebaptized tailor, Sicke Freerks, was executed in Leeuwarden, and Menno came to develop ANABAPTIST sympathies. He finally left the Catholic Church on 12 January 1536.

In the wake of the violent demise of JOHN OF LEIDEN's short-lived Kingdom of the Saints in MÜNSTER, Menno set about trying to reconcile the various Anabaptist factions. He became the leader of a small group that had previously supported the Münster kingdom, and spent the next 25 years leading an ever-expanding Anabaptist movement in the Netherlands and north-west Germany. His movements cannot be tracked with certainty, but he was in East Friesland until 1541 and from 1543 to 1545 (and in 1544 participated in a public debate with Jan ŁASKI in Emden); from 1541 to 1543 he travelled in north Holland, and seems to have lived in Amsterdam, and from 1545 to 1547 he travelled in south Holland; thereafter he moved to Germany, and lived in Lübeck before moving east to Wismar (1553–4) and finally to the village of Wüstenfelde (near Oldesloe, between Hamburg and Lübeck), where he died on 31 January 1561.

Menno's religious beliefs were similar to those of the SWISS BRETHREN, with whom his followers eventually merged: he advocated believers' baptism, the autonomy of individual congregations, and a refusal to take oaths or participate in the magistracy or to serve in armies. His view that baptism (by affusion) and the Lord's Supper (accompanied by washing of feet) were images of the believer's inward state but not mechanisms for the conferring of grace has analogies with ZWINGLI's memorialist position. The SOCINIANISM that characterizes some strands of Mennonite thought in the seventeenth century is a later accretion, but may originate in

Menno's refusal to use the term 'Trinity' on the grounds that it was unbiblical and in his insistence on the celestial origins of the flesh of Christ, a view associated with the Valentinians of late antiquity. His church discipline, which was shared by the Swiss Brethren, included prohibitions on marriage with outsiders and on the participation of women in church government; his church services were characterized by silent prayer and spontaneous sermons delivered without a written text.

Menno wrote in Low German (*Plattdeutsch*), but his writings were translated into Dutch in his *Opera omnia theologica* (Amsterdam, 1681), which contains 23 treatises. Menno insisted that he was not the founder of a sect, but he is nonetheless the eponym of the Anabaptist group now known as Mennonites, a denomination of some 850,000 members.

*NDB; NNBW* iv; *Complete Writings*, trans. from Dutch by L. Verduin and ed. J. C. Wenger with a biography by H. S. Bender (1956).

**MENSATOR, JOHANNES** (*fl.* 1507–11), German woodworker who introduced INTARSIA to Hungary in his geometrical decoration of doors and a cupboard in the Town Hall (Radnica) at Bardejov (Hungarian Bártfa, German Bartfeld), the first building in Slovakia to contain elements in the style of the Italian Renaissance (then part of Hungary).

**MENTELIN, JOHANN** (*c.*1410–1478), German printer, born in Schlettstadt (now French Sélestat). In about 1468 he became the first printer in Strassburg. In 1460 Mentelin published a 49-line Bible, which enabled him to print the entire text on 850 pages (as opposed to GUTENBERG's 1,286 pages); in 1466 he published the first Bible in GERMAN. His workshop also printed popular romances.

*NDB.*

**MERBECKE, JOHN** (1505/10–*c.*1585), English musician and author, based at St George's Chapel, Windsor. Accused of being critical of the mass and sentenced to death in 1543, he was saved by a royal pardon. His complete concordance of the English Bible (the first of its kind) was published in 1550, the same year as his *The Book of Common Prayer Noted*, set in a simple syllabic style.

**MERCATOR, GERARDUS, or (Flemish) Gerhard Kremer** (1512–94), Flemish cartographer, born in Rupelmonde (Flanders) and educated at Louvain, where in 1537 he became the assistant of GEMMA FRISIUS. In 1537 Mercator made a map of Palestine and embarked on a series of maps of Flanders (1537–40), and in 1538 produced his first map of the world. He also made maps for globes, publishing a terrestrial globe for use on board ships in 1541; in 1551 he made his first celestial globe, which he presented to the Emperor CHARLES V.

In 1552 Mercator converted to Protestantism and left Louvain to seek refuge in Duisburg, where he became professor of cosmology at the University of Duisburg and cosmographer to the duke of Cleves. In Duisburg he devised the cartographic projection that now bears his name, and in 1569 published a world map in eighteen sheets using the new projection, in which images of parallels of latitude and meridians (lines of longitude) cross each other at right angles in the finished map. In 1585 he published the first maps that were to be incorporated in his world atlas of 1594, which was published together with a collection of Mercator's cosmological essays.

The navigational advantage of Mercator's projection lay in the fact that rhumb lines (the lines of constant compass bearing that determine the most efficient course for a ship) were projected as straight lines, but maritime navigators were slow to realize how this projection could obviate the need for costly globes and complicated mathematical calculations; however, by 1640, following the lead of French mariners, maps based on Mercator's projection were in general use by European navigators.

*DSB; NBW* x; *NDB.*

**MERCHANT ADVENTURERS**. This trading company's monopoly on the export of cloth can be traced back to the thirteenth century, and lasted until 1689, when, in response to arguments for free trade, the export of cloth was made open to all. Given a charter by HENRY VIII, the company traded frequently from the Netherlands, and acted vigorously to protect its trade from rivals. Despite the loss of monopoly, the company continued to trade until the early nineteenth century.

**MERCURIALE, GIROLAMO** (1530–1603), Italian physician, born in Forlì. He studied medicine in Bologna and Pavia, and then worked as a physician in Rome. He subsequently taught at Padua and, after a period at the imperial court of MAXIMILIAN II, returned to teach at Bologna and Pisa. Mercuriale wrote widely on medical subjects; his best-known book is *De arte gymnastica* (Venice, 1573), a treatise in which Mercuriale recommends physical exercises calibrated to the age and health of his patients.

**MERULA, GIORGIO** (*c.*1430–1494), Italian humanist, born in Alessandria (near Turin) and educated in Milan under FILELFO. He subsequently taught Greek in Mantua and Venice until 1483, when he accepted the invitation of Ludovico SFORZA to return to Milan in order to write a history of the Sforza family. In 1493 Merula's secretary discovered a cache of manuscripts of classical texts in the seventh-century Abbey of San Colombano (near Piacenza). Merula published editions (with commentaries) of classical authors, including Cato, Cicero, and Plautus, and accused POLIZIANO of plagiarism.

**MERULO, CLAUDIO** (1533–1604), Italian composer and organist. He was organist at Brescia Cathedral and San Marco, Venice; he composed masses and motets not only for special sacred occasions but also for state celebrations such as the Venetian victory over the Turks at LEPANTO (1571). He wrote organ *ricercares*, toccatas, and canzonas and set ARIOSTO, BEMBO, PETRARCH, TASSO, and GUARINI in his madrigals; he also supplied music for the entertainments *Marianna* and *Le Troiane* in conjunction with Ludovico DOLCE and Antonio Molino. He worked with organ builders, and the small chamber organ he built while in the service of Duke Ottavio Farnese in Parma is still in use. He enjoyed a considerable reputation as a teacher of composition performance, and taught pupils from Italy, Germany, and Poland.

**MESTA**, the principal guild for Spanish wool. The Mesta began as an association of sheep farmers in Castile (incorporated 1273) with regulatory powers over the *cañadas*, which were the routes of the annual droving of sheep from the lowlands of the southern Meseta (New Castile and Extremadura) to the highlands of the northern Meseta (Old Castile). The Mesta promoted the interests of the sheep owners over the owners of arable farms, an economic imbalance which was to have increasingly devastating consequences on Spanish agriculture for five centuries, including the progressive deforestation and depopulation of Castile which continues to the present day.

The Mesta had its own administrative and judicial institutions, and so came into conflict with towns and the Church, who saw the privileges of the Mesta with respect to any form of enclosure or commons as an encroachment on their own powers; successive monarchs declined to curtail these privileges because the industry was an important source of income for the crown and was from the outset dominated by the most powerful grandees. In the sixteenth and seventeenth centuries the trade in wool declined and the power of the Mesta was gradually eroded; it was eventually abolished by the reforming Bourbon bureaucrats of the Enlightenment.

Julius Klein, *The Mesta: A Study in Spanish Economic History* (1920); Pedro García Martín, *La Mesta* (1990).

**METRICAL PSALMS**. In existence since the fourth century, they flourished after 1520 as LUTHER and HUS recognized their value as a vehicle for congregational singing, since they could assume the same verse form as popular song; some appear among the hymns of Lutheran chorales compiled in 1524. The development of the French metrical Psalter was supported by Calvin and the 1524 *Kirchenampt* of the Strassburg German Reformed Sect contained 22 metrical psalms. Protestant refugees worked on the Anglican-Genevan Psalter which in time influenced the Scottish Psalter of 1564. In 1566 the French Psalter replaced Susato's collections of *souterliedekins* (1556–7) in the Netherlands.

**MEZZARISA, FRANCESCO DI ANTONIO** (*fl.* 1527–81), Italian potter in FAENZA. He was initially a manufacturer of ISTORIATO ware (*c.*1527–40) but in about 1540 began to work with Virgiliotto CALAMELLI in the development of BIANCHI. Within five years he was exporting huge quantities of his characteristically florid *bianchi* to Genoa.

MDA.

**MICHELANGELO or Michelagnolo Buonarroti** (1475–1564), Italian sculptor, painter, draughtsman, architect, and poet, born on 6 March 1475 in Caprese (now Caprese

Michelangelo, *The Dying Slave*, in the Louvre, Paris

Michelangelo), the son of Ludovico Buonarroti (a Florentine nobleman working in Caprese as the *podestà* of Caprese and Chiusi) and his wife Francesca dei Neri; he was trained in the Florentine studio of Domenico GHIRLANDAIO and possibly with BERTOLDO DI GIOVANNI. His surviving early work includes a relief of *The Battle of Lapiths and Centaurs* (c.1492, Bargello, Florence).

The advent of SAVONAROLA's rule made life as an artist in Florence untenable, and in October 1494 Michelangelo left for Bologna, where he carved three figures for the shrine of St Dominic in the Church of San Domenico. By June 1496 he was in Rome, where he carved the two statues that were to establish his fame as a sculptor: the *Bacchus* (1496, Bargello) and the *Pietà* (1497–9, St Peter's Basilica, Vatican).

From 1501 to 1505 Michelangelo lived in Florence, where his principal work was *David* (1501–4, Accademia, Florence), which has become the foremost visual image of the Florentine Renaissance. During this period he also sculpted the *Madonna and Child* now in the Church of Notre Dame in Bruges and probably carved the *Madonna* relief now in the Royal Academy in London. His painting during this period includes the Doni Tondo (Uffizi) and preliminary work on a battlepiece for the Sala del Maggior Consiglio in the Palazzo Vecchio; this commission, which was shared with LEONARDO (who painted the battle of ANGHIARI), never reached the stage of painting, but a cartoon known as *The Bathers* is known from a copy (Holkham Hall, Norfolk), and some of Michelangelo's preliminary drawings survive.

In 1505 Michelangelo was called to Rome by Pope JULIUS II, who commissioned him to make his tomb. They soon quarrelled, and in April 1506 Michelangelo returned to Florence. The commission for the tomb, which involved the carving of more than 40 large figures, was quietly set aside, though it was renewed by the DELLA ROVERE family after the death of Pope Julius in February 1513, and Michelangelo carved the *Moses* and two *Slaves*. Michelangelo signed three more contracts (1516, 1532, 1542) for the tomb, each of which reduced the amount of work that he was expected to do, and in 1545 a much-reduced version of the monument was erected in the Church of San Pietro in Vincoli; the monumental *Moses* is still in the church, but the two *Slaves* are now in the Louvre.

Michelangelo returned to Rome in 1508, this time to work on the fresco cycle that covers the vault and part of the upper walls of the SISTINE CHAPEL. He worked quickly: the first half was officially unveiled on 15 August 1511, and after fresh scaffolding enabled him to complete the commission, the whole of his work was unveiled on 31 October 1512; thereafter his standing was such that he was known as Michelangelo *il divino*.

In December 1516 Pope LEO X commissioned Michelangelo to design a façade for the Church of San Lorenzo in Florence, the MEDICI church of which BRUNELLESCHI had built the interior. The façade was never built, but Michelangelo did contribute two works to San Lorenzo, the Medici chapel known

as the New Sacristy (which complemented Brunelleschi's Old Sacristy) and the Biblioteca LAURENZIANA. The New Sacristy was commissioned in November 1520, but work was suspended during the exile of the Medici (1527–30), when Michelangelo declared himself to be a firm supporter of the republic and assumed responsibility for fortifications; when the Medici were restored, Michelangelo was pardoned by Pope CLEMENT VII and resumed work on the Medici chapel.

In 1534 Michelangelo moved permanently to Rome, leaving the Medici chapel unfinished. In Rome he was immediately commissioned by Pope PAUL III to paint the *Last Judgement* on the altar wall of the Sistine Chapel; the fresco was unveiled on 31 October 1541, which was 29 years to the day after the unveiling of the ceiling. Pope Paul subsequently commissioned frescoes on *The Conversion of St Paul* and *The Crucifixion of St Peter* for the Cappella Paolina (1542–50). In 1546, at the age of 71, Michelangelo began his final architectural work, the completion of ST PETER'S BASILICA. Michelangelo designed a huge hemispherical dome, which was left unfinished at his death on 18 February 1564; the dome was completed by Giacomo DELLA PORTA and Domenico FONTANA, who altered Michelangelo's design by making the top of the dome pointed.

As work on St Peter's proceeded, Michelangelo continued to draw, to write poetry, and to sculpt. He had earlier become one of the first exponents of the presentation DRAWING (of which examples survive at Windsor Castle, the Ashmolean, and the British Museum), and in his old age turned to religious subjects, including a series on *The Crucifixion* (of which one in the British Museum is dedicated to Vittoria COLONNA). His poetry, which in his youth had consisted of amorous sonnets and a smaller number of madrigals, epigrams, and *terza rima* verses, often inspired (like many of his drawings) by his love for the youthful Tommaso de' Cavalieri, became in his final years a medium of religious expression. In the final weeks of his life Michelangelo worked on the marble *Rondanini Pietà* now in the Castello Sforzesco in Milan, which is one of the statues that led admirers to associate Michelangelo with the awesome power known as *terribilità*.

MDA; H. Hibbard, *Michelangelo* (1975).

## MICHELOZZO DI BARTOLOMEO or Michelozzi Michelozzo (1396–1472), Italian architect and sculptor, born in Florence, the son of a Burgundian. He worked as an assistant to GHIBERTI (c.1417–24) and then entered into a partnership with DONATELLO (1424–33). The niche that he is said to have designed to accommodate Donatello's statue of St Louis in Orsanmichele (1425) is one of the first examples of a design revived from Roman antiquity—but it is possible that the niche is the work of Donatello. There is no doubt that Michelozzo carved the architectural parts of Donatello's tomb for the antipope JOHN XXIII in the baptistery (1427).

Michelozzo first secured the patronage of the MEDICI family in late 1434, when he began to work on the MEDICI VILLA at Careggi, to which he added the courtyard and loggia. In 1444 he designed for Cosimo de' MEDICI the first Renaissance

Michelangelo, *Pietà*, in St Peter's Basilica, Vatican, Rome

palace, the Palazzo Medici, which is now known as the Palazzo Medici-Riccardi. This seminal building, which was judged by Flavio BIONDO to be 'comparable to the works commissioned by Roman emperors', has three storeys divided by classical string courses and graded rustication which is heavy on the ground floor and delicate on the top floor; the interior has an arcaded courtyard modelled on BRUNELLESCHI's Ospedale degli Innocenti. Michelozzo also built the Medici villas at Cafaggiolo (1451) and Fiesole (1458–61, rebuilt in the eighteenth century).

In 1437 Michelozzo began to work on the Convent of San Marco, to which he contributed the sacristy in the church, the cloisters, and the elegant three-aisled library (1437–43). He subsequently (1444–55) worked on the Church of the SS Annunziata, for which he designed the centralized tribune (later completed by ALBERTI) and the sacristy; the round choir, which is an adaptation of the design of the ancient Roman Temple of Minerva Medica, scarcely acknowledges the liturgical requirement that laity and clergy (in this case the Servite friars who used the choir) be separated by a screen. A bronze *St John* cast by Michelozzo for the Annunziata has recently been identified and is now in the Kimsell Museum in Forth Worth, Texas.

Beyond Florence, Michelozzo designed the tomb of Bartolommeo Aragazzi in Montepulciano (1427, now mostly destroyed, but two angels survive in the Victoria and Albert Museum as do several fragments in Montepulciano), the pulpit of Prato Cathedral (1428–38, a collaboration with Donatello), the square Church of Santa Maria delle Grazie in Pistoia (1452), the Portinari Chapel in Sant'Eustorgio in Milan (c.1462), which introduced the Renaissance style to Lombardy, and the Palazzo dei Rettori (1462–3, now a museum) in RAGUSA (now Dubrovnik). His only known work in silver is a statuette of *St John the Baptist* (1452) in the Museo del' Opera del Duomo in Florence.

*MDA*; Harriet Caplow, *Michelozzo* (1977); W. Ferrara and F. Quinterio, *Michelozzo di Bartolomeo* (1984).

**MIDDLE AGES or (Latin)** *medium aevum* **or (French)** *moyen âge* **or (German)** *Mittelalter* **or (Italian)** *medioevo*. The cultural model of a RENAISSANCE implies a classical age followed by a period of decline which is then reversed by a rebirth of classical values. Eighteenth- and nineteenth-century historians were often content with a very precise time-frame: the Middle Ages began in 476 with the fall of the Roman Empire in the West and ended with the fall of Constantinople in 1453. In linguistic terms, classical purity was deemed to be followed by decadence and revival: Ciceronian LATIN was seen as pure, medieval Latin as corrupt, and humanist Latin as a revival of Ciceronian purity. In religious terms, the purity of the early Church (which is normally deemed to extend to the Council of Nicaea in 325) was seen to slide into corruption, only to be restored at the REFORMATION, which is a religious Renaissance.

---

Michelangelo, *David*, in the Accademia, Florence

The importance of this model is that, however inadequate it may seem to modern eyes, it was believed by the humanists of the fifteenth and sixteenth centuries. The phrase 'Middle Ages' seems first to have been used by Flavio BIONDO in 1437, and quickly became a commonplace; thereafter the history of Europe was divided into three periods: classical antiquity, the Middle Ages, and the modern period.

The English adjective 'medieval' was formed in the nineteenth century from Latin *medius* (middle) and *aevum* (age). The term 'Dark Ages' was initially used as a descriptive synonym for 'Middle Ages', but in the nineteenth century came to refer to a period preceding the Middle Ages (which were redefined as 1000–1453). The term 'early modern', which increasingly replaces 'Renaissance' in historical writing (though similarly freighted with questionable cultural assumptions), retains the model of a 'middle age' between the ancient and the modern.

**MIDDLETON, THOMAS** (c.1580–1627), English playwright. Middleton was producing plays for HENSLOWE by 1603, working alone and in collaboration with others. Many of his plays are now lost. He worked with DEKKER on the first part of *The Honest Whore* (1604), and with ROWLEY on the tragedy *The Changeling* (1622). *Women Beware Women* (c.1621–7) is a tragedy loosely based on the story of Bianca CAPELLO and Francesco de' MEDICI. *The Revenger's Tragedy* (1607) is a disputed attribution. Seven of his other plays, including *A Chaste Maid in Cheapside* (1630), are comedies of London life. His most contentious work was the political allegory *A Game at Chess* (1624), written alone, which provoked protests from the Spanish ambassador for its treatment of Hispano-British diplomacy, and led to Middleton being summoned before the Privy Council.

*DNB*.

**MIEREVELT, MICHIEL VAN JANSZOON** (1567–1641), Dutch portrait painter, born in Delft and trained from 1581 to 1583 in the Utrecht studio of Anthonie Blocklandt (1533–83). He was appointed portrait painter to the House of Orange and, despite his ANABAPTIST sympathies, to ALBRECHT VON HABSBURG. He claimed to have painted some 10,000 portraits.

*MDA*; *NNBW* x.

**MILAN or (Italian)** Milano **or (Latin)** Mediolanum **or (German)** Mailand, a city and archiepiscopal see in Lombardy. Medieval Milan was a manufacturing city with an international reputation for its metalwork (particularly ARMS AND ARMOUR) and a substantial trade in textiles (cotton, silk, and wool). The city was ruled by the VISCONTI FAMILY from 1287 to 1447 and after the interregnum of the AMBROSIAN REPUBLIC (1447–50) was ruled by the SFORZA FAMILY from 1450 to 1515. France occupied Milan from 1500 to 1521, except for a brief interval (1512–15) when Massimiliano Sforza ruled the city, and after the French departed, Francesco II Sforza became ruler of Milan (1521–5); after the imperial occupation of 1525–9, Francesco II was reinstated (1529–35). In 1535 Milan was absorbed into the Holy Roman Empire and in 1546

CHARLES V invested his son Philip (later King PHILIP II) with the duchy of Milan. Thereafter Milan became a dependency of the Spanish crown, which it remained until the War of the Spanish Succession (1714), after which it was held by Austria.

The artistic life of Milan reached its apogee under Ludovico SFORZA and his wife Beatrice d'ESTE, who brought to their court BRAMANTE and LEONARDO DA VINCI; Bramante designed San Ambrogio and the Dominican Monastery of Santa Maria delle Grazie, where Leonardo painted the *Last Supper*. Before Bramante, the most important architects active in Milan were MICHELOZZO DI BARTOLOMEO and FILARETE. Michelozzo may have been the architect of the Medici Palace (now destroyed), the seat of the Medici bank, and was certainly the designer of the Portinari Chapel in San Eustorgio, which commemorates the bank's manager, Pigello Portinari (d. 1468). Filarete's Ospedale Maggiore (1457) uses Lombard brick and terracotta to execute a design influenced by BRUNELLESCHI; the north façade was added by Bramante. The Ospedale Maggiore was one of the earliest municipal HOSPITALS and was the first with wards laid out in a symmetrical cruciform design. The Biblioteca AMBROSIANA was founded by Cardinal Federico Borromeo, archbishop of Milan, and opened on 8 December 1609; Carlo BORROMEO, Federico's cousin, is buried in Milan Cathedral, the vast white marble cathedral commissioned by Gian Galeazzo VISCONTI in 1386.

Before Leonardo arrived, the most important painters in Milan were Vincenzo FOPPA, Ambrogio BERGOGNONE, and BRAMANTINO; subsequent artists whose work shows the influence of Leonardo include Gaudenzio FERRARI, Andrea SOLARIO, Giovanni BOLTRAFFIO, and Bernardino LUINI.

Giovanni Treccani degli Alfieri, *Storia di Milano*, vols. v–ix (1955–61); C. M. Ady, *A History of Milan under the Sforza* (1907); D. Muir, *A History of Milan under the Visconti* (1924); F. Chabod, *Il ducato di Milano e l'impero di Carlo V* (2 vols., 1961–71); Evelyn Welch, *Art and Authority in Renaissance Milan* (1995).

**MILÁN, LUIS DE** (*c*.1500–*c*.1561), Spanish composer and writer, active in Valencia. His *Libro de música de vihuela de mano intitulado El maestro* (1536) is a collection of fantasias, *tientos*, and dance movements for vihuela. It was intended as teaching material and is noteworthy for its unprecedented use of tempo markings such as 'con el compas batido' ('with an agitated beat'). His book *El cortesano* (1561), clearly influenced by CASTIGLIONE's *Il cortegiano*, illustrates Valencian court life.

**MILTITZ, KARL VON** (*c*.1490–1529), German papal nuncio, born near Meissen into a noble Saxon family. He was educated in Mainz, Trier, and Cologne and in 1514 moved to Rome, where he became a papal chamberlain and acted as the representative of FRIEDRICH III, elector of Saxony. In late 1518, after Cardinal CAJETAN's attempts to silence LUTHER had failed, Miltitz was asked to carry the Golden Rose of papal favour to Friedrich with a view to securing his assistance to contain Luther. Miltitz decided to negotiate directly, and met

Luther in Altenburg (4–6 January 1519), where Luther refused to recant but agreed to suspend his campaign until the dispute could be settled by a German bishop; Miltitz then travelled to Leipzig and, as a concession to Luther, repudiated Johann TETZEL. He subsequently met Luther at Liebenwerda (5 October 1519) and Lichtenberg, near Wittenberg (12 October 1520), but was unable to conclude an agreement.

Miltitz spent the final years of his life in Mainz and Meissen. He accidentally drowned in the Main on 20 November 1529 and was buried in Mainz Cathedral.

*NDB*; H. A. Creutzberg, *Karl von Miltitz, 1490–1529: Sein Leben und seine geschichtliche Bedeutung* (1907); P. Kalkoff, *Die Miltitziade: Eine kritische Nachlese zur Geschichte des Ablaßstreites* (1911).

**MILTON, JOHN** (*c*.1563–1647), English composer, father of the poet, a scrivener by trade, but also an amateur musician. He wrote anthems for domestic use along with other sacred works and a viol fantasia. His music was included in *The TRIUMPHS OF ORIANA* (1601), *Tears and Lamentations* (1614), *Tristitiae remedium* (1616), and RAVENSCROFT's *The Whole Book of Psalms* (1621).

**MINIATURE**. The term 'miniature' is used in art history in two distinct senses: it can denote either a picture in an illuminated manuscript or a small portrait. In manuscript illumination, the minium was the red lead colouring used by the miniator to decorate initial letters; medieval Latin *miniatura* did not refer to size, but rather derived from the verb *miniare*, to rubricate or illuminate.

A pseudo-etymological association of *miniatura* with the Latin terms that express smallness (e.g. minimum) led to the idea that a miniature was a small picture. Such miniatures were usually minutely finished portraits painted on vellum, ivory, or card. The portrait miniature did not derive (except in name) from the pictures on illuminated manuscripts, but rather has its origins in the Renaissance portrait MEDAL. The earliest portrait miniatures were painted in late fifteenth-century France, but the genre developed in the Netherlands. It may have been Flemish miniaturists in England who introduced the form to HOLBEIN. In the course of the sixteenth century the portrait miniature became an independent genre, often worn as a dress ornament, and its shape changed from round to oval. Such miniatures became particularly popular in England, where they were known as 'limnings' or 'pictures in little'; the finest English exponents of the form were Nicholas HILLIARD and Isaac OLIVER.

**MINIMS or (Italian) Minimi or (Latin) Ordo Fratrum Minimorum**, a religious ORDER founded by FRANCESCO DI PAOLO. In about 1435, the traditional date at which the Minims were founded, Francesco, who was living as a hermit near Paolo, was joined by disciples who established themselves as hermits in the vicinity. The group began to live in a community in about 1452. The Franciscans were known as the Ordo Fratrum Minorum (i.e. the 'lesser' brothers) and the new groups became known as the Ordo Fratrum Minimorum (i.e. the 'least' brothers). By 1474 the Order had secured papal recognition and established houses throughout southern Italy and Sicily.

The first rule of the Order, confirmed by Pope ALEXANDER VI in 1493, was an austere version of the Franciscan rule. The second rule, which was sanctioned by Pope Alexander in 1501, was even stricter. In addition to the usual vows of poverty, chastity, and obedience, members of the Order took a fourth vow which was, in effect, a perpetual Lenten diet: flesh, fish, and animal products (eggs, milk, butter, cheese, and dripping) were renounced in perpetuity; the monks ate only vegetables, bread, fruit, and oil, and drank only water. By the time Francesco died in 1507, the Order had established more than 30 houses in Bohemia, France, Germany, Italy, and Spain. In the seventeenth century, when the Order reached its zenith, it had 450 monasteries and had established mission stations in India. There were no houses in England, Scotland, or Ireland.

The Minims have a second order of enclosed nuns, traditionally but incorrectly said to have been established in 1495 (a letter of 1489 addresses the community in Andujar), and a mixed third order (in imitation of Franciscan secular tertiaries) for members living in the secular world; the rule of the third order was approved in 1501 and confirmed in 1506. The superiors of individual houses are called 'correctors', and the general of the Order is known as the 'corrector-general'. The habit of the Minims is black.

G. M. Roberti, *Disegno storico dell'ordine dei Minimi* (3 vols., 1902–22); P. J. S. Whitmore, *The Order of Minims in Seventeenth-Century France* (1967).

**MINO DA FIESOLE** (1429–84), Italian sculptor, trained in the Florentine studio of DESIDERIO DA SETTIGNANO. He worked in both Florence and Rome and specialized in tombs and portrait busts. He sculpted several tombs in the Church of the Badia in Florence; his Roman tombs include that of Francesco Tornabuoni in Santa Maria sopra Minerva. Mino's bust of *Piero de' MEDICI* (1453, Bargello, Florence) is the earliest dated Renaissance portrait bust. Mino da Fiesole is sometimes identified with the sculptor who designated himself 'Mino del Reame', but the name implies that this other Mino was a Neapolitan.

MDA.

**MINTURNO, ANTONIO** (d. 1579), Italian literary theorist. He was born in Traetto and moved in 1521 to Rome, where he pursued a clerical career in which he was to become bishop of Ugento and bishop of Crotone. Minturno's COUNTER-REFORMATION ideals were embodied in his two essays on literature, the Latin *De poeta* (1559) and the Italian *L'arte poetica* (1594).

OCIL; B. Weinberg, *A History of Literary Criticism in the Italian Renaissance* (2 vols., 1961).

**MIRRORS or looking-glasses.** Medieval mirrors were made either from polished metal or from glass backed by lead, and were framed ornamentally, often in ivory. Throughout the fifteenth century glassmakers in south Germany (notably Nuremberg, where a guild of mirror-makers had existed since at least 1373) produced convex mirrors known as bull's eyes (*Ochsen-Augen*), the shape being determined by the concavity of the glass from which they were blown. At the end of the fifteenth century Venetian glassmakers in Murano developed a technique (known as the 'Lorraine' or 'broad' technique) for making flat mirrors: glass was blown into a cylindrical bubble which was then cut at each end and along its axis and flattened on a stone under heat with a wooden tool; the flattened glass was then polished and bevelled before being 'silvered' with a compound of mercury and tin. This process enabled Venice (which created a corporation of mirror-makers in 1564) to dominate the European market for mirrors for two centuries, until Bernard Perrot's invention of plate glass in 1687 enabled French manufacturers to produce mirrors of a higher quality.

**MISERONI FAMILY**, a Milanese family of lapidaries, many of whose members worked in Prague or elsewhere in the imperial service. Girolamo (1522–84) and his brother Gasparo (1518–73) entered the service of COSIMO I DE MEDICI. Four of Girolamo's sons entered the imperial service: Giulio (1559–93) worked in Spain from 1582; Ottavio (1567–1624) worked from 1588 in the court of RUDOLF II in Prague, and was later joined by his brothers Giovanni Ambrogio and Alessandro. Ottavio was appointed as official lapidary to the imperial court, a post that was in due course passed to his son Dionysio (d. 1661) and his grandson Ferdinand Eusebius (d. 1684). A group portrait painted c.1653 by Karel Skréta (now in the Czech National Gallery's Convent of St George in Prague) portrays *Dionysios Miseroni and his Family* with their carved gems.

MDA.

**MISSAGLIA or Negroni da Ello FAMILY**, a family of Italian weapon-makers and armourers (see ARMS AND ARMOUR) active in Milan in the fifteenth century. The heads of the family workshop were Pietro Missaglia (d. before 1429), his son Tommaso (d. 1452), and his grandson Antonio (d. 1496), on whose death the workshop closed; their successors were the NEGROLI family. Products of the Missaglia workshops were sold all over Europe, and examples are preserved in the Kunsthistorisches Museum in Vienna, the Tower of London, the Wallace Collection in London, and the Metropolitan Museum in New York.

**MISSIONARIES.** Missionary activity has been an important aspect of territorial expansion and cultural imperialism throughout the history of Christianity and Islam. With the Reformation missionary activity declined in northern Europe, which was preoccupied with establishing defences against the forces of the Counter-Reformation. Calvinists were disinclined to sponsor missionary work because their doctrine of Predestination meant that the saving of souls was entirely in the hands of God, while Lutherans often depicted missions as an impertinent attempt to usurp the work of God.

In the Catholic Church, missions had been sent as far afield as China in the early fourteenth century, and the

Reformation gave a new urgency to missionary work, in part to compensate for the loss of northern Europe. Spain and Portugal controlled the seas and were the most active imperial powers in missionary endeavour. In America, the conquistadors were followed by missionaries from the Augustinian, Dominican, and Franciscan orders; the Dominican Bartolomé de LAS CASAS became known as the 'Apostle of the Indians'. New orders, especially the JESUITS and the CAPUCHINS, worked in America, Africa, India, China, and Japan; in Asia, the greatest missionary was Francis XAVIER; his successors, such as Roberto de Nobili and Matteo RICCI, adapted their presentation of Christianity to local conditions.

The conflict between slavery and Christian missions became the most important question in Iberian imperial policy in Spain (where a large part of the former Muslim population was enslaved), in America (where Indians suffered a *de facto* enslavement despite constant legislation to the contrary), and above all in Africa, where slavery always preceded evangelization. The only serious attempt at missionary work in Africa took place in Congo, where the king, first visited by the Portuguese in 1483, became a Christian in 1491, when he was baptized with the name João (after the Portuguese king); King João of Congo later reverted to his African religion, but his son, baptized as Afonso, remained a Christian, as did his successors, all of whom complained to Lisbon and Rome about the Portuguese treatment of their own courtiers while enthusiastically participating in the slave trade. In 1622 Pope Gregory XV formed the Congregation for the Propagation of the Faith (Congregatio de Propaganda Fide) with a view to separating missionary work from the temporal interests of Portugal and Spain and to dissociating the Church from slavery. Thereafter the 'Propaganda', as it was popularly known, controlled the missionary activities of the Church; in the mid-nineteenth century the term 'propaganda' entered English as a pejorative term.

**MOCENIGO**, the surname of a noble and ancient Venetian family and the name of a north Italian coin. The family produced statesmen, churchmen, and seven doges: Tommaso (1343–1423), Pietro (1406–76), Giovanni (d. 1475), Alvise (1507–77), and three eighteenth-century doges (Alvise II, III, and IV).

Tommaso Mocenigo was elected as doge in 1414, when he was visiting Cremona as Venetian ambassador; as doge he agreed a peace treaty with the Ottoman Sultan Mehmet I, but when the truce collapsed dispatched the Venetian fleet that defeated the Turks at Gallipoli (now Turkish Gelibolu); he also added Friuli, Istria, and Dalmatia to the territories of the republic and reconstructed the Palazzo Ducale. Tommaso is the eponym of the small Venetian COIN known as the *mocenigo*, which was first issued during his dogate.

Pietro Mocenigo was a Venetian admiral whose forces captured Smyrna (now Turkish İzmir) in 1472. The following year he placed Caterina CORNARO, queen of CYPRUS, under Venetian protection, so preparing the way for the annexation of Cyprus by Venice on her abdication in 1489. Pietro was

elected doge in 1474, and the following year raised the Ottoman siege of Scutari (now Albanian Shkodër), but soon died of an illness contracted in Dalmatia.

Giovanni Mocenigo, the younger brother of Pietro, was elected doge in 1478. He fought the Ottoman Sultan Mehmet II and also fought Ercole I d'ESTE, duke of Ferrara, from whom he captured Rovigo and the Polesine.

Alvise (or Luigi) Mocenigo became doge in 1570, the year in which the Ottoman forces of Sultan Selim II invaded Cyprus with an army of 60,000 men. Nicosia fell after a 45-day siege and its inhabitants were slaughtered; Famagusta withstood a siege for nearly a year before capitulating in August 1571, whereupon Cyprus was lost to Venice. Two months later Alvise secured a measure of revenge in the battle of LEPANTO.

Andrea Mocenigo, an early sixteenth-century historian, wrote an account of the League of CAMBRAI called *Belli memorabilis Cameracensis adversus Venetos historiae* (Venice, 1525).

**MOHÁCS, BATTLE OF**, a battle fought on 29 August 1526 near the Hungarian town of Mohács, where an Ottoman army under Süleyman I defeated a Hungarian army led by King LOUIS II, who was killed while attempting to escape. Süleyman's army then captured and occupied Buda. The battle marked the limit of Ottoman penetration into Europe.

**MOITURIER, ANTOINE** (*fl.* 1463–76), French sculptor, a native of Avignon. Several years after the departure of JUAN DE LA HUERTA from Dijon in 1457, Moiturier completed the unfinished tomb of Duke JOHN THE FEARLESS and his wife in the Chartreuse de Champmol; the Charterhouse is now a psychiatric hospital, and the tombs of the dukes of Burgundy have been moved to the Musée des Beaux-Arts in Dijon. Attributions to Moiturier include the tomb of Philippe Pot, seneschal of Burgundy, made for the Abbey of Citeaux (*c*.1477) and now in the Louvre.

**MOLCHO, SOLOMON** (*c*.1500–1532), Portuguese self-proclaimed Messiah of the Jews, the son of Portuguese MARRANOS. In 1525 he met David REUVENI in Lisbon, returned to his ancestral Judaism by performing circumcision on himself, and moved to Thessaloniki, which was an Ottoman possession and so tolerated JEWS. In 1529 he published in Thessaloniki an eschatological treatise, written in Hebrew, in which he interpreted the SACK OF ROME (1527) as a portent of the imminent redemption of the Jews.

In 1529 Molcho moved to Italy, initially to Ancona (where his sermons to the Jewish community were denounced to the Roman INQUISITION) and then to Rome (1530) and Venice (1531). On returning to Rome he was sentenced to death but released after the intervention of Pope CLEMENT VII. In 1532 he again met David Reuveni, with whom he travelled to Regensburg with a view to persuading the Emperor CHARLES V to use the Jews in order to defeat the Ottomans. On arrival in Regensburg they were both arrested: Reuveni was transported to Spain and Molcho was sent to Mantua, where he was tried by the Inquisition and burnt at the stake.

JNB; Julius Voos, *David Reubeni und Salomo Molcho: Ein Beitrage zur Geschichte der messianischen Bewegung in Judentum in der ersten Hälfte des 16 Jahrhunderts* (1933); Abraham M. Habermann, *Sippur Rabbi Yosi Dilah Reynah u-Ma'aseh Nora' mi-Shelomoh Molkho* (1942–3).

**MOLINA, LUIS DE** (1535–1600), Spanish Jesuit and the eponym of 'Molinism', born in Cuenca; he entered the JESUIT Order in 1553 and subsequently lived in Portugal, where he taught at Coimbra (1563–67) and Évora (1568–83) before moving to Lisbon, where he wrote and published his *Concordia liberi arbitrii cum gratiae donis* (1588). In 1590 he returned to live in his native Cuenca until 1600, when he was appointed as professor of moral theology at Madrid; he died within a few months of taking up his post. His principal work on political theory, *De iustitia et iure* (1593–1609), was completed, after his death, by other Jesuit hands.

The term 'Molinism' is used to denote the theology of GRACE expounded in Molina's *Concordia* of 1588. The central tenet of Molinism is the contention that the efficacy of grace lies not within grace itself (*ab intrinseco*) but rather within the divinely foreknown fact of freely given human co-operation with the workings of grace. God's foreknowledge of actions that are free is deemed to imply a 'middle knowledge' (*scientia media*), unique to him, of hypothetical future contingents. This middle knowledge enables God to arrange for human actions to occur according to his will by putting in place circumstances that will determine choice without determining the human will.

The principal proponents of Molinism were Molina's fellow Jesuits, and its principal opponents were the Dominicans, led by Domingo BÁÑEZ, who realized that if God's grace were concurrent with the act of human will and did not determine it, as Molina contended, then THOMAS AQUINAS's distinction between sufficient and efficacious grace was rendered superfluous. The debate became embittered, and the ensuing controversies became the subject of a special congregation (Congregatio de Auxiliis) in Rome (1597–1607), at the conclusion of which the debate remained unresolved and Pope Paul V declared that the Dominicans could not justly be accused of Calvinism nor the Jesuits of Pelagianism, and decreed that both sides should desist from condemning the opposing position as heretical.

The controversy was dramatized in the theological comedy *El condenado por desconfiado* (*c.*1624, published 1634) attributed to TIRSO DE MOLINA.

Frank Costello, *The Political Philosophy of Luis de Molina* (1974).

**MOLINARO, SIMONE** (*c.*1565–1615), Italian composer teacher, and lutenist who was *maestro di cappella* at the Cathedral of San Lorenzo, Genoa, and of the Cappella di Palazzo. He visited Naples in 1610 and published Carlo GESUALDO's madrigals in score form. He wrote sacred music and madrigals, and a collection of dance movements and virtuoso fantasias for lute, the *Intavolatura di liuto libro primo* (1599).

**MOLINET, JEAN** (1435–1507), French poet associated with the RHÉTORIQUEURS, born in Desvres (Pas-de-Calais) and educated in Paris. In 1464 he entered the court of CHARLES THE BOLD, and he remained at the Burgundian court for the rest of his life. His poetry includes *Le Trône d'honneur* (a long allegorical poem occasioned by the death of Duke Charles in 1477) and a large body of *ballades* and *rondeaux* characterized by salaciousness and a willingness to experiment with verse forms. His most important prose writings were a *Roman de la Rose moralisé* and an *Art de rhétorique*.

Jean Devaux, *Jean Molinet, indiciaire bourguignon* (1990).

**MOLLET FAMILY**, a dynasty of French royal gardeners. Jacques the Elder (d. *c.*1595) was gardener to the duc d'Aumale, at Aumale (north-east of Rouen); he later became head gardener at ANET. Jacques's son Claude the Elder (*c.*1564–*c.*1649) worked as his assistant at Anet, where Jacques laid out the first PARTERRES de broderie in France (*c.*1582), implementing the designs of Étienne DU PÉRAC. Parterres had previously been designed individually, but under du Pérac's influence the Mollets designed parterres as part of a unified pattern. In about 1595 Claude became gardener to HENRI IV, and in that capacity designed the gardens at FONTAINEBLEAU and SAINT-GERMAIN-EN-LAYE. He later worked on the TUILERIES, where his responsibility was the parterre to the east of the palace. Claude's designs for the parterres of the royal gardens in which he worked are included in Olivier de SERRES's *Théâtre d'agriculture* (1600); Claude's own book, the *Théâtre des plans et jardinages*, which was not published until 1652, is an important record of FRENCH GARDENS in the late sixteenth and early seventeenth centuries He was the first gardener to plant herbaceous perennials that flowered in succession against a background of evergreen shrubs, and so became the inventor of the herbaceous border.

Claude's five sons all became royal gardeners. André (d. 1655) designed gardens at St James's Palace (*c.*1630) and WIMBLEDON HOUSE (1642), and returned to St James's Palace in 1658 with his kinsman Gabriel (d. 1663; possibly Claude the Younger's son); both were described in 1661 as royal gardeners. André subsequently designed gardens in The Hague and (with his son Jean) in Stockholm; his *Le Jardin de plaisir* (Stockholm, 1651) articulates the principles that governed French garden design in the first half of the seventeenth century. André's brothers Pierre (d. 1659), Noël, and Claude the Younger (d. 1664) followed their father into positions in the gardens of the Tuileries, and Claude the Younger laid out the first *parterre de broderie* at Versailles. Another son, Jacques the Younger (d. *c.*1622), was head gardener at FONTAINEBLEAU. Claude the Younger's son Charles (*fl.* 1660–93) and grandson Armand-Claude (*c.*1670–1742) worked as royal gardeners at the Tuileries and Fontainebleau.

**MOLZA, FRANCESCO MARIA** (1489–1544), Italian poet, a native of Modena, where he lived for most of his life in a style condemned by his contemporaries as immoral. Molza wrote in both Italian and Latin; his works include elegiac verses on the desertion of CATHERINE OF ARAGON by King HENRY VIII, a collection of five novellas (1549), and a pastoral, *La ninfa tiberina* (1549).

*OCIL.*

**MOMPER, JOOS II or Josse II DE** (1564–1635), Flemish LANDSCAPE painter who worked in Antwerp. In his pictures he mediated between the formal landscapes of sixteenth-century Flemish artists and the naturalistic landscapes of early seventeenth-century Dutch artists. He expanded the range of colours used in landscape painting, supplementing the traditional blues and greens with browns, greys, and reds. In his portrayal of figures in mountain landscapes, e.g. *Mountain Landscape with a Watermill* (Gemäldegalerie, Dresden), he usually delegated the painting of the small foreground figures to assistants in his studio or to fellow artists such as Jan BRUEGHEL, and in his flat landscapes he sometimes dispensed with foreground figures altogether.

*MDA.*

**MONASTERIES, DISSOLUTION OF THE**. A central element of the Henrican Reformation, the suppression of the religious houses in England and Wales probably stemmed from both theological and financial motives. Under CROMWELL's direction, the monasteries and religious houses were systematically visited, stripped of their wealth, and partially destroyed; in 1536 an initial wave of visits closed the smaller foundations, whilst the larger establishments were forcibly surrendered in 1539. Much of their wealth was acquired by the crown, whilst land and buildings passed into aristocratic hands. The PILGRIMAGE OF GRACE represented popular resistance to this despoliation.

**MONDRAGONE, VILLA**, a VILLA in Frascati, 25 kilometres (16 miles) south-east of Rome. In 1573 Cardinal Altemps built a *CASINO* to the designs of Martino LUNGHI. The house sits on a terrace, below which an avenue of cypresses runs to the Villa Vecchia. In 1577 the cardinal commissioned a new palace, the Palazzo della Ritirata, which eventually grew to 365 rooms in commemoration of Gregory XIII being in residence when he signed the bull promulgating the Gregorian CALENDAR.

In 1613 the villa was bought by Scipione Borghese, and Giovanni FONTANA built a water-theatre, the Fontana della Girandola ('FOUNTAIN of the Catherine Wheel'), which contained polypriapic *GIOCHI D'ACQUA*. He also laid out a huge PARTERRE below the water-theatre, and at the other end constructed a *GIARDINO SEGRETO*.

C. L. Franck, *The Villas of Frascati* (1966).

**MONE, JEAN or Jan, or Jean de Metz or Jean Lartiste** (*c*.1485/90–*c*.1549), French sculptor, born in Metz. As a young man he moved to Barcelona, where he lived from 1497 (or earlier) until at least 1519 (though he was in Aix-en-Provence in 1512 and 1513 and perhaps longer); from 1517 to 1519 he worked with Bartolomé ORDÓÑEZ on the decoration of the cathedral choir. In 1521 he returned to Antwerp, where he met DÜRER, and the following year he was appointed as court sculptor to CHARLES V, in which capacity he worked

in Antwerp, Brussels, and Mechelen (French Malines). The style of his sculptures is resolutely Italianate rather than Flemish, and his preferred building material was marble. His best-known work is the altar of 1533 in the Church of Notre Dame at Halle (Brabant, near Brussels). He also sculpted the majestic tomb of Cardinal Guillaume de Croy (1525–8) for the Celestine church at Heuerlee; the tomb, which was damaged during French Revolution, is now in the Capuchin church at Enghien (Belgium). In 1524 Mone was appointed imperial artist (*artiste de l'empereur*) by MARGARET OF AUSTRIA, and moved to Mechelen, where he remained for the rest of his life.

*MDA.*

**MONLUC or Montluc, BLAISE DE LASSERAN-MASSENCÔME, SEIGNEUR DE** (1502–77), French soldier. He was born into a noble family in Condom (Gascony) and as a young man served in Italy, where he distinguished himself in his defence of Siena for eight months (1555). He also fought in the French WARS OF RELIGION and in 1574 was appointed *maréchal de France* by King HENRI III. His posthumously published *Commentaires* (Bordeaux, 1592) is a lively personal memoir and a fine account of contemporary thinking on military tactics.

Pierre Michel, *Blaise de Monluc* (1971); Jean-Charles Sournia, *Blaise de Monluc: Soldat et écrivain, 1500–1577* (1981).

**MONODY**. Sometimes used to describe music of a single line, the term specifically refers to Italian secular song (1600–40), for solo voice and continuo, played by lute, chitarrone, theorbo, harpsichord, or guitar. This style of composing, which differs from its equal-voiced polyphonic predecessors by polarizing the treble and bass lines, was to make an enormous impact on music in the baroque era. Originating in Florence and encapsulated in CACCINI's *Le nuove musiche* (1601), it quickly spread throughout northern Italy and to Rome.

**MONSON, SIR WILLIAM** (1568–1643), English admiral chiefly remembered for his *Naval Tracts* (1682), which provide a detailed account of the English war with Spain at sea between 1585 and 1603. A volunteer at sea during the ARMADA, Monson was taken prisoner for a year by the Spanish during a raid against their treasure ships in 1591. He was knighted for accompanying ESSEX on the CÁDIZ raid of 1596. In 1604 he became admiral of the 'Narrow Seas', or home waters, where, as was revealed in 1614, he was in the pay of the Spanish, and hence adopted a neutral attitude to their ships. He was briefly imprisoned for this in 1616, but later returned to service, becoming vice-admiral of the summer fleet in 1635.

**MONTAGNA, BARTOLOMEO** (*c*.1450–1523), Italian painter, born in Orzinuovi (near Brescia); he may have been a pupil of MANTEGNA. In 1482–3 he worked in Venice, where he executed large religious paintings for the Scuola di San Marco. Thereafter he lived in Vicenza, though he worked on occasion in Padua (where he contributed paintings to the Scuola del Santo) and Verona. A series of huge paintings executed about the turn of the century include *Madonna Enthroned between Four Saints* (Brera, Milan), a *Pietà* for the Monte Berico Basilica (near Vicenza), and a *Nativity* for the church in Orgiano (25 kilometres (15 miles) south of Vicenza). His monumental style was imitated by his son Benedetto Montagna (1481–1558).

*MDA*; Lionello Puppi, *Bartolomeo Montagna* (1962).

**MONTAIGNE, MICHEL EYQUEM DE** (1533–92), French essayist, born into a recently ennobled family in Gascony and educated at the Collège de Guyenne in Bordeaux. In 1557 he was appointed to a judicial post at the Parlement in Périgord, which in the following year was amalgamated with the Parlement in Bordeaux, where Étienne de LA BOËTIE became his colleague and friend. In 1570 he retired to his estate of Montaigne (Gascony), where he intended to spend the rest of his life reading and writing in the tower of the chateau (which still survives). His retirement was intermittently broken by travel (notably a journey through France, the Swiss Confederation, Bavaria, Venice, and Rome in 1580–1), by civic responsibilities (notably his service as mayor of Bordeaux from 1581 to 1585), and by diplomatic negotiations on behalf of HENRI III and Henry of Navarre (later HENRI IV).

The first two books of Montaigne's *Essais* were published in Bordeaux in 1580 (revised edition, 1582); the third book was included in the enlarged edition published in Paris in 1588. A further edition, on which Montaigne was engaged at his death, was published in 1595 by Marie de Gournay, Montaigne's adopted daughter (*fille d'alliance*). Montaigne's title, *Essais*, was wholly original, and seems to denote 'trials' or 'tests'; the modern use of *essai* (English 'essay') to mean a literary composition derives from Montaigne's title.

The topics of the *Essais* reflect traditional humanist concerns (education, morality, war, law) and Montaigne's Neostoic sympathies: his recurring themes are friendship and conversation, fear of death from a painful disease, the value of ancient literature, civic disorder, and religious uncertainty. The tone of his late essays is tolerationist, and Montaigne condemns the burning of WITCHES and Spanish maltreatment of American Indians: the whole revolves, uniquely for its time, around a realization of the relativity of observation and the resultant philosophy of *sagesse*, the antithesis of dogmatism.

Peter Burke, *Montaigne* (1982); Ian Maclean and Ian McFarlane, *Montaigne* (1982); Richard Sayce, *The Essays of Montaigne: A Critical Exploration* (1972); Hugo Friedrich, *Montaigne* (English trans, 1991).

**MONTAÑÉS, JUAN MARTÍNEZ** (1568–1649), Spanish sculptor, the most prominent member of the Seville School of SPANISH ART. His first major work was the reredos of *St Isidore* at Santiponce (near Seville), which he began in 1609, working with Francisco PACHECO as his polychromist. His finest mature work is the *Immaculate Conception* in Seville Cathedral. In 1636 he travelled to Madrid to undertake his only known secular work, a portrait head of *Philip IV* (now

lost) to be sent as a model to Florence, where Pietro Tacca was preparing an equestrian statue of the king (now in the Plaza de Oriente in Madrid). His workshop in Seville had a thriving export trade with Peru, where many of his statues and reredoses survive.

*MDA*; Beatrice Proske, *Juan Martínez Montañés: Sevillan Sculptor* (1967); José Hernández Díaz, *Juan Martínez Montañés* (1987).

**MONTCHRÉTIEN, ANTOINE DE** (*c*.1575–1621), French playwright and economist, the author of six humanist verse tragedies: *Sophonisbe* (1596; later revised as *La Carthaginoise*), *L'Écossaise* (1601; later revised as *La Reine d'Écosse*), *Les Lacènes*, *David*, *Aman* (all 1601), and *Hector* (1604). In 1615 Montchrétien published *Traité de l'économie politique*, in which he advocated a protectionist policy for French manufacturing and commerce. Montchrétien developed Protestant sympathies but seems not to have converted. He was killed in a HUGUENOT rebellion in 1621, and was posthumously tried for rebellion; he was convicted, whereupon his body was disinterred, broken on instruments of TORTURE, and burnt.

**MONTE, GUIDOBALDO DEL** (1545–1607), marchese del Monte, Italian military engineer and mathematician. He was born in Pesaro and studied mathematics at Padua and later as a private pupil of COMMANDINO (1572–5). He wrote on mechanics (1577) and on the Rojas design for a universal ASTROLABE (1579), as well as composing an important treatise on the mathematics of linear PERSPECTIVE (1600). From 1588 he was surveyor of fortifications of Tuscany. In 1592 Guidobaldo helped GALILEO obtain a chair in mathematics at Padua.

**MONTE, PHILIPPE DE** (1521–1603), Flemish composer in Naples, Cambrai, Vienna, and, after 1580, Prague. He was *Kapellmeister* at the imperial court of Maximilian II and his son Rudolf II. With Orlande de LASSUS, he composed for the wedding celebrations of the emperor's brother Archduke Karl II and Maria of Bavaria in Vienna 1571 and in 1572 for the coronation of Rudolf as king of Hungary. Realizing that Rudolf was less interested in music than his father, Monte resigned his post, staying in Prague and dedicating further sets of madrigals to patrons and possible patrons, including Cardinal Pietro Aldobrandini, Isabella de' Medici-Orsini, and Johann Fugger.

**MONTEFELTRO FAMILY**, a family of *condottieri* which ruled Urbino for most of the period from 1226 to 1508; there were nine Montefeltro counts (1226–1444), the last of whom, Oddantonio, became the first of three Montefeltro dukes. In the conflict between GUELFS AND GHIBELLINES the Montefeltro family was Ghibelline, and so supported the emperor against the pope. The family changed sides under Antonio da Montefeltro (count from 1377 to 1404), the seventh count, who recovered Urbino from the papacy in 1375 and extended the family's territories by capturing Gubbio in 1388. Antonio's son Guidantonio (count from 1404 to 1443) married a COLONNA relative of Pope MARTIN V, who supported the family in its protracted feud with the MALATESTA FAMILY of

Rimini. In 1443 Count Oddantonio da Montefeltro, the son of Guidantonio, was created duke of Urbino by Pope EUGENIUS IV. After his murder, he was succeeded by his illegitimate half-brother FEDERICO II DA MONTEFELTRO. Federico's son GUIDOBALDO DA MONTEFELTRO was deposed in 1502 by Cesare BORGIA, but recovered the duchy the following year. With his death in 1508 the Montefeltro line became extinct; thereafter Urbino was ruled by the DELLA ROVERE family.

G. Franceschini, *I Montefeltro* (1970).

**MONTELLA, GIOVANNI DOMENICO** (1570–1607), Neapolitan composer, lutenist, and organist who, in 1591, became lutenist in the Royal Chapel of the Spanish viceroy. In both his sacred music (masses, motets, and a collection of *Lamentationes*, 1602) and his numerous madrigals he shows an interest in harmonic experimentation and chromaticism.

**MONTELUPO POTTERIES**, a group of independent Tuscan potteries established in the fourteenth century in and around Montelupo, between Florence and Pisa. In the sixteenth century MAIOLICA produced by these potteries was exported throughout Europe and beyond. Since the early seventeenth century the Montelupo potteries have concentrated on brightly coloured 'peasant ware', typically depicting soldiers and animals.

Fausto Berti, *La maiolica di Montelupo* (1986), id., *Storia della ceramica di Montelupo* (2 vols., 1997).

**MONTEMAYOR, JORGE DE** (1519–61), Portuguese writer (in Spanish), born in Montemor-o-Velho (near Coimbra). He worked as a musician in the service of the Infanta Juana (daughter of CHARLES V and mother of SEBASTIAN I) and in 1554 accompanied King PHILIP II to England. He was murdered in Piedmont.

Montemayor's minor works include an *Exposición moral sobre el psalmo 86* (Alcalá de Henares, 1548) and two *Cancioneros* (Antwerp, 1554 and 1558), of which the *Segundo cancionero espiritual* was banned by the INQUISITION in 1559; he also translated the poems of the Catalan poet Ausiàs March (Valencia, 1560), on whom see CATALAN LITERATURE.

Montemayor was the author of Spain's finest pastoral romance, *Diana*, which was published in Valencia c.1559. The roots of *Diana* lie in the pastoral poems of Theocritus and Virgil and the *Arcadia* of SANNAZARO, which had been translated into Castilian in 1547. Montemayor's eponymous heroine is unhappily married to Delio and chastely loved by Sireno, and at the end of the narrative Diana remains unhappily married. Montemayor undertakes to write a sequel to finish the tale, but did not do so. Other writers were quick to oblige: Alonso Pérez wrote *La segunda parte de la Diana* (Valencia, 1564), which was often published with Montemayor's *Diana* for the next 150 years, and Gaspar Gil Polo wrote *Diana enamorada* (Valencia, 1564), an intelligent and graceful continuation of Montemayor. *Diana* was imitated by CERVANTES (*La Galatea*), Lope de VEGA (*Arcadia*), and Sir Philip SIDNEY (*Arcadia*).

Bruno Damiani, *Jorge de Montemayor* (1984).

**MONTEMURLO, BATTLE OF** (1 August 1537). The assassination of Alessandro de' MEDICI on the night of 5/6 January 1537 extinguished the elder branch of the MEDICI FAMILY; the Council of 48 elected 17-year-old COSIMO I DE MEDICI as Alessandro's successor. The exiled enemies of the Medici decided to take advantage of the ensuing period of instability to overthrow Medici rule in Florence. An army of 4,000 infantry and 300 cavalry assembled at Mirandola under the command of Piero Strozzi (whose father Filippo financed the campaign) and Bernardo Salviati. The army entered Tuscany late in July 1537, and Duke Cosimo responded by ordering Alessandro Vitelli to assemble a force of Italian, German, and Spanish infantry and to advance against the enemy force without delay. On the evening of 31 July Vitelli marched towards Prato with 700 infantry and 100 cavalry, and at dawn the following morning mounted a surprise attack on the advance guard of the enemy army near Montemurlo (a fortress near Pistoia). Having routed the advance guard, Vitelli stormed the fortress and captured the principal supporters of the invasion, Filippo Strozzi and Baccio Valori.

The main rebel army retreated, and Vitelli returned to Florence with his captives in chains. His victory is marked by the column in Piazza di Santa Trinità. On 20 August Baccio Valori was beheaded, together with his son and nephew; Filippo Strozzi was imprisoned, and was found dead in his cell on 18 December 1537.

**MONTESINOS or Montesino, ANTONIO DE** (c.1486–c.1530), Spanish friar in Hispaniola who joined the Dominican Order in 1502 and travelled to Hispaniola in 1510. His sermons against the enslavement of the Indians irritated the Spanish colonists, and Montesinos was sent back to Spain, where he became a spokesman for clerical complaints about ill treatment of the Indians. Such complaints led to the first formulation of the Laws of the INDIES, a compilation of 32 laws known as the Laws of Burgos (promulgated 1512) which gave civic protection to Indians and instituted the ENCOMIENDA (a system subsequently reformed in 1542). Montesinos wrote a tract on the legal rights of Indians (*Informatio iuridica in Indorum defensionem*, c.1516); he subsequently returned to Hispaniola for the rest of his life.

**MONTES PIETATIS or (Italian) *monti di pietà*,** Italian BANKING institutions which lent relatively small amounts of money to ordinary citizens; the loans were secured with pawned items. The first *mons* was established by the Franciscan Order in Perugia in 1461. The Franciscans championed the scheme as an antidote to usury, but their Dominican opponents condemned it as an attempt to legalize usury. In 1515 Pope LEO X and the Fifth Lateran COUNCIL ruled in favour of the *montes*, which subsequently spread to France, the Netherlands, Germany, and Spain.

H. Holzapfel, *Die Anfänge der Montes Pietatis (1462–1515)* (1903);
V. Meneghin, *Bernardino da Feltre e i monti di pietà* (1974).

**MONTEVERDI, CLAUDIO** (1567–1643), Italian composer, who studied with Marcantonio INGEGNERI in Cremona.

Having been appointed 'suonare di vivuola' to Vincenzo I Gonzaga, duke of Mantua, in 1591, he became an important member of the court music establishment. His duties required him to teach, direct a female vocal ensemble, and compose entertainments, including *Orfeo* for the 1606–7 Carnival. With the reduction of the Gonzaga court under Vincenzo's successor Francesco, by 1612 Monteverdi found himself unemployed, back in Cremona, and widowed with three children. The following year he was appointed *maestro di cappella* at San Marco, Venice. Here he provided music for feast days and state occasions while, as a Mantuan citizen and subject, he was still obliged to fulfil Gonzaga commissions.

Monteverdi's early fame grew with the publishing of several books of madrigals, dedicated to a variety of patrons, so that by 1605 his work was known all over Europe. By the end of his career he had published nine books of madrigals as well a a number of collections of sacred music including the Vespers of 1610. In 1607 he began the opera *Arianna*, first performed in 1608 to Ottavio RINUCCINI's libretto; this was revived by Monteverdi in his seventies as the inaugural piece at the 'public' opera venue the Teatro San Moisè, Venice (1639–40). He wrote both *L'incoronazione di Poppea* and *Il ritorno d'Ulisse* for the Venetian stage.

**MONTMORENCY, ANNE, DUKE OF** (1493–1567), constable of France, born into a noble family in Chantilly and named after his godmother ANNE OF BRITTANY. He was educated at court with the future King FRANCIS I and became a soldier in the WARS OF ITALY, in which he fought in the battle of Ravenna (11 April 1512) and the battle of MARIGNANO (13/14 September 1515), commanded the defence of Mézières (1521), and was taken prisoner (together with King Francis) at the battle of PAVIA (24 February 1525). From 1526 he was the architect of a short-lived reconciliation between Francis and Charles V, which culminated in the latter's journey through France in 1539–40 to quell a revolt in Ghent. In 1538 King Francis appointed Anne to the military post of constable of France.

Anne was forced to retire from the court in March 1541, but returned immediately after the accession of HENRI II (March 1547), who created him duke of Montmorency (1551). He was again taken prisoner at the battle of SAINT-QUENTIN (1557), but was released in order to represent the French crown in the negotiations that led to the Treaty of CATEAU-CAMBRÉSIS (1559).

Montmorency returned to a court dominated by the GUISES, who ensured that he was unable to secure his former pre-eminence. After the accession of CHARLES IX, however, he was invited by CATHERINE DE MÉDICIS to temper the authority of the Guises. Despite his personal antipathy for the Guises, he shared their dislike of Queen Catherine's wish to reach a compromise with the HUGUENOTS, and in April 1561 entered into a coalition (known as the Triumvirate) with the maréchal de SAINT-ANDRÉ and François, duke of GUISE. He returned to active service, and won the battle of Dreux (19 December 1562), one of the first battles of the WARS OF RELIGION, but was again captured. He was released as part

of the Treaty of Amboise (1563), and died on 12 November 1567 of wounds sustained two days earlier at the battle of Saint-Denis.

Brigitte Bedos Rezak, *Anne de Montmorency: Seigneur de la Renaissance* (1990); F. Decrue, *Anne de Montmorency* (2 vols., 1885).

**MONTORSOLI, GIOVANNI ANGELO** (*c*.1507–1563), Italian sculptor, born in Montorsoli (near Florence). He worked in the 1520s as an assistant to MICHELANGELO, and in 1531 entered the Servite ORDER, for which he executed commissions in the Church of SS Annunziata in Florence. In 1536 he moved to Naples, in 1539 to Genoa, and in 1547 to Messina, where he became master of the works (*capomaestro*) at the cathedral and made his best-known works, the Fountain of Orion on the Piazza del Duomo and the Fountain of Neptune on the nearby Piazza del Governo; the original figures of Neptune and Scylla are now in the Museo Nazionale. Montorsoli moved to Bologna in 1558 and returned to his convent in Florence in 1561.

*MDA.*

**MORAES, FRANCISCO DE** (*c*.1500–1572), Portuguese author, a treasurer in the household of King JOHN III who in 1540 moved to Paris as secretary to the Portuguese ambassador. In Paris he wrote a chivalric romance called *Palmeirim de Inglaterra*, which was first published in Spanish translation (1547) and later in the original Portuguese (1567); the *Palmeirim* enjoyed a huge success, and even drew praise from CERVANTES, who in *Don Quijote* spared only two romances from his *auto da fé* of books: AMADÍS DE GAULA and *Palmeirim*. An English translation (through French) by Anthony MUNDAY began to appear in 1581. The other writings of Moraes include three moral dialogues. He was assassinated in Évora.

**MORALES, AMBROSIO DE** (1513–91), Spanish historian and antiquary, born in Córdoba and educated at Salamanca University, where his teachers included his uncle the humanist Fernando PÉREZ DE OLIVA, whose philosophical works he was later to edit and supplement with fifteen of his own discourses. Morales's *Crónica general de España* (2 vols., Alcalá de Henares, 1574–7) takes up the romantic medieval tradition of the chronicle of Florián de OCAMPO, but Morales's analytical recourse to documents set a new standard for Spanish historical scholarship. In his *Apología* (Zaragoza, 1610), Morales defended the same historical principles in the *Anales* of his more distinguished friend Jerónimo ZURITA.

At the command of the king, Morales undertook a survey of the manuscripts, inscriptions, and relics of Asturias, Galicia, and León; his findings were published as *Las antigüedades de las ciudades de España* (Alcalá de Henares, 1575).

E. Redel, *Ambrosio de Morales* (1908).

**MORALES, CRISTÓBAL DE** (1500–53), Spanish composer who was at Ávila Cathedral and Plasencia and in 1535 joined the papal chapel of Pope PAUL III, who had serious interests in music. Following ill health he returned to Spain in 1545 where he was appointed *maestro de capilla* at Toledo Cathedral.

Serious illness caused him to resign but in 1551 he was briefy *maestro de capilla* at Málaga Cathedral. Apart from a few madrigals and *cancioneros*, his works are sacred, comprising masses, Magnificats, motets, lamentations, and a setting of the *officium defunctorum*. He saw himself as JOSQUIN's successor, was highly regarded by his contemporaries, and was cited by the theorist ZACCONI.

**MORALES, LUIS DE** (c.1520–1586), Spanish painter who worked in Extremadura, sometimes known as 'Morales el Divino' because of his predilection for devotional subjects. His paintings, which have a markedly individualistic style, include a *Pietà* and an *Ecce homo*; versions of both are in the Real Academia de Bellas Artes de San Fernando in Madrid.

MDA; Carmelo Solís Rodríguez, *Luis de Morales* (1999).

**MORAVIA or (Czech) Morava or (German) Mähren.** From the end of the twelfth century, Moravia was a margravate held as a fief of the crown of BOHEMIA, and thereafter the margravate was inevitably assigned as an apanage to one of the younger members of the Bohemian royal family. In 1410, the Margrave Jobst of Moravia, the nephew of the Emperor Charles IV, was elected as Holy Roman Emperor, but he died a few months later. In 1526, on the death of King LOUIS II of Hungary and Bohemia at the battle of MOHÁCS, Moravia passed (together with Louis's other possessions) to the Habsburg ruler FERDINAND I.

**MORE, SIR THOMAS** (1478–1535), English humanist and statesman. A brilliant lawyer and politician, More prospered in the court of HENRY VIII, succeeding WOLSEY to become lord chancellor in 1529. A humanist scholar and friend of ERASMUS, his *Utopia* (1516) is a playful account of 'no-place', where the rule of reason to determine political and private life is both celebrated and satirized. In the latter 1520s he energetically defended Catholicism against LUTHER, TYNDALE, and others. His downfall came with the breakdown of Henry's marriage to CATHERINE OF ARAGON; opposed to Henry's new religious policy, he resigned the chancellorship in 1532. Although he accepted the new Act of Succession, he refused to admit attacks on papal supremacy, and was imprisoned and executed. He was canonized in 1935.

DNB.

**MOREELSE, PAULUS JANSZOON** (1571–1638), Dutch painter and architect, born in Utrecht. He trained with MIEREVELT in Delft and on returning to Utrecht in 1596 he established himself as a painter before embarking on a visit to Italy. In 1611 he helped to found the St Lucas Guild, the Utrecht guild for painters, and became its first head. His paintings are mostly portraits, both of society figures and of shepherds and mildly erotic shepherdesses. His most important works as an architect were the façade of the meat market in Utrecht and the Catherine Gate (now destroyed, but known from drawings and prints).

MDA; NNBW x.

**MOREL, JACQUES** (*fl.* 1418, d. 1459), French sculptor, born into a family of sculptors in Lyon. In 1418 Jacques Morel was appointed master of works at Lyon Cathedral, for which he carved a monument of Cardinal de Saluces (since destroyed but known to have included an effigy of the cardinal kneeling before an angel). Morel left Lyon in the early 1420s and in 1448 he was appointed as master of works at Rodez Cathedral; while holding this post he was principally occupied with the carving of the BOURBON tombs at the Cluniac abbey of Souvigny (near Moulins), which are particularly remarkable for their ornamental treatment of drapery. His final project was the tomb of RENÉ D'ANJOU in Angers.

MDA.

**MORESQUES.** See ARABESQUES.

**MORETTO DA BRESCIA or Alessandro Bonvicino** (c.1498–1554), Italian painter, a native of Brescia, where he painted portraits such as his *Portrait of a Young Gentleman* (1526, National Gallery, London) and religious pictures for local churches, such as his series in the Cappella del Sacramento in San Giovanni Evangelista, Brescia, and *Santa Giustina* (now in the Kunsthistorisches Museum in Vienna). His pupils included Giovanni Battista MORONI.

MDA.

**MORISCOS** ('Moorish'), Muslim converts to Christianity (or the reconverted descendants of Spanish converts to Islam) who remained in Spain after the conquest of GRANADA in 1492, in violation of the terms of their surrender; many had been forcibly converted from Islam in a campaign organized by Cardinal CISNEROS. *Moriscos* are to be distinguished from the medieval MUDÉJARS (Muslims who retained their religion) and the Mozarabs (Arabic-speaking Christians living under Islamic rule).

Some *moriscos* continued to speak Arabic and to dress and eat as Arabs, as a result of which their culture was treated with contempt by the Hispanic Christians of Andalusia, who suspected that *moriscos* continued to practise Islam in secret; such suspicions were not always groundless, because Islam was openly tolerated by some noble landowners. The *moriscos* were also persecuted by the INQUISITION. The wars with Ottoman Turkey and North Africa and the continual depredations of Algerian slave traders exacerbated the hostility between the two communities, and PHILIP II decided to extirpate the threat of an Islamic fifth column among the *moriscos* by rendering their language and culture illegal in a decree of January 1567 which required them to renounce their traditional dress and customs and hand over their children to be educated by Christian priests. With the assistance of Algiers, the Granadine *moriscos* staged a rising on 24 December 1568, and it took JUAN DE AUSTRIA two years to contain the revolt. By a decree of October 1570 the *morisco* rebels and their families were deported in chains from Granada and sold as slaves all over Spain, whereupon thousands of Christian colonists were moved from northern Spain to Andalusia.

Many *moriscos* preferred to flee to North AFRICA, where some turned to piracy and others developed links with the enemies of Spain, notably France. HENRI IV incorporated a plan for a *morisco* uprising in his scheme to destroy the Spanish monarchy, but he was murdered on 14 May 1610, before he could implement his strategy.

Spain decided in 1608 to expel all *moriscos*, and the edict was proclaimed on 22 September 1609. The predicament of the *moriscos* at this time is sympathetically portrayed in *Don Quijote* and other works by CERVANTES, who had himself spent five years as a slave in Algiers. Hundreds of thousands of *moriscos* were expelled; most emigrated to North Africa, where Spanish-speaking communities of *Andalusiyyun*, as they were known, were still flourishing up to the eighteenth century. A small number returned to Spain, finding their new life under the Ottomans uncongenial, but 1609 saw the end of Islamic culture in Spain after nine centuries of uneasy coexistence.

> H. C. Lea, *The Moriscos of Spain: Their Conversion and Expulsion* (1901); Mercedes García Arenal, *Los Mariscos* (1975); Anwar Chejne, *Islam and the West: The Moriscos, a Cultural and Economic History* (1983).

**MORLEY, THOMAS** (1557/8–1602), English composer, organist at Norwich Cathedral and St Paul's Cathedral; in 1588 he graduated with a B.Mus. from Oxford and became a gentleman of the Chapel Royal in 1592. He lived in the same parish as William SHAKESPEARE which may explain his setting of 'It was a lover and his lass' in *The First Book of Ayres* (1600). In 1598 he was granted a patent enabling him to print a metrical psalter by Richard ALISON. He also published *The TRIUMPHS OF ORIANA* (1603). He was taught by William BYRD and influenced by the Italian style; his *Plain and Easy Introduction to Practical Music* (1597) details methods of composition and performance. He wrote some sacred music but is primarily remembered for his secular music, especially the madrigals written in the ballett style with dance-like rhythms and fa-la refrains.

**MORO, ANTONIO, or** (Dutch) **Antonis Mor van Dashorst** (*c.*1516/20–1576/7), Dutch portrait painter usually known by the Spanish version of his name, born in Utrecht, where he trained in the studio of Jan van SCOREL. His access to the Burgundian court and his extensive travels (he visited England, Italy, Portugal, and Spain) gave him the opportunity to paint members of many of the ruling houses of Europe. The subjects of his portraits include King PHILIP II (Escorial), Emperor MAXIMILIAN II (Prado, Madrid), Queen MARY I of England (1554, versions in the Prado and at Compton Wynyates, Warwickshire), and Sir Thomas GRESHAM (Rijksmuseum, Amsterdam). His most famous work, *Man with a Dog* (1569, National Gallery, Washington), is indebted to TITIAN's portrait of *Charles V* (Prado, Madrid).

*MDA* s.v. Mor, Antonis.

**MORO, GIACOMO** (*fl.* 1582–1610), Italian composer, possibly a Servite monk, active in Viadana, Bologna, and

Antonio Moro, *Man with a Dog* (1569), National Gallery, Washington

Fivizzano. He wrote secular and sacred music; of particular interest are his *Concerti ecclesiastici* (1604), liturgical pieces for voices and basso continuo.

**MORONE, DOMENICO** (*c.*1442–*c.*1518), Italian painter, a native of Verona, where he established a workshop in which many artists were trained. His most important surviving work is *The Victory of the Gonzaga over the Bonacolsi*, a battle-piece with townscape commissioned by Francesco GONZAGA for the Ducal Palace in Mantua.

*MDA.*

**MORONE, GIOVANNI** (1509–80), cardinal and papal legate, born in Milan on 25 January 1509, the son of the chancellor of Milan. In 1529 Pope CLEMENT VII nominated him as bishop of Modena, but the machinations of Cardinal Ippolito d'ESTE prevented him from taking possession of his see. He became a papal diplomat, and in 1536 was sent as papal nuncio to Germany; he was present at the Conference of HAGENAU (1540), the Conference of REGENSBURG (1541), and the Diet of SPEYER (1542); his conviction that the Church stood in need of reform gave him a rare measure of sympathetic understanding of the grievances of the Protestant reformers. In 1542 he was created cardinal and asked (along with Cardinals Paul Parisio and Reginald POLE) to preside over the COUNCIL OF TRENT, but in the event did not participate in the opening sessions. In 1553 he was appointed bishop of Novara by Pope JULIUS III, who in 1555 sent him (at the request of CHARLES V) to the Diet of AUGSBURG in what proved to be a vain attempt to reconcile the German Protestants with Rome.

In 1557 Morone was imprisoned by Pope PAUL IV in Castel Sant'Angelo for alleged heresy on the issues of justification, the invocation of saints, and the veneration of relics; the charges may have been false, but they point to Protestant sympathies. In 1559 he was released from prison and absolved of all charges by Pope PIUS IV, and employed by him in the closing session of the Council of Trent (of which he became, in 1563, the last president). In 1570 he was appointed bishop of Ostia, and he was later employed on diplomatic missions to Genoa (1575) and Augsburg (1576). He was appointed protector of the English in 1578, and in that capacity oversaw the activities of the ENGLISH COLLEGE in Rome. He died in Rome on 1 December 1580 and was buried in Santa Maria sopra Minerva.

NDB.

**MORONE, GIROLAMO** (1470–1529), Milanese conspirator, a civil servant in Milan through the succession of governments in power from 1499 to 1515. He was unable to secure a post with the French administration and so joined the SFORZA in exile; from 1521, he supported the attacks of the imperial army of CHARLES V on French forces in the duchy of Milan.

The decisive imperial victory at Pavia on 24 February 1525 gave rise to the conspiracy that bears Morone's name. Morone, who was by this time high chancellor of Milan, aspired to rid Italy of the armies of France, Spain, and the Empire, and to that end approached the victor of Pavia, Ferdinando Francesco d'AVALOS, marquis of Pescara, and proposed a scheme whereby the marquis would become king of Naples and Duke Francesco II Sforza would become the real ruler of Milan (rather than the obedient imperial vicar of Charles V); these *coups d'état* were to be effected with the passive acquiescence of Pope CLEMENT VII and the republic of Venice. The marquis was aggrieved by the emperor's lack of gratitude for his services and was sorely tempted by the crown of Naples, but in the event revealed the plot to the emperor.

Morone was arrested and imprisoned; the marquis of Pescara died a few months later, and in accordance with his expressed wish that Morone be freed, Charles ordered his release. He subsequently drew on Morone's assistance in the campaigns against the League of COGNAC.

**MORONI, ANDREA** (d. c.1560), Italian architect who worked principally in Padua, where he designed the colonnaded courtyard of the university (1552) and the courtyard of the Palazzo del Podestà (now the Municipio). He also built the Church of Santa Giustina, considerably modifying the plan drawn up in 1502 by Andrea RICCIO.

MDA.

**MORONI, GIOVANNI BATTISTA** (c.1520/4–1578), Italian painter, born near Bergamo and trained in the Brescia studio of MORETTO DA BRESCIA. Like Moretto, Moroni painted both religious pictures and portraits. His portraits, which were praised by the aged TITIAN, include *The Tailor* (c.1570, National Gallery, London).

MDA.

**MORTLAKE**, an English tapestry factory established in 1619 by King James I at Mortlake (a village in what is now west London). The German designer Franz Cleyn (later Sir Francis Crane), who served as director from 1619 to 1636, assembled a team of Flemish weavers to make tapestries for Prince Charles (later King Charles I) and his courtiers. The first product of the family workshop was a series of nine panels depicting the story of Venus and Vulcan. In 1622 Prince Charles purchased for the factory RAPHAEL's cartoons of *The Acts of the Apostles* (now in the Victoria and Albert Museum), from which many tapestries were woven. The other important tapestries woven before the Civil War cut off royal patronage were depictions of the story of Hero and Leander (of which a set survives in the collection of the Swedish royal family) and of the *Twelve Months*.

The factory survived the Interregnum, during which it produced a series on *The Triumph of Caesar* based on paintings by MANTEGNA that are now at Hampton Court, and carried on after the Restoration (producing a set of *Playing Boys* from a design by GIULIO ROMANO) until 1703. Mortlake tapestries are marked with a red cross on a white shield.

**MOSAIC.** The art of making pictures and geometrical patterns from pieces of coloured glass and marble fixed in a bed of cement was highly developed by the Romans and survived in Byzantine architecture. Greek mosaicists worked in Venice from the early twelfth century, and by the thirteenth century mosaic had been assimilated as a Venetian art and had started to appear in churches in Florence and Rome. In the fifteenth century Lorenzo de' MEDICI formulated a plan to cover the interior of the dome of the Duomo in Florence with mosaic; the plan was never realized, but GHIRLANDAIO designed a mosaic *Annunciation* (c.1490) for the north door of the cathedral. In the early sixteenth century Agostino CHIGI commissioned the Venetian mosaicist Luigi da Pace to make a mosaic of *God the Father* (from a cartoon by RAPHAEL) for the Chigi Chapel in the Church of Santa Maria del Popolo in Rome.

Mosaic was also used for the decoration of interiors and furniture. FLORENTINE MOSAIC is the English term for the type of decorative mosaic panels known in Italian as *commeso di pietre dure*.

**MOSER, LUKAS** (fl. 1431), German painter known only for one magnificent work, the ALTARPIECE of Tiefenbronn (near Constance), which he signed and dated 1431. The altarpiece, which depicts the story of Mary Magdalene, has an enigmatic inscription which says 'schri kunst schri und klag dich ser din begert iecz niemen mer' ('shout, Art, shout and complain; no one wants you now'); there was no icono-clastic movement in early fifteenth-century Germany, so the inscription may be Moser's complaint about being unpaid or underpaid.

*MDA*; *NDB*; Gerhard Piccard, *Der Magdalenen-altar des Lucas Moser in Tiefenbronn* (1969).

*MOS GALLICUS*, the Latin term, meaning both 'French style' and 'French custom', introduced in the 1550s to distin-guish the style of the humanist jurisprudence of ALCIATO and CUJAS at Bourges from the *mos Italicus*, the approach of medieval Italian commentators associated with Bologna.

**MOSTAERT, JAN JANSZOON** (*c*.1475–1555/6), Dutch painter, born in Haarlem; the influence of GEERTGEN TOT SINT JANS on Mostaert's style may imply that he was trained by Geertgen. Mostaert was appointed as court painter to MARGARET OF AUSTRIA, regent of the Netherlands, and painted portraits of her courtiers as he travelled with her court. His portraits include a marriage diptych of *Hendrik van Merode* and *Franziska van Brederode* (St Dimpnakerk, Geel). He never travelled to the Americas, and yet he painted scenes from the New World, such as his *Landscape of the West Indies* (Frans Hals Museum, Haarlem); these paintings may be based on sketches or oral accounts. Many of his paintings were destroyed in the Great Fire of Haarlem in 1576.

*MDA*; *NNBW*.

**MOSTO, GIOVANNI BATTISTA** (*c*.1550–1596), Italian composer and instrumentalist, who studied with Claudio MERULO and played cornett and trombone at the Munich court. He became *maestro di cappella* at Padua Cathedral in 1580 and in 1589 moved to Gyulafehérvár (Alba Iulia), where he was in the service of Prince STEFAN BATORY of Tran-sylvania. After a short period in the court of Elector Ernst von Wittelsbach in 1594, he returned to Padua. He wrote madrigals, some of which appeared in *De floridi virtuosi d'Italia* (1586) and were selected by Thomas MORLEY for pub-lication with English texts.

**MOTET**, a sacred polyphonic setting of a Latin text. Unlike the isorhythmic motets of the fourteenth century, those of the fifteenth tended to be written for four to six voices with a slow-moving *cantus firmus* in the tenor. Occasionally there are instances of polytextuality, as for instance in JOSQUIN's 'Stabat mater'. The motet became a breeding ground for new techniques of composition, particularly in the works of Josquin and GOMBERT, less so in the writing of OCKEGHEM and OBRECHT. The emphasis shifted from the Netherlandish composers as the motet spread throughout Europe after 1550. The GABRIELIS' polychoral settings in eight or more parts represent a Venetian style of motet while in England settings of vernacular texts were called anthems. In the early years of the seventeenth century the 'stile antico' manifest in PALESTRINA's motets coexisted with VIADANA's *Concerti ecclesi-astici* (1602, 1607, 1609) which include organ accompaniment. Later motets continued to keep pace with developments in musical language such as basso continuo, recitative, and solo aria.

**MOTHER-OF-PEARL or** (German) *Perlmutter*, the calcite and calcium carbonate deposits that line the shell of many types of mollusc, principally the type known as nacre (which is another name for mother-of-pearl); the deposited layers form prismatic folds that reflect light, and so the effect is slightly different from that of the pearl, which is formed from the same deposits.

Mother-of-pearl was first used in Europe by fourteenth-century German craftsmen, who used it principally as an inlay for church furniture and musical instruments but also as a medium in which crucifixes and religious medallions could be carved. In the fifteenth and sixteenth centuries German goldsmiths, notably those of the JAMNITZER family, mounted engraved and etched shells (chiefly NAUTILUS SHELLS) on gold bases.

G. E. Pazaurek, *Perlmutter* (1937); H. Grün, *Perlmuttkunst in alter und neuer Zeit* (1963).

**MOTILINÍA, TORIBIO DE** (*c*.1490–1569), Spanish mis-sionary, historian, and ethnographer in New Spain. Fray Toribio's surname, Motilinía, was a Hispanicized Huastec word meaning 'poor' which he assumed shortly after he arrived in Mexico as a Franciscan missionary in 1524. He was the first missionary to evangelize Guatemala and Nicaragua, and in 1530 founded the Mexican city of Puebla de los Ánge-les (now Puebla); he served as provincial of his Order from 1548 to 1551.

Motilinía wrote *Memoriales* in 1541 (first published 1903) but his reputation now rests on his *Historia de los indios de Nueva España*, which was completed *c*.1541 and used in manuscript by historians such as Fray Juan de TORQUEMADA, but not pub-lished until the nineteenth century (Mexico City, 1858). The *Historia*'s account of the religious observances of the Aztecs was written in the immediate aftermath of the *conquista*, and its early date gives it considerable authority as the most reliable of the Spanish accounts of the Aztecs. The *Historia* also chronicles the conversion of the Aztecs to Christianity and contains an important early account of their calendar and astronomical knowledge.

*DHE*.

**MOULINS, MASTER OF** (*fl. c*.1480–1500), Bourbon painter whose name derives from a triptych (*c*.1498) in Moulins Cathedral depicting the *Madonna and Child with Saints and Donors*. His distinctive use of luminous colours and his meticulous sculptural depiction of drapery are so indivi-dualistic that other paintings have been attributed to him with unusual confidence, including *The Meeting of Joachim and Anna* in the National Gallery in London.

*MDA*.

**MOUNT**. A garden mount is an artificial hill. The mount was often hollow, and its interior could be used for storage and to provide shelter for delicate plants. Mounts first appear in Italy, where they were a feature of both BOTANICAL GAR-DENS (where they helpfully produced differentiated microclimates) and VILLA gardens. The original mounts still survive in the botanical gardens at Padua, Montpellier (where the terraced mount is oblong), and in the Jardin des Plantes in Paris, where the mount was originally planted with vines. The garden of the Villa Quaracchi had a mount, and the one in the garden of the MEDICI VILLA in Rome survives. The fashion later spread to England, where mounts were constructed at New College, Oxford (1529, still in the garden), THEOBALDS, Lyveden New Bield, Northants (where two large mounts survive), and, most elaborate of all, Hampton Court Palace (see ENGLISH GARDENS). The mount never became fashionable in FRENCH GARDENS, despite the proselytizing efforts of Olivier de SERRES, who illustrated several mounts in his *Théâtre d'agriculture* (1600). Mounts were ascended on spiralling paths, and so were often called 'snail mounts' (e.g. the mount built at Elvetsham, Hampshire, in honour of a visit by Queen Elizabeth in 1591).

**MOUTON, JEAN** (*c.*1459–1522), French composer, and teacher of Adriaan WILLAERT. In 1500, he was *maître des enfants* at Amiens Cathedral. He became *magister capellae* to Queen ANNE OF BRITTANY and then served LOUIS XII and FRANCIS I. He wrote sacred and secular motets, Magnificats, masses, and chansons, and several pieces, such as the motet 'Domine, salvum fac regem' for the coronation of Francis I at Reims in 1515, were written for specific state occasions.

**MUDARRA, ALONSO** (*c.*1510–1580), Spanish composer and vihuelist who was brought up in the de Mendoza household. He became a canon at Seville Cathedral in 1546, where he became involved in musical matters such as the hiring of instrumentalists, the acquisition of a new organ, and commissioning music from Francisco GUERRERO. His *Tres libros de música en cifra para vihuela* (1546) contains guitar music, tablature for harp and organ, and a *fabordon* psalm. In his songs he set the poetry of GARCILASO, BOSCA, PETRARCH, SANNAZARO, Horace, Ovid, and Virgil.

**MUDD, JOHN** (1555–1631) and **THOMAS** (*c.*1560–*c.*1619), English composers, sons of the composer Henry Mudd. John was organist of Peterborough Cathedral and *rector chori* of Southwell collegiate church; the anthems 'Plead thou my cause' and 'Sing joyfully' may be by him. Thomas studied in Cambridge and wrote anthems and instrumental music; his music is mentioned in Francis Meres's *Palladis Tamia* (1598).

**MUDÉJAR**. The term *mudéjar* is a Hispanized corruption of an Arabic word meaning 'domesticated' or 'subjugated', and literally refers to the Muslims who remained under the Christian RECONQUISTA; when applied to people (as opposed to an architectural style) the term implies a continued adherence to Islam, and so is contrasted with MORISCO. The term Mudéjar is also used to denote a style of architecture and decorative art which evolved in Spain and Portugal during the period of the *reconquista*, from the twelfth to the fifteenth centuries. The style is Islamic in its origins, but was used by Spanish Christian architects; in practice, the result was often GOTHIC structures embellished with oriental motifs. When used as a stylistic term, it initially denoted the work executed by Moorish craftsmen for Spanish masters, but later came to denote the hybrid Moorish style of Christian architects, decorative artists, and craftsmen working in brick, clay (for CERAMICS), iron (for DAMASCENING), IVORY, tooled leather (for BOOK covers), plaster, wood (for FURNITURE and for wood inlays called *taraceas*), and tile (AZULEJOS). Mudéjar decoration is also an important element in the MANUELINE and PLATERESQUE styles.

The earliest significant Mudéjar building is the thirteenth-century Chapel of Alfonso VIII at the monastery of Las Huelgas (Burgos). In the fourteenth century, the finest of all Mudéjar palaces, the Alcázar, was constructed in Seville, and its Arabic elements even include Kufic inscriptions in praise of Spanish Christian rulers. In Toledo, there are two fine Mudéjar synagogues: the Sinagoga del Tránsito (1360–6), which is so called because, after the expulsion of the JEWS, it was dedicated to the death (*tránsito*) of the Virgin, and the even older synagogue now known as Santa María la Blanca, from which the Jews were expelled in 1405. In Aragon, there are many examples of Mudéjar bell towers (e.g. Calatayud, Teruel, and Zaragoza) that are clearly based on Moorish minarets.

G. G. King, *Mudéjar* (1927); F. Pérez-Embid, *El mudejarismo en la arquitectura portuguesa de la época manuelina* (1944).

**MÜHLBERG, BATTLE OF** (24 April 1547), the final battle in the SCHMALKALDIC WAR, in which the Spanish army of the Emperor CHARLES V and the army of MAURICE OF SAXONY crossed the Elbe at Mühlberg and defeated the forces of JOHANN FRIEDRICH I, who was captured and imprisoned. The decisive defeat of the Protestant army cleared the way for the emperor to impose the AUGSBURG INTERIM on the German Diet of 1548. The emperor summoned TITIAN to Augsburg in 1548 to paint an equestrian portrait, *Charles V at the Battle of Mühlberg* (Prado, Madrid).

**MULTSCHER, HANS** (*c.*1400–*c.*1467), German painter, born in Reichenhofen, Bavaria. His most important surviving works are a *Virgin and Child* (the central panel of the Werzach altarpiece of 1437 in the Church of St Maria Himmelfahrt, Landsberg am Lech, in Bavaria) and an altarpiece of 1456 in Vipiteno (German Sterzing) in Tirol, where the four panels are kept (together with sculptures from the same altarpiece) in the Multscher Museum.

MDA; NDB; Nicolò Rasmo, *Der Multscher-Altar in Sterzing* (Bozen, 1963); Irmtraud Dietrich, *Hans Multscher* (Bochum, 1992).

**MUNDAY, ANTHONY** (*c.*1560–1633), English poet, translator, and playwright. Munday's plays, which were written mainly for HENSLOWE, include *John a Kent and John a Cumber* (*c.*1594), *The Downfall of Robert, Earl of Huntington*, and *The Death* of the same. *Fedele and Fortunio* may have informed SHAKESPEARE's *Much Ado About Nothing*, whilst *John a Kent and John a Cumber*, concerning a conflict between wizards, may be a source for Bottom in his *Midsummer Night's Dream*. The transcript of *Sir Thomas More* (*c*.1593) in Munday's hand, and with revisions apparently in Shakespeare's hand, is evidence of more formal collaboration.

*DNB.*

**MUNDAY, JOHN** (*c*.1555–1630), English composer and organist, son of William MUNDAY. With Nathaniel GILES he was organist at St George's Chapel, Windsor. He graduated B.Mus. from Oxford in 1586 and wrote verse anthems, Latin sacred pieces, keyboard music, and 'In nomines' for viol consort.

**MUNDAY, WILLIAM** (*c*.1529–1591), English composer and father of John MUNDAY. He sang at Westminster Abbey and several London churches and became a gentleman of the Chapel Royal in 1564. His Latin compositions include masses, Marian antiphons, and psalm settings; he also wrote anthems and was one of the earliest composers of the verse anthem, as illustrated by his 'Ah, helpless wretch' for solo alto, choir, and instrumental accompaniment.

**MUNICH or (German) München**, a Bavarian city founded in 1157 by Duke Heinrich XIII of Bavaria, who established a mint and established Munich as an important centre for the SALT trade. In 1255 Duke Ludwig II, the Wittelsbach ruler of Upper Bavaria and the Palatinate, made Munich his capital, and thereafter Munich was the seat of the Bavarian branch of the WITTELSBACH FAMILY until 1918. The town was destroyed by fire in 1327, and rebuilt on the initiative of the Emperor Ludwig IV of Bavaria. In 1504, on the demise of the Wittelsbach line in Lower Bavaria-Landshut (see Appendix 1), Munich became the capital of a united duchy of Bavaria, and in the sixteenth century became a major centre of brewing. Throughout the turmoil of the Reformation Munich remained loyal to the Roman Church, and this loyalty made it an important centre of COUNTER-REFORMATION activities. In 1623, Munich became the seat of the electorate.

The most important Renaissance building in Munich to have survived the wars that have repeatedly destroyed the city is St Michael's Church (1583–97), which is the work of Frederick SUSTRIS; the burial vault contains more than 30 members of the Wittelsbach family.

**MUNICH SCHOOL**, a group of late sixteenth- and seventeenth-century German iron-chisellers who specialized in the decoration of arms (see ARMS AND ARMOUR). Ottmar Wetter (d. 1598) was active in Munich from 1583 to 1589 and then moved to Dresden. He was appointed as court ironworker (*Eisenarbeiter*), in which post he was succeeded by the Antwerp iron-chiseller Emanuel Sadeler (d. 1610) and then by Emmanuel's brother Daniel (d. *c*.1632) and finally by Caspar Spät (d. 1691), who had been trained by the Sadeler brothers.

The workshops of Wetter and his successors specialized in sword-hilts and firearm mounts which they decorated by chiselling reliefs of scenes and foliage, often coloured blue against a gold background. Examples of their work are preserved in the Bayerisches Nationalmuseum in Munich, the Kunsthistorisches Museum in Vienna, the British Museum, the Victoria and Albert Museum, and the Wallace Collection in London, and the Metropolitan Museum in New York.

**MÜNSTER, ANABAPTIST KINGDOM OF** (1534–5). Münster, the capital of Westphalia, was a Hansa city where Lutheran ideas made some headway in the 1520s. In January 1532 the radical preacher Berndt ROTHMANN was appointed pastor of the Lambertikirche. When a new prince-bishop directed a mandate against Rothmann (17 April 1532), Bernd KNIPPERDOLLINCK organized the group of radicals who imprisoned the nobles considering the case in nearby Telgte. Rothmann and his followers were soon able to occupy the pulpits of Münster, and their position was consolidated by the arrival in Münster of six SACRAMENTARIAN preachers from Wassenberg (Jülich). The crisis of government was temporarily resolved when PHILIP OF HESSE declared Münster to be an evangelical city in a charter of 14 February 1533.

On 1 January 1534 Heinrich Roll, an ANABAPTIST refugee, preached Anabaptist doctrines in a city church, and shortly thereafter JOHN OF LEIDEN and Jan Matthyszoon, the radical Anabaptist baker from Haarlem, arrived in the city. Knipperdollinck fell under the charismatic spell of John of Leiden, and his daughter Clara joined John's collection of wives. Matthyszoon moved into Knipperdollinck's house, which became the centre of a movement that sought to establish Münster as the New Jerusalem instead of Strassburg, which had been Melchior HOFFMAN's preferred location.

On 9 February 1534 the Anabaptists seized control of the city from the Lutheran city council and declared Münster to be the New Jerusalem which would be spared the wrath of God on the day of judgement. Matthyszoon led the rebellion, and promptly confiscated all property within the city and ordered the destruction of all books except the Bible. The prince-bishop reacted by besieging the city, and on 5 April 1534 Matthyszoon was killed while leading a sortie against the besiegers, whereupon John of Leiden became the undisputed leader of the movement. He instituted radical reforms, including polygamy, and in August 1534 declared himself to be king.

Münster fell on 25 June 1535. Many Anabaptists were massacred, but John of Leiden, Knipperdollinck, and Heinrich Krechting were taken alive. They were tried and convicted on 19 January 1536; on 22 January they were tortured and executed. Their bodies were gibbeted in iron cages on the west tower of the Lambertikirche, where the cages can still be seen.

The Anabaptist kingdom of Münster was the subject of the Latin epic *Motus monasteriensis libri decem* (1546) by Johannes Fabricius, an obscure native of Cleves who had studied at Cologne and seems to have described the uprising from personal knowledge.

R. Po-chia Hsia, 'Münster and the Anabaptists', in id. (ed.), *The German People and the Reformation* (1988); Ralf Klötzer, *Die Täuferchenschaft von Münster: Stadtreformation und Welterneuerung* (1992); James M. Stayer, *The German Peasants' War and Anabaptist Community of Goods* (1991).

**MÜNSTER, SEBASTIAN** (1488–1552), German cosmographer and Hebraist, born in Ingelheim and educated at Tübingen and Heidelberg. He entered the Franciscan Order, in which his teachers included the Hebraist Konrad PELLIKAN. In 1529 Münster repudiated his monastic vows (as had Pellikan) and in 1536 moved to Basel, where he was appointed professor of mathematics at the university. His publications as a Hebraist included the first translation of the Old Testament from Hebrew to German and grammars of Hebrew and Aramaic. His scientific works include a treatise on the mathematics of SUNDIALS (*Horologiographia*, 1531) and an important cosmographical treatise, *Cosmographia universalis* (1544), which is an illustrated geographical survey of the known world.

DSB; NDB.

**MÜNTZER or Münzer, THOMAS** (*c*.1489–1525), German revolutionary, born in Stolberg im Harz and educated in Leipzig and Frankfurt an der Oder, where he graduated in theology. In 1514 he became a chantry-priest in Brunswick, and in 1517 and 1518 attended lectures in Wittenberg on classical literature and the church fathers. He then became confessor to the Cistercian Nunnery of Benditz (Saxony) (1519–20) and immersed himself in the writings of the fourteenth-century mystics Henry Suso (German Heinrich Seuse) and Johann Tauler.

In May 1520 Müntzer became a preacher in Zwickau. He was expelled the following year for an alleged breach of the peace, not on account of his increasingly heterodox mystical theology. In 1521 he arrived in Prague, where he attempted to establish a millenarian church but was again expelled. In 1523 he secured a pulpit in Allstedt (in the electorate of Saxony), where he formed a 'Christian League' to combat Catholicism, composed new liturgies for his church (the first to be written in German), and wrote tracts which expressed doubts about infant BAPTISM; as Martin LUTHER supported infant baptism, tension was inevitable. Luther warned the Protestant princes that Müntzer was theologically unreliable, and so he was expelled from the electorate in 1524. In the first instance he went to Mülhausen (Thuringia), where he joined forces with the native reforming preacher Heinrich Pfeiffer; civil unrest ensued and both were expelled.

In September 1524 Müntzer embarked on a preaching tour of south-west Germany, where the PEASANTS' REVOLT was soon to erupt, and the following spring returned to Mülhausen, where he and Pfeiffer overthrew the city council, replacing it with a godly 'eternal council', and imposed his own church discipline on the city. As the Peasants' War engulfed Thuringia, Müntzer placed himself in command of a peasant army in the confident conviction that the millennial rule of the saints was about to begin. He established his camp at Frankenhausen, where the peasants were defeated by the forces of Hesse and Brunswick on 15 May 1525. Müntzer was captured and on 27 May tortured and executed at Mülhausen. The letter of recantation that he is said to have written before his death is inauthentic: he died impenitent.

Müntzer is the protagonist of Theodore Mundt's novel *Thomas Münzer* (1841) and of plays by Ernst Lissauer (*Luther und Thomas Münzer*, 1929), Herbert Eulenberg (*Thomas Münzer*, 1932), and Dieter Forte (*Martin Luther und Thomas Münzer oder die Einführung der Buchhaltung*, 1971).

NDB; Tom Scott, *Thomas Müntzer: Theology and Revolution in the German Reformation* (1989); Hans-Jürgen Goertz, *Thomas Müntzer: Apocalyptic Mystic and Revolutionary* (1993).

**MURET, MARC-ANTOINE DE or (Latin) Muretus** (1526–85), French humanist in France and Italy. He was born in Muret (near Limoges) and as a young man taught Latin at Villeneuve and then at the Collège de Guienne in Bordeaux, where his pupils included MONTAIGNE. He subsequently taught in Poitiers, Paris, and Toulouse (where he was accused of sexual immorality and burnt in effigy as a Huguenot) before moving to Venice, where he taught from 1555 to 1558. In 1563 he settled in Rome under the patronage of Cardinal Ippolito d'ESTE, and he remained in Rome for the rest of his life.

Muret's works include a youthful Latin tragedy and a large number of editions of classical authors (including Catullus, Cicero, Horace, and Terence) and commentaries on ancient authors (including Aristotle, Plato, and Tacitus).

Charles Dejob, *Marc-Antoine Muret, un professeur français en Italie* (1881).

**MURMELLIUS, JOHANNES** (1480–1517), Dutch humanist educator. He was born in Gelderland and studied in Deventer under HEGIUS. He later taught in Münster (at the cathedral school), Alkmaar, and Deventer. Murmellius was the author of an influential Latin grammar, *Papa puerorum*.

NDB.

**MURNER, THOMAS** (1475–1537), German Franciscan satirist, born at Oberehnheim (now French Obernai), in Alsace. He entered the Franciscan ORDER in 1490 and became a wandering student of theology, first in Freiburg im Breisgau and then in Cologne, Paris, Rostock, and Kraków. The Emperor MAXIMILIAN crowned him POET LAUREATE in 1505; he took his doctorate in theology in 1506 and, after studying jurisprudence at Basel in 1518, took his doctorate in law (1519). He travelled in Italy and England before returning to settle in Strasburg, but the advent of the Reformation obliged him to leave the city, and in 1526 he moved to Lucerne. In 1533 he was appointed priest in his native Oberehnheim, where he died in 1537.

Murner's satires take the form of corrosively embittered attacks, unmitigated by human compassion or understanding, directed against corruption, the Reformation, and Martin LUTHER; his works are illustrated with woodcuts based on his own sketches. A series of rhyming poems written between 1512 and 1515 was inaugurated with *Die Narrenbeschwörung* (1512), an imitation of BRANT's *Das Narrenschiff*, and continued with *Die Schelmenzunft* (1512), a rogues' gallery, *Die Gauchmatt* (1515, published 1519), which mocks lovers on the meadow (*matt*) of fools, and *Die Mühle von Schwindesheim* (1515), another rogues' gallery. Murner's most vitriolic satire, and arguably the most vituperative satire of the Renaissance, is his *Von dem großen Lutherischen Narren* (1522), which cruelly mocks Luther; it was this satire that led the Lutherans to refer to Murner as 'Murrnarr' ('the grumbling fool').

Murner translated VIRGIL's *Aeneid* (1515), which he dedicated to the Emperor Maximilian, and the *Institutiones* (1519) of JUSTINIAN. His lighter satires include *Chartiludium logicae* (1507) and *Ludus studentum freiburgensium* (1511).

*NDB.*

**MURRAY, JAMES STEWART, EARL OF** (*c.*1531–1570), regent of Scotland. An illegitimate son of JAMES V, James Stewart was half-brother to MARY, QUEEN OF SCOTS, whose marriage to the future FRANCIS II he helped to negotiate in 1558. From 1559, he played a key role in the Protestant rebellion against the regent MARY OF LORRAINE, and became a leading member of the government on Mary Stuart's return from France in 1561. She created him earl of Murray the following year. Mary's marriage to DARNLEY prompted his rebellion, and he was briefly in exile in England (1565–6), but later restored to favour. He was abroad during the crisis which followed Mary's marriage to BOTHWELL, and was made regent for the young JAMES VI on Mary's abdication in 1567. In May the following year he defeated Mary at Langside, and she fled to England, but she retained strong support in Scotland, and in 1570 he was assassinated by James Hamilton, whose family remained loyal to the queen.

**MUSCOVY COMPANY**, an English trading company incorporated in 1555 in the wake of Richard CHANCELLOR's journey to Russia in 1553. As Muscovy did not have access to the Baltic, the company's ships entered by the Arctic route. The company also sought to establish a NORTH-EAST PASSAGE to Asia.

**MUSIC.** The renaissance in music became evident later than that in art or literature. Both the theory and practice of music were a part of every educated person's upbringing; along with astronomy, arithmetic, and geometry, music was one of the LIBERAL ARTS. It was initially represented in the work of northern Europeans such as Guillaume DUFAY, Johannes OCKEGHEM, and the English John DUNSTAPLE. The emphasis shifted south as many composers moved to Italy, most importantly JOSQUIN DESPRÈS, whose developments of the musical language culminated in the High Renaissance polyphony of Giovanni Pierluigi PALESTRINA, Orlande de LASSUS, Tomás Luís de VICTORIA, and William BYRD. From the choral polyphony of the *ars nova* evolved large-scale forms, principally MASS settings and MOTETS, some based around secular melodies rather than plainsong. The CHORALE reflected the changes wrought by Luther's Reformation which in turn was to affect the flavour of post-Tridentine Catholic music. The Italian MADRIGAL became the most important model for secular music in many countries during the sixteenth century. The dominance of vocal music became less apparent with the evolution of families of MUSICAL INSTRUMENTS. See BOHEMIAN MUSIC; DANISH MUSIC; ENGLISH MUSIC; FLEMISH MUSIC; FRENCH MUSIC; GERMAN MUSIC; HUNGARIAN MUSIC; ITALIAN MUSIC; POLISH MUSIC; PORTUGUESE MUSIC; SPANISH MUSIC.

**MUSICAL INSTRUMENTS** took a lead from the natural distribution of sound amongst human voices (soprano, alto, tenor, bass) and were organized into families with the same instrument appearing in different sizes (e.g. VIOLS). This rationalized approach allowed for a more homogeneous sound both in purely instrumental ensemble music and later when voices and instruments were combined. Technological advances and the invention of new instruments like the HARPSICHORD inevitably informed music composition.

**MUSICAL NOTATION** in its fully developed form gives information principally about the pitch and length of a note. The two systems used during the Renaissance period, mensural notation and tablature, are markedly different from today's notation system which originated in the seventeenth century. White mensural notation (symbols outlined in black) was in use *c.*1450–1600 and replaced black mensural notation (solid black symbols) which had existed since it was established *c.*1250 by Franco of Cologne.

Mensuration refers to the relationship between note values, which could vary according to whichever special sign appeared at the start of the music and caused a note to be worth two or three times another note. This allowed the representation of different metres (i.e. all permutations of duple, triple, simple, and compound times). Note values could be further modified through the principles of 'imperfection' and 'alteration' which related to the sequence in which the note symbols appeared and the appearance of the *punctus additionis* – a dot which added to a note's duration. This was not to be confused with another dot, the *punctus divisionis*, which acted as a bar line indicating the end of a group of three *semibrevis*. Ink colour also played a part, with black notes producing the effect of either triplets or hemiola; in England the Old Hall repertory around 1400 made use of black, red, and even blue notes to facilitate notating particular rhythmic patterns. This system, while being easily read by trained singers, was not suitable for the music that appeared in score such as keyboard music. With the rise of the thoroughbass and the advent of movable type, a new system with bar lines, slurs, and other means of clarifying rhythm for quick reading was developed.

Tablature refers to notation systems which used letters, numbers, or other symbols to indicate which pitch should be sounded. Lute tablatures indicate in diagrammatic form where the player's fingers should press down on the strings. Although modern guitar and ukelele tablature resemble sixteenth-century lute tablatures, they differ considerably from German and Spanish keyboard tablatures. Modern tablature is much easier to realize than the precise and detailed Italian, Spanish, and French systems of the sixteenth and seventeenth centuries.

***MUSICA TRANSALPINA*** (1588 and 1597) was published by Nicholas YONGE. It was a collection of Italian madrigals (with

English texts) which was to have considerable impact on the English madrigal writers.

**MUSKET or (French)** *mousquet* **or (German)** *Muskete*, a hand-held gun which began to supersede the ARQUEBUS in the mid-sixteenth century. Whereas the barrel of an arquebus had to be supported by a trestle or tripod, the musket was fired from a forked 'rest' which the musketeer drove into the ground; in the seventeenth century, the technology of the musket was improved to the point where it could be fired without any support. The musket was heavier and more powerful than the arquebus: the effective range of the musket was 500 metres (550 yards), and at that distance it had sufficient power to fell a horse.

The firing mechanism of the musket was usually a matchlock, which meant that the trigger brought a match down to the GUNPOWDER in the pan; some expensive muskets used a wheel-lock, in which the trigger released a sprung wheel which rapidly revolved and emitted sparks that ignited the gunpowder, but this was eventually superseded by the snaphance, an early form of flintlock in which a flint ignited the powder by emitting sparks when struck by the trigger on a piece of furrowed steel. In about 1635 the snaphance was replaced by the flintlock which was to be in use for centuries; it differs from the snaphance in that the cover of the pan forms part of the furrowed steel struck by the flint. The musket was normally rifled: spiral grooves (German *riffeln*, 'to groove') in the bore forced the bullet (typically weighing about 40 grams (1.5 ounces)) to rotate, which diminished the effect of irregularities in weight or shape and so increased accuracy.

The musket was first deployed in battle in the 1540s by the duke of ALBA, and was soon in use throughout Europe.

**MUSURUS, MARCUS** (c.1470–1517), Greek scholar in Italy. Musurus was a native of CRETE who migrated to Florence in about 1490 to study under Janos LASCARIS. In 1503 he accepted a post in Padua, where he lectured on Greek language and literature and translated diplomatic correspondence from the sultan in Constantinople (which was written in Greek, not Turkish). Musurus moved to Venice in 1512, where he became an editor with ALDUS MANUTIUS with responsibility for Greek texts. His work in this capacity included the first printed editions of Aristophanes (1498), Euripides (1504), PLATO (2 vols., 1513), and Pausanias (1516).

After the death of Aldus in 1515, Musurus moved to Rome at the invitation of Pope LEO X, who on 19 June 1516 appointed him archbishop of the Latin archdiocese of Monemvasia (a Venetian possession in south-west Peloponnese); this post was entirely nominal, as were his two bishoprics in Crete, and Musurus remained in Rome until his death, working with Janos Lascaris on the establishment of a Greek institute.

D. Geanakoplos, *Greek Scholars in Venice* (1962), 111–66; N. G. Wilson, *From Byzantium to Italy: Greek Studies in the Italian Renaissance* (1992), 148–56.

**MUZIANO, GIROLAMO** (1532–92), Italian painter and engraver who worked in his native Brescia. His paintings often have religious subjects, but inevitably incorporate local mountain scenery into the prominent LANDSCAPE background, notably in his *Raising of Lazarus* (1555, Pinacoteca Vaticana), which was praised by MICHELANGELO, and his *St Jerome* (Accademia Carrara, Bergamo).

MDA.

**MUZIO, GIROLAMO** (1496–1576), Italian courtier, poet, and polemicist, a native of Padua who spent his life at a series of north Italian courts. His publications include several volumes of poems, controversial treatises attacking Protestantism, and a treatise on the Italian language (*Battaglie per la difesa dell'italica lingua*). In a treatise published in 1566 (*Discorso sopra il concilio che si ha da fare, e sopra la unione d'Italia*) he advocated the political unification of Italy and so became a remote progenitor of the Risorgimento.

OCIL.

**MYCONIUS or (German) Mykonius, FRIEDRICH** (1490–1546), German Protestant reformer, born at Lichtenfels am Main on 26 December 1490; he deemed his family name, Mecum, to be a temptation to pride, because it appears in the Latin of the Vulgate, and so adopted the name Myconius, an allusion to the proverbial meanness of the ancient inhabitants of the Greek island of Mykonos. He was educated in Annaberg, where he met Johann TETZEL and argued that INDULGENCES should be given to the poor rather than sold. On 14 July 1510 he entered the Franciscan ORDER, and was transferred first to Leipzig and then, in 1516, to Weimar; in 1516 he was ordained as a priest. In 1517 Martin LUTHER posted his theses on the abuse of indulgences, and Myconius became a sympathizer; he subsequently met Luther, who passed through Weimar on his way to Augsburg to answer his accusers. He was in consequence confined to various houses of his Order for the next six years.

In 1524 Myconius fled his Order and went to Gotha, where Duke Johann appointed him as preacher; there he married Margaret Jäcken and worked for the reformed cause both in the city and throughout Thuringia. He corresponded with Luther from 1525 and with MELANCHTHON from 1527, and participated in the Conferences and Colloquies of MARBURG (1529), WITTENBERG (1536), SCHMALKALDEN (1537), where he signed the Articles, and HAGENAU (1540). In 1538 he visited England as a member of the delegation that sought to induce HENRY VIII to join the SCHMALKALDIC LEAGUE, commenting memorably that the scheme would only succeed if Henry could be appointed pope. He returned to Gotha in 1540, and the following year moved to Leipzig to work for the Reformation. His heath failed in 1541, but he lived until 7 April 1546.

During his lifetime Myconius published many tracts and pamphlets in German. His principal work, which was written in collaboration with Sebastian Heller but not published until 1715, was *Historia Reformationis*, which contains a valuable first-hand account of the Reformation in Thuringia.

NDB; *Der Briefwechsel des Friedrich Mykonius (1524–1546)*, ed. H. U. Delius (1960); H. Ulbrich, *Friedrich Mykonius 1490–1546* (1962).

**MYCONIUS, OSWALD** (1488–1552), Swiss Protestant reformer, born in Lucerne, where his father was a miller. His original surname was Geisshäusler, but ERASMUS called him 'Myconius', with reference to the proverbial meanness of the ancient inhabitants of the Greek island of Mykonos; because of his father's occupation, he was also called 'Molitoris'. He was educated at the school of Rottweil, on the Neckar, and at the University of Basel (1510–14). He remained in Basel as a schoolteacher, and met Erasmus and Hans HOLBEIN; he also married while in Basel. In 1516 he moved to Zürich to teach at the cathedral school, and in 1518 encouraged the chapter to elect his friend ZWINGLI as stipendiary priest (*Leutpriester*). He taught at Lucerne from 1520 to 1522, but had to leave the city because of his Protestant sympathies, and in 1523 returned to Zürich. He worked with Zwingli until the latter's death in 1531, whereupon he moved to Basel, where he became the successor of OECOLAMPADIUS; he was the city preacher, and until 1541 was also professor of New Testament exegesis. He died in Basel on 14 October 1552.

Myconius was by conviction a Zwinglian, but he was willing to negotiate a compromise with the Lutherans on the fraught issue of the EUCHARIST; his willingness to negotiate, together with his unease about the role of the civic magistrates in matters of church discipline (such as excommunication), incurred the enmity of the Zwinglian hardliners, but also attracted the allegiance of Theodore BIBLIANDER. Myconius wrote a biography of Zwingli (1536) and was also the author of the Confession of BASEL (1534).

NDB.

**MYTH OF VENICE**, a belief, widespread amongst European intellectuals, that fifteenth- and sixteenth-century Venice represented a republican ideal of stability and justice.

The republican institutions of Venice were regarded as stable points in a world that was otherwise subject to constant political change, and the judicial system was seen as impartial. This stability was attributed by writers such as Gasparo CONTARINI, Donato GIANNOTTI, and Bernardo GIUSTINIANI to the constitution of Venice, which in its combination of a virtuous leader (the doge), a beneficent ruling class (the patricians in the Senate), and responsible representation of other citizens (the Greater Council) was deemed to satisfy the Aristotelian ideal. This sense of the uniqueness of Venice was enhanced by the uniqueness of its watery setting and the beauty of its buildings.

The myth of Venice was invoked by Dutch republicans seeking independence from Spain, by the English republicans of the Interregnum, and by secessionists in revolutionary America.

E. O. G. Haitsma Mulier, *The Myth of Venice and Dutch Republican Thought in the Seventeenth Century* (1980); C. Kallendorf, *Virgil and the Myth of Venice: Books and Readers in the Italian Renaissance* (1999); D. C. McPherson, *Shakespeare, Jonson and the Myth of Venice* (1990).

**MYTHOLOGY AND MYTHOGRAPHERS.** The principal ancient source of classical mythology was Ovid's *Metamorphoses*, which was widely studied in schools. The understanding of ancient mythology in Renaissance Europe was sometimes radically different from that of Ovid's original readers or his twenty-first-century readers, because Renaissance readers often understood the mythology as moral tales or as adumbrations of Christian truths. The most important Renaissance mythographies were BOCCACCIO's *Genealogia deorum gentilium*, Vincenzo Cartari's *Imagini*, Natale Conti's *Mythologiae*, and GIRALDI's *De deis gentium*.

# N

**NANINO, GIOVANNI BERNARDINO** (*c.*1560–1623) and **GIOVANNI MARIA** (*c.*1545–1607), Italian composers. Both brothers sang as boys at Vallerano Cathedral and held appointments as *maestro di cappella* at several different churches including San Luigi dei Francesi, Rome. Giovanni Maria joined the papal choir where he was *maestro di cappella*. Both wrote sacred and secular music and were influential teachers of a long list of early seventeenth-century Roman composers.

**NANNI DI BANCO** (*c.*1380/5–1421), Italian sculptor, born in Florence, where he trained in the studio of his father, the sculptor Antonio di Banco. Most of his sculpture was designed for two architectural settings, Florence Cathedral and the Orsanmichele. His finest work is the *Quattro santi coronati* (*c.*1411–13), a marble group for the Orsanmichele. Nanni's work for the cathedral, which began when he was apprenticed to his father, culminated in his relief of the *Assumption of the Virgin Mary* (begun 1414) over the Porta della Mandorla.

*MDA*; Mary Bergstein, *The Sculpture of Nanni di Banco* (2000).

**NANTES, EDICT OF,** or (French) **Édit de Nantes** (13 April 1598), an edict signed at Nantes by King HENRI IV, who granted the HUGUENOTS (his former co-religionists) extensive rights and confirmed earlier edicts of 1564 and 1570. Under the terms of the Edict Protestants were to be guaranteed freedom of worship (except in specified towns and cities, including Paris), equality with Catholics in matters of CIVIL LAW, and fair administration of criminal justice through the establishment of mixed Protestant and Catholic courts (in the *parlements* of Bordeaux, Paris, and Toulouse) for cases involving Huguenots; they were also to be given subsidies for their militias, clergy, and schools, and control of the universities of Montauban, Nîmes, and La Rochelle. They were also allowed to garrison at royal expense some 100 towns that were designated as *places de sûreté*. The Edict brought the French WARS OF RELIGION to a temporary conclusion; they erupted again after 1610 and a final peace was not reached until 1629.

The Edict of Nantes was revoked on 18 October 1685 by King Louis XIV in the Edict of Fontainebleau.

Janine Garrisson, *L'Édit de Nantes et sa révocation: Histoire d'une intolérance* (1985); Jean Quéniart, *La Révocation de l'Édit de Nantes* (1985); Richard Goodbar (ed.), *The Edict of Nantes: Five Essays and a New Translation* (1998).

**NAPIER, JOHN** (1550–1617), Scottish mathematician, born in Merchiston Castle in Edinburgh and educated at the University of St Andrews, after which he embarked on an extended tour of the Continent. On returning to Scotland he published a fiercely Protestant treatise entitled *The Plain Discovery of the Whole Revelation of St John* (1593) in which he denounced the pope as ANTICHRIST and predicted that the world would end between 1688 and 1700.

In 1614 Napier published his *Mirifici logarithmorum canonis descriptio* (translated by Edward WRIGHT as *A Description of the Admirable Table of Logarithms*, 1618) in which he introduced to ARITHMETIC the idea of the logarithm. In his *Rabdologiae* (1617) Napier discussed the use of a set of ten wooden or ivory rods (now known as 'Napier's bones') as the mechanical equivalent of a printed table of logarithms. Napier's logarithms were later refined by Henry BRIGGS and his calculating rods by William Oughtred (1574–1660).

*DNB*; *DSB*.

**NAPLES** or (Italian) **Napoli** or (Latin) **Neapolis**, a kingdom in southern Italy, of which the capital was the city of Naples. From 1266 to 1442 Naples was ruled by Angevin kings and queens ('Angevin' is the adjectival form of ANJOU), from 1443 to 1501 by members of the Aragonese royal family, and from 1502 to 1707 by a series of Spanish vice-regents. From 1105 to 1282 Naples was ruled jointly with SICILY, but the revolution of 1282 known as the 'Sicilian Vespers' divided Naples and Sicily into two kingdoms; they were reunited for a brief period (1443–58) under King Alfonso I (ALFONSO V of Aragon) and later under the Bourbons. Throughout the centuries when Sicily was ruled by the Aragonese, the Angevin kings of Naples continued to style themselves 'kings of Sicily'. Even within the kingdom of Naples, there was a protracted succession dispute. GIOVANNA I OF ANJOU had no sons, and her daughters both predeceased her, so she designated as her heir Louis, duc d'Anjou, brother of Charles V of France. Charles of Durazzo, great-grandson of King Carlo II of Naples, considered himself the rightful heir, and sought to assert his claim by invading Naples, ostensibly because of Giovanna's support for the antipope CLEMENT VII. In 1382 Giovanna was murdered and was succeeded by Charles as Carlo III of Durazzo (later Charles II of Hungary).

King Carlo's son LADISLAS OF DURAZZO acceded to the throne of Naples in 1386, at the age of 6, and was crowned by Pope BONIFACE IX in 1390; his claim was contested by King LOUIS II of Anjou, who had been crowned king of Naples by the antipope Clement VII. In 1404 Ladislas began to expand his realm, conquering Rome, Latium, and Umbria, and in 1409 he secured Cortona. On his death in 1414 he was succeeded by his sister GIOVANNA II. The following year she married James of Bourbon, who promptly declared himself king; the barons of Naples rebelled, forcing James to resign the crown and leave the kingdom.

Neapolitans had been expelled from Rome after the death of Ladislas, and in 1416 Giovanna sent the *condottiere* Muzio Attendolo to occupy Rome. The accession of Pope MARTIN V in 1417 changed the political climate, because he chose to enter into an alliance with Queen Giovanna, who in turn agreed to give up Rome. Pope Martin supported the claim of Louis III of Anjou to succeed Giovanna, but she declined to designate Louis II as her successor, instead nominating King Alfonso V of Aragon.

War soon broke out, and at its conclusion Alfonso entered Naples in triumph. Giovanna fled to Aversa, where, disillusioned with Alfonso, she designated Louis as her successor. Alfonso garrisoned Naples and returned to Spain, whereupon an Angevin army (assisted by a Genoese navy) retook the city. Once again there was a short period of peace, but in 1432 a revolt against Giovanna was organized in Apulia by Gian Antonio ORSINI, prince of Taranto. Louis died in 1434 while trying to suppress the rebellion, and Giovanna designated her adopted son RENÉ D'ANJOU (Louis's brother) as her successor; he was to be the last Angevin king of Naples.

Giovanna died in 1435, at which point René d'Anjou was the prisoner of PHILIP THE GOOD. René's wife Isabella claimed the inheritance of Naples on behalf of her husband, and in 1438 René joined her in Naples. In 1441 Alfonso V of Aragon besieged Naples, and six months later captured and sacked the city. René returned to France, and thereafter his claim to the throne of Naples was only nominal. At the conclusion of the war Alfonso entered Naples in triumph on 26 February 1443, and until 1458 ruled over a united kingdom of Naples and Sicily as Alfonso I. He established a magnificent court and became a generous patron of humanists. On his death in 1458 his empire was divided: he was succeeded in Aragon, Sardinia, and Sicily by his brother JOHN II and in Naples by his illegitimate son FERRANTE I.

The legitimacy of Ferrante I's rule was challenged by Pope CALLISTUS III, and although his successor, Pope PIUS II, decided to crown Ferrante as king and to dismiss the claims of his rival, René d'Anjou, there was an intervening period of instability during which Jean, duke of Calabria (René of Anjou's eldest son), invaded Naples and, with the assistance of the disaffected noblemen of Naples, defeated Ferrante at Sarno in July 1460. Ferrante secured the assistance of Alessandro

SFORZA and the Albanian leader SKANDERBEG, and by 1464 was able to re-establish his authority throughout the kingdom. He crushed a second rebellion in 1485, but died months before the invasion of CHARLES VIII caught Naples up in the WARS OF ITALY.

Ferrante was succeeded in January 1494 by his son ALFONSO II OF ARAGON, who in the 1480s had remodelled the city of Naples, straightening roads, constructing FOUNTAINS fed by an aqueduct, and building new churches. His reign was short, because he was forced to abdicate on 23 January 1495 in favour of his son FERRANTE II as the army of Charles VIII advanced on Naples. Ferrante was unable to defend the city and so fled to Ischia. King Charles garrisoned the city and then marched north to return home, whereupon Ferrante recaptured the city and in the course of the next year subdued the kingdom. He died in September 1406 and was succeeded by his uncle, FEDERICO D'ARAGONA. In the Treaty of Granada (11 November 1500) Federico partitioned Naples, abdicating some of his territories in favour of King LOUIS XII of France, who by way of recompense appointed him count of Maine.

The French conquest of Naples brought Spain and the Holy Roman Empire into the Wars of Italy, and in December 1502 the victory of Gonzalo FERNÁNDEZ DE CORDOBA on the Garigliano settled the civil war in favour of Spain and Ferdinand II of Aragón (FERDINAND V) established a Spanish administration that was to remain in place until 1707. Dissent from Spanish rule sometimes took the form of an allegiance to Protestantism, but the flowering of Naples as a Protestant centre was arrested by the INQUISITION. In 1598 an insurrection led by the philosopher Tommaso CAMPANELLA was resolutely crushed, and thereafter Naples remained peaceful until 1647, when a new fruit tax provoked riots.

F. Sabatini, *Napoli angioina* (1975); E. Pontieri (ed.), *Storia di Napoli*, vols. ii (1975) and iii (1976); Alan Ryder, *The Kingdom of Naples under Alfonso the Magnanimous* (1976); J. H. Bentley, *Politics and Culture in Renaissance Naples* (1987).

**NARDI, JACOPO** (1476–1563), Florentine chronicler who became a servant of the Florentine republic after the expulsion of the MEDICI in 1494; when they returned in 1512 he remained in public service, but in 1527 he fought to restore the republic and defeated Medicean troops under the command of Cardinal Passerini who were attacking the Palazzo della Signoria. Nardi worked for the restored republic (1527–30), but when the Medici returned in 1530, he was expelled and his property sequestrated. He spent the rest of his life in exile, principally in Venice.

While in Florence Nardi had been a member of the literary and philosophical group (which included MACHIAVELLI) that met in the RUCELLAI gardens. In exile he wrote a history of Florence from 1498 to 1538. The earlier part of his narrative is based on the diary of Biagio Buonaccorsi, but his accounts of the expulsion and restoration of the Medici vividly convey his own experience of these events in which he was a participant.

*Istorie della città di Firenze di Iacopo Nardi*, ed. A. Gelli (2 vols., 1885); Eric Cochrane, *Historians and Historiography in the Italian Renaissance* (1981).

**NARVÁEZ, PÁNFILO DE** (1470/80–1528), Spanish conquistador. He was born in Valladolid and went to America as a young man. In 1519 he took part in the conquest of Cuba under the command of Diego VELÁZQUEZ, and the following year was sent by Velázquez to Mexico with a force of 800 men with a view to intercepting CORTÉS and inducing him to resign his command. In the event, Cortés attacked the encampment of Narváez, who lost an eye in the fracas and was imprisoned for two years.

Narváez returned to Spain, and in 1528 mounted a large expedition (five ships and some 600 men) to Florida. After a fruitless exploration of the interior of Florida, during which many of his men died, Narváez returned to the coast and constructed small boats in which to sail with the survivors to Mexico. Narváez was swept out to sea and drowned. Only four men survived the expedition, including Alvar Núñez CABEZA DE VACA.

DHE.

**NASHE, THOMAS** (1567–1601), English writer. Nashe is chiefly remembered for his satirical writings. In 1589 he replied to the MARPRELATE pamphlets; *Pierce Penniless his Supplication to the Devil* (1592) attacks prevalent contemporary vices. *The Unfortunate Traveller* (1594), a picaresque prose romance, tells of the travels of Jack Wilton at the time of HENRY VIII and includes an account of the Battle of MARIGNANO. He collaborated with Marlowe on his early play *Dido*, and with JONSON on his controversial early play *Isle of Dogs*. His only sole-authored extant dramatic work is the allegorical pageant *Summer's Last Will and Testament* (c.1592–3).

DNB.

**NASI, GRACIA, or** (baptismal name) **Beatriz de Luna** (1510–68), known in Hebrew as 'ha-Geveret' (the lady), a wealthy MARRANA of Lisbon married to the banker Francisco Mendes. After the death of her husband and the establishment of the Portuguese INQUISITION in 1536, Beatriz emigrated with her children to Antwerp, where she became prominent as banker to CHARLES V. When her Christian orthodoxy became suspect she moved to Venice (where she was betrayed to the Roman INQUISITION by her sister-in-law) and subsequently to Ferrara, where Duke Ercole D'ESTE extended his protection and allowed her openly to reconvert to Judaism, taking the forename Gracia (Hebrew Hannah) and the family name Nasi (Hebrew 'prince'). In Ferrara Gracia extended her patronage to a group of leading Sephardi scholars, and was responsible for the publication of the celebrated Ferrara Bible (1553), a literal translation of the Jewish Bible into Ladino, the Spanish dialect of the *marranos*. In 1553 she moved to Istanbul (Constantinople) with her nephew Joseph NASI, where both played an outstanding part in protecting and patronizing the Sephardi Jewish community at the court of Sultan Süleyman the Magnificent, including securing an Ottoman blockade of the port of Ancona in retaliation for a pogrom.

Cecil Roth, *Dona Gracia of the House of Nasi* (1977).

**NASI, JOSEPH, or** (baptismal name) **João Miguez** (c.1520–1579), Portuguese banker and statesman. He was born into a MARRANO family, and as a young man left Portugal for Antwerp, where he founded a bank. He subsequently lived in Venice for two years before moving to Istanbul (Constantinople), where the Ottoman tradition of religious tolerance enabled him to renounce his Catholic name and proclaim his Judaism. He later founded a Jewish colony at Tiberias (Hebrew Teverya) to offer sanctuary to the JEWS of central Italy; this was one of the earliest attempts to settle Jews in Palestine.

Nasi entered the service of Sultan Süleyman and in 1566, on the accession of Selim II, was appointed as duke of Naxos. In 1571 he was instrumental in the Ottoman conquest of CYPRUS. In the 1560s and 1570s Nasi was the most important Jew in Istanbul, and foreign rulers such as the Emperor MAXIMILIAN II, WILLIAM OF ORANGE, and King SIGISMUND II AUGUSTUS of Poland consulted Nasi and used him as an intermediary with the Porte. On the death of Sultan Selim in 1574 Nasi withdrew from political activity. He and his aunt Gracia NASI were important patrons of Jewish culture in Italy and Istanbul, especially in their support for the printing of biblical texts in Hebrew and Ladino, the Spanish dialect of the *marranos*.

C. Roth, *The House of Nasi, the Duke of Naxos* (1948); P. Grunebaum-Ballin, *Joseph Nasi, Duc de Naxos* (1968).

**NATURAL LAW**, or the law of nature (Latin *ius naturae*), is the justice or set of rights derived from human reason and applicable to all of humanity; it is distinguished from positive law, which is the law enacted by particular states. In antiquity, the Stoics had articulated principles of natural law, and Roman jurists deemed natural law to be the principle underlying INTERNATIONAL LAW (*ius gentium*). Medieval and Reformation theologians tended to argue that law rested on divine authority rather than human reason, and so natural law found few advocates in Renaissance Europe. Writers such as ALTHAUS, GENTILI, and OLDENDORP wrote on natural law, but the first great exponent of the subject was GROTIUS, who argued that natural law was rooted in the peaceful human intellect, and was wholly independent of divine injunction. Natural law was the basis of Grotius' claim (in the *MARE CLAUSUM*, *MARE LIBERUM* dispute) that the seas were free to all.

**NATURE**. Philosophers such as Giordano BRUNO and a host of theologians distinguished between *natura naturans* (naturing nature) and *natura naturata* (natured nature). *Natura naturans* was described as the creative activity of God, but was not explicitly identified with God until Spinoza did so in his *Ethics*; *natura naturata* was the created world. Nature was deemed to be subordinate to and directed by God; as Dante asserted, 'natura lo suo corso prende dal divino intelletto' ('nature takes her course from the divine intellect'; *Inferno*, II. 99–100); natural phenomena such as earthquakes, eclipses, and comets, for example, were commonly taken to be expressions of the wrath of God.

Nature was described as a book in which God's ways could be discerned and in which he had left 'signatures'; this book of nature was often juxtaposed with the Bible, the book of God. One consequence of this metaphor was the emergence of an early form of natural theology, in which human reason is said to be capable of inferring divine truths from the book of nature. The first advocate of this view was Raymond of Sebonde, who proposed a natural theology based on the 'book of creatures' in his *Theologia naturalis sive Liber creaturarum* (*c*.1434–6), which was translated by MONTAIGNE, who subsequently wrote his *Apologie de Raimond Sebond* (2. 12), a statement of Pyrrhonian SCEPTICISM which is the longest of his *Essais* (2. 12). One of the consequences of this nascent natural theology was the emergence of a school of NATURAL LAW.

The created world was conceptualized as an ordered hierarchy descending from angels to humans (the middle state) to animals, plants, and inanimate nature; the dominant metaphors for this cosmic order were the chain and the staircase (the *scala naturae*). The divisions of society, such as the ESTATES, were thought to reflect this divine hierarchy, as was the subordinate status of women and infidels. The view that animals and plants had been created to satisfy the needs of humans, who enjoyed a higher position in the hierarchy of nature, moulded attitudes to animals and plants that are now denounced as cruel and wasteful but seemed entirely respectable in the fifteenth and sixteenth centuries.

CICERO had distinguished between the primal nature of wildernesses untouched by human civilization and a secondary nature in which landscapes had been altered by human constructions such as roads and buildings. In fifteenth-century Italy, humanists developed the idea of gardens being a third nature, because they combined constructed elements with a tamed version of primal nature. The garden thus occupied the honoured intermediate state, analogous to that of humans in the divine order. Many gardens, such as the garden of the Villa ALDOBRANDINI, articulated this intermediate status by beginning with formal structures close to the house and gradually softening the lines of the garden as it stretched towards a distant *bosco* or wilderness.

J. Białostocki, 'The Renaissance Concept of Nature and Antiquity', in *The Renaissance and Mannerism* (1963); John Dixon Hunt, *Greater Perfections: The Practice of Garden Theory* (2000); Keith Thomas, *Man and the Natural World* (1983).

## NAUMBURG CONVENTION or (German) Naumburgischer Fürstentag,

a meeting of Protestant princes and religious leaders held at Naumburg from 20 January to 8 February 1561. The principal purpose of the meeting was to secure agreement on the doctrine of the EUCHARIST on the basis of the AUGSBURG CONFESSION. The prospect of unity foundered on the inability of the two sides to agree on the definitive text of the Confession: the Lutherans insisted on the Invariata text of 1531 and the Calvinists adhered to the Variata text of 1540.

The Convention also considered an invitation from Pope PIUS IV to send delegates to the COUNCIL OF TRENT. The letter was returned unopened on the grounds that the form of address, *Dilecto filio* ('to my beloved son'), was unacceptable.

**NAUTILUS SHELL**, a large nacreous shell from the Indian ocean, used by goldsmiths in late sixteenth-century and seventeenth-century Europe (principally Germany, England, and the Netherlands) to fashion display cups, some of which were mounted on gold stands. The nautilus shells set by European craftsmen had sometimes been engraved by Chinese craftsmen.

**NAVAGIERO or Navagero, ANDREA** (1483–1529), Italian poet and humanist. He was born into a patrician family in Venice, where he received a humanist education and was later employed by ALDUS MANUTIUS as an editor of classical texts; he subsequently became librarian of San Marco and undertook a series of diplomatic missions on behalf of the Venetian republic. While in Spain in 1526 he became a friend of Joan BOSCÀ, whom he invited to experiment with Italian metres. Navagiero thus became the conduit by which the *ottava rima* of Italy was transmitted to Spain, where this metre (known in Spanish as *octavas reales*) was to become the dominant one in Spanish Renaissance epic.

*OCIL.*

**NAVARRE or (Spanish) Navarra**. The kingdom of Navarre, which is now divided into a Spanish province south of the Pyrenees and a French region north of the Pyrenees, was for centuries an independent Hispanic kingdom. After 1234 the crown of Navarre passed by marriage to a series of French-speaking rulers, and from 1314 to 1328 Navarre was incorporated into France. The kingdom subsequently came within the ambit of the crown of Aragon, but in 1484 the crown passed by marriage to the French house of Albret. In 1512 FERDINAND of Aragon conquered southern Navarre, which remained a viceroyalty until being made a province of Spain in 1833.

Queen JEANNE D'ALBRET and her consort King ANTOINE DE BOURBON retained as their own fief a portion of French Navarre, which remained an independent kingdom until it was absorbed into France by their son King HENRI IV in 1589.

**NAVARRO, PEDRO** (*c*.1460–1528), Spanish soldier and military engineer. He fought as a young man in North AFRICA and in 1495 joined the expedition of FERNÁNDEZ DE CÓRDOBA to Italy, where he worked as a military engineer specializing in the breaching of walls with explosives. He returned to Naples with Gonzalo on his second expedition, and in 1503 succeeded in laying mines that destroyed the defences of the French garrison. In 1509–10 he fought in Oran and Tripoli and subsequently returned to Italy, where he was captured on 11 April 1512 (along with Ferdinando AVALOS, marquis of Pescara) at the battle of Ravenna.

On his release in 1515 Navarro entered the service of FRANCIS I, where he assumed command of ARTILLERY in the French army. On 24 February 1525 he was captured by his own countrymen at the battle of PAVIA, but the following year was released under the provisions of the Treaty of Madrid.

**NAVIGATION** in the Renaissance proceeded without much attempt to take account of geographical longitude (that is,

position east–west), which in practice could not be found, though it was of course marked on geographers' maps. Latitude, that is, position north–south, could be measured, so the commonest technique was to get to the correct latitude for one's destination and then sail to it directly along the line of latitude. Finding latitude is equivalent to finding the height of the celestial pole, but the Pole Star is not very bright so at sea other stars were used, their height being taken as they crossed the meridian. The method was to establish the meridian by finding north, with the COMPASS if necessary, and then take the height of the star with a quadrant (in use from about 1450) or with a so-called mariner's ASTROLABE, a sighting instrument invented by Portuguese seafarers in the late fifteenth century, consisting of a heavy disc (usually with pieces cut away to leave a cross shape) that hung vertically from a suspension ring and carried an alidade with pinhole sights. The quadrant was fitted with a plumb line for checking that it was vertical, the mariner's astrolabe was simply heavy. After about 1470 navigators used the height of the sun, sighting being done by adjusting the alidade so that the shadow of the upper vane of the sights exactly covered the lower vane (a procedure called 'shooting the sun'). If the sun was used, north had to be found with the compass, if necessary making a correction for magnetic variation (tables were available), and astronomical tables were required to find the position of the sun relative to the pole on the day in question. Ongoing problems with the CALENDAR were irrelevant because the measurements were not very exact. Contemporary literature is much concerned with improved instruments for navigation, such as the CROSS-STAFF, long used by astronomers but introduced onto ships in the early fifteenth century, or the BACKSTAFF; the uses of new instruments, usually ones obtainable from the author, are found in many treatises on navigation, for instance one by the well-known instrument-maker Michel Coignet (1549–1623), *Onderwysinghe op de principaelste puncten der navigatien* (1580). The most famous, and probably the most useful, treatise was that of Simon STEVIN, *De Havenvinding* (1599; an English version by Edward WRIGHT, *The Haven-Finding Art*, appeared in the same year).

GLOBES and CHARTS helped track the course, and raised some interesting mathematical problems (see MERCATOR, GERARDUS), but a great deal seems to have been done by very rudimentary methods, the vessel's position being found by 'dead reckoning', that is, by assessing its speed by throwing the log overboard and counting the number of knots of its line that ran through the hand in a given time (measured by a sandglass). Simple arithmetic then established how far the ship had travelled. Underwater archaeology has shown that most ships carried very little navigating equipment, even for, say, the long voyage from the Basque country to Labrador (Canada). However, we also have evidence from lists of equipment carried by expeditions; Martin Frobisher (c.1535–1594), setting out in search of the NORTH-WEST PASSAGE in 1576, took such expensive items as a blank metal globe, presumably for calculation (cost £7 13s. 4d.), an astronomical ring-dial, for telling the time at known latitude (£1 10s.), and an astrolabe (£3 10s.), presumably a planispheric astrolabe rather than the simple mariner's astrolabe and useful for astronomical calculations. His eighteen hourglasses together cost only 17s. and his two standard texts on practical mathematics, Cunningham's *The Cosmographical Glass* (1559) and RECORDE's *The Castle of Knowledge* (1556), together cost only 10d. This kind of list shows that there was indeed a market for elaborate equipment, which no doubt not only aided the navigators but also reassured the financial backers of expeditions.

E. G. R. Taylor, *The Haven-Finding Art* (1956); D. W. Waters, *The Art of Navigation in England in Elizabethan and Early Stuart Times* (1958).

**NEAKADEMIA** (Greek; 'new academy') **or Aldine Academy**, a Greek club founded by ALDUS MANUTIUS in Venice; the precise date of its foundation is unknown, but it is first mentioned in the colophon to the Aldine Sophocles, which was published in August 1502. The Academy functioned as a learned society, an editorial board, and a dining club. The Academy's proceedings were conducted in Greek, which was also the language of its constitution (the *Neakademias Nomos*) and the publications with which it was involved through the Aldine Press. According to the constitution, members who broke the rule about speaking only in Greek during meetings of the Academy were to be fined, and proceeds were to be used to finance banquets in imitation of Platonic symposia; the tone of the document is playful, and the modest proficiency in spoken Greek amongst Venetian intellectuals makes it unlikely that such rules were to be taken seriously; in any case, the single-minded Hellenism of the constitution cannot easily be reconciled with the fact that the club also published Latin authors such as Statius and OVID. There were 35–40 members, of whom about a third were Greeks. Members of the Academy included Girolamo ALEANDRO and Pietro BEMBO, and visitors included ERASMUS and Thomas LINACRE.

Mario Brunetti, 'L'Accademia Aldina', *Rivista di Venezia*, 8 (1929); D. Geanakoplos, *Greek Scholars in Venice* (1962), 128–32.

**NEBRIJA, ANTONIO MARTÍNEZ DE CALA DE.** See LEBRIJA, ANTONIO MARTÍNEZ DE CALA DE.

**NEEDLEWORK.** The most common forms of needlework in early modern Europe were decorative EMBROIDERY and various forms of netting, knitting, and knotting.

Netting, which was used by fishermen and fowlers and for many domestic purposes, was fashioned with netting needles made from wood or bone that had been notched at either end. In the eleventh and twelfth centuries nets ceased to be purely utilitarian, and in the case of veils were darned or embroidered to enhance their appearance. In the thirteenth and fourteenth centuries increasingly elaborate decoration

A **nautilus shell cup** (c.1585–6) in the Fitzwilliam Museum in Cambridge. Neptune is holding the shell, which was carved in China

came to be known as 'spiderwork' (Latin *opus araneum*), and in the fifteenth century spiderwork evolved into LACIS and thence into the forms of LACE known as RETICELLA and PUNTO IN ARIA. Needlework CARPETS, which were popular from the sixteenth century onwards, were made by working threads through the mesh of coarse canvas, and so are a form of network.

Knitting, which was a male occupation, was effected with straight pointed needles, often used with a pegged or pinned ring. Knitting was used to make caps and pockets, but was not used for stockings until the sixteenth century; hose ordinarily consisted of pieces of fabric sewn together. The earliest known knitted stockings in England were a pair of knitted silk stockings, probably made in Italy, presented to King EDWARD VI. The first English knitted worsted stockings were made later in the sixteenth century, probably in imitation of an Italian pattern.

Knotting has been used to make cords and braids since remote antiquity. In medieval Europe weavers tied the loose ends of the warp threads of carpets, towels, and shawls into ornamental borders, so preventing fraying and giving weight to the edges. In Renaissance Europe this process evolved into a separate craft which is now known in English and French as macramé, a term derived from Turkish *makramà* ('napkin'). In macramé the thread is knotted across the width of the border, which is a laborious process. Eventually a technique was developed for working the thread along its length, so obviating the need for knotting; such borders were called bobbin lace or pillow lace.

**NEF**, a three-masted French ship of the fifteenth and sixteenth centuries, rigged with a square mainsail and topsail on the main mast, single square sails on the foremast and mizenmast, and a spritsail under the bowsprit. The largest nefs (*c*.400 tons) had a fourth mast (known as a bonaventure mizen) rigged with a single square sail. The hulls were carvel-built, which meant that the edges of the side planks were flush (many ships were clinker-built, which meant that the side planks overlapped).

The term 'nef' is also used to denote silver miniatures of ships. Late medieval silver nefs were vessels used to hold a napkin, knife, and spoon (the fork was not yet in use), but in the fifteenth and sixteenth centuries they evolved into fully rigged replicas of French nefs crewed by miniature sailors. One of the finest surviving nefs is the Burghley Nef (1482–3, Victoria and Albert Museum), in which the hull is a NAUTILUS SHELL. There is also a fine CHARLES V nef at Écouen.

Sebastian BRANT's *Das Narrenschiff* was translated into French as *La Nef des folz* (1497).

Charles Oman, *Medieval Silver Nefs* (1963).

**NEGROLI or Barini detti Negroli FAMILY**, a family of Italian weapon-makers and armourers active in Milan in the sixteenth century, when they became the successors of the MISSAGLIA family. At least 22 members of the family are known to have been employed in the family workshop, which enjoyed a European reputation for its embossed

parade armours (see ARMS AND ARMOUR), of which examples are preserved in the Armería Real in Madrid, the Kunsthistorisches Museum in Vienna, the Tower of London, and the Metropolitan Museum in New York. The most prominent member of the family was Filippo Negroli (*fl.* 1531–51), whose armours for CHARLES V are now in the Armería Real.

**NENNA, POMPONIA** (*c*.1550–1613), Italian composer, active in Naples and Rome and linked with Carlo GESUALDO. He wrote some responsories, a psalm setting, eight books of madrigals, and some villanellas.

**NEOPLATONISM.** See PLATO IN THE RENAISSANCE.

**NERI, ANTONIO** (1576–1614), Italian glassmaker. He was a priest in Florence when in 1602 he began to conduct experiments with a view to replicating precious and semi-precious stones in glass. In 1604 he visited Amsterdam to consult the Portuguese glass scientist Emmanuel Ximénes and to work in a glasshouse. In 1612 he published a treatise on glass-making, *L'arte vetraria*, which was translated into Latin, English, German, French, and Spanish. An annotated English edition published by Christopher Merrett in 1662 was translated into German and published in 1679 by the distinguished glassmaker and technologist Johann Kunckel.

**NERI, FILIPPO** (1515–95), Florentine founder of the Oratorians, born in Florence on 21 July 1515, the son of Francesco Neri, a notary, and Lucrezia Soldi, a member of a noble Florentine family who died when Filippo was a child; he was educated by the Dominican friars at San Marco. In about 1531 a fire destroyed the family's property, and Filippo was sent to San Germano (near Monte Cassino), in the kingdom of Naples, where his uncle Romolo Neri undertook to employ Filippo in his business.

Filippo resolved to enter the Church and in 1533 he moved to Rome, where he was to live for the rest of his life. In 1544 he had a vision in which a globe of fire entered his mouth and dilated his heart; this dilation was deemed to account for the two broken ribs found after his death. In 1548 Filippo founded a CONFRATERNITY of the Santissima Trinità de' Pellegrini e de' Convalescente, which was dedicated to the welfare of indigent visitors undertaking PILGRIMAGES to Rome and of impoverished convalescents.

On 23 May 1551 Filippo was ordained as a priest and moved into a community of priests at the Hospital of San Girolamo della Carità; out of this community evolved the Congregation of the Oratory, popularly known as the Oratorians (and wholly distinct from the Catholic reform movement known as the Roman Oratory or the ORATORY OF DIVINE LOVE). The evening meetings in the Oratory (the hall of San Girolamo) combined elements of worship (prayers and hymns) with religious education (readings, discussions, and lectures). The musical dramatizations of scenes from biblical history were called *oratorii*, which passed into English in the eighteenth century as 'oratorios'.

In 1564 Filippo became the priest of the Florentine church in Rome, San Giovanni del Fiorentini, but he continued to support the meetings in San Girolamo, where the nascent society was attracting distinguished members, including the historian Caesar BARONIUS. In 1574 the Florentines built accommodation for the society next to its church, and the society worked from there until it was able to construct its own church on the site of the small parish church of Santa Maria in Vallicella. When the new church was completed, Filippo secured a bull dated 15 July 1575 which authorized him to form a community of secular priests called the Congregation of the Oratory. He served as superior of the Oratory until his death on 26 May 1595. He was beatified in 1600 and canonized in 1622.

Congregations of the Oratory arose in Italy and (in 1611) France. In 1847 John Henry (later Cardinal) Newman founded an English house in Birmingham and two years later opened a second house in the Strand in London; in 1854 the London Oratory was transferred to Brompton.

L. Ponnelle and L. Bordet, *Saint Philippe Néri et la société romaine de son temps* (1928), trans. R. F. Kerr (1933).

**NERI DI BICCI** (1418–92), Italian painter, born in Florence and trained in the studio of his father Bicci di Lorenzo (1373–1452). He was a prolific painter whose surviving work includes an *Annunciation* and an *Assumption of the Virgin* in the Accademia in Florence; his Diary (*Ricordanze*) of the years 1453–75 is preserved in the Uffizi.

*MDA*; *Le Ricordanze (10 marzo 1453–24 aprile 1475)*, ed. Bruno Santi (1976).

**NEROCCIO DEI LANDI** (1447–1500), Italian painter and sculptor, born in Siena, where he remained all his life, working from 1467 to 1475 in collaboration with FRANCESCO DI GIORGIO MARTINI. His surviving work includes a *Madonna with Saints*, a CASSONE panel depicting Antony and Cleopatra, and a *Portrait of a Girl* (all in the National Gallery in Washington) and two *Madonna and Child* paintings (both in the Pinacoteca in Siena).

*MDA* s.v. Landi (del Poggio), Neroccio; Gertrude Coor, *Neroccio dei Landi* (1961).

**NETHERLANDS, THE, or Low Countries**. For much of the fourteenth century, the region now divided into the Netherlands (in English, often called Holland, after its principal province), Belgium, LUXEMBURG, and the northern *départements* of France was divided into numerous small duchies, marquisates, and counties. Towards the end of the century, the dukes of Burgundy began to consolidate these small administrative units into a single country, one which spoke FRISIAN in the north, DUTCH in the central area, FRENCH in the south, GERMAN on the eastern borders, and a form of German in Luxemburg; by the end of the following century, the Netherlands had become absorbed into the duchy of Burgundy.

The beginnings of Burgundian rule in the Netherlands can be dated to 1384, when Philip the Bold, duke of Burgundy, became count of Artois and count of Flanders by virtue of his marriage to Margaret II de Mâle. In 1404, Philip's second son Anthony (who was to die at Agincourt) succeeded his

great-aunt Margaret of Luxemburg to the duchy of Brabant, initially as regent and from 1406 as duke. The consolidation of Burgundian authority was effected by PHILIP THE GOOD, who became count of Flanders and of Artois in 1405 (by inheritance), count of Namur in 1427 (by purchase), count of Holland, Zeeland, Hainaut, and Friesland in 1428 (by forcing his cousin Jacqueline to abdicate), duke of Brabant and count of Limburg in 1430 (on the death of his cousin Philip, duke of Brabant), and duke of Luxemburg in 1443 (by purchase). Philip did not formally annex Utrecht, but arranged for his illegitimate son David to be consecrated bishop of Utrecht, and so brought it into the sphere of Burgundian influence; similarly, he arranged for two other illegitimate sons to be consecrated as bishops of Liège and for his illegitimate brother to be appointed bishop of Cambrai. The Burgundian duchy was completed by Philip's son CHARLES THE BOLD, who acquired Liège in 1468 and Gelderland in 1473.

For a brief few years, the Burgundian Netherlands seemed to be the final link in a Burgundian state that extended from the Mediterranean to the North Sea, a mighty dukedom interposed between France and the Holy Roman Empire. Deputies representing the states of the Netherlands were summoned to an Estates-General in Brussels in 1465, and a Grand Council with judicial and financial powers had its seat fixed at Mechelen (Malines) in 1473. The sense of permanence promised by such centralizing institutions quickly proved to be illusory, because no sooner had this Burgundian dream been realized than it began to disintegrate. Charles was defeated by the Swiss at Grandson (2 March 1476) and Morat (22 June 1476), and at a third engagement at Nancy on 5 January 1477, Charles was among those who perished. His death plunged the duchy into a constitutional crisis. Charles's sole heir was his 20-year-old daughter MARY OF BURGUNDY. Mary's authority was not accepted by LOUIS XI of France, who claimed the reversion of the French fiefdoms and seized Burgundy, Franche-Comté, and Artois for France.

The Netherlandic provinces, faced with the unhappy choice between French rule and Burgundian rule, chose the latter, but on terms that limited Mary's powers. Mary was trapped in Ghent, where she met the representatives of Brabant, Flanders, Hainaut, and Holland, and on 10 February 1477 she was forced to sign the *Grand Privilège*, which gave the Estates-General the right to assemble on their own initiative and to circumscribe the powers of the sovereign to marry, declare war, and raise taxes; the *Privilège* also established Dutch as the language of government and restricted appointments to high office to natives of the Netherlands.

Mary of Burgundy died in 1482, and was succeeded by her young son PHILIP THE HANDSOME. During his minority the regent was his father Maximilian of Austria (later the Emperor MAXIMILIAN I), who ruled until Philip's accession in 1493. In 1496 Philip married JUANA LA LOCA, and for the rest of his short life his interest as heir to the crown of Castile distracted him from his archducal responsibilities. On his death in 1506 the crown of Castile and the Netherlandic provinces of the duchy of Burgundy passed to his son Charles (later the Emperor CHARLES V), whose regent in the Netherlands was

Philip's sister MARGARET OF AUSTRIA. In 1530 Margaret was succeeded as regent by MARY OF HUNGARY, the sister of Charles V; she eventually resigned her regency when Charles abdicated as duke of Burgundy in 1555.

In 1512 the Netherlandic provinces were constituted as the Circle of Burgundy in the HOLY ROMAN EMPIRE, and in 1548, at the Diet of Augsburg, Charles V formally annexed the seventeen provinces of the Netherlands to the Empire. These seventeen provinces were Artois, Brabant, East Friesland, Flanders, Gelderland, Groningen, Hainaut, Holland, Limburg, Luxemburg, Mechelen (Malines), Namur, Overijssel, Tournai, Utrecht, West Friesland, and Zeeland.

Charles was succeeded as duke of Burgundy and king of Spain by his son PHILIP II, who left for Spain in August 1559 and never returned to the Netherlands. His regent was his half-sister MARGARET OF PARMA, whose administration was dominated by the religious turmoil and civil unrest that led to the REVOLT OF THE NETHERLANDS, which ended with the twelve-year truce of 1609. By the time the twelve years had elapsed, the combatants had become caught up in the THIRTY YEARS WAR, at the conclusion of which (1648) Spain formally recognized the independence of the UNITED PROVINCES.

H. G. Koenigsberger, *Monarchies, States Generals and Parliaments: The Netherlands in the Fifteenth and Sixteenth Centuries* (2002).

**NEUDÖRFER, JOHANN** (1497–1563), German type designer and biographer of artists, born in Nuremberg. His contemporary reputation centred on his mastery of CALLIGRAPHY and his views shaped the final form of Fraktur, the German 'black letter' or 'Gothic' type founts. In 1547 he published *Nachrichten von Künstlern und Werkleuten* (Nuremberg, 1547), a collection of biographical notes on German artists.

*MDA; NDB.*

**NEUMEISTER or Numeister, JOHANN** (1430/40–1512), German printer who may have been a pupil of GUTENBERG in Mainz. He worked from 1470 to 1474 in Foligno (near Assisi), where he published the first edition of DANTE's *Divine Comedy* (1472). He subsequently worked in Mainz (1479) and then moved to France, first living in Albi, north-east of Toulouse (1480), and then settling in Lyon (1483), where his press was an important element in the development of Lyon as a printing centre. The best-known products of his press were his two editions of Juan de TORQUEMADA's *Meditationes* (1479 and 1481), which were illustrated with metal cuts of paintings by Fra ANGELICO.

*NDB s.v. Numeister.*

**NICCOLI, NICCOLÒ DE'** (1364–c.1437), Italian humanist and bibliophile, a native and merchant of Florence. He eschewed public life, preferring instead to pursue his passion for manuscripts, of which he amassed a large collection: some of these were bought with credit extended by the Medici bank and others were copied by Niccolò in an elegant humanist script. On Niccolò's death, control of the library was assumed by Cosimo de' MEDICI, who wrote off Niccolò's debts and placed the 800 manuscripts in the Convent of San Marco, where they were catalogued by Tommaso Parentu-

celli (later Pope NICHOLAS V) and became the founding collection of the LIBRARY that Cosimo opened to the public.

**NICCOLÒ DA TOLENTINO or Niccolò Maruzzi della Stacciola** (c.1350–1435), Florentine *condottiere*. He spent most of his career fighting in the kingdom of Naples, and in 1426 entered the service of Florence and was deployed in the war against Filippo Maria VISCONTI. He contributed substantially to CARMAGNOLA's victory at the battle of MACLODIO in 1427 and was appointed commander-in-chief of Florence's army in 1431. In his last great battle, in 1434, he was defeated by a Milanese army commanded by Niccolò PICCININO.

On his death in 1435 Niccolò was given a state funeral in the presence of Pope EUGENIUS IV, and in 1456 ANDREA DEL CASTAGNO painted a memorial equestrian fresco in Florence Cathedral.

**NICCOLÒ DELL'ABBATE** (c.1509–1571), Italian painter, born in Modena. From 1548 to 1552 he worked in Bologna, where he decorated palaces (notably Palazzo Pozzi) and painted portraits. In 1552 he moved to France at the invitation of HENRI II to work as an assistant to PRIMATICCIO at FONTAINE-BLEAU; his work in the palace has not survived. In France Niccolò also painted LANDSCAPES peopled with mythological figures (e.g. *The Death of Eurydice*, National Gallery, London), and these paintings became the foundation of the French classical landscape painting later developed by Claude and Poussin.

**NICCOLÒ DELL'ARCA or Niccolò di Bari or Niccolò da Bologna** (fl. 1462, d. 1494), Italian sculptor who took his name from the shrine (*arca*) of St Dominic in the Church of San Domenico in Bologna, for which Niccolò carved the graceful canopy and many of the free-standing figures; he worked on the tomb from 1469 until his death 25 years later. He also sculpted the terracotta *Lamentation over the Body of Jesus* in the Church of Santa Maria della Vita in Bologna.

*MDA; Cesare Gnudi, Niccolò dell' Arca (1942).*

**NICHOLAS V** (1397–1455), pope from 6 March 1447 until his death on 24 March 1455, was born Tommaso Parentucelli in Sarzana (near La Spezia) on 13 November 1397, the son of a doctor. After taking his doctorate in theology at Bologna, Tommaso joined the staff of Bishop Niccolò Albergati of Bologna; he was to work for Bishop Niccolò for twenty years, moving with him to Rome in 1426 and so becoming an official in the curia. He attended the COUNCIL OF FLORENCE, where his negotiations with Greek delegates favourably impressed Pope EUGENIUS IV, who in 1444 appointed Tommaso to succeed Niccolò as the bishop of Bologna; he could not reside in his see, because Bologna had revolted against the papacy in 1438. In the autumn of 1446 he travelled to Frankfurt as the legate of Eugenius, and succeeded, together with his colleagues, in securing imperial recognition for the pontificate of Eugenius; his reward was to be created cardinal-priest of Santa Susanna in December 1446. On the death of Eugenius, Tommaso was elected pope, and assumed the name of his former patron.

Pope Nicholas inherited serious problems: Rome was lawless, the PAPAL STATE was fragmented and tumultuous, papal rights in the HOLY ROMAN EMPIRE had been compromised, the rump of the COUNCIL OF BASEL was still in session, and FELIX V was still claiming to be the only true pope. Nicholas had very considerable diplomatic skills, and addressed these problems imaginatively. He used his good relations with prominent Roman families to restore civil order in Rome. In the Papal State, he reined in the mercenaries, recognized local princes as his vicars, and secured rebellious cities by force or by payments. In the case of Bologna, which had rebelled against the papacy in 1438, Nicholas secured stability by appeasement, in effect acknowledging its independent status. He remained neutral when the AMBROSIAN REPUBLIC was constituted in Milan after the death of Filippo Maria VISCONTI, and when Francesco SFORZA succeeded to the dukedom of Milan, Nicholas was happy to regain undisputed possession of the March of Ancona. In the Empire, Nicholas ratified the agreement that Pope Eugenius had confirmed with the German Church and secured through the Concordat of Vienna (or Aschaffenburg) of February 1448 recognition by FRIEDRICH III of papal rights to annates (i.e. the first year's revenue from sees and benefices) and of the papal prerogative in ecclesiastical appointments in the Empire. Immediately after his election, Nicholas addressed the problem of Felix II by asking CHARLES VII of France to mediate, and in the course of the next two years made sufficient concessions to Felix to enable him to abdicate with honour and an income. Once Felix had abdicated (7 April 1449), the Council of Basel (which had migrated to Lausanne after Friedrich had withdrawn his guarantee of safe conduct) was persuaded to elect 'Tommaso of Sarzana' as pope, and then dissolved itself on 24 April 1449; Nicholas then admitted several of Felix's cardinals to the Sacred College in Rome. The restoration of unity was an occasion for thanksgiving, and Nicholas proclaimed 1450 to be a year of jubilee. The huge influx of pilgrims to Rome confirmed the Vatican's claim to be the centre of Christendom, and usefully replenished the papal treasury. In the same year Pope Nicholas canonized BERNARDINO of Siena and sent NICHOLAS OF CUSA and Giovanni di CAPISTRANO as his legates to Germany on a mission of reform. On 19 March 1452 Nicholas crowned Friedrich III as Holy Roman Emperor in a ceremony in ST PETER'S; this occasion was to be the last imperial coronation in Rome.

In 1453 the fortunes of Nicholas declined sharply. Early in January a plot on his life was exposed. The ringleader, Stefano PORCARI, was executed along with his fellow conspirators, but the episode destroyed Nicholas's peace of mind. In June the news of the fall of CONSTANTINOPLE on 29 May reached Rome, and filled the city with dread, and Nicholas felt it as a catastrophe for humanism as well as for the Church: he wrote to his friend Enea Silvio Piccolomini (later Pope PIUS II) that the fall of Constantinople was a second death to Homer and Plato. Despite the cries of horror that could be heard across Europe, Nicholas was unable to rally Christian Europe for the CRUSADE that he proclaimed on 30 September. Nicholas's attempt to convene a congress

of Italian states in Rome (with a view to negotiating peace within the peninsula) came to nothing, but the peace process continued nonetheless: secret negotiations between Milan and Venice eventually led to the Peace of LODI (9 April 1454), to which Florence soon subscribed. Nicholas was unhappy to have been excluded from the negotiations, but nonetheless agreed to subscribe to the treaty and persuaded ALFONSO V (Alfonso I of Naples) to join in the non-aggression pact. The addition on 26 June 1455 of the Papal State and the kingdom of Naples to the powers that subscribed to the treaty created the conditions for a peace that was to last until the outbreak of the Wars of Italy in 1494.

Pope Nicholas believed that the cause of the Church could be advanced if the Church was the centre of Europe's intellectual and artistic culture, and this conviction led him to become one of the greatest patrons of the period. Nicholas was an extraordinarily erudite scholar and a discriminating bibliophile who enjoyed the company of learned humanists; Enea Silvio famously remarked of Nicholas that what he did not know was outside the range of human knowledge. Nicholas commissioned the translation of classical and PATRISTIC Greek texts into Latin, and spent huge sums on the acquisition of manuscripts; the 1,200 Greek and Latin manuscripts that he collected were the foundation collection of the VATICAN LIBRARY, of which Nicholas might rightly be regarded as the founder. Pope Nicholas was also a munificent patron of architecture and the decorative arts: he commissioned churches, palaces, bridges, and fortifications in Rome, and employed the finest decorative artists for his buildings (including the Vatican Palace), notably Fra ANGELICO and his assistant Benozzo GOZZOLI.

G. Sforza, *Ricerche su Niccolò V* (1884); K. Pleyer, *Die Politik Nikolaus V* (1927).

**NICHOLAS OF CUSA** or (German) **Nicolaus von Kues** or **Khrypffs** or (Latin) **Cusanus** (1401–64), German cardinal and philosopher, born in the village of Kues (Latin Cusa) on the Moselle and educated at the Deventer school of the BRETHREN OF THE COMMON LIFE and at the universities of Heidelberg (1416) and Padua (1417–23), where he took a doctorate in CANON LAW. In 1425 he entered the University of Cologne, where he immersed himself in the writings of Albertus Magnus and Ramon Llull, and the following year he began to search for manuscripts containing classical texts; his discoveries, especially of previously unknown works of Plautus, brought him to the attention of the Italian HUMANISTS.

Nicholas was ordained as a priest in 1426 and five years later became dean of the Florinskirche in Koblenz. He was a delegate at the COUNCIL OF BASEL (1433), where he worked to reconcile the Hussites and secured the acceptance of the UTRAQUISTS through the Compactata of Prague; he dedicated to the delegates his *De concordantia Catholica*, in which he maintained the superior authority of councils over popes and argued that the principal documents that supported papal supremacy, the False Decretals and Donation of Constantine, were both spurious.

Having set out the conciliar case, Nicholas then abandoned the CONCILIAR MOVEMENT and became an advocate of papal supremacy. He represented the papal cause in Constantinople (where he was sent by Pope EUGENIUS IV to assist the process of reconciliation) and at the Diets of Mainz (1441), Frankfurt (1442), and Nuremberg (1444); in 1448, when he helped to reconcile the pope and the emperor in the Concordat of Vienna, he was officially created cardinal by a grateful Pope NICHOLAS V, having already been made one secretly by Eugenius IV. In 1450 he became bishop of Brixen (Italian Bressanone, in Tirol), despite the opposition of Archduke Sigismund (whose possessions include the county of Tirol), and was also appointed as papal legate to the German-speaking parts of the Empire. The conflict with Sigismund developed into a financial dispute, whereupon Nicholas was imprisoned, Sigismund was excommunicated, and Nicholas was expelled. He travelled to Rome, where Pope PIUS II appointed him as his vicar-general with responsibility for the governance of Rome and the patrimony of St Peter. After an abortive return to Brixen, where he was besieged by Sigismund in the fortress of Bruneck (Italian Brunico). Nicholas returned to Rome, where he spent the rest of his life as camerarius of the College of Cardinals (Sacrum Collegium). He died in Todi (Umbria).

Nicholas's principal philosophical work was *De docta ignorantia* (*c*.1440), which set out the principles of educated ignorance and the coincidence of opposites. The first principle concerns the ineffability of God which concludes that those who claim to have knowledge of God are truly ignorant, whereas those who are aware of their ignorance of God are truly knowledgeable; while the second contends that elements that are distinct in humans (such as existence and essence) are identities within God (whose existence and essence are identical) and also claims that God is both the maximal being and, because he does not occupy space, the minimal being. Nicholas's other philosophical works include *De conjecturis* (*c*.1440), which sets out the case for the unity of all knowledge, *Apologia doctae ignorantiae* (1449), a defence against the allegation of pantheism, *Idiota* (1450), four dialogues on the human mind, and *De li non aliud* (*c*.1462), which revives Proclus' term 'Not-Other' to characterize the nature of God.

Nicholas's non-philosophical works ranged from the polemical to the scientific. *Cribrationum Alcorani* was an attack on Islam intended to support a crusade against the Ottomans proposed in 1459. *Reparatio calendarii* was a proposal for a reformed CALENDAR that anticipated the Gregorian reform. In *De quadratura circuli* Nicholas claimed to have squared the circle. His *Conjectura de novissimis diebus*, which prophesied that the world would come to an end in 1734, anticipated COPERNICUS in its assertion that the earth rotated.

P. E. Sigmund, *Nicholas of Cusa and Medieval Political Thought* (1963); K. Jacobi, *Die Methode der Cusanischen Philosophie* (1969); P. M. Watts, *Nicolaus Cusanus: A Fifteenth-Century Vision of Man* (1982).

**NICHOLAS OF FLÜE or Nikolaus von Flüe or Brother Klaus** (1417–87), Swiss hermit and political negotiator, born into a family of prosperous peasants; as a young man he served as a soldier and a cantonal councillor, and in 1459 was appointed as a judge. In 1467 he left his wife and ten children (allegedly with his wife's consent) to become a hermit in the Ranft valley, east of Sachseln (in what is now St Niklausen), where he lived for the rest of his life, purportedly without food except for the EUCHARIST. His reputation for asceticism, sanctity, and wisdom made him a living shrine, and pilgrims from all over Europe sought his advice and his accounts of the visions precipitated by starvation. His finest hour was in 1481, when delegates of the SWISS CONFEDERATION meeting in Stans became embroiled in a dispute that threatened to erupt into civil war, and Nicholas intervened and settled the dispute.

Nicholas was beatified in 1669 and canonized in 1947; he is the patron saint of Switzerland. His life was the subject of a polemical biography by Hans SALAT and plays by Jakob GRETSER (*Comoedia de Nicolao Unterwaldio*, 1586) and Caesar von Arx (*Die heilige Held*, 1936).

*NDB* s.v. Flüe; R. Durrer, *Bruder Klaus: Die ältesten Quellen über den seligen Nikolaus von Flüe, sein Leben und seinen Einfluss* (2 vols., 1917–21); C. Yates, *Man of Two Worlds* (1989).

**NICHOLSON, RICHARD** (*c*.1570–1639), English composer and organist. From 1595 he was *informatur choristarum* at Magdalen College, Oxford; he took the Oxford B. Mus. in 1596 and later became the first master of the Music Praxis under William Heyther's foundation (later the chair of music). He wrote sacred and secular music including religious consort songs and a madrigal cycle; one of his madrigals appears in *The* TRIUMPHS OF ORIANA (1601).

**NICLAES, HENDRIK or (English) Henry Nicholas** (*c*.1502–1580), German Anabaptist leader in Amsterdam, a wealthy cloth merchant who arrived in Amsterdam *c*.1531 and in 1539 or 1540 founded a new church, the FAMILY OF LOVE, the radical theology of which mingled elements of mystical pantheism and antinomianism. From 1540 to 1560 Niclaes lived in Emden, where his prolific writings included *Spiegel der Gerechtigheit* ('Glass of Righteousness'), which was published in Antwerp in the late 1550s. He visited England in the early 1550s, probably 1552 or 1553. In 1560 Niclaes was obliged to flee impending arrest in Emden, and after periods in Kampen (Overijssel) and Rotterdam he moved finally to Cologne *c*.1570. His books were condemned by both Catholics and Protestants.

*DNB*; *NNBW* v; Jean Moss, 'Godded with God': *Hendrik Niclaes and his Family of Love* (1981).

**NICOLA DA GUARDIAGRELE or Nicola Gallucci** (*c*.1395–before 1462), Italian goldsmith and sculptor in the Abruzzi. His early work, such as the monstrance (1413) in Santa Maria Maggiore in Francavilla al Mare (near Pescara), is wholly Gothic in design. The Florentine elements in his later work may imply a visit to Florence in the 1420s: his enamel and niello processional cross of 1434 (Museo Diocesano, L'Aquila) shows the influence of GHIBERTI's baptistery doors, as does his silver and enamel altar front of 1448 in Teramo Cathedral. His latest surviving work, which may be unfinished, is the gilded silver and enamel processional cross (1451) for the Church of San Giovanni in Laterano in Rome.

*MDA* s.v. Gallucci, Nicola; Maria Dupré and Lorenzo Lorenzi (eds.), *Nicola da Guardiagrele e il suo tempo* (1997).

**NICOLA DA URBINO or Nicola di Gabriele Sbrage** (*fl.* 1520–37/8), Italian MAIOLICA painter in Urbino and the creator of ISTORIATO ware. The signature Nicola da Urbino on five surviving pieces was until the twentieth century thought to indicate the work of Nicolò Pellipario, an Urbino potter who was wrongly assumed to be the father of Guido Durantino and the grandfather of Orazio FONTANA. The standing of Pellipario as the inventor of istoriato ware was wholly unwarranted, because Nicola da Urbino was in fact a previously unnoticed Urbino potter called Nicola di Gabriele Sbrage, who had an independent workshop in Urbino and also decorated pottery in the workshop of Guido Durantino. In addition to the five signed pieces, which are plates now in the Bargello (1528), the Hermitage (1521), the Louvre (1525–8), the Church of San Stefano in Novellara (*c*.1530), and the British Museum (*c*.1535), Nicola is thought to have been the maker of a set of seventeen plates (*c*.1520) now in the Museo Correr in Venice and of a service (now dispersed) made for Isabella d'ESTE.

*MDA* s.v. Urbino, Nicola da.

**NICOT, JEAN** (1530–1600), French ambassador to Lisbon who sent tobacco powder to CATHERINE DE MÉDICIS in 1560 (to relieve migraines) and so created a fashion for snuff in France. He is the eponym of the tobacco plant *Nicotiana* and so of nicotine, the French (and hence English) term for the poisonous alkaloid in tobacco.

Jean Baudry, *Jean Nicot* (1988).

**NICULOSO, FRANCISCO, or Niculoso Pisano** (d. 1529), Italian potter in Spain. He was probably a native of Pisa and may have been trained in a FAENZA workshop. By 1498 he had established a workshop in Triana, a suburb of Seville, and there introduced the Italian idea of a single pictorial design made up of panels of AZULEJOS. His earliest dated work is a pictorial tomb slab (1503) in the Church of Santa Ana in Triana. In 1504 he made an altarpiece depicting *The Visitation* (framed with GROTESQUES) for the Chapel of the Catholic Kings in the Alcázar in Seville, and in the same year made the superb tiles (designed by Pedro Millán) that adorn the portal of the Convent of Santa Paula in Seville. His finest surviving work is an altarpiece of 1518 (now damaged) in the Monastery of Santa María de Tentudía in the Sierra Morena.

*MDA*; Alfredo José Morales, *Francisco Niculoso Pisano* (2nd edn. 1991).

**NIELLO**, the Italian and hence English term, derived from medieval Latin *nigellum* ('black'), for the black compound of copper, lead, silver, sulphur, and (sometimes) borax used to inlay engraved designs on precious metals; the term is also used to denote products decorated using this technique. Niello was first used in ancient Egypt, and has a continuous history thereafter. In the fifteenth century it was widely used in Germany and Italy for the decoration of rings, cups, and paxes. Maso FINIGUERRA took paper prints from his *nielli*, and so inaugurated the niello print. Niello is sometimes called Tula (because it was revived in the Russian town of Tula in the nineteenth century) or platina (though platinum was never part of the compound).

**NIFO, AGOSTINO, or (Latin) Suessanus** (*c*.1469–*c*.1546), Italian Aristotelian philosopher, born in Sessa Aurunca (Calabria) and educated at the University of Padua; he embarked on an academic career during which he taught at Padua (1492–9), Naples (1500–13, 1531–2), Pisa (1519–22), and Salerno (1522–31, 1532–5). In his *De intellectu et daemonibus* (1492) he was a proponent of AVERROËS, but by 1518 he had become a Platonizing THOMIST, and in his *De immortalitate* of that year (which was dedicated to Pope LEO X) attacked the ideas of POMPONAZZI. His *De regnandi peritia* (1523), which was dedicated to the Emperor CHARLES V, drew substantially on MACHIAVELLI's *Il principe* for its political perspective.

**NIÑO, PERO ALONSO, or El Negro** (1468–*c*.1505), Spanish explorer, born near Huelva. As a young man he sailed with several Portuguese expeditions down the coast of AFRICA, and in 1498 joined the third voyage of COLUMBUS to America. In 1498, together with Cristóbal Guerra, he explored the coast of what is now Venezuela, and returned to Spain with a cargo of pearls and dyewood. In Spain he was accused of theft and spent the rest of his life in prison.

*DHE.*

**NIZOLIO, MARIO** (1498–*c*.1566), Italian philosopher. He was born in Brescello and taught at the University of Parma. In 1536 he published *Thesaurus Ciceronianus*, a Latin lexicon derived entirely from Cicero, whom Nizolio thought the ideal model for Latin. His principal philosophical work was *De veris principiis* (1553), which distinguishes the language of ancient philosophers from the ideas that they were trying to articulate through that language; this treatise was later revived by Leibniz, who in 1670 published *De veris principiis* under the title *Antibarbarus philosophicus.*

**NÓBREGA, MANUEL DA** (1517–70), Portuguese Jesuit missionary. He was educated in CANON LAW at Coimbra and in 1549 travelled to Brazil as head of the first contingent of Jesuit missionaries to go to America; he was, together with Luis de Grã, joint provincial of Brazil. He advocated conversion by means of persuasion rather than force, and opposed the enslavement of Indians.

*DHP.*

**NOGAROLA, ISOTTA** (1418–66), Italian humanist, born in Verona, where, together with her sister Ginevra, she received a classical education under the tutelage of Martino Rizzoni, a pupil of GUARINO DA VERONA; in the 1440s she expanded her scholarly interests to include theology. Isotta

Nogarola wrote a Latin dialogue and several Latin epistles, and is now regarded as the first woman to have become an accomplished humanist scholar.

*HWWI*; M. King and A. Rabil (eds.), *Her Immaculate Hand* (1983).

**NOORT, ADAM VAN** (1561–1641), Flemish history and portrait painter, born in Antwerp, the son of the painter and stained-glass designer Lambert van Noort, who died when Adam was still a child. Adam's paintings were usually historical, but he also painted religious subjects (e.g. *Adoration of the Magi*, c.1600, Rubenshuis, Antwerp). His pupils included Rubens (for a short time) and Jacob Jordaens, who married his daughter.

*MDA* s.v. Noort (2) Adam van Noort.

**NOOT, JONKER JAN BAPTIST VAN DER** (1539–95), Flemish poet, a native of Brecht (near Antwerp) who in 1567 fled as a religious refugee to England, where he represented himself as a Calvinist. He subsequently lived in Germany and France before returning to the Netherlands and settling in Antwerp, where he represented himself as a Catholic with strong Spanish sympathies. His most important work was *Het Bosken*, which was published in London in 1570 and is the first volume of Renaissance poetry in Dutch; its principal models were the PLÉIADE poets, especially RONSARD. The only complete text of his epic *Olympiados* (which is interspersed with sonnets) is the German translation, *Das Buch Extasis* (1576).

*NBW* i.

**NORTH, SIR THOMAS** (1523–1601), English translator. His translation from AMYOT's French text of Plutarch's *Lives* (1579) was the most important source of SHAKESPEARE's Roman plays. Other translations include the *Dial of Princes* (1557) from GUEVARA's *El reloj de príncipes* and the *Moral Philosophy of Doni* (1570), Anton DONI's Italian version of the Bidpai, a collection of Sanskrit fables.

*DNB*.

**NORTH-EAST PASSAGE.** The possibility of finding a route to China by sailing around the north of Europe and Asia was first raised in Europe in the 1520s. Such a route would have the advantage of avoiding Spanish and Portuguese ships; ancient land routes to the East were from the late fifteenth century largely controlled by the Ottoman Turks. Many exploratory voyages were made throughout the sixteenth century in pursuit of such a passage, especially by the English: notable expeditions include those of WILLOUGBY and CHANCELLOR (both 1553), BOROUGHS (1556), and HUDSON (1607, 1608). WILLEM BARENTSZOON led Dutch expeditions in the area between 1594 and 1597. No north-east route was discovered, the expeditions did however make useful explorations of the Barents and White Seas.

**NORTHERN REBELLION.** The last baronial rising in England sought to release MARY, QUEEN OF SCOTS, from captivity and restore the Catholic faith. A proposed marriage between Mary and the Catholic duke of Norfolk provided the political impetus. In 1569 the duke's brother-in-law, the earl of Westmorland, and the earl of Northumberland led an army to some initial successes, occupying Durham and Ripon and hearing mass in the cathedrals. The rising was suppressed and the conspirators variously dispersed and executed.

**NORTHUMBERLAND, JOHN DUDLEY, DUKE OF** (1502–53), English lord protector. Northumberland's early career was as a soldier: he helped to suppress the PILGRIMAGE OF GRACE, served as deputy governor of Calais, and captured Boulogne. Under SOMERSET's protectorship he put down KETT's REBELLION; in 1549 he replaced him as lord protector. EDWARD VI's ill health threatened his hold on power, however, and Edward, possibly under his influence, diverted the succession from MARY and ELIZABETH to Lady Jane GREY, allowing Northumberland to marry her to his fourth son, Lord Guildford Dudley. After ten days of Lady Jane's reign, however, Mary claimed the throne at the head of an uprising, and Northumberland was executed.

*DNB* s.v. Dudley, John.

**NORTH-WEST PASSAGE.** A number of voyages in search of a sea passage from the Atlantic to the Pacific via the north of Canada were made by British seamen from the last quarter of the sixteenth century. Such a route would enable lucrative trade with the East to be opened. Ancient land routes to China and the Orient were, from the late fifteenth century, controlled by the Ottoman Turks, and other sea routes were controlled by the Spanish and Portuguese. Sir Humphrey GILBERT petitioned ELIZABETH to sanction an exploratory voyage in 1555, but significant expeditions only commenced with FROBISHER's voyages of 1576, 1577, and 1578, during which Frobisher Bay received its name. DAVIS led another three voyages between 1585 and 1587, discovering the Davis Strait. Hudson made four voyages between 1607 and 1611, discovering the Hudson river on the third, and Hudson Bay on the fourth. Between 1612 and 1616, BAFFIN made five exploratory voyages, and sailed to the north end of Baffin Bay, but it was not until 1631, with the voyages of Luke FOX and Thomas JAMES, that it was accepted that no navigable passage led from Hudson Bay through the North American continent to Asia and the Orient.

**NORTON, THOMAS** (1532–84), English playwright. Together with Thomas SACKVILLE, his fellow student at the Inner Temple, Norton wrote the first five-act English tragedy, *Gorboduc*. The play tells of King Gorboduc's division of Britain between his two sons, who quarrel over their territory and are both killed. It was first performed at the Inner Temple c.1561 in the presence of ELIZABETH I. One account suggests that Norton wrote the first three acts of the play, and Sackville the remaining two. An eyewitness account of the performance interpreted the play as a commentary on the queen's marriage plans.

*DNB*.

**NOSSENI, GIOVANNI MARIA** (1544–1620), Swiss furniture-maker, sculptor, architect, and poet, a native of Lugano who spent most of his career in Saxony; he moved to Torgau in 1575 and settled in Dresden in 1583. His best-known work is a set of twelve chairs commissioned by the Elector AUGUSTUS I in 1585; the chairs, of which seven survive in the Zwinger in Dresden, are sumptuously gilded and inlaid with semi-precious stones. After the death of Augustus in 1586 Nosseni worked as an architect and figurative sculptor.

*MDA.*

**NOSTRADAMUS or (French) Michel de Nostredame** (1503–66), French astrologer and physician, born in Saint-Rémy (Provence) and educated at Avignon and Montpellier, where he studied medicine. He practised as a physician in Agen, but in 1544 was forced to leave because the INQUISITION became suspicious of his interest in the occult and his Jewish ancestry. He settled in Salon (near Aix), where he was believed to have effected miraculous cures during an outbreak of plague. In 1547 he began to give astrological consultations, and published *Centuries*, a book of prophecies (in verse quatrains) which appeared in an expanded edition in 1566; in 1555 he began to issue annual *Prognostications*. Some of his predictions seem to have been fulfilled, which led to invitations to the courts of CATHERINE DE MÉDICIS and CHARLES IX. Belief in his prophetic powers has persisted in occult circles until the present day.

*DSB.*

**NOTKE, BERNT** (c.1440–1509), German painter and woodcarver, probably a native of Lassan (Pomerania). His most important work is a huge rood-screen (17 metres (56 feet) high) and *Triumphal Cross* group in Lübeck Cathedral (1470–7). He later carved the double-winged altarpiece in Aarhus Cathedral (1479) and the free-standing *St George and the Dragon* in the Storkyrka in Stockholm (c.1487).

*MDA*; Kerstin Petermann, *Bernt Notke* (2000).

**NOVARA, BATTLE OF.** On 6 June 1513 a French army commanded by Gian Giacomo TRIVULZIO and intent on dislodging Massimiliano SFORZA from Milan met the defending Swiss forces at Novara, 40 kilometres (25 miles) west of Milan. The battle was won by the Swiss, but fortunes were to be reversed two years later at the battle of MARIGNANO.

**NOVELLA** (Italian plural *novelle*), a short prose tale which was popular in Renaissance Italy and later developed into the modern genre of the short story. The principal model for the novella was BOCCACCIO's *Decameron*, which organized a group of tales within a narratorial frame (the *cornice*). The principal collections of novellas in fourteenth- and fifteenth-century Italy were Franco SACCHETTI's *Trecentonovelle*, Giovanni SERCAMBI's *Novelle*, and Tomasso GUARDATI's *Novellino*; in Latin, the most important novellas were the *Historia de duobus amantibus* of the future Pope PIUS II and the *Facetiae* of Poggio BRACCIOLINI.

In the sixteenth century, when the novella reached the zenith of its popularity, collections included Matteo BANDELLO's *Novelle*, Giovanni della Casa's *Galateo*, Anton Francesco DONI's *La Zucca*, FIRENZUOLA's *Ragionamenti d'amore*,

GIRALDI's *Ecatommitti*, Anton Francesco GRAZZINI's *Le cene* and STRAPAROLA's *Le piacevoli notti*. MACHIAVELLI composed a satirical novella on social climbing in Florence, *Belfagor*; the theme which attracted most writers of novellas was the tragic love of Romeo and Juliet (MASUCCIO SALERNITANO, Matteo Bandello, Luigi da Porto).

*OCIL.*

**NOYE or Noyen or Oye, SEBASTIAAN VAN** (c.1493–1557), Netherlandish architect, born in Utrecht. He worked as a military architect for the Emperor CHARLES V, in which capacity he built the star-shaped fortress at Philippeville (Flanders, now Belgium). He was also the architect of GRANVELLE's Italianate palace in Brussels.

**NUNES, PEDRO, or (Castilian) Pedro Núñez or (Latin) Petrus Nonius** (1502–78), Portuguese geographer and mathematician. He was born in Alcacer do Sal, and became professor of mathematics at Coimbra, where he remained for the rest of his life except for a six-year interlude in Spain (1538–44). In 1529 he was appointed royal cosmographer, in which capacity he demonstrated that the Spice Islands (Moluccas) were in the Portuguese sphere as defined in the Treaty of TORDESILLAS. His published works included an annotated edition of works by PTOLEMY (1537), a treatise on NAVIGATION (*De arte atque ratione navigandi*, 1546), which contains an account of the scientific equipment carried by Portuguese navigators, a treatise on the phenomenon of the second twilight (*De crepusculis*, 1542), and a book on mathematics (*Libro de algebra en arithmetica y geometria*, 1567).

*DSB.*

**NÚÑEZ CABEZA DE VACA, ÁLVAR.** See CABEZA DE VACA, ÁLVAR NÚÑEZ.

**NÚÑEZ DE TOLEDO, FERNANDO** (1475–1553), classical scholar, born in Valladolid; he was variously known as 'El Pinciano' (from his birthplace, ancient Pincia) and 'El Comendador Griego' (from his standing as a Hellenist). From 1490 to 1498 Núñez de Toledo studied at the Collegio di San Clemente in Bologna, and on returning to Spain worked as a tutor for the Mendoza family in Granada until he was recruited by Cardinal CISNEROS to work on the COMPLUTENSIAN Bible in Alcalá de Henares. He became professor of rhetoric at Alcalá de Henares, and, on the death of LEBRIJA in 1522, succeeded him as professor of Greek at Salamanca (where he also taught HEBREW).

In addition to his contributions to the Complutensian Polyglot, Núñez de Toledo published commentaries on SENECA (Basel, 1529) and PLINY THE YOUNGER (Salamanca, 1544); his geographical interests are reflected in his translation (from Latin to Spanish) of the historical geography of Bohemia by Enea Silvio Piccolomini (later Pope PIUS II) and his edition of Pomponius Mela.

**NUREMBERG or (German) Nürnberg**, a city in Franconia which became a free imperial city in 1219 and was subsequently a favourite residence of the emperors; the imperial regalia were kept in Nuremberg from 1424 to 1796. In 1356 Nuremberg was the site of the imperial diet which promulgated the Golden Bull, the constitution of the HOLY ROMAN EMPIRE. The city was ruled by a council (*kleiner Rat*) of 42 members, initially drawn from patrician families, but after a revolt in 1347 artisans secured representation. By the sixteenth century the city had become wealthy, and together with AUGSBURG had become the principal commercial and cultural link between Italy and northern Europe.

In 1525 Nuremberg became the first imperial city to adopt the Reformation, and the following year the gymnasium planned by MELANCHTHON opened. By this time the city had acquired a European reputation for the quality of its metalwork, which included gold and silver work (especially by the JAMNITZER family); the city's mechanical products included ARMOUR, GUNS (airguns and gun locks), and terrestrial and celestial globes (ASTROLABES); its inventions included the pocket watch (see CLOCKS AND WATCHES), of which the early examples were known as 'Nuremberg eggs', and BRASS. Nuremberg was the city of Hans SACHS and the school of MEISTERSINGER and of HUMANISTS such as Martin BEHAIM and Willibald PIRKHEIMER and the astronomer REGIOMANTANUS. Nuremberg's sculptors included Adam KRAFT, Veit STOSS, and the VISCHER family, and its painters and engravers included Albrecht DÜRER, Michael WOLGEMUT, and the LITTLE MASTERS. Its surviving Renaissance architecture includes tombs by Adam Krafft and Peter Vischer and two FOUNTAINS, the Fountain of Virtue (1589) and the famous Gänsemännchen Fountain (*c.*1555), which consists of a Franconian peasant carrying two geese with water flowing from their beaks.

Gerald Strauss, *Nuremberg in the Sixteenth Century* (rev. edn., 1976); J.C. Smith, *Nuremberg: a Renaissance City* (1983).

**NUREMBERG, CATHOLIC LEAGUE OF, or (German) Nürnberger Bund**, a league of German Catholic princes sponsored by FERDINAND I (brother of the Emperor CHARLES V) and constituted in 1538 as the Catholic response to the SCHMALKALDIC LEAGUE. The impending prospect of an Ottoman invasion of Austria averted an immediate conflict between the two leagues, and the decision to postpone hostilities was ratified in the 'Frankfurt Respite' of 1539.

**NUREMBERG, PEACE OF** (1532), a treaty between the Emperor CHARLES V and the SCHMALKALDIC LEAGUE concluded at Nuremberg. The treaty was a protracted ceasefire (as the German *Nürnberger Anstand* indicates) rather than an agreement, and postponed the resolution of the issues that divided the Protestant princes and the Empire until a council of the Church or a German diet could convene. Martin LUTHER welcomed the treaty, which he interpreted as a measure of recognition of Protestantism. The cessation of hostilities, together with the ensuing absence of CHARLES V from Germany for the next decade, enabled the German Protestants to expand without hindrance through much of Germany.

**NYMPHAEUM**, literally a temple of the nymphs, especially the naiads (Latin *naiades*), the goddesses of rivers and FOUNTAINS; in practice the nymphaeum was an architectural GROTTO containing fountains and statues. The nymphaeum was a Roman form which was familiar in the sixteenth century because of ancient accounts of nymphaea and the survival of the Acqua Julia, a public nymphaeum in Rome. There are Renaissance nymphaea in the FARNESE PALACE in Caprarola, the Villa d'ESTE at Tivoli, the Villa GIULIA in Rome and in the water-theatres of the Villa ALDOBRANDINI and the Villa MONDRAGONE at Frascati.

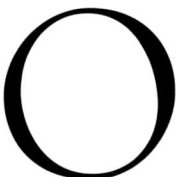

# O

**OAK-LEAF JARS.** See FLORENCE POTTERIES.

**OBRECHT, JACOB** (c.1450–1505), Flemish composer whose father was a musician in the Burgundian court. He was choirmaster at Bergen op Zoom, Cambrai Cathedral, and the Church of Our Lady in Antwerp, and was succentor at Saint-Donation, Bruges. In 1504 he became *maestro di cappella* to Duke Ercole I d'ESTE in Ferrara, where he died of the plague the following year. He was an important composer of cyclic masses and also wrote motets and songs, many of which circulated internationally.

**OCAMPO, FLORIÁN DE** (c.1495–1558), Spanish chronicler, born in Zamora and from 1509 to 1514 educated at Alcalá de Henares, where his teachers included LEBRIJA. His *Crónica general de España* (Zamora, 1543; enlarged edition, Medina, 1553) attempts to trace the HABSBURG dynasty to its roots in the ancient world through a compilation of the medieval chronicles of Castile. Ocampo also edited the chronicle of King Alfonso X of Castile (1221–84), which he published as *Los quatro libros primeros de la crónica de España* (Zamora, 1541).

**OCCITAN LANGUAGE AND LITERATURE.** The Occitan language, which is also known as Provençal, *roman*, and the *langue d'oc*, was the language of what is now southern France and part of what is now northern Italy. Occitan was distinguished from French (which was known as the *langue d'oïl*) by the two words for 'yes': northern French *oïl* (now *oui*), which derived from Latin *hoc ille*, was distinguished from Occitan *oc*, which derived from Latin *hoc*. The closest relative of Occitan is CATALAN.

Occitan was the language of the troubadours of twelfth- and thirteenth-century France, but as southern France was annexed by the French crown, the language was increasingly displaced by French. With the advent of print French became the dominant language, but books continued to be published in Occitan throughout the sixteenth century. The most important Occitan poet of the period was Pey de Garros, who published a translation of the Psalms in the Gascon dialect of Occitan (1565) and two years later published his pastoral *Poesias gasconas*. In Provence, the most important custodian (and inventor) of the Occitan literary tradition was Jean de Nostredame (brother of NOSTRADAMUS), who published *Vies des plus célèbres et anciens poètes provençaux* (1575).

**OCHINO, BERNARDINO** (1487–1564), Italian Protestant reformer, born in Siena, where he entered the austere Order of Observantine Friars, a reformed Franciscan religious ORDER. He became general of his Order, but in 1534 transferred to the newly founded CAPUCHIN Order because of his desire to submit himself to an even stricter rule; he was twice (1538 and 1541) vicar-general of the Capuchins. In 1539 he visited Venice, where his sermons adumbrated the sympathy for Luther's doctrine of JUSTIFICATION by faith that was soon committed to print in Ochino's *Dialogi sette*. Ochino established contact with Pietro Martire VERMIGLI, who encouraged his Protestant sympathies, and in 1541 Ochino became a Lutheran. When the INQUISITION was established in Rome in June 1542, Ochino was at once summoned to appear before it. He was dissuaded from doing so by Pietro Martire and by Cardinal Gasparo CONTARINI, whom he found dying of poison in Bologna, and instead fled to Geneva, where he was warmly received by CALVIN.

In the course of the next two years Ochino published six volumes of *Prediche* which explain and justify his decision to convert to Protestantism; 25 of these tracts were soon published in English translation (Ipswich, 1548). In 1545 Ochino was appointed as minister to the Italian Protestant church in Augsburg, but in January 1547 had to flee when the city was caught up in the SCHMALKALDIC WAR and occupied by imperial troops. He travelled first to Strassburg and then to England, where Thomas CRANMER secured for him a prebend of Canterbury and a royal pension.

In England Ochino wrote his most important books. The Latin original of his *Tragedy or Dialogue of the Unjust Usurped Primacy of the Bishop of Rome* is lost, but the English translation by John Ponet, bishop of Winchester, was published in 1549: the central conceit, in which Satan convokes the fallen angels in council and resolves to establish the pope as ANTICHRIST, whereupon God raises up Henry VIII and his son Edward to overthrow the conspirators, anticipates some of the episodes in Milton's *Paradise Lost*. While in England Ochino also wrote *The Labyrinth*, a treatise dedicated to Queen ELIZABETH in which he set out a doctrine of GRACE which attacked Calvinist predestination and hinted at a Christology which has affinities with SOCINIANISM.

On the accession of Queen MARY, Ochino left for Zürich, where in 1555 he became pastor of the Italian church. In 1563 he published his *Thirty Dialogues*, which were said by Ochino's detractors to advocate polygamy and to be unsound on the Trinity and on DIVORCE. He was dismissed from his post and expelled from Zürich, and eventually found refuge in Poland. An edict of 6 August 1564 banishing all foreign dissidents compelled him to flee. In Pińczów his family contracted plague, and three of his four children died; he finally reached Slavkov u Brna (Austerlitz) in Moravia, where he died late in 1564.

DNB; R. H. Bainton, *Bernardino Ochino, esule e riformatore senese del Cinquecento (1487–1563)* (1940); Bernardino Ochino, *Patterns of Perfection: Seven Sermons Preached in Patria*, ed. Philip McNair (1999)

**OCHSENKUHN, SEBASTIAN** (1521–74), German lutenist, employed by the Count Palatine Otto Heinrich at Neuberg an der Donau. His *Tabulaturbuch* (1558) contains pre-existing sacred and secular music by several composers including SENFL, MOUTON, JOSQUIN, CRÉCQUILLON, and SERMISY.

**OCKEGHEM, JOHANNES** (c.1410–1497), Flemish composer in France. In 1443 he was a *vicaire-chanteur* at the Church of Our Lady in Antwerp and was later appointed to the court of Charles I, duke of Bourbon. From 1451 he was at the royal court of CHARLES VII, by whom he was greatly rewarded by being made treasurer of Saint-Martin, Tours. His royal service continued under LOUIS XI, during whose reign he visited Spain, Dammes, Bruges (where he renewed his friendship with BUSNOIS), and Cambrai (allowing him to visit DUFAY). Considered to be one of the greatest of fifteenth-century composers, he wrote masses, motets, and songs.

**OECOLAMPADIUS, JOHANNES** (1482–1531), German Protestant reformer, born in Weinsberg (now in Württemberg but then in the Palatinate); his baptismal name was Johann Hussgen, but he later changed his name to Hausschein ('house-torch') which he then translated into Greek (with a Latin inflexion) as Oecolampadius. He was educated at schools in Weinsberg and Heilbronn and at universities in Bologna (where he studied law), Heidelberg (graduating in 1503), and Basel (where he studied theology). He became a formidable student of Greek and Hebrew, and in 1515 was appointed as preacher in Basel Cathedral. In the same year he assisted Johann FROBEN with the printing of ERASMUS' Greek–Latin New Testament, to which he contributed the supplementary notes.

In 1516 Oecolampadius was appointed cathedral preacher in Augsburg, and two years later published a tract protesting against the use of humour in Easter sermons (*De risu paschali*, 1518). In 1520 he published a grammar of GREEK and entered a Bridgettine monastery with a view to avoiding the need to take a public position on the Lutheran rebellion. His anonymous *Canonici indocti* (1519) supported Luther's call for reform, and in February 1522 Oecolampadius left the monastery and joined a small group of reformers who had been settled in Ebernburg (near Bad Kreuznach) by Franz von SICKINGEN.

In November 1522 Oecolampadius returned to Basel as priest and university lecturer in theology. He laboured with ZWINGLI to introduce the Reformation into Basel. In January 1528 Oecolampadius and Zwingli won the disputation in Bern that led to the adoption of the Reformation in that canton, and in the same year Oecolampadius married Wilibrandis Rosenblatt, a widow who later married Wolfgang CAPITO and then Martin BUCER. He participated in the Colloquy of MARBURG (1519), where he defended Zwingli's memorialist view of the EUCHARIST. Oecolampadius was a church leader rather than an innovative theologian, but he seems to have been the first reformer to have advocated lay participation in church government. He died on 24 November 1531.

NDB; J. J. Herzog, *Das Leben Johannes Oekolampads* (2 vols., 1843); E. Staehelin, *Das theologische Lebenswerk Johannes Oekolampads* (1939); E. G. Rupp, 'Johannes Oecolampadius: The Reformer as Scholar', in id., *Patterns of Reformation* (1969).

**OIL PAINTING**, a range of techniques which have in common the use of oils which when dried in air hold the particles of pigment in position and bind them to the ground. VASARI attributed the invention of oil painting to Jan van EYCK, but the attribution is a tribute to Jan van Eyck's standing rather than the identification of the inventor of a process, because although Jan van Eyck made innovative use of oils and varnishes, and so had what Vasari called a 'secret method of painting in oils', such oils had been in occasional use for generations before Jan van Eyck began to experiment with the medium.

The transmission of the technique to Italy is similarly obscure: Vasari's assertion that ANTONELLO DA MESSINA trained in the studio of Jan van Eyck and then brought oil painting to Italy is problematical, not least because no evidence survives of a visit by Antonello to the Netherlands. The technique was probably introduced in Italy by Flemish artists, and it was only adopted slowly: throughout the fifteenth century, oils were used as if they were TEMPERA, and paintings were built up in thin transparent glazes. The technique known as impasto, in which oil paint was applied in thick solid masses (which could not be done with tempera), was not developed until the end of the fifteenth century; one of the earliest impasto paintings was Giovanni BELLINI's *Doge Loredan* (c.1501, National Gallery, London). The textures that could be achieved in oils through the use of impasto led quickly to the displacement of tempera in the early decades of the sixteenth century.

**OJEDA or Hojeda, ALONSO DE** (1466/70–1515/16), Spanish explorer. He was born in Cuenca and in September 1493 sailed with COLUMBUS on his second voyage, during which he participated in the conquest of Hispaniola (1493–5). In 1499–1500 he led an expedition (accompanied by Juan de la COSA and Amerigo VESPUCCI) to the coasts of Guyana and Venezuela; he named Venezuela (the Spanish diminutive of

'Venice') after seeing Indian houses on stilts near Lake Maracaibo. Ojeda later became governor of the Caribbean coast of Colombia (from Cape Vella westward to the Gulf of Darién), and in 1509 established the settlement of San Sebastián on an island off the coast (subsequently refounded in 1533, now the city of Cartagena). Juan de la Cosa was killed in an attack by Indians, and in a second attack further along the coast Ojeda was wounded by a poisoned dart; he died shortly after returning to Hispaniola.

*DHE* s.v. Hojeda.

**OLDENBARNEVELT, JOHAN VAN** (1547–1619), Dutch statesman and Protestant leader in the final years of the REVOLT OF THE NETHERLANDS. He studied law in Louvain, Bourges, and Heidelberg and after travelling in France and Italy established a legal practice in The Hague. He became a Calvinist and a supporter of WILLIAM OF ORANGE, and in the early years of the Revolt participated in the sieges of Haarlem (1572–3) and Leiden (1574). He assisted in the formation of the Union of UTRECHT (1579), and from 1586 onwards served as pensionary (i.e. chairman) to the Estates of Holland as well as legal adviser (*Lands-advocaat*) to the province of Holland.

From 1588 to 1598 Oldenbarnevelt and MAURICE OF NASSAU were the most important political figures in the Netherlands. Oldenbarnevelt created a measure of political unity in the UNITED PROVINCES by securing appointments in each of the provinces (as captain-general and stadtholder) for Maurice, and in the 1590s they worked together to expel the Spaniards from the northern Netherlands. Oldenbarnevelt favoured carrying the war to the south, but Maurice opposed this policy. After the Spanish retook Ostend in 1604, Oldenbarnevelt began to negotiate with Spain; Maurice opposed the negotiations and the twelve-year truce, signed in April 1609.

The tensions between Oldenbarnevelt and Maurice were exacerbated by political and religious differences. Oldenbarnevelt was a republican who favoured a loose federation of provinces; Maurice was a closet monarchist who aspired to a united kingdom. In religion, Oldenbarnevelt was supported by the REMONSTRANT party (the ARMINIANS) and Maurice by the Counter-Remonstrants (the GOMARISTS), which he joined in July 1617. Oldenbarnevelt responded by persuading the Estates of Holland to adopt the 'Sharp Resolution' of August 1617, by which towns in Holland were allowed to form and finance local militias (*waardgelders*) independent of Maurice's professional multi-provincial army. Maurice saw the politics and theology of Oldenbarnevelt as a threat to the unity of the United Provinces, and ordered his arrest. He was convicted of treason and beheaded in The Hague on 13 May 1619. MASSINGER's *Barnavelt* was written and acted within months of his execution.

*NNBW* v; J. den Tex, *Oldenbarnevelt* (2 vols., 1973).

**OLDENDORP, JOHANN** (1480–1567), German jurist, professor of law at Cologne, and syndic (i.e. chief magistrate) of Rostock and Lübeck. In his *Iuris naturalis, gentium et civilis isagoge* (1539) he set out a system of legal philosophy rooted in NATURAL LAW and applicable to INTERNATIONAL LAW. He also wrote on criminal procedure in *Practica actionum forensium* (1540) and *Sylloge sive Enchiridion actionum forensium* (1552).

**OLIVER or Olivier, ISAAC** (1558/68–1617), French portrait miniaturist in England, born into a HUGUENOT family in Rouen. He was brought to England as a young child and became a pupil of Nicholas HILLIARD. He painted life-sized portraits, historical scenes, religious scenes, and portrait MINIATURES, which were usually of the head and shoulders. His miniatures include depictions of *John Donne*, *Prince Henry*, and *Anne of Denmark* (all in Windsor Castle). The Royal Collection in Windsor also holds Oliver's *Portrait of a Young Man*, which was for centuries mistakenly thought to be a portrait of Sir Philip SIDNEY. Oliver also drew a portrait (unfinished) of Queen ELIZABETH (Victoria and Albert Museum). His *Entombment of Christ* (Musée des Beaux-Arts, Angers), which was admired by his contemporaries, was completed by his son Peter Oliver (1594–1647), who was also a portrait miniaturist.

*DNB; MDA*; Raphaëlle Costa de Beauregard, *Silent Elizabethans: The Language of Colour in the Miniatures of Nicholas Hilliard and Isaac Oliver* (2000).

**OLIVÉTAN or Pierre Robert** (*c*.1506–1538), French Protestant reformer, born in Noyon (Picardy), a cousin of Jean CALVIN. He studied in Orléans, where he adopted Lutheran doctrines, in consequence of which he was obliged to flee to Strassburg, where he became a student of Greek and Hebrew. From 1532 to 1535 Olivétan lived in Neuchâtel, where he preached the Reformation to WALDENSIANS, for which purpose he translated the Bible into French (1535): his Old Testament was translated directly from the Hebrew, but his Apocrypha and New Testament are adaptations of the translations of LEFÈVRE D'ÉTAPLES. In the last years of his life he worked with Calvin on the implementation of the Reformation in Geneva.

G. Casalis and B. Roussel (eds.), *Olivétan: Traducteur de la Bible* (1987).

**OLMOS, ANDRÉS DE** (1500–71), Spanish philologist who travelled to Mexico as a Franciscan missionary in 1524. Fray Andrés became a student of Indian languages, especially Totonac, Huastec, and Nahuatl; his works on these languages are lost, except for the *Gramática mexicana* (i.e. Nahuatl), which survived in manuscript and was published in Paris in 1875, and his *Huehuetlatolli*, a collection of Nahuatl moral teachings, which was published in Mexico in 1979. He also wrote religious plays, including an AUTO on the Last Judgement which was performed for fourteen years in succession (1535–48) at the Church of San José de Naturales in Mexico City.

**OÑA, PEDRO DE** (1570–1643), Chilean poet, born into a Spanish family in Los Infantes de Angol. The conquistador García Hurtado de Mendoza, who had commissioned Alonso de ERCILLA to write his epic *La Araucana*, felt that his own role in the conquest of Chile had been given insufficient prominence by Ercilla, and so commissioned Pedro de Oña to write a rival epic. Oña's *Primera parte de Arauco domado* (Lima, 1596) is a 16,000-line epic in *octavas reales* that gives a prominent part to Hurtado de Mendoza; he never published a *segunda parte*.

Pedro de Oña also wrote a poem on the Lima earthquake (*Temblor de Lima*, 1609), a 10,000-line poem in praise of a goblet (*El vasauro*, 1635), and an unfinished elegy for IGNATIUS LOYOLA (*Ignacio de Cantabria*, 1639).

Augusto Iglesias, *Pedro de Oña* (1971).

**OPERA** grew out of Italian court theatrical entertainment, principally the pastoral and the *intermedio* (see INTERMEZZO), of which the most famous were those for *La pellegrina* (Florence, 1589). Music and its relationship to tragedy, comedy, and pastoral was the subject of treatises by Leone de' Sommi (1556) and Angelo Ingegneri (1598). The earliest operas were based on pastoral eclogues. Most important was the development of a new style of composition created by PERI, CACCINI, CAVALIERI, or GALILEI which allowed dialogue to be sung in a way which made it sound like natural speech. This *stile recitativo* was first heard at the Pitti Palace in Florence in 1600 in the Peri/Caccini/Rinuccini *Euridice*. MONTEVERDI's *Orfeo*, performed in Mantua in 1607, is musically more cohesive and dramatically realized. The increasingly expressive qualities of the developing musical language, as used in the madrigal and practised by such singers as the FERRARESE *concerti delle donne*, also played a part.

**OPORINUS, JOHANNES** (1507–68), Swiss humanist printer, born in Basel. He studied Greek in Strassburg and then returned to Basel as a teacher of Greek and as an editor for the publisher Johann FROBEN. He eventually established his own press, specializing in editions of scientific works and classical authors. His press published a Latin translation of the *Koran* (1542) with prefaces by LUTHER and MELANCHTHON and the first edition of VESALIUS' *De humani corporis fabrica* (1543), which contained many woodcut illustrations.

NDB; M. Steinmann, *Johannes Oporinus: Ein Basler Buchdrucker um die Mitte des 16 Jahrhunderts* (1967).

**OPTICS**, from the Greek word for 'eye', was the term used in antiquity for the science of sight and was reintroduced in the sixteenth century to replace the Latin name for the subject, *perspectiva*, from which we derive the term PERSPECTIVE. *Perspectiva* covered the whole science of sight, including such matters as the anatomy of the eye. It was taught in universities as part of natural philosophy, and was regarded as partly mathematical because of its use of GEOMETRY (in the area now called 'geometrical optics'). It was generally believed that sight was by the emission of eyebeams (such a theory is now called 'extramission'), but HASAN IBN HASAN IBN AL-HAYTHAM, known in the Latin West as Alhacen, preferred the theory that sight was by the reception of light into the eye (called 'intromission'). More careful dissection of the eye did not at first help: LEONARDO DA VINCI looked so carefully that he faced the unacceptable conclusion that the image on the back of the eye was inverted, which led him to introduce complications to avoid such an absurdity. In a more technical and mathematically sophisticated way, G. B. BENEDETTI did much the same in the 1560s. Better anatomical work did, however, show that the 'crystalline humour' (which we now call the lens), believed to be the source of the eyebeams, was not in the centre of the eye but rather near the front.

Aristotle had said that form follows function, so the physical similarities between the eye and a CAMERA OBSCURA were not lost upon Renaissance natural philosophers, and as it happened both were eventually explained in the same book, KEPLER's *Ad Vitellionem paralipomena . . .* (1604). Tycho BRAHE had been using a *camera obscura* for astronomy, and had obtained some unexpected results for the diameter of the moon; Kepler, then his assistant, decided that the difficulty might lie in an inadequate theory of the *camera obscura*, specifically: what was the effect of changing the size of the aperture? Kepler was good at visualizing things but this time he resorted to using string to simulate the paths of light rays to check his intuitions. He concluded that what one saw was a series of images of the aperture imposed on an image of the light source. Since he was writing on the optical part of astronomy, Kepler turned next to the human eye. He decided that the crystalline and the liquid-filled cornea in front of it must act like a thick lens, and used a spherical urine flask filled with water to do some experimental investigation. The experiments confirmed the conclusion to which he had been led by the mathematics, that the image on the back of the eye (the retina) was inverted; moreover, the analysis made it clear that sight was by the reception of light. As these conclusions had no therapeutic consequences, physicians made no difficulty about accepting them. The results introduced a permanent division between physical optics, which deals with light, and physiological optics, which deals with our perception of it.

It had been noticed since ancient times that when light went into water the direction of the ray was altered; PTOLEMY and other astronomers, noticing that there was a similar effect when light from the stars travelled through the earth's atmosphere, made attempts to quantify the phenomenon, but by the sixteenth century had got no further than producing 'tables of refraction' that showed what corrections should be imposed if star positions were measured close to the horizon. The correct law of refraction was published by Wellebrord SNEL in 1621. Surviving manuscripts show that the law had been discovered more than ten years earlier by HARRIOT, but he did not publish it.

Burning glasses, that is, concave mirrors used to focus sunlight onto something, were regularly used by anyone who required a source of intense heat; in principle the correct shape was a parabola, but the accuracy of the figuring did not matter a great deal since the sun supplied plenty of light. The same was of course true if a lens was used to focus sunlight. The performance of optical devices could be impressive but in today's terms the optical quality of the images was generally rather poor. For lenses there was also the problem of the glass having an irregular internal structure. These factors explain why, although spectacle lenses had been in use since about 1300, it was not until the 1590s that combinations of lenses were used to make spyglasses (see TELESCOPES AND MICROSCOPES).

Optical devices of many kinds are discusssed by Giambattista DELLA PORTA in his *Magia naturalis* (1558 and 1589), the emphasis generally being upon their powers of deception. A more sober treatment of optical phenomena is found in the work of the learned mathematician Francesco Maurolico of Naples (1494–1575), *Photismi de lumine et umbra* (posthumously published in 1611).

**ORATORY OF DIVINE LOVE.** The Catholic reform movement known as the Roman Oratory or the Oratory of Divine Love was inaugurated in 1517 by senior figures in the court of Pope LEO X. Its members included Gaetano da Thiene (San CAJETAN), Giampietro Carafa (later Pope PAUL IV), and Jacopo SADOLETO. Four members of the Oratory later founded the THEATINES. The Oratory arose from the fifteenth-century CONFRATERNITIES known as *compagnie del divino amore*.

**ORCAGNA or Andrea di Cione Arcagnolo** (1315/20–68), Italian painter, sculptor, and architect, the most prominent artist in Florence in the third quarter of the fourteenth century. He was admitted to the Guild of Painters in 1343 and to the Guild of Masons in 1352. In about 1350 he painted a fresco trilogy (which survives in fragments) on the *Triumph of Death*, the *Last Judgement*, and *Hell* in the Church of Santa Croce; he later painted the altarpiece of *The Redeemer* (1354–7) in the Strozzi Chapel of the Church of Santa Maria Novella. From 1355 to 1358 he worked on the marble tabernacle for the Madonna in the Orsanmichele, and from 1359 to 1362 he served as *capomaestro* of Orvieto Cathedral. At the time of his death he was working on a *St Matthew* altarpiece (Uffizi) which was finished by his brother Jacopo di Cione.

Orcagna's work was untouched by the innovations of GIOTTO; he was rather an imaginative exponent of the medieval style known as Byzantine Gothic, and his remote and dignified figures are suspended in golden space.

*MDA* s.v. Cione; Gert Kreytenberg, *Orcagna, Andrea di Cione: Ein universeller Künstler der Gotik im Florenz* (2000).

**ORDERS, ARCHITECTURAL.** An architecture order consists of a column incorporating a base (if any), shaft, and capital surmounted by its entablature (architrave, frieze, and cornice). The Doric, Ionic, and Corinthian orders are Greek in origin, and the Tuscan and Composite orders are Roman. In ancient Greece the Doric column, which had twenty broad flutes with sharp edges, had no base (though it acquired one in Roman Doric); its capital had an ovolo moulding (i.e. one whose profile was one-quarter of a circle) that in medieval and Renaissance architecture was known as quadrant moulding. The Ionic column usually had 24 flutes divided by fillets; its capital resembled a partly opened scroll, the spirals of which are known as volutes. The Corinthian order is distinguished from Ionic by its capital, which is decorated with ACANTHUS leaves. The Tuscan order was a simplified form of Doric in which the shaft was unfluted. The Italic order (which SERLIO renamed the 'Composite order')

was an elaboration of the other two Greek orders in which the capitals included both Ionian volutes and Corinthian acanthus.

The only ancient discussion of the architectural orders to survive into the Renaissance was contained in the *De architectura* of VITRUVIUS, which was first published in Rome in 1486. The most important Renaissance treatments of the orders were Serlio's *Architettura* (1559–62), VIGNOLA's *Regole delli cinque ordini d'architettura* (1562), and PALLADIO's *I quattro libri dell'architettura* (1570).

The term 'colossal order' (or 'giant order') is the modern term for any order in which columns or pilasters run through more than one storey in a façade. The finest Renaissance example is MICHELANGELO's Capitol in Rome.

R. Chilkam, *The Classical Orders of Architecture* (1985).

**ORDERS, CHIVALRIC.** The chivalric orders created in the fourteenth and fifteenth centuries differ from the military ORDERS in their class base (the chivalric orders were wholly aristocratic and royal), their relatively secular emphasis on civic virtue, and their desire to preserve the ideals of CHIVALRY through their ceremonies and rituals. The earliest chivalric order was the English Order of the Garter, which was established by King Edward III in 1348; membership consisted of the king and 25 knights; in 1362 the Order of the Annunziata was founded in Savoy by Count Amadeus VI. The Burgundian Order of the GOLDEN FLEECE (Ordre de la Toison d'Or) was created by PHILIP THE GOOD in 1530 and became the model for the Order of the Elephant founded by King CHRISTIAN I of Denmark in 1462, the Order of St Michael founded by King LOUIS XI of France in 1469, and the Order of the Holy Ghost (Saint-Esprit) founded by King HENRI III of France in 1578.

D. J. D. Boulton, *The Knights of the Crown: The Monarchical Orders of Knighthood in Later Medieval Europe, 1325–1520* (2nd edn. 2000).

**ORDERS, MILITARY**, and **ORDERS OF RANSOM.** The European CRUSADES against the Ottomans and the Spanish RECONQUISTA gave rise to military orders and to orders of ransom; these orders were in turn the antecedent institutions of the orders of CHIVALRY. The three founding military orders, all of which emerged in the twelfth century, were the Knights Templar, the Knights Hospitallers of ST JOHN, and the TEUTONIC ORDER. The Knights Templar, whose purpose was to protect the Christian shrines of Palestine, was suppressed by Pope Clement V in 1312, but the other two orders had a long afterlife. The principal orders in the Iberian peninsula were the Spanish orders of Santiago de Compostela (1175), Alcántara (c.1156), and Calatrava (1158) and the Portuguese Order of Christ. King FERDINAND II annexed the grand mastership of all three orders, and in 1523 Pope ADRIAN VI formally vested the Spanish orders in the crown of Castile. The Portuguese Order of Christ was founded in 1318 on the abolition of the Templars; both the king (then King Diniz) and the pope (John XXII) had the right to nominate to the Order; in 1522 the grand mastership of the Order was vested in the Portuguese crown. The Swedish Order of the Seraphim may have been established in 1280 and was certainly extant in 1336.

The two main orders of ransom, whose purpose was to ransom Christian prisoners from their Muslim captors, were the Trinitarians (the Order of the Most Holy Trinity) and the Mercedarians (the Order of Our Lady of Mercy). The Trinitarians (who are also known as Marthurins) were founded in 1198, and were subject to the Augustinian rule. By the fifteenth century they had grown to more than 800 houses and had ransomed huge numbers of captives. In 1596 a reformed group called the Barefooted Trinitarians was founded in Spain; the monks ransomed black slaves well into the twentieth century, and the nuns (the Barefooted Trinitarian Sisters, founded in 1612) devoted themselves to works of mercy. The Mercedarians (Orden de Nuestra Señora de la Merced) were a male order founded c.1220. The monks took a fourth vow pledging to offer themselves as hostages if necessary to redeem Christian captives. Some of their members accompanied COLUMBUS to America, and they later established houses throughout Latin America. A corresponding order of nuns was founded in Seville in 1568.

Military orders are normally readily distinguished from religious ORDERS and chivalric ORDERS, but the composite Order of St Maurice and St Lazarus (SS Maurizio e Lazzaro) contains features from all three traditions. The Order of St Maurice was founded in 1434 by Amadeus VIII of Savoy; it consisted of a small group of councillors who were to advise Amadeus on matters of governance after his withdrawal to a hermitage, and withered away when he became Pope FELIX V. The Order was revived by Pope GREGORY III in 1572 on the advice of EMANUEL PHILIBERT, duke of Savoy, and the following year Pope PIUS V united it with the Order of St Lazarus, a military and religious order that had built leper hospitals in Jerusalem, France, and Naples. Thereafter the composite Order subordinated its work amongst lepers to the task of deploying its galleys in combat against Ottomans and BARBARY PIRATES.

**ORDERS, RELIGIOUS**. Christian monasticism, which originated among the Greeks of Egypt in the late third century, was transmitted to the Western Church by Athanasius, who arrived in Rome in 340. In the late sixth century Benedictine monks brought the rule of St Benedict to Rome, whence it was diffused in the seventh century throughout Britain and Ireland by Augustine of Canterbury and his successors and in the eighth century throughout Germany by St Boniface.

Monastic orders, in the sense of corporate bodies with more than one house but with a central administration, began to emerge in the West in the tenth century. The first such order was established in 910 in Cluny, where the monks adopted the rule of St Benedict. In 1098 a new Order was founded at Citeaux (near Dijon) with a view to returning to the letter of St Benedict's rule. This order, which was called Cistercian after its mother house, reinstituted Benedict's emphasis on the importance of labour in the fields, which eventually led to the important Cistercian presence in the wool industry in England and horse and cattle breeding in northern Europe. The Benedictines had worn black, and so came to be known as Black Monks, whereas the Cistercians

wore a grey or black habit under a black scapular, and so were known as Grey Monks or White Monks. By the end of the fifteenth century the Cistercians had established some 750 houses, principally in France, but also in England, Scotland, Ireland, Sweden, Germany, Poland, Hungary, Italy, Spain, and Portugal. In 1577 a reformed order known as the FEUILLANTS emerged from the Cistercians, and in 1663 the Reformed Cistercians of the Strict Observance, popularly known as Trappists, were established at the abbey of La Trappe in Normandy. The third important order of canons, beside the Benedictines and the Cistercians, was the Augustinian canons, who were also known as Black Canons or Regular Canons (Canonici Regulares); members of this Order, which was founded c.1060, were distinguished from Benedictines and Cistercians by virtue of the fact that members were members of the clergy who lived in monasteries but served in parish churches in the patronage of their houses. They were also associated with hospitals: the two London hospitals known as St Bartholomew's and St Thomas's are both former Augustinian houses. The Victorines and Premonstratensians were independent Augustinian congregations whose way of life was influenced by the Cistercians.

The early thirteenth century saw the rise of the four mendicant orders: the Franciscans (1210), the Dominicans (1215), the Carmelites (1245), and the Augustinian hermits (1256); in 1424, the Servites (who had been founded in 1240) were recognized by Pope MARTIN V as a fifth mendicant order. The mendicant friars of these five orders were allowed to work or beg for a living, and were not tied by a vow of stability to one particular house; their privileges included exemption from episcopal jurisdiction, which for centuries led to hostility towards the mendicants on the part of the episcopate, the secular clergy, and the universities. Whereas monks remained in a particular house and worked as members of a community, friars worked independently of their convents, often assisting parochial clergy by preaching or hearing confessions.

The GREAT SCHISM divided the mendicant orders into two obediences, one consequence of which was a gradual loosening of discipline. The founding of the BRETHREN OF THE COMMON LIFE and of the WINDESHEIM CANONS may be early instances of the perception that reform was necessary. The COUNCIL OF CONSTANCE and the COUNCIL OF BASEL both instituted reforms designed to eradicate abuses and impose ascetic ideals. There were also reform movements within the orders. Within the Franciscans, a group called the Observantines (or Observants or Fratres de Observantia), who claimed to 'observe' the rule of St Francis as confirmed by Pope Honorius III on 29 November 1223, broke away from the main Order in 1368, in protest against the loss of discipline; those who remained in the main Order were thereafter called Conventual Franciscans. In the sixteenth century the Observant Franciscans were in turn divided into the CAPUCHINS, the Franciscan Recollects, and the Reformed Observantines. The other important order to derive from the Franciscans was the Ordo Fratrum Minimorum, which was founded in 1435 and is popularly known as the MINIMS. Within the Augustinian hermits, the reformed congregation known as the Discalced Augustinians or Augustinian Recollects was founded in Talavera (Spain) in 1589; there was also a German reformed congregation (founded in 1493), to which Martin LUTHER belonged. The Carmelite Order was reformed in the sixteenth century by JUAN DE LA CRUZ (St John of the Cross) in accordance with the 'Primitive Rule' prescribed by TERESA DE ÁVILA for Carmelite nuns. Members of houses who adopted the 'Teresian Reform' were thereafter called Discalced Carmelites (because they wore sandals), in contrast to the Calced Carmelites who adhered to the 'Mitigated Rule' (and wore shoes)—the Latin term *discalceare* means 'to remove shoes', and sandals were a gesture towards early eastern ascetics, who went barefoot.

In the sixteenth century, the three orders of canons and the five orders of friars were supplemented by two new kinds of religious order, the regular clerks and the secular congregations. The regular clerks took full religious vows, and devoted themselves to specialized activities such as education or missionary work. The most important orders of regular clerks were the THEATINES (1524), the BARNABITES (1530), and the JESUITS (1540). The secular congregations consisted of secular priests who lived together under temporary vows; the most important of these congregations were the Oblates of St Charles founded by Carlo BORROMEO in 1578, the Oratorians founded by Filippo NERI in about 1564, and the French Oratorians founded by Cardinal Pierre de Bérulle in 1611.

The visible history of monasticism is the history of men, because nuns were largely enclosed until the COUNCIL OF TRENT, and in some orders remained enclosed thereafter. The participation of women in the religious orders can be traced to the beginnings of monasticism: St Benedict and his sister St Scholastica founded an order of nuns who lived according to the same rule as male Benedictines; in 1425 the Oblates Regular of St Benedict (initially known as the Oblates of Mary and later as the Oblates of Tor de Specchi), an order consisting of noble Roman women, was founded by the widow Francesca of Rome (1384–1440); they were affiliated to a branch of the Benedictines known as Olivetans or White Benedictines (founded 1319). The Gilbertine Order, which was founded in the early twelfth century in Sempringham, in Lincolnshire (and is the only purely English order), was refused incorporation into the Cistercian Order (which declined to govern women) and later submitted to the spiritual direction of Augustinian canons.

Women were also represented in the mendicant orders, either in all-women 'second orders' or in mixed 'third orders'. After creating the Franciscans, St Francis and St Clare founded a 'second order' known in English as Poor Clares and in French as Clarisses; a subsidiary order with a milder rule was sanctioned by the papacy in 1262, and is known as the Urbanists. In the fifteenth century the Order was reformed on principles of strict poverty by St Colette (1381–1447), and thereafter the two main groups of Franciscan nuns were the Urbanists and the Colettines. There was also

a 'third order' of Franciscans known as Regular Tertiaries if they lived in a religious community or Secular Tertiaries if they lived as individuals in the secular world; Tertiaries included women's houses as well as men's houses. The other four mendicant orders (Dominicans, Carmelites, Augustinian hermits, and Servites) all had second and third orders.

The second order of the Dominicans remained enclosed and contemplative throughout the early modern period, and remains so today. An order of Carmelite nuns was founded in the Netherlands in 1452, spread rapidly into France, Italy, and Spain, and was later reformed by St Teresa. The second order of the Servites was founded c.1285, and the nuns of the third order were established by St Giuliana Falconieri (1270–1341) in 1306.

Women scarcely feature in the orders of regular clerks (though the Theatines founded a congregation of nuns in 1583), and although Carlo Borromeo assisted in the regulation of the URSULINES, secular congregations excluded women by virtue of the requirement of ordination. In 1610 FRANÇOIS DE SALES and Jeanne-Françoise Frémyot de Chantel (1572–1641) founded the Visitation Order (also known as the Visitandines or Salesian Sisters); a row over enclosure delayed the Order being constituted until 23 April 1618. The first women's order to eschew enclosure altogether was the Institute of Mary, a convent modelled on the rule of the Jesuits which was founded by the Englishwoman Mary Ward (1585–1645) in Munich in 1609; in 1633 her example was followed by St Vincent de Paul (1581–1660), who established the Sisters of Charity.

M. Heimbucher, *Die Orden und Kongregationen der katholischen Kirche* (2 vols., 1933–4); William Johnston (ed.), *Encyclopedia of Monasticism* (2 vols., 2000).

**ORDÓÑEZ, BARTOLOMÉ** (c.1485–c.1520), Spanish sculptor. He is known to have been working in Naples in about 1515 together with Diego de SILOÉ on the marble reredos of the Caracciolo Chapel of the Church of San Giovanni a Carbonara. By 1517 he was in Catalonia, working on the carved decoration of the choir in Barcelona Cathedral, to which he contributed the walnut screens and the *trascoro* (retrochoir) marble screen. He was commissioned by CHARLES V to carve the tomb for Charles's parents (PHILIP I and JUANA LA LOCA) for the Chapel Royal in Granada, but died while working on the tombs with his Italian assistants at Carrara.

MDA; M. Gómez-Moreno, *Las águilas del Renacimento español: Bartolomé Ordóñez, Diego Siloé, Pedro Machuca, Alonso Berruguete* (1941).

**ORELLANA, FRANCISCO DE** (1511–46), Spanish conquistador who participated in the conquest of Peru led by Francisco PIZARRO and in 1537 was given the responsibility of re-establishing the Spanish colony at Guayaquil, in what is now Ecuador. In 1540 he joined Gonzalo PIZARRO's expedition to the eastern side of the Andes in search of EL DORADO, and in December 1541 left the main party with a group of 57 men under his command. Orellana's group entered the upper reaches of the Amazon and then travelled down the river to the Atlantic, arriving in August 1542; only twelve of his men survived the journey, which was the first recorded descent of the Amazon. The river had previously been known to Europeans by a variety of names (Mar Dulce, Río Grande, and Marañón), but Orellana named the river Río de las Amazonas with reference to the female warriors of the Tapuya, who had fought alongside the men when attacking Orellan's expedition; he took the name from the female warriors described in antiquity by Herodotus and Diodorus.

In 1543 Orellana returned to Spain, where he was appointed governor of the lands that he had traversed. He led a colonizing expedition to Brazil in 1546, intending to establish a settlement at the mouth of the Amazon, but many of his prospective settlers died of plague in the Cape Verde Islands, and Orellana died shortly after arriving in Brazil.

DHE; Rafael Díaz Maderuelo, *Francisco de Orellana* (1987).

**ORESME, NICOLE** (*c*.1320–1382), French philosopher and economist, born near Caen (Normandy). He studied theology and became master of the Collège de Navarre in Paris (1356), dean of the chapter of Rouen Cathedral (1364), and bishop of Lisieux (1377). He served King Charles V as a chaplain, and at his behest translated Aristotle's *Nicomachean Ethics* and *Politics* from Latin to French. From the perspective of the early modern period his most important work was *De moneta*, a treatise on money which was first published in 1488 and remained in print for generations.

Émile Bridrey, *Nicole Oresme: La Théorie de la monnaie au XIVᵉ siècle. Étude d'histoire des doctrines et des faits économiques* (1906).

**ORLÉANS, HOUSE OF**. The title of duke of Orléans was created by the VALOIS king Philip VI of France for his son Philip, who died without issue. The second duke was Louis I, a younger son of King Charles V of France who was murdered by the duke of Burgundy (JOHN THE FEARLESS) in 1407. In 1389 Duke Louis I had married Valentina Visconti, daughter of Gian Galeazzo VISCONTI, the ruler of Milan (and from 1395 duke of Milan). Their children included the poet Duke CHARLES D'ORLÉANS (whose son Louis II acceded to the throne of France as LOUIS XII in 1498) and Jean d'Angoulême (the father of Charles d'Angoulême, whose son was King FRANCIS I).

On the death of Filippo Maria VISCONTI, third duke of Milan, on 13 August 1447, the direct male line of the Visconti became extinct, and Charles d'Orléans claimed the succession with the support of King CHARLES VII, who moved troops to Asti (which Duke Louis I had received as dowry). The claim was frustrated by the creation of the AMBROSIAN REPUBLIC and the subsequent rule of Francesco SFORZA. Charles d'Orléans died in 1465 and bequeathed his claim to Milan to his son, who as LOUIS XII invaded Italy in 1499 to claim his inheritance.

**ORLEY, BERNAERT VAN** (*c*.1488–1541), Flemish painter and designer of stained glass and tapestries. He established a studio in Brussels, where in 1518 he became a painter in the court of MARGARET OF AUSTRIA and her successor MARY OF HUNGARY. None of his paintings is dated later than 1530, and

he seems to have spent the last decade of his life designing stained-glass windows (notably the transept windows in the Church of Sainte-Gudule) and tapestries. His tapestries include a series on *The Hunts of Maximilian* (Paris, Louvre); two sets on *The Passion* (one of which survives in the Royal Palace in Madrid), an *Agony in the Garden* and a *Crucifixion* (National Gallery, Washington), a *Christ Carrying the Cross* (Musée Jacquemart-André, Paris), and a *Last Supper* (Metropolitan Museum, New York).

MDA.

**ORSI, LELIO** (1508/11–87), Italian painter and architect, born in Novellara, 20 kilometres (12 miles) north of Reggio nell'Emilia (then part of the ESTE duchy of Modena). He may have been trained in the studio of CORREGGIO. He was banished from Reggio in 1546, and after periods in Venice and Rome returned to Novellara. His frescoes in Reggio and Novellara have perished, but the delicate elegance of paintings such as *The Rest on the Flight into Egypt* (York) shows strong links with Parmesan art and a stylistic debt to PARMIGIANINO. His *Road to Emmaus* (National Gallery, London) recalls the dramatic lighting characteristic of Correggio. His only documented architectural work is the Collegiata di San Stefano in Novellara (1567), for which a study survives in Windsor Castle.

MDA; Vittoria Romani, *Lelio Orsi* (1984).

**ORSINI, VILLA**, a villa in Bomarzo, 21 kilometres (13 miles) north-east of Viterbo. The villa is a converted castle perched on top of a hill, below which a rudimentary terraced garden was constructed on the precipitous slope. The owner of the villa, a member of the ORSINI family, concentrated his imaginative energies on a second garden in the valley at the bottom of the hill, which was constructed between 1552 and 1585. This garden was not laid out, and may not have had an architect, but was instead constructed adventitiously around natural outcrops of volcanic rock protruding from the valley floor. Unknown sculptors carved these outcrops into an extraordinary range of colossal sculptures, including a temple (one of the few conventionally built structures), a leaning house, Etruscan urns, masks, giant humans, naturalistic animals such as elephants and tortoises, and many monsters. Unlike other ITALIAN GARDENS, the layout is not symmetrical, because the stone was carved wherever it was found. Vicino Orsini planted a *BOSCO* around the statues, and referred to the garden in several inscriptions as his sacred wood (*sacro bosco*), with reference to the sacred groves of classical antiquity and the *sacro bosco* of SANNAZARO's *Arcadia* (1504). The sculptors used the rock opportunistically, but it is clear that some of the statues represent the literary characters in ARIOSTO's *Orlando furioso*, and that others reflect an antiquarian interest in the funerary art of classical Rome and ancient Etruria.

The gardens were virtually unknown before the end of the Second World War, when they were described by Mario Praz and filmed by Salvador Dalí.

J. Theurillat, *Les Mystères de Bomarzo et des jardins symboliques de la Renaissance* (1973); Mark Weil and Margaretta Darnall, 'Il Sacro Bosca di Bomarzo: Its Sixteenth-Century Literary and

Antiquarian Context', in *Journal of Garden History*, 4 (1984); H. Bredekamp, *Vicino Orsini und der heilige Wald von Bomarzo* (2 vols., 1985).

**ORSINI FAMILY**, a Roman family which produced large numbers of churchmen, statesmen, and *condottieri* from the twelfth century; the churchmen included a pope in each of the twelfth century (Celestine III), the thirteenth century (Nicholas III), the fourteenth century (Benedict XII), and the eighteenth century (Benedict XIII), the statesmen included Francesco Orsini, prefect of Rome from 1435 and later duke of Gravina, and the *condottieri* included Niccolò Orsini (1442–1510), who commanded the papal army, and Lorenzo Orsini of Ceri (d. 1536), who defended Rome and Castel Sant' Angelo during the SACK OF ROME in 1527. The Orsini held vast territories in the PAPAL STATE to the north of Rome (including the county of Pitigliano), and were the avowed enemies of the COLONNA FAMILY, whose estates lay south of Rome. The fortunes of the family reached their apogee under the successive pontificates of SIXTUS IV (1471–84) and INNOCENT VIII (1484–92), but when Innocent was succeeded by Pope ALEXANDER VI (1492–1513), Cesare BORGIA attacked the Orsini and captured their fortresses at Trevignano and Bracciano; when Alexander was succeeded by JULIUS II (1503–13) and LEO X (1513–21), the fortunes (and the property) of the family were restored. In the sixteenth century the Orsini duke of Bomarzo built the ORSINI VILLA and gardens.

John Webster's *The White Devil: The Tragedy of Paulo Giordano Ursini, Duke of Brachiano* (c.1610) dramatizes a story taken from a FUGGER newsletter about a violent episode in the family's history centred on Paolo Giordano Orsini, his wife Isabella de' Medici, and his lover Vittoria ACCORAMBONI. Paolo Giordano's son Virginio, who succeeded his father as duke of Bracchiano, appears as a boy called Giovanni in the play. Don Virginio Orsini, by now 28 years old, was entertained on Twelfth Night (6 January) 1601 by Queen ELIZABETH, at the palace of Whitehall. The duke subsequently wrote to his wife describing how he had been entertained with a 'mixed comedy with music and dances' ('una commedia mescolata, con musiche e balli'). The comedy was performed by SHAKESPEARE's company, the Lord Chamberlain's Men, so it is possible that the comedy was Shakespeare's *Twelfth Night*, in which the protagonist is Duke Orsino.

G. B. Colonna, *Gli Orsini* (1955).

**ORTA, GARCIA DE** (c.1500–c.1568), Hispano-Portuguese botanist and physician. He was born into a MARRANO family in Spain and studied medicine in Salamanca and Alcalá. In 1526 he moved to Lisbon, where he taught at the university. In 1534 he travelled in the entourage of Martim Afonso de SOUSA to India, where he settled permanently in Goa and practised medicine in the viceregal court. He collected his research on the medicinal plants and drugs of India in his wide-ranging *Coloquios dos simples e drogas e cousas medicinais da India* (Goa, 1563). After his death Orta was condemned by the Portuguese INQUISITION because his profession of Christianity was said to mask a secret observance of the rites of Judaism.

*DSB.*

**ORTELIUS, ABRAHAM** (1527–98), Flemish cartographer, a native of Antwerp who trained as an engraver and in the mid-1550s became a dealer in maps (some of which he coloured), coins, and antiques. His association with MERCATOR drew Ortelius into cartography in the 1560s; his best-known design is a heart-shaped map of the world (1564). In 1570 Ortelius published *Theatrum orbis terrarum*, a collection of 53 maps by various cartographers (including himself); Ortelius later published another seventeen maps as a supplement. By the end of the century the *Theatrum* had been republished in 25 editions and translated into Dutch, French, and German. In 1575 Ortelius was appointed geographer to PHILIP II of Spain.

*DSB; MDA.*

**ORTIZ, DIEGO** (c.1510–c.1570), Spanish composer and theorist in Naples, where he was *maestro de capilla* to the Spanish viceroy Fernando Álvarez de Toledo and his successor Pedro Afan de Riviera. His *Tratado de glosas* (1553) is a didactic manual concerned with bowed string instruments. He also wrote sacred vocal music.

**ORZECHOWSKI, STANISŁAW, or (Latin) Orichovius** (1513–66), Polish writer, a native of Przemyśl who became a Catholic priest and polemicist. His Latin works include a tract opposing compulsory celibacy for the priesthood, which was an impediment for reconciliation with the RUTHENIAN Church, which had a married clergy. His Polish works, which include a defence of theocratic government and a history of Poland under the JAGIEŁŁONIAN dynasty, helped to determine the literary language of Polish prose.

*PSB.*

**OSIANDER, ANDREAS** (1496/8–1552), German Protestant reformer, born in Gunzenhausen (near Nuremberg) on 19 December 1496 (or 1498); his baptismal name was Heiligmann or Hosemann. He studied at Leipzig, Altenburg, and Ingolstadt and was ordained as a priest in 1520. He became a Hebrew tutor in the Augustinian house in Nuremberg and in 1522 was appointed preacher in the St Lorenzkirche.

Osiander became a Lutheran c.1524, and in 1525 he married. He was present at the Colloquy of MARBURG in 1529, at the Augsburg Diet of 1530 (at which the AUGSBURG CONFESSION was presented) and at the signing of the SCHMALKALDIC ARTICLES in 1537. He collaborated with Johannes BRENZ in the formulation of the church order promulgated in Ansbach, Kulmbach, and Nuremberg in 1533, and in the same year published his often-reprinted *Kinderpredigten* on the Catechism.

The introduction of the AUGSBURG INTERIM in 1548 forced Osiander to leave, initially for Breslau (now Polish Wrocław) and then for Königsberg (now Russian Kaliningrad), where ALBRECHT VON PREUSSEN appointed him to a chair in the city's new university. In 1550 he published two disputations, *De lege et evangelio* and *De iustificatione*; in the latter work he opposed Luther's doctrine of JUSTIFICATION by faith on the grounds that the righteousness of Christ is not imputed but substantially transferred to the believer.

The dispute aroused by Osiander's dismissal of Luther's doctrine of IMPUTATION, which is known as the Osiandrist Controversy, was not resolved at his death on 17 October 1552. The Osiandrist party was led by his son-in-law Johann Funck, but disappeared after his execution in 1566. Osiander's son Lukas (1534–1604), who produced an abridgement of the MAGDEBURG CENTURIES, and his grandsons Andreas (1562–1617) and Lukas (1571–1638) were all prominent theologians, and his niece Margaret Osiander married Thomas CRANMER in 1532.

NDB; W. Möller, *Andreas Osiander* (1870; repr. 1965); E. Hirsch, *Die Theologie des Andreas Osiander und ihre geschichtlichen Voraussetzungen* (1919); G. Seebas, *Das reformatorische Werk des Andreas Osiander* (1967).

**OSONA, RODRIGO DE** (c.1440–1518) and **FRANCISCO DE** (c.1465–1514), Spanish painters of the Valencian School of SPANISH ART; a third painter, Rodrigo the Younger, is a ghost, and the paintings assigned to him were executed by Francisco.

The only major painting known to have been executed by Rodrigo de Osona without the assistance of his son Francisco is the *Crucifixion* ALTARPIECE (1476) in the Church of St Nicolau in Valencia. Thereafter father and son collaborated on a series of paintings. The most distinguished paintings by Francisco working without his father are his various pictures of *The Adoration of the Magi*, notably those in the Victoria and Albert Museum in London (signed 'Lo fil de Mestre Rodrigo'), both of which were painted in the first five years of the sixteenth century.

MDA; Ximó Company i Climent, *La pintura dels Osona: Una cruïlla d'hispanismes, flamenquismes i italianismes* (1991).

**OSTENDORFER, MICHAEL** (1490/4–1559), German painter and woodcut artist who worked in Regensburg, where he may have been trained by Albrecht ALTDORFER. His best-known woodcut is a genealogy of the Ottoman sultans illustrated with imaginary portraits; his other woodcuts include many LANDSCAPES. His paintings include at least four versions of *Judith with the Head of Holofernes* (e.g. Wallraf-Richartz Museum, Cologne).

MDA; NDB.

**OTHMAYR, KASPAR** (1515–53), German composer who studied at Heidelberg University and became headmaster of the Latin school of Heilsbronn Monastery. His writing embraced both Catholic and Protestant styles as is evident in the four-part German settings of his *Epitaphium D. Martini Lutheri* (1546) and the contrapuntal, melismatic writing of *Cantilenae aliquot elegantes ac piae* (1546). In addition to his sacred writing there are also German songs and instrumental music.

**OUDENARDE TAPESTRIES**. The Flemish town of Oudenarde (now Oudenaarde) became an important centre for tapestry weaving in the fifteenth century, and by the seventeenth century it had become a rival to Brussels, 50 kilometres (80 miles) to the east. The factories of Oudenarde specialized in furniture tapestries, but also produced VERDURE TAPESTRIES and LANDSCAPES, most of which were woven in blues, greens, and yellows; the tapestries are marked with a pair of spectacles, sometimes attached to a shield. The factories declined in the late seventeenth century as the weavers migrated to France, and the last factory closed in 1787.

**OUWATER, ALBERT VAN** (*fl.* 1440–65), Dutch painter, a native of Haarlem. He was praised by Karel van MANDER as a LANDSCAPE painter, but the only work that can be confidently attributed to Ouwater, *The Raising of Lazarus* (Gemäldegalerie, Berlin), is set in the apse of an imaginary Romanesque church. It is likely that GEERTGEN TOT SINT JANS trained in his studio.

MDA; NNBW x.

**OVANDO, NICOLÁS DE** (c.1451–1511), Spanish governor of Hispaniola. He was an administrator in the military ORDER of Alcántara when in 1502 he was appointed as the third governor of Hispaniola, the successor of COLUMBUS and Francisco BOBADILLA; he left Sanlúcar de Barrameda with a fleet of 30 ships on 13 February 1502. Ovando served as governor for seven years, during which time he completed the conquest of the island and organized the ENCOMIENDAS of the Spanish settlers, for whom he supplied forced Indian labour and imported slaves from Africa and the Bahamas to work in mines and on plantations. He returned to Spain in 1509.

DHE; Ursula Lamb, *Frey Nicolás de Ovando, gobernador de las Indias 1501–1509* (1956).

**OVERBURY, SIR THOMAS** (1581–1613), English writer of characters. His *Characters* (1614–15), based on the Theophrastic model of brief sketches of character types, went through many editions, supplemented by contributions from WEBSTER, DONNE, and DEKKER. His opposition to the marriage of his patron Robert Carr (later earl of Somerset) to the divorced countess of Essex led to his imprisonment in the Tower of London. There he was slowly poisoned by agents of Lady Essex, who were later hanged; Somerset and his wife were convicted but pardoned.

DNB.

**OVID IN THE RENAISSANCE**. The Roman poet Publius Ovidius Naso (43 BC–AD 17) was probably the most widely read ancient poet of the Renaissance. The most popular works were the *Amores* (which recount Ovid's encounters with his mistress Corinna), the *Ars amatoria* (a seduction manual), the *Metamorphoses* (a collection of mythological tales), and the *Epistles from Pontus* (verse letters from his exile in Tomi, now Romanian Constanţa). Ovid's works were first printed in 1471 in two independent *editiones principes*, one published in Rome by PANNARTZ AND SWEYNHEYM and the other in Bologna by Balthazar Azoguidius. Ovid was widely read in Latin and regularly translated into European vernaculars; in England, for example, *Amores* was translated by MARLOWE (posthumously published in 1600), the *Ars amatoria* by T. Creede (1600), and the *Metamorphoses* by Arthur Golding (1567) and George Sandys (1621–6). The *Metamorphoses* is the most common source of classical MYTHOLOGY in Renaissance literature, but Ovid's tales evolved over the centuries, and many Ovidian stories appeared in distinctive versions in the works of the Renaissance mythographers. There was also a tradition of allegorical readings of Ovid, inaugurated by the fourteenth-century *Ovide moralisé* and fully realized in its fifteenth-century imitation, the *Bible des poètes* (which remained in print for much of the sixteenth century).

Ann Moss, *Ovid in Renaissance France: A Survey of the Latin Editions of Ovid and Commentaries Printed in France before 1600* (1982).

**OXENHAM, JOHN** (d. 1575), English privateer. Oxenham was with Drake at the capture of Nombre de Dios (Panama) in 1572. He returned without Drake on a later expedition, marching across the Isthmus and sailing into the Pacific. Whilst resting off the Archipiélago de las Perlas, he and his men captured two small treasure ships and returned to the mainland where they were captured by Spanish soldiers. Oxenham's men were killed at Panama; he was taken to Lima and hanged. Charles Kingsley incorporates the story into *Westward Ho!* (1855), adding a wholly fictional romance with a Spanish lady.

**OXFORD.** The university at Oxford developed in the last decades of the twelfth century, stimulated by a quarrel in 1167 between Henry II and Philip Augustus which prevented English students from attending the University of Paris. Dominican friars established a house of study at Oxford in 1221, and the Franciscans followed three years later. Colleges and halls, where students lived during the course of their studies, were endowed by wealthy patrons, beginning with University College (1249) and Merton (1264). By the mid-sixteenth century, there were fifteen colleges, including the newer foundations of All Souls (1438), Brasenose (refounded in 1502 by William Smyth, bishop of Lincoln), Corpus Christi (founded by Richard FOXE in 1517), and Christ Church (founded by WOLSEY, also in 1517). Until the dissolution of the MONASTERIES, the chancellor of the university was appointed by the bishop of Lincoln, into whose diocese Oxford fell. From the beginning of the sixteenth century, undergraduates were admitted to study at Oxford, and they increasingly began to be sons of wealthy families, rather than the poorer scholars of earlier times.

James McConica (ed.), *The Collegiate University* (1980), vol. iii of *The History of the University of Oxford*, gen. ed. T. H. Aston.

**OXFORD'S MEN.** Acting companies under the patronage of the earls of Oxford are recorded from the late fifteenth century. A new company of Oxford's Men was formed in 1580 under the patronage of Edward De Vere, seventeenth earl of Oxford, courtier, poet, and rival of Philip SIDNEY. The troupe played at the THEATRE, but was later banished to the provinces following a brawl; the group was disbanded in 1602.

# P

**PACELLO DA MERCOGLIANO** (d. 1534), Neapolitan priest and garden designer. In 1495 he entered the service of CHARLES VIII in Naples, and moved to France to work in the royal gardens at AMBOISE; he subsequently worked for LOUIS XII and FRANCIS I at BLOIS and for Cardinal Georges d'AMBOISE at GAILLON. His precise role in these gardens is not documented, but he certainly laid out the PARTERRES and introduced new fruit and vegetables, and he may have been responsible for the overall designs. He is the first gardener known to have grown citrus trees in tubs with a view to moving them into sheltered storage during the winter months.

**PACHECO, FRANCISCO** (1564–1644), Spanish painter and art historian who established a painting academy in Seville, where his pupils included Velázquez, who later married his daughter. His *El arte de la pintura, su antigüedad y grandeza* (Seville, 1649) contains unique material on the history of SPANISH ART. Pacheco also served as a censor of paintings for the INQUISITION. His own paintings, such as the *Immaculate Conception with a Portrait of Miguel Cid* (Seville Cathedral), reflect the transition from MANNERISM to BAROQUE, and their naturalistic elements reflect his conviction that art should serve the Church in its imitation of nature.
*MDA*; Enrique Valdivieso, *Francisco Pacheco* (1990).

**PACHECO PEREIRA, DUARTE.** See PEREIRA, DUARTE PACHECO.

**PACHER, MICHAEL** (*fl.* 1462–98), Austrian painter and woodcarver, a native of the Tirol. His best-known work is the high altar in the Church of St Wolfgang on the Abersee (near Salzburg), which was commissioned in 1471 and completed ten years later; it contains scenes from *The Life of the Virgin* and *The Legend of St Wolfgang*. He was also responsible for the altar at Gries (1471–88), near Bolzano, and for the central panel (*The Baptism of Christ*) of the painted ALTARPIECE (*c.*1479–82) in the north chapel of the Frauenkirche in Munich. Pacher was an innovator in his creation of pictorial space: he excelled in one-point PERSPECTIVE and foreshortening, and the low viewpoint that he habitually adopted created an illusion of monumentality.
*MDA*; *NDB*; Nicolò Rasmo, *Michael Pacher* (1971).

**PACINI, PIERO** (*c.*1440–*c.*1513), Italian printer, a native of Pescia (Tuscany) who established a printing house in Florence, where he became the city's most prominent publisher. His titles, many of which had woodcut illustrations, included Aesop's *Fables* (1496), Petrarch's *Trionfi* (1499), and PULCI's *Morgante* and *Sonetti*.

**PACIOLI, LUCA** (*c.*1445–1517), Italian mathematician. He was born in Borgo Sansepolcro and as a young man moved to Venice, where he became a tutor in the household of a prosperous merchant, Antonio Rompiasi. In 1470 he visited Rome, where he was the guest of Leon Battista ALBERTI. At some time in the early 1470s he was ordained and entered the Franciscan Order. By 1475 he was teaching mathematics at the University of Perugia. For the remainder of his life he was an itinerant teacher of mathematics, a career which took him to universities and courts throughout Italy. He worked for some time at the court of FEDERIGO DA MONTEFELTRO in Urbino and at the court of the SFORZA in Milan (1496–9). In Milan he became friends with LEONARDO DA VINCI, who made drawings of polyhedra to illustrate Pacioli's treatise *De divina proportione* (1509). The work deals with what Euclid calls 'extreme and mean proportion' (*Elements* 6, proposition 3), which in the nineteenth century was given the name 'GOLDEN SECTION'. Pacioli merely cites all the passages in which Euclid uses this proportion, providing glosses only in the form of describing the properties with terms such as 'miraculous' and referring the reader to Euclid for proofs. The connection of the proportion with regular polyhedra is that Euclid uses it to construct the regular pentagon and the regular dodecahedron (which has twelve pentagonal faces). Leonardo's drawings, which have apparently been made from models, using a sighting apparatus, are substitutes for the actual models that accompanied the manuscript of the work presented to the duke of Milan. The third part of *De divina proportione* consists of an Italian text of PIERO DELLA FRANCESCA's short book on the regular solids, presented as if it were Pacioli's own work. This text may be Piero's original vernacular (the work otherwise survives only in a Latin manuscript).

Further evidence that Pacioli may have come into possession of Piero della Francesca's mathematical manuscripts after the painter's death in 1492 is provided by Pacioli's most important work, the *Summa de arithmetica, geometria, proporzioni et proportionalità* (1494), in which the kind of textbook used in ABACUS SCHOOLS first finds its way into print. Many of the problems in the *Summa* are clearly derived from Piero della Francesca's abacus treatise, but Pacioli often provides different or neater procedures for solving them. VASARI was to complain that Pacioli had plagiarized Piero's work, but this is an anachronistic judgement. Moreover, at least in the *Summa*, Pacioli had treated Piero in the same way as Piero had treated his own predecessors. This kind of mathematics contains a very heavy element of tradition. It was once believed that Pacioli had been Piero's pupil, but recent researches have shown that this is overwhelmingly unlikely.

Pacioli was the first to write about double-entry bookkeeping, but it is not known whether he invented it.

DSB; J. B. Geijsbeek-Molenaar (ed.), *Ancient Double-Entry Bookkeeping: Luca Pacioli's Treatise* (1974); R. H. Parker and B. S. Yamey (eds.), *Accounting History: Some British Contributions* (1994); Enrico Giusti (ed.), *Luca Pacioli e la matematica del Rinascimento* (1998).

**PACIOTTO, FRANCESCO** (1521–91), Italian architect and military engineer, born in Urbino, where he was trained by Gerolamo GENGA. He worked in Rome and entered the service of the FARNESE family, acting as tutor to Alessandro FARNESE (from 1553) and designing the *cittadella* (now the Palazzo Farnese) in Piacenza (1558) for Alessandro's mother MARGARET OF PARMA; the *cittadella* has a fine arcaded courtyard, but was never completed.

In 1558, shortly after drawing up the plans for the *cittadella*, Paciotto accompanied Margaret of Parma and Alessandro Farnese to the Netherlands, where King PHILIP II (Margaret's half-brother) commissioned Paciotto to design a viceregal palace in Brussels; the palace was never built. In 1559 Paciotto built harbour defences in Nice for EMANUELE FILIBERTO, duke of Savoy, and in 1561 he went to Spain to work on designs for the ESCORIAL. In 1567 he built a military fortress in Antwerp (destroyed 1874). In 1568 he returned to Italy, and spent the rest of his career as a military architect in the service of various Italian princes.

MDA.

**PADILLA, JUAN DE** (1468–c.1522), Spanish poet also known as El Cartujano ('the Carthusian'), a monk at the Charterhouse of Santa María de las Cuevas in Seville. His surviving works include two long religious poems, the *Retablo sobre la vida de nuestro redentor Jesú Cristo* (Alcalá de Henares, 1505) and *Los doce triunfos de los doce apóstoles* (Seville, 1521); the latter poem is an allegory in imitation of DANTE.

J. Gimeno, 'Sobre el Cartujano y sus críticos', *Hispanic Review*, 29 (1961).

**PADILLA, JUAN LÓPEZ DE** (1490–1521), Spanish rebel leader, born in Toledo; he was the eldest son of the *commendador mayor* of Castile in the Order of Santiago. In May 1520 he emerged as the leader of the insurrectionists in the Revolt of the COMUNEROS against CHARLES V. His forces captured the

castle at Tordesillas where Queen JUANA LA LOCA was incarcerated, vainly hoping that she could lead a national government. Padilla subsequently proposed reforms that alienated aristocratic support for the revolt, and was deposed as leader in favour of the aristocratic Pedro Girón. After his successor's defeat, Padilla was reinstated, but after several military successes his army was defeated at Villalar (near Toro) on 23 April 1521; Padilla was captured and publicly executed the following day. His widow María Pacheco defended Toledo against the royal army for six months, but then had to flee in defeat to Portugal.

DHE.

**PADUA or (Italian) Padova or (Latin) Patavium**, a city on the river Bacchiglione, in Veneto. For most of the fourteenth century (1318–88, 1390–1405), Padua was ruled by a succession of nine members of the CARRARA FAMILY; in the two-year interregnum (1388–90), the city was held by Gian Galeazzo VISCONTI of Milan. From 1405 to 1797, except for a brief revolt in 1509 during the wars of the League of CAMBRAI, Padua was ruled by Venice. Under Venetian rule, the city was governed by two Venetian patricians (a *podestà* for civil affairs and a *capitano* for military security), each elected for a term of sixteen months.

The prosperity of the city was reflected in the grandeur of its medieval architecture. The Basilica del Santo (1232–1307) was built to contain the miracle-working bones of St Anthony of Padua (1195–1231), and became an important pilgrimage church; the preaching of BERNARDINO of Siena in the early fifteenth century enhanced St Anthony's profile and raised pilgrim numbers. The Palazzo della Ragione (1172–1210) contains on its upper floor a vast *salone* which was originally three chambers but after a fire in 1420 was converted into a single room (80 metres long, 28 metres wide, and 25 metres high (260 feet by 90 feet by 80 feet)) which is covered by a roof (built in 1306) which was for centuries the largest roof in Europe unsupported by columns. In the sixteenth century, the cathedral was rebuilt (1552) and the Palazzo del Capitano (1532) erected for the Venetian *capitani*; beside the palazzo there is an elegant Renaissance loggia called the Loggia del Consiglio.

The University of Padua was founded by the Emperor Friedrich III in 1238, and under Venetian rule the university was governed by a board of three patricians called the Riformatori dello Studio di Padova. The staff and students of the university include BEMBO, FALLOPPIO, GALILEO, Cardinal POLE, Pietro POMPONAZZI, Julius Caesar SCALIGER, Sperone SPERONI, TASSO, and VESALIUS; the university's BOTANICAL GARDEN of 1545 is arguably the oldest in Europe and its ANATOMY theatre of 1594 has been preserved.

The Paduan artist Francesco SQUARCIONE painted with an awareness of ancient art, and his influence, variously described as a Paduan style or school, can be discerned in other painters who were trained in Padua, including MANTEGNA, Giorgio SCHIAVONE, and Marco ZOPPO. The frescoes in the Arena Chapel (built in 1303 as part of a palace that was demolished in 1820) are the work of GIOTTO and the equestrian statue of the Paduan condottiere GATTAMELATA in front of the Basilica del Santo is the work of DONATELLO, as is the high altar of the basilica. In the Oratorio di San Giorgio, beside the basilica, 21 frescoes were painted in 1377 by ALTICHIERO and his pupils; in the adjoining Scuola di Sant'Antonio, four of the sixteenth-century frescoes are by TITIAN.

Padua was the headquarters of the cavalry of Venice, and the presence of large numbers of horses of high quality, together with the interest in chivalry evinced by many of the university's students, led to the establishment of many schools of equitation, which in turn secured for Padua a place on the grand tours being undertaken by young aristocrats from all over Europe. The musical life of Padua produced a form of DANCE known as the *padovano*, which evolved into the PAVAN.

Benjamin Kohl, *Padua under the Carrara, 1318–1405* (1998); id., *Culture and Politics in Early Renaissance Padua* (2001).

**PAGANO OR PAGINI, MATEO** (*fl.* 1530–59), Italian fabric designer, and the author of a series of pattern books (all published in Venice) for floral and geometrical designers in CUTWORK, LACE (including *PUNTO IN ARIA*), and RETICELLA. His books, all of which are now exceedingly rare, include *Giardinetto nuovo di punti tagliati* (1542), *Ornamento de le belle et virtudiose donne* (1543), *Il speccio di pensieri delle belle et virtudiose donne* (1544), *L'onesto essempio* (1553), *Specchio di virtù* (1554), *La gloria e l'onore de punti tagliati e punti in aere* (1558), and *Trionfo di virtù* (1559).

**PAGNINI, SANTI, or (Latin) Santes Pagninus** (d. 1541), Italian biblical scholar. He was born in Lucca and as a young man entered the Dominican Order. His formidable command of biblical Hebrew and Greek led to an invitation from Pope LEO X to teach in Rome, where in about 1518 he completed a literal translation of the Bible from Hebrew and Greek into Latin. His Bible was the first complete translation by a modern scholar, and was the first to introduce numbered verses. The first edition was published in Lyon in 1527, and the second in Cologne in 1541; it was used extensively by COVERDALE in the preparation of the Great Bible. Pagnini also compiled a Hebrew lexicon that was regularly reprinted and widely consulted all over Europe.

T. M. Centi, 'L'attività letteraria di Santi Pagnini nel campo della scienze bibliche', *Archivum Fratrum Praedicatorum*, 15 (1945).

**PAINTER, WILLIAM** (*c.*1540–1594), English translator and Clerk of the ordnance. Painter published the *Palace of Pleasure*, a collection of translations, in 1566. Twenty-five tales from BANDELLO, Livy's accounts of the origins of Rome, and histories and stories from BOCCACCIO, Herodotus, and others are included. SHAKESPEARE (*The Rape of Lucrece, All's Well That End's Well, Much Ado About Nothing*) and WEBSTER (*The Duchess of Malfi*) found source material here.

DNB.

**PALACES.** The residence of the Emperor Augustus on the Palatine Hill (Mons Palatinus) in Rome was known as the *palatium*, and it is this classical term that underlies the Renaissance idea of the palace. In Italy the term *palazzo* had no princely or gubernatorial associations, but simply meant a large city dwelling, the urban equivalent of a VILLA; many occupants of *palazzi* were wealthy merchants. In England, France, and Spain the terms 'palace', *palais*, and *palacio* were used for royal and episcopal residences; in France the term *palais* was also used for buildings representing the authority of the crown, such as courts of justice, but large urban residences were known as *hôtels* and large country houses as CHÂTEAUX; the notion of imperial or regal authority is also implied by the terms PALATINATE (German Pfalz) and palatine.

In Italy, the architecture of the Renaissance *palazzo* reflected its origins as a fortified house, characteristically with vaulted ground-floor shop fronts opening onto the street, and the main apartments on the floor above (*piano nobile*) which could be reached by a stone staircase (*scala*) rising from an inner courtyard (*cortile*). The Gothic *palazzo*, of which the finest examples are the Palazzo Vecchio and the Bargello in Florence and the older portions of the Ducal Palace in Venice, was gradually superseded by the Renaissance palace, in which the vaulted shop fronts were filled in, corner towers reduced or eliminated, and the classical ORDERS introduced in façades (e.g. ALBERTI's Palazzo Rucellai in Florence). Luciano LAURANA's Ducal Palace in Urbino (1465–72) exercised considerable influence on such Roman palaces as the papal Cancellaria and the Quirinal; the Palazzo Farnese built by Antonio SANGALLO the Younger introduced to Rome the Vitruvian idea of the symmetrical façade. The SACK OF ROME in 1527 forced patrons and architects to leave the city, and palaces with Roman features soon appeared throughout northern Italy, particularly in SANMICHELI's palaces in Verona and PALLADIO's in Vicenza. The Venetian palace remained distinctive, because the combination of political stability and the aquatic barrier of the lagoon meant that large houses had never been heavily fortified; instead, there was typically an entrance on the canal façade sufficiently capacious to accommodate the unloading of merchandise from boats, and the upper floors of the canal façade were typically pierced with glazed windows (the GLASS was made on Murano) that were virtually unknown elsewhere in Italy. Palaces designed by SANSOVINO retained these features in a classicized form, and CODUSSI's palaces introduced the classical orders. In Genoa, where a distinctive type of palace design had evolved, the Perugian architect Galeazzo ALESSI designed the palaces of the Genoese patricians in the 1550s. If villas were sufficiently large, the term *palazzo* was sometimes used, as in the Palazzo del TÈ in Mantua and the Villa FARNESE at Caprarola, which is also known as the Palazzo Farnese.

Engravings and architectural treatises disseminated Italian designs for palaces all over Europe. In France, the most important palaces were the LOUVRE, the TUILERIES (destroyed 1871), SAINT-GERMAIN-EN-LAYE and the chateaus of AMBOISE, BLOIS, CHAMBORD, CHENONCEAUX, and FONTAINEBLEAU. In Spain, the most important Renaissance palaces were the ESCORIAL and the imperial palace (now called the Palacio de Carlos V) in Granada built by Pedro MACHUCA for the

Emperor CHARLES V. In Germany, Italian ideas informed the transformation of the medieval castle in HEIDELBERG into a Renaissance palace. In England, WOLSEY's palace at Hampton Court contains some Renaissance decorative motifs, and Nonsuch Palace (1538–47) was designed in the Renaissance style. The greatest plan for an English palace, Inigo JONES's Palace of Whitehall, was never fully realized; the BANQUETING HOUSE was completed and survived the fire of 1691, but other additions, none of which was finished, were destroyed.

Christoph Frommel, *Die römische Palastbau der Hochrenaissance* (3 vols., 1973).

**PALATINA, BIBLIOTHECA.** The library of the University of Heidelberg, capital of the PALATINATE, was established in 1386, the year after the university opened, and was long housed in the Heilige-Geist-Kirche (built 1400–36). Sixteenth-century electors added substantially to the library, and in 1584 Ulrich FUGGER of the Augsburg banking dynasty donated a large collection of books and manuscripts. By the time the city fell to the forces of Maximilian I of Bavaria in 1622, the library consisted of 3,542 manuscripts and c.5,000 books. Maximilian shipped the library to Rome, where it was presented to Pope Gregory XV and housed in the VATICAN LIBRARY. Much of the library remains in the Vatican as the Biblioteca Palatina, but in 1816 the Vatican restored 852 manuscripts (which had been taken to Paris) to Heidelberg.

**PALATINATE or (German) Pfalz.** The title 'count palatine' (Latin *comes palatinus*, German *Pfalzgraf*, from Latin *palatinus*, 'belonging to the palace') is used in medieval and early modern documents for a large number of rulers whose authority derived from the HOLY ROMAN EMPIRE and included the rulers of Hungary, Poland, Lithuania, and Burgundy.

The term 'Palatinate' is usually used with reference to the Rhineland Palatinate, a large principality on both banks of the middle Rhine of which the capital is HEIDELBERG. The name was instituted in 1155, when the Emperor Friedrich Barbarossa conferred the title of 'count palatine' on his half-brother Konrad. In 1329 the Palatinate passed to the WITTELSBACH FAMILY of Bavaria, and the Golden Bull of 1356 confirmed the count palatine as the principal secular elector of the Empire. Under the Wittelsbachs the terms 'Rhenish Palatinate' and 'Electoral Palatinate' were used to distinguish this region from the Upper Palatinate (Oberpfalz) in Bavaria.

The Elector Friedrich I (elector 1449–76) extended the territories of the Palatinate of the Rhine into Alsace and north along the Rhine. In 1556 the Elector Otto Heinrich made Lutheranism the state religion of the Palatinate. He died without a male heir, and the electorate passed to another branch of the family, the dukes of Simmern. On his accession in 1561 FRIEDRICH III, duke of Simmern, established Calvinism in the Palatinate and became a supporter of the HUGUENOTS in France and the Calvinist rebels in the REVOLT OF THE NETHERLANDS. His son Ludwig VI (elector 1576–83) reverted to Lutheranism, but on his death JOHANN CASIMIR (regent 1583–92) ruled on behalf of his nephew Friedrich IV and

reintroduced Calvinism. Friedrich IV (ruled 1592–1610) was one of the architects of the German Protestant Union of 1608. In 1619, Friedrich V, the Winter King who was married to Elizabeth, daughter of King JAMES, accepted the throne of Bohemia, as a consequence of which the Palatinate suffered extensive damage during the THIRTY YEARS WAR.

In Britain the term 'Palatine' is sometimes used with reference to the six 'counties palatine' (the 'spiritual palatinates' of Durham and Ely and the 'temporal palatinates' of Lancaster, Chester, Shrewsbury, and Pembroke) and the American palatine provinces of Maryland (1632), Maine (1639), and Carolina (1663). In England the counties palatine developed independent legal systems: the palatine court of Chester survived until 1830 and Durham and Lancaster maintained independent courts of chancery until 1971.

In Rome the term *Palatine* refers to the Palatine Hill, the *Mons Palatinus* on which Augustus built the first imperial palace, and to the Biblioteca PALATINA. The cognate term 'paladin' is used in the courtly romances of Charlemagne to denote the *douzepers* (the twelve peers or paladins of Charlemagne, of whom the 'count palatine' was the foremost) and, in a transferred sense, in the romances of King Arthur to denote the knights of the Round Table.

**PALE**, a district distinguished from the surrounding country by political boundaries or by a distinct system of government; the term refers in its origins to palings, or fenceposts, and so to an enclosed area 'within the pale'. The term is often used with reference to Ireland, where from about 1395 an area around Dublin remained within the jurisdiction of ENGLISH LAW rather than the BREHON LAWS of Ireland. By 1495, when the Irish Parliament summoned by Sir Edward Poyning decreed that a double ditch be constructed around the Pale to prevent cattle-raiding, the Pale consisted of Dublin, Kildare, Louth, and Meath; in the late sixteenth century it was extended to include most of Leinster and Meath. Within the Pale, residents were required to be armed to defend the land and to be ready to undertake military duties when required to do so.

There was an English pale around CALAIS from 1347 to 1558, extending in a curve from Gravelines to Wissant, and for a short time (1545–9) there was also an English Pale of Scotland. The English phrase 'beyond the pale' gradually lost its technical sense of 'beyond the jurisdiction of English law' and came to mean 'unacceptable'.

**PALESTRINA, GIOVANNI PIERLUIGI DA** (1525/6–94), Italian composer who was first employed as organist at the cathedral in Palestrina (near Rome). From 1551 he was *magister cantorum* at the the Cappella Giulia until 1555 when he moved briefly to the Cappella Sistina. He was *maestro di cappella* at the churches of San Giovanni Laterano and Santa Maria Maggiore and at the Seminario Romano, as well as directing the music at Cardinal Ippolito d'Este's villa in Tivoli. From 1571 he was *maestro di cappella* at the Cappella Giulia where he remained, enhancing his income with freelance work elsewhere in Rome.

Palestrina was a prolific composer, his *œuvre* comprising 104 mass settings, at least 300 motets, 68 offertories, 72 hymns, 35 Magnificats, 11 litanies, several lamentations, and over 140 madrigals. His work was reprinted and his fame spread far beyond Italy. Revered by his contemporaries and recognized and republished in the nineteenth century, one of his most telling achievements was to absorb and reflect the guidelines on the style of sacred music that emerged from the 1563 COUNCIL OF TRENT, above all in his second and third books of motets (1572 and 1575). Further reform of Catholic music occurred in his revision of the plainsongs in the Roman Gradual and Antiphoner.

**PALINGENIUS or (Italian) Pier Angelo Manzoli** (*c.*1500–*c.*1543), Italian neo-Latin poet. He was born in La Stellata (near Ferrara), and became a member of the Ferrara court of RENÉE DE FRANCE, which Calvin visited in 1536. Palingenius wrote *Zodiacus vitae* (1535–6), a long poem in Latin hexameters; the poem reflects the Calvinist perspective of Palingenius, and so was suppressed by the Roman INQUISITION. The *Zodiacus vitae* was well received by Protestants elsewhere in Europe: the poem became the principal model for Mikołaj REJ's *Wizerunek* (1558), and the first six books were translated into English by Barnabe Googe (1565).

*OCIL.*

**PALISSY, BERNARD** (*c.*1510–1590), French potter and natural historian, born in Agen, where he trained as a glass painter. He established a workshop in Saintes (*c.*1542), which was on a pilgrim route to Santiago de Compostela, and in the course of sixteen years of experiments (1538–54) developed a pure white ENAMEL that could be used for the decoration of pottery. His enamelled pottery attracted the patronage of MONTMORENCY, for whom Palissy made a pottery GROTTO for the constable's château at Écouen (1555). In 1562 Palissy was imprisoned in Bordeaux for preaching HUGUENOT doctrine, but he was released through the intervention of Montmorency. Soon after his release Palissy moved to La Rochelle, where he published his *Recette véritable par laquelle tous les hommes de France pourront apprendre à multiplier leurs trésors*.

In 1566 Palissy moved to Paris, where his principal patron was CATHERINE DE MÉDICIS, who commissioned a ceramic grotto (decorated with terracotta figures) in the TUILERIES GARDENS (*c.*1573). His richly enamelled dishes and bowls were decorated with reptiles (on which he was an authority), fish, insects, and plants that (like JAMNITZER in Germany) he had cast from specimens; he also used casts of silver and pewter dishes to make pottery replicas. The quality of his reptilian dishes was recognized with the title 'inventor of the king's rustic pottery' (*inventeur des rustiques figulines du roi*), which afforded a measure of protection against the persecutors of Protestants.

In 1575 Palissy began to lecture on scientific subjects, and in 1580 he published his *Discours admirable de la nature des eaux et fontaines*, which contains an essay on 'L'Art de terre' in which Palissy describes his sixteen years as a potter. He was imprisoned for heresy in 1585 and died as a prisoner in the Bastille du Bucy. Little of his pottery has survived intact, but some 5,000 fragments have been excavated from the Tuileries and in land close to the Louvre.

*MDA*; Marguerite Boudon-Duaner, *Bernard Palissy: Le Potier du Roi* (1989); Leonard Amico, *Bernard Palissy: In Pursuit of Earthly Paradise* (1996).

**PALLADIO, ANDREA, or Andrea di Pietro della Gondola** (1508–80), Italian architect. He was born in Padua and grew up in Vicenza, where he became a stonemason. In about 1536 he secured the patronage and personal interest of Gian Giorgio TRISSINO, who named him Palladio (from Pallas, the epithet of the Roman goddess Minerva and the name of a character in *Italia liberata dai Gothi*, which Trissino was then writing) and inducted him into mathematics, music, and Latin literature (especially VITRUVIUS).

In 1545 Trissino took Palladio to Rome, where for two years he studied the surviving remains of ancient architecture. On returning to Vicenza in 1547 Palladio won the competition to recase the Palazzo della Ragione, which because of its interior design and Palladio's exterior is known as the Basilica Palladiana, even though it is a secular building. Palladio started work in 1549, surrounding the building with two superimposed galleries in the Doric and Ionic ORDERS, and the rebuilding was eventually completed in 1614; the ugly roof is not Palladio's, but is rather a product of rebuilding after the Second World War. This building established Palladio's reputation, and thereafter he was permanently engaged in the design and construction of palaces, villas, and churches.

Palladio's Vicenza buildings began with the completion of the Palazzo Thiene (started 1542), in which heavy rustication covers the entire exterior, including the Ionic columns. He then turned to Palazzo Porto (1548–52, now Palazzo Porto-Colleoni), which has a symmetrical layout and a façade which is indebted to BRAMANTE and RAPHAEL. Palazzo Chiericati (1550, now the Museo Civico) is an imitation of a Roman forum. Palazzo Valmarana (begun 1565) is a mannerist building in which pilasters and other architectural decorations cover most of the exterior. The Loggia del Capitaniato (1571) is an extravagant mannerist creation covered in relief. Palladio's last commission in Vicenza was the Teatro Olimpico, a recreation of an ancient THEATRE begun in 1580 and completed by Palladio's pupil Vincenzo SCAMOZZI.

From 1537 to 1542 Palladio built his first VILLA, the Villa Godi-Malinverni at Lonedo di Lugo (north of Vicenza), which in its walled courtyard and its symmetrical wings and façade adumbrates many of Palladio's later designs. His villas around Vicenza include the severe Villa Poiana (1540s), Villa Quinto (*c.*1550; the façade resembles an ancient temple), the austere La Malcontenta (1559–61) near Fusina on the Brenta, Villa BARBARO at Maser (late 1550s), Villa Emo at Fanzolo (1560–5; a plain building without window surrounds), and La Rotonda (1567; an elaborate building, modelled on the Roman Pantheon, with porticoes on all four sides). Most of his villas have colonnades, often curved, reaching out (in Palladio's metaphor) like arms to welcome those who approach the house.

The Villa Rotonda in Vicenza, designed by **Palladio** and completed by Vincenzo SCAMOZZI

Palladio's Venetian churches include San Giorgio Maggiore (1565–80, on an islet opposite the Doge's Palace), Il Redentore (begun 1577 in thanksgiving for deliverance from plague the previous year), and the façade of San Francesco della Vigna (1562); the façades all have porticoes like those on ancient temples.

In 1554 Palladio published *Le antichità di Roma* and *Descrizione delle chiese . . . di Roma*. He subsequently illustrated Daniele BARBARO's edition of Vitruvius (1556). In 1570 he published his *I quattro libri dell'architettura*, which sets out the principles of his architecture and illustrates many of his buildings. The far-reaching influence of this book extended to England (e.g. Inigo JONES's BANQUETING HOUSE) and the Palladian movement of the eighteenth century.

*MDA*; J. Ackerman, *Palladio* (1966); Paul Holberton, *Palladio's Villas: Life in the Renaissance Countryside* (1990); Caroline Constant, *The Palladio Guide* (2nd edn. 1993).

**PALLADIUS, PEDER** (1503–60), Danish reformer. He was a priest in Odense when he converted to Protestantism. He studied in Wittenberg from 1531 to 1537, and on returning to Denmark with BUGENHAGEN was appointed bishop of Zeeland by King CHRISTIAN III; this bishopric is the senior ecclesiastical office in Denmark, and it enabled Palladius to support Bugenhagen in his reorganization of the Danish Church and the University of Copenhagen as rigorously Lutheran institutions. His *Visitatsbog* ('Visitation Book') is one of the founding texts of Danish Lutheranism.

*DBL.*

**PALLAVICINO, BENEDETTO** (1551–1601), Italian composer and monk who was organist in Cremona and, from 1579, in the service of the Gonzaga at Sabbioneta and Mantua, where he moved in circles that included Giaches de WERT, Giovanni GASTOLDI, Salamone ROSSI, and Claudio MONTEVERDI. His secular works, which included ten books of madrigals, were popular and technically innovative; his sacred music consists of mass settings and polychoral psalms.

**PALMA GIOVANE or Jacopo Negretti** (*c.*1548–1628), Italian painter, born in Venice, the son of a painter and the great-nephew of PALMA VECCHIO; he was trained in the studios of his father and (probably) of TITIAN, whose *Pietà* (Accademia, Venice) he was to complete after Titian's death in 1576. In the mid-1560s Palma Giovane worked in Urbino and Rome, returning *c.*1570 to Venice, where his commissions included large allegorical and narrative paintings for the Sala del Maggior Consiglio in the Ducal Palace. His finest surviving work is the cycle *The Doge Pasquale Cicogna* in the Oratorio dei Crociferi (1583–95). In the first quarter of the seventeenth century he was widely regarded as the pre-eminent painter in Venice.

*MDA.*

**PALMA VECCHIO or Jacopo Negretti** (*c.*1480–1528), Italian painter. He was born in Serimalta (Lombardy) and spent his short working life in Venice, where he first appears in the documentary record in 1510. Although he painted a small number of altarpieces and portraits, most of his surviving paintings (none of which is signed or dated) are richly sensuous female half-figures, a genre introduced to Venice by GIORGIONE. Many of these paintings depict mythological figures (e.g. *Flora*, National Gallery, London) or religious scenes (e.g. *St Barbara with Four Saints*, Church of Santa Maria Formosa, Venice).

MDA; Philip Rylands, *Palma Vecchio* (1992).

**PALMEZZANO, MARCO** (*c*.1459/63–1539), Italian painter, born in Forlì, where he trained in the studio of MELOZZO DA FORLÌ, several of whose frescoes he later completed. His many surviving paintings are mostly on religious subjects, but include a small number of portraits. His best-known painting is the altarpiece of *St Anthony Abbot and Other Saints* (Pinacoteca Civile, Forlì).

MDA; Carlo Grigoni, *Marco Palmezzano pittore forlivese* (1956).

**PALMIERI, MATTEO** (1406–75), Italian humanist, born into a prosperous merchant family in Florence, where he received a humanist education and then entered the service of the republic. His historical *De temporibus suis*, which covered the 1,000 years from the Council of Ephesus in 449 to the abdication of the antipope FELIX V in 1449, was one of earliest attempts to write a comprehensive history of medieval Europe. His Italian works include a dialogue on citizenship, *Della vita civile* (in which one of the four speakers is Palmieri), and a long Dantesque poem, *La città di vita*.

**PALSGRAVE, JOHN** (*c*.1480–1554), English writer on French. Educated at Cambridge and Paris, Palsgrave was ordained and became tutor to Princess Mary, sister of HENRY VIII. He accompanied her to France on her marriage to LOUIS XII. He was later tutor to Henry Fitzroy, duke of Richmond, Henry's illegitimate son. His *L'Éclaircissement de la langue française* (1530) is the earliest French grammar in English; it is also a source for many obsolete English words and phrases.

**PALUDANUS, GULIELMUS, or (Dutch) Willem van den Broeck** (1530–80), Flemish sculptor who may have been born in Mechelen (French Malines); he joined the Guild of Artists in Antwerp in 1557 and became a burgher in 1559. He worked on Cornelis FLORIS's Town Hall for Antwerp, carving many of the architectural details. His alabaster relief of the *Crucifixion* in the Maximilianmuseum in Augsburg is one of five alabaster reliefs commissioned in 1560 for an altar in the Dominikanerkirche (now the Roman Museum) in Augsburg. Italianate elements in the work of Paludanus have been used to hypothesize an otherwise unrecorded visit to Italy, but it is equally possible that he knew the work of Italians at the imperial court in Brussels (e.g. Leone LEONI, who was there from 1556 to 1559). His terracotta statuette of *St Bartholomew* (dated 1569), now in the Kunsthistorisches Museum in Vienna, seems to imply a familiarity with the work of GIAMBOLOGNA.

BNB s.v. Paludanus, Guillaume; *MDA* s.v. Broeck, van den.

**PANELLING.** The interior walls of houses first began to be panelled in wood in fifteenth-century Flanders, and from Flanders the practice spread throughout northern Europe. The 'linenfold' panelling of the period was so named because it represents or resembles LINEN arranged in vertical folds.

Panelling was also used for the construction of FURNITURE such as beds, chests, and cupboards, and the development of joined panelling in Flanders at the beginning of the fifteenth century created lighter furniture than was possible with construction in planks. At the end of the sixteenth century the advent of the mitred diagonal joint enabled each panel to be individually framed.

**PANNARTZ, ARNOLD, AND KONRAD SWEYNHEYM** (*fl.* 1463–77), German printers. They were apprenticed in Mainz, possibly in GUTENBERG's workshop, and in 1463 moved to Italy, where they established the first printing press outside Germany in the Benedictine abbey of Subiaco (near Rome). Their publication in 1465 of an edition of CICERO's *De oratore* was set in a round type that was the first example of Roman type. The printers secured the patronage of Cardinal Juan de TORQUEMADA and so were able to move to Rome, where between 1468 and 1472 they published 46 editions of classical and patristic texts, each of which had a print run of 275 copies; prefaces to their classical texts were supplied by Giovanni BUSSI. Sweynheym prepared the copperplate maps for their press's edition of Ptolemy's *Cosmographia*, but he died before the edition was published in 1478.

Edwin Hall, *Sweynheym and Pannartz and the Origins of Printing in Italy* (1991).

**PANNEMAKER FAMILY,** Flemish weavers whose workshop produced BRUSSELS TAPESTRIES. Pieter Pannemaker the Elder (*fl.* 1517–32) worked in the tapestry factory of Pieter van Aelst (d. *c*.1530), who in 1514 received a commission from Pope LEO X to weave tapestries from RAPHAEL's cartoons of the *Acts of the Apostles*. In 1518 Pieter the Elder secured the imperial patronage of MAXIMILIAN I and he later received commissions from MARGARET OF AUSTRIA. His sons Pieter the Younger and Willem (*fl.* 1535–78) also enjoyed the patronage of the HABSBURGS. The huge output of the Pannemaker workshop included the weaving of a series of twelve tapestries designed by Jan VERMEYEN to commemorate CHARLES V's attack on TUNIS in 1535.

BNB s.v. Pannemaker, Guillaume de; *MDA*.

**PANNONIUS, JANUS, or János Česmički** (1434–72), Hungarian humanist educated in Ferrara under GUARINO DA VERONA. He subsequently studied CANON LAW in Padua. On his return to Hungary he was appointed bishop of Pécs (1459) and joined the court of MATTHIAS CORVINUS. His writings include translations of Plutarch and Homer and a corpus of Latin poems which includes an elegy addressed to MANTEGNA.

**PANORMITA, IL.** See BECCADELLI, ANTONIO.

**PANORMITANUS or Nicolò de' Tudeschi or Abbas Modernus or Siculus** (1386–1445), archbishop, cardinal, and canonist, born in Catania (Sicily). He entered the Benedictine ORDER (*c*.1400) and, after studying under the canonist Francesco Zabarella (1360–1417), taught at Bologna, Parma, Siena, and Florence. In 1425 he became abbot of Maniaco (near Messina) and in 1435 was appointed archbishop of Palermo (Latin Panormus, hence his adopted name).

In 1433 Panormitanus travelled to the COUNCIL OF BASEL as the representative of Pope EUGENIUS IV, but was persuaded by the arguments of the conciliarists and defended his position in *Tractatus de Concilia Basiliensi*, an important document in the CONCILIAR MOVEMENT. In 1436 he returned to Rome, not as the envoy of Pope Eugenius but as the ambassador of King ALFONSO V of Aragon and the champion of Alfonso's claim to the throne of Naples. Pope Eugenius favoured the candidacy of RENÉ D'ANJOU, so Panormitanus supported the rival pope, FELIX V (who raised Panormitanus to the cardinalate); once Alfonso secured the crown of Naples in 1443, and Pope Eugenius acknowledged Alfonso's right to the throne, Panormitanus (and many bishops) deserted Pope Felix in favour of Pope Eugenius.

Panormitanus wrote on a variety of topics in CANON LAW, including commentaries on the *Decretals* of Gregory IX (*In quinque decretalium libros commentaria*, 1475) and on the *Clementines* (*Glossae in Clementinas*, 1474).

K. W. Nörr, *Kirche und Konzil bei Nicolaus de Tudeschis (Panormitanus)* (1964).

**PANVINIO, ONOFRIO** (1530–68), Italian humanist, epigrapher, and antiquarian, born in Verona and educated there and in Padua and Naples. He became an Augustinian monk and entered the service of Cardinal Alessandro Farnese, who financed Panvinio's antiquarian studies. He amassed a collection of some 3,000 ancient Roman inscriptions which formed the basis of a large range of antiquarian subjects, including family history, the Roman triumph, ancient sport, the Sibylline books, and especially ancient Roman names. A portrait of Panvinio formerly attributed to TITIAN hangs in the Galleria Colonna in Rome.

*MDA.*

**PAOLO DA VERONA** (*fl.* 1470–1516), Italian embroiderer praised by VASARI as the greatest exponent of EMBROIDERY. Vasari believed Paolo to be the sole embroiderer of the scenes from the life of St John the Baptist on vestments known as the Paramento di San Giovanni, which were designed by Antonio POLLAIUOLO (and are now in the Museo dell'Opera del Duomo in Florence); in fact, work on the vestments began in 1466 and Paolo did not join the team of embroiderers until 1470.

**PAPACY**, the term that refers both to the office of pope and to the centralized church government of which the pope is the head. The term 'pontiff' (Latin *pontifex*) could be used of any bishop in the Western medieval Church, but was increasingly reserved for the pope, the 'sovereign pontiff' (Latin *pontifex maximus*, Italian *sommo pontefice*, French *souverain pontife*). The term 'pope' (Greek πάπα or πάππα, Latin *papa*), which means 'father', has been used of the bishop of Rome since the sixth century, but remained in occasional use with respect to other senior clergy until 1075, when Thesis 11 of Pope Gregory VII's *Dictatus papae* formally restricted its application to the bishop of Rome. The term 'vicar of Christ' (*vicarius Christi*), which emerged as a papal title in the eighth century, was also used by monarchs and, until the ninth century, by other bishops; by the thirteenth century the older papal title 'vicar of St Peter' had been wholly displaced by 'vicar of Christ', which by that time had become a title peculiar to the pope.

Assertions of the magisterial and jurisdictional primacy of the pope were first made explicit in the fifth century, and were later developed by Gregory VII, Innocent III, and Boniface VIII. The claim to universal jurisdiction included the right to depose temporal monarchs, a right which was last exercised by Pope PIUS V when he excommunicated Queen ELIZABETH of England on 25 February 1570. From 756 to 1871 the papacy was itself a temporal power, and the pope was head of the PAPAL STATE, a large temporal state that, like its neighbours, used DIPLOMACY and WAR as means of securing its borders and enhancing its trade and used its army to quell insurrections as well as fight enemies. On 13 May 1871 the temporal jurisdiction of the papacy was reduced to the VATICAN and its extraterritorial possessions. The spiritual authority of the papacy was long contested by general councils (see CONCILIAR MOVEMENT) and at the Reformation was repudiated by Protestant churches.

The papacy is now firmly associated with Rome, but from 330, when the capital of the Empire was removed to Constantinople, to 1527, when the SACK OF ROME left the city a smouldering ruin, the city was prey to invaders and subject to internal feuds that raged for centuries amongst the baronial families, notably the COLONNA and the ORSINI. On occasion this endemic instability led the papacy to relocate elsewhere in Italy, and from 1309 to 1377 it was located in Avignon (Provence). This period, which was described by PETRARCH and his contemporaries in exile as the 'Babylonian Captivity' (a phrase later appropriated in Luther's tract of 1520 to denounce the bondage of Catholic teaching), was followed by the GREAT SCHISM (1378–1417), in which rival popes regularly excommunicated each other. The popes of the Roman obedience were Urban VI (1378–89), BONIFACE IX, Innocent VII (1404–6), and GREGORY XII; the popes of the Avignonese obedience were CLEMENT VII and BENEDICT XIII; the popes of the Pisan obedience were Alexander V (1409–10) and JOHN XXIII.

The election of MARTIN V in 1417 concluded the Great Schism, though it was prolonged in a formal sense by the two popes of Peñiscola (CLEMENT VIII and the obscure Benedict XIV) and reopened when the COUNCIL OF BASEL deposed EUGENIUS IV, the successor of Martin V, and instead elected FELIX V, the last antipope. The court of Eugenius IV was in Florence (1435–45), but with the election of his successor NICHOLAS V in 1447, the papacy returned permanently to Rome, which, through the patronage of the papacy, became an important cultural capital. On the successors of Nicholas and their patronage, see the entries on CALLISTUS III; PIUS II; PAUL II; SIXTUS IV; INNOCENT VIII; ALEXANDER VI; PIUS III; JULIUS II; LEO X; ADRIAN VI; CLEMENT VII; PAUL III; JULIUS III; MARCELLUS II; PAUL IV; PIUS IV; PIUS V; GREGORY XIII; SIXTUS V; URBAN VII; GREGORY XIV; INNOCENT IX; CLEMENT VIII.

R. Aubenas and R. Ricard, *L'Église et la Renaissance 1449–1517* (1950).

**PAPAL ROSE.** See GOLDEN ROSE.

**PAPAL STATE or States of the Church or (ecclesiastical Latin) Patrimonium Sancti Petri or (Italian) Stato Pontifico or Stato della Chiesa or (French) *État Pontifical* or *États de l'Église* or (German) *Kirkchenstaat*.** The temporal domains of the papacy, which are now confined to the Vatican City and its extraterritorial domains (the basilicas and palaces of the Lateran and the papal villa at Castel Gandolfo), for centuries extended over much of central Italy and for a time included the Provençal territories of Avignon (bought in 1348 by Pope Clement VI from Queen GIOVANNA I of Naples) and the Venaissin (given to the papacy in 1274 by Philip III of France).

The papacy is now firmly identified with Rome, but for several periods the papal court was either elsewhere in Italy or in Provence. The Church had held land since the edict of Constantine in 321 declared the Church able to hold and transmit property. When the papacy was translated to Avignon (1309–77), its control of the papal territories in central Italy was weakened: the Marches, Romagna, and Umbria were in theory governed by papal legates but in practice were private lordships. In the early fifteenth century Pope MARTIN V reasserted papal jurisdiction; some of his gains were subsequently lost, but papal claims were renewed by Pope ALEXANDER VI, who used his son Cesare BORGIA to conquer the territories of the Papal State. The campaign was sustained by Pope JULIUS II, who regained the Romagna and acquired Bologna, so creating the State that was to dominate central Italy for four centuries. LEO X continued the process of consolidation, but the SACK OF ROME in 1527 disabled the administration of the State.

The alliance between Pope CLEMENT VII and the Emperor CHARLES V enabled subsequent popes to strengthen their rule of the Papal State. The terror of the Roman INQUISITION was used by Popes PAUL III, SIXTUS V, and CLEMENT VIII to suppress noblemen hostile to the papal regime, and the territories of the State were extended to include Modena. The State extended from sea to sea, bounded on the north-west by Venice and Lombardy, on the west by Tuscany, and on the south-east by the kingdom of Naples. Within these boundaries it included Latium, Romagna (Bologna, Ferrara, Forlì, and Rimini), Umbria (Perugia, Orvieto, Spoleto), the Marches (Ancona, Ravenna, Urbino), the duchy of Modena, and the FARNESE duchies of Parma and Piacenza; its extraterritorial domains were two Neapolitan enclaves (Benevento and Pontecorvo), Avignon, and the Venaissin.

In 1791 the papal territories in France were appropriated by the new republic; in 1870 Rome was lost to the kingdom of Italy, and the papacy withdrew to the Vatican. In 1929 the Vatican City became an independent state.

**PAPER** (Latin *papyrus*). Until the mid-fifteenth century documents were usually written on VELLUM or PARCHMENT, though the process of making paper from pulped vegetable fibres (usually extracted from linen or cotton rags, scraps of parchment, and fishing nets) was introduced into Moorish Spain in the tenth century. A paper mill was established in Sicily by 1109 (the date of the earliest surviving European paper document), and thereafter paper manufacturing was introduced in Spain (Játiva, 1150), Italy (Fabriano, 1276; Padua, 1340), France (near Troyes, 1348), and Germany (Nuremberg, 1390); in England paper was imported from the beginning of the fourteenth century, but no paper was manufactured until John Tate opened a paper mill in Hertford in 1495.

The process whereby paper was made consisted of beating boiled rags to a pulp which was then poured onto a framed sieve (known as the mould). The moisture was then drained away through the apertures in the sieve and the dried sheet was removed and pressed. Paper made by this method (which was in universal use until the invention of the paper machine in 1798) has translucent marks which become visible when sheets are held against a strong light. The thick parallel lines are called 'chain lines', the thin lines are called 'wire lines', and the decorative devices are called WATERMARKS.

Paper was occasionally used for drawing from the early fourteenth century, when CENNINI noted that paper (*carta bambagina*) was an alternative to parchment. The advent of printing led to the mass production of paper, and from the mid-fifteenth century paper was principally used for printing. Most paper was white, but coloured paper was developed in the later fifteenth century, notably the blue-toned paper (*carta azzurra*) manufactured in Venice. Grey unsized paper was used for blotting from the mid-fifteenth century, but did not displace sand for several centuries.

**PARABOSCO, GIROLAMO** (*c*.1524–1557), Italian poet, playwright, and musician, a native of Piacena. His poems include *Adonis* (a mythological poem) and a poem in praise of the women of Venice; his plays include eight comedies and a tragedy. His best-known literary work is *I diporti* (1550), a collection of seventeen comic stories. In 1551 Parabosco was appointed as organist of San Marco in Venice, where he composed motets as well as organ music.

*Grove; OCIL.*

**PARACELSUS or Philippus Aureolus Theophrastus Bombastus von Hohenheim** (1493–1541), Swiss medical alchemist, born in Einsiedeln, the son of a physician; the name that he adopted means 'above Celsus', i.e. superior to Celsus, the first-century medical writer rediscovered in the Renaissance and praised as the Cicero of physicians (*Cicero medicorum*). Paracelsus studied medicine in Ferrara, but did not complete a degree, choosing instead to live for ten years as an itinerant student; during this period he developed his interests in the occult (especially the writings of TRITHEMIUS, by whom he may have been taught) and in medical chemistry.

Paracelsus worked for several years in Villach (Austria) as the town physician, and in 1526 became a lecturer in medicine at Basel. He contravened the regulations by lecturing in German rather than Latin, and disparaged GALEN and ARISTOTLE. In 1529 he was forced to leave Basel, and again became a peripatetic physician; he died in Salzburg in mysterious circumstances.

Paracelsus' principal medical works were *Opus paramirum* and *Archidoxis*. He rejected the Galenic notion that disease could be attributed to humoral imbalance and instead argued that each disease had its own cause and cure. He also seems to have been the first physician to argue that a disease can be cured by a small dose of what caused it, in which respect his approach to therapeutics was homeopathic rather than allopathic. He eschewed herbal medicine in favour of chemical drugs, including mercury, sulphur, and iron.

*DSB*; A. G. Debus, *The English Paracelsians* (1965); id.,*The Chemical Philosophy: Paracelsan Science and Medicine* (2 vols., 1977).

**PARAGONE** (Italian; 'comparison'), a debate in Renaissance Italy about the relative merits of painting and sculpture. The topic is discussed in LEONARDO DA VINCI's notebooks and in CASTIGLIONE's *Il cortegiano*. In 1546 the historian Benedetto VARCHI gathered material on the subject by sending a set of questions to sculptors (including CELLINI and MICHELANGELO) and painters (including PONTORMO and VASARI).

I. A. Richter, *Paragone: A Comparison of the Arts by Leonardo da Vinci* (1949).

**PARCHMENT**. See VELLUM AND PARCHMENT.

**PARÉ, AMBROISE** (1510–90), French surgeon. He was born in Laval and studied medicine in Paris. In 1537 he became an army surgeon, and his experience of treating gunshot wounds by dressings rather than cauterization with burning iron or scalding oil led him to describe his innovation in *La Méthode de traiter les plaies faites par arquebustes et autres bastions à feu* (1545). In his *Dix Livres de la chirurgie* (1563) Paré described another surgical innovation in which he used ligatures to conduct amputations; this technique made thigh amputations possible. *Cinq Livres de chirurgie* (1572) dealt with fractures and dislocations, and *Deux Livres de chirurgie* (1572) with obstretrics, in which Paré explains the art of turning babies in the womb.

*DSB*; Ambroise Paré, *Ten Books of Surgery*, trans. R. W. Linker and N. Womack (1969).

**PARIS** was in antiquity a Gallo-Roman town known as Lutetia, which was confined to the island in the Seine known since 508 (when it became Clovis's capital) as La Cité. Both banks of the river were settled in the Middle Ages, but despite the growing importance of Paris, which became the capital of the duchy of France in 987, the episcopal see remained at Sens; Paris did not have its own archbishop until 1622.

The Gothic Cathedral of Notre-Dame (1163–1235) was built on the Cité, and the right bank became the centre of commerce and industry, and the site of the original LOUVRE. In 1200 the University of Paris opened on the left bank, and soon colleges were built to accommodate students from all over Europe. In 1257 the College of the Sorbonne was founded, and soon became the most important theological centre in Europe; from 1554 the name Sorbonne popularly referred to the theological faculty of the university.

In the early fifteenth century Paris was riven by the rivalry between Duke Louis of Orléans (brother of King Charles VI) and Duke JOHN THE FEARLESS of Burgundy. In November 1407 Duke John ordered the assassination of Duke Louis, and so began a rift between ARMAGNACS AND BURGUNDIANS that was to dominate public life in Paris for 28 years. In 1419 Duke John was assassinated in Montereau by a courtier of the dauphin (later CHARLES VII). Duke John's son, PHILIP THE GOOD, retaliated by supporting the claim of King Henry V of England to the throne of France, and in 1420 persuaded King CHARLES VI to accede to the Treaty of Troyes, by which Charles repudiated the dauphin and named Henry V as his successor. In December 1420 Henry V entered Paris, which remained in English hands (largely under the governorship of the duke of Bedford) until 1436; the city was unsuccessfully besieged in 1429 by JOAN OF ARC.

The English garrison was forced from Paris in April 1436, but Charles VI did not formally claim his capital until November 1437 and thereafter spent little time in Paris. Similarly, LOUIS XI, CHARLES VIII, and LOUIS XII chose to live elsewhere. FRANCIS I lived mostly at Saint-Germain-en-Laye and FONTAINEBLEAU; however, he also built the chateau of Boulogne, popularly called Madrid (destroyed 1793), then just outside Paris, and decided to build a new residence in Paris. The medieval Louvre was demolished between 1528 and 1540, and in 1541 Pierre LESCOT embarked on the construction of a new Louvre. The unfinished palace became the principal residence of FRANCIS II and CHARLES IX; however it was not until HENRI III that the French court was to settle mainly at Paris. The last French king to use the Louvre as his principal residence was LOUIS XII.

During the WARS OF RELIGION Paris was a stronghold of the CATHOLIC LEAGUE. In 1572 thousands of HUGUENOTS were killed in the ST BARTHOLOMEW'S DAY MASSACRE. In 1588 Henri III returned to the Louvre, but on 12 May, the JOURNÉE DES BARRICADES, fled from the city. The following year he returned to besiege Paris, but the siege was raised after his assassination. In 1590 King HENRI IV reimposed the siege, and four years later the city capitulated, offering the keys of the city to King Henri on 22 March 1594. His troops met resistance from a company of German LANDSKNECHTE and students of the university, but were soon in command of the city.

D. Thomson, *Renaissance Paris* (1984)

**PARKER, MATTHEW** (1504–75), English archbishop and scholar. Educated at Cambridge, Parker, sympathetic to moderate reform, held a succession of posts under HENRY VIII and EDWARD VI, including master of Corpus Christi College, Cambridge (from 1544), and dean of Lincoln (1552). Deprived under Mary, he was invited by ELIZABETH in 1559 to become archbishop of Canterbury. Here he worked to preserve the Elizabethan settlement and to oppose Puritanism, expressed in the 1572 ADMONITION TO THE PARLIAMENT. He also issued the Thirty-Nine ARTICLES and the Bishops' Bible (1568). As a scholar, he published editions of many Anglo-Saxon and medieval chroniclers, including Asser, Ælfric, Matthew of Westminster, and Matthew of Paris. His *De antiquitate*

*Britannicae ecclesiae et privilegiis ecclesiae Cantuariensis* (1572) is his most substantial work.

DNB.

**PARKINSON, JOHN** (1567–1650), English gardener and herbalist. Parkinson's life is not well documented, nor is his garden at Long Acre (near Covent Garden, in London), but he published two important horticultural books and was designated Botanicus Regius Primarius by Charles I. The title of his *Paradisi in sole, paradisus terrestris* ('The Paradise in the Sun, the Earthly Paradise', 1629) articulated the commonplace of the man-made garden as a recreation of the garden of Eden, which is depicted in a woodcut as filled with plants but devoid of animals. The book illustrates plants suitable for flower gardens, kitchen gardens, and orchards. His second book was *Theatrum botanicum: The Theatre of Plants* (1640), an illustrated herbal (see BOTANY).

DNB.

**PARLER FAMILY**, German masons in south Germany, Bohemia, and Italy; their surname derives from German *Parlier* (modern *Polier*), which means 'foreman', and in contemporary documents it is not always clear whether the reference is to members of this family, at least twelve of whom were masons. Heinrich Parler (*fl. c.*1330–1371) seems to have worked at Cologne Cathedral before his appointment as master mason of the hall church (i.e. a church in which the aisles are as high as the nave) in Schwäbisch Gmünd (40 kilometres (25 miles) east of Stuttgart); the chancel that he built had a seminal influence on the development of the south German GOTHIC style known as *Sondergotik*. The chancel of the huge minster at Ulm (which has the world's tallest spire) was also designed by one Heinrich Parler, but it is not clear whether this was the same man or a namesake. In 1391–2 another Heinrich Parler (Enrico da Gamondia, i.e. Heinrich of Gmünd) was employed at Milan Cathedral.

Two sons of Heinrich Parler of Schwäbisch Gmünd became distinguished masons. Johann Parler (*fl.* 1356–9), who is also known as Johann von Gmünd, was appointed master mason of Freiburg im Breisgau in 1359, and so is likely to have been the architect of the chancel (1354–63) of the minster. Peter Parler (*c.*1333–99), who is also known as Peter von Gmünd, was the most eminent member of the family. He lived in Nuremberg from *c.*1352, and in 1356 moved to Prague to succeed Matthias of Arras, who had begun work on Prague Cathedral in 1344. Peter Parler completed the choir (1385) and then built the south transept and the side chapels; his sculpted self-portrait in the triforium of Prague Cathedral is the earliest known self-portrait in stone. In 1373 Parler began work on the Charles Bridge (Karlův Most) in Prague. He was probably the designer and builder of St Barbara's Cathedral in Kutná Hora and of the choir of St Barthelemý in Kolín (50 kilometres (30 miles) east of Prague).

MDA; NDB; A. Legner, *Die Parler und der schöner Stil 1350–1400* (5 vols. in 6, Cologne, 1978–80).

**PARMA**, a town and episcopal see on the Lombard plain, 80 kilometres (50 miles) north-west of Bologna. From the eleventh to the thirteenth centuries Parma was one of the prizes in the struggle between GUELFS AND GHIBELLINES and oscillated in its allegiance between pope and emperor. In 1346 Parma was sold by the Correggio to the VISCONTI FAMILY; as part of the duchy of Milan, Parma passed (after a brief interval of independence during the period of the AMBROSIAN REPUBLIC) to the SFORZA FAMILY in 1450. From 1512 to 1545 Parma was incorporated in the PAPAL STATE, though it was occupied by the French from 1515 to 1521. In 1545 Pope PAUL III advanced the interests of the FARNESE FAMILY by investing his son Pierluigi Farnese with the duchies of Parma and Piacenza; a succession of eight Farnese dukes ruled until 1731.

The most prominent figures in the Parma School of art are CORREGGIO, who painted the frescoes in the domes of the cathedral and of the Church of San Giovanni Evangelista, and Il PARMIGIANINO, who painted the frescoes in the Church of Madonna della Steccata. The Palazzo della Pilotta (named after the game of pilotta played in its courts) constructed by the Farnese (1583–1622) contains the Farnese THEATRE.

A. Quondam (ed.), *Le corti farneseiane di Parma e Piacenza, 1545–1622* (2 vols., 1978).

**PARMIGIANINO, IL, or Francesco Mazzola or (Victorian English) The Parmesan** (1503–40), Italian painter and etcher, born in Parma (hence his nickname), the son of a painter. His youthful *Marriage of St Catherine* (1521, Canonica di Bardi, near Parma) shows the stylistic features that were to characterize his paintings throughout his short life: the calligraphic drawing of elongated figures positioned with an eye to linear rhythms rather than classical principles of balance. Parmigianino's early work also includes frescoes in four chapels in the north aisle of San Giovanni Evangelista, which were executed at the same time as CORREGGIO's frescoes in the dome and pendentives of the same church.

From 1524 to 1527 Parmigianino lived in Rome, where he worked primarily as an etcher; he seems to have been the first Italian artist to execute etchings and CHIAROSCURO WOODCUTS (of which he made more than any other artist) from his own designs. His few surviving paintings from this period include another *Marriage of St Catherine* and *The Vision of St Jerome* (both in the National Gallery, London).

In 1527 Parmigianino was captured in the SACK OF ROME, but escaped to Bologna, where he lived until 1531. The backgrounds of his paintings of this period show a new interest in LANDSCAPE, notably in his *Madonna with Saints* (Uffizi). His portrait paintings include an allegorical picture (now lost) of *Charles V*, who visited Bologna in 1530. While in Bologna Parmigianino painted the *Madonna della rosa* (Gemäldegalerie, Dresden); according to VASARI, Parmigianino painted this picture for Pietro ARETINO, whose tastes could account for the sensuousness of a devotional work.

In 1531 Parmigianino returned to his native Parma, where he painted his most famous work, the *Madonna dal Collo Lungo* (Uffizi), the most extreme example of Parmigianino's tendency to elongate figures, particularly the neck and hands. During this period he also painted the picture known as

*Antea* (Museo Nazionale, Naples); the subject of this painting, which is one of the finest portraits of the sixteenth century, is unknown, and there is no particular reason to identify her with the Roman courtesan Antea. He undertook to paint frescoes in the Church of Santa Maria della Steccata, but his failure to complete these frescoes within twice the contracted time led in 1539 to his imprisonment by his patrons. On his release Parmigianino moved to Casalmaggiore (15 kilometres (9 miles) from Parma), where he painted his last work, a *Madonna with Saints and a Donor* (Gemäldegalerie, Dresden), and where he died on 24 August 1540 at the age of 37.

The style of Parmigianino influenced both NICCOLÒ DELL'ABBATE and PRIMATICCIO, and through their work at FONTAINEBLEAU influenced French art.

*MDA*; Cecil Gould, *Parmigianino* (1994).

**PARRASIO, AULO GIANO, or Giovanni Paolo Parisio** (1470–1522), Italian humanist, born in Cozenza; his baptismal name was Giovanni Paolo, which he later reshaped to sound more classical. Parrasio studied Greek in Corfu and later became a member of the Accademia Pontaniana in Naples and the Roman Academy which had been founded by Julius Pomponius LAETUS, suppressed by Pope PAUL II, and reopened by Pope SIXTUS IV. He taught in Milan (1499–1506) and, at the invitation of Pope LEO X, in Rome (1514–17). Parassio recovered several ancient texts, and in 1500 published an edition of Cornelius Nepos.

**PARSONS, ROBERT** (c.1530–1570), English composer and a gentleman of the Chapel Royal from 1563; he drowned at Newark upon Trent. Well regarded as a composer, he wrote sacred music to English and Latin texts and some instrumental 'IN NOMINES' which were probably used at court.

**PARSONS, ROBERT** (1546–1610), English Catholic leader and constitutionalist. Fellow of Balliol College, Oxford (1568–74), Parsons resigned his fellowship in order to be received into the Catholic Church at Louvain (1574); the following year he became a Jesuit at Rome. In 1580 he and CAMPION led the Jesuit mission to England; Parsons's involvement in political controversies resulted in his being forced to flee the country. He spent the rest of his life pursuing Catholic concerns on the Continent: as adviser to popes and Catholic rulers, in supporting Catholic invasion of England with the ARMADA, and in working for the ENGLISH COLLEGE at Rome. His *Conference about the Next Succession to the Crown of England* (1595) sought a Catholic successor to ELIZABETH, and suggested the Infanta Isabella as the most suitable choice. His spiritual treatise *The Christian Directory* (1582) was the most influential of his writings.

*DNB.*

**PART BOOKS.** During the fifteenth and sixteenth centuries polyphonic music was published in separate books for individual voices, similar in principle to today's orchestral instrumental parts. The earliest example is the Shrewsbury fragment (c.1430), probably the survivor of a set of three.

**PARTERRE** (French *par terre*, 'on the ground'), an ornamental flower garden laid out in geometrical or botanical designs. *Parterres de broderie* or embroidered parterres (Italian *ricami*) were parterres with symmetrical botanical designs, executed in box against a background of coloured soil; the first *parterres de broderie* were constructed by Jacques MOLLET at ANET to designs by Étienne DU PÉRAC; they subsequently became central features at many gardens, notably FONTAINEBLEAU. Parterres in which the individual components of the design are flower beds rather than box, as in the designs of Jan VREDEMAN DE VRIES, are called *parterres de pièces coupées* (cutwork parterres). The late seventeenth-century *parterres à l'anglaise*, which were called 'plats' in England, were constructed with cut turf (*gazon coupé*) set against coloured stones or soil.

*PARTHENIA* (1613), a collection of virginal music by William BYRD, John BULL, and Orlando GIBBONS given to Princess Elizabeth and Count Friedrich of the Palatinate on their marriage. Its full title was *Parthenia; or, The Maidenhead of the First Music that Ever was Printed for the Virginals*. *Parthenia In-Violata* (1624) was a companion volume of anonymous dances and includes a part for bass viol.

**PARUTA, PAOLO** (1540–98), Venetian historian and statesman, born into a patrician family and educated at the University of Padua. He held a series of public positions, including historian to the republic (1579), *provveditore* to the Chamber of Loans (1580), adviser (*savio*) to the MAGGIOR CONSIGLIO (1590), governor of Brescia (1591), and superintendent of fortifications (1597). In his capacity as official historian, he continued the narrative of the history of Venice from where Pietro BEMBO had left it (in 1513) and carried it down to 1552; it was posthumously published in 1599. He also wrote a history of the war in CYPRUS (1570–2).

Paruta also wrote two books that were unrelated to his official duties. In 1579 he published *Della perfezione della vita politica*, a dialogue set in 1563 at the closing session of the COUNCIL OF TRENT, which Paruta had attended as secretary to one of the Venetian delegates; the protagonists in the dialogue represent both churchmen and secular rulers, and the issues that they consider refine the ancient debate about the relative merits of the *vita activa* and the *vita contemplativa* by defining the active life in terms of family and civic responsibilities and the contemplative life in terms of celibate religious meditation. Paruta's secularization of the *vita activa* (which had traditionally referred to Christian charity and preaching) enables him to defend the secular life of Venice against the threat posed by the oppressive sanctity of the COUNTER-REFORMATION.

Paruta's other book of political philosophy is his *Discorsi*, which covertly takes up the issues raised in MACHIAVELLI's *Discorsi* (which was on the INDEX) and reflects on matters such as the obligations of citizens, the legitimacy of political action, and the extent to which ancient Roman republicanism is an appropriate model for a modern republic.

F. Zanoni, *Paolo Paruta nella vita e nelle opere* (1904); Eric Cochrane, *Historians and Historiography in the Italian Renaissance* (1981).

**PASQUIER, ÉTIENNE** (1529–1615), French humanist jurist and historian. He was called to the Paris bar in 1549. In 1558 he ate a plate of mushrooms which poisoned him, and during the two years of his gradual recovery he wrote the first volume of his encyclopedic *Recherches de la France* (1560–1621), an unaffected and humane account of French history and literature and the University of Paris. As a historian he favoured toleration and deplored the WARS OF RELIGION, and was deeply hostile to the interference of papal legates in French affairs. As a student of literature he discusses MONTAIGNE and the poets of the PLÉIADE.

In 1565 Pasquier achieved sudden fame with his speech (which survives) pleading the case of the university of Paris to deny the right of the JESUIT Order to teach at the university. Many years later, he returned to the subject in *Catéchisme des Jésuites* (1602), an attack on the Order in the form of a dialogue. As an advocate he presided over *grands jours*, which were provincial assizes consisting of magistrates from the Parlement of Paris, convened during the summer vacations to deal with outbreaks of lawlessness or rebellion. At the *grands jours* of Poitiers in 1579 he and his judicial colleagues amused themselves with FLEA POEMS which Pasquier subsequently published. In 1585 Pasquier was appointed advocate-general of the Paris Cour des Comptes, a body that exercised financial and political functions in addition to its legal remit. In this role he resolutely opposed the corrupt system whereby hereditary offices were sold. He retired from the Cour des Comptes in 1604, aged 75, but continued to write for the next ten years. His publications include *Lettres* (1586 and 1619) which are of biographical and historical interest as well as poems in Latin and Greek and disquisitions on antiquarian subjects.

> D. Thickett, *Estienne Pasquier (1529–1615), the Versatile Barrister of 16th-Century France* (1979); Donald R. Kelley, *Foundations of Modern Historical Scholarship: Language, Law and History in the French Renaissance* (1970), 271–300.

**PASSAROTTI, BARTOLOMEO** (1529–92), Italian painter, born in Bologna, where he trained in the studio of VIGNOLA. He lived in Rome from *c*.1551 to 1565, working as an assistant to Taddeo ZUCCARO; his Roman works include the *Martyrdom of St Paul* in the Church of San Paolo alle Tre Fontane. He returned to Bologna, where he continued to paint altarpieces (e.g. *St Ursula with her Companions*, Church of Santa Maria di Pietà, Bologna) and portraits of popes and cardinals (e.g. *Pope Gregory XIII c*.1572, Schlossmuseum Gotha). He also painted a large number of pictures in a sub-genre of his own invention, a conflation of GENRE and STILL LIFE painting that depicted peasants with flowers and dead birds; these paintings include *The Butcher's Shop*, *The Fishmonger's Shop*, and *The Dog Breeder*, all in the Palazzo Barberini in Rome. Passarotti's pupils included Agostino CARRACCI.

> *MDA*; Corinna Höper, *Bartolomeo Passarotti* (2 vols., 1987).

**PASSE, CRISPIJN VAN DE** (1564–1637), Dutch engraver. He was born in Zeeland and became a member of the Antwerp guild in 1585. He subsequently worked in Cologne (1589–1611) and thereafter in Utrecht. He trained his four children (Simon, Willem, Magdalena, and Crispijn the Younger) in his studio, and the family workshop produced large numbers of engraved portraits, often of English subjects.

> *MDA*; *NNBW* v.

**PASTI, MATTEO DE'** (*c*.1420–1467), Italian illuminator, architect, and medallist. He was born in Verona and worked for a time in Venice. He illuminated Piero de' MEDICI's copy of Petrarch's *Trionfi* (now lost), built the Palazzo Rucellai in Florence (to ALBERTI's plans) and cast a series of portrait MEDALS, notably those of Sigismondo MALATESTA (for whom PISANELLO had cast a portrait medal the previous year) and Malatesta's mistress Isotta degli Atti da Rimini. His most important architectural work was the interior of the Tempio Malatestiano in Rimini, which was commissioned by Malatesta and designed by ALBERTI.

> *MDA*.

**PASTIGLIA**, a hardened paste (literally 'tablet') used to decorate the outer surface of small wooden boxes to create decorative effects imitative of those on large Renaissance CASSONI. *Pastiglia*, which typically consisted of GESSO or of a lead compound fixed with egg, was spread on the surface while still wet and then moulded in relief with small metal matrices, each of which portrayed a human figure or a plant or animal.

**PASTOR, ADAM** (d. 1560), German ANABAPTIST leader, probably born in Münster; his real name was Rudolf Martens. He was principally active in Cleves (German Kleve). In 1547 he began to work with MENNO SIMONS, but they quarrelled because of differing views on the Trinity. He later became an itinerant preacher on the lower Rhine, and died in Emden.

**PASTORAL**, a courtly imitation of rural life in which the pastoral poet, dramatist, or novelist charts the lives, loves, and deaths of shepherds and shepherdesses. The principal ancient models for the Renaissance pastoral were the *Idylls* of Theocritus and the *Eclogues* of VIRGIL. Pastoral poetry is also known as bucolic poetry.

Pastoral drama is a Renaissance genre which developed from the dialogue element in pastoral poetry. POLIZIANO's *Favola di Orfeo* (1472) was the first pastoral drama; the finest Italian examples were performed in the sixteenth century, and include GIRALDI's *Egle* (1545), Agostino Beccari's *Il sacrificio* (1554), TASSO's *Aminta* (1573), and GUARINI's *Il pastor fido* (1583). In England, the most important pastoral plays were LYLY's *Galathea* (1584), PEELE's *Arraignment of Paris* (1584), and, finest of all, FLETCHER's *Faithful Shepherdess* (1610), an imitation of Tasso's *Aminta*. There was no significant pastoral drama in France until the 1620s, when works such as Théophile de Viau's *Pyrame* (1621) and Racan's *Les Bergeries* (1623) inaugurated a short-lived fashion for the form that ended with Jean Mairet's *La Sylvie* (performed 1626).

The pastoral romance is an early form of novel in which the prose narrative is interspersed with poetry and song; the plots, which are often of extraordinary complexity, describe the amatory fortunes of characters with pastoral names (often aristocrats in disguise). The founding text was SANNAZARO's

*Arcadia* (1504), which was imitated in works such as MON-TEMAYOR's *Diana* (c.1559), CERVANTES' *Galatea* (1585), Robert GREENE's *Menaphon* (1589), Sir Philip SIDNEY's *Arcadia* (1590), Thomas LODGE's *Rosalynde* (1590), and Lope de VEGA's *La Arcadia* (1598). In France, there was a medieval tradition of *pastorelle* (Provençal *pastorela*), in which a knight and a shepherdess converse in a rural setting; pastoral romances in the tradition of Sannazaro and Montemayor include François de Belleforest's *La Pyrénée et pastorale amoureuse* (1571), Nicholas de Montreux's vast *Les Bergeries de Juliette* (5 vols., 1585–98), and Honoré d'URFÉ's *L'Astrée* (4 vols., 1607–27), which is the finest French pastoral romance.

The pastoral eclogue was an important neo-Latin genre inaugurated by poets such as DANTE (who wrote two eclogues), PETRARCH (twelve eclogues), and BOCCACCIO (*Bucolicum carmen*); in Renaissance Italy, the most important neo-Latin pastoral poets were Giovanni PONTANO and Battista MANTOVANO. In France, the PLÉIADE wrote pastoral eclogues, as did poets such as MAROT. In England, the principal pastoral poems were Alexander BARCLAY's *Eclogues* (c.1513), Edmund SPENSER's *Shepherd's Calendar* (1579), Michael DRAYTON's *Shepherd's Garland* (1593), and William Browne's *Britannia's Pastorals* (1613–16).

The two principal sub-genres of pastoral eclogue were the piscatory eclogue and the pastoral elegy. Sannazaro imitated the fisherman's idyll of Theocritus (*Idyll* 21) in his *Piscatoria* (1526) and was in turn imitated by poets such as Phineas FLETCHER (*Piscatory Eclogues*, 1633) and the Croatian poet Petar Hektorović (*Ribanje i ribarsko prigovaranje*, 1555). In pastoral elegy, the ancient models of Virgil and Theocritus were supplemented by Bion's *Lament for Adonis* and Moschus' *Lament for Bion*. Exponents of the form include Renaissance poets such as Marot and Spenser; the genre enjoyed a long afterlife in England, where pastoral elegies were written by Milton (*Lycidas*), Shelley (*Adonais*), and Arnold (*Thyrsis*).

The pastoral genre was analysed by theorists such as VIDA (*Ars poetica*, 1527), SEBILLET (*Art poétique française*, 1548), SCALIGER (*Poetices*, 1561), and the unidentified 'E.K.' who introduced and glossed Spenser's *Shepherd's Calendar*. Guarini was drawn into a debate by Giason Denores, who argued in his *Discorso* (1587) that pastoral had not been sanctioned by Aristotle as a genre and was therefore a mixed form; Guarini replied in his *Il verato* (1588) and *Il verato secundo* (1593). In the seventeenth century d'Urfé defended the pastoral genre in his *L'Auteur à la bergère Astrée* (1610). The debate about the legitimacy of pastoral continued in France throughout the seventeenth century and in England until the end of the eighteenth century, when Hugh Blair's observations on pastoral poetry (in *Lectures on Belles Lettres*, 1783) brought the debate to a close.

Renato Poggioli, *The Oaten Flute: Essays on Pastoral and the Pastoral Ideal* (1975).

**PATCHWORK**, a textile technique in which small shaped pieces of fabric are sewn together to form a cloth mosaic, often in a geometrical pattern. Patchwork has for many centuries been a peasant craft (since the eighteenth century used mainly for quilts), but in Renaissance Europe tailors also used silks and velvets to fashion patchwork ceremonial vestments for the Church and for the civil authorities.

**PATINIR or Patinier or Patenier, JOACHIM** (c.1480–c.1524), Flemish LANDSCAPE painter who first appears in the historical record when he became a member of the Guild of Painters in Antwerp in 1515. In 1521 he acted as DÜRER's host during his visit to the Netherlands; Dürer made a silverpoint drawing of Patinir in one of his sketchbooks and praised him as a 'good landscape painter' ('Maister Joachim, der gut Landschaft Mahler'). His landscape paintings are ostensibly narrative pictures, but the small human figures are typically enveloped by the landscapes in which they are situated. Many paintings are attributed to Patinir, but very few are signed, including a *Baptism of Christ* (Kunsthistorisches Museum, Vienna), a *Flight into Egypt* (Koninklijk Museum voor Schone Kunsten, Antwerp) and a *St Jerome* (Staatliche Kunsthalle, Karlsruhe). He also painted landscape backgrounds for other artists, often his friend Quentin MASSYS, such as their *Temptation of St Anthony* (Prado, Madrid).

MDA; Reindert Falkenburg, *Joachim Patinir* (1988).

**PATRISTIC SCHOLARSHIP**. In late medieval Europe the writings of the church fathers were known through three collections: the *Catena aurea* of THOMAS AQUINAS, the Decree of Gratian (the *Concordantia discordantium canonum*, popularly known as the *Decretum Gratiani*), and the Glossed Bible. All three collections remained in use throughout the fifteenth and sixteenth centuries, but there was also a humanist tradition of translation, editing, and textual commentary inaugurated by Leonardo BRUNI and GUARINO DA VERONA. In the sixteenth century a significant corpus of patristic scholarship was published, for the most part motivated by a wish to annex the church fathers to the Protestant or Catholic cause. Interest in the Greek fathers was stimulated by the debates at the COUNCIL OF FLORENCE. The conciliar translators—BESSARION, GEORGE OF TREBIZOND, TRAVERSARI—all had patristic interests, and in due course Latin translations of Eusebius of Caesaria, the Cappadocian fathers, and Cyril of Alexandria began to appear.

The printing of patristic texts began in Italy. The edition of three books by Lactantius published in Subiaco in 1465 was the first dated book to be printed in Italy; there were also early editions of Cyprian (Rome, 1471) and Ambrose (Venice, 1485). The central figure in humanist patristics was ERASMUS, who in the course of 21 years (1516–36) edited or collaborated in editions of Ambrose, Arnobius the Younger, pseudo-Athanasius, AUGUSTINE, Basil the Great, Cyprian, Hilary of Poitiers, Irenaeus, JEROME, John Chrysostom, Lactantius, and Origen. The scrupulous attention that Erasmus lavished on textual matters and problems of attribution inaugurated a tradition of patristic scholarship that culminated in the erudition of Fronto DUCAEUS and paved the way for works such as Thomas James's *Treatise of the Corruption of Scripture, Councils and Fathers* (1611).

For the reformers, the central issue with respect to the church fathers was the question of authority, and their authority was often considered to be less than that of Scripture but comparable to that of the early councils. LUTHER acknowledged the 'first fathers' in his 1523 order of service, and named many fathers in his *Von den Konziliis und Kirchen* (1539), in which he granted a limited authority to patristic teaching on the grounds of temporal proximity to the early Church. MELANCHTHON conducted a similar evaluation of patristic authority in *De ecclesia et de authoritate verbi Dei*, as did Martin CHEMNITZ in his *Loci theologici*. In the sixteenth century the authority of the fathers was often circumscribed but seldom derided, because of the importance of the early creeds in Reformation debates: the Nicene Creed was an important text all over Europe, and the Apostles' Creed was absorbed into the theological fabric of the Swiss and German churches. The medieval tradition that linked each of the twelve articles of the Apostles' Creed to one of the twelve disciples had been demolished by Erasmus (in *Conscribendarum epistolarum ratio*, 1520), who had demonstrated that the Creed was of fourth-century origin, but even the scholarship of Erasmus could not undermine popular belief.

Editions of patristic texts often had an explicit Protestant or Catholic bias. Protestants such as the ESTIENNES in Geneva, FROBEN's 'corrector' Sigismond Gelonius (who edited the 1547 edition of Chrysostom), Musculus (who translated Basil's *Ascetica magna* in 1540), Johann Lange (who translated Justin Martyr in 1565), and BEZA (who edited the *Dialogi quinque de sancta Trinitate* of pseudo-Athanasius in 1570) encouraged the view that the church fathers were proto-reformers. The greatest product of Protestant industry was the MAGDEBURG CENTURIES (13 vols., 1559–74), the Catholic response to which was the *Annales ecclesiastici* (1588–1607) of Caesar BARONIUS. In France, the cause of Protestant patristics was sustained by Abraham Scultetus' *Medulla patrum syntagma* (4 vols., 1598–1612), André Rivet's *Criticus sacer* (1612), and Jean Daillé's *Traité de l'emploi des saints pères* (1632). Catholic scholarship was less combative, though Charlotte Guillard published editions of both Greek and Latin fathers as her contribution to the war against the Protestant heresy. Most Catholic scholarship was assured rather than strident. In Italy, Cardinal Guglielmo Sirleto amassed an extensive collection of patristic manuscripts, and scholars such as Pietro Francesco Zini (who translated Greek fathers into Latin), the Jesuit Antonio POSSEVINO, and the circle of scholars associated with Cardinal Gasparo CONTARINI contributed to patristic scholarship. In France the comparable figures were the Benedictines Jacques de Billy and Joachim Perion, the humanist Gentian Hervetus (who translated Greek fathers such as Zacharias Scholasticus, Theodoret, Chrysostom, and Cyril of Alexandria), and Margarin de la Bigne, whose *Biblioteca patrum sanctorum* (1575–9) was a precursor of Migne's vast nineteenth-century editions.

**PATRIZZI or Patrizi, FRANCESCO** (1413–92), Italian humanist, a native of Siena who secured the patronage of the Sienese Pope PIUS II, who appointed Patrizzi bishop of Gaeta. In his diocese Patrizzi wrote two treatises on political theory: *De regno et regum institutione* was an analysis of the nature of monarchy and *De institutione republicae* was an analysis of republicanism, an ideology of which Patrizzi was a sympathizer. Both works were translated into several modern languages. Patrizzi is sometimes confused with his namesake, the sixteenth-century Dalmatian philosopher Francesco PATRIZZI.

**PATRIZZI or Patrizi, FRANCESCO, or (Latin) Franciscus Patritius or (Croatian) Franjo Petrić** (1529–97), Dalmatian Platonist, born in Cherso (now Cres, a Croatian island in the Adriatic) and educated in Venice (1542), Ingolstadt (1544–5), and Padua (1547–54). Thereafter he served in various noble houses in Venice and travelled extensively in the Mediterranean, including a period in Cyprus in which he improved his command of Greek. From 1577 to 1592 he worked at Ferrara as the first professor of Platonic philosophy, and in 1592 he moved to Rome at the invitation of Pope CLEMENT VIII to become professor of Platonic philosophy at the Sapienza.

Patrizzi wrote widely on philosophy, science, history, rhetoric, and military strategy, always championing Plato against Aristotle. His principal work was an encyclopedic four-part *Nova de universis philosophia* (Ferrara, 1591), a 'new philosophy of the world' which expounded his Neoplatonic theory of light metaphysics; a second edition (Venice, 1593) was revised in the vain hope of assuaging the displeasure expressed by the INQUISITION, which was about to place it on the INDEX when he died.

Patrizzi is sometimes confused with his namesake, the fifteenth-century Sienese philosopher Francesco PATRIZZI.

**PAUL II** (1417–71), pope from 30 August 1464 until his death on 26 July 1471, was born Pietro Barbo in Venice on 23 February 1417, the son of a wealthy merchant. When his uncle, Cardinal Gabriele Condulmer, was elected pope as EUGENIUS IV in 1431, Pietro took holy orders, and thereafter enjoyed the pope's nepotistic patronage. He was appointed in quick succession archdeacon of Bologna, bishop of Cervia, bishop of Vicenza, protonotary of the Roman Church, and, in 1440 (aged 23), cardinal-deacon of Santa Cecilia. He retained a prominent position in the court of Pope NICHOLAS V, who created him cardinal-deacon of San Marco in Rome. His influence was sustained during the pontificate of CALLISTUS III, but declined under Pope PIUS II; he was unexpectedly elected as Pope Pius' successor at the first ballot.

Members of the electoral college had sworn an eighteen-point pact, which included pledges to abjure nepotism and convoke regular general councils; such resolutions were clearly born of a wish to change the direction of the papacy after the pontificate of Pius II. On being elected as Pope Paul II, Pietro immediately declared that he regarded the details of the pact as advisory guidelines rather than binding principles, and shortly thereafter presented an anodyne version of the pact to the Sacred College. As pope he never practised nepotism, but he inveighed unceasingly against general councils. He also repeatedly denounced the PRAGMATIC SANCTION OF BOURGES, and so alienated King LOUIS XI of France.

Pope Paul inherited a war against the Ottomans, and quickly implemented his pledge to use income from the papal ALUM mines at Tolfa to finance the defence of Hungary and the resistance mounted by the Albanian leader SKANDER-BEG. The chief impediment to the mobilization of a crusade in central Europe was that the most able leader, GEORGE OF PODĚBRADY, the king of Bohemia, was alienated from the papacy. The permission granted by the COUNCIL OF BASEL to allow the Bohemian laity access to the chalice had been revoked in 1462, and King George had refused to implement the prohibition of this UTRAQUIST practice. Paul therefore excommunicated and deposed King George on 23 December 1466, and fifteen months later (31 March 1468) committed MATTHIAS CORVINUS, king of Hungary, to a CRUSADE against King George. The efforts of Matthias were largely ineffectual, but the problem was solved when King George died on 22 March 1471.

The advance of the Ottomans was a constant source of fear, and the fall in 1470 of Negroponte (now Greek Evvia), the last Venetian outpost in the Levant, to the forces of Sultan Mehmet II induced Pope Paul to issue a general summons for a crusade against the Ottomans. Representatives of the Italian states duly attended a congress in Rome, but all that emerged was a defensive alliance (22 December 1470) rather than an invading force. In 1471, through the offices of the Venetian envoy Caterino Zeno, Pope Paul was able to conclude an anti-Ottoman alliance with Usun Hasan, the shah of Iran. Paul also enjoyed good relations with the Emperor FRIEDRICH III, who visited Rome privately in 1468 but failed to persuade Paul to convoke a general council.

In Rome, Paul revised the civic statutes in 1469 (with the consent of the citizens of Rome), and the following year he levied a tax payable every fifteen years (and so known as the *quindemia*) by corporations that owned ecclesiastical benefices. Within the PAPAL STATE, he campaigned against the soliciting of bribes by papal officials.

Paul incurred the hostility of the humanist community by ordering the imprisonment and torture of the humanist historian PLATINA, who had protested against his abolition of the College of Abbreviators (i.e. papal draughtsmen, who were often distinguished scholars) in 1466; the humanist view that Paul was an opponent of learning was hardened by his ban on the study of the pagan poets of classical antiquity by Roman schoolchildren. In 1468 Paul suppressed the Roman ACADEMY of Julius Pomponius LAETUS on suspicion of paganism and heresy, and again the humanists were aggrieved. Platina, who had been imprisoned a second time when the Academy was closed, later had his revenge when he portrayed Paul as an illiterate antagonist of learning in his *Lives of the Popes*. It is true that Paul was not a speculative intellectual and that he was wary of secular learning, but he nonetheless promoted Christian scholarship, restored ancient monuments, collected works of art, and probably introduced printing to Rome. He also had a marked taste for sport, entertainment, and visual display: he promoted the Roman carnival, forcing JEWS to contribute to its expense, and decreed on 19 April 1470 that, henceforth, holy years would be marked by jubilees every 25 years, starting in 1475.

Pope Paul's last months were dominated by his attempt to reconcile the Russian Church to Rome by arranging for the Catholic convert Zoe (formerly Sophia) Palaiologa, daughter of Thomas Palaiologos (the exiled despot of Morea and pretender to the throne of Byzantium), to marry the widowed IVAN III, grand duke of Muscovy. The negotiations had not been completed when Paul suddenly died of a stroke on 26 July 1471; the wedding went ahead, and Zoe brought the double-headed eagle of Constantinople to the court of Muscovy, but the Russian Church did not submit to Rome.

Paul's greatest act of patronage was his commissioning of the Palazzo di San Marco, which he commissioned as a cardinal in 1455 and made his chief residence in Rome from 1466. The Sala Regia was later decorated with frescoes by BRAMANTE and the Sala del Mappomundo with frescoes by MANTEGNA. Pope PIUS IV gave the palace to Venice for use as its embassy; it housed the embassy until 1797, and so acquired its present name, the Palazzo di Venezia. It subsequently served as the Austro-Hungarian embassy (until 1915) and from 1925 to 1943 was the residence of Mussolini. It now houses a major collection of medieval and Renaissance art.

R. Weiss, *Un umanista veneziano: Papa Paolo II* (1958).

**PAUL III** (1468–1549), pope from 13 October 1534 until his death on 10 November 1549, was born Alessandro Farnese in Canino on 29 February 1468, a scion of the wealthy *condottieri* and land-owning family of the FARNESE. He received a humanist education in Rome, where his tutors included Julius Pomponius LAETUS, and in Florence, where he became a member of the circle of Lorenzo de' MEDICI. He studied at Pavia and then moved to Rome, where his sister Giulia was the mistress of Pope ALEXANDER VI. This family connection facilitated rapid advancement in the Church: he was appointed treasurer of the Roman Church in 1492 and created cardinal-deacon in 1493; because of his sister's influence, he was nicknamed 'cardinal petticoat'. He amassed a substantial collection of lucrative benefices and bishoprics, and, after the death of Pope Alexander in 1503, he enjoyed the favour of Pope Julius II, who appointed him bishop of Parma in 1509.

Cardinal Alessandro took his new diocesan duties seriously, convoking a synod and implementing the reforming decrees of the Fifth Lateran COUNCIL. This onset of religious interests was soon reflected in Cardinal Alessandro's private life: he had fathered three sons and a daughter by his Roman mistress, and in 1513 he deserted her. In June 1519 he was ordained as a priest, and he established a reputation within the curia as a reformer. When Pope CLEMENT VII died, Cardinal Alessandro was, at 67, the oldest cardinal, and dean of the Sacred College; he was elected as Pope Paul III after a two-day conclave.

Pope Paul was a flagrant nepotist who used his papacy as a means of advancing the Farnese family; he alienated huge tracts of land in the PAPAL STATE to his illegitimate children. Soon after his election he appointed his son Pierluigi Farnese as captain-general of the Church, and passed to him the duchy of Castro (in the Maremma) and a clutch of fiefdoms, including Frascati, Nepi, and Montaldo. In 1545 he created Pierluigi duke of Parma and Piacenza. He also made generous provision for Pierluigi's sons Alessandro (whom he made a cardinal at the age of 14), Ottavio, and Orazio; for details see FARNESE FAMILY.

It is paradoxical that Pope Paul's fervent desire to enrich his family was matched by a comparable passion for reform. He was the first pope to take the view that the best bulwark against Protestantism was the Catholic reform of the Church. He convoked general councils for Mantua in 1537 and Vicenza in 1538, but on both occasions the councils had to be postponed because of the objections of FRANCIS I of France and the Emperor CHARLES V, who were locked in a protracted conflict (see WARS OF ITALY). Pope Paul reduced the expenditure of the Sacred College and supplemented its membership with gifted churchmen, including Giovanni Carafa (later Pope PAUL IV), Gasparo CONTARINI, Giovanni MORONE, Reginald POLE, and Marcello Cervini (later Pope MARCELLUS II). In 1536 he established a commission to examine the state of the Church, and its report, submitted on 9 March 1537 under the title *Consilium de emendenda ecclesia*, later became the foundation of the reforms of the Council of Trent.

Pope Paul recognized that discipline had become lax in many of the religious ORDERS, and initiated a programme of reform. He also encouraged the development of new congregations, including the BARNABITES, the THEATINES, the Somaschi, the URSULINES, and, most importantly, the JESUITS, whom he approved on 27 September 1540 by the bull *Regimeni militantis ecclesiae*. On 21 July 1542 Paul established the Congregation of the Roman INQUISITION (or HOLY OFFICE) as a weapon against heresy.

When the Treaty of Crépy-en-Laonnois (18 September 1544) created a protracted lull in the wars of Europe, Pope Paul was able to revive his plan for a general council of the Church; it was to be held, at the emperor's suggestion, in Trento (German Trient), in the Austrian Tirol. The COUNCIL OF TRENT opened on 13 December 1545; Pope Paul did not attend in person, but was represented by three legates. Charles V had envisaged a council devoted to issues of reform, but Pope Paul wanted the Council to concentrate on issues of dogma. The opening seven sessions were increasingly bedevilled by the tension between emperor and pope, and on 11 March 1547 Pope Paul transferred the Council to Bologna, ostensibly on the grounds of typhus in Trento. Bologna lay within the papal sphere of influence, and Charles forbade bishops subject to him to attend; the eighth session was suspended on 1 February 1548, and the suspension was ratified on 14 September 1549.

Pope Paul's judgement in matters of foreign policy was not always vindicated by subsequent events. King HENRY VIII of England had been excommunicated by Pope Clement VII on 11 July 1533, but the sentence had been deferred and then suspended; a bull confirming the final excommunication of King Henry was prepared in August 1535, but was not promulgated until 17 December 1538, when Paul placed England under a general interdict. His hope that other European

Titian, unfinished portrait of *Pope Paul III and his Nephews*, in the Museo Nazionale in Naples

countries would respond to the interdict with trade sanctions was not realized, and the only real effect was to encourage defiance in England. Paul tried to remain neutral in the Habsburg–Valois struggle, offering support for both sides on domestic issues (he supported the campaigns of Francis against the HUGUENOTS and of Charles against the SCHMALKALDIC LEAGUE) but urged reconciliation on the grounds that a divided Europe could not resist the encroachments of the Ottomans, who were capturing Christian outposts in the Levant, advancing on central Europe, and even threatening the coast of Italy. In the event, Pope Paul's attempts to maintain good relations with both France and the Empire were compromised by his prior commitment to the advancement of his family. After the death of Pierluigi and the imperial occupation of Piacenza in 1547, Pope Paul determined to regain the duchies of Piacenza and Parma for the papacy. He therefore set aside Ottavio's claim to the dukedom of Parma and instead installed a legate; he then claimed Piacenza from the emperor. Charles V, whose illegitimate daughter was married to Ottavio, supported Ottavio's claim to the dukedom. Ottavio attempted, with the support of his brother Alessandro, to recapture Parma by military force; papal forces repelled the attack. Paul lay dying, the emperor and his own grandchildren ranged against him; before he died on 10 November 1549, Pope Paul ordered that Parma be ceded to Ottavio; in 1551 his successor JULIUS III formally restored the duchy of Parma to Ottavio.

Pope Paul was a generous patron of scholarship, art, and architecture. He restored the University of Rome, developed the holdings of the VATICAN LIBRARY, and commissioned work from artists and architects. He charged Michelangelo with the task of completing the *Last Judgement* in the SISTINE CHAPEL and placed him in charge of the construction of ST PETER'S BASILICA. He also initiated the construction of the Palazzo Farnese in Rome (which was later to be completed by his grandson Cardinal Alessandro); its architects were Antonio SANGALLO the Younger (1514–46), MICHELANGELO (till 1564), Giacomo da VIGNOLA (until 1573), and Giacomo DELLA PORTA (till 1589); the palace is now the French embassy. Pope Paul also enjoyed staging large events: in 1536 he revived the Roman Carnival, and throughout his pontificate the Vatican hosted an endless succession of banquets and masked balls.

In 1543 TITIAN embarked on a portrait of *Pope Paul III and his Nephews* (now in the Museo Nazionale in Naples); it was left unfinished, but nonetheless captures the vigour of the 75-year-old pontiff.

C. Capasso, *Paolo III, 1534–49* (1923–4); L. Dorez, *La Cour du Pape Paul III* (1932); W. H. Edwards, *Paul III oder die geistliche Gegenreformation* (1932).

**PAUL IV** (1476–1559), pope from 23 May 1555 until his death on 18 August 1559, was born Giampietro Carafa near Benevento on 28 June 1476; he was a member of the powerful Neapolitan CARAFA family. He received a humanist education (including rigorous instruction in Greek and Hebrew) in the Roman household of his uncle Cardinal Oliviero CARAFA, to whom he owed his subsequent ecclesiastical preferment. Giampietro was appointed bishop of Chieti (or 'Theate') in 1505 and served as the legate of Pope LEO X to King HENRY VIII of England in 1513–14. He was papal nuncio in Flanders and Spain 1515–20, and in 1518 he was appointed archbishop of Brindisi. By this time Giampietro's most prominent characteristics were personal asceticism, a taste for humanist scholarship (he was one of ERASMUS' many correspondents), and a characteristically Neapolitan distaste for the Spanish ascendancy in the kingdom of Naples and in the Vatican.

On returning to Rome in 1517, Giampietro joined the ORATORY OF DIVINE LOVE and devoted himself to the extirpation of abuses in his dioceses. As part of the reform programme of Pope ADRIAN VI, he renounced his bishoprics in 1524 and, together with CAJETAN and two other priests, founded a congregation known as the THEATINES (named after Giampietro's former bishopric), in which clergy bound by vows and living communally were to be engaged in preaching and pastoral work, and became the Order's first superior. He remained in Rome until the SACK OF ROME in 1527 and then lived in Venice until he returned to Rome to assume a cardinal's hat in December 1536.

The spiritual purpose of the Theatine Order was to restore apostolic purity to the clergy at a time of clerical corruption. As superior of his Order, Giampietro renounced his former humanist sympathies and became an entrenched opponent of reconciliation with the Lutheran heretics of northern Europe. He became head of the Roman INQUISITION, and in that role persecuted heretics with a savage cruelty born of reforming zeal. He became archbishop of Naples in February 1549, and in 1553 was appointed head of the HOLY OFFICE, which was responsible for the activities of the Inquisition.

On 23 May 1555, at the age of 79, Giampietro was elected as Pope Paul IV, the successor of Pope MARCELLUS II. His visceral hatred of Protestantism precluded any possibility of his reconvoking the COUNCIL OF TRENT; his preferred tool for dealing with Protestantism was the Roman Inquisition. He increased the jurisdiction and authority of the Inquisition, appointing Michele Ghislieri (later Pope PIUS V) as its head but nonetheless attending its sessions in person. His alertness to the faint whiff of heresy led him to imprison Cardinal Giovanni MORONE and to annul Cardinal Reginald POLE's legateship to England. Paul was the architect of a new instrument of the Inquisition, the *INDEX LIBRORUM PROHIBITORUM*. He suspected JEWS of secret sympathies with Protestantism, and in 1556 established the GHETTO in Rome and forced Jews to wear distinctive hats. His campaign to suppress public immorality in Rome was characteristically rigorous.

The political counterpart of Pope Paul's hatred of Protestants was his loathing for the HABSBURGS and the presence of a Spanish administration in southern Italy. He allied the papacy with France and declared war on Spain. His army was defeated by the forces of the duque de ALBA, viceroy of Naples, who occupied the Papal State and forced Pope Paul to conclude the Peace of Cave (12 September 1557), in which he acknowledged Spanish suzerainty in Naples. Pope Paul's hatred of Spain led him to fall out with a natural ally, Queen MARY I of England (who was married to King PHILIP II of Spain); when Mary died in November 1558 Pope Paul demanded the return of confiscated church lands and required Queen Elizabeth to submit to him. The widespread conviction that these demands were unreasonable hardened English opinion against the papacy and ended any hope of reconciliation. Pope Paul's dealings with crises elsewhere in northern Europe were similarly unsuccessful: he denounced the Peace of AUGSBURG as a pact with heresy, refused to acknowledge the abdication of CHARLES V (who had opposed Paul's election as pope and not sought papal sanction for his abdication), and refused to recognize the election of FERDINAND I as Holy Roman Emperor.

Pope Paul was a committed ecclesiastical reformer. He decided that the Council of Trent should be replaced by a papal council consisting initially of 60 senior Roman churchmen and then expanded by the accession of foreign bishops. This scheme was never realized, but some of his other proposals were implemented. He established a commission to reform the missal and the breviary, combated pluralism, insisted that bishops reside in their dioceses, and made his mark on monasticism by forbidding the presentation of secular clergy to monastic benefices and ordering the arrest of monks who had left their monasteries. This scrupulousness did not extend to an abjuration of the long tradition of papal nepotism, and Pope Paul unapologetically appointed his relatives to lucrative benefices; his sinister nephew, the soldier Carlo Carafa (1518–61), was raised to the cardinalate and became the pope's closest adviser. In January 1559, however, Paul acted on his growing suspicion that members of his family were behaving improperly by stripping them of their offices and expelling them from Rome.

Pope Paul was one of the most reviled of Renaissance popes. Roman citizens responded to the news of his death on 18 August 1559 with an orgy of destruction in which the headquarters of the Inquisition was destroyed and its prisoners released, and the statue of Pope Paul on the Capitol was toppled and smashed.

T. Torriani, *Una tragedia nel cinquecento romano: Paolo IV e i suoi nepoti* (1951).

**PAULI, JOHANNES** (*c*.1450–*c*.1519), German collector of SCHWÄNKE, born in Pfeddersheim (southern Palatinate). He became a monk, and assembled a collection of 232 *Schwänke* (ranging from a few lines to several pages) which was published as *Schimpf und Ernst* in 1522. This collection is characterized by religious content and a didactic tone, but is phrased in robust colloquial German and tightly structured in well-crafted narratives; it was read throughout the sixteenth and seventeenth centuries more for its value as entertainment than for its pious content.

Pauli also translated the sermons of GEILER VON KAYSERSBERG based on Sebastian BRANT's *Ship of Fools* (*Narrenschiff*) from Latin into German. He died in Thann (Alsace).

*NDB.*

**PAUMANN, KONRAD** (*c*.1410–1473), blind German composer, organist, and lutenist who was appointed official town organist of Nuremberg in 1447. Breaking his contract with the town council, he secretly fled to Munich where he entered the service of the dukes of Bavaria, Albrecht III, Sigismund, and Albrecht IV. He enjoyed an international reputation as a virtuoso performer and composer. He was possibly the inventor of German lute tablature; his *Fundamenta* are heuristic organ works.

**PAVAN**, a sixteenth-century slow, processional court dance, originally from Padua, usually followed by a faster saltarello or GALLIARD. Most pavans are in simple quadruple time, though there are examples in triple metre. Joan Ambrosio Dalza's *Intabulatura de lauto* (1508) contains an early example of the form which was to become popular throughout Europe and reached new heights in the hands of the English virginalists (BYRD, BULL, GIBBONS). The musical style of the *passamezzo* hardly differs from that of the pavan, though there may have been some slight choreographic distinctions. The *passamezzo antico* and *passamezzo moderno* refer to the two harmonic patterns used as a basis for most sixteenth-century dance compositions.

**PAVIA or** (Latin) **Ticinum**, a Lombard town on the left bank of the Ticino, 3 kilometres (2 miles) above its junction with the Po; Borgo Ticino, the suburb on the left bank, was connected to Pavia by a covered bridge (*ponte coperto*) constructed between 1351 and 1354, destroyed in 1944, and subsequently partly rebuilt. The city is dominated by the Castello Visconteo built by Galeazzo II VISCONTI in 1360. Its most important ecclesiastical buildings are the cathedral (for

which the foundation stone was laid by Cardinal Ascanio Sforza on 1488 and the dome completed in 1885), the Lombard Church of San Michele, and the Lombard-Romanesque Church of San Pietro in Cielo d'Oro, which contains the bones of AUGUSTINE and Boethius (who had been canonized as St Severinus).

In 1359 Galeazzo Visconti of Milan became lord of Pavia, and the following year was appointed imperial vicar. Pavia, which had for centuries been a rival and enemy of Milan, thereby became a Visconti possession and so was absorbed into the duchy of Milan. In 1499 King LOUIS XII of France claimed and occupied the duchy of Milan; Pavia rebelled against the French garrison and was sacked in a reprisal the following year. In 1525 the fortifications erected by the Emperor CHARLES V proved sufficient to save the city from the army of FRANCIS I, who was defeated and captured at the battle of PAVIA; two years later a French army returned and sacked the city for a week.

Pavia had been an important centre for legal studies since the early ninth century, and a school of law had been active since the eleventh century. In 1361 Galeazzo II Visconti founded a university on the site of the old law school; the main university building was built by Ludovico SFORZA in 1485. Subsidiary colleges were founded for poor students by Cardinal BORROMEO (Collegio Borromeo, 1565) and Pope PIUS V (Collegio Ghislieri, 1565).

In August 1396 Gian Galeazzo VISCONTI laid the foundation stone of the Certosa, a Carthusian monastery 8 kilometres (5 miles) north of Pavia. The nave of the church was begun in the GOTHIC style, but by the time the building had been completed in 1507, the Gothic core had been surrounded by a Renaissance church. The externally arcaded galleries, the pinnacles, the dome, and the cloisters with their 24 cells are the work of Guiniforte SOLARIO; he was succeeded in 1481 by Giovanni Antonio AMADEO, who was chief architect until 1499. By 1499 the building was complete save for the lower part of the façade, which was finished in 1507. The terracotta ornamentation in the cloisters is the work of Rinaldo de Stauris. The Certosa di Pavia represents the work of many architects and artists working in several styles, but the quality of the work makes it one of the finest Renaissance buildings in Italy and one of the most magnificent monastic complexes in the world.

**PAVIA, BATTLE OF.** At the end of 1524 a French army commanded by King FRANCIS I invaded Italy and besieged Pavia as a prelude to an attack on Milan. CHARLES V dispatched an army commanded by Charles, duke of BOURBON, and Ferdinando d'AVALOS, marquis of Pescara, to raise the siege. In the battle that ensued at Mirabello (5 kilometres (3 miles) north of Pavia) on 24 February 1525 the imperial army overwhelmed the superior French force and captured King Francis, who was taken to Spain as a prisoner.

J. Giono, *The Battle of Pavia* (1965).

**PAVILION**, a garden house, usually constructed from wood or stone. Pavilions housed FOUNTAINS in the gardens at AMBOISE, BLOIS, and GAILLON, but were normally comfortable shelters designed for viewing the gardens, and were often placed at the end of galleried promenades, as at ANET and SAINT-GERMAIN-EN-LAYE. In Italy the finest Renaissance examples are the pavilions at the Villa LANTE and the FARNESE Palace in Caprarola.

**PAZZI CONSPIRACY.** In April 1478 a group of conspirators which included Francesco and Girolamo Pazzi (members of an old Florentine banking family) and Francesco Salviati, archbishop of Pisa, plotted to assassinate Lorenzo de' MEDICI and his brother Giuliano de' MEDICI in front of the altar of the cathedral in Florence. The plot seems to have been supported by Pope SIXTUS IV, who favoured the deposition of the Medici dynasty.

In the attack on 26 April Giuliano was stabbed to death but Cosimo escaped into the sacristy with minor injuries. Attempts by the Pazzi family to rouse the people of Florence to overthrow the Medici were ignored. The subsequent execution of the conspirators (including the archbishop) and the slaughter or exile of other members of their family broke the power of the Pazzi family and consolidated the position of the Medici.

H. Acton, *The Pazzi Conspiracy* (1979).

**PEASANTS' WAR or Peasants' Revolt or (German) Bauernkrieg**, a peasants' revolt which began in June 1524 in Stühlingen (in the Black Forest) and spread the following year through the Rhineland, Swabia, Franconia, and Thuringia till it encompassed most of central and southern Germany. The revolt was the last of a series of risings that had begun with the BUNDSCHUH rising of 1493. The demands of the peasants, which were formulated in the TWELVE ARTICLES (*Die Zwölf Artikel*), ranged from the communal election of priests and control of tithing, through the abolition of serfdom, to the reduction of feudal burdens on property (rents and dues, and inheritance restrictions) and the communal usufruct of forest, water, and pasture. The principal leaders of the revolt were Hans Müller from Bulgenbach (in the Black Forest), Erasmus Gerber (in Alsace), Jäcklin Rohrbach (in Württemberg), Thomas MÜNTZER (in Thuringia), Michael GAISMAIR (in Tirol and Salzburg), with the involvement of Götz von BERLICHINGEN and Florian Geyer in Franconia.

Bands of peasants roamed the countryside pillaging monasteries and castles, though rarely committing atrocities against persons (the massacre at Weinsberg on 16 April being a signal exception). Though often well disciplined and led by those with military experience, such as former mercenaries, the peasant bands mostly lacked artillery and the capacity to organize beyond their own localities. In the course of a few weeks in 1525, the peasants were defeated by the armies of the SWABIAN LEAGUE at Böblingen (Württemberg), Königshofen, and Ingolstadt (Franconia), by Duke Antony of Lorraine at Zabern (today French Saverne) and Schwerweiler (Alsace), and, finally, on 15 May, at Frankenhausen (Thuringia), where the forces of the Protestant PHILIP OF HESSE and the Catholic GEORG DER BÄRTIGE, duke of Saxony, inflicted a decisive defeat.

The peasants cited Martin LUTHER's pleas for religious freedom, and his enemies were quick to blame the revolt on his teaching. Luther initially sought to dampen the revolt with his 'Admonitions to Peace' (*Ermahnung zum Frieden*) of April 1525, in which he acknowledged the justice of some of the peasants' demands, but then attacked them violently in his pamphlet of May 1525 'against the thieving, murdering bands of peasants' (*Wider die räuberischen und mörderischen Rotten der Bauern*).

The Peasants' War was dramatized by Goethe in *Götz von Berlichingen* (1773) and by Gerhart Hauptmann in *Florian Geyer* (1896).

Peter Blickle, *The Revolution of 1525: The German Peasants' War from a New Perspective* (1982); Tom Scott and Bob Scribner (ed. and trans.), *The German Peasants' War: A History in Documents* (1991).

**PEDERSEN, CHRISTIERN** (c.1480–1554), Danish writer, a canon of the cathedral in Lund (now in Sweden) who in 1510 moved to Paris, where he published the Danish proverbs of Peter Låle and the Latin text of the *Historia Danica* of Saxo Grammaticus (Paris, 1514), of which he wrote a continuation. He returned to Denmark, where he entered the royal service, and in 1525 followed King CHRISTIAN II into exile in the Netherlands, where Pedersen published his translations (from Latin to Danish) of the New Testament (1529) and the Psalms (1531) and converted to Lutheranism. On returning to Denmark he established a printing press in Malmö (now in Sweden), where his publications included Danish versions of the romances of Charlemagne (*Karl Magnus*), Ogier the Dane (*Krønike om Holger Danske*) and the Bible now known as 'Christian III's Bible', which was to exercise a profound influence on Danish prose.

DBL.

**PEDRO DE ALCÁNTARA or Peter of Alcantara** (1499–1562), founder of the Spanish Discalced Franciscan Order, was born in Alcántara (Extremadura), where his father was a lawyer and provincial governor. Pedro briefly attended Salamanca University (1513–14), and in 1515 entered the Observant Franciscan Order at Manjarates, where the house observed an extremely strict rule. In 1521 he was sent as the guardian of a new house at Badajoz, and in 1524 he was ordained as a priest. Thereafter he served as superior of several Spanish houses and, from 1538 to 1541, as provincial of the Observant Extremaduran province of St Gabriel. The disciplined severity of Pedro's personal life, together with his abilities as a preacher, gained him a considerable reputation, but at the conclusion of his term of office he retired to a hermitage at Arrábida (near Lisbon); the friars who gradually joined him in Portugal eventually established new communities, which in 1560 were constituted into a new province.

Pedro returned to Spain in about 1553, and in about 1556 founded a small monastery at Pedrosa, on which his congregation, the Discalced Franciscans (or Alcantarines), was later modelled. The cells were only 2 metres (6 feet) long, and Pedro strove to set an example of extreme austerity. As he explained to TERESA DE ÁVILA, he deprived himself of sleep for

40 years (allowing himself one and a half hours a night), ate only once every three days at most (sometimes fasting for eight days), wore a coarse habit (never raising the hood), and went barefoot. Pedro assisted Teresa in the reform of the Carmelite Order and became her confessor.

Pedro wrote a manual on prayer called *Tratado de la oración y meditación*, which is a condensed version of the similar treatise of Fray LUIS DE GRANADA; the accusation of plagiarism sometimes levelled at Pedro arises from an anachronistic notion of authorship and intellectual property. Pedro also wrote a *Petición especial de amor a Dios* (*c*.1560). He died in his monastery in Arenas (now Arenas de San Pedro), allegedly in a kneeling position. He was beatified in 1662, canonized in 1669, and made patron of Brazil in 1826 and of Extremadura in 1962.

Rafael Sanz Valdivieso, *Vida y escritos de San Pedro de Alcántara* (1996).

**PEELE, GEORGE** (1556–96), English playwright, educated at Oxford, and an important figure in the development of English comic drama and the dramatic use of blank verse. He worked mainly for HENSLOWE, and often in collaboration. His plays include *The Arraignment of Paris* (*c*.1584), an early pastoral drama which celebrates the beauty and virtue of ELIZABETH I; *Edward I* (*c*.1593); *The Battle of Alcazar* (published 1594), a historical dramatization of the Battle of El KSAR-EL-KEBIR; and his best-known work, *The Old Wives' Tale* (*c*.1590, published 1595), which mocks contemporary taste for romantic drama.

*DNB*.

**PEERSON, MARTIN** (*c*.1572–1651), English composer, virginalist, and organist in London. He took the Oxford B.Mus. in 1613 and was later master of the choristers at St Paul's Cathedral. He wrote sacred and secular music; his setting of 'See, O see, who is here come a-maying' was performed as part of Ben JONSON's *Private Entertainment of the King and Queen* in 1604.

**PEIRESC, NICOLE-CLAUDE-FABRI DE** (1580–1637), French humanist, botanist, and gardener. As a student in Montpellier he attended lectures at the BOTANIC GARDEN. He subsequently collected rare plants in his small garden in Aix-en-Provence. He built a large rectangular garden at his home in Belgentier (Provence), organized around a central axis; he had separate sections for flowers, medicinal plants, and rare plants. He laid out a PARTERRE in myrtle and constructed an ornamental walk 70 metres (75 yards) long lined with jasmine clipped into a green wall reaching to the ground and flanked with orange trees. He systematically collected scores of varieties of apple and pear trees.

Jacqueline Hellin, *Nicolas-Claude Fabri de Peiresc 1580–1637* (1980).

**PELETIER DU MANS, JACQUES** (1517–82), French poet, translator, and mathematician. His youthful *Œuvres poétiques* (1547) contains translations of Homer, Horace, Virgil, and Petrarch as well as original lyric poems, and his *Amour des amours* (1555) contains philosophical love poems and scientific poems typical of the PLÉIADE group with which he was associated. He contributed to the national debate about orthography in his *Dialogue* (1549), and wrote his poetic manifesto, *Art poétique* (1555), in the reformed spelling of which he was an advocate.

**PELLEGRINI, VINCENZO** (*c*.1562–1631), Italian composer, active in Pesaro and Milan, where he was *maestro di cappella* at the cathedral from 1612 and held responsible for the declining musical standards. He wrote post-Tridentine sacred music and instrumental canzonas.

**PELLIKAN, KONRAD** (1478–1556), German Hebraist, born in Rufach (now French Rouffach), in Alsace, on 8 January 1478; his original name, Kürsner, was changed to Pellikan by his maternal uncle, a cleric who intended the name to allude to the traditional Christian symbol of the pelican as an emblem of the redemptive work of Christ as mediated through the EUCHARIST. After studying for sixteen months at the University of Heidelberg (1491–2) Pellikan decided to enter the Franciscan ORDER of Friars Minor (the 'Minorites').

In 1496 Pellikan was sent to continue his education in Tübingen, where he taught himself Hebrew without the aid of a teacher or a grammar book. He eventually came to the notice of REUCHLIN, who lent him a Hebrew grammar written (in Hebrew) by Moses Qimhi. In 1503 or 1504 Pellikan published (in Strassburg) the first grammar of HEBREW to be written by a Christian and the first to be written in a European language (Latin). The culmination of Pellikan's BIBLICAL scholarship was a vast commentary on the Bible (7 vols., Zürich, 1532–9).

Pellikan served as a Minorite in Rufach, Pforzheim, and Basel until 1526, and while in Basel assisted Johann FROBEN with the preparation of his editions. He finally repudiated his monastic vows in 1526, and accepted the invitation of ZWINGLI to serve as professor of Greek and Hebrew at Zürich, where he remained until his death on 6 April 1556.

Christoph Zürcher, *Konrad Pellikans Wirken in Zürich, 1526–1556* (1975).

**PELLIPARIO.** See NICOLA DA URBINO.

**PEMBROKE'S MEN.** Formed by 1592 under the patronage of the first earl of Pembroke, it is thought that William SHAKESPEARE was associated with this acting company before joining the CHAMBERLAIN'S MEN in 1594. His plays *2* and *3 Henry VI* and *Titus Andronicus* are known to have been in their repertoire, as was Christopher MARLOWE's *Edward II*. From 1597 the group leased Philip HENSLOWE's newly built SWAN THEATRE on Bankside but disbanded the same year following the controversy surrounding their production of JONSON's *Isle of Dogs*.

**PENCZ, GEORG** (*c*.1500–1550), German painter and engraver who arrived in Nuremberg in 1523 and seems to have been trained in DÜRER's workshop. In 1525 he was accused (together with the BEHAM brothers) of blasphemy and sedition, but unlike the Behams he was allowed (on appeal) to remain near Nuremberg, in Windsheim. He seems to have lived in northern Italy in the late 1520s and to have returned to Italy c.1539–1542. The influence of BRONZINO can be discerned in his portraits, and his late work suggests a familiarity with GIULIO ROMANO. Pencz worked on a small scale, and so is numbered amongst the LITTLE MASTERS.

*MDA; NDB.*

**PENDENTIVE**, the architectural term for a concave spandrel (i.e. a curved triangular structure) that leads from the angle of two walls up to a circular dome. The domes of Florence Cathedral and St Peter's Basilica in Rome are both supported by pendentives.

**PÉNICAUD FAMILY**, a family of enamel painters in sixteenth-century Limoges. The works of Léonard (or Nardon) Pénicaud (c.1470–1542/3), who often took his designs from contemporary prints, include a *Crucifixion* (1503, Musée de Cluny, Paris) and *Deposition, Entombment,* and *Resurrection* (British Museum). Works attributed to his younger brother Jean Pénicaud (*fl.* 1510–40), including a *Flagellation* in the Victoria and Albert Museum, are distinguished by a greater attention to details such as hair and plants. Jean's son Jean II (*fl.* 1530–88), who specialized in GRISAILLES, executed both ecclesiastical works (especially reliquaries) and secular works (especially portraits, notably *Pope Clement VII* in the Louvre). In the next generation Jean III (d. 1570) and Pierre Pénicaud (d. after 1590) made enamels in the mannerist tradition of the Second School of FONTAINEBLEAU.

*MDA;* J. J. Marquet de Vasselot, *Les Émaux limousins de la fin du XV^e siècle et de la première partie du XVI^e: Nardon Pénicaud et ses contemporains* (1921).

**PENNI, GIOVAN FRANCESCO, or Il Fattore** (c.1496–after 1528), Italian painter. He was born in Florence and worked together with GIULIO ROMANO as an assistant to RAPHAEL in Rome; after Raphael's death he continued to work with Giulio Romano. His finest surviving painting is a tondo of *The Holy Family* (c.1520, Museo della Badio della Santa Trinità di Cava, Cava dei Tirreni).

*MDA.*

**PERCELLIS**. See PORCELLIS.

**PEREIRA, DUARTE PACHECO** (c.1460–1533), Portuguese explorer and geographer who sailed in 1498 along the southwest coast of AFRICA and two years later sailed with Pedro CABRAL to Brazil. He subsequently travelled to India, where he commanded the Portuguese garrison in Cochin (1503–5). While in Cochin he was attacked by the ruler of Calicut, and his successful defence of the trading colony led to his being called 'the Lusitanian Achilles' in *Os Lusíadas*, Luís de CAMÕES's epic of Portuguese exploration. From 1520 to 1522 Pereira served as governor of El Mina in Portuguese West Africa. He was an accomplished navigator, and was called upon by King AFONSO V in his negotiations leading to the Treaty of TORDESILLAS. Pereira published a celebrated navigational manual of geography called *Esmeraldo de situ orbis*, which seeks to supplement the ancients with new information on Africa.

*DHP;* Joaquim Barradas de Carvalho, *A la recherche de la spécificité de la Renaissance portugaise: L''Esmeraldo de situ orbis'* (2 vols., 1983).

**PÉREZ, ANTONIO** (1540–1611) Spanish statesman, autobiographer, and letter-writer, the illegitimate son of Gonzalo Pérez, a priest who became secretary to CHARLES V and PHILIP II. Antonio was educated in Alcalá de Henares, Louvain, Salamanca, Padua, and Venice. Pérez succeeded his father as secretary to King Philip, and was made responsible for relations with England, France, the Netherlands, and the Holy Roman Empire; he subsequently became secretary to the Council of Castile. He became the principal intermediary for royal patronage and grew wealthy on bribes.

On 29 July 1573 the prince of EBOLI died, and Pérez became the lover and political ally of the princess of EBOLI; together they assumed the leadership of the 'Eboli faction' at court, which favoured a conciliatory approach to the REVOLT OF THE NETHERLANDS. In 1578 he was implicated in the murder of Juan de Escobedo, secretary to Don JUAN DE AUSTRIA. In 1579 King Philip decided to replace Pérez with Cardinal GRANVELLE. Pérez was arrested and spent years in prison as his protracted trial slowly proceeded. On 19 July 1590 he escaped and fled to Aragon; his arrival in Zaragoza coincided with the Aragonese rebellion of 1591–2.

In Zaragoza Pérez was arraigned before the Justicia, but was acquitted because he was able to demonstrate that King Philip had been an accomplice in the murder of Escobedo. His testimony prudently libelled the king whose encroachment on Aragonese liberties was the cause of the rebellion. He was twice brought before the INQUISITION (May and September 1591) on charges fabricated for King Philip by the royal confessor, but on both occasions was rescued by Aragonese rebels. When Philip invaded Aragon in November 1591, Pérez fled to Béarn (which had become part of France in 1589), from which he mounted an abortive invasion of Aragon in 1592. He subsequently lived in France and England, and in 1598 published his *Relaciones de su vida*, which excoriated King Philip and the corruption of his court and so supported the BLACK LEGEND.

*DHE;* Gregorio Marañón, *Antonio Pérez* (2nd edn., 2 vols., 1948).

**PÉREZ DE OLIVA, FERNANDO** (c.1494–c.1531), humanist and poet, born in Córdoba and educated at Salamanca and Alcalá de Henares; he also lived in Paris for two years and spent three years in Rome at the court of Pope LEO X. His best-known work is *Diálogo de la dignidad del hombre*, the title and content of which echoes PICO's *De hominis dignitate*; the dialogue was first published in the *Obras* of the historian Francisco CERVANTES DE SALAZAR (Alcalá de Henares, 1546). He also wrote dialogues *Entre el cardenal Martínez Siliceo, la Aritmética y la Fama*. His varied interests are reflected in works such as a Latin treatise on the magnet, *Razonamiento sobre la navegación por el Guadalquivir*, and *Historia de la invención de las Indias*.

Pérez wrote adaptations of Sophocles' *Electra* (*La venganza de Agamenón*), Plautus' *Amphitryon* (*La comedia de Amphitrión*), and Euripides' *Hecuba* (*Hécuba triste*). His most famous poem is his elegy on the SACK OF ROME, entitled *Lamentación al saqueo de Roma, puesta en boca de Clemente VII*.

W. Atkinson, 'Hernán Pérez de Oliva: A Biographical and Critical Study', *Revue hispanique*, 71 (1927).

**PERI, JACOPO** (1561–1633), Florentine composer of OPERA, solo songs, and instrumental music. He was active at the Medici court where he collaborated with RINUCCINI in the pastorals *Daphne* and *Euridice*, performed at the wedding celebrations of MARIE DE MÉDICIS and HENRI IV of France in 1600. Giulio CACCINI and Emilio de' CAVALIERI were also involved. He subsequently wrote other *intermedi* (see INTERMEZZO), ballets, and equestrian displays and later collaborated with G. B. da Gagliano in the opera *La Flora* (1628). He was a member of Bardi's CAMERATA and one of the composers who claimed to be the first to have written in the new style where words are sung in a natural speech-like manner; his recitative passages in *Euridice* are both innovative and expressive.

**PERINO or Perin DEL VAGA or Pietro Buonaccorsi** (1501–47), Italian painter, born near Florence. He moved as a young man to Rome, where he worked as one of RAPHAEL's assistants (who included GIULIO ROMANO) on the stucco and fresco decoration of the Vatican Loggias. In 1527 he fled from the SACK OF ROME to Genoa, where he painted mythological frescoes in the Palazzo DORIA until *c*.1540. He then returned to Rome, where he worked with a large number of assistants on the decoration of the Vatican and Castel Sant'Angelo and several palaces, notably the Palazzo Massimo alle Colonne. Perino also designed engravings for rock crystal, notably Giovanni BERNARDI's set of rock-crystal panels of the Cassetta Farnese, for which the silver setting was made by Bastiano SBARRI (1561, Museo Nazionale, Naples).

DBI s.v. Buonaccorsi, Pietro; MDA s.v. Perino; Elena Parma Armani, *Perin del Vaga, l'anello mancante* (1986).

**PERKINS, WILLIAM** (1558–1602), English theologian. Fellow of Christ's College, Cambridge (1584–94), Perkins was an energetic anti-papist theologian, and a supporter of Puritanism. His writings include *An Exposition of the Lord's Prayer* (1592), *An Exposition of the Symbol or Creed of the Apostles* (1595), *A Discourse on Conscience* (1596), *Reformed Catholic* (1597), and *The Whole Treatise of the Cases of Conscience* (published 1606).

DNB.

**PEROTTI, NICCOLÒ** (1429–80), Italian humanist and grammarian, born in Sassaferato and educated by VITTORINO DA FELTRE in Mantua (1445–6) and then by GUARINO DA VERONA (1447). He entered the service of Cardinal BESSARION in 1447, became a papal secretary in 1455, and was consecrated archbishop of Siponto (the ancient name of Manfredonia) in 1458. Perotti was the author of the most widely diffused Latin grammar of the late fifteenth century (*Rudimenta grammatices*, 1473) and also wrote a substantial commentary on

Martial (published posthumously as *Cornucopia*, 1489) as well as translating Epictetus and Polybius.

**PERRÉAL, JEAN, or Jehan de Paris** (*fl.* 1483–1530), French painter, sculptor, architect, medallist, and decorator, the son of a court artist and poet. He became the most prominent French artist of his generation, working in the service of CHARLES VIII, LOUIS XII, and FRANCIS I, often arranging public festivities; his principal patron was ANNE OF BRITTANY. In 1494 he accompanied Charles VIII on his invasion of Italy, and returned to Italy with Louis XII in his campaigns of 1502 and 1509, but his surviving work is not markedly Italianate.

Perréal's work includes a miniature portrait of the Lyonnais poet Pierre Sala (now in the Stowe Manuscripts in the British Library) and the magnificent tomb of Duke François II of Brittany (commissioned by his daughter Anne of Brittany and executed in collaboration with Michel COLOMBE) in Nantes Cathedral. A fine portrait of Louis XII is also attributed to him.

MDA.

**PERSPECTIVE** is the name now given to constructions designed to give an effect of depth in flat pictures, or to the result of using them successfully; it is derived from the Latin term *perspectiva* which was the name given in the Middle Ages to what is now called by the Greek-derived name OPTICS. In Italian *perspectiva* is either *perspettiva* or *prospettiva*, the terms being used interchangeably. As the use of perspective in works of art became more common, in the fifteenth century, the science of vision came to be called *perspectiva communis* ('ordinary perspective') to distinguish it from the construction techniques, which were called *perspectiva artificialis* ('artificial perspective') or *perspectiva pingendi* ('perspective for painting'). By the mid-sixteenth century the medieval name *perspectiva* and its vernacular cognates was definitively established as applying to the new construction techniques and the old science of vision was known by the newer term optics.

In 1413, or shortly before, Filippo BRUNELLESCHI invented a mathematical technique for making the objects shown in a picture look three-dimensional. This invention probably arose from his interest in *perspectiva* proper, namely in thinking about how the geometry of vision would affect the perception of the proportions that had been part of the design. Unfortunately, so little is known about Brunelleschi's perspective construction that it is not even possible to decide whether his choice of subjects for his two demonstration panels, first the baptistery and second the Palazzo Vecchio seen across the square, was made because these buildings were suitable for showing off the technique or simply because they were well-known civic monuments. Matters are not greatly helped by analysis of the use of perspective in MASACCIO's *Trinity* fresco (*c*.1426), which, apart from some reliefs by DONATELLO, seems to be the earliest use of perspective construction. It seems likely that what Brunelleschi had discovered was that the perspective images of lines that in reality run perpendicular to the plane of the picture (that is, images of 'orthogonals') converge at a point that is the foot of the perpendicular from the eye of the ideal observer to the picture plane.

Perspective pictures still convey a sense of depth even if the observer is rather far from the ideal viewing position built into the construction. It is hardly surprising that painters seem to have interpreted this as an indication that getting the mathematical construction exactly right did not matter much. Correct perspective is an extreme rarity in the art of the fifteenth and sixteenth centuries, being found mainly in elaborate pieces of inlay work. In fact, perspective did not become generally fashionable, even in Florence, until the 1430s. It does, however, figure largely in ALBERTI's short treatise on painting, *De pictura* (1435), though Alberti does not give enough detail to allow one to use the rules he describes. He takes it for granted that the images of orthogonals converge, to a point he calls the 'centric point', and describes how to put in the images of lines that in reality run parallel to the picture plane ('transversals'). He gives instructions for drawing a chequerboard floor with one edge parallel to the picture plane. Alberti may have invented the method he describes, which has some connections with techniques of SURVEYING. Tiled floors are found in many fifteenth- and sixteenth-century paintings. The first detailed treatment of perspective is PIERO DELLA FRANCESCA's *De prospectiva pingendi*, which despite its Latin title was written in Italian. This analysis is rigorous and coherent; Piero proves that the construction he uses, which resembles Alberti's, is mathematically correct. The form of the treatise is that of the books for ABACUS SCHOOLS, instruction proceeding by series of worked examples. Later treatises generally omit Piero's mathematical preliminaries, and his method of using what is effectively ray-tracing to obtain images of 'more difficult' shapes; but such treatises regularly use his work, usually copying his examples. Daniele BARBARO (1568) even uses Piero's words, with an occasional modification to bring the style up to date. The earliest printed treatise was that of Viator (1505), but once illustrated books become cheaper to produce, from the 1530s onwards, perspective treatises proliferate. In the mid-sixteenth century, learned mathematicians begin to take an interest in perspective, probably because their patrons asked them for opinions on some aspect of it. G. B. BENEDETTI wrote a short essay *De rationibus operationum perspectivae* (1585) that investigates the constructions, relates them to geometrical optics, and treats everything in three dimensions, a significant mathematical advance. Unfortunately the book was too difficult for a reader in 1625 who mistakenly believed that Benedetti had proved that only the Albertian construction was correct and accordingly, in his own book, accorded it the name 'construzione legittima', by which it is still sometimes known, though it is of course by no means the only correct construction. Guidobaldo del MONTE's treatise *Perspectivae libri sex* (1600) is notable for proving that not only the images of orthogonals but those of any set of lines that in reality are parallel to one another converge to a point on the horizon. This theorem is of some use in constructing pictures, and led to important mathematical developments

when it was taken up by Girard Desargues (1591–1665), who worked on perspective and went on to invent projective geometry (1639).

During the period of the most intensive production of perspective treatises, perspective was steadily becoming less important in paintings, but it was a standard element in the design of stage set and there was a developing fashion for fictive (*trompe l'œil*) architecture. The terms 'linear perspective' and 'vanishing point', for what Alberti called the 'centric point', were introduced in 1715.

J. V. Field, *The Invention of Infinity: Mathematics and Art in the Renaissance* (1997).

**PERUGIA or (Latin) Perusia**, a city and archiepiscopal see in Umbria, formally annexed by the PAPAL STATE in 1303, but not directly administered by the papacy until 1540. From 1303 to 1540, Perugia was ruled by the College of the Ten Priors of Guilds, which worked alongside a papal legate. The powers of the college and the papacy were, however, circumscribed by *condottieri* and by oligarchical families, notably the BAGLIONI. From 1400 to 1402 the city was ruled by Gian Galeazzo VISCONTI, from 1408 to 1414 by LADISLAS OF DURAZZO, king of Naples, and from 1416 to 1424 by the *condottiere* Andrea FORTEBRACCIO. Thereafter the dominant force in the city was the Baglioni family, even though its members were never legitimized as *SIGNORIE*. In 1540, at the conclusion of the SALT WAR, the autonomy of the city was abolished by Pope PAUL III.

The University of Perugia was founded in 1308, and quickly established itself as an important centre for the study of Roman LAW: its early professors included BARTOLO DA SASSOFERRATO and his pupil Petrus Baldus de Ubaldis, a learned commentator on JUSTINIAN.

In the fifteenth century Perugia became the seat of the UMBRIAN SCHOOL of painting, with which Bartolomeo CAPORALI, PERUGINO, PINTURICCHIO, and the youthful RAPHAEL were associated. In architecture the Gothic style dominated until the mid-fifteenth century, and survives in buildings such as the cathedral (whose relics include the wedding ring of the Virgin), the Palazzo dei Priori (which now contains on its top floor the Galleria Nazionale dell' Umbria and the Biblioteca Augusta), the Loggia di Braccio, and the Great FOUNTAIN (Fontana Maggiore) with its sculptures by Niccolò and Giovanni PISANO. The Renaissance style was inaugurated by the Florentine AGOSTINO DI DUCCIO in his reliefs (some in terracotta) on the façade of the Oratory of San Bernardino (1457–61) and in his unfinished Porta San Pietro (1471); surviving examples include the Palace of the Captain of the People (Palazzo del Capitano del Popolo), the Palace of the Old University, and the Exchange Building (Collegio del Cambio, 1452–7), with frescoes by Perugino.

**PERUGINO, PIETRO VANUCCI** (*c.*1440–1523), Italian painter. He was born in Città della Pieve (near Perugia) and moved as a young man to Florence. He quickly became familiar with the new technique of OIL PAINTING; stylistic evidence suggests he worked with VERROCCHIO. By 1481 his reputation was such that he led the team invited to paint frescoes in the SISTINE CHAPEL in Rome alongside BOTTICELLI, GHIRLANDAIO, and ROSSELLI. He worked with his assistant PINTORICCHIO in the Sistine Chapel, where his frescoes, including *Jesus Delivering the Keys to St Peter* (1482), were widely acclaimed; some of his other frescoes in the chapel were destroyed to make way for MICHELANGELO's *Last Judgement*. In 1500 Perugino worked on the decoration of the Audience Chamber in the Collegio del Cambio in Perugia, by which point Agostino CHIGI could acclaim him as the finest painter in Italy. He died of the plague in Fontignano, near Perugia.

Perugino's other paintings include a *Crucifixion with Saints* (1481, National Gallery, Washington), a *Madonna with Saints* (1491–2, Louvre), a *Pietà* (1495, Pitti), a *Vision of St Bernard* (1491–4, Alte Pinakothek, Munich) and an *Assumption* (1506, Church of the SS Annunziata, Florence). His *Nativity* (1491, private collection, Rome) was painted for the future Pope JULIUS II.

The sweetness of Perugino's style led to some deprecation of his paintings, but this quality endeared him to the Pre-Raphaelites of the nineteenth century. He remains more accessible to popular taste than virtually any other painter of the Renaissance, but does not receive the sympathetic scholarly scrutiny accorded to many of his contemporaries.
MDA; Pietro Scarpellini, *Perugino* (rev. edn. 1991); Joseph Becherer, *Pietro Perugino* (1997).

**PERUZZI, BALDASSARE** (1481–1536), Italian painter, architect, and stage designer, born in Siena, where he worked as a painter. In 1503 he moved to Rome, where he was employed as an assistant to BRAMANTE on the planning of ST PETER'S BASILICA; he worked intermittently and in various capacities on the building for the rest of his life, and on the death of RAPHAEL in 1520 became its principal architect.

Peruzzi was the architect of the Villa Farnesina built in Trastevere (1509–11) for Agostino CHIGI. This VILLA, which is amongst the finest of the secular buildings of the Roman Renaissance, consists of a square block with an open loggia at the centre of the garden front and projecting wings; in a *palazzo*, the *piano nobile* is normally raised, but in this villa the main rooms are on the ground floor. Peruzzi, together with Raphael, Il SODOMA, SEBASTIANO DEL PIOMBO, and UGO DA CARPI, contributed to its decoration; the technical accomplishment of Peruzzi's Sala delle Prospettive, which has a false PERSPECTIVE view through the walls, adumbrates his later stage designs.

Peruzzi was captured by imperial troops in the SACK OF ROME (1527); he escaped to Siena, of which he became the official architect. In Siena he designed fortifications and built palaces, including the Palazzo Polini and, outside the city, the Villa Belcaro. He returned to Rome in 1530 or 1531 and there built the Palazzo Massimo alle Colonne, an early mannerist building in which Peruzzi dealt imaginatively with an awkward site by constructing a curved façade.
MDA; R. N. Adams, *Baldassare Peruzzi Architect to the Republic of Siena 1527–35* (1980); H. Wurm, *Baldassare Peruzzi Architekturzeichnungen* (1981).

**PESELLINO, FRANCESCO DI STEFANO** (c.1422–1457), Italian painter, probably trained in the Florentine studio of Fra Filippo LIPPI. His paintings include an *Annunciation* diptych (Courtauld Galleries, London) and an altarpiece of *The Trinity with Saints* which was left unfinished at his death, completed in Lippi's studio, and subsequently divided into several pieces, all bar one of which have been gradually reunited in the National Gallery in London.
MDA.

**PETIT POINT or tent stitch**, an EMBROIDERY knot stitch, in effect half of a cross stitch, which lies diagonally across the threads of the canvas. It has been used since the fifteenth century for NEEDLEWORK pictures.

**PETRARCH or (Italian) Francesco Petrarca** (1304–74), Italian poet, born in Arezzo, the son of an exiled Florentine notary. In 1311 he moved with his family to Provence, where the papacy had been exiled in 1309; Petrarch later referred to this period of exile (which extended to 1377) as the Babylonian Captivity of the Church. Although he travelled extensively in Italy and France, Petrarch's home until 1353 was Provence, where he lived in a villa near Vaucluse.

On 6 April 1327 Petrarch saw the woman whom he calls Laura in the Church of St Clare in Avignon; 21 years later, on 6 April 1348, she died of the plague. Her identity is unclear, as is the extent to which she is fact or fiction, but it is she whose presence in Petrarch's life occasioned the composition of the poems collected as *Rerum vulgarium fragmenta* ('Fragments of Vernacular Poetry') and known as the *Canzoniere* or the *Rime*.

In the course of the 1330s and 1340s Petrarch pursued humanist scholarship and wrote Italian poetry. He took minor orders and secured the patronage of the COLONNA family, who provided him with benefices which enabled Petrarch to pursue his scholarly interests. He published two of Cicero's manuscripts, one of the *Pro Archia* discovered in Liège in 1333 and the other of his *Letters to Atticus*, which Petrarch found in Verona in 1345; Petrarch's own collections of letters (350 *Familiares* and 125 *Seniles*) were inspired by and modelled on Cicero's. He also began to write poetry and prose in Latin, including *Africa* (an epic on the life of Scipio Africanus), *De viris illustribus* (biographies of famous Romans), *Rerum memorandarum libri* (an historical work about 'memorable things'), and *Secretum* (three confessional dialogues with St Augustine). His most diffused Latin work outside Italy was a collection of allegorical dialogues for treating the passions, *De remediis utriusque fortunae*. On 8 April 1341 he was crowned in Rome as poet laureate.

In Rome Petrarch supported COLA DI RIENZO's attempt to restore the ancient Roman constitution, but in the wake of Cola's fate at the hands of the Roman mob Petrarch drew back from his republican ideals and again sought the patronage of princes. In 1353 Petrarch moved permanently to Italy, initially in Milan and then in Padua, Venice, and Pavia. He finally settled in Arquà (now Arquà Petrarca) in the Euganean Hills. The works of his final years include the unfinished allegorical *Trionfi*.

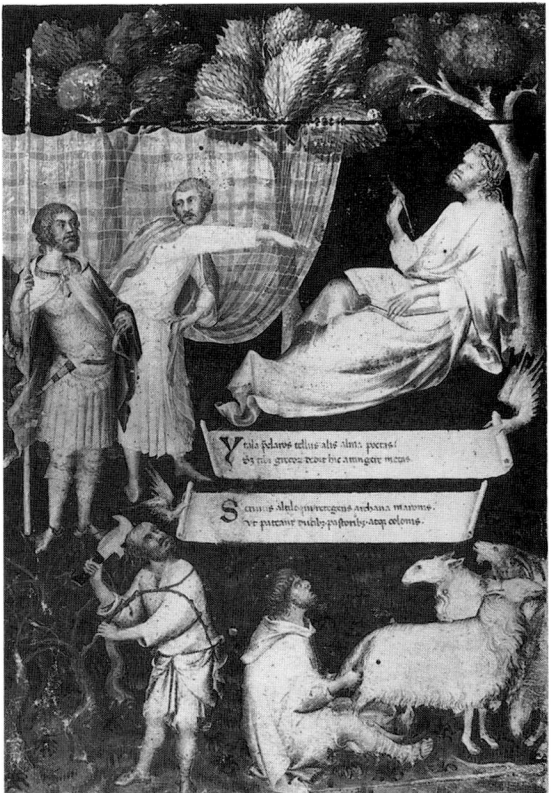

Simone Martini, the frontispiece to the copy of Servius' commentary on Virgil owned by **Petrarch**, now in the Biblioteca Ambrosiana in Milan

The sonnets of Petrarch's *Canzoniere* became the fountainhead of the European lyric; he is, after Virgil, Europe's most influential poet. His Latin scholarship provided the raw materials and the ideals of humanist pursuits for the next three centuries. Some 45 manuscripts owned by Petrarch have been identified, notably his copy of Servius' commentary on Virgil, which has a frontispiece by SIMONE MARTINI and is now in the Biblioteca Ambrosiana in Milan.

*OCIL*; P. Hainsworth, *Petrarch the Poet* (1988); N. Mann, *Petrarch* (1984).

**PETRI, OLAUS, or (Swedish) Olaf Petersson** (1493–1552), Swedish reformer and playwright, born in Örebro, the son of a blacksmith. He studied in Wittenberg (1516–18) and returned to Sweden as a disciple of LUTHER. He worked as head of the cathedral school in Strängnäs, and in 1524 became city clerk of Stockholm and began to move in court circles; he subsequently served for three years as the chancellor of GUSTAVUS VASA, and used his public prominence to preach the Reformation.

Petri published a large number of religious tracts and the first Swedish service book, *En handbok på svenska* (1529). He was responsible for the publication of a Swedish New Testament (*Thet nyia Testament på swensko*) in 1526, but there is no evidence to support the popular contention that he was the translator.

*SBL* s.v. Olavus.

**PETRUCCI, OTTAVIANO** (1466–1539), Italian music printer in Venice, whose publications of masses and motets include works by JOSQUIN DESPRÈS, WILLAERT, and FESTA. His first book, *Harmonice musices odhecaton A* (1501), contained chansons and other secular works. The year 1504 saw the publication of his first collection of FROTTOLAS and in the next five years he published ten more volumes and as many as 27 new titles. The quality of the work was high and had a reputation for reliability. His output seemed to decline both in quality and quantity after 1510 when he moved to his native Fossombrone.

**PETRUCCI FAMILY**, a dynasty that ruled SIENA from 1487 to 1524. Pandolfo Petrucci (1452–1512) returned from exile in 1487 and, assisted by his brother Giacopo (d. 1497), seized power in a *coup d'état*. Pandolfo, who enjoyed the admiration of MACHIAVELLI, assassinated his father-in-law (Niccolò Borghese) in 1500 and encouraged the Magione conspiracy against Cesare BORGIA, who exiled him from Siena in 1502; he was recalled from banishment on 29 March 1503 with the assistance of King LOUIS XII of France. Before his death on 21 May 1512 Pandolfo abdicated in favour of his son Borghese, who was exiled together with his brother Fabio in 1515; in their place Pope LEO X placed their cousin Rafaello Petrucci (d. 1522), who later became a cardinal. Alfonso Petrucci (d. 1517), the brother of Borghese and Fabio, was created cardinal by Pope JULIUS II; after the dislodgement of his brothers he conspired against Pope Leo (July 1517) and was strangled in a Roman prison. Fabio was briefly restored (1522–4) and thereafter the rule of the family came to an end.

U. Mondolfo, *Pandolfo Petrucci* (1899).

**PETTIE, GEORGE** (c.1548–1589), English writer and translator, educated at Oxford. The title of Pettie's *A Petite Palace of Pettie his Pleasure* (1576) acknowledges its debt to PAINTER's *Palace of Pleasure*, published a decade earlier. Pettie's work presents twelve stories of love, largely derived from ancient literature, in a style which anticipates EUPHUISM. He also translated books 1–3 of Stefano Guazzo's *La civile conversatione* (1581) from a French version.

*DNB.*

**PETZOLT or Petzoldt, HANS** (1551–1633), German goldsmith and silversmith who became a master of the Nuremberg Guild of Goldsmiths in 1578; on the death of Wenzel JAMNITZER in 1585, Petzolt became Nuremberg's most prominent goldsmith and thenceforth took a prominent part in civic affairs. His surviving works are mostly cups, many of which embody stylistic features associated with earlier generations of goldsmiths; some recall designs by DÜRER, and others contain Gothic elements and so are described as *Neugotik*.

*MDA.*

**PEUERL or Bäurl or Beurlin, PAUL** (1570–1625), German composer, organist, and organ builder, active in Lower and Upper Austria. Before he fled for Steyr as a religious refugee, he published four collections (1611) of his own works which include early examples of the variation suite consisting of a paduana, intrada, and galliard all based on material in the fourth movement, the 'dance'.

**PEURBACH, GEORG** (1423–61), Austrian astronomer. He was educated at the University of Vienna and for many years taught astronomy there, where his pupils included REGIOMONTANUS. At some time during the period 1448–53 Peurbach travelled through Germany, France, and Italy. He learned some Greek from BESSARION, and began work on an abridgement of PTOLEMY's *Almagest*, but this was cut short by his early death and the task was taken up by Regiomontanus.

Peurbach wrote an elementary but detailed treatise on planetary motions, using mathematical models corresponding to solid spheres rolling over one another; the treatise, which was called *Theoricae novae planetarum*, was completed in 1454, but modified later. It was printed and repeatedly reprinted with commentaries from the 1480s until the 1620s and in the sixteenth century was the standard text for teaching planetary theory.

DSB; E. J. Aiton, 'Peurbach's *Theoricae novae planetarum*: A Translation with Commentary', *Osiris*, 2nd series 3 (1987).

**PEUTINGER, CONRAD** (1465–1547), German humanist and antiquarian, born in Augsburg on 15 October 1465. After a period (1482–8) studying law in Italy, where he met POLIZIANO and PICO DELLA MIRANDOLA, Peutinger became secretary to the city council of Augsburg (1497). He married into the WELSER family and accepted the invitation of the Emperor MAXIMILIAN to join the AULIC COUNCIL. Peutinger was unsympathetic to the Reformation, and in 1534 was forced to resign as secretary to the city council because of his loyalty to the Catholic Church. He died on 28 December 1547.

Peutinger was an early student of Roman epigraphy, and was one of the first to publish Roman inscriptions. He also edited the sixth-century *Historia Gothorum* of Jordanes and the eighth-century *Historia gentis Langobardorum* of Paulus Diaconus.

In 1494 Peutinger's friend Konrad CELTIS gave him a thirteenth-century copy of a third-century map of the military roads of the western Roman Empire. This map, which is now known as the *Tabula Peutingeriana*, is composed of eleven sheets and is almost 7 metres (23 feet) long, and one of only two specimens of classical cartography to have survived; it is now in the Österreichische Nationalbibliothek in Vienna.

DLL; NDB.

**PEVERNAGE, ANDREAS** (1542/3–91), Flemish composer and choirmaster in Bruges, Kortrijk, and Antwerp. His *Cantiones sacrae* (1578) and *Laudes vespertinae*, published postumously in 1604, are collections of sacred music; his secular works appeared in four books of chansons.

**PEWTER**, an alloy which consists principally of tin and also contains lead or bismuth or copper. The proportion of tin to lead in Roman pewter was usually 7 : 3 or 4 : 1; by the fifteenth century, when the earliest surviving regulations concerning the composition of pewter were formulated, the proportion of lead had been reduced: in Montpellier in 1437 the ratio of tin to lead was fixed at 24 : 1 for dishes and bowls and 9 : 1 for salt cellars and pitchers. In 1576 Nuremberg specified a ratio of 10 : 1 for all pewter. The motive for the reduction of lead was appearance rather than health: pewter with a low proportion of lead can be polished to the point at which it resembles silver, but the admixture of lead darkens the colour to a blackish grey.

Pewter was usually moulded into functional tableware, but in the sixteenth century a more elaborate 'display pewter' was developed. Decorated display pewter originated in Lyon, where its most prominent exponent was François BRIOT. Nuremberg later became an important centre of display pewter: the city's most prominent pewterers were Nicholas Horchhaimer (d. 1583) and Albrecht Preissensein (d. 1598), who made large bowls decorated with low-relief figures; their most important successor was Caspar ENDERLEIN. In England, where London pewterers were recognized as a guild in 1348, the most outstanding pewterer whose work has survived was William Grainger (*fl.* 1616), a master of the Pewterers' Company who is the eponym of the relief cast candlestick known as the Grainger Candlestick which is now in the Victoria and Albert Museum.

English pewter was required to bear a maker's mark under a statute of 1503. Early modern marks tend to consist of an oval or circular punch surrounding initials, sometimes with a simple device. As the tables (or 'touch-plates') recording these marks and their makers perished in the fire of 1666, attribution of London pewter is sometimes problematical.

H. H. Cotterell, *Old Pewter, its Makers and Marks* (1929); V. Brett, *The Phaidon Guide to Pewter* (1981).

**PFEFFENHAUSER or Peffenhauser, ANTON** (c.1525–1603), German armourer, based in Augsburg, where he made armours (see ARMS AND ARMOURS) for the princes of Germany and the court of King PHILIP II in Spain. Examples of his armours are preserved in the Tower of London Armouries, the Wallace Collection in London, the Kunsthistorisches Museum in Vienna, Musée de l'Armée in Paris, the Real Armería in Madrid, the Historisches Museum in Dresden, and the Metropolitan Museum in New York.

NDB.

**PFEFFERKORN, JOHANNES** (1468/9–1522), German religious controversialist. He was raised as a JEW but converted to Catholicism in about 1504; after his baptism he secured the patronage of the Dominicans of Cologne, who supported his virulent diatribes against Jews and Judaism, which included attacks on the Talmud and an insistence that Jews be obliged to attend Christian sermons. In 1509 the Emperor MAXIMILIAN authorized Pfefferkorn to confiscate Jewish publications that were deemed to be hostile to Christianity. Pfefferkorn pursued this mission with such vehemence that the archbishop of Mainz asked Johann REUCHLIN to proffer his opinion on the suppression of these books. On 6 October 1510 Reuchlin replied saying that he opposed the edict on the grounds that the very few Jewish books that defamed Christianity were repudiated by most Jews, and that other Jewish books were either adjuncts to Jewish worship (which had been sanctioned by both imperial and papal dispensation) or of scholarly value. Pfefferkorn responded by circulating at the FRANKFURT fair of 1511 a pamphlet called *Handspiegel wider und gegen die Juden*, which asserted that Reuchlin had been bribed. Reuchlin replied with *Der Augenspiegel* (1511), which was pilloried by Pfefferkorn and subsequently condemned by the inquisitor Jakob von Hochstraten and the theological faculty of Cologne University; on 7 October 1512 these powerful enemies secured an imperial edict condemning the *Augenspiegel*. Eventually learned opinion turned in Reuchlin's favour, and his allies published the EPISTOLAE OBSCURORUM VIRORUM, a mimicking satire allegedly written on behalf of Pfefferkorn.

*JNB s.v. Pfefferkorn, Joseph; NDB.*

**PFISTER, ALBRECHT** (*c.*1429–*c.*1466), German printer who worked for many years as a secretary for the bishop of Bamberg before becoming a printer in Bamberg in the early 1460s. He was the first printer to use hand-coloured woodcuts as illustrations and the first to publish books in German, notably Johann von Saaz's *Der Ackermann aus Böhmen* (1460) and Ulrich Boner's *Edelstein* (1461); he also published an illustrated *Biblia pauperum* (or *Armenbibel*).

*ADB.*

**PFLUG, JULIUS VON** (1499–1564), bishop of Naumburg, educated at the universities of Leipzig, Bologna, and Padua and appointed provost of Zeitz in 1522 and dean of Meissen in 1537. Pflug's humanist sympathies and tolerant temperament led him to seek reconciliation with the Protestant party at meetings such as the Colloquy of REGENSBURG (1541), where he was willing to concede communion in both kinds and to tolerate a married clergy. In 1541 he was elected bishop of Naumburg-Zeitz, but the Lutheran elector of Saxony, JOHANN FRIEDRICH I, refused to acknowledge him, and he was not able to claim his see until the elector was defeated at the battle of MÜHLBERG in 1547. Pflug was the architect of the AUGSBURG INTERIM of 1548.

*Correspondence*, ed. J. V. Pollet (5 vols. in 6, 1969–82); J. V. Pollet, *Julius Pflug (1499–1564) et la crise religieuse dans l'Allemagne du XVIe siècle* (1990).

**PHALÈSE, PIERRE** (*c.*1505/10–*c.*1573/6), Netherlandish composer and publisher who in 1552 received the privilege to print music from movable type and published lute music, chansons, and motet collections by CLEMENS NON PAPA and CRÉCQUILLON. Later publications were more international in their outlook. A partnership with Jean Bellère (1526–95), continued by Pierre Phalèse the Younger, started in 1570, securing a supply of French and Italian works for publication. Phalèse was the first Netherlandish printer to arrange the format of lute books to allow players seated around a table to play from one copy.

**PHILIP I, THE HANDSOME, or Felipe I, El Hermoso** (1478–1506), king of Castile and founder of the Habsburg dynasty in Spain, was born in Bruges on 22 July 1478, the son of the Emperor MAXIMILIAN I and MARY OF BURGUNDY, who was the daughter of CHARLES THE BOLD. In 1482 Philip inherited the Burgundian possessions of his mother Mary (i.e. Burgundy and the Netherlands), which were placed under the guardianship of his father Maximilian, and became archduke of Burgundy. In 1496 he married JUANA LA LOCA, who was the daughter of FERDINAND V and ISABELLA. The deaths of Juana's brother Prince Juan (son and heir of Ferdinand and Isabella), of her eldest sister Isabella (queen of Portugal), and of Isabella's infant son and heir Miguel opened the succession to the crown of Spain to Princess Juana.

In 1502 Princess Juana and Archduke Philip were confirmed by the cortes of Aragon and Castile as heirs to the throne of Spain. Their marriage had by this point collapsed under the pressure of his infidelity and her insanity, and Philip returned alone to Flanders. When Juana's mother Isabella died on 24 November 1504, Ferdinand endeavoured to secure the regency of Castile, but was forced by powerful members of his court to withdraw. By this time Juana had joined Philip in Flanders, and they sailed for Spain to claim the Castilian inheritance, landing at La Coruña on 28 April 1506 with a household guard of German mercenaries. Civil war was averted through the mediation of Cardinal CISNEROS, who arranged for meetings between Ferdinand and Philip at Remesal (near Pueblo de Senabria) and Renata, and facilitated the retirement of Ferdinand from Castile.

Philip died suddenly at Burgos on 25 September 1506, probably of typhoid; his burial was delayed because Juana refused to be separated from his body. Philip and Juana were the parents of two future Holy Roman Emperors, CHARLES V and FERDINAND I.

*DBEH; DHE.*

**PHILIP II or (Spanish) Felipe II** (1527–98), king of Spain and (as Filippo I) king of Naples and (as Felipe I) king of Portugal (1527–98), was born on 21 May 1527 in Valladolid, the son of the Emperor CHARLES V and Isabella of Portugal. In 1543 he married his 16-year-old cousin Maria of Portugal (daughter of King MANUEL I), who died four days after giving birth to their son, Don CARLOS. Philip lived in Brussels for three years (1548–51), and on returning to Spain in 1551 was entrusted by his father with responsibility for its government. In July 1554 Philip married his cousin MARY I, queen of England, and was given the kingdom of Naples and the dukedom of Milan.

In 1556 Charles V abdicated, and Philip became king of Spain (i.e. king of Castile, León, and Navarre, together with Spanish America, and king of Aragon, which included Catalonia and Sardinia) and duke of Burgundy (i.e. the Netherlands). He continued to live in Brussels, and from there conducted war against France (1556–9) in the name of England and Spain; one consequence of this conflict was England's loss of Calais to France. Queen Mary and the Emperor Charles both died in 1558, but the war continued until 1559, when the Treaty of CATEAU-CAMBRÉSIS concluded the conflict, which was the final phase of the WARS OF ITALY. In fulfilment of one of the terms of the treaty, Philip married Elizabeth of Valois, daughter of King HENRI II of France and CATHERINE DE MÉDICIS; this marriage was to produce two daughters, Isabella and Catalina. Elizabeth had previously been betrothed to Don Carlos, who in 1568 was arrested at the command of his father and six months later died in prison. In the same year Elizabeth died, and in 1570 King Philip married his cousin Anna of Austria (daughter of the Emperor MAXIMILIAN II), by whom he had a son who was to succeed him as PHILIP III of Spain.

In 1559 King Philip had returned permanently to Spain, where his position was secure except for two regional rebellions, one by MORISCOS in Granada (1568–70) and the other by nobles in ARAGON (1591); beyond the boundaries of Spain, however, he faced constant conflict, some of which he initiated himself. In 1567 the REVOLT OF THE NETHERLANDS erupted, and King Philip dispatched the duke of ALBA to suppress the rebellion; in the event this costly war lasted until 1609, eleven years after the death of Philip.

King Philip's struggle against the Ottomans began with the conquest of Djerba on 13 March 1560, but the island had to be surrendered four months later (29 July). He successfully resisted the siege of Oran (April–May 1563) and the siege of Malta (May–November 1565). In 1571 it was Philip's navy that lay at the heart of the forces of the HOLY LEAGUE (commanded by his half-brother Don JUAN DE AUSTRIA) which defeated the Ottomans at the battle of LEPANTO. The victory was heralded all over Europe as the defeat of Islam by the united forces of Christendom, but within a year the Ottomans had launched another fleet: when Tunis (captured October 1573) was surrendered to the Ottomans on 13 September 1574, the Ottomans had a larger fleet than either side had had at Lepanto.

In 1580, on the death of the Cardinal-Prince HENRIQUE, Philip claimed the throne of Portugal, which he seized in an invasion commanded by the duke of Alba. In 1588 he sent the SPANISH ARMADA to invade England in the hope that a subjugated England would be the best bridgehead for an attack on the rebellious Netherlands; the attempt failed, as did attempts to send ships to assist Irish rebels in 1596 and 1597. In 1598 Philip reluctantly signed the Treaty of VERVINS, which conceded to the southern Netherlands an autonomous government under Philip's daughter Isabella and her intended husband ALBRECHT VON HABSBURG, who were to rule as sovereign princes.

Philip was a patron of art with a pronounced bias towards Italy: he bought paintings by TITIAN, but disliked the work of EL GRECO. His greatest architectural commission was the ESCORIAL (1563–83), where he spent his last years and died on 13 September 1598.

DBEH and DHE s.v. Felipe II; Geoffrey Parker, Philip II (1978); id., The Grand Strategy of Philip II (1998).

**PHILIP III or (Spanish) Felipe III** (1578–1621), king of Spain and (as Felipe II) king of Portugal, was born in Madrid on 14 April 1578, the son of King PHILIP II and his fourth wife Anna

of Austria, who was the daughter of the Emperor MAXIMILIAN II. On succeeding to the throne in 1598, he delegated the administration of the kingdom to his favourites, the most powerful of whom were the duke of LERMA and (after 1618) the duke's son, the duke of Uceda.

Philip's reign coincided with the REVOLT OF THE NETHERLANDS, the outbreak of the THIRTY YEARS WAR (in which Philip sided with the emperor and the Catholic princes), and the expulsion of the MORISCOS from Spain (1608–14), but the king left the conduct of such matters to others, and divided his time and the failing wealth of the economy between lavish court festivities and generous acts of ecclesiastical patronage. Philip died in Madrid on 31 March 1621.

DBEH; DHE; Paul Allen, Philip III and the Pax Hispanica, 1598–1621 (2000).

**PHILIP THE GOOD or (French) Philippe le Bon** (1396–1467), duke of Burgundy (from 1419), duke of Brabant (from 1430), count of Holland (from 1433), and duke of Luxemburg (from 1443), was born in Dijon, the son of JOHN THE FEARLESS, duke of Burgundy, to whose title he succeeded on the assassination of his father in 1419. He blamed the murder of his father on the dauphin (later King CHARLES VII), and retaliated by signing the Treaty of Troyes (1420), by which he recognized King Henry V of England as the heir to the French throne. He collaborated with the English for ten years, and in 1430 betrayed JOAN OF ARC to his English allies.

Philip steadily extended his domains in the Netherlands by seizing nearby duchies and counties (Brabant in 1430, Holland in 1433, Luxemburg in 1443). In 1435 he reached an accommodation with the French crown, and by the Treaty of Arras recognized Charles VII as king of France; he was rewarded for his loyalty with additional territories, including the counties of Auxerre, Bar-sur-Seine, Mâcon, and Ponthieu and the Somme towns of Montdidier, Péronne, and Roye. His Netherlandish possessions were persistently rebellious (Liège rebelled in 1430, Ghent in 1432, and Antwerp in 1435) until his victory in 1453 at the battle of Gavere (in what is now Belgium), which left 20,000 citizens of Ghent dead on the field. His vision of a crusade against the Ottoman Turks was never realized, though he did assemble the knights for a memorable banquet in 1454; after pledging to liberate the East from the infidel Turks, the knights returned home.

Philip's court was an important centre of FLEMISH ART; the artists of his court included Jan van EYCK. In 1430, on the occasion of his third marriage (to Isabella, daughter of JOHN I of Portugal), he founded the chivalric Order of the GOLDEN FLEECE. He was succeeded by his only surviving legitimate son, CHARLES THE BOLD.

Richard Vaughan, Philip the Good: The Apogee of Burgundy (1970).

**PHILIP OF HESSE or (German) Philipp von Hessen or Philip the Magnanimous or (German) Philipp der Grossmütige** (1504–67), German landgrave born in Marburg on 13 November 1504, the son of Wilhelm II, landgrave of Hesse. Philip succeeded to the landgravate on his father's death in 1509 and was declared of age in 1518. In 1523 he married Christina, daughter of GEORG DER BÄRTIGE, duke of

Saxony. In 1523 he assisted with the suppression of the rising of Franz von SICKINGEN and two years later he helped to quell the PEASANTS' REVOLT. He had no theological interests, but understood the politics of the Reformation, and in 1524 had become a Lutheran, principally because he aspired to create a league of Protestant German princes in order to overthrow the HABSBURG emperors. In Hesse, he introduced the Reformation after the Diet of SPEYER (1526) and founded the University of Marburg (1527), the first university to be founded on Protestant principles; he convened the Colloquy of MARBURG (1529) in the hope of bringing together Lutherans and Zwinglians. He subscribed to the AUGSBURG CONFESSION in 1530 and the following year became the principal architect of the SCHMALKALDIC LEAGUE, a defensive league of Protestant princes.

In 1526 Philip declared his support for the campaign to restore the duchy of Württemberg to Duke ULRICH, but the invasion was delayed until April 1534; on 13 May 1534 the Habsburg armies of CHARLES V and his brother FERDINAND I were defeated by the forces of Philip and Ulrich at the battle of Lauffen. Protestants rejoiced in the victory and declared Philip's military contribution to Protestantism to be as great as Luther's literary contribution.

In March 1540 Philip contracted a bigamous marriage to Margaret von der Saal. He had received assurances from several Protestant theologians that polygamy was not contrary to biblical teaching, and had also secured the reluctant approval of Luther and MELANCHTHON, which was given on the condition that the marriage be kept secret. When news of the marriage leaked out, the Protestant princes repudiated Philip. He responded by defecting to the Empire, and in June 1541 agreed a treaty with Charles V in Regensburg: in return for a general pardon, Philip agreed to break off relations with France and England.

The accord between Philip and the emperor lasted until the following year, when Philip persuaded the Schmalkaldic League to liberate the duchy of Brunswick-Wolfenbüttel from its Catholic duke, Heinrich II. Charles responded with a plan to destroy the League: in July 1546 he issued an imperial ban against Philip and JOHANN FRIEDRICH I, elector of Saxony. In April 1547 he captured Johann Friedrich at the battle of MÜHLBERG; two months later Philip was persuaded to surrender by his son-in-law MAURICE OF SAXONY and JOACHIM II, elector of Brandenburg, who promised Philip that he would be pardoned. In the event he was not pardoned, and was instead sentenced to fifteen years' imprisonment. He was released in 1552, when Maurice of Saxony forced the emperor to sign the Treaty of Passau, which contained a clause stipulating that Philip be released. He spent the rest of his life assisting the Protestant cause in Hesse, in France (where he sent troops to fight alongside the HUGUENOTS), and in the Netherlands (where he supported the insurgents in the REVOLT OF THE NETHERLANDS).

Philip had four sons and five daughters by Christina, and on his death partitioned his landgravate amongst his sons; by Margaret he had seven sons (all styled counts of Dietz) and one daughter. After his death he was found to have been triorches (three-testicled), which provided an explanation for his bigamy and fecundity. He died in Kassel on 31 March 1567.

NDB s.v. Philipp der Großmütige; H. J. Hillerbrand, *Landgrave Philip of Hesse* (1967).

**PHILIP OF LEIDEN** (c.1328–1382), Dutch jurist and political philosopher. His *Tractatus de cura reipublicae et sorte principantis* (c.1360) defends the authority of temporal rulers but maintains that such powers are established for the public good.

**PHILIPS, PETER** (1560/1–1628), English composer who sang as a boy at St Paul's Cathedral and studied with William BYRD. As a Catholic he fled in 1582 to the English College in Rome where he was organist and enjoyed the protection of Cardinal Alessandro Farnese. In the mid-1580s he accompanied Lord Thomas Paget, another religious refugee, to Genoa, Madrid, Paris, Brussels, and Antwerp. In 1591 he settled in Antwerp until he became organist to Archduke ALBRECHT VON HABSBURG in Brussels in 1597. He wrote secular and sacred vocal music and works for keyboard, many of which were copied into the FITZWILLIAM VIRGINAL BOOK.

**PHILOSOPHY**. The principal concerns of Renaissance philosophers were moral philosophy, political philosophy, the philosophy of nature (including metaphysics, science, and the occult), and psychology (including epistemology). The study of philosophy was linked to the HUMANIST revival of the texts of classical antiquity, and particularly of PLATO and the Neoplatonists (though the notion of the Florentine 'Platonic Academy' is something of a myth) and of other ancient philosophical traditions such as SCEPTICISM, STOICISM, and even Epicureanism (centred on the *De rerum natura* of Lucretius). Medieval scholastic philosophy was repudiated by many (but by no means all) humanists and reformers, but the ARISTOTELIAN philosophical tradition remained dominant and was even strengthened by Counter-Reformation theologians.

C. B. Schmitt and Quentin Skinner (eds.), *The Cambridge History of Renaissance Philosophy* (1988); B. P. Copenhaver and C. B. Schmitt, *Renaissance Philosophy* (1992).

**Phrantzes, Georgios** (1401–77), Greek historian. Shortly before he died in Corfu, Phrantzes completed a history of Byzantium from 1258 to his own time. This account was written independently of the history of the same period composed by DOUKAS, and so constitutes an independent witness of the events that both describe. The tone of Phrantzes' writing is xenophobic, and he disparages both west Europeans and Ottoman Turks.

Georgios Phrantzes, *Cronaca* (Greek text and Italian translation, 1990); id., *The Fall of the Byzantine Empire: A Chronicle*, trans. Marios Philippides (1980).

**PIA, VILLA**, a small VILLA with interior garden in the Vatican built in 1560 by Pirro LIGORIO as a retreat for Pope PIUS IV. The three-storeyed CASINO is one of the most elegant surviving examples of mannerist architecture. The villa faces a small oval court, 27 metres by 18 metres (30 × 20 yards), which is surrounded by three structures independent of the main building; the four buildings are linked by a low wall fitted with seats and decorated with vases. The interior court is ornamented with *stucchi* modelled on ancient Roman coins, and the decoration of the entrance loggia, which is covered in mosaics that are reflected in a pool fed by a fountain, is also based on the ancient Roman practice of combining water and mosaics.

The Villa Pia was the first *casino* in Italy to have its own GIARDINO SEGRETO, and so was an important precursor of the FARNESE Villa at Caprarola. The landscaping has been modified over the centuries, and the lower gardens have disappeared, but the villa is still, as Jakob Burckhardt observed, the 'most perfect retreat imaginable for a midsummer afternoon'.

G. Smith, *The Casino of Pius IV* (1977).

**PICARESQUE**, a literary genre in sixteenth and seventeenth-century Spain. The picaresque novel was an episodic first-person narrative that related the adventures (often criminal or sexual) of a shrewd rogue (*pícaro*) of humble origin; in this respect it was an antidote to the romance of chivalry, which celebrated the high ideals of aristocratic heroes.

The prototype of the picaresque novel was the anonymous LAZARILLO DE TORMES (1554), which was later imitated in England by Thomas NASHE (*The Unfortunate Traveller*, 1594). The most influential example of the genre is Mateo ALEMÁN's *Guzmán de Alfarache* (1599–1602), which was imitated in Germany by Johann Grimmelshausen (*Simplicissimus*, 1669), in France by Alain-René Lesage (*Gil Blas de Santillane*, 1715–35), and in England by Defoe (*Moll Flanders*, 1722). In early seventeenth-century Spain, the most important inheritors of Alemán were the pseudonymous author of *La pícara Justina* (1605), Vicente ESPINEL (*Marcos de Obregón*, 1618), Jerónimo Alcalá de Henares Yáñez (*Alonso, mozo de muchos amos*, 1624–6), and QUEVEDO, the greatest exponent of the genre (*El buscón*, 1626).

A. A. Parker, *Literature and the Delinquent: The Picaresque Novel in Spain and Europe, 1599–1753* (1967); H. Sieber, *The Picaresque* (1977); F. Rico, *The Spanish Picaresque Novel and Point of View* (1984); Giancarlo Maiorino (ed.), *The Picaresque* (1996).

**PICCININI, ALESSANDRO** (1566–*c*.1638), Italian composer, lutenist, and writer on music. He worked at the ESTE court in Ferrara and, after 1597, for Cardinal Pietro Aldobrandini in Bologna, where he was a member of the Accademia dei Filomusi. The first of his two collections of lute music (1623) contains an important preface which deals with the invention of the archlute, modifications to the chitarrone, and details of performance practice. He wrote toccatas and dances as well as the music for the first opera to be performed in Spain, *La selva sin amore*.

**PICCININO, LUCIO** (*fl.* 1578–95), Italian armour embosser, the last great Milanese manufacturer of embossed parade armours (see ARMS AND ARMOUR), and the successor to Filippo NEGROLI as Italy's most prominent armourer. An armour made for Alessandro FARNESE, duke of Parma (*c*.1578) is preserved in the Kunsthistorisches Museum in Vienna; this armour, which is decorated with scenes in relief and damascened in gold and silver, forms the basis for other attributions to Piccinino, including armours in the Wallace Collection in London, the Victoria and Albert Museum, and the Metropolitan Museum in New York.

**PICCININO, NICCOLÒ** (1386–1444), *condottiere*, born in Callisciana, near Perugia, the son of a butcher. He served a local soldier as a page, eventually becoming a cavalryman, and in 1416 entered the service of Andrea FORTEBRACCIO, who was waging war on Perugia. After the death of Fortebraccio and his son Otto in 1424, Niccolò assumed control of Fortebraccio's *condotta*. He was initially employed by Florence, but in 1426 entered the service of Filippo Maria VISCONTI, on whose behalf he fought in a series of wars against Florence, Venice, and the papacy.

Niccolò's principal antagonist was Francesco SFORZA, whom he fought in a series of campaigns in Romagna (where Francesco led a papal army) and Lombardy (where Francesco led a Venetian army) and at the battle of ANGHIARI (where Francesco led a Florentine army). Their personal rivalry was exacerbated when Filippo Maria Visconti, unnerved by the power of Niccolò Piccinino, offered his illegitimate daughter Bianca Maria as a bride for Francesco Sforza in a bid to lure him away from Venice. Francesco married Bianca Maria, and even though he did not change sides, his new relationship with Filippo Maria Visconti reduced the standing of Niccolò; his position was further weakened when he was defeated by Francesco Sforza at Monteloro in 1443. He died of dropsy the following year.

Niccolò's sons Francesco and Jacopo Piccinino were also *condottieri*. Francesco commanded the forces of the AMBROSIAN REPUBLIC against Francesco Sforza. Jacopo served Venice and then entered the service of ALFONSO V of Aragon; he later supported FERRANTE I of Naples but switched his allegiance to Jean of Anjou, and was subsequently executed for treason by Ferrante. Francesco died of dropsy in 1449.

**PICCOLOMINI, ALESSANDRO** (1508–78), Italian humanist, poet, and dramatist. He was born in Siena and became a teacher of philosophy in Padua (from 1539) and Rome (1546–58). In 1574 he was appointed archbishop of Patras and coadjutor archbishop of Siena. His works include a dialogue on women (*La Raffaella*, 1540), two comedies (*Amor costante*, 1545; *Alessandro*, 1549), a sonnet sequence (*Cento sonetti*, 1549), and treatises on natural philosophy (*Della filosofia naturale*, 1551; revised version, 1565) and moral philosophy (*Delle institutione di tutta la vita dell'uomo nato nobile et in città libera*, 1542). His Italian translations of classical literature included Aristotle's *Rhetoric* (1571) and *Poetics* (1572); his commentary on the *Poetics* (1575) became the subject of a protracted scholarly debate. Piccolomini also translated into Latin the commentary of Alexander of Aphrodisias on Aristotle's *Meteorology* (1540). His most important philosophical work is *Commentarium de certitudine mathematicarum* (1547), an examination of the basis of mathematical certainty.

*OCIL*; F. V. Carreta, *Alessandro Piccolomini, letterato e filosofo senese del Cinquecento* (1960).

**PICCOLOMINI FAMILY**, a Sienese family of merchants, landowners, *condottieri*, and churchmen which came to prominence in the thirteenth century. The enormous wealth of the family came from international trade which was organized through their branches in Genoa, Trieste, Venice, and the major cities of Germany and France. The family reached the apex of its influence in the late fifteenth century, when Enea Silvio Piccolomini was elected as Pope PIUS II and his nephew embarked on an ecclesiastical career that culminated in his election as Pope PIUS III. In 1461 King FERRANTE I of Naples conferred the dukedom of Amalfi on Antonio Piccolomini (nephew of Pope PIUS II). In 1528 Alfonso Piccolomini was appointed to a senior military command in Naples by the Emperor CHARLES V, and subsequently became *capitano del popolo* of Naples, but he was suspected of co-operation with France and relieved of his duties by Charles V in 1541.

In the sixteenth century, Alessandro PICCOLOMINI became a distinguished writer and philosopher, and in the seventeenth century Prince Ottavio Piccolomini, duke of Amalfi (1599–1656), was an important military commander in the THIRTY YEARS WAR.

**PICCOLPASSO, CIPRIANO** (*c.*1524–1579), Italian potter from CASTEL DURANTE, the author of a treatise on MAIOLICA entitled *Tre libri dell'arte del vasaio*. The treatise was written between 1556 and 1559, which makes it the earliest surviving European study of pottery, but was not published until 1860, when a French translation appeared; the Italian original was first published in 1857. The manuscript, which is illustrated, is in the Victoria and Albert Museum in London.

MDA; *Cipriano Piccolpasso's Three Books of the Potter's Art*, ed. A. Caiger-Smith and R. Lightbown (1978).

**PICO DELLA MIRANDOLA, GIANFRANCESCO** (1469–1533), Italian philosopher, born in Mirandola; he received a humanistic education at the ESTE court in Ferrara, and was also influenced by his uncle Giovanni PICO DELLA MIRANDOLA, whose life he wrote. Disputes with his brothers over the title to Mirandola led to Gianfrancesco's exile in various north Italian cities from 1502 to 1514, when he returned to Mirandola; he was assassinated by a nephew in 1533.

Gianfrancesco was a Christian SCEPTIC whose writings included treatises on astrology, epistemology, psychology, and providence. His most important philosophical work was *Examen vanitatis doctrinae gentium* (1520), which contrasts the divine knowledge embodied in the Bible with fallible and partial human knowledge.

C. B. Schmitt, *Gianfrancesco Pico della Mirandola (1469–1533) and his Critique of Aristotle* (1967).

**PICO DELLA MIRANDOLA, GIOVANNI** (1463–94), Italian syncretistic philosopher and humanist, born in Mirandola and educated in Bologna (where he studied CANON LAW) and in Ferrara and Padua (where he studied philosophy); he visited the University of Paris in 1484 and thereafter settled in Florence and Perugia. He learnt Hebrew and some Arabic and began to study AVERROËS and the CABBALA. In 1486 he proposed to defend 900 theses (his *Conclusiones*) against all comers in Rome, and in the event, thirteen were declared problematical; he vigorously stood by these thirteen in an *Apologia* which eventually led Pope INNOCENT VIII to condemn all 900. Pico fled to France, but was arrested at Vincennes in 1488. He was released at the intervention of Lorenzo de' MEDICI and returned to Florence, where he wrote a series of philosophical treatises, including *Heptaplus* (1489), an esoteric interpretation of the opening chapters of Genesis, the *De ente et uno* (1492), a treatise on ontology that attempted to reconcile Plato and Aristotle, and a huge work against the astrologers.

Pico became a follower of SAVONAROLA, and in 1493 the papal censures of Innocent VIII were lifted by Pope ALEXANDER VI. He was murdered, it seems, by a disgruntled retainer.

E. Garin, *Giovanni Pico della Mirandola* (1937); H. de Lubac, *Pic de la Mirandole: Études et discussions* (1974).

**PIENZA**, a model Renaissance town near Siena. Corsignano, the earlier name of the town, was the birthplace of Pope PIUS II, who in 1459 commissioned Bernardo ROSSELLINO to remodel the town. In the course of the next four years, Rossellino laid out the piazza (in Florentine style) and a grid of streets; the layout is the earliest example of symmetrical TOWN PLANNING. In 1462 the name of the town was changed by papal bull to Pienza, in honour of Pope Pius.

Pope Pius and Rossellino both died in 1464, when only a few houses had been completed, but the project continued. The finest buildings, grouped around the Piazza Pio II, are the Palazzo Piccolomini (also named after Pope Pius), the cathedral (with some Gothic interior features and an elegant Renaissance façade), the towered Palazzo Communale, and the Palazzo Vescovile. There is a beautiful FOUNTAIN in front of the Palazzo Piccolomini; inside the palace there is a courtyard with a two-storey loggia and hanging gardens.

E. Carli, *Pienza, la città di Pio II* (1967); C. R. Mack, *Pienza: The Creation of a Renaissance City* (1987); Andreas Tönnesmann, *Pienza: Städtebau und Humanismus* (1990); Jan Pieper, *Pienza: Il progetto di una visione umanistica del mondo* (2000).

**PIERINO DA VINCI** (*c.*1529–1553), Italian sculptor and silversmith, born in Vinci; he was the nephew of LEONARDO DA VINCI. He was trained in Florence by Baccio BANDINELLI and Niccolò TRIBOLO, and then worked in Rome for a year before settling in Pisa, where he died in his mid-twenties. His surviving works include bronze statuettes of *Pomona* and *Bacchus* (Ca' d'Oro, Venice) and a marble relief called *Pisa Restored* (*c.*1552, Vatican), in which COSIMO I DE MEDICI is shown expelling vice from Pisa.

MDA; Marco Cianchi (ed.), *Piero da Vinci* (1995).

**PIERO DELLA FRANCESCA** (1415–92), Italian painter and art theorist, born in Sansepolcro (Borgo Sansepolcro, Umbria). He first enters the documentary record in 1439, when he is recorded working with DOMENICO VENEZIANO on the frescoes of San Egidio (now lost). Thereafter his paintings include the *Baptism of Jesus* (*c.*1448–50, National Gallery, London), the polyptych of the *Madonna della Misericordia* (commissioned 1445, Palazzo Communale, Sansepolcro), the *Flagellation* (*c.*1456, Palazzo Ducale, Urbino), the fresco cycle

**Piero della Francesca,** *The Flagellation* (c.1456), in the Palazzo Ducale, Urbino

of *The Legend of the Holy Cross* (c.1455–65, in the choir of the Church of San Francesco in Arezzo), the portraits of FEDERICO II DA MONTEFELTRO and his countess *Battista Sforza* (1464, Uffizi), and a *Nativity* (c.1472, National Gallery, London). This surviving corpus is characterized by precise drawing, subtle lighting, broad masses of colour, the innovative use of PERSPECTIVE, and an emotional restraint that gives his figures great poise.

The most important of Piero's writings for an understanding of his art is *De prospectiva pigendi*, which sets out the mathematical rules of foreshortening; the treatise was written before 1482, and survives in an Italian version in Piero's hand and a Latin version annotated in his hand. He also wrote a Latin treatise on the five regular solids (*De quinque corporibus regularibus*) and Italian treatises on geometry and arithmetic, all of which survive in manuscripts that are at least partly in Piero's hand.

Piero was not placed in the highest rank by VASARI, who determined the canons of taste in Italian Renaissance art for centuries. In the early twentieth century, however, art historians reassessed Piero, and he is now acclaimed as one of the greatest of quattrocentro painters.

*MDA*; Carlo Bertelli, *Piero della Francesca* (1992); Kenneth Clark, *Piero della Francesca* (1969).

**PIERO DI COSIMO** (1461/2–1521), Italian painter, trained in the Florentine studio of Cosimo ROSSELLI; he was originally called Piero di Lorenzo, but later assumed the name of his teacher. He painted many religious pictures which, after 1500, show the influence of SIGNORELLI and LEONARDO. His most distinctive pictures are mythological fantasies, some of which are comic, such as *The Discovery of Honey* (Art Museum, Worcester, Mass.) and *The Discovery of Wine* (Fogg Museum, Cambridge, Mass.); others depict sometimes violent scenes in a spirit of sentiment or pathos, such as *Hunting Scene* (Metropolitan Museum, New York), *The Battle of the Lapiths and Centaurs* (National Gallery, London), *The Death of Procris* (National Gallery, London), *Mars and Venus* (Gemäldegalerie, Berlin), and *The Forest Fire* (Ashmolean Museum, Oxford). Piero was also a highly accomplished

**Piero della Francesca,** *The Baptism of Jesus* (c.1448–50), in the National Gallery, London

**Piero della Francesca**, *The Meeting of Solomon and the Queen of Sheba*, a fresco in the cycle on *The Legend of the Holy Cross* (*c*.1455–65) in the Church of San Francesco in Arezzo

**Piero di Cosimo**, *The Forest Fire*, in the Ashmolean Museum, Oxford

portrait painter, as is evident in his *Giuliano da Sangallo* (Rijksmuseum, Amsterdam) and his *Simonetta Vespucci* (Musée Condé, Chantilly), a nude bust in which his sitter is portrayed with a snake around her neck. Piero's pupils included ANDREA DEL SARTO.

*MDA*; Sharon Fermor, *Piero di Cosimo* (1993).

**PIETÀ**, a genre of sculpture and painting (literally 'piety') in which the Virgin Mary bears the body of Jesus on her knees or cradles him at her feet. This composition, which may originate in the Passion Plays of medieval Europe, first appears in the early fourteenth century in a limewood carving in Naumburg Cathedral. There are occasional examples of the form in France (such as the mid-fifteenth century Avignon *Pietà* in the Louvre) and Flanders (notably the *Pietà* of Petrus CHRISTUS in the Metropolitan Museum in New York), but the composition was most popular in Italy: in painting the finest examples are those by Giovanni BELLINI (Accademia, Venice) and SEBASTIANO DEL PIOMBO (Museo Civico, Viterbo), and in sculpture the greatest example of the form is MICHELANGELO's *Pietà* in St Peter's Basilica in Rome.

**PIETRE DURE** (Italian; 'hard stones'). The singular form, *pietra dura*, is used within Italy to denote a single type of stone but is widely used by non-native speakers outside Italy to denote combinations of more than one type of stone. The *pietre* are semi-precious stones, typically agate, chalcedony, jasper, and lapis lazuli, but do not include marble or precious stones (GEMS). *Pietre dure* had been carved in classical Rome, and the techniques for cutting such hard stones were revived in sixteenth-century Florence, where a workshop established under the patronage of Grand Duke COSIMO I DE' MEDICI pro-

Piero di Cosimo, *Hunting Scene*, in the Metropolitan Museum of Art, New York

duced the decorative panels known in English as FLORENTINE MOSAICS; the workshop was refounded in 1588 as the Opificio delle Pietre Dure, which still manufactures mosaics.

**PIGAFETTA, ANTONIO** ( *fl.* 1491–*c.*1526), Italian mariner, a native of Vicenza who in 1519, after an early career as a seaborne soldier in the Mediterranean, joined the expedition of MAGELLAN in Seville. He was one of the eighteen survivors of the expedition, which completed its circumnavigation of the world in 1522 under the command of Juan Sebastián ELCANO. Federico II GONZAGA commissioned Pigafetta to write an account of the voyage, which was entitled *Primo viaggio intorno al mondo*; this work may have been printed in Venice in 1524 (when Pigafetta was given permission to print the book), but the earliest surviving Italian edition was published in 1534; a French edition was published in Paris in 1525.

> *Magellan's Voyage round the World*, ed. J. A. Robertson (3 vols., 1906); Adriana Chemello (ed.), *Adriano Pigafetta e la letteratura di viaggio nel Cinquecento* (1996).

**PIGHI or Pigge, ALBERT** (*c.*1490–1542), Dutch Catholic theologian, born in Kampen (Overijssel) and educated in Louvain and Cologne. In 1522 he was called to Rome by the Dutch Pope ADRIAN VI, and spent the rest of his career as a theologian in the service of the papacy. His works include an unpublished account (which survives in manuscript in the Vatican Library) of the theology of the Orthodox Church (*Adversus Graecorum errores*) prepared with a view to facilitating reunion. His most important published theological work was *Hierarchiae ecclesiasticae assertio* (Cologne, 1538), in which Pighi contended that tradition was a legitimate authority for the formulation of doctrine, that papal pronouncements were infallible (a doctrine not formally adopted until 1870), and that a pope was incapable of personally lapsing into heresy. In 1541 Pighi attended the Conference of REGENSBURG, where his fellow delegates included Johann GROPPER, whose

doctrine of DOUBLE JUSTICE (Latin *duplex iustitia*) Pighi accepted.

> *NNBW* x; Hubert Jedin, *Studien über die Schriftstellertätigkeit Albert Pigges* (1931).

**PILGRAM, ANTON** (*c.*1450–1515), Moravian sculptor and architect, probably born in Brno, where he worked from 1502 to 1508. He moved to Heilbronn and then in 1512 to Vienna. At Heilbronn he designed the spired tabernacle for the sacrament in the Kilianskirche. In Vienna he worked on St Stephan, where his organ foot (1513) and pulpit (1514–15) each include a sculpted self-portrait.

> *BLBL*; *MDA*; *NDB*; Karl Oettinger, *Anton Pilgram und die Bildhauer von St Stephan* (1951); R. Feuchtmüller, *Die spätgotische Architektur und Anton Pilgram* (1952).

**PILGRIMAGE** or (Latin) *peregrinatio* or (French) *pèlerinage*. The tradition of pilgrimage extends from remote antiquity to the religious shrines of Varanasi, Lourdes, and Mecca. Early Christian pilgrimage grew rapidly after the visit of the Empress Helena to Bethlehem and Jerusalem in 326 and the retirement of JEROME to Bethlehem in 386. In the Middle Ages pilgrimages were organized to Palestine, to the tomb of St James (Spanish Santiago) in Compostela (in Spanish Galicia), and to the tombs of the apostles Peter and Paul in Rome. In 1300 Pope Boniface VIII instituted the JUBILEE YEAR in Rome, and thereafter large numbers of pilgrims travelled to Rome to obtain a plenary INDULGENCE whenever a jubilee year was declared; the only such year that failed to attract large numbers of pilgrims was 1525.

In 1478 pilgrimages to Santiago de Compostela were declared by Pope SIXTUS IV to be equal in efficacy to pilgrimages to Rome and Jerusalem. A second tier of local pilgrimage resorts prospered throughout Europe: in England, pilgrims travelled to Walsingham (the possessor of a phial of the Virgin's milk and the subject of a poem attributed to Sir Walter RALEGH), Peterborough, and, as Chaucer recorded in *The Canterbury Tales*, the shrine of Thomas Becket in Canterbury; in Scotland, to St Andrews; in Wales, to St Davids and Holywell; in France, to Saint-Martin-Vésubie, Saint-Maximin-la-Sainte-Baume (where Mary Magdalene was said to be buried), Chartres, and Le Puy; in Germany to Aachen and Cologne (where the bones of the Magi were brought in 1162); in the Swiss Confederation, to Einsiedeln (where Jesus was believed to have consecrated the chapel that contains a fifteenth-century black Madonna); in Italy, to Assisi (to the shrine of Francis of Assisi), Padua (the tomb of St Anthony), and, from the fifteenth century, to the Holy House of Joseph and Mary, which had been carried by angels from Nazareth to a hill near Rijeka on the coast of Dalmatia on the night of 9/10 May 1291 and thence across the Adriatic to Loreto on 7 December 1295. Construction of the Sanctuario della Santa Casa on the site where the angels lowered the house to the ground began in 1468; Giuliano SANGALLO built the dome in 1500 and Bramante added the side chapels in 1511.

Abuses arising out of the pilgrimage industry were censured by ERASMUS and by the reformers. In Protestant countries pilgrimages were discouraged and pilgrimage centres destroyed, but the popular piety of the COUNTER-REFORMATION ensured that pilgrimages survived in Catholic countries. In the sixteenth century important new pilgrimage resorts arose in Gorizia (Slovene Gorica, German Görz), north of Trieste, and in Montserrat (in Catalonia).

**PILGRIMAGE OF GRACE**, the only instance of widespread resistance to HENRY VIII's religious policy. It was sparked by opposition to the dissolution of the MONASTERIES, and sought a return to the old religion. The uprising began in Lincolnshire in 1536 and spread to Yorkshire, Cumberland, and Westmorland. Prominent among the rebel leaders was Robert Aske, a moderate lawyer who attempted to restrain the passions which had been aroused, but who was eventually executed. The pilgrims' banner, showing the five wounds of Christ, was used again in the NORTHERN REBELLION of 1569.

R. W. Hoyle, *The Pilgrimage of Grace and the Politics of the 1530s* (2001).

**PILKINGTON, FRANCIS** (*c.*1570–1638), English composer and minister at Chester Cathedral. He took the B. Mus. at Oxford in 1595. He wrote lute songs, madrigals, and some instrumental music for lute and viols. Two of his pieces are in Sir William Leighton's *Tears and Lamentations* (1614).

**PILON, GERMAIN** (1537–90), French sculptor and medallist, born in Paris. He worked as an assistant to PRIMATICCIO on the monument for the heart of King FRANCIS I in Haute-Bruyère. He contributed the kneeling bronze figures and the partly nude marble figures of HENRI II and CATHERINE DE MÉDICIS for their tomb in Saint-Denis. He later sculpted figures commissioned by Queen Catherine for the Valois Chapel (destroyed 1719) in Saint-Denis. His work for the Birague family includes *The Virgin of Pity* (Louvre), *St Francis* (Church of Saint-Jean-Saint-François), and the bronze statue of *René de Birague* (Louvre). In 1572 he was appointed master

of the mint and in 1575 he executed a series of bronze portrait medallions.

*MDA*; Geneviève Bresc-Bautier (ed.), *Germain Pilon et les sculteurs français de la Renaissance* (Paris, 1993).

**PINNACE**, a small two-masted ship introduced in the sixteenth century. The pinnace was usually square-rigged, though it occasionally had a lugsail on the main mast; the popular image of a schooner rig derives from later centuries. In fleets the pinnace was used as an advice boat and tender, which gave rise to the later use of the term for the small boat (with eight oars) carried by warships. In the sixteenth century pinnaces were also used to accompany large ships on voyages of EXPLORATION.

**PINTO, FERNÃO MENDES** (*c.*1510–1583), Portuguese traveller, a native of Montemor-o-Velho who left Portugal in 1537 on a journey that in the course of the next 21 years took him to Ethiopia, India, China, and Japan. On returning to Portugal on 22 September 1558 he composed his *Periegrinação*, a fanciful account of his travels published in 1614 and subsequently translated into Spanish, English, French, and German. The *Periegrinação* blends fact, such as his travels with Francis XAVIER, with improbable fictions, such as being sold into slavery on seventeen occasions. A Portuguese play on his name, *Fernão, Mentes? Minto!* ('Ferdinand, do you lie? I do!'), made Mendes a byword for exaggeration; as late as 1695 William Congreve could expect his audience to understand the line 'Mendez Pinto was but a type of thee, a liar of the first magnitude' (*Love for Love*).

*DHP*; François Thibaux, *La Pérégrination de Fernão Mendès Pinto* (1980); Rebecca Catz, *Fernão Mendes Pinto* (1981).

**PINTURICCHIO or Pintoricchio or Bernardino di Betto** (*c.*1452–1513), Italian painter, born in Perugia. His teachers included PERUGINO, for whom he worked as an assistant on the frescoes of the SISTINE CHAPEL (1481–2). Pinturicchio's principal works are fresco cycles in the Vatican and in Siena Cathedral: in the Vatican he painted lunettes in the Borgia apartments illustrating amongst others *The Life of Jesus* and ceiling-panel frescoes of (unusually) *Scenes from Egyptian Mythology* (1492–5); in the Piccolomini Library in Siena Cathedral he painted *Scenes from the Life of Aeneas Sylvius Piccolomini* (1503), who in 1458 had become Pope PIUS II.

*MDA*.

**PINZÓN BROTHERS**, three brothers who in 1492 accompanied COLUMBUS on his first voyage to America. On 3 August 1492 Columbus sailed from Palos (Huelva) with an expedition of some 120 men in three CARAVELS; he commanded the *Santa María*, his flagship, Martín Alonso Pinzón (*c.*1440–1493) commanded the *Pinta* (on which his brother Francisco served as pilot), and Vicente Yáñez Pinzón (*fl.* 1492–1509) commanded the smaller *Niña*. The *Santa María* was lost in Hispaniola, and on the return journey the *Pinta* was inadvertently separated from the *Niña* (on which Columbus was sailing), but nonetheless managed to land in Palos the same day; five days after the landing Martín Alonso died.

Late in 1499 Vicente Yáñez Pinzón led an expedition of four caravels across the Atlantic, arriving early in 1500 at Cape Agostinho, so reaching Brazil some three months before Pedro CABRAL claimed it for Portugal. During this voyage Vicente Yáñez explored the estuary of the Amazon and sailed along the coast of Brazil to Costa Rica. In 1507 he returned to America with Juan DÍAZ DE SOLÍS, and on this expedition reached the estuary of Río de la Plata.

DHE.

**PIRKHEIMER or Pirckheimer, WILLIBALD** (1470–1530), German humanist, born in Eichstätt and educated in Padua and Pavia. He settled in Nuremberg, where he became a city councillor in 1496. Pirkheimer collected art and books, became a close friend of DÜRER (who engraved his portrait), and knew ERASMUS, CELTIS, and REUCHLIN. He initially supported LUTHER, but in 1521 returned to Catholicism. Pirkheimer translated Greek authors into Latin, notably Ptolemy's *Geography*, and wrote original Latin treatises on history and astronomy; he also composed an ironical essay in praise of gout (*Apologia seu podagrae laus*, 1510) which is usually known as *Laus podagrae*.

**PISA**, a town and archiepiscopal see in Tuscany on the river Arno, which connects it to the sea 12 kilometres (7 miles) to the west and to Florence 80 kilometres (50 miles) to the east. Pisa's port at the mouth of the Arno, Porto Pisano, was Tuscany's most important port until it silted up in the mid-sixteenth century, after which goods were landed at Livorno and brought to Pisa by canal.

Medieval Pisa was riven by GUELF AND GHIBELLINE rivalries and constantly at war with Genoa, Florence, and Lucca. On 6 August 1284 Pisa was decisively defeated by Genoa in the naval battle of Meloria. In 1288 a civil war erupted in Pisa, and on 1 July 1288 Count Ugolino was captured by the forces of Archbishop Ruggieri and incarcerated, together with two of his adult sons and two grandsons, in the Torre della Muda, where they starved to death; the pathos of DANTE's poignant description of their deaths in the climactic final episode of the *Inferno* (32. 125–33. 87) is enhanced by the transformation of Ugolino's companions into his four small sons, who plead with their father to eat them to save his own life.

The APPIANO FAMILY, which had become prominent in public affairs in Pisa in the thirteenth century, formally assumed power in 1392, when Jacopo d'Appiano assassinated the ruler Piero Gambacorti and succeeded him as lord of Pisa. Jacopo bequeathed the state to his son Gherardo Leonardo, who in 1399 sold the city to Gian Galeazzo VIS-CONTI for 200,000 florins.

In 1406 Florence mounted a siege and naval blockade, and on 9 October entered the starving city in triumph; in 1421 Florence bought Porto Pisano from Genoa, and thereafter Florentines were encouraged by tax concessions and free housing to settle in Pisan territory. The Medici took an interest in the small university, and in 1472 re-endowed it by forcing several faculties in Florence to migrate to Pisa and temporarily forbidding Florentines to study anywhere except Pisa. In 1495 the citizens of Pisa took advantage of the pres-

ence of a French garrison in the city to mount a rebellion, and the city remained independent of Florence until 8 June 1509, when it was recaptured after the fourth siege of a protracted war; the war is examined at length in GUICCIARDINI's *Storia d'Italia*.

Piero SODERINI (GONFALONIERE of Florence) and MACHIAVELLI (secretary of the TEN OF WAR) had shown no quarter as they prosecuted the war, but in victory they proved to be magnanimous, and fed the starving citizens rather than slaughtering them. Grand Duke COSIMO I DE' MEDICI instituted a programme (the *uffizio dei fossi*) to reclaim the marshes and improve drainage and drinking water, and in 1562 he chose Pisa as the headquarters for the Order of SANTO STEFANO. By the mid-sixteenth century emigration, exile, war, and plague had reduced the population of Pisa from its peak (in 1300) of about 40,000 inhabitants to 8,574 residents in 1551.

In the thirteenth century Pisan sculpture was dominated by Nicola and Giovanni PISANO, and in the fourteenth century the cathedral complex was completed. In the sixteenth century Vasari rebuilt a palace designed by Nicola Pisano (the Palazzo della Gherardesca, which included the Torre della Muda) as the headquarters of the Order of San Stefano and also designed the Order's Church of Santo Stefano dei Cavalieri.

The most famous building in Pisa (and in Italy) is the Leaning Tower (Torre Pendente), the white marble campanile built in Romanesque style in 1174. The tower leans because of soil subsidence that became apparent when construction reached the first floor. The belfry added in 1350 does not follow the oblique angle of the lower floors, but is almost vertical, and was so designed to compensate for the tilt in the lower floors. Galileo GALILEI, a native of the city, famously dropped solid objects from the top of the tower in order to demonstrate to his colleagues the falseness of ARISTOTLE's contention that heavy objects drop with a speed proportional to their weight. In 1581, in the cathedral beside the tower, Galileo observed a swinging lamp and noted that the time of individual oscillations remained constant even though their range varied; experimental verification of this observation led Galileo to his discovery of the isochronism of the pendulum.

David Herlihy, *Pisa in the Early Renaissance* (1958).

**PISANELLO, IL,** or Antonio Pisano (c.1395–1455/6), Italian painter, draughtsman, and medallist who lived as a young man in Verona, where he may have trained in the studio of STEFANO DA ZEVIO. He collaborated with GENTILE DA FABRIANO on frescoes in the Doge's Palace in Venice (1415–20) and later completed Gentile's frescoes (left unfinished at his death in 1427) in the Lateran Basilica in Rome (1431–2).

Pisanello's surviving independent paintings consist of frescoes and a small number of panel paintings. The frescoes are an *Annunciation* in the Church of San Fermo Maggiore in Verona (c.1426), a *St George and the Princes of Trebizond* in the Church of Sant'Anastasia in Verona (1434–8), and a set of frescoes of *Scenes of War and Chivalry* (1439–42) in the castle at Mantua were rediscovered in the 1970s. The paintings include portraits of Leonello d'ESTE (c.1441, Accademia Carrara, Bergamo) and of an unidentified Este princess (c.1440, Louvre) and paintings of *The Vision of St Eustace* and *Virgin and Child with SS Anthony the Abbot and George* (both in the National Gallery, London).

Pisanello was a prolific draughtsman, and large numbers of his drawings survive, including splendid pictures of birds and animals and tinted costume studies. The finest collection is in the Codex Vallardi (Louvre); a sheet of his drawings of hanged men is in the British Museum.

Pisanello was a pioneer of the Renaissance portrait MEDAL, beginning with his medal of the Emperor JOHN VIII PALAEOLOGUS, who attended the COUNCIL OF FLORENCE in 1438. He subsequently cast medals for Sigismondo MALATESTA of Rimini, Ludovico II GONZAGA and Cecilia Gonzaga of Mantua, Lionello d'Este of Ferrara, Don Iñigo d'Avalos (grand chamberlain of Naples), and ALFONSO V of Aragon, king of Naples.

MDA; Luke Syson and Dillian Gordon, *Pisanello: Painter to the Renaissance Court* (2001).

**PISANO, ANDREA** (c.1295–1348/9) and **NINO** (d. 1368), Italian sculptors. Andrea Pisano first appears in the historical record in 1329, when he was commissioned to make a pair of bronze doors for the baptistery in Florence. The doors, which were finished in 1336, depict *The Virtues* (in eight

**Andrea Pisano**, *The Rider*, a relief sculpture carved for the campanile of Florence Cathedral and now in the Museo dell'Opera del Duomo, Florence

panels) and *The Life of John the Baptist* (in twenty panels). He succeeded GIOTTO as *capomaestro* (master mason) for the campanile of the cathedral, and carved most of the reliefs (e.g. *The Weaver* and *The Rider*); he was succeeded c.1343 by Francesco TALENTI. In 1347 Andrea was appointed *capomaestro* of Orvieto Cathedral, and on his death the following year he was succeeded by his son Nino.

There is documentary evidence that Nino Pisano worked as an architect and a goldsmith, but his only surviving works are marble sculptures, of which three are signed: a *Madonna* in Santa Maria Novella in Florence, the *Virgin* of the Cornaro monument in SS Giovanni e Paolo in Venice, and a statue of a bishop in the Church of San Francesco in Oristona (Sardinia).

Andrea and Nino Pisano were not related to Nicola and Giovanni PISANO or to Il PISANELLO.

MDA; Gert Kreytenberg, *Andrea Pisano und die toskanische Skulptur des 14. Jahrhunderts* (1984); Anita Moskowitz, *The Sculpture of Andrea and Nino Pisano* (1986).

**PISANO, NICOLA or Niccolò** (1220/5–before 1284) and **GIOVANNI** (1245/50–before 1320), Italian sculptors. Nicola Pisano moved to Pisa from his native Apulia in the mid-thirteenth century. His Gothic pulpit for the Pisa Baptistery (1260) was the first important work to revive the conventions of ancient Roman statuary: his *Simeon* derives from Dionysius, his nude *Christian Fortitude* from Hercules, and his *Virgin* from Phaedra. The naturalism and dignity of the human figures remains a feature of Pisano's subsequent work, which included the reliefs on the pulpit of Siena Cathedral (1265–8), on which he was assisted by his son Giovanni and ARNOLFO DI CAMBIO, and the decorative sculpture on the FOUNTAIN (Fontana Maggiore) in what is now the Piazza 4 Novembre in Perugia (completed 1278), on which he was again assisted by Giovanni.

Giovanni Pisano carved the saints and prophets on the exterior of the Pisa Baptistery; the project was completed by 1284, and it is possible that Giovanni had worked together with his father (whose date of death is not known). This decorative scheme was the first in Tuscany in which large-scale statuary was incorporated into the architectural design. Giovanni subsequently built the façade of Siena Cathedral (from 1284), contributed designs for Massa Marittima Cathedral (1298), and carved the reliefs for pulpits at the Church of Sant'Andrea in Pistoia (1301) and Pisa Cathedral (1302–10), all of which deploy classical motifs. Giovanni's free-standing statues include *Madonna and Child with Two Acolytes* (c.1305, Arena Chapel, Padua), the *Madonna della Cintola* (c.1312, Prato Cathedral), and the monument to Margaret of Luxemburg (wife of the Emperor Henry VII) sculpted for the Church of San Francesco in Genoa (1313; substantial fragments are preserved in the Palazzo Bianco in Genoa), the last of which was the first monument to depict its subject rising from the grave.

Nicola and Giovanni Pisano were the first sculptors to revive Roman carving, and were in effect the creators of the trecento Gothic style which was the starting point of sculptors such as JACOPO DELLA QUERCIA, GHIBERTI, and DONATELLO.

Giovanni Pisano, *The Nativity* (1301), a relief sculpture on the pulpit of the Church of Sant'Andrea in Pistoia

In the historiography of sculpture they are therefore said to be the fathers of modern sculpture.

Nicola and Giovanni Pisano were not related to Andrea and Nino PISANO or to Il PISANELLO.

*MDA*; Michael Ayrton, *Giovanni Pisano: Sculptor* (1969).

**PISTORIUS, JOHANN THE YOUNGER** (1546–1608), German theologian and Cabbalist, born in Nidda (Hessen), the son of Johann Pistorius the Elder (1503–83), one of Luther's earliest supporters. Johann the Younger studied theology, law, and medicine at Marburg and Wittenberg and in 1575 was appointed physician to the court of Karl II, margrave of Baden-Durlach. His religious allegiance shifted from Lutheranism to Calvinism, and he then became a Catholic. He published polemical religious tracts in both German and Latin and edited works of German and Polish history. In 1587 he published a collection of CABBALISTIC texts. He died in Freiburg on 18 July 1608.

*DLL*; *NDB*.

**PITHOU, PIERRE** (1539–96), French jurist. Pithou was one of four Huguenot brothers from Troyes, all of whom became prominent humanist jurists. Pithou converted to Protestantism after the outbreak of the second of the WARS OF RELIGION in 1567, but reconverted to Catholicism after the ST BARTHOLOMEW'S DAY MASSACRE (1572). When HENRI IV consolidated his support by converting to Catholicism in 1593, Pithou enjoyed royal patronage in a series of legal appointments, including attorney-general (*procureur-général*) of the Parlement of Paris. Pithou was a prolific jurist, publishing editions of the *Novellae posttheodosianae* (the constitutions of the Western Empire 438–58), the *Leges visigothorum* (the second Visigothic code, promulgated in 654), and the capitularies (ordinances of Frankish kings) of Charlemagne, Louis the Pious, and Charles the Bald; he also wrote *Observations sur le code Justinien*. He was a distinguished exponent of GALLICANISM, and his *Recueil des libertés de l'Église gallicane* (1594) ringingly declared that the papacy had no temporal jurisdiction in France and that its spiritual jurisdiction was limited to conciliar decrees recognized by the French king.

As a literary scholar Pithou published the first edition of the verse fables of Phaedrus (1596), which had previously only been known in the prose paraphrases of the 'Romulus', and edited the late Latin poem *Pervigilium Veneris* (1587) as well as Juvenal and Persius (1585). His most important literary work was his contribution to the *Satire Ménippée*

Nicola Pisano, *Christian Fortitude* (1260), on the pulpit of the Pisa Baptistery

(1594), a satirical pamphlet which supported the cause of Henri IV against the CATHOLIC LEAGUE and its Spanish allies; Pithou's contribution is the elegant indictment of the League placed in the mouth of the sieur d'Aubray, the representative of the Third ESTATE. Pithou's large library included a rich collection of manuscripts, most of which are now in the Bibliothèque Nationale.

Pithou's brother François (1543–1621) published an edition of the *Epitome Juliani* (a Latin abridgement of 124 Byzantine laws of AD 535–55) and wrote treatises on *La Grandeur des droits du royaume de France* (1587) and *De l'excommunication et de l'interdit* (1587) and *Glossarium ad libros capitularium* (1588). He also edited with his brother Pierre the *Corpus iuris canonici* (1587).

Jean Pithou (1524–1602) wrote a *Traité de police et du gouvernement des républiques*, and, together with his twin brother Nicolas (1524–98), wrote *Institution du mariage chrétien*.

Donald R. Kelley, *Foundations of Modern Historical Scholarship: Language, Law and History in the French Renaissance* (1970), 241–70.

**PITTI PALACE or (Italian) Palazzo Pitti**, a Florentine palace commissioned by Luca Pitti, a wealthy merchant; the initial plans were drawn up by BRUNELLESCHI, and construction began in 1435; it was eventually finished in 1570 by AMMANATI. In 1549 the unfinished palace was bought from Jacopo Pitti by ELEANOR OF TOLEDO, the duchess of COSIMO I DE' MEDICI, who commissioned the BOBOLI GARDENS and

extended the palace. In 1565 VASARI added a corridor over the Ponte Vecchio (which spans the Arno) in order to link the Pitti Palace with the UFFIZI PALACE, which accommodated the offices of the Medicean civic administration, and with the Palazzo della Signoria, later renamed Palazzo Vecchio. In 1550 the Medici family (who had lived in what is now the Palazzo Medici-Riccardi from 1460 to 1540) moved into the Pitti Palace, which remained the principal residence of the grand dukes of Tuscany until 1859; for the next 50 years it was owned by the Italian royal family, and in 1919 it passed to the state. The palace now houses a silver museum (Museo degli Argenti) on the ground floor and one of the world's finest collections of Renaissance art (including 11 paintings by RAPHAEL, 14 by TITIAN, 16 by ANDREA DEL SARTO, 8 by TINTORETTO, and 5 by VERONESE) in the Palatine Gallery on the first floor.

**PIUS II** (1405–64), pope from 19 August 1458 until his death on 15 August 1464, was born Enea Silvio Piccolomini in Corsignano (which was in 1462 renamed Pienza in his honour), near Siena, on 18 October 1405, the eldest of the eighteen children of an impoverished nobleman; he was later known by the Latin form of his name, Aeneas Sylvius, and assumed the papal name Pius in imitation of VIRGIL's 'Pius Aeneas'. As a boy Enea worked with his father on the family farm, but he received a humanist education in Siena and Florence (where his tutors included FILELFO); his Latin love poems of this period attest to Enea's induction into a life of sensuality.

In 1432 Enea accepted the post of secretary to Cardinal Domenico CAPRANICA, and accompanied him to the COUNCIL OF BASEL, where he stayed from 1431 to 1435 in the employment of a series of prelates. In 1435, while serving as secretary to the bishop of Novara, he was implicated in a plot against Pope EUGENIUS IV; the bishop was captured and imprisoned, but Enea escaped. He entered the service of Cardinal Niccolò Albergati at the Congress of Arras, and, after peace was agreed between France and Burgundy, Cardinal Niccolò sent Enea on a secret diplomatic mission to Scotland. In 1436 he returned to Basel and, although declining ordination because of his dissolute personal life, secured a seat at the Council, where his brilliance as an orator was widely admired.

Enea supported the opponents of Pope Eugenius, and on the election of the antipope FELIX V on 5 November 1439 was appointed as his secretary, in which capacity he wrote *Libellus dialogorum de concilii auctoritate* (1440), an eloquent defence of the CONCILIAR MOVEMENT. Felix dispatched Enea to the Diet of Frankfurt in 1442, where his eloquence and literary skills were so admired by the Emperor FRIEDRICH III that he was poached from the service of Felix to that of Friedrich, who crowned him poet laureate. During this period he enjoyed the friendship of Kaspar Schlick, the imperial chancellor, and wrote his popular Latin NOVELLA *Lucretia and Euryalus* (sometimes translated as *The Tale of Two Lovers*), which celebrated Schlick's sexual adventures, and his mildly erotic Latin COMEDY *Chrysis*.

In 1445 Enea forsook his allegiance to Felix V and was

reconciled to Pope Eugenius IV. He repudiated his life as a womanizer (during which he had fathered several illegitimate children) and, on 4 March 1446, was ordained priest. In the years to follow, he persuaded Friedrich III and the German electors to abandon their neutrality in the stand-off between pope and Council in favour of Eugenius IV. Pope NICHOLAS V acknowledged his gratitude with the conferment of the bishoprics of Trieste (1447) and Siena (1450), and Friedrich continued to employ him as a diplomat until 1455; his greatest diplomatic success for Friedrich was the signing of the Concordat of Vienna (or Concordat of Aschaffenburg) in February 1448. Enea successfully negotiated with King ALFONSO V on behalf of Pope CALLISTUS III and was rewarded on 18 December 1456 with a cardinal's hat. During this period he wrote an account (in Latin) of the reign of Friedrich. Pope Callistus died on 5 August 1548, and Enea was elected as Pope Pius II after a hotly contested conclave.

Pius came to the papacy in the aftermath of the fall of Constantinople in 1453, and since that time had worked energetically for a CRUSADE. On becoming pope he issued a crusade bull (October 1458) and summoned the Christian rulers of Europe to assemble in Mantua on 1 June 1459. Before the Congress of Mantua could assemble, Pius had to decide whom to support in the struggle for the throne of Naples: his decision to crown FERRANTE I, illegitimate son of ALFONSO V of Aragon, and to dismiss the claim of his rival RENÉ D' ANJOU, aroused the opposition of France, whose representatives at the Congress then declined to support the crusade with troops or money. At the end of the Congress Pius promulgated the bull *Execrabilis* (18 January 1460), in which he condemned all appeals from papal judgement to a future council, thus flatly repudiating the conciliar views of his tract of 1440. When Bohemia and the German princes invoked Pius' own former views in support of their arguments, he replied on 26 April 1463 with his 'bull of retraction', *In minoribus agentes*, in which occur the famous words 'Aeneam reicite, Pium suscipite' ('reject Aeneas, listen to Pius').

On returning to Rome after the Congress, Pius was faced with a baronial insurrection in the Campagna and a war between France and Spain in Naples. He quelled the baronial revolt and intervened in Naples by sending his nephew Antonio Todeschini Piccolomini to the aid of Ferdinand, who made Antonio duke of Amalfi and presented him with a bride, his illegitimate daughter Maria. The predictable effect of these developments was further to alienate the French, with whom Pius was fruitlessly negotiating for the repeal of the PRAGMATIC SANCTION OF BOURGES. When LOUIS XI succeeded to the French throne in November 1461, he announced that he had withdrawn the Pragmatic Sanction; this negotiating ploy, which was designed to elicit Pope Pius' support for the Angevin claim to Naples, failed to achieve its purpose, and so King Louis reintroduced the Gallican liberties of the French Church by royal decree.

At the Congress of Mantua, the imperial delegates had agreed to contribute funding and troops for a three-year crusade. In the event, they never delivered on their promises.

Pius' difficulties in the German lands were exacerbated when he became embroiled in an imperial quarrel with Dieter von Isenburg, archbishop of Mainz, who supported the attempt of GEORGE OF PODĚBRADY, king of Bohemia, to supplant Friedrich III as king of the Romans (i.e. emperor elect). Dieter appealed to a general council, and Pius responded by stripping him of his archbishopric (in 1464 Pius was forced to recognize him once again). Pius also drew the wrath of the king of Bohemia, not simply by supporting the imperial pretensions of Friedrich but also by refusing to accept the compacts agreed at the Council of Basel between Catholics and Hussites. Elsewhere in the German lands, trouble erupted when Duke Sigismund of Tirol objected to the reform programme instituted in Brixen by NICHOLAS OF CUSA; Pius excommunicated Duke Sigismund, who then appealed to a general council.

The cumulative effect of these difficulties was to frustrate Pius' programme of reform both within the curia and in the Church at large, and to make his grand plan for a crusade unfeasible. He nonetheless remained true to his vision of a Constantinople reclaimed for Christianity, and in 1460–1 drafted his extraordinary 'Letter to Sultan Mehmet II', which contained an exposition of Christian doctrine, a refutation of Islam, and an appeal to Mehmet to repudiate Islam, be baptized as a Christian, and accept the crown of the Eastern Empire. The letter was never sent, but is nonetheless important for its articulation of Pius' utopian aspirations. In October 1463, encouraged by the agreement of Venice and Hungary to contribute troops to a crusade, Pius once again called for Christian Europe to unite against the Ottomans. He proclaimed his intention to lead the crusade himself, and ordered the armies of Europe to assemble in Ancona. There was considerable popular support for the crusade all across Europe, but rulers were loath to commit their treasuries and their armies to a crusade. The discovery of ALUM mines at Tolfa, however, provided an unexpected source of papal revenue that could be used to finance the crusade. Pius took the cross in St Peter's in June 1464 and set out for Ancona; he was by this time seriously ill. There were very few crusaders awaiting his arrival in Ancona, but soon the Venetian galleys hove into view. At this point Pius died; his heart was interred in Ancona and his body was returned to Rome.

Pius' election as pope was acclaimed by the humanist community, but Pius' preoccupation with his dream of a crusade meant that he never became a major patron of humanist scholarship, though he did sign the foundation charter for the University of Basel (1459), which became an important humanist centre, and did offer posts in his administration to humanists such as PLATINA. He also contributed through his own wide-ranging and innovative writings to the advancement of LATIN LITERATURE. In addition to his early novella, comedy, and poems, he wrote a history of the Council of Basel, a series of biographies of contemporary figures, an educational treatise, and three important books of historical geography (on Europe, on Bohemia, and on Asia); his treatise on Asia was carefully studied by COLUMBUS. Pius' letters were deemed by his contemporaries to be models of humanist Latin. His most famous work is his *Commentarii*, a third-person autobiography of remarkable indiscretion and apparent honesty in its description of Pius' unedifying acts and ambitions. The *Commentaries* offer a unique account of the thinking of a Renaissance pope, and of a papal perspective on the workings of the Church (including a frank account of the corruption of the conclave which elected him as pope); Pius had a particular talent for evoking in a few words his impression of a scene or an individual, and his deft verbal sketches of countryside, of townscapes, and of clerical and political figures render his *Commentaries* one of the finest autobiographies of the Renaissance and, within Italy, the Latin equivalent of Benvenuto CELLINI's unpublished vernacular autobiography.

The life of Pope Pius II is the subject of a series of frescoes by PINTURICCHIO in the Piccolomini library in Siena Cathedral. His greatest architectural monument is Pienza, the model city that Pius constructed in the village of his birth, and one of the best examples of TOWN PLANNING in the period. Pius presented his cope to the cathedral in Pienza; it is one of the finest surviving examples of fourteenth-century English embroidery, and is now in the cathedral museum.

*Memoirs of a Renaissance Pope: The Commentaries of Pius II*, trans. F. A. Gragg (1959); R. J. Mitchell, *The Laurels and the Tiara: Pope Pius II* (1963); G. Paparelli, *Enea Silvio Piccolomini: L'umanesimo sul soglio di Pietro* (2nd edn, 1978).

**PIUS III** (1439–1503), pope from 22 September 1503 until his death three weeks later on 18 October, was born Francesco Todeschini-Pice in Siena on 9 May 1439. He was the nephew of Pope PIUS II (through his mother), who took Francesco into his household, allowed him to assume his family name (PICCOLOMINI) and arms, and enabled him to study CANON LAW at Perugia. After completing his doctorate he was appointed by his uncle as archbishop of Siena and, a few weeks later (5 March 1460), cardinal-deacon of Sant'Eustachio; he was 21 years old. Pius then appointed Cardinal Piccolomini as papal legate to the March of Ancona, and in 1464 made him regent of Rome and the PAPAL STATE when he left for Ancona (where he was to die) to lead the CRUSADE.

Cardinal Piccolomini's career as a papal diplomat continued under successive pontificates. He served for many years as cardinal-protector of England and Germany, and in 1471 Pope PAUL II appointed him legate in Germany, where his fluency in German was a powerful tool in his negotiations with the Emperor FRIEDRICH III and the Conference of REGENSBURG. Piccolomini's personal relations with Pope ALEXANDER VI were remote, but Alexander nonetheless sent him in November 1494 as his legate to what proved to be a fruitless meeting with CHARLES VIII. Piccolomini's disdain for his pontiff manifested itself in his indignant refusal to accept the bribe proffered by Cardinal Borgia to secure his vote at the conclave of August 1492 and surfaced again in June 1497 when he became the only cardinal in the sacred college to protest against the pope's alienation of substantial areas of the Papal State to his son Juan, duke of Gandía.

Pope Pius died ten days after his coronation on 8 October 1503. He intended to become a reforming pope and, had he lived, would have summoned a general council of the Church. As a cardinal he had been a patron of learning and the arts; in 1495 he had founded the Libreria Piccolomini in Siena Cathedral to house his uncle's library, and in 1502 had charged PINTURICCHIO to decorate it with ten frescoes that illustrate the life of Pius II.

J. Schlecht, *Pius III und die deutsche Nation* (1914).

**PIUS IV** (1499–1565), pope from 25 December 1559 until his death on 9 December 1565, was born Giovanni Angelo Medici in Milan on 31 March 1499; he was the son of a Milanese notary, and was not related to the Medici of Florence. He studied medicine and jurisprudence at Pavia and in 1527 he moved to Rome, where he embarked on a career in the curia. He served as commissioner with the papal forces in Hungary and Transylvania (1542–3) and was then appointed papal vice-legate to Bologna.

Giovanni's career prospects improved immeasurably when his elder brother married into the FARNESE family of Pope PAUL III, and the fact that he had fathered three illegitimate children was not a bar to rapid advancement. Pope Paul appointed him archbishop of RAGUSA on 14 December 1545 and created him cardinal on 8 April 1549. Under Pope JULIUS III he was appointed to the tribunal known as the Signatura Gratiae, but he became estranged from Pope PAUL IV, whose personal asceticism, judicial cruelty, and anti-Spanish sentiment he did not share, and in 1558 withdrew from Rome.

Pius brought to the papacy a genial profligacy and a tolerant temperament, both of which contrasted sharply with the austere severity of his predecessor. In the first year of his pontificate his policies consisted almost entirely of reversals of those of Paul IV. He freed Cardinal Giovanni MORONE from his incarceration in Castel Sant'Angelo (and dismissed the heresy charges against him), reduced the jurisdiction of the INQUISITION, lifted the ban on vagrant monks, and began the task of tempering the unrealistic severity of the *INDEX LIBRORUM PROHIBITORUM* of 1559. He was cheerfully nepotistic in his appointments, but his most far-reaching appointment was his advancement (on 31 January 1560) of 22-year-old Carlo BORROMEO to the cardinalate and the archbishopric of Milan.

The impetus to reverse the policies of Pius' predecessor extended to foreign policy. Pope Paul had been anti-HABSBURG, but Pius established good relations with both PHILIP II of Spain and the Emperor FERDINAND I, and filled the vacant nunciatures in Vienna, Venice, and Florence. He demonstrated his Spanish sympathies and his sensitivity to the widespread hatred of the CARAFA family by having two of Pope Paul's nephews (Cardinal Carlo Carafa and Giovanni, duke of Palino) tried and executed (on 5 March 1561) for various crimes, including instigation of the war with Spain in 1557.

The greatest accomplishment of Pope Pius was his reconvening of the COUNCIL OF TRENT (which had been suspended in 1552) and his success in bringing the Council to a conclusion. He worked together with Cardinal Borromeo to mediate between powers that wanted a new council (including France and the Empire) and those that wanted to continue the old one (notably Spain); his bull of convocation (29 November 1560) fudged the issue in contention, but when the Council met in Trento on 18 January 1562 it picked up the threads of the session that had been suspended ten years earlier. Pius kept the Council on course, appointing Cardinal Morone as its last president in 1563. On 4 December 1563, at the end of its 25th session, the Council was dissolved; Pius confirmed its decrees orally on 26 January 1564 and published the formal bull on 30 June 1564. He spent the remaining months of his pontificate persuading Catholic Europe to accept the Council's decrees.

Pius' protracted concentration on the affairs of the Council meant that he neglected the administration of the PAPAL STATE, on which he levied new taxes to pay for the Spanish war of his predecessor. One consequence of this unpopular taxation was a failed assassination attempt in the last year of Pius' life.

Pope Pius was a generous and imaginative patron of scholarship and the arts. The buildings that he commissioned include the Villa PIA in the Vatican gardens.

**PIUS V** (1504–72), pope from 7 January 1566 until his death on 1 May 1572, was born Antonio Ghislieri in Bosco (near Alessándria) on 17 January 1504, the son of impoverished parents. He worked as a shepherd until the age of 14, when he entered the Dominican Order and assumed the name Michele. He studied in Bologna and in 1528 was ordained as a priest; he was appointed master and then prior in his Order, and for sixteen years lectured on theology and philosophy at Pavia. He was then appointed inquisitor for Como and Bergamo, and his zealous prosecution of his duties brought him to the attention of Cardinal Giampietro Carafa (later Pope PAUL IV), who in 1551 persuaded Pope JULIUS III to appoint Ghislieri as commissary-general of the Roman INQUISITION. When Cardinal Carafa was elected pope, he appointed Ghislieri bishop of Nepi and Sutri (1556), cardinal (1557), and inquisitor-general of Christendom.

With the accession of Pope PIUS IV, Cardinal Ghislieri fell out of favour, partly because of his open opposition to the nepotism of the new pope, but also because of his ruthlessness as inquisitor and his links with the CARAFA family. In 1560 he was nonetheless appointed protector of the BARNABITES and bishop of Mondovi (Piedmont). On the death of Pius IV, Ghislieri became the candidate of the rigorists (led by Cardinal Carlo BORROMEO), who stood for asceticism, self-denial, and strict adherence to the decrees of the COUNCIL OF TRENT.

Election as Pius V did not compromise Ghislieri's austerity of outlook or severity of judgement. He continued to wear his rough Dominican undergarments beneath his papal robes, and, with the assistance of Cardinal Borromeo, imposed upon his court monastic standards of simple living and probity and upon the city of Rome a series of decrees against public immorality and profanation of holy days. He

opposed nepotism, and resolutely resisted family pressure to raise his grand-nephew (the Dominican Michele Bonelli) to the cardinalate, instead choosing cardinals on merit and establishing (on 3 May 1567) a commission to investigate episcopal appointments. He also enforced clerical residence (to prevent churchmen from simply collecting the revenues on benefices which they never visited) and instituted a review of religious orders, suppressing those (such as the Humiliati in 1571) in which discipline had become lax. Pius abolished the sale of indulgences and dispensations for personal gain and in a decree of 29 March 1567 banned the sale of enfeoffed estates that had reverted to the Holy See and forbade the alienation of land within the PAPAL STATE. The Council of Trent had decreed that liturgical and sacred texts should be revised, and Pius duly completed and published the Roman CATECHISM (1566) and subsequently had it translated into several languages; he also published the revised Roman breviary (1568) and the Roman missal (1570) and established commissions to revise the text of St JEROME's Vulgate (1569) and to produce a new edition of the works of THOMAS AQUINAS (published 1570).

Pius encouraged the purifying fire of the Inquisition as a tool to combat incipient Protestantism in Italy, building a new palace to house its administration, encouraging rigour in its judgements, and personally attending many of its sessions. As a result the number of prosecutions and executions of prominent intellectuals rose sharply. He regarded the presence of JEWS in the Papal State as an affront, and embarked on a programme of expulsions, excepting only those resident in the GHETTOS of Rome and Ancona who were needed to facilitate commerce. His conviction that books could subvert the faith led him in March 1571 to establish the Congregation of the Index, as a result of which hundreds of printers emigrated to Germany and Switzerland.

The foreign policy of Pope Pius was rooted in his uncompromising religious zeal rather than in political skills. His excommunication and notional deposition of Queen ELIZABETH of England on 25 February 1570 antagonized Spain, France, and the Empire and placed English Catholics under the suspicion of treason. He gave military and financial support to CATHERINE DE MÉDICIS to assist her in the campaign against the HUGUENOTS and opposed the religious freedom that they were granted in the Peace of Saint-Germain (8 August 1570). Pius was suspicious of the Emperor MAXIMILIAN II's equivocal attitude to Protestantism, and fell out with him when Maximilian trespassed on the papal prerogative by nominating COSIMO I DE MEDICI as grand duke of Tuscany. In Spain, his relations with PHILIP II were constantly strained by his opposition to royal control of the Church, and an open rift was only avoided through the diplomatic skills of Cardinal Castagna (later Pope URBAN VII). Pius' single triumph in foreign affairs was his formation of a holy league (with Venice and Spain) against the Turks, which culminated in the victory of the battle of LEPANTO on 7 October 1571.

Pope Pius was beatified by Clement X on 1 May 1672 and canonized by Clement XI on 22 May 1712.

L. Browne-Olf, *The Sword of St Michael: St Pius V* (1943); Charles Hirschauer, *La Politique de S. Pie V en France (1566–72)* (1926).

**PIZARRO, FERNANDO** (*fl.* 1530–60), Spanish conquistador, the younger half-brother of Francisco PIZARRO and the elder brother of Gonzalo PIZARRO. He travelled to America with Francisco and Gonzalo in 1529 and participated in the conquest of Peru. In 1534 he sailed to Spain with a cargo of looted gold bound for the royal treasury. He returned to Peru and in 1537 was captured (together with his brother Gonzalo) by Diego de ALMAGRO, but was soon released. In 1538 he captured and executed Almagro. In 1540 he was recalled to Spain to justify his actions; he arrived with a consignment of gold, but was arrested on arrival and imprisoned for the next twenty years.

**PIZARRO, FRANCISCO** (1476–1541), Spanish conquistador and conqueror of Peru, born in Trujillo (Extremadura), the illegitimate son of Gonzalo Pizarro, a distinguished infantry officer, and Francisca González; Francisco was the half-brother of his father's legitimate children, who included Fernando PIZARRO and Gonzalo PIZARRO. Francisco travelled to America in 1509 and accompanied BALBOA to the Pacific. He settled in Panama as a cattle farmer and together with Diego de ALMAGRO began to explore southwards along the Pacific coast of South America, eventually reaching the Inca city of Túmbez, in what is now Ecuador.

In 1528 Pizarro returned to Spain, where CHARLES V, in a *capitulación* of 26 July 1529, designated him as governor of Peru and deputed him to conquer Peru in the name of Spain. Pizarro returned to Panama with an expeditionary force that included his half-brothers Gonzalo, Fernando, and Juan. On 27 December 1530 his expedition sailed south from Panama and for unknown reasons landed far to the north of Túmbez, to which he then marched over difficult and dangerous terrain. He then advanced southwards into Peru, and at Cajamarca met Atahuallpa, the Inca ruler. On 16 November 1532 Pizarro captured Atahuallpa through a ruse. Pizarro offered Atahuallpa his freedom in exchange for enough golden artefacts to fill his cell but then reneged on his promise and executed him.

The following year (November 1533) Pizarro captured Cuzco, the Inca capital, and in 1535 founded a new capital, Lima, on the coast. The Incas subsequently besieged Cuzco, and Almagro, returning from Chile, raised the Inca siege and took possession of the city (18 April 1537). After suppressing an Indian rebellion Pizarro was supplanted in Cuzco by Almagro, who had just returned from Chile. A jurisdictional dispute between the Pizarro brothers and Almagro culminated in Almagro's defeat in the battle of Las Salinas on 26 April 1538. Almagro was captured and executed on the orders of Fernando Pizarro.

Pizarro extended the conquest of Peru to what is now Bolivia and dispatched Pedro de VALDIVIA to effect the conquest of what is now Chile. Almagro's son Diego avenged his father's death by organizing the assassination of Francisco Pizarro on 26 June 1541.

*DHE*; Rafael Varón Gabai, *Francisco Pizarro and his Brothers* (1997).

**PIZARRO, GONZALO** (1511/13–48), Spanish conquistador, the younger half-brother of Francisco PIZARRO and the younger brother of Fernando PIZARRO. He travelled to America with Francisco and Fernando in 1529 and participated in the conquest of Peru. In 1537 he was captured (together with his brother Gonzalo) by Diego de ALMAGRO, but was soon released, and contributed to Almagro's defeat the following year. In 1539 he was appointed governor of Quito. The following year he mounted an expedition to search for EL DORADO on the eastern slopes of the Andes. The expedition divided, and Francisco de ORELLANA led part of the group on the first European descent of the Amazon, while Gonzalo returned with the main party to Quito.

In 1542 the Laws of the INDIES were revised with a view to curtailing atrocities against the Indians; the 54 laws abolished Indian slavery by restricting the ENCOMIENDA. Gonzalo Pizarro led a rebellion against the Laws, and in 1546 defeated and killed the viceroy of Peru (Blasco Núñez Vela) in battle and assumed personal control of Peru. Pedro de la GASCA, who was sent by the Emperor CHARLES V to Peru as the first president of the Court of Justice (Audiencia), defeated and executed Gonzalo Pizarro.

*DHE*.

**PLACARDS, L'AFFAIRE DES**. On 18 October 1534 Protestant broadsides excoriating the Catholic mass appeared on the walls of Paris and other cities; a copy was even affixed to the door of the bedchamber of King FRANCIS I at Amboise. The king, the Parlement and the University of Paris responded with a campaign of persecution; in the course of the following year hundreds of HUGUENOTS were arrested and some were burnt at the stake. The episode marked an important turning point in the early French Reformation, by revealing the existence of a radical form of Protestantism closer to ZWINGLI than LUTHER.

**PLAGUE**. The worst epidemic in recorded European history was the Black Death, which killed some 20 million people in the years 1347–51. The Black Death was the first outbreak of European plague for 800 years, and plague was to remain endemic in Europe for the next 300 years. The plague bacterium, *Yersinia pestis*, was first identified in 1894, and the connection of this bacterium with the Black Death was strengthened in 2000, when French scientists claimed to have found the plague bacterium in the teeth of fourteenth-century victims of the Black Death; this evidence has been vigorously disputed, and some scholars contend that medieval plague was not the same disease as the modern plague caused by *Yersinia pestis*.

Plague was variously attributed to the wrath of God, planetary conjunctions, the breath of victims, and the poisoning of the air or water; during the Black Death, the belief that the air or water had been poisoned by JEWS led to massacres in cities such as Basel (where the Jews were burnt alive), Frankfurt, Mainz (12,000 deaths), and Strassburg (2,000 deaths). Public health measures developed in the fifteenth century include the imposition of quarantines (literally *quaranternaria*, 40 days), the establishment of public health commissions, and the issuing of bills of mortality.

Epidemics of plague became rarer in the late seventeenth century and disappeared in Europe in the eighteenth century. The popular English myth that the Great Fire of London (1666) killed the rats that caused the plague reflects a metropolitan parochialism in its assumption that the extermination of rats in London could account for the end of a disease that existed all over Europe.

Ann Carmichael, *Plague and the Poor in Renaissance Florence* (1986); Paul Slack, *The Impact of Plague in Tudor and Stuart England* (1985); Susan Scott and Christopher Duncan, *Biology of Plague: Evidence from Historical Populations* (2001); Samuel Cohn, *The Black Death Transformed* (2002).

**PLANTIN, CHRISTOPHE** (*c.*1520–1589), French printer in Antwerp. He was born in a village near Tours and worked in Caen and Paris before settling in Antwerp in 1549. His press specialized in classical texts, the church fathers (including AUGUSTINE and JEROME), dictionaries, medicine, science (particularly botany), and music, but the most famous of its 1,500 titles was the polyglot BIBLE commissioned by King PHILIP II of Spain and known as the *Biblia regia* (8 vols., 1568–73); Plantin was subsequently appointed as *prototypographus regius* and given the monopoly of printing all liturgical books for the territories of King Philip. The arrival of Spanish forces in November 1576 drove Plantin from Brussels (he had to pay a ransom to be allowed to leave), and he remained in exile in Paris until 1585, during which time the press was managed by his sons-in-law, Jan Moretus (1543–1610) and Franciscus Raphelengius (1539–97). He died in Antwerp on 1 July 1589. The descendants of Moretus managed the press until 1876, when the archives, library, and presses of the Plantin press were bought by the city of Antwerp and became the foundation collection of the Musée Plantin-Moretus, which opened on 19 August 1877 as Antwerp's museum of the history of printing.

*Grove* s.v. Plantin, Christopher; *NBW* v s.v. Plantijn, Christoffel; *MDA*; Colin Clair, *Christopher Plantin* (1960); Léon Voet, *The Golden Compasses: A History and Evaluation of the Printing and Publishing Activities of the Officina Plantiniana at Antwerp* (2 vols., 1969–72).

**PLAQUETTES**, the nineteenth-century term for small decorative reliefs in metal, normally bronze or lead, made from the late fourteenth to the mid-sixteenth centuries; Renaissance plaquettes were usually cast, but were occasionally struck like COINS. Plaquettes characteristically depicted mythological or religious subjects, and so may be distinguished from MEDALS (which are primarily commemorative portraits) and coins (which are primarily a medium of exchange). The plaquette was typically decorated on one side and left blank on the other.

The plaquette was often made as a cheap replica of a goldsmith's product; the rock-crystal intaglios of Valerio BELLI and Giovanni BERNARDI were particularly popular models. They were also used, notably by Peter FLÖTNER, to disseminate designs. Many plaquettes were cast as paxes, and in secular use plaquettes were incorporated into sword-hilts and inkwells.

Most plaquettes were made anonymously, but in Italy plaquettes were made by Il RICCIO and by the studio of DONATELLO, and in Germany by Flötner and 'HG', who may have been Hans JAMNITZER.

Alison Luchs (ed.), *Italian Plaquettes* (1989).

**PLATERESQUE**, a late GOTHIC and early Renaissance style in SPANISH ARCHITECTURE; the term implies a similarity to the work of a silversmith (*platero*). Architectural historians commonly distinguish two phases: the Gothic-Plateresque, which is sometimes called the 'Isabelline' style (with reference to ISABELLA THE CATHOLIC, who was an important patron of architecture), is deemed to be broadly conterminous with her reign (1474–1504); the Renaissance-Plateresque is used to describe the dominant style of the first half of the sixteenth century. The transition from Gothic-Plateresque to Renaissance-Plateresque is said to be marked by the publication of SAGREDO's *Medidas del romano* in 1526, and the end of the Renaissance-Plateresque is deemed to be marked by the publication of VILLALPANDO's translation of two books of SERLIO's *Architettura* in 1552. The Plateresque was a style used primarily in small buildings; the cathedrals of the period increasingly eschewed ornamentation, and so anticipated the unornamented style (*estilo desornamentado*) of Juan de HERRERA that was to supersede the Plateresque in the later sixteenth century.

The Plateresque in both phases is characterized by the lavish use of ornamental motifs that are often unrelated to the structural form of the surfaces on buildings, ALTARPIECES, and sculptural monuments to which they are applied: they neither repeat motifs in segments, as in common in Gothic decoration, nor derive from a unified design, as is the case in Renaissance decoration. The ornamental motifs, usually in relief, may be Gothic (in the early period), Italian Renaissance (in the later period), or MUDÉJAR (in both periods).

Gothic-Plateresque was primarily a Castilian style centred on Burgos, Toledo, and Valladolid. Its exponents, who were often of northern (especially Flemish) origin, included Simón de COLONIA, Enrique EGAS, Juan GUAS, and Gil de SILOÉ. Renaissance-Plateresque was a pan-Hispanic style that influenced Portuguese (see MANUELINE) and Latin American architecture. Its principal exponents were Alonso de COVARRUBIAS, Rodrigo GIL DE HONTAÑÓN, Diego de RIAÑO, and Diego de SILOÉ.

J. Camón Aznar, *La arquitectura plateresca* (2 vols., 1945).

**PLATINA, IL,** or **Bartolomeo Sacchi** (1421–81), Italian humanist, a native of Platina (near Cremona) who entered the service of Francesco SFORZA in Milan and then moved to Mantua, where he worked as a tutor for the GONZAGA family. He lived from 1457 to 1461 in Florence, where he studied Greek under ARGYROPOULOS. In 1462 he entered the Vatican secretariat of Pope PIUS II as a papal 'abbreviator' (i.e. a drafter of briefs). Pope PAUL II's programme of reform of the papal curia led to a reduction in the size of the secretariat, and Platina lost his job. He responded by threatening to arrange a general council of the Church to overrule the pope, and was promptly imprisoned. He was released, but his links with the Roman ACADEMY of Julius Pomponius LAETUS led him to be imprisoned again when the Academy was suppressed in 1468. During the pontificate of Pope SIXTUS IV Platina was rehabilitated and appointed Vatican librarian (1475–81); the ceremony in which Platina was appointed is depicted in a Vatican fresco by MELOZZO DA FORLÌ. Platina composed a series of papal biographies (*Liber de vita Christi ac omnium pontificum*, 1474) in which the account of Pope Paul II is markedly hostile and that of Pope Sixtus IV particularly warm.

OCIL.

**PLATO IN THE RENAISSANCE.** In later medieval Europe professional philosophy was dominated by the works of ARISTOTLE, whose thought formed the basis of scholasticism. Plato (*c*.428/7–*c*.348/7 BC), who had shaped early medieval philosophy, albeit indirectly by way of Augustinianism, was revived in the Renaissance, in some measure as a reaction against Aristotelian scholasticism, and the recovery of his texts was an important part of that enterprise. Throughout the Middle Ages Platonic thought had never been altogether lost in the West, because Neoplatonic thinking had become embedded in the patristic theology of late antiquity: Plotinus was mediated through AUGUSTINE and Proclus through pseudo-Dionysius the Areopagite. Plato was honoured in the West (Petrarch declared him to be the 'prince of philosophy'), but little read, because Plato's works, with the signal exception of the first half of the *Timaeus*, were not widely available in the Latin West. Islamic scholars had inherited a Neoplatonized Aristotle (most notable in the work of the Persian Avicenna), but their consuming interest was in science and medicine and thus in Aristotle's scientific works. In the Byzantine East, however, there was a continuous tradition of scholarship devoted to Plato, and the Greek texts of his works were everywhere available.

The earliest exponents of Platonism in Renaissance Italy were the Byzantine scholars Cardinal BESSARION and George Gemistos PLETHO, who is said to have encouraged Cosimo de' MEDICI to establish a Platonic ACADEMY in Florence in 1459. The key figure here was Marsilio FICINO, the most important Platonist of the Renaissance, who translated from Greek to Latin all of the works of Plato and, perhaps even more importantly, of Plotinus; his great editions appeared in 1484 and 1492 respectively. His other Platonic works included important commentaries; the massive *Theologica platonica* (1469–74), a defence of Plato's doctrine of the immortality of the soul and of the notion of an ancient theology that was in effect a mystical and metaphysical Platonism. The other leading Platonizing philosopher of the period was PICO DELLA MIRANDOLA, whose works, together with Ficino's, were read in learned circles all over Europe.

For the Protestant thinkers of the Reformation, Neoplatonism was suspect because of its intellectualism, its subordinationism, and its other heresies, but this taint did not necessarily extend to Plato himself. MELANCHTHON, for example, encouraged by the appropriation of Plato by Cicero,

regarded Plato as an important figure in the early history of SCEPTICISM, a view that MONTAIGNE was later to share. The recovery of Plato's original texts opened the way for Plato to be disengaged from Plotinus and Proclus, and Protestant alternatives to Ficino's translations were therefore required; the founders of this Protestant Platonism included the Huguenot Jean de Serres (Johannes Serranus, 1540–98), who provided translations and an introduction to the edition of Plato published by Henri ESTIENNE in 1578. Ficino's translations eventually prevailed because of his unrivalled scholarship and his profound understanding of Plato's thought.

In England, where John COLET, Thomas MORE, and ERASMUS were early exponents of Platonism, there arose in the mid-seventeenth century a remarkable group of Neoplatonist philosophers known as the Cambridge Platonists. Given their allegiance to the Neoplatonism of Plotinus rather than to Plato himself, they might better, as Coleridge observed, have been called the Cambridge Plotinists.

J. Hankins, *Plato in the Italian Renaissance* (2 vols., 1990); M. J. B. Allen, *Synoptic Art: Marsilio Ficino on the History of Platonic Interpretation* (1998); M. J. B. Allen and V. Rees (eds.), *Marsilio Ficino: His Theology, his Philosophy and his Legacy* (2002).

**PLATTER, THOMAS** (1499–1582), Swiss humanist. He was born into a poor family in Grächen (Valais), and spent his early years working as a goatherd and soap-maker. He moved to Basel, where he became a Zwinglian and worked as a teacher, serving more than 30 years as head of the gymnasium. He was also a printer, and in 1536 published the first edition of CALVIN's *Institutes*. At the age of 75 he wrote an autobiography (*Selbstbiographie*), which was first published in 1840.

Platter's elder son Felix (1536–1614) was city physician and professor of medicine at Basel, and the author of *Praxis medicae* (3 vols., 1602–8). His younger son, Thomas Platter the Younger (1574–1628), was a physician and traveller whose account of his travels in Europe included a description of a performance of Shakespeare's *Julius Caesar* at the GLOBE Playhouse in London on 21 September 1599.

*NDB*; A. L. Schnidrig, *Thomas Platter* (1955); H. Hecht, *Thomas Platters des Jüngeren Englandfahrt im Jahre 1599* (1929; English trans. 1937).

**PLAUTUS IN THE RENAISSANCE.** In the first century BC some 130 plays were attributed to the Roman comic dramatist Titus Maccius Plautus (before 251 BC–after 184 BC); a corpus of twenty complete plays (and one fragment) survived into the Renaissance; these texts, supplemented by the Ambrosian MS discovered by Cardinal Mai in 1815, constitute the modern canon of Plautus. In the fourteenth century, eight plays were known to survive, and in 1425 NICHOLAS OF CUSA discovered a manuscript in Cologne which contained texts of three and a half known plays and twelve plays that had been lost. This manuscript was passed to Cardinal Giovanni ORSINI, and is still in the Vatican; it formed the basis of the *editio princeps* published in Venice in 1472. The next important edition was prepared by Joachim CAMERARIUS, who drew on two additional manuscripts (one in the Vatican containing all twenty plays and another, now in Heidelberg, containing the twelve 'new' plays) for his edition of 1552. The edition of Denys LAMBIN (1552) added a learned commentary which is still consulted. The final editions in this period were those of Taubmann (1605–21) and Pareus (1619 and 1623). The fragmentary *Vidularia* survived only in the Codex Ambrosiana.

Productions of Plautus in Italy were adaptations rather than antiquarian attempts to revive classical forms. Enea Silvio Piccolomini (later PIUS II) wrote his *Chrysis* in 1444, and between 1476 and 1550 there were many adaptations for the Italian stage, beginning with the staging of a Plautus comedy in Florence in 1476. In 1486 the ESTE family of Ferrara inaugurated a long series of productions with a performance of *Menaechmi* under the patronage of Ercole I d'ESTE, duke of Ferrara; some of these plays were translated into Italian by ARIOSTO, who also acted in the productions, but his translations have not survived. In Florence, Machiavelli based his *Clizia* (1525) on Plautus' *Casina*.

The tradition of Plautine adaptations in Italy spread throughout Europe. In England, the Tudor interlude *Jack Juggler* was based on the *Amphitrio*, Nicholas UDALL's *Ralph Roister Doister* on the *Miles gloriosus*, Ben JONSON's *The Case is Altered* on *Aulularia* and the *Captivi*, SHAKESPEARE's *Comedy of Errors* on the *Menaechmi* (for the plot of the identical twins) and *Amphitruo* (for the exclusion of Antipholus of Ephesus from his own house); the influence of the *Mostellaria* can also be detected in Shakespeare's *The Taming of the Shrew*, which even borrows the names Tranio and Grumio from Plautus. As Polonius reminds Hamlet, 'Seneca cannot be too heavy, nor Plautus too light'.

**PLAYING CARDS or (Italian) *naibi* or (Spanish) *naipes*.** The early history of playing cards, which may have existed in ancient China, India, Egypt, and Arabia, is not well documented, and uncertainty about the provenance of such cards is compounded by the relation of card games to chess. Similarly, the allusions in thirteenth- and early fourteenth-century Europe to games *de rege et regina* ('of king and queen'), long understood to refer to playing cards, are probably references to chess; the earliest known European playing cards do not contain a queen.

Playing cards did not exist in classical antiquity. They seem to have been introduced into Europe (possibly by returning crusaders) in the late 1370s; the Italian and Spanish terms for playing cards are cognate with the Arabic term (*naib*). A game 'called the game of cards' (*qui ludus cartarum appellatur*) is mentioned in Germany in 1377 and a pack of playing cards (*quartspel met te copen*) is mentioned in Brabant (the Netherlands) in 1379. By the end of the fourteenth century playing cards are widely attested, often by clerical abomination.

In the early fifteenth century playing cards were manufactured in Germany and distributed throughout Europe, and by the middle of the century cards were also being printed in England, France, Italy, and the Netherlands. The earliest cards seem to have been printed from engraved wood-

blocks, and were painted either in freehand or with stencils. One of the finest sets was made by the MASTER OF THE PLAYING CARDS and another may be by Konrad WITZ.

Fifteenth-century German playing cards were divided into four suits (marked with hearts, bells, leaves, and acorns); in the sixteenth century, French playing cards were divided into *cœurs* (hearts), *trèfles* (trefoil leaves), *piques* (derived from the German leaf, *grün*), and *carreaux* (diamonds). These symbols were replicated in English cards, and in the case of *cœurs* and *carreaux* the French names were translated; French *trèfles* became known as 'clubs' (a translation of the Italian term, *bastoni*) and French *piques* became known as 'spades' (a transliteration of the Italian *spade*, i.e. swords). Each suit consisted of a numbered sequence (beginning with either an ace or a deuce) and a group of court cards. The court cards consisted of a king, a knight, and a valet; Italian and French cards gradually substituted a queen for the knight. This change was adapted in England, where the valet became the jack or knave. The design now used in the English-speaking world originates in sixteenth-century Rouen, though double-headed court cards are a nineteenth-century development, as are rounded corners.

**PLÉIADE, LA.** The Pleiades form a cluster of stars in the constellation of Taurus; only six are visible to the naked eye, but the cluster was commonly said to have seven stars. In Greek mythology the Pleiades were seven sisters, the eldest of whom, Electra, was a lost Pleiad, and so not represented by a star. In 1665 the names of the seven sisters were first applied to the individual stars in the group.

La Pléiade is a name that is now attached to a group of poets active in late sixteenth-century France (c.1549–c.1589); the central figure in the group was RONSARD. In Ronsard's accounts of the membership of the group, Joachim DU BELLAY, Jean-Antoine de BAÏF, Pontus de TYARD, and Étienne JODELLE are always listed; the other two poets are variously said to be Rémy BELLEAU, Guillaume DES AUTELS, Jean DORAT, Jean Bastien de LA PÉRUSE, and Jacques PELETIER DU MANS. The outer circle of Pléiade poets and dramatists included Nicolas DENISOT, Robert GARNIER, Jacques GRÉVIN, Amadis JAMYN, and Olivier de MAGNY.

The Pléiade was associated with two colleges in Paris. Jean Dorat was principal of the Collège de Coqueret, where Baïf, Du Bellay, and Ronsard were educated. At the Collège de Boncourt, George BUCHANAN and Marc-Antoine de MURET presided over a humanist circle which included Belleau, Grévin, Jodelle, and La Péruse.

The Pléiade may not have had the cohesion of a 'school' of poets, but its poets nonetheless represented a set of ideals that were memorably articulated in Du Bellay's *La Défence et illustration de la langue française* (1549), which was widely regarded as the manifesto of the Pléiade. This treatise, which drew heavily on Sperone SPERONI's *Delle lingue* (1542), was intended as a riposte to Thomas SEBILLET's *Art poétique* (1548). Just as Speroni had championed Italian as a noble literary language, so Du Bellay advocated a national (and nationalist) renewal of French, which he proposed to enrich by the imitation of the best writers of classical antiquity. The imitation of such writers meant that members of the Pléiade were responsible for the displacement of medieval French genres in favour of classical forms of poetry (eclogue, epic, epigram, ode, and satire) and drama (tragedy, comedy); the principal Italian genre to be taken up by the Pléiade was the sonnet, although this did not form part of the original programme.

H. Chamard, *Histoire de la Pléiade* (4 vols., 1939–40); Yvonne Bellenger, *La Pléiade: La Poésie en France autour de Ronsard* (rev. ed. 1988).

**PLETHO or (Greek) Plethon, GEORGE GEMISTOS** (c.1360–1452), Byzantine Neoplatonic philosopher. The first 50 years of his long life are not well documented. His detractor GENNADIOS II SCHOLARIOS, who is a suspect but possibly accurate source, says that Pletho studied with a Jew called Elisha at the 'barbarian court' (presumably the Ottoman court at Edirne or the old capital at Bursa), where he was tainted by Zoroastrianism. He taught in Constantinople for several years, but in 1410 he was exiled to Mistra by the Emperor MANUEL II PALAIOLOGOS because of his dangerous heresy and paganism. He lived in Mistra for the rest of his life, and became the leading intellectual at the court of the ruler (δεσπότης) of Morea (the Peloponnese).

Gemistos was almost 80 when he visited Italy to attend the COUNCIL OF FLORENCE in 1438, but his mind was reinvigorated by his meetings with Florentine humanists, out of which grew a defence of Plato entitled *On the Differences between the Philosophies of Plato and Aristotle* (1439); this book was an important influence on the nascent Platonism of humanists in Florence and Rome, and seems to have inspired Cosimo de' MEDICI to assemble his informal Platonic ACADEMY. The Platonism of Gemistos led to his adoption, while in Italy, of the name Pletho, which in its Greek form (Plethon) means 'abundance' (and so is a near-synonym for Gemistos, which means 'full') and implies that Gemistos is a second Plato (and also links him with Plotinus). Of his other writings, the two most influential were his essay on Strabo, which seems to be responsible for the revival of Strabo in the Renaissance, and his controversial *Book of Laws*, the surviving fragments of which confirm the suspicion that he espoused some form of paganism, in that Pletho explicitly affirms that Zeus is the supreme god and sets out prayers, hymns, and a liturgy designed for the worship of the gods of classical antiquity; it is not clear to what extent this paganism constitutes a repudiation of Christianity.

François Masai, *Pléthon et le platonisme de Mistra* (1956); C. M. Woodhouse, *George Gemistos Pletho* (1986); John Monfasani, 'Platonic Paganism in the Fifteenth Century', in Mario di Cesare (ed.), *Reconsidering the Renaissance* (1992).

**PLEYDENWURFF, HANS** (c.1425–1472), German painter. He was probably born in Bamberg, but was active in Nuremberg from 1457 or possibly earlier. His most important surviving works are a *Calvary* panel (Alte Pinakothek, Munich), probably from a Nuremberg church, and a pair of wings from a *Passion* altar painted in 1465 for Michaelskirche (the chapel, now destroyed, of the Residenz in Munich) and now

in the Alte Pinakothek. Pleydenwurff's son Hans (d. 1494) and Michael WOLGEMUT both trained in his studio and later collaborated on the woodcuts for the 'Nuremberg Chronicle'.
*MDA; NDB.*

**PLINY THE ELDER IN THE RENAISSANCE.** The Roman encyclopedist Gaius Plinius Secundus (AD 23–79) was a soldier and historian whose life famously ended when he was asphyxiated by fumes from the erupting Vesuvius. Most of his works are lost, but his *Historia naturalis* in 37 books was a seminal influence on the scientific writing of the Renaissance; the final books, which are concerned with the application of mineralogy to bronze statuary (34), painting and modelling (35), and sculpture in marble (36), also exercised an important influence on Renaissance theories of art: the importance accorded to mathematics for an understanding of PERSPECTIVE derives from these chapers, which were also valued by artists because of their depiction of the high social status enjoyed by artists in classical antiquity.

**PLINY THE YOUNGER IN THE RENAISSANCE.** Publius Caecilius Secundus (c. AD 61–c.112), the nephew of Pliny the Elder, was the author of nine books of literary letters and a tenth book of official correspondence; his only other work to survive into the Renaissance was a *Panegyric on Trajan*. A manuscript of books 1–7 and 9 was discovered by GUARINO DA VERONA in Venice in 1419, and it later constituted the basis of the *editio princeps* (Venice, 1471). Part of book 8 was published at the end of an edition published in Rome c.1474, and all nine books were published in their proper order by ALDUS MANUTIUS (Venice, 1508). Book 10, which is sometimes entitled *Correspondence with Trajan*, survived in a single manuscript in Paris; letters 41–121 were published by Avantius of Verona in 1502, and letters 1–40 by Aldus Manutius in 1508; the original manuscript has disappeared, but the copy from which the Aldine printers worked was discovered in the Bodleian Library in Oxford in 1888. The interest of this book for Renaissance scholars lay in the fact that it contained the first external account of the official persecution of Christians and an account of the doctrines of Christianity.

Pliny's *Panegyric on Trajan* was discovered in Mainz by Giovanni AURISPA in 1432, and was first printed in Milan in the 1480s.

**PLOTINUS IN THE RENAISSANCE.** The philosopher Plotinus (AD 205–69/70), who is sometimes described as the originator of NEOPLATONISM, was born in Lycopolis (modern Asyut, in Upper Egypt); his name implies that his family was Roman, but his native language was Greek. At the age of 40 he moved to Rome, and ten years later he began to write philosophical essays, which were collected by his pupil Porphyry in six *Enneads* (i.e. groups of nine).

Plotinus ignored Christianity, but elements in his thought were instrumental in shaping early Christian thought. The Plotinian triad, which consisted of the One (or the Good), the Mind (Νοῦς), and the Soul (ψυχή), was one of the building blocks of the Christian Trinity, and the Contemplation that Plotinus describes was an important influence on Christian mystical thought. These concepts influenced the thinking of AUGUSTINE and Pseudo-Dionysius the Areopagite, who transmitted a Christian form of Plotinian ideas to medieval, Reformation, and Counter-Reformation theologians.

The *Enneads* were first published in the Latin translation of FICINO (Florence, 1492), whose commentary on Plotinus is a central text in Renaissance Neoplatonism. The *editio princeps* of Petrus Perna's Greek text of the *Enneads* was published in Basel in 1580 together with Ficino's translation.

**PLUTARCH IN THE RENAISSANCE.** Plutarch (*c.* AD 50–*c.*120) was a Greek philosopher and historian, best known in the Renaissance for a treatise on EDUCATION (which is no longer attributed to him) and his *Lives*. The educational tract was translated into Latin by GUARINO DA VERONA as *De pueris educandis*; its emphasis on the education of the balanced individual made it a key text in humanist education. It was incorporated into Plutarch's *Moralia*, of which ALDUS MANUTIUS published the Greek text in 1509. The principal editor was Demetrius DUCAS, who was assisted by ERASMUS and Girolamo ALEANDRO. Erasmus described the *Moralia* as a holy text, and so articulated the conviction of pious humanists that Plutarch had anticipated the morality of Christianity.

Plutarch's *Lives* are comparative biographies of Greek and Roman heroes. The first translation was undertaken by SALUTATI in 1396, but his copy-text was the doubtful descendant of a version in modern Greek, and was quickly superseded when manuscripts of Plutarch's original Greek came to light. In the early fifteenth century Latin translations of individual lives or pairs of lives were produced by various humanists, and in the 1430s Pier Candido DECEMBRIO attempted to produce an *Epitome* of all the parallel lives; his successor Dario Tiberti eventually published the collection (Ferrara, 1501); the task was eased by the publication in 1470 of a collected edition of the *Lives* in Latin translations of varying quality (Rome, 1470). The first edition (*editio princeps*) of the Greek text was produced by Aldus Manutius in 1509.

The dissemination of Plutarch beyond Italy began in France with AMYOT's translations of the *Lives* (1559) and the *Moralia* (1572); in England Sir Thomas NORTH translated Amyot's version of the *Lives* (1579) and Philemon HOLLAND translated the *Moralia* (1603).

G. Resta, *Le epitome di Plutarco nel Quattrocento* (1962); R. Aulotte, *Amyot et Plutarque: La Tradition des Moralia au XVIᵉ s.* (1965); M. Manfredini, 'Codici plutarchei di umanisti Italiani', *Annali Scuola Normale Superiore di Pisa*, 17 (1987).

**PODESTÀ**, in Italian towns and cities, the title of the official responsible for the maintenance of law and order; the post could be filled by a citizen, but the *podestà* was most often an outsider, appointed as a would-be neutral to supervise the courts and the administration. The appointment was for six months to a year; the *podestà* was usually of noble birth, with some legal training and experience, and was assisted by a team of lawyers, notaries, and constables. Although intended to be neutral, the *podestà* usually reflected the views of the currently dominant party. The post could be used as a career stepping-stone by ambitious SIGNORE.

**POET LAUREATE or (German)** *Gekrönter Dichter* **or (Latin)** *poeta laureatus.* The classical and medieval tradition of creating poets laureate, famously associated with the coronation of Petrarch in Rome in 1341, was instituted in Germany in 1487, where at the Diet of Nuremberg the Emperor FRIEDRICH III crowned Konrad CELTIS as the first poet laureate of the HOLY ROMAN EMPIRE. The Emperor MAXIMILIAN authorized Celtis to create new poets laureate and also crowned poets himself. The title was intended to honour expertise in Latin verse composition and conferred the right to teach in a university. The most prominent imperial poets laureate of the sixteenth century were Heinrich BEBEL, Heinrich GLAREAN, Nikodemus FRISCHLIN, Ulrich von HUTTEN, Thomas MURNER, and VADIANUS.

In England, the first holder of the post later known as poet laureate was Ben JONSON, on whom the honour was conferred in 1617.

**POGGINI, DOMENICO** (1520–90) and **GIANPAOLO** (1518–82), Italian medallists, born in Florence, the sons of a gem engraver. Gianpaolo, the elder brother, worked in the service of King PHILIP II in Brussels and (from 1559) in Madrid; his MEDALS include two of King Philip. Domenico produced medals in Florence and also worked as a sculptor, usually in bronze. His works include a marble *Apollo* (1559) in the Boboli Gardens in Florence, a bronze *Pluto* in the Palazzo Vecchio, and portrait medals of COSIMO I DE' MEDICI and two of Benedetto VARCHI. In 1585 he moved to Rome to enter the service of Pope SIXTUS V, and cast a series of portrait medals of the pope and one of the pope's sister Camilla Peretti.

*MDA.*

**POGGIO BRACCIOLINI.** See BRACCIOLINI, POGGIO.

**POISSY, COLLOQUY OF, or (Latin)** *Disputatio Pussicena* (September–October 1561), a conference between Catholic churchmen (led by Cardinal Tournon and including Diego LAÍNEZ, general of the Jesuits) and Protestant theologians (led by Theodore BEZA and including Pietro Martire VERMIGLI) held at Poissy, near Paris. The Colloquy was convened by queen mother, CATHERINE DE MÉDICIS, in the hope that some compromise would be possible; no agreement was reached on the central issue of the EUCHARIST, but on 17 January 1562 the queen mother issued the 'January Edict', which allowed the HUGUENOTS to worship freely outside walled towns and in private houses within towns.

Donald Nugent, *Ecumenism in the Age of the Reformation: The Colloquy of Poissy* (1974).

**POLAND or (Polish)** *Polska.* Medieval and early modern Poland was a vast country which included much of what is now Ukraine, Belarus, and the Baltic states; it did not, however, include SILESIA, which became independent of Poland in 1301 and thereafter became predominantly German. In 1386 Grand Duke Jagiełło of Lithuania married Jadwiga, queen of Poland, whereupon he assumed the throne of Poland as King VLADISLAV Jagiełło II. The marriage created a dynastic link between Lithuania and Poland, and also established on the Polish throne the Lithuanian JAGIEŁŁO dynasty that was to rule Poland from 1386 to 1572. In 1501 Grand Duke Alexander of Lithuania succeeded his brother JOHN ALBERT as king of Poland, and he and his successors were both grand dukes of Lithuania and kings of Poland. The duchy of Lithuania and the kingdom of Poland were formally united by SIGISMUND II in the Treaty of LUBLIN (1569).

The Polish capital was Kraków until 1569, when it was agreed in the Union of Lublin that Warsaw would be the capital of a united Poland and Lithuania; Kraków continued to be the principal seat of the court until 1610, when SIGIS-MUND III moved the royal residence to Warsaw.

The Jagiełło kings of Poland were Vladislav II, VLADISLAV III, CASIMIR IV, John Albert, Alexander, SIGISMUND I, and Sigismund II. In 1572, on the death without an heir of Sigis-mund II, the Estates (which included the newly empowered SZLACHTA) elected Henry of Valois (from 1574 King HENRI III of France) to succeed to the Polish throne. After his departure and deposition, the Estates elected STEFAN BÁTORY, prince of Transylvania, to the throne; he added LIVONIA to the territories of Poland. On his death, the electors chose SIGISMUND III VASA, son of King JOHN III of Sweden, as king, and this decision was to lead to war with Sweden. See the individual entries for the principal events of the reigns of the kings of Poland.

In ecclesiastical politics, there was considerable sympathy for the Reformation amongst the nobility, many of whom embraced CALVINISM (though in German areas LUTHERANISM was a stronger force); there were also communities of the UNITY OF THE BROTHERS and of SOCINIANS. Under the terms of the Convention of Warsaw (1573) a measure of religious toleration was secured, but thereafter the Catholic party led by Stanislaus HOSIUS gradually became the dominant force. In 1596 the RUTHENIAN Church renounced Constantinople and submitted to the papacy, and shortly thereafter the Polish Arminians accepted UNIATE status.

See POLISH ARCHITECTURE; POLISH ART; POLISH GARDENS; POLISH LANGUAGE AND LITERATURE; POLISH MUSIC.

**POLE, REGINALD** (1500–58), archbishop of Canterbury, the son of Sir Richard Pole and his wife Margaret, countess of Salisbury, who was the niece of King EDWARD IV. He was educated at the Charterhouse at Sheen and Magdalen College, Oxford, and through the patronage of King HENRY VIII was able to study in Padua from 1521 to 1527. On his return he was appointed dean of Exeter Cathedral, but decided to continue his studies in Paris (1529–30). In 1530, after Pole had returned to England, King Henry offered him the archbishopric of York in an attempt to secure his support for the royal divorce, but Pole declined. He returned to Padua, and in 1534, at the request of the king, he embarked on his *Pro ecclesiasticae unitatis defensione* (1536), which was critical of the king's conduct.

In November 1536 Pope PAUL III summoned Pole to discuss the prospects for a general council and the following month created him cardinal. In 1537, when the Vatican was outraged by the destruction of the shrine of Thomas Becket at Canterbury, Cardinal Pole was sent as a papal legate on a mission to persuade France and Spain to sever relations with England. He was unsuccessful, but news of his mission caused an Act of Attainder to be passed against Pole and his family in 1539; his mother was executed in 1541.

In 1542 Pole was appointed as one of the three papal legates (along with Paul Parisio and Giovanni MORONE) charged with presiding over the COUNCIL OF TRENT, but the Council did not assemble until 1545. On the death of Henry VIII in 1547 Pole urged the duke of SOMERSET, protector of England, to enter into negotiations with the Holy See. In 1549, on the death of Pope PAUL III, he was in contention for the papacy, and in the ballot which elected Pope JULIUS III, Cardinal Pole lost by a single vote.

On the accession in 1553 of MARY I to the throne of England, Pope Julius III appointed Pole as his legate in England, and after the lifting of the attainder, Pole arrived in England in November 1554, formally absolved Parliament from schism, and presided over a synod of the congregations of Canterbury and York. On 22 March 1556, he succeeded CRANMER (who had been burnt at the stake) as archbishop of Canterbury. The outbreak of war between Pope PAUL IV and King PHILIP II of Spain meant that Queen Mary (Philip's wife) became the enemy of the papacy; the Pope annulled Cardinal Pole's legation and stigmatized him privately as a heretic. Pole died at Lambeth Palace on 17 November 1558, only twelve hours after the queen.

DNB; D. Fenlon, *Heresy and Obedience in Tridentine Italy: Cardinal Pole and the Counter-Reformation* (1972).

**POLIDORO DA CARAVAGGIO or Polidoro Caldara** (*c*.1500–*c*.1543), Italian painter who worked in Rome, where his contemporary reputation rested on his illusionistic façade paintings, none of which has survived; engravings and drawings of these paintings show that they often imitated classical reliefs. Of his surviving paintings, the most important is a fresco of *St Mary Magdalen* in the Church of San Silvestro al Quirinale in Rome, which is a precursor of the 'heroic' LAND-SCAPE painting which was to be developed in the seventeenth century by Poussin (who worked in Rome) and Claude. In the wake of the SACK OF ROME in 1527 Polidoro left the city and settled in Messina, where he was later murdered.

DBI s.v. Caldara; MDA; Lanfranco Raverli, *Polidoro Caldara da Caravaggio* (1978); Achim Gnann, *Polidoro da Caravaggio: Die römischen Innendekorationem* (1997).

**POLISH ARCHITECTURE.** The principal conduit of foreign architectural styles in medieval Poland was Germany, and in many respects Polish Romanesque and Gothic architecture is part of the tradition of GERMAN ARCHITECTURE. Renaissance architecture, however, may have arrived through Hungary and Bohemia, but there is also evidence of direct borrowing from Italian models. The domed Chapel of King Sigismund on the south side of Kraków Cathedral (1517–38) is the work of an Italian architect, as are the early Renaissance parts of the castle (Zamek Wawelski) in Kraków (from 1502); on the other hand, the Wawel's windows draw on Benedikt RIED VON PIESTING's Vladislav Hall in Prague and its chapel seems to be indebted to the Royal Chapel in Esztergom. Indigenous elements include the use of perforated or decorated crestings instead of crenellation on buildings such as the Cloth Hall (Sukiennice) in Kraków (1555). In Gdańsk, which was the Hanse city of Danzig, the Arsenal (1602–5), which is executed in the Flemish Renaissance style, is the work of the Fleming Antonius van Opbergen.

The most extraordinary example of Renaissance architecture in Poland is Zamość, a new town commissioned by Jan ZAMOYSKI and laid out and constructed by the Venetian architect Bernardo Morando from 1587 to 1605; Zamość is the finest example of Italian Renaissance TOWN PLANNING and architectural ensembles in northern Europe.

**POLISH ART.** The prevailing style of painting in fifteenth-century Poland was INTERNATIONAL GOTHIC; the most important regional style was Silesian art, where, because of the political alignment with Bohemia, the influence of the court painters of Prague can be discerned. Polish painting began to adopt Italian idioms in the 1460s, as is apparent in the style and settings of a triptych of the *Holy Trinity* (1467, Kraków Cathedral) by the 'Master of the Choirs' and the Augustinian Polyptych of Mikołaj Haberschrack (1468, Muzeum Narodwe, Kraków). In the late 1470s the German sculptor and woodcarver Veit STOSS (Polish Wit Stwosz) lived in Kraków, where he carved the vast ALTARPIECE for the Church of Our Lady.

In the sixteenth century Polish art was remarkable for the quality of its portraiture. The illuminator Stanisław Samostrzelnik painted full-length portraits in *Żywoty opatów mogilskich* ('Lives of the Mogiła Abbots', 1505, Muzeum Czartoryskich, Kraków). There are fine portraits (both anonymous) of King SIGISMUND I in the National Art Collection in Kraków and of the humanist Benedict of Koźmin (c.1559) in the museum of the Uniwersytet Jagielloński.

**POLISH GARDENS.** Poland has one of the richest collections of historic gardens in Europe, and the sixteenth and early seventeenth centuries are well represented. The influence of ITALIAN GARDENS is clear, both in the preference for terraces over flat sites and in the laying out of symmetrical beds on either side of an axis extending from the house. The emphasis on the view from the house anticipates the later development of the picturesque.

Seven important sixteenth-century terraced gardens have survived in Balice (1518; near Kraków), Wola Justowska (c.1540; now part of Kraków), Prądnik Biały (1551; now part of Kraków), Mogilany (c.1560; south of Kraków), Gdańsk (c.1560), Neipołomice (c.1571; east of Kraków), and Książ Wielki (c.1595; north of Kraków). Renaissance gardens have been restored at Pieskowa Skała (north-west of Kraków), Baranów, and Brzeg.

Gerard Ciołek, *Ogrody polskie* (1954), published in German as *Gärten in Polen*; Gerard Ciołek, *Zarys historii kompozycji ogrodowej w Polace* (Łódź, 1955).

**POLISH LANGUAGE AND LITERATURE.** The principal languages of what is now Poland were Polish and German;

in eastern Poland, Ukrainian and Belorussian were spoken. Kashubian, the language spoken in the area west of Gdańsk, is sometimes treated as a separate language rather than a remote dialect of Polish. The Polish language is a West Slavonic language; the other major members of the group are Czech and Slovak. In the early modern period literary Polish drew heavily on Latin for vocabulary; the substantial numbers of loanwords from French and Italian in modern Polish are more recent arrivals.

The literary languages of Poland were Polish, Latin (in which Poland has one of Europe's largest literatures), and German (especially in Silesia and the Baltic ports). In the historiography of literature in Polish, the golden age is the period from 1548 (the accession of SIGISMUND II) to 1606 (when SIGISMUND III was threatened with deposition). The greatest Polish writer of this period (who, in common with many contemporaries, also wrote in Latin) was the lyric poet Jan KOCHANOWSKI, who was educated in Padua and subsequently lived in Paris (where he met RONSARD) before returning to Poland as secretary to Sigismund II; his Polish works include *Proporzec albo hold pruski* ('The Standard of Investiture of Prussian', an account of the submission of ALBRECHT VON PREUSSEN to King SIGISMUND I in 1525), *Fraszki* ('Trifles', a set of epigrams), and *Treny* ('Lamentations'), a set of elegies on the death of his daughter Ursula. Other poets of note include Stanislaw Grochowski (1554–1614), a priest who wrote courtly panegyrics, Mikołaj Szarzyński (d. 1581), who wrote the first sonnets in Polish, and the pastoral poet Szymon Szymonowicz (1554–1624). The finest poet of the landscape was Sebastian Fabian Klonowicz (1545–1602), who described the countryside of Polish Galicia in Latin (*Rhoxolania*) and the shores of the Vistula in Polish (*Flis*, 'The Boatman').

In humanist prose, the major figures in the Polish Renaissance are Łukasz GÓRNICKI, who wrote in both Polish and Latin, and Andreas Modrevius (c.1503–72; Polish Andrzej Fryca-Modrzewski), the royal secretary and political philosopher who wrote *De republica emendanda* (Basel, 1664), a call for political reform in which the monarchy would be strengthened, the Church curbed, and the law reformed. The advent of the Reformation occasioned a series of translations, each with a confessional perspective: a Lutheran New Testament appeared in 1551, the Calvinist Bible sponsored by Mikołaj RADZIWIŁŁ in 1563, a Socinian Bible in 1578, and a Catholic Bible in 1579.

**POLISH MUSIC.** The principal centre of music in sixteenth-century Poland was the court of King SIGISMUND I in Kraków, where foreign musicians were employed in the Royal Chapel and a song school was founded in 1543. The most important Polish composer of the period to remain in Poland was Nicholas Gomółka. Prominent exiles include Nicholas Zielinski, who settled in Venice and published a collection of his compositions in 1611, and Jacob Polak or Polonais (c.1545–1605), who settled in Paris, where he performed and composed music for the lute.

**POLITIAN.** See POLIZIANO, ANGELO AMBROGINI.

**POLITIQUES.** In the French WARS OF RELIGION, the Politiques were the party that represented moderate Catholic opinion. In the early 1560s the term was used with reference to the supporters of the moderate policies of CATHERINE DE MÉDICIS and her chancellor Michel de l'HÔPITAL. The Politiques supported strong monarchical government, but argued that the role of the state was to ensure civil order rather than to extirpate heresy. In the later stages of the Wars many prominent Politiques, such as the duke of ANJOU, supported the HUGUENOTS against the CATHOLIC LEAGUE.

**POLIZIANO, ANGELO AMBROGINI, or (Latin) Angelus Ambroginus Politianus or (English exonym) Politian** (1454–94), Italian humanist, distinguished poet, and Hellenist. He was born in Montepulciano and lived for most of his life in Florence, where he secured the patronage of Lorenzo de' MEDICI and served as his private secretary and as a tutor to his son Piero until 1479, when he left for Mantua; he returned the following year and taught at the Florentine *Studio* until his early death. His works included *Lamia* (1493), on Aristotle's *Prior Analytics*, and translations into Latin of the *Enchiridion* of Epictetus and the *Problems* attributed to Alexander of Aphrodisias.

Poliziano had a passionate interest in philology and wrote accomplished poetry in Greek, Latin, and Italian; his most notable achievement is his poem on a joust for Giuliano de' MEDICI (*Stanze per la giostra del Magnifico Giuliano*) which was broken off when Giuliano was killed in the PAZZI CONSPIRACY (1478); Poliziano wrote an account of the Conspiracy modelled on Sallust. While in Mantua in 1479 he wrote *La favola d'Orfeo*, the first PASTORAL drama in Italian.

E. Bigi, *La cultura del Poliziano e altri studi umanistici* (1967); I. Maier, *Ange Politien: La Formation d'un poète humaniste, 1469–1480* (1966); V. Branca, *Poliziano e l'umanesimo della parola* (1983); Paul Colilli, *Poliziano's Science of Tropes* (1989).

**POLLAIUOLO, ANTONIO** (c.1432–1498) and **PIERO** (c.1441–1496), Italian goldsmiths, painters, and sculptors, brothers who shared a workshop in Florence. Antonio was primarily a goldsmith, bronze sculptor, engraver, and draughtsman, and Piero was primarily a painter.

In 1456 Antonio collaborated with two other artists on a silver crucifix for the Florentine baptistery, and the following year collaborated on a reliquary; this magnificent ensemble, which was completed in 1459, is now in the Museo dell'Opera del Duomo, together with another of Antonio's work for the baptistery, a silver relief of *The Birth of St John the Baptist* for the altar. He also contributed a set of candlesticks (made 1465, melted down in 1539) and the design for the finest surviving EMBROIDERY of the Renaissance, the vestments known as the Paramento di San Giovanni (1466–80, Museo dell'Opera del Duomo). Antonio's only autograph engraving is *The Battle of the Naked Men* (c.1470), suggests an interest in AMATOMY which according to VASARI extended (as it was later to do with LEONARDO) to undertaking dissections of executed criminals; however, no good evidence for such dissections exists. His bronzes include the tombs of two popes, SIXTUS V (1493, now in the Grotte Vaticane) and Innocent VIII

Antonio Pollaiuolo, *Hercules and Antaeus*, a bronze statue in the Bargello, Florence

(c.1495, now in ST PETER'S BASILICA in Rome), and a *Hercules and Antaeus* (Bargello, Florence).

Piero Pollaiuolo sometimes painted independently (e.g. six of the *Seven Virtues* of 1469/70 now in the Uffizi), but many of his paintings may be collaborations with his brother, notably *The Martyrdom of St Sebastian* (1475, National Gallery, London).

MDA; Leopold Ettlinger, *Antonio and Piero Pollaiuolo* (1978).

**POMPONAZZI, PIETRO** (1462–1525), Italian Aristotelian philosopher. He was born in Mantua and studied at Padua, where he later qualified in medicine (1496) and taught philosophy; he also taught in Ferrara (1509), Mantua (1510–11), and Bologna (1511–25). His philosophical views, which derived in significant part from Alexander of Aphrodisias, included a rejection of AVERROISM and an insistence on the need to purge Aristotelian thought from the accretions of later philosophers. His most famous work is a formidable treatise on the immortality of the soul (*De immortalitate animae*, 1516) which provoked ripostes from humanists such as Gasparo CONTARINI and Agostino NIFO; Pomponazzi replied to his detractors in an *Apologia* (1518). He also wrote a treatise on thaumaturgy (*De naturalium effectuum causis sive de incantionibus*), in which he sought to attribute miracles to natural causes, and a book on fate.

DSB; M. Pine, *Pietro Pompanozzi: Radical Philosopher of the Renaissance* (1986).

Antonio Pollaiuolo, *Battle of the Naked Men* (*c.*1470), an engraving in the Metropolitan Museum of Art, New York

**PONCE DE LEÓN, JUAN** (*c.*1460–1521), Spanish conquistador, born near Valladolid into a noble family and educated at the court; he may have accompanied COLUMBUS on his second voyage (1493), which included amongst its passengers a group of young aristocrats. In 1502 he participated in the conquest of Hispaniola under the command of Nicolás de OVANDO and in 1508 led an expedition to Buriquien (now Puerto Rico), of which he was appointed governor (*adelantado*). In 1510 he suppressed an Indian revolt, and the following year he was removed from office by Diego COLÓN, whose authority as admiral had been restored.

In 1513 Ponce de León sailed north from Puerto Rico in search of the legendary island of Bimini and the fabled fountain of youth. On 27 March (Easter Sunday) he landed near what is now St Augustine, and from this base explored the east coast of the peninsula; he named the coast 'Florida', probably because he arrived on Easter Sunday (*Pascua florida* in the ecclesiastical calendar) but possibly because there were many spring flowers on the coast. He returned to Puerto Rico and in 1521 mounted a colonizing expedition to the west coast of Florida; the precise location of the settlement is not known. The colony was soon abandoned because of Indian attacks, and Ponce de León returned to Cuba nursing a wound of which he died.

DHE.

**PONTANO, GIOVANNI, or (Latin) Pontanus** (1426/9–1503), Italian humanist, diplomat, and neo-Latin poet, born in Cerretto (Umbria) and educated in Perugia. In 1447 he entered the service of King ALFONSO I of Naples, serving as tutor to the duke of Calabria; in 1486 he was appointed chancellor of the kingdom by FERRANTE I, and in 1495 he negotiated the surrender of Naples to CHARLES VIII of France in the opening campaign of the WARS OF ITALY.

Pontano's writings included works on astrology (*De rebus coelestibus*), moral philosophy (*De prudentia* and *De fortuna*), political theory (*De principe*), and the history of the Neapolitan war in which he had played a part (*De bello Neapolitano*). He also wrote moral dialogues and Latin poetry, including lyrics and didactic verse. He was the most eminent member of the Neapolitan ACADEMY, which later became known as the Accademia Pontaniana.

J. Bentley, *Politics and Culture in Renaissance Naples* (1987).

**PONTELLI, BACCIO** (1454–1494/5), Italian architect and *intarsiatoro*, born in Florence, where he trained as a woodcarver. He worked as a young man in Pisa and subsequently worked in Urbino (1479–82) and Rome (1482–92); he was probably responsible for the INTARSIA in the *studiolo* of the Palazzo Ducale in Urbino. His greatest work as a military architect was the fortification of Ostia; in the Marches he built fortifications at Iesi, Osimo, and Senigallia and contributed to the Santuario della Santa Casa at Loreto. Roman buildings attributed to Pontelli include the papal Cancellaria (c.1485) and the Church of San Pietro in Montorio (c.1490), which was financed by FERDINAND and ISABELLA of Spain.

MDA; Gaspare de Fiore, *Baccio Pontelli, architetto fiorentino* (1963).

**PONTORMO, JACOPO DA, or Jacopo Carucci** (1494–1556), Italian mannerist painter, born near Empoli (Tuscany) and trained with ANDREA DEL SARTO in Florence, where he remained throughout his life. Pontormo's early works include the altarpiece *Holy Family Surrounded by Angels* (1518, Church of San Michele Visdomini, Florence), a *Joseph in Egypt* (1519, National Gallery, London), and *Vertumnus and Pomona*, a lunette in the MEDICI VILLA at Poggio a Caiano (1520–1).

From 1522 to 1525 Pontormo painted a fresco cycle on *The Passion* in the cloisters of Certosa del Galluzzo (near Florence); some of the designs are taken from prints by DÜRER, and so illustrate how the technology that enabled art to be reproduced mechanically was able to shape the development of original art in the sixteenth century. From 1526 to 1528 Pontormo worked in the Church of Santa Felicità (Florence), where he painted a *Deposition*, an *Annunciation*, and several roundels; the *Deposition*, which is now regarded as one of the greatest mannerist paintings, is a crowded and brightly lit composition in which elongated androgynous figures are frozen in improbable postures. Pontormo's last great commission, which occupied him from 1545 until his death, was the decoration of the choir of the Church of San Lorenzo in Florence; these frescoes were destroyed in 1738.

Pontormo's highly individualistic paintings, which are characterized by spatial distortions and elongations of the human figure, are often read through the prism of his Diary for the period 1554–6, which reveals a melancholic and hypochondriacal personality. Such oversimplified retrospective readings unhelpfully reduce fine paintings to psychological documents.

DBI s.v. Carucci; MDA; Philippe Costamagna, *Pontormo* (1994).

**PORCARI, STEFANO** (c.1400–1453), Italian republican, born into a noble Roman family. In 1427–8 he served as captain of the people (*capitano del popolo*) in Florence, where he formed friendships with Poggio BRACCIOLINI and Gianozzo MANETTI and developed republican sympathies; some of his Latin orations in praise of ancient republican liberties survive. In May 1434 the aggrieved COLONNA family established an insurrectionary republic in Rome. Pope EUGENIUS IV employed Porcari as a mediator, and subsequently appointed him as papal governor (*podestà*) of Bologna. When Eugenius died in 1447, there were riots in Rome; it is not clear that Porcari was involved, but he was exiled to Bologna the following year by Pope NICHOLAS V. In 1452 he absconded and travelled to Rome in disguise with a view to setting fire to the Vatican on 6 January 1453, capturing Pope Nicholas, his cardinals, and Castel Sant'Angelo, and proclaiming a Roman republic of which Porcari was to be tribune. Porcari dressed

for the occasion in rich robes and a gold chain, and addressed his followers in Latin on the need to cast off the priestly yoke of the pope's temporal jurisdiction. The plot was discovered, and Porcari was captured and hanged (together with nine of his followers) on 9 January 1453.

M. Miglio, ' "Viva la libertà e popolo de Roma", oratoria e politica a Roma: Stefano Porcari', *Archivio della società romana di storia patria* (1974).

**PORCELAIN**, a hard white translucent POTTERY, distinguished by the temperature of the firing into hard-paste porcelain (*pâte dure*) and soft-paste porcelain (*pâte tendre*). Hard-paste porcelain has been manufactured in China since the ninth century; Chinese hard-paste porcelain was imported into sixteenth-century Europe by Portuguese and Dutch merchants, but the technique was not rediscovered in Europe until the first decade of the eighteenth century.

Soft-paste porcelain, which is fired at a lower temperature and is not as resonant when struck, may have been first made in Europe in Venice, where an imitation *porcellana* was manufactured early in the sixteenth century; as no example of this porcelain has survived, it is possible that the reference is to LATTIMO rather than porcelain. The earliest unequivocal examples of European soft-paste porcelain are those made in the Medici factory in Florence between 1575 and 1587.

**PORCELLIS or Percellis, JAN** (c.1584–1632), Flemish painter and etcher in Holland. He was born in Ghent and migrated as a religious refugee to Rotterdam. He specialized in marine painting, and his seascapes typically depicted a small fishing boat in a choppy sea with the shoreline in the background. Whereas his predecessor Hendrik VROOM had concentrated on the depiction of ships in vivid colours, Porcellis painted monochromic images of sea and sky.

MDA; NNBW x.

**PORDENONE, IL or Giovanni Antonio de' Sacchis** (1483–1539), Italian painter, born in Pordenone (Friuli). His principal work, which shows the influence of MICHELANGELO, is a series of frescoes on *The Passion* in Cremona Cathedral (1520–2); he also painted frescoes in Treviso Cathedral (1522, now partly destroyed). In 1527 Pordenone settled in Venice, where his surviving paintings include two saints in the choir of San Rocco (1528–9) and several altarpieces, of which the best known depicts an angel showing the way to three saints (c.1535–6, Church of San Giovanni Elemosinario).

MDA; Charles Cohen, *The Art of Giovanni Antonio da Pordenone* (1996).

**PORPHYRY or (Italian) *pórfido***, a hard volcanic rock which ranges in colour from green to red; the variety used in Renaissance Florence and Venice was a deep red variety known as *pórfido rosso antico*. In ancient Egypt porphyry had been quarried at Mount Porphyrites (now Jebel Dhokan, on the west coast of the Red Sea), and when Egypt became a Roman province on the death of Cleopatra, the quarries were taken over by the Romans and used for statues, sarcophagi, and even columns. The quarries were exhausted in

Jacopo da Pontormo, *The Deposition* (1528), in the Church of Santa Felicità in Florence

the fifth century, and thereafter the only source of porphyry was Roman ruins. The excavation of ancient Rome in the sixteenth century provided the porphyry used by sculptors, of whom the most important was Francesco FERRUCCI.

**PORTA.** See DELLA PORTA.

**PORTE, THE SUBLIME, or** (French) *la sublime porte* **or** (Italian) *la porta sublima*, the western term for the government of the Ottoman Empire. The 'porte' is the gate through which ambassadors passed to attend audiences with the sultan; the term 'sublime' does not refer in a literal sense to the height of the gate, but is rather an honorific attribute. The government is sometimes called 'the Ottoman Porte', but in early modern (and modern) English is usually abbreviated to 'the Porte'.

**PORTO, LUIGI DA** (1485–1529), Italian soldier, historian, and poet, born into a prominent family in Vicenza. In the wake of the battle of AGNADELLO (1509) Vicenza was occupied by imperial troops; Luigi remained for two years in the service of the imperial administration, but then left for Venice, where he commanded a cavalry unit. He fought in the Veronese and Friuli, but in 1511 withdrew from active service after being wounded in the throat. In his forced retirement he turned to writing, and composed a series of letters (*Lettere storiche*) that describe the military history of the Venetian *terraferma* from 1509 to 1524; these letters offer a personal and markedly literary perspective on an important period in the WARS OF ITALY. He also composed the most elaborated version of the Romeo and Juliet story.

*OCIL.*

**PORTRAITS AND SELF-PORTRAITS.** A portrait is usually a painted image, but portraits can also take the form of statues (including busts, wax figures, and EQUESTRIAN STATUES), MEDALS, PRINTS, and DRAWINGS; painted portraits range from heroic representation to MINIATURES. Portraits may attempt to create a likeness of the sitter, or may be imaginary; the recently dead may have representational effigies on their tombs (sometimes made from death masks) but, in the case of long-dead saints and monarchs, the painter sometimes used a living model: DÜRER's *St Jerome* (1521, Museu de Arte Antiga, Lisbon) portrays the features of an elderly man whom Dürer sketched in Antwerp, but is nonetheless a representation of St Jerome. Such pictures can only be considered as portraits in a very limited sense.

The portraits painted by CRANACH and HOLBEIN are images of their sitters that convey a sense of character and social standing without idealizing their subjects. Portraits can be sympathetic even with the portrayal of disfiguring features; GHIRLANDAIO's *Portrait of an Old Man and a Boy* (Paris, Louvre) portrays the old man's elephantiasis, which Ghirlandaio had studied in his silverpoint preparatory sketch (Nationalmuseum, Stockholm). The sense of a portrait as an object of surrogate adoration, which originated in pictures of the Virgin Mary, was sometimes carried over into secular portraits. In WEBSTER's *White Devil* (1612) Isabella kneels before the portrait of her husband, and is killed when she kisses the poisoned lips of the portrait.

Artists are often said to have included self-portraits in crowd scenes, but documented examples are rare; one such example survives in a fresco by Benozzo GOZZOLI in the Palazzo Riccardi in Florence: the self-portrait is identified with a Latin inscription declaring the painting to be the work of Gozzoli, and so in this instance the self-portrait is a form of signature. The genre is more common in sculpture: the earliest such self-portrait is Peter PARLER's in Prague; Anton PILGRAM twice sculpted self-portraits in Vienna and GHIBERTI included his own portrait on the baptistery doors of Florence. The tradition of self-portraits as a means of depicting character was initiated in the drawings of Dürer and culminated in the etched and painted self-portraits of Rembrandt.

J. Pope-Hennessy, *The Portrait in the Renaissance* (1966); Lorne Campbell, *Renaissance Portraits: European Portrait Painting in the 14th, 15th and 16th Centuries* (1990).

**PORTUGAL.** Early modern Portugal was the kingdom at the centre of the colonial expansion of Europe into the rest of the world. The capture of Ceuta in 1415 inaugurated a period

of exploration and revived the confrontation with Islamic North Africa, the roots of which extend back to the period between Moorish invasion in 711 and the expulsion of the Muslims from the Algarve in 1249.

The royal family throughout the early modern period was the House of Avis, a dynasty founded by JOHN I (João I) in 1385 and extinguished with the death of SEBASTIAN I at the battle of KSAR-EL-KEBIR on 4 August 1578 and of his elderly and almost insane successor Cardinal-Prince HENRIQUE on 31 January 1580, when the country was annexed by Spain. The architect of the maritime expansion of Portugal was Prince HENRY THE NAVIGATOR, son of John I. Henry had been a participant in the attack on Ceuta, which had been motivated by the desire to suppress piracy and give Portugal control of the Straits of Gibraltar and access to the gold and slaves of Africa. Shortly after this campaign Henry retired to the Sagres peninsula (Ponta de Sagres), where he financed the activities of astronomers, cartographers, navigators, naval architects, and sailors. Later the Portuguese made advances in NAVIGATION by refining the design and use of the ASTROLABE and sextant and learning how to calculate latitude by reference to the position of the North Star and the sun at noon. Developments in CARTOGRAPHY and in ship design (notably the introduction of the CARAVEL) enabled Portuguese mariners to increase the range of exploration and conquest.

The voyages of EXPLORATION initiated by Prince Henry began with the discovery of Madeira in 1419 and the AZORES in 1427; in the same period a series of Portuguese expeditions began to explore the West African coast: in 1434 an expedition rounded Cape Bojador (or what is now called Cap Juby), which was the limit of the world known to Europeans; in 1482 Diogo CÃO reached the mouth of the Congo and in 1488 Bartolomeu DIAS reached the Cape of Good Hope. The Treaty of TORDESILLAS signed with Spain in 1494 delineated areas which Portugal could explore without hostility from Spain. In 1498 an expedition commanded by Vasco da GAMA rounded Africa and reached India; the voyage was celebrated by Luís CAMÕES in his epic poem *The Lusiads*. In 1500 Pedro CABRAL landed in Brazil, and in 1503 Afonso de ALBUQUERQUE reached Malacca. The colony of Macao was founded in 1557. As the coasts of Africa, Brazil, India, and Asia were explored, the Portuguese established *FEITORIAS* as a prelude to colonization. The discoveries were exploited commercially, and in the early sixteenth century the Portuguese economy flourished. This new-found wealth financed a flowering of PORTUGUESE ART, PORTUGUESE ARCHITECTURE, and PORTUGUESE LITERATURE.

In 1536 the Holy Office was instituted in Lisbon, and the Portuguese INQUISITION began the persecution of dissenters in Portugal and in India. The University of Coimbra remained a bulwark of humanist thinking for another generation, during which time its lecturers included many foreign scholars such as George BUCHANAN and the French mathematician Élie Vinet, but a series of inquisitorial trials forced many of the best scholars to leave, and in 1555 the Jesuits were appointed to reform the university, which thereafter became a strictly orthodox and conservative ecclesiastical institution.

In 1580 PHILIP II of Spain inherited the crown of Portugal, which was occupied by Spanish troops and ruled by a Spanish viceroy until the revolution of 1640 re-established the political independence of Portugal.

**PORTUGUESE ARCHITECTURE.** Until the end of the fifteenth century, the history of Portuguese architecture was part of the common architectural history of the Iberian peninsula. The Mozarabic architecture of the tenth century (e.g. Lourosa) yielded to the Romanesque of the twelfth century (e.g. the cathedrals of Braga, Coimbra, and Évora) and then to the GOTHIC, which was introduced by the Cistercians in the Abbey of Santa Maria Alcobaça (1178–1252) and flowered in the early fourteenth-century cloisters of the cathedrals in Coimbra, Évora, and Lisbon.

The advent of the late Gothic (or Flamboyant Gothic) period is marked in its triumphant expression at Batalha Monastery, where between 1402 and 1438 an architect called Huguet built the façade, the Chapel of JOHN I, and vaults for the cloister and the chapter house. In the 1490s the late Gothic idiom reached its zenith in the first distinctly Portuguese architectural style, the MANUELINE, which was a Portuguese version of the PLATERESQUE in which MUDÉJAR design inspired structures as well as decorations and so facilitated a totality of design that was uniquely Portuguese.

The influence of Renaissance ITALIAN ARCHITECTURE is most magnificently evident in the Claustro dos Felipes in the Convento de Cristo in Tomar; this large two-storeyed Palladian cloister was built by Diogo de TORRALVA between 1557 and 1566. The only cathedral built in the style of the Italian CINQUECENTO is Leiria, which was built by Afonso Álvares between 1551 and 1575. The BAROQUE did not arrive in Portugal until the mid-seventeenth century, but dominated Portuguese architecture until the Lisbon earthquake of 1755 inaugurated a period of French influence.

The Portuguese did not begin to erect significant buildings in their colonies until the last quarter of the seventeenth century. The sole exception to this late realization of the importance of colonial settlements was the west coast of India, where fortified towns were built in Damão (now Daman), Diu, Bacão (now Bessein), and Goa; the churches of Goa include important examples of Manueline (Rosário, 1543) and Renaissance architecture (cathedral, 1562–1631; Bom Jesus, 1594).

G. Kubler and M. Soria, *Art and Architecture in Spain and Portugal and their American Dominions, 1500–1800* (1959).

**PORTUGUESE ART.** The characteristics of Portuguese art before the mid-fifteenth century are virtually unknown, because only a few mural fragments precede the earliest surviving Portuguese paintings, the panels executed by Nuno GONÇALVES in the 1460s; the visit of Jan van EYCK in 1428–9 may well have made an impact on local painters, but there is no surviving example to sustain such a claim. In the sixteenth century a native school of Portuguese painters emerged; these prolific painters are often described as the 'Portuguese Primitives', but the term 'primitive' makes insufficient allowance for the pronounced influence of FLEMISH ART on their paintings, and they are more accurately described as the Luso-Flemish School of painting. During this period there were two centres of Portuguese art: in the north, at Viseu, the principal painters were Vasco Fernandes ('Grão Vasco', c.1475–1542), whose main works are two ALTARPIECES (in Freixo de Espada-à-Cinta and in the Lamego Museum) and the paintings in the Viseu Museum, and Gaspar Vaz (c.1490–1568), whose principal paintings are in the monastery Church of São João de Tarouca. The second centre was the Lisbon court, which consisted of the court painter Jorge Afonso (fl. 1508–40) and his three pupils Cristóvão de Figueiredo (fl. 1515–43), Garcia Fernandes (fl. 1514–65), and Gregório LOPES. Many of their paintings were portraits, often brightly coloured; the exception is the work of Cristóvão de Figueiredo, who used an unusual amount of black and grey, and whose preference for spots of colour over brush-strokes anticipates the techniques of the Impressionists.

Andrea SANSOVINO visited Portugal in the 1490s, but, like the earlier visit of Jan van Eyck, his presence left no visible mark on Portuguese painting. The only significant Portuguese painter to adopt an Italianate style was the miniaturist Francisco de HOLANDA. In sculpture, however, the influence of the Italian Renaissance was to become a central feature of sixteenth-century Portuguese art. The first artist to introduce the idioms of Italian Renaissance sculpture into Portugal was the French decorative sculptor Nicolas Chanterene (c.1485–c.1555), who worked on the north door of the Hieronymite monastery at Belém (which includes fine statuettes of King MANUEL and Queen Maria) before establishing himself in Coimbra, where he became the principal sculptor; his masterpiece is the pulpit in the Church of the Holy Cross in Coimbra. Under the patronage of Cardinal Georges d'AMBOISE, Chanterene became the inaugurator of the Coimbra School of sculpture which in the 1530s included the French sculptors Jean de Rouen, Jacques Buxe, and Phillippe Houdart and the Portuguese sculptors (of Castilian extraction) João and Diogo Castilho. Their sculptures, which were avowedly Italianate and erudite, created a distinctive style of sculpture in Coimbra and thence throughout Portugal.

The annexation of Portugal by Spain in 1580 shifted the centre of art to Madrid, so the finest Portuguese sculptor of the seventeenth century, Manuel Pereira, worked principally in Spain.

*MDA*; R. G. Smith, *The Art of Portugal, 1500–1800* (1968); G. Kubler and M. Soria, *Art and Architecture in Spain and Portugal and their American Dominions, 1500–1800* (1959).

**PORTUGUESE GARDENS** of the sixteenth and seventeenth centuries incorporated features that can be traced to the Roman occupation (tessellated tiles), the Moorish occupation (notably the Arabic water-tank, an architectural pool of still water), and the Spanish occupation (especially the glazed tiles known as AZULEJOS), but the design elements came from France (box PARTERRES and pleached trees) and Italy (FOUNTAINS, GROTTOES, statues, and GIARDINI SEGRETI). The fact that the terrain is hilly occasioned a natural preference for the Italian terrace rather than the flatter French garden.

The combination of *azulejos* and water-tanks was uniquely Portuguese. Arab architecture had traditionally used still water to reflect clouds and trees. The Portuguese water-tank achieves a similar effect by setting *azulejos* above the stone sides of the water-tank, so that the water is reflected in the shimmering blues, purples, yellows, greens, and oranges of the *azulejos*. And just as rich surface decoration in mosaic is an important element in Islamic architecture, so the constructed elements in Portuguese gardens (PAVILIONS, fountains, grottoes, loggias) were covered in *azulejos*. The important difference between these traditions, however, is that Suni Islamic decoration is geometrical, whereas from the mid-fifteenth century Portuguese *azulejos* were representational, depicting plants, animals, and humans; they were used, like frescoes in Italy, to illustrate classical and biblical legends.

The best surviving Renaissance gardens in Portugal are the Quinta da Bacalhoa (Estremadura) and Castelo Branco (Beira Baixa). The villa at Bacalhoa, which was built in 1480, was acquired in 1528 by Afonso de Albuquerque, the son (and namesake) of the Portuguese admiral. The garden is a square bounded on two sides by the house and on the third side by a clipped hedge. This is an open Renaissance garden rather than an enclosed medieval garden, so the fourth side is unbounded; the garden was meant to be viewed from the arcaded loggia on the first floor of the house, and the absence of a barrier on the fourth side facilitates a view of the orchards and open countryside beyond the garden. The garden is laid out in four squares of box hedging with a fountain at the centre; the layout and the planting are twentieth-century restorations, but are faithful to the Renaissance original. A long terrace leads to the pavilion and water-tank that are the glory of the garden. The huge water-tank is flanked on one side by a high wall, in front of which seats covered in green and white *azulejos* are set amongst climbing roses and jasmines. On the opposite side a low parapet topped with box obelisks supports troughs of scented herbs and flowers; this profusion of flowers is a marked contrast to the austere formality of the box hedging in the main garden. The pavilion consists of three small square buildings linked by an elegant arcaded loggia; inside, the pavilion is divided into a series of small rooms, all richly decorated with *azulejos* in blues, greens, and yellows; one of these panels depicts Susanna and the Elders; it is the earliest dated *azulejo* picture in Portugal (1565).

In 1598 the bishop of Guarda built a palace and laid out a terraced garden in Castelo Branco, a hill town in the Serra da Estrela. On the highest terrace there is an oblong water-tank surrounded by a stone balustrade; at one end a flight of steps leads down to the water. The tank was once decorated with masks and pebble mosaics and *azulejos*, most of which have disappeared, but even in its denuded state the tank is very beautiful. On the terraces below there are twin staircases lined with statues of kings on the balustrades. There is also a hidden pool, through the surface of which protrude marble flower beds; the effect of brightly coloured flowers apparently growing out of the water derives ultimately from Mughal gardens, and was probably transmitted to Portugal through Moorish influence. The main PARTERRE is laid out on a lower terrace, which is lined on three sides by clipped box walls and pleached trees; the fourth side is open, and so offers a view of the plain below. The beds in the parterre are constructed of box, and the complex symmetrical designs are complementary rather than identical; the beds are decorated with statues, and there is a fine basin with a fountain from which water shoots into the air. At the lowest level of the garden there is an ornate fountain covered in *azulejos*.

H. Carita and H. Cardoso, *Tratado da grandoza dos jardins em Portugal* (1987), trans. as *Portuguese Gardens* (1989).

**PORTUGUESE LANGUAGE.** For centuries Arabic enjoyed an important linguistic presence in Portugal, but in early modern Portugal the hegemony of Portuguese Romance was challenged only by the fashion for the SPANISH LANGUAGE in the Portuguese court, an anomaly which means that some of the finest PORTUGUESE LITERATURE is written in Spanish. A language closely related to Portuguese was (and is) also spoken in the kingdom (now province) of Galicia (and in the Bierzo district of León), where it is known as GALICIAN or Galego. Portuguese was carried around the world by Portuguese mariners, and is still an important language in South America (Brazil), North America (especially Florida), and Africa (Angola and Mozambique); it also survives in isolated outposts in Asia, including Goa, Malacca, East Timor, and Macao. Standard diachronic and diatopic developments, including interpenetration with indigenous languages, have given rise to many dialects, of which European Portuguese, Brazilian Portuguese, and African Portuguese are the principal varieties. Portuguese is written in the Latin alphabet, minus the letters *k*, *w*, and *y*; there are five diacriticals: acute accent, grave accent, circumflex, cedilla, and tilde.

The first grammar of Portuguese was published by Fernão de Oliveira in 1536. João de BARROS wrote an influential dialogue on the standardization of the literary language, and Nunes de Leão published a treatise on the orthography of Portuguese in 1576 and a philological history of the language in 1605. The first Portuguese–Latin dictionary, Jerónimo Cardoso's *Dictionarium Latinolusianicum* (1592), was soon superseded by the scholarly *Dictionarium Lusitanico-latinum* (1611) of Bishop Augustinho Barbosa.

S. Silva Neto, *História da língua portuguesa* (1952); J. M. Camara, *História e estrutura da língua portuguesa* (1975).

**PORTUGUESE LITERATURE.** The courts of John I and his sons DUARTE and Dom Pedro were the focus of early Renaissance literature in Portugal; they collected humanist manuscripts, commissioned translations of classical works into Portuguese, and wrote moral treatises themselves. The distinguished royal chroniclers of the fifteenth century include Fernão LOPES (who was famously described by Southey as the best chronicler of any age or nation), Gomes Eanes de Azurara (who described the capture of Ceuta and the African explorations of HENRY THE NAVIGATOR), Ruy de

Pina (the chronicler of Duarte and AFONSO V), and Garcia de RESENDE, the most literary of the chroniclers and the editor of the *Cancioneiro geral*, a collection of poems by some 200 poets.

The major dramatist of the early sixteenth century was Gil VICENTE, whose successors were known as the Escola Velha. Humanists such as Nicolaas Cleynaerts and Johannes Vaseus settled in Portugal, which in turn produced native humanists such as Damião de GÓIS and scientists including the astronomer Pedro Nones and the experimental scientists João de Castro and Garcia de ORTA. The presence of humanists also encouraged the flowering of neo-Latin literature.

In the sixteenth century Italian cultural influence was valued, partly as an antidote to the Castilian cultural hegemony of the previous century. The originator of Italian styles in literature and drama was SÁ DE MIRANDA, who returned from a six-year sojourn in Italy in 1526 and presided over a recasting of Portuguese literature in an Italian mode, introducing Italian verse forms such as the sonnet, the canzona, the ode, and the verse epistle in tercets and in *ottava rima*. The greatest product of the Italian school was Luís de CAMÕES, who towers over the literature of the period not only in his epic *Lusiads* but also in lyric poetry. In prose the pastoral or allegorical romance was cultivated by Bernardim RIBEIRO and João de BARROS. In drama, Sá de Miranda and his successors displaced the inheritance of Gil Vicente and introduced prose plays modelled on the plays of Terence as mediated by ARIOSTO. The greatest classical playwright was António FERREIRA, who bypassed Italian models in favour of Seneca. Many writers, notably Jorge de MONTEMAYOR, Jorge Ferreira de VASCONCELOS, Gil Vicente, and Camões, continued to write in Castilian, but their works nonetheless constitute part of the canon of Portuguese literature.

**PORTUGUESE MUSIC** thrived under JOHN I who maintained a court ensemble for ceremonial occasions. Portuguese composers of the sixteenth century include Damião de Goes (1501–74), Cosme Delgado (*c*.1530–1596), and Manuel Mendes (*c*.1550–1605). Portuguese polyphony flourished in the early seventeenth century with the school of Évora, including Duarte Lobo (*c*.1565–1646), Manuel Cardoso (1571–1650), and King John IV (1604–56), who composed sacred music and whose library was destroyed by the 1755 earthquake. Portuguese organ music is represented by Manuel RODRIGUES COELHO.

**POSSEVINO, ANTONIO** (*c*.1533–1611), Jesuit missionary and papal diplomat, born in Mantua, where he entered the Jesuits in 1559. The following year he was sent to work amongst the WALDENSES in Piedmont, and between 1563 and 1572 he lived in France, where he founded Jesuit educational institutions. In 1573 he became secretary of his Order.

King JOHN III of Sweden was a Protestant with Catholic sympathies, and opened negotiations for the reconciliation of the Swedish Church with Rome. Possevino was dispatched to Sweden in 1579 with a view to reconverting the king. In 1580 Possevino travelled to Muscovy in an unsuccessful

attempt to mediate between IVAN III and STEFAN BÁTORY, and thereafter worked in Poland. He eventually returned to Italy, and spent the rest of his career teaching at a Jesuit college in Padua. His *Moscovia* (1586) described his embassy to Russia, and his *Iudicium* (1594) attacked MACHIAVELLI.

P. Pierling, *Un nonce de la pape en Moscovie* (1884).

**POSTEL, GUILLAUME** (1510–81), French scholar and orientalist, born near Barenton (Normandy). He studied oriental languages in Paris and in 1537 became a member of the embassy sent to Constantinople by FRANCIS I; after the conclusion of the embassy he travelled extensively in the Ottoman Empire with a view to buying manuscripts for the royal library. On returning to Paris he taught Greek, Hebrew, and Arabic at the Collège de France and became the first professor of oriental languages; the first of his scholarly works on the Middle East was *De originibus seu de Hebraicae linguae et gentis antiquitate* (1538). In 1544 Postel was ordained as a priest and then returned to the Middle East; he subsequently lived for ten years in Italy where he attempted to appear before the COUNCIL OF TRENT and was imprisoned for four years by the INQUISITION; he spent the rest of his life in forced seclusion.

Postel advocated the securing of peace through a universal religion, notably in his *De orbis terrae concordia* (1544), which offended both Catholics and Protestants in its tolerance of Islam and of different forms of Christianity. His other works include *Protevangelium Jacobi, fratris Dominis, de natalibus Jesu Christi* (Basel, 1552), a translation into Latin of the Book of James, an apocryphal infancy narrative now known (because of Postel's title) as the Protevangelium.

Marion Kuntz, *Guillaume Postel* (1981).

**POTTERY**. Clay has been shaped and fired to make vessels since remote antiquity, and these have been decorated with incised or painted ornament since neolithic times. The three principal types of pottery are earthenware, STONEWARE, and PORCELAIN. Most Renaissance pottery is TIN-GLAZED EARTHENWARE, which is known in Italy as MAIOLICA and in France, Germany, Scandinavia, and Spain as FAIENCE.

**POWER, LIONEL** (d. 1445), English composer who taught the choristers in the chapel of Thomas, duke of Clarence, and was at Christ Church, Canterbury. The Old Hall manuscript contains early examples of his unified mass cycles where movements are linked through the use of related chants. It is not always clear which works are by Power, since there are similarities between his style and that of DUNSTAPLE.

**PRAETORIUS, HIERONYMUS** (1560–1629), German composer, organist, copyist, and music editor. He studied at Hamburg and Cologne, was organist at Erfurt (1580–2), and then returned to Hamburg where, in 1586, he succeeded his father Jacob as organist of the Jacobkirche. He worked on the *Melodien Gesangbuch* (1604), a compilation of German chorale settings with specific organ accompaniments. He composed masses, Magnificat settings, and motets which, despite the absence of parts, were said to have been performed with supporting instruments reminiscent of the Venetian style. His organ writing includes *cantus firmus* Magnificat settings.

## PRAETORIUS, MICHAEL, or (German) Michael Schulz

(1571–1621), German composer and music historian, educated at Torgau, Anhalt, and the University of Frankfurt an der Oder. He was organist in Frankfurt and, in 1595, to Duke Heinrich Julius of Brunswick-Wolfenbüttel. He became *Kapellmeister* in 1604. After the duke's death in 1613 he held a similar post at the electoral court of Johann Georg of Saxony, and later worked in Halle, Sondershausen, Kassel, and Magdeburg. Protestant hymns form the basis for much of his sacred music, though later works reflect Italian influence and make use of continuo. His influential *Syntagma musicum* is a theoretical work in three sections, dealing with religious music, contemporary instruments, and musical forms.

## PRAGMATIC SANCTION OF BOURGES (7 July 1438).

The term 'pragmatic sanction' (*pragmatio sanctio*) was used in Roman law of the Christian period to denote a stricture that limited the power of a prince, usually with respect to succession. The Pragmatic Sanction of Bourges, which was issued by the French clergy while the COUNCIL OF BASEL was in session, was a statement of GALLICANISM which asserted the supremacy of a council over a pope and restricted the power of the pope in France by upholding the right of the French Church to administer its temporal property without reference to the papacy and to disallow papal nominations to vacant benefices. In 1516 the Pragmatic Sanction of Bourges was annulled by the Concordat of BOLOGNA.

## PRAGUE or (Czech) Praha or (German) Prag, the ancient

capital of BOHEMIA and the seat of an archbishop. Renaissance Prague was also a seat of the Holy Roman Emperor, and so had a substantial German population living alongside native Czechs; there was also a large Jewish GHETTO (established in the tenth century) within the fortifications, but separated from the old town (Staré Město) by gates and a wall.

Much of the present appearance of central Prague can be traced to the Emperor Charles IV, who was also King Charles I of Bohemia. He is the eponym of Charles University, which he founded in 1348, and was responsible for the construction of the new town (Nové Město) that was needed because of the rapid growth of the university.

Prague was badly damaged during the HUSSITE WARS, but thereafter enjoyed a long period of prosperity until the mid-sixteenth century, when in the wake of the battle of MÜHLBERG (24 April 1547) the Emperor FERDINAND required submission, stripping the city of many of its liberties and privileges; on 20 August 1547 Ferdinand presided over a meeting of the Estates in the Hradčany Palace, while on the square outside, senior civic officials were being decapitated; the assembly came to be known as the Krvavy sněm (Bloody Diet).

In 1573 King RUDOLF II of Bohemia chose to establish his permanent residence in Prague, and as he was also king of Hungary, Holy Roman Emperor, and the senior member of the HABSBURG family whose lands stretched across Europe,

Prague became the capital of much of Europe. Rudolf brought to his court scientists such as Tycho BRAHE and Johann KEPLER, and also made Prague an important artistic centre; his agents purchased works of art from all over Europe, and Rudolf invited artists to Prague, including the painters Hans van AACHEN, Joris HOEFNAGEL, and Bartholomeus SPRANGER and the sculptor Adriaen de VRIES. Rudolf established a workshop (now known as the Prague Court Workshop) in the Hradčany Palace to produce works of art for his own collections and for use as gifts. The products of the workshop reflected Rudolf's particular interests in GEMS and ROCK CRYSTAL and ENAMEL, and the craftsmen included Christoph JAMNITZER, Kaspar LEHMANN, Paulus van VIANEN, several members of the MISERONI family and the horologist Jost BÜRGI.

In 1618 the DEFENESTRATION OF PRAGUE signalled the end of this rich period in the city's history.

## PRAGUERIE (1440), a rebellion by the French nobility

against the anti-feudal policies of CHARLES VII, who had proscribed unauthorized private militias. The name alludes to the Bohemian capital, which had recently been at the centre of the HUSSITE WARS. The rebels included the king's son Prince Louis (later King LOUIS XI), the dukes of Alençon and Bourbon, and the counts of Armagnac, DUNOIS, and Vendôme. The towns did not support the rebellion, which was soon suppressed.

## PRATOLINO, VILLA, a VILLA with gardens 13 kilometres

(8 miles) north-east of Florence. The house and garden were built between 1561 and 1581 on a 240-hectare (600-acre) site on the side of a south-facing hill. The work was commissioned by Francesco de' Medici (1541–87), and the architect and hydraulic engineer was almost certainly Bernardo BUONTALENTI. Above the house an AMPHITHEATRE was carved out of the hillside, dominated by a colossal FOUNTAIN of Apennine, probably by GIAMBOLOGNA; this statue, which is the principal surviving architectural feature of the garden, depicts Apennine pressing the head of a monster out of whose mouth the water flows. Above the fountain there was a large MAZE and a fountain that functioned as a reservoir for the waterworks that lay below.

The lower garden was not laid out in terraces. Instead it was structured by means of a central axis running through the house from the top to the bottom of the hill, but the various features of the garden were not set out symmetrically around this axis: fountains, GROTTOES, MOUNTS, PAVILIONS, and fish ponds were scattered through the garden.

The garden was chiefly remarkable for its imaginative use of water, which was said to surpass even the Villa d'ESTE. The house was surrounded by a balustraded artificial terrace, beneath which lay eight grottoes with GIOCHI D'ACQUA. In the Grotto of the Flood, the unwary visitor who sat on an inviting bench to admire the sculpture was quickly squirted with water from all directions, and retreat up the stairs to escape the drenching was inhibited by water pouring onto the staircase from hundreds of jets. The grottoes were fitted with many AUTOMATA, some based on the designs of HERON; visitors such as MONTAIGNE were particularly delighted by the animals that stooped to drink from the fountains and the sound of the water-organs. Below the house a long avenue ran down the hill, lined with free stone walls that accommodated scores of fountains. At the bottom of the avenue there was a fountain with a statue of a woman doing her laundry. Water fell from a marble cloth which she was holding, and a pot held water that seemed to be boiling.

In the sixteenth and seventeenth centuries the garden of Pratolino was the most famous in Europe; it is now the greatest of the lost gardens of Europe, because it was destroyed in 1819 to make way for a *giardino inglese*. The Renaissance garden is now being gradually restored.

Francesco de' Vieri, *Discorsi delle meravigliose opere di Pratolino* (1568); Luigi Zangheri, *Pratolino: Il giardino delle meraviglie* (2 vols., 1979).

**PREDA or Predis, AMBROGIO DA** (c.1455–after 1508), Italian painter and illuminator, appointed court painter to the SFORZA of Milan in 1482. His only fully authenticated painting is a signed and dated portrait of the *Emperor Maximilian I* (1502, Kunsthistorisches Museum, Vienna); he may have been the artist who painted a portrait of *Francesco di Bartolomeo Archinto* (1494, National Gallery, London).

Preda was named together with his elder half-brother Evangelista Preda in the contract of 1483 in which LEONARDO DA VINCI was commissioned by the Confraternity of the Immaculate Conception in Milan to paint the altarpiece known as *The Virgin of the Rocks*, of which there are versions in the National Gallery in London and the Louvre. The wings of Leonardo's altarpiece (also in the National Gallery) depict angels with musical instruments; the *Angel in Red Playing the Lute* may be the work of Ambrogio da Preda.

*MDA* s.v. Predis.

**PREDELLA.** See ALTARPIECE.

**PRESTER JOHN**, the mythical Christian ruler of a kingdom in the East; 'Prester' is a compressed form of 'presbyter' and in some documents he is called Johannes the Presbyter. In the twelfth and thirteenth centuries his kingdom was placed in central Asia or India, and he was associated with St Thomas. By the fourteenth century the consensus had shifted, and following the embassy of the Ethiopian emperor Wedem Ar'ad to Jaume II of Aragon and Pope Clement V in 1306, Prester John's kingdom was agreed to be in Ethiopia. Friar Jordanus, a Catalan who returned from the East before 1328, speaks of the Ethiopian emperor being called 'Prestre Johan'; in about 1352, the Franciscan Giovanni de' Marignolli described Ethiopia as the land of Prester John, and a Spanish Franciscan treatise of the same period describes 'Preste Juan' as the lord and patriarch of Nubia and Ethiopia; the Florentine Simone Sigoli, who visited Egypt in 1384, mentions 'Presto Giovanni' in his *Viaggio al Monte Sinai*.

In the fifteenth century, Fra MAURO's map (1459) confidently places Prester John's capital in Ethiopia, 'qui il Prete Janni fa residentia principal'. King JOHN II of Portugal attempted to correspond with Prester John about access to India, and Vasco da GAMA heard reports that Prester John was the Christian ruler of the interior of East Africa. In 1487 Pêro da COVILHÃ was dispatched to Ethiopia to establish contact with Prester John; he was discovered there in 1520 by an expedition led by Rodrigo da Lima. Francisco Álvares, a priest who accompanied Lima's expedition, published an account of the land of Prester John in his *Verdadera informaçam das terras do Preste João* (1540); this influential treatise was translated into Italian (Venice, 1550, in the *Navigationi* of G. B. RAMUSIO), Spanish (Antwerp, 1557), French (Antwerp, 1558), German (Eisleben, 1566), and English (London, 1625, in the *Pilgrims* of Samuel PURCHAS).

In the early 1520s the sultan of Adal (now Djibouti and the contiguous part of the Somali Republic) began to move his Islamic forces into Christian Ethiopia; the Portuguese believed that the Christian kingdom of Prester John was at risk, and in 1541 dispatched Cristóvão da Gama with a regiment of 400 soldiers to fight on the side of Ethiopian Christians. John Buchan's *Prester John* (1910) is a reworking of the legend for Edwardian boys.

*DHP* s.v. Preste João; L. N. Gumilev, *Searches for an Imaginary Kingdom: The Legend of the Kingdom of Prester John* (1987, trans. from Russian original of 1970); U. Knefelkamp, *Die Suche nach dem Reich des Presterkönigs Johannes* (1986).

**PREUNING FAMILY**, German potters in Nuremberg of whom the most prominent were Kunz Preuning and Paul Preuning, both of whom were active 1540–50. Since the fourteenth century relief tiles decorated with biblical subjects had been made by the stove-makers (*Hafner*) of Germany. The Preunings adapted the techniques of Hafner-ware tiles to lead-glazed earthenware jugs. Attributions are not secure, but jugs decorated with crucifixes and processions are attributed to Kunz and jugs with half-length portraits of German Protestant princes are ascribed to Paul. Jugs on which they collaborated proved to be controversial, and in 1541 they were prosecuted for depicting biblical and secular subjects on the same jug. The Victoria and Albert Museum contains examples of their work.

**PREVEZA, BATTLE OF**. On 27 September 1538 a fleet of galleys under the flags of Venice, Genoa, and Spain was defeated by an Ottoman force under the command of Barbarossa (see BARBARY PIRATES). The battle, which was the most important naval engagement of the Venetian–Ottoman war of 1537–40, took place off the coast of Preveza, on the west coast of Greece north of Levkas.

**PRIE-DIEU** (plural prie-dieux), the French term (meaning 'pray God'), first brought into English in the fourteenth century, for a praying-desk (or kneeling-desk) with a footpiece on which to kneel and a top designed to support the arms or a book. Prie-dieux were made throughout Europe from the fourteenth to the seventeenth centuries; in sixteenth-century Italy the footpiece was sometimes adapted into a chair. The prie-dieu was revived in England in the nineteenth century as part of the antiquarian impulse of the Oxford Movement.

**PRIERAS.** See MAZZOLINI.

**PRIEUR, BARTHÉLEMY** (c.1536–1611), French sculptor influenced by the Mannerism of the second School of FONTAINEBLEAU. His best-known works are the sculptures of *Peace* and *Felicity* that he carved for the monument for the heart of Anne de MONTMORENCY (Louvre), which was designed by Jean BULLANT.

MDA.

**PRIMATICCIO, FRANCESCO** (1504/5–1570), Italian painter and architect, born in Bologna. He moved to Mantua c.1526 to assist GIULIO ROMANO in the decoration of the Palazzo del TÈ. In 1532 he moved to France at the invitation of King FRANCIS I to collaborate with Il ROSSO FIORENTINO on the decoration of FONTAINEBLEAU; the precise nature of their collaboration is unclear. After Il Rosso's death in 1540 Primaticcio decorated rooms such as the Salon de la Duchesse d'Étampes (completed 1543), the Salle de Bal (1551–6), and the Galerie d'Ulysse (completed 1570), which illustrates 58 episodes from Homer's *Odyssey*. The work of Primaticcio and Il Rosso at Fontainebleau proved to be very influential, partly because of its innovative combination of stucco and paint but also because it established a preference for classical mythological instead of religious images in decorative schemes; their work eventually came to be regarded as the foundation of a style of art known as the School of FONTAINEBLEAU.

On the accession of FRANCIS II in 1559, Primaticcio succeeded Philibert DELORME as royal architect, and in this capacity designed the Valois Chapel in the Basilica at Saint-Denis (near Paris) and the rear wing (Aile de la Belle Cheminée) projecting towards the pond at Fontainebleau (1568).

MDA.

**PRINCE CHARLES'S MEN**, acting company formed by Edward ALLEYN in 1616 under the patronage of Prince Charles, the future CHARLES I. Based initially at the HOPE Theatre, the company moved in 1619 to the COCKPIT, and later played at the CURTAIN (1622) and the RED BULL. They disbanded in 1625. A later company with the same name was formed in 1631 at the SALISBURY COURT THEATRE under the patronage of the future Charles II; they performed until the closing of the theatres in 1642.

**PRINTING.** The advent of printing and of movable type gave to fifteenth-century Europe the technology requisite for the mass production of written texts and engraved pictures. Printing in Europe began with the advent of BLOCK BOOKS in the 1440s. Movable type was introduced by Johann GUTENBERG of Mainz, who developed the brass moulds known as matrices in which replicas of lead letters could be reproduced. Gutenberg also improved the process of printing by adapting the wooden screw technology of grape crushing to the needs of printing. The first book to be produced with this new technology was Gutenberg's 42-line Bible (1452–6).

Printing presses were established in Strasbourg (1460), Cologne (1464), Rome (1464), Basel (1467), and Venice (1469).

Thereafter growth was rapid: in 1470 presses were established in Nuremberg, Paris, and Utrecht; in 1471, in Milan, Naples, and Florence; in 1473, in Lyon; in 1474, in Budapest, Kraków, Valencia, Louvain, and Bruges; in 1476, in England. Most of these early books were in Latin, and the names of the cities in which the presses were located are given in Latin on title pages; for a list of the Latin names of European cities, see Appendix 2. By the late fifteenth century publishing in the vernaculars had become an important enterprise, and vernacular presses stimulated an increase in translation from the learned languages into the vernaculars and from one vernacular to another. WOODCUTS offered a cheap and technically compatible method of introducing BOOK ILLUSTRATIONS alongside print, and throughout the fifteenth and sixteenth centuries books were richly illustrated. Gothic, roman, and italic type was developed, and soon printing presses were able to produce type for Greek (1465), Hebrew (1473), MUSICAL NOTATION (1473), and mathematics (1482).

In the INCUNABULA period printers were also the publishers of the books that they printed. Germany had the largest number of publishers (and of books in print) in Europe, and printer-publishers such as Anton KÖBERGER, who owned the largest publishing empire in Germany, also operated through agents in other parts of Europe.

Printers in Germany and the Swiss Confederation, the successors of Gutenberg and his partners Johann FUST and Peter SCHÖFFER, included Johannes AMERBACH (Basel), BEATUS RHENANUS (Basel), Théodore de BRY (Frankfurt), Sigmund FEYERABEND (Frankfurt), Johann FROBEN (Basel), Christoph FROSCHAUER (Zürich), Pamphilius Gegenbach (Basel), Anton Köberger (Nuremberg), Johann MENTELIN (Strassburg), Johannes OPORINUS (Basel), Albrecht PFISTER (Bamberg), Heinrich QUENTELL (Cologne), Erhard RATDOLT (Augsburg), Berthold RUPPEL (Basel), Johann SCHÖNSPERGER (Augsburg), Günther ZAINER (Augsburg), Johann ZAINER (Ulm), and Ulrich ZELL (Cologne).

In Italy, where Venice was the most important printing centre, printers included ALDUS MANUTIUS, Zacharias CALLIERGIS, Guillaume LE BÉ, Piero PACINI (in Florence), the SONCINO family (who also worked in other parts of Europe), and the partners Arnold PANNARTZ and Konrad SWEYNHEYM (in Rome).

In France, where the principal centres of printing were Lyon and Paris, the printers included Jodocus BADIUS (Lyon), Étienne DOLET (Lyon), Jean DUPRÉ (Paris and Lyon), Johann NEUMEISTER (Lyon), Geofroy TORY (Paris), Jean de TOURNES (Lyon), Antoine VÉRARD (Paris), and members of the ESTIENNE and WECHEL families (Paris and other centres); Claude GARAMOND (Paris) seems to have been the first person to make type founding his sole profession.

In England, early printers such as Wynkyn de WORDE, Robert COPLAND, William CAXTON, and Richard PYNSON were followed by a large number of London printers, including John RASTELL, Richard TOTTEL, and the partners Richard GRAFTON and Edward WHITCHURCH.

In the Netherlands, the tradition inaugurated by Laurens KOSTER culminated in the work of printers such as Daniel BOMBERG, Christophe PLANTIN, and the ELSEVIR family.

R. Hirsch, *Printing, Selling and Reading 1450–1550* (2nd edn. 1974); S. Hindman (ed.), *Printing the Written Word: The Social History of Books, circa 1450–1520* (1991).

**PRINTS.** In typographical and artistic usage, a print is a picture or design printed from a block or a plate. The impression on the paper can be made from a design on a raised surface (e.g. WOODCUT) or a recessed surface (e.g. DRYPOINT, ENGRAVING, and ETCHING) or a flat surface (e.g. lithographs).

The methods that create recesses in the surface that are then inked are called INTAGLIO methods, and they differ in the means by which the designs are incised in the metal plates: in drypoint the surface is scratched with a steel needle; in engraving the design is engraved with a burin; in etching the design is bitten into the plate with acid.

Prints often survive in more than one 'state': a change of state occurred whenever the printer altered a plate or block to improve the quality of the print. The early states of prints are often aesthetically inferior to later states, but, as in the case of early editions of books, the early states of prints now command higher prices than do later states.

Etching was more efficient than engraving, and so was often used as a preliminary process. It is difficult for the untrained eye to distinguish etchings from engravings, even in cases in which prints were produced entirely by etching. In the case of fifteenth- and sixteenth-century prints, there is a subtle difference in the lines: etched lines have fuzzy edges of unchanging width, engraved lines have hard edges but width that varies with the pressure of the engraver's hand.

**PRIULI, GIROLAMO** (1476–1547), merchant, banker, and diarist, a Venetian patrician who kept a secret diary from 1494 to 1512; the diary has survived, except for parts of the years 1506–9. Apart from his gifts to several Venetian churches, Priuli lived a private life, and saved his vitriol for his diary. He attributed the humiliating Venetian defeat at the battle of AGNADELLO both to divine displeasure with Venice and to the ineptitude of Venice's leaders.

*I diarii*, ed. A. Segre and R. Cessi (3 vols. numbered i, ii, and iv, 1941).

**PRIVATEER.** The seventeenth-century colloquial term for 'private man of war' referred to the much older institution of licensed piracy, which included some of the depredations of the BARBARY PIRATES. A privateer was an armed ship of which the owners and officers were private citizens, but which held a commission (known as 'letters of marque') from a government authorizing the use of the ship against hostile nations, especially in the capture of merchant ships. In the late sixteenth century, privateers belonging to English, Dutch, and Huguenot owners preyed on Spanish merchant ships. The Dutch Calvinist privateers were known as Sea Beggars (French *gueux de mer*), a term proudly appropriated from an insult levied by a Spanish nobleman in response to the Compromise of BREDA, a Dutch petition for religious tolerance. Privateering was abolished by the Declaration of Paris in 1856.

The term 'privateer' was sometimes extended to the captains of privateers, notably Sir Francis DRAKE and Sir John HAWKINS.

**PROBABILISM.** See MEDINA, BARTOLOMÉ.

**PROTESTANTISM.** The term 'Protestant' derives from the *Protestatio* issued on 19 April 1529 by six Lutheran princes and fourteen cities of the HOLY ROMAN EMPIRE at the Diet of SPEYER. The Diet had called for the enforcement of the edict issued by the Diet of WORMS banning Lutheranism; the Lutherans reacted with the 'Protest', and so became the first Protestants. The term Protestant retained its specific association with Lutheranism throughout the sixteenth century, and 'Protestant churches', which were Lutheran, were distinguished from 'Reformed churches', which were Calvinist or Zwinglian. In England the term 'Protestant' was not used consistently: in the sixteenth and early seventeenth centuries it is used to refer to the members of the Church of England in contradistinction to Catholics, Presbyterians, Quakers, and Separatists, but after the Restoration in 1660 the term is understood to include nonconformists and is therefore used in contradistinction to 'papist'; the Church of England has never claimed the term, which does not appear in any edition of the Book of COMMON PRAYER.

**PROVENÇAL.** See OCCITAN LANGUAGE AND LITERATURE.

**PROVOST, JAN** (*c*.1465–1529), Flemish painter, born in Mons. In 1491 he married the widow of Simon MARMION in Valenciennes; in 1493 he was admitted to the Painters' Guild in Antwerp, and the following year he settled in Bruges, where he remained for the rest of his life. He is not known to have signed any paintings, but the attribution to him of a *Last Judgement* (1525, Groeningemuseum, Bruges) is securely rooted in contemporary documents. In 1521 he entertained DÜRER, who apparently drew his portrait (now lost).

*BNB s.v. Prévost, Jean; MDA.*

**PROVVEDITORE** (Italian), initially an *ad hoc* Venetian official, usually a noble, appointed to a position of responsibility, such as 'providing' by overseeing supplies of grain. Such a position could sometimes involve the temporary governorship of a subject city. Most commonly in the Renaissance, however, the term is used to describe a liaison official in a Venetian army, supervising the activities of the *condottieri* and representing the interests of the Venetian government in the field.

**PTOLEMY IN THE RENAISSANCE.** Claudius Ptolemy (*fl.* AD 129–41), who worked in Alexandria (Egypt), summarized the current state of Greek ASTRONOMY in a thirteen-book work whose Greek title, meaning 'Mathematical Construction', was adapted, and transliterated into Arabic, to emerge in Latin as 'Almagestum', Anglicized as *Almagest*: 'Mathematike Syntaxis' to 'Megiste Syntaxis' to 'Al-Majusti' to 'Almagestum'. The work is an advanced treatise on celestial kinematics. In the system Ptolemy describes, the earth is at rest in the centre and the rest of the universe rotates once every 24 hours; in addition to sharing the motion of the fixed stars, the sun, moon and planets move around the earth, their paths being calculated as combinations of circles. All this is in accord with the Aristotelian physics of Ptolemy's time.

Reading Ptolemy proved to be a powerful spur to astronomical research in the Renaissance. His treatise was studied by REGIOMONTANUS, whose *Epytoma* (1496) provided COPERNICUS' introduction to Ptolemy's work. The first printed edition of the *Almagest* (1514) gave the twelfth-century Latin translation of Gerard of Cremona; the next (1528) a translation made from the Greek in 1451 by GEORGE OF TREBIZOND and regarded by experts as inaccurate in its rendering of the mathematics; the Greek text was first printed in 1538.

Ptolemy also wrote on MUSIC, on ASTROLOGY, on SUNDIALS, and on geography. His *Harmonica* was first printed in Latin translation in 1562, as a contribution to an ongoing dispute in music theory. Ptolemy was, however, certainly most widely known as the author of a short treatise on astrology, the *Tetrabiblos* (Latin *Quadripartitum*), whose Greek text was first printed in 1535, and the supposed author of a hugely popular collection of astrological aphorisms, the *Centiloquium*. His work on the mathematics of sundials, *De analemmate*, was published in an edition by COMMANDINO in 1562; his *Geographia*, which uses projection to obtain flat maps of the spherical earth, was rediscovered in the early fifteenth century when it excited much interest for the information it provided about the ancient world (see CARTOGRAPHY), and sumptuous copies of it were made for princes.

*MDA*; Andrew Barker, *Greek Musical Writings* (2 vols., 1984, 1989); Claudius Ptolemy, *Almagest*, trans. G. Toomer (1984); Claudius Ptolemy, *Tetrabiblos*, ed. and trans. F. E. Robbins (1940; repr. 1994); S. J. Tester, *A History of Western Astrology* (1987).

**PUBLIC WEAL, LEAGUES OF THE, or (French) Ligues du Bien Publique**, a series of revolts extending over seven years (1465–72) mounted by the feudal lords of France against King LOUIS XI, who had alienated the clergy (by abrogating the PRAGMATIC SANCTION OF BOURGES), the University of Paris (by disregarding its views), and the nobility (by curtailing their hunting rights). On three occasions (1465, 1467, and 1472) a coalition of noblemen (including the dukes of Brittany and Bourbon and the count of Charolais) attempted to force a regency on King Louis and to gain independence from France for a group of five kingdoms.

The conflicts of the first League culminated in the battle of Montlhéry (16 July 1465), in which King Louis was defeated by CHARLES THE BOLD and so made substantial concessions in treaties signed at Conflans and Saint-Maur. The king had no intention of honouring these treaties, and provoked a second revolt in his conquest of Brittany. This revolt ended when Charles the Bold imprisoned King Louis at Péronne, releasing him only when he had undertaken by treaty to honour the terms of the treaties of Conflans and Saint-Maur, which included helping to suppress the revolt of Liège (which King

Louis had secretly encouraged) and giving Champagne as an apanage to the duke of Berry; in the event he did not relinquish Champagne, as the duchy formed a vital link between Burgundy and Flanders.

The purpose of the third League, which was supported by EDWARD IV of England, was to depose King Louis in favour of the duke of Berry. On this occasion Charles the Bold was defeated, and was forced to sign the Peace of Senlis (1472), which signalled the end of the great feudal coalitions against the crown.

**PUCELLE, JEAN or Jehan** (*c*.1300–*c*.1355), French illuminator, the head of a large workshop in Paris. His illuminated manuscripts, of which some fifteen survive, include the Hours of Jeanne d'Évreux (The Cloisters, New York), in which the iconography and perspective derive from the early period of the Italian Renaissance.

*MDA*; Kathleen Morand, *Jean Pucelle* (1962).

**PULCI, LUIGI** (1432–84), Italian poet, born into a patrician family in Florence, where he was educated in the household of Bartolomeo SCALA; he subsequently became a member of the circle of Lorenzo de' MEDICI, whose literary aspirations he shared. Pulci's finest poem is his chivalric epic *Il Morgante Maggiore* (1478; revised version, 1483), which contains memorable mock-heroic characters such as the gluttonous Morgante and the extravagantly peccant Margutte. Pulci's other works include *La Beca de Dicomano* (a parody of Lorenzo de' Medici's *La Nencia da Barberino*) and a scholarly *Lexicon* of Latinisms.

Pulci's irreverence attracted both admirers (notably RABELAIS) and detractors (notably FICINO, who thought Pulci a heretic), and on his death Pulci was denied a Christian burial.

Mark Davie, *Half-Serious Rhymes: The Narrative Poetry of Luigi Pulci* (1998).

**PUNTO IN ARIA** (Italian; 'stitch in air'), a form of needlepoint LACE in which a single thread is used to add stitch to stitch, without any background of fabric. It was first made in Venice in the fifteenth century.

**PURCHAS, SAMUEL** (*c*.1575–1626), English editor of HAKLUYT. Educated at Cambridge, Purchas became vicar of St Martin's, Ludgate (London). In 1613 he published *Purchas his Pilgrimage; or, The Relations of the World and the Religions Observed in All Ages*, followed in 1619 by *Purchas his Pilgrim: Microcosmus; or, The Histories of Man*. In 1625 he published *Hakluyt Posthumous; or, Purchas his Pilgrims: Containing a History of the World, in Sea Voyages and Land Travels by Englishmen and Others*, compiled from manuscripts left by Hakluyt, to whom he had been an assistant. It included a letter of CORYATE's from the great mogul's court at Agra.

*DNB*.

**PURGATORY or (German) Fegefeuer.** In Catholic doctrine, purgatory is the place and the state of temporal punishment, where those who have died in the grace of God (i.e. not in mortal sin) and are therefore eligible to progress to heaven are detained until they have expiated the guilt of their venial sins and suffered any pains still owing due to mortal sins that have been forgiven. Catholic teaching was amplified by THOMAS AQUINAS, immortalized in the *Purgatorio* by DANTE, and defined at the Council of Lyon (1274) and the COUNCIL OF FLORENCE (1439). At the latter Council, the official teaching was formulated with a view to reconciling the Greek Church, whose representatives baulked at the idea of material fire and contested the distinction between pain and the expiation of guilt. The Catholic representatives therefore confined the official formulation to the existence of purgatory and the efficacy of prayer and good works consecrated to the name of the dead.

The reformers demurred, denying the existence of purgatory and insisting that faith alone freed the sinner from the bondage of sin, and that the believer either went straight to heaven or, in a Lutheran variant known as psychopannychism, slept until the day of resurrection; Calvin roundly denounced this heresy in his *Psychopannychia* (1542), and Catholic apologists for purgatory, such as BELLARMINE and SUÁREZ, rejoiced that Protestants were divided on the issue. One of the earliest defences of the Catholic position was John FISHER's *Assertionis Lutheranae confutatio* (1523). The COUNCIL OF TRENT reaffirmed the decrees on purgatory of Lyon and Florence, but prudently forbade fanciful elaborations of the doctrine in public sermons. The Orthodox Church in eastern Europe retained its belief in purgatory (which it calls 'Hades'), and defined its views in a decree almost indistinguishable from the Catholic position at the Synod of Jerusalem in 1672.

**PUTTENHAM, GEORGE** (*c*.1529–1591), probable author of *The Art of English Poesy* (1589), though the work has also been attributed to his brother Richard (*c*.1520–*c*.1601). Nephew of ELYOT, Puttenham was educated at Cambridge. His treatise is a critical discussion of poetry in three parts. Book 1, 'Of Poets and Poesie', defends the dignity and worth of poetry with some similarities to SIDNEY's *Defence of Poetry*, and defines different poetic genres. Book 2, 'Of Proportion', discusses metre, anagrams, and emblems. Book 3, 'Of Ornament', addresses rhetoric and figures of speech. Puttenham also addresses linguistic change, aware of the transformation of language through the use of foreign words.

*DNB.*

**PUTTO** (plural putti), the Italian term for a young boy, used in art history to denote a small child, nude or with swaddling bands and often with wings, used in decorative art since classical antiquity but particularly characteristic of fifteenth- and sixteenth-century Italian art. Putti were sometimes called *amores* in Latin, which is indicative of their pagan origins (Amor was a Roman personification of love, usually called 'Cupid' in English), but their wings point to their Christian origins as small cherubim. The syncretic blending of angelic and pagan origins is apparent in the putti looking up from the bottom of RAPHAEL's *Sistine Madonna* (*c*.1512, Gemäldegalerie, Dresden); the fashion for using these putti on Christmas cards has made this detail of Raphael's altarpiece one of the most popular images in Renaissance art.

The putto was sometimes called a sprite (*spiritello*), and in quattrocento poetry such as POLIZIANO's *Stanze per la giostra del Magnifico Giuliano* could be a malevolent force.

Charles Dempsey, *Inventing the Renaissance Putto* (2001).

**PYGOTT, RICHARD** (*c*.1485–1549), English composer who was master of the children in Thomas WOLSEY's chapel and gentleman of the Chapel Royal. He wrote sacred music; an extract from one of his pieces appears in Thomas MORLEY's *A Plain and Easy Introduction* (1597).

**PYNAS, JAN** (1581/2–1631), Dutch painter and etcher, probably born in Alkmaar. In 1605 he travelled to Rome, where he was influenced by the work of Adam ELSHEIMER and Pieter LASTMAN. On returning to the Netherlands Pynas established a studio in Amsterdam where he produced etchings as well as paintings and where Rembrandt was for a short time his pupil. His best-known painting is the *Raising of Lazarus* (1605, Schloss Johannisburg Staatsgalerie, Aschaffenburg).

*MDA.*

**PYNSON, RICHARD** (d. 1530), Anglo-Norman printer. He was born in Normandy and became a printer in London, initially as an assistant to CAXTON. In the early 1490s he succeeded William de Machlinia as the principal printer of LAW books in London; his press also printed an illustrated edition of Chaucer's *Canterbury Tales*. On the accession of King HENRY VIII in 1509, Pynson was appointed as king's printer, and in the same year he introduced Roman type into England. In his capacity as king's printer Pynson published King Henry's *Assertio septem sacramentorum* (1521), a refutation of LUTHER's view that there were only two SACRAMENTS.

*DNB.*

**QUADRIPARTITUM**. See PTOLEMY IN THE RENAISSANCE.

**QUADRIVIUM**. See LIBERAL ARTS.

**QUARTON or Charonton, ENGUERRAND** (*c*.1410–*c*.1461), French painter. He was born in the Laonnais and worked as a painter in Avignon from the late 1440s. His paintings are executed in a syncretic style which reflects both Italian and Flemish influences. His surviving paintings include a *Virgin of Mercy* (1452, Musée Condé, Chantilly) painted in collaboration with Pierre Vilate (*fl.* 1451–95) and a *Coronation of the Virgin* (1454, Musée Municipal, Villeneuve-lès-Avignon) which includes depictions of HELL in a Flemish idiom.

DBF s.v. Charonton; *MDA*; Charles Sterling, *Enguerrand Quarton: Le Peintre de la Pieta d'Avignon* (1983).

**QUATTROCENTO**, an apheretic form of *mil quattro cento* ('one thousand four hundred'), the Italian term for the fifteenth century (14—) and for the art and architecture of the period.

**QUATUOR MARIA**, the Renaissance Latin term (the classical spelling would be *quattuor*) introduced under Queen MARY (1553–8) for the four seas surrounding Britain, i.e. the Atlantic Ocean (off the west coast of Scotland), the English Channel, the Irish Sea, and the North Sea.

**QUEEN ANNE'S MEN**, acting company formed on the accession of JAMES I in 1603, under the patronage of Queen Anne. It was based at the CURTAIN Theatre between 1603 and 1609, then at the RED BULL until 1617. In 1616, Christopher BEESTON, an actor in the troupe, became its manager and the company moved to his COCKPIT Theatre, but disbanded in 1619 on the death of the queen.

**QUEEN ELIZABETH'S MEN**, acting company formed in 1583 which played in innyards, at the THEATRE, the CURTAIN, and the ROSE. Richard TARLETON was its popular clown. In 1594 it was disbanded; many of its players joined the ADMIRAL'S MEN, formed the same year.

**QUENTELL, HEINRICH** (d. 1501), German printer, born in Strassburg. He established his workshop in Cologne, where his most successful publications were illustrated editions of

the BIBLE in Low GERMAN (1479). Quentell's press, which passed to his son and grandson, was in the first half of the sixteenth century an important publisher of Latin texts (mainly theological works) for the University of Cologne. In 1525 the press published William TYNDALE's English translation of the New Testament.

**QUERCIA, JACOPO DELLA**. See JACOPO DELLA QUERCIA.

**QUESNEL, FRANÇOIS** (1543–1619), Franco-Scottish painter, born in Edinburgh, where his father Pierre was a French painter in the service of JAMES V of Scotland. Pierre worked mainly in France as a portrait painter; his paintings include *Mary Ann Waltham* (1572, Althorp, Northants) and *Henri III* (Louvre).

*MDA*.

**QUESTIONE DELLA LINGUA or (French)** *querelle de la langue* **or (Spanish)** *problema de la lengua*. The 'language question' that was debated in Renaissance Europe was a related group of questions that centred on the preferred form of national languages. The debate was complicated by the rival claims of LATIN and the vernaculars as literary languages and by the historical question of whether educated ancient Romans spoke the *sermo litteratus* or the *sermo vulgaris*. The distinctiveness of Latin was also an important issue, and many Italian humanists contended that Latin and Italian were two forms of the same language.

The debate about a national language first emerged in Italy, where the argument was first formulated by DANTE in *De vulgare eloquentia*. Tuscan eventually emerged as the preferred form of the language, but figures such as CASTIGLIONE and TRISSINO advocated an eclectic courtly language (*lingua cortigiana*) which centred on Tuscan but took into account the language spoken in the courts of Milan, Ferrara, Urbino, and Rome. MACHIAVELLI argued that Italian should be based on spoken Florentine, but others championed literary models. BEMBO, who was a Venetian, contended in his influential *Prose della volgar lingua* (1525) that Italian should be modelled on Petrarch and Boccaccio in the same way that humanistic Latin was modelled on Cicero and Virgil. Bembo's advocacy of a language based on fourteenth-century models rather than on contemporary speech was taken up by Leonardo

SALVIATI and was eventually adoped by the Accademia della Crusca (see ACADEMIES), which in 1612 published a *Vocabulario* that stabilized the spelling, grammar, and vocabulary of literary Tuscan.

In France the most important statement of the suitability of French as a literary language was Joachim DU BELLAY's *Défense et illustration de la langue française* (1549), and in Spanish Naples Juan de VALDÉS wrote *Diálogo de la lengua* (1535, published 1737).

Cecil Grayson, *A Renaissance Controversy: Latin or Italian* (1960); M. Tavoni, *Latino, grammatica, volgare: Storia di una questione umanistica* (1984); Maurizio Vitale, *La questione della lingua* (2nd edn. 1984); Avelina Carrera de la Red, *El 'problema de la lengua' en el humanismo renacentista español* (1988).

## QUEVEDO Y VILLEGAS, FRANCISCO DE (1580–1645),

Spanish poet, satirist, and PICARESQUE novelist, born in Madrid, the son of the secretary to Princess Maria, daughter of CHARLES V. He was educated at Alcalá de Henares and Valladolid and then secured an appointment at the royal court. He established his reputation as the foremost poet in the baroque style known as *conceptismo* (from *concepto*, 'conceit'), which bears some resemblance to English metaphysical poetry. Quevedo's voluminous body of poetry ranges from moral and satirical verse to love poetry in the Petrarchan idiom. It is characterized by coruscating wit, immensely inventive verbal dexterity in every register from the vulgar and scabrous to the exalted, and above all by hyperbolic vehemence and passion. He is without contest the greatest craftsman in Spanish poetry, unequalled even by GÓNGORA and Fray LUIS DE LEÓN, both of whom he admired and imitated; he edited the latter's poems for the press, but engaged in a scurrilous pamphlet war with the former, a living rival.

In the first decade of the seventeenth century Quevedo also wrote many works in prose, the best known being the picaresque novel known as *El buscón*, which was published without his permission in Zaragoza and Barcelona in 1626 as *Historia de la vida del buscón, llamado don Pablos, exemplo de vagamundos, y espejo de tacaños*. It is now regarded as one of the finest (and certainly one of the most savage) of picaresque novels. Quevedo's other important prose works were five *Sueños* (visions) written between 1606 and 1622; these satirical prose sketches failed to secure a licence from the censor, and so remained unpublished until 1627, but they were widely circulated in manuscript. They are written in a highly artificial prose reminiscent of euphuism in England, but with an austerity of moral tone closer to that of the prose works of DONNE.

Quevedo's patron, the duke of Osuna, became viceroy of Sicily, and by 1613 Quevedo had joined him as an agent and spy; the legend that he fled to Sicily because he had murdered a man may be true, but there is no documentary evidence to substantiate the story. On 19 May 1618 Quevedo escaped an attempt on his life by agents of the Venetian COUNCIL OF TEN, and shortly thereafter returned to Spain. The duke of Osuna was imprisoned in 1620, and the following year Quevedo was confined to his estate. He returned to the court in 1632, and at first sought to curry favour with Olivares, the king's favourite (notably with his *Epístola censorial*, a verse satire calling for the reform of public morals), but in 1639 Quevedo was deemed to be the author of a poem denouncing Olivares which was found by King Philip IV under his napkin, and Quevedo was incarcerated on his own estate until 1643. In the last years of his life he wrote with undimmed genius a long series of religious and political works in the Neostoic tradition; he repudiated his early works, including *El buscón* and the *Sueños*, which are now regarded as the pinnacles of his achievement as a stylist in prose and verse, and which by that time had been widely printed and translated all over Europe.

P. J. Smith, *Quevedo on Parnassus: Allusive Context and Literary Theory in the Love-Lyric* (1987); P. Jauralde Pou, *Francisco de Quevedo, 1580–1645* (2nd edn. 1999).

**QUILTING**, the term, derived from Latin *culcita* (a stuffed cushion), for the process whereby two layers of cloth are stitched together with an interlining of flock or down; the stitches follow geometrical designs, typically a lozenge or network pattern but sometimes a complex arabesque pattern. In the early modern period it was used to make clothing and bed covers; quilted clothing included undergarments for ARMOUR and satin doublets and breeches. Quilted bed covers, sometimes decorated with EMBROIDERY or PATCHWORK, are mentioned in sixteenth-century inventories, but no examples are known to survive; such quilts were popular in early seventeenth-century England, the Netherlands, Portugal, and Italy, and later in the century became established as a folk art in America.

**QUIÑONES, FRANCISCO DE** (1480–1540), Spanish reforming cardinal. He was born in León into a noble family and entered the Franciscan ORDER in 1498, assuming the name Francisco de los Ángeles. In 1517 he was appointed definitor-general, and in 1523 minister-general of the Observant branch of his Order. During his tenure as minister-general (until 1528) Quiñones promoted internal reform (inducing many Conventual Franciscans to join the Observants) and overseas missions: in 1523 he dispatched to Mexico the group of Franciscan missionaries known to posterity as the Twelve Apostles. In 1526 and 1527, in the period of imperial–papal tensions that culminated in the SACK OF ROME and the detention of Pope CLEMENT VII, Quiñones mediated between CHARLES V and the pope. He was created cardinal late in 1527 or early in 1528. In 1529 he became an active participant in the struggle to frustrate HENRY VIII's bid to divorce CATHERINE OF ARAGON.

Cardinal Quiñones was then commanded to compile a new breviary, which was published by Pope PAUL III in 1535; it is sometimes known as the Breviary of the Holy Cross, with reference to the church of which Quiñones was cardinal-priest. This breviary reflected Cardinal Quiñones's convictions about the need for reform: it severely reduced the readings from lives of the saints and dispensed almost entirely with the ranking of festivals and the consequent ranking of antiphons (which had been 'doubled', i.e. recited both before and after the psalms or canticles, when a feast was deemed to be of double rank), versicles, and the Little Office of Our Lady (*Officium Parvum Beatae Mariae Virginis*); the Hours were almost equal in duration, each containing only three psalms, and Matins on all days containing only three lessons. In the space gained by these excisions, Cardinal Quiñones prescribed the reading of the entire Psalter during the week and of most of the Bible during the year. The breviary was both immensely popular and highly controversial: its popularity is attested by more than 100 editions between 1536 and 1558 and by its adoption in the public offices of religious orders, and its controversial status by attacks at the COUNCIL OF TRENT (for its disregard for tradition) and its proscription by Pope PAUL IV in 1558. The lasting influence of Quiñones's breviary was to be felt in England: Thomas CRANMER adapted it for his reformed service book, and so its emphasis on uniformity and the continuous reading of the Bible passed into the English Book of COMMON PRAYER.

Fernando, marquis d'Alcedo, *Le Cardinal Quiñones et la saint-Ligue* (1910).

**QUIRÓS, PEDRO FERNÁNDEZ DE**. See FERNÁNDEZ DE QUIRÓS, PEDRO.

# R

**RABELAIS, FRANÇOIS** (1483–*c*.1553), French humanist and satirist, the son of a lawyer from Chinon, in the Loire valley. In 1510 or 1511 he entered the Order of Observantine Franciscans at their convent of Le Puy Saint-Martin in Fontenay-le-Comte, where he remained until 1524. He took up the study of Greek, and seems to have embarked on a translation of Lucian into Latin. The study of Greek was regarded as heretical because of its association with the growing reformist movement, and Rabelais was threatened with imprisonment and obliged to migrate to another order. In 1524 he entered the Benedictine house at Saint-Pierre-de-Maillezais, and two years later he seems to have abandoned holy orders altogether. He studied medicine in Paris and (from 1530) in Montpellier, where he lectured on Hippocrates and Galen and in 1532 published an edited collection of medical treatises. In the same year he moved to Lyon, where he worked as a physician at the Hôtel Dieu and published *Pantagruel*.

In 1534 and 1535 Rabelais accompanied Bishop (later Cardinal) Jean DU BELLAY on two journeys to Rome, serving as his physician and secretary. During this period Rabelais published *Gargantua* (late in 1534 or early in 1535) and received papal absolution for abandoning holy orders without prior permission. On returning to France in 1536 he worked as a SECULAR priest at Du Bellay's abbey at Saint-Maur-les-Fossés, and the following year returned to academic medicine, initially in Paris and then again in Montpellier.

In the 1540s Rabelais lived in Turin (1540–2), Paris (1542–6), Metz (1546–7), and Rome (1547–9). During this period he published his *Tiers Livre* (1545) and a fragmentary *Quart Livre* (1548), the sequels to *Gargantua* and *Pantagruel*. The *Tiers Livre* was dedicated to MARGUERITE D'ANGOULÊME and enjoyed the protection afforded by a royal privilege granted by FRANCIS I, but was nonetheless condemned by the Sorbonne. An expanded version of the *Quart Livre* was published in 1552, and it too was condemned. In 1564, a decade after Rabelais's death, a fragment known as the *Île sonnante* (which constituted the first eight chapters of what was to be published as the *Cinquième Livre*) appeared.

*Pantagruel* and *Gargantua* tell the story of the giant Gargantua and his son Pantagruel; the latter story was published first, so *Gargantua* is what would now be called a 'prequel'. In the first, third, fourth, and fifth books the principal character is Pantagruel's companion Panurge. The narrative, with its constant shifts of time and scale, is peculiar to its author, but running through the whole is the comic vision of *Pantagruélisme*, i.e. 'living in good cheer'. Seen from a modern perspective, Rabelais can appear to be an irreligious writer, but the contention that he was an atheist is no longer accepted; on the contrary, he is seen as a disciple of ERASMUS, a spokesman in his own manner for evangelical reform.

Lucien Febvre, *The Problem of Unbelief in the Sixteenth Century* (1942; English trans. 1982); M. A. Screech, *Rabelais* (1979); M. Bakhtin, *Rabelais and his World* (English trans. 1968).

**RACKET**, a double reed woodwind instrument. It existed in four different sizes and had a short cylindrical body made of solid wood bored with ten channels making a continuous tube. It produced deeper sounding notes than any other instrument except the organ, and could sound effective when played with other woodwind instruments or strings. Its limitations in producing a strong tone or being expressive contributed to its obsolesence.

**RACOVIAN CATECHISM**, a doctrinal statement of the UNITARIAN principles of SOCINIANISM, prepared by Valentin Schmalz and Johannes Völkel on the basis of earlier versions drafted by Faustus SOCINUS. The earliest printed text was the Polish version which was published in Raców, in southern Poland, in 1605. A German translation was published in 1608, a Latin translation in 1609. An edition of the Latin translation with an unauthorized dedication to King JAMES I of England was publicly burnt in London in 1614. The English Unitarian John Biddle published an English translation in Amsterdam in 1652.

The Racovian Catechism is a manual of instruction rather than a confession of faith. Its eight sections deal with the unique authority of the Bible, SOTERIOLOGY (emphasizing holiness of life), the doctrine of GOD (rejecting the Trinity), Christ as person (a man raised to divine power), prophet, king, and priest, and, finally, the Church.

**RADEWIJNS, FLORENS, or (Latin) Florentius** (1350–1400), Dutch religious leader, a follower of Geert de GROOTE, on whose death in 1384 Radewijns succeeded Groote as leader of the BRETHREN OF THE COMMON LIFE. In 1387 he was instrumental in the founding of the WINDESHEIM CANONS at a house near Zwolle, and so became one of the progenitors of the DEVOTIO MODERNA.

*NNBW* v.

**RADZIWIŁŁ, MIKOŁAJ** (1515–65), Polish-Lithuanian statesman and soldier, born into a noble Lithuanian family. In 1547 the Emperor CHARLES V conferred on him the title of imperial prince, and four years later he became palatine of Vilnius. He was by conviction a Calvinist, and while on embassies in France and Germany for King SIGISMUND II helped to promote the cause of the Reformation. In Lithuania his work for the Protestant cause culminated in the publication in 1563 of the first Polish translation of the Bible, which is now known as the Radziwiłł Bible. In the final months of his life he defended Livonia against a Russian invasion.

*PSB.*

**RAFFAELLO DA MONTELUPO** (1504–66), Italian sculptor and architect, born in Florence, the son of the sculptor BACCIO DA MONTELUPO. He worked in Rome from 1524 to 1527, when he fled from the SACK OF ROME. He subsequently lived in Loreto, Florence, and Orvieto before returning to Rome (1543–52) to serve as architect of Castel Sant'Angelo and finally settling in Orvieto, where he became *capomaestro* of the cathedral. His best-known statue is a depiction of *St Damian* for the New Sacristy of the Church of San Lorenzo in Florence; the design is an adaptation of one by MICHELANGELO.

MDA s.v. Montelupo; Riccardo Gatteschi, *Vita di Raffaello da Montelupo* (1998).

**RAGUSA**, the Italian name for the DALMATIAN port now known by the Croatian name of Dubrovnik. The city was ruled by BYZANTIUM until 1205, when it became a Venetian protectorate with considerable autonomy under the light hand of a Venetian governor with the title count of Ragusa. During this period the territory of Ragusa expanded inland, and trans-Adriatic trade links were developed, especially with ANCONA and Otranto.

In 1378 Venice ceded its Dalmatian ports to Hungary under the terms of the Peace of Zara. In 1409 LADISLAS OF DURAZZO, king of Naples and pretender to the Hungarian throne, sold his presumptive title to the Dalmatian ports, which thereby gained their independence. In the period of confusion within Hungary that followed, Venice took advantage of the political vacuum and between 1409 and 1420 reoccupied all the ports except Ragusa, which had declined to acknowledge the suzerainty of Ladislas and remained loyal to SIGISMUND of Hungary, who in return ensured that Venice did not renew the protectorate by force of arms.

For the next century Ragusa was a city dominated but not governed by Venice. The city grew rapidly because of its policy of accepting Christian refugees from areas of the Balkans conquered by the Ottomans; the city also accepted Italian refugees, notably Piero SODERINI in 1512. Relations with Venice were strained after 1526, when Ragusa began to pay an annual tribute to the Ottoman government in Constantinople in return for the right to trade in Ottoman domains.

The chartering of ships made Ragusa wealthy, and the lavish expenditure on palaces (such as the Sponza Palace, now the state archives, and the Rector's Palace, now a museum) and works of art, together with public funding for street planning and paving and for fountains (notably the Onofrio Fountain of 1438), created a city of great beauty. Many of these buildings in what is now the Old Town (*Stari Grad*) were damaged or destroyed in the bombardment of 1991.

There were few open spaces within the city walls, but in the surrounding hills there were VILLAS with large GARDENS. In 1440 a traveller described the countryside around the city as embellished with vineyards, huge palaces, and wonderful gardens. By the mid-sixteenth century, garden design typically included terraces, pergolas, and fruit trees. Gardens were laid out geometrically (typically in four rectangles), but the shortage of water made FOUNTAINS in the Italian style impracticable, so the style more closely resembled the sculptural form of French fountains. Most of the Renaissance gardens have disappeared, though structures are often still visible, notably in the garden at Trsteno built in 1502 for the Gučetić family. Four important gardens survive in varying states of disrepair: on the mainland, the villas and gardens of the Sorkočević family on the Lapad peninsula and at Rijecka still retain many original features; the villa on Lapad has a fine loggia, and Rijecka Dubrovacka still has its four-part parterre and its stone-pillared pergolas; on the island of Šipan (20 kilometres (12 miles) from the city) the two important gardens of the Skočibuha family are derelict, but nonetheless retain their terraces and pergolas.

The literature of Renaissance Ragusa was written in Croatian: the poet Menchetic (1457–1501) wrote hundreds of Ovidian love poems and elegies, and the poet and playwright George Drzhic (1460–1510) also wrote erotic Ovidian poems. The masterpiece of the Ragusan nobleman Stepan Gučetić (1495–1525) is the satirical poem *Dervishiyada*. The goldsmith and lyric poet Andrija Cubranović (1500–50) wrote *Jedupka*, a poem about a Gipsy woman. The poet Petar Hektorović (1486–1572) wrote a piscatory eclogue called *Ribanye*, which was influenced by SANNAZARO, and also inaugurated a nationalist tradition in Croatian poetry by publishing three songs that he had heard being performed by the popular singers known as *guslars*. Ragusan literature culminated in the poetry of Ivan Gundulic (1558–1638), who was known in Italian as Giovanni Gondola. Three of his eleven plays have survived, as does most of his nationalist epic *Osman*, which was first published in 1826.

The Venetian form of the word 'Ragusa' was 'Ragusi', which was used to describe the place and, when absorbed into other languages, to denote the large merchant vessels of Ragusa. Metathesis of the first two letters of 'Ragusi' produced the English word 'argosy' to denote such ships.

B. Krékic, *Dubrovnik in the 14th and 15th Centuries* (1972);

M. Aymard, *Venise, Ragusa et la commerce du blé pendant la seconde moitié du XIVᵉ siècle* (1966).

**RAIMONDI, MARCANTONIO** (*c*.1470/82–*c*.1527/34), Italian engraver, born near Bologna and trained in the Bolognese studio of Il FRANCIA. He travelled to Venice c.1505 and there copied some woodcuts by DÜRER (who would later accuse him of plagiarism), notably his *Life of the Virgin*. He subsequently worked in Rome (c.1510–27) as an engraver; many of his designs were copies of paintings and designs by RAPHAEL and GIULIO ROMANO. Raimondi established the ENGRAVING as a reproductive medium that could be achieved in a workshop, and through his engravings the work of Raphael, Giulio Romano, and other Italian artists became known throughout Europe. His copies were in turn used as designs for MAIOLICA dishes.

> MDA; Innis Shoemaker and Elizabeth Broun, *The Engravings of Marcantonio Raimondi* (1981).

**RAINOLDS, JOHN** (1549–1607), English Calvinist, educated at Oxford, where he was a fellow of Corpus Christi College from 1568. Rainolds came to prominence through his lectures on Aristotle's *Rhetoric*. In 1593 he was made dean of Lincoln, and in 1598 became president of his old Cambridge college. As a leading proponent of Calvinism, he led the Puritan cause at the HAMPTON COURT CONFERENCE (1604). Although the Puritan petition came to nothing, Rainolds was held in high respect by his theological opponents, and participated in preparing the Authorized Version of the Bible. He was also responsible for the anti-theatrical *Th'Overthrow of Stage-Plays* (1599).

> DNB.

**RAIS, GILLES DE.** See GILLES DE RETZ.

**RALEGH or Raleigh, SIR WALTER** (1552–1618), English naval commander, courtier, and historian. The half-brother of Sir Humphrey GILBERT, Ralegh began his career as explorer and colonizer in his company, after serving four years as a soldier in France. He initially enjoyed favour at court, being knighted and granted land in Ireland; an affair with one of ELIZABETH's maids of honour, Elizabeth Throckmorton (whom he subsequently married), however, led to a fall from grace. His expedition to Virginia to establish a colony was not successful, but did result in the introduction of tobacco and potatoes to England. An expedition in 1595 to Suyana (now Venezuela) was motivated by a search for gold; he also sailed with ESSEX in 1596 to attack Cádiz. Ralegh's detractors won the ear of JAMES VI on his succession, and Ralegh was imprisoned with his family in the Tower of London on charges of treason. While imprisoned he wrote an ambitious *History of the World*, which became popular though it progressed no further than 168 BC. A petition for release to resume his search for gold was eventually granted, but the second expedition was as fruitless as the first, and Ralegh was executed on his return.

> DNB.

**RAMELLI, AGOSTINO** (c.1537–c.1608), Italian engineer. He was born in Ponte Tresa (near Como) and entered the service of Gian Giacomo de' Medici, marquis of Marignano, for whom he worked as a military engineer. In about 1570 he moved to France to enter the military service of the duke of Anjou (later King HENRI III), and in 1572 was captured at the siege of La Rochelle; after his release he settled in France.

Ramelli was the author of *Le diverse et articiose machine* (Paris, 1588), which was printed in Italian and French on facing pages. The 'various and ingenious machines' described and depicted in the 195 full- or double-page illustrations include pumps (the subject of half the illustrations), AUTOMATA, revolving bookcases, cranes, dams, military bridges, screwjacks, tilt hammers, watermills, and windmills.

> *Le diverse et articiose machine*, English trans. M. T. Gnudi, ed.
> E. S. Ferguson (1976).

**RAMOS DE PAREJA, BARTOLOMÉ, or (Italian) Bartolomeo Ramos de Pareia** (c.1440–after 1490), Spanish musical theorist and composer in Salamanca, Bologna, and Rome. He wrote some sacred music, including a perpetual canon, 'Mundus et musica et totu concentus'. He did not attract a strong following, as his theoretical *Musica practica* (1482) demonstrates; he held opposing views to those of respected forebears like Boethius and Guido d'Arezzo and, although his ideas look ahead to mean-tone temperament, they fly in the face of accepted harmonic wisdom.

**RAMUS, PETRUS, or (French) Pierre de la Ramée** (1515–72), French humanist logician, professor of philosophy at the Collège Royal in Paris. His writings, most of which were in Latin, centre on the reformation of Aristotelian logic. His early writings, such as *Dialecticae partitiones* and *Aristotelicae animadversiones* (both 1543), were aggressively anti-Aristotelian. In 1555 he published his *Dialectique*, which was the first philosophical treatise to be written in French; in this treatise Ramus develops a process of logical deduction which he presents as an extension rather than a repudiation of Aristotelian logic. The method of Ramus was subsequently absorbed into the Protestant exegetical tradition, one strand of which evolved in the eighteenth century into Methodism. Ramus also applied his method to cognate disciplines such as RHETORIC (on which he published in collaboration with Omer Talon), grammar, and mathematics. He developed Protestant sympathies, and was killed in the ST BARTHOLOMEW'S DAY MASSACRE; his death was dramatized in MARLOWE's *Massacre at Paris*.

> N. Bruyère, *Methode et dialectique dans l'œuvre de La Ramée* (1984);
> Walter Ong, *Ramus: Method and the Decay of Dialogue* (1958).

**RAMUSIO, GIOVANNI BATTISTA** (1485–1577), Italian historical geographer, born in Treviso and educated in Padua. He entered the service of the Venetian republic, first as a diplomat and subsequently as secretary of the Senate and of the COUNCIL OF TEN. He assembled a collection of travellers' reports (some of which he translated from French and Spanish) and published them as *Delle navigationi et viaggi* (1550–9), devoting each of its massive three volumes to a continent (Africa, Asia, America); the *Navigationi*, which was dedicated to Ramusio's friend FRACASTORO, became a model for later historical geographers, including Richard HAKLUYT. Ramusio later published editions of Quintilian and of book 3 of Livy's history of Rome for the ALDINE Press.

> DSB.

Raphael, *Parnassus*, in the Stanza della Segnatura, Vatican, Rome

**RAPHAEL or (Italian) Raffaello Sanzio** (1483–1520), Italian painter, born in Urbino, where his father Giovanni SANTI was a painter in the court of FEDERICO DA MONTEFELTRO; Giovanni Santi died in 1494, when Raphael was 11, and the palpable influence of PERUGINO in Raphael's early paintings, such as *The Coronation of the Virgin* (1502–3, Vatican), *The Crucifixion* (1503, National Gallery, London), and *The Marriage of the Virgin* (1504, Brera, Milan), may imply that shortly after his father's death he became a pupil in Perugino's studio in Perugia.

In 1504 Raphael visited Florence, where he fell under the influence of LEONARDO DA VINCI and MICHELANGELO. The works of his Florentine period include many of his greatest Madonnas; these paintings, in which the Madonna and Child are variously painted in the company of the infant John and his mother Elizabeth and the aged Joseph, include the *Madonna del Granduca* (c.1505, Pitti Palace, Florence), *La Belle Jardinière* (1507, Louvre, Paris), and the 'Canigiani' *Holy Family* (c.1507, Alte Pinakothek, Munich).

In 1508 Raphael was invited to Rome by Pope JULIUS II, who commissioned him to paint the frescoes in the room that he had designated as his library; this room is now known as the Stanza della Segnatura because it was later used by the Signatura Gratiae (which, together with the Signatura Iustitiae, made up the Apostolic Signatura, the supreme tribunal of the Church). On the ceiling Raphael painted four women whose attributes associate them with Theology, Poetry, Philosophy, and Jurisprudence; the wall below each figure amplifies these personified abstractions. The wall beneath Theology contains the *Disputa* and depicts the fathers of the Church discussing the doctrine of transubstantiation, watched from above by the Trinity; the wall beneath

Poetry shows the poets on Parnassus; the wall beneath Philosophy, traditionally known as the *School of Athens*, depicts ancient philosophers in an architectural setting; the wall beneath Jurisprudence depicts personifications of the cardinal virtues (Fortitude, Prudence, and Temperance), below which JUSTINIAN is shown with the *Pandects* and Pope Gregory IX with the *Decretals*. These paintings are one of the supreme achievements of western art, and were influential in shaping the future development of that art. Raphael subsequently decorated two other rooms in the papal apartments, the Stanza d'Eliodoro (1511–14) and (together with his assistants) the Stanza dell'Incendio (1515–17); he also designed the ceiling and wall arabesques in the Vatican Loggie, and these designs were to have a lasting influence on interior decoration.

Raphael remained in Rome for the rest of his short life, during which he worked as a painter of Madonnas, altarpieces, and portraits, an architect, a tapestry designer, and a draughtsman. His Madonnas from this period include the *Madonna Alba* (c.1511, National Gallery, Washington), the *Madonna di Loreto* (c.1511, Musée Condé, Chantilly), and the *Madonna della Sedia* (c.1514, Palazzo Pitti). His altarpieces include the *Sistine Madonna* (c.1512, Gemäldegalerie, Dresden) and the *Transfiguration* (Vatican), on which he was working when he died (and which was displayed over his coffin in the Pantheon). His portraits include *Pope Julius II* (c.1511, National Gallery, London), *Baldassare Castiglione* (c.1515, Louvre), and *Pope Leo X with Cardinals Giulio de' Medici and Luigi de' Rossi* (1518, Uffizi).

In 1514 Raphael was appointed architect of ST PETER'S BASILICA and later designed the Villa MADAMA (c.1518); his work for Agostino CHIGI included the design for the Chigi Chapel in

Raphael, *La Belle Jardinère* (1507), in the Louvre, Paris

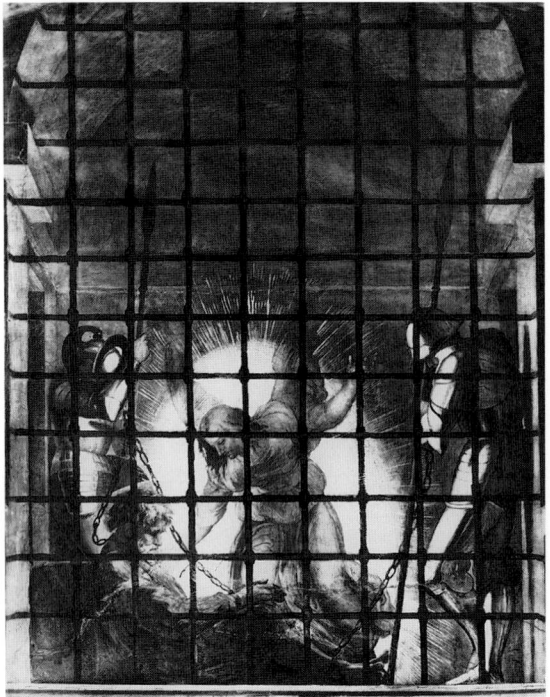

**Raphael**, *The Deliverance of St Peter* (central section), in the Stanza d'Eliodoro, Vatican, Rome

Santa Maria del Popolo (*c*.1513–16), the decoration of the Villa Farnesina in Trastevere with a wall fresco (*Galatea*, *c*.1512) and of its garden loggia with a fresco cycle of *Cupid and Psyche* (*c*.1518), and the design for the Chigi Stables (1514–18, now destroyed). Pope LEO X commissioned Raphael to design and prepare cartoons of *The Lives of SS Peter and Paul* to be woven in Brussels; the cartoons are now in the Victoria and Albert Museum and the tapestries in the Vatican, where they were for centuries hung in the Sistine Chapel on ceremonial occasions.

Raphael was one of the greatest draughtsmen of the Renaissance. He worked with pen and ink in drawings such as his *Study of Leonardo's Leda* (*c*.1506, Royal Library, Windsor) and *Nude Male Warriors* (Ashmolean Museum, Oxford), but also used black chalk (e.g. *Study for the Head of a Muse*, *c*.1510, Horne Museum, Florence) and red chalk, notably in *Jupiter and Cupid* and, on the verso, *Girl Holding a Mirror* (*c*.1517–18, Louvre).

MDA; Francis Ames-Lewis, *The Draftsman Raphael* (1986);
R. Jones and N. Penny, *Raphael* (1983).

**RAPIN, NICOLAS** (1538–1608), French poet. He was born in Fontenay-le-Comte and studied law at Poitiers. His career in legal administration and local government was disrupted by the WARS OF RELIGION, in which Rapin's sympathies lay with the POLITIQUES and the cause of Henry of Navarre (later HENRI IV), for whom he fought at Ivry, a victory which he was to commemorate in verse (1590). He collaborated with other poets (including Pierre PITHOU) on the *Satire ménippée* (which in its first edition of 1594 was entitled *La Vertu du Catholicon d'Espagne*), a satire which begins with the attempt of charlatans representing Spain and the CATHOLIC LEAGUE to sell the miracle potion of extreme Catholicism. Rapin's other works include an erotic FLEA POEM (1583), a Horatian *Plaisirs du gentilhomme champêtre* (1575, expanded in 1581 and 1583), and a French translation of canto 18 of ARIOSTO's *Orlando furioso* (1572).

**RASI, FRANCESCO** (1574–*c*.1620), Italian singer, composer, chitarrone player, and poet. He studied at Pisa and sang at the premières of PERI's *Euridice*, CACCINI's *Il rapimento di Cefalo*, and MONTEVERDI's *Orfeo* (the title role was created for him) and *Arianna*. His *Vaghezze di musica* (1608) and *Madrigali* (1610) are in a monodic style and reflect the influence of Caccini, with whom he studied. He also wrote Latin motets and poetry, published at Mantua in 1614.

**RASTELL, JOHN** (*c*.1475–1536), English printer and playwright. His works include the INTERLUDE *The Nature of the Four Elements* (*c*.1520), and the comedies *Calisto and Melibea* and *The Dialogue of Gentleness and Nobility* (both *c*.1525). He also printed the work of other writers. His son William took over the press and published the interludes of John HEYWOOD, and many of MORE's polemical works.

DNB.

**RATDOLT, ERHARD** (1447–1527/8), German printer. He was born in Augsburg, but while still a child moved to Mainz, where he trained as a printer, probably in the workshop of GUTENBERG. In the 1470s and early 1480s he worked as a printer in Venice, and in 1486 he accepted an invitation to return to his native Augsburg, where his workshop became the most important producer of colour printing in Germany. Ratdolt's many innovations include the first title page, the first type-face catalogue, the first texts of geometry and astronomy to be illustrated with diagrams, and the first books with illustrations in three colours. He first printed music in 1487, using WOODCUTS, and in 1491 began to use movable type to print music.

Grove; E. D. C. McMurtrie, *Erhard Ratdolt, the Father of Typographical Decoration* (1936).

**RATGEB, JERG or Jörg** (*c*.1480–1526), German painter. He was born in Herrenberg and was active there and in Stuttgart, Frankfurt, and finally Pforzheim, where he died. His experience of the political and social unrest that eventually led to the PEASANTS' WAR is reflected in his most famous painting, the Herrenberg altarpiece (1514–17), which is now in the Stuttgart Staatsgalerie.

MDA.

**RATISBON, CONFERENCE OF**. See REGENSBURG, CONFERENCE OF.

**RAVENSCROFT, THOMAS** (*c*.1582–*c*.1633), English composer, publisher, and theorist, who sang at St Paul's

Cathedral and composed for the CHILDREN OF PAUL'S. His involvement with the theatre is evident in *Pammelia* which he edited in 1609. This collection contains songs from theatrical shows, tavern songs, street vendors' cries, rounds, and catches, such as 'Hold thy peace knave' from SHAKESPEARE'S *Twelfth Night*. *A Brief Discourse* (1614) is a theoretical work on the subject of mensuration, and includes madrigals, play songs, and consort songs.

**RECEPTION.** In legal history, the term 'Reception' denotes the gradual process whereby Roman law, together with a measure of CANON LAW and Lombard FEUDAL LAW, was absorbed into the legal systems of the Germanic territories, including the Netherlands. The process, which lasted from the beginning of the fifteenth century to the end of the seventeenth, displaced the regional legal systems which had evolved unevenly from a blend of ancient tribal law and the capitulary legislation (both ecclesiastical and secular) introduced by Charlemagne and developed by his successors. The Reception originated in the study of Roman law alongside canon law in German universities, an innovation grounded in the belief that the Holy Roman Empire of the German nation was the successor to the Roman Empire of antiquity, and so should be regulated by Roman law. When MAXIMILIAN I established the Imperial Chamber of Justice (the REICHS-KAMMERGERICHT) in 1495, he stipulated that eight of its seventeen members be doctors of law and that the court's judgments be based on the JUSTINIAN formulation of Roman law, the *Corpus iuris civilis*. The importance of the Justinian *Corpus* declined, and it was gradually supplanted by recourse to legal commentaries produced by jurists within and outwith the universities. Roman law filtered down to the lower courts, and in the course of the next century Roman law displaced Germanic law in Germanic regions subject to the Imperial Chamber, with the notable exception of Saxony, which remained wedded to the thirteenth-century *Sachsenspiegel* of Eike von Repgow until the end of the nineteenth century; areas beyond the jurisdiction of the Imperial Chamber, such as Schleswig and the Swiss cantons, remained largely unaffected by the process, but the Netherlands, which was largely independent of the Imperial Chamber, was nonetheless strongly influenced by the Reception.

The impact of the reception was chiefly felt in the area of private law, the branch of Roman law that governs relations between individuals and between individuals and the state; it did not have as strong an impact on public law (either administrative or criminal). See DUTCH LAW; GERMAN LAW.

**RECONQUISTA.** The Muslim conquest of the Iberian peninsula began with the invasion of 711; the peninsula was largely subdued by 718, when the mixed Arab and Berber army crossed the Pyrenees and advanced north until they were finally turned back at Poitiers in 732. Except for the mountainous regions of the Asturias, Spain and Portugal were divided into a series of Islamic, Arabic-speaking emirates known collectively as al-Andalus. The term *reconquista* ('reconquest') is used to denote the conquest of the

peninsula by Latin Christians in the twelfth, thirteenth, and fifteenth centuries. Portugal became an independent kingdom in 1139, and in the thirteenth century Christian forces recaptured Córdoba (1236), Valencia (1238), Murcia (1243), Seville (1248), and Cádiz (1262). By 1275 only the sultanate of GRANADA remained in Muslim hands. For patriotic Christian chroniclers, the fall of Granada in 1492 marked the culmination of the *reconquista* of Visigothic Spain.

*DHE.*

**RECORDE, ROBERT** (*c.*1510–1558), Welsh mathematician and physician, born in Tenby and educated at Oxford (BA 1531) and Cambridge (MD 1545). His medical treatise *The Urinal of Physic* was published in 1547, at which time he was practising as a physician in London. From 1551 to 1553 he was surveyor of the mines and monies of Ireland.

Recorde's mathematical writings include *The Ground of Arts, Teaching the Work and Practice of Arithmetic, Both in Whole Numbers and Fractions* (1540), which deals with ARITHMETIC; *The Pathway to Knowledge* (1551), on GEOMETRY; *The Castle of Knowledge* (1556), on ASTRONOMY; and *The Whetstone of Wit* (1557), the first English book on ALGEBRA, in which Recorde introduced the equality sign (=).

*DNB; DSB.*

**RECUSANTS**, the term used to denote those who in the wake of the English Reformation refused to acknowledge royal supremacy and refused to attend the services of the Church of England. The Act of Uniformity of 1558 imposed penalties (chiefly fines) on recusants. Later statutes distinguished between Catholics (who continued to be called recusants) and Protestant dissenters and nonconformists. On 25 February 1570 Pope PIUS V excommunicated and formally deposed Queen ELIZABETH, and thereafter recusancy became an important force in England, especially in Lancashire, but also in Durham, Derbyshire, Warwickshire, Staffordshire, Herefordshire, Monmouthshire, and Hampshire.

The perceived threat of armed rebellion supported by the papacy led to the formulation of a succession of penal laws, of which the first were the three penal laws of 1571 (the result of the NORTHERN REBELLION of 1569) and the most extreme was that of 1581, which imposed a fine of £20 a month for recusancy and declared any attempt to seek reconciliation with the Roman Church to be treasonous; in practice such laws were at best irregularly enforced, and in any case only the wealthiest members of society could afford to pay such huge fines. In 1585 a penal Act made it treason for a Catholic priest to enter or remain in England, and in 1593 the proffering of assistance to recusants became an offence. Another set of penal laws was imposed after the GUNPOWDER PLOT of 1605. In Scotland, an Act passed by the Reformation Parliament of 1560 made the saying or hearing of mass punishable by death.

Anti-Catholic legislation remained in place until the relief Acts of 1778 (England), 1791 (Ireland), and 1793 (Scotland), and Catholic emancipation was finally achieved in 1829, but the bigotry of anti-Catholic legislation lives on in the Act of

Settlement of 1701, which provides that the monarch will vacate the throne on becoming or marrying a Catholic.

**RED BULL THEATRE.** Originally an inn in Clerkenwell, London, in whose yard plays were performed, the building was adapted for use as a theatre in 1605, and occupied by QUEEN ANNE'S MEN until 1617. It was regarded disparagingly by other acting troupes, and had a reputation for shocking or sensational, but insubstantial, drama, with generous use of effects.

**REDFORD, JOHN** (c.1485–1547), English composer, poet, and dramatist. He was a vicar-choral and later master of the choristers at St Paul's Cathedral. Mentioned by MORLEY in his *Plain and Easy Introduction* (1597), he is notable as one of the earliest composers, rather than improvisers, of organ music.

**REDMAN, HENRY** (*fl.* 1496, d. 1528), English master mason, the son of the master mason of Westminster Abbey; he worked as a mason at the abbey from 1496 (or earlier), and in 1516 succeeded his father as master mason. In 1519 he became king's master mason, initially with William VERTUE and then alone. He visited the chapel of King's College, Cambridge, with Vertue in 1507, but the extent to which their views affected the construction of the fan vaulting is not clear. Redman and Vertue collaborated on a design for Lupton's Tower (1516) at Eton College (though it is unclear whether theirs was the design that was built) and on the fan-vaulted cloister of St Stephen's Chapel in the Palace of Westminster (c.1526). Redman was appointed as Cardinal WOLSEY's architect, so he may have been the designer of Hampton Court. He was, together with John Lebons, the architect of Cardinal College (later Christ Church), Oxford.

MDA.

**REFORMATION**, the religious reform movement of the early sixteenth century which began with the reform of abuses in the Catholic Church and culminated in the emergence of PROTESTANTISM and the secession of reformed churches in central and north-west Europe. The leaders of the Reformation churches, such as LUTHER, CALVIN, and ZWINGLI, are known as the reformers, and the movement of Catholic renewal in reaction to Protestantism is known as the COUNTER-REFORMATION. In the 1990s historians began to dissent from the singular form of the term, preferring instead to speak of 'reformations'; the plural form is now particularly favoured by Catholic historians who wish to depict the secession of Protestant churches as only one stage in a movement of Catholic reform that began in the eleventh century and extended to the eighteenth.

In the model that conceives of the Reformation as an early sixteenth-century movement centred in Germany and inaugurated by Luther, the precursors of the Reformation are deemed to be the reform movements initiated by John WYCLIFFE and the LOLLARDS in England and Jan HUS in Bohemia. In early modern England, it was Wycliffe rather than Luther who was deemed to be the first of the reformers;

as John Milton explained in *Areopagitica*, God reveals himself 'first to his Englishmen'.

The reformers of the early sixteenth century, not all of whom became Protestants, deemed both the practices and the doctrines of the Church to stand in need of reform. Practices such as the sale of INDULGENCES were excoriated, and many doctrines were reassessed in the BIBLICAL scholarship of the HUMANISTS. In popular historiography, the act that inaugurated the Reformation was Luther's nailing of his 95 Theses to the door of the castle church in WITTENBERG on 31 October 1517. The widely held sentiments that prompted this act led to the confrontation at the Diet of WORMS in 1521; popular support for the Reformation was marked by the outbreak of the PEASANTS' WAR in 1524. Luther was not a revolutionary, and his refusal to support the peasant rebellion gained powerful supporters of the Reformation amongst the German princes, notably the rulers of Saxony (the Elector Johann der Beständige), Hesse (PHILIP OF HESSE), and the German provinces in the Baltic (ALBRECHT VON PREUSSEN). LUTHERANISM quickly spread to SWEDEN (see GUSTAVUS VASA) and DENMARK and also to German states such as BRANDENBURG, Brunswick, and Württemberg (see ULRICH). The doctrine of the Lutheran Reformation is articulated in the AUGSBURG CONFESSION (1530), and the Lutheran Church secured official recognition in the Religious Peace of AUGSBURG (1555).

The Swiss Reformation was led by Ulrich ZWINGLI, and spread from Zürich to other cantons in the SWISS CONFEDERATION. Zwingli's theology was less scholastic than Luther's, especially in the doctrine of the EUCHARIST, and the two churches divided on this issue. The Zwinglian Reformation was established in STRASSBURG (by Martin BUCER), BASEL (by OECOLAMPADIUS), and Neuchâtel (by Guillaume FAREL). After the death of Zwingli in 1531, leadership of the Swiss Reformation passed to GENEVA.

In 1541 Jean Calvin reconstituted Geneva as a theocratic city-state. The determinist theological doctrine of GRACE that Calvin described in his *Institutio christianae religionis* (1536) found sympathizers and champions all over Europe, including Germany, France, the Netherlands, England, and Scotland. In France, hostility to the Calvinists, who were known as HUGUENOTS, eventually led to the WARS OF RELIGION; in the Netherlands, where the Reformation is usually said to have begun in the 'wonder year' of 1566, the religious cause became caught up in political rebellion which culminated in the REVOLT OF THE NETHERLANDS. In Scotland, the Reformation was led by the Calvinist John KNOX. Calvinist churches are usually known as Reformed churches (French *Églises réformées*, German *reformierte Kirchen*), whereas Lutheran churches are usually known as Evangelical churches.

In England the Reformation was a halting and insular process. King HENRY VIII, who was Catholic in doctrine and in church government, overthrew the papacy and suppressed the MONASTERIES for political and personal reasons, not because he felt a strong need for reform. Queen MARY suppressed the Reformation, but it was reinstituted under Queen ELIZABETH. Calvinism had many adherents in the

Church and the universities, but the queen resisted any reformation in church government. The theology of the Church of England, as articulated in the Thirty-Nine ARTICLES, contains Calvinist, Lutheran, and Catholic elements, and this eclectic theology was grafted onto ecclesiastical structures that are essentially Roman, save that the monarch rather than the pope is head of the Church.

Leopold von Ranke, *Deutsche Geschichte im Zeitalter der Reformation* (6 vols., 1839–47; English trans of vols. i–iii, 1845–7); G. R. Elton (ed.), *The Reformation 1520–1559* (2nd edn., 1990); A. G. Dickens, *The English Reformation* (1964); Euan Cameron, *The European Reformation* (1991).

## REGENSBURG, CONFERENCE OF or Colloquy of, or (German) Regensburger Religiongespräch, formerly known in English as the Conference of Ratisbon (from Latin Ratisbona).

The city of Regensburg was an important imperial residence, and so was the setting of many imperial diets. The Conference was a meeting of six theologians convened at Regensburg from 27 April to 22 May 1541 by the Emperor CHARLES V; its purpose was to establish doctrinal agreement and to work towards ecclesiastical reunion.

The three Catholic participants were Johann ECK, Julius von PFLUG, and Johann GROPPER; the Catholic side was led by the papal legate Gasparo CONTARINI, who was present but not a delegate. The Protestants were Philipp MELANCHTHON, Martin BUCER, and Johann Pistorius the Elder (1503–68). Negotiations followed the *Regensburger Buch*, a discussion document that had been produced in secret preliminary meetings. The theologians agreed on a statement on JUSTIFICATION, but were unable to resolve issues such as papal authority and the standing of the SACRAMENTS. Martin LUTHER and the Protestant princes of Germany opposed the concessions made by the Protestant side at the Conference, and reunion was not achieved.

The *Acta* were published by Martin Bucer (Strassburg, 1541) and translated into English by Miles COVERDALE (1541, probably published in Geneva).

P. Matheson, *Cardinal Contarini at Regensburg* (1972).

## REGIOMONTANUS or (German) Johannes Müller (1436–76),

German astronomer and mathematician, born in Königsberg (Franconia). In Latin he called himself Joannes de Monte Regio, which later becomes Regiomontanus. He was educated first at the local university in Leipzig (1447–50) and then at the University of Vienna (1450–61), where he rapidly became a colleague rather than a pupil of the professor of astronomy, Georg PEURBACH. In about 1460 Regiomontanus began to learn Greek from BESSARION. Together with Peurbach, he accompanied Bessarion to Italy in search of Greek manuscripts, and remained there, chiefly in Padua and Rome, for six years. After a short period as royal librarian at the court of MATTHIAS CORVINUS in Buda, Regiomontanus settled in 1471 in Nuremberg, where he built an observatory and set up a printing press for publishing his writings. In 1475 Pope SIXTUS IV called him to Rome to advise on CALENDAR REFORM. However, Regiomontanus died shortly after arriving in the city.

Regiomontanus must have known from his student days that there were difficulties with the current (Julian) calendar. The date of the equinox, which Julius Caesar had intended to fix at 21 March, was obviously not properly fixed, which was to say that the estimate of the length of the year, as measured from equinox to equinox, must be incorrect. Peurbach and Regiomontanus hoped that this and other matters might be remedied by returning to the true text of PTOLEMY rather than relying upon translations of the *Almagest* that seemed to have been made from texts already corrupted by later accretions. That is, they proposed a thoroughly humanistic solution to the astronomical problems. Unfortunately, Peurbach died in 1461, so Regiomontanus was left to carry on the task of interpretation and commentary alone. It was still unfinished at his death, but his work was nevertheless printed in 1496 as *Epytoma Ioannis de monte regio in almagestum ptolemei*. This book proved to be very valuable to later generations of astronomers, for whom it provided a properly technical account of Ptolemy's methods, in a modernized form that made their relevance clear.

The *Epytoma* was certainly seen as Regiomontanus' greatest achievement, but he also wrote a short treatise on triangles which, as the preface tells us, needs to be read before coming to grips with Ptolemy's mathematics. This book, probably written about 1462, but published posthumously in 1533, is called *De triangulis omnimodis libri quinque* and deals not only with plane triangles (the kind one finds in EUCLID) but also with spherical ones, which are necessary for astronomy. It was much used by later generations of students and is notable for introducing, and proving, the Sine Rule, which Regiomontanus probably knew from the work of Levi ben Gerson (1288–1344) on the CROSS-STAFF. In its treatment of plane triangles, the content of *De triangulis* shows some overlap with the geometry taught in ABACUS SCHOOLS and Regiomontanus makes a little use of ALGEBRA to solve a problem for which, he says, he has not yet found a geometrical solution.

*DSB*; Ernst Zinner, *Regiomontanus: His Life and Work*, trans. Ezra Brown, Studies in the History and Philosophy of Mathematics 1 (1990); a translation of Zinner's second edition of 1968, with additional essays by various scholars to bring the work up to date; 1st edn. was 1938.

## RÉGNIER, MATHURIN (1573–1613),

French satirist, the nephew of Philippe DESPORTES, whose wealthy abbacies he inherited. He used his fortune to lead a profligate life on the fringes of the court of HENRI IV, for whom he wrote court poems for ceremonial occasions. Régnier's principal poems are a collection of seventeen verse satires addressed to members of the court. The poems, which have a moral dimension apparently at odds with Régnier's own deportment, attempt to raise vernacular satire to the literary dignity of Horatian satire, and so use a formal alexandrine metre.

Petra Strien-Bourmer, *Mathurin Régnier und die Verssatire seit der Pléiade* (1992).

## REICHSKAMMERGERICHT, the Imperial Chamber Court

founded by MAXIMILIAN I in 1495 as the permanent high court

of the HOLY ROMAN EMPIRE. The court consisted of eight noblemen and eight doctors of law appointed by the Empire, i.e. by the electors, and a president nominated by the emperor; the name *Reich* represented the court's standing as the court of the Empire rather than the personal court of the emperor. The Reichskammergericht was financed by a general tax (known in English as the Common Penny) voted by the ESTATES. Maximilian required that the judgments of the court be based on JUSTINIAN's *Corpus iuris civilis*, and so accelerated the RECEPTION of Roman law in Germany and shaped the future development of GERMAN LAW. The court initially sat at Frankfurt, but in 1527 moved to Speyer, where it remained until 1693. The judicial competence of the Reichskammergericht encompassed breaches of the peace, arbitrary seizure of goods (known in law as 'distraint') and arbitrary imprisonment, pleas relating to the imperial treasury, violations of the decrees of the emperor or the statutes of the Diet, and certain classes of property disputes and suits against immediate tenants of the Empire.

The Reichskammergericht was reformed in the mid-sixteenth century by the Emperor FERDINAND I, who expanded the number of judges to 24, insisted that the noblemen be competent in Roman law, and inaugurated an annual review of the proceedings of the court by an appellate committee of the Reichstag. The review procedure lapsed in 1588, and thereafter the court stagnated, weighed down by a huge amount of litigation and encumbered by its own laborious procedures.

The jurisdiction of the Reichskammergericht overlapped with the AULIC COUNCIL (German Reichshofrat) founded by Maximilian I in 1498 as the supreme executive and judicial council of the Empire. In 1648 the Treaty of Westphalia regulated the competition between the two courts by stipulating that only the court which had first dealt with a case should have competence to pursue it; thereafter, the inefficiency of the Reichskammergericht meant that most litigation was instead channelled through the Aulic Council, but the Reichskammergericht continued to sit until the dissolution of the Empire in 1806.

**REICHSTAG**, the Diet or Assembly of the HOLY ROMAN EMPIRE. By the end of the fifteenth century it had become the principal executive authority of the Empire. The Reichstag was not a standing body, but assembled at the behest of the emperor for short periods. It nominally represented the ESTATES, but in fact consisted of three curias: the electors, the princes, and the free imperial cities. When the emperor summoned the Reichstag he would present proposals for discussion by each of the three curias, which would then formulate an agreed view of which the emperor would be informed.

At the Diet of Worms (Wormser Reichstag) of 1495 the powers of the Reichstag were extended to include the maintenance of peace and declaration of war, the determination of foreign policy, and the regulation of tax collection. In the sixteenth century it met regularly to decide on the military and financial measures necessary to defend imperial territory against Ottoman incursions.

**REINHOLD, ERASMUS** (1511–53), German astronomer. He was born in Saalfeld and became professor of mathematics at Wittenberg, where, together with his colleague Georg RHETICUS, he became interested in the heliocentric cosmology of COPERNICUS and persuaded MELANCHTHON and CRUCIGER to support the publication of Copernicus' *De revolutionibus* (1543). Reinhold then set about constructing astronomical tables based on Copernicus' work; these tables, called *Tabulae Prutenicae* (that is 'Prussian tables'), were published in 1551. Like all tables that used relatively recent observations, they were at first more accurate than older ones, but within about twenty years they began to be noticeably inadequate. This stimulated Tycho BRAHE to attempt a reform of his own.
    *DSB.*

**REJ, MIKOŁAJ** (1505–69), Polish writer, a courtier and landowner who in 1546 became a Calvinist. Poland had a strong culture of literary Latin, but, in common with many Protestants, Rej was an advocate of the vernacular, and soon became a champion of Polish as a literary language. His writings include several plays based on classical models, poetry in several genres (notably the epigram), and a prose paraphrase of the Psalms. He is now honoured as the father of Polish literature.
    *PSB.*

*REJA* (Spanish; 'lattice'). In sixteenth-century Spain the finest iron products were *rejas*, the tiered gridiron screens of up to 10 metres (30 feet) in height that were installed in between nave and choir in churches and chapels. Some of the finest examples are in Toledo Cathedral, in which wrought-iron *rejas* enclose the chancel and the chapels; the hammered iron spindled balusters are plated with silver. Wrought-iron *rejas* were also used as window grilles in civic buildings such as the Casa de las Conchas in Salamanca.

**RELIEF or** (Italian) *relievo*, the art-historical term for a work of sculpture in which figures stand out from a plane and the dimension of depth is reduced; the term is not peculiar to any medium, and is used with reference to sculptures in stone, wood, metal (e.g. GHIBERTI's bronze doors on the Florentine baptistery), and gems (see CAMEO). The term 'high relief' (*alto relievo*) is used when the scale of projection (i.e. the dimension of depth) is more than half of the other two dimensions; in the case of architectural decoration the term is used more loosely to denote sculpture carved fully in the round (i.e. when the scale of projection equals the other dimensions). The Italian term *mezzo relievo* is used when the scale of projection is approximately half that of the other dimensions. The term 'low relief' (Italian *basso relievo*, French *bas-relief*) is used when the scale of projection is less than half of the other dimensions and there is no undercutting. In Italian, the very low relief used by sculptors such as DONATELLO and DESIDERIO DA SETTIGNANO is known as *relievo stiacciato* or simply *stiacciato*.

**REMONSTRANTS**, members of the ARMINIAN party in the Dutch Reformed Church. The term derives from the

Remonstrance (Dutch *Remonstrantie*) of 1610, a statement of theological principles formulated shortly after Arminius' death by his friend Johannes Uitenbogaert and signed by 44 Arminians. The Remonstrance cites the five articles from Arminius' *Declaratio sententiae* (1608) that constitute the core of Remonstrant belief. The rejection of the Calvinist doctrines of predestination (in both its supralapsarian and sublapsarian forms), the limited atonement (i.e. Jesus died only for the elect), and the irresistibility and indefectibility of GRACE brought the Remonstrants into conflict with followers of Francis GOMAR, who were known as Counter-Remonstrants. Remonstrants did not secure full toleration until 1795.

**RENAISSANCE or (Italian) *Rinascimento*,** a model of cultural descent in which the culture of fifteenth- and sixteenth-century Europe is represented as a repudiation of medieval values in favour of the revival of the culture of ancient Greece and Rome. The parallel religious model is the REFORMATION, in which the Church is represented as repudiating its medieval degeneracy in favour of a renewal of the purity of the early Church. The idea of the MIDDLE AGES (*medium aevum*) was introduced to European HISTORIOGRAPHY by Flavio BIONDI. In the arts, it was VASARI who used the term *rinascità* to denote the period from CIMABUE and GIOTTO to his own time.

The broadening of the term 'renaissance' to encompass a period and a cultural model is a product of the nineteenth century. In 1855 Jules Michelet used the term Renaissance as the title of a volume on sixteenth-century France. Five years later Jakob Burckhardt published *Die Cultur der Renaissance in Italien* ('The Civilization of the Renaissance in Italy'), in which he identified the idea of a Renaissance with a set of cultural concepts, such as individualism and the idea of the universal man. Vasari's designation of a movement in art had become the term for an epoch in history associated with a particular set of cultural values. In late twentieth-century historiography, the idea that the Renaissance marked the beginning of the modern age evolved into the representation of the fifteenth and sixteenth centuries as the early modern period; this notion is as fraught with ideological baggage as is the term Renaissance.

The idea of a Renaissance is of considerable use when referring to the scholarly, courtly, and even military cultures of the fifteenth and sixteenth centuries, because members of those elites were consciously emulating classical antiquity, but it is of little value as a model for popular culture and the everyday life of most Europeans. The idea of historical periods, which is emphasized by the use of centuries or rulers as boundaries, is particularly problematical in the case of the Renaissance, because a model that assumes the repudiation of the immediate past is insufficiently attentive to cultural continuities.

**RENÉ D'ANJOU** (1409–80), duke of Anjou, Lorraine, and Bar, count of Provence and Piedmont, king of Naples, and nominal king of Sicily and Jerusalem, born in Angers on 16

January 1409, the second son of LOUIS II OF ANJOU, king of Sicily and claimant to the throne of Naples. When Louis II died in 1417, his elder son Louis III succeeded to the duchy of Anjou and inherited his claim to Sicily (which was ruled by Spain); René's title during this period was count of Guise. In 1419, at the age of 10, René was betrothed to Isabelle, daughter of Charles II, duke of Lorraine. By the terms of the marriage contract, he became heir to the duchy of Bar (which was claimed as the inheritance of his mother Yolande) and heir to the duchy of Lorraine (which was claimed as the inheritance of his wife); he succeeded to the duchy of Bar in 1430 and to the duchy of Lorraine in 1431.

The inheritance of Lorraine was disputed by Antoine de Vaudémont, who, supported by PHILIP THE GOOD of Burgundy, defeated and captured René in July 1431. He was conditionally released the following April after handing over two of his sons (Jean and Louis) as hostages. When his claim to be duke of Lorraine was recognized by the Emperor SIGISMUND in 1434, René was again imprisoned by Philip the Good, and remained in captivity until 1436, when he was released on payment of a large ransom. The restoration of good relations between Philip and René was signalled by the marriage of Marie de Bourbon (Philip's niece) to Jean, duke of Calabria (René's eldest son).

In 1435, whilst still in prison, René succeeded to the duchy of Anjou and the county of Provence on the death of his brother Louis III, and also succeeded to the throne of Naples through the death of Queen GIOVANNA II. His wife Isabelle claimed the inheritance of Naples on behalf of her husband, and in 1438 René joined her in Naples. In 1441 ALFONSO V of Aragon besieged Naples, and six months later captured and sacked the city. René returned to France, and thereafter his claim to the throne of Naples was only nominal.

Queen Isabelle died in 1453. René then married Jeanne de Laval and withdrew from public life. He was a lavish patron of the arts, and was also a writer: his works include a treatise on tournament ritual (*Traité de la forme et devis d'un tournoi*, c.1444) and two allegorical works, the *Mortification de vaine plaisance* (c.1453) and *Le Livre du cœur d'amour épris* (c.1460).

Margaret, René's daughter by Isabelle, had married HENRY VI of England, and their son Prince Edward was murdered in 1471. René appears (as Reignier) in Shakespeare's *1 Henry VI*, and Margaret is a major figure in the three parts of *Henry VI*.

A. Lecoy de la Marche, *Le Roi René: Sa Vie, son administration, ses travaux artistiques et littéraires* (2 vols., 1875).

**RENÉE DE FRANCE** (1510–74), duchess of Ferrara, was born in Blois, the daughter of King LOUIS XI and ANNE OF BRITTANY. In 1528 she married Ercole II d'ESTE, who acceded to the dukedom of Ferrara in 1534. In Ferrara Renée (Italian Renata) became a patron of humanist learning and a protector of French Protestant refugees; in 1536 Jean CALVIN visited her to seek her support. Her conversion to Protestantism under the influence of Calvin and Clément MAROT displeased her husband, who in 1554 removed her children and briefly imprisoned Renée; she recanted to secure her release, but subsequently reaffirmed her Protestantism.

Duke Ercole died in 1560, whereupon Renée returned to France and settled in her chateau in Montargis (Loiret), which became an important Protestant centre and refuge. In 1562, in the first of the French WARS OF RELIGION, her chateau was besieged by her son-in-law François, duke of GUISE.

**REQUESENS Y ZÚÑIGA, LUIS DE** (1528–76), Spanish governor of the Netherlands. He represented King PHILIP II in Rome (1563) and in 1568 was charged by King Philip with the suppression of the MORISCO rebellion in Granada (1568–70), and so became the superior of DON JUAN OF AUSTRIA, who commanded the royal troops. He was subsequently appointed viceroy of Milan and in 1573 was chosen by King Philip to succeed the duke of ALBA as governor-general of the Netherlands. Requesens initially attempted to negotiate with the rebels leading the REVOLT OF THE NETHERLANDS, but he soon renewed the war, defeating LOUIS OF NASSAU at Mook on 14 April 1574 and then besieging Leiden (May–October 1574); the siege was raised by insurgents who opened the dykes to flood the area and allow sea beggars (see PRIVATEERS) to bring in relief. In a peace conference convened at Breda (February–July 1575) Requesens agreed to withdraw Spanish troops and to dismantle the Spanish administration, but the talks failed when he insisted that Protestantism could not be tolerated. Early in 1576 Requesens besieged Zierikzee, but was recalled to Brussels because of insubordination in the Spanish cavalry; he died of fever on 4 March 1576, before he reached Brussels. The army, which was leaderless and unpaid, became anarchic, and in November sacked Antwerp in the episode known as the 'Spanish fury'. Requesens was succeeded as governor-general by Don Juan of Austria.

DHE; Aldo Xavier, *Luis de Requesens en la Europa del siglo XVI* (1984).

**REREDOS.** See ALTARPIECE.

**RESENDE, GARCIA DE** (c.1470–1536), Portuguese chronicler and poet, born in Évora. He served at the court of JOHN II as a chronicler and (from 1491) as a private secretary to the king. His *Vida de Dom João II* (1545) is derivative, but nonetheless contains personal recollections and observations that make it an important document of social history. After the death of John II, Resende served in the courts of MANUEL I (whom he accompanied in 1498 to Castile and Aragon) and JOHN III, and in 1513 he accompanied the Portuguese ambassador Tristão da CUNHA on a visit to Pope LEO X. Garcia's *Miscellânea e variedade de histórias* (first published in 1798) contains a continuation of his chronicle.

Garcia de Resende printed poems by some 200 poets (mostly of the previous century, but up to and including himself and SÁ DE MIRANDA) in his *Cancioneiro geral* (1516), which is sometimes called the *Cancioneiro de Resende* to avoid confusion with Fernando del CASTILLO's Spanish *Cancionero general* (1511), on which it is modelled.

DHP; André Crabbé Rocha, *Garcia de Resende e o Cancioneiro geral* (1979).

**RETABLE.** See ALTARPIECE.

**RETICELLA**, a form of needlepoint LACE used in sixteenth- and early seventeenth-century Italy for civil and ecclesiastical ceremonial garments. The technique involved cutting away portions of woven linen fabric and then filling the gaps with openwork patterns worked in buttonhole stitching. It differs from CUTWORK in that it makes less use of the linen threads of the fabric and more use of free needlework.

**RETZ, GILLES DE**. See GILLES DE RETZ.

**REUCHLIN, JOHANN**, or Capnio Phorcensis (1455–1522), German humanist and Hebraist. He was born in Pforzheim, in the Black Forest, and studied in Freiburg (1470–74), Basel (1474–77) and Paris (1478), where he learnt Greek. He published a Latin lexicon (*Vocabularis breviloquus*, 1475–76) when he was only 20, and then turned to the study of law in Orléans (1479) and Poitiers (1480–1). From 1484 to 1496 he was an interpreter and lawyer in the service of Eberhard im Bart, duke of Württemberg, and he twice travelled to Italy in this period. Eberhard died in 1496, and Reuchlin moved to Heidelberg, where he translated Greek authors and taught Greek, even though he did not have a formal teaching position. His position on the pronunciation of the GREEK LANGUAGE was that it should be pronounced as if it were modern Greek; this contention, which he articulated in *Dialogus de recta Latini Graecique sermonis pronunciatione* (1519), was in direct opposition to the view of ERASMUS (who was to publish his *De recta Latini Graecique sermonis pronunciatione* in 1528) and so the two pronunciations of ancient Greek are sometimes called Erasmian and Reuchlinian. In Heidelberg he also wrote two Latin comedies: *Sergius oder Capitus caput* (1496) was a satire on monasticism and the trade in relics and *Scena progymnasmata sive Henno* (1497) was a farce which proved to be seminal in the development of comic drama in Germany.

In 1502 Reuchlin returned to Stuttgart, and until 1513 he served as a senior judge for the SWABIAN LEAGUE. For many years Reuchlin had been studying Hebrew, and in 1498 he had returned from Italy with a large consignment of Hebrew books. Reuchlin was dauntingly learned in many fields of humanist endeavour, especially in the study of Greek, but it was his establishment (and subsequent defence) of HEBREW SCHOLARSHIP in Germany that was to prove to be his most important contribution to humanist scholarship. His *De rudimentis Hebraicis* (1506) and *De accentibus et orthographia linguae Hebraicae* (1518) are the founding texts of Hebrew studies in Germany.

Reuchlin had met PICO when visiting Italy in 1490, and under his influence developed a scholarly interest in the CABBALA, on which he wrote two books, *De verbo mirifico* (1494) and *De arte cabbalistica* (1517), both of which strive to reconcile the Cabbala with Christianity.

In 1510 Reuchlin became embroiled in a controversy with PFEFFERKORN and the Dominicans of Cologne which was to dominate the rest of his life. In 1509, at Pfefferkorn's instigation, the Emperor MAXIMILIAN I had agreed that, as a preliminary to the conversion of the JEWS to Christianity, all Jewish books directed against Christianity should be confiscated. The following year Reuchlin was instructed by imperial command to proffer his opinion on the suppression of these books, and on 6 October 1510 he replied from Stuttgart opposing the proposed edict on the grounds that the very few Jewish books that defamed Christianity were repudiated by most Jews, and that other Jewish books were either adjuncts to Jewish worship (which had been sanctioned by both imperial and papal dispensation) or of scholarly value; taking the offensive, Reuchlin proposed that two ten-year professorships in Hebrew studies should be established by imperial edict at every German university, and that books should be supplied by Jews. In the face of this proposal, the emperor equivocated, and Reuchlin's opponents laid the blame at his feet for frustrating their plans. Pfefferkorn responded by circulating at the FRANKFURT fair of 1511 a pamphlet called *Handspiegel wider und gegen die Juden*, which asserted that Reuchlin had been bribed. Reuchlin replied with *Der Augenspiegel* (1511), which was pilloried by Pfefferkorn and subsequently condemned by the inquisitor Jakob von Hochstraten and the theological faculty of Cologne University; on 7 October 1512 these powerful enemies secured an imperial edict condemning the *Augenspiegel*. European universities were consulted, and so Reuchlin shifted the debate into Latin when he fought back with his *Defensio contra calumniatores* (1513). Hochstraten initiated an inquisitorial investigation in Mainz, but Reuchlin succeeded in having the case transferred to Rome, where in July 1516 the trial was terminated, which was in effect an unarticulated victory for Reuchlin. In Germany learned opinion had turned in Reuchlin's favour, and his allies published the EPISTOLAE OBSCURORUM VIRORUM.

In 1520 a commission in Frankfurt found in Reuchlin's favour against Hochstraten, but by this time the debate had been overtaken by the more pressing concern of the Lutheran question. Reuchlin was rumoured to be sympathetic to Luther, and he enjoyed the support of many prominent reformers, but he remained loyal to Rome, and tried to dissuade MELANCHTHON (his sister's grandson) from defecting to the Lutheran cause. In 1519 Reuchlin fled from the famine, plague, and civil war that had been visited on Stuttgart, and took refuge as professor of Greek and Hebrew at Ingolstadt; when the plague arrived in Ingolstadt in 1521, Reuchlin moved to Tübingen, where he taught for the last year of his life. He was, like Erasmus, a relentless writer of letters, and through his correspondence he disseminated his views throughout Europe.

M. Krebs (ed.), *Johannes Reuchlin, 1455–1522* (1955); A. Herzig and J. Schoeps (eds.), *Reuchlin und die Juden* (1993).

**REUVENI, DAVID** (*c*.1485–*c*.1538), Jewish messianic leader in Italy and Portugal who claimed to be the ambassador of the lost tribes of Reuben, Gad, and Manasseh. He first appeared in Venice in 1523; his origins are unknown, but he had lived for several years in the Levant, including Jerusalem and Alexandria. In 1524 he travelled to Rome and secured an audience with Pope CLEMENT VII, to whom he proposed an anti-Ottoman alliance with his brother Joseph, king of a Jewish country in the east.

Furnished with a letter of commendation from Pope Clement, Reuveni travelled in 1525 to Portugal, where he lived for two years. He established contact with Solomon MOLCHO, whom he encouraged to revert publicly to Judaism, and also excited messianic expectations amongst the MARRANOS of Portugal and North Africa. He was expelled from Portugal and travelled to Provence, where he was imprisoned and then ransomed by local JEWS. He returned to Venice in 1530, and was denounced as an impostor by Federico II GONZAGA to Pope Clement and the Emperor CHARLES V. In 1532 he travelled with Molcho to meet the emperor in Regensburg, where they were both arrested: Molcho was sent to Mantua and burnt at the stake, and Reuveni was transported to Spain, where he died.

**REUWICH, ERHARD** (*c*.1455–*c*.1490), Dutch engraver, born in Utrecht. In 1483 he accompanied Canon Bernhard von Breydenbach (chamberlain to the archbishop of Mainz), Graaf Johann zu Solms-Lich, and the Ritter Philipp von Bicken on a pilgrimage to Jerusalem. Reuwich's sketches, which included a map of Venice and views of Corfu and Rhodes, were made into woodcuts and incorporated by Breydenbach in his *Peregrinationes in Terram Sanctam*, which was published in Mainz by Peter SCHÖFFER in 1486 and was subsequently translated into other languages, including German (1486), Dutch (1488), French (1488), Spanish (1497), and Italian (1500).

*MDA.*

**REVOLT OF THE NETHERLANDS** (1567–1609). In the early 1550s the seventeen provinces of the NETHERLANDS were territories of the duchy of Burgundy. The duke was the Emperor CHARLES V, and the duchy of Burgundy was part of the HOLY ROMAN EMPIRE; the regent of the Netherlands was Charles's sister MARY OF HUNGARY. In October 1555 Charles abdicated his dukedom and Mary resigned her regency. The new duke of Burgundy was Charles's son King PHILIP II of Spain. In August 1559 Philip left the Netherlands, never to return, and appointed as his regent his half-sister MARGARET OF PARMA; her chief minister, and head of the Council of State, was Cardinal GRANVELLE, who loyally implemented King Philip's religious policies. On his accession Philip had promptly admitted the JESUITS to the Netherlands with a view to combating Protestantism, and papal bulls of 1559 and 1561 established a Catholic university in DOUAI and reorganized the structure of the Church to make it more amenable to control from Madrid. The Spanish INQUISITION was also implemented in the Netherlands.

The Netherlandish subjects of King Philip included Lutherans, Calvinists, Anabaptists, and moderate Catholics (including humanists), and all of these groups dissented from policies that they regarded as abhorrent. In July 1563 WILLIAM OF ORANGE and the count of EGMONT resigned from the Council in protest at these policies; the support of Walloon aristocrats led by the duke of AERSCHOT enabled Granvelle to survive in post for several months, but he was nonetheless forced to resign in January 1564, and was succeeded the following year by Aerschot. King Philip was unrelenting, and ordered the implementation of the decrees of the COUNCIL OF TRENT in the Netherlands. The WARS OF RELIGION had begun in France in 1562, and fears of a religious war in the Netherlands emboldened noblemen led by William of Orange to appeal to the king for religious toleration. King Philip replied to the regent from Segovia in two letters of October 1565, ordering that heresy be extirpated.

A group of some 200 members of the lesser nobility, both Catholic and Protestant, formed an alliance known as the Compromise and on 5 April 1566, led by LOUIS OF NASSAU (younger brother of William of Orange) and Henry of Brederode, processed into Brussels to demand religious toleration. One of Margaret of Austria's councillors dismissed the protesters as *gueux* (beggars), a term which they promptly appropriated for themselves. There were also signs of rebellion amongst ordinary citizens. The Catholic Church had for centuries valued sacred art, but Dutch Protestantism was markedly iconoclastic and many Protestants thought that religious images were idolatrous. In August 1566 iconoclastic attacks on churches and monasteries spread from Steenvoorde (Flanders) to centres such as Amsterdam, Antwerp, and Ghent.

In 1567 King Philip responded to these rebellions by recalling the duke of ALBA from Italy and sending him to the Netherlands to quell civil unrest and religious dissent. He arrived with an army of 9,000 troops, whereupon the regent resigned and both William of Orange and Louis of Nassau went into exile to organize armed resistance, so leaving Alba, as governor-general, as the unchallenged head of government. Alba used the tribunal known as the COUNCIL OF BLOOD to remove all opponents of Spanish rule, and in 1568 arrested and executed the leaders of the rebellion, the count of Egmont and the count of HOORNE.

In 1572 Alba moved troops south in anticipation of a French invasion led by the Huguenot leader Gaspard de COLIGNY, whereupon Protestants led by William of Orange took advantage of the reduction of troops in the north to capture the provinces of Holland and Zeeland and to defeat the Spanish fleet dispatched to regain the lost provinces. By the time the ST BARTHOLOMEW'S DAY MASSACRE had alleviated the French threat, the sea beggars (*Gueux de Mer*) had established a defensive cordon, and Alba did not have sufficient naval power to attempt another sea attack, because Spanish naval resources had been diverted to the Mediterranean to participate in the campaign against the Ottomans that culminated in the battle of LEPANTO.

In November 1573 King Philip replaced Alba as governor-general with Luis de REQUESENS, who defeated (and killed) Louis of Nassau at Mook (near Nijmegen) on 14 April 1574 and then besieged Leiden (May–October 1574); the siege was raised by insurgents who opened the dykes to flood the area and allow Sea Beggars to bring in relief. In a peace conference convened at Breda (February–July 1575) Requesens agreed to withdraw Spanish troops and to dismantle the Spanish

administration, but the talks failed when he insisted that Protestantism could not be tolerated. Requesens unexpectedly died of fever on 4 March 1576; his army, which was leaderless and unpaid, became anarchic, and in eleven days (4–14 November 1576) sacked Antwerp in the episode known as the 'Spanish fury', in which thousands of citizens were slaughtered and much of the city was destroyed.

As the devastation proceeded the duke of Aerschot, who had distanced himself from the brutality of the duke of Alba, was able to negotiate the Pacification of GHENT (8 November 1576), which called for the withdrawal of foreign troops and deferred the issue of religious toleration. Requesens was succeeded as governor-general by Don JUAN DE AUSTRIA, who on arrival ratified the Pacification of Ghent in the 'Eternal Edict' of February 1577, by which he pledged to withdraw the Spanish army and the Dutch signatories agreed to return the Netherlands to Catholicism. Holland and Zeeland declined to sign the Edict or to recognize Don Juan's authority as governor-general.

On 24 July 1577 Don Juan occupied Namur, and the following month churches were sacked in iconoclastic riots in Flemish towns such as Antwerp, Brussels, Bruges, and Ghent. In December 1577 the Estates-General withdrew their recognition of Don Juan and the next month appointed Archduke (later Emperor) MATTHIAS as governor and William of Orange as lieutenant-governor. Don Juan was joined by his nephew Alessandro FARNESE, with whom he defeated a northern army at Gembloux (Brabant) on 31 January 1578. The involvement of foreigners continued as Walloon noblemen in the south formed the anti-Calvinist coalition known as the 'Malcontents' and invited François, duc d'ANJOU, to be their leader, declaring him to be duke of Brabant. JOHANN CASIMIR arrived from the Palatinate to command an army (in part financed by Queen ELIZABETH of England) sent by Dutch Calvinists to relieve GHENT. The death of Don Juan de Austria on 1 October 1578 left a vacuum into which Alessandro Farnese quickly stepped, and for the next fourteen years he was the most important military figure in the Netherlands.

On 7 January 1579 three southern provinces (Hainaut, Artois, and Douai) formed the Catholic and pro-Spanish Union of ARRAS, and on 23 January 1579 five northern provinces (Friesland, Gelderland, Holland, Utrecht, and Zeeland) responded by forming the Union of UTRECHT, which Groningen and Overijssel later joined. William of Orange, who preferred the prospect of a political compromise to an invasion of the northern provinces by Farnese (who had captured Maastricht on 29 June 1579), offered the throne of the Netherlands to François, duc d'Anjou (brother of King HENRI III of France, a potential ally against Spain). King Philip accused William of Orange of treason (June 1580), and the following year the Estates-General of the Union of Utrecht formally deposed King Philip as head of state in the Act of Abjuration (July 1581). The enforced abjuration of Philip ended the governorship of Archduke Matthias (and his hope of a Netherlandish throne), and the new state, the UNITED PROVINCES, became independent.

Duke François arrived to claim his throne, and on 17 January 1583 he attacked Antwerp in an episode known as the 'French fury'; he was eventually repelled and returned to France, where he died on 10 June 1584. A month later, on 10 July 1584, William of Orange was assassinated. Farnese's military campaign in Flanders continued apace with the capture of Oudenaarde (1582), Dunkirk (1583), Bruges (1584), Ghent (1584), Brussels (1585) and, after a fourteen-month siege, Antwerp (1585), which he required all Protestant citizens to leave within two years.

In August 1585 England entered the conflict when Queen Elizabeth, fearing that the fall of Antwerp could portend a Spanish victory, agreed in the Treaty of Nonsuch to dispatch to the aid of the Protestants an expeditionary force of 7,000 troops under the command of the earl of Leicester. The English army landed at Vlissingen (English exonym Flushing) on 10/20 December 1585, and the following month Leicester accepted the governor-generalship of the United Provinces. He was, however, helpless in the face of Farnese's advance. Farnese captured Grave and Venloo (June 1586) and then took towns defended by the English, including ZUTPHEN (October 1586), where Sir Philip SIDNEY was killed, and Deventer (January 1587). Leicester left at the end of 1587, but English troops were left behind to garrison towns such as Gertruidenberg, which Farnese captured in April 1589.

In 1588 Farnese was poised to conquer the United Provinces, but King Philip ordered him to lead his armies to Dunkirk and Nieuwpoort with a view to boarding the ships of the Spanish ARMADA and invading England. Other opportunities for the conquest of the north arose, but Farnese was repeatedly ordered to invade France to assist the CATHOLIC LEAGUE, first to relieve Paris (September 1590) and then Rouen (April 1592); on his third expedition to France (December 1592) he died near Arras.

The final years of the rebellion were dominated by Johan van OLDENBARNEVELT, the pensionary (i.e. chairman) of the Estates of Holland, and MAURICE OF NASSAU, son of William of Orange. Oldenbarnevelt created a measure of political unity in the United Provinces by securing the appointment (as captain-general and stadtholder) of Maurice of Nassau in all but one of the provinces (Friesland), thus obviating the need for a foreign prince to unite the country. Maurice of Nassau created a professional army, and in the course of the 1590s expelled the Spanish from every town and bridgehead in the north. Spain negotiated treaties with France (May 1598) and England (August 1604), and in April 1609 agreed to a twelve-year truce with the United Provinces; the provisions of the truce, which had been negotiated by Oldenbarnevelt and opposed by Maurice of Nassau, obliged Spain to close the river Scheldt (a concession that was ruinous to Antwerp) and to give the Dutch fleet trading access to the West Indies. At the conclusion of the twelve-year truce in 1621 neither side was willing to countenance a renewal, so fighting began again in the broader context of the THIRTY YEARS WAR. In the Treaty of Münster (January 1648) Spain recognized the independence of the United Provinces, which formally ceased to be part of the Holy Roman Empire.

Pieter Geyl, *The Revolt of the Netherlands, 1555–1609* (1932).

**REYMOND, PIERRE** (1513–84), French enamel painter, the head of a large workshop in LIMOGES; the products of his workshop bear his initials but are not necessarily his work. He specialized in tableware (cups, ewers, plates, dishes, etc.) decorated with mythological scenes, typically in GRISAILLE against a dark blue background. Reymond also made the enamelled altarpiece commissioned by Anne de MONT-MORENCY for the chapel of his Château d'Écouen (now the Musée de la Renaissance).

**RHENANUS, BEATUS**. See BEATUS RHENANUS.

**RHETICUS, GEORG** (1514–74), German mathematician and astronomer, born in Feldkirch, in Rhaetia (a region of the Tirol), from which he took his name; in 1528 his father, a physician, was beheaded for sorcery. In 1536 Rheticus was appointed professor of mathematics at Wittenberg, and in 1539 visited COPERNICUS in Frauenburg (now Polish Frombork). He greatly admired Copernicus' work, and in 1540 published the first account of the heliocentric cosmology Copernicus proposed (*Narratio prima de libris revolutionum Copernici*). Rheticus subsequently persuaded Copernicus to publish his own full account of this work, *De revolutionibus*, which Copernicus had been engaged upon for many years. The work appeared in 1543, edited and with a misleading preface by Andreas OSIANDER. It is not entirely clear whether Rheticus, like Osiander and REINHOLD, believed that Copernicus' system was proposed as merely another mathematical model for the purposes of calculation rather than as physically true.

In 1542 Rheticus left Wittenberg to become professor of mathematics at Leipzig. He was forced to resign in 1551 because of a sexual scandal, and thereafter worked in Poland and Hungary as a physician. He also wrote on spherical triangles and compiled tables of circular functions (sine, cosine, tangent).

*DSB*; R. S. Westman, 'The Melanchthon Circle, Rheticus and the Wittenberg Interpretation of the Copernican Theory', *Isis*, 66 (1975).

**RHETORIC**. In medieval and Renaissance Europe rhetoric was one of the seven LIBERAL ARTS, and was a central subject in schools and universities. Rhetoric was defined as the art of speaking well (or the art of persuasion), and encompassed the learning of the Latin language and the use of Latin literature as a model for style. The precepts of rhetoric were those articulated in antiquity by Quintilian and Aristotle, and the most important model for prose was Cicero. The educational purpose of dramatic productions of Latin plays in educational institutions was to enhance the command of rhetoric, which was the art that underlay public speaking (including the delivery of sermons and of disputations) and the writing of letters.

Rhetoric was deemed to have five parts: invention (the ascertaining of the materials of persuasion), disposition (the placing of the materials in an appropriate order), elocution (the study of figures of speech), memory (the methods used to commit complex subjects to memory), and 'action' (the action of speaking and the use of gesture). The principal centre of rhetoric was France, where in the sixteenth century Petrus RAMUS reformed the subject, transferring invention and disposition from the discipline of rhetoric to the sister discipline of logic. The effect of this shift was an emphasis on practical skills rather than speculative thought.

At the beginning of the sixteenth century, rhetoric was focused on Latin and (in small measure) Greek. The advent of the Reformation created a new emphasis on the use of vernacular languages, and by the end of the sixteenth century rhetoric had become the subject of vernacular preaching manuals.

Brian Vickers, *In Defence of Rhetoric* (1988); Peter Mack (ed.), *Renaissance Rhetoric* (1994).

**RHÉTORIQUEURS or *Grands Rhétoriqueurs* or (Dutch) *Rederijkers*,** groups of middle-class poets in France and the Netherlands, often organized into literary societies. On the Dutch societies (*Geschiedenis der Rederijkers*), see CHAMBERS OF RHETORIC. In France and French Flanders the term is used to denote a group of poets active in the late fifteenth and early sixteenth centuries, including Jean BOUCHET, Georges CHASTELLAIN, Guillaume CRÉTIN, Pierre GRINGORE, Jean LEMAIRES DE BELGES, Jean MAROT, Jean MOLINET, and Octavien de SAINT-GELAIS.

Kathleen Chesney (ed.), *Fleurs de rhétorique* (1950).

**RIAÑO, DIEGO DE** (d. 1534), Spanish architect who served as cathedral architect in Seville, where he designed and built the chapter house and sacristy; he also designed the elaborately decorated Seville Town Hall, which was constructed after his death according to his plans (1534–72). He is regarded as the most important exponent of the Renaissance-PLATERESQUE style in Andalusia.

MDA.

**RIARIO FAMILY,** a family of modest origins that rose to become *signori* of Imola and Forlì through their connections through marriage to the DELLA ROVERE family. Francesco della Rovere was elected as Pope SIXTUS IV in 1471, thanks in large part to the efforts of his nephew the Franciscan Pietro Riario, who bribed voters with the promises of future benefices. The pope's sister Bianca was married to Paolo Riario, and their children were the beneficiaries of papal nepotism. Pietro Riario (1445–74) was created cardinal and appointed archbishop of Florence and papal legate for all of Italy; the voracity of his sexual and financial appetites was remarkable even by the standards of papal nephews.

In 1473 Pope Sixtus bought Imola from Galeazzo Maria SFORZA, duke of Milan, and appointed Pietro's brother Girolamo as count; as part of the transaction the pope arranged for Girolamo to marry Caterina SFORZA, the duke's illegitimate daughter; in 1480 Girolamo and Caterina were

also invested with Forlì. In 1474 Pietro succumbed to his dissipations, and his place as the malevolent counsellor of Sixtus was taken by Count Girolamo; it was he who persuaded Pope Sixtus to participate in the PAZZI CONSPIRACY (1478) and to provoke a conflict with Ferrara (1482–4). Girolomo was assassinated (possibly with the connivance of Lorenzo de' MEDICI) on 14 April 1488; his widow Caterina promptly occupied the fortress of Forlì, deployed troops to subdue the city, and then governed both Forlì and Imola as regent for her son Ottaviano until they surrendered to Cesare BORGIA on 22 January 1500.

Raffaelo Riario (1461–1521), the son of Valentina Riario and Antonio Sansoni, also benefited from his uncle's position as pope. He was laden with benefices by Pope Sixtus, who in 1477 created him cardinal. He was caught up in the violent aftermath of the Pazzi Conspiracy and narrowly escaped. In 1517 he was implicated in the conspiracy against Pope LEO X mounted by Alfonso PETRUCCI, but was pardoned after paying a large fine.

**RIBADENEIRA, PEDRO DE** (1527–1611), Spanish hagiographer and historian, born in Toledo on 1 November 1527; his baptismal name was Pedro Ortiz de Cisneros, but he later adopted the surname of his maternal grandmother. He was sent to Rome to study, and on 18 September 1540, at the age of 12, was admitted by IGNATIUS LOYOLA to the nascent JESUIT Order. In 1542 he was sent to Paris to continue his studies, and in 1555 he was appointed head of the Jesuit mission in the Spanish Netherlands. He visited England in 1558 (the last year of MARY I's reign) and subsequently wrote a two-volume history of the English schism, the *Historia eclesiástica del scisma del reino de Inglaterra* (1588–93), which was regularly reprinted and later incorporated into the *De origine et progressu schismatis Anglicani* of Nicholas SANDERS.

In 1560 Ribadeneira was appointed provincial of the Jesuit Order in Tuscany, and he was subsequently transferred to Sicily, Flanders, and Spain. In 1574 he settled permanently in Madrid, where he died on 10 September 1611. His writings include a classic biography of Ignatius Loyola, which was published in Latin (*Vita Ignatii Loyolae*, Naples, 1572) and then in his own Spanish translation (1583); Ribadeneira denied that Ignatius had wrought any miracle other than the creation of the Jesuits, but when the process of canonization began to gather pace, he was able to publish a revised account (1609) which attested the requisite number of miracles. His other important works were a consolatory treatise addressed to the Spanish people in the wake of the defeat of the Spanish ARMADA (*Tratado de la tribulación*, 1589), a refutation of MACHIAVELLI's *Prince* (*Tratado de la religión*, 1595), and two volumes of saints' lives (*Flos sanctorum*, 1599 and 1601).

**RIBALTA, FRANCISCO** (1565–1628), Spanish painter, probably trained at the ESCORIAL under Juan FERNÁNDEZ DE NAVARRETE. By 1599 he was living and working in Valencia, where his style gradually changed from MANNERIST to Spanish BAROQUE. His paintings include *The Vision of Father Francisco Jerónimo Simó* (1612, National Gallery, London) and two works made for the CAPUCHINS, *St Francis Comforted by an Angel* (*c*.1620, Prado) and *St Francis Embracing Christ* (*c*.1620, Museo de Bellas Artes, Valencia).

*MDA*; D. F. Darby, *Francisco Ribalta and his School* (1938); C. G. Espresati, *Ribalta* (1948); David Kowal, *Ribalta y los Ribaltescos* (1985).

**RIBAUT or Ribault, JEAN** (1520–65), French colonizer, a native of Dieppe. On the eve of the outbreak of the WARS OF RELIGION, Ribaut was appointed by Admiral Gaspard de COLIGNY as the commander of an expedition travelling to America with the purpose of establishing a colony (and refuge) for French HUGUENOTS. He sailed with two ships on 18 February 1562, and on 1 May landed in Florida at the mouth of a river which he named Rivière de Mai (now St Johns river, near Jacksonville). He travelled up the coast and settled his colonists on what is now Parris Island (near Beaufort, South Carolina), constructing for their protection Fort Charles at nearby Port Royal. Ribaut returned to France, which was now engulfed in civil war, and the following year may have travelled to England, where his *True and Last Discovery of Florida* was published in 1563.

The Parris Island colony failed, in part because the war cut off supplies from the colonists, who rebelled against the governor and sailed back to Europe. In 1565 Coligny again sent Ribaut to America, this time to inspect and assist the colony established by René de Laudonnière on the Rivière de Mai. While he was visiting the colony, it was attacked by the Spanish forces of Pedro MENÉNDEZ DE AVILÉS, who murdered the colonists and the garrison. Two of Ribaut's ships escaped, but they were shipwrecked and the crews and surviving colonists surrendered to Menéndez on the strength of his promise that they would be spared; Menéndez then ordered Ribaut and the other survivors to be executed, and gibbeted their bodies with the inscription 'no por franceses sino por herejes' ('not as Frenchmen but as heretics', i.e. Protestants). The attack was avenged by Dominique de Gourges three years later: he hanged the Spanish garrison at Fort San Mateo (as the fort had been renamed) and inscribed on a pine tablet the words 'non comme Espagnoles mais comme assassins' ('not as Spaniards but as murderers').

**RIBEIRO, BERNARDIM** (*c*.1482–1552), Portuguese poet and novelist. He was born in Torrão (Alentejo) and studied law at Lisbon (1507–12). His early poems were published in Garcia de RESENDE's *Cancioneiro geral* (1516). Joana Zagola, the lady whom he aspired to marry, was snatched away, first by marriage to another and then, after she was widowed, to a convent; Ribeiro responded with his octosyllabic *Éclogas*, which were among the first PASTORAL poems to be written in Portuguese. In about 1522 Ribeiro travelled to Italy, where he wrote his semi-autobiographical chivalric pastoral romance *Menina e Moça* (sometimes called the *Saudades*), which was posthumously published in Ferrara in 1554 together with a continuation called the *Crisfal*, which is attributed to Cristóvão Falcão (*c*.1518–*c*.1554); the *Crisfal* is so close to the style and sentiment of Ribeiro's work that it is difficult to ascertain whether it is a skilful imitation or another work by

Ribeiro. Ribeiro returned to Lisbon in 1524 and entered the secretariat of the new king, JOHN III; towards the end of his life he fell prey to mental illness.

Izabel Margato, *As saudades da 'Menina e Moça'* (1988); Paulo Meneses, '*Menina e Moça' de Bernardim Ribeiro* (1998); Helder Macedo, *Do significado oculto da 'Menina e Moça'* (2nd edn. 1999).

**RICCI, MATTEO** (1552–1610), missionary in China, born in Macerata (in the March of Ancona) on 7 October 1552; he entered the JESUIT College in Rome in 1571, where he specialized in the study of the natural sciences. In 1578 he was sent by his Order to Goa and in 1582 to Macao, where he studied the Chinese language. In 1583 he moved to Zhaoqing, 65 kilometres (40 miles) west of Guangzhou (Canton). Ricci's collection of scientific instruments (including clocks, optical devices, and cosmographical instruments), globes, maps (including a map of the world), and books of European engravings excited the interest of the viceregal court, and feats of memory and his knowledge of the application of mathematics to map projection and sundials made him welcome amongst Chinese scientists. Ricci was forced to leave the country in 1589 and migrated, with the permission of the viceroy, to Shaoguan, 185 kilometres (115 miles) north of Guangzhou. In 1595 he moved to northern China, first to Nan-ch'eng (Kiangsi province), then to Nanching (Nanking) and finally to Beijing (Peking), where he was welcomed by the emperor on 24 January 1601 and remained until his death on 11 May 1610.

Ricci wrote prolifically in Chinese, publishing proselytizing books on Christianity and treatises on geography, geometry, and cosmology. His missionary work was controversial, because he allowed converts to practise Confucian rites of ancestor worship (on the grounds that the ceremonies were civil rather than religious in character). The controversy about the propriety of his concessions to Confucian practices continued long after his death, and was finally decided against him by Pope Clement IX in judgments of 1704 and 1715.

Vincent Cronin, *The Wise Man from the West* (1955).

**RICCIO, IL, or Andrea Briosco** (1470–1532), Italian sculptor, a native of Trento who spent his working life in Padua as a sculptor in bronze and terracotta. He specialized in small bronzes, sometimes for churches but often for domestic use in objects such as inkwells and firedogs or for display as statuettes. His finest surviving work is a bronze paschal candlestick (1507–16, Basilica del Santo, Padua) which combines classical and Christian ornament in a profusion of figures and relief scenes. He also made PLAQUETTES based on engravings by MANTEGNA.

*MDA* s.v. Riccio, Andrea.

**RICH, BARNABE** (*c*.1540–1617), English writer. From 1562 Rich was in military service in France and the Low Countries, and served for a decade in Ireland from 1572. From 1574 he turned to writing, producing 25 books, including romances, in the style of EUPHUISM, discussions of military affairs and Irish government, and satires. His *Rich His Farewell* *to the Military Profession* (1581) included 'Apollonius and Silla', the source for SHAKESPEARE's *Twelfth Night*.

*DNB.*

**RICHARD III** (1452–85), king of England. A brother of EDWARD IV, Richard proved loyal during the crisis of 1470–1, when Edward briefly lost his throne to the restored HENRY VI. As Edward re-established his hold over his kingdom, Richard secured a power base in the north, was granted land in Cumberland, and led English forces against the Scots in 1480. On the death of Edward in 1483, he made a bid for the throne, capturing and imprisoning Edward's sons, EDWARD V and his brother Richard. Opposition in the south was led by Henry Tudor, later HENRY VII, but Richard retained the crown. In 1485, Henry Tudor challenged him again, with French support; Richard was defeated and killed at Bosworth, and Henry claimed the throne. Represented as one of SHAKESPEARE's most memorable villains, Richard's reputation is still much debated; certainly the hunchback which Shakespeare ascribed to him is an invention. It is difficult however to exonerate him from at least some complicity in the murder of Edward V and his brother.

*DNB.*

**RICHIER, LIGIER** (*c*.1500–1567), French sculptor, born into a family of sculptors in Lorraine. His best-known sculpture is the group carved in 1553 for the Easter Sepulchre in the Church of Saint-Étienne in Saint-Mihiel (Lorraine), in which Gothic figures are combined with Italianate drapery. In these statues, and in the skeleton statue on the tomb of René de Châlons (now in the Church of Saint-Pierre in Bar-le-Duc) the religious intensity and grim naturalism of the figures takes the Gothic idom to a macabre extreme. Richier became a Huguenot, and in 1564 left France as a religious refugee and settled in Geneva.

*MDA*; Catherine Bourdieu, *Ligier Richier: Sculpteur lorrain* (1998).

**RIDLEY, NICHOLAS** (1500–55), English reformer. Educated at Cambridge, Ridley was successively fellow of Pembroke Hall, Cambridge (*c*.1530), chaplain to CRANMER (1537), master of Pembroke (1540), bishop of Rochester (1547), and bishop of London (1550). His reformist opinions were especially influential in shaping the development of the Church in the reign of EDWARD VI. He assisted Cranmer in the preparation of the first Book of COMMON PRAYER, and promulgated Protestant doctrines in his London diocese. He was deprived under MARY and imprisoned; with LATIMER he defended reformist religion in disputation at Oxford but was burnt at the stake for heresy.

*DNB.*

**RIDOLFI CONSPIRACY**, one of many attempts to free MARY, QUEEN OF SCOTS, during her imprisonment in England, and hence aid the restoration of Catholicism. In 1571 Roberto Ridolfi, an Italian banker, plotted with the duke of Norfolk and others to this end, but their plans came to the attention of CECIL and were thwarted. Norfolk, who had also been implicated in the NORTHERN REBELLION, was executed, but Ridolfi escaped.

**RIED or Rieth VON PIESTING, BENEDIKT** (*c*.1454–1534), German mason and architect who served as master of the king's works in Bohemia. His structures mediate between the GOTHIC style that he inherited and the Renaissance Italian style that he introduced into BOHEMIAN ARCHITECTURE. Ried's greatest work is the Vladislav Hall (1493–1502) in the Old Royal Palace (Starý Královský Palác) on the Hradčany in Prague; this vast room is remarkable both for its ribbed Gothic vaulting, in which the structural ribs are supplemented with liernes (decorative tertiary ribs), and for the resolutely Italianate decoration of the windows and doorways. The late Gothic organ gallery constructed in Prague Cathedral in the early 1490s, in which the vault ribs imitate the branches of a tree, also seems to be Ried's work, but the attribution is not secure.

Ried was also responsible for the design of the vault of the magnificent Gothic Cathedral of St Barbara in Kutná Hora, in which the ribs resemble a network of lozenges (the vault was constructed in the 1540s to his design), and for the design and construction of the similarly exuberant vault in the Church of St Nicholas at Louny.

G. Fehr, *Benedikt Rieth* (1961).

**RIEMENSCHNEIDER, TILMAN** (*c*.1460–1531), German sculptor and woodcarver. He was born in Osterode am Harz, the son of the master of the mint in Würzburg, where he moved in 1483 and opened a workshop; he served on the town council (1504–20) and eventually became burgomaster (1520–1); he was imprisoned during the PEASANTS' WAR.

Riemenschneider worked in wood, marble, limestone, and sandstone. His best-known work is the marble tomb (completed 1513) of the Emperor Henry II (d. 1024) and his Empress Kunigunde in Bamberg Cathedral (of which Henry was the founder). His other works include the ALTARPIECE of *Mary Magdalene* for the high altar at Münnerstadt (1490–2; two panels remain in the church, but the carving of *St Mary Magdalene with Six Angels* is now in the Bayerisches Nationalmuseum in Munich), limestone statues of *Adam and Eve* for Würzburg town council (1491–3, Mainfränkisches Museum, Würzburg), the *Altar of the Holy Blood* for the Jakobskirche in Rothenburg ob der Tauber (1501–5), a triptych for Windsheim (*c*.1508), an altarpiece of the *Twelve Apostles* for St Kilian, Windsheim (1507–9, now in the Kurpfälzisches Museum in Heidelberg), and a sandstone *Lamentation* group (1520–5) for the high altar of the Cistercian abbey (now the Pfarrkirche) at Maidbronn (near Würzburg).

*MDA*; Julien Chapuis (ed.), *Tilman Riemenschneider: Master Sculptor of the Late Middle Ages* (1999).

**RIMINI or (Latin) Ariminium**, a port and bishopric in the Romagna, on the Adriatic coast of Italy. In 1237, the election of Giovanni Malatesta as PODESTÀ inaugurated a long period of rule by the MALATESTA FAMILY. The city was subjected to more than 400 air raids in 1943 and 1944, and much of its fabric (including the Palazzo Comunale of 1562) was destroyed;

the principal surviving monuments of Malatesta rule are the castle built for Sigismondo Malatesta in 1446 and ALBERTI's Malatesta Temple (Tempio Malatestiano), which was badly damaged during the war; the Temple contains allegorical paintings by AGOSTINO DI DUCCIO and a portrait of Sigismondo MALATESTA by PIERO DELLA FRANCESCA. The city was briefly ruled by Cesare BORGIA (1500–3) and by Venice (1503–9), and after 1527 was directly governed by the papacy.

Philip Jones, *The Malatesta of Rimini and the Papal State* (1974).

**RINUCCINI, OTTAVIO** (1562–1621), Italian poet and librettist, born into a prominent family in Florence. He wrote three melodramas that are among the earliest operatic libretti: his *Dafne* (1594) and *Euridice* (1600) were set to music by Jacopo PERI (the latter in collaboration with Giuglio CACCINI) and his *Arianna* (1607) by MONTEVERDI.

OCIL.

**RINUCCINI FAMILY**, Florentine family of statesmen, churchmen, humanists, and *condottieri*. Alamanno Rinuccini (1419–99) wrote a dialogue against the MEDICI, *De libertate*. Alessandro Rinuccini (1555–1622) was a Latin poet whose *Diva Catharina martyr* reflected the cult of Catherine of Alexandria. Ottavio RINUCCINI was a poet and librettist. In the seventeenth century, Archbishop Giovanni Battista Rinuccini (1592–1653), who was born into a Roman branch of the family, was sent to Ireland as a papal nuncio (1645–9) and played a prominent role in the civil war.

**RITTER FAMILY**, a late sixteenth- and seventeenth-century family of German goldsmiths based in Nuremberg. The founder of the family was Christoph Ritter the Elder (d. 1572), whose best-known surviving work is a salt cellar topped with an enamelled *Crucifixion* group (now in a private collection in London) which he made in 1551 for the Nuremberg city treasury. His son Christoph the Younger (1548–1616) and grandson Jeremias (1582–1646) both made covered cups. Another member of the family, Wolf Christoph Ritter (1592–1634), made a table-fountain shaped like an elephant (Germanisches Nationalmuseum, Nuremberg) and a remarkable basin and bird-shaped ewer in which both pieces are covered with rock crystal (Schatzkammer der Residenz, Munich).

**RIVAUDEAU, ANDRÉ DE** (*c.*1540–1580), French Protestant playwright and poet, a native of Poitou, where his play *Aman* (1566) was performed; the subject of the play is biblical (the story of Haman, in the Book of Esther), but its form is that of ancient tragedy, though it has a happy ending. Rivaudeau's other works include biblical poems and a translation of Epictetus.

**RIZZIO, DAVID** (1533–66). Secretary to MARY, QUEEN OF SCOTS, Rizzio was murdered in the presence of the queen in 1566. The murder, in which her alienated husband DARNLEY was implicated, was a demonstration by the Protestant nobility against the Catholic succession. It achieved little in itself, but signalled Protestant dissatisfaction with Mary's reign,

which, more forcefully expressed, would later force her to abdicate.

DNB.

**RIZZO, ANTONIO DI GIOVANNI** (*c.*1439–*c.*1499), Italian sculptor and architect, a native of Verona. In 1466 he settled permanently in Venice, though he worked for a time with Giovanni AMADEO on the Certosa di Pavia. In Venice Rizzo carved the tomb of Doge Niccolò Tron in Santa Maria Gloriosa dei Frari and collaborated with Andrea BREGNO on the *Adam* and *Eve* sculpted for niches in the Arco Foscari (*c.*1485, now in the Doge's Palace); they are among the earliest nude statues of the Venetian Renaissance. His architectural work in the Doge's Palace includes the Scala de' Giganti (named after the giants carved by SANSOVINO) and the façade on the eastern side of the courtyard, which had been damaged in the fire of 1483.

MDA; Anne Markham Schulz, *Antonio Rizzo: Sculptor and Architect* (1983).

**ROBERTI, ERCOLE DE'**. See ERCOLE DE ROBERTI.

**ROBIN, JEAN** (1550–1629), French botanist, herbalist, and gardener. He constructed a garden at the downstream end of the Île de la Cité in Paris. The garden was at first named after HENRI IV, who had commissioned it, but since the early seventeenth century it has been known as Place Dauphine; the dauphin was Henri IV's son, the future Louis XIII. The garden was used to develop and display Robin's collection of ornamental plants, many of which were illustrated (as botanical designs for needlework) in Pierre Vallet's *florilegium* of 1608 (*Le Jardin du roi très chrétien Henri IV*), which illustrated the plants on 75 plates. Robin grew the first false acacia in Europe from seeds collected in Virginia, and so became the eponym of *Robinia pseudoacacia*; he also popularized the tuberose (*Polianthes tuberosa*), and this interest in scented flowers led eventually to his (anonymous) publication of the *Histoire des plantes aromatiques*. He also published catalogues of his plants (*Catalogus stirpium*) in 1601 and 1619.

HENRI III conferred the title of *arboriste et simpliciste du roi* on Robin, and made him responsible for the gardens of the LOUVRE; these posts were subsequently renewed by Henri IV and Louis XIII. When the University of Paris decided in 1597 to create a BOTANICAL GARDEN, Robin was commissioned to design it. The garden, which was known as the Jardin Royal des Plantes Médicinales, was eventually constructed by Guy de la Brosse in 1626, and Robin's son Vespasian (1597–1662) was appointed head gardener; in 1718 its name was changed to Jardin Royal des Plantes, and after the Revolution it became the Jardin des Plantes.

**ROBINSON, THOMAS** (*fl.* 1589–1609), English composer, lutenist, cittern player, and teacher. His playing technique is outlined in *The School of Music* (1603) in which he suggests more consistent use of the right thumb and the innovative idea of also making use of the third finger.

**ROBORTELLI, FRANCESCO** (1516–67), Italian classical scholar, born in Udine; he studied in Bologna and subsequently taught in Lucca, Pisa, Venice, and Padua. Robortelli edited Greek and Roman texts, most notably Aristotle's *Poetics*, which he published in an annotated Latin edition (Florence, 1548).

**ROCK CRYSTAL**, the lapidary term for silicon dioxide, popularly known as quartz, of which it is a variety. Its transparency commended it to GEM carvers, who found it particularly suitable for objects decorated in INTAGLIO; its hardness meant that it was usually ground with a wheel rather than carved. The grinding of rock crystal has a continuous history in Europe since antiquity. The most important engravers of rock crystal were Valerio BELLI, Giovanni BERNARDI, Annibale FONTANA, the MISERONI FAMILY (who worked in the imperial service), and the SARACCHI FAMILY. Crystal glass (Italian *vetro di cristallo*) was developed to imitate the qualities of rock crystal, and the relative lightness of crystal glass meant that it eventually displaced rock crystal.

**RODRIGUES COELHO, MANUEL** (1583–1635), Portuguese composer and organist of Elvas Cathedral. He became organist and chaplain to the king at Lisbon in 1602. His music, published in *Flores de musica pera o instrumento de tecla & harpa* (1620), was influenced by CABEZON, SWEELINCK, and the English virginalists.

**RODRÍGUEZ DE FONSECA, JUAN** (1451–1524), Spanish bishop and statesman, born into a distinguished ecclesiastical family. He served as a chaplain to Queen ISABELLA and was appointed bishop of Badajoz (1494), Córdoba (1499), Palencia (1505), and Burgos (1514), and archbishop of Rossano, in Italy (1519). He travelled as a diplomat in the service of FERDINAND and Isabella, and from 1493 he was responsible for affairs of state relating to the exploration, conquest, and settlement of Spanish AMERICA. In the course of his political duties, Fonseca established the Council of the INDIES and the CASA DE CONTRATACIÓN DE LAS INDIAS.

*DHE.*

**ROELAS, JUAN DE LAS** (c.1560–1624), Spanish painter who entered holy orders at an unknown date before 1602, and thereafter painted for churches and monasteries in Seville. His works include *The Circumcision* (c.1606, University Church, Seville) and *The Martyrdom of St Andrew* (1609–13, Museo de Bellas Artes, Seville).

*MDA*; Enrique Val Diviesco, *Juan de Roelas* (1978).

**ROGERS, JOHN** (c.1500–1555) English publisher of Matthews's Bible. Educated at Pembroke Hall, Cambridge, Rogers was from 1534 chaplain to English merchants at Antwerp. Here he met TYNDALE and adopted Protestant principles under his influence; he also prepared his translation of the Bible for the English press. In 1537, 'Matthews's Bible' appeared under the pseudonym Thomas Matthews; Rogers contributed prefaces and some marginal notes. He returned to England in EDWARD VI's reign and was given preferments in London, becoming prebendary and then divinity lecturer at St Paul's Cathedral. He preached prominently against the papacy under MARY, and became the first Protestant martyr of her reign, burnt for heresy at Smithfield, London.

*DNB.*

**ROGERS, WILLIAM** (*fl.* 1589–1604), the first known professional English engraver. He may have been trained in the Netherlands, possibly in the studio of the WIERIX FAMILY in Antwerp. He specialized in portraits and title pages; his portraits include Queen ELIZABETH, the earl of ESSEX, and King HENRI IV of France, and his title pages CAMDEN's *Britannia* (1600) and GERARD's *Herbal* (1597).

*DNB*; *MDA* s.v. Rogers, William (i).

**ROJAS, FERNANDO DE** (c.1465–1541), Spanish playwright, born into a *converso* family in Puebla de Montalbán (Toledo). He studied at Salamanca, but on returning to his birthplace found his family under investigation by the Spanish INQUISITION. He later moved to Talavera, where he became a successful judge and where he lived for the rest of his life.

Fernando de Rojas was the author of the *Tragicomedia de Calisto y Melibea*, popularly known as *Celestina*, the pre-eminent literary work of fifteenth-century Spain; the earliest surviving edition was published in Burgos in 1499. The play, which exists in versions of sixteen acts (*auctos*) and 21 acts, recounts through dialogues the story of the love affair of the noble youth Calisto and the girl Melibea, and of the band of cheating servants, prostitutes, and ruffians, led by the aged procuress Celestina, who facilitate the seduction. The work is richly comic, but ends with the violent death of all the protagonists. Though based on Roman and Italian humanist comedy, *Celestina* is a totally original work in style, genre, and tone. It quickly proved to be enormously popular: in the course of the sixteenth century some 60 editions and six sequels were published. Its sexual explicitness and amoral pessimism did not trouble the Spanish INQUISITION, which was content simply to excise anticlerical passages.

Peter Dunn, *Fernando de Rojas* (1975); Ricardo Castells, *Fernando de Rojas and the Renaissance Vision* (2000).

**ROLLENHAGEN, GABRIEL** (1583–1619), German playwright and writer on EMBLEMS. He was born in Magdeburg, the son of Georg ROLLENHAGEN, and became a lawyer in the employment of the Church. His comedy *Amantes amentes* (1609) is a dramatization in German (with comic scenes in Low German) of the Latin version of the story of Euryalus and Lucretia by Piccolomini (later Pope PIUS II). He also compiled an influential book of emblems, *Nucleus emblematum selectissimorum* (2 vols., 1610–13).

*DLL.*

**ROLLENHAGEN, GEORG** (1542–1609), German dramatist who was born in Bernau (near Berlin) and studied theology at Wittenberg. He became a teacher in Halberstadt in 1563 and returned to Wittenberg as a private tutor in 1566. In 1573 he settled in Magdeburg as a Lutheran pastor and (two years later) headmaster.

Rollenhagen wrote *Froschmeuseler*, a moralistic animal epic loosely based on *Batrachomyomachia*, the pseudo-Homeric battle of the frogs and mice. He also wrote three biblical dramas which were intended for performance by his pupils: *Abraham* (1569), *Tobias* (1576), and *Vom reichen Manne und armen Lazaro* (1590), the last of which shows how the lives of rich and poor on earth will be reversed in heaven.

DLL.

**ROMANINO, GIROLAMO** (1484/7–1559/61), Italian painter, a native of Brescia and a contemporary of MORETTO DA BRESCIA. The influence of GIORGIONE on his style was so marked that problems of attribution arise. His surviving religious paintings include the *Enthroned Madonna with Saints and Angels* (Museo Civico, Padua) and *St Matthew and the Angel* (San Giovanni Evangelista, Cremona). His finest work is a mythological cycle of frescoes in the Castello del Buon Consiglio in Trento.

MDA; Alessandro Nova, *Girolamo Romanino* (1994).

**ROMANO, GIAN CRISTOFORO, or Giovanni Cristoforo Ganti** (c.1465–1512), Italian sculptor, born in Rome, where he trained in the studio of Andrea BREGNO. He subsequently worked in a series of north Italian cities. In Milan he carved the tomb of Gian Galeazzo VISCONTI for the Certosa di Pavia (1493–7) and executed a sculpted portrait of Francesco SFORZA (Bargello, Florence); in Mantua he executed a marble bust of Isabella d'ESTE (Louvre); in Urbino he sculpted FEDERICO DA MONTEFELTRO (Bargello, Florence).

DBI s.v. Ganti; MDA s.v. Gian Cristoforo Romano.

**ROME.** In 330 the capital of the Empire was removed from Rome to Constantinople, and thereafter the city declined in importance. Medieval Rome was a small city within the PAPAL STATE characterized by lawlessness and the feuds of its noble families, especially the COLONNA and the ORSINI. For most of the fourteenth century the papacy was seated in Avignon, and it did not return permanently to Rome until the accession of Pope NICHOLAS V in 1447. Pope Nicholas, who is sometimes described as the first of the Renaissance popes, inherited a city that had been sacked in 1413 by the forces of LADISLAS OF DURAZZO, and set about creating a papal capital out of the ruins.

From 1447 to 1527, when the SACK OF ROME left the city a smouldering ruin, Pope Nicholas and his successors rebuilt Rome. The most important of the Renaissance popes with respect to the fabric of the city was SIXTUS IV, who widened and paved the streets, commissioned new buildings (including the SISTINE CHAPEL), and encouraged scholarship and art on an unprecedented scale. Sixtus was the first of a succession of popes who lived and governed like secular Renaissance princes.

The period known as the High Renaissance in Rome corresponds to the pontificates of JULIUS II (1503–13) and LEO X (1513–21), when the city's architects and artists included BRAMANTE, MICHELANGELO, RAPHAEL, and (for a short period) LEONARDO DA VINCI and its writers included BANDELLO, BEMBO, and TRISSINO. The most important Roman building of this period was ST PETER'S BASILICA, for which Bramante and Raphael were the first architects.

Many of the palaces and churches of Rome were destroyed in the sack of 1527–8, but the city was slowly rebuilt. Reconstruction began with PAUL III (1534–39), who commissioned Michelangelo to complete the *Last Judgement* in the SISTINE CHAPEL and to supervise the reconstruction of St Peter's. Later in the century, SIXTUS V (1585–90), the architect of BAROQUE Rome, commissioned Domenico FONTANA to build new streets to link the seven pilgrimage churches and supplied the city with clean drinking water piped in by an aqueduct. Sixtus rebuilt the Lateran Palace and the VATICAN LIBRARY and completed the dome of St Peter's. St Peter's Basilica was completed in 1614 and consecrated in 1626; Bernini's colonnade in the piazza of St Peter's was added between 1656 and 1671.

P. Partner, *Renaissance Rome* (1976).

**RONCALLI, CRISTOFORO, or Il Pomarancio** (1553–1626), Italian painter, born in Pomarancio (near Volterra). He worked for twenty years (1590–1610) painting frescoes in the Vatican and the Palazzo del Quirinale. He also attracted the patronage of Marchese Vicenzo GIUSTINIANI, whom he accompanied in 1606 on a journey to Germany, the Netherlands, England, and France.

MDA.

**RONDELET, GUILLAUME** (1507–66), French physician and marine zoologist, a native of Montpellier who travelled widely in Europe before returning in 1545 to Montpellier, where he taught medicine. His principal works of ichthyology were *De piscibus marinis* (Lyon, 1554) and *Universae aquatilium historiae* (Lyon, 1555), both of which are greatly expanded versions of the *De aquatilibus* (Paris, 1553) of Pierre Belon, who had described some 110 fish; Rondelet described 197 marine fish and 47 freshwater fish, and his early training in anatomy enabled him to describe fish in unprecedented detail.

DSB.

**RONSARD, PIERRE DE** (1524–85), French poet and leader of the PLÉIADE. He was born in Manoir de la Possonière (near Vendôme) and became a page at the royal court. He accompanied Madeleine d'Orléans (daughter of FRANCIS I) to Scotland after her marriage to King JAMES V (1537) and later accompanied Lazare de BAÏF on a diplomatic mission to Alsace (1540). On returning to Paris from Alsace his hopes of a military career were frustrated by the onset of a serious illness which left him partially deaf. In about 1547 Ronsard began to study at the Collège de Coqueret, where his tutors included DORAT.

Ronsard contributed to the *Défence et illustration de la langue française* (1549), which appeared under Joachim DU BELLAY's name, and in 1550 published his first collection, *Les Quatre Premiers Livres des Odes*; this collection was faithful to the precepts of the *Défence* and was divided between imitation of the Pindaric and Horatian odes. In 1552 Ronsard published a fifth book of odes and *Les Amours* (a cycle of 183 Petrarchan love sonnets), accompanied by musical settings;

in a revised edition published the following year Ronsard added new poems and a commentary by MURET.

In the mid-1550s Ronsard published two further cycles of love poems and two books of *Hymns*. The love poems (chansons and sonnets), entitled the *Continuation des amours* (1555) and the *Nouvelle Continuation des Amours* (1556), are addressed to a peasant girl called Marie, and turn away from the Petrarchism of *Les Amours* (which was in the tradition of *amour courtois*) towards a more direct and erotic portrayal of love in the spirit of the *Greek Anthology*. The *Hymnes* of 1555–6 are not Christian hymns, but are rather celebrations of important men, natural phenomena, and idealized abstractions (e.g. Justice), in the tradition, at least in part, of Marullus.

Ronsard's late poetry reflects the confessional rift that led to the outbreak of the WARS OF RELIGION in 1562. He turned his pen to the service of the Church and the crown and wrote works such as the *Remonstrance au peuple de France* (1562), which led to his becoming embroiled in debate with Protestant polemicists. In 1564 he published *Élégies, mascarades et bergerie*, a collection of verse written for the court entertainments commissioned by CATHERINE DE MÉDICIS.

From the mid-1560s Ronsard was preoccupied with the collective editions of his work, of which six were published between 1560 and 1587. During this period he also wrote the first four books of a national epic, *La Franciade* (1572; the remaining twenty books were never written), and a third cycle of love poems, the *Sonnets pour Hélène* (dedicated to a lady-in-waiting at the court of Queen Catherine), which mark both a return to the Petrarchan style and something of a poetic retrospective.

Terence Cave (ed.), *Ronsard the Poet* (1973); Daniel Ménager, *Ronsard* (1979); Michel Simonin, *Pierre de Ronsard* (1990).

**RORE, CIPRIANO DE** (*c*.1515/16–1565), Netherlandish composer active in Brescia, Ferrara, Venice, and Parma. From 1546 he was *maestro di cappella* at the court of Duke Ercole II d'ESTE; during the following decade he wrote masses for specific occasions for the Este household, and madrigals which bear all the chromatic hallmarks of the Ferrarese school of this period. His international reputation grew and he was commissioned by Duke ALBRECHT V of Bavaria to write motets. He is principally known as a madrigalist.

**RORITZER or Roriczer FAMILY**, a dynasty of German architects in fifteenth- and early sixteenth-century Regensburg, where they built the cathedral; Wenzel, the first master mason, died in 1419 and was succeeded by his son Konrad (*c*.1419–1477) and his grandson Mathäus (d. 1495). The family also contributed to the Frauenkirche in Munich, the Lorenzkirche in Nuremberg, and the Stefansdom in Vienna. In 1486 Mathäus published *Büchlein von der Fialen Gerechtigkeit*, a treatise on Gothic finials, the ornamental pieces (usually in the form of a fleur-de-lis) at the top of canopies and pinnacles. Mathäus was succeeded by his brother Wolfgang, who was executed in 1514, thus bringing the dynasty to an end.

*MDA*; L. R. Shelby, *Gothic Design Techniques: The Fifteenth-Century Design Booklets of Mathäus Roritzer and Hans Schuttermayer* (1977).

**ROSE**, an octagonal Elizabethan playhouse in Bankside, the earliest of the three theatres (the others were the SWAN and the GLOBE) on the south bank of the Thames close to what is now Southwark Bridge. It was built in 1586–7 by Philip HENSLOWE. It is not clear how the building was used for the first five years of its short life, but from 1592, when the building was substantially altered, it was occupied by STRANGE'S MEN; from 1564 to 1600 it provided a base for the ADMIRAL'S MEN, thereafter being occupied by a number of different companies. Plays by Christopher MARLOWE and the first performances of William SHAKESPEARE's *Henry VI* were given here. In 1604 Henslowe's lease expired and the following year the building was demolished. The site of the Rose was uncovered in 1989 and plans exist for re-excavation.

www.rosetheatre.org.uk.

**ROSENPLÜT or Rosenblut, HANS** (*c*.1400–*c*.1470), Nuremberg poet and playwright, a brass-founder who in 1444 was appointed master gunner (*Büchsenmeister*) of the city. He was the author of the earliest surviving FASTNACHTSPIELE, which include a play called *Des Türken Vasnachtspil* (1456) which favourably compares the orderliness of Ottoman government with the oppressive governments of the HOLY ROMAN EMPIRE. He wrote SPRÜCHE on the same subject and on the HUSSITE WARS, and also composed many SCHWÄNKE and drinking songs (*Weinsegen* and *Weingrüsse*) and was the finest exponent of the *Priameln*, a verse form in which an elaborate preamble leads to a sharp punch-line. Rosenplüt eschewed conventional poetic diction, preferring instead to lace his verse with demotic crudities and obscenities designed to delight his readers.

**ROSICRUCIANS**, a secret society whose members venerated the rose (as an emblem of resurrection) and the cross (as an emblem of redemption). The founding documents of the society were two anonymous documents published in Germany, the *Fama fraternitatis* (1614) and the *Confessio fraternitatis* (1615); it is possible that these works were written by the Lutheran pastor Johann Valentin Andreæa (1586–1654), who in 1616 published the *Chymische Hochzeit Christiani Rosenkreutz*. All three works are indebted to John DEE's *Monas hieroglyphica*, which circulated in manuscript until it was published in 1654.

**ROSSELLI, COSIMO** (1439–1507), Italian artist, a native of Florence who trained in the studio of Benozzo GOZZOLI. His surviving paintings include an *Annunciation* (1473, Louvre), frescoes in the cloister of the Church of the SS Annunziata and the Church of Sant'Ambrogio in Florence, and frescoes in the SISTINE CHAPEL in Rome (1481). His own pupils included Fra BARTOLOMEO and PIERO DI COSIMO.

*MDA*; Arthur Blumenthal (ed.), *Cosimo Rosselli: Painter of the Sistine Chapel* (2001).

**ROSSELLI, FRANCESCO, or (French) FRANÇOIS ROUSSEL** (*c*.1510–after 1577), French composer, active in Lyon until he was appointed *magister puerorum* at the Cappella Giulia (1548) and *maestro di cappella* of San Lorenzo in Damaso (1564). He wrote madrigals and chansons and his sacred music comprises masses and motets.

**ROSSELLINO, ANTONIO** (1427/8–79), Italian sculptor, born in Florence; he was the younger brother of Bernardo ROSSELLINO. His principal surviving work is the tomb of the cardinal-prince of Portugal in San Miniato al Monte (1461–6), Florence. The tomb was admired by Antonio PICCOLOMINI, duke of Amalfi, who commissioned a replica for the Church of Monte Oliveto in Naples to commemorate his wife Maria of Aragon (d. 1470). A terracotta *Madonna and Child*, presumably made in preparation for a now unknown marble statue, is in the Victoria and Albert Museum.

MDA.

**ROSSELLINO, BERNARDO** (*c*.1407/10–1464), Italian architect and sculptor, born in Florence. In the early 1430s he worked as a sculptor in Arezzo, where his surviving work includes a terracotta *Annunciation* in the cathedral and the *Madonna della Misericordia* relief in the tympanum of the Palazzo della Fraternità. His principal work of the 1440s was the architectural tomb of Leonardo BRUNI (1444–50), in Santa Croce, Florence.

In the second half of his career Rossellino worked primarily as an architect. In the 1450s he worked in Rome as *ingegnere di palazzo* to Pope NICHOLAS V, and on returning to

The lantern surmounting BRUNELLESCHI's dome on Florence Cathedral. The lantern was built by **Bernardo Rossellino**

Florence he built the Palazzo Rucellai (to ALBERTI's design) and added the lantern to BRUNELLESCHI's dome on the cathedral.

Rossellino's most important work as an architect and town planner was the remodelling of PIENZA (1459–64) for Pope PIUS II. Rossellino laid out the piazza (in Florentine style) and a grid of streets; the layout is the earliest example of symmetrical TOWN PLANNING. When Pope Pius and Rossellino died in 1464, only a few houses had been completed, but the project continued, and Rossellino's plans were implemented in the buildings grouped around the Piazza Pio II, including Palazzo Piccolomini and the cathedral.

MDA; C. R. Meek, *Studies in the Architectural Career of Bernardo di Matteo Gamberelli called Rossellino* (1980); Anne Markham Schulz, *The Sculpture of Bernardo Rossellino and his Workshop* (1977).

**ROSSETER, PHILIP** (1567/8–1623), English composer, lutenist at the court of JAMES I from 1603; he worked with John DOWLAND and Thomas FORD. His *Book of Ayres* (1601) is a collection of songs by CAMPION and Rosseter; they have lute and bass viol accompaniment, while his *Lessons for Consort* (1609) are written for lute, bandora, cittern flute, and treble and bass viols. With Robert Keystar he managed the former Children of the Queen's Revels at the WHITEFRIARS Theatre.

**ROSSETTI, BIAGIO** (1447–1516), Italian architect and town planner. He became ducal architect of FERRARA in 1483, and in that capacity designed an extension to the city of Ferrara that trebled the space within the walls; his extension is called the *Addizione Erculea* (Herculean Addition) in honour of his patron Ercole I d'ESTE. The most important building in the *Addizione* is Rossetti's Palazzo dei Diamanti, which owes its name to the 12,500 diamond-shaped blocks of marble in its façade; it is now the city art gallery. He also designed the principal buildings in the Piazza Nuova: Palazzo Bevilacqua, Palazzo Rondinelli, and his own house, Casa Rossetti. Of the four very different churches that he designed for the *Addizione*, San Cristoforo and San Francesco have been relatively unchanged, but San Benedetto and Santa Maria in Vado have been damaged and rebuilt.

MDA; B. Zevi, *Biagio Rossetti, architetto ferrarese* (1960); Ada Marcianò, *L'età di Biagio Rossetti* (1991).

**ROSSETTO, STEFANO** (*fl.* 1560–80), Italian composer. While he was in the service of Cardinal Ferdinando de' Medici in Florence he wrote madrigals, motets, and music for the 1567 Carnival. His *Lamento d'Olimpia* (1567) is characteristic of his interest in madrigal cycles. He was later court organist at Munich.

**ROSSI, SALOMONE** (*c*.1570–*c*.1630), Italian composer, held in sufficiently high esteem at the Gonzaga court in Mantua that he did not have to wear the yellow badge which marked out members of the Jewish community. He wrote secular vocal and instrumental music and his *Hashirim asher lish'lomo* ('The Songs of Solomon', 1622) contains polyphonic settings of Hebrew psalms, hymns, and synagogal songs.

**ROSSO FIORENTINO, IL, or Giovanni Battista di Jacopo** (1494–1540), Italian painter, a native of Florence, where he probably trained alongside PONTORMO in the studio of ANDREA DEL SARTO. He worked in Florence (1413–23) and Rome (1423–7) and elsewhere in Italy before accepting the invitation of FRANCIS I to decorate FONTAINEBLEAU in collaboration with PRIMATICCIO. Their work proved to be very influential, and eventually came to be regarded as the foundation of a style of art known as the School of FONTAINEBLEAU.

The paintings of Il Rosso's Italian period, such as his *Deposition* (1521, Palazzo dei Priori, Volterra) and *Moses and Jethro's Daughters* (1523, Uffizi), are characterized by distorted figures and daring colour contrasts which combine to create an atmosphere of dramatic intensity. At Fontainebleau Il Rosso was responsible for the decoration of the Galerie François I, which includes the first STRAPWORK, a decorative motif that Il Rosso seems to have invented. The paintings of his French period, such as the *Pietà* executed for the Constable Anne de Montmorency (now in the Louvre), have an individualistic style, albeit one adapted to the tastes of the French court.

*MDA*; David Franklin, *Rosso in Italy* (1994).

**ROTA, BERNARDINO** (1508–75), Italian poet and dramatist, born in Naples, where he became a prominent literary figure. He wrote poetry in both Latin and Italian; his best-known poems are 26 sonnets expressing his grief at the death of his wife. Rota also wrote two comedies, *Scilinguato* and *Strabalzi*.

*OCIL*.

**ROTHMANN, BERNDT or Bernhard** (*c.*1495–*c.*1535), German ANABAPTIST leader, born in Münster, the son of a blacksmith, and educated by the BRETHREN OF THE COMMON LIFE. In 1529 he was appointed chaplain of the Church of St Mauritz in Warendorf (near Münster). In 1531 he visited Wittenberg (where he met MELANCHTHON) and Strassburg (where he met Wolfgang CAPITO) and returned to Warendorf as a Lutheran convert. That autumn he took part in a public debate on the subject of PURGATORY, whereupon he was silenced by his bishop but supported by the council and guilds of Münster.

In January 1532 Rothmann moved from Warendorf to Münster, where he became minister of the Church of St Lambert. A few months later he published his Confession of Faith, which was broadly Lutheran, but on the subject of the EUCHARIST resolutely Zwinglian. In June of the same year he successfully opposed the Lutherans of Marburg in a disputation held in Münster, and so was able, together with his followers, to occupy the pulpits of Münster. His position was consolidated by the arrival in Münster of six SACRAMENTARIAN preachers from Wassenberg (Jülich).

In 1533 Rothmann replied to the Marburg Lutherans in his *Bekenntnisse van beiden Sacramenten*, which rejected infant BAPTISM and so aligned him with the Anabaptists and against the Lutherans and Zwinglians. In 1534 Rothmann and his followers were rebaptized by the followers of Melchior HOFF-MAN, by which time Münster had become an Anabaptist city-state.

Rothmann's precise role in the Anabaptist kingdom of MÜNSTER led by JOHN OF LEIDEN is uncertain, but at the least he defended the notion of Münster as the New Jerusalem in two tracts published in 1534, *Restitution rechter und gesunder christlicher Lehre* and *Bericht von der Wrake*. The city fell in June 1535, but it is not known whether Rothmann was killed or managed to escape.

*Die Schriften Bernhard Rothmanns*, ed. R. Stupperich (1970).

**ROTTENHAMMER, JOHANN** (1564/5–1625), German painter, trained in Rome, where he worked with Paul BRIL. He specialized in mythological subjects set against LAND-SCAPE backgrounds (e.g. *Fall of Phaethon*, *c.*1604, Mauritshuis, The Hague) and religious paintings (e.g. *Coronation of the Virgin*, National Gallery, London). His pictures were usually small, and were often painted on copper.

*MDA*.

**ROUSSEL, GÉRARD** (*c.*1500–1555), French humanist and reformer. He was born near Amiens and became a follower of Jacques LEFÈVRE D'ÉTAPLES, under whose guidance he edited works by Boethius and Aristotle. He followed Lefèvre to Meaux, where he became a canon at the cathedral and preached the need for ecclesiastical reform. In 1524 he was suspended by Bishop BRIÇONNET, who feared that Roussel's preaching could endanger the diocese. Roussel left France for Strassburg, and returned eleven years later at the invitation of King FRANCIS I. In 1536 he was consecrated as bishop of Oloron, where he enjoyed the patronage and protection of MARGUERITE D'ANGOULÊME. His sermons in Oloron advocated biblical study, and he began to administer the EUCHARIST in both kinds (i.e. wine as well as bread was given to communicants), for which he was censured by the University of Paris. He was killed in 1555 (the traditional date of 1550 is wrong) by an attacker who chopped down his pulpit as he was preaching.

Charles Schmidt, *Gérard Roussel: Prédicateur de la reine Marguerite de Navarre* (1845).

**ROWLEY, WILLIAM** (*c.*1585–*c.*1637), English actor and playwright. Following early plays for QUEEN ANNE'S MEN, Rowley worked in collaboration with other dramatists, typically providing comic subplots. He wrote five plays with Thomas MIDDLETON, including *The Changeling* (1622); he also collaborated with DEKKER, FORD, FLETCHER, and WEBSTER. As an actor, he specialized in clowning roles. From 1609 he was a member of PRINCE CHARLES'S MEN, becoming leader in 1616.

*DNB*.

**RUCELLAI, BERNARDO** (1448–1514), historian and garden designer, the son of Giovanni RUCELLAI. He was a confidant and supporter of Lorenzo de' MEDICI, and the author of *De bello Italico*, an account of CHARLES VIII's invasion of 1494–5 (published 1724); the importance of this book extends well beyond the chronicle of events, because it introduced to political theory the notion of the balance of power. Rucellai also laid out the gardens known in English as the Rucellai Gardens and in Italian as the Orti Oricellari; these gardens, just off the Via della Scala in Florence (between what is now the Via Bernardo Rucellai and the Via degli Orti Oricellari), were famous for their TOPIARY, which was used to create plants shaped as humans, animals (apes, donkeys, and a bear), buildings (porticoes and temples), geometrical shapes, urns, and giants. The gardens later became the setting for an outdoor academy convened by Rucellai's grandson Cosimo; MACHIAVELLI, who was one of the participants, set the dialogues in his *Libro dell'arte della guerra* ('Book of the Art of War', 1521) in the gardens.

Guglielmo Pellegrini, *L'umanista Bernardo Rucellai e le sua opera storiche* (1920); Felix Gilbert, 'Bernardo Rucellai and the Orti Oricellari', *Journal of the Warburg and Courtauld Institutes* (1949); Leandro Maria Bartoli and Gabriella Contorni, *Gli Orti Oricellari a Firenze: Un giardino, una città* (1991).

**RUCELLAI, GIOVANNI** (1475–1525), Italian humanist, poet, and dramatist, a member of the prominent Florentine Rucellai family. His poetry includes a georgic *Le api* (1539) modelled on Virgil's fourth *Georgic*; his plays include *Rosamunda* (1525), an adaptation of Sophocles' *Antigone*, and *Oreste*, which is based on Euripides' *Iphigenia in Tauris*.

OCIL.

**RUCKER, THOMAS** (*c.*1532–1606), German sword cutler (*Schwertfeger*). The most famous product of his Augsburg workshop is a chair made in 1574 for the Emperor RUDOLF II in Prague and kept in his Kunstkammer. The chair, which is now in Longford Castle (Wiltshire), is made of wrought and chiselled iron, and is decorated with more than 100 reliefs, each of which is enclosed within a strapwork frame.

**RUCKERS FAMILY**, Antwerp makers of harpsichords and virginals (1579–1667) including Hans (*c.*1550–1598), Johannes (1578–1643), and Andreas (1579–after 1645). The quality of their craftsmanship was evident in the beauty of their instruments and the sound they produced. The surviving virginals are rectangular, with one set of strings that runs across the player, who would sit against the long side of the instrument. The harpsichords were set up with two sets of strings, an octave apart. The double manual instruments were constructed with offset keyboards sounding a fourth apart; further complex designs were also present in compound instruments where a virginal was combined with a harpsichord.

**RUDOLF II or Rudolph II** (1552–1612), Holy Roman Emperor, was born in Vienna on 18 July 1552, the son of the HABSBURG Emperor MAXIMILIAN II and his wife Maria, daughter of the Emperor CHARLES V. In 1563 Rudolf was sent to Spain to be educated at the court of his uncle PHILIP II of Spain. In September 1572 he was crowned king of Hungary and in September 1575 king of Bohemia. The next month he was chosen king of the Romans at Regensburg and in October 1576 he succeeded his father as Holy Roman Emperor. He deputed the governance of Austria to his brothers Ernst (until his death in 1595) and MATTHIAS and personally attended to the suppression of the REVOLT IN THE NETHERLANDS and the

An iron chair made by **Thomas Rucker** for the Emperor **Rudolf II**, now in Longford Castle, Wiltshire

defence of the Empire against the Ottomans, a struggle that culminated in the TURKISH WAR (1593–1606). In order to finance the war, Rudolf had to make concessions to the ESTATES, who represented not only the various class interests, but also the various parties of the Reformation and Counter-Reformation and the regional interests of various provinces, which included AUSTRIA, BOHEMIA and MORAVIA, HUNGARY (including TRANSYLVANIA), and SILESIA. When Rudolf began to suppress Protestantism in Hungary, the Hungarian Protestant Estates rebelled in alliance with István Bocskai, the Calvinist *voivode* of Transylvania, whom they elected as a rival king of Hungary. Members of the Habsburg family had watched with alarm as Rudolf had sunk from eccentricity into insanity in the early years of the seventeenth century, and on 25 April 1606 they met in Vienna and appointed Matthias as head of the family, with full authority in the Habsburg domains. Matthias secured recognition by the Estates of Austria, Hungary, and Moravia in exchange for religious freedom and political concessions (Treaty of Libeň,

June 1608), but Bohemia and Silesia remained loyal to Rudolf in exchange for the concessions formulated in the MAJESTÄTS-BRIEF (July 1609). In the final years of his reign, Rudolf was preoccupied with the War of the JÜLICH-CLEVES SUCCESSION (1609–14). He died in Prague on 20 January 1612, refusing the last rites of the Church, and was succeeded by his brother Matthias.

In 1573 Rudolf had established his court in Prague, and thereafter he exercised his patronage in many areas of the arts and sciences. His interest in ASTRONOMY brought both Tycho BRAHE and Johann KEPLER to Prague, and he is the eponym of Kepler's *Rudolphine Tables* (Ulm, 1627), which map the position of 1005 stars; he also brought Giordano BRUNO to his court. His scientific interests included ALCHEMY AND CHEMISTRY, ASTROLOGY, BOTANY, MATHEMATICS, gemmology (see GEMS), and ornithology. He was Europe's greatest collector, and his agents travelled all over Europe in pursuit of ancient and contemporary art.

MEL; MDA s.v. Habsburg; R. Evans, *Rudolph II and his World: A Study in Intellectual History 1576–1612* (1973).

**RUEDA, LOPE DE** (*c.*1505–1565), Spanish playwright and actor-manager, born in Seville, where he worked as a metal-beater. He is first recorded as an actor in 1551, when he performed before the future PHILIP II. He subsequently acted in Benavente (1554), and from 1558 to 1561 worked as actor-manager (*autor de comedias*) for a company of strolling players in Segovia (1558), Seville (1559), Toledo (1561), and Madrid (1561); he later returned to Seville (1564) and Córdoba (1565). He seems to have been too ill to sign his will, which is dated 21 March 1565.

After Lope de Rueda's death, his friend Juan Timoneda published his plays in three volumes (1567, 1567, and 1570). His prose *comedias* are imitations of their Italian originals: *Eufemia* is based on BOCCACCIO, *Medora* on Gigio Artemio Giancarli, *Armelina* on Giovanni Maria Cecchi, and *Los engañados* (which introduced the motif of the woman disguised as a man to Spanish drama) on *Gl'ingannati*, an anonymous comedy produced in 1531 by the Intronati, a learned society in Siena. The most original part of these plays are the fourteen prose interludes (*pasos*) that Lope interpolated into his comedies; another ten of his 40 *pasos* survive independently, and they are all still performed, attracting audiences because of their reliance on farce and their depiction of the clever peasant. Rueda also wrote verse plays and pastoral dialogues.

Rueda shifted the centre of Spanish drama away from the court by creating plays for a middle-class audience. After his death an actor in his company was instrumental in opening the Teatro de la Cruz, the first permanent theatre in Madrid, in 1579, as a result of which Rueda is often deemed to be the founder of Spain's national theatre.

E. Cotarelo y Mori, *Lope de Rueda y el teatro de su tiempo* (1898); S. Salazar, *Lope de Rueda y su teatro* (1911).

**RUFFO, VINCENZO** (*c.*1510–1587) Italian composer, active in Verona, Savona, Milan, and Pistoia. Giovanni Mateo ASOLA and Marcantonio INGEGNERI were amongst his pupils.

The textural clarity in his masses demonstrates Counter-Reformation ideals; he was also a prolific composer of madrigals.

**RUGGERI, UGO** (*c.*1450–*c.*1508), Italian printer and caster of cannons. He was born in Reggio Emilia and studied law in Bologna, where he became a printer in about 1473; his press published law books in Latin and popular literature in Italian. He also cast cannons for Giovanni BENTIVOGLIO.

**RUGGLE, GEORGE** (1575–1622), Anglo-Latin dramatist. He was educated at Cambridge (St John's and Trinity), and from *c.*1598 to 1620 was a fellow of Clare College. His only extant play is a Latin comedy called *Ignoramus* (in legal Latin, 'We take no notice of [it]'), a satire occasioned by a dispute (1611–12) about precedence between the mayor of Cambridge and the vice-chancellor of the university. Ruggle's mockery of the mayor's legal representative was rightly understood to be an attack on common lawyers; such an attack on the practice of COMMON LAW emanating from one of the bastions of CIVIL LAW inevitably antagonized the legal profession. The common lawyers had incurred the enmity of King James, who was therefore predisposed to enjoy the satire, and in the event so enjoyed the performance presented before him in 1615 that he attended another production later in the year. The play was printed in 1630.

DNB; E. F. J. Tucker, '*Ignoramus* and Seventeenth-Century Satire of the Law', *Harvard Library Bulletin*, 19 (1971).

**RUIZ DE ALARCÓN Y MENDOZA, JUAN** (1580–1639), playwright, born in Taxco (Mexico), where his father was superintendent of mines. He left for Spain in 1600, studying law in Salamanca and then living in Seville (1606–8) before returning to Mexico City with a view to assuming an academic career. In 1611 he returned to Madrid, where he entered the household of the marquis of Salinas, under whose patronage he embarked on a twin career as an official in the Council of the INDIES (from 1614 until his death) and as a playwright (1615–25). He died in Madrid on 4 August 1639.

Alarcón published most of his plays in a two-part collection. The *Parte primera de las comedias* (1628) contains eight plays. The protagonist of the didactic comedy *Los favores del mundo* is, like his creator, called Ruiz de Alarcón. This autobiographical strain is made more explicit in *Las paredes oyen* (first performed 1617), in which a hunchback called Juan courts a young widow and is cruelly mocked for his deformity; Alarcón was himself a hunchback, and was pitilessly scorned for his deformity by his contemporaries, including Lope de VEGA, Luis de GÓNGORA, Luis VÉLEZ DE GUEVERA, and Francisco QUEVEDO. The collection also included two *comedias de enredo* ('comedies of intrigue') entitled *La industria y la suerte* and *El semejante a sí mismo*, a fantasy called *La cueva de Salamanca*, a play on the fortunes of love entitled *Mudarse por mejorarse*, a moral drama called *El desdichado en fingir*, and a comedy entitled *Todo es ventura* (of which Alarcón's authorship has been doubted).

The *Parte segunda de las comedias* (Barcelona, 1634) contains thirteen plays. The collection includes classical plays on

Lycurgus of Sparta (*Los empeños de un engaño: El dueño de las estrellas*) and Dion of Sicily (*La amistad castigada*), a hostage drama in which Christians are enslaved by Moors (*La manganilla de Melilla*), a moral drama set in the reign of Pedro the Cruel (*Ganar amigos*) which was initially attributed to Lope de Vega, a two-part revenge play (*El tejedor de Segovia*) of which Alarcón probably only wrote the second part, a moral play that places patriotism above love and directs remorseless invective against Lope (*Los pechos privilegiados*), and dramatizations of a fable from the fourteenth-century *El conde Lucanor* (*La prueba de las promesas*) and of an anecdote from the *Anales* of Jerónimo ZURITA (*La crueldad por el honor*). The collection also includes *El examen de maridos*, which had been published in 1630 as the work of Lope de Vega, and Alarcón's greatest play (also previously attributed to Lope), the moral comedy *La verdad sospechosa*, which was later to be adapted by Pierre Corneille in *Le Menteur* and Carlo Goldoni in *Il bugiardo*. Alarcón wrote six other *comedias* which were published long after his death.

Alarcón's plays are constructed around a casuistical notion of stereotyped characters ('humours') and social dilemmas ('comedy of manners') which are not congenial to modern tastes, but his plays are valued for their skilfully constructed plots and for the memorable characterization of figures such as Don Fadrique in *Ganar amigos*.

*Obras completas* (3 vols., 1957–68); Ellen Clayton, *Juan Ruiz de Alarcón, Baroque Dramatist* (1970).

**RUPPEL, BERTHOLD** (d. 1495), German printer. He was trained in GUTENBERG's workshop in Mainz and in 1464 established the first printing workshop in Basel. One of his most popular publications was an edition of Gregory of Nyssa's *Commentary on Job* (1467).

**RUSTICI, GIOVANNI FRANCESCO** (1474–1554), Italian sculptor, born into a prosperous family in Florence and trained in the studio of VERROCCHIO. His finest surviving work, which reflects the influence of LEONARDO, is the bronze group *John the Baptist Preaching* (which includes figures of a Levite and a Pharisee) which was mounted in 1515 above the north entrance of the Florentine Baptistery. He also worked in marble (e.g. *Virgin and Child with Infant St John*, Bargello, Florence) and in terracotta (e.g. *Victorious Knight*, Museo Horne, Florence). In 1528 Rustici moved to France at the invitation of FRANCIS I, and remained there for the rest of his life; he died in Tours. No work from his long residence in France is known to have survived.

*MDA.*

**RUTHENIAN CHURCHES.** Ruthenia is a Carpathian region now divided between the Ukraine (centred on L'viv, Polish Lwów) and the Polish district of Galicia and bordering on Romania, Hungary, and Slovakia. Ruthenia was annexed by Lithuania in 1366, and so in 1569, when Poland and Lithuania were united in the Union of LUBLIN, it became part of the united state.

Until 1485 the Ruthenians were part of the Russian Church under the jurisdiction of the metropolitan of Kiev. When the metropolitan was expelled from the COUNCIL OF FLORENCE in 1443 on the promulgation of the union of eastern and western churches, the Ruthenians lost the prospect of communion with Rome. In 1485, however, Pope PIUS II appointed a Catholic metropolitan of Kiev with responsibility for the eight eparchies of the province that were in Poland-Lithuania. For the next century, the churches remained Orthodox but their metropolitan was Catholic. The anomaly was resolved by the Union of BREST-LITOVSK (1596), in which the Ruthenian Church became a UNIATE CHURCH that retained the Orthodox rite but nonetheless became part of the Catholic Church.

**RUTTIER or (early modern English) rutter or (Flemish) leeskaertan or (Spanish) derroterro**, a type of navigational chart containing tide tables and (from 1521) woodcut views of coastlines and ports as seen from the sea. The term derives from the use of French *routier* in the title of *Le Grand Routier et pilotage*, a pilot book for the Atlantic coast of France published in 1483 and subsequently translated into English. In 1521 Richard Proude published *The New Rutter of the Sea for the North Parts*, which covered the entire coast of Britain. Ruttiers continued in use until the end of the seventeenth century.

**RUZANTE.** See BEOLCO, ANGELO.

# S

**SÁ, MANUEL DE** (*c*.1530–1596), Portuguese Jesuit scholar who entered the JESUIT Order at Coimbra in 1545. In 1551 he was appointed professor of philosophy at Alcalá de Henares, and in 1557 he was summoned to Rome to teach at the Roman College. He was appointed by Pope PIUS V to serve on the commission investigating the Septuagint text of the BIBLE with Juan MALDONADO. He spent the final years of his career as a papal representative in Loreto and Genoa.

Sá published several biblical commentaries, but his best-known work was his dictionary of casuistry, *Aphorismi confessariorum* (1595). The *Aphorismi* was placed on the INDEX LIBRORUM PROHIBITORUM in 1603 because it allowed confession and absolution by exchange of letters, but after this epistolary heresy was excised in the edition of 1608, the *Aphorismi* became a standard text in moral theology.

**SÁ, MEM DE** (*c*.1500–1572), Portuguese governor of Brazil, the illegitimate son of a Coimbra canon and the younger brother of the poet Francisco de SÁ DE MIRANDA. In 1557 he was appointed governor of Brazil, where his raids of 1560 and 1567 destroyed the French island colony of Fort Coligny and mainland colony of La France Antarctique; the victory of 1567 was accomplished on 20 January, the Feast of St Sebastian, and so the new Portuguese colony was named São Sebastião do Rio de Janeiro. In the course of his fourteen years as governor Mem de Sá supported Portuguese colonization and the missionary endeavours of the JESUITS.

DHP; L. Norton, *A dinastia dos Sás no Brasil* (1965); Herbert Wetzel, *Mem de Sá, terceiro governador geral* (1972).

**SABELLICUS or (Italian) Marcantonio Coccio** (1436–1506), Italian humanist and historian, a native of Vicovaro who became a prominent member of the Roman ACADEMY and later became a member of the circle of ALDUS MANUTIUS in Venice, where he became the librarian of San Marco with responsibility for the library of Cardinal BESSARION. His works included a history of Venice (*Rerum Venetarum ab urbe condita*, 1486) and a history of the world in 92 books (*Enneades sive rapsodiae historiarum*, 1504).

OCIL.

**SABINUS, GEORGIUS, or (German) Georg Schüler** (1508–60), German humanist and neo-Latin poet. He was born in Brandenburg and studied under MELANCHTHON at WITTENBERG; in 1536 he married Melanchthon's daughter Anna. He became professor of Latin at Frankfurt an der Oder, and subsequently was appointed as the first rector of the new Lutheran university in Königsberg, which had been founded in 1544. He edited CICERO (1554) and wrote a commentary on Ovid (1554). His own Latin poems, in elegiacs, were published in 1550.

DLL.

**SACCHETTI, FRANCO** (*c*.1330–*c*.1400), Italian writer, born in Ragusa (now Dubrovnik) into a prominent Florentine family. He travelled extensively in his youth, and in the early 1360s settled in Florence, where he held a series of civic appointments. His works include lyrics (*Libro delle rime*, *c*.1362) and a vernacular commentary on the Gospels (*Sposizioni di Vangeli*, 1381). Sacchetti's most important work is a collection of 300 tales (*Trecentonovelle*, composed 1392–7, printed 1724) modelled loosely on BOCCACCIO's *Decameron* but without a narrative frame; only 223 of the tales survive in a complete form. Sacchetti's tales lack the imaginative and stylistic accomplishment of Boccaccio's, but he had a fine ear for linguistic registers, and could render speech as various as domestic conversations and pulpit oratory more vividly than many literary authors.

OCIL; *Tales from Sacchetti*, ed. M. Steegmann (1978).

**SACHS, HANS** (1494–1576), German poet and dramatist, born in Nuremberg on 5 November 1494, the son of a tailor. He was educated in the Latin school of Nuremberg and in 1509 was apprenticed to a shoemaker. From 1511 to 1516 he practised his trade as a wandering journeyman in Regensburg, Frankfurt, Passau, Salzburg, Munich, Osnabrück, Vienna, Lübeck, and Leipzig, and on the completion of his *Wanderjahre* returned to Nuremberg for the rest of his life. He had been trained in MEISTERGESANG in his teens, and on settling in Nuremberg he resumed both his trade as a shoemaker and his avocation as a writer of *Meisterleider*, SPRUCHGEDICHTE, SCHWÄNKE, and verse plays. He welcomed the advent of the Reformation and wrote in Luther's honour *Die wittenbergisch Nachtigall* (1523), a 700-line poem in KNITTELVERSE which praises Luther the nightingale and denounces the pope as a lion (Luther's adversary had been Pope LEO X); the town council of Nuremberg promptly forbade Sachs to publish any more *Büchlein oder Reimen*, but the interdiction was soon lifted when the council declared for the Reformation.

Sachs was one of the most prolific writers of the century. By 1567, according to the tally given in *Summe aller meiner Gedichte* (which Sachs wrote in the belief that he was dying), he had written 4,275 *Meisterlieder* (which were performed by the Nuremberg Meistersinger school but not printed), 1,700 *Spruchgedichte* and *Schwänke*, and 208 plays, including comedies, tragedies, and FASTNACHTSPIELE. The terms 'comedy' and 'tragedy' gesture towards the classical genres, but the plays are simply narrative dialogues, and are not constructed like the plays of antiquity or the Renaissance.

In 1519 Sachs married Kunigunde Kreutzer, and when she died in 1560 he married Barbara Harscher, a young widow. His friends included DÜRER, Willibald PIRKHEIMER, Jost AMMAN (who executed his portrait in woodcut), and the VISCHER family (especially Peter the Elder). He died in Nuremberg on 19 January 1576. His writing was not highly valued during the seventeenth and early eighteenth centuries, but Goethe restored his standing in his poem *Hans Sachsens poetische Sendung* (1776) and Wagner made him a national hero through his opera *Die Meistersinger von Nürnberg* (1868).

*DLL.*

**SACK OF ROME or (Italian)** *Sacco di Roma*. Rome was twice sacked in late antiquity (410 and 455) and twice in the early modern period (1413 and 1527). On 8 June 1413 the forces of LADISLAS OF DURAZZO, king of Naples, entered the city, expelled Pope JOHN XXIII, and pillaged the city. The term 'Sack of Rome' is used in Renaissance historiography to designate the capture and destructive occupation of Rome by imperial troops from May 1527 to February 1528. In this central episode in the WARS OF ITALY, King FRANCIS I, who had recently been released from captivity, formed the League of COGNAC (22 May 1526), an anti-imperial pact between France, Venice, the papacy (Pope CLEMENT VII), and Francesco SFORZA of Milan. In the war that followed, an imperial army consisting of Lutheran *Landsknechte* and Spanish troops stormed and captured Rome on 6 May 1527; in the first assault the imperial commander, the duc de BOURBON, was killed, and in the following week the army of 30,000 troops devastated the city. By mid-May military discipline had been reestablished, and the city settled into a brutal occupation that lasted until February 1528, when the imperial army left the city; much of the physical fabric of Rome was destroyed during the occupation, and the economy of the city was broken.

J. Hook, *The Sack of Rome* (1978); M. Lenzi, *Il Sacco di Roma* (1978).

**SACKVILLE, THOMAS, EARL OF DORSET** (1536–1608), English statesman, playwright, and poet. Whilst a student at the Inner Temple, Sackville was the co-author, with Thomas NORTON, of the first five-act tragedy in English, *Gorboduc* (c.1561), to which he contributed the last two acts. Having trained as a barrister, he entered Parliament in 1557 and was raised to the peerage a decade later. In 1563 he contributed the 'Induction' and 'The Complaint of Buckingham' to the second edition of *A Mirror for Magistrates*, a collection of verse laments from famous historical figures. In the 'Induction', Sorrow leads the Poet to the realms of the dead; in his 'Complaint', the decapitated head of the duke of Buckingham tells of his rebellion against RICHARD III and laments his betrayal by a trusted dependant.

*DNB.*

**SACRA CONVERSAZIONE**, a painting in which the Virgin MARY and the infant Jesus are portrayed together with saints; the form is distinguished from the Holy Family (*Sacra Famiglia*), in which the Virgin and Child are accompanied by Joseph and sometimes by other relatives. The *sacra conversazione* became very popular in fifteenth-century Italy, where its exponents included Fra ANGELICO, Giovanni BELLINI, Fra Filippo LIPPI, MANTEGNA, PIERO DELLA FRANCESCA, RAPHAEL, TINTORETTO, TITIAN, and DOMENICO VENEZIANO. The Virgin's role as a divine protector meant that the form was often chosen to acknowledge divine assistance in war, as in Mantegna's *Madonna of Victory* (Louvre) and Titian's *Pesaro Madonna* (Santa Maria dei Frari, Venice), and in recovery from disease, as in HOLBEIN's painting for the burgomaster of Basel (Darmstadt Museum).

When the saint portrayed in a *sacra conversazione* is St Catherine, as in Gérard DAVID's *Sacra Conversazione* (National Gallery, London) and Tintoretto's *Sacra Conversazione* (Palazzo Ducale, Venice), she is represented receiving her wedding ring from the infant Jesus; a painting containing this image is known as a 'Mystic Marriage of St Catherine'.

**SACRAMENTARIANS**, the name given by Martin LUTHER to theologians such as ZWINGLI and OECOLAMPADIUS who maintained that, in the EUCHARIST, the bread and wine were only transformed into the body and blood of Christ in what Zwingli called a 'sacramental or metaphorical sense' (*sacramentaliter sive* μετωνυμικός). In common and polemical use, the term was used to denote anyone who denied the 'real presence' (i.e. actual presence) of Christ in the sacraments. Sacramentarians believed that the celebration of the eucharist was a commemorative act, and so are also known as memorialists.

**SACRAMENTS**. In the twelfth century the notion of a sacrament (Latin *sacramentum*) came to be restricted in the Western Church to rites instituted by Jesus, and in the same period the number of sacraments was fixed at seven: BAPTISM, confirmation, the EUCHARIST, penance, extreme unction, ordination, and matrimony. This list was formally affirmed in the COUNCIL OF FLORENCE (in the *Decretum pro Armenis*) and the COUNCIL OF TRENT.

Protestant churches demurred, and for the most part were only willing to recognize two sacraments, baptism and the eucharist. Article 25 of the Thirty-Nine ARTICLES of the Church of England adopts a similar position, distinguishing these two sacraments from the other 'five commonly called sacraments' on the grounds that only baptism and the eucharist were clearly authorized by Jesus. The number of sacraments was a subject of controversy: in 1537, for example, Alexander ALESIUS and John Stokesley, bishop of London, held a debate on the number of sacraments.

The sacraments were deemed in the Catholic Church to work *ex opere operato* ('through the act performed'), so their efficacy was thought to be independent of the moral state of the priest administering the sacraments. Similarly, three of the sacraments (baptism, confirmation, and ordination) were thought by Catholic theologians to imprint an indelible mark (*character indelibilis*) on the soul of the recipient. Protestants disputed both contentions.

**SACRA RAPPRESENTAZIONE**, a civic religious play of fifteenth-century Italy, similar to the AUTO SACRAMENTAL in Spain and the mystery play in England and France. The subjects of the plays were initially biblical, but later included saints' lives; the usual metre was *ottava rima*. Within Italy the genre was most highly developed in Tuscany, where *rappresentazioni* were mounted by CONFRATERNITIES and by princely patrons. Many of the plays were anonymous, but those of which the authors are known include Lorenzo de' MEDICI's *Rappresentazione dei Santi Giovani e Paolo*, which was performed in 1491 by the children of the Compagnia del Vangelista.

L. Banfi (ed.), *Sacre rappresentazioni del Quattrocento* (1963).

**SACROBOSCO, JOHANNES DE** (*fl. c.*1250); his vernacular name was probably John of Holywood. He was the author of a short treatise on 'the [heavenly] sphere' (*De sphaera*) which was the standard textbook of elementary ASTRONOMY. Many astronomers published commentaries on it.

Lynn Thorndike, *The Sphere of Sacrobosco and its Commentators* (1949).

**SADELER FAMILY**, a dynasty of Flemish engravers whose huge output consists mostly of reproductions of paintings by other artists rather than original designs. The founder of the family was Johannes (Dutch Jan) Sadeler the Elder (1550–*c.*1600), a native of Brussels who became a member of the Antwerp guild and later worked in Frankfurt, Munich, Florence, Verona, Rome, and Venice; his brother Raphael the Elder (1560/1–*c.*1630), a native of Antwerp, accompanied Johannes to Frankfurt. In the next generation, Justus (1583–1620), the son of Johannes, was an engraver and Aegidius (*c.*1570–1629), a nephew of Johannes, was a painter and engraver who *c.*1579 accompanied Johannes to Cologne and later travelled to Munich, Antwerp, and Rome. He eventually settled in Prague, where he worked as imperial engraver at the courts of RUDOLF II, MATTHIAS, and FERDINAND II. The three sons of Raphael the Elder, Raphael the Younger (1584–1632), Philip (*fl.* 1620s), and Johannes the Younger (1588–1665), all worked in Munich. Many of the prints produced in the family's workshops are signed only with a single initial, so precise attribution is often problematic.

MDA.

**SÁ DE MIRANDA, FRANCISCO DE** (1485–1558), Portuguese poet, born into an ancient and noble family in Coimbra.

In 1505 he moved to Lisbon, where he attended the university and participated in the life of the royal court. He was awarded a doctorate in law in 1516 and embarked on a legal career. He travelled from 1520 to 1526 in Italy, visiting Milan, Venice, Florence, Rome, Naples, and Sicily; the Italians that he met included Giovanni RUCELLAI, SANNAZARO, and Vittoria COLONNA. In 1526 he returned to Portugal as an exponent of Italian forms, and there presided over a recasting of Portuguese literature in the Renaissance mode, introducing verse forms such as the sonnet, the canzona, the ode, and the verse epistle in tercets and in *ottava rima*.

Sá de Miranda settled in Coimbra, where he wrote *Os estrangeiros* (produced *c.*1527), a classical comedy in the Italian style and the first Portuguese prose comedy. In poetry, he wrote a canzona entitled *Fábula de Mondego* in Spanish (1528) and a pastoral eclogue entitled *Aleixo* in Portuguese (*c.*1531); *Aleixo* was the first poem in Portuguese to be written in *ottava rima*. In 1534 Sá withdrew from the court and retired to an estate on the river Neira (near the Galician border), where he wrote five eclogues, four in Spanish and one in Portuguese (1535–8). In 1538 he wrote his second prose comedy, *Vilhalpandos*, which was performed before Cardinal-Prince HENRIQUE, who after Sá's death printed both comedies.

José V. de Pina Martins, *Sá de Miranda e a cultura do Rinascimento* (1972); Thomas Earle, *Theme and Image in the Poetry of Sá de Miranda* (1980).

**SADOLETO, JACOPO** (1477–1547), reforming cardinal and humanist, born in Ferrara, the son of a jurist. He acquired a reputation as a Latin stylist; the subject of his best-known poem is the marble *Laocoön* group rediscovered in 1506 and now in the Vatican. He moved to Rome to pursue a career in the Church and secured the patronage of Cardinal Oliviero CARAFA. Sadoleto served as secretary to Pope LEO X (along with Pietro BEMBO) and Pope CLEMENT VII, and in 1517 was appointed bishop of Carpentras; in 1536 he was created cardinal together with Reginald POLE and in 1537 was appointed to the commission charged with the preparation of a general council (which was eventually convoked as the COUNCIL OF TRENT). In 1542 he was appointed as a papal legate and charged with what proved to be the fruitless task of reconciling King FRANCIS I of France and the Emperor CHARLES V. His writings include treatises on original sin (*De peccato originali*) and on the education of boys (*De pueris recte instituendis*), a letter to the citizens of Geneva pleading for reconciliation (1539), and a controversial commentary on Romans, which was placed on the INDEX until its doctrine of GRACE, which was suspected of semi-Pelagianism, was reformulated in Thomistic (i.e. neo-Augustinian) terms.

R. M. Douglas, *Jacopo Sadoleto (1477–1547) Humanist and Reformer* (1959).

**SAGREDO, DIEGO DE** (*fl.* 1526), Spanish architectural theorist, a chaplain at the court of Queen JUANA LA LOCA and the author of *Medidas del Romano*, the first Spanish book on Renaissance architecture. The treatise was first published in Toledo in 1526; a French translation, *Raison d'architecture*, followed in 1530. The treatise is a commentary on VITRUVIUS, illustrated with woodcuts, and advocates a return to the purity of the ancient Roman style leavened by an admixture of the Spanish PLATERESQUE.

**SAGRERA, GUILLEM** (*fl.* 1416–50), Catalan architect and decorative sculptor, one of the twelve architects assembled in 1416 to plan the construction of the monumental nave of Girona Cathedral (the widest of any Gothic cathedral in Europe). In 1422 he carved the statues for the Porta del Mirador, the south door of Palma Cathedral in Majorca, and in 1426 he began work on the sculpted decoration for the Merchants' Exchange in Palma. Sagrera left Palma for Naples in 1449, and he was thereafter employed by ALFONSO V on the reconstruction of the Castel Nuovo; the large square hall is Sagrera's finest accomplishment.

DBC; MDA; Gabriel Alomar Esteve, *Guillem Sagrera y la arquitectura gótica del siglo XV* (1970).

**SAHAGÚN, BERNARDINO DE** (1499/1500–1590), Spanish philologist, historian, and ethnographer. He was born in Sahagún (León), entered the Franciscan Order in 1524, and sailed for Mexico as a missionary in 1529. While teaching the sons of the Aztec nobility at the College of Santiago Tlaltelolco, Fray Bernardino developed a learned interest in the Aztec and Nahuatl languages, and collected the materials for his *Historia general de las cosas de Nueva España*, which he wrote in Spanish and Nahuatl. He used oral as well as written sources, interviewing elderly Indians to secure information about Aztec society before the Spanish conquest and to formulate an account of the conquest from an Aztec perspective. The *Historia* was completed in 1577, but permission to print was not granted, and so it secured its limited influence through manuscript transmission; it was eventually published in 1892.

DHE; M. S. Edmondson (ed.), *Sixteenth-Century Mexico: The Work of Sahagún* (1974).

**SAINT-ANDRÉ, JACQUES D'ALBON, MARÉCHAL DE** (*c.*1505–1562), French soldier. He fought against Spain in the WARS OF ITALY and was appointed *maréchal de France* and governor of Lyonnais by King HENRI II. He was captured at the battle of SAINT-QUENTIN (1557) but soon released and so was able to participate in the negotiations which led to the Treaty of CATEAU-CAMBRÉSIS (1559). In April 1561 he joined forces with MONTMORENCY and François, duke of GUISE, in a triumvirate opposed to the efforts of the regent CATHERINE DE MÉDICIS to appease the HUGUENOTS. He was killed on 19 December 1562 at the battle of Dreux, one of the earliest battles in the WARS OF RELIGION. His death, together with the capture of Montmorency by the Protestants and the capture of ANTOINE DE BOURBON by the Catholics, enabled Queen Catherine to negotiate the Treaty of AMBOISE.

Lucien Romier, *La Carrière d'un favori: Jacques d'Albon de Saint-André, maréchal de France, 1512–1562* (1909).

**ST BARTHOLOMEW'S DAY MASSACRE** (23–4 August 1572), a massacre of French Protestants in Paris in which thousands of HUGUENOTS were killed in the city and thousands more elsewhere in France; the massacre is sometimes called the St Bartholomew's Eve Massacre, because the killing began on 23 August 1572, the day before the Feast of St Bartholomew (whose emblem is a flaying knife).

The number of prominent Huguenots in Paris was swollen by the marriage on 18 August of Henry of Navarre (later King HENRI IV) and MARGUERITE DE VALOIS. On 22 August the Guise faction wounded but failed to kill Gaspard de COLIGNY, the Huguenot leader. In the early morning of 24 August, Henri, duke of Guise, succeeded in killing Coligny, whereupon the ringing of church bells gave the signal to begin the slaughter of Protestants. The killing continued in Paris until 17 September and spread to other cities in France, where it continued until 3 October. Catherine de Médicis was congratulated by the theologians of the University of Paris, and Pope GREGORY XIII celebrated with Te Deums in thanksgiving for the victory of the Church in France over infidelity and joyfully ordered bonfires to be lit and a commemorative medal struck.

The events of the massacre were dramatized by Christopher MARLOWE in *The Massacre of Paris* (written *c.*1592), which includes a memorable scene in which Petrus RAMUS is killed by Henri, duke of Guise, after a verbal attack on his misappropriation of Aristotle.

Philippe Erlanger, *St Bartholomew's Night: The Massacre of Saint Bartholomew* (1962); Robert Kingdon, *Myths about the St. Bartholomew's Day Massacres, 1572–1576* (1988).

**SAINT-GELAIS, MELLIN DE** (1487–1558), French poet, born in Angoulême, the son of Octavien de SAINT-GELAIS. He studied in Italy, and became well known as a musician, astrologer, and poet. He was a court poet at the courts of FRANCIS I and HENRI II, and specialized in semi-dramatic and musical performances of his own compositions, which were typically satirical or amorous. He wrote in many genres, and may have been the first to write sonnets in French, though he was preceded in publication by MAROT. In 1554 his translation of TRISSINO's *Sofonisba* was staged before CATHERINE DE MÉDICIS. Towards the end of his career he was displaced in the royal favour by his young rival Pierre de RONSARD.

**SAINT-GELAIS, OCTAVIEN DE** (1468–1502), French poet associated with the RHÉTORIQUEURS. He was born into a prominent family in Cognac and entered the Church; his career culminated with his appointment as bishop of Angoulême. Saint-Gelais translated Ovid's *Heroides* and Virgil's *Aeneid* and also wrote original verse, notably the *Séjour d'honneur*, an allegorical account of a poet's journey to the royal court.

**SAINT-GERMAIN-EN-LAYE**, a royal estate overlooking the Seine at Yvelines, 18 kilometres (11 miles) west of Paris. From 1282 until 1682, when Louis XIV moved the court to Versailles, Saint-Germain-en-Laye was the summer palace of the kings of France. The twelfth-century castle was built by Louis VI, and, except for the chapel, was destroyed by the Black Prince and rebuilt by Charles V in 1368; in 1539 FRANCIS I commissioned the architect Pierre Chambiges to rebuild the castle, retaining only the chapel (*c.*1235) and the keep

(1368), which he capped with a turret. This is the pentangular building with towers at each of its five corners known as the Old Chateau. In terms of the development of FRENCH ARCHITECTURE, it is important as the first flat-roofed building in Europe; the roofs are edged by a stone balustrade surmounted with urns. The Old Chateau was the birthplace of HENRI II and CHARLES IX and was for ten years the childhood home of MARY, QUEEN OF SCOTS; it later served as a Napoleonic prison and is now the Museum of National Antiquities.

The New Chateau (Château Neuf) was begun in 1557 by Philibert DELORME at the command of Henri II; Delorme was succeeded by Francesco PRIMATICCIO in 1559, and construction continued for 50 years. Henri II laid out gardens descending in seven terraces linked by staircases to the river below; these gardens were completed by Henri IV, who installed water-driven AUTOMATA (designed by Thomas FRANCINI) depicting mythological figures in the GROTTOES; these automata included GIOCHI D'ACQUA with which the king delighted in spraying his guests. In the Grotte des Flambeaux, special effects created the illusion of a storm with thunder and lightning. The fourth terrace was a promenade that extended at each end towards the river, on the roofs of two galleries that projected out onto the fifth terrace and terminated in twin PAVILIONS; this U-shaped promenade looked down on the Jardins des Dentelles; below this garden the slope was planted with fruit trees. The Château Neuf was the favourite residence of Louis XIII; after his death in 1643 it was neglected, though it served as the residence of Henrietta Maria (daughter of Henri IV and queen of Charles I) from 1645 to 1648. The terraces collapsed in 1661, and were rebuilt by Louis XIV, and new gardens were laid out. The chateau was given to the exiled James II in 1688; it was demolished between 1777 and 1782, and all that remains is the two pavilions: the Pavillon Henri IV is now a hotel, and the Pavillon du Jardinier, now called Pavilion de Sully, is a private residence. The huge terrace promenade survives because it was incorporated into Le Nôtre's redesigned gardens (1663–75).

G. Houdard, *Les Châteaux royaux de Saint-Germain-en-Laye* (2 vols., 1909–11); Kenneth Woodbridge, *Princely Gardens: The Origins and Development of the French Formal Style* (1986).

## ST JOHN, KNIGHTS HOSPITALLERS OF THE ORDER OF.

The Ordo Fratrum Hospitalariorum Hierosolymitanorum or Ordo Militiae Sancti Johannis Baptistae Hospitalis Hierosolymitani or Johanniter Orden, later known as the Knights of Rhodes and the Sovereign Order of the Knights of Malta (*Malteser Orden*) and now known in English as the Venerable Order of the Hospital of St John of Jerusalem, was established in Jerusalem in 1087 to attend to the medical and defensive needs of Christian pilgrims. After the fall of the Latin kingdom in 1291, the Order was expelled from Jerusalem, and in the first instance re-established itself in Cyprus. In 1310 the Order migrated to Rhodes, which it defended against Turkish attacks from 1480 until 1523, when the victorious Sultan Süleyman I the Magnificent allowed the Order to retreat to Candia (CRETE). In 1530 the Emperor CHARLES V presented MALTA and Tripoli (now the capital of Libya) to the Order. In 1551 Tripoli fell to the Ottomans and the Order consolidated all its forces in Malta, where they withstood a famous Ottoman siege (18 May–8 September 1565); the Order remained in Malta until 1798.

The Hospitallers differed from the Templars in two important respects. First, the Templars were a purely military order of warrior monks but the Hospitallers were committed to both nursing and warfare. Second, the Templars were an all-male order, whereas the Hospitallers welcomed the affiliation of women's houses; until 1187 women Hospitallers cared for the sick in a women's hospital in Jerusalem, but after the fall of Jerusalem the nuns returned to Europe, where they became an entirely contemplative order; their rule, which dates from 1188, does not mention nursing.

The rule of the Hospitallers was that of the Augustinian canons. Their habit was originally a black monastic coat (*cappa clausa*) with slits for the arms and a white 'Maltese cross' (as it later came to be called) on the breast. As this habit impeded combat, Pope Alexander IV approved in 1264 a wartime habit of a red surcoat with a large white cross; both conventual and military habits are illustrated in paintings by PINTURICCHIO in the Piccolomini Library in Siena Cathedral.

At the Reformation, most bailiwicks of the Order remained loyal to Rome, but there were two important exceptions. The master and knights of the bailiwick of Brandenburg converted to Lutheranism, and in England the refusal of the master and knights to acknowledge the royal supremacy led to its suppression; its revival in 1834 led to the establishment in 1877 of the St John's Ambulance Association and its offshoot the St John's Ambulance Brigade.

## ST PETER'S BASILICA or (Italian) Basilica di San Pietro in Vaticano.

The first church of Catholic Christendom is named after St Peter because it was erected over the place where he was believed to have been buried. It is called a basilica because of the shape of the original church on the site, an oblong consisting (from west to east) of a porch, an atrium flanked by cloisters, a narthex, and a nave flanked by four aisles; at the east end, behind the altar, the pontifical chair was accommodated in an apse. This church, which is known in English as Old St Peter's, was built *c.*AD 330 and demolished early in the sixteenth century to make way for its successor.

In the mid-fifteenth century Pope NICHOLAS V had commanded his architect (*ingegnere di palazzo*) Bernardo ROSSELLINO to draw up plans for a new church in the form of a Latin cross, but the project was abandoned on the death of Pope Nicholas. It was Pope JULIUS II who revived the project by commissioning BRAMANTE to design a new church, which was to be shaped like a Greek cross; Pope Julius laid the foundation stone on 18 April 1506. The cost of the building could not be met from current reserves, so in 1516 Pope LEO X issued an indulgence to raise money for the project. In Germany Archbishop ALBRECHT VON MAINZ charged Johann TETZEL with the responsibility for preaching the indulgence, the income from which was to be divided between the archbishop and the Vatican. Martin LUTHER was so scandalized by Tetzel's assurances that cash payments would deliver donors

A medal (c.1506) made by CARADOSSO showing BRAMANTE's design for **St Peter's Basilica** (British Museum)

from PURGATORY that he returned to Wittenberg and issued his 95 Theses. The financing of the new church proved to be the touchpaper of the REFORMATION.

Bramante died in 1514 and was succeeded by RAPHAEL (d. 1520), Baldassare PERUZZI (d. 1536), Antonio da SANGALLO the Younger (d. 1546), and MICHELANGELO (d. 1564), each of whom modified Bramante's plans as construction proceeded. In 1546, when Michelangelo was appointed as chief architect, he enlarged the plan and redesigned the dome. The dome was completed after Michelangelo's death by Giacomo DELLA PORTA and Domenico FONTANA, who altered his design for a hemispherical dome by making the top of the dome pointed. The two smaller domes were added by Giacomo VIGNOLA. The Egyptian obelisk on the square was erected by Domenico Fontana in 1586.

In the early seventeenth century Carlo Maderno altered Michelangelo's centralized plan by adding a nave (which blocked the view of the dome from the piazza) and a façade on which work began in 1607. The building was finished in 1614 and consecrated by Pope Urban VIII on 18 November 1626. Gianlorenzo Bernini framed the Piazza di San Pietro with his colonnade between 1656 and 1667.

E. Francia, *1505–1606: Storia della costruzione del nuovo San Pietro* (1977).

**SAINT-QUENTIN, BATTLE OF** (10 August 1557). In February 1556, in the final years of the WARS OF ITALY, King PHILIP II signed the Truce of Vaucelles with HENRI II. The following year King Henri violated the truce by forming an alliance with Pope PAUL IV and dispatching a force commanded by François de GUISE to invade Italy and reconquer Naples for the French crown. Spanish forces in the Netherlands commanded by EMANUELE FILIBERTO responded with

an invasion of France, and besieged the fortress of Saint-Quentin (Picardy), where the defences were commanded by Gaspard de COLIGNY. On 10 August 1557 a French relief force commanded by Anne de MONTMORENCY was destroyed by the Spanish army. The road to Paris lay open, but Spain was unable to pay for its troops to march on and attack Paris.

**SALAMANCA or (Latin) Salamantica or Helmantica**, a city and bishopric in western Spain on the right bank of the river Tormes, which is spanned by a bridge of 26 arches, of which fifteen are Roman and nine were built in the sixteenth century. The population in the sixteenth century was about 50,000, of whom some 10,000 were students at the university, which had been founded in about 1230 and had subsequently developed an international reputation for CANON LAW, CIVIL LAW, and theology; in the fifteenth and sixteenth centuries, the university was widely regarded as one of the greatest in Europe. Its sumptuous entrance (1534) is a fine example of PLATERESQUE architecture, and the lecture room in which Fray LUIS DE LEÓN taught has been preserved with its original furnishings, a professor's desk (with a sounding board) and benches for students. The city began to decline in importance in the mid-sixteenth century, and in 1593 Valladolid, which had hitherto been subject to the see of Salamanca, gained its own bishop, and so further reduced the standing of Salamanca.

The greatest Renaissance building in Salamanca is the New Cathedral (Catedral Nueva); the nine architects assembled in 1512 to discuss the construction of the new cathedral included Juan GIL DE HONTAÑÓN the Elder, who was subsequently commissioned to build the cathedral. His son Juan Gil the Younger succeeded his father as architect at Salamanca, where he worked from 1526 to 1531; another son, Rodrigo Gil, worked as cathedral architect at Salamanca from 1538; the cathedral was eventually completed in 1734.

**SALAT, HANS** (1498–1561), Swiss playwright and Catholic polemicist, born in Sursee. He fought the reformers in 1529, and subsequently became clerk of the law courts in Lucerne, but he was dismissed from this post in 1540. His literary works, which were all directed against the Reformation, include satires and historical works (*Der Tanngrotz*, 1531; *Triumphans Herculis Helvetici*, 1532; a *Chronik* of the Reformation, 1536), a biography of NICHOLAS OF FLÜE (*Des frommen Bruder Clausen Leben*, 1536), and the polemical plays *Judith* (1534) and *Der verlorene Sohn* (1535), the latter of which was adapted (using the same title) by Caesar von Arx in 1935.

Hans Salat, *Reformationschronik 1517–1534*, ed. Ruth Jörg (3 vols., 1986).

**SALINAS, FRANCISCO DE** (1513–90), Spanish music theorist and organist. Blind since childhood, he attended the University of Salamanca where he studied philosophy, Greek, and liberal arts. He travelled to Rome where he studied music theory, and became organist at Sigüenza and later León. He returned to Salamanca where he held the chair of theoretical and practical music from 1569. *De musica*

(1577) is a theoretical work about proportion, harmony, and rhythm with reference to the theoretical systems of the ancient Greeks.

**SALISBURY COURT THEATRE.** Built of brick in 1629 on a site off Fleet Street, the Salisbury Court Theatre was successively occupied by the King's Men (see CHAMBERLAIN'S MEN) (1629–31), who performed FORD's *The Broken Heart* there, PRINCE CHARLES'S MEN (1631–5), and Queen Henrietta's Men (1637–42). The last theatre built in London before the Civil War, and reopened in 1660 by Christopher BEESTON's son William, it provided, together with the COCKPIT, an important link between the theatre of the post-Elizabethan age and that of the Restoration.

**SALMASIUS, CLAUDIUS, or (French) Claude Saumaise** (1588–1653), French classical scholar, born in Saumur and educated in Paris, where he became a friend of Isaac CASAUBON and converted to Protestantism. He established his European reputation as a scholar when at the age of 19 he discovered in Heidelberg the manuscript that later became the basis of the *Palatine Anthology*. In the course of his career he wrote some 80 learned treatises, including a vast edition of the *Polyhistoria* of Solinus, which is a reworking of the *Historia naturalis* of PLINY THE ELDER (*Plinianae Exercitationes in Solini Polyhistoria*, Paris, 1629). He became professor of Greek at Leiden (1632) and later entered the service of Queen Christina of Sweden. His attack on the execution of Charles I of England in 1649 provoked a riposte from John Milton.

**SALT WAR.** In 1540 Pope PAUL III ordered that the price of salt be raised in the Papal State, and the citizens of PERUGIA rebelled in protest; in the ensuing Salt War, a papal army forced the city to surrender.

**SALUTATI, COLUCCIO** (1331–1406), influential Italian humanist. He was born in Stignano in Florentine territory near Lucca (Valdinievole), and spent his youth in Bologna, where his family lived in exile. From 1375 until his death Salutati served as chancellor of Florence, and during this period he helped to establish Florence as the most important centre for humanist endeavour; the teachers that he brought to the city included CHRYSOLORAS. He wrote treatises on political and moral philosophy and composed poetry, but his finest literary works are his letters; his correspondents included Petrarch, though they never met.

B. L. Ullmann, *The Humanism of Coluccio Salutati* (1963);
R. G. Witt, *Colucci Salutati and his Public Letters* (1976); R. G. Witt, *Hercules at the Crossroads: The Life, Works and Thought of Coluccio Salutati* (1983).

**SALVIATI or Francesco de' Rossi** (1510–63), Italian painter and friend of VASARI. He was a native of Florence, where he trained in the studio of ANDREA DEL SARTO. He migrated to Rome *c.*1530 and entered the service of Cardinal Salviati, whose name he adopted. His first important painting, a fresco of the *Visitation* (1538) in the Oratory of San Giovanni Decollato, established his reputation as an artist. In 1539 he

travelled to Venice; the subsequent influence of PARMIGIANINO on his paintings may indicate that he visited Parma on his way to or from Venice. He worked for several years (1544–8) for COSIMO I DE' MEDICI on the decoration of the Sala dell'Udienza in the Palazzo della Signoria in Florence. In 1544 he visited France, where he worked for the cardinal of Lorraine, and then returned to Rome, where his principal commission was a set of frescoes in the Palazzo Farnese in Rome depicting the history of the FARNESE FAMILY. His other commissions included tapestry designs and portraits.

*MDA*; Anna Coliva, *Francesco Salviati: I affreschi romani* (1998).

**SALVIATI, LEONARDO** (1540–89), Italian writer and academician. He was educated under Piero VETTORI and became a prominent member of the Accademia della Crusca (see ACADEMIES). His work on BOCCACCIO's *Decameron* included an expurgated edition (1582) designed to bring the work back into print (it had been placed on the INDEX in 1559) and a linguistic analysis (*Avertimenti della lingua sopra 'l Decamerone*, 1584–6); he also collaborated with a fellow academician on an analysis of TASSO's *Gerusalemme liberata*. Salviati was the author of two comedies, *Il granchio* ('The Crab') and *La spina* ('The Thorn'), both of which are modelled on the comedies of Roman antiquity.

In the debate known as the QUESTIONE DELLA LINGUA Salviati was an uncompromising supporter of Tuscan. As a young man he had set out his intention of becoming a champion of the Tuscan language in his *Orazione in lode della fiorentina favella* (1564). He was one of the organizers of the Crusca's *Vocabulario*, which in its published form (1612) incorporated many of Salviati's linguistic convictions.

*OCIL*; P. M. Brown, *Leonardo Salviati: A Critical Biography* (1974).

**SAMBIN, HUGUES** (1515/20–1601/2), French architect, sculptor, woodcarver, and furniture designer. He was born in Gray (Burgundy) and worked throughout Burgundy, where architects and woodcarvers associated with his Dijon workshop created a distinctive decorative style characterized by fanciful high-relief sculpture (e.g. Maison Milsand, Dijon, *c.*1561) and intricate rustication (e.g. the Petit Château at Tanlay, *c.*1568). His principal building was the Palais de Justice in Besançon (1581), and his carved work includes a walnut cupboard of 1570 (now in the Louvre). His *Œuvre de la diversité des termes, dont on use en architecture* (1572) contains his fine engravings of sculptural forms, especially caryatides.

*MDA*; A. Castan, *L'Architecteur Hugues Sambin* (1891).

**SAMBUCUS, JOHANNES, or (Hungarian) Zsámboki János** (1531–84), Hungarian humanist, physician, and jurist, who studied in Wittenberg, Ingolstadt, Strassburg, and Paris. In 1553 he moved to Italy, where he studied medicine in Padua and taught at Bologna. He subsequently joined the HABSBURG court in Vienna, where he worked as a physician and librarian. His publications include an EMBLEM book (1564), a commentary on Dioscorides (1577), and works on law and the interpretation of dreams.

*MEL* s.v. Zsámboki János; *Die Briefe des Johannes Sambucus*, ed. H. Gerstinger (1968).

**SAMPIERO DA BASTELICA or Sampiero Corso** (1498–1567), Corsican *condottiere* and patriot who served as a mercenary under Giovanni de' MEDICI and subsequently fought for France before returning to his native CORSICA in 1545. He was imprisoned by the Genoese government of the island and on his release travelled to France to persuade HENRI II of France to conquer Corsica by entering into a military alliance with the Ottoman Sultan Süleyman I. In February 1553 the combined forces of France and the Ottomans quickly overran the island; only Calvi remained in Genoese hands. The Emperor CHARLES V decided to intervene on behalf of Genoa, and invaded with an army of Genoese and imperial forces.

The next three years were a bloodbath, during which Sampiero fought for the French. The French won the war, but in 1559 Corsica was again passed to Genoa, which promptly levied a tax on Corsica and (in violation of the Treaty of CATEAU-CAMBRÉSIS) confiscated the property of Sampiero, who responded to these two impositions by organizing a national uprising. Sampiero visited Constantinople in an attempt to place Corsica under Ottoman suzerainty, but this plan failed, and in June 1564 Sampiero landed in Valinco with a band of 50 men; his forces, which quickly grew to 8,000 men, waged war against Genoa until 1567, when the rebellion was broken by the assassination of Sampiero.

**SAMPLER**, a cloth panel worked with various types of stitches in EMBROIDERY. The sampler was a means by which stitches were taught to beginners (usually young girls), and also helped the embroiderers to learn letters and numbers; professional samplers, like pattern books, were a means by which exemplary designs and motifs could be displayed, and it is this sense that is embedded in the word 'sampler'. In the sixteenth century designs were taken from pattern books that were printed in Germany and Italy from the 1520s, in France from the 1580s, and in England from the 1590s.

The sampler first appeared in late fifteenth-century Europe, and so coincides with the emergence of the idea that NEEDLEWORK was an appropriate pastime for women of leisure. Characters such as Hermia and Helena in SHAKESPEARE's *Midsummer Night's Dream* could recall how they had 'with our needles created both one flower, Both on one sampler'. Of the seven samplers known to survive from the sixteenth century (mostly now in the Victoria and Albert Museum), one is German, one Italian, and five English (including the earliest dated example, made in 1598 and discovered in 1960).

**SÁNCHEZ, TOMÁS** (1550–1610), Spanish theologian and jurist. Sánchez was born in Córdoba and in 1567 joined the Jesuit Order; he eventually became master of the novices at Granada. His *Disputationes de sancto matrimonii sacramento* (Genoa, 1592), published in Spanish as *Tratado sobre el matrimonio*, was a comprehensive analysis of the spiritual and moral aspects of marriage. It was widely read all over Europe, and is now regarded by Catholic authorities as a classic work on marriage and reviled by divorce reformers within and outside the Church.

Melchor Bajen Espãnol, *Pensamiento de Tomás Sánchez, S. I., sobre moral sexual* (1976).

**SÁNCHEZ COELLO, ALONSO** (*c.*1531–1588), Spanish painter of Portuguese parentage, born in Benifaró de Valls (Valencia) and educated in Brussels, where in 1571 he succeeded Antonio MORO as court painter to PHILIP II. He painted many formal court portraits, including *Joanna of Austria* (1557, Kunsthistorisches Museum, Vienna), *Infante Don Carlos* (*c.*1558, Prado), and a double portrait of *The Infantas Isabella Clara Eugenia and Catalina Micaela* (*c.*1575, Prado).
MDA.

**SÁNCHEZ COTÁN, JUAN** (1561–1627), Spanish painter, born near Toledo and trained in the Toledo studio of the still life painter Blas de Prado. His early pictures are still lifes of food (especially vegetables), a genre known in Spain as the *bodegón*. His pictures in this genre include *Still Life with Quince, Cabbage, Melon, and Cucumber* (*c.*1602, Museum of Art, San Diego, California). In 1604 he entered a Carthusian monastery, and thereafter painted religious subjects; between 1615 and 1617 he painted a cycle of pictures illustrating the life of St Bruno and the history of the Carthusian Order for the monastery in Granada, where the pictures remain.
MDA; Emilio Orozco Díaz, *El pintor Fray Juan Sánchez Cotán* (1993).

**SANDERS, NICHOLAS** (*c.*1530–1581), English Catholic polemicist. Sanders was educated at Oxford; on graduating he lectured in canon law (1551). On the accession of ELIZABETH he left England for the Continent, and was ordained at Rome in 1560. He attended the COUNCIL OF TRENT and performed diplomatic missions to Poland and Prussia before in 1565 becoming professor of theology at Louvain. Here he opposed JEWEL's *Apologia*, a defence of the Elizabethan settlements, in various writings, including *The Supper of our Lord* (1565), *The Rock of our Church* (1567), and *De visibili monarchia ecclesiae* (1571). From 1572 he became involved in Catholic politics, serving as adviser to Pope Gregory XIII, supporting Spanish war with England, and travelling to Ireland in 1579 to foment rebellion against English rule. His *De origine ac progressu schismatis Anglicani* was translated into Italian by DAVANZATI.
DNB.

**SANGALLO, ANTONIO DA, THE ELDER** (*c.*1460–1534), Italian architect, born in the Sangallo district of Florence, the son of a woodworker; he was the younger brother of Giuliano da SANGALLO and the uncle of Antonio da SANGALLO the Younger. His best surviving work is the Church of San Biagio in Montepulciano (1518–45), which is one of the finest centrally planned Renaissance churches; it is loosely modelled on BRAMANTE's plan for ST PETER'S BASILICA, and so takes the form of a Greek cross surmounted by a dome. He also built the Palazzo Nobili-Tarugi and the Palazzo Conducci in Montepulciano.
MDA; Georg Satzinger, *Antonio da Sangallo der Ältere und die Madonna di San Biagio bei Montepulciano* (1990).

**SANGALLO, ANTONIO DA, THE YOUNGER** (1484–1546), Italian architect, born in the Sangallo district of Florence; he was the nephew of Giuliano da SANGALLO and of Antonio da SANGALLO the Elder. He was trained by his uncles and then moved to Rome, where by 1503 he was working as a carpenter for BRAMANTE in the workshop of ST PETER'S BASILICA. His earliest building in Rome was probably the Church of Santa Maria di Loreto (c.1507), to which Giacomo del DUCA later added the cupola.

In 1516 Sangallo succeeded his uncle Giuliano da Sangallo as architect of St Peter's Basilica; he held the post for 30 years, and although he made extensive plans (and built an elaborate model which is now in the museum of St Peter's), he built relatively little, and most of what he did build was lost in the redesign of his successor, MICHELANGELO. He designed the interior of the Cappella Paolina in the Vatican and also built the Banco di San Spirito and the Palazzo Baldassini in Rome. His works as a military engineer include fortifications at Florence (notably the Fortezza da Basso, 1534–7) and Rome and St Patrick's Well (Pozzo di San Patrizio) at Orvieto (1537), which was commissioned by Pope CLEMENT VII to supply the town with water in the event of a siege.

Sangallo's principal patrons were the FARNESE FAMILY, particularly Cardinal Alessandro Farnese (later Pope PAUL III), for whom he designed the Palazzo Farnese in Rome. He was succeeded as architect of the palace (which is now the French embassy) by Michelangelo (till 1564), Giacomo da VIGNOLA (until 1573), and Giacomo DELLA PORTA (till 1589); in 1837 the façade was imitated (but not duplicated) for the Reform Club in London. Sangallo also built the foundations of Villa FARNESE at Caprarola, which was later completed by Vignola.

MDA; Christoph Frommel, *The Architectural Drawings of Antonio Sangallo the Younger and his Circle* (2 vols., 1994).

**SANGALLO, GIULIANO DA** (c.1445–1516), Italian architect, military engineer, and sculptor, born in the Sangallo district of Florence, the son of a woodworker. Giuliano was the elder brother of Antonio da SANGALLO the Elder and the uncle of Antonio da SANGALLO the Younger; he became the favourite architect of Lorenzo de' MEDICI. The influence of BRUNELLESCHI is apparent in his small church of Santa Maria delle Carceri in Prato (1484–91), which was among the first Renaissance churches to be designed on a Greek cross plan. Sangallo's Florentine buildings include the Palazzo Gondi (begun 1490), the Palazzo Corsi (now the Museo Horne), the sacristy in Brunelleschi's Church of Santo Spirito (1492–4, in collaboration with Il CRONACA), the atrium of Santa Maria Maddalena de' Pazzi (c.1490–5), and a design for the façade of Brunelleschi's Church of San Lorenzo (1516), for which MICHELANGELO also produced designs. Elsewhere in Tuscany, he built the MEDICI VILLA at Poggio a Caiano. His work as a military engineer for Lorenzo de' Medici includes the fortifications at Sarzana and Poggio Imperiale.

In 1514 Sangallo succeeded BRAMANTE as architect of ST PETER'S BASILICA, where he was soon succeeded by his nephew Antonio the Younger. His most important Roman building is the Church of Santa Maria dell'Anima (1514).

Sangallo also designed the Palazzo della Rovere (1496) in Savona for the future Pope JULIUS II; the façade remains, but the rest of the palace is now much altered.

MDA; Giancarlo Severini, *Architettura militari di Giovanni da Sangallo: I disegni di architettura e dell'antico* (1985).

**SAN MARCO, BIBLIOTECA DI, or Biblioteca Marciana, or St Mark's Library (Florence).** On the death of Niccolò NICCOLI in 1437, his library of c.800 volumes was bought by Cosimo de' MEDICI, who passed it to the Dominicans. The collection was placed in the Library of the Convent of San Marco, which was rebuilt by Michelozzi MICHELOZZO between 1436 and 1443. The collection expanded, but suffered at the hands of SAVONAROLA. The books that escaped destruction were bought by Pope LEO X in 1508 and returned to Florence in 1532 by Pope CLEMENT VII. In 1571 Duke COSIMO I DE' MEDICI declared the Biblioteca di San Marco to be a public library. In 1808 the collection was merged with the Bibliotheca LAURENZIANA.

**SANMICHELI or Sanmichele, MICHELE** (c.1487–1559), Italian architect and military engineer, born in Verona, the son of an architect. In about 1500 he moved to Rome, where he may have worked as an assistant to Antonio da SANGALLO the Younger. Within the Papal State he supervised the construction of the central and right gables of the Gothic façade and the campanile of Orvieto Cathedral (1510–24), in which he built the Petrucci Chapel (c.1516), and later worked with Sangallo on the fortifications of Parma and Piacenza (1526).

The SACK OF ROME ended Sanmicheli's papal patronage, and in 1527 he returned to Verona, where he became a military engineer in the service of the Venetian republic. He designed fortifications for Verona (Porta Nuova, 1539–50; Porta San Zeno, 1547–50; Porta Palio, 1548–9), Venice, and the Venetian dependencies of Corfu, Crete, Cyprus, and the Dalmatian coast; in Venice he built the Forte di San Andrea on the Lido (1535–40), now neglected but in the sixteenth century described by VASARI as one of the most imposing fortresses in Europe.

Sanmicheli was also a designer of palaces. In Venice he built Palazzo Corner-Mocenigo (c.1543) and Palazzo Grimani (c.1566, now the Court of Appeal), on the Grand Canal. In Verona he built Palazzo Pompei (c.1527–57, now the Natural History Museum), Palazzo Canossa (c.1530), and Palazzo Bevilacqua (c.1530). His Veronese buildings also include the Pellegrini Chapel (c.1528) in the Church of San Bernardino, and the round Church of the Madonna di Campagna (1559).

MDA; Lionello Puppi, *Michele Sanmicheli architetto: Opera completa* (1986).

**SANNAZARO, JACOPO** (1457–1530), Italian poet, born into a noble family in Naples, where he lived for many years at the court. In 1501 he followed King FEDERICO into exile in France, returning to Naples after the king's death in 1504. With the support of PONTANO, Sannazaro became a member of the Neapolitan Academy (see ACADEMIES).

Sannazaro wrote in both Latin and Italian. His most important Latin poem was *De partu Virginis* (1526), an epic on the birth of Jesus. His principal work in Italian was *L'Arcadia*, a pastoral romance in which verse eclogues are linked by a prose narrative. *L'Arcadia* proved to be enormously popular, and established the shape of European PASTORAL for the next two centuries.

*OCIL*; C. Kidwell, *Sannazaro and Arcadia* (1993).

**SANO DI PIETRO or (formally) Ansano di Pietro di Mencio** (1405–81), Italian painter and the head of the largest workshop in fifteenth-century Siena. The workshop produced ALTARPIECES in the style of SASSETTA for village churches near Siena.

*MDA*.

**SAN PEDRO, DIEGO DE** (*c*.1437–*c*.1498), Spanish writer of prose fiction and poetry. He was by profession the administrator of Peñafiel and by virtue of his literary gifts a seminal figure in the history of courtly romance. His *Tratado de amores de Arnalte e Lucenda* (Burgos, 1493) is a conventional courtly romance, but *La cárcel de amor* (Seville, 1492), in which the lover is taken by Desire to the 'prison of love' of the title, is the most important Spanish sentimental romance of the fifteenth century, and its popularity is attested by the 24 editions and 20 translations of the sixteenth century; the English version by Lord Berners is thought to be in part responsible for the English literary style known as EUPHUISM. San Pedro's love poems were printed in the *Cancionero general* of Fernando de CASTILLO.

Keith Whinnom, *Diego de San Pedro* (1974).

**SANSEVERINO FAMILY**, an ancient Neapolitan family, from the eleventh century the leading family of the kingdom of Naples; the family's fiefs, which numbered more than 300 landholdings, were in effect governed independently of the machinery of government (which they also dominated). In the struggle between the Aragonese and the Angevins for the throne of Naples, the family was divided: Roberto Sanseverino, count of Caiazzo (d. 1487), supported FERRANTE I of Aragon, but his son Galeazzo (d. 1525), who was married to a daughter of Ludovico SFORZA, died fighting for the French at the battle of PAVIA. The *condottiere* Ferrante Sanseverino, prince of Salerno (d. 1507), who was the patron of Bernardo TASSO, fought in the imperial army of CHARLES V. Ferrante was a resolute defender of Neapolitan rights in the face of imposed Spanish institutions and when the Spanish INQUISITION was introduced in Naples in 1552 he was obliged to flee to France to avoid becoming one of its victims.

**SANSOVINO, ANDREA, or Andrea Contucci** (*c*.1457–1529), Italian sculptor and architect, born in a Tuscan village near Monte San Savino and trained in the Florentine studio of Antonio POLLAIUOLO. He worked in Portugal from 1491 to 1501, but no work from this period is known to survive. He subsequently moved to Rome, where he sculpted the companion tombs for Cardinal Ascanio Sforza and Cardinal Basso della Rovere (1505–9, Church of Santa Maria del Popolo) and *The Virgin and Child with St Anne* (1512, Church of Sant'Agostino). Sansovino worked from 1513 to 1527 in

Loreto, where he was responsible for the sculpture of the shrine of the Holy House (Sanctuario della Santa Casa). The finest surviving example of his architecture is the courtyard of the Palazzo della Signoria in Jesi.

*DBI* s.v. Contucci; *MDA*; G. H. Huntley, *Andrea Sansovino, Sculptor and Architect of the Italian Renaissance* (1935); Nicoletta Baldini and Renato Giulietti (eds.), *Andrea Sansovino: I documenti* (1999).

**SANSOVINO, FRANCESCO** (1521–86), Italian political philosopher, historian, poet, and recorder of art and architecture, born in Venice, the son of Jacopo SANSOVINO. His works include a treatise on forms of government in Italy (*Del governo dei regni e delle repubbliche*, 1561), a history of the noble families and cities of Italy (1576), and *Venetia* (1581), a fourteen-volume artistic and architectural survey of Venice.

*OCIL*.

**SANSOVINO, JACOPO TATTI** (1486–1570), Italian architect and sculptor, born in Florence, where he trained in the studio of Andrea SANSOVINO, whose surname he assumed. He lived in Rome from *c*.1505, working as a sculptor and a restorer of antique statues, and in 1517 had a well-publicized quarrel with MICHELANGELO; his principal architectural project in Rome was Palazzo Gaddi.

In 1527 the SACK OF ROME forced Sansovino to leave the city, whereupon he moved to Venice, where he was appointed *protomagister* of San Marco (in effect, city architect) in 1529. He began work on the Church of San Francesco della Vigna (to which PALLADIO was to add the façade) in 1534, and in the late 1530s embarked on a series of important buildings now known as the Libreria Vecchia, the Palazzo della Zecca, and the Loggetta. The Libreria Vecchia, which was long known as the Libreria del Sansovino, was built to house the Biblioteca MARCIANA and now houses the Museum of Archaeology; Palladio praised the building as the finest since classical antiquity. The adjoining Palazzo della Zecca was the mint, which now houses the Biblioteca Marciana. His other buildings in Venice include the façade of the Church of San Giuliano (1553–55), Palazzo Corner della Ca' Grande (*c*.1550, now the seat of the Prefecture), and, on the mainland, Villa Garzoni, Pontecasale (*c*.1530). His best-known sculptures in Venice are the statues of *Mars* and *Neptune* (1550), the 'giants' at the top of Antonio RIZZO's Scala de' Giganti in the Doge's Palace.

*MDA*; Deborah Howard, *Jacopo Sansovino* (1975); Bruce Boucher, *The Sculpture of Jacopo Sansovino* (2 vols., 1991); Manuela Morresi, *Jacopo Sansovino* (2000).

**SANTA CRUZ, ÁLVARO DE BAZÁN, MARQUIS OF** (1526–88), Spanish admiral, born at Granada on 12 December 1526, the son and grandson of military men who were also called Álvaro de Bazán; Don Álvaro's grandfather had taken part in the conquest of Granada in 1492, and his father entered the service of CHARLES V and rose to become commander-in-chief of the Mediterranean fleet of the Spanish navy.

Bazán joined the military ORDER of Santiago and followed his father into the navy. In 1564 he took part in the capture of

Vélez del Peñon de la Gomera (Arabic Badis) on the north coast of AFRICA, and he subsequently commanded a fleet of galleys in the blockade of Tétouan. In 1568 PHILIP II appointed Bazán as commander of the Neapolitan fleet of galleys, and the following year created him marquis of Santa Cruz. At the battle of LEPANTO (7 October 1571), in which he commanded the reserve fleet, the commander of the Ottoman left wing outflanked the Christian right wing commanded by Gian Andrea DORIA, and Santa Cruz's rapid response was deemed to have averted a defeat. In 1573 he supported Don JUAN DE AUSTRIA in his attack on TUNIS.

In 1580 Santa Cruz participated in the subjugation of POR-TUGAL; he was subsequently appointed admiral of the ocean and charged with subduing Portugal's island possessions in the Atlantic, which continued to support a pretender to the Portuguese throne. The fleet of the Portuguese pretender, which was supported by English and French privateers, was defeated off Terceira (in the AZORES) by Santa Cruz in 1583. On 9 August 1583 he wrote to Philip II from Angra (Terceira) proposing an invasion of England, an idea that subsequently led to the raising of the Spanish ARMADA. He returned to Lisbon to prosecute his plan, and was appointed commander of the Armada. He was held to account for Sir Francis DRAKE's destruction of the Spanish fleet at Cádiz in 1587, but nonetheless continued to prepare the Armada to invade England. He died in Lisbon on 9 February 1588, a few months before the Armada sailed to defeat under the command of the count of MEDINA SIDONIA.

*DBEH* s.v. Bazán; *DHE.*

**SANTI, GIOVANNI** (c.1435/40–1494), Italian painter and writer who worked as court painter and chronicler for the ducal court in Urbino. His surviving paintings include a *Madonna* in the Ducal Palace in Urbino and an *Annunciation* in the Brera (Milan). His verse chronicle in 23,000 verses, *La vita e le geste di Federico di Montefeltro* (composed 1484–7), is a history of the dukes of Urbino dedicated to GUIDOBALDO DA MONTEFELTRO; it also contains incidental comments about many contemporary artists in its 'Disputa della pictura' (chapter 91). Santi is now principally known as the father of RAPHAEL.

*MDA*; Ranieri Varese, *Giovanni Santi* (1994).

**SANTI DI TITO** (1536–1602), Italian painter, born in Sansepolcro (Borgo San Sepolcro, Umbria) and trained in the Florentine studio of BRONZINO. He worked in Rome with Federico BAROCCI and Federico ZUCCARO before returning to Florence and establishing himself as a painter of ALTARPIECES for churches such as Santa Maria Novella, Santa Croce, San Salvatore, San Giuseppe, and, in his later years, for churches in the *contado* (dependent territory) of Florence.

*MDA* s.v. Tito, Santi di.

**SANTILLANA, ÍÑIGO LÓPEZ DE MENDOZA, MARQUIS OF** (1398–1458), Spanish statesman, poet, and literary theor-ist, the son of the admiral of Castile, who died when Íñigo was 6 years old. He was raised by his grandmother, the formidable Doña Mencía de Cisneros, and lived at the court

of Aragon from 1412 to 1418. During this period he began to assemble his private library, part of which is now in the Biblioteca Nacional de Madrid; his collection included many classical manuscripts, though he could not read Latin or Greek. In 1445 Mendoza fought alongside his nephew Gómez MANRIQUE at the battle of Olmedo (1445), where his side was defeated; in the same year he became count of Real de Manzanares and marquis of Santillana.

In 1449 Santillana collected his poems at the request of Don Pedro de Portugal, and prefaced the collection with an essay on poetry (*Prohemio e carta que el marqués de Santillana envió al condestable de Portugal*) which ranges from a taxon-omy of poetry (sublime poetry in the learned languages, mediocre poetry in the vernaculars, and low poetry in ballads and popular songs) and the first history of vernacular verse to a defence of the nobility and civic utility of poetry.

Santillana's own poetry includes 42 Petrarchan sonnets (*Sonetos, hechos al itálico modo*), which are the first sonnets in the Spanish language, an allegorical *Comedieta de Ponça* (which celebrates the defeat of ALFONSO V of Aragon by the Genoese in a naval battle of 1535 off the coast of Ponza), a collection of moral apophthegms (*Proverbios de gloriosa doctrina e fructuosa*), a consolation to his cousin the count of Alba in prison (*Diálogo de Bías contra Fortuna*), and an attack against Álvaro de LUNA (*Doctrinal de privados*). Santillana also wrote a number of songs in traditional style, of which the early examples are rooted in the troubadour tradition of Galicia (one is written in Galician) and the late examples are Italianate.

*DHE* s.v. López de Mendoza; R. Lapesa, *La obra literaria del marqués de Santillana* (1957); D. W. Foster, *The Marqués de Santillana* (1971).

**SANTO STEFANO, ORDER OF THE KNIGHTS OF, or (Italian) Cavalieri di Santo Stefano**, an order of CHIVALRY founded by COSIMO I DE' MEDICI in 1562 to defend the coast of Tuscany against pirates.

G. Guarnieri, *I cavalieri di Santo Stefano nella storia della marina italiana 1562–1859* (1960).

**SANUTO or Sanudo, MARINO THE YOUNGER** (1466–1536), Venetian diarist and historian, born on 22 May 1466, the son of the Venetian senator Leonardo Sanuto; he was orphaned at the age of 8, and his inheritance was misspent by his guardian; his lack of wealth permanently hampered his prospects for advancement. He was elected to the Maggior Consiglio in 1486 and from 1498 was regularly elected *savio di ordeni*, which gave him a seat in the Senate, but was twice passed over for the post of official historiographer, first when SABELLICUS was succeeded by NAVAGIERO and again when Navagiero was succeeded by Pietro BEMBO. His friends included ALDUS MANUTIUS, who dedicated his editions of POLIZIANO and OVID to Sanuto. In 1531 he was granted an annual pension of 150 gold ducats.

Sanuto published nothing during his lifetime, but he was a prolific writer. In 1483 he accompanied his cousin Mario (who was one of the three *sindici inquisitori* and was hearing appeals from the decisions of the *rettori*) on a journey through Istria and the *terraferma* of Venice, and as he travelled he visited scholars and their libraries and transcribed inscriptions; his *Itinerario per la terrafirma veneziana* was eventually published in 1847. He also wrote a continuation of a chronicle of the lives of the doges (*Le vite dei dogi*, 1733), an account of the War of FERRARA in 1482–4 (*Comentarii della guerra di Ferrara*, 1829), and an account of CHARLES VIII's invasion of Italy in 1494–5 (*La spedizione di Carlo VIII*, 1873).

Sanuto's *Diaries*, which in their printed form fill 58 volumes, are a minute account of his life and times from 1 January 1496 until September 1533. The diary, in which the tone of personal passages is often bitter, is a compendium of daily events and gossip that also contains transcriptions of personal and official correspondence and of government records ranging from committee minutes to polling lists to international treaties; much of this material survives in no other source.

*I diarii*, ed. R. Fulin et al. (58 vols., 1879–1903); Eric Cochrane, *Historians and Historiography in the Italian Renaissance* (1981).

**SARACCHI FAMILY**, a family of goldsmiths and ROCK-CRYSTAL engravers in late sixteenth- and early seventeenth-century Milan. In the late sixteenth century Giovanni Ambrogio (1540/1–after 1595), the head of the family business from 1579, worked in partnership with his four brothers, Simone (1547/8–before 1595), Stefano (1550/1–before 1595), Michele (after 1550–after 1595), and Raffaello (c.1550–before 1595). The next generation consisted of Giovanni Ambrogio's four sons: Gabriele (who became court jeweller in Mantua in 1617), Pietro Antonio, Gasparo, and Costanzo.

The products of the family workshop, especially engraved rock-crystal vases, were collected by courts in Italy and Germany. Examples of the family's work are preserved in the Pitti Palace in Florence, the Residenzmuseum in Munich, and the Kunsthistorisches Museum in Vienna.

*MDA.*

**SARACENI, CARLO** (c.1579–1620), Italian painter. He was born in Venice, but spent most of his short life in Rome. The influence of ELSHEIMER (whose pupil he may have been) and CARAVAGGIO is particularly apparent in his LANDSCAPES on copper (of which nine survive in the Museo Nazionale in Naples), typically portraying mythological scenes. Saraceni contributed to the decorative frescoes in the Quirinal Palace and also painted altarpieces for Roman churches.

*MDA*; Anna Ottani Cavina, *Carlo Saraceni* (1968).

**SARAVIA, ADRIAEN** (1530–1613) Flemish Protestant theologian. He was born into a Hispano-Flemish family in Artois, and as a young man entered the Franciscan ORDER in Saint-Omer. He was converted to Protestantism in 1557, and from 1559 to 1562 lived as a religious refugee in London, where he was a member of the Dutch Reformed Church in Austin Friars. After a brief period as minister of the Walloon congregation in Antwerp, Saravia was appointed as the first master of Elizabeth College in Guernsey (1568), and four years later moved to Southampton as master of King Edward

VI School. Saravia returned to the Netherlands in 1578, working as a reformed minister in Ghent (1578–82) and Leiden (1582–4) and as professor of theology at Leiden (1584–7). The recall of his patron Robert Dudley, earl of Leicester, caused Saravia to flee once again to England, where he held a series of ecclesiastical appointments.

Saravia's principal theological work was a treatise on episcopacy, *De diversis ministrorum evangelii gradibus* (1590), in which he based his advocacy of episcopacy on divine law (*ius divinum*). The treatise (which later became important in the English debate about episcopacy) was implicitly directed against BEZA, who replied in 1592; Saravia in turn replied in 1594. In the first decade of the seventeenth century Saravia served on the London committee responsible for the translation of the Bible.

*DNB*; *NNBW* ix; W. Nijenhuis, *Adrianus Saravia* (1980).

**SARDINIA or (Italian) Sardegna**. The Mediterranean island of Sardinia, which lies 12 kilometres (7 miles) south of CORSICA, was in the Middle Ages a pawn in the protracted struggle between Pisa and Genoa. In 1297 Pope Boniface VIII invested King James II of Aragon with Sardinia, but he did not attempt to claim the island until 1323, when he mounted an invasion; by 1326, the Aragonese conquest was complete. In 1403 a feudal marquisate (the marquisate of Oristano) was imposed on the island, and in 1421, when ALFONSO V of Aragon visited Sardinia, the Cortes (which consisted of the three ESTATES of nobles, clergy, and burghers) ratified a legal code (*carta de logu*) that thereafter applied to the whole island. In 1478 the marquisate was abolished in favour of viceregal rule, which was administered by feudal lords and by assemblies of the Cortes, which was convoked every ten years; the language of Spanish administration was CATALAN, a dialect of which is still spoken in Cagliari. Sardinia remained a Spanish province until 1708, after which it passed to Austria and thence to Savoy, Piedmont, and Italy.

**SARMIENTO DE GAMBOA, PEDRO** (1532–92), Spanish seaman and historian, born in Alcalá de Henares. He served as a soldier and (from 1555) as a seaman, and developed a reputation for his skills in NAVIGATION. He participated in the expedition of Álvaro de Mendaña in the Pacific (1567–9) and accompanied Francisco de TOLEDO on his viceregal tour of Peru (1570–2), out of which came Gamboa's *Historia Indica*, an account of the Incas which emphasized their cruelty and contrived to demonstrate the illegality of the Inca empire; the *Historia* remained in manuscript until it was published in 1906.

After Sir Francis DRAKE's appearance on the Peruvian coast, Gamboa was sent in pursuit of Drake, departing from Callao in October 1579 and surveying the Strait of Magellan (through which Drake had passed) with a view to fortifying it against further incursions. He proceeded to Spain, where PHILIP II appointed Gamboa as governor of the Strait and dispatched him with sixteen ships laden with settlers and supplies with a view to establishing a colony on the western side of the Strait. A colony was established close to what is now Punta Arenas, but it failed within a few years; when Thomas CAVENDISH arrived in 1587, he found the starving survivors of the settlement, which he named 'the Town of Famine' and which was later known in English as 'Port Famine'.

Gamboa sailed for Spain in 1586, but was intercepted by English ships and taken as a prisoner to England; he was released after an audience with Queen ELIZABETH. He again sailed for Spain, and was again captured, this time by HUGUENOTS, who ransomed him to Spain in 1590.

DHE; Stephen Clissold, *Conquistador: The Life of Don Pedro Sarmiento de Gamboa* (1954); Rosa Arciniega, *Pedro Sarmiento de Gamboa, el Ulises de América* (1956).

**SARPI, PAOLO** (1552–1623), Italian philosopher and historian, born in Venice; his baptismal name was Pietro, which he changed to Paolo when he became a Servite friar. He developed interests in OPTICS and magnetism, and in the 1590s was drawn into the patrician society of Venice. In 1606 Venice fell under a papal interdict promulgated by Pope PAUL V because the Senate had enacted laws restricting the right of the Church to own property, whereupon the Senate asked Fra Paolo to advise on the points in dispute and appointed him as consultant in theology and canon law to the republic. Throughout the confrontation with the papacy it was Sarpi who issued the propaganda that championed the Venetian position.

The interdict was lifted in 1607, but Sarpi was permanently estranged from the papacy. Thereafter he worked to create an international network of allies, who included Protestants, GALLICANS and dissident Catholic CONCILIARISTS. In his principal scholarly work, the *Istoria del concilio tridentino*, Sarpi sought to expose the process by which the papacy, abetted by the JESUITS, manipulated the COUNCIL OF TRENT in order to subvert the process of reform. The manuscript of the treatise was smuggled to England, where it was published under the pseudonym Pietro Soave Polano. It is an outstanding example of late humanist historical writing.

**SASSETTA, IL,** or **Stefano di Giovanni** (c.1400–1450), Italian painter, a native of Siena, where his first recorded work is an altarpiece (now dispersed; panels for the predella are now in the Pinacoteca in Siena, the Vatican, the Museum of Fine Arts in Budapest, and the Bowes Museum in Barnard Castle) for the Arte della Lana Chapel (1423–6). His *Madonna of the Snow* (1432), an early SACRA CONVERSAZIONE, is now in the Pitti Palace in Florence. His most famous work is an altarpiece depicting *The Life of St Francis of Assisi* painted in 1444 for the Church of San Francesco at Sansepolcro (Borgo San Sepolcro, Umbria), of which seven small panels survive in the National Gallery in London and one in the Musée Condé in Chantilly.

*MDA.*

**SATTLER, MICHAEL** (c.1490–1527), German Anabaptist leader, born near Freiburg, where he became a Benedictine monk and rose to become prior of the Monastery of St Peter, in the Black Forest. In 1525 he left his monastery,

married, and fled to Zürich, where he joined a group of Swiss ANABAPTISTS. He was expelled by the town council (which was dominated by Zwinglians) in 1525 and the following year travelled to Strassburg, where he was welcomed by Wolfgang CAPITO and Martin BUCER. In February 1527 he chaired a meeting of Swiss and German Anabaptists which adopted the SCHLEITHEIM CONFESSION, which he probably wrote. Soon after, he and his wife were arrested in Horb, where he had many followers, and taken to Rottenburg for trial. Both were convicted of heresy: Sattler was burnt at the stake on 20 May 1527 and two days later his wife Margaretha was executed by drowning.

J. H. Yoder, *The Legacy of Michael Sattler* (1973); C. A. Snyder, *The Life and Thought of Michael Sattler* (1984).

**SAVERY, ROELANDT** (c.1576–1639), Flemish painter and etcher. He was born in Kortrijk (French Courtrai) and worked in the Amsterdam studio of his brother Jacques (and possibly in the court of HENRI IV of France) before travelling to Prague (c.1604) to enter the service of RUDOLF II. He painted many of the animals in the emperor's menagerie (e.g. *Paradise*, in the National Gallery in Prague), and his drawings include a dodo drawn from a living specimen. He travelled with the imperial court in Tirol and the Alps, where he executed many LANDSCAPE paintings and drawings. From 1612 to 1616 he worked in Vienna in the service of the Emperor MATTHIAS, and in 1619 he settled in Utrecht, where he remained for the rest of his life and became a distinguished painter of STILL LIFES, particularly flower paintings in the Flemish tradition.

*BNB s.v. Savery, Roland; MDA.*

**SAVILLE, SIR HENRY** (1549–1622), English scholar, educator, and collector of manuscripts. Educated at Oxford, Saville travelled on the Continent in 1578, where he began to collect manuscripts. He became tutor in Greek to ELIZABETH on his return. In 1585, partly through the influence of CECIL, he was appointed warden of Merton College, Oxford, which flourished under his leadership. In 1591 his translation of four books of TACITUS was published. In 1596, after some manoeuvring, he became provost of Eton (whilst maintaining the wardenship of Merton). In 1604 he was knighted by JAMES VI; he corrected the Latin translation of James's *Apology for the Oath of Allegiance* (1609) and was involved with the production of the authorized translation of the Bible. In 1610 the first volume of his edition of Chrysostom was printed at Eton, with a press Saville acquired for that purpose; the remainder of the work appeared by 1613. He also edited Xenophon's *Cyropaedia* (1613). He assisted Thomas BODLEY in the establishment of the Bodleian Library, and founded the Savillean chairs of astronomy and geometry at Oxford.

**SAVOLDO, GIOVANNI GIROLAMO** (*fl.* 1506–48), Italian painter, born in Brescia; he trained in Florence and worked principally in Venice. His few surviving paintings, which show the influence of TITIAN, include a *Transfiguration* (Uffizi) and a *Mary Magdalene* (National Gallery, London). His portrait of *Gaston de Foix* (Louvre) uses the device of the double mirror reflection to illustrate the PARAGONE, the debate about the relative merits of painting and sculpture.

*MDA*; Antonio Boschetto, *Giovan Gerolamo Savoldo* (1963).

**SAVONAROLA, GIROLAMO** (1452–98), Dominican friar, born in Ferrara on 21 September 1452, the son of a courtier and the grandson of a famous physician. In 1475, after a sudden conversion, Savonarola left Ferrara for Bologna, where he entered the Dominican monastery. He became a preacher in Florence (1482–4), San Gimignano (1484–5), and Brescia (1486), and in 1490, at the request of Lorenzo de' MEDICI, he returned to Florence, where he became prior of the monastery of San Marco in July 1491.

Savonarola developed an increasingly apocalyptic style of preaching and, after the death of Lorenzo in 1492, became a prominent critic of the Medici family. In 1493 Savonarola separated his monastery from the Reformed Congregation of Lombardy, and thereafter resisted the efforts of Pope ALEXANDER VI to return the monastery to the jurisdiction of Lombardy; Savonarola became vicar-general of his new congregation, to which additional priories were soon added.

In 1494 Piero II de' MEDICI was exiled and Savonarola became the principal political figure in the republic, on which he imposed a theocratic government that retained some elements of democracy. On 13 May 1497 he was excommunicated by Pope Alexander, but declined to accept his excommunication and continued to preach, affirming his orthodoxy by the publication of his Catholic apology, 'The Triumph of the Cross' (Latin *Triumphus Crucis*, Italian *Il trionfo della Croce*). In 1498 the government of Florence joined forces with the Church and arrested Savonarola, who confessed to heresy under TORTURE and was burnt at the stake on 23 May 1498. The memory of Savonarola was revived when the republic of 1527–30 proclaimed Christ to be its king, and he is now being considered for canonization.

D. Weinstein, *Savonarola and Florence* (1970).

**SAVORGNAN FAMILY**, Friulian family of *condottieri* and military engineers in the service of Venice; the seat of the family was Osoppo, on the Austrian border. The most prominent Savorgnan *condottieri* were Girolamo (1466–1529), who is buried in an exquisite sarcophagus in Osoppo, his son Mario (d. 1594), and Giulio Savorgnan (1516–95), who as superintendent of fortifications designed defence installations on the Venetian *terraferma* and in Venetian possessions overseas, including Corfu, Crete, and Cyprus.

E. Salaris, *Una famiglia di militari italiani . . . I Savorgnani* (1913).

**SAVOY or (French) Savoie or (Italian) Savoia or Savoy-Piedmont, DUCHY OF**, a mountainous principality which in the late fourteenth century, when it was a county (i.e. ruled by a count of the House of SAVOY), included what are now the French *départements* of Savoie and Haute-Savoie, the Swiss cantons of Geneva and Vaud (which includes Lausanne), and the Italian regions of Valle d'Aosta and Piedmont (which includes Turin) and part of Liguria; Savoy extended south in a narrow corridor to the Mediterranean, where its port was Nice. In 1416 the status of Savoy was raised from county to duchy by the Emperor SIGISMUND, and Amadeus VIII became the first duke of Savoy; in 1440 he was elected as Pope FELIX V.

After the death of Pope Felix V in 1451, Savoy began to decline: the SWISS CONFEDERATION acquired Vaud and the lower Valais (1475–6), Geneva became independent (1533), and Savoy became a battleground in the WARS OF ITALY, as a consequence of which it ceased to exist as an independent state when the remaining territories of the principality were occupied by the army of FRANCIS I (1536). Under the Treaty of CATEAU-CAMBRÉSIS (1559), Savoy was restored to EMANUELE FILIBERTO, who attempted to convert the WALDENSES by force. In 1563 he moved the capital from Chambéry (where the ducal chateau, now the Prefecture, still stands) to Turin, so inaugurating the gradual process by which the culture of the duchy became more Italian than French.

Savoy was ruled by a single dynasty for almost a thousand years: in 1000, Umberto I became count of Savoy and in 1946 Umberto II was deposed as king of Italy. Members of the family were counts of Piedmont from 1043, dukes of Savoy from 1391, kings of Sardinia (1720–1861), kings of Italy (1861–1946), king of Albania (1939–43), and emperor of Ethiopia (1936–43), and from the fifteenth century also styled themselves kings of CYPRUS and of the (non-existent) crusader kingdoms of Jerusalem and Lesser Armenia.

F. Cognasso, *I Savoia* (1971).

**SAXONY**, an electoral duchy in eastern Germany. The early medieval duchy consisted of what is now Lower Saxony (Niedersachsen), but the area now known as Saxony is the territorial inheritance of the electorate created in 1423 when the Emperor SIGISMUND granted Friedrich I of Saxony (Friedrich der Streitbare, i.e. 'the Quarrelsome', who was also Friedrich IV of Meissen) the duchy of Saxony-Wittenberg and endowed the duchy with the electoral privilege. From 1423 to 1918, Saxony was ruled by members of the WETTIN family. The principal cities of Saxony were Dresden, LEIPZIG, Meissen, Chemnitz (1953–90, Karl-Marx-Stadt), and Zwickau.

In 1485 the duchy was divided between two of the sons of Friedrich II, each of whom was styled 'duke of Saxony' (*Herzog von Sachsen*): Ernst, the founder of the Ernestine line, inherited Saxony-Wittenberg and Thuringia, and also inherited the electorship; his brother ALBRECHT III ANIMOSUS, the founder of the Albertine line, inherited Meissen and Osterland. On the succession of the Ernestine and Albertine lines, see Appendix I. The territories under Ernestine rule came to be known as the electorate of Saxony, and those under Albertine rule as the duchy of Saxony.

Ernst was succeeded as elector by FRIEDRICH III, who in 1502 founded the University of WITTENBERG and appointed Martin LUTHER to the staff; the eventual consequence of this appointment was that the electorate of Saxony became the cradle of the REFORMATION.

On 19 May 1547, in an agreement known as the Capitulation of Wittenberg, the Ernestine Elector JOHANN FRIEDRICH I surrendered the electoral dignity and the province that contained Wittenberg to MAURICE OF SAXONY, head of the Albertine branch of the Wettin family; this capitulation had been occasioned by the defeat of the electorate in the SCHMALKALDIC WAR, when Johann Friedrich was captured by the Emperor CHARLES V. Thereafter the duchy and electorate were united, except for Thuringia, which remained an Ernestine possession and was eventually divided into five principalities: Saxe-Weimar, Saxe-Eisenach, Saxe-Gotha, Saxe-Meiningen, and Saxe-Altenburg.

The united duchy and electorate (except for Thuringia) passed in 1553 to AUGUSTUS I, who secured recognition of his legitimacy as elector from Johann Friedrich in the Naumburg Treaty of February 1554, but his fear of an Ernestine coup long remained an important influence on his domestic and foreign policies. In 1567 Matthias FLACIUS ILLYRICUS supported the Ernestine cause by preaching against Augustus, and Johann Friedrich's champion Wilhelm von GRUMBACH led a rebellion, for which he was tortured and executed.

The electorate and the duchy were thereafter united until the dissolution of the HOLY ROMAN EMPIRE in 1806, when Saxony became a kingdom that survived until the proclamation of the republic in 1918. In the twentieth century Saxony disappeared as an official territorial designation when the *Länder* of the German Democratic Republic were dissolved in 1952, but Saxony and Saxony-Anhalt were revived together with the other three *Länder* in the GDR when Germany was reunified in 1990.

R. Kötzschke and H. Krezschmar, *Sächsische Geschichte* (2 vols., 1935).

**SAXTON, CHRISTOPHER** (c.1542–1611), English cartographer, born in Yorkshire and educated at Cambridge. In 1572 he received a commission to survey and draw maps of every county in England and Wales. His *Atlas of the Counties of England and Wales* was published in 1579, and was the first provincial atlas of any country. Saxton subsequently engraved an influential map of England and Wales (1583).

*DNB.*

**SBARRI, MANNO DI BASTIANO** (1536–76), Italian goldsmith, a native of Florence; he may have been trained in the studio of Benvenuto CELLINI. His best-known work is the silver setting of the Cassetta Farnese, a set of rock-crystal panels engraved by Giovanni BERNARDI (1561, Museo Nazionale, Naples). In 1561 Cardinal Alessandro FARNESE commissioned a crucifix and a pair of candlesticks for St Peter's Basilica in Rome. Two years after Sbarri's death in 1576, Cardinal Farnese passed the commission for three pieces to Antonio GENTILI, who completed the task (1581) and signed the altar set before it was placed in the sacristy of St Peter's in 1582; the role of each artist in this collaborative work has been the subject of scholarly debate, but Sbarri is usually thought to have been responsible for the figures in the style of MICHELANGELO at the base of each piece.

**SCALA, BARTOLOMEO** (1430–97), Italian humanist, born in Florence, the son of a miller. He studied law in Florence and then in Milan under Francesco FILELFO. On returning to Florence he joined the household of Piero I de' MEDICI, and in 1459 became secretary of the GUELF party. Piero was succeeded in 1469 by his son Lorenzo de' MEDICI, and Scala served as Lorenzo's treasurer. Despite this extended service to the Medici, Scala later wrote a defence of the republic under SAVONAROLA, in whose administration he had worked after the exile of the Medici. Scala also wrote a history of Florence from its remote beginnings to 1450.

Alison Brown, *Bartolomeo Scala 1430–1497* (1979); *Bartolomeo Scala: Humanistic and Political Writings*, ed. Alison Brown (1997).

**SCALIGER, JOSEPH JUSTUS** (1540–1609), French classical scholar, born in Agen, the tenth child of Julius Caesar SCALIGER. He was educated at home and (from 1552) at the College of Guienne in Bordeaux. He returned home in 1555 because of an epidemic of plague, and for the next three years worked with his father, who inducted Joseph into classical scholarship. On his father's death in 1558 Joseph moved to Paris, where he was taught by Adrien TURNÈBE, Jean DORAT, and Guillaume POSTEL, and studied Hebrew and Arabic as well as Greek and Latin.

In 1563 Scaliger secured the patronage of Louis de Chastaigner, sieur de La Roche Pozay, with whom he travelled to Rome (where they met Marc-Antoine de MURET) and then across Europe to England and Scotland; their association lasted until the death of Louis in 1595. On returning to France Scaliger studied law with CUJAS for three years. Scaliger had converted to Protestantism, and on the outbreak of the WARS OF RELIGION fought on the Huguenot side (1567–70) before taking up a teaching post in Geneva (1572–4). Thereafter he lived in France until 1593, travelling with the household of Chastaigner in response to the vicissitudes of the wars. In 1593 Scaliger moved to Leiden, where he lived for the last thirteen years of his life; he held a chair at the University of Leiden, where he was the successor of LIPSIUS, but ensured before taking up the appointment that he would not be required to teach, because he greatly disliked lecturing.

Scaliger's scholarly works include editions of the *Catalecta* (1575), Festus (1575), Catullus, Tibullus, and Propertius (1577), Manilius (1579), Apuleius (1600), and Julius Caesar (1606). Scaliger also wrote a chronology of antiquity (*De emendatione temporum*, 1583), which, drawing on his knowledge of Manilius and of Copernican astronomy, revolutionized the received chronology of the ancient world; *De emendatione temporum* is also remarkable for its integration of biblical chronology into the history of the classical world and for its pioneering use of Persian, Babylonian, and Egyptian history. The apogee of Scaliger's chronological scholarship was his *Thesaurus temporum* (1606), a comprehensive chronicle of the ancient world which includes an extraordinary reconstruction of the lost chronicle of Eusebius.

In the last years of his life Scaliger, who was the most eminent Protestant scholar in Europe, became the target of Catholic controversialists. Scaliger imprudently published a boastful account of his life and family (*Epistola de vetustate et splendore gentis Scaligerae*, 1594), which was mercilessly attacked by Gaspar Scioppius in *Scaliger hypobolimaeus* ('The

Suppositious Scaliger', 1607); Scioppius was later to boast that his book had killed Scaliger, who replied with a *Confutatio fabulae Burdonum* (1608) and died five months later.

A. T. Grafton, *Joseph Scaliger: A Study in the History of Classical Scholarship* (2 vols., 1983–93).

**SCALIGER, JULIUS CAESAR, or (French) Jules-César Scaliger or (Italian) Giulio Cesare Scaligero** (1484–1558), Italian scholar, physician, and literary theorist in France. He claimed to be a descendant of the Veronese DELLA SCALA family. As a young man he entered the Franciscan Order, and later became a soldier. His best-known works were *Oratorio pro M. Tullio Cicerone* (1531), an embittered attack on ERASMUS, and *Poetices libri septem* (1561), an Aristotelian treatise on literary theory which proved to be a seminal influence on notions of decorum in seventeenth-century French drama.

*Acta Scaligeriana*, ed. J. Cubelier de Beynac and M. Magnien (1986).

**SCAMOZZI, VINCENZO** (1548–1616), Italian architect and architectural theorist, born in Vicenza, the son of a builder; he was trained by PALLADIO, whose principal successor he became in northern Italy. His finest early work is the Rocca Pisana, a hilltop VILLA at Lonigo, near Vicenza (1575–8). After Palladio's death in 1580 Scamozzi completed several of his unfinished buildings, including La Rotunda and the Teatro Olimpico (to which he added the permanent stage set) in Vicenza (1583–4) and San Giorgio Maggiore in Venice. His most important independent works are the Procuratie Nuove in Venice (c.1584), a Palladian building designed to complement the style of SANSOVINO's adjoining library, the THEATRE in Sabbioneta (1588), and the Palazzo Trissino (now the Palazzo del Comune) in Vicenza (1592).

Scamozzi's *Discorsi sopra le antichità di Roma* (1582) describes the surviving antiquities of Rome. His influential architectural treatise *L'idea dell'architettura universale* (Venice, 1615) is a defence of Palladian principles which hardly mentions Palladio and an attack on the baroque style; this treatise contained the codification of the architectural ORDERS that was to remain authoritative for centuries.

*MDA*; Rainald Franz, *Vincenzo Scamozzi* (1999).

**SCARSELLINO or Scarsella, Ippolito** (c.1550–1620), Italian painter, draughtsman, and miniaturist, born in Ferrara and trained in Bologna and Venice; he worked in several north Italian towns, but mainly in Ferrara. Large numbers of his paintings survive, including a fine *Nativity* (Brera, Milan) and an allegorical *Fame Conquering Time* (Wadsworth Atheneum, Hartford, Connecticut).

*MDA*; Maria Novelli, *Lo Scarsellino* (1964).

**SCENERY, THEATRICAL.** The origins of stage scenery lie in the perspective paintings on the walls behind the actors in late fifteenth-century dramatic performances in Italy. The first artist to construct decorated theatrical scenery was Baldassare PERUZZI, who, according to VASARI, based his designs (for plays to be performed for Popes LEO X and

CLEMENT VII) on VITRUVIUS. Sebastiano SERLIO, who was Peruzzi's pupil, inherited his notes and drawings and used them in his *Architettura*. In the section dealing with perspective (published in 1545) Serlio describes the theatrical scenery required for different dramatic genres; the model was of a street receding from the front of the stage and flanked on either side by paintings of houses, which were appropriately foreshortened. Theatrical scenery modelled on Serlio was installed in a hall in Siena which was converted into a theatre in 1560.

The alternative to the Serlian model was an adaptation of the ancient practice of acting in front of a background that in Roman antiquity had evolved into a huge architectural façade. In theatres such as SCAMOZZI's Olimpico at Vicenza and his *teatro all'antica* in Sabbioneta, each of the arches in the façade opened into a perspectival painting of a receding street.

Theatrical scenery was further developed by Bernardo BUONTALENTI for his lavish entertainments for the grandducal court of Tuscany. The engravings illustrating his *Intermezzi* of 1589 depict painted scenes at the sides of his stages, but it is not clear whether these were portable wings that could be replaced with each new scene. Buontalenti's innovations passed through his successor Giulio Parigi to Inigo JONES, who became the most accomplished stage designer of seventeenth-century England. The public theatres in England did not use scenery, but the courtly masques and entertainments mounted by Inigo Jones had elaborate scenery (and costumes), details of which are recorded in a series of drawings now at Chatsworth.

**SCEPTICISM**, a philosophical tradition characterized by an epistemology centred on doubt about human ability to obtain knowledge. The principal exponent of scepticism in antiquity was Pyrrho of Elias (hence the term Pyrrhonism to denote a particular school of scepticism), whose teachings were embodied in the writings of Sextus Empiricus and the biography of Pyrrho by Diogenes Laertius. The revival of scepticism in fifteenth- and sixteenth-century Europe was occasioned by the rediscovery of the writings of Sextus Empiricus; its decline in the seventeenth century was symbolized by Descartes's declaration that the defeat of scepticism was the first obligation of philosophy.

Renaissance scepticism had a religious dimension, and was concerned to examine the criteria for religious truth as well as scientific issues such as the cosmology of Copernicus. The most prominent sceptics were ERASMUS and MONTAIGNE. Erasmus deployed sceptical arguments to combat LUTHER, arguing (like Sextus) in favour of conformity to traditional practices on the grounds that no reliable criterion of truth could be deployed to invalidate those practices. Montaigne, who had a medal struck with the sceptical motto 'Que sçay-je?' (modern French *sais-je*), made sceptical arguments available in the vernacular in his *Apologie de Raymond Sebonde* (*Essais* 2. 12).

R. H. Popkin, *The History of Scepticism from Erasmus to Spinoza* (1979).

**SCÈVE, MAURICE** (*c*.1510–1564), French poet and humanist, born in Lyon. His best-known work is *Délie, objet de plus haute vertu* (1544), which was the first collection of French love poems on the Petrarchan model; the collection is illustrated by some 50 emblematic WOODCUTS. Scève also wrote *La Saulsaye, églogue de la vie solitaire* (1547), a PASTORAL debate in the tradition of SANNAZARO, and *Microcosme* (1562), a scientific hexameral poem which extends from the Creation to the death of Adam and (through Adam's prophetic dream) to the coming of Christ.

Dorothy Coleman, *Maurice Scève, Poet of Love* (1975).

**SCHAFFNER, MARTIN** (1477/8–1549), German painter and medallist, a native of Ulm. For most of his career Schaffner specialized in ALTARPIECES, and when the Reformation destroyed that market, he turned to portraiture. His paintings show the influence of Hans BURGKMAIR and Hans SCHÄUFELIN, but also contain Italian elements drawn from LEONARDO DA VINCI. His religious paintings include *Descent into Limbo* (1519, Staatsgalerie, Stuttgart, on loan to Ulmer Museum in Ulm), and his portraits include *Eitel Besserer* (1516, Ulmer Museum) and *Eitel Hans Besserer* (1529–30, Alte Pinakothek, Munich).

MDA.

**SCHAPPELER, CHRISTOPH** (*c*.1472–1551), Swiss reformer in Memmingen. He was born in St Gallen and in 1513 became a priest at St Martin's Church in Memmingen, an imperial free city in southern Swabia. In 1517 he met KARLSTADT, who dedicated his first publication to Schappeler. By 1521 Schappeler was advocating the cause of reform in his sermons, not because he dissented from Catholic theology but rather because he thought that the Church exacerbated the plight of the poor. He was expelled by his bishop in February 1524, and thereafter became a public opponent of tithing (largely on social grounds) and began to develop sympathies for Reformation theology.

In January 1525 Schappeler proposed a series of reformation theses for a disputation, rejecting tithing, auricular confession (i.e. confession to the ear of a priest), the invocation of the Virgin Mary and the saints, and the Catholic doctrines of the EUCHARIST and PURGATORY; he supported the call for communion in both kinds and endorsed the doctrinal formulations of the TWELVE ARTICLES, to which he may have contributed the marginal annotations. Schappeler's precise confessional allegiance is not clear, but the configuration of his doctrinal positions is redolent of the UTRAQUISTS. In January 1525 Schappeler escaped the suppression of the PEASANTS' REVOLT by returning to St Gallen, where he served as minister until his death on 25 August 1551.

**SCHARDT, JAN JORISZOON VAN DER** (*c*.1530–after 1581), Netherlandish sculptor, born in Nijmegen. He lived in Italy in the 1560s, and in 1569 entered the service of MAXIMILIAN II in Vienna. In the early 1570s he was often in Nuremberg, and from 1576 to 1579 worked at the Danish court. His best-known works are terracotta busts of the Nuremberg merchant and art collector *Willibald Imhoff* (1570) and his wife *Anna Imhoff* (1581), both now in the Gemäldegalerie in Berlin.

MDA.

**SCHÄUFELIN** or **Schäufelein, HANS LEONHARD** (*c*.1480–1538), German painter and wood engraver, a native of Nuremberg, where he worked in the studio of DÜRER. In 1505 he moved to Augsburg, and later settled permanently in Nördlingen, of which he became a citizen in 1515. The best-known products of his workshop were the illustrations for the *Teuerdank* (1517) of the Emperor MAXIMILIAN I. His paintings include ALTARPIECES and other pictures for churches (notably the *Christgärteneraltar* in the Bayerisches Staatsgemäldesammlung in Munich, of which six panels are on loan to the Schaezlerpalais in Augsburg) and civic buildings (notably the fresco of *The Siege of Bethulia* in the Nördlingen Town Hall, 1515). Schäufelin's son Hans the Younger also became an engraver.

MDA s.v. Schäufelein; Christof Metzger, *Der Christgartener Altar des Hans Schäufelin* (1996).

**SCHEDEL, HARTMANN** (1440–1514), German humanist, born on 13 February 1440 in Nuremberg and educated at the University of Leipzig (1456–60). In 1563 he moved to Padua, where he studied medicine; he returned to Nuremberg in 1480 and worked there as a physician for the rest of his life; he died on 28 November 1514.

Schedel was a member of the circle of humanists, artists, and printers in Nuremberg and a collector of manuscripts and printed books. His *Liber chronicarum*, popularly known as the 'Nuremberg Chronicle', was published in 1493 by Anton KÖBERGER and illustrated with 1,809 woodcuts by Michael WOLGEMUT and his stepson Wilhelm Pleydenwurff (son of Hans PLEYDENWURFF); a German version, the *Weltchronik*, was published in the same year by Simon (or Georg) Alt.

DLL.

**SCHEDONI** or **Schidone, BARTOLOMEO** (1578–1615), Italian painter, born near Modena; by 1597 he had moved to Parma, where he spent his career in the service of the FARNESE family except for an interlude (1602–6) at the ducal court in Modena, where he executed an emblematical series on *The Life of Coriolanus* in the Palazzo Pubblico. Many of his other paintings survive in the Galleria Nazionale in Parma and the Museo Nazionale in Naples.

MDA; Federica Dallasta, *Bartolomeo Schedoni: Pittore emiliano* (1999).

**SCHEIDT** or **Scheid** or **Scheit, KASPAR** (*c*.1520–1565), German satirist, a schoolmaster in WORMS and the uncle of Johann FISCHART, who was educated in his house. In 1551 Scheidt published a loose translation of Friedrich DEDEKIND's Latin satire *Grobianus* into German rhyming verse, entitling it *Grobianus: Von groben sitten und unhöfflichen geberden*. Scheidt's version of the satire is much earthier than the Latin original; it enjoyed huge popularity in Germany and was translated into other modern European languages. Scheidt also wrote a consolatory poem on the death of a wife, *Frölich Heimfahrt* (1552).

DLL.

**SCHEIN, JOHANN HERMANN** (1586–1630), German composer who was educated as a boy soprano in the elector of Saxony's Hofkapelle, and later at the University of Leipzig and the specialist music and humanities Schulpforta near Naumburg. He wrote sacred music which reflects the influence of VIADANA, and Lutheran chorales and secular music setting his own texts.

**SCHEINER, CHRISTOPH** (1573–1650), German astronomer. He entered the JESUIT Order and in 1610 became professor of mathematics and Hebrew at Ingolstadt. In 1612 one of his correspondents published a booklet which contained some letters about sunspots sent to him by Scheiner, writing under the pseudonym Apelles, the first account of this phenomenon; this work brought Scheiner into a protracted dispute with Galileo GALILEI. Scheiner returned to the subject at much greater length in his *Rosa ursina* (1630), in which he also described his experiments in 1612 on the use of a CAMERA OBSCURA for solar observation. Scheiner's treatise on OPTICS (*Oculus*, 1619) confirmed the view of Felix Plater (1536–1614), whose anatomical work had been used by KEPLER, that the retina was the site of image formation.

*DSB.*

**SCHIAVONE or Andrea Meldolla or (Croatian) Andrija Medulić** (c.1510–1563), Dalmatian painter, engraver, and etcher, born into an Italian family in Zara (then a Venetian possession, now Croatian Zadar). He settled in Venice, where he painted two of the pictures of philosophers in the Great Hall of the Biblioteca MARCIANA. He also painted frescoes on the façades of Venetian palaces, but none has survived. Of his panel paintings the best known is *Christ before Herod* (c.1560, Museo Nazionale, Naples).

*MDA; Francis Richardson, Andrea Schiavone (1980).*

**SCHIAVONE, GIORGIO or (Croatian) Juraj Ćulinović** (c.1433/6–1504), Dalmatian painter, born in Sebenico (then a Venetian possession, now Croatian Šibenik); his surname reflects his Slavic origins. Schiavone worked with SQUARCIONE in Padua from 1456 to 1461, during which time he painted the polyptych *Virgin and Child with Saints* (National Gallery, London). He then returned to Dalmatia, where he worked in Zara (now Croatian Zadar) for two years before settling in Sebenico; his paintings for Sebenico Cathedral have been destroyed, but the *Virgin and Child Enthroned* in the Church of St Louro in Sebenico is probably a late work by Schiavone.

*DBI s.v. Ćulinović, Juraj; MDA.*

**SCHICKHARDT, HEINRICH** (1558–1635), German architect, a distinguished exponent of the Italian Renaissance style whose historical importance is occluded by virtue of the historical accident that none of his buildings survives. He worked with his mentor Georg Beer (d. 1600) on the Neues Lusthaus at Stuttgart (1584–93, since demolished) and in 1590 was appointed as the official architect to Ludwig, duke of Württemberg; he subsequently accompanied Ludwig's nephew and successor, Friedrich I of Mömpelgard, on a protracted visit to Italy (1598–1600).

Schickhardt returned to Germany with an informed understanding of Italian Renaissance architecture and immediately began work on an Italianate wing for Stuttgart Castle (1600–9, destroyed 1777); the extension was a symmetrical building with scores of Tuscan columns. Schickhardt also contributed to the development of TOWN PLANNING by designing the town of Freudenstadt; its many unusual features include an L-shaped church (1601–9) with separate naves for men and women and an altar and pulpit at the corner. The town was destroyed in April 1945 but has been rebuilt from the ashes.

*MDA; Ehrenfried Kluckert, Heinrich Schickhardt: Architekt und Ingenieur (1992).*

**SCHINER, MATTHÄUS** (1456–1522), Swiss cardinal, statesman and soldier, born in Mühlbach and educated in Zürich; he was appointed bishop of Sitten (Sion) in 1500 and about eight years later was secretly made a cardinal. In 1509 Schiner became JULIUS II's legate to the SWISS CONFEDERATION and in 1511 his cardinalate was made public. Two years later he mobilized Swiss troops to support the SFORZA, and his army defeated the French at the battle of NOVARA. In 1515 he commanded the Swiss forces that were defeated at the battle of MARIGNANO. He supported the election of the Emperor CHARLES V in 1519, and in 1521 commanded a Swiss army in the Spanish conquest of Milan.

*A. Büchi, Kardinal Matthäus Schiner als Staatsmann und Kirchenfürst (1937).*

**SCHLEITHEIM CONFESSION or Schleitheim Articles**, a confession of faith, probably drafted by Michael SATTLER, adopted on 24 February 1527 by an assembly of SWISS BRETHREN at Schleitheim, a border town near Schaffhausen. The Confession, which was entitled *Brüderliche Vereinigung etlicher Kinder Gottes* ('Fraternal Union of Some of the Children of God'), contained seven articles which affirmed (1) believers' baptism; (2) excommunication only after two private admonitions and one public admonition had failed; (3) that the Lord's Supper, which is described in terms of Zwinglian memorialism (see EUCHARIST), is restricted to those who have undergone believers' baptism; (4) abstinence from worldly pleasures, including visits to taverns; (5) that pastors were to be chosen for their honesty and integrity; (6) a refusal to bear arms and to participate in government or the administration of justice; (7) a refusal to take oaths.

The Confession was quickly controverted by ZWINGLI and, in 1544, by CALVIN.

**SCHLICK, ARNOLDT** (c.1460–c.1521), German composer, organist, and author of a treatise on organs. He acted as organ consultant in Hagenau, Speyer, and Neustadt an der Haardt (now Neustadt an der Weinstrasse). He wrote about both building and playing organs in *Spiegel der Orgelmacher und Organisten* (1511), and his *Tabulaturen etlicher Lobgesang* includes some of his own compositions as well as the first printed German organ tablatures.

**SCHMALKALDIC ARTICLES or (German) Schmalkaldische Artikel**, a doctrinal statement drawn up by Martin LUTHER in 1536 at the behest of JOHANN FRIEDRICH, elector of Saxony, for presentation to the General Council convoked in Mantua by Pope PAUL III for 23 May 1537. The name derives from the fact that the Articles were approved by an assembly of Protestant princes (the SCHMALKALDIC LEAGUE) and Lutheran theologians that met at Schmalkalden (Thuringia) on 23 February 1537.

Luther's version of the text consisted of three sections. First, he used an exposition of the creeds to delineate the doctrines on which there was no disagreement. Second, he set out a long and detailed account of the matters on which there was no agreement, attacking the Roman doctrines of the EUCHARIST, PURGATORY, the authority of the pope, the invocation of saints, and the corruption of the religious ORDERS. Third, he described the doctrines on which Protestants were divided amongst themselves, such as the eucharist.

The Schmalkalden Assembly approved Luther's text, but also approved a conciliatory appendix at the request of MELANCHTHON, who was willing to concede limited authority to the pope. In 1538 Luther printed the Articles without Melanchthon's appendix as *Artikel christlicher Lehre*, and in 1580 this version was incorporated into the Book of CONCORD. The Latin title *Articuli Smalcaldici* was first used in an edition of 1553.

**SCHMALKALDIC LEAGUE or League of Schmalkalden or (German) Schmalkaldischer Bund**, a Protestant alliance formed in Schmalkalden (Thuringia) on 27 February 1531 to defend Protestant states and towns against the forces of the Emperor CHARLES V; the leaders of the League were JOHANN FRIEDRICH I, elector of Saxony, and PHILIP OF HESSE. In 1532, when the imperial forces were threatened by the advance of the Ottomans, Charles V and the League signed a treaty known as the Peace of NUREMBERG. The German Catholic princes responded to the threat of the League by forming the Catholic League of NUREMBERG in 1538. The refusal of the Protestants to participate in the COUNCIL OF TRENT led to a revival of hostilities, and the League was defeated in the SCHMALKALDIC WAR.

**SCHMALKALDIC WAR or (German) Schmalkaldischer Krieg** (1546–7), a war between the Emperor CHARLES V and the SCHMALKALDIC LEAGUE of Protestant princes of Germany. The turning point in the war was Charles's conclusion of a secret agreement with MAURICE OF SAXONY, which eased the imperial conquest of southern Germany. Charles then advanced north, and the League was defeated at the battle of MÜHLBERG on 24 April 1547.

**SCHÖFFER, PETER** (*c*.1425–*c*.1503), German printer. He was born in Gernsheim (Rhine) and by 1449 was working as a scriptor (i.e. manuscript copyist) in Paris. He later married Dyna (or Christina), the daughter of Johann FUST, and in 1466 succeeded his late father-in-law in his PRINTING business in Mainz. He was, together with GUTENBERG, one of the earliest printers, and he is said to be the first printer to have developed a satisfactory method of stamping matrices.

On 14 August 1457 Schöffer and Fust published the elegant Mainz Psalter, which was the first book to use colours, and in 1462 a two-volume Latin Bible. Their edition of CICERO's *De officiis* (1465) was the first book to contain Greek characters. After Schöffer inherited the business he printed the first book advertisements and the first title pages. His son Johann inherited the business and ran it until his death in 1531; his best-known books are an edition of Johannes TRITHEMIUS' *Compendium* and a complete LIVY (1518–19).

**SCHOLASTICISM IN THE RENAISSANCE.** Scholasticism is a method of scholarly enquiry which resolves apparent contradictions in ancient (and so authoritative) works by recourse to logic (see LIBERAL ARTS), which enables the scholar to discern the underlying truth (*veritas rerum*) to which the authoritative texts bear witness. The revival of scholasticism in the Catholic Church in the late nineteenth and early twentieth centuries created an anachronistic synonymity between medieval theology and the scholastic method. In fact not all medieval theology was scholastic (William of Ockham declared logic to be of limited use for theology), and the scholastic method was used in many disciplines, including law and medicine.

The humanists of fifteenth-century Italy were the most influential detractors of scholasticism. The central antischolastic work was the *Dialecticae disputationes* of Lorenzo VALLA, who argued that language was more remarkable for its persuasive power than for its embodiment of logical certainty. The influence of Valla and his successors eventually extended to the UNIVERSITIES, where the study of logic was gradually replaced by the analysis of RHETORIC in the literature of classical antiquity.

**SCHONGAUER, MARTIN** (1435/50–1491), German engraver and painter, born in Colmar (Alsace), the son of a goldsmith from Augsburg; except for a brief spell at the University of Leipzig in 1465, he lived in Colmar throughout his life. Schongauer's contemporary reputation as Germany's greatest artist was based on his engravings (which he always initialled), in which he endowed popular religious subjects with the dignity of his lyrical idiom. Of his few surviving paintings, the best known is the *Madonna in the Rose Garden* (or *Virgin and the Rosebush*) of 1473 (Church of St Martin, Colmar). Schongauer's fame attracted the young DÜRER, but by the time he reached Colmar in 1492, Schongauer had died.
MDA.

**SCHÖNSPERGER, JOHANN** (1481–1523), German printer in Augsburg. Schönsperger was appointed imperial court printer to MAXIMILIAN I, for whom he published a magnificent prayer book (1513) set in a specially designed Gothic type and printed in ten copies on vellum. He also published the emperor's *Teuerdank* (1517).

**SCHOUTEN, WILLEM CORNELISZOON** (*fl.* 1590–1619), DUTCH EAST INDIA COMPANY captain who was appointed as commander of two Dutch ships bound for South America with a view to finding a route to ASIA further south than that used by the Spanish; the expedition was sponsored by Isaac Le Maire, a former director of the DUTCH EAST INDIA COMPANY, and the head of the expeditionary mission was his son Jacob Le Maire. The *Eendracht* and the *Hoorn* sailed out of the Texel on 14 June 1615; the *Hoorn* was accidentally burnt in Deseado (Argentina) while being breamed (i.e. having encrusted seaweed burnt off the hull), so Schouten proceeded south in the *Eendracht* and on 29 January 1616 rounded the tip of South America, passing south of Tierra del Fuego; the southern extremity was named Cape Horn, with reference to the town of Hoorn (West Friesland), of which Captain Schouten was a native. They named Staaten Island (now Isla de los Estados), at the eastern extremity of Tierra del Fuego, after the ESTATES-GENERAL of the Netherlands, and named the channel (now Estrecho de la Maire) after the Le Maire family. Schouten sailed across the Pacific and along the coast of New Guinea before reaching the Moluccas. The resident governor of the Dutch East India Company refused to believe that Schouten and Le Maire had found a new route into the Pacific and declared the ship's logbook to be a forgery.

NNBW vii; Edward Duyker (ed.), *Mirror of the Australian Navigation* (1999).

**SCHWANK** (plural *Schwänke*), a literary and dramatic German genre. Until the sixteenth century, the *Schwank* was a narrative form (in verse or prose) consisting of humorous episodic narratives connected only by a central character who is a practical joker (e.g. TILL EULENSPIEGEL). In the sixteenth century, the narrative *Schwank* were supplemented by a new form, the dramatic *Schwank*, of which the most distinguished exponent was Hans SACHS.

H. Fischer (ed.), *Schwankerzählungen des deutschen Mittelalters* (1967); E. Strassner, *Schwank* (1968).

**SCHWARZ, HANS** (*c*.1492–*c*.1522), German medallist and sculptor, born in Augsburg. He was the first German exponent of the portrait MEDAL, an art that had been revived in Italy; the faces of Schwarz's sitters are shown in profile or in three-quarters view, which was the Italian style. His subjects included the imperial councillor Kunz von der Rosen (*c*.1519), Lucia Dorer (1522), and three members of the Schauderspacher family (1522), Magdalena, her son Georg, and her daughter Ursula.

Schwarz's sculptures, which are usually in low relief, include work for the FUGGER family chapel in the Church of St Anne in Augsburg, executed to designs by DÜRER.

MDA.

**SCHWENCKFELD, KASPAR** (1489–1561), German radical reformer and mystic. He was born into a noble family on their estate in Lower Silesia, and after studying in Cologne entered the service of the duke of Liegnitz (now Polish Legnica). His mysticism drew on the sermons of the fourteenth-century Dominican Johann Tauler, and his incipient Protestantism was developed through an immersion in the writings of LUTHER. In 1522 he went on a pilgrimage to Wittenberg, where he met KARLSTADT.

On returning to SILESIA Schwenckfeld preached the Reformation and imposed a strict rule of church discipline on his followers, but refused to assent to Luther's doctrines of the EUCHARIST and of JUSTIFICATION by faith. This position incurred the enmity of both Protestants and Catholics, and in 1529 Schwenckfeld left Silesia for Strassburg. In the 1530s Schwenckfeld's theology became more heterodox, and from 1533 to 1535 he lived in exile in a succession of south German cities.

Schwenckfeld's heterodoxy centred on his Christology: he developed a doctrine of the deification or glorification of Christ's humanity (*Vergötterung des Fleisches Christi*), which led to his expulsion from Ulm. In 1540 he published an elaborate defence of his Christology in *Konfession und Erklärung*, as a result of which he became a religious outcast: an anathema was issued from Schmalkalden and his books were banned in Protestant centres. Schwenckfeld spent the rest of his life evading the authorities, and died in Ulm on 10 December 1561.

After Schwenckfeld's death, his followers, who called themselves the 'Confessors of the Glory of Christ', continued to propagate his teaching, and in 1564 inaugurated a four-volume collection of his writings. They evolved into a distinctive sect which in the seventeenth century developed an allegiance to the writings of Jacob BÖHME. In 1720 a commission of JESUITS was dispatched to Silesia to convert the sect by force, and many fled abroad. The group that in 1734 reached Philadelphia, where they still survive, are known as Schwenckfelders; the sect survived in Silesia until 1826.

*Corpus Schwenckfeldianorum* (19 vols.; vols. i–xv, 1907–39; vols. xvi–xix, 1959–61); P. C. Erb, *Schwenckfeld in his Reformation Setting* (1978); P. C. Erb (ed.), *Schwenckfeld and Early Schwenckfeldianism* (1986); R. E. McLaughlin, *Caspar Schwenckfeld, Reluctant Radical: His Life to 1540* (1986).

**SCOREL, JAN VAN** (1495–1562), Dutch painter and humanist, born in Schoorl (near Alkmaar) on 1 August 1495, the son of a priest: an imperial Act of 1541 rescinded his illegitimacy. He worked for a period in 1516–17 in the Utrecht studio of Jan GOSSAERT and in 1519 set out on a journey that was to take him as far as Jerusalem. He stopped for long periods in Speyer, Strassburg, Basel, and Nuremberg and finally reached Venice, where he joined a party of Dutch pilgrims and sailed to Crete, Rhodes, Cyprus, and Jerusalem; his portraits of *Twelve Members of the Haarlem Brotherhood of Jerusalem Pilgrims* (*c*.1528, Frans Halsmuseum, Haarlem) and his series of Utrecht Pilgrim portraits (Central Museum, Utrecht) are early examples of the Dutch tradition of group portraiture; some sheets from his sketchbook survive in the British Museum. After returning to Venice he travelled to Rome, where he was warmly received by Pope ADRIAN VI (a native of Utrecht), whose portrait (now lost) he painted. In 1524 Jan returned to Utrecht, where he was appointed a canon and remained for the rest of his life.

Jan van Scorel painted ALTARPIECES (mostly destroyed or lost) which show that while in Rome he had studied antique sculpture and the work of RAPHAEL and MICHELANGELO. His LANDSCAPES are rooted in a Netherlandish tradition, but also show the influence of Italian painting. In addition to painting, Jan van Scorel worked on the restoration of St Mary's Church in Utrecht and cleaned the Ghent altarpiece of Hubert and Jan van EYCK.

*MDA*; *NNBW* x; G. J. Hoogewerf, *Jan van Scorel* (1923).

**SCOT, REGINALD** (1538–99), English writer on hops and witchcraft. Educated at Oxford, Scot married in 1568 and lived as a country gentleman, serving as MP 1588–9. He is noted for two works. The first, published in 1574, with further editions in 1576 and 1578, is the *Perfect Platform of a Hop-Garden*, the first treatise on hop growing produced in England. In 1584 his *Discourse of Witchcraft* was published; this denounced belief in WITCHCRAFT as contrary to both reason and religion.

**SCOTLAND**. At the outset of the fifteenth century, Scotland was in civil war, as the rule of Robert III was disputed. His son James was captured and passed to King Henry IV of England; he remained in English hands for eighteen years. On his return to Scotland as James I in 1424, he attempted to establish there the centralized monarchical rule which he had witnessed in England, striking against enemies amongst the Scottish lords. He was murdered in 1437 as part of a failed coup by opponents of this newly asserted royal power. His son James II continued to break the power of Scottish lords, precipitating three years of civil war from 1452 with his murder of the eighth earl of Douglas, head of the family of his chief opponents. James III's exalted sense of personal authority perhaps stemmed from these efforts of his father and grandfather. His marriage to Margaret of Denmark, who brought Orkney and Shetland with her as dowry, saw Scotland's borders extended to the north; to the south, however, Berwick was lost to the English in 1482, and James himself was imprisoned in Edinburgh Castle for a time. His reign ended in 1488 as his 18-year-old son, the future JAMES IV, claimed the throne from his unpopular father. James IV's reign saw Scotland benefit from a programme of royal expenditure and patronage which sought to emulate those of the greatest Renaissance princes.

An invasion of Northumberland in 1496–7 brought the retaliation of HENRY VII; James's marriage with Margaret Tudor, Henry's daughter, did not bring lasting peace with England, but did ensure the eventual union of the two crowns through the succession of their great-grandson JAMES VI to the English throne in 1603. For the present, however, the Scottish allegiance with France, which funded the expansion of the Scottish navy, proved stronger than peace with England. In 1513, with HENRY VIII occupied in France, Scotland invaded England; the English retaliated with the destruction of the Scottish king and the cream of the nobility at the battle of Flodden in the same year.

James IV's death brought his son JAMES V to the throne in his infancy. A magnatial power struggle occupied the regency, but James asserted royal authority on coming of age

in 1528, and pursued a programme of royal aggrandizement. He exploited the emergence of reformist opinion in the 1530s to counter the power and wealth of the Church, and renewed the traditional alliance with France through his marriage with MARY OF LORRAINE. He died shortly after the defeat of his army by the English at Solway Moss in 1542, leaving the dowager queen to reign as regent until the majority of his daughter MARY, QUEEN OF SCOTS. Mary's marriage would determine the future of Scotland, and although initially engaged to the future EDWARD VI of England, in 1558 she married the future FRANCIS II of France, thus seemingly binding Scotland to the French monarchy and Catholicism. A brief Protestant rebellion ensued, but the death of Francis in 1560 saw Mary return to Scotland alone. A claimant to the English throne through her grandmother Margaret Tudor, she was a threat to ELIZABETH, and when she abdicated her throne in 1567, following the murder of DARNLEY and her marriage to BOTHWELL, she was imprisoned and eventually executed in England. The earl of MURRAY served as regent during the infancy of James VI, through whom the crowns, if not the governments, of England and Scotland were united in 1603.

J. McQueen (ed.), *Humanism in Renaissance Scotland* (1990).

**SCOTTISH ARCHITECTURE**. Renaissance architecture in Scotland was primarily a decorative form applied to existing buildings rather than a structural form, and the most important influence is French (particularly the chateaus of the Loire) rather than Italian. The idiom of the French Renaissance can be seen in the great halls of Edinburgh Castle (especially the carved stone corbels), Falkirk Palace, and Stirling Castle, for example, which are all decorated in a French Renaissance idiom. A rare example of what appears to be Italian influence is the façade of Crichton Castle (1581–91), which is made from diamond-shaped ashlar blocks redolent of the Palazzo dei Diamanti in FERRARA.

Richard Fawcett, *Scottish Architecture: From the Accession of the Stewarts to the Reformation, 1371–1560* (1994); Deborah Howard, *Scottish Architecture: Reformation to Restoration* (1995).

**SCOTTISH GARDENS**. Scottish Renaissance gardens were constructed on the French model, though the hilly landscape of Scotland meant that some gardens were terraced in the Italian style, notably the lost royal garden at Linlithgow. There is little detailed documentation of Scottish gardens before the end of the sixteenth century, and very few gardens have survived, even in attenuated form. Falkland Palace, in Fife, had a royal gardener amongst its employees from 1456, but he and his successors seem to have grown little other than onions. In 1513 the wooden trellis that enclosed the garden was replaced by a stone wall, and in 1628 a plan for 'planting and contriving the garden anew' was effected, but little is known of the layout and contents, save that it included a real tennis court. The gardens are now laid out brilliantly in the style of the seventeenth century, but this is entirely the work of the twentieth-century designer Percy Cane. Similarly, the garden of Edzell Castle (Angus), the seat of the Lindsay family, is largely lost. It was constructed in 1604, possibly to the design of the then owner, the poet Sir

David Lindsay, but nothing is known of the original layout. What do survive, however, are the stone sculptured walls that enclosed the original garden. The walls are faced with panels in which bas-relief sculpture alternates with either flower boxes or birds' nests. The sculptures on the east wall depict the planetary deities (Mercury, Venus, Mars, etc.); those on the west wall show the four cardinal virtues (prudence, temperance, fortitude, and justice), and those on the south the LIBERAL ARTS.

The only Scottish Renaissance garden to have survived in substantially unaltered form (though not content) is the King's Knot at Stirling Castle. The garden was laid out c.1540, and was long known as the New Garden, to distinguish it from the King's Privy Garden, which was a KNOT GARDEN laid out in 1532. There is no documentary evidence of the original plantations of the New Garden, but the surviving terraces and ramps show that this was a garden on the grand scale. The garden was laid out in a long rectangle with a central square of turf terraces rising in the form of an octagon. At the top there is a MOUNT which is the King's Knot, which would originally have been surmounted with a PAVILION from which to view the garden.

E. H. M. Cox, *A History of Gardening in Scotland* (1935).

**SCOTTISH LANGUAGES.** Three languages were spoken in early modern Scotland. In the lowlands of the south, the language was Scots, a close relative of English (or, as some would have it, a dialect of English) which is variously known as Lowland Scots (the academic term) or Lallans (the nationalist term) or 'the Doric' (the term used in the north-east); Scots was also spoken in Orkney and Shetland and in parts of Ulster.

In the highlands of northern Scotland, the principal language was Scots Gaelic, one of the three languages (together with Irish Gaelic and Manx Gaelic) of the Goidelic group of Celtic languages. Scots Gaelic now survives only on the west coast and in the Western Isles.

The Northern Isles (Orkney and Shetland) had been Norwegian possessions until they were pledged to the Scottish crown in 1468. Until that date the language of the Northern Isles was Norn, a Scandinavian language that did not die out until the eighteenth century. In the intervening centuries, Norn was gradually displaced by Scots, which was the language of the Church.

**SCOTTISH LAW.** Scotland has shared a monarch with England since 1603, and in 1707 Scottish and English parliaments were fused into a single British Parliament, which in 1801 merged with the Parliament of Ireland to become the Parliament of the United Kingdom. Despite these constitutional ties, Scottish law is of a quite different character from ENGLISH LAW, and, except in the area of FEUDAL LAW, was not significantly influenced by English law until the nineteenth century. The fundamental distinction between COMMON LAW and equitable jurisdictions in England has never existed in Scotland. Similarly, the Roman law that stood at the heart of Scottish law until the nineteenth century has never been a significant presence in English law. One consequence of this distinction is that Scottish law has long been codified, initially on the Justinian model. In practice this distinction means that English judges search for appropriate precedent, whereas Scottish judges base their reasoned judgments on codified principles.

Roman law and CANON LAW were introduced into medieval Scotland by the Church. The administration of the law was in the hands of the king's council, one branch of which evolved into a parliament which was legislating by the twelfth century and declaring, changing, and applying the law by the end of the thirteenth century. By 1425 there was a firmly established royal court of justice. In 1426 a common law of Scotland was declared, by which all Scots were deemed to be subject to the king's national laws rather than to particular laws and privileges. The royal court of justice and the ecclesiastical courts were both influenced by Roman law, which entered Scotland from France, with which Scotland had long enjoyed a firm alliance. The other important elements in Scottish law were indigenous CUSTOMARY LAW, the LAW MERCHANT, international MARITIME LAW, and FEUDAL LAW.

In 1532 the College of Justice was formed, consisting of seven lay judges, seven clerical judges, and a clerical president; this structure remained unaltered until 1808. The College discharged its civil responsibilities by establishing the Court of Session, which was a permanent civil court. The Court of Session has never had a criminal jurisdiction; from the early sixteenth century till the establishment of the High Court of Justiciary in 1672, criminal justice was administered by special commissions or local 'deputes'. In 1563 ecclesiastical courts were replaced by the Commissary Court of Edinburgh, the jurisdiction of which included marriage, divorce, and bastardy; in 1573 the Commissary Court introduced divorce on the basis of desertion.

Until 1468, when Orkney and Shetland were impignorated to the Scottish Crown, the legal code in force in the Northern Isles was udal law, which derived from the Norse Magnus Code of 1274. During the period from 1468 to 1615 (the end of the Sinclair earldom), udal law was gradually supplanted by Scottish law, though in certain important areas, including land tenure (which is feudal in Scottish law but allodial in udal law), the udal system remained (and remains) in force.

David Walker, *A Legal History of Scotland* (5 vols. to date, 1988–98).

**SCOTTISH LITERATURE.** The literary languages of fifteenth- and sixteenth-century Scotland were Scots and Latin; very little Gaelic literature survives, though there is an important collection of ballads in the manuscript known as the Book of the Dean of Lismore. In both Scots and Latin most imaginative writing was associated with the court. In Scots, the principal poets (Scots 'makars') were King James I, Robert Henryson, William Dunbar, and Gawin Douglas. King James was almost certainly the author of *The King's Quire*; Henryson wrote a sequel to Chaucer's *Troilus and Criseyde* entitled *The Testament of Cresseid*; Dunbar's poems include the powerful 'Lament for the Makars'; Gawin Douglas wrote original verse and also translated the *Aeneid* (*Eneados*, 1553). The most important vernacular playwright (who was also a poet) was Sir David Lindsay, whose morality play *A Satire of the Three Estates* was performed before the court in 1540 and 1552. In Latin, the principal writers were the humanists George BUCHANAN, Hector BOECE, and John MAJOR and the jurists William BARCLAY and Sir Thomas CRAIG.

**SCROTS or Scrotes or Stretes, GUILLIM** (*fl.* 1537–53), Flemish painter. He was court painter to MARY OF HUNGARY (regent of the Netherlands) in 1537 and by 1546 had entered the service of King HENRY VIII of England. His paintings include the distorted portrait of King EDWARD VI in the National Portrait Gallery in London (see ANAMORPHOSIS).

MDA.

**SCULPTURE IN STONE.** The rediscovery of ANTIQUE SCULPTURE meant that Italian sculpture was the most classical of Renaissance art forms. The study of the CONTRAPPOSTO of antiquity caused the composition of classical sculptures to be revived, but the absence of paint on any surviving ancient sculpture misled Renaissance artists into thinking that ancient sculptors had not coloured their statues, and Renaissance statues, in marble and bronze at least, were therefore normally unpainted. In northern Europe, sculpted tombs and religious statues had been painted since late antiquity, and the fashion for unpainted sculpture came from Italy.

Sculpture in stone (usually MARBLE), like BRONZE SCULPTURE but unlike TERRACOTTA sculpture, usually began with the construction of a three-dimensional model, which was typically executed in wax, clay, or plaster. The proportions of the model were then transferred to stone by the process known as 'pointing': the sculptor chooses a series of points on the model and measures the distances between them with calipers; he then transfers the measurements (usually in a multiple) to the block of stone, making marks at the corresponding points, and uses these marks to guide his chisel. This was the method described by CELLINI and VASARI and used by Italian sculptors such as MICHELANGELO.

The methodology of stone sculpture was to some extent at odds with its ideology, because the figure was deemed to lie latent in the stone: Michelangelo proclaimed in the opening quatrain of a sonnet for Vittoria Colonna that

> Non ha l'ottimo artista alcun concetto
> C'un marmo solo in se non circonscriva
> Col suo soverchio, e solo a quello arriva
> La man, che ubbidisce all'intelletto.

(Even the greatest artist cannot conceive anything that a block of marble does not contain within itself, and only the hand that obeys the intellect can penetrate to this image.)

**SEA BEGGARS.** See PRIVATEERS.

**SEBASTIAN I or (Portuguese) Sebastião I** (1554–78), king of Portugal, was born in Lisbon, the posthumous son of Prince John (João) of Portugal and his wife Juana, daughter of CHARLES V. In 1557, at the age of 3, he became king of Portugal on the death of his grandfather JOHN III of Portugal. During his minority, Portugal was ruled through the co-regency of his grandmother Queen Catherine and his great-uncle the Cardinal-Prince HENRIQUE.

Sebastian was by temperament a mystic and an ascetic. On assuming the throne in 1568, he left the government of the country to others (chiefly the Jesuits) and led a life that combined personal austerity and military training, driven by a wish to lead a CRUSADE against the Moors of North Africa; his single-mindedness extended to a refusal to marry, despite the risk that failure to produce an heir would lead to the Portuguese crown passing to a foreigner. He first led an expedition to Morocco in 1574. In his second expedition, which culminated in the battle of KSAR-EL-KEBIR on 4 August 1578, Sebastian was killed and his army utterly defeated.

Sebastian's body was buried first at Ksar-el-Kebir, then at Ceuta, and finally in the Hieronymite convent in Belém (near Lisbon), but many Portuguese refused to acknowledge his death, as a result of which Sebastian came to be venerated as the hidden king (*rei encuberto*); this cult of Sebastianism was an important force in the revolution of 1640 and in the civil war of 1822–34, and still survives as a folk tradition in Portugal. Sebastian's failure to return alive from Ksar-el-Kebir opened the way for four pretenders to the throne to impersonate him: the so-called 'king of Penamacor' and 'king of Ericeira' were captured in 1584 and 1585; Gabriel Espinosa, whose claim was supported by the Portuguese Jesuits and by members of the Spanish and imperial courts, was captured and executed in 1594; Marco Tullio, a Calabrian who knew no Portuguese, was welcomed in Venice in 1603 as the hidden king, but was later captured and executed.

King Sebastian is the protagonist of John Dryden's tragedy *Don Sebastian, King of Portugal* (London, 1692).

DHP; António Cândido Franco, *Vida de Sebastião, rei de Portúgal* (1993).

**SEBASTIÁN DE ALMONACID or Sebastián de Toledo** (*fl.* 1482–9), Spanish sculptor also known as 'El Maestro Sebastián'. He contributed to the main reredos at Toledo Cathedral, where he or one of his pupils also made the tomb of Álvaro de LUNA and his wife (1489). His other Castilian tombs, all in the Flemish late Gothic style, include the splendid tomb of Archbishop Alfonso Carrillo (d. 1482) in the Iglesia Magistral in Alcalá de Henares; the church and the tomb were badly damaged in the Spanish Civil War, but the tomb has been restored and placed in a side chapel.

MDA s.v. Sebastián de Toledo.

**SEBASTIANO DEL PIOMBO or Sebastiano Luciani** (1485/6–1547), Italian painter, born in Venice, where he initially trained as a musician and then trained as a painter in the studio of Giovanni BELLINI and subsequently became a disciple and friend of GIORGIONE. In 1511 he moved to Rome under the patronage of Agostino CHIGI, and lived there for the rest of his life except for a brief return to Venice in 1528–9. In 1531 he was appointed keeper of the seal for the papal curia; he took religious orders, abandoned painting for a comfortable life in the Church, and was thereafter known as 'del Piombo' ('of the lead [seal]').

The paintings of Sebastiano's Venetian youth, such as *Salome* (National Gallery, London), show the strong influence of Giorgione. On arriving in Rome he worked alongside RAPHAEL, PERUZZI, and Il SODOMA on the decoration of Chigi's villa (now known as the Villa Farnesina). He subsequently concentrated on portraiture, a genre in which his painting retained some Venetian features, such as a preference for the half-length portrait (e.g. *Portrait of a Young Woman*, 1512, Uffizi) and the dramatic use of CHIAROSCURO (e.g. *Portrait of a Young Man*, 1514, Uffizi). His finest surviving portraits are those of *Andrea* DORIA (Palazzo Doria, Rome) and *Pope* CLEMENT VII (Museo Nazionale, Naples).

Sebastiano was befriended by MICHELANGELO, who assisted him in works such as *The Raising of Lazarus* (1516–18, National Gallery, London), which was painted in competition with Raphael's *Transfiguration* (Vatican); Michelangelo's drawings for the figure of Lazarus are preserved in the British Museum. According to VASARI, Michelangelo also provided the design for Sebastiano's famous *Pietà* (c.1520–5, Museo Civico, Viterbo); the influence of Michelangelo is also apparent in the *Holy Family with Donor* (1517–18, National Gallery, London).

*MDA*; Michael Hirst, *Sebastiano del Piombo* (1981).

**SEBILLET, THOMAS** (1512–89), French literary theorist and translator, the author of *L'Art poétique français* (1548), a poetic manifesto which provoked Joachim DU BELLAY's *Défence et illustration*, published in the following year. In his *L'Art poétique français* Sebillet anticipates Du Bellay's emphasis on the inspiration of the poet, but the models he recommends are medieval as well as classical. In 1549 he published a French translation of the *Iphigenia* of Euripides in which he adapted Greek metres to French verse.

*SECCO* (Italian; 'dry'), the term for wall painting executed on plaster that had completely dried; *secco* was thereby distinguished from FRESCO, which was painted on wet plaster. The pigments were applied to the wall either in TEMPERA (which was applied to dry plaster) or suspended in limewater (which was applied to dampened plaster). In frescoes such as Fra ANGELICO's series in the Convent of San Marco in Florence, *a secco* colours were added to the dried frescoes to delineate points of detail.

**SECULAR CLERGY**. From the twelfth century, and possibly earlier, the term 'secular clergy' was used to denote priests living in the secular (ecclesiastical Latin *saecularis*) world, as opposed to 'regular clergy' who lived according to the rule (Latin *regula*) of a religious ORDER. In contrast to regular clergy, the secular clergy took no vows and could own property. In early modern ecclesiastical English, 'secular' often follows the substantive, as in 'priest secular' and 'canon secular'.

**SECUNDUS, JANUS or Johannes, or (Dutch) Jan Nicolaeszoon Everaerts** (1511–36), Dutch neo-Latin poet, born into a prominent family in The Hague. He studied law at Bourges. In 1533 he was appointed secretary to the cardinal-archbishop of Toledo, and while in Spain composed the series of amatory neo-Latin poems collected as *Basia*, which was subsequently translated into many modern languages. In 1534 Janus accompanied the Emperor CHARLES V on his expedition to TUNIS, and then returned to the Netherlands to become secretary to the bishop of Utrecht. Charles V invited Janus to become his Latin secretary, but he died of fever in Saint-Amand (near Tournai) while travelling to meet the emperor in Italy. Janus was one of the finest love-poets in Latin of any period, and his surviving verse includes elegies, epigrams, and odes.

J. P. Guépin, *De kunst van Janus Secundus* (1991); David Price, *Janus Secundus* (1995).

**SEGNI, BERNARDO** (1504–58), Florentine humanist and historian who held a series of public offices culminating in a period as the ambassador of COSIMO I DE' MEDICI to the imperial court (1541). He published translations of Aristotle and Sophocles, and also wrote a history of Florence from 1527 to 1555 (*Istorie fiorentine*, 1723) and a biography of his uncle Niccolò CAPPONI (*Vita di Niccolò Capponi*, 1723).

Eric Cochrane, *Historians and Historiography in the Italian Renaissance* (1981).

**SEISENEGGER, JAKOB** (1505–67), German painter, appointed court painter to the HABSBURGS in 1531; his principal patron was Archduke FERDINAND, brother of the emperor. Seisenegger's portrait of *The Emperor Charles V with his Hunting Dog* (1532, Kunsthistorisches Museum, Vienna) was the model for TITIAN's celebrated portrait (now in the Prado in Madrid) which so impressed the emperor that he appointed Titian as his court painter.

*MDA*; Kurt Löchner, *Jakob Seisenegger* (1962).

**SELDEN, JOHN** (1584–1654), English orientalist and jurist. Selden was educated at Hart Hall, Oxford, and studied law at Clifford's Inn and the Inner Temple; he became a barrister of the Inner Temple in 1612 and a bencher in 1633. His early studies in legal history include *The Duello* (1610), a study of trial by combat, *Janus Anglorum; Facies altera* (1610), a study of English legal history up to the reign of Henry II, *Titles of Honour* (1614), an edition of FORTESCUE's *De laudibus legum Angliae* (1616), and *The Office of Lord Chancellor of England* (1617). In this period he was also bringing his prodigious learning to bear on orientalist and antiquarian interests. His *De diis Syriis* (1617), which established his reputation all over Europe, pioneered the use of a comparative methodology in its examination of Semitic mythology. In 1621 he was imprisoned for his role in the Protestation of the Commons; his jailer lent him a manuscript of the *Historia novorum* of the twelfth-century monk Eadmer, and Selden used his period of incarceration to prepare the first printed edition of Eadmer, which was published in 1623.

In 1623 Selden entered Parliament as burgess for Lancaster, and subsequently served as MP for several constituencies, sitting for Oxford University in the Long Parliament. In 1643 he became a member of the Westminster Assembly of Divines. He entered fully into public life, taking a prominent part in the impeachment of Buckingham, acting as legal counsel to Sir Edmund Hampden when Hampden was imprisoned for refusing to pay ship-money, supporting printers and book-sellers against Laud's interventions, and participating in the preparation of articles to impeach Laud. After 1649 he withdrew from public life. The *Table Talk* of his last twenty years was collected by his amanuensis and published in 1689; it was Selden's most widely read book for 200 years.

Selden continued to write throughout his period as a public figure. His legal writings include *Mare clausum* (1635), a reply to GROTIUS (see *MARE CLAUSUM, MARE LIBERUM*), a treatise on *Privileges of the Baronage of England* (1641), and an edition of the *Fleta* (1647), a thirteenth-century treatise on English law which, its title suggests, may have been written in the Fleet Prison; his treatise *On the Judicature in Parliaments* was published posthumously. His orientalist and juridical interests were combined in his publications on Jewish law, notably *De iure naturali et gentium iuxta disciplinam Ebraeorum* (1640), a study of the Jewish law of marriage and divorce, *Uxor Ebraica* (1646), and the three volumes of *De synedriis et prefecturis iuridicis veterum Ebraeorum* (1650, 1653, 1655).

**SELF-PORTRAITS.** See PORTRAITS AND SELF-PORTRAITS.

**SELLAIO, JACOPO DEL.** See JACOPO DEL SELLAIO.

**SELLYNG, WILLIAM, or William of Selling** (d. 1494), English humanist and Benedictine monk. He became a monk *c.*1448 and subsequently studied at Canterbury College, Oxford (BD, 1458). In 1464 he travelled to Italy, where he studied at Padua and Bologna (DD, 1466) for three years. He returned to Italy in 1469 on a mission to secure indulgences from Pope PAUL II for the forthcoming tercentenary of Thomas Becket's death. In 1487 he again travelled to Rome, this time as the representative of HENRY VII; on this occasion he may have been accompanied by his nephew Thomas LINACRE.

Sellyng was the finest Latin scholar of the Englishmen of his generation, and enjoyed a high reputation as a Latin orator. He is sometimes described as the first Englishman to have studied Greek; that is not the case, but he is certainly among the first known to have studied Greek in Italy, and the monastery of Christ Church in Canterbury, of which he was prior from 1472 to 1494, was one of the earliest English centres in which Greek texts were studied; the manuscripts that he collected include manuscripts of HOMER and Euripides that passed into the collection of Archbishop Parker and are now in Corpus Christi College, Cambridge.

Roberto Weiss, *Humanism in England during the Fifteenth Century* (3rd edn., 1967), 153–9.

**SENDIVOGIUS or (Polish) Michael Sędzimir or Sędziwoj** (1556–*c.*1630), Polish alchemist. He enjoyed a popular reputation as the possessor of a powder (secured from the Scottish alchemist Alexander Seton) capable of transmuting lead into gold; he gave demonstrations of the efficacy of this powder

to King SIGISMUND III VASA and the Emperor RUDOLF II, but in 1607 lost the remainder of his stock. In learned circles the reputation of Sendivogius rested on the theory of metals that he expounded in his *Novum lumen chemicum* (1604), which was translated into English as *A New Light of Alchemy* in 1650.
DSB.

**SENECA THE YOUNGER IN THE RENAISSANCE.** The Roman statesman, Stoic philosopher, and tragedian Lucius Annaeus Seneca was born in Córdoba (Spain) between 4 BC and AD 1, the second son of a rhetorician also called Lucius Annaeus Seneca; the works of Seneca the Elder were first published in Paris in 1587.

Sidonius Apollinaris, the fifth-century bishop of Clermont, had distinguished between Seneca the Stoic philosopher and Seneca the tragedian (*Carmina* 9. 230–8), and this erroneous splitting of Seneca the Younger persisted in medieval and Renaissance Europe. As late as 1671, John Milton could say uncertainly (in the preface to *Samson Agonistes*) that 'Seneca the philosopher is by some thought the author of those tragedies (at least the best of them) that go under that name'. As a philosopher, Seneca the Younger was chiefly influential as the exponent of STOICISM.

The nine tragedies of Seneca the Younger shaped the revival of TRAGEDY in Renaissance Europe. He was deemed to be a model playwright, because he wrote in crisp, clear Latin and organized his plays in five acts, in conformity with Horace's precept. Elements such as horror, grotesque, ghosts, witches, tyrants, and bloodshed all appealed to contemporary tastes. In Italy the effect of Seneca on vernacular drama was facilitated by the translation of his tragedies into Italian in 1497; the most important Senecan dramatist in Italy was GIRALDI, whose tragedies exulted in bloodshed. In England, Seneca's *Troades* was performed at Trinity College, Cambridge, in 1552, and corpse-strewn vernacular plays such as Kyd's *The Spanish Tragedy* (*c.*1585) and Shakespeare's *Titus Andronicus* and *Richard III* were heavily influenced by Seneca.

J. Jacquot (ed.), *Les Tragédies de Sénèque et le théâtre de la Renaissance* (1964); K. Blüher, *Seneca in Spanien* (1969); J. W. Binns, 'Seneca and Neo-Latin Tragedy in England', in C. D. N. Costa (ed.), *Seneca* (1974); E. Lefèvre (ed.), *Der Einfluss Senecas auf das europäische Drama* (1978).

**SENFL, LUDWIG** (*c.*1486–1542/3), Swiss composer who sang as a boy in Emperor MAXIMILIAN I's Hofkapelle in Augsburg and Vienna. He remained with the Hofkapelle in Konstanz and by 1513 succeeded ISAAC as court composer. He was one of several imperial musicians dismissed by CHARLES V and, by 1523, was composer in the Hofkapelle of Duke Wilhelm of Bavaria in Munich, He wrote sacred and secular music including motets ('Non moriar sed vivam' and 'In pace in idipsum') for Luther at the Diet of Augsburg in 1530 and several lieder and motets for Duke ALBRECHT VON PREUSSEN.

**SEPÚLVEDA, JUAN GINÉS DE** (*c.*1490–1573), Spanish humanist, born in Pozo Blanco (Córdoba) and educated in Córdoba, Alcalá de Henares, and Bologna. He published a translation into Ciceronian Latin of ARISTOTLE's *Politics* (Paris, 1548), and became well known as a Latin stylist. He had a taste for controversy, initially with ERASMUS and then with Bartolomé de LAS CASAS, whose protest against the Spanish treatment of American Indians Sepúlveda answered with a Latin dialogue entitled *Democrates alter; sive, De iusti belli causis*. He also gave evidence at the imperial tribunal arising out of Las Casas's complaints about Spanish brutality in America, citing in defence of the *CONQUISTADORES* the principles articulated by Aristotle justifying the conquest and enslavement of inferior races. The tribunal dissociated itself from Sepúlveda's views, and the revision of the Laws of the INDIES in 1543 implemented the views of Las Casas.

Sepúlveda was appointed as court historian by CHARLES V, and in that capacity wrote Latin biographies of both Charles (*De rebus gestis Caroli V*, 1556) and PHILIP II (*De rebus gestis Philippi II*, 1564).

DHE; A. F. Bell, *Juan Ginés de Sepúlveda* (1925).

**SERAFINO AQUILANO** (1466–1500), poet and musician from Aquila who was active in Rome, Milan, and Naples. His *Rappresentazione allegorica della Volutta, Virtu e Famma* was performed at Mantua in 1494. Well known as a poet and highly skilled 'improvvisatore', his improvised style can be divined from the *strambotti* published by PETRUCCI, some of which may be by Serafino himself.

**SERAFINO DE' CIMINELLI**. See CIMINELLI, SERAFINO DE'.

**SERCAMBI, GIOVANNI** (1348–1424), Italian author, a native of Lucca, where he worked as a soldier and administrator for the Guinigi family. His *Novelle* is a collection of 155 short tales modelled on BOCCACCIO's *Decameron*. His other works include a chronicle of Lucca from 1164 to 1423 (*Croniche della cose di Lucca*) and *Monito*, a treatise on government.

OCIL.

**SERIPANDO, GIROLAMO** (1493–1563), cardinal and theologian, probably born in Naples, where he entered the Augustinian Monastery of San Giovanni a Carbonara in 1507. He rose to become general of the Order in 1539. He served as a theological adviser in the opening sessions of the COUNCIL OF TRENT, showing some sympathy for Protestant perspectives in his view that the Bible should be studied in its original languages and that the Bible had a claim to authority greater than that of the traditions of the Church.

In 1554 Girolamo was elected archbishop of Salerno, and in 1561 he was created cardinal by Pope PIUS IV and sent back to the Council of Trent, this time as a papal legate. Once again his theological expertise was put to good use, in that he was put in charge of the group responsible for the formulation of decrees relating to dogma. His reformist view that a bishop should reside in his diocese led to a rift with the pope, who recalled him to Rome; Girolamo died suddenly in Trento, before he could return.

Girolamo wrote prolifically; including commentaries on the New Testament and the Council of Trent.

**SERLIO, SEBASTIANO** (1475–c.1554), Italian architect, architectural theorist, and painter, born in Bologna, where he trained with his father as a painter; he subsequently moved to Rome, where he studied architecture and antiquities in the studio of Baldassare PERUZZI. In 1527 Serlio fled the SACK OF ROME and settled in Venice, where he lived until 1541, when he moved to France at the invitation of FRANCIS I to work on FONTAINEBLEAU. Serlio's only known surviving architectural works are a doorway at Fontainebleau (the only surviving portion of a house known as the Grande Ferrare) and the chateau of ANCY-LE-FRANC.

Serlio published the first volume of his monumental treatise *Tutte l'opere d'architettura e prospettiva* in Venice in 1537; this volume, which was book 4 of the planned treatise, was devoted to the architectural ORDERS. Book 3, on antiquities, followed in 1540. While at Fontainebleau he published book 1 (1545, on geometry), book 2 (1545, on perspective), and book 5 (1547, on churches). On being superseded by Philibert DELORME at Fontainebleau, Serlio moved to Lyon, where he wrote book 6 (on domestic architecture); this book was not published, and the first of the two known manuscripts was discovered in 1925. In 1575 Jacopo strada published book 7, which supplemented the first six books with Serlio's drawings, many of which derive from plans that Serlio had inherited from Peruzzi. An extra book, the *Libro extraordinario* (1551), was devoted to portals.

Serlio's *Architettura* was enormously influential. It was the first treatise to codify the five architectural orders, and diffused the style of BRAMANTE and RAPHAEL throughout Europe. Translations of parts of the treatise were published in various languages, including Dutch (1539 and 1606), French (1542), Spanish (1563), and English (1611).

MDA; Sabine Frommel, *Sebastiano Serlio architetturo* (1998).

**SERMISY, CLAUDIN DE** (c.1490–1562), French composer who was a musician in the Royal Chapel of Queen Anne and LOUIS XII and was involved with the musical festivities at the FIELD OF THE CLOTH OF GOLD (1520). He was *sous-maître* from 1533. He wrote polyphonic masses and motets and over 200 chansons.

**SERRES, OLIVIER DE** (1539–1619), French Huguenot horticulturist and writer on gardens. He published three books on agriculture, of which the best known was *Théâtre d'agriculture et ménage des champs* (1600), a huge volume on estate management. The agricultural material is based on his experience of managing an estate at Pradel (near Villeneuve-de-Berg), but the material on gardens derives from Claude MOLLET, who supplied diagrams of his PARTERRES at FONTAINEBLEAU, SAINT-GERMAIN-EN-LAYE, and the TUILERIES.

**SERVETUS, MICHAEL, or (Spanish) Miguel Serveto or (French) Michel de Villeneuve** (1511–53), physician and UNITARIAN theologian. He was born in Tuleda (Navarre), the son of a notary, and studied law in Toulouse. He travelled to Italy in the train of Juan de Quintana, the Franciscan who was soon to be appointed confessor to the Emperor CHARLES V, and in February 1530 witnessed the coronation of Charles

V in Bologna. He travelled north to Lyon and Geneva and thence to Basel (where he met OECOLAMPADIUS) and Strassburg (where he met BUCER).

Servetus' first publication was a learned anti-Trinitarian essay, *De Trinitatis erroribus libri VII* (Hagenau, 1531), which he refashioned the following year into a DIALOGUE. From *c*.1535 to 1537 he worked as an editor and proofreader of scientific treatises in Lyon, where he adopted his father's surname, Villanueva, as Latin 'Villanovanus' and French 'de Villeneuve'. He decided to study medicine, and to that end first moved to Paris (where he met CALVIN, who attempted to win him back to Trinitarianism) and then to Louvain and Montpellier; in 1542 he was appointed physician to Pierre Paulmier, archbishop of Vienne, a post that he held for the rest of his life. He continued to work as an editor, and wrote the annotations for the Latin translation of the Bible by Santi PAGNINI (Lyon, 1542).

In 1541 Servetus opened a fatal correspondence with Calvin, forwarding to him a manuscript of his treatise calling for the 'Restoration of Christianity' (*Christianismi restitutio*) and expressing a wish to visit Geneva. Calvin disapproved of the treatise's Unitarianism and of its heterodox view of the incarnation, and used his influence to block its publication in Basel. Servetus arranged for the treatise to be printed secretly in Vienne, and on 3 January 1553 copies of the treatise were shipped to Lyon and Frankfurt for the Easter book fairs. The treatise was anonymous, although the name of Servetus appears in the text (page 196) and the initials MSV are appended at the end. In a rare instance of co-operation across confessional lines, Calvin denounced Servetus to the INQUISITION, contributing to the dossier that revealed Servetus' authorship of the treatise to the inquisitor-general of Lyon, Matthieu Ory (RABELAIS's 'Doribus'), who interrogated (16 March) and arrested (4 April) Servetus. At 4.00 a.m. on 7 April Servetus escaped from prison, and thenceforth became a fugitive. On 17 June he was sentenced in his absence to be burnt slowly at the stake.

On the morning of Sunday, 13 August, Servetus walked into Geneva with a view to travelling on by boat towards Zürich and thence to Naples. On discovering that there was no boat until the next day, he decided to stay overnight at an inn called the Rose, and then attended Sunday afternoon service in Saint-Pierre, as was required. He was arrested, convicted, and burnt at the stake at Champel (near Geneva) on 27 October 1553.

In 1535 Geneva had repealed all existing laws on the subject of religion; its edicts of 1543 had legitimized the practice of banishment, but did not provide for the death sentence for heresy. The Evangelical Swiss Cantons had all been consulted, and all condemned Servetus, but none demanded the death penalty. Servetus seems to have been condemned according to the JUSTINIAN code, which was revived for the occasion. These legal anomalies provoked a protracted controversy on the moral question of whether heretics should be executed. In his *Defensio orthodoxae fidei* Calvin set out his position on the execution of Servetus (in response to a request from the Protestant cities of Germany), arguing that it was indeed lawful for Christian princes and magistrates to punish heretics with death.

R. H. Bainton, *Hunted Heretic: The Life and Death of Michael Servetus* (1953); C. Manzoni, *Umanesimo ed cressia: Michele Serveto* (1974); J. Friedman, *Michael Servetus: A Case Study in Total Heresy* (1978).

**SETTLES.** See CHAIRS, SETTLES, AND STOOLS.

**SEUSENHOFER FAMILY**, a German dynasty of armourers. Konrad Seusenhofer (1450/60–1517), a native of Augsburg, moved in 1504 to Innsbruck, where he established an imperial armoury for MAXIMILIAN I. He was succeeded as court armourer by his brother Hans (1470–1555) and Hans's son Jörg (1500/5–80). In the course of the sixteenth century plate armour evolved from a kind of protective clothing to an emblem of rank and standing, and the armour of the Seusenhofer family became increasingly elaborate in its decorative details (see ARMS AND ARMOUR). Examples of Seusenhofer armours are preserved in the Tower of London Armouries, the Kunsthistorisches Museum in Vienna, the Musée de l'Armée (Les Invalides, Paris), and the Metropolitan Museum in New York.

**SEVILLE or (Spanish) Sevilla or (Arabic) Ishbiliya or (Latin) Hispalis**, the principal city of Andalusia, is a port on the river Guadalquivir 85 kilometres (55 miles) from the Atlantic. Seville was a Muslim city until 1248, when the forces of Ferdinand III conquered the city. By the fifteenth century it had become an important Mediterranean commercial centre whose wealth was built on the trade in slaves, olive oil, wine, grain, SILK, and woollen textiles. The establishment of the CASA DE CONTRATACIÓN in Seville in 1505 ushered in a period of unprecedented prosperity, because the city thereafter enjoyed a monopoly of trade with Spanish America, and in particular of its silver bullion. In 1517 the city had a population of about 25,000, but the influx of foreign merchants who saw the city as the hub of European and Atlantic trade increased the population to 90,000 by 1594, making Seville the largest city in the western Mediterranean.

This prosperity was marked by the completion of what was then the largest cathedral in Europe (built 1403–1519) and is still one of the largest in the world, and by a burgeoning of poetry, woodcarving, and painting (which Francisco PACHECO later encouraged with his art academy). The most important private building of this period is the Casa de Pilatos, an early sixteenth-century palace which combines Renaissance, Gothic, and MUDÉJAR elements and was believed to be based on Pontius Pilate's gubernatorial residence in Palestine. Of the civic buildings, the best example of Renaissance architecture is the east face of the Casa de Ayuntamiento (Town Hall), which was constructed between 1527 and 1534. The end of the sixteenth century marked the zenith of Seville's fortunes, because thereafter competition from Cádiz sapped its economic strength.

Seville was an important centre for the INQUISITION. An expulsion of JEWS occurred in 1483 and again in the national expulsion of 1492. The AUTOS-DA-FÉ of the 1480s, during which some 2,000 convicted heretics were burnt, were revived in 1559 and 1560 by PHILIP II as a mechanism for suppressing the city's burgeoning Protestant movement.

H. and P. Chaunu, *Séville et l'Atlantique, 1504–1650* (8 vols., 1955).

**SEYSSEL, CLAUDE DE** (*c*.1450–1520), Savoyard political theorist. He was born in Aix-les-Bains (Savoy), and in the course of his career became bishop of Marseille, archbishop of Turin, a minister of King LOUIS XII, chancellor of France, and ambassador to England. He collaborated with Janos LASCARIS on translations of ancient Greek works, and also wrote panegyrics to the king which were published in 1508 as the *Histoire singulière de Louis XII* and *Les Louanges de Louis XII*. He retired from the court, but at the request of King FRANCIS I, Louis's successor, wrote *La Grande Monarchie de France* (1519), a seminal treatise in which Seyssel argued that the king's authority was sufficiently circumscribed by Christian principles and existing rules and customs.

Alberto Caviglia, *Claudio di Seyssel (1450–1520): La vita nella storia de' suoi tempi* (1928); J. H. Hexter, *The Vision of Politics on the Eve of Reformation: More, Machiavelli and Seyssel* (1973).

**SFORZA, CATERINA** (*c*.1462–1509), countess of Forlì, the illegitimate daughter of Duke Gian Galeazzo SFORZA of Milan. In 1473 she married Girolamo RIARIO as part of a transaction by which Pope SIXTUS V bought Imola from Duke Gian Galeazzo and presented it to Girolamo and Caterina; in 1480 they were presented with Forlì. When Girolamo was assassinated in April 1488, Caterina promptly occupied the fortress of Forlì, deployed troops to subdue the city, and then governed both Forlì and Imola as regent for her son Ottaviano until they surrendered to Cesare BORGIA on 22 January 1500. She was taken as a prisoner to Rome, and after resigning her claims to Forlì and Imola was released, whereupon she retired to Florence.

In 1496 Caterina had secretly married Giovanni de' Medici, a member of a cadet branch of the MEDICI family; their son was Giovanni de' Medici (Giovanni della Banda Nere).

E. Breisach, *Caterina Sforza, a Renaissance Virago* (1967).

**SFORZA, FRANCESCO I** (1401–66), first Sforza duke of Milan, the illegitimate son of the Romagnol *condottiere* Muzio Attendolo. On his father's death in battle on 4 January 1424, Francesco inherited Muzio's troops, with whom he fought in the service of Filippo Maria VISCONTI against Venice and then with Venice against the Visconti; similarly, he drove papal forces from the Romagna and the Marches, and subsequently fought for the papacy. In 1441 Francesco married Bianca, the daughter of Filippo Maria Visconti, and received for his dowry the lordships of Pontremoli and Cremona and the promise of succession to the duchy of Milan. Filippo died in 1447, but Francesco was denied his inheritance by the establishment of the AMBROSIAN REPUBLIC. On the collapse of the republic, Francesco entered Milan in triumph on 25 March 1450.

As duke of Milan Francesco entered into strategic alliances with Cosimo de' MEDICI of Florence (with whose support he was able to impose the Peace of LODI) and King LOUIS XI

of France, and extended the authority and territories of the duchy to include Genoa and much of Lombardy. His construction projects included the canal of the Martesana (which gave Milan access to the Adda river), the Ospedale Maggiore (now the faculty of medicine of the University of Milan), which was designed by FILARETE, and the restoration of the Visconti fortress of Porta Giovia (reconstructed in the nineteenth century as the Castello Sforzesco and now Milan's Museo d'Arte Antica); in 1499 the castle was betrayed by its castellan, and in *The Prince* MACHIAVELLI regretted Francesco's decision to restore the fortress, although he praised Francesco's success as a ruler. Francesco's court attracted Italian and Greek scholars and quickly became an important humanist centre. His daughter Ippolita became well known for her Latin discourses. The humanist Francesco FILELFO celebrated his career as a *condottiere* in his *Sforziade*.

In the 1470s Francesco's son Galeazzo Maria commissioned an equestrian statue of his father; LEONARDO took over the original commission and prepared designs for a bronze statue, and he was succeeded by Antonio POLLAIUOLO; a full-scale clay model was damaged by the French and eventually disintegrated, and the statue was never cast.

**SFORZA, GALEAZZO MARIA** (1444–76), second Sforza duke of Milan, the son of Francesco SFORZA and Maria Bianca VISCONTI. In 1466 he was in France fighting in support of King LOUIS XI against the Leagues of the PUBLIC WEAL when he learnt that he had succeeded his father Francesco as duke of Milan. He returned to Milan and inaugurated a period of stern rule during which peace was maintained by force; his legendary cruelty may even have extended to the murder of his mother, who was poisoned in 1468. Galeazzo Maria was a generous patron of humanist scholarship and the arts, and also supported the SILK industry and the cultivation of rice. He was assassinated in the porch of Milan Cathedral on 26 December 1476; his murder by three Milanese noblemen who styled themselves latter-day incarnations of Brutus and Cassius may be the only assassination of the Renaissance to have been modelled on classical precedent.

Evelyn Welch, *Art and Authority in Renaissance Milan* (1995).

**SFORZA, GIAN GALEAZZO** (1469–94), third Sforza duke of Milan, the son of Galeazzo Maria SFORZA, whom he succeeded at the age of 7 under the regency of his mother Bona of Savoy, who in 1481 was displaced by Gian Galeazzo's uncle Ludovico SFORZA. In 1489 Ludovico arranged the marriage of Gian Galeazzo to Isabella of Aragon, granddaughter of King FERRANTE I of Naples; in 1518 their daughter Bona Sforza (1493–1557) married King SIGISMUND I of Poland. Gian Galeazzo died suddenly in 1484, and his death was widely believed to have been arranged by his protector (and successor) Ludovico Sforza.

**SFORZA, LUDOVICO, IL MORO or (English) the Moor** (1451–1508), fourth Sforza duke of Milan, the second son of Francesco SFORZA and Bianca Maria VISCONTI. The origin of the term *il Moro* is uncertain: he may have been dark-skinned, or his second name may have been Mauro. When his elder brother Galeazzo Maria SFORZA was assassinated in 1476, the dukedom of Milan passed to Gian Galeazzo SFORZA; the regency was initially held by Ludovico's sister-in-law Bona of Savoy, but in 1481 Ludovico assumed the regency and became the ruler of the duchy of Milan. In January 1491 he married Beatrice d'ESTE, who died in childbirth in 1497. On the death of Gian Galeazzo in mysterious circumstances (he may have been murdered by Ludovico) in 1494, Ludovico became duke of Milan; he received the ducal crown on 22 October 1494.

Milan was an important focus of the WARS OF ITALY, and Ludovico was inevitably drawn into the conflict. Initially he sought an alliance with Naples, and to that end arranged for his nephew Gian Galeazzo to marry Isabella of Aragon, granddaughter of King FERRANTE I of Naples (1489); similarly, he later sought to maintain good relations with the Emperor MAXIMILIAN I, and so arranged for his niece Bianca Maria Sforza (Gian Galeazzo's daughter) to marry the emperor (1494), to whom he paid a dowry of 440,000 ducats. In 1491 his own marriage to 15-year-old Beatrice d'Este strengthened an alliance with Ferrara.

In 1493 Ludovico repudiated the long-standing Sforza alliances with Naples and Florence and instead declared his support for Venice and the papacy. He was aware of the danger posed by the Orléanist claim to Milan, but nonetheless encouraged King CHARLES VIII of France to invade Naples. In 1494 Charles VIII invaded Italy with a view to implementing the Angevin claim to the throne of Naples; the French army captured and garrisoned Naples. Ludovico played a leading role in the formation of the HOLY LEAGUE (Pope ALEXANDER VI, the Emperor MAXIMILIAN I, King FERDINAND II of Spain, Venice, and Milan), but did not contribute troops. Similarly, in 1496 he supported the emperor's expedition to assist Pisa in its war with Florence, but once again did not offer military assistance.

In 1499 LOUIS XII of Orléans, the new king of France, invaded Italy in support of his family's claim to the duchy of Milan, which originated in the marriage of his grandfather (Louis I, duke of Orléans) to Valentina Visconti, daughter of Gian Galeazzo VISCONTI, duke of Milan. The French army and its Venetian allies captured Milan on 6 October 1499 and went on to occupy Genoa. Ludovico Sforza retook Milan on 5 January 1500, but his army was defeated at Novara on 8 April 1500; Ludovico was taken as a prisoner to France, where he died in the castle of Loches (near Tours) eight years later. MACHIAVELLI was later to criticize the series of misjudgements that led to Ludovico's loss of his duchy.

Ludovico's patronage extended to music, scholarship, science, architecture, and art; he was famously the patron of LEONARDO DA VINCI, with whom he shared scientific as well as artistic interests. Ludovico's architecture commissions include the completion of the Certosa di Pavia and Pavia Cathedral and BRAMANTE's additions to Sant'Ambrogio (where he built the unfinished Portico della Canonica) and Santa Maria delle Grazie, in which Bramante built the dome

and cloisters and Leonardo painted the *Last Supper*. The dispersal of Ludovico's court in 1499 was lamented by many literary courtiers, notably CASTIGLIONE.

F. Malaguzzi Valeri, *La corte di Ludovico il Moro* (4 vols., 1913–24); D. M. Bueno de Mesquita, 'Ludovico Sforza and his Vassals', in E. F. Jacob (ed.), *Italian Renaissance Studies* (1960); id., 'The Conscience of the Prince', *Proceedings of the British Academy*, 65 (1979).

**SFORZA FAMILY**, a Milanese dynasty of six dukes descended from the Romagnol *condottiere* Muzio Attendolo (1369–1424), a kinsman of Micheletto ATTENDOLO. Muzio's illegitimate son Francesco took his father's *nom de guerre* (*sforzo* means 'struggle'), and so became Francesco SFORZA. Through his marriage in 1441 to Bianca, daughter of Filippo Maria VISCONTI, he claimed the dukedom of Milan after the collapse of the AMBROSIAN REPUBLIC in 1450. In 1445 Francesco's brother Alessandro (1408–73) became ruler of Pesaro (in the PAPAL STATE), which he and his descendants ruled until 1512; in 1493 Alessandro's grandson Giovanni of Pesaro married Lucrezia BORGIA.

Francesco's sons included Galeazzo Maria SFORZA, who succeeded his father to the duchy and was assassinated in 1476, Ludovico SFORZA, who succeeded his nephew Gian Galeazzo SFORZA as duke, and Ascanio (d. 1505), who became a cardinal. Caterina SFORZA, the illegitimate daughter of Galeazzo Maria and the wife of Girolamo RIARIO, achieved fame as both warrior and lover. Bona Sforza, Gian Galeazzo's legitimate daughter, married King SIGISMUND I of Poland in 1518; on the death of her husband she returned to Italy, where she was murdered in 1557 by her lover. Francesco, the son of Galeazzo Maria, was taken to France as a prisoner, but eventually became abbot of Marmoutier (near Strasbourg).

The sons of Ludovico Sforza, Massimiliano (1493–1530) and Francesco (1495–1535), took refuge in Germany after the fall of Milan. Massimiliano was reinstalled as the fifth Sforza duke of Milan by the Swiss in 1512, but after the defeat of his allies at the battle of MARIGNANO (1515) accepted the offer of FRANCIS I of a pension of 30,000 ducats and retired to Paris. After the defeat of the French at the battle of BICOCCA (1522) Francesco was installed as Duke Francesco II, the sixth and last Sforza duke of Milan; he was deposed during the imperial occupation of 1525–9. On his death on 24 October 1535 the duchy was absorbed into the empire of CHARLES V and the direct male line of the Sforza became extinct.

C. M. Ady, *History of Milan under the Sforza* (1907); G. Franciosi, *Gli Sforza* (1931); C. Santoro, *Gli Sforza* (1968).

**SFUMATO**. In VASARI's account of the development of painting, the transition from early quattrocento paintings in which colours were separated by lines to later paintings by LEONARDO DA VINCI and GIORGIONE in which colours were elided and transitions imperceptible was deemed to have been effected by the use of *sfumato*, a technique (mentioned by Leonardo) analogous to the disappearance of smoke (Italian *fumo*) into the air.

**SGRAFFITO**. See GRAFFITO.

**SHAKESPEARE, WILLIAM** (1564–1616), English dramatist and poet. He was born in Stratford and in the late 1580s moved to London, where he worked as an actor and playwright. For most of his career he was associated with the CHAMBERLAIN'S MEN, which was refounded in 1594 and after the accession of King JAMES became the King's Men. This company occupied the GLOBE Playhouse from 1599, and in 1608 acquired the BLACKFRIARS.

Shakespeare's earliest plays, which he began to write in the late 1580s, were a trilogy on the reign of Henry VI and a sequel on Richard III; in the 1590s he wrote a second cycle of history plays on the reigns of Richard II, Henry IV (two plays), and Henry V, and also wrote a play about King John. His tragedies from the 1590s include *Titus Andronicus*, *Romeo and Juliet*, and *Julius Caesar*. This was also the period during which Shakespeare wrote a series of ten comedies: in the early 1590s he wrote *Two Gentlemen of Verona*, *The Taming of the Shrew*, *The Comedy of Errors*, and *Love's Labour's Lost*, and in the late 1590s he wrote *A Midsummer Night's Dream*, *The Merchant of Venice*, *The Merry Wives of Windsor*, *Much Ado About Nothing*, and *As You Like It*; *Twelfth Night* followed in 1600 or 1601. His poems from the 1590s include *Venus and Adonis* and *The Rape of Lucrece*.

In the first five years of the seventeenth century Shakespeare wrote his principal tragedies (*Hamlet*, *Othello*, and *King Lear*) and the plays which have been known since the late nineteenth century as the 'problem plays' (*Troilus and Cressida*, *All's Well That Ends Well*, and *Measure for Measure*). In the course of the next three years (1606–8) he wrote tragedies set in the ancient world (*Timon of Athens*, *Antony and Cleopatra*, and *Coriolanus*) or in Scotland (*Macbeth*) and probably composed many of his *Sonnets* (published 1609). In the final years of his career (1609–11) he wrote four romances (*Pericles*, *Cymbeline*, *The Winter's Tale*, and *The Tempest*), whereupon he retired to Stratford. In retirement he collaborated with John FLETCHER on *Henry VIII*, *Cardenio* (now lost), and *The Two Noble Kinsmen*. In 1616, shortly after his death, 36 of his plays were collected in the volume now known as the First Folio.

**SHELDON TAPESTRIES.** The first professional TAPESTRY workshops in England were established in the early 1560s by William Sheldon (d. 1570) on his estates at Barcheston (Warwickshire) and Bordesley (Worcestershire); after Sheldon's death the ownership of the workshops passed to his son Ralph Sheldon (1537–1613) and his grandson Ralph Sheldon the Younger. The workshops were managed by Richard Hyckes (c.1524–1621) and his son Francis (c.1566–1630), who had been trained in tapestry weaving in the Netherlands.

Of the tapestries that can be shown to be products of the factory, the best known is a set of pictorial maps of English counties centred on Warwickshire (1588, Bodleian Library, Oxford). The most important attributions to the Sheldon factory are the *Judgement of Paris* (Victoria and Albert Museum) and the *Four Seasons* (Hatfield House).

> E. A. B. Barnard and A. J. B. Wace, *The Sheldon Tapestry Weavers and their Work* (1928).

**SHELL CAMEOS.** The carving of cameos in sea-shells began in the sixteenth century, when merchants returning from the Caribbean began to import Helmet shells, of which the principal species are the Horned Helmet, the Red Helmet, the King Helmet, and the King Conch. Benvenuto CELLINI's account of his experiments in carving cameos from shells, together with his reflections on ancient shell cameos (which he thought were Roman amulets), constitute the first description of shell cameos. The subjects of these cameos were usually religious; there is, for example, a set of eight German shell cameos in the Victoria and Albert Museum (dated 1571) that depict the lives of Jesus and the Virgin Mary.

**SHEPHERD or Sheppard, JOHN** (c.1515–1558), English composer and organist. He was *informatur choristarum* at Magdalen College, Oxford, from 1543 and a gentleman of the Chapel Royal by 1552. Some of his Latin church music, such as the six-part Magnificat, is in a florid style reminiscent of the ETON CHOIRBOOK, while other examples, like the *Western Wind* mass are rhythmically less complex. There are also some English anthems and services dating from the reign of EDWARD VI.

**SHIPS AND SHIPBUILDING.** The principal innovations in the design of ships in Renaissance Europe were prompted by the introduction of the lateen sail and the development of naval ARTILLERY. Medieval ships were square-rigged, but the advent of the lateen sail, which had long been the typical sail of the Mediterranean felucca (which now survives only on the Nile) and the Arab dhow (which survives on the coastal waters of the Indian Ocean), enabled ships to sail under a much larger range of wind conditions. When cannon were first introduced, they were placed in fixed positions on the high forecastles and aftercastles; the instabilities caused by carrying heavy guns in such a position limited the amount of artillery that a ship could carry, and in new designs cannon were placed on lower decks and fired through portholes.

The largest shipyard in Europe was the ARSENALE in Venice. The main types of ships were the CARAVEL, the CARRACK, the COG, the GALLEASS, the GALLEON, the GALLEY, and the PINNACE. The largest warship of Renaissance Europe was *HENRY GRÂCE A DIEU*. See also MARY ROSE, HMS; FIGUREHEADS.

> F. C. Lane, *Venetian Ships and Shipbuilders of the Renaissance* (1934).

**SHUTE, JOHN** (d. 1563), English writer on architecture who worked in the service of the duke of Northumberland, who in 1550 sent him to Italy. Shute's *First and Chief Grounds of Architecture* (1563) was the first published English treatise on architecture and the only one to be published in the sixteenth century; it contains annotated engravings of the architectural ORDERS. Shute describes himself in the treatise as a painter and architect, but no painting or building by him is known.
> MDA.

**SICILY or (Italian) Sicilia or (literary Latin) Trinacria.** The Mediterranean island of Sicily was from 1282 (the date of the rebellion known as the Sicilian Vespers) to 1410 a kingdom, and, after a two-year interregnum, was from 1412 to 1713 ruled by Spanish viceroys. During the fourteenth century, the kings of Naples repeatedly attempted to conquer Sicily; in the fifteenth century, particularly during the reign of ALFONSO V, the avarice flowed in the other direction, in that Sicily was seen by Spanish kings as the key to the acquisition of the kingdom of Naples. Alfonso inherited a culturally isolated and impoverished island whose trade was in the hands of Catalan merchants, and proceeded to establish institutions that would develop Sicily: he established a university in Catania in 1434 and reformed its institutions of government.

Development was structured along Spanish lines, not always to the benefit of Sicily: the Spanish INQUISITION was introduced in 1487, eight years after it was established in Spain, and in 1492 JEWS were expelled. In the sixteenth century, when the coasts of Sicily were subject to the depredations of BARBARY PIRATES, the economy stagnated; the exception to this overall decline was Messina, which established a SILK industry and in 1548 acquired a university. During this period the advance of the Ottomans into the Balkans created waves of refugees; the descendants of the Greeks and Christian Albanians who settled in Sicily still form distinctive communities.

Denis Mack Smith, *Medieval Sicily 800–1713* (1968).

**SICKINGEN, FRANZ VON** (1481–1523), German soldier, born on 2 March 1481 in Ebernburg, near Worms. He embarked on a career as a soldier, fighting in 1508 for the imperial army of MAXIMILIAN I against the army of Venice. He inherited substantial estates on the Rhine, and sought to increase his holdings by private warfare. In 1513 he took up the cause of Balthazar Schlör, an exiled citizen of Worms, and defied an imperial ban by attacking the city with a private army of 7,000 men, destroying both its commerce and the agriculture of his territories. He subsequently attacked Anthony, duke of Lorraine, and forced PHILIP OF HESSE to pay him 35,000 gulden. In 1518 Sickingen sided with the citizens of Mainz in their rebellion against the governing oligarchy, leading an army of 20,000 men in an attack on the city and extracting from the governors 20,000 gold gulden for himself and a month's pay for his private army.

Maximilian recognized Sickingen's military capabilities and in 1518 released him from the imperial ban against his campaign of private warfare in order to deploy his skills in the interests of the Empire. The following year he led the forces of the SWABIAN LEAGUE against ULRICH, duke of Württemberg, who had murdered Hans von Hutten during a hunting party; this expedition brought Sickingen into contact with Ulrich von HUTTEN, under whose influence Sickingen eventually became a champion of the Protestant cause. In 1519, however, he was more fully occupied with the succession to the imperial throne on the death of Maximilian: he accepted a large bribe from FRANCIS I, but when the election took place, he took his army to Frankfurt, where its presence helped to ensure the election of CHARLES V. Sickingen's support was rewarded with his appointment as imperial chamberlain and councillor, and in 1521 he led an imperial

army in an invasion of France, but was forced to retreat at Mézières. Sickingen's sympathy for the reformed cause first became apparent in 1519 when he succeeded (through intimidation) in freeing Johann REUCHLIN from the Dominicans. He subsequently offered refuge to the reformers (including Martin LUTHER) in his castles, and appointed Martin BUCER as his chaplain.

Sickingen shared with Luther an ambition to overthrow the 'spiritual princes' (the churchmen who wielded secular power in northern Europe) and to strengthen the military ORDERS that had declared for the Reformation. In 1522, with the aid of Hutten, he initiated the KNIGHTS' WAR, leading a peasant army against the forces of the archbishop of Trier. His attack was repelled, and Sickingen retreated to his castle at Landstuhl, near Kaiserslautern. On 22 October 1522 the Council of Regency placed him under an imperial interdict, to which he defiantly replied in the spring of 1523 by sacking Kaiserslautern. The combined forces of Trier, Hesse, and the Palatinate, which had successfully defended Trier, now marched on Landstuhl. Their attack on the castle was one of the first in which ARTILLERY was used, and the fortress was soon breached. Sickingen was wounded in the attack, and on 6 May 1523 he surrendered; he died of his wounds the following day.

**SIDNEY, SIR PHILIP** (1554–86), English courtier, writer, and soldier. Lacking any official court position, Sidney spent much of his youth studying and travelling on the Continent. In 1585 he joined his uncle LEICESTER's campaign against Spain in the Low Countries, and was made governor of Vlissingen (English exonym Flushing). His premature death came from an infected wound sustained whilst on campaign. He is remembered as the perfect Renaissance courtier and patron, as well as for his own writings. These include a *Defence of Poetry*, which argues for poetry's superiority to history or philosophy for the teaching of virtue; a sonnet sequence, *Astrophel and Stella*, which in a remarkably varied use of the Italian sonnet form tells of the former's unrequited love for the latter; and a prose romance, *Arcadia*.

DNB.

**SIENA**, a city-state and archiepiscopal see, the economic rival and political enemy of Florence, which blocked Siena's trade routes to the north. From 1348, when the Black Death killed half its population, till 1559, when it was absorbed into the grand duchy of Tuscany, Siena was constantly in a state of turmoil which was sustained by internal divisions and external warfare. Pandolfo Petrucci seized power in 1487, and sought to restore stability through external alliances with Florence and France and severe repression of dissent within the city; he ruled until 1512 and the PETRUCCI FAMILY continued to rule until 1524, when Fabio Petrucci was driven from the city.

The expulsion of the last Petrucci was a matter for rejoicing. The city placed itself under imperial protection, created a government of 'ten conservators of the liberties of the state', and thereafter dated their annual public records by years reckoned 'from the restoration of liberty' (*ab instaurata liberate*). This government lasted for 27 years, but the protection of the imperial Spanish guard gradually became a tyranny. On 26 July 1552 an army of Sienese exiles in Rome led by Aeneas Piccolomini (a scion of the PICCOLOMINI FAMILY and a descendant of Pope PIUS II) entered Siena and disarmed the Spanish garrison, which retreated to its citadel; a peace treaty was brokered by Duke COSIMO I DE' MEDICI, and on 5 August 1552 the Spanish garrison surrendered the fortress to the Sienese.

Duke Cosimo aspired to absorb Siena into his grand duchy. Siena sought to defend itself through an alliance with France, but Duke Cosimo fought with the assistance of Spanish imperial troops. In the battle of Marciana (2 August 1554) Cosimo defeated the Sienese and French army commanded by Piero STROZZI, the Florentine exile and *maréchal de France*, and went on to besiege Siena, which surrendered on 21 April 1555. Accounts of the siege have survived in the *Diario dell'ultima guerra senese* of the Sienese historian Alessandro Sozzini di Girolamo and the *Commentaires* of Blaise de MONLUC. A Sienese republic in exile was established in Montalcino and survived for another four years, but Duke Cosimo took formal possession of Siena on 19 July 1555. Thereafter the city was administered as part of the grand duchy of Tuscany.

Despite its continuous history of civil strife, Siena was an important centre for the arts. The Sienese School of painting had a long and distinguished history. In the art of the sermon, the most important figure was San BERNARDINO. The Piccolomini family produced a humanist pope (Pius II) and, in the sixteenth century, Bishop Alessandro Piccolomini, author of a dialogue on women, *Della bella creanza delle donne*; the other important religious figure in Siena was CATHERINE OF SIENA. Eminent members of the Sozzini family included several prominent jurists as well as Faustus SOCINUS and Laelius SOCINUS. In science the most prominent Sienese of the period was the botanist Pierandrea MATTIOLI.

The festival of *Palio delle Contrade*, in which riders from seventeen wards (*contrade*) of Siena compete in a horse race for the prize banner (*palio*) has only existed in its present form since the mid-seventeenth century. In the fifteenth and sixteenth centuries the celebrations of *Palio* consisted of bullfights, which in the early seventeenth century were replaced by races with mounted buffaloes.

William Bowsky, *The Finance of the Commune of Siena, 1287–1355* (1970); Judith Hook, *Siena, a City and its History* (1979).

**SIGISMONDO D'INDIA** (c.1582–c.1629), Italian composer from Naples who was active in Florence, Mantua, and Rome. In 1611 he was at the Savoy court of CARLO EMANUELE I in Turin. He wrote some sacred music and many secular songs and madrigals.

**SIGISMUND or (German) Siegmund** (1368–1437), Holy Roman Emperor and king of Hungary and Bohemia, was born in Nuremberg on 15 February 1368, a younger son of the Emperor Charles IV and Elizabeth, daughter of the duke of Pomerania. Sigismund was educated at the Hungarian court and in 1385 married Maria, elder daughter of Louis the Great, king of Hungary and Poland, to whom he had been betrothed since 1374. On Louis's death the Polish crown passed to his younger daughter Jadwiga, and the throne of Hungary passed to Sigismund, who was crowned on 31 March 1387. For the next nine years Sigismund sought to secure his kingdom in the face of the rival claim of King Ladislas of Naples, son of Charles II of Hungary.

In 1396 Sigismund led a crusade against the Ottomans, whose forces had conquered Serbia (1389) and Bulgaria (1393). His army of 90,000 men, which contained noblemen and soldiers from all over Europe, captured Vidin (Bulgaria) and marched east along the Danube, supported by 70 galleys, to besiege Nicopolis (Bulgarian Nikopol). Sultan Beyazit responded by raising the siege of Constantinople and leading his army of 140,000 troops to Nicopolis, where in the course of a four-day battle (25–8 September 1396) he crushed the army of Sigismund.

For the next fourteen years Sigismund struggled to re-establish his authority in Hungary, where in 1401 he was imprisoned and twice deposed. His half-brother Emperor WENCESLAS IV was deposed in 1400, and his successor, Ruprecht of the Palatinate, died in 1410. Sigismund was elected king of the Romans by three electors on 20 September 1410, and after the death of his rival Jobst of Moravia was again elected on 21 July 1411. He was crowned as king of the Romans in Aachen on 8 November 1414.

The GREAT SCHISM had by 1414 produced three rival popes, and Sigismund convened the COUNCIL OF CONSTANCE to resolve the schism. Sigismund invited Jan HUS to defend his views at the Council, and granted him a safe conduct. The extent of his complicity in the subsequent trial and execution of Hus is not clear: he attempted to have Hus freed from the conventual prison of the Franciscans in which he was incarcerated, and was abroad when Hus was executed, but he accepted the verdict of the tribunal.

When Wenceslas died in 1419 Sigismund inherited the crown of Bohemia, but the HUSSITE WARS prevented him from claiming his kingdom for seventeen years. He was crowned in Milan as king of Lombardy on 25 November 1431, and was finally crowned as HOLY ROMAN EMPEROR by Pope EUGENIUS IV on 31 May 1433. He returned to Bohemia, and his claim to that crown was finally recognized in the Compactata of Prague (5 July 1436). He died in Znojmo (German Znaim) in Moravia on 9 December 1437 and was buried in Oradea (German Grosswardein, Hungarian Nagyvárad), in Transylvania.

Sigismund appears amongst the dramatis personae of MARLOWE's *Tamburlaine*, part II; Sigismund was a contemporary of Timur (1336–1405), but the events that Marlowe portrays are actually taken from the life of VLADISLAV III; the treachery that Marlowe attributes to Sigismund may reflect the common Protestant conviction that he dishonoured the safe conduct that he had granted to Hus.

**SIGISMUND I or Zygmunt I** (1467–1548), king of Poland, was the son of King CASIMIR IV JAGIEŁŁO and the younger brother of Alexander, who succeeded their father as king. In 1506 Sigismund succeeded Alexander as king. Throughout his reign Sigismund was at war. The conflict with the TEUTONIC Knights ended with Poland's suppression of the Order in 1521. On the eastern front, Sigismund fought a protracted war with IVAN IV of Russia. Within Poland, Sigismund enjoyed the support of the aristocracy but had a hostile relationship with the SZLACHTA. In ecclesiastical politics, Sigismund was tolerant of Protestants, Jews, and RUTHENIANS. His marriage to Bona Sforza, daughter of Gian Galeazzo SFORZA, created a link with the culture of the Italian Renaissance.

**SIGISMUND II AUGUSTUS or Zygmunt II** (1520–72), king of Poland, was the son of SIGISMUND I and Bona Sforza. In 1530, at the age of 10, he was declared co-ruler with his father, and in 1544 he became ruler of Lithuania; he succeeded his father to the Polish throne in 1548. In 1561 he negotiated the Treaty of Vilnius, which integrated Livonia into Lithuania and ended Russian attacks on Livonia. In 1569 he secured the Treaty of LUBLIN, by which the union of the kingdom of Poland and the duchy of Lithuania became a permanent union rather than a personal union dependent on the same person serving as king and duke. In ecclesiastical politics, Sigismund continued the tolerationist policies of his father. Among his cultural concerns, he encouraged GÓRNICKI to adapt the work of CASTIGLIONE into Polish. There were no children by his three marriages, so Sigismund was the last member of the JAGIEŁŁO dynasty.

**SIGISMUND III VASA or Zygmunt III** (1566–1632), king of Poland and Sweden, was the son of King JOHN III of Sweden and Catherine JAGIEŁŁO of Poland. He was raised as a Catholic, which eased his election to the Polish throne in 1587. In 1592 he married Anna of Styria, sister of the future Emperor FERDINAND II, and later in the year succeeded to the throne of Sweden. Sigismund's Catholic convictions and imperial marriage made his accession unpopular in Sweden, and in 1598 the regent (his uncle, later CHARLES IX of Sweden) mounted a rebellion that led to the deposition of Sigismund the following year.

Sigismund refused to renounce his claim to the Swedish throne and embarked on a Swedish–Polish War that was to persist until the Peace of Altmark in 1629. Sigismund's claim to the tsardom of Russia on behalf of his son caused another war; Polish forces occupied Moscow for three years (1610–12) and were to retain Smolensk until 1654. Sigismund also mounted a campaign against the Turks in Moldavia. In domestic politics, Sigismund moved his royal residence from Kraków to Warsaw in 1610.

**SIGLO DE ORO** (Spanish; 'golden century' or 'golden age'). The term RENAISSANCE has long been resisted by cultural historians of Spain, because its association with the influence of Italian models occludes the large body of literature and art not influenced by Italian models. In poetry, for example, the blank verse (*versos sueltos*) introduced by Joan BOSCÀ (*Leandro*, 1543) in imitation of the *versi sciolti* of Gian Giorgio TRISSINO

was used on occasion by GARCILASO DE LA VEGA and fully achieved by Francisco de Figueroa in his *Tirsi*, but the form never became an important presence in Spanish poetry, which continued to be rhymed.

The term *Siglo de Oro* was originally coined in the court of FERDINAND and ISABELLA as a description of their own reign in terms of the classical golden age of Augustus, but the boundaries of the *Siglo de Oro* have since been variously and more generously defined. In the nineteenth century the model proposed by Prosper Mérimée gained wide assent. Mérimée defined the Golden Age as running from 1517 to 1681, and distinguished three periods: 1517–98 (i.e. the reigns of CHARLES V and PHILIP II), the apogee of 1598–1635 (ending with the death of Lope de VEGA), and the decline and decadence of 1635–81 (ending with the death of Calderón). This model of the *Siglo de Oro*, like that of the Renaissance, may now be old-fashioned, but it has nonetheless become a useful feature of the landscape of Spanish literary and cultural history.

**SIGNORE or (English) lord or (Latin) dominus**, most commonly used to describe the ruler of an Italian commune which had ceased to function as a republic and had become subject to a lordship or *signoria*. Contemporaries hostile to such regimes often referred to them as 'tyrannies', while later historians sought to demonize them as 'despotisms'. *Signori* (plural) often sought to legitimize and perpetuate their rule by acquiring prestigious, feudal, hereditary titles from their imperial or papal overlords: count (*conte*), marquis (*marchese*), or duke (*duca*), as in the case of the GONZAGA and the ESTE. *Signori* generally came from prominent local or regional families, such as the DELLA SCALA; less often they were, like the SFORZA, *condottieri*.

J. E. Law, *The Lords of Renaissance Italy* (1981).

**SIGNORELLI, LUCA** (c.1450–1523), Italian painter, born in Cortona and, according to VASARI, trained in the studio of PIERO DELLA FRANCESCA. His paintings include a *Flagellation* (c.1475, Brera, Milan) and the *School of Pan* (c.1490, destroyed in Berlin during the Second World War), both of which depict sculptural figures. His finest surviving work is the fresco series *The Apocalypse* in the Chapel of San Brizio in Orvieto Cathedral; the series was begun in 1447 by Fra ANGELICO and Benozzo GOZZOLI and finished by Signorelli (1499–1504).

MDA; Jonathan Riess, *The Renaissance Antichrist: Luca Signorelli's Orvieto Frescoes* (1995).

**SIGONIUS, CAROLUS, or (Italian) Carlo Sigonio or Sigone** (1520–84), Italian humanist and historian. He was born in Modena and became a student of GREEK, in which he later held professorships in Modena, Venice, Padua, and Bologna. Sigonius published widely on ancient history (both Greek and Roman) and philology. His *Fasti consulares* (1550), which was based on ancient bronze tablets excavated in the Forum in 1547, was the first chronological account of Roman history; his writings on the ancient world, which include *De antiquo iure Romanorum, Italiae, provinciarum* (1560), *De republica Atheniensium* (1564), *De Atheniensium et Lacedaemoniorum*

Luca **Signorelli**, *The School of Pan*
(1490); the painting was
destroyed in Berlin in 1945

*temporis* (1565), and *De Romanae iurisprudentiae iudiciis* (1574),
are important accounts of the constitutional and legal history
of Rome, Athens, and Sparta, and his *De republica Eboracum*
(1582) is a comprehensive account of the religious, civil, and
military institutions of the JEWS. *De regno Italiae* (1574) records
the history of Italy from 570 (the Lombard invasion) to
1200, and a companion volume, *De occidentali imperia* (1579),
narrates the history of the Western Empire. Sigonius also
published an important edition of LIVY with the *scholia*.

In 1583 Sigonius published in Venice an edition of what
purported to be the *Consolatio* of CICERO; the authenticity
of the work was challenged by scholars (including Justus
LIPSIUS), and it is now regarded as a forgery. Sigonius died
near Modena in August 1584.

> Eric Cochrane, *Historians and Historiography in the Italian
> Renaissance* (1981).

**SIGÜENZA, JOSÉ DE** (*c.*1544–1606), Spanish historian and
poet, born in Sigüenza. He succeeded Benito ARIAS MONTANO
as librarian of the ESCORIAL and later served as prior of the
Hieronymite monastery at the Escorial, which he had joined
in 1567. His three-volume *Historia de la Orden de San Jerónimo*
(1595, 1600, 1605) sets out the life of St JEROME in the first
volume, and delineates the history of the ORDER in the second
and third volumes; the third volume contains an important
account of the construction of the Escorial and PHILIP II's
relations with its various architects. The reputation of the
*Historia* has never recovered from its description by Miguel
de Unamuno as 'the Escorial ['rubbish heap'] of Spanish
prose', a phrase that acknowledges its scale and solidity but
also skewers its prose as flat, dull, and unemotional. The

description is wholly unjustified; Sigüenza's style is rich and
intelligent. He was also the author of a small volume of
poems collected under the Augustinian title *Ciudad de Dios*.

> M. A. Menger, *Fray José de Sigüenza, poeta e historiador* (1944);
> L. Rubio González, *Valores literarios del Padre Sigüenza* (1976).

**SILESIA or (Polish) Śląsk or (German) Schlesien**, a region
in what is now south-west Poland, the principal city of which
is Breslau (now Wrocław, Latin Vratislavia), in Lower Silesia.
Medieval Silesia's population was Slavic, and in about 1000
the Silesian clans were incorporated into the kingdom of
Poland. When the territories of the Polish crown were partitioned in 1138, Silesia became a separate principality, and in
1201 it became entirely independent of Poland. In the course
of the twelfth century, control of Silesia gradually passed
to Germany, and in 1163 the Emperor Friedrich I Barbarossa
created dukedoms of Upper and Lower Silesia and invited
German colonists to settle in their domains. Breslau was
refounded as a German town subject to GERMAN LAW, and
by the end of the thirteenth century Silesia had become predominantly German.

By the end of the fourteenth century, a series of partitions
had divided Silesia into eighteen principalities. The lack of
a central government, together with an unwillingness to
return to Polish rule, led the rulers of Silesia to seek the protection of the German rulers of BOHEMIA. King John the Blind
and King Charles (later the Emperor Charles IV) imposed
civil order and created a central administration, but the link
with Bohemia eventually drew Silesia into the HUSSITE WARS.
Silesia declared for SIGISMUND against the Hussites, and so
was subjected to a series of devastating invasions (1425–35). In

Upper Silesia, many German settlers were either killed or left for safe havens, and the ethnic balance was altered in favour of the Slavs. The accession of the Hussite GEORGE OF PODĚBRADY to the Bohemian throne led to a rebellion in Breslau, but before George could subdue the rebellion he was displaced by the Hungarian King MATTHIAS CORVINUS, whose suzerainty the burghers of Breslau readily acknowledged in 1469. Matthias restored civil order, appointed a vice-regent, and instituted a permanent diet of princes and ESTATES. Under his ineffectual successor LADISLAS II, Silesia managed to achieve a measure of autonomy and so reduce the tax burden exacted by the king.

At the Reformation, Silesia, despite its loyalty to Sigismund during the Hussite Wars, accepted the Lutheran Church with little resistance from within and none from without. The accession of FERDINAND I as king of Bohemia and Hungary in 1526 initially had little effect on Silesia, because Ferdinand was too preoccupied with the Hungarian insurrection and Ottoman threat to be able to attend to the suppression of the Reformation in regions such as Silesia. In the second half of his reign, however, he restricted the powers of the Silesian Diet, removed all Silesian authority in matters relating to foreign affairs, and systematically annexed the territories of extinct Silesian dynasties. By 1550, Silesia had lost most of its autonomy, and was for most purposes administered from Prague. Under the Habsburgs, Silesia was absorbed into the kingdom of Bohemia, the archduchy of Austria, and the Holy Roman Empire, but it enjoyed a period of peace until the outbreak of the THIRTY YEARS WAR in 1618, during which Silesia was occupied by a succession of mercenary armies; by the end of hostilities in 1648, some three-quarters of the population of Silesia had been killed.

N. Davis and R. Moorhouse, *Microcosm* (2002).

**SILK** is a fibrous substance produced by a moth (*Bombyx mori*) that during its larval stage (when it is known as a silkworm) feeds on mulberry leaves. Until the fifteenth century, the main species of mulberry cultivated for sericulture (the art of rearing silkworms) was the black mulberry (*Morus nigra*), but thereafter it was displaced by the white mulberry (*Morus alba*), which originated in Asia and began to be cultivated in southern Europe in the twelfth century.

For centuries silk was imported from China along the overland trade route known as the Silk Road. European sericulture seems to have begun in the twelfth century in Sicily, and slowly spread to north Italian centres such as Florence, Genoa, Milan, and Venice. In France, silk weaving began in Tours in 1480, and sericulture began in 1520, when FRANCIS I brought silkworm eggs from Milan to be reared in the Rhône valley. In England sericulture was introduced in the mid-fifteenth century, but remained a small industry until about 1585, when a large number of Flemish weavers escaping from the REVOLT OF THE NETHERLANDS and French HUGUENOT weavers escaping from the WARS OF RELIGION settled in the Spitalfields area of London, where they were formed into a corporation in 1629.

In the Americas, CORTÉS organized the planting of mul-

berry plantations in Mexico in 1522 and subsequently imported silkworm eggs from Spain, but the industry failed before the end of the century. James I (JAMES VI) exported silkworms to Virginia in 1609, but the ship sank, and a second attempt was not made until 1619; thereafter the Virginia settlers successfully established a sericulture industry.

Luca Molà, *The Silk Industry of Renaissance Venice* (2001).

**SILOÉ, DIEGO DE** (*c*.1495–1563), Spanish architect and decorative sculptor, born in Burgos; he was the son of the sculptor Gil de SILOÉ. Diego studied in Florence, where he learnt to sculpt in the style of MICHELANGELO and to design buildings in the idiom of the Italian Renaissance.

On returning to Spain Diego embarked on his finest work both as architect and decorative sculptor, the gilded staircase (Escalera Dorada) in Burgos Cathedral, which is modelled on the staircase designed by BRAMANTE to link the terraces of the BELVEDERE COURT; this debt may imply that Diego had worked in Rome as well as Florence while studying in Italy. The staircase is decorated with a profusion of putti and carved heads in the Renaissance manner.

In 1528 Diego succeeded Enrique EGAS as architect of Granada Cathedral, and so embarked on the greatest project of his career. He inherited the Gothic foundations of his predecessor, and daringly decided to impose a vast domed chancel with ribbed vaults over the sanctuary apse; the cathedral was finally completed in 1561.

Diego repeated his idea of a circular domed sanctuary imposed on a rectangular nave in the Church of El Salvador in Úbeda (1536), which was built by Andrés VANDELVIRA. His other important buildings are the tower of Santa María del Campo (1527), near Burgos, the courtyard of the Colegio Fonseca in Salamanca (1529–34), and the Church of San Gabriel in Loja (1552–68); he is also credited with the designs of Guadix Cathedral (1549) and, less certainly, Málaga Cathedral (1538).

*MDA*; M. Gómez-Moreno, *Las águilas del Renacimento español: Bartolomé Ordóñez, Diego Siloé, Pedro Machuca, Alonzo Berruguete* (1941); E. E. Rosenthal, *The Cathedral of Granada* (1961).

**SILOÉ, GIL DE** (*fl*. 1486–99), French sculptor and woodcarver in Spain, a native of Orléans. He carved the central section of the façade of the Colegio de San Gregorio (now the Museo Nacional de Escultura) in Valladolid and designed the reredoses for two churches in Burgos (San Gil and San Nicolás) and the tombs (1489–93) of JOHN II and Queen Isabella of Portugal and of their son Prince Alfonso in the Carthusian monastery of Miraflores near Burgos. The style of his sculptures is Gothic, with recollections of Flemish conventions and a marked MUDÉJAR influence. Gil is regarded as the last great exponent of the Gothic in Spain, just as his son Diego de SILOÉ is regarded as one of the earliest exponents of the Renaissance style.

*MDA*; Joaquin Yarza Luaces, *Gil de Siloé: El retablo de la Concepción en la capilla de obispo Acuña* (2000).

**SILVER.** In late medieval Europe the supply of silver from the mines of Germany and Austria was diminishing, but the discovery of silver in the Americas (which now supply two-thirds of the world's silver) led to both an increase in availability and a decrease in price; in the first instance silver was mined in the Spanish viceroyalty of Peru, where the mines in Potosí (in what is now Bolivia) were opened in 1545. Silver is too soft to be used in its pure state for the manufacture of plate, coin, and jewellery, and so was mixed with an alloy (usually copper) to lower its melting point; on the proportions of the alloy and the assaying of silver, see HALLMARK.

**SIMONE MARTINI** (c.1284–1344), Italian painter, a native of Siena, where he trained in the studio or circle of DUCCIO. His earliest surviving painting is *The Virgin in Majesty* (1315; reworked 1321) in the Palazzo Pubblico in Siena. He may have painted the equestrian portrait (the earliest surviving example of this genre) of the soldier Guidoriccio da Fogliano on the opposite wall (1328); the attribution to Simone has recently become controversial. At an unknown date he painted scenes illustrating *The Life of St Martin* in Lower Church of San Francesco in Assisi.

In 1317 Simone was in Naples, where he painted an altarpiece (Museo Nazionale, Naples) depicting St Louis of Toulouse resigning his crown to his brother Robert of Anjou. He subsequently painted altarpieces for Pisa (1320, Museo Civico, Pisa) and Orvieto (1320, Museo dell'Opera del Duomo), both of which may be collaborations with LIPPO MEMMI, his brother-in-law; Simone and Lippo later signed their collaborative *Annunciation* (1333, Uffizi), painted as an alterpiece for the cathedral in Siena: this was the first altarpiece with a narrative subject in Italian art. In 1340 or 1341 Simone joined the papal court in Avignon, where he painted *Jesus Reproved by his Parents* (1342, Walker Art Gallery, Liverpool) and the frontispiece to the copy of Servius' commentary on Virgil owned by PETRARCH (Biblioteca Ambrosiana, Milan), whom Simone met in Avignon.

*MDA* s.v. Martine; Andrew Martindale, *Simone Martine* (1988).

**SIMPSON, THOMAS** (1582–c.1630), English composer, viol player, and editor. He was employed at the elector palatine's court in Heidelberg and, by 1615, by Count Ernst III of Holstein-Schaumburg at Buckeburg. He later worked at the Danish court. He wrote dance music for viol or violin consorts; *Opusculum neuwer Pavanen* (1610), which also includes arrangements of works by John DOWLAND, John Farmer, and Thomas TOMKINS, is the earliest collection.

**SIRMOND, JACQUES** (1559–1651), French Jesuit educator and patristic scholar who entered the JESUIT Order in 1576. He served as professor of rhetoric at the Collège de Clermont in Paris (1581–90), where his pupils included FRANÇOIS DE SALES, and then became secretary to the Jesuit general Claudio AQUAVIVA in Rome (1590–1608), where he also assisted BARONIUS in his historical works. On returning to France he became rector of the Jesuit college in Paris (1617) and

**Simone Martini** and Lippo Memmi, *The Annunciation* (1333), in the Uffizi, Florence

MICHELANGELO, *The Last Judgement*,
**Sistine Chapel**, Vatican, Rome

confessor to King Louis XIII (1637–43). His principal works were editions of the church fathers (Fulgentius, Paschasius Radbertus, Theodoret of Cyrrhus, Rufinus, and the *Opuscula* then attributed to Eusebius of Caesarea and now believed to be the work of Eusebius of Emesa). His *Dionysii Parisiensis et Dionysii Areopagitae discrimen* (1641) prompted a protracted controversy in its refusal to identity Dionysius of Paris (St Denis, the patron saint of France) with Dionysius the Areopagite.

**SISTINE CHAPEL**, the principal chapel of the VATICAN, so called from the adjectival form of Sisto, the Italian name of Pope SIXTUS IV, who in 1473 commissioned the construction of the chapel, which since its completion has been used as the meeting place of the conclave of cardinals during the election of new popes. In 1476 Pope Sixtus commissioned a series of sixteen frescoed scenes and a frescoed alterpiece; these were painted (1481–3) by BOTTICELLI, GHIRLANDAIO, PERUGINO, PINTURICCHIO, ROSSELLI, and SIGNORELLI. Bartolomeo DELLA GATTA and PIERO DI COSIMO also contributed. The north and south walls still retain six frescoes each; the liturgical frescoes on the east and west walls were later lost (the former, by Perugino, to MICHELANGELO's *The Last Judgement*).

MICHELANGELO, *The Fall of Man and the Expulsion from the Garden of Eden* (1508–12), on the ceiling of the **Sistine Chapel** in the Vatican

Pope JULIUS II engaged Michelangelo to paint the ceiling (1508–12); 30 years later Michelangelo returned to paint *The Last Judgement* on the altar wall (1533–41). On ceremonial occasions the side walls were covered by the tapestries commissioned by Pope LEO X, designed by RAPHAEL (whose cartoons are in the Victoria and Albert Museum in London), and woven in Brussels (1515–19). The marble screen and cantoria were made in the workshop of Andrea BREGNO.

**SIXTUS IV** (1414–84), pope from 9 August 1471 until his death on 12 August 1484, was born Francesco della Rovere in Celle (near Savona) on 21 July 1414, the son of poor parents. He entered the Franciscan Order, and after studying at Bologna and Padua, pursued an academic career. He served as provincial of Liguria and on 19 May 1464 was elected general of his Order. His scholarship was admired by BESSARION, on whose recommendation he was created cardinal of San Pietro in Vincoli on 18 September 1467. On the death of Pope PAUL II, Francesco bought the influential support of Galeazzo Maria SFORZA, duke of Milan, with lavish gifts, and Francesco's nephew the Franciscan Pietro RIARIO secured the backing of important cardinals with promises of lucrative benefices. Having successfully suborned the electorate, Francesco was elected as Pope Sixtus IV.

On his election, Sixtus IV proposed to organize a CRUSADE against the Turks. He paid for the preparation of a crusading fleet, but the European powers failed to rally to his call, and in the event he achieved only a few local successes, such as the establishment of a bridgehead in Smyrna (now İzmir) in 1472. The fall of Otranto to the Ottomans on 11 August 1480 prompted Sixtus to proclaim another crusade the following year; the papal galleys did manage to recapture Otranto in September 1482, but this victory probably owed more to the sudden death of Sultan Mehmet II on 3 May 1481 than to the military might of the papal forces.

In foreign policy, Sixtus had to deal with the intractable problem of France's desire for ecclesiastical autonomy. King LOUIS XI of France upheld the provisions of the PRAGMATIC SANCTION OF BOURGES (1438) and angered Sixtus with an ordinance of 8 January 1475 requiring royal approval for the publication of papal decrees in France. In 1474 and 1476 Sixtus revived the negotiations (initiated by Paul II) with Grand Duke IVAN III of Muscovy in a fruitless attempt to reconcile the Russian Orthodox Church with Rome and to secure Russian support for the struggle against the Turks. In Spain, Sixtus acquiesced in the royal request that the Spanish INQUISITION be established, promulgating his bull on 1 November 1478, and after a period in 1482–3 in which he sought to check the abuses of the Inquisition, he confirmed Tomás de TORQUEMADA as grand inquisitor. In 1478 he annulled the decrees of the COUNCIL OF CONSTANCE.

The domestic policy of Sixtus was aimed at aggrandizing the PAPAL STATE and advancing the interests of his family. He quickly abjured his election oath by appointing his two young nephews, Pietro Riario and Giuliano della Rovere (later Pope JULIUS II), as cardinals and lavishing lucrative benefices on them. When Cardinal Riario succumbed to his

dissipation in 1474, his place as the malevolent councillor of Sixtus was taken by his brother Count Girolamo Riario, who was the son-in-law of Galeazzo Maria SFORZA, duke of Milan. Girolamo, often abetted by Galeazzo, embroiled Sixtus in the violent political struggles of Italy, most infamously in the PAZZI CONSPIRACY. Sixtus was dragged along with Naples into a pointless war with Florence (1478–80) and then, at the instigation of Girolamo, into a conflict with Ferrara (1482–4) which began with Sixtus inciting Venice to attack Ferrara and changed course when Sixtus turned against Venice. The Peace of Bagnolo (1484), which was intended by Sixtus and Girolamo to consolidate their control of Romagna, resulted instead in rebellions in Rome and elsewhere in Latium.

Sixtus's unblushing generosity to members of his family, which included the appointment of six nephews to the cardinalate, was papal nepotism on an unprecedented scale, and set the standard for pontificates to come. The widespread discontent at the management of the papacy as a family business came to a head in March 1482 when the Croatian archbishop Andrea Zamometič attempted to reconvene the COUNCIL OF BASEL and have Sixtus suspended until the Council could pass judgement on him. Sixtus responded by renewing the ban on appeals to general councils.

Sixtus was a generous patron of scholarship and the arts. He founded the Sistine choir, built the SISTINE CHAPEL, refounded the VATICAN LIBRARY, and organized the Vatican archives. Beyond the Vatican, he was largely responsible for the transformation of Rome into a Renaissance city, widening and paving streets, building the bridge now known as the Ponte Sisto, building new churches (notably Baccio PONTELLI's Santa Maria della Pace), rebuilding old churches (notably Pontelli's Santa Maria del Popolo, where the family of Sixtus is buried), and attracting to Rome Europe's greatest artists. He is buried in a magnificent bronze tomb by Antonio Pollaiuolo in the Vatican Grottoes.

E. Lee, *Sixtus IV and Men of Letters* (1978).

**SIXTUS V** (1525–90), pope from 24 April 1585 until his death on 27 August 1590, was born Felice Peretti in Grottammare (in the March of Ancona) on 13 December 1520. He was the son of an agricultural labourer, and was educated with the assistance of an uncle who was a Franciscan. At the age of 12 Peretti entered the Franciscan Order at nearby Montalto; he was later to be known as Cardinal Montalto. Peretti was ordained as a priest at Siena in 1547 and the following year graduated doctor of theology at Fermo (which had a university until 1826). In 1552 Peretti moved to Rome at the behest of Cardinal Carpi, protector of the Franciscans, and there consolidated his reputation as an outstanding preacher; his friends included IGNATIUS LOYOLA and Filippo NERI. He was appointed inquisitor for Venice in 1557 by Pope PAUL IV; he was recalled because of his severity, but reappointed by Pope PIUS IV in 1560.

In 1566 PIUS V, who as grand inquisitor had come to admire Peretti's management of the Inquisition in Venice, appointed him vicar-general of the Franciscans and bishop of Sant'Agata dei Goti (near Caserta); In 1570 Pius created Peretti (who was his confessor) cardinal, and the following year appointed him bishop of Fermo (1571–7). Cardinal Montalto fell out of favour during the pontificate of pope GREGORY XIII, and retired to his villa to prepare an edition of St Ambrose. On being elected pope he assumed the name Sixtus as a gesture of respect towards his fellow Franciscan Pope SIXTUS IV. As pope Sixtus retained his allegiance to the Franciscans, keeping the JESUITS at arm's length but declaring (in 1588) the thirteenth-century Franciscan theologian St Bonaventura (whom Sixtus IV had canonized in 1482) a doctor of the Church.

During the pontificate of Pope Gregory much of the PAPAL STATE had fallen into the hands of bandits, and in the course of the next two years Sixtus brutally reasserted papal authority by executing thousands of bandits (and the noblemen who sheltered them). He set about restoring the economy of the Papal State by draining marshes, regulating food prices, and encouraging agriculture and the wool and SILK industries. Gregory had left the papal treasury depleted, and Sixtus restored financial stability by selling ecclesiastical offices, imposing taxes, and establishing new MONTES PIETATIS. Despite huge expenditure on public works, Pius amassed a fortune of more than 4 million scudi, which made him one of the richest men in Europe.

Sixtus reformed the papal curia, and in a bull of 3 December 1586 set the number of cardinals at 70 (6 bishops, 50 priests, and 14 deacons), an arrangement that remained in place until 1958. On 22 January 1588 he established fifteen permanent cardinalitial congregations (known as 'Roman congregations'), six to oversee secular affairs and nine for spiritual affairs (including the inquisitorial HOLY OFFICE, the Congregation of Sacred Rites, and the Sacred Congregation of Propaganda); these congregations remained virtually unchanged until the twentieth century, when they were reorganized by Pius X (1908) and Vatican II (1962–5).

The foreign policy of Sixtus was imaginative and wide-ranging. He promoted missions in Japan, China, the Philippines, and South America, and, closer to home, skilfully tried to maintain Catholic unity in Europe. Although he inherited the traditional papal mistrust of Spanish domination, he assisted PHILIP II of Spain in his struggle against the Huguenot Henry of Navarre (later HENRI IV), excommunicating him in 1585; he also promised to support Philip's invasion of England, but refused to pay after his ARMADA was defeated in 1588. Sixtus also supported STEFAN BÁTORY and SIGISMUND III VASA to win Poland for the Catholic cause and induced CARLO EMANUELE I, duke of Savoy, to incorporate Geneva into his realm.

Sixtus attended to the needs of his family, even elevating his 15-year-old nephew Alessandro to the cardinalate, and was also a generous patron of learning and the arts. As a scholar he inaugurated a revision of the Latin text of St JEROME's Vulgate (published on 2 May 1590 and later revised under CLEMENT VIII) and established the Vatican press, which in 1587 published an edition of the Septuagint, the Greek version of the BIBLE. Sixtus was a modernizer, so he did not place a high value on the preservation of the antiquities of

Rome; instead he remodelled the city, and was responsible for its transformation into Europe's finest BAROQUE city. He drove boulevards through the city to connect the seven pilgrimage churches, constructed the Acqua Felice aqueduct to increase the supply of fresh water to the city, rebuilt the Lateran Palace, completed the dome of ST PETER'S BASILICA, and constructed a new VATICAN LIBRARY.

Sixtus was detested by the people of Rome, largely because of the tax burden that he had imposed, and when he died of malaria in August 1590 a Roman mob tore down his statue on the Capitol.

R. Canestrari, *Sisto Quinto* (1935); R. Canestrari, *Sisto V* (1954).

**SKANDERBEG or Scanderbeg or (Albanian) Skënderbeu or (Turkish) Iskander Bey** (1405–68), Albanian national leader. He was born Gjergj Kastrioti in Albania and raised as a Muslim in the Ottoman court in Constantinople, where he joined the Ottoman army and was known as Iskander Bey (Prince Alexander). In 1443 he deserted, and, converting to Catholicism, began a guerrilla war against the Ottomans in his native Albania. With the support of Venice and (later) the papacy, he succeeded in resisting the Ottoman advance until his death.

I. Ajeti (ed.), *Simpoziumi për Skënderbeun/Simpozijum o Skënderbegu* (Proceedings of the Skanderbeg Symposium of 9–12 May 1968, 1969).

**SKARGA, PIOTR** (1536–1612), Polish theologian and nationalist, a native of Grójec who joined the JESUIT Order in 1569 and ten years later became head of the Jesuit Academy at Vilnius. In 1588 he became a preacher at the court of King SIGISMUND III VASA, where he resisted any extension of toleration to non-Catholics. His parliamentary sermons (*Kasania Sejmowe*, 1579) are imbued with patriotic sentiments that appealed strongly to Polish nationalists.

**SKELTON, JOHN** (c.1460–1529), English poet. Educated probably at Cambridge, Skelton was awarded the 'laureate', an academic honour, from Oxford (1488), Cambridge (1493), and Louvain (1492). From 1489 he was a court poet to HENRY VII; he was tutor to the future HENRY VIII between 1496 and 1501. Ordained in 1498, he was the rector of Diss in Norfolk from c.1503 until his death, but appears to have lived in Westminster from 1511. His poems include: *The Bowge of Court* (1499), a satirical dream-allegory of the court of Henry VII; the lamentation *Philip Sparrow* (1505); the *Ballad of the Scottish King* (1513), celebrating the English victory at Flodden; *The Tunning of Elynour Rummyng* (c.1521); and the self-laudatory *Garland of Laurel* (1523). His secular morality play *Magnificence* was written c.1518. In the early 1520s, he attacked WOLSEY in a series of poems, including *Speak Parrot, Colin Clout*, and *Why Come ye Not to Court*. His fast-flowing and irregular verse form is known as 'skeltonics'.

DNB; Greg Walker, *John Skelton and the Politics of the 1520s* (1988).

**SLAVERY.** The slavery of classical antiquity survived in attenuated form in the serfdom of the feudal system, but the more brutal forms of slavery disappeared from much of

Europe, persisting only in areas occupied by the Ottomans or the Moors. In Spain, both Moors and Spaniards kept captives as slaves during the RECONQUISTA, and elsewhere in Europe the practice of keeping slaves was revived after the Ottoman conquest of Constantinople. Thereafter Christians who were captured and taken to areas occupied by the Ottomans were variously used as agricultural workers, GALLEY slaves, or (when castrated) harem attendants, and European households, particularly in Italy, used captured Turks and Arabs as house servants. Captives were sold by both sides, and in Europe members of the orders of ransom (principally Trinitarians and Mercedarians) negotiated ransoms and offered themelves in exchange for captives.

Portuguese contacts with sub-Saharan Africans inaugurated a revival of the slave trade, and in the last half of the fifteenth century the Portuguese imported some 140,000 slaves from Africa to Portugal. The European discovery of America accelerated the growth of the African slave trade and inaugurated the trade in American Indians. In the Laws of the INDIES and the institutions of the ENCOMIENDA and the *repartimiento* (see LAS CASAS, FRAY BARTOLOMÉ DE) Spain sanctioned the forced labour of Indians but forbade their outright sale, but offered no comparable rights to Africans.

Slavery was condemned by missionaries (notably LAS CASAS) and by Popes PAUL III (1537) and PIUS V (1567), and the Jesuits even attempted to establish a model slaveless colony in Paraguay, but the slave trade nonetheless grew apace, and soon England, France, and the Netherlands were engaged in the transatlantic slave trade, which was not finally abolished until the nineteenth century.

Hugh Thomas, *The History of the Atlantic Slave Trade, 1440–1870* (1998).

**SLAVONIA.** The modern state of Slovenia (Slovenian Slovenija) inherits part of the area formerly known as Slavonia, but the region occupied by the Slovenes also included Carinthia, Styria, and Carniola, which were part of the duchy of Austria. The Slovenes (*Slovenci*, German *Winden*), who in nineteenth-century historical works are called 'Wends', are sometimes confused with the Slovaks (see SLOVAKIA) and with the Slovinci of eastern Pomerania.

Slovene is an ancient literary language (the earliest surviving manuscripts date from *c.*1000), and at the Reformation was thought to be a suitable language for religious texts. Between 1550 and 1582, Primoz Truber, a Slovene Protestant refugee in Tübingen, published Slovene translations of a catechism, a New Testament, and several Protestant works of theology, and in 1584 J. Dalmatin of Wittenberg published a sumptuous edition of a complete Slovene Bible. At the same time, Adam Bohorič produced a grammar of Slovene (*Arcticae Horulae succisivae de Latinocarniolana literatura*, Wittenberg, 1584). The Catholic Church responded by translating into Slovene *Principiorum fidei doctrinalium demonstratio* (1578), a treatise on the authority of the Church and the apostolic succession by the English Catholic apologist Thomas Stapleton.

In the early modern period there were no princely courts and no large cities (Ljubljana only became a bishopric in 1461)

in Slavonia, so the humanists tended to migrate to large cities such as Venice or Vienna; the Slavonian origins of such authors are indicated by the use of the epithets Carnus and Carniolanus in their surnames. The most celebrated Slavonian of the period, the reformer Pietro Paolo VERGERIO the Younger, came from Capodistria (Slovenian Koper), but he came from an Italian rather than a Slavonic family.

P. Simoniti, *Humanizem na Slovenskem in Slovenski Humanisti do srede XVI Stoletja* (1979).

**SLEIDANUS, JOHANNES** (1506–56), German historian, born Johann Philippson at Schleiden (from which he derived his Latin name) in the Eifel. He studied classical languages at Liège and Cologne and jurisprudence at Paris and Orléans. In 1536 he entered the service of Cardinal Jean DU BELLAY and was involved with the (fruitless) negotiations to align France with the SCHMALKALDIC LEAGUE. The date of his conversion to Protestantism is not known, but by 1542 he had settled in the Protestant city of STRASSBURG and had embarked on a history of the Reformation commissioned by PHILIP OF HESSE and the Schmalkaldic League on the recommendation of Martin BUCER and Johannes STURM.

Sleidanus completed the first volume of his history in 1545, when he was sent to England as an emissary to HENRY VIII. On his return he represented Strassburg at the diets of Frankfurt and Worms and travelled to Marburg to work in the archives of Philip of Hesse. The SCHMALKALDIC WAR interrupted Sleidanus' research and truncated his stipend, so in 1551 he wrote to ask EDWARD VI of England for an annual pension, which was granted at the behest of Thomas CRANMER but soon discontinued. Sleidanus returned to the Continent, representing a group of imperial cities (Esslingen, Ravensburg, Reutlingen, Biberach, and Lindau) at the COUNCIL OF TRENT (1551–2) and participating later in 1552 in the negotiations between HENRI II of France and the German Protestants.

In 1554 Sleidanus was appointed professor of law at Strassburg, where he completed his history of the Reformation, which was published as *De statu religionis et reipublicae Carolo V Caesare commentarii* (2 vols., Strassburg, 1555; English translation by John Dawes, 1560). Sleidanus' account of the Reformation was not sufficiently partisan to gain the approval of any of the combatants, and even MELANCHTHON expressed dissatisfaction; it is, however, still valued for the large number of contemporary documents that it contains. In October 1556 Sleidanus died in straitened circumstances in Strassburg.

W. Friedensburg, *Johannes Sleidanus* (1935).

**SLOVAKIA** or Slovensko. From 1308 until 1918, Slovakia was part of Hungary. The Slovaks (*Slovák*, feminine *Slovenko*, adjective *Slovenský*, Hungarian *Tót*) are sometimes called 'Slovenes' in nineteenth-century historical works, a usage that unhelpfully encourages confusion with the Slovenes of Carinthia, Styria, and Carniola (on whom see SLAVONIA). The Slovak language is a close relative of the CZECH LANGUAGE, especially in the Moravian dialect. Because the Reformation came to Slovakia from Bohemia, Czech became (and remained for centuries) the church language of Slovak Protestants and the language in which they read their Bibles.

Slovak was not a written language until the eighteenth century.

The Ottoman defeat of Hungary at the battle of MOHÁCS in 1526 meant that Slovakia, which became a bulwark of Christian Europe against the Turks, passed from the control of the kings of Hungary to that of the HABSBURGS. The conflict between the Lutheranism and Calvinism of the Slovaks (and of the German and many of the Magyar residents of the region) and the Catholicism of the Habsburgs eventually led to religious wars in 1603 and in 1669–71.

**SLUTER, CLAUS** (*c*.1360–1406), Netherlandish sculptor. He was born in Haarlem and entered the service of Philip the Bold, duke of Burgundy, for whom he worked on the Chartreuse de Champmol (near Dijon), which was built as a ducal mausoleum and is now a psychiatric hospital; in 1389 he succeeded Jean de Marville as master sculptor. Sluter built the chapel doorway, which contains a complex programme of sculpture, and also constructed the *Calvary*, of which the base, known as the *Puits de Moïse*, survived the despoliation of the French Revolution as a mutilated but magnificent fragment; he also designed the duke's tomb, which was built by Sluter's nephew Claux de WERVE and is now in the Musée des Beaux-Arts in Dijon. In 1404 Sluter retired to the Monastery of Saint-Étienne in Dijon.

MDA; NNBW iii; Hella Schreckenberg, *Claus Sluter* (1987); Kathleen Morand, *Claus Sluter: Artist at the Court of Burgundy* (1991).

**SMITH, SIR THOMAS** (1513–77), English jurist and statesman. Smith was educated at Cambridge, where he became a fellow of Queens' College before travelling to Paris and then to Padua, where he received a DCL. On returning to Cambridge he attempted to reform the pronunciation of ancient GREEK in the university, and after much debate succeeded; his epistle on the subject, *De recta et emendata linguae Graecae pronunciatione*, was published in Paris in 1568; the same volume contains his dialogue on the writing of English, *De recta et emendata linguae Anglicanae scriptione*. He was appointed as the first Regius professor of civil law at Cambridge in 1544 and became secretary of state in 1548. He became a Protestant, and so was deprived of his offices during Mary's reign, but returned to public life under Elizabeth as her ambassador to France, where he lived from 1562 to 1566. He was reappointed secretary of state in 1572.

Smith's principal publication was *De republica Anglorum: The Manner of Government or the Policy of the Realm of England*, which was published posthumously in 1583. This treatise is the most important contemporary work on the Tudor constitution; it was often reprinted, and the interest that it aroused elsewhere in Europe occasioned translations into Latin, Dutch, and German.

DNB; Mary Dewar, *Sir Thomas Smith: A Tudor Intellectual in Office* (1964).

**SMYTH, JOHN** (*c*.1554–1612), English Baptist leader in Amsterdam. Educated at Cambridge, where he became a fellow of Christ's College in 1594, Smyth was ordained and began preaching Puritan teachings in Lincoln (*c*.1600–2). By 1607 he was the leader of a separatist congregation at Gainsborough, and the following year he led a group of followers to Amsterdam, where he established the first Baptist church. In the year of his death, his associates established the first English Baptist church in London. He is remembered as the reputed founder of the General Baptists, who believe that baptism, involving immersion in water, should be performed only when the subject is old enough to understand the significance of the ceremony.

DNB.

**SMYTHSON or Smithson, ROBERT** (*c*.1535–1614), English architect, the most important exponent of the Elizabethan country-house style. He worked as principal mason at Longleat (1568–75) before embarking on his most original building, WOLLATON HALL (1580–8), in Nottinghamshire. This innovative building, which may have derived from a plan by Sebastiano SERLIO, is a single monumental pile organized internally around the two axes which meet in a large central hall; the building is now a natural history museum. Plans and drawings by Smythson (now in the Royal Institute of British Architects in London) show that he designed Worksop Manor (*c*.1585, now destroyed) in Nottinghamshire, Hardwick Hall (1590–7) in Derbyshire, and Burton Agnes (1601–10) in Yorkshire. Houses attributed to Smythson on stylistic grounds include Barlborough (Derbyshire), Wootton Lodge (Staffordshire), and Fountains Hall (Yorkshire).

John Smythson (*c*.1570–1634), Robert's son, designed several of the buildings at Welbeck Abbey, Nottinghamshire (including the riding school, 1622–3), and most of the buildings at Bolsover Castle (1612–34). His papers (also in the RIBA) include a narrative of a journey to London in 1618.

MDA; M. Girouard, *Robert Smythson: The Elizabethan Country House* (1983).

**SNEL VAN ROYEN, WILLEBRORD** (1581–1626), Dutch natural philosopher and mathematician, born in Leiden, the son of a mathematician whom he succeeded in 1613 as professor of mathematics at the University of Leiden. In 1615 he conducted a series of experiments designed to measure the size of the earth, using triangulation to determine the length of a meridian degree; he published details of his calculations in *Eratosthenes Batavus* (1617). In 1621 Snel's work on optics led to his formulation of the law of refraction now known in English as Snell's Law, according to which the ratio of the sine of the angle of incidence to the sine of the angle of refraction remains constant in a given medium; Snell's Law was first published by Descartes in *Dioptrique* (1637).

DSB.

**SOCINIANISM**, the heretical denial of the divinity of Christ, so called from its immediate origins in the teachings of Laelius and Faustus SOCINUS; the doctrine derived ultimately from the Arian heresy of the fourth century. The differences between classical Arianism and reformed Socinianism became apparent in sixteenth-century Poland, when Faustus Socinus debated with the Arians. The Arians believed that the Son of God existed prior to his incarnation, and the Socinians did not; thus, in the Arian view, Christ was eternal, but in the Socinian view he was only perpetual. The other point of contention concerned prayer: the Polish Arians thought that direct prayer (the *invocatio Christi*) was unacceptable, whereas Socinus argued that it was acceptable but not obligatory; in his view, the only obligatory element was worship, the *adoratio Christi*, a point that he debated with the non-adorationist Francis DÁVID. The first systematic statement of Socianism was the RACOVIAN CATECHISM of 1605. Socinianism is a specific form of UNITARIANISM, but in the early modern period Socianians and other Unitarian groups were sometimes estranged.

## SOCINUS, FAUSTUS, or (Italian) Fausto Paolo Sozzini

(1539–1604), Italian Protestant reformer and nephew of Laelius SOCINUS, born in Siena on 5 December 1539. His eminent father Alessandro Sozzini died in 1541, aged 31, and Fausto was raised in great comfort but with little formal education. In 1558 he and members of his family began to be suspected of Lutheran sympathies, in part because of the activities of Laelius in northern Europe. In 1561 Fausto travelled to Lyon, probably as a merchant; his name appears on the list of members of the Italian congregation in Geneva in 1562, but he was back in Lyon in 1563. At the end of 1563 he returned to Italy, and for the next twelve years lived as a conforming Catholic in the service of Isabella de' Medici, granddaughter of Grand Duke COSIMO I DE' MEDICI. He left Italy for Basel at the end of 1575, where on 12 July 1578 he finished a treatise on soteriology entitled *De Jesu Christo servatore*.

A manuscript copy of this unpublished treatise aroused the interest of Giorgio Blandrata, who invited Socinus to Transylvania. Blandrata had attempted to persuade the anti-Trinitarian bishop Francis DÁVID, who had renounced the worship of Christ, to return to a less extreme form of anti-Trinitarianism, but their negotiations had broken off because Blandrata had been accused of sodomy. Blandrata therefore invited Socinus to negotiate in his stead. Socinus travelled to Poland and thence to Transylvania, arriving in Kolozsvár (Romanian Cluj, German Klausenburg) in November 1578. For the next four months Socinus and Dávid debated the finer points of the doctrine of invocation. Socinus failed to win Dávid over to his view that the worship of Christ (*adoratio Christi*) was obligatory for Christians even though prayer to Christ (*invocatio Christi*) was simply permissive, because Dávid's radical anti-Trinitarianism extended to non-adorationism. At the end of their fruitless negotiations, Socinus left for Poland and Dávid was tried for heresy and imprisoned; he died in prison three months later.

Socinus spent the last fifteen years of his life in Poland. He settled in Kraków, where he was at first excluded from the anti-Trinitarian reformed 'Minor Church' because of his unacceptable views on adult baptism (which he thought appropriate only to Gentile converts). He was eventually admitted to the Church and soon became an important presence in the Church's synods and the principal combatant of what he saw as the Arian heresy (for the points at issue,

see SOCINIANISM); although he did not return to Transylvania, he continued to exert an important influence on the anti-Trinitarian Church there. He was forced to leave Kraków in 1583, and in 1586 married a Polish noblewoman, Elizabeth Morsztyn. After the death of his wife and birth of his daughter the following year, he returned to Kraków. By 1598 Socinus was publishing theological works over his own name, and on Ascension Day (25 May) a mob wrecked his house and beat Socinus, forcing him to flee. He sought refuge in Lucławice, 50 kilometres (30 miles) east of Kraków, where he lived until his death on 4 March 1604.

Socinus' works were collected by his grandson and published in Amsterdam in 1656. His most important surviving works are a treatise on the authority of scripture (*De auctoritate s. scripturae*, 1570, first published over the name of a Spanish Jesuit in 1588) and *De Jesu Christo servatore*. His name is irrevocably associated with a heresy, but he never led a heretical sect. His Christology may not have been acceptable to mainstream opinion in the Catholic Church, but in the context of Polish Christianity was not unorthodox. His most unusual belief was in the sanctity of human life: he not only thought that war was unlawful, but also argued that no circumstances could justify the taking of human life.

G. Pioli, *Fausto Socino: Vita, opere, fortunata* (1952).

## SOCINUS, LAELIUS, or (Italian) Lelio Francesco Maria

Sozini (1525–62), Italian Protestant reformer, born in Siena on 29 January 1525, the sixth son of a jurist, and educated as a lawyer in Bologna. He moved to Venice, which was then the principal centre of Protestantism in Italy, and in 1547 left Italy, meeting prominent reformers in France, the United Provinces, and England before settling in Switzerland, where he lived until 1550. Thereafter he visited Wittenberg, where he became a guest of MELANCHTHON, and then travelled to Prague, Vienna, and Kraków. He returned to Italy in 1552 and inducted his young nephew Fausto Sozzini (who always spelt his name with a double *z*) into his radical Protestant ideas. In 1554 he returned to Switzerland, and in Geneva (where he met CALVIN) he was challenged in the wake of the recent execution of SERVETUS on the soundness of his doctrine of the Trinity; he managed to satisfy Heinrich BULLINGER that he was not a heretic, drawing up an orthodox confession of faith on 15 July 1555, while nonetheless securing the right to enquire further into issues of Christology. He died in Zürich on 14 May 1562. His principal writings were a Confession of Faith (1555), a treatise on the SACRAMENTS (*De sacramentis dissertatio*, 1560), and a fragmentary *De resurrectione* (1654).

It is not entirely clear whether Laelius Socinus subscribed to the SOCINIAN heresy with which he is associated. BEZA and ZANCHI attributed to Laelius anonymous heretical works which were in fact written by CASTELLIO (*De haereticis*, 1553; *Contra libellum Calvini*, 1554) and Fausto Socinus (an *Explicatio* of the proem to John's Gospel, 1562); he was certainly a radical, enquiring theologian, but none of the works that can be confidently attributed to him demonstrates that Laelius Socinus was a Socinian.

**SODERINI, PIERO DI TOMMASO** (1452–1522), Florentine *GONFALONIERE*. He began his political career in the service of Lorenzo de' MEDICI and Piero II de' MEDICI, and, when Piero was expelled from Florence in 1494, emerged as one of the most powerful figures in the republic. In 1502 Soderini was elected *gonfaloniere di giustizia* for life (Latin *vexilifer perpetuus*), a newly created office modelled on the dogeship of Venice. In the course of his ten years as head of the republic, Soderini reformed public sector finance and the judiciary and instituted a national militia to replace the *ad hoc* regiments of foreign mercenaries; in 1509 he triumphed in the war against Pisa by capturing the city.

In 1512 a chapter in the WARS OF ITALY ended with the withdrawal of French troops from Italy, whereupon the victorious papal-Spanish army advanced on Florence. In August this army captured Prato and demanded that Soderini resign in favour of the Medici. He accepted and left the city as a permanent exile, first in Siena, then in RAGUSA (now Dubrovnik), and finally in Rome, where he died.

R. S. Cooper, 'Pier Soderini: Aspiring Prince or Civic Leader?', *Studies in Medieval and Renaissance History*, II (1978).

**SODOMA, IL, or Giovanni Antonio Bazzi** (1477–1549), Savoyard painter. He was born in Vercelli (which was then in Savoy) and worked in the vicinity of Siena except for a three-year sojourn in Rome (1508–10). VASARI attributed his nickname to pederasty; this may be true, but he also fathered at least two children and enjoyed both civic and ecclesiastical patronage, which implies that Vasari's account of his reputation may be exaggerated.

Il Sodoma painted frescoes in the Olivetan Convent of Sant'Anna in Camprena, near Pienza (1503–4) and in the Abbey of Monte Oliveto Maggiore (1505–8). In Rome, where his painting took on some of the characteristics of RAPHAEL and LEONARDO, he painted a fresco illustrating *The Marriage of Alexander and Roxana* in Agostino CHIGI's Roman villa, now known as the Farnesina (1516). After his return to Siena Il Sodoma painted his finest fresco cycle, *The Life of St Catherine* (1526), in the Church of San Domenico in Siena.

*DBI* s.v. Bazzi; *MDA*.

**SOLARIO or Solari, ANDREA** (c.1465–c.1524), Italian painter. He was a native of Milan and was influenced by LEONARDO DA VINCI, who lived in Milan, with a break of seven years, from 1482 to 1509. His best-known painting is *Madonna with a Green Cushion* (1509), which was once in the collection of MARIE DE MÉDICIS and is now in the Louvre. Andrea was the younger brother of Cristoforo Solario (c.1460–1524), a sculptor and architect who worked for the SFORZA in Milan and the ESTE in Ferrara.

*MDA*; David Brown, *Andrea Solario* (1987).

**SOLARIO or Solari, GUINIFORTE** (1429–81), Italian architect and sculptor, born in Milan, the son of Giovanni Solario (1410–80), the architect of the Certosa di Pavia. Guiniforte was a resolutely Gothic architect, and when he succeeded FILARETE as architect of the Ospedale Maggiore, he completed Filarete's Renaissance building as a Gothic building.

He worked on Milan Cathedral and, in succession to his father, on the Certosa di Pavia; he also built the Gothic nave of the Church of Santa Maria delle Grazie (1465–90), which was completed by BRAMANTE.

*MDA* s.v. Solari.

**SOLARIO or Solari, PIETRO ANTONIO** (c.1450–1493), Italian architect and sculptor, the son of Guiniforte SOLARIO; he worked with his father in Milan until 1490, when he moved to Russia, where he designed three of the fortification towers in the Moscow Kremlin (Nikol'skaya, Spasskaya, and Borovitskaya). He collaborated with an otherwise unknown Italian architect called Marco Ruffo on the uncompromisingly Italianate Granovitaya Palata ('faceted palace', so called from its diamond-shaped stone facings) in the Kremlin (1487–91).

*MDA* s.v. Solari.

**SOLIS, VIRGILIUS** (1514–62), German engraver, book illustrator (especially of bibles), and prolific designer. His Nuremberg workshop produced more than 600 ornamental and figurative prints, many of which were intended for use by German silversmiths in chalices and ewers but were also used for a century after his death by woodcarvers, furniture designers, and decorative artists working in stucco. His large number of children included Virgilius Solis the Younger, who worked as a painter and designer in the court of RUDOLF II in Prague, and Nikolaus Solis, a printmaker.

*MDA*; I. O'Dell-Franke, *Kupferstiche und Radierungen aus Werkstatt des Virgil Solis* (1977).

**SOMATIANS or (Italian) Somaschi**, a religious ORDER of clerks regular founded in 1532 by St Jerome Emiliani (1481–1537), a former officer in the Venetian army who had been captured at Castelnuovo (Treviso) by the forces of the League of CAMBRAI and subsequently escaped from his dungeon. Jerome was ordained priest in 1518, and in 1531, after he had recovered from plague, he founded a series of orphanages, hospitals, and refuges for prostitutes. In order to administer these institutions, Jerome founded the congregation known as the Somaschi because of their mother house in Somasca (between Milan and Bergamo). He took a particular interest in the education of orphans and abandoned children, and seems to have been the first to use the technique of the CATECHISM to instruct children. Jerome died on 8 February 1537 and was canonized in 1767. The Somatians were approved by Pope PIUS V in 1568.

P. Paschini, *L'Ordine dei Chierici Regolari Somaschi, 1528–1928* (1928).

**SOMER, PAUL VAN** (1576–1621), Flemish portrait painter. He was born in Antwerp and in 1604 established a studio in Amsterdam. In 1616 he settled in London as a court painter. His best-known painting is a portrait of *Queen Anne of Denmark* (1617), which is now in the Royal Collection.

*BNB*; *DNB* s.v. Van Somer; *MDA*.

**SOMERSET, EDWARD SEYMOUR, DUKE OF** (c.1500–1552), protector of England. Brother of JANE SEYMOUR,

Somerset benefited from the honours showered on Jane's family on her marriage to HENRY VIII. On Henry's death in 1547, he became lord protector in the reign of his young nephew EDWARD VI, effectively governing the country for two years. Two rebellions in 1549 (KETT'S REBELLION in Norfolk, and disturbances in the West Country) however, threatened his position, and he was replaced by NORTHUMBERLAND. He was imprisoned and executed in 1552.

*DNB* s.v. Seymour, Edward.

**SONCINO FAMILY**, a dynasty of Jewish printers in Germany, Italy, Bohemia, and the Ottoman Empire. The family settled in Soncino (near Cremona) in 1454, and the press was inaugurated by Joshua Solomon (d. 1493) in 1484 with the publication of *Berakhot*, a Talmudic treatise; in 1488 he published the first printed edition of the complete Hebrew BIBLE.

Joshua's nephew Gershom ben Moses (d. 1534) printed more than 100 HEBREW texts (both sacred and secular) and a similar number of works in Greek, Latin, and Italian; he was an innovator in the nascent field of Hebrew typography and was the first printer to use woodcut illustrations in Hebrew works. He printed books in several Italian cities (including Brescia, Fano, Pesaro, and Rimini) before establishing presses in the Ottoman Empire, first in Thessaloniki (from 1527) and then in Istanbul (from 1530).

Gershom's son Eliezer (d. 1547) inherited his father's business in Istanbul. Eliezer's son Gershom (d. 1562) established a branch of the family business in Cairo. Another branch of the family settled in Prague, where they established a Hebrew press in 1512.

JNB; MDA; M. Marx, *Gershom Soncino's Wanderyears in Italy, 1498–1527* (1936).

**SONNET**, a poetic form that originated in thirteenth-century Provence and Italy. Petrarch's sonnets, which consisted of fourteen lines of iambic pentameter verse (or alexandrines in France) divided into an octave (eight lines rhymed *abba abba*) and a sestet (six lines variously rhymed); there was typically a turn (Italian *volta*) in sense and tone after the octave. Petrarch's sonnets were imitated for centuries; Italian Renaissance sonneteers include BEMBO, CASTIGLIONE, MICHELANGELO, and TASSO. Some sonneteers, including Michelangelo, add extra verses to make a *sonetto caudate* ('tailed sonnet').

In the fifteenth and sixteenth centuries sonnets were introduced in other European countries, notably England, France, the Netherlands, Poland, Portugal, and Spain, and were written in Latin as well as in vernaculars; the form was subsequently introduced in Denmark, Germany, Russia, and Sweden.

In France the sonnet was introduced by Mellin de SAINT-GELAIS (1533–4), but the first to be published was written by Clément MAROT (1538). Both used the rhyme scheme *ccd eed* for their sestets; this pattern was eventually displaced by Jacques PELETIER DU MANS's *ccd ede*, which became the standard rhyme scheme for the French sonnet, and was used by RONSARD (*Les Amours*, 1552–3) and Joachim DU BELLAY (*Les Regrets*, 1558). Ronsard, followed at the end of the century by

MALHERBE, inaugurated the French convention of writing sonnets in alexandrines, the standard metre of French poetry.

In Spain the sonnet was introduced by the marqués de SANTILLANA, and its exponents included Joan BOSCÀ, GARCILASO DE LA VEGA, and Lope de VEGA. In Portugal the sonnet was introduced by SÁ DE MIRANDA and Antonio FERREIRA, and found its finest exponent in CAMÕES.

In England the sonnet was introduced by Thomas WYATT and the earl of SURREY. The English sonnet is divided into three quatrains (rhymed *abab bcbc cdcd* by SPENSER and *abab cdcd efef* by SHAKESPEARE) and a concluding rhymed couplet. The turn is placed at the end of the third quatrain (line 12) rather than the end of the octave (line 8). The traditional subject of the sonnet was romantic love, but John DONNE used the form for devotional purposes in his *Holy Sonnets*.

Sonnets are sometimes organized as sonnet sequences, in which case individual sonnets resemble stanzas in a long poem. The first important sequence, DANTE's *Vita nuova*, contained linking passages in prose (as well as other verse forms) that explain the narrative to the reader. In Petrarch's *Canzoniere*, however, there is no linking prose, so the reader must infer the plot from individual sonnets that are only loosely connected. In this respect individual sonnets are not linked as closely as stanzas in a long poem, and they also stand alone to an extent that is not normally the case with stanzas. The first non-Italian sonnet sequence was Joachim Du Bellay's *L'Olive* (1549 or 1550). Elsewhere in Europe, the most important sonnet sequences were Camões's *Rimos*, Spenser's *Amoretti*, and Shakespeare's *Sonnets*.

Michael Spiller, *The Development of the Sonnet* (1992).

**SORBS AND SORBIAN**. The Sorbs are a Slavonic people who are now surrounded entirely by German speakers; in Germany they are known as Wends. Sorbs live in Lusatia (German Lausitz), to the north-east of Dresden, and call themselves Lužičane or Serbs; in the early modern period both Dresden and LEIPZIG had substantial Sorbian populations. In English the language is variously called Sorbian or Wendish or Lusatian. The Sorbian community consists of two principal groups: the High Sorbs live in Oberlausitz and the Low Sorbs in Niederlausitz. The Sorbian capital is Bautzen (Sorbian Budyšin), in Oberlausitz. In the Reformation period, the high and low dialects of Sorbian were recognized by the publication of separate translations of LUTHER's *Kleiner Katechismus* into High Sorbian and Low Sorbian.

**SORG, JÖRG THE YOUNGER** (d. 1603), German armour etcher, the son and grandson of Augsburg armourers; his maternal grandfather was Kolman HELMSCHMIED. Examples of armour (see ARMS AND ARMOUR) etched to Sorg's designs are preserved in the Tower of London Armouries, the Kunsthistorisches Museum in Vienna, and the Metropolitan Museum in New York. These armours are not signed, but can be identified from an album of pen and wash drawings (now in the Staatsbibliothek in Stuttgart) that depict 45 armours decorated by Sorg between 1548 and 1563; each armour is marked with the names of the armourer who made it and the owner for whom it was made.

**SOTERIOLOGY**, the doctrine of salvation (Greek σωτηρία), which in early modern theological treatises always includes the doctrines of ATONEMENT and GRACE and sometimes extends backwards to the doctrine of sin and forwards to eschatology (heaven, PURGATORY, and HELL).

*SOTIE* or *sottie*, a kind of satirical play popular in France in the fifteenth and sixteenth centuries. The characters were known as *sots* (i.e. fools); their costume consisted of a grey robe, a hood with asses' ears, and bells on the legs. The normal practice was for each *sot* to be given a number rather than a name, though sometimes *sots* with allegorical names were led by a Mère Sotte. The texts of some 60 *soties* survive; the most famous are those of Pierre GRINGORE.

Jean-Claude Aubailly, *Le Monologue, le dialogue et la sottie* (1976).

**SOTO, DOMINGO DE** (1494–1560), Spanish theologian and jurist. He studied at the universities of Alcalá and Paris, and in 1524 entered the Dominican Order. In 1532 he became professor of theology at Salamanca. In 1545 he was sent at the behest of CHARLES V to the COUNCIL OF TRENT, and he subsequently served as the emperor's confessor. In 1552 he succeeded Melchor CANO as the principal theologian at Salamanca. His most important jurisprudential work was *De iustitia et de iure* (1555), in which he proposed that the ordinance of reason (*rationis ordinatio*) was the mechanism by which laws could be evaluated. He also took the view that INTERNATIONAL LAW (*ius gentium*) was a part of the law of specific communities (later termed positive law) rather than a moral or NATURAL LAW.

Soto's erudition, which was distinguished even by the standards of those in attendance at the Council of Trent, ranged far beyond theology and law. In his commentaries on Aristotle (1545) he outlined a theory of the trajectory of missiles that anticipated (and may have influenced) Galileo's theories.

**SOTO, FERNANDO DE** (*c*.1500–1542), Spanish explorer, born in Jerez de los Caballeros (Extremadura) and educated at the University of Salamanca at the expense of his patron, Pedrarias DÁVILA. In 1519 he accompanied Dávila on his second expedition to Darién, and so participated in the conquest and subsequent pacification of what is now Nicaragua. In 1528 Soto explored the coast of Guatemala and Yucatán, and in 1532 led a relief force of 300 troops to reinforce PIZARRO in Peru, where he helped to capture Atahuallpa in Cajamarca; he subsequently discovered a route through the mountains to Cuzco, and led the advance party of the first Europeans to enter the Inca capital.

The looting of Inca wealth was prodigious, and Soto returned to Spain with a fortune of 180,000 ducats and with the attendant social standing that enabled him to marry the daughter of his patron Dávila. He was soon made restless by the reports of Alvar Núñez CABEZA DE VACA and others of the wealth of the lands of Florida (then a vaguely defined area

considerably larger than the present state), and so sold much of his property to raise an expedition of four ships, 620 soldiers, and 123 horses. He sailed from Sanlúcar de Barrameda in April 1538, carrying an imperial warrant from CHARLES V naming him as governor of Cuba and royal captain (*adelantado*) of the lands of Florida. He established his advance base in Havana, and left on 12 May 1539 for the Florida peninsula. For the next three years he explored what is now the southeastern United States. His precise route is not known, but he certainly reached the Mississippi river early in 1541, and spent the winter of 1541/2 west of the Mississippi, in what is now Arkansas and Louisiana. Returning along the Mississippi to the Gulf of Mexico in the early summer of 1542, Soto died (possibly on 25 June), and his body was committed to the waters of the river.

There are three independent (and often contradictory) narratives of Soto's expedition. The first was written by an anonymous Portuguese gentleman who claimed to have accompanied the expedition: *Relaçam verdadeira dos trabalhos que passarom no descobrimento da Província da Florida* (Évora, 1557) was subsequently published in English translation by HAKLUYT in 1609; the second was a reported account secured by El Inca GARCILASO DE LA VEGA from a Spanish cavalier on the expedition and included in his *La Florida del Inca* (Lisbon, 1605); the third is the report submitted in 1544 (but unpublished until 1850) by Luis Hernández de Biedma to Charles V's Council of the INDIES.

De Soto is the eponym of a famous American motor car.
DHE; E. G. Bourne (ed.), *Narratives of the Career of Hernando de Soto in the Conquest of Florida* (2 vols., 1904); David Duncan, *Hernando de Soto: A Savage Quest in the Americas* (1997); Patricia Galloway (ed.), *The Hernando de Soto Expedition: History, Historiography and 'Discovery' in the Southeast* (1997); Charles Hudson, *Knights of Spain, Warriors of the Sun: Hernando de Soto and the South's Ancient Chiefdoms* (1997).

**SOUSA, MARTIM AFONSO DE** (1500–64), Portuguese colonial administrator in Brazil and India. He was born into an aristocratic family and served as a soldier before travelling to Brazil in 1531 as the head of a naval expedition. He explored the coast of Brazil, and founded a colony on the island of São Vicente, near what is now São Paulo.

Sousa returned to Portugal, and in 1534 was appointed governor of India. He was active on the coast of Kerala, intervening in the wars between Cochin and Calicut, and then again returned to Portugal. In 1542 he was appointed viceroy of India, and in the course of his three-year tenure of office presided over an administration which is widely characterized as corrupt and ineffectual. In 1543 he led an expedition to destroy the Hindu temples in the holy city of Kanchipuram in the southern kingdom of Vijayanagar (near what is now Chennai). Sousa was eventually dismissed.

DHP; Luís de Albuquerque and Maria do Anjo Ramos (eds.), *Martim Afonso de Sousa* (1989).

**SOUTHWELL, ROBERT** (1561–95), English Catholic poet. Educated at Louvain and Paris, Southwell became a Jesuit in 1580 and was ordained four years later. After a period as prefect of studies at the ENGLISH COLLEGE, Rome, he was sent to England. Here he visited Catholics and celebrated mass, travelling in disguise and using false identities. In 1592 he was betrayed, imprisoned, and tortured, and finally hanged and quartered in 1595. Much of his poetry, which became popular when published on his death, was written in prison. It includes the long narrative *St Peter's Complaint*, an account in Peter's voice of the Passion of Christ, and other devotional poems, of which 'The Burning Babe' is perhaps the best known. He was canonized in 1970.

*DNB.*

**SPAGNOLI, GIOVANNI BATTISTA.** See MANTOVANO, BATTISTA.

**SPAIN.** Early fifteenth-century Spain consisted of four independent kingdoms: Castile, ARAGON (including the kingdoms of Valencia, Majorca, SARDINIA, NAPLES, and SICILY and the principality of Catalonia), NAVARRE, and the Islamic sultanate of GRANADA. By the end of the fifteenth century Spain had in some measure been unified: the union by marriage of Castile and Aragon (1479) and the conquest of Granada (1492) created a more homogeneous state than had hitherto existed, albeit one with significant regional differences. The use of the Arabic language was suppressed, but Spaniards still spoke four languages (Castilian, Catalan-Valencian, Galician, and Basque), and culture was markedly regional in character. In the sixteenth century Spain added the viceregal states of New Spain (1519, now Mexico), Peru (1543), and PORTUGAL (1580); when Burgundy (which included the NETHERLANDS) was acquired in the early sixteenth century, it was ruled by governors-general rather than vice-regents.

The largest kingdom in fifteenth-century Spain was Castile, which for the first half of the century was nominally ruled by King JOHN II (Juan II) and in practice ruled by a series of regents and favourites, of whom the most powerful were Álvaro de LUNA and Juan Pacheco, marquis of Villena. King John was succeeded by HENRY IV (Enrique IV), his son by his first wife Maria; ISABELLA I was his daughter by his second wife Isabella of Portugal. Princess Isabella assumed the throne of Castile after the defeat of Henry IV's daughter JUANA LA BELTRANEJA at the battle of Toro in 1476.

In Aragon, ALFONSO V acceded to the throne in 1416, but spent much of his reign in Naples, where he ruled as Alfonso I. His younger brother Prince John acted as lieutenant-general in Aragon and became king of Navarre in 1425; in 1458 he succeeded his brother as King JOHN II of Aragon, Sardinia, and Sicily. King John was succeeded in 1479 by his son Ferdinand II, who was already king consort of Castile (as FERDINAND V).

The unification of Castile and Aragon under Ferdinand and Isabella was a united monarchy, but each state maintained its own local institutions. Royal authority was asserted through institutions such as the Santa Hermandad (a militia created in 1476) and the Spanish INQUISITION, though these were administered separately in each of the royal possessions. In towns a representative of the crown was established in 1480 with the reform of the *corregidor* system, and there

were significant reforms of the Church, of justice, and of royal administration, notably in the creation of a standing army and navy and the institution of a system of bureaucracy based in councils for war, the Inquisition, finance, and the INDIES.

In the sixteenth century Spain began to colonize its American possessions and to intervene in the WARS OF ITALY, and in the first half of the century became the most powerful country in Europe. Ferdinand and Isabella were succeeded by their daughter JUANA LA LOCA, who was married to Philip of Habsburg, who became PHILIP I of Spain, the founder of the Habsburg dynasty in Spain. In 1482 Philip had inherited the Burgundian archduchy of his mother MARY OF BURGUNDY (i.e. Burgundy and the Netherlands), which was placed under the guardianship of his father Maximilian, and on his accession to the throne of Castile, Burgundy and the Netherlands were added to the territories of Spain.

The most important figure in early sixteenth-century Europe was CHARLES V, the son of Philip I and Juana; his accession to the throne of Spain as Carlos I provoked the Revolt of the COMUNEROS, in part because of the cost of Charles's pretensions to the title of Holy Roman Emperor, which he obtained in 1519. Charles's various European inheritances meant that his role as king of Spain was only one of many claims on his attention and presence. In all he paid seven visits to Spain and lived there for a total of eighteen years (he lived in Germany for eight years and in the Netherlands for 28 years); his principal concerns were combating Protestantism in Germany, establishing imperial rule in Italy and the Netherlands, and fighting the Ottoman Turks in the Habsburg homelands of Austria and Hungary, campaigns in which Spanish forces played the leading role, as they also did in the conquest of America.

Charles was succeeded as king of Spain by his son PHILIP II, who had been given the responsibility for the government of Spain in 1551 and on the abdication of his father in 1556 became king of Spain (i.e. king of Castile, León, and Navarre, together with Spanish America, and king of Aragon, which included Catalonia and Sardinia) and duke of Burgundy (i.e. the Netherlands). In 1559 King Philip left Brussels and returned permanently to Spain, where his position was secure except for two regional rebellions, one by MORISCOS in Granada (1568–70) and the other by nobles in Aragon (1591); beyond the boundaries of Spain, he had to contend with the REVOLT OF THE NETHERLANDS (to which he dispatched the duke of ALBA) and the Ottoman threat. In 1571 it was Philip's navy that lay at the heart of the forces of the HOLY LEAGUE (commanded by his half-brother Don JUAN DE AUSTRIA) which defeated the Ottomans at the battle of LEPANTO. In 1580, on the death of Cardinal-Prince HENRIQUE, Philip claimed the throne of Portugal, which he seized in an invasion commanded by the duke of Alba. In 1588 he sent the Spanish ARMADA to invade England in the hope that a subjugated England would be the best bridgehead for an attack on the rebellious Netherlands.

In 1598 Philip II was succeeded by his son PHILIP III, whose reign was marked by the continuation of the Revolt of the

Netherlands, the expulsion of the *moriscos* from Spain (1608–14), and the outbreak of the THIRTY YEARS WAR (in which Philip sided with the emperor and the Catholic princes).

See the separate entries on SPANISH ARCHITECTURE; SPANISH ART; SPANISH DRAMA; SPANISH GARDENS; SPANISH LANGUAGE; SPANISH LAW; SPANISH LITERATURE; SPANISH MUSIC.

**SPALATIN, GEORG** (1484–1545), German humanist and reformer, born on 14 January 1484 at Spalt (near Nuremberg), the son of a tanner; his name was Georg Burkhardt, but he later derived his adoptive surname from Spalt, both in Latin (Spalatinus) and German. He was educated in Nuremberg before attending the University of Erfurt and migrating in 1502 to the new University of Wittenberg. From 1505 to 1507 he taught at the Cistercian monastery at Georgenthal. He was ordained as a priest in 1508 and the following year entered the service of FRIEDRICH III, elector of Saxony, initially as tutor to his nephews (including the future Elector JOHANN FRIEDRICH I) and then as court chaplain, librarian, and secretary. He became a formidable scholar, and was an unusually competent student of GREEK.

In 1511 Spalatin was sent back to Wittenberg, where he met Luther; his letters to Luther have been lost, but Luther's replies survive. Spalatin subsequently became the conduit through whom Luther's ideas were presented to the elector; he read Luther's works to Friedrich, and in the case of the Latin works translated into German. In 1518 he accompanied Friedrich to the Diet of AUGSBURG and in 1521 to the Diet of WORMS, and was with Friedrich when CHARLES V was elected as emperor and when Charles was crowned.

Friedrich died in 1525, and in the same year Spalatin married and moved to Altenburg (where he had been a canon for many years) in order to implement the Reformation. Although he no longer lived at the electoral court, Spalatin acted as an adviser to Friedrich's successors, his son Johann and his nephew JOHANN FRIEDRICH I.

Spalatin worked for the rest of his life overseeing the transition from Catholicism to Lutheranism in electoral Saxony and, subsequently, in ducal Saxony. He suffered from severe depression in his later years, and died in Altenburg on 16 January 1545. He compiled *Annales Reformationis* (published in 1718) and a *Chronicon et annales* covering the period 1463–1525; the portion of his *Historischer Nachlaß und Briefe* describing the life of Friedrich III (*Das Leben und die Zeitgeschichte Friedrichs des Weisen*) was published in 1851.

*CoE*; I. Höss, *Georg Spalatin, 1484–1545* (1956; 2nd edn. 1989).

**SPANISH ARCHITECTURE.** The substantial Moorish presence in late medieval Spain meant that there was a significant Islamic element in Spanish architecture. As late as the fourteenth century, it was possible to have in the Alhambra of Granada a Moorish building that was virtually untouched by the architectural traditions of Europe. In areas where the RECONQUISTA had been completed in the thirteenth century, however, there was a tradition of Christian architecture, albeit transformed by MUDÉJAR traditions into distinctively Hispanic forms: the thirteenth-century Mudéjar

towers of Calatayud, Teruel, and Zaragoza are Christian belfries, but they are unmistakably based on minaret design.

In the eleventh century, the Lombard Romanesque style appeared in Catalonia, first in Ripoll (the heavily restored Church of Santa Maria, built 1010–32) and then in Cardona (San Vicenç, consecrated 1040); French Romanesque architecture started at its highest point with Santiago de Compostela (c.1075–1188). In the thirteenth century, French Romanesque yielded to French GOTHIC (e.g. Burgos, León, and Toledo), except in Catalonia, where a distinctive style of Catalan Gothic emerged in the cathedrals and churches of Barcelona and Palma (Majorca). The late Gothic style in Spain was inaugurated by masons from the Netherlands and Germany, most distinctively in Juan de COLONIA's Germanic spires on Burgos Cathedral.

Despite these important northern influences, the handling of space in Spanish cathedrals remained unique because of its debt to the tradition of mosque architecture which reaches back to the eighth-century mosque of Córdoba. The combination of Islamic floor space and Gothic height produced the largest cathedrals in Europe in Seville (from 1402), Salamanca (1512), and Segovia (1525). The spirit of Islam also lived on in the PLATERESQUE architectural decoration of the late fifteenth and early sixteenth centuries.

The influence of Renaissance ITALIAN ARCHITECTURE can be discerned in the early sixteenth century in the staircase (1504) of the Hospital de Santa Cruz in Toledo (now the Museo Provincial) and in the courtyard of the Castle of La Calahorra (1509–12). The most Italianate of Spain's palaces is Pedro MACHUCA's unfinished palace for CHARLES V in the grounds of the Alhambra in Granada (1526–68). The structural features of the palace, which is designed around a circular courtyard, are entirely Italian, but some of the decorative features, such as the garlanded window frames, are Plateresque.

The last great Italianate building to be built in Spain was the ESCORIAL, which in its final form was the work of Juan de HERRERA. The Herreran style, which may reflect the austerity of PHILIP II as much as the predilections of the architect of the Escorial, draws on the principles of Italian MANNERISM, and is chiefly remarkable for its uncompromising lines and avoidance of ornament. The eschewing of ornament has given the style its Spanish name, *estilo desornamentado*. At its best, as in the Escorial, the Herreran style can be noble, even magnificent, but to some eyes and in some buildings it can be cold, forbidding, and monotonous. The Herreran style remained the dominant style of Spanish architecture throughout the seventeenth century, especially in cathedral architecture: the cathedral in Valladolid was not completed to his vast designs, but is unmistakably Herrera's building. Herreran monumental severity also characterizes the style of the cathedrals of Salamanca and, in Spanish America, Mexico City, Puebla, and Lima.

G. Kubler and M. Soria, *Art and Architecture in Spain and Portugal and their American Dominions, 1500–1800* (1959); M. Gómez-Moreno, *Las águilas del Renacimento español: Bartolomé Ordóñez, Diego Siloé, Pedro Machuca, Alonzo Berruguete* (1941).

**SPANISH ART**. With the exception of the Asturias, early medieval Spain was under Islamic domination, and the earliest distinctively Hispanic art is the hybrid form known as Mozarabic, the art of Spanish Christians in Moorish Spain. In the course of the RECONQUISTA it was Moors who were the most skilled craftsmen, and their MUDÉJAR architecture and architectural decoration inevitably influenced the development of Spanish art. The POTTERY of fifteenth- and sixteenth-century Spain, for example, is known as 'Hispano-Moresque', and the fine tiles known as AZULEJOS are clearly Moorish in origin.

Spain was not a unified country until the late fifteenth century, and artistic culture was markedly regional in character. The principal schools of art in fourteenth- and fifteenth-century Spain are known as the Catalan School and the Hispano-Flemish School.

The founders of the Catalan School were Ferrer Bassa (d. 1348), who painted the Italianate frescoes in the cell of St Michael in the Monastery of Santa Maria de Pedralbes (Barcelona) in about 1346, and his contemporary the Barcelona miniaturist Ramon Destorrents, whose pupils Jaume and Pere Serra were influenced by the style of Sienese art. Pere Serra's pupil Lluís Borrassà, who painted the ALTARPIECE of *St Michael* (1416–17) now in the Museu Diocesà in Girona, was the most important painter of the early fifteenth century. By the 1430s the dominant figures in Catalan art were Bernat MARTORELL and Lluís DALMAU. The art of the Catalan School culminated in the paintings of Jaume HUGUET. In the Valencian School, which is sometimes distinguished from the Catalan School, the principal artist was JACOMART, whose stylist influence can be discerned in the surviving altarpiece of Rodrigo de OSONA.

In the fifteenth century, Castile and León had important commercial links with Flanders, and FLEMISH ART became fashionable in the court of Queen ISABELLA, who collected Flemish paintings and appointed one Fleming as her royal architect (Juan GUAS) and another, JUAN DE FLANDES, as her court painter. The gradual blending of Flemish styles with the native traditions of Mudéjar architectural decoration produced the distinctive style known as Hispano-Flemish or Hispano-Flamencan, which is characterized by a sombre palette, a love of architectural settings, and a demotic realism in portraiture and narrative composition. The cultural hegemony of Castile gave Hispano-Flemish art a national standing; the greatest artists in this tradition were Fernando GALLEGO and Bartolomé BERMEJO.

In the first half of the sixteenth century, the PLATERESQUE dominated architecture and decorative art. In painting and sculpture, the other important stylistic presence was Italian MANNERISM. The most prominent mannerist sculptors were JUAN DE JUNI, Alonso de BERRUGUETE, and Gaspar BECERRA. In painting, the principal exponents of the mannerist style were Pedro de CAMPAÑA, Joan Vicent MAÇIP, and, above all, Pedro BERRUGUETE.

In the second half of the sixteenth century, Spanish art was dominated by the patronage of PHILIP II, who was preoccupied with the construction and decoration of the ESCORIAL.

King Philip employed many foreign artists for his monastery-palace, but the small number of Spanish artists that he employed included the mannerist Juan FERNÁNDEZ DE NAVARRETE. Philip also introduced the tradition of the court PORTRAIT to Spain, employing the Dutch artist Antonio MORO and then the Portuguese Alonso SÁNCHEZ COELLO as court portraitists, so inaugurating the tradition that was to culminate in Velázquez and introducing the first wholly secular genre in Spanish art. Philip's patronage did not extend to those of whose style he did not approve, so neither Luis de MORALES nor El GRECO received the call to the Escorial.

In the late sixteenth and early seventeenth centuries, a new style of naturalistic Spanish painting emerged, anticipated by Juan Fernández de Navarrete's dramatic use of shading (*tenebrismo*) and characterized by the use of light and shade to portray three-dimensional shapes which were often sculptural in form. The principal exponents of this style were the painters Francisco RIBALTA, Juan Bautista Maíno (1578–1649), and Juan SÁNCHEZ COTÁN, who before he became a monk painted still lifes of food.

G. Kubler and M. Soria, *Art and Architecture in Spain and Portugal and their American Dominions, 1500–1800* (1959).

**SPANISH DRAMA**. In medieval Spain, drama was associated with the Church, and the liturgical drama (re-enactments in dialogue of religious stories such as the Nativity and the Passion) was performed on carts (*carros*) in towns and villages on feast days. Apart from a fragmentary *Auto de los Reyes Magos* from the mid-twelfth century, the texts of these medieval *autos* are lost, though documentary sources give a strong sense of the continuity of the tradition. In the sixteenth and seventeenth centuries, the finest writers of *autos* were Lucas FERNÁNDEZ (especially his *Auto de la Pasión, c.*1500) and Gil VICENTE (in whose *Auto de la Fe* a personified Faith explains the incarnation to shepherds). Fernando LÓPEZ DE YANGUAS inaugurated the Renaissance form of liturgical drama with his *Farsa sacramental* (1520), which took the mystery of the EUCHARIST as its central theme, thereby inaugurating the AUTOS SACRAMENTALES, one-act allegorical dramas performed on the Feast of Corpus Christi. The *auto sacramental* attracted all the leading playwrights of the Golden Age, including Lope de VEGA (*Las aventuras del hombre*), TIRSO DE MOLINA (*El colmenero divino*), and Calderón, the greatest exponent of the genre.

In the fifteenth century a court drama developed alongside the liturgical drama of the *autos*. Religious themes dominate the allegorical masquerades (*momos*) and Christmas and Easter plays of Gómez MANRIQUE, but their courtly elegance reflects secular patronage. The religious theme persists in the work of the dominant playwright of the next generation, Juan del ENCINA, but his plays also embody the traditions of ITALIAN DRAMA, particularly in his dramatic eclogues.

In the early sixteenth century, the most important secular dramatists were Bartolomé de TORRES NAHARRO (most of whose plays were produced in Rome) and the Portuguese playwright Gil VICENTE, some of whose plays are written in Castilian, which was the second language of the Portuguese court. In Spain there was also a tradition of learned drama, which sometimes took the form of translations to be read rather than performed (such as Pedro Simón ABRIL's translation of Terence) but also included imitations of classical drama which could be performed, such as Lupercio Leonardo de ARGENSOLA's Senecan tragedies of *Filis* (now lost), *Isabela*, and *Alejandra*.

Until the late sixteenth century there were no permanent public theatres in Spain. In the early part of the century, Lope de RUEDA, Spain's first professional actor-manager, mounted performances of his plays in public squares and innyards; CERVANTES saw one such performance in the square in front of the cathedral in Segovia, and Agustín de Rojas, who had been one of Rueda's actors, dramatized the life of a travelling company in his *El viaje entretenido* (1630). In the late sixteenth century public theatres known as *corrales* (because they were located in the large open yards of Spanish inns and houses) were built in Seville, Valencia, and Madrid. The principal theatres of late sixteenth-century Madrid were the Corral de la Pacheca (rebuilt in 1582 as the Corral del Príncipe, which was later roofed) and the Corral de la Cruz (built in 1579). In Alcalá de Henares, the Corral de Zapateros was built in 1601, and remained in continuous use as a theatre until 1945, when it was converted into a cinema; it has been restored, and reopened in 1999 as El Teatro Pequeño. In Mexico, where the earliest recorded European play was performed in 1538, a theatre was built in 1597.

Public theatres fostered the growth of a national drama that in late sixteenth- and early seventeenth-century Europe was rivalled only by ENGLISH DRAMA. The finest playwrights of the period were Juan de la CUEVA, Guillén de CASTRO, Cervantes, and Luis VÉLEZ DE GUEVERA. Their accomplishments were overshadowed by a generation of Europe's finest dramatists, working in the tradition of the *comedia nueva* pioneered by Spain's greatest playwright, Lope de Vega. Among his numerous followers were Juan RUIZ DE ALARCÓN, Tirso de Molina, and Calderón.

Margaret Wilson, *Spanish Drama of the Golden Age* (1969);
N. D. Shergold, *A History of the Spanish Stage* (1969); Melveena McKendrick, *Theatre in Spain 1490–1700* (1992).

**SPANISH GARDENS.** Spain was for centuries an important centre of Islamic horticulture, and the oldest surviving gardens in Europe are the thirteenth-century gardens of the Alhambra and the Generalife; both are in Granada, which remained under Moorish administration until 1492. In the fourteenth century Christian adaptations of Moorish gardens began to appear, complementing buildings constructed in the MUDÉJAR style. The garden of the Alcázar in Seville is the largest of surviving gardens to have retained Moorish features, which include raised paths, geometrical AZULEJOS, and the use of reflective still water as well as running water in FOUNTAINS. The arcaded courts with a pool at the centre preserve the original design, but there is an overlay of Italian Renaissance features in the enclosed Garden of Maria Padilla including *GIOCHI D'ACQUA* (Spanish *burladores*) and a PAVILION installed in the early sixteenth century by the Emperor CHARLES V.

Charles V's garden at ARANJUEZ is lost beneath that of his son, but his influence can be felt in other Spanish gardens. At the Alhambra Charles added a fountain to the Moorish garden, and in his final retreat at the monastery at Yuste he established a small garden in which he grew plants collected from all over his former empire; he also installed a pool which he stocked with tench, for which he could fish from a balcony (*mirador*) off his study, directly above the pool.

The two greatest gardens of Renaissance Spain were commissioned by PHILIP II at Aranjuez and the ESCORIAL. The gardens of the Escorial were laid out by the architect Juan de HERRARA and the gardener Marcos de Cordona. The gardens outside the palace are not well documented, save for a hanging garden of which early travellers speak, but the original terraces on which the gardens were built have survived. Inside the palace there are gardens in the courtyards; the finest of the courtyards is the vast Court of the Evangelists (Patio de los Evangelistas), which has at its centre an octagonal temple surrounded by four square pools fed by small fountains built into the statues of the evangelists, each of whom holds his Gospel in an appropriate language: Matthew in HEBREW, Mark in LATIN, Luke in GREEK, and John in SYRIAC; the original geometrical parterres that filled the court were replaced in the eighteenth century by an arabesque box garden which is more subdued than was its predecessor. The other courtyards of the Escorial also contain gardens, all of which originally looked more Italianate than they do now, because they contained 76 fountains and 73 statues, many imported from Italy.

In the early seventeenth century the garden of Buen Retiro was laid out on the eastern edge of Madrid; the designer was the Florentine Cosimo Lotti, who began work in 1628 and later went on to contribute to Aranjuez. The garden was the setting for meetings of literary ACADEMIES, and in the mid-seventeenth century accommodated at least seven hermits; these genuine hermits were the predecessors of the ornamental hermits of eighteenth-century English gardens.

G. Gromart, *Jardins d'Espagne* (2 vols., 1926); Marquesa de Casa Caldés, *Jardines de España* (1973), trans. as *Spanish Gardens* (1987).

**SPANISH LANGUAGE.** Five major languages were spoken in fifteenth-century Spain: Arabic, Basque, Castilian, the CATALAN group, and GALICIAN. The fall of the emirate of GRANADA in 1492 led to a huge reduction in native speakers of Arabic, though the last Arabic-speaking MORISCOS were not expelled until 1611. Basque, for which the Basque name is Euskera, was confined to an area close to the western end of the Pyrenees, and to the contiguous area on the French side of the border; the first Basque book was published in 1545.

In the fifteenth century, Castilian was the language of central and southern Christian Spain, but the unification of Spain in 1497 heightened its importance, and Castilian gradually became the dominant language of government and culture, and so came to be known as 'Spanish'. Linguists recognize two dialect groups (Peninsular and Spanish American) and many regional sub-dialects. Early modern Spain had three additional romance languages, all now moribund: Leonese was spoken in western Spain and Aragonese was spoken in Aragon and Navarre, and Jews and Muslims spoke varieties of Ladino. There are some early examples of Spanish being written in Arabic script, but the universal convention in sixteenth-century Spain was to use the Latin alphabet plus the tilde and the acute accent, which remain the only diacriticals other than the dieresis.

Scholarship on the Spanish language was inaugurated by LEBRIJA, whose *Gramática* (1492) was the first published grammar of a modern European language. Several important Spanish bilingual dictionaries were published at the end of the fifteenth century and in the sixteenth; the first monolingual thesaurus was the *Tesoro de la lengua castellana o española* (1611) of Sebastián de Covarrúbias y Orozco.

W. J. Entwistle, *The Spanish Language* (1962); Rafael Lapesa, *Historia de la lengua española* (9th edn. 1981).

**SPANISH LAW.** From the beginning of the eighth century to the middle of the thirteenth century, most of Spain was occupied by Arab forces and administered by the Umayyad caliphate; for much of this period only the kingdom of Asturias remained independent. During these centuries Arab and Iberian Muslims were subject to Islamic law, and Christians were subject to an attenuated form of Visigothic law which incorporated many elements of German CUSTOM-ARY LAW. The *reconquista*, the process by which the peninsula was reconquered, began with the defeat of the Arab army at Las Navas de Tolosa in 1212 and concluded with the expulsion of the Arabs in 1492. Portugal had been an independent kingdom since 1139, and, as the Arabs were driven south, Christian kingdoms emerged in Aragon, Castile, and Navarre. Legal systems evolved independently in each kingdom, and local law was formulated in municipal statutes known as *fueros* (from the Latin *forum*, the place in Rome where the law courts sat). Grants of municipal *fueros* were initially given to facilitate the resettlement of property vacated by Arabs, but they long outlived their original purpose, and remained a powerful element in Spanish law for centuries; the unification of Spain gradually subverted the power of the *fueros*, but they did not disappear altogether until the Basque *fueros* were extinguished in 1876.

The influence of Roman law began to be felt in the thirteenth century, when Spanish jurists began to study Roman law in Italy and France. In 1255 Alfonso X of Castile issued a code of law known as the *Fuero real* or the *Fuero de las leyes*, which codified local *fueros* and customary law, but also incorporated elements of Roman law. In the course of the next ten years Alfonso promulgated the compilation officially entitled the *Libro de las leyes* but popularly known (because of its seven parts) as the *Código de las siete partidas*. The *Partidas* includes municipal charters and customary law, but is primarily a systematic and comprehensive codification of CANON LAW and Roman law; the Roman law is centred on the Justinian *Corpus*. The *Partidas* was studied in the universities and consulted in the courts, and in 1348 it was declared authoritative in all spheres save that of municipal *fueros*. It eventually became the basis of law in the Spanish colonies,

and its influence can still be felt in the legal systems of central and South America, and in the states of the American southwest that were formerly part of Mexico.

In 1485 Ferdinand and Isabella issued a compilation of 1,163 laws entitled *Ordenanzas reales de Castilla*, which is normally called (with reference to its eponymous compiler, Alfonso Díaz de Montalvo) the *Libro de Montalvo*; this collection codified all laws promulgated since the *Partidas*. Points of conflict between the two codifications were resolved in the *Legas de Toro* of 1505.

Beyond the borders of Spain, the most influential body of medieval Spanish law was the compilation of Catalan MARITIME LAW known as the *Libre del consolato del mare* which appeared c.1370 and after it was published in Barcelona in 1494 quickly became the basis of maritime law throughout the Mediterranean.

Sixteenth- and seventeenth-century Habsburg Spain produced many distinguished jurists. In INTERNATIONAL LAW the most important figure was Fray Francisco de VITORIA, but significant contributions were made by Balthazar AYALA, Diego de Covarrubias y Lieva (known as the Spanish BARTOLO), Domingo de SOTO, and Arias de Valderas (author of *De bello et ejus iustitia*, 1533). Public law was dominated by Juan de MARIANA, Luis de MOLINA, and Francisco SUÁREZ; in private law the major figures were Antonio Gomez, Juan Lopez de Viveros (editor of the *Leyes de Toro*), and Molina. Molina, Soto, and Vitoria were also prominent in criminal law. The most important canonists were Antonio Agustín, Martin Azpilcueta (author of the classic *Manuale sive Encheiridion confessoriorum et paenitentium*), and Covarrubias.

Román Riaza and Alfonso García Gallo, *Manual de historia del derecho español* (1934).

**SPANISH LITERATURE.** Castilian was the dominant language of fifteenth- and sixteenth-century Spain (where Arabic, Basque, CATALAN, and GALICIAN were also spoken) and was also the medium of the most considerable literature. Under the patronage of King JOHN II (Juan II) of Castile (1407–54), the troubadour lyric of courtly love flourished; these poems were collected in *cancioneros* ('songbooks'), of which some 60 survive in manuscript. The most important was the *Cancionero de Baena*, an anthology presented to King John in 1445 by Juan Alfonso de BAENA; the collection contains 612 poems by 54 named poets. Another notable anthology, *Cancionero de Estúñiga*, is a collection by the poet Lope de Estúñiga (c.1415–1465) of poems written by the courtiers who followed ALFONSO V to Naples. In the sixteenth century, Fernando del CASTILLO compiled the first printed collection, *Cancionero general* (Valencia, 1511), which contains 1,033 poems by 128 named poets and many unnamed poets.

The Italianate school of Castilian writing was inaugurated by Juan de MENA and the marquis of SANTILLANA, and, in the next generation, Gómez MANRIQUE and Jorge MANRIQUE. In the sixteenth century they were followed by Joan BOSCÁ and GARCILASO DE LA VEGA. The true introduction of the Renaissance style, and in particular the hendecasyllabic and strophic forms such as the sonnet, octet, and *terza rima*, together with the associated themes of Petrarchanism and Neoplatonism and the use of classical *imitatio*, was the work of Diego HURTADO DE MENDOZA and, in the next generation, Fernando de ACUÑA, Fernando de HERRERA, Francisco de ALDANA, Fray LUIS DE LEÓN, JUAN DE LA CRUZ, and Lope de VEGA. Of the poets who championed Spanish traditions and opposed the Italian style, the most prominent was Cristóbal de CASTILLEJO. In the early seventeenth century, the dominant poets were GÓNGORA, the eponym of GONGORISM, and QUEVEDO, the master of the baroque metaphysical style.

In prose, Spain was responsible for the invention of almost every form of early modern fiction, from the sentimental and epistolary novel to the pastoral romance and the PICARESQUE novel. The seminal figure in the Castilian PASTORAL was the Portuguese MONTEMAYOR, whose *Diana* (which is indebted to SANNAZARO's *Arcadia*) was imitated by CERVANTES (*La Galatea*) and Lope de Vega (*Arcadia*). The prototype of the picaresque novel was the anonymous *LAZARILLO DE TORMES* (1554), which was later imitated by Mateo ALÉMAN in *Guzmán de Alfarache* (1599–1602), Vicente ESPINEL (*Marcos de Obregón*, 1618), and Quevedo (*El buscón*, 1626). The finest literary work of Golden Age Spain, however, is Cervantes' *Don Quijote* (1605–15), which draws on both the romance and the picaresque traditions to produce a totally original comic work which transcends all Renaissance generic categories and points forward to the modern novel. Other forms of realism were represented by Fernando de ROJAS's *Celestina* and Cervantes' short stories (*Novelas ejemplares*, 1613). Romance was represented by AMADÍS DE GAULA, one of the most widely read works of fiction of the century, while in non-fiction the enormously popular essays of Antonio de GUEVARA and the devotional works of LUIS DE GRANADA, Luis de León, TERESA DE ÁVILA, and Juan de la Cruz were immensely influential.

**SPANISH MUSIC.** The patronage of King John I of Aragon (1350–96) inaugurated the fine tradition of European musicians, instruments, and musical repertoire that existed in Spain at the beginning of the Renaissance period. Sacred music was written by Juan de Anchieta (1462–1523) and Francisco de Peñalosa (c.1470–1535); the *Cancionero músico de Palacio* contains over 460 Spanish folk songs. Instrumental music, principally for organ and VIHUELA, was written by Antonio de CABÉZON and Luis MILÁN respectively, while a substantial amount of sacred vocal polyphony was composed by Cristóbal de MORALES, Francisco GUERRERO, and Tomás Luís de VICTORIA, regarded as the 'Spanish Palestrina'.

**SPEED, JOHN** (c.1552–1629), English cartographer and historian, born in Farrington (Cheshire), where he trained as a tailor in his father's workshop. He moved to London and settled in Moorfields, working from 1598 in the custom house. He began to design maps, one of which he presented to Queen Elizabeth, and, with the support of friends in the Society of Antiquaries such as CAMDEN and COTTON, also wrote a *History of Great Britain* (1611). His principal cartographical works were *The Theatre of the Empire of Great Britain* (1611) and a world atlas, *A Prospect of the Most Famous Parts of the World* (1627).
*DNB.*

**SPELMAN, SIR HENRY** (c.1564–1641), English antiquarian. Educated at Cambridge, Spelman studied at Lincoln's Inn (1585–6) before returning to Norfolk where he lived as a country gentleman. He was elected MP in 1597, and in 1604 served as high sheriff of Norfolk, but also devoted himself to antiquarian studies, being a member of the Society of Antiquaries from 1593 to its discontinuation in 1604. His *Aspilogia*, a Latin treatise on coats of armour, was probably written before 1595; it was published in 1654. He transcribed many deeds and charters relating to the monasteries in Norfolk and Suffolk, and his dialogue on coins of 1594 was probably read before the antiquarian society. In 1612 he moved with his family to London; five years later his appointment as commissioner to determine unsettled titles to lands and manors in Ireland necessitated three visits there. Further work includes *De non temerandis ecclesiis: A Tract of the Rights and Respect Due unto Churches* (1613); a glossary of ancient legal terms (1626; 1664); and a compilation of the *Councils, Decrees, Laws and Constitutions of the English Church* (1639). He also established a lectureship in Anglo-Saxon at Cambridge, but the position lapsed after the death of the first incumbent.

**SPENGLER, LAZARUS** (1479–1534), German Protestant leader, born in Nuremberg; he studied law at Leipzig and then returned to Nuremberg, where he became town clerk (1507) and a member of the ruling council (1516). He became an early adherent of the Reformation and in 1519 published his first Lutheran tract. He was denounced by Johann ECK and named in *EXSURGE DOMINE* (1520), the bull which threatened LUTHER with excommunication. Thereafter Spengler remained silent until 1525, when he again began to publish tracts advancing the cause of the Reformation. He participated in the implementation of the Reformation in Nuremberg, but politically was timid rather than defiant, advising the Council of Nuremberg against joining the SCHMALKALDIC LEAGUE.
Harold J. Grimm, *Lazarus Spengler: A Lay Leader of the Reformation* (1978).

**SPENSER, EDMUND** (c.1552–1599), English poet. Of relatively humble origin, Spenser rose through patronage (including that of LEICESTER) to a position as colonial administrator in Ireland. Here he produced some of the key poetic texts of the Elizabethan age. *The Shepherd's Calendar* (published 1579), modelled on classical authors, consists of twelve eclogues with dialogues between shepherds on such subjects as love, poetry, and Queen Elizabeth. *The Fairy Queen* (published 1590 and 1596) offers a more extended celebration of Spenser's monarch, in the form of chivalric allegory. His house in Ireland was attacked and burned in TYRONE's rebellion; Spenser and his family returned to London, where he died.
*DNB.*

**SPERANDIO, SAVELLI** (1425–1504), Italian medallist, goldsmith, and sculptor who may have been a native of Mantua. He worked variously in Mantua, Ferrara, Faenza, and Bologna and finally settled in Venice in 1496. He made several portrait MEDALS, notably those of the merchant

Bartolomeo Pendaglia and Giovanni II BENTIVOGLIO of Bologna; his best-known sculpture is the terracotta monument to the antipope Alexander V in the Church of San Francesco in Bologna (where Alexander had been buried after his death on 3 May 1410).

MDA.

**SPERONI, SPERONE** (1500–88), Italian humanist, born in Padua and educated in Bologna under POMPONAZZI. Speroni was a prolific writer of dialogues, and also composed commentaries on poets such as Virgil, Dante, and Ariosto. His *Della lingua* (1542) was an exposition of BEMBO's position in the debate known as the QUESTIONE DELLA LINGUA, and became the principal model for Joachim DU BELLAY's *Défence et illustration de la langue française* (1549). The Aristotelian precepts that underlay Speroni's tragedy *Canaca* (1546) led him into a protracted debate about the nature of TRAGEDY.

OCIL.

**SPEYER, DIETS OF.** The German city of Speyer (Latin Augusta Nemetum, English exonym Spires) on the left bank of the Rhine was an imperial free city from 1294 to 1797, the seat of the REICHSKAMMERGERICHT from 1527 to 1693, and the host of many imperial diets (German *Reichstage*), of which the most important were the diets of 1526, 1529, and 1544. The Diet of June 1526, at which the Protestant minority was led by PHILIP OF HESSE, issued an edict which allowed each state or city to choose a form of religion that could be justified before God and the emperor; this edict was the first official recognition of Lutheranism.

The Diet of 1529 issued an edict on 21 February which rescinded the edict of the previous diet and instead called for the enforcement of the edict issued by the Diet of WORMS banning Lutheranism; the Lutherans reacted with the 'Protest' signed in April 1521 by six Lutheran princes and fourteen Protestant cities, and so became the first PROTESTANTS. In June 1530 CHARLES V tried to reconcile the two sides by convoking the Diet of Augsburg, where he was given the AUGSBURG CONFESSION.

The Diet of 1544 concluded a treaty on 23 May which settled the dispute between Charles V and King CHRISTIAN III of Denmark.

**SPEYER, JOHANN VON** and **WENDELIN VON**. See JOHANN VON SPEYER.

**SPIEGEL** or Spieghel, HENDRICK LAURENSZOON (1549–1612), Dutch poet and humanist, a member of the Amsterdam CHAMBER OF RHETORIC known as De Egelantier. He wrote a philological treatise, *Tweespraeck van de nederduytsche letterkunst*, in which he called on his countrymen to enrich the literary form of their language with the Latin and Greek of classical antiquity. His own poetry included an epic (*Hertspiegbel*, 1614) and a poem in praise of dancing.

NNBW ii.

**SPIERA, FRANCESCO, or (English) Francis Spira** (1502–48), Italian Protestant who practised as a lawyer in Cittadella (near Padua). On converting to Protestantism he was arraigned before the Roman INQUISITION in Venice; he publicly recanted, and was allowed to return to Cittadella, where he became depressed and committed suicide. His name became a byword in Protestant Europe for the fate that awaited those who had discovered true Christianity and subsequently repudiated it.

Emilio Comba, *Francesco Spiera: Episodio della riforma religiosa in Italia* (1872); Carl Roenneke, *Francesco Spiera: Eine Geschichte aus der Zeit der Reformation in Italien* (1874).

**SPINELLO or Spinelli ARETINO** (1350/2–1410), Italian painter, born in Arezzo and probably trained in Florence. He was primarily a narrative painter of fresco cycles. His four principal cycles were the series on St Benedict for the sacristy of San Miniato al Monte in Florence, on St Catherine of Alexandria for the Church of San Francesco in Arezzo, on SS Ephysius and Potitus for the loggia of the Campo Santo in Pisa (now partly ruined) and on Pope Alexander III in the Palazzo Pubblico in Siena.

MDA s.v. Spinelli; Anna Rosa Calderoni Masetti, *Spinello Aretino giovane* (1973).

**SPRANGER, BARTHOLOMÄUS** (1546–1611), Flemish painter, born in Antwerp, the son of a wealthy merchant; he trained in several Antwerp studios, notably that of Frans FLORIS. Spranger travelled widely in France and Italy (where he was influenced by the paintings of CORREGGIO and PARMIGIANINO) before settling in Prague in 1581 as court painter to the Emperor RUDOLF II. He became a prominent mannerist artist whose paintings included many erotically charged nudes; the formality of his compositions, which are often structured as a spiral, seems to derive from Correggio. Spranger's friend Karel van MANDER, whom he had met in Rome, returned to Haarlem as Spranger's avowed disciple, and so many features of Spranger's style became prominent elements in the painting of the Haarlem Academy.

BNB, s.v. Spranger, Barthélemy; MDA; Michael Henning, *Die Tafelbilder Bartholomäus Sprangers* (1987).

**SPREZZATURA or (Spanish) despejo**, a courtly aspiration to measured nonchalance with respect to artistic accomplishment; the aspiration derives from the ideal in ancient philosophy (particularly Cicero) of restrained and modest behaviour. The most influential elucidation of *sprezzatura* is contained in CASTIGLIONE's *Il cortegiano*.

**SPRUCH** (plural *Sprüche*) and **SPRUCHDICHTUNG**. The *Spruch* is a Middle High German poetic form which consisted of one or more strophes and was usually sung; its subject matter was usually the effect of social and political conditions on the individual. The terms *Spruchdichtung* and *Gnomische Dichtung* are sometimes used as synonyms for *Spruch*, but are also used to refer to short poems of a didactic character which were recited rather than read; in the sixteenth century, Hans SACHS extended the term *Spruchdichtung* to include his plays as well as his poems.

**SPURS, BATTLE OF THE** (16 August 1513). In October 1511 a HOLY LEAGUE consisting of Pope JULIUS II, King FERDINAND II of Spain, King HENRY VIII of England, and the republic of Venice was formed to fight France and its Italian allies in the WARS OF ITALY. In 1513 King Henry VIII, whose army was supplemented by imperial troops and continental mercenaries, invaded France on behalf of the League, and besieged the town of Thérouanne/Guinegate. On 16 August a column of French cavalry attempted to lift the siege, but was dispersed in disarray by the English army, which captured many prisoners; fleeing French soldiers were alleged to have lost their spurs. English accounts of the incident magnified the skirmish into a battle with a view to asserting the military capabilities of the youthful King Henry.

**SQUARCIALUPI, ANTONIO** (1416–80), Italian organist and composer. He was well known in Italy as an organist, having been appointed to Orsanmichele in Florence in 1431, and in 1432 at the Cathedral of Santa Maria del Fiore. He was the owner of the fifteenth-century manuscript now known as the 'Squarcialupi Codex'.

**SQUARCIONE, FRANCESCO** (c.1395–1468), Italian painter and tailor, born in Padua, the son of a notary. He worked as a tailor until his mid-thirties, when he became a painter. He is said to have amassed a large collection of antique art while travelling as a young man in Italy and Greece, but no trace of such a collection survives. He trained scores of painters in his workshop (including MANTEGNA) and is regarded as the founder of the Paduan school of painting. No surviving painting is known to represent the unassisted work of Squarcione; the three surviving products of his workshop are a half-length *Madonna* (Gemäldegalerie, Berlin), a damaged polyptych (Museo Civico, Padua), and a fragmentary fresco cycle on *The Life of St Francis* on the exterior of the Church of San Francesco in Padua.

*MDA*; Alberta De Nicolò Salmazo (ed.), *Francesco Squarcione: Pictorum gymnasiarcha singularis* (1999).

**STADLMAYER, JOHANN** (c.1575–1648), German composer who was *magister capellae* at the court of Ludwig II in Ofen in Hungary from 1522; he drowned in the Taja. He wrote masses, motets, hymns, and part songs and was widely known throughout the German-speaking world; of particular interest are his large-scale psalm motets on Luther's translation of the Psalter.

**STADTHOLDER or Stadholder**, the English exonyms for Dutch *stadhouder* and its equivalents in other Germanic languages such as German (*Statthalter*) and Danish (*statholder*). The term means 'viceroy' or 'lord lieutenant', but in the Netherlands has a precise historical sense, because *stadhouder* was the title of the head of state of the Dutch republic from 1580 until its abolition in 1802. When the title was conferred by the Estates-General on WILLIAM OF ORANGE in 1580 it implied a nominal recognition of the suzerainty of King PHILIP II of Spain over the Netherlands. Although the stadtholder had to be elected by each province separately, the title became dynastic, and was in effect vested in the House of Orange.

**STAINED GLASS**, glass dyed with coloured oxides while still in its molten state or (in the sixteenth century) painted on its dried and hardened surface. Stained-glass windows normally consist of pieces of glass of various shapes and sizes held together by a lead framework. From the eleventh century the stained glass of churches was arranged in representational designs, and in the twelfth and thirteenth centuries huge stained-glass windows were installed in the Gothic cathedrals of Europe. In the fourteenth century, advances in the technology of glass meant that the glass panels could be larger, which afforded painters the opportunity of enhancing details of the design with the use of enamels; in this period stained-glass windows began to appear in French houses. The size of the glass panels again increased in the fifteenth century, by which time designs had become the province of fresco painters and domestic installations of stained glass had extended to England, Germany, the Netherlands, and the Swiss Confederation.

In the sixteenth century the technology of glass painting underwent a significant change, in that transparent enamel pigments could be painted onto sheets of clear glass. The finest surviving stained glass of the early sixteenth century is that in the chapel of King's College, Cambridge, which was designed by Dirick VELLERT and made by the glass stainers Bernard FLOWER and Galyon HONE. In the second half of the century, the most remarkable surviving stained glass is the series of windows installed by the CRABETH brothers in St Jans Church in Gouda.

**STAMPA, GASPARA** (1523–54), Italian poet and courtesan, a native of Padua who lived from 1531 in Venice, where she presided over a literary salon and was a member of the Accademia dei Pellegrini. Her poems were Petrarchan lyrics (mostly sonnets) inspired by her love for Collaltino di Collalto, count of Treviso, who eventually deserted her. The poems, which were published (*Rime*, 1554) shortly after her death by her sister Cassandra, are characterized by a lightness and delicacy wholly at odds with the grave and sometimes stolid humanist poetry then in fashion, and she is now regarded as one of Italy's finest lyric poets.

*HWWI*; F. Bassanese, *Gaspara Stampa* (1982).

**STANCARO, FRANCESCO** (1501–74), Italian theologian, born in Mantua and educated at Padua, where he was ordained as a priest and taught at the university. He converted to Protestantism in 1540 and fled to Vienna (1544) and then to Basel, where he published a Hebrew grammar (1547). He then moved to Kraków, where he published a set of 50 theological propositions (*Canones reformationis*, 1548). He was arrested as a heretic but escaped and fled in 1551 to Königsberg (now Russian Kaliningrad), where he entered into a public debate with Andreas OSIANDER and published his *Apologia contra Ostiandrum*. In his final years Stancaro visited Protestants in Poland, Hungary, and Transylvania.

**STARKEY, THOMAS** (c.1490–1538), English humanist and political theorist. Educated at Oxford, Starkey was in the early 1530s a member of Reginald POLE's household in Padua and Venice. In 1534, returning to London, he became chaplain to Pole's mother, the countess of Salisbury, and a chaplain to HENRY VIII. He was commissioned by the king to write to Pole for his opinion on divorce and papal authority; Starkey's links with Pole, who opposed Henry's divorce, put him in some jeopardy. His two best-known works are the *Exhortation to Christian Unity* (also known as *A Treatise against Papal Supremacy*), written in 1534, and the *Dialogue between Pole and Lupset*, which remained in manuscript in Starkey's lifetime, and which attempts to define the state of a true commonwealth. He also wrote an *Essay on Preaching* (1535).

**STAUPITZ, JOHANN VON** (*c.*1470–1524), German Augustinian who studied at the University of Leipzig before joining the Augustinian ORDER in 1490. He became prior of an Augustinian house in Tübingen in 1497, and in 1503 accepted the invitation of FRIEDRICH III, elector of Saxony, to become the first dean of the faculty of theology at the new University of Wittenberg. In the same year Staupitz became vicar-general of the Augustinian friars in Germany. He remained loyal to Luther even after Luther's attack on the sale of INDULGENCES, and refused to discipline him. Staupitz served as dean at Wittenberg until 1512 and as vicar of the Observant Augustinians until 1520. In 1523 Cardinal Matthäus appointed him as abbot of the Benedictine Abbey of St Peter at Salzburg. In Nuremberg he was the centre of a circle called the Sodalitas Staupitziana, whose members included Lazarus SPENGLER and Albrecht DÜRER. In the last year of his life Staupitz preached against the Reformation. He died on 28 December 1524.

E. Wolf, *Staupitz and Luther* (1927).

**STEENWYCK, HENDRICK VAN, THE ELDER** (*c.*1550–*c.*1600), and **HENDRICK VAN, THE YOUNGER** (*c.*1580–*c.*1649), Netherlandish painters of architectural views. Hendrick the Elder, who was probably a pupil of Jan VREDEMAN DE VRIES, is said to have been the first painter to develop the painting of church interiors as a distinctive form (e.g. *Interior of a Church*, Musée d'Art Ancien, Brussels). Hendrick the Younger lived from 1617 to 1637 in England, where he painted architectural interiors in the pictures produced by Anthony Van Dyck's studio (e.g. *Charles I* and *Queen Henrietta Maria*, Gemäldegalerie, Dresden).

*MDA* s.v. Steenwijk; *NNBW* x (Hendrick the Younger).

**STEFAN BÁTORY or István Báthory** (1533–86), king of Poland and prince of Transylvania, spent his youth at the imperial court of the Emperor FERDINAND I and subsequently secured the patronage of János ZÁPOLYA, who secured Stefan's appointment as *voivode* of Transylvania; the reaction of MAXIMILIAN, the new emperor, was to imprison Stefan for two years. On 25 May 1571, on the death of Zápolya's son János Sigismund, Stefan was elected prince of Transylvania by the Hungarian Estates, much to the displeasure of the imperial court in Vienna. As Stefan's claim was contested, a civil war ensued.

In 1574 Henry of Valois left Poland for France (where he had become King HENRI IV), and the following year the Polish nobility elected Stefan as king of Poland, on condition that he marry the elderly sister of SIGISMUND II AUGUSTUS, the last reigning member of the JAGIEŁŁO dynasty. He was crowned in Kraków on 1 May 1575 and proceeded to claim his new kingdom; Danzig (now Polish Gdańsk) resisted, but fell to Stefan after a six-month siege in 1577. He reached an accommodation with the Ottomans and, after a costly war with Russia, made peace with Muscovy, which yielded LIVONIA to him. Stefan admitted the JESUITS to Poland, in part because the Order was sympathetic to his vision of a union of Muscovy, Poland, and Transylvania that could drive the Ottomans from Europe.

**STEFANO DA ZEVIO or Stefano (di Giovanni) da Verona** (*c.*1375–*c.*1438), Italian painter, a native of Verona who became a major Italian exponent of the INTERNATIONAL GOTHIC style. His two finest surviving works are a *Virgin and Child with St Catherine in a Rose Garden* (Castelvecchio, Verona) and an *Adoration of the Magi* (Brera, Milan).

*MDA* s.v. Stefano da Verona.

**STEINHÖWEL, HEINRICH** (1412–82), German physician and humanist. He was born in Weil der Stadt (Württemberg) and studied in Vienna and Padua before practising as a physician in Esslingen and in Ulm. His translations into German include the *Historia Hierosolymitana* of Robertus Monachus (*Historia von der Kreuzfahrt Herzog Friedrichs*, 1461), the tale of *Apollonius von Tyros* (translated from the Latin version in the *Gesta Romanorum*), BOCCACCIO's tales of *Griselda*, *De claribus mulieribus* (*Von den sinnrychen erluchten Wyben*), and *Guiscardo und Sigismunda* (all 1473), a collection of Aesop's fables (1473), and POGGIO's *Facetiae* (1476 ff.). These translations exerted an important influence on the development of vernacular German prose.

Steinhöwel's medical works include treatises on hygiene (*Regimen sanitatis*, 1472) and on plague (*Das Büchlein von der Pestilenz*, 1473).

*DLL.*

**STERNHOLD, THOMAS** (*c.*1500–1549), and **JOHN HOPKINS** (d. 1570), English writers of metrical psalms, who collaborated on a collection of 44 psalms which was published in 1549; the music was first supplied in the Geneva edition of 1556. In 1562 the expanded collection (which includes psalms versified by other writers) was added to the Book of COMMON PRAYER.

**STETHAIMER or Stetthaimer, HANS, or Hans von Burghausen** (*c.*1360–1432), German architect who designed churches in a late Gothic style; in his brick 'hall-churches', the aisles are approximately the same height as the naves, and so the naves are lit from the windows of the aisles rather than from above. His tomb in St Martin's, Landshut (Bavaria), lists seven churches which he had built in Landshut and Salzburg, notably St Martin's in Landshut and the chancel of the Franciscan church in Salzburg.

*MDA* s.v. Hans von Burghausen; T. Herzog, *Meister Hans von Burghausen* (1958); Harriet Brinkmöller, *Die Raumauffassung des Meisters Hans von Burghausen in Seinen Hauptwerken* (1985).

**STEVIN, SIMON** (1548–1620), Flemish engineer and mathematician, born in Bruges. He entered the service of MAURICE OF NASSAU as a military engineer, in which capacity he improved the defensive capabilities of the sluices in the dykes; these innovations made possible the flooding of the lowlands to halt the progress of invading Spanish troops or (as in the case of the siege of Leiden in 1574) admit sea beggars (see PRIVATEERS) with relief supplies.

In 1585, when Stevin was teaching mathematics in Leiden, he published *De Thiende* ('The Tenth', translated into French as *La Disme*, 1585), which used decimal fractions in its ARITHMETIC, helping to make them popular; Stevin points out that decimals have the great advantage of allowing one to handle fractions in the same way as whole numbers. This work also introduced some advances in ALGEBRA. The following year he published a work on mechanics and hydrostatics. This proved to be of great importance, but attracted little attention before the appearance of the Latin edition, entitled *Mechanica*, in 1605. Stevin had confirmed, by experiment, that G. B. BENEDETTI had been correct in concluding, from a thought experiment, that speed of fall was independent of the weight of the falling body. In hydrostatics Stevin demonstrated principles for finding the force exerted by a fluid and hence formed the concept of pressure in a fluid. Stevin also wrote about FORTIFICATION (1617) and published an influential treatise on NAVIGATION, *De Havenvinding* (1599; an English version by E. WRIGHT, *The Haven-Finding Art*, appeared in the same year), as well as a learned treatise on OPTICS and PERSPECTIVE, *De Duersightighe* (1605; Latin translation by W. SNEL, *Sciagraphia*, in the same year). He also wrote on ASTRONOMY and on MUSIC.

DSB; NNBW v; E. J. Dijksterhuis, *Simon Stevin: Science in the Netherlands around 1600* (1970).

**STIEFEL or Stifel or Styfel, MICHAEL** (1486/7–1567), German mathematician, an Augustinian monk who was an early supporter of Martin LUTHER. Stiefel, who was one of the first German writers on ALGEBRA, became professor of mathematics at Jena. He was the author of a poem about Luther (1522) and several mathematical works, including *Arithmetica integra* (1544), which has an introduction by MELANCHTHON, *Deutsche Arithmetica* (1545), and an edition of Christoff Rudolff's *Die Coss* (1553).

**STILL LIFE or (Dutch) *stilleven* or (formerly) *stilstaand leven* or *stilliggend leven* or (German) *stilleben* or *stilliegende sachen* or (French) *nature morte*,** the term (plural 'still lifes') for a painting of inanimate objects (typically fruit, flowers, dead game, or vessels), usually displayed on a table. From the fifteenth century paintings contained elements of still life, notably Giovanni da UDINE's preparatory studies (later executed as GROTESQUES) of fruit and birds. The earliest still life is sometimes said to be Jacopo de' BARBARI's portrayal (1504) of a dead partridge and a pair of gauntlets (Alte Pinakothek, Munich), but this too may be a preparatory study.

Still life painting became an important part of DUTCH ART and FLEMISH ART. In the sixteenth century painters such as Pieter AERTSEN and his nephew Joachim BEUCKELAER showed the kitchen of Martha (in the house of Mary and Martha visited by Jesus) piled high with vegetables and kitchenware. By the end of the sixteenth century, the portrayal of a meal on a table (known as a 'banquet piece') had become a popular NETHERLANDISH genre. In Antwerp, the studios of Rubens, Jan BRUEGHEL (who specialized in flowers), and Frans Snyders (who painted animals exuberantly) all produced still lifes, and in the Protestant north, the form often incorporated didactic elements such as the skull and the hourglass, though Catholic Utrecht perpetuated the Flemish tradition of flower painting without any overt moral purpose.

MDA.

**STIMMER, TOBIAS** (1539–84), Swiss painter, engraver, and book illustrator who designed the paintings and sculptures on the astronomical clock in Strassburg Cathedral. He also painted a large number of Italianate FRESCOES, notably at Haus zum Ritter in Schaffhausen and the Altes Castle (now in ruins) in Hohenbaden, near Baden-Baden. His woodcuts included the illustrations in two books by Paolo GIOVIO and a new edition of Sebastian BRANT's *Narrenschiff* (Basel, 1574).

MDA.

**STOICISM AND NEOSTOICISM.** Stoicism is a philosophical tradition founded in antiquity by Zeno of Citium (*c*.300 BC); the term derives from the painted porch (*stoa poikile*) in Athens under which Zeno and his disciples taught. The most important Latin Stoic philosophers were Cicero (though he called himself a Platonist), Seneca, and Epictetus; and the last major classical figure for whom Stoicism was a governing ideology and a way of life was the Emperor Marcus Aurelius (second century AD). Stoic metaphysics contributed to the development of both Neoplatonic and Christian thought, but the aspect of Stoicism most important in the Renaissance was ethics.

Neostoicism was a late sixteenth-century school of philosophy which attempted to reconcile Stoic virtue and Christian ethics. The founding text of Neostoicism was LIPSIUS' *De constantia in publicis malis* (1584), a dialogue that explores the ethical issues raised by the REVOLT OF THE NETHERLANDS. The Stoicism of Lipsius was adapted by Guillaume DU VAIR to the context of the French WARS OF RELIGION in his *Philosophie moral des Stoïques*, which was first printed as a preface to his translation of Epictetus into French.

J. Eymard d'Angers, *Recherches sur le stoicisme au XVI*ᵉ *et XVII*ᵉ *siècles* (1976); M. Morford, *Stoics and Neostoics: Rubens and the Circle of Lipsius* (1991).

**STONE, NICHOLAS** (1586/7–1647), English sculptor and mason, born in Devon, the son of a quarryman. In 1606 he travelled to Amsterdam, where he trained in the workshop of Hendrick de KEYSER, whose daughter he married. He returned to England in 1613 and settled in London as a sculptor of TOMBS, notably his effigies of Francis Hollis (d. 1622) in Westminster Abbey (the first English example of a contemporary figure shown in Roman armour) and of John DONNE in St Paul's Cathedral (which shows Donne standing in his shroud); his workshop also produced the monuments to Edmund SPENSER (1620) and Isaac CASAUBON (1634) in Westminster Abbey. The activities of Stone's workshop are well documented, because his Notebook and Account Book survive in Sir John Soane's Museum (London).

In 1619 Stone was appointed master mason of Inigo JONES's BANQUETING HOUSE in Whitehall and in 1632 became the king's master mason, in which capacity he worked on Inigo Jones's portico for St Paul's Cathedral and on the Goldsmiths' Hall, both of which were destroyed in the fire of 1666.

*DNB* s.v. Stone, Nicholas the Elder; *MDA*; John Havill, *Nicholas Stone: Statuary Mason and Architect* (1982).

**STONEWARE or (German) *Steinzeug* or (French) *grès*,** pottery made of clay and a fusible stone (usually feldspar) fired at high temperatures to achieve vitrification of the stone (but not the clay). Stoneware is non-porous, and glazing is added only for decorative effect. Stoneware was produced in ancient China, but the technique seems to have been reinvented in the twelfth century in the Rhineland, which remained the principal centre of production until the late seventeenth century, after which it was made in England (Nottinghamshire and Staffordshire) and the Netherlands (Delft). Early modern Rhenish stoneware, which was produced in Cologne, Raeren (near Aachen in what is now Belgium), and Siegburg, was usually covered with a salt glaze: salt (sodium chloride) was thrown into the heated kiln, whereupon the chlorine evaporated and the sodium combined with the silicates in the pot to form a glaze with a pitted surface. Sixteenth-century Siegburg stoneware was usually white, and typically took the form of *Sturzbecher*, which were drinking-cups in which the stem was shaped as an inverted human head or body. Cologne and Raeren stoneware often had a brown and yellow surface (and so came to be known as tiger ware in England); in Raeren the outstanding craftsmen were members of the MENNICKEN FAMILY. The most distinctive product of the Cologne potteries was the BELLARMINE.

**STOOLS.** See CHAIRS, SETTLES, AND STOOLS.

**STORCH, NICHOLAS** (d. after 1536), German ANABAPTIST, a Swabian wool weaver who became the leader of the ZWICKAU PROPHETS. Storch and his fellow prophets were expelled from Zwickau and on 27 December 1521 appeared in WITTENBERG, where they were interrogated by MELANCHTHON and AMSDORF, who were impressed by their learning. In 1523 Storch was living in west Thuringia, and after the PEASANTS' WAR he became the leader of an Anabaptist sect in north Franconia. He seems to have returned to Zwickau in 1536, but thereafter he disappears from the historical record. Much ink has been spilt on the mutual influence of Storch and MÜNTZER, but it seems likely that Storch was an adherent of the libertine doctrines of the Brethren of the Free Spirit, and hence entirely at odds with Müntzer's theology, which derived from the mystical theology of the fourteenth-century Dominican Johann Tauler.

**STOSS, VEIT, or (Polish) Wit Stwosz** (*c.*1450–1533), German sculptor and woodcarver, a native of Horb am Neckar (Swabia). He lived from 1477 to 1479 in Kraków, where he carved the vast ALTARPIECE for the Church of Our Lady, which is one of Poland's most important works of art. The central panel dramatically portrays *The Dormition of the Virgin* below *The Assumption of the Virgin*; the figures of the mourning apostles, some larger than life size, are carved in the round, and their faces are highly individual, often with exaggerated gestures and facial expressions. The bodies of his figures are not carved with close attention to human anatomy, but rather as dramatic figures in which light and shade are controlled through the adept use of intricately folded drapery, of which Stoss was a master. He later carved the tomb of King CASIMIR IV Jagiełło for the Wawel Cathedral in Kraków; the tomb is signed and dated 1492, but as that was the year of Casimir's death, it seems likely that the tomb was sculpted in the course of the next few years.

Stoss returned to Nuremberg in 1489 and worked as a carver and sculptor for the city's churches. He was accused of forging a document, and thereafter his life in Nuremberg was dominated by criminal proceedings. His unpainted limewood carving of *St Roch* (*c.*1523, SS Annunziata, Florence) was proclaimed by VASARI as a 'miracle in wood'.

*MDA*; Veit Funk, *Veit Stoss, der Krakauer Marienaltar* (1985), trans. as *Le Rétable de Cracovie: L'Œuvre de Veit Stoss* (1986).

**STOW, JOHN** (*c.*1525–1605), English antiquarian. Originally a tailor, Stow began collecting manuscripts and writing historical works in 1564. His *Survey of London* (1598) is remarkable as a detailed description of Elizabethan London. Other publications include *The Works of Geoffrey Chaucer* (1561), *Summary of English Chronicles* (1565), and the second edition of HOLINSHED's *Chronicles*.

*DNB*.

**STRADA, JACOPO** (*c.*1515–1588), Italian artist and antiquarian. He was born into a Netherlandish family in Mantua and moved in the late 1540s to Augsburg, where he lived in the house of Johan Jakob FUGGER; he subsequently moved to Paris and Lyon, and in 1554 returned to Rome and entered the papal secretariat. He soon left for Nuremberg, where he initially worked for the Fuggers as an artist and goldsmith and from 1557 worked in the service of the HABSBURG Emperors FERDINAND I, MAXIMILIAN II, and RUDOLF II (who was the father of several children by Strada's daughter Katharina), rising to the post of court antiquary, in which capacity he collected art, books, and antiquities for the imperial collections. His huge private library consisted of some 3,000 books in thirteen languages. His portrait by TITIAN (1567/8, Kunsthistoriches Museum, Vienna) shows Strada holding an ancient statuette behind a table on which ancient coins can be seen.

Strada's scholarly command of ancient coins, which he had collected from his youth, informed his account of imperial Rome, *Epitome thesauri antiquitatum* (Lyon, 1553). In France Strada had acquired from SERLIO the seventh book of his *Architettura* (which supplemented the first six books with

Serlio's drawings), which he published in 1575. His posthumous publications include *Künstliche Abriss allerhand Wasser-, Wind-, Ross- und Hand Mühlen* (Frankfurt, 1617), a treatise on mills published by his grandson Ottavio Strada.

*MDA.*

**STRADIOTS or (Italian)** *stradiotti*, Venetian light cavalry armed with lance, scimitar, and shield. The regiments were originally raised in Greece in return for land grants, and in the fifteenth century the recruitment base was expanded to include Albanians, Cypriots, and Croatians (though most Croatians were organized in a separate cavalry regiment called the *Crovati*). Stradiots were regarded as too untrustworthy to garrison Venetian outposts in the areas from which they had been recruited, and so were used in battle in the WARS OF ITALY and, in places other than their homes, as garrison troops; they usually fought for Venice, but also served as mercenaries in France and Germany. In the late sixteenth century they were also deployed in police work in Venice's mainland territories, mainly in the suppression of banditry. Venice encouraged loyalty by recruiting from successive generations of the same families and by the use of honours and pensions.

**STRAET, JAN VAN DER or (Italian) Giovanni Stradano** (1523–1605), Dutch painter and TAPESTRY designer, born in Bruges and trained as a painter in the Antwerp studio of Pieter AERTSEN. Shortly after becoming a master in the Bruges Guild of Painters in 1545, he moved to Florence, working as assistant to VASARI on the fresco decoration of the Palazzo Vecchio and designed tapestries, including a series of hunting scenes for the MEDICI VILLA at Poggio a Caiano (1567). He returned to the Netherlands for a protracted visit (1576–8), but spent the rest of his life in Florence.

*MDA; Alessandra Baroni Vannucci, Jan van der Straet detto Giovanni Stradano: Flandrus pictor et inventor (1997).*

**STRANGE'S MEN,** Elizabethan acting company, first recorded in 1582 as performing at court. The company may have partly merged with the ADMIRAL'S MEN between 1590 and 1594, performing at the THEATRE in 1590–1 and the ROSE in 1592–3. The early career of William SHAKESPEARE may have been with this company; the first part of his *Henry VI*, *The Comedy of Errors*, and *Titus Andronicus* were in their repertoire. They disbanded in 1594 on the death of Lord Strange.

**STRAPAROLA, GIANFRANCESCO** (c.1490–1557), Italian author, a native of Caravaggio. He published a collection of *Sonetti* (1508), but his most important work is a collection of 75 stories about 'pleasant nights' (*Piacevoli notti*, published in two parts, 1550 and 1553); the fictional framework is a gathering during Carnival on the island of Murano, where in the course of thirteen evenings the stories are recounted. The stories, which include supernatural elements, oriental tales, and animal fables, were widely translated, and became an important model as the folk tale assumed a literary form in the course of the seventeenth century. In England, where some of the tales were translated in William PAINTER's *Palace*

*of Pleasure* (1566), several have been adduced as sources for Shakespeare's plays, particularly *Merry Wives of Windsor*. Straparola's collection contains the earliest known version of the story known in English as *Puss in Boots*.

*OCIL.*

**STRAPWORK or rollwork**, a decorative pattern in architectural ornamentation consisting of interlacing bands which resemble leather straps or carved fretwork. The earliest use of strapwork is a stucco frieze (1533–5) in the Galerie François I at FONTAINEBLEAU; the frieze was designed by Il ROSSO FIORENTINO as a frame for a group of paintings. Thereafter strapwork decoration, which was typically used in ceilings and funerary ornaments, is associated primarily with designers in the Netherlands (e.g. Cornelis BOS, Cornelis FLORIS DE VRIENDT, and Jan VREDEMAN DE VRIES) and Germany (e.g. Wendel DIETTERLIN). Strapwork was widely used in Elizabethan England and had a long afterlife in both England and America as a motif in furniture decoration, particularly in Chippendale designs.

**STRASSBURG or (French) Strasbourg or (Latin) Argentoratum**, which is now in France, was in early modern Europe a German city which had for centuries been a free imperial city. In 1262 the long struggle between the bishop and the citizens was settled at the battle of Oberhausbergen in favour of the citizens, whose power was ratified in the constitution of 1332, which admitted the guilds to the government of the city. In 1348–9 an outbreak of plague was blamed on the JEWS, who were said to have poisoned the wells, and 2,000 Jews were burnt; during this period the mystic Johann Tauler (c.1300–1361) was instrumental in caring for Christian victims of the plague. In 1381 the city joined the SWABIAN LEAGUE.

In the late fifteenth century Strassburg became an important centre of HUMANISM; the most prominent humanist was Sebastian BRANT. The cathedral preacher Johann GEILER VON KAYSERSBERG enjoyed good relations with the humanist community. From 1474 to 1477 the city's army fought with the SWISS CONFEDERATION in its war against CHARLES THE BOLD.

By 1523 Strassburg had become a Reformation city. In the first half of the sixteenth century the most important reformer was Martin BUCER, whose civic counterpart was Jakob STURM VON STURMECK. Under Bucer's leadership Strassburg had become a Protestant city by 1523, and in 1529 the mass was abolished and the monasteries suppressed. Jakob Sturm was responsible for the city's policies during the PEASANTS' WAR and represented the city at a series of diets, including the Diet of SPEYER (1526) and the Colloquy of MARBURG (1529). In 1531 Sturm brought Strassburg into the SCHMALKALDIC LEAGUE. In 1546 he dispatched Strassburg troops to fight alongside other members of the League against the Emperor CHARLES V, but in February 1547 Strassburg was forced to submit, and Sturm negotiated favourable terms with Charles V. In May 1548 he negotiated for Strassburg to mitigate the effects of the AUGSBURG INTERIM. Strassburg did not participate in the THIRTY YEARS WAR.

The principal Renaissance structure in Strassburg is the astronomical CLOCK in the Cathedral; the figures were designed and painted by Tobias STIMMER.

Miriam Chrisman, *Strasbourg and the Reform* (1957); id., *Lay Culture, Learned Culture: Books and Social Change in Strasbourg, 1490–1599* (1982); Lorna J. Abray, *The People's Reformation: Magistrates, Clergy and Commons in Strasbourg 1500–1598* (1985).

**STRIGEL, BERNHARD** (1460–1528), German painter, born in Memmingen (near Ulm) and trained in the studio of his father and uncle, whom he assisted on their ALTAR-PIECES for Disentis and Obersaxen. His work in the 1490s was influenced by ZEITBLOM, in whose studio he may have worked. He held several municipal and guild offices in Memmingen, where he continued to paint altarpieces (notably those in the Germanisches Nationalmuseum in Nuremberg and the wings of the Schusseuried altarpiece now in the Gemäldegalerie in Berlin). From 1499 he also worked as a painter in the service of the Emperor MAXIMILIAN I, whose portrait he painted many times.

*MDA*; Gertrud Otto, *Bernhard Strigel* (1964).

**STRIGEL, VIKTORIN** (1524–69), German theologian and biblical scholar, born in Kaufbeuren (Swabia) and educated at Freiburg and Wittenberg, where he became a disciple of MELANCHTHON. His first teaching post was in Erfurt, and in 1548 he moved to Jena as the founding professor and rector. He established a reputation for inter-confessional sympathies and as an advocate of SYNERGISM, both of which brought him into conflict with FLACIUS ILLYRICUS. In August 1560 he was required to participate in a disputation with Flacius before a court in Weimar on the issue of the place of the human will in relation to GRACE in the process of conversion. It was this occasion that led Flacius to coin his aphorism that original sin is the substance of the natural man.

In 1563 Strigel was appointed to a chair at Leipzig, but opposition to his tolerationist views eventually forced him to resign his post, and in 1567 he took up a professorship in Heidelberg. His publications range through philological, historical, and theological subjects, and include a vast commentary that covers most of the Bible.

**STRIGGIO, ALESSANDRO THE ELDER** (*c.*1540–1592), composer who moved in the aristocratic circles of the Gonzaga court in Mantua. He enjoyed a reputation as a skilful instrumentalist, playing the lira and the eighteen-stringed lirone. He was in the 1560s attached to the Medici court where he wrote music for intermedi (see INTERMEZZO). His madrigals reflect the influence of the virtuoso *concerto delle donne* at FERRARA which he heard during a visit in 1584, and the new monodic style favoured by Vincenzo GALILEI, whom he met in the 1570s. Thereafter he returned to Mantua.

**STRIGGIO, ALESSANDRO THE YOUNGER** (*c.*1573–1630), Italian musician, diplomat, librettist, and son of Alessandro STRIGGIO the Elder, whose works he published posthumously.

He studied law at Mantua, carried out ambassadorial duties for the Gonzaga in Milan, and was subsequently promoted, finally becoming chancellor in 1628. He was a member of the Accademia degli Invaghiti which promoted the première of MONTEVERDI'S OPERA *Orfeo* (1607) for which he wrote the libretto. He was also the librettist for Marco da Gagliano's *Il trionfo d'onore* and *Il sacrificio d'Ifigenia*, which were both performed in Mantua in 1608.

**STROZZI, PALLA** (*c.*1373–1462), Italian humanist. Strozzi was a member of the mercantile STROZZI FAMILY of Florence. He energetically supported SALUTATI's invitation to CHRYSOLORAS to lecture in Florence, and subsequently learnt Greek from him; he played a similar role in attracting FILELFO to Florence in 1428. Strozzi contributed to the place of Florence as a centre for GREEK SCHOLARSHIP by buying a substantial number of Greek manuscripts, which he placed at the disposal of Florentine Hellenists. When Cosimo de' MEDICI returned from exile in Padua in 1434, he banished Strozzi, who spent the rest of his life in Padua, where he continued to support humanist studies and to assist Byzantine refugees, including John ARGYROPOULOS.

**STROZZI FAMILY**, a Florentine mercantile and banking family, prominent from the thirteenth to the mid-sixteenth centuries. By the early fifteenth century the wealth and political standing of the family made them the principal rivals of the MEDICI FAMILY. The humanist Palla STROZZI was one of those banished by Cosimo de' MEDICI 'Il Vecchio' in 1434. Filippo Strozzi (1428–91) returned from banishment in 1466 and became an adviser to Lorenzo de' MEDICI; in 1489 Filippo commissioned the family's Florentine palace, the Palazzo Strozzi, which was the work of BENEDETTO DA MAIANO and Il CRONACA. Filippo's son and namesake Filippo Strozzi (1489–1538) was exiled by Alessandro de' MEDICI in 1533, and, after Alessandro's death in 1537, attempted to overthrow COSIMO I DE' MEDICI; he was captured after his defeat in the battle of MONTEMURLO, and died in prison, either by suicide or by assassination.

The sons of Filippo the Younger, Piero Strozzi (*c.*1510–38) and Leone Strozzi (1515–54) both fought in the service of France in the WARS OF ITALY. Elsewhere in Italy, members of the family included the poets Tito Vespiano Strozzi (1424–1505) and his son Ercole Strozzi (*c.*1473–1508), both of whom lived at the ESTE court in Ferrara.

M. M. Bullard, *Filippo Strozzi and the Medici* (1980).

**STUART, ALEXANDER** (*c.*1493–1513), Scottish humanist. An illegitimate son of JAMES IV, he was educated at home and on the Continent, studying rhetoric and logic under ERASMUS, who praised his quick learning, at Padua from 1508. Created archbishop of St Andrews in 1505, he became lord chancellor of Scotland *c.*1510, and was a patron of learning, co-founding St Leonard's College at St Andrews in 1512. The following year he was killed with his father at the battle of Flodden.

**STUDIOLO**. See CABINET.

**STUMPF, JOHANN** (1500–78), Swiss geographer, historian, and theologian, born at Bruchsal (between Karlsruhe and Heidelberg) and educated in Strassburg and Heidelberg. In 1520 he joined the Knights of ST JOHN, who sent him in 1521 to their preceptory in Freiburg im Breisgau; he was ordained as a priest in Basel, and in 1522 was appointed head of the Order's preceptory at Bubikon, in the canton of Zürich.

Stumpf soon defected to the Protestant cause, attending the Bern Disputation of 1528 and fighting in the first Kappel War in 1529. Many of his parishioners in Bubikon had left the Catholic Church with Stumpf, and he continued to work in the same parish as its Protestant pastor until 1543; from 1543 until 1561 he worked as pastor in Stammheim (in the canton of Zürich), and in 1561 he retired to Zürich, where he lived for the rest of his life.

The first of Stumpf's four wives was the daughter of a historian called Heinrich Brennwald (1478–1551), who had written an unpublished treatise on Swiss history (eventually published in Basel, 2 vols., 1908–10) and encouraged his son-in-law to study Swiss history. In 1546 he finished his huge chronicle of Swiss history, which was published in a sumptuous illustrated 934-page folio as *Germeiner lobicher Eidgenossenschaft Städten, Landen und Völkern chronikwürdiger Taten Beschreibung* (Zürich, 1568); enlarged editions were published in 1586 and 1606.

Stumpf also published a biography of the eleventh-century Emperor Henry IV (1556), laudatory poems (*Lobsprüche*) on each of the thirteen cantons in the SWISS CONFEDERATION (1573), and an account of the Swiss Reformation, *Schweizer und Reformationschronik,* which contains the first biography of ZWINGLI.

*DHBS.*

**STURE, STEN THE ELDER** (*c.*1440–1503), **SVANTE** (*c.*1460–1512), and **STEN THE YOUNGER** (*c.*1492–1520), a dynasty of Swedish regents (Swedish *riksföres*) who led the resistance to Danish rule in Sweden. In 1471 Sten Sture the Elder defeated an invasion mounted by King CHRISTIAN I of Denmark. He was succeeded by Svante and Sten the Younger, both of whom tried to reduce the power of the pro-Danish nobility. Sten the Younger died of wounds sustained while trying to repel the invasion of CHRISTIAN II that marked the end of the reign of the Sture dynasty.

**STURM or Sturm von Sturmeck, JAKOB** (1489–1553), reformer and statesman, born in Strassburg on 10 August 1489 and educated at the universities of Heidelberg and Freiburg. He subsequently embraced the reformed faith and in 1517 entered the service of the provost of Strassburg (a member of the WITTELSBACH family). In 1524 Sturm left this post to become a member of the city's ruling council. He was responsible for the city's policies during the PEASANTS' WAR and represented the city at a series of diets, beginning with the Diet of SPEYER in 1526. He signed the 'protest' at the Diet of Speyer of 1529, and so became one of the first PROTESTANTS. Sturm attended the Colloquy of MARBURG in 1529 in the hope of contributing to reconciliation between Lutherans and Zwinglians, and when the attempt failed, he presented the Zwinglian *Confessio tetrapolitana* to the Augsburg Diet of 1530.

Sturm enjoyed good relations with PHILIP OF HESSE, and in 1531 brought Strassburg into the SCHMALKALDIC LEAGUE. In 1546 he dispatched Strassburg troops to fight alongside other members of the League against the Emperor CHARLES V, but in February 1547 Strassburg was forced to submit, and Sturm negotiated favourable terms with Charles V. In May 1548 he was able to negotiate special terms for Strassburg to mitigate the effects of the AUGSBURG INTERIM. He died in Strassburg on 30 October 1553.

Thomas Brady, Jr., *Protestant Poetics: Jakob Sturm (1489–1553) and the German Reformation* (1994).

**STURM, JOHANNES** (1507–89), Protestant reformer and educationalist, educated in Liège at the school of the BRETHREN OF THE COMMON LIFE and at Louvain University. He lived in Paris from 1530 to 1536, moving in humanist circles and lecturing on classical literature; during this period he came under the influence of Martin BUCER, and converted to Protestantism.

In 1537 Sturm moved to Strassburg, where he worked for the Reformation cause and in 1538 founded a gymnasium (with himself as rector) which was to become one of the most important humanist schools in Europe; in 1564 he founded an ACADEMY in the city. Sturm's inter-confessional reformed sympathies alienated uncompromising Lutherans in Strassburg, and in 1581 he was forced into temporary exile. His writings included a biography of BEATUS RHENANUS.

J. Rott, 'Le Recteur strasbourgeois Jean Sturm et les Protestants français' and 'Bibliographie des œuvres imprimées du recteur strasbourgeois Jean Sturm', in M. de Kroon and M. Lienhard (eds.), *Investigationes historicae*, vol. ii (1986).

**STYFEL, MICHAEL.** See STIEFEL, MICHAEL.

**SUÁREZ, FRANCISCO** (1548–1617), Spanish theologian, philosopher, and jurist, born in Granada on 5 January 1548 and educated at Salamanca. He entered the JESUIT Order in 1564 and was ordained in 1572. He taught philosophy at Segovia (1571–4), and subsequently taught theology at Valladolid (1574–5, 1576–80), Segovia and Ávila (1575–6), the College of Rome (1580–5), Alcalá de Henares (1585–93), Salamanca (1593–7), and Coimbra (1597–1616, intermitted with a sojourn in Rome, 1604–6). He died in Lisbon on 25 September 1617.

Suárez is in many ways the last great exponent of SCHOLAS-TICISM. As a philosopher, he was a reflective follower of THOMAS AQUINAS, and he published a vast corpus of commentaries and treatises on ARISTOTLE. As a jurist, he is one of the founders of INTERNATIONAL LAW, in that his *De legibus* (1612) proposed natural law as the basis of international law, an idea that grew out of the work of Francisco de VITORIA and later shaped the thinking of GROTIUS and Samuel von Pufendorf. In his *De bello et de Indis* Suárez, again drawing on Vitoria, criticized Spanish practices of enslavement, forced labour, and summary execution in Spanish America on the grounds that the Indians enjoyed natural rights of life, liberty, and property.

In 1613, at the behest of Pope Paul V, Suárez published his *Defensio catholicae fidei contra Anglicanae sectae errores*, a polemical attack on the Oath of Allegiance exacted by James I (JAMES VI) in England; King James protested to PHILIP III that he was harbouring a detractor of the divine right of kings, and ordered that the book be burnt by the common hangman.

Reijo Wilenius, *The Social and Political Theory of Francisco Suárez* (1963); Josef Soder, *Francisco Suárez und das Völkerrecht* (1973); Carlos Larrainsar, *Una introducción a Francisco Suárez* (1977); Antonio Molina Meliá, *Iglesia y estado en el Siglo de Oro español: El pensamiento de Francisco Suárez* (1977).

## SULLY, MAXIMILIEN DE BÉTHUNE, BARON DE ROSNY, DUKE OF

(1560–1641), French HUGUENOT statesman, born into a noble Huguenot family in Rosny-sur-Seine. In 1572 he was sent to the court of Henry of Navarre (later King HENRI IV) in Paris to continue his education; his two Protestant tutors were killed in the ST BARTHOLOMEW'S DAY MASSACRE, but Maximilien was sheltered by the principal of the Collège de Bourgogne. He fought for King Henri in the WARS OF RELIGION (1562–98) and was wounded in the battle of Ivry (1590).

In 1598 Maximilien was appointed to the *conseil des finances* as head of the revenue system, and two years later he became what would now be called minister of finance (*surintendant des finances*), and so responsible for the rebuilding of the French economy after the depredations of a long war; his other appointments included *grand maître de l'artillerie* (1599; master of artillery), *grand voyer* (1599; minister of transport), *surintendant des bâtiments* (1600; superintendent of public buildings), governor of the Bastille (1602), and governor of Poitou (1603).

In his role as *surintendant des finances* Maximilien increased the efficiency of the taxation system and in 1604 introduced the tax known as the Paulette, an annual tax on office-holders of one-sixtieth of the value of the office, in exchange for which taxed offices could be made hereditary. As *grand maître de l'artillerie* he chose to make his Paris home the Arsenal, and during the war with Savoy he commanded the artillery at the sieges of Charbonnières (September 1600) and Montmélian (October–November 1600), and at the conclusion of hostilities negotiated the Peace of Savoy. As *grand voyer* he greatly improved the infrastructure of marine transport (bridges, rivers, and canals), notably the digging of the Briare Canal, which connects the Loire with the Seine. As *surintendant des bâtiments* he oversaw the construction of the LOUVRE, completed the Pont Neuf (1606), and built the Place Royale (1605–12; now the Place des Vosges).

As a member of the inner cabinet (*conseil des affaires*) Maximilien helped to arrange the marriage of Henri with MARIE DE MÉDICIS (October 1600) and, on the accession of James I of England (see JAMES VI), became Henri's ambassador to England (June–July 1603). In 1606 he was created duke of Sully and a peer of France. King Henri was assassinated in 1610, and the following year Sully was forced from public office. In the course of his long retirement he dictated

his memoirs, the *Économies royales d'état, domestiques, politiques et militaires* (1638), which contains an account of the *grand dessein*, a plan for a United States of Europe which Sully attributed to King Henri. His memoirs also helped to create the legendary image of Sully.

Laurent Arezou, *Sully à travers l'histoire* (2001); B. Barbiche and Ségolène de Dainville-Barbiche, *Sully* (1997).

## SUMMENHART, KONRAD

(*c.*1450–1502), German theologian, born in Württemberg and educated at the University of Paris. From 1489 he lectured on philosophy and theology at Tübingen. In theology his allegiance was to the traditions of SCHOLASTICISM rather than to the HUMANIST school of BIBLICAL scholarship that was gaining ground in Germany, but Summenhart was nonetheless an advocate of reform, particularly with respect to monastic abuse.

## SUMPTUARY LAWS.

Codified laws designed to regulate consumption first appeared in twelfth-century France and Italy; in the thirteenth century sumptuary laws were promulgated in Spain, in the fourteenth century in England and Switzerland, and in the fifteenth century in Germany and Scotland. At first such laws emanated from the Church: in 1274 Gregory X banned excessive ornamentation in clothing, and in 1279 the papal legate in Genoa regulated women's clothing. The Church retained an interest in sumptuary legislation relating to matters such as travel on Sundays, but by the fourteenth century most such legislation was promulgated by the civil authorities.

The most common subject of sumptuary legislation was clothing regulation, but there were also extensive regulations governing expenditure at marriages, baptisms, and burials and various alimentary restrictions, such as compulsory fasting and eating of fish. In the regulation of clothing, restrictions either took the form of limits on expenditure (on cloth or specified items of clothing) or of the reservation of certain types of cloth or clothing for designated social or professional groups: the wearing of ermine, for example, was often restricted to the nobility, and at the other end of the social scale there were restrictions on the clothing (extending to colours, cloth, and style) that could be worn by groups such as servants, apprentices, and prostitutes.

The range of sumptuary legislation can be seen in four well-documented states: Scotland, Venice, Switzerland, and England. In Scotland an Act of 1429 stipulated that all gentlemen with an annual income in excess of £20 had to wear a fur hat; an Act of 1551 specified the number of dishes at a meal that could be consumed by each noble rank, ranging from three for burghers to eight for earls; an Act of 1581 forbade the feeding of oats to horses during the summer; an Act of 1681 restrained the expenditure on marriages, baptisms, and burials.

In Venice, expenses on weddings and funerals were regulated in 1299, excesses in women's dress were checked in 1323, and ceremonial dress for patricians was prescribed in 1334. After the plague of 1347–8 green and dark-blue clothing was forbidden, with a view to lifting morale; dowry limits were set in the fifteenth century, and in the sixteenth century men were required to close their shirts at the neck. In Switzerland there were various regulations on dress, including a requirement that men's coats cover their genitals, and a few rules that were uniquely Swiss, such as the curfew for children (who were not allowed on the streets after the 'bed-bell' had rung) and the interdiction forbidding unaccompanied women to travel in sleighs. In England, an Act of 1337 forbade the wearing of fur by anyone below the rank of knight, though this was eased in 1363 to allow labourers to wear the fur of cats, foxes, rabbits, and sheep. In 1541 CRANMER set out detailed alimentary rules specifying the number of courses and dishes appropriate to members of each level of the ecclesiastical hierarchy. A series of early sixteenth-century regulations stipulating dress codes culminated in an Act of 1553 'for the reformation of excess in apparel', which regulated the wearing of silk.

Alan Hunt, *Governance of the Consuming Passions: A History of Sumptuary Laws* (1996); Diane Hughes, 'Sumptuary Laws and Social Relations in Renaissance Italy', in John Bossy (ed.), *Disputes and Settlements: Law and Human Relations in the West* (1983); Frances Baldwin, *Sumptuary Legislation and Personal Regulation in England* (1926); John Vincent, *Costume and Conduct in the Laws of Basel, Bern and Zurich, 1370–1800* (1935); K. R. Greenfield, *Sumptuary Law in Nürnberg* (1918).

**SUNDIALS** provided the commonest means of telling the time. Designs are so numerous and so diverse that the different types should be considered as distinct instruments. Several new types were introduced in the Renaissance. Sundials are discussed by VITRUVIUS, but the surviving text appears to be defective. Philological exegesis led to mathematical investigation—the curve described by the shadow of the tip of the gnomon on a flat dial is a conic section (a circle, ellipse, parabola, or hyperbola)—and important work was done by, among others, COMMANDINO and G. B. BENEDETTI.

**SUPREMACY, ACT OF**, the name of two Acts asserting the authority of the English crown in ecclesiastical as well as temporal matters. The statute of November 1534 conferred on the king and his successors the title of 'only supreme head on earth of the Church of England, called *Anglicana Ecclesia*'. This statute was repealed by MARY I but restored in revised form by ELIZABETH I in 1559, claiming her as 'supreme governor' of the Church. The Act was extended and its provisions made more stringent in 1563.

**SURREY, HENRY HOWARD, EARL OF** (1516–47), English poet. Until 1546 Surrey was held in high favour by HENRY VIII, receiving honours and serving as governor of Boulogne. In December 1546, however, his enemies worked to accuse him of treason and he was executed. He is remembered as the institutor, possibly inventor, of the English SONNET form (with *abab cdcd efef gg* rhyme scheme) which was later used by SHAKESPEARE. His elegant sonnets and poems also benefit from his study of French and Italian models; a blank verse translation of books 2 and 4 of the *Aeneid* is also remembered.

*DNB* s.v. Henry Howard.

**SURVEYING** was always of social significance because of the need to define the boundaries of plots of land. In the Renaissance, taxes on agricultural produce, including such relatively expensive crops as the dyestuff indigo (*isaïtis tinctoris*), were regularly assessed according to the area under cultivation, which of course led to landowners taking an interest in surveying rather than leaving it all to the official appointed by the tax authorities. This interest in surveying is seen in the GEOMETRY taught in ABACUS SCHOOLS, which is very largely concerned with problems leading to the finding of areas of triangles. Unless the shape includes precise right angles (which is not very likely for a plot of land) breaking the shape down into triangles is the most reliable way of finding the area. The calculations in abacus books always relate to measurements of length, never using angles except for the right angles involved in constructing perpendiculars. This probably reflects actual practice, since measuring a length was straightforward whereas instruments capable of measuring an angle other than a right angle to a useful degree of accuracy were relatively uncommon, and probably expensive; the one most often referred to in early surveying texts is the ASTROLABE (that is, the planispheric astrolabe). Moreover, once the angle was taken one would need tables of trigonometric functions such as, say, tangents of angles in order to carry out the further calculation.

Until late in the sixteenth century, it was only to astronomers that such tables were commonplace. ALBERTI is credited with having used a specially designed sighting instrument to make a plan of a city, and from the little we know about the instrument its design seems to have been derived from the astrolabe, and the apparatus may even have used parts of an actual astrolabe since astrolabes were constructed so as to make it easy to take them apart. The instrument used by Alberti seems to be an ancestor of the plane table, which was introduced in the sixteenth century and was the commonest surveying instrument for about 200 years. A plane table consisted of a flat horizontal plate attached at right angles to a pole that could be driven into the earth; a plumb line was attached to the plate to provide a vertical for purposes of adjustment, and there was usually a compass for orientation; the horizontal plate was fitted with an alidade with pinhole sights, and marked with a scale against which one could read off the position of the alidade; this arrangement provided for horizontal sightings through 360 degrees. As cannon came increasingly into use, in the sixteenth century, surveying acquired more importance in warfare, particularly in laying out the plans of the elaborately shaped forts that were designed to withstand the battery of cannon by never presenting them with a wall at which they could fire straight on.

It was no doubt partly because of this military connection that so many elaborate surveying instruments were invented in the Renaissance, each promising to be easier to use and to provide more exact results more quickly than any of its predecessors. The inventors and makers of these devices, who were usually one and the same, wrote treatises about them, often lavishly illustrated. One relatively simple instrument, which seems to have been invented in the 1580s, in English called a 'sector', was the subject of a treatise by GALILEO, *Del compasso geometrico e militare* (1598); he also made and sold the instrument and provided tuition on its use.

Alberti wrote a book of supposedly recreational mathematics, *Ludi matematici*, which contains a number of standard surveying problems, such as finding the height of an inaccessible tower, or using a quadrant to take angles. Treatises on surveying were written in the vernacular and therefore generally for only local circulation.

**SUSSEX'S MEN**, Elizabethan acting company founded *c.*1569 under the patronage of the third earl of Sussex. In 1572 their patron was made lord chamberlain and the group performed at court for the first time; they subsequently toured the provinces. In 1583, the earl of Sussex died and the group came under the patronage of his son, the fourth earl. In 1593–4 they were at the ROSE Theatre under Philip HENSLOWE's management, performing William SHAKESPEARE's *Titus Andronicus* amongst other works. In 1594 their patron died and the group disbanded shortly afterwards.

**SUSTRIS, FREDERICH LAMBERTSZOON** (*c.*1540–1599), Italian painter of Dutch descent, born in Padua, the son of Lambert SUSTRIS. After training in his father's studio in Padua, Sustris visited Rome (1560) and for several years lived in Florence (1563–7), where he worked as an assistant to VASARI on the decoration of the Palazzo Vecchio. In 1568 he moved to Augsburg, initially in the service of Anton FUGGER, for whom he worked with other Italian painters on the decoration of the Fugger palace in Munich; only fragments of two interiors survived the Second World War. From 1573 Sustris worked in Landshut and (from 1580) in Munich in the service of Wilhelm von Landshut (later duke of Bavaria), for whom he probably decorated the Jesuit Michaelkirche (1583) in Munich and designed the garden and GROTTO (Grottenhof) of the ducal Residenz (1582–86) in Munich; he also worked with Pieter de WITTE on the decoration of the Munich Antiquarium.

*MDA*; Vincenzo Mancini, *Lambert Sustris a Padova: La Villa Bigolin a Selvazzano* (1993).

**SUSTRIS, LAMBERT** (*c.*1515/20–*c.*1584), Dutch painter, a native of Amsterdam who by the mid-1540s was living in Venice and working as a painter of landscape backgrounds in the workshop of TITIAN; in 1548 and again in 1550–1 Sustris accompanied Titian to Augsburg, where he painted several portraits, including those of Hans Christoff Vohlin and Veronika Vohlin (Alte Pinakothek, Munich). He moved to Padua in 1554 and returned some fifteen years later to Venice. The few works that can confidently be assigned to his late Venetian period include *The Bath* (Kusthistorisches Museum, Vienna).

*MDA*.

**SWABIA or (German) Schwaben or (Latin) Suevia**. The term 'Swabia' designates both the province of Bayrisch Schwaben centred on AUGSBURG (Bavarian Swabia, east of the river Lech), and the region of Upper Swabia to the west, but the medieval duchy of Swabia and the Swabian Circle of the HOLY ROMAN EMPIRE established by MAXIMILIAN I in 1512 (which was almost conterminous with the duchy) covered a much larger area, which included territories held by the rulers of Württemberg, Hesse, Baden, and Tübingen and the counts of HOHENZOLLERN.

**SWABIAN LEAGUE or (German) Schwäbischer Städtebund**, a series of confederations of south German cities, principally in the territories of the duchy of SWABIA. In English-language historiography, the term is normally used to designate the confederation of 1488, but German historians also use the term to describe earlier Swabian confederations. In 1331, 22 Swabian cities, joined by Württemberg in 1340, formed a league at the request of the Emperor Louis IV of Bavaria; in 1376, fourteen Swabian cities led by Ulm formed a federation that spread over the Rhineland, Bavaria, and Franconia; in 1392, twelve Swabian cities united in defence of their liberties; in 1441, twelve Swabian cities, expanding to 31 in 1446, united in the first instance to suppress highway robbery, but in 1441 waged war on ALBRECHT ACHILLES.

On 14 February 1488 FRIEDRICH III, king of the Romans, constituted a federation, sometimes known as the Great Swabian League to distinguish it from its more ephemeral predecessors, which brought together four constituent parties: a coalition of 22 Swabian cities, Archduke Sigismund of Tirol, the Bavarian military ORDER of the Knights of St George, and Count (later Duke) Eberhard V of Württemberg, who became the first captain of the League. The League was endowed with an armed force (12,000 infantry and 1,200 cavalry) with which to police and defend Swabia, and was administered through a constitution which gave it a captain, a federal council (consisting of three colleges of nine councillors each), and a federal court with both judicial and executive powers. The League rapidly expanded, and by 1490 included AUGSBURG and other Swabian cities, the margraves of Brandenburg-Ansbach, Bayreuth, and Baden, the four Rhenish electors, and MAXIMILIAN, king of the Romans, who had been released from incarceration in Bruges with the assistance of the armed forces of the League; by 1500 Bavaria was also a member.

The League imposed peace on southern Germany, sometimes by force of arms, and settled a series of internal disputes. In 1492 the League forced Duke Albrecht IV of Bavaria to renounce his claim to Regensburg. In 1518 a League army led by Franz von SICKINGEN attacked Duke ULRICH of Württemberg (because he had seized Reutlingen), and the following year expelled him from the League and sold his duchy to CHARLES V, whose imperial forces garrisoned the duchy until 1534. In 1523 the army of the League quelled the KNIGHTS' REVOLT led by Franz von Sickingen. In 1525, Georg Truchsess von Waldburg, captain of the League, joined forces with the Palatinate to suppress the PEASANTS' REVOLT.

The Swabian League was finally destroyed by internal divisions arising from the Reformation, and formally expired on 2 February 1534.

**SWABIAN WAR or (recte) Swiss War** (1499), a war between the Emperor MAXIMILIAN I and the SWISS CONFEDERATION. The emperor was supported by the SWABIAN LEAGUE in his attempt to subjugate the Rhaetian leagues in the east (modern Graubünden, in French Grisons) to imperial jurisdiction, but was defeated by the Swiss in the Calven Gorge (above Mals) on 22 May 1499 and again at Donach in July 1499. The peace treaty which was signed in Basel on 22 September 1499 referred matters in dispute to arbitration. The emperor annulled all imperial decisions directed against the Confederation, and thereafter made no attempt to interfere in its affairs. In effect, the Confederation became an autonomous state allied with the Empire; the alliance was to be fractured by the Reformation, and autonomy did not become independence until 1648.

**SWANENBURGH, JACOB ISAACZSOON VAN** (1571–1638), Dutch painter, born in Leiden. He lived in Italy for some fifteen years, and painted many architectural views. He also painted pictures of HELL (e.g. *Charon's Boat*, Stedelijk Museum de Lakenhal, Leiden) and the WITCHES' Sabbath. He was the first teacher of Rembrandt.

MDA.

**SWAN THEATRE**, theatre built in London, *c*.1595, on Bankside. It had no established acting company, and was used for sporting and other events, as well as play performances. A description and sketch of the interior was given in a letter by a visitor to London, Johannes de Witt, to a friend in 1596; he describes it as a circular building with a brick foundation and wooden pillars painted to look like marble, and estimates its capacity as 3,000 spectators. Until the discovery of the archaeological remains of the ROSE and GLOBE theatres in the late twentieth century, this sketch was the only substantial evidence of the internal configuration of Elizabethan theatres. In 1614, on the opening of the HOPE Theatre, the building was no longer used for theatrical performances.

**SWART VAN GRONINGEN, JAN** (*c*.1500–*c*.1553), Netherlandish book illustrator, painter, and designer of stained-glass windows. He worked in Gouda (from 1522) and later in Antwerp, where he died; his familiarity with the conventions of Venetian art may imply that he visited Venice. Swart made 73 of the 97 woodcuts in the Dutch BIBLE published in Antwerp in 1528. The most distinctive aspect of his paintings is a penchant for unusual head-coverings, including turbans and high hats. His designs for stained glass include drawings for a series of three windows illustrating the story of Ruth (*c*.1535–40, Albertina, Vienna).

MDA; NNBW x.

**SWEATING SICKNESS or English sweat or (Latin)** *sudor Anglicus*, an unidentified disease, probably a form of influenza, that emerged as an epidemic in England in 1485 (when it caused a postponement of the coronation of King HENRY VII) and recurred in 1507, 1517 (when it spread to Calais and Antwerp), 1528 (when it spread in the course of the following year to Hamburg and thence across northern Europe, Scandinavia, and Russia), 1551 (when it was confined

to England), and 1578. In the wake of the 1551 epidemic John CAIUS wrote his *Book of Counsel against the Disease Commonly Called the Sweat or the Sweating Sickness* (1552). The disease normally killed its victims within hours, and so was thought to be more lethal than PLAGUE, which took several days to kill those who contracted it. The disease seems to have disappeared in the sixteenth century.

**SWEDEN or (Swedish) Sverige.** From 1397 to 1448, Sweden was a member of the Scandinavian Union (later called the Kalmar Union), and was ruled from Copenhagen. In 1448, King ERIC was deposed, and Karl Knutsson Bonde, the Swedish *rikis forstandere* (modern Swedish *riksförestândare*, 'director of the realm'), was crowned as King CHARLES VIII of Sweden. The throne was also claimed by King CHRISTIAN I of Denmark, and Charles's tenure of the throne was never secure: Charles was still king when he died in 1470, but he had been constantly at war and had twice been exiled.

During the reign of Charles VIII the STURE family rivalled the authority of the king, and from 1470 till 1520 ruled as *riksforestândarer* appointed by the Swedish royal council. In 1520 CHRISTIAN II of Denmark defeated the Stures in battle and ordered the execution of 80 Swedish noblemen. This massacre (8 November 1520), known as the Stockholm Bloodbath (Stockholms blodbad), precipitated a nationalist uprising led by GUSTAVUS VASA, who was supported by the wealthy merchants of LÜBECK. The rising was successful, and on 6 June 1523 Gustavus was elected king at Strängnäs.

Gustavus inaugurated a Protestant dynasty of Vasa monarchs who were to rule Sweden until the abdication of Queen Christina in 1654. Under Gustavus, Sweden became the first country in Europe to renounce papal supremacy and establish an independent Reformation church. In June 1527, at the Riksdag of Vesterås, Sweden sequestered all church property, including the monasteries, and transferred its ownership to the crown; at the same time, the *Denarius Sancti Petri* (the papal tax known in English as 'Peter's Pence') was discontinued. In the course of the next few years, the liturgy was reformed, Olaus and Laurentius PETRI and Laurentius ANDREAE shaped the Church along Lutheran lines, and the Swedish translation of the New Testament published in 1526 was widely disseminated. Dissent was not tolerated, and on 18 February 1527 two bishops who had remained faithful to Rome were gibbeted in Stockholm. In 1529 the Swedish Reformed Church was established as the national church of Sweden, and in 1531 Laurentius Petri was consecrated as archbishop of Uppsala, and so became the first Protestant primate of Sweden. In 1528 Gustavus Adolphus introduced the Reformation into Finland, where the most important Reformer, now a national hero, was Mikael AGRICOLA.

The reign of Gustavus was troubled by peasant risings (the peasantry remained loyal to Rome) and war, including war with Lübeck (resolved in the truce of 28 August 1537) and with Tsar IVAN IV of Russia. The Riksdag decreed the monarchy to be hereditary rather than elective, and so Gustavus was succeeded by his son ERIC XIV, whose short reign (1560–8) was dominated by wars with Denmark (1563–70) and

Poland. In 1568 Eric was deposed by his half-brother JOHN III, who reigned from 1569 to 1592. The first decade of John's reign was dominated by war with Russia (1571–7) over the possession of ESTONIA and LIVONIA. Decades of confrontation with Ivan IV of Russia finally ended with the truce signed at Plyussa (Russia) on 5 August 1582.

King John was a learned student of theology, and while remaining nominally Protestant he had many Catholic sympathies, and explored the possibility of reuniting the Swedish Church with Rome. On 4 October 1562, long before his accession to the throne, he had married Catherine Jagiełłonica, sister of King SIGISMUND II of Poland. This alliance raised the prospect of Sweden's eventual reversion to Catholicism, a possibility which would have been realized had his Catholic son Sigismund, who was elected as King SIGISMUND III of Poland on 19 August 1587, succeeded him to the throne of Sweden. In the event, when King John died, his brother Charles presented himself as the champion of Swedish Protestantism and Sigismund was unable to rule Sweden; Sigismund was an entirely nominal monarch, and his attempt to enter Sweden in order to claim his throne was rebuffed by the forces of Charles Vasa at the battle of Stångåbro on 25 September 1598. Charles ruled as regent throughout this period, formally deposing Sigismund in 1599; on 9 March 1600 he was elected by the Riksdag as King CHARLES IX, but he declined to use the title of king until King John's son Duke John formally renounced his claim on 6 March 1604. His reign (1604–11) was dominated by a series of defeats in wars with Poland, Russia, and then Denmark (the 'War of Kalmar', which was concluded by the Peace of Knåred on 20 January 1613). In 1611 King Charles was succeeded by his son Gustavus II Adolphus, the statesman and warrior king who is celebrated in Swedish popular historiography as the greatest of Swedish kings.

From 1157 to 1809, the territory of Sweden included most of what is now Finland. Throughout this period, Scania (Swedish Skåne) and Blekinge, in what is now southern Sweden, belonged to Denmark, and Bohuslän and Halland (the coastal territories to the north and south of Gothenburg) belonged to Norway. All four territories passed to Sweden (together with the island of Bornholm, which was subsequently returned to Denmark) in the Treaty of Roskilde (1658).

**SWEDISH ART AND ARCHITECTURE.** The principal citizens of the seaports of fifteenth-century Sweden were German traders, and the art that they installed in their churches was German, notably Bernt NOTKE's free-standing group of *St George* in Stockholm Cathedral. With the advent of the Reformation in 1529, art and architecture became secularized. In the sixteenth century the royal castles in Stockholm and Kalmar were refashioned under Dutch influence, and new castles, notably the royal palace at Vadstena (1545–1620) were built. The great period of Swedish architecture was the seventeenth century, when the cities were laid out on grids (Stockholm in 1625, Kalmar in 1647, Karlskrona in 1679) and many fine buildings erected.

**SWEDISH LANGUAGE AND LITERATURE.** Swedish is a Scandinavian language that was spoken in what is now central Sweden and in the coastal regions of Finland, Estonia, and LIVONIA. The language of northern Sweden was Saami (formerly called Lapp), and in the southern territories of Scania (Swedish Skåne) and Blekinge a dialect of DANISH was spoken. In the middle of the fourteenth century, a standard form of Swedish emerged, and so consolidated what had been a coherent system of dialects; this national language (*riksspråk*) is known as Late Old Swedish, and is conventionally dated 1375–1526; the only area not to be absorbed into this common language was the island of Gotland, which continued to speak a dialect (or language) known as *Forngutniska*. Modern Swedish is conventionally dated from the publication of the first Swedish translation of the New Testament— hence the improbably precise date of 1526.

The first Swedish dictionaries were the anonymous *Variarum rerum vocabula cum Sueca interpretatione* (1538) and the *Synonymorum libellus* of Elaus Petri Helsingius (1587), both of which were modelled on German originals. The first Swedish grammar was written in Latin in 1664; the first to be written in Swedish was published in 1696.

The rich literary tradition of medieval Sweden was terminated by the advent of the Reformation, because the reformers controlled the printing presses. The literary language of modern Swedish was created by the publication of a Swedish New Testament in 1526 (*Thet nyia Testament på swensko*) and of a complete Bible in 1541 (*Biblia, thet är, all then helgha schriff på swensko*). For the rest of the century the major figure in Swedish literature was the reformer Olaus PETRI.

**SWEELINCK, JAN PIETERSZOON** (1562–1621), Dutch composer, organist, and teacher whose entire life was spent in Amsterdam, apart from visits to Haarlem, Rotterdam, and other Dutch cities where he acted as an organ consultant. He was appointed organist at the Oude Kerk, where he was required to play the organ twice daily rather than during services where, according to post-Reformation Calvinist rules, the organ was considered too secular. He was highly regarded as a teacher and composed sacred and secular music, including 70 fantasias, toccatas, and variations for keyboard. Honoured by his friend John BULL, who wrote a fantasia based on a Sweelinck melody after his death, his influence is also apparent in the work of Samuel Scheidt.

**SWEYNHEYM, KONRAD.** See PANNARTZ, ARNOLD.

**SWISS BRETHREN**, an ANABAPTIST community founded at Zollikon (near Zürich) in January 1525. Members of the group, which included Georg BLAUROCK, Conrad GREBEL, and Felix MANTZ, regarded believers' BAPTISM as the basis of church membership. Similar congregations arose in German-speaking areas of Switzerland and in the Rhineland, Alsace, south-west Germany, and the Austrian Tirol; the term 'Swiss Brethren' was increasingly extended to include members of these congregations formed outside Switzerland.

The Brethren shared with other Anabaptists a belief in believers' baptism, but differed on other issues: they were pacifists, refused to participate in government, and, unlike the followers of Jakob HUTTER, did not share their possessions. The confession of faith of the Swiss Brethren was the SCHLEITHEIM CONFESSION of 1527, which was drafted by Michael SATTLER; it was quickly controverted by ZWINGLI and later by CALVIN.

On 7 March 1526 the Zürich authorities issued an edict making rebaptism punishable by drowning, and at the Diet of Speyer in 1529 CHARLES V authorized the execution of Anabaptists by fire and sword without recourse to a trial. In the persecution that followed, Mantz was drowned and Sattler, Blaurock, and Balthasar HUBMAIER were tortured and burnt. The historian Sebastian FRANCK estimated that 2,000 Anabaptists were killed before 1530.

Many Swiss Brethren escaped persecution over the next two centuries by migrating to Germany, the Netherlands, and America, where they merged with the followers of MENNO SIMONS and are known as Mennonites. The descendants of those who remained in the mountains of the canton of Bern are now also known as Mennonites.

F. Blanke, *Brüder in Christo: Die Geschichte der ältesten Täufergemeinde (Zollikon 1525)* (1955), trans. as *Brothers in Christ: The History of the Oldest Anabaptist Congregation* (1961).

## SWISS CONFEDERATION or Helvetia (1291–1798).

On 1 August 1291 the three contiguous forest cantons of Schwyz, Uri, and Nidwalden formed a 'perpetual league' for mutual defence. The view that this act represented a conscious rejection of the authority of the HABSBURGS, the Alemannic dynasty which ruled the German-speaking cantons north of the Alps, is romantic legend. After the decisive defeat of Austria at the battle of Morgarten (1315), five more cantons joined the Confederation: Lucerne (1332), ZÜRICH (1351), Glarus (1352), Zug (1352), and Bern (1353). This expansion led to a renewed threat from Leopold II of Swabia, who was defeated at the battles of Sempach (1386) and Näfels (1388), which marked the end of effective Habsburg hegemony in the Swiss lands. After the battle of Sempach, the cantonal name 'Schwyz' began to be used for the entire confederation; it was not until 1785 that the Swiss historian Johannes von Müller formulated the distinction between the canton ('Schwyz') and the country ('Schweiz'). In 1803 Schweiz (English 'Switzerland') became the official name of the country. The term 'canton' was not officially sanctioned until 1798, but had been used by foreigners such as MACHIAVELLI and Philippe de COMMINES and appears in the French treaty of 1452 and in the Treaties of Westphalia (1648).

In the early fifteenth century, the Confederation was divided by a dispute between Zürich and the other seven cantons over the succession in Toggenburg, and in 1436 civil war broke out. Zürich had a powerful ally in Austria, but was nonetheless defeated, and peace was restored in 1450. This is the period that gave rise to the legend of Wilhelm Tell, which represents many features of popular Swiss historiography, including the folk-beliefs that Swiss freedom was an ancient tradition and that the Scandinavian origins of the Swiss made them a race superior to the Germanic Austrians (represented by Gessler the bailiff) who occupied their cities. The most familiar versions of the legend, Schiller's play *Wilhelm Tell* (1804) and Rossini's opera *Guglielmo Tell* (1829), derive from the chronicle of Ägidius TSCHUDI, the earliest version of which was published in 1538; the story first appears in *Das Weiße Buch von Sarnen* (*c*.1470), and subsequently formed the subject of two ballads and a folk-play, *Das Urner Tellenspiel* (*c*.1511).

Between 1481 and 1513, another five cantons joined the Confederation: Freiburg/Fribourg (1481), Solothurn (1481), BASEL (1501), Schaffhausen (1501), and Appenzell (1513). Between 1450 and 1513, the Confederation established itself as an important military power. The war against CHARLES THE BOLD of Burgundy (1474–7) culminated in Swiss victories at Grandson (2 March 1456), Morat/Murten (22 June 1476), and Nancy (5 January 1477); in the last of these battles Charles was killed. At the end of the century, Swiss forces defeated the imperial army of MAXIMILIAN in the Swiss War (1499), which led to a *de facto* recognition of Swiss independence in the Treaty of Basel (*de jure* recognition had to await the Treaty of Westphalia in 1648). The reputation established at these battles meant that for the rest of the century, the rulers of Europe (especially the French) sought the services of Swiss mercenaries; in 1510 Pope JULIUS II acknowledged this reputation in his establishing of the papal SWISS GUARD. In 1511 the Confederation joined the HOLY LEAGUE, helped to drive the French out of Italy, and then occupied northern Italy. In 1515, however, the Swiss were defeated by the invading army of FRANCIS I at the battle of MARIGNANO, and this defeat tarnished the image of the Swiss as Europe's finest soldiers.

The thirteen cantons which constituted the Confederation between 1513 and 1798 were not conterminous with the modern state of Switzerland, nor were the boundaries of the cantons the same as the modern boundaries. Until 1798, the cantons were all contained within the Rhine basin, and the territories acquired by peaceful annexation or military conquest in the fifteenth and early sixteenth centuries—Aargau (1415), Thurgau (1460), Ticino/Tessin (1440, 1500, 1512), and Vaud (1536)—were protectorates or subject lands, and were not full members of the Confederation until 1798. As these territories contained most of the French, Italian, and Romansch speakers of the Swiss lands, and as the Valais, Neuchâtel, and Geneva remained outside the confederation until 1815, the medieval and early modern Confederation was essentially German and German-speaking; Fribourg had been partly French-speaking on its accession in 1481, but German quickly became the dominant language. Throughout this period, St Gallen and Graubünden were independent associates of the Confederation, and did not join until 1798. Mülhausen (French Mulhouse) formed an alliance with the Confederation in 1466, and from 1515 to 1648 it was an associate member of the Confederation, but thereafter it became an independent ally of the Confederation (1648–1797), French (1797–1871) and German (1871–1918), and has since 1918 been French. Rottweil in Württemberg was also an associate member from 1456, but in the Reformation years remained Catholic.

The fragile unity of the Confederation as it stood in 1513 was ended by the Reformation, which divided the Confederation along confessional lines. ZWINGLI inaugurated the Swiss Reformation in Zürich, and in the course of five years (1518–23) Zürich changed from a loyal Catholic canton to a Protestant stronghold in which Catholic practices were prohibited. The Swiss Reformation spread from Zürich to Schaffhausen, Glarus, Appenzell, Basel, and Bern, and these six cantons came to be known as the Evangelical Swiss Cantons. The cantons of Lucerne, Uri, Schwyz, Unterwalden (comprising the two half-cantons of Obwalden and Nidwalden), and Zug, which remained faithful to the Catholic Church, formed an alliance and attacked Zürich. They were met at nearby Kappel on 11 October 1531 by a defensive force and Zwingli was killed. The Peace of Kappel which signalled an end to hostilities also formalized the religious division of the cantons: the seven Catholic Cantons (Uri, Schwyz, Unterwalden, Lucerne, Zug, Fribourg, and Solothurn) could outvote the six Evangelical Cantons, and were therefore able to refuse admission to Geneva and Strassburg and restrict Mülhausen to associate membership. One of the effects of the religious divisions between and within cantons was that the change from the Julian to the Gregorian calendar was the most irregular in Europe; for details see Appendix 3.

## SWISS GUARD or (Italian) Guardia Svizzera Pontificia.

The corps of military guardians of the Vatican was instituted by Pope JULIUS II, who agreed to pay the Swiss cantons of Lucerne and Zürich to supply 250 guardsmen. The choice of Swiss troops was based on the belief that they were the finest soldiers in Europe and would remain neutral in Roman politics. The reputation for invincibility was to be tarnished by the battle of MARIGNANO, but the Guard did not become involved in politics, and has survived in unbroken succession until the present day (there are now about 100 guards, mostly from Valais). The parade uniform of the Swiss Guard (tunic with puffed sleeves, breeches, and stockings striped in wide bands of red, yellow, and blue), which is still worn during daylight hours, was designed by MICHELANGELO.

The French Gardes Suisses was a Swiss mercenary regiment raised to fight in the WARS OF RELIGION. The distinguished service of the regiment in the battle of Arques (21 September 1589) led King HENRI IV to incorporate it into his army, and in 1615 the regiment became one of the *Gardes du Corps*; its members remained loyal to the royal family at the Revolution, and were wiped out by the Marseillais and the mob on 10 August 1792.

P. Krieg, *Die päpstliche Schweizergarde* (1948).

## SWORDS.

In fourteenth- and fifteenth-century Europe the cruciform sword was the characteristic weapon of knights. It consisted of a double-edged blade, a cross-guard (consisting of two 'quillons'), a handle (sometimes long enough to be gripped with two hands), and a 'pommel' at the top of the handle (acting as a counterweight to the blade). In the course of the fifteenth century the guards were elaborated, initially in Spanish swords: curved bars were fitted over the quillons to protect the forefingers when hooked over a quillon, and a curved bar was sometimes added to protect the knuckles. In the second half of the fifteenth century swords began to be decorated: blades were engraved or inlaid in copper or brass, and hilts were inlaid with precious metals, gems, or enamels.

In the early sixteenth century the sword, which had hitherto been a military weapon, became a civilian dress accessory. The civilian sword, which was called a rapier, thereafter developed separately from the military sword. The rapier, which was used without armour, soon acquired a comprehensive hand-guard (the predecessor of the modern cup-hilt) and decoration included the DAMASCENING of the hilt and chiselling of the blade; the art of iron-chiselling reached its apogee with the MUNICH SCHOOL. The rapier was used with a left-hand DAGGER with matching decoration, or with a cloak wrapped around the left arm. Refinements in the style of the rapier and in the conventions for its use evolved into the martial art of fencing, i.e. the art of (de)fence and (of)fence. The other civilian sword was the falchion, a medieval sword with a blade like a cleaver, which developed in the late fifteenth century into a curved sword with the edge on the convex side used by civilians when travelling or hunting.

The military sword was heavier than the rapier and had a broader blade. In the fifteenth century Swiss infantry had used a short sword in which the quillons were shaped like the letter S; in the early sixteenth century the quillons of this sword, which was by then used by German LANDSKNECHTE as well as Swiss infantry, evolved into a figure of eight, and in the late sixteenth century bars protecting the back of the hand were gradually extended into basket-guards which completely enveloped the hand. During the THIRTY YEARS WAR this sword was adapted as a cavalry weapon. The sabre, which was a curved cavalry sword, developed in eastern Europe in the sixteenth century under Ottoman influence, but was not used in western Europe until the eighteenth century.

## SYLBURG, FRIEDRICH

(1536–96), German classical scholar, born near Marburg. He lived and taught in Heidelberg, and edited classical texts, notably all of ARISTOTLE and Dionysius of Halicarnassus (the rhetor and historian of Rome). His edition of Clement of Alexandria was an important contribution to PATRISTIC SCHOLARSHIP.

## SYLVIUS, JACOBUS or (French) Jacques Dubois

(c.1489–1555), French neo-Latin poet and medical humanist, born in Amiens, the son of a weaver, and educated by his brother François, who taught him Latin, Greek, and Hebrew. Sylvius studied medicine in Paris and Montpellier and in 1550 was appointed professor of medicine at the Collège Royal; he subsequently became an outspoken critic of the ANATOMY of VESALIUS. His writings include an annotated edition of GALEN, the first grammar of French (*In linguam Gallicum isagoge*, 1531), and a recently discovered Latin poem in which he provides an eyewitness account of the FIELD OF THE CLOTH OF GOLD.

*DBF* s.v. Dubois 67; Stephen Bamforth and Jean Dupèbe, 'Médicins', in *Prosateurs latins en France au XVIᵉ siècle* (1987); *Francisci Francorum regis et henrici Anglorum Colloquium*, ed. Stephen Bamforth and Jean Dupèbe, *Renaissance Studies*, 5 (1991).

**SYNERGISM**, the theological contention, associated with Philipp MELANCHTHON and his followers (notably Viktorin STRIGEL), that in the act of conversion the human will can comply with the grace of God exercised through the Holy Spirit. This view, in the context of theological debate about the doctrine of GRACE, has its origins in the semi-Pelagianism of the fifth century. Melanchthon's detractors, the GNESIO-LUTHERANS, accused him of Pelagianism, but he evaded the charge by insisting that the primary cause of conversion was the action of the Holy Spirit rather than the exercise of the human will. The debate about synergism was finally settled by the Formula of CONCORD in 1577.

**SYPHILIS**, a disease which, like TYPHUS, first appeared in Europe at the end of the fifteenth century. Gonorrhoea, the other common venereal disease, has a continous history in Europe since classical antiquity, but syphilis first appeared during the first campaign of the WARS OF ITALY. The French army of CHARLES VIII occupied Naples in 1495, and both French and Spanish troops contracted syphilis. As the soldiers and their camp followers travelled throughout Europe and around the world, they created an epidemic of syphilis. It was originally called the Neapolitan disease, but soon became known in Italy as the French disease (*mal francese*), which passed into medical Latin as *morbus Gallicus*; in English it was usually called the pox. It carried a social stigma, like leprosy, and so was often blamed on other countries: it was called the Spanish disease in the Netherlands, the Polish disease in Russia, the Portuguese disease in India and Japan, and the Christian disease in the Ottoman Empire. Men were quick to blame the disease on women, and Gaspar Torrella proposed that it be called *pudendagra* because it was a disease of the *pudenda* (*Tractatus cum conciliis contra Pudendagram seu Morba Gallicum*, Rome, 1497). The term 'syphilis' derived from the protagonist of FRACASTORO's Latin poem *Syphilis sive Morbus Gallicus* (1530).

The historical epidemiology of syphilis is not clearly understood. The fact that some of the Spanish soldiers in Naples had visited America with COLUMBUS may imply that one effect of the conquest was a new disease created by the mingling of related American and European treponemal infections. The rapidity with which syphilis spread throughout Europe implies that it was a new disease; it is possible, however, that European treponemal infections (including pinta and yaws as well as syphilis) had long been extant as mild childhood diseases for which natural immunities developed, and that improved living standards meant that treponemes spread by skin contact were displaced by stronger and more virulent sexually transmitted strains.

Syphilis was widely thought by those who had not contracted it to be God's punishment for sin. The Emperor MAXIMILIAN declared in 1495 that syphilis was a divine reproach to blasphemy, but when he contracted the disease himself, he began to think of it as a medical condition that might be cured. His preferred cure was guaiac wood, which was the remedy recommended by the imperial physician Nicolaus Pol (whose report, completed in 1517, was published in Venice in 1535 as *De cura morbu Gallici per lignum guaycanum*); Ulrich von HUTTEN, a fellow sufferer, attributed his cure to guaiac in *De guaiaci medicina et morbo Gallico* (Mainz, 1519), but died of the disease four years later.

Physicians whose patients could not afford costly imported guaiac wood instead prescribed mercury, which had long been used for diseases of the skin, but mercury had the disadvantage of deleterious side effects. The origins of the guaiac cure lay in the observation by Spaniards in America that American Indians used guaiac wood to cure the disease that the Spaniards took to be syphilis; in the belief that an American disease required an American remedy, Spaniards (and then other Europeans) began to use guaiac. When it was eventually realized that guaiac was ineffective, mercury again came back into use.

Jon Arrizabalanga, John Henderson, and Roger French, *The Great Pox: The French Disease in Renaissance Europe* (1997).

**SYRIAC SCHOLARSHIP**. Syriac is an eastern dialect of Aramaic, and, until it was superseded by Arabic, was the literary language of Christian writers east of the Euphrates; its main centres were at Edessa and Nisibis. Syriac was used for various early translations of the Bible (the Diatessaron, the Old Syriac, the Peshitta, and the Syro-hexaplar), for translations of Greek patristic works (a large number of which survive only in Syriac versions), and for original Christian writings by church fathers such as Aphraates and St Ephrem Syrus. It has a consonantal alphabet which is written in three scripts: Estrangelo, Nestorian, and Jacobite (which is sometimes called Serto); in some texts, Syriac is printed in Hebrew characters.

Syriac was of interest to Renaissance scholars principally because the Peshitta, the Syriac version of the Bible authorized in Syriac-speaking churches, contains readings that are earlier than those in the earliest surviving Greek manuscripts of the New Testament. The Syriac New Testament was first published (Vienna, 1555) by Johann Albrecht Widmanstadt (or Widmanstetter), who also published a Syriac grammar (1556). TREMELLIUS subsequently published a Syriac New Testament together with a translation into Latin (1569). The Syriac text of the Old Testament, edited by Andreas Masius, was first published in PLANTIN's *Biblia regia* (Antwerp, 1645), whose text formed the basis of Brian Walton's *Polyglot* (London, 1657).

**SYRLIN, JÖRG** (*c*.1425–*c*.1491), Swabian woodcarver, a native of Ulm, where he carved the magnificent Gothic choir stalls in the cathedral (*c*.1469–75). The human figures of prophets and sibyls on the bench-ends are not distinguished simply by inscriptions or traditional attributes: they have also been endowed with individual faces, each of which expresses strong emotion.

*MDA*; David Gropp, *Das Ulmer Chorgestühl und Jörg Syrlin der Ältere* (Berlin, 1999).

**SZEKLERS or (Hungarian) Székely or (Latin) Siculi**, a Finno-Ugrian people who lived (and still live) in TRANSYLVANIA. Their provenance, which has been the subject of much scholarly debate, is unknown; their folk traditions trace their descent to Attila's Huns. The Szekler language is a dialect of Hungarian, and in the early modern period was written in runes of Turkic origin.

*SZLACHTA*, the Polish ESTATE of the gentry, which was an important force in the 37 small assemblies (*sejmiki*) which sent delegates to the provincial and national assemblies. The *szlachta* constituted the Chamber of Deputies of the national Diet (*Seym*) and contributed some 150 delegates to the Senate. In 1573 the *szlachta* acquired the privilege of participating with the aristocracy in the right to elect the kings of Poland.

# T

**TABLE CLOCKS AND TABERNACLE CLOCKS**. The term table clock could now be used to denote any clock that is ordinarily kept on a table, but in the technical language of horology the term refers specifically to spring-driven clocks in gilt-metal cases shaped like drums. In the first half of the sixteenth century, the German and French manufacturers of table clocks designed the drum, which was typically 5 centimetres (2 inches) high, to sit on a flat surface; the dial of these horizontal table clocks was on the top surface and was usually fitted with an hour hand and touch-pins to enable the time to be ascertained at night without the need to strike a light.

In the mid-sixteenth century, the dials began to be moved to the side of the drum, and such clocks were known as tabernacle clocks. French tabernacle clocks typically took the form of a hexagonal tower, whereas German tabernacle clocks usually consisted of a square tower surmounted by an open spire or a pierced dome covering the bell.

**TABLES**. The large communal dining table consisting of boards on trestles originated in the practice of north European tribes and was the most common form of dining table from the Middle Ages to the eighteenth century. As such tables became objects of display when not in use, they were sometimes waxed on one surface, and the table top was turned upside down (with the waxed surface facing down) when the table was to be used for eating. Such tables were usually called 'boards' in early modern English, a terminology that survives in phrases such as 'bed and board' and 'board of directors'.

In the fifteenth century furniture-makers revived the design of the Roman table, an oblong or rectangle resting on two upright supports, though they usually used wood rather than marble, as the Romans had done; the marble-topped table was revived in the late sixteenth century and was often inlaid with PIETRE DURE. The sixteenth-century hall table (i.e. a table designed for use in the hall, the principal room of a house) usually had carved baluster-shaped legs, and sometimes had flaps beneath the surface which could be drawn out to extend its length; such tables were called draw tables. In English houses the nearby serving table, which typically had cupboards below its long, narrow surface, was called a hutch table.

In wealthy households diners sat along one side of the table, leaving the other side free for service. This convention was convenient for artists, who in paintings such as LEONARDO's *Last Supper* were able to depict the faces of everyone at the table. When large tables were used by peasants, however, diners sat on both sides, as in Pieter BRUEGEL's *Peasant Wedding*.

**TABORITES**, a Bohemian Hussite group that took its name from Mount Tabor, their fortified base 100 kilometres (60 miles) south of Prague. The Taborites had no churches and rejected the EUCHARISTIC doctrine of transubstantiation. Their priests, who did not wear vestments, blessed the bread and wine at an ordinary table rather than at an altar, and during the blessing the people recited the Lord's Prayer. Like many radical groups in succeeding centuries, they refused to take oaths and to recognize the legitimacy of courts.

After the death of King WENCESLAS IV in 1419, the Taborites began to spread their version of the kingdom of God by brute force; their extreme cruelty was denounced as inhuman by equally cruel defenders of orthodoxy. After the death of their leader Jan ŽIŽKA in 1424, the Taborites divided into two groups. One group joined the UTRAQUISTS after the Compactata of Prague in 1433, and the other, under the command of their new leader Procopius the Bald, were utterly defeated at the battle of Lipany (near Český Brod) on 30 May 1434, and thereafter disappeared from history.

Thomas Fudge, *The Magnificent Ride: The First Reformation in Hussite Bohemia* (1998).

**TACCOLA, MARIANO** (1382–before 1458), Italian civil and hydraulic engineer and sculptor, a native of Siena who in 1432 secured the patronage of the Emperor SIGISMUND, with whom he seems to have served in the campaigns against the Ottomans. Taccola's sketches of civil and military structures (Latin *machinae*) began in 1427 with pictures of bridges and harbour works, and expanded to include both pictures of existing structures and original designs for new ones. In 1449 Taccola collected these drawings into a ten-book treatise, *De machinis libri decem*, which was never printed but nonetheless became very influential. He also wrote an early treatise (c.1419) on 'engines' (*De ingeneis*) such as watermills and river works.

DSB; MDA; De machinis libri decem, ed. Giustina Scaglia (2 vols., 1971); Frank Prager and Giustina Scaglia, Mariano Taccola and his Book 'De ingeneis', books III and IV (1972); L'Art de la guerre: Machines et stratagems de Taccola, ingénieur de la Renaissance, ed. Eberhard Knobloch (1992).

**TACITUS IN THE RENAISSANCE.** The works of the Roman historian Cornelius Tacitus (c.AD 56–120) included an ethnological treatise on the tribes of northern Europe (De origine et situ Germanorum, usually known as the Germania) and two untitled treatises that chronicle the history of imperial Rome from AD 14 to 96. The treatise now known as the Annals began with the accession of Tiberius in AD 14 and continued until AD 69, the year of the four emperors; this work had at least sixteen books, but books 7–10 have never been recovered, books 5 and 6 survive only in part, and book 16 breaks off in AD 66, two years before the suicide of Nero. The treatise subsequently known as the Histories began in AD 69 and probably ended with the assassination of Domitian on 18 September 96; of this treatise four complete books and 26 chapters of a fifth book survive. The total number of books in these two treatises was 30, according to St Jerome, but the division of books between the two treatises is uncertain.

Tacitus was little known in late antiquity, and for almost a millennium his works were forgotten, although in the ninth century there were copies of the Annals and the early books of the Germania at the monastery in Fulda. Between 1355 and 1357 Zanobi di Strada discovered a manuscript of Tacitus in the library of the abbey at Montecassino, and reported his discovery to BOCCACCIO, who mentioned Tacitus in the revised version of his Amorosa visione and drew examples from Tacitus for his treatise on famous women (De claris mulieribus). In about 1430 the manuscript known as the Second Medicean was discovered; it contained Annals 11–16 and Histories 1–5. Eighty years later the discovery of another manuscript supplied Annals 1–6, which was printed in an edition of 1515. The Histories was translated into Italian in 1544 and the Annals in 1563. The transmission of Tacitus beyond Italy began with the edition by BEATUS RHENANUS in 1519 and culminated in the magisterial edition published by LIPSIUS in 1575.

P. Burke, 'Tacitism', in T. A. Dorey (ed.), Tacitus (1969);
K. C. Schellhase, Tacitus in Renaissance Political Thought (1976).

**TADDEO DI BARTOLO** (c.1363–c.1422), Italian painter, born in Siena, where he painted the frescoes in the chapel of the Palazzo Pubblico (1407–14) and in the Palazzo Piccolomini. His paintings include a polyptych (now dismembered) of The Virgin and Child and St Francis Trampling the Vices (1403) in the Galleria Nazionale dell'Umbria in Perugia.

MDA.

**TALAVERA DE LA REINA POTTERIES.** The Castilian town of Talavera de la Reina, so called because from the reign of Alfonso XI (1312–50) it was deemed to be the marriage portion of the queens of Castile, became an important centre for the manufacturing of TIN-GLAZED EARTHENWARE in the mid-sixteenth century. In 1562 King PHILIP II appointed the Fleming Jan FLORIS to make tiles (AZULEJOS) in Talavera for his royal palaces. Four years later Jerónimo Montero, a potter from Seville, was brought by royal command to Talavera to offer tuition in the painting and glazing of pottery. In 1570 the Talavera workshop of Juan Fernández (fl. 1570–1603) received a commission to manufacture 24,800 tiles for the ESCORIAL, and three years later received a supplementary order for 136 vessels (jars, pots, and vases). Tiles from the Fernández workshop are typically decorated with white ACANTHUS leaves set against a blue background, and its early pots and jars are decorated with STRAPWORK and GROTESQUE motifs in yellow and blue, usually set against a white background. Talavera factories also made large pictorial panels for the churches of Castile.

In the early seventeenth century Talavera factories continued to make tiles (notably the order for 102,980 tiles for the Dominican Convent of Porta Coeli in Valladolid) and pots (notably the flower pots made for the palace of the dukes of Lerma in Valladolid), but a new market in domestic tableware was occasioned in 1601 by a SUMPTUARY LAW restricting the use of table silver; thereafter the Talavera factories made large numbers of plates, jars, ewers, and basins. The industry has survived until the present day.

A. W. Frothingham, Talavera Pottery (1944); B. Martínez Caviro, Ceramica de Talavera (2nd edn. 1984).

**TALENTI, FRANCESCO** (fl. 1325–69), Italian architect, a native of Florence who is first recorded working in Orvieto in 1325, presumably as an assistant to Lorenzo Maitani (c.1275–1330), who was building Orvieto Cathedral. By 1343 Talenti had returned to Florence and was working on the cathedral campanile, to which he contributed the windowed upper storeys. In 1350 he was appointed capomaestro of the cathedral, and in this capacity modified the original plans of ARNOLFO DI CAMBIO, significantly altering, and probably extending, Arnolfo's façade; this façade was destroyed in the sixteenth century.

**TALLIS, THOMAS** (c.1505–1585), English composer and organist in Dover, London, and Waltham Abbey, Essex. Following the dissolution of the Abbey in 1540 he sang at Canterbury Cathedral and was a member of the Chapel Royal under HENRY VIII, EDWARD VI, MARY TUDOR, and ELIZABETH I, who granted him and William BYRD an exclusive licence allowing them to print music. The Cantiones sacrae (1575) was the first publication to appear from this arrangement. The style of his sacred music reflects both the changing requirements of a politically influenced liturgy and the influence of continental music. His versatility is in evidence in a range of works from the grandeur of the 40-part 'Spem in alium' through the complexity of 'Gaude gloriosa Dei mater' to the direct simplicity of 'O nata lux'.

**TANSILLO, LUIGI** (1510–68), Italian poet, soldier, and courtier, born in Venosa. In 1535 he entered the service of the Spanish viceregal court in Naples, serving as a soldier (fighting the Ottomans) and administrator (notably as governor of

Gaeta). In his poetry he wrote in many genres (including the sonnet, the pastoral eclogue, the didactic poem, and the epic) and ranged from robustly secular subjects such as *Il vendemmiatore* ('The Grape Gatherer', 1532), which was placed on the INDEX, to pious works such as his epic *Le lagrime de San Pietro* (1585), which is now best known as the model for MALHERBE's *Les Larmes de saint Pierre* (1587). His didactic poem on the wet-nurse (*La balia*, 1566) attempted to persuade mothers to feed their babies themselves.

*OCIL.*

**TAPESTRY**, a decorative woven fabric with a pictorial or ornamental design. In wealthy households tapestries were hung on walls and draped over beds and tables; like carpets, they were not used on floors, which were covered with rush matting. In churches tapestries were draped over altars and choir stalls.

In the process of WEAVING tapestries the coloured weft threads were passed alternatively over and under the warps; the wefts do not pass from selvage to selvage, but are rather checked by the requirements of the pattern and then battened down so that in the finished product the warps are not visible. Tapestries were woven on high-warp or low-warp looms, and in both cases the weaver worked from the back of the tapestry. A high-warp tapestry (*tapisserie de haute lice* or *lisse*) was woven on a upright loom in which the threads were wound on rollers arranged in a vertical row, and the threads were parted manually; the cartoon stood behind the weaver (and so could be checked for points of detail against the design that he had transferred to the warp threads) and on the other side of the loom mirrors were placed to enable the weaver to see the front of the tapestry as he worked. A low-warp tapestry (*tapisserie de basse lice* or *lisse*) was woven on a horizontal loom in which the warps were controlled by harnesses attached to treadles; this method was faster and cheaper, but in the hands of all but the most skilled craftsmen the quality of the tapestries was compromised by two problems of visibility: the cartoon, which was placed underneath the warp, was not easily visible, and the front of the tapestry could not be seen at all. Warp threads were typically made of linen or hemp, but wefts, which would be visible in the finished product, were usually wool or even silk, and silver and gold threads were sometimes added to the weft.

The earliest surviving European tapestry was woven in the eleventh century for the Church of St Gereon in Cologne; it is now divided between the Germanisches Museum in Nuremberg, the Musée des Tissues in Lyon, and the Victoria and Albert Museum in London. For the next three centuries, tapestries were produced throughout the German lands, and although many seem to have been woven in monastic workshops, the designs were often secular: the chivalric narratives of the *Minnesang* (see MEISTERGESANG) were visualized in woven *Minneteppiche*.

In the last quarter of the fourteenth century Burgundy and France emerged as the most important European centres for the production of tapestry. Nicolas Bataille produced tapestries for the courts of King Charles V of France and his three brothers, the dukes of Anjou, Berry, and Burgundy. The *Apocalypse* tapestries (1375–9) produced for the duke of Anjou were 152 metres (500 feet) long; most of the set survives in the Musée des Tapisseries in Angers. Between 1387 and 1400, Bataille's workshop produced more than 250 tapestries for his royal patrons.

In 1384 Artois was annexed to the duchy of Burgundy and Arras became an important centre of weaving. Many of its tapestries were exported to England, and the name of the town passed into English as a generic name for tapestry; when Shakespeare's Polonius hides behind the arras, he is hiding behind a tapestry suspended from a ceiling close to a wall. Several important tapestry sets are thought to have been woven in Arras, but the only one known to have been made in Arras is *The Story of St Piat and Eleuthère* (1402) in Tournai Cathedral.

After the sack of Arras in 1477 the Burgundian centre for the manufacturing of tapestries shifted to Tournai (Hainaut), where tapestries had been made since the early fourteenth century. In the fifteenth century the stylistic similarities between tapestries woven in Arras and Tournai make it difficult to attribute tapestries to one centre or another on the basis of style; the four panels of the *Chatsworth Hunts* (Victoria and Albert Museum, London), for example, could have been made in either town. The tapestries of Pasquier GRENIER, however, can confidently be assigned to Tournai. The provenance of a large group of tapestries known as *milles-fleurs* is disputed. These tapestries, which acquired their name from the brightly coloured flowers in the background of the courtly and pastoral scenes which they depict, were woven in the late fifteenth and early sixteenth centuries; they may have been woven at workshops in Tournai, but it is also possible that they are the work of itinerant weavers in the Loire valley or of urban centres such as Brussels. The most famous of the *milles-fleurs* tapestries is the series known as *La Dame à la licorne* (*c*.1495, Musée de Cluny, Paris). The dominance of Arras and Tournai in the French-speaking lands meant that the tapestry industry in Paris did not recover its ascendancy until the seventeenth century. Elsewhere in France, the only important centre was the temporary workshop established by King FRANCIS I in about 1540 at FONTAINEBLEAU in order to weave one set of tapestries (now in the Kunsthistorisches Museum in Vienna); the patterns reproduce the decorations on the walls of the Galerie François I at Fontainebleau.

From the early sixteenth century the European tapestry industry was dominated by the factories of Flanders. The most important centres were Brussels, Bruges, Ghent, Lille, Louvain, Oudenarde, and Valenciennes. The OUDENARDE TAPESTRIES were marked with a pair of spectacles; in 1528, BRUSSELS TAPESTRIES first began to include the well-known mark of a shield between two Bs. In the late sixteenth century some Flemish weavers migrated to the northern Netherlands, where the most prominent weaver was Frans Spierinc, whose Delft workshop, founded in 1591, produced tapestries for export to England (such as the *Story of Diana* at Knole) and to the Danish court.

In Italy the manufacturing of tapestries began in the mid-fifteenth century, when Flemish weavers began to work in Milan and Ferrara. In Milan, where a tapestry workshop was established by Francesco SFORZA in 1455, the most important surviving product of the workshop is an early sixteenth-century *Caesar Receiving Pompey's Head* (Musée des Arts Décoratifs, Paris). Benedetto da Milano, who trained in the Milan factory, established a workshop in Vigevano, where in the first decade of the sixteenth century he wove a set of *Months* (Museo Castello Sforzesco, Milan) modelled on BRAMANTINO; these are the earliest surviving tapestries to show the influence of Italian Renaissance art. In Ferrara a workshop was established by Leonello d'ESTE in the mid-1450s; in the mid-sixteenth century this workshop was operated by Hans and Nicolas KARCHER. Nicolas Karcher twice (1539–45, 1553–6) worked in the service of the GONZAGA family in Mantua; this workshop is the likely provenance of the series of *Playing Boys* now divided between the Gulbenkian Museum in Lisbon and the Museo Poldi Pezzoli in Milan. In 1546 Nicolas Karcher founded a workshop in Florence for Duke COSIMO I DE' MEDICI; the first and most important product of this workshop was the sumptuous twenty-piece *History of Joseph* (1546–52) designed by BRONZINO, PONTORMO, and SALVIATI and now in the Palazzo Vecchio in Florence.

In northern Europe buyers were long content to import Flemish tapestries, sometimes in large numbers: King HENRY VIII owned more than 2,000 tapestries. The indigenous English industry began with the SHELDON TAPESTRIES in the sixteenth century and the MORTLAKE TAPESTRIES of the seventeenth century. Denmark also imported Flemish tapestries, but in the 1580s an important set known as the ELSINORE TAPESTRIES was woven in Denmark.

Thomas Campbell et al., *Tapestry in the Renaissance* (2002).

**TARLETON, RICHARD** (d. 1588). Together with KEMPE, Tarleton was one of the most popular clowns in Elizabethan theatre. He joined QUEEN ELIZABETH'S MEN on their formation in 1583, and gained a strong following due both to his extemporizing and to his performance of jigs, or farcial afterpieces which followed the main performance. The popularity of Tarleton and other clowns may partly explain the mixture of comedy and tragedy in many of the dramas of this period.

*DNB.*

**TARTAGLIA, NICCOLÒ, or Niccolò Fontana** (c.1499–1557), Italian mathematician and engineer, born into a poor family in Brescia; his family name was Fontana, but he became known as Tartaglia ('stammerer') because of a speech impediment acquired after he was cut across the face by French soldiers while he, his mother, and her sister were taking sanctuary in a church during the sack of Brescia in 1512. Portraits show him with a beard that covers the scars.

According to his own account, Tartaglia was largely self-taught. By 1521 he was established as a teacher of mathematics in Verona. As was usual at the time (see ABACUS SCHOOLS), Tartaglia engaged in public equation-solving contests. It was in the course of one such that he noticed his opponent,

Francesco Maria Fiore, was able to solve some cubic equations, and he managed to work out how Fiore was doing it. It seems that Fiore had inherited this method of solution, as a piece of possibly lucrative intellectual property, from his teacher Scipione dal Ferro (1465–1526), who had taught mathematics in Bologna. This is, at least, what Tartaglia was to tell CARDANO in the late 1530s. He also passed on a general method of solving cubic equations, asking Cardano to keep it secret. According to his own account, Cardano did so for several years, but when Tartaglia had still not published the method, Cardano, reflecting that it was not in any case original to Tartaglia, published it himself, in his *Ars magna* (1545). The preface does indeed explain that Cardano learnt the solution from Tartaglia, but the method nevertheless became known as 'Cardano's method'. The ensuing priority dispute was fiery. It included a public exchange of problems between the antagonists (Cardano had the support of Lodovico FERRARI), carried out in print. This is of interest as preserving something of equation-solving contests. Tartaglia's reluctance to publish his method of solving cubic equations may be connected with the fact that it involves square roots of negative quantities; Cardano rides roughshod over this difficulty (with some justification since one can check that the results are correct); the first rigorous treatment of such roots was by BOMBELLI (1572). See also ALGEBRA.

By 1534 Tartaglia had moved to Venice, where he continued to teach mathematics, and made the acquaintance of Giuliano Savorgnan, who was then in charge of the defence of the republic. The military man asked the mathematician for help with calculations of the range of cannon. Tartaglia's attack on the problem, based on Aristotelian physics, came up with the answer that (one suspects) the gunners had already arrived at empirically, namely that maximum range was obtained by setting the barrel at an elevation of 45 degrees. This work, the first application of mathematics to gunnery, was published in a treatise called *La nova scientia* ('The New Science', 1537); see ARTILLERY. In 1543 Tartaglia published an Italian translation of EUCLID, and a version of some of the works of ARCHIMEDES.

Tartaglia finally published his method of solving cubic equations in the form of a rhyme (no doubt for ease in memorizing it) in a book of mixed problems, some put to him by Savorgnan, called *Quesiti et invenzioni diverse* (1546). The book, whose problems range over gunnery and FORTIFICATION as well as algebra, is dedicated to HENRY VIII of England, but its close-packed italic type and octavo format mark it as a handbook. Tartaglia later wrote a much more formal mathematical treatise, *General trattato di numeri e misure* (1556 and 1560). This impressive and lucid summary of the mathematics of the day (including GEOMETRY) was published as a two-volume folio, and has every right to take itself seriously.

Lodovico Ferrari and Niccolò Tartaglia, *Cartelli di sfida matematica, riproduzione infacsimile delle edizioni originali 1547–1548*, introd. Arnaldo Masotti (1974).

**TASSO, BERNARDO** (c.1493–1569), Italian poet, a native of Salerno who entered the service of Ferrante Sanseverino, prince of Salerno; in 1552 he followed Sanseverino into exile in Rome. In 1557 he moved to the court of Guidobaldo II DELLA ROVERE, duke of Urbino. Guglielmo Gonzaga, duke of Mantua, appointed Tasso as governor of Ostiglia, where he lived for the rest of his life.

The principal model for Tasso's verse was Horace, as is apparent in his *Odi* and *Salmi* (both 1560). He translated and expanded Montalvo's AMADÍS DE GAULA as *Amadigi de Gaula* (1560). His *Floridante* was completed and published in 1587 by his son, the poet Torquato TASSO.

**TASSO, TORQUATO** (1544–95), Italian poet, dramatist, and literary theorist, born in Sorrento and educated at a Jesuit school in Naples. In 1554 he joined his father Bernardo TASSO in Rome, and subsequently moved with him to Pesaro (1556), Venice (1559), and Padua (1560), where he studied at the university. In 1562, aged 18, he published his romance epic *Rinaldo*. Three years later he entered the service of Cardinal Luigi d'Este, whom he was to accompany to France (where he met RONSARD) in 1570.

From 1565 to 1586 Tasso was associated with the ESTE court of Ferrara, where in 1572 he was appointed court poet to Alfonso II d'ESTE, for whom he wrote his PASTORAL drama *Aminta*, which was performed by I GELOSI in 1573 and published in 1581. During this period he also wrote *Gerusalemme liberata*, an epic on the capture of Jerusalem by Christian forces in the First Crusade; the poem was circulated in manuscript from 1575, published in part as *Il Goffredo* (Venice, 1580), and published in its entirety as *Gerusalemme liberata* in Ferrara in 1581.

In the late 1570s Tasso began to suffer from the onset of insanity. He was incarcerated in 1577 in Ferrara, but escaped to his sister's house in Sorrento. On returning to Ferrara in 1579, he was confined in the Hospital of Santa Anna for the next seven years. On his release in 1586 Tasso moved to the GONZAGA court in Mantua, where he wrote *Re Torrismondo* (1587), a tragedy of incest and betrayal. After an itinerant period he finally settled in the Monastery of Sant'Onofrio near Rome, where he produced a revised version of *Gerusalemme liberata* entitled *Gerusalemme conquistata* (1593) in which he purged the original version of its sensuousness. Tasso's other works include a collection of more than 1,000 short poems (*Rime*, 1593), a hexameral epic (*Il mondo creato*, 1594), 28 dialogues, a treatise on epic (*Discorsi del poema eroico*, 1594), and almost 2,000 elegantly crafted letters.

OCIL; Peter Brand, *Torquato Tasso* (1965).

**TAUSEN, HANS** (1494–1561), Danish Protestant reformer, born in Birkende (near Odense, on Fyn), the son of a peasant. He entered the Franciscan monastery at Antvorshov (now a suburb of Slagelse, on Sjælland) and subsequently studied at Leiden, where he met Dutch humanists and demonstrated an excellent command of Latin and Hebrew (he was later to translate the Pentateuch). In May 1523 Tausen became a student at WITTENBERG, where he became a disciple of LUTHER. On returning to Denmark he proclaimed his newly acquired Lutheran ideas, and was imprisoned in his monastery for

advocating unsound doctrines. After his release he preached in Viborg in favour of the Reformation and discarded his monastic habit. On being appointed chaplain to King FREDERICK I in October 1526, he used Danish rather than Latin in the church services. He subsequently married Dorothea Viberg, the sister of the Danish reformer known as Sadolin, and so became the first Danish priest to marry.

In 1529 Tausen was appointed by the king to preach in Copenhagen, and together with his followers formulated a reformed 'Confession of Faith' in 43 articles. On 2 July 1530 he secured the support of the National Assembly of Noblemen (Herredag) to contain the opposition of Bishop Rönne of Roskilde, but three years later, when King Frederick died, Rönne persuaded the Herredag to reverse its earlier decision. Tausen was convicted of blasphemy, but a popular rising in his defence (during which Tausen saved the bishop from death at the hands of the enraged mob) led to his punishment being reduced to a warning. In 1542 Tausen was appointed bishop of Ribe in the Reformed Danish Church, and served in that post for twenty years. His 'Confession' was superseded by the adoption of the less aggressive AUGSBURG CONFESSION.

DBL.

**TAVERNER, JOHN** (c.1490–1545), English composer from Lincolnshire who moved from the collegiate choir at Tattershall to Cardinal (now Christ Church) College, Oxford, to become the first choirmaster in 1526. Following WOLSEY's fall, he was based at the financially well-supported Church of St Botolph, Boston, where he is buried. His sacred music comprises masses, votive antiphons, Magnificats, and liturgical pieces; he also composed secular songs. The 'in nomine tibi' section of his *Gloria tibi Trinitas* mass provided the melody of the 'IN NOMINE' tradition.

**TÈ, PALAZZO DEL**, a palatial VILLA in Mantua converted from stables between 1525 and 1535 for Federico II GONZAGA, marquis of Mantua; the architect was GIULIO ROMANO. The villa is a single-storeyed square building with a plain exterior that gives little hint of the mannerist palace that lies within. The finest room, the Sala di Psiche, is decorated with frescoes by Giulio Romano and Rinaldo Mantovano illustrating the legend of Psyche; other rooms were decorated by GIOVANNI DA UDINE and Francesco PRIMATICCIO.

The three subdued arches of the *cortile d'onore*, the court in which important visitors (such as CHARLES V in 1530) were received, lead through a richly sculpted and stuccoed loggia to the gardens. The GIARDINO SEGRETO and its GROTTO survive, but the original PARTERRES have been replaced with a herb garden; early visitors also reported mock naval battles being fought on two lakes in the garden, both of which have disappeared.

**TEBALDEO, ANTONIO** (1463–1537), Italian poet, born in Ferrara, where his responsibilities in the ESTE court included serving as a tutor to Isabella d'ESTE and acting as personal secretary to Lucrezia BORGIA. He subsequently lived in Rome in the court of Pope LEO X. Tebaldeo's poems include pastoral poems (in both Latin and Italian) and Petrarchan sonnets. His verse was first collected in an unauthorized edition in 1499 and remained in print throughout the sixteenth century.

*OCIL.*

**TECHNOLOGY.** The principal technological innovations of the Renaissance were in the areas of PRINTING, GUNPOWDER, NAVIGATION, and timekeeping with mechanical CLOCKS AND WATCHES. In regard to machines, the medieval technologies for using the power of wind and water were considerably refined. In the Netherlands the design of the windmill developed from the tower mill of the fourteenth century (in which only the cap carrying the wind shaft had to be realigned, but the linkage which took motion from the sails to the millstones in the base of the structure had to be made capable of accommodating the additional motion of the top piece) to the post-mill of the sixteenth century (in which the whole mill is turned and the linkage stays as before); this improvement meant that mills could readily be used for pumping water as well as grinding corn. Similarly, improvements in the technology of water wheels (which in northern Europe were usually undershot, that is, driven from below) enabled engineers to convert the rotary motion of the medieval mill into the reciprocating motion required for tools such as tilt hammers, mechanical saws, bellows, pumps, and beaters; these tools facilitated growth in industries such as iron-making, tanning, and, perhaps most importantly, papermaking.

B. Gille, *Les Ingénieurs de la Renaissance* (1964).

**TELESCOPES AND MICROSCOPES.** Small spyglasses that used more than one lens and were the ancestors of the telescope appeared in Italy in the 1590s, as fairground toys. Making good lenses depended first upon getting GLASS that was properly transparent and free of striations and other irregularities, which meant that one needed to be able to control the temperature while the glass cooled, and second on being able to grind the blank accurately. These conditions seem to have first been met in the Netherlands, and in the summer of 1609 a visitor brought a telescope to Venice. Galileo GALILEI, who was then in Padua, heard of the instrument and, using his understanding of the relevant OPTICS, made himself an improved version. This type of telescope, variously known as the Dutch or Galilean or terrestrial telescope, has a convex object glass and a concave eyepiece. The images are erect but the magnification is not very high. Moreover, the field of view is small, so some skill is required to use the instrument for astronomical observation, but Galileo himself acquired the necessary skill and published an account of his observations of the moon, Jupiter and its moons, and the Milky Way; this book, *Sidereus nuncius* (1610), was greeted with huge enthusiasm and pirated editions started to appear almost immediately. The telescope was obviously useful to the military; Galileo sent telescopes to various ruling princes; KEPLER was able to use one presented to the elector of Cologne and published a short account of his observations of the planets, noting that the images were crossed by bright lines at right angles, one reddish and one bluish, but he was clearly delighted by the effect of magnification. Kepler then started to think about how lenses might be combined, a purely theoretical matter since he said that good glass was not obtainable in Prague, and in his *Dioptrice* (1611) suggested using two convex lenses, a combination that produces an inverted image; it also turned out to produce a much wider field of view and rapidly found such favour with astronomers that it became known not only as the Keplerian but also simply as the astronomical telescope. In fact the advantage of the wider field was such that instruments were later made with an additional lens to give an erect image for terrestrial applications.

The development of the microscope from the magnifying glass of the Middle Ages was another product of research in optics. The first compound microscopes were constructed in the first decade of the seventeenth century; the earliest recorded use of the microscope to produce printed illustrations was the set of drawings of bees for Francesco Stelluti's *Descrizzione dell'ape* (1625). However, the quality of the images in Galilean compound microscopes was not very good, and the important microscopical work of the seventeenth century, by Leeuwenhoek (1632–1723) and later by Hooke (1635–1703), was carried out with simple microscopes.

**TELESIO, BERNARDINO** (*c.*1509–1588), Italian natural philosopher and anti-Aristotelian. He was born in Cozenza and studied mathematics and philosophy at Padua. Apart from several protracted visits to Naples, Telesio spent his life in Cozenza, where the ACADEMY that he founded, the Accademia Cosentina, promoted the study of natural philosophy in accordance with his principles. Telesio rejected Aristotelian doctrines in favour of a system of his own devising based on sense experience and nature. His principal work was *De rerum natura*, which was published in 1565, revised in an edition of 1570 and substantially expanded in an edition of 1586.

**TEMPERA**, a kind of paint and method of painting, sometimes called 'distemper' in English and *détrempe* in French; the most common form is egg tempera, in which the pigments of the paint are mixed (or 'tempered') with egg yolks. Tempera was the most common technique for painting wooden panels from the late twelfth to the early sixteenth centuries, by which time it had been superseded by OIL PAINTING. Even after oil painting had become well established, artists such as MICHELANGELO and RAPHAEL continued *pingere a tempera* ('to paint in tempera') as well as oils. The effect of tempera differs from oils in being more vivid and luminous (which suited the hieratic style of trecento painting) and in its restricted colour range, which meant that it could not achieve the naturalistic illusions of oils. When tempera was used for wall painting, it was known as *fresco a secco* (see SECCO).

**TEMPESTA, ANTONIO** (1555–1630), Italian painter and engraver, a native of Florence, where he assisted VASARI in the decoration of the Palazzo Vecchio. He moved to Rome, where he entered the service of Pope GREGORY XIII, for whom Tempesta decorated buildings in the Vatican; he also worked in the villas of Tivoli and Caprarola. His engravings, of which almost 2,000 are known, usually depict scenes from mythology, the Bible, and history; his particular skill lay in the depiction of horses, which are often portrayed in battlepieces and hunting scenes.

*MDA.*

**TEN OF WAR** or (Italian) Dieci di libertà e pace, the Florentine council responsible for diplomacy and warfare. MACHIAVELLI was its secretary for fourteen years (1498–1512), and his letters contain detailed accounts of the work of the council.

**TERBRUGGHEN or ter Bruggen, HENDRICK JANSOON** (1588–1629), Dutch painter, a native of The Hague who from 1604 to 1614 lived in Italy, where he joined the circle of CARAVAGGIO. He returned to Utrecht in 1616, and together with Gerrit van Honthorst (1590–1656) introduced Caravaggio's style (especially his use of light colours) into Dutch painting; the two painters are regarded as the founders of the Utrecht School. Of his religious paintings, the best known is *Jacob and Laban* (National Gallery, London); his finest GENRE PAINTINGS are the two pictures of *A Flute Player* (Schlossmuseum, Kassel).

*MDA s.v. Brugghen, Hendrick ter; Benedict Nicolson, Hendrick Terbrugghen (1958).*

**TERENCE IN THE RENAISSANCE.** The Roman comic dramatist Publius Terentius Afer (*c.*190 BC–159 BC) was brought to Rome as a slave from North Africa and, when he was eventually manumitted, adopted the name of his owner. The plays of Terence were quoted and imitated by later authors such as Cicero, Horace, Persius, and Quintilian, and subsequently by grammarians and patristic writers. The tenth-century German nun Roswitha (or Hrotswit) of Gandersheim wrote six Latin comedies which were Christian versions of Terence's comedies; her plays were published in 1501 by Konrad CELTIS. The series of productions of PLAUTUS and Terence which began in 1486 at the ESTE court included three plays by Terence translated by ARIOSTO. Terence was also widely taught in schools, and was often the first author to be studied; educational humanists such as ERASMUS declared both the Latinity and the morality of Terence to be appropriate for the education of children, and this theme was taken up by MELANCHTHON, CASAUBON (who urged his son to model his Latin on that of Terence), and MONTAIGNE. The *editio princeps* was published in Strassburg in 1470.

H. W. Lawton, *Térence en France au XVIᵉ siècle* (2 vols., 1970–2); S. Prete, 'Terenzio e le sue commedie: Dal Petrarca al Poliziano', *Arcadia: Accademia lett. Italiana atti e memorie*, 8 (1981–2).

**TERESA DE ÁVILA or Teresa de Jesús** (1515–82), Spanish mystic and religious reformer, born into an aristocratic Castilian family in Gotarrendura, a village near Ávila. Her secular name was Teresa Sánchez de Cepeda y Ahumada; in Latin (and English) her name is often spelt 'Theresa'. Her religious fervour developed early: at the age of 7 she tried to run away to Morocco with her younger brother Rodrigo to die as martyrs. She was educated by Augustinian nuns and in 1533 entered the Carmelite Convent of the Incarnation at Ávila. After a year in the convent she suffered a recurrence of a childhood illness (possibly malaria), and spent the next three years recovering at home.

The convent life to which Teresa returned was relaxed in its attention to traditional disciplines: in their 'mitigated observance', nuns were free to leave their enclosure, and the convent was a social centre for the wealthy families of Ávila. Teresa lived in these unreformed Carmelite surroundings for 25 years, in the course of which she became a mystic: she began with constant mental prayer, and in 1555 began to experience visions.

In 1562 Teresa founded a reformed congregation at her house of San José in Ávila, and lived with thirteen nuns in uncompromising poverty, hardship, and solitude. The nuns subsisted on a meagre vegetarian diet and wore a coarse brown woollen habit and leather sandals; the term 'Discalced' (from Latin *discalceare*, to make unshod) refers to the practice of wearing sandals rather than shoes, as Jesus enjoined his disciples (Matthew 10: 10). By the time of her death, there were sixteen new Discalced Carmelite houses modelled on Teresa's reforms, mostly in Castile and Andalusia, and a similar number of established houses which adopted her reformed rule. In the late 1560s Teresa supported JUAN DE LA CRUZ in his reform of the Carmelite friars.

Teresa did not write voluntarily, but rather because she was commanded to do so. Her autobiographical *Vida* (of which the first draft was completed *c.*1561) was denounced to the INQUISITION by Calced Carmelites, who tried to have Teresa deported to Spanish America. They managed only to have her immured in Toledo, where in 1577 she wrote *El castillo interior* ('The Interior Castle', also known as *Las moradas*, i.e. the seven 'dwellings' leading to union with God), which was published in Salamanca in 1588. Her *Libro de las fundaciones* (Brussels, 1613) describes her programme of reform and her *Libro de las relaciones* describes her spiritual progress to various confessors. *El camino de perfección* ('The Way of Perfection', Évora, 1583) is a spiritual guide for nuns, as is her less well-known *Avisos espirituales* (Córdoba, 1598). Teresa also wrote a mystical commentary on the Song of Solomon, *Conceptos del amor de Dios sobre algunas palabras de los Cantares de Salomón* (Brussels, 1611).

Teresa died on 4 October 1582 while travelling from Burgos to Ávila; she was buried where she died, in Alba de Tormes. She was beatified in 1614 and canonized in 1622; in 1970 she became the first woman saint to be declared a doctor of the Church. A portrait painted in 1570 by Fray Juan de la Miseria survives at Ávila. The most famous representation of St Teresa, Gianlorenzo Bernini's sculpture in the church of Santa Maria della Victoria in Rome, endows her with a sensuality that derives from Teresa's writings on mystic marriage and is shaped by a tradition that conflates spiritual and sexual ecstasy.

747

*Obras*, ed. P. Silverio de Santa Teresa (9 vols., 1915–24); Silverio de Santa Teresa, *Vida de Santa Teresa* (5 vols., 1935–7); Fr. Thomas and Fr. Gabriel, *Saint Theresa of Avila: Studies in her Life, Doctrine and Times* (1963); Gillian Ahlgren, *Teresa of Avila and the Politics of Sanctity* (1996); Cathleen Medwick, *Teresa of Avila* (2000).

**TERRACOTTA or (Latin) *terra cocta* or (French) *terre cuite***, the term (from Italian, meaning 'baked earth') for a red unglazed pottery used mostly for bricks and decorative tiles but also as a medium for sculpture. The term is sometimes used with reference to the glazed earthenware associated with the DELLA ROBBIA workshop in Florence. This oxymoronic sense has developed because Luca della Robbia invented a technique of using vitreous glazes to colour his terracotta sculptures; this 'glazed terracotta', which was impervious to damp and so could be used in outdoor architectural settings, is distinct from the TIN-GLAZED EARTHENWARE which in Italy is known as MAIOLICA.

**TERZI or Tércio, FILIPPO** (1520–97), Italian architect and engineer who moved to Portugal in 1576 to enter the service of King SEBASTIAN I. In 1578 he accompanied the king to North Africa as a captain of artillery, and was present at the battle of KSAR-EL-KEBIR, where the king was killed and Terzi was captured. Attempts to ransom Terzi failed, but he escaped and returned to Portugal, where he entered the service of Cardinal-Prince HENRIQUE. His buildings, which include the Church of São Vicente de Fora in Lisbon and the fortifications north and south of Lisbon, were important influences on later PORTUGUESE ARCHITECTURE, as was the school that he founded for the training of architects.

*DHP; MDA.*

**TERZI or Terzio, FRANCESCO** (*c*.1523–1591), Italian painter and draughtsman. He was born in Bergamo and as a young man painted a large *Crucifixion* in the Church of SS Bartolomeo e Stefano in Lallo (near Bergamo). In 1551 he became court painter to Ferdinand I (later the Emperor FERDINAND) and spent more than 25 years in the imperial service in Austria and Bohemia and executed many portraits of the imperial family and associated figures such as Andrea DORIA and Ferrante GONZAGA; these portraits are mostly in Schloss Ambras in Innsbruck or the Kunsthistorisches Museum in Vienna.

*MDA s.v. Terzio.*

**TETRABIBLOS**. See PTOLEMY IN THE RENAISSANCE.

**TETRAPOLITAN CONFESSION**, a Protestant confession of faith drafted by Martin BUCER and Wolfgang CAPITO at the Diet of Augsburg and presented to the Emperor CHARLES V on 9 July 1530; the four south German cities after which the confession was named were Strassburg, Konstans, Lindau, and Memmingen. The theological formulations are based on the AUGSBURG CONFESSION (a draft of which had been passed in confidence to the compilers), but are rephrased to accommodate Zwinglian sensibilities.

**TETZEL, JOHANN** (*c*.1465–1519), German preacher and promoter of the sale of INDULGENCES, born in Leipzig, the son of a goldsmith. He was educated at the university (1482–87) and in about 1490 entered the Dominican Order. In 1502 he became a preacher of indulgences, travelling widely in Germany. In 1516, when Pope LEO X issued the indulgence to finance the rebuilding of ST PETER'S BASILICA in Rome, Tetzel was charged by his archbishop ALBRECHT OF MAINZ with the responsibility for preaching the indulgence in Magdeburg and Halberstadt, the income from which was to be divided between the archbishop and the Vatican. Tetzel undertook his task in the spirit of an auctioneer, setting aside theological nuances in favour of assurances that cash payments would automatically deliver donors from PURGATORY.

The indulgence had been forbidden in Saxony by the elector, so Tetzel could not preach in Wittenberg. He therefore decided enterprisingly to preach in Jüterbog, just outside the electoral boundary. Martin LUTHER travelled to Jüterbog to hear Tetzel preach, and was so scandalized by the extravagant commercialism of Tetzel's sermon that he was prompted to issue his 95 Theses in Wittenberg on 31 October 1517. Tetzel responded in January 1518 with 106 counter-theses drawn up with the assistance of Konrad WIMPINA, and the papal diplomat Karl von MILTITZ tried in vain to constrain Tetzel in order to placate Luther, but Luther was fast moving towards the point at which he would not consider reconciliation. Tetzel withdrew to the Dominican convent in Leipzig, where he died on 4 July 1519.

Nikolaus Paulus, *Johann Tetzel der Ablaßprediger* (1899).

**TEUTONIC ORDER**. The military ORDER of German knights, priests, and lay brothers known in German as the Deutschorden and in Latin as the Ordo Fratrum Domus Hospitalis Sanctae Mariae Teutonicorum Ierosolymitani developed from a hospital community founded in Acre (Palestine) in 1190 and in 1198 was converted into a military order, initially under the rule of the Templars and from 1245 under its own rule.

The Order sought to advance the front line of Christendom, initially in Palestine, Syria, and Hungary, and then in Prussia (from 1231) and LIVONIA (from 1236). The Order's work in the Baltic extended beyond evangelism to civic administration and colonization by German settlers, who established German towns in the regions administered by the Order. In Prussia these towns included Thorn (1231, now Polish Toruń), Kulm (1232, now Polish Chełmno), Memel (1252, now Lithuanian Klaipeda), Königsberg (1255, now Russian Kaliningrad), Elbing (1327, now Polish Elbląg) and Marienwerder (1327, now Polish Kwidzyn); in 1309 the Order moved the seat of its grand masters (which had been moved from Acre to Venice in 1291) to Prussian Marienburg (now Polish Malbork). In COURLAND, the Order founded Windau (1237, now Latvian Ventspils) and Pilten (now Latvian Piltene), and in Semgallen (formerly called Semigallia) it founded Dünaburg (1274, Russian Dvinsk, later Daugavpils). In Livonia the Order established colonies in the already-established towns of Riga (which resisted the authority of the knights) and Wenden (now Latvian Cesis), and established the town of Dorpat (1224, Russian Yuryev, later Tartu). In

1309 the Order extended its rule to the west by conquering Pomerania, and in 1346 it reached the limit of its expansion eastwards with the conquest of ESTONIA. Ivangorod (now Polish Dęblin) was occupied by the Order from 1329 to 1383, and Samogitia (now Lithuanian Zemaitija) from 1398 to 1411.

The union of Poland and Lithuania in 1386 signalled the acceptance of Catholicism throughout the territories controlled by the Order, and also set the secular authorities against the Order. In 1410 the army of the Order was defeated by Polish-Lithuanian forces at the battle of Tannenberg (Polish Stębark), and thereafter the authority of the Order diminished and resistance to its administration increased. In 1525, ALBRECHT VON PREUSSEN, the grand master of the Order, converted to Lutheranism, resigned his office, and became the first HOHENZOLLERN duke of Prussia. The Order soon lost its possessions in Livonia, and the removal of its headquarters from Marienburg to Mergentheim (Swabia) signalled the end of its hegemony in the Baltic. The Order still survives, but its most prominent members are the women who work in military hospitals.

**THEATINES,** a religious order, also known as Clerks Regular of the Divine Providence, founded in Rome in 1524 by CAJETAN, Giampietro Carafa (later Pope PAUL IV), and two other members of the ORATORY OF DIVINE LOVE; the Order was named after Giampietro's episcopal see of Chieti, or 'Theate'. The purpose of the Order was to purge the Church of abuses and ecclesiastical scandals. Theatines abjured personal property and were forbidden to beg; their lives were characterized by uncompromising personal austerity. The only feature of their habit that distinguished them from secular priests was the wearing of white socks. The Order quickly spread throughout Italy, and to Spain and central Europe, but it never became large. In 1583 a congregation of Theatine nuns was established.

**THEATRE.** The Theatre vies with the problematic case of the Red Lion (1567) for the claim to be the first purpose-built public playhouse. Opened in 1576, it was built in Shoreditch, London, by James Burbage, member of LEICESTER'S MEN and father of Richard BURBAGE. It was located outside the City boundary owing to the lord mayor's opposition to theatre, but nevertheless experienced some harassment from the authorities. The theatre was a circular, wooden, and roofless building, with a raised platform stage; admission was a penny for standing room, two pennies for admission to the galleries. It was used for fencing, sporting, and other entertainments, as well as for play performances. In 1594 it became the base for the CHAMBERLAIN'S MEN. In 1597 Burbage's lease on the land came to an end; the following year, the building was dismantled and the materials taken across the river to Bankside, to be used in the construction of the GLOBE.

**THEATRE IN LONDON INNS.** Before the widespread availability of purpose-built theatres, itinerant companies of players often performed in innyards; trestle tables might provide a temporary and improvised stage. Play performances are recorded in a number of London inns throughout the last

quarter of the sixteenth century. In the City, the Bel Savage on Ludgate Hill (1579–88), the Bell (1576–83), the Bull Inn on Bishopsgate Street (1575–94), and the Cross Keys (1579–c.1596) saw performances, as did the Boar's Head in Aldgate, the Red Lion in Stepney, and the Saracen's Head in Islington. The RED BULL Inn in Clerkenwell, in whose yard plays were performed, was converted into a theatre in 1605 and became a base for QUEEN ANNE'S MEN.

**THEATRES AND THEATRE ARCHITECTURE.** The revival of interest in classical drama in the Renaissance led in turn to a growth in theatre building. In sixteenth-century Italy, theatre architecture was based on classical models, most notably in PALLADIO's Teatro Olimpico at Vicenza. First used in 1585, its acting area was backed by a *scaenae frons*, with five openings for entrances and exits, and faced an orchestra space and semicircular seating for the audience. Serlio, the most important writer on theatre architecture, developed the perspective scenery; his *Second Book of Architecture* was published in French in 1545 and in English in 1611.

Outdoor theatre in England had rather different origins, developing from the *ad hoc* arrangements for plays in innyards (see THEATRE IN LONDON INNS), great halls, pageant wagons, and other spaces. Such playhouses as the GLOBE had a thrust or apron stage surrounded by a courtyard and galleries; there was little or no representative scenery. Indoor theatres were more influenced by Italian models; the COCKPIT Theatre, for instance, on which Inigo Jones collaborated, drew on Jones's findings during his visit to Vicenza. Other characteristics of Italian theatre—elaborate stage LIGHTING and perspective scenery—were used by Jones in his productions of court MASQUES.

**THEOBALDS,** a palace and garden near Waltham Cross, in Hertfordshire, built between 1575 and 1585 for William CECIL, Lord Burghley. The two gardens were both square, and were laid out beneath the principal apartments of the house; in this respect they imitated the royal gardens (see ENGLISH GARDENS), albeit on a grander scale. The design of the gardens was probably the work of Cecil and the herbalist John GERARD. The private garden (Privy Garden) to the west, which was overlooked by the rooms of the Cecil family, was laid out in hedges and knots (see KNOT GARDENS). The Great Garden, to the south, which was overlooked by the state apartments, was a garden of more than 1 hectare (2 acres) divided into nine squares, with a FOUNTAIN in the central square. Paul Hentzner, a German traveller who attended Cecil's funeral in 1598, described MAZES, a fountain with a *jet d'eau*, and a semicircular PAVILION with marble busts of the twelve Roman emperors (*Itinerarium Germaniae, Galliae, Angliae, Italiae*, 1612). The canal which surrounded the Great Garden when Hentzner visited was supplemented a few years later by two artificial rivers and a MOUNT.

The palace was dismantled in the seventeenth century, and replaced by four houses, of which one remains (Old Palace House); the site of the gardens is now a park.

Roy Strong, *The Renaissance Garden in England* (1979).

**THEOPHRASTUS IN THE RENAISSANCE.** Theophrastus (*c.*372 BC–287 BC) was the successor to Aristotle as scholarch of the Peripatos. He was primarily a scientist rather than a philosopher; his main scientific treatises centred on botany (especially taxonomy and physiology), but he also wrote on natural phenomena and human physiology. In the late Renaissance it was his *Characters*, a collection of 30 character sketches, which created a new genre, initially in English literature; the distinctive feature of the Theophrastian character is that it describes types rather than individuals.

English character-writing originates in Isaac CASAUBON's edition of the *Characters*, with Latin translations (1592). In 1608 Joseph Hall published his *Characters of Virtues and Vices*, so bringing the form into English. Sir Thomas OVERBURY produced a volume of *Characters* (1614) in collaboration with John DONNE, Thomas DEKKER, and John WEBSTER, and this collection ran through many editions. In 1628 John Earle published a collection of Theophrastian characters called *Microcosmographie*, which responded to Overbury by proposing alternatives to some of his characters.

On the Continent the form was slow to develop, but it took root in France, where Jean de la Bruyère published his *Caractères de Théophrastes, traduits du grec, avec les caractères ou les mœurs de ce siècle* (1688).

**THEORBO,** a member of the lute family similar to, and sometimes synonymous with, the CHITTARONE. The neck extends beyond the pegbox to a further pegbox, allowing for additional bass strings, which are slightly offset to avoid crossing the shorter strings which were stopped by the player's left hand. It is first mentioned in Bastiano de' Rossi's *Descrizione dell'apparato, e degl'intermedi* (1589), which describes the Medici wedding celebrations.

**THERMES, PAUL DE LA BARTHE, SEIGNEUR DE** (1482–1562), French soldier, born in Gascony. He fought in Naples (1528) and was subsequently captured by BARBARY PIRATES; he was released after the payment of a ransom. In 1544 he was captured by imperial forces during the course of the French victory at Ceresole (French Cérisoles), and in 1550 successfully defended Parma against the imperial army. In 1558, at the age of 76, he led the French army to defeat at the battle of Gravelines, in which he was captured by the Flemish forces of the count of EGMONT.

**THIRTY YEARS WAR or (German) Dreißigjähriger Krieg,** a series of wars that began with the DEFENESTRATION OF PRAGUE in 1618 and spread throughout the HOLY ROMAN EMPIRE, eventually enveloping most of continental Europe. The fighting is conventionally distinguished into five phases: first, the Bohemian War (1618–20), in which the Emperor Ferdinand II, with the assistance of Spanish finance and troops, Bavarian Catholics, and the papacy, defeated the Bohemian Protestants led by Friedrich V, elector palatine of the Rhine and king of Bohemia; second, the Palatinate War (1621–3), in which a Bavarian army under Johann Tzerclaes, Graf von Tilly, and Spanish troops under Ambrogio di Spinola conquered the Upper Palatinate, and Spain and the Nether-

lands renewed the REVOLT OF THE NETHERLANDS, which had been suspended in 1609; third, the Danish War (1624–29), in which the imperial army of Albrecht Eusebius von Wallenstein defeated a coalition led by CHRISTIAN IV of Denmark; fourth, the Swedish War (1630–5), in which Gustavus II Adolphus of Sweden conquered north Germany and defeated Wallenstein at the cost of his own life; fifth, the Franco-Habsburg War (1635–48), a pan-European war in which the French fought the Spanish in France, Italy, Spain, and (with Swedish assistance) along the Rhine, the Dutch fought the Spanish in the southern Netherlands, the Swedes reconquered north Germany and repeatedly invaded Bohemia and Moravia, the Danes fought the Swedes in the second Swedish-Danish War, and the French and Swedish armies advanced through Bavaria and Bohemia to Vienna, which was saved by news of the Treaty of Westphalia (Westfälischer Friede, 14/24 October 1648), which concluded the Thirty Years War, though France and Spain remained at war until 1659.

**THOMAS À KEMPIS or Thomas van Kempen** (*c.*1380–1471), Netherlandish devotional writer, born into a peasant family in Kempen (near Krefeld), the son of Johann and Gertrude Hemerken. At the age of 12 he was sent to a monastery in Deventer (in the Netherlands) to be educated. In 1399 he entered the new Augustinian monastery at St Agnietenberg (near Zwolle, in the Netherlands), where his brother Johan was prior. There he spent the rest of his life as a monk, taking vows in 1407, being ordained as a priest in 1413, becoming sub-prior in 1425 and dying at the age of 91 on 8 August 1471.

Thomas was a prolific writer of devotional works, hymns, and sermons. His most famous work, the *Imitatio Christi* (of which his authorship is a likelihood rather than a certainty), is said to have been translated into more languages than any book except for the Bible.

**THOMAS AQUINAS IN THE RENAISSANCE.** The memory of the Dominican friar and theologian Thomas (the adjectival Latin form of whose birthplace, Aquino, is sometimes treated as a surname) was kept alive after his death in 1274 by his two most important theological works, *Summa contra gentiles* ('A Compendium to Confute the Pagans') and *Summa theologica*, by his canonization in 1323, and by a succession of learned Dominican commentaries on his works. The origins of Renaissance Thomism can be traced to 1403, when the Thomists of the University of Paris, who had been expelled in 1387, were readmitted. The first great exponent of Thomism was the Dominican John Capreolus (*c.*1378–1444), whose *Defensiones theologiae divi Thomae Aquinatus* (1409–33) against the attacks of detractors such as Henry of Ghent, Duns Scotus, Durandus of Saint-Pourçain, and William of Ockham revived the authority of Thomism after a century of relative obscurity and secured for Capreolus the sobriquet *Thomistarum princeps*. The other seminal figure in the Thomism of this period was Henry of Gorkum (*c.*1378–1421), whose *Quaestiones in summa sancti Thomae*, which was a popular version of Thomas's *Summa theologica*, greatly increased awareness of Thomas's teachings. Henry's migration from Paris to Cologne in 1419 created a second centre for Thomist studies, and the Cologne school of Thomists which emerged in the late fifeenth century was destined to nurture a formidable enemy in Martin LUTHER.

Luther was unusual amongst reformers in engaging seriously with Thomism, though he had a worthy successor in Martin BUCER; contemporaries such as CALVIN and ZWINGLI showed little interest in Thomism. Luther's confrontation with the Thomists was both sudden and sustained. On 1 November 1517 Luther pinned his theses to the door of the castle church in Wittenberg. In 1518 alone, he was attacked by Thomists such as Konrad WIMPINA (who wrote a set of theses to counter Luther's), Johann TETZEL (who defended Wimpina and exchanged pamphlet attacks with Luther), Silvestre MAZZOLINI, and Cardinal CAJETAN. This formidable Thomist quartet was a harbinger of some 30 Dominican Thomists who were to attack Luther in years to come.

The growth of Thomism in Catholic circles continued unchecked by Luther's fulminations, and may even have been fuelled by the emergence of such an opponent. In the first half of the sixteenth century the most distinguished scholars were the Spanish Thomists, who included Domingo de SOTO, Melchor CANO, Bartolomé MEDINA, and Francisco de VITORIA. At the COUNCIL OF TRENT Thomas's *Summa theologica* was accorded particular authority, and prominent Thomists at the Council ensured that many of the Tridentine decrees reflected the doctrine and even the phrasing of the *Summa theologica*. In 1567, four years after the Council, Pope PIUS V declared Thomas to be a doctor of the Church and ranked his festival (which was fixed at 7 March until 1970) equal to those of the four original *doctores ecclesiae* (Gregory, Ambrose, Augustine, and Jerome). Several religious orders arising out of the Counter-Reformation claimed Thomas as a progenitor, and in the case of the JESUITS this appropriation of Thomas created a new generation of Thomist scholars, including Luis de MOLINA, Francisco SUÁREZ, Roberto BELLARMINO, and their opponent (in the theological debate about congruism) Gabriel VÁZQUEZ.

**THORN, PEACE OF** (1411 and 1466), the English name of two treaties concluded in Thorn (now Polish Toruń) between Poland and the TEUTONIC knights. The first treaty (1411) followed the defeat of the knights by VLADISLAV II at the battle of Tannenberg (1410; now Polish Stębark), and under its terms the knights paid indemnities and transferred land to Poland. By the terms of the second treaty (1466), which concluded a thirteen-year war (1454–66), the knights forfeited much of their western territories to Poland, including Elbing (now Polish Elbląg), Kulm (now Polish Chełmno), Marienburg (now Polish Malbork), and Pomerania. The knights lost their border with the German lands and the Poles gained access to the Baltic Sea.

**THORPE, JOHN** (*c.*1565–1655), English surveyor, born into a family of stonemasons in the village of King's Cliffe (Northants). In 1570, while still a young child, he laid the foundation stone at Kirby Hall (Northants), where his father was employed as a mason. He was employed by the Office of Works from 1584 to 1601 and then established himself as an independent land surveyor.

A book of Thorpe's plans and drawings in Sir John Soane's Museum (London) gave rise to the view that Thorpe was the architect of many of the great houses of England, including Audley End (Essex), Longford Castle (Wilts.), Longleat (Wilts.), Rushton Hall (Northants), WOLLATON (Notts.), and the first version of Holland House (Kensington). Investigation of the houses whose plans and elevations are represented in the volume has shown that many were built before or soon after his birth, and that Thorpe was surveying existing buildings rather than designing new ones. A few of the designs do not describe any known house of the period, and so may be original, but there is no documentary evidence that Thorpe was an architect.

*DNB; MDA; The Book of Architecture of John Thorpe in Sir John Soane's Museum*, ed. John Summerson (1966).

**THUANUS or Jacques Auguste de Thou** (1555–1617), French historian, born into a family of jurists; he was the son and grandson of presidents of the Parlement of Paris. He studied law at Orléans, Bourges (where he met HOTMAN), and Valence (where he was taught by CUJAS and became a friend of Joseph SCALIGER). After an early career in the Church he moved to a secular career, and in 1588 he married, entered the Parlement, and became a *conseiller d'état*. His *Historia sui temporis* (5 vols., 1604–20), a survey of French history from 1545 to 1584, is the most detailed contemporary account of the WARS OF RELIGION. In his analysis Thuanus gives a particularly sympathetic role to his patron King HENRI IV, but nonetheless tries to remain just and impartial in his judgements. Part II of the Historia, which covered the period 1560–72, was placed on the INDEX on 9 November 1609, and in 1614 Thuanus was accused of heresy by a Jesuit. After the death of King Henri he was excluded from public life; he died in Paris on 7 May 1617.

*S. Kinser, The Works of J.-A. de Thou* (1966).

**TIBALDI or Pellegrino Pellegrini** (1527–96), Italian painter, sculptor, and architect, a native of Bologna who from 1549 to 1553 lived in Rome, where he fell under the influence of MICHELANGELO. On returning to Bologna he painted his finest work, a series of scenes from the *Odyssey* in Palazzo Poggi, which is now part of Bologna University. In the 1560s and 1570s Tibaldi worked as an architect, usually under the patronage of Cardinal Carlo BORROMEO, for whom he built the Collegio Borromeo in Pavia (1564), the Jesuit Church of San Fidele in Milan (1569, one year after the construction of the Gesù in Rome), the round Church of San Sebastiano in Milan (1576), and the austere Canonica courtyard of the Archiepiscopal Palace in Milan (commissioned 1565, begun 1572). From 1567 to 1576 he served as principal architect of Milan Cathedral, in which capacity he built the crypt under the choir and erected the barriers between the choir and the ambulatory.

In 1587 Tibaldi travelled to Madrid to supervise the decorative works of the ESCORIAL, to which he contributed sculptural decoration and a series of 46 frescoes in the library. He returned to Milan a few months before his death.

*MDA; Michael Scholz-Hänsel, Eine spanische Wissenschaftsutopie am Ende des 16. Jahrhunderts: Die Bibliothekfresken von Pellegrino Pelligrini im Escorial (1987); A. Mazzotta and G. Panizza, Pellegrino Pellegrini: L'architettura (1990); Stefano della Torre, Pellegrino Tibaldi architetto e il S. Fedele di Milano (1994).*

**TILES.** Glazed pottery tiles were manufactured for use as pavement in the ancient Middle East, but not in ancient Greece and Rome. The art of making such tiles in early modern Europe was not revived from classical antiquity, but was rather adopted from the Arabic tradition which was transmitted through Portugal and Spain to the rest of Europe. The tiles that embodied both the technology and the designs were the AZULEJOS of Portugal and Spain, which were exported throughout the Mediterranean. In the fifteenth century, Italian potteries in FAENZA and Naples responded to the importation of Spanish tiles by manufacturing their own MAIOLICA tiles. Italian tiles were made for floors rather than for the decoration of walls, and they differed from *azulejos* in that each tile had a complete design.

Italian techniques facilitated a broader range of colours than was available to Iberian potters, and by the early sixteenth century Italian technology had been carried to Spain and Portugal by potters such as Francisco NICULOSO of Pisa, who opened a pottery in Seville and introduced the idea of a single pictorial design made up of panels of *azulejos*. Such designs were taken up by other potters, including Cristóbal de AUGUSTA and Jan FLORIS DE VRIENDT. The fashion for pictorial tiles spread to Flanders and thence to Friesland and Holland. In these northern centres polychrome was eventually abandoned in favour of the blue monochrome which became associated with Delft, which dominated the European tile industry from the seventeenth to the nineteenth centuries.

Early examples of floor tiles survive in France, notably the twelfth-century tiles in the Basilica (now Cathedral) of Saint-Denis (now a suburb of Paris), but it only became a significant art form in the sixteenth century; the finest example is the tile pavement attributed to Masséot ABAQUESNE and made for the Château d'Écouen (now the Musée de la Renaissance) between 1542 and 1549.

**TILL EULENSPIEGEL.** In sixteenth-century Germany the most important form of popular literature was the *Volksbuch*, a prose narrative genre that could be structured either as a single continuous narrative or as a series of episodes. The most popular of the *Volksbücher* was *Till Eulenspiegel*, a collection of comic stories connected only by the presence of the eponymous hero; the lack of any narrative thread means that *Till Eulenspiegel* is in effect a collection of SCHWÄNKE. Till is a clever peasant and practical joker who victimizes the rich, and so resembles the *pícaro* of Spanish PICARESQUE literature. The historical Till with whom the stories came to be associated was a peasant from Kneitlingen (Brunswick) who died

in Mölln in 1350, but the stories seem to have been kept alive solely by oral transmission for more than a century. The earliest surviving edition is a High German version of 1515, but details of spelling have led scholars to believe that this text derives from a lost Low German original of about 1480.

Richard Strauss wrote his *Tondichtung* (tone-poem) *Till Eulenspiegels lustige Streiche* in 1895, and in 1928 the Nobel laureate Gerhart Hauptmann published a modern *Eulenspiegel*, a verse epic in hexameters.

**TINCTORIS, JOHANNES DE** (*c.*1435–1511), Flemish musical theorist, composer, painter, lawyer, and mathematician who was *petit vicaire* at Cambrai and responsible for the choirboys at Chartres Cathedral. In 1463 he became procurator of the German nation at Orléans where he studied law. He became legal adviser and teacher of theoretical and practical music at the court of FERRANTE I in Naples in the early 1470s. During his time in Italy he moved in intellectual humanist circles. His twelve surviving treatises cover musical pitch, rhythmic notation, the modal system, contrapuntal writing, and musical terms. *De inventione et usu musicae* (1481–3) is concerned with the origins of music and performance practice. His theoretical work was highly regarded throughout Europe and influenced Franchino GAFFURIO.

**TIN-GLAZED EARTHENWARE,** pottery decorated with a technique that originated in the Islamic world and entered medieval Europe through Spain. After the pottery has been fired it is dipped in a glaze consisting of lead and tin oxides mixed with potash. The resultant glaze is white, but may be coloured with designs in pigments derived from metallic oxides. The vessel is then fired again, which fixes the glaze.

Italian tin-glazed earthenware is called MAIOLICA, but in France, Germany, Scandinavia, and Spain it is called FAIENCE, a term derived from the Italian potteries in FAENZA.

**TINO DI CAMAINO** (*c.*1280–1337), Italian sculptor and architect, a native of Siena who worked in Siena, Pisa, Florence, and (from 1324 until his death) Naples. Tino was primarily a carver of tombs, including those of the Emperor Henry VII (of which the surviving portions are in the Museo dell'Opera del Duomo in Pisa), Bishop Orso (Florence Cathedral), and, one of his most important works, Cardinal Riccardo Petroni (Siena Cathedral). The seated effigy of Bishop Orso is the earliest known example, and it is possible that Tino invented this memorial pose. In Naples Tino carved tabernacled tombs for the Angevin court (including Queen Mary of Hungary's tomb in Santa Maria Donna Regina) and worked as an architect on the reconstruction of the Monastery of San Martino.

*MDA; Wilhelm Valentiner, Tino di Camaino, a Sienese Sculptor of the Fourteenth Century (1935).*

**TINTORETTO or Jacopo Robusti** (1519–94), Italian painter, born in Venice, the son of a dyer (Italian *tintore*, hence *tintoretto*, 'little dyer'). Tintoretto's early life is not well documented, but he seems to have trained for a short period in the studio of TITIAN; by 1539 he was established as an

Tintoretto, *Susanna and the Elders* (*c.*1556), in the Kunsthistorisches Museum, Vienna

independent artist. In 1547 he painted *The Last Supper* (also known as *The Institution of the Eucharist*) in the Church of San Marcuola, and the following year he painted *St Mark Rescuing a Slave* (1548, Accademia, Venice; also known as *The Miracle of the Slave*), one of four paintings commissioned by the Scuola di San Marco; this painting is an early product of Tintoretto's unusual method of composition, whereby he made small wax models of his figures and then experimented with various possibilities for composition and lighting. He sometimes reused these models, which is why Tintoretto's pictures sometimes repeat the same figures but portray them from different angles.

In the 1550s and early 1560s Tintoretto painted *Cain and Abel* (*c.*1550, Accademia, Venice), *The Discovery of the Body of St Mark* (1562, Brera, Milan), and one of his most famous works, *Susanna and the Elders* (*c.*1556, Kunsthistorisches Museum, Vienna); variations on the voluptuous nude figure of Susanna appear in *The Liberation of Arsinoë* (1554–6, Gemäldegalerie, Dresden) and *The Origin of the Milky Way* (*c.*1575, National Gallery, London). During this period Tintoretto also painted three vast pictures for the Church of Madonna dell'Orto

(where he is buried): *The Worship of the Golden Calf* and *The Last Judgement*, on either side of the altar, are 15 metres (50 feet) high; the finest of the three pictures is *The Presentation of the Virgin* (1551), which hangs over the sacristy door.

From 1565 to 1587 Tintoretto worked on a series of more than 50 paintings on biblical themes for the Scuola di San Rocco; excellently restored in recent decades, these paintings provide evidence to counter the tenacious view that MANNERIST art represents a decline from the standards of the High Renaissance, and the series should be valued (as it was by Ruskin) for its grandeur of conception alongside MICHELANGELO's Sistine Chapel ceiling and RAPHAEL's Vatican *Stanze*. During the latter part of his work on the Scuola di San Rocco Tintoretto also worked with VERONESE on the redecoration of the Doge's palace after the fire of 1577. His paintings in the Palace include huge works on *The Siege of Zara* (1584–7) and *Paradise* (1588).

Tintoretto's son Domenico (1562–1635) worked as an assistant to his father and executed many portraits, but the canon of his work is uncertain; Jacopo was commissioned to paint the portrait sequence of 76 doges in the Sala del Maggior

Tintoretto, *The Crucifixion* (1565), on the end wall of the Sala dell'Albergo in the Scuola di San Rocco, Venice

Consiglio of the Ducal Palace, but the portraits are substantially the work of Domenico and the Tintoretto studio.

MDA; Giandomenico Romanelli, *Tintoretto: La Scuola grande di San Rocco* (1994).

**TIRSO DE MOLINA or Fray Gabriel Téllez or El Mercedario** (1583–1648), Spanish playwright and novelist. He was educated at Alcalá de Henares and joined the Mercedarian Order in 1601, after which he continued his studies in Guadalajara. From 1605 to 1615 he was based in Toledo, where he began to write plays and prose fiction under the pseudonym 'Tirso de Molina', by which he is now known; in 1621 he was to claim in his *Los cigarreles de Toledo* (published 1624) that he had already written 300 *comedias*. He travelled in Galicia and Portugal and in 1616 travelled to Hispaniola for two years, after which he lived for a time in Madrid. In 1625 he was censured by the Council of Castile for his depictions of vice on the stage and ordered to refrain from writing secular plays. His final years were spent as a friar in his Order, of which he wrote a history (*Historia general de la Orden de Nuestra Señora de la Merced*) that remained unpublished until 1974.

As a friar, Tirso was known as Fray Gabriel or El Mercedario ('the Mercedarian'). His pseudonym was an allusion to Luis de MOLINA and his doctrine of GRACE; Tirso's *molinista* sympathies are readily apparent in his theological comedy *El condenado por desconfiado*.

Tirso wrote more than 400 plays, and some 85 surviving plays are attributed to him. His most important play is *El burlador de Sevilla y convividado de piedra*, which introduced the story of the womanizing Don Juan and the statue of the Comendador into European literature.

**TISSARD, FRANÇOIS** (d. 1508), French humanist. He was born in Amboise and educated in Paris and Orléans before moving to Italy to study Greek and Hebrew. He was

appointed to a chair at the University of Paris, where he edited works by ancient Greek authors, including Pythagoras. In 1508, shortly before his death, Tissard published the first Hebrew grammar in France.

**TITIAN or (Italian) Tiziano Vecellio** (c.1489–1576), Italian painter, born in Pieve di Cadore (Veneto); he trained in the Venetian studio of Giovanni BELLINI and subsequently worked on the external decoration of the Fondaco dei Tedeschi as an assistant to GIORGIONE, whose style he emulated so exactly that some paintings (e.g. *Concert champêtre*, Louvre) could be by either artist.

Titian's earliest documented work is a group of three frescoes in the Scuola del Santo in Padua (1511). On returning to Venice, Titian painted the altarpiece of *St Mark with Four Saints* (c.1511; now housed in the Santa Maria della Salute) and his first masterpiece, *Sacred and Profane Love* (c.1514, Galleria Borghese, Rome). In the ten-year period between 1516 and 1525 Titian painted the works that were to establish him as the principal painter in Venice for the next 50 years. The best-known portrait of this period is *Man with a Glove* (c.1520, Louvre). A series of altarpieces includes his *Assumption* (1516–18, Santa Maria dei Frari, Venice), a *Resurrection* triptych with a magnificent *St Sebastian* (1518–22, SS Nazaro e Celso, Brescia), a *Madonna and Saints with a Donor* (1520, Galleria Comunale Francesco Podesti, Ancona), the *Pesaro Madonna* (1519–26, Santa Maria dei Frari, Venice), and the celebrated *St Peter Martyr* (1525–30, painted for the Venetian Church of SS Giovanni e Paolo but now lost and known only from copies). Secular pictures from this period include allegories, notably *Three Ages of Man* (c.1514, National Gallery, Edinburgh), portraits, and three mythological pictures (1518–23) commissioned by Alfonso I d'ESTE for the Camerino d'Alabastro in the castle in Ferrara: *Worship of Venus* (Prado, Madrid), *Bacchanal* (Prado), and *Bacchus and Ariadne* (National Gallery, London).

In the 1530s the style of Titian's paintings changed: compositions became less flamboyant and more contemplative, and juxtaposed colours were increasingly used to complement rather than contrast. His paintings during this decade include a portrait of CHARLES V with his dog (1533, Prado), based on one by Jakob SEISENEGGER, a portrait of Doge Andrea GRITTI (National Gallery, Washington), and portraits of Francesco Maria DELLA ROVERE, duke of Urbino, and of his duchess (1536–8, Uffizi). During this period he also painted the *Presentation of the Virgin* (1534–8, Accademia, Venice), the *Pardo Venus* (*c.*1535–40, Louvre), and the *Venus of Urbino* (*c.*1538, Uffizi).

In the early 1540s Titian painted his *Ecce homo* (Kunsthistorisches Museum, Vienna), a *Crowning with Thorns* (Louvre), and three large ceiling canvases of biblical figures (*c.*1543–4; now in Santa Maria della Salute) for SANSOVINO's Church of Santo Spirito, which was demolished in the late seventeenth century. In 1545 Titian made his only journey to Rome, where his paintings were admired; his *Danaë* (Museo Nazionale, Naples) was praised for its colour, but, according to VASARI, criticized by MICHELANGELO for poor draughtsmanship. While in Rome he painted his unfinished portrait of *Pope Paul III and his Nephews* (Museo Nazionale, Naples). Titian returned to Venice in 1546, and two years later was summoned by Charles V to Augsburg, where he painted two portraits of the emperor: the EQUESTRIAN PORTRAIT of Charles at the battle of MÜHLBERG (Prado) and a seated portrait (Alte Pinakothek, Munich).

In the 1550s Titian's most important patron was Philip of Spain (later King PHILIP II), of whom he painted several portraits (notably *Philip of Spain in Armour*, 1550–1, Prado) and for whom he painted in 1554 a series of mythological pictures that Titian described as *poesie*, including another *Danaë* (Prado), *Venus and Adonis* (Prado), and *Perseus and Andromeda* (1554, Wallace Collection, London); in the same year he painted *La Gloria* (Prado), a double portrait of the emperor (in his death shroud) and his dead consort, Isabella of

**Titian**, *The Assumption of the Virgin* (1516–18), in the Church of Santa Maria dei Frari, in Venice

**Titian**, *Sacred and Profane Love* (*c.*1514), Galleria Borghese, Rome

Titian, *Bacchus and Ariadne* (1521–3), in the National Gallery, London

Portugal, being presented to God. In 1559–60 Titian executed two more *poesie* for King Philip, the *Rape of Europa* (Isabella Stewart Gardner Museum, Boston) and *Diana and Actaeon* (London, National Gallery). His most important religious picture of this decade was a *Martyrdom of St Lawrence* (Gesuiti, Venice).

In the 1560s and 1570s Titian worked primarily as a studio painter. His own paintings included a second version of the *Martyrdom of St Lawrence* (c.1570, Escorial), a second version of the *Crowning of Thorns* (c.1570, Alte Pinakothek, Munich), the pastoral idyll *Shepherd and Nymph* (c.1570, Alte Pinakothek, Munich), and the *Pietà* (c.1573–6, Accademia, Venice) left unfinished at his death and completed by PALMA GIOVANE.

*MDA*; Charles Hope, *Titian* (1980).

**TOEPUT, LODEWIJK, or Il Pozzoserrato** (c.1550–c.1603/5), Flemish painter who moved to Venice in the mid-1570s, and may have seen the fire in the Doge's Palace which he subsequently painted (1577, Museo Civico Bailo Treviso). After periods of residence in Florence (late 1570s) and Rome (1581) Toeput settled in Treviso (Veneto). He was primarily a painter of LANDSCAPES (e.g. *Landscape with a Hermit*, 1601, Alte Pinakothek, Munich). Several of his paintings depict COMMEDIA DELL'ARTE performances.

*MDA*.

**TOLEDO or (Latin) Toletum or (Arabic) Tulaitula or (Hebrew) Toledoth**, an ancient city and archbishopric on the Tagus in central Spain and the capital of Visigothic Spain, was once a Roman colonia and in late antiquity was the host of some 30 church councils between the fifth and sixteenth centuries; the city was also the centre of an ancient Jewish settlement. In 712 Toledo was occupied by the Moors, becoming an important city in the caliphate of Córdoba (712–1035) and then an independent emirate (1035–85). In 1085 Toledo was captured by King Alfonso VI of León and Castile, who made Toledo his capital in 1087. Islamic tolerance of Judaism was maintained by Christian rulers for several centuries, but gradually gave way to Christian intolerance: there was a pogrom in 1391 and in 1492 the JEWS were finally expelled; in 1502 Islam was also proscribed. The city had an important Mozarabic community (Arabic-speaking Christians), which abandoned the use of Arabic in the twelfth century but retained its own special liturgy, the Mozarabic rite, which elsewhere had been replaced by the Roman rite. In 1580 the community was granted a special licence to use the Mozarabic rite in church services, a privilege that has been exercised to the present day.

The archbishops of Toledo, who at the Council of 681 became the primates of the Spanish Church, enjoyed wealth and power that was virtually unrivalled. Cardinal CISNEROS, the most prominent of the archbishops, was one of the most powerful figures in Spain, and even commanded its armies. The University of Toledo was founded in 1498, and remained in the city until 1845. In 1520–1 Toledo was the seat of the Revolt of the COMUNEROS, which was precipitated by the accession of Charles I (later CHARLES V) to the throne of Castile. In 1560 PHILIP II established his capital in nearby Madrid, and thereafter the political and commercial importance of Toledo declined. Toledo was the setting of many of the plays of Lope de VEGA (who was a Toledan), and its covered Zocodover is described by CERVANTES in his *Novelas ejemplares*.

The city is dominated by the Gothic cathedral and by the Alcázar, a Moorish citadel that was converted into a palace by FERDINAND and ISABELLA, Charles V, and Philip II; it was destroyed by fire in 1710, 1810, and 1887 and left in ruins by the shelling of the siege of 1936, but the restorations have re-created important Renaissance features, including the façade of Juan de HERRERA, the Bisagra Gate of Alonso de COVARRUBIAS, and the staircase of Herrera and Francisco de Villalpando.

In the cathedral, Covarrubias built the magnificent Chapel of the New Kings (Capilla de los Reyes Nuevos, 1531–4); his other works in Toledo include the Hospital de Tavera (from 1537). Renaissance work in the cathedral includes some 750 Flemish stained-glass windows (1418–1561). The City Hall (Ayuntamiento) was remodelled by El GRECO. The Monasterio de San Juan de los Reyes, which has one of the finest cloisters in Spain, was commissioned by Ferdinand and Isabella in thanksgiving for the victory over the Portuguese at the battle of Toro in 1476, and built by Juan GUAS; the chains on the façade were taken from the Christians freed from Moorish captivity after the conquest of GRANADA.

Toledo swords have been famous for millennia: the *culter toletanus* is mentioned in the *Cynegetica* of Grattius Faliscus (a contemporary of Ovid), and the industry, which flourished under the Moors, reached the peak of its reputation in the sixteenth century.

**TOLEDO, FRANCISCO DE** (1515–82), the fifth Spanish viceroy of Peru, the second son of the count of Oropesa. His early career was spent as a soldier in the service of CHARLES V. In 1568 Don Francisco was appointed viceroy of Peru by King PHILIP II. He arrived in Lima on 26 November 1569, and immediately embarked on a two-year tour of his viceregal domain, attending in particular to the development of mining and the organization of local administration, in which he reverted in some measure to the indigenous system of governance by native chiefs, who were required to raise tribute money and discharge magisterial functions, including the organization of forced labour.

In 1570 Toledo established a tribunal of the Spanish INQUISITION in Peru. He also ordered the ferocious suppression of Indian rebellions, culminating in the execution in 1572 of Tupac Amaru, the last descendant of the Inca emperors, and the destruction of the most holy religious relics of the Incas. In 1581 Don Francisco retired to Spain.

DHE; Roberto Levillier, *Don Francisco de Toledo, supremo organizador del Perú: Su vida, su obra* (vol. i, 1935; vols. ii and iii, 1940–2); León Gómez Rivas, *El virrey del Perú don Francisco de Toledo* (1994).

**TOLEDO, JUAN BAUTISTA DE** (d. 1567), Spanish architect, philosopher, and mathematician who studied in Rome, where he is said to have assisted MICHELANGELO at ST PETER'S. He worked as viceregal architect in Naples before being recalled to Spain in 1559 by King PHILIP II to serve as royal architect in Madrid. He built the façade of the Church of the Convento de Descalzas Reales in Madrid, and in 1563 began work on the ESCORIAL, for which he drew the ground plan but built only the two-storeyed Patio de los Evangelistas (modelled on SANGALLO's Palazzo Farnese in Rome) and the forbiddingly severe south façade. On his death in 1567 he was succeeded by his assistant Juan de HERRERA, who in completing the building modified the plans, but the basic design is nonetheless that of Juan Bautista de Toledo.

G. Kubler, *Building the Escorial* (1982); José Javier Rivera Blanco, *Juan Bautista de Toledo y Felipe II* (1984).

**TOLEDO, PEDRO ÁLVAREZ DE** (1484–1553), Spanish viceroy of Naples, the son of the second duke of Alba. He served as a page to FERDINAND V, and inaugurated a distinguished military career in 1512 by participating in the conquest of Navarre; he subsequently fought in Germany and Italy, and in 1532 was appointed viceroy of Naples by CHARLES V.

Pedro de Toledo was a firm administrator: he suppressed banditry, expelled the JEWS in 1540, and instituted a tribunal of the INQUISITION, which led in 1547 to a popular revolt. He was also a patron of letters; writers at his court included GARCILASO DE LA VEGA, Juan de VALDÉS, and many Italian writers. His standing in Italy was reflected in the marriage of his daughter Eleanor to COSIMO I DE' MEDICI in 1539.

DHE; J. M. del Moral, *El virrey de Nápoles: Don Pedro de Toledo y la guerra contra el turco* (1966); Carlos José Hernando Sánchez, *Castilla y Nápoles en siglo XVI: El virrey Pedro de Toledo* (1994).

**TOLOMEI, CLAUDIO** (1492–1555), Italian poet, born in Siena, from which he was banished in 1526 because of his support for the MEDICI family. Thereafter he lived in Rome, Piacenza, and Siena (of which he became bishop in 1549), before returning to Siena as an honoured citizen; he subsequently led a Sienese diplomatic mission to France.

Tolomei's poems were avowedly Tuscan in language, and in the debate known as the QUESTIONE DELLA LINGUA he attempted to demonstrate the suitability of Tuscan as a literary language by applying Latin metres to vernacular poetry, as is evident in his *Versi e regole della nuova poesia toscana* (1539) and his *Il Cesano* (1555).

OCIL.

**TOMÁS DE JESÚS or Thomas à Jesu** (1564–1627), Spanish mystic who entered the Discalced Carmelite Order in 1587, and soon rose to become professor of theology at Seville, prior of Zaragoza, and provincial of Old Castile; he lived austerely (and at times as a hermit) in various Carmelite monasteries. In 1607 Tomás was called to Rome by Pope Paul V to expand the missionary work of his Order; in the short term his efforts were frustrated by the opposition of senior Spanish and Italian prelates, but his ideas were sustained in a cardinalitial commission (*De propaganda fide*) and eventually realized in the establishment of the Congregation for the Propagation of the Faith (Congregatio de Propaganda Fide) in 1622.

The literary results of Tomás's thinking about missionary endeavour were theoretical works entitled *Stimulus missionum* (1610) and *De procuranda salute omnium gentium* (1613). His best-known work, *De contemplatione divina* (Spanish *Sobre la contemplación divina*, 1620), is a spiritual guide in the tradition of Spanish mysticism.

**TOMBS AND MAUSOLEUMS.** The tomb re-emerged as an important art form in the eleventh century, when burials began to take place in churches; such tombs took the form of a sarcophagus or of an inscribed slab laid on the church floor. The term 'mausoleum' to denote a tomb of particular magnificence was revived in the Renaissance in allusion to the Mausoleum of Halicarnassus, which survived until 1522 in what is now Bodrum, in Turkey. Tombs were usually made of stone, though ALABASTER was sometimes used in England and BRASS was occasionally used in England and in Germany. In Italy, tombs tended to be attached to a wall, with the sarcophagus mounted within a niche, but in northern Europe they were usually free-standing.

Tombs often included an effigy in which the figure was shown in death as if asleep or, occasionally, as in life. Antonio POLLAIUOLO's tomb of Pope INNOCENT VIII (1492) in St Peter's Basilica in Rome depicts the pope seated as in life and lying recumbent as in death. In the sixteenth century, the representation typically (as in the French royal tombs at Saint-Denis) took the form of a *gisant*, in which the deceased was shown in death (sometimes as a skeleton or a mouldering corpse), above which was an *orant*, which was a depiction of the deceased as if alive.

In the late Middle Ages, the tombs of important personages were often surmounted by a canopy and the figure of the deceased was attended by small figures of mourners or, at a later stage, by angels. In Italian tombs, sculpted curtains sometimes hang from the canopy, and the curtains are parted by figures standing beside the sarcophagus. The small mourners, who are known as 'weepers', reached their apogee in the work of Claus SLUTER in Dijon (c.1404–11). By the end of the fifteenth century weepers had begun to carry the effigy of the deceased on a slab, and in sixteenth- and early seventeenth-century England and Flanders, the weepers were replaced as bearers by angels (who in the seventeenth century wore Roman armour) or by representations of the theological virtues (faith, hope, and charity) or the cardinal virtues (prudence, justice, temperance and fortitude). The number of mourners gradually increased, so that by the sixteenth century the tomb of the Emperor MAXIMILIAN I in Innsbruck consists of a sarcophagus (which is empty) surrounded by 24 figures of his ancestors.

In fourteenth-century Italy, tombs began to be erected outside churches, usually mounted on colonnettes in public squares. In 1380 PETRARCH's sarcophagus was mounted on the square outside the church in what is now Arquà Petrarca, and the DELLA SCALA family tombs were erected between 1277 and 1387 in the churchyard of Santa Maria Anticà in Verona.

The art of the tomb culminated in the early sixteenth century with MICHELANGELO's tombs for the MEDICI (1521–34) in the Church of San Lorenzo in Florence.

**TOMKINS, THOMAS** (1572–1656), Welsh composer who studied with William BYRD and, indirectly (through the pages of the *Plain and Easy Introduction*), with Thomas MORLEY. He was organist of Worcester Cathedral and a gentleman of the Chapel Royal, providing music for both. He wrote services, anthems, verse anthems, keyboard works, consort music, and madrigals; 'The fauns and satyrs tripping' appears in The TRIUMPHS OF ORIANA (1601).

**TOPIARY.** The art of shaping plants by clipping and training was practised in classical antiquity and revived in the late fifteenth century. The term derives from PLINY THE ELDER, who used the phrase *topiarium opus* (plural *topiaria opera*) both as a generic term for ornamental gardening and as a specific term for intricate tableaux carved from cypresses to depict fleets of ships, hunting scenes, and various natural and constructed landscapes such as woods, hills, lakes, canals, and streams. Topiary was revived in fifteenth-century Italy. The woodcuts in the *Hypnerotomachia Polifili* (1499) of Francesco COLONNA depicted elaborate topiary designs both in geometrical shapes and in representational images of humans, animals, and architectural forms. The most elaborate topiary known to have been executed in Italy was in the Orti Oricellari created by Bernardo RUCELLAI in the late fifteenth century. Among ENGLISH GARDENS, the best example of such topiary seems to have been in the Privy Garden at Hampton Court. The topiary described by English writers of the period is chiefly remarkable for the wide range of plants that were clipped and trained: the poet Barnabe Googe mentions in his translation of the *Four Books of Husbandry* (1577) from the Latin of *Rei rusticae libri quatuor* (Cologne, 1570) by Konrad Heresbach (1496–1576) that rosemary was popular with women gardeners, who clipped it in such shapes as carts and peacocks; John PARKINSON recommends privet, deprecates box as a novelty, and acknowledges the popularity of thrift (sea-pink), hyssop, lavender, germander, and thyme. Francis BACON, in his essay *Of Gardens* (1625), describes the fashion for topiary cut in juniper; he dismisses representational topiary as childish, but advocates the use of geometrical topiary to define borders ('welts'), and to create shapes such as pyramids and columns. This preference adumbrates the later fashion for what came to be known as 'hortulan architecture'.

**TOPSELL, EDWARD** (1572–*c*.1638), English zoologist and divine. Little is known of his life except for a series of ecclesiastical posts. His two zoological works, *The History of Four-Footed Beasts* (1607) and *The History of Serpents* (1608), are principally concerned with the elucidation of animals mentioned in the Bible. These books, which draw heavily on GESNER, were the first illustrated manuals of natural history to be published in English.

*DNB.*

**TORDESILLAS, TREATY OF**, a treaty between Spain and Portugal delimiting spheres of influence in the Americas. In 1454 Pope NICHOLAS V had given Portugal the exclusive right to explore and exploit the route to 'the Indies' (India and its adjacent regions), which was assumed to lie along the coast of AFRICA. The Portuguese had inaugurated the eastern route to the Indies, and in 1488 Bartolomeu DIAS rounded the Cape of Good Hope. The return of Columbus from his first voyage in March 1493 was thought to have demonstrated that the Indies could be reached by sailing west, and gave Spain a presence in the route to the Indies. The kings of Spain and Portugal applied to Pope ALEXANDER VI to divide the world in half for purposes of exploration.

On 4 May 1493 Pope Alexander issued a bull that drew the dividing line from pole to pole 100 leagues west of the Azores and the Cape Verde Islands; Portugal was to have the right of exploration and conquest in lands to the east, and Spain would have the same right in lands to the west. The Portuguese protested, and the two sides met in Tordesillas to settle the dispute. On 7 June 1494 the treaty was signed, shifting the line 270 leagues further west, approximately the 50th degree of longitude west of Greenwich, which strikes the mainland of South America close to the mouth of the Amazon. This new arrangement allowed Portugal to claim Brazil on 22 April 1500.

The treaty had to be modified when Portuguese ships sailing east started to encounter Spanish ships sailing west in the disputed territories of the Pacific. The dispute came to a head when MAGELLAN, sailing west under a Spanish flag, reached the Moluccas in November 1521. The dispute was settled in April 1529 with the Treaty of Zaragoza, which awarded the Moluccas to Portugal and fixed the dividing line 297.5 leagues east of the Moluccas, compensating Spain for its loss with a payment of 350,000 ducats. Other European powers, including England, France, and the Netherlands, saw no need to abide by any of the provisions of either treaty.

**TORELLI, LUDOVICA** (1500–69), Italian patron of religious associations for women, the daughter of the duke of Guastella. In 1529, having been twice widowed, she submitted herself to the tutelage of BATTISTA DA CREMA, under whose guidance she developed with Antonio ZACCARIA (who was also a disciple of Battista) a women's order for the BARNABITES; she built the Angeliche, which was the first convent for the women's order. In 1538 Ludovica Torelli repudiated her titles and worldly possessions; thereafter she was known as Paula, and devoted herself to the spiritual education of women. In 1557 she founded a Jesuit school in Milan for the education of young noblewomen.

*HWWI*; L. Scaraffia and G. Zarri, *Women and Faith in Italy* (1999).

**TORQUEMADA, ANTONIO DE** (1530–90), Spanish humanist who may have been a native of León. His most celebrated work was his *Jardín de flores curiosas, en que se tratan algunas materias de humanidad, filosofía, teología y geografía, con otras curiosas y apacibles* (Salamanca, 1570), a delightful and ill-disciplined miscellany whose exotic flowers included facts and fictions culled from authors ranging from Aristotle to the writers of chivalric romances. The *Jardín* was translated into French (1582), Italian (1596), and English (1600); Lewis Lewkenor's English translation was called *The Spanish Mandeville of Miracles; or, The Garden of Curious Flowers*.

CERVANTES mocked the *Jardín*, but also borrowed substantially from it for his *Persiles y Sigismunda*. Torquemada also wrote a chivalric romance (*libro de caballerías*) entitled *Historia del invencible caballero don Olivante de Laura* (Barcelona, 1564), which was burnt by the curate in *Don Quijote*. Torquemada also published a collection of seven moral DIALOGUES called *Los coloquios satíricos, con un coloquio pastoril y gracioso al cabo dellos* (Mondoñedo, 1553).

J. H. Elsdon, *On the Life and Work of the Spanish Humanist Antonio de Torquemada* (1937); Lina Rodríguez Cacho, *Pecados sociales y literatura satírica en el siglo XVI: Los 'Coloquios' de Torquemada* (1989).

**TORQUEMADA, JUAN DE**, or (Latin) **Johannes de Turrecremata** (1388–1468), Spanish cardinal and theologian, born in Valladolid, where he was educated and in 1403 joined the Dominican Order. In 1417 he accompanied his provincial to the COUNCIL OF CONSTANCE, and thence travelled to Paris, where he studied and took his doctorate (1423). On returning to Spain he became prior of the Dominican house in Valladolid and then of the house in Toledo. In 1431 he was called to Rome by Pope EUGENIUS IV and appointed master of the sacred palace (*magister sancti palatii*). In 1433 he was sent as a papal theologian to the COUNCIL OF BASEL, and in 1439 he was created cardinal. He died in Rome on 26 September 1468.

Torquemada's principal works were a contribution to CANON LAW, *In Gratiani Decretum commentarii* (4 vols., 1519), a systematic analysis of the Church and papal authority, *Summa ecclesiastica* (Salamanca, 1550), and a treatise denying the immaculate conception of the Virgin Mary (*De conceptione deiparae Mariae*, Rome, 1547), which was edited by Edward Pusey in 1869, and so was appropriated for his campaign to discredit the popular Mariolatry that unnecessarily separated the Roman and Anglican communions.

DHE; Karl Binder, *Konzilsgedanken bei Kardinal Juan de Torquemada* (1976); Thomas Izbicki, *Protector of the Faith: Cardinal Johannes de Turrecremata and the Defense of the Institutional Church* (1981).

**TORQUEMADA, FRAY JUAN DE** (1563–1624), historian of Aztec Mexico. He was born in Spain but migrated as a child to Mexico, where in 1583 he entered the Franciscan Order, eventually rising to become its provincial. His *Monarquía indiana*, which was completed in 1612 and published in Seville in 1615, is a history and ethnography of the Aztecs under Spanish rule. The *Monarquía* is essentially a compilation of earlier works on the subject: many chapters are simply unacknowledged translations of Jerónimo de MENDIETA's unpublished *Historia eclesiástica indiana*, the only significant changes being the pruning of criticisms whenever Mendieta criticized the conquistadors; there are also significant debts to Bernardino de SAHAGÚN, MOTOLINÍA, and Andrés de OLMOS.

The charge of plagiarism which is routinely levied against Torquemada reflects anachronistic assumptions about intellectual property. His sources were mostly unpublished, so his treatise was important as one of the few on its subject (together with that of José de ACOSTA) that was available in print for contemporary readers.

Alejandra Moreno Toscana, *Fray Juan de Torquemada y su 'Monarquía indiana'* (1963).

**TORQUEMADA, TOMÁS DE** (1420–98), Dominican inquisitor-general, born in Valladolid, the son of the lord of Torquemada (a small town in Castile) and the nephew of Cardinal Juan de TORQUEMADA, whom he followed into the Dominican ORDER, joining the Friars Preachers in their monastery in Valladolid. He was appointed prior of the Convento de Santa Cruz in Segovia, where he remained for 22 years, and where he served as confessor to the Infanta ISABELLA.

In 1474 Isabella succeeded to the throne of Castile and, on the advice of Torquemada, married FERDINAND, the future king of Aragon. Torquemada persuaded Ferdinand and Isabella to revive the INQUISITION, which had been instituted in Spain in 1236 but had become moribund. The establishment of a Spanish Inquisition in Castile and its territories was approved by Pope SIXTUS V in 1478; proceedings began in 1480, and in 1483 Torquemada was appointed as its first inquisitor-general, a post that he held until his death in 1498. In 1484, despite the reluctance of the papacy, the Inquisition was extended to Aragon and all of its territories except for Naples, which remained subject to the Roman INQUISITION. Between 1484 and 1498 Torquemada issued a series of protocols on the conduct of the Inquisition; these documents were collected after his death and published in 1537 as *Copilación de las instrucciones del Officio de la Sancta Inquisición*. During Torquemada's eighteen years as inquisitor-general, his tribunals, according to one set of calculations, burnt 10,220 victims, condemned 6,860 to be burnt in effigy, and reconciled 97,321; those who were reconciled were forbidden entry to the professions and subjected to SUMPTUARY LAWS. His *Copilación* stipulated that TORTURE could be administered in the event of *semiplena probatio*, i.e. evidence inducing a reasonable belief of guilt but falling short of conclusive evidence.

In his last years Torquemada retained the office of inquisitor-general but gradually withdrew to his friar's cell in Ávila, where he died on 16 September 1498.

DHE; Rafael Sabatini, *Torquemada and the Spanish Inquisition* (7th edn. 1929); Lionel Dumarcet, *Tomás de Torquemada* (1999).

**TORRALVA, DIOGO DE** (*c.*1500–1566), Portuguese architect, the son-in-law of Diogo ARRUDA. His early buildings, such as the Graça Church in Évora, contain MANUELINE elements but are essentially Italian Renaissance structures. His most celebrated building is the two-storeyed Palladian cloister of the Convento de Cristo in Tomar, in which a Serlian motif (an arch with three openings, the central one arched and wider than the others, so called from its illustration in SERLIO's *Architettura*) is used as an open arcade on the upper floor; the name of the cloister (Claustro dos Felipes) recalls that this was the place where PHILIP II was proclaimed king after the death of SEBASTIAN I at the battle of KSAR-EL-KEBIR. Diogo also designed the apse of the Jeronimite church in the Lisbon district of Belém (1540–41), and the octagonal Church of Nossa Senhora da Consolação in the Dominican convent at Elvas (1543–7) is often attributed to him. Diogo is widely regarded as the leading architect of the Portuguese Renaissance.

MDA.

**TORRENTIUS, JOHANNES, or (Dutch) Jan Simonszoon van der Beeck** (1589–1644), Dutch painter in Haarlem and London who specialized in STILL LIFES and in erotic GENRE scenes. In 1627 he was tried in Haarlem as a suspected ROSICRUCIAN; he was tortured and sentenced to be burnt at the stake, but the sentence was commuted to twenty years in jail. He was freed through the intercession of King Charles I of England, and lived in England from 1630 until *c.*1641, when he returned to Amsterdam. The only picture that can be attributed to Torrentius with confidence is a *Still Life* organized as an emblem of temperance (1614) which belonged to Charles I and is now in the Rijksmuseum in Amsterdam.

MDA; NNBW iv.

**TORRES, FRANCISCO, or (Latin) Franciscus Turrianus** (*c.*1504–1584), Jesuit polemicist and PATRISTIC SCHOLAR. After studying in Salamanca Torres moved to Rome, where he established a reputation as a polemicist, championing in his writings the immaculate conception of the Virgin Mary (a doctrine often defended by the JESUITS), episcopal authority, and the supremacy of the pope over councils. From 1562 to 1563 he served as a papal theologian at the COUNCIL OF TRENT, and then published the *editio princeps* of the Apostolic Constitutions (Venice, 1563), a fourth-century body of ecclesiastical law of Syrian provenance which Torres attributed to St Clement of Rome (it is now attributed to the anonymous interpolator of the epistles of St Ignatius).

In 1566 Torres entered the Jesuit Order, and was later appointed as a professor at the Roman College, where he worked on the revision of JEROME's Vulgate translation of the Bible. He defended the contested authenticity of the 85 Apostolic Canons (now believed to date from the late fourth century), the False Decretals (said to be the work of Isidore of Seville but now thought to be a French work of the ninth century), the 80 Nicene Canons (now classified as *spuria*), and the *Acta* of the sixth and seventh general councils of the Church (Constantinople III and Nicaea II), which are still thought to be genuine.

**TORRES NAHARRO, BARTOLOMÉ DE** (*c*.1485–*c*.1524), Spanish playwright and poet, born in La Torre de Miguel Sesmero (30 kilometres (18 miles) south-east of Badajoz) and educated at Salamanca. He was ordained as a priest but then became a soldier; he was captured by BARBARY PIRATES and sold into slavery in Algiers. Torres Naharro was ransomed in 1511 and travelled to Rome, where he renewed his ties with the Church, and thence to Naples, where he entered the household of Fabrizio COLONNA. He disappears from the historical record in 1524, and is assumed, in absence of evidence to the contrary, to have returned to Spain and died shortly thereafter.

Torres collected his poems and seven of his plays in a volume entitled *Propalladia* (Naples, 1517); these 'first works of Pallas' were supplemented by a second edition (Seville, 1520) containing an eighth play (*Calamita*) and a third edition (Naples, 1524) containing a ninth (*Aquilina*). Torres's introduction to the *Propalladia* contains the first theorized account of Spanish drama. The broad frame of reference is classical: plays are either *comedias* or *tragedias*, and, in keeping with the Horatian precept, are not to extend beyond five acts; he translates Horace's *actus* as *jornada* rather than *acto*, so introducing a vernacular term that was to be revived at the end of the century by Juan de la CUEVA and Cristóbal de VIRUÉS. He also proposes a taxonomy of comedy that distinguishes realistic *comedias a noticia*, such as his semi-autobiographical *Soldatesca* (in which the protagonist is a Spanish recruiting officer) and *Tinellaria* from fanciful *comedias a fantasía*, such as his *Serafina*, *Himenea* (a dramatization of acts 12, 14, and 15 of Fernando de ROJAS's *La Celestina*), *Calamita*, and *Aquilana*. His early *Diálogo de nacimiento* and *Trofea* are imitations of Juan del ENCINA and his *Jacinta* is an entertainment written in honour of Isabella d'ESTE on the occasion of her visit to Rome in the winter of 1514–15.

The plays of Torres Naharro are not remarkable for their stagecraft or the majesty of their language, but the characterization is vivid and the dramatic effects deftly contrived. The diction of Spanish plays had traditionally been standard Castilian, but Torres Naharro introduced characters speaking in dialect and in foreign accents, costume scenes (*cuadros de costumbres*), and realistic settings, such as the cardinal's kitchen (*tinello*) in *Tinellaria*. The plays were placed on the INDEX in 1559, but the publication of slightly censored editions was allowed in 1573.

The poems in *Propalladia* consist of four ballads, three Italianate *lamentaciones de amor*, and a triumphalist 'Psalmo en la gloriosa victoria que los españoles ovieron contra los venecianos'.

John Lihani, *Bartolomé de Torres Naharro* (1979).

**TORRIGIANO or Torrigiani, PIETRO** (1472–1528), Italian sculptor, born in Florence, where he was trained in the Medici sculpture collection by BERTOLDO DI GIOVANNI and later specialized in terracotta statues and busts. He famously broke the nose of MICHELANGELO (who may have been his fellow student) in a fight, and so incurred the obloquy of writers such as CELLINI and VASARI, both of whom vilify Torrigiano. He left Florence for Rome (where he worked in the Borgia apartments in the Vatican in 1493), Bologna, and Siena, becoming a soldier and then travelling to Antwerp in 1509 to enter the service of MARGARET OF AUSTRIA.

In 1511 Torrigiano moved to England, where he was to produce his finest work. He carved the marble and gilt-bronze tomb of King HENRY VII and his queen Elizabeth of York in Westminster Abbey (1512), the finest example of Italian Renaissance sculpture in England; he also carved the nearby tomb of Lady Margaret Beaufort, King Henry's mother and the eponym of the Lady Margaret professorships at Oxford and Cambridge. The figures portrayed in his terracotta portrait busts include Henry VII (Victoria and Albert Museum), Henry VIII, and Bishop John Fisher (both in Metropolitan Museum in New York).

In about 1520 Torrigiano left England for Spain, where he worked in Seville, as a sculptor of painted terracotta statues, including *St Jerome* kneeling in penitence and a *Virgin and Child* (both in the Museo de Bellas Artes in Seville). He was arrested and imprisoned by the INQUISITION and died in prison, apparently by starving himself to death.

DNB; MDA.

**TORTOISESHELL.** The carapace of the hawksbill turtle (*Chelonia imbricata*), which was hunted in the tropical seas of the West Indies and the coast of Brazil, is covered with thirteen overlapping epidermic plates (five in the centre and four on each side). These plates were removed and moulded under heat and pressure, a process which produced a brittle translucent yellow material mottled with brown tints. Tortoiseshell was used as an inlay in furniture and as a veneer for caskets and small boxes.

**TORTURE.** One of the consequences of the RECEPTION of Roman law in the twelfth century is that trial by ordeal (itself a form of torture) was gradually displaced by the inquisitorial torture enshrined in Roman law; ordeal had to be administered in the presence of a priest, so the interdiction of the fourth Lateran Council in 1215 forbidding priests to participate in trials by ordeal led quickly to its final demise. By the fourteenth century torture had been enshrined in criminal inquisitorial procedure all across Europe. Torture was also recognized in CANON LAW, and so could be used to elicit confessions from heretics: a bull of 1282 directed that heretics be tortured by the civil power (as murderers of souls), and inquisitorial torture was not repudiated by the Vatican until 1816, when it was decreed that the accused should instead be confronted by the accuser.

In Italy, jurisprudential discussion of torture began in earnest with BARTOLO. In 1528 Hippolytus de Marsiliis (1450–1529) offered a full analysis of torture in his *Practica causarum criminalium*, in which he claims credit for inventing the torture of sleep deprivation. Italian scholarship on the subject culminated in 1616 with the publication of the definitive systematic work on torture, Prospero Farinacci's *Praxis et theorica criminalis*. More than any other country, Italy produced distinguished juridical apologists for torture, but in the eighteenth century it also produced the book that led to its abolition across Europe, the marchese de Beccaria's *Dei delitti e delle pene* (1764).

In France, royal *ordonnances* recognized the legitimacy of torture from the thirteenth century. In the taxonomy of torture which developed in early modern France, torture was divided into ordinary and extraordinary (according to severity), and preparatory torture (*question préparatoire*) used to elicit confessions was distinguished from preliminary torture (*question préalable*), which was administered to condemned prisoners as the first stage of their execution to encourage them to incriminate their accomplices in crime. Procedures for regulating torture adopted by the Parlement of Paris in 1707 were adopted in other jurisdictions, but until then the practice and modes of torture varied considerably: many areas favoured water torture and the use of the boot (an iron boot which crushed the legs as wedges were hammered in), but courts in Brittany roasted the feet of suspects and used machines to crush hands and feet, while in Besançon joints were pulled apart and in Autun limbs were dipped into boiling oil. Enlightenment voices condemned judicial torture, but it was not abolished until 1789.

In SPANISH LAW torture was enshrined in the thirteenth-century *Código de las siete partidas*, and was widely used during the INQUISITION; the *Instrucciones* drawn up by TORQUEMADA in 1484 (published 1592) stipulated that torture could be administered in the event of *semiplena probatio*, i.e. evidence inducing a reasonable belief of guilt but falling short of conclusive evidence; it was normally used when there was only one witness to attest heresy. In 1558 Philip II decreed that torture could only be administered with the authority of his council, but this injunction was ignored, and in 1561 the inquisitor Valdés ruled that torture was to be left to the discretion of the judges. The rules of torture codified by Torquemada and Valdés extended beyond Spain to other countries where the Inquisition was established. The comparable text for the Roman INQUISITION was the *Sacro arsenale* (1558, and frequently reprinted till 1730).

In Germany torture was regulated by the CAROLINA of 1532, which stipulated that, in the absence of credible witnesses to

a crime, torture could be used to elicit confessions; it was abolished in 1776. The Netherlands submitted to Philip II's decree of 1570 setting out criminal procedure, but Brabant insisted on retaining its right to torture suspects in the event of *semiplena probatio*. In Scotland torture was used in cases of WITCHCRAFT, and in the seventeenth century it was deployed extensively, usually in the form of the thumbscrew and the boot, to elicit renunciations from covenanters; it was abolished in 1708. In Scandinavia, Denmark allowed judicial torture, but it was increasingly restricted to cases of treason. Sweden seems to be unique in Europe in never having incorporated torture into its legal procedures; torture was instead administered by extra-judicial 'secret committees'. In Russia torture was regulated in an ordinance of 1556, but in practice it was widely used outside the judicial system, even for debt collection.

In England torture never played an important role in criminal procedure, because medieval English criminal law was accusatory rather than inquisitorial in nature, which meant that the accuser had to prove guilt rather than the accused innocence; in the sixteenth century, however, the Privy Council inaugurated torture as a means of eliciting essential facts from accused persons, and later torture was used by the Star Chamber; throughout the sixteenth century, torture had been used extra-judicially, especially by agents of the crown. Common lawyers argued that torture was ordinarily illegal, but conceded that it could be administered under the extraordinary powers of the crown to supersede the COMMON LAW in the event of a national emergency; even COKE acquiesced in torture under these circumstances, but he later changed his mind on the grounds that torture was inconsistent with the liberty of the subject; judicial torture disappeared in England in about 1640.

**TORY, GEOFROY** (c.1480–1533), French humanist printer and woodcut artist. He was born in Bourges and studied in Rome and Bologna. From 1507 to 1515 he taught in Paris and worked as an editor for Henri ESTIENNE, and in 1516 he returned to Rome to study classical remains. On returning to France (c.1518) Tory became an exponent of printing in roman founts, and in 1530 he was appointed royal printer and engraver (in which capacity he also designed book bindings).

In 1529 Tory published *Le Champfleury*, a treatise of aesthetics in which he related the proportions of letters of the alphabet to those of the natural world and advocated the use of punctuation marks. Although he was a noted classical scholar with particular expertise in Greek, Tory was also an impassioned advocate of literary French.

*MDA.*

**TOSCANELLI, PAOLO DAL POZZO** (1397–1482), Italian mathematician and geographer, born in Florence and educated in Padua, where he studied medicine and became a friend of NICHOLAS OF CUSA. On returning to Florence he was appointed astrologer to the Signoria and moved in humanist circles; his friends included ALBERTI, BRUNELLESCHI, and LANDINO, and his correspondents included REGIOMONTANUS.

In 1472 he was given permission to set a ring into the sill of one of the windows in the lantern of the dome of Florence Cathredral to make an aperture to admit sunlight into the body of the church for a few days around the summer solstice, allowing him to make very precise measurements of the height of the sun. This kind of arrangement, called a gnomon, turns the building into a CAMERA OBSCURA. To supplement Toscanelli's results, Egnazio DANTI set up two gnomons in Santa Maria Novella (Florence) in the 1570s. Cusanus, who made several attempts to square the circle by exact geometrical methods, consulted Toscanelli on the subject; some of the correspondence was published in Regiomontanus' *De quadratura circuli* (1533).

On 14 June 1474 Toscanelli sent a letter and map to AFONSO V of Portugal, to whom he explained his 'small earth' hypothesis and suggested that Asia might be reached by sailing westwards across the Atlantic; COLUMBUS gained access to the information in the letter and map in the early 1480s, and concluded that the distance from the CANARY ISLANDS to Cathay was no more than 6,000 kilometres (3,700 miles). The estimate proved to be wrong, but may have been a significant encouragement for Columbus.

DSB; G. Uzielli, *La vita e i tempi di Paolo Pozzo Toscanelli* (1894).

**TOTTEL, RICHARD** (d. 1954), English stationer and printer. He is the eponym of the so-called 'Tottel's Miscellany', a collection of *Songs and Sonnets* (1557) which contained 40 poems by SURREY and the major works of WYATT. He also published Thomas MORE's *Dialogue of Comfort* (1553), Surrey's *Aeneid* (1557), and a large number of law books.

DNB.

**TOURNES, JEAN DE** (1504–64), French printer, a native of Noyon who established a printing workshop in Lyon *c.*1540. His books include elegant editions of Petrarch (1550) and Vitruvius (1552). His son and namesake Jean de Tournes the Younger (1539–1615) became a Protestant and in 1585 left Lyon for Geneva, where he re-established the family printing workshop.

**TOURNEUR, CYRIL** (*c.*1575–1626), English playwright. Details of Tournur's biography are obscure although he is known to have participated in an unsuccessful raid on Spanish treasure ships in Cádiz in 1625. He is the author of two tragedies, one of which, *The Nobleman* (1612), is lost; the other is *The Atheist's Tragedy* which, with echoes of SHAKESPEARE's *King Lear* (1605), was probably written sometime after that date; it was published in 1611. The influential *Revenger's Tragedy* (published 1607) was for a long time attributed to Tourneur. Critical opinion now favours MIDDLETON as the author, though the issue is not resolved.

DNB.

**TOWN PLANNING** In the early fourteenth century ARNOLFO DI CAMBIO, who helped to design Florence Cathedral, also designed building restrictions for the area surrounding it and made decisions about the complete layout of the small city of San Giovanni Valdarno. The notion of the ideal city is a prominent feature of utopian writing, and also appears intermittently in Renaissance architectural treatises, including ALBERTI's *De re aedificatoria* and FRANCESCO DI GIORGIO's *Trattato di architettura civile e militari*. Of practising architects, the most utopian was FILARETE, who in his *Il trattato d'architettura* devised symmetrical plans for a star-shaped city called Sforzinda and a coastal town called Plousiapolis.

The principal surviving planned towns of Renaissance Europe are PIENZA (near Siena), Zamość (in south-eastern Poland), and Freudenstadt (in the Black Forest). Pienza was commissioned by Pope PIUS II in 1459 and laid out by Bernardo ROSSELLINO. Zamość was commissioned by Jan ZAMOYSKI and laid out and constructed by the Venetian architect Bernardo Morando from 1587 to 1605. Freudenstadt was laid out by Heinrich SCHICKHARDT in the first decade of the seventeenth century; it was destroyed in April 1945 but has since been rebuilt. Of planned interventions in existing cities, the most important was the rebuilding of ROME by Pope SIXTUS V.

**TRABACI, GIOVANNI MARIA** (*c.*1575–1647), Italian composer and organist in Naples who became *maestro di cappella* at the Royal Chapel of the Spanish viceroys in 1614. He was also associated with the household of the Capoa di Balzo family. He was a prolific composer, writing both sacred and secular music; in its expressive chromaticism, the earlier work suggests the influence of Carlo GESUALDO.

**TRADESCANT, JOHN** (*c.*1570–1638), English traveller, gardener, and collector of plants and curiosities, who established a famous physic garden in Lambeth. He was employed by Robert Cecil, for whom he laid out the gardens at HATFIELD HOUSE, and subsequently worked for Lord Wotton and the duke of Buckingham; after the assassination of Buckingham he became royal gardener to Charles I and Henrietta Maria. Aristocratic and royal patronage enabled Tradescant to travel abroad, and he used such journeys to collect new plants. He travelled in the Netherlands and France in 1609 and 1611, and acquired a large collection of trees (mostly fruit trees), 65 of which are portrayed in a manuscript known as 'Tradescant's Orchard', which is now in the Bodleian Library in Oxford. In 1618 he travelled to Archangel with Sir Dudley Digges, and his diary of the voyage ('A Voyage of Ambassade'), which is also in the Bodleian Library, is the earliest extant account of Russian flora; his trophies included the Siberian larch and the purple geranium (cranesbill). He joined the fleet that blockaded Algiers in 1620–1, and used the occasion to collect North African plants. In 1627 he took part in the siege of La Rochelle, and again returned with a booty of plants, this time including 'sea-stock gillyflower' (*Matthiola sinuata*) and several varieties of rock rose (*cistus*). Tradescant's membership of the Virginia Company provided yet another conduit for new plants: his North American trophies included spiderwort (*Tradescantia virginiana*), Virginia creeper (*Parthenocissus quinquefolia*), and stag's horn sumach (*Rhus typhina*).

Tradescant's son John (1608–62) succeeded his father as royal gardener at Oatlands; he undertook three voyages to Virginia, which enabled him to add considerably to the range of American plants cultivated in England. His *Museum Tradescantianum* (1656) notes the acquisition of the American cowslip (*Dodecatheon meadia*) and the swamp cypress (*Taxodium distichum*).

The collections of the Tradescants, which included large numbers of curiosities as well as botanical specimens, passed on the death of John the Younger to Elias Ashmole, who gave them to the University of Oxford, where they form part of the foundation collection of the Ashmolean Museum.

Mea Allan, *The Tradescants: Their Plants, Gardens and Museum, 1570–1662* (1964); M. Welch, *The Tradescants and the Foundation of the Ashmolean Museum* (1978); A. Macgregor (ed.), *Tradescant's Rarities* (1983); Prudence Leith-Ross, *The John Tradescants: Gardeners to the Rose and Lily Queen* (1984).

**TRAGEDY.** In late medieval literature tragedy was a literary rather than a dramatic genre, and typically took the form of moralizing poems or treatises that described the fall of great men as illustrations of the mutability of fortune and the need for Christian faith. In the early sixteenth century, tragedy was revived as a dramatic genre in which the principal models were SENECA the Younger and, to a lesser extent, the Greek tragedians. ARISTOTLE was not an important influence: the *Poetics*, which survived only in a mutilated form, did not begin to influence plays (as opposed to scholarly thinking) until the end of the sixteenth century, and even in the early seventeenth century most dramatists were unaware of Aristotelian notions such as the tragic flaw and of his analysis of tragedy in terms of emotional effects such as pity, fear, and catharsis.

The first Renaissance tragedy was TRISSINO's *La Sofonisba* (1515), which was modelled on Sophocles and Euripides. In the early 1540s the Latin plays of George Buchanan (who was living in Bordeaux) introduced drama in the Greek style to France. In 1541 GIRALDI inaugurated the tradition of Senecan tragedy with his *Orbecche* (1541). Senecan motifs such as horror, ghosts, witches, tyrants, and bloodshed all appealed to contemporary tastes and were incorporated into Senecan tragedy. In England, plays such as NORTON and SACKVILLE's *Gorboduc* (1562), KYD's *The Spanish Tragedy* (c.1585), and SHAKESPEARE's *Titus Andronicus* and *Richard III* were heavily influenced by Seneca; in France Senecan tragedy was introduced by Étienne JODELLE in *Cléopâtre captive* (1552). In Spain Seneca was the principal model for playwrights such as Lupercio ARGENSOLA and Cristóbal de VIRUÉS.

As vernacular tragedy developed, Senecan influences gradually faded. The prevailing tone became one of grandeur rather than horror, and Senecan figures such as the ghost increasingly became a psychological rather than a physical presence on the stage. France produced some fine tragedies (notably Robert GARNIER's *Les Juives*), as did Italy (where playwrights such as Luigi ALAMANNI, Pietro ARETINO, Luigi GROTO, Giovanni RUCELLAI, Sperone SPERONI, and Torquato TASSO remained more faithful to classical models than was the case elsewhere in Europe), but the countries in which tragedy developed into national genres were Spain, which produced tragedians such as Juan de la CUEVA, CERVANTES (especially *El cerco de Numancia*), and Lope de VEGA, and England, where the accomplishment of Shakespeare eventually overshadowed the tragedies of other very skilled playwrights.

**TRANSYLVANIA or (German) Grossfürstentum or (later) Siebenbürgen or (Hungarian) Erdély or (Romanian) Ardeal**, now a province of Romania but from 1004 to 1918 a principality in eastern Hungary; the principality was larger than the present province, and at various times included Maramures, Crişana, and Banat. In the twelfth century, King Géza II added to the established populations of SZEKLERS, Magyars, and Romanians a new wave of immigrants from Flanders and the Lower Rhine; since the thirteenth century, these German-speaking immigrants have been known as Saxons. By 1417, a fifth ethnic group, the GIPSIES, was sufficiently well established to have its own *voivode* or prince. The Szeklers, Magyars, and Saxons all had political rights, but Romanians, who constituted the largest community, had no political power.

In 1211 King Andrew II invited members of the TEUTONIC ORDER to settle in Transylvania, so swelling the number of German speakers. The Saxons were given special privileges, and founded German towns. The German name for Transylvania (Siebenbürgen) refers to the seven principal German towns, each of which has a German name, a Hungarian name, a Romanian name, and a Latin name: German Klausenburg is Hungarian Kolozsvár, Romanian Cluj (now Cluj-Napoca), and Latin Claudiopolis; German Kronstadt is Hungarian Brassó, Romanian Braşov, and Latin Corona; German Hermannstadt is Hungarian Nagyszeben, Romanian Sibiu, and Latin Cibinium; German Schässburg is Hungarian Segesvár and Romanian Sighişoara; the other three towns are Bistritz (Bistrita), Medisch (Medias), and Muhlbach (Sebes).

In 1526, on the death of King Louis II of Hungary and Bohemia, the throne passed to the Habsburgs. There was resistance in Hungary to the accession of FERDINAND, and the Transylvanian *voivode*, János ZÁPOLYA, was able to secure a measure of independence from the rest of Hungary by placing Transylvania under the protection of the Ottomans. Zápolya's infant son János Sigismund Zápolya retained a measure of independence throughout his reign; in 1570 he abdicated as king of Hungary, but remained *voivode* of Transylvania for another year. His successor was STEFAN BÁTORY.

Transylvania is popularly associated with vampires and with Dracula. The historical figure in the distant background of Bram Stoker's *Dracula* (1897) is Vlad III, the fifteenth-century lord of Wallachia who was known as Vlad Dracul ('Vlad the Devil') and Vlad Ţepeş ('Vlad the Impaler'); both epithets reflect his reputation for dealing harshly with his enemies. In the autumn of 1442 Vlad travelled with his army to Transylvania and fought alongside the Transylvanian army of the *voivode* Iancu of Hunedoara and defeated the Ottomans in a battle near Ialomiţa.

**TRAVERSARI, AMBROGIO** (1386–1439), Italian humanist, a Camaldolese monk at the Convent of Santa Maria degli Angeli in Florence. He was a distinguished churchman, serving as general of his Order (from 1431), papal legate at the COUNCIL OF BASEL, and translator at the COUNCIL OF FLORENCE, where he drafted the Greek text proclaiming the union of the Byzantine and Roman churches.

Traversari was an accomplished Hellenist and was one of the first humanists to study HEBREW. His initial interest in Greek was in New Testament Greek rather than classical Greek, and he was later drawn to PATRISTIC SCHOLARSHIP and to the translation of the Greek fathers. His involvement in the humanist circles of Niccoli and Cosimo de' MEDICI led him to the study of classical Greek, and he translated Diogenes Laertius' *Lives of the Philosophers*.

C. H. Stinger, *Humanism and the Church Fathers: Ambrogio Traversari (1386–1439) and Christian Antiquity in the Italian Renaissance* (1977); G. C. Garfagnini (ed.), *Ambrogio Traversari nel VI centenario della nascita* (1988); S. Frigerio (ed.), *Ambrogio Traversari: Un monaco e un monastero nell' Umanesimo fiorentino* (1988).

**TRECENTO**, an apheretic form of *mil tre cento* ('one thousand three hundred'), the Italian term for the fourteenth century (13—) and for the art and architecture of the period.

**TREMELLIUS, IMMANUEL** (1510–80), Italian Hebrew scholar, born into a Jewish family in Ferrara and educated at Pavia. He converted to Catholicism in 1540 under the guidance of Cardinal POLE, and the following year became a Protestant under the guidance of Pietro Martire VERMIGLI. He taught at Strassburg and in 1553 moved to England at the invitation of Thomas CRANMER. He was appointed Regius reader in Hebrew at Cambridge in 1549, but on the accession of MARY in 1553 returned to the Continent. In 1561 he was appointed to a chair of Hebrew at Heidelberg, but in 1577 he was expelled because of his Calvinist theology by the Lutheran count palatine. He finished his career as a Hebrew teacher in Sedan. Tremellius translated the Old Testament from Hebrew to Latin in collaboration with Franciscus JUNIUS (5 vols., 1575–9) and the New Testament from Syriac to Latin (1569). The Junius–Tremellius Bible became the standard Protestant Latin Bible, and retained this status throughout the seventeenth century; sometimes this Bible is confused with a composite Bible that consists of a Junius–Tremellius Old Testament bound together with BEZA's Latin translation of the New Testament from the Greek. Tremellius' other works include a Hebrew and Greek catechism (1551) and an Aramaic and Syriac grammar (1569).

ADB; DNB; JNB.

**TRIBOLO, NICCOLÒ, or Niccolò di Raffaello de' Pericoli** (1500–50), Italian sculptor and garden designer, a native of Florence. He designed the BOBOLI GARDENS in Florence and the garden of the MEDICI VILLA at Castello. As a sculptor his finest original works were FOUNTAINS, including the Fountain of Hercules and Cacus at Castello; he also copied works by MICHELANGELO (Bargello, Florence).

MDA.

**TRIDENTINE or (Italian) Tridentino**, the adjectival form of 'Trento' (Latin *Tridentum*), used with specific reference to the COUNCIL OF TRENT, and to its decrees.

**TRINITY HOUSE**. Originally a guild for mariners established in 1514, its duties were extended by ELIZABETH to include the construction of 'sea-marks' such as lighthouses and buoys, to aid the safe navigation of shipping around the English coasts.

**TRISSINO, GIAN GIORGIO** (1478–1550), Italian dramatist, poet, and linguistic theorist, born into a patrician family in Vicenza and educated in Milan, where he studied Greek. After periods at the ESTE court in Ferrara (1512) and the restored MEDICI court in Florence (1513), where he attended the meetings of Bernardo RUCELLAI's Accademia Platonica in the Orti Oricellari, Trissino moved to the court of Pope LEO X in Rome, where he became a papal diplomat; he subsequently enjoyed the patronage of CLEMENT VII and PAUL III.

Trissino's plays include *Sofonisba* (1515), which was the first TRAGEDY to eschew the Senecan tradition in favour of Greek models and Aristotelian precepts, and *I simillimi* (1548), a comedy that drew on Aristophanes as well as Plautus. His poems include Horatian odes (the earliest example in Italian), Pindaric odes, Petrarchan sonnets, and a historical blank-verse epic, *L'Italia liberata da' Gotti* (1547–8).

Trissino's linguistic works include an epistle to Pope Clement VII on orthographic reform (1524), two treatises on grammar, a treatise on poetry which deals extensively with metre (*La poetica*, 1529), and a translation into Italian of Dante's *De vulgari eloquentia* (1529), which was a central document in the debate known as the QUESTIONE DELLA LINGUA, to which Trissino contributed *Il castellano della lingua italiana* (1529).

**TRISTÃO, NUNO** (d. 1446), Portuguese explorer who undertook four voyages along the west coast of AFRICA under the patronage of HENRY THE NAVIGATOR. In 1441 he reached Rio de Oro and Cape Blanco, and probed further south in 1443. In his third voyage, in 1444, he reached the mouth of the Senegal river. On his final voyage in 1446 he sailed past Cape Verde and reached the mouth of the Gambia river, where he was killed by the poisoned darts of Africans whom he was attempting to capture for sale into slavery.

DHP.

**TRITHEMIUS, JOHANNES** (1462–1516), German humanist, abbot, occultist, and cryptographer, born in Trittenheim (on the Moselle), from which he took his name. He was orphaned as a young man and fled from his stepfather to Würzburg, where he acquired a humanist education. In 1482 he entered the Benedictine monastery at Sponheim, and the following year was elected as its abbot. In the course of the next 23 years he reformed the monastery and amassed a library of manuscripts that soon had a European reputation. In 1506 complaints about the harshness of the discipline that he imposed on the house led to his resignation, and thereafter he served as abbot of the Scottish Abbey of St Jakob at Würzburg. His writings include historical works (notably *De viris illustribus Germaniae*, 1495), several treatises on demonology, treatises on CRYPTOGRAPHY (*Stenographia*, 1606; *Polygraphia*, 1518), and a large corpus of sermons. AGRIPPA dedicated his *De occulta philosophia* (1510) to Trithemius.

K. Arnold, *Johannes Trithemius* (1971).

**TRIUMPH.** In classical Rome, a triumph (Latin *triumphus*) was the highest honour that could be bestowed on a victorious general; it took the form of a processional entry into Rome and a slow parade to the Capitol in which the victorious general (*triumphator*), crowned with laurel, was carried in a chariot and accompanied by his army and prominent captives.

The Roman triumph was not replicated on the streets of Renaissance Europe, but was echoed in the ceremonial entries of rulers into cities: in 1443 ALFONSO I entered his newly conquered capital of Naples in a procession modelled on an ancient triumph, and King LOUIS XII's victorious entry into Milan in 1509 was planned as a triumph by LEONARDO DA VINCI. The triumph also became an important motif in the literature and art of the period. DANTE installed Beatrice in a triumphator's chariot in *Purgatorio* 29, and PETRARCH wrote a series of influential poetical *Trionfi* which depict the processional triumphs of love, chastity, death, fame, time, and eternity.

The pictorial reconstruction of the triumphs of antiquity began with the carvings on the triumphal arch at Castelnuovo (1452–66), in Naples, which honours Alfonso I of Naples, and culminated in GIULIO ROMANO's *Triumph of Scipio Africanus*, DÜRER's woodcut series *The Triumph of Maximilian*, and MANTEGNA's *Triumph of Caesar* cartoons (Hampton Court). Petrarch's allegorical triumphs were soon illustrated in illuminated manuscripts, and so became a popular motif in woodcuts, tapestries, and CASSONE paintings. The finest examples are arguably PIERO DELLA FRANCESCA's illustrations on the backs of his portraits of FEDERICO DA MONTEFELTRO and his wife Battista Sforza (Uffizi).

The triumph motif also entered the religious and mythological traditions. SAVONAROLA wrote a *Triumphis Crucis* in which Jesus was the triumphator, and TITIAN explored the same theme in his woodcut *The Triumph of Faith*. Mantegna painted a *Triumph of Virtue* (Louvre) and HOLBEIN painted a *Triumph of Riches and Poverty* (destroyed 1666). English MASQUES such as *The* TRIUMPHS OF ORIANA brought the form to the stage.

**TRIUMPHS OF ORIANA, THE** (1601), a collection of 29 madrigals by MORLEY, WEELKES, GIBBONS, and others, published by Thomas MORLEY in 1603 though it was due to appear in 1601. It is dedicated to Queen Elizabeth, who is eulogized in the refrain 'Long live fair Oriana' which appears in all but three of the madrigals, mirroring the 'Viva la bella Dori' of *Il trionfo di Dori* (1592) upon which it is modelled.

**TRIVIUM.** See LIBERAL ARTS.

**TRIVULZIO FAMILY,** a Milanese noble family which was already prominent in the twelfth century and subsequently produced generations of *condottieri* and prelates.

Gian Giacomo Trivulzio (1441–1518), a highly educated soldier, commanded troops for King LOUIS XI in Brittany and later served as a *condottiere* under the SFORZA. After falling out with Ludovico SFORZA in 1483, Gian Giacomo returned to the service of France, initially for King CHARLES VIII and then as the commander of LOUIS XII's army in its attacks on Milan in 1499–1500. He was appointed as the French governor in Milan, and led the forces of the League of CAMBRAI to victory over Venice at the battle of AGNADELLO (1509). His army was defeated at the battle of NOVARA (1513), but victorious at the battle of MARIGNANO. In about 1511 he commissioned an equestrian statue of himself from LEONARDO DA VINCI, but the statue was never completed.

Teodoro Trivulzio (1474–1551) was another soldier in the service of France; his most difficult task was reconstituting the French army after the catastrophic battle of PAVIA in 1525. The prelates in the family, including Gian Giacomo's brother Cardinal Antonio (d. 1508), shared this allegiance to France. Cardinal Scaramuccia (d. 1527), count of Melzo, was an adviser to King Louis XII, and Cardinal Agostino (d. 1548) served as a papal legate in France. The most prominent political figure in the family was Antonio Trivulzio, an opponent of the VISCONTI who supported the AMBROSIAN REPUBLIC of 1447–50.

The family assembled a large collection of books, manuscripts, and works of art. The Trivulzio Collection is in part dispersed, but is mostly in the Castello Sforzesco in Milan.

**TROLLE, HERLUF** (1516–65), Danish admiral, a diplomat in the service of CHRISTIAN III and FREDERICK II. He had no naval experience, but in 1559 was nonetheless appointed admiral of the fleet and four years later became admiral-in-chief. In 1563 he embarked with a fleet of 27 ships and in a battle off the island of Öland defeated a Swedish fleet of 38 ships, capturing Jacob Bagge, the Swedish commander; later in the year he fought an indecisive battle with a Swedish fleet commanded by Klas Horn. In 1563 Trolle put to sea with a fresh fleet and off Fehmann again encountered Horn, who on this occasion had a much larger fleet. The ensuing battle was indecisive but immensely destructive, and both fleets retreated to their home ports. Trolle had been wounded in the battle and died shortly after reaching Copenhagen.

DBL.

**TROMBONCINO, BARTOLOMEO** (*c*.1470–*c*.1535), Venetian composer who played trombone at Mantua for Francesco II Gonzaga and murdered his wife on discovering her infidelity. He also worked for Isabella d'ESTE, marchioness of Mantua, and Lucrezia BORGIA in Ferrara. By 1518 he was teaching lute and singing in Venice, for which he was famous even after his death. He wrote some sacred music and, more importantly, 170 FROTTOLAS setting Renaissance and classical poets including Petrarch, Galeotto, Dall'Aquila, Sannazaro, Ariosto, Bembo, and Ovid.

*TROMPE L'ŒIL*, French art-historical term for a painting that deceives the viewer into thinking that represented objects are real. Perspectival *trompe-l'œil* effects could be achieved most effectively with INTARSIA. In the STUDIOLO of the Ducal Palace in Urbino, intarsia in some 30 different woods gives the illusion of cupboards, writing desks, musical instruments, and built-in bookshelves stocked with books. Such deception can rarely be achieved in painting, but illusionistic ceilings such as MANTEGNA's Camera degli Sposi in the Palazzo Ducale in Mantua give the impression that the ceiling is open to the sky, though the viewer always remains aware that the image has been created through art.

**TSCHUDI or Schudy, ÄGIDIUS or Gilg or Giles** (1505–72), Swiss historian, born into an ancient family in Glarus and educated in Zürich (where he was taught by ZWINGLI), Basel, and Paris (where he was taught by LEFÈVRE D'ÉTAPLES). Tschudi returned to Glarus, of which he became chief magistrate (*Landamman*) in 1558. He remained loyal to the Catholic Church and was ennobled by the Emperor FERDINAND in 1559; thereafter he promoted the cause of the COUNTER-REFORMATION throughout the Swiss cantons.

In the course of his extensive travels through the Swiss cantons Tschudi gathered the materials for his works of Swiss history. In 1528 he completed a book on Rhaetia, which was published in 1538 in both Latin (*De prisca ac vera Alpina Rhaetia*) and German (*Die uralt wahrhaftig Alpische Rhätia*); this is the chronicle that first set out the familiar version of the story of Wilhelm Tell (see SWISS CONFEDERATION). Tschudi's other historical works were published in the eighteenth century: his magisterial *Chronicon Helveticum*, the history of the Swiss cantons from 1001 to 1470, was published in two sumptuous folios in Basel in 1734 and 1736, and *Beschreibung Gallicae Comatae*, an account of ancient Helvetia and Rhaetia, was published in 1758. The discovery in the nineteenth century that Tschudi had forged some of the documents on which his histories were based meant that historians could no longer rely on Tschudi's histories or his manuscripts as sources for medieval Swiss history.

**TUDOR, HOUSE OF,** English royal family. The Tudor royal dynasty was founded by HENRY VII, nephew of HENRY VI, who claimed the throne from RICHARD III at the battle of Bosworth in 1485; two generations of his descendents occupied the throne until the death of ELIZABETH in 1603. The Tudor name reflects the marriage of HENRY V's widow Catherine de Valois to the Welsh courtier Owen Tudor. Their son Edmund, created earl of Richmond in 1452, was half-brother to Henry VI; he married Margaret Beaufort, descendant of John of Gaunt, and their son Henry Tudor became Henry VII. Henry VII's marriage to Elizabeth of York, daughter of EDWARD IV, united the warring houses of Lancaster and York. The reign of his son HENRY VIII (reigned 1509–47) was marked by the break with Rome, and, notwithstanding the efforts of MARY (1553–8), the turn to Protestantism was consolidated in the reigns of EDWARD VI (1547–3) and Elizabeth (1558–1603). On the death of Elizabeth,

the crown passed to her Stuart cousin JAMES VI of Scotland, whose great-grandfather James IV had married Henry VIII's sister Margaret.

**TUILERIES GARDENS or (French) Jardins des Tuileries**. In 1563 CATHERINE DE MÉDICIS commissioned a new palace to be built beside the LOUVRE, on a site that had been used to make tiles (French *tuiles*). The palace was never finished, and was eventually burnt in the Commune of 1871, but the gardens still survive, albeit in a French classical form. The gardens were created on the model of ITALIAN GARDENS between 1564 and 1572; the gardens were destroyed during the siege of Paris (1590–4) and restored by HENRI IV between 1594 and 1609. These early gardens were subsumed into the grand design of André Le Nôtre, who rebuilt the gardens for Louis XIV between 1666 and 1671.

The original gardens were laid out in rectangles by Pierre Le Nôtre; each of the three broad paths (*allées*) that separate the rows of rectangles was lined with a different species of tree: fir, elm, and sycamore. Close to the palace the size of the plants diminished, and dwarf shrubs and flowers were laid out in PARTERRES surrounded by trellis-work PAVILIONS and arbours. The lines of this garden were preserved in André Le Nôtre's design, and so survive today in attenuated form, but there is no continuity in the plantings. The rectangular compartments of Catherine's gardens contained features such as FOUNTAINS, a MAZE, and an enormous SUNDIAL. Some compartments contained fruit trees, and there were also trees planted *in quincunx* (Latin; 'by fives'), with one tree at each corner and the fifth in the middle; the decussation (if viewed from above) was significant in the numerology of the period, and the feature subsequently appeared in ENGLISH GARDENS of the sixteenth and seventeenth centuries. Elsewhere in Catherine's garden there was a ceramic GROTTO decorated with terracotta figures by the potter and naturalist Bernard PALISSY. In 1573, shortly after the gardens were completed, they were used as the setting for an entertainment mounted for the ambassadors of Poland on the occasion of their presentation of the crown of Poland to Henri (later HENRI III of France).

Henri IV restored the gardens, and added the Terrace des Feuillants, which runs along what is now the rue de Rivoli. Henri's gardeners, who included Claude MOLLET and Jean Le Nôtre (father of André and son or nephew of Pierre), planted some 20,000 mulberry trees in the garden (including a double row along the terrace), and introduced silkworms; SILK was manufactured in a building in the gardens. The main structural features of Henri IV's gardens were palisades and vaulted trellises (*berceaux*); the palisades were rows of jasmine, judas trees, pomegranate, and quince elaborately clipped into green walls. The main *berceau* was 550 metres (600 yards) long, and ran parallel to the terrace; at the end of each of the eight formal paths running across the garden from the terrace, the *berceau* was broken by a pavilion.

The garden now survives vestigially in the André Le Nôtre design for Louis XIV, in which a terrace was built alongside the river and the parterres were aligned along a central axis which extended beyond the walls of the garden to an avenue which later became the Champs-Élysées.

**TULLIA D'ARAGONA** (c.1508–1558), Italian poet and courtesan whose name derives from the supposition that she was the illegitimate daughter of Cardinal Luigi of Aragon, whose mistress was Tullia's mother. Her *Rime* (1547), a collection of Petrarchan poems, was dedicated to her patron Eleanor of Toledo, the first wife of Duke COSIMO I DE' MEDICI. Tullia also published a Neoplatonic essay on love, the *Dialogo dell'infinità d'amore* (1547), which was dedicated to Duke Cosimo. Tullia was a prominent figure in Brescia, Ferrara, Florence, Rome, and Venice. Her admirers and clients (who were not always synonymous) included bankers, churchmen, courtiers, and a host of writers who praised her, including the historians Jacopo NARDI and Benedetto VARCHI and the poet Girolamo MUZIANO.

HWWI; Georgina Masson, *Courtesans of the Italian Renaissance* (1975).

**TUNIS, BATTLE OF.** In 1535 BARBAROSSA conquered Tunis in the name of the Ottoman sultan. Mohammed al-Hafsi, the Berber claimant to the caliphate, appealed to CHARLES V for assistance. In July 1535 an invasion led in person by Charles V, whose admiral of the fleet was Andrea DORIA and whose commander of land forces was Alfonso D'AVALOS, stormed Tunis and installed Mohammed VI as a Spanish vassal. The victory in the battle of Tunis was acclaimed all over Europe as a Christian triumph over the infidel, but the occupation of the city was never consolidated: the Spaniards garrisoned the fort of La Golette (Halq el Qued, 'the throat', at the mouth of the port of Tunis) and the island of Djerba, but Tunis remained easy prey. In 1570 the pasha of Algiers occupied the city on behalf of the Ottomans, deposing Ahmet III (the son and successor of Mohammed VII). In 1573 the Ottomans lost the city to Don JUAN DE AUSTRIA, who aspired to be king of Tunis, but Spain was finally expelled in 1574, and Tunis became an Ottoman province.

**TURA, COSIMO or Cosmè** (*fl.* 1450–95), Italian painter, the first great painter of Ferrara. He served as court painter to the ESTE FAMILY, for whom he executed wall paintings in the Palazzo Schifanoia (1469–70), now in poor condition. His surviving paintings include *An Allegorical Figure*, a *Virgin and Child Enthroned* (the central panel of an altarpiece), a *St Jerome* (all in the National Gallery in London), and a pair of organ shutters depicting *St George* (1469, Museo del Duomo, Ferrara). The sculpted quality of his paintings evinces a debt to MANTEGNA, Francesco SQUARCIONE, and PIERO DELLA FRANCESCA, but his use of metallic colours and the nervous energy of his painting characterize his individualistic style, which has sometimes been described as a precursor to twentieth-century Expressionism. In 1486 he was dismissed as court painter in favour of Ercole de' ROBERTI, and died in poverty.

MDA; S. Campbell, *Cosmè Tura of Ferrara: Style, Politics and the Renaissance City* (1997); J. Manca, *Cosmè Tura: The Life and Art of a Painter in Estense Ferrara* (2000).

**TURKISH WAR** (1593–1606), a war between HUNGARY and the Ottoman Empire. In 1590 the Ottomans concluded their long war with Persia (1578–90), so freeing their armies to attend to disturbances in Hungary and the Danubian provinces. In June 1593 an Ottoman army besieged Sisak (Croatia; Hungarian Sziszek); Austrian and Hungarian troops were promptly deployed to raise the siege, and on 22 June slaughtered the Ottoman army. Sinan, the 80-year-old Ottoman vizier, took personal command of an army intent on subduing Hungary, and left Constantinople dragging the Austrian ambassador in chains alongside him. In 1594 the Ottomans captured Veszprém and Györ (German Raab) and held Esztergom (German Gran) against a vigorous assult by the forces of Archduke MATTHIAS.

Murat III, the Ottoman sultan, died on 16 January 1595, and was succeeded by his son Mehmet III, who personally led his Janissaries into the war, capturing Eger (German Erlau) in October 1596 and decisively defeating the allied armies of the Archduke Maximilian and Sigismund, *voivode* of Transylvania, at the battle of Keresztes (23–6 October 1596). Thereafter Sultan Mehmet returned to Constantinople and left the conduct of the war to his generals. In 1598 the tide of the war turned, and the Ottomans lost Györ, Tata (German Dotis or Totis), Veszprém, and Pápa; in October the cutting of supply lines and a revolt by the Janissaries forced the Ottomans to retreat to winter quarters in Belgrade. In September 1600 the Ottomans captured Stara Kanjiža (Vojvodina; Hungarian Magyarkanissa), and the following year Archduke Ferdinand led an army of 30,000 troops in an unsuccessful attempt to retake the city. In August 1602 the Ottomans recaptured Székesfehérvár (German Stuhlweis). Archduke Matthias captured Pest and besieged Buda, but in November 1602 the Ottomans successfully raised the siege.

The war was finally concluded in a treaty (12 November 1606) that abolished the annual tribute which had been paid by Austria since 1547. Austria compounded the tribute with a single payment of 200,000 florins, and received official recognition by the Ottomans of the Holy Roman Emperor, who was thereafter to be given the imperial title of *padişáh* in official Ottoman documents. The treaty marked the end of Ottoman expansion in Europe.

**TURNÈBE, ADRIEN, or (Latin) Adrianus Turnebus** (1512–65), French classical philologist. He was born at Les Andelys in Normandy, and at the age of 12 moved to Paris to continue his education. He was appointed professor of rhetoric at the University of Toulouse and in 1547 returned to Paris as reader in Greek at the Collège Royal. From 1552 to 1556 he served as royal printer of Greek, and in that capacity printed editions of Aeschylus, Sophocles, and Homer's *Iliad*. His voluminous writings, which were collected by his son Étienne (3 vols., Strassburg, 1600), range from translations of Greek authors into Latin and French to philological treatises and commentaries on Theophrastus, Philo, and Cicero. Another son, Adrien, collected his *Adversaria* (1581), a miscellany of textual criticism of classical authors.

John Lewis, *Adrien Turnèbe (1512–65): A Humanist Observed* (1998).

**TURNÈBE, ODET DE** (1552–81), French humanist, lawyer, poet, and dramatist, son of Adrien TURNÈBE. His life is not well documented, but it is known that he studied law at Toulouse and that shortly before his premature death he was appointed *premier président de la Cour des Monnaies*. Turnèbe composed poetry in French, Spanish, and Italian and in about 1580 wrote a learned and bawdy prose comedy, *Les Contents*, which was published in 1584.

**TURNER, WILLIAM** (1508–68), English herbalist. He twice lived on the Continent for protracted periods, during which he studied botany and met prominent botanists such as GESNER. His publications on botany began with *Libellus de re herbaria* (Cambridge, 1538), but thereafter he wrote in English with a view to introducing the medicinal botany of the Continent to English physicians. His *New Herbal* (1551) was illustrated with woodcuts taken from the 1545 edition of Leonhard FUCH's *De historia stirpium*.
*DNB; DSB.*

**TUSSER, THOMAS** (*c.*1524–1580), English poet and agricultural writer. Educated at Cambridge, Tusser farmed in Suffolk, where he introduced the cultivation of barley to England. His *A Hundred Points of Good Husbandry* (1557, enlarged in later editions) is a manual in verse on gardening and farming, together with more general advice on conduct, expressed in maxims and proverbs.
*DNB.*

**TWELVE ARTICLES or (German) *Zwölf Artikel***, the manifesto of the PEASANTS' REVOLT, adopted at Memmingen in March 1525. The Articles, which were drafted by Christoph SCHAPPELER or Sebastian LOTZER, set out the peasants' demands, which included the abolition of serfdom, the right to fish in streams (but not ponds), to hunt game, and to cut wood, the autonomy of individual congregations, controlled rents, a fair judicial system, and the abolition of heriot (German *Todfall*), which was the right of a feudal lord to take a tenant's best beast or other chattel on the death of the tenant. Martin LUTHER formally assented to the Articles, but nonetheless opposed the peasants' attempt to achieve their demands by rebellion.
M. Brecht, 'Der theologische Hintergrund der Zwölf Artikel der Bauernschaft Schwaben von 1525', *Zeitschrift für Kirchengeschichte*, 85 (1974).

**TYARD or Thyard, PONTUS DE** (1521–1605), French poet and philosopher. He was born in his noble family's chateau in Bissy (Mâcon) and studied at the Collège de Cocqueret in Paris, where he became associated with the poets of the PLÉIADE. He subsequently entered the Church and in 1578 was consecrated as bishop of Chalon-sur-Saône; in 1589 he was driven from his diocese by the CATHOLIC LEAGUE because of his support for King HENRI III, whereupon he withdrew from public life.

Tyard collected his youthful poems as three books of *Erreurs amoureuses* (1549, 1551, 1555) and *Livre de vers lyriques* (1555); the latter collection shows the influence of RONSARD.

His third collection, *Œuvres poétiques* (1573), included its two predecessors and added the *Recueil des nouvelles œuvres poétiques*. In philosophy Tyard translated the *Dialoghi di amore* of LEONE EBREO into French (1551) and collected his own works in *Discours philosophiques* (1587), which includes treatises on poetry (*Solitaire premier, ou prose des muses, et de la fureur poétique*, 1552), music (*Solitaire second*, 1552), time (*Discours du temps, de l'an, et de ses parties*, 1556), the spiritual and corporeal universe (*L'Univers*, 1557), and astrology (*Mantice*, 1558). The treatise on poetry is, together with Girolamo Fracchetta's *Dialogo del furore poetico* (1581), the fullest treatment in Renaissance literature of the Neoplatonic theory that poets are inspired by a divine fury, the *furor poeticus*.
K. M. Hall, *Pontus de Tyard and his 'Discours philosophiques'* (1963); Sylviane Bokdam, *Pontus de Tyard* (1997).

**TYE, CHRISTOPHER** (*c.*1505–*c.*1572), English composer who was a lay clerk at King's College, Cambridge, in 1537, having taken a B.Mus. the previous year, and who became *magister choristarum* at Ely Cathedral by 1543. His connections with the royal court were made through Dr Richard Cox (later chancellor of Oxford and bishop of Ely). Like William BYRD and Thomas TALLIS, he lived through the changing religious policies of EDWARD VI, MARY TUDOR, and ELIZABETH I. His sacred music adapted itself to the needs of the time, ranging from syllabic Edwardian anthems to Latin psalm settings and MAGNIFICATS composed during Mary's reign. The *Acts of the Apostles* (1553) are metrical settings of biblical texts, dedicated to Edward VI.

**TYNDALE, WILLIAM** (*c.*1494–1516), English Bible translator. Educated at Oxford, Tyndale moved to the Continent in the early 1520s, and from there worked on an English translation of the Bible. Published in Cologne in 1525, copies were smuggled into England, but destroyed when they came into the hands of the authorities. Tyndale was himself accused of heresy in the Low Countries and was burnt at the stake. Parts of his translation were incorporated into the Henrican Great Bible and the Authorized Bible of 1611, and thus have attained great familiarity over the centuries.
*DNB.*

**TYPHUS.** Of the diseases new to Europe in the early modern period, the most important were typhus and SYPHILIS. Typhus, which is a water-borne disease, was not distinguished from typhoid, which is transmitted through faeces, until 1849.

The earliest recorded instance of typhus in Europe occurred in Spain, where in 1489 the Spanish army was besieging GRANADA. Spanish soldiers quickly became infected with the new disease, and the number of troops killed in battle (*c.*3,000) was eclipsed by the number killed by typhus (*c.*18,000). The cause of the outbreak is not known with certainty, but epidemiologists have noted that the Spanish army had augmented its numbers with mercenaries who had recently been in CYPRUS fighting the Ottomans and so have suggested that the disease had arrived in the Levant from an unknown source during the later CRUSADES.

From Spain, typhus spread initially to NAPLES, where in 1528 the Neapolitan garrison of CHARLES V was under siege from a French army of 28,000 troops (see WARS OF ITALY); within a month of typhus breaking out, more than half of the French army had died of typhus, and the siege collapsed.

Typhus next occurred in the Balkans, where imperial armies were struggling to contain the Ottoman advance. In 1542, 30,000 imperial soldiers in the Balkans succumbed to typhus; in 1546, at the siege of Belgrade, it was the besieging Ottoman army that became infected, and, as in Naples in 1528, it was typhus that caused the siege to be lifted. When the imperial armies returned to Europe, they brought typhus with them; some soldiers went on to Spanish possessions in America, and so exported the disease to the Aztecs and Incas who were already suffering from epidemics of diseases that had arrived earlier (principally smallpox and measles). Typhus flourishes in the squalid conditions of warfare, and repeatedly ravaged the combatants in the THIRTY YEARS WAR.

The term 'typhus' was coined from the Greek word for smoke (an allusion to the stupor characteristic of the disease) in the late eighteenth century. In earlier English it was known as 'pestilential fever' or 'putrid fever', and was also named after the squalid conditions in which it arose, hence 'camp fever', 'hospital fever', 'ship fever', and 'jail fever'; English writers were particularly conscious of the threat posed by 'jail fever', because typhus was brought to court by prisoners and passed to court officials and juries.

**TYPOGRAPHY.** See PRINTING.

**TYRONE, HUGH O'NEILL, EARL OF** (*c*.1540–1616), Irish rebel. Raised in England, O'Neill became earl of Tyrone on the death of his brother in 1562. In 1568 he was sent to Ireland to impose order on the fractious O'Neill family. By 1595, however, he was himself in rebellion against ELIZABETH, with support from Catholic Europe. At the battle of Yellow Ford (the battle of the Blackwater) in 1598, he led a skilled army to victory over the English, and he maintained resistance to England until finally defeated in 1602. Five years later, he fled the country, and died in Rome.

*DNB* s.v. O'Neill, Hugh.

# U

**UBERTINO, FRANCESCO DI**. See BACCHIACCA.

**UBIQUITARIANISM**, the doctrine, mainly associated with Luther and his followers, that Jesus Christ in his human nature is everywhere present. Luther's belief in Ubiquitarianism lay at the heart of his belief in the 'real presence' of Christ in the EUCHARIST. The doctrine was the subject of heated controversies in the 1560s, when its champions were Johannes BRENZ (who had defended the doctrine at a Lutheran synod in Stuttgart in 1559) and Jakob Andreae and its principal detractors were BEZA and BULLINGER.

**UCCELLO, PAOLO, or Paolo di Dono** (*c*.1397–1475), Italian painter, a native of Florence, where he trained in the workshop of GHIBERTI (1407–15); he subsequently worked in Venice as a mosaicist at San Marco. In 1436 Paolo was invited to execute a frescoed equestrian monument to Sir John HAWKWOOD for Florence Cathedral; this fresco, in which the horse is modelled on the ancient bronze horses that surmount the central doorway of San Marco in Venice, demonstrates Paolo's interest in PERSPECTIVE.

In the 1440s Paolo accepted two more commissions from the cathedral, a frescoed clock face depicting the heads of four prophets and designs for stained-glass rondels (depicting a *Nativity* and a *Resurrection*) to be mounted in the drum of BRUNELLESCHI's dome. It may have been in this decade that he painted a fresco of the *Flood* (now damaged) in the cloister of Santa Maria Novella; this picture is a virtuoso demonstration of Paolo's mastery of foreshortening and of complex drawing.

In the 1450s Paolo painted *St George and the Dragon* (*c*.1455, National Gallery, London) and completed the three large battlepieces (*c*.1455) painted for the MEDICI Palace depicting *The Rout of San Romano*, a minor battle in which the Florentines defeated the Sienese on 1 June 1432; the three panels are now divided between the Louvre, the Uffizi, and the National Gallery in London. Paolo's *Hunt in the Forest* (*c*.1460, Ashmolean Museum, Oxford) testifies to his ability as an evocative painter of animals and to his abiding interest in perspective; in the face of such a painting VASARI's damaging condemnation of Paolo Uccello as an artist excessively preoccupied with geometry and perspective seems unnecessarily harsh.

MDA; Franco and Stefano Borsi, *Paolo Uccello* (1992; English trans. 1994).

Paolo Uccello, *The Hunt in the Forest* (*c*.1460), Ashmolean Museum, Oxford

Paolo Uccello, *The Rout of San Romano* (c.1450–60), National Gallery, London. The central figure (on the white charger) is NICCOLÒ DA TOLENTINO

**UDALL, NICHOLAS** (c.1505–1556), English educator and playwright. Headmaster of Eton College and later Westminster, Udall is remembered as the author of the earliest known English comedy, *Ralph Roister Doister*. Printed c.1566, the dates of its composition and first performance are uncertain; performances c.1534–41 at Eton, or c.1552 at Westminster, have both been suggested. The play, in short rhyming verse, dramatizes the unsuccessful wooing of a wealthy London widow by the fool Roister. Other plays written by Udall are either lost or survive in fragments only. The anonymous political allegory *Respublica* is probably his work.

*DNB.*

**UDINE, GIOVANNI DA.** See GIOVANNI DA UDINE.

**UFFIZI PALACE**, the Florentine palace designed by VASARI for Grand Duke COSIMO I DE' MEDICI to accommodate the public offices of his administration. Construction began in 1560, and in 1565 Vasari added a corridor over the Ponte Vecchio (which spans the Arno) in order to link the Uffizi with the PITTI PALACE; Bernardo BUONTALENTI later added the loggia. In the 1570s and 1580s the art collection of the MEDICI FAMILY was moved to the Uffizi by Grand Duke Francesco I de' Medici. These collections were expanded by successive grand dukes, and formed the basis of the present collection, which is the world's finest collection of Italian Renaissance art.

**UGO DA CARPI** (*fl.* 1502–32), Italian painter and wood engraver. He was born in Carpi (near Modena) and became

Italy's most important exponent of the CHIAROSCURO WOODCUT. His application of 1516 to the Venetian Senate for a patent on his method of using woodcuts to make PRINTS that seem to be painted may imply that he had invented the process independently of German artists. Many of his prints were designed by PARMIGIANINO (the most prolific chiaroscuro woodcut designer of the Renaissance); Ugo also used drawings of RAPHAEL as the basis of his prints.

*MDA s.v. Carpi, Ugo da.*

**UGOLINO DA SIENA or Ugolino di Nerio** (*fl.* 1317–39), Italian painter whose principal surviving work, an ALTARPIECE of *The Virgin and Child with Saints*, painted for the Church of Santa Croce in Florence, was dispersed in the nineteenth century. There are fragments in private collections, in the National Gallery in London, and in the Gemäldegalerie in Berlin, but substantial parts of the altarpiece have been lost.

*MDA s.v. Ugolino di Nerio.*

**UGOLINO DI VIERI** (*fl.* 1329–80), Italian goldsmith in Siena, the maker of the gilt-brass reliquary of the Sacro Corporale (1337–8) in Orvieto Cathedral. The reliquary, which is shaped like the Gothic façade of the cathedral, is enriched with precious stones and enamel panels; it contains the bloodstained cloth in which the host was wrapped in the Miracle of Bolsena (in 1263 the host bled to reassure a doubting Bohemian priest about the doctrine of transubstantiation). Ugolino's only other surviving work is the reliquary of

San Savino (Museo dell'Opera del Duomo, Orvieto), on which he collaborated with Viva di Lando.

*MDA*; P. Dal Poggetto, *Ugolino di Vieri: Gli smalti di Orvieto* (1965).

**ULRICH** (1487–1550), duke of Württemberg, succeeded his uncle Eberhard II as duke of Württemberg in 1498 and was declared of age in 1503. He embarked upon a military career in the service of the Emperor MAXIMILIAN, fighting with the imperial army in Bavaria in 1504, accompanying the emperor on his unfinished journey to Rome in 1508 and marching with the imperial army to France in 1513. His imperial ties were confirmed when in 1511 Ulrich married Sabina, daughter of Albrecht III, duke of Upper Bavaria-Munich, and niece of the Emperor Maximilian.

Ulrich's domestic policies were inept and his methods for raising taxes widely resented, and in 1514 a rising known as the 'poor Conrad' (*armer Konrad*) was suppressed only after Ulrich had made concessions to the ESTATES in return for financial assistance. He embarked on an affair with the wife of a knight, Hans von Hutten, and in 1515 killed the jealous husband in the course of a violent argument. Ulrich's wife Sabina and her supporters sought refuge under the protection of her brother Duke WILHELM IV of Bavaria and persuaded the emperor to place Ulrich under imperial interdiction, and Hans's relative Ulrich von HUTTEN excoriated Ulrich in print. On the death of Maximilian in January 1519, Ulrich supported the candidacy of FRANCIS I and occupied Reutlingen; the SWABIAN LEAGUE mobilized its forces and drove Ulrich from Württemberg, which was subsequently sold by the League to the Emperor CHARLES V. The imperial occupation of the duchy was to continue until 1534.

Ulrich spent his years of exile in the Swiss Confederation, France, and Germany. He initially fought in the army of Francis I, and in 1523 converted to Protestantism under the influence of OECOLAMPADIUS. At the outbreak of the PEASANTS' WAR he styled himself 'Ulrich the Peasant', raised an army from the Swiss cantons and adjoining areas north of the Rhine, and invaded Württemberg in February 1525; his Swiss mercenaries were recalled because of the defeat of Francis I at the battle of PAVIA, and Ulrich was forced to withdraw. In 1526 PHILIP OF HESSE declared his support for the campaign to restore the duchy to Ulrich, but the invasion was delayed until April 1534; on 13 May 1534 the Habsburg armies of Charles V and his brother FERDINAND I were defeated by the forces of Ulrich and Philip of Hesse at the battle of Lauffen. In February 1535 Ulrich was formally restored to the duchy under the terms negotiated in June 1534 in the Treaty of Kaaden, under which Ulrich was recognized as the lawful duke but was subject to the suzerainty of Austria.

Ulrich promptly introduced the Reformation into Württemberg, suppressing the monasteries and sequestering church property as a means of replenishing his treasury. In April 1536 he joined the SCHMALKALDIC LEAGUE and in 1546 fought against the emperor in the SCHMALKALDIC WAR. He was quickly defeated by the duque de ALBA, whose army occupied Württemberg; under the humiliating terms of the Treaty of Heilbronn signed in January 1547, Ulrich was allowed to keep his duchy (despite the protestations of Ferdinand) but was forced to hand over large sums of money and control of his defensive fortresses and to appear as a suppliant before the emperor at Ulm. He was subsequently obliged to submit to the AUGSBURG INTERIM in May 1548. Ulrich died on 6 November 1550 at Tübingen and was buried in the Stiftskirche.

**UMBRELLAS AND PARASOLS.** The purpose of the modern umbrella is to protect its holder from rain, but, as the etymology of the word (Latin *umbra*, i.e. shade) indicates, it was originally intended to afford protection from the heat of the sun; similarly, a parasol (Italian *parasole*) is, etymologically, a cover that 'defends' (Latin *parare*) its user from the sun (Latin *sol*). The modern distinction between the umbrella (for rain) and the parasol (for sun) was not established until the eighteenth century, when French ladies began to distinguish between the *parasol* and the *parapluie*. In medieval and early modern Europe umbrellas had a social significance, in that they were indicative of rank or high office: in 1177 Pope Alexander III gave the doge of Venice the privilege of protection by an umbrella, and until 1797 the doge walked or rode under a sumptuous state umbrella. Umbrellas also appear in religious contexts and have the same symbolic function as the BALDACCHINO: a large umbrella hangs in each of the basilican churches of Rome, and in the fifteenth century an umbrella was incorporated into the heraldic device of the PAPAL STATE; a fresco by Francesco SALVIATI in the Farnese Palace in Rome depicts Pope EUGENIUS IV beneath the banner of the Papal State on which an umbrella shelters the crossed keys.

The parasol was introduced in sixteenth-century Europe by aristocratic women in Italy, Portugal, and Spain. CATHERINE DE MÉDICIS brought her parasol to France when she married the future King HENRI II in 1533, and Henri's mistress DIANE DE POITIERS owned a parasol of which fragments still survive. The parasol was nonetheless not in common use amongst aristocratic French women: in 1578 Henri ESTIENNE argued in his *Deux Dialogues du nouveau français italianisé* that the parasol was an Italian affectation that had never become fashionable in France and in 1580 MONTAIGNE observed in one of his *Essais* that the carrying of parasols was an Italian custom of great antiquity. In 1562 MARY, QUEEN OF SCOTS, owned a silk parasol with fringes and tassels; it is not known when the first umbrella reached England, but one was first portrayed in art in a portrait of the diplomat Sir Henry Unton (c.1596, National Portrait Gallery, London). In 1608 Thomas CORYATE brought a leather umbrella with a gold fringe back from Italy, and regarded it as a possession sufficiently important to be mentioned in his will.

T. S. Crawford, *A History of the Umbrella* (1970).

**UMBRIAN SCHOOL.** In the nineteenth century the association of Umbria with St Francis of Assisi led to the notion of an Umbrian School of painting in which the assumed characteristics of St Francis were imposed on the painting of Umbria, which was thus said to be sweet and soft. These characteristics have nothing to do with the eirenic temperament of St Francis, but rather derive from the influence of Florentine artists such as Fra ANGELICO, Fra Filippo LIPPI, Benozzo GOZZOLI, Domenico VENEZIANO, and, most importantly, PIERO DELLA FRANCESCA.

The artistic centre of fifteenth- and early sixteenth-century Umbria was Perugia, where the most important painters were PERUGINO and PINTORICCHIO, both of whom were influenced by Piero. The quality of their painting in turn had an effect on the art of Rome and Tuscany. Pintoricchio worked in Rome and Siena and Perugino's pupils included RAPHAEL, whose art softened that of FRANCIA, who then introduced the traditions of Umbrian art into the Bolognese School of painting.

**UNIATE CHURCHES** are the eastern churches in communion with the Catholic Church but nonetheless retaining their own ecclesiastical languages, rites, and CANON LAW. The term 'uniate' (Latin *unio*, Polish *unia*) was first used by opponents of the Union of BREST-LITOVSK (1596), which brought the RUTHENIAN CHURCH of Poland into communion with the Church of Rome.

**UNIFORMITY, ACTS OF**. The term refers to legislative Acts passed in England in 1549, 1552, 1559, and 1662, all of which related to the enforcement of Protestantism. The Act of 21 January 1549 (repealed 1553) imposed the use of the Book of COMMON PRAYER and specified penalties for those who refused to use it. Public services were required to be in English, except in the universities, where Latin, Greek, or Hebrew could be used.

The Act of 14 April 1552 (repealed 1553) imposed the use of the revised Book of Common Prayer, and also specified penalties for absence from church on Sundays and holy days.

The Act of 8 May 1559, which was later incorporated into the 1662 edition of the Book of Common Prayer, repealed the ecclesiastical legislation of Queen MARY and reimposed the 1552 revision of the Book of Common Prayer, though the 'Declaration on Kneeling' (known since the nineteenth century as the Black Rubric) was removed from the end of the communion service. Absence from church became punishable by a financial penalty fixed at 12 pence.

The Act of 1662, which reintroduced the Book of Common Prayer in a slightly modified edition, was part of the Restoration settlement, and still remains on the Statute Book, though it has been modified on points of detail in 1865 (Clerical Subscription Act), 1871 (Universities Test Acts), and 1872 (Act of Uniformity Amendment Act, repealed 1974).

**UNITARIANISM AND ANTI-TRINITARIANISM**. The modern Christian Trinity did not become the official doctrine of the Church until the Council of Constantinople in 381. Prior to that date, the process by which monotheistic Judaic Christianity absorbed the Trinitarian formulations of middle Platonism had not been unchallenged: in the second and third centuries, theologians eager to preserve monotheism and to safeguard the unity (or 'monarchy') of God resisted the emerging consensus that God was triune.

Tertullian, who was the first to use the term *trinitas* of the Godhead, excoriated the unitary heresy as monarchianism.

The revival of monarchianism at the Reformation is called Unitarianism; like their counterparts in late antiquity, Unitarians insisted on the unipersonality of God. The earliest Reformation Unitarian to commit his views to print was Martin Cellarius (1499–1564), a pupil of Johann REUCHLIN who advanced Unitarian views in his *De operibus Dei* (Strassburg, 1527); similar views were soon expressed by Juan de VALDÉS, Michael SERVETUS, and Bernardino OCHINO.

In 1558 Giorgio BIANDRATA formed a Unitarian congregation in Poland; the Church grew rapidly over the next seven years, but in 1565 it was excluded from the synod of the reformed Church, and thereafter convened its own synods as the 'Minor Church' of Poland. Faustus SOCINUS led the Unitarian Church from 1579 until his death in 1604, and so Unitarianism came to be known as SOCINIANISM. In 1605, the Polish Minor Church issued the RACOVIAN CATECHISM, an influential statement of the Unitarian position. The Unitarian College at Racow was closed by the Jesuits in 1638 and in 1658 all Unitarians were expelled from Poland.

Biandrata arrived in Hungary in 1563 and spread the Unitarian message so successfully that the king, János Sigismund Zápolya, was converted. By the 1570s TRANSYLVANIA had become a semi-independent Turkish dependency, but Unitarianism had taken root there and is still a significant presence in the religious life of what is now a Romanian province.

In England, Unitarian sentiments emerged during the Interregnum. The founder of modern English Unitarianism was John Biddle (1615–62), who published an English translation of the Racovian Catechism in Amsterdam in 1652.

**UNITED PROVINCES or Dutch republic**. In 1579 the seven northern provinces of the NETHERLANDS (initially Friesland, Gelderland, Holland, Utrecht, and Zeeland and subsequently Groningen and Overijssel) formed a federation known as the Union of UTRECHT. In 1581 the Union proclaimed its independence from Spain, nominally under the rule of Francis, duke of ANJOU, but in fact led by WILLIAM OF ORANGE, stadtholder of the powerful provinces of Holland and Zeeland. After William's death the fledgling state was temporarily led by the earl of LEICESTER, the commander of the British forces in the Netherlands. Leicester was unable to rule effectively, and in 1588 power passed to William's son MAURICE OF NASSAU, who became the military leader, and to Jan van OLDENBARNEVELT, who became the public face of the federation for purposes of international relations. In 1596 the new state secured its first foreign recognition, which took the form of the 'Triple Alliance' with England and France. The twelve-year truce signed with Spain in April 1609 was a military truce rather than a legal acknowledgement of independence, and when the truce expired, hostilities again broke out. The United Provinces finally achieved formal independence in the Treaty of Münster in 1648.

In constitutional terms, the United Provinces was a loose confederation; each province appointed a stadtholder who assumed responsibility for all internal affairs; defence of the state, however, remained the prerogative of the central government. The highest national institution was the Estates-General (Dutch Staaten Generaal; see ESTATE), to which each province sent deputies. The republican character of the constitution was subverted by the success of the House of Orange in securing the stadtholderships of individual provinces and the senior military posts of the federation: when Maurice died on 23 April 1625, his brother Frederick Henry succeeded as stadtholder of five of the seven provinces and as captain-general of land forces and admiral-general of the republic's navy; in the 1631 Act of Survivance Frederick Henry's titles became hereditary and in 1637 he assumed the title of 'Highness'. By independence in 1648, the Dutch republic had in a limited sense become a monarchy, though the House of Orange was excluded from public office at the conclusion of the first Anglo-Dutch War in 1654.

J. L. Motley, *The Rise of the Dutch Republic* (3 vols., 1864).

**UNITY OF THE BROTHERS or Bohemian Brethren or Czech Brethren or (Latin) Unitas Fratrum or (Czech) Jednota Bratrská**, a group of UTRAQUISTS loyal to the teaching of Peter CHELČICKÝ (d. *c.*1460). The Brethren rejected oaths and military service and eschewed urban life and private property in favour of rural communities with shared ownership; in the 1460s the leader was 'Brother Gregory' who in 1467 organized the formal secession of the group from the Utraquist Church.

At the end of the century the leadership of the Brethren was assumed by Lucáš of Prague, who arranged for the writings of Chelčický and Brother Gregory to be condemned by the Synod of Rychnov in 1494 and in the 1520s began to advocate the Lutheran doctrine of GRACE (justification by faith alone). At this stage the theology of the Brethren was still Catholic in its insistence on a celibate priesthood and seven SACRAMENTS, but after the death of Lucáš in 1528 the drift towards Lutheran theology accelerated; in 1542 the Brethren formally accepted Luther's doctrines of grace and the EUCHARIST, but retained their insistence on confession.

In the wake of the battle of MÜHLBERG (1547) the Emperor FERDINAND began to persecute the Brethren, many of whom emigrated to Poland, where they formed an alliance with the Calvinists at the Synod of Koźminek (1555). The theology of those who remained in the Czech lands also became more Calvinist than Lutheran. In 1575 the Brethren were given the freedom to practise their religion by the emperor and established the seat of their Church in Moravia; thereafter they became known as the Moravian Brethren. In 1609 RUDOLF II presented the Brethren and the Utraquists with the University of Prague, but the subjugation of Bohemia in the wake of the battle of the White Mountain (Bila Hora) on 8 November 1620 led to the expulsion from the Czech lands of all Protestants, including the last bishop of the Brethren, the educationalist Jan Comenius. Thereafter the descendants of the Brethren scattered over Europe, America, and Africa; the Moravian Church still survives, and more than a quarter of its members are in Tanzania.

P. Brock, *The Political and Social Doctrines of the Unity of Czech Brethren* (1957).

**UNIVERSITIES.** In medieval Europe universities were centres for the study of theology, LAW, and MEDICINE. A medieval university was known either as a *studium particulare*, which was a local institution, or a *studium generalia*, which was a national or international institution. The later term *universitas* was initially the designation for a corporate body, but gradually came to be associated with educational institutions, for which the usual term was *universitas magistrorum et scholarium* ('community of teachers and scholars'); the abbreviated term *universitas* and its vernacular equivalents were first used in Germany, and then spread throughout Europe. From the thirteenth century onwards, many of these universities secured papal, imperial, or royal licences to award degrees, which were essentially teaching qualifications.

By 1400 there were some 65 universities in Europe, and by 1500 there were about 100 universities. Instruction was invariably in Latin, which allowed scholars to migrate easily to universities in other countries: ERASMUS taught in Cambridge, BUCHANAN in Coimbra, and ALCIATO in Bourges. The movement of students across the borders of Europe is attested by the presence in large universities of 'nations'; the University of Paris, for example, consisted of four nations: French (which included Spaniards, Italians, and Greeks), Picard (which included Netherlandish students), English (which included students from Ireland, Scotland, Germany, and the English enclaves in France), and Norman. Universities were usually divided into four faculties, which were sometimes called 'colleges', a sense that coexisted with the use of the term 'college' to describe a place of residence for scholars. The lower or elementary faculty was that of arts, which awarded the degree of *magister*, or master of arts; the seven LIBERAL ARTS (*artes liberales*) were organized into the humanities of the trivium (logic, rhetoric, and grammar) and the mathematical sciences of the quadrivium (arithmetic, astronomy, geometry, and music). The three higher faculties, which awarded doctorates, were theology, law, and medicine. This organization was normal but not universal: sometimes CANON LAW and CIVIL LAW were separate faculties, and medicine and the arts were sometimes combined into a single faculty. Universities sometimes began as single-faculty institutions: Salerno was a medical school, Bologna and Bourges were colleges of law, Seville was a centre for philological study, and the Sorbonne was a college of logic.

There had been a continuous tradition of learned institutions in Europe since classical antiquity, but the earliest surviving institution to have evolved into what would now be called a university was the ninth-century medical school in Salerno. The universities in Bologna and Paris, both of which were established in the twelfth century, claim to be Europe's first universities. By the beginning of the thirteenth century, there were eight institutions described as *studia generalia*: in Italy, Salerno, Bologna, Reggio Emilia, and Vicenza; in France, Paris and Montpellier; in Spain, Palencia; in England,

Oxford. In the course of the thirteenth century, *studia generalia* were established elsewhere in Italy (Modena, Padua, Vercelli, and Naples), and in England (Cambridge), France (Toulouse), Spain (Salamanca and Lleida), and Portugal (Coimbra); there were also important specialized institutions, such as the university founded in Seville in 1254 for the study of Semitic languages (especially Arabic). In the fourteenth century, universities spread throughout Europe, in Italy (Piacenza, Pavia, Arezzo, Rome, Perugia, Treviso, Florence, Siena, and Ferrara), France (Orléans, Angers, Avignon, Cahors, Grenoble, Perpignan, and Orange), Spain (Huesca and Valladolid), Hungary (Pécs), and Poland (Kraków). In the German lands (which included Bohemia) the first university was established in Prague in 1348 (and named after the Emperor Charles IV), and similar institutions were soon established in Vienna (1365), Heidelberg (1386), Cologne (1388), and Erfurt (1392). Another twelve German universities were founded before the REFORMATION, including Leipzig (1409), Trier (1450), Basel (1456), Freiburg (1457), Ingolstadt (1472), Mainz (1476), Tübingen (1477), Wittenberg (1502), and Frankfurt an der Oder (1506), and universities on the German model were established in Copenhagen (1475) and Uppsala (1477). In France, new universities were founded in Aix-en-Provence (1409), Poitiers (1431), Caen (1437), Bordeaux (1441), Valance (1452), Nantes (1463), and Bourges (1465). In Scotland, universities were established in St Andrews (1411), Glasgow (1453), and Aberdeen (1494). In Brabant, the University of Louvain, which was later to become an important centre of Counter-Reformation scholarship, was founded in 1423.

In the early sixteenth century the universities were subjected to the twin pressures of HUMANISM and the Reformation. The humanist revival of classical learning was initially felt in the newer universities, such as the University of Alcalá (1508), and was for long resisted in the medieval universities. The Reformation produced Protestant universities, of which the first was in Marburg (1527); Lutheran universities were also established in Königsberg (1544; now Kaliningrad), Jena (1558), and Helmstedt (1575). A Calvinist institution was founded in Geneva (1559; see ACADEMY) and Protestant universities were established in Leiden (1575), Franeker (1585), Harderwijk (1600), and Groningen (1614); in 1621, the Academy in Strassburg (which by 1578 had more than 1,000 students) was formally constituted as a university. In Ireland, a Protestant university (Trinity College, Dublin) was founded in 1591. The most important of the Counter-Reformation universities were Louvain, Altdorf (1578; in Germany, not Switzerland), and the Jesuit Collegium Romanum (1551, later refounded as the Pontificia Università Gregoriana); Catholic scholarship was also championed at the new universities in Valencia (1501), Seville (1505), Santiago (1526), Granada (1531), and Oviedo (1574).

Throughout the early modern period, universities excluded experimental sciences from their purview; there are occasional exceptions (notably Leiden in the seventeenth century), but for the most part scientific research was conducted in private institutions, such as GRESHAM COLLEGE in London.

**URBAN VII** (1521–90), pope for thirteen days (15–27 September 1590), was born Giambattista Castagna in Rome on 4 August 1521, the son of a Genoese nobleman and his Roman wife. He studied CANON LAW at Perugia, Padua, and Bologna, and in 1551 travelled to France in the train of his uncle Cardinal Girolamo Verallo, papal legate to HENRI II. On his return to Rome he was assigned to a senior position in the tribunal known as the Signatura Gratiae and in 1553 was appointed archbishop of Rossano (Calabria). He was for a short time governor of the PAPAL STATE and in 1562–3 took part in the closing sessions of the COUNCIL OF TRENT. In 1564 he accompanied Cardinal Boncompagni (later Pope GREGORY XIII) on a papal legation to Spain, and remained in Spain as a papal nuncio until 1572, on occasion calming the strained relations between Pope PIUS V and King PHILIP II caused by the control exercised by the Spanish crown over the Church.

In 1573 Castagna resigned his bishopric and became nuncio to Venice, and he subsequently served as governor of Bologna. Pope Gregory XIII created him cardinal-priest on 12 December 1583. Pope SIXTUS V confirmed Castagna's appointment as governor of Bologna and appointed him to the Inquisition.

Castagna was elected as Pope Urban VII on 15 September 1590, and the following day collapsed with malaria; he died before he could be crowned, and bequeathed his fortune (30,000 *scudi*) to be used as dowries for poor Roman girls.

**URFÉ, HONORÉ D'** (1567–1625), French novelist and playwright, born into a prominent family in Marseille. His first important poem was *Sireine* (completed 1594, published 1604), which was modelled on MONTEMAYOR's *Diana*. Urfé became caught up in the WARS OF RELIGION, in which he was a supporter of the CATHOLIC LEAGUE; he was twice captured and imprisoned, and while in jail he composed the first volume of his *Épîtres morales* (1598), which articulate the principle of STOIC fortitude in adversity. The second volume of *Épîtres morales* (1610) reflects an interest in mystical Platonism and the CABBALA. Urfé's final work was *L'Astrée* (1607–27), which became the model for the French PASTORAL novel of the seventeenth century.

Louise Horowitz, *Honoré d'Urfé* (1984).

**URSINUS, ZACHARIAS** (1534–83), Calvinist theologian, born in Breslau, Silesia (now Wrocław, in Poland), on 18 July 1534. He studied at Wittenberg (1550–7), where he became a disciple of MELANCHTHON, but his subsequent experience of Geneva (where he studied under CALVIN) and Paris (where he studied Hebrew under Jean Mercier) and his meetings with BULLINGER and CASTELLIO gradually shifted the balance of his theology from Lutheran to Calvinist.

In 1561 Ursinus was appointed professor at the Collegium Sapientiae at Heidelberg, where, in 1563, he collaborated with Kaspar Olevian on the composition of the HEIDELBERG CATECHISM. On the death of the Elector FRIEDRICH III and the succession of Ludwig VI, Ursinus was dismissed from his post, and in 1578 became professor at Neustadt-an-der-Haardt (now Neustadt an der Weinstrasse), where he remained for the rest of his life. In 1581 Ursinus published his *Admonitio christiana* (known from its place of publication as the *Neostadiensium admonitio*), which was published on behalf of the Reformed (i.e. Calvinist) Church at Heidelberg as a rejoinder to the Formula of CONCORD. The twelve chapters of the *Admonitio* are an important formulation of Calvinist theology.

E. K. Sturm, *Der junge Zacharias Ursin: Sein Weg vom Philippismus zum Calvinismus (1534–1562)* (1972); D. Visser, *Zacharias Ursinus: The Reluctant Reformer. His Life and Times* (1983).

**URSO or Ursoni, FILIPPO** (*fl.* 1554), the Italian author of an album of pen and ink designs for parade armour, now in the Victoria and Albert Museum. The album is dated 1554, and its otherwise unknown author is said in the manuscript to be a native of Mantua.

**URSULINES.** The Ursuline Order was founded by ANGELA MERICI in Brescia in November 1535. In the first instance the Order was a society of virgins who took no vows, but lived in their own homes and dedicated themselves to the education of poor girls and the care of sick women. The order was approved by Pope PAUL III in 1544. In 1572, Cardinal Carlo BORROMEO persuaded Pope GREGORY XIII to declare the Ursulines a religious order under the rule of St Augustine and to introduce simple vows and communal living. The order expanded under the powerful patronage of FRANÇOIS DE SALES. In 1612 Pope PAUL V allowed the Ursulines of Paris to take solemn vows and to adopt strict enclosure; convents deriving from this reform were called Religious Ursulines, and those who derived from the original Congregation were called Congregated Ursulines. In 1639 Marie Guyard ('la vénérable Mère Marie de l'Incarnation'), a French Religious Ursuline, founded a convent in Québec, where the sisters worked (and continue to work) among the Indians and the French community.

The order is named after St Ursula, a British princess who was believed to have perished in Cologne along with 11,000 virgins. This capacious number may have been generated by a tenth-century transcription error, in which the abbreviation XIMV (*undecim martyres virgines*, i.e. eleven virgin-martyrs) was unwittingly thought to mean *undecim milia virgines* (i.e. 11,000 virgins). Her cult was widespread in the Netherlands, the Rhineland, northern France, and Venice. There are at least 25 surviving painted cycles of her life dating from the fourteenth to the sixteenth centuries, including one by Vittore CARPACCIO, now in the Accademia di Belle Arti in Venice.

**USCOKS or Uskoks or (Italian) Uscocchi.** The Ottoman occupation of the Balkan peninsula in the late fifteenth and early sixteenth centuries produced large numbers of Christian refugees who sought sanctuary in the West. 'Uskok' is the Croatian, Serbian, and Slovene word for 'fugitive'. A body of Uscoks established itself in the Dalmatian fortress of Klis, which lay within the Venetian enclave of Spalato (now Split), and there fought a rearguard action against the Ottomans. When Klis became indefensible in the mid-sixteenth century, the Uscoks retreated some 400

kilometres (250 miles) along the coast to the Croatian port of Senj, which then lay on the Habsburg–Ottoman frontier, and was subject to a separate legal code, the *Militärgrenze*. Under the terms of this code, the Uscoks were promised an annual subsidy in return for military service.

The imperial subsidy was rarely paid, and the Uscoks turned to piracy. After 1540, Venice guaranteed the safety of Ottoman merchant vessels with escorts of galleys, but the draught of the galleys was too deep for them to mount a challenge to the light boats of the Uscoks amongst the shoals and islets of the Kvarnerić. Initially the Uscok pirates had only preyed on Ottoman vessels, but the provocation of Venetian escorts led the Uscoks to pillage the Venetian islands of Arbe, Pago, and Veglia (now the Croatian islands of Rab, Pag, and Krk) and to use the Venetian enclaves on the Dalmatian coast as bridgeheads for attacks on the Ottomans. Uscok pirates ranged across the Adriatic, and were joined by BARBARY PIRATES along the southern shores of Italy.

Uscok pirates raided the vessels of the PAPAL STATE and the kingdom of NAPLES as well as Ottoman and Venetian vessels, and when the pope and the king of Spain complained to Venice, the appeals were passed to Austria. The Habsburg view, which may have been encouraged by a share of the spoils, was that Uscok assaults on the Ottomans outweighed the irritation of their piracy.

In 1577 Venice mounted a protracted campaign against the Uscoks, and succeeded for a time in suppressing raids during daylight, in the summer, and on calm seas, though the Uscoks continued to venture out on foul winter nights. In 1592 an Ottoman army invaded Croatia, hoping to capture Senj, but the mountains and forests around the town precluded the use of artillery and cavalry, and the following year the army was beaten back by Austrian troops. Venice became involved in the war when Admiral Giovanni Bembo blockaded Trieste and Fiume, which were the main points of sale for pirated goods. In 1602 an Uscok raid on Istria united Venice and Austria against the Uscoks. Venice sent a heavily guarded commissioner to Senj, but he was murdered before he could restore order. In 1615 the tensions generated by Uscoks led to a war between Venice and Austria, and in the peace that was negotiated in Madrid in 1617, it was agreed that the Uscoks should be disbanded and transported with their families to the interior of Croatia, and that their boats should be destroyed.

The first history of the Uscoks was Minuccio Minucci's *Istoria degli Uscochi* (Venice, 1603), which was later continued by Paolo SARPI.

**UTENS, GIUSTO** (1558–1609), an Italian painter of Flemish origin who between 1599 and 1602 painted a series of lunettes depicting VILLAS with their gardens near Florence; the fourteen lunettes (tempera on canvas) were executed for the *salone grande* of the Villa di Artimino, and are now in the Museo di Firenze Com'era. The paintings emphasize structural patterns, so all trees, for example, are the same height, regardless of age or species, but this artistic failing renders the paintings particularly valuable to historians of villas and gardens, because they preserve intention as well as realization. The ITALIAN GARDENS depicted in the lunettes include the BOBOLI GARDENS, PRATOLINO, and the MEDICI VILLAS at Castello and Poggio a Caiano.

Daniela Mignani, *Le Ville Medicee di Giusto Utens* (1980).

**UTRAQUISTS or Calixtines or (Czech) Podoboji**. Utraquism is the belief that communion *sub utraque specie* ('under both kinds'), i.e. the 'species' of both bread and wine, should be taken by the laity as well as by the clergy. The idea was first advocated formally in 1414 by Jakob of Meis, a professor at University of Prague. Jan HUS did not openly advocate the practice, but it was demanded by many of his followers, the Bohemian Hussites, despite its condemnation at the COUNCIL OF CONSTANCE in 1415 and at the COUNCIL OF BASEL in 1432. The Utraquists were sometimes called Calixtines, because they demanded the communion cup (Greek and Latin *calix*) which was restricted to the celebrant; Bohemians who defended communion in one kind (*sub una specie*) were called Subunists or Subunites.

In 1433 the Compactata of Prague recognized both Utraquists and Subunists, and this recognition was ratified in Moravia at Jihlava (German Iglau) on 5 July 1436 in the treaty with the Hussites that acknowledged SIGISMUND as king of Bohemia; in 1437 the Council of Basel revoked its earlier decision and conceded the chalice. These decisions never received papal ratification, and were formally revoked by Pope PIUS II in 1462, but were nonetheless maintained by the Bohemian Diet until 1567.

G. Constant, *Concession à l'Allemagne de la communion sous les deux espèces* (2 vols., 1923).

**UTRECHT, UNION OF** (23 January 1579), a confederation, arising out of the Union of ARRAS, of the northern states of the Netherlands, initially consisting of Friesland, Gelderland, Holland, Utrecht, and Zeeland and later incorporating Groningen and Overijssel. The federation marked an important stage in the REVOLT OF THE NETHERLANDS, because two years later it proclaimed its independence from Spain and so became the antecedent state of the UNITED PROVINCES. Other provinces were soon brought into the Union, and the document of Union became the written constitution of the republic.

**UYTEWAEL or Wtewael, JOACHIM** (1566–1638), Dutch painter, born in Utrecht. As a young man he travelled to Flanders, Italy, and France, returning to Utrecht in 1592. He was a mannerist in style with a pronounced sense of the dramatic value of contrasting light and shade, and his favoured subjects were biblical and mythological themes. His surviving paintings include *The Deluge* (1592–5, Germanisches Nationalmuseum, Nuremberg) and *Kitchen Scene with the Parable of the Great Supper* (1605; Gemäldegalerie, Berlin).

MDA; Anne Lowenthal, *Joachim Wtewael and Dutch Mannerism* (1986).

# V

**VACA DE CASTRO, CRISTÓBAL** (*c*.1492–1566), governor of Peru. He was born into a noble family in León, and served as a court official before being sent to Peru by CHARLES V to settle the jurisdictional dispute between Francisco PIZARRO and Almagro, the illegitimate son of Diego de ALMAGRO. By the time he arrived, Pizarro had been assassinated (26 June 1541). Vaca de Castro assumed the government of the country and raised an army of conquistadors which defeated the forces of Almagro in the battle of Chupas (near Guamanga); Almagro was subsequently beheaded as a traitor.

The proclamation of the 'New Laws' that reformed the Laws of the INDIES provoked another rebellion, this time led by Gonzalo PIZARRO, who entered Lima on 28 October 1544. Vaca de Castro fell out with the newly arrived viceroy, Blasco Nuñez de Vela, on the question of how to deal with the rebellion. Vaca de Castro was arrested, but escaped from prison and made his way to Spain, where he was again imprisoned; three years later he was pardoned and released.

*DHE*; Casiano García Rodriguez, *Vida de Don Cristóbal Vaca de Castro* (1957).

**VADIANUS or Vadian or Joachim von Watt** (1484–1551), Swiss humanist and reformer, born in St Gallen and educated at the University of Vienna, where he was taught by Konrad CELTIS, appointed to a professorship, and in 1516 appointed as rector; in 1514 he was crowned POET LAUREATE by the Emperor MAXIMILIAN. In 1518 Vadianus returned to St Gallen as city physician, and the following year began to espouse the cause of the Reformation. He became a friend and supporter of ZWINGLI, and may be the author of the Zwinglian tract *Karsthans und Kegelhans* (1521). In 1526 he became burgomaster of St Gallen, and subsequently wrote a history of its monastery. He also wrote a treatise on literature (*De poetica carminis ratione liber*, 1518) and commentaries on classical authors.

W. Näf, *Vadian und seine Stadt St Gallen* (2 vols., 1944–57).

**VALCKENBORCH or Valkenborgh FAMILY**, Flemish painters of LANDSCAPE and GENRE PAINTINGS. Lucas Valckenborch (*c*.1535–1597) joined the guild of his native Mechelen (French Malines) in 1560 and subsequently moved to Antwerp, from which he fled to Aachen in 1565 to avoid persecution as a Protestant. He entered the service of Archduke (later Emperor) MATTHIAS, travelling with him to Linz (*c*.1582),

and spent his final years (from 1593) in Frankfurt. His elder brother Marten Valckenborch (1524–1612) fled with Lucas but subsequently returned to Antwerp before leaving for Frankfurt to meet his brother and then travelling to Venice (1602) and Rome (1604).

Both Lucas and Marten painted series of *The Seasons* and both painted genre pictures in the tradition of BRUEGEL. The brothers returned repeatedly to the subject of the Tower of Babel: there are examples by Lucas in the Alte Pinakothek in Munich and the Louvre in Paris and by Marten in the Gemäldegalerie Alte Meister in Dresden.

*MDA*; Alexander Wied, *Lucas und Marten van Valckenborch* (1990).

**VALDÉS, ALFONSO DE** (*c*.1490–1532), Spanish satirist, born in Cuenca, the elder of the twin sons of the *regidor* of Cuenca. Alfonso entered the service of CHARLES V, and was in his entourage at his coronation in Aachen in 1520. He served as Latin secretary of state from 1524, left Spain with the court in 1529, and died of the plague in Vienna in 1532.

Alfonso was the author of two Erasmian dialogues (published 1530 and often reprinted) for which he was denounced to the INQUISITION as a Lutheran; the fact that he was a known friend of Erasmus made him liable to such accusations. The *Diálogo de las cosas ocurridas en Roma* (also known as the *Diálogo de Lactancio y un arcediano*) is a defence of the SACK OF ROME by imperial troops in 1527, which Alfonso understood as a divine punishment for the corruption of the papacy. The *Diálogo de Mercurio y Carón*, which was attributed to Alfonso's brother Juan until the twentieth century, is a Lucianic dialogue in two books which sustains the defence of Charles V's imperial policies and contrasts the corruption of cruel princes and wealthy clerics (in book 1) with humane rulers and conscientious clergy (in book 2). Alfonso also wrote commentaries on Romans and 1 Corinthians (published posthumously in 1556 and 1557) and a translation of Matthew's Gospel into Spanish. The religious principles articulated in *Ciento y diez consideraciones divinas* (1539), written with his brother Juan, align both brothers with the religious movement of ALUMBRISMO.

M. Carrasco, *Alfonso et Juan de Valdés: Leur Vie et leurs écrits réligieux* (1880); Dorothy Donald, *Alfonso de Valdés y su época* (1983).

**VALDÉS, JUAN DE** (*c.*1491–1541), Spanish humanist, born in Cuenca, the younger of the twin sons of the *regidor* of Cuenca. He studied Latin and Greek at Alcalá de Henares, and became interested in the thought of ERASMUS, with whom he corresponded. His Erasmian *Diálogo de doctrina cristiana* (Alcalá de Henares, 1529) was denounced to the INQUISITION. Juan fled to Rome in 1531, and later settled in Naples, where he became the central figure in a group of Erasmian sympathizers that included future Protestants such as Bernardino OCHINO and Pietro Martire VERMIGLI and the Catholic reformers Giulia GONZAGA and the ill-fated Pietro CARNESECCHI. He died in Naples in May 1541.

Juan's *Alfabeto cristiano* (1546) is a defence of the Lutheran doctrine of JUSTIFICATION by faith. The religious principles articulated in *Ciento y diez consideraciones divinas* (1539), written with his brother Alfonso VALDÉS, align both brothers with the religious movement of ALUMBRISMO.

Juan's most important work in the humanist philological tradition is his *Diálogo de la lengua* (*c.*1535, published 1737), which draws on the example of BEMBO's *Prose della volgar lingua* (1525) to discuss the lexis, spelling, syntax, and stylistic range of the SPANISH LANGUAGE. In the dialogue two Spaniards (one called Valdés) encourage two Italian interlocutors to improve their Spanish by imitating works such as the AMADÍS DE GAULA and *Celestina* of Fernando de ROJAS and by considering the elegant concision and directness of expression of some 200 Castilian proverbs; Valdés mocks the stylistic excesses of the chivalric romances (*libros de caballerías*) then in fashion.

M. Carrasco, *Alfonso et Juan de Valdés: Leur Vie et leur écrits religieux* (1880); D. Ricart, *Juan de Valdés y el pensamiento religioso europeo en los siglos XVI y XVII* (1958); J. N. Bakhuizen van den Brink, *Juan de Valdés, réformateur en Espagne et en Italie, 1529–1541* (1969); José C. Nieto, *Juan de Valdés and the Origins of the Spanish and Italian Reformation* (1970).

**VALDIVIA, PEDRO DE** (1497–53), Spanish conqueror of Chile, born in Extremadura. He joined the imperial army and fought at the battle of PAVIA (1525) before crossing the Atlantic to participate in the conquest of Venezuela in 1535. In 1537 he joined PIZARRO in Peru, and received from him the commission to conquer Chile in the wake of the abortive invasion by Diego de ALMAGRO in 1535.

In 1540 Valdivia marched south with a force of 150 Spaniards and 1,000 Indians, and in February 1541 founded Santiago de Nuevo Extremo (now Santiago de Chile). In 1548 he returned to Peru and assisted Pedro de la GASCA to suppress the rebellion of Gonzalo PIZARRO. On his return to Chile, he faced a rebellion by Mapuche Indians. In 1550 he marched south and founded La Concepción del Nuevo Extremo (now Penco, near Concepción), Villarrica, Imperial (now Nueva Imperial), Angol, and Valdivia, with a view to subduing the country. The Indians refused to submit to the conquistadors, and in 1553 there was a general rising during which Valdivia was captured, tortured, and murdered by a rebel group led by Lautaro, his former Indian servant. Indian resistance was to continue until 1640.

*DHE*; Gerardo Larraín Valdés, *Pedro de Valdivia: Biografía* (1996).

**VALENCIA**, a city and archbishopric on the Mediterranean coast of Spain, since 1238 a kingdom in the crown of Aragon, though at the end of the fifteenth century united with Castile and thereafter ruled by a viceroy. In the fifteenth century the city was an important centre for the manufacture of MAIOLICA, and in 1474 became the first Spanish city to acquire a printing press. The university was founded in about 1500, but its antecedent institutions (a civic college of arts, medicine, and law and an episcopal school of theology) date from the mid-fourteenth century. In the fifteenth century, when Valencia's writers included Ausiàs March, the city became an important cultural and literary centre. The Valencian School of painting inaugurated by Vicent MAÇIP and his son Joan Vicent included Lluís DALMAU, Pedro Orrente (1560–1644), Francisco RIBALTA and his son Juan (1597–1628), and José Ribera (1591–1662).

**VALENCIA, FRAY MARTÍN DE** (*c.*1474–1534), Spanish missionary in Mexico. He was born near León, where he joined the Observant Franciscans. In 1524 he was chosen as the leader of the 'Twelve Apostles to Mexico', who arrived in Veracruz in 1524. In the last ten years of his life he was responsible for the conversion of thousands of Indians.

*DHE*; S. Escalante Plancarte, *Fray Martín de Valencia* (1945).

**VALERIANO, PIETRO, or Giovanni Pietro delle Fosse** (1477–1558), Italian humanist and poet, born in Belluno and educated in Venice. He entered the service of Giulio de' MEDICI (later Pope CLEMENT VII), who in 1509 sent Valeriano to Rome, where he was appointed tutor to Giulio's nephews Ippolito and Alessandro de' MEDICI; on Giulio's accession Valeriano became his apostolic protonotary. In 1527 he moved to Florence in the wake of the SACK OF ROME; he died in Padua.

Valeriano collected his Latin love poems in *Amorum libri* (1549). He contributed to the QUESTIONE DELLA LINGUA debate with a *Dialogo della lingua volgare* (posthumously published in 1620) in which he argued in favour of a literary form of Italian based on philological principles and the *lingua cortigiana* rather than any particular dialect. His *De literatorum infelicitate* (published posthumously in 1620) is an account of intellectual life in Rome during his years there. Valeriano also wrote *Hieroglyphica* (1556), a treatise on the writing system of ancient Egypt based on his study (and that of his uncle Valeriano Bolzanio) of inscriptions on obelisks in Rome, the *Hieroglyphica* attributed to Horapollo, and the Bembine Table (see EGYPTOLOGY).

*OCIL.*

**VALLA, LORENZO** (1407–57), major Italian humanist. Valla was born and educated in Rome, and from 1429 to 1433 lectured on eloquence in Pavia. He served as secretary to ALFONSO V of Aragon from 1437 to 1448, and then returned to Rome, where he worked as a papal secretary and as a professor of eloquence at the university; he had a good command of Greek, and during this period became part of the circle of BESSARION.

Valla deployed his brilliant philological and historical scholarship in the study of logic and RHETORIC, moral philosophy, and ancient history. In his important *Dialecticae disputationes* (1439) he violently attacked scholastic and Aristotelian logic and proposed instead a system of logic symbiotically related to rhetoric. His *De voluptate* (1431, later revised as *De vero bono*) is a dialogue on the idea of the good in STOICISM, Epicureanism (see EPICURUS), and Christianity. His greatest historical triumph was his proof that the Donation of Constantine, the apparently fourth-century text used to justify papal claims to temporal power, was a medieval forgery (*De falso credita et ementita Constantini donatione declamatio*, 1440). He completed a draft of his masterpiece, a work on humanist LATIN (*De elegantiis linguae Latinae*), in 1440, and thereafter revised and supplemented it for many years.

Valla's Greek scholarship included translations of Homer (sixteen books of the *Iliad*), Aesop, Herodotus, Xenophon, and Thucydides. He also published a comparison of the Latin and Greek texts of the New Testament (*Collatio Novi Testamenti*, 1444). This philological scholarship, together with Valla's analysis of the irreconcilability of divine omnipotence and human free will (*De libero arbitrio*, posthumously published in 1493), led initially to suspicions of heresy and eventually to acclamation by reformers, especially Martin LUTHER.

M. Fois, *Il pensiero cristiano di Lorenzo Valla* (1969); S. I. Camporeale, *Lorenzo Valla, umanesimo e teologia* (1972); O. Besomi and M. Regoliosi (eds.), *Lorenzo Valla e l'umanesimo italiano* (1986); Peter Mack, *Renaissance Argument: Valla and Agricola in the Traditions of Renaissance Rhetoric* (1993).

**VALLADOLID**, a town and bishopric in north-west Spain, since 1208 a possession of the crown of Castile. It was for centuries the chief commercial and political centre of Castile and the seat of the Castilian chancery and royal courts (audiencia). The town occasionally served as a royal residence, and Ferdinand II of Aragon (FERDINAND V) and ISABELLA of Castile were married there in 1469. In 1520–1 Valladolid was the centre of the Revolt of the COMUNEROS and later of Protestant groups which were crushed by the INQUISITION in the late 1550s. PHILIP II established his court in Valladolid (where he had been born), but the town proved to be unhealthy and in 1560 Philip transferred the court to Madrid, where it has remained ever since, except for a brief return to Valladolid in 1600–6. COLUMBUS died in the town (1506); CERVANTES lived there (1603–6), and his house is now a museum and library. Artists who worked in the town include the painter Alonso BERRUGUETE and the sculptors JUAN DE JUNI and Gregorio FERNÁNDEZ.

The finest Renaissance building in Valladolid is the cathedral, which was begun by Juan de HERRERA in 1585; his original model is now preserved in the muniment room. All that was built according to his design was the nave and one tower (out of four), which collapsed in 1841. The Colegio de Santa Cruz (1479–92) was built in the PLATERESQUE style by Enrique EGAS. The late fifteenth-century Colegio de San Gregorio was badly damaged by the French in 1808, but still retains its fine late Gothic façade. The university was a powerful institution throughout the sixteenth and seventeenth centuries but its present buildings are later. Philip II granted Valladolid a city charter in 1596, from which time it declined steadily in importance until the industrial revival of modern times. It is now an archdiocese and provincial capital.

Bartolomé Bennassar, *Valladolid au siècle d'or* (1967); Luis Antonio Ribot García (ed.), *Valladolid, corazón del mundo hispánico, siglo XVI* (1981).

**VALOIS, HOUSE OF**, the ruling dynasty of France from 1328 (the accession of Philip VI) to 1589 (the accession of the House of BOURBON); see Appendix 1 and the entries on LOUIS XI, CHARLES VIII, LOUIS XII, FRANCIS I, HENRI II, FRANCIS II, CHARLES IX, and HENRI III. Other prominent branches of the family are the dukes of ALENÇON, ANJOU, and BURGUNDY. On the wars sometimes known as the Habsburg–Valois Wars, see WARS OF ITALY.

G. Dodu, *Les Valois* (1934).

**VALTURIO, ROBERTO** (1405–75), writer on warfare. He was born in Rimini, and in 1438 moved to Rome, where he worked in the papal Office of Abbreviators as a legal draughtsman. He returned to Rimini and entered the service of Sigismondo MALATESTA as an adviser and diplomat. In about 1450 he wrote a twelve-book treatise on the art of war, which was eventually published as *De re militari lib. XII* (Verona, 1472) with a dedication to Malatesta. The treatise is chiefly remarkable for the 82 woodcuts used to illustrate military machines; these illustrations, which may have been executed by Matteo de' PASTI, set a new standard for illustrated books. The text is a detailed analysis of warfare, and its humanist bias means that many of the illustrative examples are drawn from the campaigns of classical antiquity. There are also detailed discussions of strategy, tactics, weaponry, and the qualities of an ideal *condottiere*.

*De re militari* was widely influential in military circles. The Latin version was read all over Europe, and translations appeared in Italian (1483) and French (1532); it was an important precursor of MACHIAVELLI's *Della arte della guerra*.

**VANDELVIRA, ANDRÉS DE** (1509–75), Spanish architect, apprenticed to Diego de SILOÉ. He was the last exponent in peninsular Spain of the style of SPANISH ARCHITECTURE known as Granadine Renaissance. His masterpiece is Jaén Cathedral (1532–48), which influenced the redesign of Mexico Cathedral by Claudio de ARCINIEGA in 1584 and Francisco BECERRA's designs for the Peruvian cathedrals of Lima and Cuzco. Vandelvira's final building was the Chapel of El Salvador in the Santiago Hospital at Úbeda (1562–75).

*MDA.*

**VANNI, ANDREA** (c.1330–1413), Italian painter, a native of Siena, where he held several civic offices. Apart from a period in Naples and Sicily (1384–91), he remained in Siena throughout his life. His most important painting is a portable tryptych originally in Naples and now in the Corcoran Gallery in Washington. The fresco of *St Catherine* in the conventual Church of San Domenico is usually attributed to Andrea.

**VARCHI, BENEDETTO** (1503–65), Florentine historian who studied law in Pisa and on returning to Florence became a notary. His principled republicanism led Varchi to support the expulsion of the MEDICI from Florence in 1527, and on their restoration in 1530 he was exiled. In 1537 he took part in Piero STROZZI's unsuccessful attempt to depose the Medici, but in 1543 was nonetheless invited by Duke COSIMO I DE' MEDICI to return to the city in order to write a history of Florence from 1527 to 1538. Varchi's carefully documented sixteen-book *Storia fiorentina* is a model of balanced historical scholarship, except in its adulation of Duke Cosimo, but nonetheless remained unpublished until 1721.

Varchi was also a poet (*Sonnetti*, 1555–7), a playwright, and a translator of classical texts. His *L'Ercolano* (1560) champions the Tuscan vernacular as a literary language.

Eric Cochrane, *Historians and Historiography in the Italian Renaissance* (1981).

**VARTHEMA, LUDOVICO DE** (*c*.1470–1517), Italian traveller and travel writer. He was apparently born in Bologna and as a young man may have served as a soldier. In 1502 he embarked on a journey that took him across the Mediterranean to Alexandria and on to Cairo, Beirut, Tripoli (the Lebanese city), Aleppo, and Damascus, where he became a soldier in the Mameluke garrison.

Varthema seems to have become a Muslim, at least temporarily, because in 1503 he was one of the soldiers that accompanied pilgrims on the Haj, in which capacity he visited Medina and Mecca. He departed from the Haj port of Jeddah for India, but in Aden he was arrested as a Christian spy; after his release, which he attributed to the affections of one of the sultanas of Yemen, he visited south Arabian cities such as Sana'a and then sailed via the horn of Africa to India, landing at the Gujarati port of Diu. He then retraced his steps to the Persian Gulf, stopping at Muscat and the island of Ormuz (which was in 1507 to be overrun by ALBUQUERQUE) before striking inland across Persia to Herat, the seat of the fifteenth-century Timurid Renaissance (and now in Afghanistan), before returning via Shiraz and the Gulf to India, where he sailed down the west coast to Ceylon (now Sri Lanka).

By this point Varthema was beginning to approximate the route taken half a century earlier by the Venetian traveller Niccolò de' CONTI. He travelled on to Pegu (near Rangoon), where Conti had lived, and thence to Malacca (now Melaka, on the Malay peninsula), Pedir (a sultanate on the north coast of Sumatra), and finally to the Moluccas. He returned to India via Java (where Conti had lived), and in Cannanore (now Kannur, on the Kerala coast) joined the Portuguese garrison. His military service was of sufficient distinction for him to be knighted by the viceroy, Francisco de ALMEIDA; his sponsor was Tristão da CUNHA. He subsequently served for more than a year as factor of the *FEITORIA* at Cochin (Kochi), and in December 1507 left for Portugal by the Cape route. In Portugal Varthema's knighthood was confirmed by King MANUEL I, and Varthema then left for Rome.

Varthema's *Itinerario* (Rome, 1510; Venice, 1511) contains detailed observations of the people and places that he visited.

His descriptions are on the whole scrupulous, though his eyes are those of a European male; his understanding of the motives of the Yemeni sultana, for example, occasions reflections on 'the desire of the women of Arabia Felix for white men', an early statement of what is now called Orientalism. The *Itinerario* soon proved to be immensely popular, and was read all over Europe in translations into Latin (Milan, 1511; Nuremberg, 1610), German (Augsburg, 1515; Strassburg, 1516), Spanish (Seville, 1520; from the Latin), Flemish (Antwerp, 1554); French (Lyon, 1556); and English (1577, in Richard Eden's *History of Travel*).

**VASA**, a royal dynasty that ruled Sweden from 1523 until the abdication of Queen Christina in 1654; its members included GUSTAVUS VASA, ERIK XIV, JOHN, and SIGISMUND III, who was also the first of three Vasa kings of Poland.

**VASARI, GIORGIO** (1511–74), Italian painter, architect, and biographer, born in Arezzo, the son of a potter; he received his first lessons in drawing from Luca SIGNORELLI, to whom he was distantly related. In 1524 his precocity attracted the patronage of Cardinal Silvio Passerini, who was the guardian of the youthful Alessandro de' MEDICI and his cousin Cardinal Ippolito de' Medici, the nominal joint rulers of Florence; Cardinal Silvio decided to educate the three boys together, so giving Vasari access to the Medici patronage that was to sustain him throughout his life. Vasari subsequently trained as a painter with ANDREA DEL SARTO and as a sculptor with Baccio BANDINELLI; while an apprentice Vasari briefly met MICHELANGELO, whose biographer he was later to become.

In 1555 Duke Cosimo de' MEDICI appointed Vasari as *capomaestro* of the Palazzo della Signoria (1555), to which he contributed the decoration of several rooms, notably the room now known as the Salone del Cinquecento. His other work in Florence includes the altarpiece of the *Immaculate Conception* in the Church of SS Apostoli and a posthumous portrait of Lorenzo de' MEDICI (1534, Uffizi). In architecture his most important work in Florence was the UFFIZI PALACE. He also renovated the interiors of the churches of Santa Maria Novella (1565–72) and Santa Croce (1566–84), creating large open spaces in conformity with the prescripts of the COUNCIL OF TRENT.

In Rome Vasari collaborated with Bartolomeo AMMANATI and Giacomo VIGNOLA on the design of the Villa GIULIA (1551–5). He also decorated the Sala dei Cento Giorni (so named because Vasari took 100 days to paint it) in the Palazzo della Cancellaria and the Sala Regia in the Vatican. In Pisa Vasari designed the Palazzo dei Cavalieri, and in his native Arezzo he decorated his family home (now a museum) and designed the abbey Church of SS Fiora e Lucilla (begun 1566) and the loggias (now known as the Logge Vasariane) on the Piazza Grande.

In 1543 Vasari began to plan a book on the lives of 'the most excellent painters, sculptors and architects', and in 1550 the first edition of *Vite de' più eccellenti architetti, pittori e scultori* was published; a heavily revised and substantially enlarged edition was published in 1568. Vasari's *Vite* was the first narrative history of art, and the model that he proposed has been qualified but never fully dislodged, and continues to exert a powerful influence on the canon of popular and academic taste. Art was reborn in Tuscany in the 1250s and there grew in three stages to a peak of perfection in the sixteenth century. The first stage of the revival, in which artists began to imitate nature, was inaugurated by GIOTTO; the second stage was the fifteenth century, in which the new understanding of perspective and anatomy was inaugurated by MASACCIO; the final stage, in which artists mastered and then surpassed nature, reaching the 'summit of perfection', was the age of LEONARDO DA VINCI, RAPHAEL, and Michelangelo.

*MDA*; Patricia Rubin, *Giorgio Vasari: Art and History* (1995).

**VASCO DA GAMA.** See GAMA, VASCO DA.

**VASCONCELOS, JORGE FERREIRA DE** (*c*.1515–*c*.1563), Portuguese playwright and novelist. His familiarity with Coimbra has been taken to imply that he was educated there, but no verifiable facts are known about the period before he entered the court of King JOHN III as a gentleman-in-waiting (*moço da câmara*) to Prince Duarte sometime in the 1530s. In 1540, on the death of Prince Duarte, he became secretary of the royal treasury (*escrivão do Tesouro*), and in 1563 was appointed secretary of the Casa da Moeda.

Vasconcelos was the author of three prose comedies that were intended to be read as dramatic dialogues rather than performed on the stage. *Eufrosina*, which was written in the late 1530s or early 1540s (published 1561), is a love story set in Coimbra, and draws on the structure and content of Fernando de ROJAS's *La Celestina*. *Ulisipo* (i.e. Lisbon) is a love story that mocks the avariciousness of the Lisbon middle class, and *Aulegrafia* is a comedy about the fading ideals of courtly love; both plays were probably written in the mid-1550s, but they were not published until the next century (1618–19).

Vasconcelos also wrote *Memorial da segunda távola redonda* (*c*.1554, published 1567), a chivalric romance that mingles the gods of classical antiquity with the Arthurian knights of the Round Table.

Jean Subirats, *Jorge Ferreira de Vasconcelos* (2 vols., 1982).

**VATABLE, FRANÇOIS** (*c*.1495–1547), French classical scholar and pioneer of HEBREW SCHOLARSHIP in France. Vatable was born in Picardy, and in about 1530 was appointed to one of the two founding chairs of Hebrew at the Collège de France. He combined classical and Semitic interests, translating both ancient philosophers (notably Aristotle) and the Hebrew scriptures (notably his *Biblia sacra Hebraica*, 1539–43). Some of his publications were based on notes taken by his students that found their way into the hands of Robert ESTIENNE, and Vatable subsequently dissociated himself from such works because he thought that they had been tainted by Protestantism.

**VATICAN.** In 1308 the papacy was exiled to Avignon, and the following year the Lateran Palace was seriously damaged by fire. When the papacy returned to Rome in 1377, the build-

ings of the Vatican were badly in need of repair and restoration. This process began in 1410, when the antipope JOHN XXIII restored the covered passage from the Vatican to Castel Sant'Angelo. In 1447 Pope NICHOLAS V drew up a comprehensive building plan which included residential accommodation for cardinals and the Vatican secretariat. This plan was implemented by Pope Nicholas's successors: Pope SIXTUS IV built the SISTINE CHAPEL, Pope INNOCENT VIII built the Villa Belvedere (since destroyed) and the BELVEDERE COURT, Popes JULIUS II and LEO X built BRAMANTE's *cortile* and RAPHAEL's *Stanze*, Pope PAUL III built the Sala Regia and Pope PIUS IV added the Villa PIA.

The plans of Nicholas V had also including the replacement of ST PETER's BASILICA with a new building, but that plan did not begin to bear fruit until 1506, when Pope Julius II commissioned Bramante to design a new church. Construction proceeded under a distinguished series of architects that included Raphael, Baldassare PERUZZI, Antonio SANGALLO the Younger, MICHELANGELO (who designed the dome), Giacomo DELLA PORTA, Domenico FONTANA (who built the VATICAN LIBRARY), Giacomo VIGNOLA, and Carlo Maderno; the building was finished in 1614 and consecrated by Pope Paul V in 18 November 1616.

**VATICAN LIBRARY or Biblioteca Apostolica Vaticana.** Documentation of the Vatican Library begins in 1295 with an inventory that lists 443 manuscripts. This library was taken to Avignon and was not returned when the GREAT SCHISM was concluded. What is now the Vatican Library began with the humanist popes of the mid-fifteenth century, notably NICHOLAS V, who assembled a collection of manuscripts from all over Europe and made them accessible to scholars, and SIXTUS IV, who appointed PLATINA as his librarian. The first *Cardinale Bibliotecario* was Marcello Cervini (later Pope MARCELLUS II). The collection expanded under successive popes, and in 1600 was augmented by the library of Fulvio ORSINI. In this period the collection was accommodated in the Floreria, beneath the Borgia apartments.

The building that now houses the Library was designed by Domenico FONTANA and built in 1587–9; it bisects (and diminishes the effect of) the BELVEDERE COURT built by BRAMANTE.

A. T. Grafton (ed.), *Rome Reborn: The Vatican Library and Renaissance Culture* (1993).

**VÁZQUEZ, GABRIEL** (1549–1604), Spanish Thomist, born in Belmonte, hence his Latin name of Bellomontanus. He entered the JESUIT Order in 1569, and taught moral theology at the colleges of Madrid, Ocaña, and Alcalá de Henares. He held a chair at Rome from 1585 to 1591, and then returned to Alcalá de Henares, where he taught for the rest of his life.

Vázquez was a scholar of immense learning, and had a remarkable command of PATRISTIC SCHOLARSHIP. His most important work is his *Commentarii ac disputationes*, a huge commentary on the *Summa theologica* of THOMAS AQUINAS (8 vols., 1598–1615). He was a passionate controversialist in the debate on the nature of GRACE.

Michael Lapierre, *The Noetical Theory of Gabriel Vasquez* (1999).

**VÁZQUEZ, LORENZO** (*c*.1450–*c*.1514), Spanish master mason and architect, probably born in Segovia, to whom the earliest Spanish buildings in the Renaissance style are attributed. From 1489 he was employed as a master mason by Cardinal MENDOZA, initially at the Colegio de Santa Cruz at Valladolid, which had been started in 1486 and was transformed by Vázquez in 1491 into a Renaissance building with an Italianate frontispiece medallion. His subsequent Mendoza commissions were the palace at Cogulludo (1495), which mingles Renaissance elements with Gothic windows, the palace at Guadalajara (completed before 1507), and (together with Michele Carloni of Genoa) the castle of La Calahorra, near Guadix (1509–12).

MDA.

**VÁZQUEZ DE CORONADO, FRANCISCO** (*c*.1510–1554), Spanish explorer born in Salamanca who in 1535 travelled in the suite of Antonio de MENDOZA to Mexico, where he married advantageously and in 1538 became governor of the province of New Galicia. In February 1540 he undertook an expedition to the kingdom of Cíbola in search of the legendary wealth of its seven cities. His substantial force, which included some 250 Spanish cavalry, several hundred Indians, droves of livestock, and even some Spanish footmen and priests, descended on the seven cities, which were probably the Zuñi pueblos of what is now New Mexico, but found no evidence of the fabled wealth. Expeditions sent in various directions explored the Hopi territory of north-eastern Arizona, the Grand Canyon in Colorado (later described by the expedition leader, Garcia López de Cárdenas), and the Rio Grande. Tales of riches in a place called Quivira inspired an expedition which set out for the north-east in April 1541, and on this journey Vázquez seems to have reached what is now central Kansas. A planned rendezvous with the maritime expedition of Fernando de ALARCÓN did not come to fruition. In the spring of 1542 Vázquez returned with his expedition to Compostela; he was relieved of his governorship in 1544 and thereafter lived obscurely until his death in Mexico City. The written accounts of the Coronado Expedition, as it is called in English, created lasting European images of the bison-covered plains of the southern United States, of the Grand Canyon, and of the Zuñi pueblos. The priests accompanying the expedition remained as missionaries, and so extended the domain of the Spanish Church into new territories.

F. W. Hodge (ed.), *Spanish Explorers in the Southern United States, 1528–1543* (1907).

**VECCHI, ORAZIO** (1550–1605), Modenese composer who was *maestro di cappella* at the cathedrals of Salò, Modena, and Reggio. In 1598 he was appointed *maestro di corte* at Modena, a city where his abilities were recognized by the general council. He collaborated with composers such as Andrea GABRIELI and Claudio MERULO in writing for a Medici wedding in 1579 and worked with Giovanni GABRIELI and Ludovico BALBI on revising the Roman Gradual in 1591. His sacred music includes mass settings and motets, some using the Gabrieli-like *CORI SPEZZATI* techniques. He also wrote canzonettas and madrigals and is best remembered for his madrigal comedy *L'Amfiparnaso* (1594), based on well-known *commedia dell'arte* characters.

**VECCHIETTA or Lorenzo di Pietro di Giovanni** (1410–80), Italian painter, sculptor, and architect, a native of Siena, where he was probably trained in the workshop of Stefano di SASSETTA. His surviving sculptures, such as his *SS Peter and Paul* (1458–62) in the Loggia della Mercanzia, reflect the influence of DONATELLO, who had visited Siena in 1457. His paintings include *St Catherine* (1461/2, Palazzo Pubblico, Siena) and an *Assumption* (1461/2, Pienza Cathedral). His most celebrated work is the bronze ciborium (1467–72) made for the high altar of Santa Maria della Scala in Siena and in 1506 moved to the high altar of Siena Cathedral to replace DUCCIO's *Maestà*. His other great work in bronze is the full-sized *Risen Christ* (1476) now on the high altar of Santa Maria della Scala in Siena.

MDA.

**VEEN, OTTO VAN, or** (Latin) **Vaenius** (*c*.1556–1629), Netherlandish painter, born into a noble family in Leiden. He studied in Italy (*c*.1575–*c*.1580) with Federico ZUCCARO and then returned to the Netherlands. He worked in Brussels (from 1585) as court painter to Alessandro FARNESE and in 1592 settled in Antwerp, where he became court painter to ALBRECHT VON HABSBURG. Otto van Veen's paintings drew heavily on Italian mannerist traditions, some features of which he commended to Rubens, who was for a time his pupil. His paintings include *The Mystic Marriage of St Catherine* (1589), an altarpiece commissioned for the Capuchin church in Brussels and now in the Musée d'Art Ancien in Brussels.

MDA; NNBW vi.

**VEGA CARPIO, LOPE DE** (1562–1635), Spanish playwright, born in Madrid, where he was educated in the Theatine college. He entered the service of the bishop of Ávila and then studied at Alcalá de Henares and Salamanca. In 1583 he sailed with the marquis of SANTA CRUZ to Terceira (the island in the Azores that remained faithful to the Portuguese pretender after the Spanish annexation of Portugal), and was present at the naval battle at which the navy of the pretender (supported by English and French privateers) was defeated. On returning to Spain he entered into a prolonged affair with a married woman called Elena Osorio (the daughter of a theatre director), who became the Filis of Lope's early lyrics. In 1587 he was exiled from Madrid for four years for writing libellous verses, and then married the 16-year-old Isabel de Urbina, the Belisa of his lyrics. He spent the years of his exile in Valencia, living in the ducal residence at Alba de Tormes (near Salamanca); he may have sailed with the Spanish ARMADA in 1588. He then lived in Seville before returning to Madrid. On the death of Isabel in 1594 Lope acquired a mistress, the married actress Micaela de Luján (by whom he had five children); in his love poetry Micaela is addressed as Camila Lucinda. He had married Juana de Guardo (by whom he had three children), and on the break-up of his affair with Micaela Lope returned to his wife. On Juana's death Lope was ordained as a priest (1614), but his vow of celibacy proved not to be an impediment to his further affairs with actresses, the last and most tragic being with 26-year-old Marta de Nevares. Throughout his eventful life Lope struggled with poverty, with the difficulty of finding a patron and a secure post, and with the illnesses and deaths of his wives, mistresses, and children; he also struggled with his conscience. His astounding literary output earned him the sobriquet *monstruo de naturaleza* ('monster of nature').

Lope's poetry ranges through a large number of forms, including sonnets (of which he was Spain's most prolific composer), ballads, *canciones*, epistles, eclogues, odes, and epics. His epics include *La Dragontea* (1598, on Sir Francis DRAKE and other English villains), *La hermosura de Angélica* (1602, modelled on ARIOSTO), and *Jerusalén conquistada* (1609, an imitation of TASSO which represents Spain as the heart of Christendom). His prose works consist of pastoral romances (such as *La Arcadia*, 1598), *novelas* (short stories), and *La Dorotea* (1632), a fine dialogue novel in the tradition of Fernando de ROJAS's *La Celestina*.

These formidable accomplishments in poetry and prose are eclipsed by Lope's standing as Spain's national playwright and one of the world's greatest dramatists. He claimed to have written more than 1,400 plays, of which more than 300 survive; another 200 plays are attributed to Lope with varying degrees of probability. He wrote comic 'cloak-and-dagger plays' (*comedias de capa y espada*, notably *El perro del hortelano* and *La dama boba*), plays based on romances of chivalry, plays about biblical characters (e.g. *La hermosa Ester*) and saints (e.g. *La buena guarda*, in which an angel replaces a nun who elopes with her lover), history plays (notably *Fuenteovejuna*, Lope's best-known play), and many fine tragedies (notably *El caballero de Olmedo* and *El castigo sin venganza*), an uncommon genre in Golden Age drama.

**VEGETIUS IN THE RENAISSANCE.** Flavius Vegetius Renatus is the otherwise unknown author of the *Epitoma rei militaris*, the only military manual to have survived intact from late antiquity, probably from the late fourth century. The four books of the treatise deal with (1) the induction of recruits, (2) the organization of the army, (3) tactics and strategy, and (4) fortifications and naval warfare. Vegetius exercised an important influence on the military thinking of the Renaissance, in part because his background as an administrator rather than a soldier fostered an antiquarian impulse that led him to look to the past for examples of exemplary military practice; this approach struck a sympathetic chord with humanist military thinkers of the Renaissance. His treatise shaped practical warfare, in that the seven Vegetian military formations (e.g. the 'A', the 'L', the wedge, and the saw) were used on the battlefields of Europe. The treatise also became a seminal presence in the literature of war, notably MACHIAVELLI's *Arte della guerra*. Vegetius' notion that citizens should be fit for both peace and war filtered into educational theory and practice, and so the ideal of the citizens' army gradually supplanted the preference for mercenaries. The treatise was translated into various vernaculars (including

English and French) before the advent of printing, and in the late fifteenth century Latin versions were printed in Utrecht (1473), Cologne (1476), Paris (1478), Rome (1487), and Pisa (1488); a German translation was printed in Ulm (1475), and CAXTON published an English version (translated from French) in 1489.

**VEGIO, MAFFEO** (1407–58), Italian humanist, born in Lodi and educated in Milan and Pavia. He moved to Rome, where he became a member of the papal courts of EUGENIUS IV and MARTIN V. His principal work is a humanist treatise on education, *De educatione liberorum* (1445–8), in which he advocates the early structure of a wide range of subjects and gradual specialization; he recommends for special study the works of Aesop, Sallust, Seneca (the tragedies), and VIRGIL. His devotion to Virgil led Vegio to compose a sequel (in the form of a thirteenth book) to Virgil's *Aeneid* (1427) in which he describes the death and deification of Aeneas and the greatness of ancient Rome; this sequel was printed as Virgil's in many editions of the *Aeneid* in the fifteenth and sixteenth centuries. His Latin verse included epigrams, a four-book poem on the Golden Fleece, and a description of Old St Peter's Basilica. He also wrote treatises on archaeology and philology.

*OCIL.*

**VELASCO, LUIS DE** (*c*.1511–1564), second Spanish viceroy of Mexico. He was born into an ancient and noble Castilian family, and in 1550 travelled to Mexico (New Spain) to succeed Antonio de MENDOZA as viceroy. Velasco enforced the 'New Laws' of 1542 (see INDIES, LAWS OF THE) which had virtually abolished the enslavement of Indians; the landowners reacted to enforcement by conspiring to enthrone Cortés's son as king of New Spain, and Velasco crushed the revolt with uncompromising severity. In 1553 he presided over the opening of the University of Mexico. His attempt to extend the Spanish conquest to Florida in an expedition of 1559 ended in failure. Shortly before his death, he fitted out the expedition of Miguel López de Legaspi to the Philippines.

Velasco's son and namesake Luis (1539–1616) was twice viceroy of Mexico and once viceroy of Peru.

*DHE*; María Justina Sarabia Viejo, *Don Luis de Velasco, virrey de Nueva España, 1550–1564* (1978).

**VELÁZQUEZ DE CUÉLLAR, DIEGO** (1461/6–1524), Spanish conquistador. He was born in Cuéllar (Castile), and travelled with COLUMBUS on his second voyage (1494). In Hispaniola he entered the service of Nicolás de OVANDO, and in that capacity led the force that invaded Cuba in 1511. The conquest of Cuba was completed by 1514; Velázquez became governor of the island and founded the first European settlements at Baracao (where he had first landed), Bayamo, Santiago de Cuba, Puerto Príncipe, Santo Espíritu, Trinidad, and the original Havana, all of which were founded by 1515.

In 1517 Velázquez sent the expedition that discovered Yucatán, and the following year another of his expeditions explored the coast of Mexico. In 1519 he equipped the force led by CORTÉS (to whom he was related) which invaded

VÉLEZ DE GUEVARA, LUIS

Mexico and destroyed the Aztec empire. In 1520 he sent Pánfilo de NARVÁEZ (who had assisted in the conquest of Cuba) with a force of 800 men to intercept Cortés; the mission ended in disaster as the two forces turned against each other, and Velázquez was relieved of his governorship. He was reinstated shortly before his death.

*DHE.*

**VÉLEZ DE GUEVARA, LUIS** (1579–1644), Spanish playwright, poet, and satirist, born in Écija (near Seville) and educated at the University of Osuna; on graduating in 1596, he entered the service of Cardinal Rodrigo de Castro, archbishop of Seville. On the death of the cardinal in 1600, Guevara became a soldier, fighting for the next five years as far afield as Italy and Algiers. On returning to Spain in 1600 he served various noblemen before securing a position in the household of King Philip IV. He was profligate by nature, spending extravagantly and marrying four times.

Vélez wrote some 400 plays; the 80 plays that survive include INTERLUDES (Spanish *entremeses*), biblical plays, history plays, and *AUTOS SACRAMENTALES*. His imitation of the style of Lope de VEGA is so successful that it causes problems of attribution. His best-known plays are *La serrana de la Vera* (in which a bandit-heroine wreaks revenge on her seducer), *Más pesa el rey que la sangre* (which dramatizes the loyalty of Guzmán el Bueno, a patriotic hero of medieval Seville), and *Reinar después de morir* (which portrays the legendary love of Prince Pedro of Portugal for Inés de Castro). Vélez also wrote a satirical novel called *El diablo cojuelo* (1641), which Lesage adapted as his classic *Le Diable boiteux* (1707).

F. E. Spencer and R. Schevill, *The Dramatic Works of Luis Vélez de Guevara* (1937); P. Bolaños Donoso and M. Martín Ojeda (eds.), *Luis Vélez de Guevara y su época* (1996).

**VELLERT, DIRICK** (1480/5–1548), Flemish glass designer, glass painter, etcher, and engraver who worked in Antwerp. He designed several of the windows for the Chapel of King's College, Cambridge, including the great east window; the windows were constructed to Vellert's designs by Galyon HONE. Vellert's own glass painting, which was executed in a markedly Italianate style, includes a set of glass roundels now in the Musée du Cinquantenaire in Brussels.

*MDA.*

**VELLUM** (French *velin*) **AND PARCHMENT**, the untanned skins of animals which were bathed in lime, scraped, polished with pumice, and stretched before being used as luxurious surfaces for writing or printing or painting (usually for portrait MINIATURES) or as materials for bookbinding. The term 'parchment' normally denotes sheepskin or goatskin, whereas 'vellum' is normally the softer unsplit skin of a calf, lamb, or kid. In Renaissance Europe particularly sumptuous volumes were printed on white uterine vellum made from the skin of still-born or newly born animals.

**VENEZIANO, ANTONIO** (1543–93), Italian poet, born in Monreale (Sicily). In 1578 he was captured by BARBARY PIRATES. He later visited Spain, where he died in prison. He wrote poetry both in his Sicilian dialect (notably his Petrarchan *Celia*) and in Latin (in which he wrote epigrams).

*OCIL.*

**VENICE or (Italian) Venezia.** Renaissance Venice was a maritime city-state with an empire. Its territories on the Italian mainland extended to the plains of Lombardy, and included Belluno, Bergamo, BRESCIA, CREMONA, Feltre, PADUA, Treviso, Udine, VERONA, and VICENZA; on the Adriatic rim, it governed Istria and DALMATIA; further to the south-east, Venice guarded the strategically important Strait of Otranto by fortifying Scutari (Albanian Shkodër), Vallona (Albanian Vlorë), Parga (Greek Párga), and the islands of Corfu (Greek Kérika), Santa Maura (Greek Levkás), Cefalonia (Greek Kefallinía), and Zante (Greek Zákinthos); on the Gulf of Corinth it fortified Lepanto (Greek Návpactos), and on the southern coast of the Morea (Peloponnese), it held Navarino (Greek Pylos), Modon (Greek Methóni), Corone (Greek Koróni), Malvasia (Greek Monemvasia), and the nearby island of Cerigo (Greek Kíthira); its most far-flung island possessions were CRETE (Italian Candia), Naxos (from 1207–1566), and CYPRUS.

In the fourteenth century Venice became embroiled in a protracted struggle with Genoa. At the conclusion of the War of Chioggia (1378–81) Venice emerged as the victor and thereafter became the most important maritime power in the eastern Mediterranean. Thereafter Venice faced an increasingly threatening enemy in the Ottomans, whose expansionist policies included the occupation of the Balkans and the appropriation of Venice's Aegean outposts. The conflict that began with wars in 1416 and 1425–30 was revived in 1499 and again in 1537–40 (when Venice joined in a HOLY LEAGUE with Pope PAUL III and the Emperor CHARLES V to fight BARBAROSSA and the Ottomans) and eventually culminated in another Turkish War (1570–3) in which Venice and its allies won the battle of LEPANTO in 1571 and lost Cyprus to the Ottomans in 1573. Venice retained Crete and a few Aegean islands until the war of 1645–64. The GALLEYS and other armaments for these wars were produced on the ARSENALE, the seat of a vast shipbuilding industry.

In the course of the fifteenth century Venice lost many of its offshore possessions to the Ottomans, but during the same period it made substantial territorial gains on the mainland; these possessions, which are collectively known as the Venetian *terraferma*, were expanded by the incorporation of Padua (taken from the CARRARA in 1405), Vicenza and Verona (1405), Brescia (1426), and Bergamo (1428), the spoils of a war with Filippo Maria VISCONTI of Milan. In the sixteenth century Venice suffered at the hands of the League of CAMBRAI but managed to retain its independence during most of the campaigns in the WARS OF ITALY.

The stability of Venice was attributed by its admirers to its republican constitution; this admiration eventually gave birth to the MYTH OF VENICE. The principal institutions of government were the Greater Council (MAGGIOR CONSIGLIO), the Senate (which had *c.*300 members), the College (which prepared the Senate's business and implemented its decisions), the COUNCIL OF TEN, and an elected DOGE. The wealth of Venice, which derived from its trade with the Levant and western Europe and from industries such as SILK, GLASS, and PRINTING, was protected by Europe's most sophisticated BANKING system.

Renaissance Venice was an important centre of printing (notably the Aldine Press of ALDUS MANUTIUS and the GIOLITO PRESS), painting (including the BELLINI family, CARPACCIO, GIORGIONE, PALMA GIOVANNI, PALMA VECCHIO, TINTORETTO, TITIAN, VERONESE, and, in Murano, VIVARINI), sculpture (notably VITTORIA), architecture (notably PALLADIO and Jacopo SANSOVINO), music (notably GABRIELI and MONTEVERDI), and literature (including ARETINO and BEMBO and the Greek scholars of the NEAKADEMIA). The JEWS of Venice, who were confined to a GHETTO, were successful merchants who were at once despised for the ancestral crime of deicide and valued by scholars for their learning.

The city of Venice is built on islands separated by waterways that form a magnificent setting for the city's buildings, from the Cathedral of San Marco to the late sixteenth-century Rialto Bridge (c.1590) and the Bridge of Sighs (1600). Renaissance buildings include the Doge's Palace, the Biblioteca Marciana, and a series of palaces on the right (east) bank of the Grand Canal: Sansovino's Palazzo Corner della Ca' Grande, the Palazzo Corner-Spinelli, the Palazzo Grimani, the Palazzo Vendramin-Calergi, and the Ca' d'Oro, Venice's elegant 'golden house'. The finest of the Renaissance churches are San Zaccaria, which contains a fresco (a rare medium in Venice) by ANDREA DEL CASTAGNO, and San Giorgio Maggiore, which was begun by Palladio in 1566 and completed by SCAMOZZI in 1610.

> D. S. Chambers, *The Imperial Age of Venice, 1380–1580* (1970); Edward Muir, *Civic Ritual in Renaissance Venice* (1981); F. C. Lane, *Money and Banking in Medieval and Renaissance Venice* (1985); Norbert Huse, *The Art of Renaissance Venice* (1990); J. E. Law, *Venice and the Veneto in the Early Renaissance* (2000).

**VENIER or Veniero FAMILY**, a Venetian family that produced three DOGES. Antonio Venier was doge from 1382 to 1400, and extended Venice's empire in the east, notably by the acquisition of Corfu and the Aegean Islands. Francesco Venier was elected as doge in 1554 and died in office in 1556. Sebastiano Venier (doge from 1557 to 1558) had been appointed captain of the sea (*generale da mar*) in 1570 (aged 74), and was in significant measure responsible for the Venetian victory over the Ottomans at the battle of LEPANTO (1571). He was elected doge in 1557, aged 82.

> P. Molmenti, *Sebastiano Veniero* (1889).

**VÉRARD, ANTOINE** (d. 1513), French printer, probably a native of Tours. He settled in Paris, where his workshop made illuminated manuscripts. In 1485 Vérard became a printer, specializing in illustrated books. He published some 250 books, including many romances, religious works, and translations of classical literature.

**VERDELOT, PHILIPPE** (c.1470/80–before 1552) French composer in Italy, where, in the 1520s, he was appointed

*maestro di cappella* at both the baptistery of Santa Maria del Fiore and the cathedral. He wrote masses, motets, chansons, and some early examples of the madrigal. He set a variety of Petrarchist texts such as *ballate*, canzonias, and sonnets. His madrigals were popular throughout the sixteenth century, being arranged by Adriaan WILLAERT and Claudio MERULO and parodied by ARCADELT and others.

**VERDURE TAPESTRIES**, a type of TAPESTRY woven at various tapestry centres, notably OUDENARDE, from the fifteenth to the eighteenth centuries. Verdure tapestries either depicted a landscape with leafy plants (sometimes with birds and animals) or consisted of a design depicting leaves. Tapestries in which the leaves are larger than they are in life are known as large-leaf verdures.

**VERGERIO, PIETRO PAOLO THE ELDER** (1370–1444), Italian humanist educator and biographer of the Carrara despots, born in Capodistria (now Koper, in Slovenia). He was educated in Padua and subsequently taught in Florence (1386), Bologna (1388–90), and Padua (1390–7, 1400–5). From 1398 to 1400 he lived in Florence, where he studied Greek under CHRYSOLORAS. He served in the papal courts of INNOCENT VII and GREGORY XII from 1406 to 1409, and attended the COUNCIL OF CONSTANCE (1414–18). In 1418 he accompanied King SIGISMUND (later Holy Roman Emperor) to Bohemia and Hungary, and remained in the imperial court for the rest of his life. Vergerio's *De ingenuis moribus et liberalibus studiis* (c.1402) was the first Renaissance treatise to set out an integrated programme of education, and it exercised a significant influence on educational thinking for three centuries. Vergerio also wrote on PETRARCH, whose *Africa* he published.

> John M. McManamon, *Pierpaolo Vergerio the Elder (c.1369–1444): The Humanist as Orator* (1996).

**VERGERIO, PIETRO PAOLO THE YOUNGER** (1498–1565), Italian Protestant reformer. He was born in Capodistria (now Koper, in Slovenia) and studied law at Padua, where be became a judge. In 1527 he entered the service of the Church as a layman and in 1533 was appointed papal nuncio to the Holy Roman Empire, where he met LUTHER. He was finally ordained, and in 1536 was appointed bishop of Capodistria by Pope PAUL III. He gradually developed Protestant sympathies and in 1549 fled to Switzerland. He became a Protestant minister, and worked in the Swiss Confederation and in Poland before moving in 1553 to Tübingen, where he wrote and translated polemical Protestant literature.

**VERGIL, POLYDORE, or (Italian) Polidoro Vergilio** (c.1470–c.1555), Italian historian in England. He came to England in 1502 and held various church positions, becoming archdeacon of Wells in 1508. His chronicle *Anglicae historiae libri XXVI* was published between 1534 and 1555.

> DNB; Denys Hay, *Polydore Vergil* (1952).

**VERMEYEN, JAN CORNELISZOON** (c.1500–c.1559), Netherlandish painter and designer of tapestries and engravings, a native of Beverwijk. His long beard occasioned the nicknames Barbalonga and Jan met de Baard. Vermeyen travelled as court painter in the peripatetic courts of MAR-GARET OF AUSTRIA (1525–9), MARY OF HUNGARY (1530), and the Emperor CHARLES V, in whose entourage he visited TUNIS in 1535; he subsequently designed the twelve tapestries (executed in the PANNEMAKER workshop) that commemorated the campaign. Vermeyen's style as a painter was similar to that of his friend Jan van SCOREL, and it has not always been possible to be certain which of them was the painter of a picture; the *Portrait of Evrard de la Marck* (Pannwitz Collection, Heemstede, Holland), long attributed to Scorel, is now thought to be by Vermeyen.

*MDA*; Hendrick Horn, *Jan Cornelisz Vermeyen* (2 vols., 1989).

## VERMIGLI, PIETRO MARTIRE (1499–1562), the Protestant theologian known in English as Peter Martyr, born in Florence on 8 May 1500, the son of Stefano Vermigli (a disciple of SAVONAROLA) and his first wife Maria Fumantina; he was named after the thirteenth-century Dominican saint Peter the Martyr (San Pietro Martire). He was educated in Fiesole by the Augustinians of the Latin Congregation, and subsequently joined the order. In 1519 he was transferred to the Convent of San Giovanni de Vedara near Padua, where he formed a friendship with Reginald POLE and took his doctorate. During the 1520s Pietro worked as a public preacher in Brescia, Pisa, Rome, and Venice, and also mastered biblical Greek and Hebrew. In 1530 he was elected abbot of the Augustinian monastery in Spoleto, and in 1533 he became prior of St Petrus-ad-arum in Naples.

At Naples Pietro continued to study the Bible in its original languages and also read Martin BUCER's commentaries on the Gospels and on the Psalms and ZWINGLI's *De vera et falsa religione*. When his sympathies for the Protestant reformers became apparent in his sermons and lectures, he was forbidden by the Spanish viceroy in Naples to preach in public. Pietro appealed to Rome, where friends such as Cardinal Pole interceded on his behalf, and the ban was lifted. In 1541 he was appointed as abbot of the Monastery of San Frediano in Lucca, where he openly supported the considerable Protestant movement. When summoned to appear before the chapter of his Order in Genoa, Pietro decided to flee. He initially travelled to Pisa, and thence to Florence, with a view to seeking refuge with Bernardino OCHINO, who was similarly inclined to Protestantism.

By 1542 it had become clear that Pietro had to leave Italy or die at the hands of the INQUISITION. He escaped to Zürich, and thence to Basel and finally to Strassburg, where Bucer secured for him a chair in theology. In Strassburg Pietro married Catherine Dammartin, a former nun from Metz. In 1547 Archbishop CRANMER invited Pietro and Bernardino Ochino (who had escaped to Geneva) to England, where they were each awarded a pension of 40 marks. In 1548 Pietro was appointed Regius professor of divinity at Oxford, and the following year took part in a famous disputation on the EUCHARIST: he had by this point abandoned both the Catholic doctrine of transubstantiation and the Lutheran doctrine of consubstantiation, instead advocating the virtualism of

Calvin and the English reformers (including Cranmer). Pietro was consulted on the 1552 revision of the Book of Common Prayer, but there is no readily apparent mark of his influence on the revised version; he was also appointed to the commission charged with the reformation of CANON LAW.

On the accession of Queen MARY I, Pietro was imprisoned, and after six months was permitted to return to Strassburg. On 15 February 1553 his wife had died in Oxford, where she had been buried in Christ Church Cathedral, close to the tomb of St Frideswide. In 1557 Cardinal Pole ordered that her remains be disinterred and that her corpse be tried for heresy; the case collapsed, because witnesses could not understand her German or her heavily accented English, and her body was thrown on a dunghill in the stables of the dean of Christ Church. In 1558 the Calvinist divine James Calfhill recovered the body, mixed the remains of Catherine with those of St Frideswide, and reburied them in Christ Church, where they still share a common grave. It was this bizarre episode that occasioned Nicholas SANDERS's once-famous epigram 'hic requiescat religio cum superstitione' ('here rests religion alongside superstition').

In Strassburg Pietro's professorship was revived, but his alienation from Lutheranism, particularly on the doctrine of the eucharist, led to his migration to Zürich, where he was appointed professor of Hebrew and married Catherina Merenda. He declined invitations to Geneva (1557) and England (1561), but continued to correspond with reformers (including Bishop JEWEL) until his death on 12 November 1562.

Pietro wrote prolifically, mostly biblical commentaries and polemical works in defence of Zwinglian sacramental theology. His posthumous *Loci communes* (1561) was read by learned Protestants for generations.

*DNB*; Philip McNair, *Peter Martyr in Italy: An Anatomy of an Apostacy* (1967).

## VERNICLE or (Latin) *sudarium*, a cloth impressed with an image of the face of Jesus. The original vernicle was first mentioned in late antiquity, when a woman subsequently known as St Veronica was said to have wiped the face of Jesus with her veil as he stumbled on the road to Calvary; the cloth was imprinted with an image of Jesus, and subsequently the name Veronica was popularly said to mean 'true image' (*vera icon*). A cloth said to be the vernicle has been preserved in St Peter's Basilica in Rome since the eighth century; it was first displayed for veneration during Holy Week in 1292.

In the fourteenth and fifteenth centuries this vernicle, which seems to be the work of a Byzantine artist, was much venerated as a relic. Its significance for both theologians and artists was that it accorded with a new emphasis on the humanity of Jesus and of his physical suffering. The vernicle became a popular subject of painting from the fifteenth to the seventeenth centuries. The two best-known representations of the vernicle are Hans MEMLING's painting (1470–5, National Gallery, Washington) and DÜRER's woodcut of *The Sudarium Spread out by an Angel* (1516).

The Turin Shroud is another sudarium, in this case the cloth in which Joseph of Arimathea is said to have wrapped the body of Jesus. The shroud, which has been in Turin since 1578, was carbon-dated in 1988 by laboratories in Britain, Switzerland, and the United States; the tests in all three laboratories produced dates between 1260 and 1390 for the harvesting of the flax from which the shroud is woven.

**VERONA**, a city and episcopal see in Venetia, is built on a loop in the Adige (Latin Athesis). From the late thirteenth century until 1387 the city was dominated by the DELLA SCALA family, whose Gothic tomb monuments (the *Arche Scaligeri*) are now among the finest works of art in the city. The city was the focus of the struggle between the GUELFS AND GHIBELLINES, whose factionalism is the basis of the story of Romeo and Juliet: the Montecchi (Montagues) were Guelfs who supported the pope and the Capuleti were Ghibellines who supported the emperor. The cult status of SHAKESPEARE's version of the story has led to the whimsical identification of Juliet's tomb (*Tomba di Giulietta*) in the CAPUCHIN cloisters and of an improbably picturesque balcony in the 'Casa de Giulietta'.

In 1387 Gian Galeazzo VISCONTI captured the city; after his death in 1402, the city passed by treacherous means into the hands of Francesco II de CARRARA, *signore* of Padua. In 1405 Verona was annexed (together with Padua) by Venice, and remained under Venetian administration under 1797 with only a single break, which was the occupation (by invitation) of the imperial army (1509–17) after the battle of AGNADELLO.

The strategic importance of Verona, with imperial Austria to the north and Spanish Milan to the west, occasioned a renewal of its defences after the city was recovered in 1517. In the 1530s Venice surrounded the city with new fortifications, the first stage of which was designed by Michele SANMICHELI. The city was badly damaged during the Second World War, but much remains of the innovatory buildings of Sanmicheli, including his fortifications, gates (especially the rusticated Porta del Palio), the *enceinte*, and palaces such as the Palazzo Bevilacqua (1527) and the Palazzo Pompei (1530). The faceted rustications which gave rise to the name of the Palazzo dei Diamanti (1582) also show it to be a late imitation of the style of Sanmicheli; the Gran Guardia Vecchia (1609) is an even later imitation, in this case by Sanmicheli's nephew Domenico Curtoni. Fra GIOCONDO, who seems to have been associated with Sanmicheli, designed the Palazzo del Consiglio (1476), which has a splendid arcade (with columns directly supporting arches) modelled on the Ospedale degli Innocenti in Florence.

Verona was one of Italy's most important cultural centres; its educators included GUARINO DA VERONA; the artists who lived and worked in the city range from PISANELLO to VERONESE; the musicians of Verona formed one of the earliest musical academies, the Accademia Filarmonice.

C. Cipolla, *Compendio della storia politica di Verona* (1889); A. M. Allen, *A History of Verona* (1910); *Verona e il suo territorio*, iii.1 (1975) and iii.2 (1969).

**VERONESE or Paolo Caliari** (1528–88), Italian painter, born in Verona, the son of a sculptor; he was trained as a painter in the studio of a local painter, Antonio Badile (1486–1541). In the early 1550s Veronese moved to Venice, where his first important commission (*c*.1555) was the decoration of the Church of San Sebastiano, where he was to work intermittently for the next ten years (and where he is buried); he began with the ceiling of the sacristy with paintings of *The Coronation of the Virgin* and the four evangelists, and then turned to the ceiling of the church (a cycle on *Esther and Ahasuerus*), the upper choir (two paintings of *St Sebastian*), the altarpiece (*The Virgin in Glory with Four Saints*), the doors of the organ (*The Purification of the Virgin* on the outside and *The Pool of Bethesda* on the inside), the front of the organ loft (the *Nativity*), and the chancel (two paintings on *The Life of St Sebastian*). These exuberantly sensuous paintings, crowded with processions, give San Sebastiano one of the finest interiors in Venice.

In the 1560s Veronese decorated several villas on the mainland, notably PALLADIO's Villa BARBARO in Maser. He also began to paint religious feast scenes, notably his huge *Marriage Feast at Cana* (1562, Louvre), which was painted for the refectory (now a conference hall) of the monastic Church of San Giorgio Maggiore. A later feast scene, *The Last Supper*, attracted the unwelcome attention of the INQUISITION, before which Veronese was summoned on a charge of irreverence because of his inclusion of figures such as a dog and soldiers; Veronese defended himself successfully, by changing the title of the picture to *The Feast in the House of Levi* (1573, Accademia, Venice). One of the finest paintings of Veronese's maturity is *The Family of Darius before Alexander* (*c*.1570, National Gallery).

In his last years the scale of Veronese's commissions (which came from as far away as Prague) meant that he increasingly worked as a workshop painter, assisted in his studio by his sons Gabriele and Carletto and his brother Benedetto Caliari. His last major commission, which he shared with TINTORETTO, was the redecoration of the Doge's palace after the serious fire of 1577. His finest painting in the palace, executed with his brother, is *The Apotheosis of Venice* (*c*.1585) in the ceiling of the Sala del Maggior Consiglio.

*MDA*; Terizio Pignatti, *Veronese* (2 vols., 1995).

**VERRAZZANO, GIOVANNI DA** (1485–1528), Italian explorer, born into a noble Tuscan family. As a young man he moved to Dieppe, and from that base undertook several trading expeditions to the Levant. In 1523 he entered the service of FRANCIS I, who appointed him as the commander of a French expedition of two ships commissioned to search for a NORTH-WEST PASSAGE to Asia. His fleet sailed to what is now South Carolina and then turned north along the coast to the New York Bay and Maine; he was the first European to visit what is now New York, where he is commemorated by the Verrazzano Narrows and the bridge linking Staten Island and Brooklyn. On returning to France he composed an account of his voyage in a letter to King Francis.

In 1527 Verrazzano led a second expedition across the Atlantic, but was forced to turn back from Brazil by a

Veronese, *The Marriage Feast at Cana* (1562), in the Louvre, Paris

mutinous crew. On his third expedition, in 1528, he sailed to the Bahamas and then an island in the Lower Antilles that was probably Guadeloupe. Verrazzano rowed to the beach with his brother and waded ashore, whereupon he was killed by Caribs; his brother, who survived the attack, reported that Verrazzano was promptly butchered and eaten by Caribs as his brother watched, but such stories of cannibalism are not always grounded in fact.

The planisphere of Verrazzano's first voyage is now in the National Maritime Museum in Greenwich, and there are contemporary copies in the Vatican Library and in the library of the Hispanic Society in New York.

L. C. Wroth, *The Voyages of Giovanni da Verrazzano 1524–28* (1970).

**VERROCCHIO, ANDREA DEL** (1435–88), Italian sculptor and painter, born in Florence. He trained initially as a goldsmith and then as a sculptor, possibly in the studio of DONATELLO. His expertise as a metalworker is apparent in his decoration (with ACANTHUS leaves) of the bronze tomb of Piero and Cosimo de' MEDICI in the Church of San Lorenzo (1470). His bronze sculptures include *Boy with a Dolphin*

Veronese, *The Triumph of Mordecai*, in the cycle on *Esther and Ahasuerus* on the ceiling of the Church of San Sebastiano in Venice

(*c.*1480, Palazzo Vecchio), a *David* (*c.*1475, Bargello), and the EQUESTRIAN STATUE of Bartolomeo COLLEONI in Venice (1470–88); his terracotta works include a fine portrait bust of Lorenzo de' MEDICI (National Gallery, Washington). Verrocchio's workshop produced many paintings, such as *Madonna and Child with Two Angels* (National Gallery, London), but no surviving painting is known to be the unaided work of Verrocchio. The breadth of Verrocchio's interests and abilities adumbrates that of his most famous pupil, LEONARDO DA VINCI.

MDA; Andrew Butterfield, *The Sculptures of Andrea del Verrocchio* (1997).

**VERTUE, ROBERT** (*fl.* 1475, d. 1506) and **WILLIAM** (*fl.* 1501, d. 1527), English masons, the sons of Adam Vertue, a mason at Westminster Abbey; Robert became king's master mason in 1487 and William in 1510. In 1501 the brothers were joint master masons of Bath Abbey, and were responsible for the fan vaulting. As king's master masons (together with Robert Janyns and John Lebons) they probably contributed to the vaults of King's College Chapel (which William visited in 1507) in Cambridge, Henry VII's Chapel in Westminster Abbey, and St George's Chapel in Windsor, but their precise role is not documented, even though William was a signatory to the Windsor contract.

Robert Vertue died in 1506, and thereafter William worked alone or with Henry REDMAN, who in 1515 became joint king's mason with William Vertue. He collaborated with Redman on a design for Lupton's Tower (1516) in Eton College (though it is unclear whether theirs was the design that was built) and on the fan-vaulted cloister of St Stephen's Chapel in the Palace of Westminster (c.1526). He seems also to have been the architect of St Peter in Vincula in the Tower of London (1512) and of the first two-storey range of buildings at Corpus Christi College, Oxford (1512–18). In 1520 he played a prominent role in the preparations for the FIELD OF THE CLOTH OF GOLD.

*MDA.*

**VERVINS, PEACE OF**, a treaty signed on 2 May 1598 by King HENRI IV of France and King PHILIP II of Spain. The treaty restored the territorial arrangements of the Treaty of CATEAU-CAMBRÉSIS (1559). France regained most of its territories in French Flanders (though Spain retained Cambrai). Spain was left free to prosecute its war against Dutch rebels, but King Philip was obliged to surrender control of the Spanish Netherlands to his daughter Isabella and her intended husband ALBRECHT VON HABSBURG, who were to rule as sovereign princes.

**VERZELINI, GIACOMO** (1522–1606), Italian glassmaker who became the most important manufacturer of glass in Elizabethan England. After training in his native Venice, Verzelini worked in Antwerp before moving in 1571 to CRUTCHED FRIARS (London), where he was employed by Jean Carré to make crystal glass in the style of Venetian crystal. The following year he succeeded Carré as the proprietor of the factory and in 1575 Queen Elizabeth awarded him a 21-year monopoly for the manufacture of Venetian-style glass in England; the value of the monopoly was enhanced by the imposition of an import ban on Venetian glass, though the ban proved to be ineffective. He retired to his estate in Kent in 1592.

Verzelini produced large goblets made from soda-lime; the eight surviving examples are engraved with diamond-point ornament, and some are dated (1577–90).

*MDA.*

**VESALIUS, ANDREAS, or (Flemish) Andreas van Wesele** (1514–64), Flemist anatomist, born in Brussels, the son of an imperial apothecary. He studied at Louvain, Paris, and then Padua, where he was appointed to a lectureship in anatomy in 1537. In 1538 Vesalius published *Tabulae anatomicae sex*, a set of six anatomical illustrations designed for medical students. The drawings (of which the first three were by Vesalius) are based on observation, but at this stage Vesalius saw his cadavers through Galenic eyes, and so he drew a five-lobed liver, the heart of an ape, and, ignoring the strictures of BERENGARIO DA CARPI, a *rete mirabile* (a network of blood vessels at the base of the brain that exists in some animals but not in humans).

In 1539 Vesalius acquired a new supply of executed criminals, and in the course of the next three years conducted the research on which his *De humani corporis fabrica* was based. This treatise, which is known as *De fabrica*, was published in Basel in 1543 (revised edition, 1555) and has fine illustrations by Jan Steven van CALCAR. *De fabrica* is not a repudiation of GALEN, but rather an interpretation of his anatomy (which was largely based on dissections of apes and other animals) by reference to observation-based anatomy.

The publication of *De fabrica* created a European reputation for Vesalius, who was appointed as physician to CHARLES V and (from 1559) PHILIP II. Vesalius undertook a pilgrimage to Jeruslem and died while travelling home on the Venetian island of Zante (now Greek Zakinthos).

*DSB*; C. D. O'Malley, *Andreas Vesalius of Brussels 1514–1564* (1964).

**VESPUCCI, AMERIGO** (1454–1512), Florentine explorer and the eponym of America, born in Florence on 9 March 1451 into an old but impoverished merchant family; he was the son of a notary and the nephew of a scholarly Dominican who provided for his education. He was placed by his family as a clerk in the trading firm of Lorenzo di Pierfrancesco de' Medici. In 1494 he was sent to Seville, where he became the company's shipping agent. In December 1495 the death of the Florentine merchant who had been fitting out twelve ships for the royal fleet (and who had previously fitted out the second expedition of COLUMBUS) led to the commission of Amerigo to complete the contract.

On 10 April 1495 King FERDINAND rescinded the monopoly of exploration held by Columbus; this order was to be abrogated on 2 June 1497, but in the interim, private voyages were permitted. Amerigo is said to have sailed on one of these expeditions on 10 May 1497, reaching a land mass 1,000 leagues west of Grand Canary on 16 June 1497 and exploring this previously unknown continent before returning to Cádiz on 15 October 1498. Longitude is notoriously difficult to gauge, but Amerigo's statements of longitude and latitude fail to inspire confidence that this voyage ever took place.

Amerigo's second voyage is easier to document. Late in 1498 news reached Spain that Columbus had discovered a large land mass near Trinidad, and on 16 May 1499 an expedition consisting of three ships under the command of Alonso de OJEDA set out to explore this new coast more fully; Amerigo was captain of one of the ships. On reaching the coast, Ojeda turned westwards, leaving Amerigo to explore the coast to the east. Amerigo and his crew were the first Europeans known to have visited the mouth of the Amazon. The expedition returned to Cádiz on 8 September 1500.

Amerigo's third voyage is problematical, because his two accounts give discrepant dates and distances. He claims to have entered the service of King MANUEL I of Portugal, and to have sailed from Lisbon in May 1501, first to the Brazilian coast and then south to 13 degrees from the South Pole (which would place him deep in the Antarctic continent) before returning via Sierra Leone (10 June 1502) to Lisbon (7 September 1502).

Amerigo's fourth voyage to America, and his second for Portugal, began with his departure from Lisbon in a fleet of six ships on 10 May 1503. His intended destination was

Malacca, which he believed to be at a latitude of 33 degrees south (it is actually 2 degrees 14 minutes north). He reached Bahia (in Brazil) and built a fort in a harbour at 18 degrees south before returning to Lisbon on 18 June 1504.

In 1505 Amerigo visited Columbus in Spain, and was entrusted with a letter for Columbus' son Diego. On 24 April 1505 Amerigo was granted Spanish citizenship, and on 6 August 1508 he was appointed principal navigator (*piloto mayor*) of the CASA DE CONTRATACIÓN in Seville, where he died on 22 February 1522.

There are no surviving journals to document any of Amerigo's voyages; the only surviving accounts are contained in four letters written by Amerigo. Three letters (describing two voyages) written to Pierfrancesco de' Medici were printed in an elaborated Latin translation in 1504; one issue was entitled *Mundus novus* ('The New World') and another *Epistola Albericii de novo mundo* ('The Letter of Amerigo on the New World'); an Italian translation of the Latin published in Vicenza in 1507 was entitled *Novo mondo da Alb. Vesputio*, and so associated Amerigo with the new continent.

The fourth letter was written from Lisbon to Piero SODERINI in September 1504. In this letter, Amerigo claims to have made four voyages between 1497 and 1504. A printed version of the Italian text of this letter was translated into French, and thence into Latin as *Quatuor Americi navigationes*. The cartographer Martin WALDSEEMÜLLER, who was then working in the University of Saint-Dié (Lorraine), used the Latin version of the letter in his *Cosmographiae introductio* (Saint-Dié, 1507), which showed the Americas as a separate continent, and proposed that this newly discovered fourth continent should be called 'America, because Americus discovered it'. The success of this misguided suggestion, together with scepticism about Amerigo's first voyage, has led to the deprecation of Amerigo and so has obscured his achievement as the first European to realize that the lands described by Columbus constituted a separate continent.

A. Magnaghi, *Amerigo Vespucci: Studio critico* (1926); F. J. Pohl, *Amerigo Vespucci, pilot major* (1944); G. Arciniegas, *Amerigo and the New World* (1955).

## VESTMENTS AND VESTIARIAN CONTROVERSY.

Vestments are the distinctive dress worn by the clergy when exercising their liturgical functions. Distinctive priestly costumes developed between the fourth and ninth centuries, and by the tenth century the Western Church had developed the liturgical vestments that have remained in use throughout the subsequent millennium. The principal vestments of the late medieval and Renaissance Church were wholly stable in design. The white linen alb, a narrow-sleeved garment which extended from the neck to the ankles, was worn by priests at mass; the surplice (Latin *superpelliceum*, 'over a fur garment') was an alb with wide sleeves, which could be worn over fur while the priest celebrated mass; the chasuble was an overgarment with the sides cut away, only worn during the celebration of the mass; the dalmatic, a striped overtunic reaching to the knees, was worn by deacons, bishops,

and (in England) by monarchs at their coronations; and the tunicle, a cloak without a girdle, was worn as an outer liturgical garment by subdeacons underneath the dalmatic and chasuble by bishops. The vestments of bishops also included sandals, mitres, and gloves. Within the Catholic Church, the material, colour, and cut of vestments were regulated by detailed legislation set out in the missal and the *Caeremoniale episcoporum* (most fully in the edition promulgated by Pope CLEMENT VIII in 1600); mass vestments had to be blessed and prayers recited as the priest dressed.

In the Lutheran Church, vestments were regarded as ADIAPHORA, and in practice many traditional Catholic vestments were retained. In Calvin's Geneva, however, vestments were abolished as inconsistent with the goal of simplicity of worship, and ministers instead wore a black gown, sometimes with white bands. This 'Geneva gown' was gradually adopted in reformed congregations throughout Europe.

In England, the question of vestments became the subject of a debate known as the Vestiarian controversy. Vestments were specified in the Book of COMMON PRAYER of 1549, but the following year John Hooper refused to wear the surplice and rochet prescribed in the Prayer Book at his consecration as bishop of Gloucester. A compromise was eventually reached, and for the rest of the decade the requirements for vestments were not enforced. The restoration of vestments in 1559, especially in the Chapel Royal, reignited the controversy. At the convocation of 1563, there was strong opposition to the requirement that priests had to wear a cope while celebrating communion and a surplice at other times. In 1564 Matthew PARKER's attempts to negotiate a compromise failed, and two years later he issued his statutory *Book of ADVERTISEMENTS*, which required the wearing of a square cap and scholar's gown, of a surplice in church, and of a cope in cathedrals and in collegiate churches. A rebellion amongst London clergy who refused to comply led to 37 clergy being deprived. The controversy produced a substantial controversial literature, and towards the end of the sixteenth century shifted its focus from the specific issue of vestments to the general principle of episcopal authority; in the seventeenth century, the disputed right of bishops to enforce conformity became part of the larger debate about church government, and the surplice and square cap became symbols in a larger battle. The debate about vestments was not settled until the secession of the nonconformist clergy in 1662; thereafter it remained dormant until the issue was revived by the Oxford Movement of the nineteenth century.

**VETTORI, FRANCESCO** (1474–1539), Florentine statesman, diplomat, and historian who entered the civic government after the expulsion of the MEDICI in 1494. He became a member of the Signoria in 1503 and in 1507 represented Florence in the imperial Diet of Constance. He became disenchanted with the administration of SODERINI, and plotted against him in 1512 on behalf of the Medici. He served as Florentine ambassador to the court of Pope LEO X, representing a Medici government at the court of a Medici pope. He later became ambassador to France (1515–18) and returned to

Rome as ambassador to Pope CLEMENT VII in 1529. He was the author of a history of Italy from 1511 to 1527.

Vettori was a friend and correspondent of MACHIAVELLI, who famously wrote to Vettori on 10 December 1513 describing his circumstances as he composed *Il principe*; the letter is often reprinted in modern editions of *The Prince*.

R. D. Jones, *Francesco Vettori: Florentine Citizen and Medici Servant* (1972).

**VETTORI, PIERO, or (Latin) Petrus Victorius** (1499–1585), Italian humanist, born into a noble family in Florence. His principled republicanism and opposition to the MEDICI led to his exile in San Casciano from 1530 to 1534. On returning to Florence he prepared an edition of Cicero; he became professor of Latin at the Florentine *Studio* in 1538, professor of Greek in 1543, and professor of moral philosophy in 1548. His principal works were commentaries on Aristotle, including the *Rhetoric* (1548), *Poetics* (1560), *Politics* (1576), and *Nicomachean Ethics* (1584).

**VIADANA, LODOVICO** (*c*.1560–1627), Italian Franciscan composer who was born into the Grossi family and entered the order of Minor Observants, for whom he became *diffinitor* for the province of Bologna in 1614. He was also *maestro di cappella* at Mantua Cathedral, the convent of San Luca, Cremona, Concordia Cathedral, and Fano Cathedral. Both his sacred and secular music demonstrate an interest in using instrumental groups and basso continuo. The *Concerti ecclesiastici* (1602) include *concerti* for three voices and figured basso continuo; the *concertato* style is also evident in the *Salmi a 4 cori*, scored for a group of five solo singers, three four-part choirs, and three organs, a CHITTARONE, strings, CORNETTS, bassoons, and trombones which double the vocal parts.

**VIANEN, PAULUS VAN** (*c*.1570–1613), Dutch silversmith in Munich and Prague, the originator of the AURICULAR STYLE in silver. Paulus was trained in his father's workshop in Utrecht and subsequently worked at the ducal court in Munich (1596–1601), the archiepiscopal court in Salzburg (1601–3), and the imperial court of RUDOLF II in Prague (1603–13), where he was court goldsmith. After his death in 1613, his designs were returned to his family in Utrecht, where his brother Adam (*c*.1569–1627) and Adam's son Christiaen (*c*.1600–1667) quickly adopted the auricular style. Christiaen worked in the English court of Charles I (1635–9) and subsequently twice returned to England (1652, *c*.1660–6).

MDA; J. R. ter Molen, *Van Vianen een Utrechtse familie van zilversmeden met een internationale faam* (2 vols., 1984); Teréz Gerszi, *Paulus van Vianen, Handzeihnungen* (1982).

**VICENTE, GIL** (*c*.1465–*c*.1537), Portuguese dramatist and poet, celebrated as the father of PORTUGUESE DRAMA, one of the greatest European dramatists of the early sixteenth century, and his country's greatest poet after CAMÕES. He lived so obscurely that details of his life have eluded the assiduous efforts of scholars. He may have been born in Guimarães and educated in Coimbra and he may have been the goldsmith who in 1506 fashioned the gold and enamel Belém monstrance now in the Museu Nacional de Arte Antiga in Lisbon and who served as master of the mint from 1513 to 1517.

Between 1502 and 1536, Vicente wrote 44 plays, which were published by his son Luis as *Copilação de todas las obras* (Lisbon, 1562); of these, sixteen are in Portuguese, eleven in Spanish, and seventeen in a macaronic mixture of the two languages. The use of Spanish in court plays may in part have been an act of deference to Queen Maria (queen 1500–16), who was the daughter of FERDINAND and ISABELLA of Spain, but also reflects the fashion for Spanish amongst the Portuguese aristocracy and the bilingualism of the court. The plays include AUTOS, tragicomedies for the courts of MANUEL I and JOHN III, and comedies and farces for popular and courtly audiences. His best-known *autos*, which often censure the clergy for immorality, are the *Auto dos Reis Magos* (1503; 'of the Three Kings'), the *Auto da alma* (1516; 'of the Soul'), the three *Autos das barcas* (1517–19; the boats are of hell, purgatory, and heaven), and the *Auto da feira* (1528; of the fair). The tragicomedy often said to be his masterpiece is *Dom Duardos* (1525), a Spanish play that draws on the chivalric romance *Primaleón* (1512); his Spanish plays also include a dramatization of AMADÍS DE GAULA (1533). His comedies include *Comedia del viudo* (1514) and *Comedia de Rubena* (1521).

DHP; Anselmo Braamcamp Freire, *Vida e obras de Gil Vicente, 'Trovador, mestre da Balança'* (1920; rev. edn. 1944); J. H. Parker, *Gil Vicente* (1967); Paul Teyssier, *La Langue de Gil Vicente* (1959).

**VICENTINO, NICOLÀ** (1511–*c*.1576), Italian composer and theorist who studied with Adriaan WILLAERT. He was in Ferrara, Siena, and Rome while in the service of Cardinal Ippolito II d'ESTE and was briefly *maestro di cappella* at Vicenza Cathedral; he then held minor ecclesiastical appointments in Milan where he died in the plague of 1575–6. He wrote some madrigals, but became famous for his treatise *L'antica musica ridotta alla moderna prattica* (1555), following a notorious debate in 1551 with Vicente Lusitano. The work outlines his theories concerning chromaticism and diatonicism which were further supported by a specially constructed *arcicembalo* and *arciorgano* capable of reproducing microtones.

**VICENZA or (Latin) Vicentia**, a city and episcopal see in the Veneto, was ruled successively by the DELLA SCALA family of Verona (1311–87), by the VISCONTI family of Milan, and by Venice (from 1405). Prominent Vicentines include the dramatist Gian Giorgio TRISSINO and the navigator Antonio PIGAFETTA; the painter Bartolommeo MONTAGNA spent much of his working life in Vicenza. The most famous son of Vicenza is Andrea PALLADIO, whose buildings were continued by Vincenzo SCAMOZZI. Palladian buildings in the city include the arcades of the Basilica (not a church, but a transformation of the Palazzo della Ragione of 1444), the Palazzo Chiericati (now a museum and art gallery), the Palazzo Barbarano, the Palazzo Civena-Trissino, the Palazzo Thiene, the Palazzo Valmarana, the Casa del Diavolo, the Loggia del Capitano (i.e. of the Venetian governor), and the Teatro Olimpico (see THEATRES AND THEATRE ARCHITECTURE).

One of Palladio's most famous buildings, the Villa Capra (also known as La Rotonda), is 2 kilometres (1 mile) south of the city; it was begun by Palladio in 1549 and completed by Scamozzi in 1606. The villa is a square building with a pillared portico on each face; inside the square, a series of rectangular rooms surrounds a central circular hall with a low dome. The design was often copied, notably at Château de Marly (near Paris), Chiswick House (London), and Mereworth Castle (Kent).

James Grubb, *Firstborn of Venice: Vicenza in the Early Renaissance* (1988).

**VICTORIA, TOMÁS LUÍS DE** (1548–1611), Spanish composer who was educated at Ávila Cathedral and the Jesuit Collegio Germánico in Rome where, in 1573, he was appointed *maestro di cappella*. In the mid-1570s he graduated to the priesthood and joined the Congregazione dell'Oratorio in Rome. He returned to Spain in 1587 where he was chaplain to the Dowager Empress María and *maestro* of the convent choir at the Monasterio de las Descalzas de Santa Clara in Madrid. Here he enjoyed financial security and the benefits of well-supported musical forces, both vocal and instrumental. His wrote masses, motets, Magnificats, psalms, Passions, and other liturgical music; he set only Latin texts and his style reflects his early study of Palestrina.

**VIDA, MARCO GIROLAMO** (1485–1566), neo-Latin poet, born in Cremona and baptized as Marcantonio. In about 1510 he entered the order of the Canonici Regolari Lateranensi, where he assumed the name Marco Girolamo. During this period he established his reputation as a Latin poet with two elegant didactic poems called *Scacchiae ludus* ('The Game of Chess') and *Bombyx* ('The Silkworm'). He moved to the papal court in Rome c.1513 and secured the patronage of Pope LEO X, who bestowed the Priory of St Sylvester at Frascati on Vida, and commissioned an epic on the life of Jesus; the *Christiad* was published in six books of Virgilian hexameters in 1535, and such was its popularity that it was republished in some 60 editions before the end of the century. The poem's description of the Council in hell, which had been adumbrated in Herodotus, CLAUDIAN, and BOCCACCIO's *Filocolo*, became the model for a new generation of imitations by Erasmo di Valvasone (*Angeleide*, 1590), Taubmanus (*Bellum angelicum*, 1597), TASSO, Abraham Cowley, and John Milton. Sometime before 1520 Vida began another important long Latin poem, the *Ars poetica* (1527), which is a defence of poetic imitation, particularly the imitation of Virgil. He also wrote hymns in the Virgilian style, some of which are among his finest poems.

On the accession of Clement VII in 1523, Vida became an apostolic protonotary, and in 1532 he was appointed bishop of Alba; he moved after the death of Clement in 1534, and lived there for the rest of his long life. He attended the COUNCIL OF TRENT, where he enjoyed the learned conversations of the poet Marcantonio FLAMINIO and of Cardinals Cervini, del Monte, and POLE; his stylized record of their conversations was published in *Dialogi de dignitate reipublicae* (1556), which

embodies the common sixteenth-century identification of prelapsarian Eden with the golden age of classical antiquity.

Mario di Cesare, *Vida's 'Christiad' and Vergilian Epic* (1964); id., *Bibliotheca Vidiana: A Bibliography of Marco Girolamo Vida* (1974); id., 'From Vergil to Vida to Milton', in J.-C. Margolin (ed.), *Conventus Neo-Latini Turonensis* (1976).

**VIDIUS, VIDUS**. See GUIDI, GUIDO.

**VIENNA or (German) Wien or (Hungarian) Becs or (Latin) Vindobona**. The city of Vienna became the HABSBURG capital in 1276. From the perspective of Christian Europe, Vienna was the most advanced bulwark against the Ottoman threat; it was also the contested territory of two Christian nations, Hungary and the duchy of Austria. In the early modern period Vienna was besieged on six occasions, In 1477 it was unsuccessfully besieged by a Hungarian army, and in 1485, at the conclusion of a second siege, it fell to the army of MATTHIAS CORVINUS. In 1529 and 1532 Vienna was besieged by the Ottomans, in 1619 the city was besieged by Bethlen Gábor, and in 1683 the Ottomans made their final assault on the city.

The term 'siege of Vienna' usually refers to the first of the Ottoman sieges. On 21 September 1529 the forces of the Ottoman Sultan Süleyman I the Magnificent besieged the city, which was garrisoned with some 20,000 troops. The Ottoman army consisted of at least 200,000 troops, but its supply lines were too overstretched to sustain a long siege, so Süleyman decided to attack. On 9 October his army overwhelmed the front line of the city's defences and penetrated the walls before being repulsed; in the course of the next five days, repeated assaults were repelled by ARTILLERY and hand-to-hand combat. The prospective arrival of an imperial army to lift the siege, together with the onset of winter, occasioned Süleyman's decision to lift the siege and withdraw his troops.

**VIÈTE, FRANÇOIS** (1540–1603), French mathematician, born in Fontenay-le-Comte and trained in law at the University of Poitiers. He entered public life as a member of the Parlement of Brittany and in 1580 was appointed to a position in the Paris Parlement. Viète was an accomplished breaker of ciphers (see CRYPTOGRAPHY), and was employed in this capacity by HENRI IV. There is clearly a possible analogy between such work with ciphers, in which one handles symbols that are of unknown significance, and work in ALGEBRA, which involves formal manipulation of equations in which there are symbols whose numerical value is unknown. Unfortunately for historians, but naturally enough since the work was secret, we have little information about Viète's work with ciphers.

As a mathematician, Viète's main interest was in algebra. The importance of his contribution does not seem to have been widely recognized until after his death. The Greek in the title of his treatise *In artem analyticum isagoge* (1591) is a deliberate reference to the Greek origins of algebra and the rediscovered *Arithmetica* of Diophantus (see BOMBELLI, RAFAELLE). Viète indeed makes considerable use of Diophantus' vocabulary, as well as adopting the rigorous ancient style of presentation. Viète's work is notable for its systematic exploration of the characteristics of various forms of equation. One element in the orderliness of Viète's approach is in his notation. He consistently uses vowels to stand for the unknown quantity and consonants to stand for numbers that are already given. This distinction proved useful and eventually became universal, but in the form it was given by Descartes in his *Geometrie* (1637), in which letters from the end of the alphabet (x, y, z) were used where Viète had employed vowels, and letters from the beginning (a, b, c ...) took the place he had given to consonants. Viète makes maximum use of the various symbols that had been introduced, such as plus (+), minus (−), and equals (=). This tends to make his equations distinguishable from the surrounding prose. This was increasingly the case in learned algebra, but in Viète's work it also has a deeper significance: Viète is, for the first time, treating equations as if they were entities in their own right. Thus an equation has the same ontological status as, say, a triangle and, like a triangle, may be thought of as having properties. So in Viète's work it is clear that, in his mind, algebra now has the same status as GEOMETRY.

Viète seems to have been less interested in geometry than in algebra. However, like several of his contemporaries, he reacted to the incompleteness of the then-known text of Apollonius' *Conica* (edited by COMMANDINO, 1566) by attempting to reconstruct some of the missing theorems. This work was published as *Apollonius Gallus* (1600).

An edition of Viète's complete works appeared in 1646, edited and with substantial commentary notes by a leading mathematician of the time, Franz van Schooten (1615–60).
 DSB.

**VIGARNY or Biguerny, FELIPE** (*c.*1480–1543), Burgundian sculptor, architect, and medallist in Spain who migrated from his native Langres to Burgos in about 1498. He carved the relief *Christ Bearing the Cross* for the enclosure that surrounds the high altar of Burgos Cathedral and then, together with his partner Alfonso BERRUGUETE, carved the reredos for the Chapel Royal at Granada (1520–1). In 1539 Vigarny and Berruguete worked together on the carving of the upper part of the choir stalls in Toledo Cathedral. His medals include a portrait head of Cardinal CISNEROS (now in the Complutensian University in Madrid). The architectural theorist Diego de SAGREDO praises Vigarny's art in his *Medidas del Romano* (1526), particularly in respect of the rule of proportion that he used when carving the human form.
 MDA.

**VIGENÈRE, BLAISE DE** (1523–96), French diplomat and cryptographer, born in Saint-Pourçain. After a brief period in the secretariat of FRANCIS I in 1540, Vigenère entered the service of the duke of Nevers, for whom he worked for almost 30 years. He retired in 1570 in order to write, and by the end of his life had published 22 books. While in Rome on a diplomatic visit in 1549 he became interested in CRYPTOGRAPHY, and in 1586 he published his *Traité des chiffres*, a seminal work in which he presented ciphers so secure that many were not

deciphered until the nineteenth century. In 1587 he published his *Traité des comètes*, in which he described comets as entirely natural phenomena and attempted to dispel the porpular belief that the appearance of a comet portended the death of a monarch.

**VIGNOLA, GIACOMO or Jacopo BAROZZI DA** (1507–73), Italian architect, garden designer, and architectural theorist. He was born in Vignola (near Modena) and studied painting and architecture in Bologna. In 1530 he settled in Rome, where he became architect to Pope JULIUS III. He collaborated with Bartolomeo AMMANATI and VASARI on the Villa GIULIA (1551–5) and in 1559 began work on the Villa FARNESE PALACE at Caprarola.

The first of Vignola's Roman churches was the Tempietto di Sant'Andrea, which was built for Pope Julius; this church had the first oval dome in Christendom. Vignola repeated the design on a larger scale in his late Sant'Anna dei Palafrenieri (begun 1573), which was to be extensively imitated by BAROQUE architects. His most influential church was Il Gesù, the mother church of the JESUIT Order, on which work was started in 1568. This is shaped like a Latin cross, and has a broad nave and a large dome area; the façade was added after Vignola's death by Giacomo DELLA PORTA. Il Gesù has been copied in Jesuit churches all over the world, and is probably the world's most imitated church. Its plan also sowed the seeds for the layout of the Baroque church of the seventeenth century.

In 1562 Vignola published *Regole delle cinque ordini d'architettura*, which was widely regarded as the definitive codification of the five architectural ORDERS.
 MDA; W. Lotz et al., *La vita e le opere di Jacopo Barozzi da Vignola* (1974).

**VIGO, GIOVANNI DA** (1450–1525), Italian surgeon. He was born in Rapallo and practised in Genoa and Savona. He was appointed physician to Pope JULIUS II on his accession in 1503. His medical writings, which draw on his early experience of civilian and military surgery and his subsequent work as a physician in noble households, include *Practica in arte chirurgica copiosa* ('Abundant Practice in Surgery', Rome, 1514) and a surgical manual called *Practica compendiosa* (Rome and Pavia, 1518), which was translated into French, Italian, and English.
 DSB.

**VIHUELA**, a guitar-like member of the viol family, but related to the lute in that its six or seven courses of strings were plucked, except for the *vihuela de arco* which was played with a bow. The *vihuela de mano* was plucked with the fingers while a quill was used as a plectrum on the *vihuela de pendola*. Further similarities to the lute exist in its tuning, the presence of up to ten frets, and the use of tablature. It was prevalent in Spain in the fifteenth and sixteenth centuries where composers such as Luis MILÁN and Alonso MUDARRA wrote about playing techniques and performance practice; Italian and Portuguese versions were known as 'violas'.

**VILLA.** A villa is an Italian country house and its estate (including garden spaces), the rural or suburban version of the PALACE (Italian *palazzo*); in practice the two terms overlap: a large villa in the country, such as the Farnese villa at Caprarola, is sometimes called a *palazzo* and a grand city house in a garden setting is often called a villa. ALBERTI's revival of the ancient idea of the *villa suburbana* further blurred the distinction, so that the suburban villa of the Gonzaga family on the edge of Mantua is called Palazzo del TÈ, and the Doria villa on the edge of Genoa is called the Palazzo DORIA PRINCIPE. Until 1700 the term 'villa' was used in vernacular languages only of houses in Italy. If the house was small, or small in comparison to the scale of the garden, it was sometimes known as a *CASINO*.

The revival of the Roman ideal of a house in the country fit for the leisure of the man of letters does not derive from VITRUVIUS, who does not mention the villa, but rather from literary sources such as the letters of Pliny the Younger and from archaeological excavations of ancient villas, such as Hadrian's villa at Tivoli. Pliny's idea of separate summer and winter dining rooms, for example, was implemented in the Villa MADAMA, and the influence of Hadrian's villa can be seen in the Ocean Fountain in the BOBOLI GARDENS and the statuary in the gardens of the Villa d'ESTE at Tivoli.

Early villas were fortified houses with utilitarian designs, but Renaissance architects refined the form, and built elegant houses on hilltop or hillside sites, with views of gardens and distant vistas. The designs of house and garden were fully integrated, and architects contrived to achieve an interpenetration of house and garden (see ITALIAN GARDENS).

The first villas to realize the humanist ideal of the retreat for the civilized man were the MEDICI VILLAS at Careggi and Fiesole, both of which provided settings for learned debate. In Rome, the first villa to be built outside the city walls was the Villa Madama, the classical design of which was to prove enormously influential. Of the villas around Rome, the most important were the Villa GIULIA (then on the edge of Rome), the Villa FARNESE at Caprarola, the Villa d'Este at Tivoli, the Villa LANTE near Viterbo, the Villa ORSINI at Bomarzo, and the villas of Frascati (including ALDOBRANDINI and MONDRAGONE); within the Vatican, the Villa PIA is a tiny rural retreat in the city.

In the 1520s the influence of Roman villas began to be felt in regions to the north of Rome (there were no significant villas to the south). The most important villas of northern Italy were the Villa PRATOLINO (Tuscany), the Villa BARBARO (Veneto), the Villa CICOGNA (Piedmont), and the Villa BRENZONE (Lombardy).

Georgina Masson, *Italian Villas and Palaces* (1959); David Coffin, *The Villa in the Life of Renaissance Rome* (1979); A. Tantillo Mignosi, *Ville e paese* (1980); J. S. Ackermann, *The Villa: Form and Ideology in Country Houses* (1990); Paul Holberton, *Palladio's Villas: Life in the Renaissance Countryside* (1990); P. van der Ree, G. Schmienk, and G. Stenbergen, *Italian Villas and Gardens* (1992); Mirka Benes, *Villas and Gardens in Early Modern Italy and France* (2001).

**VILLALPANDO, FRANCISCO CORRAL DE** (d. 1561), Spanish architect and metalworker, born in Palencia into a family of decorative artists working in plaster. In 1548 he built the chancel screen (plated in silver and gold) in Toledo Cathedral in a style that combines Renaissance and PLATERESQUE elements. In 1553 he was appointed as royal architect to CHARLES V, and in that capacity built the great staircase of the Alcázar in Toledo. He translated from Italian to Spanish two books of SERLIO's *Architettura*: books 3 (on the ORDERS of architecture) and 4 (on the architecture of antiquity).

MDA.

**VILLAMEDIANA, JUAN DE TASSIS Y PERALTA, COUNT OF** (1580–1622), Spanish poet and courtier, born in Lisbon, the son of a diplomat. He was educated in Salamanca, married in 1601, and succeeded to the title of count on the death of his father in 1607. His gambling and sexual profligacy led to his exclusion from the court in 1608; he was initially exiled to Valladolid, and from 1611 to 1617 lived and worked as a soldier in Italy, where he met Giambattista MARINO. On returning to Madrid in 1617 his savage satires offended the influential objects of his caustic inventive, and in 1621 he was again exiled, this time to Andalusia. On the death of PHILIP III later that year, he returned to Madrid, where he was appointed as gentleman-in-waiting to Isabella of Bourbon, Philip IV's young queen, whom he imprudently attempted to seduce. It was widely believed that on 15 May 1622 he had set the theatre at ARANJUEZ on fire during a performance of his masque *La gloria de Niquea* in order to be able to carry off the queen in his arms. He was assassinated on 21 August 1622 while stepping out of his coach after returning home from the royal palace, apparently at the instigation of the jealous king or his minister Olivares.

Villamediana was a friend and disciple of Luis de GÓNGORA, and his own *Fábulas* represent the zenith of GONGORISM. His poetry ranges from elegant but venomous court satires to a collection of more than 200 polished love sonnets. Villamediana's colourful life was the subject of *Son mis amores* (Barcelona, 1944), a historical novel by Albert Torrella.

DHE; E. Cotarelo y Mori, *El conde de Villamediana* (1886); Luis Rosales, *Pasión y muerte del conde de Villamediana* (1969).

**VILLANELLA.** The villanella originated in the sixteenth century as the *villanella alla napoletana* and in Cotgrave's *Dictionnaire* (1611) was defined as 'a country dance, round or song'. They were sung at the court of FRANCIS I in 1544 by Ferrante Sanseverino, prince of Salerno, and grew in popularity, with collections by ARCADELT and CLEREAU published in Paris in the 1550s. They were characterized by three-part chordal writing, with 'forbidden' parallel fifths often employed to enhance its 'rustic' qualities. Derivative forms were, in Germany, drinking songs and, in Italy, the *greghesca* (created by Antonio Molino and favoured by Venetian composers), the *GIUSTINIANA*, and the *mascherata* (for use during a ball or procession).

**VILLANI, GIOVANNI** (*c.*1276–1348), Italian merchant banker and chronicler, born in Florence, the son of Villano di

Stoldo, whom he followed into commerce. In the early years of the fourteenth century he travelled in France, the Netherlands, and Italy. In about 1315 he began to take part in civic affairs: he served as a *priore* (i.e. a member of the Signoria) in 1316, 1317, and 1321, and in 1317 became master of the mint, in which capacity he assembled its archives and compiled a record of all the COINS that had been struck in Florence. In the early 1320s he became involved in the project to reconstruct the city's walls, and was afterwards accused of embezzlement, but managed to prove his innocence. He fought with the Florentine army against Lucca, and was present at the defeat of the Florentine army by Castruccio Castracani's forces at Altopascio in 1325. He became involved in famine relief in 1328, negotiated (unsuccessfully) for the acquisition of Lucca by Florence in 1339, and supervised the construction of Andrea PISANO's doors for the Florentine baptistery in 1340. The following year negotiations with Lucca were reopened, and Villani spent several months as a hostage in Ferrara. Towards the end of his life he was implicated in a series of commercial failures in Florence, and was for a period imprisoned. He died in the plague of 1348.

Villani recorded these contemporary events in the chronicle known as the *Istorie fiorentine* or *Cronica universale*. The chronicle, which is written in Italian (Villani had little Latin), places the rise of Florence in the context of world (i.e. biblical and European) history. After Giovanni's death the chronicle was continued by his brother Matteo and thereafter by Matteo's son Filippo.

Villani claimed to have been inspired to write his chronicle while in Rome for the jubilee of 1300, when he explored the classical remains and read the historians of ancient Rome. The history of Rome, he explained, had been celebrated by Virgil, Sallust, Lucan, and Livy, and he proposed to perform the same service for Florence, the daughter of Rome; Rome was in decline, but Florence was in the ascendant. This passage anticipates Gibbon's experience in the ruins of the Capitol.

*Croniche fiorentine*, ed. I. Moutier (1823); *Selections from the First Nine Books of the Croniche fiorentine*, trans. R. E. Selfe (1896); Eric Cochrane, *Historians and Historiography in the Italian Renaissance* (1981).

**VILLEGAIGNON, NICOLAS DURAND DE** (1510–71), French colonizer. He participated in the expedition of CHARLES V to ALGIERS (1541) and was later appointed naval commander of the Brittany coast by King HENRI II. In 1555 he sailed from Le Havre as the head of a colonizing mission to Brazil. A settlement called Fort Coligny (named after the expedition's patron Gaspard de COLIGNY) was established on an island (now called Villegaignon) near what is now Rio de Janeiro. Once the colony had been established and its Protestant orthodoxy ensured by the arrival in 1557 of missionaries sent from Geneva by Calvin, Villegaignon returned to France to raise more settlers; he was preceded, however, by returning settlers who discouraged potential emigrants with their reports of the tyranny and brutality of Villegaignon. The failure of the colony to attract a substan-

tial number of settlers made it vulnerable to attack, and in 1560 Mem de SÁ, the governor of Brazil, mounted a raid on the colony; the surviving colonists dispersed and then reassembled at Fort Coligny, but in 1567 Sá returned and destroyed the remnants of the colony.

DBF s.v. Durand; Frank Lestringant, *Le Huguenot et Le Souvage* (1990).

**VILLON, FRANÇOIS** (*c*.1431–after 1463), French poet, educated at the University of Paris, where he led a riotous life. In 1455 he killed a priest and two years later he was involved in an armed robbery of the Collège de Navarre. In November 1462 Villon was sentenced to hang for his part in a riot; he was banished (on appeal) in January 1463, whereupon he disappears from the historical record.

Villon's poetry repudiates courtly ideals of service to aristocratic women in favour of an appetite for low-born women; he was, however, also capable of writing devotional poetry to the Virgin Mary. Villon's most important poem is the *Grand Testament* (1461), a mock will which consists of two sections: in the first Villon dictates his will to his clerk, and in the second half he announces a series of burlesque bequests. His short poems include the 'Ballade des pendus', a description of his own hanging body in which the poet appeals for a sympathetic understanding of the executed criminal.

Michael Freeman, *François Villon in his Works: The Villain's Tale* (2000).

**VINCI, LEONARDO DA**. See LEONARDO DA VINCI.

**VINCI, PIERINO DA**. See PIERINO DA VINCI.

**VINCKBOONS, DAVID** (1576–1632), Flemish painter and print designer in Amsterdam, born on 13 August 1576 in Mechelen (French Malines), the son of a watercolourist. In 1579 the family moved to Antwerp and in 1591 fled the advancing Spanish army and settled in Amsterdam. Vinckboons trained in the studio of his fellow émigré Gillis van CONINXLOO, from whom he inherited an enthusiasm for landscapes peopled by tiny figures. The depictions of peasant festivals in Vinckboons's GENRE pictures show the influence of Pieter BRUEGEL the Elder. Vinckboons sometimes punned on his name by including in his landscapes a finch (*vinck*) in a tree (*boom*).

MDA; NBW iii.

***VINDICIAE CONTRA TYRANNOS***, an influential treatise on political theory printed in 1579, allegedly in Edinburgh but actually on the Continent, probably in Basel or in France. The treatise was published under the pseudonym Stephanus Junius Brutus, and has been variously attributed to Hubert LANGUET, Philippe DUPLESSIS-MORNAY, Théodore de BEZA, François HOTMAN, and Isaac CASAUBON. The treatise articulates a HUGUENOT perspective on the WARS OF RELIGION, and sets out the case for resisting royal authority on religious and civil grounds.

**VIOL** was a generic term referring to Renaissance string instruments but was more specifically a six-stringed instrument with frets played with a bow, which was held in such a way that the player could alter the tension of the hair and thus affect the timbre of the music. It was originally called a viola da gamba or 'leg viol' because it was held between the player's legs, like a cello but without a supporting spike; smaller versions were rested on the player's knees; the viola da braccio was played on the arm. It was used as both a solo and ensemble instrument; a viol consort or chest of viols was made up of different-sized instruments (treble, tenor, and bass). Specific types of viol included the lyra viol designed for virtuoso playing and the viola d'amore which had sympathetic strings and produced a particularly sweet sound.

**VIRDUNG, SEBASTIAN** (c.1465–after 1511), German priest, composer, and author of a treatise on musical instruments. His university education was at Heidelberg where he sang in the chapel of Count Philip; the organist there was Arnoldt SCHLICK, with whom he later bitterly and publicly exchanged views. By 1505 he was in Stuttgart in Duke ULRICH's chapel and two years later was succentor at Konstanz Cathedral. His *Musica getutscht* ('Music Translated into German', 1511) is an illustrated treatise, presented in the form of a dialogue, on musical instruments, with information about keyboard and lute tablatures, recorder fingering charts, and performance practice. Instruments are categorized and advice is given on playing clavichord, lute, and recorder.

**VIRET, PIERRE** (1511–71), French Protestant reformer, born in Orbe (Vaud, which was then independent of the SWISS CONFEDERATION) and educated in Paris, where he became a Protestant. On returning to Orbe in 1530 Viret was ordained by Guillaume FAREL, whom he assisted in the implementation of the Reformation in Geneva and in Vaud (1534–36), which became a protectorate of Bern in 1536 (and in 1798 was to become a Swiss canton). He served as pastor of the church in Lausanne for 23 years (1537–59), but in 1559 was expelled because of his attempt to impose the Genevan form of church discipline on Lausanne. He subsequently became an intinerant preacher in centres such as Geneva, Montpellier, and Lyon. He eventually settled in Béarn under the protection of JEANNE D'ALBRET.

Viret's writings included satires, dialogues, exhortations to the faithful (*Remonstrances aux fidèles*, 1547), excoriations of opponents (*L'Interim*, 1565), and a popular version of the theology of Calvin's *Institutes*, the *Instruction chrétienne* (1564).

Jean Barnaud, *Pierre Viret: Sa Vie et son œuvre (1511–1571)* (1911); R. D. Linder, *The Political Ideas of Pierre Viret* (1964).

**VIRGIL IN THE RENAISSANCE.** The Roman poet Publius Vergilius Maro (70–19 BC), who was born near Mantua, was the author of *Eclogues* (ten PASTORAL poems), *Georgics* (four agricultural poems), and the epic *Aeneid*. Within a century of his death the poems (and the tomb) of Virgil were objects of veneration, and poets such as Statius referred to the *Aeneid* as divine. Virgil was absorbed into the Christian tradition, a process facilitated by the interpretation of *Eclogue 4* (which predicts the virgin birth of a child who would bring peace and a return to the golden age) as a prophecy of the birth of Jesus; this messianic reading was sanctioned by the Emperor

Constantine at the Council of Nicaea (325) and, despite the ambivalence of AUGUSTINE and the hostility of JEROME, became the accepted interpretation in late antiquity; it was later to be accepted by some Renaissance humanists and rejected by others.

In the Middle Ages the aspects of Virgil that were ill suited to incorporation into Christian thought were interpreted in allegorical terms by writers such as John of Salisbury, and Virgil himself came to be seen as a proto-Christian (*anima naturaliter Christiana*) who was separated only by a short period of time from the Christianity that he would surely have embraced. In the *Divine Comedy* Dante's Virgil is the poet's guide through hell and purgatory, and although he is responsible for the conversion of Statius (whom Dante regarded as a Christian), he is not redeemed, and returns to limbo rather than entering paradise.

The Renaissance Virgil was read through the prism of centuries of commentaries, a tradition that began with the scholiasts and Christian allegorists (e.g. Fulgentius) of late antiquity and extended to learned contemporary commentary (e.g. the commentary of Cristoforo LANDINO), but there was also a popular tradition that associated Virgil with magic (e.g. the French chapbook *Les Faits merveilleux de Virgile*, c.1499) which was translated into English in 1520. Many editions of the *Aeneid* in the fifteenth and sixteenth centuries printed Maffeo VEGIO's sequel as a thirteenth book of the *Aeneid*, and many began with four lines (possibly Virgilian in origin) in which Virgil forsakes pastoral in favour of epic. These lines (which are translated by SPENSER in the opening stanza of *The Fairy Queen* and paraphrased by Milton at the beginning of *Paradise Regained*) were taken as exemplary by Renaissance poets who emulated Virgil by writing pastoral eclogues when young and turning to the epic in maturity.

V. Zabughin, *Vergilio nel Rinascimento italiano* (2 vols., 1921–23); J. W. Spargo, *Virgil the Necromancer* (1934); A. L. Pellegrini (ed.), *The Early Renaissance: Virgil and the Classical Tradition* (1985); Craig Kallendorf, *A Bibliography of Renaissance Italian Translations of Virgil* (1994).

**VIRGINALS.** As early as 1511, when they were mentioned in Sebastian VIRDUNG's *Musica getutscht*, the virginals were a rectangular keyboard instrument, small enough to be placed on a table or the player's lap. Later the term referred to all types of harpsichord although now it tends to refer to those instruments whose metal strings are set at right angles to the keys. The lowest strings are at the front and the jacks are set diagonally across the instrument. The origin of the term is unclear but is likely to be to do with its use by female players. Since it is described by Paulus Paulirinus as early as 1460 it cannot refer to any specific connection with 'the virgin queen', ELIZABETH I.

**VIRGIN MARY.** See MARY.

**VIRTÙ.** The Italian term *virtù* is cognate with English 'virtue', but retained in early modern Italian the force of its origins in Latin *virtus*, which carries the senses of 'excellence' and 'manliness'. It also carries a meaning in the natural

sciences of 'innate power or property' of a mineral or vegetable. The term was intensified by MACHIAVELLI to convey
the notion of a virtue that was energetic rather than passive,
one that prompted imaginative statecraft and military
prowess. This active sense of the term is preserved in the
modern English use of the loanword 'virtuoso'.

**VIRUÉS, CRISTÓBAL DE** (*c.*1550–*c.*1614), epic poet, playwright and soldier. He was born in Valencia, served as a
soldier in the battle of LEPANTO and in the defence of MILAN
(which was then a Spanish dependency), and returned to
Valencia in about 1585. After publishing the first part of his
epic *El Monserrate* (1587), Virués returned to Milan, where
he published a sequel, *El Monserrate segundo* (1602). The
poems are accounts, from the perspective of the COUNTER-
REFORMATION, of the legendary Spanish hermit Juan Garín; in
the book-burning scene in *Don Quijote*, this poem is saved
from the flames.

In 1609 Virués published a collection of five tragedies
(*La gran Semíramis*, *La cruel Casandra*, *Atila furioso*, *La infelice
Marcela*, and *Elisa Dido*) written in the 1570s and 1580s entitled
*Obras trágicas y líricas del capitán Cristóbal de Virués.*

C. V. Sargent, *A Study of the Dramatic Works of Cristóbal de Virués*
(1930); John Weiger, *Cristóbal de Virués* (1978).

**VISCHER FAMILY**, a family of Nuremberg sculptors and
bronze-founders. The greatest product of their workshop is
the bronze shrine mounted over the silver sarcophagus of
St Sebaldus (1490) in the Sebalduskirche in Nuremberg. The
initial design (now in the Gemäldegalerie in Vienna), which
was prepared by Peter Vischer the Elder (*c.*1460–1529) in 1488,
shows a three-bayed BALDACCHINO sheltering the sarcophagus. By the time the shrine was constructed (1508–19) the
Italian experience of his sons Hermann the Younger (*c.*1486–
1517) and Peter the Younger (1487–1528)—and their influence
on their brother Hans (*c.*1489–1550)—meant that Renaissance
elements were introduced: the canopy is Gothic, as are the
figures of the apostles, but the base and the baldacchino
depict biblical and mythological figures in a Renaissance
idiom.

Hermann Vischer the Elder (*fl.* 1453, d. 1488) was responsible for the bronze font in the Stadtkirche in Wittenberg.
His son Peter the Elder contributed the bronze figures of
Theodoric and King Arthur to the tomb of the Emperor MAX-
IMILIAN I in Innsbruck (1513). Hans Vischer may have been the
designer of the Apollo FOUNTAIN (1523) in the courtyard of the
old Town Hall (Altes Rathaus) in Nuremberg; the figure
of Apollo, which derives from an Italian engraving, is the earl-
iest surviving free-standing nude to have been cast outside
Italy. Hans was certainly responsible for three tombs in the
Wittenberg Schlosskirche, including the tomb of the Elector
FRIEDRICH III (1527), and for reliefs in the FUGGER Chapel in
Augsburg. Hans's son Georg Vischer (*c.*1520–1592) specialized in small decorative bronzes such as inkwells.
MDA.

**VISCONTI, BERNABÒ** (1323–85), *signore* of Milan who
assumed control of Milan on the death of his uncle Giovanni

Visconti in 1354. The following year he arranged with his
brother Galeazzo for their brother Matteo to be assassinated,
and thereafter governed Matteo's territories (Bologna, Lodi,
Piacenza, and Parma) jointly with Galeazzo. He also held
Milan and Genoa in common with Galeazzo, but was sole
lord of Bergamo, Brescia, and Como. When Galeazzo withdrew from political life in 1360, Bernabò became the most
powerful overlord in northern Italy. He was constantly
engaged in warfare, and financed his wars with heavy taxes:
he fought Popes Innocent VI and Urban V, who proclaimed
a crusade against him, and he fought the Emperor Charles
IV, who declared the forfeiture of his fief. He lost Genoa to
Simone BOCCANEGRA in 1358, but gained Reggio nell'Emilia in
1371. On the death of his brother Galeazzo in 1378, Bernabò
sought to succeed to his possessions, but his nephew Gian
Galeazzo VISCONTI deposed and imprisoned him, and he died
in prison.

Bernabò was a man of voracious appetites with a reputation for coarseness, cruelty, and concupiscence: at one
point he was estimated to be the father of 37 living children and to have been responsible for the condition of 18
women who were then pregnant; Chaucer describes him in
'The Monk's Tale' as the 'god of delight and scourge of
Lombardy'.

**VISCONTI, FILIPPO MARIA** (1392–1447), third duke of
Milan. He became nominal ruler of Pavia in 1402, and succeeded his brother Giovanni Maria, the second duke, in 1412.
The cruelty that he shared with his brother was exacerbated
by ill health, obsessive suspicion, and a malevolent sensitivity about his unattractive appearance. On succeeding to the
dukedom, Filippo Maria promptly married Beatrice Tenola,
the widow of Facino CANE, who had kept Giovanni Maria in
power. This marriage ensured the loyalty of Facino's troops,
and also gave him control of Alessandria, Novara, Pavia, and
Tortona, all of which Facino had controlled; in 1418 Filippo
Maria arranged for the judicial execution of his duchess on a
fabricated charge of adultery.

Filippo Maria committed himself to an unceasing
campaign to reconquer the Visconti territories lost by his
brother. He employed able *condottieri*, including Francesco
CARMAGNOLA, Niccolò PICCININO, and Francesco SFORZA, and
so managed to recover the Lombard portion of his father's
duchy. He conquered Genoa in 1412, and extended his rule
into the Val Levantina in a victory over the Swiss at the
battle of ARBEDO. These conquests marked the limit of expansion without confrontation with Florence and Venice. War
with Florence broke out in 1423, and two years later Venice
became involved; there was a short-lived peace between 1428
and 1431, but thereafter hostilities continued until 1444. In the
course of these wars, Filippo Maria lost Bergamo, Brescia,
Genoa, and Vercelli.

Filippo Maria died on 13 August 1447, the last of the
Visconti in the direct male line. His government was suc-
ceeded by the AMBROSIAN REPUBLIC and then by Francesco
Sforza, who in 1441 had married Filippo Maria's daughter
Bianca.

**VISCONTI, GIAN GALEAZZO** (1351–1402), first duke of Milan, the son of Galeazzo II Visconti and Blanche of Savoy. In 1360 (aged 9) he married Isabelle de Valois, daughter of King Jean II of France, and received as dowry the county of Vertus, in Champagne; he was thereafter known as the conte di Virtù. On the death of his father in 1378, Gian Galeazzo succeeded to the lordships of Alessandria, Asti, Casale, Novara, Padua, Tortona, Valenza, and Vercelli. His wife Isabelle died in 1372, and in 1380 Gian Galeazzo married his cousin Caterina Visconti, the daughter of his uncle Bernabò. In 1385 Gian Galeazzo deposed and imprisoned Bernabò and so consolidated all territories subject to Visconti rule. Two years later he married his daughter Valentina to Louis de Valois, duc d'Orléans; this marriage was later to form the basis of King LOUIS XII's claim to Milan. In 1395 the Emperor WENCESLAS conferred on Gian Galeazzo the title duke of Milan, for which the new duke paid 100,000 florins.

By 1385 Gian Galeazzo had brought together all the Visconti lands under his rule, but he aspired to still more territory. In 1387 he joined forces with the CARRARA family of Padua and seized Verona and Vicenza from Antonio DELLA SCALA; the following year he allied himself with the Venetians and turned against the Carrara family, occupying Padua, Bassano, Belluno, and Feltre. His aspirations in Romagna, Umbria, and Tuscany aroused the enmity of Florence, but in the three wars that followed (1390–2, 1397–8, 1400–2), Gian Galeazzo relentlessly subdued the armies of Florence, and he acquired the lordships of Lunigiana (1398), Pisa and Siena (1399), Assisi, Perugia, and Spoleto (1400), and Bologna (1402). Florence was by now a besieged island in a northern Italy controlled by Gian Galeazzo, but it was spared what could have been a successful assault by his death from plague on 3 September 1402.

Duke Gian Galeazzo was an important patron of scholarship and architecture. He employed humanist secretaries, supported the universities of Pavia and Piacenza, fostered the manuscript illumination of the Lombard School, encouraged the building of the cathedral in Milan, and commissioned the Certosa di Pavia (one of the greatest buildings of Renaissance Italy, and the burial place of the Visconti). He completed the Castello Visconteo (in Pavia) which had been commissioned by his father; two of its corner towers were destroyed by French artillery in 1525. The castle now contains a museum of archaeology and sculpture and a Risorgimento museum. Gian Galeazzo's library is in the Bibliothèque Nationale in Paris.

D. M. Bueno de Mesquita, *Giangaleazzo Visconti* (1941); Hans Baron, *The Crisis of the Early Italian Renaissance* (1955).

**VISCONTI, GIOVANNI MARIA** (1389–1412), second duke of Milan; he succeeded to the dukedom on the death of his father on 3 September 1402. His guardian, and the *de facto* ruler of the Visconti territories, was Facino CANE, the chief arbiter in the succession crisis that ensued in the wake of the death of Duke Gian Galeazzo. Even after the young duke finally secured his position in 1404, it was Facino and his *condottieri* who kept him in office and advised on every aspect of government. This arrangement did not succeed in holding the Visconti empire together, and in the course of Giovanni Maria's ten-year reign, most of the territories conquered by his father were lost.

The extremity of Duke Giovanni Maria's cruelty may have been pathogenetic. He was murdered by Ghibelline noblemen and succeeded by his brother Filippo Maria.

**VISCONTI FAMILY**, a Milanese family which rose to prominence in the late thirteenth century and governed Milan from 1277 to 1447, except for the years 1302–10. Ottone Visconti (d. 1295) was appointed archbishop of Milan by Pope Urban IV in 1262, but was unable to occupy his see until 1277, when his coalition of Milanese noblemen defeated the forces of the *signore*, Napoleon della Torre, at Decio. Ottone imprisoned the six leading members of the della Torre family in cages, and installed himself as *signore*.

Ottone was the first of the twelve Visconti lords of Milan. The second was Ottone's great-nephew Matteo Visconti (1255–1322), who became captain of the people (*capitano del popolo*) in 1287 but was forced to flee to Verona in 1302 because of a revolt by the della Torre family. Matteo's imperial loyalties led to Henry VII, king of the Romans (i.e. emperor elect), restoring him to Milan and appointing him as imperial vicar of Lombardy (1310–12). Matteo extended his realm by bribery, diplomacy, and military conquest to include Alessandro, Bergamo, Cremona, Piacenza, Pavia, Tortona, and Vercelli. In 1322 a quarrel with Pope John XXII led to Matteo's excommunication, and he at once abdicated in favour of his son Galeazzo (1277–1328). Matteo died shortly thereafter (24 June 1322), leaving five sons who were to feature in the subsequent history of the family: Galeazzo, Marco, Lucchino, Giovanni, and Stefano.

The tenure of Galeazzo I Visconti as *signore* (1322–8) was challenged by an invading papal army, which he defeated in 1324 at Vaprio d'Adda with the assistance of the imperial forces of Ludwig IV of Bavaria, king of the Romans. In 1327 he was imprisoned in Monza by King Ludwig, who suspected that Galeazzo had arranged a secret peace with the papacy. He was released through the intercession of Castruccio Castracani, duke of Lucca (whose biography was later to be written by MACHIAVELLI). Galeazzo's son by his wife Beatrice d'Este (namesake of the later Beatrice d'ESTE, duchess of Milan) was Azzone (1301–39), who succeeded his father and became the fourth Visconti lord of Milan. Azzone purchased the title of imperial vicar for 25,000 florins from Ludwig IV; he extended the Visconti realm by the conquest of another ten towns, murdered his uncle Marco (who had commanded an imperial army and captured Pisa and Lucca for the Visconti), and was succeeded as *signore* by his uncles Lucchino (in 1339) and Giovanni (in 1349).

Lucchino Visconti, the fifth lord, made peace with the papacy in 1341, bought Parma from Obizzo d'Este, and subjected Pisa to the rule of Milan; he was poisoned by his wife Isabella Fieschi (a member of the prominent Genoese family) in 1349 and succeeded by his brother Giovanni. Giovanni, who became archbishop of Milan, was a friend of PETRARCH and an enemy of Pope Clement VI; he greatly expanded the

Visconti realm, acquiring Bologna (1350) and Genoa (1353) and so extending Visconti rule to all of northern Italy except for Ferrara, Mantua, Piedmont, Verona, and Venice.

After Giovanni's death on 5 October 1354, the state was partitioned amongst his three nephews (the sons of his brother Stefano), Matteo II, Galeazzo II, and Bernabò VISCONTI. Matteo II, who inherited Bologna, Lodi, Piacenza, and Parma, carried licentiousness to a rare extreme and was murdered in 1355 by his brothers, who thereafter governed his territories conjointly. Galeazzo II, whose court was in Pavia, was a patron of Petrarch and by an imperial Act of 27 October 1361 (confirmed in 1399 by Pope BONIFACE IX) founded the University of Pavia. In 1360 Galeazzo married his son Gian Galeazzo VISCONTI to Isabelle de Valois, daughter of Jean II, king of France, and in 1368 he married his daughter Violante to the duke of Clarence (son of King Edward III of England); through these marriages Galeazzo II confirmed the standing of the family as a European power. On the last two Visconti dukes of Milan, see VISCONTI, GIOVANNI MARIA; VISCONTI, FILIPPO MARIA.

F. Cognasso, *I Visconti* (1966).

**VISSCHER, PIETER ROEMER** (1547–1620), Dutch poet and humanist, a native of Amsterdam. His epigrams led his contemporaries to praise him as the Dutch Martial, but in the history of DUTCH LITERATURE he is more important as the head of a literary and artistic household which included his daughters Anna Roemers Visscher and Maria Tesselschade Roemers Visscher. Anna (1583–1651) was the author of a fine descriptive poem on the glory of the Amstel (*De Roemster van den Aemstel*) and a highly skilled glass engraver; her younger sister Maria (1595–1649) was also a glass engraver, an accomplished lyric poet, and the Dutch translator of TASSO.

NNBW v.

**VITÉZ, JÁNOS** (c.1408–1472), Hungarian humanist, appointed secretary to the Emperor SIGISMUND in 1433 and bishop of Várad (Romanian Vărădia de Mureş) in 1445. He was appointed as tutor to the future MATTHIAS CORVINUS, who as king appointed Vitéz as his chancellor and raised him to the nobility. In 1465 Vitéz became archbishop of Esztergom.

Vitéz was the progenitor of Hungarian humanism. He corresponded with leading humanists elsewhere in Europe, wrote elegant Latin discourses, and was instrumental in the establishment of the university in Pressburg (Bratislava).

MEL.

**VITORIA, FRANCISCO DE** (1483/6–1546), Spanish jurist and theologian who entered the Dominican Order as a young man, and studied at the Convent of San Pablo in Burgos before moving to Paris in 1506. He studied at the University of Paris until 1512, being ordained in 1509; he taught philosophy at the university from 1512 to 1517, and was awarded his doctorate in theology in 1523, whereupon he returned to Spain. He taught at Valladolid from 1523 to 1526, and then moved to the Dominican house of San Esteban in Salamanca, where he became the professor of theology. At Salamanca he reformed the syllabus, placing at its centre the study of the *Summa theologica* of THOMAS AQUINAS (on which he wrote a series of lectures) and encouraging in his students a humanistic approach to textual and philological questions. His pupils included Domingo SOTO and Melchor CANO.

Vitoria's *De Indis et de iure belli relectiones* (1557) is one of the founding texts of INTERNATIONAL LAW. Vitoria argued that the temporal jurisdiction of the papacy did not extend beyond the boundaries of Christendom, and so contested the right of the pope to assign non-Christian lands and people in the Americas to the dominion of any prince; papal authority, in his view, sanctioned the sending of missionaries, and armed force could be used to protect those missionaries, but no violence could be justified against pagan non-combatants. He also maintained that killing, looting, and SLAVERY were unjustifiable on the grounds that pagans enjoyed rights of life, property, and liberty.

DHE; C. B. Tralles, *Francisco de Vitoria, fundador del derecho internacional moderno* (1927); J. B. Scott, *The Spanish Origin of International Law: Francisco de Vitoria and his Law of Nations* (1934); Francisco de Vitoria, *Political Writings*, ed. Anthony Pagden and Jeremy Lawrance (1991).

**VITRUVIUS IN THE RENAISSANCE.** The Roman architect and military engineer Vitruvius (*fl.* 46–30 BC), who in the Renaissance was identified as Marcus Vitruvius Pollo, was in his own time a minor figure known to have designed the basilica (now lost) at Fanum Fortunae (later Colonia, now Fano). In retirement he wrote the architectural treatise *De architectura*, which centuries later, as the only surviving ancient text on any of the visual arts, became the founding text of Renaissance architecture. The ten books of *De architectura* deal with TOWN PLANNING (1), building materials (2), temples, architectural ORDERS, and the rules of PROPORTION (3 and 4), secular civic buildings (5), domestic buildings (6), pavements and decorative plaster (7), water supplies (8), the mathematical sciences of GEOMETRY, mensuration, and ASTRONOMY (9), and civic and military machines (10).

*De architectura* never disappeared entirely from public view, but in the fifteenth century it re-emerged as an important record of antiquity. The discovery in St Gallen of a manuscript of *De architectura* by Poggio BRACCIOLINI in 1414 excited considerable interest. ALBERTI and FRANCESCO DI GIORGIO drew on the treatise for both their buildings and their architectural theory. *De architectura* was first printed in Rome c.1486 and appeared in an illustrated edition by Fra GIOCONDO in 1511; it appeared in an Italian translation overseen by RAPHAEL (c.1520) and in 1521 was published with the first of many commentaries. The learned edition and translation of Daniele BARBARO (1556, 1566) became the standard ones for later generations. It was subsequently translated into every major European language, and has remained permanently in print. In the sixteenth century the most important exponent of Vitruvian architecture was PALLADIO.

Manfredo Tafuri, *Venezia e il Rinascimento: Religione, scienza, architettura* (1985).

**VITTORIA, ALESSANDRO** (1525–1608), Italian sculptor in marble, bronze, and terracotta, born in Trento; in 1543 he moved to Venice, where he was trained in the workshop of Jacopo SANSOVINO. He worked for many years in the Palazzo Ducale, where his work includes the stuccoed ceiling of the Scala d'Oro (1555–9) and three statues in the Sala delle Quattro Porte (1587); he was also heavily involved in the repairs after the fire of 1577. He also contributed to the Villa BARBARO at Maser (Veneto), where his stuccoes are combined with frescoes by VERONESE. His monumental sculptures are to be found in many Venetian churches, and there are examples of his bronze figures and portrait busts in the Ca' d'Oro and the Seminario Patriarcale.

MDA; Martin Thomas, *Alessandro Vittoria and the Portrait Bust in Renaissance Venice* (1998); Lorenzo Finocchi Ghersi, *Alessandro Vittoria: Architettura, scultura e decorazione nella venezia del tardo Rinascimento* (1988).

**VITTORINO DA FELTRE** (1378–1446), humanist educator. He was born in Feltre (80 kilometres (50 miles) north of Padua) and as a young man moved to Padua, where he studied and subsequently taught grammar and mathematics. He lived in Venice from c.1415 to 1419, learning Greek from GUARINO DA VERONA. He returned to Padua in 1419, and two years later was appointed professor of rhetoric; the following year he again moved to Venice, and in 1423 he opened a school in Venice. Later that year he accepted the invitation of Gianfrancesco GONZAGA to teach in Mantua.

The school that Vittorino founded in Mantua, Casa Giocosa, was attended by the children (including girls) of patrician families and of humanists such as POGGIO and FILELFO; other pupils included Niccolò PEROTTI and Lorenzo VALLA. Children were required to learn mathematics, natural science, music, and logic as well as Latin. The school was the first in Europe to teach Greek texts (both classical and patristic) in the original language, and its teachers included expatriate Greeks such as GEORGE OF TREBIZOND and Theodore GAZA. The study of Greek and Latin history, philosophy, and literature (and especially of Cicero and Virgil) at La Giocosa (and at Guarino's school in Ferrara) inaugurated a curriculum that was to dominate education in Europe for centuries. Famous pupils included VALLA and FEDERICO DA MONTEFELTRO as well as the GONZAGA and other princes.

N. Giannetto (ed.), *Vittorino da Feltre e la sua scuola: Umanesimo, pedagogia, arti* (1981); G. Müller, *Mensch und Bildung im italienischen Renaissance-Humanismus: Vittorino da Feltre und die humanistischen Erziehungsdenker* (1984). Paul Grendler, *Schooling in Renaissance Italy: Literacy and Learning 1300–1600* (1989).

**VIVARINI FAMILY**, a family of painters in fifteenth-century Venice; their workshop was on the island of Murano. Antonio Vivarini (c.1415–76/84), who was also known as Antonio da Murano, worked with his brother-in-law Giovanni d'Alemagna (d. 1450); the ALTARPIECES that they produced together include the polyptych *Virgin and Child Enthroned with Saints* (1448, Pinacoteca Nazionale, Bologna), to which Antonio's younger brother Bartolomeo Vivarini (c.1432–c.1501) may have contributed. Antonio's son Alvise Luigi (1442/53–1503/5) was trained by his uncle Bartolomeo but was also influenced by Giovanni BELLINI, whose style he

imitated; his finest paintings are portraits of contemporary and historical figures, notably his *St Anthony of Padua* (Correr, Venice).

MDA; R. Pallucchini, *I Vivarini* (1962); John Steer, *Alvise Vivarini* (1982).

**VIVES, JUAN LUÍS** (1492–1540), Spanish humanist and philosopher, born in Valencia and educated there and at the Collège de Montaigu in Paris (1509–12). He subsequently worked as a private tutor in Bruges (1512–16) and Louvain (1517–23), and then moved to England, where he taught at Corpus Christi College in Oxford (1523–5) and lived in the royal court as councillor to CATHERINE OF ARAGON (1526–8). His support for Queen Catherine in the matter of the royal divorce incurred the displeasure of King HENRY VIII, and c.1529 Vives returned to Bruges, where in 1537 he became a councillor to the countess of Nassau.

As a philosopher Vives was a disciple of Lorenzo VALLA and an opponent of scholasticism, on which his principal work was *De causis corruptarum artium* (1531). His works on education include the influential treatise *De tradendis disciplinis* (1531), a set of dialogues for learners of Latin (*Linguae Latinae exercitatio*, 1539), *De institutione feminae christianae*, a book on the education of women which was translated into Spanish (1528) and English (*The Instruction of a Christian Woman*, 1540), and an extensive commentary on Augustine's *City of God* (1522).

C. G. Noreña, *Juan Luís Vives* (1970).

**VLADISLAV II or (Polish) Władysław II Jagiełło** (c.1351–1434), king of Poland, was the son of the grand duke of Lithuania. He inherited the dukedom (as Duke Jagiełło) in 1377, and thereafter became embroiled in wars with the TEUTONIC ORDER. Lithuania was a pagan duchy, but Jagiełło decided that it was expedient to convert the duchy to Christianity and (in 1386) to marry Jadwiga, queen of Poland; he assumed the crown of Poland as King Władysław II Jagiełło and founded the Jagiełło dynasty that was to rule Poland until 1572. In 1410 he defeated the Teutonic Order at the battle of Tannenberg (now Polish Stêbark), and the following year signed the Treaty of THORN. Vladislav was the father (by his third wife) of VLADISLAV III and CASIMIR IV.

**VLADISLAV III or (Polish) Władysław III Jagiełło** (1424–44), king of Poland and Hungary, was the son of King VLADISLAV II of Poland, whom he succeeded in 1434, aged 10; six years later he was elected and crowned as King Vladislas I of Hungary. At the urging of Pope EUGENIUS IV and with the assistance of János HUNYADI, Vladislav mounted a crusade against the Ottomans. In 1443 his army defeated the forces of Murat II at Niş (then in Bulgaria, now in Serbia) and in the treaty that followed Vladislav regained a substantial amount of territory. He then violated the terms of peace by renewing hostilities, and on 10 November 1444 was killed when his army was defeated at the battle of Varna (Bulgaria).

**VOLKSBUCH** (plural *Volksbücher*), a form of popular German literature consisting of prose narratives which may be continuous or episodic. The narratives are often translations of late medieval French and German verse romances. *Volksbücher* were produced in large numbers throughout the sixteenth century, and some remained in print for more than 200 years. Considered in terms of dramatic progeny, the most important *Volksbuch* of the sixteenth century is the *Historia von D. Johann Fausten* (1587), which is known in German as the *Spieß'sches Faustbuch* (with reference to the Frankfurt printer Johann Spiess); this *Volksbuch* was (in an English translation) the source of MARLOWE's *Doctor Faustus* and later became the remote original of Goethe's *Faust*.

**VOLTERRA, WAR OF** (1472), The ancient city of Volterra (which had been numbered among the towns of Etruria by PLINY) enjoyed independence in the twelfth and thirteenth centuries, but in 1361 it was formally subjugated by Florence. In 1470 a group of Volterran merchants formed a company to extract ALUM from the nearby deposits of alunite. The venture was financed by Lorenzo de' MEDICI of Florence.

Lorenzo's decision to set the price of alum at a level that suited his family's financial interests (which included the only other alunite mine, in the PAPAL STATE) was greeted with strenuous protests from the Volterrans, and this protest quickly grew into a rebellion. In 1472 the Florentine Signoria, encouraged by Lorenzo, engaged FEDERICO II DA MONTEFELTRO to crush the rebellion. His troops defeated the Volterran forces and sacked and pillaged the town, murdering many of its inhabitants. Widespread unease in Florence about the brutality of the attack may have misled the PAZZI family into thinking that their conspiracy to assassinate Lorenzo would be followed by a popular uprising against the Medici.

E. Fiumi, *L'impresa di Lorenzo de' Medici contro Volterra* (1948).

**VORSTIUS, CONRADUS, or Konrad von der Vorst** (1569–1622), Arminian theologian. He was born in Cologne to Dutch parents and studied theology in Heidelberg. He subsequently moved to Basel and then Geneva, where he enjoyed the patronage of BEZA. In 1596 he accepted a post at a private academy in Steinfurt, where his writings attracted the accusation of SOCINIANISM. He was acquitted of this charge by the theological faculty of Heidelberg University, and so was able to remain in his post at Steinfurt.

The death of ARMINIUS in 1609 left a vacancy at Leiden, and in 1610 Vorstius accepted an invitation to fill the chair. Before he could take up the chair, however, his publication of a theological treatise (*Tractatus theologicus de Deo, sive de natura et attributis Dei*, 1610) excited opposition to his appointment on the grounds of the treatise's rationalism. Dutch Calvinists led by Francis GOMAR declared the treatise to be heretical, the theologians of Heidelberg expressed their horror, and in England Adriaen SARAVIA denounced the treatise. Even King JAMES I of England took a horrified interest in the treatise, drawing up a list of its theological errors and instructing his ambassador at The Hague to oppose Vorstius' appointment.

In 1612 Vorstius withdrew from Leiden to Gouda, but created a new storm of controversy by translating works by Faustus SOCINUS. He was condemned as a heretic by the Synod of DORT and banished from the United Provinces. He died in Tönningen on 29 September 1622.

**VOS, MAARTEN PIETERSZOON DE** (1532–1603), Flemish painter. He was trained in the Antwerp studio of Frans FLORIS and in 1552 travelled to Italy, where he studied in Rome and Florence and then in TINTORETTO's studio in Venice. He returned to Antwerp in 1558, and worked there for the rest of his life. He painted ALTARPIECES that are characterized by the elongation of the figures that he portrayed and the skilful use of light to suggest spaciousness. Vos also painted portraits of Flemish burghers.

*MDA.*

**VOSS, GERHARD JAN, or (Latin) Vossius** (1577–1649), Dutch classical scholar, born in the Palatinate, where his Dutch father Johannes was in exile. In 1578 the Voss family returned to Leiden, where Johannes studied theology, and subsequently moved to Dordrecht, where he became a pastor. Gerhard was educated in Dordrecht, and in 1595 matriculated at the University of Leiden, where he began his long friendship with GROTIUS. In 1600 he returned to Dordrecht as rector of the school, and spent his private hours consolidating his formidable knowledge of classical philology and historical theology. He returned to Leiden in 1614 as regent of the theological college, but his scholarly history of Pelagianism (*Historia Pelagiana*, 1618) brought him under suspicion of Remonstrant (Arminian) tendencies, and in 1619 he resigned before he could be dismissed for heresy. In 1622 he was appointed to a chair at Leiden, initially of rhetoric and chronology, and afterwards of Greek. Voss corresponded with Bishop William Laud, and in 1629, as a result of Laud's patronage, he travelled to England to be installed as a non-residential prebend in Canterbury Cathedral and to receive the degree of LLD from Oxford. His last post was in Amsterdam, where he moved in 1632 to take up the founding professorship of ecclesiastical history at the newly founded Athenaeum, and held that post for the rest of his life.

Voss contributed substantially to both classical and theological scholarship. He described the history of Greek literature (*De historicis Graecis*, 1624) and Latin literature (*De historicis Latinis*, 1627). His *Aristarchus, sive de arte grammatica* appeared in 1635. In 1642 he published *Dissertationes tres de tribus symbolis, Apostolico, Athanasiano et Constantinopolitano*, which decisively discredited the traditional attribution of the Athanasian Creed by demonstrating that it contained phrases that arose out of later doctrinal controversies.

The strong historical temper of Voss's theological writing, which led him to consider both Christian dogma and the claims of non-Christian religions as objects of historical enquiry, renders him one of the founders of historical theology.

Nicholas Wickenden, *G. J. Vossius and the Humanist Concept of History* (1993).

**VREDEMAN DE VRIES, JAN or Hans** (1527–*c*.1606), Frisian painter, architect, and garden designer. He was born in Leeuwarden (Friesland) and worked in Antwerp, Aachen, Liège, Wolfenbüttel, Hamburg, Danzig, Prague, Amsterdam, and The Hague. He published a series of influential pattern books containing perspective drawings of buildings, gardens, and furniture as well as decorative ornaments. His book of garden plans (*Hortorum viridariorumque elegantes et multiplicis formae*, 1583) was the channel by which the designs of DUTCH GARDENS and FLEMISH GARDENS were disseminated throughout Europe.

The gardens which Vredeman designed himself were laid out with a painterly attention to detail and form; he was the first landscape architect to present the garden as a work of art. The most important architectonic element in his gardens was the gallery, which overlooked complementary structures containing FOUNTAINS and PARTERRES. His use of *parterres de pièces coupées* to exhibit exotic plants to best advantage was subsequently copied all over northern Europe.

Vredeman's own designs included the royal gardens in Prague, which subsequently set the style for other BOHEMIAN GARDENS. His innovative experiments with PERSPECTIVE include *trompe-l'œil* panels of garden vistas, a two-part collection of illusionist art (*Perspective id est celeberrima ars inspicient is*, Leiden, 1604 and 1605), and a treatise on architecture (*Architectura*, 1606).

*MDA; NNBW* vii.

**VRELANT, WILLEM, or (French) Guillaume Wielant** (d. *c*.1481), Netherlandish miniaturist. He was born in Utrecht, but spent most of his life in Bruges, where he was a friend and neighbour of Hans MEMLING. His most famous work is the *Mirror of Humility*, which was commissioned by PHILIP THE GOOD and is now in the Bibliothèque Municipale in Valenciennes.

*MDA.*

**VRIENDT**. See FLORIS DE VRIENDT FAMILY.

**VRIES, ADRIAEN DE** (*c*.1545–1625), Dutch sculptor in Italy and Bohemia. He was born in The Hague but moved as a young man to Florence, where he trained as a sculptor and bronze-founder in the studio of his countryman GIAMBOLOGNA; he subsequently worked in Rome and Prague. His greatest works are FOUNTAINS, notably those commissioned for Augsburg (1598 and 1602) and Copenhagen; the Copenhagen fountain was taken as war booty to Stockholm in 1660 and is now in the Palace of Drottningholm.

*MDA; NNBW* ix; L. O. Larsson, *Adrian de Vries, 1545–1626* (1967).

**VROOM, HENDRIK CORNELISZOON** (*c*.1563–1640), Dutch marine artist and tapestry-maker, the first painter to specialize in seascapes and in the depiction of ships. He was commissioned to design tapestries for the Palace of Westminster depicting the defeat of the Spanish ARMADA; the tapestries were executed by Francis Spiring but were destroyed in the fire that consumed the palace on 16 October 1834.

*MDA*; Margarita Russell, *Visions of the Sea: Hendrick C. Vroom and the Origins of Dutch Marine Painting* (1983).

**WAELRANT, HUBERT** (*c*.1516/17–1595), Flemish composer, editor, singer, and teacher, based in Antwerp where he sang at the cathedral and the St Jacobskerk, and taught in a school. He worked with the printer Jean de Laet during the 1550s, and in 1585 edited PHALÈSE and Bellère's madrigal collection *Symphonica angelica*, to which he contributed five compositions. His work is notable for the attention he paid to text, either as a printer where notes and syllables are accurately aligned or as a composer where, as in 'Ferma speranz'e fe pur' (from his first book of madrigals), he effectively reflects the meaning of the words through his handling of harmony and chromaticism.

**WAGHENAER or Wagenaer, LUCAS JANSZOON** (*c*.1534–1605), Dutch seaman and cartographer who in 1585 published a sea atlas entitled *Spieghel der Zeevaerdt*, which was translated into English in 1588 as *The Mariner's Mirrour*. The charts, which cover the Baltic and North Sea coasts, the English channel, and the Atlantic coasts of France, Spain, and Portugal, were widely used by British mariners throughout the next century. The name *Mariner's Mirror* was revived in 1911 as the title of the journal of the Society for Nautical Research in Greenwich.

    *NNBW* vii.

**WALDENSES or Vaudois.** The Waldenses are a Christian community with its origins in a twelfth-century anti-sacerdotal sect founded by Peter Waldo of Lyon. They were energetically persecuted in the thirteenth century, and fled to centres in Provence, Dauphiné, Piedmont, Lombardy, Germany, and Spain. Peter Waldo died in Bohemia, and the Waldensian community there was later absorbed into the Hussites. In the fifteenth century the principal community of Waldenses was in SAVOY, where they were savagely persecuted by the ruling house. In 1487 Pope INNOCENT VIII issued a bull ordering that the Waldenses be exterminated.

With the advent of the Reformation, the Waldenses quickly joined forces with the reformers, some of whom (including BEZA and OLIVÉTAN) believed that the medieval Waldenses were Protestants *avant la lettre* who had kept the flame of the early Church alive through the Catholic centuries. In 1522 the Bohemian Hussites (who were popularly called 'Waldenses') made their first approach to LUTHER. In 1530 Georges Morel and Pierre Masson, who represented the Waldenses of Dauphiné and Provence, established contact with south German and Swiss reformers, of whom the key figure was Johann OECOLAMPADIUS (who instructed the Waldensian leaders in the finer points of Protestant doctrine, especially the iniquity of submission to the ordinances of the Catholic Church). In 1532 a synod was held at Chanforans; the Protestant representatives in attendance included Guillaume FAREL and Olivetan. The synod adopted a Confession of Faith which affirmed the doctrine of predestination, sanctioned clerical marriage, and repudiated the Catholic Church. Thereafter Piedmontese Waldenses worshipped openly in churches that they called 'temples'. In 1545 thousands of Waldenses were massacred in Provence in a campaign mounted by FRANCIS I.

A massacre of 1655 perpetrated by the duke of Savoy prompted John Milton's sonnet 'Avenge, O Lord, thy slaughtered saints'. There is still a small Waldensian community in Italy, known as the Chiesa Evangelica Valdese.

**WALDIS, BURKARD** (*c*.1490–*c*.1556), German fabulist. He was born in Allendorf and became a Franciscan monk in Riga (then a Hansa city administered by the LIVONIAN ORDER). While travelling to Rome in 1524 he was converted to Lutheranism, and on returning to Riga he renounced his vows and married. Riga was under the control of its bishop, who twice imprisoned Waldis. On being released in 1540 he moved to Hesse, where he became pastor of Abterode.

Waldis's versions of Aesop's *Fables* (*Esopas*, 1548) are exuberantly coarse elaborations set in German localities. His Low German *De Parabell vam vorlorn Szohn* (1527) is a FAST-NACHTSPIEL turned to the service of religious polemic in which the prodigal son is a proto-Lutheran whose faith triumphs over the good works of his proto-Catholic brother.

**WALDSEEMÜLLER, MARTIN, or (Latin) Hylacomylus** (1470–1518), German cartographer, born in Baden and educated at the University of Freiburg im Breisgau; he later taught at the University of Saint-Dié (Lorraine, not then part of France). In 1508 Waldseemüller published *Cosmographiae introductio*, which included a twelve-page map of the world which showed the Americas as a separate continent which he called America on the grounds that Amerigo VESPUCCI had discovered it. He subsequently published a four-page map of Europe (1511).

DSB.

**WALES or (Welsh) Cymru or (Latin) Cambria**. The English King Edward I completed the conquest of Wales in 1283 and formally united Wales to England in the Statute of Wales of 1284. On 7 February 1301 the king's son, Edward of Caernarfon (later King Edward II), was created prince of Wales by his father, and thereafter the principality of Wales was formally vested in the heir to the English crown. The fortified towns of Wales became English colonies: within the towns English was spoken and English law was administered; in the countryside, Welsh was spoken and the law was Cymric CUSTOMARY LAW, in which land tenure was by gavelkind (which meant that land could be willed and that intestate lands descended to all legitimate sons equally) rather than by primogeniture. The most significant rebellion against English rule was that of Owain Glyndŵr, a courtier of the English King Richard II, who from 1401 to 1406 pillaged the towns and castles of Wales; the rebellion was dramatized from an English perspective by SHAKESPEARE in *1 Henry IV*, where the Welsh rebel is called Owen Glendower.

In 1485 Henry Tudor, earl of Richmond, the grandson of Owen Tudor of Anglesey and his wife Catherine of France (widow of the English King Henry V), defeated Richard III and became King HENRY VII, and so a dynasty that could be claimed as Welsh secured the throne of England. His son HENRY VIII consolidated the incorporation of Wales into England with the Union of Wales and England Act of 1537 (27 Henry VIII), which was an Act of the English Parliament; from an English perspective, the purpose of the Act was to grant the Welsh people the same political and legal rights as those enjoyed by the English people. The marcher lordships were dissolved; most of their territory was assigned to five new Welsh counties, and the remainder was annexed either to contiguous English counties (Gloucestershire, Hereford-shire, and Shropshire) or to existing Welsh shires (Cardigan, Carmarthen, Glamorgan, and Pembroke). Thereafter Wales sent 24 MPs to the English Parliament. In an Act of 1542, ENGLISH LAW was imposed on all residents of the principality, both English and Welsh, and responsibility for its administration was entrusted to the Council of Wales and the Marches; Cymric land tenure by gavelkind was abolished, and the sole language of legal procedure was thereafter to be English.

**WALLPAPER**. Until the end of the fifteenth century, interior walls in large houses were covered with tapestries or linen wall hangings (e.g. the Wienhausen hangings, near Celle), leather hangings (e.g. GUADAMECI), or painted cloths. Wallpapers were a less costly substitute for such wall coverings, and first began to appear in England and France in the 1480s; a century later they were widely used, though they did not replace tapestries in the houses of the aristocracy. Early wallpapers may have been painted, but there are no surviving examples to confirm that hypothesis. In the late sixteenth century, surviving examples are printed from wood blocks and characteristically display black coats of arms and floral patterns on a white or pale background.

Françoise Teynac, *Wallpaper: A History* (1982); Lesley Hoskins, *The Papered Wall* (1994).

**WALTHER, JOHANN** (1496–1570), German singer, composer, and poet who sang at the elector of Saxony's Hofkapelle and matriculated at Leipzig University in 1527. From 1535 he ran a *Kantorei* which performed at public occasions at Torgau until he moved to the Dresden Hofkapelle in 1548. He was a Lutheran who, in 1525, advised Luther on the German mass and wrote CHORALES. He produced an early Protestant *tenorlied* hymnbook used in the Hofkapelle and in schools.

**WAR AND WARFARE**. Renaissance Europe was never at peace. The hundreds of states that constituted the Holy Roman Empire were constantly engaged in local wars. The Hundred Years War, a protracted but intermittent conflict between England and France, lasted from 1337 until 1453. The WARS OF ITALY (1494–1559) were the central conflicts in the Habsburg–Valois Wars that spread across much of Europe between 1494 and 1559, and the REVOLT OF THE NETHERLANDS lasted from 1567 to 1648. Within France, Protestants fought Catholics in the WARS OF RELIGION, which lasted from 1562 to 1598. Christians fought Muslims in Spain until the final expulsion of the Moors in 1492, and on the eastern frontiers of Europe the Ottomans occupied the Balkan peninsula and twice (1529 and 1532) stood at the gates of Vienna.

The technology of war developed rapidly from the fourteenth to the sixteenth centuries. At the beginning of the fourteenth century, the English longbow and the continental crossbow were still Europe's most formidable weapons. The introduction of GUNPOWDER into warfare, possibly by the English at the battle of Crécy (26 August 1346), exacerbated the human costs of war, though its high cost ensured that it never entirely superseded the pikes used by infantrymen to lethal effect. The combination of pike and gun ensured the eventual victory of infantry over armoured cavalry in the vanguard of war. Advances in ARTILLERY in the fifteenth century transformed siege warfare, because a cannon could breach the walls of a castle; these developments also transformed the art of FORTIFICATION. In the same period, the ARQUEBUS, the first hand-held firearm, could be used by cavalry but was essentially an infantry weapon. In the sixteenth century, the MUSKET and the pistol were invented; the deployment of the musket by Spanish forces at the battle of PAVIA was an important factor in the comprehensive defeat of the French army. In naval warfare, GUNS were mounted in fixed positions on the bows of war GALLEYS, which had to be manoeuvred so that the guns could be fired directly ahead. The development of light ships that could manoeuvre quickly famously enabled the English to defeat the Spanish ARMADA.

The armies of medieval Europe were raised through feudal levies, but in fourteenth-century Italy the mercenary bands of the *condottieri* emerged as a new kind of army. The rise of Swiss and German mercenaries was a parallel development. In 1476 and 1477 Swiss mercenaries defeated the armies of CHARLES THE BOLD in three successive battles, in the last of which, at Nancy, Charles was killed. These battles, in which the Swiss carried pikes (many of which were 3 metres (10 feet) long), were among the earliest engagements in which infantry battalions defeated armoured cavalry. The reputation established at these battles meant that, for the rest of the century, the rulers of Europe (especially the French) sought the services of Swiss mercenaries. The defeat of the Swiss at the battle of MARIGNANO in 1515 tarnished the image of the Swiss as Europe's finest mercenaries, and thereafter pride of place was taken by the German LANDSKNECHTE, whose victory at the battle of Ravenna (1512) established their reputation as Europe's best infantry.

A continent constantly at war produced a multitude of able military commanders, including the duke of ALBA, Micheletto ATTENDOLO, Ferdinando d'AVALOS, BARTOLOMEO D'ALVIANO, BAYARD, Facino CANE, CARDONA, Francesco CARMAGNOLA, Bartolomeo COLLEONI, FERNÁNDEZ DE CÓRDOBA, Jean DUNOIS, EGMONT, Alessandro FARNESE, Francesco FERRUCI, Gaston de FOIX, Georg von FRUNDSBERG, Il GATTAMELATA, John HAWKWOOD, János HUNYADI, François LA NOUE, MAURICE OF NASSAU, NICCOLÒ DA TOLENTINO, Giovanni de' MEDICI, Niccolò PICCININO, Mikołaj RADZIWIŁŁ, Jacques SAINT-ANDRÉ, THERMES, and Alfonso d'AVALOS. At sea, the great naval commanders included BARBAROSSA, Cristoforo da CANAL, Andrea DORIA, Sir Francis DRAKE, Lord HOWARD, JUAN DE AUSTRIA, Pedro MENÉNDEZ DE AVILÉS, and Sir Walter RALEGH.

The methods according to which war was conducted drew heavily on classical precedent. On the battlefield, armies moved in formations; in the case of the Swiss mercenaries, such offensive or defensive formations could consist of some 6,000 pikemen. In Spain the Swiss phalanx evolved into a tactical formation known as the *tercio*, a square of 2,500 men armed with pikes, swords, and guns (the name, which literally means 'bale', survives in Los Tercios, the Spanish Foreign Legion).

The literature of war included practical manuals, theoretical treatises, and accounts of ancient and contemporary battles. VALTURIO's *De re militari* and MACHIAVELLI's *Della arte della guerra* were read all over Europe. Such treatises were often written with an eye to the citizen armies of classical antiquity, and so the employment of mercenaries was often denounced. In Renaissance art, the battlepiece was an important genre.

C. Oman, *A History of the Art of War in the Sixteenth Century* (2 vols., 1937); J. R. Hale, *War and Society in Renaissance Europe, 1450–1620* (1985); M. Mallett, *Mercenaries and their Masters: Warfare in Renaissance Italy* (1974).

**WARD, JOHN** (1571–1638), English composer who sang at Canterbury Cathedral and was a king's scholar at the grammar school. He subsequently worked in the musical household of Sir Henry Fanshawe to whom he dedicated his 1613 book of madrigals. He was well known for his ayres and five- and six-part fantasias for viols; some of his sacred music requires viol accompaniment.

**WARS OF ITALY** (1494–1559). Italy was the main theatre of the series of wars sometimes described in a wider European context as the Habsburg–Valois Wars. The chief protagonists were Spain, France, the HOLY ROMAN EMPIRE, the SWISS CONFEDERATION, England, and the various states of Italy, and in the later stages Denmark, Sweden, and the Ottoman Empire became involved. At the heart of the conflicts there were dynastic rivalries between the HABSBURGS and the VALOIS and territorial disputes between France and the duchy of BURGUNDY over Flanders, Artois, and the Netherlandish territories of the duchy, between France and the Empire over Milan, and between France and Spain over the kingdom of NAPLES, Roussillon, and Cerdagne. The reason that Italy became the main theatre of the wars was that the fragile comity of its principal states (Milan, Venice, Florence, Genoa, Savoy, the Papal State, and the kingdom of Naples) was destroyed by territorial ambitions that were often advanced by calling on the assistance of other European states.

War was endemic in Italy, but the Peace of LODI (1454) had restricted hostilities to local disputes such as the War of VOLTERRA (1472), the War of FERRARA (1482–4) and the war waged by Naples and the Papal State against Florence (1478–80). The term 'Wars of Italy' is used to refer to the renewal of national and international conflict that began with the invasion of Italy by King CHARLES VIII of France in 1494 and concluded with the Treaty of CATEAU-CAMBRÉSIS in 1559.

In 1494 Charles VIII invaded Italy with a view to implementing the Angevin claim to the throne of Naples; he was invited to do so by Ludovico SFORZA, despite the claim of the related House of ORLÉANS to the duchy of Milan. The French army marched through Sforza, Florentine, and papal territory without encountering significant resistance and captured Naples without a battle on 22 February 1495. After being crowned as king of Naples, Charles withdrew, leaving the kingdom garrisoned. The French occupation of Naples united the enemies of France, including the pope (ALEXANDER VI), the emperor (MAXIMILIAN I), and the king of Spain (FERDINAND II), who, together with Milan and Venice, formed a HOLY LEAGUE, which was constituted in Venice on 31 March 1495. On 6 July 1495 an attempt was made by the army of the League to block the French retreat at a battlefield near Parma; both sides claimed victory after the ensuing battle of FORNOVO, but King Charles was able to resume his march homeward. In the kingdom of Naples, however, Spanish troops under the command of Gonzalo de CÓRDOBA overcame the French garrisons and restored the throne to Ferdinand II of Aragon.

In 1499 LOUIS XII of Orléans, the new king of France, invaded Italy in support of his family's claim to the duchy of Milan, which originated in the marriage of his grandfather (Louis I, duke of Orléans) to Valentina Visconti, daughter of

Gian Galeazzo VISCONTI, duke of Milan. The French army and its Venetian allies captured Milan on 6 October 1499 and went on to occupy Genoa. Ludovico Sforza retook Milan on 5 January 1500, but his army was defeated at Novara on 8 April 1500; Ludovico was taken as a prisoner to France, where he died eight years later. Milan was an imperial fief, and its occupation by France was sanctioned by the Emperor Maximilian in the Treaty of BLOIS (September 1504), as part of a projected arrangement in which King Louis's daughter Claude would marry Maximilian's grandson, the future CHARLES V. King Louis and King Ferdinand then partitioned Naples in the Treaty of Granada (1500), but a boundary dispute renewed hostilities; the Spanish army was victorious in the battles of CERIGNOLA (28 April 1503) and GARIGLIANO (29 December 1503), and in a second Treaty of BLOIS (1505) King Louis renounced his claim to Naples, leaving the kingdom in the control of King Ferdinand.

On 10 December 1508 King Louis and the Emperor Maximilian joined forces in the League of CAMBRAI, and, together with the forces of Pope JULIUS II, invaded the Veneto. The victory of the League at the battle of AGNADELLO on 14 May 1509 was followed by the occupation of the entire Venetian *terraferma* (except for Treviso). The Venetians quickly recaptured Padua and in October 1511 formed the HOLY LEAGUE, which consisted of Venice, the Empire, Spain, Pope Julius II (who had changed sides), and HENRY VIII of England. At the battle of Ravenna on 11 April 1512, the French lost their initial advantage when their commander Gaston de FOIX was killed, and the French army had to retreat. The following year, a French army intent on dislodging Massimiliano Sforza from Milan was defeated by the Swiss troops protecting him at the battle of Novara on 6 June 1513. By this time members of the Holy League had begun to attack France itself: in 1512 an Anglo-Spanish force attempted to invade Aquitaine and Ferdinand's army occupied Navarre, and the following year Henry VIII invaded northern France, defeating a French army at the battle of the SPURS near Thérouanne (Artois) on 16 August 1513, and the Swiss Confederation, which had entered the fray when it was forced out of Lombardy, invaded Burgundy as far as Dijon.

In 1515, FRANCIS I, the new French king, invaded Milan, defeating the Swiss protectors of Massimiliano Sforza at the battle of MARIGNANO on 13/14 September 1515, after which Massimiliano ceded the dukedom of Milan to King Francis. The defeat at Marignano drove the Swiss out of Italy, and Francis consolidated his control of the region by persuading Maximilian to withdraw his imperial garrisons from the Venetian *terraferma*, which enabled Venice to regain its mainland territory. French success was crowned by the Concordat of BOLOGNA, in which Pope LEO X ceded considerable ecclesiastical powers to the French crown, and by the Treaty of Noyen (August 1516), in which the new king of Spain, Charles I (later the Emperor CHARLES V), acknowledged the legitimacy of the French claim to Milan.

These settlements signalled a suspension of hostilities that lasted until the death of the Emperor Maximilian; in Italy, independent states separated the Spanish-controlled south from the French-occupied north-west, an arrangement that gave the peninsula a moment of unhappy stability. This balance was upset when Charles I was elected king of the Romans (i.e. emperor elect) on 28 June 1519, because Spain and the Empire suddenly had a common ruler, and between Charles's German and Spanish positions lay French-controlled Genoa and Milan, which impeded communications and gave his opponents a base from which to strike at Charles's possessions in Burgundy and the Netherlands. From the perspective of Francis I, his Italian territories assumed an importance far beyond his ancestral claims, because they constituted the last barrier to complete encirclement on his land frontiers from Provence to Artois. Spanish, imperial, and French security all hung on the possession of north-west Italy. For the next 40 years, from the accession of Charles V in 1519 to the battle of SAINT-QUENTIN in 1557, Europe was to live with the bloody consequences of the rivalry between Charles V and Francis I.

Francis declared war on 22 April 1521, and Charles V, with the assistance of King Henry VIII and Pope Leo X, captured Milan on 19 November 1521 and defeated the French at the battle of BICOCCA on 24 June 1522. By 1523 the French had been expelled from Genoa and the Milanese. The imperial army, commanded by the disaffected duc de BOURBON, invaded Provence as far as Marseille; on failing to take the city (September 1524) it retreated. The French invaded Italy in 1523 and the following year returned under the command of King Francis. The French army retook Milan on 26 October 1524, but was comprehensively defeated at the battle of PAVIA, at which Francis was captured and dispatched to Spain as a prisoner. He eventually secured his release by signing the Treaty of Madrid (January 1526), which made four important concessions: in the north, Francis surrendered his claims to Flanders and Artois; in Italy, he surrendered his claims to Milan, Genoa, Asti, and the kingdom of Naples; he surrendered Burgundy to Charles V; he agreed to restore to the duc de Bourbon his lands and titles.

In April 1526 Francis was released. and he promptly repudiated the Treaty of Madrid on the grounds that he had signed under duress. The following month he formed the League of COGNAC (22 May), an anti-imperial pact between France, Venice, the papacy (Pope CLEMENT VII), and Francesco SFORZA of Milan. In the war that followed, the imperial army, commanded by the duc de Bourbon, perpetrated the SACK OF ROME (May 1527–February 1528). A French army dislodged the imperial garrison in Genoa and forged an alliance with Andrea DORIA, the commander of Genoa's navy. The Genoese fleet blockaded Naples, but in July 1528 Andrea Doria changed sides, aggrieved that the French had given commercial privileges to Savona at the expense of Genoa. The effect of his defection to the Empire was the lifting of the French siege of Naples, partly because of the death of their commander Odet de Lautrec on 16 August, but also because the end of the blockade would allow Spanish reinforcements to gain access to the beleaguered garrison. Andrea Doria returned to Genoa, evicted the French garrison, and established a semi-independent republican state under Spanish protection. The final blow in this stage of the Habsburg–Valois struggle was delivered on 21 June 1529, when the French army in Milan was defeated at the battle of Ladriano. In the Treaty of Barcelona and its successor the Peace of CAMBRAI (3 August 1529), France acknowledged the Spanish claim to Naples and withdrew its claim to Milan, which was returned to the new duke, Francesco II Sforza, under the watchful eye of the emperor. These concessions in effect reinstituted the terms of the Treaty of Madrid, except that Charles V renounced his claims to Burgundy, Provence, and Languedoc.

On 1 November 1535 Francesco Sforza died without leaving an heir, and Charles V promptly installed an imperial governor in Milan. Francis retaliated by forming an alliance with the Ottoman Emperor Süleyman and the Protestant princes of Germany and mounting an invasion of Savoy and Piedmont, capturing Turin on 3 April 1536; Charles responded with an unproductive counter-invasion of Provence. Peace was restored by the intervention of Pope PAUL III, who negotiated the Truce of Nice in June 1538 and the following month arranged a meeting of Francis and Charles at Aigues-Mortes (in the Camargue); the pope's arrival in Nice was marked by the erection of a marble cross, after which the *quartier* known as Croix de Marbre is named.

The truce was intended to last for ten years, but in 1542 hostilities recommenced on a European scale when King Francis formed an alliance with Cleves (a Protestant duchy since 1533), Denmark, Sweden, and the Ottoman Empire, and attacked Luxemburg, Brabant, Roussillon, and Navarre. A combined French and Ottoman fleet captured Nice (then part of the duchy of SAVOY) on 6 September 1543; the Ottoman commander, Barbarossa (see BARBARY PIRATES), was allowed to sack the city and enslave 2,500 of its inhabitants. In the same month the French garrison evacuated Toulon (which was already an important naval base) to enable the Ottoman fleet to winter there until February 1544. The empire struck back through the alliance between Charles V and Henry VIII, whose forces attacked France simultaneously. Imperial troops advanced on Paris, reaching Soissons on 12 September 1544, and English troops captured Boulogne on 18 September 1544. Francis dealt separately with these two invaders. On 18 September 1544 Francis signed with Charles the Treaty of Crépy-en-Laonnois, which reaffirmed the territorial concessions of the Treaties of Madrid and Cambrai, proposed conciliatory Habsburg–Valois marriages, and committed France to assist the Empire to repel the Ottoman invaders on its eastern flank; the treaty also contained secret clauses in which Francis undertook to assist Charles in his efforts to bring the Protestants of Germany back into the Catholic Church and to persuade the pope to convene a general council of the Church. Two years later, in June 1546, Francis made peace with Henry VIII in the Treaty of Ardes (or Guines), according to which Boulogne would revert to France in 1554 on payment of 2 million crowns.

One again treaties secured a temporary peace in Europe, and Charles was able to concentrate his efforts on the conquest of Germany: In the campaign of 1546–7 known as the SCHMALKALDIC WAR, Charles inflicted a decisive defeat on the Protestant princes at the battle of MÜHLBERG on 24 April 1547. In January 1552, HENRI II, the new French king, signed the Treaty of Chambord with MAURICE OF SAXONY (who represented the Protestant princes), pledging financial help to the German Protestants in return for French acquisition of the imperial bishoprics of Metz, Toul, and Verdun. Charles tried to recapture Metz (November 1552–January 1553), but the renewed strength of the Protestant forces sapped his will to continue the campaign. Hostilities ceased in Germany with the signing of the PEACE OF AUGSBURG in 1555.

The war continued in other theatres. In 1552 the Sienese expelled the imperial troops which had been garrisoned in Siena by Charles to ensure secure communications between Naples and Milan, and called on France to ensure that the city was not reoccupied. In 1555, Duke COSIMO I DE' MEDICI retook Siena, nominally on behalf of the Empire but in fact for his own benefit. In northern Europe, Charles supplemented the weapons of war by marrying his son Philip (the future PHILIP II) to Queen MARY I of England on 25 July 1554, so gaining the alliance of England; he then renounced his suzerainty of the Netherlands (October 1555) and Spain (January 1556) in favour of Philip. In February 1556 Philip signed the Truce of Vaucelles with Henri II. The following year King Henri violated the truce by forming an alliance with Pope PAUL IV and dispatching a force commanded by François de GUISE to invade Italy and reconquer Naples for the French crown. Spanish forces in the Netherlands responded with an invasion of France, and defeated a French army at the battle of SAINT-QUENTIN on 10 August 1567; the duc de Guise was thereby forced to withdraw his troops from Italy. He was redeployed to Calais, which he captured on 7 January 1558. Domestic pressures meant that neither Henri nor Philip had the will to continue the wars, which were finally concluded by the two-part Treaty of CATEAU-CAMBRÉSIS: on 2 April 1559 a treaty with England allowed France to keep Calais for eight years (in the event it was never returned); the following day, a treaty with Spain acknowledged Spanish supremacy in Italy by reducing the military presence of France to a garrison in Saluzzo and a few fortresses while allowing Spain control of Naples, Sicily, SARDINIA, and Milan; Duke Cosimo was also obliged to relinquish the strategic Sienese dependencies of Orbetello, Talamone, and Porto Ercole, which were thereafter garrisoned by Spain; CORSICA was returned to Genoa. France was allowed to retain the imperial bishoprics of Metz, Toul, and Verdun (all of which are still in France), but was obliged to surrender the sovereignty of Piedmont and Savoy to EMANUELE FILIBERTO, who created an independent buffer state (see SAVOY) between France and the Spanish territories in Italy.

The wars left Italy, both north and south, dominated by foreign powers; the physical and psychological ravages of the wars found their greatest historian in Francesco GUICCIARDINI.

**WARS OF RELIGION or (French) Guerres de Religion** (1562–98), a series of eight civil wars in which France was divided on confessional lines and noble houses fought for control of the crown. The Protestants (HUGUENOTS) found allies in England, the Netherlands, and the German Protestant princes; the Catholics, who formed the CATHOLIC LEAGUE, were supported by Savoy, Spain, and the papacy.

The premature and accidental death of King HENRI II in July 1559 left France in control of his widow CATHERINE DE MÉDICIS and their four sons: François (who succeeded his father as FRANCIS II), Charles (later King CHARLES IX), Henri (later HENRI III), and François, duke of Alençon (later duc d'ANJOU). On the accession of Francis II Anne de MONT-MORENCY was displaced by François de GUISE and his brother Cardinal Charles de GUISE, who mounted a campaign to extirpate the Protestant heresy. The principal opponents of the Guises were Louis de Bourbon, prince of CONDÉ, and his brother ANTOINE DE BOURBON, king of Navarre. Condé became the military protector of the Protestants and may have helped to organize the Conspiracy of AMBOISE to capture the young king and displace the Guises. The Conspiracy failed, and Condé escaped execution only because of the death of King Francis II, who was succeeded by his 10-year-old brother Charles IX. The regent was Queen Catherine, who sought compromise with the Huguenots in the Colloquy of POISSY (1561) and the January Edict (1562); the duke of Guise responded by massacring a Protestant congregation in Vassy, Champagne (1 March 1562), and then taking control of the government in Paris (15 March 1562), where he brought the queen mother and the king.

The first war (March 1562–March 1563) began with Condé's response to the seizure of control at Paris: he occupied Orléans (April 1562), which in effect became the Huguenot capital. This was followed by an outbreak of Protestant rebellions in provincial centres such as Lyon, Rouen, and Tours. In September 1562 Condé concluded the Treaty of Richmond with England, which agreed to provide troops and finance in return for the temporary possession of Le Havre, which would be exchanged for Calais at the cessation of hostilities. In the battle of Dreux (19 December 1562) Guise defeated the Huguenots, but Condé was captured by the Catholics and Montmorency by the Protestants. The incarceration of the military leaders gave Queen Catherine the opportunity to negotiate the Treaty of AMBOISE (19 March 1563), which made concessions to Protestants and concluded the first war. The two sides then united to expel the English from Le Havre (July 1563) and to force Queen ELIZABETH to abandon her claim to Calais (Treaty of Troyes, April 1564).

The origins of the second war (September 1567–March 1568) lay in a meeting in Bayonne in the summer of 1565 between Queen Catherine and her daughter Queen Elizabeth of Spain, who was accompanied by the duke of ALBA. The meeting provoked Protestant fears of a Spanish attack on French Protestants. Two years later, in the summer of 1567, the duke of Alba marched his army from Milan to the Netherlands, and Huguenots began to fear a two-pronged attack on the Protestants of the Netherlands and France. In September Condé and Gaspard de COLIGNY attempted (and failed) to capture the king in an episode known as the Conspiracy of Meaux. As fighting intensified, Spain intervened on behalf of the Catholics and JOHANN CASIMIR (count palatine of the Rhine) on behalf of the Protestants. Condé marched on Paris but was defeated at the battle of Saint-Denis (10 November 1567), at which Montmorency was mortally wounded. The war was concluded with the Treaty of Longjumeau (March 1568), which reconfirmed the concessions of the Treaty of Amboise.

In the third war (September 1568–August 1570) the duke of Anjou (later King HENRI III) defeated the Huguenots at the battle of Jarnac (Poitou), at which Condé was killed (13 March 1569), and then went on to a second victory at the battle of Montcontour, in Poitou (3 October 1569). With the death of Condé Coligny became the sole commander of the Huguenot forces. Despite suffering defeats in the north, he enjoyed considerable support in the south, and was able to negotiate the Treaty of Saint-Germain (August 1570), which concluded the third war and again reconfirmed the Treaty of Amboise, but also allowed the Protestants to fortify and garrison Cognac, La Charité, Montauban, and La Rochelle. Thereafter Coligny displaced the Guises at court and the moderate Catholic party of POLITIQUES emerged. The marriage of Henry of Navarre (later King HENRI IV) and MARGUERITE DE VALOIS (18 August 1572) in Paris attracted many prominent Huguenots to the city. The Guise faction reacted to this sequence of events by assassinating Coligny and unleasing the ST BARTHOLOMEW'S DAY MASSACRE, which in the course of the next six weeks spread throughout France and claimed the lives of thousands of Huguenots.

The fourth war (October 1572–July 1573) consisted of a series of Protestant risings south of the Loire and of the (unsuccessful) siege of La Rochelle by the duke of Anjou (later Henri III) from December 1572 to June 1573. The defences of La Rochelle were commanded by François de LA NOUE, who was determined to retain control of the port, which was an important base for Dutch SEA BEGGARS and Huguenot PRIVATEERS. The siege was lifted when Duke Henri was elected as king of Poland and concluded the Treaty of La Rochelle (June 1573), which reaffirmed the conditions of the Treaty of Saint-Germain, whereupon Henri hurried to Poland to claim his throne.

The principal protagonists of the fifth war (November 1574–May 1576) were King Henri III (who had returned from Poland on the death of his brother) and the duke of Montmorency-Damville (governor of Languedoc), who aspired to create an autonomous Protestant region in southern France, and to that end convened the assembly of Huguenots and Politiques that met in Nîmes in December 1574. Henri, duc de GUISE, defeated the German army of JOHANN CASIMIR at the battle of Dormans (on the Marne) on 10 October 1575, but was unable to breach the defences of Montmorency-Damville. The war concluded with the Treaty of Monsieur (May 1576), which is so called because it was negotiated by François, duc d'ANJOU, who was known as 'Monsieur'. This treaty made additional concessions to the Huguenots, including freedom of worship everywhere in France except at the royal court and within two leagues of

Paris; they were also allowed to fortify and garrison eight 'security zones' (*places de sûreté*) and to establish separate Protestant courts (called *chambres-mi-parties*) in all *parlements*.

The sixth war (August 1576–December 1577) was prompted by Catholic dissent from the concessions embodied in the Treaty of Monsieur. Henri de Guise formed the CATHOLIC LEAGUE (1576) and the Estates-General of Blois voted to withdraw the privileges extended to Protestants in the Treaty of Monsieur. At this stage King Henri supported the League and its campaign to suppress Protestantism. The campaign ended with the Treaty of Bergerac (September 1577), in which many Protestant privileges were withdrawn and freedom of worship was restricted to the suburbs of one town in each judicial district; the terms of the treaty were ratified in the Edict of Poitiers.

The seventh war (November 1579–November 1580), which is also known as the Lovers' War (*Guerre des Amoureux*), was a violent interlude in a period of fragile peace that lasted from the autumn of 1577 till the spring of 1585. The principal event of the seventh war was the capture of Cahors by Henry of Navarre (31 May 1580). The war ended with the Treaty of Fleix (26 November 1580), which reaffirmed the Edict of Poitiers.

The cause of the eighth war (September 1585–April 1598), which is also known as the War of the Three Henrys (Henri III, Henry of Navarre, and Henri, duc de Guise), was the death of François, duc d'Anjou, on 10 June 1584. When he died François was heir to the throne, and thereafter the heir presumptive was the Protestant Henry of Navarre. King Henri and his mother Queen Catherine recognized Henry of Navarre, but the Catholic League instead recognized Henry's uncle Cardinal Charles de Bourbon, and this choice was ratified in a secret treaty with Spain (Treaty of Joinville, December 1584). Henri, duc de Guise, revived the Catholic League, which mounted attacks on Protestant centres and governed Paris through a uncompromisingly Catholic council known as the Sixteen (the number of administrative districts into which the city was divided). In the Treaty of Nemours (July 1585) King Henri in effect surrendered, revoking all concessions to Protestants and recognizing Cardinal de Bourbon as the rightful heir to the French throne. Pope SIXTUS V excommunicated King Henri, and Duke CARLO EMANUELE I of Savoy entered the war on the Catholic side and captured the French fortress of Saluzzo (in Piedmont). Henri decided that the Guises had to be killed, and to that end invited Henri, duc de Guise, to Blois, where he was assassinated; Guise's brother, Cardinal Louis de Lorraine, was killed the next day, and Cardinal de Bourbon was arrested. Leadership of the Catholic League passed to the surviving Guise brother, Charles de Lorraine, duke of MAYENNE. Henri III joined Henry of Navarre in an attack on Paris, but the king was assassinated at Saint-Cloud on 2 August 1589, and Henry of Navarre acceded to the throne as King Henri IV.

A struggle between King Henri IV and the League, which was supported by PHILIP II of Spain, contributed to a second phase of this war. At the outset large parts of France were controlled by members of the League who were implacably hostile to the Protestant king: the duke of Mercœur held Brittany, the duke of Mayenne held Burgundy and Normandy, the duke of Savoy captured Dauphiné and Provence, and the Sixteen held Paris. King Henri established his headquarters at Tours, and after securing victories in Normandy at the battle of Arques (21 September 1589) and the battle of Ivry (14 March 1590), besieged Paris. He was close to starving the city into submission when Philip II of Spain intervened by ordering Alessandro FARNESE to withdraw from his suppression of the REVOLT OF THE NETHERLANDS in order to assist the League in France. Farnese relieved Paris (which he subsequently garrisoned) and later returned to relieve Rouen (April 1592); Spanish troops also invaded Brittany (October 1590) and Languedoc (March 1591). The crisis was resolved when King Henri converted to Catholicism at Saint-Denis on 23 July 1593. He entered Paris in March 1594, received absolution from Pope CLEMENT VIII in 1595. The Catholic League was dissolved, and for the next three years Henri fought to drive the armies of Spain from France. In 1595 he fought Spanish troops in Brittany, Marseille, Burgundy, and Picardy, and subsequently fought in Calais (April 1596) and Amiens (March and October 1597).

The Wars of Religion were concluded, at least temporarily, with the Edict of NANTES (13 April 1598); a lasting peace was not reached until 1629. War with Spain came to an end with the Peace of VERVINS (2 May 1598).

Mack Holt, *The French Wars of Religion, 1562–1629* (1995);
R. J. Knecht, *The French Wars of Religion, 1559–1598* (2nd edn. 1996).

**WASTELL, JOHN** (*fl.* 1485–1518), English builder, the successor of Simon Clark (*fl.* 1445–89) as master mason of the Abbey of Bury St Edmunds and of King's College, Cambridge. He was master mason of the King's College Chapel from 1486, and so is likely to have been the designer of the fan-vaulted ceiling. He later became master mason of Canterbury Cathedral, where he was probably the designer of the crossing tower (1494–7). Many buildings are attributed to Wastell on stylistic grounds, including the retrochoir of the Abbey (now Cathedral) of Peterborough.

*MDA.*

**WATERCOLOUR PAINTING.** A watercolour is a painting in which the pigment, or colouring substance, is held in suspension with a medium (usually a plant gum) which is soluble in water rather than in oil; it is distinguished from other kinds of painting that use water by the fact that lighter tones are achieved by thinning with water rather than the admixture of a white pigment. The technique has a continuous history from antiquity (on the papyrus rolls of Egypt) to its apogee in nineteenth-century England. In the Renaissance, watercolour painting derives from the related art of manuscript illumination.

The use of watercolour apart from manuscript illumination is unusual in Renaissance art. The best-known watercolours of the period are the landscape pictures that DÜRER executed in the course of his visit to Italy in 1495 and the miniatures of Isaac and Peter OLIVER.

**WATERMARKS**, transparent designs embedded in PAPER during the manufacturing process, formed from the impression of bent wire fashioned into an emblem or monograph or personal mark and sewn to the wires of the mould. The wires from which the design is made render the paper on which they are impressed thinner and hence less opaque; the watermark is usually invisible, but can be seen if the sheet of paper is held against strong light. The earliest watermarks appear in Italian paper manufactured in 1282, and by the end of the next century they were commonplace throughout Europe. The purpose of watermarks was to identify the manufacturer and to denote the size and quality of the paper; scholars can use watermarks to establish the provenance and date of paper, and, because books consist of folded sheets of paper, can also detect whether additional sheets have been added to a book.

**WEAVING**, the process of manufacturing textile fabrics by interlacing twisted or spun threads in a continuous web; the warp threads are stretched on a loom and the weft threads are passed by turns above and below the warp threads. Weaving was practised in ancient civilizations such as Egypt and China, and has a continuous history in western Europe since antiquity. In the late Middle Ages the horizontal ground loom was fitted with legs, thus enabling the weaver to use treadles to adjust the heddles which created a space (by lifting some of the warp threads) through which the weft could be passed. Horizontal looms, which are also known as low-warp looms, were used for the manufacture of plain and geometrical fabrics, and upright looms, which are also known as high-warp looms, were used to weave high-quality TAPESTRIES. Italian SILK weavers introduced the draw-loom, in which complex machinery manipulated by a draw-boy enabled the weaver to vary the number of warp threads raised each time the weft threads were passed through the warp. LEONARDO DA VINCI designed an automated loom (c.1490), but automation did not begin to affect the practice of weaving until the seventeenth century, when the introduction of automatic looms caused civil disturbances in England, Germany, and the Netherlands.

**WEBSTER, JOHN** (c.1578–c.1626), English playwright. Webster's reputation rests on two tragedies: *The White Devil* (1609–12; published 1612) is a powerful treatment of the life of Vittoria ACCORAMBONI and *The Duchess of Malfi* (c.1613, published 1623) dramatizes a tale by BANDELLO. He also collaborated with other playwrights, notably with DEKKER on the comedies *Westward Hoe* (1604) and *Northward Hoe* (1605), the latter a light-hearted response to MARSTON, JONSON, and CHAPMAN's *Eastward Hoe*; *A Cure for a Cuckhold* (c.1625) was written with ROWLEY.
    *DNB.*

**WECHEL FAMILY**, a dynasty of German humanist printers active in Paris from the 1520s, in Frankfurt from 1572, and subsequently in Hanau and Basel. Christian Wechel (*fl.* 1520–54) inaugurated the publishing house in Paris, where he specialized in bilingual (Greek and Latin) editions of classical texts and also published contemporary books, including AGRIPPA's *De occulta philosophia* (1531), book 3 of RABELAIS's *Pantagruel* (1546), several editions of ALCIATI's emblem books (in French, German, and Latin), and a large number of medical treatises.

In 1554 Christian's son Andreas Wechel (d. 1581) inherited the business, and in 1572 he moved to Frankfurt to escape persecution as a Protestant in the WARS OF RELIGION. Like his father, Andreas published both ancient and modern authors; contemporary authors published by the press, many of whom were radical thinkers, included Giordano BRUNO, George BUCHANAN, John DEE, Giambattista DELLA PORTA, Philippe DUPLESSIS-MORNAY, Gabriele FALLOPPIO, Jean François FERNEL, PARACELSUS, Petrus RAMUS, Jacopo SADOLETO, Sebastiano SERLIO, and Giacomo ZABARELLA.

**WECHTER, GEORG THE ELDER** (c.1526–1586), German painter and printmaker in Nuremberg. In 1579 Wechter published a set of 30 designs of cups and tankards that remained in use for many years. One of the most influential designs is of a COLUMBINE CUP, which Wechter is sometimes said (in error) to have invented.
    *MDA.*

**WEDDERBURN, JAMES** (c.1495–1553), Scottish poet and playwright. Educated at St Andrews, where he became sympathetic to reformist opinion, Wedderburn was intended to follow his father as a merchant, and was sent to France, where there was family business, for this purpose. Returning to the family home in Dundee, he wrote two plays, a tragedy on the beheading of John the Baptist and a comedy, *Dionysius the Tyrant*. Both plays, which satirized abuses in the Catholic Church, were performed in the open air near Dundee in 1539–40; both are now lost. With his brothers John (c.1500–1556) and Robert (c.1510–c.1557) he wrote sacred parodies of popular ballads, which were collected and published in 1567 as *A Compendious Book of Godly and Spiritual Songs Collected out of Sundry Parts of the Scripture*. These activities brought him to the attention of ecclesiastical authorities, and in 1539 he left Scotland for France, where he lived until his death.

**WEELKES, THOMAS** (c.1576–1623), English composer who in 1598 was organist of Winchester College and in 1602 became organist and *informatur choristarum* at Chichester Cathedral. In the same year he was awarded the B.Mus. from New College, Oxford, and later was gentleman extraordinary of the Chapel Royal. He was dismissed from Chichester in 1617 for drunkenness. His reputation as a madrigalist rests on his *Balletts and Madrigals to Five Voices* (1598) and *Madrigals of 5. and 6. Parts* (1600). He was a master of imitative contrapuntal techniques as is apparent in 'As Vesta was, from Latmos hill descending', which was published in MORLEY's *The TRIUMPHS OF ORIANA* (1601); he was also skilled in imaginative word painting, as is shown by his 'Thule the period of cosmography'. This expressive style is also to be found in some of his sacred music, including 'When David heard'.

**WEERBEKE, GASPAR VAN** (c.1445–after 1517), Flemish composer in Italy. He was at the Sforza court in Milan from

1472; from 1480, and again in 1500, he sang in the papal choir in Rome under Sixtus IV and Innocent VIII. He also maintained links with the Burgundian court choir of PHILIP THE HANDSOME. His sacred music, predominantly masses and motets, reflects the Franco-Flemish polyphonic influence of DUFAY blended with the Italian style.

**WEIDITZ, HANS** (*c.*1500–*c.*1536), German engraver of woodcuts and book illustrator, who may have been born in Strassburg. He was trained in the Augsburg workshop of Hans BURGKMAIR. He designed and engraved many devotional woodcuts and illustrated large numbers of devotional and scientific books and editions of classical authors.
*MDA.*

**WEIGEL, VALENTIN** (1535–88), Lutheran mystic, pastor at the church of Zschopau (near Chemnitz). His influence was entirely local until 1609, when his writings (not all of which are now thought to be genuine) began to be published in Halle. He attacked the Bibliolaters (*Buchstabentheologen*) who, in Weigel's view, venerated the letter of Scripture rather than its spirit as revealed to the believer, and proposed a cosmology that was antipathetical to Lutheranism.

Weigel's mysticism drew on that of pseudo-Dionysius the Areopagite and PARACELSUS, and was in turn an important influence on the mystical views of Jacob BÖHME.

**WELSER FAMILY**, an Augsburg banking dynasty which was prominent in city affairs in the thirteenth century and rose to importance as European merchants and bankers in the fifteenth century, when the brothers Bartolomäus (d. 1484), Jakob (d. 1483), Lukas (d. 1494), and Ulrich (d. 1497/8) Welser established branches in Antwerp, Lisbon, and London and in the commercial centres of Italy and south Germany. Trade with the Levant established in the fifteenth century expanded in the early sixteenth century under Lucas's son Anton (d. 1518), who exploited the sea route to Asia discovered by Vasco da GAMA. By this time the family had become important bankers to the Empire, and the scale of their loans to the emperors was second only to those of their Augsburg rivals, the FUGGER family.

Anton Welser's sons Bartolomäus (1488–1561) and Anton (1486–1557) developed the family's interests in mining, and in return for large loans to the Emperor CHARLES V were given mineral rights in the Caribbean and allowed to establish a colony in Venezuela. They dispatched an expedition to Venezuela led by Ambrosius Dalfinger (d. 1532), who seized the province of Caracas in 1528; in 1530 Nikolaus FEDERMANN was appointed as governor. The family ruled and exploited the province until 1555, when it reverted to Spain. Thereafter the commercial fortunes of the Welsers declined, and the business became bankrupt in 1614.

The commercial successes of the family were accompanied by a commensurate elevation in social position. Bartolomäus's niece Philippine (1527–80) married Archduke Ferdinand, the second son of the Emperor FERDINAND I. Anton's grandson Marcus Welser (1558–1614) became burgomaster of AUGSBURG and became a prominent historian

and philologist. He published a five-volume history of early Bavaria (*Rerum Boicarum*, Augsburg, 1602) which was translated into German by his brother Paul, and his works were eventually collected as *Opera historica et philologica* (Nuremberg, 1682). The Augsburg branch of the Welser family became extinct in 1797.

**WENCESLAS IV or (Czech) Václav IV** (1361–1419), king of Bohemia and Holy Roman Emperor, was the son of the Emperor Charles IV. He was elected as king of the Romans in 1376, and on his father's death in 1378 became emperor. He lacked the political skills to govern the Empire, and in 1389 withdrew to Prague. In 1400 he was deposed as emperor in favour of Ruprecht of the Palatinate, and two years later he was deposed as king of Bohemia by his brother SIGISMUND. He was reinstated in 1404, but never regained full political authority. He expelled Jan HUS from Prague and silently acquiesced in his execution.

**WERT, GIACHES DE** (1535–95), Flemish composer active in Mantua, Ferrara, and Novellara. In 1565 he was appointed *maestro di cappella* at the Gonzaga court in Milan and the ducal chapel of Santa Barbara in Mantua, for which some of his sacred music (notably the hymns) was written. He also had connections with the Este court at FERRARA where he absorbed the cultural atmosphere charged by the presence of the *concerto delle donne*, to whom he dedicated his eighth book of madrigals. Influenced by RORE and an influence in turn on MONTEVERDI, he was an important madrigalist, setting PETRARCH, BEMBO, TANSILLO, TASSO, and GUARINI. He also composed the music for Guarini's abandoned production of *Il pastor fido* (1592).

**WERVE, CLAUX DE, or (English) Nicholas of Werve** (1396–1439), Dutch sculptor, born in Haarlem. In 1404 he succeeded his uncle Claus SLUTER as court sculptor to the dukes of Burgundy, and remained faithful to Sluter's style. He completed Sluter's tomb for Duke Philip the Bold at Dijon. He was commissioned to build a tomb for Duke JOHN THE FEARLESS (d. 1419) and his duchess, but died before work began; work on the tomb was continued by the Spanish sculptor Juan de la Huerta (*fl.* 1431–62), and after he abandoned the project in 1457 it was completed by Antoine MOITURIER. The tombs were designed for the Chartreuse de Champmol but are now in the Musée des Beaux-Arts in Dijon.
*NNBW* iii; *MDA* s.v. Claus de Werve.

**WESSEL GANSFORT** (1420–89), Dutch humanist and theologian; his baptismal name was Wessel, and he is sometimes called Johann Wessel (or John of Wessel) by confusion with his contemporary Johann von Wesel (or John of Wesel), a German ecclesiastical reformer from Oberwesel am Rhein. Wessel Gansfort was educated by the BRETHREN OF THE COMMON LIFE at Deventer, and subsequently studied and taught in Paris for sixteen years. After a protracted visit to Italy, where he adopted the values of Renaissance HUMANISM, he returned to the Netherlands for the rest of his life. In the

Protestant historiography of the Reformation, Wessel Gansfort has long been regarded as a proto-Protestant; this view originated in LUTHER's edition of a collection of Wessel Gansfort's writings in 1521.

E. W. Miller, *Wessel Gansfort: Life and Writings* (2 vols., 1917); F. Akkerman et al. (eds.), *Wessel Gansfort and Northern Humanism* (1993).

**WETTIN FAMILY**, a dynasty of German rulers and electors whose nobility can be traced to the eleventh century, when they became counts of Meissen and of the East Mark of SAXONY. In 1423 the Emperor SIGISMUND granted Friedrich I of Saxony (who was also Friedrich IV of Meissen) the dukedom of Saxony-Wittenberg and endowed the duchy with the electoral privilege.

In 1485 the duchy was divided between two of the sons of Friedrich II, each of whom was styled 'duke of Saxony': Ernst, the founder of the Ernestine line, inherited Saxony-Wittenberg and Thuringia, and also inherited the electorship; his brother ALBRECHT III ANIMOSUS, the founder of the Albertine line, inherited Meissen and Osterland. On the succession of the Ernestine and Albertine lines, see Appendix 1.

On 19 May 1547, in an agreement known as the Capitulation of Wittenberg, the Ernestine Elector JOHANN FRIEDRICH I surrendered the electoral dignity and the province that contained WITTENBERG TO MAURICE OF SAXONY, head of the Albertine branch of the Wettin family. The united duchy and electorate passed in 1553 to AUGUSTUS I, who secured recognition of his legitimacy as elector from Johann Friedrich in the Naumburg Treaty of February 1554, but his fear of an Ernestine coup long remained an important influence on his domestic and foreign policies. In 1567 Matthias FLACIUS ILLYRICUS supported the Ernestine cause by preaching against Augustus, and Johann Friedrich's champion Wilhelm von GRUMBACH led a rebellion, for which he was tortured and executed.

The electorate and the duchy were thereafter united until the dissolution of the HOLY ROMAN EMPIRE in 1806, whereupon members of the family reigned as kings of Saxony until the proclamation of the republic in 1918.

**WEYDEN, ROGIER VAN DER** (*c.*1399–1464), Flemish painter, almost certainly the otherwise unknown Rogelet de la Pâture who joined the Tournai workshop of Robert CAMPIN in 1426 and emerged as Maistre Rogier in 1432. In 1435 Rogier van der Weyden was appointed by the city of Brussels as its official painter, and, apart from a visit to Italy in the jubilee year of 1450, remained in the city for the rest of his life. The canon and chronology of his work are both problematical, because none of the pictures attributed to him is signed or dated.

Rogier had a particularly large workshop, and his paintings exercised a profound influence on Netherlandish art. His key works include a dramatic *Deposition* (Prado, Madrid), which is attributed to Rogier in late fifteenth-century documents and can be shown to be an early work by virtue of the fact that a dated copy was made in 1443. Other pictures executed before 1450 include the Miraflores altarpiece (Gemäldegalerie, Berlin) and *St Luke Painting the Virgin* (Museum of Fine Arts, Boston). It was probably in the 1450s that he painted the Frankfurt altarpiece (Städelsches Kunstinstitut und Städtische Galerie, Frankfurt) and the *Entombment* (Uffizi). The most important work of Rogier's final years is a *Crucifixion* (*c.*1460, Escorial). Products of his workshop include the *St Columba* altarpiece (Alte Pinakothek, Munich), the Bladelin Triptych (Gemäldegalerie, Berlin), and the polyptych of *The Last Judgement* in the chapel of the Hôtel Dieu (les Hospices de Beaune) in Beaune.

MDA; Dirk de Vos, *Rogier van der Weyden: The Complete Works* (1999).

**WHITCHURCH, EDWARD** (d. 1561), English Protestant publisher, a London grocer who entered into a partnership with Richard GRAFTON, with whom he distributed the English Bible (printed in Antwerp) known as 'Thomas Matthews's Bible', the first complete Bible in English. Together with Grafton he distributed the corrected version of COVERDALE's New Testament (Paris, 1538); they then established a press at which they printed the 'Great Bible' (1539) and the first edition of the Book of COMMON PRAYER (1549).

DNB.

**WHITE, ROBERT** (*c.*1538–1574), English composer who in 1560 was granted a B.Mus. at Cambridge where he sang at Trinity College. He was master of the choristers at Ely (1562) and Chester Cathedral (1567), where he was also involved in the mystery plays, and at Westminster Abbey from 1569. He wrote keyboard, viol, and lute music and his sacred vocal music comprises Latin psalms, antiphons, lamentations, psalm motets, and English anthems.

**WHITEFRIARS PLAYHOUSE**, private theatre in the converted refectory hall of the old Whitefriars monastery, London. It was in use between 1606 and 1629, when it was succeeded by the SALISBURY COURT THEATRE. Initially used by child acting companies, it was also occupied from 1613 to 1614 by LADY ELIZABETH'S MEN.

**WHITGIFT, JOHN** (*c.*1530–1604), English archbishop. Educated at Cambridge, Whitgift's career included positions as professor of divinity (1563), master of Trinity (1567), dean of Lincoln (1571), and bishop of Worcester (1577). Although strongly Calvinist, he opposed Puritanism, and expelled CARTWRIGHT from the professorship of divinity at Cambridge; he continued this opposition to both Puritanism and papacy when made archbishop of Canterbury in 1583. His Eleven Articles of 1583 uphold the Elizabethan settlement, reinforce the Thirty-Nine ARTICLES, and defend Anglican liturgy and ritual. The LAMBETH ARTICLES of 1595 upheld Calvinist doctrines of predestination.

DNB.

**WHYTHORNE, THOMAS** (1528–96), English composer and lutenist who studied at Magdalen College School and Magdalen College, Oxford. He worked as a music tutor to

Rogier van der Weyden, *The Deposition*, in the Prado, Madrid

various noble families and, after 1571, became master of the music in Archbishop PARKER's chapel. His *Duos, of Songs for Two Voices* (1590) was intended for children as well as adults and could be either played or sung. He also wrote some sacred music, 200 poems, and an autobiography.

**WICKRAM, GEORG or Jörg** (*c.*1505–*c.*1561), German novelist, playwright, goldsmith, and painter, born in Colmar (Alsace), the illegitimate son of a municipal official. He became a civic official in Colmar, where his enthusiasm for MEISTERGESANG led him to found a Meistersinger school in 1549; he later became town clerk of Burkheim (Rhein), where he died before 1562.

Wickram contributed to many genres of literature. His editions included an adaptation of Albrecht von Halberstadt's Middle High German translation of Ovid's *Metamorphoses* (1545) and a collection of tales and SCHWÄNKE for stagecoach travellers, *Das Rollwagenbüchlein* (1555). As a playwright, Wickram wrote FASTNACHTSPIELE (*Die Zehen Alter*, 1531; *Das Narrengieße*, 1538; *List der Weiber*, 1543) and biblical dramas (*Der verlorene Sohn*, 1540; *Tobias*, 1551). His poems, which

include *Von der Trunkenheit* and *Der irrereittende Pilger* (1556), are satirical and moralizing.

Wickram's most important literary works were novels. *Ritter Galmy* (1539) and *Gabriotto und Reinhart* (1551) are both descendants of the medieval romances of chivalry; *Der Jungen Knaben Spiegel* (1554), *Der Goldtfaden* (1554, printed 1557), and *Von guten und bösen Nachbarn* (1560) all contain central characters who are burghers, and are regarded as the earliest examples of middle-class fiction. In the historiography of the novel, *Der Goldtfaden* is sometimes said to be the first important German novel.

**WIERIX FAMILY**, Netherlandish engravers whose workshop was in Antwerp. Anthonie Wierix the Elder (*c.*1520/5–*c.*1572) was a painter and engraver; his three sons, Anthonie the Younger (*c.*1555/9–1604), Hieronymus (*c.*1553–1619), and Johan (1549–1618), were trained as engravers in their father's studio. The three brothers began to engrave complex designs when they were still very young, and their precocity was accentuated by the declaration of their ages (using the Latin formula *anno aetatis*, 'in the year of [his] age') on their

*The Adoration of the Magi*, the central panel of the Columba Triptych in the Alte Pinakothek, Munich; attributed to **Rogier van der Weyden** and his workshop

engravings. Hieronymus copied DÜRER's *St George* when he was 12 and his *St Jerome* when he was 13; similarly, Johan copied Marcantonio RAIMONDI's *Venus and Cupid* at 14 and Dürer's *Fall of Man* at 16. In addition to these famous copies, the brothers produced more than 2,000 original engravings, many of which were devotional prints distributed by the Jesuits.

*MDA s.v. Wierix.*

**WILBYE, JOHN** (1574–1638), English composer who was employed by the Kitsons of Hengrave Hall, near Bury St Edmunds. He published two books of madrigals, contributed to MORLEY's *The TRIUMPHS OF ORIANA* (1601) and Leighton's *Tears or Lamentations* (1614), and, with Edward JOHNSON, worked on the publication of DOWLAND's second book of lute songs in 1600. His writing was influenced by Morley, Alfonso FERRABOSCO (I), and KIRBYE and, like Thomas WEELKES, he composed some five- and six-voice settings.

**WILHELM IV** (1493–1550), second duke of Bavaria, the son of Albrecht IV of WITTELSBACH and Kunigunde, daughter of the Emperor FRIEDRICH III. In March 1508, on the death of Albrecht IV, Wilhelm succeeded to the dukedom, but from 1516 he had to share the government with his brother Ludwig. On Ludwig's death in 1545, Wilhelm became the sole ruler of Bavaria, and on the death of Wilhelm in March 1550 the entire duchy passed to his son Albrecht V.

Wilhelm was a loyal Catholic and a steadfast opponent of the Reformation. He invited the Jesuits to establish at the University of Ingolstadt their headquarters for all of Germany and in 1546 he assisted CHARLES V in the SCHMALKALDIC WAR. Wilhelm was the patron of AVENTINUS, and commissioned his history of Bavaria.

**WILHELM IV, LANDGRAVE OF HESSE** (1532–92), son of PHILIP OF HESSE, combined the activities of a successful reigning prince with a serious interest in ASTRONOMY. As an astronomer he set up a well-equipped observatory at Kassel (antedating that of Tycho BRAHE at Uraniborg) and, not always having time to make sustained series of observations in person, employed astronomers to help him, among them Christoph Rothmann (*c.*1550–1605), one of the foremost observers of the time. The observatory instruments were of the highest quality, many of them made by the leading clock and precision instrument-maker of the day, Jost BÜRGI. The landgrave's programme was to study the fixed stars (the stars that form the patterns of the constellations) so as to provide a more exact basis for observing motions. In this period, positions of other objects, such as planets, were generally measured by taking their distances from three nearby fixed stars. Thus the landgrave's work on the fixed stars made a vital contribution to Tycho Brahe's work on the planets. The landgrave's observations of the New Star of 1572 helped to prove that it belonged among the fixed stars;

Galileo GALILEI considered these observations more exact than Tycho's.

John Leopold, *Astronomen, Sterne, Geräte: Landgrad Wilhelm IV und seine sich selbst bewegenden Globen* (1986); L. von Mackensen, *Die erste Sternwarte Europas mit ihren Instrumenten und Uhren. 400 Jahre Jost Bürgi in Kassel* (2nd edn. 1982).

**WILHELM V VON KLEVE or William V of Cleves** (1516–92) succeeded his father Johann as duke (*Herzog*) of Cleves in 1539. Since 1521 the duchy of Cleves, on the Lower Rhine, had been a principality which included the duchies of Cleves, Jülich, and Berg, and the counties of Ravensberg and Mark. The Reformation was introduced to Cleves in 1533, and Wilhelm ruled as a Protestant, but he soon fell into conflict with CHARLES V over the imperial claim to the disputed duchy of Gelderland, and allied himself with FRANCIS I, placing Gelderland under French protection. The ensuing conflict lasted until Wilhelm was forced by the terms of the Treaty of Venlo (7 September 1543) to cede the duchy to Charles and to prohibit the spread of the Reformation in his territories. In 1566 Wilhelm suffered the first of a protracted series of mental breakdowns, and the population divided into warring factions of Calvinists, Lutherans, and Catholics. These tensions eventually led to the War of the JÜLICH-CLEVES SUCCESSION (1609–14).

**WILKINSON, ROBERT** (*c*.1475/80–*c*.1515), English composer at Eton where he was *informatur choristarum* (*c*.1500–15) and constable in 1502. His large-scale, intricate, contrapuntal sacred music (including the nine-voice 'Salve regina') is contained in the ETON CHOIRBOOK.

**WILLAERT, ADRIAAN** (*c*.1490–1562), Netherlandish composer in Italy. At Paris to read law at the university, he met Jean MOUTON, with whom he studied music. He went to Rome in 1514 and was a singer at Ferrara in the service of Cardinal Ippolito II d'ESTE, with whom he later travelled to Hungary. In 1527 he was appointed *maestro di cappella* at San Marco, Venice, where he remained until his death. Amongst his pupils were Cipriano de RORE, Baldassare DONATO, and ZARLINO. He wrote sacred and secular music including masses, motets, madrigals, and instrumental *ricercares*. His polychoral psalm settings, with their use of *CORI SPEZZATI* techniques, provided models for later Venetian composers, including the GABRIELI.

**WILLIAM OF ORANGE or William the Silent or (Dutch) Willem den Eerste** (1533–84), prince of Orange (in Provence), count of Nassau (in Germany), Dutch leader in the REVOLT OF THE NETHERLANDS, and stadtholder of the United Provinces, born in Dillenburg (Germany), the son of the count of Nassau-Dillenburg, who was a Lutheran. William was raised as a Lutheran until he inherited vast territories in Burgundy (including parts of the Netherlands and the principality of Orange) in 1544, whereupon he was sent to Brussels at the command of the Emperor CHARLES V to be educated in the resolutely Catholic court of the regent MARY OF HUNGARY. He became a page of the emperor, and when Charles abdi-

cated as duke of Burgundy in October 1555, William stood beside him. In the same year William commanded an imperial army in France and was appointed to the Council of State of the Netherlands by PHILIP II. In 1559 he was one of the principal negotiators of the Treaty of CATEAU-CAMBRÉSIS, and when four months later Philip left permanently for Spain, William was appointed as lord lieutenant (stadtholder) of the northern provinces of Holland, Zeeland, and Utrecht, and a member of the Council of State of the Netherlands.

In the four years between the departure of King Philip for Spain in August 1559 and William's resignation from the Council of State in July 1563, William moved from unquestioning loyalty to the Habsburgs to an overtly oppositional position. The reasons for this shift are complex, but certainly include William's growing unease about the repressive measures used to enforce Catholicism by Cardinal GRANVELLE, and the shift of religious allegiance consequent upon his marriage to Anna, the Lutheran daughter of MAURICE OF SAXONY. The resignation of William and the count of EGMONT from the Council led the following year to the dismissal of Granvelle (March 1564). In 1567 Philip sent the Duke of ALBA to restore civil order. Egmont and the count of HOORNE remained in the Netherlands, and were executed; William prudently withdrew to his Dillenburg estate to prepare for war.

On 6 October 1568 William and his brother LOUIS OF NASSAU invaded the Netherlands with an army of German mercenaries, but a lack of local support forced them to retreat before they reached Brussels. The following year he fought alongside the HUGUENOTS in the hope of receiving reciprocal assistance, and Louis pursued a parallel diplomatic initiative. The most significant product of this collaboration was the action by which the sea beggars (see PRIVATEERS), working from the Huguenot port of La Rochelle, captured Brill, in Zeeland (1 April 1572). On 19 July 1572 William was proclaimed as stadtholder of Holland, and eight days later he again invaded the southern Netherlands, this time with a view to relieving the siege of Mons (Hainaut), which had been captured by Louis of Nassau on 23 May. A few months later the French alliance collapsed because of the ST BARTHOLOMEW'S DAY MASSACRE.

William joined the rebel coalition in the north in October 1572, and in April 1573 was received into the Dutch Reformed Church, an act that in theory represented a movement away from the Lutheranism of his early childhood (revived by his marriage to Anna of Saxony) towards the Calvinism of the Dutch Reformed Church, but in practice represented a realignment that was more political than religious. He was one of the negotiators of the Pacification of GHENT, which briefly brought together the northern and southern provinces in an anti-Spanish alliance. Despite his efforts to hold the seventeen provinces together, the south formed the Union of ARRAS (7 January 1579) and the north the Union of UTRECHT (23 January 1579). King Philip proclaimed William to be a traitor (June 1580), and William responded by publishing an *Apology* (December 1580) which defended his political career and accused Spain of inhuman crimes in the Netherlands, in Spain, and in Spanish America. On 18 March 1582 William was wounded in an attempt on his life in Antwerp. Two years later, on 10 July 1584, he was assassinated in the Prinsenhof in Delft by a pro-Spanish cabinetmaker.

William was married to Anne van Buren (an Egmont noblewoman who died in 1558), Anna of Saxony (whose habitual infidelities led to their divorce in 1571), Charlotte de Bourbon-Monpensier (who died in 1582), and Louise, daughter of Gaspard COLIGNY; by these four wives he had ten daughters and three sons. His eldest son, Philip William, who succeeded him as prince of Orange, was kidnapped as a child and spent his life as a Spanish hostage; his second son was MAURICE OF SAXONY, and his third son, Frederick Henry (1584–1647), led the United Provinces throughout the THIRTY YEARS WAR. In 1689 William's great-grandson, the third William of Orange, became King William III of England, Scotland, and Ireland.

C. V. Wedgwood, *William the Silent* (1956).

**WILLOUGHBY, SIR HUGH** (d. 1554), English explorer. Despite lacking navigational experience, Willoughby led the expedition of 1553, funded by London merchants, to find the North-East Passage to India. Although CHANCELLOR sailed into the White Sea, Willoughby's ship became lost and eventually perished.

*DNB.*

**WIMBLEDON HOUSE**, a lost house and garden in what is now south London, was built for Thomas Cecil, earl of Exeter (1542–1622); construction began in 1588. A drawing by Robert SMYTHSON made in 1609 shows that the gardens had been laid out in squares and rectangles (like those at THEOBALDS), and that there was a banqueting house in the garden. Shortly after the drawing was made, the planting was extended with an orchard, a vineyard, and a lime walk, all of which were formally organized to facilitate views of and from the garden. These Jacobean plantings were retained when Charles I bought Wimbledon House for Henrietta Maria and commissioned André MOLLET to redesign the gardens; in 1642 Mollet added a MAZE and the first English wilderness, the descendant of the Italian BOSCO. The Elizabethan gardens, however, were replaced by four PARTERRES, two of which had fountains and *parterres de broderie*.

C. S. S. Higham, *Wimbledon Manor House under the Cecils* (1962); Roy Strong, *The Renaissance Garden in England* (1979).

**WIMPFELING, JAKOB** (1450–1528), prolific German humanist, born in Schlettstadt (now French Sélestat), in Alsace, and educated at the universities of Freiburg, Erfurt, and Heidelberg. In 1484, by which time he had become rector of Heidelberg University, he resigned his academic offices and moved to Speier, where he worked as a preacher at the cathedral church until 1498. He returned for a time to Heidelberg (1498–1501) and subsequently lived in Strassburg (1501–15) before retiring to Schlettstadt.

Wimpfeling's writings include a Terentian play, two treatises on education, and a plea for religious reform, *Apologia pro republica christiana* (1506). His most important work was his *Epitome rerum Germanicarum* (1505), the first general

history of Germany. He was a fierce and influential critic of church abuses.

Lewis Spitz, *The Religious Reformation of the German Humanists* (1963).

**WIMPINA, KONRAD** (1460–1531), German humanist and Catholic theologian. He was born in Buchen (Baden) to a family called Koch (his later name was taken from Wimpfen, in Württemberg, where he held a canonry) and educated at the University of Leipzig, where he became a professor in 1491 and rector in 1494. He was ordained in 1500 and in 1505 accepted an invitation to serve as the first rector of the new University of Frankfurt an der Oder.

Wimpina was one of LUTHER's first opponents, and in January 1515 helped Johann TETZEL to draw up his counter-theses against Luther. His *Anacephalaeosis sectarium* (1530) is a comprehensive attack on Luther's theology. In 1530 he was a member of the group of Catholic theologians charged by the Emperor CHARLES V with refuting the AUGSBURG CONFESSION.

*ADB.*

**WINDESHEIM CANONS.** In the twelfth century, the houses of the Augustinian ORDER coalesced into congregations which developed constitutions which were supplementary to the rule of St Augustine. The Windesheim canons began as a house established near Zwolle (Netherlands) in 1387; their founding members, disciples of Geert de GROOTE and Florens RADEWIJNS, were associated with the BRETHREN OF THE COMMON LIFE. Their constitution was approved by Pope BONIFACE IX in 1395, and under Johan Vos (1391–1424), the second prior of the house, they joined three other Dutch houses to form the Windesheim canons. In 1413 the congregation absorbed the seven houses of the Groenendael canons, and in 1430 the canons of Neuss. In the course of the fifteenth century houses were established throughout the Netherlands, northern Germany, and Switzerland. The most prominent canons in the order were Gabriel BIEL, Jan BUSCH, and THOMAS À KEMPIS.

The Windesheim canons were the principal exponents of the DEVOTIO MODERNA, the spiritualism of which they practised and taught to the secular clergy and the laity. The reforms enjoined by Jan Busch in his *De reformatione monasteriorum* were at best a partial success, and the Order began to contract under the onslaught of the Reformation. By the end of the sixteenth century the Dutch houses had all been disbanded, Windesheim itself succumbing in 1581. In 1573 the Order was reorganized under a prior-general, and it lived on in the Spanish Netherlands, Austria, and the Catholic parts of Germany until the secularization of the monasteries in 1802.

**WITCHCRAFT.** The exercise of demonic powers, known variously as sorcery and witchcraft, was for many centuries a marginal issue in the Church; the small number of people accused of witchcraft were tried by bishops' courts and punished by the secular authorities, and from 1258 the INQUISITION was forbidden to examine cases of witchcraft unless they also involved heresy. In the course of the fourteenth century ecclesiastical opinion changed, and in 1398 the jurisdictional powers of the Inquisition were extended to include witchcraft.

In 1484 the German inquisitors Heinrich Kramer and Jacob Sprenger secured from Pope INNOCENT VIII a bull giving their courts jurisdiction over witchcraft, and they printed the bull at the front of their *Malleus maleficarum* ('Hammer of Evils'), which was published in Speyer in 1487. In the course of the next century prosecutions increased steadily. In northern Europe the 'witch-craze' reached its apogee in the half-century from 1580 to 1630, though in England the greatest number of executions occurred in the mid-1640s; the last judicial hanging of a witch in England was in 1685 (though occasional lynchings occurred until the early twentieth century), and the last burning of a witch in Scotland was in 1727. American persecution of witches culminated in the trials in Salem (Massachusetts) in 1692; in Hungary and Poland the most intensive period of persecution was the early eighteenth century; and in Latin America witches were burnt until the mid-nineteenth century. In the Mediterranean countries of Europe, there was no witch-hunting and hardly any prosecution. In all some 50,000 people, overwhelmingly women, were executed for witchcraft. The literature of witchcraft included Johann Weier's *De praestigiis daemonum* (1563) and Reginald SCOT's *Discovery of Witchcraft* (1563).

B. Ankarloo and G. Henningsen (eds.), *Häxornas Europa, 1400–1700*, English trans. *Early Modern Witchcraft* (1990); B. P. Levack, *The Witch-Hunt in Early Modern Europe* (1987); G. Scarre, *Witchcraft and Magic in Sixteenth- and Seventeenth-Century Europe* (1987); A. Macfarlane, *Witchcraft in Tudor and Stuart England* (1970); Keith Thomas, *Religion and the Decline of Magic* (1971); Sydney Anglo (ed.), *The Damned Art: Essays in the Literature of Witchcraft* (1977); Carlo Ginzburg, *Storia notturna*, trans. as *Ecstasies: Deciphering the Witches' Sabbath* (1991); Lyndal Roper, *Oedipus and the Devil: Witchcraft, Sexuality and Religion in Early Modern Europe* (1994).

**WITTE, PIETER DE, or (Italian) Pietro Candido or (English and German exonym) Peter Candid** (*c.*1548–1628), Netherlandish painter. He was born in Bruges and moved *c.*1570 to Italy, where he worked in Florence, Rome, and Volterra. In 1586 he moved to Munich, where he worked for the rest of his life. He collaborated with Frederick SUSTRIS on the decoration of the Antiquarium, Europe's first museum of antiquities; it was destroyed by Allied bombs during the Second World War. He painted a *Martyrdom of St Ursula* for the Michaelskirche (1588) and the main ALTARPIECE for the Frauenkirche (1620). He was also a designer of tapestries, and produced four series between 1604 and 1618, on *The Months* (of which *March* is in the Residenzmuseum in Munich), *The Deeds of Otto of Wittelsbach*, *The Seasons*, and *The Times of Day*.

*MDA* s.v. Candid, Peter.

**WITTELSBACH FAMILY**, the ruling house of BAVARIA from 1124 and electors of the PALATINATE of the Rhine from 1329 (see Appendix 1 for lists of rulers); the divisions of both Bavaria and the Palatinate meant that the Wittelsbach territories were not ruled as a single principality until the union of Bavaria and the Palatinate in 1777. By the Treaty of Pavia in 1329, the Wittelsbach Emperor Ludwig IV resigned

the Palatinate and Upper Bavaria to his nephews Rudolf II and Ruprecht; Rudolf died in 1353, and his brother Ruprecht was the sole ruler until 1390.

The descendants of Ludwig IV continued to rule Lower Bavaria, which was repeatedly partitioned, but finally reunited within itself and with Upper Bavaria by Albrecht IV (1447–1508), the first duke of a united Bavaria. The line of Wittelsbach dukes of Bavaria included Albrecht's sons WILHELM IV and Ludwig X (1516–45), Wilhelm's son ALBRECHT V, and Albrecht's son Wilhelm V, who abdicated in 1597 in favour of his son Maximilian, who in 1623 became the first of a succession of Wittelsbach electors of Bavaria.

Members of the Wittelsbach dynasty ruled as the electors of the Palatinate from 1329 until 1777, when the Palatinate and Bavaria were united, and from 1799 ruled as kings of Bavaria until the proclamation of the republic in 1918, when Ludwig III, the last of the Wittelsbach rulers, was deposed.

**WITTENBERG**, the capital of Saxony and the seat of the electors of the Ernestine branch of the WETTIN dynasty until 1547. The university was founded by FRIEDRICH III in 1502, and Martin LUTHER was appointed to a professorship in philosophy in 1508. On 31 October 1517 Luther affixed his 95 Theses to the wooden doors of the Gothic Schlosskirche (remodelled in the nineteenth century and now called the Reformation Memorial Church); these doors were burnt in 1760 and replaced in 1858 by bronze doors bearing the Latin text of the Theses, but the church (built 1439–99) survives, and contains the tombs of Friedrich III (by Peter VISCHER the Younger), Luther, and MELANCHTHON. For the next 30 years, under the leadership of Luther and Melanchthon, the town was the centre of the Reformation, and during this period it became an important centre for PRINTING. The engraver and painter Lucas CRANACH the Elder lived in the city from 1505 to 1547, and served for a time as burgomaster. The most important surviving Renaissance building is the Town Hall (Rathaus, 1524–40), which combines Gothic windows with Renaissance gables and a fine balcony added in 1573. The association of the city with the Reformation gave the university a European reputation; Shakespeare made Hamlet and Horatio students at Wittenberg. The WITTENBERG CONCORD was signed in the town in 1536.

On 19 May 1547, in an agreement known as the Capitulation of Wittenberg, the Ernestine Elector JOHANN FRIEDRICH I surrendered the electoral dignity and the province that contained Wittenberg to MAURICE OF SAXONY, head of the Albertine branch of the Wettin family.

In the popular historiography of the Reformation, Luther is deemed to be the first reformer and Wittenberg the cradle of the Reformation. The Augustinian monastery where Luther lived is now a museum (the Lutherhalle), as are the houses of Cranach and Melanchthon, and in 1922 the town was officially renamed Lutherstadt Wittenberg.

H. Junghans, *Wittenberg als Lutherstadt* (1979); W. Friedensburg, *Geschichte der Universität Wittenberg* (1917); K. Aland et al. (eds.), *450 Jahre Martin-Luther-Universität, Halle-Wittenberg* (3 vols., 1952–3).

**WITTENBERG CONCORD**, an agreement reached in May 1536 by Lutherans and Zwinglians on the fraught subject of the EUCHARIST. A preliminary meeting was held in December 1534 in Kassel, where the Lutherans were represented by MELANCHTHON and the Zwinglians by Martin BUCER. In May 1536 a full-scale meeting attended by Martin LUTHER was convened at Wittenberg. Both sides agreed on a doctrinal statement which had been drafted by Melanchthon; it was essentially a statement of the Lutheran position, but did not insist on the UBIQUITARIANISM that underpinned Luther's consubstantiation.

The Concord was not ratified by the Swiss Zwinglians, and so the reunion of the two churches proved to be impermanent.

**WITTENWEILER, HEINRICH** (*fl.* early fifteenth century), poet of *Der Ring*, a citizen of Wyl, in St Gallen (Swiss Confederation); his surname reflects the origins of his family in the Thurgau town of Wittenweil, from which his ancestors had moved to Wyl in the thirteenth century. Wittenweiler was the author of a comic EPIC known as *Der Ring*. In the course of almost 10,000 lines, Wittenweiler tells the story of a peasant courtship and wedding and of the consequent celebrations and feuds. The tale of Bertschi Triefnas and his bride Mätzli Rüerenzumpf is markedly didactic in its commendation of good conduct, but is nonetheless so exuberantly coarse that it has at times been condemned as obscene. The satire is mainly directed at the peasantry, but courtly life does not escape the acidic eye of Wittenweiler.

**WITZ, KONRAD** (*c.*1400/10–1445/7), German painter. He was born in Rottweil (Swabia), but worked principally in Basel and Geneva. Witz's most important work is the Heilspiegel altarpiece (*c.*1435), a polyptych in sixteen panels; the twelve surviving scenes are now divided between the Kunstmuseum in Basel, the Musée des Beaux-Arts in Dijon, and the Gemäldegalerie in Berlin. Witz's last major work was his altarpiece of *Christ Walking on the Waters* (1444, Musée d'Art et d'Histoire, Geneva), which is celebrated for its depiction of landscape. Witz was also the artist who painted one of the earliest surviving sets of PLAYING CARDS (Kunsthistorisches Museum, Vienna).

*MDA.*

**WOLF, HIERONYMUS** (1516–80), German humanist scholar. He was born in Oettingen and studied under MELANCHTHON and CAMERARIUS. In 1551 he became secretary and librarian to the FUGGER family in Augsburg, and from 1557 worked as the headmaster of the Protestant school in Augsburg. As a scholar Wolf specialized in Greek; his publications include editions of the orators Isocrates (1548) and Demosthenes (1549) and of the Stoic lectures of Epictetus, and a long series of editions of works by Byzantine historians.

**WOLGEMUT, MICHAEL** (*c.*1434–1519), German painter and woodcut engraver, a native of Nuremberg. He specialized in the design of WOODCUT illustrations for printed books. He was employed by Anton KÖBERGER to design the wood-cuts for Hartmann Schedel's *Weltchronik* (1493). His most important surviving paintings are ALTARPIECES in Schwabach and Zwickau (Saxony).

*MDA.*

**WOLLATON HALL**, which has now been absorbed into Nottingham, was built between 1580 and 1588 by Robert SMYTHSON for Sir Francis Willoughby (*c.*1546–1596). The house is square, and its two high storeys rise to a third in the corner pavilions. The exterior is richly decorated with gables, pinnacles, and more than 200 statues. Many of the architectural details derive from the treatises of Sebastiano SERLIO and Jan VREDEMAN DE VRIES.

The gardens, which are now lost, are known from a plan by John Smythson (Robert's son) and a painting at Yale University; the plan shows that the gardens, which consisted of three adjoining squares extending from the back of the house, were organized symmetrically around an axis running squarely through the house. Although this arrangement is common in ITALIAN GARDENS and FRENCH GARDENS, this is the only Renaissance garden in England known to have been organized in this way; the design derives ultimately from Serlio, as mediated by Jacques DUCERCEAU's *Les Plus Excellents Bâtiments de France* (1576 and 1579).

Alice Freedman, *House and Household in Elizabethan England: Wollaton Hall and the Willoughby Family* (1989); Mark Girouard, *Robert Smythson and the Architecture of the Elizabethan Era* (1966).

**WOLSEY, THOMAS** (*c.*1474–1530), English cardinal and statesman. Wolsey rose from humble origins to be the key minister of the first half of HENRY VIII's reign. He served HENRY VII as chaplain and was retained by Henry VIII, successively becoming bishop of Lincoln, archbishop of York (both 1514), cardinal, and lord chancellor (1515); as chancellor, he administered both government and church business. He was the target of a considerable body of satirical verse from authors such as SKELTON, Roye, and Barlow. Henry's wish to rid himself of CATHERINE OF ARAGON ultimately proved Wolsey's downfall. Unable to negotiate with the papacy the annulment Henry sought, he was removed from office and later charged with treason. He died at Leicester Abbey on the way to answer the charges.

*DNB.*

**WOODCUT or (early modern English) wooden cut**, a design cut in relief on a block of wood for the purpose of making PRINTS and the term used to denote the print obtained from this process. The artist draws a design on the flattened surface of a block of wood and then uses knives and gouges to cut away the parts that are to be left white in the print. The design, which stands proud in a relief, is then inked and pressed on a sheet of paper. The ensuing print bears a design which is the mirror image of that drawn by the artist. The technique is to be distinguished from ETCHING and ENGRAVING, which are both intaglio processes in which designs are printed from the grooves incised in the plate.

The woodcut has existed in the Middle East and China since antiquity, but in Europe the earliest woodcuts date from the beginning of the fifteenth century; the delay may have been occasioned by the lack of any western technology for making PAPER until the end of the fourteenth century. In the course of the fifteenth century woodcuts came to be produced all over Europe, and were used extensively for the production of religious prints, PLAYING CARDS and BLOCK BOOKS. With the advent of printing, woodcuts became the ideal process for the production of book illustrations, because the relief surface of the block could be made the same height as the type, which meant that engraved blocks could be locked together with movable type in the press. The most celebrated woodcut illustrations of the fifteenth century are DÜRER's *Apocalypse* woodcuts of 1499 and those contained in the *Hypnerotomachia Polifili* (also 1499) of Francesco COLONNA.

In the sixteenth century, when illustrated books were produced in large numbers, the various stages in the process became the province of specialized craftsmen: the designer of the print was sometimes a prominent artist such as Hans BALDUNG GRIEN, CRANACH, Dürer, Urs GRAF, or HOLBEIN; the artist's drawing was transferred to the engraver's block by a specialist in such transfers, and another artisan gouged the wood, whereupon the block was passed to the printer; the names of the printers are usually known, as are those of many of the artists, but block cutters are normally anonymous.

Woodcuts were ideally suited to Gothic designs with strong lines, but were inferior to engravings and etchings as a means of reproducing complex shaded designs, in part because the woodcut is not amenable to cross-hatching. In the seventeenth century the use of woodcuts came to be restricted to utilitarian purposes such as printers' devices and the production of broadsheets.

**WORDE, WYNKYN DE, or Jan van Wynkyn** (d. 1535), Alsatian printer in England. Worde became assistant to CAXTON in 1476 on the latter's establishment of a printing press in London. He inherited the business on Caxton's death in 1492, continuing to run it from a new base in Fleet Street until his own demise. His catalogue of books published is an important record of the early book trade.

*DNB.*

**WORMS, CONFERENCE OF, or (German) Wormser Religionsgespräche** (1540–1), the colloquy arranged in the wake of the failure of the Conference of HAGENAU in the hope of reconciling the Protestants and Catholics of Germany. Eleven delegates from each side met on 25 November 1540. Johann ECK spoke for the Catholics and MELANCHTHON for the Protestants. Early in January a statement on original sin was agreed by both sides, but before discussions could proceed further it was decided on 18 January that the Conference should be suspended in deference to the forthcoming Conference of REGENSBURG.

**WORMS, DIET OF, or (German) Wormser Reichstag** (1521). Worms was the seat of a long series of imperial diets, of which the most important was convened in 1521 in order for LUTHER to defend himself before the Emperor CHARLES V. The Diet took place in the Bischofshof from 27 January to 25 May. The papal legate Girolamo ALEANDRO presented the case against Luther on 13 February, whereupon Luther was summoned to appear. He arrived on 16 April and gave his testimony on 17 and 18 April. On 19 April Charles announced his decision to suppress Luther's doctrines, and on 26 April Luther left Worms with the promise of a safe conduct from the emperor. On 26 May Luther's doctrines were formally condemned in the Edict of Worms, which imposed an imperial ban on Luther and condemned him as the devil incarnate. Charles left Germany at the conclusion of the Diet, and did not return for nine years, so allowing Luther and his followers to spread the Reformation.

Gordon Rupp, *Luther's Progress to the Diet of Worms, 1521* (1951).

**WOTTON, SIR HENRY** (1568–1639), English diplomat, poet, and architectural theorist. Educated at Oxford, Wotton was an agent for ESSEX in 1595, and a friend of DONNE. He served as ambassador to Venice and on other diplomatic missions between 1604 and 1624; he then became provost of Eton until his death. His *Elements of Architecture* appeared in 1624. The *Reliquiae Wottonianae*, containing poems and other writings, first appeared in 1651, and was enlarged in later editions.

*DNB.*

**WOTTON, THOMAS** (1521–87), English book collector (and the father of Sir Henry WOTTON), the son of the treasurer of Calais and sheriff of Kent. He was imprisoned in 1554, probably because of his Protestantism; he served as sheriff of Kent in 1558 and 1579. Wotton was a bibliophile and the eponym of the 'Wotton bindings', the BOOK BINDINGS that he commissioned from workshops in Paris or from French craftsmen in London. These bindings combine French decorative detail with armorial stamps. The wording 'Thomas Wottoni et amicorum' (i.e. 'this is the book of Thomas Wotton and his friends') is an adaptation of the phrase used by GROLIER, and so Wotton came to be known as 'The English Grolier'. Wotton's library passed through the female line to the earls of Chesterfield and of Carnarvon, and was sold and dispersed in 1919. Some 135 Wotton bindings are known to survive.

*DNB.*

**WRIGHT, EDWARD** (1558–1615), English mathematician, born in Garveston (Norfolk) and educated at Caius College, Cambridge, where he afterwards held a fellowship from 1587 to 1596. In 1589 he accompanied the earl of Cumberland on a voyage to the Azores, an experience that made him aware of shortcomings in navigational practice occasioned by charts with parallel lines of latitude and longitude and the forbidding nature of the complex innovations of MERCATOR.

In 1599 Wright published *Certain Errors in Navigation Detected and Corrected*, a treatise in which he explained Mercator's projection by analogy to a bladder being inflated in a cylinder and demonstrated its principal advantage, which is that rhumb lines could be drawn as straight lines; the treatise also includes a Mercator projection of the North Atlantic.

In 1614 Wright began to lecture on navigational mathematics to the EAST INDIA COMPANY. His translation of John NAPIER's *Mirifici logarithmorum canonis descriptio* was posthumously published as *A Description of the Admirable Table of Logarithms* in 1618.

*DNB; DSB.*

**WÜRTTEMBERG CONFESSION**, a Protestant confession of faith in 35 articles compiled by Johannes BRENZ for presentation to the COUNCIL OF TRENT in 1552. It is loosely modelled on the AUGSBURG CONFESSION, and in doctrine is diplomatically Lutheran; its theological formulations seek to accommodate the CALVINIST view on several key doctrines, but in its language it is conciliatory towards Catholic statements of doctrine. Many elements in the Württemberg Confession were absorbed into the Thirty-Nine ARTICLES.

**WYATT, SIR THOMAS** (1503–42), English poet. Educated at Cambridge, Wyatt served HENRY VIII as diplomat, ambassador, and in other offices. He was arrested and imprisoned during ANNE BOLEYN's fall from favour in 1536, but later released, becoming ambassador to CHARLES V the following year. In 1541 he was arrested again, and accused of ambassadorial misconduct, but again released. A selection of his poems first appeared in print in TOTTEL's *Miscellany* (1557), where their Italianate metre was altered to the conventional iambic; others remained in manuscript until the nineteenth and twentieth centuries. With SURREY, Wyatt developed the English form of the sonnet, contributing the final rhyming couplet to the form; other poems develop the English lyric tradition.

*DNB.*

**WYCLIFFE, JOHN** (*c.*1328–1384), English reformer. Educated at Oxford where he lived until the last years of his life, Wycliffe was a fellow of Merton College (1356), master of Balliol (1360), and warden of Canterbury Hall (1365–7). He served the government as propagandist and diplomatic messenger and later received protection for his controversial writings. Published from the mid-1360s, these offered various attacks on church doctrine. Wycliffe argued that the Bible provided the sole authority for religious doctrine, that clergy not in a state of grace could be removed from office, and that the pope's authority had little scriptural basis; he also attacked the doctrine of transubstantiation as encouraging superstition. Although these teachings, combined with a call for church reform, gained him followers, Wycliffe was forced to leave Oxford after his attack on the eucharist. His writings were condemned by the Church, but inspired later groups, including the LOLLARDS and Czech reformers, notably Jan HUS.

*DNB.*

**WYNGAERDE, ANTHONIS VAN DEN** (*c.*1525–1571), Flemish painter, draughtsman, and etcher who travelled throughout the Netherlands and in England, France, Italy, and Spain. In the course of his travels he made many topographical drawings, of which the principal collections are in Antwerp (Plantin-Moretus Museum), London (Victoria and Albert Museum), Oxford (Ashmolean Museum), and Vienna (Österreichische Nationalbibliothek). The largest drawings are those of Spain, made when PHILIP II commissioned Wyngaerde to draw all the principal towns and cities in the country; more than 60 of these Spanish topographical drawings survive.

*The Panorama of London circa 1544 by Anthonis van den Wyngaerde,* ed. Howard Colvin and Susan Foister (1996); Richard Kagan (ed.), *Spanish Cities of the Golden Age: The Views of Anton van den Wyngaerde* (1989).

**WYTTENBACH, THOMAS** (1472–1526), Swiss humanist and reformer. He was born in Biel (Swiss Confederation) and studied at Tübingen; he subsequently taught at Basel, where ZWINGLI became one of his pupils. At Basel Wyttenbach became interested in the BIBLICAL scholarship of the HUMANISTS, and on returning to Biel became embroiled in ecclesiastical disputes. He became pastor at Biel in 1515, and in 1523 declared his support for the REFORMATION. His marriage in 1524 led to his deposition. On his death Biel was still not fully committed to the Reformation, which was finally implemented by Jakob Würben, Wyttenbach's successor.

# X

**XANTO AVELLI, FRANCESCO.** See AVELLI, FRANCESCO XANTO.

**XAVIER, FRANCIS or Francisco de** (1506–52), Basque Jesuit missionary, born on 7 April 1506 in the Castle of Xavier (Javier), near Sangüesa, in Navarre; his father, Juan de Jasso, was privy counsellor to the king of Navarre, and his mother, Maria de Azpilcueta y Xavier, was the sole heiress of two noble families. Francis was educated from 1524 at the University of Paris, where he became one of the six disciples of his fellow Basque IGNATIUS LOYOLA. The seven students took their vows together at Montmartre on 15 August 1534 and met again in 1537 in Venice, where they were ordained as priests. Unable to proceed to Palestine because of the outbreak of hostilities between Venice and the Ottomans, they went to Rome, determined to start a new religious ORDER. In 1540 the JESUIT Order was approved by Pope PAUL III, and set about its task of establishing foreign missions. Francis joined Simão Rodrigues (a Portuguese Jesuit) in Lisbon, and on 7 April 1541, at the invitation of King JOHN III, they sailed for Goa with the intention of evangelizing Asia, to which Francis had been appointed apostolic nuncio. Francis chose to live among the sailors, endeavouring to renew their spiritual lives. The voyage was broken for five months in Mozambique, and Francis finally reached Goa on 6 May 1542, after a journey of thirteen months.

Francis established his mission base in Goa, where he determined to reform the lapsed Portuguese Catholics, who kept mistresses and slaves, spurned the poor, and neglected their religious obligations. After five months in Goa, Francis travelled to Kerala, where he evangelized the Paravas, a tribe of pearl fishers who had repudiated Christianity; after fifteen months he returned to Goa having accomplished his mission —the Paravas are still Catholics. Francis then travelled to Ceylon (now Sri Lanka) and to Mylapore (now a coastal suburb of Madras), the traditional burial site of St Thomas; he arrived at Mylapore (Portuguese São Tomé) in April 1544, and remained for four months. He sailed to Malacca, arriving on 25 September 1544, but his visit was not a success. While in Malacca he wrote to King John of Portugal urging him to establish the INQUISITION in Goa with a view to suppressing the JEWS; the tribunal was eventually established in 1560.

Francis sailed on to Amboina and the Moluccas (now Indonesian Ambon and Maluku) before returning to Malacca in July 1547. The story of how Francis saved the city from a naval attack by the Achinese sultan of Pedir (on the north coast of Sumatra) is a hagiographical legend.

In 1549 Francis travelled to Japan, arriving in Kagoshima (Kyushu) on 15 August 1549; in the course of his year in Kagoshima he made 150 converts, but his aggressive evangelism and intolerance of Buddhism offended the daimyo of Satsuma, who forbade his subjects to convert to Christianity on pain of death. Francis moved on to Hirado (then a Portuguese outpost), where he conducted 100 baptisms in a few days, and then travelled on to Yamaguchi (where he made no converts) and thence to Kyoto. The winter journey across Chugoku-sanchi was undertaken on foot, and Francis and his companion Fernández suffered terribly. When they finally arrived in Kyoto, which had never before been visited by a European, they found a city reduced to ruins by civil war; neither the mikado nor the shogun would grant an audience to the two missionaries, so they reverted to preaching on the streets. Francis was an incompetent linguist, and after a fruitless fortnight trying to expound the recondite dogmas of his faith in a language of which he had no mastery, he returned to Yamaguchi. On this occasion Ouchi (the ruler of the Choshu fief of which Yamaguchi was the capital), who was skilfully wooed by Francis and Fernández, gave permission to his subjects to embrace Christianity, and the missionaries baptized 500 converts. Finally, Francis travelled to Bungo (now Bungo-Takada, on Kyushu), where he successfully cultivated Otomo, the young feudal ruler, and preached for four months before embarking for Malacca on 20 November 1551.

Francis had worked in Japan for 27 months, during which time he won some 760 converts. He had converted the first tranche of 150 (in Kagoshima) with the assistance of the bilingual Japanese Christian Yajiro (known in Portuguese as Angero or Anjiro) who had been baptized as 'Paul of the Holy Faith'. Francis left Yajiro in Kagoshima to attend to the converts, and set off to evangelize with no knowledge of Japanese. It seems scarcely credible that hundreds of conversions from Buddhism to Christianity could have been achieved by sermons preached in Portuguese or Latin to Japanese audiences who understood neither language; it seems much more likely that conversions were made at the behest of local rulers eager to enhance trading relations with the Portuguese. The mission inaugurated by Francis produced some 300,000 converts by the end of the century, but Christianity was banned by imperial decree on 27 January 1614, and most of the Christians who refused to repudiate their faith were killed at the massacre at Hara on 12 April 1638.

Francis reached Goa in February 1552, but was soon eager to depart again. On the voyage from Japan to Malacca he had conceived the plan of a diplomatic mission to China, in which he would travel in the train of Diogo Pereira, who was then captain of the *Santa Cruz*, the ship on which Francis had sailed from Japan to Malacca. In Goa Francis secured from the viceroy permission for the enterprise and the nomination of Pereira as the viceregal ambassador, and then left for Malacca on 25 April 1552. The governor of Malacca, Álvaro de Ataíde (a son of Vasco da GAMA), refused to recognize Pereira's diplomatic status, and detained Francis and Pereira. On 16 July 1552 Francis left without Pereira (who remained in detention) for Singapore, and late in August reached the island of Changhsu Shan (now held by Taiwan), which was the closest point to the Chinese mainland where Europeans were permitted to visit. There Francis died of a fever, probably on 2 December 1551.

Francis's body was taken to Malacca and thence to Goa, where it was entombed in a shrine now in the magnificent Renaissance church of Bom Jesus (built 1594–1603). His right arm was detached in 1615 and is now in the Chiesa del Gesù in Rome. The rest of his body is said to have remained incorrupt for centuries, but is now succumbing to the climate of India. Francis was beatified by Pope Paul V in 1619 and canonized by Pope Gregory XV in 1622.

G. Schurhammer, *Franz Xavier* (2 vols., 1955), English trans. as *Francis Xavier* (4 vols., 1973–82).

**XEBEC**, a type of small three-masted vessel used in the Mediterranean from the sixteenth to the nineteenth centuries. The xebec was commonly used as a corsair, and the need of the PRIVATEER to be able to travel faster than his prey was an important element in design, so the xebec had a comparatively narrow floor (i.e. the lower section of its transverse frames) to achieve speed but a comparatively wide beam that would sustain a large area of sail; the rigs of the xebec varied with the wind. When sailing as corsairs xebecs carried crews of several hundred men and were armed with up to 24 guns.

**XIMÉNEZ DE CISNEROS, CARDINAL FRANCISCO**. See CISNEROS, CARDINAL FRANCISCO JIMÉNEZ DE.

**XYLANDER, WILHELM** (1532–76), German classical philologist. He was born in Augsburg and studied in Heidelberg, where he was professor of Greek 1558–76. He edited several ancient mathematical texts, and in 1552 published the first translation of EUCLID into German.

*ADB.*

# Y

**YÁÑEZ DE LA ALMEDINA, FERNANDO** (*fl.* 1506–31), Spanish painter who collaborated with Fernando de Llanos (*fl.* 1506–16) on twelve panels depicting *The Life of the Virgin Mary* on the ALTARPIECE of Valencia Cathedral. The style of the paintings is the basis for the suggestion that one of these Fernandos is the 'Ferrando Spagnolo' who was working with LEONARDO in 1505 on his painting of the battle of ANGHIARI. The two painters separated in 1513, and the last reference to Yáñez is to work being undertaken in 1526 on the altarpiece of Cuenca Cathedral.

MDA s.v. Llanos and Yáñez; P. M. Ibáñez Martínez, *Fernando Yáñez de Almedina* (1999).

**YONGE, NICOLAS** (d. 1619), English musician, editor, and singer in London where he sang at St Paul's Cathedral (1594–1618). Inspired by Phalèse's three madrigal anthologies of 1583 and 1585, he edited two anthologies of Italian madrigals (*Musica transalpina*) which were published with English texts in 1588 and 1597. These collections reflect the popularity of the Italian madrigal and were to influence the English madrigalists.

**YSENBRANDT, ADRIAEN** (d. 1551), Flemish painter. He worked in Bruges, where he was admitted to the guild as a master in 1510. He was a pupil of Gérard DAVID, and the pictures that have been attributed to Ysenbrandt, such as *Mary Magdalene in a Landscape* (National Gallery, London), are painted in the style of David and in some cases imitate works by David.

MDA.

# Z

**ZABARELLA, GIACOMO or Jacopo** (1533–89), Italian Aristotelian philosopher and logician, born in Padua, where he was educated at the university and remained all his life, finally becoming professor of logic and natural philosophy; he was also an influential member of the Accademia degli Stabili. His writings include commentaries on Aristotle and treatises on logic (*Opera logica*, 1578; *Tabulae logicae*, 1580) and natural philosophy (*De naturalis scientiae constitutione*, 1586; *De rebus naturalibus*, 1590).

  Heikki Mikkeli, *An Aristotelian Response to Renaissance Humanism: Giacomo Zabarella on the Nature of the Arts and Sciences* (1992); A. Poppi, *La dottrina della scienza in Giacomo Zabarella* (1972).

**ZACCARIA, ANTONIO MARIA** (1502–39), founder of the BARNABITES. He was born in Cremona and studied MEDICINE at the University of Padua. He subsequently practised medicine among the poor of Cremona, where his mentor was BATTISTA DA CREMA. He was ordained as a priest in 1528, and in 1530 he was appointed chaplain to Ludovica TORELLI in Milan, who assisted Zaccaria in the foundation of the Barnabite Order. He conducted religious missions in Milan and Vicenza, and died in Cremona. After his death he became the object of an unofficial cult, and he was canonized in 1897.

  G. Chastel, *Saint Antoine-Marie Zaccaria, Barnabite* (1930).

**ZACCONI, LUDOVICO** (1555–1627), Italian musical theorist in Pesaro, San Severino Marche, and Venice, where he studied counterpoint with Andrea GABRIELI. He supplemented his income as a priest by playing harpsichord, lute, and viola da gamba, and singing. In 1585 he was employed as a singer by Archduke Karl of Austria in Graz and in 1590 in Munich by Duke Wilhelm V of Bavaria. Despite an incomplete musical training, he wrote the *Prattica di musica* (1585). This treatise covers mensural notation and acceptable ways of decorating a vocal melodic line.

**ZACUTO OF SALAMANCA or (Hebrew) Abraham ben Shmuel Zacuth** (*c*.1450–*c*.1515), Spanish astronomer, mathematician, and historian, born into a Jewish family in Salamanca, where he studied and afterwards worked at the university. In the 1470s Zacuto wrote an astronomical treatise, *Ha-Hibbur Ha-Gadol*, which was later translated into Latin and Spanish. He later compiled a set of astronomical tables, copies of which COLUMBUS carried on his voyages. When the JEWS were expelled from Spain in 1492, Zacuto sought refuge in Portugal, where he advised Vasco da GAMA on the use of astronomical instruments. When the Jews were expelled from Portugal in 1497, he sought refuge in Tunis, where he wrote *Sefer Yohasin*, a history of the world. He died in Damascus.

  DSB; JNB.

**ZAINER, GÜNTHER** (d. 1478), German printer, born in Reutlingen; he was probably the brother of Johann ZAINER. He seems to have been trained in the workshop of Johann MENTELIN in Strassburg, and in 1468 he established the first printing workshop in Augsburg. His publications include the first illustrated Bible (1475), the first printed edition of the *De imitatione Christi* of THOMAS À KEMPIS, and an edition of the thirteenth-century *Golden Legend* (*Lombardica historia*) of the Genoese hagiographer Jacobus de Voragine in which the lives of the saints are illustrated with 231 woodcuts.

**ZAINER, JOHANN** (d. *c*.1500), German printer, born in Reutlingen; he was probably the brother of Günther ZAINER. In the early 1470s Zainer moved to Ulm, where he established a printing workshop that specialized in illustrated books. In 1476 he published the first edition of Aesop's *Fables* in German.

**ZAMORA, ALFONSO DE** (1474–1531), Spanish Hebraist. He was born into a Jewish family and given a rabbinical education, but converted to Christianity in 1506 and was appointed as the founding professor of HEBREW at Salamanca University. He wrote a Hebrew grammar and a Hebrew dictionary, and was engaged by Cardinal CISNEROS to edit the Hebrew texts of the COMPLUTENSIAN POLYGLOT. He also published an open letter to Spanish Jews urging them to convert to Christianity.

**ZAMOYSKI, JAN** (1542–1605), Polish statesman. He was educated in Padua and Paris, and on returning to Poland in 1565 was appointed as secretary to King SIGISMUND II. He subsequently supported the election of Henry of Valois (later HENRI III of France) as king of Poland (1573); after Henry's departure and deposition, Zamoyski supported the candidacy of STEFAN BÁTORY (1575). He commanded the Polish army in the war with Russia and in 1587 secured the election of SIGISMUND III as king of Poland. When Sigismund began to negotiate with the HABSBURGS over the Polish succession, Zamoyski led a rebellion of noblemen in defence of the elective monarchy.

The Italianate town of Zamość (see POLISH ARCHITECTURE) was commissioned by Jan Zamoyski.

**ZANCHI, GIROLAMO** (1516–90), Italian Protestant reformer, born near Brescia. He entered the Augustinian Order, and in 1531 was sent to Lucca, where he met Pietro Martire VERMIGLI and began to read BULLINGER and CALVIN. He fled Italy in 1551, first visiting Calvin in Geneva and then settling in Strassburg, where he was appointed professor of biblical exegesis in 1553. In 1561 Zanchi became involved in a theological debate about the EUCHARIST (he was an advocate of the Calvinist position) and in consequence left in 1563 for a post at Chiavenna. In 1568 he was appointed professor of dogmatics at the University of Heidelberg, but when Lutheranism was imposed on the Palatinate in 1568, he left for Neustadt. His most important publication was a theological treatise, *De religione christiana* (Neustadt, 1585; English translation, 1599), which set out his position on predestination.

C. J. Burchill, 'Girolamo Zanchi: Portrait of a Reformed Theologian and his Work', *Sixteenth Century Journal*, 15 (1984).

**ZANOTTI, CAMILLO** (c.1545–1591), Italian composer who was *maestro di cappella* at Cesena Cathedral and vice-*Kapellmeister* to the Habsburg Emperor RUDOLF II in Prague. He wrote madrigals and masses dedicated to his imperial patron.

**ZÁPOLYA, JÁNOS** (1487–1540), king of Hungary, born into a noble Hungarian family. He became a soldier, in which capacity he successfully crushed the rebellion of György DÓZSA (1514) but failed to defend Belgrade against the Ottoman onslaught (1521). In 1526 he was censured for failing to relieve the Hungarian forces at the battle of MOHÁCS, at which King LOUIS II was killed. In the ensuing struggle for the succession, both Zápolya and Archduke FERDINAND (brother of the emperor) secured the support of sections of the nobility, and they became rival kings. In 1528 Zápolya formed an alliance with the Ottomans against Ferdinand and so was able to hold part of the country. In 1538 conditions for peace were agreed in the Treaty of Nagyvarad (now Oradea), in which Zápolya conceded that Ferdinand would be his heir. He swiftly repudiated this agreement, naming his infant son János Sigismund Zápolya as his successor and guaranteeing the succession by placing him under Ottoman protection.

**ZÁRATE, AGUSTÍN DE** (c.1506–c.1565), historian of Peru who served as secretary to the Council of Castile for at least fifteen years before being sent by CHARLES V to Peru as a royal accountant. He witnessed the rebellion of Gonzalo PIZARRO, but remained loyal to the emperor, and included an account of what he saw in his history of the fall of the Inca empire,

*Historia del descubrimiento y conquista del Perú*, which was first published in Antwerp in 1555 and subsequently republished in Seville and Venice. The first English translation appeared in 1581.

**ZARLINO, GIOSEFFE** (1517–90), Franciscan music theorist and composer who was a singer and organist at Chioggia Cathedral. He studed counterpoint with WILLAERT in Venice from 1541 and succeeded RORE as *maestro di cappella* at San Marco in 1565. His pupils included Claudio MERULO, Giovanni CROCE, and Vincenzo GALILEI. His theoretical *Le istitutioni harmoniche* (1558) is concerned with a philosophical and mathematical approach to music, and covers both ancient Greek and contemporary methods of tuning; together with Heinrich GLAREAN's *Dodecachordon* (1547), it is one of the most important sixteenth-century music treatises.

**ZASIUS or** (German) **Zäsy, ULRICH** (1461–1536), German humanist and jurist, born in Konstanz, where he worked as an ecclesiastical notary. In 1494 he moved to Freiburg, where he was headmaster of the grammar school, town clerk, and (from 1506) professor of law at the university; his students included Johann ECK. In the course of his career Zasius became the most important early humanist jurist in the German lands, and enjoyed a standing comparable to that of Guillaume BUDÉ in France. His publications include his 'nocturnal studies' (*Lucubraciones*, 1518) and a study of the JUSTINIAN Pandects (*In titulos aliquot Pandectarum*, 1543).

**ZEINER, LUCAS** (*fl.* 1479–1512), Swiss glass stainer in Zürich who specialized in small glass panels with heraldic designs. The intricate detail of his designs was achieved by using a quill to scratch the thin layer of coloured glass that covered the clear glass below.

**ZEITBLOM, BARTHOLOMAUS** (c.1460–c.1520), German painter. He was born in Nördlingen, and may have been a pupil of Martin SCHONGAUER before settling in Ulm (c.1482), where he supplied large ALTARPIECES painted in a Gothic idiom to various towns in Swabia. The lyrical element in his work attracted the enthusiasm of nineteenth-century German Romantics, who described Zeitblom as the 'German Perugino' and even the 'German Leonardo'.

*MDA.*

**ZELL, MATTHÄUS** (1477–1548) and **KATHARINA** (c.1497–1562), German reformers. Matthäus Zell was educated in Freiburg, where in 1511 he became a professor of theology and in 1517 became rector. In 1518 he moved to Strassburg as a priest and penitentiary (i.e. a priest with special responsibility for matters of penance), and in 1521 converted to Protestantism. In 1523 he married Katharina Schütz, defending his decision to marry in *Appelatio sacerdotum maritorum* (1524). He was the most popular preacher of his generation in Strassburg.

Katharina Zell was a reformer in her own right. She organized the care of religious refugees who arrived in Strassburg in large numbers, wrote on theological issues (including her marriage to a priest), and corresponded with reformers such as LUTHER and Ambrosius BLARER.

**ZELL, ULRICH** (d. 1507), German printer who established the first printing workshop in Cologne in 1464. In the course of his career he printed more than 200 titles, mostly works of theology published for the benefit of members of Cologne University. His edition of the *Cologne Chronicle* (1499) contains an account of the invention of printing in which he claims that GUTENBERG was anticipated in his use of movable type by printers in Haarlem.

**ZENALE, BERNARDINO** (*c.*1464–1526), Italian painter, born in Treviglio (near Bergamo), where he collaborated with his fellow citizen Bernardino Butinone (*c.*1450–*c.*1507) on the polyptych for the cathedral. They also worked together on a fresco cycle depicting *The Life of St Ambrose* for the Church of San Pietro in Gessate in Milan. Near the end of his life Zenale wrote a treatise on PERSPECTIVE, but it was not published and no manuscript copy is known to survive.
    *MDA.*

**ZIMARA, MARCANTONIO** (*c.*1460–1532), Italian philosopher. He was born in San Pietro in Galatina (Lecce) and from 1497 studied philosophy at Padua under Agostino NIFO and POMPONAZZI. He subsequently taught logic while studying medicine at Padua (1501–5), and in 1509 was appointed professor of natural philosophy. From 1509 to 1518 he lived in San Pietro in Galatina, after which he taught in Salerno (1518–22), Naples (1522–3), and again at Padua (1525–8).

Zimara edited works by medieval philosophers (notably Albertus Magnus) and edited and wrote commentaries on Aristotle and AVERROËS. His *Tabula dilucidationum in dictis Aristotelis et Averrois* (1537), which long remained in print, became the principal scholarly tool for searching the works of Aristotle and Averroës.

**ZIMBELSTERN**, a toy organ-stop used in north European organs in the sixteenth and seventeenth centuries. It consisted of a revolving star with bells attached, and was driven by a pneumatically powered wheel behind the case, which was mounted on or near the top of the organ. There is a Zimbelstern on the organ in the chapel of St John's College, Cambridge.

**ŽIŽKA, JAN** (1376–1424), Bohemian soldier. He fought against the TEUTONIC knights and in 1410 lost an eye in the battle of Tannenberg (now Polish Stębark). On returning to Prague he became a follower of Jan HUS, and *c.*1420 became leader of the TABORITES. By 1421 he had become completely blind, but he nonetheless continued to lead his army to a series of victories against the forces of the Emperor SIGISMUND. In 1423 he defeated the UTRAQUISTS and so for a time unified the Hussites. He then invaded Moravia, but died of plague before his conquest had been completed.
    F. G. Heymann, *John Zizka and the Hussite Revolution* (1955).

**ZOOLOGY**. The study of animals in Renaissance Europe inherited the taxonomies of classical antiquity (principally those of the *Historia animalium* of Aristotle and the *Historia naturalis* of PLINY THE ELDER) and the medieval bestiary tradition (which had a pronounced moral element). Zoological description was characterized by exhaustive accounts of physical characteristics, but also included extended accounts of folklore associated with each animal. The most original aspect of Renaissance zoology was the exploration of embryology, of which the most distinguished student was FABRICI (*De formato foetu*, 1600). Of the descriptive zoologists, the most important were ALDROVANDI and GESNER.

**ZOPPO, MARCO** (1432–78), Italian painter and draughtsman, born near Bologna and trained in the workshop of SQUARCIONE in Padua. Zoppo pursued his career in Venice (1455 and 1468–73) and in Bologna, where he painted a triptych for the Collegio di Spagna. Fragments of his altarpiece for the Church of San Giustina in Venice (1468) survive in the National Gallery in London (*St Augustine*) and the Ashmolean Museum in Oxford (*St Paul*). A large collection of his drawings is preserved in the British Museum
    *MDA*; Berenice Vigi (ed.), *Marco Zoppo e il suo tempore* (1993); Hugh Chapman, *Padua in the 1450s: Marco Zoppo and his Contemporaries* (1998).

**ZUCCARO or Zuccari, FEDERICO** (*c.*1540–1609), Italian painter and art theorist and the younger brother of Taddeo ZUCCARO, born in Vado (near Urbino) and trained in his brother's studio in Rome. He lived for a time in Venice, where he painted the fresco of *Barbarossa Kissing the Foot of the Pope* (1582) in the Palazzo Ducale. He returned to Rome in 1566, and on the death of his brother in the same year assumed control of the studio and of Taddeo's unfinished commissions, including the decoration of the Villa FARNESE in Caprarola, the Farnese Palace in Rome, and the Sala Regia in the Vatican.

In 1573 or 1574 Zuccaro travelled to England, where he drew Queen Elizabeth and the earl of Leicester (both drawings are in the British Museum) and is said to have painted portraits of the queen and members of her court, all of which are now lost. He later travelled and painted in Venice, Loreto, and Rome before accepting the invitation of PHILIP II of Spain to the ESCORIAL, where he painted several ALTARPIECES (1585–8). He returned to Rome and became the founding president of the Accademia di San Luca, to which he later donated his house. In 1607 he published a theoretical treatise entitled *L'idea de' pittori, scultori ed architetti*.
    *MDA*; E. James Mundy, *Renaissance into Baroque: Italian Master Drawings by the Zuccari, 1550–1600* (1989); Michael Brunner (ed.), *Federico Zuccaro: Kunst zwischen Ideal und Reform* (2000).

**ZUCCARO or Zuccari, TADDEO** (1529–66), Italian painter, born in Vado (near Urbino). In 1551 he moved to Rome, where he decorated the Cappella Mattei (completed 1556) in the Church of Santa Maria della Consolazione. He became an exponent of history painting, which he produced in his large studio; his apprentices included his younger brother Federico ZUCARO. Taddeo's commissions included the decoration of the Villa FARNESE in Caprarola, the Farnese

Palace in Rome, and the Sala Regia in the Vatican; all three were completed by his brother after his death.

Zuccaro was the most important artist to have made designs for ISTORIATO wares. VASARI records that Zuccaro designed the table-service commissioned by Guidobaldo II della Rovere, duke of Urbino, for presentation to King PHILIP II of Spain; the designs, which depict scenes from the life of Julius Caesar, were executed in MAIOLICA, apparently at the FONTANA factory in Urbino, and some of the plates survive in museums, including the Bargello in Florence.

MDA; John Gere, *Taddeo Zuccaro: His Development Studied in his Drawings* (1969); E. James Mundy, *Renaissance into Baroque: Italian Master Drawings by the Zuccari, 1550–1600* (1989).

**ZUICHEMUS or Viglius d'Aytta de Zuichem** (1507–77), Flemish jurist, successor of ALCIATO at Bourges. He became president of the Council of Justice (the Groot Raad) in the Netherlands and adviser to the regent, Margaret of Parma. He prepared the first edition of the paraphrase of the JUSTINIAN *Institutes* written in 534 by Theophilus, a professor of law at Constantinople. He also wrote *De institutione iurisconsulti* (1530) and a study of part of the Justinian *Digest* entitled *Praelectiones in titulum Pandectarum de rebus creditis* (1582).

BNB, s.v. Aytta de Zuichem; NBW viii, s.v. Viglius Zuichemus ab Aytta.

**ZUMÁRRAGA, JUAN DE** (*c*.1475/6–1548), archbishop and inquisitor in Mexico. He was born into a Spanish family in Vizcaíno (Baja California) and entered the Franciscan Order, rising to become provincial of Concepción in 1520. In 1527 CHARLES V appointed him as the first bishop of Mexico, in which capacity Zumárraga organized parishes, encouraged the conversion of the Indians, and (in 1531) dedicated the shrine of Our Lady of Guadalupe, which was to become the national shrine of Mexico.

Zumárraga quarrelled with the civil authorities and placed them under an interdict, as a result of which he was recalled to Spain in 1532. He returned to Mexico in 1534, and instituted a series of schools designed to educate the sons of the Aztec nobility. He served as inquisitor from 1536 to 1543, and in this capacity destroyed many Aztec temples. He was created archbishop in 1547.

DHE; R. E. Greenleaf, *Zumárraga and the Mexican Inquisition, 1536–43* (1961); Fernando Gil, *Primeras 'doctrinas' del Nuevo Mundo: Estudio de fray Juan de Zumárraga* (1993).

**ZÜNDT, MATHIAS** (*c*.1498–1572), German goldsmith, etcher, and draughtsman who trained in the JAMNITZER workshop in Nuremberg and subsequently worked in Prague. None of his work is known to survive, but many of his engraved designs for jewellery and silver were implemented by other artisans. His etchings, which were published between 1565 and 1571, include maps, battlepieces, and portraits.

MDA.

**ZURARA or Azurara, GOMES EANES DE** (1410/20–1473/4), Portuguese historian who succeeded Fernão LOPES as royal chronicler in 1454. His *Crónica da tomada de Ceuta* is a continuation of his predecessor's account of the reign of King JOHN I, and records the conquest of Ceuta, on the north coast of AFRICA, in 1415. His *Crónica do descobrimento e conquista de Guiné* was the first account of the Portuguese exploration of the West African coast, and initiated the historiographical tradition that attributes the success of the early voyages to the guiding hand of Prince HENRY THE NAVIGATOR.

DHP; E. Prestage, *The Chronicles of Fernão Lopes and Gomes Eanes de Zurara* (1928).

**ZÜRICH or (French) Zurich or (Italian) Zurigo**, a city and canton in the SWISS CONFEDERATION. The canton grew steadily from the fourteenth to the sixteenth century as the city of Zürich acquired the southern part of the Zürich-See (1362) and the towns of Küsnacht (1384), Thalwil (1385), Erlenbach (1400), Greifensee (1402), Horgen (1406), Grüningen (1408), Stäfa (1408), Bülach (1409), Regensberg (1409), Wald (1425), Kyburg (1452), Winterthur (purchased from the HABSBURGS in 1467), Eglisau (1496), Stein (1498), Konau (1512), and Wädenswil (1549). The modern canton does not include Stein (which joined Thurgau in 1798), but does include the lower Stammheim valley (added 1798) and Rheinau (added 1803). This process of acquisition precipitated the first civil war in the Confederation, the 'Old Zürich War' of 1436–50.

The city of Zürich had become a member of the Swiss Confederation in 1491, but nonetheless remained a free imperial city. This dual allegiance created tensions that were not resolved until 1400, when the city received from the Emperor WENCESLAS the *Reichsvogtei*, which gave it immunity from imperial prosecution and its own criminal jurisdiction. In the course of the fifteenth century civic power gradually passed into the hands of the guilds, and towards the end of the century Hans Waldmann, leader of the Swiss Confederation in its victory against CHARLES THE BOLD and burgomaster of Zürich from 1483 to 1489, introduced financial and administrative reforms that laid the foundations for the commercial prosperity of Zürich. Under Waldmann's rule, Zürich became the unofficial capital of the Confederation. Waldmann's reforms excited opposition, and he was deposed and executed, but the constitution of 1498, which remained in force till 1798, was an embodiment of his ideas and ideals.

In 1519 ZWINGLI inaugurated the Reformation in Zürich, and in the course of the next five years Zürich changed from a loyal Catholic canton to a Protestant stronghold in which Catholic practices were prohibited. As the Reformation spread to other cantons, Zürich soon complemented its commercial supremacy by becoming the leader of the Protestant cantons. On Zwingli's death in 1531, he was succeeded by BULLINGER, who welcomed religious refugees from all over Europe and established Zürich as a European centre of Protestantism, the Zwinglian rival to the Calvinist stronghold of Geneva.

**ZÜRICH AGREEMENT or (Latin) Consensus Tigurinus**, a statement of faith agreed in May 1549 by the French Protestants of Geneva and the SWISS CONFEDERATION (represented by CALVIN and Guillaume FAREL) and the German Protestants of the Swiss Confederation (represented by Heinrich BULLINGER, who was ZWINGLI's successor at Zürich). The 26 articles of the Agreement were mainly concerned with the doctrine of the EUCHARIST, articulating Calvin's virtualism in a way that permitted the Zwinglian party to agree without compromising their memorialist position. The agreement brought the Calvinists and the Zwinglians closer together, but drove the Calvinists and the Lutherans further apart.

**ZURITA, JERÓNIMO DE** (1512–80), Spanish historian, born in Zaragoza and educated at Alcalá de Henares, where his teachers included Fernando NÚÑEZ DE TOLEDO. His father Miguel was a physician at the court of CHARLES V, and through his father's influence Zurita became a magistrate at Barbastro and in 1537 was appointed as an assistant secretary to the INQUISITION.

In 1548 Zurita was appointed as official chronicler of Aragon, the duties of which he fulfilled with his *Anales de la corona de Aragón* (6 vols., Zaragoza, 1562–80; index, 1604), which chronicles the history of Aragón from the Arab invasion to 1516. His task was not yet completed when PHILIP II appointed him as secretary to the Council of the Inquisition in 1566 with particular responsibility for matters requiring the king's signature. Progress on the *Anales* was inevitably slowed, and on 21 January 1571 Zurita resigned his post and obtained a sinecure in Zaragoza which would enable him to complete his chronicle. The final volume was printed on 22 April 1580, and Zurita died six months later, on 3 November 1580. His successor was the poet and historian Bartolomé Leonardo de ARGENSOLA, who carried the narrative from 1516 to 1520; his final volume, which extended to 1525, was published by Francisco Diego de Sayas in 1667.

Zurita was a workmanlike prose stylist, but he is, together with Ambrosio de MORALES, one of the founding fathers of Spanish historical scholarship. His *Anales* were grounded in archival research, not only in Zaragoza, but as far afield as Rome, Naples, and Sicily. He ignored the usual convention of beginning with the creation of the world, instead using the wholly historical Arab invasion as his starting point. He also exercised historical judgement, reconciling conflicting evidence and tracing the origins of events to natural causes rather than supernatural interventions. Part of Zurita's private library is now in the ESCORIAL.

A. Canellas, *Fuentes de Zurita* (1974).

**ZUTPHEN, BATTLE OF.** On 22 September 1586 the Spanish forces commanded by Alessandro FARNESE engaged the 6,000 English troops under the command of the earl of LEICESTER, who had been besieging the town of Zutphen in the Dutch province of Gelderland. The battle was indecisive, but is remembered because of the death of Sir Philip SIDNEY. The city fell to the Spaniards the following year, but was recaptured by the army of MAURICE OF NASSAU in 1591.

**ZWICK, JOHANNES** (*c.*1496–1542), Swiss-German Protestant reformer. He was born into a patrician family in Constance and studied law at Freiburg and Siena, where he finished his doctorate in CIVIL LAW and CANON LAW in 1520. He

briefly converted to Lutheranism, but by 1522 had joined ZWINGLI in Zürich. He was ordained and was appointed priest at Riedlingen, and in 1527 became a minister in Constance, where he worked with Ambrosius BLARER. After Blaurer's departure in 1531, Zwick became the religious leader of Constance. In 1542 he accepted an invitation to become a preacher in Bischofszell (Thurgau), but he died of the plague shortly after his arrival.

Zwick was an educator and a composer of hymns (seventeen of which were printed in the *Neue Gesangbuch* of 1540) and the reforms that he introduced were implemented in southern Germany as well as in the Evangelical Swiss Cantons. His younger brother Konrad (d. 1557) was also an influential reformer.

**ZWICKAU PROPHETS**, an ANABAPTIST group which attempted to establish a community of the godly elect in Zwickau (Saxony). During his stay in Zwickau Thomas MÜNTZER was in close contact with the group, but how far they influenced each other theologically remains uncertain. The Prophets claimed direct and immediate divine inspiration for their rejection of traditional doctrines and practices, including infant BAPTISM. On 27 December 1521 three of the Prophets—Thomas Drechsel, Nicholas STORCH, and Mark Thoma (called Stübner because his father owned a bathhouse in Elsterberg)—appeared in WITTENBERG, where they attracted the sympathetic attention of KARLSTADT and Nicholas von AMSDORF and the reluctant tolerance of MELANCHTHON.

**ZWILLING, GABRIEL** (*c.*1487–1558), surnamed Didymus (Greek; 'twin'), German reformer. He was born near Annaberg and studied at Prague and Wittenberg, where he lived in the Augustinian monastery and there met LUTHER. He embraced the Reformation, and served as Luther's deputy when Luther was absent at his retreat in the Wartburg in 1521. He worked with KARLSTADT to introduce radical reforms which led in January 1522 to riots provoked by their advocacy of iconoclasm. On Luther's return, Zwilling's reforms were reversed. He later served as pastor of the church in Torgau.

*ADB* s.v. Gabriel Didymus.

**ZWINGLI, ULRICH or Huldrych** (1484–1531), Swiss Reformation leader, born in Wildhaus (in the Toggenburg valley in St Gallen) on 1 January 1484, the son of a peasant who had become the clerk (*Amtmann*) of his village and his wife Margaret Meili, the sister of the abbot of Fischingen in Thurgau. He was educated at schools in Wesen and Basel and Bern and at the universities of Vienna and Basel. On graduating in 1506 from Basel, where he had studied under Thomas WYTTENBACH, Zwingli was ordained as a priest and appointed as parish priest of Glarus; his appointment was opposed by Heinrich Goldi, a Zürich priest (and pluralist) who had been nominated by Pope JULIUS II, but Zwingli secured his post by bribing Goldi, and remained in his post at Glarus until 1516.

At Glarus Zwingli learnt Greek and immersed himself in HUMANIST scholarship, especially the work of ERASMUS and PICO DELLA MIRANDOLA. In 1513 and 1514 he served as a military chaplain to Swiss mercenaries in Italy, and was present at the battle of MARIGNANO. In 1516 Zwingli left Glarus to become parish priest at Einsiedeln, where he remained until 1518; Einsiedeln was a pilgrimage centre and the site of an important Benedictine abbey, and during his years there Zwingli became discontented by the ecclesiastical abuses at the shrine.

On 11 December 1518 Zwingli was elected as stipendiary priest (*Leutpriester*) in the Old Minster at Zürich, where he was to remain for the rest of his life. His sermons on the New Testament in 1519 mark the beginning of the REFORMATION in the SWISS CONFEDERATION. In the course of the next three years, Zwingli used his pulpit to inveigh against the monastic ORDERS, fasting, the invocation of saints, and the doctrine of PURGATORY. In April 1522 he published his first Reformation tract, *Von Erkiesen und Freiheit der Speisen*, which defended those who had eaten meat during Lent against an attack mounted by the monasteries and the bishop of Konstanz. A few months later, on 22 August, he published *Architeles*, which advocated freedom for believers from the control of bishops and the papacy.

The break with Rome was precipitated by the issue of priestly celibacy. Zwingli was one of the signatories of a letter to the bishop of Konstanz asking him to countenance a married clergy on the grounds that chastity was unnatural and that the signatories were in any case already married in the eyes of God. Pope ADRIAN VI reacted by asking the council of Zürich to repudiate Zwingli, who in turn managed to persuade the council that the dispute should be settled by a public disputation, which was held on 20 January 1523 before an audience of 600, including the council. Zwingli introduced and successfully upheld 67 theses against the papal disputant, Johann FABER (the vicar-general of the bishop of Konstanz). The council adopted the theses and reconstituted the Minster chapter independent of episcopal control. A second disputation, held on 26 October 1523, provided the material for Zwingli's treatise for clergy on the gospel and the law, *Eine kurze christliche Einleitung*. In the months that followed the mass was abolished (though not formally suppressed until April 1525), pictures and statues were removed from the churches of Zürich, and daily meetings for prayer and Bible study (the 'Prophezey') were instituted. On 2 April 1524 Zwingli publicly celebrated his marriage to Anna Meyer

(née Reinhart) in the cathedral, so consecrating a union that was at least two years old and inaugurating a series of public professions of marriage amongst his priestly colleagues. In August of the same year he published the first of a series of pamphlets on the EUCHARIST, and so initiated a conflict with LUTHER that was never resolved: Lutheran consubstantiation could not be reconciled with Zwingli's view that the eucharist was simply a commemorative rite, and that the bread and wine were not changed in any way. Luther described Zwingli's position as SACRAMENTARIANISM; it is now known as memorialism. Attempts were made, notably at the Colloquy of MARBURG in 1529, to heal the rift between the Lutheran and Zwinglian positions, but to no avail; the eucharist remained the theological issue that was permanently to divide the reformed churches of Germany and the Swiss Confederation, and the Zwinglian Church refused to join Protestant alliances such as the SCHMALKALDIC LEAGUE.

The eucharist was the defining difference between Zwingli and Luther, but they also disagreed on other theological matters. Zwingli's Christology, as articulated in his *Responsio brevis* of 1526, proposes a separation of the divine and human natures of Christ that is much sharper than Luther's. On BAPTISM, Luther had ceased to believe in infant baptism, but Zwingli's debates with the ANABAPTISTS had led him to formulate a defence of infant baptism as the Christian successor to the Jewish circumcision of infants. Luther believed that the secular authorities had no jurisdiction over religious matters, but Zwingli defended the right of the magistracy to legislate and to judge, and so approved of the execution by drowning of an Anabaptist in 1527 at the command of the council of Zürich.

The Reformation spread from Zürich to Schaffhausen, Glarus, Appenzell, Basel, and Bern (later known as the Evangelical Swiss Cantons), but the cantons of Lucerne, Uri, Schwyz, Unterwalden, and Zug, which remained faithful to the Catholic Church, formed an alliance and attacked Zürich. They were met at nearby Kappel on 11 October 1531 by a small defensive force. Zwingli was the chaplain, and so carried the banner of Zürich, and in the course of the battle he was killed.

U. Gäbler, *Huldrych Zwingli: Eine Einfuhrung in sein Leben und sein Werk* (1983; English trans. 1987); G. W. Locher, *Huldrych Zwingli in neuer Sicht: Zehn Beiträge zur Theologie der Zürcher Reformation* (1969; English trans. 1981); id., *Die Zwinglische Reformation im Rahmen der europäische Kirchengeschichte* (1979); G. R. Potter, *Zwingli* (1975); W. P. Stephens, *The Theology of Huldrich Zwingli* (1986).

# APPENDIX 1
# TABLES OF RULING HOUSES

Individuals and dynasties in bold are the subjects of entries in the main text. Where names are listed in the main language of the ruled country or territory, rulers of more than one territory are entered under more than one form of their names and titles. Thus James VI of Scotland also appears as James I of England, Władisław II Jagiełło of Poland also appears as Jogaila of Lithuania, and Enrique III, king of Navarre, also appears as Henri IV, king of France. In cases where local names would cause confusion (e.g. Bohemia and Byzantium), forms of names familiar to readers of English are used. For full accounts of Renaissance dynasties see D. Schwennicke (ed.), *Europäische Stammtafeln* (11 vols. in 13 parts, Marburg, 1978–88); see also John Morby, *Dynasties of the World* (Oxford, 1989 and 2002).

## POPES AND ANTIPOPES
(Antipopes are in square brackets)

| | |
|---|---|
| 1303–4 | Benedict XI |
| 1305–14 | Clement V |
| 1316–34 | John XXII |
| [1328–30] | [Nicholas V] |
| 1334–42 | Benedict XII |
| 1342–52 | Clement VI |
| 1352–62 | Innocent VI |
| 1362–70 | Urban V |
| 1370–8 | Gregory XI |
| 1378–89 | Urban VI |
| [1378–94] | [Clement VII] |
| 1389–1404 | **Boniface IX** |
| [1394–1417] | **[Benedict XIII]** |
| 1404–6 | Innocent VII |
| 1406–15 | **Gregory XII** |
| [1409–10] | [Alexander V] |
| [1410–15] | **[John XXIII]** |
| 1417–31 | **Martin V** |
| [1423–9] | **[Clement VIII]** |
| [1425–?] | [Benedict XIV] |
| 1431–47 | **Eugenius IV** |
| [1439–49] | **[Felix V]** |
| 1447–55 | **Nicholas V** |
| 1455–8 | **Callistus III** |
| 1458–64 | **Pius II** |
| 1464–71 | **Paul II** |
| 1471–84 | **Sixtus IV** |
| 1484–92 | **Innocent VIII** |
| 1492–1503 | **Alexander VI** |
| 1503 | **Pius III** |
| 1503–13 | **Julius II** |
| 1513–21 | **Leo X** |

| | |
|---|---|
| 1522–3 | **Adrian VI** |
| 1523–34 | **Clement VII** |
| 1534–49 | **Paul III** |
| 1550–5 | **Julius III** |
| 1555 | **Marcellus II** |
| 1555–9 | **Paul IV** |
| 1559–65 | **Pius IV** |
| 1566–72 | **Pius V** |
| 1572–85 | **Gregory XIII** |
| 1585–90 | **Sixtus V** |
| 1590 | **Urban VII** |
| 1590–1 | **Gregory XIV** |
| 1591 | **Innocent IX** |
| 1592–1605 | **Clement VIII** |
| 1605 | Leo XI |
| 1605–21 | Paul V |
| 1621–3 | Gregory XV |
| 1623–44 | Urban VIII |

Franz Xaver Seppelt, *Geschichte der Päpste* (5 vols., Munich, 1933–9); J. N. Kelly, *A Dictionary of Popes* (Oxford, 1986 and 1996).

## AUSTRIA
### DUKES OF AUSTRIA
*House of Habsburg*

| | |
|---|---|
| 1298–1330 | Friedrich III (king of the Romans, 1314) |
| 1326–58 | Albrecht II (brother; 'Albrecht the Lame') |
| 1330–9 | Otto (brother) |
| 1358–1365 | Rudolf IV (son of Albrecht II; 'Rudolf the Founder') |

*Albertine Line (Austria)*

| | |
|---|---|
| 1365–95 | Albrecht III (brother; ruler of Austria after partition in 1379) |

| | |
|---|---|
| 1395–1404 | Albrecht IV (son; 'Albrecht the Patient') |
| 1404–39 | Albrecht V (son; king of the Romans, 1438) |
| 1440–57 | **Ladislas Posthumus** (king of Hungary, 1445) |

*Leopoldine Line (Carinthia, Styria, Tirol)*

| | |
|---|---|
| 1365–86 | Leopold III (son of Albrecht II; ruler of Tirol, Styria, and Carinthia after partition in 1379) |
| 1386–1406 | Wilhelm (son) |
| 1386–1411 | Leopold IV (brother; 'Leopold the Fat') |

*Line of Tirol (counts of Tirol)*

| | |
|---|---|
| 1406–39 | Friedrich IV (brother; ruler of Tirol after partition in 1411) |
| 1439–90 | Sigismund (son; archduke 1477; abdicated 1490) |

*Line of Styria (dukes of Styria and Carinthia)*

| | |
|---|---|
| 1406–24 | Ernst (son of Leopold III; duke from 1411; 'Ernst the Iron') |
| 1424–63 | Albrecht VI (son; archduke 1453) |
| 1424–93 | Friedrich IV (brother; king of the Romans, 1440; archduke 1453) |
| [1490] | [reunion of Habsburg territories under Maximilian, king of the Romans] |

## BOHEMIA
### KINGS OF BOHEMIA
*House of Habsburg*

| | |
|---|---|
| 1306–7 | Rudolf of Austria (married Elizabeth, widow of Wenceslas II) |

*House of Carinthia*

| | |
|---|---|
| 1307–10 | Henry (married Anne, daughter of Wenceslas II; deposed 1310) |

*House of Luxemburg*

| | |
|---|---|
| 1310–46 | John the Blind (married Elizabeth, daughter of Wenceslas II) |
| 1346–78 | Charles (son; later the Emperor Charles IV) |
| 1378–1419 | **Wenceslas IV** (son; co-regent 1363, emperor 1378–1400) |
| 1419–37 | **Sigismund** (brother; king of Hungary from 1387, king of the Romans from 1410; duke of Luxemburg from 1419) |

*House of Habsburg*

| | |
|---|---|
| 1437–9 | Albrecht of Austria (married Elizabeth, daughter of Sigismund; Emperor Albrecht II, 1438–9) |
| [1439–53] | [interregnum] |
| 1453–7 | **Ladislas Posthumus** |

*House of Poděbrady*

| | |
|---|---|
| 1458–71 | George of Poděbrady |

*House of Poland*

| | |
|---|---|
| 1471–1516 | Vladislav II (son of Casimir IV of Poland and Elizabeth, daughter of Albrecht of Austria) |
| 1516–26 | Louis (son; co-regent from 1509) |

*House of Habsburg*

| | |
|---|---|
| 1526–64 | **Ferdinand I** (married Anne, daughter of Vladislav II; emperor from 1558) |

## BYZANTIUM
### EMPERORS (CONSTANTINOPLE)
*Palaiologos Dynasty*

| | |
|---|---|
| 1259–82 | Michael VIII |
| 1282–1328 | Andronicus II (son; deposed) |
| 1294–1320 | Michael IX (son) |
| 1328–41 | Andronicus III (son) |
| 1341–76 | John V (son; deposed) |
| 1347–54 | John VI Kantakouzenos (co-emperor; deposed) |
| 1353–7 | Matthew (son; deposed) |
| 1376–9 | Andronicus IV (son of John V; co-emperor; deposed) |
| 1379–90 | John V (restored; deposed) |
| 1390 | John VII (son of Andronicus IV; co-emperor; deposed) |
| 1390–1 | John V (restored) |
| 1391–1425 | **Manuel II** |
| 1399–1408 | John VII (restored; co-emperor) |
| 1425–48 | **John VIII** (son of Manuel II) |
| 1449–53 | Constantine XI (brother) |
| [29 May 1453] | [Ottoman capture of Constantinople] |

### EMPERORS, EMPRESSES, AND GRAND KOMNENOI OF TREBIZOND

| | |
|---|---|
| 1204–22 | Alexius I (captured Trebizond 1204) |
| 1222–35 | Andronicus I Gidos (son-in-law) |
| 1235–8 | John I Axouch (son of Alexius I) |
| 1238–63 | Manuel I (brother) |
| 1263–6 | Andronicus II (son) |
| 1266–80 | George (brother; deposed) |
| 1280–4 | John II (brother; deposed) |
| 1284–5 | Theodora (sister; deposed) |
| 1285–97 | John II (restored) |
| 1297–1330 | Alexius II (son) |
| 1330–2 | Andronicus III (son) |
| 1332 | Manuel II (son; deposed) |
| 1332–40 | Basil (son of Alexius II) |
| 1340–1 | Irene Palaiologina (widow; deposed) |
| 17–30 July 1341 | Anna Anachoutlou (daughter of Alexius II; deposed) |
| 30 July–7 Aug. 1341 | Michael (son of John II; deposed) |
| 1341–2 | Anna (restored) |
| 1342–4 | John III (son of Michael; deposed) |
| 1344–9 | Michael (restored and deposed) |
| 1349–90 | Alexius III (son of Basil) |
| 1390–1417 | Manuel III (son) |
| 1417–29 | Alexius IV (son) |
| 1429–58 | John IV (son) |
| 1458–61 | David I (brother; deposed) |
| [1461] | [Ottoman capture of Trebizond] |

## CYPRUS
### KINGS AND QUEENS OF CYPRUS
*House of Antioch-Lusignan*

| | |
|---|---|
| 1267–84 | Hugh III |
| 1284–5 | John I (son) |
| 1285–1306, 1310–24 | Henry II (brother; deposed 1306, restored 1310) |
| 1306–10 | Amalric (brother; governor only) |
| 1324–59 | Hugh IV (nephew of Henry II) |
| 1359–69 | Peter I (son; co-regent from 1358) |
| 1369–82 | Peter II (son; 'Peter the Fat') |
| 1382–98 | James I (son of Hugh IV) |
| 1398–1432 | Janus (son) |
| 1432–58 | John II (son) |
| 1458–64 | Charlotte (daughter; deposed) |
| 1464–73 | James II (brother; 'James the Bastard') |
| 1473–4 | James III (son) |
| 1473–89 | Caterina **Cornaro** (mother; abdicated) |
| [1489–1571] | [Venetian rule of Cyprus] |
| [1571–1878] | [Turkish rule of Cyprus] |

## DENMARK AND NORWAY
### KINGS OF DENMARK AND NORWAY (united 1380–1814)
*House of Pomerania*

| | |
|---|---|
| 1396–1439 | Erik VII |

*House of the Palatinate*

| | |
|---|---|
| 1440–8 | Kristian III of Bavaria (son of Catherine, sister of Erik VII) |

*House of Oldenburg*

| | |
|---|---|
| 1448–81 | Kristian I (count of Oldenburg, descended through female line from Erik V, 1259–86; **Christian I**) |
| [1481–3] | [interregnum] |
| 1483–1513 | Hans (son; **John**) |
| 1513–23 | Kristian II (son; deposed 1523; **Christian II**) |
| 1523–33 | Frederik I (son of Kristian I; **Frederick I**) |
| 1534–59 | Kristian III (son; **Christian III**) |
| 1559–88 | Frederik II (son; **Frederick II**) |
| 1588–1648 | Kristian IV (son; **Christian IV**) |

## ENGLAND
### KINGS AND QUEENS OF ENGLAND
*House of Plantagenet*

| | |
|---|---|
| 1327–77 | Edward III |
| 1377–99 | Richard II (grandson; deposed) |

*House of Lancaster*

| | |
|---|---|
| 1399–1413 | Henry IV (grandson of Edward III; duke of Lancaster) |
| 1413–22 | Henry V (son) |
| 1422–61, 1470–1 | **Henry VI** (son; deposed 1461, restored 1470, deposed 1471) |

*House of York*

| | |
|---|---|
| 1461–70, 1471–83 | **Edward IV** (great-great-grandson of Edward III; deposed 1470, restored 1471) |
| 1483 | **Edward V** (son; deposed) |
| 1483–5 | **Richard III** (brother of Edward IV) |

*House of Tudor*

| | |
|---|---|
| 1485–1509 | **Henry VII** (great-great-grandson of Edward III) |
| 1509–47 | **Henry VIII** (son) |
| 1547–53 | **Edward VI** (son) |

*House of Suffolk*

| | |
|---|---|
| 1553 | Jane (great-granddaughter of Henry VII; Lady Jane **Grey**) |

*House of Tudor*

| | |
|---|---|
| 1553–8 | **Mary I** (daughter of Henry VIII; married Philip II of Spain, who was king-consort, 1554–8) |
| 1558–1603 | **Elizabeth I** (half-sister) |

*House of Stuart*

| | |
|---|---|
| 1603–25 | James I (grandson of Henry VII; **James VI** of Scotland) |
| 1625–49 | Charles I (son) |

## FRANCE
### KINGS OF FRANCE
*House of Valois*

| | |
|---|---|
| 1328–50 | Philippe VI |
| 1350–64 | Jean II (son; 'John the Good') |
| 1364–80 | Charles V (son; 'Charles the Wise') |
| 1380–1422 | Charles VI (son; 'Charles the Mad') |
| 1422–61 | **Charles VII** (son; 'Charles the Victorious') |
| 1461–83 | **Louis XI** (son) |
| 1483–98 | **Charles VIII** (son) |

*Line of Orléans*

| | |
|---|---|
| 1498–1515 | **Louis XII** (great-grandson of Charles V) |

*Line of Angoulême*

| | |
|---|---|
| 1515–47 | François I (great-great-grandson of Charles V; **Francis I**) |
| 1547–59 | **Henri II** (son) |
| 1559–60 | François II (son; **Francis II**) |
| 1560–74 | **Charles IX** (brother) |
| 1574–89 | **Henri III** (brother) |

*House of Bourbon*

| | |
|---|---|
| 1589–1610 | **Henri IV** (tenth in descent from Louis IX, king 1226–70) |
| 1610–43 | Louis XIII (son) |

### DUKES OF ANJOU

| | |
|---|---|
| 1360–84 | Louis I |
| 1384–1417 | Louis II (son) |
| 1417–34 | Louis III (son) |
| 1434–80 | **René** (brother; king of Naples, 1435–42) |
| [1480] | [union with France] |

### DUKES OF BOURBONNAIS
*House of Bourbon*

| | |
|---|---|
| 1310–42 | Louis I |
| 1342–56 | Pierre I (son) |

| | |
|---|---|
| 1356–1410 | Louis II (son; 'Louis the Good') |
| 1410–34 | Jean I (son) |
| 1434–56 | Charles I (son) |
| 1456–88 | Jean II (son) |
| 1488 | Charles II (brother; abdicated) |
| 1488–1503 | Pierre II (brother; 'Pierre of Beaujeu') |
| 1503–21 | Suzanne (daughter) |

*Line of Montpensier*

| | |
|---|---|
| 1505–27 | Charles III (husband of Suzanne) |
| [1527] | [union with France] |

### DUKES OF BRITTANY
*House of Montfort*

| | |
|---|---|
| 1364–99 | Jean IV ('Jean the Conqueror') |
| 1399–1422 | Jean V (son) |
| 1422–50 | François I (son) |
| 1450–7 | Pierre II (son) |
| 1457–8 | Arthur III (son of John IV; 'Arthur of Richmond') |
| 1458–88 | François II (nephew) |
| 1488–1514 | Anne (daughter; married Louis XII of France) |
| [1514] | [union with France] |

### COUNTS OF PROVENCE
*Valois House of Anjou*

| | |
|---|---|
| 1382–4 | Louis I |
| 1384–1417 | Louis II (son) |
| 1417–34 | Louis III (son) |
| 1434–80 | **René** (brother) |
| 1480–1 | Charles III of Maine (nephew) |
| [1481] | [union of Provence and Maine with France] |

## GERMANY
### HOLY ROMAN EMPERORS
Before their imperial coronations, monarchs were styled 'king of the Romans' (*Romanorum Rex*); thereafter they were styled 'Holy Roman Emperor' (*Romanorum Imperator*)

*House of Luxemburg*

| | |
|---|---|
| 1308–13 | Henry VII (crowned 1312) |

*House of Wittelsbach*

| | |
|---|---|
| 1314–47 | Ludwig IV of Bavaria (crowned 1328) |
| [1314–30] | [Frederick of Austria] |

*House of Luxemburg*

| | |
|---|---|
| 1347–78 | Charles IV (grandson of Henry VII; crowned 1355) |
| [1349] | [Günther of Schwarzburg (abdicated)] |
| 1378–1400 | Wenceslas (**Wenceslas IV** of Bohemia; son of Charles IV; co-regent 1376; deposed 1400) |

*House of Wittelsbach*

| | |
|---|---|
| 1400–10 | Ruprecht of the Palatinate |

*House of Luxemburg*

| | |
|---|---|
| 1410–37 | Sigmund or **Sigismund** (son of Charles IV; crowned 1433) |
| [1410–11] | [Jobst of Moravia (nephew of Charles IV)] |

*House of Habsburg*

| | |
|---|---|
| 1438–9 | Albrecht II (great-great-grandson of Albrecht I of Austria, 1298–1308) |
| 1440–93 | Friedrich III (second cousin; crowned 1452) |
| 1493–1519 | **Maximilian I** (son; co-regent from 1486; crowned 1508) |
| 1519–58 | **Charles V** (grandson; crowned 1530; abdicated 1558) |
| 1558–64 | **Ferdinand I** (brother) |
| 1564–76 | **Maximilian II** (son) |
| 1576–1612 | **Rudolf II** (son) |
| 1612–19 | Matthias (brother) |
| 1619–37 | Ferdinand II (grandson of Ferdinand I) |

### DUKES OF LORRAINE
*House of Châtenois*

| | |
|---|---|
| 1303–12 | Thiébaut II |
| 1312–29 | Ferry IV (son) |
| 1329–46 | Rudolf (son) |
| 1346–90 | John I (son) |
| 1390–1431 | Charles II (son) |

*House of Anjou*

| | |
|---|---|
| 1431–53 | René I (married Isabelle, daughter of Charles II; 'René the Good') |
| 1453–70 | John II (son) |
| 1470–3 | Nicolas (son) |

*House of Vaudémont*

| | |
|---|---|
| 1473–1508 | René II (grandson of René I) |
| 1508–44 | Anthony (son) |
| 1544–5 | Francis I (son) |
| 1545–1608 | Charles III (son; 'Charles the Great') |
| 1608–24 | Henry II (son) |

### DUKES OF BRUNSWICK AND LÜNEBURG
*Old Line of Brunswick*

| | |
|---|---|
| 1369–73 | Magnus II ('Magnus the Younger') |
| 1373–1400 | Friedrich (son) |
| [1400] | [union of Brunswick and Lüneburg] |

*Middle Line of Lüneburg*

| | |
|---|---|
| 1388–1416 | Heinrich (brother; joint ruler of Lüneburg from 1388; joint ruler of Brunswick from 1400; ruler of Lüneburg after partition in 1409) |
| 1416–28 | Wilhelm I (son; ruler of Brunswick after 1428; 'Wilhelm the Victorious') |
| 1428–34 | Bernhardt I (son of Magnus II; ruler of Brunswick 1409–28) |
| 1434–41, 1446–58 | Friedrich (son; abdicated 1441 and 1458; 'Friedrich the Pious') |
| 1434–46 | Otto I (brother; 'Otto the Lame') |
| 1458–64 | Bernhardt II (son of Friedrich) |
| 1464–71 | Otto II (brother) |
| 1471–1522 | Heinrich (son; abdicated 1522; 'Heinrich the Middle') |
| 1522–7 | Otto III (son; ruler of Harburg, 1527–49) |
| 1522–46 | Ernst I (brother; 'Ernst the Confessor') |

| | |
|---|---|
| 1536–9 | Franz (brother; ruler of Gifhorn, 1539–49) |
| 1546–59 | Franz Otto (son of Ernst I) |
| 1559–98 | Heinrich (brother; ruler of Dannenberg after partition in 1569) |

*Middle Line of Brunswick*

| | |
|---|---|
| 1388–1428 | Bernhardt I (son of Magnus II; joint ruler of Lüneburg from 1388 and of Brunswick from 1400; ruler of Brunswick from 1409 and Lüneburg from 1428) |
| 1428–82 | Wilhelm (nephew; ruler of Lüneburg 1416–28; ruler of Calenberg from 1432; 'Wilhelm the Victorious') |
| 1432–73 | Heinrich (brother; ruler of Wolfenbüttel; 'Heinrich the Pacific') |
| 1482–4 | Friedrich (son of Wilhelm I; ruler of Calenberg from 1483; deposed 1484) |
| 1482–95 | Wilhelm II (brother; ruler of Göttingen from 1483; abdicated; 'Wilhelm the Younger') |

*Line of Calenberg-Göttingen*

| | |
|---|---|
| 1495–1540 | Erik I (son of Wilhelm II; ruler of Calenberg-Göttingen after partition in 1495; 'Erik the Elder') |
| 1540–84 | Erik II (son; 'Erik the Younger') |
| [1585] | [union with Wolfenbüttel] |

*Line of Wolfenbüttel*

| | |
|---|---|
| 1495–1514 | Heinrich I (son of Wilhelm II; ruler of Wolfenbüttel from 1495) |
| 1514–68 | Heinrich II (son; 'Heinrich the Younger') |
| 1568–89 | Julius (son; ruler of Calenberg from 1585) |
| 1589–1613 | Heinrich Julius (son) |
| 1613–34 | Friedrich Ulrich (son) |

*New Line of Lüneburg*

| | |
|---|---|
| 1559–92 | Wilhelm (son of Ernst I; ruler of Lüneburg-Celle from 1569; 'Wilhelm the Younger') |
| 1592–1611 | Ernst II (son) |
| 1611–33 | Kristian (brother) |

LANDGRAVES OF HESSE

| | |
|---|---|
| 1264–1308 | Heinrich I ('Heinrich the Child') |
| 1284–98 | Heinrich the Younger (son; co-regent) |
| 1308–11 | Johann (brother; Lower Hesse) |
| 1308–28 | Otto (brother; Upper Hesse) |
| 1328–76 | Heinrich II (son; 'Heinrich the Iron') |
| 1376–1413 | Herman the Learned (nephew; co-regent from 1367) |
| 1413–58 | Ludwig II (son; 'Ludwig the Peaceful') |
| 1458–83 | Heinrich III (son; Upper Hesse; 'Heinrich the Rich') |
| 1483–1500 | Wilhelm III (son; Upper Hesse; 'Wilhelm the Younger') |
| 1458–71 | Ludwig III (son of Ludwig II; Lower Hesse; 'Ludwig the Frank') |
| 1471–93 | Wilhelm I (son; Lower Hesse; abdicated; 'Wilhelm the Elder') |
| 1493–1509 | Wilhelm II (brother; Lower Hesse from 1493, Upper from 1500; 'Wilhelm the Middle') |
| 1509–67 | Philipp (son; **Philip of Hesse**) |
| 1567–92 | **Wilhelm IV** (son; Hesse-Cassel; 'Wilhelm the Wise') |
| 1592–1627 | Moritz the Learned (son; Hesse-Cassel; abdicated) |

ELECTORS OF BRANDENBURG
*House of Hohenzollern*

| | |
|---|---|
| 1415–40 | Friedrich I |
| 1440–63 | Friedrich the Fat (son; margrave only, Old Mark and Prignitz) |
| 1440–70 | Friedrich II (brother; Middle and New Marks; 'the Iron Margrave') |
| 1470–86 | **Albrecht Achilles** (brother) |
| 1486–99 | Johann Cicero (son) |
| 1499–1535 | Joachim I, Nestor (son) |
| 1535–71 | Johann (son; margrave only; New Mark) |
| 1535–71 | Joachim II, Hector (brother; Old Mark and Prignitz, Middle Mark) |
| 1571–98 | Johann Georg (son) |
| 1598–1608 | Joachim Friedrich (son) |
| 1608–20 | Johann Sigmund (son; duke of Prussia, 1618) |
| 1620–40 | Georg Wilhelm (son) |

ELECTORS AND DUKES OF SAXONY
*House of Wettin*
Electors of Saxony

| | |
|---|---|
| 1423–28 | Friedrich I (Frederick IV of Meissen; 'Friedrich the Warlike') |
| 1428–64 | Friedrich II ('Friedrich the Gentle') |

Electors of Saxony (Ernestine Line)

| | |
|---|---|
| 1464–86 | Ernst (son) |
| 1484–1525 | Friedrich III (son; 'Friedrich the Wise') |
| 1525–32 | Johann the Constant (brother) |
| 1532–47 | **Johann Friedrich I, the Magnanimous** (son; deprived of the electorate by Charles V in 1547) |

Dukes of Saxony (Albertine Line)

| | |
|---|---|
| 1464–1500 | Albrecht (son of Friedrich II: 'Albrecht the Bold') |
| 1500–39 | **Georg der Bärtige** (son) |
| 1539–41 | Heinrich the Pious (brother) |

Electors of Saxony

| | |
|---|---|
| 1541–53 | Moritz (**Maurice of Saxony**; son; elector from 1547) |
| 1553–86 | Augustus (brother) |
| 1586–91 | Christian I (son) |
| 1591–1611 | Christian II (son) |
| 1611–56 | Johann Georg I (brother) |

DUKES OF BAVARIA
*House of Wittelsbach*

| | |
|---|---|
| 1294–1347 | Ludwig IV (king of the Romans 1314; resigned Palatinate 1329; ruler of Lower Bavaria from 1341; 'Ludwig the Bavarian') |

*Line of Upper Bavaria*

| | |
|---|---|
| 1347–51 | Ludwig VI (son; joint ruler of Upper Bavaria after partition in 1349; abdicated 1351; 'Ludwig the Roman') |
| 1347–51 | Otto V (brother; joint ruler of Upper Bavaria after partition in 1349; abdicated 1351; joint ruler of Lower Bavaria-Landshut, 1376–9) |
| 1347–61 | Ludwig V (brother; joint ruler of Upper Bavaria after partition in 1649; 'Ludwig the Brandenburger') |
| 1361–3 | Meinhard (son) |
| [1363] | [union with Lower Bavaria-Landshut] |

*Line of Lower Bavaria-Straubing*

| | |
|---|---|
| 1347–58 | Wilhelm I (son of Ludwig IV; joint ruler of Lower Bavaria after partition in 1349; joint ruler of Lower Bavaria-Straubing after union in 1353; deposed 1358) |
| 1347–1404 | Albrecht I (brother; joint ruler of Lower Bavaria after partition in 1349; joint ruler of Lower Bavaria-Straubing after union in 1353) |
| 1387–97 | Albrecht II (son; co-regent) |
| 1404–35 | Johann/Hans III (brother; co-regent from 1397; John III) |

*Line of Lower Bavaria-Landshut*

| | |
|---|---|
| 1347–75 | Stefan II (son of Ludwig IV; joint ruler of Lower Bavaria after partition in 1349; ruler of Lower Bavaria-Landshut from 1353; ruler of Upper Bavaria from 1363) |
| 1375–93 | Friedrich (son; joint ruler of Lower Bavaria-Landshut from 1376; ruler of Lower Bavaria-Landshut after partition in 1392) |
| 1393–1450 | Heinrich XVI (son; ruler of Upper Bavaria-Ingolstadt from 1447; 'Heinrich the Rich') |
| 1450–79 | Ludwig IX (son; 'Ludwig the Rich') |
| 1479–1503 | Georg (son; 'Georg the Rich') |
| [1504] | [union with Upper Bavaria-Munich] |

*Line of Upper Bavaria-Ingolstadt*

| | |
|---|---|
| 1375–1413 | Stefan III (son of Stefan II; joint ruler of Upper Bavaria from 1376; ruler of Bavaria-Ingolstadt from 1392; 'Stefan the Magnificent') |
| 1413–43 | Ludwig VII (son; deposed 1443; 'Ludwig the Bearded') |
| 1443–5 | Ludwig VIII (son; 'Ludwig the Younger') |
| [1447] | [union with Lower Bavaria-Landshut] |

*Line of Upper Bavaria-Munich*

| | |
|---|---|
| 1375–97 | Johann/Hans II (son of Stefan II; joint ruler of Upper Bavaria from 1376; ruler of Upper Bavaria-Munich from 1392) |
| 1397–1435 | Wilhelm III (son) |
| 1397–1438 | Ernst (brother) |
| 1438–60 | Albrecht III (son; 'Albrecht the Pious') |
| 1460–3 | Johann/Hans IV (son) |
| 1460–67 | Sigismund (brother; abdicated) |

*Dukes of Bavaria*

| | |
|---|---|
| 1467–1508 | Albrecht IV (brother; ruler of Lower Bavaria-Landshut from 1504; 'Albrecht the Wise') |
| 1508–50 | Wilhelm IV (son) |
| 1516–45 | Ludwig X (brother) |
| 1550–79 | Albrecht V (son of Wilhelm IV) |
| 1579–97 | Wilhelm V (son; abdicated; 'Wilhelm the Pious') |

*Elector of Bavaria*

| | |
|---|---|
| 1597–1651 | Maximilian I (son; regent 1595–7; elector from 1623) |

ELECTORS OF THE PALATINATE
*House of Wittelsbach*

| | |
|---|---|
| 1329–53 | Rudolf II |
| 1353–90 | Ruprecht I (brother) |
| 1390–8 | Ruprecht II (nephew) |
| 1398–1410 | Ruprecht III (son; king of the Romans, 1400) |
| 1410–36 | Ludwig III (son) |
| 1436–49 | Ludwig IV (son; 'Ludwig the Gentle') |
| 1452–76 | Friedrich I (brother; regent 1449–52) |
| 1476–1508 | Philipp (son of Ludwig IV; 'Philipp the Upright') |
| 1508–44 | Ludwig V (son; 'Ludwig the Pacific') |
| 1544–56 | Friedrich II (brother) |
| 1556–9 | Otto Heinrich (nephew) |

*Line of Simmern*

| | |
|---|---|
| 1559–76 | Friedrich III (duke of Simmern; fifth in descent from Ruprecht III; 'Friedrich the Pious') |
| 1576–83 | Ludwig VI (son) |
| 1583–1610 | Friedrich IV (son) |
| 1610–23 | Friedrich V (son; king of Bohemia, 1619–20; deposed on award of electorate to Bavaria; 'the Winter King') |

COUNTS AND DUKES OF WÜRTTEMBERG
*Counts of Württemberg*

| | |
|---|---|
| 1241–65 | Ulrich I ('Ulrich the Founder') |
| 1265–79 | Ulrich II (son) |
| 1279–1325 | Eberhard I (brother; 'Eberhard the Noble') |
| 1325–44 | Ulrich III (son) |
| 1344–62 | Ulrich IV (son; abdicated) |
| 1344–92 | Eberhard II (brother; 'Eberhard the Quarrelsome') |
| 1392–1417 | Eberhard III (grandson; 'Eberhard the Mild') |
| 1417–19 | Eberhard IV (son; 'Eberhard the Younger') |

*Line of Stuttgart*

| | |
|---|---|
| 1419–80 | Ulrich V (son; ruler of Württemberg-Stuttgart after partition in 1442; 'Ulrich the Beloved') |
| 1480–2 | Eberhard VI (son; abdicated; 'Eberhard the Younger') |
| [1482] | [union with Urach] |

*Line of Urach*

| | |
|---|---|
| 1419–50 | Ludwig I (son of Eberhard IV; ruler of Württemberg-Stuttgart after partition in 1442; 'Ludwig the Elder') |
| 1450–57 | Ludwig II (son; 'Ludwig the Younger') |

*Dukes of Württemberg*

| | |
|---|---|
| 1457–96 | Count Eberhard V, the Bearded (Duke Eberhard I from 1495) |
| 1496–8 | Eberhard II (formerly Eberhard VI of Stuttgart; deposed) |
| 1498–1519, 1534–50 | Ulrich |
| [1519–34] | [imperial occupation] |
| 1550–68 | Christoph (son) |
| 1568–93 | Ludwig (son) |
| 1593–1608 | Friedrich I of Mömpelgard (nephew of Ulrich) |
| 1608–28 | Johann Friedrich (son) |
| 1628–74 | Eberhard III (son) |

MARGRAVES OF BADEN
*House of Zähringen*

| | |
|---|---|
| 1288–1332 | Rudolf III (son of Herman VII, 1288–91) |
| 1291–1333 | Friedrich II (brother) |
| 1291–1348 | Rudolf IV (brother) |
| 1297–1335 | Rudolf Hesso (son of Hesso, 1288–97) |
| 1333–53 | Herman VIII (son of Friedrich II) |
| 1348–53 | Friedrich III (son of Rudolf IV; 'Friedrich the Pacific') |
| 1348–61 | Rudolf V (brother) |
| 1353–72 | Rudolf VI (son of Friedrich III) |
| 1372–91 | Rudolf VII (son) |
| 1372–1431 | Bernhardt I (brother) |
| 1431–53 | Jakob I (son) |
| 1453–4 | Georg (son; abdicated) |
| 1453–8 | Bernhardt II (brother) |
| 1453–75 | Karl I (brother) |
| 1475–1515 | Christoph I (son; abdicated) |
| 1515–33 | Filipp I (son) |

*Margraves of Baden-Baden*

| | |
|---|---|
| 1515–36 | Bernhardt III (brother) |
| 1536–56 | Christoph II (son; abdicated) |
| 1536–69 | Philibert (brother) |
| 1569–88 | Filipp II (son) |
| 1588–94 | Edward Fortunatus (son of Christoph II; deposed) |
| [1594–1622] | [union with Baden-Durlach] |

*Margraves of Baden-Durlach*

| | |
|---|---|
| 1515–52 | Ernst (Baden-Durlach from 1535) |
| 1552–3 | Bernhardt IV (son) |
| 1552–77 | Karl II (brother) |
| 1577–90 | Jakob III (son) |
| 1577–1604 | Ernst Friedrich (brother) |
| 1577–1622 | Georg Friedrich (brother; abdicated) |
| 1590–1 | Ernst Jakob (son of Jakob III) |
| 1622–59 | Friedrich V (son of Georg Friedrich) |

HUNGARY
KINGS AND QUEEN OF HUNGARY
*House of Anjou*

| | |
|---|---|
| 1307–42 | Charles I (grandson of Charles II of Naples) |
| 1342–82 | Louis I (son; king of Poland from 1370) |
| 1382–5, 1386–95 | Mary (daughter; deposed 1385, restored 1386) |
| 1385–6 | Charles III of Durazzo (great-grandson of Charles II of Naples; king of Naples 1381–6) |

*House of Luxemburg*

| | |
|---|---|
| 1387–1437 | **Sigismund** (married Mary; king of the Romans from 1410; king of Bohemia from 1419) |

*House of Habsburg*

| | |
|---|---|
| 1437–9 | Albrecht of Austria (king of Bohemia; married Elizabeth, daughter of Sigismund) |

*House of Poland*

| | |
|---|---|
| 1440–4 | Vladislas I (king of Poland from 1434) |

*House of Habsburg*

| | |
|---|---|
| 1445–57 | **Ladislas V Posthumus** (son of Albrecht; king of Bohemia from 1453) |

*House of Hunyadi*

| | |
|---|---|
| 1458–90 | **Matthias I Corvinus** (Mátyás Hunyadi) |

*House of Poland*

| | |
|---|---|
| 1490–1516 | Vladislas II (son of Elizabeth, daughter of Albrecht; king of Bohemia from 1471 as **Ladislas II**) |
| 1516–26 | Louis II (son; co-regent from 1508; king of Bohemia) |

*House of Habsburg*

| | |
|---|---|
| 1526–64 | Ferdinand I (married Anne, daughter of Vladislas II; emperor from 1558) |

*House of Zápolyai (rival kings)*

| | |
|---|---|
| 1526–40 | János **Zápolya** |
| 1540–70 | János Sigismund (son; abdicated; *voivode* of Transylvania 1570–1) |

ITALY
KINGS OF NAPLES AND SICILY
*House of Anjou—Kings and Queens of Naples*

| | |
|---|---|
| 1266–85 | Carlo I (lost Sicily to Peter I in 1282) |
| 1285–1309 | Carlo II (son; 'Carlo the Lame') |
| 1309–43 | Roberto the Wise (son) |
| 1343–81 | **Giovanna I** (granddaughter; deposed) |
| 1381–6 | Carlo III of Durazzo (great-grandson of Carlo II; king of Hungary 1385–6) |
| 1386–1400 | Luigi II of Anjou |
| 1400–14 | **Ladislas of Durazzo** |
| 1414–35 | **Giovanna II** (sister; reigned with Louis III, 1424–34) |
| 1435–42 | **René** the Good (adopted son; deposed) |

*House of Aragon*

| | |
|---|---|
| 1443–58 | Alfonso I (**Alfonso V** of Aragon, from 1416; 'Alfonso the Magnanimous') |

| | |
|---|---|
| 1458–94 | **Ferrante I** (illegitimate son) |
| 1494–5 | **Alfonso II** (son; abdicated) |
| [1495] | [**Charles VIII** of France] |
| 1495–6 | **Ferrante II** (son) |
| 1496–1501 | **Federico** (son of Ferrante I; deposed) |
| [1501–3] | [**Louis XII** of France] |
| [1503–1707] | [Spanish governors] |

*House of Aragon—Kings and Queen of Sicily*

| | |
|---|---|
| 1282–5 | Piero I (king of Aragon from 1276) |
| 1285–95 | Jacopo the Just (son; abdicated; king of Aragon 1291–1327) |
| 1296–1337 | Federico II (brother) |
| 1337–42 | Piero II (son) |
| 1342–55 | Luigi (son) |
| 1355–77 | Federico III (brother; 'Federico the Simple') |
| 1377–1401 | Maria (daughter) |
| 1390–1409 | Martino I (husband of Maria; 'Martino the Younger') |
| 1409–10 | Martino II (father of Martino I; 'Martino the Humane') |
| [1410–12] | [interregnum] |
| [1412–1713] | [Aragonese and then Spanish governors] |

## DOGES OF VENICE

| | |
|---|---|
| 1312–28 | Giovanni Soranzo |
| 1329–39 | Francesco Dandolo |
| 1339–42 | Bartolomeo Gradenigo |
| 1343–54 | Andrea Dandolo |
| 1354–5 | Marin **Falier** |
| 1355–6 | Giovanni Gradenigo |
| 1356–61 | Giovanni Dolfin |
| 1361–5 | Lorenzo Celsi |
| 1365–8 | Marco Cornaro |
| 1368–82 | Andrea Contarini |
| 1382 | Michele Morosini |
| 1382–1400 | Antonio **Venier** |
| 1400–13 | Michele Steno |
| 1414–23 | Tommaso **Mocenigo** |
| 1423–57 | Francesco Foscari (deposed) |
| 1457–62 | Pasquale Malipiero |
| 1462–71 | Cristoforo Moro |
| 1471–3 | Niccolò Tron |
| 1473–4 | Niccolò Marcello |
| 1474–6 | Pietro **Mocenigo** |
| 1476–8 | Andrea Vendramin |
| 1478–85 | Giovanni **Mocenigo** |
| 1485–6 | Marco **Barbarigo** |
| 1486–1501 | Agostino **Barbarigo** |
| 1501–21 | Leonardo **Loredan** |
| 1521–3 | Antonio Grimani |
| 1523–38 | Andrea **Gritti** |
| 1539–45 | Pietro Lando |
| 1545–53 | Francesco Donato |
| 1553–4 | Marcantonio Trevisan |
| 1554–6 | Francesco **Venier** |
| 1556–9 | Lorenzo Priuli |
| 1559–67 | Girolamo Priuli |
| 1567–70 | Pietro **Loredan** |
| 1570–7 | Alvise **Mocenigo** |
| 1577–8 | Sebastiano **Venier** |
| 1578–85 | Niccolò da Ponte |
| 1585–95 | Pasquale Cicogna |
| 1595–1605 | Marino Grimani |
| 1606–12 | Leonardo Donato |
| 1612–15 | Marcantonio Memmo |
| 1615–18 | Giovanni Bembo |
| 1618 | Niccolò Donato |
| 1618–23 | Antonio Priuli |
| 1623–4 | Francesco Contarini |
| 1625–9 | Giovanni Cornaro I |
| 1630–1 | Niccolò Contarini |
| 1631–46 | Francesco Erizzo |

## COUNTS AND DUKES OF SAVOY
*Dukes of Savoy*

| | |
|---|---|
| 1391–1440 | Amadeus VIII (Antipope **Felix V** 1439–49) |
| 1440–65 | Louis (son) |
| 1465–72 | Amadeus IX (son) |
| 1472–82 | Philibert I (son; 'Philibert the Hunter') |
| 1482–90 | Charles I (brother; 'Charles the Warrior') |
| 1490–6 | Charles II (son; 'Charles John Amadeus') |
| 1496–7 | Philip II of Bresse (son of Louis) |
| 1497–1504 | Philibert II (son; 'Philibert the Handsome') |
| 1504–53 | Charles III (brother; 'Charles the Good') |
| 1553–80 | Emmanuel Philibert (son; **Emanuele Filiberto**) |
| 1580–1630 | Charles Emmanuel I (son; 'Charles Emmanuel the Great') |
| 1630–7 | Victor Amadeus I (son) |
| 1637–8 | Francis Hyacinth (son) |
| 1638–75 | Charles Emmanuel II (brother) |

## COUNTS AND DUKES OF URBINO
*Counts of Urbino*
House of **Montefeltro**

| | |
|---|---|
| 1226–41 | Buonconte |
| 1241–53 | Montefeltrano (son) |
| 1253–85, 1294–6 | Guido (son; abdicated 1296) |
| [1285–94] | [papal rule] |
| 1296–1322 | Federico I (son) |
| [1322–34] | [papal rule] |
| 1324–59 | Nolfo (son) |
| [1359–77] | [papal rule] |
| 1377–1404 | Antonio (grandson) |
| 1404–43 | Guido Antonio (son) |

*Dukes of Urbino*
House of Montefeltro

| | |
|---|---|
| 1443–4 | Oddantonio (son; created duke of Urbino in 1443) |
| 1444–82 | **Federico** II (illegitmate brother; created duke of Urbino in 1474) |
| 1482–1508 | **Guidobaldo I** (son) |
| [1502–3] | [Cesare **Borgia**] |

House of **della Rovere**

| | |
|---|---|
| 1508–16, 1521–38 | Francesco Maria I |
| [1516–19] | [Lorenzo de' **Medici**] |

| | |
|---|---|
| [1519–20] | [papal rule] |
| 1538–74 | Guidobaldo II (son of Francesco Maria I) |
| 1574–1621 | Francesco Maria II (son; abdicated) |

SIGNORI, MARQUISES, AND DUKES OF FERRARA
*House of Este*
*Signori* of Ferrara

| | |
|---|---|
| 1196–1212 | Azzo I |
| 1212–15 | Aldobrandino (son) |
| 1215–64 | Azzo II (brother; 'Azzo the Younger') |
| 1264–93 | Obizzo I (grandson) |
| 1293–1308 | Azzo III (son) |
| 1308 | Fresco (son; deposed) |
| [1308–17] | [papal rule] |
| 1317–35 | Rinaldo (grandson of Obizzo I) |
| 1317–44 | Niccolò I (brother) |
| 1317–52 | Obizzo II (brother) |
| 1352–61 | Aldobrandino III (son) |
| 1361–88 | Niccolò II (brother; 'Niccolò the Lame') |
| 1388–93 | Alberto (brother) |

Marquises of Ferrara

| | |
|---|---|
| 1393–1441 | Niccolò III (son) |
| 1441–50 | Leonello (son) |

Dukes of Ferrara

| | |
|---|---|
| 1450–71 | **Borso** (brother; duke of Modena 1452; duke of Ferrara 1471) |
| 1471–1505 | **Ercole I** (brother) |
| 1505–34 | **Alfonso I** (son) |
| 1534–59 | **Ercole II** (son) |
| 1559–97 | **Alfonso II** (son) |
| [1598] | [union of Ferrara with **Papal State**] |

DUKES OF MILAN
*House of Visconti*

| | |
|---|---|
| 1378–1402 | **Gian Galeazzo** (*signore* of Milan; duke from 1395) |
| 1402–12 | **Giovanni Maria** (son) |
| 1412–47 | **Filippo Maria** (brother) |
| [1447–50] | [**Ambrosian Republic**] |

*House of Sforza*

| | |
|---|---|
| 1450–66 | **Francesco I** (son-in-law) |
| 1466–76 | **Galeazzo Maria** (son) |
| 1476–94 | **Gian Galeazzo** (son) |
| 1494–9 | **Ludovico, Il Moro** (son of [Francesco I; deposed) |
| [1499–1512] | [**Louis XII of France**] |
| 1512–15 | Massimiliano (son; deposed) |
| [1515–21, 1525] | [**Francis I of France**] |
| 1521–5, 1529–35 | Francesco II (brother) |
| [1525–9] | [**Charles V of Habsburg**] |
| [1535] | [union with Empire] |

SIGNORI, MARQUISES, AND DUKES OF MANTUA
*House of Gonzaga*
*Signori* of Mantua

| | |
|---|---|
| 1328–60 | Luigi I |
| 1360–9 | Guido (son) |

| | |
|---|---|
| 1369–82 | Luigi II (son; also called Ludovico I) |
| 1382–1407 | **Francesco I** (son) |

Marquises of Mantua

| | |
|---|---|
| 1407–44 | **Gianfrancesco I** (son; marquis from 1433) |
| 1444–78 | Luigi III (son; also called **Ludovico II**) |
| 1478–84 | **Federico I** (son) |
| 1484–1519 | **Gianfrancesco II** (son) |

Dukes of Mantua

| | |
|---|---|
| 1519–40 | **Federico II** (son; duke from 1530) |
| 1540–50 | Francesco III (son) |
| 1550–87 | Guglielmo (brother) |
| 1587–1612 | Vincenzo I (son) |
| 1612 | Francesco IV (son) |
| 1612–26 | Ferdinando (brother) |
| 1626–7 | Vincenzo II (brother) |
| [1628–31] | [War of the Mantuan Succession] |

RULERS OF FLORENCE AND TUSCANY
*House of Medici*
Rulers of Florence

| | |
|---|---|
| 1434–64 | **Cosimo** the Elder |
| 1464–9 | **Piero I**, the Gouty (son) |
| 1469–92 | **Lorenzo** the Magnificent (son) |
| 1492–4 | **Piero II**, the Younger (son; deposed) |
| [1494–1512] | [republican rule] |
| 1512–13 | Giovanni (brother; later Pope **Leo X**) |
| 1513 | **Giuliano**, duke of Nemours (brother) |
| 1513–19 | Lorenzo, duke of Urbino (son of Piero the Younger) |
| 1519–23 | Giulio (grandson of Piero I; later **Clement VII**) |
| 1523–7 | Ippolito (illegitimate son of Giuliano) |
| [1527–30] | [republican rule] |

DUKES OF FLORENCE
*House of Medici*

| | |
|---|---|
| 1531–7 | **Alessandro** (illegitimate son of Giulio) |

GRAND DUKES OF TUSCANY
*House of Medici*

| | |
|---|---|
| 1537–74 | **Cosimo I** (illegitimate descendant of Cosimo the Elder; grand duke from 1569) |
| 1574–87 | Francesco (son) |
| 1587–1609 | Ferdinando I (brother) |
| 1609–21 | Cosimo II (son) |
| 1621–70 | Ferdinando II (son) |

DUKES OF PARMA AND PIACENZA
*House of Farnese*

| | |
|---|---|
| 1545–7 | Pierluigi (son of Pope **Paul III**) |
| 1547–9, 1550–86 | Ottavio (son) |
| [1549–50] | [papal rule] |
| 1586–92 | Alessandro (son) |
| 1599–1622 | Ranuccio I (son) |
| 1622–46 | Odoardo (son) |

## LITHUANIA
### GRAND DUKES OF LITHUANIA
*House of Liutauras*

| | |
|---|---|
| 1295–1316 | Vytenis |
| 1316–41 | Gediminas (brother) |
| 1341–5 | Jaunutis (son; deposed) |
| 1345–77 | Algirdas (brother) |
| 1345–77 | Kęstutis (brother) |
| 1377–92 | Jogaila (son of Algirdas; king of Poland, as **Vladislav II**, 1386–1434) |
| 1392–1430 | Vytautas the Great (son of Kęstutis) |
| 1430–2 | Švitrigaila (son of Algirdas; deposed) |
| 1432–40 | Sigismund (son of Kęstutis) |
| 1440–92 | **Casimir** (son of Jogaila; king of Poland from 1446) |
| 1492–1506 | Alexander (son; king of Poland from 1501) |
| [1501] | [union with Poland] |

## MONACO
### HOUSE OF GRIMALDI
*Lords of Monaco*

| | |
|---|---|
| 1458–94 | Lambert Grimaldi |
| 1494–1505 | Jean II (son) |
| 1505–23 | Lucien (brother) |
| 1523–32 | Augustin (brother) |
| 1532–81 | Honoré I (son of Lucien) |
| 1581–9 | Charles II (son) |
| 1589–1604 | Hercule (brother) |

*Princes of Monaco*

| | |
|---|---|
| 1604–62 | Honoré II (son; prince from 1612) |
| [1641] | [becomes French protectorate] |

## THE NETHERLANDS
### DUKES OF LUXEMBURG
*House of Limburg*

| | |
|---|---|
| 1353–83 | Wenceslas I (count of Luxemburg; duke from 1354) |
| 1383–1419 | Wenceslas II (nephew; king of the Romans 1378–1400; king of Bohemia as **Wenceslas IV** from 1378) |
| 1419–37 | **Sigismund** (brother; king of Hungary from 1387; king of the Romans from 1410; king of Bohemia from 1419) |

*House of Habsburg*

| | |
|---|---|
| 1437–9 | Albrecht of Austria (married Elizabeth, daughter of Sigismund; king of Hungary and Bohemia from 1437; king of the Romans from 1438) |

*House of Wettin*

| | |
|---|---|
| 1439–43 | Wilhelm of Saxony (married Anna, daughter of Albrecht; abdicated) |
| [1443] | [union with Burgundy] |

### DUKES OF BRABANT
*House of Luxemburg*

| | |
|---|---|
| 1355–83 | Wenceslas (Duke of Luxemburg) |
| 1355–1404 | Johanna (daughter of Johann III, duke of Brabant, and wife of Wenceslas; abdicated) |

*House of Burgundy*

| | |
|---|---|
| 1405–15 | Anthony |
| 1415–27 | John IV (son) |
| 1427–30 | Philip of Saint-Pol (brother) |
| [1430] | [union of Brabant with Burgundy] |

### DUKES OF BURGUNDY
*House of Valois*

| | |
|---|---|
| 1363–1404 | Philip the Bold |
| 1404–19 | John the Fearless (son) |
| 1419–67 | **Philip the Good** (son; duke of Brabant from 1430; count of Holland from 1433; duke of Luxemburg from 1443) |
| 1467–77 | Charles the Rash (son) |
| 1477–82 | Mary (daughter) |
| [1477] | [French conquest of Burgundy] |

*House of Habsburg*

| | |
|---|---|
| 1482–1506 | **Philip the Handsome** (son of Mary and Emperor **Maximilian I**; king of Castile from 1504) |
| 1506–55 | Charles (son; king of Spain 1516–56; emperor as **Charles V** from 1519; abdicated) |
| [1555] | [union of Low Countries with Spain] |

### COUNTS OF HOLLAND
*House of Bavaria*

| | |
|---|---|
| 1354–58 | William V (deposed) |
| 1389–1404 | Athert (brother) |
| 1404–17 | William VI (son) |
| 1417–33 | Jacqueline (daughter; abdicated) |
| [1433] | [union of Holland with Burgundy] |

### STADHOLDERS OF THE UNITED PROVINCES
*House of Orange-Nassau*

| | |
|---|---|
| 1572–84 | **William I** ('William the Silent') |
| 1585–1625 | **Maurice** (son) |
| 1625–47 | Frederik Hendrik (brother) |

## OTTOMAN EMPIRE
### SULTANS OF THE OTTOMAN TURKS

| | |
|---|---|
| 1280–1324 | Osman I |
| 1324–62 | Orhan (son) |
| 1362–89 | Murat I (son) |
| 1389–1403 | Beyazit I (son; deposed) |
| [1403–13] | [interregnum] |
| 1413–21 | Mehmet I (son) |
| 1421–44, 1446–51 | Murat II (son; abdicated 1444–46) |
| 1444–6, 1451–81 | Mehmet II, the Conqueror (son) |
| 1481–1512 | Beyazit II (son; deposed) |
| 1512–20 | Selim I (son; 'Selim the Grim') |
| 1520–66 | Süleyman the Magnificent (son) |
| 1566–74 | Selim II (son; 'Selim the Sot') |
| 1574–95 | Murat III (son) |
| 1595–1603 | Mehmet III (son) |

| | |
|---|---|
| 1603–17 | Ahmet I (son) |
| 1617–18, 1622–3 | Mustafa I (brother; deposed 1618, restored 1622) |
| 1618–22 | Osman II (son of Ahmet I) |
| 1623–40 | Murat IV (son of Ahmet I) |

## POLAND
### KINGS AND QUEEN OF POLAND
*House of Piast*

| | |
|---|---|
| 1305–33 | Władysław I (crowned 1320; 'Władysław the Short') |
| 1333–70 | Casimir III (son; 'Casimir the Great') |

*House of Anjou*

| | |
|---|---|
| 1370–82 | Louis the Great (son of Elizabeth, daughter of Władysław I, and Charles I of Hungary) |
| 1382–99 | Jadwiga (daughter) |

*House of Lithuania*

| | |
|---|---|
| 1386–1434 | Władysław II Jagiełło (**Vladislav II** married Jadwiga; grand duke of Lithuania, 1377–92) |
| 1434–44 | Władysław III (son; **Vladislav III**) |
| [1444–6] | [interregnum] |
| 1446–92 | **Casimir IV** (brother) |
| 1492–1501 | **John I Albert** (son) |
| 1501–6 | Alexander (brother) |
| 1506–48 | **Sigismund I** or Zygmunt I (brother; 'Sigismund the Elder') |
| 1548–72 | **Sigismund II** or Zygmunt II Augustus (son) |

*House of France*

| | |
|---|---|
| 1573–5 | Henry (deposed; **Henri III** of France, 1574–89) |

*House of Transylvania*

| | |
|---|---|
| 1575–86 | **Stefan Bátory** (prince of Transylvania; married Anna, daughter of Sigismund I) |

*House of Sweden*

| | |
|---|---|
| 1587–1632 | **Sigismund III Vasa** or Zygmunt III (son of Catherine, daughter of Sigismund I, and **John III** of Sweden) |
| 1632–48 | Władysław IV (son) |

## PORTUGAL
### KINGS OF PORTUGAL
*House of Avis*

| | |
|---|---|
| 1385–1433 | João I (**John I**) |
| 1433–8 | **Duarte** (son) |
| 1438–81 | **Afonso V** (son; 'Afonso the African') |
| 1481–95 | João II (son; '**John II, the Perfect**') |
| 1495–1521 | Manuel I (grandson of Duarte; 'Manuel the Fortunate') |
| 1521–57 | João III (son; **John III**) |
| 1557–78 | Sebastião I (grandson; **Sebastian I**) |
| 1578–80 | Henry the Cardinal (son of Manuel I; **Henrique, Cardeal**) |
| [1580–1640] | [Spanish rule] |

## RUSSIA
### GRAND PRINCES OF MOSCOW-VLADIMIR
*House of Rurik*

| | |
|---|---|
| 1359–89 | Dimitri Donskoi |
| 1389–1425 | Basil I (son) |
| 1425–62 | Basil II, the Blind (son) |
| 1462–1505 | **Ivan III** (son; 'Ivan the Great') |
| 1471–90 | Ivan the Younger (son; co-regent) |
| 1505–33 | Basil III (brother) |

*Tsars of Russia*

| | |
|---|---|
| 1533–84 | **Ivan IV**, the Terrible (son; tsar from 1547) |
| 1584–98 | Theodore I (son) |

*House of Godunov*

| | |
|---|---|
| 1598–1605 | Boris **Godunov** |
| 1605 | Theodore II (son) |
| 1605–6 | Dimitri [false Dimitri]; pretended son of Ivan IV |

*House of Shuiskii*

| | |
|---|---|
| 1606–10 | Basil IV (deposed) |
| [1610–13] | [interregnum] |

*House of Romanov*

| | |
|---|---|
| 1613–45 | Michael Romanov |

## SCOTLAND
### HOUSE OF STUART

| | |
|---|---|
| 1371–90 | Robert II |
| 1390–1406 | Robert III (son) |
| 1406–37 | James I (son) |
| 1437–60 | James II (son) |
| 1460–88 | James III (son) |
| 1488–1513 | James IV (son) |
| 1513–42 | James V (son) |
| 1542–67 | **Mary** (daughter; deposed) |
| 1567–1621 | **James VI** (son of Mary; king of England as James I from 1603) |

## SERBIA
### TSARS OF SERBIA
*House of Branković*

| | |
|---|---|
| 1427–56 | George Branković |
| 1456–8 | Lazar (son) |
| 1458–9 | Stephen the Blind (brother; deposed) |
| 1459 | Stephen Tomašević (son-in-law of Lazar; deposed) |
| [1459] | [Ottoman conquest of Serbia] |

## SPAIN
### KINGS OF SPAIN
*House of Habsburg*

| | |
|---|---|
| 1516–56 | Carlos I (son of Felipe I and Joanna of Castile; abdicated; Emperor as **Charles V**, 1519–58) |
| 1556–98 | Felipe II (son; **Philip II**) |
| 1598–1621 | Felipe III (son; **Philip III**) |
| 1621–65 | Felipe IV (son) |

KINGS OF CASTILE AND LEÓN

*House of Trastámara*

| | |
|---|---|
| 1369–79 | Enrique II |
| 1379–90 | Juan I (son) |
| 1390–1406 | Enrique III (son; 'Enrique the Sickly') |
| 1406–54 | Juan II (son; **John II**) |
| 1454–74 | Enrique IV (son; '**Henry IV**, the Impotent') |

*House of Aragon*

| | |
|---|---|
| 1474–1504 | Fernando V (**Ferdinand II** of Aragon, 1479–1516) and Isabel I (daughter of John II; '**Isabella the Catholic**') |

*House of Habsburg*

| | |
|---|---|
| 1504–6 | Felipe I ('**Philip I** the Handsome') and **Juana la Loca** |

KINGS OF NAVARRE (PAMPLONA)

*House of Évreux*

| | |
|---|---|
| [1314–28] | [union with France] |
| 1328–43 | Philip III |
| 1343–9 | Joan II (daughter of Louis X of France; widow of Philip III) |
| 1349–87 | Charles II (son; 'Charles the Bad') |
| 1387–1425 | Charles III (son; 'Charles the Noble') |

*House of Aragon*

| | |
|---|---|
| 1425–79 | John II (king of Aragon, 1458–79) |
| 1425–41 | Blanche (daughter of Charles III; wife of John II) |
| 1479 | Eleanor (daughter) |

*House of Fois*

| | |
|---|---|
| 1479–83 | Francis Phoebus (grandson of Eleanor) |

*House of Albret*

| | |
|---|---|
| 1484–1516 | John III (from 1512, French Navarre only; Spanish Navarre was annexed by King Ferdinand V of Castile) |
| 1483–1517 | Catherine (sister of Francis; wife of John III) |
| 1517–55 | Henry II (son) |

*House of Bourbon*

| | |
|---|---|
| 1555–62 | Anthony (**Antoine de Bourbon**) |
| 1555–72 | Joan III (**Jeanne d'Albret**; daughter of Henry II; wife of Anthony) |
| 1572–1610 | Henry III (son; king of France as **Henri IV**, 1589–1610) |

KINGS OF ARAGON

*House of Trastámara*

| | |
|---|---|
| 1412–16 | Fernando I |
| 1416–58 | **Alfonso V** (son; 'Alfonso the Magnanimous') |
| 1458–79 | Juan II (brother) |
| [1479–1504] | [union with Castile] |
| 1479–1516 | Fernando II (son; married **Isabella the Catholic**; '**Ferdinand II** the Catholic') |
| [1516] | [union with Castile] |

KINGS OF GRANADA

*House of Nasrid*

| | |
|---|---|
| 1232–73 | Mohammed I |
| 1273–1302 | Mohammed II (son) |
| 1302–9 | Mohammed III (son; deposed) |
| 1309–14 | Nasir (brother; deposed) |
| 1314–25 | Ismail I (great-grandson of father of Mohammed I) |
| 1325–33 | Mohammed IV (son) |
| 1333–54 | Yusuf I (brother) |
| 1354–9 | Mohammed V (son; deposed) |
| 1359–60 | Ismail II (brother) |
| 1360–2 | Mohammed VI (grand-nephew of Ismail I; deposed) |
| 1362–91 | Mohammed V (restored) |
| 1391–2 | Yusuf II (son) |
| 1392–1408 | Mohammed VII (son) |
| 1408–17 | Yusuf III (brother) |
| 1417–19 | Mohammed VIII (son; deposed) |
| 1419–27 | Mohammed IX (grandson of Mohammed V; deposed) |
| 1427–9 | Mohammed VIII (restored and deposed again) |
| 1429–31 | Mohammed IX (restored and deposed again) |
| 1432 | Yusuf IV (maternal grandson of Mohammed VI) |
| 1432–45 | Mohammed IX (restored and deposed) |
| 1445 | Mohammed X (nephew; deposed) |
| 1445–6 | Yusuf V (grandson of Yusuf II; deposed) |
| 1446–8 | Mohammed X (restored and deposed again) |
| 1448–53 | Mohammed IX (restored) |
| 1453–5 | Mohammed XI (son of Mohammed VIII; deposed) |
| 1455–62 | Said (grandson of Yusuf II; deposed) |
| 1462 | Yusuf V (restored and deposed again) |
| 1462–4 | Said (restored and deposed again) |
| 1464–82 | Ali (son; deposed) |
| 1482–3 | Mohammed XII (son; deposed) |
| 1483–5 | Ali (restored and deposed again) |
| 1485–7 | Mohammed XIII (brother; deposed) |
| 1487–92 | Mohammed XII (restored and deposed again) |
| [1492] | [Castilian conquest of Granada] |

SWEDEN

| | |
|---|---|
| [1389–1448] | [Danish rule] |

*House of Denmark*

| | |
|---|---|
| 1448–57, 1464–5, 1457–70 | Karl VIII Knutsson (twice deposed and restored; **Charles VIII**) |
| 1457–64, 1465–7 | Kristian I (deposed and restored; king of Denmark 1448–81; **Christian I**) |
| 1471–97, 1501–3 | Sten Sture the Elder (deposed and restored) |
| 1497–1501 | Hans II (king of Denmark, 1413–1513) |
| 1504–12 | Svante Nilsson (regent) |
| 1512–20 | Sten Sture the Younger (son; regent) |

| | |
|---|---|
| 1520–1 | Kristian II (deposed; king of Denmark, 1513–23; **Christian II**) |

*House of Vasa*

| | |
|---|---|
| 1523–60 | Gustavus I (regent 1521–3; '**Gustavus Vasa**') |
| 1560–8 | Erik XIV (son; deposed; **Eric XIV**) |
| 1568–92 | Johan III (half-brother; **John III**) |
| 1592–9 | Sigismund (son; deposed; king of Poland, 1587–1632; '**Sigismund III Vasa**') |
| 1604–11 | Karl IX (son of Gustavus I; regent 1599–1604; **Charles IX**) |
| 1611–32 | Gustavus II Adolphus (son) |
| 1632–54 | Christina (daughter; abdicated) |

## TRANSYLVANIA

*VOIVODES* (PRINCES)

| | |
|---|---|
| [1004–1526] | [Hungarian rule] |
| 1526–40 | János **Zápolya** |
| 1540–71 | János Sigismund Zápolya |
| 1570–86 | István (or **Stefan**) Bátory |
| 1581–99 | Sigismund Bátory (abdicated 1599; died 1613) |
| 1599–1604 | Andreas Bátory |
| 1605–6 | István (or Stefan) Bocskai |
| 1606–8 | Sigismund Rákoczi |
| 1608–13 | Gabor Bátory |

# APPENDIX 2
# PLACE NAMES IN IMPRINTS

The place of publication in Latin books is usually given in Latin, but the Latin names for Renaissance towns and cities are not necessarily those bestowed by the Romans; in the case of the Netherlands and Germany, the vernacular place names are sometimes retained and Latin inflections added. Academic publications in Germany present a special problem, because the name of the academy is given, but the name of the city is often missing, so I have listed academies as if they were place names; similarly, I have listed as place names the names of printers who customarily omitted the location of their presses from their imprints. I have not included names in which the Latin form is close to the vernacular (e.g. Londinium) unless there is some possibility of confusion: Latin 'Vienna' for example, is sometimes thought to be the Vienna in Austria, but it in fact refers to Vienne, in France (the Austrian Vienna is Vindobona); similarly, Mantua Carpetanorum is Madrid, not Mantua. Imprint names are given in Latin unless otherwise indicated. In areas in which the dominant language has changed (e.g. Silesia and Transylvania) I give more than one vernacular form. Towns and cities with the same vernacular names (e.g. Zell, of which there were at least eight in the German lands) are often similarly indistinguishable in Latin, so I give a single Latin equivalent (in this case Cella).

I have printed Latin place names in the nominative form, but in imprints first- and second-declension place names normally appear in the genitive singular form; other place names appear as ablatives. Many of the place names appear in several variants: Amsterdam, for example, appears as Amstelaedamum, Amsteladamum, Amstelodamum, Amstelredamum, Amstelredamense oppidum, Amstelrodami, and Amsterodamum. In such cases I have usually printed only one form of the Latin name. Variants may be found in the fuller lists provided in Henry Cotton, *Typographical Gazetteer* (2nd edn., London, 1831), J. G. Th. Graesse, *Orbis Latinus oder Verzeichnis der wichtigsten lateinischen Orts- und Ländernamen*, ed. Friedrich Benedict (Berlin, 1909 and 1980) and *Orbis Latinus: Lexikon lateinischer geographischer Namen des Mittelalters und der Neuzeit* (3 vols., Budapest, 1972). Graesse is available on-line at <http://www.Columbia.edu/acis/ets/Graesse/contents.html>. My treatment of vernacular names, which is described in the Introduction, is designed to be helpful rather than consistent, and in these lists I often supply the German names for bilingual areas such as Alsace, Bohemia, Silesia, and Transylvania.

| | | | |
|---|---|---|---|
| Abbatis Villa | Abbeville | Academia ad Rhenum | Duisburg |
| Aboa | Turku (Finnish); | Teutopolit | |
| | Åbo (Swedish) | Academia ad Varnam | Rostock |
| Abredonia | Aberdeen | Academia ad Visurgim | Rinteln |
| Abrincae | Avranches | Academia Agrippina | Cologne |
| Academia ad Albim | Wittenberg | Academia Albertina | Königsberg (now |
| Academia ad Elmum Julia | Helmstedt | | Kaliningrad) |
| Academia ad Geram | Erfurt | Academia Albipolitana | Wittenberg |
| Academia ad Nicrum | Heidelberg | Academia Archipalatina | Heidelberg |
| Academia ad Pregolam Regia | Königsberg (now | Academia Caroliniana | Szczecin (Poland; |
| | Kaliningrad) | | German Stettin) |

| | | | |
|---|---|---|---|
| Academia Casimiriana | Coburg | Aginum, Agenno, Agensinatium civitas | Agen |
| Academia Cattorum | Marburg | Agria | Eger (Hungary; German Erlau) |
| Academia Christiano-Albertina | Kiel | Agrippina Colonia | Cologne |
| Academia Eberhardina-Carolina | Tübingen | Aix-la-Chapelle (French) | Aachen |
| Academia Electoralis-Brandenburgica | Duisburg | Alba | Acqui (Piedmont) |
| Academia Electoralis-Palatina | Heidelberg | Alba Graeca | Belgrade (Serbian Beograd) |
| Academia Emmericiana | Erfurt | Alba Julia | Alba Iulia (Romanian); Karlsburg (modern German); Weissenburg (Renaissance German); Gyulafehérvár (Hungarian) |
| Academia Ernestina | Rinteln | | |
| Academia Francovadana | Frankfurt an der Oder | | |
| Academia Fridericiana-Alexandrina | Erlangen | | |
| Academia Fridericiana-Mecklenburgensis | Bützow | Alba Regalis | Székesfehérvár (Hungary), formerly Fehérvár (German Stuhlweissenburg) |
| Academia Frisiorum | Franeker (Friesland) | | |
| Academia Georgia Augusta | Göttingen | | |
| Academia Hassiaca | Marburg an der Lahn | | |
| Academia Hasso-Schaumburgica | Rinteln | Alcobaziense Monasterium | Benedictine abbey in Alcobaça (Portugal) |
| Academia Herbipolensis | Würzburg | Aldenarda | Oudenaarde (Flemish); Audenarde (French) |
| Academia Herbornensis | Herborn | | |
| Academia Holsatorum | Ratzeburg | Alenconium | Alençon |
| Academia Julia | Helmstedt | Alisum | Heilbronn |
| Academia Julia Ducalis | Würzburg | Alta Villa | Elfeld |
| Academia Julio-Friderciana Ostro-Ducalis | Würzburg | Amacao | Macao (Chinese Aomenkow) |
| Academia Ludoviciana | Giessen | Amacusa | Amakusa-to (Japan) |
| Academia Marchiarum (or Marchica) | Frankfurt an der Oder or Berlin | Amberes (Spanish) | Antwerp (Flemish Antwerpen; French Anvers) |
| Academia Mecklenburgensium | Rostock | | |
| Academia Megapolensium | Rostock | Ambiani | Amiens |
| Academia Nassaviensis | Herborn | Amboyna | Amboina or Ambon (Indonesia) |
| Academia Noribergensis | Nuremberg (German Nürnberg) | Amstelodamum | Amsterdam |
| Academia Noricorum | Altdorf | Amursfortum | Amersfoort (Utrecht) |
| Academia Palatino-Electoralis | Heidelberg or Mannheim | Andeguum | Angiers |
| | | Andreopolis | St Andrews |
| Academia Philurea | Leipzig | Aneda | Edinburgh |
| Academia Rauracorum | Basel (Switzerland) | Angelopolis | Puebla de los Ángeles (Mexico) |
| Academia Regiomontana | Königsberg (now Kaliningrad) | Anglostadium | Ingolstadt |
| Academia Rhodopolitana | Rostock | Angolismum | Angoulême |
| Academia Ruperto-Carolina | Heidelberg | Annecium | Annecy |
| Academia Salana | Jena | Ansloga | Oslo |
| Academia Saxonum-Ducalis | Jena | Antiquaria | Antequera |
| Academia Soraborum | Halle an der Saale | Antissiodorum | Auxerre |
| Academia Teutoburgensium | Duisburg | Anvers (French) | Antwerp |
| Academia Thuringorum | Erfurt | Aquae-Granum | Aachen |
| Academia Varno-Balthica | Rostock | Aquae Sextiae | Aix-en-Provence |
| Academia Venedorum | Halle | Aquae Statiella | Acqui |
| Academia Viadrina | Frankfurt an der Oder | Arae Flaviae | Blaubeuren |
| Academia Wilhelmiana | Marburg | Arausio | Orange |
| Adrianopolis | Adrianople (Turkish Edirne; Bulgarian Odrin) | Arctaunum Francorum | Ortenburg (near Frankfurt) |
| | | Arelatae | Arles |
| Aesium | Iesi | Arenacum | Arnhem |

| | | | |
|---|---|---|---|
| Argentina | Strassburg (French Strasbourg) | Basti | Baça (near Granada) |
| | | Baudissa | Bautzen |
| Argentoratum | Strassburg (French Strasbourg) | Bellositum Dobunorum | Oxford |
| | | Bellovacum | Beauvais |
| Ariminum | Rimini | Berolinum | Berlin |
| Arnoldi villa | Arnhem | Berona | Beromünster |
| Arosia | Västerå | | (Switzerland) *or* |
| Asculum | Ascoli | | Verona |
| Asta | Asti | Beuthania | Bytom (Silesia; |
| Asta | Jerez de la Frontera | | German Beuthen) |
| Astigium | Ecija | Bipontium | Zweibrucken |
| Asturica | Astorga | | (Germany; French |
| Athenae Balthicae | Rostock | | Deuxponts) |
| Athenae Carolinae | Szczecin (Poland; German Stettin) | Bistrovitzium | Bistreț (Romania; German Bistritz, |
| Athenae Gelrorum | Harderwijk | | Hungarian Bistercze) |
| Athenae Rauracae | Basel | Bisuntia | Besançon |
| Athum | Ath (Flemish Aat) | Biterra | Beziers |
| Atrebatum | Arras | Biturgia | Borgo di San Sepolcro |
| Audomaropolis | Saint-Omer | Biturigiae | Bourges |
| Audomarum | Saint-Omer | Blabyria | Blaubeuren |
| Augusta | Augsburg | Blesae | Blois |
| Augusta Munatiana | Augst (Switzerland; also known as Baselaugst) | Bliterae | Beziers |
| | | Bois-le-Duc | 's-Hertogenbosch |
| | | Boleslavia | Bolesławiec (German |
| Augusta Perusia | Perugia | | Buntzlau) |
| Augusta Rauracorum | Augst (Switzerland; also known as Baselaugst) | Bonna | Bonn |
| | | Bononia | Bologna |
| | | Borbetomagus | Worms |
| Augusta Taurinorum | Turin | Brachara | Braga |
| Augusta Trebocorum | Strassburg (French Strasbourg) | Braclara | Braga |
| | | Braunsperga | Braniewo (Poland; |
| Augusta Trecarum | Troyes | | German Braunsberg) |
| Augusta Treverorum | Treves (Germany; in French, Treves) *or* Trèves (France) | Brauum Burgi | Burgos |
| | | Brecennum | Bracciano |
| | | Breidabolstad | Breiðabólsstaður |
| Augusta Tricassiorum | Saint-Paul Trois Châteaux | | (Iceland) |
| | | Breslavia | Wrocław (German |
| Augusta Trinobantum | London | | Breslau) |
| Augusta Vangionum | Worms | Brestia | Brest (now Belarus); |
| Augusta Vindelicorum | Augsburg | | Polish Brześć |
| Augustodunum | Autun | Briga | Brzeg (Silesia; German |
| Augustoritum (Pictonum) | Limoges | | Brieg) |
| Auracum | Aurach | Brixia | Brescia |
| Aurelia | Orléans | Brujas (Spanish) | Bruges |
| Aurelia Allobrogum | Geneva | Brunna | Brno (Moravia; |
| Aureliacum | Orléans | | German Brünn) |
| Aureliani | Orléans | Brunonia | Braunschweig |
| Austrae Civitas | Cividale del Friuli | | (English Brunswick) |
| Autissiodorum | Auxerre | Brunopolis | Braniewo (Polish; |
| Avaricum | Bourges | | German Braunsberg) |
| Avenio | Avignon | Brunstrutum | Portentrui |
| Babenberga | Bamberg | | (Switzerland, near |
| Barcino | Barcelona | | Bern) |
| Baruthum | Bayreuth | Brunsvicum | Braunschweig |
| Barxino | Barcelona | | (English Brunswick) |
| Basatum | Bazas | Bruxellae | Brussels |
| Basilea | Basel | Budissina | Bautzen |

| | | | |
|---|---|---|---|
| Burdigala | Bordeaux | Ciudad de los Reyes | Lima (Peru) |
| Burgum Auracense | Aurach | Civitas Austriae | Cividale |
| Burgum Uxomense | Osma (Soria, Spain) | Civitas Portugalensis | Oporto |
| Burgus (Sebusianorum) | Bourge-en-Bresse | Ciza | Zeitz |
| Buscum-Ducis | 's-Hertogenbosch | Claromontium | Clermont-Ferrand |
| Cabelium | Chablis | Clarus Mons | Clermont *or* |
| Cabillonum | Chalons-sur-Saône | | Chiaramonte Gulfi |
| Cadomum | Caen | | (Sicily) |
| Cadurcum | Cahors | Claudiopolis | Cluj-Napoca |
| Caerffyrthin (Welsh) | Carmarthen | | (Romania; German |
| Caerfrangon (Welsh) | Worcester | | Klausenburg; |
| Caer-Graunt (Welsh) | Cambridge | | Hungarian Kolozsvár) |
| Caer-Ludd (Welsh) | London | Clausenburg | Cluj-Napoca |
| Caesaraugusta | Zaragoza | | (Romania; German |
| Caesarodunum Turonum | Tours | | Klausenburg; |
| Calaris | Cagliari (Sardinia) | | Hungarian Kolozsvár) |
| Calceata | San Domingo de | Clavasium | Chivazzo |
| | Calzada | Clivia | Cleves |
| Caletum | Calais | Cluniacum | Cluny |
| Calissium | Kalisz | Codania | Copenhagen |
| Callium | Cagli | Colonia Allobrogum | Geneva |
| Camberiacum | Chambéry | Colonia Claudia | Cologne |
| Cameracum | Cambrai | Colonia Julia Romana | Seville |
| Camora | Zamora | Colonia Munatiana | Basel |
| Campi | Kampen (Overijssel) | Colonia Ubiorum | Cologne |
| Campidunum | Kempten (Swabia) | Colonia Venetorum | Cologna |
| Canicopolis | Kilkenny | Colonia Viriata | Madrid |
| Cantabrigia | Cambridge | Coloswar | Cluj-Napoca |
| Carantonus | Charenton | | (Romania; German |
| Carnutum | Chartres | | Klausenburg; |
| Carolsruha | Karlsruhe | | Hungarian Kolozsvár) |
| Caropolis | Charleville | Columbaria | Colmar |
| Caropolis | Compiègne | Commelinus | printer in Heidelberg |
| Casale Major | Casal-Maggiore | Complutum | Alcalá de Henares |
| Casale S. Evaxii | Casal de S. Vaso | Concha | Cuença |
| Casinas Monasterium | Monte Cassino | Condivincum Nannetum | Nantes |
| Benedictinorum | | Confluentes | Koblenz |
| Cassela | Caselle (Piedmont) | Conimbrica | Coimbra |
| Cassellae | Kassel (Germany) | Corcagia | Cork |
| Cassovia | Szikszó (Hungary; | Corispitium | Quimper (Breton |
| | German Caschau) | | Kemper) |
| Casurgis | Prague | Corona | Braşov (Romania; |
| Catalaunum | Chalons-sur-Marne | | German Kronstadt; |
| Catuapolis | Douai | | Hungarian Brassó) |
| Cella | Zell | Cosminecum | Koźmin (Poland; |
| Cellae | Selles | | German Koschmin) |
| Cenomanum | Le Mans | Cotonium | Codogno |
| Cetobrica | Setúbal | Cracovia | Kraków |
| Ceulen (Dutch) | Cologne | Crispinus | printer in Geneva |
| Cherium, Carea | Chieri | Cuelen (Dutch) | Cologne |
| Chilonium | Kiel | Curia Rhaetorum | Coire |
| Christiania | Oslo | Curia Variscorum | Hof, Stadthamhof, |
| Cibinium | Sibiu (Romania; | | Bayern (Oberpfalz) |
| | German | Cusentia | Cosenza |
| | Hermannstadt; | Cutna | Kutná Hora (Bohemia; |
| | Hungarian | | German Kuttenberg) |
| | Nagyszeben) | Cygnea | Zwickau |
| Citizum | Zeitz | Danhusium | Dannhausen |

| | | | |
|---|---|---|---|
| Dantiscum | Gdańsk (German Danzig) | Frisinga | Freising |
| | | Fulgineum | Foligno |
| Daventria | Deventer | Gades | Cádiz |
| Delfi | Delft | Gallio | Gaillon (Normandy) |
| Delphi | Delft | Ganabum | Orléans |
| Dertona | Tortona | Gandavum | Ghent |
| Dertosa | Tortosa | Gauda | Gouda |
| Dessavia | Dessau | Gedanum | Gdańsk (German Danzig) |
| Dia August Vocontiorum | Die | | |
| Dionysium | Saint-Denis | Genabum | Orléans |
| Divio | Dijon | Gera ad Elistrum | Gera (Germany, not Italy) |
| Divodurum | Metz | | |
| Divona Cadurci | Cahors | Gerunda | Gerona |
| Dordracum | Dort (German Dordrecht) | Ghiessa Cattorum | Giessen |
| | | Giasium | Iaşi |
| Duacum | Douai | Giennium | Jaén |
| Durocortorum | Reims | Gippesvicum | Ipswich |
| Eblana | Dublin | Gissa Hassorum | Giessen |
| Ebora | Évora | Glascua | Glasgow |
| Eboracum | York | Gorlicium Lusatiorum | Görlitz |
| Ebrodunum | Yverdon | Gratianopolis | Grenoble |
| Ebroicum | Évreux | Gravionarium | Bamberg |
| Eisteta | Eichstätt | Gripswaldia | Greifswald |
| Elna | Perpignan | Grodiscum | Grodzisk |
| Eltwilla | Eltville | Guelpherbytum | Wolfenbüttel |
| Elvetiorum Argentina | Strassburg | Gymnasium Hagense | Rinteln |
| Embrica | Emmerich | Hafnia | Copenhagen |
| Emdanum | Emden | Haga Comitum | The Hague |
| Emerita | Mérida | Hagenau | Haguenau (now in France) |
| Enchusa | Enkhuisen | | |
| Engadi Vallis | Engadine (Switzerland; Romansh Engiadina) | Hailbruna | Heilbronn |
| | | Hala Hermundurorum | Halle (Saxony) |
| | | Hala Magdeburgica | Halle (Saxony) |
| Engolismum | Angoulême | Hala Saxonum | Halle (Saxony) |
| Erfordia | Erfurt | Hala Soraborum | Halle (Saxony) |
| Essium | Iesi | Hala Suevorum | Halle (Swabia) |
| Eustadium | Eichstätt | Halebum | Hamburg |
| Evie | village near Vilnius (Lithuania) | Hannovera | Hanover |
| | | Hanovia (ad Maenum) | Hanau |
| Faesulae | Fiesole | Harderovicum Gelrorum | Harderwijk |
| Fanum Caesaris | Fano | Harderovocum Sycambrorum | Harderwijk |
| Fanum Lucerferi | Sanlúcar de Barrameda | Helenopolis | Frankfurt am Main |
| | | Helsingora | Elsinore (Danish Helsingør) |
| Faventia | Faenza (Italy) or Fayence (France) | | |
| | | Herbipolis | Würzburg |
| Felsina | Bologna | Hermannstadt | Sibiu (Romania; German Hermannstadt; Hungarian Nagyszeben) |
| Flaviobriga | Bilboa | | |
| Flenopolis | Flensburg | | |
| Flexia | La Flèche | | |
| Fontanetum Comitis | Fontenay-le-Comte | | |
| Forum Cornelii | Imola | Hermanopolis | Sibiu (Romania; German Hermannstadt; Hungarian Nagyszeben) |
| Forum Julium | Friuli | | |
| Forum Livii | Forlì | | |
| Francofurtum Marchionum | Frankfurt an der Oder | | |
| Fraustadium | Wschowa (German Fraustadt) | Hispalis | Seville |
| | | Holmia | Stockholm |
| Friburgum Brisgoviae | Freiburg im Breisgau | Homborgum ad Clivum | Homberg |

| | | | |
|---|---|---|---|
| Ilarda | Lleida (Catalonia; Spanish Lérida) | Liburnum | Libourne |
| | | Liburnus | Livorno |
| Insula ad lacum Acronium | 'an island in Lake Constance', i.e. Lindau | Licium | Lecce |
| | | Lignicium | Legnica (Poland; German Liegnitz) |
| Insulae | Lille | Ligurnus | Livorno |
| Interamum | Terni | Lincium Austriae | Linz |
| Iprae | Ypres | Lingones | Langres |
| Isca Damnoniorum | Exeter | Lipsia | Leipzig |
| Isenacum | Eisenach | Literomericium | Litoměřice |
| Isidis Vadum | Oxford | Llondain (Welsh) | London |
| Islebia | Eisleben | Londinium | London |
| Isna | Isny | Losana (Italian) | Lausanne |
| Iuli Pueblo | Juli (Peru) | Lovanium | Louvain |
| Jassium | Iaşi | Lubeca | Lübeck or Lyubcha (Belarus; German Lubiecz) |
| Javrinum | Györ (Hungary; German Raab) | | |
| Juliobriga | Logroño | Lubiana | Laubach |
| Juliomagnum | Angiers | Lubinum | Lübben or Lübbenau |
| Junecopia | Jönköping | Lucanum | Lugano |
| Kahira | Cairo | Lucronium | Logroño |
| Kassa | Szikszó (Hungary; German Caschau) | Lugdunum | Lyon or Leiden |
| | | Lugdunum Batavorum | Leiden |
| Keulen (Dutch) | Cologne | Lunnyng (Manx) | London |
| Kilia Holsatorum | Kiel | Lutetia | Paris |
| Kilonium | Kiel | Luteva | Lodève |
| Kuttenberga | Kutná Hora (Bohemia; German Kuttenberg) | Luynk (Flemish) | Liège |
| | | Lyceum Ernestinum | Rinteln |
| Labacum | Laubach | Lycium | Lecce |
| Labodunum | Ladenburg | Macloviopolis | Saint-Malo |
| Labronis Portus | Livorno | Maclovium | Saint-Malo |
| La Haye (French) | The Hague | Mancunium | Manchester |
| L'Aia (Italian) | The Hague | Mantua Carpetanorum | Madrid |
| Landessuta | Landshut | Marsipolis | Merseburg |
| Lantenacum | Loudéac | Martisburgum | Marburg |
| Lantrigvierum | Tréguier (Breton Landreger) | Massilia | Marseille |
| | | Matisco | Mâcon |
| Laudunum | Laon | Matritum | Madrid |
| Lauretum | Loreto | Mayence (French) | Mainz |
| Lauri | Leerdam | Medioburgum Zelandorum | Middelburg |
| Laus Pompeia | Lodi | Mediolanum | Milan |
| Lavginga | Lauingen | Mediomatrices | Metz |
| Legio | León | Meldae | Mieux |
| Leida | Leiden | Metae | Metz |
| Lemovicense Castrum | Limoges | Methymna | Medina del Campo |
| Lentia | Linz (Austria) | Mindona | Mondoñedo |
| Leodicum Eburonum | Liège (Flemish Luik) | Misena | Meissen |
| Leodium | Liège (Flemish Luik) | Misna | Meissen |
| Leopolis | L'viv or L'vov (Ukraine; Polish Lwów; German Lemberg) | Moguntiacum | Mainz |
| | | Molinae | Moulins |
| Leovardia | Leeuwarden (Dutch; Frisian Leiuwert) | Mompelgartum | Montbéliard |
| | | Monachium | Munich |
| Le Preux | printer in Paris | Monaco (Italian) | Munich or Monaco |
| Lesna | Leszno (Poland; German Lissa) | Monasterium | Münster |
| | | Monspelius | Montpellier |
| Leucopetra | Weissenfels | Mons Pessulanus | Montpellier |
| Leucorea | Wittenberg | Mons Regalis | Mondovi or Monreale (Sicily) |

| Latin | Modern |
|---|---|
| Mons Regius | Monterrey (Spain) or Kaliningrad (German Königsberg) |
| Montes | Mons |
| Mussipontum | Pont-à-Mousson |
| Mutina | Modena |
| Mwythig (Welsh) | Shrewsbury |
| Nannetae | Nantes |
| Nannetum | Nantes |
| Neapolis | Naples |
| Neapolis Casimiriana | Neustadt (Rheinland) |
| Neapolis Nemetum | Neustadt (Rheinland) |
| Neapolis Palatinorum | Neustadt (Rheinland) |
| Neocomum | Neuchâtel (Switzerland) |
| Neostadium ad Hartam | Neustadt (Rheinland) |
| Neostadium in Paltinatu | Neustadt (Rheinland) |
| Nerolinga | Nordlingen |
| Nidrosia | Trondheim |
| Nordovicium | Norwich |
| Norimberga | Nuremberg |
| Nova Plzna | Pilsen (Czech Plzeň) |
| Noviomagium | Nijmegen |
| Noviomagus | Nijmegen |
| Oenipons | Innsbruck |
| Offen | Buda |
| Ognata | Oñate |
| Olomutium | Olomouc (Moravia; German Olmütz) |
| Olyssipo | Lisbon |
| Onoldium | Ansbach |
| Onoltzbachium | Ansbach |
| Ortesium | Orthez |
| Osca | Huesca |
| Othonia | Odense |
| Otthinium | Odense |
| Ottinpurra | Benedictine monastery in Swabia |
| Ovetum | Oviedo |
| Oxoma | Osma (Soria, Spain) |
| Oxomense Burgum | Osma (Soria, Spain) |
| Oxonia or Oxonium | Oxford |
| Padeborna | Paderborn |
| Paleopraga | Prague |
| Palma Balearium | Palma |
| Palthenius | Zacharias Palthenius, printer of Frankfurt am Main |
| Palum | Pau |
| Panormum | Palermo |
| Papia | Pavia |
| Parisii | Paris |
| Parthenopa | Naples |
| Parthenope | Naples |
| Parthenopolis | Magdeburg |
| Patavia | Passau |
| Patavium | Padua |
| Pelsna | Pilsen (Czech Plzeň) |
| Perusia | Perugia |
| Pesclavium | Poschiavo (Switzerland; German Puschlav) |
| Petracora | Périgueux |
| Petrocorium | Périgueux |
| Pferda | Fürth |
| Pheibia | Piove de Sacco |
| Phorca | Pforzheim |
| Pictavia or Pictavium | Poitiers |
| Pinarolium | Pinerola |
| Pincia | Valladolid |
| Pisae | Pisa |
| Pisaurum | Pesaro |
| Piscia | Pescia |
| Pistoria | Pistoia |
| Placentia | Piacenza |
| Plantiniana Officina | Antwerp or Leiden |
| Plavia Variscorum | Plauen |
| Plebisacium | Piove de Sacco |
| Poczatec | Počátky (Bohemia; German Potschatek) |
| Pompeiopolis | Pamplona |
| Pons Oeni | Innsbruck |
| Portus Cale | Oporto |
| Portus Lusitaniae | Oporto |
| Posonium | Bratislava (German Pressburg) |
| Pratum Albuini | Prato (Brescia) |
| Pressburg (German) | Bratislava |
| Prostitium | Prostějov (Moravia; German Prossnitz) |
| Quinque Ecclesiae | Pécs (Hungary; German Fünfkirchen) |
| Racovia | Raków (near Kraków) |
| Ratiasyum Lemonvicum | Limoges |
| Ratisbona | Regensburg (Bavaria) |
| Reginohradecium | Hradec Králové (Bohemia; German Königgrätz) |
| Regiomontium | Königsberg (now Kaliningrad) |
| Regium | Reggio |
| Revalia | Tallinn |
| Rhedones | Rennes |
| Rhetianus Typis | Leiden |
| Rhodopolis | Rostock |
| Rhyd-y-chen (Welsh) | Oxford |
| Rigiacum Artrebatium | Arras |
| Ripa | Riba (Denmark) or Riva (Italy) |
| Rivus Siccus | Medina de Ríoseco |
| Rothomagnum | Rouen |
| Ruan (Portuguese) | Rouen |
| Rubeus Mons | Rougemont (Burgundy) |
| Rupella | La Rochelle (France) |

| | |
|---|---|
| Rutheni | Rodez |
| Saganum Silesiae | Zagań (Poland; German Sagan) |
| Sagium | Sées (Normandy) |
| S. Albani Villa | St Albans (England) |
| Salisburgum | Salzburg |
| Salmantica | Salamanca |
| Salmurium | Saumur |
| Salutiae | Saluzzo |
| Samarobrina | Amiens |
| Sanctandreana Officina | Heidelberg |
| S. Blasii Monasterium | Benedictine abbey in Black Forest |
| Scaphusia | Schaffhausen |
| S. Cucufatis Monasterium | Monastery of Sant Cugat del Valles, near Barcelona |
| S. Deodati Fanum | Saint-Dié |
| Secerrae | Cerera |
| Sedinum | Szczecin (Poland; German Stettin) |
| Segobia | Segovia |
| Segobrica | Segorbe |
| Segodunum | Rodez |
| Segontia | Sigüenza |
| Seguntum | Sigüenza |
| Senae | Siena |
| Senones | Sens |
| Servesta | Zerbst |
| S. Galli Fanum | St Gallen |
| 's-Gravenhage (Dutch) | The Hague |
| S. Jacobus de Tlatilulco | Franciscan monastery in Mexico City |
| Spira | Speyer |
| Stella Navarrorum | Estella |
| St Ubes | Setúbal |
| Subdinnum | Le Mans |
| Sublacense Monasterium | monastery near Subiaco |
| Svollae | Zwolle |
| Sylva-Ducalis | 's-Hertogenbosch |
| Taraco | Tarragona |
| Tarvisium | Treviso |
| Taurinum | Turin |
| Taurum | Toro |
| Teate | Chieti |
| Telo Martius | Toulon |
| Tergeste | Trieste |
| Testaria | Wetzlar |
| Teutoburgum | Duisburg |
| Tholosa | Toulouse |
| Tigurinus Pagus | Zürich |
| Tigurum | Zürich |
| Tincinum | Pavia |
| Tirasso | Tarazona |
| Toletum | Toledo |
| Tolosa Palladia | Toulouse |
| Tolosa Tectosagum | Toulouse |

| | |
|---|---|
| Tornacum Nerviorum | Tournai (Flemish Doornik) |
| Tornesius | printer in Lyon |
| Torunium | Toruń (Poland; German Thorn) |
| Trajectum ad Mosam | Maastricht |
| Trajectum ad Rhenum | Utrecht |
| Trajectum superius | Maastricht |
| Trecae | Troyes |
| Tremonia | Dortmund |
| Treviri | Trier |
| Tricasses | Troyes |
| Tridentum | Trento |
| Tridinum | Trino |
| Tugenus Pagus | Zug |
| Tugium | Zug |
| Tullum Leucorum | Toul |
| Turiaso | Tarazona |
| Turones | Tours |
| Turonium | Tours |
| Turrelacum | Durlach |
| Turris Julia | Trujillo |
| Tusculanum Lacus Benaci | Toscolano (Lago di Garda) |
| Tutela | Tulle (France) *or* Tudela (Navarre) |
| Typis Clarendonianus | Oxford |
| Typis Hendelianus | Jena |
| Typis Orphanotrophei | Halle |
| Typis San-Blasianis | Benedictine abbey in Black Forest |
| Ultrajectum | Utrecht |
| Ulyssipo | Lisbon |
| Uraniburgum | Tycho Brahe's castle on the Danish (now Swedish) island of Hveen |
| Urbs vetus | Orvieto |
| Urso | Osuna |
| Utinum | Udine |
| Valentia Edetanorum | Valencia |
| Valentia Segalaunorum | Valence |
| Valentinianae | Valenciennes |
| Vallisoletum | Valladolid |
| Varsavia | Warsaw |
| Vasatum | Bazas |
| Veneti | Vannes |
| Venetiae | Venice |
| Venetiae Dariorigum | Vannes |
| Vesalia Clivorum | Wesel |
| Vesantio | Besançon |
| Vibiscus | Vevey |
| Vienna | Vienne (France) |
| Vignon | printer in Geneva |
| Vigornia | Worcester |
| Vinaria | Weimar |
| Vincensius | printer in Lyon |
| Vindinum | Le Mans |

| | | | |
|---|---|---|---|
| Vindobona | Vienna | Westmonasterium | Westminster |
| Virmaranum | Guimarães | | (London) |
| Voegel | printer in Leipzig | Winterberga | Vimperk (Bohemia; |
| Vormatia | Worms | | German Winterberg) |
| Vratislavia | Wrocław (German | Wintonia | Winchester |
| | Breslau) | Wurmacia | Worms |
| Vuormacium Vangionum | Worms | Xerezium | Jerez de la Frontera |

# APPENDIX 3

# DATES AT WHICH STATES, CITIES, AND TERRITORIES IN EUROPE ADOPTED THE GREGORIAN CALENDAR

From 1582 till 1700 the difference between the Julian and Gregorian calendars was ten days. In Italy, Poland, Spain, and Portugal the day after Thursday, 4 October 1582 was declared to be Friday, 15 October 1582; the ten suppressed days (listed below) were 5–14 October. The year 1700 was a leap year in the Gregorian calendar but a common year in the Julian, so the discrepancy increased to 11 days; in 1800 the gap increased to 12 days and in 1900 to 13 days. I have listed suppressed days whenever possible, but when territories changed hands by force or treaty, calendars changed without a formal declaration of suppressed days. See CALENDARS in main text.

| State, etc. | Date | Days suppressed | State, etc. | Date | Days suppressed |
|---|---|---|---|---|---|
| Albania | 1913 | | Bishoprics: | | |
| Alsace | | | Augsburg | 1583 | 14–23 February |
| Catholic | 1584 | | Eichstadt | 1583 | 6–15 October |
| Protestant | 1648 | | Freising | 1583 | 6–15 October |
| Artois/Picardy | 1582 | 22–31 December | Cologne | 1583 | 3–12 November |
| Austria (except Brixen, | | | Mainz | 1583 | 12–21 November |
| Salzburg, and Styria) | 1584 | 7–16 January | Münster | 1583 | 18–27 November |
| Brixen and Salzburg | 1583 | 6–15 October | Paderborn | 1585 | 17–26 June |
| Styria | 1583 | 15–24 December | Ratisbon/Regensburg | 1583 | 6–15 October |
| Baltic States | | | Trier | 1583 | 5–14 October |
| Courland | | | Würzburg | 1583 | 5–14 November |
| adopts Gregorian | 1617 | | Duchies: | | |
| reverts to Julian | 1795 | | Bavaria | 1583 | 6–15 October |
| Estonia | 1918 | 1–13 February | Cleves | 1583 | 18–27 November |
| Livonia | | | Jülich | 1583 | 3–12 November |
| adopts Gregorian | 1582 | 5–14 October | Westphalia | 1584 | 2–11 July |
| reverts to Julian | 1629 | | Margravates: | | |
| adopts Gregorian | 1918 | 1–13 February | Baden | 1583 | 17–26 November |
| Lithuania | | | Lusatia | 1584 | 7–16 January |
| adopts Gregorian | 1586 | | Prussia | 1610 | 23 August– |
| reverts to Julian | 1795 | | | | 1 September |
| Bohemia | 1584 | 7–16 January | Germany (Protestant) | 1700 | 18–28 February |
| Bulgaria | 1916 | 1–13 April | Greece | | |
| Denmark (incl. Iceland) | 1700 | 18–28 February | Civil calendar | 1923 | 16–28 February |
| England and Wales | 1752 | 3–13 September | Church calendar | 1924 | 11–22 March |
| France | 1582 | 10–19 December | Hungary | 1587 | 22–31 October |
| Germany (Catholic) | 1583–5 | | Ireland | 1752 | 3–13 September |

855

| State, etc. | Date | Days suppressed |
|---|---|---|
| Italy | 1582 | 5–14 October |
| Florence and Pisa adopt 1 January New Year[1] | 1750 | |
| Liège | 1583 | 11–20 February |
| Lorraine | 1582 | 10–19 December |
| Luxemburg | 1582 | 22–31 December |
| Moravia | 1584 | 7–16 January |
| Norway | 1700 | 18–28 February |
| Poland | 1582 | 5–14 October |
| Portugal | 1582 | 5–14 October |
| Russia | 1918 | 1–13 February |
| Romania | | |
| Civil calendar | 1919 | 19–31 January |
| Church calendar | 1924 | 1–13 October |
| Savoy | 1582 | 22–31 December |
| Scotland | 1752 | 3–13 September |
| adopts 1 January New Year | 1600 | |
| Silesia | 1584 | 13–22 January |
| Slovakia | 1587 | 22–31 October |
| Spain | 1582 | 5–14 October |
| Spanish Netherlands | | |
| Brabant (incl. Antwerp) | 1583 | 22–31 December |
| Flanders | 1582 | 22–31 December |
| Hainaut | 1582 | 22–31 December |
| Limburg | 1582 | 22–31 December |
| Namur | 1582 | 22–31 December |
| Strassburg | | |
| Bishopric | 1583 | 12–21 November |
| City | 1682 | 19–28 February |
| Sweden (incl. Finland) | | |
| Court | | |
| adopts Gregorian | 1590 | |
| reverts to Julian | 1604 | |
| Country | 1753 | 18–28 February |
| Switzerland | | |
| Catholic cantons: | | |
| Freiburg, Lucerne, Schwyz, Solothurn, Uri, Zug, Unterwalden | 1584 | 12–21 January |
| Protestant cantons: | | |
| Zürich, Bern, Basel, Schaffhausen | 1701 | 1–11 January |
| Mixed cantons: | | |
| Appenzell (divided 1597) | | |
| Inner Appenzell | 1584 (confirmed 1590) | |
| Outer Appenzell | | |
| adopts Gregorian | 1584 | 12–21 January |
| reverts to Julian | 1597 | |
| adopts Gregorian | 1798 (Christmas) | |
| Glarus | | |
| Catholic communes | 1701 | 1–11 January |
| Protestant communes | 1798 | |
| *Territories allied to one canton* | | |
| Grisons | | |
| Catholic communes | 1623–4 | |
| Protestant communes | 1783–1812 | |
| Mixed communes | c.1650–1750 | |

| State, etc. | Date | Days suppressed |
|---|---|---|
| Valese (regions subject to St Moritz and Monthey) | 1622 | |
| Valese (remainder) | 1656 | 11–20 March |
| St Gallen | | |
| Principality | 1584 | 12–21 January |
| City | 1724 | |
| Toggenburg | 1724 | |
| Bern | | |
| Bishopric (Catholic) | 1584 | 12–21 January |
| Neuchâtel | | |
| Protestant | 1701 | 1–11 January |
| Catholic (Solothurn) | 1584 | 12–21 January |
| Geneva | 1701 | 12–21 January |
| Biel | 1701 | 12–21 January |
| *Territories subject to several cantons* | | |
| Baden | | |
| Protestant communes | 1701 | 1–11 January |
| Catholic communes | 1585 | |
| St Gallen | | |
| Rheintal | 1585 | |
| Sargans | 1584 | 12–21 January |
| Thurgau | | |
| Catholics | 1584/5 | |
| Protestants retain Julian for festivals | | |
| Uznach | 1584 | 12–21 January |
| Gaster | 1584 | 12–21 January |
| Ticino | 1584 | 12–21 January |
| Mülhausen | 1701 | |
| Transylvania | 1590 | 15–24 December |
| Turkey[2] | 1925 | |
| United Provinces: | | |
| Friesland | 1701 | 2–12 January |
| Gelderland (Catholic including Nijmegen) | 1582 | 22–31 December |
| Gelderland (Protestant including Zutphen) | 1700 | 1–11 July |
| Groningen | | |
| adopts Gregorian | 1583 | 1–10 March |
| reverts to Julian | 1594 | 24 June |
| adopts Gregorian | 1701 | 1–11 January |
| Holland | 1582 | 22–31 December |
| Overijssel | 1701 | 1–11 January |
| Utrecht | 1700 | 1–11 December |
| Zeeland | 1582 | 22–31 December |
| Yugoslavia | | |
| Bosnia, Croatia, Dalmatia, Herzegovina, Slovenia | 1919 | 15–27 January |
| Montenegro | 1916 | |
| Serbia | 1919 | 19–31 January |

1 Until 1750 the Florentines dated the new year from the 25 March following and the Pisans from the 25 March preceding the beginning of the common year.

2 Until 1917 the Ottoman calendar was exactly 584 years behind the Julian calendar and the new year began on 1 March. In 1917 thirteen days were suppressed and this change brought the dates (but not the years) in line with the Gregorian calendar. In 1925 the 584-year discrepancy was resolved, and 1341 became 1925.

# Appendix 4

# Ligatures and Contractions in Renaissance Greek

The first Greek founts to achieve commercial success were those of ALDUS MANUTIUS. Aldus eschewed the practice of his contemporaries, who had imitated the uncial forms found in manuscripts of classical texts, and instead modelled his type on the cursive hands of contemporary commercial Greek. The freehand features of this living Greek included a large number of abbreviations and contractions inherited from late Byzantine Greek. Printers following the tradition established by Aldus developed ligatures to represent both these abbreviated forms and sequences of letters that were by convention tied together in forms in which the original letters are not always readily apparent. The ever-expanding number of ligatures reached its apogee with the Greek type designed and manufactured by Claude GARAMOND for Robert ESTIENNE between 1541 and 1544. These Royal Greek founts, which were known as *characteres regii*, contained virtually all known ligatures. The influence of these founts exceeded even that of their Aldine originals, for they not only fixed the form of printed Greek for two centuries, but they also became the model for handwritten Greek in western Europe. As a result, many of the forms that appear in the printed and handwritten Greek of the sixteenth century cannot now be read by scholars trained only to read the modern forms in which classical and demotic Greek are now printed. On the early printing of Greek, see Robert Proctor, *The Printing of Greek in the Fifteenth Century* (Oxford, 1900), Victor Scholderer, *Greek Printing Types, 1465–1927* (London, 1927) and Nicolas Barker, *Aldus Manutius and the Development of Greek Script and Type in the Fifteenth Century* (2nd edn., New York, 1992).

In this table I have reproduced a selection of the ligatures and contractions that modern readers might find difficult to read. The collection of these ligatures was undertaken by William H. Ingram for an article entitled 'The Ligatures of Early Printed Greek', in *Greek, Roman and Byzantine Studies* 7 (1966), 371–89. Professor Ingram photographed ligatures from a series of alphabet books ranging from Aldus' *De literis Graecis* (Venice, 1501) to the various editions of Estienne's *Alphabetum Graecum* (Paris, 1539–1580), and then reduced the photographs to a common type size and printed them as an appendix to his article. I have, with the permission of the editors, reproduced the photographs in the article, albeit in a different order and arrangement, and in a few instances have differed from Professor Ingram in matters of interpretation.

## Contractions at end of words

ιν

μάτων

ον

όν

ους

ούς

τικὴ

ως

ῶς

## Superscribed contractions at ends of words

αις

αῖς

αν

ας

ᾶς

ειν

εῖν

εις

εῖς

εν

ες

ῆς

ις

οις

οῖς

ος

ὸς

ων

## Superscribed contractions above letters

ὸν   \\ (e.g. τ̈ = τὸν)

ϖν   ~ (e.g. τ̃ = τϖν)

## Ligatures and contractions

ά

αι

αλ

αλλ

αν

ἀντί

ἀντὶ τοῦ

αξ

αο

ἀόριστος

ἀορίστου

απ

ἀπο

ἀπὸ

αρ

ἀρ

αὐ

αὐτὸ

αὐτοῦ

αὐτῷ

γα

γαι

γαν

γὰρ

γας

γγ

γε

γει

γελ

γελλ

γεν

γενικὴ

γενικῆ

γενικὴν

γενικῆς

γερ

γευ

γην

γι

γίνεται

γκ

γλ

γμ

γν

γο

γρ

γράμμα

γρι

γρο

γυ

γυι

γυν

γω

δα

| Greek | | Greek | | Greek | |
|---|---|---|---|---|---|
| δαι | | ει | | θη | |
| δαν | | εἶ | | θην | |
| δαυ | | εἶν | | θι | |
| δέ | | εἶναι | | θν | |
| δει | | ἐκ | | θο | |
| δεξ | | ελ | | θρ | |
| δευ | | ελλ | | θρο | |
| δευρ | | εν | | θρω | |
| δη | | ἐν | | θυ | |
| δην | | ἐξ | | θω | |
| δι | | ἐξάλιον | | κα | |
| δια | | ἐπειδὴ | | καθω | |
| διὰ | | επευ | | καί | |
| διο | | ἐπι | | | |
| δίφθογγον | | ἐπὶ | | καν | |
| δίφθογγος | | ερ | | καϲ | |
| διφθόγγου | | ες | | κατὰ | |
| διφθόγγῳ | | ἐστι | | κεράτιον | |
| δο | | ἐστὶ | | κεφάλαιον | |
| δοτικὴ | | ετο | | κο | |
| δρ | | ευ | | κοτύλη | |
| δραχμή | | εὐθεῖα | | κρ | |
| δρι | | ευς | | κρα | |
| δρο | | ἥμιϲυ | | κυ | |
| δρω | | ην | | κύαθος | |
| δυ | | θα | | κυι | |
| δυι | | θαι | | κῶν | |
| δυν | | θαυ | | λα | |
| δυς | | θε | | λίτρα | |
| ἐγῶ | | θει | | λλ | |

| | | |
|---|---|---|
| λο | ον | ππω |
| λω | ορ (cf ρος) | πρ |
| μα | ος | πρα |
| μαι | ὅτι | πρι |
| μαν | ου | προ |
| μαρ | οὐγγία | πρω |
| μαυ | οὐδε | πτ |
| μεθ | οὐκ | πυ |
| μελ | οὐκα | πυι |
| μελλ | οὖν | πυν |
| μέλλων | οὗτος | πω |
| μὲν | πα | ρα |
| μένος | παι | ρι |
| μέσον | παν | ρο |
| μέσος | παρ | ρος (cf ορ) |
| μέσου | παρα | σα |
| μετὰ | παρακείμενος | σαι |
| μην | παρατατικός | σαν |
| μνᾶ | παυ | σαρ |
| μο | περ | σαυτα |
| μυ | περι | σβ |
| μυι | | σε |
| μυν | περὶ | σει |
| μω | πευ | σθ |
| μῶν | πι | σθα |
| ν | πο | σθαι |
| ξεστὴ | ππε | σθε |
| οι | ππευς | σθη |
| οἷον | ππι | σθην |
| ὁλκὴ | ππο | σθι |

| | | | | | |
|---|---|---|---|---|---|
| σθλ | | στ | | ταῖς | |
| σθο | | στα | | ταν | |
| σθω | | σται | | τας | |
| σκη | | στας | | ταυ | |
| σκο | | σταυ | | ταῦτα | |
| σμι | | στε | | τε | |
| σο | | στει | | τερ | |
| σου | | στη | | τὴν | |
| σπ | | στι | | τῆς | |
| σπα | | στο | | τι | |
| σπαι | | στρ | | το | |
| σπαν | | στυ | | τὸν | |
| σπε | | στω | | τοῦ | |
| σπει | | συ | | τούς | |
| σπη | | συν | | τοῦτο | |
| σπι | | σφ | | τρ | |
| σπλ | | σχα | | τρι | |
| σπο | | σχε | | τρο | |
| σπυ | | σξει | | ττ | |
| σπω | | σξη | | τυν | |
| σσ | | σχην | | τω | |
| σσα | | σχι | | τῷ | |
| σσαι | | σξν | | των | |
| σσαν | | σχο | | ὑ | |
| σσας | | σχρ | | ὐ | |
| σσε | | σχυ | | υι | |
| σση | | σχυν | | υν | |
| σσι | | σω | | ὖν | |
| σσο | | τα | | ὑπ | |
| σσω | | ται | | ὑπερ | |

| | | | | | |
|---|---|---|---|---|---|
| ὑπερσυνελικὸς | | χει | | χθυς | |
| ὑπο | | χην | | χθω | |
| ὑπὸ | | χθ | | χο | |
| υς | | χθα | | χόα | |
| υσι | | χθαι | | χοῖνιξ | |
| φι | | χθας | | χρ | |
| φρ | | χθε | | χρι | |
| χαι | | χθη | | χνν | |
| χαν | | χθην | | ψαι | |
| χαρ | | χθι | | ψαν | |
| χαρι | | χθο | | ψει | |
| χας | | χθυ | | ϖ | |
| χαυ | | χθυν | | | |

# PICTURE ACKNOWLEDGEMENTS

Albertina, Vienna 114; Archivi Alinari 13, 14, 33 t & b, 105 t & b, 108, 117, 222, 223, 230, 330, 331 t & b, 332, 333, 336, 338, 339, 451, 461, 468, 469, 475, 490, 495 t, 508, 530, 581, 592, 608, 610 t, 614, 615, 616, 628, 650, 667, 707, 755 t, 755 b, 790; Ashmolean Museum, Oxford, UK/Bridgeman Art Library 610 b, 771; © Ch. Bastin & J. Evrard, Brussels 289; Bayerische Staatsgemäldesammlungen, Alte Pinakothek, Munich 161, 817; Biblioteca Ambrosiana, Milan (A 79 INF, f.1v) 601; Bildarchiv Foto Marburg 365; Bildarchiv Preussischer Kulturbesitz 705; © Osvaldo Bohm, Venice 754; © The British Museum 517 t, 517 b, 677; Capponi Chapel, Santa Felicità, Florence, Italy/Bridgeman Art Library 631; Fitzwilliam Museum, Cambridge 554; Gabinetto Fotografico, Piazzale degli Uffizi, Florence 476, 509; Gemäldegalerie Alte Meister, Staatliche Kunstsammlungen Dresden 337; Glasgow Museums: The Burrell Collection 77; Institut Amatller d'Art Hispànic, Barcelona 102; Copyright IRPA-KIK, Brussels 266; Kunsthistorisches Museum Vienna 78, 156, 753; Louvre, Paris, France/Bridgeman Art Library 35, 460, 510, 527, 649, 791; Louvre, Paris, France/Giraudon/Bridgeman Art Library 259; © LSH Foto, Stockholm 43; The Metropolitan Museum of Art, Gift of Robert Gordon, 1875 (75.7.2) 611; The Metropolitan Museum of Art, Purchase, Joseph Pulitzer Bequest, 1917 (17.50.99) 629; Musée Condé, Chantilly, France/Bridgeman Art Library 466; Musée des Beaux-Arts, Dijon, France/Bridgeman Art Library 135; © Museo del Prado, Madrid 816; © National Gallery, London 136, 267, 459, 495 b, 609, 756, 772; National Gallery of Art, Washington, Andrew W. Mellon Collection, Photograph © 2002 Board of Trustees, National Gallery of Art, Washington 541; National Gallery of Art, Washington, Samuel H. Kress Collection, Photograph © 2002 Board of Trustees, National Gallery of Art, Washington 361; By courtesy of the National Portrait Gallery, London 329; Private Collection. Photograph: Photographic Survey, Courtauld Institute of Art 669; © Rijksmuseum Amsterdam 415; Scala, Florence 116; 216, 321, 404, 470; Vatican Museums and Galleries, Vatican City 528, 648, 708; Vatican Museums and Galleries, Vatican City, Italy/Bridgeman Art Library 709.